COLUMBIA COLLEGE
3 2711 00024 0645

W9-CZU-709

A CONCORDANCE TO THE POETRY OF LANGSTON HUGHES

A Concordance to the Poetry of Langston Hughes

Compiled by Peter Mandelik and Stanley Schatt
University of Houston

GALE RESEARCH COMPANY
Book Tower
Detroit, Michigan 48226

Library of Congress Cataloging in Publication Data

Mandelik, Peter.

A concordance to the poetry of Langston Hughes.

1. Hughes, Langston, 1902-1967--Concordances. I. Schatt, Stanley, joint author. II. Hughes, Langston, 1902-1967. III. Title.

PS3515.U274Z49 1974 811'.5'2 74-11251

ISBN 0-8103-1011-2

CONTENTS

Introduction vii

Identification Code Used in This Concordance - Table 1

Abbreviations of Poetry Volumes xi

An Index to Poem Titles xiii

A Concordance to the Poetry of Langston Hughes 3

Numerical Keywords 279

Colloquial Contractions 280

Statistical Summary - Table 2

Word Frequencies in Rank Order 285

Words Omitted from This Concordance 296

INTRODUCTION

James Mercer Langston Hughes (1902-1967) was a prolific poet, short story writer, dramatist, essayist, and editor. In forty years of writing he published forty-five books and hundreds of poems. Because he was a Black man writing during a period when Afro-American literature was viewed by many literary critics more as a curiosity than as a subject to be treated seriously, many of Hughes' books are now out of print and available only in special collections. With the re-examination of Afro-American culture during the past two decades, Hughes' critical reputation has soared to the point that he is now acknowledged as America's most significant Black poet.

Influenced in his early years by the poetry of Walt Whitman and Carl Sandburg, Hughes later experimented with jazz and blues rhythms. Rather than write the Negro dialect poetry many critics expected him to produce, he wrote poetry utilizing the actual language of Harlem with its slang and jive talk. Hughes' poetry thus provides a storehouse of material for both the linguist and the social historian. Perhaps because of the limited amount of Hughes' poetry in print, recent critics have tended to emphasize his themes rather than his imagery; hopefully this concordance will focus attention on the complexity of the imagery patterns found in the poems.

Langston Hughes spent forty years revising his poetry, and the problems inherent in the compilation of any concordance were augmented by the lack of a standard edition of the poems. Hughes revised many of his earliest poems by eliminating the Dunbar-like dialect found in both *The Weary Blues* (1926) and *Fine Clothes To The Jew* (1932). In his final volumes of poetry, *Selected Poems* (1959) and *The Panther And The Lash* (1967), he eliminated many of the now obscure political references from poems written during the thirties. We have used the most recent appearance of a poem as the standard edition. Table 1 includes a list of Hughes' volumes of poetry and the computer abbreviations we have used. It also lists the 572 titles of the poems Hughes published, abbreviated to fifteen characters in the concordance, but printed here in full. The poems included are those most recently edited as found in Donald Dickinson's *A Bio-Bibliography Of Langston Hughes;* poems in which a change in title and in accidentals is not substantial replace the earlier poems. Those poems dropped from the concordance for this reason are listed below. The children's poems found in *The Langston Hughes Reader* are not included in the concordance. In all cases of removal of a poem from the list, the most recent authorial revision replaces all earlier versions.

POEMS INCLUDED	
STONY LONESOME	SP
HARLEM	PL
NEGRO	SP
CORNER MEETING	PL
JIM CROW CAR	PL
NIGHT AND MORN	DK
NIGHT AND MORN	DK
WORDS LIKE FREEDOM	PL
MIDNIGHT DANCER	SP
HEAVEN	SP
MILITANT	PL
WARNING	PL
GARDEN	SP
DREAM DEFERRED	PL
ARDELLA	SP
YOUTH	DK
TRUMPET PLAYER	SP

POEMS REMOVED	
DEATH CHANT	SH
PUZZLED	SP
PROEM	WB
CORNER MEETING	SP
LUNCH IN A JIM CROW CAR	SP
HEY!	FC
HEY! HEY!	FC
REFUGEE IN AMERICA	SP
TO A BLACK DANCER	WB
REPRISE	FW
PRIDE	ANS
ROLAND HAYES BEATEN	SP
POEM	DLD
HARLEM	SP
QUIET GIRL	DK
WE HAVE TOMORROW	WB
TRUMPET PLAYER: 52nd STREET	FW

Three sort keys control each word occurrence group: volume publication date, alphabetic order of title, and numerical order of line. Only in *"The Negro Mother"* are line numbers duplicated--the lines of prose introduction are numbered "1" where they precede the actual poem.

Table 2 lists the twenty-three words not printed in the sorted list, the number of times each word occurs and its relative percentage of occurrence in the corpus of 48,490 words. The decision on whether or not to eliminate a word was based upon criteria established previously by editors of both the Cornell University Press and Wisconsin University Press series of concordances.

Sorting of multiple-occurring words is arranged according to these rules: the year of publication of the volume according to the list in Table 1, the alphabetic order of the title, and the numerical sequence of lines. The most recent editorial alteration of Hughes' texts were chosen for inclusion in the concordance, so that his revision of word-use and imagery can be traced.

The sorted words are restricted to thirty-four letters. Hyphenated strings of words exceeding this length are truncated but appear complete in the second column within their original context. The hyphen and the apostrophe are the only retained punctuation in the first column, but all punctuation is retained in the second column. It is ironic that a poet who was described decades ago as primitive by some critics should require the most sophisticated computing resources to analyze his work.

We are grateful to the University of Houston Office of Research for providing the necessary funds for xeroxing all Hughes' published poems.

Peter Mandelik and Stanley Schatt
May, 1974

TABLE 1 - IDENTIFICATION CODE USED IN THIS CONCORDANCE

Abbreviations of Poetry Volumes

An Index to Poem Titles

Abbreviations of Poetry Volumes

ANS *A New Song.* New York: International Workers Order, 1938.

AYM *Ask Your Mama.* New York: Alfred A. Knopf, 1961.

DK *The Dream Keeper.* New York: Alfred A. Knopf, 1932.

DLD *Dear Lovely Death.* Amenia, New York: Troutbeck Press, 1931.

FC *Fine Clothes to the Jew.* New York: Alfred A. Knopf, 1927.

FW *Fields of Wonder.* New York: Alfred A. Knopf, 1947.

JC *Jim Crow's Last Stand.* Atlanta: Negro Publication Society of America, 1943.

LHR *Langston Hughes Reader.* New York: Braziller, 1958.

NM *The Negro Mother.* New York: Alfred A. Knopf, 1932.

OWT *One Way Ticket.* New York: Alfred A. Knopf, 1949.

PL *The Panther and the Lash.* New York: Alfred A. Knopf, 1967.

SH *Shakespeare in Harlem.* New York: Alfred A. Knopf, 1942.

SL *Scottsboro Limited.* New York: Golden Stair Press, 1932.

SP* *Selected Poems of Langston Hughes.* New York: Alfred A. Knopf, 1959.

WB *The Weary Blues.* New York: Alfred A. Knopf, 1926.

**Montage of a Dream Deferred.* New York: Henry Holt, 1951. This volume does not appear in the concordance because it was reprinted as part of *Selected Poems.*

A BLACK PIERROT	SP	
A FAREWELL	WB	
A HOUSE IN TAOS	SP	
A NEW SONG	ANS	
A RUINED GAL	FC	
ACCEPTANCE	LHR	
ADVICE	SP	
AESTHETE IN HARLEM	OLD	AESTHETE HARLEM
AFRAID	WB	
AFRICA	SP	
AFRO-AMERICAN FRAGMENT	SP	AFRO-AMER FRAG
AFTER MANY SPRINGS	DK	AFTR MNY SPRNGS
ALABAMA EARTH	DK	
AMERICAN HEARTBREAK	FL	AMER HEARTBREAK
ANGELS WINGS	SP	
ANGOLA QUESTION MARK	FL	ANGOLA QUESTION
ANNOUNCEMENT	SH	
APRIL RAIN SONG	DK	
ARDELLA	SP	
ARGUMENT	SP	
AS BEFITS A MAN	SP	
AS I GREW OLDER	SP	
ASK YOUR MAMA	AYM	
ASPIRATION	SH	
AUNT SUE'S STORIES	SP	AUNTSUE'S STORI
AUTUMN THOUGHT	DK	
BABY	SP	
BAD LUCK CARD	SP	
BAD MAN	FC	
BAD MORNING	SP	
BALLAD OF GIN MARY	FC	BLD OF GIN MARY
BALLAD OF SAM SOLOMON	JC	BLD SAM SOLOMON
BALLAD OF THE PAWNBROKER	SH	BLD PAWNBROKER
BALLAD OF THE KILLER BOY	SH	BLD THE KILLER
BALLAD OF THE SINNER	SH	BLD THE SINNER
BALLAD OF THE GIRL WHOSE NAME IS MU	SP	BLD OF THE GIRL
BALLAD OF THE FORTUNE TELLER	SP	BLD FORTUNE TEL
BALLAD OF THE GYPSY	SP	BLD THE GYPSY
BALLAD OF THE LANDLORD	SP	BLD LANDLORD
BALLAD OF THE MAN WHO'S GONE	SP	BLD OF THE MAN
BALLAD OF OZZIE POWELL	ANS	BLD OZZIE POWEL
BALLAD OF MARY'S SON	LHR	BLD MARY'S SON
BALLADS OF LENIN	ANS	BLDS OF LENIN
BAR	SP	
BEALE STREET LOVE	FC	BEALE ST. LOVE
BEALE STREET	SP	
BED TIME	SH	
BEGGAR BOY	DK	
BE-BOP BOYS	SP	
BIBLE BELT	FL	
BIG BUDDY	JC	
BIG SUR	FW	
BIG-TIMER THE POEM	NM	BIG-TIMER POEM
BIG-TIMER THE MOOD	NM	BIG-TIMER MOOD
BIRD IN ORBIT	AYM	
BIRMINGHAM SUNDAY	FL	BIRMINGHAM SUND
BIRTH	FW	
BLACK CLOWN THE MOOD	NM	BLACK CLWN MOOD
BLACK CLOWN THE POEM	NM	BLACK CLWN POEM
BLACK GAL	FC	
BLACK MARIA	SP	
BLACK PANTHER	FL	
BLUE BAYOU	SP	
BLUE MONDAY	SP	
BLUES AT DAWN	SP	
BLUES FANTASY	WB	
BLUES IN STEREO	AYM	
BLUES ON A BOX	OWT	
BOARDING HOUSE	OWT	
BOMBINGS IN DIXIE	FL	BOMBINGS DIXIE
BOOGIE 1 A.M.	SP	
BORDER LINE	FW	
BOUND NO'TH BLUES	SP	BOUND NO'TH BLS
BRASS SPITOONS	FC	
BRIEF ENCOUNTER	SH	
BROKE	NM	
BROTHERS	SP	
BUDDY	SP	
BURDEN	FW	
CABARET	WB	
CABARET GIRL DIES ON WELFARE ISLAND	SH	CABARET GIRL
CAFE: 3 A.M.	SP	
CARIBBEAN SUNSET	WB	CARIBBEAN SUNST
CAROLINA CABIN	FW	
CASUALTY	SP	
CATCH	SP	
CHANT FOR MAY DAY	ANS	CHANT MAY DAY
CHANT FOR TOM MOONEY	ANS	CHANT TOM MOONY
CHILDREN'S RHYMES	PL	CHILDREN'S RYME
CHILDREN'S RHYMES	SP	CHILDREN'S RYME
CHIPPY	FW	
CHORD	SP	
CHRIST IN ALABAMA	PL	CHRIST IN ALA.
CIRCLES	FW	
CLOSING TIME	FC	
COLLEGE FORMAL: RENAISSANCE CASINO	SP	COLLEGE FORMAL
COLOR	PL	
COLORED SOLDIER THE POEM	NM	COLORED SL POEM
COLORED SOLDIER THE MOOD	NM	COLORED SL MOOD
COMMENT ON CURB	SP	
COMMUNION	FW	
CONSERVATORY STUDENT STRUGGLES WITH	LHR	CONSERVATORY
CONSIDER ME	SP	
CONVENT	FW	
CORA	SP	
CORNER MEETING	FL	
COULD BE	SP	
CRAP GAME	FC	
CROON	SP	
CROSS	SP	
CROSSING	SP	
CROWNS AND GARLANDS	FL	CROWNS GARLANDS
CULTURAL EXCHANGE	PL	CULTURAL EXCHNG
CURIOUS	OWT	
DANCER	SP	
DANCERS	FW	
DANSE AFRICAINE	SP	
DARK YOUTH OF THE U.S.A.	NM	DARK YOUTH USA
DAYBREAK IN ALABAMA	PL	DAYBREAK IN ALA
DAYBREAK	SH	
DEAD IN THERE	SP	
DEAR LOVELY DEATH	LHR	DEAR LVLY DEATH
DEATH IN YORKVILLE	PL	DEATH YORKVILLE
DEATH IN HARLEM	SH	
DEATH OF AN OLD SEAMAN	DK	DEATH SEAMAN
DEATH OF DO DIRTY: A ROUNDER'S SONG	FC	DEATH DO DIRTY
DECEASED	OWT	
DECLARATION	SH	
DEFERRED	SP	
DELINQUENT	SP	
DEMAND	SP	
DEMOCRACY	SP	
DESERT	SP	
DESIRE	SP	
DIME	SP	
DIMOUT IN HARLEM	FW	DIMOUT IN HARLM
DINNER GUEST: ME	PL	DINNER GUEST ME
DISILLUSION	WB	
DIVE	SP	
DOWN AND OUT	SP	
DOWN WHERE I AM	PL	
DREAM	SP	
DREAM BOOGIE	SP	
DREAM BOOGIE: VARIATION	SP	DREAM BOOGE VAR
DREAM DEFERRED	PL	
DREAM DUST	FL	
DREAM VARIATIONS	SP	DREAM VARIATION
DREAMS	DK	
DRESSED UP	DK	
DRUM	SP	
DRUNKARD	SP	
DUSK	FW	
DUSTBOWL	FW	
EARLY EVENING QUARREL	SP	EARLY EVENING '
EARTH SONG	FW	
EASY BOOGIE	SP	
ELDERLY LEADERS	PL	
ELEVATOR BOY	SP	
END	SP	
ENNUI	SP	
EVENING SONG	SP	
EVENIN' AIR BLUES	SH	EVENIN' BLUES
EVIL	SP	
EVIL MORNING	SH	
EVIL WOMAN	FC	
EXITS	FW	
FACT	SP	
FAIRIES	DK	
FAITHFUL ONE	FW	
FANTASY IN PURPLE	SP	FATASY PURPLE
FEET O' JESUS	SP	
FINAL CALL	FL	
FINAL CURVE	SP	
FIRE	SP	
FIRED	SP	
FLATTED FIFTHS	SP	
FLIGHT	OWT	
FLORIDA ROAD WORKERS	FL	FLORIDA WORKERS
FOR DEAD MIMES	FW	
FOR THE PORTRAIT OF AN AFRICAN BOY	WB	FOR PORTRAIT OF
FRAGMENTS	FW	
FREDERICK DOUGLASS: 1817-1895	FL	FREDRK DOUGLASS
FREE MAN	SH	
FREEDOM	JC	
FREEDOM	PL	
FREEDOM TRAIN	SP	

AN INDEX TO POEM TITLES

Title	Code	Short title
FREEDOM'S PLOW	SP	
FROSTING	FL	
FULFILMENT	SP	
FUNERAL	CWT	
GAL'S CRY FOR A DYING LOVER	FC	GAL'S CRY DYING
GARDEN	SP	
GAUGE	SP	
GENIUS CHILD	SP	
GEORGIA DUSK	PL	
GHOSTS OF 1619	FL	
GIFTS	FW	
GIRL	FW	
GO SLOW	PL	
GONE BOY	SP	
GOOD MORNING STALINGRAD	JC	GOOD MORN STLIN
GOOD MORNING	SP	
GOSPEL CHA-CHA	AYM	
GRADUATION	SP	
GRAVE YARD	FW	
GREEN MEMORY	SP	
GRIEF	FW	
GYPSY MAN	FC	
GYPSY MELODIES	SP	
HARD DADDY	SP	
HARD LUCK	FC	
HARLEM	FL	
HARLEM	SP	
HARLEM DANCE HALL	FW	HARLEM DANCE HA
HARLEM NIGHT SONG	SP	HARLEM NIGHT SO
HARLEM NIGHT CLUB	WB	HARLEM NIGHT CL
HARLEM SWEETIES	SH	
HAVANA DREAMS	SP	
HEART	FW	
HEAVEN	SP	
HEY-HEY BLUES	SH	
HIGH TO LOW	SP	
HISTORY	PL	
HOMECOMING	SP	
HOMESICK BLUES	DK	
HONEY BABE	CWT	
HOPE	SP	
HOPE	SP	
HORN OF PLENTY	AYM	
HOW ABOUT IT, DIXIE	JC	HOW ABOUT DIXIE
I LOVED MY FRIEND	DK	I LOVED FRIEND
IF-ING	SH	
IMPASSE	PL	
IN A TROUBLED KEY	SH	IN TROUBLED KEY
IN EXPLANATION OF OUR TIMES	SP	IN EXPLANATION
IN TIME OF SILVER RAIN	SP	IN TIME SILVER
INTERNE AT PROVIDENT	SP	INTERNE AT PROV
IRISH WAKE	DK	
IS IT TRUE?	AYM	
ISLAND	SP	
ISLAND	SP	
I, TOO	SP	
JAIME	FW	
JAM SESSION	SP	
JAZZ BAND IN A PARISIAN CABARET	FC	JAZZ BAND
JAZZONIA	WB	
JAZZTET MUTED	AYM	
JIM CROW CAR	FL	
JIM CROW'S LAST STAND	JC	JIM CROW'S LAST
JITNEY	CWT	
JOE LOUIS	SP	
JOY	SP	
JUDGMENT DAY	SP	
JUICE JOINT: NORTHERN CITY	CWT	JUICE JOINT
JUKE BOX LOVE SONG	SP	JUKE BOX LOVE
JULIET	SP	
JUNIOR ADDICT	PL	
JUSTICE	FL	
KID IN THE PARK	SP	
KID SLEEPY	SP	
KIDS WHO DIE	ANS	
KU KLUX	FL	
LADY'S BOOGIE	SP	
LAMENT FOR DARK PEOPLES	WB	LAMENT DARK PEO
LAMENT OVER LOVE	SP	LAMENT OVER LOV
LAST PRINCE OF THE EAST	FL	LAST PRINCE
LATE LAST NIGHT	SP	
LAUGHERS	FC	
LENOX AVENUE BAR	PL	LENOX AVE. BAR
LENOX AVENUE: MIDNIGHT	WB	LENOX AVE MIDNT
LET AMERICA BE AMERICA AGAIN	ANS	LET AMERICA BE
LETTER	SH	
LETTER	SP	
LIFE IS FINE	SP	
LIKEWISE	SP	
LINCOLN MONUMENT: WASHINGTON	DK	LINCOLN MONUMNT
LINCOLN THEATRE	CWT	
LISTEN HERE BLUES	FC	LISTEN HERE
LITANY	SP	
LITTLE GREEN TREE	SP	LITTLE GRN TREE
LITTLE LYRIC (OF GREAT IMPORTANCE)	SP	LITTLE LYRIC
LITTLE OLD LETTER	SP	LITTLE OLD LETT
LITTLE SONG	FW	

Title	Code	Short title
LITTLE SONG ON HOUSING	FL	LITTLE SNG HOUS
LIVE AND LET LIVE	SP	LIVE LET LIVE
LONESOME CORNER	CWT	
LONG TRIP	SP	
LONG VIEW: NEGRO	FL	LONG VIEW NEGRO
LOVE	SP	
LOVE AGAIN BLUES	SH	LOVE AGAIN BLUS
LOVER'S RETURN	SP	
LOW TO HIGH	SP	
LUCK	SP	
LULLABY	DK	
LUMUMBA'S GRAVE	PL	
LYNCHING SONG	ANS	
MA LORD	DK	
MA MAN	FC	
MADAM AND HER MADAM	SP	MADAM HER MADAM
MADAM AND THE RENT MAN	SP	MADAM RENT MAN
MADAM AND THE PHONE BILL	SP	MADAM PHONE BIL
MADAM AND THE MINISTER	SP	MADAM MINISTER
MADAM AND THE WRONG VISITOR	SP	MADAM WRONG VIS
MADAM AND THE CENSUS MAN	SP	MADAM CENSUS
MADAM AND THE NUMBER WRITER	SP	MADAM NUMBER WR
MADAM AND THE CHARITY CHILD	SP	MADAM CHARTY CH
MADAM AND HER MIGHT-HAVE-BEEN	SP	MADAM MIGHT-HAV
MADAM AND THE FORTUNE TELLER	SP	MADAM FORT TELL
MADAM'S CALLING CARDS	SP	MADAM'S CALLING
MADAM'S PAST HISTORY	SP	MADAM'S PAST HI
MAGNOLIA FLOWERS	SP	MAGNOLIA FLOWER
MAMA AND DAUGHTER	SP	MAMA AND DAUGHT
MAMMY	FC	
MAN	FW	
MAN INTO MEN	CWT	
MARCH MOON	SP	
MAYBE	SP	
ME AND MY SONG	JC	
ME AND THE MULE	SP	
MELLOW	SP	
MERRY-GO-ROUND	PL	
MEXICAN MARKET WOMAN	SP	MEXICAN MARKET
MIDNIGHT CHIPPIE'S LAMENT	SH	MIDNIGHT CHIPPI
MIDNIGHT DANCER	SP	
MIDNIGHT RAFFLE	SP	
MIDWINTER BLUES	SP	
MIGRANT	SP	
MIGRATION	FW	
MILITANT	PL	
MINNIE SINGS HER BLUES	FC	MINNIE SINGS
MINSTREL MAN	DK	
MISERY	SP	
MISS BLUES'ES CHILD	SP	MISS BLUES'ES
MISSISSIPPI	FL	
MISSISSIPPI LEVEE	SH	MISSISSIPPI LEV
MOAN	FC	
MONROE'S BLUES	SP	
MONTMARTRE	FW	
MOONLIGHT NIGHT: CARMEL	SP	MOONLIGHT NIGHT
MORNING AFTER	SP	
MOTHER IN WARTIME	PL	MOTHER IN WAR
MOTHER TO SON	SP	
MOTHERLAND	FW	
MOTTO	FL	
MOVIES	SP	
MULATTO	SP	
MY PEOPLE	SP	
MYSTERY	SP	
NATCHA	SP	
NECESSITY	SP	
NEGRO	SP	
NEGRO DANCERS	DK	
NEGRO GHETTO	ANS	
NEGRO SERVANT	CWT	
NEIGHBOR	SP	
NEON SIGNS	SP	
NEW MOON	FW	
NEW YORKERS	SP	
NIGHT AND MORN	DK	
NIGHT FUNERAL IN HARLEM	SP	NIGHT FUNERAL
NIGHT SONG	FW	
NIGHTMARE BOOGIE	SP	NIGHTMARE BOOGE
NIGHT: FOUR SONGS	SP	NIGHT FOUR SONG
NO REGRETS	SP	
NORTHERN LIBERAL	PL	NORTHERN LIBERL
NOT A MOVIE	SP	
NOTE ON COMMERCIAL THEATRE	SP	NOTE COMM THEAT
NOTE TO ALL NAZIS FACISTS AND KLANS	JC	NOTE TO NAZIS
NUDE YOUNG DANCER	WB	NUDE YOUNG DANC
NUMBERS	SP	
OCTOBER 16: THE RAID	PL	OCTOBER 16 RAID
ODE TO DINAH	AYM	
OFFICE BUILDING: EVENING	PL	OFFICE BUILDING
OFFICIAL NOTICE	FL	
OLD SAILOR	FW	
OLD WALT	SP	
ONE	SP	
ONE-WAY TICKET	SP	
ONLY WOMAN BLUES	SH	ONLY WOMAN BLUS
OPEN LETTER TO THE SOUTH	ANS	OPEN LETTER

Title	Code	Short title
OPPRESSION	PL	
OUR LAND	WB	
OUT OF WORK	SH	
PARADE	SP	
PARISIAN BEGGAR WOMAN	DK	PARISIAN BEGGAR
PARK BENCH	ANS	
PASSING	SP	
PASSING LOVE	DK	
PASTORAL	LHR	
PAY DAY	SH	
PEACE	PL	
PERSONAL	SP	
PIERROT	WB	
POEM	WB	
POEME D'AUTOMNE	WB	
POET TO BIGOT	LHR	
POPPY FLOWER	FW	
PORT TOWN	SP	
PORTER	SP	
PO' BOY BLUES	DK	
PRAYER	FW	
PRAYER	SP	
PRAYER MEETING	SP	
PREFERENCE	SP	
PRESENT	SH	
PRIME	FL	
PRIZE FIGHTER	FC	
PROJECTION	SP	
QUESTION AND ANSWER	PL	QUESTION ANSWER
QUESTION	SP	
QUIET GIRL	DK	
RAID	CWT	
RAILROAD AVENUE	SP	
REASONS WHY	DK	
RED CROSS	JC	
RED SILK STOCKINGS	FC	RED SILK STOCK
RELIEF	SP	
REMEMBRANCE	FW	
REQUEST	SP	
REQUEST FOR REQUIEMS	CWT	REQUEST REQUIEM
RESTRICTIVE COVENANTS	OWT	RESTRICTIVE
REVERIE ON THE HARLEM RIVER	SP	REVERIE HARLEM
RIDE, RED, RIDE	AYM	
RUBY BROWN	SP	
SAILING DATE	FW	
SAILOR	DK	
SAME IN BLUES	SP	
SATURDAY NIGHT	FC	
SCOTTSBORO	SL	
SEA CALM	SP	
SEA CHARM	DK	
SEASCAPE	SP	
SEASHORE THROUGH DARK GLASSES (ATLA	SP	SEASHORE THROUG
SHADES OF PIGMEAT	AYM	SHADES OF PIG
SHAKESPEARE IN HARLEM	SH	SHAKESPEARE
SHALIMAR	SP	
SHAME ON YOU	SP	
SHARE-CROPPERS	SP	
SHOUT	SP	
SHOW FARE, PLEASE	AYM	SHOW FARE PLESE
SICK ROOM	WB	
SILENCE	FW	
SILHOUETTE	SP	
SINNER	SP	
SISTER	SP	
SISTER JOHNSON MARCHES	ANS	SISTER JOHNSON
SITUATION	SP	
SIX-BITS BLUES	SH	
SLAVE	PL	
SLEEP	FW	
SLIVER	SP	
SLIVER OF SERMON	SP	SLIVER SERMON
SLUM DREAMS	PL	
SNAIL	SP	
SNAKE	FW	
SNOB	SH	
SO LONG	SP	
SOLEDAD	WB	
SONG	DK	
SONG FOR A BANJO DANCE	DK	SONG BANJO DANC
SONG FOR A DARK GIRL	SP	SONG DARK GIRL
SONG FOR BILLIE HOLIDAY	SP	SONG BILLIE HOL
SONG OF SPAIN	ANS	
SONGS	FW	
SONGS TO THE DARK VIRGIN	WB	SONGS DARK VIRG
SOUTHERN MAMMY SINGS	SP	SOUTHERN MAMMY
SPECIAL BULLETIN	PL	SPECIAL BULLTIN
SPIRITUALS	SP	
SPORT	FC	
STARS	SP	
STATEMENT	SH	
STILL HERE	FL	
STOKELY MALCOLM ME	PL	STOKELY MALCOLM
STONY LONESOME	SP	
STRANGE HURT	SP	
STRANGER IN TOWN	CWT	STRANGER IN TWN
STREET SONG	SP	
SUBWAY RUSH HOUR	SP	SUBWAY RUSH HOU
SUICIDE	FC	
SUICIDE'S NOTE	SP	
SUMMER EVENING (CALUMET AVENUE)	SP	SUMMER EVENING
SUMMER NIGHT	WB	
SUN SONG	SP	
SUNDAY	SH	
SUNDAY BY THE COMBINATION	SP	SUNDAY BY COMB
SUNDAY MORNING PROPHECY	SP	SUNDAY MORNING
SUPPER TIME	SH	
SWEET WORDS ON RACE	FL	SWEET WORDS RAC
SYLVESTER'S DYING BED	SP	SYLVESTER'S BED
S-SSS-SS-SH!	SP	
TAG	SP	
TAMBOURINES	SP	
TELL ME	SP	
TESTAMENT	LHR	
TESTIMONIAL	SP	
THE BACKLASH BLUES	FL	BACKLASH BLUES
THE BALLAD OF MARGIE POLITE	OWT	BLD MARGE POLIT
THE BITTER RIVER	JC	THE BITTER RIVR
THE BLACK MAN SPEAKS	JC	BLACK MAN SPEAK
THE CAT AND THE SAXOPHONE (2 A.M.)	WB	CAT AND SAXOPHN
THE CONSUMPTIVE	DLD	
THE DOVE	FL	
THE DREAM KEEPER	DK	DREAM KEEPER
THE JESTER	WB	
THE NEGRO SPEAKS OF RIVERS	SP	NEGRO SPEAKS OF
THE NEGRO MOTHER	SP	THE NEGRO MOTHE
THE NEW CABARET GIRL	FC	NEW CABARET GRL
THE SOUTH	SP	
THE TOWN OF SCOTTSBORO	SL	TOWN OF SCOTTSB
THE WEARY BLUES	SP	
THE WHITE ONES	WB	
THEME FOR ENGLISH B	SP	THEME FOR ENG B
THERE	FW	
THIRD DEGREE	FL	
TO A LITTLE LOVER-LASS, DEAD	WB	TO LITTLE LOVER
TO ARTINA	SP	
TO BE SOMEBODY	SP	
TO CAPTAIN MULZAC	JC	TO CAPTAIN MULZ
TO MIDNIGHT NAN AT LEROY'S	WB	TO MIDNIGHT NAN
TO THE DARK MERCEDES OF (EL PALACIO	WB	TO DARK MERCEDE
TODAY	FW	
TOMORROW	SP	
TOO BLUE	OWT	
TOWER	DLD	
TROUBLED WOMAN	SP	
TRUMPET PLAYER	SP	
TWILIGHT REVERIE	SH	TWILIGHT REVERI
TWO THINGS	DLD	
ULTIMATUM	SP	
UNCLE TOM	SP	
UNDERTOW	PL	
UNION	ANS	
UN-AMERICAN INVESTIGATORS	PL	UN-AMERICAN
UP-BEAT	SP	
VAGABONDS	SP	
VARI-COLORED SONG	FL	VARI-COLORED
VISITORS TO THE BLACK BELT	OWT	VISITORS
WAKE	SP	
WALKERS WITH THE DAWN	DK	WALKERS WITH
WALLS	FW	
WAR	PL	
WARNING	FL	
WARNING	SP	
WARNING: AUGMENTED	SP	WARNING AUGMENT
WATER-FRONT STREETS	SP	WATER-FRONT STR
WEST TEXAS	SP	
WHAT?	SP	
WHAT? SO SOON!	SP	
WHEN SUE WEARS RED	SP	WHEN SUE WEARS
WHEN THE ARMIES PASSED	FW	WHEN ARMIES PAS
WHERE? WHEN? WHICH?	PL	WHERE WHEN WHCH
WHO BUT THE LORD?	FL	WHO BUT TH LORD
WIDE RIVER	DK	
WIDOW WOMAN	SP	
WINE-O	SP	
WINTER MOON	SP	
WINTER SWEETNESS	DK	WINTER SWEEETNS
WISDOM	FW	
WITHOUT BENEFIT OF DECLARATION	PL	WITHOUT BENEFIT
WONDER	SP	
WORDS LIKE FREEDOM	PL	WORDS LIKE FREE
WORKIN' MAN	FC	
WORLD WAR II	SP	
YESTERDAY AND TODAY	CWT	YESTERDAY TODAY
YOUNG BRIDE	WB	
YOUNG GAL'S BLUES	SP	YOUNG GAL'S BLS
YOUNG NEGRO GIRL	SH	YOUNG NEGRO GRL
YOUNG PROSTITUTE	WB	YOUNG PROSTITUT
YOUNG SAILOR	SP	
YOUTH	DK	
125TH STREET	SP	
50 - 50	SP	

A CONCORDANCE TO THE POETRY OF LANGSTON HUGHES

ABE 5

ABE LINCOLN DONE SET ME FREE - . . NM BLACK CLWN POEM 30
LET'S GO SEE OLD ABE . . . . DK LINCOLN MONUMNT 1
QUIET FOR TEN THOUSAND CENTURIES,
OLD ABE. . . . . DK LINCOLN MONUMNT 4
OLD ABE. . . . . DK LINCOLN MONUMNT 11
I HEARD THE SINGING OF THE
MISSISSIPPI WHEN ABE LINCOLN . . SP NEGRO SPEAKS OF 8

ABIDE 1

THAT RIGHT MIGHT ABIDE . . . . . . NM DARK YOUTH USA 14

ABLE 1

YOU AIN'T GONNA BE ABLE TO SAY A
WORD . . . . SP BLD LANDLORD 19

ABOARD 1

IS THAT THE WAY TO GET ABOARD THE
FREEDOM TRAIN? . . . . SP FREEDOM TRAIN 28

ABOLISH 1

ABOLISH POLL TAX SO FOLKS CAN VOTE. JC JIM CROW'S LAST 24

ABOMINATIONS 1

WOMEN'S ABOMINATIONS! JUST LIKE A
CURSE! . . . . SH PAY DAY 19

ABOUT 63

ABOUT TOMORROW . . . . WB HARLEM NIGHT CL 16
LIKE A SWEET VEIL ABOUT YOUR BOWER? WB NUDE YOUNG DANC 4
MIGHT WRAP ABOUT THY BODY. . . . . WB SONGS DARK VIRG 11
BARREL-HOUSE JAZZ. SHOWING-OFF.
STRUTTING ABOUT PROUDLY, BRAGGING
AND . . . . NM BIG-TIMER MOOD 4
BUT THEY GIVIN' 'EM TO SCHOOL BOYS
NOW AND PAYIN' JUST ABOUT HALF. NM BROKE 43
HUNG ABOUT MY NECK. . . . . ANS A NEW SONG 19
AND THE PRISON WALLS WRAP YOU ABOUT. ANS CHANT TOM MOONY 8
HOW ABOUT THIS NECKLACE? . . . . . SH BLD PAWNBROKER 5
I'M ABOUT TO LOSE MY MIND. . . . . SH EVENIN' BLUES 6
SO LET'S JUST FORGET WHAT THIS FUSS
WAS ABOUT. . . . . SH LETTER 15
ABOUT TWO KINDS O' PISTOLS THAT I
AIN'T GOT. . . . . SH TWILIGH, REVERI 10
ABOUT FREEDOM'S WAYS. . . . . JC HOW ABOUT DIXIE 16
ABOUT LIVING AND DYING - . . . . . FW BORDER LINE 2
ABOUT HERE AND THERE - . . . . . . FW BORDER LINE 6
ABOUT THIS LITTLE CABIN . . . . . . FW CAROLINA CABIN 4
WHAT IT WAS ALL ABOUT . . . . FW COMMUNION 2
WHAT IT WAS ALL ABOUT . . . . FW COMMUNION 4
WHAT ABOUT . . . . OWT BLD MARGE POLIT 36
IS WHAT I LIKE ABOUT YOU. . . . . . OWT HONEY BABE 8
ABOUT TWO-THREE A.M. . . . . OWT HONEY BABE 10
SEE WHAT THIS WEEK'S JIVE IS ALL
ABOUT: . . . . OWT JITNEY 25
TO SING ABOUT THE MEN WHO'VE DONE
THEM WRONG - . . . . OWT JUICE JOINT 24
WONDERING ABOUT FUR COATS . . . . . OWT MAN INTO MEN 9
NOBODY CARES ABOUT YOU . . . . . . OWT TOO BLUE 4
YOU CAN TALK ABOUT . . . . OWT VISITORS 1
YOU CAN TALK ABOUT . . . . OWT VISITORS 5
I'LL LEAVE HER MORE TO NAG ABOUT . LHR TESTAMENT 11
ABOUT THIS HOUSE IN TAOS . . . . . SP A HOUSE IN TAOS 17
SHE COULD TELL YOU ABOUT LOVE. . . SP BLD FORTUNE TEL 5
DON'T YOU 'MEMBER I TOLD YOU ABOUT
IT . . . . SP BLD LANDLORD 3
I THOUGHT ABOUT OLD GREELEY . . . . SP BLUE BAYOU 4
AND I THOUGHT ABOUT LOU . . . . . . SP BLUE BAYOU 5
BUT I'M TALKING ABOUT . . . . SP COMMENT ON CURB 6
I DREAMED ABOUT WHEN WE FIRST FELL
IN LOVE . . . . SP DEFERRED 9
NOBODY GIVES A DAMN ABOUT. . . . . SP DOWN AND OUT 6
I READ IN THE PAPERS ABOUT THE . . SP FREEDOM TRAIN 1
I HEARD ON THE RADIO ABOUT THE . . SP FREEDOM TRAIN 3
I SEEN FOLKS TALKIN' ABOUT THE . . SP FREEDOM TRAIN 5
SOMEBODY TELL ME ABOUT THIS . . . . SP FREEDOM TRAIN 23
I GOT TO KNOW ABOUT THIS . . . . . SP FREEDOM TRAIN 29
JIMMY WANTS TO KNOW ABOUT THE . . . SP FREEDOM TRAIN 47
AND I'M GOIN' THERE TO THINK ABOUT
HIM. . . . . SP LAMENT OVER LOV 12
GONNA THINK ABOUT MY MAN - . . . . SP LAMENT OVER LOV 23
I THOUGHT ABOUT MY BABY . . . . . . SP LIFE IS FINE 14
NOTHING ABOUT MY . . . . SP MADAM PHONE BIL 33
WELL, EVEN LESS ABOUT YOUR . . . . SP MADAM PHONE BIL 35
I FELT LIKE THAT ABOUT HIM. . . . . SP MAMA AND DAUGHT 12
HE'S FORGOT ABOUT HIS RACE. . . . . SP ME AND THE MULE 4
AND IN EVERYTHING BUT WHAT'S ABOUT
ME - . . . . SP NOTE COMM THEAT 11
STAND UP AND TALK ABOUT ME. . . . . SP NOTE COMM THEAT 13
AND WRITE ABOUT ME - . . . . SP NOTE COMM THEAT 14
AND SING ABOUT ME. . . . . SP NOTE COMM THEAT 16
AND PUT ON PLAYS ABOUT ME! . . . . SP NOTE COMM THEAT 17
DID YOU EVER THINK ABOUT YOUR
MOTHER? . . . . SP REVERIE HARLEM 5
DID YOU EVER THINK ABOUT YOUR
SWEETHEART . . . . SP REVERIE HARLEM 7
KNOW MORE ABOUT THIS PRETTY RUBY
BROWN. . . . . SP RUBY BROWN 17
ABOUT MARRIAGE . . . . SP S-SSS-SS-SH! 10
ABOUT HIS THIGHS. . . . . SP TRUMPET PLAYER 8
WHAT SHE SAID ABOUT HER CHILDREN . AYM BIRD IN ORBIT 51
HOW ABOUT THAT N.A.A.C.P. . . . . . AYM BIRD IN ORBIT 79
AND HANG IT ABOUT YOUR NECK . . . . PL CROWNS GARLANDS 2
I'M GONNA WRITE ME SOME MUSIC ABOUT PL DAYBREAK IN ALA 2
AND WRITE ABOUT DAYBREAK . . . . . PL DAYBREAK IN ALA 22

ABOVE 11

BROAD ARCH ABOVE THE ROAD WE CAME. DK YOUTH 3
THAT ANY MAN BE CRUSHED BY ONE
ABOVE. . . . . ANS LET AMERICA BE 9
NO LOVE FROM ABOVE. . . . . FW PRAYER 12
ABOVE A CROWD OF BLACK FOLK, HUMBLE,
MEAN. . . . . OWT LINCOLN THEATRE 4
ABOVE ME. . . . . SP AS I GREW OLDER 21
SIXTEEN FLOORS ABOVE THE GROUND. . SP LIFE IS FINE 13
NO LOVE FROM ABOVE. . . . . SP LITANY 12
I LOOKED UPON THE NILE AND RAISED
THE PYRAMIDS ABOVE IT. . . . . . SP NEGRO SPEAKS OF 7
TO THIS COLLEGE ON THE HILL ABOVE
HARLEM. . . . . SP THEME FOR ENG B 9
WHITE MASTER ABOVE . . . . PL CHRIST IN ALA. 8
ABOVE THE STRUGGLE . . . . PL NORTHERN LIBERL 11

ABSORB 1

ABSORB THY BODY. . . . . WB SONGS DARK VIRG 12

ABUELA 2

TU ABUELA, DONDE ESTA? . . . . . . AYM RIDE, RED, RIDE 11
TU ABUELA, DONDE ESTA? . . . . . . AYM RIDE, RED, RIDE 13

ABYSSINIA 1

ON THAT DAY WHEN ABYSSINIA BAPTIST
CHURCH . . . . SP PROJECTION 5

ACCEPTING 1

SHOULDERS AT FATE, ACCEPTING HIS
POSITION - BUT INSIDE HIMSELF
UNHAPPY . . . . NM BIG-TIMER MOOD 6

ACCLIMATED 1

WHERE TO SNOW NOW ACCLIMATED . . . AYM ODE TO DINAH 2

ACCOMPANY 1

MAY ACCOMPANY THE RECITATION -
ECHOING SOFTLY, OVER THERE,
THERE'S A ROSE . . . . NM COLORED SL MOOD 4

ACCORDION 1

AND A BLIND MAN PLAYS AN ACCORDION SP SUMMER EVENING 16

ACCOUNT 2

ON ACCOUNT OF . . . . SP LATE LAST NIGHT 10
ON ACCOUNT OF THE DODGERS ON THE
RADIO. . . . . SP PASSING 5

ACE-BOY 1

HE'S MY ACE-BOY. . . . . SP DEAD IN THERE 14

ACHE 2

WHAT MAKES LOVE SUCH AN ACHE AND
PAIN? . . . . SH LOVE AGAIN BLUS 14
LOVE SUCH AN ACHE AND PAIN? . . . . SH LOVE AGAIN BLUS 16

ACHIEVE 1

TO ACHIEVE . . . . SP BE-BOP BOYS 2

ACHING 2

ACHING EMPTINESS. . . . . WB SUMMER NIGHT 16
MY HEART IS ACHING . . . . SP RELIEF 1

ACID 1

AND A POISON ACID BURNS - . . . . . FW EXITS 3

ACORDARME 1

CUYO NOMBRE NO QUIERO ACORDARME. . .
. . . . ANS SONG OF SPAIN 28

ACQUIRED 1

KNOWLEDGE ACQUIRED BUT THROWN AWAY. JC THE BITTER RIVR 20

ACRES 1

BACK FROM THE ACRES OF CROSSES IN
FRANCE. . . . . NM COLORED SL POEM 15

ACROSS 22

BLOOD COUGHED ACROSS THE SKY. . . . WB CARIBBEAN SUNST 2
MA BABY LIVES ACROSS DE RIVER . . . DK WIDE RIVER 1
SHE LIVES ACROSS DE RIVER. . . . . DK WIDE RIVER 3
NO SHAME IS WRIT ACROSS ITS FACE - SL TOWN OF SCOTTSB 2
AND WHO ARE YOU THAT DRAWS YOUR VEIL
ACROSS THE STARS? . . . . ANS LET AMERICA BE 18
WHEN I COME ACROSS THAT WOMAN . . . SH BRIEF ENCOUNTER 5
SHE LOOKED ACROSS THE PLACE - . . . SH DEATH IN HARLEM 94
I CAN LOOK WAY ACROSS THE SEA . . . JC GOOD MORN STLIN 31
ACROSS THE SKY. . . . . FW THERE 4
ACROSS THE RAILROAD TRACKS - . . . OWT VISITORS 2

ACROSS THE FLOOR. . . . . SP END 6
SHIPS CAME FROM ACROSS THE SEA . . SP FREEDOM'S PLOW 29
ACROSS THE PLAINS OF AMERICA. . . . SP FREEDOM'S PLOW 60
ACROSS THE FIELD OF HISTORY. . . . SP FREEDOM'S PLOW 133
ACROSS THE MIDDLE OF MANHATTAN . . SP GOOD MORNING 6
DUSKY SASH ACROSS MANHATTAN . . . . SP GOOD MORNING 16
ACROSS . . . . SP HARLEM NIGHT SO 5
ARE SMEARED ACROSS . . . . SP JULIET 9
ON RELIEF WAY ACROSS THE SEA . . . SP RELIEF 3
THAT STRETCHES PADDLE-TAILED ACROSS
THE FLOOR. . . . . SP TO BE SOMEBODY 5
FILLMORE OUT IN FRISCO. 7TH ACROSS
THE BAY. . . . . AYM ASK YOUR MAMA 31
ALL ACROSS THE COUNTRY. EUROPE - . AYM HORN OF PLENTY 41

ACT 3
I DID NOT ACT LIKE . . . . SH BLD THE SINNER 11
HE STILL TRIES TO ACT IN THE SAME
OLD WAY. . . . . JC JIM CROW'S LAST 12
ACT ROUGH AND TOUGH. . . . . SP WARNING AUGMENT 6

ACTING 1
KEEP FEELING LIKE THIS I'M GONNA
START ACTING BAD. . . . . SH TWILIGHT REVERI 4

ACTION 1
AWAKENING TO ACTION. . . . . ANS A NEW SONG 2

ACTIONS 1
SO WHEN MY ACTIONS ARE STUPID . . . LHR ACCEPTANCE 3

ACTS 1
GRANDMA ACTS LIKE . . . . SP DIME 4

ADAM 2
WITH ADAM POWELL FOR CHAUFFEUR . . AYM RIDE. RED. RIDE 32
SEND FOR ADAM POWELL ON A
NON-SUBPOENA DAY. . . . . PL FINAL CALL 37

ADDED 1
ADDED TO DE TROUBLE THAT I GOT. . . SH LOVE AGAIN BLUS 6

ADDRESSED 1
GOD ADDRESSED ME A LETTER. . . . . SP PERSONAL 7

ADELE 1
ADELE RAMONA MICHAEL SERVE BAKOKO
TEA . . . . AYM BIRD IN ORBIT 20

ADOPTED 2
ONCE I ADOPTED . . . . SP MADAM CHARTY CH 1
THEN I ADOPTED . . . . SP MADAM CHARTY CH 5

ADVENTURE 1
HER GREAT ADVENTURE ENDED . . . . . SP S-SSS-SS-SH! 1

ADVENTURERS 1
ADVENTURERS AND BOOTY SEEKERS. . . SP FREEDOM'S PLOW 31

ADVENTURES 1
AS GREAT ADVENTURES SHOULD . . . . SP S-SSS-SS-SH! 2

ADVENTUROUS 2
IN INDENTURED HANDS AND ADVENTUROUS
HANDS. . . . . SP FREEDOM'S PLOW 51
INDENTURED HANDS. ADVENTUROUS HANDS. SP FREEDOM'S PLOW 62

ADVISER 1
DR. RUFUS CLEMENT HIS CHIEF ADVISER. PL CULTURAL EXCHNG 44

AEONS 1
THAT CHINA MADE AEONS AGO - . . . . PL BIRMINGHAM SUND 9

AFFAIR 1
PRIVATE AFFAIR? . . . . SP MADAM PHONE BIL 34

AFFORD 1
I CAN QUITE AFFORD TO BE: . . . . . PL NORTHERN LIBERL 12

AFRAID 8
AND WE'RE AFRAID. . . . . WB AFRAID 6
I AM AFRAID OF THIS CIVILIZATION - WB FOR PORTRAIT OF 3
DO NOT BE AFRAID OF LIGHT. . . . . DK SONG 3
WE ARE NOT AFRAID OF NIGHT. . . . . DK WALKERS WITH 3
SAY. AIN'T YOU AFRAID . . . . ANS PARK BENCH 8
WAS NOT AFRAID. . . . . JC BLD SAM SOLOMON 44
AND IS AFRAID TO PLAY . . . . FW MIGRATION 3
AND AFRAID. . . . . SP ONE-WAY TICKET 19

AFRICA 18
CRIED AMONG THE PALMS IN AFRICA . . WB AFRAID 3
FROM AFRICA TO GEORGIA . . . . . . NM BLACK CLWN POEM 57
FROM AFRICA TO CHINA. . . . . ANS CHANT TOM MOONY 18
OUT OF AFRICA . . . . JC ME AND MY SONG 8
AFRICA . . . . JC ME AND MY SONG 12
OUT OF AFRICA . . . . JC ME AND MY SONG 14
OF AFRICA . . . . JC ME AND MY SONG 24
OUT OF AFRICA . . . . JC ME AND MY SONG 32
AFRICA IMPRISONED . . . . FW MOTHERLAND 3
IS AFRICA. . . . . SP AFRO-AMER FRAG 3
IS AFRICA. . . . . SP AFRO-AMER FRAG 12
YOU FROM AFRICA. . . . . SP BROTHERS 5
TO CURE ILLS OF AFRICA. . . . . . . SP INTERNE AT PROV 13
BLACK LIKE THE DEPTHS OF MY AFRICA. SP NEGRO 3
ALL THE WAY FROM AFRICA TO GEORGIA SP NEGRO 11
BLACK LIKE THE DEPTHS OF MY AFRICA. SP NEGRO 19
DARK ONES OF AFRICA. . . . . SP SUN SONG 5
SUNRISE OUT OF AFRICA. . . . . . . PL JUNIOR ADDICT 36

AFRICA'S 3
AND TORN FROM BLACK AFRICA'S STRAND
I CAME . . . . ANS LET AMERICA BE 49
IS AFRICA'S . . . . SP AFRO-AMER FRAG 23
THREE HUNDRED YEARS AGO IN AFRICA'S
LAND. . . . . SP THE NEGRO MOTHE 8

AFTER 18
AFTER DE BOAT'S DONE GONE. . . . . FC A RUINED GAL 2
DAY AFTER DAY . . . . NM BLACK CLWN POEM 47
AFTER ALL THEM DOLLARS I GIVED HER
THESE LAST TWO YEARS. . . . . . NM BROKE 23
I SUFFER AFTER . . . . DK MINSTREL MAN 6
JUST ONE THING AFTER 'NOTHER . . . SH LOVE AGAIN BLUS 5
AFTER AWHILE. . . . . FW MIGRATION 10
STILL AFTER HOURS POURING DRINKS THE
LAW FORBIDS - . . . . OWT JUICE JOINT 38
O. DRUMS OF LIFE IN HARLEM AFTER
DARK! . . . . OWT NEGRO SERVANT 15
BUT AFTER I BEEN HERE AWHILE . . . OWT STRANGER IN TWN 15
AFTER DARK. . . . . SP DIVE 6
AFTER BITTER THRUST OF BEARING . . SP INTERNE AT PROV 28
AFTER REV. BUTLER . . . . SP MADAM MINISTER 30
HAVE TO WORK AFTER ALL. . . . . . . SP NECESSITY 12
AND THE DAY AFTER TOMORROW. . . . . SP NIGHT FOUR SONG 4
A MOVIE HOUSE IN HARLEM NAMED AFTER
LINCOLN. . . . . SP SHAME ON YOU 6
NOTHING AT ALL NAMED AFTER JOHN
BROWN. . . . . SP SHAME ON YOU 7
IN A TOWN NAMED AFTER STANLEY . . . AYM BLUES IN STEREO 21
AND THE SMELL OF RED CLAY AFTER RAIN PL DAYBREAK IN ALA 9

AFTERNOONS 2
ON SUNNY SUMMER SUNDAY AFTERNOONS IN
HARLEM . . . . SP PASSING 1
ON SUNNY SUNDAY AFTERNOONS . . . . SP PASSING 6

AGAIN 49
AGAIN. . . . . WB BLUES FANTASY 19
I WOULD BE SIMPLE AGAIN. . . . . . WB DISILLUSION 1
TO YOU AGAIN. . . . . WB DISILLUSION 15
SHALL I BE WISE AGAIN? . . . . . . WB THE JESTER 19
HIT ME AGAIN. . . . . FC BEALE ST. LOVE 6
I SEES YO' FACE AGAIN. . . . . . . FC BLD OF GIN MARY 8
PULLING HIMSELF TOGETHER. BOASTING
LOUDLY AGAIN. BUT REALIZING
WITHIN THE . . . . NM BIG-TIMER MOOD 11
AND AGAIN MONEY'S SHORT. . . . . . NM BIG-TIMER POEM 40
HUMOROUS DEFIANCE. MELANCHOLY JAZZ.
THEN DEFIANCE AGAIN FOLLOWED BY
LOUD . . . . NM BLACK CLWN MOOD 2
JOY. A BURST OF MUSIC. STRUTTING AND
DANCING. THEN SUDDEN SADNESS
AGAIN. . . . . NM BLACK CLWN MOOD 3
I RISE AGAIN - A BLACK CLOWN. . . . NM BLACK CLWN POEM 11
THEN SADNESS AGAIN - . . . . NM BLACK CLWN POEM 33
WILL KISS YOU AGAIN. . . . . DK PARISIAN BEGGAR 12
LET AMERICA BE AMERICA AGAIN. . . . ANS LET AMERICA BE 1
O. LET AMERICA BE AMERICA AGAIN - ANS LET AMERICA BE 52
MUST BRING BACK OUR MIGHTY DREAM
AGAIN. . . . . ANS LET AMERICA BE 69
WE MUST TAKE BACK OUR LAND AGAIN. ANS LET AMERICA BE 72
AND MAKE AMERICA AGAIN! . . . . . . ANS LET AMERICA BE 86
WILL I MAKE THEM AGAIN. AND YET
AGAIN? . . . . ANS SONG OF SPAIN 47
WILL I MAKE THEM AGAIN. AND YET
AGAIN? . . . . ANS SONG OF SPAIN 47
WORKERS. MAKE NO BOMBS AGAIN! . . . ANS SONG OF SPAIN 54
WORKERS. MINE NO GOLD AGAIN! . . . ANS SONG OF SPAIN 55
WORKERS. LIFT NO HAND AGAIN . . . . ANS SONG OF SPAIN 56
WORKERS. MAKE NO BOMBS AGAIN . . . ANS SONG OF SPAIN 63
I MUST NOT DO IT AGAIN. . . . . . . ANS SONG OF SPAIN 72
I MUST NOT DO IT AGAIN. . . . . . . ANS SONG OF SPAIN 74
I MUST NEVER DO THAT AGAIN. . . . . ANS SONG OF SPAIN 78
I MUST TAKE THE WORLD FOR MY OWN
AGAIN - . . . . ANS SONG OF SPAIN 81
BUT YOU GOT TO LOVE AGAIN. . . . . SH LOVE AGAIN BLUS 18
AGAIN MANKIND HAS LOST ITS COURSE. JC TO CAPTAIN MULZ 6
AND TYRANNY AGAIN IS BOLD. . . . . JC TO CAPTAIN MULZ 28
WE WILL NOT BE AGAIN. . . . . JC TO CAPTAIN MULZ 34
WHEN I COME AGAIN. . . . . FW FAITHFUL ONE 8
SHE WAS COMING BACK AGAIN. . . . . FW GIRL 8
BUT NOT AGAIN THE SAME. . . . . . . LHR DEAR LVLY DEATH 8
THE CHILD. COME BACK AGAIN. . . . . LHR PASTORAL 9
"LATE TO WORK AGAIN." . . . . SP FIRED 4
IS IT FOR REAL - OR JUST A SHOW
AGAIN? . . . . SP FREEDOM TRAIN 46

PUTS FORTH NEW LIFE AGAIN. . . . . SP IN TIME SILVER 3
NOW, I'M ALMOST BACK IN THE BARREL AGAIN. . . . . SP RELIEF 10
IT WILL AGAIN . . . . SP SUMMER EVENING 37
AGAIN. . . . . SP TROUBLED WOMAN 12
PREGNANT AGAIN! . . . . SP WHAT? SO SOON! 2
WALKS ONCE AGAIN. . . . . SP WHEN SUE WEARS 8
MELT TO WATER ONCE AGAIN . . . . . AYM ODE TO DINAH 36
AGAIN. . . . . PL LONG VIEW NEGRO 13
AND TERROR COME AGAIN . . . . PL MISSISSIPPI 6
AGAIN? . . . . PL MISSISSIPPI 8
COME AGAIN TO TOWN - . . . . PL OCTOBER 16 RAID 26

AGAINST 16
TWO AGAINST THE MOON . . . . WB TO MIDNIGHT NAN 15
I GUESS I KNOW WHAT I'M UP AGAINST. NM BIG-TIMER POEM 57
AGAINST THE . . . . DK LINCOLN MONUMNT 8
ITS COURT, TOO WEAK TO STAND AGAINST A MOB, ... SL TOWN OF SCOTTSB 3
AGAINST THE SUN! . . . . ANS A NEW SONG 54
WILL ALL RAISE THEIR HANDS AGAINST THE KIDS WHO DIE. . . . . ANS KIDS WHO DIE 29
RACE AGAINST RACE. . . . . ANS OPEN LETTER 29
AGAINST SPAIN. . . . . ANS SONG OF SPAIN 77
AGAINST THE WALL. . . . . FW DUSK 6
AGAINST THE WALL - . . . . FW DUSK 8
WORK WITH ME AND NOT AGAINST ME. SAY. . . . . SP DEFERRED 37
CLANG AGAINST THE TREES WENT THE AX IN MANY HANDS . . . . SP FREEDOM'S PLOW 55
AGAINST BLACK FENCES. . . . . SP MULATTO 15
ETCHED AGAINST THE SKY. . . . . . . SP SEASCAPE 4
COMMENT AGAINST LAMP POST . . . . . SP WHAT? SO SOON! 7
AGAINST MY FELLOW MAN . . . . PL ANGOLA QUESTION 12

AGE 2
NOW OLD AGE HAS . . . . SP LITTLE GRN TREE 7
AT TWENTY-TWO, MY AGE. BUT I GUESS I'M WHAT . . . . SP THEME FOR ENG B 17

AGENT 1
I'M JUST THE AGENT. . . . . SP MADAM RENT MAN 21

AGES 1
TURNED BROWN BY THE AGES. . . . . . SP WHEN SUE WEARS 3

AGE-LESS 2
ECHO THE AGE-LESS, AGE-LONG OLD DESPAIR . . . . OWT JUICE JOINT 27
THAT FILLS A WOMAN'S AGE-LESS, AGE-LONG PAIN - . . . . OWT JUICE JOINT 28

AGE-LONG 2
ECHO THE AGE-LESS, AGE-LONG OLD DESPAIR . . . . OWT JUICE JOINT 27
THAT FILLS A WOMAN'S AGE-LESS, AGE-LONG PAIN - . . . . OWT JUICE JOINT 28

AGING 1
PREMIER DOWNING AGING . . . . AYM SHADES OF PIG 3

AGIN' 1
SHE'D DO IT AGIN'! . . . . SP BLD OF THE GIRL 16

AGITATOR 1
"DISRUPTOR! AGITATOR! . . . . JC THE BITTER RIVR 47

AGO 21
AGO. . . . . FC SPORT 16
YEARS AGO AT THE NATION'S START . . NM DARK YOUTH USA 12
I BOUGHT TWO WEEKS AGO? . . . . . . SH BLD PAWNBROKER 10
A FEW YEARS AGO. . . . . JC BLD SAM SOLOMON 6
LONG AGO, LONG AGO - THE WHIP AND STEEL BARS - . . . . JC THE BITTER RIVR 37
LONG AGO, LONG AGO - THE WHIP AND STEEL BARS - . . . . JC THE BITTER RIVR 37
IT WAS A LONG TIME AGO. . . . . . . SP AS I GREW OLDER 1
EIGHTEEN YEARS AGO. . . . . SP DEFERRED 10
IT WAS A LONG TIME AGO. . . . . . . SP FREEDOM'S PLOW 100
BUT NOT SO LONG AGO AT THAT, LINCOLN SAID: . . . . SP FREEDOM'S PLOW 101
A LONG TIME AGO, BUT NOT TOO LONG AGO, ... SP FREEDOM'S PLOW 28
A LONG TIME AGO, BUT NOT TOO LONG AGO, ... SP FREEDOM'S PLOW 28
A LONG TIME AGO, ... SP FREEDOM'S PLOW 188
A LONG TIME AGO, BUT NOT TOO LONG AGO, A MAN SAID: . . . . SP FREEDOM'S PLOW 90
A LONG TIME AGO, BUT NOT TOO LONG AGO, A MAN SAID: . . . . SP FREEDOM'S PLOW 90
LONG AGO. . . . . SP MADAM MINISTER 12
BUT IT WAS A LONG TIME AGO . . . . SP MAMA AND DAUGHT 13
THREE HUNDRED YEARS AGO IN AFRICA'S LAND. . . . . SP THE NEGRO MOTHE 8
LONG AGO . . . . SP UNCLE TOM 9
LONG AGO. . . . . PL AMER HEARTBREAK 6
THAT CHINA MADE AEONS AGO - . . . . PL BIRMINGHAM SUND 9

AGREE 1
NEVER TO AGREE. . . . . LHR POET TO BIGOT 6

AGREES 1
SO WE AGREES! . . . . SP MADAM RENT MAN 30

AH 4
AH, WE SHOULD HAVE A LAND OF JOY, WB OUR LAND 13
AH, MY BELOVED ONE, AWAY! . . . . . WB OUR LAND 17
AH, ... WB POEM 2
AH, ... WB POEM 14

AHEAD 5
BOASTING, LIKE A CHEAP BULLY, BUT SUDDENLY LOOKING AHEAD: SHRUGGING HIS . . . . NM BIG-TIMER MOOD 5
I AM THE MAN WHO NEVER GOT AHEAD, ANS LET AMERICA BE 37
STILL AHEAD SOMEHOW. . . . . SP ISLAND 4
IF THESE WHITE FOLKS WANT TO GO AHEAD . . . . SP RELIEF 12
JUST GO AHEAD AND DIE. . . . . . . PL WITHOUT BENEFIT 13

AIDS 1
AIDS TRIUMPHANT ENTRY SQUALLING . . SP INTERNE AT PROV 27

AIME 1
ALIOUNE AIME SEDAR SIPS HIS NEGRITUDE. . . . . AYM BIRD IN ORBIT 23

AIMED 1
AIMED AT OZIE POWELL. . . . . ANS BLD OZZIE POWEL 16

AINT 1
BUT I AINT GOT NOTHIN' REAL . . . . NM BIG-TIMER POEM 47

AIN'T 172
SWEETIE, AIN'T I? . . . . WB CAT AND SAXOPHN 21
CAUSE I AIN'T GOT NO FRIEND. . . . FC A RUINED GAL 10
AIN'T NOTHIN' FOR A RUINED GAL . . FC A RUINED GAL 13
AIN'T CUT HIM WID NO RAZOR, ... FC BLACK GAL 3
AIN'T NEVER BEEN UNKIND. . . . . . FC BLACK GAL 4
YET I AIN'T NEVER BEEN NO BAD ONE. FC BLACK GAL 13
'LEVEN AIN'T FAR AWAY. . . . . . . FC CRAP GAME 4
WHEN YOU AIN'T GOT A DIME. . . . . FC DEATH DO DIRTY 4
HE AIN'T GOT A CHANCE. . . . . . . FC DEATH DO DIRTY 29
I AIN'T GONNA MISTREAT MA . . . . . FC EVIL WOMAN 1
AIN'T DE STYLE NOW DAYS. . . . . . FC EVIL WOMAN 12
AIN'T EVEN GOT A STALL. . . . . . . FC HARD LUCK 18
IF HER DADDY AIN'T WHITE . . . . . FC NEW CABARET GRL 3
IF HER DADDY AIN'T 'FAY . . . . . . FC NEW CABARET GRL 15
AIN'T NOTHIN' TO DO FOR YOU, NOHOW. FC RED SILK STOCK 5
IT AIN'T NOTHIN' BUT A HOVEL. . . . FC WORKIN' MAN 4
AIN'T NOTHIN' BUT A 'HORE. . . . . FC WORKIN' MAN 8
CAUSE SHE AIN'T DE RIGHT KIND. . . FC WORKIN' MAN 12
IT AIN'T SO DEEP: . . . . NM BIG-TIMER POEM 2
BUT - AIN'T MY LIFE MINE? . . . . . NM BIG-TIMER POEM 20
UP AND DOWN, AND THEY JUST AIN'T NO JOBS IN THIS MAN'S TOWN. . . . . NM BROKE 3
YOU ALL OUT THERE LAUGHIN', BUT THAT AIN'T NO JOKE - . . . . NM BROKE 10
SO I SAY, "MISTER, I AIN'T NO SWEEPIN' MACHINE." . . . . NM BROKE 16
LANDLADY 'LOWED TO ME LAST WEEK, "SAM, AIN'T YOU GOT NO MONEY?" . NM BROKE 19
I SAY, "NOW, BABY, YOU KNOW I AIN'T GOT NONE, HONEY." . . . . NM BROKE 20
WELL, AIN'T NEVER DONE IT, BUT FOR TO KEEP BODY AND SOUL . . . . . NM BROKE 29
WHAT I DON'T KNOW 'BOUT SHOVELIN' COAL, AIN'T NO MO' TO KNOW! . . NM BROKE 32
AND DE MAN COME TELLIN' ME THEY AIN'T HIRIN' NO MO' COLORED - JUST WHITE. . . . . NM BROKE 45
AND SHE COME TELLIN' ME, SHE AIN'T GOT NO MO' EVENINGS FREE! . . . NM BROKE 53
ALL THIS TALKIN' AIN'T NOTHIN' BUT TINKLIN' SYMBOLS AND SOUNDIN' BRASS: . . . . NM BROKE 58
(AIN'T SEEN HER IN SIX YEARS! USED TO GO WITH HER, TOO!) . . . . . NM BROKE 63
BUT I AIN'T GOT NOBODY . . . . . . DK DRESSED UP 11
MA LORD AIN'T NO STUCK-UP MAN. . . DK MA LORD 1
MA LORD, HE AIN'T PROUD. . . . . . DK MA LORD 2
MA LORD AIN'T NO STUCK-UP MAN. . . DK MA LORD 10
AN' I AIN'T GOT NO BOAT. . . . . . DK WIDE RIVER 2
I AIN'T GOT NO BOAT. . . . . DK WIDE RIVER 4
I AIN'T A GOOD SWIMMER . . . . . . DK WIDE RIVER 5
SAY, AIN'T YOU AFRAID . . . . ANS PARK BENCH 8
A HUMAN GETS LONESOME IF THERE AIN'T TWO. . . . . SH BED TIME 15
IT AIN'T STOLE. . . . . SH BLD PAWNBROKER 16
THERE AIN'T NO REASON . . . . SH BLD THE KILLER 21
YOU AIN'T GOT TO WAKE UP NO BODY BUT ME. . . . . SH DAYBREAK 5
DIXIE'S AIN'T NO PLACE FOR A GANG THAT'S SLOW. . . . . SH DEATH IN HARLEM 38

Line	Book	Poem	Line No.
AND A WOMAN CROSS THE TABLE WHEN A MAN AIN'T BROKE -	SH	DEATH IN HARLEM	54
AIN'T YOU SHAKE?	SH	DEATH IN HARLEM	76
(I KNOW IT AIN'T TODAY)	SH	EVIL MORNING	2
BUT I AIN'T GOT A MILLION,	SH	IF-ING	13
FACT IS, AIN'T GOT A DIME -	SH	IF-ING	14
MY LIFE AIN'T NOTHIN'	SH	LOVE AGAIN BLUS	1
I SAY MY LIFE AIN'T NOTHIN'	SH	LOVE AGAIN BLUS	3
AIN'T GONNA PAY A CENT ON THAT RADIO	SH	PAY DAY	7
AIN'T EVEN GONNA DREAM 'BOUT THE WOMENS I HAD.	SH	PAY DAY	18
AIN'T THAT TOO BAD?	SH	SUNDAY	14
I WOULD MAKE A FIRE BUT THERE AIN'T NO WOOD.	SH	SUPPER TIME	4
THAT PLACE WHERE YOUR TRUNK WAS, AIN'T NO TRUNK NO MORE.	SH	SUPPER TIME	8
ABOUT TWO KINDS O' PISTOLS THAT I AIN'T GOT.	SH	TWILIGHT REVERI	10
BUT I AIN'T GOT NO OWL HEAD AND YOU DONE LEFT TOWN	SH	TWILIGHT REVERI	13
AIN'T YOU GONNA STAND BY ME?	JC	BIG BUDDY	2
AIN'T YOU GONNA STAND BY ME?	JC	BIG BUDDY	4
AIN'T YOU GONNA STAND BY ME?	JC	BIG BUDDY	9
AIN'T DUE TO LAST.	JC	BLD SAM SOLOMON	16
AIN'T NO TELLING WHAT	JC	BLD SAM SOLOMON	27
BUT YOU AIN'T DEAD!	JC	GOOD MORN STLIN	4
BUT YOU AIN'T DEAD!	JC	GOOD MORN STLIN	40
YOU AIN'T DEAD!	JC	GOOD MORN STLIN	53
YOU AIN'T TELLING NOTHING BUT YOUR JIM CROW LIES -	JC	JIM CROW'S LAST	22
BUT SHE AIN'T JUST NOBODY	OWT	BLD MARGE POLIT	23
AIN'T NO MORE!	OWT	BLUES ON A BOX	8
I AIN'T GONNA	OWT	BOARDING HOUSE	11
WHITE FOLKS AIN'T FOR ME.	OWT	FLIGHT	6
GIRL, AIN'T YOU HEARD?	OWT	JITNEY	9
NO, MARTHA, I AIN'T HEARD.	OWT	JITNEY	10
CHILD, AIN'T YOU HEARD?	OWT	JITNEY	18
HONEY, AIN'T YOU HEARD?	OWT	JITNEY	47
BABY, AIN'T YOU HEARD?	OWT	JITNEY	52
CAUSE THERE AIN'T A GOOD MAN	OWT	REQUEST REQUIEM	7
CAUSE I AIN'T NOBODY'S BEAU.	OWT	STRANGER IN TWN	10
I AIN'T NOBODY'S BEAU.	OWT	STRANGER IN TWN	12
BUT I AIN'T GOT	OWT	TOO BLUE	14
THERE AIN'T NO WAY FOR ME	OWT	YESTERDAY TODAY	7
FOR WHICH THERE AIN'T NO HOPE.	SP	ARGUMENT	7
THERE AIN'T NO GOOD LEFT	SP	BAD LUCK CARD	5
AIN'T COMIN' FOR ME.	SP	BLACK MARIA	5
YOU AIN'T GONNA BE ABLE TO SAY A WORD	SP	BLD LANDLORD	19
AIN'T EVEN HEARD HER MURMUR.	SP	BLD OF THE GIRL	11
A POOR MAN AIN'T GOT	SP	BLD OF THE MAN	27
AND SHE AIN'T COME HOME YET.	SP	BLD THE GYPSY	15
THESE MISSISSIPPI TOWNS AIN'T	SP	BOUND NO'TH BLS	23
I AIN'T SENT!	SP	CHILDREN'S RYME	7
AIN'T FREE!	SP	CHILDREN'S RYME	16
AIN'T FOR US A-TALL!	SP	CHILDREN'S RYME	22
AIN'T GOT NO HEART NO MORE.	SP	CORA	2
THERE AIN'T NO STOVE -	SP	DEFERRED	19
I AIN'T NEVER	SP	DEFERRED	46
SHE AIN'T HEARD.	SP	DIME	5
CHILE, GRANNY AIN'T GOT NO DIME.	SP	DIME	6
AIN'T YOU HEARD	SP	DREAM BOOGIE	2
AIN'T YOU HEARD	SP	DREAM BOOGIE	11
I AIN'T GOT NO SUGAR, HATTIE.	SP	EARLY EVENING	7
AIN'T GOT NO SUGAR, I	SP	EARLY EVENING	9
YOU AIN'T GONNA HAVE NOTHIN TO SAY.	SP	EARLY EVENING	12
I AIN'T NO WISE WOMAN, HAMMOND.	SP	EARLY EVENING	13
AIN'T NO SENSE IN A GOOD WOMAN	SP	EARLY EVENING	15
JOB AIN'T NO GOOD THOUGH.	SP	ELEVATOR BOY	4
BUT I AIN'T NOBODY'S SISTER.	SP	EVENING SONG	7
BUT THERE AIN'T NO EAGLE	SP	FACT	3
I AIN'T BEEN GOOD,	SP	FIRE	4
I AIN'T BEEN CLEAN -	SP	FIRE	5
I HOPE THERE AIN'T NO JIM CROW ON THE FREEDOM TRAIN,	SP	FREEDOM TRAIN	11
'CAUSE FREEDOM AIN'T FREEDOM WHEN A MAN AIN'T FREE.	SP	FREEDOM TRAIN	34
'CAUSE FREEDOM AIN'T FREEDOM WHEN A MAN AIN'T FREE.	SP	FREEDOM TRAIN	34
BLACK MEN AND WHITE WILL SAY, AIN'T IT FINE?	SP	FREEDOM TRAIN	61
HE AIN'T GONE.	SP	GONE BOY	9
DADDY, AIN'T YOU HEARD?	SP	GOOD MORNING	28
AIN'T YOU HEARD?	SP	ISLAND	12
CAUSE YOU AIN'T DEAD.	SP	JUDGMENT DAY	9
SHE AIN'T GOT BOOGIE-WOOGIE	SP	LADY'S BOOGIE	3
AN' I AIN'T GOIN' THERE TO SWIM;	SP	LAMENT OVER LOV	8
AIN'T GOIN' THERE TO SWIM.	SP	LAMENT OVER LOV	10
MAYBE IT AIN'T RIGHT -	SP	LIVE LET LIVE	1
YOU AIN'T DEAD.	SP	MADAM FORT TELL	4
MADAM, YOU AIN'T WISE.	SP	MADAM FORT TELL	8
AIN'T HAD NO LUCK	SP	MADAM CHARTY CH	11
AND YOU AIN'T DONE A THING	SP	MADAM RENT MAN	13
AIN'T FREE.	SP	MADAM PHONE BIL	18
YOU AIN'T GONNA FIND IT	SP	MADAM FORT TELL	19
AIN'T GOIN' WITH YOU TODAY!	SP	MADAM WRONG VIS	20
AIN'T GONNA PLAY NO MORE	SP	MADAM NUMBER WR	22
I AIN'T PLEASED!	SP	MADAM RENT MAN	28
SO I AIN'T IN NO MOOD	SP	MADAM MINISTER	32
BUT I SURE AIN'T GONNA PAY!	SP	MADAM PHONE BIL	40
THAT AIN'T NO TIME TO GO.	SP	MIDWINTER BLUES	12
LIFE FOR ME AIN'T BEEN NO CRYSTAL STAIR.	SP	MOTHER TO SON	2
WHERE THERE AIN'T BEEN NO LIGHT.	SP	MOTHER TO SON	13
AND LIFE FOR ME AIN'T BEEN NO CRYSTAL STAIR.	SP	MOTHER TO SON	20
NAW, YOU AIN'T MY BROTHER.	SP	MULATTO	27
NIGGERS AIN'T MY BROTHER.	SP	MULATTO	28
NIGGERS AIN'T MY BROTHER.	SP	MULATTO	30
YOU AIN'T WHITE.	SP	MULATTO	38
AND AIN'T SEEN CHRIST YET,	SP	MYSTERY	2
AND YOUNGER THAN HE AIN'T.	SP	NEIGHBOR	8
HE AIN'T SMART.	SP	NEIGHBOR	11
NAW, HE AIN'T NEITHER.	SP	NEIGHBOR	13
AND THERE AIN'T NO KU KLUX	SP	NOT A MOVIE	14
I AIN'T GONNA	SP	NUMBERS	4
IT AIN'T FOREVER, GIMME!	SP	PREFERENCE	14
AND AIN'T THERE ANY JOY IN THIS TOWN?	SP	RUBY BROWN	15
LORD, AIN'T MINE!	SP	SAME IN BLUES	25
AIN'T WORTH A LITTLE BIT.	SP	SOUTHERN MAMMY	10
AIN'T WORTH A LITTLE BIT.	SP	SOUTHERN MAMMY	12
THAT COLORED BOY AIN'T SAID A THING	SP	SOUTHERN MAMMY	15
JUST AIN'T GOT NO HEART.	SP	SOUTHERN MAMMY	22
JUST AIN'T GOT NO HEART.	SP	SOUTHERN MAMMY	24
"AIN'T GOT NOBODY IN ALL THIS WORLD,	SP	THE WEARY BLUES	19
AIN'T GOT NOBODY BUT MA SELF.	SP	THE WEARY BLUES	20
I AIN'T HAPPY NO MO'	SP	THE WEARY BLUES	29
CAUSE THERE AIN'T NO SENSE	SP	WAKE	3
AIN'T NO PLACE	SP	WEST TEXAS	18
LIGHTS AIN'T COME ON YET.	SP	WONDER	2
AIN'T GOT NOBODY TO SHARE MY BED,	SP	50 - 50	2
AIN'T GOT NOBODY TO HOLD MY HAND -	SP	50 - 50	3
I AIN'T GOT NO MAN.	SP	50 - 50	5
YOU AIN'T GOT NO HEAD!	SP	50 - 50	8
AIN'T YOU GOT NO INFORMATION	AYM	BIRD IN ORBIT	82
(AND AIN'T NEVER HAD A BLACK HOUSE)	AYM	SHADES OF PIG	42
I AIN'T SENT!	PL	CHILDREN'S RYME	3
AIN'T FREE.	PL	CHILDREN'S RYME	10
AIN'T FOR US A-TALL!	PL	CHILDREN'S RYME	13
DEATH AIN'T	PL	DEATH YORKVILLE	19
I AIN'T NEVER SEEN NOBODY	PL	FLORIDA WORKERS	17
BUT THERE AIN'T NO BACK	PL	MERRY-GO-ROUND	12

AIR 24

Line	Book	Poem	Line No.
A SAD SONG IN DE AIR.	DK	HOMESICK BLUES	2
A SAD SONG IN DE AIR.	DK	HOMESICK BLUES	4
EQUALITY IS IN THE AIR WE BREATHE.	ANS	LET AMERICA BE	14
I CHAWED DE MORNIN' AIR.	SH	EVENIN' BLUES	8
CHAWED DE MORNIN' AIR.	SH	EVENIN' BLUES	10
I GOT EVENIN' AIR TO SPARE.	SH	EVENIN' BLUES	12
CAN'T SEND NO MESSAGES THROUGH THE AIR.	JC	GOOD MORN STLIN	50
AND AIR,	FW	HARLEM DANCE HA	6
WHILE BLUES AS MELLOW AS THE SOUTHERN AIR	OWT	JUICE JOINT	25
SHRUNKEN LIKE A BALLOON WITHOUT AIR,	SP	A BLACK PIERROT	13
AND THERE IS NO AIR	SP	DRUM	10
STOPPIN' IN THE COUNTRY IN THE WIDE-OPEN AIR	SP	FREEDOM TRAIN	53
THE SCENT OF PINE WOOD STINGS THE SOFT NIGHT AIR.	SP	MULATTO	18
SHARP PINE SCENT IN THE EVENING AIR.	SP	MULATTO	22
PINE WOOD SCENT IN THE EVENING AIR.	SP	MULATTO	40
WHEN THE AIR IS ONE INTERMINABLE BALL GAME	SP	PASSING	2
COLD BRASS IN WARM AIR.	SP	SONG BILLIE HOL	17
(BRUISED BODY HIGH IN AIR)	SP	SONG DARK GIRL	6
THE VERY ROOM IN WHICH TODAY THE AIR	PL	JUNIOR ADDICT	13
POLLUTES HIS STINKING AIR	PL	JUNIOR ADDICT	21
FOR AIR IS HIS GRAVE.	PL	LUMUMBA'S GRAVE	16
BUD IN SUNNY AIR	PL	SLUM DREAMS	3
ON AIR ALONE	PL	SLUM DREAMS	11
SULTRY AIR OF FEAR.	PL	SWEET WORDS RAC	8

AIRPLANES 1

Line	Book	Poem	Line No.
SEE THE AIRPLANES IN THE SKY?	SP	KID IN THE PARK	4

AISLE 1

Line	Book	Poem	Line No.
CARRIED LONELY UP THE AISLE	OWT	FUNERAL	1

AL 1

Line	Book	Poem	Line No.
KATHERINE DUNHAM AL AND LEON $ $ $ $ $	AYM	HORN OF PLENTY	6

ALABAMA 9

Line	Book	Poem	Line No.
DEEP IN ALABAMA EARTH	DK	ALABAMA EARTH	2
AND OUT OF ALABAMA EARTH	DK	ALABAMA EARTH	6
WHILE OVER ALABAMA EARTH	DK	ALABAMA EARTH	10
RED IS THE ALABAMA ROAD,	ANS	BLD OZZIE POWEL	1
AND RED IS THAT ALABAMA ROAD,	ANS	BLD OZZIE POWEL	29
TO TAKE AWAY TO ALABAMA.	SP	INTERNE AT PROV	6
OR ZIK TO ALABAMA	AYM	SHADES OF PIG	28
DAYBREAK IN ALABAMA	PL	DAYBREAK IN ALA	3
IN ALABAMA.	PL	DAYBREAK IN ALA	23

ALABAM' 3

Context	Poem	Line
TOOK HER TO ALABAM'.	SH ONLY WOMAN BLUS	20
FOR ALABAM'	SP CROON	2
(EVEN VOTE FOR REAL IN ALABAM')	PL GHOSTS OF 1619	8

ALAN 1

Context	Poem	Line
BY MOE ASCH OR ALAN LOMAX	AYM IS IT TRUE?	10

ALARM 2

Context	Poem	Line
ALARM CLOCK HERE RINGING SO DAMN LOUD	SH DAYBREAK	3
CAUSE THAT OLD ALARM CLOCK SHO HURTS MY EARS.	SH LETTER	19

ALBANS 3

Context	Poem	Line
TO MOVE OUT TO ST. ALBANS $ $ $ $ $ $ $ $	AYM HORN OF PLENTY	22
EVEN FARTHER THAN ST. ALBANS	AYM HORN OF PLENTY	31
LIVING IN ST. ALBANS	AYM HORN OF PLENTY	59

ALBERT 6

Context	Poem	Line
I TREATED ALBERT FINE.	FC BLACK GAL	2
I DRESSED UP ALBERT JOHNSON.	FC BLACK GAL	9
AN' I WANTS MA ALBERT BACK.	FC BLACK GAL	16
ALBERT!	SP BABY	1
HEY, ALBERT!	SP BABY	2
ALBERT, DON'T YOU PLAY IN DAT ROAD.	SP BABY	8

ALBERTA 10

Context	Poem	Line
ALBERTA K.	SP MADAM CENSUS	6
MADAM ALBERTA K.?	SP MADAM WRONG VIS	18
ALBERTA K.	SP MADAM CENSUS	18
YOU KNOW, ALBERTA,	SP MADAM HER MADAM	19
I SAID, YES - BUT ALBERTA	SP MADAM WRONG VIS	19
THAT ALBERTA K. JOHNSON	SP MADAM PHONE BIL	29
MADAM ALBERTA K.	SP MADAM'S PAST HI	2
ALBERTA K.	SP MADAM'S CALLING	10
ALBERTA K. JOHNSON -	SP MADAM'S CALLING	19
ALBERTA K. JOHNSON -	SP MADAM'S PAST HI	25

ALETHA 1

Context	Poem	Line
THERESA BELLE ALETHA	SP SUMMER EVENING	18

ALEXANDER 1

Context	Poem	Line
I QUIT ALEXANDER!	OWT JITNEY	46

ALEXANDER'S 1

Context	Poem	Line
ALEXANDER'S QUIT LUCY!	OWT JITNEY	51

ALHAMBRA 1

Context	Poem	Line
THE ROOSEVELT, RENAISSANCE, GEM, ALHAMBRA:	SP MOVIES	1

ALI 1

Context	Poem	Line
PLUS CASSIUS MOHAMMED ALI CLAY.	PL CROWNS GARLANDS	5

ALIKE 1

Context	Poem	Line
ALIKE WILL SHARE.	OWT BOARDING HOUSE	6

ALIOUNE 1

Context	Poem	Line
ALIOUNE AIME SEDAR SIPS HIS NEGRITUDE.	AYM BIRD IN ORBIT	23

ALIVE 9

Context	Poem	Line
ALIVE IN A MARBLE TOMB.	ANS BLDS OF LENIN	10
IF I WAS ALIVE	OWT FUNERAL	5
NOT EVEN MEMORIES ALIVE	SP AFRO-AMER FRAG	4
AND PRAISE HIM ALIVE.	SP BLD OF THE MAN	20
IF YOU'RE NOT ALIVE AND KICKING,	SP SHAME ON YOU	10
STILL ALIVE?	PL DEATH YORKVILLE	17
I STAY ALIVE.	PL MOTTO	4
IS ALIVE WITH GHOSTS TODAY,	PL OCTOBER 16 RAID	24
FOR THE DEAD BECOME ALIVE.	PL SPECIAL BULLTIN	2

ALIVENESS 3

Context	Poem	Line
DEAR DREAM OF UTTER ALIVENESS -	SP DEMAND	2
TELL ME, O QUICKLY! DREAM OF ALIVENESS,	SP DEMAND	4
TELL ME, O DREAM OF UTTER ALIVENESS -	SP DEMAND	6

ALL 229

Context	Poem	Line
ALL THE TOM-TOMS OF THE JUNGLES BEAT IN MY BLOOD,	WB FOR PORTRAIT OF	1
AND ALL THE WILD HOT MOONS OF THE JUNGLES SHINE IN MY SOUL.	WB FOR PORTRAIT OF	2
WHERE ALL PATHS GO?	WB HARLEM NIGHT CL	17
I WORK ALL DAY,	WB PIERROT	1
I WORK ALL DAY,	WB PIERROT	4
AND PIERROT THOUGHT ALL MAIDENS FAIR	WB PIERROT	19
AND ALL THREE COVERED WITH A SHEET OF PAIN.	WB SICK ROOM	6
THAT ALL MY SHINING BRILLIANTS	WB SONGS DARK VIRG	4
THAT ALL MY FOLDS	WB SONGS DARK VIRG	10
MEN TAKES ALL THEY CAN FROM ME	FC BLACK GAL	6
LOCKED ALL AROUND ME.	FC BLD OF GIN MARY	3
ALL MIXED UP WITH DIMES AND	FC BRASS SPITOONS	28
A CLEAN BRIGHT SPITOON ALL NEWLY POLISHED, -	FC BRASS SPITOONS	38
DON'T LAST ALL DE TIME.	FC CRAP GAME	8
DREAM-SINGERS ALL, -	FC LAUGHERS	19
STORY-TELLERS ALL, -	FC LAUGHERS	21
ALL YOU SWEET GIRLS.	FC LISTEN HERE	3
A LOOKIN' ALL SAD	FC NEW CABARET GRL	19
ALL NIGHT LONG.	FC SATURDAY NIGHT	24
AND THERE IS NO MUSIC AT ALL	FC SPORT	9
I WORKS ALL DAY	FC WORKIN' MAN	1
ALL DAY IN THE SUN	OLD THE CONSUMPTIVE	1
ALL NIGHT IN BED	OLD THE CONSUMPTIVE	5
TWO THINGS CAST OFF ALL SHAME.	OLD TWO THINGS	6
AND ALL THAT KIND O' THING.	NM BIG-TIMER POEM	24
CAUSE I'M ALL RIGHT.	NM BIG-TIMER POEM	50
OR THINKIN' AT ALL?	NM BIG-TIMER POEM	70
AND I GUESS THAT ONE'S ALL -	NM BIG-TIMER POEM	72
THAT'S ALL I AM!	NM BIG-TIMER POEM	76
THAT'S . . . ALL . . . I . . . AM.	NM BIG-TIMER POEM	77
ALL THE WORLD ROUND -	NM BLACK CLWN POEM	56
SAY TO ALL FOEMEN:	NM BLACK CLWN POEM	67
THAT ALL MIGHT UNDERSTAND:	NM BLACK CLWN POEM	76
YOU ALL OUT THERE LAUGHIN', BUT THAT AIN'T NO JOKE -	NM BROKE	10
AFTER ALL THEM DOLLARS I GIVED HER THESE LAST TWO YEARS.	NM BROKE	23
I SAID, "BABY, YOU KNOW I LOVES YOU, AND ALL LIKE THAT	NM BROKE	50
ALL THIS TALKIN' AIN'T NOTHIN' BUT TINKLIN' SYMBOLS AND SOUNDIN' BRASS:	NM BROKE	58
ALL THESE YEARS YOU SAY YOU BEEN WORKIN' HERE?	NM BROKE	68
IS I MARRIED? NO, ALL THESE-HERE GIRLS UP NORTH IS TOO LIGHT.	NM BROKE	70
DIDN'T HAVE ANY SCHOOLS; AND THERE WERE ALL SORTS OF	NM COLORED SL POEM	25
IN HIS SOLDIER'S UNIFORM, AND ALL.	NM COLORED SL POEM	38
AND IT'S A GOOD THING ALL THE BLACK BOYS LYING DEAD	NM COLORED SL POEM	51
SEEKING THE KNOWLEDGE THAT RIGHTS ALL WRONG -	NM DARK YOUTH USA	17
TO ALL THE WORLD THERE GOES	DK ALABAMA EARTH	7
I KNOW, FOR I HEARD, WHEN ALL WAS STILL,	DK DEATH SEAMAN	3
BRING ME ALL OF YOUR DREAMS,	DK DREAM KEEPER	1
BRING ME ALL OF YOUR	DK DREAM KEEPER	3
ALL THE DOORYARD BRIGHT AND CLEAR	DK IRISH WAKE	6
I BEEN BLUE ALL NIGHT LONG.	DK NIGHT AND MORN	12
LET ALL OTHERS KEEP SILENT A MOMENT.	ANS A NEW SONG	3
BOOTS ALL MUDDY WITH SOIL.	ANS BLDS OF LENIN	6
40-VOICES: GROW STRONG WITH UNION, ALL HANDS TOGETHER -	ANS CHANT MAY DAY	11
TO BEAUTIFY THIS HOUR, THIS SPRING, AND ALL THE SPRINGS TO COME	ANS CHANT MAY DAY	12
THAT ALL OVER THE EARTH TODAY	ANS CHANT TOM MOONY	12
50-VOICES: REACHING ALL THE WORLD.	ANS CHANT MAY DAY	18
WORKER: ALL WORKERS:	ANS CHANT MAY DAY	19
HE WON'T MATTER AT ALL.	ANS CHANT TOM MOONY	29
WORKER: PROLETARIANS OF ALL THE WORLD:	ANS CHANT MAY DAY	31
AND ALL OVER THE WORLD -	ANS CHANT TOM MOONY	42
ALL KINDS OF KIDS WILL DIE	ANS KIDS WHO DIE	16
WILL ALL RAISE THEIR HANDS AGAINST THE KIDS WHO DIE.	ANS KIDS WHO DIE	29
I AM THE NEGRO, SERVANT TO YOU ALL.	ANS LET AMERICA BE	33
FOR ALL THE DREAMS WE'VE DREAMED	ANS LET AMERICA BE	56
AND ALL THE SONGS WE'VE SUNG	ANS LET AMERICA BE	57
AND ALL THE HOPES WE'VE HELD	ANS LET AMERICA BE	58
AND ALL THE FLAGS WE'VE HUNG,	ANS LET AMERICA BE	59
ALL, ALL THE STRETCH OF THESE GREAT GREEN STATES -	ANS LET AMERICA BE	85
ALL, ALL THE STRETCH OF THESE GREAT GREEN STATES -	ANS LET AMERICA BE	85
ALL WORKERS,	ANS OPEN LETTER	33
WHO ARE ALL THEM PEOPLE	ANS SISTER JOHNSON	9
COME NOW, ALL YOU WHO ARE SINGERS,	ANS SONG OF SPAIN	1
BUT ALL THE WHOLE OPPRESSED	ANS UNION	3
IT TOOK ALL I HAD.	SH ANNOUNCEMENT	6
ALL DRESSED TO KILL -	SH BLD THE SINNER	18
ALL UNSUSPECTIN OF THE CHIPPIE ON HIS LEFT -	SH DEATH IN HARLEM	80
ALL THOSE SWEET COLORS	SH HARLEM SWEETIES	27
ALL THROUGH THE SPECTRUM	SH HARLEM SWEETIES	39
THEN WHIP 'EM ALL NIGHT LONG.	SH HEY-HEY BLUES	8
THEN WHIP 'EM ALL NIGHT LONG.	SH HEY-HEY BLUES	10
"THIS WEEK I NEED IT ALL."	SH PAY DAY	4
AND TAKE BACK ALL THEM THINGS WE HAD	SH PAY DAY	12
ALL DAY SUNDAY DIDN'T EVEN DRESS UP.	SH SUNDAY	1
BUT THE BOYS IS ALL MARRIED! PSHAW!	SH SUNDAY	13
AND SHOOT ALL KINDS O' SHELLS INTO YOU.	SH TWILIGHT REVERI	8
UNTIL WE ALL ARE FREE.	JC GOOD MORN STLIN	27
ALL OVER THE WORLD, WHO CARE.	JC GOOD MORN STLIN	45
DON'T KEEP 'EM ALL FOR YOU.	JC HOW ABOUT DIXIE	8
AND ALL BECAUSE OF	JC RED CROSS	3
AND ALL THE WATERS OF THE WORLD.	JC TO CAPTAIN MULZ	4

MANY BLOODS - YET ALL OF ONE BLOOD
STILL: JC TO CAPTAIN MULZ 48
WHAT IT WAS ALL ABOUT FW COMMUNION 2
WHAT IT WAS ALL ABOUT FW COMMUNION 4
BUT THEY ALL BRING REST. FW EXITS 4
THEY ALL BRING PEACE FW EXITS 5
THEY ALL BRING REST FW EXITS 8
NO ONE CARED AT ALL FW HEART 9
AND TO ALL FW OLD SAILOR 10
ALL THE SCUM FW PRAYER 5
IS ALL. FW THERE 6
ALL STAINED FW WHEN ARMIES PAS 7
SCATTERED ALL OVER THE SNOW. FW WHEN ARMIES PAS 13
UP ALL NIGHT! OWT BLD MARGE POLIT 51
WE'LL ALL BOARD THERE. OWT BOARDING HOUSE 4
SEE WHAT THIS WEEK'S JIVE IS ALL
ABOUT: OWT JITNEY 25
31ST! ALL OUT! OWT JITNEY 36
AND DAWN COMES DOWN THE STREET ALL
WANLY WHITE. OWT JUICE JOINT 4
LET YOUR SONGS HOLD ALL THE SUNNY
JOYS OWT JUICE JOINT 19
STRIKES UP A TUNE ALL GAY AND BRIGHT
AND GLAD OWT JUICE JOINT 43
AND CRIES. ALL CARELESS-LIKE FROM
REDDENED LIPS! OWT LINCOLN THEATRE 10
KNOWING ALL THINGS OWT MAN INTO MEN 16
ALL DAY SUBDUED. POLITE. OWT NEGRO SERVANT 1
YOU'VE WORKED ALL DAY. OWT NEGRO SERVANT 10
I WALKED ALL OVER THE ZOO AND THE
PARK. OWT STRANGER IN TWN 1
THAT TAKETH ALL THINGS UNDER WING - LHP DEAR LVLY DEATH 2
BUT ALL ONE SNARL OF SOULS. SP A HOUSE IN TAOS 40
ALL THROUGH THE FIRE. SP ANGELS WINGS 10
BUT I'D HATE TO DIE ALL ALONE! SP AS BEFITS A MAN 2
OUT OF ANY BOOK AT ALL. SP AUNTSUE'S STORI 20
AND ALL CONFUSED SP BEALE STREET 2
STOLE ALL SHE HAD. SP BLD FORTUNE TEL 24
A GIRL WITH ALL THAT RAISING. SP BLD OF THE GIRL 1
THE GUY SHE GAVE HER ALL TO SP BLD OF THE GIRL 5
GYPSY SETTIN' ALL ALONE. SP BLD THE GYPSY 2
AND TELL YOU ALL I CAN. SP BLD THE GYPSY 8
MAKES ME WORK ALL DAY SP BLUE BAYOU 8
HUH - FOR ALL." SP CHILDREN'S RYME 24
FOR ALL THE STUFF SP CONSIDER ME 31
WHEN I WALKED ALL BY MYSELF. SP CROSSING 2
MY FRIENDS WAS ALL AROUND ME SP CROSSING 3
I WALKED ALL BY MYSELF: SP CROSSING 20
COLD-WATER FLAT AND ALL THAT. SP DEFERRED 14
ALL I WANT IS SP DEFERRED 32
ALL I WANT IS TO SEE SP DEFERRED 34
ALL I WANT IS A WIFE WHO WILL SP DEFERRED 36
TO STAY HOME AT ALL. SP DELINQUENT 4
IT ALL THE TIME. SP DIME 8
BUT YOU WERE NOT THERE AT ALL! SP DREAM 14
IS NO ATOM AT ALL. SP DRUM 8
ALL THE CORNERS THAT ARE LEFT. SP FINAL CURVE 4
AWAKE ALL NIGHT WITH LOVING SP FIRED 1
AND DIG ALL PLAYS. SP FLATTED FIFTHS 19
BELONGING TO ALL THE HANDS WHO
BUILD. SP FREEDOM'S PLOW 27
SLAVE MEN AND SLAVE MASTERS. ALL NEW
- SP FREEDOM'S PLOW 33
BUT NOW WE KNOW HOW IT ALL CAME OUT. SP FREEDOM'S PLOW 136
ALL MEN ARE CREATED EQUAL. SP FREEDOM'S PLOW 168
ALL THESE HANDS MADE AMERICA. SP FREEDOM'S PLOW 69
TO ALL THE ENEMIES OF THESE GREAT
WORDS: SP FREEDOM'S PLOW 186
ALL MEN ARE CREATED EQUAL SP FREEDOM'S PLOW 91
FOR ALL AMERICA. FOR ALL THE WORLD. SP FREEDOM'S PLOW 197
FOR ALL AMERICA. FOR ALL THE WORLD. SP FREEDOM'S PLOW 197
UNTIL ALL RACES AND ALL PEOPLES KNOW
ITS SHADE. SP FREEDOM'S PLOW 199
UNTIL ALL RACES AND ALL PEOPLES KNOW
ITS SHADE. SP FREEDOM'S PLOW 199
OUT ALL NIGHT SP GONE BOY 3
BUT MOST OF ALL TO HARLEM SP GOOD MORNING 15
WHERE THE PEOPLE ALL ARE ICEBERGS SP GRADUATION 8
ALL HER CLOTHES WAS GONE: SP HOMECOMING 3
ALL OVER THE WORLD SP IN EXPLANATION 2
SO ALL OVER THE WORLD TODAY SP IN EXPLANATION 18
AND OVER ALL THE PLAIN SP IN TIME SILVER 6
AMONG ALL WHO STAND ON TWO FEET. SP INTERNE AT PROV 17
YOU GOT TO LOVE ALL THE TIME. SP LAMENT OVER LOV 18
HERE. WELL. THAT IS ALL SO I WILL
CLOSE. SP LETTER 9
SHOPS ALL OVER HARLEM SP LIKEWISE 10
ALL THE SCUM SP LITANY 5
HE WORKED ALL THE TIME. SP MADAM MIGHT-HAV 9
ALL I WANT IS YOU. SP MADAM MIGHT-HAV 18
THAT'S ALL VERY WELL - SP MADAM NUMBER WR 30
THE WIND HAS BLOWN ALL THE
CLOUD-GARMENTS SP MARCH MOON 3
LIKE THE PILLOWS OF ALL SWEET
DREAMS. SP MIDNIGHT DANCER 6
SNOW ALL OVER THE GROUND. SP MIDWINTER BLUES 2
SNOW ALL OVER THE GROUND - SP MIDWINTER BLUES 4
BUT ALL THE TIME SP MOTHER TO SON 8
HARLEM LAUGHING IN ALL THE WRONG
PLACES SP MOVIES 2
HER FEATURES IS ALL RUN TOGETHER SP NECESSITY 9
HAVE TO WORK AFTER ALL. SP NECESSITY 12
BOSOM TURN ALL GOLDEN IN THE SUNSET. SP NEGRO SPEAKS OF 10
ALL THE WAY FROM AFRICA TO GEORGIA SP NEGRO 11
ALL THEIR LIVES SP NEW YORKERS 8
WHEN IT WAS ALL OVER SP NIGHT FUNERAL 27
IT WAS ALL THEIR TEARS THAT MADE SP NIGHT FUNERAL 42
ALL THEM FACES SP NIGHTMARE BOOGE 7
AND ALL KINDS OF SWING MIKADOS SP NOTE COMM THEAT 10
ALL BY ITSELF. SP ONE 8
WHEN THE KIDS LOOK ALL NEW SP PASSING 7
TO YOU ALL THE TIME. SP PORTER 3
ALL MY DAYS SP PORTER 6
AND IT'S ALL YOUR'N. SP PREFERENCE 10
ALL I WANT IS YOU. SP SAME IN BLUES 16
NOTHING AT ALL NAMED AFTER JOHN
BROWN. SP SHAME ON YOU 7
IS ALL YOU KNOW. SP SNAIL 4
IS ALL YOU SEE. SP SNAIL 6
BUT WE ALL SHOULD BE FREE. SP SOUTHERN MAMMY 16
WE ALL SHOULD BE FREE. SP SOUTHERN MAMMY 18
SUN AND THE SONG OF ALL THE
SUN-STARS SP SUN SONG 3
AND ALL THE LITTLE DEVILS SP SUNDAY MORNING 9
ALL THE WOMENS IN TOWN SP SYLVESTER'S BED 3
ALL YOU DARK CHILDREN IN THE WORLD
OUT THERE. SP THE NEGRO MOTHE 35
"AIN'T GOT NOBODY IN ALL THIS WORLD. SP THE WEARY BLUES 19
TELL ALL MY MOURNERS SP WAKE 1
LOOK ALL SCRAGGLY AND BAD. SP WARNING AUGMENT 10
WON'T COVER IT ALL - SP WHAT? 4
I'M ALL ALONE IN THIS WORLD. SHE
SAID. SP 50 - 50 1
ALL THE TIME. SP 50 - 50 11
AND SMITTY HAS NOT CHANGED AT ALL. AYM BIRD IN ORBIT 22
ALL SOLD DOWN THE RIVER. AYM BIRD IN ORBIT 52
ALL ACROSS THE COUNTRY. EUROPE - AYM HORN OF PLENTY 41
LIVE ALL THAT WHILE IN PARIS AYM HORN OF PLENTY 53
WITH ALL DELIBERATE SPEED A AYM ODE TO DINAH 100
WHERE THE PEOPLE ALL ARE DARKER AYM ODE TO DINAH 121
TRIBAL NOW NO LONGER ONE FOR ALL AYM ODE TO DINAH 88
AND ALL FOR ONE NO LONGER AYM ODE TO DINAH 89
ALL THAT MUSIC. ALL THAT DANCING AYM SHOW FARE PLESE 12
ALL THAT MUSIC. ALL THAT DANCING AYM SHOW FARE PLESE 12
ALL YOU GOT TO OFFER PL BACKLASH BLUES 17
AND NEVER CAME BACK HOME AT ALL PL BIRMINGHAM SUND 3
BEFORE CHINA WAS EVER RED AT ALL PL BIRMINGHAM SUND 12
HUH! - FOR ALL? PL CHILDREN'S RYME 15
VOTED ALL THE DIXIECRATS PL CULTURAL EXCHNG 40
TO MAKE US ALL INTO PRINCES AND
PRINCESSES. PL FINAL CALL 7
TO ALL THE WORLD CRIED. PL FREDRK DOUGLASS 14
GHOSTS OF ALL TOO SOLID FLESH. PL GHOSTS OF 1619 1
ARE ALL ON YOUR SIDE. PL LAST PRINCE 7
BEEN SAVING ALL MY LIFE PL LITTLE SNG HOUS 2
OUR NEIGHBORS ALL COLORED ARE. PL LITTLE SNG HOUS 19
THE WHORES ALL POWDERED PL LUMUMBA'S GRAVE 3
LET ALL WHO WILL PL MILITANT 1
AND DIG ALL JIVE - PL MOTTO 2
OH. RUN. ALL WHO HAVE NOT PL SPECIAL BULLTIN 16
ALL DAY EVERYDAY. PL WORDS LIKE FREE 4

ALLEY 1
I WENT BACK IN THE ALLEY SP HOMECOMING 1

ALLIES 1
FOR YOU HAVE ALLIES EVERYWHERE. JC GOOD MORN STLIN 44

ALLY 2
THAT YOU'RE OUR ALLY JUST FOR TODAY. JC GOOD MORN STLIN 24
BUT AS FOR ME - YOU'RE MY ALLY JC GOOD MORN STLIN 26

ALL-REET 1
WHAT COULD POSSIBLY BE ALL-REET? SP DANCER 22

ALMOST 13
WALKING PROUDLY. ALMOST PRANCING.
BUT GRADUALLY SUBDUED TO A SLOW.
HEAVY NM BLACK CLWN MOOD 7
AN' ALMOST LOSE MA MIND. DK PO' BOY BLUES 18
EXCEPT THE DREAM THAT'S ALMOST DEAD
TODAY. ANS LET AMERICA BE 61
HAVE ALMOST FORGOTTEN THEIR NAMES SH YOUNG NEGRO GRL 4
I HAVE ALMOST FORGOTTEN MY DREAM. SP AS I GREW OLDER 2
ALMOST MADE ME BLIND. SP MORNING AFTER 6
NOW. I'M ALMOST BACK IN THE BARREL
AGAIN. SP RELIEF 10
ALMOST WITH THE SUN. SP S-SSS-SS-SH! 16
HAS ALMOST FORGOTTEN MEALIE. AYM ASK YOUR MAMA 58
DISTANT ALMOST NOW AS DISTANT AYM ODE TO DINAH 39
YES ALMOST FORGOT PL STOKELY MALCOLM 9
SMUG. ALMOST SECURE PL UN-AMERICAN 2
THAT ALMOST MAKE ME CRY. PL WORDS LIKE FREE 6

ALONE 24
BECAUSE WE ARE ALONE. WB AFRAID 4

FER I CAN'T STAY HERE ALONE. . . . FC GYPSY MAN 6
AND FIGHT IT OUT ALONE. . . . . . . NM BIG-TIMER POEM 56
WHO FOUGHT ALONE. . . . . SL SCOTTSBORO 11
HELPLESS, STUPID, SCATTERED, AND ALONE - AS NOW - . . . . ANS OPEN LETTER 28
NOT ME ALONE - . . . . ANS UNION 1
SHE WAS DRIVING ALONE, ... SH ANNOUNCEMENT 2
DON'T LEAVE ME HERE ALONE. . . . . SH MIDNIGHT CHIPPI 12
AND I WON'T NEED NO FURNITURE LIVING ALONE - . . . . SH PAY DAY 15
TO WHITE FOLKS ALONE. . . . . JC BLD SAM SOLOMON 12
BUT STOOD, INDIVIDUAL AND ALONE, . JC TO CAPTAIN MULZ 22
ALONE, I KNOW, NO ONE IS FREE. . . JC TO CAPTAIN MULZ 35
LET ME ALONE. . . . . LHR CONSERVATORY 4
BUT I'D HATE TO DIE ALL ALONE! . . SP AS BEFITS A MAN 2
GYPSY SETTIN' ALL ALONE. . . . . . SP BLD THE GYPSY 2
THUS THE DREAM BECOMES NOT ONE MAN'S DREAM ALONE. . . . . SP FREEDOM'S PLOW 22
NOT MY DREAM ALONE, BUT OUR DREAM. SP FREEDOM'S PLOW 24
NOT MY WORLD ALONE, ... SP FREEDOM'S PLOW 25
MY PHONE ALONE. . . . . SP MADAM PHONE BIL 13
FOR YOURSELF ALONE. . . . . SP MADAM MIGHT-HAV 28
NOR THE SWEET OF YOUR LIPS ALONE. SP TO ARTINA 8
I'M ALL ALONE IN THIS WORLD, SHE SAID. . . . . SP 50 - 50 1
WHERE NO SHADOW WALKS ALONE . . . . AYM ASK YOUR MAMA 75
ON AIR ALONE . . . . PL SLUM DREAMS 11

ALONG 3

A COMPLAINT TO B GIVEN BY A DEJECTED LOOKING FELLOW SHUFFLING ALONG . NM BROKE 1
I CAN'T GET ALONG WITH YOU, I CAN'T GET ALONG WITHOUT - . . . . . . SH LETTER 14
I CAN'T GET ALONG WITH YOU, I CAN'T GET ALONG WITHOUT - . . . . . . SH LETTER 14
SO I CAN ROLL ALONG. . . . . . . SH SIX-BITS BLUES 12
I GOT TO ROLL ALONG! . . . . SH SIX-BITS BLUES 13
ALONG. . . . . FW NIGHT SONG 7
TO COME ALONG AN' TALK. . . . . . SP BOUND NO'TH BLS 12
AND I'LL GET ALONG. . . . . SP MADAM'S PAST HI 22
IF THE WAR HADN'T COME ALONG . . . SP RELIEF 8

ALREADY 2

I'M ALREADY TWO YEARS LATE. . . . SP DEFERRED 2
ALREADY THERE WAS THREE - . . . . . AYM GOSPEL CHA-CHA 60

ALRIGHT 1

SHE WOULD BE ALRIGHT IF SHE WASN'T SO BOW-LEGGED, AND CROSS-EYED, . NM BROKE 64

ALSO 7

DESCENDED ALSO . . . . SP CONSIDER ME 50
ALSO LENOX AVENUE. . . . . SP COULD BE 14
THAT WHAT HE SAID WAS ALSO MEANT FOR THEM. . . . . SP FREEDOM'S PLOW 99
ALSO ILLS QUITE COMMON . . . . . . SP INTERNE AT PROV 16
BEAUTIFUL, ALSO, IS THE SUN. . . . SP MY PEOPLE 5
BEAUTIFUL, ALSO, ARE THE SOULS OF MY PEOPLE. . . . . SP MY PEOPLE 6
YOU ALSO TOOK MY SPIRITUALS AND GONE. . . . . SP NOTE COMM THEAT 8

ALTAR 4

YET AN ALTAR OF JEWELS. . . . . . . WB POEM 17
AN ALTAR OF SHIMMERING JEWELS, . . WB POEM 18
A CLEAN SPITOON ON THE ALTAR OF THE LORD. . . . . FC BRASS SPITOONS 37
(ANCIENT ALTAR OF THELONIOUS) . . . SP NEON SIGNS 5

ALTARS 1

AND WORN-OUT ALTARS STAND . . . . . ANS UNION 9

ALTER 1

RESTING NEAR THE ALTER WHERE . . . OWT FUNERAL 3

ALTHOUGH 4

ALTHOUGH I DO NOT KNOW, ... WB YOUNG BRIDE 2
ALTHOUGH RIGHT NOW, EVEN YET TODAY, JC JIM CROW'S LAST 11
ALTHOUGH YOU'RE OLDER - AND WHITE - SP THEME FOR ENG B 39
ALTHOUGH MINORITY, ... PL GHOSTS OF 1619 17

ALVIN 1

ARTHUR CARMEN ALVIN MARY $ $ $ $ $ $ $ $ . . . . AYM HORN OF PLENTY 7

ALWAYS 20

I'S ALWAYS BEEN A WORKIN' GIRL. . . FC BLACK GAL 1
YET IT SEEMS LIKE ALWAYS . . . . . FC BLACK GAL 5
ALWAYS IN SUNDAY SCHOOL. . . . . . FC LISTEN HERE 10
CERTAINLY, CHILE, I ALWAYS WAS CRAZY 'BOUT YOU! . . . . NM BROKE 74
AS ALWAYS. . . . . ANS KIDS WHO DIE 5
THEY ALWAYS TREAT ME MEAN. . . . . SP CORA 7
ME, I ALWAYS DID WANT TO STUDY FRENCH. . . . . SP DEFERRED 21
BEING ALWAYS . . . . SP ENNUI 3
SOME THERE WERE, AS ALWAYS, ... SP FREEDOM'S PLOW 132
THE PEOPLE DO NOT ALWAYS SAY THINGS OUT LOUD, ... SP FREEDOM'S PLOW 145
BUT THE WORD WAS THERE ALWAYS: . . SP FREEDOM'S PLOW 47
THE PEOPLE DO NOT ALWAYS UNDERSTAND EACH OTHER. . . . . SP FREEDOM'S PLOW 152
ALWAYS THE TRYING TO UNDERSTAND, . SP FREEDOM'S PLOW 154
YOU'RE ALWAYS GIVING . . . . SP MADAM MIGHT-HAV 15
ALWAYS COMING AROUND . . . . SP MADAM CHARTY CH 23
IT'S ALWAYS A STONE - . . . . SP MADAM MIGHT-HAV 26
THERE'S ALWAYS ROOM. . . . . SP TO BE SOMEBODY 21
IS ALWAYS FOUR YEARS . . . . AYM HORN OF PLENTY 30
ALWAYS TOOK THE OTHER SIDE.) . . . AYM RIDE, RED, RIDE 18
WHY DOWN SOUTH IS ALWAYS DOWN. . . PL VARI-COLORED 15

AM 81

I AM AFRAID OF THIS CIVILIZATION - WB FOR PORTRAIT OF 3
OH, I AM GOOD, ... WB PIERROT 21
YES, I AM GOOD, ... WB PIERROT 24
I AM THE BLACK JESTER. . . . . . . WB THE JESTER 15
WHO AM I? . . . . NM BIG-TIMER POEM 1
THAT'S ALL I AM! . . . . NM BIG-TIMER POEM 76
THAT'S . . . ALL . . . I . . . AM. NM BIG-TIMER POEM 77
I AM THE FOOL OF THE WHOLE WORLD. NM BLACK CLWN POEM 8
WORKER AND CLOWN AM I . . . . NM BLACK CLWN POEM 49
UH! I SHO AM TIRED. . . . . NM BROKE 1
YOU GOT A GOOD JOB? YES! WELL, I SHO AM GLAD TO SEE YOU, DEAR! . . . NM BROKE 69
AMERICAN AM I, NONE CAN DENY: . . . NM DARK YOUTH USA 6
I AM DARK YOUTH . . . . NM DARK YOUTH USA 8
AM I TOO OLD TO SEE THE FAIRIES DANCE? . . . . DK AFTR MNY SPRNGS 7
FOR I AM HAPPY WITH MY SEA. . . . DK DEATH SEAMAN 10
I AM IVAN, THE PEASANT, ... ANS BLDS OF LENIN 5
I AM CHICO, THE NEGRO, ... ANS BLDS OF LENIN 13
I AM CHANG FROM THE FOUNDRIES . . ANS BLDS OF LENIN 21
I AM THE POOR WHITE, FOOLED AND PUSHED APART, ... ANS LET AMERICA BE 19
I AM THE NEGRO BEARING SLAVERY'S SCARS. . . . . ANS LET AMERICA BE 20
I AM THE RED MAN DRIVEN FROM THE LAND. . . . . ANS LET AMERICA BE 21
I AM THE IMMIGRANT CLUTCHING THE HOPE I SEEK - . . . . ANS LET AMERICA BE 22
I AM THE YOUNG MAN, FULL OF STRENGTH AND HOPE, ... ANS LET AMERICA BE 25
I AM THE FARMER, BONDSMAN TO THE SOIL. . . . . ANS LET AMERICA BE 31
I AM THE WORKER SOLD TO THE MACHINE. ANS LET AMERICA BE 32
I AM THE NEGRO, SERVANT TO YOU ALL. ANS LET AMERICA BE 33
I AM THE PEOPLE, HUMBLE, HUNGRY, MEAN - . . . . ANS LET AMERICA BE 34
I AM THE MAN WHO NEVER GOT AHEAD, ANS LET AMERICA BE 37
I AM THE BLACK WORKER, ... ANS OPEN LETTER 12
HERE I AM WITH MY HEAD HELD HIGH! ANS SISTER JOHNSON 1
AS LONG AS I AM YOU . . . . JC GOOD MORN STLIN 42
THAT I AM HALF ASHAMED . . . . . . FW SNAKE 5
WHO AM NOBODY, ... FW THERE 8
ASK ME WHO AM I. . . . . OWT VISITORS 18
WHEN I AM DEAD AND GONE? . . . . . LHR TESTAMENT 2
I AM A BLACK PIERROT: . . . . SP A BLACK PIERROT 1
I AM A BLACK PIERROT: . . . . SP A BLACK PIERROT 5
I AM A BLACK PIERROT: . . . . SP A BLACK PIERROT 10
I AM BLACK. . . . . SP AS I GREW OLDER 18
YOU KNOW, AS OLD AS I AM, ... SP DEFERRED 45
I AM EVIL AND MAD. . . . . SP EARLY EVENING 14
DON'T TURN OUT LIKE I AM. . . . . SP EVENING SONG 12
OR AM I STILL A PORTER ON THE FREEDOM TRAIN? . . . . SP FREEDOM TRAIN 19
I AM THE DARKER BROTHER. . . . . . SP I, TOO 2
THEY'LL SEE HOW BEAUTIFUL I AM . . SP I, TOO 16
I, TOO, AM AMERICA. . . . . SP I, TOO 18
HE SAID, I AM INTERESTED . . . . . SP MADAM MINISTER 5
OR AM I MISTAKEN? . . . . SP MADAM MIGHT-HAV 14
JUST LIKE I AM! . . . . SP MADAM CENSUS 28
I SAID, NEITHER AM I. . . . . . . SP MADAM RENT MAN 29
LIKE I AM. . . . . SP ME AND THE MULE 8
I AM YOUR SON, WHITE MAN! . . . . . SP MULATTO 1
I AM YOUR SON, WHITE MAN! . . . . . SP MULATTO 43
I AM A NEGRO: . . . . SP NEGRO 1
I AM A NEGRO: . . . . SP NEGRO 17
I AM FED UP . . . . SP ONE-WAY TICKET 16
AND I AM GETTIN' TIRED! . . . . . . SP SOUTHERN MAMMY 4
I AM GETTIN' TIRED! . . . . SP SOUTHERN MAMMY 6
THAT I WHO AM THY SHEPHERD . . . . SP SUNDAY MORNING 41
I AM THE CHILD THEY STOLE FROM THE SAND . . . . SP THE NEGRO MOTHE 7
I AM THE DARK GIRL WHO CROSSED THE WIDE SEA . . . . SP THE NEGRO MOTHE 9
I AM THE WOMAN WHO WORKED IN THE FIELD . . . . SP THE NEGRO MOTHE 11
I AM THE ONE WHO LABORED AS A SLAVE, SP THE NEGRO MOTHE 13
AND I, WHO AM BLACK, WOULD LOVE HER SP THE SOUTH 18
AND I, WHO AM BLACK, ... SP THE SOUTH 20
I AM TWENTY-TWO, COLORED, BORN IN WINSTON-SALEM. . . . . SP THEME FOR ENG B 7
I AM THE ONLY COLORED STUDENT IN MY CLASS. . . . . SP THEME FOR ENG B 10

YET A PART OF ME, AS I AM A PART OF YOU. . . . SP THEME FOR ENG B 32
FROM NOBODY AND NOTHING TO WHERE I AM. . . . AYM HORN OF PLENTY 39
I AM THE AMERICAN HEARTBREAK - . . PL AMER HEARTBREAK 1
JUST WHO DO YOU THINK I AM? . . . PL BACKLASH BLUES 2
WHO DO YOU THINK I AM? . . . PL BACKLASH BLUES 4
I KNOW I AM . . . PL DINNER GUEST ME 1
AM I SUPPOSED TO BE GOD, . . . PL GO SLOW 11
AM I SUPPOSED TO FORGIVE . . . PL GO SLOW 15
WHAT I AM. . . . PL IMPASSE 4
HERE AM I! . . . PL LITTLE SNG HOUS 28
TO SHOW HOW LIBERAL I AM? . . . PL NORTHERN LIBERL 10
AM. . . . PL NORTHERN LIBERL 23
AND THAT I AM HONORED, TOO, . . . PL OFFICIAL NOTICE 9
BECAUSE I AM HERE - . . . PL WAR 20

AMBITION 2
IS MY AMBITION. . . . NM DARK YOUTH USA 21
AMBITION BATTERED AND BRUISED. . . JC THE BITTER RIVR 21

AMBULANCE 1
AN' SEEN DE AMBULANCE . . . FC DEATH DO DIRTY 27

AMEKA 1
AZIKIWE'S SON, AMEKA, . . . AYM ASK YOUR MAMA 65

AMEN 4
AMEN! HALLELUJAH! . . . SP MYSTERY 8
AMEN! . . . SP SUNDAY MORNING 43
AMEN IS NOT AN ENDING . . . AYM ODE TO DINAH 123
AMEN! . . . AYM SHADES OF PIG 45

AMENDMENT 1
DON'T TAKE THE FIFTH AMENDMENT. . . AYM RIDE, RED, RIDE 28

AMEN-CORNER 1
IN THE AMEN-CORNER OF THE . . . SP PRAYER MEETING 6

AMERICA 35
UNITED STATES OF AMERICA. MARTIAL MUSIC ON A PIANO, OR BY AN ORCHESTRA. . . . NM COLORED SL MOOD 3
THEY TOLD US AMERICA WOULD KNOW NO BLACK OR WHITE: . . . NM COLORED SL POEM 11
AND I'M STILL JUST A "NIGGER" IN AMERICA TONIGHT. . . . NM COLORED SL POEM 47
LET AMERICA BE AMERICA AGAIN. . . . ANS LET AMERICA BE 1
LET AMERICA BE AMERICA AGAIN. . . . ANS LET AMERICA BE 1
(AMERICA NEVER WAS AMERICA TO ME.) ANS LET AMERICA BE 5
(AMERICA NEVER WAS AMERICA TO ME.) ANS LET AMERICA BE 5
LET AMERICA BE THE DREAM THE DREAMERS DREAMED - . . . ANS LET AMERICA BE 6
(IT NEVER WAS AMERICA TO ME.) . . . ANS LET AMERICA BE 10
THAT'S MADE AMERICA THE LAND IT HAS BECOME. . . . ANS LET AMERICA BE 44
O, LET AMERICA BE AMERICA AGAIN - ANS LET AMERICA BE 62
O, LET AMERICA BE AMERICA AGAIN - ANS LET AMERICA BE 62
WHO MADE AMERICA, . . . ANS LET AMERICA BE 66
AMERICA! . . . ANS LET AMERICA BE 74
AMERICA NEVER WAS AMERICA TO ME, . ANS LET AMERICA BE 77
AMERICA NEVER WAS AMERICA TO ME, . ANS LET AMERICA BE 77
AMERICA WILL BE! . . . ANS LET AMERICA BE 79
AND MAKE AMERICA AGAIN! . . . ANS LET AMERICA BE 86
TO A NEW WORLD, AMERICA! . . . SP FREEDOM'S PLOW 34
AMERICA IS A DREAM. . . . SP FREEDOM'S PLOW 142
AND THE COTTON THAT CLOTHED AMERICA. SP FREEDOM'S PLOW 54
THAT HEWED AND SHAPED THE ROOFTOPS OF AMERICA. . . . SP FREEDOM'S PLOW 56
AMERICA! . . . SP FREEDOM'S PLOW 157
THAT MOVED AND TRANSPORTED AMERICA. SP FREEDOM'S PLOW 58
ACROSS THE PLAINS OF AMERICA. . . . SP FREEDOM'S PLOW 60
INTO THE WARP AND WOOF OF AMERICA: SP FREEDOM'S PLOW 167
THAT FED AND HOUSED AND MOVED AMERICA. . . . SP FREEDOM'S PLOW 67
ALL THESE HANDS MADE AMERICA. . . . SP FREEDOM'S PLOW 69
WHO OWNS THOSE WORDS? AMERICA! . . SP FREEDOM'S PLOW 175
WHO IS AMERICA? YOU, ME! . . . SP FREEDOM'S PLOW 176
WE ARE AMERICA! . . . SP FREEDOM'S PLOW 177
AND THE WAY TO BUILD AMERICA. . . . SP FREEDOM'S PLOW 84
FOR ALL AMERICA, FOR ALL THE WORLD. SP FREEDOM'S PLOW 197
I, TOO, SING AMERICA. . . . SP I, TOO 1
I, TOO, AM AMERICA. . . . SP I, TOO 18

AMERICAN 7
FOR THE AMERICAN MILLIONAIRES, . . FC JAZZ BAND 6
AMERICAN AM I, NONE CAN DENY: . . . NM DARK YOUTH USA 6
THE AMERICAN YOUTH OF TODAY. . . . NM DARK YOUTH USA 25
I SAID, USE AMERICAN. . . . SP MADAM'S CALLING 15
AMERICAN THAT'S ME. . . . SP MADAM'S CALLING 20
THAT'S AMERICAN. . . . SP THEME FOR ENG B 33
I AM THE AMERICAN HEARTBREAK - . . PL AMER HEARTBREAK 1

AMERICANS 1
WHO SAID THOSE THINGS? AMERICANS! SP FREEDOM'S PLOW 174

AMERICAN'S 1
AMERICAN'S BETTER. . . . SP MADAM'S CALLING 16

AMERICA'D 1
AND EVERYBODY IN AMERICA'D . . . SH IF-ING 11

AMERICA'S 1
IN AMERICA'S MAGIC LAND. . . . NM DARK YOUTH USA 5

AMONG 7
WE CRY AMONG THE SKYSCRAPERS . . . WB AFRAID 1
CRIED AMONG THE PALMS IN AFRICA . . WB AFRAID 3
AMONG THESE LIFE, LIBERTY . . . SP FREEDOM'S PLOW 94
AMONG ALL WHO STAND ON TWO FEET. . SP INTERNE AT PROV 17
WHO TIPS AMONG THE SHADOWS . . . AYM BIRD IN ORBIT 67
TIPS AMONG THE SHADOWS . . . AYM BIRD IN ORBIT 30
AS YET UNFELT AMONG MAGNOLIA TREES. PL BIRMINGHAM SUND 27

AMONGST 1
NOW AMONGST DECENT PEOPLE, . . . SP BLD OF THE GIRL 7

AMORPHOUS 1
AMORPHOUS JACK-O'-LANTERNS CAPER . PL CULTURAL EXCHNG 5

AMOUNT 3
AMOUNT OF TRAVELING . . . SP SAME IN BLUES 6
AMOUNT OF NOTHING . . . SP SAME IN BLUES 13
AMOUNT OF IMPOTENCE . . . SP SAME IN BLUES 20

AMPHITHEATRE 1
OF THE AMPHITHEATRE . . . SP INTERNE AT PROV 38

AMPLIFIER 1
LADDER, FLAG, AND AMPLIFIER . . . PL CORNER MEETING 1

AN 54
YET AN ALTAR OF JEWELS, . . . WB POEM 17
AN ALTAR OF SHIMMERING JEWELS, . . WB POEM 18
AN ENDLESS STREET . . . WB TO LITTLE LOVER 10
AN EMPTY CABARET . . . FC SPORT 11
AND ETERNITY AN UNBLOWN SAXOPHONE FC SPORT 12
SUIT AND HAT OF A CLOWN, TO THE MUSIC OF A PIANO, OR AN ORCHESTRA. . . . NM BLACK CLWN MOOD 1
IN AN OLD SUIT AND A BATTERED HAT, TO THE TUNE OF A SLOW DRAG STOMP NM BROKE 1
UNITED STATES OF AMERICA. MARTIAL MUSIC ON A PIANO, OR BY AN ORCHESTRA. . . . NM COLORED SL MOOD 3
AN ANCHOR ON HIS BREAST. . . . OK SAILOR 6
THE LAW'S A KLANSMAN WITH AN EVIL WILL, . . . ANS BLD OZZIE POWEL 11
THE DEVIL'S A KLEAGLE WITH AN EVIL WILL, . . . ANS BLD OZZIE POWEL 25
TO BELIEVE AN ANGELO HERNDON, OF EVER GET TOGETHER. . . . ANS KIDS WHO DIE 36
FOR AN OLD NIGHT-BIRD. . . . SH DEATH IN HARLEM 26
IN AN ERMINE CAPE . . . SH DEATH IN HARLEM 65
THOUGHT I HAD AN ANGEL-CHILE. . . . SH LOVE AGAIN BLUS 8
THOUGHT I HAD AN ANGEL-CHILE. . . . SH LOVE AGAIN BLUS 10
WHAT MAKES LOVE SUCH AN ACHE AND PAIN? . . . SH LOVE AGAIN BLUS 14
LOVE SUCH AN ACHE AND PAIN? . . . SH LOVE AGAIN BLUS 16
THERE WAS AN OLD CROW BY THE NAME OF JIM. . . . JC JIM CROW'S LAST 1
LOSER FROM AN EMPTY POCKET . . . JC THE BITTER RIVR 69
IT'S AN EARTH SONG - . . . FW EARTH SONG 1
FOR AN EARTH SONG. . . . FW EARTH SONG 3
AN EARTH SONG! . . . FW EARTH SONG 11
FOR AN EARTH SONG. . . . FW EARTH SONG 15
BUT AN AWFUL THING . . . LHR BLD MARY'S SON 4
AN INSTRUMENT . . . LHR CONSERVATORY 10
AN HOUR. . . . LHR POET TO BIGOT 13
AND I CROSSED AN ICY STREAM . . . SP CROSSING 10
A TIGER, A LION, AND AN OWL . . . SP DELINQUENT 11
OF AN UNKNOWN STRANGE PERFUME . . . SP DESIRE 6
RUNNIN' AN ELEVATOR . . . SP ELEVATOR BOY 2
THERE'S BEEN AN EAGLE ON A NICKEL, SP FACT 1
AN EAGLE ON A QUARTER, TOO. . . . SP FACT 2
AN ENSLAVED PEOPLE HEADING TOWARD FREEDOM . . . SP FREEDOM'S PLOW 189
LIKE AN OLD GRANDMOTHER, . . . SP FULFILMENT 17
CAN YOU LOVE AN EAGLE, . . . SP GENIUS CHILD 6
ON RED HEART BECOME AN ANVIL . . . SP MIGRANT 20
IN AN ENVELOPE MARKED: . . . SP PERSONAL 1
IN AN ENVELOPE MARKED: . . . SP PERSONAL 4
SEEKING AN ANSWER TO HER QUESTIONS. SP RUBY BROWN 20
WE SAW AN INDIAN MERCHANTMAN . . . SP SEASCAPE 7
AND A BLIND MAN PLAYS AN ACCORDION SP SUMMER EVENING 16
AN OLD NEGRO MINISTER CONCLUDES HIS SERMON IN HIS LOUDEST VOICE. . . SP SUNDAY MORNING 1
BY THE PALE DULL PALLOR OF AN OLD GAS LIGHT . . . SP THE WEARY BLUES 5
LIKE AN . . . SP TROUBLED WOMAN 6
HER FACE IS LIKE AN ANCIENT CAMEO SP WHEN SUE WEARS 2
WHERE AN ANCIENT RIVER FLOWS . . . AYM BLUES IN STEREO 14
AMEN IS NOT AN ENDING . . . AYM ODE TO DINAH 123
OR AN ANGEL WITH WINGS . . . PL GO SLOW 12
AND, LIKE AN ATOM BOMB, BURSTS APART. . . . PL JIM CROW CAR 4

AND SEEKS AN OUT IN OTHER WORLDLY DREAMS. . . . . PL JUNIOR ADDICT 3
WHO SEEKS AN OUT IN EYES THAT DROOP PL JUNIOR ADDICT 4
IN AN UNMARKED GRAVE. . . . . PL LUMUMBA'S GRAVE 14
WITH AN EDGE LIKE APARTHEID. . . . PL WHERE WHEN WHCH 6

ANCESTORS 1
AS OUR ANCESTORS . . . . WB AFRAID 2

ANCHOR 1
AN ANCHOR ON HIS BREAST. . . . . . DK SAILOR 6

ANCIENT 8
TANGLED IN THAT ANCIENT ENDLESS CHAIN . . . . ANS LET AMERICA BE 26
THIS ANCIENT HAG . . . . SP MEXICAN MARKET 1
I'VE KNOWN RIVERS ANCIENT AS THE WORLD AND OLDER THAN THE . . . . SP NEGRO SPEAKS OF 2
ANCIENT, DUSKY RIVERS. . . . . . . SP NEGRO SPEAKS OF 12
(ANCIENT ALTAR OF THELONIOUS) . . . SP NEON SIGNS 5
HER FACE IS LIKE AN ANCIENT CAMEO SP WHEN SUE WEARS 2
WHERE AN ANCIENT RIVER FLOWS . . . AYM BLUES IN STEREO 14
FROM ANCIENT EVENINGS) . . . . . . PL LENOX AVE. BAR 9

ANDERSON 2
MARION ANDERSON SAID TO THE DAR. . JC JIM CROW'S LAST 17
SAMMY DAVIS AND MARIAN ANDERSON . . SP PROJECTION 16

ANEW 2
ANEW - AND GOOD. . . . . SP S-SSS-SS-SH! 4
WERE PLED ANEW AT SOME HEROIC BAR. PL MOTHER IN WAR 4

ANGEL 2
THE ANGEL OF MERCY'S . . . . JC RED CROSS 1
OR AN ANGEL WITH WINGS . . . . . . PL GO SLOW 12

ANGELES 2
FROM LOS ANGELES TO LONDON . . . . JC BLACK MAN SPEAK 15
TO LOS ANGELES, BAKERSFIELD, . . . SP ONE-WAY TICKET 11

ANGELO 1
TO BELIEVE AN ANGELO HERNDON, OR EVER GET TOGETHER. . . . . ANS KIDS WHO DIE 36

ANGELS 3
THE ANGELS WINGS IS WHITE AS SNOW, SP ANGELS WINGS 1
THE ANGELS WINGS IS WHITE AS SNOW, SP ANGELS WINGS 6
BUT THE ANGELS WINGS IS WHITE AS SNOW. . . . . SP ANGELS WINGS 11

ANGEL-CHILE 2
THOUGHT I HAD AN ANGEL-CHILE. . . . SH LOVE AGAIN BLUS 8
THOUGHT I HAD AN ANGEL-CHILE. . . . SH LOVE AGAIN BLUS 10

ANGRILY 1
THE MUSIC, OVER-BURDENED, BACKING AWAY ANGRILY, FRANTIC WITH HUMILIATION . . . . NM BLACK CLWN MOOD 10

ANGRY 1
AND BOWING HIS HEAD IN SHAME, BECOMES SUDDENLY FIERCE AND ANGRY, THEN HE . . . . NM COLORED SL MOOD 11

ANIMALS 1
ANIMALS . . . . SP HEAVEN 5

ANKLES 1
DONE BROKE MY ANKLES DOWN. . . . . PL DOWN WHERE I AM 7

ANNIHILATE 1
TO ANNIHILATE THY BODY. . . . . . . WB SONGS DARK VIRG 18

ANOTHER 19
ANOTHER WHITE OF FACE. . . . . . . ANS OPEN LETTER 31
SHE HAD ANOTHER JOKER . . . . SH ANNOUNCEMENT 11
IS ANOTHER DESIRE. . . . . SH ASPIRATION 6
PICKED UP ANOTHER WOMAN AND . . . . SH DEATH IN HARLEM 141
THEY LOVED ONE ANOTHER TILL . . . . SH DEATH IN HARLEM 39
OR JUST ANOTHER . . . . FW SAILING DATE 16
THERE'S MANY ANOTHER WOMAN . . . . OWT HONEY BABE 13
ANOTHER PADDY. . . . . SP DEAD IN THERE 9
TOMORROW IS ANOTHER DAY. . . . . . SP DEMOCRACY 12
TO GOVERN ANOTHER MAN . . . . SP FREEDOM'S PLOW 103
TO GOVERN ANOTHER MAN . . . . SP FREEDOM'S PLOW 170
AND FIGHT ANOTHER WAR. . . . . . . SP RELIEF 13
AND IN ANOTHER WEEK . . . . SP SUMMER EVENING 32
NOTHING BUT ANOTHER SHADOW . . . . AYM HORN OF PLENTY 43
FROM ANOTHER DISTANT QUARTER . . . AYM ODE TO DINAH 17
SAVE FOR ANOTHER DAY. . . . . PL BOMBINGS DIXIE 4
TOMORROW IS ANOTHER DAY. . . . . . PL FREEDOM 12
SAYS SUGAR'S GONE UP ANOTHER TWO CENTS. . . . . PL HARLEM 9
LOOK SLOW AT ONE ANOTHER - . . . . PL OCTOBER 16 RAID 12

ANSWER 8
FOR WHAT COULD I ANSWER HIM, EXCEPT, "IT'S A LIE!" . . . . NM COLORED SL POEM 43
TO ANSWER ITS CALL. . . . . SP DRUM 5
BUT IN HARLEM THEY DON'T ANSWER BACK. . . . . SP LIKEWISE 14
I HAVE GIVEN MY ANSWER. . . . . . . SP PERSONAL 6
SEEKING AN ANSWER TO HER QUESTIONS. SP RUBY BROWN 20
ANSWER QUESTIONS ANSWER . . . . . . AYM SHADES OF PIG 22
ANSWER QUESTIONS ANSWER . . . . . . AYM SHADES OF PIG 22
IS THE ANSWER TO THE CHILD. . . . . AYM SHOW FARE PLESE 19

ANSWERED 2
SAM SOLOMON ANSWERED. . . . . JC BLD SAM SOLOMON 29
SHE ANSWERED, BABE, WHAT MUST I DO? SP 50 - 50 12

ANSWERING 1
ANSWERING THE USUAL QUESTIONS . . . PL DINNER GUEST ME 4

ANSWERIN' 1
ANSWERIN' THEM WANT-ADS' NOT NARY BIT O' FUN. . . . . NM BROKE 4

ANSWERS 2
STONE ANSWERS BACK. . . . . SP HEAVEN 11
AND ANSWERS WITH A QUESTION . . . . AYM SHADES OF PIG 23

ANTENNA 1
BUT I GOT TO GET A NEW ANTENNA, LORD - . . . . AYM BLUES IN STEREO 36

ANTI-POVERTY 1
SEND FOR ROBIN HOOD TO CLINCH THE ANTI-POVERTY . . . . PL FINAL CALL 3

ANVIL 1
ON RED HEART BECOME AN ANVIL . . . SP MIGRANT 20

ANY 19
ANY OLD TIME . . . . FC DEATH DO DIRTY 2
GOOD GAL ANY MORE. . . . . FC EVIL WOMAN 2
AND ONE OLD FUNNY BOY SAID, "I'LL WORK AT ANY PRICE . . . . NM BROKE 8
DIDN'T HAVE ANY SCHOOLS; AND THERE WERE ALL SORTS OF . . . . NM COLORED SL POEM 25
SO NOW I KNOW WE BLACKS ARE JUST LIKE ANY OTHER - . . . . NM COLORED SL POEM 35
I CANNOT FIND THEM ANY MORE. . . . DK AFTR MNY SPRNGS 8
THAT ANY MAN BE CRUSHED BY ONE ABOVE. . . . . ANS LET AMERICA BE 9
SURE, CALL ME ANY UGLY NAME YOU CHOOSE - . . . . ANS LET AMERICA BE 70
ANY OLD THING TO EAT. . . . . SH BRIEF ENCOUNTER 2
LOOKIN' FOR ANY OLD THING TO EAT - SH BRIEF ENCOUNTER 4
ON STATE STREET ANY DAY. . . . . . SH MIDNIGHT CHIPPI 18
MAKE YOU WALK LIKE A GHOST IF YOU BOTHER ME ANY MORE. . . . . SH TWILIGHT REVERI 6
OUT OF ANY BOOK AT ALL. . . . . . . SP AUNTSUE'S STORI 20
ANY PLACE IS DREARY . . . . SP COULD BE 15
ANY PLACE THAT IS . . . . SP ONE-WAY TICKET 6
ANY PLACE THAT IS . . . . SP ONE-WAY TICKET 13
AND AIN'T THERE ANY JOY IN THIS TOWN? . . . . SP RUBY BROWN 15
HER NAME ANY MORE. . . . . SP RUBY BROWN 22
ANY BETTER THAN WHITE. . . . . . . SP SHAME ON YOU 9

ANYBODY 2
IF THERE'S ANYBODY ON THIS EARTH, JUDGE. . . . . SH BRIEF ENCOUNTER 11
ANYBODY . . . . SP DESERT 1

ANYBODY'S 1
IF I WAS ANYBODY'S SISTER. . . . . SP EVENING SONG 5

ANYHOW 6
ANYHOW, AWAY OFF THERE. . . . . . . JC GOOD MORN STLIN 52
BUT IS TRUE ANYHOW: . . . . SP IN EXPLANATION 34
TRUE ANYHOW NO MATTER HOW MANY . . SP IN EXPLANATION 38
BUT I'M ASKING ANYHOW. . . . . . . AYM BLUES IN STEREO 31
GONNA LOVE YOU ANYHOW . . . . AYM ODE TO DINAH 67
SACKCLOTH AND ASHES, ANYHOW. . . . PL BOMBINGS DIXIE 3

ANYMORE 1
ANYMORE. . . . . PL SWEET WORDS RAC 15

ANYONE 2
AND WOMEN, TOO, WHOM ANYONE MAY MEET OWT JUICE JOINT 35
ELSE IT HAD NO MEANING FOR ANYONE. SP FREEDOM'S PLOW 108

ANYTHING 5
ANYTHING HE WANTS OUT OF IT. . . . SP BUDDY 10
MO'N ANYTHING ELSE CAN. . . . . . . SP LAMENT OVER LOV 6
I HAD ANYTHING FREE. . . . . SP MADAM MIGHT-HAV 12
ANYTHING BUT A SLAVE! HE SAID. . . PL FREDRK DOUGLASS 17
I'D BELIEVE IN ANYTHING . . . . . . PL KU KLUX 7

ANYWAY 1
WELL, ANYWAY, IT DON'T HAVE TO BE A MARRIED MAN. . . . . SP SISTER 12

ANYWHERE 5

Context	Poem	Line
BLACK BOYS COULDN'T WORK THEN ANYWHERE LIKE THEY CAN	NM COLORED SL POEM	19
DID HE GET ANYWHERE? NO!	SP DANCER	23
ANYWHERE.	SP DELINQUENT	17
DON'T GET ANYWHERE.	SP HIGH TO LOW	7
ANYWHERE.	SP KID IN THE PARK	13

ANZIO 2

Context	Poem	Line
HER GRANDSON'S NAME WAS JIMMY. HE DIED AT ANZIO.	SP FREEDOM TRAIN	43
THEN MAYBE FROM THEIR GRAVES IN ANZIO	SP FREEDOM TRAIN	59

AN' 86

Context	Poem	Line
BUT JUMP OVERBOARD AN' DROWN. . . .	FC A RUINED GAL	14
I BEATS MA WIFE AN'	FC BAD MAN	7
BEATS MA WIFE AN'	FC BAD MAN	9
I'M GOIN' TO DE DEVIL AN'	FC BAD MAN	17
THEN THEY GOES AN' FINDS A YALLER GAL	FC BLACK GAL	7
AN' LETS ME BE.	FC BLACK GAL	8
AN' SOON AS HE GOT OUT DE BARREL .	FC BLACK GAL	11
AN' I WANTS MA ALBERT BACK.	FC BLACK GAL	16
AN' IF I CRAPS.	FC CRAP GAME	5
AN' HAD CUT HIS GAL	FC DEATH DO DIRTY	8
AN' SHOT A MAN IN DE BACK.	FC DEATH DO DIRTY	9
AN' A STEW O' MEAT.	FC DEATH DO DIRTY	14
AN' WHEN DE COPS GOT ME	FC DEATH DO DIRTY	16
AN' PUT ME IN JAIL	FC DEATH DO DIRTY	17
AN' SAYS YO' BOY IS GETTIN' BEAT.	FC DEATH DO DIRTY	24
AN' SEEN DE AMBULANCE	FC DEATH DO DIRTY	27
AN' DE ONES THAT KILT HIM. - . . .	FC DEATH DO DIRTY	31
SHE FIGHTS AN' QUARRELS MOST . . .	FC EVIL WOMAN	7
AN' SHE'S GOIN' ON BACK	FC EVIL WOMAN	14
STARTED IN TO MOAN AN' CRY.	FC GAL'S CRY DYING	6
BLACK AN' UGLY	FC GAL'S CRY DYING	13
I'M BLACK AN' UGLY	FC GAL'S CRY DYING	15
AN' SELL 'EM TO DE JEW.	FC HARD LUCK	6
GIVES YOU A DOLLAR AN' A HALF. . .	FC HARD LUCK	8
GIVES YOU A DOLLAR AN' A HALF. . .	FC HARD LUCK	10
GIN AN' WHISKEY	FC LISTEN HERE	5
HE'S GOT THOSE 'LECTRIC-SHOCKIN' EYES AN'	FC MA MAN	5
AN' BETTER. BETTER. BETTER WHEN HE'S DRUNK.	FC MA MAN	12
COME AN' EAGLE-ROCK WITH ME. . . .	FC MA MAN	16
THAT'S WHERE MA MAN AN' ME GO. . .	FC MINNIE SINGS	2
AN' OUR TROUBLES AT DE DOOR. . . .	FC MINNIE SINGS	6
MA MAN AN' ME DANCE.	FC MINNIE SINGS	8
AN' DIG ME A GRAVE THIS VERY DAY.	FC MINNIE SINGS	17
AN' SHE DON'T LIKE CORN.	FC NEW CABARET GRL	6
AN' SHE SAY. HONEY.	FC NEW CABARET GRL	9
AN' THERE SHE SETS A CRYIN'	FC NEW CABARET GRL	17
GO OUT AN' LET DE WHITE BOYS . . .	FC RED SILK STOCK	3
AN' TOMORROW'S CHILE'LL	FC RED SILK STOCK	9
GO OUT AN' LET DE WHITE BOYS . . .	FC RED SILK STOCK	11
AN' SADIE IS A WHORE.	FC SATURDAY NIGHT	4
AN' A GLASS O' GIN:	FC SATURDAY NIGHT	6
AN' DIAMOND RING.	FC SATURDAY NIGHT	10
AN' YOU'S A LONG TIME	FC SATURDAY NIGHT	17
SHAKE 'EM UP AN' SHAKE 'EM UP . . .	FC SATURDAY NIGHT	23
AN' A PO'. PO' GAL CAN SLEEP. . . .	FC SUICIDE	18
WID A PICK AN' A SHOVEL.	FC WORKIN' MAN	2
AN' I TREATS HER FINE.	FC WORKIN' MAN	10
AN' I SHO PAYS DOUBLE	FC WORKIN' MAN	14
AN' GITS NOTHIN' BUT TROUBLE. . . .	FC WORKIN' MAN	16
I OPENS MA MOUTH AN' LAUGHS. . . .	DK HOMESICK BLUES	18
AN' BE MA FRIEND THROUGH ETERNITY."	DK MA LORD	16
"ME AN' MA BABY'S	DK NEGRO DANCERS	1
"ME AN' MA BABY'S	DK NEGRO DANCERS	13
AN' DE ROAD IS HARD AN' LONG. . . .	DK PO' BOY BLUES	12
AN' DE ROAD IS HARD AN' LONG. . . .	DK PO' BOY BLUES	12
AN' ALMOST LOSE MA MIND.	DK PO' BOY BLUES	18
AN' I AIN'T GOT NO BOAT.	DK WIDE RIVER	2
AN' I DON'T KNOW HOW TO FLOAT. . .	DK WIDE RIVER	6
'TWIXT MA LOVE AN' ME.	DK WIDE RIVER	8
'TWIXT MA LOVE AN' ME.	DK WIDE RIVER	10
AN' GIT TO MA BABY SOMEHOW.	DK WIDE RIVER	14
I'LL LAY DOWN AN' DIE RIGHT NOW. .	DK WIDE RIVER	18
AN' YOU DIE.	SP BABY	7
WALK . . . AN' WALK . . . AN' WALK.	SP BOUND NO'TH BLS	10
WALK . . . AN' WALK . . . AN' WALK.	SP BOUND NO'TH BLS	10
TO COME ALONG AN' TALK.	SP BOUND NO'TH BLS	12
HATES TO BE LONELY AN' SAD.	SP BOUND NO'TH BLS	16
GONNA SHUT AN' LOCK MY DOOR	SP CORA	4
AN' I NEED A DIME FO' BEER.	SP DOWN AND OUT	10
TWO NEW SUITS AN'	SP ELEVATOR BOY	12
GOIN' UP AN' DOWN.	SP ELEVATOR BOY	16
UP AN' DOWN.	SP ELEVATOR BOY	17
GOT TO MOAN AN' GRIEVE?	SP FIRE	13
I'D FLY ON MA MAN AN'	SP HARD DADDY	17
WENT FLYIN' TO THE STARS AN' MOON	SP JUDGMENT DAY	3
AN' NOW I'M SETTIN' CLEAN AN' BRIGHT	SP JUDGMENT DAY	11
AN' NOW I'M SETTIN' CLEAN AN' BRIGHT	SP JUDGMENT DAY	11
CLEAN AN' BRIGHT.	SP JUDGMENT DAY	13
CLEAN AN' BRIGHT.	SP JUDGMENT DAY	14
AN' I AIN'T GOIN' THERE TO SWIM; .	SP LAMENT OVER LOV	8
AN' PLANT IT AT MY BACK DOOR. . . .	SP MIDWINTER BLUES	20
PO' AN' BLACK	SP SINNER	2
AN' A SINNER IN YO' SIGHT.	SP SINNER	4
WHEN I'M OLD AN' UGLY	SP YOUNG GAL'S BLS	11
AN' THE GRAVE IS COLD.	SP YOUNG GAL'S BLS	14
TO BE UGLY AN' OLD.	SP YOUNG GAL'S BLS	18

APART 2

Context	Poem	Line
I AM THE POOR WHITE. FOOLED AND PUSHED APART.	ANS LET AMERICA BE	19
AND. LIKE AN ATOM BOMB. BURSTS APART.	PL JIM CROW CAR	4

APARTHEID 2

Context	Poem	Line
WITH AN EDGE LIKE APARTHEID. . . .	PL WHERE WHEN WHCH	6
APARTHEID?	PL WHERE WHEN WHCH	16

APPALLS 1

Context	Poem	Line
THAT APPALLS?	FW CONVENT	9

APPEAL 1

Context	Poem	Line
APPEAL TO ME.	JC HOW ABOUT DIXIE	2

APPEARS 1

Context	Poem	Line
AND WAKE ME UP GENTLE WHEN THE DAWN APPEARS	SH LETTER	18

APPENDIX 1

Context	Poem	Line
PRACTICE ON THE SMALL APPENDIX . .	SP INTERNE AT PROV	9

APPLAUDS 1

Context	Poem	Line
THE CROWD APPLAUDS A PLUMP BROWN-SKIN BLEACHED BLONDE . . .	OWT LINCOLN THEATRE	7

APPLE 1

Context	Poem	Line
THE APPLE OF MY EYE?	LHR TESTAMENT	6

APPLY 1

Context	Poem	Line
WHY FREEDOM DON'T APPLY	JC BLACK MAN SPEAK	7

APPRECIATES 1

Context	Poem	Line
TO SHOW YOU I STILL APPRECIATES YOU.	SP LETTER	5

APPRECIATE 1

Context	Poem	Line
WHO CAN APPRECIATE ME:	SP PREFERENCE	12

APRONS 1

Context	Poem	Line
WHITE APRONS	SP INTERNE AT PROV	2

AQUEL 1

Context	Poem	Line
AQUEL RINCON DE LA MANCHA DE . . .	ANS SONG OF SPAIN	27

ARABELLA 9

Context	Poem	Line
ARABELLA JOHNSON AND THE TEXAS KID	SH DEATH IN HARLEM	1
AND ARABELLA JOHNSON HAD HER . . .	SH DEATH IN HARLEM	8
BUT ARABELLA HAD HER GUN.	SH DEATH IN HARLEM	105
DO IT. ARABELLA!	SH DEATH IN HARLEM	20
OH. THEY NABBED ARABELLA	SH DEATH IN HARLEM	131
ROCK IT. ARABELLA.	SH DEATH IN HARLEM	39
WHEN ARABELLA WENT TO THE LADIES' ROOM.	SH DEATH IN HARLEM	78
AND ARABELLA WAS BUSY IN THE LADIES' ROOM.	SH DEATH IN HARLEM	92
ARABELLA DREW HER PISTOL.	SH DEATH IN HARLEM	99

ARC 2

Context	Poem	Line
THAT GROWS IN NO-MAN'S LAND. JOAN OF ARC. AND VARIOUS OTHER WAR-TIME	NM COLORED SL MOOD	5
JEANNE D' ARC.	SL SCOTTSBORO	17

ARCH 1

Context	Poem	Line
BROAD ARCH ABOVE THE ROAD WE CAME.	DK YOUTH	8

AREAWAY 1

Context	Poem	Line
WHICH AREAWAY. OR BAR.	PL WHERE WHEN WHCH	11

ARGENTINE 1

Context	Poem	Line
RUSSIA TO THE ARGENTINE.	ANS CHANT TOM MOONY	20

ARISE 2

Context	Poem	Line
REVOLT! ARISE!	ANS A NEW SONG	47
20-VOICES: ARISE.	ANS CHANT MAY DAY	32

ARKANSAS 1

Context	Poem	Line
BY WAY OF ARKANSAS	SP CONSIDER ME	39

ARM 4

Context	Poem	Line
HE HAD A MERMAID ON HIS ARM. . . .	DK SAILOR	5
BENEATH HIS ARM.	SP CATCH	7
WITH CALEDONIA'S ARM	SP FIRED	9
WHO STICKS A NEEDLE IN HIS ARM . .	PL JUNIOR ADDICT	2

ARMS 16

Context	Poem	Line
IN BLOND MEN'S ARMS.	WB HARLEM NIGHT CL	11
AND IN THE EARTH-DARK ARMS OF DEATH	WB YOUNG BRIDE	4
OPEN WIDE YOUR ARMS TO LIFE. . . .	DK SONG	5
LIFT ARMS IN VAIN. RUN. HIDE. DIE:	ANS SONG OF SPAIN	60
IN THE ARMS OF YOUR PITY	FW PRAYER	2
IN THE ARMS OF YOUR PITY.	FW PRAYER	8

IN THE ARMS OF YOUR LOVE - . . . . FW PRAYER 10
TO FLING MY ARMS WIDE . . . . SP DREAM VARIATION 1
TO FLING MY ARMS WIDE . . . . SP DREAM VARIATION 10
IN THE ARMS OF THE BUTCHER BOY! . . SP JOY 7
IN THE ARMS OF YOUR PITY . . . . . SP LITANY 2
IN THE ARMS OF YOUR PITY. . . . . . SP LITANY 8
IN THE ARMS OF YOUR LOVE - . . . . SP LITANY 10
THROWS HER ENORMOUS ARMS AROUND . . SP PROJECTION 6
AND BIG BROWN ARMS . . . . PL DAYBREAK IN ALA 12
PRESENT ARMS . . . . PL SPECIAL BULLTIN 11

ARMSTRONG 1

LUMUMBA LOUIS ARMSTRONG . . . . . . AYM ASK YOUR MAMA 39

ARMY 2

JIM CROW ARMY. . . . . JC BLACK MAN SPEAK 17
HE WAS A SOLDIER IN THE ARMY. . . . SP CASUALTY 1

AROSE 1

UNDER MY HAND THE PYRAMIDS AROSE. SP NEGRO 8

AROUND 29

LOOKED ALL AROUND ME. . . . . FC BLD OF GIN MARY 3
LIKE ME LEFT AROUND. . . . . OWT REQUEST REQUIEM 8
I'LL KNOW MY WAY AROUND. . . . . . OWT STRANGER IN TWN 16
MY WAY AROUND. . . . . OWT STRANGER IN TWN 18
AND WENT AROUND. . . . . SP BLD OF THE MAN 10
FUN TO SPORT AROUND. . . . . SP BLUE MONDAY 7
THEM BOTH AROUND . . . . SP COLLEGE FORMAL 10
DREAMS AROUND . . . . SP COMMENT ON CURB 3
MY FRIENDS WAS ALL AROUND ME . . . SP CROSSING 3
LIKE A WISP OF SMOKE AROUND THE FIRE - . . . . SP DANSE AFRICAINE 11
NO MONEY AROUND. . . . . SP ELEVATOR BOY 5
AND WRAP AROUND YOU. . . . . SP JUKE BOX LOVE 2
HOME'S JUST AROUND . . . . SP KID IN THE PARK 9
DON'T YOU WANT TO RUN AROUND . . . SP KID SLEEPY 2
WALK THE DOG AROUND - . . . . SP MADAM HER MADAM 10
ALWAYS COMING AROUND . . . . SP MADAM CHARTY CH 23
TURN AROUND - I'LL BRUSH BEHIND. . SP MAMA AND DAUGHT 6
TURN AROUND! . . . . SP MAMA AND DAUGHT 20
WOKE UP AND LOOKED AROUND ME - . . SP MORNING AFTER 11
THROWS HER ENORMOUS ARMS AROUND . . SP PROJECTION 6
WHEN A DREAM GETS KICKED AROUND. . SP SAME IN BLUES 32
WHY DOES HE KEEP ON FOOLIN' AROUND MARIE? . . . . SP SISTER 2
BUT WHY DOES HE KEEP ON FOOLIN' AROUND MARIE? . . . . SP SISTER 4
THE REASON MARIE RUNS AROUND WITH TRASH . . . . SP SISTER 8
AND WRAP A STRING AROUND ITS FINGER SP SUMMER EVENING 26
BUT TURN THE TELESCOPE AROUND. . . PL LONG VIEW NEGRO 8
THE EARTH AROUND . . . . PL QUESTION ANSWER 4
BUT IT MUST BE AROUND . . . . PL STOKELY MALCOLM 4
SOMEWHERE AROUND. . . . . PL STOKELY MALCOLM 12

ARRAYED 1

AT EITHER SIDE ARRAYED . . . . . . AYM JAZZTET MUTED 15

ARREST 1

ARREST. . . . . SP BLD LANDLORD 27

ARROGANT 1

WITH ARROGANT EYES AND SCORNFUL LIPS: . . . . ANS A NEW SONG 31

ART 4

THOU ART NOT BEAUTIFUL . . . . . . WB POEM 4
THOU ART NOT GOOD . . . . WB POEM 10
THOU ART NOT LUMINOUS . . . . WB POEM 16
OF CROCODILE ART . . . . SP MOVIES 4

ARTHUR 2

ARTHUR CARMEN ALVIN MARY $ $ $ $ $ $ $ $ . . . . AYM HORN OF PLENTY 7
SEND FOR KING ARTHUR TO BRING THE HOLY GRAIL. . . . . PL FINAL CALL 8

ARTIC 1

ON ARTIC AVENUE . . . . SP SEASHORE THROUG 10

AS 167

AS OUR ANCESTORS . . . . WB AFRAID 2
YET AS THE VULGAR DANCERS WHIRLED WB CABARET 3
BRILLIANT AS THE DAY. . . . . WB OUR LAND 11
AS FLOWERS IN THE SUN. . . . . . . WB PIERROT 20
STILL AS A WHISPERING HEARTBEAT. . WB SUMMER NIGHT 9
WEARY AS THE TIRED NIGHT. . . . . . WB SUMMER NIGHT 12
EMPTY AS THE SILENCE. . . . . WB SUMMER NIGHT 14
AN' SOON AS HE GOT OUT DE BARREL . FC BLACK GAL 11
EAGLE-ROCKISH AS I KIN BE! . . . . FC MA MAN 18
CARELESS, AND HALF-DEFIANT ECHOES OF THE "ST. JAMES INFIRMARY" AS THE NM BIG-TIMER MOOD 2
AND BLUE. HIDING HIS DISCONTENT AS THOUGHTS OF A BETTER LIFE OVERCOME . . . . NM BIG-TIMER MOOD 7
NOT THE SAME AS YOU - . . . . NM BLACK CLWN POEM 3
BACK BENT AS IN THE FIELDS. THE SLOW STEP. THE BOWED HEAD. "NOBODY KNOWS . . . . NM BLACK CLWN MOOD 4
EMPTY HANDED AS I BEGAN. . . . . . NM BLACK CLWN POEM 20
AND ME AND MY BROTHER WERE HAPPY AS YOU PLEASE . . . . NM COLORED SL POEM 6
AS IF FATE HAD NOT BLED HIM WITH HER KNIFE! . . . . DK BEGGAR BOY 8
SOFT AS IT BEGAN - . . . . DK I LOVED FRIEND 5
LIKE A MIGHTY HEART-BEAT AS THEY COME? . . . . SL SCOTTSBORO 8
MY WOMEN TAKEN AS THE BODY-TOYS . . ANS A NEW SONG 14
DARK AS THE EARTH. . . . . ANS A NEW SONG 27
AS ALWAYS. . . . . ANS KIDS WHO DIE 5
AND BLACK HANDS AND WHITE HANDS CLASPED AS ONE. . . . . ANS KIDS WHO DIE 48
AS THE BLACK BOY SPINS . . . . . . ANS LYNCHING SONG 7
"SEPARATE AS THE FINGERS." . . . . ANS OPEN LETTER 20
HELPLESS, STUPID, SCATTERED, AND ALONE - AS NOW - . . . . ANS OPEN LETTER 28
WORKERS, SEE YOURSELVES AS SPAIN! ANS SONG OF SPAIN 58
I MIGHT AS WELL PUT IT ON IN THE HAY. . . . . SH BED TIME 10
EVERYBODY DODGED AS . . . . SH DEATH IN HARLEM 101
AS THE SHOTS RANG OUT. . . . . . . SH DEATH IN HARLEM 113
AS THE SHOTS RANG OUT. . . . . . . SH DEATH IN HARLEM 118
JUST AS THE SKY IN THE . . . . . . SH DEATH IN HARLEM 133
(IT WAS JUST AS IF SOMEBODY . . . . SH DEATH IN HARLEM 97
SAME AS I CAN HEY-HEY ON BEER. . . SH HEY-HEY BLUES 2
SAME AS I CAN HEY-HEY ON BEER. . . SH HEY-HEY BLUES 4
BUT YOU JUST AS WELL BE HERE WHERE YOU DUE TO LIVE. . . . . SH LETTER 11
HERE BY MYSELF. I DO AS I PLEASE. SH SUNDAY 2
SET ON THE FRONT PORCH AS LONG AS I PLEASE. . . . . SH SUNDAY 8
SET ON THE FRONT PORCH AS LONG AS I PLEASE. . . . . SH SUNDAY 8
THAT AS LONG AS YOUR RED STAR . . . JC GOOD MORN STLIN 13
THAT AS LONG AS YOUR RED STAR . . . JC GOOD MORN STLIN 13
BUT AS FOR ME - YOU'RE MY ALLY . . JC GOOD MORN STLIN 26
AS LONG AS I AM YOU . . . . JC GOOD MORN STLIN 42
AS LONG AS I AM YOU . . . . JC GOOD MORN STLIN 42
AS THE GENTLE NIGHT . . . . JC ME AND MY SONG 2
AS THE KIND AND QUIET NIGHT . . . . JC ME AND MY SONG 4
AS THE DEEP PRODUCTIVE EARTH . . . JC ME AND MY SONG 6
AS IRON . . . . JC ME AND MY SONG 10
AS THE BLACK EARTH . . . . JC ME AND MY SONG 17
AS BLACK IRON . . . . JC ME AND MY SONG 19
AS THE BLACK NIGHT . . . . JC ME AND MY SONG 21
AS THE RICH EARTH . . . . JC ME AND MY SONG 26
AS THE BLACK NIGHT . . . . JC ME AND MY SONG 28
AS THE FIRST IRON . . . . JC ME AND MY SONG 30
AS A GIFT FROM YOU. . . . . JC THE BITTER RIVR 54
AND ME AS WELL. . . . . FW BIRTH 5
AS DOWN THE ROAD . . . . FW CAROLINA CABIN 15
SOFT AS DUSK THE DARKNESS . . . . . FW DIMOUT IN HARLM 7
STRONG AS THE BURSTING OF YOUNG BUDS. . . . . FW EARTH SONG 7
STRONG AS THE SHOOTS OF A NEW PLANT. FW EARTH SONG 8
STRONG AS THE COMING OF THE FIRST CHILD . . . . FW EARTH SONG 9
AS THE DREAMED OF SKIES. . . . . . FW WISDOM 8
AS DECREED BY FATE . . . . OWT BLD MARGE POLIT 30
OF WHISKEY AS THEY START OUT FOR A BALL. . . . . OWT JUICE JOINT 8
WHILE BLUES AS MELLOW AS THE SOUTHERN AIR . . . . OWT JUICE JOINT 25
WHILE BLUES AS MELLOW AS THE SOUTHERN AIR . . . . OWT JUICE JOINT 25
AND WEARY AS A DROWSY SOUTHERN RAIN OWT JUICE JOINT 26
AS EVERY SWAYING . . . . OWT JUICE JOINT 29
THEN DROWSY AS THE RAIN . . . . . . OWT JUICE JOINT 45
AS HARD AS MY HEAD IS. . . . . . . OWT TOO BLUE 12
AS HARD AS MY HEAD IS. . . . . . . OWT TOO BLUE 12
AS THOUGH YOU COULD KEEP. . . . . . SP A HOUSE IN TAOS 27
THE ANGELS WINGS IS WHITE AS SNOW. SP ANGELS WINGS 1
O. WHITE AS SNOW. . . . . SP ANGELS WINGS 2
AS . . . . SP ANGELS WINGS 4
THE ANGELS WINGS IS WHITE AS SNOW. SP ANGELS WINGS 6
BUT THE ANGELS WINGS IS WHITE AS SNOW. . . . . SP ANGELS WINGS 11
AS . . . . SP ANGELS WINGS 13
UNLUCKY AS CAN BE. . . . . SP BAD LUCK CARD 8
AND SHARP AS FLAME. . . . . SP BEALE STREET 8
JUST AS THOUGH IT WAS NO SIN - . . SP BLD OF THE GIRL 14
TURNS RED AS FIRE. . . . . SP BLUE BAYOU 15
LIKE AS NOT YOU WON'T. . . . . . . SP COULD BE 12
BUT IT WAS AS IF THEY'D LEFT. . . . SP CROSSING 4
AND AS FAR AS I COULD SEE . . . . . SP CROSSING 16
AND AS FAR AS I COULD SEE . . . . . SP CROSSING 16
BUT WAS JUST AS IF THEY'D LEFT. . . SP CROSSING 22
YOU KNOW, AS OLD AS I AM, ... SP DEFERRED 45
YOU KNOW, AS OLD AS I AM, ... SP DEFERRED 45
I HAVE AS MUCH RIGHT . . . . SP DEMOCRACY 5
AS THE OTHER FELLOW HAS . . . . . . SP DEMOCRACY 6
JUST AS YOU. . . . . SP DEMOCRACY 21
AS SONG GROWS STRONGER . . . . . . SP DRUNKARD 2
AS TIME GROWS LONGER UNTIL DAY . . SP DRUNKARD 3

Line	Source	No.
SOME THERE WERE, AS ALWAYS,	SP FREEDOM'S PLOW	132
AND MEN UNITED AS A NATION.	SP FREEDOM'S PLOW	141
SING IT SOFTLY AS EVER YOU CAN -	SP GENIUS CHILD	3
AS DOES	SP HEAVEN	7
JUST AS IF YOU WERE DOWN SOUTH,	SP HIGH TO LOW	16
AS DOWN THE ROADWAY	SP IN TIME SILVER	18
AS KEEPS THIS YOUNG NYMPH, JOY!	SP JOY	9
TALL AS A TREE IS TALL,	SP LAMENT OVER LOV	20
TALL AS A TREE IS TALL.	SP LAMENT OVER LOV	22
RESPECTABLY AS EVER,	SP LETTER	11
FINE AS WINE!	SP LIFE IS FINE	32
SWEET AS PURPLE DEW,	SP MIDNIGHT DANCER	4
I COULD JUST AS WELL'VE	SP MIDNIGHT RAFFLE	13
AS HE RIDES OUT ON THE PRAIRIE,	SP MIGRANT	11
O, SWEET AS EARTH,	SP MULATTO	32
YET OLD AS MYSTERY,	SP MYSTERY	13
AND LOST AS MY NEED.	SP MYSTERY	16
AS BLACK WAS BORN,	SP MYSTERY	23
BLACK AS THE NIGHT IS BLACK,	SP NEGRO	2
I'VE KNOWN RIVERS ANCIENT AS THE WORLD AND OLDER THAN THE	SP NEGRO SPEAKS OF	2
BLACK AS THE NIGHT IS BLACK,	SP NEGRO	18
BLACK AS ME!	SP NIGHTMARE BOOGE	4
IN SEEKING AS IN FINDING,	SP OLD WALT	8
AS THE WIND	SP ONE	2
AS A BOTTLE OF LICKER	SP ONE	6
AS OUR SHIP PASSED BY	SP SEASCAPE	2
AS WE RODE THE FOAM	SP SEASCAPE	6
AS WE WERE BEFORE.	SP SHARE-CROPPERS	10
ARE SOMETIMES AS DANGEROUS	SP SLIVER	3
AS A SLIVER OF THE MOON.	SP SLIVER	4
SO AS NOT TO FORGET	SP SUMMER EVENING	27
YES, SIR! LONG AS LIFE DO LAST!	SP SYLVESTER'S BED	22
AS GREAT ADVENTURES SHOULD	SP S-SSS-SS-SH!	2
LOOK AT MY FACE - DARK AS THE NIGHT -	SP THE NEGRO MOTHE	5
I AM THE ONE WHO LABORED AS A SLAVE,	SP THE NEGRO MOTHE	13
SEDUCTIVE AS A DARK-EYED WHORE,	SP THE SOUTH	14
YET A PART OF ME, AS I AM A PART OF YOU.	SP THEME FOR ENG B	32
AS I LEARN FROM YOU,	SP THEME FOR ENG B	37
AS THOUGH I WERE GOD.	SP TO ARTINA	3
AS THE TUNE COMES FROM HIS THROAT	SP TRUMPET PLAYER	42
AS OUT OF THE GUTTER	SP UP-BEAT	5
AS LEOLA PASSES BY	AYM ASK YOUR MAMA	36
IRENE AND HELEN ARE AS THEY USED TO BE	AYM BIRD IN ORBIT	21
AS LEDA STREW HER CORN	AYM BIRD IN ORBIT	29
WAS BLACK AS ME.	AYM GOSPEL CHA-CHA	62
LOVE THY NEIGHBOR AS THYSELF	AYM HORN OF PLENTY	85
AS A SILVER UNICORN	AYM IS IT TRUE?	13
AS IS CUSTOM BELOW ZERO.	AYM ODE TO DINAH	12
CRUMBLES AS IT'S NIBBLED	AYM ODE TO DINAH	14
DISTANT ALMOST NOW AS DISTANT	AYM ODE TO DINAH	39
AS FORGOTTEN PAIN IN THE QUARTER	AYM ODE TO DINAH	40
AS EACH QUARTER CLINKS	AYM ODE TO DINAH	55
AS NORTH POLE IS TO SOUTH	AYM SHADES OF PIG	27
AS YET UNFELT AMONG MAGNOLIA TREES.	PL BIRMINGHAM SUND	27
AND TOUCHING EACH OTHER NATURAL AS DEW	PL DAYBREAK IN ALA	19
I HAVE AS MUCH RIGHT	PL FREEDOM	5
AS THE OTHER FELLOW HAS	PL FREEDOM	6
JUST AS YOU.	PL FREEDOM	21
AS SOON AS YOU SEE	PL LITTLE SNG HOUS	6
AS SOON AS YOU SEE	PL LITTLE SNG HOUS	8
SOON AS YOU SPY	PL LITTLE SNG HOUS	15
AS IF IT WERE SOME NOBLE THING,	PL MOTHER IN WAR	1
AS IF FREEDOM'S CAUSE	PL MOTHER IN WAR	3
AS IF THE WEAPONS USED TODAY	PL MOTHER IN WAR	5
AS IF TECHNICOLOR BANNERS FLEW	PL MOTHER IN WAR	7
AS I LIVE AND LEARN	PL MOTTO	6
AS FOR YOU OTHERS -	PL SPECIAL BULLTIN	18
I'D JUST AS LEAVE	PL SWEET WORDS RAC	13
AND DREAMS AS FRAGILE	PL THE DOVE	3
AS POTTERY WITH DOVE	PL THE DOVE	4
DARK BROWN AS	PL THE DOVE	6
AS THOSE INVESTIGATED -	PL UN-AMERICAN	6
AS HAVE SOME FOLKS I KNOW,	PL VARI-COLORED	2
SHARP AS INTEGRATION	PL WHERE WHEN WHCH	5

ASCENDS 1

Line	Source	No.
TO WHICH THE SOUL ASCENDS	OLD TOWER	2

ASCH 1

Line	Source	No.
BY MOE ASCH OR ALAN LOMAX	AYM IS IT TRUE?	10

ASHAMED 3

Line	Source	No.
THAT I AM HALF ASHAMED	FW SNAKE	5
AND BE ASHAMED -	SP I, TOO	17
"I'M SO ASHAMED OF BEING WHITE."	PL DINNER GUEST ME	14

ASHES 2

Line	Source	No.
SCRATCHING IN THE DEAD FIRE'S ASHES	SP THE SOUTH	7
SACKCLOTH AND ASHES, ANYHOW.	PL BOMBINGS DIXIE	3

ASIDE 2

Line	Source	No.
I'LL CAST MY BLUES ASIDE.	WB BLUES FANTASY	26
GOT A JIM CROW CAR SET ASIDE FOR ME.	SP FREEDOM TRAIN	10

ASK 20

Line	Source	No.
ASK HIM TO GIMME HIS HAND.	FC MOAN	8
ASK THAT WOMAN -	SH BLD THE KILLER	28
BUT IF YOU WAS TO ASK ME	SH EVENIN' BLUES	19
SAYS IF YOU WAS TO ASK ME	SH EVENIN' BLUES	21
YOU WOULDN'T NEED TO ASK ME:	SH EVENIN' BLUES	27
I DID NOT ASK FOR THIS RIVER	JC THE BITTER RIVR	51
ASK ME WHO AM I.	OWT VISITORS	18
DID YOU ASK FOR THE BEATEN BRASS OF THE MOON?	SP A HOUSE IN TAOS	23
IF MY CHILDREN ASK ME, DADDY, PLEASE EXPLAIN	SP FREEDOM TRAIN	31
I DIDN'T ASK HIM	SP MADAM PHONE BIL	14
ASK YOU WHY!	SP MADAM MINISTER	24
I ASK YOU THIS:	SP PRAYER	1
I ASK YOU THIS:	SP PRAYER	3
THEY RUNG MY BELL TO ASK ME	AYM HORN OF PLENTY	96
I SAID, ASK YOUR MAMA.	AYM IS IT TRUE?	56
WHEN THEY ASK YOU IF YOU KNEW ME,	AYM RIDE, RED, RIDE	27
GOT TO ASK YOU - GOT TO ASK!	AYM SHOW FARE PLESE	10
GOT TO ASK YOU - GOT TO ASK!	AYM SHOW FARE PLESE	10
I SAID, ASK YOUR MAMA.	PL CULTURAL EXCHNG	35
DON'T ASK ME WHY.	PL WITHOUT BENEFIT	12

ASKED 14

Line	Source	No.
I ASKED HER ONE NIGHT	FC NEW CABARET GRL	7
I ASKED YOU FOR A DOLLAR.	OWT HONEY BABE	5
I ASKED MY LANDLADY DID I HAVE PRIVILEGES.	OWT STRANGER IN TWN	7
AND ASKED FOR FISH.	SP HOPE	2
I ASKED YOU, BABY,	SP MAYBE	1
SHE ASKED HERSELF TWO QUESTIONS	SP RUBY BROWN	11
I ASKED THE WHITE LORD JESUS	SP SONG DARK GIRL	7
ASKED ME FOR A KISS.	SP SUICIDE'S NOTE	3
THEY ASKED ME AT THANKSGIVING	AYM BIRD IN ORBIT	15
ASKED ME RIGHT AT CHRISTMAS	AYM BIRD IN ORBIT	69
YET THEY ASKED ME OUT ON MY PATIO	AYM HORN OF PLENTY	45
THEY ASKED ME AT THE PTA	AYM IS IT TRUE?	54
THEY ASKED ME RIGHT AT CHRISTMAS.	AYM ODE TO DINAH	127
THEY ASKED ME IF MY BLACKNESS,	PL CULTURAL EXCHNG	33

ASKING 4

Line	Source	No.
I'M ASKING, GRANDPA, ASKING.	AYM BIRD IN ORBIT	36
I'M ASKING, GRANDPA, ASKING.	AYM BIRD IN ORBIT	38
BUT I'M ASKING ANYHOW.	AYM BLUES IN STEREO	31
GOT TIRED OF ASKING, WHEN?	PL GHOSTS OF 1619	16

ASLEEP 2

Line	Source	No.
ASLEEP,	SP DREAM	9
UNAWARES - ASLEEP.	SP FIRED	3

ASPEN 1

Line	Source	No.
MA HEART'S A FLUTTERING ASPEN LEAF	DK REASONS WHY	7

ASSORTED 1

Line	Source	No.
BETWEEN ASSORTED TERRORS	PL LENOX AVE. BAR	2

ASSUMING 1

Line	Source	No.
HIM, ASSUMING A FALSE AND BRAGGING SELF-ASSURANCE, AND A PRETENDED	NM BIG-TIMER MOOD	8

ASTONISHED 1

Line	Source	No.
AND THE NIGHT MIGHT BE ASTONISHED	AYM BLUES IN STEREO	19

ASTRAY 1

Line	Source	No.
GONE ASTRAY -	JC TO CAPTAIN MULZ	9

ASUNDER 2

Line	Source	No.
ROCKS THAT BURST ASUNDER	SP LOVE	3
DREAMS KICKED ASUNDER.	PL QUESTION ANSWER	11

AT 158

Line	Source	No.
THE GODS ARE LAUGHING AT US.	WB LENOX AVE MIDNT	4
AND THE GODS ARE LAUGHING AT US.	WB LENOX AVE MIDNT	14
MIGHT FALL AT THY FEET.	WB SONGS DARK VIRG	5
CRY AT MY GRINNING MOUTH,	WB THE JESTER	12
LAUGH AT MY SORROW'S REIGN.	WB THE JESTER	14
WILL FALL AT THE FEET OF YOUR BEAUTY,	WB TO DARK MERCEDE	5
AT LEAST I CAN OFFER THAT.	FC BRASS SPITOONS	39
THAT LAUGHS AND CRIES AT THE SAME TIME.	FC JAZZ BAND	12
WHEN MA MAN LOOKS AT ME	FC MA MAN	1
WHEN MA MAN LOOKS AT ME	FC MA MAN	7
AN' OUR TROUBLES AT DE DOOR.	FC MINNIE SINGS	6
LOOK AT YO' LEGS.	FC RED SILK STOCK	4
LOOK AT YO' LEGS.	FC RED SILK STOCK	12
THEN AT THE CLOSING HOUR	FC SPORT	7
AND THERE IS NO MUSIC AT ALL	FC SPORT	9
COMES HOME AT NIGHT, -	FC WORKIN' MAN	7
SHOULDERS AT FATE, ACCEPTING HIS POSITION - BUT INSIDE HIMSELF UNHAPPY	NM BIG-TIMER MOOD	6
LOOK AT ME NOW AND	NM BIG-TIMER POEM	7
FOLKS, DOWN YONDER AT HOME.	NM BIG-TIMER POEM	54
OR THINKIN' AT ALL?	NM BIG-TIMER POEM	70
LAUGH AT ME! LAUGH AT ME!	NM BLACK CLWN POEM	33

LAUGH AT ME! LAUGH AT ME! . . . . . . NM BLACK CLWN POEM 53
LAUGH AT ME THEN. . . . . NM BLACK CLWN POEM 55
LOOK AT THE STARS YONDER . . . . . NM BLACK CLWN POEM 73
AND ONE OLD FUNNY BOY SAID, "I'LL WORK AT ANY PRICE . . . . NM BROKE 8
LAST JOB I HAD, WENT TO WORK AT FIVE IN DE MORNIN', OR LITTLE MO' . . NM BROKE 12
AND DE MAN COME TELLIN' ME I BETTER GET THERE AT FO'. . . . . NM BROKE 13
SO I WENT DOWN TOWN TO A HOTEL WHERE I USED TO WORK AT NIGHT, ... NM BROKE 44
(IS YOU LOOKIN' AT ME, BABY, OR SOME OTHER WAY?) . . . . NM BROKE 76
THEN HIS DARK FACE SMILED AT ME IN THE NIGHT - . . . . NM COLORED SL POEM 39
YEARS AGO AT THE NATION'S START . . NM DARK YOUTH USA 12
(AT BOOKER WASHINGTON'S GRAVE) . . DK ALABAMA EARTH 1
THE RAIN PLAYS A LITTLE SLEEP-SONG ON OUR ROOF AT NIGHT - . . . . . DK APRIL RAIN SONG 6
PUT NO TOMBSTONE AT MY HEAD, . . . DK DEATH SEAMAN 5
AIMED AT OZIE POWELL. . . . . ANS BLD OZZIE POWEL 16
STARE AT OZIE POWELL. . . . . ANS BLD OZZIE POWEL 20
HE WON'T MATTER AT ALL. . . . . . . ANS CHANT TOM MOONY 29
WHOSE HAND AT THE FOUNDRY, WHOSE PLOW IN THE RAIN. . . . . ANS LET AMERICA BE 68
PULL AT THE ROPE! OH! . . . . ANS LYNCHING SONG 1
I LOOKED AT THEIR BLACK FACES . . . ANS NEGRO GHETTO 1
AT HARLAN, RICHMOND, GASTONIA, ATLANTA, NEW-ORLEANS; . . . . . ANS OPEN LETTER 16
BUT SINCE I GOT TO GET UP AT DAY, SH BED TIME 9
HOUSE IS SO QUIET! . . . LISTEN AT THEM MICE. . . . . SH BED TIME 12
AT A BIG PIANO A LITTLE DARK GIRL SH DEATH IN HARLEM 10
BESSIE STARED AT BELLA . . . . . . SH DEATH IN HARLEM 111
FOLKS AT THE TABLES DRINK AND GRIN. SH DEATH IN HARLEM 31
(DIXIE RENTS ROOMS AT A BUCK A BREAK.) . . . . SH DEATH IN HARLEM 34
LOUNGERS AT THE BAR LAUGH OUT LOUD. SH DEATH IN HARLEM 35
LOOKED AT THE BLACKS AND . . . . . SH DEATH IN HARLEM 66
LOOKED AT THE BLACKS AND . . . . . SH DEATH IN HARLEM 68
LOOKED AT THE BLACKS AND . . . . . SH DEATH IN HARLEM 70
JUST LOOK AT ME AND SEE! . . . . . SH EVENIN' BLUES 24
HOW DID I KNOW WHERE YOU GONE GONE AT? . . . . SH LETTER 5
I'LL MEET YOU AT THE BUS STATION. SH LETTER 21
LOOK AT THAT WATER DRIPPING IN THE SINK. . . . . SH SUPPER TIME 5
LISTEN AT MY HEARTBEATS TRYING TO THINK. . . . . SH SUPPER TIME 6
LISTEN AT MY FOOTPRINTS WALKING ON THE FLOOR. . . . . SH SUPPER TIME 7
TO VOTE AT THE POLLS. . . . . . . JC BLD SAM SOLOMON 23
IT MEANS FREEDOM AT HOME, TOO - . . JC HOW ABOUT DIXIE 23
AT MAKING MINCE-MEAT . . . . JC NOTE TO NAZIS 3
I HAVE DRUNK AT THE RIVER TOO LONG: JC THE BITTER RIVR 66
I'VE DRUNK AT THE BITTER RIVER . . JC THE BITTER RIVR 73
AT THE END OF DAY. . . . . FW FAITHFUL ONE 12
NO ONE CARED AT ALL . . . . FW HEART 9
AT FIRST THEY ARE NICE TO HIM. . . FW MIGRATION 5
AT DAWN . . . . FW MONTMARTRE 4
THE HOUNDS ARE AT YOUR BACK. . . . OWT FLIGHT 4
PRESS HANDS TOGETHER, LAUGHING AT HER SONG. . . . . OWT LINCOLN THEATRE 15
O, VELOT AT NIGHT! . . . . OWT NEGRO SERVANT 5
AT SIX O'CLOCK, OR SEVEN, OR EIGHT. OWT NEGRO SERVANT 8
O, SAXOPHONES AT NIGHT! . . . . . . OWT NEGRO SERVANT 18
LATE AT NIGHT . . . . OWT RAID 1
CLUTCHING AT A . . . . LHR POET TO BIGOT 10
OUT OF ANY BOOK AT ALL. . . . . . . SP AUNTSUE'S STORI 20
RISE AT DAWNIN' FULL OF FUN? . . . SP BLACK MARIA 13
LISTEN AT THEM LITTLE VARMINTS! . . SP CHILDREN'S RYME 4
DOWNTOWN AT EIGHT. . . . . SP CONSIDER ME 18
TO WORK AT EIGHT. . . . . SP CONSIDER ME 46
HE WAS NO GOOD AT MAKING LOVE . . . SP DANCER 7
AND NO GOOD AT MAKING MONEY. . . . SP DANCER 8
AT THAT BOY! . . . . SP DANCER 16
BUT BEING NO GOOD AT LOVIN' - . . . SP DANCER 18
TO GET THROUGH HIGH AT TWENTY'S KIND OF LATE - . . . . SP DEFERRED 6
NOW AT LAST I'VE GOT A JOB . . . . SP DEFERRED 25
WHERE I GET OFF AT FIVE. . . . . . SP DEFERRED 26
AT ONCE! . . . . SP DEFERRED 31
TO STAY HOME AT ALL. . . . . SP DELINQUENT 4
THEN REST AT COOL EVENING . . . . . SP DREAM VARIATION 5
REST AT PALE EVENING . . . . SP DREAM VARIATION 14
BUT YOU WERE NOT THERE AT ALL! . . SP DREAM 14
IS NO ATOM AT ALL. . . . . SP DRUM 8
BUT I'M GONNA KEEP ON AT IT . . . . SP EVIL 3
AT THE FEET O' JESUS, ... SP FEET O' JESUS 1
AT THE FEET O' JESUS . . . . SP FEET O' JESUS 5
AT YO' FEET I STAND. . . . . SP FEET O' JESUS 6
THAT AT A SUDDEN CHANGE BECOME . . SP FLATTED FIFTHS 6
BUT NOT SO LONG AGO AT THAT, LINCOLN SAID: . . . . SP FREEDOM'S PLOW 101
WITH JOHN BROWN AT HARPER'S FERRY, NEGROES DIED. . . . . SP FREEDOM'S PLOW 116
HER GRANDSON'S NAME WAS JIMMY. HE DIED AT ANZIO. . . . . SP FREEDOM TRAIN 43
NOT STOPPIN' AT NO STATIONS MARKED COLORED NOR WHITE. . . . . SP FREEDOM TRAIN 51
AT HOME THEY GOT A TRAIN THAT'S YOURS AND MINE! . . . . SP FREEDOM TRAIN 62
AT EACH GATE. . . . . SP GOOD MORNING 25
AT HER THIGHS. . . . . SP GRADUATION 5
THE DREAM IS A COCKTAIL AT SLOPPY JOE'S - . . . . SP HAVANA DREAMS 1
(NOT AT 409) . . . . SP HIGH TO LOW 17
AT THE MISTERS, LORDS, GENERALS, VICEROYS, ... SP IN EXPLANATION 42
OF 26-GIRL AT THE CORNER, ... SP INTERNE AT PROV 10
I'LL BE AT THE TABLE . . . . SP I, TOO 9
YOU LOOKED AT ME CROSS-EYED . . . . SP LATE LAST NIGHT 7
I LOOKED AT MY DADDY - . . . . . . SP LOVER'S RETURN 13
WHERE YOUR FORTUNE'S AT. . . . . . SP MADAM FORT TELL 12
WHERE IS MY FORTUNE AT? . . . . . . SP MADAM FORT TELL 15
AN' PLANT IT AT MY BACK DOOR, . . . SP MIDWINTER BLUES 20
PLANT IT AT MY BACK DOOR, ... SP MIDWINTER BLUES 22
WORKS AT THE FOUNDRY. . . . . . . SP MIGRANT 4
AT NIGHT MY WISHING STAR. . . . . . SP MISS BLUES'ES 8
AT THE CROCODILE TEARS . . . . . . SP MOVIES 3
LAUGHS AT ME. . . . . SP MOVIES 9
AT HIS CORNER . . . . SP NIGHT FUNERAL 36
AT THE ELKS CLUB LOUNGE . . . . . . SP PARADE 3
AT CLUB HARLEM IT'S ELEVEN . . . . SP SEASHORE THROUG 3
NOTHING AT ALL NAMED AFTER JOHN BROWN. . . . . SP SHAME ON YOU 7
MISS MICHAELMAS IS AT DE MASS . . . SP SOUTHERN MAMMY 3
MAKIN' ROUNDS AT NIGHT. . . . . . . SP STREET SONG 4
FROM A TENT AT THE CORNER . . . . . SP SUMMER EVENING 12
BOTH AT MA DO'. . . . . SP SYLVESTER'S BED 12
LOOK AT MY FACE - DARK AS THE NIGHT - . . . . SP THE NEGRO MOTHE 5
LOOK EVER UPWARD AT THE SUN AND THE STARS. . . . . SP THE NEGRO MOTHE 48
AT TWENTY-TWO, MY AGE. BUT I GUESS I'M WHAT . . . . SP THEME FOR ENG B 17
AT THE TOP. . . . . SP TO BE SOMEBODY 23
WITH THE TRUMPET AT HIS LIPS . . . SP TRUMPET PLAYER 2
WITH THE TRUMPET AT HIS LIPS . . . SP TRUMPET PLAYER 10
FROM THE TRUMPET AT HIS LIPS . . . SP TRUMPET PLAYER 18
FROM THE TRUMPET AT HIS LIPS . . . SP TRUMPET PLAYER 22
WITH THE TRUMPET AT HIS LIPS . . . SP TRUMPET PLAYER 34
AT THE PICTURE SHOW. . . . . AYM ASK YOUR MAMA 24
AT THE DOME VINGT FRANCS WILL DO . AYM ASK YOUR MAMA 50
WHO AT THE SORBONNE HAS SIX CLASSES. AYM ASK YOUR MAMA 54
THEY ASKED ME AT THANKSGIVING . . . AYM BIRD IN ORBIT 15
AND SMITTY HAS NOT CHANGED AT ALL. AYM BIRD IN ORBIT 22
AT MOTHER BETHEL'S IN THE MORNING? AYM BIRD IN ORBIT 35
I LOOK AT THE STARS . . . . AYM BIRD IN ORBIT 53
AND THEY LOOK AT THE STARS, ... AYM BIRD IN ORBIT 54
STARS AT STARS STARS. . . . . AYM BIRD IN ORBIT 57
ASKED ME RIGHT AT CHRISTMAS . . . . AYM BIRD IN ORBIT 69
THEY ASKED ME AT THE PTA . . . . . AYM IS IT TRUE? 54
AT EITHER SIDE ARRAYED . . . . . . AYM JAZZTET MUTED 15
THEY ASKED ME RIGHT AT CHRISTMAS, AYM ODE TO DINAH 127
WHEN THE MAN SHOT AT THE WOMAN . . AYM ODE TO DINAH 131
PAID AT THE BOX OFFICE . . . . . . AYM SHOW FARE PLESE 15
AND NEVER CAME BACK HOME AT ALL . . PL BIRMINGHAM SUND 3
BEFORE CHINA WAS EVER RED AT ALL . PL BIRMINGHAM SUND 12
LOOKING AT LISTENERS' FACES. . . . PL CORNER MEETING 5
YOU KNOW, RIGHT AT CHRISTMAS . . . PL CULTURAL EXCHNG 32
AT THE DAMASK TABLE, MINE. . . . . PL DINNER GUEST ME 18
PARK AVENUE AT EIGHT . . . . PL DINNER GUEST ME 20
BEATIN' AT THE DOOR - . . . . PL DOWN WHERE I AM 2
THEY CLUTCH AT THE EGG . . . . . . PL ELDERLY LEADERS 8
LOOK AT ME! . . . . PL FLORIDA WORKERS 2
NOW WHEN THE MAN AT THE CORNER STORE PL HARLEM 8
AT CARNIVAL . . . . PL MERRY-GO-ROUND 2
SHE SPOKE OF SONS AT WAR, ... PL MOTHER IN WAR 2
WERE PLED ANEW AT SOME HEROIC BAR, PL MOTHER IN WAR 4
WE LICK OUR CHOPS AT BIRMINGHAM . . PL NORTHERN LIBERL 2
AT JIM CROW LAWS . . . . PL NORTHERN LIBERL 19
LOOK SLOW AT ONE ANOTHER - . . . . PL OCTOBER 16 RAID 12
HAS LONG BEEN TRIED AT LAW, ... PL OCTOBER 16 RAID 20
DOWN THE STREET AT ME! . . . . . . PL WHO BUT TH LORD 4

ATAVISTIC 1

THIS SONG OF ATAVISTIC LAND, . . . SP AFRO-AMER FRAG 18

ATLANTA 4

AT HARLAN, RICHMOND, GASTONIA, ATLANTA, NEW-ORLEANS; . . . . . ANS OPEN LETTER 16
WHEN MY GRANDMOTHER IN ATLANTA, 83 AND BLACK, ... SP FREEDOM TRAIN 37
CAPE TOWN, ATLANTA, ... PL QUESTION ANSWER 2
MADE IN ATLANTA, ... PL SPECIAL BULLTIN 13

ATLANTIC 2

ATLANTIC CITY, ... FC BRASS SPITOONS 4
BINOCULAR THE ATLANTIC. . . . . . . SP SEASHORE THROUG 2

ATOM 3

UNTIL THE LAST ATOM . . . . SP DRUM 7
IS NO ATOM AT ALL. . . . . SP DRUM 8
AND, LIKE AN ATOM BOMB, BURSTS APART. . . . . PL JIM CROW CAR 4

ATOMS 1
DUST OF DINGY ATOMS . . . . PL CULTURAL EXCHNG 3

ATTENTION 1
AND CENTER OF ATTENTION . . . . . . PL DINNER GUEST ME 17

ATTIC 1
AND THE ATTIC LEAKS. . . . . SP MADAM RENT MAN 18

ATTUCKS 1
ATTUCKS DIED . . . . NM DARK YOUTH USA 13

AUGUST 2
AUGUST 1ST IS . . . . OWT BLD MARGE POLIT 27
MARK AUGUST 1ST . . . . OWT BLD MARGE POLIT 29

AUNT 10
AUNT SUE HAS A HEAD FULL OF STORIES. SP AUNTSUE'S STORI 1
AUNT SUE HAS A WHOLE HEART FULL OF STORIES. . . . . SP AUNTSUE'S STORI 2
AUNT SUE CUDDLES A BROWN-FACED CHILD TO HER BOSOM . . . . SP AUNTSUE'S STORI 4
IN THE FLOW OF OLD AUNT SUE'S VOICE. SP AUNTSUE'S STORI 13
AUNT SUE'S STORIES. . . . . SP AUNTSUE'S STORI 16
KNOWS THAT AUNT SUE'S STORIES ARE REAL STORIES. . . . . SP AUNTSUE'S STORI 18
HE KNOWS THAT AUNT SUE NEVER GOT HER STORIES . . . . SP AUNTSUE'S STORI 19
LISTENING TO AUNT SUE'S STORIES. . SP AUNTSUE'S STORI 25
TO SEE MA OLD AUNT CLEW. . . . . . SP YOUNG GAL'S BLS 8
TO SEE MA OLD AUNT CLEW. . . . . . SP YOUNG GAL'S BLS 10

AUSTRALIA 1
IN AUSTRALIA, TOO, THEY SAY. . . . SP MIGRANT 26

AUTHORITY 1
IN SEEKING AUTHORITY? . . . . PL GHOSTS OF 1619 20

AUTUMN 7
THE AUTUMN LEAVES . . . . WB POEME D'AUTOMNE 1
IN AUTUMN THEY DIE AND ARE BLOWN AWAY. . . . . DK AUTUMN THOUGHT 2
TO A HANDFUL OF DUST IN AUTUMN. . . FW DUSTBOWL 3
AUTUMN FLOWER . . . . SP TROUBLED WOMAN 7
WIND-BLOWN AUTUMN FLOWER . . . . . SP TROUBLED WOMAN 10
AUTUMN LEAVES IN AUTUMN . . . . . . AYM HORN OF PLENTY 73
AUTUMN LEAVES IN AUTUMN . . . . . . AYM HORN OF PLENTY 73

AVAILABLE 1
ARE NOT AVAILABLE . . . . PL OPPRESSION 2

AVENUE 18
LENOX AVENUE, ... WB LENOX AVE MIDNT 11
YOU, PARK AVENUE. . . . . ANS PARK BENCH 2
TO PARK AVENUE? . . . . ANS PARK BENCH 12
A PARTY OF WHITES FROM FIFTH AVENUE SH DEATH IN HARLEM 58
THERE IS A GIN MILL ON THE AVENUE OWT JUICE JOINT 1
TO LENOX AVENUE. . . . . SP CONSIDER ME 40
OR LENOX AVENUE. . . . . SP COULD BE 2
ALSO LENOX AVENUE. . . . . SP COULD BE 14
LENOX AVENUE . . . . SP DIVE 1
TAKE THE LENOX AVENUE BUSSES, . . . SP JUKE BOX LOVE 4
AND OFF DOWN LENOX AVENUE . . . . . SP NIGHT FUNERAL 33
LEAPS CLEAN OVER TO SEVENTH AVENUE SP PROJECTION 2
ON RAILROAD AVENUE. . . . . SP RAILROAD AVENUE 2
ON ARTIC AVENUE . . . . SP SEASHORE THROUG 10
DOWN ON LENOX AVENUE THE OTHER NIGHT SP THE WEARY BLUES 4
EIGHTH AVENUE, SEVENTH, AND I COME TO THE Y. . . . . SP THEME FOR ENG B 13
PARK AVENUE AT EIGHT . . . . PL DINNER GUEST ME 20
UPTOWN ON LENOX AVENUE . . . . . . PL PRIME 1

AW 6
AW, PICK THAT RAG! . . . . SH DEATH IN HARLEM 13
AW, PICK IT, MISS LUCY! . . . . . . SH DEATH IN HARLEM 27
AW, PLUNK IT, MISS LUCY, ... SH DEATH IN HARLEM 56
AW, PLAY IT, MISS LUCY! . . . . . . SH DEATH IN HARLEM 74
AW, MY HEART IS . . . . SP BLACK MARIA 7
AW, WHAT A LIE! . . . . SP BLD THE GYPSY 13

AWAIT 2
AWAIT THEIR DAY . . . . ANS SONG OF SPAIN 51
IN LITTLE GRAVES TODAY AWAIT . . . PL BIRMINGHAM SUND 17

AWAITING 1
AND THE FOUR BELLS SHE'S AWAITING SP SUMMER EVENING 20

AWAKE 2
AWAKE, ... SP DREAM 6
AWAKE ALL NIGHT WITH LOVING . . . . SP FIRED 1

AWAKENED 1
MIGHT BE AWAKENED SOMEDAY SOON . . PL BIRMINGHAM SUND 25

AWAKENING 1
AWAKENING TO ACTION. . . . . ANS A NEW SONG 2

AWAY 72
CHILE, HE'S GONE AWAY. . . . . . . WB BLUES FANTASY 8
BABE, HE'S GONE AWAY. . . . . WB BLUES FANTASY 10
AND THE WAN NIGHT WORE AWAY. . . . WB CABARET 4
THEY TOOK ME AWAY FROM THE JUNGLES. WB LAMENT DARK PEO 6
OH, SWEET, AWAY! . . . . WB OUR LAND 15
AH, MY BELOVED ONE, AWAY! . . . . . WB OUR LAND 17
'LEVEN AIN'T FAR AWAY. . . . . . . FC CRAP GAME 4
I'D GO AWAY . . . . FC MINNIE SINGS 16
I RAN AWAY. . . . . NM BIG-TIMER POEM 5
THE MUSIC, OVER-BURDENED, BACKING AWAY ANGRILY, FRANTIC WITH HUMILIATION . . . . NM BLACK CLWN MOOD 10
AND THAT OUR DARK BLOOD WOULD WIPE AWAY THE STAIN . . . . NM COLORED SL POEM 8
IN AUTUMN THEY DIE AND ARE BLOWN AWAY. . . . . DK AUTUMN THOUGHT 2
AWAY FROM THE TOO-ROUGH FINGERS . . DK DREAM KEEPER 7
HE WENT AWAY FROM ME. . . . . DK I LOVED FRIEND 2
FOR THE DEAD WHO'D GONE AWAY, . . . DK IRISH WAKE 2
HALF A WORLD AWAY FROM HOME, . . . DK SAILOR 2
I CAN SLEEP SO GOOD WITH YOU AWAY! SH BED TIME 11
FAR AWAY. . . . . SH DEATH IN HARLEM 127
SLIPPED AWAY . . . . SH DEATH IN HARLEM 135
FLY AWAY FROM YOU. . . . . SH DECLARATION 18
AWAY . . . . SH DECLARATION 20
JUST TO DRIVE MY BLUES AWAY - . . . SH EVENIN' BLUES 14
TO DRIVE MY BLUES AWAY. . . . . . . SH EVENIN' BLUES 16
GIVES LOVE AWAY SHE'S THROUGH. . . SH MIDNIGHT CHIPPI 24
JUST SO IT GOES AWAY FROM HERE. . . SH SIX-BITS BLUES 6
STAY AWAY IF YOU WANT TO, AND SEE IF I CARE! . . . . SH SUPPER TIME 10
YOU'RE HALF A WORLD AWAY OR MORE . JC GOOD MORN STLIN 17
ANYHOW, AWAY OFF THERE. . . . . . . JC GOOD MORN STLIN 52
TO KEEP THE KLAN AWAY) . . . . . . JC GOOD MORN STLIN 56
KNOWLEDGE ACQUIRED BUT THROWN AWAY, JC THE BITTER RIVR 20
TAKES YOUR WORDS AWAY. . . . . . . JC THE BITTER RIVR 42
CARRIES YOUR "PATIENCE" AWAY . . . JC THE BITTER RIVR 46
SWEEPS YOUR LIES AWAY. . . . . . . JC THE BITTER RIVR 50
FAR AWAY. . . . . FW HEART 16
THEIR DREAM AWAY. . . . . FW LITTLE SONG 8
FAINTED AWAY . . . . FW NIGHT SONG 20
SEE! WHEN YOU WIPE THE MUD AWAY. . FW WHEN ARMIES PAS 21
TAKEN MARGIE AWAY - . . . . OWT BLD MARGE POLIT 53
AND PUT MYSELF AWAY? . . . . OWT TOO BLUE 9
TODAY YOU GONE AWAY. . . . . OWT YESTERDAY TODAY 4
AND TOOK MY LORD AWAY. . . . . . . LHR BLD MARY'S SON 26
SO I CREPT AWAY INTO THE NIGHT . . SP A BLACK PIERROT 3
SO FAR AWAY . . . . SP AFRO-AMER FRAG 2
SO FAR AWAY . . . . SP AFRO-AMER FRAG 11
SO FAR AWAY . . . . SP AFRO-AMER FRAG 22
PLEASE DON'T TAKE HIM AWAY! . . . . SP AS BEFITS A MAN 16
DON'T TAKE DADDY AWAY! . . . . . . SP AS BEFITS A MAN 18
TAKES MY WOMAN AWAY. . . . . SP BLUE BAYOU 12
TO SPORT AWAY, ... SP CONSIDER ME 21
GONE AWAY. . . . . SP DEAD IN THERE 15
TAKE IT AWAY! . . . . SP DREAM BOOGIE 17
I GAMBLED YOUR DIME AWAY. . . . . . SP EARLY EVENING 8
DONE GAMBLED THAT DIME AWAY. . . . SP EARLY EVENING 10
BUT HAD RUN AWAY TO FREEDOM. . . . SP FREEDOM'S PLOW 113
THERE WAS LIGHT WHEN THE BATTLE CLOUDS ROLLED AWAY. . . . . . . SP FREEDOM'S PLOW 139
WAS FAR AWAY . . . . SP GREEN MEMORY 5
TO TAKE AWAY TO ALABAMA. . . . . . SP INTERNE AT PROV 6
AND ROT AWAY! . . . . SP MADAM RENT MAN 10
WENT AWAY - . . . . SP MADAM MINISTER 31
A THOUSAND MILES AWAY. . . . . . . SP MIGRANT 24
PREACHED THAT BOY AWAY - . . . . . SP NIGHT FUNERAL 22
GONNA SALT EVERY DIME AWAY . . . . SP NUMBERS 2
AND TAKE IT AWAY . . . . SP ONE-WAY TICKET 24
PLOWING LIFE AWAY . . . . SP SHARE-CROPPERS 15
CHILDREN SOLD AWAY FROM ME, HUSBAND SOLD, TOO. . . . . SP THE NEGRO MOTHE 15
BUT DREAM SHIPS SAIL AWAY . . . . . SP WATER-FRONT STR 2
WHO BREAK AWAY LIKE COMETS $ $ $ $ $ $ . . . . AYM HORN OF PLENTY 20
AWAY. . . . . PL CROWNS GARLANDS 11
AWAY. . . . . PL FINAL CALL 2
SEND FOR THE PIED PIPER TO PIPE OUR RATS AWAY. . . . . PL FINAL CALL 38
HAS PASSED AWAY, ... PL OCTOBER 16 RAID 18
AWAY THEY GO: . . . . PL OFFICE BUILDING 6

AWFUL 6
I TELL YOU IT'S AWFUL, WHEN YOU'RE BROKE. . . . . NM BROKE 47
IT WAS AWFUL - FACING THAT BOY WHO WENT OUT TO DIE. . . . . NM COLORED SL POEM 42
UH! IT SURE IS AWFUL TO . . . . . . SH EVIL MORNING 13
BUT AN AWFUL THING . . . . LHR BLD MARY'S SON 4
IS AWFUL, AWFUL HARD. . . . . SP BAD LUCK CARD 2
IS AWFUL, AWFUL HARD. . . . . SP BAD LUCK CARD 2

AWHILE 7
THE OLD AND RICH WILL LIVE ON AWHILE, ... ANS KIDS WHO DIE 4
AFTER AWHILE. . . . . FW MIGRATION 10

BUT AFTER I BEEN HERE AWHILE . . . OWT STRANGER IN TWN 15
YOU'VE BEEN RESTING AWHILE. . . . . SP AFRICA 2
GOT TO CLEAN AWHILE. . . . . PL OFFICE BUILDING 3
YOU CLEAN AWHILE. . . . . PL OFFICE BUILDING 7
CLEANING AWHILE. . . . . PL OFFICE BUILDING 10

AWOKE 2
I THOUGHT LOVE WAS A DREAM, BUT I
SHO HAVE AWOKE - . . . . NM BROKE 54
THAN I AWOKE. . . . . SP MADAM WRONG VIS 22

AW-OO 1
AW-OO! YONDER COMES A WOMAN I USED
TO KNOW WAY DOWN SOUTH. . . . . NM BROKE 62

AX 3
CLANG AGAINST THE TREES WENT THE AX
IN MANY HANDS . . . . SP FREEDOM'S PLOW 55
AX HANDLES, HAMMER HANDLES, ... SP FREEDOM'S PLOW 65
WITH AX HANDLES . . . . PL SPECIAL BULLTIN 12

AY 8
AY, MI NEGRA! . . . . AYM BIRD IN ORBIT 32
AY, MORENA! . . . . AYM BIRD IN ORBIT 33
AY, BAHIA! . . . . AYM GOSPEL CHA-CHA 27
AY, BAHIA! . . . . AYM GOSPEL CHA-CHA 28
AY, DIOS! . . . . AYM IS IT TRUE? 20
AY, DIOS! . . . . AYM IS IT TRUE? 21
AY, DIOS! . . . . AYM IS IT TRUE? 22
AY, MORENA, DONDE ESTA? . . . . . . AYM RIDE, RED, RIDE 20

AY-LORD 3
AY-LORD! . . . . SP STONY LONESOME 9
AY-LORD! . . . . SP STONY LONESOME 10
AY-LORD! . . . . SP STONY LONESOME 11

AZIKIWE'S 1
AZIKIWE'S SON, AMEKA, ... AYM ASK YOUR MAMA 65

A-BASSIN 1
LUCY WAS A-BASSIN IT, BOOM, BOOM,
BOOM. . . . . SH DEATH IN HARLEM 77

A-BEEN 2
IF THAT WATER HADN'T A-BEEN SO COLD SP LIFE IS FINE 7
IF IT HADN'T A-BEEN SO HIGH . . . . SP LIFE IS FINE 18

A-BEGGIN' 1
BLACK GALS WAS A-BEGGIN', ... SP SYLVESTER'S BED 13

A-CLIMBIN' 1
I'SE BEEN A-CLIMBIN' ON, ... SP MOTHER TO SON 9

A-COMIN' 4
THE DAWN'S A-COMIN'! . . . . SP PRAYER MEETING 2
THE DAWN'S A-COMIN'! . . . . SP PRAYER MEETING 4
THE DAWN'S A-COMIN'! . . . . SP PRAYER MEETING 9
BUT I FELT MA TIME'S A-COMIN'. . . SP SYLVESTER'S BED 17

A-CREEPIN' 1
A-CREEPIN' MUDDY PAST - . . . . . . SP SYLVESTER'S BED 20

A-CRYING 1
IN THE DARK THEY FELL A-CRYING . . DK IRISH WAKE 1

A-GOIN' 1
A-GOIN' BY. . . . . SP BABY 5

A-HUMMIN' 1
AND I SWING IT A-HUMMIN', ... NM BIG-TIMER POEM 30

A-LOVIN' 1
KEEP ON A-LOVIN' ME, DADDY, ... SP YOUNG GAL'S BLS 23

A-MOANIN' 1
SWEET GALS WAS A-MOANIN', ... SP SYLVESTER'S BED 5

A-ONLY 1
(IF I'D A-ONLY KNEW IT) . . . . . . SH ANNOUNCEMENT 10

A-PLAYIN' 1
I'D RATHER DIE WHERE THE BAND'S
A-PLAYIN' . . . . SH CABARET GIRL 3

A-SASSIN' 1
A-SASSIN' ME?" . . . . PL KU KLUX 10

A-SHOUTIN' 1
A-SHOUTIN', GOD, IT'S COMIN' SOON. SP JUDGMENT DAY 4

A-STANDIN' 1
YOU'RE A-STANDIN' THERE . . . . . . PL KU KLUX 11

A-TALL 5
DON'T HAVE TO SHARE IT A-TALL. . . SH PAY DAY 2
NOT NARY ONE A-TALL. . . . . OWT STRANGER IN TWN 6
NOBODY A-TALL - . . . . OWT STRANGER IN TWN 11
AIN'T FOR US A-TALL: . . . . SP CHILDREN'S RYME 22
AIN'T FOR US A-TALL: . . . . PL CHILDREN'S RYME 13

A-WAITIN' 2
I BEEN WAITIN' AND A-WAITIN' . . . SP OLD THE GYPSY 14
LORD, I BEEN A-WAITIN' FOR THE . . SP FREEDOM TRAIN 7

A-WALKIN' 1
WHEN HE GOES A-WALKIN' . . . . . . DK MA LORD 3

A-WAY 1
I STARTED FEELING THIS A-WAY. . . . SH EVIL MORNING 4

A.M 5
WENT BUSTIN INTO DIXIE'S BOUT ONE
A.M. . . . . SH DEATH IN HARLEM 2
ABOUT TWO-THREE A.M. . . . . OWT HONEY BABE 10
UNTIL 12 - 1 - 2 A.M. . . . . . . SP GONE BOY 4
TWO A.M. MIDNIGHT BY YOUR SELF? . . SP REVERIE HARLEM 2
TWO A.M. . . . . SP REVERIE HARLEM 10

B 3
A COMPLAINT TO B GIVEN BY A DEJECTED
LOOKING FELLOW SHUFFLING ALONG . NM BROKE 1
THIS IS MY PAGE FOR ENGLISH B. . . SP THEME FOR ENG B 41
SEND FOR DEAD BLIND LEMON TO SING
THE B FLAT . . . . PL FINAL CALL 13

BABA-RE-BOP 1
HEY! BABA-RE-BOP! MOP! ON A BE-BOP
KICK! . . . . SP LIKEWISE 23

BABE 11
BABE, HE'S GONE AWAY. . . . . WB BLUES FANTASY 10
BABE, YOU CAN'T . . . . FC NEW CABARET GRL 23
BABE, YOU SHO CAN GO! . . . . SH DEATH IN HARLEM 40
A LITTLE LOVIN', BABE, BUT . . . . SH SIX-BITS BLUES 9
I CAN SEE YOUR HOUSE, BABE, ... OWT CURIOUS 1
HONEY BABE, ... OWT HONEY BABE 1
THAT, HONEY BABE, ... OWT HONEY BABE 7
BABE, AND CALL ON YOU, ... OWT LONESOME CORNER 4
BABE, DID YOU EVER . . . . SP BLACK MARIA 11
BABE, YOUR MOUTH WAS OPEN LIKE A
WELL. . . . . SP MORNING AFTER 12
SHE ANSWERED, BABE, WHAT MUST I DO? SP 50 - 50 12

BABIES 5
BABIES AND GIN AND CHURCH . . . . . FC BRASS SPITOONS 26
NURSES OF BABIES. . . . . FC LAUGHERS 13
SO I HOLLERS, "COM'ERE, BABIES, . . SP SYLVESTER'S BED 23
BUT BABIES BORN IN SHADOWS . . . . AYM ODE TO DINAH 70
CHOCOLATE BABIES BORN IN SHADOWS . AYM ODE TO DINAH 76

BABY 61
LOVES MY BABY . . . . WB CAT AND SAXOPHN 6
BUT MY BABY . . . . WB CAT AND SAXOPHN 10
WANTS MY BABY . . . . WB CAT AND SAXOPHN 18
BUT MY BABY . . . . WB CAT AND SAXOPHN 20
THE LAST CRYING BABY SLEEPS . . . . WB SUMMER NIGHT 7
PRETTY BABY, ... WB TO MIDNIGHT NAN 10
BUYS SHOES FOR THE BABY. . . . . . FC BRASS SPITOONS 21
DARK BABY, ... FC CRAP GAME 6
HONEY BABY, ... FC MA MAN 17
BABY, O, BABY, ... FC MINNIE SINGS 11
BABY, O, BABY, ... FC MINNIE SINGS 11
I SAY, "NOW, BABY, YOU KNOW I AIN'T
GOT NONE, HONEY." . . . . NM BROKE 20
I SAID, "BABY, YOU KNOW I LOVES YOU,
AND ALL LIKE THAT . . . . NM BROKE 50
(IS YOU LOOKIN' AT ME, BABY, OR SOME
OTHER WAY?) . . . . NM BROKE 76
MY LITTLE DARK BABY, ... DK LULLABY 2
MY LITTLE BLACK BABY, ... DK LULLABY 11
MY DARK BODY'S BABY, ... DK LULLABY 12
OH, LITTLE DARK BABY, ... DK LULLABY 19
NIGHT BLACK BABY, ... DK LULLABY 20
MA BABY LIVES ACROSS DE RIVER . . . DK WIDE RIVER 1
AN' GIT TO MA BABY SOMEHOW. . . . . DK WIDE RIVER 14
GIT TO MA BABY SOMEHOW - . . . . . DK WIDE RIVER 16
CAUSE IF I DON'T SEE MA BABY . . . DK WIDE RIVER 17
I SAID, BABY, ... SH OLD THE KILLER 3
HONEY BABY, SOCK IT! . . . . SH DEATH IN HARLEM 21
HONEY-GOLD BABY . . . . SH HARLEM SWEETIES 7
DRIVE THAT BABY BACKWARD. . . . . . SH IF-ING 8
DO NOT SELL ME OUT, BABY, ... SH IN TROUBLED KEY 1
DO NOT SELL ME OUT, BABY. . . . . . SH IN TROUBLED KEY 3
I USED TO BELIEVE IN YOU, BABY, . . SH IN TROUBLED KEY 5
YOUR BABY, ... SH LETTER 22
BABY, GIMME A LITTLE LOVIN', . . . SH SIX-BITS BLUES 7
WHEN YOU'RE IN YOUR HOUSE, BABY . . OWT CURIOUS 5
BABY, AIN'T YOU HEARD? . . . . . . OWT JITNEY 52
BABY, SAY WHEN. . . . . OWT RAID 5
BUT BABY . . . . OWT RAID 6
BUT, BABY, I FEEL BLUE. . . . . . . OWT YESTERDAY TODAY 12
BABY, COULD YOU SEE YOUR WAY CLEAR? SP DEFERRED 38
BABY, IF YOU LOVE ME . . . . SP DOWN AND OUT 1
IF YOU LOVE ME, BABY, ... SP DOWN AND OUT 3
COME HERE, BABY, DARLIN'! . . . . . SP EVENING SONG 3
YOUR SON BABY . . . . SP LETTER 10

I THOUGHT ABOUT MY BABY . . . . . . SP LIFE IS FINE 14
I'LL BE DOGGED, SWEET BABY, ... SP LIFE IS FINE 29
I ASKED YOU, BABY, ... SP MAYBE 1
I SAID, BABY! BABY! . . . . SP MORNING AFTER 13
I SAID, BABY! BABY! . . . . SP MORNING AFTER 13
I SAID, BABY! BABY! . . . . SP MORNING AFTER 15
BABY! PLEASE! . . . . SP SAME IN BLUES 1
I SAID TO MY BABY, ... SP SAME IN BLUES 2
BABY, TAKE IT SLOW. . . . . SP SAME IN BLUES 17
YOU CAN HAVE ME, BABY - . . . . . . SP SUMMER EVENING 2
SWEET WATERMELON IN A BABY CARRIAGE, SP SUNDAY BY COMB 1
I FEEL LIKE DANCIN', BABY, ... SP SUNDAY BY COMB 7
BABY, DANCE WITH ME! . . . . SP SYLVESTER'S BED 16
HONEY! BABY! DON'T GO, DEAR!" . . . SP S-SSS-SS-SH! 15
THE BABY CAME ONE MORNING, ... SP TO BE SOMEBODY 2
DREAMING OF A BABY GRAND PIANO . . SP TO BE SOMEBODY 4
DREAMING OF A BABY GRAND TO PLAY . . SP ULTIMATUM 1
BABY, HOW COME YOU CAN'T SEE ME . . SP WIDOW WOMAN 15
A MIGHTY LOVER, BABY, CAUSE YOU . . AYM ODE TO DINAH 96
NO SHOW FARE, BABY - . . . .

2

BABY'S

"ME AN' MA BABY'S . . . . DK NEGRO DANCERS 1
"ME AN' MA BABY'S . . . . DK NEGRO DANCERS 13

2

BACH

I'D LIKE TO TAKE UP BACH. . . . . . SP DEFERRED 48
OR RECORDS - BESSIE, BOP, OR BACH. SP THEME FOR ENG B 24

97

BACK

AN' I WANTS MA ALBERT BACK. . . . . FC BLACK GAL 16
OH, GOD, I WANTS HIM BACK! . . . . FC BLACK GAL 18
AN' SHOT A MAN IN DE BACK. . . . . FC DEATH DO DIRTY 9
AN' SHE'S GOIN' ON BACK . . . . . . FC EVIL WOMAN 14
BACK BENT AS IN THE FIELDS. THE SLOW STEP. THE BOWED HEAD. "NOBODY KNOWS . . . . NM BLACK CLWN MOOD 4
MY BROTHER DIED IN FRANCE - BUT I CAME BACK. . . . . NM COLORED SL POEM 1
BACK, AND EYES SHINING. QUIETLY RECALLING THE VISION. THE DEAD MAN SPEAKS . . . . NM COLORED SL MOOD 8
BACK FROM THE ACRES OF CROSSES IN FRANCE. . . . . NM COLORED SL POEM 15
OF BEING HELD BACK, OF HAVING NO CHANCE - . . . . NM COLORED SL POEM 31
WITH THE WHITE AND THE BLACK WHOM NOTHING HOLDS BACK - . . . . . . NM DARK YOUTH USA 24
I'VE GONE BACK TO THE WIND AND WAVE. DK DEATH SEAMAN 8
BUT I WISH I HAD BACK THAT . . . . DK DRESSED UP 7
AND TATTOOED ON HIS BACK HE HAD . . DK SAILOR 7
GET WAY BACK, HONEY, ... DK SONG BANJO DANC 5
WHEN I BOWED MY BACK . . . . ANS A NEW SONG 8
WHEN THE BIRDS COME BACK FROM THE SOUTH. . . . . ANS CHANT MAY DAY 6
MUST BRING BACK OUR MIGHTY DREAM AGAIN. . . . . ANS LET AMERICA BE 69
WE MUST TAKE BACK OUR LAND AGAIN, ANS LET AMERICA BE 73
A KNIFE IN THE BACK . . . . ANS SONG OF SPAIN 36
JITTERBUGGING BACK. . . . . SH BLD THE SINNER 16
STAND BACK FOLKSES, LET US . . . . SH DEATH IN HARLEM 106
DOWN IN A CELLAR BACK FROM THE STREET. . . . . SH DEATH IN HARLEM 23
YAL, COME ON BACK - I KNOW YOU WANT TO. . . . . SH LETTER 9
HERE'S FIVE DOLLARS, CASSIE, BUY A TICKET BACK. . . . . SH LETTER 20
AND TAKE BACK ALL THEM THINGS WE HAD SH PAY DAY 12
CAUSE I'M GOING BACK TO ROOMING AND BE A FREE MAN. . . . . SH PAY DAY 16
I WOULDN'T TAKE YOU BACK IF YOU COME ON YOUR KNEES. . . . . SH SUNDAY 9
AND MY GRANDFATHER'S BACK WITH ITS LADDER OF SCARS. . . . . JC THE BITTER RIVR 36
TO FORCE MY BACK TO THE WALL. . . . JC THE BITTER RIVR 56
TIRED NOW OF THE PAT ON THE BACK, JC THE BITTER RIVR 76
FOR ME GIVES BACK NO STARS. . . . JC THE BITTER RIVR 88
WANTS ME TO COME BACK . . . . FW DUSTBOWL 2
WANTS ME TO COME BACK . . . . FW DUSTBOWL 8
TO COME BACK. . . . . FW DUSTBOWL 13
SHE WAS COMING BACK AGAIN. . . . . FW GIRL 8
BACK INTO THE GRASS - . . . . FW SNAKE 2
HE GOT SHOT IN THE BACK . . . . . . OWT BLD MARGE POLIT 10
BACK DOOR . . . . OWT BLUES ON A BOX 5
THE HOUNDS ARE AT YOUR BACK. . . . OWT FLIGHT 4
WHOSE LANGUID LEAN BRINGS BACK THE SUNNY SOUTH . . . . OWT JUICE JOINT 42
THE CHILD, COME BACK AGAIN. . . . LHR PASTORAL 9
BEFORE WE RUN BACK . . . . SP A HOUSE IN TAOS 42
BEAT BACK INTO THE BLOOD - . . . . SP AFRO-AMER FRAG 7
BLACK, GET BACK! . . . . SP ARGUMENT 3
SO ON BACK . . . . SP CONSIDER ME 10
MIGHT BE THAT YOU'LL COME BACK, . . SP COULD BE 11
I TAKE MY CURSES BACK. . . . . . . SP CROSS 4
THEN GOT PUT BACK WHEN WE COME NORTH. . . . . SP DEFERRED 5
SO I WENT ON BACK TO BED - . . . . SP FIRED 7
NO BACK DOOR ENTRANCE TO THE FREEDOM TRAIN. . . . . SP FREEDOM TRAIN 12
WILL SOME WHITE MAN YELL, GET BACK! SP FREEDOM TRAIN 39
HE TURNED HIS BACK ON ME. . . . . . SP HARD DADDY 8
HE TURNED HIS BACK ON ME. . . . . . SP HARD DADDY 10
STONE ANSWERS BACK, ... SP HEAVEN 11
I WENT BACK IN THE ALLEY . . . . . SP HOMECOMING 1
I PULLED BACK THE COVERS, ... SP HOMECOMING 5
ARE RARING UP AND TALKING BACK . . SP IN EXPLANATION 7
ARE RARING UP AND TALKING BACK . . SP IN EXPLANATION 20
FROM HARLEM PAST HONG KONG TALKING BACK. . . . . SP IN EXPLANATION 22
HELL, NO! IT'S TIME TO TALK BACK NOW! . . . . SP IN EXPLANATION 29
HEAR THOSE WORDS AND SHOUT THEM BACK SP IN EXPLANATION 41
BUT IN HARLEM THEY DON'T ANSWER BACK, ... SP LIKEWISE 14
NOT A WORD WRIT ON THE BACK. . . . SP LITTLE OLD LETT 10
CAME BACK HOME LAST NIGHT. . . . . SP LOVER'S RETURN 2
I STEPPED BACK . . . . SP MADAM WRONG VIS 9
BACK WINDOW'S CRACKED, ... SP MADAM RENT MAN 15
SO I CAN BRUSH YOUR BACK, I SAY! . SP MAMA AND DAUGHT 21
I GOT BACK HOME . . . . SP MIDNIGHT RAFFLE 7
AN' PLANT IT AT MY BACK DOOR, . . . SP MIDWINTER BLUES 20
PLANT IT AT MY BACK DOOR, ... SP MIDWINTER BLUES 22
SO BOY, DON'T YOU TURN BACK. . . . SP MOTHER TO SON 14
BACK.) . . . . SP MOVIES 12
GIT ON BACK THERE IN THE NIGHT, . . SP MULATTO 37
PLAY BACK A CENT. . . . . SP NUMBERS 5
NOW, I'M ALMOST BACK IN THE BARREL AGAIN. . . . . SP RELIEF 10
SITTING ON OLD MRS. LATHAM'S BACK PORCH . . . . SP RUBY BROWN 9
YOU WILL TURN BACK . . . . SP SUNDAY MORNING 17
YOU WILL TURN BACK . . . . SP SUNDAY MORNING 19
CHILDREN, I COME BACK TODAY . . . . SP THE NEGRO MOTHE 1
I HAD NOTHING, BACK THERE IN THE NIGHT. . . . . SP THE NEGRO MOTHE 24
BELIEVE IN THE RIGHT, LET NONE PUSH YOU BACK. . . . . SP THE NEGRO MOTHE 43
BUT SHE TURNS HER BACK UPON ME. . . SP THE SOUTH 22
ROCKING BACK AND FORTH TO A MELLOW CROON, ... SP THE WEARY BLUES 2
ITS BACK! . . . . AYM IS IT TRUE? 48
YET THE HORSE WHOSE BACK IS BROKEN AYM IS IT TRUE? 52
AND YOUR HAIR WAS BLOWING BACK . . AYM RIDE, RED, RIDE 33
BLOWING BACK IN THE WIND . . . . . AYM SHADES OF PIG 35
WITH MY BACK . . . . PL ANGOLA QUESTION 4
WERE TO COME BACK BLACK. . . . . . PL BIBLE BELT 2
AND NEVER CAME BACK HOME AT ALL . . PL BIRMINGHAM SUND 3
OH, BARE YOUR BACK! . . . . PL CHRIST IN ALA. 3
DARK GHOSTS COME BACK TO HAUNT YOU NOW, ... PL GHOSTS OF 1619 2
THE OLD KICKS IN THE BACK, ... PL HARLEM 4
ON THE BUS WE'RE PUT IN THE BACK - PL MERRY-GO-ROUND 11
BUT THERE AIN'T NO BACK . . . . . . PL MERRY-GO-ROUND 12
WILL COME BACK, ... PL OPPRESSION 11
I'VE NO WEAPON TO STRIKE BACK . . . PL WHO BUT TH LORD 20

1

BACKGROUND

TO BE READ BY A WORKMAN WITH, FOR BACKGROUND, THE RHYTHMIC . . . . ANS CHANT MAY DAY 1

1

BACKING

THE MUSIC, OVER-BURDENED, BACKING AWAY ANGRILY, FRANTIC WITH HUMILIATION . . . . NM BLACK CLWN MOOD 10

10

BACKLASH

MISTER BACKLASH, MISTER BACKLASH, PL BACKLASH BLUES 1
MISTER BACKLASH, MISTER BACKLASH, PL BACKLASH BLUES 1
TELL ME, MISTER BACKLASH, ... PL BACKLASH BLUES 3
IS A WHITE BACKLASH. . . . . PL BACKLASH BLUES 18
GREAT BIG WORLD, MISTER BACKLASH, PL BACKLASH BLUES 21
MISTER BACKLASH, MISTER BACKLASH, PL BACKLASH BLUES 25
MISTER BACKLASH, MISTER BACKLASH, PL BACKLASH BLUES 25
TELL ME, MISTER BACKLASH, ... PL BACKLASH BLUES 27
I'M GONNA LEAVE YOU, MISTER BACKLASH, ... PL BACKLASH BLUES 29
SINGING YOUR MEAN OLD BACKLASH BLUES. . . . . PL BACKLASH BLUES 30

1

BACKSTAGE

STRAYHORN HID BACKSTAGE WITH LUTHER $ $ . . . . AYM HORN OF PLENTY 10

2

BACKWARD

DRIVE THAT BABY BACKWARD. . . . . . SH IF-ING 8
BUT BACKWARD IN THE LANDS WHERE FACIST FEAR . . . . JC TO CAPTAIN MULZ 26

1

BACKYARD

LEST SOME FRANCO STEAL INTO OUR BACKYARD . . . . ANS SONG OF SPAIN 66

1

BACK-SLID

HAVE YOU BACK-SLID? . . . . SP MADAM MINISTER 18

40

BAD

I'M A BAD, BAD MAN . . . . FC BAD MAN 1

I'M A BAD, BAD MAN . . . . FC BAD MAN 1
I'M A BAD, BAD MAN. . . . . FC BAD MAN 3
I'M A BAD, BAD MAN. . . . . FC BAD MAN 3
I'M SO BAD I . . . . FC BAD MAN 13
SO BAD, BAD, BAD I . . . . FC BAD MAN 15
SO BAD, BAD, BAD I . . . . FC BAD MAN 15
SO BAD, BAD, BAD I . . . . FC BAD MAN 15
YET I AIN'T NEVER BEEN NO BAD ONE. FC BLACK GAL 13
SEEMS LIKE BAD LICKER, ... FC BLD OF GIN MARY 11
WON'T BE SO BAD IN JAIL . . . . FC BLD OF GIN MARY 19
I'M THE BAD EGG, SEE! . . . . NM BIG-TIMER POEM 9
YOU SAY I'LL MEET A BAD ENDIN', HEH? NM BIG-TIMER POEM 33
BUT BROKEN WAS THE SOLDIER'S DREAM,
TOO BAD TO BE . . . . NM COLORED SL POEM 49
TREAT A MAN SO BAD? . . . . SH ANNOUNCEMENT 8
I WONDER IF WHITE FOLKS EVER FEEL
BAD. . . . . SH DAYBREAK 12
THE PICKIN'S WEREN'T BAD ON A 133RD. SH DEATH IN HARLEM 5
THE PICKIN'S WEREN'T BAD - . . . . SH DEATH IN HARLEM 6
FEEL BAD TWO DAYS STRAIGHT. . . . . SH EVIL MORNING 14
TURNED OUT SO BAD. . . . . SH PAY DAY 10
AIN'T THAT TOO BAD? . . . . SH SUNDAY 14
KEEP FEELING LIKE THIS I'M GONNA
START ACTING BAD. . . . . SH TWILIGHT REVERI 4
THINGS IS BAD - . . . . JC GOOD MORN STLIN 7
BUT THEY'RE NOT SO BAD . . . . JC GOOD MORN STLIN 8
LIFT THEIR HEADS AND THINGS IS BAD, JC GOOD MORN STLIN 30
I MISS YOU SO BAD - . . . . OWT YESTERDAY TODAY 6
MY BAD LUCK CARD. . . . . SP BAD LUCK CARD 4
BEAT HER UP BAD. . . . . SP BLD FORTUNE TEL 22
LIKE THEY TRY TO DO YOU BAD. . . . SP BOUND NO'TH BLS 18
SOME OF THESE YOUNG ONES IS CERT'LY
BAD - . . . . SP CHILDREN'S RYME 17
BEIN TREATED SO BAD. . . . . SP EARLY EVENING 16
I DON'T TREAT YOU BAD, HATTIE. . . SP EARLY EVENING 17
CHILDREN SO BAD? . . . . SP MADAM CHARTY CH 10
THINGS IS BAD - . . . . SP MADAM CHARTY CH 27
BAD THAT WAY. . . . . SP MIGRANT 40
I DRUNK SOME BAD LICKER THAT . . . SP MORNING AFTER 5
LIKE A BAD BOY IN THE CORNER. . . . SP TO BE SOMEBODY 7
LOOK ALL SCRAGGLY AND BAD. . . . . SP WARNING AUGMENT 10
IT WOULD BE TOO BAD IF JESUS . . . PL BIBLE BELT 1
IS NOT SO BAD. . . . . PL DINNER GUEST ME 21

BAD-LUCK 1
DEALT MY BAD-LUCK CARD. . . . . . . SP LITTLE GRN TREE 8

BAGS 1
I PACK A MILLION BAGS O' SAND . . . SH MISSISSIPPI LEV 11

BAG'S 1
WHERE CAME TO BAG'S ILLUSIVE . . . AYM IS IT TRUE? 12

BAHIA 4
BAHIA LAGOS DAKAR LENOX . . . . . . AYM ASK YOUR MAMA 47
AY, BAHIA! . . . . AYM GOSPEL CHA-CHA 27
AY, BAHIA! . . . . AYM GOSPEL CHA-CHA 28
A LONG WAY TO BAHIA - . . . . AYM GOSPEL CHA-CHA 39

BAIL 3
HE'D GO MA BAIL. . . . . FC DEATH DO DIRTY 19
TENANT HELD NO BAIL . . . . SP BLD LANDLORD 32
OUT ON BAIL . . . . SP JAM SESSION 2

BAILEY 1
FAILS TO GET PEARL BAILEY. . . . . AYM ODE TO DINAH 6

BAKE 2
COME ON HOME AND BAKE SOME CORN
BREAD. . . . . SH LETTER 16
BAKE. . . . . PL FROSTING 8

BAKED 1
SUN HAS BAKED ME. . . . . PL STILL HERE 4

BAKERSFIELD 1
TO LOS ANGELES, BAKERSFIELD. . . . SP ONE-WAY TICKET 11

BAKES 1
YOU STILL BAKES BISCUITS? FRIED
CHICKEN EVERY NIGHT? IS THAT
TRUE? . . . . NM BROKE 73

BAKOKO 1
ADELE RAMONA MICHAEL SERVE BAKOKO
TEA . . . . AYM BIRD IN ORBIT 20

BALL 5
A BALL PASSED BY. . . . . SH DEATH IN HARLEM 102
OF WHISKEY AS THEY START OUT FOR A
BALL. . . . . OWT JUICE JOINT 8
ONE BATTED A HARD BALL RIGHT THROUGH
MY WINDOW . . . . SP CHILDREN'S RYME 18
BECAME A BRIGHT BALL OF LIGHT . . . SP FULFILMENT 10
WHEN THE AIR IS ONE INTERMINABLE
BALL GAME . . . . SP PASSING 2

BALLOON 1
SHRUNKEN LIKE A BALLOON WITHOUT AIR. SP A BLACK PIERROT 13

BALLOONS 1
STONES BURST LIKE BALLOONS . . . . AYM ASK YOUR MAMA 68

BALLOT 1
IS THERE BALLOT BOXES ON THE FREEDOM
TRAIN? . . . . SP FREEDOM TRAIN 20

BALLOTS 1
AND BALLOTS DROP IN BOXES . . . . . AYM BIRD IN ORBIT 13

BALLS 3
ROLLING WHITE BALLS IN THE POOL
ROOMS. . . . . SP RAILROAD AVENUE 27
HIGH BALLS, LOW BALLS: . . . . . . AYM ASK YOUR MAMA 18
HIGH BALLS, LOW BALLS: . . . . . . AYM ASK YOUR MAMA 18

BALTIMORE 1
AND HE DIDN'T STOP IN BALTIMORE . . SP NOT A MOVIE 10

BAM 1
BAM! BOP! MOP! . . . . SP TO BE SOMEBODY 20

BAND 12
JAZZ BAND! . . . . FC JAZZ BAND 2
JAZZ BAND! . . . . FC JAZZ BAND 10
PLAY IT, JAZZ BAND! . . . . FC JAZZ BAND 18
JAZZ BAND, JAZZ BAND! . . . . FC MINNIE SINGS 7
JAZZ BAND, JAZZ BAND! . . . . FC MINNIE SINGS 7
A MORAL POEM TO BE RENDERED BY A MAN
IN A STRAW HAT WITH A BRIGHT
BAND, A . . . . NM BIG-TIMER MOOD 1
BUT WHEN THE BAND BEGAN TO PLAY, . FW HARLEM DANCE HA 2
THE BAND DOWN IN THE PIT BURSTS INTO
JAZZ. . . . . OWT LINCOLN THEATRE 6
A BIG BRASS BAND . . . . SP AS BEFITS A MAN 11
A BAND IS PLAYING. . . . . SP HARLEM NIGHT SO 12
WITH BAND AND DRUM . . . . SP PARADE 10
TO A BAND THAT ONCE PASSED OVER . . AYM ODE TO DINAH 27

BANDAGE 1
HER BANDAGE HIDES TWO FESTERING
SORES . . . . PL JUSTICE 3

BANDANNA 1
IS A SOFT BANDANNA HANDKERCHIEF . . WB OUR LAND 5

BANDS 1
IN LITTLE BANDS TOGETHER. . . . . . SP FREEDOM'S PLOW 37

BAND-MEN 1
AND BAND-MEN IN CIRCUSES - . . . . FC LAUGHERS 13

BAND'S 1
I'D RATHER DIE WHERE THE BAND'S
A-PLAYIN' . . . . SH CABARET GIRL 3

BANG 1
BIG BEN, I'M GONNA BUST YOU BANG UP
SIDE THE WALL! . . . . SH DAYBREAK 1

BANJO 2
HE KIN PLAY A BANJO. . . . . FC MA MAN 7
HE KIN PLAY A BANJO. . . . . FC MA MAN 9

BANJO'S 2
(THE BANJO'S SOBBING LOW) . . . . . DK SONG BANJO DANC 17
(THE BANJO'S SOBBING LOW) . . . . . DK SONG BANJO DANC 25

BANK 2
A BANK FULL OF CASH. . . . . SH BLD THE KILLER 10
I SET DOWN ON THE BANK. . . . . . . SP LIFE IS FINE 2

BANKS 2
TAKES TOOLS AND BANKS AND MINES, . ANS OPEN LETTER 61
SINGING SORROW SONGS ON THE BANKS OF
A MIGHTY RIVER . . . . SP AUNTSUE'S STORI 11

BANNER 4
BANNER OF FORCE AND LABOR, STRENGTH
AND UNION. . . . . ANS CHANT TOM MOONY 43
HERE I GO WITH MY BANNER IN MY HAND! ANS SISTER JOHNSON 5
LIFT HIGH MY BANNER OUT OF THE DUST. SP THE NEGRO MOTHE 41
LIKE A BANNER . . . . PL COLOR 2

BANNERS 1
AS IF TECHNICOLOR BANNERS FLEW . . PL MOTHER IN WAR 7

BAPTIST 2
EBECANEEZER BAPTIST CHURCH. . . . . SP PRAYER MEETING 7
ON THAT DAY WHEN ABYSSINIA BAPTIST
CHURCH . . . . SP PROJECTION 5

BAPTIZED 1
I WAS BAPTIZED . . . . SP MADAM MINISTER 11

BAR 17

LOUNGERS AT THE BAR LAUGH OUT LOUD. . . . SH DEATH IN HARLEM 35
YOU SPREAD YOUR COLOR BAR. . . . . JC BLACK MAN SPEAK 16
I'LL SING FOR YOU - BUT DROP THAT COLOR BAR. . . . . JC JIM CROW'S LAST 18
OF THE BAR STOOLS . . . . FW CHIPPY 7
TURN FROM THE BAR AND JOIN YOU IN YOUR SONG. . . . . OWT JUICE JOINT 22
WHERE TWO OLD BROWN MEN STAND BEHIND THE BAR - . . . . OWT JUICE JOINT 37
SATURDAY LAUGHTER, A BAR, A BED. . SP CONSIDER ME 43
HE SITS IN A BAR WITH A BEER. . . . SP NEIGHBOR 6
WONDER BAR . . . . SP NEON SIGNS 1
STILL BAR YOU THE WAY, AND DENY YOU LIFE - . . . . SP THE NEGRO MOTHE 46
FACE LIKE A CHOCOLATE BAR . . . . . SP 125TH STREET 1
POOL HALL OR BAR ON CORNER . . . . AYM HORN OF PLENTY 70
THERE'S A BAR WITH WINDOWS FROSTED AYM ODE TO DINAH 24
WITH A BAR WITH FROSTED WINDOWS . . AYM ODE TO DINAH 42
TURNED INTO A BAR: . . . . PL LITTLE SNC HOUS 21
WERE PLED ANEW AT SOME HEROIC BAR. PL MOTHER IN WAR 4
WHICH AREAWAY, OR BAR. . . . . . . FL WHERE WHEN WHCH 11

BARBECUE 1

BARBECUE STAND . . . . SP MADAM'S PAST HI 11

BARE 8

WILL STRIP THEIR BODIES BARE . . . WR POEME D'AUTOMNE 10
BARE YOUR BOSOM TO THE SUN. . . . . DK SONG 2
BEAT WITH BARE, BROWN FISTS - . . . DK SONG 8
PLACE WHERE YOUR CLOTHES HUNG'S EMPTY AND BARE. . . . . SH SUPPER TIME 9
THAT GOOD BLACK FEET TO DANCING ON BARE FLOORS. . . . . OWT JUICE JOINT 20
BARE. . . . . SP MOTHER TO SON 7
BARE FEET TO BEAT THE GREAT DRUMBEAT AYM BLUES IN STEREO 9
OH, BARE YOUR BACK! . . . . PL CHRIST IN ALA. 3

BARED 2

BARED HER BOSOMS, BARED IN PUBLIC AYM BIRD IN ORBIT 49
BARED HER BOSOMS, BARED IN PUBLIC AYM BIRD IN ORBIT 49

BAREFOOT 1

YOU BAREFOOT, TOO. . . . . AYM BLUES IN STEREO 12

BARING 1

STRENGTH HE DOESN'T REALLY FEEL. GAY, LOUD, UNHAPPY JAZZ, BARING HIS . . . . NM BIG-TIMER MOOD 9

BARK 1

BARK LIKE A DOG. . . . . SH ONLY WOMAN BLUS 8

BARKIN' 2

HOUND DAWG'S BARKIN' . . . . FC GAL'S CRY DYING 7
HOUND DAWG'S BARKIN' . . . . FC GAL'S CRY DYING 9

BARRED 2

THE UNIONS BARRED US: THE FACTORIES, TOO. . . . . NM COLORED SL POEM 22
MARY MCLEOD BETHUNE BARRED BY . . . AYM BIRD IN ORBIT 76

BARREL 4

AN' SOON AS HE GOT OUT OF BARREL . FC BLACK GAL 11
STEP OUT O' THE BARREL, BOY. . . . SP ELEVATOR BOY 11
I WOULDN'T BE OUT THE BARREL YET. SP RELIEF 9
NOW, I'M ALMOST BACK IN THE BARREL AGAIN. . . . . SP RELIEF 10

BARREL-HOUSE 1

BARREL-HOUSE JAZZ, SHOWING-OFF, STRUTTING ABOUT PROUDLY, BRAGGING AND . . . . NM BIG-TIMER MOOD 4

BARREN 4

LIFE IS A BARREN FIELD . . . . . . DK DREAMS 7
THAT THERE SHOULD BE A BARREN GARDEN SP A HOUSE IN TAOS 16
BUT THAT THERE SHOULD BE THREE BARREN HEARTS . . . . SP A HOUSE IN TAOS 19
IN THE BARREN DUSK . . . . SP DESERT 4

BARRIERS 1

TO SPROUT THEIR BITTER BARRIERS . . PL GEORGIA DUSK 11

BARS 21

BARS . . . . NM COLORED SL POEM 26
WHEN BEYOND STEEL BARS SOUND THE DEATHLESS DRUMS . . . . SL SCOTTSBORO 7
STRONG ARE THE BARS AND STEEL THE GATE. . . . . ANS BLD OZZIE POWEL 5
AND THE STEEL BARS SURROUND YOU. . ANS CHANT TOM MOONY 7
SHAKING THE BARS. . . . . ANS CHANT TOM MOONY 21
IT GIVES ONLY THE GLINT OF STEEL BARS . . . . JC THE BITTER RIVR 27
AND DARK BITTER FACES BEHIND STEEL BARS: . . . . JC THE BITTER RIVR 28
THE SCOTTSBORO BOYS BEHIND STEEL BARS. . . . . JC THE BITTER RIVR 29
LEWIS JONES BEHIND STEEL BARS. . . JC THE BITTER RIVR 30
THE VOTELESS SHARE-CROPPER BEHIND STEEL BARS. . . . . JC THE BITTER RIVR 31
THE LABOR LEADER BEHIND STEEL BARS. JC THE BITTER RIVR 32
THE SOLDIER THROWN FROM A JIM CROW BUS BEHIND STEEL BARS. . . . . . JC THE BITTER RIVR 33
THE 15¢ MUGGER BEHIND STEEL BARS. JC THE BITTER RIVR 34
THE GIRL WHO SELLS HER BODY BEHIND STEEL BARS. . . . . JC THE BITTER RIVR 35
LONG AGO, LONG AGO - THE WHIP AND STEEL BARS - . . . . JC THE BITTER RIVR 37
TIRED NOW OF THE STEEL BARS . . . . JC THE BITTER RIVR 77
TIRED OF THE BARS! . . . . JC THE BITTER RIVR 80
THE YEARS BUILD THEIR BARS . . . . FW CIRCLES 5
YET THERE'RE BARS . . . . SP GOOD MORNING 24
BUT MARCH EVER FORWARD, BREAKING DOWN BARS. . . . . SP THE NEGRO MOTHE 47
BARS AND FLOOR SKYROCKET . . . . . . FL THIRD DEGREE 13

BARTERED 1

THE POOREST WORKER BARTERED THROUGH THE YEARS. . . . . ANS LET AMERICA BE 38

BAR-GLASS 1

WHERE THE SEA'S A BAR-GLASS . . . . SP TRUMPET PLAYER 31

BASEBALL 1

GLOBAL TROTTERS BASEBALL BATTERS $ $ . . . . AYM HORN OF PLENTY 16

BASIC 3

YET I'M THE ONE WHO DREAMT OUR BASIC DREAM . . . . ANS LET AMERICA BE 39
FAR REMOVED FROM BASIC OVEN. . . . SP GRADUATION 17
BASIC AND WONDERING . . . . SP MYSTERY 15

BASIE'S 1

AND SEE WHAT COUNT BASIE'S PLAYING NEW. . . . . SH BED TIME 2

BASKET 1

IN THE COLLECTION BASKET . . . . . SP SUNDAY MORNING 40

BASS 6

BASS SO LOW! . . . . SH DEATH IN HARLEM 30
AND TWINING THE BASS . . . . SP BOOGIE 1 A.M. 6
ROLLING BASS. . . . . SP DREAM BOOGIE VAR 2
DOWN IN THE BASS . . . . SP EASY BOOGIE 1
DOWN IN THE BASS . . . . SP EASY BOOGIE 5
ROLLING BASS. . . . . SP NIGHTMARE BOOGE 10

BASTARD 5

O, YOU LITTLE BASTARD BOY, ... SP MULATTO 16
BASTARD BOY, ... SP MULATTO 26
TO LITTLE YELLOW BASTARD BOYS. . . SP MULATTO 36
BASTARD BOY, ... SP MULATTO 45
MOST HOLY BASTARD . . . . PL CHRIST IN ALA. 10

BASTILE 1

THAT TORE THE BASTILE DOWN . . . . SL SCOTTSBORO 14

BATABANO 1

THE DREAM IS THE ROAD TO BATABANO. SP HAVANA DREAMS 3

BATHED 2

LAUGHED AND BATHED . . . . SP FULFILMENT 7
I BATHED IN THE EUPHRATES WHEN DAWNS WERE YOUNG. . . . . SP NEGRO SPEAKS OF 5

BATHMATS 1

BATHMATS OF PRIDE. . . . . PL UNDERTOW 5

BATHROBES 1

SILKEN BATHROBES WITH GOLD TWINES SP FLATTED FIFTHS 5

BATTED 1

ONE BATTED A HARD BALL RIGHT THROUGH MY WINDOW . . . . SP CHILDREN'S RYME 18

BATTERED 3

IN AN OLD SUIT AND A BATTERED HAT, TO THE TUNE OF A SLOW DRAG STOMP NM BROKE 1
AMBITION BATTERED AND BRUISED. . . JC THE BITTER RIVR 21
I BEEN SCARED AND BATTERED. . . . . PL STILL HERE 1

BATTERS 1

GLOBAL TROTTERS BASEBALL BATTERS $ $ . . . . AYM HORN OF PLENTY 16

BATTLE 4

OUR BATTLE YET IS FAR FROM WON . . JC JIM CROW'S LAST 30
THERE WAS LIGHT WHEN THE BATTLE CLOUDS ROLLED AWAY. . . . . SP FREEDOM'S PLOW 139
OF BLOOD AND BATTLE . . . . PL LAST PRINCE 11
BATTLE GROUND . . . . PL THE DOVE 9

BATTLEFIELD 1

ON THE BATTLEFIELD. . . . . PL OFFICIAL NOTICE 8

BAWLIN' 1

COME BAWLIN' ME OUT, 'CAUSE I'M BROKE. . . . . . NM BROKE 26

BAY 1

FILLMORE OUT IN FRISCO, 7TH ACROSS THE BAY. . . . . . AYM ASK YOUR MAMA 31

BAYONETS 1

BEATING THEM WITH LAWS AND CLUBS AND BAYONETS AND BULLETS . . . . . ANS KIDS WHO DIE 30

BAYOU 2

BY THE BLUE BAYOU . . . . . SP BLUE BAYOU 2

THE BLUE BAYOU . . . . . SP BLUE BAYOU 14

BAYOU'S 1

THE BLUE BAYOU'S . . . . . SP BLUE BAYOU 22

BE 240

I WOULD BE SIMPLE AGAIN. . . . . . WB DISILLUSION 1

BE KIND TO ME. . . . . . WB DISILLUSION 11

WILL BE THEIR ONLY . . . . . WB POEME D'AUTOMNE 14

SHALL I BE WISE AGAIN? . . . . . WB THE JESTER 19

BE YOUR PAL. . . . . . WB TO MIDNIGHT NAN 4

BE YOUR MAN. . . . . . WB TO MIDNIGHT NAN 20

WON'T BE NOBODY'S BRIDE . . . . . FC A RUINED GAL 4

DON'T EVEN WANT TO BE GOOD. . . . . . FC BAD MAN 14

DON'T EVEN WANT TO BE GOOD. . . . . . FC BAD MAN 16

AN' LETS ME BE. . . . . . FC BLACK GAL 8

JUDGE, WON'T LET ME BE. . . . . . FC BLD OF GIN MARY 12

SO LICKER'LL LET YOU BE. . . . . . FC BLD OF GIN MARY 16

WON'T BE SO BAD IN JAIL . . . . . FC BLD OF GIN MARY 19

TILL LICKER'LL LET YOU BE. . . . . . FC BLD OF GIN MARY 24

DEATH, BE KIND . . . . . FC CLOSING TIME 13

I'M GONNA BE A GYPSY WOMAN . . . . . FC GYPSY MAN 5

I USED TO BE A GOOD CHILE, ... FC LISTEN HERE 7

USED TO BE A GOOD CHILE, - . . . . . FC LISTEN HERE 9

EAGLE-ROCKISH AS I KIN BE! . . . . . FC MA MAN 13

IT SHO WOULD BE SAD. . . . . . FC MINNIE SINGS 14

SHO, THERE MUST BE PEACE, ... FC MOAN 16

WOULD BE A SURPRISE. . . . . . FC NEW CABARET GRL 4

WOULD BE A SURPRISE. . . . . . FC NEW CABARET GRL 16

I WOULDN'T BE FIGHTIN'. . . . . . FC PRIZE FIGHTER 3

BE A HIGH YALLER, ... FC RED SILK STOCK 10

WON'T BE NOTHIN' LEFT . . . . . FC SATURDAY NIGHT 15

MUST BE . . . . . FC SPORT 3

CAUSE I TRIES TO BE GOOD . . . . . FC WORKIN' MAN 15

A MORAL POEM TO BE RENDERED BY A MAN IN A STRAW HAT WITH A BRIGHT BAND, A . . . . . NM BIG-TIMER MOOD 1

A DRAMATIC MONOLOGUE TO BE SPOKEN BY A PURE-BLOODED NEGRO IN THE WHITE NM BLACK CLWN MOOD 1

LET IT BE GAY. . . . . . NM BLACK CLWN POEM 13

LIKE THIS WILL I BE: . . . . . NM BLACK CLWN POEM 60

SO WHEN I GOT READY TO GO, I SAID, "I'LL BE SEEIN' YOU SOON, MARIE." NM BROKE 52

SHE WOULD BE ALRIGHT IF SHE WASN'T SO BOW-LEGGED, AND CROSS-EYED. NM BROKE 54

A DRAMATIC RECITATION TO BE DONE IN THE HALF-DARK BY A YOUNG BROWN FELLOW . . . . . NM COLORED SL MOOD 1

DIDN'T OUR GOVERNMENT TELL US THINGS WOULD BE FINE . . . . . NM COLORED SL POEM 37

BUT BROKEN WAS THE SOLDIER'S DREAM, TOO BAD TO BE . . . . . NM COLORED SL POEM 49

A RECITATION TO BE DELIVERED BY A NEGRO BOY, BRIGHT, CLEAN, AND NEATLY . . . . . NM DARK YOUTH USA 1

TO BE WISE AND STRONG, THEN, STUDYING LONG, NM DARK YOUTH USA 16

AN' BE MA FRIEND THROUGH ETERNITY." DK MA LORD 16

THIS IS GONNA BE MA SONG. . . . . . DK NIGHT AND MORN 8

THIS IS GONNA BE MA SONG: . . . . . DK NIGHT AND MORN 10

I COULD BE BLUE BUT . . . . . DK NIGHT AND MORN 11

DO NOT BE AFRAID OF LIGHT. . . . . . DK SONG 3

WIDE A RIVER CAN BE. . . . . . DK WIDE RIVER 12

SHALL BE ONE! . . . . . ANS A NEW SONG 50

TO BE READ BY A WORKMAN WITH, FOR BACKGROUND, THE RHYTHMIC . . . . . ANS CHANT MAY DAY 1

BE LIKE THE FLOWERS. . . . . . ANS CHANT MAY DAY 3

10-VOICES: BE LIKE THE SAP RISING IN THE TREES, ... ANS CHANT MAY DAY 15

WILL BE FORGOTTEN THEN . . . . . ANS CHANT TOM MOONY 27

BUT REMEMBERED FOREVER WILL BE THE NAME: . . . . . ANS CHANT TOM MOONY 30

SCHOOLS WILL BE NAMED: . . . . . ANS CHANT TOM MOONY 32

FARMS WILL BE NAMED: . . . . . ANS CHANT TOM MOONY 34

DAMS WILL BE NAMED: . . . . . ANS CHANT TOM MOONY 36

SHIPS WILL BE NAMED: . . . . . ANS CHANT TOM MOONY 38

FACTORIES WILL BE NAMED: . . . . . ANS CHANT TOM MOONY 40

WILL BE THE NAME: . . . . . ANS CHANT TOM MOONY 45

MAYBE, NOW, THERE WILL BE NO MONUMENT FOR YOU . . . . . ANS KIDS WHO DIE 38

MAYBE YOUR BODIES'LL BE LOST IN A SWAMP. . . . . . ANS KIDS WHO DIE 40

LET AMERICA BE AMERICA AGAIN. . . . . ANS LET AMERICA BE 1

LET IT BE THE DREAM IT USED TO BE. ANS LET AMERICA BE 2

LET IT BE THE DREAM IT USED TO BE. ANS LET AMERICA BE 2

LET IT BE THE PIONEER ON THE PLAIN ANS LET AMERICA BE 3

LET AMERICA BE THE DREAM THE DREAMERS DREAMED - . . . . . ANS LET AMERICA BE 6

LET IT BE THAT GREAT STRONG LAND OF LOVE . . . . . ANS LET AMERICA BE 7

THAT ANY MAN BE CRUSHED BY ONE ABOVE. . . . . . ANS LET AMERICA BE 9

O, LET MY LAND BE A LAND WHERE LIBERTY . . . . . ANS LET AMERICA BE 11

IN SEARCH OF WHAT I MEANT TO BE MY HOME - . . . . . ANS LET AMERICA BE 46

O, LET AMERICA BE AMERICA AGAIN - ANS LET AMERICA BE 62

AND YET MUST BE - THE LAND WHERE EVERY MAN IS FREE. . . . . . ANS LET AMERICA BE 64

AMERICA WILL BE! . . . . . ANS LET AMERICA BE 79

THAT THE LAND MIGHT BE OURS. . . . ANS OPEN LETTER 14

BE OURS: . . . . . ANS OPEN LETTER 18

LET UNION BE . . . . . ANS OPEN LETTER 55

EXCEPT THAT THEY BE MADE FOR US . . ANS SONG OF SPAIN 64

THAT MUST BE ENDED. . . . . . ANS UNION 12

AND BE A WHITE MAN THE REST OF MY DAYS! . . . . . SH DAYBREAK 11

HOW DE BLUES THEY COME TO BE, . . . SH EVENIN' BLUES 20

HOW DE BLUES THEY COME TO BE - . . SH EVENIN' BLUES 22

BUT YOU JUST AS WELL BE HERE WHERE YOU DUE TO LIVE. . . . . . SH LETTER 11

I'LL TRY NOT TO BE THAT MEAN NO MORE. . . . . . SH LETTER 13

YOU TURNED OUT TO BE A DEVIL . . . SH LOVE AGAIN BLUS 11

HOW HIGH HAVE YOU GOT TO BE? . . . SH MISSISSIPPI LEV 14

HOW HIGH HAVE YOU GOT TO BE . . . SH MISSISSIPPI LEV 16

CAUSE I'M GOING BACK TO ROOMING AND BE A FREE MAN. . . . . . SH PAY DAY 16

IT MIGHT BE MISUNDERSTOOD - . . . . SH SNOB 4

THEY OUGHT TO BE SOME NOISE. . . . SH SUNDAY 11

THEY OUGHT TO BE LIKE ME SETTING HERE - FEELING GLAD! . . . . . SH SUNDAY 15

AND BE UP AND OUT AND READY . . . . JC BLD SAM SOLOMON 21

WHO WANTS TO BE FREE. . . . . . JC GOOD MORN STLIN 21

THAT MAY BE SO - FOR THOSE WHO WANT IT SO. . . . . . JC GOOD MORN STLIN 25

AND YOU WON'T BE . . . . . JC GOOD MORN STLIN 41

COME TO BE. . . . . . JC HOW ABOUT DIXIE 4

TO BE WON OVER THERE. . . . . . JC HOW ABOUT DIXIE 22

AND BE THE SAME OLD CROW HE USED TO BE - . . . . . JC JIM CROW'S LAST 10

AND BE THE SAME OLD CROW HE USED TO BE - . . . . . JC JIM CROW'S LAST 10

BUT WHEN IT IS, JIM CROW'LL BE DONE. JC JIM CROW'S LAST 31

"WAIT, BE PATIENT," YOU SAY. . . . JC THE BITTER RIVR 39

DREAMER OF DREAMS TO BE BROKEN, . . JC THE BITTER RIVR 67

BUILDER OF HOPES TO BE SMASHED. . . JC THE BITTER RIVR 68

WE WILL NOT BE AGAIN. . . . . . JC TO CAPTAIN MULZ 34

CAN BE FREE. . . . . . JC TO CAPTAIN MULZ 61

AND CHAINS BE GONE! . . . . . FW DUSK 13

THAT WILL NEVER BE. . . . . . FW JAIME 8

I THOUGHT THAT LOVE MUST BE . . . . FW MAN 5

LET THE GRAVEYARD BE THE . . . . . OWT BOARDING HOUSE 13

WHO WOULD BE MY VERY OWN - . . . . OWT STRANGER IN TWN 4

WILL BE A SIGN. . . . . . LHR BLD MARY'S SON 21

HE SAID, OH, LORD, THY WILL BE DONE! LHR BLD MARY'S SON 24

THAT MY SOUL SHOULD NOT BE LOST. . LHR BLD MARY'S SON 33

TO BE SOUVENIRS OF JESUS, ... LHR PASTORAL 8

THAT THERE SHOULD BE A BARREN GARDEN SP A HOUSE IN TAOS 16

BUT THAT THERE SHOULD BE THREE BARREN HEARTS . . . . . SP A HOUSE IN TAOS 19

BUT I WANT MY FUNERAL TO BE FINE: SP AS BEFITS A MAN 6

UNLUCKY AS CAN BE. . . . . . SP BAD LUCK CARD 8

MUST BE THE BLACK MARIA . . . . . SP BLACK MARIA 1

YOU AIN'T GONNA BE ABLE TO SAY A WORD . . . . . SP BLD LANDLORD 19

WHEN WILL MY GAL BE HOME? . . . . . SP BLD THE GYPSY 4

SHE'LL BE HERE BY AND BY. . . . . . SP BLD THE GYPSY 12

HATES TO BE LONELY, ... SP BOUND NO'TH BLS 13

LAWD, I HATES TO BE SAD. . . . . . SP BOUND NO'TH BLS 14

SAYS I HATES TO BE LONELY, ... SP BOUND NO'TH BLS 15

HATES TO BE LONELY AN' SAD, ... SP BOUND NO'TH BLS 16

BE PRESIDENT. . . . . . SP CHILDREN'S RYME 9

COULD BE HASTINGS STREET, ... SP COULD BE 1

COULD BE 18TH & VINE . . . . . SP COULD BE 3

AND STILL BE TRUE. . . . . . SP COULD BE 4

COULD BE 5TH & MOUND, ... SP COULD BE 5

COULD BE RAMPART: . . . . . SP COULD BE 6

COULD BE YOU LOVE ME, ... SP COULD BE 9

COULD BE THAT YOU DON'T. . . . . . SP COULD BE 10

MIGHT BE THAT YOU'LL COME BACK. . . SP COULD BE 11

WHAT COULD POSSIBLY BE ALL-FEET? . SP DANCER 22

WHAT DID NOT SEEM COULD EVER BE: . SP DREAM 4

WHAT HE SAID MUST BE MEANT FOR EVERY HUMAN BEING - . . . . . SP FREEDOM'S PLOW 107

WHEN IT STOPS IN MISSISSIPPI WILL IT BE MADE PLAIN . . . . . SP FREEDOM TRAIN 21

THAT THE SLAVES WOULD BE FREE. . . SP FREEDOM'S PLOW 134

FOR THE FREEDOM TRAIN WILL BE YOURS AND MINE! . . . . . SP FREEDOM TRAIN 58

DON'T BE DISCOURAGED, BUILDER! . . SP FREEDOM'S PLOW 162

DON'T BE WEARY, SOLDIER! . . . . . . SP FREEDOM'S PLOW 164
WHEN HE SHOULD BE GONE . . . . . . SP GONE BOY 6
KEEP THINKIN' I WON'T BE LONELY . . SP HOPE 3
I'LL BE AT THE TABLE . . . . SP I, TOO 3
AND BE ASHAMED - . . . . SP I, TOO 17
SAYS DON'T BE 'FRAID . . . . SP JUDGMENT DAY 8
IF YOU WANT TO BE HAPPY . . . . . . SP LAMENT OVER LOV 17
I'LL BE DOGGED, SWEET BABY, ... SP LIFE IS FINE 29
WHAT'S TOO GOOD TO BE TRUE, ... SP MADAM MIGHT-HAV 7
JUST MIGHT BE SO. . . . . SP MADAM MIGHT-HAV 8
BE A HIT FOR ME. . . . . SP MADAM NUMBER WR 12
CAN IT BE . . . . SP MADAM HER MADAM 14
THAT MAY BE TRUE - . . . . SP MADAM HER MADAM 22
SHE SAID, MADAM! BE CALM - . . . . SP MADAM FORT TELL 22
BUT I'LL BE DOGGED . . . . SP MADAM HER MADAM 23
THERE OUGHT TO BE MAGNOLIAS . . . . SP MAGNOLIA FLOWER 10
MAMA, DAD COULDN'T BE STILL YOUNG. SP MAMA AND DAUGHT 17
IT ISN'T NICE TO BE NAKED? . . . . SP MARCH MOON 10
I MUST BE MISS BLUES'ES CHILD. . . SP MISS BLUES'ES 6
WHEN A CHILE GETS TO BE THIRTEEN . SP MYSTERY 1
BE WASTED FOREVER. . . . . SP NO REGRETS 4
BE NEVER. . . . . SP NO REGRETS 9
I RECKON IT'LL BE . . . . SP NOTE COMM THEAT 18
YES, IT'LL BE ME. . . . . SP NOTE COMM THEAT 20
CAN'T BE RIGHT. . . . . SP PARADE 19
COME AND BE MINE. . . . . SP PORT TOWN 8
I KNOW WHAT RELIEF CAN BE - . . . . SP RELIEF 6
I WOULDN'T BE OUT THE BARREL YET. SP RELIEF 9
THE ONE TO STOP 'EM WON'T BE ME. . SP RELIEF 15
TO BE CONFUSION . . . . SP SAME IN BLUES 27
THERE'S LIABLE TO BE CONFUSION . . SP SAME IN BLUES 31
TO BE SO STILL THAT WAY. . . . . . SP SEA CALM 6
BE GOOD! . . . . SP SILHOUETTE 12
BE GOOD! . . . . SP SILHOUETTE 13
WELL, ANYWAY, IT DON'T HAVE TO BE A MARRIED MAN. . . . . SP SISTER 12
BUT WE ALL SHOULD BE FREE. . . . . SP SOUTHERN MAMMY 16
WE ALL SHOULD BE FREE. . . . . . . SP SOUTHERN MAMMY 18
NOT MEANIN' TO BE SASSY . . . . . . SP SOUTHERN MAMMY 19
AND NOT MEANIN' TO BE SMART - . . . SP SOUTHERN MAMMY 20
JACK, IF YOU GOT TO BE A ROUNDER SP STREET SONG 1
BE A ROUNDER RIGHT - . . . . SP STREET SONG 2
BE SUNDAY. . . . . SP SUMMER EVENING 34
MONDAY MORNING'S GONNA BE? . . . . SP SUNDAY BY COMB 5
WILL BE LOST! . . . . SP SUNDAY MORNING 35
AND BE SAVED - . . . . SP SUNDAY MORNING 38
WHY SHOULD IT BE MY LONELINESS, . . SP TELL ME 1
WHY SHOULD IT BE MY SONG, ... SP TELL ME 2
WHY SHOULD IT BE MY DREAM . . . . . SP TELL ME 3
FOR I WILL BE WITH YOU TILL NO WHITE BROTHER . . . . SP THE NEGRO MOTHE 51
AND I CAN'T BE SATISFIED. . . . . . SP THE WEARY BLUES 26
AND CAN'T BE SATISFIED - . . . . . SP THE WEARY BLUES 28
THEN, IT WILL BE TRUE. . . . . . . SP THEME FOR ENG B 5
WELL, I LIKE TO EAT, SLEEP, DRINK, AND BE IN LOVE. . . . . SP THEME FOR ENG B 21
SO WILL MY PAGE BE COLORED THAT I WRITE? . . . . SP THEME FOR ENG B 27
BEING ME, IT WILL NOT BE WHITE. . . SP THEME FOR ENG B 28
BUT IT WILL BE . . . . SP THEME FOR ENG B 29
SOMETIMES PERHAPS YOU DON'T WANT TO BE A PART OF ME. . . . . SP THEME FOR ENG B 34
NOR DO I OFTEN WANT TO BE A PART OF YOU. . . . . SP THEME FOR ENG B 35
I WILL NOT BE SATISFIED . . . . . . SP TO ARTINA 4
I WILL NOT BE SATISFIED . . . . . . SP TO ARTINA 6
I WILL BE GOD WHEN IT COMES TO YOU. SP TO ARTINA 11
WHO MIGHT BE PASSING! . . . . . . SP TO BE SOMEBODY 12
TOMORROW MAY BE . . . . SP TOMORROW 1
IF I LIVE TO BE A THOUSAND . . . . SP WIDOW WOMAN 17
BUT I'D RATHER BE DEAD THAN . . . . SP YOUNG GAL'S BLS 17
TO BE UGLY AN' OLD. . . . . SP YOUNG GAL'S BLS 18
CAUSE I DON'T WANT TO BE BLUE. . . SP YOUNG GAL'S BLS 24
PERHAPS IF IT BE GOD'S WILL . . . . AYM ASK YOUR MAMA 54
IRENE AND HELEN ARE AS THEY USED TO BE . . . . AYM BIRD IN ORBIT 21
AND THEY WONDER WHERE I BE . . . . AYM BIRD IN ORBIT 55
AND I WONDER WHERE THEY BE. . . . . AYM BIRD IN ORBIT 56
MUST BE RED! . . . . AYM BIRD IN ORBIT 72
WOULD BE TOO TAME - . . . . AYM BLUES IN STEREO 6
AND THE NIGHT MIGHT BE ASTONISHED AYM BLUES IN STEREO 19
ME WHO USED TO BE NOBODY, ... AYM HORN OF PLENTY 42
STILL TO BE INVENTED, ... AYM IS IT TRUE? 15
FOR THE MILL WHEEL TO BE MILL WHEEL AYM IS IT TRUE? 24
FOR THE BISCUIT TO BE BREAD . . . . AYM IS IT TRUE? 26
FOR THE SADNESS TO BE SORROW, . . . AYM IS IT TRUE? 28
WILL EVENTUALLY BE . . . . AYM IS IT TRUE? 36
TO BE CARTED OFF BY BRINK'S, . . . AYM ODE TO DINAH 57
YOU'LL BE CALLED BY EASTLAND. . . . AYM RIDE, RED, RIDE 26
IT WOULD BE TOO BAD IF JESUS . . . PL BIBLE BELT 1
YOU MAY BE . . . . PL BIBLE BELT 12
MIGHT BE AWAKENED SOMEDAY SOON . . PL BIRMINGHAM SUND 25
THAT MEN BE BURNED TO DEATH - . . . PL BOMBINGS DIXIE 7
BE PRESIDENT. . . . . PL CHILDREN'S RYME 5
USED TO BE. . . . . PL CORNER MEETING 3
WHEN I GET TO BE A COMPOSER . . . . PL DAYBREAK IN ALA 1
GET TO BE A COMPOSER . . . . PL DAYBREAK IN ALA 21
TO BE A PROBLEM ON . . . . PL DINNER GUEST ME 19
MIGHT BE DEAD, ... PL FREDRK DOUGLASS 5
BUT INSTEAD DECIDED TO BE BOLD . . PL FREDRK DOUGLASS 7
OH, TO BE A BEAST, A BIRD, ... PL FREDRK DOUGLASS 16
WHO WOULD BE FREE . . . . PL FREDRK DOUGLASS 18
AND SO MUST BE . . . . PL FROSTING 5
HOW CAN ONE MAN BE TEN? . . . . . PL GHOSTS OF 1619 21
OR TEN BE A HUNDRED AND TEN? . . . PL GHOSTS OF 1619 22
AM I SUPPOSED TO BE GOD, ... PL GO SLOW 11
THE OLD "BE PATIENT" . . . . PL HARLEM 5
THAT MUST NOT BE . . . . PL HISTORY 3
CAN IT BE . . . . PL KU KLUX 10
THAN TRUTH CAN BE. . . . . PL LONG VIEW NEGRO 7
DIG AND BE DUG . . . . PL MOTTO 8
BUT WHO ARE WE TO BE . . . . PL NORTHERN LIBERL 6
I CAN QUITE AFFORD TO BE: . . . . PL NORTHERN LIBERL 12
BUT IT MUST BE AROUND . . . . . . PL STOKELY MALCOLM 4
BUT I KNOW IT MUST BE . . . . . . PL STOKELY MALCOLM 11
TOMORROW YOU'LL BE DEAD . . . . . PL WITHOUT BENEFIT 9

BEACH 1
PALM BEACH. . . . . FC BRASS SPITTOONS 5

BEAR 3
EVEN TAME A BEAR, ... SH FREE MAN 6
BEAR IN MIND . . . . SP DRUM 1
WHICH SIN TO BEAR? . . . . SP PRAYER 4

BEARD 2
SPEAK OF FREDERICK DOUGLASS'S BEARD AYM BIRD IN ORBIT 44
LOST IN CASTRO'S BEARD? . . . . . . AYM RIDE, RED, RIDE 12

BEARDS 1
LITTLE CULLUD BOYS WITH BEARDS . . SP FLATTED FIFTHS 1

BEARER 1
BITTER BEARER OF BURDENS . . . . . JC THE BITTER RIVR 71

BEARING 2
I AM THE NEGRO BEARING SLAVERY'S SCARS. . . . . ANS LET AMERICA BE 20
AFTER BITTER THRUST OF BEARING . . SP INTERNE AT PROV 28

BEAST 1
OH, TO BE A BEAST, A BIRD, ... PL FREDRK DOUGLASS 16

BEAST-STRONG 1
BEAST-STRONG, ... SP THE SOUTH 4

BEAT 26
ALL THE TOM-TOMS OF THE JUNGLES BEAT IN MY BLOOD, ... WB FOR PORTRAIT OF 1
AN' SAYS YO' BOY IS GETTIN' BEAT. FC DEATH SO DIRTY 24
SO BEAT DAT DRUM, BOY! . . . . . . FC SATURDAY NIGHT 21
DONE BEAT YOU TO DE PLACE, STANDIN' OUT SIDE DE DO' . . . . NM BROKE 6
LET THE RAIN BEAT UPON YOUR HEAD WITH SILVER LIQUID DROPS. . . . . OK APRIL RAIN SONG 2
BEAT WITH BARE, BROWN FISTS - . . . OK SONG 8
I'M BEAT TO MY KNEES. . . . . . . JC HOW ABOUT DIXIE 10
IT'S HARD TO BEAT HITLER . . . . . JC HOW ABOUT DIXIE 19
LET THE GREAT WAVES BEAT! . . . . JC TO CAPTAIN MULZ 72
BEAT BACK INTO THE BLOOD - . . . . SP AFRO-AMER FRAG 7
BEAT OUT OF BLOOD WITH WORDS SAD-SUNG . . . . SP AFRO-AMER FRAG 8
BEAT HER UP BAD. . . . . SP BLD FORTUNE TEL 22
AND THE TOM-TOMS BEAT, ... SP DANSE AFRICAINE 12
AND THE TOM-TOMS BEAT, ... SP DANSE AFRICAINE 13
IT'S A HAPPY BEAT? . . . . SP DREAM BOOGIE 9
THAT STEADY BEAT . . . . SP EASY BOOGIE 2
BEAT THE DRUMS OF TRAGEDY FOR ME. SP FATASY PURPLE 1
BEAT THE DRUMS OF TRAGEDY AND DEATH. SP FATASY PURPLE 2
BEAT THE DRUMS OF TRAGEDY FOR ME, SP FATASY PURPLE 5
MAKES HAMMER BEAT OF DRUM BEAT . . SP MIGRANT 17
MAKES HAMMER BEAT OF DRUM BEAT . . SP MIGRANT 17
BARE FEET TO BEAT THE GREAT DRUMBEAT AYM BLUES IN STEREO 9
I DONE BEAT MY . . . . PL DOWN WHERE I AM 3
NOT BEAT - ELITE, ... PL NORTHERN LIBERL 14
SLUG ME! BEAT ME! . . . . PL THIRD DEGREE 7
AND BEAT THE LIVING HELL . . . . . PL WHO BUT TH LORD 14

BEATEN 9
BEATEN WITH SWIFT STICKS . . . . . FC SPORT 6
BEATEN AND SORE. . . . . NM BLACK CLWN POEM 22
BEATEN YET TODAY - O, PIONEERS! . . ANS LET AMERICA BE 36
FORMERLY THE BEATEN AND THE POOR . JC TO CAPTAIN MULZ 19
DID YOU ASK FOR THE BEATEN BRASS OF THE MOON? . . . . SP A HOUSE IN TAOS 23
SUN AND THE BEATEN HARDNESS OF THE EARTH, ... SP SUN SONG 2
BEATEN AND MISTREATED FOR THE WORK THAT I GAVE - . . . . SP THE NEGRO MOTHE 14
THE BEATEN PRIDE. . . . . SP UNCLE TOM 2
BEATEN AND BLACK: . . . . PL CHRIST IN ALA. 2

BEATING 10
BEATING THEM WITH LAWS AND CLUBS AND BAYONETS AND BULLETS . . . . . . ANS KIDS WHO DIE 30
BEATING YOUR FISTS . . . . FW DUSK 5

THE LOW BEATING OF THE TOM-TOMS. . SP DANSE AFRICAINE 1
THE SLOW BEATING OF THE TOM-TOMS. SP DANSE AFRICAINE 2
AND THE LOW BEATING OF THE TOM-TOMS SP DANSE AFRICAINE 14
BEATING OUT AND BEATING OUT A - . . SP DREAM BOOGIE 7
BEATING OUT AND BEATING OUT A - . . SP DREAM BOOGIE 7
BEATING FOREVER . . . . SP DRUM 3
AND BEATING THE LAND'S . . . . SP MOONLIGHT NIGHT 7
BUT HEARTS KEEP DOGGED BEATING . . AYM ASK YOUR MAMA 69

BEATIN' 1
BEATIN' AT THE DOOR - . . . . PL DOWN WHERE I AM 2

BEATS 5
I BEATS MA WIFE AN' . . . . FC BAD MAN 7
I BEATS MA SIDE GAL TOO. . . . . . . FC BAD MAN 8
BEATS MA WIFE AN' . . . . FC BAD MAN 9
BEATS MA SIDE GAL TOO. . . . . FC BAD MAN 10
AND BEATS A DRUM . . . . FW JAIME 2

BEAU 2
CAUSE I AIN'T NOBODY'S BEAU. . . . . OWT STRANGER IN TWN 10
I AIN'T NOBODY'S BEAU. . . . . OWT STRANGER IN TWN 12

BEAUTIES 1
WHO CARRY BEAUTIES IN THEIR HEARTS SP WATER-FRONT STR 7

BEAUTIFUL 15
THOU ART NOT BEAUTIFUL . . . . WB POEM 4
FOR YOUR FACES ARE BEAUTIFUL, TOO. WB THE WHITE ONES 2
A BRIGHT BOWL OF BRASS IS BEAUTIFUL TO THE LORD. . . . . FC BRASS SPITOONS 32
ONCE YOU WERE BEAUTIFUL. . . . . . . DK PARISIAN BEGGAR 5
BEAUTIFUL . . . . JC ME AND MY SONG 27
THEY'LL SEE HOW BEAUTIFUL I AM . . SP I, TOO 16
THE NIGHT IS BEAUTIFUL. . . . . . . SP MY PEOPLE 1
THE STARS ARE BEAUTIFUL. . . . . . SP MY PEOPLE 3
BEAUTIFUL, ALSO, IS THE SUN. . . . SP MY PEOPLE 5
BEAUTIFUL, ALSO, ARE THE SOULS OF MY PEOPLE. . . . . SP MY PEOPLE 6
BLACK AND BEAUTIFUL - . . . . SP NOTE COMM THEAT 15
SHE WAS YOUNG AND BEAUTIFUL . . . . SP RUBY BROWN 1
BEAUTIFUL, LIKE A WOMAN. . . . . . SP THE SOUTH 13
THE SPRING IS NOT SO BEAUTIFUL THERE - . . . . SP WATER-FRONT STR 1
THE SPRING IS NOT SO BEAUTIFUL THERE - . . . . SP WATER-FRONT STR 5

BEAUTIFY 1
TO BEAUTIFY THIS HOUR, THIS SPRING, AND ALL THE SPRINGS TO COME . . ANS CHANT MAY DAY 12

BEAUTY 5
SURPASSING BEAUTY. . . . . WB POEM 7
WILL FALL AT THE FEET OF YOUR BEAUTY. . . . . WB TO DARK MERCEDES 5
TILL BEAUTY AND PRIDE FILLS EACH DARK FACE . . . . NM DARK YOUTH USA 20
SMITTEN BY BEAUTY. . . . . SP A HOUSE IN TAOS 4
AND THE BEAUTY OF SUSANNA JONES IN RED . . . . SP WHEN SUE WEARS 10

BEAUTY'S 1
SO IF YOU WANT TO KNOW BEAUTY'S . . SH HARLEM SWEETIES 41

BECAME 3
BECAME A BRIGHT BALL OF LIGHT . . . SP FULFILMENT 10
BECAME FLESH-AND-BLOOD MEN? . . . . PL GHOSTS OF 1619 15
SUDDENLY BECAME MAJORITY . . . . . . PL GHOSTS OF 1619 18

BECAUSE 24
BECAUSE WE ARE ALONE. . . . . WB AFRAID 4
BECAUSE I'M POOR AND BLACK AND FUNNY - . . . . NM BLACK CLWN POEM 2
BECAUSE MY MIND IS DULL . . . . NM BLACK CLWN POEM 4
BECAUSE MY MOUTH . . . . DK MINSTREL MAN 1
BECAUSE MY MOUTH . . . . DK MINSTREL MAN 9
BECAUSE MY FEET . . . . DK MINSTREL MAN 13
BECAUSE YOU ARE TO ME A SONG . . . . DK PASSING LOVE 1
BECAUSE YOU ARE TO ME A PRAYER . . DK PASSING LOVE 3
BECAUSE YOU ARE TO ME A ROSE - . . DK PASSING LOVE 5
JUST BECAUSE I LOVES YOU - . . . . . DK REASONS WHY 1
JUST BECAUSE I LOVES YOU . . . . . . DK REASONS WHY 5
BECAUSE ONE IS BLACK. . . . . ANS OPEN LETTER 30
BECAUSE, O POOR WHITE WORKERS, . . ANS OPEN LETTER 45
BECAUSE A GOOD REPUTATION . . . . . SH SNOB 5
AND ALL BECAUSE OF . . . . JC RED CROSS 7
BECAUSE MY FACE IS BLACK. . . . . . JC THE BITTER RIVR 78
BECAUSE SHE'S TIRED. . . . . SP GRADUATION 30
BECAUSE OF PEOPLE WITH NO TITLES . SP IN EXPLANATION 60
BECAUSE HE TRIED TO VOTE . . . . . . SP NOT A MOVIE 2
BECAUSE I WAS ON RELIEF . . . . . . SP RELIEF 4
AND BECAUSE SHE WAS COLORED . . . . SP RUBY BROWN 4
BECAUSE WE'RE COLORED. . . . . PL HARLEM 15
BECAUSE YOU ARE THERE. . . . . PL WAR 17
BECAUSE I AM HERE - . . . . PL WAR 20

BECKON 1
INSISTENCE BECKON . . . . FW CONVENT 7

BECOME 3
THAT'S MADE AMERICA THE LAND IT HAS BECOME. . . . . ANS LET AMERICA BE 44
LET US BECOME INSTEAD, YOU AND I, ANS OPEN LETTER 21
WILL BECOME INFINITY. . . . . FW THERE 9
THAT AT A SUDDEN CHANGE BECOME . . SP FLATTED FIFTHS 6
ON RED HEART BECOME AN ANVIL . . . SP MIGRANT 20
DARK SHADOWS BECOME DARKER BY A SHADE . . . . AYM ODE TO DINAH 51
BECOME JEWISH . . . . AYM SHADES OF PIG 18
FOR THE DEAD BECOME ALIVE. . . . . PL SPECIAL BULLTIN 2

BECOMES 7
AND THE NIGHT BECOMES . . . . WB SUMMER NIGHT 8
AND DEATH BECOMES . . . . FC SPORT 10
AND BOWING HIS HEAD IN SHAME, BECOMES SUDDENLY FIERCE AND ANGRY. THEN HE . . . . NM COLORED SL MOOD 11
WHO BECOMES . . . . OWT MAN INTO MEN 19
THUS THE DREAM BECOMES NOT ONE MAN'S DREAM ALONE. . . . . SP FREEDOM'S PLOW 22
BEFORE THE PRESENT BECOMES WHEN . . AYM ODE TO DINAH 104
BECOMES SO SMALL . . . . PL LONG VIEW NEGRO 12

BED 19
WHERE ON THE BED . . . . WB SICK ROOM 3
ALL NIGHT IN BED . . . . OLD THE CONSUMPTIVE 5
FOR HERE I DO NOT MAKE MY BED. . . DK DEATH SEAMAN 6
WENT TO BED. . . . . SH DEATH IN HARLEM 142
LEFT ME BY MYSELF IN A DOUBLE BED. SH LETTER 7
AND CROCHET A QUILT FOR OUR DOUBLE BED. . . . . SH LETTER 17
I'M GONNA RENT ME A CUBBY-HOLE WITH A SINGLE BED. . . . . SH PAY DAY 17
YOU JUMP OUT OF BED. . . . . OWT HONEY BABE 11
WALNUT BED. . . . . SP BLD FORTUNE TEL 16
IF I THOUGHT THOUGHTS IN BED, . . . SP BLUES AT DAWN 3
SATURDAY LAUGHTER, A BAR, A BED. . SP CONSIDER ME 43
IN MY BED! . . . . SP EASY BOOGIE 13
SO I WENT ON BACK TO BED - . . . . SP FIRED 7
I MADE DOWN THE BED. . . . . SP HOMECOMING 6
HE ROSE UP ON HIS DYING BED . . . . SP HOPE 1
THE SINGER STOPPED PLAYING AND WENT TO BED . . . . SP THE WEARY BLUES 33
AIN'T GOT NOBODY TO SHARE MY BED. SP 50 - 50 2
HE SAID, SHARE YOUR BED - . . . . SP 50 - 50 13
ON YOUR BED OF WHISPERED ECHOES: . AYM IS IT TRUE? 19

BEDLOE'S 1
ON BEDLOE'S ISLAND MANAGED BY SOL HUROK . . . . AYM HORN OF PLENTY 4

BEDWARD 2
BEDWARD! POCOMANIA! WEDO! OGOUN! . AYM GOSPEL CHA-CHA 36
DAMBALLA WEDO! THE VIRGIN! BEDWARD! AYM GOSPEL CHA-CHA 43

BEECHER 1
SEND FOR FREDERICK DOUGLASS, GARRISON, BEECHER, ... PL FINAL CALL 30

BEEN 73
WHAT STAR-WHITE MOON HAS BEEN YOUR MOTHER? . . . . WB NUDE YOUNG DANC 7
IT'S ALWAYS BEEN A WORKIN' GIRL. . . FC BLACK GAL 1
AIN'T NEVER BEEN UNKIND. . . . . . FC BLACK GAL 4
YET I AIN'T NEVER BEEN NO BAD ONE. FC BLACK GAL 13
WHEN FOR YEARS, I HAD BEEN SEEKING OLD AESTHETE HARLEM 4
BEEN WALKIN' SINCE FIVE THIS MORNIN'. . . . . NM BROKE 2
AND SHE BEEN HOLDIN' 'EM SO TIGHT TILL BE EAGLE'S IN TEARS - . . . . NM BROKE 24
BUT I SHO BEEN LOOKIN' ROUND HARD LATELY FOR WAYS AND MEANS . . . NM BROKE 39
IT'S DONE GOT ME SO CRAZY, FEEL LIKE I BEEN TAKIN' COKE. . . . . NM BROKE 60
ALL THESE YEARS YOU SAY YOU BEEN WORKIN' HERE? . . . . NM BROKE 68
BEEN MADE, PROUD AND SMILING, BUT THE LIVING, REMEMBERING WITH A HALF-SOB . . . . NM COLORED SL MOOD 10
THE WORLD'S BEEN MADE SAFE FOR DEMOCRACY . . . . NM COLORED SL POEM 29
I BEEN BLUE ALL NIGHT LONG. . . . . DK NIGHT AND MORN 12
I WISH I'D NEVER BEEN BORN. . . . . DK PO' BOY BLUES 24
(THERE'S NEVER BEEN EQUALITY FOR ME, ANS LET AMERICA BE 15
THE LAND THAT NEVER HAS BEEN YET - ANS LET AMERICA BE 63
BEEN UP HERE SIX MONTHS - . . . . . SH EVENIN' BLUES 5
IT MUST HAVE BEEN YESTERDAY. . . . SH EVIL MORNING 1
MUST HAVE BEEN YESTERDAY . . . . . SH EVIL MORNING 3
AND IF YOU THINK I BEEN TOO MEAN BEFORE. . . . . SH LETTER 12
BEEN WORKIN' ON DE LEVEE. . . . . . SH MISSISSIPPI LEV 1
BEEN LOOKIN' FOR A JOB . . . . . . SH OUT OF WORK 5
THAT'S BEEN KEEPING MY NOSE TO THE GRINDSTONE. . . . . SH PAY DAY 13
BEEN IN MY MOUTH. . . . . JC THE BITTER RIVR 5
YOURS HAS BEEN THE POWER . . . . . JC THE BITTER RIVR 35

Line	Poem	No.
BEEN DRIVEN OFF ITS WAY.	JC TO CAPTAIN MULZ	7
WE NEGROES HAVE BEEN SLAVES BEFORE.	JC TO CAPTAIN MULZ	33
WALLS HAVE BEEN KNOWN	FW DUSK	10
AND I'VE BEEN WAITING LONG	FW EARTH SONG	2
I'VE BEEN WAITING LONG	FW EARTH SONG	5
AND I'VE BEEN WAITING LONG	FW EARTH SONG	14
HE HAS BEEN	FW OLD SAILOR	1
IT MIGHT HAVE BEEN	FW WHEN ARMIES PAS	17
HAD OF BEEN WHITE	OWT BLD MARGE POLIT	2
BUT AFTER I BEEN HERE AWHILE	OWT STRANGER IN TWN	15
I'D NEVER BEEN	LHR CONSERVATORY	12
YOU'VE BEEN RESTING AWHILE.	SP AFRICA	2
I BEEN WAITIN' AND A-WAITIN'	SP BLD THE GYPSY	14
I BEEN RUNNIN' THIS	SP ELEVATOR BOY	21
THERE'S BEEN AN EAGLE ON A NICKEL.	SP FACT	1
I AIN'T BEEN GOOD.	SP FIRE	4
I AIN'T BEEN CLEAN -	SP FIRE	5
I BEEN STINKIN', LOW-DOWN, MEAN.	SP FIRE	6
I BEEN STEALIN'.	SP FIRE	17
BEEN TELLIN' LIES.	SP FIRE	18
LORD, I BEEN A-WAITIN' FOR THE	SP FREEDOM TRAIN	7
HE WAS A COLORED MAN WHO HAD BEEN A SLAVE	SP FREEDOM'S PLOW	112
HAVING BEEN	SP JAM SESSION	4
MAMA, IT HAS BEEN RAINING CATS AND DOGS UP	SP LETTER	8
HAS IT BEEN SAVED.	SP MADAM MINISTER	7
HE'S BEEN A MULE SO LONG	SP ME AND THE MULE	3
BUT HE MUST A BEEN TELLIN' A LIE.	SP MIDWINTER BLUES	14
HE MUST A BEEN TELLIN' A LIE.	SP MIDWINTER BLUES	16
LIFE FOR ME AIN'T BEEN NO CRYSTAL STAIR.	SP MOTHER TO SON	2
I'SE BEEN A-CLIMBIN' ON.	SP MOTHER TO SON	9
WHERE THERE AIN'T BEEN NO LIGHT.	SP MOTHER TO SON	13
AND LIFE FOR ME AIN'T BEEN NO CRYSTAL STAIR.	SP MOTHER TO SON	20
I'VE BEEN A SLAVE:	SP NEGRO	4
I'VE BEEN A WORKER:	SP NEGRO	7
I'VE BEEN A SINGER:	SP NEGRO	10
I'VE BEEN A VICTIM:	SP NEGRO	14
AND THE LAST PRAYERS BEEN SAID	SP NIGHT FUNERAL	30
AND WISH SHE'D NEVER BEEN BORN?	SP REVERIE HARLEM	8
YES, HE'S DONE BEEN LEFT.	SP STONY LONESOME	15
DOWN THE LONG HARD ROW THAT I BEEN HOEING	AYM BLUES IN STEREO	34
THE PAST HAS BEEN A MINT	PL HISTORY	1
BEEN SAVING ALL MY LIFE	PL LITTLE SNG HOUS	2
WHERE HAS TERROR BEEN?	PL MISSISSIPPI	9
HAS LONG BEEN TRIED AT LAW.	PL OCTOBER 16 RAID	20
I BEEN SCARED AND BATTERED.	PL STILL HERE	1
I HAVE BEEN SEEKING	PL STOKELY MALCOLM	1
I BEEN UPSET	PL STOKELY MALCOLM	5
IT'S BEEN SAID	PL WITHOUT BENEFIT	8

BEER 5

Line	Poem	No.
SAME AS I CAN HEY-HEY ON BEER.	SH HEY-HEY BLUES	2
SAME AS I CAN HEY-HEY ON BEER.	SH HEY-HEY BLUES	4
I SAID HEY-HEY ON BEER -	SH HEY-HEY BLUES	20
AND HEY-HEY ON BEER -	SH HEY-HEY BLUES	22
THEY SELL BEER FOAMING THERE IN MUG-LIKE CUPS.	OWT JUICE JOINT	5
AN' I NEED A DIME FO' BEER.	SP DOWN AND OUT	10
I NEED A DIME FO' BEER.	SP DOWN AND OUT	11
HE SETS IN A BAR WITH A BEER.	SP NEIGHBOR	6
AND IF UNCLE MAC BRINGS BEER	SP SUMMER EVENING	24

BEERS 1

Line	Poem	No.
INTO FLATTED FIFTHS AND FLATTER BEERS	SP FLATTED FIFTHS	5

BEFORE 45

Line	Poem	No.
I MEAN FOUR - BEFORE DAYLIGHT - S'POSE TO'VE DONE HIT YO' FIRST STROKE -	NM BROKE	14
BRIGHT BEFORE US	DK YOUTH	2
IN THIS WORLD BEFORE	SH ASPIRATION	7
BUT BEFORE I'D BITE A NAIL	SH EVIL MORNING	7
AND IF YOU THINK I BEEN TOO MEAN BEFORE.	SH LETTER	12
BEFORE THE HOT NIGHTS OF SUMMER	SH YOUNG NEGRO GRL	8
NEHRU SAID, BEFORE HE WENT TO JAIL.	JC JIM CROW'S LAST	15
BEFORE YOU'RE THROUGH.	JC NOTE TO NAZIS	6
WE NEGROES HAVE BEEN SLAVES BEFORE.	JC TO CAPTAIN MULZ	33
IT HAD NO DIGNITY BEFORE.	FW HARLEM DANCE HA	1
THAT HAD NO DIGNITY BEFORE!	FW HARLEM DANCE HA	8
BEFORE THE TALL	FW NIGHT SONG	2
BEFORE THE TALL	FW NIGHT SONG	9
BEFORE THE TALL	FW NIGHT SONG	16
BEFORE YOU SPEAK.	FW SILENCE	3
BEFORE MAN'S WISDOM.	FW WISDOM	2
IMPORTANT BEFORE -	OWT BLD MARGE POLIT	22
BEFORE THIS LONG HEGIRA HAD BEGUN	OWT JUICE JOINT	12
BEFORE WE RUN BACK	SP A HOUSE IN TAOS	42
NO LONGER THE LIGHT OF MY DREAM BEFORE ME.	SP AS I GREW OLDER	20
NEVER SEEN YOU BEFORE -	SP BLD FORTUNE TEL	2
IF I RECALL THE DAY BEFORE.	SP BLUES AT DAWN	8
BEFORE THE EARLY DAWN	SP CHORD	3
BEFORE ME	SP CONSIDER ME	7
BEFORE THE CIVIL WAR, DAYS WERE DARK.	SP FREEDOM'S PLOW	113
IN CHINA BEFORE WHAT HAPPENED	SP IN EXPLANATION	6
BEFORE	SP KID IN THE PARK	7
I NEVER SEEN HIM BEFORE.	SP MADAM WRONG VIS	2
BEFORE I'D PAY	SP MADAM RENT MAN	9
BEFORE NIGHT.	SP MADAM WRONG VIS	16
BEFORE	SP MADAM'S PAST HI	7
NIGHT OF THE DAY BEFORE YESTERDAY	SP NIGHT FOUR SONG	3
THAN THEY EVER DID BEFORE.	SP RUBY BROWN	26
AS WE WERE BEFORE.	SP SHARE-CROPPERS	10
BUT MAYBE BEFORE MIDNIGHT	SP SUMMER EVENING	22
BEFORE THE PRESENT BECOMES WHEN	AYM ODE TO DINAH	104
BEFORE TAKING BESS TO WIFE	AYM SHADES OF PIG	16
BEFORE CHINA WAS EVER RED AT ALL	PL BIRMINGHAM SUND	12
THEN BEFORE YOU CAN WALK	PL CROWNS GARLANDS	3
RIDE SO FINE BEFORE.	PL FLORIDA WORKERS	18
THEY TOLD US BEFORE.	PL HARLEM	6
BEFORE THE MUSHROOM BOMB	PL JUNIOR ADDICT	20
BEFORE YOU ARE KING.	PL LAST PRINCE	14
SINCE THE DAY BEFORE LAST	PL STOKELY MALCOLM	6
SO MANY TIMES BEFORE.	PL SWEET WORDS PAC	12

BEFO' 2

Line	Poem	No.
HAS I DID IT BEFO'? CERTAINLY!	NM BROKE	31
'TWAS THE NIGHT BEFO' CHRISTMAS	SP MIDWINTER BLUES	5

BEG 1

Line	Poem	No.
I BEG A DIME FOR DINNER -	ANS PARK BENCH	5

BEGAN 6

Line	Poem	No.
EMPTY HANDED AS I BEGAN.	NM BLACK CLWN POEM	20
SOFT AS IT BEGAN -	DK I LOVED FRIEND	5
SOME BEGAN TO TREMBLE AND	SH DEATH IN HARLEM	109
SOME BEGAN TO SCREAM.	SH DEATH IN HARLEM	110
BUT WHEN THE BAND BEGAN TO PLAY.	FW HARLEM DANCE HA	2
THEY BEGAN TO BUILD OUR LAND.	SP FREEDOM'S PLOW	40

BEGGAR 1

Line	Poem	No.
WHAT IS THERE WITHIN THIS BEGGAR LAD	DK BEGGAR BOY	1

BEGGED 1

Line	Poem	No.
SHE BEGGED ME, PLEASE.	SH BLD THE SINNER	13

BEGINNING 2

Line	Poem	No.
WOVEN FROM THE BEGINNING	SP FREEDOM'S PLOW	136
BEGINNING IN SOME OTHER LAND -	PL JUNIOR ADDICT	9

BEGINS 1

Line	Poem	No.
NOW I BEGINS TO DOUBT.	SH IN TROUBLED KEY	6

BEGUN 4

Line	Poem	No.
NOW THAT CROW'S BEGUN TO LOOK LIKE HELL.	JC JIM CROW'S LAST	6
BEFORE THIS LONG HEGIRA HAD BEGUN	OWT JUICE JOINT	12
DONE BEGUN.	SP BLACK MARIA	17
DONE BEGUN!	SP BLACK MARIA	22

BEHIND 16

Line	Poem	No.
AND DARK BITTER FACES BEHIND STEEL BARS:	JC THE BITTER RIVR	28
THE SCOTTSBORO BOYS BEHIND STEEL BARS.	JC THE BITTER RIVR	29
LEWIS JONES BEHIND STEEL BARS.	JC THE BITTER RIVR	30
THE VOTELESS SHARE-CROPPER BEHIND STEEL BARS.	JC THE BITTER RIVR	31
THE LABOR LEADER BEHIND STEEL BARS.	JC THE BITTER RIVR	32
THE SOLDIER THROWN FROM A JIM CROW BUS BEHIND STEEL BARS.	JC THE BITTER RIVR	33
THE 15¢ MUGGER BEHIND STEEL BARS.	JC THE BITTER RIVR	34
THE GIRL WHO SELLS HER BODY BEHIND STEEL BARS.	JC THE BITTER RIVR	35
BEHIND YOUR HIGH STONE WALLS -	FW CONVENT	3
WHERE TWO OLD BROWN MEN STAND BEHIND THE BAR -	OWT JUICE JOINT	37
THIS WORLD I'LL LEAVE BEHIND	SP DEFERRED	40
BORN BEHIND THE 8-ROCK.	SP MADAM CHARTY CH	14
TURN AROUND - I'LL BRUSH BEHIND.	SP MAMA AND DAUGHT	6
AND BEHIND WILL COME	SP PARADE	9
BODY'LL HAVE TO WALK BEHIND ME.	SP YOUNG GAL'S BLS	6
IN THE POT BEHIND THE PAPER DOORS	PL CULTURAL EXCHNG	26

BEIGE 2

Line	Poem	No.
BEIGE SAILORS WITH LARGE NOSES	SP SEASHORE THROUG	1
BLACK, YELLOW, BEIGE, AND BROWN.	PL BACKLASH BLUES	24

BEIN 1

Line	Poem	No.
BEIN TREATED SO BAD.	SP EARLY EVENING	16

BEING 20

Line	Poem	No.
OF BEING HELD BACK, OF HAVING NO CHANCE -	NM COLORED SL POEM	31
BEING WALKERS WITH THE DAWN AND MORNING.	DK WALKERS WITH	1
BEING WALKERS WITH THE SUN AND MORNING.	DK WALKERS WITH	6
BEING THIS-A WAY!	OWT FUNERAL	8

BEING A FISHER BOY. . . . . SP CATCH 8
BEING MYSTERY.) . . . . SP CONSIDER ME 15
BEING NEITHER WHITE NOR BLACK? . . SP CROSS 12
BUT BEING NO GOOD AT LOVIN' - . . . SP DANCER 18
BEING ALWAYS . . . . SP ENNUI 3
WHAT HE SAID MUST BE MEANT FOR EVERY HUMAN BEING - . . . . SP FREEDOM'S PLOW 107
IN LIFE BEING CREATED . . . . SP S-SSS-SS-SH! 3
I GUESS BEING COLORED DOESN'T MAKE ME NOT LIKE . . . . SP THEME FOR ENG B 25
BEING ME, IT WILL NOT BE WHITE. . . SP THEME FOR ENG B 28
AND BEING SO . . . . PL ANGOLA QUESTION 15
BEING WINED AND DINED, ... PL DINNER GUEST ME 3
"I'M SO ASHAMED OF BEING WHITE." . PL DINNER GUEST ME 14
BEING GHOSTS . . . . PL GHOSTS OF 1619 29
AND FOR BEING A MAN . . . . PL LUMUMBA'S GRAVE 11
OF BEING LAID OUT COLD AND DEAD, . PL WHO BUT TH LORD 6
BEING POOR AND BLACK. . . . . . . PL WHO BUT TH LORD 19

BEIN' 1

IN MY BEIN' DEAD. . . . . SP WAKE 4

BELAFONTE 1

BELAFONTE FRISCO JOSEPHINE . . . . AYM BIRD IN ORBIT 5

BELATED 1

PAYMENTS NOT BELATED - . . . . . . AYM HORN OF PLENTY 78

BELEAGUERED 1

GENERAL BOURSE BELEAGUERED . . . . AYM SHADES OF PIG 4

BELGIANS 1

THE BELGIANS CUT OFF MY HANDS IN THE CONGO. . . . . SP NEGRO 15

BELGIUM 1

BELGIUM SHADOWS LEOPOLD . . . . . . AYM SHADES OF PIG 2

BELIE 1

BELIE THE BUDDING PROMISE . . . . . PL SWEET WORDS RAC 5

BELIEVE 16

WHO DON'T BELIEVE IN LIES, AND BRIBES AND CONTENTMENT, ... ANS KIDS WHO DIE 17
TO BELIEVE AN ANGELO HERNDON, OR EVER GET TOGETHER. . . . . . . ANS KIDS WHO DIE 36
SAY! YOU KNOW I BELIEVE I'LL CHANGE MY NAME. . . . . SH DAYBREAK 9
BELIEVE I'LL DO A LITTLE DANCIN' . SH EVENIN' BLUES 13
I USED TO BELIEVE IN YOU, BABY. . . SH IN TROUBLED KEY 5
IF YOU BELIEVE . . . . JC HOW ABOUT DIXIE 5
DO YOU BELIEVE THAT, JACK? . . . . SP ARGUMENT 4
IN THIS BLOCK, I DO BELIEVE! . . . SP CHILDREN'S RYME 11
IT'S HARD TO BELIEVE. . . . . . . SP DEAD IN THERE 10
DO YOU BELIEVE . . . . SP FIRE 11
BELIEVE IN THE RIGHT, LET NONE PUSH YOU BACK. . . . . SP THE NEGRO MOTHE 43
I BELIEVE MY OLD LADY'S . . . . . . SP WHAT? SO SOON! 1
THEY SAID, "DO YOU BELIEVE . . . . PL KU KLUX 3
I'D BELIEVE IN ANYTHING . . . . . . PL KU KLUX 7
AND TELL ME YOU BELIEVE IN . . . . PL KU KLUX 19
AND HE DIDN'T BELIEVE . . . . PL LUMUMBA'S GRAVE 6

BELIEVED 2

AND BELIEVED THE TINY FLOWERS . . . LHR PASTORAL 6
BUT IN THEIR HEARTS THE SLAVES BELIEVED HIM, TOO. . . . . SP FREEDOM'S PLOW 97

BELIEVING 1

BELIEVING EVERYTHING SHE READ . . . PL MOTHER IN WAR 9

BELL 3

PATROL BELL! . . . . SP BLD LANDLORD 26
EVEN RUNG THIS BELL ON SUNDAY, YET AYM ASK YOUR MAMA 8
THEY RUNG MY BELL TO ASK ME . . . . AYM HORN OF PLENTY 96

BELLA 1

BESSIE STARED AT BELLA . . . . . . SH DEATH IN HARLEM 111

BELLE 1

THERESA BELLE ALETHA . . . . SP SUMMER EVENING 18

BELLOWING 1

THE BELLOWING BULL, THE RED CAPE, ANS SONG OF SPAIN 13

BELLS 1

AND THE FOUR BELLS SHE'S AWAITING SP SUMMER EVENING 20

BELL-BOUY 1

OUR CHARTS, OUR COMPASS AND BELL-BOUY . . . . JC TO CAPTAIN MULZ 53

BELONG 1

BELONG . . . . OWT MAN INTO MEN 17

BELONGED 1

THAT BELONGED TO MY FATHER? . . . . SH BLD PAWNBROKER 2

BELONGING 1

BELONGING TO ALL THE HANDS WHO BUILD. . . . . SP FREEDOM'S PLOW 27

BELOVED 2

AH, MY BELOVED ONE, AWAY! . . . . . WB OUR LAND 17
TO THE BLACK BELOVED . . . . WB POEM 1

BELOW 1

AS IS CUSTOM BELOW ZERO. . . . . . AYM ODE TO DINAH 12

BEN 1

BIG BEN, I'M GONNA BUST YOU BANG UP SIDE THE WALL! . . . . SH DAYBREAK 1

BENCH 4

EVER TIME I MOUNTS THIS BENCH . . . FC BLD OF GIN MARY 7
I LIVE ON A PARK BENCH. . . . . . . ANS PARK BENCH 1
ON A BENCH IN THE PARK: . . . . . . SP KID IN THE PARK 2
SHE NEEDS TO SET ON DE MOANER'S BENCH . . . . SP MYSTERY 3

BENEATH 12

HAVE FALLEN BENEATH YOUR EYES. . . WB SOLEDAD 4
OF A FREE LIFE BENEATH OUR GREAT SKY. . . . . NM DARK YOUTH USA 10
BENEATH THE SLAVER'S WHIP. . . . . ANS A NEW SONG 9
THE PEOPLE BENEATH THAT BOMBING PLANE . . . . ANS SONG OF SPAIN 41
EACH FOURTEEN YEARS OLD WHEN LYNCHED TOGETHER BENEATH THE . . . . . . JC THE BITTER RIVR 1
THAT ONCE WAS SUNG BENEATH THE SUN OWT JUICE JOINT 10
BENEATH HIS ARM. . . . . SP CATCH 7
BENEATH A TALL TREE . . . . SP DREAM VARIATION 6
BENEATH MY HEAD. . . . . SP FIRED 10
IN JOY BENEATH THE SKY . . . . . . SP IN TIME SILVER 17
RIGHT HERE BENEATH GOD'S SKY. . . . SP NEW YORKERS 3
BENEATH HIS EYES . . . . SP TRUMPET PLAYER 4

BENIGHTED 1

IN THE EYES ONCE SOFT BENIGHTED . . SP MIGRANT 22

BENT 2

BACK BENT AS IN THE FIELDS. THE SLOW STEP. THE BOWED HEAD. "NOBODY KNOWS . . . . NM BLACK CLWN MOOD 4
BLACK BROWN YELLOW BENT DOWN WORKING SP IN EXPLANATION 52

BERETS 1

LITTLE CULLUD BOYS IN BERETS . . . SP FLATTED FIFTHS 15

BERNICE 3

BERNICE SAID SHE WANTED . . . . . . SH BLD THE KILLER 1
BERNICE SAID SHE WANTED . . . . . . SH BLD THE KILLER 5
BERNICE SAID SHE NEEDED . . . . . . SH BLD THE KILLER 9

BESIDES 1

BESIDES. . . . . SP I, TOO 15

BESS 2

PORGY AND BESS . . . . AYM ASK YOUR MAMA 23
BEFORE TAKING BESS TO WIFE . . . . AYM SHADES OF PIG 16

BESSIE 9

BESSIE PULLED A KNIFE. . . . . . . SH DEATH IN HARLEM 104
BESSIE STARED AT BELLA . . . . . . SH DEATH IN HARLEM 111
BUT BESSIE TOOK A BULLET TO HER . . SH DEATH IN HARLEM 116
AND LEFT POOR BESSIE BLEEDIN . . . SH DEATH IN HARLEM 121
AND WHOEVER LOVED BESSIE WAS . . . SH DEATH IN HARLEM 126
HER NAME WAS BESSIE. SHE WAS BROWN AND BOLD. . . . . SH DEATH IN HARLEM 81
BESSIE WAS, TOO. . . . . SH DEATH IN HARLEM 88
AND THERE WAS BESSIE . . . . SH DEATH IN HARLEM 95
OR RECORDS - BESSIE, BOP, OR BACH. SP THEME FOR ENG B 24

BEST 4

BEST FRIEND O' MINE. . . . . FC DEATH DO DIRTY 30
YOU WAS THE BEST - BUT YOU THE WORST. . . . . SH PAY DAY 20
IS JIM CROW FREEDOM THE BEST . . . JC BLACK MAN SPEAK 19
THAT A WOMAN DOES THE BEST SHE CAN? SP SISTER 14

BET 1

I BET SHE'D HEAR. . . . . SP LADY'S BOOGIE 6

BETHEL'S 1

AT MOTHER BETHEL'S IN THE MORNING? AYM BIRD IN ORBIT 35

BETHUNE 2

MRS. BETHUNE TOLD MARTIN DIES. . . JC JIM CROW'S LAST 21
MARY MCLEOD BETHUNE BARRED BY . . . AYM BIRD IN ORBIT 76

BETTER 29

BETTER LISTEN TO ME! . . . . FC LISTEN HERE 16
AN' BETTER, BETTER, BETTER WHEN HE'S DRUNK. . . . . FC MA MAN 12

AN' BETTER, BETTER, BETTER WHEN HE'S DRUNK. — FC MA MAN 12
AN' BETTER, BETTER, BETTER WHEN HE'S DRUNK. — FC MA MAN 12
AND BLUE, HIDING HIS DISCONTENT AS THOUGHTS OF A BETTER LIFE OVERCOME — NM BIG-TIMER MOOD 7
AND DE MAN COME TELLIN' ME I BETTER GET THERE AT FO'. — NM BROKE 13
AND TOLD ME I'D BETTER PAY HER FOR MY ROOM RENT AND BOARD! — NM BROKE 22
AND IT'S BETTER A THOUSAND TIMES YOU'RE IN FRANCE DEAD. — NM COLORED SL POEM 45
SOMETHING IN MY MIND BETTER I FORGOT. — SH TWILIGHT REVERI 2
"YOUR FOLKS WILL HAVE A BETTER DAY." — JC THE BITTER RIVR 40
WILL BRING A BETTER DAY." — JC THE BITTER RIVR 44
FOR A BETTER WAY - — JC TO CAPTAIN MULZ 12
BETTER THAN — SP DESERT 2
BETTER THAN NOBODY — SP DESERT 8
BETTER TO DIE FREE — SP FREEDOM'S PLOW 110
BETTER DIE FREE, — SP FREEDOM'S PLOW 172
CAN'T YOU BRING NO BETTER NEWS? — SP HARD DADDY 6
YOU BETTER LET — SP MADAM PHONE BIL 12
YOU BETTER LEAVE - — SP MADAM MIGHT-HAV 22
I SAID, BETTER BUY TWO - — SP MADAM WRONG VIS 27
AMERICAN'S BETTER. — SP MADAM'S CALLING 16
ANY BETTER THAN WHITE. — SP SHAME ON YOU 9
"YOU'LL FIND RAIN BETTER — SP STRANGE HURT 4
SCHOOLS ARE BETTER FOR THEIR CHILDREN $ — AYM HORN OF PLENTY 24
BUT SCRIPT-WRITERS WHO KNOW BETTER — AYM IS IT TRUE? 49
BETTER HURRY, BETTER HURRY — AYM ODE TO DINAH 103
BETTER HURRY, BETTER HURRY — AYM ODE TO DINAH 103
AND WE BETTER FIND OUT, MAMA. — PL CULTURAL EXCHNG 23
WITH BETTER DEATH — PL JUNIOR ADDICT 22

BETWEEN 15
YOU WHO LIVE BETWEEN THE HILLS — WB A FAREWELL 7
A SILENT WOMAN LIES BETWEEN TWO LOVERS - — WB SICK ROOM 4
BETWEEN US TWO. — ANS PARK BENCH 4
YOU'VE STOOD BETWEEN US WELL. — JC GOOD MORN STLIN 35
BETWEEN TEARS AND CRYING. — FW BORDER LINE 4
BETWEEN THE LITTLE CLOUDS OF HEAVEN — LHR PASTORAL 1
IN BETWEEN. — SP ADVICE 6
BETWEEN ME AND MY DREAM. — SP AS I GREW OLDER 10
BETWEEN US QUICKLY — SP DESIRE 7
BETWEEN TWO RIVERS, — SP ISLAND 1
BETWEEN ASSORTED TERRORS — PL LENOX AVE. BAR 2
LOOKS LIKE BETWEEN 'EM THEY DONE — PL STILL HERE 5
THREE KICKS BETWEEN THE LEGS — PL THIRD DEGREE 10
CAUGHT BETWEEN — PL UNDERTOW 3
BETWEEN SELMA, PEKING, — PL UNDERTOW 12

BEWARE 2
BEWARE THE DAY — PL WARNING 4
BEWARE THE HOUR — PL WARNING 9

BEYOND 7
BEYOND THE RIM OF DAY. — WB TO LITTLE LOVER 7
WHEN BEYOND STEEL BARS SOUND THE DEATHLESS DRUMS — SL SCOTTSBORO 7
BEYOND A HIGH TENSION WALL — SP MELLOW 5
BEYOND ITS MASK OF WHITENESS — AYM BLUES IN STEREO 18
THE BOAT BEYOND THE FORTALEZA — AYM GOSPEL CHA-CHA 27
INTEREST BEYOND CARING? — AYM SHOW FARE PLESE 25
BEYOND THE HOLY GHOST. — AYM SHOW FARE PLESE 30

BE- 1
GET OUT O' MY SIGHT BE- — SH EVIL MORNING 15

BE-BACH 1
BE-BACH! — SP LADY'S BOOGIE 9

BE-BOP 3
BE-BOP! — SP CHILDREN'S RYME 27
RE-BOP BE-BOP MOP AND STOP. — SP FLATTED FIFTHS 2
HEY! BABA-RE-BOP! MOP! ON A BE-BOP KICK! — SP LIKEWISE 23

BIBS 1
GET OUT THEIR BIBS — SP SUNDAY MORNING 10

BIG 29
I GOT A BIG CAR — NM BIG-TIMER POEM 25
AND DIDN'T HAVE SUCH A BIG MOUTH. — NM BROKE 65
BIG BEN, I'M GONNA BUST YOU BANG UP SIDE THE WALL! — SH DAYBREAK 1
TOGETHER IN MY BIG OLD DOWN-HOME FRAME. — SH DAYBREAK 3
AT A BIG PIANO A LITTLE DARK GIRL — SH DEATH IN HARLEM 10
BIG TIME SPORTS AND GIRLS WHO KNOW — SH DEATH IN HARLEM 37
WHEN A MAN'S WON A FIGHT IN A BIG MAN'S TOWN - — SH DEATH IN HARLEM 35
BIG BLACK EYES. — SH ONLY WOMAN BLUS 14
IN THIS GREAT BIG LONESOME TOWN! — SH OUT OF WORK 14
GREAT BIG LONESOME TOWN! — SH OUT OF WORK 16
BIG BUDDY, BIG BUDDY, — JC BIG BUDDY 1
BIG BUDDY, BIG BUDDY, — JC BIG BUDDY 1
BIG BUDDY, BIG BUDDY, — JC BIG BUDDY 3
BIG BUDDY, BIG BUDDY, — JC BIG BUDDY 3
BUT SAY, BIG BUDDY, — JC BIG BUDDY 7
BIG BUDDY BIG BUDDY, — JC BIG BUDDY 10
BIG BUDDY BIG BUDDY, — JC BIG BUDDY 10
HEY, BIG BUDDY, — JC BIG BUDDY 12
SAY BIG BUDDY, — JC BIG BUDDY 13
A BIG BRASS BAND — SP AS BEFITS A MAN 11
BIG BOY CAME — SP CATCH 1
OF THE WHOLE BIG TOWN — SP COLLEGE FORMAL 14
MY OLD MAN DIED IN A FINE BIG HOUSE. — SP CROSS 9
ON GREAT BIG HANDS, — SP DREAM BOOGE VAR 6
SOUND LIKE A GREAT BIG CROWD. — SP MORNING AFTER 18
GREAT BIG YELLOW STARS. — SP MULATTO 10
GREAT BIG YELLOW STARS. — SP MULATTO 32
CLIMBING UP A GREAT BIG MOUNTAIN — SP PORTER 7
IN A GREAT . . . BIG . . . NIGHT. — SP SYLVESTER'S BED 28
BIG BOY OPENED HIS MOUTH AND SAID, — SP 50 - 50 6
FROM THE BIG GLASS SHOPPING CENTER — AYM HORN OF PLENTY 34
ON THE BIG SCREEN OF THE WELFARE CHECK — AYM ODE TO DINAH 93
OR BIG MAYBELL TO — AYM SHADES OF PIG 29
BUT THE WORLD IS BIG. — PL BACKLASH BLUES 19
THE WORLD IS BIG AND ROUND, — PL BACKLASH BLUES 20
GREAT BIG WORLD, MISTER BACKLASH, — PL BACKLASH BLUES 21
BIG AND BRIGHT AND ROUND - — PL BACKLASH BLUES 22
AND BIG BROWN ARMS — PL DAYBREAK IN ALA 12
IN THEIR BIG CARS — PL FLORIDA WORKERS 11

BIGGER 2
(NOT KNOWING THERE'S A STEINWAY BIGGER, BIGGER) — SP TO BE SOMEBODY 3
(NOT KNOWING THERE'S A STEINWAY BIGGER, BIGGER) — SP TO BE SOMEBODY 3

BIG-TIMER 1
I'M JUST A BIG-TIMER, — NM BIG-TIMER POEM 75

BILL 2
SHE BOUGHT A NEW HAT LAST WEEK AND COME SENDIN' ME THE BILL. — NM BROKE 49
PHONE BILL DOES I CARE! — SP MADAM PHONE BIL 36

BILLINGTON'S 1
IN BILLINGTON'S CHURCH OF RUBBER. — AYM HORN OF PLENTY 84

BILLOWING 1
WITH BILLOWING SAILS THE GALLEONS CAME — SP FREEDOM'S PLOW 75

BILLS 2
A ROLL OF BILLS IN HIS LEFT-HAND POCKET. — SH DEATH IN HARLEM 19
WHEN I'M PAYING YOUR BILLS — SP ULTIMATUM 2

BIND 2
BOUNDARIES BIND UNBINDING — PL CULTURAL EXCHNG 10
TO BIND MY MIND - CHAIN MY FEET - — PL DEATH YORKVILLE 6

BINOCULAR 1
BINOCULAR THE ATLANTIC. — SP SEASHORE THROUG 2

BIRD 5
LIFE IS A BROKEN-WINGED BIRD — DK DREAMS 3
A BLUE BIRD IN A NEST. — DK SAILOR 8
IF I WAS A BIRD I'D — SH DECLARATION 17
CATCH THAT JIM CROW BIRD, PULL THE FEATHERS OUT HIS TAIL! — JC JIM CROW'S LAST 16
OH, TO BE A BEAST, A BIRD, — PL FREDRK DOUGLASS 16

BIRDS 6
AND NOT THIS LAND WHERE BIRDS ARE GREY. — WB OUR LAND 12
WHEN THE BIRDS COME BACK FROM THE SOUTH. — ANS CHANT MAY DAY 6
AND BIRDS SING - — SP HEAVEN 6
SEE THE BIRDS — SP KID IN THE PARK 5
BIRDS THAT REALLY SING — AYM HORN OF PLENTY 76
BIRDS THAT REALLY SING. — AYM HORN OF PLENTY 87

BIRMINGHAM 1
THE BIRMINGHAM STATION'S MARKED COLORED AND WHITE. — SP FREEDOM TRAIN 25

BIRMINGHAM-ON-SUNDAY 1
THIS BIRMINGHAM-ON-SUNDAY WALL. — PL BIRMINGHAM SUND 14

BIRMINGHAM 3
WE LICK OUR CHOPS AT BIRMINGHAM — PL NORTHERN LIBERL 2
AND BIRMINGHAM - — PL NORTHERN LIBERL 20
DURBAN, BIRMINGHAM, — PL QUESTION ANSWER 1

BIRTH 2
BRINGS NEW BIRTH. — FW GIRL 13
GIVE SWEET BIRTH — SP MULATTO 35

BIRTHING 1

BIRTHING IS HARD . . . . SP ADVICE 2

BISCUITS 1

YOU STILL BAKES BISCUITS? FRIED CHICKEN EVERY NIGHT? IS THAT TRUE? . . . . NM BROKE 73

BISHOP 1

FATHER BISHOP, EFFENDI, MOTHER HORNE. . . . . SP MYSTERY 21

BISQUIT 1

FOR THE BISQUIT TO BE BREAD . . . . AYM IS IT TRUE? 26

BIT 6

JUST A BIT TOO BOLD? . . . . WB JAZZONIA 11
ANSWERIN' THEM WANT-ADS' NOT NARY BIT O' FUN. . . . . NM BROKE 4
A BIT OF CLAY, BROWN, UGLY, GIVEN LIFE? . . . . DK BEGGAR BOY 5
YOU JEST A LITTLE BIT O' WOMAN BUT YOU . . . . SP MORNING AFTER 17
AIN'T WORTH A LITTLE BIT. . . . . . SP SOUTHERN MAMMY 10
AIN'T WORTH A LITTLE BIT. . . . . . SP SOUTHERN MAMMY 12

BITE 6

IF A PRETTY GAL LIKE YOU WAS WILLIN', I'D BITE. . . . . NM BROKE 72
BITE A NAIL IN TWO. . . . . SH EVIL MORNING 6
BUT BEFORE I'D BITE A NAIL . . . . SH EVIL MORNING 7
NEVER MISSED A BITE . . . . AYM ODE TO DINAH 130
WHILE THE BITE . . . . PL GO SLOW 2
AND BITE INTO THE SANDWICH OF YOUR HEART. . . . . PL JIM CROW CAR 2

BITING 1

TO KEEP THE BALL FROM BITING IN HIS MOUTH. . . . . OWT JUICE JOINT 44

BITLESS 1

RIDE ON BITLESS HORSES . . . . PL WHERE WHEN WHCH 9

BITS 1

OR BITS OF DUST IN EYES . . . . SP SONG BILLIE HOL 12

BITTER 40

FROM ONE SIDE TO THE OTHER, BUT NOW A HARSH AND BITTER NOTE CREEPS INTO . . . . NM BLACK CLWN MOOD 9
BUT THE DREAM WAS CRUEL - AND BITTER - AND SOMEHOW . . . . NM COLORED SL POEM 40
BITTER WAS THE DAY . . . . ANS A NEW SONG 7
BITTER WAS THE DAY . . . . ANS A NEW SONG 11
BITTER WAS THE DAY, I SAY. . . . . ANS A NEW SONG 17
BITTER . . . . ANS A NEW SONG 39
HERE I SET WITH A BITTER OLD THOUGHT. . . . . SH TWILIGHT REVERI 1
YAL, HERE I SET THINKING - A BITTER OLD THOUGHT . . . . SH TWILIGHT REVERI 9
AND HERE I SET THINKING WITH A BITTER OLD FROWN. . . . . SH TWILIGHT REVERI 14
THERE IS A BITTER RIVER . . . . . . JC THE BITTER RIVR 2
THERE IS A BITTER RIVER . . . . . . JC THE BITTER RIVR 6
I'VE DRUNK OF THE BITTER RIVER . . JC THE BITTER RIVR 10
WHERE I DRANK OF THE BITTER RIVER JC THE BITTER RIVR 16
OH, WATER OF THE BITTER RIVER . . . JC THE BITTER RIVR 22
THE BITTER RIVER REFLECTS NO STARS - JC THE BITTER RIVR 26
AND DARK BITTER FACES BEHIND STEEL BARS: . . . . JC THE BITTER RIVR 28
THE BITTER RIVER REFLECTS NO STARS. JC THE BITTER RIVR 38
BUT THE SWIRL OF THE BITTER RIVER JC THE BITTER RIVR 41
THE SWIRL OF THE BITTER RIVER . . . JC THE BITTER RIVR 45
THE SWIRL OF THE BITTER RIVER . . . JC THE BITTER RIVR 49
NOR THE TASTE OF ITS BITTER BREW. JC THE BITTER RIVR 52
AND MAKE ME DRINK OF THE BITTER CUP JC THE BITTER RIVR 57
YOU FORCED ME TO THE BITTER RIVER JC THE BITTER RIVR 63
BITTER BEARER OF BURDENS . . . . JC THE BITTER RIVR 71
I'VE DRUNK AT THE BITTER RIVER . . JC THE BITTER RIVR 73
TIRED NOW OF THE BITTER RIVER. . . JC THE BITTER RIVR 75
I'VE DRUNK OF THE BITTER RIVER . . JC THE BITTER RIVR 81
OH, TRAGIC BITTER RIVER . . . . . . JC THE BITTER RIVR 83
THE CALL OF YOUR BITTER WATER . . . JC THE BITTER RIVR 85
THE BLOOD OF YOUR BITTER WATER . . JC THE BITTER RIVR 87
I'M TIRED OF THE BITTER RIVER! . . JC THE BITTER RIVR 89
TOO BITTER TO REMEMBER - . . . . . . FW CHIPPY 5
IN HER BITTER SORROW. . . . . FW MOTHERLAND 4
WITH BITTER RANCE . . . . FW SAILING DATE 3
OF BITTER YEARNINGS LOST . . . . . SP AFRO-AMER FRAG 19
AFTER BITTER THRUST OF BEARING . . SP INTERNE AT PROV 28
HARLEM OF THE BITTER DREAM, ... SP PASSING 14
BITTER TELEVISION BLURRED . . . . . SP SONG BILLIE HOL 18
TO SPROUT THEIR BITTER BARRIERS . . PL GEORGIA DUSK 11
WITH A BITTER FRAGRANCE . . . . . . PL WHERE WHEN WHCH 2

BITTERNESS 1

TASTING ITS BITTERNESS IN MY THROAT. PL MILITANT 5

BLACK 172

SLEEK BLACK BOYS IN A CABARET. . . WB HARLEM NIGHT CL 1
CALL GAY BLACK BOYS. . . . . WB HARLEM NIGHT CL 7
BLACK BOYS' LIPS . . . . WB HARLEM NIGHT CL 8
I WAS A BLACK MAN, TOO. . . . . . . WB LAMENT DARK PEO 3
TO THE BLACK BELOVED . . . . WB POEM 1
MY BLACK ONE. . . . . WB POEM 3
MY BLACK ONE. . . . . WB POEM 9
MY BLACK ONE. . . . . WB POEM 15
I AM THE BLACK JESTER. . . . . . . WB THE JESTER 15
NIGHT BLACK BOY. . . . . WB TO MIDNIGHT NAN 14
DAMN MA BLACK OLD MAMMY'S SOUL . . FC A RUINED GAL 17
CAN'T HELP IT CAUSE I'M BLACK. . . FC BLACK GAL 14
CAUSE HE WAS BLACK . . . . FC DEATH DO DIRTY 7
ON A PO' BLACK GIRL. . . . . FC GAL'S CRY DYING 12
BLACK AN' UGLY . . . . FC GAL'S CRY DYING 13
I'M BLACK AN' UGLY . . . . FC GAL'S CRY DYING 15
BLACK GAL. . . . . FC RED SILK STOCK 2
THE BLACK SHEEP. . . . . NM BIG-TIMER POEM 4
BECAUSE I'M POOR AND BLACK AND FUNNY - . . . . NM BLACK CLWN POEM 2
I RISE AGAIN - A BLACK CLOWN. . . . NM BLACK CLWN POEM 11
BLACK - IN A WHITE WORLD . . . . . NM BLACK CLWN POEM 36
BLACK - YOU CAN DIE. . . . . NM BLACK CLWN POEM 41
JUST A BLACK CLOWN! . . . . NM BLACK CLWN POEM 54
I WAS ONCE A BLACK CLOWN . . . . . NM BLACK CLWN POEM 77
WE WERE JUST TWO COLORED BOYS, BROWN AND BLACK. . . . . NM COLORED SL POEM 2
THEY TOLD US AMERICA WOULD KNOW NO BLACK OR WHITE: . . . . NM COLORED SL POEM 11
BLACK BOYS COULDN'T WORK THEN ANYWHERE LIKE THEY CAN . . . . . NM COLORED SL POEM 19
AND IT'S A GOOD THING ALL THE BLACK BOYS LYING DEAD . . . . NM COLORED SL POEM 51
WITH THE WHITE AND THE BLACK WHOM NOTHING HOLDS BACK - . . . . . . NM DARK YOUTH USA 24
(FOR A BLACK MOTHER) . . . . DK LULLABY 1
MY LITTLE BLACK BABY. . . . . DK LULLABY 11
NIGHT BLACK BABY. . . . . DK LULLABY 20
8 BLACK BOYS IN A SOUTHERN JAIL. . SL SCOTTSBORO 1
8 BLACK BOYS AND ONE WHITE LIE. . . SL SCOTTSBORO 3
8 BLACK BOYS IN A SOUTHERN JAIL. . SL SCOTTSBORO 28
I SPEAK IN THE NAME OF THE BLACK MILLIONS . . . . ANS A NEW SONG 1
"YOU ARE MY SERVANT, BLACK MAN - I, THE FREE!" . . . . ANS A NEW SONG 32
THE BLACK . . . . ANS A NEW SONG 48
BLACK YOUNG OZIE POWELL. . . . . . ANS BLD OZZIE POWEL 10
BUT NINE BLACK BOYS KNOW FULL WELL. ANS BLD OZZIE POWEL 21
BLACK YOUNG OZIE POWELL. . . . . . ANS BLD OZZIE POWEL 28
10-OTHERS: BLACK WORKERS. . . . . . ANS CHANT MAY DAY 21
BLACK AND WHITE. . . . . ANS KIDS WHO DIE 2
WHITE AND BLACK. . . . . ANS KIDS WHO DIE 22
AND BLACK HANDS AND WHITE HANDS CLASPED AS ONE. . . . . ANS KIDS WHO DIE 48
AND TORN FROM BLACK AFRICA'S STRAND I CAME . . . . ANS LET AMERICA BE 49
AND THE BLACK BOY DIE. . . . . . . ANS LYNCHING SONG 4
AS THE BLACK BOY SPINS . . . . . . ANS LYNCHING SONG 7
THAT BLACK BOY'S . . . . ANS LYNCHING SONG 12
I LOOKED AT THEIR BLACK FACES . . . ANS NEGRO GHETTO 1
I AM THE BLACK WORKER. . . . . . . ANS OPEN LETTER 12
BECAUSE ONE IS BLACK. . . . . ANS OPEN LETTER 30
"YOU ARE MY BROTHER, BLACK OR WHITE." . . . . ANS OPEN LETTER 39
WHITE AND BLACK. . . . . ANS UNION 5
A BLACK WOMAN CRIED. . . . . SH DEATH IN HARLEM 115
TO PLUM-TINTED BLACK. . . . . SH HARLEM SWEETIES 18
SHE HAD LONG BLACK HAIR. . . . . . SH ONLY WOMAN BLUS 13
BIG BLACK EYES. . . . . SH ONLY WOMAN BLUS 14
TO THE BLACK MAN. . . . . JC BLACK MAN SPEAK 8
BLACK . . . . JC ME AND MY SONG 1
BLACK . . . . JC ME AND MY SONG 3
BLACK . . . . JC ME AND MY SONG 5
STRONG AND BLACK . . . . JC ME AND MY SONG 9
AS THE BLACK EARTH . . . . JC ME AND MY SONG 17
AS BLACK IRON . . . . JC ME AND MY SONG 19
AS THE BLACK NIGHT . . . . JC ME AND MY SONG 21
AS THE BLACK NIGHT . . . . JC ME AND MY SONG 28
BLACK . . . . JC ME AND MY SONG 31
BECAUSE MY FACE IS BLACK. . . . . . JC THE BITTER RIVR 78
BLACK WORKERS WITH WHITE WORKERS - JC TO CAPTAIN MULZ 37
AND I, BLACK MAN, ... JC TO CAPTAIN MULZ 60
WITH A ROUND BLACK FACE . . . . . . FW MIGRATION 12
THE SOLDIER WERE BLACK. . . . . . . OWT BLD MARGE POLIT 12
BLACK CAT . . . . OWT BLUES ON A BOX 3
HURRY, BLACK BOY, HURRY! . . . . . OWT FLIGHT 7
WHERE SINGING BLACK BOYS DANCE AND PLAY EACH NIGHT . . . . OWT JUICE JOINT 2
SOMETIMES A BLACK BOY PLAYS A SONG OWT JUICE JOINT 9
THAT GOOD BLACK FEET TO DANCING ON BARE FLOORS. . . . . OWT JUICE JOINT 20
WHERE BLACK MEN COME TO DRINK AND PLAY AND SING. . . . . OWT JUICE JOINT 34
SOFT SAD BLACK FEET . . . . OWT JUICE JOINT 46
ABOVE A CROWD OF BLACK FOLK, HUMBLE, MEAN. . . . . OWT LINCOLN THEATRE 4

Line	Poem	Line no.
BLACK SKINS	OWT MAN INTO MEN	12
I AM A BLACK PIERROT:	SP A BLACK PIERROT	1
AND THE NIGHT WAS BLACK, TOO. . . .	SP A BLACK PIERROT	4
I AM A BLACK PIERROT:	SP A BLACK PIERROT	5
I AM A BLACK PIERROT:	SP A BLACK PIERROT	10
BLACK, GET BACK!	SP ARGUMENT	3
BLACK IS FINE!	SP ARGUMENT	8
I AM BLACK.	SP AS I GREW OLDER	18
BLACK SLAVES	SP AUNTSUE'S STORI	6
AND BLACK SLAVES	SP AUNTSUE'S STORI	8
AND BLACK SLAVES	SP AUNTSUE'S STORI	10
MUST BE THE BLACK MARIA	SP BLACK MARIA	1
THE BLACK MARIA THAT I SEE -	SP BLACK MARIA	3
BLACK MARIA PASSIN' BY	SP BLACK MARIA	18
PUT THE BLACK MAN	SP BLUE BAYOU	16
BLACK.	SP CONSIDER ME	35
AND MY OLD MOTHER'S BLACK.	SP CROSS	2
IF EVER I CURSED MY BLACK OLD MOTHER	SP CROSS	5
BEING NEITHER WHITE NOR BLACK? . .	SP CROSS	12
BLACK LIKE ME.	SP DREAM VARIATION	17
CAN A COAL BLACK MAN DRIVE THE FREEDOM TRAIN?	SP FREEDOM TRAIN	18
WHEN MY GRANDMOTHER IN ATLANTA, 83 AND BLACK, ...	SP FREEDOM TRAIN	37
GLEAMIN' IN THE SUNLIGHT FOR WHITE AND BLACK?	SP FREEDOM TRAIN	50
BLACK MEN AND WHITE WILL SAY, AIN'T IT FINE?	SP FREEDOM TRAIN	61
WHITE HANDS AND BLACK HANDS	SP FREEDOM'S PLOW	67
OUT OF LABOR - WHITE HANDS AND BLACK HANDS -	SP FREEDOM'S PLOW	82
LOOK TOO BLACK, ...	SP HIGH TO LOW	6
BLACK BROWN YELLOW BENT DOWN WORKING	SP IN EXPLANATION	52
BLACK HANDS	SP INTERNE AT PROV	19
BLACK AND WHITE, ...	SP ISLAND	5
SINCE I WAS BORN BLACK.	SP LITTLE OLD LETT	12
YOU DONE FORGOT THAT YOU ARE BLACK.	SP LOW TO HIGH	6
BLACK - AND DON'T GIVE A DAMN! . .	SP ME AND THE MULE	6
OF BLACK CELEBRITIES	SP MELLOW	2
BLACK GAL LIKE ME, ...	SP MISERY	13
BLACK GAL LIKE ME	SP MISERY	14
BLACK -	SP MOVIES	10
BLUE BLACK	SP MULATTO	14
AGAINST BLACK FENCES.	SP MULATTO	15
FATHER DIVINE, A RABBI BLACK . . .	SP MYSTERY	22
AS BLACK WAS BORN, ...	SP MYSTERY	23
BUT EAT, DRINK, STAY BLACK, AND DIE.	SP NECESSITY	4
BLACK AS THE NIGHT IS BLACK, . . .	SP NEGRO	2
BLACK AS THE NIGHT IS BLACK, . . .	SP NEGRO	2
BLACK LIKE THE DEPTHS OF MY AFRICA.	SP NEGRO	3
BLACK AS THE NIGHT IS BLACK, . . .	SP NEGRO	18
BLACK AS THE NIGHT IS BLACK, . . .	SP NEGRO	18
BLACK LIKE THE DEPTHS OF MY AFRICA.	SP NEGRO	19
BLACK BOY TO HIS GRAVE?	SP NIGHT FUNERAL	20
THAT LONG BLACK HEARSE DONE SPED,	SP NIGHT FUNERAL	34
BLACK AS ME!	SP NIGHTMARE BOOGE	4
BLACK AND BEAUTIFUL -	SP NOTE COMM THEAT	15
SOLID BLACK, ...	SP PARADE	18
OLD BLACK ME!	SP PARADE	33
A BLACK OLD WOMAN CROONS	SP PRAYER MEETING	5
A BLACK OLD WOMAN CROONS -	SP PRAYER MEETING	8
BLACK PEOPLE DON'T REMEMBER	SP SHAME ON YOU	8
THEY'VE JUST HUNG A BLACK MAN . . .	SP SILHOUETTE	3
THEY'VE HUNG A BLACK MAN	SP SILHOUETTE	5
PO' AN' BLACK	SP SINNER	2
THEY HUNG MY BLACK YOUNG LOVER . .	SP SONG DARK GIRL	3
SING, O BLACK MOTHER!	SP SPIRITUALS	15
BLACK AND WHITE	SP SUBWAY RUSH HOU	5
BLACK SEED FOR EYES	SP SUMMER EVENING	3
BLACK GALS WAS A-BEGGIN', ...	SP SYLVESTER'S BED	13
AND I, WHO AM BLACK, WOULD LOVE HER	SP THE SOUTH	18
AND I, WHO AM BLACK, ...	SP THE SOUTH	20
COMING FROM A BLACK MAN'S SOUL. . .	SP THE WEARY BLUES	15
TALL BLACK STUDENT	AYM ASK YOUR MAMA	32
WAS BLACK AS ME.	AYM GOSPEL CHA-CHA	62
WHERE BLACK SHADOWS MOVE LIKE SHADOWS	AYM JAZZTET MUTED	4
(AND AIN'T NEVER HAD A BLACK HOUSE)	AYM SHADES OF PIG	42
BLACK, ...	PL ANGOLA QUESTION	2
BLACK, YELLOW, BEIGE, AND BROWN. .	PL BACKLASH BLUES	24
WERE TO COME BACK BLACK.	PL BIBLE BELT	2
BEATEN AND BLACK:	PL CHRIST IN ALA.	2
WHITE SHARECROPPERS WORK THE BLACK PLANTATIONS, ...	PL CULTURAL EXCHNG	49
OF BLACK AND WHITE BLACK WHITE BLACK PEOPLE	PL DAYBREAK IN ALA	14
OF BLACK AND WHITE BLACK WHITE BLACK PEOPLE	PL DAYBREAK IN ALA	14
OF BLACK AND WHITE BLACK WHITE BLACK PEOPLE	PL DAYBREAK IN ALA	14
AND BLACK HANDS AND BROWN AND YELLOW HANDS	PL DAYBREAK IN ALA	16
IS A THING TO WHICH WE BLACK ARE WISE:	PL JUSTICE	2
TO MY BLACK SELF.	PL LITTLE SNC HOUS	24
LUMUMBA WAS BLACK	PL LUMUMBA'S GRAVE	1
LUMUMBA WAS BLACK	PL LUMUMBA'S GRAVE	5
LUMUMBA WAS BLACK.	PL LUMUMBA'S GRAVE	9
FOR A KID THAT'S BLACK?	PL MERRY-GO-ROUND	15
WHITE AND BLACK, ...	PL OCTOBER 16 RAID	7
I, BLACK, COME TO MY PRIME	PL PRIME	9
THE SKIN ON YOUR BLACK FACE, . . .	PL SPECIAL BULLTIN	19
BROWN, BLACK, WHITE -	PL WAR	6
BEING POOR AND BLACK, ...	PL WHO BUT TH LORD	19

BLACKBERRY 2

Line	Poem	Line no.
BLACKBERRY CORDIAL, ...	SH HARLEM SWEETIES	25
PERSIMMON, BLACKBERRY, ...	SH HARLEM SWEETIES	38

BLACKENING 1

Line	Poem	Line no.
BLACKENING THE EYES, -	FC BEALE ST. LOVE	5

BLACKNESS 1

Line	Poem	Line no.
THEY ASKED ME IF MY BLACKNESS, . .	PL CULTURAL EXCHNG	33

BLACKS 7

Line	Poem	Line no.
SO NOW I KNOW WE BLACKS ARE JUST LIKE ANY OTHER -	NM COLORED SL POEM	35
LOOKED AT THE BLACKS AND	SH DEATH IN HARLEM	66
LOOKED AT THE BLACKS AND	SH DEATH IN HARLEM	68
LOOKED AT THE BLACKS AND	SH DEATH IN HARLEM	70
MADE FROM THE HIDES OF BLACKS . . .	AYM BIRD IN ORBIT	66
MADE FROM THE HIDES OF BLACKS . . .	AYM BIRD IN ORBIT	89
PAST HUTS THAT HOUSE A MILLION BLACKS	AYM BLUES IN STEREO	15

BLADE 2

Line	Poem	Line no.
A BLADE TEN INCHES LONG.	FC SUICIDE	8
A BLADE TEN INCHES LONG.	FC SUICIDE	10

BLADES 1

Line	Poem	Line no.
DISTORTED BLADES OF GRASS, ...	SP GARDEN	2

BLAME 4

Line	Poem	Line no.
SOME FOLKS BLAME HIGH PRICES ON THE JEWS.	SP LIKEWISE	12
(SOME FOLKS BLAME TOO MUCH ON JEWS.)	SP LIKEWISE	13
AND BLAME YOU FOR THIS, ...	PL WAR	16
IT'S HARD TO BLAME ME, ...	PL WAR	19

BLARING 1

Line	Poem	Line no.
BUT BLOW ONE BLARING TRUMPET NOTE OF SUN	SP FATASY PURPLE	7

BLAST 1

Line	Poem	Line no.
COME WITH A BLAST OF TRUMPETS, . .	SP WHEN SUE WEARS	4

BLAZED 1

Line	Poem	Line no.
BLAZED TO THE CRACK OF WHIPS . . .	SP TRUMPET PLAYER	7

BLEACHED 1

Line	Poem	Line no.
THE CROWD APPLAUDS A PLUMP BROWN-SKIN BLEACHED BLONDE . . .	OWT LINCOLN THEATRE	7

BLED 2

Line	Poem	Line no.
AS IF FATE HAD NOT BLED HIM WITH HER KNIFE!	DK BEGGAR BOY	8
IS THE BLOOD HE BLED.	PL OFFICIAL NOTICE	6

BLEED 1

Line	Poem	Line no.
WHERE THE SUNSETS BLEED.	PL GEORGIA DUSK	12

BLEEDIN 1

Line	Poem	Line no.
AND LEFT POOR BESSIE BLEEDIN . . .	SH DEATH IN HARLEM	121

BLEEDING 2

Line	Poem	Line no.
AND MY HEART WAS BLEEDING, TOO. . .	SP A BLACK PIERROT	9
OF THE BLEEDING MOUTH, ...	PL CHRIST IN ALA.	11

BLESS 4

Line	Poem	Line no.
BLESS GOD!	OWT JITNEY	34
TO BLESS HIM DEAD	SP BLD OF THE MAN	19
GOD BLESS HER, DEAD AND GONE! . . .	SP REVERIE HARLEM	6
AND BLESS THE FIRE.	PL BOMBINGS DIXIE	8

BLESSED 1

Line	Poem	Line no.
BLESSED US WITH A KISS	SP FULFILMENT	18

BLESSINGS 1

Line	Poem	Line no.
I REALIZE THE BLESSINGS DENIED TO ME.	SP THE NEGRO MOTHE	22

BLIND 8

Line	Poem	Line no.
ARE YOU DEAF, DUMB, AND BLIND? . .	JC BLD SAM SOLOMON	32
ALMOST MADE ME BLIND.	SP MORNING AFTER	6
AND MAYBE WAS I BLIND	SP SO LONG	6
AND A BLIND MAN PLAYS AN ACCORDION	SP SUMMER EVENING	16
STEP-FATHERED BY BLIND LEMON . . .	AYM ODE TO DINAH	20
BLIND LEMON.	AYM ODE TO DINAH	22
SEND FOR DEAD BLIND LEMON TO SING THE B FLAT	PL FINAL CALL	13
THAT JUSTICE IS A BLIND GODDESS . .	PL JUSTICE	1

BLOCK 2

Line	Poem	Line no.
IN THIS BLOCK, I DO BELIEVE! . . .	SP CHILDREN'S RYME	11
BLOCK.	SP RAILROAD AVENUE	3

THE ONLY NEGROES IN THE BLOCK . . . AYM HORN OF PLENTY 79

BLOND 1

IN BLOND MEN'S ARMS. . . . WB HARLEM NIGHT CL 11

BLONDE 1

THE CROWD APPLAUDS A PLUMP BROWN-SKIN BLEACHED BLONDE . . . OWT LINCOLN THEATRE 7

BLOOD 58

BLOOD COUGHED ACROSS THE SKY. . . . WB CARIBBEAN SUNST 2
ALL THE TOM-TOMS OF THE JUNGLES BEAT IN MY BLOOD. . . . WB FOR PORTRAIT OF 1
HER LIPS BLOOD RED . . . FC CLOSING TIME 4
AND THAT OUR DARK BLOOD WOULD WIPE AWAY THE STAIN . . . NM COLORED SL POEM 8
LENIN WITH THE FLAG BLOOD RED. . . . SL SCOTTSBORO 21
REDDER NOW WHERE YOUR BLOOD HAS FLOWED. . . . ANS BLD OZZIE POWEL 3
BUT REDDER NOW WHERE YOUR LIFE'S BLOOD FLOWED. . . . ANS BLD OZZIE POWEL 31
EATING BLOOD AND GOLD. . . . ANS KIDS WHO DIE 6
FOR THE KIDS WHO DIE ARE LIKE IRON IN THE BLOOD OF THE PEOPLE - . . . ANS KIDS WHO DIE 32
WHOSE SWEAT AND BLOOD, WHOSE FAITH AND PAIN. . . . ANS LET AMERICA BE 67
BLOOD ON THE SAND . . . ANS SONG OF SPAIN 16
NEGRO BLOOD. . . . JC RED CROSS 4
POISONED MY BLOOD. . . . JC THE BITTER RIVR 9
MIXED WITH THE BLOOD OF THE LYNCHED BOYS . . . JC THE BITTER RIVR 12
WITH YOUR TASTE OF BLOOD AND CLAY, . . . JC THE BITTER RIVR 23
MIXED WITH BLOOD AND GALL. . . . JC THE BITTER RIVR 58
AND IT'S TURNED TO STEEL IN MY BLOOD. . . . JC THE BITTER RIVR 82
THE BLOOD OF YOUR BITTER WATER . . . JC THE BITTER RIVR 87
MANY BLOODS - YET ALL OF ONE BLOOD STILL: . . . JC TO CAPTAIN MULZ 48
THE BLOOD OF BROTHERHOOD. . . . JC TO CAPTAIN MULZ 49
IT IS NOT BLOOD? . . . FW WHEN ARMIES PAS 11
BUT IF THEY WERE BLOOD, MOTHER - . . . FW WHEN ARMIES PAS 14
YOUR FATHER'S BLOOD. . . . FW WHEN ARMIES PAS 18
PERHAPS BLOOD . . . FW WHEN ARMIES PAS 19
AND THIS IS MY BLOOD, HE SAID. . . . LHR BLD MARY'S SON 19
AND THIS IS MY BLOOD! . . . LHR BLD MARY'S SON 30
HIS BODY AND HIS BLOOD DIVINE! . . . LHR BLD MARY'S SON 31
HIS BODY AND HIS BLOOD . . . LHR BLD MARY'S SON 34
DRIPPED BLOOD OVER THE EASTERN HILLS SP A BLACK PIERROT 8
BEAT BACK INTO THE BLOOD - . . . SP AFRO-AMER FRAG 7
BEAT OUT OF BLOOD WITH WORDS SAD-SUNG . . . SP AFRO-AMER FRAG 8
STIRS YOUR BLOOD. . . . SP DANSE AFRICAINE 5
STIRS YOUR BLOOD. . . . SP DANSE AFRICAINE 15
AND BLOOD ROLLED OUT. . . . SP GREEN MEMORY 3
BUT BLOOD . . . SP GREEN MEMORY 4
CHOCOLATE AND BLOOD: . . . SP INTERNE AT PROV 29
FLOW OF HUMAN BLOOD IN HUMAN VEINS. SP NEGRO SPEAKS OF 3
WITH BLOOD ON ITS MOUTH. . . . SP THE SOUTH 2
OBLIVIOUS TO BLOOD . . . AYM BIRD IN ORBIT 28
SUNSETS STAINED WITH BLOOD . . . AYM GOSPEL CHA-CHA 29
PRESSURE OF THE BLOOD IS SLIGHTLY HIGHER . . . AYM JAZZTET MUTED 2
WHERE THE PRESSURE OF THE BLOOD . . . AYM JAZZTET MUTED 18
THEIR BLOOD UPON THE WALL . . . PL BIRMINGHAM SUND 5
WOULD REDDEN WITH THEIR BLOOD . . . PL BIRMINGHAM SUND 13
WHO LEFT THEIR BLOOD UPON THAT WALL. PL BIRMINGHAM SUND 16
SOMETIMES THERE'S BLOOD IN THE GEORGIA DUSK . . . PL GEORGIA DUSK 5
WHOSE BLOOD? . . . EVERYONE'S. . . . PL GEORGIA DUSK 8
OF BLOOD AND SORROW. . . . PL HISTORY 2
OF BLOOD AND BATTLE . . . PL LAST PRINCE 11
HIS BLOOD WAS RED - . . . PL LUMUMBA'S GRAVE 10
THAT TEARS AND BLOOD . . . PL MISSISSIPPI 4
THAT TEARS AND BLOOD . . . PL MISSISSIPPI 18
IS THE BLOOD HE BLED. . . . PL OFFICIAL NOTICE 6
SIGNED IN BLOOD. . . . PL OFFICIAL NOTICE 12
WITH HIS BLOOD . . . PL OFFICIAL NOTICE 13
BLOOD ON MY SPORT SHIRT . . . PL THIRD DEGREE 3
I DIP MY BROOM IN BLOOD. . . . PL WAR 14
MY MOP IN BLOOD - . . . PL WAR 15

BLOODIED 1

AND BLOODIED SUNDAY DRESSES . . . PL BIRMINGHAM SUND 7

BLOODS 1

MANY BLOODS - YET ALL OF ONE BLOOD STILL: . . . JC TO CAPTAIN MULZ 48

BLOODY 3

WITH A BLOODY CRY . . . ANS LYNCHING SONG 6
OUT OF WAR IT CAME, BLOODY AND TERRIBLE! . . . SP FREEDOM'S PLOW 130
BY THIS BLOODY YIELD. . . . PL OFFICIAL NOTICE 10

BLOOD-LOVING 1

AND THE BLOOD-LOVING GENERALS. . . . ANS KIDS WHO DIE 27

BLOOM 2

10-VOICES: BLOOM IN THE STRENGTH OF YOUR UNKNOWN POWER. . . . ANS CHANT MAY DAY 9
AND THE DEEP RED ROSES BLOOM. . . . SH YOUNG NEGRO GRL 5

BLOTS 1

BLOTS COLORS OFF THE MAP. . . . AYM ASK YOUR MAMA 63

BLOW 10

WHERE COLD WINDS BLOW. . . . NM BLACK CLWN POEM 37
AND THE WINDS BLOW FREE! . . . JC TO CAPTAIN MULZ 76
BUT BLOW QUICKLY . . . SP A HOUSE IN TAOS 33
BLOW QUICKLY, WIND. . . . SP A HOUSE IN TAOS 41
BUT BLOW ONE BLARING TRUMPET NOTE OF SUN . . . SP FATASY PURPLE 7
I'LL HOLLER, BLOW YOUR WHISTLE. . . SP FREEDOM TRAIN 65
BLOW TRUMPETS, JESUS! . . . SP WHEN SUE WEARS 9
FOR FUN TO BLOW DOORS DOWN. . . . PL CULTURAL EXCHNG 7
THE FIRST BLOW, HE SAID. . . . PL FREDRK DOUGLASS 20
THE STEEL WINDS BLOW? . . . PL WITHOUT BENEFIT 6

BLOWING 4

I THOUGHT I HEARD THE HORN OF PLENTY BLOWING. . . . AYM BLUES IN STEREO 35
AND YOUR HAIR WAS BLOWING BACK . . . AYM RIDE, RED, RIDE 33
BLOWING BACK IN THE WIND . . . AYM SHADES OF PIG 35
A WHIRL OF WHISTLES BLOWING. . . . PL CULTURAL EXCHNG 11

BLOWN 3

IN AUTUMN THEY DIE AND ARE BLOWN AWAY. . . . DK AUTUMN THOUGHT 2
THE WIND HAS BLOWN ALL THE CLOUD-GARMENTS . . . SP MARCH MOON 3
BLOWN SKY HIGH BY MONT PELEE? . . . AYM RIDE, RED, RIDE 14

BLOWS 4

BUT THE WIND BLOWS THERE. . . . OWT RESTRICTIVE 15
A CHANCE WIND BLOWS THERE. . . . SP SONG BILLIE HOL 13
BLOWS A SCRATCHY SOUND. . . . PL CULTURAL EXCHNG 4
AND THE WIND BLOWS . . . PL WHERE WHEN WHCH 4

BLOWTORCH 1

LIKE BLOWTORCH. . . . PL THIRD DEGREE 9

BLUE 31

IT KEEPS ME FROM FEELIN' BLUE. . . FC BAD MAN 12
AND HER SKIN BLUE WHITE. . . . FC CLOSING TIME 5
BLUE, BLUE, BLUES! . . . FC MINNIE SINGS 19
BLUE, BLUE, BLUES! . . . FC MINNIE SINGS 19
AND BLUE, HIDING HIS DISCONTENT AS THOUGHTS OF A BETTER LIFE OVERCOME . . . NM BIG-TIMER MOOD 7
FILLED WITH BLUE STARS. . . . DK AFTR MNY SPRNGS 4
IN A BLUE CLOUD-CLOTH . . . DK DREAM KEEPER 6
I STILL FEELS BLUE. . . . DK DRESSED UP 4
I COULD BE BLUE BUT . . . DK NIGHT AND MORN 11
I BEEN BLUE ALL NIGHT LONG. . . . DK NIGHT AND MORN 12
AND WATCHED THE BLUE WAVES TIPPED WITH FOAM. . . . DK SAILOR 4
A BLUE BIRD IN A NEST. . . . DK SAILOR 8
NOT A SOUL BUT LONESOME BLUE. . . . SH MIDNIGHT CHIPPI 2
NOBODY BUT LONESOME BLUE. . . . SH MIDNIGHT CHIPPI 4
CRYIN' TO NO LONESOME BLUE! . . . SH MIDNIGHT CHIPPI 26
CRYIN' TO NO LONESOME BLUE! . . . SH MIDNIGHT CHIPPI 28
UNTIL THE STARS PALE AND THE SKY TURNS BLUE . . . OWT JUICE JOINT 3
I STOOD THERE FEELIN' BLUE - . . . OWT LONESOME CORNER 2
AND I'M TOO BLUE . . . OWT TOO BLUE 16
BUT, BABY, I FEEL BLUE. . . . OWT YESTERDAY TODAY 12
BY THE BLUE BAYOU . . . SP BLUE BAYOU 2
THE BLUE BAYOU . . . SP BLUE BAYOU 14
THE BLUE BAYOU'S . . . SP BLUE BAYOU 22
THAT OLD BLUE MONDAY . . . SP BLUE MONDAY 10
NIGHT SKY IS BLUE. . . . SP HARLEM NIGHT SO 8
BLUE BLACK . . . SP MULATTO 14
CUR DOG, FICE DOG, KERRY BLUE - . . . SP WARNING AUGMENT 13
EARLY BLUE EVENING. . . . SP WONDER 1
CAUSE I DON'T WANT TO BE BLUE. . . . SP YOUNG GAL'S BLS 24
AND GEORGIA SKIES SO BLUE. . . . PL VARI-COLORED 10
I WONDER WHY THE SKY'S SO BLUE . . . PL VARI-COLORED 13

BLUES 43

BLUES SINGERS SAY. . . . WB BLUES FANTASY 3
NOW THE CRYIN' BLUES . . . WB BLUES FANTASY 11
I'LL CAST MY BLUES ASIDE. . . . WB BLUES FANTASY 26
"JAZZ BOY BLUES." . . . WB SUMMER NIGHT 6
SING YOUR BLUES SONG. . . . WB TO MIDNIGHT NAN 9
BLUES . . . BLUES! . . . FC MINNIE SINGS 18
BLUES . . . BLUES! . . . FC MINNIE SINGS 18
BLUE, BLUE, BLUES! . . . FC MINNIE SINGS 19
I'D SHO HAVE THEM BLUES. . . . FC MINNIE SINGS 20
MUSIC TAKES ON A BLUES STRAIN, GRADUALLY RETURNING TO A SORT OF . . . NM BIG-TIMER MOOD 3
A GAY AND LOW-DOWN BLUES. COMIC ENTRANCE LIKE THE CLOWNS IN THE CIRCUS. . . . NM BLACK CLWN MOOD 1
OR A WEARY BLUES. . . . NM BROKE 1
HOMESICK BLUES, LAWD. . . . DK HOMESICK BLUES 13
HOMESICK BLUES IS . . . DK HOMESICK BLUES 15

I FEELS DE BLUES A COMIN'. . . . . DK NIGHT AND MORN 5
JUST TO DRIVE MY BLUES AWAY - . . . SH EVENIN' BLUES 14
TO DRIVE MY BLUES AWAY. . . . . . . SH EVENIN' BLUES 16
DE BLUES FORGETS TO STAY. . . . . . SH EVENIN' BLUES 18
HOW DE BLUES THEY COME TO BE. . . . SH EVENIN' BLUES 20
HOW DE BLUES THEY COME TO BE - . . SH EVENIN' BLUES 22
IF YOU CAN WHIP DE BLUES, BOY. . . SH HEY-HEY BLUES 7
BOY, IF YOU CAN WHIP DE BLUES. . . SH HEY-HEY BLUES 9
WHILE BLUES AS MELLOW AS THE SOUTHERN AIR . . . . OWT JUICE JOINT 25
PLAY THE ST. LOUIS BLUES . . . . . OWT REQUEST REQUIEM 1
I GOT THOSE SAD OLD WEARY BLUES. . OWT TOO BLUE 1
SAYS DADDY I HAVE GOT THE BLUES. . SP HARD DADDY 2
SAYS DADDY I HAVE GOT THE BLUES. . SP HARD DADDY 4
PLAY THE BLUES FOR ME. . . . . . . SP MISERY 1
PLAY THE BLUES FOR ME. . . . . . . SP MISERY 2
'S GOT TO HEAR A BLUES . . . . . . SP MISERY 15
IF THE BLUES WOULD LET ME. . . . . SP MISS BLUES'ES 1
IF THE BLUES WOULD LET ME. . . . . SP MISS BLUES'ES 3
MONROE SINGS A LITTLE BLUES. . . . SP MONROE'S BLUES 5
HIS LITTLE BLUES IS SAD. . . . . . SP MONROE'S BLUES 6
MONROE SINGS A LITTLE BLUES - . . . SP MONROE'S BLUES 7
YOU'VE TAKEN MY BLUES AND GONE - . SP NOTE COMM THEAT 1
YEP, YOU DONE TAKEN MY BLUES AND GONE. . . . . SP NOTE COMM THEAT 7
TO THE TUNE O' THOSE WEARY BLUES. SP THE WEARY BLUES 8
O BLUES! . . . . SP THE WEARY BLUES 11
SWEET BLUES! . . . . SP THE WEARY BLUES 14
O BLUES! . . . . SP THE WEARY BLUES 16
"I GOT THE WEARY BLUES . . . . . . SP THE WEARY BLUES 25
GOT THE WEARY BLUES . . . . SP THE WEARY BLUES 27
WHILE THE WEARY BLUES ECHOED THROUGH HIS HEAD. . . . . SP THE WEARY BLUES 34
TO THE SHADOW OF THE BLUES. . . . . AYM ODE TO DINAH 112
DEEP IN THE BLUES . . . . AYM SHADES OF PIG 32
SINGING YOUR MEAN OLD BACKLASH BLUES. . . . . PL BACKLASH BLUES 30
WILL HAVE THE BLUES. . . . . PL BACKLASH BLUES 37
BLUES. . . . . PL FINAL CALL 14

BLUES'ES 2
I MUST BE MISS BLUES'ES CHILD. . . SP MISS BLUES'ES 6
I'M JUST MISS BLUES'ES CHILD! . . . SP MISS BLUES'ES 14

BLUES'LL 1
WONDER WHAT DE BLUES'LL BRING? . . DK NIGHT AND MORN 6

BLUE-GREEN 2
WID BLUE-GREEN EYES: . . . . FC NEW CABARET GRL 2
WID BLUE-GREEN EYES: . . . . FC NEW CABARET GRL 14

BLUE-GUMMED 1
CAUSE A BLUE-GUMMED WOMAN . . . . . FC EVIL WOMAN 11

BLUFF 1
CALLED THEIR BLUFF. . . . . JC BLD SAM SOLOMON 52

BLUNDERINGLY 1
AND SOMETIMES ONLY BLUNDERINGLY EXPRESS THEM. . . . . SP FREEDOM'S PLOW 149

BLURRED 1
BITTER TELEVISION BLURRED . . . . . SP SONG BILLIE HOL 18

BLUSH 2
TO BLUSH OF THE ROSE. . . . . SH HARLEM SWEETIES 22
BUT WHY DON'T YOU BLUSH. . . . . . SP MARCH MOON 7

BOARD 4
AND TOLD ME I'D BETTER PAY HER FOR MY ROOM RENT AND BOARD! . . . . NM BROKE 22
WE'LL ALL BOARD THERE. . . . . . . OWT BOARDING HOUSE 4
EVERYBODY'S GOT A RIGHT TO BOARD THE FREEDOM TRAIN? . . . . SP FREEDOM TRAIN 22
GET ON BOARD OUR FREEDOM TRAIN! . . SP FREEDOM TRAIN 69

BOARDING 3
CHEAPEST BOARDING HOUSE: . . . . . OWT BOARDING HOUSE 2
CHEAPEST BOARDING HOUSE. . . . . . OWT BOARDING HOUSE 8
CHEAPEST BOARDING HOUSE! . . . . . OWT BOARDING HOUSE 14

BOARDS 1
AND BOARDS TORN UP. . . . . SP MOTHER TO SON 5

BOASTING 2
BOASTING, LIKE A CHEAP BULLY, BUT SUDDENLY LOOKING AHEAD: SHRUGGING HIS . . . . NM BIG-TIMER MOOD 5
PULLING HIMSELF TOGETHER, BOASTING LOUDLY AGAIN, BUT REALIZING WITHIN THE . . . . NM BIG-TIMER MOOD 11

BOAT 4
WHEN DE BOAT COMES IN. . . . . . . FC A RUINED GAL 7
AN' I AIN'T GOT NO BOAT. . . . . . DK WIDE RIVER 2
I AIN'T GOT NO BOAT. . . . . DK WIDE RIVER 4
THE BOAT BEYOND THE FORTALEZA . . . AYM GOSPEL CHA-CHA 37

BOATS 2
LAUNCHED THE BOATS AND WHIPPED THE HORSES . . . . SP FREEDOM'S PLOW 58
AND HOLDS OF BOATS, CHICO. . . . . SP GOOD MORNING 10

BOAT-HULLS 1
SPLASH INTO THE RIVERS AND THE SEAS WENT THE BOAT-HULLS . . . . . . SP FREEDOM'S PLOW 57

BOAT'S 1
AFTER DE BOAT'S DONE GONE. . . . . FC A RUINED GAL 2

BODDIDLY 1
JOCKO BODDIDLY LIL GREENWOOD . . . AYM BIRD IN ORBIT 4

BODIES 8
WILL STRIP THEIR BODIES BARE . . . WB POEME D'AUTOMNE 10
TOUCH OUR BODIES, WIND. . . . . . . SP A HOUSE IN TAOS 30
OUR BODIES ARE SEPARATE, INDIVIDUAL THINGS. . . . . SP A HOUSE IN TAOS 31
TOUCH OUR BODIES, WIND. . . . . . . SP A HOUSE IN TAOS 32
OF OUR BODIES . . . . SP A HOUSE IN TAOS 35
WITH OUR BODIES - . . . . SP A HOUSE IN TAOS 44
JUICY BODIES . . . . SP MULATTO 12
DUSK DARK BODIES . . . . SP MULATTO 34

BODIES'LL 1
MAYBE YOUR BODIES'LL BE LOST IN A SWAMP. . . . . ANS KIDS WHO DIE 40

BODY 31
MIGHT WRAP ABOUT THY BODY. . . . . WB SONGS DARK VIRG 11
ABSORB THY BODY. . . . . WB SONGS DARK VIRG 12
HOLD AND HIDE THY BODY. . . . . . . WB SONGS DARK VIRG 13
TO ANNIHILATE THY BODY. . . . . . . WB SONGS DARK VIRG 18
WELL, AIN'T NEVER DONE IT, BUT FOR TO KEEP BODY AND SOUL . . . . . NM BROKE 29
HIS BURIED BODY LIES - . . . . . . DK ALABAMA EARTH 3
STILL BODY . . . . ANS LYNCHING SONG 13
YOU AIN'T GOT TO WAKE UP NO BODY BUT ME. . . . . SH DAYBREAK 5
MAKE THIS EARLY MORNING TIME TO KEEP BODY AND SOUL . . . . SH DAYBREAK 7
BODY . . . . JC ME AND MY SONG 7
THE GIRL WHO SELLS HER BODY BEHIND STEEL BARS. . . . . JC THE BITTER RIVR 35
A BODY SONG! . . . . FW EARTH SONG 12
MY BODY . . . . FW GIRL 12
HER BODY CLOSE TO MINE. . . . . . . FW MAN 6
AND THE BODY . . . . FW SLEEP 2
AND THE BODY . . . . FW SLEEP 10
THIS IS MY BODY . . . . LHR BLD MARY'S SON 13
THIS IS MY BODY . . . . LHR BLD MARY'S SON 29
HIS BODY AND HIS BLOOD DIVINE! . . LHR BLD MARY'S SON 31
HIS BODY AND HIS BLOOD . . . . . . LHR BLD MARY'S SON 34
TOUCHING MY BODY OF UTTER DEATH - SP DEMAND 3
THEY PUT MA BODY IN THE GROUND. . . SP JUDGMENT DAY 1
OFF THE BODY OF THE MOON . . . . . SP MARCH MOON 4
WHAT'S A BODY BUT A TOY? . . . . . SP MULATTO 11
WHAT'S A BODY BUT A TOY? . . . . . SP MULATTO 17
WHAT'S THE BODY OF YOUR MOTHER? . . SP MULATTO 19
WHAT'S THE BODY OF YOUR MOTHER? . . SP MULATTO 21
THAT WARMED HER BODY. . . . . SP RUBY BROWN 3
(BRUISED BODY HIGH IN AIR) . . . . SP SONG DARK GIRL 6
CARRYING IN MY BODY THE SEED OF THE FREE. . . . . SP THE NEGRO MOTHE 10
I WILL TAKE YOUR SOUL OUT OF YOUR BODY . . . . SP TO ARTINA 2

BODY-TOYS 1
MY WOMEN TAKEN AS THE BODY-TOYS . . ANS A NEW SONG 14

BODY'LL 1
BODY'LL HAVE TO WALK BEHIND ME. . . SP YOUNG GAL'S BLS 6

BODY'S 1
MY DARK BODY'S BABY. . . . . DK LULLABY 12

BOG 1
AND MY HEART IN A BOG. . . . . . . SH EVIL MORNING 12

BOHUNK 1
POLISH, BOHUNK, IRISH. . . . . . . SP MIGRANT 9

BOIL 1
I BOIL A FISH AND SALT IT . . . . . AYM GOSPEL CHA-CHA 24

BOIS 1
OVER FRAISES DU BOIS. . . . . PL DINNER GUEST ME 13

BOJANGLES 1
DANCERS BOJANGLES LATE LAMENTED $ $ $ $ . . . . AYM HORN OF PLENTY 5

BOLD 6
A DANCING GIRL WHOSE EYES ARE BOLD WB JAZZONIA 5
JUST A BIT TOO BOLD? . . . . WB JAZZONIA 11

BUT I WAS BOLD. . . . . SH BLD THE SINNER 9
HER NAME WAS BESSIE, SHE WAS BROWN AND BOLD. . . . . SH DEATH IN HARLEM 81
AND TYRANNY AGAIN IS BOLD. . . . . JC TO CAPTAIN MULZ 28
BUT INSTEAD DECIDED TO BE BOLD . . PL FREDRK DOUGLASS 7

BOLDNESS 1
THE PANTHER IN HIS DESPERATE BOLDNESS . . . . PL BLACK PANTHER 8

BOMB 2
AND, LIKE AN ATOM BOMB, BURSTS APART. . . . . PL JIM CROW CAR 4
BEFORE THE MUSHROOM BOMB . . . . . . PL JUNIOR ADDICT 20

BOMBAY 1
CAUSE FROM BOMBAY TO GEORGIA . . . JC HOW ABOUT DIXIE 11

BOMBERS 2
I MUST DRIVE THE BOMBERS OUT OF SPAIN! . . . . ANS SONG OF SPAIN 79
I MUST DRIVE THE BOMBERS OUT OF THE WORLD! . . . . ANS SONG OF SPAIN 80

BOMBING 4
A BOMBING PLANE'S . . . . ANS SONG OF SPAIN 31
THE PEOPLE BENEATH THAT BOMBING PLANE . . . . ANS SONG OF SPAIN 41
THE BOMBING PLANE! . . . . ANS SONG OF SPAIN 62
I MADE THOSE BOMBING PLANES. . . . ANS SONG OF SPAIN 73

BOMBS 7
UP MILLIONS FOR BOMBS TO KILL A CHILD - . . . . ANS SONG OF SPAIN 44
I BOUGHT THOSE BOMBS FOR SPAIN! . . ANS SONG OF SPAIN 45
WORKERS MADE THOSE BOMBS FOR A FACIST SPAIN! . . . . ANS SONG OF SPAIN 46
WORKERS, MAKE NO BOMBS AGAIN! . . . ANS SONG OF SPAIN 54
WORKERS, MAKE NO BOMBS AGAIN . . . ANS SONG OF SPAIN 63
AND DROPPING BOMBS FROM A CHRISTIAN STEEPLE . . . . ANS SONG OF SPAIN 69
I MADE THOSE BOMBS FOR SPAIN. . . . ANS SONG OF SPAIN 71

BOMBS'LL 1
WHEN BOMBS'LL FALL NOT ONLY ON SPAIN - . . . . ANS SONG OF SPAIN 32

BONDS 1
BONDS AND STILL AND MARGARET STILL $ $ . . . . AYM HORN OF PLENTY 15

BONDSMAN 1
I AM THE FARMER, BONDSMAN TO THE SOIL. . . . . ANS LET AMERICA BE 31

BONE 2
OF THE BONE . . . . SP JULIET 7
SOMETIMES A BONE . . . . SP LUCK 3

BONES 5
HIT 'EM, BONES! . . . . FC CRAP GAME 9
YOU BREAK YOUR BONES . . . . FW DUSK 7
FULL OF CHINE BONES IN DARK GLASSES. SP SUMMER EVENING 15
TO DEVOUR THE CORRUPT BONES . . . . SP SUNDAY MORNING 11
FOR A NEGRO'S BONES. . . . . SP THE SOUTH 8

BONGO 3
ON THE BONGO OF THE MOON. . . . . . AYM GOSPEL CHA-CHA 8
BUFFALO AND BONGO! . . . . AYM ODE TO DINAH 45
IBM ELECTRIC BONGO DRUMS ARE COSTLY. AYM SHOW FARE PLESE 7

BONGO-BONGO 1
BONGO-BONGO! CONGO! . . . . AYM ODE TO DINAH 44

BOOGIED 1
BOOGIED. . . . . SP DANCER 11

BOOGIE-WOOGIE 4
THE BOOGIE-WOOGIE RUMBLE . . . . . SP BOOGIE 1 A.M. 3
THE BOOGIE-WOOGIE RUMBLE . . . . . SP DREAM BOOGIE 3
SHE AIN'T GOT BOOGIE-WOOGIE . . . . SP LADY'S BOOGIE 3
BOOGIE-WOOGIE. . . . . SP NIGHTMARE BOOGIE 9

BOOK 3
THE BOOK STUDIED - BUT USELESS. . . JC THE BITTER RIVR 18
OUT OF ANY BOOK AT ALL. . . . . . . SP AUNTSUE'S STORI 20
HIS WIFE LOOKED IT UP IN HER DREAM BOOK . . . . SP HOPE 3

BOOKER 3
(AT BOOKER WASHINGTON'S GRAVE) . . DK ALABAMA EARTH 1
(NEGRO SKIPPER OF THE BOOKER T. WASHINGTON SAILING WITH A MIXED CREW) . . . . JC TO CAPTAIN MULZ 1
IS THE BOOKER T.. . . . . JC TO CAPTAIN MULZ 64

BOOKER-T 1
LET US FORGET WHAT BOOKER-T. SAID. ANS OPEN LETTER 19

BOOKS 8
AND DICE INSTEAD OF BOOKS WILL DO NM BLACK CLWN POEM 5
DRESSED, CARRYING HIS BOOKS TO SCHOOL. . . . . NM DARK YOUTH USA 1
STURDY I STAND, BOOKS IN MY HAND - NM DARK YOUTH USA 1
WHO MAKE SURVEYS AND WRITE BOOKS. ANS KIDS WHO DIE 23
TOROS, FLAMENCO, PAINTINGS, BOOKS - ANS SONG OF SPAIN 38
BY BURNING BOOKS . . . . JC FREEDOM 2
SAVE THOSE THAT HISTORY BOOKS CREATE. . . . . SP AFRO-AMER FRAG 5
BUT YOUR GIFT BOOKS ARE SUBVERSIVE. AYM RIDE, RED, RIDE 24

BOOK-OF-THE-MONTH 1
BOOK-OF-THE-MONTH IN CASES . . . . AYM HORN OF PLENTY 68

BOOM 6
LUCY WAS A-BASSIN IT, BOOM, BOOM, BOOM, ... SH DEATH IN HARLEM 77
LUCY WAS A-BASSIN IT, BOOM, BOOM, BOOM, ... SH DEATH IN HARLEM 77
LUCY WAS A-BASSIN IT, BOOM, BOOM, BOOM, ... SH DEATH IN HARLEM 77
WHILE MISS LUCY PLAYED IT, BOOM, BOOM, BOOM, ... SH DEATH IN HARLEM 91
WHILE MISS LUCY PLAYED IT, BOOM, BOOM, BOOM, ... SH DEATH IN HARLEM 91
WHILE MISS LUCY PLAYED IT, BOOM, BOOM, BOOM, ... SH DEATH IN HARLEM 91

BOOT 2
(AND I NEVER HAD A HIP BOOT ON) . . AYM SHADES OF PIG 33
OF THE HOBNAILED BOOT, ... PL BLACK PANTHER 2

BOOTED 3
THE BOOTED, BOOTED FOOL OF SILLY MEN. . . . . WB THE JESTER 17
THE BOOTED, BOOTED FOOL OF SILLY MEN. . . . . WB THE JESTER 17
SPOTS WHERE THE BOOTED . . . . SP NEON SIGNS 7

BOOTLEG'S 1
GO TO DE BOOTLEG'S. . . . . FC HARD LUCK 11

BOOTS 4
BOOTS ALL MUDDY WITH SOIL. . . . . ANS BLDS OF LENIN 6
I BRUSHED THE BOOTS OF WASHINGTON. SP NEGRO 6
BOOTS POLISHED LIKE A MURRAY HEAD. SP SUMMER EVENING 6
HIP BOOTS . . . . AYM SHADES OF PIG 31

BOOTY 1
ADVENTURERS AND BOOTY SEEKERS. . . SP FREEDOM'S PLOW 31

BOOZE 1
AND JAZZ AND BOOZE. . . . . SP BEALE STREET 4

BOP 3
A COOL BOP DADDY. . . . . SP DEAD IN THERE 5
OR RECORDS - BESSIE, BOP, OR BACH. SP THEME FOR ENG B 24
BAM! BOP! MOP! . . . . SP TO BE SOMEBODY 20

BOPS 1
BOPS BRIGHT. . . . . SP CHORD 4

BORE 2
BORE . . . . SP ENNUI 2
MORE THAN GERMAN EVER BORE. . . . PL CULTURAL EXCHNG 16

BORN 17
WHERE SHE WAS BORN. . . . . FC NEW CABARET GRL 8
I WISH I'D NEVER BEEN BORN. . . . . DK PO' BOY BLUES 24
STARS ARE BORN. . . . . FW BIRTH 3
I WAS BORN HERE, HE SAID. . . . . . SP GOOD MORNING 2
BUT FOR LIVIN' I WAS BORN. . . . . SP LIFE IS FINE 26
SINCE I WAS BORN BLACK. . . . . . . SP LITTLE OLD LETT 12
BORN BEHIND THE 8-ROCK. . . . . . . SP MADAM CHARTY CH 14
AS BLACK WAS BORN. . . . . SP MYSTERY 23
I WAS BORN HERE. . . . . SP NEW YORKERS 1
I WASN'T BORN HERE, SHE SAID. . . . SP NEW YORKERS 4
AND WISH SHE'D NEVER BEEN BORN? . . SP REVERIE HARLEM 8
I AM TWENTY-TWO, COLORED, BORN IN WINSTON-SALEM. . . . . SP THEME FOR ENG B 7
BUT BABIES BORN IN SHADOWS . . . . AYM ODE TO DINAH 70
IF BORN PREMATURE . . . . AYM ODE TO DINAH 72
CHOCOLATE BABIES BORN IN SHADOWS . AYM ODE TO DINAH 76
BORN TO GROW UP WILD - . . . . . . AYM ODE TO DINAH 87
BORN JEW. . . . . PL UN-AMERICAN 11

BORROWED 1
BORROWED FOR THE HORNS . . . . . . AYM BLUES IN STEREO 24

BOSOM 4
BARE YOUR BOSOM TO THE SUN. . . . . DK SONG 2
AUNT SUE CUDDLES A BROWN-FACED CHILD TO HER BOSOM . . . . SP AUNTSUE'S STORI 4
LET ME TO THY BOSOM FLY! . . . . . SP MYSTERY 7
BOSOM TURN ALL GOLDEN IN THE SUNSET. SP NEGRO SPEAKS OF 10

BOSOMS 1
BARED HER BOSOMS. BARED IN PUBLIC . . . AYM BIRD IN ORBIT 49

BOSS 3
JUST ONLY PROVIDIN' DE BOSS MAN IS NICE!" . . . NM BROKE 3
THE BOSS MAN SAID. . . . SP FIRED 5
BOSS MAN TAKES THE MONEY . . . SP SHARE-CROPPERS 7

BOSTON 1
BOSTON AND EL PASO - . . . SP FREEDOM'S PLOW 88

BOTH 8
THEM BOTH AROUND . . . SP COLLEGE FORMAL 10
TOOK US BOTH IN . . . SP FULFILMENT 20
I'D SCRATCH OUT BOTH HIS EYES. . . . SP HARD DADDY 18
AND WE BOTH WAS IN . . . SP MADAM NUMBER WR 19
BOTH AT MA DO'. . . . SP SYLVESTER'S BED 12
BOTH CAN RISE: . . . SP UP-BEAT 10
BOTH FISTS SORE. . . . PL DOWN WHERE I AM 4
NOT THAT BOTH . . . PL MOTHER IN WAR 14

BOTHER 4
NEVER MIND! DON'T BOTHER. . . . SH OLD PAWNBROKER 4
MAKE YOU WALK LIKE A GHOST IF YOU BOTHER ME ANY MORE. . . . SH TWILIGHT REVERI 6
NEVER GONNA BOTHER ME. . . . SP HARD DADDY 12
WON'T BOTHER ME. . . . SP REQUEST 6

BOTTLE 3
IN A CHAMPAGNE BOTTLE. . . . FW MONTMARTRE 3
ONE MORE BOTTLE OF GIN. . . . SP DEFERRED 33
AS A BOTTLE OF LICKER . . . SP ONE 6

BOTTLES 1
A DIME ON THOSE TWO BOTTLES. . . . SP SUMMER EVENING 29

BOTTOM 1
RISE FROM THE BOTTOM. . . . NM BLACK CLWN POEM 71

BOTTOMS 1
AND THE SINISTER SHUTTERED HOUSES OF THE BOTTOMS . . . SP RUBY BROWN 18

BOUGHT 8
I BOUGHT HIM SUITS O' CLOTHES. . . . FC BLACK GAL 10
HE BOUGHT ME CORN BREAD . . . FC DEATH DO DIRTY 13
SHE BOUGHT A NEW HAT LAST WEEK AND COME SENDIN' ME THE BILL. . . . NM BROKE 49
I BOUGHT A NEW HAT. . . . OK DRESSED UP 5
I BOUGHT THOSE BOMBS FOR SPAIN! . . . ANS SONG OF SPAIN 45
I BOUGHT TWO WEEKS AGO? . . . SH OLD PAWNBROKER 10
WE BOUGHT FOR THE WEDDING THAT'S . . . SH PAY DAY 9
BOUGHT A DOBERMAN PINSCHER. . . . AYM BIRD IN ORBIT 37

BOUND 1
THE SUN BOUND DOWN BY LAW. . . . ANS NEGRO GHETTO 4

BOUNDARIES 1
BOUNDARIES BIND UNBINDING . . . PL CULTURAL EXCHNG 10

BOUQUETS 1
BOUQUETS I'LL SEND YOU . . . AYM BLUES IN STEREO 2

BOURSE 1
GENERAL BOURSE BELEAGUERED . . . AYM SHADES OF PIG 4

BOUT 1
WENT BUSTIN INTO DIXIE'S BOUT ONE A.M. . . . SH DEATH IN HARLEM 2

BOW 1
DOUBLE BOW. . . . SP UNCLE TOM 6

BOWED 6
BOWED DOWN WITH CHATTERING PARROTS . . . WB OUR LAND 10
BACK BENT AS IN THE FIELDS. THE SLOW STEP. THE BOWED HEAD. "NOBODY KNOWS . . . NM BLACK CLWN MOOD 4
WHEN I BOWED MY BACK . . . ANS A NEW SONG 8
DIXIE GRINNED. DIXIE BOWED. . . . SH DEATH IN HARLEM 62
BOWED THEIR HEADS TO CRY. . . . SP SYLVESTER'S BED 8
BOWED BY . . . SP TROUBLED WOMAN 4

BOWER 1
LIKE A SWEET VEIL ABOUT YOUR BOWER? . . . WB NUDE YOUNG DANC 4

BOWING 1
AND BOWING HIS HEAD IN SHAME. BECOMES SUDDENLY FIERCE AND ANGRY. THEN HE . . . NM COLORED SL MOOD 11

BOWL 3
A BRIGHT BOWL OF BRASS IS BEAUTIFUL TO THE LORD. . . . FC BRASS SPITOONS 32
OF THIS SILVER BOWL. . . . SH OLD PAWNBROKER 14
AND YOU SING 'EM IN HOLLYWOOD BOWL. . . . SP NOTE COMM THEAT 3

BOWS 1
THAT BOWS ME DOWN. . . . FW BURDEN 2

BOW-LEGGED 1
SHE WOULD BE ALRIGHT IF SHE WASN'T SO BOW-LEGGED. AND CROSS-EYED. . . . NM BROKE 64

BOX 9
LOOKIN' FOR A BOX CAR . . . OK HOMESICK BLUES 11
LOOK IN THE BREAD BOX. NOTHING BUT A FLY. . . . SH SUPPER TIME 2
IN A LONG BOX - . . . OWT DECEASED 3
IN A BOX WITHOUT A SMILE. . . . OWT FUNERAL 2
AND THE SONGS ON THE JUKE BOX . . . OWT RAID 3
I LOOKED IN MY BOX FOR MATL. . . . SP LITTLE OLD LETT 2
YET THEY GOT A SATIN BOX . . . SP NIGHT FUNERAL 7
PAID AT THE BOX OFFICE . . . AYM SHOW FARE PLESE 15
NOW ARE WHAT THE SOAP BOX . . . PL CORNER MEETING 2

BOXED 1
THEN WE BOXED 'EM. . . . SP MADAM NUMBER WR 15

BOXES 2
IS THERE BALLOT BOXES ON THE FREEDOM TRAIN? . . . SP FREEDOM TRAIN 20
AND BALLOTS DROP IN BOXES . . . AYM BIRD IN ORBIT 13

BOXING 1
DREAMING OF THE BOXING GLOVES . . . SP TO BE SOMEBODY 15

BOX-CAR 2
A BOX-CAR SOME TRAIN . . . SP RAILROAD AVENUE 5
AND LEAVING UNTOUCHED THE BOX-CAR . . . SP RAILROAD AVENUE 28

BOY 69
TO WHAT CLEAN BOY HAVE YOU OFFERED YOUR LIPS? . . . WB NUDE YOUNG DANC 8
"JAZZ BOY BLUES." . . . WB SUMMER NIGHT 6
NIGHT BLACK BOY. . . . WB TO MIDNIGHT NAN 14
MA LITTLE. SHORT. SWEET. BROWNSKIN BOY. - . . . FC BLACK GAL 17
CLEAN THE SPITOONS. BOY. . . . FC BRASS SPITOONS 1
HEY. BOY! . . . FC BRASS SPITOONS 11
HEY. BOY! . . . FC BRASS SPITOONS 16
HEY. BOY! . . . FC BRASS SPITOONS 31
HEY. BOY! . . . FC BRASS SPITOONS 36
COM' HERE. BOY! . . . FC BRASS SPITOONS 40
LEMME ROLL 'EM. BOY. . . . FC CRAP GAME 1
AN' SAYS YO' BOY IS GETTIN' BEAT. . . . FC DEATH DO DIRTY 24
SO BEAT DAT DRUM. BOY! . . . FC SATURDAY NIGHT 21
AND ONE OLD FUNNY BOY SAID. "I'LL WORK AT ANY PRICE . . . NM BROKE 8
IT WAS AWFUL - FACING THAT BOY WHO WENT OUT TO DIE. . . . NM COLORED SL POEM 42
A RECITATION TO BE DELIVERED BY A NEGRO BOY. BRIGHT. CLEAN. AND NEATLY . . . NM DARK YOUTH USA 1
I WAS A GOOD BOY. . . . OK PO' BOY BLUES 7
YES. I WAS A GOOD BOY. . . . OK PO' BOY BLUES 9
AND THE BLACK BOY DIE. . . . ANS LYNCHING SONG 4
AS THE BLACK BOY SPINS . . . ANS LYNCHING SONG 7
BOY. YOU'RE SWEET! . . . SH DEATH IN HARLEM 50
LISTEN. BOY. . . . SH DEATH IN HARLEM 84
IF I WAS A RICH BOY . . . SH DECLARATION 8
IF YOU CAN WHIP DE BLUES. BOY. . . . SH HEY-HEY BLUES 7
BOY. IF YOU CAN WHIP DE BLUES. . . . SH HEY-HEY BLUES 9
THE CRACKERS SAID. BOY. . . . JC OLD SAM SOLOMON 31
I WAS A BOY THEN. . . . FW MAN 1
BUT I WAS A BOY THEN. . . . FW MAN 10
HE IS A LITTLE DARK BOY . . . FW MIGRATION 11
PLAY YOUR GUITAR. BOY. . . . OWT BLUES ON A BOX 1
HURRY. BLACK BOY. HURRY! . . . OWT FLIGHT 7
SOMETIMES A BLACK BOY PLAYS A SONG OWT JUICE JOINT 9
GUITAR-PLAYING BOY . . . OWT JUICE JOINT 30
KILLED MARY'S BOY. . . . LHR OLD MARY'S SON 7
FOR MARY'S BOY. . . . LHR OLD MARY'S SON 14
BIG BOY CAME . . . SP CATCH 1
BEING A FISHER BOY. . . . SP CATCH 8
COLLEGE BOY SMART . . . SP COLLEGE FORMAL 7
A COLORED BOY. . . . SP CONSIDER ME 2
COLORED BOY. . . . SP CONSIDER ME 17
AT THAT BOY! . . . SP DANCER 16
STEP OUT O' THE BARREL. BOY. . . . SP ELEVATOR BOY 11
HURRY UP. BOY! . . . SP IN EXPLANATION 15
GEORGE SALLIE COOLIE BOY GETS TIRED SOMETIMES. . . . SP IN EXPLANATION 17
SHUT UP. BOY! . . . SP IN EXPLANATION 20
GEORGE SALLIE COOLIE INDIAN BOY . . . SP IN EXPLANATION 51
IN THE ARMS OF THE BUTCHER BOY! . . . SP JOY 7
A LITTLE BOY. . . . SP MADAM CHARTY CH 6
SO BOY. DON'T YOU TURN BACK. . . . SP MOTHER TO SON 14
O. YOU LITTLE BASTARD BOY. . . . SP MULATTO 16
BASTARD BOY. . . . SP MULATTO 26
BASTARD BOY. . . . SP MULATTO 45
BLACK BOY TO HIS GRAVE? . . . SP NIGHT FUNERAL 20
PREACHED THAT BOY AWAY - . . . SP NIGHT FUNERAL 22
THAT BOY THAT THEY WAS MOURNIN' . . . SP NIGHT FUNERAL 28

HELLO, SAILOR BOY. . . . . SP PORT TOWN 1
LIGHTS, SAILOR BOY. . . . . SP PORT TOWN 9
A BOY . . . . SP RAILROAD AVENUE 13
DID IT EVER OCCUR TO YOU, BOY. . . SP SISTER 13
LAST WEEK THEY LYNCHED A COLORED BOY. . . . . SP SOUTHERN MAMMY 13
THAT COLORED BOY AIN'T SAID A THING SP SOUTHERN MAMMY 15
REACH UP YOUR HAND, DARK BOY, AND TAKE A STAR. . . . . SP STARS 7
LIKE A BAD BOY IN THE CORNER. . . . SP TO BE SOMEBODY 7
LITTLE BOY . . . . SP TO BE SOMEBODY 14
BIG BOY OPENED HIS MOUTH AND SAID. SP ED - ED 6
DRESSED LIKE A TEDDY BOY . . . . . AYM ASK YOUR MAMA 62
IRA! BOY, IRA! . . . . AYM RIDE, RED, RIDE 5
THE LITTLE BOY . . . . PL JUNIOR ADDICT 1
THE WHITE MAN SAID, "BOY, ... PL KU KLUX 9

BOYS 29

SLEEK BLACK BOYS IN A CABARET. . . WB HARLEM NIGHT CL 1
CALL GAY BLACK BOYS. . . . . WB HARLEM NIGHT CL 7
GO OUT AN' LET DE WHITE BOYS . . . FC RED SILK STOCK 3
GO OUT AN' LET DE WHITE BOYS . . . FC RED SILK STOCK 11
BUT THEY GIVIN' 'EM TO SCHOOL BOYS NOW AND PAYIN' JUST ABOUT HALF. NM BROKE 43
WE WERE JUST TWO COLORED BOYS, BROWN AND BLACK. . . . . NM COLORED SL POEM 2
BLACK BOYS COULDN'T WORK THEN ANYWHERE LIKE THEY CAN . . . . . NM COLORED SL POEM 19
AND IT'S A GOOD THING ALL THE BLACK BOYS LYING DEAD . . . . NM COLORED SL POEM 51
8 BLACK BOYS IN A SOUTHERN JAIL. . SL SCOTTSBORO 1
8 BLACK BOYS AND ONE WHITE LIE. . . SL SCOTTSBORO 3
8 BLACK BOYS IN A SOUTHERN JAIL. . SL SCOTTSBORO 28
BUT NINE BLACK BOYS KNOW FULL WELL. ANS BLD OZZIE POWEL 21
PULL IT, BOYS. . . . . ANS LYNCHING SONG 5
I'M GONNA GET UP A POKER GAME AND INVITE THE BOYS. . . . . SH SUNDAY 12
BUT THE BOYS IS ALL MARRIED! PSHAW! SH SUNDAY 13
MIXED WITH THE BLOOD OF THE LYNCHED BOYS . . . . JC THE BITTER RIVR 12
THE SCOTTSBORO BOYS BEHIND STEEL BARS. . . . . JC THE BITTER RIVR 29
WHERE THE LYNCHED BOYS HUNG. . . . JC THE BITTER RIVR 34
WHERE SINGING BLACK BOYS DANCE AND PLAY EACH NIGHT . . . . OWT JUICE JOINT 2
PLAY YOUR GUITARS, GRINNING NIGHT-DARK BOYS. . . . . OWT JUICE JOINT 17
AND SLEEK-HAIRED BOYS WHO DEAL IN LOVE FOR PAY . . . . OWT LINCOLN THEATRE 14
LITTLE CULLUD BOYS WITH BEARDS . . SP FLATTED FIFTHS 1
LITTLE CULLUD BOYS WITH FEARS, . . SP FLATTED FIFTHS 3
LITTLE CULLUD BOYS IN BERETS . . . SP FLATTED FIFTHS 15
PASSING BOYS AND GIRLS . . . . . . SP IN TIME SILVER 19
TO LITTLE YELLOW BASTARD BOYS. . . SP MULATTO 36
LITTLE CULLUD BOYS . . . . SP TAG 1
BOYS WHO TRY . . . . SP UP-BEAT 2
MAY MEET BOYS . . . . SP UP-BEAT 7

BOYS' 1

BLACK BOYS' LIPS . . . . WB HARLEM NIGHT CL 8

BOY-FRIEND 2

I GOT A CHINESE BOY-FRIEND . . . . OWT JITNEY 11
WHY DON'T SHE GET A BOY-FRIEND . . SP SISTER 5

BOY'S 5

TO A COLORED BOY'S RISING IN WEALTH OR STATION - . . . . NM COLORED SL POEM 27
THAT BLACK BOY'S . . . . ANS LYNCHING SONG 12
AND MY BOY'S MOST GROWN - . . . . . SP DEFERRED 16
FROM THAT POOR BOY'S FRIENDS - . . SP NIGHT FUNERAL 14
THAT POOR BOY'S . . . . SP NIGHT FUNERAL 43

BRADDOCK 1

OF THE BRADDOCK HOTEL . . . . OWT BLD MARGE POLIT 6

BRAGGING 2

BARREL-HOUSE JAZZ, SHOWING-OFF, STRUTTING ABOUT PROUDLY, BRAGGING AND . . . . NM BIG-TIMER MOOD 4
HIM, ASSUMING A FALSE AND BRAGGING SELF-ASSURANCE, AND A PRETENDED NM BIG-TIMER MOOD 8

BRAID 1

YOU BRAID YOUR HAIR TOO TIGHT - . . OWT HONEY BABE 2

BRANCH 2

20-VOICES: STRENGTHENING EACH BRANCH, ... ANS CHANT MAY DAY 16
THE HARLEM BRANCH Y, WHERE I TAKE THE ELEVATOR . . . . SP THEME FOR ENG B 14

BRANCHES 2

MAY ITS BRANCHES SPREAD AND ITS SHELTER GROW . . . . SP FREEDOM'S PLOW 198
THE BRANCHES RISE . . . . SP SPIRITUALS 9

BRASS 6

A BRIGHT BOWL OF BRASS IS BEAUTIFUL TO THE LORD. . . . . FC BRASS SPITOONS 32
BRIGHT POLISHED BRASS LIKE THE CYMBALS . . . . FC BRASS SPITOONS 33
ALL THIS TALKIN' AIN'T NOTHIN' BUT TINKLIN' SYMBOLS AND SOUNDIN' BRASS: . . . . NM BROKE 58
DID YOU ASK FOR THE BEATEN BRASS OF THE MOON? . . . . SP A HOUSE IN TAOS 23
A BIG BRASS BAND . . . . SP AS BEFITS A MAN 11
COLD BRASS IN WARM AIR. . . . . . . SP SONG BILLIE HOL 17

BRAVE 3

WHO DREAMT A DREAM SO STRONG, SO BRAVE, SO TRUE. . . . . ANS LET AMERICA BE 41
SWEET WORDS SO BRAVE . . . . PL SWEET WORDS RAC 9
TOO BRAVE TO NAME A NAME - . . . . PL UN-AMERICAN 7

BRAZEN 1

SYNCOPATED MUSIC, TELLING HIS STORY IN A HARD, BRAZEN, CYNICAL FASHION. . . . . NM BIG-TIMER MOOD 1

BREAD 14

HE BOUGHT ME CORN BREAD . . . . . . FC DEATH DO DIRTY 13
COME ON HOME AND BAKE SOME CORN BREAD. . . . . SH LETTER 16
LOOK IN THE BREAD BOX, NOTHING BUT A FLY. . . . . SH SUPPER TIME 2
HE GAVE THEM OF HIS BREAD. . . . . LHR BLD MARY'S SON 16
SHE GAVE HIM BREAD. . . . . SP BLD FORTUNE TEL 14
I CANNOT LIVE ON TOMORROW'S BREAD. SP DEMOCRACY 14
WHEN YOU THINK YOU GOT BREAD . . . SP MADAM MIGHT-HAV 25
MY BREAD WASN'T BUTTERED . . . . . SP MIDNIGHT RAFFLE 15
CAN'T HARDLY GET HIS BREAD. . . . . SP MONROE'S BLUES 4
FOR THE BISQUIT TO BE BREAD . . . . AYM IS IT TRUE? 26
NOR TAKE THE PLACE OF MEAT OR BREAD PL CROWNS GARLANDS 15
I CANNOT LIVE ON TOMORROW'S BREAD. PL FREEDOM 14
AND BREAD ONE. . . . . PL HARLEM 10
EAT QUIETLY THE BREAD OF SHAME. . . PL MILITANT 2

BREAK 13

WHEN THE FLOWERS BREAK THROUGH THE EARTH. . . . . ANS CHANT MAY DAY 4
(DIXIE RENTS ROOMS AT A BUCK A BREAK.) . . . . SH DEATH IN HARLEM 34
YOU BREAK YOUR BONES . . . . FW DUSK 7
BREAK THROUGH THE WALL! . . . . . . SP AS I GREW OLDER 26
TO BREAK THIS SHADOW . . . . SP AS I GREW OLDER 30
SONGS THAT BREAK . . . . SP GYPSY MELODIES 1
A BREAK. . . . . SP LIVE LET LIVE 5
(BREAK THE HEART OF ME) . . . . . . SP SONG DARK GIRL 2
(BREAK THE HEART OF ME) . . . . . . SP SONG DARK GIRL 10
SHE'D BREAK DOWN DOORS . . . . . . SP STRANGE HURT 13
WHO BREAK AWAY LIKE COMETS $ $ $ $ $ $ . . . . AYM HORN OF PLENTY 20
SLIP AND BREAK . . . . AYM IS IT TRUE? 47
BREAK . . . . PL OPPRESSION 13

BREAKFAST 3

THIS MORNIN' FOR BREAKFAST . . . . SH EVENIN' BLUES 7
THIS MORNIN' FOR BREAKFAST . . . . SH EVENIN' BLUES 9
HAD TO GET BREAKFAST. . . . . SP MADAM HER MADAM 5

BREAKING 1

BUT MARCH EVER FORWARD, BREAKING DOWN BARS. . . . . SP THE NEGRO MOTHE 47

BREAKS 4

THE FORCE THAT BREAKS THE TIME-CLOCK. . . . . ANS OPEN LETTER 56
IT TAKES YOU AND IT BREAKS YOU - . SH LOVE AGAIN BLUS 17
RIFFS, SMEARS, BREAKS. . . . . . . SP EASY BOOGIE 9
AND HELL BREAKS OUT . . . . SP SUNDAY MORNING 5

BREAST 2

AN ANCHOR ON HIS BREAST. . . . . . DK SAILOR 6
DEEP IN MY BREAST - THE NEGRO MOTHER. . . . . SP THE NEGRO MOTHE 32

BREASTED 1

HAS BREASTED . . . . FW OLD SAILOR 8

BREASTS 1

BREASTS . . . . SP MIDNIGHT DANCER 5

BREATH 13

AND THE BREATH OF A ROSE IN JUNE. WB PIERROT 10
CHOKING HIS BREATH . . . . OLD THE CONSUMPTIVE 11
LIKE GOD'S BREATH. . . . . DK SEA CHARM 9
THAN SHE'S GOT BREATH. . . . . . . LHR TESTAMENT 12
THE FLAMING SOURCE OF YOUR BRIGHT BREATH. . . . . SP DEMAND 5
OF OUR MINGLED BREATH. . . . . . . SP DESIRE 4
TO DROWN THE RATTLE OF MY DYING BREATH. . . . . SP FATASY PURPLE 4
O, LITTLE BREATH OF OBLIVION THAT IS NIGHT. . . . . SP STARS 2

OUT OF THE LITTLE BREATH OF OBLIVION SP STARS 8
BREATH AND SMELL . . . . SP SUBWAY RUSH HOU 2
ON THE BREATH OF ORNETTE COLEMAN. AYM JAZZTET MUTED 9
'BOUT OUT OF BREATH. . . . . PL DOWN WHERE I AM 11
HAVING GIVEN UP BREATH - . . . . . PL SLAVE 5

BREATHE 2
EQUALITY IS IN THE AIR WE BREATHE. ANS LET AMERICA BE 14
CAN'T BREATHE FREE. . . . . OWT RESTRICTIVE 14

BREEZE 3
TO SWAY IN THE BREEZE. . . . . . . FW GIRL 17
BY SONGS UPON THE BREEZE . . . . . PL BIRMINGHAM SUND 26
GENTLE BREEZE: . . . . PL WARNING 8

BREW 1
NOR THE TASTE OF ITS BITTER BREW. JC THE BITTER RIVR 52

BRIBES 1
WHO DON'T BELIEVE IN LIES, AND
BRIBES AND CONTENTMENT. . . . . ANS KIDS WHO DIE 17

BRIBE-REACHING 1
AND THE BRIBE-REACHING POLICE. . . ANS KIDS WHO DIE 26

BRICK 1
IN EVERY BRICK AND STONE, IN EVERY
FURROW TURNED . . . . ANS LET AMERICA BE 43

BRICKBATS 2
BRICKBATS BURST LIKE BUBBLES . . . AYM ASK YOUR MAMA 67
UNLIKE BRICKBATS . . . . AYM ASK YOUR MAMA 72

BRICKTOP 1
BRICKTOP INEZ MABEL MERCER . . . . AYM BIRD IN ORBIT 6

BRIDE 1
WON'T BE NOBODY'S BRIDE . . . . . . FC A RUINED GAL 4

BRIDGE 4
SHUBUTA BRIDGE OVER THE CHICASAWHAY
RIVER IN MISSISSIPPI. . . . . . JC THE BITTER RIVR 1
FROM ITS IRON BRIDGE HUNG. . . . . JC THE BITTER RIVR 13
WHERE THE IRON BRIDGE CROSSES THE
STREAM. . . . . JC THE BITTER RIVR 60
WE'VE PUT A CAPTAIN ON THAT SHIP'S
BRIDGE THERE. . . . . JC TO CAPTAIN MULZ 43

BRIDGE'S 2
DE RAILROAD BRIDGE'S . . . . DK HOMESICK BLUES 1
DE RAILROAD BRIDGE'S . . . . DK HOMESICK BLUES 3

BRIGHT 19
A BRIGHT BOWL OF BRASS IS BEAUTIFUL
TO THE LORD. . . . . FC BRASS SPITOONS 32
BRIGHT POLISHED BRASS LIKE THE
CYMBALS . . . . FC BRASS SPITOONS 33
A CLEAN BRIGHT SPITOON ALL NEWLY
POLISHED. - . . . . FC BRASS SPITOONS 38
A MORAL POEM TO BE PENDERED BY A MAN
IN A STRAW HAT WITH A BRIGHT
BAND, A . . . . NM BIG-TIMER MOOD 1
A RECITATION TO BE DELIVERED BY A
NEGRO BOY, BRIGHT, CLEAN, AND
NEATLY . . . . NM DARK YOUTH USA 1
ALL THE DOORYARD BRIGHT AND CLEAR DK IRISH WAKE 6
BRIGHT BEFORE US . . . . DK YOUTH 2
STRIKES UP A TUNE ALL GAY AND BRIGHT
AND GLAD . . . . OWT JUICE JOINT 43
BRIGHT LIKE A SUN - . . . . SP AS I GREW OLDER 5
BOPS BRIGHT. . . . . SP CHORD 4
THE FLAMING SOURCE OF YOUR BRIGHT
BREATH. . . . . SP DEMAND 5
THE BRIGHT DAY CAUGHT ME . . . . . SP FIRED 2
BECAME A BRIGHT BALL OF LIGHT . . . SP FULFILMENT 10
AN' NOW I'M SETTIN' CLEAN AN' BRIGHT SP JUDGMENT DAY 11
CLEAN AN' BRIGHT, ... SP JUDGMENT DAY 13
CLEAN AN' BRIGHT. . . . . SP JUDGMENT DAY 14
THE BRIGHT STARS SCATTER EVERYWHERE. SP MULATTO 39
IN THE EARLY BRIGHT . . . . SP SHALIMAR 3
BIG AND BRIGHT AND ROUND - . . . . PL BACKLASH BLUES 22

BRIGHTER 1
TO A BRIGHTER DAY. . . . . JC TO CAPTAIN MULZ 15

BRIGHT-EYED 1
BRIGHT-EYED JOY - . . . . SP JOY 4

BRILLIANT 1
BRILLIANT AS THE DAY. . . . . WB OUR LAND 11

BRILLIANTS 1
THAT ALL MY SHINING BRILLIANTS . . WB SONGS DARK VIRG 4

BRING 17
THEY'LL BRING YOU MISERY. . . . . . FC LISTEN HERE 18
BRING ME ALL OF YOUR DREAMS. . . . DK DREAM KEEPER 1
BRING ME ALL OF YOUR . . . . DK DREAM KEEPER 3
WONDER WHAT DE BLUES'LL BRING? . . DK NIGHT AND MORN 6
I HAVE THIS WORD TO BRING. . . . . ANS A NEW SONG 4
MUST BRING BACK OUR MIGHTY DREAM
AGAIN. . . . . ANS LET AMERICA BE 69
WILL BRING A BETTER DAY." . . . . . JC THE BITTER RIVR 44
BUT THEY ALL BRING REST. . . . . . FW EXITS 4
THEY ALL BRING PEACE . . . . FW EXITS 5
THEY ALL BRING REST . . . . FW EXITS 8
SENT TO BRING THE WHOLE WORLD JOY. LHR BLD MARY'S SON 10
I'LL BRING HOME CHICKEN! . . . . . SP GRADUATION 22
CAN'T YOU BRING NO BETTER NEWS? . . SP HARD DADDY 6
I BRING YOU MY SONGS . . . . SP SUN SONG 6
BRING WELFARE CHECKS MUCH SOONER . AYM ODE TO DINAH 73
SEND FOR KING ARTHUR TO BRING THE
HOLY GRAIL. . . . . PL FINAL CALL 8
THAN BRING TODAY'S RELEASE . . . . PL JUNIOR ADDICT 25

BRINGING 3
BRINGING PILGRIMS AND PRAYER-MAKERS. SP FREEDOM'S PLOW 30
BRINGING MEN AND DREAMS, WOMEN AND
DREAMS. . . . . SP FREEDOM'S PLOW 36
BRINGING THE COTTON AND THE CORN TO
YIELD. . . . . SP THE NEGRO MOTHE 12

BRINGS 4
BRINGS NEW BIRTH. . . . . FW GIRL 13
WHOSE LANGUID LEAN BRINGS BACK THE
SUNNY SOUTH . . . . OWT JUICE JOINT 42
BRINGS REMAINDERS FROM THE KITCHEN SP GRADUATION 7
AND IF UNCLE MAC BRINGS BEER . . . SP SUMMER EVENING 24

BRINK'S 1
TO BE CARTED OFF BY BRINK'S. . . . AYM ODE TO DINAH 57

BROAD 4
BROAD ARCH ABOVE THE ROAD WE CAME. DK YOUTH 8
AND JIVE SOME OLD BROAD I MIGHT
MEET. . . . . SH BED TIME 4
IN THE BROAD DAYLIGHT. . . . . . . SH BLD THE KILLER 14
JUST STOPPIN' IN THE FIELDS IN THE
BROAD DAYLIGHT. . . . . SP FREEDOM TRAIN 52

BROADWAY 1
YOU SING 'EM ON BROADWAY . . . . . SP NOTE COMM THEAT 2

BROKE 18
WHEN YOU'RE BROKE. . . . . NM BROKE 11
FOLKS WHO IS GETTIN' HARD ON YOU -
JUST 'CAUSE YOU BROKE. . . . . . NM BROKE 15
SO HERE I IS, BROKE. . . . . NM BROKE 18
COME BAWLIN' ME OUT, 'CAUSE I'M
BROKE. . . . . NM BROKE 28
EVEN IF I IS BROKE. . . . . NM BROKE 38
I TELL YOU IT'S AWFUL, WHEN YOU'RE
BROKE. . . . . NM BROKE 47
SINCE I'M BROKE. . . . . NM BROKE 55
BUT I CAN'T EVEN BUY A PAPER - I'M
SO BROKE. . . . . NM BROKE 61
'CAUSE I'M BROKE. . . . . NM BROKE 79
AND A WOMAN CROSS THE TABLE WHEN A
MAN AIN'T BROKE - . . . . SH DEATH IN HARLEM 54
I BROKE MY HEART THIS MORNIN', . . SP CORA 1
LIKE A MULE BROKE TO THE HALTER. . SP INTERNE AT PROV 25
CAUSE YOU BROKE MY HEART IN TWO. . SP LATE LAST NIGHT 6
AND BROKE MY HEART IN TWO - . . . . SP LATE LAST NIGHT 8
THE SINK IS BROKE. . . . . SP MADAM RENT MAN 11
NEARLY BROKE ME DOWN. . . . . SP MADAM HER MADAM 12
YOUR FEVER'S BROKE - . . . . SP MADAM WRONG VIS 24
DONE BROKE MY ANKLES DOWN. . . . . PL DOWN WHERE I AM 7

BROKEN 10
THE BROKEN HEART OF LOVE. . . . . . WB LENOX AVE MIDNT 5
ON A BROKEN STEM. . . . . WB YOUNG PROSTITUT 3
BUT BROKEN WAS THE SOLDIER'S DREAM.
TOO BAD TO BE . . . . NM COLORED SL POEM 49
AND BROKEN SHAFTS OF MOON-GLIMMER DK AFTR MNY SPRNGS 5
LOVE - AND CHAINS ARE BROKEN. . . . DK ALABAMA EARTH 13
DREAMER OF DREAMS TO BE BROKEN. . . JC THE BITTER RIVR 67
TO A BROKEN SONG IN OCTOBER. . . . FW DUSTBOWL 9
THESE STEPS IS BROKEN DOWN. . . . . SP BLD LANDLORD 6
WHERE A BROKEN GLASS . . . . SP SHALIMAR 2
YET THE HORSE WHOSE BACK IS BROKEN AYM IS IT TRUE? 52

BROKEN-WINGED 1
LIFE IS A BROKEN-WINGED BIRD . . . DK DREAMS 3

BRONX 2
TO HARLEM BROOKLYN THE BRONX . . . SP GOOD MORNING 14
YOU LIVE IN THE BRONX . . . . PL STOKELY MALCOLM 13

BRONZE 1
PERSIMMON BRONZE . . . . SH HARLEM SWEETIES 23

BROOKLYN 1
TO HARLEM BROOKLYN THE BRONX . . . SP GOOD MORNING 14

BROOM 2
DEATH IS THE BROOM . . . . PL WAR 8

I DIP MY BROOM IN BLOOD. . . . . . PL WAR 14

BROTHER 15
MY BROTHER DIED IN FRANCE - BUT I CAME BACK. . . . . NM COLORED SL POEM 1
WHO HAS A VISION OF HIS BROTHER KILLED IN FRANCE WHILE FIGHTING FOR THE . . . . NM COLORED SL MOOD 2
AND ME AND MY BROTHER WERE HAPPY AS YOU PLEASE . . . . NM COLORED SL POEM 6
LAST NIGHT IN A DREAM MY BROTHER CAME TO ME . . . . NM COLORED SL POEM 13
AND SAID TO ME, "BROTHER, YOU'VE GOT YOUR CHANCE. . . . . NM COLORED SL POEM 16
'CAUSE THAT'S WHAT I DIED FOR - ISN'T IT, BROTHER?" . . . . . . NM COLORED SL POEM 36
"YOU ARE MY BROTHER, BLACK OR WHITE," . . . . ANS OPEN LETTER 39
ON ELECTION DAY, BROTHER. . . . . . JC BLD SAM SOLOMON 36
OF YOUR BROTHER. . . . . FW WHEN ARMIES PAS 20
TELL ME, BROTHER, ... SP FIRE 10
I AM THE DARKER BROTHER. . . . . . SP I, TOO 2
NAW, YOU AIN'T MY BROTHER. . . . . SP MULATTO 27
NIGGERS AIN'T MY BROTHER. . . . . . SP MULATTO 28
NIGGERS AIN'T MY BROTHER. . . . . . SP MULATTO 30
FOR I WILL BE WITH YOU TILL NO WHITE BROTHER . . . . SP THE NEGRO MOTHE 51

BROTHERHOOD 4
OUT OF THAT BROTHERHOOD . . . . . . ANS OPEN LETTER 49
THE BLOOD OF BROTHERHOOD. . . . . . JC TO CAPTAIN MULZ 49
BROTHERHOOD. . . . . JC TO CAPTAIN MULZ 79
BROTHERHOOD! . . . . SP FREEDOM'S PLOW 134

BROTHERS 3
WE DID NOT KNOW THAT WE WERE BROTHERS. . . . . ANS OPEN LETTER 47
BROTHERS - YOU AND I. . . . . SP BROTHERS 7
BROTHERS AND SISTERS. . . . . SP SUNDAY MORNING 37

BROTHER'S 1
ONCE YOUR BROTHER'S KEEPER . . . . AYM ODE TO DINAH 84

BROUGHT 4
I BROUGHT HER FROM DE SOUTH . . . . FC EVIL WOMAN 13
THAT BROUGHT DARK FACES . . . . . . OWT JUICE JOINT 13
HIS BUDDIES BROUGHT FLOWERS. . . . SP BLD OF THE MAN 15
TO THEM FOLKS THAT BROUGHT THE FLOWERS. . . . . SP NIGHT FUNERAL 40

BROW 1
PUT THEIR LAURELS ON YOUR BROW . . PL CROWNS GARLANDS 6

BROWN 49
DARK BROWN GIRLS . . . . WB HARLEM NIGHT CL 10
WHITE ONES, BROWN ONES, ... WB HARLEM NIGHT CL 14
HER DARK BROWN FACE . . . . WB YOUNG PROSTITUT 1
IS A BROWN MAN'S FIST . . . . FC BEALE ST. LOVE 2
A DRAMATIC RECITATION TO BE DONE IN THE HALF-DARK BY A YOUNG BROWN FELLOW . . . . NM COLORED SL MOOD 1
WE WERE JUST TWO COLORED BOYS, BROWN AND BLACK, ... NM COLORED SL POEM 2
LIKE LITTLE BROWN BUTTERFLIES. . . DK AUTUMN THOUGHT 5
A BIT OF CLAY, BROWN, UGLY, GIVEN LIFE? . . . . DK BEGGAR BOY 6
BEAT WITH BARE, BROWN FISTS - . . . DK SONG 8
SHAKE YOUR BROWN FEET, HONEY, . . . DK SONG BANJO DANC 1
SHAKE YOUR BROWN FEET, CHILE, . . . DK SONG BANJO DANC 2
SHAKE YOUR BROWN FEET, HONEY, . . . DK SONG BANJO DANC 3
SHAKE YOUR BROWN FEET, HONEY, . . . DK SONG BANJO DANC 10
SHAKE YOUR BROWN FEET, LIZA, . . . DK SONG BANJO DANC 20
SHAKE YOUR BROWN FEET, LIZA, . . . DK SONG BANJO DANC 22
SHAKE YOUR BROWN FEET, LIZA, . . . DK SONG BANJO DANC 24
JOHN BROWN. . . . . SL SCOTTSBORO 12
HER NAME WAS BESSIE. SHE WAS BROWN AND BOLD. . . . . SH DEATH IN HARLEM 81
BROWN SUGAR LASSIE, ... SH HARLEM SWEETIES 5
OR COCOA BROWN, ... SH HARLEM SWEETIES 14
CARAMEL, BROWN SUGAR, ... SH HARLEM SWEETIES 31
WHERE TWO OLD BROWN MEN STAND BEHIND THE BAR - . . . . OWT JUICE JOINT 37
TO SEEK A NEW BROWN LOVE. . . . . . SP A BLACK PIERROT 15
LAD TALL AND BROWN . . . . SP COLLEGE FORMAL 5
GOLD AND BROWN . . . . SP COLLEGE FORMAL 15
WITH JOHN BROWN AT HARPER'S FERRY, NEGROES DIED. . . . . SP FREEDOM'S PLOW 116
JOHN BROWN WAS HUNG. . . . . SP FREEDOM'S PLOW 117
BLACK BROWN YELLOW BENT DOWN WORKING SP IN EXPLANATION 52
BROWN AND WONDERFUL WITH LONGING . SP INTERNE AT PROV 12
BROWN HANDS . . . . SP INTERNE AT PROV 18
COLD AND BROWN - . . . . SP ISLAND 6
DANCE WITH YOU, MY SWEET BROWN HARLEM GIRL. . . . . SP JUKE BOX LOVE 12
HER SKIN SO BROWN. . . . . SP MEXICAN MARKET 7
KNOW MORE ABOUT THIS PRETTY RUBY BROWN. . . . . SP RUBY BROWN 17
NOTHING AT ALL NAMED AFTER JOHN BROWN. . . . . SP SHAME ON YOU 7
TURNED BROWN BY THE AGES. . . . . . SP WHEN SUE WEARS 3
AND THE BROWN LAND . . . . SP YOUNG SAILOR 18
BLACK, YELLOW, BEIGE, AND BROWN. . PL BACKLASH BLUES 24
AND BIG BROWN ARMS . . . . PL DAYBREAK IN ALA 12
AND BLACK HANDS AND BROWN AND YELLOW HANDS . . . . PL DAYBREAK IN ALA 16
FOR OLD JOHN BROWN WHO KNEW SLAVERY COULDN'T . . . . PL FINAL CALL 22
LAST LITTLE BROWN PRINCE . . . . . PL LAST PRINCE 2
JOHN BROWN. . . . . PL OCTOBER 16 RAID 3
JOHN BROWN . . . . PL OCTOBER 16 RAID 4
AND BROWN HIMSELF . . . . PL OCTOBER 16 RAID 19
JOHN BROWN. . . . . PL OCTOBER 16 RAID 29
DARK BROWN AS . . . . PL THE DOVE 6
EARTH IS BROWN . . . . PL THE DOVE 7
BROWN, BLACK, WHITE - . . . . PL WAR 6

BROWNSKIN 1
MA LITTLE, SHORT, SWEET, BROWNSKIN BOY, - . . . . FC BLACK GAL 17

BROWN-FACED 1
AUNT SUE CUDDLES A BROWN-FACED CHILD TO HER BOSOM . . . . SP AUNTSUE'S STORI 4

BROWN-SKIN 2
BROWN-SKIN STEPPERS . . . . DK NEGRO DANCERS 9
THE CROWD APPLAUDS A PLUMP BROWN-SKIN BLEACHED BLONDE . . . OWT LINCOLN THEATRE 7

BROWN-SKINS 1
BROWN-SKINS CRYIN', "DADDY! . . . . SP SYLVESTER'S BED 15

BROWN'S 1
AND JOHN BROWN'S WHITE AND LONGER AYM BIRD IN ORBIT 45

BRUISED 2
AMBITION BATTERED AND BRUISED. . . JC THE BITTER RIVR 21
(BRUISED BODY HIGH IN AIR) . . . . SP SONG DARK GIRL 6

BRUSH 4
MAMA, PLEASE BRUSH OFF MY COAT. . . SP MAMA AND DAUGHT 1
TURN AROUND - I'LL BRUSH BEHIND. . SP MAMA AND DAUGHT 6
LET ME BRUSH THE HEM - . . . . . . SP MAMA AND DAUGHT 10
SO I CAN BRUSH YOUR BACK, I SAY! . SP MAMA AND DAUGHT 21

BRUSHED 1
I BRUSHED THE BOOTS OF WASHINGTON. SP NEGRO 6

BRUTALITY 1
FROM POLICE BRUTALITY. . . . . . . PL WHO BUT TH LORD 18

BUBBLES 3
BUST 'EM LIKE BUBBLES. . . . . . . NM BIG-TIMER POEM 60
BRICKBATS BURST LIKE BUBBLES . . . AYM ASK YOUR MAMA 67
UNLIKE BUBBLES . . . . AYM ASK YOUR MAMA 71

BUCK 2
(DIXIE RENTS ROOMS AT A BUCK A BREAK.) . . . . SH DEATH IN HARLEM 34
YOU PASS THE BUCK. . . . . SP MADAM RENT MAN 24

BUCKLE 1
"ONE - TWO - BUCKLE MY SHOE!" . . . SP CHILDREN'S RYME 2

BUCKS 5
TWO BUCKS ON IT? . . . . SH BLD PAWNBROKER 3
TEN BUCKS YOU SAY I OWE YOU? . . . SP BLD LANDLORD 9
TEN BUCKS YOU SAY IS DUE? . . . . . SP BLD LANDLORD 10
WELL, THAT'S TEN BUCKS MORE'N I'LL PAY YOU . . . . SP BLD LANDLORD 11
BUT A FEW BUCKS A WEEK. . . . . . . SP MADAM CHARTY CH 18

BUD 3
I'M GONNA BUY ME A ROSE BUD . . . . SP MIDWINTER BLUES 19
BUY ME A ROSE BUD. . . . . SP MIDWINTER BLUES 21
BUD IN SUNNY AIR . . . . PL SLUM DREAMS 3

BUDDIES 1
HIS BUDDIES BROUGHT FLOWERS. . . . SP BLD OF THE MAN 15

BUDDING 1
BELIE THE BUDDING PROMISE . . . . . PL SWEET WORDS RAC 5

BUDDY 16
O, YOU CAN'T FIND A BUDDY . . . . . FC DEATH DO DIRTY 1
BIG BUDDY, BIG BUDDY, ... JC BIG BUDDY 1
BIG BUDDY, BIG BUDDY, ... JC BIG BUDDY 1
BIG BUDDY, BIG BUDDY, ... JC BIG BUDDY 3
BIG BUDDY, BIG BUDDY, ... JC BIG BUDDY 3
BUT SAY, BIG BUDDY, ... JC BIG BUDDY 7
BIG BUDDY BIG BUDDY, ... JC BIG BUDDY 10
BIG BUDDY BIG BUDDY, ... JC BIG BUDDY 10
HEY, BIG BUDDY, ... JC BIG BUDDY 12
SAY BIG BUDDY, ... JC BIG BUDDY 18
THAT KID'S MY BUDDY, ... SP BUDDY 1

BUDDY, HAVE YOU HEARD? . . . . SP DEFERRED 52
SHE DONE LEFT PO' BUDDY . . . . SP STONY LONESOME 12
PO' BUDDY JONES. . . . . SP STONY LONESOME 14
HEY, BUDDY! . . . . PL FLORIDA WORKERS 1
HEY, BUDDY, LOOK! . . . . PL FLORIDA WORKERS 19

BUDDY-O 3
BUDDY-O . . . . SP MIGRANT 3
BUDDY-O . . . . SP MIGRANT 6
BUDDY-O . . . . SP MIGRANT 34

BUDS 1
STRONG AS THE BURSTING OF YOUNG
BUDS. . . . . FW EARTH SONG 7

BUFFALO 3
BUFFALO, SCRANTON, ... SP ONE-WAY TICKET 5
BUFFALO AND BONGO! . . . . AYM ODE TO DINAH 45
BUFFALO TO HARLEM'S OVERNIGHT: . . AYM ODE TO DINAH 48

BUG 2
WHAT DON'T BUG . . . . SP CHILDREN'S RYME 12
WHAT DON'T BUG . . . . PL CHILDREN'S RYME 6

BUGLE 1
SYNCOPATED. DETERMINED TO LAUGH. A
BUGLE CALL. GAY. MARTIAL MUSIC. NM BLACK CLWN MOOD 6

BUGS 2
SURE BUGS ME: . . . . SP CHILDREN'S RYME 14
SURE BUGS ME: . . . . PL CHILDREN'S RYME 8

BUICK 1
IN MY BUICK! . . . . SH ANNOUNCEMENT 12

BUILD 10
TO BUILD A "HOMELAND FOR THE FREE." ANS LET AMERICA BE 50
TO BUILD UP PROFITS FOR THE RAPE OF
SPAIN! . . . . ANS SONG OF SPAIN 57
DON'T KNOW WHY I BUILD THIS LEVEE SH MISSISSIPPI LEV 7
DON'T KNOW WHY I BUILD THIS LEVEE SH MISSISSIPPI LEV 9
THE YEARS BUILD THEIR BARS . . . . FW CIRCLES 5
WHEN A MAN STARTS OUT TO BUILD A
WORLD. . . . . SP FREEDOM'S PLOW 4
THE WILL THERE TO BUILD. . . . . . SP FREEDOM'S PLOW 8
BELONGING TO ALL THE HANDS WHO
BUILD. . . . . SP FREEDOM'S PLOW 27
THEY BEGAN TO BUILD OUR LAND. . . . SP FREEDOM'S PLOW 40
AND THE WAY TO BUILD AMERICA. . . . SP FREEDOM'S PLOW 84

BUILDER 2
BUILDER OF HOPES TO BE SMASHED, . . JC THE BITTER RIVR 68
DON'T BE DISCOURAGED, BUILDER! . . SP FREEDOM'S PLOW 162

BUILDING 5
THE EYES SEE THERE MATERIALS FOR
BUILDING, ... SP FREEDOM'S PLOW 15
"YOU ARE A MAN. TOGETHER WE ARE
BUILDING OUR LAND." . . . . . . SP FREEDOM'S PLOW 156
THE LIGHT ON THE PALMOLIVE BUILDING SP INTERNE AT PROV 40
I MADE MORTAR FOR THE WOOLWORTH
BUILDING. . . . . SP NEGRO 9
A CITY BUILDING . . . . SP STARS 3

BUILT 2
SO THEY BUILT A CROSS . . . . LHR BLD MARY'S SON 13
I BUILT MY HUT NEAR THE CONGO AND IT
LULLED ME TO SLEEP. . . . . . . SP NEGRO SPEAKS OF 6

BULBS 1
HOLLAND BULBS IN SPRING . . . . . . AYM HORN OF PLENTY 74

BULL 1
THE BELLOWING BULL, THE RED CAPE, ANS SONG OF SPAIN 13

BULLET 4
BULLET HOLES. . . . . FC DEATH DO DIRTY 34
BUT BESSIE TOOK A BULLET TO HER . . SH DEATH IN HARLEM 116
ONE BULLET WOULD DO? . . . . OWT TOO BLUE 11
NEITHER BULLET NOR GUN - . . . . . OWT TOO BLUE 15

BULLETS 6
BEATING THEM WITH LAWS AND CLUBS AND
BAYONETS AND BULLETS . . . . . . ANS KIDS WHO DIE 30
BULLETS LIKE RAIN'S . . . . ANS SONG OF SPAIN 33
WHERE BULLETS ARE THE TELLERS. . . AYM BIRD IN ORBIT 14
HOW MANY BULLETS DOES IT TAKE . . . PL DEATH YORKVILLE 3
TO THE BULLETS OF YORKVILLE, . . . PL DEATH YORKVILLE 10
HOW MANY BULLETS DOES IT TAKE . . . PL DREAM DEFERRED 1

BULLY 1
BOASTING, LIKE A CHEAP BULLY. BUT
SUDDENLY LOOKING AHEAD: SHRUGGING
HIS . . . . NM BIG-TIMER MOOD 5

BUNCHE 2
RALPH BUNCHE INVESTIGATED! . . . . AYM BIRD IN ORBIT 75
I LOVE RALPH BUNCHE - . . . . PL CROWNS GARLANDS 19

BURDENS 1
BITTER BEARER OF BURDENS . . . . . JC THE BITTER RIVR 71

BURGHER'S 1
WITH THE BURGHER'S WIFE ONE JUNE. WB PIERROT 30

BURIED 6
HIS BURIED BODY LIES - . . . . . . DK ALABAMA EARTH 3
WE BURIED HIM HIGH ON THE WINDY
HILL. . . . . DK DEATH SEAMAN 1
NOW THAT HE'S BURIED - . . . . . . SP BLD OF THE MAN 21
SOMETIMES EVEN BURIED WITH OUR
FAMILY. . . . . PL CULTURAL EXCHNG 55
THEY BURIED LUMUMBA . . . . PL LUMUMBA'S GRAVE 13
AND BURIED IN THE GROUND - . . . . PL OCTOBER 16 RAID 27

BURN 9
DARK MOUTHS WHERE RED TONGUES BURN ANS A NEW SONG 36
BURN WHITE WITH STARS. . . . . . . SH YOUNG NEGRO GRL 9
THEY BURN FREEDOM. . . . . JC FREEDOM 3
FIRE GONNA BURN MA SOUL! . . . . . SP FIRE 3
FIRE GONNA BURN MA SOUL! . . . . . SP FIRE 9
FIRE GONNA BURN MA SOUL! . . . . . SP FIRE 16
FIRE GONNA BURN MA SOUL! . . . . . SP FIRE 22
FIRE GONNA BURN MA SOUL! . . . . . SP FIRE 25
THAT TRIED TO BURN WITHIN HER SOUL. SP RUBY BROWN 7

BURNED 1
THAT MEN BE BURNED TO DEATH - . . . PL BOMBINGS DIXIE 7

BURNING 3
AND BURNING THE DARK. . . . . DLD THE CONSUMPTIVE 12
BY BURNING BOOKS . . . . JC FREEDOM 2
HER SEEK THE BURNING SUNLIGHT . . . SP STRANGE HURT 9

BURNS 3
UNTIL THE FUTURE BURNS OUT . . . . ANS OPEN LETTER 36
AND A POISON ACID BURNS - . . . . . FW EXITS 3
BURNS IN MY HEART A LOVE-FIRE SHARP
LIKE PAIN. . . . . SP WHEN SUE WEARS 11

BURST 5
JOY. A BURST OF MUSIC. STRUTTING AND
DANCING. THEN SUDDEN SADNESS
AGAIN. . . . . NM BLACK CLWN MOOD 3
ROCKS THAT BURST ASUNDER . . . . . SP LOVE 3
BRICKBATS BURST LIKE BUBBLES . . . AYM ASK YOUR MAMA 67
STONES BURST LIKE BALLOONS . . . . AYM ASK YOUR MAMA 68
AND BURST LIKE ROMAN CANDLES. . . . PL THIRD DEGREE 14

BURSTING 2
STRONG AS THE BURSTING OF YOUNG
BUDS. . . . . FW EARTH SONG 7
SELDOM BURSTING . . . . AYM ASK YOUR MAMA 70

BURSTS 3
THE BAND DOWN IN THE PIT BURSTS INTO
JAZZ. . . . . OWT LINCOLN THEATRE 6
THE DIPLOMA BURSTS ITS FRAME . . . SP GRADUATION 23
AND, LIKE AN ATOM BOMB, BURSTS
APART. . . . . PL JIM CROW CAR 4

BURY 2
WE GONNA BURY THAT SON-OF-A-GUN! . JC JIM CROW'S LAST 32
NO MONEY TO BURY HIM. . . . . SP BLD OF THE MAN 1

BUS 4
I'LL MEET YOU AT THE BUS STATION. SH LETTER 21
THE SOLDIER THROWN FROM A JIM CROW
BUS BEHIND STEEL BARS, ... JC THE BITTER RIVR 33
THE BUS, THE SUB - . . . . OWT NEGRO SERVANT 12
ON THE BUS WE'RE PUT IN THE BACK - PL MERRY-GO-ROUND 11

BUSES 1
IN BUSES MARKED NEW YORK . . . . . SP GOOD MORNING 12

BUSINESS 4
NO BUSINESS TO DIE. . . . . SP BLD OF THE MAN 28
A NEGRO'S GOT NO BUSINESS ON THE
FREEDOM TRACK! . . . . SP FREEDOM TRAIN 40
BUSINESS, FRIEND. . . . . SP MADAM MINISTER 16
THE MADAM STANDS FOR BUSINESS. . . SP MADAM'S PAST HI 3

BUSSES 1
TAKE THE LENOX AVENUE BUSSES. . . . SP JUKE BOX LOVE 4

BUST 4
BUST 'EM LIKE BUBBLES. . . . . . . NM BIG-TIMER POEM 60
BIG BEN, I'M GONNA BUST YOU BANG UP
SIDE THE WALL! . . . . SH DAYBREAK 1
THEM THOUGHTS WOULD BUST MY HEAD - SP BLUES AT DAWN 4
MY HEART TO BUST. . . . . SP MADAM MIGHT-HAV 32

BUSTIN 1
WENT BUSTIN INTO DIXIE'S BOUT ONE
A.M. . . . . SH DEATH IN HARLEM 2

BUSY 1
AND ARABELLA WAS BUSY IN THE LADIES'
ROOM. . . . . SH DEATH IN HARLEM 92

BUT 366
BUT YOU WILL NOT MISS ME. - . . . . WB A FAREWELL 6
BUT MY BABY . . . . WB CAT AND SAXOPHN 10
BUT ME. . . . . WB CAT AND SAXOPHN 14
BUT MY BABY . . . . WB CAT AND SAXOPHN 20
BUT . . . . WB CAT AND SAXOPHN 24
BUT THE WHITE MEN CAME. . . . . . . WB LAMENT DARK PEO 2
BUT THE WHITE MEN CAME. . . . . . . WB LAMENT DARK PEO 4
BUT PIERROT WONDERED WHY. . . . . . WB PIERROT 6
BUT PIERROT LEFT PIERRETTE. . . . . WB PIERROT 16
BUT PIERROT'S STEEPED IN SIN. . . . WB PIERROT 26
BUT SOON . . . . WB POEME D'AUTOMNE 8
BUT ONE SHARP, LEAPING FLAME . . . WB SONGS DARK VIRG 17
BUT JUMP OVERBOARD AN' DROWN. . . . FC A RUINED GAL 14
DON'T KNOW WHY I DO IT BUT . . . . FC BAD MAN 11
BUT I'LL MISS MA GIN. . . . . FC BLD OF GIN MARY 20
BUT WHEN I WAS HUNGRY, ... FC DEATH DO DIRTY 11
BUT WHEN I GOT THERE . . . . FC DEATH DO DIRTY 26
I TREATS HER KIND BUT . . . . FC EVIL WOMAN 5
BUT HE SHO DO TREAT ME KIND. . . . FC GAL'S CRY DYING 14
BUT HE SHO DO TREAT ME KIND. . . . FC GAL'S CRY DYING 16
BUT I HAD TO LEAVE CAUSE . . . . . FC GYPSY MAN 11
BUT I'LL HAVE MO' SENSE NEXT TIME. FC GYPSY MAN 18
IT AIN'T NOTHIN' BUT A HOVEL. . . . FC WORKIN' MAN 4
AIN'T NOTHIN' BUT A 'HORE. . . . . FC WORKIN' MAN 8
BUT SHE DON'T GIMME LOVIN' . . . . FC WORKIN' MAN 11
AN' GITS NOTHIN' BUT TROUBLE. . . . FC WORKIN' MAN 16
BOASTING, LIKE A CHEAP BULLY. BUT
SUDDENLY LOOKING AHEAD: SHRUGGING
HIS . . . . NM BIG-TIMER MOOD 5
SHOULDERS AT FATE, ACCEPTING HIS
POSITION - BUT INSIDE HIMSELF
UNHAPPY . . . . NM BIG-TIMER MOOD 6
PULLING HIMSELF TOGETHER, BOASTING
LOUDLY AGAIN, BUT REALIZING
WITHIN THE . . . . NM BIG-TIMER MOOD 11
BUT - AIN'T MY LIFE MINE? . . . . . NM BIG-TIMER POEM 20
BUT WHILE I'M LIVIN' - I'M LIVIN'! NM BIG-TIMER POEM 35
BUT IF I WANTED TO GO STRAIGHT . . NM BIG-TIMER POEM 41
BUT I AINT GOT NOTHIN' REAL . . . . NM BIG-TIMER POEM 47
BUT DON'T LET IT MATTER TO YOU. . . NM BIG-TIMER POEM 49
WALKING PROUDLY, ALMOST PRANCING,
BUT GRADUALLY SUBDUED TO A SLOW,
HEAVY . . . . NM BLACK CLWN MOOD 7
FROM ONE SIDE TO THE OTHER. BUT NOW
A HARSH AND BITTER NOTE CREEPS
INTO . . . . NM BLACK CLWN MOOD 9
AND HELPLESSNESS. THE MUSIC IS LIKE
A MOURNFUL TOM-TOM IN THE DARK!
BUT . . . . NM BLACK CLWN MOOD 11
BUT NO! NOT FOREVER . . . . NM BLACK CLWN POEM 59
BUT NOW - . . . . NM BLACK CLWN POEM 78
YOU ALL OUT THERE LAUGHIN', BUT THAT
AIN'T NO JOKE - . . . . NM BROKE 10
WELL, AIN'T NEVER DONE IT, BUT FOR
TO KEEP BODY AND SOUL . . . . . NM BROKE 29
BUT I SHO BEEN LOOKIN' ROUND HARD
LATELY FOR WAYS AND MEANS . . . NM BROKE 39
BUT THEY GIVIN' 'EM TO SCHOOL BOYS
NOW AND PAYIN' JUST ABOUT HALF. NM BROKE 43
BUT RIGHT LONG THROUGH HERE NOW, I
CAN'T 'FORD TO BUY YOU NO HAT." NM BROKE 51
I THOUGHT LOVE WAS A DREAM, BUT I
SHO HAVE AWOKE - . . . . NM BROKE 54
BUT YOU DON'T SEE NO PRESIDENTS
DYIN' O' GRIEF - . . . . NM BROKE 57
ALL THIS TALKIN' AIN'T NOTHIN' BUT
TINKLIN' SYMBOLS AND SOUNDIN'
BRASS: . . . . NM BROKE 58
BUT I CAN'T EVEN BUY A PAPER - I'M
SO BROKE. . . . . NM BROKE 61
DOES I WANTA? WELL, CAN'T SAY BUT
WHAT I MIGHT - . . . . NM BROKE 71
MY BROTHER DIED IN FRANCE - BUT I
CAME BACK. . . . . NM COLORED SL POEM 1
BEEN MADE, PROUD AND SMILING. BUT
THE LIVING, REMEMBERING WITH A
HALF-SOB . . . . NM COLORED SL MOOD 10
BUT NOW I KNOW WE'VE GOT PLENTY TO
DO. . . . . NM COLORED SL POEM 23
BUT NOW I KNOW WELL THAT'S NOT OUR
SITUATION: . . . . NM COLORED SL POEM 28
BUT THE DREAM WAS CRUEL - AND BITTER
- AND SOMEHOW . . . . NM COLORED SL POEM 40
BUT BROKEN WAS THE SOLDIER'S DREAM,
TOO BAD TO BE . . . . NM COLORED SL POEM 49
BUT HIGHER THAN THE SINGING PINES DK ALABAMA EARTH 4
IS NOT HE BUT A SHADOW IN THE SUN - DK BEGGAR BOY 5
BUT HIS SOUL WENT OUT TO SEA. . . . DK DEATH SEAMAN 2
I PUT 'EM ON BUT . . . . DK DRESSED UP 3
BUT I WISH I HAD BACK THAT . . . . DK DRESSED UP 7
BUT I AIN'T GOT NOBODY . . . . . . DK DRESSED UP 11
BUT WHEN THE SUN ROSE MAKING . . . DK IRISH WAKE 5

I COULD BE BLUE BUT . . . . DK NIGHT AND MORN 11
NOBODY BUT DEATH . . . . DK PARISIAN BEGGAR 11
BUT THIS WORLD IS WEARY . . . . . . DK PO' BOY BLUES 11
BUT THAT THE SEA IS STRONG . . . . DK SEA CHARM 5
BUT THAT SEA WIND IS SWEET . . . . DK SEA CHARM 9
BUT SWEET . . . . ANS A NEW SONG 41
BUT NINE BLACK BOYS KNOW FULL WELL. ANS BLD OZZIE POWEL 21
BUT REDDER NOW WHERE YOUR LIFE'S
BLOOD FLOWED. . . . . ANS BLD OZZIE POWEL 31
BUT THE MAN WITH THE TITLE OF
GOVERNOR . . . . ANS CHANT TOM MOONY 10
BUT REMEMBERED FOREVER WILL BE THE
NAME: . . . . ANS CHANT TOM MOONY 30
BUT THE DAY WILL COME - . . . . . . ANS KIDS WHO DIE 43
BUT OPPORTUNITY IS REAL, AND LIFE IS
FREE, ... ANS LET AMERICA BE 13
BUT I'M WAKIN' UP! . . . . ANS PARK BENCH 7
BUT ON ME AND YOU! . . . . ANS SONG OF SPAIN 53
BUT ALL THE WHOLE OPPRESSED . . . . ANS UNION 3
BUT SINCE I GOT TO GET UP AT DAY, SH BED TIME 9
BUT A MAN'S GOT TO LIVE. . . . . . SH BLD PAWNBROKER 19
BUT I WAS BOLD. . . . . SH BLD THE SINNER 9
THAT'S NOTHING BUT TRASH. . . . . . SH BLD THE KILLER 12
BUT I WAS DRINKING LICKER. . . . . SH BLD THE SINNER 15
YOU AIN'T GOT TO WAKE UP NO BODY BUT
ME. . . . . SH DAYBREAK 5
BUT FOR A WISE NIGHT-BIRD . . . . . SH DEATH IN HARLEM 4
BUT ARABELLA HAD HER GUN. . . . . . SH DEATH IN HARLEM 105
BUT BESSIE TOOK A BULLET TO HER . . SH DEATH IN HARLEM 116
BUT THE TEXAS KID, ... SH DEATH IN HARLEM 139
BUT THIS EVENIN' FOR SUPPER, . . . SH EVENIN' BLUES 11
BUT IF YOU WAS TO ASK ME . . . . . SH EVENIN' BLUES 19
BUT BEFORE I'D BITE A NAIL . . . . SH EVIL MORNING 7
BUT YOU CAN'T, PRETTY MAMA, ... SH FREE MAN 3
BUT YOU'LL NEVER, PRETTY MAMA, . . SH FREE MAN 7
BUT IF YOU GIMME GOOD CORN WHISKY SH HEY-HEY BLUES 5
BUT GIMME GOOD CORN WHISKY . . . . SH HEY-HEY BLUES 23
BUT I AIN'T GOT A MILLION. . . . . SH IF-ING 13
BUT MY LOVE MIGHT TURN INTO A KNIFE SH IN TROUBLED KEY 11
SURE, I MISSED YOUR TRUNK - BUT I
DIDN'T MISS YOU. . . . . SH LETTER 8
BUT YOU JUST AS WELL BE HERE WHERE
YOU DUE TO LIVE. . . . . SH LETTER 11
BUT A LOT O' GAWD-KNOWS-WHAT. . . . SH LOVE AGAIN BLUS 2
BUT A LOT O' GAWD-KNOWS-WHAT. . . . SH LOVE AGAIN BLUS 4
BUT YOU GOT TO LOVE AGAIN. . . . . SH LOVE AGAIN BLUS 18
NOT A SOUL BUT LONESOME BLUE. . . . SH MIDNIGHT CHIPPI 2
NOBODY BUT LONESOME BLUE. . . . . . SH MIDNIGHT CHIPPI 4
BUT DE WATER STILL MAKES A FLOOD. SH MISSISSIPPI LEV 12
BUT SHE'S DE ONLY . . . . SH ONLY WOMAN BLUS 5
I MIGHT STARVE FOR A YEAR BUT . . . SH OUT OF WORK 17
YOU WAS THE BEST - BUT YOU THE
WORST. . . . . SH PAY DAY 20
BUT DE DAMN FOOL . . . . SH PRESENT 5
BUT DON'T MAKE IT TOO LONG. . . . . SH SIX-BITS BLUES 8
A LITTLE LOVIN', BABE, BUT . . . . SH SIX-BITS BLUES 9
BUT THIS HOUSE IS MIGHTY QUIET! . . SH SUNDAY 10
BUT THE BOYS IS ALL MARRIED! PSHAW! SH SUNDAY 17
LOOK IN THE BREAD BOX, NOTHING BUT A
FLY. . . . . SH SUPPER TIME 2
I WOULD MAKE A FIRE BUT THERE AIN'T
NO WOOD. . . . . SH SUPPER TIME 4
BUT I AIN'T GOT NO OWL HEAD AND YOU
DONE LEFT TOWN . . . . SH TWILIGHT REVERI 13
BUT SAY, BIG BUDDY, ... JC BIG BUDDY 7
EVERYBODY BUT ME. . . . . JC BLACK MAN SPEAK 4
BUT YOU MUST'VE FORGOT . . . . . . JC BLD SAM SOLOMON 3
NEGROES NEVER VOTED BUT . . . . . . JC BLD SAM SOLOMON 7
BUT WE INTEND TO VOTE . . . . JC BLD SAM SOLOMON 35
CAN'T DIE BUT ONCE. . . . . JC BLD SAM SOLOMON 40
BUT SAM SOLOMON . . . . JC BLD SAM SOLOMON 43
BUT THE NEGROES IN MIAMI . . . . . JC BLD SAM SOLOMON 51
BUT YOU MUST'VE FORGOTTEN . . . . . JC BLD SAM SOLOMON 55
BUT FREEDOM . . . . JC FREEDOM 10
BUT YOU AIN'T DEAD! . . . . JC GOOD MORN STLIN 4
BUT THEY'RE NOT SO BAD . . . . . . JC GOOD MORN STLIN 8
BUT WHEN YOUR GUNS ROAR, ... JC GOOD MORN STLIN 18
BUT AS FOR ME - YOU'RE MY ALLY . . JC GOOD MORN STLIN 26
BUT YOU AIN'T DEAD! . . . . JC GOOD MORN STLIN 40
BUT I RECKON YOU CAN HEAR ME. . . . JC GOOD MORN STLIN 51
BUT SOMETHING HAPPENED, JIM'S
FEATHERS FELL. . . . . JC JIM CROW'S LAST 5
BUT INDIA AND CHINA AND HARLEM, TOO. JC JIM CROW'S LAST 13
I'LL SING FOR YOU - BUT DROP THAT
COLOR BAR. . . . . JC JIM CROW'S LAST 18
YOU AIN'T TELLING NOTHING BUT YOUR
JIM CROW LIES - . . . . JC JIM CROW'S LAST 22
BUT WHEN IT IS, JIM CROW'LL BE DONE. JC JIM CROW'S LAST 31
THE BOOK STUDIED - BUT USELESS, . . JC THE BITTER RIVR 18
TOOLS HANDLED - BUT UNUSED, ... JC THE BITTER RIVR 19
KNOWLEDGE ACQUIRED BUT THROWN AWAY. JC THE BITTER RIVR 20
BUT THE SWIRL OF THE BITTER RIVER JC THE BITTER RIVR 41
BUT THERE ARE THOSE WHO STILL HOLD
CUT . . . . JC TO CAPTAIN MULZ 10
BUT STOOD, INDIVIDUAL AND ALONE, . JC TO CAPTAIN MULZ 22
BUT BACKWARD IN THE LANDS WHERE
FACIST FEAR . . . . JC TO CAPTAIN MULZ 26
BUT WE HAVE JOINED HANDS - . . . . JC TO CAPTAIN MULZ 36

BUT MORE THAN SHIP. . . . JC TO CAPTAIN MULZ 41
BUT MORE THAN THESE. . . . JC TO CAPTAIN MULZ 45
BUT SUDDEN NEARNESS . . . FW BURDEN 3
BUT HERE THERE'S PEACE . . . FW CAROLINA CABIN 18
POSE OF NOTHING BUT YESTERDAYS . . FW CHIPPY 4
BUT I COULD NOT FIGURE OUT . . . FW COMMUNION 2
BUT SOMETIMES NOT. . . . FW DUSK 9
BUT THEY ALL BRING REST. . . . FW EXITS 4
BUT SHE TOLD EVERYBODY . . . FW GIRL 7
BUT WHEN THE BAND BEGAN TO PLAY. . FW HARLEM DANCE HA 2
BUT NO ONE WAS CURIOUS. . . . FW HEART 8
BUT I WAS A BOY THEN. . . . FW MAN 10
BUT FINALLY THEY TAUNT HIM . . . FW MIGRATION 6
BUT THE NIGHT-PEOPLE CRIED. . . . FW POPPY FLOWER 4
BUT IT HAS A RED STAR ON IT! . . . FW WHEN ARMIES PAS 9
BUT IF THEY WERE BLOOD, MOTHER - . FW WHEN ARMIES PAS 14
BUT SHE AIN'T JUST NOBODY . . . OWT BLD MARGE POLIT 23
NAW! BUT THEY TRIED! . . . OWT BLD MARGE POLIT 45
BUT ME - IF I CAN . . . OWT BOARDING HOUSE 9
BUT I CAN'T SEE YOU. . . . OWT CURIOUS 2
BUT I CAN'T SEE YOU. . . . OWT CURIOUS 4
BUT I WOULD GIVE A DAMN. . . . OWT FUNERAL 9
BUT THE GOOD LORD KNOWS . . . OWT HONEY BABE 3
BUT NARY A ONE . . . OWT HONEY BABE 15
BUT SUDDENLY A GUITAR-PLAYING LAD OWT JUICE JOINT 41
BUT NONE OF THEM PEOPLES . . . OWT LONESOME CORNER 7
BUT BABY . . . OWT RAID 6
BUT THE WIND BLOWS THERE. . . . OWT RESTRICTIVE 15
BUT I DIDN'T HAVE NARY ONE. . . . OWT STRANGER IN TWN 5
BUT AFTER I BEEN HERE AWHILE . . . OWT STRANGER IN TWN 15
BUT I AIN'T GOT . . . OWT TOO BLUE 14
BUT, BABY, I FEEL BLUE. . . . OWT YESTERDAY TODAY 12
BUT AN AWFUL THING . . . LHR BLD MARY'S SON 4
BUT NOT AGAIN THE SAME. . . . LHR DEAR LVLY DEATH 8
BUT YOUR HOUR IS . . . LHR POET TO BIGOT 14
BUT THAT THERE SHOULD BE THREE BARREN HEARTS . . . SP A HOUSE IN TAOS 19
BUT BLOW QUICKLY . . . SP A HOUSE IN TAOS 33
BUT ALL ONE SNARL OF SOULS. . . . SP A HOUSE IN TAOS 40
BUT I DRUG MA WINGS . . . SP ANGELS WINGS 7
BUT THE ANGELS WINGS IS WHITE AS SNOW. . . . SP ANGELS WINGS 11
BUT I'D HATE TO DIE ALL ALONE! . . SP AS BEFITS A MAN 2
BUT I WANT MY FUNERAL TO BE FINE: SP AS BEFITS A MAN 6
BUT IT WAS THERE THEN. . . . SP AS I GREW OLDER 3
BUT THAT THEY CAME . . . SP AUNTSUE'S STORI 21
BUT I HOPE IT . . . SP BLACK MARIA 4
BUT THAT MUSIC PLAYIN' UPSTAIRS . . SP BLACK MARIA 9
BUT NOBODY'S SEEN HER SHED A TEAR. SP BLD OF THE GIRL 9
BUT IF I WAS A GYPSY . . . SP BLD THE GYPSY 22
BUT NO USE DENYING - . . . SP BLUE MONDAY 8
NOTHIN' TO DO BUT WALK. . . . SP BOUND NO'TH BLS 8
BUT EVER FRIEND YOU FINDS SEEMS . . SP BOUND NO'TH BLS 17
BUT GOD, NATURE, . . . SP CAFE: 3 A.M. 6
BUT HE DOESN'T WALK LIKE ONE. . . . SP CASUALTY 2
AND THINGS LIKE THAT. BUT NOW, LORD, SP CHILDREN'S RYME 3
BUT I'M TALKING ABOUT . . . SP COMMENT ON CURB 6
BUT IT WAS AS IF THEY'D LEFT. . . . SP CROSSING 4
BUT WAS JUST AS IF THEY'D LEFT. . . SP CROSSING 22
BUT BEING NO GOOD AT LOVIN' - . . . SP DANCER 18
BUT DEAD IN THERE. . . . SP DEAD IN THERE 11
BUT MAYBE THIS YEAR I CAN GRADUATE. SP DEFERRED 7
BUT YOU KNOW. . . . SP DEFERRED 11
BUT NOW MY DAUGHTER'S MARRIED . . . SP DEFERRED 15
BUT NIGHT SCHOOLS TEACH FRENCH. . . SP DEFERRED 24
BUT FASTER . . . SP DIVE 4
BUT YOU WERE NOT THERE AT ALL! . . SP DREAM 14
BUT I RECKON I COULD TREAT YOU . . SP EARLY EVENING 19
BUT I AIN'T NOBODY'S SISTER. . . . SP EVENING SONG 7
BUT I'M GONNA KEEP ON AT IT . . . SP EVIL 2
BUT THERE AIN'T NO EAGLE . . . SP FACT 7
BUT BLOW ONE BLARING TRUMPET NOTE OF SUN . . . SP FATASY PURPLE 7
EMPTY, BUT CLEAN. . . . SP FREEDOM'S PLOW 3
BUT NOT SO LONG AGO AT THAT, LINCOLN SAID: . . . SP FREEDOM'S PLOW 101
BUT IN THEIR HEARTS THE SLAVES KNEW SP FREEDOM'S PLOW 106
BUT HAD RUN AWAY TO FREEDOM. . . . SP FREEDOM'S PLOW 113
BUT OTHERS KNEW IT HAD TO TRIUMPH. SP FREEDOM'S PLOW 122
BUT A COMMUNITY DREAM. . . . SP FREEDOM'S PLOW 27
NOT MY DREAM ALONE, BUT OUR DREAM. SP FREEDOM'S PLOW 24
BUT YOUR WORLD AND MY WORLD. . . . SP FREEDOM'S PLOW 26
A LONG TIME AGO, BUT NOT TOO LONG AGO. . . . SP FREEDOM'S PLOW 28
BUT IT CAME! . . . SP FREEDOM'S PLOW 131
BUT MAYBE THEY EXPLAINS IT ON THE SP FREEDOM TRAIN 35
BUT NOW WE KNOW HOW IT ALL CAME OUT. SP FREEDOM'S PLOW 136
BUT THE WORD WAS THERE ALWAYS: . . SP FREEDOM'S PLOW 47
BUT THERE IS, SOMEWHERE THERE, . . SP FREEDOM'S PLOW 133
A LONG TIME AGO, BUT NOT TOO LONG AGO, A MAN SAID: . . . SP FREEDOM'S PLOW 90
BUT IN THEIR HEARTS THE SLAVES BELIEVED HIM, TOO, . . . SP FREEDOM'S PLOW 97
BUT MOST OF ALL TO HARLEM . . . SP GOOD MORNING 15
BUT THE TRAINS ARE LATE. . . . SP GOOD MORNING 22
BUT BLOOD . . . SP GREEN MEMORY 4
I CRIED ON HIS SHOULDER BUT . . . SP HARD DADDY 7
CRIED ON HIS SHOULDER BUT . . . SP HARD DADDY 9
(BUT NOBODY KNOWS IF THAT IS SO.) SP HAVANA DREAMS 4
BUT IS TRUE ANYHOW: . . . SP IN EXPLANATION 34
BUT I LAUGH. . . . SP I, TOO 5
BUT THE GOSSIPS HAD NO . . . SP JOE LOUIS 9
BUT NOT REALLY . . . SP KID IN THE PARK 12
BUT IF SHE WAS TO LISTEN . . . SP LADY'S BOOGIE 5
BUT HERE IS FIVE DOLLARS FOR YOU . SP LETTER 4
I TRIED TO THINK BUT COULDN'T. . . SP LIFE IS FINE 3
BUT IT WAS . . . SP LIFE IS FINE 9
BUT IT WAS . . . SP LIFE IS FINE 20
BUT FOR LIVIN' I WAS BORN. . . . SP LIFE IS FINE 26
BUT IN HARLEM THEY DON'T ANSWER BACK. . . . SP LIKEWISE 14
BUT IT MADE ME WISH . . . SP LITTLE OLD LETT 7
BUT THE PEOPLE OF THE NIGHT . . . SP LIVE LET LIVE 2
BUT THE DEVIL TOLD ME: . . . SP LOVER'S RETURN 17
BUT YOU DO! . . . SP LOW TO HIGH 2
BUT YOU DO. . . . SP LOW TO HIGH 9
BUT YOU DO. . . . SP LOW TO HIGH 17
BUT SHE HAD A TWELVE-ROOM . . . SP MADAM HER MADAM 3
BUT MY MIGHT-HAVE-BEEN . . . SP MADAM MIGHT-HAV 3
BUT I'VE COME TO CALL . . . SP MADAM WRONG VIS 7
BUT HE HATED TO WRITE . . . SP MADAM CENSUS 7
BUT THE NUMBER THAT DAY . . . SP MADAM NUMBER WR 17
BUT A FEW BUCKS A WEEK. . . . SP MADAM CHARTY CH 18
I SAID, YES - BUT ALBERTA . . . SP MADAM WRONG VIS 19
BUT I'LL BE DOGGED . . . SP MADAM HER MADAM 23
COMES OUT - BUT REPEATS! . . . SP MADAM NUMBER WR 28
BUT SUPPOSE . . . SP MADAM NUMBER WR 31
BUT I SURE AIN'T GONNA PAY! . . . SP MADAM PHONE BIL 40
BUT I HANKERED TO SEE . . . SP MADAM'S CALLING 7
BUT I DIDN'T FIND 'EM. . . . SP MAGNOLIA FLOWER 4
BUT IT WAS A LONG TIME AGO . . . SP MAMA AND DAUGHT 13
BUT WHY DON'T YOU BLUSH. . . . SP MARCH MOON 7
BUT YOU THOUGHT YOU WOULD. . . . SP MAYBE 4
BUT HE LEFT ME WHEN THE COAL WAS LOW. . . . SP MIDWINTER BLUES 8
BUT HE LEFT WHEN THE COAL WAS LOW. SP MIDWINTER BLUES 10
BUT HE MUST A BEEN TELLIN' A LIE. SP MIDWINTER BLUES 14
BUT HE'S THE ONLY MAN I'LL . . . SP MIDWINTER BLUES 17
BUT IF HE WASN'T IN A HURRY . . . SP MIGRANT 38
BUT YOU HAVE GONE SO FAR! . . . SP MISS BLUES'ES 10
YOU JEST A LITTLE BIT O' WOMAN BUT YOU . . . SP MORNING AFTER 17
BUT ALL THE TIME . . . SP MOTHER TO SON 8
WHAT'S A BODY BUT A TOY? . . . SP MULATTO 11
WHAT'S A BODY BUT A TOY? . . . SP MULATTO 17
BUT EAT, DRINK, STAY BLACK, AND DIE. SP NECESSITY 4
BUT WHEN HE DRINKS. . . . SP NEIGHBOR 17
BUT, THANK GOD, HE WASN'T DEAD! . . SP NOT A MOVIE 13
AND IN EVERYTHING BUT WHAT'S ABOUT ME - . . . SP NOTE COMM THEAT 11
BUT SOMEDAY SOMEBODY'LL . . . SP NOTE COMM THEAT 12
BUT A OLD WOMAN'LL SAY, . . . SP PREFERENCE 7
BUT WHO WOULD MISS ME IF I LEFT? . SP REVERIE HARLEM 14
BUT THE WHITE MEN. . . . SP RUBY BROWN 23
BUT MY LOVIN' DAYS IS THROUGH. . . SP SAME IN BLUES 18
BUT THAT THIRD PARTY. . . . SP SAME IN BLUES 24
BUT THE PEOPLE WILL FORGET - . . . SP SHAME ON YOU 4
BUT WHY DOES HE KEEP ON FOOLIN' AROUND MARIE? . . . SP SISTER 4
BUT IT'S LIKE A FOREIGN LANGUAGE . SP SO LONG 4
BUT THE SONG . . . SP SONG BILLIE HOL 5
BUT WE ALL SHOULD BE FREE. . . . SP SOUTHERN MAMMY 16
BUT SOMETIMES I THINK THAT WHITE FOLKS . . . SP SOUTHERN MAMMY 21
BUT MAYBE BEFORE MIDNIGHT . . . SP SUMMER EVENING 22
BUT I WONDER WHERE . . . SP SUNDAY BY COMB 3
BUT I FELT MA TIME'S A-COMIN'. . . SP SYLVESTER'S BED 17
BUT I'S STILL SWEET PAPA 'VESTER. SP SYLVESTER'S BED 21
BUT THE NEIGHBORS . . . SP S-SSS-SS-SH! 12
BUT MOTHER AND CHILD . . . SP S-SSS-SS-SH! 20
BUT GOD IS LONG! . . . SP TAMBOURINES 10
BUT I DON'T NEED NO PIANO. . . . SP TESTIMONIAL 5
BUT GOD PUT A SONG AND A PRAYER IN MY MOUTH. . . . SP THE NEGRO MOTHE 18
BUT I KEPT TRUDGING ON THROUGH THE LONELY YEARS. . . . SP THE NEGRO MOTHE 26
BUT I HAD TO KEEP ON TILL MY WORK WAS DONE: . . . SP THE NEGRO MOTHE 28
I HAD ONLY HOPE THEN, BUT NOW THROUGH YOU, . . . SP THE NEGRO MOTHE 33
BUT MARCH EVER FORWARD, BREAKING DOWN BARS. . . . SP THE NEGRO MOTHE 47
BUT SHE SPITS IN MY FACE. . . . SP THE SOUTH 19
BUT SHE TURNS HER BACK UPON ME. . . SP THE SOUTH 22
AIN'T GOT NOBODY BUT MA SELF. . . . SP THE WEARY BLUES 20
AT TWENTY-TWO, MY AGE. BUT I GUESS I'M WHAT . . . SP THEME FOR ENG B 17
BUT IT WILL BE . . . SP THEME FOR ENG B 29
BUT WE ARE, THAT'S TRUE! . . . SP THEME FOR ENG B 36
BUT SENDING MUSIC . . . SP TO BE SOMEBODY 8
WHERE THE MOONLIGHT'S BUT A SPOTLIGHT . . . SP TRUMPET PLAYER 27
BUT SOFTLY . . . SP TRUMPET PLAYER 41
BUT IT REQUIRES . . . SP UP-BEAT 11
BUT DON'T LET THAT DOG CURB YOU! . SP WARNING AUGMENT 4
BUT A DOG CAN TELL . . . SP WARNING AUGMENT 7

BUT THEY GOT MORE SENSE . . . . . . SP WARNING AUGMENT 11
BUT DREAM SHIPS SAIL AWAY . . . . . SP WATER-FRONT STR 2
BUT LADS PUT OUT TO SEA . . . . . . SP WATER-FRONT STR 6
BUT WEST TEXAS WHERE THE SUN . . . SP WEST TEXAS 16
BUT I'D RATHER BE DEAD THAN . . . . SP YOUNG GAL'S BLS 17
HAS NO RECOURSE NOW BUT TO THE LAW? AYM ASK YOUR MAMA 11
BUT I WILL. . . . . AYM ASK YOUR MAMA 26
BUT WHY RIDE ON MULE OR DONKEY . . AYM ASK YOUR MAMA 59
BUT HEARTS KEEP DOGGED BEATING . . AYM ASK YOUR MAMA 69
BUT I'M ASKING ANYHOW. . . . . . . AYM BLUES IN STEREO 31
BUT I GOT TO GET A NEW ANTENNA, LORD
- . . . . AYM BLUES IN STEREO 36
BUT WHEN I GOT . . . . AYM GOSPEL CHA-CHA 56
NOTHING BUT ANOTHER SHADOW . . . . AYM HORN OF PLENTY 43
BUT SCRIPT-WRITERS WHO KNOW BETTER AYM IS IT TRUE? 49
BUT JUST A PUNCTUATION. . . . . . . AYM ODE TO DINAH 124
BUT BABIES BORN IN SHADOWS . . . . AYM ODE TO DINAH 70
BUT YOUR GIFT BOOKS ARE SUBVERSIVE. AYM RIDE, RED, RIDE 24
SINCE BUT TWO EXIST . . . . AYM SHOW FARE PLESE 29
BUT IT IS SO - . . . . PL ANGOLA QUESTION 14
BUT THE WORLD IS BIG, ... PL BACKLASH BLUES 19
BUT SAY IT - . . . . PL BIBLE BELT 11
BUT LEFT INSTEAD . . . . PL BIRMINGHAM SUND 4
BUT I CAN'T EAT HIM FOR LUNCH. . . PL CROWNS GARLANDS 20
BUT INSTEAD DECIDED TO BE BOLD . . PL FREDRK DOUGLASS 7
ANYTHING BUT A SLAVE! HE SAID. . . PL FREDRK DOUGLASS 17
BUT RAPE, ROB, STEAL, ... PL GHOSTS OF 1619 6
ARE BUT A THOUSAND AND TEN . . . . PL GHOSTS OF 1619 25
BUT I DON'T . . . . PL IMPASSE 5
BUT DESTINED SURE TO FLOOD - AND
SOON - . . . . PL JUNIOR ADDICT 10
BUT THE HOUSE IS OLD. . . . . PL LITTLE SNG HOUS 10
BUT TURN THE TELESCOPE AROUND, . . PL LONG VIEW NEGRO 8
BUT HE NEEDS NO MARKER - . . . . . PL LUMUMBA'S GRAVE 15
BUT THERE AIN'T NO BACK . . . . . . PL MERRY-GO-ROUND 12
BUT WHO ARE WE TO BE . . . . PL NORTHERN LIBERL 6
"BUT JUST WAIT, CHILE . . . " . . . PL OFFICE BUILDING 11
BUT THE DREAM . . . . PL OPPRESSION 10
BUT WON'T LET ME . . . . PL PRIME 7
BUT SUPPOSE I DON'T WANT IT, . . . PL QUESTION ANSWER 14
BUT I DON'T CARE! . . . . PL STILL HERE 8
BUT IT MUST BE AROUND . . . . PL STOKELY MALCOLM 4
BUT THAT DAY WAS SO LONG . . . . . PL STOKELY MALCOLM 7
BUT I KNOW IT MUST BE . . . . PL STOKELY MALCOLM 11
BUT I DON'T HAVE A HEART OF GOLD. PL VARI-COLORED 5
BUT YES, SIR, SIR, TO YOU. . . . . PL VARI-COLORED 12
BUT THE LORD HE WAS NOT QUICK. . . PL WHO BUT TH LORD 12
SO WHO BUT THE LORD . . . . PL WHO BUT TH LORD 21

BUTCHER 1

IN THE ARMS OF THE BUTCHER BOY! . . SP JOY 7

BUTCHER'S 1

DRIVING THE BUTCHER'S CART . . . . SP JOY 6

BUTLER 3

YOU GOT A BUTLER AND MAID. . . . . ANS PARK BENCH 6
REVEREND BUTLER CAME BY . . . . . . SP MADAM MINISTER 1
AFTER REV. BUTLER . . . . SP MADAM MINISTER 30

BUTTERED 1

MY BREAD WASN'T BUTTERED . . . . . SP MIDNIGHT RAFFLE 15

BUTTERFLIES 2

LIKE LITTLE BROWN BUTTERFLIES. . . DK AUTUMN THOUGHT 5
THE BUTTERFLIES . . . . SP IN TIME SILVER 12

BUTTERFLY 1

LIKE DE WINGS OF A BUTTERFLY. . . . DK REASONS WHY 4

BUY 25

MYSELF A HOUSE TO BUY. . . . . . . WB PIERROT 3
I'M GONNA BUY ME A KNIFE WITH . . . FC SUICIDE 7
GONNA BUY A KNIFE WITH . . . . . . FC SUICIDE 9
I CAN'T EVEN GET DE MONEY FOR TO BUY
MYSELF A SMOKE. . . . . NM BROKE 46
BUT RIGHT LONG THROUGH HERE NOW, I
CAN'T 'FORD TO BUY YOU NO HAT." NM BROKE 51
BUT I CAN'T EVEN BUY A PAPER - I'M
SO BROKE. . . . . NM BROKE 61
KNOWIN THEY CAN BUY A DOZEN COLORED
PLACES. . . . . SH DEATH IN HARLEM 61
I'D BUY MYSELF A CAR, ... SH DECLARATION 9
I'D BUY ME A MULE. . . . . SH IF-ING 2
I'D BUY ME A PACKARD. . . . . SH IF-ING 6
HERE'S FIVE DOLLARS, CASSIE. BUY A
TICKET BACK. . . . . SH LETTER 20
BUY YOU TWO FOR A QUARTER . . . . . SH MIDNIGHT CHIPPI 17
BUY ME A FEW THINGS. . . . . SH PAY DAY 6
WE CAN BUY LOVELY THINGS WITH MONEY. SP A HOUSE IN TAOS 24
TO PAY HIS CARFARE, BUY A SUIT, . . SP BUDDY 8
MAYBE I CAN BUY THAT WHITE ENAMEL
STOVE! . . . . SP DEFERRED 20
I'M GONNA BUY TWO NEW SUITS . . . . SP DEFERRED 30
I'D LIKE TO BUY A STRAIGHTENIN'
COMB, ... SP DOWN AND OUT 9
I SENT YOU THIS MORNING TO BUY? . . SP EARLY EVENING 2
I SENT YOU THIS MORNING TO BUY? . . SP EARLY EVENING 4
AND BUY HER SOME CHICKEN. . . . . . SP MADAM WRONG VIS 26
I SAID, BETTER BUY TWO - . . . . . SP MADAM WRONG VIS 27
I'M GONNA BUY ME A ROSE BUD . . . . SP MIDWINTER BLUES 19
BUY ME A ROSE BUD. . . . . SP MIDWINTER BLUES 21
STILL I BUY. . . . . PL LITTLE SNG HOUS 13

BUYS 1

BUYS SHOES FOR THE BABY. . . . . . FC BRASS SPITOONS 21

BY 116

DROP ONE BY ONE INTO STILLNESS. . . WB SUMMER NIGHT 3
STANDIN' BY DE LONESOME RIVERSIDE FC A RUINED GAL 1
STANDIN' BY DE WEARY RIVERSIDE . . FC A RUINED GAL 6
BY DE EDGE O' DE WEARY RIVERSIDE . FC A RUINED GAL 11
SOMEBODY COMES BY . . . . FC DEATH DO DIRTY 23
ONE IS KNOWN BY THE NAME OF DEATH. DLD TWO THINGS 7
A MORAL POEM TO BE RENDERED BY A MAN
IN A STRAW HAT WITH A BRIGHT
BAND. A . . . . NM BIG-TIMER MOOD 1
A DRAMATIC MONOLOGUE TO BE SPOKEN BY
A PURE-BLOODED NEGRO IN THE WHITE NM BLACK CLWN MOOD 1
HUMOROUS DEFIANCE. MELANCHOLY JAZZ.
THEN DEFIANCE AGAIN FOLLOWED BY
LOUD . . . . NM BLACK CLWN MOOD 2
ROUND BY ROUND. . . . . NM BLACK CLWN POEM 44
A COMPLAINT TO B GIVEN BY A DEJECTED
LOOKING FELLOW SHUFFLING ALONG . NM BROKE 1
A DRAMATIC RECITATION TO BE DONE IN
THE HALF-DARK BY A YOUNG BROWN
FELLOW . . . . NM COLORED SL MOOD 1
UNITED STATES OF AMERICA. MARTIAL
MUSIC ON A PIANO, OR BY AN
ORCHESTRA. . . . . NM COLORED SL MOOD 3
A RECITATION TO BE DELIVERED BY A
NEGRO BOY, BRIGHT, CLEAN, AND
NEATLY . . . . NM DARK YOUTH USA 1
WHEN YOU PASS BY. . . . . DK REASONS WHY 8
STONE BY STONE. . . . . SL SCOTTSBORO 15
TO BE READ BY A WORKMAN WITH, FOR
BACKGROUND, THE RHYTHMIC . . . . ANS CHANT MAY DAY 1
THAT ANY MAN BE CRUSHED BY ONE
ABOVE. . . . . ANS LET AMERICA BE 9
THE SUN BOUND DOWN BY LAW. . . . . ANS NEGRO GHETTO 4
A BALL PASSED BY. . . . . SH DEATH IN HARLEM 102
SHE LEFT THE TEXAS KID SETTIN BY
HIMSELF . . . . SH DEATH IN HARLEM 79
SO JUST BY IF-ING . . . . SH IF-ING 15
LEFT ME BY MYSELF IN A DOUBLE BED. SH LETTER 7
CRY BY YOURSELF, GIRLS, ... SH MIDNIGHT CHIPPI 29
BY HOLDING ITS HEAD . . . . SH SNOB 7
HERE BY MYSELF, I DO AS I PLEASE. SH SUNDAY 2
AIN'T YOU GONNA STAND BY ME? . . . JC BIG BUDDY 2
AIN'T YOU GONNA STAND BY ME? . . . JC BIG BUDDY 4
AIN'T YOU GONNA STAND BY ME? . . . JC BIG BUDDY 9
STAND BY MY SIDE. . . . . JC BIG BUDDY 17
I SWEAR, BY GUM, ... JC BLACK MAN SPEAK 9
BY BURNING BOOKS . . . . JC FREEDOM 2
BY IMPRISONING NEHRU . . . . JC FREEDOM 5
BY LYNCHING A NEGRO . . . . JC FREEDOM 8
LOOKS LIKE BY NOW . . . . JC HOW ABOUT DIXIE 17
THERE WAS AN OLD CROW BY THE NAME OF
JIM. . . . . JC JIM CROW'S LAST 1
YOU REFLECT NO STARS BY NIGHT, . . JC THE BITTER RIVR 24
NO SUN BY DAY. . . . . JC THE BITTER RIVR 25
MENACED BY THE WILL . . . . JC TO CAPTAIN MULZ 30
VEILING SHADOWS CUT BY LAUGHTER . . FW DIMOUT IN HARLM 8
BY A WHITE COP - . . . . OWT BLD MARGE POLIT 11
AS DECREED BY FATE . . . . OWT BLD MARGE POLIT 30
FOLKS PASS BY AND STARE - . . . . . OWT FUNERAL 4
WOMEN OF THE STREETS STOP BY FOR
SUPS . . . . OWT JUICE JOINT 7
WHILE GIRLS WHO WASH RICH WHITE
FOLKS CLOTHES BY DAY . . . . . . OWT LINCOLN THEATRE 13
PEOPLE PASS BY ME - . . . . OWT LONESOME CORNER 6
THEY HARDLY TAKE GOD BY SURPRISE. LHR ACCEPTANCE 4
BY WHICH I WISH . . . . LHR CONSERVATORY 11
SMITTEN BY BEAUTY. . . . . SP A HOUSE IN TAOS 4
A-GOIN' BY. . . . . SP BABY 5
BLACK MARIA PASSIN' BY . . . . . . SP BLACK MARIA 18
SHE'LL BE HERE BY AND BY. . . . . . SP BLD THE GYPSY 12
SHE'LL BE HERE BY AND BY. . . . . . SP BLD THE GYPSY 12
BY THE BLUE BAYOU . . . . SP BLUE BAYOU 2
BY WHAT SENDS . . . . SP CHILDREN'S RYME 5
BY WAY OF ARKANSAS . . . . SP CONSIDER ME 39
WHEN I WALKED ALL BY MYSELF. . . . SP CROSSING 2
I WALKED ALL BY MYSELF: . . . . . . SP CROSSING 20
GOING BY . . . . SP DEAD IN THERE 3
BY DAYLIGHT . . . . SP DIVE 2
ENDOWED BY THEIR CREATOR . . . . . SP FREEDOM'S PLOW 92
BY AND BY. . . . . SP HOPE 4
BY AND BY. . . . . SP HOPE 4
SEE THE PEOPLE PASSING BY? . . . . SP KID IN THE PARK 3
REVEREND BUTLER CAME BY . . . . . . SP MADAM MINISTER 1
WHAT YOU MEAN BY THAT? . . . . . . SP MADAM FORT TELL 10
STILL LEFT BY V-J DAY. . . . . . . SP MIGRANT 29
AND WATCHES THE SUN GO BY. . . . . SP NEIGHBOR 3
ALL BY ITSELF. . . . . SP ONE 8
PLAYED BY INEZ AND TIMME. . . . . . SP PROJECTION 14

TWO A.M. MIDNIGHT BY YOUR SELF? . . SP REVERIE HARLEM 2
SIT DOWN BY THE RIVER . . . . SP REVERIE HARLEM 3
BY YOUR SELF! . . . . SP REVERIE HARLEM 12
NOW THE STREETS DOWN BY THE RIVER SP RUBY BROWN 16
AS OUR SHIP PASSED BY . . . . SP SEASCAPE 2
YEAR BY YEAR GOES BY . . . . SP SHARE-CROPPERS 11
YEAR BY YEAR GOES BY . . . . SP SHARE-CROPPERS 11
BY SOUND THAT SHIMMERS - . . . . . SP SONG BILLIE HOL 19
TO STRUGGLE BY HIS SELF. . . . . . SP STONY LONESOME 13
LORDY! SLEEPIN' BY HERSELF. . . . . SP STONY LONESOME 17
PIMPS IN GRAY GO BY. . . . . SP SUMMER EVENING 5
JITNEYS GO BY . . . . SP SUMMER EVENING 14
THE TAMALE MAN WILL COME BY. . . . SP SUMMER EVENING 23
BY THE PALE DULL PALLOR OF AN OLD GAS LIGHT . . . . SP THE WEARY BLUES 5
BOWED BY . . . . SP TROUBLED WOMAN 4
TURNED BROWN BY THE AGES. . . . . . SP WHEN SUE WEARS 3
AS LEOLA PASSES BY . . . . AYM ASK YOUR MAMA 36
BY THOSE YET UNINDUCTED . . . . . . AYM BIRD IN ORBIT 12
WERE YOU MARRIED BY JOHN JASPER . . AYM BIRD IN ORBIT 37
MARY MCLEOD BETHUNE BARRED BY . . . AYM BIRD IN ORBIT 76
ON BEDLOE'S ISLAND MANAGED BY SOL HUROK . . . . AYM HORN OF PLENTY 4
BY MOE ASCH OR ALAN LOMAX . . . . . AYM IS IT TRUE? 10
TO A DISC BY DINAH . . . . AYM ODE TO DINAH 15
IF PUSHED BY HURRIED ENTRANCE. . . AYM ODE TO DINAH 119
STEP-FATHERED BY BLIND LEMON . . . AYM ODE TO DINAH 20
STEP-FATHERED BY . . . . AYM ODE TO DINAH 21
AND BY MISTAKE SHOT OUT THE LIGHT. AYM ODE TO DINAH 132
DARK SHADOWS BECOME DARKER BY A SHADE . . . . AYM ODE TO DINAH 51
SUCKED IN BY FAT JUKEBOXES . . . . AYM ODE TO DINAH 52
TO BE CARTED OFF BY BRINK'S. . . . AYM ODE TO DINAH 57
BLOWN SKY HIGH BY MONT PELEE? . . . AYM RIDE, RED, RIDE 14
YOU'LL BE CALLED BY EASTLAND. . . . AYM RIDE, RED, RIDE 26
BY A STUDENT IN A FEZ . . . . AYM SHADES OF PIG 25
WHERE THE MASK IS PLACED BY OTHERS AYM SHOW FARE PLESE 6
TORN TO SHREDS BY DYNAMITE . . . . PL BIRMINGHAM SUND 8
BY SONGS UPON THE BREEZE . . . . . PL BIRMINGHAM SUND 26
MOTIVATED BY THE TRUEST . . . . . . PL BLACK PANTHER 10
BY WHAT SENDS . . . . PL CHILDREN'S RYME 1
BY THE RIVER AND THE RAILROAD . . . PL CULTURAL EXCHNG 8
FOR THE CARS TO FLY BY ON. . . . . PL FLORIDA WORKERS 4
LEFT BY A STREAK OF SUN. . . . . . PL GEORGIA DUSK 6
CAN'T SIT SIDE BY SIDE. . . . . . . PL MERRY-GO-ROUND 8
HANGED BY THE NECK. . . . . PL OCTOBER 16 RAID 21
BY THIS BLOODY YIELD. . . . . PL OFFICIAL NOTICE 10
TETHERED BY SOMETHING WORSE THAN PRIDE. . . . . PL WHERE WHEN WHCH 10
BY THE THIRD DECREE. . . . . PL WHO BUT TH LORD 8

CA 5
CA IRA! CA IRA! . . . . AYM RIDE, RED, RIDE 7
CA IRA! CA IRA! . . . . AYM RIDE, RED, RIDE 7
SEND FOR ROBESPIERRE TO SCREAM, "CA IRA! CA IRA! . . . . PL FINAL CALL 15
SEND FOR ROBESPIERRE TO SCREAM, "CA IRA! CA IRA! . . . . PL FINAL CALL 15
CA IRA!" . . . . PL FINAL CALL 16

CAB 4
CAB! . . . . OWT JITNEY 4
CAB! . . . . OWT JITNEY 54
CAB! . . . . OWT JITNEY 60
CAB! . . . . OWT JITNEY 66

CABARET 10
SLEEK BLACK BOYS IN A CABARET. . . WB HARLEM NIGHT CL 1
IN A HARLEM CABARET . . . . WB JAZZONIA 3
IN A WHIRLING CABARET . . . . WB JAZZONIA 16
CABARET, CABARET! . . . . FC MINNIE SINGS 1
CABARET, CABARET! . . . . FC MINNIE SINGS 1
CABARET, CABARET! . . . . FC MINNIE SINGS 3
CABARET, CABARET! . . . . FC MINNIE SINGS 3
IN DE CABARET . . . . FC NEW CABARET GRL 18
AN EMPTY CABARET . . . . FC SPORT 11
IN A CABARET. . . . . DK NEGRO DANCERS 10

CABIN 1
ABOUT THIS LITTLE CABIN . . . . . . FW CAROLINA CABIN 4

CADILLAC 2
NOW YOU'VE GOT YOUR CADILLAC. . . . SP LOW TO HIGH 5
GOLDEN CROSSES TO A CADILLAC $ $ $ $ $ $ . . . . AYM HORN OF PLENTY 14

CADILLACS 1
CADILLACS WITH DIGNITARIES . . . . SP PARADE 7

CAESAR 1
CAESAR TOLD ME TO KEEP HIS DOOR-STEPS CLEAN. . . . . SP NEGRO 5

CAGE 1
LIKE A SQUIRREL IN A CAGE - . . . . FW CIRCLES 7

CAGED 3
NOW THEY'VE CAGED ME . . . . WB LAMENT DARK PEO 9
CAGED IN THE CIRCUS OF CIVILIZATION. WB LAMENT DARK PEO 12
KEEP ME CAGED UP HERE. . . . . . . SH FREE MAN 8

CAGES 1
IN SILVER CAGES SINGING. . . . . . AYM ODE TO DINAH 61

CAKE 1
CAKE - . . . . PL FROSTING 4

CALEDONIA 1
HOWDY-DO, DAUGHTER! CALEDONIA, HOW ARE YOU? . . . . NM BROKE 66

CALEDONIA'S 1
WITH CALEDONIA'S ARM . . . . SP FIRED 9

CALIFORNIA 1
KIDS WILL DIE IN THE ORANGE GROVES OF CALIFORNIA . . . . ANS KIDS WHO DIE 12

CALL 19
CALL GAY BLACK BOYS. . . . . WB HARLEM NIGHT CL 7
I'M THE GUY THE HOME FOLKS CALL - NM BIG-TIMER POEM 3
THAT I CAN CALL MINE. . . . . NM BIG-TIMER POEM 48
CALL IN A GANG O' WOMEN . . . . . . NM BIG-TIMER POEM 65
SYNCOPATED, DETERMINED TO LAUGH. A BUGLE CALL. GAY, MARTIAL MUSIC. NM BLACK CLWN MOOD 6
FOR TO CALL ME SWEET. . . . . DK DRESSED UP 12
SURE, CALL ME ANY UGLY NAME YOU CHOOSE - . . . . ANS LET AMERICA BE 70
YOU MAY CALL OUT THE KLAN . . . . . JC BLD SAM SOLOMON 2
COULD NOT CALL THEIR HOUSE, THEIR HOUSE, ... JC TO CAPTAIN MULZ 17
AND CALL HIM "NIGGER." . . . . . . FW MIGRATION 7
BABE, AND CALL ON YOU. . . . . . . OWT LONESOME CORNER 4
TO ANSWER ITS CALL. . . . . SP DRUM 5
DON'T YOU HEAR ME CALL? . . . . . . SP EVENING SONG 4
IN DIXIE, OFTEN THEY WON'T CALL NEGROES MISTER. . . . . SP IN EXPLANATION 7
THE MISTERS WON'T CALL LOTS OF OTHER FOLKS MISTER. . . . . SP IN EXPLANATION 11
THEY CALL THEM, HEY GEORGE! . . . . SP IN EXPLANATION 12
BUT I'VE COME TO CALL . . . . SP MADAM WRONG VIS 7
YOU CALL IT FATE? . . . . SP WHAT? SO SOON! 8
THAT MAN THEY CALL THE LAW. . . . . PL WHO BUT TH LORD 2

CALLED 11
THEY CALLED HIM DO DIRTY . . . . . FC DEATH DO DIRTY 6
WHEN THE NATION CALLED US THAT MIGHTY DAY. . . . . NM COLORED SL POEM 4
SAM SOLOMON CALLED ON . . . . JC BLD SAM SOLOMON 17
THEY CALLED OUT THE KLAN. . . . . . JC BLD SAM SOLOMON 41
CALLED THEIR BLUFF. . . . . JC BLD SAM SOLOMON 52
TO THE FOLKS CALLED MISTER. . . . . SP IN EXPLANATION 4
YOU SAY YOU THOUGHT EVERYBODY WAS CALLED MISTER? . . . . SP IN EXPLANATION 5
TO THOSE CALLED MISTER. . . . . . . SP IN EXPLANATION 21
I'VE WRITTEN, CALLED REPEATEDLY. . AYM ASK YOUR MAMA 7
WHEN THE ROLL IS CALLED UP YONDER AYM RIDE, RED, RIDE 2
YOU'LL BE CALLED BY EASTLAND. . . . AYM RIDE, RED, RIDE 26

CALLING 4
CALLING THROUGH TIME! . . . . NM BLACK CLWN POEM 74
CALLING LIFE . . . . SP DRUM 15
THEY HAD NO INTENTION OF CALLING COOLIES MISTER. . . . . SP IN EXPLANATION 9
CALLING ME UP . . . . SP MADAM PHONE BIL 21

CALLIN' 1
WHEN THEY CALLIN' ME HONEY. . . . . NM BIG-TIMER POEM 68

CALLS 3
I CALLS FOR MA WOMAN . . . . FC WORKIN' MAN 5
AND STILL IT CALLS TO ME? . . . . . DK BEGGAR BOY 4
WHERE NO WORLDLY DUTY CALLS - . . . FW CONVENT 5

CALM 3
SOUGHT CALM RELIEF. . . . . WB YOUNG BRIDE 5
SHE SAID, MADAM! BE CALM - . . . . SP MADAM FORT TELL 22
THE CALM. . . . . SP SUICIDE'S NOTE 1

CALMLY 1
CALMLY TELLING THE STORY. PROUDLY AND EXPECTANTLY WITH HEAD UP. SHOULDERS . . . . NM COLORED SL MOOD 7

CALVARY 1
WHEN I GOT TO CALVARY . . . . AYM GOSPEL CHA-CHA 58

CAME 41
BUT THE WHITE MEN CAME. . . . . . . WB LAMENT DARK PEO 2
BUT THE WHITE MEN CAME. . . . . . . WB LAMENT DARK PEO 4
UNTIL I CAME TO THIS NEAR STREET . DLD AESTHETE HARLEM 6
MY BROTHER DIED IN FRANCE - BUT I CAME BACK. . . . . NM COLORED SL POEM 1
LAST NIGHT IN A DREAM MY BROTHER CAME TO ME . . . . NM COLORED SL POEM 13

SINCE THE COLORED SOLDIERS CAME HOME FROM FRANCE. . . . . NM COLORED SL POEM 32
BROAD ARCH ABOVE THE ROAD WE CAME. OK YOUTH 8
AND TORN FROM BLACK AFRICA'S STRAND I CAME . . . . ANS LET AMERICA BE 49
AND THE SUN CAME UP AND . . . . . . SH DEATH IN HARLEM 137
CAME TIPPIN INTO DIXIE'S TO GET A VIEW. . . . . SH DEATH IN HARLEM 59
CAME TIPPIN INTO DIXIE'S WITH SMILES ON THEIR FACES. . . . . SH DEATH IN HARLEM 60
MOON CAME. . . . . FW NIGHT SONG 3
MOON CAME. . . . . FW NIGHT SONG 10
MOON CAME. . . . . FW NIGHT SONG 17
THE SOLDIERS CAME . . . . LHR BLD MARY'S SON 25
BUT THAT THEY CAME . . . . SP AUNTSUE'S STORI 21
A FELLOW CAME ONE DAY. . . . . . . SP BLD FORTUNE TEL 9
BIG BOY CAME . . . . SP CATCH 1
SHIPS CAME FROM ACROSS THE SEA . . SP FREEDOM'S PLOW 29
OUT OF WAR IT CAME, BLOODY AND TERRIBLE! . . . . SP FREEDOM'S PLOW 130
BUT IT CAME! . . . . SP FREEDOM'S PLOW 131
WITH BILLOWING SAILS THE GALLEONS CAME . . . . SP FREEDOM'S PLOW 35
BUT NOW WE KNOW HOW IT ALL CAME OUT. SP FREEDOM'S PLOW 136
WE KNOW NOW HOW IT CAME OUT. . . . SP FREEDOM'S PLOW 138
LABOR! OUT OF LABOR CAME THE VILLAGES . . . . SP FREEDOM'S PLOW 70
LABOR! OUT OF LABOR CAME THE ROWBOATS . . . . SP FREEDOM'S PLOW 72
CAME THE WAGONS AND THE COACHES. . SP FREEDOM'S PLOW 74
OUT OF LABOR CAME THE FACTORIES. . SP FREEDOM'S PLOW 76
CAME THE FOUNDRIES. CAME THE RAILROADS. . . . . SP FREEDOM'S PLOW 77
CAME THE FOUNDRIES. CAME THE RAILROADS. . . . . SP FREEDOM'S PLOW 77
CAME THE MARTS AND MARKETS, SHOPS AND STORES. . . . . SP FREEDOM'S PLOW 78
CAME THE MIGHTY PRODUCTS MOULDED, MANUFACTURED. . . . . SP FREEDOM'S PLOW 79
CAME THE DREAM, THE STRENGTH, THE WILL. . . . . SP FREEDOM'S PLOW 83
I CAME UP ONCE AND HOLLERED! . . . SP LIFE IS FINE 5
I CAME UP TWICE AND CRIED! . . . . SP LIFE IS FINE 6
CAME BACK HOME LAST NIGHT. . . . . SP LOVER'S RETURN 2
REVEREND BUTLER CAME BY . . . . . . SP MADAM MINISTER 1
THE DAY HE CAME ROUND, ... SP MADAM CENSUS 2
THEM FLOWERS CAME . . . . SP NIGHT FUNERAL 13
THE BABY CAME ONE MORNING. . . . . SP S-SSS-SS-SH! 15
AND NEVER CAME BACK HOME AT ALL . . PL BIRMINGHAM SUND 3

CAMEO 1

HER FACE IS LIKE AN ANCIENT CAMEO SP WHEN SUE WEARS 2

CAMP 1

WE WERE SENT TO TRAINING CAMP, THEN OVERSEAS - . . . . NM COLORED SL POEM 5

CAMPAIGN 1

CAMPAIGN. . . . . PL FINAL CALL 4

CAMPANELLA 1

JACKIE WILLIE CAMPANELLA $ $ $ $ $ $ $ $ $ . . . . AYM HORN OF PLENTY 17

CAN 109

MEN TAKES ALL THEY CAN FROM ME . . FC BLACK GAL 6
AT LEAST I CAN OFFER THAT. . . . . FC BRASS SPITOONS 39
CAN I GO HOME WID YUH, SWEETIE? . . FC JAZZ BAND 22
AN' A PO', PO' GAL CAN SLEEP. . . . FC SUICIDE 18
TWO THINGS CAN REAWAKEN . . . . . . DLD TWO THINGS 3
THAT I CAN CALL MINE. . . . . NM BIG-TIMER POEM 48
I GUESS I CAN STAND THE RACKET . . NM BIG-TIMER POEM 55
CAN A CLOWN HAVE HIS DAY. . . . . . NM BLACK CLWN POEM 15
THAT I CAN STAND MORE. . . . . . . NM BLACK CLWN POEM 24
BLACK - YOU CAN DIE. . . . . NM BLACK CLWN POEM 41
THAT CAN REALLY MAKE ME FREE! . . . NM BLACK CLWN POEM 62
YOU CAN TAKE THAT JOB AND GO TO - I HOPE YOU CHOKE. . . . . NM BROKE 37
YES, UM-HUM! YOU SHO IS SWEET! CAN YOU PAY FO' DE LICENSE, DEAR? . NM BROKE 78
BLACK BOYS COULDN'T WORK THEN ANYWHERE LIKE THEY CAN . . . . . NM COLORED SL POEM 19
AMERICAN AM I, NONE CAN DENY: . . . NM DARK YOUTH USA 6
THAT I CAN NEITHER HEAR NOR FEEL NOR SEE. . . . . OK BEGGAR BOY 2
THAT I CAN NEITHER KNOW NOR UNDERSTAND . . . . OK BEGGAR BOY 3
WIDE A RIVER CAN BE. . . . . OK WIDE RIVER 12
CAN MAKE MY EARTH-BODY FREE. . . . ANS A NEW SONG 28
THAT CAN UNITED RISE . . . . ANS OPEN LETTER 27
WORKERS, KNOW THAT WE TOO CAN CRY. ANS SONG OF SPAIN 59
I CAN SLEEP SO GOOD WITH YOU AWAY! SH BED TIME 11
CAN I GET TEN ON THIS SUIT . . . . SH BLD PAWNBROKER 9
BABE, YOU SHO CAN GO! . . . . SH DEATH IN HARLEM 40
KNOWIN THEY CAN BUY A DOZEN COLORED PLACES. . . . . SH DEATH IN HARLEM 61
YOU CAN CATCH THE WIND. . . . . . . SH FREE MAN 1
YOU CAN CATCH THE SEA. . . . . . . SH FREE MAN 2
YOU CAN TAME A RABBIT. . . . . . . SH FREE MAN 5
I CAN HEY ON WATER . . . . SH HEY-HEY BLUES 1
SAME AS I CAN HEY-HEY ON BEER. . . SH HEY-HEY BLUES 2
SAME AS I CAN HEY-HEY ON BEER. . . SH HEY-HEY BLUES 4
I CAN HEY-HEY-HEY - AND CHEER! . . SH HEY-HEY BLUES 6
IF YOU CAN WHIP DE BLUES, BOY, . . SH HEY-HEY BLUES 7
BOY, IF YOU CAN WHIP DE BLUES, . . SH HEY-HEY BLUES 9
CAUSE I CAN HEY ON WATER. . . . . . SH HEY-HEY BLUES 19
SO I CAN ROLL ALONG. . . . . SH SIX-BITS BLUES 12
CAN COMMIT SUICIDE . . . . SH SNOB 6
I CAN EXPECT FROM YOU? . . . . . . JC BLACK MAN SPEAK 20
I CAN LOOK WAY ACROSS THE SEA . . . JC GOOD MORN STLIN 31
BUT I RECKON YOU CAN HEAR ME. . . . JC GOOD MORN STLIN 51
ABOLISH POLL TAX SO FOLKS CAN VOTE. JC JIM CROW'S LAST 24
CAN BE FREE. . . . . JC TO CAPTAIN MULZ 61
FOUR WALLS CAN HOLD . . . . FW WALLS 1
FOUR WALLS CAN SHELTER . . . . . . FW WALLS 5
BUT ME - IF I CAN . . . . OWT BOARDING HOUSE 9
I CAN SEE YOUR HOUSE, BABE, ... OWT CURIOUS 1
I CAN SEE YOUR HOUSE. . . . . OWT CURIOUS 3
THAT CAN MOVE, MOVES. . . . . OWT RESTRICTIVE 5
YOU CAN TALK ABOUT . . . . OWT VISITORS 1
YOU CAN TALK ABOUT . . . . OWT VISITORS 5
YOU CAN SAY . . . . OWT VISITORS 9
WE CAN BUY LOVELY THINGS WITH MONEY. SP A HOUSE IN TAOS 24
UNLUCKY AS CAN BE. . . . . SP BAD LUCK CARD 8
PO' WEARY ME CAN DO. . . . . SP BAD LUCK CARD 10
AND TELL YOU ALL I CAN. . . . . . . SP BLD THE GYPSY 8
SHE SAYS HE CAN HAVE . . . . SP BUDDY 6
THIS YEAR MAYBE, DO YOU THINK I CAN GRADUATE? . . . . SP DEFERRED 1
BUT MAYBE THIS YEAR I CAN GRADUATE. SP DEFERRED 7
MAYBE NOW I CAN HAVE THAT WHITE ENAMEL STOVE . . . . SP DEFERRED 8
MAYBE I CAN BUY THAT WHITE ENAMEL STOVE! . . . . SP DEFERRED 20
CAN LIE! . . . . SP DREAM 13
CAN A COAL BLACK MAN DRIVE THE FREEDOM TRAIN? . . . . SP FREEDOM TRAIN 18
SING IT SOFTLY AS EVER YOU CAN - . SP GENIUS CHILD 3
CAN YOU LOVE AN EAGLE, ... SP GENIUS CHILD 6
CAN YOU LOVE A MONSTER . . . . . . SP GENIUS CHILD 9
WELL, YOU CAN SEE. . . . . SP HIGH TO LOW 23
LOVE CAN HURT YOU . . . . SP LAMENT OVER LOV 5
MO'N ANYTHING ELSE CAN. . . . . . . SP LAMENT OVER LOV 6
CAN TAKE A PERSON'S LIFE. . . . . . SP LITTLE OLD LETT 16
HOW CAN YOU FORGET ME? . . . . . . SP LOW TO HIGH 1
HOW CAN YOU FORGET ME . . . . SP LOW TO HIGH 7
HOW CAN YOU FORGET ME. . . . . . . SP LOW TO HIGH 10
HOW CAN YOU LOW-RATE ME . . . . . . SP LOW TO HIGH 12
HOW CAN YOU FORGET ME? . . . . . . SP LOW TO HIGH 16
CAN I DO FOR YOU? . . . . SP MADAM RENT MAN 4
CAN IT BE . . . . SP MADAM HER MADAM 14
THEN I CAN PLAY . . . . SP MADAM NUMBER WR 25
FOR INSTANCE, WHAT CAN . . . . . . SP MADAM PHONE BIL 27
SO I CAN BRUSH YOUR BACK, I SAY! . SP MAMA AND DAUGHT 21
AND GOD KNOWS SHE SURE CAN OVERCHARGE - . . . . SP NECESSITY 10
IF THEY CAN: . . . . SP PARADE 17
WHO CAN APPRECIATE ME: . . . . . . SP PREFERENCE 12
SAID THE LADY, CAN YOU DO . . . . . SP QUESTION 1
I KNOW WHAT RELIEF CAN BE - . . . . SP RELIEF 6
WHAT CAN A COLORED GIRL DO . . . . SP RUBY BROWN 13
YOU CAN HAVE ME, BABY - . . . . . . SP SAME IN BLUES 17
I CAN UNDERSTAND - SOME DECENT MAN? SP SISTER 6
THAT A WOMAN DOES THE BEST SHE CAN? SP SISTER 14
CAN CUT A MAN'S . . . . SP SLIVER 7
WHAT CAN PURGE MY HEART . . . . . . SP SONG BILLIE HOL 1
WHAT CAN PURGE MY HEART . . . . . . SP SONG BILLIE HOL 4
WHAT CAN PURGE MY HEART . . . . . . SP SONG BILLIE HOL 7
BOTH CAN RISE: . . . . SP UP-BEAT 10
BUT A DOG CAN TELL . . . . SP WARNING AUGMENT 7
YET YOU NEVER CAN TELL WHEN A . . . SP WIDOW WOMAN 23
CAN A YOUNG GAL DO? . . . . SP YOUNG GAL'S BLS 20
WHAT CAN A YOUNG GAL DO? . . . . . SP YOUNG GAL'S BLS 22
THE MEN CAN ONLY MURMUR . . . . . . AYM ASK YOUR MAMA 37
AND CAN KNOCK THE HADES . . . . . . AYM ODE TO DINAH 117
CAN I GET IT NOW? . . . . AYM RIDE, RED, RIDE 6
TELL ME, MAMA, CAN I GET MY SHOW . AYM SHOW FARE PLESE 1
THEN BEFORE YOU CAN WALK . . . . . PL CROWNS GARLANDS 8
HOW CAN ONE MAN BE TEN? . . . . . . PL GHOSTS OF 1619 21
(YET LITTLE CAN . . . . PL JUNIOR ADDICT 16
CAN IT BE . . . . PL KU KLUX 10
THAN TRUTH CAN BE. . . . . PL LONG VIEW NEGRO 7
I CAN QUITE AFFORD TO BE: . . . . . PL NORTHERN LIBERL 12
I SAID, O, LORD, IF YOU CAN, . . . PL WHO BUT TH LORD 9
CAN PROTECT ME? . . . . PL WHO BUT TH LORD 22

CANAAN 1

WESTPORT AND NEW CANAAN . . . . . . AYM HORN OF PLENTY 81

CANARIES 1

TO KEEP FAR-OFF CANARIES . . . . . AYM ODE TO DINAH 60

CANCER 1

PRACTICE ON A STATE STREET CANCER. SP INTERNE AT PROV 7

CANDLE 1
CANDLE INSIDE. . . . SP 125TH STREET 4

CANDLES 1
AND BURST LIKE ROMAN CANDLES. . . . PL THIRD DEGREE 14

CANDY 1
THE CANDY STORE'S . . . . PL LITTLE SNG HOUS 20

CANE 4
DIAMOND RING, CIGARETTE HOLDER, AND
A CANE, TO THE MUSIC OF PIANO OR NM BIG-TIMER MOOD 1
IN THE COTTON AND THE CANE. . . . NM BLACK CLWN POEM 17
CUTTING CANE IN THE SUN. . . . ANS BLDS OF LENIN 14
HOW TALL HOW TALL THE CANE GREW . . AYM BIRD IN ORBIT 41

CANNOT 11
I CANNOT FIND THEM ANY MORE. . . . OK AFTR MNY SPRNGS 8
THAT CANNOT FLY. . . . OK DREAMS 4
I CANNOT SAY YOU EVERYWHERE. . . . OK PASSING LOVE 4
I CANNOT LIVE ON TOMORROW'S BREAD. SP DEMOCRACY 14
AND GRANDMA CANNOT GET HER GOSPEL
HYMNS . . . . SP PASSING 3
WHO CANNOT . . . . SP VAGABONDS 8
AND I CANNOT WRITE COMMERCIALS - . AYM IS IT TRUE? 31
I CANNOT LIVE ON TOMORROW'S BREAD. PL FREEDOM 14
CANNOT KNOW, OF COURSE, ... PL JUNIOR ADDICT 6
A SUNRISE THAT HE CANNOT SEE . . . PL JUNIOR ADDICT 8
I CANNOT. . . . PL MILITANT 3

CANVASS 1
SPLASH OF COLOR ON CANVASS. . . . ANS SONG OF SPAIN 21

CAN'T 57
CAN'T HELP IT CAUSE I'M BLACK. . . FC BLACK GAL 14
O, YOU CAN'T FIND A BUDDY . . . . FC DEATH DO DIRTY 1
I CAN'T HAVE NO WOMAN'S . . . . FC EVIL WOMAN 9
FER I CAN'T STAY HERE ALONE. . . . FC GYPSY MAN 6
SHO CAN'T FIND NO EASE. . . . FC GYPSY MAN 24
YOU CAN'T LIVE THAT WAY! . . . . FC NEW CABARET GRL 22
BABE, YOU CAN'T . . . . FC NEW CABARET GRL 23
YOU CAN'T KEEP ME DOWN! . . . . NM BLACK CLWN POEM 68
TALKIN' 'BOUT "WE'LL WORK FOR 50¢ A
DAY, IF WE CAN'T GET NO MO'." . NM BROKE 7
I CAN'T EVEN GET DE MONEY FOR TO BUY
MYSELF A SMOKE. . . . NM BROKE 46
BUT RIGHT LONG THROUGH HERE NOW, I
CAN'T 'FORD TO BUY YOU NO HAT." NM BROKE 51
BUT I CAN'T EVEN BUY A PAPER - I'M
SO BROKE. . . . NM BROKE 61
DOES I WANTA? WELL, CAN'T SAY BUT
WHAT I MIGHT - . . . . NM BROKE 71
CAN'T SEE! AND DON'T KNOW! AND WON'T
EVER CARE! . . . . NM COLORED SL POEM 53
BUT YOU CAN'T, PRETTY MAMA, ... SH FREE MAN 3
STILL I CAN'T HELP LOVIN' YOU. . . SH IN TROUBLED KEY 7
SAYS I CAN'T HELP LOVIN' YOU . . . SH IN TROUBLED KEY 9
I CAN'T GET ALONG WITH YOU, I CAN'T
GET ALONG WITHOUT - . . . . SH LETTER 14
I CAN'T GET ALONG WITH YOU, I CAN'T
GET ALONG WITHOUT - . . . . SH LETTER 14
SO NOBODY CAN'T LOW-RATE YOU. . . . SH MIDNIGHT CHIPPI 30
I STILL CAN'T SEE . . . . JC BLACK MAN SPEAK 2
I CAN'T UNDERSTAND . . . . JC BLACK MAN SPEAK 6
CAN'T DIE BUT ONCE. . . . JC BLD SAM SOLOMON 40
I STILL CAN'T SAY, ... JC GOOD MORN STLIN 9
CAN'T SEND NO MESSAGES THROUGH THE
AIR. . . . . JC GOOD MORN STLIN 50
YOU CAN'T LOCK UP GANDHI, ... JC HOW ABOUT DIXIE 13
THAT CROW CAN'T FIGHT FOR DEMOCRACY JC JIM CROW'S LAST 9
BUT I CAN'T SEE YOU. . . . OWT CURIOUS 2
BUT I CAN'T SEE YOU. . . . OWT CURIOUS 4
CAN'T BREATHE FREE. . . . OWT RESTRICTIVE 14
I KNOW I CAN'T . . . . SP CHILDREN'S RYME 8
CAN'T C.P.T. . . . . SP DANCER 25
NO MAYORS AND SUCH FOR WHICH COLORED
CAN'T VOTE, ... SP FREEDOM TRAIN 56
CAN'T YOU BRING NO BETTER NEWS? . . SP HARD DADDY 6
CAN'T RAISE NO CHILD ON THAT. . . . SP MADAM CHARTY CH 19
CAN'T DO - AND MORE, TOO? . . . . SP MADAM PHONE BIL 30
SAID, WE CAN'T USE YOU . . . . SP MADAM'S PAST HI 16
I CAN'T GET OFF MY MIND. . . . SP MAMA AND DAUGHT 8
CAN'T YOU UNDERSTAND. . . . SP MISERY 9
CAN'T HARDLY GET HIS BREAD. . . . SP MONROE'S BLUES 4
SO SMALL I CAN'T WHIP A CAT . . . . SP NECESSITY 6
CAN'T BE RIGHT. . . . SP PARADE 19
WHAT MY OTHER MAN CAN'T DO - . . . SP QUESTION 2
I CAN'T, SHE SAID, I CAN'T! . . . . SP SAME IN BLUES 3
I CAN'T, SHE SAID, I CAN'T! . . . . SP SAME IN BLUES 3
"YOU CAN'T LEAVE US HERE!" . . . . SP SYLVESTER'S BED 14
AND I CAN'T BE SATISFIED. . . . SP THE WEARY BLUES 26
AND CAN'T BE SATISFIED - . . . . SP THE WEARY BLUES 28
BABY, HOW COME YOU CAN'T SEE ME . . SP ULTIMATUM 1
I KNOW I CAN'T . . . . PL CHILDREN'S RYME 4
BUT I CAN'T EAT HIM FOR LUNCH. . . PL CROWNS GARLANDS 20
SEND FOR LENIN! (DON'T YOU DARE! -
HE CAN'T COME . . . . PL FINAL CALL 24
YOU CAN'T EAT HERE! . . . . PL GO SLOW 6
YOU CAN'T LIVE HERE! . . . . PL GO SLOW 7
YOU CAN'T WORK HERE! . . . . PL GO SLOW 8
AND CAN'T HAVE NOW . . . . PL HARLEM 14
CAN'T SIT SIDE BY SIDE. . . . PL MERRY-GO-ROUND 8

CAP 3
MAMA, I FOUND THIS SOLDIER'S CAP . FW WHEN ARMIES PAS 1
WHOSE CAP IT IS, SON. . . . FW WHEN ARMIES PAS 6
NIGHT IN A SEKOU TOURE CAP . . . . AYM ASK YOUR MAMA 61

CAPE 4
THE BELLOWING BULL, THE RED CAPE, ANS SONG OF SPAIN 13
IN AN ERMINE CAPE . . . . SH DEATH IN HARLEM 65
DIXIE TO SINGAPORE, CAPE TOWN TO
HONG KONG . . . . SP IN EXPLANATION 10
CAPE TOWN, ATLANTA, ... PL QUESTION ANSWER 2

CAPER 1
AMORPHOUS JACK-O'-LANTERNS CAPER . PL CULTURAL EXCHNG 5

CAPITAL 1
(A CAPITAL LETTER THERE, ... SP CONSIDER ME 13

CAPSTAN 1
AND SMOKED A CAPSTAN CIGARETTE . . OK SAILOR 3

CAPTAIN 3
WE'VE PUT A CAPTAIN ON THAT SHIP'S
BRIDGE THERE, ... JC TO CAPTAIN MULZ 43
CAPTAIN MULZAC, ... JC TO CAPTAIN MULZ 63
AND MORE THAN CAPTAIN . . . . JC TO CAPTAIN MULZ 65

CAPTAIN'S 1
THEIR CAPTAIN'S . . . . FW SAILING DATE 20

CAPTURE 1
AND CAPTURE EVERY STREET . . . . PL FREDRK DOUGLASS 8

CAPTURED 1
NOT EVEN FOLKWAYS CAPTURED . . . . AYM IS IT TRUE? 9

CAR 13
I GOT A BIG CAR . . . . NM BIG-TIMER POEM 25
LOOKIN' FOR A BOX CAR . . . . OK HOMESICK BLUES 11
CAR NO MORE. . . . SH ANNOUNCEMENT 16
A PACKARD CAR. . . . SH BLD THE KILLER 6
I'D BUY MYSELF A CAR. . . . SH DECLARATION 9
IN A JIM CROW CAR. . . . JC BLACK MAN SPEAK 14
WHEN THE PD CAR . . . . OWT BLD MARGE POLIT 52
TAKE A STREET CAR . . . . OWT JITNEY 41
GOT A JIM CROW CAR SET ASIDE FOR ME. SP FREEDOM TRAIN 10
FOR LUNCHES AND CAR FARE? . . . . SP KID SLEEPY 15
RIDES THE STATE STREET STREET CAR, SP MIGRANT 7
AND RIDE THE JIM CROW CAR UNTIL IT
SCREAMS . . . . PL JIM CROW CAR 3
THERE'S A JIM CROW CAR. . . . PL MERRY-GO-ROUND 10

CARAMEL 2
CARAMEL TREAT, ... SH HARLEM SWEETIES 6
CARAMEL, BROWN SUGAR, ... SH HARLEM SWEETIES 31

CARD 2
MY BAD LUCK CARD. . . . SP BAD LUCK CARD 4
DEALT MY BAD-LUCK CARD. . . . SP LITTLE GRN TREE 8

CARDS 1
I HAD SOME CARDS PRINTED . . . . SP MADAM'S CALLING 1

CARE 23
NOBODY WILL CARE - . . . . NM BLACK CLWN POEM 42
(I DON'T CARE NOTHIN' 'BOUT HER
MYSELF!) . . . . NM BROKE 27
CAN'T SEE! AND DON'T KNOW! AND WON'T
EVER CARE! . . . . NM COLORED SL POEM 53
I DON'T CARE HOW YOU PLAY 'EM . . . SH HEY-HEY BLUES 17
I DON'T CARE WHERE IT'S GOIN' . . . SH SIX-BITS BLUES 5
I WISH I COULD TELL YOU HOW MUCH I
DON'T CARE . . . . SH SUNDAY 5
STAY AWAY IF YOU WANT TO, AND SEE IF
I CARE! . . . . SH SUPPER TIME 10
ALL OVER THE WORLD, WHO CARE. . . . JC GOOD MORN STLIN 45
WHY CARE? . . . . FW SAILING DATE 18
O, SONGS THAT DO NOT CARE! . . . . OWT NEGRO SERVANT 7
MUST CARE. . . . OWT RESTRICTIVE 17
SAYS SHE DON'T CARE! . . . . SP DELINQUENT 14
YOU DON'T EVEN CARE. . . . SP HIGH TO LOW 9
I DON'T CARE. . . . SP KID SLEEPY 9
I DON'T CARE. . . . SP KID SLEEPY 17
THEN TAKE CARE OF HER CHILDREN . . SP MADAM HER MADAM 7
YOU SAY YOU DON'T CARE . . . . SP MADAM PHONE BIL 32
PHONE BILL DOES I CARE! . . . . SP MADAM PHONE BIL 36
YOU WPA FOLKS TAKE CARE OF YOURSELF
- . . . . SP MADAM'S PAST HI 21
WHO DO NOT CARE, ... SP VAGABONDS 2
DON'T CARE WHAT TIME IT IS - . . . AYM ODE TO DINAH 66
DID NOT CARE. . . . PL PEACE 4
BUT I DON'T CARE! . . . . PL STILL HERE 8

CARED 2
- NO ONE CARED AT ALL — FW HEART 9
- CARED VERY MUCH! — SP S-SSS-SS-SH! 14

CARELESS 1
- CARELESS, AND HALF-DEFIANT ECHOES OF THE "ST. JAMES INFIRMARY" AS THE — NM BIG-TIMER MOOD 2

CARELESS-LIKE 1
- AND CRIES, ALL CARELESS-LIKE FROM REDDENED LIPS! — OWT LINCOLN THEATRE 10

CARES 5
- NOBODY CARES JUST WHY. — FC MOAN 11
- NOBODY CARES — DK PARISIAN BEGGAR 3
- NOBODY CARES ABOUT YOU — OWT TOO BLUE 4
- FULL OF CARES - — SP BLACK MARIA 8
- NOBODY CARES — SP DELINQUENT 16

CARESSES 1
- CARESSES OF THE COLD — WB POEME D'AUTOMNE 13

CARFARE 1
- TO PAY HIS CARFARE, BUY A SUIT. — SP BUDDY 8

CARIBBEAN 1
- THAT IS SUNSET IN THE CARIBBEAN. — WB CARIBBEAN SUNST 4

CARING 2
- OF NOT CARING MUCH — SP S-SSS-SS-SH! 9
- INTEREST BEYOND CARING? — AYM SHOW FARE PLESE 25

CARMEN 2
- YOU PUT ME IN MACBETH AND CARMEN JONES — SP NOTE COMM THEAT 9
- ARTHUR CARMEN ALVIN MARY $ $ $ $ $ $ $ $ — AYM HORN OF PLENTY 7

CARNIVAL 2
- WHERE THE CARNIVAL IS CHRISTIAN. — SP SUMMER EVENING 13
- AT CARNIVAL — PL MERRY-GO-ROUND 2

CAROLINA 2
- SHUT UP, SAYS THE GOVERNOR OF SOUTH CAROLINA. — SP IN EXPLANATION 24
- GOVERNORS OF SOUTH CAROLINA, GERALD L.K. STRYDOMS. — SP IN EXPLANATION 43

CARPET 2
- FOR A CARPET TACK. — FC EVIL WOMAN 16
- AND PLACES WITH NO CARPET ON THE FLOOR - — SP MOTHER TO SON 6

CARRIAGE 1
- SWEET WATERMELON IN A BABY CARRIAGE, — SP SUMMER EVENING 2

CARRIED 4
- CARRIED ME TO DE COURT, — FC BLD OF GIN MARY 1
- CARRIED LONELY UP THE AISLE — OWT FUNERAL 1
- I CARRIED MY SORROW SONGS. — SP NEGRO 12
- CARRIED HIM OUT FOR DEAD — SP NIGHT FUNERAL 32

CARRIES 5
- 'CAUSE I CARRIES A SWITCH-BLADE — NM BIG-TIMER POEM 29
- CARRIES YOUR "PATIENCE" AWAY — JC THE BITTER RIVR 46
- WHO CARRIES UGLY THINGS TO SHOW THE SUN? — SP A HOUSE IN TAOS 21
- CARRIES HOME — SP DEAD IN THERE 4
- HE CARRIES — SP YOUNG SAILOR 1

CARRY 6
- IF YOU CARRY THIS THROUGH, — JC BLD SAM SOLOMON 26
- TO HELP ME CARRY THIS LOAD. — SP BOUND NO'TH BLS 6
- TO CARRY - — SP CATCH 10
- HAS A LUNCH TO CARRY. — SP MIGRANT 13
- COMING FOR TO CARRY ME HOME. — SP MYSTERY 10
- WHO CARRY BEAUTIES IN THEIR HEARTS — SP WATER-FRONT STR 7

CARRYING 5
- DRESSED, CARRYING HIS BOOKS TO SCHOOL. — NM DARK YOUTH USA 1
- CARRYING A MERMAID — SP CATCH 2
- CARRYING IN MY BODY THE SEED OF THE FREE. — SP THE NEGRO MOTHE 10
- SHOUTS ARE WHISPERS CARRYING — AYM ASK YOUR MAMA 2
- SHOUTS ARE WHISPERS CARRYING — AYM IS IT TRUE? 2

CARRYIN' 1
- THE FREEDOM THAT THEY CARRYIN' ON THIS FREEDOM TRAIN, — SP FREEDOM TRAIN 45

CARS 7
- TO THE RUMBLE OF STREET CARS, — WB LENOX AVE MIDNT 9
- WE COULDN'T EAT IN RESTAURANTS; HAD JIM CROW CARS; — NM COLORED SL POEM 24
- AND SIXTEEN FISH-TAIL CARS, — SP AS BEFITS A MAN 10
- A HEARSE AND TWO CARS - — SP BLD OF THE MAN 6
- THEM TWO FINE CARS? — SP NIGHT FUNERAL 4
- FOR THE CARS TO FLY BY ON, — PL FLORIDA WORKERS 4
- IN THEIR BIG CARS — PL FLORIDA WORKERS 11

CART 2
- TO DO CART WHEELS? — SH ASPIRATION 2
- DRIVING THE BUTCHER'S CART — SP JOY 6

CARTED 1
- TO BE CARTED OFF BY BRINK'S. — AYM ODE TO DINAH 57

CARVE 1
- SHALL I CARVE MA SELF OR — FC SUICIDE 11

CASBAH 1
- CASBAH — SP NEON SIGNS 10

CASES 2
- CONGRESS CASES RUSSIA. — SP MIGRANT 30
- BOOK-OF-THE-MONTH IN CASES — AYM HORN OF PLENTY 68

CASH 5
- A BANK FULL OF CASH. — SH BLD THE KILLER 10
- OF MY MEAGRE CASH, — JC THE BITTER RIVR 70
- IS SHE WANTS SOME CASH? — SP SISTER 9
- TO EARN A LITTLE CASH, — PL BACKLASH BLUES 14
- TO EARN A LITTLE CASH, — PL BACKLASH BLUES 16

CASHED 1
- I'M GONNA GET IT CASHED, — SH PAY DAY 5

CASHIER 1
- THE CASHIER TREMBLED — SH BLD THE KILLER 15

CASSIE 2
- DEAR CASSIE: YES, I GOT YOUR LETTER. — SH LETTER 1
- HERE'S FIVE DOLLARS, CASSIE, BUY A TICKET BACK. — SH LETTER 20

CASSIUS 1
- PLUS CASSIUS MOHAMMED ALI CLAY. — PL CROWNS GARLANDS 5

CAST 5
- I'LL CAST MY BLUES ASIDE. — WB BLUES FANTASY 26
- TWO THINGS CAST OFF ALL SHAME. — OLD TWO THINGS 6
- SHE CAST HER EYES ON TEXAS, HOLLERED, — SH DEATH IN HARLEM 83
- CAST YOUR DIMS — SH HARLEM SWEETIES 3
- DEAD OR LIVE THEIR GHOSTS CAST SHADOWS — AYM SHADES OF PIG 6

CASTANETS 1
- CHA-CHA LIKE CASTANETS — AYM GOSPEL CHA-CHA 3

CASTRO 1
- KENYATTA RED! CASTRO RED! — AYM BIRD IN ORBIT 73

CASTRO'S 1
- LOST IN CASTRO'S BEARD? — AYM RIDE, RED, RIDE 12

CAT 3
- BLACK CAT — OWT BLUES ON A BOX 3
- SO SMALL I CAN'T WHIP A CAT — SP NECESSITY 6
- IN FACT, HE'S A GREAT CAT. — SP NEIGHBOR 16

CATCH 9
- YOU CAN CATCH THE WIND, — SH FREE MAN 1
- YOU CAN CATCH THE SEA, — SH FREE MAN 2
- EVER CATCH ME. — SH FREE MAN 4
- CATCH THAT JIM CROW BIRD, PULL THE FEATHERS OUT HIS TAIL! — JC JIM CROW'S LAST 16
- I CATCH THE PATTERN — FW SILENCE 1
- TO CATCH A RAINBOW CRY, — SP IN TIME SILVER 14
- IF I EVER CATCH HIM, — SP MADAM PHONE BIL 19
- JUST DON'T LET MAMA CATCH YOU — SP STREET SONG 3
- TO CATCH UP WITH TOMORROW — AYM IS IT TRUE? 30

CATCHES 1
- THE SPEAKER CATCHES FIRE, — PL CORNER MEETING 4

CATCHING 1
- SUDDENLY CATCHING FIRE — AYM JAZZTET MUTED 7

CATS 2
- MAMA, IT HAS BEEN RAINING CATS AND DOGS UP — SP LETTER 8
- AND SEVEN CATS GO FRANTIC. — SP SEASHORE THROUG 4

CAT-GUT 2
- OF CAT-GUT LACE. — SP BOOGIE 1 A.M. 8
- OF CAT-GUT LACE. — SP NIGHTMARE BOOGE 12

CAT'S 1
- THAT CAT'S A FOOL. — SP NEIGHBOR 12

CAUGHT 3
- CAUGHT IN A CRACK — SP CONSIDER ME 26
- THE BRIGHT DAY CAUGHT ME — SP FIRED 2
- CAUGHT BETWEEN — PL UNDERTOW 3

CAUSE 47
CAUSE I IS LONG GONE WRONG. . . . . FC A RUINED GAL 5
CAUSE I AIN'T GOT NO FRIEND. . . . FC A RUINED GAL 10
CAUSE EVERBODY TELLS ME SO. . . . . FC BAD MAN 2
CAN'T HELP IT CAUSE I'M BLACK. . . FC BLACK GAL 14
CAUSE HE WAS BLACK . . . . FC DEATH DO DIRTY 7
CAUSE A BLUE-GUMMED WOMAN . . . . . FC EVIL WOMAN 11
CAUSE HE NEVER DOES COME HOME. . . FC GYPSY MAN 2
BUT I HAD TO LEAVE CAUSE . . . . . FC GYPSY MAN 11
I GIVE IT TO HIM CAUSE I LOVED HIM FC GYPSY MAN 17
DON'T YOU FOOL WID NO MEN CAUSE . . FC LISTEN HERE 17
CAUSE DE RIVER'S QUIET . . . . . . FC SUICIDE 17
CAUSE SHE AIN'T DE RIGHT KIND. . . FC WORKIN' MAN 12
CAUSE I TRIES TO BE GOOD . . . . . FC WORKIN' MAN 15
CAUSE I'M ALL RIGHT. . . . . NM BIG-TIMER POEM 50
CAUSE IF I DON'T SEE MA BABY . . . OK WIDE RIVER 17
CAUSE WE DANCIN DOWN! . . . . SH DEATH IN HARLEM 57
CAUSE THEY TOLD ME DE NORTH WAS FINE. . . . . SH EVENIN' BLUES 2
CAUSE THEY TOLD ME DE NORTH WAS FINE. . . . . SH EVENIN' BLUES 4
CAUSE WHEN I'M DANCIN' . . . . . . SH EVENIN' BLUES 17
YOU'RE THE CAUSE . . . . SH EVIL MORNING 9
CAUSE I CAN HEY ON WATER. . . . . . SH HEY-HEY BLUES 19
CAUSE THAT OLD ALARM CLOCK SHO HURTS MY EARS. . . . . SH LETTER 19
CAUSE SHE'S DE ONLY . . . . SH ONLY WOMAN BLUS 11
CAUSE I'M GOING BACK TO ROOMING AND BE A FREE MAN. . . . . SH PAY DAY 16
CAUSE I'M SURE ENJOYING MYSELF TODAY! . . . . SH SUNDAY 7
CAUSE IF I DON'T THEY'LL CUT DOWN MY PAY. . . . . SH SUPPER TIME 14
CAUSE I'D TAKE THAT OWL HEAD AND FIRE ON YOU. . . . . SH TWILIGHT REVERI 12
CAUSE I WANT YOU TO STATE . . . . . JC BLACK MAN SPEAK 22
CAUSE THE VOTE IS NOT RESTRICTED . JC BLD SAM SOLOMON 11
CAUSE FROM BOMBAY TO GEORGIA . . . JC HOW ABOUT DIXIE 11
CAUSE THE GOOD LORD KNOWS WHAT WE'RE FIGHTING FOR! . . . . JC JIM CROW'S LAST 26
CAUSE THERE AIN'T A GOOD MAN . . . OWT REQUEST REQUIEM 7
CAUSE I AIN'T NOBODY'S BEAU. . . . OWT STRANGER IN TWN 10
CAUSE YOU DON'T LOVE ME . . . . . . SP BAD LUCK CARD 1
CAUSE THEY TREAT ME MEAN - . . . . SP CORA 5
CAUSE YOU AIN'T DEAD. . . . . SP JUDGMENT DAY 9
CAUSE YOU BROKE MY HEART IN TWO. . SP LATE LAST NIGHT 6
CAUSE I'M STILL HERE KICKIN'! . . . SP MADAM WRONG VIS 28
CAUSE I HAD A INSURANCE . . . . . . SP MADAM'S PAST HI 14
CAUSE THE MAN I LOVE'S DONE . . . . SP MISERY 7
CAUSE THERE AIN'T NO SENSE . . . . SP WAKE 3
A MIGHTY LOVER, BABY, CAUSE YOU . . SP WIDOW WOMAN 15
CAUSE WHEN I'M DEAD SOME . . . . . SP YOUNG GAL'S BLS 5
CAUSE I DON'T WANT TO BE BLUE. . . SP YOUNG GAL'S BLS 24
MISTER, CAUSE I WANT TO RIDE? . . . PL MERRY-GO-ROUND 5
AS IF FREEDOM'S CAUSE . . . . PL MOTHER IN WAR 3
SUPPORT YOUR CAUSE. . . . . PL NORTHERN LIBERL 17

CAUTIOUS 1
THE OLD, THE CAUTIOUS, THE OVER-WISE - . . . . PL ELDERLY LEADERS 1

CEASES 1
THE LAST VICTROLA CEASES WITH THE WR SUMMER NIGHT 5

CELEBRITIES 1
OF BLACK CELEBRITIES . . . . SP MELLOW 2

CELL 1
IRON CELL. . . . . SP BLD LANDLORD 29

CELLAR 3
IN THAT CELLAR ON THE FLOOR . . . . SH DEATH IN HARLEM 122
DOWN IN A CELLAR BACK FROM THE STREET. . . . . SH DEATH IN HARLEM 23
THERE'S RATS IN THE CELLAR. . . . . SP MADAM RENT MAN 17

CELLOPHANES 2
CELLOPHANES HIS LONG STRIDE. . . . SP INTERNE AT PROV 46
CELLOPHANES HIS FUTURE. . . . . . . SP INTERNE AT PROV 47

CENSUS 1
THE CENSUS MAN. . . . . SP MADAM CENSUS 1

CENT 3
AIN'T GONNA PAY A CENT ON THAT RADIO SH PAY DAY 7
PLAY BACK A CENT. . . . . SP NUMBERS 5
WITHOUT A CENT. . . . . SP ULTIMATUM 9

CENTENNIAL 4
THIS LAST QUARTER OF CENTENNIAL . . AYM ODE TO DINAH 8
THIS LAST QUARTER OF CENTENNIAL: . AYM ODE TO DINAH 93
EMANCIPATION CENTENNIAL - . . . . . PL DEATH YORKVILLE 12
CIVIL WAR CENTENNIAL: 1965. . . . . PL DEATH YORKVILLE 14

CENTENNIALS 1
HOW MANY CENTENNIALS DOES IT TAKE PL DEATH YORKVILLE 15

CENTER 2
FROM THE BIG GLASS SHOPPING CENTER AYM HORN OF PLENTY 94
AND CENTER OF ATTENTION . . . . . . PL DINNER GUEST ME 17

CENTRAL 3
MY GOODNESS, CENTRAL, ... SP MADAM PHONE BIL 4
WHAT'S THAT, CENTRAL? . . . . SP MADAM PHONE BIL 31
23RD AND CENTRAL, 18TH STREET AND VINE. . . . . AYM ASK YOUR MAMA 6

CENTS 1
SAYS SUGAR'S GONE UP ANOTHER TWO CENTS. . . . . PL HARLEM 9

CENTURIES 3
QUIET FOR TEN THOUSAND CENTURIES, OLD ABE. . . . . OK LINCOLN MONUMNT 4
THE FUSE OF CENTURIES OF DRAGON KINGS . . . . PL BIRMINGHAM SUND 19
HOW MANY CENTURIES DOES IT TAKE . . PL DEATH YORKVILLE 5

CERTAIN 4
WITH CERTAIN UNALIENABLE RIGHTS . . . . SP FREEDOM'S PLOW 93
THERE'S A CERTAIN . . . . SP SAME IN BLUES 5
A CERTAIN . . . . SP SAME IN BLUES 12
A CERTAIN . . . . SP SAME IN BLUES 19

CERTAINLY 3
HAS I DID IT BEFO'? CERTAINLY! . . NM BROKE 21
CERTAINLY, CHILE, I ALWAYS WAS CRAZY 'BOUT YOU! . . . . NM BROKE 74
FOR KIDS WILL DIE CERTAINLY. . . . ANS KIDS WHO DIE 3

CERT'LY 1
SOME OF THESE YOUNG ONES IS CERT'LY BAD - . . . . SP CHILDREN'S RYME 17

CHA 1
CHA. . . . . AYM GOSPEL CHA-CHA 64

CHAGRIN 1
TO MY CHAGRIN - NOT EVEN SINGING - AYM IS IT TRUE? 32

CHAIN 4
TANGLED IN THAT ANCIENT ENDLESS CHAIN . . . . ANS LET AMERICA BE 26
THIS GOLD WATCH AND CHAIN . . . . . SH BLD PAWNBROKER 1
TO BIND MY MIND - CHAIN MY FEET - PL DEATH YORKVILLE 6
FROM THE SLAVE CHAIN TO THE LYNCH ROPE . . . . PL DEATH YORKVILLE 9

CHAINS 2
LOVE - AND CHAINS ARE BROKEN. . . . OK ALABAMA EARTH 13
AND CHAINS BE GONE! . . . . FW DUSK 13

CHAIR 2
AND SHE SAT ON HER CHAIR LIKE A SWEET JELLY ROLL. . . . . SH DEATH IN HARLEM 82
IN CHARITY'S POOR CHAIR - . . . . . FW OLD SAILOR 16

CHALLENGE 1
WITH A CHALLENGE . . . . FW CONVENT 8

CHAMPAGNE 1
IN A CHAMPAGNE BOTTLE. . . . . . . FW MONTMARTRE 3

CHANCE 7
HE AIN'T GOT A CHANCE. . . . . . . FC DEATH DO DIRTY 29
NO OTHER GAL'S GOT A CHANCE. . . . FC MINNIE SINGS 10
AND SAID TO ME, "BROTHER, YOU'VE GOT YOUR CHANCE, ... NM COLORED SL POEM 16
OF BEING HELD BACK, OF HAVING NO CHANCE - . . . . NM COLORED SL POEM 31
THAT IF SHE HAD A CHANCE . . . . . SP BLD OF THE GIRL 15
A CHANCE TO LET . . . . SP PARADE 29
A CHANCE WIND BLOWS THERE. . . . . SP SONG BILLIE HOL 13

CHANCES 1
JOBS ARE JUST CHANCES . . . . SP ELEVATOR BOY 6

CHANG 1
I AM CHANG FROM THE FOUNDRIES . . ANS BLDS OF LENIN 21

CHANGE 11
SAY! YOU KNOW I BELIEVE I'LL CHANGE MY NAME, ... SH DAYBREAK 9
CHANGE MY COLOR, CHANGE MY WAYS. . SH DAYBREAK 10
CHANGE MY COLOR, CHANGE MY WAYS. . SH DAYBREAK 10
IF I HAD SOME SMALL CHANGE . . . . SH IF-ING 1
ONLY TO CHANGE . . . . LHR DEAR LVLY DEATH 4
CHANGE IS THY OTHER NAME. . . . . . LHR DEAR LVLY DEATH 10
THAT AT A SUDDEN CHANGE BECOME . . SP FLATTED FIFTHS 6
AND THE CHANGE. . . . . SP REQUEST 2
GOT CHANGE IN HIS LONG POCKET? . . AYM SHOW FARE PLESE 4
DID YOU NOT CHANGE IT . . . . PL UN-AMERICAN 15
THEY CHANGE THEIR MIND! . . . . . . PL WARNING 5

CHANGED 3
AND SMITTY HAS NOT CHANGED AT ALL. AYM BIRD IN ORBIT 22
CHANGED INTO "EYE FOR EYE," . . . . PL BLACK PANTHER 7
CHANGED YOUR NAMES. . . . . PL SPECIAL BULLTIN 17

CHARGE 3
WHAT WAS THE COVER CHARGE, KID? . . FC CLOSING TIME 14
CHARGE YOU MUCH. . . . . SP BLD FORTUNE TEL 8
RECKON THERE'S NO CHARGE . . . . . SP BLD OF THE MAN 23

CHARGED 2
AND CHARGED FIVE . . . . SP BLD OF THE MAN 18
CHARGED FIVE DOLLARS . . . . SP NIGHT FUNERAL 23

CHARGES 2
THE CHARGES SWEAR. . . . . OWT BLD MARGE POLIT 20
CHARGES NOHOW. . . . . SP MADAM PHONE BIL 9

CHARIOT 2
SWING LOW, SWEET CHARIOT, ... SP MYSTERY 9
GONNA RIDE IN MY CHARIOT SOME DAY! SP SPIRITUALS 8

CHARITY 1
WHAT MAKES THESE CHARITY . . . . . SP MADAM CHARTY CH 9

CHARITY'S 2
IN CHARITY'S POOR CHAIR - . . . . . FW OLD SAILOR 15
CHARITY'S CHECKED MONEY . . . . . . SP INTERNE AT PROV 26

CHARLESTON 4
CHARLESTON. . . . . WB CAT AND SAXOPHN 29
TWO MO' WAYS TO DO DE CHARLESTON! DK NEGRO DANCERS 2
TWO MO' WAYS TO DO DE CHARLESTON!" DK NEGRO DANCERS 6
TWO MO' WAYS TO DO DE CHARLESTON!" DK NEGRO DANCERS 15

CHARLIE 6
CHARLIE IS A GAMBLER . . . . FC SATURDAY NIGHT 3
STRUT, MR. CHARLIE. . . . . FC SATURDAY NIGHT 7
DO, IT, MR. CHARLIE. . . . . FC SATURDAY NIGHT 27
(DEDICATED TO THE MEMORY OF CHARLIE LANG AND ERNEST GREEN. . . . . . JC THE BITTER RIVR 1
AND CHARLIE YARDBIRD PARKER . . . . AYM BIRD IN ORBIT 30
DID I KNOW CHARLIE MINGUS? . . . . AYM HORN OF PLENTY 51

CHARM 2
SEA CHARM . . . . DK SEA CHARM 1
LIKE HE HAD A CHARM. . . . . SP MADAM WRONG VIS 10

CHARMS 1
SING EVE'S CHARMS! . . . . WB HARLEM NIGHT CL 13

CHARNEL 1
MERCEDES IS CHARNEL ROSE. . . . . . WB TO DARK MERCEDE 3

CHART 1
A CHART AND COMPASS . . . . JC TO CAPTAIN MULZ 11

CHARTING 1
CHARTING TOMORROW. . . . . FW MIGRATION 17

CHARTS 1
OUR CHARTS, OUR COMPASS AND BELL-BOUY . . . . JC TO CAPTAIN MULZ 53

CHASE 1
SHE COULD CHASE ME UP A TREE . . . SH ONLY WOMAN BLUS 9

CHATTERING 1
BOWED DOWN WITH CHATTERING PARROTS WB OUR LAND 10

CHAUFFEUR 1
WITH ADAM POWELL FOR CHAUFFEUR . . AYM RIDE, RED, RIDE 32

CHAWED 2
I CHAWED DE MORNIN' AIR. . . . . . SH EVENIN' BLUES 8
CHAWED DE MORNIN' AIR. . . . . . . SH EVENIN' BLUES 10

CHA-CHA 3
CHA-CHA LIKE CASTANETS . . . . . . AYM GOSPEL CHA-CHA 3
CHA-CHA . . . CHA-CHA . . . . AYM GOSPEL CHA-CHA 63
CHA-CHA . . . CHA-CHA . . . . AYM GOSPEL CHA-CHA 63

CHEAP 7
THOSE KIND COME CHEAP IN HARLEM . . WB YOUNG PROSTITUT 4
BOASTING, LIKE A CHEAP BULLY. BUT SUDDENLY LOOKING AHEAD: SHRUGGING HIS . . . . NM BIG-TIMER MOOD 5
CHEAP LITTLE RHYMES . . . . SP SLIVER 1
A CHEAP LITTLE TUNE . . . . SP SLIVER 2
A CHEAP LITTLE TUNE . . . . SP SLIVER 5
TO CHEAP LITTLE RHYMES . . . . . . SP SLIVER 6
YOU MAY PLAY FOLKS CHEAP. . . . . . SP WARNING AUGMENT 5

CHEAPEST 3
CHEAPEST BOARDING HOUSE: . . . . . OWT BOARDING HOUSE 2
CHEAPEST BOARDING HOUSE. . . . . . OWT BOARDING HOUSE 8
CHEAPEST BOARDING HOUSE! . . . . . OWT BOARDING HOUSE 14

CHECK 3
I'M GONNA CHECK UP ON THIS . . . . SP FREEDOM TRAIN 15
ON THE CHECK THAT IS HIS PAY. . . . SP MIGRANT 37
ON THE BIG SCREEN OF THE WELFARE CHECK . . . . AYM ODE TO DINAH 98

CHECKED 1
CHARITY'S CHECKED MONEY . . . . . . SP INTERNE AT PROV 26

CHECKS 3
WRAPPED IN CHECKS AND WEALTHY. . . SP GRADUATION 9
BRING WELFARE CHECKS MUCH SOONER . AYM ODE TO DINAH 73
I SEND CHECKS. . . . . PL NORTHERN LIBERL 16

CHECK'S 1
THIS WHOLE PAY CHECK'S JUST FOR ME. SH PAY DAY 1

CHEER 2
I CAN HEY-HEY-HEY - AND CHEER! . . SH HEY-HEY BLUES 6
AND I'LL HEY-HEY-HEY - AND CHEER! SH HEY-HEY BLUES 24

CHERUB-FACES 1
WHIRL OF CHERUB-FACES. . . . . . . ANS SONG OF SPAIN 22

CHI 2
5TH AND MOUND IN CINCI, 63RD IN CHI, AYM ASK YOUR MAMA 5
18TH AND VINE IN K.C., 63RD IN CHI. AYM ASK YOUR MAMA 32

CHICAGO 7
CHICAGO. . . . . FC BRASS SPITOONS 3
KIDS WILL DIE IN THE STREETS OF CHICAGO . . . . ANS KIDS WHO DIE 10
IN CHICAGO . . . . OWT RESTRICTIVE 9
NOW IT'S MANHATTAN, CHICAGO, . . . SP FREEDOM'S PLOW 86
(CHICAGO) . . . . SP MIGRANT 1
CHICAGO, DETROIT, ... SP ONE-WAY TICKET 4
IN HARLEM OR THE SOUTH SIDE OF CHICAGO . . . . AYM HORN OF PLENTY 55

CHICASAWHAY 1
SHUBUTA BRIDGE OVER THE CHICASAWHAY RIVER IN MISSISSIPPI, ... JC THE BITTER RIVR 1

CHICKEN 6
YOU STILL BAKES BISCUITS? FRIED CHICKEN EVERY NIGHT? IS THAT TRUE? . . . . NM BROKE 73
IF YOU WANT A GOOD CHICKEN . . . . OWT JITNEY 55
EATING CHICKEN. . . . . SP GRADUATION 12
I'LL BRING HOME CHICKEN! . . . . . SP GRADUATION 22
AND BUY HER SOME CHICKEN. . . . . . SP MADAM WRONG VIS 26
MEANWHILE DINAH EATING CHICKEN . . AYM ODE TO DINAH 129

CHICO 2
I AM CHICO, THE NEGRO, ... ANS BLDS OF LENIN 13
AND HOLDS OF BOATS, CHICO, ... SP GOOD MORNING 10

CHIEF 1
DR. RUFUS CLEMENT HIS CHIEF ADVISER. PL CULTURAL EXCHNG 44

CHILD 28
TODAY'S DARK CHILD, TOMORROW'S STRONG MAN: . . . . NM DARK YOUTH USA 2
YOU WHO ARE A CHILD OF NIGHT. . . . DK SONG 4
PEEPS A MAPLE-SUGAR CHILD. . . . . DK WINTER SWEEETNS 4
UP MILLIONS FOR BOMBS TO KILL A CHILD - . . . . ANS SONG OF SPAIN 44
MY MOTHER'S CHILD. . . . . SH BLD THE SINNER 12
STRONG AS THE COMING OF THE FIRST CHILD . . . . FW EARTH SONG 9
A LITTLE SOUTHERN COLORED CHILD . . FW MIGRATION 1
LITTLE FRIGHTENED CHILD . . . . . . FW MIGRATION 15
CHILD, AIN'T YOU HEARD? . . . . . . OWT JITNEY 18
I'M GOING SHOPPING NOW, CHILD. . . OWT JITNEY 58
THE CHILD, COME BACK AGAIN. . . . . LHR PASTORAL 9
AUNT SUE CUDDLES A BROWN-FACED CHILD TO HER BOSOM . . . . SP AUNTSUE'S STORI 4
AND THE DARK-FACED CHILD, LISTENING, SP AUNTSUE'S STORI 17
THE DARK-FACED CHILD IS QUIET . . . SP AUNTSUE'S STORI 23
THIS IS A SONG FOR THE GENIUS CHILD. SP GENIUS CHILD 1
NOBODY LOVES A GENIUS CHILD. . . . SP GENIUS CHILD 5
NOBODY LOVES A GENIUS CHILD. . . . SP GENIUS CHILD 11
A LITTLE GIRL CHILD. . . . . SP MADAM CHARTY CH 2
CAN'T RAISE NO CHILD ON THAT. . . . SP MADAM CHARTY CH 19
I MUST BE MISS BLUES'ES CHILD. . . SP MISS BLUES'ES 6
I'M JUST MISS BLUES'ES CHILD! . . . SP MISS BLUES'ES 14
BUT MOTHER AND CHILD . . . . SP S-SSS-SS-SH! 20
I AM THE CHILD THEY STOLE FROM THE SAND . . . . SP THE NEGRO MOTHE 7
WHERE THE CHRIST CHILD ONCE HAD LAIN. . . . . AYM ODE TO DINAH 34
IN RELATION TO THE CHILD, ... AYM ODE TO DINAH 83
NOW NOT EVEN KEEPER TO YOUR CHILD - AYM ODE TO DINAH 85
IS THE ANSWER TO THE CHILD. . . . . AYM SHOW FARE PLESE 19
COLORED CHILD . . . . PL MERRY-GO-ROUND 1

CHILDREN 20
THE SEA'S OWN CHILDREN . . . . . . DK SEA CHARM 2
WHEN I SAW MY CHILDREN UNSCHOOLED. ANS A NEW SONG 12
WITH THE WHITE CHILDREN . . . . . . FW MIGRATION 4
THE COLORED CHILDREN . . . . FW MIGRATION 8
THERE IS TWO THOUSAND CHILDREN . . SP CHILDREN'S RYME 10
IF MY CHILDREN ASK ME, DADDY, PLEASE
EXPLAIN . . . . SP FREEDOM TRAIN 31
WHAT SHALL I TELL MY CHILDREN? . . .
YOU TELL ME - . . . . SP FREEDOM TRAIN 33
THEN TAKE CARE OF HER CHILDREN . . SP MADAM HER MADAM 7
CHILDREN SO BAD? . . . . SP MADAM CHARTY CH 10
CHILDREN, I COME BACK TODAY . . . . SP THE NEGRO MOTHE 1
CHILDREN SOLD AWAY FROM ME, HUSBAND
SOLD, TOO. . . . . SP THE NEGRO MOTHE 15
NOW, THROUGH MY CHILDREN, I'M
REACHING THE GOAL. . . . . SP THE NEGRO MOTHE 20
NOW, THROUGH MY CHILDREN, YOUNG AND
FREE, ... SP THE NEGRO MOTHE 21
ALL YOU DARK CHILDREN IN THE WORLD
CUT THERE, ... SP THE NEGRO MOTHE 35
OH, MY DARK CHILDREN, MAY MY DREAMS
AND MY PRAYERS . . . . SP THE NEGRO MOTHE 49
DARES KEEP DOWN THE CHILDREN OF THE
NEGRO MOTHER. . . . . SP THE NEGRO MOTHE 52
AND IN HER HOUSE MY CHILDREN . . . SP THE SOUTH 27
WHAT SHE SAID ABOUT HER CHILDREN . AYM BIRD IN ORBIT 51
SCHOOLS ARE BETTER FOR THEIR
CHILDREN $ . . . . AYM HORN OF PLENTY 24
AND COLORED CHILDREN HAVE WHITE
MAMMIES: . . . . PL CULTURAL EXCHNG 50

CHILD-MINDED 1
THE CHILD-MINDED SOUTH . . . . . . SP THE SOUTH 6

CHILD'LL 2
I HOPE MY CHILD'LL . . . . SP LAMENT OVER LOV 1
I SAY I HOPE MY CHILD'LL . . . . . SP LAMENT OVER LOV 3

CHILE 14
CHILE, HE'S GONE AWAY. . . . . . . WB BLUES FANTASY 8
I USED TO BE A GOOD CHILE, ... FC LISTEN HERE 7
USED TO BE A GOOD CHILE, - . . . . FC LISTEN HERE 9
PACE. "SOMETIMES I FEEL LIKE A
MOTHER-LESS CHILE." TURNING
FUTILELY . . . . NM BLACK CLWN MOOD 8
CERTAINLY, CHILE, I ALWAYS WAS CRAZY
'BOUT YOU! . . . . NM BROKE 74
SHAKE YOUR BROWN FEET, CHILE, . . . DK SONG BANJO DANC 2
SHAKE 'EM, HONEY CHILE. . . . . . . DK SONG BANJO DANC 11
SHAKE 'EM, LIZA, CHILE, ... DK SONG BANJO DANC 21
WHAT'S DE MATTER, CHILE? . . . . . ANS SISTER JOHNSON 6
WHEN I WAS A CHILE WE USED TO PLAY. SP CHILDREN'S RYME 1
CHILE, THESE STEPS IS HARD TO CLIMB. SP DIME 1
CHILE, GRANNY AIN'T GOT NO DIME. . SP DIME 6
WHEN A CHILE GETS TO BE THIRTEEN . SP MYSTERY 1
"BUT JUST WAIT, CHILE . . . " . . . PL OFFICE BUILDING 11

CHILE'LL 1
AN' TOMORROW'S CHILE'LL . . . . . . FC RED SILK STOCK 9

CHIMNEY 1
YET NO PRESENTS DOWN THE CHIMNEY. AYM ODE TO DINAH 74

CHINA 8
FROM AFRICA TO CHINA, ... ANS CHANT TOM MOONY 18
I WOULD SWIM TO CHINA . . . . SH DECLARATION 3
BUT INDIA AND CHINA AND HARLEM, TOO, JC JIM CROW'S LAST 13
FROM CHINA . . . . SP CONSIDER ME 38
IN CHINA BEFORE WHAT HAPPENED . . . SP IN EXPLANATION 8
THAT CHINA MADE AEONS AGO - . . . . PL BIRMINGHAM SUND 9
THAT WHAT CHINA MADE . . . . PL BIRMINGHAM SUND 11
BEFORE CHINA WAS EVER RED AT ALL . PL BIRMINGHAM SUND 12

CHINE 1
FULL OF CHINE BONES IN DARK GLASSES. SP SUMMER EVENING 15

CHINESE 3
CHINESE? . . . HELL, NO! . . . . . SH OLD PAWNBROKER 7
I GOT A CHINESE BOY-FRIEND . . . . OWT JITNEY 11
THE MISSIONARIES NEVER TAUGHT
CHINESE . . . . PL BIRMINGHAM SUND 21

CHIP 1
AND HAD A CHIP ON SHOULDER? . . . . AYM HORN OF PLENTY 50

CHIPPIE 1
ALL UNSUSPECTIN OF THE CHIPPIE ON
HIS LEFT - . . . . SH DEATH IN HARLEM 80

CHOCOLATE 8
CHOCOLATE DARLING . . . . SH HARLEM SWEETIES 11
A CHOCOLATE TREAT. . . . . SH HARLEM SWEETIES 32
CHOCOLATE AND BLOOD: . . . . SP INTERNE AT PROV 29
MAKES IRON OF CHOCOLATE MUSCLES. . SP MIGRANT 15
FACE LIKE A CHOCOLATE BAR . . . . . SP 125TH STREET 1
CHOCOLATE BABIES BORN IN SHADOWS . AYM ODE TO DINAH 76
THE CHOCOLATE GANGRENOUS ICING OF AYM ODE TO DINAH 30
UMBILICAL IN SULPHUROUS CHOCOLATE: AYM ODE TO DINAH 91

CHOCOLATE-CUSTARD 1
CHOCOLATE-CUSTARD . . . . SP ISLAND 7

CHOICE 2
AND MAKE YOUR CHOICE KNOWN . . . . JC BLD SAM SOLOMON 10
CHOOSE HIS COMPASS' CHOICE, ... PL FREDRK DOUGLASS 13

CHOIR 1
AND LET THE CHOIR SING A STORMY SONG SP FATASY PURPLE 3

CHOKE 1
YOU CAN TAKE THAT JOB AND GO TO - I
HOPE YOU CHOKE. . . . . NM BROKE 37

CHOKING 1
CHOKING HIS BREATH . . . . OLD THE CONSUMPTIVE 11

CHOOSE 5
SAY IT VERY SLOWLY IF YOU CHOOSE. FC MAMMY 4
SURE, CALL ME ANY UGLY NAME YOU
CHOOSE - . . . . ANS LET AMERICA BE 70
DOES 'EM LIKE YOU CHOOSE. . . . . . SP LOVER'S RETURN 12
CHOOSE HIS COMPASS' CHOICE, ... PL FREDRK DOUGLASS 13
(NO IN-BETWEEN TO CHOOSE) . . . . . PL MOTHER IN WAR 11

CHOPS 3
AND THE DEVIL LICKS HIS CHOPS . . . SP SUNDAY MORNING 7
WE LICK OUR CHOPS AT BIRMINGHAM . . PL NORTHERN LIBERL 2
AND LICK MY CHOPS . . . . PL NORTHERN LIBERL 18

CHORDS 1
HE PLAYED A FEW CHORDS THEN HE SANG
SOME MORE - . . . . SP THE WEARY BLUES 24

CHRIST 7
CHRIST, ... SL SCOTTSBORO 10
AND AIN'T SEEN CHRIST YET, ... SP MYSTERY 2
CHRIST! . . . . SP MYSTERY 20
FROM THE SAINTS OF GOD IN CHRIST . SP PASSING 4
WHERE THE CHRIST CHILD ONCE HAD
LAIN. . . . . AYM ODE TO DINAH 34
CHRIST IS A NIGGER, ... PL CHRIST IN ALA. 1
NIGGER CHRIST . . . . PL CHRIST IN ALA. 12

CHRISTENED 1
MY MOTHER CHRISTENED ME . . . . . . SP MADAM CENSUS 17

CHRISTIAN 3
AND DROPPING BOMBS FROM A CHRISTIAN
STEEPLE . . . . ANS SONG OF SPAIN 69
WHERE THE CARNIVAL IS CHRISTIAN. . SP SUMMER EVENING 13
IN CHRISTIAN SUNDAY SCHOOL . . . . PL BIRMINGHAM SUND 22

CHRISTMAS 5
'TWAS THE NIGHT BEFO' CHRISTMAS . . SP MIDWINTER BLUES 5
I LIKE A PIPE FOR A CHRISTMAS
PRESENT, ... SP THEME FOR ENG B 23
ASKED ME RIGHT AT CHRISTMAS . . . . AYM BIRD IN ORBIT 69
THEY ASKED ME RIGHT AT CHRISTMAS. AYM ODE TO DINAH 127
YOU KNOW, RIGHT AT CHRISTMAS . . . PL CULTURAL EXCHNG 32

CHUMPS 1
AND START A SKIN GAME WITH SOME
CHUMPS I KNOW. . . . . SH BED TIME 6

CHURCH 9
CHURCH ON SUNDAY. . . . . FC BRASS SPITOONS 24
BABIES AND GIN AND CHURCH . . . . . FC BRASS SPITOONS 26
DON'T HAVE TO GO TO CHURCH. . . . . SH SUNDAY 3
THE WAY YOU SHOUT OUT LOUD IN
CHURCH, ... SP HIGH TO LOW 13
EBECANEEZER BAPTIST CHURCH. . . . . SP PRAYER MEETING 7
ON THAT DAY WHEN ABYSSINIA BAPTIST
CHURCH . . . . SP PROJECTION 5
THE GOOD CHURCH FOLK DO NOT MENTION SP RUBY BROWN 21
COME INTO THE CHURCH THIS MORNING. SP SUNDAY MORNING 36
IN BILLINGTON'S CHURCH OF RUBBER. AYM HORN OF PLENTY 84

CHURCHES 1
THERE ARE SO MANY CHURCHES . . . . PL BIBLE BELT 3

CIGARETTE 3
DIAMOND RING, CIGARETTE HOLDER, AND
A CANE, TO THE MUSIC OF PIANO OR NM BIG-TIMER MOOD 1
AND SMOKED A CAPSTAN CIGARETTE . . DK SAILOR 3
CIGARETTE MACHINE. . . . . SP TOMORROW 5

CIGARETTES 1
AND THERE'S A NEW TAX ON CIGARETTES
- . . . . PL HARLEM 11

CINCI 1
5TH AND MOUND IN CINCI, EZRD IN CHI. AYM ASK YOUR MAMA 5

CINNAMON 2
TO CINNAMON TOES. . . . . SH HARLEM SWEETIES 24
LICORICE, CLOVE, CINNAMON . . . . . SH HARLEM SWEETIES 35

CINNAMON AND RAYON. . . . . SP GRADUATION 1

CINQUE 1
FOR CINQUE SAYING, "RUN A NEW FLAG UP THE MAST." . . . . PL FINAL CALL 21

CIRCLE 1
CIRCLE OF LIGHT. . . . . SP DANSE AFRICAINE 9

CIRCLES 2
THE CIRCLES SPIN ROUND . . . . . . FW CIRCLES 1
AND THE CIRCLES SPIN ROUND . . . . FW CIRCLES 2

CIRCUS 3
IN THE CIRCUS OF CIVILIZATION. . . WB LAMENT DARK PEO 10
CAGED IN THE CIRCUS OF CIVILIZATION. WB LAMENT DARK PEO 12
A GAY AND LOW-DOWN BLUES. COMIC ENTRANCE LIKE THE CLOWNS IN THE CIRCUS. . . . . NM BLACK CLWN MOOD 1

CIRCUSES 1
AND BAND-MEN IN CIRCUSES - . . . . FC LAUGHERS 18

CITADELLE 1
TO THE CITADELLE OF SHADOWS SHADOWS AYM GOSPEL CHA-CHA 18

CITIES 2
IN ORIENTAL CITIES . . . . FW OLD SAILOR 7
AND THE TOWNS THAT GREW TO CITIES. SP FREEDOM'S PLOW 71

CITIZENS 1
THE SOLID CITIZENS . . . . PL UNDERTOW 1

CITY 12
OH, GREAT DARK CITY. . . . . WB DISILLUSION 12
ATLANTIC CITY. . . . . FC BRASS SPITOONS 4
WENT TO THE CITY. . . . . NM BIG-TIMER POEM 6
PAUL ROBESON SAID, OUT IN KANSAS CITY. . . . . JC JIM CROW'S LAST 19
OF OUR WEARY CITY . . . . FW PRAYER 6
ON THIS CITY STREET. . . . . OWT JUICE JOINT 16
O, IN THIS TAVERN ON THE CITY STREET OWT JUICE JOINT 33
ON THE CITY STREET. . . . . OWT JUICE JOINT 48
OF OUR WEARY CITY . . . . SP LITANY 6
FROM KANSAS CITY . . . . SP MADAM PHONE BIL 22
A CITY BUILDING . . . . SP STARS 3
A CITY DREAMING . . . . SP STARS 5

CIVIL 4
I WANT TO PASS THE CIVIL SERVICE. SP DEFERRED 43
BEFORE THE CIVIL WAR, DAYS WERE DARK. . . . . SP FREEDOM'S PLOW 118
CIVIL WAR CENTENNIAL: 1965. . . . . PL DEATH YORKVILLE 14
AND THE ECHO OF THE CIVIL WAR . . . PL OCTOBER 16 RAID 17

CIVILIZATION 4
I AM AFRAID OF THIS CIVILIZATION - WB FOR PORTRAIT OF 3
IN THE CIRCUS OF CIVILIZATION. . . WB LAMENT DARK PEO 10
CAGED IN THE CIRCUS OF CIVILIZATION. WB LAMENT DARK PEO 12
FOR LIGHT AND CIVILIZATION . . . . PL FLORIDA WORKERS 7

CIVILIZED 1
FOR THE "CIVILIZED" RACE. . . . . . NM BLACK CLWN POEM 50

CLANG 1
CLANG AGAINST THE TREES WENT THE AX IN MANY HANDS . . . . SP FREEDOM'S PLOW 55

CLASPED 1
AND BLACK HANDS AND WHITE HANDS CLASPED AS ONE. . . . . ANS KIDS WHO DIE 48

CLASS 3
I'M A FIRST CLASS HUSTLER. . . . . NM BIG-TIMER POEM 37
THAT'S DE WORKING CLASS! . . . . . ANS SISTER JOHNSON 12
I AM THE ONLY COLORED STUDENT IN MY CLASS. . . . . SP THEME FOR ENG B 10

CLASSES 1
WHO AT THE SORBONNE HAS SIX CLASSES. AYM ASK YOUR MAMA 54

CLAUS 4
INVESTIGATE THAT SANTA CLAUS . . . AYM BIRD IN ORBIT 84
SANTA CLAUS, FORGIVE ME, ... AYM ODE TO DINAH 69
SANTA CLAUS, FORGIVE ME, ... AYM RIDE, RED, RIDE 23
RIDING IN A JAGUAR, SANTA CLAUS. . AYM RIDE, RED, RIDE 30

CLAVES 1
MAKE CLAVES OF MY SORROWS . . . . . AYM GOSPEL CHA-CHA 33

CLAY 8
A BIT OF CLAY, BROWN, UGLY, GIVEN LIFE? . . . . DK BEGGAR BOY 6
WITH YOUR TASTE OF BLOOD AND CLAY. JC THE BITTER RIVR 23
DOWN INTO THE CLAY. . . . . SP AS BEFITS A MAN 14
PLUS CASSIUS MOHAMMED ALI CLAY. . . PL CROWNS GARLANDS 5
AND THE SMELL OF RED CLAY AFTER RAIN PL DAYBREAK IN ALA 9
AND RED CLAY EARTH HANDS IN IT . . PL DAYBREAK IN ALA 17
IN WHITE ON CLAY . . . . PL THE DOVE 5
IT'S MADE OF PLAIN OLD GEORGIA CLAY. PL VARI-COLORED 7

CLAY'S 2
I WONDER WHY RED CLAY'S SO RED . . PL VARI-COLORED 9
AND WHY THE CLAY'S SO RED. . . . . PL VARI-COLORED 14

CLEAN 23
SIMPLE AND CLEAN . . . . WB DISILLUSION 2
TO WHAT CLEAN BOY HAVE YOU OFFERED YOUR LIPS? . . . . WB NUDE YOUNG DANC 8
CLEAN THE SPITOONS, BOY. . . . . . FC BRASS SPITOONS 1
CLEAN THE SPITOONS. . . . . FC BRASS SPITOONS 6
DOLLARS AND CLEAN SPITOONS . . . . FC BRASS SPITOONS 29
A CLEAN SPITOON ON THE ALTAR OF THE LORD. . . . . FC BRASS SPITOONS 37
A CLEAN BRIGHT SPITOON ALL NEWLY POLISHED, - . . . . FC BRASS SPITOONS 38
SO DE MAN SAY, "I'LL GET SOMEBODY ELSE, THEN, TO CLEAN." - . . . . NM BROKE 17
A RECITATION TO BE DELIVERED BY A NEGRO BOY, BRIGHT, CLEAN, AND NEATLY . . . . NM DARK YOUTH USA 1
I AIN'T BEEN CLEAN - . . . . SP FIRE 5
EMPTY, BUT CLEAN. . . . . SP FREEDOM'S PLOW 3
AN' NOW I'M SETTIN' CLEAN AN' BRIGHT SP JUDGMENT DAY 11
CLEAN AN' BRIGHT, ... SP JUDGMENT DAY 13
CLEAN AN' BRIGHT. . . . . SP JUDGMENT DAY 14
HOUSE TO CLEAN. . . . . SP MADAM HER MADAM 4
CAESAR TOLD ME TO KEEP HIS DOOR-STEPS CLEAN. . . . . SP NEGRO 5
AND FAR TOO CLEAN TO STAY THAT WAY. SP PASSING 8
LEAPS CLEAN OVER TO SEVENTH AVENUE SP PROJECTION 2
NOR FUEL FOR THE CLEAN FLAME OF JOY SP RUBY BROWN 6
NEIGHBORHOOD'S CLEAN. . . . . PL LITTLE SNG HOUS 9
GOT TO CLEAN AWHILE. . . . . PL OFFICE BUILDING 3
YOU CLEAN AWHILE. . . . . PL OFFICE BUILDING 7
CLEAN. . . . . PL WAR 11

CLEANED 2
O' GETTIN' A NEW WINTER COAT, OR HAVIN' THAT OLD ONE CLEANED. . . NM BROKE 40
I HAD MA CLOTHES CLEANED . . . . . DK DRESSED UP 1

CLEANING 1
CLEANING AWHILE. . . . . PL OFFICE BUILDING 10

CLEAR 3
ALL THE DOORYARD BRIGHT AND CLEAR DK IRISH WAKE 6
BABY, COULD YOU SEE YOUR WAY CLEAR? SP DEFERRED 38
CLEAR GREEN CRYSTAL WATER . . . . . AYM GOSPEL CHA-CHA 30

CLEMENT 1
DR. RUFUS CLEMENT HIS CHIEF ADVISER. PL CULTURAL EXCHNG 44

CLENCHED 1
AND SO MY FIST IS CLENCHED . . . . PL MILITANT 12

CLEOPATRA 1
WAS CLEOPATRA GORGEOUS . . . . . . WB JAZZONIA 12

CLEVER 1
AND CLEVER ENOUGH . . . . SP SHAME ON YOU 7

CLEW 2
TO SEE MA OLD AUNT CLEW. . . . . . SP YOUNG GAL'S BLS 8
TO SEE MA OLD AUNT CLEW. . . . . . SP YOUNG GAL'S BLS 10

CLICKING 1
AND THE CLICKING OF THE KEYS . . . SP GRADUATION 14

CLIMB 4
TRYING TO CLIMB UP. . . . . NM BLACK CLWN POEM 45
SO I CLIMB TOWARD TOMORROW, OUT OF PAST SORROW. . . . . NM DARK YOUTH USA 22
CHILE, THESE STEPS IS HARD TO CLIMB. SP DIME 1
THAT I HAD TO CLIMB, THAT I HAD TO KNOW . . . . SP THE NEGRO MOTHE 3

CLIMBED 2
I CLIMBED . . . . AYM GOSPEL CHA-CHA 51
LORD KNOWS I CLIMBED . . . . AYM GOSPEL CHA-CHA 55

CLIMBING 1
CLIMBING UP A GREAT BIG MOUNTAIN . SP PORTER 7

CLIMBIN' 2
I'SE STILL CLIMBIN', ... SP MOTHER TO SON 19
CLIMBIN' THAT HILL. . . . . PL DOWN WHERE I AM 10

CLINCH 1
SEND FOR ROBIN HOOD TO CLINCH THE ANTI-POVERTY . . . . PL FINAL CALL 3

CLINGING 1
YET CLINGING TO THE LADDER. . . . . NM BLACK CLWN POEM 43

CLINKS 1
- CH QUARTER CLINKS . . . AYM ODE TO DINAH 55

CLOCK 3
- ALARM CLOCK HERE RINGING SO DAMN LOUD . . . SH DAYBREAK 3
- CAUSE THAT OLD ALARM CLOCK SHO HURTS MY EARS. . . . SH LETTER 19
- THE CLOCK IS MOVING FORWARD HERE - JC TO CAPTAIN MULZ 25

CLOCKS 1
- NO CLOCKS ON THE WALL. . . . SP END 2

CLORINDA 1
- SAYS CLORINDA. . . . FC BEALE ST. LOVE 7

CLOSE 6
- DANCIN CLOSE, AND DANCIN SWEET, . . SH DEATH IN HARLEM 22
- HER BODY CLOSE TO MINE. . . . FW MAN 6
- HERE. WELL, THAT IS ALL SO I WILL CLOSE. . . . SP LETTER 9
- CLOSE UP TIGHT THAT NIGHT. . . . SP LIKEWISE 11
- SO CLOSE . . . SP SUBWAY RUSH HOU 3
- AND EARS THAT CLOSE TO HARLEM SCREAMS. . . . PL JUNIOR ADDICT 5

CLOSED 2
- THE LAST PLAYER-PIANO IS CLOSED. . WB SUMMER NIGHT 4
- FACE THE WALL WITH THE DARK CLOSED GATE. . . . DK SONG 7

CLOSELY 2
- LISTEN CLOSELY: . . . SP DREAM BOOGIE 5
- LISTEN TO IT CLOSELY: . . . SP DREAM BOOGIE 10

CLOSING 1
- THEN AT THE CLOSING HOUR . . . FC SPORT 7

CLOTH 1
- INTO CLOTH OF DOLLARS . . . AYM SHOW FARE PLESE 22

CLOTHED 1
- AND THE COTTON THAT CLOTHED AMERICA. SP FREEDOM'S PLOW 54

CLOTHES 10
- I BOUGHT HIM SUITS O' CLOTHES, . . FC BLACK GAL 10
- GATHER UP YO' FINE CLOTHES . . . FC HARD LUCK 5
- JEW TAKES YO' FINE CLOTHES, . . . FC HARD LUCK 7
- JEW TAKES YO' FINE CLOTHES, . . . FC HARD LUCK 9
- IN THE CLOTHES OF A MODERN MAN, HE PROCLAIMS HIMSELF. . . . NM BLACK CLWN MOOD 15
- I HAD MA CLOTHES CLEANED . . . DK DRESSED UP 1
- PLACE WHERE YOUR CLOTHES HUNG'S EMPTY AND BARE. . . . SH SUPPER TIME 9
- WHILE GIRLS WHO WASH RICH WHITE FOLKS CLOTHES BY DAY . . . OWT LINCOLN THEATRE 13
- THE CREDIT MAN'S DONE TOOK MA CLOTHES . . . SP DOWN AND OUT 7
- ALL HER CLOTHES WAS GONE: . . . SP HOMECOMING 3

CLOTHESBRUSH 1
- LINCOLN'S LIKE A CLOTHESBRUSH . . . AYM BIRD IN ORBIT 46

CLOUDS 5
- STORM CLOUDS MOVE FAST. . . . ANS SONG OF SPAIN 48
- EXPLORING THE CLOUDS. . . . FW NEW MOON 4
- BETWEEN THE LITTLE CLOUDS OF HEAVEN LHR PASTORAL 1
- THE STORM CLOUDS . . . SP AFRICA 7
- THERE WAS LIGHT WHEN THE BATTLE CLOUDS ROLLED AWAY. . . . SP FREEDOM'S PLOW 139

CLOUD-CLOTH 1
- IN A BLUE CLOUD-CLOTH . . . DK DREAM KEEPER 6

CLOUD-DUST 1
- CLOUD-DUST. . . . PL DREAM DUST 3

CLOUD-GARMENTS 1
- THE WIND HAS BLOWN ALL THE CLOUD-GARMENTS . . . SP MARCH MOON 3

CLOVE 1
- LICORICE, CLOVE, CINNAMON . . . SH HARLEM SWEETIES 35

CLOWN 11
- THE DUMB CLOWN OF THE WORLD, . . . WB THE JESTER 16
- SUIT AND HAT OF A CLOWN, TO THE MUSIC OF A PIANO, OR AN ORCHESTRA. . . . NM BLACK CLWN MOOD 1
- I RISE AGAIN - A BLACK CLOWN. . . . NM BLACK CLWN POEM 11
- CAN A CLOWN HAVE HIS DAY. . . . NM BLACK CLWN POEM 15
- GARMENTS OF A CLOWN . . . NM BLACK CLWN POEM 26
- WORKER AND CLOWN AM I . . . NM BLACK CLWN POEM 49
- JUST A BLACK CLOWN! . . . NM BLACK CLWN POEM 54
- I'M ONLY A CLOWN! . . . NM BLACK CLWN POEM 58
- THAT MAKE ME A CLOWN! . . . NM BLACK CLWN POEM 70
- I WAS ONCE A BLACK CLOWN . . . NM BLACK CLWN POEM 77
- THE WAY YOU CLOWN - . . . SP HIGH TO LOW 18

CLOWNS 1
- A GAY AND LOW-DOWN BLUES. COMIC ENTRANCE LIKE THE CLOWNS IN THE CIRCUS. . . . NM BLACK CLWN MOOD 1

CLOWN'S 1
- ECHOES THE FIGHTING "MARSEILLAISE." TEARING OFF HIS CLOWN'S SUIT, . NM BLACK CLWN MOOD 13

CLUB 5
- CLUB ROLAND HAYES, . . . JC HOW ABOUT DIXIE 14
- AT THE ELKS CLUB LOUNGE . . . SP PARADE 3
- AT CLUB HARLEM IT'S ELEVEN . . . SP SEASHORE THROUG 3
- OF THE COUNTRY CLUB SET. . . . PL UNDERTOW 2
- EVEN SOGGY COUNTRY CLUB . . . PL UNDERTOW 7

CLUBS 2
- BEATING THEM WITH LAWS AND CLUBS AND BAYONETS AND BULLETS . . . ANS KIDS WHO DIE 30
- AND WHIPPED HIS HEAD WITH CLUBS . . SP NOT A MOVIE 3

CLUNY 1
- IN THE SHADOW OF THE CLUNY . . . AYM ASK YOUR MAMA 55

CLUTCH 1
- THEY CLUTCH AT THE EGG . . . PL ELDERLY LEADERS 8

CLUTCHING 2
- I AM THE IMMIGRANT CLUTCHING THE HOPE I SEEK - . . . ANS LET AMERICA BE 22
- CLUTCHING AT A . . . LHR POET TO BIGOT 10

COACHES 2
- CAME THE WAGONS AND THE COACHES. . SP FREEDOM'S PLOW 74
- COVERED WAGONS, STAGE COACHES, . . SP FREEDOM'S PLOW 75

COAL 5
- UM-MM! SIGN HERE SAYS THEY WANTS SOMEBODY TO SHOVEL COAL. . . . NM BROKE 28
- WHAT I DON'T KNOW 'BOUT SHOVELIN' COAL, AIN'T NO MO' TO KNOW! . . NM BROKE 32
- CAN A COAL BLACK MAN DRIVE THE FREEDOM TRAIN? . . . SP FREEDOM TRAIN 18
- BUT HE LEFT ME WHEN THE COAL WAS LOW. . . . SP MIDWINTER BLUES 8
- BUT HE LEFT WHEN THE COAL WAS LOW. SP MIDWINTER BLUES 10

COAST 2
- OFF THE COAST OF IRELAND . . . SP SEASCAPE 1
- OFF THE COAST OF ENGLAND . . . SP SEASCAPE 5

COAT 6
- O' GETTIN' A NEW WINTER COAT, OR HAVIN' THAT OLD ONE CLEANED. . . NM BROKE 40
- A FUR COAT! . . . SH PRESENT 7
- COAT, SHOES, . . . SP BUDDY 9
- AND THE COAT THAT I WAS WEARING . . SP CROSSING 7
- GOLDEN HANDS IN WHITE COAT, . . . SP INTERNE AT PROV 20
- MAMA, PLEASE BRUSH OFF MY COAT. . . SP MAMA AND DAUGHT 1

COATS 8
- AND ITS GALL COATS THE RED OF MY TONGUE, . . . JC THE BITTER RIVR 11
- COATS MY TONGUE. . . . JC THE BITTER RIVR 86
- JOSTLE OF FUR COATS . . . OWT MAN INTO MEN 2
- JOSTLE OF DIRTY COATS . . . OWT MAN INTO MEN 3
- WONDERING ABOUT FUR COATS . . . OWT MAN INTO MEN 9
- DIRTY COATS . . . OWT MAN INTO MEN 10
- HOWARD COATS. . . . SP FLATTED FIFTHS 14
- WHITE COATS . . . SP INTERNE AT PROV 1

COCA-COLA 1
- AND COCA-COLA . . . SP INTERNE AT PROV 32

COCKTAIL 1
- THE DREAM IS A COCKTAIL AT SLOPPY JOE'S - . . . SP HAVANA DREAMS 1

COCOA 2
- OR COCOA BROWN, . . . SH HARLEM SWEETIES 14
- WALNUT OR COCOA, . . . SH HARLEM SWEETIES 29

COCONUT 1
- JET AND COCONUT EYES, . . . SP GRADUATION 2

COCONUTS 1
- WHERE THE PALMS AND COCONUTS . . . AYM GOSPEL CHA-CHA 2

COFFEE 3
- COFFEE AND CREAM. . . . SH HARLEM SWEETIES 10
- COFFEE AND CREAM, . . . SH HARLEM SWEETIES 24
- COFFEE WITHOUT SUGAR . . . SP EARLY EVENING 5

COFFIN 1
- FOLKS MADE A COFFIN . . . FW GIRL 9

COGNAC 1
COME ON DRINK COGNAC. . . . . SP PORT TOWN 5

COIN 1
THE ONE COIN IN THE METER . . . . . AYM ODE TO DINAH 4

COKE 1
IT'S DONE GOT ME SO CRAZY, FEEL LIKE
I BEEN TAKIN' COKE. . . . . . . NM BROKE 60

COLD 22
SO COLD. . . . . WB FOR PORTRAIT OF 6
AND NOT THIS LAND WHERE LIFE IS
COLD. . . . . WB OUR LAND 7
CARESSES OF THE COLD . . . . WB POEME D'AUTOMNE 13
WHERE COLD WINDS BLOW. . . . . . . NM BLACK CLWN POEM 37
NOW, HUNCHED IN THE COLD, ... DK PARISIAN BEGGAR 2
WHOLE WIDE WORLD'S TURNED COLD. . . DK PO' BOY BLUES 6
I'M THE ONLY ONE'S GOT TO PILE OUT
IN THE COLD. . . . . SH DAYBREAK 6
TO KEEP THEM COLD MUDDY WATERS . . SH MISSISSIPPI LEV 17
THE WINDS OF WINTER COLD. . . . . . FW CAROLINA CABIN 14
IN A HIGH COLD WIND . . . . SP CROSSING 6
IF THAT WATER HADN'T A-BEEN SO COLD SP LIFE IS FINE 7
COLD IN THAT WATER! . . . . SP LIFE IS FINE 10
IT WAS COLD! . . . . SP LIFE IS FINE 11
COLD BRASS IN WARM AIR. . . . . . . SP SONG BILLIE HOL 17
IN THE COLD. . . . . SP STRANGE HURT 15
AN' THE GRAVE IS COLD. . . . . . . SP YOUNG GAL'S BLS 14
THE GRAVEYARD GRAVE IS COLD. . . . SP YOUNG GAL'S BLS 16
FROM THE COLD THAT MAKES NIAGARA . AYM ODE TO DINAH 25
AND COLD STEEL . . . . PL OPPRESSION 8
COLD WATER ON ME. . . . . PL THIRD DEGREE 16
WHEN THE COLD COMES . . . . PL WHERE WHEN WHCH 1
OF BEING LAID OUT COLD AND DEAD. . PL WHO BUT TH LORD 6

COLD-FACED 1
THE COLD-FACED NORTH. . . . . SP THE SOUTH 24

COLD-WATER 1
COLD-WATER FLAT AND ALL THAT. . . . SP DEFERRED 14

COLE 1
KING COLE JUKEBOX PAYOLA . . . . . . AYM ASK YOUR MAMA 42

COLEMAN 1
ON THE BREATH OF ORNETTE COLEMAN. AYM JAZZTET MUTED 9

COLLAR 1
AND A WHITE EMBROIDERED COLLAR. . . FW MIGRATION 13

COLLARD 2
IN A POT OF COLLARD GREENS . . . . PL CULTURAL EXCHNG 19
AND A LEAF OF COLLARD GREEN. . . . PL CULTURAL EXCHNG 30

COLLARS 1
WHEN WHITE COLLARS GET DONE, . . . PL OFFICE BUILDING 8

COLLECTION 1
IN THE COLLECTION BASKET . . . . . SP SUNDAY MORNING 40

COLLEGE 2
COLLEGE BOY SMART . . . . SP COLLEGE FORMAL 7
TO THIS COLLEGE ON THE HILL ABOVE
HARLEM. . . . . SP THEME FOR ENG B 9

COLOR 10
ARE TOO HEAVY WITH COLOR. . . . . . WB POEME D'AUTOMNE 2
OF PREJUDICE, AND HATE, AND THE
FALSE COLOR LINE - . . . . NM COLORED SL POEM 9
MA SOUL IS FULL OF COLOR . . . . . DK REASONS WHY 3
TO KILL THE LIES OF COLOR . . . . . ANS OPEN LETTER 25
SPLASH OF COLOR ON CANVASS, ... ANS SONG OF SPAIN 21
CHANGE MY COLOR, CHANGE MY WAYS. . SH DAYBREAK 10
YOU SPREAD YOUR COLOR BAR. . . . . JC BLACK MAN SPEAK 16
I'LL SING FOR YOU - BUT DROP THAT
COLOR BAR. . . . . JC JIM CROW'S LAST 18
AND NARY A SIGN OF A COLOR LINE - SP FREEDOM TRAIN 57
WHAT COLOR . . . . PL WAR 3

COLORED 42
AND DE MAN COME TELLIN' ME THEY
AIN'T HIRIN' NO MO' COLORED -
JUST WHITE. . . . . NM BROKE 45
WE WERE JUST TWO COLORED BOYS, BROWN
AND BLACK. . . . . NM COLORED SL POEM 2
TO A COLORED BOY'S RISING IN WEALTH
OR STATION - . . . . NM COLORED SL POEM 27
SINCE THE COLORED SOLDIERS CAME HOME
FROM FRANCE. . . . . NM COLORED SL POEM 32
KNOWIN THEY CAN BUY A DOZEN COLORED
PLACES. . . . . SH DEATH IN HARLEM 61
RICH CREAM COLORED . . . . SH HARLEM SWEETIES 17
EVERY COLORED MAN . . . . JC BLD SAM SOLOMON 18
HE LED HIS COLORED DELEGATION . . . JC BLD SAM SOLOMON 46
A LITTLE SOUTHERN COLORED CHILD . . FW MIGRATION 1
THE COLORED CHILDREN . . . . FW MIGRATION 8
THEY KILLED A COLORED SOLDIER! . . OWT BLD MARGE POLIT 13
COLORED LEADERS . . . . OWT BLD MARGE POLIT 38
A COLORED BOY, ... SP CONSIDER ME 2
COLORED BOY, ... SP CONSIDER ME 17
HE WAS A COLORED MAN WHO HAD BEEN A
SLAVE . . . . SP FREEDOM'S PLOW 112
NO SIGNS FOR COLORED ON THE FREEDOM
TRAIN. . . . . SP FREEDOM TRAIN 13
THE BIRMINGHAM STATION'S MARKED
COLORED AND WHITE. . . . . SP FREEDOM TRAIN 25
THE WHITE FOLKS GO LEFT, THE COLORED
GO RIGHT - . . . . SP FREEDOM TRAIN 26
NOT STOPPIN' AT NO STATIONS MARKED
COLORED NOR WHITE. . . . . SP FREEDOM TRAIN 51
NO MAYORS AND SUCH FOR WHICH COLORED
CAN'T VOTE. . . . . SP FREEDOM TRAIN 56
UNTIL COLORED FOLKS SPREAD . . . . SP GOOD MORNING 4
THE COLORED RACE WILL RISE! . . . . SP GRADUATION 26
AND BECAUSE SHE WAS COLORED . . . . SP RUBY BROWN 4
WHAT CAN A COLORED GIRL DO . . . . SP RUBY BROWN 13
LAST WEEK THEY LYNCHED A COLORED
BOY. . . . . SP SOUTHERN MAMMY 13
THAT COLORED BOY AIN'T SAID A THING SP SOUTHERN MAMMY 15
I AM TWENTY-TWO, COLORED, BORN IN
WINSTON-SALEM. . . . . SP THEME FOR ENG B 7
I AM THE ONLY COLORED STUDENT IN MY
CLASS. . . . . SP THEME FOR ENG B 10
I GUESS BEING COLORED DOESN'T MAKE
ME NOT LIKE . . . . SP THEME FOR ENG B 25
SO WILL MY PAGE BE COLORED THAT I
WRITE? . . . . SP THEME FOR ENG B 27
FOR A COLORED . . . . SP WEST TEXAS 19
AND I'M THE ONLY COLORED. . . . . . AYM HORN OF PLENTY 35
IS COLORED FOLKS' DEPRESSION. . . . AYM ODE TO DINAH 126
YOU MUST THINK US COLORED FOLKS . . PL BACKLASH BLUES 11
WHERE IS THE COLORED LAUNDROMAT . . PL CULTURAL EXCHNG 24
COMES THE COLORED HOUR: . . . . . . PL CULTURAL EXCHNG 42
AND COLORED CHILDREN HAVE WHITE
MAMMIES: . . . . PL CULTURAL EXCHNG 50
AND POPPY COLORED FACES . . . . . . PL DAYBREAK IN ALA 11
BECAUSE WE'RE COLORED. . . . . . . PL HARLEM 15
OUR NEIGHBORS ALL COLORED ARE. . . PL LITTLE SNG HOUS 19
COLORED CHILD . . . . PL MERRY-GO-ROUND 1
WHITE AND COLORED . . . . PL MERRY-GO-ROUND 7

COLORS 2
ALL THOSE SWEET COLORS . . . . . . SH HARLEM SWEETIES 27
BLOTS COLORS OFF THE MAP. . . . . . AYM ASK YOUR MAMA 63

COLUMN 1
IN GEORGE SOKOLSKY'S COLUMN. . . . AYM HORN OF PLENTY 86

COMB 1
I'D LIKE TO BUY A STRAIGHTENIN'
COMB. . . . . SP DOWN AND OUT 9

COMBINATE 1
COMBINATE A LITTLE . . . . SP NUMBERS 7

COMBINES 1
NAT-UNDREAMED-OF LEWIS COMBINES . . SP FLATTED FIFTHS 11

COME 117
I WILL NOT COME . . . . WB DISILLUSION 14
THOSE KIND COME CHEAP IN HARLEM . . WB YOUNG PROSTITUT 4
IF A SEVEN DON'T COME . . . . FC CRAP GAME 3
CAUSE HE NEVER DOES COME HOME. . . FC GYPSY MAN 2
HE NEVER DOES COME HOME. . . . . . FC GYPSY MAN 4
EVEN IF YOU DO COME FROM GEORGIA. FC JAZZ BAND 21
COME AN' EAGLE-ROCK WITH ME. . . . FC MA MAN 16
WHERE I COME FROM . . . . FC NEW CABARET GRL 11
TILL DE RED DAWN COME. . . . . . . FC SATURDAY NIGHT 28
AND DE MAN COME TELLIN' ME I BETTER
GET THERE AT FO'. . . . . NM BROKE 13
COME BAWLIN' ME OUT, 'CAUSE I'M
BROKE. . . . . NM BROKE 26
AND DE MAN COME TELLIN' ME THEY
AIN'T HIRIN' NO MO' COLORED -
JUST WHITE. . . . . NM BROKE 45
SHE BOUGHT A NEW HAT LAST WEEK AND
COME SENDIN' ME THE BILL. . . . NM BROKE 49
AND SHE COME TELLIN' ME, SHE AIN'T
GOT NO MO' EVENINGS FREE! . . . NM BROKE 53
HE SAID, "SHO YOU'LL COME WID ME . DK MA LORD 15
SINCE I COME UP NORTH DE . . . . . DK PO' BOY BLUES 5
NOW! COME OUT . . . . DK SONG BANJO DANC 8
LIKE A MIGHTY HEART-BEAT AS THEY
COME? . . . . SL SCOTTSBORO 3
WHEN THE BIRDS COME BACK FROM THE
SOUTH. . . . . ANS CHANT MAY DAY 6
TO BEAUTIFY THIS HOUR, THIS SPRING,
AND ALL THE SPRINGS TO COME . . ANS CHANT MAY DAY 12
BUT THE DAY WILL COME - . . . . . . ANS KIDS WHO DIE 43
COME NOW, ALL YOU WHO ARE SINGERS. ANS SONG OF SPAIN 1
COME TO FIND OUT . . . . SH ANNOUNCEMENT 9
WHEN I COME ACROSS THAT WOMAN . . . SH BRIEF ENCOUNTER 5
WHEN SHE COME OUT . . . . SH DEATH IN HARLEM 93
FOLKS, I COME UP NORTH . . . . . . SH EVENIN' BLUES 1
I COME UP NORTH . . . . SH EVENIN' BLUES 3
HOW DE BLUES THEY COME TO BE. . . . SH EVENIN' BLUES 20

HOW DE BLUES THEY COME TO BE - . . SH EVENIN' BLUES 22
IT COME LAST NIGHT. . . . . SH LETTER 2
YAL, COME ON BACK - I KNOW YOU WANT TO. . . . . SH LETTER 9
COME ON HOME AND BAKE SOME CORN BREAD. . . . . SH LETTER 16
I SAID COME HERE, LONESOME. . . . . SH MIDNIGHT CHIPPI 5
I'M GONNA TELL THE FURNITURE MAN TO COME . . . . SH PAY DAY 11
I WOULDN'T TAKE YOU BACK IF YOU COME ON YOUR KNEES. . . . . SH SUNDAY 9
COME WHAT MAY. . . . . JC BLD SAM SOLOMON 24
COME TO BE. . . . . JC HOW ABOUT DIXIE 4
SEASONS COME, SEASONS GO. . . . . . FW CIRCLES 4
WANTS ME TO COME BACK . . . . FW DUSTBOWL 2
WANTS ME TO COME BACK . . . . FW DUSTBOWL 8
TO COME BACK. . . . . FW DUSTBOWL 13
WHEN I COME AGAIN. . . . . FW FAITHFUL ONE 8
THAT NEVER COME. . . . . FW JAIME 4
WHERE BLACK MEN COME TO DRINK AND PLAY AND SING. . . . . OWT JUICE JOINT 34
THE PASSOVER HAD COME. . . . . . . LHR BLD MARY'S SON 2
THE CHILD, COME BACK AGAIN. . . . . LHR PASTORAL 9
WHEN YOU COME UP YOURSELF . . . . . SP BLD LANDLORD 7
COME AND GET THIS MAN! . . . . . . SP BLD LANDLORD 22
AND SHE AIN'T COME HOME YET. . . . SP BLD THE GYPSY 15
TO COME ALONG AN' TALK. . . . . . . SP BOUND NO'TH BLS 12
MIGHT BE THAT YOU'LL COME BACK. . . SP COULD BE 11
THEN GOT PUT BACK WHEN WE COME NORTH. . . . . SP DEFERRED 5
DEMOCRACY WILL NOT COME . . . . . . SP DEMOCRACY 1
TILL THE LAST WORMS COME . . . . . SP DRUM 4
TO COME! . . . . SP DRUM 16
COME! . . . . SP DRUM 17
COME! . . . . SP DRUM 18
COME HERE, BABY, DARLIN'! . . . . . SP EVENING SONG 3
COME DRIFTIN' DOWN ON ME. . . . . . SP FEET O' JESUS 4
FREEDOM WILL COME! . . . . SP FREEDOM'S PLOW 128
THE PEOPLE SAY IT IS PROMISES - THAT WILL COME TRUE. . . . . SP FREEDOM'S PLOW 144
WILL HIS FREEDOM TRAIN COME ZOOMIN' DOWN THE TRACK . . . . SP FREEDOM TRAIN 49
I'VE SEEN THEM COME DARK . . . . . SP GOOD MORNING 17
COME. . . . . SP HARLEM NIGHT SO 1
COME. . . . . SP HARLEM NIGHT SO 14
COME HOME TO DIE! . . . . SP LOVER'S RETURN 19
COME TO MY DOOR. . . . . SP MADAM NUMBER WR 2
BUT I'VE COME TO CALL . . . . SP MADAM WRONG VIS 7
COME TIME TO DIE. . . . . SP MADAM MINISTER 22
COME, DRINK PALM WINE. . . . . . . SP NATCHA 5
COME, DRINK KISSES. . . . . SP NATCHA 6
I COME - AND WHY? . . . . SP NEW YORKERS 5
WHERE I COME FROM . . . . SP NEW YORKERS 6
SO I COME UP HERE. . . . . SP NEW YORKERS 12
AND BEHIND WILL COME . . . . SP PARADE 9
COME TRUE. . . . . SP PASSING 15
COME WITH ME! . . . . SP PORT TOWN 4
COME ON DRINK COGNAC. . . . . SP PORT TOWN 5
COME HERE, I LOVE YOU. . . . . . . SP PORT TOWN 7
COME AND BE MINE. . . . . SP PORT TOWN 8
COME ON, SAILOR. . . . . SP PORT TOWN 13
COME WITH ME. . . . . SP PORT TOWN 16
IF THE WAR HADN'T COME ALONG . . . SP RELIEF 8
THE TAMALE MAN WILL COME BY. . . . SP SUMMER EVENING 23
COME INTO THE CHURCH THIS MORNING. SP SUNDAY MORNING 36
CHILDREN, I COME BACK TODAY . . . . SP THE NEGRO MOTHE 1
DARK ONES OF TODAY, MY DREAMS MUST COME TRUE: . . . . SP THE NEGRO MOTHE 34
AND LET THAT PAGE COME OUT OF YOU - SP THEME FOR ENG B 4
EIGHTH AVENUE, SEVENTH, AND I COME TO THE Y. . . . . SP THEME FOR ENG B 13
BABY, HOW COME YOU CAN'T SEE ME . . SP ULTIMATUM 1
COME WITH A BLAST OF TRUMPETS. . . SP WHEN SUE WEARS 4
WAITING FOR TOMORROW TO COME - . . SP WINE-O 3
LIGHTS AIN'T COME ON YET. . . . . . SP WONDER 2
THEY COME ON NOW! . . . . SP WONDER 4
COME 7! . . . . AYM ASK YOUR MAMA 22
WERE TO COME BACK BLACK. . . . . . PL BIBLE BELT 2
WHEN THE LONG HOT SUMMERS COME . . PL DEATH YORKVILLE 18
THAT COME TO WHITE MIND . . . . . . PL DINNER GUEST ME 5
COME DOWN. . . . . PL DOWN WHERE I AM 16
SEND FOR LENIN! (DON'T YOU DARE! - HE CAN'T COME . . . . PL FINAL CALL 24
FREEDOM WILL NOT COME . . . . PL FREEDOM 1
DARK GHOSTS COME BACK TO HAUNT YOU NOW. . . . . PL GHOSTS OF 1619 2
QUICK, SUNRISE, COME - . . . . . . PL JUNIOR ADDICT 19
QUICK, SUNRISE, COME! . . . . PL JUNIOR ADDICT 35
QUICK, COME! . . . . PL JUNIOR ADDICT 37
SUNRISE, PLEASE COME! . . . . PL JUNIOR ADDICT 38
COME! COME! . . . . PL JUNIOR ADDICT 39
COME! COME! . . . . PL JUNIOR ADDICT 39
HE'LL COME TO TOWN. . . . . PL LAST PRINCE 15
HERE I COME! . . . . PL LITTLE SNO HOUS 1
DOWN SOUTH WHERE I COME FROM . . . PL MERRY-GO-ROUND 6
AND TERROR COME AGAIN . . . . PL MISSISSIPPI 6
I KNEW THAT THIS WOULD COME." . . . PL NORTHERN LIBERL 5
COME AGAIN TO TOWN - . . . . PL OCTOBER 16 RAID 26
HERE COME YOU: . . . . PL OFFICE BUILDING 2
WILL COME BACK. . . . . PL OPPRESSION 11
I, BLACK, COME TO MY PRIME . . . . PL PRIME 9

COMEDIANS 1
COMEDIANS IN VAUDEVILLE . . . . . . FC LAUGHERS 17

COMEDY 1
COMEDY. - . . . . WB THE JESTER 4

COMES 26
WHEN DE BOAT COMES IN. . . . . . . FC A RUINED GAL 7
SOMEBODY COMES BY . . . . FC DEATH DO DIRTY 27
TILL DE DAWN COMES IN. . . . . . . FC SATURDAY NIGHT 8
COMES HOME AT NIGHT, - . . . . . . FC WORKIN' MAN 3
AW-OO! YONDER COMES A WOMAN I USED TO KNOW WAY DOWN SOUTH. . . . . NM BROKE 62
WHO COMES? . . . . SL SCOTTSBORO 9
COMES TO A NORTHERN SCHOOL . . . . FW MIGRATION 2
AND SLEEP COMES. . . . . FW SLEEP 6
AND DAWN COMES DOWN THE STREET ALL WANLY WHITE. . . . . OWT JUICE JOINT 4
A NIGGER COMES HOME FROM WORK: . . OWT MAN INTO MEN 1
A NEGRO COMES HOME FROM WORK: . . . OWT MAN INTO MEN 8
A MAN COMES HOME FROM WORK: . . . . OWT MAN INTO MEN 15
THERE COMES THIS SONG . . . . SP AFRO-AMER FRAG 16
MONDAY COMES. . . . . SP CONSIDER ME 45
NEXT TIME A MAN COMES NEAR ME . . . SP CORA 3
WHILE NIGHT COMES ON GENTLY. . . . SP DREAM VARIATION 7
WHEN COMPANY COMES. . . . . SP I, TOO 4
WHEN COMPANY COMES. . . . . SP I, TOO 10
COMES OUT - BUT REPEATS! . . . . . SP MADAM NUMBER WR 28
I WILL BE GOD WHEN IT COMES TO YOU. SP TO ARTINA 11
AS THE TUNE COMES FROM HIS THROAT SP TRUMPET PLAYER 42
SINCE THE MONEY THAT COMES IN . . . SP WHAT? 3
NIGHT EACH NIGHT COMES NIGHTLY . . AYM BLUES IN STEREO 22
COMES THE COLORED HOUR: . . . . . . PL CULTURAL EXCHNG 42
(AND IF NOBODY COMES, SEND FOR ME.) PL FINAL CALL 39
WHEN THE COLD COMES . . . . PL WHERE WHEN WHCH 1

COMETS 1
WHO BREAK AWAY LIKE COMETS $ $ $ $ $ $ . . . . AYM HORN OF PLENTY 20

COMIC 1
A GAY AND LOW-DOWN BLUES. COMIC ENTRANCE LIKE THE CLOWNS IN THE CIRCUS. . . . . NM BLACK CLWN MOOD 1

COMING 12
YOU ARE SURE YOURSELVES THAT IT IS COMING - . . . . ANS KIDS WHO DIE 44
STRONG AS THE COMING OF THE FIRST CHILD . . . . FW EARTH SONG 9
SHE WAS COMING BACK AGAIN. . . . . FW GIRL 8
NIGHT COMING TENDERLY . . . . SP DREAM VARIATION 16
ALWAYS COMING AROUND . . . . SP MADAM CHARTY CH 23
COMING FOR TO CARRY ME HOME. . . . SP MYSTERY 10
COMING HOME. . . . . SP SEASCAPE 8
I WAS THE SEED OF THE COMING FREE. SP THE NEGRO MOTHE 30
COMING FROM A BLACK MAN'S SOUL. . . SP THE WEARY BLUES 15
YOUR NUMBER'S COMING OUT! . . . . . AYM BLUES IN STEREO 1
INSTEAD OF COMING HOME TO DECENT DIE AYM HORN OF PLENTY 54
HE WAS COMING . . . . PL WHO BUT TH LORD 3

COMIN' 6
NIGHT-TIME'S COMIN' DOWN. . . . . . FC A RUINED GAL 12
I'LL CUT YOU DOWN COMIN'. . . . . . NM BIG-TIMER POEM 32
I FEELS DE BLUES A COMIN'. . . . . DK NIGHT AND MORN 5
AIN'T COMIN' FOR ME. . . . . SP BLACK MARIA 5
A-SHOUTIN', GOD, I'S COMIN' SOON. SP JUDGMENT DAY 4
COMIN' HOME TO YOU - . . . . SP LOVER'S RETURN 6

COMMENT 2
COMMENT ON STOOP . . . . SP SISTER 15
COMMENT AGAINST LAMP POST . . . . . SP WHAT? SO SOON! 7

COMMERCIALS 1
AND I CANNOT WRITE COMMERCIALS - . AYM IS IT TRUE? 31

COMMIT 1
CAN COMMIT SUICIDE . . . . SH SNOB 6

COMMITTEE 1
THE COMMITTEE SHIVERS . . . . PL UN-AMERICAN 21

COMMITTEES 1
NO WELCOMIN' COMMITTEES, NOR POLITICIANS OF NOTE. . . . . SP FREEDOM TRAIN 55

COMMITTEE'S 1
THE COMMITTEE'S FAT. . . . . PL UN-AMERICAN 1

COMMON 3
LAND CREATED IN COMMON. . . . . . . SP FREEDOM'S PLOW 158
DREAM NOURISHED IN COMMON. . . . . SP FREEDOM'S PLOW 159
ALSO ILLS QUITE COMMON . . . . . . SP INTERNE AT PROV 16

COMMUNITY 3
IN THE COMMUNITY IS GOOD . . . . . SH SNOB 2
A COMMUNITY OF HANDS TO HELP - . . SP FREEDOM'S PLOW 21
BUT A COMMUNITY DREAM. . . . . . . SP FREEDOM'S PLOW 23

COMPANIONS 1
TOOK TWENTY-ONE COMPANIONS . . . . PL OCTOBER 16 RAID 6

COMPANY 4
WHEN COMPANY COMES. . . . . SP I. TOO 4
WHEN COMPANY COMES. . . . . SP I. TOO 10
SUCH COMPANY. SUCH COMPANY. . . . . SP JOY 8
SUCH COMPANY. SUCH COMPANY. . . . . SP JOY 8

COMPASS 3
A CHART AND COMPASS . . . . JC TO CAPTAIN MULZ 11
OUR CHARTS. OUR COMPASS AND
BELL-BOUY . . . . JC TO CAPTAIN MULZ 53
COMPASS POINTS. . . . . SP SEASHORE THROUG 13

COMPASS' 1
CHOOSE HIS COMPASS' CHOICE. . . . . PL FREDRK DOUGLASS 13

COMPELLED 1
OF THOSE COMPELLED TO STAY - . . . DK IRISH WAKE 4

COMPLAINING 1
WITHOUT COMPLAINING LOUD AND LONG. PL MILITANT 4

COMPLAINT 1
A COMPLAINT TO B GIVEN BY A DEJECTED
LOOKING FELLOW SHUFFLING ALONG . NM BROKE 1

COMPOSER 2
WHEN I GET TO BE A COMPOSER . . . . PL DAYBREAK IN ALA 1
GET TO BE A COMPOSER . . . . PL DAYBREAK IN ALA 21

COMPROMISE 2
THROUGH COMPROMISE AND FEAR. . . . SP DEMOCRACY 4
THROUGH COMPROMISE AND FEAR. . . . PL FREEDOM 4

COMRADE 9
COMRADE LENIN OF RUSSIA. . . . . . ANS BLDS OF LENIN 1
MOVE OVER. COMRADE LENIN. . . . . . ANS BLDS OF LENIN 3
I FOUGHT WITH YOU. COMRADE LENIN. ANS BLDS OF LENIN 7
COMRADE LENIN OF RUSSIA. . . . . . ANS BLDS OF LENIN 9
MOVE OVER. COMRADE LENIN. . . . . . ANS BLDS OF LENIN 11
I LIVED FOR YOU. COMRADE LENIN . . ANS BLDS OF LENIN 15
COMRADE LENIN OF RUSSIA. . . . . . ANS BLDS OF LENIN 17
MOVE OVER. COMRADE LENIN. . . . . . ANS BLDS OF LENIN 19
COMRADE LENIN OF RUSSIA . . . . . . ANS BLDS OF LENIN 25

COMRADES 1
YOU HAVE LYNCHED MY COMRADES . . . JC THE BITTER RIVR 59

COM' 1
COM' HERE. BOY! . . . . FC BRASS SPITOONS 40

COM'ERE 1
SO I HOLLERS. "COM'ERE. BABIES. . . SP SYLVESTER'S BED 23

CONCENTRATED 1
CONCENTRATED TO THE ESSENCE . . . . AYM SHOW FARE PLESE 13

CONCERNING 1
CONCERNING THIS . . . . FW MIGRATION 14

CONCLUDES 1
AN OLD NEGRO MINISTER CONCLUDES HIS
SERMON IN HIS LOUDEST VOICE. . . SP SUNDAY MORNING 1

CONDUCT 1
DISORDERLY CONDUCT . . . . OWT BLD MARGE POLIT 19

CONDUCTED 1
WHERE SIT-INS ARE CONDUCTED . . . . AYM BIRD IN ORBIT 11

CONDUCTOR 1
NO CONDUCTOR AND NO TRAIN. . . . . AYM ODE TO DINAH 43

CONFERENCE 1
THERE SOUTHERN CONFERENCE? . . . . AYM BIRD IN ORBIT 81

CONFIDENT 1
WITH HIS FACE FULL OF LIGHT AND
FAITH. CONFIDENT THAT A NEW WORLD
HAS . . . . NM COLORED SL MOOD 9

CONFOUND 1
TO CONFOUND EVEN HAZEL SCOTT . . . SP TO BE SOMEBODY 11

CONFUSE 1
SEND FOR TROTSKY! (WHAT? DON'T
CONFUSE THE ISSUE. . . . . PL FINAL CALL 26

CONFUSED 1
AND ALL CONFUSED . . . . SP BEALE STREET 2

CONFUSION 2
TO BE CONFUSION . . . . SP SAME IN BLUES 27
THERE'S LIABLE TO BE CONFUSION . . SP SAME IN BLUES 31

CONGO 5
I BUILT MY HUT NEAR THE CONGO AND IT
LULLED ME TO SLEEP. . . . . . . SP NEGRO SPEAKS OF 6
THE BELGIANS CUT OFF MY HANDS IN THE
CONGO. . . . . SP NEGRO 15
LUMUMBA IN THE CONGO . . . . AYM BIRD IN ORBIT 59
BONGO-BONGO! CONGO! . . . . AYM ODE TO DINAH 44
NIAGARA OF THE CONGO! . . . . AYM ODE TO DINAH 47

CONGRESS 1
CONGRESS CASES RUSSIA. . . . . . . SP MIGRANT 30

CONJURES 1
CONJURES UNICORN. . . . . AYM ASK YOUR MAMA 56

CONNIVE 1
WHERE NEVER KINGS CONNIVE NOR
TYRANTS SCHEME . . . . ANS LET AMERICA BE 8

CONQUER 2
TO THE ENEMY WHO WOULD CONQUER US
FROM WITHOUT. . . . . SP FREEDOM'S PLOW 178
AND CONQUER US FROM WITHIN. . . . . SP FREEDOM'S PLOW 181

CONSCIENCE 1
OF THE DO-MOVE COSMIC CONSCIENCE? AYM BIRD IN ORBIT 38

CONSENT 2
WITHOUT THAT OTHER'S CONSENT. . . . SP FREEDOM'S PLOW 104
WITHOUT THAT OTHER'S CONSENT. . . . SP FREEDOM'S PLOW 171

CONSIDER 5
CONSIDER ME. . . . . SP CONSIDER ME 1
CONSIDER ME. . . . . SP CONSIDER ME 16
CONSIDER HER . . . . SP CONSIDER ME 27
CONSIDER ME. . . . . SP CONSIDER ME 41
CONSIDER ME. . . . . SP CONSIDER ME 49

CONTENTMENT 1
WHO DON'T BELIEVE IN LIES. AND
BRIBES AND CONTENTMENT. . . . . ANS KIDS WHO DIE 17

CONTROL 1
WHILE YOU CONTROL . . . . LHP POET TO BIGOT 12

CONVENIENT 1
OPPORTUNISTIC. CONVENIENT EVASION. PL ELDERLY LEADERS 4

CONVERSATIONS 1
WHEN SHE CONVERSATIONS YOU . . . . SP PREFERENCE 13

COOK 2
THAT WHISKEY WILL COOK THE EGG. . . SP BAR 1
WILL COOK THE WHISKEY. . . . . . . SP BAR 4

COOKING 2
I DO COOKING. . . . . SP MADAM'S PAST HI 23
ON THE OLD IRON STOVE WHAT'S
COOKING? . . . . PL CULTURAL EXCHNG 27

COOKS 1
COOKS. . . . . FC LAUGHERS 10

COOKSTOVES 1
COOKSTOVES. . . . . SP GRADUATION 18

COOL 6
PLANT YOUR TOES IN THE COOL SWAMP
MUD. . . . . OWT FLIGHT 1
A COOL BOP DADDY. . . . . SP DEAD IN THERE 5
THEN REST AT COOL EVENING . . . . . SP DREAM VARIATION 5
THEM COOL GREEN LEAVES . . . . . . SP LITTLE GRN TREE 13
COOL FACE OF THE RIVER . . . . . . SP SUICIDE'S NOTE 2
I PLAY IT COOL . . . . PL MOTTO 1

COOLIE 4
LISTEN. COOLIE! . . . . SP IN EXPLANATION 14
GEORGE SALLIE COOLIE BOY GETS TIRED
SOMETIMES. . . . . SP IN EXPLANATION 17
SHUT UP. COOLIE! . . . . SP IN EXPLANATION 48
GEORGE SALLIE COOLIE INDIAN BOY . . SP IN EXPLANATION 51

COOLIES 1
THEY HAD NO INTENTION OF CALLING
COOLIES MISTER. . . . . SP IN EXPLANATION 9

COP 2
OUT THE COP THAT NIGHT. . . . . . . OWT BLD MARGE POLIT 4
BY A WHITE COP - . . . . OWT BLD MARGE POLIT 11

COPPER'S 1
COPPER'S WHISTLE! . . . . SP BLD LANDLORD 25

COPPING 1
COPPING A THRILL . . . . SP UP-BEAT 8

COPS 2
AN' WHEN DE COPS GOT ME . . . . . . FC DEATH DO DIRTY 16
MOTORCYCLE COPS. . . . . SP PARADE 13

CORA 2
'HIND MA FRIEND MISS CORA LEE. . . SP YOUNG GAL'S BLS 2
'HIND MA DEAR FRIEND CORA LEE . . . SP YOUNG GAL'S BLS 4

CORDELIA 3
THEY DONE TOOK CORDELIA . . . . . . SP STONY LONESOME 1
DONE TOOK CORDELIA . . . . SP STONY LONESOME 3
THEY DONE PUT CORDELIA . . . . . . SP STONY LONESOME 6

CORDELIA'S 1
CORDELIA'S . . . . SP STONY LONESOME 18

CORDIAL 1
BLACKBERRY CORDIAL. . . . . SH HARLEM SWEETIES 25

CORN 8
CORN. YOU LIKE . . . . WB CAT AND SAXOPHN 7
HE BOUGHT ME CORN BREAD . . . . . . FC DEATH DO DIRTY 13
AN' SHE DON'T LIKE CORN. . . . . . FC NEW CABARET GRL 6
BUT IF YOU GIMME GOOD CORN WHISKY SH HEY-HEY BLUES 5
BUT GIMME GOOD CORN WHISKY . . . . SH HEY-HEY BLUES 23
COME ON HOME AND BAKE SOME CORN BREAD. . . . . SH LETTER 16
BRINGING THE COTTON AND THE CORN TO YIELD. . . . . SP THE NEGRO MOTHE 12
AS LEDA STREW HER CORN . . . . . . AYM BIRD IN ORBIT 29

CORNER 21
GIRLS. DON'T STAND ON NO CORNER . . SH MIDNIGHT CHIPPI 25
I SAY DON'T STAND ON NO CORNER . . SH MIDNIGHT CHIPPI 27
I WENT DOWN TO THE CORNER. . . . . OWT LONESOME CORNER 1
I USED TO GO ROUND THE CORNER. . . OWT LONESOME CORNER 3
OLD LONESOME CORNER! . . . . OWT LONESOME CORNER 5
WHEN YOU TURN THE CORNER . . . . . SP FINAL CURVE 1
OF 26-GIRL AT THE CORNER. . . . . . SP INTERNE AT PROV 10
THE CORNER . . . . SP KID IN THE PARK 10
IN A CORNER FULL OF UGLINESS. . . . SP MAGNOLIA FLOWER 2
AND THERE WAS ONLY THIS CORNER . . SP MAGNOLIA FLOWER 6
AT HIS CORNER . . . . SP NIGHT FUNERAL 36
LOUNGING ON A CORNER. . . . . SP RAILROAD AVENUE 14
FROM A TENT AT THE CORNER . . . . . SP SUMMER EVENING 12
LIKE A BAD BOY IN THE CORNER. . . . SP TO BE SOMEBODY 7
ON THE CORNER PICKING SPLINTERS . . AYM ASK YOUR MAMA 33
POOL HALL OR BAR ON CORNER . . . . AYM HORN OF PLENTY 70
PUSHED INTO THE CORNER . . . . . . PL BLACK PANTHER 1
PUSHED INTO THE CORNER OF THE . . . PL BLACK PANTHER 3
PUSHED INTO THE CORNER OF . . . . . PL BLACK PANTHER 5
TO THE NEIGHBORHOOD CORNER. . . . . PL CROWNS GARLANDS 9
NOW WHEN THE MAN AT THE CORNER STORE PL HARLEM 8

CORNERS 5
CORNERS . . . . OWT JITNEY 1
ALL THE CORNERS THAT ARE LEFT. . . SP FINAL CURVE 4
AND TURNIN' CORNERS. . . . . SP MOTHER TO SON 11
TO THE FARTHEREST CORNERS . . . . . AYM ASK YOUR MAMA 3
TO THE FARTHEREST CORNERS SOMETIMES AYM IS IT TRUE? 3

CORNETS 1
CORNETS PLAY. . . . . FC CLOSING TIME 11

CORRECTED 1
AND THE TALMUD IS CORRECTED . . . . AYM SHADES OF PIG 24

CORRIDORS 1
OPENING INTO CORRIDORS. . . . . . . SP INTERNE AT PROV 43

CORRUPT 1
TO DEVOUR THE CORRUPT BONES . . . . SP SUNDAY MORNING 11

COSMIC 1
OF THE DO-MOVE COSMIC CONSCIENCE? AYM BIRD IN ORBIT 38

COST 1
THEY COST ME MORE . . . . SP MADAM'S CALLING 3

COSTLY 1
IBM ELECTRIC BONGO DRUMS ARE COSTLY. AYM SHOW FARE PLESE 7

COSTS 2
WHERE A NICKEL COSTS A DIME. . . . PL PRIME 2
WHERE A NICKEL COSTS A DIME. . . . PL PRIME 11

COTTON 11
IN THE COTTON AND THE CANE. . . . . NM BLACK CLWN POEM 17
AND THE COTTON THAT CLOTHED AMERICA. SP FREEDOM'S PLOW 54
AND THE COTTON FIELD IS FRIGHTENED SP MIGRANT 23
TO MAKE THE COTTON YIELD. . . . . . SP SHARE-CROPPERS 4
TO MAKE THE COTTON YIELD. . . . . . SP SHARE-CROPPERS 16
BRINGING THE COTTON AND THE CORN TO YIELD. . . . . SP THE NEGRO MOTHE 12
COTTON AND THE MOON. . . . . SP THE SOUTH 9
PICKIN' COTTON IN THE FIELD . . . . SP WEST TEXAS 6
SAY HOW WHITE THE COTTON COTTON AYM BIRD IN ORBIT 42
SAY HOW WHITE THE COTTON COTTON . . AYM BIRD IN ORBIT 42
IN THE COTTON FIELDS. . . . . PL WARNING 7

COTTON'S 1
WHEN THE COTTON'S PICKED . . . . . SP SHARE-CROPPERS 5

COUGHED 1
BLOOD COUGHED ACROSS THE SKY. . . . WB CARIBBEAN SUNST 2

COULD 47
I WOULDN'T GO TO HEABEN IF I COULD. FC BAD MAN 18
FEELS LIKE I COULD DIE. . . . . . . FC MOAN 14
I COULD MAKE SIX DOLLARS A DAY . . FC PRIZE FIGHTER 4
COULD HARDLY FIND A JOB THAT OFFERED DECENT PAY. . . . . NM COLORED SL POEM 21
FOR WHAT COULD I ANSWER HIM. EXCEPT. "IT'S A LIE!" . . . . NM COLORED SL POEM 43
AND YOU COULD HEAR THE DROWSY WAILING . . . . DK IRISH WAKE 3
I COULD BE BLUE BUT . . . . DK NIGHT AND MORN 11
I FEEL SO MEAN I COULD . . . . . . SH EVIL MORNING 5
WOMAN THAT COULD MISTREAT ME! . . . SH ONLY WOMAN BLUS 6
SHE COULD MAKE ME HOLLER LIKE A SISSIE. . . . . SH ONLY WOMAN BLUS 7
SHE COULD CHASE ME UP A TREE . . . SH ONLY WOMAN BLUS 9
WOMAN THAT COULD MISTREAT ME. . . . SH ONLY WOMAN BLUS 12
SO'S THAT I COULD EAT. . . . . . . SH OUT OF WORK 6
I WISH I COULD TELL YOU HOW MUCH I DON'T CARE . . . . SH SUNDAY 5
COULD NOT CALL THEIR HOUSE. THEIR HOUSE. . . . . JC TO CAPTAIN MULZ 17
BUT I COULD NOT FIGURE OUT . . . . FW COMMUNION 3
THERE WERE SOME WHO COULD NOT HEAR. LHP BLD MARY'S SON 11
AS THOUGH YOU COULD KEEP. . . . . . SP A HOUSE IN TAOS 27
MADAM COULD LOOK IN YOUR HAND - . . SP BLD FORTUNE TEL 1
SHE COULD TELL YOU ABOUT LOVE. . . SP BLD FORTUNE TEL 5
THAT WOMAN WHO COULD FORESEE . . . SP BLD FORTUNE TEL 29
HOW SHE COULD GET IN TROUBLE . . . SP BLD OF THE GIRL 3
COULD BE HASTINGS STREET. . . . . . SP COULD BE 1
COULD BE 18TH & VINE . . . . SP COULD BE 3
COULD BE 5TH & MOUND. . . . . SP COULD BE 5
COULD BE RAMPART: . . . . SP COULD BE 6
COULD BE YOU LOVE ME. . . . . SP COULD BE 9
COULD BE THAT YOU DON'T. . . . . . SP COULD BE 10
AND AS FAR AS I COULD SEE . . . . . SP CROSSING 16
WHAT COULD POSSIBLY BE ALL-REET? . SP DANCER 22
BABY. COULD YOU SEE YOUR WAY CLEAR? SP DEFERRED 38
WHAT DID NOT SEEM COULD EVER BE: . SP DREAM 4
BUT I RECKON I COULD TREAT YOU . . SP EARLY EVENING 19
I COULD TAKE THE HARLEM NIGHT . . . SP JUKE BOX LOVE 1
I COULD OF HAD THREE - . . . . . . SP MADAM MIGHT-HAV 2
I COULD JUST AS WELL'VE . . . . . . SP MIDNIGHT RAFFLE 13
AND I COULD SEE . . . . SP NIGHTMARE BOOGE 2
LAWD. I WISH I COULD DIE - . . . . SP REVERIE HARLEM 13
I COULD NOT SEE . . . . SP SO LONG 7
HOW I COULD PRAISE MY LORD! . . . . SP TESTIMONIAL 4
I NOURISHED THE DREAM THAT NOTHING COULD SMOTHER . . . . SP THE NEGRO MOTHE 31
YOU COULD HAVE ME WITH YOU . . . . SP 50 - 50 10
COULD I RECOMMEND A MATO. . . . . . AYM HORN OF PLENTY 97
WHERE HE COULD NOT PRAY . . . . . . PL BIBLE BELT 4
NEVER COULD GET. . . . . PL HARLEM 13
I COULD TELL YOU. . . . . PL IMPASSE 1
THEY COULD NOT SEE . . . . PL PEACE 6

COULDN'T 12
BLACK BOYS COULDN'T WORK THEN ANYWHERE LIKE THEY CAN . . . . . . NM COLORED SL POEM 19
WE COULDN'T EAT IN RESTAURANTS; HAD JIM CROW CARS; . . . . NM COLORED SL POEM 24
I COULDN'T FIND NO JOB . . . . . . SH OUT OF WORK 7
COULDN'T FIND NO JOB . . . . SH OUT OF WORK 9
THEY LIKED HIM SO WELL THEY COULDN'T STAND . . . . JC JIM CROW'S LAST 3
COULDN'T TELL. TO SAVE HER. . . . . SP BLD FORTUNE TEL 31
WHO COULDN'T DIG HIM. . . . . SP DEAD IN THERE 19
I TRIED TO THINK BUT COULDN'T. . . SP LIFE IS FINE 3
MAMA. DAD COULDN'T BE STILL YOUNG. SP MAMA AND DAUGHT 17
I COULDN'T READ THEN. I COULDN'T WRITE. . . . . SP THE NEGRO MOTHE 23
I COULDN'T READ THEN. I COULDN'T WRITE. . . . . SP THE NEGRO MOTHE 23
FOR OLD JOHN BROWN WHO KNEW SLAVERY COULDN'T . . . . PL FINAL CALL 22

COULD'VE 2
LOOKS LIKE SHE COULD'VE KNOWED IT SP BLD FORTUNE TEL 19
I COULD'VE DIED FOR LOVE - . . . . SP LIFE IS FINE 25

COUNT 2
AND SEE WHAT COUNT BASIE'S PLAYING NEW. . . . . SH BED TIME 2
DO I SEE A COUPLE? OR DID I COUNT TWICE? . . . . SH BED TIME 13

COUNTRY 6
STOPPIN' IN THE COUNTRY IN THE WIDE-OPEN AIR . . . . SP FREEDOM TRAIN 53
ALL ACROSS THE COUNTRY, EUROPE - . AYM HORN OF PLENTY 41
AND ONE SHOULD LOVE ONE'S COUNTRY AYM HORN OF PLENTY 57
FOR ONE'S COUNTRY IS YOUR MAMA. . . AYM HORN OF PLENTY 58
OF THE COUNTRY CLUB SET. . . . . . PL UNDERTOW 2
EVEN SOGGY COUNTRY CLUB . . . . . . PL UNDERTOW 7

COUNTS 1
FOR THE DUKES AND COUNTS. . . . . . FC JAZZ BAND 4

COUNTY 2
JUDGE GIVES NEGRO 90 DAYS IN COUNTY JAIL . . . . SP BLD LANDLORD 33
THE COUNTY WON'T PAY ME . . . . . . SP MADAM CHARTY CH 17

COUPLE 1
DO I SEE A COUPLE? OR DID I COUNT TWICE? . . . . SH BED TIME 13

COUPLES 1
COUPLES ON THE FLOOR ROCK AND SHAKE. SH DEATH IN HARLEM 33

COURAGE 1
OF COURAGE, OF GOOD-WILL. . . . . . JC TO CAPTAIN MULZ 50

COURSE 13
OF COURSE, THE MAN WITH THE TITLE OF GOVERNOR . . . . ANS CHANT TOM MOONY 26
OF COURSE, THE WISE AND THE LEARNED ANS KIDS WHO DIE 19
AGAIN MANKIND HAS LOST ITS COURSE. JC TO CAPTAIN MULZ 6
OF COURSE, I'M JUST A STRANGER . . OWT STRANGER IN TWN 13
LET THINGS TAKE THEIR COURSE. . . . SP DEMOCRACY 11
(OF COURSE, I MIGHT . . . . SP NUMBERS 6
OF COURSE . . . . AYM IS IT TRUE? 39
OF COURSE . . . . AYM IS IT TRUE? 40
OF COURSE . . . . AYM IS IT TRUE? 41
OF COURSE, WAIT. . . . . PL DINNER GUEST ME 23
LET THINGS TAKE THEIR COURSE. . . . PL FREEDOM 11
CANNOT KNOW, OF COURSE. . . . . . . PL JUNIOR ADDICT 6
OF COURSE - . . . . PL SLAVE 7

COURT 3
CARRIED ME TO DE COURT. . . . . . . FC BLD OF GIN MARY 1
ITS COURT, TOO WEAK TO STAND AGAINST A MOB, ... SL TOWN OF SCOTTSB 3
JUVENILE COURT . . . . SP MADAM CHARTY CH 22

COURTESANS 1
LIKE YOUNG COURTESANS . . . . WB POEME D'AUTOMNE 6

COURTESY 1
GIVES ME THE COURTESY OF ROAD . . . FW SNAKE 3

COURTS 1
AND THE SLEAZY COURTS. . . . . . . ANS KIDS WHO DIE 25

COURT-YARD 1
INTO THE COURT-YARD. . . . . WB SUMMER NIGHT 25

COUSIN 1
WHAT'S HIS NAME, MY COUSIN. . . . . AYM GOSPEL CHA-CHA 41

COUSINS 1
AND THE COUSINS OF THE TOO-THIN SUITS . . . . PL WHERE WHEN WHCH 8

COVENANTS 2
THEY'VE GOT COVENANTS . . . . OWT RESTRICTIVE 10
THEY DRAW UP RESTRICTIVE COVENANTS SP MIGRANT 25

COVER 3
WHAT WAS THE COVER CHARGE, KID? . . FC CLOSING TIME 14
COVER YOU . . . . FW FOR DEAD MIMES 3
WON'T COVER IT ALL - . . . . SP WHAT? 4

COVERED 2
AND ALL THREE COVERED WITH A SHEET OF PAIN. . . . . WB SICK ROOM 6
COVERED WAGONS, STAGE COACHES. . . SP FREEDOM'S PLOW 75

COVERS 1
I PULLED BACK THE COVERS. . . . . . SP HOMECOMING 5

COZY 1
WHEN COZY HOUSES HOLD. . . . . . . SP STRANGE HURT 12

CO-RELIGIONISTS 1
CO-RELIGIONISTS . . . . PL UN-AMERICAN 3

CRACK 3
CAUGHT IN A CRACK . . . . SP CONSIDER ME 36
CRACK WENT THE WHIPS THAT DROVE THE HORSES . . . . SP FREEDOM'S PLOW 59
BLAZED TO THE CRACK OF WHIPS . . . SP TRUMPET PLAYER 7

CRACKED 1
BACK WINDOW'S CRACKED. . . . . . . SP MADAM RENT MAN 15

CRACKERS 5
THE CRACKERS SAID, SAM, ... JC BLD SAM SOLOMON 25
THE CRACKERS SAID, BOY, ... JC BLD SAM SOLOMON 31
THE CRACKERS SAID, SAM, ... JC BLD SAM SOLOMON 37
THE CRACKERS THOUGHT . . . . JC BLD SAM SOLOMON 49
THE CRACKERS WERE IN LOVE WITH HIM. JC JIM CROW'S LAST 2

CRACKLING 1
A CRACKLING FIRE, ... FW CAROLINA CABIN 7

CRADLE 1
SO YOU LIE IN YOUR CRADLE . . . . . PL LAST PRINCE 8

CRANKED 1
SO WE CRANKED UP OUR OLD FORD . . . SP WEST TEXAS 11

CRAPS 1
AN' IF I CRAPS. . . . . FC CRAP GAME 5

CRAP-SHOOTERS 1
CRAP-SHOOTERS. . . . . FC LAUGHERS 9

CRAWFORD 1
AND HEILBRONER, CRAWFORD, ... SP FLATTED FIFTHS 10

CRAWLED 1
AND HE CRAWLED ON HIS KNEES TO HIS HOUSE . . . . SP NOT A MOVIE 4

CRAZY 5
THAT CRAZY LITTLE YALLER GAL . . . FC NEW CABARET GRL 13
IT'S DONE GOT ME SO CRAZY, FEEL LIKE I BEEN TAKIN' COKE, ... NM BROKE 60
CERTAINLY, CHILE, I ALWAYS WAS CRAZY 'BOUT YOU! . . . . NM BROKE 74
LOOKS LIKE WHAT DRIVES ME CRAZY . . SP EVIL 1
TILL IT DRIVES YOU CRAZY, TOO. . . SP EVIL 4

CREAM 3
COFFEE AND CREAM. . . . . SH HARLEM SWEETIES 10
RICH CREAM COLORED . . . . SH HARLEM SWEETIES 17
COFFEE AND CREAM, ... SH HARLEM SWEETIES 34

CREATE 3
WE'RE FIGHTING TO CREATE. . . . . . JC BLACK MAN SPEAK 24
IF WE'RE FIGHTING TO CREATE . . . . JC BLACK MAN SPEAK 25
SAVE THOSE THAT HISTORY BOOKS CREATE. . . . . SP AFRO-AMER FRAG 5

CREATED 4
LAND CREATED IN COMMON, ... SP FREEDOM'S PLOW 158
ALL MEN ARE CREATED EQUAL. . . . . SP FREEDOM'S PLOW 168
ALL MEN ARE CREATED EQUAL . . . . . SP FREEDOM'S PLOW 91
IN LIFE BEING CREATED . . . . SP S-SSS-SS-SH! 3

CREATOR 1
ENDOWED BY THEIR CREATOR . . . . . SP FREEDOM'S PLOW 92

CREDIT 4
THE CREDIT MAN'S DONE TOOK MA CLOTHES . . . . SP DOWN AND OUT 7
DID YOU TELL HER THAT OUR CREDIT OFFICE . . . . AYM ASK YOUR MAMA 10
CUTS MY HAIR ON CREDIT. . . . . . . AYM HORN OF PLENTY 95
WEAVING OUT OF LONG-TERM CREDIT . . AYM SHOW FARE PLESE 24

CREED 1
OLDER THAN CREED. . . . . SP MYSTERY 14

CREEP 1
FEELING DEATH CREEP - . . . . OLD THE CONSUMPTIVE 8

CREEPING 2
CREEPING LIKE FIRE . . . . OLD THE CONSUMPTIVE 9
CREEPING LIKE FIRE FROM A SLOW SPARK OLD THE CONSUMPTIVE 10

CREEPS 1
FROM ONE SIDE TO THE OTHER. BUT NOW A HARSH AND BITTER NOTE CREEPS INTO . . . . NM BLACK CLWN MOOD 9

CREPT 1
SO I CREPT AWAY INTO THE NIGHT . . SP A BLACK PIERROT 3

CREW 2
(NEGRO SKIPPER OF THE BOOKER T. WASHINGTON SAILING WITH A MIXED CREW) . . . . JC TO CAPTAIN MULZ 1
THERE IS A CREW OF MANY RACES, TOO. JC TO CAPTAIN MULZ 47

CRIED 11
CRIED AMONG THE PALMS IN AFRICA . . WB AFRAID 3
A BLACK WOMAN CRIED. . . . . SH DEATH IN HARLEM 115
BUT THE NIGHT-PEOPLE CRIED. . . . . FW POPPY FLOWER 4

A RACE LEADER CRIED. OWT BLD MARGE POLIT 43
I CRIED ON HIS SHOULDER BUT SP HARD DADDY 7
CRIED ON HIS SHOULDER BUT SP HARD DADDY 9
SET ON MY STEPS AND CRIED. SP LATE LAST NIGHT 2
I CAME UP TWICE AND CRIED! SP LIFE IS FINE 6
I STOOD THERE AND I CRIED! SP LIFE IS FINE 17
SHE CRIED, OH, NO! SP MADAM HER MADAM 18
TO ALL THE WORLD CRIED, PL FREDRK DOUGLASS 14

CRIES 6
SO STILL WITH SILENT CRIES. WB SOLEDAD 11
THAT LAUGHS AND CRIES AT THE SAME TIME. FC JAZZ BAND 12
AND CRIES, ALL CARELESS-LIKE FROM REDDENED LIPS! OWT LINCOLN THEATRE 10
THAT CRIES AND CRIES AND CRIES PL GEORGIA DUSK 2
THAT CRIES AND CRIES AND CRIES PL GEORGIA DUSK 2
THAT CRIES AND CRIES AND CRIES PL GEORGIA DUSK 2

CRIMSON 2
LIKE CRIMSON FW FOR DEAD MIMES 4
A CRIMSON TRICKLE IN THE GEORGIA DUSK. PL GEORGIA DUSK 7

CRIPPLE 1
CRIPPLE MR. LONESOME, SH MIDNIGHT CHIPPI 21

CROAK 1
I WOULDN'T PAY HER A PENNY NOW IF I WAS TO CROAK - NM BROKE 25

CROCHET 1
AND CROCHET A QUILT FOR OUR DOUBLE BED, SH LETTER 17

CROCODILE 3
AT THE CROCODILE TEARS SP MOVIES 3
OF CROCODILE ART SP MOVIES 4
IS CROCODILE: SP MOVIES 7

CROOK 1
IS THE SLIM CURVED CROOK OF THE MOON TONIGHT! SP WINTER MOON 3

CROOKS 1
WHEN CROOKS AND KLANSMEN JC GOOD MORN STLIN 29

CROON 1
ROCKING BACK AND FORTH TO A MELLOW CROON, SP THE WEARY BLUES 2

CROONED 1
AND FAR INTO THE NIGHT HE CROONED THAT TUNE. SP THE WEARY BLUES 31

CROONS 2
A BLACK OLD WOMAN CROONS SP PRAYER MEETING 5
A BLACK OLD WOMAN CROONS - SP PRAYER MEETING 8

CROSS 13
GOT TO CROSS THAT RIVER DK WIDE RIVER 13
CROSS THAT RIVER, DK WIDE RIVER 15
AND A WOMAN CROSS THE TABLE WHEN A MAN AIN'T BROKE - SH DEATH IN HARLEM 54
THAT CROSS THE SEA, FW OLD SAILOR 4
SO THEY BUILT A CROSS LHR BLD MARY'S SON 13
MY CROSS FOR YOU LHR BLD MARY'S SON 20
THEY MADE A CROSS LHR BLD MARY'S SON 27
HE DIED ON THE CROSS LHR BLD MARY'S SON 32
IN THE DARK SHADOWS THAT CROSS AND RECROSS SP AUNTSUE'S STORI 15
TO A CROSS ROADS TREE. SP SONG DARK GIRL 4
THROUGH A PARK, THEN I CROSS ST. NICHOLAS, SP THEME FOR ENG B 12
WITH A CROSS AYM GOSPEL CHA-CHA 54
ON THE CROSS PL CHRIST IN ALA. 13

CROSSED 5
I CROSSED HER PALM WITH SILVER, SP BLD THE GYPSY 9
AND I CROSSED AN ICY STREAM SP CROSSING 10
AND HE CROSSED THAT DIXIE LINE SP NOT A MOVIE 6
THE ONES WHO'VE CROSSED THE LINE SP PASSING 11
I AM THE DARK GIRL WHO CROSSED THE WIDE SEA SP THE NEGRO MOTHE 9

CROSSES 4
SADLY RECALLS THE ROWS OF WHITE CROSSES IN FRANCE. NM COLORED SL MOOD 12
BACK FROM THE ACRES OF CROSSES IN FRANCE, NM COLORED SL POEM 15
WHERE THE IRON BRIDGE CROSSES THE STREAM, JC THE BITTER RIVR 60
GOLDEN CROSSES TO A CADILLAC $ $ $ $ $ $ AYM HORN OF PLENTY 14

CROSSING 1
AND THE WATER I WAS CROSSING SP CROSSING 11

CROSS-EYED 2
SHE WOULD BE ALRIGHT IF SHE WASN'T SO BOW-LEGGED, AND CROSS-EYED, NM BROKE 64
YOU LOOKED AT ME CROSS-EYED SP LATE LAST NIGHT 7

CROW 25
WE COULDN'T EAT IN RESTAURANTS; HAD JIM CROW CARS; NM COLORED SL POEM 24
IN A JIM CROW CAP. JC BLACK MAN SPEAK 14
JIM CROW ARMY, JC BLACK MAN SPEAK 17
IS JIM CROW FREEDOM THE BEST JC BLACK MAN SPEAK 19
PROTECTING JIM CROW. JC HOW ABOUT DIXIE 20
THERE WAS AN OLD CROW BY THE NAME OF JIM. JC JIM CROW'S LAST 1
TO SEE JIM CROW GET OUT OF HAND. JC JIM CROW'S LAST 4
PEARL HARBOR PUT JIM CROW ON THE RUN. JC JIM CROW'S LAST 8
THAT CROW CAN'T FIGHT FOR DEMOCRACY JC JIM CROW'S LAST 9
AND BE THE SAME OLD CROW HE USED TO BE - JC JIM CROW'S LAST 10
HAVE MADE UP THEIR MINDS JIM CROW IS THROUGH. JC JIM CROW'S LAST 14
CATCH THAT JIM CROW BIRD, PULL THE FEATHERS OUT HIS TAIL! JC JIM CROW'S LAST 16
TO JIM CROW MY PEOPLE IS A PITY. JC JIM CROW'S LAST 20
YOU AIN'T TELLING NOTHING BUT YOUR JIM CROW LIES - JC JIM CROW'S LAST 22
JIM CROW STARTED HIS LAST STAND. JC JIM CROW'S LAST 29
THE SOLDIER THROWN FROM A JIM CROW BUS BEHIND STEEL BARS, JC THE BITTER RIVR 33
GOT A JIM CROW CAR SET ASIDE FOR ME. SP FREEDOM TRAIN 10
I HOPE THERE AIN'T NO JIM CROW ON THE FREEDOM TRAIN, SP FREEDOM TRAIN 11
WHY THERE'S JIM CROW STATIONS FOR THE FREEDOM TRAIN? SP FREEDOM TRAIN 32
WHERE THERE NEVER WAS NO JIM CROW SIGNS NOWHERE, SP FREEDOM TRAIN 54
WITH JIM CROW LAWS, SP ONE-WAY TICKET 17
AND RIDE THE JIM CROW CAR UNTIL IT SCREAMS PL JIM CROW CAR 3
WHERE IS THE JIM CROW SECTION PL MERRY-GO-ROUND 3
THERE'S A JIM CROW CAR. PL MERRY-GO-ROUND 10
AT JIM CROW LAWS PL NORTHERN LIBERL 19

CROWD 5
YOU MUST THINK YOU GOT TO WAKE UP A CROWD! SH DAYBREAK 4
EVERYBODY'S HAPPY, IT'S A SPENDIN CROWD - SP DEATH IN HARLEM 36
ABOVE A CROWD OF BLACK FOLK, HUMBLE, MEAN. OWT LINCOLN THEATRE 4
THE CROWD APPLAUDS A PLUMP BROWN-SKIN BLEACHED BLONDE OWT LINCOLN THEATRE 7
SOUND LIKE A GREAT BIG CROWD. SP MORNING AFTER 18

CROWN 6
A CROWN OF SWEAT SP INTERNE AT PROV 35
CROWN ON HIS HEAD, SP JUDGMENT DAY 7
TAKE THE NEON LIGHTS AND MAKE A CROWN, SP JUKE BOX LOVE 3
WHICH CROWN TO PUT SP PRAYER 5
WERE JET A CROWN. SP TRUMPET PLAYER 16
MAKE A CROWN OF SAMMYS, SIDNEYS, HARRYS, PL CROWNS GARLANDS 4

CROWNED 1
IS CROWNED WITH NO FALSE PATRIOTIC WREATH, ANS LET AMERICA BE 12

CROWNS 1
GREAT NAMES FOR CROWNS AND GARLANDS! PL CROWNS GARLANDS 17

CROW'LL 1
BUT WHEN IT IS, JIM CROW'LL BE DONE. JC JIM CROW'S LAST 31

CROW'S 2
OLD JIM CROW'S SORROW? JC BLACK MAN SPEAK 28
NOW THAT CROW'S BEGUN TO LOOK LIKE HELL. JC JIM CROW'S LAST 6

CRUCIFIED 1
CRUCIFIED. PL BIBLE BELT 13

CRUEL 3
BUT THE DREAM WAS CRUEL - AND BITTER - AND SOMEHOW NM COLORED SL POEM 40
PEOPLE WHO ARE CRUEL SP ONE-WAY TICKET 18
PASSIONATE, CRUEL, SP THE SOUTH 15

CRUMB 1
SOMETIMES A CRUMB FALLS SP LUCK 1

CRUMBLES 1
CRUMBLES AS IT'S NIBBLED AYM ODE TO DINAH 14

CRUSH 1
OF DOG EAT DOG, OF MIGHTY CRUSH THE WEAK. . . . ANS LET AMERICA BE 24

CRUSHED 2
THAT ANY MAN BE CRUSHED BY ONE ABOVE. . . . ANS LET AMERICA BE 9
WHO CRUSHED . . . SP MIDNIGHT DANCER 7

CRUSHING 2
CRUSHING THE LIPS. . . . FC BEALE ST. LOVE 4
SCORN CRUSHING ME DOWN. . . . NM BLACK CLWN POEM 52

CRUST 2
OR CRUST AND SUGAR OVER - . . . SP HARLEM 7
OR CRUST AND SUGAR OVER - . . . PL DREAM DEFERRED 7

CRY 30
WE CRY AMONG THE SKYSCRAPERS . . . WB AFRAID 1
CRY AT MY GRINNING MOUTH. . . . WB THE JESTER 12
STARTED IN TO MOAN AN' CRY. . . . FC GAL'S CRY DYING 6
I DON'T CRY OVER TROUBLES. . . . NM BIG-TIMER POEM 58
CRY TO THE WORLD . . . NM BLACK CLWN POEM 75
MY INNER CRY? . . . DK MINSTREL MAN 12
WITH A BLOODY CRY . . . ANS LYNCHING SONG 6
I JUST WANT TO CRY: . . . ANS SISTER JOHNSON 3
WORKERS, KNOW THAT WE TOO CAN CRY. ANS SONG OF SPAIN 59
SHE UTTERED A CRY. . . . SH DEATH IN HARLEM 100
CRY BY YOURSELF, GIRLS. . . . SH MIDNIGHT CHIPPI 29
FOLKS STARTED TO CRY IT - . . . OWT BLD MARGE POLIT 14
THE CRY SPREAD OVER HARLEM . . . OWT BLD MARGE POLIT 15
FOR TEARS IF SHE SHOULD CRY. . . . LHR TESTAMENT 8
TO HOLLER, CRY, AND MOAN. . . . SP AS BEFITS A MAN 4
MAKES A GOOD WOMAN CRY. . . . SP EARLY EVENING 6
TO CATCH A RAINBOW CRY. . . . SP IN TIME SILVER 14
AND YOU MAY SEE ME CRY - . . . SP LIFE IS FINE 28
LAWD! AND I WANTED TO CRY. . . . SP LOVER'S RETURN 14
LAWD! THAT I WANTED TO CRY. . . . SP LOVER'S RETURN 16
WHEN PIMPS OUT OF LONELINESS CRY: SP SLIVER SERMON 1
BOWED THEIR HEADS TO CRY. . . . SP SYLVESTER'S BED 8
AND THE CRY THAT TURNED TO MUSIC . AYM GOSPEL CHA-CHA 31
"I-DON'T-WANT-TO-DIE" CRY. . . . PL BLACK PANTHER 4
NOT MOAN OR CRY. . . . PL COLOR 8
SEND FOR DREYFUS TO CRY, "J'ACCUSE!" PL FINAL CALL 12
FOR LUMUMBA TO CRY "FREEDOM NOW!" PL FINAL CALL 18
TO THE JINGO CRY . . . PL LAST PRINCE 10
MAMA, DON'T CRY. . . . PL WITHOUT BENEFIT 19
THAT ALMOST MAKE ME CRY. . . . PL WORDS LIKE FREE 6

CRYING 7
THE LAST CRYING BABY SLEEPS . . . WB SUMMER NIGHT 7
ON EVERY LYNCHING TREE, A POSTER CRYING FREE . . . ANS OPEN LETTER 44
BETWEEN TEARS AND CRYING. . . . FW BORDER LINE 4
FROM NOT CRYING. . . . FW GRIEF 3
FAINTING, FANNING, AND CRYING. . . SP AS BEFITS A MAN 8
IN MY HEART I'M CRYING. . . . SP MISS BLUES'ES 13
SEND FOR DENMARK VESEY CRYING, "FREE!" . . . PL FINAL CALL 20

CRYIN' 10
NOW THE CRYIN' BLUES . . . WB BLUES FANTASY 11
AN' THERE SHE SETS A CRYIN' . . . FC NEW CABARET GRL 17
TO KEEP FROM CRYIN' . . . DK HOMESICK BLUES 17
CRYIN' TO NO LONESOME BLUE! . . . SH MIDNIGHT CHIPPI 26
CRYIN' TO NO LONESOME BLUE! . . . SH MIDNIGHT CHIPPI 28
I WAS CRYIN' . . . SP LATE LAST NIGHT 5
SO I WAS CRYIN' . . . SP LATE LAST NIGHT 9
A GOOD WOMAN'S CRYIN' . . . SP MISERY 11
INSTEAD OF THAT I'M CRYIN' - . . . SP MISS BLUES'ES 5
BROWN-SKINS CRYIN', "DADDY! . . . SP SYLVESTER'S BED 15

CRYIN'S 1
HE SAID A WOMAN'S CRYIN'S . . . SP HARD DADDY 11

CRYSTAL 3
LIFE FOR ME AIN'T BEEN NO CRYSTAL STAIR. . . . SP MOTHER TO SON 2
AND LIFE FOR ME AIN'T BEEN NO CRYSTAL STAIR. . . . SP MOTHER TO SON 20
CLEAR GREEN CRYSTAL WATER . . . AYM GOSPEL CHA-CHA 30

CUBA 1
UP FROM CUBA HAITI JAMAICA, . . . SP GOOD MORNING 11

CUBAN 1
A CUBAN PORTRAIT . . . WB SOLEDAD 1

CUBBY-HOLE 1
I'M GONNA RENT ME A CUBBY-HOLE WITH A SINGLE BED. . . . SH PAY DAY 17

CUDDLES 2
WHEN I CUDDLES UP TO HIM . . . FC MINNIE SINGS 9
AUNT SUE CUDDLES A BROWN-FACED CHILD TO HER BOSOM . . . SP AUNTSUE'S STORI 4

CULLUD 5
LITTLE CULLUD BOYS WITH BEARDS . . SP FLATTED FIFTHS 1
LITTLE CULLUD BOYS WITH FEARS. . . SP FLATTED FIFTHS 3
LITTLE CULLUD BOYS IN BERETS . . . SP FLATTED FIFTHS 15
LITTLE CULLUD BOYS . . . SP TAG 1
CULLUD NATION! . . . SP WHAT? SO SOON! 6

CULTURE 2
(NOT ETHICAL CULTURE) . . . SP HIGH TO LOW 12
CULTURE, THEY SAY, IS A TWO-WAY STREET: . . . PL CULTURAL EXCHNG 58

CUP 1
AND MAKE ME DRINK OF THE BITTER CUP JC THE BITTER RIVR 57

CUPS 2
LIKE THE WINE CUPS OF SOLOMON. . . FC BRASS SPITOONS 35
THEY SELL BEER FOAMING THERE IN MUG-LIKE CUPS. . . . OWT JUICE JOINT 5

CUR 1
CUR DOG, FICE DOG, KERRY BLUE - . . SP WARNING AUGMENT 13

CURB 5
DON'T LET YOUR DOG CURB YOU! . . . SP WARNING AUGMENT 1
CURB YOUR DOGGIE . . . SP WARNING AUGMENT 2
CURB YOU! . . . SP WARNING 3
BUT DON'T LET THAT DOG CURB YOU! . SP WARNING AUGMENT 4
JUST DON'T LET YOUR DOG CURB YOU! SP WARNING AUGMENT 14

CURE 1
TO CURE ILLS OF AFRICA, . . . SP INTERNE AT PROV 13

CURIOUS 1
BUT NO ONE WAS CURIOUS. . . . FW HEART 8

CURLED 1
I GOT MA TAIL CURLED! . . . FC CRAP GAME 2

CURRENT 1
IN CURRENT DEMOCRATIC NIGHT, . . . PL DINNER GUEST ME 11

CURSE 2
GOD! WHY DID YOU EVER CURSE ME . . SH CABARET GIRL 7
WOMEN'S ABOMINATIONS! JUST LIKE A CURSE! . . . SH PAY DAY 19

CURSED 2
IF EVER I CURSED MY WHITE OLD MAN SP CROSS 3
IF EVER I CURSED MY BLACK OLD MOTHER SP CROSS 5

CURSES 1
I TAKE MY CURSES BACK. . . . SP CROSS 4

CURTAIN 1
A YELLOW CURTAIN, . . . SP FULFILMENT 13

CURVED 2
CURVED . . . SP CATCH 6
IS THE SLIM CURVED CROOK OF THE MOON TONIGHT! . . . SP WINTER MOON 3

CUSS 1
CUSS TOO LOUD, . . . SP HIGH TO LOW 5

CUSSED 1
SHE MIGHT NOT'VE CUSSED . . . OWT BLD MARGE POLIT 3

CUSTOM 1
AS IS CUSTOM BELOW ZERO. . . . AYM ODE TO DINAH 12

CUT 14
AIN'T CUT HIM WID NO RAZOR, . . . FC BLACK GAL 3
AN' HAD CUT HIS GAL . . . FC DEATH DO DIRTY 8
I'LL CUT YOU DOWN COMIN'. . . . NM BIG-TIMER POEM 32
AND THEN CUT DOWN DE LOG - . . . SH ONLY WOMAN BLUS 10
THEY CUT YOU . . . SH STATEMENT 2
CAUSE IF I DON'T THEY'LL CUT DOWN MY PAY. . . . SH SUPPER TIME 14
VEILING SHADOWS CUT BY LAUGHTER . . FW DIMOUT IN HARLM 8
YOU GONNA CUT OFF MY HEAT? . . . SP BLD LANDLORD 14
THE HAND SEEKS TOOLS TO CUT THE WOOD. . . . SP FREEDOM'S PLOW 18
THE BELGIANS CUT OFF MY HANDS IN THE CONGO. . . . SP NEGRO 15
CAN CUT A MAN'S . . . SP SLIVER 7
ELSE I'LL CUT YOU OFF . . . SP ULTIMATUM 6
CUT FROM SHADOWS CUT FROM SHADE . . AYM JAZZTET MUTED 5
CUT FROM SHADOWS CUT FROM SHADE . . AYM JAZZTET MUTED 5

CUTS 1
CUTS MY HAIR ON CREDIT. . . . AYM HORN OF PLENTY 35

CUTTING 3
CUTTING CANE IN THE SUN. . . . ANS BLDS OF LENIN 14
CUTTING THE DARKNESS . . . SP MOONLIGHT NIGHT 3
CUTTING THE DARKNESS . . . SP MOONLIGHT NIGHT 5

CUYO 1
CUYO NOMBRE NO QUIERO ACORDARME. . . . . ANS SONG OF SPAIN 28

CYMBALS 1
BRIGHT POLISHED BRASS LIKE THE CYMBALS . . . . . FC BRASS SPITOONS 33

CYNICAL 1
SYNCOPATED MUSIC, TELLING HIS STORY IN A HARD, BRAZEN, CYNICAL FASHION. . . . . NM BIG-TIMER MOOD 1

C.P.T 1
CAN'T C.P.T. . . . . . SP DANCER 25

DA 5
DA, DA, ... DK NEGRO DANCERS 4
DA, DA, ... DK NEGRO DANCERS 4
DA, DA, DA! . . . . . DK NEGRO DANCERS 5
DA, DA, DA! . . . . . DK NEGRO DANCERS 5
DA, DA, DA! . . . . . DK NEGRO DANCERS 5

DAD 1
MAMA, DAD COULDN'T BE STILL YOUNG. SP MAMA AND DAUGHT 17

DADDLE-DE-DO 1
SKEE! DADDLE-DE-DO! . . . . . SP CHILDREN'S RYME 26

DADDY 31
DADDY. . . . . . WB CAT AND SAXOPHN 13
DADDY, EAGLE-ROCK WITH ME. . . . . FC MA MAN 14
IF MA DADDY DIDN'T LOVE ME . . . . FC MINNIE SINGS 13
IF HER DADDY AIN'T WHITE . . . . . FC NEW CABARET GRL 3
IF HER DADDY AIN'T 'FAY . . . . . FC NEW CABARET GRL 15
DON'T TAKE DADDY AWAY! . . . . . SP AS BEFITS A MAN 18
GOOD EVENING, DADDY! . . . . . SP BOOGIE 1 A.M. 1
A COOL BOP DADDY. . . . . . SP DEAD IN THERE 5
GOOD MORNING, DADDY! . . . . . SP DREAM BOOGIE 1
IF MY CHILDREN ASK ME, DADDY, PLEASE EXPLAIN . . . . . SP FREEDOM TRAIN 31
GOOD MORNING, DADDY! . . . . . SP GOOD MORNING 1
DADDY, AIN'T YOU HEARD? . . . . . SP GOOD MORNING 28
I WENT TO MA DADDY, ... SP HARD DADDY 1
SAYS DADDY I HAVE GOT THE BLUES. . SP HARD DADDY 2
WENT TO MA DADDY, ... SP HARD DADDY 3
SAYS DADDY I HAVE GOT THE BLUES. . SP HARD DADDY 4
MA DADDY SAYS, HONEY, ... SP HARD DADDY 5
GOOD MORNING, DADDY! . . . . . SP ISLAND 11
MY OLD TIME DADDY . . . . . SP LOVER'S RETURN 1
I LOCKED AT MY DADDY - . . . . . SP LOVER'S RETURN 13
DADDY, I WANT SO-AND-SO. . . . . SP PREFERENCE 5
LOVE ME, DADDY - . . . . . SP QUESTION 4
DADDY, DADDY, DADDY. . . . . SP SAME IN BLUES 15
DADDY, DADDY, DADDY. . . . . SP SAME IN BLUES 15
DADDY, DADDY, DADDY. . . . . SP SAME IN BLUES 15
BROWN-SKINS CRYIN', "DADDY! . . . . SP SYLVESTER'S BED 15
FO' TO LOVE YO' DADDY RIGHT!" . . . SP SYLVESTER'S BED 24
DADDY. . . . . . SP WARNING 1
KEEP ON A-LOVIN' ME, DADDY, ... SP YOUNG GAL'S BLS 23
JOHN JASPER! JESUS! DADDY GRACE! . AYM GOSPEL CHA-CHA 44
DADDY . . . . . AYM GOSPEL CHA-CHA 50

DADDY-O 4
DADDY-O . . . . . SP MIGRANT 2
DADDY-O . . . . . SP MIGRANT 5
DADDY-O . . . . . SP MIGRANT 33
DADDY-O. . . . . . SP MIGRANT 41

DAILY 2
THE DAILY NEWS . . . . . SP LIKEWISE 7
IN THE DAILY NEWS. . . . . . PL MOTHER IN WAR 10

DAISY 1
AND THE FIELD DAISY EYES . . . . . PL DAYBREAK IN ALA 13

DAKAR 1
BAHIA LAGOS DAKAR LENOX . . . . . AYM ASK YOUR MAMA 47

DAMASK 1
AT THE DAMASK TABLE, MINE. . . . . PL DINNER GUEST ME 18

DAMBALLA 3
DAMBALLA WEDO OGOUN AND THE HORSE AYM GOSPEL CHA-CHA 15
DAMBALLA WEDO! THE VIRGIN! BEDWARD! AYM GOSPEL CHA-CHA 43
DAMBALLA . . . . . AYM GOSPEL CHA-CHA 47

DAMN 16
DAMN MA BLACK OLD MAMMY'S SOUL . . FC A RUINED GAL 17
DAMN THEIR SOULS, - . . . . . FC DEATH DO DIRTY 32
AND I DON'T GIVE A DAMN - . . . . . NM BIG-TIMER POEM 74
ALARM CLOCK HERE RINGING SO DAMN LOUD . . . . . SH DAYBREAK 3
I SAID, GO, HOT DAMN! . . . . . SH ONLY WOMAN BLUS 22
BUT DE DAMN FOOL . . . . . SH PRESENT 5
I DON'T GIVE A DAMN . . . . . OWT FUNERAL 7
BUT I WOULD GIVE A DAMN. . . . . . OWT FUNERAL 9
I DON'T GIVE A DAMN . . . . . SP CROON 1
NOBODY GIVES A DAMN ABOUT. . . . . SP DOWN AND OUT 6
DAMN A LOVER . . . . . SP LOVER'S RETURN 18
YOU TREAT ME LIKE YOU DAMN WELL PLEASE. . . . . . SP LOW TO HIGH 14
GIVE A DAMN! . . . . . SP MADAM CENSUS 26
BLACK - AND DON'T GIVE A DAMN! . . SP ME AND THE MULE 6
AND IN VOTING NOT GIVE A DAMN . . . PL GHOSTS OF 1619 9
GIVE A DAMN. . . . . . PL IMPASSE 8

DAMS 2
DAMS WILL BE NAMED: . . . . . ANS CHANT TOM MOONY 36
RAILROADS, SHIPS AND DAMS. . . . . ANS OPEN LETTER 62

DANCE 21
DANCE TODAY! . . . . . WB HARLEM NIGHT CL 5
MA MAN AN' ME DANCE. . . . . . FC MINNIE SINGS 8
TO DANCE WITH GLEE. . . . . . NM BLACK CLWN POEM 32
AM I TOO OLD TO SEE THE FAIRIES DANCE? . . . . . DK AFTR MNY SPRNGS 7
THEIR PETALS DANCE ON THE WIND . . DK AUTUMN THOUGHT 4
SO DANCE WITH SWIFT FEET, HONEY, . DK SONG BANJO DANC 16
DANCE WITH SWIFT FEET, HONEY - . . DK SONG BANJO DANC 18
MIGHT NEVER DANCE NO MO'. . . . . . DK SONG BANJO DANC 19
HOW'D A DANCE STRIKE YOU? . . . . . SH DEATH IN HARLEM 44
AND DANCE IN RAIN. . . . . . FW GIRL 22
WHERE SINGING BLACK BOYS DANCE AND PLAY EACH NIGHT . . . . . OWT JUICE JOINT 2
DARK DANCERS DANCE AND DREAMERS SEEK A STAR . . . . . OWT JUICE JOINT 39
DANCE IN THIS JUICE JOINT . . . . . OWT JUICE JOINT 47
O, TRIBAL DANCE! . . . . . OWT NEGRO SERVANT 3
DANCE! . . . . . SP DANSE AFRICAINE 6
TO WHIRL AND TO DANCE . . . . . SP DREAM VARIATION 3
DANCE! WHIRL! WHIRL! . . . . . SP DREAM VARIATION 12
DANCE WITH YOU TILL DAY - . . . . . SP JUKE BOX LOVE 11
DANCE WITH YOU, MY SWEET BROWN HARLEM GIRL. . . . . . SP JUKE BOX LOVE 12
BABY, DANCE WITH ME! . . . . . SP SUNDAY BY COMB 7
THAT HOODED SERPENTS MAY DANCE. . . PL SPECIAL BULLTIN 4

DANCED 1
SHE DANCED IN SUNSHINE . . . . . FW GIRL 3

DANCER 2
MIDNIGHT DANCER OF THE JAZZY HOUR? WB NUDE YOUNG DANC 2
EVEN A GREAT DANCER . . . . . SP DANCER 24

DANCERS 10
YET AS THE VULGAR DANCERS WHIRLED WB CABARET 3
OF KING DAVID'S DANCERS. . . . . . FC BRASS SPITOONS 34
DANCERS WHIRL. . . . . . FC CLOSING TIME 12
DANCERS, ... FC LAUGHERS 3
DANCERS - . . . . . FC LAUGHERS 23
GOD! WHAT DANCERS! . . . . . FC LAUGHERS 24
SINGERS AND DANCERS. . . . . . FC LAUGHERS 27
DANCERS AND LAUGHERS. . . . . . FC LAUGHERS 28
DARK DANCERS DANCE AND DREAMERS SEEK A STAR . . . . . OWT JUICE JOINT 39
DANCERS BOJANGLES LATE LAMENTED $ $ $ $ . . . . . AYM HORN OF PLENTY 5

DANCIN 3
DANCIN CLOSE, AND DANCIN SWEET, . . SH DEATH IN HARLEM 22
DANCIN CLOSE, AND DANCIN SWEET, . . SH DEATH IN HARLEM 22
CAUSE WE DANCIN DOWN! . . . . . SH DEATH IN HARLEM 57

DANCING 9
A DANCING GIRL WHOSE EYES ARE BOLD WB JAZZONIA 5
JOY, A BURST OF MUSIC, STRUTTING AND DANCING, THEN SUDDEN SADNESS AGAIN. . . . . . NM BLACK CLWN MOOD 3
ARE GAY WITH DANCING, ... DK MINSTREL MAN 14
GYPSIES, GUITARS, DANCING . . . . . ANS SONG OF SPAIN 6
AND GAY DANCING FEET . . . . . OWT JUICE JOINT 14
THAT GOAD BLACK FEET TO DANCING ON BARE FLOORS. . . . . . OWT JUICE JOINT 20
OF DANCING SOUND . . . . . SP COLLEGE FORMAL 12
SLIM, DANCING JOY, ... SP JOY 2
ALL THAT MUSIC, ALL THAT DANCING . AYM SHOW FARE PLESE 12

DANCIN' 5
BELIEVE I'LL DO A LITTLE DANCIN' . SH EVENIN' BLUES 13
A LITTLE DANCIN' . . . . . SH EVENIN' BLUES 15
CAUSE WHEN I'M DANCIN' . . . . . SH EVENIN' BLUES 17
I FEEL LIKE DANCIN', BABY, ... SP SUNDAY BY COMB 1
I FEEL LIKE DANCIN'! . . . . . SP SUNDAY BY COMB 6

DANGER 2
THROUGH THE JUNGLE OF WHITE DANGER AYM ODE TO DINAH 31
WHEN DANGER IS NOT NEAR, ... PL SWEET WORDS RAC 10

DANGEROUS 4
DANGEROUS . . . . . JC TO CAPTAIN MULZ 2
YES, DANGEROUS ARE THE WIDE WORLD'S WATERS STILL. . . . . . JC TO CAPTAIN MULZ 29
THAT SAILS THESE DANGEROUS SEAS - JC TO CAPTAIN MULZ 40
ARE SOMETIMES AS DANGEROUS . . . . SP SLIVER 3

DAR 1

MARION ANDERSON SAID TO THE DAR. . . . JC JIM CROW'S LAST 17

DARE 9

VIRGINIA DARE WINE - . . . . SH HARLEM SWEETIES 26
I DON'T DARE START THINKING IN THE MORNING. . . . . SP BLUES AT DAWN 1
I DON'T DARE START THINKING IN THE MORNING. . . . . SP BLUES AT DAWN 2
SO I DON'T DARE START THINKING IN THE MORNING. . . . . SP BLUES AT DAWN 5
I DON'T DARE REMEMBER IN THE MORNING SP BLUES AT DAWN 6
DON'T DARE REMEMBER IN THE MORNING. SP BLUES AT DAWN 7
SO I DON'T DARE REMEMBER IN THE MORNING. . . . . SP BLUES AT DAWN 10
NOBODY'LL DARE . . . . SP I, TOO 11
SEND FOR LENIN! (DON'T YOU DARE! - HE CAN'T COME . . . . PL FINAL CALL 24

DARES 1

DARES KEEP DOWN THE CHILDREN OF THE NEGRO MOTHER. . . . . SP THE NEGRO MOTHE 52

DARING 2

THAT EVEN YET ITS MIGHTY DARING SINGS . . . . ANS LET AMERICA BE 42
DARING THE SEA - . . . . JC TO CAPTAIN MULZ 68

DARK 83

STAINING THE DARK SEA RED. . . . . WB CARIBBEAN SUNST 3
DARK HARLEM. . . . . WB DISILLUSION 6
OH, GREAT DARK CITY. . . . . WB DISILLUSION 12
DARK BROWN GIRLS . . . . WB HARLEM NIGHT CL 10
THOU DARK ONE. . . . . WB SONGS DARK VIRG 6
THOU DARK ONE. . . . . WB SONGS DARK VIRG 14
THOU DARK ONE. . . . . WB SONGS DARK VIRG 19
DARK LAND OF DEATH . . . . WB TO LITTLE LOVER 6
HER DARK BROWN FACE . . . . WB YOUNG PROSTITUT 1
DARK BABY. . . . . FC CRAP GAME 6
AND BURNING THE DARK. . . . . OLD THE CONSUMPTIVE 12
AND HELPLESSNESS. THE MUSIC IS LIKE A MOURNFUL TOM-TOM IN THE DARK! BUT . . . . NM BLACK CLWN MOOD 11
AND THAT OUR DARK BLOOD WOULD WIPE AWAY THE STAIN . . . . NM COLORED SL POEM 8
AND NO LONGER DO WE KNOW THE DARK MISERY . . . . NM COLORED SL POEM 30
THEN HIS DARK FACE SMILED AT ME IN THE NIGHT - . . . . NM COLORED SL POEM 39
TODAY'S DARK CHILD, TOMORROW'S STRONG MAN: . . . . NM DARK YOUTH USA 2
I AM DARK YOUTH . . . . NM DARK YOUTH USA 8
TILL BEAUTY AND PRIDE FILLS EACH DARK FACE . . . . NM DARK YOUTH USA 20
IN THE DARK THEY FELL A-CRYING . . DK IRISH WAKE 1
MY LITTLE DARK BABY. . . . . DK LULLABY 2
MY DARK BODY'S BABY. . . . . DK LULLABY 12
OH, LITTLE DARK BABY. . . . . DK LULLABY 19
LOVELY, DARK, AND LONELY ONE. . . . DK SONG 1
FACE THE WALL WITH THE DARK CLOSED GATE. . . . . DK SONG 7
DARK AS THE EARTH. . . . . ANS A NEW SONG 27
DARK MOUTHS WHERE RED TONGUES BURN ANS A NEW SONG 36
SAY WHO ARE YOU THAT MUMBLES IN THE DARK? . . . . ANS LET AMERICA BE 17
FOR I'M THE ONE WHO LEFT DARK IRELAND'S SHORE. . . . . ANS LET AMERICA BE 47
AT A BIG PIANO A LITTLE DARK GIRL SH DEATH IN HARLEM 10
IT'S DARK ON THIS STOOP, LAWD! THE SUN'S GONE DOWN! . . . . SH TWILIGHT REVERI 15
YOU ARE LIKE A WARM DARK DUSK . . . SH YOUNG NEGRO GRL 1
YOU ARE LIKE A WARM DARK DUSK . . . SH YOUNG NEGRO GRL 6
FROM THE DARK LIPS . . . . JC ME AND MY SONG 23
DARK WITH FILTH AND MUD. . . . . . JC THE BITTER RIVR 7
AND DARK BITTER FACES BEHIND STEEL BARS: . . . . JC THE BITTER RIVR 28
IN THE DARK . . . . FW DIMOUT IN HARLM 17
HE IS A LITTLE DARK BOY . . . . . . FW MIGRATION 11
IN THE DARK . . . . FW NIGHT SONG 1
IN THE DARK . . . . FW NIGHT SONG 8
IN THE DARK . . . . FW NIGHT SONG 15
DARK. . . . . FW NIGHT SONG 22
SONGS IN THE DARK. . . . . FW SONGS 2
THAT BROUGHT DARK FACES . . . . . . OWT JUICE JOINT 13
DARK DANCERS DANCE AND DREAMERS SEEK A STAR . . . . OWT JUICE JOINT 39
DARK HARLEM WAITS FOR YOU. . . . . OWT NEGRO SERVANT 11
O, DRUMS OF LIFE IN HARLEM AFTER DARK! . . . . OWT NEGRO SERVANT 15
DARK FACE. . . . . SP AFRO-AMER FRAG 24
MY DARK HANDS! . . . . SP AS I GREW OLDER 25
IN THE DARK SHADOWS THAT CROSS AND RECROSS . . . . SP AUNTSUE'S STORI 15
AFTER DARK. . . . . SP DIVE 6
DARK LIKE ME - . . . . SP DREAM VARIATION 8
NOR DARK . . . . SP END 8
BEFORE THE CIVIL WAR, DAYS WERE DARK. . . . . SP FREEDOM'S PLOW 118
IN THOSE DARK DAYS OF SLAVERY. . . SP FREEDOM'S PLOW 123
DARK TENTH OF A NATION. . . . . . . SP GOOD MORNING 8
I'VE SEEN THEM COME DARK . . . . . SP GOOD MORNING 17
THE STREETS ARE DARK. . . . . SP ISLAND 4
DARK? . . . . SP KID IN THE PARK 8
DYING IN THE DARK. . . . . SP LOVE 8
AND SOMETIMES GOIN' IN THE DARK . . SP MOTHER TO SON 12
DUSK DARK BODIES . . . . SP MULATTO 34
IN THE DARK: . . . . SP NEW YORKERS 16
DUSK DARK . . . . SP RAILROAD AVENUE 1
HARDENING THE DUSK DARK EVENING. . SP RAILROAD AVENUE 24
IN THE DARK OF THE MOON. . . . . . SP SILHOUETTE 4
IN THE DARK OF THE MOON . . . . . . SP SILHOUETTE 7
REACH UP YOUR HAND, DARK BOY, AND TAKE A STAR. . . . . SP STARS 7
FULL OF CHINE BONES IN DARK GLASSES. SP SUMMER EVENING 15
DARK ONES OF AFRICA. . . . . SP SUN SONG 5
TO TELL YOU A STORY OF THE LONG DARK WAY . . . . SP THE NEGRO MOTHE 2
LOOK AT MY FACE - DARK AS THE NIGHT - . . . . SP THE NEGRO MOTHE 5
I AM THE DARK GIRL WHO CROSSED THE WIDE SEA . . . . SP THE NEGRO MOTHE 9
DARK ONES OF TODAY, MY DREAMS MUST COME TRUE: . . . . SP THE NEGRO MOTHE 34
ALL YOU DARK CHILDREN IN THE WORLD OUT THERE. . . . . SP THE NEGRO MOTHE 35
OH, MY DARK CHILDREN, MAY MY DREAMS AND MY PRAYERS . . . . SP THE NEGRO MOTHE 49
HAS DARK MOONS OF WEARINESS . . . . SP TRUMPET PLAYER 3
TURN, OH, TURN, DARK LOVERS . . . . AYM IS IT TRUE? 18
DARK SHADOWS BECOME DARKER BY A SHADE . . . . AYM ODE TO DINAH 51
DARK GHOSTS COME BACK TO HAUNT YOU NOW, ... PL GHOSTS OF 1619 2
THESE DARK GHOSTS TO TAUNT YOU - . PL GHOSTS OF 1619 3
DARK NIGHT . . . . PL OPPRESSION 7
IN THE DARK . . . . PL PEACE 5
DARK BROWN AS . . . . PL THE DOVE 6

DARKER 6

LIKE DARKER RIVERS . . . . SP ISLAND 3
I AM THE DARKER BROTHER. . . . . . SP I, TOO 2
HE LOOKS DARKER THAN HE IS, TOO. . SP NEIGHBOR 9
WHERE THE PEOPLE ALL ARE DARKER . . AYM ODE TO DINAH 121
DARK SHADOWS BECOME DARKER BY A SHADE . . . . AYM ODE TO DINAH 51
WHERE THE LIGHTER IS THE DARKER . . AYM SHOW FARE PLESE 16

DARKEST 1

CUT OF THE DARKEST DAYS FOR A PEOPLE AND A NATION. . . . . SP FREEDOM'S PLOW 137

DARKNESS 19

TOMORROW. . . . IS DARKNESS. . . . WB HARLEM NIGHT CL 20
OF THY DARKNESS. . . . . WB POEM 20
WITHOUT REST IN THE DARKNESS. . . . WB SUMMER NIGHT 11
IN THE DARKNESS . . . . WB SUMMER NIGHT 21
NOR DARKNESS - . . . . DK WALKERS WITH 5
DOWN PATHS OF DEATH AND DARKNESS . JC TO CAPTAIN MULZ 8
ROSE OF NEON DARKNESS. . . . . . . FW CHIPPY 1
SHADOWS VEIL HIS DARKNESS . . . . . FW DIMOUT IN HARLM 5
SOFT AS DUSK THE DARKNESS . . . . . FW DIMOUT IN HARLM 7
HELP ME TO SHATTER THIS DARKNESS. SP AS I GREW OLDER 28
TO THE DARKNESS . . . . SP FATASY PURPLE 9
CUTTING THE DARKNESS . . . . SP MOONLIGHT NIGHT 3
CUTTING THE DARKNESS . . . . SP MOONLIGHT NIGHT 5
AND THE DARKNESS . . . . SP MYSTERY 26
THEN EVERYTHING WAS DARKNESS . . . SP SYLVESTER'S BED 27
OUT OF THE DARKNESS, THE IGNORANCE, THE NIGHT. . . . . SP THE NEGRO MOTHE 40
IN THE QUIET DARKNESS. . . . . . . SP TROUBLED WOMAN 2
OF DARKNESS U.S.A. - . . . . PL DINNER GUEST ME 9
VEILING WHAT THE DARKNESS HIDES. . PL GEORGIA DUSK 4

DARK-EYED 1

SEDUCTIVE AS A DARK-EYED WHORE. . . SP THE SOUTH 14

DARK-FACED 2

AND THE DARK-FACED CHILD, LISTENING. SP AUNTSUE'S STORI 17
THE DARK-FACED CHILD IS QUIET . . . SP AUNTSUE'S STORI 23

DARLING 3

SLIDE ON OVER, DARLING. . . . . . . DK SONG BANJO DANC 7
CHOCOLATE DARLING . . . . SH HARLEM SWEETIES 11
DEAR, DEAR DARLING OLD WHITE MAMMIES - . . . . PL CULTURAL EXCHNG 54

DARLIN' 1

COME HERE, BABY, DARLIN'! . . . . . SP EVENING SONG 3

DARN 1

ROSCOE KNOWS DARN WELL . . . . . . SP MADAM PHONE BIL 16

DAT 7

HEAR DAT MUSIC. . . . . WB TO MIDNIGHT NAN 5
HEAR DAT MUSIC. . . . . WB TO MIDNIGHT NAN 7
LET'S SHAKE DAT THING! . . . . . . FC SATURDAY NIGHT 12
SO BEAT DAT DRUM, BOY! . . . . . . FC SATURDAY NIGHT 21

SHOUT DAT SONG: . . . . FC SATURDAY NIGHT 22
DON'T YOU PLAY IN DAT ROAD. . . . . SP BABY 3
ALBERT, DON'T YOU PLAY IN DAT ROAD. SP BABY 8

DATE 3
ON SAILING DATE. . . . . FW SAILING DATE 6
IT'S SAILING DATE. . . . . FW SAILING DATE 19
TO HAVE A DATE. . . . . OWT BLD MARGE POLIT 32

DATES 1
ON GRAVESTONES DATES ARE PLAYED. . AYM JAZZTET MUTED 13

DAUGHTER 6
FOR EVER HAVIN' A DAUGHTER. . . . . FC A RUINED GAL 18
HOWDY-DO, DAUGHTER! CALEDONIA, HOW
ARE YOU? . . . . NM BROKE 66
WHAT SHALL I LEAVE MY DAUGHTER, . . LHR TESTAMENT 5
WHERE'RE YOU GOING, DAUGHTER? . . . SP MAMA AND DAUGHT 3
DAUGHTER, ONCE UPON A TIME - . . . SP MAMA AND DAUGHT 9
WHERE THE SONG'S MAHALIA'S DAUGHTER AYM ODE TO DINAH 19

DAUGHTER'S 1
BUT NOW MY DAUGHTER'S MARRIED . . . SP DEFERRED 15

DAVE 2
DAVE MEANT HER NO GOOD. . . . . . . SP BLD FORTUNE TEL 18
WHERE DAVE WENT. . . . . SP BLD FORTUNE TEL 32

DAVID'S 1
OF KING DAVID'S DANCERS. . . . . . FC BRASS SPITOONS 34

DAVIS 1
SAMMY DAVIS AND MARIAN ANDERSON . . SP PROJECTION 16

DAWG'S 2
HOUND DAWG'S BARKIN' . . . . FC GAL'S CRY DYING 7
HOUND DAWG'S BARKIN' . . . . FC GAL'S CRY DYING 9

DAWN 14
WHEN THE LITTLE DAWN WAS GREY. . . WB CABARET 6
UNTIL THE NEW DAWN. . . . . WB SUMMER NIGHT 22
TILL DE DAWN COMES IN. . . . . . . FC SATURDAY NIGHT 8
TILL DE RED DAWN COME. . . . . . . FC SATURDAY NIGHT 28
BEING WALKERS WITH THE DAWN AND
MORNING. . . . . DK WALKERS WITH 1
AND WAKE ME UP GENTLE WHEN THE DAWN
APPEARS . . . . SH LETTER 18
DUSK TURN TO DAWN. . . . . FW DUSK 12
AT DAWN . . . . FW MONTMARTRE 4
AND DAWN COMES DOWN THE STREET ALL
WANLY WHITE. . . . . OWT JUICE JOINT 4
SO I WEPT UNTIL THE DAWN . . . . . SP A BLACK PIERROT 7
BEFORE THE EARLY DAWN . . . . SP CHORD 3
FROM DAWN TO DUSK . . . . SP END 5
PLAYBOY OF THE DAWN. . . . . SP GONE BOY 1
IN THAT DAWN OF MUSIC WHEN I . . . PL DAYBREAK IN ALA 20

DAWNIN' 1
RISE AT DAWNIN' FULL OF FUN? . . . SP BLACK MARIA 13

DAWNS 2
I BATHED IN THE EUPHRATES WHEN DAWNS
WERE YOUNG. . . . . SP NEGRO SPEAKS OF 5
SOME DAWNS . . . . SP TOMORROW 7

DAWN-TODAY 1
AND DAWN-TODAY . . . . DK YOUTH 7

DAWN'S 3
THE DAWN'S A-COMIN'! . . . . SP PRAYER MEETING 2
THE DAWN'S A-COMIN'! . . . . SP PRAYER MEETING 4
THE DAWN'S A-COMIN'! . . . . SP PRAYER MEETING 9

DAY 101
HAUNTS ME NIGHT AND DAY. . . . . . WB BLUES FANTASY 12
BRILLIANT AS THE DAY. . . . . WB OUR LAND 11
I WORK ALL DAY. . . . . WB PIERROT 1
I WORK ALL DAY. . . . . WB PIERROT 4
BEYOND THE RIM OF DAY. . . . . . . WB TO LITTLE LOVER 7
TWO DOLLARS A DAY. . . . . FC BRASS SPITOONS 15
AN' DIG ME A GRAVE THIS VERY DAY. FC MINNIE SINGS 17
I COULD MAKE SIX DOLLARS A DAY . . FC PRIZE FIGHTER 4
I WORKS ALL DAY . . . . FC WORKIN' MAN 1
ALL DAY IN THE SUN . . . . OLD THE CONSUMPTIVE 1
WHEN THE DAY IS THROUGH. . . . . . NM BLACK CLWN POEM 7
CAN A CLOWN HAVE HIS DAY. . . . . . NM BLACK CLWN POEM 15
DAY AFTER DAY . . . . NM BLACK CLWN POEM 47
DAY AFTER DAY . . . . NM BLACK CLWN POEM 47
TALKIN' 'BOUT "WE'LL WORK FOR 50¢ A
DAY, IF WE CAN'T GET NO MO'." . NM BROKE 7
DE TIME IS FOURTEEN HOURS A DAY? . NM BROKE 34
WHEN THE NATION CALLED US THAT
MIGHTY DAY. . . . . NM COLORED SL POEM 4
TROUBLE EVER DAY. . . . . DK MA LORD 9
BITTER WAS THE DAY . . . . ANS A NEW SONG 7
THE DAY IS PAST. . . . . ANS A NEW SONG 10
BITTER WAS THE DAY . . . . ANS A NEW SONG 11
THAT DAY IS PAST. . . . . ANS A NEW SONG 16
BITTER WAS THE DAY, I SAY. . . . . ANS A NEW SONG 17
THAT DAY IS PAST. . . . . ANS A NEW SONG 24
THAT DAY IS PAST . . . . ANS A NEW SONG 33
10-VOICES: MAY DAY! . . . . ANS CHANT MAY DAY 27
20-VOICES: MAY DAY! . . . . ANS CHANT MAY DAY 28
40-VOICES: MAY DAY! . . . . ANS CHANT MAY DAY 29
BUT THE DAY WILL COME - . . . . . . ANS KIDS WHO DIE 43
AWAIT THEIR DAY . . . . ANS SONG OF SPAIN 51
BUT SINCE I GOT TO GET UP AT DAY. SH BED TIME 9
IT WAS DAY - . . . . SH DEATH IN HARLEM 138
ON STATE STREET ANY DAY. . . . . . SH MIDNIGHT CHIPPI 18
YOU GOT TO LIVE HERE A YEAR AND A
DAY. . . . . SH OUT OF WORK 12
A YEAR AND A DAY, LAWD. . . . . . . SH OUT OF WORK 13
A YEAR AND A DAY IN THIS . . . . . SH OUT OF WORK 15
THAT EXTRA DAY WOULD GET ME DOWN. SH OUT OF WORK 18
ALL DAY SUNDAY DIDN'T EVEN DRESS UP. SH SUNDAY 1
TO THE POLLS ELECTION DAY . . . . . JC BLD SAM SOLOMON 9
ON ELECTION DAY . . . . JC BLD SAM SOLOMON 22
ON ELECTION DAY, BROTHER. . . . . . JC BLD SAM SOLOMON 36
ON ELECTION DAY . . . . JC BLD SAM SOLOMON 45
NO SUN BY DAY. . . . . JC THE BITTER RIVR 25
"YOUR FOLKS WILL HAVE A BETTER DAY." JC THE BITTER RIVR 40
WILL BRING A BETTER DAY." . . . . . JC THE BITTER RIVR 44
TO A BRIGHTER DAY. . . . . JC TO CAPTAIN MULZ 15
OF A NEWER DAY. . . . . JC TO CAPTAIN MULZ 70
AT THE END OF DAY. . . . . FW FAITHFUL ONE 12
IN THE LONELY DAY . . . . FW LITTLE SONG 6
DAY . . . . FW NIGHT SONG 19
MARGIE'S DAY. . . . . OWT BLD MARGE POLIT 28
MARGIE'S DAY! . . . . OWT BLD MARGE POLIT 57
WHILE GIRLS WHO WASH RICH WHITE
FOLKS CLOTHES BY DAY . . . . . . OWT LINCOLN THEATRE 13
ALL DAY SUBDUED, POLITE, ... OWT NEGRO SERVANT 1
YOU'VE WORKED ALL DAY. . . . . . . OWT NEGRO SERVANT 10
AND A NEW DAY. . . . . SP BLACK MARIA 20
A FELLOW CAME ONE DAY. . . . . . . SP BLD FORTUNE TEL 9
MAKES ME WORK ALL DAY . . . . SP BLUE BAYOU 8
IF I RECALL THE DAY BEFORE. . . . . SP BLUES AT DAWN 8
IT WAS THAT LONELY DAY, FOLKS. . . SP CROSSING 1
IT WAS THAT LONELY DAY, FOLKS. . . SP CROSSING 19
TOMORROW IS ANOTHER DAY. . . . . . SP DEMOCRACY 12
TILL THE WHITE DAY IS DONE. . . . . SP DREAM VARIATION 4
TILL THE QUICK DAY IS DONE. . . . . SP DREAM VARIATION 13
AS TIME GROWS LONGER UNTIL DAY . . SP DRUNKARD 3
THE TASTE OF DAY. . . . . SP DRUNKARD 5
THE BRIGHT DAY CAUGHT ME . . . . . SP FIRED 2
DAY . . . . SP FULFILMENT 9
NEXT DAY . . . . SP GONE BOY 5
PROJECTION OF A DAY! . . . . SP INTERNE AT PROV 30
DANCE WITH YOU TILL DAY - . . . . . SP JUKE BOX LOVE 11
DAY, NIGHT. . . . . SP LONG TRIP 7
NIGHT, DAY. . . . . SP LONG TRIP 8
THE DAY HE CAME ROUND. . . . . . . SP MADAM CENSUS 2
BUT THE NUMBER THAT DAY . . . . . . SP MADAM NUMBER WR 17
THE OTHER DAY. . . . . SP MADAM'S CALLING 2
DAY IN, DAY ROUND. . . . . SP MEXICAN MARKET 4
DAY IN, DAY ROUND. . . . . SP MEXICAN MARKET 4
LOVE TILL THE DAY I DIE. . . . . . SP MIDWINTER BLUES 18
STILL LEFT BY V-J DAY. . . . . . . SP MIGRANT 29
NIGHT AND DAY. . . . . SP MYSTERY 4
NIGHT OF THE DAY BEFORE YESTERDAY SP NIGHT FOUR SONG 3
AND THE DAY AFTER TOMORROW. . . . . SP NIGHT FOUR SONG 4
HIS INSURANCE LAPSED THE OTHER DAY - SP NIGHT FUNERAL 6
IN THE POST OFFICE FOR A RAINY DAY. SP NUMBERS 3
ON THE DAY WHEN THE SAVOY . . . . . SP PROJECTION 1
ON THAT DAY WHEN ABYSSINIA BAPTIST
CHURCH . . . . SP PROJECTION 5
ON THAT DAY - . . . . SP PROJECTION 10
ON THAT DAY, LORD. . . . . SP PROJECTION 15
ONE DAY. . . . . SP RUBY BROWN 8
GONNA RIDE IN MY CHARIOT SOME DAY! SP SPIRITUALS 8
NAME IN THE PAPERS EVERY DAY! . . . AYM HORN OF PLENTY 37
WHO WENT TO SUNDAY SCHOOL THAT DAY PL BIRMINGHAM SUND 2
SAVE FOR ANOTHER DAY. . . . . PL BOMBINGS DIXIE 4
THEY DO NOT LAST A DAY - . . . . . PL CROWNS GARLANDS 13
SEND FOR ADAM POWELL ON A
NON-SUBPOENA DAY. . . . . PL FINAL CALL 37
TOMORROW IS ANOTHER DAY. . . . . . PL FREEDOM 12
SINCE THE DAY BEFORE LAST . . . . . PL STOKELY MALCOLM 6
BUT THAT DAY WAS SO LONG . . . . . PL STOKELY MALCOLM 7
BEWARE THE DAY . . . . PL WARNING 4
ALL DAY EVERYDAY. . . . . PL WORDS LIKE FREE 4

DAYBREAK 2
DAYBREAK IN ALABAMA . . . . PL DAYBREAK IN ALA 3
AND WRITE ABOUT DAYBREAK . . . . . PL DAYBREAK IN ALA 22

DAYLIGHT 4
I MEAN FOUR - BEFORE DAYLIGHT -
S'POSE TO'VE DONE HIT YO' FIRST
STROKE - . . . . NM BROKE 14
IN THE BROAD DAYLIGHT. . . . . . . SH BLD THE KILLER 14
BY DAYLIGHT . . . . SP DIVE 2
JUST STOPPIN' IN THE FIELDS IN THE
BROAD DAYLIGHT. . . . . SP FREEDOM TRAIN 52

DAYS 25

AIN'T DE STYLE NOW DAYS. FC EVIL WOMAN 12
NOR DAYS OF GLOOM. DK WALKERS WITH 4
AND BE A WHITE MAN THE REST OF MY DAYS! SH DAYBREAK 11
FEEL BAD TWO DAYS STRAIGHT. SH EVIL MORNING 14
DESPERATE DAYS FW DANCERS 7
SOME OF THESE DAYS OWT BOARDING HOUSE 3
IN LAZY FAR-OFF DROWSY SOUTHERN DAYS OWT JUICE JOINT 11
JUDGE GIVES NEGRO 90 DAYS IN COUNTY JAIL SP BLD LANDLORD 33
DAYS ARE DONE. SP CASUALTY 4
HORSE A FANTASY OF DAYS SP FLATTED FIFTHS 17
BEFORE THE CIVIL WAR, DAYS WERE DARK. SP FREEDOM'S PLOW 118
IN THOSE DARK DAYS OF SLAVERY, SP FREEDOM'S PLOW 123
OUT OF THE DARKEST DAYS FOR A PEOPLE AND A NATION. SP FREEDOM'S PLOW 137
MY GOOD-TIME DAYS DONE PAST. SP LITTLE GRN TREE 2
NOW MY DAYS ARE LONELY. SP MISS BLUES'ES 11
MONROE'S FELL ON EVIL DAYS - SP MONROE'S BLUES 1
MONROE'S FELL ON EVIL DAYS. SP MONROE'S BLUES 3
ALL MY DAYS SP PORTER 6
BUT MY LOVIN' DAYS IS THROUGH. SP SAME IN BLUES 18
DAYS FILLED WITH FIERY SUNSHINE SP STRANGE HURT 6
IN THE DAYS OF YOUR GREATNESS SP SUNDAY MORNING 26
IN THE DAYS OF YOUR RICHNESS SP SUNDAY MORNING 29
WAITED TWENTY DAYS AYM IS IT TRUE? 25
NOT THESE DAYS. AYM ODE TO DINAH 97
IN THESE LUSH AND THEIVING DAYS PL PRIME 3

DAYTIME 2

DAYTIME OR NIGHTIME JOB. PL JUNIOR ADDICT 32
WHEN DAYTIME FOLKS PL OFFICE BUILDING 4

DAY-PEOPLE 1

THE DAY-PEOPLE LAUGHED - FW POPPY FLOWER 3

DAY'S 4

THEN YOU KNOW A NEW DAY'S SP BLACK MARIA 16
YES, A NEW DAY'S SP BLACK MARIA 21
DAY'S WORK, TOO! SP MADAM'S PAST HI 24
EVERY DAY'S TOMORROW AYM HORN OF PLENTY 88

DEAD 55

DEAD FC SATURDAY NIGHT 18
DEAD, TOO. FC SATURDAY NIGHT 20
AND WHEN I'M DEAD - I'LL KEEP STILL. NM BIG-TIMER POEM 36
BACK, AND EYES SHINING, QUIETLY RECALLING THE VISION, THE DEAD MAN SPEAKS NM COLORED SL MOOD 8
AND IT'S BETTER A THOUSAND TIMES YOU'RE IN FRANCE DEAD. NM COLORED SL POEM 45
AND IT'S A GOOD THING ALL THE BLACK BOYS LYING DEAD NM COLORED SL POEM 51
FOR THE DEAD WHO'D GONE AWAY. DK IRISH WAKE 2
(NOT DEAD! NOT DEAD! SL SCOTTSBORO 22
(NOT DEAD! NOT DEAD! SL SCOTTSBORO 22
NONE OF THOSE IS DEAD.) SL SCOTTSBORO 23
EXCEPT THE DREAM THAT'S ALMOST DEAD TODAY. ANS LET AMERICA BE 61
TO SMASH THE OLD DEAD DOGMAS OF THE PAST - ANS OPEN LETTER 24
AND TURNED DEAD WHITE. SH BLD THE KILLER 16
DE FACT THAT SHE IS DEAD. SH BRIEF ENCOUNTER 14
FACT THAT SHE IS DEAD - SH BRIEF ENCOUNTER 16
HAD GIVE YOU UP FOR DEAD. JC GOOD MORN STLIN 3
BUT YOU AIN'T DEAD! JC GOOD MORN STLIN 4
DONE GIVE YOU UP FOR DEAD - JC GOOD MORN STLIN 38
BUT YOU AIN'T DEAD! JC GOOD MORN STLIN 40
YOU AIN'T DEAD! JC GOOD MORN STLIN 59
TOO DEAD OWT DECEASED 4
WHEN I AM DEAD AND GONE? LHR TESTAMENT 2
LORD, I WISH I WAS DEAD! SP BLD OF THE GIRL 12
FOR HER MAN THAT WAS DEAD. SP BLD OF THE MAN 14
TO BLESS HIM DEAD SP BLD OF THE MAN 19
BUT DEAD IN THERE. SP DEAD IN THERE 11
I DO NOT NEED MY FREEDOM WHEN I'M DEAD. SP DEMOCRACY 13
CAUSE YOU AIN'T DEAD. SP JUDGMENT DAY 9
YOU AIN'T DEAD. SP MADAM FORT TELL 4
SO WHEN I'M DEAD THEY WON'T NEED SP MIDWINTER BLUES 23
HIS WOMAN AND HIS FRIEND IS DEAD. SP MONROE'S BLUES 2
MY WOMAN AND MY FRIEND IS DEAD. SP MONROE'S BLUES 8
CARRIED HIM OUT FOR DEAD SP NIGHT FUNERAL 32
TURNED DEAD WHITE! SP NIGHTMARE BOOGE 8
BUT, THANK GOD, HE WASN'T DEAD! SP NOT A MOVIE 13
GOD BLESS HER, DEAD AND GONE! SP REVERIE HARLEM 6
FROM THE DEAD WEIGHT OF SEA. SP SPIRITUALS 14
SCRATCHING IN THE DEAD FIRE'S ASHES SP THE SOUTH 7
HE SLEPT LIKE A ROCK OR A MAN THAT'S DEAD. SP THE WEARY BLUES 35
IN MY BEIN' DEAD. SP WAKE 4
CAUSE WHEN I'M DEAD SOME SP YOUNG GAL'S BLS 5
BUT I'D RATHER BE DEAD THAN SP YOUNG GAL'S BLS 17
DEAD OR LIVE THEIR GHOSTS CAST SHADOWS AYM SHADES OF PIG 6
SEND FOR DEAD BLIND LEMON TO SING THE B FLAT PL FINAL CALL 13
SEND (GOD FORBID - HE'S NOT DEAD LONG ENOUGH!) PL FINAL CALL 17
MIGHT BE DEAD. PL FREDRK DOUGLASS 5
HE IS NOT DEAD. PL FREDRK DOUGLASS 22
I DO NOT NEED MY FREEDOM WHEN I'M DEAD. PL FREEDOM 13
WHILE JOBLESS I STARVE DEAD? PL GO SLOW 14
THEY KILLED HIM DEAD. PL LUMUMBA'S GRAVE 12
THAT MY SON IS DEAD. PL OFFICIAL NOTICE 3
THE DEAD MEN THERE. PL PEACE 2
FOR THE DEAD BECOME ALIVE. PL SPECIAL BULLTIN 2
OF BEING LAID OUT COLD AND DEAD. PL WHO BUT TH LORD 6
TOMORROW YOU'LL BE DEAD PL WITHOUT BENEFIT 9

DEAF 1

ARE YOU DEAF, DUMB, AND BLIND? JC BLD SAM SOLOMON 32

DEAL 1

AND SLEEK-HAIRED BOYS WHO DEAL IN LOVE FOR PAY OWT LINCOLN THEATRE 14

DEALT 1

DEALT MY BAD-LUCK CARD. SP LITTLE GRN TREE 8

DEAR 15

YOU GOT A GOOD JOB? YES! WELL, I SHO AM GLAD TO SEE YOU, DEAR! NM BROKE 69
YES, UM-HUM! YOU SHO IS SWEET! CAN YOU PAY FO' DE LICENSE, DEAR? NM BROKE 78
DEAR CASSIE: YES, I GOT YOUR LETTER. SH LETTER 1
DEAR LOVELY DEATH LHR DEAR LVLY DEATH 1
DEAR LOVELY DEATH, LHR DEAR LVLY DEATH 9
DEAR DREAM OF UTTER ALIVENESS - SP DEMAND 2
DEAR MAMA, SP LETTER 1
WAS SO DEAR, SO DEAR SP NIGHT FUNERAL 39
WAS SO DEAR, SO DEAR SP NIGHT FUNERAL 39
HONEY! BABY! DON'T GO, DEAR!" SP SYLVESTER'S BED 16
'HIND MA DEAR FRIEND CORA LEE SP YOUNG GAL'S BLS 4
DEAR, DEAR DARLING OLD WHITE MAMMIES - PL CULTURAL EXCHNG 54
DEAR, DEAR DARLING OLD WHITE MAMMIES - PL CULTURAL EXCHNG 54
DEAR OLD PL CULTURAL EXCHNG 56
DEAR DEATH: PL OFFICIAL NOTICE 1

DEATH 38

LIFE AND DEATH, WB SICK ROOM 5
MERCEDES IS A JUNGLE-LILY IN A DEATH HOUSE. WB TO DARK MERCEDE 1
DARK LAND OF DEATH WB TO LITTLE LOVER 6
AND IN THE EARTH-DARK ARMS OF DEATH WB YOUNG BRIDE 4
DEATH, BE KIND FC CLOSING TIME 13
SHE IS DEATH. FC MAMMY 2
DEATH. FC MAMMY 6
AND DEATH BECOMES FC SPORT 10
FEELING DEATH CREEP - DLD THE CONSUMPTIVE 8
DEATH IS A TOWER DLD TOWER 1
ONE IS KNOWN BY THE NAME OF DEATH. DLD TWO THINGS 7
NOBODY BUT DEATH DK PARISIAN BEGGAR 11
A WIDE, DEEP DEATH. DK SEA CHARM 11
CUR OF THE RACK AND RUIN OF OUR GANGSTER DEATH, ANS LET AMERICA BE 80
DEATH AND LOVE AND HEARTBREAK ANS SONG OF SPAIN 7
IN THE DEATH HOUSE. SH BLD THE KILLER 26
DOWN PATHS OF DEATH AND DARKNESS JC TO CAPTAIN MULZ 8
STEALING FROM DEATH FW DANCERS 5
DEATH IN THE NIGHT. FW FRAGMENTS 3
WHERE DEATH FW THERE 1
DEAR LOVELY DEATH LHR DEAR LVLY DEATH 1
DEAR LOVELY DEATH, LHR DEAR LVLY DEATH 9
WHO NAGGED ME TO MY DEATH? LHR TESTAMENT 10
TOUCHING MY BODY OF UTTER DEATH - SP DEMAND 3
WAS LIKE A DOUBLE DEATH, SP DESIRE 2
THAT DEATH IS A DRUM SP DRUM 2
DEATH IS A DRUM, SP DRUM 13
BEAT THE DRUMS OF TRAGEDY AND DEATH. SP FATASY PURPLE 2
I'M JUST OLD DEATH SP MADAM WRONG VIS 13
WHEN THE RUMBLE OF DEATH SP SUNDAY MORNING 2
THAT MEN BE BURNED TO DEATH - PL BOMBINGS DIXIE 7
DEATH AIN'T PL DEATH YORKVILLE 19
WITH BETTER DEATH PL JUNIOR ADDICT 22
DEAR DEATH: PL OFFICIAL NOTICE 1
TO THE MARKET OF DEATH PL SLAVE 2
TO THE MARKET OF DEATH PL SLAVE 13
OF DEATH RATTLES. PL SPECIAL BULLTIN 8
DEATH IS THE BROOM PL WAR 8

DEATHLESS 1

WHEN BEYOND STEEL BARS SOUND THE DEATHLESS DRUMS SL SCOTTSBORO 7

DECCA 1

WITH DECCA. SP BE-BOP BOYS 4

DECEASED 1

EASTLAND AND MALAN DECEASED AYM SHADES OF PIG 5

DECEMBER 3
DECEMBER 7,1941: . . . . JC JIM CROW'S LAST 7
DECEMBER 7,1941: . . . . JC JIM CROW'S LAST 27
DECEMBER. . . . . FW CHIPPY 9

DECENT 7
COULD HARDLY FIND A JOB THAT OFFERED DECENT PAY. . . . . NM COLORED SL POEM 21
NOW AMONGST DECENT PEOPLE. . . . . SP BLD OF THE GIRL 7
OWNED A DECENT RADIO YET? . . . . . SP DEFERRED 47
I CAN UNDERSTAND - SOME DECENT MAN? SP SISTER 6
DON'T DECENT FOLKS HAVE DOUGH? . . SP SISTER 10
INSTEAD OF COMING HOME TO DECENT DIE AYM HORN OF PLENTY 54
DECENT GARBAGE SERVICE . . . . . . AYM HORN OF PLENTY 75

DECIDED 1
BUT INSTEAD DECIDED TO BE BOLD . . PL FREDRK DOUGLASS 7

DECK 1
HE SAT UPON THE ROLLING DECK . . . DK SAILOR 1

DECREED 1
AS DECREED BY FATE . . . . OWT BLD MARGE POLIT 30

DEDICATED 1
(DEDICATED TO THE MEMORY OF CHARLIE LANG AND ERNEST GREEN. . . . . . JC THE BITTER RIVR 1

DEEP 21
DEEP . . . RIVER. . . . . FC CLOSING TIME 8
I'M DEEP IN TROUBLE. . . . . FC MOAN 1
DEEP IN TROUBLE. . . . . FC MOAN 4
EIGHTY-NINE FEET DEEP. . . . . . . FC SUICIDE 14
EIGHTY-NINE FEET DEEP. . . . . . . FC SUICIDE 16
IT AIN'T SO DEEP: . . . . NM BIG-TIMER POEM 2
DEEP IN ALABAMA EARTH . . . . DK ALABAMA EARTH 2
IS DEEP WITH SONG. . . . . DK MINSTREL MAN 4
A WIDE, DEEP DEATH. . . . . DK SEA CHARM 11
AND THE DEEP RED ROSES BLOOM. . . . SH YOUNG NEGRO GRL 5
AS THE DEEP PRODUCTIVE EARTH . . . JC ME AND MY SONG 6
DEEP AND MELLOW SONG . . . . JC ME AND MY SONG 15
DEEP . . . . JC ME AND MY SONG 25
AND DEEP DETERMINATION GEARED TO KILL . . . . JC TO CAPTAIN MULZ 51
THE SEA IS DEEP. . . . . FW EXITS 1
AND HID HER DEEP IN EARTH. . . . . FW GIRL 10
MY SOUL HAS GROWN DEEP LIKE THE RIVERS. . . . . SP NEGRO SPEAKS OF 4
MY SOUL HAS GROWN DEEP LIKE THE RIVERS. . . . . SP NEGRO SPEAKS OF 13
DEEP IN MY BREAST - THE NEGRO MOTHER. . . . . SP THE NEGRO MOTHE 32
IN A DEEP SONG VOICE WITH A MELANCHOLY TONE . . . . SP THE WEARY BLUES 17
DEEP IN THE BLUES . . . . AYM SHADES OF PIG 32

DEEPEST 3
YOUR SHIP IS MANKIND'S DEEPEST DREAM JC TO CAPTAIN MULZ 67
GREAT THOUGHTS IN THEIR DEEPEST HEARTS . . . . SP FREEDOM'S PLOW 148
THREE HUNDRED YEARS IN THE DEEPEST SOUTH: . . . . SP THE NEGRO MOTHE 17

DEEPLY 1
SO DEEPLY SCARRED. . . . . WB SOLEDAD 10

DEFEAT 1
AND NOT DEFEAT. . . . . JC TO CAPTAIN MULZ 74

DEFENDED 1
TOO WELL DEFENDED. . . . . ANS UNION 10

DEFERRED 14
OF A DREAM DEFERRED . . . . SP BOOGIE 1 A.M. 4
DEFERRED. . . . . SP DEFERRED 51
MONTAGE OF A DREAM DEFERRED: . . . SP DIME 3
OF A DREAM DEFERRED? . . . . SP DREAM BOOGIE 4
TO A DREAM DEFERRED? . . . . SP GOOD MORNING 27
WHAT HAPPENS TO A DREAM DEFERRED? SP HARLEM 1
OUR DREAM DEFERRED. . . . . SP ISLAND 10
DREAM DEFERRED. . . . . SP LIKEWISE 27
IN A DREAM DEFERRED. . . . . SP SAME IN BLUES 7
IN A DREAM DEFERRED. . . . . SP SAME IN BLUES 14
IN A DREAM DEFERRED. . . . . SP SAME IN BLUES 21
IN A DREAM DEFERRED. . . . . SP SAME IN BLUES 28
DEFERRED . . . . SP TELL ME 4
WHAT HAPPENS TO A DREAM DEFERRED? PL DREAM DEFERRED 1

DEFIANCE 3
HUMOROUS DEFIANCE. MELANCHOLY JAZZ. THEN DEFIANCE AGAIN FOLLOWED BY LOUD . . . . NM BLACK CLWN MOOD 2
HUMOROUS DEFIANCE. MELANCHOLY JAZZ. THEN DEFIANCE AGAIN FOLLOWED BY LOUD . . . . NM BLACK CLWN MOOD 2
OUT OF SADNESS IT RISES TO DEFIANCE AND DETERMINATION. A HYMN OF FAITH . . . . NM BLACK CLWN MOOD 12

DEFY 1
HE WHO OPPRESSES ME, HIM I DEFY! . NM DARK YOUTH USA 7

DEGENERATES 1
DEGENERATES, ... SP CAFE: 3 A.M. 4

DEGREE 1
BY THE THIRD DEGREE. . . . . PL WHO BUT TH LORD 8

DEGREED 1
WELL-FED, DEGREED, ... PL NORTHERN LIBERL 13

DEJECTED 1
A COMPLAINT TO B GIVEN BY A DEJECTED LOOKING FELLOW SHUFFLING ALONG . NM BROKE 1

DELEGATION 1
HE LED HIS COLORED DELEGATION . . . JC BLD SAM SOLOMON 46

DELIBERATE 1
WITH ALL DELIBERATE SPEED A . . . . AYM ODE TO DINAH 100

DELICIOUS 2
DELICIOUS, FINE SUGAR HILL. . . . . SH HARLEM SWEETIES 44
THE LOBSTER IS DELICIOUS, ... PL DINNER GUEST ME 15

DELIGHT 4
YOU DELIGHT. . . . . JC NOTE TO NAZIS 1
DELIGHT - . . . . AYM BIRD IN ORBIT 2
SHIVER WITH DELIGHT . . . . PL UN-AMERICAN 4
WITH DELIGHT IN . . . . PL UN-AMERICAN 22

DELIGHTED 1
DELIGHTED! INTRODUCE ME TO EARTHA AYM BIRD IN ORBIT 3

DELIVERED 1
A RECITATION TO BE DELIVERED BY A NEGRO BOY, BRIGHT, CLEAN, AND NEATLY . . . . NM DARK YOUTH USA 1

DEM 1
YOU SEE DEM TRUCKS . . . . SP BABY 4

DEMOCRACY 9
THE WORLD'S BEEN MADE SAFE FOR DEMOCRACY . . . . NM COLORED SL POEM 29
WHY DEMOCRACY MEANS . . . . JC BLACK MAN SPEAK 3
DEMOCRACY, PLEASE - . . . . JC HOW ABOUT DIXIE 10
THAT CROW CAN'T FIGHT FOR DEMOCRACY JC JIM CROW'S LAST 9
DEMOCRACY! . . . . JC TO CAPTAIN MULZ 30
DEMOCRACY WILL NOT COME . . . . . . SP DEMOCRACY 1
DEMOCRACY! . . . . SP FREEDOM'S PLOW 185
DEMOCRACY! . . . . SP IN EXPLANATION 37
DEMOCRACY. . . . . SP INTERNE AT PROV 14

DEMOCRACY'S 1
THINKING WE WERE FIGHTING FOR DEMOCRACY'S TRUE REIGN . . . . . . NM COLORED SL POEM 7

DEMOCRATIC 1
IN CURRENT DEMOCRATIC NIGHT. . . . PL DINNER GUEST ME 11

DEMONSTRATE 1
DON'T DEMONSTRATE! WAIT! - . . . . PL GO SLOW 9

DEMURELY 1
WHICH SEEKS DEMURELY . . . . PL DINNER GUEST ME 6

DENIED 2
I REALIZE THE BLESSINGS DENIED TO ME. . . . . SP THE NEGRO MOTHE 22
IS DENIED. . . . . PL BIBLE BELT 8

DENMARK 1
SEND FOR DENMARK VESEY CRYING, "FREE!" . . . . PL FINAL CALL 20

DENNISON 1
IN THE DENNISON HOTEL IN JERSEY. . SP ELEVATOR BOY 3

DENY 2
AMERICAN AM I, NONE CAN DENY: . . . NM DARK YOUTH USA 6
STILL BAR YOU THE WAY, AND DENY YOU LIFE - . . . . SP THE NEGRO MOTHE 46

DENYING 1
BUT NO USE DENYING - . . . . SP BLUE MONDAY 8

DEPRAVED 2
THE SICK, THE DEPRAVED, ... FW PRAYER 3
THE SICK, THE DEPRAVED. . . . . . . SP LITANY 3

DEPRESSION 2
THE DEPRESSION PUT . . . . SP MADAM'S PAST HI 8
IS COLORED FOLKS' DEPRESSION. . . . AYM ODE TO DINAH 126

DEPTHS 2
BLACK LIKE THE DEPTHS OF MY AFRICA. SP NEGRO 7
BLACK LIKE THE DEPTHS OF MY AFRICA. SP NEGRO 19

DESCENDED 1
DESCENDED ALSO . . . . SP CONSIDER ME 50

DESCENDS 1
DESCENDS LIKE A WHITE MIST . . . . WB SUMMER NIGHT 24

DESERT 3
A DESERT OF WATER. . . . . SP LONG TRIP 2
THE SEA IS A DESERT OF WAVES. . . . SP LONG TRIP 9
TO FERTILIZE THE DESERT . . . . . . AYM IS IT TRUE? 16

DESERVE 1
TWO THINGS DESERVE THE NAME. . . . OUD TWO THINGS 2

DESIRE 6
IS ANOTHER DESIRE. . . . . SH ASPIRATION 6
DESIRE TO US . . . . SP DESIRE 1
DISTILLED FROM OLD DESIRE - . . . . SP TRUMPET PLAYER 24
DESIRE . . . . SP TRUMPET PLAYER 25
DESIRE . . . . SP TRUMPET PLAYER 29
WOULD HARDLY DESIRE . . . . PL BOMBINGS DIXIE 6

DESIRING 1
DESIRING. . . . . WB SUMMER NIGHT 17

DESNUDA'S 1
LA MAJA DESNUDA'S . . . . ANS SONG OF SPAIN 23

DESPAIR 4
ECHO THE AGE-LESS, AGE-LONG OLD
DESPAIR . . . . OWT JUICE JOINT 27
IS DUSTED WITH DESPAIR. . . . . . . SP SONG BILLIE HOL 15
REMEMBER MY SWEAT, MY PAIN, MY
DESPAIR. . . . . SP THE NEGRO MOTHE 36
OF HIS DESPAIR. . . . . PL JUNIOR ADDICT 15

DESPERATE 6
DESPERATE HOURS . . . . FW DANCERS 3
DESPERATE DAYS . . . . FW DANCERS 7
THE DESPERATE, THE TIRED, ... FW PRAYER 4
THE DESPERATE, THE TIRED, ... SP LITANY 4
WE ARE THE DESPERATE . . . . SP VAGABONDS 1
THE PANTHER IN HIS DESPERATE
BOLDNESS . . . . PL BLACK PANTHER 8

DESPITE 1
HUNGRY YET TODAY DESPITE THE DREAM. ANS LET AMERICA BE 35

DESSALINES 1
DESSALINES. . . . . SL SCOTTSBORO 18

DESTINED 1
BUT DESTINED SURE TO FLOOD - AND
SOON - . . . . PL JUNIOR ADDICT 10

DESTROY 1
THE EVIL FORCES THAT WOULD DESTROY JC TO CAPTAIN MULZ 52

DETACHED 1
DETACHED. . . . . PL SLUM DREAMS 8

DETAIL 2
EVERY DETAIL MINDING . . . . SP OLD WALT 5
EACH DETAIL MINDING. . . . . SP OLD WALT 9

DETAINED 1
DETAINED IN JAIL . . . . SP JAM SESSION 5

DETECTIVES 1
DETECTIVES FROM THE VICE SQUAD . . SP CAFE: 3 A.M. 1

DETERMINATION 2
CUT OF SADNESS IT RISES TO DEFIANCE
AND DETERMINATION. A HYMN OF
FAITH . . . . NM BLACK CLWN MOOD 12
AND DEEP DETERMINATION GEARED TO
KILL . . . . JC TO CAPTAIN MULZ 51

DETERMINED 1
SYNCOPATED, DETERMINED TO LAUGH. A
BUGLE CALL. GAY, MARTIAL MUSIC. NM BLACK CLWN MOOD 6

DETROIT 2
DETROIT. . . . . FC BRASS SPITOONS 2
CHICAGO, DETROIT. . . . . SP ONE-WAY TICKET 4

DEUM 1
TE DEUM! . . . . SP MYSTERY 18

DEVIL 4
I'M GOIN' TO DE DEVIL AN' . . . . . FC BAD MAN 17
YOU TURNED OUT TO BE A DEVIL . . . SH LOVE AGAIN BLUS 11
BUT THE DEVIL TOLD ME: . . . . . . SP LOVER'S RETURN 17
AND THE DEVIL LICKS HIS CHOPS . . . SP SUNDAY MORNING 7

DEVILS 2
THE WHITE DEVILS OF THE TERROR . . ANS SONG OF SPAIN 50
AND ALL THE LITTLE DEVILS . . . . . SP SUNDAY MORNING 9

DEVIL'S 1
THE DEVIL'S A KLEAGLE WITH AN EVIL
WILL. . . . . ANS BLD OZZIE POWEL 25

DEVOUR 1
TO DEVOUR THE CORRUPT BONES . . . . SP SUNDAY MORNING 11

DEW 5
THEY MISTOOK THE GENTLE DEW, . . . LHR PASTORAL 5
OF GOLDEN DEW. . . . . SP HARLEM NIGHT SO 10
SWEET AS PURPLE DEW. . . . . SP MIDNIGHT DANCER 4
AND FALLING OUT OF HEAVEN LIKE SOFT
DEW. . . . . PL DAYBREAK IN ALA 6
AND TOUCHING EACH OTHER NATURAL AS
DEW . . . . PL DAYBREAK IN ALA 19

DEWDROP'S 1
THE DEWDROP'S . . . . SP SNAIL 8

DEWY 1
WALKING IN THE DEWY NIGHT. . . . . SP AUNTSUE'S STORI 9

DE-DAD 1
SKEE-DE-DAD! DE-DAD! . . . . FC SATURDAY NIGHT 13

DE-DADDLE-DY 1
DE-DADDLE-DY! . . . . SP WHAT? SO SOON! 10

DE-DOP 3
DE-DOP! . . . . SP CHILDREN'S RYME 29
DE-DOP! . . . . SP QUESTION 7
DE-DOP! . . . . SP WHAT? SO SOON! 11

DIAMOND 10
AN' DIAMOND RING. . . . . FC SATURDAY NIGHT 10
DIAMOND RING, CIGARETTE HOLDER, AND
A CANE, TO THE MUSIC OF PIANO OR NM BIG-TIMER MOOD 1
GOT A DIAMOND RING. . . . . NM BIG-TIMER POEM 22
GREAT DIAMOND MOON. . . . . OK LULLABY 17
A DIAMOND OR TWO. . . . . SH BLD THE KILLER 2
NOR THEM TWO DIAMOND RINGS . . . . SH PAY DAY 8
IN SILVER THREAD AND DIAMOND NOTES SP FLATTED FIFTHS 12
DIAMOND RINGS . . . . SP LIKEWISE 6
I WANT A DIAMOND RING. . . . . . . SP SAME IN BLUES 9
(AND I NEVER HAD A DIAMOND . . . . AYM SHADES OF PIG 38

DIAMONDS 1
DIAMONDS IN PAWN . . . . AYM SHADES OF PIG 37

DICE 2
AND DICE INSTEAD OF BOOKS WILL DO NM BLACK CLWN POEM 5
WITH DICE AND WOMEN . . . . SP BEALE STREET 3

DID 63
HAS I DID IT BEFO'? CERTAINLY! . . NM BROKE 31
WE DID NOT KNOW THAT WE WERE
BROTHERS. . . . . ANS OPEN LETTER 47
WE DID NOT KNOW . . . . ANS OPEN LETTER 51
DO I SEE A COUPLE? OR DID I COUNT
TWICE? . . . . SH BED TIME 13
I DID NOT ACT LIKE . . . . SH BLD THE SINNER 11
GOD! WHY DID YOU EVER CURSE ME . . SH CABARET GIRL 7
HOW DID I KNOW WHERE YOU DONE GONE
AT? . . . . SH LETTER 5
AND EVEN IF I DID, I WAS MAD - . . SH LETTER 6
I EVER DID SEE. . . . . SH ONLY WOMAN BLUS 4
DID YOU EVER TRY LIVIN' . . . . . . SH OUT OF WORK 19
I SAY DID YOU EVER TRY LIVIN' . . . SH OUT OF WORK 21
I NEVER DID LIKE THE INSTALLMENT
PLAN . . . . SH PAY DAY 14
HE DID! . . . . SH PRESENT 9
DID MY SWEET MAMA GO? . . . . SH SHAKESPEARE 4
I DID NOT ASK FOR THIS RIVER . . . JC THE BITTER RIVR 51
WHO DID NOT OWN . . . . JC TO CAPTAIN MULZ 20
I DID NOT UNDERSTAND - . . . . . . FW MAN 2
I ASKED MY LANDLADY DID I HAVE
PRIVILEGES. . . . . OWT STRANGER IN TWN 7
DID NOT MAKE ME VERY WISE - . . . . LHR ACCEPTANCE 2
MEN WHO KNEW NOT WHAT THEY DID . . LHR BLD MARY'S SON 6
SHE DID NOT LOVE ME. . . . . SP A BLACK PIERROT 2
SHE DID NOT LOVE ME. . . . . SP A BLACK PIERROT 6
SHE DID NOT LOVE ME. . . . . SP A BLACK PIERROT 11
DID YOU ASK FOR THE BEATEN BRASS OF
THE MOON? . . . . SP A HOUSE IN TAOS 23
BABE, DID YOU EVER . . . . SP BLACK MARIA 11
SAYS, DID YOU EVER SEE THE SUN RISE SP BLACK MARIA 14
DID HE GET ANYWHERE? NO! . . . . . SP DANCER 23
ME, I ALWAYS DID WANT TO STUDY
FRENCH. . . . . SP DEFERRED 21
WHAT DID NOT SEEM COULD EVER BE: . SP DREAM 4
WHAT DID I SAY? . . . . SP DREAM BOOGIE 14
IF I DID! . . . . SP MADAM MINISTER 20
WHERE DID THEY GET . . . . SP NIGHT FUNERAL 3

INSURANCE MAN, HE DID NOT PAY -	SP NIGHT FUNERAL	5
DID YOU?	SP PARADE	26
DID YOU EVER GO DOWN TO THE RIVER -	SP REVERIE HARLEM	1
DID YOU EVER THINK ABOUT YOUR MOTHER?	SP REVERIE HARLEM	5
DID YOU EVER THINK ABOUT YOUR SWEETHEART	SP REVERIE HARLEM	7
THAN THEY EVER DID BEFORE.	SP RUBY BROWN	25
DID IT EVER OCCUR TO YOU, SON.	SP SISTER	7
DID IT EVER OCCUR TO YOU, BOY.	SP SISTER	13
I DID NOT SEE YOUR FACE!	SP SUNDAY MORNING	30
DID NOT THINK IT GOOD!	SP S-SSS-SS-SH!	7
HE DID A LAZY SWAY.	SP THE WEARY BLUES	6
HE DID A LAZY SWAY.	SP THE WEARY BLUES	7
THE STARS WENT OUT AND SO DID THE MOON.	SP THE WEARY BLUES	32
DID	SP WORLD WAR II	10
DID YOU TELL HER THAT OUR CREDIT OFFICE	AYM ASK YOUR MAMA	10
WHAT DID SHE SAY?	AYM ASK YOUR MAMA	13
DID I VOTE FOR NIXON?	AYM BIRD IN ORBIT	16
GRANDPA, WHERE DID YOU MEET MY GRANDMA?	AYM BIRD IN ORBIT	34
GRANDPA, DID YOU HEAR THE	AYM BIRD IN ORBIT	39
GRANDPA, DID YOU FIND HER IN THE TV SILENCE	AYM BIRD IN ORBIT	61
DID YOU EVER FIND HER?	AYM BIRD IN ORBIT	64
DID I WANT TO EAT WITH WHITE FOLKS?	AYM BIRD IN ORBIT	70
WHERE DID I GET MY MONEY!	AYM HORN OF PLENTY	47
DID I KNOW CHARLIE MINGUS?	AYM HORN OF PLENTY	51
AND WHY DID RICHARD WRIGHT	AYM HORN OF PLENTY	52
DID YOU EVER SEE TEN NEGROES	AYM SHOW FARE PLESE	20
DID NOT KNOW	PL BIRMINGHAM SUND	10
DID NOT CARE.	PL PEACE	4
DID I EVER LIVE	PL STOKELY MALCOLM	16
MAKE ME SAY I DID IT.	PL THIRD DEGREE	2
DID YOU NOT CHANGE IT	PL UN-AMERICAN	15

34

DIDN'T

DIDN'T HAVE A FRIEND NOWHERE.	FC BLD OF GIN MARY	4
IF MA DADDY DIDN'T LOVE ME	FC MINNIE SINGS	13
IF HE DIDN'T LOVE ME	FC MINNIE SINGS	15
DIDN'T TURN OUT RIGHT.	NM BIG-TIMER POEM	10
AND DIDN'T HAVE SUCH A BIG MOUTH.	NM BROKE	65
'CAUSE WHEN I WAS LIVING, I DIDN'T HAVE MINE.	NM COLORED SL POEM	18
DIDN'T HAVE ANY SCHOOLS; AND THERE WERE ALL SORTS OF	NM COLORED SL POEM	25
DIDN'T OUR GOVERNMENT TELL US THINGS WOULD BE FINE	NM COLORED SL POEM	33
THAT I DIDN'T WANT TO MEET.	SH BRIEF ENCOUNTER	6
I DIDN'T WANT TO SEE!	SH BRIEF ENCOUNTER	12
NO MUSIC DIDN'T PLAY,	SH DEATH IN HARLEM	125
WHAT DO YOU MEAN, WHY I DIDN'T WRITE?	SH LETTER	3
SURE, I MISSED YOUR TRUNK - BUT I DIDN'T MISS YOU.	SH LETTER	8
ALL DAY SUNDAY DIDN'T EVEN DRESS UP.	SH SUNDAY	1
I DIDN'T UNDERSTAND	FW MAN	11
THEY DIDN'T KILL THE SOLDIER,	OWT BLD MARGE POLIT	42
NO, I DIDN'T TOUCH HER.	OWT FLIGHT	5
BUT I DIDN'T HAVE NARY ONE.	OWT STRANGER IN TWN	5
HE DIDN'T HAVE MUCH SENSE.	SP DANCER	6
HIS EYES DIDN'T LOOK JUST RIGHT.	SP LOVER'S RETURN	4
I DIDN'T ASK HIM	SP MADAM PHONE BIL	14
WHY DIDN'T HE TELL ME SOME'N	SP MADAM PHONE BIL	25
BUT I DIDN'T FIND 'EM.	SP MAGNOLIA FLOWER	4
I DIDN'T MEAN TO STUMP MA TOE ON YOU, LADY.	SP MAGNOLIA FLOWER	9
I DIDN'T MEAN TO STUMP MA TOE ON YOU.	SP MAGNOLIA FLOWER	13
YOU TOLD ME THAT YOU DIDN'T.	SP MAYBE	3
DIDN'T TURN OUT RIGHT.	SP MIDNIGHT RAFFLE	4
DIDN'T HARDLY KNOW MY MIND.	SP MORNING AFTER	2
DIDN'T KNOW MY MIND.	SP MORNING AFTER	4
HE DIDN'T STOP IN WASHINGTON	SP NOT A MOVIE	9
AND HE DIDN'T STOP IN BALTIMORE	SP NOT A MOVIE	10
WE DIDN'T KNOW -	SP WEST TEXAS	14
AND HE DIDN'T TRUST	PL LUMUMBA'S GRAVE	2
AND HE DIDN'T BELIEVE	PL LUMUMBA'S GRAVE	6

56

DIE

KNOWED SOMEBODY'S 'BOUT TO DIE.	FC GAL'S CRY DYING	2
KNOWED SOMEBODY'S 'BOUT TO DIE.	FC GAL'S CRY DYING	4
FEELS LIKE I COULD DIE.	FC MOAN	14
BLACK - YOU CAN DIE.	NM BLACK CLWN POEM	41
IT WAS AWFUL - FACING THAT BOY WHO WENT OUT TO DIE.	NM COLORED SL POEM	42
SERVE - AND HATE WILL DIE UNBORN.	DK ALABAMA EARTH	12
IN AUTUMN THEY DIE AND ARE BLOWN AWAY.	DK AUTUMN THOUGHT	2
FOR IF DREAMS DIE	DK DREAMS	2
I DIE?	DK MINSTREL MAN	16
I'LL LAY DOWN AN' DIE RIGHT NOW.	DK WIDE RIVER	13
IS IT MUCH TO DIE?	SL SCOTTSBORO	4
IS IT MUCH TO DIE WHEN IMMORTAL FEET	SL SCOTTSBORO	5
I FIGHT, I STARVE, I DIE.	ANS BLDS OF LENIN	24
THIS IS FOR THE KIDS WHO DIE.	ANS KIDS WHO DIE	1
FOR KIDS WILL DIE CERTAINLY.	ANS KIDS WHO DIE	3
LETTING KIDS DIE.	ANS KIDS WHO DIE	7
KIDS WILL DIE IN THE SWAMPS OF MISSISSIPPI	ANS KIDS WHO DIE	8
KIDS WILL DIE IN THE STREETS OF CHICAGO	ANS KIDS WHO DIE	10
KIDS WILL DIE IN THE ORANGE GROVES OF CALIFORNIA	ANS KIDS WHO DIE	12
ALL KINDS OF KIDS WILL DIE	ANS KIDS WHO DIE	16
WILL LIVE ON WEAVING WORDS TO SMOTHER THE KIDS WHO DIE.	ANS KIDS WHO DIE	24
WILL ALL RAISE THEIR HANDS AGAINST THE KIDS WHO DIE.	ANS KIDS WHO DIE	29
FOR THE KIDS WHO DIE ARE LIKE IRON IN THE BLOOD OF THE PEOPLE -	ANS KIDS WHO DIE	32
TO TASTE THE IRON OF THE KIDS WHO DIE.	ANS KIDS WHO DIE	34
LISTEN, KIDS WHO DIE -	ANS KIDS WHO DIE	37
THROUGH THE KIDS WHO DIE.	ANS KIDS WHO DIE	51
AND THE BLACK BOY DIE.	ANS LYNCHING SONG	4
AND THE WHITE FOLKS DIE.	ANS LYNCHING SONG	8
THE WHITE FOLKS DIE?	ANS LYNCHING SONG	9
THE WHITE FOLKS DIE?	ANS LYNCHING SONG	11
LIFT ARMS IN VAIN, RUN, HIDE, DIE:	ANS SONG OF SPAIN	60
I'M GONNA DIE!	SH BLD THE KILLER	27
I HATE TO DIE THIS WAY WITH THE QUIET	SH CABARET GIRL	1
I'D RATHER DIE WHERE THE BAND'S A-PLAYIN'	SH CABARET GIRL	3
RATHER DIE THE WAY I LIVED -	SH CABARET GIRL	5
MAKIN' ME DIE THIS WAY?	SH CABARET GIRL	8
CAN'T DIE BUT ONCE.	JC BLD SAM SOLOMON	40
WE WON'T DIE.	JC GOOD MORN STLIN	15
FOR ME WHEN I DIE.	OWT REQUEST REQUIEM	2
BUT I'D HATE TO DIE ALL ALONE!	SP AS BEFITS A MAN	2
AN' YOU DIE.	SP BABY	7
NO BUSINESS TO DIE.	SP BLD OF THE MAN	28
I WONDER WHERE I'M GONNA DIE,	SP CROSS	11
BETTER TO DIE FREE	SP FREEDOM'S PLOW	110
BETTER DIE FREE.	SP FREEDOM'S PLOW	172
IF YOU GONNA SEE ME DIE.	SP LIFE IS FINE	30
COME HOME TO DIE!	SP LOVER'S RETURN	19
COME TIME TO DIE.	SP MADAM MINISTER	22
LOVE TILL THE DAY I DIE.	SP MIDWINTER BLUES	18
BUT EAT, DRINK, STAY BLACK, AND DIE.	SP NECESSITY	4
UNTIL THEY DIE	SP NEW YORKERS	9
LAWD, I WISH I COULD DIE -	SP REVERIE HARLEM	13
"SYLVESTER'S GONNA DIE!"	SP SYLVESTER'S BED	6
DIE?	SP WORLD WAR II	12
INSTEAD OF COMING HOME TO DECENT DIE	AYM HORN OF PLENTY	54
JUST GO AHEAD AND DIE.	PL WITHOUT BENEFIT	13

25

DIED

THEY SAY SHE DIED, -	WB YOUNG BRIDE	1
THEY SAY SHE DIED OF GRIEF	WB YOUNG BRIDE	3
MY BROTHER DIED IN FRANCE - BUT I CAME BACK.	NM COLORED SL POEM	1
'CAUSE THAT'S WHAT I DIED FOR - ISN'T IT, BROTHER?"	NM COLORED SL POEM	36
ATTUCKS DIED	NM DARK YOUTH USA	13
HEART AND DIED	SH DEATH IN HARLEM	117
AND DIED IN PAIN.	FW GIRL	2
WITHERED AND DIED.	FW POPPY FLOWER	2
WITHERED AND DIED.	FW POPPY FLOWER	6
HE DIED ON THE CROSS	LHR BLD MARY'S SON	32
MY OLD MAN DIED IN A FINE BIG HOUSE.	SP CROSS	9
MY MA DIED IN A SHACK.	SP CROSS	10
WITH JOHN BROWN AT HARPER'S FERRY, NEGROES DIED.	SP FREEDOM'S PLOW	116
HER GRANDSON'S NAME WAS JIMMY. HE DIED AT ANZIO.	SP FREEDOM TRAIN	43
HE DIED FOR REAL. IT WARN'T NO SHOW.	SP FREEDOM TRAIN	44
NEITHER HAD NOBODY DIED.	SP LATE LAST NIGHT	4
I MIGHT'VE SUNK AND DIED.	SP LIFE IS FINE	8
I MIGHT'VE JUMPED AND DIED.	SP LIFE IS FINE	19
I COULD'VE DIED FOR LOVE -	SP LIFE IS FINE	25
AND I WISH THAT I HAD DIED."	SP THE WEARY BLUES	30
HE DIED IN 1895.	PL FREDRK DOUGLASS	21
AND DIED	PL OCTOBER 16 RAID	13
YOU SAY HE DIED WITH HONOR	PL OFFICIAL NOTICE	7
A SLAVE WHO DIED YOUNG.	PL SLAVE	4
A SLAVE WHO DIED YOUNG.	PL SLAVE	8

1

DIES

MRS. BETHUNE TOLD MARTIN DIES.	JC JIM CROW'S LAST	21

1

DIET

NURSE, PUT HER ON A DIET.	SP MADAM WRONG VIS	25

3

DIFFERENCE

I THINK THE DIFFERENCE LIES	FW BORDER LINE	3
I SAID, IT DON'T MAKE NO DIFFERENCE NOHOW.	OWT STRANGER IN TWN	9
MAKES NO DIFFERENCE TO ME -	AYM BLUES IN STEREO	30

1

DIFFICULTIES

SEE THE DIFFICULTIES, TOO, AND THE OBSTACLES.	SP FREEDOM'S PLOW	16

DIFF' 1
NO DIFF' NO HOW. . . . . SP DEAD IN THERE 22

DIG 5
AN' DIG ME A GRAVE THIS VERY DAY. FC MINNIE SINGS 17
WHO COULDN'T DIG HIM. . . . . SP DEAD IN THERE 19
AND DIG ALL PLAYS. . . . . SP FLATTED FIFTHS 19
AND DIG ALL JIVE - . . . . PL MOTTO 2
DIG AND BE DUG . . . . PL MOTTO 8

DIGNIFY 1
DIGNIFY THE PLACE . . . . SP SEASHORE THROUG 6

DIGNITARIES 1
CADILLACS WITH DIGNITARIES . . . . SP PARADE 7

DIGNITY 2
IT HAD NO DIGNITY BEFORE. . . . . . FW HARLEM DANCE HA 1
THAT HAD NO DIGNITY BEFORE! . . . . FW HARLEM DANCE HA 8

DIME 22
A DIME. . . . . FC BRASS SPITOONS 13
A DIME. . . . . FC BRASS SPITOONS 18
WHEN YOU AIN'T GOT A DIME. . . . . FC DEATH DO DIRTY 4
HE TOOK MA LAST THIN DIME. . . . . FC GYPSY MAN 14
HE TOOK MA LAST THIN DIME. . . . . FC GYPSY MAN 16
I BEG A DIME FOR DINNER - . . . . . ANS PARK BENCH 5
FACT IS. AIN'T GOT A DIME - . . . . SH IF-ING 14
GRANDMA. LEND ME A DIME. . . . . . SP DIME 2
CHILE. GRANNY AIN'T GOT NO DIME. . SP DIME 6
AN' I NEED A DIME FO' BEER. . . . . SP DOWN AND OUT 10
I NEED A DIME FO' BEER. . . . . . . SP DOWN AND OUT 11
I GAMBLED YOUR DIME AWAY. . . . . . SP EARLY EVENING 8
DONE GAMBLED THAT DIME AWAY. . . . SP EARLY EVENING 10
ON A DIME. . . . . SP FACT 4
HE PLAYED A DIME. . . . . SP MADAM NUMBER WR 13
WITHOUT A DIME. . . . . SP MIDNIGHT RAFFLE 8
GONNA SALT EVERY DIME AWAY . . . . SP NUMBERS 2
A DIME ON THOSE TWO BOTTLES. . . . SP SUMMER EVENING 29
VINGT FRANCS NICKEL DIME . . . . . AYM ASK YOUR MAMA 46
WHERE A NICKEL COSTS A DIME. . . . PL PRIME 2
SKIM EVEN A DIME - . . . . PL PRIME 8
WHERE A NICKEL COSTS A DIME. . . . PL PRIME 11

DIMES 2
ALL MIXED UP WITH DIMES AND . . . . FC BRASS SPITOONS 28
TWO DIMES AND A NICKLE ONLY . . . . SP TOMORROW 3

DIMMED 1
DIMMED TOO SOON. . . . . SP GYPSY MELODIES 5

DIMMING 1
DIMMING. . . . . SP AS I GREW OLDER 12

DIMOUT 1
IN THE DUSKY DIMOUT . . . . FW DIMOUT IN HARLM 3

DINAH 2
TO A DISC BY DINAH . . . . AYM ODE TO DINAH 15
MEANWHILE DINAH EATING CHICKEN . . AYM ODE TO DINAH 129

DINAH'S 2
WHERE DINAH'S SONGS ARE MADE . . . AYM ODE TO DINAH 53
THE SHADES OF DINAH'S SINGING . . . AYM ODE TO DINAH 58

DINED 1
BEING WINED AND DINED. . . . . PL DINNER GUEST ME 3

DINGY 1
DUST OF DINGY ATOMS . . . . PL CULTURAL EXCHNG 3

DINNER 2
I BEG A DIME FOR DINNER - . . . . . ANS PARK BENCH 5
DINNER. AND SUPPER. TOO - . . . . . SP MADAM HER MADAM 6

DIOS 3
AY. DIOS! . . . . AYM IS IT TRUE? 20
AY. DIOS! . . . . AYM IS IT TRUE? 21
AY. DIOS! . . . . AYM IS IT TRUE? 22

DIP 2
WE DIP AND DIVE. . . . . SP LONG TRIP 3
I DIP MY BROOM IN BLOOD. . . . . . PL WAR 14

DIPLOMA 2
DIPLOMA IN ITS NEW FRAME: . . . . . SP GRADUATION 10
THE DIPLOMA BURSTS ITS FRAME . . . SP GRADUATION 23

DIRGES 1
PLAY HILLBILLY DIRGES . . . . PL SPECIAL BULLTIN 3

DIRT 2
THEY THROW DIRT IN YOUR FACE. . . . SP WIDOW WOMAN 8
THROW DIRT IN YOUR FACE. . . . . . SP WIDOW WOMAN 10

DIRTY 6
THEY CALLED HIM DO DIRTY . . . . . FC DEATH DO DIRTY 6
IF DIRTY HAD DE MONEY . . . . FC DEATH DO DIRTY 18
JOSTLE OF DIRTY COATS . . . . OWT MAN INTO MEN 3
DIRTY COATS . . . . OWT MAN INTO MEN 10
IN THE DIRTY MIRE. . . . . SP ANGELS WINGS 8
OR GREASY POTS IN A DIRTY KITCHEN. SP ELEVATOR BOY 20

DISC 1
TO A DISC BY DINAH . . . . AYM ODE TO DINAH 15

DISCIPLES 1
TO HIS TWELVE DISCIPLES . . . . . . LHR BLD MARY'S SON 15

DISCONTENT 1
AND BLUE. HIDING HIS DISCONTENT AS THOUGHTS OF A BETTER LIFE OVERCOME . . . . NM BIG-TIMER MOOD 7

DISCOURAGED 1
DON'T BE DISCOURAGED. BUILDER! . . SP FREEDOM'S PLOW 162

DISCS 1
SIX DISCS . . . . SP BE-BOP BOYS 3

DISEASE 2
SUCH A STRANGE DISEASE. . . . . . . FC GYPSY MAN 20
SUCH A STRANGE DISEASE. . . . . . . FC GYPSY MAN 22

DISGRACE 1
DISGRACE THE RACE! . . . . SP SEASHORE THROUG 9

DISGUISE 1
WEARS NO DISGUISE. . . . . PL BLACK PANTHER 9

DISGUSTED 1
I'M MAD AND DISGUSTED . . . . SP MADAM PHONE BIL 6

DISH-WASHERS 1
DISH-WASHERS. . . . . FC LAUGHERS 6

DISORDERLY 1
DISORDERLY CONDUCT . . . . OWT BLD MARGE POLIT 19

DISOWNED 1
MY PEOPLE DISOWNED ME - . . . . . . NM BIG-TIMER POEM 11

DISRUPTOR 1
"DISRUPTOR! AGITATOR! . . . . JC THE BITTER RIVR 47

DISTANCE 4
HELL OF A DISTANCE . . . . ANS PARK BENCH 3
I THINK THE DISTANCE . . . . FW BORDER LINE 7
LONG DISTANCE? . . . . SP MADAM PHONE BIL 2
LONG DISTANCE . . . . SP MADAM PHONE BIL 17

DISTANT 3
FROM ANOTHER DISTANT QUARTER . . . AYM ODE TO DINAH 17
DISTANT ALMOST NOW AS DISTANT . . . AYM ODE TO DINAH 39
DISTANT ALMOST NOW AS DISTANT . . . AYM ODE TO DINAH 39

DISTILLED 1
DISTILLED FROM OLD DESIRE - . . . . SP TRUMPET PLAYER 24

DISTORTED 3
DISTORTED BLADES OF GRASS. . . . . SP GARDEN 2
DISTORTED TREES. . . . . SP GARDEN 4
DISTORTED TULIPS . . . . SP GARDEN 6

DITCHES 2
JOSTLE OF MEN IN THE DITCHES. . . . OWT MAN INTO MEN 7
DITCHES . . . . OWT MAN INTO MEN 14

DIVE 2
RUNS TO DIVE IN THE PARK . . . . . SP DIVE 3
WE DIP AND DIVE. . . . . SP LONG TRIP 3

DIVIDE 1
TO THE ENEMY WHO WOULD DIVIDE . . . SP FREEDOM'S PLOW 180

DIVIDENDS 1
FEEL THE RUG OF DIVIDENDS. . . . . PL UNDERTOW 5

DIVINE 5
HIS BODY AND HIS BLOOD DIVINE! . . LHR BLD MARY'S SON 31
FATHER DIVINE. A RABBI BLACK . . . SP MYSTERY 22
AND FATHER DIVINE WILL SAY IN TRUTH. SP PROJECTION 20
THE WINE DIVINE. . . . . PL DINNER GUEST ME 16
FATHER DIVINE (WHERE?) . . . . . . PL FINAL CALL 34

DIVINITY 1
DIVINITY. . . . . FW THERE 11

DIXIE 15
(DIXIE MAKES HIS MONEY ON TWO-BIT GIN.) . . . . SH DEATH IN HARLEM 32
(DIXIE RENTS ROOMS AT A BUCK A BREAK.) . . . . SH DEATH IN HARLEM 34
DIXIE GRINNED. DIXIE BOWED. . . . . SH DEATH IN HARLEM 62
DIXIE GRINNED. DIXIE BOWED. . . . . SH DEATH IN HARLEM 62

DIXIE RUBBED HIS HANDS AND LAUGHED OUT LOUD -	SH DEATH IN HARLEM	63
WHERE I LIVE DOWN IN DIXIE	JC GOOD MORN STLIN	6
DOWN SOUTH IN DIXIE ONLY TRAIN I SEE'S	SP FREEDOM TRAIN	9
IN DIXIE, OFTEN THEY WON'T CALL NEGROES MISTER.	SP IN EXPLANATION	7
DIXIE TO SINGAPORE, CAPE TOWN TO HONG KONG	SP IN EXPLANATION	10
AND HE CROSSED THAT DIXIE LINE	SP NOT A MOVIE	6
AND NOT DIXIE.	SP ONE-WAY TICKET	8
HOW DIXIE PROTECTS	SP SILHOUETTE	9
WAY DOWN SOUTH IN DIXIE	SP SONG DARK GIRL	1
WAY DOWN SOUTH IN DIXIE	SP SONG DARK GIRL	5
WAY DOWN SOUTH IN DIXIE	SP SONG DARK GIRL	9

DIXIECRATS 1

VOTED ALL THE DIXIECRATS	PL CULTURAL EXCHNG	40

DIXIE'S 5

WENT BUSTIN INTO DIXIE'S BOUT ONE A.M.	SH DEATH IN HARLEM	2
IN DIXIE'S PLACE ON 133RD	SH DEATH IN HARLEM	24
DIXIE'S AIN'T NO PLACE FOR A GANG THAT'S SLOW.	SH DEATH IN HARLEM	38
CAME TIPPIN INTO DIXIE'S TO GET A VIEW.	SH DEATH IN HARLEM	59
CAME TIPPIN INTO DIXIE'S WITH SMILES ON THEIR FACES.	SH DEATH IN HARLEM	60

DIZZY 2

LIKE A DIZZY GILLESPIE TRANSCRIPTION	SP PROJECTION	13
JAZZERS DUKE AND DIZZY ERIC DOLPHY $ $ $	AYM HORN OF PLENTY	8

DO 133

DO IT!	WB CAT AND SAXOPHN	27
WHAT DO YOU KNOW	WB HARLEM NIGHT CL	15
I DO NOT HATE YOU.	WB THE WHITE ONES	1
I DO NOT HATE YOU,	WB THE WHITE ONES	3
YET WHY DO YOU TORTURE ME.	WB THE WHITE ONES	5
WHY DO YOU TORTURE ME?	WB THE WHITE ONES	7
ALTHOUGH I DO NOT KNOW.	WB YOUNG BRIDE	2
DON'T KNOW WHY I DO IT BUT	FC BAD MAN	11
THEY CALLED HIM DO DIRTY	FC DEATH DO DIRTY	6
SHE DON'T DO ME RIGHT.	FC EVIL WOMAN	6
BUT HE SHO DO TREAT ME KIND.	FC GAL'S CRY DYING	14
BUT HE SHO DO TREAT ME KIND.	FC GAL'S CRY DYING	16
NOTHIN' FOR YOU TO DO.	FC HARD LUCK	2
NOTHIN' FOR YOU TO DO.	FC HARD LUCK	4
EVEN IF YOU DO COME FROM GEORGIA.	FC JAZZ BAND	21
AND I'D SAVE MORE THAN I DO NOW.	FC PRIZE FIGHTER	6
AIN'T NOTHIN' TO DO FOR YOU. NOHOW.	FC RED SILK STOCK	5
DO, IT, MR. CHARLIE.	FC SATURDAY NIGHT	27
AND DICE INSTEAD OF BOCKS WILL DO	NM BLACK CLWN POEM	5
LET'S GET MARRIED RIGHT NOW! YES! WHAT DO YOU SAY?	NM BROKE	75
BUT NOW I KNOW WE'VE GOT PLENTY TO DO.	NM COLORED SL POEM	23
AND NO LONGER DO WE KNOW THE DARK MISERY	NM COLORED SL POEM	30
FOR HERE I DO NOT MAKE MY BED.	DK DEATH SEAMAN	6
DO NOT, DO NOT WEEP FOR ME.	DK DEATH SEAMAN	9
DO NOT, DO NOT WEEP FOR ME.	DK DEATH SEAMAN	9
YOU DO NOT THINK	DK MINSTREL MAN	5
YOU DO NOT HEAR	DK MINSTREL MAN	11
YOU DO NOT KNOW	DK MINSTREL MAN	15
TWO MO' WAYS TO DO DE CHARLESTON!	DK NEGRO DANCERS	3
TWO MO' WAYS TO DO DE CHARLESTON!"	DK NEGRO DANCERS	6
TWO MO' WAYS TO DO DE CHARLESTON!"	DK NEGRO DANCERS	15
DO NOT UNDERSTAND.	DK SEA CHARM	3
DO NOT BE AFRAID OF LIGHT.	DK SONG	3
DO THAT ROCKIN' STEP.	DK SONG BANJO DANC	6
AND YOU DO NOT GO FREE.	ANS CHANT TOM MOONY	5
AND YOU DO NOT GO FREE.	ANS CHANT TOM MOONY	9
WHAT DO YOU MEAN -	ANS LYNCHING SONG	10
I DO NOT UNDERSTAND.	ANS SONG OF SPAIN	11
I DO NOT UNDERSTAND.	ANS SONG OF SPAIN	18
I MUST NOT DO IT AGAIN.	ANS SONG OF SPAIN	72
I MUST NOT DO IT AGAIN.	ANS SONG OF SPAIN	74
I MUST NEVER DO THAT AGAIN.	ANS SONG OF SPAIN	78
TO DO CART WHEELS?	SH ASPIRATION	2
DO I SEE A COUPLE? OR DID I COUNT TWICE?	SH BED TIME	13
DO IT, ARABELLA!	SH DEATH IN HARLEM	20
BELIEVE I'LL DO A LITTLE DANCIN'	SH EVENIN' BLUES	13
DO NOT SELL ME OUT, BABY,	SH IN TROUBLED KEY	1
PLEASE DO NOT SELL ME OUT.	SH IN TROUBLED KEY	2
DO NOT SELL ME OUT, BABY.	SH IN TROUBLED KEY	3
DO NOT SELL ME OUT.	SH IN TROUBLED KEY	4
EVEN THOUGH YOU DO ME WRONG.	SH IN TROUBLED KEY	8
THOUGH YOU DO ME WRONG -	SH IN TROUBLED KEY	10
WHAT DO YOU MEAN, WHY I DIDN'T WRITE?	SH LETTER	3
WHAT DO YOU MEAN, JUST A LITTLE SPAT?	SH LETTER	4
DON'T IG ME LIKE YOU DO.	SH MIDNIGHT CHIPPI	20
PLEASE DON'T IG ME LIKE YOU DO.	SH MIDNIGHT CHIPPI	22
AND DE LEVEE DON'T DO NO GOOD.	SH MISSISSIPPI LEV	8
WHEN DE LEVEE DON'T DO NO GOOD.	SH MISSISSIPPI LEV	10
AND SEE WHAT IT WOULD DO TO YOU?	SH OUT OF WORK	24
HERE BY MYSELF, I DO AS I PLEASE.	SH SUNDAY	2
IF I JUST HAD A OWL HEAD, OLD OWL HEAD WOULD DO.	SH TWILIGHT REVERI	11
WE'LL DO TO YOU.	JC BLD SAM SOLOMON	28
I DO OR SAY.	FW FAITHFUL ONE	10
I DO NOT NEED	FW SILENCE	4
I DO NOT UNDERSTAND	FW SONGS	4
WHOSE IS IT, DO YOU KNOW?	FW WHEN ARMIES PAS	4
I DO NOT KNOW	FW WHEN ARMIES PAS	5
SON, I DO NOT KNOW.	FW WHEN ARMIES PAS	16
TELL ME, WHAT DO YOU DO?	OWT CURIOUS	5
TELL ME, WHAT DO YOU DO?	OWT CURIOUS	6
O, SONGS THAT DO NOT CARE!	OWT NEGRO SERVANT	7
WHAT SHALL I DO?	OWT TOO BLUE	6
ONE BULLET WOULD DO?	OWT TOO BLUE	11
DO YOU UNDERSTAND THE STILLNESS	SP A HOUSE IN TAOS	11
I DO NOT UNDERSTAND.	SP AFRO-AMER FRAG	17
DO YOU BELIEVE THAT, JACK?	SP ARGUMENT	4
SURE DO!	SP ARGUMENT	5
PO' WEARY ME CAN DO.	SP BAD LUCK CARD	10
SHE'D DO IT AGIN'!	SP BLD OF THE GIRL	16
NOTHIN' TO DO BUT WALK.	SP BOUND NO'TH BLS	8
LIKE THEY TRY TO DO YOU BAD.	SP BOUND NO'TH BLS	18
IN THIS BLOCK, I DO BELIEVE!	SP CHILDREN'S RYME	11
I EXPECT THEY DO -	SP COMMENT ON CURB	5
THIS YEAR MAYBE, DO YOU THINK I CAN GRADUATE?	SP DEFERRED	1
I DO NOT NEED MY FREEDOM WHEN I'M DEAD.	SP DEMOCRACY	13
DO YOU HEAR WHAT I SAID?	SP EASY BOOGIE	11
DO YOU BELIEVE	SP FIRE	11
THE PEOPLE DO NOT ALWAYS SAY THINGS OUT LOUD.	SP FREEDOM'S PLOW	145
THE PEOPLE DO NOT ALWAYS UNDERSTAND EACH OTHER.	SP FREEDOM'S PLOW	152
DO NOT DROWN ME NOW:	SP ISLAND	2
I DON'T KNOW WHAT TO DO."	SP LOVER'S RETURN	8
BUT YOU DO!	SP LOW TO HIGH	2
BUT YOU DO.	SP LOW TO HIGH	9
BUT YOU DO.	SP LOW TO HIGH	17
CAN I DO FOR YOU?	SP MADAM RENT MAN	4
I SAID, DO YOU LOVE ME?	SP MADAM MIGHT-HAV	13
I SAID, IF YOU DO,	SP MADAM CENSUS	15
THEM OTHER GIRLS DO	SP MADAM PHONE BIL	28
CAN'T DO - AND MORE, TOO?	SP MADAM PHONE BIL	30
I DO COOKING,	SP MADAM'S PAST HI	23
I DON'T HAVE TO DO NOTHING	SP NECESSITY	3
I DO NOT KNOW.	SP PRAYER	7
I DO NOT KNOW.	SP PRAYER	9
DO, JESUS!	SP PROJECTION	11
SAID THE LADY, CAN YOU DO	SP QUESTION	1
WHAT MY OTHER MAN CAN'T DO -	SP QUESTION	2
WHAT CAN A COLORED GIRL DO	SP RUBY BROWN	13
THE GOOD CHURCH FOLK DO NOT MENTION	SP RUBY BROWN	21
DO NOT SWOON.	SP SILHOUETTE	2
DO NOT SPEAK OF SORROW	SP SONG BILLIE HOL	10
DO NOT RING, NOT EVEN MURMUR.	SP SUMMER EVENING	21
WHAT WILL YOU DO?	SP SUNDAY MORNING	16
YES, SIR! LONG AS LIFE DO LAST!	SP SYLVESTER'S BED	22
NOR DO I OFTEN WANT TO BE A PART OF YOU.	SP THEME FOR ENG B	35
WHO DO NOT CARE.	SP VAGABONDS	2
LIKE YOU OUGHT TO DO.	SP WARNING AUGMENT	3
SO WHAT WOULD YOU DO?	SP WHAT?	8
CAN A YOUNG GAL DO?	SP YOUNG GAL'S BLS	20
WHAT CAN A YOUNG GAL DO?	SP YOUNG GAL'S BLS	22
SHE ANSWERED, BABE, WHAT MUST I DO?	SP 50 - 50	12
AT THE DOME VINGT FRANCS WILL DO	AYM ASK YOUR MAMA	50
DO YOU READ MUSIC? AND LOUIS SAYING $ $	AYM HORN OF PLENTY	11
AND THE GUN TO DO THE KILLING'S	AYM IS IT TRUE?	14
DO, JESUS!	AYM SHADES OF PIC	43
OR DO YOU THINK THAT PAPA'S	AYM SHOW FARE PLESE	3
JUST WHO DO YOU THINK I AM?	PL BACKLASH BLUES	2
WHO DO YOU THINK I AM?	PL BACKLASH BLUES	4
WHAT DO YOU THINK I GOT TO LOSE?	PL BACKLASH BLUES	26
THEY DO NOT LAST A DAY -	PL CROWNS GARLANDS	13
I DO NOT NEED MY FREEDOM WHEN I'M DEAD.	PL FREEDOM	13
WHAT WE'RE GONNA DO	PL HARLEM	21
THEY SAID, "DO YOU BELIEVE	PL KU KLUX	3
NOW I DO NOT UNDERSTAND	PL WHO BUT TH LORD	16

DOBERMAN 1

BOUGHT A DOBERMAN PINSCHER.	AYM BIRD IN ORBIT	87

DOCILE 1

SWEET AND DOCILE.	PL WARNING	2

DOCKS 1

ON THE DOCKS	FC PRIZE FIGHTER	5

DOCTOR 3

FOLLOWS THE YOUNG DOCTOR.	SP INTERNE AT PROV	45
THE DOCTOR SAID, MADAM,	SP MADAM WRONG VIS	23

THE DOCTOR 'N' UNDERTAKER'S . . . . SP SYLVESTER'S BED 11

DODGED 1

EVERYBODY DODGED AS . . . . SH DEATH IN HARLEM 101

DODGERS 1

ON ACCOUNT OF THE DODGERS ON THE RADIO. . . . . SP PASSING 5

DOES 32

DOES A JAZZ-BAND EVER SOB? . . . . WB CABARET 1
CAUSE HE NEVER DOES COME HOME. . . FC GYPSY MAN 2
HE NEVER DOES COME HOME. . . . . . FC GYPSY MAN 4
I DOES HER GOOD . . . . FC WORKIN' MAN 9
WELL. ER - ER . . . HOW MUCH DOES YOU PAY? . . . . NM BROKE 35
DOES I WANTA? WELL. CAN'T SAY BUT WHAT I MIGHT - . . . . NM BROKE 71
DOES NOT KNOW . . . . ANS CHANT TOM MOONY 11
THE STEEL OF FREEDOM DOES NOT STAIN. ANS LET AMERICA BE 71
OR DOES SOME STRANGE . . . . FW CONVENT 6
NEITHER DOES THE SUN. . . . . OWT RESTRICTIVE 8
NEITHER DOES I TREAT YOU GOOD. . . SP EARLY EVENING 18
DOES IT DRY UP . . . . SP HARLEM 2
DOES IT STINK LIKE ROTTEN MEAT? . . SP HARLEM 6
OR DOES IT EXPLODE? . . . . SP HARLEM 11
AS DOES . . . . SP HEAVEN 7
DOES 'EM LIKE YOU CHOOSE. . . . . . SP LOVER'S RETURN 12
DOES K STAND FOR? . . . . SP MADAM CENSUS 10
PHONE BILL DOES I CARE! . . . . . . SP MADAM PHONE BIL 36
WHICH IS WHY I RECKON I DOES . . . SP NECESSITY 11
HONEY. WHAT DOES YOU NEED? . . . . SP PREFERENCE 8
WHY DOES HE KEEP ON FOOLIN' AROUND MARIE? . . . . SP SISTER 2
BUT WHY DOES HE KEEP ON FOOLIN' AROUND MARIE? . . . . SP SISTER 4
THAT A WOMAN DOES THE BEST SHE CAN? SP SISTER 14
SO DOES A MAN. . . . . SP SISTER 16
DOES NOT KNOW . . . . SP TRUMPET PLAYER 37
HOW MANY BULLETS DOES IT TAKE . . . PL DEATH YORKVILLE 3
HOW MANY CENTURIES DOES IT TAKE . . PL DEATH YORKVILLE 5
HOW MANY CENTENNIALS DOES IT TAKE PL DEATH YORKVILLE 15
HOW MANY BULLETS DOES IT TAKE . . . PL DREAM DEFERRED 1
DOES IT DRY UP . . . . PL DREAM DEFERRED 2
DOES IT STINK LIKE ROTTEN MEAT? . . PL DREAM DEFERRED 6
OR DOES IT EXPLODE? . . . . PL DREAM DEFERRED 11

DOESN'T 5

STRENGTH HE DOESN'T REALLY FEEL. GAY. LOUD. UNHAPPY JAZZ. BARING HIS . . . . NM BIG-TIMER MOOD 9
DOESN'T SAY WHEN. . . . . OWT RAID 7
THE MOON DOESN'T RUN. . . . . OWT RESTRICTIVE 7
BUT HE DOESN'T WALK LIKE ONE. . . . SP CASUALTY 2
I GUESS BEING COLORED DOESN'T MAKE ME NOT LIKE . . . . SP THEME FOR ENG B 25

DOG 15

OF DOG EAT DOG. OF MIGHTY CRUSH THE WEAK. . . . . ANS LET AMERICA BE 24
OF DOG EAT DOG. OF MIGHTY CRUSH THE WEAK. . . . . ANS LET AMERICA BE 24
O' MY FEELING LIKE A DOG . . . . . SH EVIL MORNING 10
WORKIN' LIKE A TUCK-TAIL DOG. . . . SH MISSISSIPPI LEV 2
LIKE A TUCK-TAIL DOG. . . . . SH MISSISSIPPI LEV 4
BARK LIKE A DOG. . . . . SH ONLY WOMAN BLUS 8
WALK THE DOG AROUND - . . . . SP MADAM HER MADAM 10
DON'T LET YOUR DOG CURB YOU! . . . SP WARNING AUGMENT 1
DON'T LET YOUR DOG . . . . SP WARNING 2
BUT DON'T LET THAT DOG CURB YOU! . SP WARNING AUGMENT 4
BUT A DOG CAN TELL . . . . SP WARNING AUGMENT 7
CUR DOG. FICE DOG. KERRY BLUE - . . SP WARNING AUGMENT 13
CUR DOG. FICE DOG. KERRY BLUE - . . SP WARNING AUGMENT 13
JUST DON'T LET YOUR DOG CURB YOU! SP WARNING AUGMENT 14
OF THE DOG IS FAST. . . . . PL GO SLOW 3

DOGGED 3

I'LL BE DOGGED. SWEET BABY. . . . . SP LIFE IS FINE 29
BUT I'LL BE DOGGED . . . . SP MADAM HER MADAM 23
BUT HEARTS KEEP DOGGED BEATING . . AYM ASK YOUR MAMA 69

DOGGIE 1

CURB YOUR DOGGIE . . . . SP WARNING AUGMENT 2

DOGMAS 1

TO SMASH THE OLD DEAD DOGMAS OF THE PAST - . . . . ANS OPEN LETTER 24

DOGS 2

MAMA. IT HAS BEEN RAINING CATS AND DOGS UP . . . . SP LETTER 8
SOUTHERN DOGS HAVE VINDICATED ME - PL NORTHERN LIBERL 4

DOG-GONE 3

DOG-GONE LITTLE MOUSES! I WISH I WAS YOU! . . . . SH BED TIME 14
DOG-GONE! . . . . SP GONE BOY 8
AND I PLAYED SO DOG-GONE HARD. . . SP LITTLE GRN TREE 6

DOING 3

AND I HOPE YOU'RE MAKING GOOD. AND DOING FINE - . . . . NM COLORED SL POEM 17
DOING EIGHTY . . . . SH ANNOUNCEMENT 3
NOT OF HER OWN DOING - . . . . . . PL CULTURAL EXCHNG 18

DOLLAR 9

A DOLLAR. . . . . FC BRASS SPITOONS 14
A DOLLAR. . . . . FC BRASS SPITOONS 19
GIVES YOU A DOLLAR AN' A HALF. . . FC HARD LUCK 8
GIVES YOU A DOLLAR AN' A HALF. . . FC HARD LUCK 10
LITTLE DOLLAR ROSE . . . . FW CHIPPY 6
I ASKED YOU FOR A DOLLAR. . . . . . OWT HONEY BABE 5
FOR ONE MORE DOLLAR AND A HALF. . . SP MADAM FORT TELL 23
IF I EVER HIT FOR A DOLLAR . . . . SP NUMBERS 1
OF THE SHADOW OF A DOLLAR . . . . . AYM SHOW FARE PLESE 14

DOLLARS 10

TWO DOLLARS A DAY. . . . . FC BRASS SPITOONS 15
TWO DOLLARS . . . . FC BRASS SPITOONS 20
DOLLARS AND CLEAN SPITOONS . . . . FC BRASS SPITOONS 29
I COULD MAKE SIX DOLLARS A DAY . . FC PRIZE FIGHTER 4
AFTER ALL THEM DOLLARS I GIVED HER THESE LAST TWO YEARS. . . . . . NM BROKE 23
SIX DOLLARS A WEEK? WHEE-OOO! YOU SHO PAYS WELL! . . . . NM BROKE 36
HERE'S FIVE DOLLARS. CASSIE. BUY A TICKET BACK. . . . . SH LETTER 20
BUT HERE IS FIVE DOLLARS FOR YOU . SP LETTER 4
CHARGED FIVE DOLLARS . . . . SP NIGHT FUNERAL 23
INTO CLOTH OF DOLLARS . . . . AYM SHOW FARE PLESE 22

DOLLS 2

WHOSE DOLLS ARE INTERRACIAL! . . . AYM BIRD IN ORBIT 85
YOUR DOLLS ARE INTERRACIAL. . . . . AYM RIDE. RED. RIDE 25

DOLPHY 1

JAZZERS DUKE AND DIZZY ERIC DOLPHY $ $ $ . . . . AYM HORN OF PLENTY 8

DOME 1

AT THE DOME VINGT FRANCS WILL DO . AYM ASK YOUR MAMA 50

DON 1

DON QUIXOTE! ESPANA! . . . . ANS SONG OF SPAIN 26

DONDE 5

TU ABUELA. DONDE ESTA? . . . . . . AYM RIDE. RED. RIDE 11
TU ABUELA. DONDE ESTA? . . . . . . AYM RIDE. RED. RIDE 13
DONDE ESTA? DONDE ESTA? . . . . . . AYM RIDE. RED. RIDE 15
DONDE ESTA? DONDE ESTA? . . . . . . AYM RIDE. RED. RIDE 15
AY. MORENA. DONDE ESTA? . . . . . . AYM RIDE. RED. RIDE 20

DONE 60

MY MAN'S DONE LEFT ME. . . . . . . WB BLUES FANTASY 7
AFTER DE BOAT'S DONE GONE. . . . . FC A RUINED GAL 2
THAT MAN THAT DONE ME WRONG? . . . FC SUICIDE 12
ABE LINCOLN DONE SET ME FREE - . . NM BLACK CLWN POEM 30
DONE BEAT YOU TO DE PLACE. STANDIN' OUT SIDE DE DO' . . . . NM BROKE 6
I MEAN FOUR - BEFORE DAYLIGHT - S'POSE TO'VE DONE HIT YO' FIRST STROKE - . . . . NM BROKE 14
WELL. AIN'T NEVER DONE IT. BUT FOR TO KEEP BODY AND SOUL . . . . . NM BROKE 29
IT'S DONE GOT ME SO CRAZY. FEEL LIKE I BEEN TAKIN' COKE. . . . . . . NM BROKE 60
A DRAMATIC RECITATION TO BE DONE IN THE HALF-DARK BY A YOUNG BROWN FELLOW . . . . NM COLORED SL MOOD 1
NEVER DONE NO WRONG. . . . . DK PO' BOY BLUES 8
NEVER DONE NO WRONG. . . . . DK PO' BOY BLUES 10
THE PAST IS DONE! . . . . ANS A NEW SONG 52
NOW MY WORK IS DONE. . . . . ANS BLDS OF LENIN 16
HOW DID I KNOW WHERE YOU DONE GONE AT? . . . . SH LETTER 5
I DONE WALKED DE STREETS TILL . . . SH OUT OF WORK 3
BUT I AIN'T GOT NO OWL HEAD AND YOU DONE LEFT TOWN . . . . SH TWILIGHT REVERI 13
DONE GIVE YOU UP FOR DEAD - . . . . JC GOOD MORN STLIN 38
BUT WHEN IT IS. JIM CROW'LL BE DONE. JC JIM CROW'S LAST 31
ARE DONE . . . . FW SLEEP 3
ARE DONE. . . . . FW SLEEP 11
TO SING ABOUT THE MEN WHO'VE DONE THEM WRONG - . . . . OWT JUICE JOINT 24
GONE AND DONE ME WRONG . . . . . . OWT LINCOLN THEATRE 12
HE SAID. OH. LORD. THY WILL BE DONE! LHR BLD MARY'S SON 24
I HAVE DONE SO LITTLE . . . . LHR POET TO BIGOT 1
AND YOU HAVE DONE SO LITTLE . . . . LHR POET TO BIGOT 3
GYPSY DONE SHOWED ME . . . . SP BAD LUCK CARD 3
GYPSY DONE TOLE ME - . . . . SP BAD LUCK CARD 7
DONE BEGUN. . . . . SP BLACK MARIA 17
DONE BEGUN! . . . . SP BLACK MARIA 22
DAYS ARE DONE. . . . . SP CASUALTY 4
THE CREDIT MAN'S DONE TOOK MA CLOTHES . . . . SP DOWN AND OUT 7
TILL THE WHITE DAY IS DONE. . . . . SP DREAM VARIATION 4

TILL THE QUICK DAY IS DONE. SP DREAM VARIATION 13
DONE GAMBLED THAT DIME AWAY. SP EARLY EVENING 10
MY GOOD-TIME DAYS DONE PAST. SP LITTLE GRN TREE 2
YOU DONE FORGOT THAT YOU ARE BLACK. SP LOW TO HIGH 6
AND YOU AIN'T DONE A THING SP MADAM RENT MAN 13
YOU PROMISED TO'VE DONE. SP MADAM RENT MAN 14
DONE SINCE THEN? SP MADAM MINISTER 14
CAUSE THE MAN I LOVE'S DONE SP MISERY 7
DONE ME WRONG. SP MISERY 8
WHEN HIS WORK IS DONE SP NEIGHBOR 5
AND THE ORGAN HAD DONE PLAYED SP NIGHT FUNERAL 29
THAT LONG BLACK HEARSE DONE SPED. SP NIGHT FUNERAL 34
YEP. YOU DONE TAKEN MY BLUES AND GONE. SP NOTE COMM THEAT 7
AND THE WORK IS DONE SP SHARE-CROPPERS 6
AND THE NATIONS THEY DONE FIT. SP SOUTHERN MAMMY 8
THEY DONE TOOK CORDELIA SP STONY LONESOME 1
DONE TOOK CORDELIA SP STONY LONESOME 3
THEY DONE PUT CORDELIA SP STONY LONESOME 6
SHE DONE LEFT PO' BUDDY SP STONY LONESOME 12
YES. HE'S DONE BEEN LEFT. SP STONY LONESOME 15
BUT I HAD TO KEEP ON TILL MY WORK WAS DONE: SP THE NEGRO MOTHE 28
SORRY THAT OLD WAR IS DONE! SP WORLD WAR II 6
I DONE BEAT MY PL DOWN WHERE I AM 3
DONE BROKE MY ANKLES DOWN. PL DOWN WHERE I AM 7
WHEN WHITE COLLARS GET DONE. PL OFFICE BUILDING 8
MY HOPES THE WIND DONE SCATTERED. PL STILL HERE 2
LOOKS LIKE BETWEEN 'EM THEY DONE PL STILL HERE 5
I DONE FORGOT WHEN IT PASSED PL STOKELY MALCOLM 8

DONKEY 1

BUT WHY RIDE ON MULE OR DONKEY AYM ASK YOUR MAMA 59

DONKEYS 1

LITTLE MULES AND DONKEYS SHARE AYM ASK YOUR MAMA 76

DON'T 189

DON'T YOU, HONEY? WB CAT AND SAXOPHN 9
DON'T LOVE NOBODY WB CAT AND SAXOPHN 12
DON'T WANT NOBODY WB CAT AND SAXOPHN 22
AND YOU DON'T MEAN MAYBE. WB TO MIDNIGHT NAN 12
DON'T KNOW WHY I DO IT BUT FC BAD MAN 11
DON'T EVEN WANT TO BE GOOD. FC BAD MAN 14
DON'T EVEN WANT TO BE GOOD. FC BAD MAN 16
IF A SEVEN DON'T COME FC CRAP GAME 3
DON'T LAST ALL DE TIME. FC CRAP GAME 8
SHE DON'T DO ME RIGHT. FC EVIL WOMAN 6
PLEASE DON'T TAKE THIS MAN O' MINE. FC GAL'S CRY DYING 18
DON'T YOU FOOL WID NO MEN CAUSE FC LISTEN HERE 17
SHE DON'T DRINK GIN FC NEW CABARET GRL 5
AN' SHE DON'T LIKE CORN. FC NEW CABARET GRL 6
I DON'T KNOW FC NEW CABARET GRL 10
BUT SHE DON'T GIMME LOVIN' FC WORKIN' MAN 11
AND WHOEVER DON'T LIKE IT NM BIG-TIMER POEM 27
AND IF I DON'T GET YOU GOIN'. NM BIG-TIMER POEM 31
BUT DON'T LET IT MATTER TO YOU. NM BIG-TIMER POEM 49
SO DON'T WORRY 'BOUT ME. NM BIG-TIMER POEM 53
I DON'T CRY OVER TROUBLES. NM BIG-TIMER POEM 58
THEN I DON'T HAVE TO THINK. NM BIG-TIMER POEM 64
AND I DON'T GIVE A DAMN - NM BIG-TIMER POEM 74
AND DON'T YOU KNOW THAT OLD WOMAN SWELLED UP LIKE A SPECKLED TOAD NM BROKE 21
(I DON'T CARE NOTHIN' 'BOUT HER MYSELF!) NM BROKE 27
WHAT I DON'T KNOW 'BOUT SHOVELIN' COAL, AIN'T NO MO' TO KNOW! NM BROKE 32
BUT YOU DON'T SEE NO PRESIDENTS DYIN' O' GRIEF - NM BROKE 57
CAN'T SEE! AND DON'T KNOW! AND WON'T EVER CARE! NM COLORED SL POEM 53
THEY DON'T HURT MA FEET. DK DRESSED UP 10
AN' I DON'T KNOW HOW TO FLOAT. DK WIDE RIVER 6
CAUSE IF I DON'T SEE MA BABY DK WIDE RIVER 17
DON'T THEY, OZZIE POWELL? ANS BLD OZZIE POWEL 22
WHO DON'T BELIEVE IN LIES. AND BRIBES AND CONTENTMENT. ANS KIDS WHO DIE 17
AND THE OLD AND RICH DON'T WANT THE PEOPLE ANS KIDS WHO DIE 33
DON'T WANT THE PEOPLE TO GET WISE TO THEIR OWN POWER. ANS KIDS WHO DIE 35
LAWD! DON'T YOU KNOW? ANS SISTER JOHNSON 11
THAT GAL DON'T DRIVE MY SH ANNOUNCEMENT 15
NEVER MIND! DON'T BOTHER. SH BLD PAWNBROKER 4
I DON'T KNOW WHY IT LOOKS SH BLD PAWNBROKER 11
O.K. YOU DON'T WANT IT? SH BLD PAWNBROKER 17
TILL YOU DON'T KNOW RIGHT FROM WRONG. SH HEY-HEY BLUES 12
I DON'T CARE HOW YOU PLAY 'EM SH HEY-HEY BLUES 17
DON'T LEAVE ME HERE ALONE. SH MIDNIGHT CHIPPI 12
DON'T IG ME LIKE YOU DO. SH MIDNIGHT CHIPPI 20
PLEASE DON'T IG ME LIKE YOU DO. SH MIDNIGHT CHIPPI 22
GIRLS. DON'T STAND ON NO CORNER SH MIDNIGHT CHIPPI 25
I SAY DON'T STAND ON NO CORNER SH MIDNIGHT CHIPPI 27
DON'T KNOW WHY I BUILD THIS LEVEE SH MISSISSIPPI LEV 7
AND DE LEVEE DON'T DO NO GOOD. SH MISSISSIPPI LEV 8
DON'T KNOW WHY I BUILD THIS LEVEE SH MISSISSIPPI LEV 9
WHEN DE LEVEE DON'T DO NO GOOD. SH MISSISSIPPI LEV 10
WHY DON'T YOU TRY IT. FOLKS. SH OUT OF WORK 23
DON'T HAVE TO SHARE IT A-TALL. SH PAY DAY 2
DON'T HAVE TO HEAR NOBODY SAY. SH PAY DAY 3
I DON'T CARE WHERE IT'S GOIN' SH SIX-BITS BLUES 5
BUT DON'T MAKE IT TOO LONG. SH SIX-BITS BLUES 8
DON'T MAKE IT TOO LONG. SH SIX-BITS BLUES 10
DON'T SNUB THE OTHER FELLOW - SH SNOB 3
DON'T HAVE TO GO TO CHURCH. SH SUNDAY 3
DON'T HAVE TO GO NOWHERE. SH SUNDAY 4
I WISH I COULD TELL YOU HOW MUCH I DON'T CARE SH SUNDAY 5
CAUSE IF I DON'T THEY'LL CUT DOWN MY PAY. SH SUPPER TIME 14
DON'T YOU HEAR THIS HAMMER RING? JC BIG BUDDY 11
DON'T YOU HEAR THIS HAMMER RING? JC BIG BUDDY 13
DON'T YOU HEAR THIS HAMMER RING? JC BIG BUDDY 19
WHY FREEDOM DON'T APPLY JC BLACK MAN SPEAK 7
I REALLY DON'T KNOW JC BLACK MAN SPEAK 10
I DON'T PAY YOU NO MIND. JC BLD SAM SOLOMON 30
LOTS OF FOLKS WHO DON'T LIKE YOU JC GOOD MORN STLIN 2
I STILL DON'T KNOW JC GOOD MORN STLIN 12
LISTEN! I DON'T OWN NO RADIO - JC GOOD MORN STLIN 49
DON'T KEEP 'EM ALL FOR YOU. JC HOW ABOUT DIXIE 8
I DON'T GIVE A DAMN OWT FUNERAL 7
I DON'T TURN. MADAM! OWT JITNEY 39
I SAID. IT DON'T MAKE NO DIFFERENCE NOHOW. OWT STRANGER IN TWN 9
I DON'T KNOW WHERE TO TURN. OWT TOO BLUE 2
I DON'T KNOW WHERE TO GO. OWT TOO BLUE 3
I DON'T KNOW HOW YOU FEEL TODAY - OWT YESTERDAY TODAY 11
I DON'T MIND DYING - SP AS BEFITS A MAN 1
I DON'T MIND DYING SP AS BEFITS A MAN 5
PLEASE DON'T TAKE HIM AWAY! SP AS BEFITS A MAN 16
DON'T TAKE DADDY AWAY! SP AS BEFITS A MAN 18
DON'T YOU PLAY IN DAT ROAD. SP BABY 3
ALBERT. DON'T YOU PLAY IN DAT ROAD. SP BABY 8
CAUSE YOU DON'T LOVE ME SP BAD LUCK CARD 1
I DON'T KNOW WHAT SP BAD LUCK CARD 9
DON'T YOU 'MEMBER I TOLD YOU ABOUT IT SP BLD LANDLORD 3
IT'S A WONDER YOU DON'T FALL DOWN. SP BLD LANDLORD 8
I DON'T DARE START THINKING IN THE MORNING. SP BLUES AT DAWN 1
I DON'T DARE START THINKING IN THE MORNING. SP BLUES AT DAWN 2
SO I DON'T DARE START THINKING IN THE MORNING. SP BLUES AT DAWN 5
I DON'T DARE REMEMBER IN THE MORNING SP BLUES AT DAWN 6
DON'T DARE REMEMBER IN THE MORNING. SP BLUES AT DAWN 7
SO I DON'T DARE REMEMBER IN THE MORNING. SP BLUES AT DAWN 10
I DON'T SEE HIM MUCH. SP BUDDY 3
WHAT DON'T BUG SP CHILDREN'S RYME 12
THEY DON'T KICK SP COMMENT ON CURB 2
ONE DON'T MAKE ENOUGH SP CONSIDER ME 30
COULD BE THAT YOU DON'T. SP COULD BE 10
I DON'T GIVE A DAMN SP CROON 1
IT DON'T MAKE SENSE - SP DEFERRED 22
FOLKS SAY SHE DON'T LIKE SP DELINQUENT 7
SAYS SHE DON'T CARE! SP DELINQUENT 14
I DON'T TREAT YOU BAD. HATTIE. SP EARLY EVENING 17
DON'T YOU HEAR ME CALL? SP EVENING SONG 4
DON'T TURN OUT LIKE I AM. SP EVENING SONG 12
DON'T HAVE NO EFFECT ON YOU - SP EVIL 2
DON'T BE DISCOURAGED. BUILDER! SP FREEDOM'S PLOW 162
DON'T BE WEARY. SOLDIER! SP FREEDOM'S PLOW 164
DON'T GET ANYWHERE. SP HIGH TO LOW 7
YOU DON'T EVEN CARE. SP HIGH TO LOW 9
DON'T KNOW WHY. SP HOPE 2
AND DON'T MEAN HALF IT SAYS - SP IN EXPLANATION 33
SO MANY GODS DON'T KNOW. SP JOE LOUIS 7
SAYS DON'T BE 'FRAID SP JUDGMENT DAY 8
DON'T YOU WANT TO RUN AROUND SP KID SLEEPY 2
I DON'T CARE. SP KID SLEEPY 9
DON'T YOU WANT TO GET UP SP KID SLEEPY 11
I DON'T CARE. SP KID SLEEPY 17
AND LAUNDRY I DON'T HAVE MUCH LEFT SP LETTER 3
BUT IN HARLEM THEY DON'T ANSWER BACK. SP LIKEWISE 14
YOU DON'T NEED NO GUN NOR KNIFE - SP LITTLE OLD LETT 14
I DON'T KNOW WHAT TO DO." SP LOVER'S RETURN 6
YOU DON'T KNOW MY NAME. SP MADAM WRONG VIS 6
SOMETIMES YOU DON'T KNOW SP MADAM MIGHT-HAV 6
I DON'T PAY NO REVERSED SP MADAM PHONE BIL 8
THE WATER DON'T RUN. SP MADAM RENT MAN 12
DON'T MEAN NO HARM. SP MADAM WRONG VIS 12
WITH PARENTS THAT DON'T EVEN SP MADAM CHARTY CH 15
DON'T YOU SEE? SP MADAM RENT MAN 22
I SAID. I DON'T SP MADAM CENSUS 25
I DON'T KNOW? SP MADAM PHONE BIL 26
I SAID. I DON'T WANT SP MADAM MIGHT-HAV 31
YOU SAY YOU DON'T CARE SP MADAM PHONE BIL 32
DON'T WORRY 'BOUT ME! SP MADAM'S PAST HI 19
BUT WHY DON'T YOU BLUSH. SP MARCH MOON 7
DON'T YOU KNOW SP MARCH MOON 9
BLACK - AND DON'T GIVE A DAMN! SP ME AND THE MULE 6
DON'T KNOW'S I'D MIND HIS GOIN' SP MIDWINTER BLUES 7
DON'T KNOW'S I'D MIND HIS GOIN' SP MIDWINTER BLUES 9

PLEASE DON'T SNORE SO LOUD. SP MORNING AFTER 14
PLEASE DON'T SNORE SO LOUD. SP MORNING AFTER 16
SO BOY, DON'T YOU TURN BACK. SP MOTHER TO SON 14
DON'T YOU SET DOWN ON THE STEPS SP MOTHER TO SON 15
DON'T YOU FALL NOW - SP MOTHER TO SON 17
I DON'T HAVE TO WORK. SP NECESSITY 2
I DON'T HAVE TO DO NOTHING SP NECESSITY 3
HE DON'T DRINK. SP NEIGHBOR 20
SO THEY DON'T SOUND LIKE ME. SP NOTE COMM THEAT 6
I DON'T FOOL WITH THESE YOUNG GIRLS. SP PREFERENCE 3
BLACK PEOPLE DON'T REMEMBER SP SHAME ON YOU 8
WHY DON'T SHE GET A BOY-FRIEND SP SISTER 5
DON'T DECENT FOLKS HAVE DOUGH? SP SISTER 10
WELL, ANYWAY, IT DON'T HAVE TO BE A
MARRIED MAN. SP SISTER 12
JUST DON'T LET MAMA CATCH YOU SP STREET SONG 3
HONEY! BABY! DON'T GO, DEAR!" SP SYLVESTER'S BED 16
BUT I DON'T NEED NO PIANO, SP TESTIMONIAL 5
SOMETIMES PERHAPS YOU DON'T WANT TO
BE A PART OF ME. SP THEME FOR ENG B 34
DON'T LET YOUR DOG CURB YOU! SP WARNING AUGMENT 1
DON'T LET YOUR DOG SP WARNING 2
BUT DON'T LET THAT DOG CURB YOU! SP WARNING AUGMENT 4
JUST DON'T LET YOUR DOG CURB YOU! SP WARNING AUGMENT 14
I DON'T WANT NOBODY ELSE AND SP WIDOW WOMAN 19
DON'T NOBODY ELSE WANT ME. SP WIDOW WOMAN 20
I SAY DON'T WANT NOBODY ELSE SP WIDOW WOMAN 21
AND DON'T NOBODY ELSE WANT ME - SP WIDOW WOMAN 22
CAUSE I DON'T WANT TO BE BLUE. SP YOUNG GAL'S BLS 24
THAT DON'T KNOW HOW TO PLAY AYM BLUES IN STEREO 25
HOW I GOT THERE I DON'T KNOW. AYM GOSPEL CHA-CHA 40
DON'T CARE WHAT TIME IT IS - AYM ODE TO DINAH 66
DON'T TAKE THE FIFTH AMENDMENT. AYM RIDE, RED, RIDE 28
DON'T KNOW WHY I, PL ANGOLA QUESTION 1
DON'T KNOW WHY I PL ANGOLA QUESTION 8
"I DON'T WANT TO STUDY WAR NO MORE." PL BLACK PANTHER 6
WHAT DON'T BUG PL CHILDREN'S RYME 6
SEND FOR LENIN! (DON'T YOU DARE! -
HE CAN'T COME PL FINAL CALL 24
SEND FOR TROTSKY! (WHAT? DON'T
CONFUSE THE ISSUE. PL FINAL CALL 26
DON'T DEMONSTRATE! WAIT! - PL GO SLOW 9
BUT I DON'T PL IMPASSE 5
AND YOU DON'T PL IMPASSE 7
BUT SUPPOSE I DON'T WANT IT, PL QUESTION ANSWER 14
BUT I DON'T CARE! PL STILL HERE 8
WHAT I DON'T KNOW WHAT I WANT PL STOKELY MALCOLM 3
BUT I DON'T HAVE A HEART OF GOLD. PL VARI-COLORED 5
DON'T LET HIM MAKE A PULP OUT OF ME! PL WHO BUT TH LORD 11
WHY GOD DON'T PROTECT A MAN PL WHO BUT TH LORD 17
DON'T YOU KNOW PL WITHOUT BENEFIT 2
DON'T ASK ME WHY. PL WITHOUT BENEFIT 12
MAMA, DON'T CRY. PL WITHOUT BENEFIT 19

DOOMED 1
MERCEDES IS A DOOMED STAR. WB TO DARK MERCEDE 2

DOOR 18
THEN OUT MA DOOR HE GOES. FC BLACK GAL 12
AN' OUR TROUBLES AT DE DOOR. FC MINNIE SINGS 6
WHEN I OPENS DE DOOR. FC WORKIN' MAN 6
WENT RUSHIN FOR THE DOOR SH DEATH IN HARLEM 120
TO HER DOOR. FW FAITHFUL ONE 2
BACK DOOR OWT BLUES ON A BOX 5
I KNOCK ON YOUR DOOR OWT HONEY BABE 9
GONNA SHUT AN' LOCK MY DOOR SP CORA 4
OUTSIDE THE DOOR. SP END 9
THERE IS NO DOOR! SP END 10
NO BACK DOOR ENTRANCE TO THE FREEDOM
TRAIN. SP FREEDOM TRAIN 12
AND I OPENED UP MY DOOR. SP HOMECOMING 2
COME TO MY DOOR. SP MADAM NUMBER WR 2
AN' PLANT IT AT MY BACK DOOR. SP MIDWINTER BLUES 20
PLANT IT AT MY BACK DOOR. SP MIDWINTER BLUES 22
AND OUT THE DOOR SP TO BE SOMEBODY 10
THE DOOR MARKED LADIES OPENS INWARD AYM ODE TO DINAH 115
BEATIN' AT THE DOOR - PL DOWN WHERE I AM 2

DOORKNOB 1
WHERE THE DOORKNOB LETS IN LIEDER PL CULTURAL EXCHNG 15

DOORKNOBS 1
NURSES TURN GLASS DOORKNOBS SP INTERNE AT PROV 42

DOORS 7
AND LET YOUR SONGS DRIFT THROUGH THE
SWINGING DOORS. OWT JUICE JOINT 18
SHE'D BREAK DOWN DOORS SP STRANGE HURT 13
HAVE DOORS THAT OPEN OUTWARD AYM JAZZTET MUTED 16
WHERE THE DOORS ARE DOORS OF PAPER PL CULTURAL EXCHNG 2
WHERE THE DOORS ARE DOORS OF PAPER PL CULTURAL EXCHNG 2
FOR FUN TO BLOW DOORS DOWN. PL CULTURAL EXCHNG 7
IN THE POT BEHIND THE PAPER DOORS PL CULTURAL EXCHNG 26

DOORSTEPS 1
AND THE WAY YOU LOUNGE ON DOORSTEPS SP HIGH TO LOW 15

DOORWAY 2
IN THE DOORWAY LIGHT. FC CLOSING TIME 3
A WOMAN STANDING IN THE DOORWAY SP EVENING SONG 1

DOORYARD 1
ALL THE DOORYARD BRIGHT AND CLEAR DK IRISH WAKE 6

DOOR-STEPS 1
CAESAR TOLD ME TO KEEP HIS
DOOR-STEPS CLEAN. SP NEGRO 5

DOO-DOO-DOO 1
DOO-DOO-DOO! FC SATURDAY NIGHT 14

DOPE 3
THEN YOU'RE A DOPE SP ARGUMENT 6
"IT'S EASIER TO GET DOPE PL JUNIOR ADDICT 28
YES, EASIER TO GET DOPE PL JUNIOR ADDICT 30

DORIE 1
WHEN DORIE MILLER TOOK GUN IN HAND - JC JIM CROW'S LAST 28

DOROTHY'S 1
DOROTHY'S NAME IS MUD. SP BLD OF THE GIRL 8

DOUBLE 5
AN' I SHO PAYS DOUBLE FC WORKIN' MAN 14
LEFT ME BY MYSELF IN A DOUBLE BED. SH LETTER 7
AND CROCHET A QUILT FOR OUR DOUBLE
BED, SH LETTER 17
WAS LIKE A DOUBLE DEATH, SP DESIRE 2
DOUBLE BOW, SP UNCLE TOM 6

DOUBLED 1
PRICES ARE DOUBLED PL LITTLE SNG HOUS 11

DOUBT 1
NOW I BEGINS TO DOUBT. SH IN TROUBLED KEY 6

DOUBTED 1
WHO DOUBTED THAT THE WAR WOULD END
RIGHT, SP FREEDOM'S PLOW 133

DOUGH 5
(WHEN YOU'RE NO GOOD FOR DOUGH THEY
GO.) SP DANCER 20
DON'T DECENT FOLKS HAVE DOUGH? SP SISTER 10
WITH THE DOUGH. SP SITUATION 4
HAVE MADE THEIR DOUGH, PL OFFICE BUILDING 5
AND HEAD NORTH WITH THE DOUGH. PL VARI-COLORED 4

DOUGLASS 3
WHAT FREDERICK DOUGLASS SAID WAS
TRUE. SP FREEDOM'S PLOW 115
SEND FOR FREDERICK DOUGLASS,
GARRISON, BEECHER, PL FINAL CALL 30
DOUGLASS WAS SOMEONE WHO, PL FREDRK DOUGLASS 1

DOUGLASS'S 1
SPEAK OF FREDERICK DOUGLASS'S BEARD AYM BIRD IN ORBIT 44

DOVE 2
OLD PICASSO AND THE DOVE PL THE DOVE 2
AS POTTERY WITH DOVE PL THE DOVE 4

DOWN 156
BOWED DOWN WITH CHATTERING PARROTS WB OUR LAND 10
AND PIERROT RAN DOWN THE LONG WHITE
ROAD WB PIERROT 29
NIGHT-TIME'S COMIN' DOWN. FC A RUINED GAL 12
I'LL CUT YOU DOWN COMIN'. NM BIG-TIMER POEM 32
FOLKS, DOWN YONDER AT HOME. NM BIG-TIMER POEM 54
LAUGH AND PUSH ME DOWN. NM BLACK CLWN POEM 9
THROWING DOWN THE HAT OF A FOOL, AND
STANDING FORTH, STRAIGHT AND
STRONG, NM BLACK CLWN MOOD 14
WILL NOT PULL ME DOWN. NM BLACK CLWN POEM 28
FOREVER PUSHED DOWN. NM BLACK CLWN POEM 46
SCORN CRUSHING ME DOWN. NM BLACK CLWN POEM 52
YOU CAN'T KEEP ME DOWN! NM BLACK CLWN POEM 68
UP AND DOWN, AND THEY JUST AIN'T NO
JOBS IN THIS MAN'S TOWN. NM BROKE 3
SO I WENT DOWN TOWN TO A HOTEL WHERE
I USED TO WORK AT NIGHT, NM BROKE 44
AW-OO! YONDER COMES A WOMAN I USED
TO KNOW WAY DOWN SOUTH. NM BROKE 62
I WENT DOWN TO DE STATION. DK HOMESICK BLUES 7
WENT DOWN TO DE STATION. DK HOMESICK BLUES 9
SUN'S GOING DOWN THIS EVENING - DK SONG BANJO DANC 12
THE SUN'S GOING DOWN THIS VERY NIGHT
\- DK SONG BANJO DANC 14
THE SUN'S GOING DOWN THIS VERY NIGHT
\- DK SONG BANJO DANC 26
I'LL LAY DOWN AN' DIE RIGHT NOW. DK WIDE RIVER 18
MARCH WITH YOU DOWN TIME'S STREET, SL SCOTTSBORO 6
THAT TORE THE BASTILE DOWN SL SCOTTSBORO 14
THE MILLIONS SHOT DOWN WHEN WE
STRIKE? ANS LET AMERICA BE 54
THE SUN BOUND DOWN BY LAW. ANS NEGRO GHETTO 4

LIKE WATER DOWN THE STREET.	ANS NEGRO GHETTO	6
IF I HAD SOME MONEY I'D STROLL DOWN THE STREET	SH BED TIME	3
I WENT DOWN THE ROAD.	SH BLD THE SINNER	1
STRAIGHT DOWN THE ROAD	SH BLD THE SINNER	3
GOING DOWN THAT ROAD.	SH BLD THE SINNER	17
I WAS WALKIN' DOWN DE STREET, JUDGE.	SH BRIEF ENCOUNTER	3
DOWN IN A CELLAR BACK FROM THE STREET.	SH DEATH IN HARLEM	23
CAUSE WE DANCIN DOWN!	SH DEATH IN HARLEM	57
STROLL DOWN LUSCIOUS.	SH HARLEM SWEETIES	43
I LOOKED DOWN 31ST STREET.	SH MIDNIGHT CHIPPI	1
DOWN ON 31ST STREET.	SH MIDNIGHT CHIPPI	3
AND THEN CUT DOWN DE LOG -	SH ONLY WOMAN BLUS	10
THAT EXTRA DAY WOULD GET ME DOWN.	SH OUT OF WORK	18
DOWN ON '33RD STREET	SH STATEMENT	1
AND SET DOWN AND DRINK IT, MYSELF AND ME.	SH SUPPER TIME	12
CAUSE IF I DON'T THEY'LL CUT DOWN MY PAY.	SH SUPPER TIME	14
IT'S DARK ON THIS STOOP, LAWD! THE SUN'S GONE DOWN!	SH TWILIGHT REVERI	15
DOWN SOUTH YOU MAKE ME RIDE	JC BLACK MAN SPEAK	13
IT WAS DOWN IN MIAMI	JC BLD SAM SOLOMON	5
WHERE I LIVE DOWN IN DIXIE	JC GOOD MORN STLIN	6
SOME FOLKS TRY TO TELL ME DOWN THIS WAY	JC GOOD MORN STLIN	23
DOWN PATHS OF DEATH AND DARKNESS	JC TO CAPTAIN MULZ	8
THAT BOWS ME DOWN.	FW BURDEN	2
AS DOWN THE ROAD	FW CAROLINA CABIN	15
OURSELVES UPSIDE DOWN.	FW CIRCLES	10
DOWN THE STREET YOUNG HARLEM	FW DIMOUT IN HARLM	1
DOWN THE STREET IS WALKING	FW DIMOUT IN HARLM	4
DOWN THE STREET YOUNG HARLEM	FW DIMOUT IN HARLM	16
RIDING UP AND DOWN.	OWT BLD MARGE POLIT	34
DOWN ON 43RD.	OWT JITNEY	12
AND DAWN COMES DOWN THE STREET ALL WANLY WHITE.	OWT JUICE JOINT	4
THE HEAD OF LINCOLN LOOKS DOWN FROM THE WALL	OWT LINCOLN THEATRE	1
THE BAND DOWN IN THE PIT BURSTS INTO JAZZ.	OWT LINCOLN THEATRE	6
I WENT DOWN TO THE CORNER.	OWT LONESOME CORNER	1
WHEN YOU LET ME DOWN -	OWT REQUEST REQUIEM	6
I SET DOWN ON A STONE.	OWT STRANGER IN TWN	2
WHEN THEY LET ME DOWN.	SP AS BEFITS A MAN	13
DOWN INTO THE CLAY.	SP AS BEFITS A MAN	14
I LIE DOWN IN THE SHADOW.	SP AS I GREW OLDER	19
THESE STEPS IS BROKEN DOWN.	SP BLD LANDLORD	6
IT'S A WONDER YOU DON'T FALL DOWN.	SP BLD LANDLORD	8
SHE PUT 'EM DOWN.	SP BLD OF THE MAN	12
AND I SAW THE SUN GO DOWN.	SP BLUE BAYOU	3
AND I SAW THE SUN GO DOWN.	SP BLUE BAYOU	6
I SAW THE SUN GO DOWN.	SP BLUE BAYOU	19
AND I SAW THE SUN GO DOWN.	SP BLUE BAYOU	24
DOWN.	SP BLUE BAYOU	25
DOWN.	SP BLUE BAYOU	26
LAWD, I SAW THE SUN GO DOWN!	SP BLUE BAYOU	27
AND IT'S MARKED DOWN THAT-A-WAY.	SP BLUE MONDAY	5
MONDAY'LL GET YOU DOWN.	SP BLUE MONDAY	9
WILL SURELY GET YOU DOWN.	SP BLUE MONDAY	11
GOIN' DOWN THE ROAD, LAWD,	SP BOUND NO'TH BLS	1
GOIN' DOWN THE ROAD.	SP BOUND NO'TH BLS	2
DOWN THE ROAD, LAWD,	SP BOUND NO'TH BLS	3
WAY, WAY DOWN THE ROAD.	SP BOUND NO'TH BLS	4
WHAT'S WRITTEN DOWN	SP CHILDREN'S RYME	20
I WENT DOWN IN THE VALLEY	SP CROSSING	9
HELP ME WHEN I'M DOWN AND OUT.	SP DOWN AND OUT	2
HELP ME WHEN I'M DOWN AND OUT.	SP DOWN AND OUT	4
DOWN IN THE BASS	SP EASY BOOGIE	1
DOWN IN THE BASS	SP EASY BOOGIE	5
GOIN' UP AN' DOWN.	SP ELEVATOR BOY	16
UP AN' DOWN.	SP ELEVATOR BOY	17
COME DRIFTIN' DOWN ON ME.	SP FEET O' JESUS	4
DOWN SOUTH IN DIXIE ONLY TRAIN I SEE'S	SP FREEDOM TRAIN	9
NOR WRITE THEM DOWN ON PAPER.	SP FREEDOM'S PLOW	146
WILL HIS FREEDOM TRAIN COME ZOOMIN' DOWN THE TRACK	SP FREEDOM TRAIN	49
DOWN INTO THE EARTH WENT THE PLOW	SP FREEDOM'S PLOW	49
DOWN THE STREET	SP HARLEM NIGHT SO	11
STOCKINGS DOWN.	SP HIGH TO LOW	11
JUST AS IF YOU WERE DOWN SOUTH.	SP HIGH TO LOW	16
YOU LET ME DOWN -	SP HIGH TO LOW	20
I MADE DOWN THE BED.	SP HOMECOMING	6
BLACK BROWN YELLOW BENT DOWN WORKING	SP IN EXPLANATION	52
AS DOWN THE ROADWAY	SP IN TIME SILVER	18
AND FOR YOUR LOVE SONG TONE THEIR RUMBLE DOWN.	SP JUKE BOX LOVE	6
I'M GOIN' DOWN TO THE RIVER	SP LAMENT OVER LOV	7
DOWN TO THE RIVER.	SP LAMENT OVER LOV	9
I WENT DOWN TO THE RIVER.	SP LIFE IS FINE	1
I SET DOWN ON THE BANK.	SP LIFE IS FINE	2
AND THOUGHT I WOULD JUMP DOWN.	SP LIFE IS FINE	15
I LOOK DOWN THE ROAD	SP LITTLE GRN TREE	9
A LITTLE PIECE DOWN THE ROAD.	SP LITTLE GRN TREE	11
TO PUT IT DOWN.	SP MADAM CENSUS	4
NEARLY BROKE ME DOWN.	SP MADAM HER MADAM	12
I'M GOING DOWN THE STREET.	SP MAMA AND DAUGHT	2
MY GOOD MAN TURNED ME DOWN.	SP MIDWINTER BLUES	6
DON'T YOU SET DOWN ON THE STEPS	SP MOTHER TO SON	15
WENT DOWN TO NEW ORLEANS, AND I'VE SEEN ITS MUDDY	SP NEGRO SPEAKS OF	9
DOWN HOME	SP NEIGHBOR	1
AND OFF DOWN LENOX AVENUE	SP NIGHT FUNERAL	33
AND I PUT IT DOWN IN	SP ONE-WAY TICKET	3
DID YOU EVER GO DOWN TO THE RIVER -	SP REVERIE HARLEM	1
SIT DOWN BY THE RIVER	SP REVERIE HARLEM	3
DOWN ON THE HARLEM RIVER:	SP REVERIE HARLEM	9
NOW THE STREETS DOWN BY THE RIVER	SP RUBY BROWN	16
UPTOWN AND DOWN.	SP SAME IN BLUES	30
WAY DOWN SOUTH IN DIXIE	SP SONG DARK GIRL	1
WAY DOWN SOUTH IN DIXIE	SP SONG DARK GIRL	5
WAY DOWN SOUTH IN DIXIE	SP SONG DARK GIRL	9
LAID HER DOWN.	SP STONY LONESOME	5
SHE'D BREAK DOWN DOORS	SP STRANGE HURT	13
TILL THE SUN GOES DOWN.	SP SUNDAY BY COMB	2
RUSHES DOWN THE DRAIN	SP SUNDAY MORNING	3
BUT MARCH EVER FORWARD, BREAKING DOWN BARS.	SP THE NEGRO MOTHE	47
CARES KEEP DOWN THE CHILDREN OF THE NEGRO MOTHER.	SP THE NEGRO MOTHE	52
DOWN ON LENOX AVENUE THE OTHER NIGHT	SP THE WEARY BLUES	4
THE STEPS FROM THE HILL LEAD DOWN INTO HARLEM.	SP THEME FOR ENG B	11
UP TO MY ROOM, SIT DOWN, AND WRITE THIS PAGE:	SP THEME FOR ENG B	15
UP THE STAIRS AND DOWN THE STAIRS	SP TO BE SOMEBODY	9
TAMED DOWN.	SP TRUMPET PLAYER	12
DOWN IN WEST TEXAS WHERE THE SUN	SP WEST TEXAS	1
AND WE STARTED DOWN THE ROAD	SP WEST TEXAS	12
SPEAK OF RICE DOWN IN THE MARSHALND	AYM BIRD IN ORBIT	43
ALL SOLD DOWN THE RIVER.	AYM BIRD IN ORBIT	52
TOURE DOWN IN GUINEA	AYM BIRD IN ORBIT	58
DOWN THE LONG HARD ROW THAT I BEEN HOEING	AYM BLUES IN STEREO	34
UNTAKEN DOWN ON TAPE -	AYM IS IT TRUE?	8
YET NO PRESENTS DOWN THE CHIMNEY.	AYM ODE TO DINAH	74
LIES WRITTEN DOWN	PL CHILDREN'S RYME	11
HIS WORDS JUMP DOWN	PL CORNER MEETING	6
FOR FUN TO BLOW DOORS DOWN.	PL CULTURAL EXCHNG	7
DONE BROKE MY ANKLES DOWN.	PL DOWN WHERE I AM	7
COME DOWN.	PL DOWN WHERE I AM	16
SEND FOR OLD MAN MOSES TO LAY DOWN THE LAW.	PL FINAL CALL	9
AND KNOCKED ME DOWN.	PL KU KLUX	14
DOWN SOUTH WHERE I COME FROM	PL MERRY-GO-ROUND	6
DOWN SOUTH ON THE TRAIN	PL MERRY-GO-ROUND	9
WHY DOWN SOUTH IS ALWAYS DOWN.	PL VARI-COLORED	15
WHY DOWN SOUTH IS ALWAYS DOWN.	PL VARI-COLORED	15
DOWN THE STREET AT ME!	PL WHO BUT TH LORD	4

DOWNING 1

PREMIER DOWNING AGING	AYM SHADES OF PIG	3

DOWNTOWN 6

DOWNTOWN TO WORK TODAY.	SP BLUE MONDAY	2
HE WORKS DOWNTOWN FOR TWELVE A WEEK.	SP BUDDY	4
DOWNTOWN.	SP COMMENT ON CURB	4
DOWNTOWN AT EIGHT.	SP CONSIDER ME	18
TO LIVE DOWNTOWN	SP PASSING	12
THEY KNOW ME, TOO, DOWNTOWN.	AYM HORN OF PLENTY	40

DOWN- 1

AND GO TO WORK DOWN-	SP KID SLEEPY	12

DOWN-HOME 1

TOGETHER IN MY BIG OLD DOWN-HOME FRAME.	SH DAYBREAK	8

DOZEN 3

KNOWIN THEY CAN BUY A DOZEN COLORED PLACES.	SH DEATH IN HARLEM	61
I WANT A DOZEN PRETTY WOMEN	SP AS BEFITS A MAN	3
TWO DOZEN MEN TO THE FLOOR.	SP TO BE SOMEBODY	18

DO-MOVE 1

OF THE DO-MOVE COSMIC CONSCIENCE?	AYM BIRD IN ORBIT	38

DO-RIGHT 1

DO-RIGHT MAN?	SP EARLY EVENING	24

DO' 2

DONE BEAT YOU TO DE PLACE, STANDIN' OUT SIDE DE DO'	NM BROKE	6
BOTH AT MA DO'.	SP SYLVESTER'S BED	12

DR 3

AND THE GENTLEMEN WITH DR. IN FRONT OF THEIR NAMES.	ANS KIDS WHO DIE	21
ON DR. ROBERT WEAVER?	AYM BIRD IN ORBIT	83
DR. RUFUS CLEMENT HIS CHIEF ADVISER.	PL CULTURAL EXCHNG	44

DRAFTEE 2

FRANTIC, KICK THEIR DRAFTEE YEARS	SP FLATTED FIFTHS	4
NUDGE THEIR DRAFTEE YEARS.	SP TAG	4

DRAG 1
IN AN OLD SUIT AND A BATTERED HAT, TO THE TUNE OF A SLOW DRAG STOMP NM BROKE 1

DRAGON 1
THE FUSE OF CENTURIES OF DRAGON KINGS . . . . PL BIRMINGHAM SUND 19

DRAIN 1
RUSHES DOWN THE DRAIN . . . . SP SUNDAY MORNING 3

DRAMAS 1
WHILE MOVIES ECHO DRAMAS ON THE SCREEN. . . . . OWT LINCOLN THEATRE 2

DRAMATIC 2
A DRAMATIC MONOLOGUE TO BE SPOKEN BY A PURE-BLOODED NEGRO IN THE WHITE NM BLACK CLWN MOOD 1
A DRAMATIC RECITATION TO BE DONE IN THE HALF-DARK BY A YOUNG BROWN FELLOW . . . . NM COLORED SL MOOD 1

DRANK 1
WHERE I DRANK OF THE BITTER RIVER JC THE BITTER RIVR 16

DRAW 1
THEY DRAW UP RESTRICTIVE COVENANTS SP MIGRANT 25

DRAWED 1
I JUST DRAWED MY MONEY TONIGHT . . SP PREFERENCE 9

DRAWS 1
AND WHO ARE YOU THAT DRAWS YOUR VEIL ACROSS THE STARS? . . . . ANS LET AMERICA BE 18

DREAM 82
DREAM SINGERS. . . . . FC LAUGHERS 1
I THOUGHT LOVE WAS A DREAM, BUT I SHO HAVE AWOKE - . . . . NM BROKE 54
LAST NIGHT IN A DREAM MY BROTHER CAME TO ME . . . . NM COLORED SL POEM 13
BUT THE DREAM WAS CRUEL - AND BITTER - AND SOMEHOW . . . . NM COLORED SL POEM 40
THEN I WOKE UP, AND THE DREAM WAS ENDED - . . . . NM COLORED SL POEM 48
BUT BROKEN WAS THE SOLDIER'S DREAM, TOO BAD TO BE . . . . NM COLORED SL POEM 49
WITH THE DREAM. . . . . ANS A NEW SONG 42
A NEW DREAM FLAMES . . . . ANS A NEW SONG 53
LET IT BE THE DREAM IT USED TO BE. ANS LET AMERICA BE 2
LET AMERICA BE THE DREAM THE DREAMERS DREAMED - . . . . ANS LET AMERICA BE 6
HUNGRY YET TODAY DESPITE THE DREAM. ANS LET AMERICA BE 35
YET I'M THE ONE WHO DREAMT OUR BASIC DREAM . . . . ANS LET AMERICA BE 39
WHO DREAMT A DREAM SO STRONG, SO BRAVE, SO TRUE, ... ANS LET AMERICA BE 41
EXCEPT THE DREAM THAT'S ALMOST DEAD TODAY. . . . . ANS LET AMERICA BE 61
MUST BRING BACK OUR MIGHTY DREAM AGAIN. . . . . ANS LET AMERICA BE 69
LIKE A WOMAN IN A DREAM . . . . . . SH DEATH IN HARLEM 112
OUT OF A DREAM. . . . . SH HARLEM SWEETIES 12
TO A HONEY-BROWN DREAM. . . . . . . SH HARLEM SWEETIES 36
AIN'T EVEN GONNA DREAM 'BOUT THE WOMENS I HAD. . . . . SH PAY DAY 18
OF MY DREAM. . . . . JC NOTE TO NAZIS 4
THAT STRANGLED MY DREAM: . . . . . JC THE BITTER RIVR 17
AND SPIT IN THE FACE OF MY DREAM. JC THE BITTER RIVR 62
YOUR SHIP IS MANKIND'S DEEPEST DREAM JC TO CAPTAIN MULZ 67
GRAB A LONELY DREAM . . . . FW LITTLE SONG 3
THEIR DREAM AWAY. . . . . FW LITTLE SONG 8
DREAM OF YESTERDAY . . . . FW MOTHERLAND 1
I HAVE ALMOST FORGOTTEN MY DREAM. SP AS I GREW OLDER 2
MY DREAM. . . . . SP AS I GREW OLDER 6
BETWEEN ME AND MY DREAM. . . . . . SP AS I GREW OLDER 10
THE LIGHT OF MY DREAM. . . . . . . SP AS I GREW OLDER 14
NO LONGER THE LIGHT OF MY DREAM BEFORE ME. . . . . SP AS I GREW OLDER 20
FIND MY DREAM! . . . . SP AS I GREW OLDER 27
THE DREAM IS VAGUE . . . . SP BEALE STREET 1
THE DREAM IS VAGUE. . . . . SP BEALE STREET 5
OF THE DREAM . . . . SP BEALE STREET 10
OF A DREAM DEFERRED . . . . SP BOOGIE 1 A.M. 4
WAS NO WATER IN A DREAM . . . . . . SP CROSSING 12
OF A DREAM . . . . SP DEFERRED 50
DEAR DREAM OF UTTER ALIVENESS - . . SP DEMAND 2
TELL ME, O QUICKLY! DREAM OF ALIVENESS. . . . . SP DEMAND 4
TELL ME, O DREAM OF UTTER ALIVENESS - . . . . SP DEMAND 6
MONTAGE OF A DREAM DEFERRED: . . . SP DIME 3
THIS MOST STRANGE DREAM. . . . . . SP DREAM 2
OF A DREAM DEFERRED? . . . . SP DREAM BOOGIE 4
THAT IS MY DREAM! . . . . SP DREAM VARIATION 9
AND DREAMED THE SWEETEST DREAM . . SP FIRED 8
FIRST IN THE HEART IS THE DREAM - SP FREEDOM'S PLOW 9
THUS THE DREAM BECOMES NOT ONE MAN'S DREAM ALONE. . . . . SP FREEDOM'S PLOW 22
THUS THE DREAM BECOMES NOT ONE MAN'S DREAM ALONE. . . . . SP FREEDOM'S PLOW 22
BUT A COMMUNITY DREAM. . . . . . . SP FREEDOM'S PLOW 23
NOT MY DREAM ALONE, BUT OUR DREAM. SP FREEDOM'S PLOW 24
NOT MY DREAM ALONE, BUT OUR DREAM. SP FREEDOM'S PLOW 24
AMERICA IS A DREAM. . . . . SP FREEDOM'S PLOW 142
DREAM NOURISHED IN COMMON, ... SP FREEDOM'S PLOW 159
CAME THE DREAM, THE STRENGTH, THE WILL, ... SP FREEDOM'S PLOW 83
TO A DREAM DEFERRED? . . . . SP GOOD MORNING 27
WHAT HAPPENS TO A DREAM DEFERRED? SP HARLEM 1
THE DREAM IS A COCKTAIL AT SLOPPY JOE'S - . . . . SP HAVANA DREAMS 1
THE DREAM IS THE ROAD TO BATABANO. SP HAVANA DREAMS 3
PERHAPS THE DREAM IS ONLY HER FACE - SP HAVANA DREAMS 5
HIS WIFE LOOKED IT UP IN HER DREAM BOOK . . . . SP HOPE 3
DREAM WITHIN A DREAM. . . . . SP ISLAND 9
DREAM WITHIN A DREAM. . . . . SP ISLAND 9
OUR DREAM DEFERRED. . . . . SP ISLAND 10
DREAM DEFERRED. . . . . SP LIKEWISE 27
HAD A DREAM LAST NIGHT I . . . . . SP MORNING AFTER 7
A LONG, DREAM NIGHT WITH ME. . . . SP NATCHA 7
I HAD A DREAM . . . . SP NIGHTMARE BOOGIE 1
A NIGHTMARE DREAM: . . . . SP NIGHTMARE BOOGIE 5
HARLEM OF THE BITTER DREAM. . . . . SP PASSING 14
SINCE THEIR DREAM HAS . . . . SP PASSING 15
IN A DREAM DEFERRED. . . . . SP SAME IN BLUES 7
IN A DREAM DEFERRED. . . . . SP SAME IN BLUES 14
IN A DREAM DEFERRED. . . . . SP SAME IN BLUES 21
IN A DREAM DEFERRED. . . . . SP SAME IN BLUES 28
WHEN A DREAM GETS KICKED AROUND. . SP SAME IN BLUES 32
WHY SHOULD IT BE MY DREAM . . . . . SP TELL ME 3
GOD PUT A DREAM LIKE STEEL IN MY SOUL. . . . . SP THE NEGRO MOTHE 19
I NOURISHED THE DREAM THAT NOTHING COULD SMOTHER . . . . SP THE NEGRO MOTHE 31
BUT DREAM SHIPS SAIL AWAY . . . . . SP WATER-FRONT STR 2
WHAT HAPPENS TO A DREAM DEFERRED? PL DREAM DEFERRED 1
BUT THE DREAM . . . . PL OPPRESSION 10

DREAMED 6
LET AMERICA BE THE DREAM THE DREAMERS DREAMED - . . . . ANS LET AMERICA BE 6
FOR ALL THE DREAMS WE'VE DREAMED . ANS LET AMERICA BE 56
AS THE DREAMED OF SKIES. . . . . . FW WISDOM 8
I DREAMED ABOUT WHEN WE FIRST FELL IN LOVE . . . . SP DEFERRED 9
AND DREAMED THE SWEETEST DREAM . . SP FIRED 8
I DREAMED 7-0-3. . . . . SP MADAM NUMBER WR 10

DREAMER 1
DREAMER OF DREAMS TO BE BROKEN. . . JC THE BITTER RIVR 67

DREAMERS 4
YOU DREAMERS. . . . . DK DREAM KEEPER 2
LET AMERICA BE THE DREAM THE DREAMERS DREAMED - . . . . ANS LET AMERICA BE 6
DARK DANCERS DANCE AND DREAMERS SEEK A STAR . . . . OWT JUICE JOINT 39
TO THE DREAMERS. . . . . PL OPPRESSION 3

DREAMER'S 1
ON A DREAMER'S TAIL . . . . SP JAM SESSION 8

DREAMING 7
DREAMING . . . . SP GOOD MORNING 20
DREAMING YOU GO. . . . . SP SNAIL 2
A CITY DREAMING . . . . SP STARS 5
DREAMING OF A BABY GRAND PIANO . . SP TO BE SOMEBODY 2
DREAMING OF A BABY GRAND TO PLAY . SP TO BE SOMEBODY 4
DREAMING OF THE BOXING GLOVES . . . SP TO BE SOMEBODY 15
DREAMING THAT THE NEGROES . . . . . PL CULTURAL EXCHNG 38

DREAMS 33
BRING ME ALL OF YOUR DREAMS. . . . DK DREAM KEEPER 1
HOLD FAST TO DREAMS . . . . DK DREAMS 1
FOR IF DREAMS DIE . . . . DK DREAMS 2
HOLD FAST TO DREAMS . . . . DK DREAMS 5
FOR WHEN DREAMS GO . . . . DK DREAMS 6
OUT OF THE DUST OF DREAMS . . . . . DK FAIRIES 1
TO A SLEEP WITHOUT DREAMS . . . . . DK QUIET GIRL 5
FOR ALL THE DREAMS WE'VE DREAMED . ANS LET AMERICA BE 56
DREAMER OF DREAMS TO BE BROKEN. . . JC THE BITTER RIVR 67
AND DREAMS . . . . FW OLD SAILOR 17
AND WITHOUT DREAMS. . . . . FW SLEEP 8
O, DREAMS! . . . . OWT NEGRO SERVANT 16
TO A SLEEP WITHOUT DREAMS . . . . . SP ARDELLA 5
INTO A THOUSAND WHIRLING DREAMS . . SP AS I GREW OLDER 32
DREAMS AROUND . . . . SP COMMENT ON CURB 3
HOW DREAMS . . . . SP DREAM 12
BRINGING MEN AND DREAMS, WOMEN AND DREAMS. . . . . SP FREEDOM'S PLOW 36
BRINGING MEN AND DREAMS, WOMEN AND DREAMS. . . . . SP FREEDOM'S PLOW 36

LIKE THE PILLOWS OF ALL SWEET DREAMS. . . . . . SP MIDNIGHT DANCER 6
DARK ONES OF TODAY. MY DREAMS MUST COME TRUE: . . . . . SP THE NEGRO MOTHE 34
OH. MY DARK CHILDREN. MAY MY DREAMS AND MY PRAYERS . . . . . SP THE NEGRO MOTHE 49
AND DREAMS. LIKE ME. . . . . . SP WATER-FRONT STR 8
AND DREAMS I'LL SEND YOU . . . . . AYM BLUES IN STEREO 3
DREAMS AND NIGHTMARES! . . . . . PL CULTURAL EXCHNG 36
NIGHTMARES. DREAMS. OH! . . . . . PL CULTURAL EXCHNG 37
GET OUT THE LUNCH-BOX OF YOUR DREAMS PL JIM CROW CAR 1
AND SEEKS AN OUT IN OTHER WORLDLY DREAMS. . . . . . PL JUNIOR ADDICT 3
TELESCOPE OF DREAMS . . . . . PL LONG VIEW NEGRO 3
FOR HONEST DREAMS . . . . . PL MILITANT 10
NOW DREAMS . . . . . PL OPPRESSION 1
DREAMS KICKED ASUNDER. . . . . . PL QUESTION ANSWER 11
LITTLE DREAMS . . . . . PL SLUM DREAMS 1
AND DREAMS AS FRAGILE . . . . . PL THE DOVE 3

DREAMT 3
YET I'M THE ONE WHO DREAMT OUR BASIC DREAM . . . . . ANS LET AMERICA BE 39
WHO DREAMT A DREAM SO STRONG. SO BRAVE. SO TRUE. . . . . . ANS LET AMERICA BE 41
LAST NIGHT I DREAMT . . . . . SP DREAM 1

DREAM-DUST 1
ONE HANDFUL OF DREAM-DUST . . . . . PL DREAM DUST 5

DREAM-SINGERS 1
DREAM-SINGERS ALL. - . . . . . FC LAUGHERS 19

DREAM'S 1
OR MAYBE THE DREAM'S A VEDADO ROSE - SP HAVANA DREAMS 7

DREARY 1
ANY PLACE IS DREARY . . . . . SP COULD BE 15

DREMPT 1
I DREMPT LAST NIGHT I . . . . . SP MORNING AFTER 9

DRESS 3
LIFTS HIGH A DRESS OF SILKEN GOLD. WB JAZZONIA 6
ALL DAY SUNDAY DIDN'T EVEN DRESS UP. SH SUNDAY 1
IN TIME TO WASH AND DRESS. . . . . SP DEFERRED 27

DRESSED 7
ARE DRESSED IN SCARLET AND GOLD . . WB POEME D'AUTOMNE 5
I DRESSED UP ALBERT JOHNSON. . . . FC BLACK GAL 9
DRESSED. CARRYING HIS BOOKS TO SCHOOL. . . . . . NM DARK YOUTH USA 1
DRESSED TO KILL - . . . . . SH BLD THE SINNER 2
ALL DRESSED TO KILL - . . . . . SH BLD THE SINNER 18
DRESSED SO FINE? . . . . . SP LADY'S BOOGIE 2
DRESSED LIKE A TEDDY BOY . . . . . AYM ASK YOUR MAMA 62

DRESSES 2
WHITE DRESSES . . . . . SP INTERNE AT PROV 3
AND BLOODIED SUNDAY DRESSES . . . . PL BIRMINGHAM SUND 7

DREW 1
ARABELLA DREW HER PISTOL. . . . . . SH DEATH IN HARLEM 99

DREYFUS 1
SEND FOR DREYFUS TO CRY. "J'ACCUSE!" PL FINAL CALL 12

DRIFT 1
AND LET YOUR SONGS DRIFT THROUGH THE SWINGING DOORS. . . . . . OWT JUICE JOINT 18

DRIFTIN' 1
COME DRIFTIN' DOWN ON ME. . . . . . SP FEET O' JESUS 4

DRINK 14
SHE DON'T DRINK GIN . . . . . FC NEW CABARET GRL 5
MIX UP A DRINK. . . . . . NM BIG-TIMER POEM 62
FOLKS AT THE TABLES DRINK AND GRIN. SH DEATH IN HARLEM 31
AND SET DOWN AND DRINK IT. MYSELF AND ME. . . . . . SH SUPPER TIME 12
AND MAKE ME DRINK OF THE BITTER CUP JC THE BITTER RIVR 57
WHERE BLACK MEN COME TO DRINK AND PLAY AND SING. . . . . . OWT JUICE JOINT 34
HE GAVE THEM TO DRINK OF HIS WINE. LHR BLD MARY'S SON 17
COME. DRINK PALM WINE. . . . . . SP NATCHA 5
COME. DRINK KISSES. . . . . . SP NATCHA 6
BUT EAT. DRINK. STAY BLACK. AND DIE. SP NECESSITY 4
HE DON'T DRINK. . . . . . SP NEIGHBOR 20
COME ON DRINK COGNAC. . . . . . SP PORT TOWN 5
WELL. I LIKE TO EAT. SLEEP. DRINK. AND BE IN LOVE. . . . . . SP THEME FOR ENG B 21
TO DRINK. . . . . . SP YOUNG SAILOR 11

DRINKING 2
BUT I WAS DRINKING LICKER. . . . . SH BLD THE SINNER 15
DRINKING . . . . . SP SNAIL 7

DRINKIN' 2
DRINKIN' AND GAMBLIN' NOW. . . . . NM BIG-TIMER POEM 13
DRINKIN' LIFE LIKE WINE. . . . . . NM BIG-TIMER POEM 18

DRINKS 3
STILL AFTER HOURS POURING DRINKS THE LAW FORBIDS - . . . . . OWT JUICE JOINT 38
BUT WHEN HE DRINKS. . . . . . SP NEIGHBOR 17
HE DRINKS FAST. . . . . . SP NEIGHBOR 18

DRIPPED 2
DRIPPED BLOOD OVER THE EASTERN HILLS SP A BLACK PIERROT 8
AND DRIPPED THEIR JUICE . . . . . SP MIDNIGHT DANCER 9

DRIPPING 1
LOOK AT THAT WATER DRIPPING IN THE SINK. . . . . . SH SUPPER TIME 5

DRIVE 11
AND DRIVE US TO THE TIME-CLOCK AND THE PLOW . . . . . ANS OPEN LETTER 27
I MUST DRIVE THE BOMBERS OUT OF SPAIN! . . . . . ANS SONG OF SPAIN 79
I MUST DRIVE THE BOMBERS OUT OF THE WORLD! . . . . . ANS SONG OF SPAIN 80
THAT GAL DON'T DRIVE MY . . . . . SH ANNOUNCEMENT 15
AND DRIVE SO FAR. SO FAR. . . . . . SH DECLARATION 11
I WOULD DRIVE . . . . . SH DECLARATION 13
JUST TO DRIVE MY BLUES AWAY - . . . SH EVENIN' BLUES 14
TO DRIVE MY BLUES AWAY. . . . . . SH EVENIN' BLUES 16
DRIVE THAT BABY BACKWARD. . . . . . SH IF-ING 8
TO DRIVE THE FICISTS FROM THE LAND. JC GOOD MORN STLIN 34
CAN A COAL BLACK MAN DRIVE THE FREEDOM TRAIN? . . . . . SP FREEDOM TRAIN 18

DRIVEN 4
I AM THE RED MAN DRIVEN FROM THE LAND. . . . . . ANS LET AMERICA BE 21
BEEN DRIVEN OFF ITS WAY. . . . . . JC TO CAPTAIN MULZ 7
DRIVEN TO THE FIELD. . . . . . SP SHARE-CROPPERS 2
DRIVEN TO THE FIELD - . . . . . SP SHARE-CROPPERS 14

DRIVES 3
LOOKS LIKE WHAT DRIVES ME CRAZY . . SP EVIL 1
TILL IT DRIVES YOU CRAZY. TOO. . . SP EVIL 4
AND NIGHT-TIME DRIVES ME WILD. . . SP MISS BLUES'ES 12

DRIVING 2
SHE WAS DRIVING ALONE. . . . . . SH ANNOUNCEMENT 2
DRIVING THE BUTCHER'S CART . . . . SP JOY 6

DRONING 1
DRONING A DROWSY SYNCOPATED TUNE. SP THE WEARY BLUES 1

DROOP 2
WATCH THEM DROOP. WILT. FADE . . . PL CROWNS GARLANDS 10
WHO SEEKS AN OUT IN EYES THAT DROOP PL JUNIOR ADDICT 4

DROP 4
DROP ONE BY ONE INTO STILLNESS. . . WB SUMMER NIGHT 3
I'LL SING FOR YOU - BUT DROP THAT COLOR BAR. . . . . . JC JIM CROW'S LAST 18
GOD WILLING DROP A SHILLING . . . . AYM ASK YOUR MAMA 44
AND BALLOTS DROP IN BOXES . . . . . AYM BIRD IN ORBIT 13

DROPPED 6
DROPPED HER WITH A THUD. . . . . . SP BLD OF THE GIRL 6
DROPPED OUT SIX MONTHS WHEN I WAS SEVEN. . . . . . SP DEFERRED 3
INTO THAT FURROW THE FREEDOM SEED WAS DROPPED. . . . . . SP FREEDOM'S PLOW 194
WHEN I DROPPED THAT NICKEL . . . . SP MIDNIGHT RAFFLE 9
I WOULDN'T HAVE DROPPED IT. . . . . SP MIDNIGHT RAFFLE 11
DROPPED ON THE MEN'S ROOM FLOOR . . PL UNDERTOW 9

DROPPING 1
AND DROPPING BOMBS FROM A CHRISTIAN STEEPLE . . . . . ANS SONG OF SPAIN 69

DROPS 2
LET THE RAIN BEAT UPON YOUR HEAD WITH SILVER LIQUID DROPS. . . . DK APRIL RAIN SONG 2
STARS ARE GREAT DROPS . . . . . SP HARLEM NIGHT SO 9

DROUGHT 1
WITH THE DROUGHT. . . . . . SP JULIET 15

DROVE 5
THEY DROVE ME OUT OF THE FOREST. . WB LAMENT DARK PEO 5
AND DROVE HER OFF TO JAIL . . . . . SH DEATH IN HARLEM 132
THAT MIGHTY NIGH DROVE ME WILD! . . SH LOVE AGAIN BLUS 12
CRACK WENT THE WHIPS THAT DROVE THE HORSES . . . . . SP FREEDOM'S PLOW 59
NEARLY DROVE ME WILD. . . . . . SP MADAM CHARTY CH 4

DROWN 3
BUT JUMP OVERBOARD AN' DROWN. . . . FC A RUINED GAL 14
TO DROWN THE RATTLE OF MY DYING BREATH. . . . . . SP FATASY PURPLE 4

DO NOT DROWN ME NOW: . . . . SP ISLAND 2

DROWNED 3

TO A LITTLE DROWNED GIRL. . . . . . . FC CLOSING TIME 15
OR THE RIVERS WHERE YOU'RE DROWNED LIKE LIEBKNECHT. . . . . ANS KIDS WHO DIE 42
MIXED WITH THE HOPES THAT ARE DROWNED THERE . . . . JC THE BITTER RIVR 14

DROWNS 1

DROWNS THE RUMBLE OF THAT TRAIN . . AYM ODE TO DINAH 38

DROWSY 6

AND YOU COULD HEAR THE DROWSY WAILING . . . . DK IRISH WAKE 3
OR IF I WASN'T SO DROWSY I'D LOOK UP JOE . . . . SH BED TIME 5
IN LAZY FAR-OFF DROWSY SOUTHERN DAYS OWT JUICE JOINT 11
AND WEARY AS A DROWSY SOUTHERN RAIN OWT JUICE JOINT 26
THEN DROWSY AS THE RAIN . . . . . . OWT JUICE JOINT 45
DRONING A DROWSY SYNCOPATED TUNE. SP THE WEARY BLUES 1

DRUG 3

BUT I DRUG MA WINGS . . . . SP ANGELS WINGS 7
O. I DRUG MA WINGS . . . . SP ANGELS WINGS 9
IS HEAVY WITH THE DRUG . . . . PL JUNIOR ADDICT 14

DRUGS 1

WITH VILER DRUGS . . . . PL JUNIOR ADDICT 24

DRUM 13

SO BEAT DAT DRUM. BOY! . . . . FC SATURDAY NIGHT 21
A GREAT DRUM . . . . FC SPORT 5
AND BEATS A DRUM . . . . FW JAIME 2
THAT DEATH IS A DRUM . . . . SP DRUM 2
DEATH IS A DRUM. . . . . SP DRUM 13
A SIGNAL DRUM. . . . . SP DRUM 14
MAKES HAMMER BEAT OF DRUM BEAT . . SP MIGRANT 17
WITH BAND AND DRUM . . . . SP PARADE 10
LIKE A TAUT DRUM. . . . . SP RAILROAD AVENUE 19
IF I JUST HAD A DRUM. . . . . SP TESTIMONIAL 3
NOR DRUM . . . . SP TESTIMONIAL 7
THE PAPA DRUM OF SUN . . . . AYM GOSPEL CHA-CHA 9
AND THE MOTHER DRUM OF EARTH . . . AYM GOSPEL CHA-CHA 10

DRUMBEAT 2

MAKE A DRUMBEAT. . . . . SP JUKE BOX LOVE 8
BARE FEET TO BEAT THE GREAT DRUMBEAT AYM BLUES IN STEREO 9

DRUMS 9

WHEN BEYOND STEEL BARS SOUND THE DEATHLESS DRUMS . . . . SL SCOTTSBORO 7
O. DRUMS! . . . . OWT NEGRO SERVANT 4
O. DRUMS OF LIFE IN HARLEM AFTER DARK! . . . . OWT NEGRO SERVANT 15
ARE THE DRUMS - AND YET . . . . . . SP AFRO-AMER FRAG 14
BEAT THE DRUMS OF TRAGEDY FOR ME. SP FATASY PURPLE 1
BEAT THE DRUMS OF TRAGEDY AND DEATH. SP FATASY PURPLE 2
BEAT THE DRUMS OF TRAGEDY FOR ME. SP FATASY PURPLE 5
IBM ELECTRIC BONGO DRUMS ARE COSTLY. AYM SHOW FARE PLESE 7
MUFFLED DRUMS IN SWANEE RIVER TEMPO. PL SPECIAL BULLTIN 9

DRUNK 8

AN' BETTER. BETTER. BETTER WHEN HE'S DRUNK. . . . . FC MA MAN 12
DRUNK LONG . . . . FC SPORT 15
DRUNK AND ROWDY AND GAY! . . . . . . SH CABARET GIRL 6
I'VE DRUNK OF THE BITTER RIVER . . JC THE BITTER RIVR 10
I HAVE DRUNK AT THE RIVER TOO LONG: JC THE BITTER RIVR 66
I'VE DRUNK AT THE BITTER RIVER . . JC THE BITTER RIVR 73
I'VE DRUNK OF THE BITTER RIVER . . JC THE BITTER RIVR 81
I DRUNK SOME BAD LICKER THAT . . . SP MORNING AFTER 5

DRUNKARD 1

OLD JUDGE SAYS YOU'S A DRUNKARD. . FC BLD OF GIN MARY 13

DRUNKEN 1

THOUGH I GO DRUNKEN . . . . FW FAITHFUL ONE 1

DRUNKENNESS 1

I THOUGHT THAT DRUNKENNESS . . . . FW MAN 7

DRY 5

DRY AND WITHERED. . . . . DK AUTUMN THOUGHT 3
I LOOK IN THE KETTLE. THE KETTLE IS DRY. . . . . SH SUPPER TIME 1
DOES IT DRY UP . . . . SP HARLEM 2
I'LL NEVER DRY THESE TEARS. . . . . SP WIDOW WOMAN 18
DOES IT DRY UP . . . . PL DREAM DEFERRED 2

DU 1

OVER FRAISES DU BOIS. . . . . PL DINNER GUEST ME 13

DUBOIS 1

DUBOIS (WHEN?) MALCOLM (OH!) SEND FOR STOKELY. . . . . PL FINAL CALL 35

DUE 7

BUT YOU JUST AS WELL BE HERE WHERE YOU DUE TO LIVE. . . . . SH LETTER 11
AIN'T DUE TO LAST. . . . . JC BLD SAM SOLOMON 16
TEN BUCKS YOU SAY IS DUE? . . . . . SP BLD LANDLORD 10
IS DUE TO LAST. . . . . SP LITTLE GRN TREE 4
YOUR RENT IS DUE. . . . . SP MADAM RENT MAN 6
NO SAFETY. NO LOVE. NO RESPECT WAS I DUE. . . . . SP THE NEGRO MOTHE 16
DUE TO SMOLDERING SHADOWS . . . . . AYM JAZZTET MUTED 20

DUET 1

WILL SING A DUET. . . . . SP PROJECTION 17

DUG 2

HAVE YOU DUG THE SPILL . . . . . . SH HARLEM SWEETIES 1
DIG AND BE DUG . . . . PL MOTTO 8

DUKE 2

THE DUKE IS MELLOW! . . . . OWT JITNEY 26
JAZZERS DUKE AND DIZZY ERIC DOLPHY $ $ $ . . . . AYM HORN OF PLENTY 8

DUKES 1

FOR THE DUKES AND COUNTS. . . . . . FC JAZZ BAND 4

DULL 2

BECAUSE MY MIND IS DULL . . . . . . NM BLACK CLWN POEM 4
BY THE PALE DULL PALLOR OF AN OLD GAS LIGHT . . . . SP THE WEARY BLUES 5

DUMB 7

THE DUMB CLOWN OF THE WORLD. . . . WB THE JESTER 16
ONLY DUMB GUYS FIGHT. . . . . FC PRIZE FIGHTER 1
IF I WASN'T DUMB . . . . FC PRIZE FIGHTER 2
ONLY DUMB GUYS FIGHT. . . . . FC PRIZE FIGHTER 7
A DUMB LITTLE JIGABOO FROM . . . . SH DEATH IN HARLEM 16
ARE YOU DEAF. DUMB. AND BLIND? . . JC BLD SAM SOLOMON 32
AND I'M NOT SO DUMB . . . . JC GOOD MORN STLIN 11

DUNCE 1

ARE YOU A FOOL OR A DUNCE? . . . . JC BLD SAM SOLOMON 38

DUNHAM 1

KATHERINE DUNHAM AL AND LEON $ $ $ $ $ . . . . AYM HORN OF PLENTY 6

DUPONT 1

ROTONDE SELECT DUPONT FLORE . . . . AYM ASK YOUR MAMA 51

DURBAN 1

DURBAN. BIRMINGHAM. . . . . PL QUESTION ANSWER 1

DURHAM 1

I WENT TO SCHOOL THERE. THEN DURHAM. THEN HERE . . . . SP THEME FOR ENG B 8

DUSABLE 1

NEVER KNEW DUSABLE. . . . . SP MIGRANT 12

DUSK 22

YOU ARE LIKE A WARM DARK DUSK . . . SH YOUNG NEGRO GRL 1
YOU ARE LIKE A WARM DARK DUSK . . . SH YOUNG NEGRO GRL 6
IN THE DUSK IS WALKING . . . . . . FW DIMOUT IN HARLM 2
SOFT AS DUSK THE DARKNESS . . . . . FW DIMOUT IN HARLM 7
WANDERING IN THE DUSK. . . . . . . FW DUSK 1
YOU GET LOST IN THE DUSK - . . . . FW DUSK 3
DUSK TURN TO DAWN. . . . . FW DUSK 12
DUSK . . . . FW NIGHT SONG 5
DUSK . . . . FW NIGHT SONG 12
IN THE BARREN DUSK . . . . SP DESERT 4
FROM DAWN TO DUSK . . . . SP END 5
I WENT LOOKIN' FOR MAGNOLIA FLOWERS IN THE DUSK . . . . SP MAGNOLIA FLOWER 5
SOMEWHERE IN THIS DUSK. . . . . . . SP MAGNOLIA FLOWER 11
GEORGIA DUSK . . . . SP MULATTO 2
DUSK DARK BODIES . . . . SP MULATTO 34
DUSK DARK . . . . SP RAILROAD AVENUE 1
HARDENING THE DUSK DARK EVENING. . SP RAILROAD AVENUE 24
SOMETIMES THERE'S A WIND IN THE GEORGIA DUSK . . . . PL GEORGIA DUSK 1
IN LONELY PITY THROUGH THE GEORGIA DUSK . . . . PL GEORGIA DUSK 3
SOMETIMES THERE'S BLOOD IN THE GEORGIA DUSK . . . . PL GEORGIA DUSK 5
A CRIMSON TRICKLE IN THE GEORGIA DUSK. . . . . PL GEORGIA DUSK 7
SOMETIMES A WIND IN THE GEORGIA DUSK PL GEORGIA DUSK 9

DUSKY 3

IN THE DUSKY DIMOUT . . . . FW DIMOUT IN HARLM 3
DUSKY SASH ACROSS MANHATTAN . . . . SP GOOD MORNING 16
ANCIENT. DUSKY RIVERS. . . . . . . SP NEGRO SPEAKS OF 12

DUST 7

OUT OF THE DUST OF DREAMS . . . . . DK FAIRIES 1
TO A HANDFUL OF DUST IN AUTUMN. . . FW DUSTBOWL 3
WITH DUST IN HER HAIR. . . . . . . SP SONG BILLIE HOL 11
OR BITS OF DUST IN EYES . . . . . . SP SONG BILLIE HOL 12

LIFT HIGH MY BANNER OUT OF THE DUST.	SP	THE NEGRO MOTHE	41
DUST OF DINGY ATOMS	PL	CULTURAL EXCHNG	3
WITH URANIUM DUST.	PL	LUMUMBA'S GRAVE	4

DUSTED 1

IS DUSTED WITH DESPAIR.	SP	SONG BILLIE HOL	15

DUSTY 1

IS DUSTY	SP	JULIET	14

DUTY 1

WHERE NO WORLDLY DUTY CALLS -	FW	CONVENT	5

DWELL 1

WHEREIN THE FALSE GODS DWELL	ANS	UNION	8

DYING 11

WHEN WE GOT THROUGH FIGHTING, OVER THERE, AND DYING?	NM	COLORED SL POEM	34
ABOUT LIVING AND DYING -	FW	BORDER LINE	2
NO WAY OF DYING.	FW	GRIEF	6
AND DYING IS MEAN -	SP	ADVICE	3
I DON'T MIND DYING -	SP	AS BEFITS A MAN	1
I DON'T MIND DYING	SP	AS BEFITS A MAN	5
SWIFT DYING	SP	DESIRE	3
TO DROWN THE RATTLE OF MY DYING BREATH.	SP	FATASY PURPLE	4
HE ROSE UP ON HIS DYING BED	SP	HOPE	1
DYING IN THE DARK.	SP	LOVE	8
DYING - FOR WHAT?	PL	QUESTION ANSWER	6

DYIN' 3

BUT YOU DON'T SEE NO PRESIDENTS DYIN' O' GRIEF -	NM	BROKE	57
'CAUSE I'M JUST DYIN' TO TAKE ON THAT THERE MARRIAGE YOKE.	NM	BROKE	77
AND I KNOW'D I'S DYIN' FAST.	SP	SYLVESTER'S BED	18

DYNAMITE 2

TORN TO SHREDS BY DYNAMITE	PL	BIRMINGHAM SUND	8
THE DYNAMITE THAT MIGHT IGNITE	PL	BIRMINGHAM SUND	18

D' 1

JEANNE D' ARC.	SL	SCOTTSBORO	17

EACH 17

AND PIERROT LOVED EACH ONE,	WB	PIERROT	18
EXCEPT THE NAME EACH GIVES IT -	OLD	TWO THINGS	9
TILL BEAUTY AND PRIDE FILLS EACH DARK FACE	NM	DARK YOUTH USA	20
20-VOICES: STRENGTHENING EACH BRANCH,	ANS	CHANT MAY DAY	16
EACH FOURTEEN YEARS OLD WHEN LYNCHED TOGETHER BENEATH THE	JC	THE BITTER RIVR	1
WHERE SINGING BLACK BOYS DANCE AND PLAY EACH NIGHT	OWT	JUICE JOINT	2
THE PEOPLE DO NOT ALWAYS UNDERSTAND EACH OTHER.	SP	FREEDOM'S PLOW	152
AT EACH GATE.	SP	GOOD MORNING	25
TO EACH STONE,	SP	HEAVEN	9
EACH DETAIL MINDING,	SP	OLD WALT	9
WITH HIS EBONY HANDS ON EACH IVORY KEY	SP	THE WEARY BLUES	9
EACH AND EVERY WEEK?	SP	ULTIMATUM	3
NIGHT EACH NIGHT COMES NIGHTLY	AYM	BLUES IN STEREO	22
AS EACH QUARTER CLINKS	AYM	ODE TO DINAH	55
AND TOUCHING EACH OTHER NATURAL AS DEW	PL	DAYBREAK IN ALA	19
TO ROUTE EACH PATH	PL	FREDRK DOUGLASS	10
TO MAKE EACH HIGHWAY	PL	FREDRK DOUGLASS	12

EAGLE 8

EAGLE ROCKIN'.	FC	MA MAN	15
ON FRIDAY THE EAGLE FLIES.	SP	CONSIDER ME	42
THERE'S BEEN AN EAGLE ON A NICKEL,	SP	FACT	1
AN EAGLE ON A QUARTER, TOO.	SP	FACT	2
BUT THERE AIN'T NO EAGLE	SP	FACT	3
CAN YOU LOVE AN EAGLE,	SP	GENIUS CHILD	6
FLY LIKE THE EAGLE FLIES.	SP	HARD DADDY	14
FLY LIKE THE EAGLE FLIES.	SP	HARD DADDY	16

EAGLE-ROCKIN' 1

EAGLE-ROCKIN'.	FC	MA MAN	13

EAGLE-ROCK 2

DADDY, EAGLE-ROCK WITH ME.	FC	MA MAN	14
COME AN' EAGLE-ROCK WITH ME.	FC	MA MAN	16

EAGLE-ROCKISH 1

EAGLE-ROCKISH AS I KIN BE!	FC	MA MAN	18

EAGLE'S 1

AND SHE BEEN HOLDIN' 'EM SO TIGHT TILL DE EAGLE'S IN TEARS -	NM	BROKE	24

EAR 1

WITHIN THE INNER EAR.	PL	SWEET WORDS RAC	4

EARLY 9

WEARY EARLY IN DE MORN.	DK	PO' BOY BLUES	20
EARLY, EARLY IN DE MORN.	DK	PO' BOY BLUES	22
EARLY, EARLY IN DE MORN.	DK	PO' BOY BLUES	22
O, I'M THE MAN WHO SAILED THOSE EARLY SEAS	ANS	LET AMERICA BE	45
MAKE THIS EARLY MORNING TIME TO KEEP BODY AND SOUL	SH	DAYBREAK	7
YOU HAVE TO GET THERE EARLY	OWT	JITNEY	56
BEFORE THE EARLY DAWN	SP	CHORD	3
IN THE EARLY BRIGHT	SP	SHALIMAR	3
EARLY BLUE EVENING.	SP	WONDER	1

EARN 3

TO EARN ENOUGH	SP	KID SLEEPY	14
TO EARN A LITTLE CASH,	PL	BACKLASH BLUES	14
TO EARN A LITTLE CASH,	PL	BACKLASH BLUES	16

EARNING 1

EARNING RICHES FOR THE WHOLE WORLD	SP	IN EXPLANATION	53

EARS 2

CAUSE THAT OLD ALARM CLOCK SHO HURTS MY EARS.	SH	LETTER	19
AND EARS THAT CLOSE TO HARLEM SCREAMS,	PL	JUNIOR ADDICT	5

EARTH 38

LIKE THE EARTH,	WB	DISILLUSION	3
FALL UPON THE EARTH,	DK	AFTR MNY SPRNGS	6
DEEP IN ALABAMA EARTH	DK	ALABAMA EARTH	2
AND OUT OF ALABAMA EARTH	DK	ALABAMA EARTH	6
WHILE OVER ALABAMA EARTH	DK	ALABAMA EARTH	10
DARK AS THE EARTH,	ANS	A NEW SONG	27
THEY SWEEP THE EARTH -	ANS	A NEW SONG	46
WHEN THE FLOWERS BREAK THROUGH THE EARTH,	ANS	CHANT MAY DAY	4
20-VOICES: GROW OUT OF THE PASSIVE EARTH,	ANS	CHANT MAY DAY	10
THAT ALL OVER THE EARTH TODAY	ANS	CHANT TOM MOONY	12
SHAKING THE EARTH	ANS	CHANT TOM MOONY	23
50-VOICES: WHEN THE EARTH IS NEW,	ANS	CHANT MAY DAY	30
80-VOICES: TILL THE FORCES OF THE EARTH ARE YOURS	ANS	CHANT MAY DAY	35
IF THERE'S ANYBODY ON THIS EARTH, JUDGE,	SH	BRIEF ENCOUNTER	11
AS THE DEEP PRODUCTIVE EARTH	JC	ME AND MY SONG	6
AS THE BLACK EARTH	JC	ME AND MY SONG	17
AS THE RICH EARTH	JC	ME AND MY SONG	26
IT'S AN EARTH SONG -	FW	EARTH SONG	1
FOR AN EARTH SONG.	FW	EARTH SONG	3
AN EARTH SONG!	FW	EARTH SONG	11
FOR AN EARTH SONG.	FW	EARTH SONG	15
AND HID HER DEEP IN EARTH.	FW	GIRL	10
SUDDENLY THE EARTH WAS THERE,	FW	HARLEM DANCE HA	3
FOR THE GREAT EARTH SPIRITS	FW	JAIME	3
AND MAKE EARTH HAPPY	FW	WISDOM	7
DOWN INTO THE EARTH WENT THE PLOW	SP	FREEDOM'S PLOW	49
THE EARTH	SP	IN TIME SILVER	2
O, SWEET AS EARTH,	SP	MULATTO	33
OF EARTH NOR SKY	SP	NEW YORKERS	11
WERE ON EARTH,	SP	PARADE	25
FROM THE SOLID LAP OF EARTH.	SP	SPIRITUALS	12
SUN AND THE BEATEN HARDNESS OF THE EARTH,	SP	SUN SONG	2
WARMTH, EARTH, WARMTH,	SP	THE SOUTH	10
SHOUTS FROM THE EARTH ITSELF	AYM	BLUES IN STEREO	8
AND THE MOTHER DRUM OF EARTH	AYM	GOSPEL CHA-CHA	10
AND RED CLAY EARTH HANDS IN IT	PL	DAYBREAK IN ALA	17
THE EARTH AROUND	PL	QUESTION ANSWER	4
EARTH IS BROWN	PL	THE DOVE	7

EARTHA 1

DELIGHTED! INTRODUCE ME TO EARTHA	AYM	BIRD IN ORBIT	3

EARTHQUAKE 1

THIS IS EARTHQUAKE	FW	TODAY	1

EARTH-BODY 1

CAN MAKE MY EARTH-BODY FREE.	ANS	A NEW SONG	28

EARTH-DARK 1

AND IN THE EARTH-DARK ARMS OF DEATH	WB	YOUNG BRIDE	4

EARTH-DUST 1

EARTH-DUST,	PL	DREAM DUST	2

EARTH-MEANING 1

THE EARTH-MEANING	SP	FULFILMENT	1

EARTH-THING 1

MY LITTLE EARTH-THING,	DK	LULLABY	3

EASE 2

SHO CAN'T FIND NO EASE.	FC	GYPSY MAN	24
'LL EASE MY MISERY.	SP	MISERY	4

EASIER 2
"IT'S EASIER TO GET DOPE . . . . . PL JUNIOR ADDICT 28
YES, EASIER TO GET DOPE . . . . . . PL JUNIOR ADDICT 30

EAST 3
EAST TURNED PALE . . . . SH DEATH IN HARLEM 134
SHINES LIKE A STAR IN THE EAST. . . SP INTERNE AT PROV 41
NORTH AND EAST - . . . . SP ONE-WAY TICKET 7

EASTERN 1
DRIPPED BLOOD OVER THE EASTERN HILLS SP A BLACK PIERROT 8

EASTLAND 3
YOU'LL BE CALLED BY EASTLAND. . . . AYM RIDE, RED, RIDE 26
EASTLAND AND MALAN DECEASED . . . . AYM SHADES OF PIC 5
MAMMY EASTLAND . . . . PL CULTURAL EXCHNG 52

EASY 5
SO I'M TAKIN' IT EASY . . . . NM BIG-TIMER POEM 73
AND HANDLE EASY LIKE A PURCHASED THING, ... OWT JUICE JOINT 36
THAT EASY ROLL, ... SP EASY BOOGIE 6
EASY LIKE I ROCK IT . . . . SP EASY BOOGIE 12
IT'S NOT EASY TO KNOW WHAT IS TRUE FOR YOU OR ME . . . . SP THEME FOR ENG B 16

EAT 13
HAD NOTHIN' TO EAT, ... FC DEATH DO DIRTY 12
WE COULDN'T EAT IN RESTAURANTS; HAD JIM CROW CARS; . . . . NM COLORED SL POEM 24
OF DOG EAT DOG, OF MIGHTY CRUSH THE WEAK. . . . . ANS LET AMERICA BE 24
ANY OLD THING TO EAT. . . . . SH BRIEF ENCOUNTER 2
LOOKIN' FOR ANY OLD THING TO EAT - SH BRIEF ENCOUNTER 4
WHAT YOU LIKE TO EAT? . . . . SH DEATH IN HARLEM 52
SWEET ENOUGH TO EAT. . . . . SH HARLEM SWEETIES 8
SO'S THAT I COULD EAT. . . . . . . SH OUT OF WORK 6
THEY SEND ME TO EAT IN THE KITCHEN SP I, TOO 3
AND EAT WELL, ... SP I, TOO 6
"EAT IN THE KITCHEN," . . . . SP I, TOO 13
BUT EAT, DRINK, STAY BLACK, AND DIE. SP NECESSITY 4
WELL, I LIKE TO EAT, SLEEP, DRINK, AND BE IN LOVE. . . . . SP THEME FOR ENG B 21
TO EAT. . . . . SP VAGABONDS 5
DID I WANT TO EAT WITH WHITE FOLKS? AYM BIRD IN ORBIT 70
BUT I CAN'T EAT HIM FOR LUNCH. . . PL CROWNS GARLANDS 20
YOU CAN'T EAT HERE! . . . . PL GO SLOW 6
EAT QUIETLY THE BREAD OF SHAME. . . PL MILITANT 2

EATING 3
EATING BLOOD AND GOLD. . . . . . . ANS KIDS WHO DIE 6
EATING CHICKEN. . . . . SP GRADUATION 12
MEANWHILE DINAH EATING CHICKEN . . AYM ODE TO DINAH 129

EATIN' 1
I'M EATIN' AND LOVIN', ... NM BIG-TIMER POEM 51

EBECANEEZER 1
EBECANEEZER BAPTIST CHURCH. . . . . SP PRAYER MEETING 7

EBONY 1
WITH HIS EBONY HANDS ON EACH IVORY KEY . . . . SP THE WEARY BLUES 9

ECHO 4
ECHO THE AGE-LESS, AGE-LONG OLD DESPAIR . . . . OWT JUICE JOINT 27
WHILE MOVIES ECHO DRAMAS ON THE SCREEN. . . . . OWT LINCOLN THEATRE 2
ECHO: . . . . SP WORLD WAR II 9
AND THE ECHO OF THE CIVIL WAR . . . PL OCTOBER 16 RAID 17

ECHOED 1
WHILE THE WEARY BLUES ECHOED THROUGH HIS HEAD. . . . . SP THE WEARY BLUES 34

ECHOES 3
CARELESS, AND HALF-DEFIANT ECHOES OF THE "ST. JAMES INFIRMARY" AS THE NM BIG-TIMER MOOD 2
ECHOES THE FIGHTING "MARSEILLAISE." TEARING OFF HIS CLOWN'S SUIT. . NM BLACK CLWN MOOD 13
ON YOUR BED OF WHISPERED ECHOES: . AYM IS IT TRUE? 19

ECHOING 1
MAY ACCOMPANY THE RECITATION - ECHOING SOFTLY, OVER THERE, THERE'S A ROSE . . . . NM COLORED SL MOOD 4

ECSTASY 1
IS ECSTASY . . . . SP TRUMPET PLAYER 23

EDGE 5
BY DE EDGE O' DE WEARY RIVERSIDE . FC A RUINED GAL 11
EDGE INTO A SWOON. . . . . SP MOONLIGHT NIGHT 8
HERE ON THE EDGE OF HELL . . . . . PL HARLEM 1
ON THE EDGE OF HELL . . . . PL HARLEM 17
WITH AN EDGE LIKE APARTHEID. . . . PL WHERE WHEN WHCH 6

EDGECOMBE 1
AND 409 EDGECOMBE . . . . SP PROJECTION 8

EDITORIALS 1
WHO PEN EDITORIALS IN THE PAPERS, ANS KIDS WHO DIE 20

EDUCATION 1
"WORK, EDUCATION, PATIENCE . . . . JC THE BITTER RIVR 43

EEEEOOOOO 1
EEEEOOOOO! . . . . OWT JITNEY 59

EEEOOOOOO 1
EEEOOOOOO! . . . . OWT JITNEY 3

EEEOOOOOOOOOO 1
EEEOOOOOOOOOO! . . . . OWT JITNEY 53

EFFECT 1
DON'T HAVE NO EFFECT ON YOU - . . . SP EVIL 2

EFFENDI 1
FATHER BISHOP, EFFENDI, MOTHER HORNE, ... SP MYSTERY 21

EGG 4
I'M THE BAD EGG, SEE! . . . . NM BIG-TIMER POEM 9
THAT WHISKEY WILL COOK THE EGG. . . SP BAR 1
MAYBE THE EGG . . . . SP BAR 3
THEY CLUTCH AT THE EGG . . . . . . PL ELDERLY LEADERS 8

EGYPTIAN 1
A QUEEN FROM SOME TIME-DEAD EGYPTIAN NIGHT . . . . SP WHEN SUE WEARS 7

EIGHT 6
AT SIX O'CLOCK, OR SEVEN, OR EIGHT, OWT NEGRO SERVANT 8
IT'S EIGHT, ... SP BLUE MONDAY 3
DOWNTOWN AT EIGHT, ... SP CONSIDER ME 18
TO WORK AT EIGHT, ... SP CONSIDER ME 46
SIX OR EIGHT AND TEN YEARS OLDER'N MYSELF. . . . . SP PREFERENCE 2
PARK AVENUE AT EIGHT . . . . PL DINNER GUEST ME 20

EIGHTEEN 5
GWINE GIVE YOU EIGHTEEN MONTHS . . FC BLD OF GIN MARY 15
EIGHTEEN MONTHS IN JAIL! . . . . . FC BLD OF GIN MARY 17
O, EIGHTEEN MONTHS LOCKED IN! . . . FC BLD OF GIN MARY 18
OLD HARD-FACED JUDGE SAYS EIGHTEEN MONTHS . . . . FC BLD OF GIN MARY 23
EIGHTEEN YEARS AGO. . . . . SP DEFERRED 10

EIGHTH 1
EIGHTH AVENUE, SEVENTH, AND I COME TO THE Y, ... SP THEME FOR ENG B 13

EIGHTY 1
DOING EIGHTY . . . . SH ANNOUNCEMENT 3

EIGHTY-NINE 2
EIGHTY-NINE FEET DEEP. . . . . . . FC SUICIDE 14
EIGHTY-NINE FEET DEEP. . . . . . . FC SUICIDE 16

EITHER 2
TO MAKE IT EITHER MORE OR LESS, . . LHR DEAR LVLY DEATH 7
AT EITHER SIDE ARRAYED . . . . . . AYM JAZZTET MUTED 15

EL 1
BOSTON AND EL PASO - . . . . SP FREEDOM'S PLOW 88

ELAN 1
KILLED WITH GREAT ELAN, ... PL MOTHER IN WAR 6

ELDERLY 1
ELDERLY, ... PL ELDERLY LEADERS 5

ELECTION 5
TO THE POLLS ELECTION DAY . . . . . JC BLD SAM SOLOMON 9
ON ELECTION DAY . . . . JC BLD SAM SOLOMON 22
ON ELECTION DAY, BROTHER. . . . . . JC BLD SAM SOLOMON 36
ON ELECTION DAY . . . . JC BLD SAM SOLOMON 45
AND ELECTION TIME . . . . AYM HORN OF PLENTY 89

ELECTRIC 1
IBM ELECTRIC BONGO DRUMS ARE COSTLY. AYM SHOW FARE PLESE 7

ELEVATOR 5
TRIED TO FIND ONE O' THEM LITTLE ELEVATOR AND SWITCHBOARD JOBS THEY USED . . . . NM BROKE 41
RUNNIN' AN ELEVATOR . . . . SP ELEVATOR BOY 2
ELEVATOR TOO LONG. . . . . SP ELEVATOR BOY 22
I TOOK THE ELEVATOR . . . . SP LIFE IS FINE 12
THE HARLEM BRANCH Y, WHERE I TAKE THE ELEVATOR. . . . . SP THEME FOR ENG B 14

ELEVATORS 1
ONLY THE ELEVATORS SP ELEVATOR BOY 15

ELEVATOR-BOYS 1
ELEVATOR-BOYS. FC LAUGHERS 7

ELEVEN 2
A YEAR WHEN I WAS ELEVEN. SP DEFERRED 4
AT CLUB HARLEM IT'S ELEVEN SP SEASHORE THROUG 7

ELI 2
ELI. ELI! SP MYSTERY 17
ELI. ELI! SP MYSTERY 17

ELITE 1
NOT BEAT - ELITE. PL NORTHERN LIBERL 14

ELKS 1
AT THE ELKS CLUB LOUNGE SP PARADE 3

ELLA 1
MILES AND ELLA AND MISS NINA $ $ $
$ $ $ $ AYM HORN OF PLENTY 9

ELSE 14
ELSE I'LL USE HER HEAD FC EVIL WOMAN 15
SO DE MAN SAY. "I'LL GET SOMEBODY
ELSE. THEN. TO CLEAN." - NM BROKE 17
LIKE EVERYTHING ELSE. SP ELEVATOR BOY 7
ELSE IT HAD NO MEANING FOR ANYONE. SP FREEDOM'S PLOW 108
MO'N ANYTHING ELSE CAN. SP LAMENT OVER LOV 6
ELSE YOU'LL TAKE OUT MY PHONE? SP MADAM PHONE BIL 11
YOU GOT SOME'N ELSE SP MADAM MIGHT-HAV 23
IF YOU GOT SOMEBODY ELSE. SP ULTIMATUM 4
ELSE I'LL CUT YOU OFF SP ULTIMATUM 6
I DON'T WANT NOBODY ELSE AND SP WIDOW WOMAN 19
DON'T NOBODY ELSE WANT ME. SP WIDOW WOMAN 20
I SAY DON'T WANT NOBODY ELSE SP WIDOW WOMAN 21
AND DON'T NOBODY ELSE WANT ME - SP WIDOW WOMAN 22
OR ELSE MURDERED PL WHO BUT TH LORD 7

ELSE'S 3
OR SOMEBODY ELSE'S SHOES SP ELEVATOR BOY 18
ON NOBODY ELSE'S SHELF. SP MADAM FORT TELL 20
ON SOMEBODY ELSE'S PL FROSTING 7

EMANCIPATION 3
100-YEARS EMANCIPATION AYM ODE TO DINAH 9
EMANCIPATION CENTENNIAL - PL DEATH YORKVILLE 12
EMANCIPATION: 1865 PL LONG VIEW NEGRO 1

EMBROIDERED 1
AND A WHITE EMBROIDERED COLLAR. FW MIGRATION 13

EMBROIDERIES 1
EMBROIDERIES PL LENOX AVE. BAR 7

EMERGING 1
EMERGING TO THE FANFARE PL SPECIAL BULLTIN 7

EMMETT 1
SHAKES HANDS WITH EMMETT TILL. AYM ASK YOUR MAMA 66

EMPTINESS 2
ACHING EMPTINESS. WB SUMMER NIGHT 16
TRAGIC EMPTINESS OF HIS LIFE. NM BIG-TIMER MOOD 12

EMPTY 8
EMPTY AS THE SILENCE. WB SUMMER NIGHT 14
EMPTY WITH A VAGUE. WB SUMMER NIGHT 15
AN EMPTY CABARET FC SPORT 11
EMPTY HANDED AS I BEGAN. NM BLACK CLWN POEM 20
THEN THE PLACE WAS EMPTY. SH DEATH IN HARLEM 124
PLACE WHERE YOUR CLOTHES HUNG'S
EMPTY AND BARE. SH SUPPER TIME 9
LOSER FROM AN EMPTY POCKET JC THE BITTER RIVR 69
EMPTY. BUT CLEAN. SP FREEDOM'S PLOW 3

ENAMEL 2
MAYBE NOW I CAN HAVE THAT WHITE
ENAMEL STOVE SP DEFERRED 8
MAYBE I CAN BUY THAT WHITE ENAMEL
STOVE! SP DEFERRED 20

ENCLOSES 1
THE FLOWER NO SCENT ENCLOSES. FW REMEMBRANCE 4

END 5
WHY NOT END RIGHT NOW JC BLACK MAN SPEAK 27
AT THE END OF DAY. FW FAITHFUL ONE 12
THE MOVIES END. THE LIGHTS FLASH
GAILY ON. OWT LINCOLN THEATRE 5
WHO DOUBTED THAT THE WAR WOULD END
RIGHT. SP FREEDOM'S PLOW 133
LOOK THROUGH THE LARGER END - PL LONG VIEW NEGRO 9

ENDED 3
THEN I WOKE UP. AND THE DREAM WAS
ENDED - NM COLORED SL POEM 48
THAT MUST BE ENDED. ANS UNION 12
HER GREAT ADVENTURE ENDED SP S-SSS-SS-SH! 1

ENDING 1
AMEN IS NOT AN ENDING AYM ODE TO DINAH 127

ENDIN' 1
YOU SAY I'LL MEET A BAD ENDIN'. HEH? NM BIG-TIMER POEM 37

ENDLESS 3
AN ENDLESS STREET WB TO LITTLE LOVER 10
TANGLED IN THAT ANCIENT ENDLESS
CHAIN ANS LET AMERICA BE 26
THE MOUNTAINS AND THE ENDLESS PLAIN
- ANS LET AMERICA BE 84

ENDOWED 1
ENDOWED BY THEIR CREATOR SP FREEDOM'S PLOW 92

ENDS 3
THAT NEVER ENDS. OLD TOWER 4
THE POEM ENDS. OK I LOVED FRIEND 4
WHEN THEY MEET THEIR ENDS. SP NIGHT FUNERAL 16

ENEMIES 1
TO ALL THE ENEMIES OF THESE GREAT
WORDS: SP FREEDOM'S PLOW 186

ENEMY 3
TO THE ENEMY WHO WOULD CONQUER US
FROM WITHOUT. SP FREEDOM'S PLOW 178
TO THE ENEMY WHO WOULD DIVIDE SP FREEDOM'S PLOW 180
ENEMY. PL WAR 18

ENGINEER 1
WHO'S THE ENGINEER ON THE FREEDOM
TRAIN? SP FREEDOM TRAIN 17

ENGLAND 1
OFF THE COAST OF ENGLAND SP SEASCAPE 5

ENGLAND'S 1
AND POLAND'S PLAIN. AND ENGLAND'S
GRASSY LEA. ANS LET AMERICA BE 48

ENGLEWOOD 1
THE LEGION FROM ENGLEWOOD AYM BIRD IN ORBIT 77

ENGLISH 3
SHALL I USE OLD ENGLISH SP MADAM'S CALLING 13
THIS IS MY PAGE FOR ENGLISH B. SP THEME FOR ENG B 41
SPEAKS ENGLISH FRENCH SWAHILI AYM ASK YOUR MAMA 57

ENJOYING 1
CAUSE I'M SURE ENJOYING MYSELF
TODAY! SH SUNDAY 7

ENORMOUS 1
THROWS HER ENORMOUS ARMS AROUND SP PROJECTION 6

ENOUGH 12
SWEET ENOUGH TO EAT. SH HARLEM SWEETIES 8
ONE DON'T MAKE ENOUGH SP CONSIDER ME 30
NO MAN IS GOOD ENOUGH SP FREEDOM'S PLOW 102
NO MAN IS GOOD ENOUGH SP FREEDOM'S PLOW 169
JOE HAS SENSE ENOUGH TO KNOW SP JOE LOUIS 5
TO EARN ENOUGH SP KID SLEEPY 14
IF YOU'RE GREAT ENOUGH SP SHAME ON YOU 1
AND CLEVER ENOUGH SP SHAME ON YOU 2
NOT ENOUGH TO HURT MY PLAYING $ $ $
$ $ AYM HORN OF PLENTY 12
IT'S NOT ENOUGH TO MOURN PL BOMBINGS DIXIE 1
AND NOT ENOUGH TO PRAY. PL BOMBINGS DIXIE 2
SEND (GOD FORBID - HE'S NOT DEAD
LONG ENOUGH!) PL FINAL CALL 17

ENSLAVED 1
AN ENSLAVED PEOPLE HEADING TOWARD
FREEDOM SP FREEDOM'S PLOW 189

ENTHRONED 1
THAT KEEP THE RICH ENTHRONED ANS OPEN LETTER 26

ENTRANCE 5
A GAY AND LOW-DOWN BLUES. COMIC
ENTRANCE LIKE THE CLOWNS IN THE
CIRCUS. NM BLACK CLWN MOOD 1
TO GUARD THE HARBOR ENTRANCE JC TO CAPTAIN MULZ 14
NO BACK DOOR ENTRANCE TO THE FREEDOM
TRAIN. SP FREEDOM TRAIN 12
IF PUSHED BY HURRIED ENTRANCE. AYM ODE TO DINAH 119
WHERE ENTRANCE TO NEGROES. PL BIBLE BELT 5

ENTRY 2
AIDS TRIUMPHANT ENTRY SQUALLING SP INTERNE AT PROV 27
TRIUMPHAL ENTRY SEND YOU - AYM BLUES IN STEREO 7

ENVELOPE 2
IN AN ENVELOPE MARKED: . . . . . . SP PERSONAL 1
IN AN ENVELOPE MARKED: . . . . . . SP PERSONAL 4

EQUAL 2
ALL MEN ARE CREATED EQUAL. . . . . SP FREEDOM'S PLOW 168
ALL MEN ARE CREATED EQUAL . . . . . SP FREEDOM'S PLOW 31

EQUALITY 2
EQUALITY IS IN THE AIR WE BREATHE. ANS LET AMERICA BE 14
(THERE'S NEVER BEEN EQUALITY FOR ME. ANS LET AMERICA BE 15

EQUALLY 1
PLEASURED EQUALLY . . . . SP OLD WALT 7

EQUATION 1
WISDOM REDUCED TO THE PERSONAL
EQUATION: . . . . PL ELDERLY LEADERS 2

ER 2
WELL, ER - ER . . . HOW MUCH DOES
YOU PAY? . . . . NM BROKE 35
WELL, ER - ER . . . HOW MUCH DOES
YOU PAY? . . . . NM BROKE 35

ERIC 1
JAZZERS DUKE AND DIZZY ERIC DOLPHY
$ $ $ . . . . AYM HORN OF PLENTY 8

ERMINE 1
IN AN ERMINE CAPE . . . . SH DEATH IN HARLEM 65

ERNEST 1
(DEDICATED TO THE MEMORY OF CHARLIE
LANG AND ERNEST GREEN. . . . . . JC THE BITTER RIVR 1

ERZULIE 1
ERZULIE PLAYS A TUNE . . . . AYM GOSPEL CHA-CHA 7

ES 1
DE SANGRE ES LA GOTA? . . . . AYM RIDE, RED, RIDE 22

ESCAPE 1
MAY ESCAPE THE SPELL OF THE SOUTH. SP THE SOUTH 28

ESCROW 1
IN ESCROW TO JOE GLASSER. . . . . . AYM HORN OF PLENTY 82

ESPANA 1
DON QUIXOTE! ESPANA! . . . . ANS SONG OF SPAIN 26

ESPECIALLY 1
ESPECIALLY FOR THE FIRST ONES . . . AYM HORN OF PLENTY 66

ESSENCE 1
CONCENTRATED TO THE ESSENCE . . . . AYM SHOW FARE PLESE 13

ESTA 5
TU ABUELA, DONDE ESTA? . . . . . . AYM RIDE, RED, RIDE 11
TU ABUELA, DONDE ESTA? . . . . . . AYM RIDE, RED, RIDE 13
DONDE ESTA? DONDE ESTA? . . . . . . AYM RIDE, RED, RIDE 15
DONDE ESTA? DONDE ESTA? . . . . . . AYM RIDE, RED, RIDE 15
AY, MORENA, DONDE ESTA? . . . . . . AYM RIDE, RED, RIDE 20

ET 1
AND MY GOLD FISH ET THE GLASS. . . SP CHILDREN'S RYME 19

ETCHED 1
ETCHED AGAINST THE SKY. . . . . . . SP SEASCAPE 4

ETERNITY 3
AND ETERNITY AN UNBLOWN SAXOPHONE FC SPORT 12
AN' BE MA FRIEND THROUGH ETERNITY." DK MA LORD 16
PIPE OF ETERNITY. . . . . SP SUNDAY MORNING 4

ETHER 1
A MIST OF IODINE AND ETHER . . . . SP INTERNE AT PROV 44

ETHICAL 1
(NOT ETHICAL CULTURE) . . . . SP HIGH TO LOW 12

EUPHRATES 1
I BATHED IN THE EUPHRATES WHEN DAWNS
WERE YOUNG. . . . . SP NEGRO SPEAKS OF 5

EUROPE 1
ALL ACROSS THE COUNTRY, EUROPE - . AYM HORN OF PLENTY 41

EVANGELISTA 1
EVANGELISTA, TOO. . . . . SL SCOTTSBORO 26

EVAPORATION 1
EVAPORATION . . . . SP DESIRE 5

EVASION 1
OPPORTUNISTIC, CONVENIENT EVASION. PL ELDERLY LEADERS 4

EVEN 45
DON'T EVEN WANT TO BE GOOD. . . . . FC BAD MAN 14
DON'T EVEN WANT TO BE GOOD. . . . . FC BAD MAN 16
AIN'T EVEN GOT A STALL. . . . . . . FC HARD LUCK 18
EVEN IF YOU DO COME FROM GEORGIA. FC JAZZ BAND 21
EVEN IF I IS BROKE. . . . . NM BROKE 38
I CAN'T EVEN GET DE MONEY FOR TO BUY
MYSELF A SMOKE. . . . . NM BROKE 46
BUT I CAN'T EVEN BUY A PAPER - I'M
SO BROKE. . . . . NM BROKE 61
THAT EVEN YET ITS MIGHTY DARING
SINGS . . . . ANS LET AMERICA BE 42
EVEN TAME A BEAR. . . . . SH FREE MAN 6
EVEN THOUGH YOU DO ME WRONG. . . . SH IN TROUBLED KEY 8
AND EVEN IF I DID, I WAS MAD - . . SH LETTER 6
AIN'T EVEN GONNA DREAM 'BOUT THE
WOMENS I HAD. . . . . SH PAY DAY 18
ALL DAY SUNDAY DIDN'T EVEN DRESS UP. SH SUNDAY 1
ALTHOUGH RIGHT NOW, EVEN YET TODAY, JC JIM CROW'S LAST 11
EVEN PERHAPS . . . . FW THERE 10
EVEN EVERY FOREIGNER . . . . OWT RESTRICTIVE 4
NOT EVEN MEMORIES ALIVE . . . . . . SP AFRO-AMER FRAG 4
AIN'T EVEN HEARD HER MURMUR, . . . SP BLD OF THE GIRL 11
EVEN IF IT IS MY HOME. . . . . . . SP CROON 3
EVEN A GREAT DANCER . . . . SP DANCER 24
EVEN THE SNAKE . . . . SP DESERT 5
THEY EVEN GOT A SEGREGATED LANE. . SP FREEDOM TRAIN 27
YOU DON'T EVEN CARE. . . . . SP HIGH TO LOW 9
FOLKS WITH NOT EVEN MISTER IN FRONT
OF THEIR NAMES . . . . SP IN EXPLANATION 19
WASN'T EVEN ONE PACE LONG - . . . . SP LITTLE OLD LETT 6
WILL GIVE EVEN . . . . SP LIVE LET LIVE 3
WITH PARENTS THAT DON'T EVEN . . . SP MADAM CHARTY CH 15
WELL, EVEN LESS ABOUT YOUR . . . . SP MADAM PHONE BIL 35
OR EVEN TWO, ... SP RELIEF 14
DO NOT RING, NOT EVEN MURMUR. . . . SP SUMMER EVENING 21
TO CONFOUND EVEN HAZEL SCOTT . . . SP TO BE SOMEBODY 11
EVEN RUNG THIS BELL ON SUNDAY, YET AYM ASK YOUR MAMA 8
EVEN FARTHER THAN ST. ALBANS . . . AYM HORN OF PLENTY 31
I MOVED OUT EVEN FARTHER FURTHER
FARTHER . . . . AYM HORN OF PLENTY 33
EVEN FOR THE NEGROES - . . . . . . AYM HORN OF PLENTY 65
NOT EVEN FOLKWAYS CAPTURED . . . . AYM IS IT TRUE? 9
TO MY CHAGRIN - NOT EVEN SINGING - AYM IS IT TRUE? 32
ON THE TAPES - NOT EVEN FOLKWAYS. AYM IS IT TRUE? 34
EVEN WHEN YOU'RE WINNING . . . . . AYM ODE TO DINAH 113
NOW NOT EVEN KEEPER TO YOUR CHILD - AYM ODE TO DINAH 85
SOMETIMES EVEN BURIED WITH OUR
FAMILY. . . . . PL CULTURAL EXCHNG 55
(EVEN VOTE FOR REAL IN ALABAM') . . PL GHOSTS OF 1619 8
SKIM EVEN A DIME - . . . . PL PRIME 8
EVEN SOGGY COUNTRY CLUB . . . . . . PL UNDERTOW 7
MY HEART'S NOT EVEN LEAD. . . . . . PL VARI-COLORED 6

EVENING 9
SUN'S GOING DOWN THIS EVENING - . . DK SONG BANJO DANC 12
GOOD EVENING, DADDY! . . . . SP BOOGIE 1 A.M. 1
THEN REST AT COOL EVENING . . . . . SP DREAM VARIATION 5
REST AT PALE EVENING . . . . SP DREAM VARIATION 14
SHARP PINE SCENT IN THE EVENING AIR. SP MULATTO 22
PINE WOOD SCENT IN THE EVENING AIR. SP MULATTO 40
HARDENING THE DUSK DARK EVENING. . SP RAILROAD AVENUE 24
AND THE EVENING . . . . SP REQUEST 5
EARLY BLUE EVENING. . . . . SP WONDER 1

EVENINGS 2
AND SHE COME TELLIN' ME, SHE AIN'T
GOT NO MO' EVENINGS FREE! . . . NM BROKE 53
FROM ANCIENT EVENINGS) . . . . . . PL LENOX AVE. BAR 9

EVENIN' 2
BUT THIS EVENIN' FOR SUPPER. . . . SH EVENIN' BLUES 11
I GOT EVENIN' AIR TO SPARE. . . . . SH EVENIN' BLUES 12

EVENTUALLY 1
WILL EVENTUALLY BE . . . . AYM IS IT TRUE? 36

EVER 48
DOES A JAZZ-BAND EVER SOB? . . . . WB CABARET 1
NOR EVER KNOW. . . . . WB DISILLUSION 5
FOR EVER HAVIN' A DAUGHTER. . . . . FC A RUINED GAL 18
EVER TIME I MOUNTS THIS BENCH . . . FC BLD OF GIN MARY 7
EVER NIGHT. . . . . FC EVIL WOMAN 8
CAN'T SEE! AND DON'T KNOW! AND WON'T
EVER CARE! . . . . NM COLORED SL POEM 53
EVER TIME DE TRAINS PASS . . . . . DK HOMESICK BLUES 5
TROUBLE EVER DAY. . . . . DK MA LORD 9
TO BELIEVE AN ANGELO HERNDON, OR
EVER GET TOGETHER. . . . . ANS KIDS WHO DIE 36
THAT I EVER HAD! . . . . SH BRIEF ENCOUNTER 18
GOD! WHY DID YOU EVER CURSE ME . . SH CABARET GIRL 7
I WONDER IF WHITE FOLKS EVER FEEL
BAD, ... SH DAYBREAK 12
EVER CATCH ME. . . . . SH FREE MAN 4
I EVER DID SEE. . . . . SH ONLY WOMAN BLUS 4
DID YOU EVER TRY LIVIN' . . . . . . SH OUT OF WORK 19
I SAY DID YOU EVER TRY LIVIN' . . . SH OUT OF WORK 21
I'M EVER SO SURE . . . . FW FAITHFUL ONE 3
FORGETS HE EVER SANG . . . . OWT JUICE JOINT 31
BABE, DID YOU EVER . . . . SP BLACK MARIA 11

SAYS. DID YOU EVER SEE THE SUN RISE SP BLACK MARIA 14
BUT EVER FRIEND YOU FINDS SEEMS SP BOUND NO'TH BLS 17
IF EVER I CURSED MY WHITE OLD MAN SP CROSS 3
IF EVER I CURSED MY BLACK OLD MOTHER SP CROSS 5
NOR EVER SP DEMOCRACY 3
WHAT DID NOT SEEM COULD EVER BE: SP DREAM 4
FROM THAT SEED A TREE GREW. IS GROWING. WILL EVER GROW. SP FREEDOM'S PLOW 135
SING IT SOFTLY AS EVER YOU CAN - SP GENIUS CHILD 3
RESPECTABLY AS EVER. SP LETTER 11
IF I EVER CATCH HIM. SP MADAM PHONE BIL 19
NOT EVER. SP MULATTO 29
IF I EVER HIT FOR A DOLLAR SP NUMBERS 1
DID YOU EVER GO DOWN TO THE RIVER - SP REVERIE HARLEM 1
DID YOU EVER THINK ABOUT YOUR MOTHER? SP REVERIE HARLEM 5
DID YOU EVER THINK ABOUT YOUR SWEETHEART SP REVERIE HARLEM 7
THAN THEY EVER DID BEFORE. SP RUBY BROWN 26
DID IT EVER OCCUR TO YOU. SON. SP SISTER 7
DID IT EVER OCCUR TO YOU. BOY. SP SISTER 13
BUT MARCH EVER FORWARD. BREAKING DOWN BARS. SP THE NEGRO MOTHE 47
LOOK EVER UPWARD AT THE SUN AND THE STARS. SP THE NEGRO MOTHE 48
THAN SOME PEOPLE EVER HAD. SP WARNING AUGMENT 12
DID YOU EVER FIND HER? AYM BIRD IN ORBIT 64
HOW THEY EVER GOT THAT WAY. AYM BLUES IN STEREO 27
AND WAS PORGY EVER MARRIED AYM SHADES OF PIG 15
DID YOU EVER SEE TEN NEGROES AYM SHOW FARE PLESE 20
BEFORE CHINA WAS EVER RED AT ALL PL BIRMINGHAM SUND 12
MORE THAN GERMAN EVER BORE. PL CULTURAL EXCHNG 16
NOR EVER PL FREEDOM 3
DID I EVER LIVE PL STOKELY MALCOLM 16

EVERBODY 2
CAUSE EVERBODY TELLS ME SO. FC BAD MAN 2
EVERBODY TELLS ME SO. FC BAD MAN 4

EVERBODY'S 1
MADE ME EVERBODY'S FOOL. FC LISTEN HERE 12

EVERWHERE 1
EVERWHERE I GO. FC BAD MAN 6

EVERY 22
YOU STILL BAKES BISCUITS? FRIED CHICKEN EVERY NIGHT? IS THAT TRUE? NM BROKE 73
IT'S A LIE! IT'S A LIE! EVERY WORD THEY SAID. NM COLORED SL POEM 44
IN EVERY BRICK AND STONE. IN EVERY FURROW TURNED ANS LET AMERICA BE 43
IN EVERY BRICK AND STONE. IN EVERY FURROW TURNED ANS LET AMERICA BE 43
AND YET MUST BE - THE LAND WHERE EVERY MAN IS FREE. ANS LET AMERICA BE 64
EVERY PAST MISTAKE ANS OPEN LETTER 37
ON EVERY LYNCHING TREE. A POSTER CRYING FREE ANS OPEN LETTER 44
EVERY WAY THEY IS. SH STATEMENT 3
EVERY COLORED MAN JC BLD SAM SOLOMON 18
THE WORLD WHERE EVERY UGLY PAST MISTAKE JC TO CAPTAIN MULZ 56
EVERY TONE I SEEK FW SILENCE 7
AS EVERY SWAYING OWT JUICE JOINT 29
WHO SINGS THE TROUBLES EVERY WOMAN HAS. OWT LINCOLN THEATRE 8
EVEN EVERY FOREIGNER OWT RESTRICTIVE 4
YOUR EVERY STEP REVEALS SP AFRICA 13
WHAT HE SAID MUST BE MEANT FOR EVERY HUMAN BEING - SP FREEDOM'S PLOW 107
GONNA SALT EVERY DIME AWAY SP NUMBERS 2
EVERY DETAIL MINDING SP OLD WALT 5
EACH AND EVERY WEEK? SP ULTIMATUM 3
NAME IN THE PAPERS EVERY DAY! AYM HORN OF PLENTY 37
EVERY DAY'S TOMORROW AYM HORN OF PLENTY 68
AND CAPTURE EVERY STREET PL FREDRK DOUGLASS 8

EVERYBODY 20
EVERYBODY WB CAT AND SAXOPHN 2
EVERYBODY WB CAT AND SAXOPHN 16
EVERYBODY DODGED AS SH DEATH IN HARLEM 101
AND EVERYBODY IN AMERICA'D SH IF-ING 11
EVERYBODY BUT ME. JC BLACK MAN SPEAK 4
AND FOR EVERYBODY JC GOOD MORN STLIN 20
BUT SHE TOLD EVERYBODY FW GIRL 7
AND EVERYBODY OWT BLD MARGE POLIT 50
EVERYBODY THAT GAVE SOMETHING SP BLD OF THE MAN 11
NO! THE HUSSY'S TELLING EVERYBODY - SP BLD OF THE GIRL 13
WE KNOWS EVERYBODY SP CHILDREN'S RYME 15
THAT TREE IS FOR EVERYBODY. SP FREEDOM'S PLOW 196
YOU SAY YOU THOUGHT EVERYBODY WAS CALLED MISTER? SP IN EXPLANATION 5
NO. SON. NOT EVERYBODY. SP IN EXPLANATION 6
RIDE EVERYBODY MUST TAKE. SP WIDOW WOMAN 2
RIDE EVERYBODY MUST TAKE. SP WIDOW WOMAN 4
STOP EVERYBODY MUST MAKE. SP WIDOW WOMAN 6
WE KNOW EVERYBODY PL CHILDREN'S RYME 9
TOUCHING EVERYBODY WITH KIND FINGERS PL DAYBREAK IN ALA 18
A ROAD HELPS EVERYBODY. PL FLORIDA WORKERS 14

EVERYBODY'S 2
EVERYBODY'S HAPPY. IT'S A SPENDIN CROWD - SH DEATH IN HARLEM 36
EVERYBODY'S GOT A RIGHT TO BOARD THE FREEDOM TRAIN? SP FREEDOM TRAIN 22

EVERYDAY 1
ALL DAY EVERYDAY. PL WORDS LIKE FREE 4

EVERYONE'S 1
WHOSE BLOOD? . . . EVERYONE'S. PL GEORGIA DUSK 8

EVERYTHING 9
HOME. KIDS. AND EVERYTHING FINE. NM BIG-TIMER POEM 46
OF OWNING EVERYTHING FOR ONE'S OWN GREED! ANS LET AMERICA BE 30
OVER EVERYTHING LIKE A SHROUD. SH CABARET GIRL 2
ROOMING AND EVERYTHING SP DEFERRED 12
LIKE EVERYTHING ELSE. SP ELEVATOR BOY 7
EVERYTHING. SP HEAVEN 8
AND IN EVERYTHING BUT WHAT'S ABOUT ME - SP NOTE COMM THEAT 11
THEN EVERYTHING WAS DARKNESS SP SYLVESTER'S BED 27
BELIEVING EVERYTHING SHE READ PL MOTHER IN WAR 9

EVERYWHERE 10
I CANNOT SAY YOU EVERYWHERE. OK PASSING LOVE 4
50-VOICES: LIFE IS EVERYWHERE FOR YOU. ANS CHANT MAY DAY 24
50-VOICES: LIFE IS EVERYWHERE. ANS CHANT MAY DAY 26
FOR YOU HAVE ALLIES EVERYWHERE. JC GOOD MORN STLIN 44
EVERYWHERE. FW OLD SAILOR 20
AND EVERYWHERE I SAW SP DREAM 3
EVERYWHERE. SP HEAVEN 4
SILVER MOONLIGHT EVERYWHERE. SP MULATTO 20
THE BRIGHT STARS SCATTER EVERYWHERE. SP MULATTO 39
IT EVERYWHERE. PL LUMUMBA'S GRAVE 23

EVE'S 2
SING EVE'S CHARMS! WB HARLEM NIGHT CL 13
WERE EVE'S EYES WB JAZZONIA 9

EVICTION 1
WHAT? YOU GONNA GET EVICTION ORDERS? SP BLD LANDLORD 13

EVIL 11
THE LAW'S A KLANSMAN WITH AN EVIL WILL. ANS BLD OZZIE POWEL 11
THE DEVIL'S A KLEAGLE WITH AN EVIL WILL. ANS BLD OZZIE POWEL 25
TOO LONG HAS ITS EVIL POISON JC THE BITTER RIVR 8
THE EVIL FORCES THAT WOULD DESTROY JC TO CAPTAIN MULZ 52
AND EVIL OLD OWT BLUES ON A BOX 6
I'M SORRY FOR THAT EVIL WISH SP CROSS 7
I AM EVIL AND MAD. SP EARLY EVENING 14
MONROE'S FELL ON EVIL DAYS - SP MONROE'S BLUES 1
MONROE'S FELL ON EVIL DAYS. SP MONROE'S BLUES 3
SHINES LIKE THE EVIL ONE SP WEST TEXAS 2
SHINES LIKE THE EVIL ONE SP WEST TEXAS 17

EXCEPT 9
EXCEPT THE NAME EACH GIVES IT - DLD TWO THINGS 9
FOR WHAT COULD I ANSWER HIM. EXCEPT. "IT'S A LIE!" NM COLORED SL POEM 43
EXCEPT IN OUR HEARTS. ANS KIDS WHO DIE 39
EXCEPT THE DREAM THAT'S ALMOST DEAD TODAY. ANS LET AMERICA BE 61
EXCEPT THAT THEY BE MADE FOR US ANS SONG OF SPAIN 64
EXCEPT THAT HE TALKS TOO MUCH. SP NEIGHBOR 15
EXCEPT ON HOLIDAYS. SP SHAME ON YOU 5
EXCEPT THE NEIGHBORS SP S-SSS-SS-SH! 5
EXCEPT IN MEMORIES OF HATE AYM ODE TO DINAH 90

EXCHANGE 1
IN EXCHANGE FOR PL WITHOUT BENEFIT 17

EXIST 1
SINCE BUT TWO EXIST AYM SHOW FARE PLESE 29

EXIT 1
OUT OF ONE IN EXIT AYM ODE TO DINAH 118

EXPECT 4
I CAN EXPECT FROM YOU? JC BLACK MAN SPEAK 20
THOSE WHO EXPECT FW PRAYER 11
I EXPECT THEY DO - SP COMMENT ON CURB 5
THOSE WHO EXPECT SP LITANY 11

EXPECTANTLY 1
CALMLY TELLING THE STORY. PROUDLY AND EXPECTANTLY WITH HEAD UP. SHOULDERS NM COLORED SL MOOD 7

EXPENSIVE 2

Line	Source	Poem	Line No.
THAT GENTLEMAN IN EXPENSIVE SHOES	AYM	BIRD IN ORBIT	65
THAT GENTLEMAN IN EXPENSIVE SHOES	AYM	BIRD IN ORBIT	88

EXPLAIN 2

Line	Source	Poem	Line No.
IF MY CHILDREN ASK ME, DADDY, PLEASE EXPLAIN	SP	FREEDOM TRAIN	31
I SAID, PLEASE EXPLAIN TO ME	SP	MADAM FORT TELL	9

EXPLAINS 1

Line	Source	Poem	Line No.
BUT MAYBE THEY EXPLAINS IT ON THE	SP	FREEDOM TRAIN	35

EXPLODE 2

Line	Source	Poem	Line No.
OR DOES IT EXPLODE?	SP	HARLEM	11
OR DOES IT EXPLODE?	PL	DREAM DEFERRED	11

EXPLOITERS 1

Line	Source	Poem	Line No.
C, THIEVES, EXPLOITERS, KILLERS,	ANS	A NEW SONG	29

EXPLORING 1

Line	Source	Poem	Line No.
EXPLORING THE CLOUDS.	FW	NEW MOON	4

EXPRESS 1

Line	Source	Poem	Line No.
AND SOMETIMES ONLY BLUNDERINGLY EXPRESS THEM,	SP	FREEDOM'S PLOW	149

EXTRA 1

Line	Source	Poem	Line No.
THAT EXTRA DAY WOULD GET ME DOWN.	SH	OUT OF WORK	18

EXTRA-LARGE 1

Line	Source	Poem	Line No.
EXTRA-LARGE THE KINGS AND QUEENS	AYM	JAZZTET MUTED	14

EYE 4

Line	Source	Poem	Line No.
THE APPLE OF MY EYE?	LHR	TESTAMENT	6
REPORT, MY EYE!	SP	MADAM CHARTY CH	25
CHANGED INTO "EYE FOR EYE,"	PL	BLACK PANTHER	7
CHANGED INTO "EYE FOR EYE,"	PL	BLACK PANTHER	7

EYES 44

Line	Source	Poem	Line No.
WHITE GIRLS' EYES	WB	HARLEM NIGHT CL	6
A DANCING GIRL WHOSE EYES ARE BOLD	WB	JAZZONIA	5
WERE EVE'S EYES	WB	JAZZONIA	9
HAVE FALLEN BENEATH YOUR EYES.	WB	SOLEDAD	4
YOUR EYES,	WB	SOLEDAD	5
BLACKENING THE EYES, -	FC	BEALE ST. LOVE	5
HE'S GOT THOSE 'LECTRIC-SHOCKIN' EYES AN'	FC	MA MAN	5
WID BLUE-GREEN EYES:	FC	NEW CABARET GRL	2
WID BLUE-GREEN EYES:	FC	NEW CABARET GRL	14
BACK, AND EYES SHINING, QUIETLY RECALLING THE VISION, THE DEAD MAN SPEAKS	NM	COLORED SL MOOD	8
WERE IT NOT FOR YOUR EYES.	DK	QUIET GIRL	3
WITH ARROGANT EYES AND SCORNFUL LIPS:	ANS	A NEW SONG	31
THE HIGH SHERIFF'S EYES ARE FILLED WITH HATE,	ANS	BLD OZZIE POWEL	7
THEY NEVER SAW THE HIGH SHERIFF'S EYES	ANS	BLD OZZIE POWEL	19
SHE CAST HER EYES ON TEXAS, HOLLERED,	SH	DEATH IN HARLEM	83
BIG BLACK EYES,	SH	ONLY WOMAN BLUS	14
EYES	FW	GRIEF	1
IN YOUR WAKING EYES:	SP	AFRICA	8
WERE IT NOT FOR YOUR EYES.	SP	ARDELLA	3
WITH WEARY SADISTIC EYES	SP	CAFE: 3 A.M.	2
EYES IN EYES	SP	COLLEGE FORMAL	8
EYES IN EYES	SP	COLLEGE FORMAL	8
IN HER EYES.	SP	DELINQUENT	12
YOUR EYES SEE FOREVER?	SP	DEMAND	9
LOOKS LIKE HIS EYES	SP	DREAM BOOGE VAR	9
HIS EYES LOOK OUT ON THE WORLD,	SP	FREEDOM'S PLOW	11
THE EYES SEE THERE MATERIALS FOR BUILDING,	SP	FREEDOM'S PLOW	15
JET AND COCONUT EYES,	SP	GRADUATION	2
TO SCATTER STAR-DUST IN THEIR EYES.	SP	GRADUATION	24
I'D SCRATCH OUT BOTH HIS EYES.	SP	HARD DADDY	18
SHE HOPES TO LAY EYES ON YOU SOMETIME IN LIFE.	SP	LETTER	7
HIS EYES DIDN'T LOOK JUST RIGHT.	SP	LOVER'S RETURN	4
SHE SQUINTED UP HER EYES.	SP	MADAM FORT TELL	6
IN THE EYES ONCE SOFT BENIGHTED	SP	MIGRANT	22
SO THE EYES OF MY PEOPLE.	SP	MY PEOPLE	4
OR BITS OF DUST IN EYES	SP	SONG BILLIE HOL	12
BLACK SEED FOR EYES	SP	SUMMER EVENING	3
BENEATH HIS EYES	SP	TRUMPET PLAYER	4
IN HIS EYES,	SP	TRUMPET PLAYER	28
PLENTY EYES.	SP	UP-BEAT	12
AND THE FIELD DAISY EYES	PL	DAYBREAK IN ALA	13
WHO SEEKS AN OUT IN EYES THAT DROOP	PL	JUNIOR ADDICT	4
THAT ONCE PERHAPS WERE EYES.	PL	JUSTICE	4
JAUNDICED EYES SHOWING	PL	MISSISSIPPI	15

FACE 49

Line	Source	Poem	Line No.
HER DARK BROWN FACE	WB	YOUNG PROSTITUT	1
I SEES YO' FACE AGAIN.	FC	BLD OF GIN MARY	8
HER FACE IS PALE	FC	CLOSING TIME	2
I SHOULD MEET LIFE FACE TO FACE	OLD	AESTHETE HARLEM	3
I SHOULD MEET LIFE FACE TO FACE	OLD	AESTHETE HARLEM	3
LOOK 'EM IN THE FACE AND	NM	BIG-TIMER POEM	59
WHITE SPIT IN MY FACE -	NM	BLACK CLWN POEM	48
WITH HIS FACE FULL OF LIGHT AND FAITH, CONFIDENT THAT A NEW WORLD HAS	NM	COLORED SL MOOD	9
THEN HIS DARK FACE SMILED AT ME IN THE NIGHT -	NM	COLORED SL POEM	39
TILL BEAUTY AND PRIDE FILLS EACH DARK FACE	NM	DARK YOUTH USA	20
FACE THE WALL WITH THE DARK CLOSED GATE,	DK	SONG	7
NO SHAME IS WRIT ACROSS ITS FACE -	SL	TOWN OF SCOTTSB	2
ANOTHER WHITE OF FACE.	ANS	OPEN LETTER	31
GONNA HIT YOU IN THE FACE AND LET YOU FALL!	SH	DAYBREAK	2
KICKED HER IN THE FACE.)	SH	DEATH IN HARLEM	98
AND SPIT IN THE FACE OF MY DREAM.	JC	THE BITTER RIVR	62
BECAUSE MY FACE IS BLACK,	JC	THE BITTER RIVR	78
WITH A ROUND BLACK FACE	FW	MIGRATION	12
VEILING HER FACE LIKE A VIRGIN	FW	NEW MOON	6
DARK FACE.	SP	AFRO-AMER FRAG	24
IN A MIDNIGHT FACE,	SP	DREAM BOOGE VAR	4
FACE TO THE WALL.	SP	DREAM	10
IN THE FACE OF THE SUN,	SP	DREAM VARIATION	11
PERHAPS THE DREAM IS ONLY HER FACE -	SP	HAVANA DREAMS	5
HIS FACE WAS PALE AND	SP	LOVER'S RETURN	3
HE'S GOT A GRIN ON HIS FACE.	SP	ME AND THE MULE	2
COOL FACE OF THE RIVER	SP	SUICIDE'S NOTE	2
I DID NOT SEE YOUR FACE!	SP	SUNDAY MORNING	30
LOOK AT MY FACE - DARK AS THE NIGHT -	SP	THE NEGRO MOTHE	5
BUT SHE SPITS IN MY FACE.	SP	THE SOUTH	19
THE GRINNING FACE,	SP	UNCLE TOM	4
HER FACE IS LIKE AN ANCIENT CAMEO	SP	WHEN SUE WEARS	2
THEY THROW DIRT IN YOUR FACE,	SP	WIDOW WOMAN	8
THROW DIRT IN YOUR FACE,	SP	WIDOW WOMAN	10
FACE LIKE A CHOCOLATE BAR	SP	125TH STREET	1
FACE LIKE A JACK-O'-LANTERN,	SP	125TH STREET	3
FACE LIKE SLICE OF MELON,	SP	125TH STREET	5
IN THE FACE OF WHAT	PL	HARLEM	22
LOOK ME IN THE FACE -	PL	KU KLUX	18
YOUR SPIT IS MY FACE,	PL	MILITANT	11
TO STRIKE YOUR FACE.	PL	MILITANT	14
THE SKIN ON YOUR BLACK FACE,	PL	SPECIAL BULLTIN	19
THE FACE OF WAR IS MY FACE.	PL	THE DOVE	1
THE FACE OF WAR IS MY FACE.	PL	THE DOVE	1
THE FACE OF WAR IS YOUR FACE.	PL	WAR	2
THE FACE OF WAR IS YOUR FACE.	PL	WAR	2
IS THE FACE	PL	WAR	4
YOUR FACE AND MY FACE.	PL	WAR	7
YOUR FACE AND MY FACE.	PL	WAR	7

FACES 17

Line	Source	Poem	Line No.
FOR YOUR FACES ARE BEAUTIFUL, TOO.	WB	THE WHITE ONES	2
YOUR FACES ARE WHIRLING LIGHTS OF LOVELINESS AND SPLENDOR, TOO.	WB	THE WHITE ONES	4
I LOOKED AT THEIR BLACK FACES	ANS	NEGRO GHETTO	1
CAME TIPPIN INTO DIXIE'S WITH SMILES ON THEIR FACES,	SH	DEATH IN HARLEM	60
IN THEIR FACES	JC	FREEDOM	12
AND DARK BITTER FACES BEHIND STEEL BARS:	JC	THE BITTER RIVR	28
HAS STUDIED VARIED FACES,	FW	OLD SAILOR	5
THAT BROUGHT DARK FACES	OWT	JUICE JOINT	13
KIND, THOUGHTFUL TO THE FACES THAT ARE WHITE.	OWT	NEGRO SERVANT	2
O, SWEET RELIEF FROM FACES THAT ARE WHITE!	OWT	NEGRO SERVANT	19
SHADOW FACES	SP	CHORD	1
SO THE FACES OF MY PEOPLE.	SP	MY PEOPLE	2
A MILLION FACES	SP	NIGHTMARE BOOGE	3
ALL THEM FACES	SP	NIGHTMARE BOOGE	7
LOOKING AT LISTENERS' FACES.	PL	CORNER MEETING	5
AND POPPY COLORED FACES	PL	DAYBREAK IN ALA	11
FACES LIKE JACK-O'-LANTERNS	PL	THIRD DEGREE	5

FACING 2

Line	Source	Poem	Line No.
IT WAS AWFUL - FACING THAT BOY WHO WENT OUT TO DIE.	NM	COLORED SL POEM	42
FACING A TWO-BIT	FW	CHIPPY	8

FACIST 2

Line	Source	Poem	Line No.
WORKERS MADE THOSE BOMBS FOR A FACIST SPAIN!	ANS	SONG OF SPAIN	46
BUT BACKWARD IN THE LANDS WHERE FACIST FEAR	JC	TO CAPTAIN MULZ	26

FACT 9

Line	Source	Poem	Line No.
FACT IS YOU WORRIES ME.	FC	BLD OF GIN MARY	14
FACT THAT I HURT HER, JUDGE,	SH	BRIEF ENCOUNTER	13
DE FACT THAT SHE IS DEAD,	SH	BRIEF ENCOUNTER	14
FACT THAT I HURT HER,	SH	BRIEF ENCOUNTER	15
FACT THAT SHE IS DEAD -	SH	BRIEF ENCOUNTER	16
FACT IS, AIN'T GOT A DIME -	SH	IF-ING	14
THE FACT WE NEVER VOTED	JC	BLD SAM SOLOMON	13
IN FACT, HE'S A GREAT CAT.	SP	NEIGHBOR	16
FOR THE FACT THAT WHITE WAS RIGHT	PL	GHOSTS OF 1619	10

FACTORIES 5
THE UNIONS BARRED US; THE FACTORIES, TOO, ... NM COLORED SL POEM 22
FACTORIES WILL BE NAMED: . . . . . ANS CHANT TOM MOONY 40
AND THE MINES AND THE FACTORIES AND THE OFFICE TOWERS . . . . ANS OPEN LETTER 15
TAKES FACTORIES, ... ANS OPEN LETTER 59
OUT OF LABOR CAME THE FACTORIES, . SP FREEDOM'S PLOW 76

FADE 1
WATCH THEM DROOP, WILT, FADE . . . PL CROWNS GARLANDS 10

FADING 1
THE QUIET FADING OUT OF LIFE . . . SP MAGNOLIA FLOWER 1

FAILED 2
FAILED HIM . . . . SP DANCER 2
THAT HAD NOT FAILED PEOPLE . . . . SP DANCER 3

FAILS 1
FAILS TO GET PEARL BAILEY. . . . . AYM ODE TO DINAH 6

FAINTED 2
A WHITE LADY FAINTED. . . . . SH DEATH IN HARLEM 114
FAINTED AWAY . . . . FW NIGHT SONG 20

FAINTING 1
FAINTING, FANNING, AND CRYING. . . SP AS BEFITS A MAN 8

FAIR 3
WITH PIOUS FOLK AND FAIR . . . . . WB A FAREWELL 4
AND PIERROT THOUGHT ALL MAIDENS FAIR WB PIERROT 19
AND ITS SANDS ARE FAIR: . . . . . . SP ISLAND 6

FAIRIES 3
AM I TOO OLD TO SEE THE FAIRIES DANCE? . . . . DK AFTR MNY SPRNGS 7
FAIRIES WEAVE THEIR GARMENTS. . . . DK FAIRIES 2
SPOTTING FAIRIES. . . . . SP CAFE: 3 A.M. 3

FAIRY 1
SEND FOR THE FAIRY QUEEN WITH A WAVE OF THE . . . . PL FINAL CALL 5

FAITH 5
AND, FAITH, I LOVE HER YET. . . . . WB PIERROT 13
OUT OF SADNESS IT RISES TO DEFIANCE AND DETERMINATION. A HYMN OF FAITH . . . . NM BLACK CLWN MOOD 12
WITH HIS FACE FULL OF LIGHT AND FAITH, CONFIDENT THAT A NEW WORLD HAS . . . . NM COLORED SL MOOD 9
WHOSE SWEAT AND BLOOD, WHOSE FAITH AND PAIN, ... ANS LET AMERICA BE 67
AND THE FAITH THAT IS IN HIS HEART - SP FREEDOM'S PLOW 6

FAITHFUL 1
THE FAITHFUL, ... FW FOR DEAD MIMES 7

FALL 13
MIGHT FALL AT THY FEET, ... WB SONGS DARK VIRG 5
WILL FALL AT THE FEET OF YOUR BEAUTY, ... WB TO DARK MERCEDE 5
FALL UPON THE EARTH, ... DK AFTR MNY SPRNGS 6
WHEN BOMBS'LL FALL NOT ONLY ON SPAIN - . . . . ANS SONG OF SPAIN 52
GONNA HIT YOU IN THE FACE AND LET YOU FALL! . . . . SH DAYBREAK 2
TO FALL, ... FW DUSK 11
FALL. . . . . FW MONTMARTRE 6
IT'S A WONDER YOU DON'T FALL DOWN. SP BLD LANDLORD 8
TILL THE LAST STARS FALL, ... SP DRUM 6
AND LET MY FOOL-SELF FALL. . . . . SP LAMENT OVER LOV 24
WHITE GIRLS FALL . . . . SP MELLOW 3
DON'T YOU FALL NOW . . . . SP MOTHER TO SON 17
INTO LATE FALL . . . . SP WHAT? 2

FALLEN 1
HAVE FALLEN BENEATH YOUR EYES. . . WB SOLEDAD 4

FALLING 1
AND FALLING OUT OF HEAVEN LIKE SOFT DEW. . . . . PL DAYBREAK IN ALA 6

FALLOUT 1
IN POISON FROM THE FALLOUT . . . . PL JUNIOR ADDICT 26

FALLS 6
UNTIL THE WHOLE WORLD FALLS INTO THE HANDS OF . . . . ANS CHANT TOM MOONY 24
SOMETIMES A CRUMB FALLS . . . . . . SP LUCK 1
AND NIAGARA FALLS IS FROZEN ¢ ¢ ¢ ¢ ¢ ¢ ¢ . . . . AYM HORN OF PLENTY 28
FOR NIAGARA FALLS IS FROZEN . . . . AYM ODE TO DINAH 11
WHEN NIAGARA FALLS IS FROZEN . . . AYM ODE TO DINAH 23
WHILE NIAGARA FALLS IS FROZEN. . . AYM ODE TO DINAH 68

FALSE 4
HIM, ASSUMING A FALSE AND BRAGGING SELF-ASSURANCE, AND A PRETENDED NM BIG-TIMER MOOD 8
OF PREJUDICE, AND HATE, AND THE FALSE COLOR LINE - . . . . NM COLORED SL POEM 9
IS CROWNED WITH NO FALSE PATRIOTIC WREATH, ... ANS LET AMERICA BE 12
WHEREIN THE FALSE GODS DWELL . . . ANS UNION 8

FAMILY 2
SOMETIMES EVEN BURIED WITH OUR FAMILY. . . . . PL CULTURAL EXCHNG 55
A MEDAL TO YOUR FAMILY - . . . . . PL WITHOUT BENEFIT 16

FAMOUS 2
FAMOUS - THE HARD WAY - . . . . . . AYM HORN OF PLENTY 38
FAMOUS, ... PL ELDERLY LEADERS 6

FAN 1
PERHAPS IT'S A FAN OF SILVER LACE - SP HAVANA DREAMS 6

FANFARE 1
EMERGING TO THE FANFARE . . . . . . PL SPECIAL BULLTIN 7

FANNING 1
FAINTING, FANNING, AND CRYING. . . SP AS BEFITS A MAN 8

FANTASY 1
HORSE A FANTASY OF DAYS . . . . . . SP FLATTED FIFTHS 17

FAR 19
'LEVEN AIN'T FAR AWAY. . . . . . . FC CRAP GAME 4
FAR AWAY. . . . . SH DEATH IN HARLEM 127
AND DRIVE SO FAR, SO FAR. . . . . . SH DECLARATION 11
AND DRIVE SO FAR, SO FAR. . . . . . SH DECLARATION 11
SO FAR. . . . . SH DECLARATION 14
TOO FAR TO ONE SIDE. . . . . SH SNOB 8
HOW FAR YOU GO, NOR HOW LONG YOU STAY - . . . . SH SUNDAY 6
OUR BATTLE YET IS FAR FROM WON . . JC JIM CROW'S LAST 30
FAR AWAY. . . . . FW HEART 16
SO FAR AWAY . . . . SP AFRO-AMER FRAG 2
SO FAR AWAY . . . . SP AFRO-AMER FRAG 11
SO FAR AWAY . . . . SP AFRO-AMER FRAG 22
AND AS FAR AS I COULD SEE . . . . . SP CROSSING 16
FAR REMOVED FROM BASIC OVEN, . . . SP GRADUATION 17
WAS FAR AWAY . . . . SP GREEN MEMORY 5
BUT YOU HAVE GONE SO FAR! . . . . . SP MISS BLUES'ES 10
AND FAR TOO CLEAN TO STAY THAT WAY, SP PASSING 8
AND FAR INTO THE NIGHT HE CROONED THAT TUNE. . . . . SP THE WEARY BLUES 31
FAR FROM STONE. . . . . AYM ASK YOUR MAMA 73

FARE 7
HERE'S YOUR FARE! . . . . OWT JITNEY 22
FOR LUNCHES AND CAR FARE? . . . . . SP KID SLEEPY 15
NO SHOW FARE, BABY - . . . . AYM ODE TO DINAH 96
TELL ME FARE FROM YOU? . . . . . . AYM SHOW FARE PLESE 2
SHOW FARE, MAMA, PLEASE. . . . . . AYM SHOW FARE PLESE 35
SHOW FARE, MAMA. . . . . AYM SHOW FARE PLESE 36
SHOW FARE! . . . . AYM SHOW FARE PLESE 37

FARE'S 1
IF SHOW FARE'S MORE THAN 30¢ ¢ ¢ ¢ ¢ ¢ ¢ ¢ . . . . AYM HORN OF PLENTY 29

FARMER 1
I AM THE FARMER, BONDSMAN TO THE SOIL. . . . . ANS LET AMERICA BE 31

FARMERS 1
FARMERS, ... ANS OPEN LETTER 3

FARMS 1
FARMS WILL BE NAMED: . . . . ANS CHANT TOM MOONY 34

FARTHER 3
EVEN FARTHER THAN ST. ALBANS . . . AYM HORN OF PLENTY 31
I MOVED OUT EVEN FARTHER FURTHER FARTHER . . . . AYM HORN OF PLENTY 33
I MOVED OUT EVEN FARTHER FURTHER FARTHER . . . . AYM HORN OF PLENTY 33

FARTHEREST 2
TO THE FARTHEREST CORNERS . . . . . AYM ASK YOUR MAMA 3
TO THE FARTHEREST CORNERS SOMETIMES AYM IS IT TRUE? 3

FAR-OFF 4
AND FAR-OFF LONG TOMORROW: . . . . FW MOTHERLAND 2
IN LAZY FAR-OFF DROWSY SOUTHERN DAYS OWT JUICE JOINT 11
TO KEEP FAR-OFF CANARIES . . . . . AYM ODE TO DINAH 60
WITH FLUID FAR-OFF GOING . . . . . PL CULTURAL EXCHNG 9

FAR-TOO-HUMBLE 1
THEIR FAR-TOO-HUMBLE FEET. . . . . ANS NEGRO GHETTO 8

FASHION 1
SYNCOPATED MUSIC. TELLING HIS STORY IN A HARD, BRAZEN, CYNICAL FASHION. . . . . NM BIG-TIMER MOOD 1

FAST 6
HOLD FAST TO DREAMS . . . . DK DREAMS 1
HOLD FAST TO DREAMS . . . . DK DREAMS 5
STORM CLOUDS MOVE FAST. . . . . ANS SONG OF SPAIN 48
HE DRINKS FAST. . . . . SP NEIGHBOR 18
AND I KNOW'D I'S DYIN' FAST. . . . SP SYLVESTER'S BED 18
OF THE DOG IS FAST. . . . . PL GO SLOW 3

FASTER 2
BUT FASTER . . . . SP DIVE 4
FASTER . . . . SP DIVE 5

FASTING 1
THERE WAS FASTING IN THE STREETS AND JOY. . . . . LHR BLD MARY'S SON 3

FAT 2
SUCKED IN BY FAT JUKEBOXES . . . . AYM ODE TO DINAH 52
THE COMMITTEE'S FAT. . . . . PL UN-AMERICAN 1

FATE 7
LOUD LAUGHERS IN THE HANDS OF FATE - FC LAUGHERS 4
OF FATE. . . . . FC LAUGHERS 32
SHOULDERS AT FATE. ACCEPTING HIS POSITION - BUT INSIDE HIMSELF UNHAPPY . . . . NM BIG-TIMER MOOD 6
AS IF FATE HAD NOT BLED HIM WITH HER KNIFE! . . . . DK BEGGAR BOY 8
AS DECREED BY FATE . . . . OWT BLD MARGE POLIT 30
FATE MUST HAVE . . . . SP WHAT? SO SOON! 3
YOU CALL IT FATE? . . . . SP WHAT? SO SOON! 8

FATHER 8
THAT BELONGED TO MY FATHER? . . . . SH BLD PAWNBROKER 2
FATHER WARNED ME. . . . . SH BLD THE SINNER 7
YOUR FATHER, YES, HE WAS THE ONE! SP MAMA AND DAUGHT 11
FATHER BISHOP, EFFENDI, MOTHER HORNE. . . . . SP MYSTERY 21
FATHER DIVINE, A RABBI BLACK . . . SP MYSTERY 22
AND FATHER DIVINE WILL SAY IN TRUTH. SP PROJECTION 20
GOD IS HIS FATHER: . . . . PL CHRIST IN ALA. 7
FATHER DIVINE (WHERE?) . . . . PL FINAL CALL 34

FATHER'S 2
YOUR FATHER'S BLOOD. . . . . FW WHEN ARMIES PAS 18
NOR FATHER'S - . . . . OWT BLD MARGE POLIT 55

FAUBUS 2
MAMMY FAUBUS . . . . PL CULTURAL EXCHNG 51
MAMMY FAUBUS! . . . . PL CULTURAL EXCHNG 57

FAULTILY 1
AND FAULTILY PUT THEM INTO PRACTICE. SP FREEDOM'S PLOW 151

FEAR 7
BUT BACKWARD IN THE LANDS WHERE FACIST FEAR . . . . JC TO CAPTAIN MULZ 26
AND SOME WERE FILLED WITH FEAR - . . LHR BLD MARY'S SON 12
THROUGH COMPROMISE AND FEAR. . . . SP DEMOCRACY 4
NO ROOM FOR FEAR. . . . . SP SUBWAY RUSH HOU 7
OF FEAR . . . . PL ANGOLA QUESTION 6
THROUGH COMPROMISE AND FEAR. . . . PL FREEDOM 4
SULTRY AIR OF FEAR. . . . . PL SWEET WORDS RAC 8

FEARS 2
LITTLE CULLUD BOYS WITH FEARS. . . SP FLATTED FIFTHS 3
WITH FEARS. . . . . SP TAG 2

FEAST 1
PREPARING TO FEAST ON LIFE. . . . . SP SUNDAY MORNING 8

FEATHERS 2
BUT SOMETHING HAPPENED, JIM'S FEATHERS FELL. . . . . JC JIM CROW'S LAST 5
CATCH THAT JIM CROW BIRD, PULL THE FEATHERS OUT HIS TAIL! . . . . . JC JIM CROW'S LAST 16

FEATURES 1
HER FEATURES IS ALL RUN TOGETHER . SP NECESSITY 9

FED 3
THAT PLANTED AND HARVESTED THE FOOD THAT FED . . . . SP FREEDOM'S PLOW 53
THAT FED AND HOUSED AND MOVED AMERICA. . . . . SP FREEDOM'S PLOW 67
I AM FED UP . . . . SP ONE-WAY TICKET 16

FEED 1
AND FEED ME, TOO? . . . . SP QUESTION 5

FEEL 15
STRENGTH HE DOESN'T REALLY FEEL. GAY, LOUD, UNHAPPY JAZZ, BARING HIS . . . . NM BIG-TIMER MOOD 9
FACE. "SOMETIMES I FEEL LIKE A MOTHER-LESS CHILE." TURNING FUTILELY . . . . NM BLACK CLWN MOOD 8
IT'S DONE GOT ME SO CRAZY, FEEL LIKE I BEEN TAKIN' COKE. . . . . . . NM BROKE 60
THAT I CAN NEITHER HEAR NOR FEEL NOR SEE. . . . . DK BEGGAR BOY 2
FEEL THE WEIGHT, MR. LEVY. . . . . SH BLD PAWNBROKER 13
I WONDER IF WHITE FOLKS EVER FEEL BAD. . . . . SH DAYBREAK 12
I FEEL SO MEAN I COULD . . . . . . SH EVIL MORNING 5
FEEL BAD TWO DAYS STRAIGHT. . . . . SH EVIL MORNING 14
I DON'T KNOW HOW YOU FEEL TODAY - OWT YESTERDAY TODAY 11
BUT, BABY, I FEEL BLUE. . . . . . . OWT YESTERDAY TODAY 12
I FEEL LIKE DANCIN', BABY, ... SP SUNDAY BY COMB 1
I FEEL LIKE DANCIN'! . . . . SP SUNDAY BY COMB 6
I FEEL AND SEE AND HEAR, HARLEM, I HEAR YOU: . . . . SP THEME FOR ENG B 18
JOE SAID I WONDER HOW IT WOULD FEEL SP WEST TEXAS 7
FEEL THE RUG OF DIVIDENDS. . . . . PL UNDERTOW 5

FEELING 8
FEELING LIFE GO. . . . . DLD THE CONSUMPTIVE 4
FEELING DEATH CREEP - . . . . DLD THE CONSUMPTIVE 8
I STARTED FEELING THIS A-WAY. . . . SH EVIL MORNING 4
O' MY FEELING LIKE A DOG . . . . . SH EVIL MORNING 10
THEY OUGHT TO BE LIKE ME SETTING HERE - FEELING GLAD! . . . . . . SH SUNDAY 15
SETTING HERE THINKING FEELING SAD. SH TWILIGHT REVERI 3
KEEP FEELING LIKE THIS I'M GONNA START ACTING BAD. . . . . SH TWILIGHT REVERI 4
AND FEELING TO MY VERY SOUL . . . . PL MILITANT 6

FEELIN' 4
IT KEEPS ME FROM FEELIN' BLUE. . . FC BAD MAN 12
FEELIN' SO SAD, LAWD, ... SH MIDNIGHT CHIPPI 7
FEELIN' SO SAD AND LONE. . . . . . SH MIDNIGHT CHIPPI 8
I STOOD THERE FEELIN' BLUE - . . . OWT LONESOME CORNER 2

FEELS 4
FEELS LIKE I COULD DIE. . . . . . . FC MOAN 14
I STILL FEELS BLUE. . . . . DK DRESSED UP 4
I FEELS DE BLUES A COMIN', ... DK NIGHT AND MORN 5
I WONDER HOW IT FEELS . . . . SH ASPIRATION 1

FEES 1
IGNORE ME - THOUGH I PAY YOUR FEES. SP LOW TO HIGH 15

FEET 42
MIGHT FALL AT THY FEET. . . . . . . WB SONGS DARK VIRG 5
WILL FALL AT THE FEET OF YOUR BEAUTY. . . . . WB TO DARK MERCEDE 5
HE KNOCKS ME OFF MA FEET. . . . . . FC MA MAN 2
HE KNOCKS ME OFF MA FEET. . . . . . FC MA MAN 4
EIGHTY-NINE FEET DEEP. . . . . . . FC SUICIDE 14
EIGHTY-NINE FEET DEEP. . . . . . . FC SUICIDE 16
AND FOUND LIFE - STEPPING ON MY FEET! . . . . DLD AESTHETE HARLEM 7
THEY DON'T HURT MA FEET. . . . . . DK DRESSED UP 10
BECAUSE MY FEET . . . . DK MINSTREL MAN 13
SHAKE YOUR BROWN FEET, HONEY, . . . DK SONG BANJO DANC 1
SHAKE YOUR BROWN FEET, CHILE, . . . DK SONG BANJO DANC 2
SHAKE YOUR BROWN FEET, HONEY, . . . DK SONG BANJO DANC 3
SHAKE YOUR BROWN FEET, HONEY, . . . DK SONG BANJO DANC 10
SO DANCE WITH SWIFT FEET, HONEY, . DK SONG BANJO DANC 16
DANCE WITH SWIFT FEET, HONEY - . . DK SONG BANJO DANC 18
SHAKE YOUR BROWN FEET, LIZA, . . . DK SONG BANJO DANC 20
SHAKE YOUR BROWN FEET, LIZA, . . . DK SONG BANJO DANC 22
SHAKE YOUR BROWN FEET, LIZA, . . . DK SONG BANJO DANC 24
IS IT MUCH TO DIE WHEN IMMORTAL FEET SL SCOTTSBORO 5
AND THE FIRE SCORCHED MY FEET. . . ANS A NEW SONG 20
WHEN THE MARCHING FEET OF THE MASSES ANS KIDS WHO DIE 45
THEIR FAR-TOO-HUMBLE FEET. . . . . ANS NEGRO GHETTO 8
WITH MY FEET IN THE MIRE . . . . . SH EVIL MORNING 11
DE SHOES WORE OFF MY FEET. . . . . SH OUT OF WORK 2
DE SHOES WORE OFF MY FEET. . . . . SH OUT OF WORK 4
AND GAY DANCING FEET . . . . OWT JUICE JOINT 14
THAT GOAD BLACK FEET TO DANCING ON BARE FLOORS. . . . . OWT JUICE JOINT 20
SOFT SAD BLACK FEET . . . . OWT JUICE JOINT 46
WITH NO SENSE, JUST WONDERFUL FEET. SP DANCER 21
WHEN I SET MY FEET IN GLORY . . . . SP DEFERRED 41
ON MY TWO FEET . . . . SP DEMOCRACY 8
YOU'LL HEAR THEIR FEET . . . . . . SP DREAM BOOGIE 6
LIKE MARCHING FEET. . . . . SP EASY BOOGIE 4
AT THE FEET O' JESUS, ... SP FEET O' JESUS 1
AT THE FEET O' JESUS . . . . SP FEET O' JESUS 5
AT YO' FEET I STAND. . . . . SP FEET O' JESUS 6
AMONG ALL WHO STAND ON TWO FEET. . SP INTERNE AT PROV 17
BARE FEET TO BEAT THE GREAT DRUMBEAT AYM BLUES IN STEREO 9
TO BIND MY MIND - CHAIN MY FEET - PL DEATH YORKVILLE 6
I'M GONNA PLANT MY FEET . . . . . . PL DOWN WHERE I AM 13
ON WHICH HE SET HIS FEET. . . . . . PL FREDRK DOUGLASS 9
ON MY TWO FEET . . . . PL FREEDOM 8

FELL 8
IN THE DARK THEY FELL A-CRYING . . DK IRISH WAKE 1
I FELL IN LOVE WITH . . . . DK PO' BOY BLUES 13

FELL IN LOVE WITH . . . . DK PO' BOY BLUES 15
BUT SOMETHING HAPPENED. JIM'S FEATHERS FELL. . . . . JC JIM CROW'S LAST 5
I DREAMED ABOUT WHEN WE FIRST FELL IN LOVE . . . . SP DEFERRED 9
MONROE'S FELL ON EVIL DAYS - . . . SP MONROE'S BLUES 1
MONROE'S FELL ON EVIL DAYS. . . . . SP MONROE'S BLUES 3
ONE OF THE PILLARS OF THE TEMPLE FELL. . . . . SP MULATTO 4

FELLOW 10
WOULDN'T NO GOOD FELLOW . . . . . . WB TO MIDNIGHT NAN 3
WOULDN'T NO GOOD FELLOW . . . . . . WB TO MIDNIGHT NAN 19
A COMPLAINT TO.B GIVEN BY A DEJECTED LOOKING FELLOW SHUFFLING ALONG . NM BROKE 1
A DRAMATIC RECITATION TO BE DONE IN THE HALF-DARK BY A YOUNG BROWN FELLOW . . . . NM COLORED SL MOOD 1
DON'T SNUB THE OTHER FELLOW - . . . SH SNOB 3
A FELLOW CAME ONE DAY. . . . . . . SP BLD FORTUNE TEL 9
AS THE OTHER FELLOW HAS . . . . . . SP DEMOCRACY 6
FELLOW, SAY? . . . . SP LOW TO HIGH 11
AGAINST MY FELLOW MAN . . . . PL ANGOLA QUESTION 12
AS THE OTHER FELLOW HAS . . . . . . PL FREEDOM 6

FELT 8
IT FELT GOOD TO SHOUT! . . . . . . FW COMMUNION 8
SHE MIGHT NOT'VE FELT . . . . OWT BLD MARGE POLIT 7
I NEVER FELT SO LONESOME . . . . . SP LITTLE OLD LETT 11
I SAID, IT FELT GOOD - . . . . . . SP MADAM MINISTER 19
I FELT KINDER SORRY . . . . SP MADAM MINISTER 28
I FELT LIKE THAT ABOUT HIM. . . . . SP MAMA AND DAUGHT 12
SHE FELT QUEER PAIN . . . . SP STRANGE HURT 2
BUT I FELT MA TIME'S A-COMIN'. . . SP SYLVESTER'S BED 17

FEMININE 1
FEMININE SWEETNESS . . . . SH HARLEM SWEETIES 19

FENCES 1
AGAINST BLACK FENCES. . . . . SP MULATTO 15

FER 2
FER I CAN'T STAY HERE ALONE. . . . FC GYPSY MAN 6
FIT FER A HOPPIN' TOAD. . . . . . . SP BOUND NO'TH BLS 24

FERRY 2
WITH JOHN BROWN AT HARPER'S FERRY, NEGROES DIED. . . . . SP FREEDOM'S PLOW 116
SINCE HARPERS FERRY . . . . PL OCTOBER 16 RAID 23

FERTILIZE 1
TO FERTILIZE THE DESERT . . . . . . AYM IS IT TRUE? 16

FESTER 2
OR FESTER LIKE A SORE - . . . . . . SP HARLEM 4
OR FESTER LIKE A SORE - . . . . . . PL DREAM DEFERRED 4

FESTERING 1
HER BANDAGE HIDES TWO FESTERING SORES . . . . PL JUSTICE 3

FEVER'S 1
YOUR FEVER'S BROKE - . . . . SP MADAM WRONG VIS 24

FEW 7
BUY ME A FEW THINGS. . . . . SH PAY DAY 6
A FEW YEARS AGO. . . . . JC BLD SAM SOLOMON 6
A FEW . . . . FW DANCERS 2
A FEW . . . . FW DANCERS 6
A FEW MINUTES LATE . . . . SP DREAM BOOGE VAR 11
BUT A FEW BUCKS A WEEK. . . . . . . SP MADAM CHARTY CH 18
HE PLAYED A FEW CHORDS THEN HE SANG SOME MORE - . . . . SP THE WEARY BLUES 24

FEZ 1
BY A STUDENT IN A FEZ . . . . AYM SHADES OF PIG 25

FICE 1
CUR DOG, FICE DOG, KERRY BLUE - . . SP WARNING AUGMENT 13

FICISTS 1
TO DRIVE THE FICISTS FROM THE LAND. JC GOOD MORN STLIN 34

FIELD 9
LIFE IS A BARREN FIELD . . . . . . DK DREAMS 7
OR A PRISON GRAVE, OR THE POTTER'S FIELD. . . . . ANS KIDS WHO DIE 41
ACROSS THE FIELD OF HISTORY. . . . SP FREEDOM'S PLOW 193
AND THE COTTON FIELD IS FRIGHTENED SP MIGRANT 23
DRIVEN TO THE FIELD. . . . . SP SHARE-CROPPERS 2
DRIVEN TO THE FIELD - . . . . SP SHARE-CROPPERS 14
I AM THE WOMAN WHO WORKED IN THE FIELD . . . . SP THE NEGRO MOTHE 11
PICKIN' COTTON IN THE FIELD . . . . SP WEST TEXAS 6
AND THE FIELD DAISY EYES . . . . . PL DAYBREAK IN ALA 13

FIELDS 5
BACK BENT AS IN THE FIELDS. THE SLOW STEP. THE BOWED HEAD. "NOBODY KNOWS . . . . NM BLACK CLWN MOOD 4
OH, FIELDS OF WONDER . . . . FW BIRTH 1
JUST STOPPIN' IN THE FIELDS IN THE BROAD DAYLIGHT. . . . . SP FREEDOM TRAIN 52
WHILE REVOLT IN THE RICE FIELDS . . PL LAST PRINCE 12
IN THE COTTON FIELDS. . . . . PL WARNING 7

FIERCE 1
AND BOWING HIS HEAD IN SHAME, BECOMES SUDDENLY FIERCE AND ANGRY. THEN HE . . . . NM COLORED SL MOOD 11

FIERY 1
DAYS FILLED WITH FIERY SUNSHINE . . SP STRANGE HURT 6

FIFTEEN-YEAR-OLD 1
TO KILL A FIFTEEN-YEAR-OLD KID? . . PL DREAM DEFERRED 2

FIFTH 2
A PARTY OF WHITES FROM FIFTH AVENUE SH DEATH IN HARLEM 58
DON'T TAKE THE FIFTH AMENDMENT. . . AYM RIDE, RED, RIDE 28

FIFTHS 1
INTO FLATTED FIFTHS AND FLATTER BEERS . . . . SP FLATTED FIFTHS 5

FIFTY 1
FIFTY NEGROES! . . . . PL LENOX AVE. BAR 6

FIGHT 14
ONLY DUMB GUYS FIGHT. . . . . FC PRIZE FIGHTER 1
ONLY DUMB GUYS FIGHT. . . . . FC PRIZE FIGHTER 7
AND FIGHT IT OUT ALONE. . . . . . . NM BIG-TIMER POEM 36
WORK, PRAY, AND FIGHT. . . . . . . NM BLACK CLWN POEM 64
WHO JOINED UP TO FIGHT FOR THE U.S.A. . . . . NM COLORED SL POEM 3
SO WE MARCHED TO THE FRONT, HAPPY TO FIGHT. . . . . NM COLORED SL POEM 12
I FIGHT, I STARVE, I DIE. . . . . . ANS BLDS OF LENIN 24
WHEN A MAN'S WON A FIGHT IN A BIG MAN'S TOWN - . . . . SH DEATH IN HARLEM 55
IF I GOT TO FIGHT, ... JC BIG BUDDY 5
I'LL FIGHT LIKE A MAN. . . . . . . JC BIG BUDDY 6
THAT CROW CAN'T FIGHT FOR DEMOCRACY JC JIM CROW'S LAST 9
AND THERE ARE THOSE WHO FIGHT . . . JC TO CAPTAIN MULZ 13
IF THE FIGHT IS NOT YET WON, . . . SP FREEDOM'S PLOW 163
AND FIGHT ANOTHER WAR. . . . . . . SP RELIEF 13

FIGHTERS 1
FIGHTERS FOR THE FREE. . . . . . . SL SCOTTSBORO 20

FIGHTING 8
ECHOES THE FIGHTING "MARSEILLAISE." TEARING OFF HIS CLOWN'S SUIT. . NM BLACK CLWN MOOD 13
WHO HAS A VISION OF HIS BROTHER KILLED IN FRANCE WHILE FIGHTING FOR THE . . . . NM COLORED SL MOOD 2
THINKING WE WERE FIGHTING FOR DEMOCRACY'S TRUE REIGN . . . . . NM COLORED SL POEM 7
WHEN WE GOT THROUGH FIGHTING, OVER THERE, AND DYING? . . . . NM COLORED SL POEM 34
WE'RE FIGHTING TO CREATE. . . . . . JC BLACK MAN SPEAK 24
IF WE'RE FIGHTING TO CREATE . . . . JC BLACK MAN SPEAK 25
CAUSE THE GOOD LORD KNOWS WHAT WE'RE FIGHTING FOR! . . . . JC JIM CROW'S LAST 26
STRUGGLING, FIGHTING, ... PL QUESTION ANSWER 5

FIGHTIN' 2
I WOULDN'T BE FIGHTIN'. . . . . . . FC PRIZE FIGHTER 3
THE NATIONS THEY IS FIGHTIN' . . . SP SOUTHERN MAMMY 7

FIGHTS 1
SHE FIGHTS AN' QUARRELS MOST . . . FC EVIL WOMAN 7

FIGURE 3
I WAS TRYING TO FIGURE OUT . . . . FW COMMUNION 1
BUT I COULD NOT FIGURE OUT . . . . FW COMMUNION 3
YOU FIGURE OUT WHY! . . . . SP MADAM CHARTY CH 28

FIGURETTE 1
FIGURETTE . . . . SP WHAT? SO SOON! 9

FIGURINE 1
FIGURINE . . . . SP QUESTION 6

FILIPINOS 1
WHITES AND FILIPINOS. . . . . ANS KIDS WHO DIE 14

FILL 4
I'M GONNA FILL 'EM UP FULL O' . . . FC DEATH DO DIRTY 33
FILL IT UP WITH GAS . . . . SH DECLARATION 10
FILL IT UP WITH GAS AND . . . . . . SH IF-ING 7
I GOT MY FILL. . . . . PL DOWN WHERE I AM 12

FILLED 6
FILLED WITH BLUE STARS. . . . . . . DK AFTR MNY SPRNGS 4

THE HIGH SHERIFF'S EYES ARE FILLED WITH HATE. . . . ANS BLD OZZIE POWEL 7
I FILLED HIM FULL OF HOLES . . . . SH BLD THE KILLER 23
AND SOME WERE FILLED WITH FEAR - . LHR BLD MARY'S SON 12
DAYS FILLED WITH FIERY SUNSHINE . . SP STRANGE HURT 6
SOMETIMES, THE VALLEY WAS FILLED WITH TEARS. . . . SP THE NEGRO MOTHE 25

FILLMORE 1

FILLMORE OUT IN FRISCO, 7TH ACROSS THE BAY. . . . AYM ASK YOUR MAMA 31

FILLS 2

TILL BEAUTY AND PRIDE FILLS EACH DARK FACE . . . NM DARK YOUTH USA 20
THAT FILLS A WOMAN'S AGE-LESS, AGE-LONG PAIN - . . . OWT JUICE JOINT 28

FILTH 3

DARK WITH FILTH AND MUD. . . . JC THE BITTER RIVR 7
WITH ITS FILTH AND ITS MUD TOO LONG. JC THE BITTER RIVR 74
TIRED OF FILTH AND MUD. . . . JC THE BITTER RIVR 80

FINAL 2

WHORES IN FINAL WEARINESS SAY: . . SP SLIVER SERMON 3
AND THAT FINAL STOP IS A . . . SP WIDOW WOMAN 5

FINALLY 1

BUT FINALLY THEY TAUNT HIM . . . . FW MIGRATION 6

FIND 24

O, YOU CAN'T FIND A BUDDY . . . . FC DEATH DO DIRTY 1
SHO CAN'T FIND NO EASE. . . . FC GYPSY MAN 24
TRIED TO FIND ONE O' THEM LITTLE ELEVATOR AND SWITCHBOARD JOBS THEY USED . . . NM BROKE 41
COULD HARDLY FIND A JOB THAT OFFERED DECENT PAY. . . . NM COLORED SL POEM 21
I CANNOT FIND THEM ANY MORE. . . . OK AFTR MNY SPRNGS 8
NO WONDER WE FIND THEM SUCH MARVELLOUS THINGS! . . . OK FAIRIES 5
COME TO FIND OUT . . . SH ANNOUNCEMENT 9
AND FIND SOMEBODY TO KID AND TALK. SH BED TIME 8
I COULDN'T FIND NO JOB . . . SH OUT OF WORK 7
COULDN'T FIND NO JOB . . . SH OUT OF WORK 9
LAWD! I GOT TO FIND ME A WOMAN FOR THE WPA - . . . SH SUPPER TIME 13
WE SOMETIMES FIND . . . FW CIRCLES 9
FIND MY DREAM! . . . SP AS I GREW OLDER 27
SHE TRIED TO FIND OUT . . . SP BLD FORTUNE TEL 25
GOT TO FIND SOMEBODY . . . SP BOUND NO'TH BLS 5
HOPING TO FIND THEIR FREEDOM, . . . SP FREEDOM'S PLOW 44
YOU AIN'T GONNA FIND IT . . . SP MADAM FORT TELL 19
BUT I DIDN'T FIND 'EM. . . . SP MAGNOLIA FLOWER 4
"YOU'LL FIND RAIN BETTER . . . SP STRANGE HURT 4
GRANDPA, DID YOU FIND HER IN THE TV SILENCE . . . AYM BIRD IN ORBIT 61
DID YOU EVER FIND HER? . . . AYM BIRD IN ORBIT 64
WHEN I TRY TO FIND A JOB . . . PL BACKLASH BLUES 13
TRY TO FIND MYSELF A JOB . . . PL BACKLASH BLUES 15
AND WE BETTER FIND OUT, MAMA, . . . PL CULTURAL EXCHNG 23

FINDING 6

AND FINDING ONLY THE SAME OLD STUPID PLAN. . . . ANS LET AMERICA BE 23
WENT FINDING AND SEEKING. . . . SP OLD WALT 2
FINDING LESS THAN SOUGHT . . . SP OLD WALT 3
OF THE SEEKING OR THE FINDING. . . SP OLD WALT 6
IN SEEKING AS IN FINDING. . . . SP OLD WALT 8
AND FINDING. . . . SP OLD WALT 11

FINDS 3

THEN THEY GOES AN' FINDS A YALLER GAL . . . FC BLACK GAL 7
BUT EVER FRIEND YOU FINDS SEEMS . . SP BOUND NO'TH BLS 17
'CAUSE YOU FINDS IT'S KINDER HARD. SP MOTHER TO SON 16

FINE 26

I TREATED ALBERT FINE. . . . FC BLACK GAL 2
GATHER UP YO' FINE CLOTHES . . . FC HARD LUCK 5
JEW TAKES YO' FINE CLOTHES, . . . FC HARD LUCK 7
JEW TAKES YO' FINE CLOTHES, . . . FC HARD LUCK 9
AN' I TREATS HER FINE, . . . FC WORKIN' MAN 10
HOME, KIDS, AND EVERYTHING FINE. . NM BIG-TIMER POEM 46
AND I HOPE YOU'RE MAKING GOOD, AND DOING FINE - . . . NM COLORED SL POEM 17
DIDN'T OUR GOVERNMENT TELL US THINGS WOULD BE FINE . . . NM COLORED SL POEM 33
SHO IS FINE. . . . OK DRESSED UP 6
CAUSE THEY TOLD ME DE NORTH WAS FINE. . . . SH EVENIN' BLUES 2
CAUSE THEY TOLD ME DE NORTH WAS FINE. . . . SH EVENIN' BLUES 4
DELICIOUS, FINE SUGAR HILL. . . . SH HARLEM SWEETIES 44
THEN MAKE FINE SPEECHES . . . JC HOW ABOUT DIXIE 15
I WANT SOME FINE MUSIC . . . OWT REQUEST REQUIEM 3
BLACK IS FINE! . . . SP ARGUMENT 8
BUT I WANT MY FUNERAL TO BE FINE: SP AS BEFITS A MAN 6
MY OLD MAN DIED IN A FINE BIG HOUSE. SP CROSS 9
BLACK MEN AND WHITE WILL SAY, AIN'T IT FINE? . . . SP FREEDOM TRAIN 61
OF A JOB IN A FINE OFFICE . . . SP GRADUATION 16
DRESSED SO FINE? . . . SP LADY'S BOOGIE 2
LIFE IS FINE! . . . SP LIFE IS FINE 31
FINE AS WINE! . . . SP LIFE IS FINE 32
LIFE IS FINE! . . . SP LIFE IS FINE 33
THEM TWO FINE CARS? . . . SP NIGHT FUNERAL 4
HAS A FINE ONE-BUTTON ROLL, . . . SP TRUMPET PLAYER 36
RIDE SO FINE BEFORE. . . . PL FLORIDA WORKERS 18

FINGER 1

AND WRAP A STRING AROUND ITS FINGER SP SUMMER EVENING 26

FINGERS 6

AWAY FROM THE TOO-ROUGH FINGERS . . OK DREAM KEEPER 7
"SEPARATE AS THE FINGERS." . . . ANS OPEN LETTER 20
TO A HEEL TAP AND A SWIRL OF FINGERS ANS SONG OF SPAIN 8
SHE SNAPS HER FINGERS, SLOWLY SHAKES HER HIPS, . . . OWT LINCOLN THEATRE 9
GREAT LONG FINGERS . . . SP DREAM BOOGE VAR 5
TOUCHING EVERYBODY WITH KIND FINGERS PL DAYBREAK IN ALA 18

FINGER-TALL 1

GIN IS SOLD IN GLASSES FINGER-TALL. OWT JUICE JOINT 6

FINISHED 2

NOW I HAVE FINISHED MY TOIL. . . . ANS BLDS OF LENIN 8
IF THE HOUSE IS NOT YET FINISHED, SP FREEDOM'S PLOW 161

FIRE 31

CREEPING LIKE FIRE . . . OLD THE CONSUMPTIVE 9
CREEPING LIKE FIRE FROM A SLOW SPARK OLD THE CONSUMPTIVE 10
HIS SOUL ON FIRE. . . . OK MA LORD 13
AND THE FIRE SCORCHED MY FEET. . . ANS A NEW SONG 20
I WOULD MAKE A FIRE BUT THERE AIN'T NO WOOD. . . . SH SUPPER TIME 4
IF I HAD A FIRE I'D MAKE ME SOME TEA SH SUPPER TIME 11
CAUSE I'D TAKE THAT OWL HEAD AND FIRE ON YOU. . . . SH TWILIGHT REVERI 12
A CRACKLING FIRE, . . . FW CAROLINA CABIN 7
ALL THROUGH THE FIRE. . . . SP ANGELS WINGS 10
TURNS RED AS FIRE. . . . SP BLUE BAYOU 15
A POOL OF FIRE. . . . SP BLUE BAYOU 23
LIKE A WISP OF SMOKE AROUND THE FIRE - . . . SP DANSE AFRICAINE 11
FIRE, . . . SP FIRE 1
FIRE, LORD! . . . SP FIRE 2
FIRE GONNA BURN MA SOUL! . . . SP FIRE 3
FIRE, . . . SP FIRE 7
FIRE, LORD! . . . SP FIRE 8
FIRE GONNA BURN MA SOUL! . . . SP FIRE 9
FIRE, . . . SP FIRE 14
FIRE, LORD! . . . SP FIRE 15
FIRE GONNA BURN MA SOUL! . . . SP FIRE 16
FIRE, . . . SP FIRE 21
FIRE, LORD! . . . SP FIRE 22
FIRE GONNA BURN MA SOUL! . . . SP FIRE 23
I MEANS FIRE, LORD! . . . SP FIRE 24
FIRE GONNA BURN MA SOUL! . . . SP FIRE 25
MIXED WITH LIQUID FIRE. . . . SP TRUMPET PLAYER 20
SUDDENLY CATCHING FIRE . . . AYM JAZZTET MUTED 7
THAT SOMETIMES TURN TO FIRE. . . . AYM JAZZTET MUTED 21
AND BLESS THE FIRE. . . . PL BOMBINGS DIXIE 8
THE SPEAKER CATCHES FIRE, . . . PL CORNER MEETING 4

FIRED 1

"YOU'RE FIRED!" . . . SP FIRED 6

FIRE'S 1

SCRATCHING IN THE DEAD FIRE'S ASHES SP THE SOUTH 7

FIRM 2

ROCKS AND THE FIRM ROOTS OF TREES. SP SPIRITUALS 1
FROM THE FIRM ROOTS OF TREES. . . . SP SPIRITUALS 10

FIRST 22

IN THE FIRST GARDEN . . . WB JAZZONIA 10
I'M A FIRST CLASS HUSTLER. . . . NM BIG-TIMER POEM 37
I MEAN FOUR - BEFORE DAYLIGHT - S'POSE TO'VE DONE HIT YO' FIRST STROKE - . . . NM BROKE 14
WORKER: THE FIRST OF MAY: . . . ANS CHANT MAY DAY 3
IT'S DE FIRST OF MAY! . . . ANS SISTER JOHNSON 4
IT'S DE FIRST OF MAY! . . . ANS SISTER JOHNSON 8
IT'S DE FIRST OF MAY! . . . ANS SISTER JOHNSON 13
WHEN THE FIRST VIOLETS . . . SH YOUNG NEGRO GRL 3
FIRST SMELTED IN . . . JC ME AND MY SONG 11
AS THE FIRST IRON . . . JC ME AND MY SONG 30
STRONG AS THE COMING OF THE FIRST CHILD . . . FW EARTH SONG 9
AT FIRST THEY ARE NICE TO HIM. . . FW MIGRATION 5
IN THE FIRST PLACE . . . SP DANCER 5
I DREAMED ABOUT WHEN WE FIRST FELL IN LOVE . . . SP DEFERRED 9
HE STARTS FIRST WITH HIMSELF . . . SP FREEDOM'S PLOW 5
FIRST IN THE HEART IS THE DREAM - SP FREEDOM'S PLOW 9

FIRST TIME IN MY LIFE . . . . SP MADAM MIGHT-HAV 11
FIRST GRADE IN NEW ORLEANS . . . . AYM BIRD IN ORBIT 9
THAT LUGGED THE FIRST WHITE . . . . AYM GOSPEL CHA-CHA 16
FIRST WHITE TOURIST UP THE MOUNTAIN AYM GOSPEL CHA-CHA 17
ESPECIALLY FOR THE FIRST ONES . . . AYM HORN OF PLENTY 66
THE FIRST BLOW, HE SAID. . . . . . PL FREDRK DOUGLASS 20

FIRST-CLASS 1
FOR A FIRST-CLASS FUNERAL, ... SP BLD OF THE MAN 5

FISH 7
HE'D FOUND A FISH . . . . SP CATCH 9
HALF FISH, ... SP CATCH 11
AND MY COLD FISH ET THE GLASS. . . SP CHILDREN'S RYME 19
AND ASKED FOR FISH. . . . . SP HOPE 2
LIGHTS IN THE FISH JOINTS, ... SP RAILROAD AVENUE 3
SHAKING THE LIGHTS IN THE FISH JOINTS, ... SP RAILROAD AVENUE 26
I BOIL A FISH AND SALT IT . . . . . AYM GOSPEL CHA-CHA 24

FISHER 1
BEING A FISHER BOY, ... SP CATCH 8

FISHING 1
WE SAW A LINE OF FISHING SHIPS . . SP SEASCAPE 3

FISH-TAIL 2
I WANT A FISH-TAIL HEARSE . . . . . SP AS BEFITS A MAN 9
AND SIXTEEN FISH-TAIL CARS, ... SP AS BEFITS A MAN 10

FIST 3
IS A BROWN MAN'S FIST . . . . FC BEALE ST. LOVE 2
IF I LAND MY FIST ON YOU. . . . . . SP BLD LANDLORD 20
AND SO MY FIST IS CLENCHED . . . . PL MILITANT 12

FISTS 5
BEAT WITH BARE, BROWN FISTS - . . . DK SONG 8
BEATING YOUR FISTS . . . . FW DUSK 5
IN THE WIND'S FRENETIC FISTS . . . AYM GOSPEL CHA-CHA 4
IN THE WIND'S FRENETIC FISTS. . . . AYM GOSPEL CHA-CHA 34
BOTH FISTS SORE. . . . . PL DOWN WHERE I AM 4

FIT 2
FIT FER A HOPPIN' TOAD. . . . . . . SP BOUND NO'TH BLS 24
AND THE NATIONS THEY DONE FIT. . . SP SOUTHERN MAMMY 8

FIVE 8
BEEN WALKIN' SINCE FIVE THIS MORNIN'. . . . . NM BROKE 2
LAST JOB I HAD, WENT TO WORK AT FIVE IN DE MORNIN', OR LITTLE MO' . . NM BROKE 12
HERE'S FIVE DOLLARS, CASSIE, BUY A TICKET BACK. . . . . SH LETTER 20
AND CHARGED FIVE . . . . SP BLD OF THE MAN 18
ONCE FIVE, ONCE THREE, ... SP CONSIDER ME 4
WHERE I GET OFF AT FIVE, ... SP DEFERRED 26
BUT HERE IS FIVE DOLLARS FOR YOU . SP LETTER 4
CHARGED FIVE DOLLARS . . . . SP NIGHT FUNERAL 23

FIX 3
TILL YOU FIX THIS HOUSE UP NEW. . . SP BLD LANDLORD 12
THE SAME OLD FIX. . . . . SP MADAM NUMBER WR 20
PERHAPS FROM A FIX . . . . PL SLAVE 9

FIXED 1
AND YOU FIXED 'EM . . . . SP NOTE COMM THEAT 5

FLAG 5
LENIN WITH THE FLAG BLOOD RED. . . SL SCOTTSBORO 21
TUSKEGEE WITH A NEW FLAG ON THE TOWER! . . . . ANS OPEN LETTER 43
WAVING A FLAG AND MOUTHING ROT . . ANS SONG OF SPAIN 68
LADDER, FLAG, AND AMPLIFIER . . . . PL CORNER MEETING 1
FOR CINQUE SAYING, "RUN A NEW FLAG UP THE MAST." . . . . PL FINAL CALL 21

FLAGS 2
AND ALL THE FLAGS WE'VE HUNG, . . . ANS LET AMERICA BE 59
LOWER THE FLAGS . . . . PL SPECIAL BULLTIN 1

FLAGSHIP 1
YOUR SHIP IS FLAGSHIP . . . . JC TO CAPTAIN MULZ 69

FLAME 7
THAT I WERE A FLAME, ... WB SONGS DARK VIRG 16
BUT ONE SHARP, LEAPING FLAME . . . WB SONGS DARK VIRG 17
PERPETUALLY THE FLAME. . . . . . . DUD TWO THINGS 4
LIKE A FLAME. . . . . DK YOUTH 3
THOUGHT OF FLAME, ... SH DEATH IN HARLEM 71
AND SHARP AS FLAME. . . . . SP BEALE STREET 8
NOR FUEL FOR THE CLEAN FLAME OF JOY SP RUBY BROWN 6

FLAMENCO 3
FLAMENCO IS THE SONG OF SPAIN: . . ANS SONG OF SPAIN 5
FLAMENCO IS THE SONG OF SPAIN. . . ANS SONG OF SPAIN 10
TOROS, FLAMENCO, PAINTINGS, BOOKS - ANS SONG OF SPAIN 38

FLAMES 1
A NEW DREAM FLAMES . . . . ANS A NEW SONG 53

FLAMING 1
THE FLAMING SOURCE OF YOUR BRIGHT BREATH. . . . . SP DEMAND 5

FLASH 1
THE MOVIES END. THE LIGHTS FLASH GAILY ON. . . . . OWT LINCOLN THEATRE 5

FLAT 3
I GOT A FURNISHED-UP FLAT, ... NM BIG-TIMER POEM 23
COLD-WATER FLAT AND ALL THAT. . . . SP DEFERRED 14
SEND FOR DEAD BLIND LEMON TO SING THE B FLAT . . . . PL FINAL CALL 13

FLATTED 1
INTO FLATTED FIFTHS AND FLATTER BEERS . . . . SP FLATTED FIFTHS 5

FLATTER 1
INTO FLATTED FIFTHS AND FLATTER BEERS . . . . SP FLATTED FIFTHS 5

FLAVOR 1
FLAVOR HARLEM OF MINE! . . . . . . SH HARLEM SWEETIES 28

FLEE 2
WHITE FOLKS FLEE - . . . . PL LITTLE SNG HOUS 5
WHITE FOLKS, FLEE! . . . . PL LITTLE SNG HOUS 25

FLEEING 1
WAS SHE FLEEING WITH LUMUMBA? . . . AYM RIDE, RED, RIDE 16

FLESH 4
THE WIND IMPRISONED IN THE FLESH, ANS NEGRO GHETTO 3
THIS SUFFERING FLESH, ... LHR DEAR LVLY DEATH 6
WITH SPATTERED FLESH . . . . PL BIRMINGHAM SUND 6
GHOSTS OF ALL TOO SOLID FLESH, . . PL GHOSTS OF 1619 1

FLESHLY 1
FLESHLY PLEASURES . . . . FW OLD SAILOR 11

FLESH-AND-BLOOD 2
FLESH-AND-BLOOD GHOSTS . . . . . . PL GHOSTS OF 1619 14
BECAME FLESH-AND-BLOOD MEN? . . . . PL GHOSTS OF 1619 15

FLEW 1
AS IF TECHNICOLOR BANNERS FLEW . . PL MOTHER IN WAR 7

FLIES 3
ON FRIDAY THE EAGLE FLIES. . . . . SP CONSIDER ME 42
FLY LIKE THE EAGLE FLIES. . . . . . SP HARD DADDY 14
FLY LIKE THE EAGLE FLIES. . . . . . SP HARD DADDY 16

FLINCHING 1
DE TROUBLE I'VE HAD." FLINCHING UNDER THE WHIP. THE SPIRITUAL . NM BLACK CLWN MOOD 5

FLING 2
TO FLING MY ARMS WIDE . . . . SP DREAM VARIATION 1
TO FLING MY ARMS WIDE . . . . SP DREAM VARIATION 10

FLOAT 1
AN' I DON'T KNOW HOW TO FLOAT. . . DK WIDE RIVER 6

FLOOD 3
WHEN THIS FLOOD IS OVER, ... SH MISSISSIPPI LEV 5
BUT DE WATER STILL MAKES A FLOOD. SH MISSISSIPPI LEV 12
BUT DESTINED SURE TO FLOOD - AND SOON - . . . . PL JUNIOR ADDICT 10

FLOOR 12
IN THAT CELLAR ON THE FLOOR . . . . SH DEATH IN HARLEM 122
COUPLES ON THE FLOOR ROCK AND SHAKE. SH DEATH IN HARLEM 33
LISTEN AT MY FOOTPRINTS WALKING ON THE FLOOR. . . . . SH SUPPER TIME 7
AND LIKE A WAVE THE FLOOR - . . . . FW HARLEM DANCE HA 7
ACROSS THE FLOOR. . . . . SP END 6
KITCHEN FLOOR SQUEAKS, ... SP MADAM RENT MAN 16
AND PLACES WITH NO CARPET ON THE FLOOR - . . . . SP MOTHER TO SON 6
THUMP, THUMP, THUMP, WENT HIS FOOT ON THE FLOOR. . . . . SP THE WEARY BLUES 23
THAT STRETCHES PADDLE-TAILED ACROSS THE FLOOR. . . . . SP TO BE SOMEBODY 5
TWO DOZEN MEN TO THE FLOOR. . . . . SP TO BE SOMEBODY 18
BARS AND FLOOR SKYROCKET . . . . . PL THIRD DEGREE 13
DROPPED ON THE MEN'S ROOM FLOOR . . PL UNDERTOW 9

FLOORS 2
THAT GOAD BLACK FEET TO DANCING ON BARE FLOORS. . . . . OWT JUICE JOINT 20
SIXTEEN FLOORS ABOVE THE GROUND. . SP LIFE IS FINE 13

FLORE 1
ROTONDE SELECT DUPONT FLORE . . . . AYM ASK YOUR MAMA 51

FLORIDA 1
- FROM GEORGIA FLORIDA LOUISIANA . . SP GOOD MORNING 13

FLOW 2
- IN THE FLOW OF OLD AUNT SUE'S VOICE. SP AUNTSUE'S STORI 13
- FLOW OF HUMAN BLOOD IN HUMAN VEINS. SP NEGRO SPEAKS OF 3

FLOWED 2
- REDDER NOW WHERE YOUR BLOOD HAS FLOWED. . . . . ANS BLD OZZIE POWEL 3
- BUT REDDER NOW WHERE YOUR LIFE'S BLOOD FLOWED. . . . . ANS BLD OZZIE POWEL 31

FLOWER 6
- IS LIKE A WITHERED FLOWER . . . . . WB YOUNG PROSTITUT 2
- THE FLOWER NO SCENT ENCLOSES. . . . FW REMEMBRANCE 4
- A FLOWER. . . . . LHR POET TO BIGOT 17
- AUTUMN FLOWER . . . . SP TROUBLED WOMAN 7
- WIND-BLOWN AUTUMN FLOWER . . . . . SP TROUBLED WOMAN 10
- THEIR OWN SWEET TIME TO FLOWER . . PL SWEET WORDS RAC 2

FLOWERS 21
- AS FLOWERS IN THE SUN. . . . . . . WB PIERROT 20
- FLOWERS ARE HAPPY IN SUMMER. . . . DK AUTUMN THOUGHT 1
- STREW NO FLOWERS ON MY GRAVE. . . . DK DEATH SEAMAN 7
- WHEN THE FLOWERS BREAK THROUGH THE EARTH. . . . . ANS CHANT MAY DAY 4
- BE LIKE THE FLOWERS. . . . . ANS CHANT MAY DAY 8
- WHEN FLOWERS SPREAD THE PLAIN. . . FW GIRL 6
- FOR SURE THERE GREW FLOWERS . . . . FW GIRL 14
- AND FLOWERS. . . . . FW HARLEM DANCE HA 4
- AND BELIEVED THE TINY FLOWERS . . . LHR PASTORAL 6
- AND A WHOLE TRUCK LOAD OF FLOWERS. SP AS BEFITS A MAN 12
- SEND SOME FLOWERS. . . . . SP BLD OF THE MAN 8
- HIS BUDDIES BROUGHT FLOWERS. . . . SP BLD OF THE MAN 15
- HEARSE AND FLOWERS . . . . SP DEAD IN THERE 6
- AND FLOWERS LIFT THEIR HEADS. . . . SP IN TIME SILVER 5
- I WENT LOOKIN' FOR MAGNOLIA FLOWERS SP MAGNOLIA FLOWER 3
- I WENT LOOKIN' FOR MAGNOLIA FLOWERS IN THE DUSK . . . . SP MAGNOLIA FLOWER 5
- NO FLOWERS FROM THE STORE. . . . . SP MIDWINTER BLUES 24
- THAT WREATH OF FLOWERS? . . . . . . SP NIGHT FUNERAL 12
- THEM FLOWERS CAME . . . . SP NIGHT FUNERAL 13
- THEY'LL WANT FLOWERS, TOO. . . . . SP NIGHT FUNERAL 15
- TO THEM FOLKS THAT BROUGHT THE FLOWERS. . . . . SP NIGHT FUNERAL 40

FLOWING 1
- FLOWING THROUGH THE SOUTH. . . . . JC THE BITTER RIVR 3

FLOWS 2
- SUNDAY MORNING WHERE THE RHYTHM FLOWS. . . . . SP MYSTERY 11
- WHERE AN ANCIENT RIVER FLOWS . . . AYM BLUES IN STEREO 14

FLUID 1
- WITH FLUID FAR-OFF GOING . . . . . PL CULTURAL EXCHNG 9

FLUNG 1
- IS FLUNG. . . . . SP LUCK 4

FLUTE 1
- AND YET HE PLAYS UPON HIS FLUTE A WILD FREE TUNE . . . . DK BEGGAR BOY 7

FLUTTERING 1
- MA HEART'S A FLUTTERING ASPEN LEAF DK REASONS WHY 7

FLY 12
- THAT CANNOT FLY. . . . . DK DREAMS 4
- FLY AWAY FROM YOU. . . . . SH DECLARATION 18
- LOOK IN THE BREAD BOX, NOTHING BUT A FLY. . . . . SH SUPPER TIME 2
- FOLKS FLY. . . . . OWT RESTRICTIVE 3
- FLY LIKE THE EAGLE FLIES. . . . . . SP HARD DADDY 14
- FLY LIKE THE EAGLE FLIES. . . . . . SP HARD DADDY 16
- I'D FLY ON MA MAN AN' . . . . SP HARD DADDY 17
- LET ME TO THY BOSOM FLY! . . . . . SP MYSTERY 7
- ON THE FLY . . . . SP UP-BEAT 4
- FOR THE CARS TO FLY BY ON. . . . . PL FLORIDA WORKERS 4
- WHITE FOLKS FLY - . . . . PL LITTLE SNG HOUS 14
- WHITE FOLKS, FLY! . . . . PL LITTLE SNG HOUS 27

FLYING 1
- FLYING HOME . . . . SP KID IN THE PARK 6

FLYIN' 2
- MA SOUL WENT FLYIN' O' THE TOWN. . SP JUDGMENT DAY 2
- WENT FLYIN' TO THE STARS AN' MOON SP JUDGMENT DAY 3

FOAM 2
- AND WATCHED THE BLUE WAVES TIPPED WITH FOAM. . . . . DK SAILOR 4
- AS WE RODE THE FOAM . . . . SP SEASCAPE 6

FOAMING 1
- THEY SELL BEER FOAMING THERE IN MUG-LIKE CUPS. . . . . OWT JUICE JOINT 5

FOEMEN 1
- SAY TO ALL FOEMEN: . . . . NM BLACK CLWN POEM 67

FOGGY 1
- AND THE RADIO, TOO, FOGGY WITH PROPAGANDA . . . . SP IN EXPLANATION 31

FOLD 1
- PUSHCARTS FOLD AND UNFOLD . . . . . PL CULTURAL EXCHNG 21

FOLDS 1
- THAT ALL MY FOLDS . . . . WB SONGS DARK VIRG 10

FOLK 3
- WITH PIOUS FOLK AND FAIR . . . . . WB A FAREWELL 4
- ABOVE A CROWD OF BLACK FOLK, HUMBLE, MEAN. . . . . OWT LINCOLN THEATRE 4
- THE GOOD CHURCH FOLK DO NOT MENTION SP RUBY BROWN 21

FOLKS 73
- I'M THE GUY THE HOME FOLKS CALL - NM BIG-TIMER POEM 3
- FOLKS, DOWN YONDER AT HOME. . . . . NM BIG-TIMER POEM 54
- FOLKS SHO IS GETTIN' HARD ON YOU - JUST 'CAUSE YOU BROKE. . . . . . NM BROKE 15
- WHITE FOLKS, LAUGH! . . . . DK NEGRO DANCERS 11
- WHITE FOLKS, PRAY! . . . . DK NEGRO DANCERS 12
- LET THE WHITE FOLKS LIVE . . . . . ANS LYNCHING SONG 3
- AND THE WHITE FOLKS DIE. . . . . . ANS LYNCHING SONG 8
- THE WHITE FOLKS DIE? . . . . ANS LYNCHING SONG 9
- THE WHITE FOLKS DIE? . . . . ANS LYNCHING SONG 11
- I WONDER IF WHITE FOLKS EVER FEEL BAD. . . . . SH DAYBREAK 12
- FOLKS AT THE TABLES DRINK AND GRIN. SH DEATH IN HARLEM 31
- FOLKS, I COME UP NORTH . . . . . . SH EVENIN' BLUES 1
- WHY DON'T YOU TRY IT, FOLKS. . . . SH OUT OF WORK 23
- TO WHITE FOLKS ALONE. . . . . JC BLD SAM SOLOMON 12
- SOME FOLKS THINK . . . . JC FREEDOM 1
- SOME FOLKS THINK . . . . JC FREEDOM 4
- SOME FOLKS THINK . . . . JC FREEDOM 7
- LOTS OF FOLKS WHO DON'T LIKE YOU . JC GOOD MORN STLIN 2
- SOME FOLKS TRY TO TELL ME DOWN THIS WAY . . . . JC GOOD MORN STLIN 23
- AND SEE WHERE SIMPLE WORKING FOLKS LIKE ME . . . . JC GOOD MORN STLIN 32
- THE FOLKS WHO HATE YOU'D . . . . . JC GOOD MORN STLIN 37
- FOLKS OUGHT TO KNOW . . . . JC HOW ABOUT DIXIE 18
- ABOLISH POLL TAX SO FOLKS CAN VOTE. JC JIM CROW'S LAST 24
- "YOUR FOLKS WILL HAVE A BETTER DAY." JC THE BITTER RIVR 40
- FOLKS MADE A COFFIN . . . . FW GIRL 9
- FOLKS STARTED TO CRY IT - . . . . . OWT BLD MARGE POLIT 14
- WHITE FOLKS AIN'T FOR ME. . . . . . OWT FLIGHT 6
- FOLKS PASS BY AND STARE - . . . . . OWT FUNERAL 4
- WHILE GIRLS WHO WASH RICH WHITE FOLKS CLOTHES BY DAY . . . . OWT LINCOLN THEATRE 13
- FOLKS FLY. . . . . OWT RESTRICTIVE 3
- FOLKS, I'M TELLING YOU. . . . . . . SP ADVICE 1
- SOME FOLKS SAY. . . . . SP CAFE: 3 A.M. 5
- FOR WHITE FOLKS . . . . SP CHILDREN'S RYME 21
- IT WAS THAT LONELY DAY, FOLKS. . . SP CROSSING 1
- IT WAS THAT LONELY DAY, FOLKS. . . SP CROSSING 19
- UNTIL HE MADE FOLKS SAY. . . . . . SP DANCER 14
- FOLKS SAY SHE DON'T LIKE . . . . . SP DELINQUENT 3
- FOLKS SAY IT'S NOT JUST . . . . . . SP DELINQUENT 7
- I SEEN FOLKS TALKIN' ABOUT THE . . SP FREEDOM TRAIN 5
- NO WHITE FOLKS ONLY ON THE FREEDOM TRAIN. . . . . SP FREEDOM TRAIN 14
- THE WHITE FOLKS GO LEFT, THE COLORED GO RIGHT - . . . . SP FREEDOM TRAIN 26
- UNTIL COLORED FOLKS SPREAD . . . . SP GOOD MORNING 4
- THE FOLKS WITH NO TITLES IN FRONT OF THEIR NAMES . . . . SP IN EXPLANATION 1
- TO THE FOLKS CALLED MISTER. . . . . SP IN EXPLANATION 4
- THE MISTERS WON'T CALL LOTS OF OTHER FOLKS MISTER. . . . . SP IN EXPLANATION 11
- FOLKS WITH NOT EVEN MISTER IN FRONT OF THEIR NAMES . . . . SP IN EXPLANATION 19
- SOME FOLKS BLAME HIGH PRICES ON THE JEWS. . . . . SP LIKEWISE 12
- (SOME FOLKS BLAME TOO MUCH ON JEWS.) SP LIKEWISE 13
- YOU WPA FOLKS TAKE CARE OF YOURSELF - . . . . SP MADAM'S PAST HI 21
- FOLKS WORK HARD . . . . SP NEW YORKERS 7
- TO THEM FOLKS THAT BROUGHT THE FLOWERS. . . . . SP NIGHT FUNERAL 40
- IF THESE WHITE FOLKS WANT TO GO AHEAD . . . . SP RELIEF 12
- DON'T DECENT FOLKS HAVE DOUGH? . . SP SISTER 10
- SOMETIMES I THINK THAT WHITE FOLKS SP SOUTHERN MAMMY 9
- BUT SOMETIMES I THINK THAT WHITE FOLKS . . . . SP SOUTHERN MAMMY 21
- THE SAME THINGS OTHER FOLKS LIKE WHO ARE OTHER RACES. . . . . SP THEME FOR ENG B 26
- OF ONE THE WHITE FOLKS . . . . . . SP UNCLE TOM 8
- YOU MAY PLAY FOLKS CHEAP. . . . . . SP WARNING AUGMENT 5
- HEAR THE OLD FOLKS SAY HOW . . . . AYM BIRD IN ORBIT 40

DID I WANT TO EAT WITH WHITE FOLKS? AYM BIRD IN ORBIT 70
YOU MUST THINK US COLORED FOLKS . . PL BACKLASH BLUES 11
AND IT'S FULL OF FOLKS LIKE ME WHO ARE . . . . PL BACKLASH BLUES 23
FOR WHITE FOLKS . . . . PL CHILDREN'S RYME 12
RICH FOLKS RIDE - . . . . PL FLORIDA WORKERS 15
WHITE FOLKS FLEE - . . . . PL LITTLE SNG HOUS 5
WHITE FOLKS FLY - . . . . PL LITTLE SNG HOUS 14
WHITE FOLKS HAVE LEFT . . . . PL LITTLE SNG HOUS 22
WHITE FOLKS, FLEE! . . . . PL LITTLE SNG HOUS 25
WHITE FOLKS, FLY! . . . . PL LITTLE SNG HOUS 27
WHEN THE WHITE FOLKS GET THROUGH . PL OFFICE BUILDING 1
WHEN DAYTIME FOLKS . . . . PL OFFICE BUILDING 4
SO FOLKS SAY. . . . . PL STOKELY MALCOLM 14
AS HAVE SOME FOLKS I KNOW. . . . . PL VARI-COLORED 2

FOLKSES 2
LAWD, FOLKSES, HOW MUCH LONGER IS THIS GONNA LAST? . . . . NM BROKE 59
STAND BACK FOLKSES, LET US . . . . SH DEATH IN HARLEM 106

FOLKS' 2
WHITE FOLKS' RECESSION . . . . . . AYM ODE TO DINAH 125
IS COLORED FOLKS' DEPRESSION. . . . AYM ODE TO DINAH 126

FOLKWAYS 2
NOT EVEN FOLKWAYS CAPTURED . . . . AYM IS IT TRUE? 9
ON THE TAPES - NOT EVEN FOLKWAYS. AYM IS IT TRUE? 34

FOLLOWED 1
HUMOROUS DEFIANCE. MELANCHOLY JAZZ. THEN DEFIANCE AGAIN FOLLOWED BY LOUD . . . . NM BLACK CLWN MOOD 2

FOLLOWS 1
FOLLOWS THE YOUNG DOCTOR. . . . . . SP INTERNE AT PROV 45

FONTAINE 1
OF RUE FONTAINE. . . . . DK PARISIAN BEGGAR 10

FOOD 3
THAT PLANTED AND HARVESTED THE FOOD THAT FED . . . . SP FREEDOM'S PLOW 53
TIME I PAY RENT AND GET MY FOOD . . SP LETTER 2
SEA FOOD JOINTS . . . . SP SEASHORE THROUG 11

FOOL 11
THE BOOTED, BOOTED FOOL OF SILLY MEN. . . . . WB THE JESTER 17
MADE ME EVERBODY'S FOOL. . . . . . FC LISTEN HERE 12
DON'T YOU FOOL WID NO MEN CAUSE . . FC LISTEN HERE 17
I AM THE FOOL OF THE WHOLE WORLD. NM BLACK CLWN POEM 8
THROWING DOWN THE HAT OF A FOOL, AND STANDING FORTH, STRAIGHT AND STRONG. . . . . NM BLACK CLWN MOOD 14
RIDE LIKE A FOOL. . . . . SH IF-ING 4
BUT DE DAMN FOOL . . . . SH PRESENT 5
ARE YOU A FOOL OR A DUNCE? . . . . JC BLD SAM SOLOMON 38
THAT CAT'S A FOOL. . . . . SP NEIGHBOR 12
I DON'T FOOL WITH THESE YOUNG GIRLS. SP PREFERENCE 3
HE PLAYED THAT SAD RAGGY TUNE LIKE A MUSICAL FOOL. . . . . SP THE WEARY BLUES 13

FOOLED 1
I AM THE POOR WHITE, FOOLED AND PUSHED APART. . . . . ANS LET AMERICA BE 19

FOOLIN' 2
WHY DOES HE KEEP ON FOOLIN' AROUND MARIE? . . . . SP SISTER 2
BUT WHY DOES HE KEEP ON FOOLIN' AROUND MARIE? . . . . SP SISTER 4

FOOLS 1
ARE SECOND-CLASS FOOLS. . . . . . . PL BACKLASH BLUES 12

FOOL-SELF 1
AND LET MY FOOL-SELF FALL. . . . . SP LAMENT OVER LOV 24

FOOT 5
ON FOOT . . . ON FOOT . . . . SP PARADE 11
ON FOOT . . . ON FOOT . . . . SP PARADE 11
ON FOOT . . . . SP PARADE 12
THUMP, THUMP, THUMP, WENT HIS FOOT ON THE FLOOR. . . . . SP THE WEARY BLUES 23
HAD HE WALKED WITH WARY FOOT . . . PL FREDRK DOUGLASS 2

FOOTBALL 1
FOOTBALL PLAYERS LEATHER PUNCHERS $ $ $ . . . . AYM HORN OF PLENTY 18

FOOTPRINTS 1
LISTEN AT MY FOOTPRINTS WALKING ON THE FLOOR. . . . . SH SUPPER TIME 7

FORBID 1
SEND (GOD FORBID - HE'S NOT DEAD LONG ENOUGH!) . . . . PL FINAL CALL 17

FORBIDS 1
STILL AFTER HOURS POURING DRINKS THE LAW FORBIDS - . . . . OWT JUICE JOINT 38

FORCE 4
BANNER OF FORCE AND LABOR, STRENGTH AND UNION. . . . . ANS CHANT TOM MOONY 43
INSTEAD: MIGRATION INTO FORCE AND POWER - . . . . ANS OPEN LETTER 42
THE FORCE THAT BREAKS THE TIME-CLOCK, ... ANS OPEN LETTER 56
TO FORCE MY BACK TO THE WALL . . . JC THE BITTER RIVR 56

FORCED 1
YOU FORCED ME TO THE BITTER RIVER JC THE BITTER RIVR 63

FORCES 3
80-VOICES: TILL THE FORCES OF THE EARTH ARE YOURS . . . . ANS CHANT MAY DAY 35
UNTIL THE FORCES OF THE WORLD . . . ANS OPEN LETTER 63
THE EVIL FORCES THAT WOULD DESTROY JC TO CAPTAIN MULZ 52

FORD 1
SO WE CRANKED UP OUR OLD FORD . . . SP WEST TEXAS 11

FORE 1
FORE IT IS TOO LATE! . . . . SH EVIL MORNING 16

FOREHEAD 1
GLEAMS ON HIS FOREHEAD. . . . . . . SP INTERNE AT PROV 36

FOREIGN 2
THERE'S NOTHING FOREIGN . . . . . . SP MADAM'S CALLING 17
BUT IT'S LIKE A FOREIGN LANGUAGE . SP SO LONG 4

FOREIGNER 1
EVEN EVERY FOREIGNER . . . . OWT RESTRICTIVE 4

FORESEE 1
THAT WOMAN WHO COULD FORESEE . . . SP BLD FORTUNE TEL 29

FOREST 2
THEY DROVE ME OUT OF THE FOREST. . WB LAMENT DARK PEO 5
WHAT GREAT FOREST HAS HUNG ITS PERFUME . . . . WB NUDE YOUNG DANC 3

FOREVER 13
FOREVER PUSHED DOWN. . . . . NM BLACK CLWN POEM 46
BUT NO! NOT FOREVER . . . . NM BLACK CLWN POEM 59
AND YET A VOICE FOREVER . . . . . . DK LINCOLN MONUMNT 7
ON GUARD WITH THE WORKERS FOREVER - ANS BLDS OF LENIN 27
50-VOICES: FOREVER FOR THE WORKERS! ANS CHANT MAY DAY 13
BUT REMEMBERED FOREVER WILL BE THE NAME: . . . . ANS CHANT TOM MOONY 30
LIFE FOREVER THROUGH THE WORKERS' POWER - . . . . ANS CHANT TOM MOONY 44
REST FOREVER . . . . FW FOR DEAD MIMES 8
YOUR EYES SEE FOREVER? . . . . . . SP DEMAND 9
BEATING FOREVER . . . . SP DRUM 3
BE WASTED FOREVER. . . . . SP NO REGRETS 4
IT AIN'T FOREVER, GIMME! . . . . . SP PREFERENCE 14
IMPEL YOU FOREVER UP THE GREAT STAIRS - . . . . SP THE NEGRO MOTHE 50

FORGET 14
LET ME FORGET. . . . . WB DISILLUSION 13
AND FORGET THAT THEY LYIN' . . . . NM BIG-TIMER POEM 67
LET US FORGET WHAT BOOKER-T. SAID, ANS OPEN LETTER 19
I MIGHT NOT FORGET AND I MIGHT NOT FORGIVE. . . . . SH LETTER 10
SO LET'S JUST FORGET WHAT THIS FUSS WAS ABOUT. . . . . SH LETTER 15
AND SOME FORGET TO LAUGH WHO STILL ARE KIDS. . . . . OWT JUICE JOINT 40
TO MAKE MY GAL FORGET. . . . . . . SP BLD THE GYPSY 17
TRYING TO FORGET TO REMEMBER . . . SP DRUNKARD 4
HOW CAN YOU FORGET ME? . . . . . . SP LOW TO HIGH 1
HOW CAN YOU FORGET ME . . . . SP LOW TO HIGH 7
HOW CAN YOU FORGET ME. . . . . . . SP LOW TO HIGH 10
HOW CAN YOU FORGET ME? . . . . . . SP LOW TO HIGH 16
BUT THE PEOPLE WILL FORGET - . . . SP SHAME ON YOU 4
SO AS NOT TO FORGET . . . . SP SUMMER EVENING 27

FORGETS 2
DE BLUES FORGETS TO STAY. . . . . . SH EVENIN' BLUES 18
FORGETS HE EVER SANG . . . . OWT JUICE JOINT 31

FORGIVE 6
I MIGHT NOT FORGET AND I MIGHT NOT FORGIVE. . . . . SH LETTER 10
FORGIVE THEM LIES! . . . . SH ONLY WOMAN BLUS 16
FORGIVE ME . . . . SP CONSIDER ME 33
SANTA CLAUS, FORGIVE ME. . . . . . AYM ODE TO DINAH 69
SANTA CLAUS, FORGIVE ME. . . . . . AYM RIDE, RED, RIDE 23
AM I SUPPOSED TO FORGIVE . . . . . PL GO SLOW 15

FORGOT 6
SOMETHING IN MY MIND BETTER I FORGOT. ... SH TWILIGHT REVERI 2
BUT YOU MUST'VE FORGOT ... JC BLD SAM SOLOMON 3
YOU DONE FORGOT THAT YOU ARE BLACK. SP LOW TO HIGH 6
HE'S FORGOT ABOUT HIS RACE. ... SP ME AND THE MULE 4
I DONE FORGOT WHEN IT PASSED ... PL STOKELY MALCOLM 8
YES ALMOST FORGOT ... PL STOKELY MALCOLM 9

FORGOTTEN 9
WILL BE FORGOTTEN THEN ... ANS CHANT TOM MOONY 27
HAVE ALMOST FORGOTTEN THEIR NAMES SH YOUNG NEGRO GRL 4
BUT YOU MUST'VE FORGOTTEN ... JC BLD SAM SOLOMON 55
FORGOTTEN WATCH-FIRES ON A HILL SOMEWHERE! ... OWT NEGRO SERVANT 6
I HAVE ALMOST FORGOTTEN MY DREAM. SP AS I GREW OLDER 2
HAS FORGOTTEN ... SP RAILROAD AVENUE 6
SOME TRAIN HAS FORGOTTEN. ... SP RAILROAD AVENUE 29
HAS ALMOST FORGOTTEN MEALIE. ... AYM ASK YOUR MAMA 58
AS FORGOTTEN PAIN IN THE QUARTER . AYM ODE TO DINAH 40

FORM 1
ONE UNION FORM: ... ANS OPEN LETTER 35

FORMED 1
NEW WORDS ARE FORMED. ... ANS A NEW SONG 38

FORMER 1
ARE THE GHOSTS OF FORMER GLORY . . AYM GOSPEL CHA-CHA 20

FORMERLY 1
FORMERLY THE BEATEN AND THE POOR . JC TO CAPTAIN MULZ 19

FORT 1
FORT DE FRANCE. PLACE PIGALLE ... AYM ASK YOUR MAMA 45

FORTALEZA 1
THE BOAT BEYOND THE FORTALEZA ... AYM GOSPEL CHA-CHA 37

FORTH 5
THROWING DOWN THE HAT OF A FOOL. AND STANDING FORTH. STRAIGHT AND STRONG. ... NM BLACK CLWN MOOD 14
I WENT FORTH IN THE MORNING ... SP A BLACK PIERROT 14
PUTS FORTH NEW LIFE AGAIN. ... SP IN TIME SILVER 3
AND TREES PUT FORTH ... SP IN TIME SILVER 15
ROCKING BACK AND FORTH TO A MELLOW CROON. ... SP THE WEARY BLUES 2

FORTUNE 7
I GO TO SEEK MY FORTUNE. ... WB A FAREWELL 3
FORTUNE TELLER LOOKED IN MY HAND. SP MADAM FORT TELL 1
FORTUNE TELLER SAID. ... SP MADAM FORT TELL 2
FORTUNE TELLER SQUEEZE MY HAND. . . SP MADAM FORT TELL 5
FORTUNE TELLER SAID. ... SP MADAM FORT TELL 7
WHERE IS MY FORTUNE AT? ... SP MADAM FORT TELL 15
SHE SAID. YOUR FORTUNE. HONEY. . . SP MADAM FORT TELL 17

FORTUNE'S 1
WHERE YOUR FORTUNE'S AT. ... SP MADAM FORT TELL 12

FORTY-FOUR 2
GONNA GO GET MY PISTOL. I SAID FORTY-FOUR - ... SH TWILIGHT REVERI 5
THE RELIEF GAVE FORTY-FOUR. ... SP BLD OF THE MAN 2

FORWARD 2
THE CLOCK IS MOVING FORWARD HERE - JC TO CAPTAIN MULZ 25
BUT MARCH EVER FORWARD. BREAKING DOWN BARS. ... SP THE NEGRO MOTHE 47

FOUGHT 3
WHO FOUGHT ALONE. ... SL SCOTTSBORO 11
I FOUGHT WITH YOU. COMRADE LENIN. ANS BLDS OF LENIN 7
THE G.I.'S WHO FOUGHT WILL SAY. WE WANTED IT SO! ... SP FREEDOM TRAIN 60

FOUND 10
AND FOUND LIFE - STEPPING ON MY FEET! ... OLD AESTHETE HARLEM 7
RELIEF WAS FOUND. ... ANS A NEW SONG 23
THEY HAVE FOUND THEIR HOUR. ... JC TO CAPTAIN MULZ 24
MAMA. I FOUND THIS SOLDIER'S CAP . FW WHEN ARMIES PAS 1
HE'D FOUND A FISH ... SP CATCH 9
AND I FOUND HER ... SP JOY 5
THE LETTER THAT I FOUND THERE ... SP LITTLE OLD LETT 3
SEEKING MORE THAN FOUND. ... SP OLD WALT 4
WHAT I HAVE NEVER FOUND ... PL STOKELY MALCOLM 2
WHAT I HAVE NOT FOUND ... PL STOKELY MALCOLM 10

FOUNDRIES 2
I AM CHANG FROM THE FOUNDRIES . . ANS BLDS OF LENIN 21
CAME THE FOUNDRIES. CAME THE RAILROADS. ... SP FREEDOM'S PLOW 77

FOUNDRY 2
WHOSE HAND AT THE FOUNDRY. WHOSE PLOW IN THE RAIN. ... ANS LET AMERICA BE 68
WORKS AT THE FOUNDRY. ... SP MIGRANT 4

FOUR 12
I MEAN FOUR - BEFORE DAYLIGHT - S'POSE TO'VE DONE HIT YO' FIRST STROKE - ... NM BROKE 14
THE PRESIDENT'S FOUR FREEDOMS ... JC HOW ABOUT DIXIE 1
IN THE FOUR FREEDOMS. TOO. ... JC HOW ABOUT DIXIE 6
FOUR WALLS CAN HOLD ... FW WALLS 1
FOUR WALLS THAT SHIELD ... FW WALLS 3
FOUR WALLS CAN SHELTER ... FW WALLS 5
NIGHT OF THE FOUR SONGS UNSUNG: . . SP NIGHT FOUR SONG 5
AND THE FOUR BELLS SHE'S AWAITING SP SUMMER EVENING 20
IS ALWAYS FOUR YEARS ... AYM HORN OF PLENTY 90
FOUR LITTLE GIRLS ... PL BIRMINGHAM SUND 1
FOUR TINY GIRLS ... PL BIRMINGHAM SUND 15
FOUR LITTLE GIRLS ... PL BIRMINGHAM SUND 24

FOURSQUARE 1
A MAN. SPARE. SWARTHY. STRONG FOURSQUARE - ... JC TO CAPTAIN MULZ 44

FOURTEEN 2
DE TIME IS FOURTEEN HOURS A DAY? . NM BROKE 34
EACH FOURTEEN YEARS OLD WHEN LYNCHED TOGETHER BENEATH THE ... JC THE BITTER RIVR 1

FO' 6
AND DE MAN COME TELLIN' ME I BETTER GET THERE AT FO'. ... NM BROKE 13
YES. UM-HUM! YOU SHO IS SWEET! CAN YOU PAY FO' DE LICENSE. DEAR? . NM BROKE 78
AN' I NEED A DIME FO' BEER. ... SP DOWN AND OUT 10
I NEED A DIME FO' BEER. ... SP DOWN AND OUT 11
'BOUT HALF-PAST FO'. ... SP SYLVESTER'S BED 10
FO' TO LOVE YO' DADDY RIGHT!" ... SP SYLVESTER'S BED 24

FRAGILE 1
AND DREAMS AS FRAGILE ... PL THE DOVE 3

FRAGRANCE 2
IS TO REMEMBER FRAGRANCE WHERE . . FW REMEMBRANCE 3
WITH A BITTER FRAGRANCE ... PL WHERE WHEN WHCH 2

FRAGRANT 1
AND A LAND OF FRAGRANT WATER ... WB OUR LAND 3

FRAISES 1
OVER FRAISES DU BOIS. ... PL DINNER GUEST ME 13

FRAME 3
TOGETHER IN MY BIG OLD DOWN-HOME FRAME. ... SH DAYBREAK 8
DIPLOMA IN ITS NEW FRAME: ... SP GRADUATION 10
THE DIPLOMA BURSTS ITS FRAME ... SP GRADUATION 23

FRANCE 8
MY BROTHER DIED IN FRANCE - BUT I CAME BACK. ... NM COLORED SL POEM 1
WHO HAS A VISION OF HIS BROTHER KILLED IN FRANCE WHILE FIGHTING FOR THE ... NM COLORED SL MOOD 2
SADLY RECALLS THE ROWS OF WHITE CROSSES IN FRANCE. ... NM COLORED SL MOOD 12
BACK FROM THE ACRES OF CROSSES IN FRANCE. ... NM COLORED SL POEM 15
SINCE THE COLORED SOLDIERS CAME HOME FROM FRANCE. ... NM COLORED SL POEM 32
AND IT'S BETTER A THOUSAND TIMES YOU'RE IN FRANCE DEAD. ... NM COLORED SL POEM 45
I'LL NEVER GO TO FRANCE. ... SP DEFERRED 23
FORT DE FRANCE. PLACE PIGALLE ... AYM ASK YOUR MAMA 45

FRANCO 2
LEST SOME FRANCO STEAL INTO OUR BACKYARD ... ANS SONG OF SPAIN 66
WHO HIRE FRANCO TO LEAD HIS GANG-HORDES ... ANS SONG OF SPAIN 76

FRANCS 2
VINGT FRANCS NICKEL DIME ... AYM ASK YOUR MAMA 46
AT THE DOME VINGT FRANCS WILL DO . AYM ASK YOUR MAMA 50

FRANTIC 4
THE MUSIC. OVER-BURDENED. BACKING AWAY ANGRILY. FRANTIC WITH HUMILIATION ... NM BLACK CLWN MOOD 10
FRANTIC. KICK THEIR DRAFTEE YEARS SP FLATTED FIFTHS 4
AND SEVEN CATS GO FRANTIC. ... SP SEASHORE THROUG 4
FRANTIC. ... SP TAG 3

FREDERICK 3
WHAT FREDERICK DOUGLASS SAID WAS TRUE. ... SP FREEDOM'S PLOW 115
SPEAK OF FREDERICK DOUGLASS'S BEARD AYM BIRD IN ORBIT 44
SEND FOR FREDERICK DOUGLASS. GARRISON. BEECHER. ... PL FINAL CALL 30

FREE 50

Line	Poem	Line no.
ABE LINCOLN DONE SET ME FREE -	NM BLACK CLWN POEM	30
THAT CAN REALLY MAKE ME FREE!	NM BLACK CLWN POEM	62
AND SHE COME TELLIN' ME, SHE AIN'T GOT NO MO' EVENINGS FREE!	NM BROKE	53
OF A FREE LIFE BENEATH OUR GREAT SKY.	NM DARK YOUTH USA	10
AND YET HE PLAYS UPON HIS FLUTE A WILD FREE TUNE	DK BEGGAR BOY	7
FIGHTERS FOR THE FREE.	SL SCOTTSBORO	20
CAN MAKE MY EARTH-BODY FREE.	ANS A NEW SONG	28
"YOU ARE MY SERVANT, BLACK MAN - I, THE FREE!"	ANS A NEW SONG	32
AND YOU DO NOT GO FREE.	ANS CHANT TOM MOONY	5
AND YOU DO NOT GO FREE.	ANS CHANT TOM MOONY	9
SEEKING A HOME WHERE HE HIMSELF IS FREE.	ANS LET AMERICA BE	4
BUT OPPORTUNITY IS REAL, AND LIFE IS FREE.	ANS LET AMERICA BE	13
NOR FREEDOM IN THIS "HOMELAND OF THE FREE.")	ANS LET AMERICA BE	16
TO BUILD A "HOMELAND FOR THE FREE."	ANS LET AMERICA BE	50
THE FREE?	ANS LET AMERICA BE	51
WHO SAID THE FREE? NOT ME?	ANS LET AMERICA BE	52
AND YET MUST BE - THE LAND WHERE EVERY MAN IS FREE.	ANS LET AMERICA BE	64
ON EVERY LYNCHING TREE, A POSTER CRYING FREE	ANS OPEN LETTER	44
CAUSE I'M GOING BACK TO ROOMING AND BE A FREE MAN.	SH PAY DAY	16
A FREE WORLD TOMORROW.	JC BLACK MAN SPEAK	26
WHO WANTS TO BE FREE.	JC GOOD MORN STLIN	21
UNTIL WE ALL ARE FREE.	JC GOOD MORN STLIN	27
ALONE, I KNOW, NO ONE IS FREE.	JC TO CAPTAIN MULZ	35
CAN BE FREE.	JC TO CAPTAIN MULZ	61
AND THE WINDS BLOW FREE!	JC TO CAPTAIN MULZ	76
CAN'T BREATHE FREE.	OWT RESTRICTIVE	14
AIN'T FREE!	SP CHILDREN'S RYME	16
BETTER TO DIE FREE	SP FREEDOM'S PLOW	110
FREE MEN AND INDENTURED SERVANTS,	SP FREEDOM'S PLOW	32
'CAUSE FREEDOM AIN'T FREEDOM WHEN A MAN AIN'T FREE.	SP FREEDOM TRAIN	34
THAT THE SLAVES WOULD BE FREE.	SP FREEDOM'S PLOW	134
SOME WERE FREE HANDS	SP FREEDOM'S PLOW	41
IN THE FREE HANDS AND THE SLAVE HANDS.	SP FREEDOM'S PLOW	50
FREE HANDS AND SLAVE HANDS.	SP FREEDOM'S PLOW	61
BETTER DIE FREE,	SP FREEDOM'S PLOW	172
I HAD ANYTHING FREE.	SP MADAM MIGHT-HAV	12
AIN'T FREE.	SP MADAM PHONE BIL	18
BUT WE ALL SHOULD BE FREE.	SP SOUTHERN MAMMY	16
WE ALL SHOULD BE FREE.	SP SOUTHERN MAMMY	18
CARRYING IN MY BODY THE SEED OF THE FREE.	SP THE NEGRO MOTHE	10
NOW, THROUGH MY CHILDREN, YOUNG AND FREE,	SP THE NEGRO MOTHE	21
I WAS THE SEED OF THE COMING FREE.	SP THE NEGRO MOTHE	30
STAND LIKE FREE MEN SUPPORTING MY TRUST.	SP THE NEGRO MOTHE	42
AND SOMEWHAT MORE FREE.	SP THEME FOR ENG B	40
WOMAN LIKE ME IS FREE!	SP WIDOW WOMAN	24
AIN'T FREE.	PL CHILDREN'S RYME	10
100 YEARS NOT FREE.	PL DEATH YORKVILLE	13
SEND FOR DENMARK VESEY CRYING, "FREE!"	PL FINAL CALL	20
WHO WOULD BE FREE	PL FREDRK DOUGLASS	18
MANY YEARS FREE.	PL OCTOBER 16 RAID	16

FREEDOM 72

Line	Poem	Line no.
FREEDOM!	NM BLACK CLWN POEM	29
NOR FREEDOM IN THIS "HOMELAND OF THE FREE.")	ANS LET AMERICA BE	16
THE STEEL OF FREEDOM DOES NOT STAIN.	ANS LET AMERICA BE	71
WHY FREEDOM DON'T APPLY	JC BLACK MAN SPEAK	7
IS JIM CROW FREEDOM THE BEST	JC BLACK MAN SPEAK	13
THEY BURN FREEDOM.	JC FREEDOM	3
THEY IMPRISON FREEDOM.	JC FREEDOM	6
THEY LYNCH FREEDOM.	JC FREEDOM	9
BUT FREEDOM	JC FREEDOM	10
IT MEANS FREEDOM AT HOME, TOO -	JC HOW ABOUT DIXIE	23
FREEDOM.	JC TO CAPTAIN MULZ	73
I DO NOT NEED MY FREEDOM WHEN I'M DEAD.	SP DEMOCRACY	13
FREEDOM	SP DEMOCRACY	15
I WANT FREEDOM	SP DEMOCRACY	20
FOR THE FREEDOM TRAIN.	SP DREAM BOOGE VAR	12
FREEDOM TRAIN.	SP FREEDOM TRAIN	2
FREEDOM TRAIN.	SP FREEDOM TRAIN	4
FREEDOM TRAIN.	SP FREEDOM TRAIN	6
FREEDOM TRAIN!	SP FREEDOM TRAIN	8
I HOPE THERE AIN'T NO JIM CROW ON THE FREEDOM TRAIN.	SP FREEDOM TRAIN	11
NO BACK DOOR ENTRANCE TO THE FREEDOM TRAIN.	SP FREEDOM TRAIN	12
NO SIGNS FOR COLORED ON THE FREEDOM TRAIN.	SP FREEDOM TRAIN	13
BUT HAD RUN AWAY TO FREEDOM.	SP FREEDOM'S PLOW	113
NO WHITE FOLKS ONLY ON THE FREEDOM TRAIN.	SP FREEDOM TRAIN	14
FREEDOM TRAIN.	SP FREEDOM TRAIN	16
WHO'S THE ENGINEER ON THE FREEDOM TRAIN?	SP FREEDOM TRAIN	17
CAN A COAL BLACK MAN DRIVE THE FREEDOM TRAIN?	SP FREEDOM TRAIN	18
OR AM I STILL A PORTER ON THE FREEDOM TRAIN?	SP FREEDOM TRAIN	19
IS THERE BALLOT BOXES ON THE FREEDOM TRAIN?	SP FREEDOM TRAIN	20
WHEN FREEDOM WOULD TRIUMPH.	SP FREEDOM'S PLOW	120
EVERYBODY'S GOT A RIGHT TO BOARD THE FREEDOM TRAIN?	SP FREEDOM TRAIN	22
FREEDOM TRAIN!	SP FREEDOM TRAIN	24
GUARDING IN THEIR HEARTS THE SEED OF FREEDOM.	SP FREEDOM'S PLOW	124
IS THAT THE WAY TO GET ABOARD THE FREEDOM TRAIN?	SP FREEDOM TRAIN	28
FREEDOM WILL COME!	SP FREEDOM'S PLOW	128
FREEDOM TRAIN!	SP FREEDOM TRAIN	30
WHY THERE'S JIM CROW STATIONS FOR THE FREEDOM TRAIN?	SP FREEDOM TRAIN	32
'CAUSE FREEDOM AIN'T FREEDOM WHEN A MAN AIN'T FREE.	SP FREEDOM TRAIN	34
'CAUSE FREEDOM AIN'T FREEDOM WHEN A MAN AIN'T FREE.	SP FREEDOM TRAIN	34
FREEDOM TRAIN.	SP FREEDOM TRAIN	36
GETS IN LINE TO SEE THE FREEDOM.	SP FREEDOM TRAIN	38
A NEGRO'S GOT NO BUSINESS ON THE FREEDOM TRACK!	SP FREEDOM TRAIN	40
FREEDOM TRAIN!	SP FREEDOM TRAIN	42
SEEKING A GREATER FREEDOM.	SP FREEDOM'S PLOW	42
HOPING TO FIND THEIR FREEDOM.	SP FREEDOM'S PLOW	44
THE FREEDOM THAT THEY CARRYIN' ON THIS FREEDOM TRAIN.	SP FREEDOM TRAIN	45
THE FREEDOM THAT THEY CARRYIN' ON THIS FREEDOM TRAIN.	SP FREEDOM TRAIN	45
GUARDING IN THEIR HEARTS THE SEED OF FREEDOM.	SP FREEDOM'S PLOW	46
FREEDOM TRAIN.	SP FREEDOM TRAIN	48
FREEDOM.	SP FREEDOM'S PLOW	48
WILL HIS FREEDOM TRAIN COME ZOOMIN' DOWN THE TRACK	SP FREEDOM TRAIN	49
FOR THE FREEDOM TRAIN WILL BE YOURS AND MINE!	SP FREEDOM TRAIN	58
FREEDOM TRAIN!	SP FREEDOM TRAIN	64
FREEDOM TRAIN!	SP FREEDOM TRAIN	66
FREEDOM TRAIN!	SP FREEDOM TRAIN	68
GET ON BOARD OUR FREEDOM TRAIN!	SP FREEDOM TRAIN	69
FREEDOM!	SP FREEDOM'S PLOW	183
AN ENSLAVED PEOPLE HEADING TOWARD FREEDOM	SP FREEDOM'S PLOW	189
INTO THAT FURROW THE FREEDOM SEED WAS DROPPED.	SP FREEDOM'S PLOW	194
FREEDOM!	SP IN EXPLANATION	36
ON THE LINE WHOSE ROUTE WAS FREEDOM	AYM ODE TO DINAH	30
THE ROCK ON WHICH FREEDOM	PL AMER HEARTBREAK	2
FOR LUMUMBA TO CRY "FREEDOM NOW!"	PL FINAL CALL	18
FREEDOM WILL NOT COME	PL FREEDOM	1
I DO NOT NEED MY FREEDOM WHEN I'M DEAD.	PL FREEDOM	13
FREEDOM	PL FREEDOM	15
I WANT FREEDOM	PL FREEDOM	20
FREEDOM	PL FROSTING	1
THROUGH THEIR "FREEDOM" SIEVE.	PL LUMUMBA'S GRAVE	8
WANT TO SHOOT YOUR WAY TO FREEDOM	PL OCTOBER 16 RAID	8
THERE ARE WORDS LIKE FREEDOM	PL WORDS LIKE FREE	1
ON MY HEARTSTRINGS FREEDOM SINGS	PL WORDS LIKE FREE	3

FREEDOMS 3

Line	Poem	Line no.
THE PRESIDENT'S FOUR FREEDOMS	JC HOW ABOUT DIXIE	1
I WOULD LIKE TO SEE THOSE FREEDOMS	JC HOW ABOUT DIXIE	3
IN THE FOUR FREEDOMS, TOO.	JC HOW ABOUT DIXIE	6

FREEDOM'S 4

Line	Poem	Line no.
ABOUT FREEDOM'S WAYS.	JC HOW ABOUT DIXIE	16
FREEDOM'S NOT JUST	JC HOW ABOUT DIXIE	21
TOWARD FREEDOM'S GOAL.	PL FREDRK DOUGLASS	11
AS IF FREEDOM'S CAUSE	PL MOTHER IN WAR	7

FREELY 1

Line	Poem	Line no.
AND GIVE FREELY	SP SUNDAY MORNING	39

FREEZE 1

Line	Poem	Line no.
YOU RAISE MY TAXES, FREEZE MY WAGES,	PL BACKLASH BLUES	5

FREE-DELIVERY 1

Line	Poem	Line no.
AND FREE-DELIVERY TV SETS	AYM JAZZTET MUTED	12

FRENCH 5

Line	Poem	Line no.
ME, I ALWAYS DID WANT TO STUDY FRENCH.	SP DEFERRED	21
BUT NIGHT SCHOOLS TEACH FRENCH.	SP DEFERRED	24
SO, SI'L-VOUS PLAIT, I'LL STUDY FRENCH!	SP DEFERRED	28
SPEAKS ENGLISH FRENCH SWAHILI	AYM ASK YOUR MAMA	57
THE FRENCH MAY HAVE THE SECRET.	AYM IS IT TRUE?	17

FRENETIC 2
IN THE WIND'S FRENETIC FISTS . . . AYM GOSPEL CHA-CHA 4
IN THE WIND'S FRENETIC FISTS. . . . AYM GOSPEL CHA-CHA 34

FRIDAY 1
ON FRIDAY THE EAGLE FLIES. . . . . SP CONSIDER ME 42

FRIED 1
YOU STILL BAKES BISCUITS? FRIED CHICKEN EVERY NIGHT? IS THAT TRUE? . . . . NM BROKE 73

FRIEND 23
CAUSE I AIN'T GOT NO FRIEND. . . . FC A RUINED GAL 10
DIDN'T HAVE A FRIEND NOWHERE. . . . FC BLD OF GIN MARY 4
HE WAS A FRIEND O' MINE. . . . . . FC DEATH DO DIRTY 5
MA FRIEND O' MINE. . . . . FC DEATH DO DIRTY 10
GOOD FRIEND O' MINE. . . . . FC DEATH DO DIRTY 15
O. FRIEND O' MINE. . . . . FC DEATH DO DIRTY 20
MA FRIEND O' MINE. . . . . FC DEATH DO DIRTY 25
BEST FRIEND O' MINE. . . . . FC DEATH DO DIRTY 30
MA FRIEND O' MINE. . . . . FC DEATH DO DIRTY 35
I LOVED MY FRIEND. . . . . DK I LOVED FRIEND 1
I LOVED MY FRIEND. . . . . DK I LOVED FRIEND 6
"YOU MA FRIEND," HE 'LOWED. . . . . DK MA LORD 5
HE'S A FRIEND O' MINE. . . . . . . DK MA LORD 11
AN' BE MA FRIEND THROUGH ETERNITY." DK MA LORD 16
PAWNBROKER, OLD FRIEND - . . . . . SH OLD PAWNBROKER 22
I'D LIKE TO MEET A GOOD FRIEND . . SP BOUND NO'TH BLS 11
BUT EVER FRIEND YOU FINDS SEEMS . . SP BOUND NO'TH BLS 17
BUSINESS, FRIEND. . . . . SP MADAM MINISTER 16
HIS WOMAN AND HIS FRIEND IS DEAD. . SP MONROE'S BLUES 2
MY WOMAN AND MY FRIEND IS DEAD. . . SP MONROE'S BLUES 8
HIS GIRL FRIEND HAD TO PAY. . . . . SP NIGHT FUNERAL 24
'HIND MA FRIEND MISS CORA LEE. . . SP YOUNG GAL'S BLS 2
'HIND MA DEAR FRIEND CORA LEE . . . SP YOUNG GAL'S BLS 4

FRIENDS 5
FRIENDS TRIED TO TELL HER . . . . . SP BLD FORTUNE TEL 17
MY FRIENDS WAS ALL AROUND ME . . . SP CROSSING 3
MY FRIENDS WAS RIGHT THERE WITH ME SP CROSSING 21
FROM THAT POOR BOY'S FRIENDS - . . SP NIGHT FUNERAL 14
THEN MY FRIENDS! . . . . SP SUNDAY MORNING 14

FRIENDSHIP 1
I THOUGHT THAT FRIENDSHIP LAY . . . FW MAN 7

FRIENDS'LL 1
AND MAYBE YOUR FRIENDS'LL . . . . . SP BLD OF THE MAN 7

FRIGHTEN 1
TO FRIGHTEN THE PEOPLE - . . . . . ANS KIDS WHO DIE 31

FRIGHTENED 3
LITTLE FRIGHTENED CHILD . . . . . . FW MIGRATION 15
AND THE COTTON FIELD TO FRIGHTENED SP MIGRANT 23
AND FRIGHTENED TREAD. . . . . PL FREDRK DOUGLASS 3

FRIGHTENING 1
OF FRIGHTENING NAME? . . . . SP GENIUS CHILD 10

FRISCO 2
FILLMORE OUT IN FRISCO, 7TH ACROSS THE BAY, ... AYM ASK YOUR MAMA 31
BELAFONTE FRISCO JOSEPHINE . . . . AYM BIRD IN ORBIT 5

FRIZ 1
SNOW HAS FRIZ ME. . . . . PL STILL HERE 3

FRO 1
SWAYING TO AND FRO ON HIS RICKETY STOOL . . . . SP THE WEARY BLUES 12

FROM 155
THEY TOOK ME AWAY FROM THE JUNGLES. WB LAMENT DARK PEO 6
AND REST FROM PAIN OF LOVE . . . . WB YOUNG BRIDE 6
IT KEEPS ME FROM FEELIN' BLUE. . . FC BAD MAN 12
MEN TAKES ALL THEY CAN FROM ME . . FC BLACK GAL 6
I BROUGHT HER FROM DE SOUTH . . . . FC EVIL WOMAN 13
EVEN IF YOU DO COME FROM GEORGIA. FC JAZZ BAND 21
WHERE I COME FROM . . . . FC NEW CABARET GRL 11
CREEPING LIKE FIRE FROM A SLOW SPARK OLD THE CONSUMPTIVE 10
FROM ONE SIDE TO THE OTHER. BUT NOW A HARSH AND BITTER NOTE CREEPS INTO . . . . NM BLACK CLWN MOOD 9
FROM AFRICA TO GEORGIA . . . . . . NM BLACK CLWN POEM 57
RISE FROM THE BOTTOM. . . . . NM BLACK CLWN POEM 71
OUT OF HIS GRAVE FROM OVER THE SEA. NM COLORED SL POEM 14
BACK FROM THE ACRES OF CROSSES IN FRANCE. . . . . NM COLORED SL POEM 15
SINCE THE COLORED SOLDIERS CAME HOME FROM FRANCE. . . . . NM COLORED SL POEM 32
AWAY FROM THE TOO-ROUGH FINGERS . . DK DREAM KEEPER 7
TO KEEP FROM CRYIN' . . . . DK HOMESICK BLUES 17
HE WENT AWAY FROM ME. . . . . DK I LOVED FRIEND 2
HALF A WORLD AWAY FROM HOME. . . . DK SAILOR 2
AND FROM ITS TINY WINDOW . . . . . DK WINTER SWEETNS 3
I AM CHANG FROM THE FOUNDRIES . . ANS BLDS OF LENIN 21
SPEAKS FROM THE MARBLE: . . . . . . ANS BLDS OF LENIN 26
WHEN THE BIRDS COME BACK FROM THE SOUTH. . . . . ANS CHANT MAY DAY 6
FROM AFRICA TO CHINA. . . . . ANS CHANT TOM MOONY 18
100-VOICES: FROM THIS HOUR. . . . . ANS CHANT MAY DAY 36
I AM THE RED MAN DRIVEN FROM THE LAND. . . . . ANS LET AMERICA BE 21
AND TORN FROM BLACK AFRICA'S STRAND I CAME . . . . ANS LET AMERICA BE 49
FROM THOSE WHO LIVE LIKE LEECHES ON THE PEOPLE'S LIVES. . . . . . . ANS LET AMERICA BE 72
AND DROPPING BOMBS FROM A CHRISTIAN STEEPLE . . . . ANS SONG OF SPAIN 69
SO FROM NOW ON. . . . . SH ANNOUNCEMENT 13
A DUMB LITTLE JIGABOO FROM . . . . SH DEATH IN HARLEM 16
DOWN IN A CELLAR BACK FROM THE STREET. . . . . SH DEATH IN HARLEM 23
A PARTY OF WHITES FROM FIFTH AVENUE SH DEATH IN HARLEM 58
FLY AWAY FROM YOU. . . . . SH DECLARATION 18
FROM . . . . SH DECLARATION 21
TILL YOU DON'T KNOW RIGHT FROM WRONG. . . . . SH HEY-HEY BLUES 12
FROM WASHIN' OVER ME? . . . . SH MISSISSIPPI LEV 18
JUST SO IT GOES AWAY FROM HERE. . . SH SIX-BITS BLUES 6
FROM LOS ANGELES TO LONDON . . . . JC BLACK MAN SPEAK 15
I CAN EXPECT FROM YOU? . . . . . . JC BLACK MAN SPEAK 20
TO DRIVE THE FACISTS FROM THE LAND. JC GOOD MORN STLIN 34
CAUSE FROM BOMBAY TO GEORGIA . . . JC HOW ABOUT DIXIE 11
OUR BATTLE YET IS FAR FROM WON . . JC JIM CROW'S LAST 30
FROM THE DARK LIPS . . . . JC ME AND MY SONG 23
FROM ITS IRON BRIDGE HUNG. . . . . JC THE BITTER RIVR 13
THE SOLDIER THROWN FROM A JIM CROW BUS BEHIND STEEL BARS. . . . . . JC THE BITTER RIVR 33
AS A GIFT FROM YOU. . . . . JC THE BITTER RIVR 54
LOSER FROM AN EMPTY POCKET . . . . JC THE BITTER RIVR 69
STEALING FROM THE NIGHT . . . . . . FW DANCERS 1
STEALING FROM DEATH . . . . FW DANCERS 5
FROM ITS MOTHER'S WOMB - . . . . . FW EARTH SONG 10
FROM WHERE . . . . FW EXITS 10
FROM NOT CRYING. . . . . FW GRIEF 3
NO LOVE FROM ABOVE. . . . . FW PRAYER 12
FROM SALT SEA WATER . . . . FW SAILING DATE 4
FROM HERE TO THERE. . . . . FW SAILING DATE 12
FROM THE WIND AND RAIN. . . . . . . FW WALLS 4
GARNERED FROM YESTERDAY . . . . . . FW WALLS 7
TURN FROM THE BAR AND JOIN YOU IN YOUR SONG. . . . . OWT JUICE JOINT 22
TO KEEP THE GALL FROM BITING IN HIS MOUTH. . . . . OWT JUICE JOINT 44
THE HEAD OF LINCOLN LOOKS DOWN FROM THE WALL . . . . OWT LINCOLN THEATRE 1
AND CRIES, ALL CARELESS-LIKE FROM REDDENED LIPS! . . . . OWT LINCOLN THEATRE 10
A NIGGER COMES HOME FROM WORK: . . OWT MAN INTO MEN 1
A NEGRO COMES HOME FROM WORK: . . . OWT MAN INTO MEN 8
A MAN COMES HOME FROM WORK: . . . . OWT MAN INTO MEN 15
O, SWEET RELIEF FROM FACES THAT ARE WHITE! . . . . OWT NEGRO SERVANT 19
WILL TAKE GOOD MONEY FROM YOU, . . SP BLD THE GYPSY 19
AND TAKE YOUR MONEY FROM YOU - . . SP BLD THE GYPSY 21
YOU FROM THE WEST INDIES. . . . . . SP BROTHERS 2
I FROM KENTUCKY. . . . . SP BROTHERS 3
YOU FROM AFRICA. . . . . SP BROTHERS 5
I FROM THE U.S.A. . . . . SP BROTHERS 6
DETECTIVES FROM THE VICE SQUAD . . SP CAFE: 3 A.M. 1
FROM CHINA . . . . SP CONSIDER ME 38
FROM THE . . . . SP CONSIDER ME 51
FROM DAWN TO DUSK . . . . SP END 5
SHIPS CAME FROM ACROSS THE SEA . . SP FREEDOM'S PLOW 29
THEN MAYBE FROM THEIR GRAVES IN ANZIO . . . . SP FREEDOM TRAIN 59
WOVEN FROM THE BEGINNING . . . . . SP FREEDOM'S PLOW 166
TO THE ENEMY WHO WOULD CONQUER US FROM WITHOUT, ... SP FREEDOM'S PLOW 178
AND CONQUER US FROM WITHIN, ... SP FREEDOM'S PLOW 181
FROM THAT SEED A TREE GREW, IS GROWING, WILL EVER GROW. . . . . . SP FREEDOM'S PLOW 195
FROM RIVER TO RIVER . . . . SP GOOD MORNING 5
PLANES FROM PUERTO RICO, ... SP GOOD MORNING 9
UP FROM CUBA HAITI JAMAICA, ... SP GOOD MORNING 11
FROM GEORGIA FLORIDA LOUISIANA . . SP GOOD MORNING 13
BRINGS REMAINDERS FROM THE KITCHEN SP GRADUATION 7
FAR REMOVED FROM BASIC OVEN. . . . SP GRADUATION 17
FROM HERE - . . . . SP GREEN MEMORY 6
FROM HARLEM PAST HONG KONG TALKING BACK. . . . . SP IN EXPLANATION 22
FROM VERONA . . . . SP JULIET 12
NO LOVE FROM ABOVE. . . . . SP LITANY 12
FROM THE TABLES OF JOY. . . . . . . SP LUCK 2
AND THE LADY FROM THE . . . . SP MADAM CHARTY CH 21
FROM KANSAS CITY . . . . SP MADAM PHONE BIL 22
LIKE PALE PLUMS FROM A TREE . . . . SP MELLOW 4
NO FLOWERS FROM THE STORE. . . . . SP MIDWINTER BLUES 24
ALL THE WAY FROM AFRICA TO GEORGIA SP NEGRO 11
WHERE I COME FROM . . . . SP NEW YORKERS 6
FROM THAT POOR BOY'S FRIENDS - . . SP NIGHT FUNERAL 14
FROM THE SAINTS OF GOD IN CHRIST . SP PASSING 4
IN FROM THE SEA! . . . . SP PORT TOWN 2

ON THE MONEY FROM A WHITE WOMAN'S KITCHEN?	SP RUBY BROWN	14
FROM RIVER TO RIVER.	SP SAME IN BLUES	29
TWO PARTIES FROM PHILADELPHIA	SP SEASHORE THROUG	5
FROM THE FIRM ROOTS OF TREES.	SP SPIRITUALS	10
FROM THE SOLID LAP OF EARTH.	SP SPIRITUALS	12
FROM THE DEAD WEIGHT OF SEA.	SP SPIRITUALS	14
THAN SHELTER FROM THE RAIN."	SP STRANGE HURT	5
FROM A TENT AT THE CORNER	SP SUMMER EVENING	12
THROWS A TOOTHPICK FROM HER WINDOW.	SP SUMMER EVENING	19
I AM THE CHILD THEY STOLE FROM THE SAND	SP THE NEGRO MOTHE	7
CHILDREN SOLD AWAY FROM ME, HUSBAND SOLD, TOO.	SP THE NEGRO MOTHE	15
COMING FROM A BLACK MAN'S SOUL.	SP THE WEARY BLUES	15
THE STEPS FROM THE HILL LEAD DOWN INTO HARLEM.	SP THEME FOR ENG B	11
AS I LEARN FROM YOU,	SP THEME FOR ENG B	37
I GUESS YOU LEARN FROM ME -	SP THEME FOR ENG B	38
FROM THE TRUMPET AT HIS LIPS	SP TRUMPET PLAYER	18
FROM THE TRUMPET AT HIS LIPS	SP TRUMPET PLAYER	22
DISTILLED FROM OLD DESIRE -	SP TRUMPET PLAYER	24
AS THE TUNE COMES FROM HIS THROAT	SP TRUMPET PLAYER	42
WHILE FROM THE GUTTER	SP UP-BEAT	9
A QUEEN FROM SOME TIME-DEAD EGYPTIAN NIGHT	SP WHEN SUE WEARS	7
FROM THE SHADOWS OF THE QUARTER	AYM ASK YOUR MAMA	1
FAR FROM STONE.	AYM ASK YOUR MAMA	73
MADE FROM THE HIDES OF BLACKS	AYM BIRD IN ORBIT	66
THE LEGION FROM ENGLEWOOD	AYM BIRD IN ORBIT	77
MADE FROM THE HIDES OF BLACKS	AYM BIRD IN ORBIT	89
SHOUTS FROM THE EARTH ITSELF	AYM BLUES IN STEREO	8
FROM LESSER STARS IN ORBIT $ $ $ $ $ $ $	AYM HORN OF PLENTY	21
FROM NOBODY AND NOTHING TO WHERE I AM.	AYM HORN OF PLENTY	39
I SAID, FROM YOUR MAMA!	AYM HORN OF PLENTY	48
FROM THE OTHER	AYM HORN OF PLENTY	91
FROM THE BIG GLASS SHOPPING CENTER	AYM HORN OF PLENTY	94
FROM THE SHADOWS OF THE QUARTER	AYM IS IT TRUE?	1
CUT FROM SHADOWS CUT FROM SHADE	AYM JAZZTET MUTED	5
CUT FROM SHADOWS CUT FROM SHADE	AYM JAZZTET MUTED	5
FROM THE WING TIP OF A MATCH TIP	AYM JAZZTET MUTED	8
FROM JUKEBOX JOINTS IS LAID	AYM JAZZTET MUTED	11
MAMA'S FRUITCAKE SENT FROM GEORGIA	AYM ODE TO DINAH	13
FROM ANOTHER DISTANT QUARTER	AYM ODE TO DINAH	17
FROM THE COLD THAT MAKES NIAGARA	AYM ODE TO DINAH	25
FROM SLABS OF SILVER SHADOWS.	AYM ODE TO DINAH	54
TELL ME FARE FROM YOU?	AYM SHOW FARE PLESE	2
WEAVING METAL FROM TWO QUARTERS	AYM SHOW FARE PLESE	21
FROM THE SLAVE CHAIN TO THE LYNCH ROPE	PL DEATH YORKVILLE	9
FROM VERY INDECISION	PL FREDRK DOUGLASS	4
IN POISON FROM THE FALLOUT	PL JUNIOR ADDICT	26
FROM ANCIENT EVENINGS)	PL LENOX AVE. BAR	9
DOWN SOUTH WHERE I COME FROM	PL MERRY-GO-ROUND	6
PERHAPS FROM A FIX	PL SLAVE	9
FROM OUR OLD	PL THE DOVE	8
SLIPPING OUT FROM UNDER THEM	PL UNDERTOW	10
SAVE ME FROM THAT MAN!	PL WHO BUT TH LORD	10
FROM POLICE BRUTALITY.	PL WHO BUT TH LORD	18
HIDDEN FROM THE SKY	PL WITHOUT BENEFIT	14

FRONT 13

SO WE MARCHED TO THE FRONT, HAPPY TO FIGHT.	NM COLORED SL POEM	12
AND THE GENTLEMEN WITH DR. IN FRONT OF THEIR NAMES.	ANS KIDS WHO DIE	21
SET ON THE FRONT PORCH AS LONG AS I PLEASE.	SH SUNDAY	8
IN FRONT OF ME.	SP AS I GREW OLDER	4
SUMMER NIGHTS ON THE FRONT PORCH	SP AUNTSUE'S STORI	3
ROAD'S IN FRONT O' ME,	SP BOUND NO'TH BLS	7
ROAD'S IN FRONT O' ME.	SP BOUND NO'TH BLS	9
THE FOLKS WITH NO TITLES IN FRONT OF THEIR NAMES	SP IN EXPLANATION	1
FOLKS WITH NOT EVEN MISTER IN FRONT OF THEIR NAMES	SP IN EXPLANATION	19
WITH NO TITLES IN FRONT OF THEIR NAMES.	SP IN EXPLANATION	28
THE PEOPLE WITH NO TITLES IN FRONT OF THEIR NAMES	SP IN EXPLANATION	40
WITH NO TITLE IN FRONT OF NAME	SP IN EXPLANATION	54
IN FRONT OF THEIR NAMES.	SP IN EXPLANATION	61

FRONTIER 1

TO THE LAST FRONTIER	PL ANGOLA QUESTION	5

FROSTED 2

THERE'S A BAR WITH WINDOWS FROSTED	AYM ODE TO DINAH	24
WITH A BAR WITH FROSTED WINDOWS	AYM ODE TO DINAH	42

FROSTING 1

IS JUST FROSTING	PL FROSTING	2

FROWN 1

AND HERE I SET THINKING WITH A BITTER OLD FROWN.	SH TWILIGHT REVERI	14

FROWNIN' 1

I'S GWINE TO QUIT MA FROWNIN'	SP THE WEARY BLUES	21

FROZEN 7

FROZEN WITH SNOW.	DK DREAMS	8
THAT ARE FROZEN	FW GRIEF	2
IN THE FROZEN RAIN,	SP TROUBLED WOMAN	3
AND NIAGARA FALLS IS FROZEN ¢ ¢ ¢ ¢ ¢ ¢ ¢	AYM HORN OF PLENTY	28
FOR NIAGARA FALLS IS FROZEN	AYM ODE TO DINAH	11
WHEN NIAGARA FALLS IS FROZEN	AYM ODE TO DINAH	23
WHILE NIAGARA FALLS IS FROZEN.	AYM ODE TO DINAH	68

FRUITCAKE 1

MAMA'S FRUITCAKE SENT FROM GEORGIA	AYM ODE TO DINAH	13

FRUITS 1

FRUITS	SP LIKEWISE	4

FRUSTRATED 1

I'S FRUSTRATED!	SP BAD MORNING	4

FUEL 1

NOR FUEL FOR THE CLEAN FLAME OF JOY	SP RUBY BROWN	6

FULFILLED 1

WAS FULFILLED.	SP FULFILMENT	3

FULL 26

SO FULL OF PAIN AND PASSION,	WB SOLEDAD	6
SO FULL OF LIES.	WB SOLEDAD	7
SO FULL OF PAIN AND PASSION.	WB SOLEDAD	8
I'M GONNA FILL 'EM UP FULL O'	FC DEATH DO DIRTY	33
TWO THINGS ARE FULL OF WONDER.	OLD TWO THINGS	5
WITH HIS FACE FULL OF LIGHT AND FAITH, CONFIDENT THAT A NEW WORLD HAS	NM COLORED SL MOOD	9
MA SOUL IS FULL OF COLOR	DK REASONS WHY	3
I KNOW FULL WELL NOW	ANS A NEW SONG	25
BUT NINE BLACK BOYS KNOW FULL WELL,	ANS BLD OZZIE POWEL	21
I AM THE YOUNG MAN, FULL OF STRENGTH AND HOPE.	ANS LET AMERICA BE	25
A BANK FULL OF CASH,	SH BLD THE KILLER	10
I FILLED HIM FULL OF HOLES	SH BLD THE KILLER	23
AUNT SUE HAS A HEAD FULL OF STORIES.	SP AUNTSUE'S STORI	1
AUNT SUE HAS A WHOLE HEART FULL OF STORIES.	SP AUNTSUE'S STORI	2
FULL OF CARES -	SP BLACK MARIA	8
RISE AT DAWNIN' FULL OF FUN?	SP BLACK MARIA	13
FULL OF FUN, FULL OF FUN?	SP BLACK MARIA	15
FULL OF FUN, FULL OF FUN?	SP BLACK MARIA	15
IN A CORNER FULL OF UGLINESS.	SP MAGNOLIA FLOWER	2
FULL OF UGLINESS.	SP MAGNOLIA FLOWER	7
FULL OF STARS.	SP MULATTO	9
THE SOUTHERN NIGHT IS FULL OF STARS,	SP MULATTO	31
FULL OF CHINE BONES IN DARK GLASSES.	SP SUMMER EVENING	15
WHEN YOU'RE FULL OF STUFF.	SP WARNING AUGMENT	8
FULL OF NUTS AND SWEET.	SP 125TH STREET	2
AND IT'S FULL OF FOLKS LIKE ME WHO ARE	PL BACKLASH BLUES	23

FUN 10

ANSWERIN' THEM WANT-ADS' NOT NARY BIT O' FUN.	NM BROKE	4
HAVE OUR FUN.	SH DEATH IN HARLEM	107
RISE AT DAWNIN' FULL OF FUN?	SP BLACK MARIA	13
FULL OF FUN, FULL OF FUN?	SP BLACK MARIA	15
FULL OF FUN, FULL OF FUN?	SP BLACK MARIA	15
FUN TO SPORT AROUND.	SP BLUE MONDAY	7
THOUGHT IT FUN.	SP S-SSS-SS-SH!	21
IN WARTIME WE HAD FUN.	SP WORLD WAR II	5
FOR FUN TO BLOW DOORS DOWN.	PL CULTURAL EXCHNG	7
YOU HAVE YOUR "FUN"	PL OFFICE BUILDING	3

FUNERAL 11

BUT I WANT MY FUNERAL TO BE FINE:	SP AS BEFITS A MAN	6
FOR A FIRST-CLASS FUNERAL,	SP BLD OF THE MAN	5
A FUNERAL WAS HAD.	SP BLD OF THE MAN	16
A FUNERAL SO HIGH?	SP BLD OF THE MAN	26
A NIGHT FUNERAL	SP DEAD IN THERE	2
NIGHT FUNERAL	SP NIGHT FUNERAL	1
NIGHT FUNERAL	SP NIGHT FUNERAL	9
NIGHT FUNERAL	SP NIGHT FUNERAL	17
NIGHT FUNERAL	SP NIGHT FUNERAL	25
FUNERAL GRAND.	SP NIGHT FUNERAL	44
NIGHT FUNERAL	SP NIGHT FUNERAL	45

FUNNY 2

BECAUSE I'M POOR AND BLACK AND FUNNY -	NM BLACK CLWN POEM	2
AND ONE OLD FUNNY BOY SAID, "I'LL WORK AT ANY PRICE	NM BROKE	8

FUR 4

A FUR COAT!	SH PRESENT	7
JOSTLE OF FUR COATS	OWT MAN INTO MEN	2
WONDERING ABOUT FUR COATS	OWT MAN INTO MEN	9

WITHOUT GETTING FUR IN MY MOUTH . . SP NECESSITY 7

FURNISHED 1
THIS LITTLE OLD FURNISHED ROOM'S . SP NECESSITY 5

FURNISHED-UP 1
I GOT A FURNISHED-UP FLAT. . . . . NM BIG-TIMER POEM 23

FURNITURE 4
I'M GONNA TELL THE FURNITURE MAN TO COME . . . . SH PAY DAY 11
AND I WON'T NEED NO FURNITURE LIVING ALONE - . . . . SH PAY DAY 15
YOU GONNA TAKE MY FURNITURE AND . . SP BLD LANDLORD 15
MY FURNITURE PAID FOR. . . . . . . SP DEFERRED 35

FURROW 3
IN EVERY BRICK AND STONE, IN EVERY FURROW TURNED . . . . ANS LET AMERICA BE 43
THE PLOW PLOWED A NEW FURROW . . . SP FREEDOM'S PLOW 132
INTO THAT FURROW THE FREEDOM SEED WAS DROPPED. . . . . SP FREEDOM'S PLOW 134

FURTHER 1
I MOVED OUT EVEN FARTHER FURTHER FARTHER . . . . AYM HORN OF PLENTY 33

FURTHERMORE 1
- FURTHERMORE, RUB OUT . . . . SP MADAM CENSUS 29

FUSE 1
THE FUSE OF CENTURIES OF DRAGON KINGS . . . . PL BIRMINGHAM SUND 19

FUSS 1
SO LET'S JUST FORGET WHAT THIS FUSS WAS ABOUT. . . . . SH LETTER 15

FUTILE 1
FUTILE OF ME TO OFFER YOU MY HAND. PL LAST PRINCE 1

FUTILELY 1
PACE. "SOMETIMES I FEEL LIKE A MOTHER-LESS CHILE." TURNING FUTILELY . . . . NM BLACK CLWN MOOD 8

FUTURE 4
UNTIL THE FUTURE BURNS OUT . . . . ANS OPEN LETTER 36
WHAT YOUR FUTURE MEANT. . . . . . . SP BLD FORTUNE TEL 30
AND I'LL LOOK INTO THE FUTURE . . . SP BLD THE GYPSY 7
CELLOPHANES HIS FUTURE. . . . . . . SP INTERNE AT PROV 47

GAIETY 1
INNER HEARTACHES AND LONELINESS TO THE IRONIC GAIETY OF THE MUSIC. THEN . . . . NM BIG-TIMER MOOD 10

GAILY 1
THE MOVIES END. THE LIGHTS FLASH GAILY ON. . . . . OWT LINCOLN THEATRE 5

GAIN 6
WITH NO GAIN - . . . . NM BLACK CLWN POEM 19
OF PROFIT, POWER, GAIN, OF GRAB THE LAND! . . . . ANS LET AMERICA BE 27
A WORLD TO GAIN. . . . . PL QUESTION ANSWER 7
A WORLD TO GAIN. . . . . PL QUESTION ANSWER 10
THERE'S A WORLD TO GAIN. . . . . . PL QUESTION ANSWER 13
FOR NEFARIOUS GAIN? . . . . PL UN-AMERICAN 18

GAINED 1
WHO HAD GAINED . . . . PL PEACE 7

GAL 27
SHAMELESS GAL. . . . . WB TO MIDNIGHT NAN 2
AIN'T NOTHIN' FOR A RUINED GAL . . FC A RUINED GAL 13
I BEATS MA SIDE GAL TOO. . . . . . FC BAD MAN 3
BEATS MA SIDE GAL TOO. . . . . . . FC BAD MAN 10
THEN THEY GOES AN' FINDS A YALLER GAL . . . . FC BLACK GAL 7
AN' HAD CUT HIS GAL . . . . FC DEATH DO DIRTY 3
GOOD GAL ANY MORE. . . . . FC EVIL WOMAN 2
THAT LITTLE YALLER GAL . . . . . . FC NEW CABARET GRL 1
THAT CRAZY LITTLE YALLER GAL . . . FC NEW CABARET GRL 13
BLACK GAL. . . . . FC RED SILK STOCK 2
PUT ON YO' RED SILK STOCKINGS, GAL. FC RED SILK STOCK 8
AN' A PO', PO' GAL CAN SLEEP. . . . FC SUICIDE 18
AND I SHO HAD A PRETTY GAL, TOO, UP YONDER ON SUGAR HILL. . . . . . NM BROKE 48
IF A PRETTY GAL LIKE YOU WAS WILLIN', I'D BITE. . . . . NM BROKE 72
OLD GAL O' MINE. . . . . DK DRESSED UP 8
A GAL I THOUGHT WAS KIND. . . . . . DK PO' BOY BLUES 14
A GAL I THOUGHT WAS KIND. . . . . . DK PO' BOY BLUES 16
I HAD A GAL. . . . . SH ANNOUNCEMENT 1
THAT GAL DON'T DRIVE MY . . . . . . SH ANNOUNCEMENT 15
PLAY A LONG TIME, GAL! . . . . . . SH DEATH IN HARLEM 46
WHEN WILL MY GAL BE HOME? . . . . . SP BLD THE GYPSY 4
TO MAKE MY GAL FORGET. . . . . . . SP BLD THE GYPSY 17
I'M A PO' GAL . . . . SP DOWN AND OUT 5
BLACK GAL LIKE ME. . . . . SP MISERY 13
BLACK GAL LIKE ME . . . . SP MISERY 14
CAN A YOUNG GAL DO? . . . . SP YOUNG GAL'S BLS 20
WHAT CAN A YOUNG GAL DO? . . . . . SP YOUNG GAL'S BLS 22

GALL 4
AND ITS GALL COATS THE RED OF MY TONGUE. . . . . JC THE BITTER RIVR 11
MIXED WITH BLOOD AND GALL. . . . . JC THE BITTER RIVR 58
THE GALL OF YOUR BITTER WATER . . . JC THE BITTER RIVR 85
TO KEEP THE GALL FROM BITING IN HIS MOUTH. . . . . OWT JUICE JOINT 44

GALLEONS 1
WITH BILLOWING SAILS THE GALLEONS CAME . . . . SP FREEDOM'S PLOW 35

GALLOPS 1
AND THE SUN GALLOPS NO MORE . . . . FW THERE 3

GALS 4
I HATES THEM SKINNEY YALLER GALS . . FC BLACK GAL 15
AND LIVIN' ON GALS. . . . . NM BIG-TIMER POEM 14
SWEET GALS WAS A-MOANIN'. . . . . . SP SYLVESTER'S BED 5
BLACK GALS WAS A-BEGGIN'. . . . . . SP SYLVESTER'S BED 13

GAL'S 1
NO OTHER GAL'S GOT A CHANCE. . . . FC MINNIE SINGS 10

GAMBLE 1
GAVE HIM MONEY TO GAMBLE. . . . . . SP BLD FORTUNE TEL 13

GAMBLED 2
I GAMBLED YOUR DIME AWAY. . . . . . SP EARLY EVENING 8
DONE GAMBLED THAT DIME AWAY. . . . SP EARLY EVENING 10

GAMBLER 1
CHARLIE IS A GAMBLER . . . . FC SATURDAY NIGHT 3

GAMBLIN' 1
DRINKIN' AND GAMBLIN' NOW. . . . . NM BIG-TIMER POEM 13

GAME 5
AND START A SKIN GAME WITH SOME CHUMPS I KNOW. . . . . SH BED TIME 6
I'M GONNA GET UP A POKER GAME AND INVITE THE BOYS. . . . . SH SUNDAY 12
WHEN THE AIR IS ONE INTERMINABLE BALL GAME . . . . SP PASSING 2
WHERE CAME TO BAG'S ILLUSIVE . . . AYM IS IT TRUE? 12
IN GENTILE GAME . . . . PL UN-AMERICAN 9

GANDHI 2
GANDHI. . . . . SL SCOTTSBORO 24
YOU CAN'T LOCK UP GANDHI. . . . . . JC HOW ABOUT DIXIE 13

GANG 2
CALL IN A GANG O' WOMEN . . . . . . NM BIG-TIMER POEM 65
DIXIE'S AIN'T NO PLACE FOR A GANG THAT'S SLOW. . . . . SH DEATH IN HARLEM 38

GANGPLANK 1
GO UP THE GANGPLANK . . . . FW SAILING DATE 13

GANGRENOUS 2
SAVE IN MEMORIES OF GANGRENOUS ICING AYM ODE TO DINAH 78
THE CHOCOLATE GANGRENOUS ICING OF AYM ODE TO DINAH 80

GANGSTER 1
OUR OF THE RACK AND RUIN OF OUR GANGSTER DEATH. . . . . ANS LET AMERICA BE 80

GANG-HORDES 1
WHO HIRE FRANCO TO LEAD HIS GANG-HORDES . . . . ANS SONG OF SPAIN 76

GARBAGE 2
AND GARBAGE . . . . OWT VISITORS 15
DECENT GARBAGE SERVICE . . . . AYM HORN OF PLENTY 75

GARDEN 4
IN THE FIRST GARDEN . . . . WB JAZZONIA 10
HE WENT INTO THE GARDEN . . . . . . LHR BLD MARY'S SON 22
THAT THERE SHOULD BE A BARREN GARDEN SP A HOUSE IN TAOS 16
MISS GARDNER'S IN HER GARDEN. . . . SP SOUTHERN MAMMY 1

GARDNER'S 1
MISS GARDNER'S IN HER GARDEN. . . . SP SOUTHERN MAMMY 1

GARLAND 1
MAKE A GARLAND OF LEONTYNES AND LENAS . . . . PL CROWNS GARLANDS 1

GARLANDS 1
GREAT NAMES FOR CROWNS AND GARLANDS! PL CROWNS GARLANDS 17

GARMENT 2
THAT I WERE A GARMENT, ... WB SONGS DARK VIRG 8
A SHIMMERING, SILKEN GARMENT, ... WB SONGS DARK VIRG 9

GARMENTS 3
GARMENTS OF A CLOWN . . . . NM BLACK CLWN POEM 26
TEAR OFF THE GARMENTS . . . . NM BLACK CLWN POEM 69
FAIRIES WEAVE THEIR GARMENTS. . . . DK FAIRIES 2

GARNERED 1
GARNERED FROM YESTERDAY . . . . FW WALLS 7

GARRISON 1
SEND FOR FREDERICK DOUGLASS, GARRISON, BEECHER, ... PL FINAL CALL 30

GARVEY 1
SEND FOR MARCUS GARVEY (WHAT?) SUFI (WHO?) . . . . PL FINAL CALL 33

GAS 6
AND I STEPS ON THE GAS, ... NM BIG-TIMER POEM 26
POISON GAS IS SPAIN. . . . . ANS SONG OF SPAIN 35
FILL IT UP WITH GAS . . . . SH DECLARATION 10
FILL IT UP WITH GAS AND . . . . . . SH IF-INC 7
BY THE PALE DULL PALLOR OF AN OLD GAS LIGHT . . . . SP THE WEARY BLUES 5
KEEPS THE GAS ON WHILE THE TV . . . AYM ODE TO DINAH 5

GASTONIA 1
AT HARLAN, RICHMOND, GASTONIA, ATLANTA, NEW-ORLEANS; . . . . . ANS OPEN LETTER 16

GATE 4
FACE THE WALL WITH THE DARK CLOSED GATE, ... DK SONG 7
STRONG ARE THE BARS AND STEEL THE GATE, ... ANS BLD OZZIE POWEL 5
AT EACH GATE. . . . . SP GOOD MORNING 25
WHILE THEY LOCK THE GATE. . . . . . PL GO SLOW 10

GATES 1
THE GATES OPEN - . . . . SP GOOD MORNING 23

GATHER 8
GATHER UP YO' FINE CLOTHES . . . . FC HARD LUCK 5
GATHER UP . . . . FW PRAYER 1
GATHER UP . . . . FW PRAYER 7
GATHER UP . . . . FW PRAYER 9
GATHER UP . . . . SP LITANY 1
GATHER UP . . . . SP LITANY 7
GATHER UP . . . . SP LITANY 9
GATHER OUT OF STAR-DUST . . . . PL DREAM DUST 1

GATHERED 2
GATHERED TOGETHER - . . . . SP SUN SONG 4
WAS GATHERED ROUND ME. . . . . SP SYLVESTER'S BED 4

GAVE 10
SO I GAVE UP AND WENT . . . . FW COMMUNION 5
HE GAVE THEM OF HIS BREAD. . . . . LHP BLD MARY'S SON 16
HE GAVE THEM TO DRINK OF HIS WINE. LHP BLD MARY'S SON 17
GAVE HIM MONEY TO GAMBLE. . . . . . SP BLD FORTUNE TEL 13
SHE GAVE HIM BREAD. . . . . SP BLD FORTUNE TEL 14
THE RELIEF GAVE FORTY-FOUR. . . . . SP BLD OF THE MAN 2
THE GUY SHE GAVE HER ALL TO . . . . SP BLD OF THE GIRL 5
EVERYBODY THAT GAVE SOMETHING . . . SP BLD OF THE MAN 11
YOU SAY I GAVE MY O.K.? . . . . . . SP MADAM PHONE BIL 38
BEATEN AND MISTREATED FOR THE WORK THAT I GAVE - . . . . SP THE NEGRO MOTHE 14

GAWD-KNOWS-WHAT 2
BUT A LOT O' GAWD-KNOWS-WHAT. . . . SH LOVE AGAIN BLUS 2
BUT A LOT O' GAWD-KNOWS-WHAT. . . . SH LOVE AGAIN BLUS 4

GAY 13
THEY SAY A JAZZ-BAND'S GAY. . . . . WB CABARET 2
CALL GAY BLACK BOYS. . . . . WB HARLEM NIGHT CL 7
STRENGTH HE DOESN'T REALLY FEEL. GAY, LOUD, UNHAPPY JAZZ, BARING HIS . . . . NM BIG-TIMER MOOD 9
A GAY AND LOW-DOWN BLUES, COMIC ENTRANCE LIKE THE CLOWNS IN THE CIRCUS. . . . . NM BLACK CLWN MOOD 1
SYNCOPATED, DETERMINED TO LAUGH. A BUGLE CALL, GAY, MARTIAL MUSIC. NM BLACK CLWN MOOD 6
LET IT BE GAY. . . . . NM BLACK CLWN POEM 13
ARE GAY WITH DANCING, ... DK MINSTREL MAN 14
MUSIC GAY, ... DK NEGRO DANCERS 8
DRUNK AND ROWDY AND GAY! . . . . . . SH CABARET GIRL 6
AND GAY DANCING FEET . . . . CWT JUICE JOINT 14
STRIKES UP A TUNE ALL GAY AND BRIGHT AND GLAD . . . . CWT JUICE JOINT 43
GAY, LAUGHING JOY, ... SP JOY 3
AND LIFE IS GAY. . . . . SP WATER-FRONT STR 4

GAY-COLORED 1
SO WITH MY ONCE GAY-COLORED SOUL . SP A BLACK PIERROT 12

GEARED 1
AND DEEP DETERMINATION GEARED TO KILL . . . . JC TO CAPTAIN MULZ 51

GEM 1
THE ROOSEVELT, RENAISSANCE, GEM, ALHAMBRA: . . . . SP MOVIES 1

GENERAL 1
GENERAL BOURSE BELEAGUERED . . . . AYM SHADES OF PIC 4

GENERALS 2
AND THE BLOOD-LOVING GENERALS, . . ANS KIDS WHO DIE 27
AT THE MISTERS, LORDS, GENERALS, VICEROYS, ... SP IN EXPLANATION 42

GENIUS 4
OF LESSER GENIUS. . . . . SP DANCER 4
THIS IS A SONG FOR THE GENIUS CHILD. SP GENIUS CHILD 1
NOBODY LOVES A GENIUS CHILD. . . . SP GENIUS CHILD 5
NOBODY LOVES A GENIUS CHILD. . . . SP GENIUS CHILD 11

GENTILE 1
IN GENTILE GAME . . . . PL UN-AMERICAN 9

GENTLE 7
AND WAKE ME UP GENTLE WHEN THE DAWN APPEARS . . . . SH LETTER 18
AS THE GENTLE NIGHT . . . . JC ME AND MY SONG 2
THEY MISTOOK THE GENTLE DEW, . . . LHP PASTORAL 5
SOUTHERN GENTLE LADY, ... SP SILHOUETTE 1
SOUTHERN GENTLE LADY, ... SP SILHOUETTE 11
GENTLE BREEZE: . . . . PL WARNING 8
WITH OLD AND NOT TOO GENTLE . . . . PL WHERE WHEN WHCH 15

GENTLEMAN 2
THAT GENTLEMAN IN EXPENSIVE SHOES AYM BIRD IN ORBIT 55
THAT GENTLEMAN IN EXPENSIVE SHOES AYM BIRD IN ORBIT 88

GENTLEMEN 2
AND THE GENTLEMEN WITH DR. IN FRONT OF THEIR NAMES, ... ANS KIDS WHO DIE 21
AND SEVENTEEN GENTLEMEN . . . . . . SP PARADE 2

GENTLER 1
LIFE IN PLACES GENTLER SPEAKING . . OLD AESTHETE HARLEM 5

GENTLY 4
THESE WORDS ARE GENTLY SPOKEN: . . DK ALABAMA EARTH 11
WHILE NIGHT COMES ON GENTLY, . . . SP DREAM VARIATION 7
IS GENTLY STEWING. . . . . PL CULTURAL EXCHNG 20
MURMURING GENTLY . . . . PL DINNER GUEST ME 12

GEORGE 5
THEY CALL THEM, HEY GEORGE! . . . . SP IN EXPLANATION 12
GEORGE SALLIE COOLIE BOY GETS TIRED SOMETIMES. . . . . SP IN EXPLANATION 17
SHUT UP, GEORGE! . . . . SP IN EXPLANATION 46
GEORGE SALLIE COOLIE INDIAN BOY . . SP IN EXPLANATION 51
IN GEORGE SOKOLSKY'S COLUMN. . . . AYM HORN OF PLENTY 86

GEORGIA 15
EVEN IF YOU DO COME FROM GEORGIA. FC JAZZ BAND 21
FROM AFRICA TO GEORGIA . . . . . . NM BLACK CLWN POEM 57
CAUSE FROM BOMBAY TO GEORGIA . . . JC HOW ABOUT DIXIE 11
FROM GEORGIA FLORIDA LOUISIANA . . SP GOOD MORNING 13
GEORGIA DUSK . . . . SP MULATTO 2
ALL THE WAY FROM AFRICA TO GEORGIA SP NEGRO 11
TO SING ON THE GEORGIA ROADS. . . . SP SUN SONG 7
MAMA'S FRUITCAKE SENT FROM GEORGIA AYM ODE TO DINAH 13
MARTIN LUTHER KING IS GOVERNOR OF GEORGIA, ... PL CULTURAL EXCHNG 43
SOMETIMES THERE'S A WIND IN THE GEORGIA DUSK . . . . PL GEORGIA DUSK 1
IN LONELY PITY THROUGH THE GEORGIA DUSK . . . . PL GEORGIA DUSK 3
SOMETIMES THERE'S BLOOD IN THE GEORGIA DUSK . . . . PL GEORGIA DUSK 5
A CRIMSON TRICKLE IN THE GEORGIA DUSK. . . . . PL GEORGIA DUSK 7
SOMETIMES A WIND IN THE GEORGIA DUSK PL GEORGIA DUSK 9
IT'S MADE OF PLAIN OLD GEORGIA CLAY. PL VARI-COLORED 7
AND GEORGIA SKIES SO BLUE. . . . . PL VARI-COLORED 10

GERALD 2
SHUT UP, SAYS GERALD L.K. SMITH. . SP IN EXPLANATION 23
GOVERNORS OF SOUTH CAROLINA, GERALD L.K. STRYDOMS. . . . . SP IN EXPLANATION 43

GERMAN 1
MORE THAN GERMAN EVER BORE, ... PL CULTURAL EXCHNG 16

GERMANY 1
INDIA TO GERMANY, ... ANS CHANT TOM MOONY 19

GET 85

AND WHEN I GET ON THE TRAIN . . . . WB BLUES FANTASY 25
AND IF I DON'T GET YOU GOIN'. . . . NM BIG-TIMER POEM 31
TALKIN' 'BOUT "WE'LL WORK FOR 50¢ A DAY, IF WE CAN'T GET NO MO'." . NM BROKE 7
AND DE MAN COME TELLIN' ME I BETTER GET THERE AT FO'. . . . . NM BROKE 13
SO DE MAN SAY, "I'LL GET SOMEBODY ELSE, THEN, TO CLEAN." - . . . . NM BROKE 17
I CAN'T EVEN GET DE MONEY FOR TO BUY MYSELF A SMOKE. . . . . NM BROKE 46
LET'S GET MARRIED RIGHT NOW! YES! WHAT DO YOU SAY? . . . . NM BROKE 75
GET WAY BACK, HONEY. . . . . DK SONG BANJO DANC 5
TELLING OTHERS TO GET TOGETHER. . . ANS KIDS WHO DIE 13
DON'T WANT THE PEOPLE TO GET WISE TO THEIR OWN POWER. . . . . ANS KIDS WHO DIE 35
TO BELIEVE AN ANGELO HERNDON, OR EVER GET TOGETHER. . . . . ANS KIDS WHO DIE 36
IF THIS RADIO WAS GOOD I'D GET WOO SH BED TIME 1
BUT SINCE I GOT TO GET UP AT DAY. SH BED TIME 9
CAN I GET TEN ON THIS SUIT . . . . SH BLD PAWNBROKER 9
I'LL GET 'EM FOR YOU. . . . . SH BLD THE KILLER 4
CAME TIPPIN INTO DIXIE'S TO GET A VIEW. . . . . SH DEATH IN HARLEM 59
GET OUT O' MY SIGHT BE- . . . . . . SH EVIL MORNING 15
GET ON THAT MULE AND . . . . SH IF-ING 3
I'D GET ME A PLANE . . . . SH IF-ING 10
I CAN'T GET ALONG WITH YOU, I CAN'T GET ALONG WITHOUT - . . . . . . SH LETTER 14
I CAN'T GET ALONG WITH YOU, I CAN'T GET ALONG WITHOUT - . . . . . . SH LETTER 14
THAT EXTRA DAY WOULD GET ME DOWN. SH OUT OF WORK 18
I'M GONNA GET IT CASHED. . . . . . SH PAY DAY 5
I'M GONNA GET UP A POKER GAME AND INVITE THE BOYS. . . . . SH SUNDAY 12
GONNA GO GET MY PISTOL, I SAID FORTY-FOUR - . . . . SH TWILIGHT REVERI 5
GONNA GO GET MY PISTOL, I MEAN THIRTY-TWO. . . . . SH TWILIGHT REVERI 7
GO GET OUT YOUR KLAN - . . . . . . JC BLD SAM SOLOMON 54
TO SEE JIM CROW GET OUT OF HAND. . JC JIM CROW'S LAST 4
IF YOU WANT TO GET OLD HITLER'S GOAT. . . . . JC JIM CROW'S LAST 23
YOU GET LOST IN THE DUSK - . . . . FW DUSK 3
GOTTA GET MY TEACHING! . . . . . . OWT JITNEY 31
I WANT TO GET OVER TO STATE. . . . OWT JITNEY 38
YOU HAVE TO GET THERE EARLY . . . . OWT JITNEY 56
GET SHORTER AND SHORTER. . . . . . OWT RAID 4
TO GET YOU OUT OF MY HEAD. . . . . OWT YESTERDAY TODAY 8
SO GET YOURSELF . . . . SP ADVICE 4
BLACK, GET BACK! . . . . SP ARGUMENT 3
WHAT? YOU GONNA GET EVICTION ORDERS? SP BLD LANDLORD 13
TALK ON - TILL YOU GET THROUGH. . . SP BLD LANDLORD 18
COME AND GET THIS MAN! . . . . . . SP BLD LANDLORD 22
HOW SHE COULD GET IN TROUBLE . . . SP BLD OF THE GIRL 3
MONDAY'LL GET YOU DOWN. . . . . . . SP BLUE MONDAY 9
WILL SURELY GET YOU DOWN. . . . . . SP BLUE MONDAY 11
I WOULDN'T GET UP NO MORE - . . . . SP BLUES AT DAWN 9
DID HE GET ANYWHERE? NO! . . . . . SP DANCER 23
TO GET THROUGH HIGH AT TWENTY'S KIND OF LATE - . . . . SP DEFERRED 6
WHERE I GET OFF AT FIVE. . . . . . SP DEFERRED 26
IS THAT THE WAY TO GET ABOARD THE FREEDOM TRAIN? . . . . SP FREEDOM TRAIN 28
WILL SOME WHITE MAN YELL, GET BACK! SP FREEDOM TRAIN 39
GET ON BOARD OUR FREEDOM TRAIN! . . SP FREEDOM TRAIN 69
LEST THE SONG GET OUT OF HAND. . . SP GENIUS CHILD 4
DON'T GET ANYWHERE. . . . . SP HIGH TO LOW 7
DON'T YOU WANT TO GET UP . . . . . SP KID SLEEPY 11
TIME I PAY RENT AND GET MY FOOD . . SP LETTER 2
HAD TO GET BREAKFAST. . . . . SP MADAM HER MADAM 5
TILL I GET OVER . . . . SP MADAM NUMBER WR 23
AND I'LL GET ALONG. . . . . SP MADAM'S PAST HI 22
I CAN'T GET OFF MY MIND. . . . . . SP MAMA AND DAUGHT 8
CAN'T HARDLY GET HIS BREAD. . . . . SP MONROE'S BLUES 4
WHERE DID THEY GET . . . . SP NIGHT FUNERAL 3
AND GRANDMA CANNOT GET HER GOSPEL HYMNS . . . . SP PASSING 3
IT TOOK ME TWO YEARS TO GET ON WPA. SP RELIEF 7
YOU WON'T GET A GODDAMN THING! . . SP SAME IN BLUES 11
AND WE GET NONE. . . . . SP SHARE-CROPPERS 8
WHY DON'T SHE GET A BOY-FRIEND . . SP SISTER 5
GET OUT THEIR BIBS . . . . SP SUNDAY MORNING 10
BUT I GOT TO GET A NEW ANTENNA, LORD - . . . . AYM BLUES IN STEREO 36
WHERE DID I GET MY MONEY! . . . . . AYM HORN OF PLENTY 47
FAILS TO GET PEARL BAILEY. . . . . AYM ODE TO DINAH 6
CAN I GET IT NOW? . . . . AYM RIDE, RED, RIDE 6
TELL ME, MAMA, CAN I GET MY SHOW . AYM SHOW FARE PLESE 1
WHEN I GET TO BE A COMPOSER . . . . PL DAYBREAK IN ALA 1
GET TO BE A COMPOSER . . . . PL DAYBREAK IN ALA 21
TRYIN' TO GET UP THERE - . . . . . PL DOWN WHERE I AM 6
AND I GET TO SEE 'EM RIDE. . . . . PL FLORIDA WORKERS 16
NEVER COULD GET. . . . . PL HARLEM 13
GET OUT THE LUNCH-BOX OF YOUR DREAMS PL JIM CROW CAR 1
"IT'S EASIER TO GET DOPE . . . . . PL JUNIOR ADDICT 28
THAN IT IS TO GET A JOB." . . . . . PL JUNIOR ADDICT 29
YES, EASIER TO GET DOPE . . . . . . PL JUNIOR ADDICT 30
THAN TO GET A JOB - . . . . PL JUNIOR ADDICT 31
TO GET A NICE HOME . . . . PL LITTLE SNG HOUS 3
WHEN I GET SOLD: . . . . PL LITTLE SNG HOUS 12
WHEN THE WHITE FOLKS GET THROUGH . PL OFFICE BUILDING 1
WHEN WHITE COLLARS GET DONE. . . . PL OFFICE BUILDING 8

GETS 7

'CAUSE 'FORE YOU GETS THERE, TEN THOUSAND AND ONE . . . . NM BROKE 5
A HUMAN GETS LONESOME IF THERE AIN'T TWO. . . . . SH BED TIME 15
GETS IN LINE TO SEE THE FREEDOM. . SP FREEDOM TRAIN 38
GEORGE SALLIE COOLIE BOY GETS TIRED SOMETIMES. . . . . SP IN EXPLANATION 17
WHEN A CHILE GETS TO BE THIRTEEN . SP MYSTERY 1
WHEN A DREAM GETS KICKED AROUND. . SP SAME IN BLUES 32
GETS SHOT RIGHT INTO GLORY. . . . . AYM IS IT TRUE? 53

GETTING 2

GETTING UP IN THE MORNING LONESOME AND SAD? . . . . SH DAYBREAK 13
WITHOUT GETTING FUR IN MY MOUTH . . SP NECESSITY 7

GETTIN' 5

AN' SAYS YO' BOY IS GETTIN' BEAT. FC DEATH DO DIRTY 24
FOLKS SHO IS GETTIN' HARD ON YOU - JUST 'CAUSE YOU BROKE. . . . . . NM BROKE 15
O' GETTIN' A NEW WINTER COAT, OR HAVIN' THAT OLD ONE CLEANED. . . NM BROKE 40
AND I AM GETTIN' TIRED! . . . . . . SP SOUTHERN MAMMY 4
I AM GETTIN' TIRED! . . . . SP SOUTHERN MAMMY 6

GHOST 2

MAKE YOU WALK LIKE A GHOST IF YOU BOTHER ME ANY MORE. . . . . . . SH TWILIGHT REVERI 6
BEYOND THE HOLY GHOST. . . . . . . AYM SHOW FARE PLESE 30

GHOSTLY 2

HOW THIN AND SHARP AND GHOSTLY WHITE SP WINTER MOON 2
GHOSTLY MONUMENT OF WINTER . . . . AYM ODE TO DINAH 26

GHOSTS 10

ARE THE GHOSTS OF FORMER GLORY . . AYM GOSPEL CHA-CHA 20
DEAD OR LIVE THEIR GHOSTS CAST SHADOWS . . . . AYM SHADES OF PIC 6
GHOSTS OF ALL TOO SOLID FLESH. . . PL GHOSTS OF 1619 1
DARK GHOSTS COME BACK TO HAUNT YOU NOW. . . . . PL GHOSTS OF 1619 2
THESE DARK GHOSTS TO TAUNT YOU - . PL GHOSTS OF 1619 3
YET GHOSTS SO SOLID, GHOSTS SO REAL PL GHOSTS OF 1619 4
YET GHOSTS SO SOLID, GHOSTS SO REAL PL GHOSTS OF 1619 4
FLESH-AND-BLOOD GHOSTS . . . . . . PL GHOSTS OF 1619 14
BEING GHOSTS . . . . PL GHOSTS OF 1619 29
IS ALIVE WITH GHOSTS TODAY. . . . . PL OCTOBER 16 RAID 24

GIANT 1

SLEEPY GIANT. . . . . SP AFRICA 1

GIFT 2

AS A GIFT FROM YOU. . . . . JC THE BITTER RIVR 54
BUT YOUR GIFT BOOKS ARE SUBVERSIVE. AYM RIDE, RED, RIDE 24

GIFTS 1

WOULD GIVE HER MANY RARE GIFTS . . SP THE SOUTH 21

GIGOLOS 1

FOR THE WHORES AND GIGOLOS. . . . . FC JAZZ BAND 5

GILLESPIE 1

LIKE A DIZZY GILLESPIE TRANSCRIPTION SP PROJECTION 13

GIMME 12

ASK HIM TO GIMME HIS HAND. . . . . FC MOAN 8
BUT SHE DON'T GIMME LOVIN' . . . . FC WORKIN' MAN 11
JUST GIMME SOME SASS. . . . . NM BIG-TIMER POEM 28
BUT IF YOU GIMME GOOD CORN WHISKY SH HEY-HEY BLUES 5
BUT GIMME GOOD CORN WHISKY . . . . SH HEY-HEY BLUES 23
GIMME SIX-BITS' WORTH O' TICKET . . SH SIX-BITS BLUES 1
BABY, GIMME A LITTLE LOVIN'. . . . SH SIX-BITS BLUES 7
YOU GIMME TWO. . . . . OWT HONEY BABE 6
I'D TELL HER, GIMME A PLACE TO SLEEP. . . . . SP EVENING SONG 6
GIMME YO' SHOES . . . . SP PORTER 11
IT AIN'T FOREVER, GIMME! . . . . . SP PREFERENCE 14
GIMME $25.00 . . . . SP REQUEST 1

GIMS 1

CAST YOUR GIMS . . . . SH HARLEM SWEETIES 3

GIN 16

GIN? . . . . WB CAT AND SAXOPHN 4
BUT I'LL MISS MA GIN. . . . . FC BLD OF GIN MARY 20
GIN ON SATURDAY. . . . . FC BRASS SPITOONS 23
BABIES AND GIN AND CHURCH . . . . . FC BRASS SPITOONS 26
GIT SOME GIN TO MAKE YOU LAUGH. . . FC HARD LUCK 12
GIN AN' WHISKEY . . . . FC LISTEN HERE 5
SHE DON'T DRINK GIN . . . . FC NEW CABARET GRL 5
AN' A GLASS O' GIN: . . . . FC SATURDAY NIGHT 6

A GLASS OF GIN — FC SPORT 14
(DIXIE MAKES HIS MONEY ON TWO-BIT GIN.) — SH DEATH IN HARLEM 32
GIN RICKEYS FOR TWO. — SH DEATH IN HARLEM 42
SPAGHETTI AND GIN, MUSIC AND SMOKE. — SH DEATH IN HARLEM 53
THERE IS A GIN MILL ON THE AVENUE — OWT JUICE JOINT 1
GIN IS SOLD IN GLASSES FINGER-TALL. — OWT JUICE JOINT 6
INTO THIS GIN MILL — OWT JUICE JOINT 15
ONE MORE BOTTLE OF GIN. — SP DEFERRED 33

GINGER 1
GINGER, WINE-GOLD. — SH HARLEM SWEETIES 37

GIRL 22
A DANCING GIRL WHOSE EYES ARE BOLD — WB JAZZONIA 5
NIGHT-DARK GIRL OF THE SWAYING HIPS? — WB NUDE YOUNG DANC 6
I'S ALWAYS BEEN A WORKIN' GIRL. — FC BLACK GAL 1
TO A LITTLE DROWNED GIRL. — FC CLOSING TIME 15
ON A PO' BLACK GIRL. — FC GAL'S CRY DYING 12
AT A BIG PIANO A LITTLE DARK GIRL — SH DEATH IN HARLEM 10
THE GIRL WHO SELLS HER BODY BEHIND STEEL BARS, — JC THE BITTER RIVR 35
LIKE MY LITTLE GIRL. — OWT HONEY BABE 16
GIRL, AIN'T YOU HEARD? — OWT JITNEY 9
A GIRL WITH ALL THAT RAISING, — SP BLD OF THE GIRL 1
HALF GIRL — SP CATCH 12
GOLDEN GIRL — SP COLLEGE FORMAL 1
A NIGHT-VEILED GIRL — SP DANSE AFRICAINE 7
DANCE WITH YOU, MY SWEET BROWN HARLEM GIRL. — SP JUKE BOX LOVE 12
A LITTLE GIRL CHILD. — SP MADAM CHARTY CH 2
HIS GIRL FRIEND HAD TO PAY. — SP NIGHT FUNERAL 24
TO THAT GIRL WHO PAID THE PREACHER MAN - — SP NIGHT FUNERAL 41
A PASSING GIRL — SP RAILROAD AVENUE 15
WHAT CAN A COLORED GIRL DO — SP RUBY BROWN 13
HOLD A YELLOW GIRL — SP RUBY BROWN 19
I AM THE DARK GIRL WHO CROSSED THE WIDE SEA — SP THE NEGRO MOTHE 9
LITTLE GIRL — SP TO BE SOMEBODY 1

GIRLIE 1
PEACH-SKINNED GIRLIE. — SH HARLEM SWEETIES 9

GIRLS 25
DARK BROWN GIRLS — WB HARLEM NIGHT CL 10
FOR PIERROT SAW A WORLD OF GIRLS. — WB PIERROT 17
SWEET GIRLS, SWEET GIRLS, — FC LISTEN HERE 1
SWEET GIRLS, SWEET GIRLS. — FC LISTEN HERE 1
ALL YOU SWEET GIRLS. — FC LISTEN HERE 3
GOOD GIRLS, GOOD GIRLS, — FC LISTEN HERE 13
GOOD GIRLS, GOOD GIRLS. — FC LISTEN HERE 13
OH, YOU GOOD GIRLS, — FC LISTEN HERE 15
IS I MARRIED? NO, ALL THESE-HERE GIRLS UP NORTH IS TOO LIGHT. — NM BROKE 70
SHOP GIRLS, — ANS OPEN LETTER 6
BIG TIME SPORTS AND GIRLS WHO KNOW — SH DEATH IN HARLEM 37
HARLEM GIRLS VARY - — SH HARLEM SWEETIES 40
GIRLS, DON'T STAND ON NO CORNER — SH MIDNIGHT CHIPPI 25
CRY BY YOURSELF, GIRLS, — SH MIDNIGHT CHIPPI 29
WHILE GIRLS WHO WASH RICH WHITE FOLKS CLOTHES BY DAY — OWT LINCOLN THEATRE 13
THE GIRLS LEFT HIM. — SP DANCER 19
PASSING BOYS AND GIRLS — SP IN TIME SILVER 19
THEM OTHER GIRLS DO — SP MADAM PHONE BIL 28
WHITE GIRLS FALL — SP MELLOW 3
I DON'T FOOL WITH THESE YOUNG GIRLS. — SP PREFERENCE 3
MIGHT MEET GIRLS — SP UP-BEAT 3
GIRLS WHO WILL — SP UP-BEAT 6
FOUR LITTLE GIRLS — PL BIRMINGHAM SUND 1
FOUR TINY GIRLS — PL BIRMINGHAM SUND 15
FOUR LITTLE GIRLS — PL BIRMINGHAM SUND 24

GIRLS' 1
WHITE GIRLS' EYES — WB HARLEM NIGHT CL 6

GIRL-FRIEND 2
I KEPT WISHING I HAD A GIRL-FRIEND — OWT STRANGER IN TWN 3
MY GIRL-FRIEND SEND HER LOVE AND SAY — SP LETTER 6

GIRL'LL 1
YOUNG GIRL'LL SAY. — SP PREFERENCE 4

GIT 8
GIT SOME GIN TO MAKE YOU LAUGH. — FC HARD LUCK 12
GIT ME A WAGGON TO HAUL. — FC HARD LUCK 14
GIT A WAGGON TO HAUL. — FC HARD LUCK 16
GIT A QUART O' LICKER. — FC SATURDAY NIGHT 11
WHEN DE WORMS GIT THROUGH — FC SATURDAY NIGHT 16
AN' GIT TO MA BABY SOMEHOW. — DK WIDE RIVER 14
GIT TO MA BABY SOMEHOW - — DK WIDE RIVER 16
GIT ON BACK THERE IN THE NIGHT. — SP MULATTO 37

GITS 1
AN' GITS NOTHIN' BUT TROUBLE. — FC WORKIN' MAN 16

GIVE 26
GWINE GIVE YOU EIGHTEEN MONTHS — FC BLD OF GIN MARY 15
I GIVE IT TO HIM CAUSE I LOVED HIM — FC GYPSY MAN 17
AND I DON'T GIVE A DAMN - — NM BIG-TIMER POEM 74
GOD! GIVE ME LAUGHTER — NM BLACK CLWN POEM 23
GOD! GIVE ME THE SPOTTED — NM BLACK CLWN POEM 25
AND GIVE US THE RIGHTS THAT ARE YOURS AND MINE. — NM COLORED SL POEM 10
AND GIVE ME ROOM. — ANS BLDS OF LENIN 4
GIVE HER — SH PRESENT 6
HAD GIVE YOU UP FOR DEAD. — JC GOOD MORN STLIN 3
DONE GIVE YOU UP FOR DEAD - — JC GOOD MORN STLIN 38
I DON'T GIVE A DAMN — OWT FUNERAL 7
BUT I WOULD GIVE A DAMN. — OWT FUNERAL 9
HAS TO GIVE HIS MOTHER TEN - — SP BUDDY 5
OR GIVE MY SUGAR — SP CONSIDER ME 23
I DON'T GIVE A DAMN — SP CROON 1
WILL GIVE EVEN — SP LIVE LET LIVE 3
GIVE A DAMN! — SP MADAM CENSUS 26
BLACK - AND DON'T GIVE A DAMN! — SP ME AND THE MULE 6
GIVE SWEET BIRTH — SP MULATTO 35
AND GIVE FREELY — SP SUNDAY MORNING 39
WOULD GIVE HER MANY RARE GIFTS — SP THE SOUTH 21
YOU GIVE ME SECOND-CLASS HOUSES, — PL BACKLASH BLUES 7
GIVE ME SECOND-CLASS SCHOOLS, — PL BACKLASH BLUES 8
AND IN VOTING NOT GIVE A DAMN — PL GHOSTS OF 1619 9
GIVE A DAMN. — PL IMPASSE 8
TOMORROW'S SUNSHINE GIVE — PL JUNIOR ADDICT 17

GIVED 1
AFTER ALL THEM DOLLARS I GIVED HER THESE LAST TWO YEARS, — NM BROKE 23

GIVEN 7
A COMPLAINT TO B GIVEN BY A DEJECTED LOOKING FELLOW SHUFFLING ALONG — NM BROKE 1
A BIT OF CLAY, BROWN, UGLY, GIVEN LIFE? — DK BEGGAR BOY 6
I WAS GIVEN ITS WATER — JC THE BITTER RIVR 53
LOVE IS GIVEN. — FW GIFTS 2
LOVE IS GIVEN. — SP LUCK 5
I HAVE GIVEN MY ANSWER. — SP PERSONAL 6
HAVING GIVEN UP BREATH - — PL SLAVE 5

GIVES 11
AND GIVES HER KISS TO NOTHINGNESS. — WB TO LITTLE LOVER 11
GIVES YOU A DOLLAR AN' A HALF. — FC HARD LUCK 8
GIVES YOU A DOLLAR AN' A HALF. — FC HARD LUCK 10
EXCEPT THE NAME EACH GIVES IT - — DLD TWO THINGS 9
HE GIVES ME HIS HAND. — DK MA LORD 4
GIVES LOVE AWAY SHE'S THROUGH. — SH MIDNIGHT CHIPPI 24
IT GIVES ONLY THE GLINT OF STEEL BARS — JC THE BITTER RIVR 27
FOR HE GIVES BACK NO STARS. — JC THE BITTER RIVR 38
GIVES ME THE COURTESY OF ROAD — FW SNAKE 3
JUDGE GIVES NEGRO 90 DAYS IN COUNTY JAIL — SP BLD LANDLORD 33
NOBODY GIVES A DAMN ABOUT. — SP DOWN AND OUT 6

GIVING 2
HIBBLER'S GIVING OUT! — OWT JITNEY 27
YOU'RE ALWAYS GIVING — SP MADAM MIGHT-HAV 15

GIVIN' 1
BUT THEY GIVIN' 'EM TO SCHOOL BOYS NOW AND PAYIN' JUST ABOUT HALF. — NM BROKE 43

GLAD 5
YOU GOT A GOOD JOB? YES! WELL, I SHO AM GLAD TO SEE YOU, DEAR! — NM BROKE 69
THEY OUGHT TO BE LIKE ME SETTING HERE - FEELING GLAD! — SH SUNDAY 15
THEY WERE GLAD. — JC GOOD MORN STLIN 39
I'M GLAD — JC GOOD MORN STLIN 58
STRIKES UP A TUNE ALL GAY AND BRIGHT AND GLAD — OWT JUICE JOINT 43

GLASS 8
A GLASS O' WHISKEY — FC SATURDAY NIGHT 5
AN' A GLASS O' GIN: — FC SATURDAY NIGHT 6
A GLASS OF GIN — FC SPORT 14
AND MY GOLD FISH ET THE GLASS. — SP CHILDREN'S RYME 19
NURSES TURN GLASS DOORKNOBS — SP INTERNE AT PROV 42
LETS HIS GLASS — SP NEIGHBOR 23
WHERE A BROKEN GLASS — SP SHALIMAR 2
FROM THE BIG GLASS SHOPPING CENTER — AYM HORN OF PLENTY 94

GLASSER 1
IN ESCROW TO JOE GLASSER. — AYM HORN OF PLENTY 82

GLASSES 3
GIN IS SOLD IN GLASSES FINGER-TALL. — OWT JUICE JOINT 6
FULL OF CHINE BONES IN DARK GLASSES. — SP SUMMER EVENING 15
IN HORN-RIM GLASSES. — AYM ASK YOUR MAMA 53

GLEAM 1
AND WHITE TEETH GLEAM - — ANS A NEW SONG 37

GLEAMIN' 1

GLEAMIN' IN THE SUNLIGHT FOR WHITE AND BLACK? . . . SP FREEDOM TRAIN 50

GLEAMS 2

GLEAMS ON HIS FOREHEAD. . . . SP INTERNE AT PROV 36
UNTIL IT GLEAMS . . . SP TRUMPET PLAYER 14

GLEE 1

TO DANCE WITH GLEE. . . . NM BLACK CLWN POEM 32

GLIDES 1

HE GLIDES SO SWIFTLY . . . FW SNAKE 1

GLINT 1

IT GIVES ONLY THE GLINT OF STEEL BARS . . . JC THE BITTER RIVR 27

GLOBAL 1

GLOBAL TROTTERS BASEBALL BATTERS C $ $ . . . AYM HORN OF PLENTY 16

GLOOM 1

NOR DAYS OF GLOOM. . . . OK WALKERS WITH 4

GLOOMY 1

THE WORLD IS GLOOMY. . . . FW CAROLINA CABIN 13

GLORIFIED 1

IS GLORIFIED. . . . PL BIBLE BELT 10

GLORIFY 1

GLORIFY THEIR MILLION-DOLLAR WAYS PL PRIME 5

GLORY 14

GLORY! HALLELUJAH! . . . SH ONLY WOMAN BLUS 15
SUNDAY PRAYERS SYNCOPATE GLORY. . . . SP CONSIDER ME 44
WHEN I SET MY FEET IN GLORY . . . SP DEFERRED 41
THEN I'LL SHOUT, GLORY FOR THE . . SP FREEDOM TRAIN 63
GLORY! HALLELUJAH! . . . SP PRAYER MEETING 1
GLORY! HALLELUJAH! . . . SP PRAYER MEETING 3
TO THE GLORY OF GOD! . . . SP TAMBOURINES 4
TO GLORY! . . . SP TAMBOURINES 6
TO GLORY! . . . SP TAMBOURINES 14
OF GLORY TO YOUR NAME AND MINE . . AYM BLUES IN STEREO 10
ARE THE GHOSTS OF FORMER GLORY . . AYM GOSPEL CHA-CHA 20
WITH HIS GLORY. . . . AYM GOSPEL CHA-CHA 25
GETS SHOT RIGHT INTO GLORY. . . . AYM IS IT TRUE? 53
THOUGH WORN IN GLORY ON MY HEAD. . PL CROWNS GARLANDS 12

GLOVES 3

TWINKLE ON THE RUBBER GLOVES . . . SP INTERNE AT PROV 33
DREAMING OF THE BOXING GLOVES . . . SP TO BE SOMEBODY 15
THE GLOVES THAT SENT . . . SP TO BE SOMEBODY 17

GLOW 2

GLOW OF THE QUINCE . . . SH HARLEM SWEETIES 21
UNTIL A GLOW IS LIGHTED . . . SP MIGRANT 21

GNARLED 1

ON A GNARLED AND NAKED TREE. . . . SP SONG DARK GIRL 12

GO 85

I GO TO SEEK MY FORTUNE. . . . WB A FAREWELL 3
WHERE ALL PATHS GO? . . . WB HARLEM NIGHT CL 17
GO WHERE GOLD . . . WB TO DARK MERCEDE 4
GO WHERE THEY WILL PAY YOU WELL . . WB TO DARK MERCEDE 7
EVERYWHERE I GO. . . . FC BAD MAN 6
I WOULDN'T GO TO HEABEN IF I COULD. FC BAD MAN 18
HE'D GO MA BAIL. . . . FC DEATH DO DIRTY 19
GO TO DE BOOTLEG'S. . . . FC HARD LUCK 11
CAN I GO HOME WID YUH, SWEETIE? . . FC JAZZ BAND 22
THAT'S WHERE MA MAN AN' ME GO. . . FC MINNIE SINGS 2
THAT'S WHERE WE GO. - . . . FC MINNIE SINGS 4
I'D GO AWAY . . . FC MINNIE SINGS 16
OR WHERE I GO. . . . FC NEW CABARET GRL 12
GO OUT AN' LET DE WHITE BOYS . . . FC RED SILK STOCK 3
GO OUT AN' LET DE WHITE BOYS . . . FC RED SILK STOCK 11
THE LIGHTS GO OUT . . . FC SPORT 8
FEELING LIFE GO. . . . OLD THE CONSUMPTIVE 4
BUT IF I WANTED TO GO STRAIGHT . . NM BIG-TIMER POEM 41
NO PLACE TO GO. . . . NM BLACK CLWN POEM 35
YOU CAN TAKE THAT JOB AND GO TO - I HOPE YOU CHOKE. . . . NM BROKE 37
SO WHEN I GOT READY TO GO, I SAID, "I'LL BE SEEIN' YOU SOON, MARIE." NM BROKE 52
(AIN'T SEEN HER IN SIX YEARS! USED TO GO WITH HER, TOO!) . . . NM BROKE 63
FOR WHEN DREAMS GO . . . OK DREAMS 6
I WANTS TO GO SOMEWHERE. . . . OK HOMESICK BLUES 6
LET'S GO SEE OLD ABE . . . OK LINCOLN MONUMNT 1
AND YOU DO NOT GO FREE. . . . ANS CHANT TOM MOONY 5
AND YOU DO NOT GO FREE. . . . ANS CHANT TOM MOONY 9
HERE I GO WITH MY BANNER IN MY HAND! ANS SISTER JOHNSON 5
I GO. . . . SH ASPIRATION 8
THEN I'LL GO. . . . SH BLD PAWNBROKER 18
BABE, YOU WHO CAN GO! . . . SH DEATH IN HARLEM 40
I SAID, GO, HOT DAMN! . . . SH ONLY WOMAN BLUS 22
DID MY SWEET MAMA GO? . . . SH SHAKESPEARE 4
DON'T HAVE TO GO TO CHURCH. . . . SH SUNDAY 3
DON'T HAVE TO GO NOWHERE. . . . SH SUNDAY 4
HOW FAR YOU GO, NOR HOW LONG YOU STAY - . . . SH SUNDAY 6
GONNA GO GET MY PISTOL, I SAID FORTY-FOUR - . . . SH TWILIGHT REVERI 5
GONNA GO GET MY PISTOL, I MEAN THIRTY-TWO, . . . SH TWILIGHT REVERI 7
SAM SAID, IT'S TIME TO GO . . . JC BLD SAM SOLOMON 8
GO GET OUT YOUR KLAN - . . . JC BLD SAM SOLOMON 54
SEASONS COME, SEASONS GO, . . . FW CIRCLES 4
THOUGH I GO DRUNKEN . . . FW FAITHFUL ONE 1
GO UP THE GANGPLANK . . . FW SAILING DATE 13
GO HOME, YOU HUCKS! . . . OWT BLD MARGE POLIT 41
GO OUT THERE. . . . OWT BOARDING HOUSE 12
I USED TO GO ROUND THE CORNER, . . OWT LONESOME CORNER 3
IT'S TIME TO GO. . . . OWT RAID 9
I DON'T KNOW WHERE TO GO. . . . OWT TOO BLUE 3
AND I SAW THE SUN GO DOWN. . . . SP BLUE BAYOU 3
AND I SAW THE SUN GO DOWN. . . . SP BLUE BAYOU 6
I SAW THE SUN GO DOWN. . . . SP BLUE BAYOU 19
AND I SAW THE SUN GO DOWN, . . . SP BLUE BAYOU 24
LAWD, I SAW THE SUN GO DOWN! . . . SP BLUE BAYOU 27
(WHEN YOU'RE NO GOOD FOR DOUGH THEY GO.) . . . SP DANCER 20
I'LL NEVER GO TO FRANCE, . . . SP DEFERRED 23
TO GO WITH ME . . . SP FATASY PURPLE 8
WHERE I GO. . . . SP FATASY PURPLE 10
IF YOU WANTA GO TO HEABEN . . . SP FIRE 12
THE WHITE FOLKS GO LEFT, THE COLORED GO RIGHT - . . . SP FREEDOM TRAIN 26
THE WHITE FOLKS GO LEFT, THE COLORED GO RIGHT - . . . SP FREEDOM TRAIN 26
GO SINGING, TOO, . . . SP IN TIME SILVER 20
AND GO TO WORK DOWN- . . . SP KID SLEEPY 12
I'D GO TO HADES . . . SP MADAM RENT MAN 9
THAT AIN'T NO TIME TO GO. . . . SP MIDWINTER BLUES 12
AND WATCHES THE SUN GO BY. . . . SP NEIGHBOR 3
LET'S GO, SWEETIE! . . . SP PORT TOWN 15
WHICH WAY TO GO? . . . SP PRAYER 2
IF THESE WHITE FOLKS WANT TO GO AHEAD . . . SP RELIEF 12
DID YOU EVER GO DOWN TO THE RIVER - SP REVERIE HARLEM 1
I GOT TO GO! . . . SP SAME IN BLUES 4
AND SEVEN CATS GO FRANTIC. . . . SP SEASHORE THROUG 4
DREAMING YOU GO. . . . SP SNAIL 2
PIMPS IN GRAY GO BY, . . . SP SUMMER EVENING 5
JITNEYS GO BY . . . SP SUMMER EVENING 14
HONEY! BABY! DON'T GO, DEAR!" . . . SP SYLVESTER'S BED 16
GO HOME AND WRITE . . . SP THEME FOR ENG B 2
AND GO? . . . SP WEST TEXAS 10
TO GO. . . . AYM ASK YOUR MAMA 30
I WANT TO GO TO THE SHOW, MAMA. . . AYM ODE TO DINAH 95
GO SLOW, THEY SAY - . . . PL GO SLOW 1
GO SLOW, I HEAR - . . . PL GO SLOW 4
AWAY THEY GO: . . . PL OFFICE BUILDING 6
WHY NOT GO UNDER? . . . PL QUESTION ANSWER 12
YOU GOT TO GO . . . PL WITHOUT BENEFIT 4
JUST GO AHEAD AND DIE. . . . PL WITHOUT BENEFIT 13

GOAD 1

THAT GOAD BLACK FEET TO DANCING ON BARE FLOORS. . . . OWT JUICE JOINT 20

GOAL 2

NOW, THROUGH MY CHILDREN, I'M REACHING THE GOAL. . . . SP THE NEGRO MOTHE 20
TOWARD FREEDOM'S GOAL, . . . PL FREDRK DOUGLASS 11

GOAT 1

IF YOU WANT TO GET OLD HITLER'S GOAT, . . . JC JIM CROW'S LAST 23

GOD 51

GOD HAVING A HEMORRHAGE, . . . WB CARIBBEAN SUNST 1
WOULD GOD HIS LIPS WERE SWEET! . . WB TO LITTLE LOVER 12
OH, GOD, I WANTS HIM BACK! . . . FC BLACK GAL 18
MY GOD! . . . FC BRASS SPITOONS 25
O, GOD, PLEASE! . . . FC CLOSING TIME 9
GOD! WHAT DANCERS! . . . FC LAUGHERS 24
GOD! WHAT SINGERS! . . . FC LAUGHERS 26
MY GOD, I SAYS, . . . FC NEW CABARET GRL 21
GOD! GIVE ME LAUGHTER . . . NM BLACK CLWN POEM 23
GOD! GIVE ME THE SPOTTED . . . NM BLACK CLWN POEM 25
GOD! WHY DID YOU EVER CURSE ME . . SH CABARET GIRL 7
BLESS GOD! . . . OWT JITNEY 34
GOD, IN HIS INFINITE WISDOM . . . LHR ACCEPTANCE 1
THEY HARDLY TAKE GOD BY SURPRISE. LHR ACCEPTANCE 4
AND THE SON OF GOD WAS HE - . . . LHR BLD MARY'S SON 9
THUNDER OF THE RAIN GOD: . . . SP A HOUSE IN TAOS 2
THUNDER OF THE RAIN GOD: . . . SP A HOUSE IN TAOS 5
THUNDER OF THE RAIN GOD: . . . SP A HOUSE IN TAOS 8
UNDER THE THUNDER OF THE RAIN GOD? SP A HOUSE IN TAOS 14
AND, GOD KNOWS, . . . SP ARGUMENT 9
GOD REST HIS SOUL - . . . SP BLD OF THE MAN 22
BUT GOD, NATURE, . . . SP CAFE: 3 A.M. 6
GOD KNOWS . . . SP HIGH TO LOW 1
HE IS A GOD. . . . SP JOE LOUIS 6

A-SHOUTIN', GOD, I'S COMIN' SOON. . SP JUDGMENT DAY 4
HAIL, MARY, MOTHER OF GOD! . . . . SP MYSTERY 6
AND GOD KNOWS SHE SURE CAN
OVERCHARGE - . . . . SP NECESSITY 10
BUT, THANK GOD, HE WASN'T DEAD! . . SP NOT A MOVIE 13
FROM THE SAINTS OF GOD IN CHRIST . SP PASSING 4
GOD ADDRESSED ME A LETTER. . . . . SP PERSONAL 3
LORD GOD, ... SP PRAYER 8
GOD BLESS HER, DEAD AND GONE! . . . SP REVERIE HARLEM 6
GREAT GOD! . . . . SP SLIVER SERMON 2
GREAT GOD! . . . . SP SLIVER SERMON 4
OH, GOD! . . . . SP SLIVER SERMON 5
MY GOD! . . . . SP SLIVER SERMON 6
GOD! . . . . SP SLIVER SERMON 8
TO THE GLORY OF GOD! . . . . SP TAMBOURINES 4
BUT GOD IS LONG! . . . . SP TAMBOURINES 10
BUT GOD PUT A SONG AND A PRAYER IN
MY MOUTH. . . . . SP THE NEGRO MOTHE 18
GOD PUT A DREAM LIKE STEEL IN MY
SOUL. . . . . SP THE NEGRO MOTHE 19
AS THOUGH I WERE GOD. . . . . SP TO ARTINA 3
I WILL BE GOD WHEN IT COMES TO YOU. SP TO ARTINA 11
GOD WILLING DROP A SHILLING . . . . AYM ASK YOUR MAMA 44
KINGSTON TOO GOD WILLING . . . . . AYM ASK YOUR MAMA 48
AND THE WHITE GOD NEVER GOES . . . AYM BLUES IN STEREO 10
THE LORD GOD HIMSELF . . . . PL BOMBINGS DIXIE 5
GOD IS HIS FATHER: . . . . PL CHRIST IN ALA. 7
SEND (GOD FORBID - HE'S NOT DEAD
LONG ENOUGH!) . . . . PL FINAL CALL 17
AM I SUPPOSED TO BE GOD. . . . . . PL GO SLOW 11
WHY GOD DON'T PROTECT A MAN . . . . PL WHO BUT TH LORD 17

GODDAMN 1
YOU WON'T GET A GODDAMN THING! . . SP SAME IN BLUES 11

GODDESS 1
THAT JUSTICE IS A BLIND GODDESS . . PL JUSTICE 1

GODS 4
THE GODS ARE LAUGHING AT US. . . . WB LENOX AVE MIDNT 4
AND THE GODS ARE LAUGHING AT US. . WB LENOX AVE MIDNT 14
WHEREIN THE FALSE GODS DWELL . . . ANS UNION 8
SO MANY GODS DON'T KNOW. . . . . . SP JOE LOUIS 7

GOD-A-MIGHTY 1
THANK GOD-A-MIGHTY! HERE'S THE . . SP FREEDOM TRAIN 67

GOD'S 4
LIKE GOD'S HAND. . . . . DK SEA CHARM 6
LIKE GOD'S BREATH. . . . . DK SEA CHARM 9
RIGHT HERE BENEATH GOD'S SKY. . . . SP NEW YORKERS 3
PERHAPS IF IT BE GOD'S WILL . . . . AYM ASK YOUR MAMA 64

GOES 10
THEN THEY GOES AN' FINDS A YALLER
GAL . . . . FC BLACK GAL 7
THEN OUT MA DOOR HE GOES. . . . . . FC BLACK GAL 12
TO ALL THE WORLD THERE GOES . . . . DK ALABAMA EARTH 7
WHEN HE GOES A-WALKIN' . . . . . . DK MA LORD 3
YOU WILL NOT STAY WHEN SUMMER GOES. DK PASSING LOVE 6
JUST SO IT GOES AWAY FROM HERE. . . SH SIX-BITS BLUES 6
YOU GOES TO HELL? . . . . SP MADAM NUMBER WR 32
YEAR BY YEAR GOES BY . . . . SP SHARE-CROPPERS 11
TILL THE SUN GOES DOWN. . . . . . . SP SUNDAY BY COMB 2
AND THE WHITE GOD NEVER GOES . . . AYM BLUES IN STEREO 16

GOING 15
SUN'S GOING DOWN THIS EVENING - . . DK SONG BANJO DANC 12
THE SUN'S GOING DOWN THIS VERY NIGHT
- . . . . DK SONG BANJO DANC 14
THE SUN'S GOING DOWN THIS VERY NIGHT
- . . . . DK SONG BANJO DANC 25
GOING DOWN THAT ROAD. . . . . SH BLD THE SINNER 17
CAUSE I'M GOING BACK TO ROOMING AND
BE A FREE MAN. . . . . SH PAY DAY 16
I'M GOING TO THE REGAL. . . . . . . OWT JITNEY 24
I'M GOING SHOPPING NOW, CHILD. . . OWT JITNEY 58
NO USE IN MY GOING . . . . SP BLUE MONDAY 1
GOING BY . . . . SP DEAD IN THERE 3
I'M GOING DOWN THE STREET. . . . . SP MAMA AND DAUGHT 2
WHERE'RE YOU GOING, DAUGHTER? . . . SP MAMA AND DAUGHT 3
I'M GOING . . . . SP REQUEST 3
WITH FLUID FAR-OFF GOING . . . . . PL CULTURAL EXCHNG 9
NO TRAINS OR STEAMBOATS GOING - . . PL CULTURAL EXCHNG 12
GOING SLOW, SLOW, SLOW. . . . . . . PL GO SLOW 17

GOIN' 20
I'M GOIN' TO DE DEVIL AN' . . . . . FC BAD MAN 17
AN' SHE'S GOIN' ON BACK . . . . . . FC EVIL WOMAN 14
AND IF I DON'T GET YOU GOIN', . . . NM BIG-TIMER POEM 31
I DON'T CARE WHERE IT'S GOIN' . . . SH SIX-BITS BLUES 5
GOIN' DOWN THE ROAD, LAWD, ... SP BOUND NO'TH BLS 1
GOIN' DOWN THE ROAD. . . . . SP BOUND NO'TH BLS 2
GOIN' UP AN' DOWN. . . . . SP ELEVATOR BOY 16
I'M GOIN' DOWN TO THE RIVER . . . . SP LAMENT OVER LOV 7
AN' I AIN'T GOIN' THERE TO SWIM; . SP LAMENT OVER LOV 8
AIN'T GOIN' THERE TO SWIM. . . . . SP LAMENT OVER LOV 10
AND I'M GOIN' THERE TO THINK ABOUT
HIM. . . . . SP LAMENT OVER LOV 12
I'M GOIN' UP IN A TOWER . . . . . . SP LAMENT OVER LOV 19
AIN'T GOIN' WITH YOU TODAY! . . . . SP MADAM WRONG VIS 20
DON'T KNOW'S I'D MIND HIS GOIN' . . SP MIDWINTER BLUES 7
DON'T KNOW'S I'D MIND HIS GOIN' . . SP MIDWINTER BLUES 9
AND SOMETIMES GOIN' IN THE DARK . . SP MOTHER TO SON 12
FOR I'SE STILL GOIN', HONEY, . . . SP MOTHER TO SON 18
WHERE WE WAS GOIN' . . . . SP WEST TEXAS 13
I'M GOIN' TO THE PO' HOUSE . . . . SP YOUNG GAL'S BLS 7
GOIN' TO THE PO' HOUSE . . . . . . SP YOUNG GAL'S BLS 9

GOLD 24
LIFTS HIGH A DRESS OF SILKEN GOLD. WB JAZZONIA 6
IN A GOWN OF GOLD? . . . . WB JAZZONIA 13
OF ROSE AND GOLD. . . . . WB OUR LAND 6
ARE DRESSED IN SCARLET AND GOLD . . WB POEME D'AUTOMNE 5
GO WHERE GOLD . . . . WB TO DARK MERCEDE 4
PAWN YO' GOLD WATCH . . . . FC SATURDAY NIGHT 9
SUNSHINE SEEMED LIKE GOLD. . . . . DK PO' BOY BLUES 2
SUNSHINE SEEMED LIKE GOLD. . . . . DK PO' BOY BLUES 4
EATING BLOOD AND GOLD. . . . . . . ANS KIDS WHO DIE 6
OF GRAB THE GOLD! OF GRAB THE WAYS
OF SATISFYING NEED! . . . . . . ANS LET AMERICA BE 28
THE TORN SUIT OF SATIN AND GOLD, . ANS SONG OF SPAIN 15
WITH ITS WINGS OF GOLD FOR WHICH I
PAY - . . . . ANS SONG OF SPAIN 42
WORKERS, MINE NO GOLD AGAIN! . . . ANS SONG OF SPAIN 55
THIS GOLD WATCH AND CHAIN . . . . . SH BLD PAWNBROKER 1
OTHER PEOPLE'S GOLD. . . . . SH BLD THE KILLER 18
A ROW OF GOLD IN HIS UPPER MOUTH. SH DEATH IN HARLEM 18
AND MY GOLD FISH ET THE GLASS. . . SP CHILDREN'S RYME 19
GOLD AND BROWN . . . . SP COLLEGE FORMAL 15
SILKEN BATHROBES WITH GOLD TWINES SP FLATTED FIFTHS 9
GOLD AND BROWN - . . . . SP ISLAND 6
AND HORSES SHOD WITH GOLD . . . . . AYM BLUES IN STEREO 4
IF I HAD A HEART OF GOLD, ... PL VARI-COLORED 1
I'D UP AND SELL MY HEART OF GOLD . PL VARI-COLORED 3
BUT I DON'T HAVE A HEART OF GOLD. PL VARI-COLORED 5

GOLDEN 10
GOLDEN GIRL . . . . SP COLLEGE FORMAL 1
IN A GOLDEN GOWN . . . . SP COLLEGE FORMAL 2
OF GOLDEN DEW. . . . . SP HARLEM NIGHT SO 10
GOLDEN HANDS IN WHITE COAT. . . . . SP INTERNE AT PROV 20
ON THEM GOLDEN STREETS . . . . . . SP MADAM NUMBER WR 26
BOSOM TURN ALL GOLDEN IN THE SUNSET. SP NEGRO SPEAKS OF 10
AND GOLDEN LIKE THE SUNSHINE . . . SP RUBY BROWN 2
MELLOWS TO A GOLDEN NOTE. . . . . . SP TRUMPET PLAYER 44
GOLDEN CROSSES TO A CADILLAC $ $ $
$ $ $ . . . . AYM HORN OF PLENTY 14
TO IMPLEMENT THE GOLDEN RULE. . . . PL BIRMINGHAM SUND 22

GONE 35
CHILE, HE'S GONE AWAY. . . . . . . WB BLUES FANTASY 8
BABE, HE'S GONE AWAY. . . . . WB BLUES FANTASY 10
HAS GONE THE QUIET WAY . . . . . . WB TO LITTLE LOVER 4
AFTER DE BOAT'S DONE GONE. . . . . FC A RUINED GAL 2
CAUSE I IS LONG GONE WRONG. . . . . FC A RUINED GAL 5
I'VE GONE BACK TO THE WIND AND WAVE. DK DEATH SEAMAN 8
FOR THE DEAD WHO'D GONE AWAY, . . . DK IRISH WAKE 2
HOW DID I KNOW WHERE YOU DONE GONE
AT? . . . . SH LETTER 5
IT'S DARK ON THIS STOOP, LAWD! THE
SUN'S GONE DOWN! . . . . SH TWILIGHT REVERI 15
GONE ASTRAY - . . . . JC TO CAPTAIN MULZ 9
AND CHAINS BE GONE! . . . . FW DUSK 13
GONE AND DONE ME WRONG . . . . . . OWT LINCOLN THEATRE 12
WHEN THE WINE'S GONE TO YOUR HEAD OWT RAID 2
TODAY YOU GONE AWAY. . . . . OWT YESTERDAY TODAY 4
WHEN I AM DEAD AND GONE? . . . . . LHR TESTAMENT 2
GONE AWAY. . . . . SP DEAD IN THERE 15
SOLID GONE! . . . . SP GONE BOY 2
WHEN HE SHOULD BE GONE . . . . . . SP GONE BOY 6
HE AIN'T GONE. . . . . SP GONE BOY 9
ALL HER CLOTHES WAS GONE: . . . . . SP HOMECOMING 3
WASN'T NOBODY GONE. . . . . SP LATE LAST NIGHT 3
I WAS IN MY GRAVE AND GONE. . . . . SP LITTLE OLD LETT 8
BUT YOU HAVE GONE SO FAR! . . . . . SP MISS BLUES'ES 10
YOU'VE TAKEN MY BLUES AND GONE - . SP NOTE COMM THEAT 1
YEP, YOU DONE TAKEN MY BLUES AND
GONE. . . . . SP NOTE COMM THEAT 7
YOU ALSO TOOK MY SPIRITUALS AND
GONE. . . . . SP NOTE COMM THEAT 8
GONE UP NORTH. . . . . SP ONE-WAY TICKET 26
GONE OUT WEST. . . . . SP ONE-WAY TICKET 27
GONE! . . . . SP ONE-WAY TICKET 28
GOD BLESS HER, DEAD AND GONE! . . . SP REVERIE HARLEM 6
AND IT'S IN THE WAY YOU'RE GONE . . SP SO LONG 3
YOU'RE GONE SO LONG . . . . SP SO LONG 9
WHEN LOVE IS GONE WHAT . . . . . . SP YOUNG GAL'S BLS 19
WHEN LOVE IS GONE, O, ... SP YOUNG GAL'S BLS 21
SAYS SUGAR'S GONE UP ANOTHER TWO
CENTS, ... PL HARLEM 9

GONNA 73
SUN'S GONNA SHINE . . . . WB BLUES FANTASY 17
I'M GONNA FILL 'EM UP FULL O' . . . FC DEATH DO DIRTY 33

Line	Poem	No.
I AIN'T GONNA MISTREAT MA	FC EVIL WOMAN	1
I'M JUST GONNA KILL HER	FC EVIL WOMAN	3
MEANS HE'S GONNA LEAVE THIS WORLD.	FC GAL'S CRY DYING	8
MEANS HE'S GONNA LEAVE THIS WORLD.	FC GAL'S CRY DYING	10
I'M GONNA BE A GYPSY WOMAN	FC GYPSY MAN	5
GONNA PRAY TO MA JESUS.	FC MOAN	7
I'M GONNA KILL MA SELF.	FC SUICIDE	5
I'M GONNA BUY ME A KNIFE WITH . . .	FC SUICIDE	7
GONNA BUY A KNIFE WITH	FC SUICIDE	9
LAWD, FOLKSES, HOW MUCH LONGER IS THIS GONNA LAST?	NM BROKE	59
THIS IS WHAT I'M GONNA SING. . . .	DK NIGHT AND MORN	2
THIS IS WHAT I'M GONNA SING: . . .	DK NIGHT AND MORN	4
THIS IS GONNA BE MA SONG.	DK NIGHT AND MORN	8
THIS IS GONNA BE MA SONG:	DK NIGHT AND MORN	10
I'M GONNA DIE!	SH BLD THE KILLER	27
BIG BEN, I'M GONNA BUST YOU BANG UP SIDE THE WALL!	SH DAYBREAK	1
GONNA HIT YOU IN THE FACE AND LET YOU FALL!	SH DAYBREAK	2
GONNA SLEEP LIKE A WATER-LOG. . . .	SH MISSISSIPPI LEV	6
WOMAN'S GONNA MISTREAT ME.	SH ONLY WOMAN BLUS	18
WOMAN'S GONNA MISTREAT ME.	SH ONLY WOMAN BLUS	24
I'M GONNA GET IT CASHED.	SH PAY DAY	5
AIN'T GONNA PAY A CENT ON THAT RADIO	SH PAY DAY	7
I'M GONNA TELL THE FURNITURE MAN TO COME	SH PAY DAY	11
I'M GONNA RENT ME A CUBBY-HOLE WITH A SINGLE BED.	SH PAY DAY	17
AIN'T EVEN GONNA DREAM 'BOUT THE WOMENS I HAD.	SH PAY DAY	18
I'M GONNA GET UP A POKER GAME AND INVITE THE BOYS.	SH SUNDAY	12
KEEP FEELING LIKE THIS I'M GONNA START ACTING BAD.	SH TWILIGHT REVERI	4
GONNA GO GET MY PISTOL, I SAID FORTY-FOUR -	SH TWILIGHT REVERI	5
GONNA GO GET MY PISTOL, I MEAN THIRTY-TWO.	SH TWILIGHT REVERI	7
AIN'T YOU GONNA STAND BY ME? . . .	JC BIG BUDDY	2
AIN'T YOU GONNA STAND BY ME? . . .	JC BIG BUDDY	4
AIN'T YOU GONNA STAND BY ME? . . .	JC BIG BUDDY	9
I'M GONNA SPLIT THIS ROCK	JC BIG BUDDY	14
JOE LOUIS SAID, WE GONNA WIN THIS WAR	JC JIM CROW'S LAST	25
WE GONNA BURY THAT SON-OF-A-GUN! .	JC JIM CROW'S LAST	32
I AIN'T GONNA	OWT BOARDING HOUSE	11
WHAT? YOU GONNA GET EVICTION ORDERS?	SP BLD LANDLORD	13
YOU GONNA CUT OFF MY HEAT?	SP BLD LANDLORD	14
YOU GONNA TAKE MY FURNITURE AND . .	SP BLD LANDLORD	15
YOU AIN'T GONNA BE ABLE TO SAY A WORD	SP BLD LANDLORD	19
GONNA SHUT AN' LOCK MY DOOR	SP CORA	4
I WONDER WHERE I'M GONNA DIE. . . .	SP CROSS	11
I'M GONNA BUY TWO NEW SUITS	SP DEFERRED	30
YOU AIN'T GONNA HAVE NOTHIN TO SAY.	SP EARLY EVENING	12
BUT I'M GONNA KEEP ON AT IT	SP EVIL	3
FIRE GONNA BURN MA SOUL!	SP FIRE	3
FIRE GONNA BURN MA SOUL!	SP FIRE	9
FIRE GONNA BURN MA SOUL!	SP FIRE	16
FIRE GONNA BURN MA SOUL!	SP FIRE	23
FIRE GONNA BURN MA SOUL!	SP FIRE	25
I'M GONNA CHECK UP ON THIS	SP FREEDOM TRAIN	15
NEVER GONNA BOTHER ME.	SP HARD DADDY	12
GONNA THINK ABOUT MY MAN -	SP LAMENT OVER LOV	23
IF YOU GONNA SEE ME DIE.	SP LIFE IS FINE	30
YOU SAID YOU WAS GONNA TAKE ME . .	SP LOW TO HIGH	3
HE SAID, I'M GONNA PUT IT	SP MADAM CENSUS	13
YOU AIN'T GONNA FIND IT	SP MADAM FORT TELL	19
AIN'T GONNA PLAY NO MORE	SP MADAM NUMBER WR	22
I'M GONNA PRAY	SP MADAM MINISTER	25
BUT I SURE AIN'T GONNA PAY!	SP MADAM PHONE BIL	40
I'M GONNA BUY ME A ROSE BUD	SP MIDWINTER BLUES	19
GONNA SALT EVERY DIME AWAY	SP NUMBERS	2
I AIN'T GONNA	SP NUMBERS	4
GONNA RIDE IN MY CHARIOT SOME DAY!	SP SPIRITUALS	8
MONDAY MORNING'S GONNA BE?	SP SUNDAY BY COMB	5
"SYLVESTER'S GONNA DIE!"	SP SYLVESTER'S BED	6
I'M GONNA WALK TO THE GRAVEYARD . .	SP YOUNG GAL'S BLS	1
GONNA WALK TO THE GRAVEYARD	SP YOUNG GAL'S BLS	3
GONNA LOVE YOU ANYHOW	AYM ODE TO DINAH	67
I'M GONNA LEAVE YOU, MISTER BACKLASH.	PL BACKLASH BLUES	29
I'M GONNA WRITE ME SOME MUSIC ABOUT	PL DAYBREAK IN ALA	2
AND I'M GONNA PUT THE PURTIEST SONGS IN IT	PL DAYBREAK IN ALA	4
I'M GONNA PUT SOME TALL TALL TREES IN IT	PL DAYBREAK IN ALA	7
AND I'M GONNA PUT WHITE HANDS . . .	PL DAYBREAK IN ALA	15
I'M GONNA PLANT MY FEET	PL DOWN WHERE I AM	13
WHAT WE'RE GONNA DO	PL HARLEM	21

GOOD 81

Line	Poem	No.
MY GOOD MAN'S LEFT ME.	WB BLUES FANTASY	9
OH, I AM GOOD.	WB PIERROT	21
YES, I AM GOOD.	WB PIERROT	24
THOU ART NOT GOOD	WB POEM	10
WOULDN'T NO GOOD FELLOW	WB TO MIDNIGHT NAN	3
WOULDN'T NO GOOD FELLOW	WB TO MIDNIGHT NAN	19
DON'T EVEN WANT TO BE GOOD.	FC BAD MAN	14
DON'T EVEN WANT TO BE GOOD.	FC BAD MAN	16
GOOD FRIEND O' MINE.	FC DEATH DO DIRTY	15
GOOD GAL ANY MORE.	FC EVIL WOMAN	2
NOBODY THERE WAS GOOD TO ME. . . .	FC GYPSY MAN	12
I USED TO BE A GOOD CHILE.	FC LISTEN HERE	7
USED TO BE A GOOD CHILE. -	FC LISTEN HERE	9
GOOD GIRLS, GOOD GIRLS, ...	FC LISTEN HERE	13
GOOD GIRLS, GOOD GIRLS.	FC LISTEN HERE	13
OH, YOU GOOD GIRLS, ...	FC LISTEN HERE	15
HE PLAYS GOOD WHEN HE'S SOBER . . .	FC MA MAN	11
MA SWEET GOOD MAN HAS	FC SUICIDE	1
MA SWEET GOOD MAN HAS	FC SUICIDE	3
I DOES HER GOOD	FC WORKIN' MAN	9
CAUSE I TRIES TO BE GOOD	FC WORKIN' MAN	15
YOU GOT A GOOD JOB? YES! WELL, I SHO AM GLAD TO SEE YOU, DEAR! . . .	NM BROKE	69
AND I HOPE YOU'RE MAKING GOOD, AND DOING FINE -	NM COLORED SL POEM	17
AND IT'S A GOOD THING ALL THE BLACK BOYS LYING DEAD	NM COLORED SL POEM	51
I WAS A GOOD BOY, ...	DK PO' BOY BLUES	7
YES, I WAS A GOOD BOY, ...	DK PO' BOY BLUES	9
I AIN'T A GOOD SWIMMER	DK WIDE RIVER	5
IF THIS RADIO WAS GOOD I'D GET KDQ	SH BED TIME	1
I CAN SLEEP SO GOOD WITH YOU AWAY!	SH BED TIME	11
IT'S GOOD LIKE THAT WHEN YOU . . .	SH DEATH IN HARLEM	29
BUT IF YOU GIMME GOOD CORN WHISKY	SH HEY-HEY BLUES	5
BUT GIMME GOOD CORN WHISKY	SH HEY-HEY BLUES	23
I HAVE A GOOD TIME!	SH IF-ING	16
AND DE LEVEE DON'T DO NO GOOD. . .	SH MISSISSIPPI LEV	8
WHEN DE LEVEE DON'T DO NO GOOD. . .	SH MISSISSIPPI LEV	10
IN THE COMMUNITY IS GOOD	SH SNOB	2
BECAUSE A GOOD REPUTATION	SH SNOB	5
TURN ON THE LIGHT AND LOOK REAL GOOD!	SH SUPPER TIME	3
CAUSE THE GOOD LORD KNOWS WHAT WE'RE FIGHTING FOR!	JC JIM CROW'S LAST	26
THAT IS GOOD.	FW CAROLINA CABIN	11
IT FELT GOOD TO SHOUT!	FW COMMUNION	8
BUT THE GOOD LORD KNOWS	OWT HONEY BABE	3
IF YOU WANT A GOOD CHICKEN	OWT JITNEY	55
JOSTLE OF MEN WITH GOOD JOBS . . .	OWT MAN INTO MEN	6
GOOD JOBS	OWT MAN INTO MEN	13
CAUSE THERE AIN'T A GOOD MAN . . .	OWT REQUEST REQUIEM	7
THAT WE HAVE GOOD REASON	LHR POET TO BIGOT	5
THERE AIN'T NO GOOD LEFT	SP BAD LUCK CARD	5
DAVE MEANT HER NO GOOD.	SP BLD FORTUNE TEL	18
WILL TAKE GOOD MONEY FROM YOU. . .	SP BLD THE GYPSY	19
GOOD EVENING, DADDY!	SP BOOGIE 1 A.M.	1
I'D LIKE TO MEET A GOOD FRIEND . .	SP BOUND NO'TH BLS	11
HE WAS NO GOOD AT MAKING LOVE . . .	SP DANCER	7
AND NO GOOD AT MAKING MONEY. . . .	SP DANCER	8
BUT BEING NO GOOD AT LOVIN' - . . .	SP DANCER	18
(WHEN YOU'RE NO GOOD FOR DOUGH THEY GO.)	SP DANCER	20
GOOD MORNING, DADDY!	SP DREAM BOOGIE	1
MAKES A GOOD WOMAN CRY.	SP EARLY EVENING	6
AIN'T NO SENSE IN A GOOD WOMAN . .	SP EARLY EVENING	15
NEITHER DOES I TREAT YOU GOOD. . .	SP EARLY EVENING	18
JOB AIN'T NO GOOD THOUGH.	SP ELEVATOR BOY	4
MAYBE A GOOD JOB SOMETIMES:	SP ELEVATOR BOY	10
I AIN'T BEEN GOOD, ...	SP FIRE	4
NO MAN IS GOOD ENOUGH	SP FREEDOM'S PLOW	102
NO MAN IS GOOD ENOUGH	SP FREEDOM'S PLOW	169
GOOD MORNING, DADDY!	SP GOOD MORNING	1
GOOD MORNING, DADDY!	SP ISLAND	11
MADAM, IT'S JUST GOOD LUCK	SP MADAM FORT TELL	3
WAS TOO GOOD FOR ME.	SP MADAM MIGHT-HAV	4
WHAT'S TOO GOOD TO BE TRUE.	SP MADAM MIGHT-HAV	7
I SAID, IT FELT GOOD -	SP MADAM MINISTER	19
HE SAID, YOUR NAME LOOKS GOOD . . .	SP MADAM'S CALLING	11
MY GOOD MAN TURNED ME DOWN.	SP MIDWINTER BLUES	6
A GOOD WOMAN'S CRYIN'	SP MISERY	11
HE'S A GOOD MAN.	SP NEIGHBOR	14
THE GOOD CHURCH FOLK DO NOT MENTION	SP RUBY BROWN	21
IT IS NOT GOOD	SP SEA CALM	4
BE GOOD!	SP SILHOUETTE	12
BE GOOD!	SP SILHOUETTE	13
ANEW - AND GOOD.	SP S-SSS-SS-SH!	4
DID NOT THINK IT GOOD!	SP S-SSS-SS-SH!	7

GOODBYE 1

Line	Poem	No.
GOODBYE!	SP MADAM MINISTER	27

GOODMORNING 8

Line	Poem	No.
GOODMORNING, STALINGRAD!	JC GOOD MORN STLIN	1
GOODMORNING, STALINGRAD!	JC GOOD MORN STLIN	5
GOODMORNING, STALINGRAD!	JC GOOD MORN STLIN	10
GOODMORNING, STALINGRAD!	JC GOOD MORN STLIN	16
GOODMORNING, STALINGRAD!	JC GOOD MORN STLIN	22
GOODMORNING, STALINGRAD!	JC GOOD MORN STLIN	28
GOODMORNING, STALINGRAD!	JC GOOD MORN STLIN	57
GOODMORNING, STALINGRAD!	JC GOOD MORN STLIN	60

GOODNESS 1

Line	Poem	No.
SURPASSING GOODNESS.	WB POEM	13

MY GOODNESS, CENTRAL, ... SP MADAM PHONE BIL 4
THOUGH THE GOODNESS . . . . SF NO REGRETS 3

GOOD-TIME 2
MY GOOD-TIME DAYS DONE PAST. . . . SP LITTLE GRN TREE 2
FOR A SUIT OF GOOD-TIME WEARING? . AYM SHOW FARE PLESE 23

GOOD-TIMER 1
I'M JUST A GOOD-TIMER . . . . NM BIG-TIMER POEM 43

GOOD-WILL 1
OF COURAGE, OF GOOD-WILL, ... JC TO CAPTAIN MULZ 50

GOOSE 1
GOOSE LAID: . . . . PL ELDERLY LEADERS 10

GORGEOUS 2
WAS CLEOPATRA GORGEOUS . . . . . . WB JAZZONIA 12
OF GORGEOUS SUN. . . . . WB OUR LAND 2

GOSPEL 5
AND GRANDMA CANNOT GET HER GOSPEL HYMNS . . . . SP PASSING 3
STOPS TO LISTEN TO GOSPEL SONGS . . SP SUMMER EVENING 11
A GOSPEL SHOUT . . . . SP TAMBOURINES 7
AND A GOSPEL SONG: . . . . SP TAMBOURINES 8
GOSPEL SINGERS WHO PANT TO PACK $ $ $ $ . . . . AYM HORN OF PLENTY 17

GOSSIPS 1
BUT THE GOSSIPS HAD NO . . . . . . SP JOE LOUIS 9

GOT 148
I GOT A RAILROAD TICKET, ... WB BLUES FANTASY 20
GOT A RAILROAD TICKET, ... WB BLUES FANTASY 23
CAUSE I AIN'T GOT NO FRIEND. . . . FC A RUINED GAL 10
AN' SOON AS HE GOT OUT DE BARREL . FC BLACK GAL 11
I GOT MA TAIL CURLED! . . . . FC CRAP GAME 2
WHEN YOU AIN'T GOT A DIME. . . . . FC DEATH DO DIRTY 4
AN' WHEN DE COPS GOT ME . . . . . . FC DEATH DO DIRTY 16
THAT NIGHT HE GOT KILT . . . . . . FC DEATH DO DIRTY 21
BUT WHEN I GOT THERE . . . . FC DEATH DO DIRTY 26
HE AIN'T GOT A CHANCE. . . . . . . FC DEATH DO DIRTY 29
GOT SUCH LOW-DOWN WAYS. . . . . . . FC EVIL WOMAN 10
AIN'T EVEN GOT A STALL. . . . . . . FC HARD LUCK 18
YOU'VE GOT SEVEN LANGUAGES TO SPEAK IN . . . . FC JAZZ BAND 19
HE'S GOT THOSE 'LECTRIC-SHOCKIN' EYES AN' . . . . FC MA MAN 5
NO OTHER GAL'S GOT A CHANCE. . . . FC MINNIE SINGS 10
I GOT A HIGH-YALLER; . . . . NM BIG-TIMER POEM 21
GOT A DIAMOND RING. . . . . NM BIG-TIMER POEM 22
I GOT A FURNISHED-UP FLAT. . . . . NM BIG-TIMER POEM 23
I GOT A BIG CAR . . . . NM BIG-TIMER POEM 25
BUT I AINT GOT NOTHIN' REAL . . . . NM BIG-TIMER POEM 47
WE ONLY GOT ONE LIFE . . . . NM BIG-TIMER POEM 71
LANDLADY 'LOWED TO ME LAST WEEK, "SAM, AIN'T YOU GOT NO MONEY?" . NM BROKE 19
I SAY, "NOW, BABY, YOU KNOW I AIN'T GOT NONE, HONEY." . . . . NM BROKE 20
SO WHEN I GOT READY TO GO, I SAID, "I'LL BE SEEIN' YOU SOON, MARIE." NM BROKE 52
AND SHE COME TELLIN' ME, SHE AIN'T GOT NO MO' EVENINGS FREE! . . . NM BROKE 53
IT'S DONE GOT ME SO CRAZY, FEEL LIKE I BEEN TAKIN' COKE. . . . . . NM BROKE 60
YOU GOT A GOOD JOB? YES! WELL, I SHO AM GLAD TO SEE YOU, DEAR! . . . NM BROKE 69
AND SAID TO ME, "BROTHER, YOU'VE GOT YOUR CHANCE. . . . . NM COLORED SL POEM 16
BUT NOW I KNOW WE'VE GOT PLENTY TO DO. . . . . NM COLORED SL POEM 23
WHEN WE GOT THROUGH FIGHTING, OVER THERE, AND DYING? . . . . NM COLORED SL POEM 34
I GOT NEW SHOES - . . . . DK DRESSED UP 9
BUT I AIN'T GOT NOBODY . . . . . . DK DRESSED UP 11
THE MOURNERS GOT UP SMILING. . . . DK IRISH WAKE 7
GOT TWO MO' WAYS. . . . . DK NEGRO DANCERS 2
GOT TWO MO' WAYS. . . . . DK NEGRO DANCERS 14
AN' I AIN'T GOT NO BOAT. . . . . . DK WIDE RIVER 2
I AIN'T GOT NO BOAT. . . . . DK WIDE RIVER 4
GOT TO CROSS THAT RIVER . . . . . . DK WIDE RIVER 17
I AM THE MAN WHO NEVER GOT AHEAD, ANS LET AMERICA BE 37
YOU GOT A BUTLER AND MAID. . . . ANS PARK BENCH 6
BUT SINCE I GOT TO GET UP AT DAY, SH BED TIME 9
BUT A MAN'S GOT TO LIVE. . . . . . SH BLD PAWNBROKER 19
YOU MUST THINK YOU GOT TO WAKE UP A CROWD! . . . . SH DAYBREAK 4
YOU AIN'T GOT TO WAKE UP NO BODY BUT ME. . . . . SH DAYBREAK 5
I'M THE ONLY ONE'S GOT TO PILE OUT IN THE COLD. . . . . SH DAYBREAK 6
THE MUSIC GOT THROUGH. . . . . . . SH DEATH IN HARLEM 90
I GOT EVENIN' AIR TO SPARE. . . . . SH EVENIN' BLUES 12
BUT I AIN'T GOT A MILLION. . . . . SH IF-ING 13
FACT IS, AIN'T GOT A DIME - . . . . SH IF-ING 14
DEAR CASSIE: YES, I GOT YOUR LETTER. SH LETTER 1
ADDED TO DE TROUBLE THAT I GOT. . . SH LOVE AGAIN BLUS 6
WHEN I GOT YOU I . . . . SH LOVE AGAIN BLUS 7
WHEN I GOT YOU . . . . SH LOVE AGAIN BLUS 9
BUT YOU GOT TO LOVE AGAIN. . . . . SH LOVE AGAIN BLUS 18
HOW HIGH HAVE YOU GOT TO BE? . . . SH MISSISSIPPI LEV 14
HOW HIGH HAVE YOU GOT TO BE . . . . SH MISSISSIPPI LEV 16
I GOT HER IN MISSISSIPPI. . . . . . SH ONLY WOMAN BLUS 19
YOU GOT TO LIVE HERE A YEAR AND A DAY. . . . . SH OUT OF WORK 12
I GOT TO ROLL ALONG! . . . . SH SIX-BITS BLUES 13
LAWD! I GOT TO FIND ME A WOMAN FOR THE WPA - . . . . SH SUPPER TIME 13
ABOUT TWO KINDS O' PISTOLS THAT I AIN'T GOT. . . . . SH TWILIGHT REVERI 10
BUT I AIN'T GOT NO OWL HEAD AND YOU DONE LEFT TOWN . . . . SH TWILIGHT REVERI 13
IF I GOT TO FIGHT, ... JC BIG BUDDY 5
GOT WINGS IN THE MUD, ... JC RED CROSS 2
HE GOT SHOT IN THE BACK . . . . . OWT BLD MARGE POLIT 10
I GOT A CHINESE BOY-FRIEND . . . . OWT JITNEY 11
MARTHA'S GOT A JAPANESE! . . . . . OWT JITNEY 17
THEY'VE GOT COVENANTS . . . . . . OWT RESTRICTIVE 10
I GOT THOSE SAD OLD WEARY BLUES. . OWT TOO BLUE 1
BUT I AIN'T GOT . . . . OWT TOO BLUE 14
THAN SHE'S GOT BREATH. . . . . . . LHR TESTAMENT 12
HE KNOWS THAT AUNT SUE NEVER GOT HER STORIES . . . . SP AUNTSUE'S STORI 19
A POOR MAN AIN'T GOT . . . . SP BLD OF THE MAN 27
GOT TO FIND SOMEBODY . . . . SP BOUND NO'TH BLS 5
AIN'T GOT NO HEART NO MORE. . . . SP CORA 2
THEN GOT PUT BACK WHEN WE COME NORTH. . . . . SP DEFERRED 5
NOW AT LAST I'VE GOT A JOB . . . . SP DEFERRED 25
CHILE, GRANNY AIN'T GOT NO DIME. . SP DIME 6
I AIN'T GOT NO SUGAR, HATTIE, . . . SP EARLY EVENING 7
AIN'T GOT NO SUGAR, I . . . . SP EARLY EVENING 9
I GOT A JOB NOW . . . . SP ELEVATOR BOY 1
GOT TO MOAN AN' GRIEVE? . . . . . . SP FIRE 13
GOT A JIM CROW CAR SET ASIDE FOR ME. SP FREEDOM TRAIN 10
EVERYBODY'S GOT A RIGHT TO BOARD THE FREEDOM TRAIN? . . . . SP FREEDOM TRAIN 22
THEY EVEN GOT A SEGREGATED LANE. . SP FREEDOM TRAIN 27
I GOT TO KNOW ABOUT THIS . . . . . SP FREEDOM TRAIN 29
A NEGRO'S GOT NO BUSINESS ON THE FREEDOM TRACK! . . . . SP FREEDOM TRAIN 40
AT HOME THEY GOT A TRAIN THAT'S YOURS AND MINE! . . . . SP FREEDOM TRAIN 62
WE GOT UP . . . . SP FULFILMENT 4
SAYS DADDY I HAVE GOT THE BLUES. . SP HARD DADDY 2
SAYS DADDY I HAVE GOT THE BLUES. . SP HARD DADDY 4
SHE AIN'T GOT BOOGIE-WOOGIE . . . . SP LADY'S BOOGIE 3
YOU GOT TO LOVE ALL THE TIME. . . . SP LAMENT OVER LOV 18
NOW YOU'VE GOT YOUR CADILLAC, . . . SP LOW TO HIGH 5
SHE GREW UP AND GOT RUINT. . . . . SP MADAM CHARITY CH 3
HE SAID, HAVE YOU GOT . . . . SP MADAM MINISTER 3
WHEN I GOT THROUGH. . . . . SP MADAM HER MADAM 9
YOU GOT SOME'N ELSE . . . . SP MADAM MIGHT-HAV 22
WHEN YOU THINK YOU GOT BREAD . . . SP MADAM MIGHT-HAV 25
YOU'VE GOT NO TRUST. . . . . SP MADAM MIGHT-HAV 30
TILL I GOT MIXED UP . . . . SP MADAM'S PAST HI 12
HE'S GOT A GRIN ON HIS FACE. . . . SP ME AND THE MULE 2
YOU GOT TO TAKE ME . . . . SP ME AND THE MULE 7
I GOT BACK HOME . . . . SP MIDNIGHT RAFFLE 7
KNOWING WHAT I GOT. . . . . SP MIDNIGHT RAFFLE 12
'S GOT TO HEAR A BLUES . . . . . . SP MISERY 15
NOW WHAT'VE I GOT? . . . . SP NEW YORKERS 13
YET THEY GOT A SATIN BOX . . . . . SP NIGHT FUNERAL 7
AND HE GOT THE MIDNIGHT TRAIN . . . SP NOT A MOVIE 5
AND WONDER WHAT YOU GOT LEFT? . . . SP REVERIE HARLEM 4
I GOT TO GO! . . . . SP SAME IN BLUES 4
THAT LITTLE NEGRO'S MARRIED AND GOT A KID. . . . . SP SISTER 1
JUST AIN'T GOT NO HEART. . . . . . SP SOUTHERN MAMMY 22
JUST AIN'T GOT NO HEART. . . . . . SP SOUTHERN MAMMY 24
JACK, IF YOU GOT TO BE A ROUNDER . SP STREET SONG 1
"AIN'T GOT NOBODY IN ALL THIS WORLD, SP THE WEARY BLUES 13
AIN'T GOT NOBODY BUT MA SELF. . . . SP THE WEARY BLUES 20
"I GOT THE WEARY BLUES . . . . . . SP THE WEARY BLUES 25
GOT THE WEARY BLUES . . . . SP THE WEARY BLUES 27
IF YOU GOT SOMEBODY ELSE, ... SP ULTIMATUM 4
BUT THEY GOT MORE SENSE . . . . . . SP WARNING AUGMENT 11
GOT TO NEGLECT SOMETHING, ... SP WHAT? 7
AIN'T GOT NOBODY TO SHARE MY BED, SP 50 - 50 2
AIN'T GOT NOBODY TO HOLD MY HAND - SP 50 - 50 3
I AIN'T GOT NO MAN. . . . . SP 50 - 50 5
YOU AIN'T GOT NO HEAD! . . . . . . SP 50 - 50 3
AIN'T YOU GOT NO INFORMATION . . . AYM BIRD IN ORBIT 82
HOW THEY EVER GOT THAT WAY. . . . AYM BLUES IN STEREO 27
BUT I GOT TO GET A NEW ANTENNA, LORD - . . . . AYM BLUES IN STEREO 36
HOW I GOT THERE I DON'T KNOW. . . AYM GOSPEL CHA-CHA 40
BUT WHEN I GOT . . . . AYM GOSPEL CHA-CHA 56
WHEN I GOT TO CALVARY . . . . . . AYM GOSPEL CHA-CHA 58
GOT THERE! YES, I MADE IT! . . . . AYM HORN OF PLENTY 38
GOT TO WAIT - . . . . AYM ODE TO DINAH 92
GOT TO WAIT. . . . . AYM ODE TO DINAH 34
GOT CHANGE IN HIS LONG POCKET? . . AYM SHOW FARE PLESE 4
GOT TO ASK YOU - GOT TO ASK! . . . AYM SHOW FARE PLESE 10
GOT TO ASK YOU - GOT TO ASK! . . . AYM SHOW FARE PLESE 10

ALL YOU GOT TO OFFER . . . . PL BACKLASH BLUES 17
WHAT DO YOU THINK I GOT TO LOSE? . PL BACKLASH BLUES 26
WHAT YOU THINK I GOT TO LOSE? . . . PL BACKLASH BLUES 28
WONDERING HOW THINGS GOT THIS WAY PL DINNER GUEST ME 10
GOT NOWHERE. . . . . PL DOWN WHERE I AM 8
I GOT MY FILL. . . . . PL DOWN WHERE I AM 12
GOT TIRED OF ASKING, WHEN? . . . . PL GHOSTS OF 1619 16
GOT TO CLEAN AWHILE. . . . . PL OFFICE BUILDING 3
I GOT YOUR MESSAGE . . . . PL OFFICIAL NOTICE 2
YOU GOT TO GO . . . . PL WITHOUT BENEFIT 4

GOTA 1
DE SANGRE ES LA GOTA? . . . . AYM RIDE, RED, RIDE 22

GOTT 1
MIEN GOTT! . . . . FC JAZZ BAND 16

GOTTA 1
GOTTA GET MY TEACHING! . . . . OWT JITNEY 31

GOURDS 2
SEA GOURDS MAKE MARACAS OUT OF ME. AYM GOSPEL CHA-CHA 6
WHERE THE SEA SAND AND THE SEA
GOURDS . . . . AYM GOSPEL CHA-CHA 32

GOVERN 2
TO GOVERN ANOTHER MAN . . . . SP FREEDOM'S PLOW 103
TO GOVERN ANOTHER MAN . . . . SP FREEDOM'S PLOW 170

GOVERNMENT 3
DIDN'T OUR GOVERNMENT TELL US THINGS
WOULD BE FINE . . . . NM COLORED SL POEM 33
HE'S TRYING TO RUIN THE GOVERNMENT SP BLD LANDLORD 23
THE GOVERNMENT MIGHT HONOR YOU. . . SP SHAME ON YOU 3

GOVERNOR 7
A MAN WITH THE TITLE OF GOVERNOR HAS
SPOKEN: . . . . ANS CHANT TOM MOONY 4
A MAN WITH THE TITLE OF GOVERNOR HAS
SPOKEN: . . . . ANS CHANT TOM MOONY 6
BUT THE MAN WITH THE TITLE OF
GOVERNOR . . . . ANS CHANT TOM MOONY 10
OF COURSE, THE MAN WITH THE TITLE OF
GOVERNOR . . . . ANS CHANT TOM MOONY 26
SHUT UP, SAYS THE GOVERNOR OF SOUTH
CAROLINA. . . . . SP IN EXPLANATION 24
SHUT UP, SAYS THE GOVERNOR OF
SINGAPORE. . . . . SP IN EXPLANATION 25
MARTIN LUTHER KING IS GOVERNOR OF
GEORGIA. . . . . PL CULTURAL EXCHNG 43

GOVERNORS 1
GOVERNORS OF SOUTH CAROLINA, GERALD
L.K. STRYDOMS. . . . . SP IN EXPLANATION 42

GOWN 3
IN A GOWN OF GOLD? . . . . WB JAZZONIA 13
IN A GOLDEN GOWN . . . . SP COLLEGE FORMAL 2
PUTS ON A RED GOWN. . . . . PL LAST PRINCE 13

GOYA 1
GOYA, VELASQUEZ, MURILLO, ... ANS SONG OF SPAIN 20

GRAB 5
OF PROFIT, POWER, GAIN, OF GRAB THE
LAND! . . . . ANS LET AMERICA BE 27
OF GRAB THE GOLD! OF GRAB THE WAYS
OF SATISFYING NEED! . . . . ANS LET AMERICA BE 28
OF GRAB THE GOLD! OF GRAB THE WAYS
OF SATISFYING NEED! . . . . ANS LET AMERICA BE 28
GRAB A LONELY DREAM . . . . FW LITTLE SONG 3
AND PUSH AND SHOVE AND GRAB! . . . OWT JITNEY 57

GRABS 1
GRABS A LOAD OF SUNRISE . . . . . . SP MIGRANT 10

GRACE 2
THE SLY AND SERVILE GRACE . . . . . SP UNCLE TOM 7
JOHN JASPER! JESUS! DADDY GRACE! . AYM GOSPEL CHA-CHA 44

GRADE 1
FIRST GRADE IN NEW ORLEANS . . . . AYM BIRD IN ORBIT 9

GRADUALLY 2
MUSIC TAKES ON A BLUES STRAIN,
GRADUALLY RETURNING TO A SORT OF NM BIG-TIMER MOOD 3
WALKING PROUDLY, ALMOST PRANCING.
BUT GRADUALLY SUBDUED TO A SLOW,
HEAVY . . . . NM BLACK CLWN MOOD 7

GRADUATE 2
THIS YEAR MAYBE, DO YOU THINK I CAN
GRADUATE? . . . . SP DEFERRED 1
BUT MAYBE THIS YEAR I CAN GRADUATE. SP DEFERRED 7

GRAFT 1
THE RAPE AND ROT OF GRAFT, AND
STEALTH, AND LIES, ... ANS LET AMERICA BE 81

GRAIL 1
SEND FOR KING ARTHUR TO BRING THE
HOLY GRAIL. . . . . PL FINAL CALL 8

GRANADA 1
GRENADINE GRANADA OR . . . . AYM RIDE, RED, RIDE 21

GRAND 9
OVER TO THE GRAND. . . . . OWT JITNEY 42
FUNERAL GRAND. . . . . SP NIGHT FUNERAL 44
GRAND MARSHAL IN HIS WHITE SUIT . . SP PARADE 5
DREAMING OF A BABY GRAND PIANO . . SP TO BE SOMEBODY 2
DREAMING OF A BABY GRAND TO PLAY . . SP TO BE SOMEBODY 4
WHAT A GRAND TIME WAS THE WAR! . . SP WORLD WAR II 1
WHAT A GRAND TIME WAS THE WAR! . . SP WORLD WAR II 3
WHAT A GRAND TIME WAS THE WAR, . . SP WORLD WAR II 7
A. PHILIP RANDOLPH THE HIGH GRAND
WORTHY. . . . . PL CULTURAL EXCHNG 45

GRANDEES 1
I MADE RICH THE GRANDEES AND LORDS ANS SONG OF SPAIN 75

GRANDFATHER'S 1
AND MY GRANDFATHER'S BACK WITH ITS
LADDER OF SCARS, ... JC THE BITTER RIVR 36

GRANDMA 6
GRANDPA, GRANDMA, ... SP CONSIDER ME 9
GRANDMA, LEND ME A DIME. . . . . . SP DIME 2
GRANDMA ACTS LIKE . . . . SP DIME 4
AND GRANDMA CANNOT GET HER GOSPEL
HYMNS . . . . SP PASSING 3
AND ITS GRANDMA - . . . . SP S-SSS-SS-SH! 18
GRANDPA, WHERE DID YOU MEET MY
GRANDMA? . . . . AYM BIRD IN ORBIT 34

GRANDMA'S 1
(GRANDPA'S GRANDMA'S GRANNY . . . . AYM RIDE, RED, RIDE 17

GRANDMOTHER 2
WHEN MY GRANDMOTHER IN ATLANTA, 83
AND BLACK, ... SP FREEDOM TRAIN 37
LIKE AN OLD GRANDMOTHER, ... SP FULFILMENT 17

GRANDPA 6
GRANDPA, GRANDMA, ... SP CONSIDER ME 9
GRANDPA, WHERE DID YOU MEET MY
GRANDMA? . . . . AYM BIRD IN ORBIT 34
I'M ASKING, GRANDPA, ASKING. . . . AYM BIRD IN ORBIT 36
GRANDPA, DID YOU HEAR THE . . . . . AYM BIRD IN ORBIT 39
GRANDPA, DID YOU FIND HER IN THE TV
SILENCE . . . . AYM BIRD IN ORBIT 61
HER YESTERDAY PAST GRANDPA - . . . PL CULTURAL EXCHNG 17

GRANDPA'S 1
(GRANDPA'S GRANDMA'S GRANNY . . . . AYM RIDE, RED, RIDE 17

GRANDSON'S 1
HER GRANDSON'S NAME WAS JIMMY. HE
DIED AT ANZIO. . . . . SP FREEDOM TRAIN 43

GRANNY 2
CHILE, GRANNY AIN'T GOT NO DIME. . SP DIME 6
(GRANDPA'S GRANDMA'S GRANNY . . . . AYM RIDE, RED, RIDE 17

GRANT 2
GRANT HIM YOUR LOVE. . . . . PL CHRIST IN ALA. 9
SEND FOR LINCOLN, SEND FOR GRANT. PL FINAL CALL 29

GRANTED 1
AND SILENTLY TOOK FOR GRANTED . . . SP FREEDOM'S PLOW 98

GRAPES 1
THE GRAPES OF JOY . . . . SP MIDNIGHT DANCER 8

GRASP 1
AND GRASP FOR A STRAW. . . . . . . SP SUNDAY MORNING 20

GRASS 4
BACK INTO THE GRASS - . . . . FW SNAKE 2
DISTORTED BLADES OF GRASS, ... SP GARDEN 2
THEIR GRASS WITH UNICORNS. . . . . AYM ASK YOUR MAMA 77
WHERE THE GRASS IS GREENER $ $ $ $
$ $ $ . . . . AYM HORN OF PLENTY 23

GRASSES 2
AND STURDY WEEDS AND GRASSES . . . FW GIRL 16
GREEN GRASSES GROW . . . . SP IN TIME SILVER 4

GRASSLESS 1
GRASSLESS MOUND. . . . . SP STONY LONESOME 8

GRASSY 1
AND POLAND'S PLAIN, AND ENGLAND'S
GRASSY LEA, ... ANS LET AMERICA BE 48

GRAVE 14
AN' DIG ME A GRAVE THIS VERY DAY. — FC MINNIE SINGS 17
OUT OF HIS GRAVE FROM OVER THE SEA. — NM COLORED SL POEM 14
(AT BOOKER WASHINGTON'S GRAVE) — DK ALABAMA EARTH 1
STREW NO FLOWERS ON MY GRAVE, — DK DEATH SEAMAN 7
OR A PRISON GRAVE, OR THE POTTER'S FIELD, — ANS KIDS WHO DIE 41
I WAS IN MY GRAVE AND GONE. — SP LITTLE OLD LETT 8
BLACK BOY TO HIS GRAVE? — SP NIGHT FUNERAL 20
AN' THE GRAVE IS COLD. — SP YOUNG GAL'S BLS 14
THE GRAVEYARD GRAVE IS COLD. — SP YOUNG GAL'S BLS 16
IN AN UNMARKED GRAVE. — PL LUMUMBA'S GRAVE 14
FOR AIR IS HIS GRAVE. — PL LUMUMBA'S GRAVE 16
SUN IS HIS GRAVE, — PL LUMUMBA'S GRAVE 17
SPACE IS HIS GRAVE. — PL LUMUMBA'S GRAVE 19
MY HEART'S HIS GRAVE, — PL LUMUMBA'S GRAVE 20

GRAVES 3
THEN MAYBE FROM THEIR GRAVES IN ANZIO — SP FREEDOM TRAIN 59
IN LITTLE GRAVES TODAY AWAIT — PL BIRMINGHAM SUND 17
WE PASSED THEIR GRAVES: — PL PEACE 1

GRAVESTONES 1
ON GRAVESTONES DATES ARE PLAYED. — AYM JAZZTET MUTED 13

GRAVEYARD 7
THE GRAVEYARD IS THE — OWT BOARDING HOUSE 1
THE GRAVEYARD IS THE — OWT BOARDING HOUSE 7
LET THE GRAVEYARD BE THE — OWT BOARDING HOUSE 13
FOR GRAVEYARD MOLD. — SP BLD OF THE MAN 24
I'M GONNA WALK TO THE GRAVEYARD — SP YOUNG GAL'S BLS 1
GONNA WALK TO THE GRAVEYARD — SP YOUNG GAL'S BLS 3
THE GRAVEYARD GRAVE IS COLD. — SP YOUNG GAL'S BLS 16

GRAY 5
OUR SKY IS GRAY. — ANS SONG OF SPAIN 49
WHOSE HAIR WAS GRAY — SP JOE LOUIS 3
TURNS GRAY. — SP MIGRANT 32
PIMPS IN GRAY GO BY, — SP SUMMER EVENING 5
IN GRAY SLOUCH HATS. — PL THIRD DEGREE 6

GREASY 1
OR GREASY POTS IN A DIRTY KITCHEN. — SP ELEVATOR BOY 20

GREAT 45
OH, GREAT DARK CITY. — WB DISILLUSION 12
WHAT GREAT FOREST HAS HUNG ITS PERFUME — WB NUDE YOUNG DANC 3
A GREAT DRUM — FC SPORT 5
OF A FREE LIFE BENEATH OUR GREAT SKY. — NM DARK YOUTH USA 10
GREAT DIAMOND MOON, — DK LULLABY 17
LET IT BE THAT GREAT STRONG LAND OF LOVE — ANS LET AMERICA BE 7
ALL, ALL THE STRETCH OF THESE GREAT GREEN STATES — — ANS LET AMERICA BE 85
FOR ME, NO MORE, THE GREAT MIGRATION TO THE NORTH. — ANS OPEN LETTER 41
IN THIS GREAT BIG LONESOME TOWN! — SH OUT OF WORK 14
GREAT BIG LONESOME TOWN! — SH OUT OF WORK 16
LET THE GREAT WAVES BEAT! — JC TO CAPTAIN MULZ 72
LET THE GREAT WAVES RISE — JC TO CAPTAIN MULZ 75
GREAT LONELY HILLS. — FW BIG SUR 1
GREAT MOUNTAINS. — FW BIG SUR 2
FOR THE GREAT EARTH SPIRITS — FW JAIME 3
EVEN A GREAT DANCER — SP DANCER 24
IN A GREAT NEED. — SP DEMOCRACY 18
GREAT LONG FINGERS — SP DREAM BOOGE VAR 5
ON GREAT BIG HANDS, — SP DREAM BOOGE VAR 6
ON THE GREAT WOODED WORLD, — SP FREEDOM'S PLOW 12
THERE WAS A GREAT WOODED LAND, — SP FREEDOM'S PLOW 140
GREAT THOUGHTS IN THEIR DEEPEST HEARTS — SP FREEDOM'S PLOW 148
TO ALL THE ENEMIES OF THESE GREAT WORDS: — SP FREEDOM'S PLOW 186
STARS ARE GREAT DROPS — SP HARLEM NIGHT SO 9
SOUND LIKE A GREAT BIG CROWD. — SP MORNING AFTER 18
GREAT BIG YELLOW STARS. — SP MULATTO 10
GREAT BIG YELLOW STARS. — SP MULATTO 32
IN FACT, HE'S A GREAT CAT. — SP NEIGHBOR 16
CLIMBING UP A GREAT BIG MOUNTAIN — SP PORTER 7
IF YOU'RE GREAT ENOUGH — SP SHAME ON YOU 1
GREAT GOD! — SP SLIVER SERMON 2
GREAT GOD! — SP SLIVER SERMON 4
GREAT — SP SLIVER SERMON 7
IN A GREAT . . . BIG . . . NIGHT. — SP SYLVESTER'S BED 28
HER GREAT ADVENTURE ENDED — SP S-SSS-SS-SH! 1
AS GREAT ADVENTURES SHOULD — SP S-SSS-SS-SH! 2
IMPEL YOU FOREVER UP THE GREAT STAIRS — — SP THE NEGRO MOTHE 50
BARE FEET TO BEAT THE GREAT DRUMBEAT — AYM BLUES IN STEREO 9
THE GREAT MISTAKE — PL AMER HEARTBREAK 4
GREAT BIG WORLD, MISTER BACKLASH, — PL BACKLASH BLUES 21
GREAT NAMES FOR CROWNS AND GARLANDS! — PL CROWNS GARLANDS 17
IN A GREAT NEED. — PL FREEDOM 18
IN THE GREAT WHITE RACE?" — PL KU KLUX 4
THE GREAT WHITE RACE." — PL KU KLUX 20
KILLED WITH GREAT ELAN, — PL MOTHER IN WAR 6

GREATER 1
SEEKING A GREATER FREEDOM, — SP FREEDOM'S PLOW 42

GREATNESS 1
IN THE DAYS OF YOUR GREATNESS — SP SUNDAY MORNING 26

GREED 2
OF OWNING EVERYTHING FOR ONE'S OWN GREED! — ANS LET AMERICA BE 30
OF HATE AND GREED AND RACE — JC TO CAPTAIN MULZ 57

GREED'S 1
AND THE RULE OF GREED'S UPHELD — — ANS UNION 11

GREEKS 1
FOR THEM POLES AND GREEKS — SP RELIEF 2

GREELEY 2
I THOUGHT ABOUT OLD GREELEY — SP BLUE BAYOU 4
I'LL KILL OLD GREELEY. — SP BLUE BAYOU 13

GREEN 7
ALL, ALL THE STRETCH OF THESE GREAT GREEN STATES — — ANS LET AMERICA BE 85
(DEDICATED TO THE MEMORY OF CHARLIE LANG AND ERNEST GREEN, — JC THE BITTER RIVR 1
GREEN GRASSES GROW — SP IN TIME SILVER 4
THEM COOL GREEN LEAVES — SP LITTLE GRN TREE 13
AND THE GREEN SEA — SP YOUNG SAILOR 16
CLEAR GREEN CRYSTAL WATER — AYM GOSPEL CHA-CHA 30
AND A LEAF OF COLLARD GREEN. — PL CULTURAL EXCHNG 30

GREENBACKS 1
IF I HAD SOME GREENBACKS — SH IF-ING 5

GREENER 1
WHERE THE GRASS IS GREENER $ $ $ $ $ $ $ — AYM HORN OF PLENTY 23

GREENS 1
IN A POT OF COLLARD GREENS — PL CULTURAL EXCHNG 19

GREENWOOD 1
JOCKO BODDIDLY LIL GREENWOOD — AYM BIRD IN ORBIT 4

GREETINGS 1
GREETINGS! — ANS OPEN LETTER 11

GRENADINE 1
GRENADINE GRANADA OR — AYM RIDE, RED, RIDE 21

GREW 6
FOR SURE THERE GREW FLOWERS — FW GIRL 14
THAT GREW UPON THE PLAIN — LHR PASTORAL 7
AND THE TOWNS THAT GREW TO CITIES. — SP FREEDOM'S PLOW 71
FROM THAT SEED A TREE GREW, IS GROWING, WILL EVER GROW. — SP FREEDOM'S PLOW 195
SHE GREW UP AND GOT RUINT. — SP MADAM CHARTY CH 3
HOW TALL HOW TALL THE CANE GREW — AYM BIRD IN ORBIT 41

GREY 2
WHEN THE LITTLE DAWN WAS GREY. — WB CABARET 6
AND NOT THIS LAND WHERE BIRDS ARE GREY. — WB OUR LAND 12

GRIEF 2
THEY SAY SHE DIED OF GRIEF — WB YOUNG BRIDE 3
BUT YOU DON'T SEE NO PRESIDENTS DYIN' O' GRIEF — — NM BROKE 57

GRIEVE 1
GOT TO MOAN AN' GRIEVE? — SP FIRE 13

GRIN 4
GRIN JUNGLE JOYS. — WB HARLEM NIGHT CL 5
FOLKS AT THE TABLES DRINK AND GRIN. — SH DEATH IN HARLEM 31
HE'S GOT A GRIN ON HIS FACE. — SP ME AND THE MULE 2
GRIN THAT WIDE. — SP 125TH STREET 6

GRINDSTONE 1
THAT'S BEEN KEEPING MY NOSE TO THE GRINDSTONE. — SH PAY DAY 13

GRINNED 1
DIXIE GRINNED, DIXIE BOWED. — SH DEATH IN HARLEM 63

GRINNING 3
CRY AT MY GRINNING MOUTH, — WB THE JESTER 12
PLAY YOUR GUITARS, GRINNING NIGHT-DARK BOYS, — OWT JUICE JOINT 17
THE GRINNING FACE, — SP UNCLE TOM 4

GRIP 1
IN THE GRIP OF HAND TO HAND. — FW MAN 4

GROCERIES 1
GROCERIES — SP LIKEWISE 2

GROPING 1
GROPING, HOPING. . . . . PL QUESTION ANSWER 8

GROUND 14
THEY PUT MA BODY IN THE GROUND. . . SP JUDGMENT DAY 1
SIXTEEN FLOORS ABOVE THE GROUND. . SP LIFE IS FINE 13
WHO SITS UPON THE GROUND . . . . . SP MEXICAN MARKET 2
SNOW ALL OVER THE GROUND. . . . . . SP MIDWINTER BLUES 2
SNOW ALL OVER THE GROUND - . . . . SP MIDWINTER BLUES 4
OUT TO STONY LONESOME GROUND. . . . SP STONY LONESOME 2
GROUND! . . . . SP STONY LONESOME 21
WHEN THEY PUT YOU IN THE GROUND AND SP WIDOW WOMAN 7
I SAY PUT YOU IN THE GROUND AND . . SP WIDOW WOMAN 9
RISING OUT OF THE GROUND LIKE A SWAMP MIST . . . . PL DAYBREAK IN ALA 5
ON SOLID GROUND. . . . . PL DOWN WHERE I AM 14
ON THE GROUND. . . . . PL KU KLUX 16
AND BURIED IN THE GROUND - . . . . PL OCTOBER 16 RAID 22
BATTLE GROUND . . . . PL THE DOVE 9

GROVES 1
KIDS WILL DIE IN THE ORANGE GROVES OF CALIFORNIA . . . . ANS KIDS WHO DIE 12

GROW 12
20-VOICES: GROW OUT OF THE PASSIVE EARTH. . . . . ANS CHANT MAY DAY 10
40-VOICES: GROW STRONG WITH UNION. ALL HANDS TOGETHER - . . . . . . ANS CHANT MAY DAY 11
40-VOICES: GROW STRONG. . . . . . . ANS CHANT MAY DAY 33
LET POWER GROW! . . . . ANS OPEN LETTER 50
FROM THAT SEED A TREE GREW, IS GROWING, WILL EVER GROW. . . . . SP FREEDOM'S PLOW 195
MAY ITS BRANCHES SPREAD AND ITS SHELTER GROW . . . . SP FREEDOM'S PLOW 198
WATCHED HARLEM GROW . . . . SP GOOD MORNING 3
GREEN GRASSES GROW . . . . SP IN TIME SILVER 4
AND GROW STRONG. . . . . SP I, TOO 7
WHEN YOU GROW UP THE HARD WAY . . . SP MADAM MIGHT-HAV 5
IN ORDER THAT THE RACE MIGHT LIVE AND GROW. . . . . SP THE NEGRO MOTHE 4
BORN TO GROW UP WILD - . . . . . . AYM ODE TO DINAH 37

GROWING 2
IN GROWING THINGS . . . . FW GIRL 19
FROM THAT SEED A TREE GREW, IS GROWING, WILL EVER GROW. . . . . SP FREEDOM'S PLOW 195

GROWN 6
AND MY BOY'S MOST GROWN - . . . . . SP DEFERRED 16
HAS GROWN QUITE TALL. . . . . SP DELINQUENT 2
HAS GROWN QUITE STOUT. . . . . . . SP DELINQUENT 6
HAS GROWN QUITE WISE - . . . . . . SP DELINQUENT 10
MY SOUL HAS GROWN DEEP LIKE THE RIVERS. . . . . SP NEGRO SPEAKS OF 4
MY SOUL HAS GROWN DEEP LIKE THE RIVERS. . . . . SP NEGRO SPEAKS OF 13

GROWS 4
THAT GROWS IN NO-MAN'S LAND, JOAN OF ARC, AND VARIOUS OTHER WAR-TIME NM COLORED SL MOOD 5
VOICE GROWS THICKER . . . . SP DRUNKARD 1
AS SONG GROWS STRONGER . . . . . . SP DRUNKARD 2
AS TIME GROWS LONGER UNTIL DAY . . SP DRUNKARD 3

GUARANTEE 1
GUARANTEE . . . . SP DEAD IN THERE 7

GUARD 4
ON GUARD WITH THE WORKERS FOREVER - ANS BLDS OF LENIN 27
TO HOLD AND GUARD . . . . ANS SONG OF SPAIN 65
HE TRIED TO GUARD . . . . SH BLD THE KILLER 17
TO GUARD THE HARBOR ENTRANCE . . . JC TO CAPTAIN MULZ 14

GUARDIA 1
MAYOR LA GUARDIA . . . . OWT BLD MARGE POLIT 33

GUARDING 2
GUARDING IN THEIR HEARTS THE SEED OF FREEDOM. . . . . SP FREEDOM'S PLOW 124
GUARDING IN THEIR HEARTS THE SEED OF FREEDOM. . . . . SP FREEDOM'S PLOW 46

GUESS 6
I GUESS I CAN STAND THE RACKET . . NM BIG-TIMER POEM 55
I GUESS I KNOW WHAT I'M UP AGAINST. NM BIG-TIMER POEM 57
AND I GUESS THAT ONE'S ALL - . . . NM BIG-TIMER POEM 72
GUESS I'LL QUIT NOW. . . . . SP ELEVATOR BOY 23
I GUESS I WILL LIVE ON. . . . . . . SP LIFE IS FINE 24
AT TWENTY-TWO, MY AGE. BUT I GUESS I'M WHAT . . . . SP THEME FOR ENG B 17
I GUESS BEING COLORED DOESN'T MAKE ME NOT LIKE . . . . SP THEME FOR ENG B 25
I GUESS YOU LEARN FROM ME - . . . . SP THEME FOR ENG B 38

GUIDE 2
THAT GUIDE US TOWARD THE HARBOR OF THE NEW WORLD . . . . JC TO CAPTAIN MULZ 54
YOU WHO GUIDE IT ON ITS WAY. . . . JC TO CAPTAIN MULZ 66

GUINEA 1
TOURE DOWN IN GUINEA . . . . AYM BIRD IN ORBIT 58

GUISE 1
UNDER THE GUISE OF A PATRIOT . . . ANS SONG OF SPAIN 67

GUITAR 2
FOR PIERROT PLAYED ON A SLIM GUITAR. WB PIERROT 27
PLAY YOUR GUITAR, BOY. . . . . . . OWT BLUES ON A BOX 1

GUITARS 2
GYPSIES, GUITARS, DANCING . . . . . ANS SONG OF SPAIN 6
PLAY YOUR GUITARS, GRINNING NIGHT-DARK BOYS. . . . . OWT JUICE JOINT 17

GUITAR-PLAYING 2
GUITAR-PLAYING BOY . . . . OWT JUICE JOINT 30
BUT SUDDENLY A GUITAR-PLAYING LAD OWT JUICE JOINT 41

GUM 1
I SWEAR, BY GUM. . . . . JC BLACK MAN SPEAK 9

GUN 9
NEVER SAW THE HIGH SHERIFF'S GUN . ANS BLD OZZIE POWEL 15
BUT ARABELLA HAD HER GUN. . . . . . SH DEATH IN HARLEM 105
LIFT THEIR HEADS, TOO, WITH GUN IN HAND . . . . JC GOOD MORN STLIN 32
WHEN DORIE MILLER TOOK GUN IN HAND - JC JIM CROW'S LAST 28
SHALL I TAKE A GUN . . . . OWT TOO BLUE 8
NEITHER BULLET NOR GUN - . . . . . OWT TOO BLUE 15
YOU DON'T NEED NO GUN NOR KNIFE - SP LITTLE OLD LETT 14
AND THE GUN TO DO THE KILLING'S . . AYM IS IT TRUE? 14
WHO TOOK HIS GUN, ... PL OCTOBER 16 RAID 5

GUNBOATS 1
FOR THE WHITE WORLD'S GUNBOATS . . PL LAST PRINCE 6

GUNS 1
BUT WHEN YOUR GUNS ROAR, ... JC GOOD MORN STLIN 18

GURGLES 1
SHE GURGLES TO TEXAS. . . . . SH DEATH IN HARLEM 51

GURGLING 1
GURGLING JERICHO. . . . . SP SUMMER EVENING 17

GUTTER 4
THE RAIN MAKES RUNNING POOLS IN THE GUTTER. . . . . DK APRIL RAIN SONG 5
IN THE GUTTER . . . . SP UP-BEAT 1
AS OUT OF THE GUTTER . . . . SP UP-BEAT 5
WHILE FROM THE GUTTER . . . . SP UP-BEAT 9

GUY 4
A GUY WAS SAYIN' . . . . FC DEATH DO DIRTY 28
I'M THE GUY THE HOME FOLKS CALL - NM BIG-TIMER POEM 3
THE GUY SHE GAVE HER ALL TO . . . . SP BLD OF THE GIRL 5
A GUY. . . . . PL WITHOUT BENEFIT 18

GUYS 2
ONLY DUMB GUYS FIGHT. . . . . FC PRIZE FIGHTER 1
ONLY DUMB GUYS FIGHT. . . . . FC PRIZE FIGHTER 7

GWINE 3
GWINE GIVE YOU EIGHTEEN MONTHS . . FC BLD OF GIN MARY 15
HE TOLE ME I WAS GWINE. . . . . . . DK MA LORD 14
I'S GWINE TO QUIT MA FROWNIN' . . . SP THE WEARY BLUES 21

GYPSIES 2
WITH GYPSIES AND SAILORS. . . . . . WB A FAREWELL 1
GYPSIES, GUITARS, DANCING . . . . . ANS SONG OF SPAIN 6

GYPSY 11
MA MAN'S A GYPSY . . . . FC GYPSY MAN 1
MA MAN'S A GYPSY, - . . . . FC GYPSY MAN 3
I'M GONNA BE A GYPSY WOMAN . . . . FC GYPSY MAN 5
GYPSY DONE SHOWED ME . . . . SP BAD LUCK CARD 3
GYPSY DONE TOLE ME - . . . . SP BAD LUCK CARD 7
GYPSY SAYS I'D KILL MY SELF . . . . SP BAD LUCK CARD 11
GYPSY SETTIN' ALL ALONE. . . . . . SP BLD THE GYPSY 2
I SAID, TELL ME, GYPSY. . . . . . . SP BLD THE GYPSY 3
GYPSY SAID, SILVER. . . . . SP BLD THE GYPSY 5
UH! I HATES A LYIN' GYPSY . . . . . SP BLD THE GYPSY 18
BUT IF I WAS A GYPSY . . . . SP BLD THE GYPSY 22

GYPSY'S 1
I WENT TO THE GYPSY'S. . . . . . . SP BLD THE GYPSY 1

G.I 1
THE G.I.'S WHO FOUGHT WILL SAY, WE WANTED IT SO! . . . . SP FREEDOM TRAIN 60

HABITUES 1

HABITUES OF THE HIGH SHUTTERED HOUSES. . . . . SP RUBY BROWN 24

HAD 105

AN' HAD CUT HIS GAL . . . . FC DEATH DO DIRTY 8
HAD NOTHIN' TO EAT. . . . . FC DEATH DO DIRTY 12
IF DIRTY HAD DE MONEY . . . . FC DEATH DO DIRTY 18
BUT I HAD TO LEAVE CAUSE . . . . . FC GYPSY MAN 11
WHEN FOR YEARS. I HAD BEEN SEEKING OLD AESTHETE HARLEM 4
DE TROUBLE I'VE HAD." FLINCHING UNDER THE WHIP. THE SPIRITUAL . NM BLACK CLWN MOOD 5
LAST JOB I HAD. WENT TO WORK AT FIVE IN DE MORNIN'. OR LITTLE MO' . . NM BROKE 12
AND I SHO HAD A PRETTY GAL. TOO. UP YONDER ON SUGAR HILL. . . . . . NM BROKE 48
WE COULDN'T EAT IN RESTAURANTS: HAD JIM CROW CARS: . . . . NM COLORED SL POEM 24
AS IF FATE HAD NOT BLED HIM WITH HER KNIFE! . . . . DK BEGGAR BOY 8
I HAD MA CLOTHES CLEANED . . . . . DK DRESSED UP 1
BUT I WISH I HAD BACK THAT . . . . DK DRESSED UP 7
HE HAD A MERMAID ON HIS ARM. . . . DK SAILOR 5
AND TATTOOED ON HIS BACK HE HAD . . DK SAILOR 7
AND THE OPPRESSORS HAD NO PITY. . . ANS A NEW SONG 21
I HAD A GAL. . . . . SH ANNOUNCEMENT 1
HAD TO PAY HER TICKET. . . . . . . SH ANNOUNCEMENT 5
IT TOOK ALL I HAD. . . . . SH ANNOUNCEMENT 6
SHE HAD ANOTHER JOKER . . . . SH ANNOUNCEMENT 11
IF I HAD SOME MONEY I'D STROLL DOWN THE STREET . . . . SH BED TIME 3
THAT I EVER HAD! . . . . SH BRIEF ENCOUNTER 18
AND ARABELLA JOHNSON HAD HER . . . SH DEATH IN HARLEM 8
BUT ARABELLA HAD HER GUN. . . . . . SH DEATH IN HARLEM 105
IF I HAD SOME SMALL CHANGE . . . . SH IF-ING 1
IF I HAD SOME GREENBACKS . . . . . SH IF-ING 5
IF I HAD A MILLION . . . . SH IF-ING 9
THOUGHT I HAD AN ANGEL-CHILE. . . . SH LOVE AGAIN BLUS 8
THOUGHT I HAD AN ANGEL-CHILE. . . . SH LOVE AGAIN BLUS 10
SHE HAD LONG BLACK HAIR. . . . . . SH ONLY WOMAN BLUS 13
AND TAKE BACK ALL THEM THINGS WE HAD SH PAY DAY 12
AIN'T EVEN GONNA DREAM 'BOUT THE WOMENS I HAD. . . . . SH PAY DAY 18
IF I HAD A FIRE I'D MAKE ME SOME TEA SH SUPPER TIME 11
IF I JUST HAD A OWL HEAD. OLD OWL HEAD WOULD DO. . . . . SH TWILIGHT REVERI 11
THEY HAD A PARADE. . . . . JC BLD SAM SOLOMON 42
HAD GIVE YOU UP FOR DEAD. . . . . . JC GOOD MORN STLIN 3
IT HAD NO DIGNITY BEFORE. . . . . . FW HARLEM DANCE HA 1
THAT HAD NO DIGNITY BEFORE! . . . . FW HARLEM DANCE HA 8
HAD OF BEEN WHITE . . . . OWT BLD MARGE POLIT 2
BEFORE THIS LONG HEGIRA HAD BEGUN OWT JUICE JOINT 12
I KEPT WISHING I HAD A GIRL-FRIEND OWT STRANGER IN TWN 3
THE PASSOVER HAD COME. . . . . . . LHR BLD MARY'S SON 2
STOLE ALL SHE HAD. . . . . SP BLD FORTUNE TEL 24
THAT IF SHE HAD A CHANCE . . . . . SP BLD OF THE GIRL 15
A FUNERAL WAS HAD. . . . . SP BLD OF THE MAN 16
HAD HER TAIL . . . . SP CATCH 5
THAT HAD NOT FAILED PEOPLE . . . . SP DANCER 3
HAD A LITTLE LAMB. . . . . SP EVENING SONG 10
HAD MORE WOMEN . . . . SP FIRE 19
THAN PHARAOH HAD WIVES. . . . . . . SP FIRE 20
ELSE IT HAD NO MEANING FOR ANYONE. SP FREEDOM'S PLOW 108
HE WAS A COLORED MAN WHO HAD BEEN A SLAVE . . . . SP FREEDOM'S PLOW 112
BUT HAD RUN AWAY TO FREEDOM. . . . SP FREEDOM'S PLOW 113
BUT OTHERS KNEW IT HAD TO TRIUMPH. SP FREEDOM'S PLOW 122
I WISH I HAD WINGS TO . . . . SP HARD DADDY 13
WISH I HAD WINGS TO . . . . SP HARD DADDY 15
WAS THE ONLY THING I HAD. . . . . . SP HOMECOMING 8
THEY HAD NO INTENTION OF CALLING COOLIES MISTER. . . . . SP IN EXPLANATION 9
BUT THE GOSSIPS HAD NO . . . . . . SP JOE LOUIS 9
NEITHER HAD NOBODY DIED. . . . . . SP LATE LAST NIGHT 4
I HAD TWO HUSBANDS. . . . . SP MADAM MIGHT-HAV 1
I COULD OF HAD THREE - . . . . . . SP MADAM MIGHT-HAV 2
BUT SHE HAD A TWELVE-ROOM . . . . . SP MADAM HER MADAM 3
I HAD SWORE . . . . SP MADAM NUMBER WR 3
HAD TO GET BREAKFAST. . . . . SP MADAM HER MADAM 5
LIKE HE HAD A CHARM. . . . . SP MADAM WRONG VIS 10
AIN'T HAD NO LUCK . . . . SP MADAM CHARTY CH 11
I HAD ANYTHING FREE. . . . . SP MADAM MIGHT-HAV 12
WITH NONE I HAD. . . . . SP MADAM CHARTY CH 12
NO SOONER HAD I TOLD HIM . . . . . SP MADAM WRONG VIS 21
I HAD SOME CARDS PRINTED . . . . . SP MADAM'S CALLING 1
I HAD A . . . . SP MADAM'S PAST HI 5
THEN I HAD A . . . . SP MADAM'S PAST HI 10
CAUSE I HAD A INSURANCE . . . . . . SP MADAM'S PAST HI 14
HAD A DREAM LAST NIGHT I . . . . . SP MORNING AFTER 7
IT'S HAD TACKS IN IT. . . . . SP MOTHER TO SON 3
HIS GIRL FRIEND HAD TO PAY. . . . . SP NIGHT FUNERAL 24
AND THE ORGAN HAD DONE PLAYED . . . SP NIGHT FUNERAL 29
I HAD A DREAM . . . . SP NIGHTMARE BOOGE 1
MAYVILLE HAD NO PLACE TO OFFER HER. SP RUBY BROWN 5
IF I JUST HAD A PIANO. . . . . . . SP TESTIMONIAL 1
IF I JUST HAD A ORGAN. . . . . . . SP TESTIMONIAL 2
IF I JUST HAD A DRUM. . . . . SP TESTIMONIAL 3
THAT I HAD TO CLIMB. THAT I HAD TO KNOW . . . . SP THE NEGRO MOTHE 7
THAT I HAD TO CLIMB. THAT I HAD TO KNOW . . . . SP THE NEGRO MOTHE 7
I HAD NOTHING. BACK THERE IN THE NIGHT. . . . . SP THE NEGRO MOTHE 24
BUT I HAD TO KEEP ON TILL MY WORK WAS DONE: . . . . SP THE NEGRO MOTHE 28
I HAD TO KEEP ON! NO STOPPING FOR ME - . . . . SP THE NEGRO MOTHE 29
I HAD ONLY HOPE THEN. BUT NOW THROUGH YOU. . . . . SP THE NEGRO MOTHE 33
AND I WISH THAT I HAD DIED." . . . SP THE WEARY BLUES 30
THAN SOME PEOPLE EVER HAD. . . . . SP WARNING AUGMENT 12
I HAD A WOMAN . . . . SP WEST TEXAS 3
IN WARTIME WE HAD FUN. . . . . . . SP WORLD WAR II 5
IF YOU HAD A HEAD AND USED YOUR MIND SP 50 - 50 9
AND HAD A CHIP ON SHOULDER? . . . . AYM HORN OF PLENTY 50
WHERE THE CHRIST CHILD ONCE HAD LAIN. . . . . AYM ODE TO DINAH 34
(AND I NEVER HAD A HIP BOOT ON) . . AYM SHADES OF PIG 33
(AND I NEVER HAD THAT MUCH HAIR) . . AYM SHADES OF PIG 36
(AND I NEVER HAD A DIAMOND . . . . AYM SHADES OF PIG 38
(AND AIN'T NEVER HAD A BLACK HOUSE) AYM SHADES OF PIG 42
HAD HE WALKED WITH WARY FOOT . . . PL FREDRK DOUGLASS 2
WE REMEMBER THE JOB WE NEVER HAD. PL HARLEM 12
WHO HAD GAINED . . . . PL PEACE 7
IF I HAD A HEART OF GOLD. . . . . . PL VARI-COLORED 1
I HAD VISIONS IN MY HEAD . . . . . PL WHO BUT TH LORD 5
IF YOU HAD KNOWN WHAT I KNOW . . . PL WORDS LIKE FREE 7

HADES 2

I'D GO TO HADES . . . . SP MADAM RENT MAN 9
AND CAN KNOCK THE HADES . . . . . . AYM ODE TO DINAH 117

HADN'T 3

IF THAT WATER HADN'T A-BEEN SO COLD SP LIFE IS FINE 7
IF IT HADN'T A-BEEN SO HIGH . . . . SP LIFE IS FINE 18
IF THE WAR HADN'T COME ALONG . . . SP RELIEF 8

HAG 1

THIS ANCIENT HAG . . . . SP MEXICAN MARKET 1

HAIL 2

HAIL. MARY. MOTHER OF GOD! . . . . SP MYSTERY 6
AND SPLINTERS OF HAIL. . . . . . . PL DREAM DUST 4

HAIR 11

SHE HAD LONG BLACK HAIR. . . . . . SH ONLY WOMAN BLUS 13
YOU BRAID YOUR HAIR TOO TIGHT - . . OWT HONEY BABE 2
WHOSE HAIR WAS GRAY . . . . SP JOE LOUIS 3
THE TRIBUNE'S HAIR . . . . SP MIGRANT 31
UPON MY HAIR? . . . . SP PRAYER 5
WITH DUST IN HER HAIR. . . . . . . SP SONG BILLIE HOL 11
HAS A HEAD OF VIBRANT HAIR . . . . SP TRUMPET PLAYER 11
CUTS MY HAIR ON CREDIT. . . . . . . AYM HORN OF PLENTY 95
AND YOUR HAIR WAS BLOWING BACK . . AYM RIDE. RED. RIDE 33
HAIR . . . . AYM SHADES OF PIG 34
(AND I NEVER HAD THAT MUCH HAIR) . AYM SHADES OF PIG 36

HAIR-DRESSING 1

HAIR-DRESSING PARLOR . . . . SP MADAM'S PAST HI 6

HAITI 1

UP FROM CUBA HAITI JAMAICA. . . . . SP GOOD MORNING 11

HALF 10

GIVES YOU A DOLLAR AN' A HALF. . . FC HARD LUCK 8
GIVES YOU A DOLLAR AN' A HALF. . . FC HARD LUCK 10
BUT THEY GIVIN' 'EM TO SCHOOL BOYS NOW AND PAYIN' JUST ABOUT HALF. NM BROKE 43
HALF A WORLD AWAY FROM HOME. . . . DK SAILOR 2
YOU'RE HALF A WORLD AWAY OR MORE . JC GOOD MORN STLIN 17
THAT I AM HALF ASHAMED . . . . . . FW SNAKE 5
HALF FISH. . . . . SP CATCH 11
HALF GIRL . . . . SP CATCH 12
AND DON'T MEAN HALF IT SAYS - . . . SP IN EXPLANATION 33
FOR ONE MORE DOLLAR AND A HALF. . . SP MADAM FORT TELL 23

HALF-DARK 1

A DRAMATIC RECITATION TO BE DONE IN THE HALF-DARK BY A YOUNG BROWN FELLOW . . . . NM COLORED SL MOOD 1

HALF-DEFIANT 1

CARELESS. AND HALF-DEFIANT ECHOES OF THE "ST. JAMES INFIRMARY" AS THE NM BIG-TIMER MOOD 2

HALF-PAST 2

'BOUT HALF-PAST THREE. . . . . . . SP SYLVESTER'S BED 2
'BOUT HALF-PAST FO'. . . . . SP SYLVESTER'S BED 10

HALF-PINT 1

HALF-PINT. - . . . . WB CAT AND SAXOPHN 3

HALF-SHY 1

THERE'S A HALF-SHY YOUNG MOON . . . FW NEW MOON 5

HALF-SOB 1
BEEN MADE. PROUD AND SMILING. BUT THE LIVING. REMEMBERING WITH A HALF-SOB . . . . NM COLORED SL MOOD 10

HALF-TRUTHS 1
LIFE IS A SYSTEM OF HALF-TRUTHS AND LIES. . . . . PL ELDERLY LEADERS 3

HALL 1
POOL HALL OR BAR ON CORNER . . . . AYM HORN OF PLENTY 70

HALLELUJAH 4
GLORY! HALLELUJAH! . . . . SH ONLY WOMAN BLUS 15
AMEN! HALLELUJAH! . . . . SP MYSTERY 8
GLORY! HALLELUJAH! . . . . SP PRAYER MEETING 1
GLORY! HALLELUJAH! . . . . SP PRAYER MEETING 3

HALLS 1
IN THE HALLS. . . . . OWT VISITORS 16

HALO 1
AND A HALO ON MY HEAD . . . . PL GO SLOW 13

HALTER 1
LIKE A MULE BROKE TO THE HALTER. . SP INTERNE AT PROV 25

HALTINGLY 1
HALTINGLY AND STUMBLINGLY SAY THEM. SP FREEDOM'S PLOW 150

HAMBURGERS 1
HAMBURGERS PEPSI-COLA . . . . AYM ASK YOUR MAMA 41

HAMMER 6
DON'T YOU HEAR THIS HAMMER RING? . JC BIG BUDDY 11
DON'T YOU HEAR THIS HAMMER RING? . JC BIG BUDDY 13
DON'T YOU HEAR THIS HAMMER RING? . JC BIG BUDDY 19
AX HANDLES. HAMMER HANDLES. . . . . SP FREEDOM'S PLOW 65
JOHN HENRY WITH HIS HAMMER . . . . SP LOVE 5
MAKES HAMMER BEAT OF DRUM BEAT . . SP MIGRANT 17

HAMMOND 2
WHERE IS THAT SUGAR. HAMMOND. . . . SP EARLY EVENING 1
I AIN'T NO WISE WOMAN. HAMMOND. . . SP EARLY EVENING 13

HAND 41
IN ONE HAND . . . . WB THE JESTER 1
ASK HIM TO GIMME HIS HAND. . . . . FC MOAN 8
STURDY I STAND. BOOKS IN MY HAND - NM DARK YOUTH USA 1
AND THE STRENGTH A STRONG HAND KNOWS. . . . . OK ALABAMA EARTH 9
HE GIVES ME HIS HAND. . . . . OK MA LORD 4
LIKE GOD'S HAND. . . . . OK TEA CHARM 6
WHOSE HAND AT THE FOUNDRY. WHOSE PLOW IN THE RAIN. . . . . ANS LET AMERICA BE 68
ONE SINGLE HAND . . . . ANS OPEN LETTER 22
HERE IS MY HAND. . . . . ANS OPEN LETTER 56
HERE I GO WITH MY BANNER IN MY HAND! ANS SISTER JOHNSON 5
WORKERS. LIFT NO HAND AGAIN . . . . ANS SONG OF SPAIN 56
WON'T YOU LEND A HAND? . . . . . . JC BIG BUDDY 8
LIFT THEIR HEADS. TOO. WITH GUN IN HAND . . . . JC GOOD MORN STLIN 33
TO SEE JIM CROW GET OUT OF HAND. . JC JIM CROW'S LAST 4
WHEN DORIE MILLER TOOK GUN IN HAND - JC JIM CROW'S LAST 28
IN THE PALM OF MY HAND . . . . . . FW DUSTBOWL 5
IN THE GRIP OF HAND TO HAND. . . . FW MAN 4
IN THE GRIP OF HAND TO HAND. . . . FW MAN 4
SHE SEEKS YOUR HAND. . . . . FW SLEEP 4
MADAM COULD LOOK IN YOUR HAND - . . SP BLD FORTUNE TEL 1
PUT SOME SILVER IN MY HAND . . . . SP BLD THE GYPSY 6
PLEASE REACH OUT YO' HAND. . . . . SP FEET O' JESUS 8
KEEP YOUR HAND ON THE PLOW! HOLD ON! SP FREEDOM'S PLOW 200
THE HAND SEEKS TOOLS TO CUT THE WOOD. . . . . SP FREEDOM'S PLOW 18
THEN THE HAND SEEKS OTHER HANDS TO HELP. . . . . SP FREEDOM'S PLOW 20
KEEP YOUR HAND ON THE PLOW! HOLD ON! SP FREEDOM'S PLOW 126
KEEP YOUR HAND ON THE PLOW! HOLD ON! SP FREEDOM'S PLOW 129
HAND REACHING OUT TO HAND. . . . . SP FREEDOM'S PLOW 39
HAND REACHING OUT TO HAND. . . . . SP FREEDOM'S PLOW 39
KEEP YOUR HAND ON THE PLOW! HOLD ON! SP FREEDOM'S PLOW 160
KEEP YOUR HAND ON THE PLOW! HOLD ON! SP FREEDOM'S PLOW 191
LEST THE SONG GET OUT OF HAND. . . SP GENIUS CHILD 4
FORTUNE TELLER LOCKED IN MY HAND. SP MADAM FORT TELL 1
FORTUNE TELLER SQUEEZE MY HAND. . . SP MADAM FORT TELL 5
UNDER MY HAND THE PYRAMIDS AROSE. SP NEGRO 8
REACH UP YOUR HAND. DARK BOY. AND TAKE A STAR. . . . . SP STARS 7
WITH THE TOUCH OF YOUR HAND . . . . SP TO ARTINA 7
AIN'T GOT NOBODY TO HOLD MY HAND - SP 50 - 50 2
AND LIFT MY HAND . . . . PL ANGOLA QUESTION 11
HAND ME MY MINT JULEP. MAMMY. . . . PL CULTURAL EXCHNG 59
FUTILE OF ME TO OFFER YOU MY HAND. PL LAST PRINCE 1

HANDED 1
EMPTY HANDED AS I BEGAN. . . . . . NM BLACK CLWN POEM 20

HANDFUL 2
TO A HANDFUL OF DUST IN AUTUMN. . . FW DUSTBOWL 3
ONE HANDFUL OF DREAM-DUST . . . . . PL DREAM DUST 5

HANDKERCHIEF 1
IS A SOFT BANDANNA HANDKERCHIEF . . WB OUR LAND 5

HANDLE 1
AND HANDLE EASY LIKE A PURCHASED THING. . . . . OWT JUICE JOINT 36

HANDLED 1
TOOLS HANDLED - BUT UNUSED. . . . . JC THE BITTER RIVR 19

HANDLES 4
HELD THE PLOW HANDLES. . . . . . . SP FREEDOM'S PLOW 64
AX HANDLES. HAMMER HANDLES. . . . . SP FREEDOM'S PLOW 65
AX HANDLES. HAMMER HANDLES. . . . . SP FREEDOM'S PLOW 65
WITH AX HANDLES . . . . PL SPECIAL BULLTIN 12

HANDS 54
LOUD LAUGHERS IN THE HANDS OF FATE - FC LAUGHERS 4
LOUD-MOUTHED LAUGHERS IN THE HANDS FC LAUGHERS 31
HERE ARE MY HANDS . . . . NM BLACK CLWN POEM 61
ONLY MY OWN HANDS. . . . . ANS A NEW SONG 26
40-VOICES: GROW STRONG WITH UNION. ALL HANDS TOGETHER - . . . . . . ANS CHANT MAY DAY 11
UNTIL THE WHOLE WORLD FALLS INTO THE HANDS OF . . . . ANS CHANT TOM MOONY 24
WILL ALL RAISE THEIR HANDS AGAINST THE KIDS WHO DIE. . . . . ANS KIDS WHO DIE 29
AND BLACK HANDS AND WHITE HANDS CLASPED AS ONE. . . . . ANS KIDS WHO DIE 48
AND BLACK HANDS AND WHITE HANDS CLASPED AS ONE. . . . . ANS KIDS WHO DIE 48
MILL HANDS. . . . . ANS OPEN LETTER 5
YOU HAVE LINKED YOUR HANDS WITH ME. ANS OPEN LETTER 46
MUST PUT THEIR HANDS WITH MINE . . ANS UNION 6
HANDS ON HIM. . . . . SH DEATH IN HARLEM 9
DIXIE RUBBED HIS HANDS AND LAUGHED OUT LOUD - . . . . SH DEATH IN HARLEM 63
BUT WE HAVE JOINED HANDS - . . . . JC TO CAPTAIN MULZ 36
PRESS HANDS TOGETHER. LAUGHING AT HER SONG. . . . . OWT LINCOLN THEATRE 15
MY HANDS! . . . . SP AS I GREW OLDER 24
MY DARK HANDS! . . . . SP AS I GREW OLDER 25
ON GREAT BIG HANDS. . . . . SP DREAM BOOGE VAR 6
WHEN A MAN STARTS OUT WITH HIS HANDS SP FREEDOM'S PLOW 2
THEN THE HAND SEEKS OTHER HANDS TO HELP. . . . . SP FREEDOM'S PLOW 20
A COMMUNITY OF HANDS TO HELP - . . SP FREEDOM'S PLOW 21
BELONGING TO ALL THE HANDS WHO BUILD. . . . . SP FREEDOM'S PLOW 27
SOME WERE FREE HANDS . . . . SP FREEDOM'S PLOW 41
SOME WERE INDENTURED HANDS . . . . SP FREEDOM'S PLOW 43
SOME WERE SLAVE HANDS . . . . SP FREEDOM'S PLOW 45
IN THE FREE HANDS AND THE SLAVE HANDS. . . . . SP FREEDOM'S PLOW 50
IN THE FREE HANDS AND THE SLAVE HANDS. . . . . SP FREEDOM'S PLOW 50
IN INDENTURED HANDS AND ADVENTUROUS HANDS. . . . . SP FREEDOM'S PLOW 51
IN INDENTURED HANDS AND ADVENTUROUS HANDS. . . . . SP FREEDOM'S PLOW 51
TURNING THE RICH SOIL WENT THE PLOW IN MANY HANDS . . . . SP FREEDOM'S PLOW 52
CLANG AGAINST THE TREES WENT THE AX IN MANY HANDS . . . . SP FREEDOM'S PLOW 55
FREE HANDS AND SLAVE HANDS. . . . . SP FREEDOM'S PLOW 61
FREE HANDS AND SLAVE HANDS. . . . . SP FREEDOM'S PLOW 61
INDENTURED HANDS. ADVENTUROUS HANDS. SP FREEDOM'S PLOW 62
INDENTURED HANDS. ADVENTUROUS HANDS. SP FREEDOM'S PLOW 62
WHITE HANDS AND BLACK HANDS . . . . SP FREEDOM'S PLOW 63
WHITE HANDS AND BLACK HANDS . . . . SP FREEDOM'S PLOW 63
ALL THESE HANDS MADE AMERICA. . . . SP FREEDOM'S PLOW 69
OUT OF LABOR - WHITE HANDS AND BLACK HANDS - . . . . SP FREEDOM'S PLOW 82
OUT OF LABOR - WHITE HANDS AND BLACK HANDS - . . . . SP FREEDOM'S PLOW 82
BROWN HANDS . . . . SP INTERNE AT PROV 18
BLACK HANDS . . . . SP INTERNE AT PROV 19
GOLDEN HANDS IN WHITE COAT. . . . . SP INTERNE AT PROV 20
NURSES' HANDS ON SUTURE. . . . . . SP INTERNE AT PROV 21
THE BELGIANS CUT OFF MY HANDS IN THE CONGO. . . . . SP NEGRO 15
SOMETHING STRONG TO PUT MY HANDS ON. SP SPIRITUALS 3
WITH HIS EBONY HANDS ON EACH IVORY KEY . . . . SP THE WEARY BLUES 9
SHAKES HANDS WITH EMMETT TILL. . . AYM ASK YOUR MAMA 66
AND I'M GONNA PUT WHITE HANDS . . . PL DAYBREAK IN ALA 15
AND BLACK HANDS AND BROWN AND YELLOW HANDS . . . . PL DAYBREAK IN ALA 16
AND BLACK HANDS AND BROWN AND YELLOW HANDS . . . . PL DAYBREAK IN ALA 16
AND RED CLAY EARTH HANDS IN IT . . PL DAYBREAK IN ALA 17
I TAKE IN MY HANDS . . . . PL WAR 9

HAND-HIGH 1
HAND-HIGH SALUTES - HEIL! . . . . . PL SPECIAL BULLTIN 10

HANG 4
HANG ON HERE. . . . . OWT BOARDING HOUSE 10
OR THEY'LL HANG YOU TO A TREE! . . OWT FLIGHT 8
NOR SEEN HER HANG HER HEAD. . . . . SP BLD OF THE GIRL 10
AND HANG IT ABOUT YOUR NECK . . . . PL CROWNS GARLANDS 2

HANGED 1
HANGED BY THE NECK. . . . . PL OCTOBER 16 RAID 21

HANGING 1
THERE'S HANGING MOSS . . . . FW CAROLINA CABIN 1

HANKERED 1
BUT I HANKERED TO SEE . . . . SP MADAM'S CALLING 7

HAPPENED 5
BUT SOMETHING HAPPENED, JIM'S FEATHERS FELL. . . . . JC JIM CROW'S LAST 5
HAPPENED IN THE SPRING - . . . . . LHR BLD MARY'S SON 5
SOMETHING MUSTA HAPPENED . . . . . SP BLD THE GYPSY 16
IN CHINA BEFORE WHAT HAPPENED . . . SP IN EXPLANATION 8
WHAT HAPPENED THEN? . . . . PL GHOSTS OF 1619 13

HAPPENS 3
WHAT HAPPENS . . . . SP GOOD MORNING 26
WHAT HAPPENS TO A DREAM DEFERRED? SP HARLEM 1
WHAT HAPPENS TO A DREAM DEFERRED? PL DREAM DEFERRED 1

HAPPINESS 3
SHE LIVED IN SINFUL HAPPINESS . . . FW GIRL 1
AND THE PURSUIT OF HAPPINESS. . . . SP FREEDOM'S PLOW 95
HAPPINESS IS . . . . SP HEAVEN 3

HAPPY 13
AND ME AND MY BROTHER WERE HAPPY AS YOU PLEASE . . . . NM COLORED SL POEM 6
SO WE MARCHED TO THE FRONT, HAPPY TO FIGHT. . . . . NM COLORED SL POEM 12
FLOWERS ARE HAPPY IN SUMMER. . . . DK AUTUMN THOUGHT 1
FOR I AM HAPPY WITH MY SEA. . . . . DK DEATH SEAMAN 10
HAPPY THEY WERE HERE. . . . . DK IRISH WAKE 8
EVERYBODY'S HAPPY. IT'S A SPENDIN CROWD - . . . . SH DEATH IN HARLEM 36
AND MAKE EARTH HAPPY . . . . FW WISDOM 7
YESTERDAY I WAS HAPPY. . . . . . . OWT YESTERDAY TODAY 9
I THOUGHT YOU WAS HAPPY, TOO. . . . OWT YESTERDAY TODAY 10
IT'S A HAPPY BEAT? . . . . SP DREAM BOOGIE 9
I'M HAPPY! . . . . SP DREAM BOOGIE 16
IF YOU WANT TO BE HAPPY . . . . . . SP LAMENT OVER LOV 17
I AIN'T HAPPY NO MO' . . . . SP THE WEARY BLUES 29

HARBOR 3
PEARL HARBOR PUT JIM CROW ON THE RUN. . . . . JC JIM CROW'S LAST 8
TO GUARD THE HARBOR ENTRANCE . . . JC TO CAPTAIN MULZ 14
THAT GUIDE US TOWARD THE HARBOR OF THE NEW WORLD . . . . JC TO CAPTAIN MULZ 54

HARD 27
SO HARD. . . . . WB FOR PORTRAIT OF 4
WITH HARD KNUCKLES . . . . FC BEALE ST. LOVE 3
WHEN HARD LUCK OVERTAKES YOU . . . FC HARD LUCK 1
WHEN HARD LUCK OVERTAKES YOU . . . FC HARD LUCK 3
I'M A HARD WORKIN' MAN . . . . . . FC WORKIN' MAN 13
SYNCOPATED MUSIC, TELLING HIS STORY IN A HARD, BRAZEN, CYNICAL FASHION. . . . . NM BIG-TIMER MOOD 1
FOLKS SHO IS GETTIN' HARD ON YOU - JUST 'CAUSE YOU BROKE. . . . . . NM BROKE 15
BUT I SHO BEEN LOOKIN' ROUND HARD LATELY FOR WAYS AND MEANS . . . NM BROKE 39
AN' DE ROAD IS HARD AN' LONG. . . . DK PO' BOY BLUES 12
IT'S HARD TO BEAT HITLER . . . . . JC HOW ABOUT DIXIE 19
HARD LUCK . . . . OWT BLUES ON A BOX 7
AS HARD AS MY HEAD IS. . . . . . . OWT TOO BLUE 12
BIRTHING IS HARD . . . . SP ADVICE 2
IS AWFUL, AWFUL HARD. . . . . SP BAD LUCK CARD 2
IT'S HARD TO UNDERSTAND . . . . . . SP BLD OF THE GIRL 2
AND I WORK TOO HARD . . . . SP BLUE BAYOU 9
ONE BATTED A HARD BALL RIGHT THROUGH MY WINDOW . . . . SP CHILDREN'S RYME 18
IT'S HARD TO BELIEVE. . . . . SP DEAD IN THERE 10
CHILE, THESE STEPS IS HARD TO CLIMB. SP DIME 1
AND I PLAYED SO DOG-GONE HARD. . . SP LITTLE GRN TREE 6
WHEN YOU GROW UP THE HARD WAY . . . SP MADAM NIGHT-HAV 5
'CAUSE YOU FINDS IT'S KINDER HARD. SP MOTHER TO SON 16
FOLKS WORK HARD . . . . SP NEW YORKERS 7
DOWN THE LONG HARD ROW THAT I BEEN HOEING . . . . AYM BLUES IN STEREO 34
FAMOUS - THE HARD WAY - . . . . . . AYM HORN OF PLENTY 38
THE HARD . . . . AYM SHADES OF PIG 19
IT'S HARD TO BLAME ME. . . . . . . PL WAR 13

HARDENING 1
HARDENING THE DUSK DARK EVENING. . SP RAILROAD AVENUE 24

HARDLY 6
COULD HARDLY FIND A JOB THAT OFFERED DECENT PAY. . . . . NM COLORED SL POEM 21
THEY HARDLY TAKE GOD BY SURPRISE. LHR ACCEPTANCE 4
CAN'T HARDLY GET HIS BREAD. . . . . SP MONROE'S BLUES 4
DIDN'T HARDLY KNOW MY MIND. . . . . SP MORNING AFTER 2
WOULD HARDLY WRITE IT IN THE SCRIPT - . . . . AYM IS IT TRUE? 30
WOULD HARDLY DESIRE . . . . PL BOMBINGS DIXIE 6

HARDNESS 1
SUN AND THE BEATEN HARDNESS OF THE EARTH. . . . . SP SUN SONG 2

HARD-FACED 1
OLD HARD-FACED JUDGE SAYS EIGHTEEN MONTHS . . . . FC BLD OF GIN MARY 23

HARD-HEARTED 2
HARD-HEARTED AND UNLOVING! . . . . SH DECLARATION 15
HARD-HEARTED AND UNTRUE! . . . . . SH DECLARATION 16

HARLAN 1
AT HARLAN, RICHMOND, GASTONIA, ATLANTA, NEW-ORLEANS; . . . . . . ANS OPEN LETTER 16

HARLEM 51
DARK HARLEM. . . . . WB DISILLUSION 6
IN A HARLEM CABARET . . . . WB JAZZONIA 3
OF THE HARLEM NIGHT . . . . WB SUMMER NIGHT 2
THOSE KIND COME CHEAP IN HARLEM . . WB YOUNG PROSTITUT 4
FLAVOR HARLEM OF MINE! . . . . . . SH HARLEM SWEETIES 28
HARLEM GIRLS VARY - . . . . SH HARLEM SWEETIES 40
BUT INDIA AND CHINA AND HARLEM, TOO. JC JIM CROW'S LAST 13
DOWN THE STREET YOUNG HARLEM . . . FW DIMOUT IN HARLM 1
DOWN THE STREET YOUNG HARLEM . . . FW DIMOUT IN HARLM 15
THE CRY SPREAD OVER HARLEM . . . . OWT BLD MARGE POLIT 15
HARLEM . . . . OWT DECEASED 1
DARK HARLEM WAITS FOR YOU. . . . . OWT NEGRO SERVANT 11
O, DRUMS OF LIFE IN HARLEM AFTER DARK! . . . . OWT NEGRO SERVANT 15
UP IN HARLEM - . . . . OWT VISITORS 6
IN HARLEM. . . . . OWT VISITORS 8
IN HARLEM TOWN . . . . SP COLLEGE FORMAL 4
HARLEM TO YOU! . . . . SP COMMENT ON CURB 7
WATCHED HARLEM GROW . . . . SP GOOD MORNING 3
TO HARLEM BROOKLYN THE BRONX . . . SP GOOD MORNING 14
BUT MOST OF ALL TO HARLEM . . . . . SP GOOD MORNING 15
THE HARLEM ROOF-TOPS . . . . SP HARLEM NIGHT SO 6
FROM HARLEM PAST HONG KONG TALKING BACK. . . . . SP IN EXPLANATION 22
I COULD TAKE THE HARLEM NIGHT . . . SP JUKE BOX LOVE 1
DANCE WITH YOU, MY SWEET BROWN HARLEM GIRL. . . . . SP JUKE BOX LOVE 12
SHOPS ALL OVER HARLEM . . . . SP LIKEWISE 10
BUT IN HARLEM THEY DON'T ANSWER BACK. . . . . SP LIKEWISE 14
IN HARLEM? . . . . SP LIKEWISE 18
WHAT'S THE HARLEM . . . . SP LIKEWISE 20
USE IN HARLEM . . . . SP LIKEWISE 21
HARLEM LAUGHING IN ALL THE WRONG PLACES . . . . SP MOVIES 2
IN HARLEM . . . . SP NEIGHBOR 4
IN HARLEM: . . . . SP NIGHT FUNERAL 2
IN HARLEM: . . . . SP NIGHT FUNERAL 10
IN HARLEM: . . . . SP NIGHT FUNERAL 18
IN HARLEM: . . . . SP NIGHT FUNERAL 28
IN HARLEM. . . . . SP NIGHT FUNERAL 46
ON SUNNY SUMMER SUNDAY AFTERNOONS IN HARLEM . . . . SP PASSING 1
AND HARLEM HAS ITS . . . . SP PASSING 9
HARLEM OF THE BITTER DREAM. . . . . SP PASSING 14
DOWN ON THE HARLEM RIVER: . . . . . SP REVERIE HARLEM 9
AT CLUB HARLEM IT'S ELEVEN . . . . SP SEASHORE THROUG 3
A MOVIE HOUSE IN HARLEM NAMED AFTER LINCOLN. . . . . SP SHAME ON YOU 6
O, SWEEP OF STARS OVER HARLEM STREETS. . . . . SP STARS 1
TO THIS COLLEGE ON THE HILL ABOVE HARLEM. . . . . SP THEME FOR ENG B 9
THE STEPS FROM THE HILL LEAD DOWN INTO HARLEM. . . . . SP THEME FOR ENG B 11
THE HARLEM BRANCH Y, WHERE I TAKE THE ELEVATOR . . . . SP THEME FOR ENG B 14
I FEEL AND SEE AND HEAR, HARLEM, I HEAR YOU: . . . . SP THEME FOR ENG B 18
IN HARLEM OR THE SOUTH SIDE OF CHICAGO . . . . AYM HORN OF PLENTY 55
STANDS HARLEM - . . . . PL HARLEM 2
IN HARLEM . . . . PL HARLEM 13
AND EARS THAT CLOSE TO HARLEM SCREAMS. . . . . PL JUNIOR ADDICT 5

HARLEMITES 1
HARLEMITES SAY . . . . OWT BLD MARGE POLIT 26

HARLEM'S 4
IN HARLEM'S NO LACK. . . . . SH HARLEM SWEETIES 20
VEILING HARLEM'S LAUGHTER . . . . . FW DIMOUT IN HARLM 13

TAKE HARLEM'S HEARTBEAT. . . . . . SP JUKE BOX LOVE 7
BUFFALO TO HARLEM'S OVERNIGHT: . . AYM ODE TO DINAH 48

HARM 1
DON'T MEAN NO HARM. . . . . SP MADAM WRONG VIS 12

HARNESS 1
TO TILL THE SOIL, AND HARNESS THE POWER OF THE WATERS. . . . . . . SP FREEDOM'S PLOW 19

HARPER 1
I.W. HARPER . . . . SP SUMMER EVENING 10

HARPERS 1
SINCE HARPERS FERRY . . . . PL OCTOBER 16 RAID 23

HARPER'S 1
WITH JOHN BROWN AT HARPER'S FERRY, NEGROES DIED. . . . . SP FREEDOM'S PLOW 116

HARRIETT 1
SEND FOR HARRIETT TUBMAN, OLD SOJOURNER TRUTH. . . . . PL FINAL CALL 32

HARRYS 1
MAKE A CROWN OF SAMMYS, SIDNEYS, HARRYS. . . . . PL CROWNS GARLANDS 4

HARSH 1
FROM ONE SIDE TO THE OTHER, BUT NOW A HARSH AND BITTER NOTE CREEPS INTO . . . . NM BLACK CLWN MOOD 9

HARVESTED 1
THAT PLANTED AND HARVESTED THE FOOD THAT FED . . . . SP FREEDOM'S PLOW 53

HAS 70
WHAT GREAT FOREST HAS HUNG ITS PERFUME . . . . WB NUDE YOUNG DANC 3
WHAT STAR-WHITE MOON HAS BEEN YOUR MOTHER? . . . . WB NUDE YOUNG DANC 7
HAS GONE THE QUIET WAY . . . . . . WB TO LITTLE LOVER 4
MA SWEET GOOD MAN HAS . . . . FC SUICIDE 1
MA SWEET GOOD MAN HAS . . . . FC SUICIDE 3
AND THE OTHER HAS NO NAME . . . . . OLD TWO THINGS 8
HAS I DID IT BEFO'? CERTAINLY! . . NM BROKE 31
WHO HAS A VISION OF HIS BROTHER KILLED IN FRANCE WHILE FIGHTING FOR THE . . . . NM COLORED SL MOOD 2
WITH HIS FACE FULL OF LIGHT AND FAITH, CONFIDENT THAT A NEW WORLD HAS . . . . NM COLORED SL MOOD 9
THE TRUTH A SIMPLE HEART HAS HELD OK ALABAMA EARTH 8
REDDER NOW WHERE YOUR BLOOD HAS FLOWED. . . . . ANS BLD OZZIE POWEL 3
A MAN WITH THE TITLE OF GOVERNOR HAS SPOKEN: . . . . ANS CHANT TOM MOONY 4
A MAN WITH THE TITLE OF GOVERNOR HAS SPOKEN: . . . . ANS CHANT TOM MOONY 6
THAT'S MADE AMERICA THE LAND IT HAS BECOME. . . . . ANS LET AMERICA BE 44
THE LAND THAT NEVER HAS BEEN YET - ANS LET AMERICA BE 63
TOO LONG HAS THE TASTE OF ITS WATER JC THE BITTER RIVR 4
TOO LONG HAS ITS EVIL POISON . . . JC THE BITTER RIVR 8
YOURS HAS BEEN THE POWER . . . . . JC THE BITTER RIVR 55
AGAIN MANKIND HAS LOST ITS COURSE. JC TO CAPTAIN MULZ 6
HAS TAKEN HOLD. . . . . JC TO CAPTAIN MULZ 27
HE HAS BEEN . . . . FW OLD SAILOR 1
HAS STUDIED VARIED FACES. . . . . . FW OLD SAILOR 5
HAS TASTED MYSTERY. . . . . FW OLD SAILOR 6
HAS BREASTED . . . . FW OLD SAILOR 8
THAT WOMEN HE HAS LEFT . . . . . . FW OLD SAILOR 18
IT HAS A RED STAR ON IT. . . . . . FW WHEN ARMIES PAS 3
BUT IT HAS A RED STAR ON IT! . . . FW WHEN ARMIES PAS 9
WHO SINGS THE TROUBLES EVERY WOMAN HAS. . . . . OWT LINCOLN THEATRE 8
DE MAN I LOVES HAS . . . . OWT LINCOLN THEATRE 11
HAS A VULGAR TONE. . . . . LHR CONSERVATORY 2
AUNT SUE HAS A HEAD FULL OF STORIES. SP AUNTSUE'S STORI 1
AUNT SUE HAS A WHOLE HEART FULL OF STORIES. . . . . SP AUNTSUE'S STORI 2
MY ROOF HAS SPRUNG A LEAK. . . . . . SP BLD LANDLORD 2
HAS TO GIVE HIS MOTHER TEN - . . . SP BUDDY 5
HAS TO. . . . . SP CONSIDER ME 29
HAS GROWN QUITE TALL. . . . . SP DELINQUENT 2
HAS GROWN QUITE STOUT. . . . . . . SP DELINQUENT 6
HAS GROWN QUITE WISE - . . . . . . SP DELINQUENT 10
AS THE OTHER FELLOW HAS . . . . . . SP DEMOCRACY 6
JOE HAS SENSE ENOUGH TO KNOW . . . SP JOE LOUIS 5
MAMA, IT HAS BEEN RAINING CATS AND DOGS UP . . . . SP LETTER 8
NOW OLD AGE HAS . . . . SP LITTLE GRN TREE 7
HAS IT BEEN SAVED. . . . . SP MADAM MINISTER 7
THE WIND HAS UNDRESSED THE MOON. . SP MARCH MOON 2
THE WIND HAS BLOWN ALL THE CLOUD-GARMENTS . . . . SP MARCH MOON 3
HAS KNOWN HIGH WIND-SWEPT MOUNTAINS. SP MEXICAN MARKET 5
AND THE SUN HAS MADE . . . . SP MEXICAN MARKET 6
HAS A LUNCH TO CARRY. . . . . SP MIGRANT 13
MY SOUL HAS GROWN DEEP LIKE THE RIVERS. . . . . SP NEGRO SPEAKS OF 4
MY SOUL HAS GROWN DEEP LIKE THE RIVERS. . . . . SP NEGRO SPEAKS OF 13
AND HARLEM HAS ITS . . . . SP PASSING 9
SINCE THEIR DREAM HAS . . . . SP PASSING 15
HAS FORGOTTEN . . . . SP RAILROAD AVENUE 6
SOME TRAIN HAS FORGOTTEN. . . . . . SP RAILROAD AVENUE 29
NATURE HAS A WAY . . . . SP S-SSS-SS-SH! 8
HAS DARK MOONS OF WEARINESS . . . . SP TRUMPET PLAYER 3
HAS A HEAD OF VIBRANT HAIR . . . . SP TRUMPET PLAYER 11
HAS A FINE ONE-BUTTON ROLL, ... SP TRUMPET PLAYER 26
HAS NO RECOURSE NOW BUT TO THE LAW? AYM ASK YOUR MAMA 11
WHO AT THE SORBONNE HAS SIX CLASSES. AYM ASK YOUR MAMA 54
HAS ALMOST FORGOTTEN MEALIE. . . . AYM ASK YOUR MAMA 58
AND SMITTY HAS NOT CHANGED AT ALL. AYM BIRD IN ORBIT 22
AS THE OTHER FELLOW HAS . . . . . . PL FREEDOM 6
THE PAST HAS BEEN A MINT . . . . . PL HISTORY 1
(AND HAS NO WAY TO UNDERSTAND) . . PL JUNIOR ADDICT 7
WHERE HAS TERROR BEEN? . . . . . . PL MISSISSIPPI 9
HAS PASSED AWAY. . . . . PL OCTOBER 16 RAID 18
HAS LONG BEEN TRIED AT LAW. . . . . PL OCTOBER 16 RAID 20
SNOW HAS FRIZ ME. . . . . PL STILL HERE 3
SUN HAS BAKED ME. . . . . PL STILL HERE 4

HAST 2
YET THOU HAST . . . . WB POEM 5
YET THOU HAST . . . . WB POEM 11

HASTE 1
MAKE HASTE! . . . . PL CULTURAL EXCHNG 61

HASTINGS 2
COULD BE HASTINGS STREET. . . . . . SP COULD BE 1
HASTINGS STREET IS WEARY. . . . . . SP COULD BE 13

HAT 8
A MORAL POEM TO BE RENDERED BY A MAN IN A STRAW HAT WITH A BRIGHT BAND, A . . . . NM BIG-TIMER MOOD 1
SUIT AND HAT OF A CLOWN, TO THE MUSIC OF A PIANO, OR AN ORCHESTRA. . . . . . . NM BLACK CLWN MOOD 1
THROWING DOWN THE HAT OF A FOOL, AND STANDING FORTH, STRAIGHT AND STRONG. . . . . NM BLACK CLWN MOOD 14
IN AN OLD SUIT AND A BATTERED HAT, TO THE TUNE OF A SLOW DRAG STOMP NM BROKE 1
SHE BOUGHT A NEW HAT LAST WEEK AND COME SENDIN' ME THE BILL. . . . NM BROKE 49
BUT RIGHT LONG THROUGH HERE NOW, I CAN'T 'FORD TO BUY YOU NO HAT." NM BROKE 51
I BOUGHT A NEW HAT. . . . . OK DRESSED UP 5
AND HAT, TOO! . . . . SP WHAT? 6

HATE 12
I DO NOT HATE YOU. . . . . WB THE WHITE ONES 1
I DO NOT HATE YOU. . . . . WB THE WHITE ONES 3
OF PREJUDICE, AND HATE, AND THE FALSE COLOR LINE - . . . . NM COLORED SL POEM 9
SERVE - AND HATE WILL DIE UNBORN. OK ALABAMA EARTH 12
THE HIGH SHERIFF'S EYES ARE FILLED WITH HATE. . . . . ANS BLD OZZIE POWEL 7
I HATE TO DIE THIS WAY WITH THE QUIET . . . . SH CABARET GIRL 1
THE FOLKS WHO HATE YOU'D . . . . . JC GOOD MORN STLIN 37
OF HATE AND GREED AND RACE . . . . JC TO CAPTAIN MULZ 57
HATE HIM, TOO. . . . . FW MIGRATION 9
BUT I'D HATE TO DIE ALL ALONE! . . SP AS BEFITS A MAN 2
EXCEPT IN MEMORIES OF HATE . . . . AYM ODE TO DINAH 90
SCATTERS HATE LIKE SEED . . . . . . PL GEORGIA DUSK 10

HATED 1
BUT HE HATED TO WRITE . . . . SP MADAM CENSUS 7

HATES 6
I HATES THEM RINNEY YALLER GALS . . FC BLACK GAL 15
UH! I HATES A LYIN' GYPSY . . . . . SP BLD THE GYPSY 18
HATES TO BE LONELY. . . . . SP BOUND NO'TH BLS 13
LAWD, I HATES TO BE SAD. . . . . . SP BOUND NO'TH BLS 14
SAYS I HATES TO BE LONELY. . . . . SP BOUND NO'TH BLS 15
HATES TO BE LONELY AN' SAD. . . . . SP BOUND NO'TH BLS 16

HATS 2
SOME PIMPS WEAR SUMMER HATS . . . . SP WHAT? 1
IN GRAY SLOUCH HATS. . . . . PL THIRD DEGREE 6

HATTIE 3
I AIN'T GOT NO SUGAR, HATTIE. . . . SP EARLY EVENING 7
IF YOU'S A WISE WOMAN, HATTIE. . . SP EARLY EVENING 11
I DON'T TREAT YOU BAD, HATTIE. . . SP EARLY EVENING 17

HAUL 2
GIT ME A WAGGON TO HAUL. . . . . . FC HARD LUCK 14
GIT A WÀGGON TO HAUL. . . . . FC HARD LUCK 16

HAUNT 2
DARK GHOSTS COME BACK TO HAUNT YOU NOW. . . . . PL GHOSTS OF 1619 2
THEY MAY NOT ONLY HAUNT YOU - . . . PL GHOSTS OF 1619 5

HAUNTS 1
HAUNTS ME NIGHT AND DAY. . . . . WB BLUES FANTASY 12

HAVE 130
I MUST HAVE A PARTING. . . . . WB A FAREWELL 5
AND HAVE NEVER SEEN THE SEAS. . . . WB A FAREWELL 8
WHAT JUNGLE TREE HAVE YOU SLEPT UNDER. . . . . WB NUDE YOUNG DANC 1
WHAT JUNGLE TREE HAVE YOU SLEPT UNDER. . . . . WB NUDE YOUNG DANC 5
TO WHAT CLEAN BOY HAVE YOU OFFERED YOUR LIPS? . . . . WB NUDE YOUNG DANC 8
WE SHOULD HAVE A LAND OF SUN. . . . WB OUR LAND 1
WE SHOULD HAVE A LAND OF TREES. . . WB OUR LAND 8
AH, WE SHOULD HAVE A LAND OF JOY. . WB OUR LAND 13
I HAVE ONE WIFE. . . . . WB PIERROT 11
I HAVE ONE WIFE. . . . . WB PIERROT 14
HAVE FALLEN BENEATH YOUR EYES. . . WB SOLEDAD 4
DIDN'T HAVE A FRIEND NOWHERE. . . . FC BLD OF GIN MARY 4
O, PLEASE SIR, JUDGE, HAVE MERCY! FC BLD OF GIN MARY 21
HAVE MERCY, PLEASE, ON ME! . . . . FC BLD OF GIN MARY 22
I CAN'T HAVE NO WOMAN'S . . . . . FC EVIL WOMAN 9
O, LAWD HAVE MERCY . . . . . FC GAL'S CRY DYING 11
BUT I'LL HAVE MO' SENSE NEXT TIME. FC GYPSY MAN 18
I'D SHO HAVE THEM BLUES. . . . . FC MINNIE SINGS 20
THEN I DON'T HAVE TO THINK. . . . NM BIG-TIMER POEM 64
AND LET 'EM HAVE MY MONEY. . . . NM BIG-TIMER POEM 66
CAN A CLOWN HAVE HIS DAY. . . . . NM BLACK CLWN POEM 15
TO HAVE. . . . . NM BROKE 42
I THOUGHT LOVE WAS A DREAM, BUT I SHO HAVE AWOKE - . . . . NM BROKE 54
AND DIDN'T HAVE SUCH A BIG MOUTH. NM BROKE 65
YES, INDEEDY, I SHO HAVE MISSED YOU. TOO! . . . . NM BROKE 67
'CAUSE WHEN I WAS LIVING, I DIDN'T HAVE MINE. . . . . NM COLORED SL POEM 18
DIDN'T HAVE ANY SCHOOLS; AND THERE WERE ALL SORTS OF . . . . NM COLORED SL POEM 25
'S A TERRIBLE THING TO HAVE. . . . DK HOMESICK BLUES 14
A TERRIBLE THING TO HAVE. . . . . DK HOMESICK BLUES 16
I HAVE HELD MY PAIN . . . . . DK MINSTREL MAN 7
WE HAVE TOMORROW . . . . . DK YOUTH 1
I HAVE THIS WORD TO BRING. . . . ANS A NEW SONG 4
NOW I HAVE FINISHED MY TOIL. . . . ANS BLDS OF LENIN 8
THE MILLIONS WHO HAVE NOTHING FOR OUR PAY? . . . . ANS LET AMERICA BE 55
THE MILLIONS WHO HAVE NOTHING FOR OUR PAY? . . . . ANS LET AMERICA BE 60
YOU HAVE LINKED YOUR HANDS WITH ME. ANS OPEN LETTER 46
HAVE OUR FUN. . . . . SH DEATH IN HARLEM 107
IT MUST HAVE BEEN YESTERDAY. . . . SH EVIL MORNING 1
MUST HAVE BEEN YESTERDAY . . . . SH EVIL MORNING 3
HAVE YOU DUG THE SPILL . . . . SH HARLEM SWEETIES 1
I HAVE A GOOD TIME! . . . . SH IF-ING 16
HOW HIGH HAVE YOU GOT TO BE? . . . SH MISSISSIPPI LEV 14
HOW HIGH HAVE YOU GOT TO BE . . . . SH MISSISSIPPI LEV 16
DON'T HAVE TO SHARE IT A-TALL. . . SH PAY DAY 2
DON'T HAVE TO HEAR NOBODY SAY. . . SH PAY DAY 3
DON'T HAVE TO GO TO CHURCH. . . . . SH SUNDAY 3
DON'T HAVE TO GO NOWHERE. . . . . SH SUNDAY 4
HAVE ALMOST FORGOTTEN THEIR NAMES SH YOUNG NEGRO GRL 4
FOR YOU HAVE ALLIES EVERYWHERE. . . JC GOOD MORN STLIN 44
HAVE MADE UP THEIR MINDS JIM CROW IS THROUGH. . . . . JC JIM CROW'S LAST 14
"YOUR FOLKS WILL HAVE A BETTER DAY." JC THE BITTER RIVR 40
YOU HAVE LYNCHED MY COMRADES . . . JC THE BITTER RIVR 59
NOW YOUR WORDS NO LONGER HAVE MEANING - . . . . JC THE BITTER RIVR 65
I HAVE DRUNK AT THE RIVER TOO LONG: JC THE BITTER RIVR 66
THEY HAVE FOUND THEIR HOUR. . . . JC TO CAPTAIN MULZ 24
WE NEGROES HAVE BEEN SLAVES BEFORE. JC TO CAPTAIN MULZ 33
BUT WE HAVE JOINED HANDS - . . . . JC TO CAPTAIN MULZ 36
TOGETHER WE HAVE LAUNCHED A SHIP . JC TO CAPTAIN MULZ 39
WILL HAVE NO PLACE. . . . . JC TO CAPTAIN MULZ 58
WALLS HAVE BEEN KNOWN . . . . . FW DUSK 10
IT MIGHT HAVE BEEN . . . . . FW WHEN ARMIES PAS 17
TO HAVE A DATE. . . . . OWT BLD MARGE POLIT 32
YOU HAVE TO GET THERE EARLY . . . . OWT JITNEY 56
BUT I DIDN'T HAVE NARY ONE. . . . . OWT STRANGER IN TWN 5
I ASKED MY LANDLADY DID I HAVE PRIVILEGES. . . . . OWT STRANGER IN TWN 7
I HAVE DONE SO LITTLE . . . . . LHR POET TO BIGOT 1
AND YOU HAVE DONE SO LITTLE . . . . LHR POET TO BIGOT 3
THAT WE HAVE GOOD REASON . . . . . LHR POET TO BIGOT 5
HAVE SUCH MEAGRE . . . . . LHR POET TO BIGOT 8
I HAVE ALMOST FORGOTTEN MY DREAM. SP AS I GREW OLDER 2
SHE SAYS HE CAN HAVE . . . . . SP BUDDY 6
HE DIDN'T HAVE MUCH SENSE. . . . . SP DANCER 6
MAYBE NOW I CAN HAVE THAT WHITE ENAMEL STOVE . . . . . SP DEFERRED 8
I'LL HAVE A THRONE FOR MINE! . . . SP DEFERRED 42
BUDDY, HAVE YOU HEARD? . . . . . SP DEFERRED 52
I HAVE AS MUCH RIGHT . . . . . SP DEMOCRACY 5
YOU AIN'T GONNA HAVE NOTHIN TO SAY. SP EARLY EVENING 12
HAVE TO STAND! . . . . . SP EARLY EVENING 22
DON'T HAVE NO EFFECT ON YOU - . . . SP EVIL 2
THEN YOU KNOW THAT YOU HAVE TURNED SP FINAL CURVE 3
SAYS DADDY I HAVE GOT THE BLUES. . SP HARD DADDY 2
SAYS DADDY I HAVE GOT THE BLUES. . SP HARD DADDY 4
WE HAVE OUR TROUBLES, TOO - . . . . SP HIGH TO LOW 2
WE HAVE OUR PROBLEMS. . . . . SP HIGH TO LOW 24
AND LAUNDRY I DON'T HAVE MUCH LEFT SP LETTER 3
JEWS MUST HAVE HEARD . . . . . SP LIKEWISE 25
HE SAID, HAVE YOU GOT . . . . . SP MADAM MINISTER 3
I'LL HAVE YOU KNOW . . . . . SP MADAM MINISTER 10
HE SAID, WHAT HAVE YOU . . . . . SP MADAM MINISTER 13
HAVE YOU BACK-SLID? . . . . . SP MADAM MINISTER 18
LAWD, HAVE PITY! . . . . . SP MADAM PHONE BIL 20
I'LL HAVE YOU KNOW . . . . . SP MADAM CENSUS 31
I WOULDN'T HAVE DROPPED IT, ... SP MIDNIGHT RAFFLE 11
BUT YOU HAVE GONE SO FAR! . . . . . SP MISS BLUES'ES 10
I DON'T HAVE TO WORK. . . . . SP NECESSITY 2
I DON'T HAVE TO DO NOTHING . . . . SP NECESSITY 3
HAVE TO WORK AFTER ALL. . . . . SP NECESSITY 12
I HAVE GIVEN MY ANSWER. . . . . SP PERSONAL 8
RATHER HAVE WINE? . . . . . SP PORT TOWN 6
YOU CAN HAVE ME, BABY - . . . . . SP SAME IN BLUES 17
HAVE MERCY, LORD! . . . . . SP SINNER 1
HAVE MERCY, LORD! . . . . . SP SINNER 5
DON'T DECENT FOLKS HAVE DOUGH? . . SP SISTER 10
WELL, ANYWAY, IT DON'T HAVE TO BE A MARRIED MAN. . . . . SP SISTER 12
WHO HAVE NOWHERE . . . . . SP VAGABONDS 4
FATE MUST HAVE . . . . . SP WHAT? SO SOON! 3
BODY'LL HAVE TO WALK BEHIND ME. . . SP YOUNG GAL'S BLS 8
YOU COULD HAVE ME WITH YOU . . . . SP 50 - 50 10
IF I HAVE . . . . . AYM ASK YOUR MAMA 28
THE FRENCH MAY HAVE THE SECRET. . . AYM IS IT TRUE? 17
HAVE DOORS THAT OPEN OUTWARD . . . AYM JAZZTET MUTED 16
WILL HAVE THE BLUES. . . . . PL BACKLASH BLUES 33
OF THE SOUTH HAVE TAKEN OVER - . . PL CULTURAL EXCHNG 39
WEALTHY NEGROES HAVE WHITE SERVANTS. PL CULTURAL EXCHNG 48
AND COLORED CHILDREN HAVE WHITE MAMMIES: . . . . . PL CULTURAL EXCHNG 50
MIGHT HAVE LOST HIS SOUL. . . . . PL FREDRK DOUGLASS 6
I HAVE AS MUCH RIGHT . . . . . PL FREEDOM 5
AND CAN'T HAVE NOW . . . . . PL HARLEM 14
WHITE FOLKS HAVE LEFT . . . . . PL LITTLE SNG HOUS 22
SOUTHERN DOGS HAVE VINDICATED ME - PL NORTHERN LIBERL 4
HAVE PROVEN A POINT . . . . . PL NORTHERN LIBERL 8
HAVE MADE THEIR DOUGH. . . . . PL OFFICE BUILDING 5
YOU HAVE YOUR "FUN" . . . . . PL OFFICE BUILDING 9
OH, RUN, ALL WHO HAVE NOT . . . . PL SPECIAL BULLTIN 16
I HAVE BEEN SEEKING . . . . . PL STOKELY MALCOLM 1
WHAT I HAVE NEVER FOUND . . . . . PL STOKELY MALCOLM 2
WHAT I HAVE NOT FOUND . . . . . PL STOKELY MALCOLM 10
HAVE PSEUDONYMS REVEALED . . . . . PL UN-AMERICAN 8
AS HAVE SOME FOLKS I KNOW, ... PL VARI-COLORED 2
BUT I DON'T HAVE A HEART OF GOLD. PL VARI-COLORED 5

HAVEN 1
TO THE HAVEN OF WHITE QUAKERS . . . AYM ODE TO DINAH 32

HAVING 5
GOD HAVING A HEMORRHAGE. . . . . WB CARIBBEAN SUNST 1
OF BEING HELD BACK, OF HAVING NO CHANCE - . . . . . NM COLORED SL POEM 31
HAVING BEEN . . . . . SP JAM SESSION 4
HAVING PREVIOUSLY POINTED OUT THE SINS OF THIS WORLD: . . . . SP SUNDAY MORNING 1
HAVING GIVEN UP BREATH - . . . . . PL SLAVE 5

HAVIN' 2
FOR EVER HAVIN' A DAUGHTER. . . . . FC A RUINED GAL 18
O' GETTIN' A NEW WINTER COAT, OR HAVIN' THAT OLD ONE CLEANED. . . NM BROKE 40

HAWKINS 1
WHERE WINTER'S NAME IS HAWKINS ¢ ¢ ¢ ¢ . . . . . AYM HORN OF PLENTY 27

HAY 1
I MIGHT AS WELL PUT IT ON IN THE HAY. . . . . SH BED TIME 10

HAYES 1
CLUB ROLAND HAYES. . . . . JC HOW ABOUT DIXIE 14

HAYMOW 1
WHOSE HAYMOW WAS A MANGER MANGER . AYM ODE TO DINAH 33

HAZEL 1
TO CONFOUND EVEN HAZEL SCOTT . . . SP TO BE SOMEBODY 11

HE 207
AN' SOON AS HE GOT OUT DE BARREL . FC BLACK GAL 11
THEN OUT MA DOOR HE GOES. . . . . FC BLACK GAL 12
JUDGE PIERCE HE SAYS, MARY. . . . . FC BLD OF GIN MARY 5
HE WAS A FRIEND O' MINE. . . . . FC DEATH DO DIRTY 5
CAUSE HE WAS BLACK . . . . . FC DEATH DO DIRTY 7

HE BOUGHT ME CORN BREAD	FC DEATH DO DIRTY	13
THAT NIGHT HE GOT KILT	FC DEATH DO DIRTY	21
HE AIN'T GOT A CHANCE.	FC DEATH DO DIRTY	29
BUT HE SHO DO TREAT ME KIND.	FC GAL'S CRY DYING	14
BUT HE SHO DO TREAT ME KIND.	FC GAL'S CRY DYING	16
CAUSE HE NEVER DOES COME HOME.	FC GYPSY MAN	2
HE NEVER DOES COME HOME.	FC GYPSY MAN	4
HE TOOK MA LAST THIN DIME.	FC GYPSY MAN	14
HE TOOK MA LAST THIN DIME.	FC GYPSY MAN	16
HE KNOCKS ME OFF MA FEET.	FC MA MAN	2
HE KNOCKS ME OFF MA FEET.	FC MA MAN	4
DE WAY HE SHOCKS ME SHO IS SWEET.	FC MA MAN	6
HE KIN PLAY A BANJO.	FC MA MAN	7
LORDY, HE KIN PLUNK, PLUNK, PLUNK.	FC MA MAN	8
HE KIN PLAY A BANJO.	FC MA MAN	9
HE PLAYS GOOD WHEN HE'S SOBER	FC MA MAN	11
IF HE DIDN'T LOVE ME	FC MINNIE SINGS	15
THAT HE LOVED SO	OLD THE CONSUMPTIVE	2
HE SAT,	OLD THE CONSUMPTIVE	3
HE LAY,	OLD THE CONSUMPTIVE	7
STRENGTH HE DOESN'T REALLY FEEL. GAY, LOUD, UNHAPPY JAZZ, BARING HIS	NM BIG-TIMER MOOD	9
IN THE CLOTHES OF A MODERN MAN, HE PROCLAIMS HIMSELF.	NM BLACK CLWN MOOD	15
AND BOWING HIS HEAD IN SHAME, BECOMES SUDDENLY FIERCE AND ANGRY, THEN HE	NM COLORED SL MOOD	11
HE WHO OPPRESSES ME, HIM I DEFY!	NM DARK YOUTH USA	7
IS NOT HE BUT A SHADOW IN THE SUN -	DK BEGGAR BOY	5
AND YET HE PLAYS UPON HIS FLUTE A WILD FREE TUNE	DK BEGGAR BOY	7
HE WENT AWAY FROM ME.	DK I LOVED FRIEND	2
MA LORD, HE AIN'T PROUD.	DK MA LORD	2
WHEN HE GOES A-WALKIN'	DK MA LORD	3
HE GIVES ME HIS HAND.	DK MA LORD	4
"YOU MA FRIEND," HE 'LOWED.	DK MA LORD	5
HE KNOWED HOW TO PRAY.	DK MA LORD	7
WHEN HE WENT TO HEAVEN.	DK MA LORD	12
HE TOLE ME I WAS SWINE.	DK MA LORD	14
HE SAID, "SHO YOU'LL COME WID ME	DK MA LORD	15
HE SAT UPON THE ROLLING DECK	DK SAILOR	1
HE HAD A MERMAID ON HIS ARM,	DK SAILOR	5
AND TATTOOED ON HIS BACK HE HAD	DK SAILOR	7
THE HIGH SHERIFF SHOOTS AND HE SHOOTS TO KILL	ANS BLD OZZIE POWEL	9
HE WON'T MATTER AT ALL.	ANS CHANT TOM MOONY	29
SEEKING A HOME WHERE HE HIMSELF IS FREE.	ANS LET AMERICA BE	4
HE TRIED TO GUARD	SH BLD THE KILLER	17
HE DID!	SH PRESENT	9
HE LED HIS COLORED DELEGATION	JC BLD SAM SOLOMON	46
AND BE THE SAME OLD CROW HE USED TO BE -	JC JIM CROW'S LAST	10
HE STILL TRIES TO ACT IN THE SAME OLD WAY.	JC JIM CROW'S LAST	12
NEHRU SAID, BEFORE HE WENT TO JAIL.	JC JIM CROW'S LAST	15
HE, TOO, A SYMBOL OF NEW LIBERTIES.	JC TO CAPTAIN MULZ	46
HE SAID,	FW HEART	5
HE SITS ON A HILL	FW JAIME	1
HE SITS ON A HILL	FW JAIME	5
HE IS A LITTLE DARK BOY	FW MIGRATION	11
HE HAS BEEN	FW OLD SAILOR	1
HE SUNS HIMSELF	FW OLD SAILOR	15
THAT WOMEN HE HAS LEFT	FW OLD SAILOR	18
HE GLIDES SO SWIFTLY	FW SNAKE	1
HE GOT SHOT IN THE BACK	OWT BLD MARGE POLIT	10
FORGETS HE EVER SANG	OWT JUICE JOINT	31
HE WAS MARY'S SON,	LHR BLD MARY'S SON	8
AND THE SON OF GOD WAS HE -	LHR BLD MARY'S SON	9
HE GAVE THEM OF HIS BREAD.	LHR BLD MARY'S SON	16
HE GAVE THEM TO DRINK OF HIS WINE.	LHR BLD MARY'S SON	17
AND THIS IS MY BLOOD, HE SAID.	LHR BLD MARY'S SON	19
HE WENT INTO THE GARDEN	LHR BLD MARY'S SON	22
AND HE KNELT THERE TO PRAY.	LHR BLD MARY'S SON	23
HE SAID, OH, LORD, THY WILL BE DONE!	LHR BLD MARY'S SON	24
HE DIED ON THE CROSS	LHR BLD MARY'S SON	32
WHEN HE PASSES ON.	LHR TESTAMENT	4
HE KNOWS THAT AUNT SUE NEVER GOT HER STORIES	SP AUNTSUE'S STORI	19
HE WAS HER KIN.	SP BLD FORTUNE TEL	12
HE MISTREATED HER TERRIBLE.	SP BLD FORTUNE TEL	21
WHAT ROAD HE TOOK.	SP BLD FORTUNE TEL	26
HE WORKS DOWNTOWN FOR TWELVE A WEEK.	SP BUDDY	4
SHE SAYS HE CAN HAVE	SP BUDDY	6
ANYTHING HE WANTS OUT OF IT.	SP BUDDY	10
HE WAS A SOLDIER IN THE ARMY,	SP CASUALTY	1
BUT HE DOESN'T WALK LIKE ONE.	SP CASUALTY	2
HE WALKS LIKE HIS SOLDIERING	SP CASUALTY	3
HE	SP CONSIDER ME	14
HE DIDN'T HAVE MUCH SENSE.	SP DANCER	6
HE WAS NO GOOD AT MAKING LOVE	SP DANCER	7
SO HE TAPPED,	SP DANCER	9
UNTIL HE MADE FOLKS SAY,	SP DANCER	14
DID HE GET ANYWHERE? NO!	SP DANCER	23
HE USED TO SAY.	SP DEAD IN THERE	17
HE STARTS FIRST WITH HIMSELF	SP FREEDOM'S PLOW	5
WHAT HE SAID MUST BE MEANT FOR EVERY HUMAN BEING -	SP FREEDOM'S PLOW	107
HE WAS A COLORED MAN WHO HAD BEEN A SLAVE	SP FREEDOM'S PLOW	112
HER GRANDSON'S NAME WAS JIMMY. HE DIED AT ANZIO.	SP FREEDOM TRAIN	43
HE DIED FOR REAL. IT WARN'T NO SHOW.	SP FREEDOM TRAIN	44
THAT WHAT HE SAID WAS ALSO MEANT FOR THEM.	SP FREEDOM'S PLOW	39
WHEN HE SHOULD BE GONE	SP GONE BOY	6
HE AIN'T GONE.	SP GONE BOY	9
I WAS BORN HERE, HE SAID,	SP GOOD MORNING	2
HE TURNED HIS BACK ON ME.	SP HARD DADDY	8
HE TURNED HIS BACK ON ME.	SP HARD DADDY	10
HE SAID A WOMAN'S CRYIN'S	SP HARD DADDY	11
HE ROSE UP ON HIS DYING BED	SP HOPE	1
HE IS A GOD.	SP JOE LOUIS	6
HE SAYS, "MARY, I'M	SP LOVER'S RETURN	5
HE LOOKED SO THIN -	SP LOVER'S RETURN	15
HE SAID, HOWDY-DO?	SP MADAM RENT MAN	2
THE DAY HE CAME ROUND,	SP MADAM CENSUS	2
HE SAID, ARE YOU MADAM?	SP MADAM WRONG VIS	3
HE SAID, HAVE YOU GOT	SP MADAM MINISTER	3
HE SAID, YOU KNOW	SP MADAM RENT MAN	5
HE SAID, MADAM,	SP MADAM NUMBER WR	5
HE SAID, I AM INTERESTED	SP MADAM MINISTER	5
HE SAID, I RECKON	SP MADAM WRONG VIS	5
BUT HE HATED TO WRITE	SP MADAM CENSUS	7
HE USED A SWITCH-BLADE	SP MADAM CHARTY CH	7
HE WORKED ALL THE TIME,	SP MADAM MIGHT-HAV	9
HE SAID, WHAT	SP MADAM CENSUS	9
LIKE HE HAD A CHARM.	SP MADAM WRONG VIS	10
HE SAID, THAT MIGHT	SP MADAM NUMBER WR	11
HE SAID, I REALLY	SP MADAM WRONG VIS	11
HE PLAYED A DIME,	SP MADAM NUMBER WR	13
HE SAID, WHAT HAVE YOU	SP MADAM MINISTER	13
HE SAID, I'M GONNA PUT IT	SP MADAM CENSUS	13
HE SAID, YOU'RE JOHNSON -	SP MADAM WRONG VIS	17
HE SAID, SISTER	SP MADAM MINISTER	17
HE SAID, MADAM, I SWEAR	SP MADAM MIGHT-HAV	17
HE SAID, MADAM,	SP MADAM RENT MAN	19
HE SAID, MRS.,	SP MADAM CENSUS	21
HE SAID, SISTER,	SP MADAM MINISTER	21
JUST TO SAY HE LOVES ME!	SP MADAM PHONE BIL	23
WHY DIDN'T HE TELL ME SOME'N	SP MADAM PHONE BIL	25
HE SAID, MADAM,	SP MADAM RENT MAN	27
HE SAID, IN ME	SP MADAM MIGHT-HAV	29
HE SAID, YOUR NAME LOOKS GOOD	SP MADAM'S CALLING	11
HE IS THAT YOUNG MAN, MAMA,	SP MAMA AND DAUGHT	7
YOUR FATHER, YES, HE WAS THE ONE!	SP MAMA AND DAUGHT	11
HE UP AND WENT HIS WAY.	SP MAMA AND DAUGHT	14
HE WAS YOUNG YESTERDAY.	SP MAMA AND DAUGHT	18
HE WAS YOUNG WHEN HE -	SP MAMA AND DAUGHT	19
HE WAS YOUNG WHEN HE -	SP MAMA AND DAUGHT	19
BUT HE LEFT ME WHEN THE COAL WAS LOW.	SP MIDWINTER BLUES	8
BUT HE LEFT WHEN THE COAL WAS LOW.	SP MIDWINTER BLUES	10
HE TOLD ME THAT HE LOVED ME	SP MIDWINTER BLUES	13
HE TOLD ME THAT HE LOVED ME	SP MIDWINTER BLUES	13
BUT HE MUST A BEEN TELLIN' A LIE.	SP MIDWINTER BLUES	14
HE TOLD ME THAT HE LOVED ME.	SP MIDWINTER BLUES	15
HE TOLD ME THAT HE LOVED ME.	SP MIDWINTER BLUES	15
HE MUST A BEEN TELLIN' A LIE.	SP MIDWINTER BLUES	16
AS HE RIDES OUT ON THE PRAIRIE.	SP MIGRANT	11
BUT IF HE WASN'T IN A HURRY	SP MIGRANT	38
HE WOULDN'T WRITE SO	SP MIGRANT	39
HE SETS ON A STOOP	SP NEIGHBOR	2
HE SETS IN A BAR WITH A BEER.	SP NEIGHBOR	6
HE LOOKS TALLER THAN HE IS	SP NEIGHBOR	7
HE LOOKS TALLER THAN HE IS	SP NEIGHBOR	7
AND YOUNGER THAN HE AIN'T.	SP NEIGHBOR	8
HE LOOKS DARKER THAN HE IS, TOO.	SP NEIGHBOR	9
HE LOOKS DARKER THAN HE IS, TOO.	SP NEIGHBOR	9
AND HE'S SMARTER THAN HE LOOKS.	SP NEIGHBOR	10
HE AIN'T SMART.	SP NEIGHBOR	11
NAW, HE AIN'T NEITHER.	SP NEIGHBOR	13
EXCEPT THAT HE TALKS TOO MUCH.	SP NEIGHBOR	15
BUT WHEN HE DRINKS,	SP NEIGHBOR	17
HE DRINKS FAST.	SP NEIGHBOR	18
HE DON'T DRINK.	SP NEIGHBOR	20
HE JUST	SP NEIGHBOR	22
THAT'S NO LIE, HE SAID,	SP NEW YORKERS	2
INSURANCE MAN, HE DID NOT PAY -	SP NIGHT FUNERAL	5
BECAUSE HE TRIED TO VOTE	SP NOT A MOVIE	2
AND HE CRAWLED ON HIS KNEES TO HIS HOUSE	SP NOT A MOVIE	4
AND HE GOT THE MIDNIGHT TRAIN	SP NOT A MOVIE	5
AND HE CROSSED THAT DIXIE LINE	SP NOT A MOVIE	6
HE DIDN'T STOP IN WASHINGTON	SP NOT A MOVIE	9
AND HE DIDN'T STOP IN BALTIMORE	SP NOT A MOVIE	10
BUT, THANK GOD, HE WASN'T DEAD!	SP NOT A MOVIE	13
WHY DOES HE KEEP ON FOOLIN' AROUND MARIE?	SP SISTER	2
BUT WHY DOES HE KEEP ON FOOLIN' AROUND MARIE?	SP SISTER	4
HE DID A LAZY SWAY.	SP THE WEARY BLUES	6
HE DID A LAZY SWAY.	SP THE WEARY BLUES	7

HE MADE THAT POOR PIANO MOAN WITH MELODY. . . . . SP THE WEARY BLUES 10
HE PLAYED THAT SAD RAGGY TUNE LIKE A MUSICAL FOOL. . . . . SP THE WEARY BLUES 13
HE PLAYED A FEW CHORDS THEN HE SANG SOME MORE - . . . . SP THE WEARY BLUES 24
HE PLAYED A FEW CHORDS THEN HE SANG SOME MORE - . . . . SP THE WEARY BLUES 24
AND FAR INTO THE NIGHT HE CROONED THAT TUNE. . . . . SP THE WEARY BLUES 31
HE SLEPT LIKE A ROCK OR A MAN THAT'S DEAD. . . . . SP THE WEARY BLUES 35
HE CARRIES . . . . SP YOUNG SAILOR 1
TO SPEND, HE SAYS. . . . . SP YOUNG SAILOR 9
HE SAID, SHARE YOUR BED - . . . . . SP 50 - 50 13
THOSE SIT-IN KIDS, HE SAID. . . . . AYM BIRD IN ORBIT 71
WHERE HE COULD NOT PRAY . . . . . . PL BIBLE BELT 4
SEND FOR LENIN! (DON'T YOU DARE! - HE CAN'T COME . . . . PL FINAL CALL 24
HAD HE WALKED WITH WARY FOOT . . . PL FREDRK DOUGLASS 2
ON WHICH HE SET HIS FEET, ... PL FREDRK DOUGLASS 9
ANYTHING BUT A SLAVE! HE SAID. . . PL FREDRK DOUGLASS 17
THE FIRST BLOW, HE SAID. . . . . . PL FREDRK DOUGLASS 20
HE DIED IN 1895. . . . . PL FREDRK DOUGLASS 21
HE IS NOT DEAD. . . . . PL FREDRK DOUGLASS 22
A SUNRISE THAT HE CANNOT SEE . . . PL JUNIOR ADDICT 8
THE VERY ROOM IN WHICH HE LEAVES . PL JUNIOR ADDICT 11
AND HE DIDN'T TRUST . . . . PL LUMUMBA'S GRAVE 2
AND HE DIDN'T BELIEVE . . . . . . PL LUMUMBA'S GRAVE 6
BUT HE NEEDS NO MARKER - . . . . . PL LUMUMBA'S GRAVE 15
IS THE BLOOD HE BLED. . . . . . . PL OFFICIAL NOTICE 6
YOU SAY HE DIED WITH HONOR . . . . PL OFFICIAL NOTICE 7
HE WAS COMING . . . . PL WHO BUT TH LORD 3
BUT THE LORD HE WAS NOT QUICK. . . PL WHO BUT TH LORD 12

HEABEN 3

I WOULDN'T GO TO HEABEN IF I COULD. FC BAD MAN 18
WHEN HE WENT TO HEABEN. . . . . . . OK MA LORD 12
IF YOU WANTA GO TO HEABEN . . . . . SP FIRE 12

HEAD 39

ELSE I'LL USE HER HEAD . . . . . . FC EVIL WOMAN 15
PUT MA HEAD UN'NEATH DE KIVER. . . FC GAL'S CRY DYING 5
BACK BENT AS IN THE FIELDS. THE SLOW STEP. THE BOWED HEAD. "NOBODY KNOWS . . . . NM BLACK CLWN MOOD 4
CALMLY TELLING THE STORY. PROUDLY AND EXPECTANTLY WITH HEAD UP. SHOULDERS . . . . NM COLORED SL MOOD 7
AND BOWING HIS HEAD IN SHAME. BECOMES SUDDENLY FIERCE AND ANGRY. THEN HE . . . . NM COLORED SL MOOD 11
LET THE RAIN BEAT UPON YOUR HEAD WITH SILVER LIQUID DROPS. . . . OK APRIL RAIN SONG 2
PUT NO TOMBSTONE AT MY HEAD. . . . OK DEATH SEAMAN 5
HERE I AM WITH MY HEAD HELD HIGH! ANS SISTER JOHNSON 1
WITH LOVIN IN HIS HEAD. . . . . . . SH DEATH IN HARLEM 140
BY HOLDING ITS HEAD . . . . SH SNOB 7
IF I JUST HAD A OWL HEAD, OLD OWL HEAD WOULD DO. . . . . SH TWILIGHT REVERI 11
IF I JUST HAD A OWL HEAD, OLD OWL HEAD WOULD DO. . . . . SH TWILIGHT REVERI 11
CAUSE I'D TAKE THAT OWL HEAD AND FIRE ON YOU. . . . . SH TWILIGHT REVERI 12
BUT I AIN'T GOT NO OWL HEAD AND YOU DONE LEFT TOWN . . . . SH TWILIGHT REVERI 13
THE HEAD OF LINCOLN LOOKS DOWN FROM THE WALL . . . . OWT LINCOLN THEATRE 1
THE HEAD OF LINCOLN IS SERENELY TALL OWT LINCOLN THEATRE 3
WHEN THE WINE'S GONE TO YOUR HEAD OWT RAID 2
AS HARD AS MY HEAD IS. . . . . . . OWT TOO BLUE 12
TO GET YOU OUT OF MY HEAD. . . . . OWT YESTERDAY TODAY 8
AUNT SUE HAS A HEAD FULL OF STORIES. SP AUNTSUE'S STORI 1
NOR SEEN HER HANG HER HEAD. . . . . SP BLD OF THE GIRL 10
THEM THOUGHTS WOULD BUST MY HEAD - SP BLUES AT DAWN 4
BENEATH MY HEAD. . . . . SP FIRED 10
CROWN ON HIS HEAD. . . . . SP JUDGMENT DAY 7
FOR HIS HEAD TO LAY. . . . . SP NIGHT FUNERAL 8
AND THE LID SHUT ON HIS HEAD . . . SP NIGHT FUNERAL 28
AND WHIPPED HIS HEAD WITH CLUBS . . SP NOT A MOVIE 3
SIX KNOTS WAS ON HIS HEAD . . . . . SP NOT A MOVIE 12
BOOTS POLISHED LIKE A MURRAY HEAD. SP SUMMER EVENING 6
WHILE THE WEARY BLUES ECHOED THROUGH HIS HEAD. . . . . SP THE WEARY BLUES 34
THAT NEVER LIFTS ITS HEAD . . . . . SP TROUBLED WOMAN 11
HAS A HEAD OF VIBRANT HAIR . . . . SP TRUMPET PLAYER 11
YOU AIN'T GOT NO HEAD! . . . . . . SP 50 - 50 8
IF YOU HAD A HEAD AND USED YOUR MIND SP 50 - 50 9
THOUGH WORN IN GLORY ON MY HEAD. . PL CROWNS GARLANDS 12
AND A HALO ON MY HEAD . . . . PL GO SLOW 13
THEY HIT ME IN THE HEAD . . . . . . PL KU KLUX 13
AND HEAD NORTH WITH THE DOUGH. . . PL VARI-COLORED 4
I HAD VISIONS IN MY HEAD . . . . . PL WHO BUT TH LORD 5

HEADING 1

AN ENSLAVED PEOPLE HEADING TOWARD FREEDOM . . . . SP FREEDOM'S PLOW 189

HEADLINES 1

HEADLINES IN PRESS: . . . . SP BLD LANDLORD 30

HEADS 6

LIFT THEIR HEADS AND THINGS IS BAD. JC GOOD MORN STLIN 20
LIFT THEIR HEADS, TOO, WITH GUN IN HAND . . . . JC GOOD MORN STLIN 33
AND SWITCH THEIR SKIRTS AND LIFT THEIR STRAIGHTENED HEADS . . . . OWT JUICE JOINT 22
AND FLOWERS LIFT THEIR HEADS. . . . SP IN TIME SILVER 5
BOWED THEIR HEADS TO CRY. . . . . . SP SYLVESTER'S BED 8
THE HEADS ON THESE TWO QUARTERS . . AYM SHOW FARE PLESE 26

HEADSTRONG 1

HEADSTRONG AND WILD. . . . . SH BLD THE SINNER 10

HEAP 1

ON THE SCRAP HEAP OF TIME - . . . . ANS CHANT TOM MOONY 28

HEAR 30

HEAR DAT MUSIC. . . . . WB TO MIDNIGHT NAN 5
HEAR DAT MUSIC. . . . . WB TO MIDNIGHT NAN 7
THAT I CAN NEITHER HEAR NOR FEEL NOR SEE. . . . . OK BEGGAR BOY 2
AND YOU COULD HEAR THE DROWSY WAILING . . . . OK IRISH WAKE 3
YOU DO NOT HEAR . . . . OK MINSTREL MAN 11
DON'T HAVE TO HEAR NOBODY SAY. . . SH PAY DAY 3
DON'T YOU HEAR THIS HAMMER RING? . JC BIG BUDDY 11
DON'T YOU HEAR THIS HAMMER RING? . JC BIG BUDDY 13
DON'T YOU HEAR THIS HAMMER RING? . JC BIG BUDDY 19
BUT I RECKON YOU CAN HEAR ME. . . . JC GOOD MORN STLIN 51
TO HEAR A WORD. . . . . FW SILENCE 5
THERE WERE SOME WHO COULD NOT HEAR. LHP BLD MARY'S SON 11
HEAR THAT MUSIC PLAYIN' UPSTAIRS? SP BLACK MARIA 6
YOU'LL HEAR THEIR FEET . . . . . . SP DREAM BOOGIE 6
DO YOU HEAR WHAT I SAID? . . . . . SP EASY BOOGIE 11
DON'T YOU HEAR ME CALL? . . . . . . SP EVENING SONG 4
HEAR THOSE WORDS AND SHOUT THEM BACK SP IN EXPLANATION 41
I BET SHE'D HEAR. . . . . SP LADY'S BOOGIE 6
THOUGH YOU MAY HEAR ME HOLLER. . . SP LIFE IS FINE 27
'S GOT TO HEAR A BLUES . . . . . . SP MISERY 15
I FEEL AND SEE AND HEAR, HARLEM, I HEAR YOU: . . . . SP THEME FOR ENG B 18
I FEEL AND SEE AND HEAR, HARLEM, I HEAR YOU: . . . . SP THEME FOR ENG B 18
HEAR YOU, HEAR ME - WE TWO - YOU, ME, TALK ON THIS PAGE. . . . . . SP THEME FOR ENG B 19
HEAR YOU, HEAR ME - WE TWO - YOU, ME, TALK ON THIS PAGE. . . . . . SP THEME FOR ENG B 19
(I HEAR NEW YORK, TOO.) ME - WHO? SP THEME FOR ENG B 20
GRANDPA, DID YOU HEAR THE . . . . . AYM BIRD IN ORBIT 39
HEAR THE OLD FOLKS SAY HOW . . . . AYM BIRD IN ORBIT 40
HEAR MY VOICE! . . . . PL FREDRK DOUGLASS 15
GO SLOW, I HEAR - . . . . PL GO SLOW 4
NOT HEAR THEM . . . . PL SWEET WORDS RAC 14

HEARD 28

ONE SAID SHE HEARD THE JAZZ-BAND SOB WB CABARET 5
HEARD DE OWL A HOOTIN'. . . . . . . FC GAL'S CRY DYING 1
HEARD DE OWL A HOOTIN'. . . . . . . FC GAL'S CRY DYING 3
I KNOW, FOR I HEARD, WHEN ALL WAS STILL. . . . . OK DEATH SEAMAN 3
IS HEARD. . . . . FW SILENCE 8
GIRL, AIN'T YOU HEARD? . . . . OWT JITNEY 9
NO, MARTHA, I AIN'T HEARD. . . . . OWT JITNEY 10
CHILD, AIN'T YOU HEARD? . . . . . . OWT JITNEY 18
HONEY, AIN'T YOU HEARD? . . . . . . OWT JITNEY 47
BABY, AIN'T YOU HEARD? . . . . . . OWT JITNEY 52
AIN'T EVEN HEARD HER MURMUR. . . . SP BLD OF THE GIRL 11
I KNOW YOU'VE HEARD . . . . SP BOOGIE 1 A.M. 2
BUDDY, HAVE YOU HEARD? . . . . . . SP DEFERRED 52
SHE AIN'T HEARD. . . . . SP DIME 5
AIN'T YOU HEARD . . . . SP DREAM BOOGIE 2
AIN'T YOU HEARD . . . . SP DREAM BOOGIE 11
I HEARD ON THE RADIO ABOUT THE . . SP FREEDOM TRAIN 3
DADDY, AIN'T YOU HEARD? . . . . . . SP GOOD MORNING 28
AIN'T YOU HEARD? . . . . SP ISLAND 12
JEWS MUST HAVE HEARD . . . . SP LIKEWISE 25
I HEARD THE SINGING OF THE MISSISSIPPI WHEN ABE LINCOLN . . SP NEGRO SPEAKS OF 8
I HEARD MY MOTHER SINGING . . . . . SP SPIRITUALS 6
I HEARD A NEGRO PLAY. . . . . SP THE WEARY BLUES 3
I HEARD THAT NEGRO SING, THAT OLD PIANO MOAN - . . . . SP THE WEARY BLUES 18
I THOUGHT I HEARD THE HORN OF PLENTY BLOWING. . . . . AYM BLUES IN STEREO 35
I'VE HEARD . . . . PL SWEET WORDS RAC 11

HEARING 2

I TIRE SO OF HEARING PEOPLE SAY. . SP DEMOCRACY 10
I TIRE SO OF HEARING PEOPLE SAY. . PL FREEDOM 10

HEARS 1

'COURSE, YOU HEARS PLENTY 'BOUT THIS-HERE UNEMPLOYMENT RELIEF - NM BROKE 55

HEARSE 4
I WANT A FISH-TAIL HEARSE . . . . . SP AS BEFITS A MAN 9
A HEARSE AND TWO CARS - . . . . . . SP BLD OF THE MAN 6
HEARSE AND FLOWERS . . . . SP DEAD IN THERE 6
THAT LONG BLACK HEARSE DONE SPED. SP NIGHT FUNERAL 34

HEART 52
THE BROKEN HEART OF LOVE. . . . . . WB LENOX AVE MIDNT 5
THE WEARY, WEARY HEART OF PAIN. - WB LENOX AVE MIDNT 6
WHEN IT HURTS YO' HEART YOU . . . . FC GYPSY MAN 23
LONG A PART OF THE UNION'S HEART - NM DARK YOUTH USA 11
THE TRUTH A SIMPLE HEART HAS HELD DK ALABAMA EARTH 8
HEART MELODIES . . . . DK DREAM KEEPER 4
MA HEART WAS IN MA MOUTH. . . . . . DK HOMESICK BLUES 8
HEART WAS IN MA MOUTH. . . . . . DK HOMESICK BLUES 10
ITS PEOPLE'S HEART, TOO SMALL TO
HOLD A SOB. . . . . SL TOWN OF SCOTTSB 4
AND THIS IS WHAT MOVED IN MY HEART: ANS NEGRO GHETTO 7
HEART AND DIED . . . . SH DEATH IN HARLEM 117
AND MY HEART IN A BOG. . . . . . SH EVIL MORNING 12
HEART . . . . FW GRIEF 4
TOOK HIS HEART . . . . FW HEART 2
HERE IS MY HEART!" . . . . FW HEART 7
PIERROT'S HEART . . . . FW HEART 11
TOOK HIS HEART . . . . FW HEART 14
WHERE HIS HEART IS . . . . FW HEART 18
YOUR HEART IS RIGHT. . . . . OWT HONEY BABE 4
AND MY HEART WAS BLEEDING, TOO. . . SP A BLACK PIERROT 9
AUNT SUE HAS A WHOLE HEART FULL OF
STORIES. . . . . SP AUNTSUE'S STORI 2
AW, MY HEART IS . . . . SP BLACK MARIA 7
TILL THEY'RE THE HEART . . . . . . SP COLLEGE FORMAL 13
I BROKE MY HEART THIS MORNIN', . . SP CORA 1
AIN'T GOT NO HEART NO MORE. . . . . SP CORA 2
YOU PAWNED MY HEART. . . . . . . SP COULD BE 8
AND THE FAITH THAT IS IN HIS HEART - SP FREEDOM'S PLOW 6
FIRST IN THE HEART IS THE DREAM - SP FREEDOM'S PLOW 9
HEART REACHING OUT TO HEART. . . . SP FREEDOM'S PLOW 36
HEART REACHING OUT TO HEART. . . . SP FREEDOM'S PLOW 38
CAUSE YOU BROKE MY HEART IN TWO. . SP LATE LAST NIGHT 6
AND BROKE MY HEART IN TWO - . . . . SP LATE LAST NIGHT 8
OR IS YOUR HEART STONE-COLD? . . . SP MADAM MINISTER 8
MY HEART TO BUST. . . . . SP MADAM MIGHT-HAV 32
OR RED HEART BECOME AN ANVIL . . . SP MIGRANT 20
IN MY HEART I'M CRYING. . . . . . . SP MISS BLUES'ES 13
IN YOUR HEART . . . . SP MOVIES 6
MY HEART IS ACHING . . . . SP RELIEF 1
WHAT CAN PURGE MY HEART . . . . . . SP SONG BILLIE HOL 1
WHAT CAN PURGE MY HEART . . . . . . SP SONG BILLIE HOL 4
WHAT CAN PURGE MY HEART . . . . . . SP SONG BILLIE HOL 7
(BREAK THE HEART OF ME) . . . . . . SP SONG DARK GIRL 2
(BREAK THE HEART OF ME) . . . . . . SP SONG DARK GIRL 10
JUST AIN'T GOT NO HEART. . . . . . SP SOUTHERN MAMMY 22
JUST AIN'T GOT NO HEART. . . . . . SP SOUTHERN MAMMY 24
I WILL TAKE YOUR HEART. . . . . . . SP TO ARTINA 1
I WILL TAKE YOUR HEART FOR MINE. . SP TO ARTINA 9
BURNS IN MY HEART A LOVE-FIRE SHARP
LIKE PAIN. . . . . SP WHEN SUE WEARS 11
AND BITE INTO THE SANDWICH OF YOUR
HEART. . . . . PL JIM CROW CAR 2
IF I HAD A HEART OF GOLD. . . . . . PL VARI-COLORED 1
I'D UP AND SELL MY HEART OF GOLD . PL VARI-COLORED 3
BUT I DON'T HAVE A HEART OF GOLD. PL VARI-COLORED 5
THAT'S WHY MY HEART IS RED. . . . . PL VARI-COLORED 8

HEARTACHES 1
INNER HEARTACHES AND LONELINESS TO
THE IRONIC GAIETY OF THE MUSIC.
THEN . . . . NM BIG-TIMER MOOD 10

HEARTBEAT 2
STILL AS A WHISPERING HEARTBEAT. . WB SUMMER NIGHT 9
TAKE HARLEM'S HEARTBEAT, ... SP JUKE BOX LOVE 7

HEARTBEATS 1
LISTEN AT MY HEARTBEATS TRYING TO
THINK. . . . . SH SUPPER TIME 6

HEARTBREAK 2
DEATH AND LOVE AND HEARTBREAK . . . ANS SONG OF SPAIN 7
I AM THE AMERICAN HEARTBREAK - . . PL AMER HEARTBREAK 1

HEARTS 9
EXCEPT IN OUR HEARTS. . . . . ANS KIDS WHO DIE 39
BUT THAT THERE SHOULD BE THREE
BARREN HEARTS . . . . SP A HOUSE IN TAOS 19
BUT IN THEIR HEARTS THE SLAVES KNEW SP FREEDOM'S PLOW 106
GUARDING IN THEIR HEARTS THE SEED OF
FREEDOM. . . . . SP FREEDOM'S PLOW 124
GUARDING IN THEIR HEARTS THE SEED OF
FREEDOM. . . . . SP FREEDOM'S PLOW 46
GREAT THOUGHTS IN THEIR DEEPEST
HEARTS . . . . SP FREEDOM'S PLOW 148
BUT IN THEIR HEARTS THE SLAVES
BELIEVED HIM, TOO. . . . . SP FREEDOM'S PLOW 97
WHO CARRY BEAUTIES IN THEIR HEARTS SP WATER-FRONT STR 7
BUT HEARTS KEEP DOGGED BEATING . . AYM ASK YOUR MAMA 69

HEARTSTRINGS 1
ON MY HEARTSTRINGS FREEDOM SINGS . PL WORDS LIKE FREE 3

HEART-BEAT 1
LIKE A MIGHTY HEART-BEAT AS THEY
COME? . . . . SL SCOTTSBORO 8

HEART'S 3
MA HEART'S A FLUTTERING ASPEN LEAF DK REASONS WHY 7
MY HEART'S HIS GRAVE. . . . . PL LUMUMBA'S GRAVE 20
MY HEART'S NOT EVEN LEAD. . . . . . PL VARI-COLORED 6

HEAT 3
WITH NO HEAT . . . . OWT VISITORS 14
YOU GONNA CUT OFF MY HEAT? . . . . SP BLD LANDLORD 14
AND THE HEAT . . . . SP MIGRANT 18

HEAVEN 10
ONLY HEAVEN. . . . . FW GIFTS 4
BETWEEN THE LITTLE CLOUDS OF HEAVEN LHR PASTORAL 1
FOR LITTLE TEARS OF HEAVEN . . . . LHR PASTORAL 4
HEAVEN, HEAVEN, IS MY HOME! . . . . SP DEFERRED 39
HEAVEN, HEAVEN, IS MY HOME! . . . . SP DEFERRED 39
HEAVEN IS . . . . SP HEAVEN 1
LORD IN HEAVEN, ... SP JUDGMENT DAY 6
WAS HEAVEN SENT. . . . . SP LITTLE LYRIC 2
ONLY HEAVEN. . . . . SP LUCK 8
AND FALLING OUT OF HEAVEN LIKE SOFT
DEW. . . . . PL DAYBREAK IN ALA 6

HEAVY 6
ARE TOO HEAVY WITH COLOR. . . . . . WB POEME D'AUTOMNE 2
WALKING PROUDLY, ALMOST PRANCING,
BUT GRADUALLY SUBDUED TO A SLOW,
HEAVY . . . . NM BLACK CLWN MOOD 7
LIKE A HEAVY LOAD. . . . . SP HARLEM 10
REMEMBER MY YEARS, HEAVY WITH SORROW
- . . . . SP THE NEGRO MOTHE 37
LIKE A HEAVY LOAD. . . . . PL DREAM DEFERRED 10
IS HEAVY WITH THE DRUG . . . . . . PL JUNIOR ADDICT 14

HEEL 1
TO A HEEL TAP AND A SWIRL OF FINGERS ANS SONG OF SPAIN 8

HEGIRA 1
BEFORE THIS LONG HEGIRA HAD BEGUN OWT JUICE JOINT 12

HEH 1
YOU SAY I'LL MEET A BAD ENDIN', HEH? NM BIG-TIMER POEM 33

HEIL 2
HAND-HIGH SALUTES - HEIL! . . . . . PL SPECIAL BULLTIN 10
HEIL! . . . . PL SPECIAL BULLTIN 15

HEILBRONER 1
AND HEILBRONER, CRAWFORD, ... SP FLATTED FIFTHS 10

HEIRLOOMED 1
(HEIRLOOMED . . . . PL LENOX AVE. BAR 8

HELD 8
OF BEING HELD BACK, OF HAVING NO
CHANCE - . . . . NM COLORED SL POEM 21
THE TRUTH A SIMPLE HEART HAS HELD DK ALABAMA EARTH 8
I HAVE HELD MY PAIN . . . . DK MINSTREL MAN 7
AND ALL THE HOPES WE'VE HELD . . . ANS LET AMERICA BE 58
HERE I AM WITH MY HEAD HELD HIGH! ANS SISTER JOHNSON 1
AND HELD FOR TOMORROW. . . . . . . FW WALLS 8
TENANT HELD NO BAIL . . . . SP BLD LANDLORD 32
HELD THE PLOW HANDLES. . . . . . . SP FREEDOM'S PLOW 64

HELEN 1
IRENE AND HELEN ARE AS THEY USED TO
BE . . . . AYM BIRD IN ORBIT 21

HELL 24
ON MY ROAD TO HELL. . . . . NM BIG-TIMER POEM 44
WHAT IT IS TO LIVE IN HELL. . . . . ANS BLD OZZIE POWEL 23
HELL OF A DISTANCE . . . . ANS PARK BENCH 3
CHINESE? . . . HELL, NO! . . . . . . SH BLD PAWNBROKER 7
THAT LEADS TO HELL. . . . . SH BLD THE SINNER 4
I SAID TO HELL . . . . SH BLD THE KILLER 19
RIGHT STRAIGHT TO HELL. . . . . . . SH BLD THE SINNER 20
NOW THAT CROW'S BEGUN TO LOOK LIKE
HELL. . . . . JC JIM CROW'S LAST 6
THE URGE TO RAISE HELL. . . . . . . OWT BLD MARGE POLIT 8
TO ME IT'S HELL . . . . OWT VISITORS 11
ROOM IN HELL TO JOIN ME . . . . . . LHR TESTAMENT 3
AND WISHED SHE WERE IN HELL. . . . SP CROSS 6
HELL NO SHUT UP! SAY THE PEOPLE . . SP IN EXPLANATION 27
HELL, NO! IT'S TIME TO TALK BACK
NOW! . . . . SP IN EXPLANATION 29
HELL NO SHUT UP! . . . . SP IN EXPLANATION 57
YOU GOES TO HELL? . . . . SP MADAM NUMBER WR 32
ROTS IN HELL TODAY! . . . . SP MAMA AND DAUGHT 16
THOUGHT I WAS IN HELL. . . . . . . SP MORNING AFTER 8
THOUGHT I WAS IN HELL. . . . . . . SP MORNING AFTER 10

LIKE HELL! . . . . SP MULATTO 6
AND HELL BREAKS OUT . . . . SP SUNDAY MORNING 5
HERE ON THE EDGE OF HELL . . . . . PL HARLEM 1
ON THE EDGE OF HELL . . . . PL HARLEM 17
AND BEAT THE LIVING HELL . . . . . PL WHO BUT TH LORD 14

HELLO 2
HELLO, SAILOR BOY, ... SP PORT TOWN 1
HELLO, SAILOR, ... SP PORT TOWN 3

HELP 14
CAN'T HELP IT CAUSE I'M BLACK. . . FC BLACK GAL 14
'LL HELP YOU OUT . . . . FC DEATH DO DIRTY 3
STILL I CAN'T HELP LOVIN' YOU, . . SH IN TROUBLED KEY 7
SAYS I CAN'T HELP LOVIN' YOU . . . SH IN TROUBLED KEY 9
HELP ME TO SHATTER THIS DARKNESS, SP AS I GREW OLDER 28
TO HELP ME CARRY THIS LOAD. . . . . SP BOUND NO'TH BLS 6
HELP ME WHEN I'M DOWN AND OUT. . . SP DOWN AND OUT 2
HELP ME WHEN I'M DOWN AND OUT, . . SP DOWN AND OUT 4
THEN THE HAND SEEKS OTHER HANDS TO HELP. . . . . SP FREEDOM'S PLOW 20
A COMMUNITY OF HANDS TO HELP - . . SP FREEDOM'S PLOW 21
HELP ME, YARDBIRD! . . . . AYM JAZZTET MUTED 22
HELP ME! . . . . AYM JAZZTET MUTED 23
SEND FOR LAFAYETTE AND TELL HIM, "HELP! HELP ME!" . . . . PL FINAL CALL 19
SEND FOR LAFAYETTE AND TELL HIM, "HELP! HELP ME!" . . . . PL FINAL CALL 19

HELPLESS 1
HELPLESS, STUPID, SCATTERED, AND ALONE - AS NOW - . . . . ANS OPEN LETTER 28

HELPLESSNESS 1
AND HELPLESSNESS. THE MUSIC IS LIKE A MOURNFUL TOM-TOM IN THE DARK! BUT . . . . NM BLACK CLWN MOOD 11

HELPS 1
A ROAD HELPS EVERYBODY. . . . . . . PL FLORIDA WORKERS 14

HEM 1
LET ME BRUSH THE HEM - . . . . . . SP MAMA AND DAUGHT 10

HEMMED 1
HEMMED IN . . . . OWT RESTRICTIVE 12

HEMORRHAGE 1
GOD HAVING A HEMORRHAGE, ... WB CARIBBEAN SUNST 1

HEMP 1
HEMP . . . . SP GAUGE 1

HENRY 1
JOHN HENRY WITH HIS HAMMER . . . . SP LOVE 5

HER 136
AND, FAITH, I LOVE HER YET. . . . . WB PIERROT 13
AND GIVES HER KISS TO NOTHINGNESS. WB TO LITTLE LOVER 11
HER DARK BROWN FACE . . . . WB YOUNG PROSTITUT 1
HER FACE IS PALE . . . . FC CLOSING TIME 2
HER LIPS BLOOD RED . . . . FC CLOSING TIME 4
AND HER SKIN BLUE WHITE. . . . . . FC CLOSING TIME 5
I'M JUST GONNA KILL HER . . . . . . FC EVIL WOMAN 3
I TREATS HER KIND BUT . . . . FC EVIL WOMAN 5
I BROUGHT HER FROM DE SOUTH . . . . FC EVIL WOMAN 13
ELSE I'LL USE HER HEAD . . . . . . FC EVIL WOMAN 15
IF HER DADDY AIN'T WHITE . . . . . FC NEW CABARET GRL 3
I ASKED HER ONE NIGHT . . . . FC NEW CABARET GRL 7
IF HER DADDY AIN'T 'FAY . . . . . . FC NEW CABARET GRL 15
I DOES HER GOOD . . . . FC WORKIN' MAN 9
AN' I TREATS HER FINE. . . . . . . FC WORKIN' MAN 10
AND TOLD ME I'D BETTER PAY HER FOR MY ROOM RENT AND BOARD! . . . . NM BROKE 22
AFTER ALL THEM DOLLARS I GIVED HER THESE LAST TWO YEARS. . . . . . NM BROKE 23
I WOULDN'T PAY HER A PENNY NOW IF I WAS TO CROAK - . . . . NM BROKE 25
(I DON'T CARE NOTHIN' 'BOUT HER MYSELF!) . . . . NM BROKE 27
(AIN'T SEEN HER IN SIX YEARS! USED TO GO WITH HER, TOO!) . . . . . NM BROKE 63
(AIN'T SEEN HER IN SIX YEARS! USED TO GO WITH HER, TOO!) . . . . . NM BROKE 63
AS IF FATE HAD NOT BLED HIM WITH HER KNIFE! . . . . OK BEGGAR BOY 8
HAD TO PAY HER TICKET. . . . . . . SH ANNOUNCEMENT 5
FACT THAT I HURT HER, JUDGE. . . . SH BRIEF ENCOUNTER 13
FACT THAT I HURT HER. . . . . SH BRIEF ENCOUNTER 15
AND ARABELLA JOHNSON HAD HER . . . SH DEATH IN HARLEM 8
BUT ARABELLA HAD HER GUN. . . . . . SH DEATH IN HARLEM 105
BUT BESSIE TOOK A BULLET TO HER . . SH DEATH IN HARLEM 116
AND DROVE HER OFF TO JAIL . . . . . SH DEATH IN HARLEM 132
HER NAME WAS BESSIE. SHE WAS BROWN AND BOLD. . . . . SH DEATH IN HARLEM 31
AND SHE SAT ON HER CHAIR LIKE A SWEET JELLY ROLL. . . . . SH DEATH IN HARLEM 32
SHE CAST HER EYES ON TEXAS, HOLLERED, ... SH DEATH IN HARLEM 83
SETTIN IN HER PLACE! . . . . SH DEATH IN HARLEM 96
KICKED HER IN THE FACE.) . . . . . SH DEATH IN HARLEM 98
ARABELLA DREW HER PISTOL. . . . . . SH DEATH IN HARLEM 99
I GOT HER IN MISSISSIPPI. . . . . . SH ONLY WOMAN BLUS 19
TOOK HER TO ALABAM'. . . . . SH ONLY WOMAN BLUS 20
TOLD HER HUSBAND . . . . SH PRESENT 2
GIVE HER . . . . SH PRESENT 6
WENT HOME TO HER MA. . . . . SH SHAKESPEARE 8
THE GIRL WHO SELLS HER BODY BEHIND STEEL BARS. . . . . JC THE BITTER RIVR 35
TO HER DOOR. . . . . FW FAITHFUL ONE 2
AND WOUND HER SORE. . . . . FW FAITHFUL ONE 6
AND HID HER DEEP IN EARTH. . . . . FW GIRL 10
HER BODY CLOSE TO MINE. . . . . . . FW MAN 6
IN HER BITTER SORROW. . . . . FW MOTHERLAND 4
VEILING HER FACE LIKE A VIRGIN . . FW NEW MOON 6
I SAT THERE SINGING HER . . . . . . FW SONGS 1
A SOLDIER TOOK HER PART. . . . . . OWT BLD MARGE POLIT 9
AND KEPT HER THERE. . . . . OWT BLD MARGE POLIT 18
NO, I DIDN'T TOUCH HER. . . . . . . OWT FLIGHT 5
SHE SNAPS HER FINGERS, SLOWLY SHAKES HER HIPS. . . . . OWT LINCOLN THEATRE 9
SHE SNAPS HER FINGERS, SLOWLY SHAKES HER HIPS. . . . . OWT LINCOLN THEATRE 9
PRESS HANDS TOGETHER, LAUGHING AT HER SONG. . . . . OWT LINCOLN THEATRE 15
I'LL LEAVE HER MORE TO NAG ABOUT . LHR TESTAMENT 11
AUNT SUE CUDDLES A BROWN-FACED CHILD TO HER BOSOM . . . . SP AUNTSUE'S STORI 4
HE KNOWS THAT AUNT SUE NEVER GOT HER STORIES . . . . SP AUNTSUE'S STORI 19
RIGHT OUT OF HER OWN LIFE. . . . . SP AUNTSUE'S STORI 22
HE WAS HER KIN. . . . . SP BLD FORTUNE TEL 12
AND LET HIM SLEEP IN HER . . . . . SP BLD FORTUNE TEL 15
FRIENDS TRIED TO TELL HER . . . . . SP BLD FORTUNE TEL 17
DAVE MEANT HER NO GOOD. . . . . . . SP BLD FORTUNE TEL 18
HE MISTREATED HER TERRIBLE. . . . . SP BLD FORTUNE TEL 21
BEAT HER UP BAD. . . . . SP BLD FORTUNE TEL 22
THEN WENT OFF AND LEFT HER. . . . . SP BLD FORTUNE TEL 23
COULDN'T TELL, TO SAVE HER, ... SP BLD FORTUNE TEL 31
THE GUY SHE GAVE HER ALL TO . . . . SP BLD OF THE GIRL 5
DROPPED HER WITH A THUD. . . . . . SP BLD OF THE GIRL 6
BUT NOBODY'S SEEN HER SHED A TEAR. SP BLD OF THE GIRL 9
NOR SEEN HER HANG HER HEAD. . . . . SP BLD OF THE GIRL 10
NOR SEEN HER HANG HER HEAD. . . . . SP BLD OF THE GIRL 10
AIN'T EVEN HEARD HER MURMUR. . . . SP BLD OF THE GIRL 11
FOR HER MAN THAT WAS DEAD. . . . . SP BLD OF THE MAN 14
I CROSSED HER PALM WITH SILVER. . . SP BLD THE GYPSY 9
HAD HER TAIL . . . . SP CATCH 5
CONSIDER HER . . . . SP CONSIDER ME 27
AND NOW I WISH HER WELL. . . . . . SP CROSS 8
IN HER EYES. . . . . SP DELINQUENT 12
TRYING TO MAKE HER WHERE-WITH-ALL: SP EVENING SONG 2
I'D TELL HER, GIMME A PLACE TO SLEEP. . . . . SP EVENING SONG 6
HER GRANDSON'S NAME WAS JIMMY. HE DIED AT ANZIO. . . . . SP FREEDOM TRAIN 43
AT HER THIGHS. . . . . SP GRADUATION 5
TELLS HER MAMA SHE'S A TYPIST . . . SP GRADUATION 13
PERHAPS THE DREAM IS ONLY HER FACE - SP HAVANA DREAMS 5
ALL HER CLOTHES WAS GONE: . . . . . SP HOMECOMING 3
HIS WIFE LOOKED IT UP IN HER DREAM BOOK . . . . SP HOPE 3
AND I FOUND HER . . . . SP JOY 5
HER MOUTH. . . . . SP JULIET 10
ON HER MIND - . . . . SP LADY'S BOOGIE 4
MY GIRL-FRIEND SEND HER LOVE AND SAY SP LETTER 6
SHE SQUINTED UP HER EYES. . . . . . SP MADAM FORT TELL 6
THEN TAKE CARE OF HER CHILDREN . . SP MADAM HER MADAM 7
SHE OPENED HER MOUTH. . . . . SP MADAM HER MADAM 17
LAST TIME I TOLD HER. . . . . SP MADAM CHARTY CH 25
NURSE, PUT HER ON A DIET, ... SP MADAM WRONG VIS 25
AND BUY HER SOME CHICKEN. . . . . . SP MADAM WRONG VIS 26
SELLING HER SCANTY WARES . . . . . SP MEXICAN MARKET 3
HER SKIN SO BROWN. . . . . SP MEXICAN MARKET 7
FOR HER MISERY. . . . . SP MISERY 16
HER FEATURES IS ALL RUN TOGETHER . SP NECESSITY 9
SHE LIFTED UP HER LIPS . . . . . . SP NEW YORKERS 15
AND GRANDMA CANNOT GET HER GOSPEL HYMNS . . . . SP PASSING 3
THROWS HER ENORMOUS ARMS AROUND . . SP PROJECTION 6
GOD BLESS HER, DEAD AND GONE! . . . SP REVERIE HARLEM 6
THAT WARMED HER BODY. . . . . SP RUBY BROWN 3
MAYVILLE HAD NO PLACE TO OFFER HER, SP RUBY BROWN 5
THAT TRIED TO BURN WITHIN HER SOUL. SP RUBY BROWN 7
SEEKING AN ANSWER TO HER QUESTIONS. SP RUBY BROWN 20
HER NAME ANY MORE. . . . . SP RUBY BROWN 22
PAY MORE MONEY TO HER NOW . . . . . SP RUBY BROWN 25
WITH DUST IN HER HAIR. . . . . . . SP SONG BILLIE HOL 11
MISS GARDNER'S IN HER GARDEN. . . . SP SOUTHERN MAMMY 1
MISS YARDMAN'S IN HER YARD. . . . . SP SOUTHERN MAMMY 2
WHEN LIFE HURT HER: . . . . SP SPIRITUALS 7
LAID HER DOWN. . . . . SP STONY LONESOME 5
HER SEEK THE BURNING SUNLIGHT . . . SP STRANGE HURT 9
THROWS A TOOTHPICK FROM HER WINDOW. SP SUMMER EVENING 19
HER GREAT ADVENTURE ENDED . . . . . SP S-SSS-SS-SH! 1

AND HER MOTHER . . . . SP S-SSS-SS-SH! 6
AND HER MOTHER . . . . SP S-SSS-SS-SH! 13
AND I, WHO AM BLACK, WOULD LOVE HER SP THE SOUTH 18
WOULD GIVE HER MANY RARE GIFTS . . SP THE SOUTH 21
BUT SHE TURNS HER BACK UPON ME. . . SP THE SOUTH 22
AND IN HER HOUSE MY CHILDREN . . . SP THE SOUTH 27
AND HER NAME . . . . SP WEST TEXAS 4
HER FACE IS LIKE AN ANCIENT CAMEO SP WHEN SUE WEARS 2
DID YOU TELL HER THAT OUR CREDIT
OFFICE . . . . AYM ASK YOUR MAMA 10
YES, SIR, I TOLD HER. . . . . AYM ASK YOUR MAMA 12
AS LEDA STREW HER CORN . . . . . . AYM BIRD IN ORBIT 29
BARED HER BOSOMS, BARED IN PUBLIC AYM BIRD IN ORBIT 49
WHAT SHE SAID ABOUT HER CHILDREN . AYM BIRD IN ORBIT 51
GRANDPA, DID YOU FIND HER IN THE TV
SILENCE . . . . AYM BIRD IN ORBIT 61
DID YOU EVER FIND HER? . . . . . . AYM BIRD IN ORBIT 64
HER YESTERDAY PAST GRANDPA - . . . PL CULTURAL EXCHNG 17
NOT OF HER OWN DOING - . . . . . . PL CULTURAL EXCHNG 18
HER BANDAGE HIDES TWO FESTERING
SORES . . . . PL JUSTICE 3

HERD 3

NOW I HERD WITH THE MANY - . . . . WB LAMENT DARK PEO 11
JUST A HERD OF NEGROES . . . . . . SP SHARE-CROPPERS 1
THAN A HERD OF NEGROES . . . . . . SP SHARE-CROPPERS 13

HERE 85

FER I CAN'T STAY HERE ALONE. . . . FC GYPSY MAN 6
LISTEN HERE TO ME. . . . . FC LISTEN HERE 2
LISTEN HERE TO ME: . . . . FC LISTEN HERE 4
LISTEN HERE TO ME. . . . . FC LISTEN HERE 14
NOT WANTED HERE; NOT NEEDED THERE - NM BLACK CLWN POEM 40
HERE ARE MY HANDS . . . . NM BLACK CLWN POEM 61
SO HERE I IS, BROKE. . . . . NM BROKE 18
UM-MM! SIGN HERE SAYS THEY WANTS
SOMEBODY TO SHOVEL COAL. . . . . NM BROKE 28
BUT RIGHT LONG THROUGH HERE NOW, I
CAN'T 'FORD TO BUY YOU NO HAT." NM BROKE 51
ALL THESE YEARS YOU SAY YOU BEEN
WORKIN' HERE? . . . . NM BROKE 68
FOR HERE IN THE SOUTH THERE'S NO
VOTES AND NO RIGHT. . . . . . . NM COLORED SL POEM 46
FOR HERE I DO NOT MAKE MY BED. . . OK DEATH SEAMAN 6
HAPPY THEY WERE HERE. . . . . OK IRISH WAKE 8
HERE IS MY HAND. . . . . ANS OPEN LETTER 66
HERE I AM WITH MY HEAD HELD HIGH! ANS SISTER JOHNSON 1
HERE I GO WITH MY BANNER IN MY HAND! ANS SISTER JOHNSON 5
HERE YOU ARE. . . . . SH BLD THE KILLER 8
ALARM CLOCK HERE RINGING SO DAMN
LOUD . . . . SH DAYBREAK 3
BEEN UP HERE SIX MONTHS - . . . . . SH EVENIN' BLUES 5
KEEP ME CAGED UP HERE. . . . . . . SH FREE MAN 8
BUT YOU JUST AS WELL BE HERE WHERE
YOU DUE TO LIVE. . . . . SH LETTER 11
I SAID COME HERE, LONESOME, ... SH MIDNIGHT CHIPPI 5
DON'T LEAVE ME HERE ALONE. . . . . SH MIDNIGHT CHIPPI 12
YOU GOT TO LIVE HERE A YEAR AND A
DAY. . . . . SH OUT OF WORK 12
JUST SO IT GOES AWAY FROM HERE. . . SH SIX-BITS BLUES 6
HERE BY MYSELF, I DO AS I PLEASE. SH SUNDAY 2
THEY OUGHT TO BE LIKE ME SETTING
HERE - FEELING GLAD! . . . . . . SH SUNDAY 15
HERE I SET WITH A BITTER OLD
THOUGHT, ... SH TWILIGHT REVERI 1
SETTING HERE THINKING FEELING SAD. SH TWILIGHT REVERI 3
YAL, HERE I SET THINKING - A BITTER
OLD THOUGHT . . . . SH TWILIGHT REVERI 9
AND HERE I SET THINKING WITH A
BITTER OLD FROWN. . . . . SH TWILIGHT REVERI 14
NOW - RIGHT HERE! . . . . JC HOW ABOUT DIXIE 24
THE CLOCK IS MOVING FORWARD HERE - JC TO CAPTAIN MULZ 25
ABOUT HERE AND THERE - . . . . . . FW BORDER LINE 6
BUT HERE THERE'S PEACE . . . . . . FW CAROLINA CABIN 18
HERE IS THAT SLEEPING PLACE, . . . FW GRAVE YARD 1
IS HERE. . . . . FW GRAVE YARD 6
HERE IS MY HEART!" . . . . FW HEART 7
FROM HERE TO THERE, ... FW SAILING DATE 12
HANG ON HERE, ... OWT BOARDING HOUSE 10
BUT AFTER I BEEN HERE AWHILE . . . OWT STRANGER IN TWN 15
TO ME IT'S HERE . . . . OWT VISITORS 3
TO ME IT'S HERE . . . . OWT VISITORS 7
YESTERDAY YOU WAS HERE. . . . . . . OWT YESTERDAY TODAY 3
HERE I SIT . . . . SP BAD MORNING 1
SHE'LL BE HERE BY AND BY. . . . . SP BLD THE GYPSY 12
I LIVE HERE, TOO. . . . . SP DEMOCRACY 19
AND RENT TIME'S NEARLY HERE. . . . SP DOWN AND OUT 8
COME HERE, BABY, DARLIN'! . . . . . SP EVENING SONG 3
THE PLAN AND THE PATTERN IS HERE, SP FREEDOM'S PLOW 165
NOW IT IS ME HERE, AND YOU THERE. SP FREEDOM'S PLOW 85
I WAS BORN HERE, HE SAID, ... SP GOOD MORNING 2
FROM HERE - . . . . SP GREEN MEMORY 6
HERE, SALLIE! . . . . SP IN EXPLANATION 13
IT'S SUNNY HERE . . . . SP KID SLEEPY 5
STAY HERE? . . . . SP KID SLEEPY 20
STAY HERE. . . . . SP KID SLEEPY 22
BUT HERE IS FIVE DOLLARS FOR YOU . SP LETTER 4
HERE, WELL, THAT IS ALL SO I WILL
CLOSE. . . . . SP LETTER 9
SO SINCE I'M STILL HERE LIVIN', . . SP LIFE IS FINE 23
CAUSE I'M STILL HERE KICKIN'! . . . SP MADAM WRONG VIS 28
I WAS BORN HERE, ... SP NEW YORKERS 1
RIGHT HERE BENEATH GOD'S SKY. . . . SP NEW YORKERS 3
I WASN'T BORN HERE, SHE SAID, . . . SP NEW YORKERS 4
SO I COME UP HERE. . . . . SP NEW YORKERS 12
COME HERE, I LOVE YOU. . . . . . . SP PORT TOWN 7
"YOU CAN'T LEAVE US HERE!" . . . . SP SYLVESTER'S BED 14
I WENT TO SCHOOL THERE, THEN DURHAM,
THEN HERE . . . . SP THEME FOR ENG B 8
HERE!) . . . . PL FINAL CALL 25
AND LEAVE ME STANDIN' HERE. . . . . PL FLORIDA WORKERS 12
I LIVE HERE, TOO. . . . . PL FREEDOM 19
YOU CAN'T EAT HERE! . . . . PL GO SLOW 6
YOU CAN'T LIVE HERE! . . . . PL GO SLOW 7
YOU CAN'T WORK HERE! . . . . PL GO SLOW 8
HERE ON THE EDGE OF HELL . . . . . PL HARLEM 1
SO WE STAND HERE . . . . PL HARLEM 16
THAN IS HIS LIVING HERE, ... PL JUNIOR ADDICT 23
HERE I COME! . . . . PL LITTLE SNG HOUS 1
HERE AM I! . . . . PL LITTLE SNG HOUS 28
HERE COME YOU: . . . . PL OFFICE BUILDING 2
I'M STILL HERE! . . . . PL STILL HERE 9
. . . AND HERE IS . . . . PL THE DOVE 1
BECAUSE I AM HERE - . . . . PL WAR 20
LISTEN HERE, JOE, ... PL WITHOUT BENEFIT 1
LISTEN HERE, KID, ... PL WITHOUT BENEFIT 7

HEREAFTER 2

AND HIS OWN HEREAFTER - . . . . . . SP YOUNG SAILOR 5
AND NOTHING HEREAFTER. . . . . . . SP YOUNG SAILOR 20

HERE'S 4

HERE'S MY SUGAR-DADDY PAL. . . . . SH DEATH IN HARLEM 48
HERE'S FIVE DOLLARS, CASSIE, BUY A
TICKET BACK. . . . . SH LETTER 20
HERE'S YOUR FARE! . . . . OWT JITNEY 22
THANK GOD-A-MIGHTY! HERE'S THE . . SP FREEDOM TRAIN 67

HERNDON 1

TO BELIEVE AN ANGELO HERNDON, OR
EVER GET TOGETHER. . . . . ANS KIDS WHO DIE 36

HEROIC 1

WERE PLED ANEW AT SOME HEROIC BAR, PL MOTHER IN WAR 4

HERS 1

NOT HERS, ... SP A HOUSE IN TAOS 39

HERSELF 2

SHE ASKED HERSELF TWO QUESTIONS . . SP RUBY BROWN 11
LORDY! SLEEPIN' BY HERSELF. . . . . SP STONY LONESOME 17

HESITATE 1

OR MUST I HESITATE? . . . . AYM RIDE, RED, RIDE 8

HEWED 1

THAT HEWED AND SHAPED THE ROOFTOPS
OF AMERICA. . . . . SP FREEDOM'S PLOW 56

HEY 35

HEY! HEY! . . . . WB BLUES FANTASY 1
HEY! HEY! . . . . WB BLUES FANTASY 1
HEY! HEY! . . . . WB BLUES FANTASY 6
HEY! HEY! . . . . WB BLUES FANTASY 6
HEY! . . . HEY! . . . . WB BLUES FANTASY 13
HEY! . . . HEY! . . . . WB BLUES FANTASY 13
HEY! . . . HEY! . . . . WB BLUES FANTASY 28
HEY! . . . HEY! . . . . WB BLUES FANTASY 28
HEY! HEY! . . . . WB BLUES FANTASY 30
HEY! HEY! . . . . WB BLUES FANTASY 30
HEY, BOY! . . . . FC BRASS SPITOONS 11
HEY, BOY! . . . . FC BRASS SPITOONS 16
HEY, BOY! . . . . FC BRASS SPITOONS 31
HEY, BOY! . . . . FC BRASS SPITOONS 36
HEY! HEY! . . . . FC SATURDAY NIGHT 25
HEY! HEY! . . . . FC SATURDAY NIGHT 25
I CAN HEY ON WATER . . . . SH HEY-HEY BLUES 1
HEY ON WATER . . . . SH HEY-HEY BLUES 3
CAUSE I CAN HEY ON WATER, ... SH HEY-HEY BLUES 19
HEY ON WATER . . . . SH HEY-HEY BLUES 21
SAID, LISTEN! HEY! . . . . SH MIDNIGHT CHIPPI 14
HEY NINNY NEIGH! . . . . SH SHAKESPEARE 1
AND A HEY NONNY NOE! . . . . SH SHAKESPEARE 2
HEY NINNY NEIGH . . . . SH SHAKESPEARE 5
HEY, BIG BUDDY, ... JC BIG BUDDY 12
HEY, MISTER, WAIT! . . . . OWT JITNEY 37
HEY! . . . . OWT JITNEY 65
HEY, ALBERT! . . . . SP BABY 2
HEY! . . . . SP DANCER 17
HEY, POP! . . . . SP DREAM BOOGIE 18
HEY, LAWDY, MAMA! . . . . SP EASY BOOGIE 10
THEY CALL THEM, HEY GEORGE! . . . . SP IN EXPLANATION 12
HEY! BABA-RE-BOP! MOP! ON A BE-BOP
KICK! . . . . SP LIKEWISE 23
HEY, BUDDY! . . . . PL FLORIDA WORKERS 1

HEY, BUDDY, LOOK! . . . . PL FLORIDA WORKERS 19

HEY-HEY 4

SAME AS I CAN HEY-HEY ON BEER. . . SH HEY-HEY BLUES 2
SAME AS I CAN HEY-HEY ON BEER. . . SH HEY-HEY BLUES 4
I SAID HEY-HEY ON BEER - . . . . . SH HEY-HEY BLUES 20
AND HEY-HEY ON BEER - . . . . SH HEY-HEY BLUES 22

HEY-HEY-HEY 2

I CAN HEY-HEY-HEY - AND CHEER! . . SH HEY-HEY BLUES 6
AND I'LL HEY-HEY-HEY - AND CHEER! SH HEY-HEY BLUES 24

HE'D 2

HE'D GO MA BAIL. . . . . FC DEATH DO DIRTY 19
HE'D FOUND A FISH . . . . SP CATCH 9

HE'LL 3

HE'LL NEVER HYPE . . . . SP DEAD IN THERE 8
HE'LL NEVER LAY A . . . . SP DEAD IN THERE 12
HE'LL COME TO TOWN. . . . . PL LAST PRINCE 15

HE'S 23

CHILE, HE'S GONE AWAY. . . . . . . WB BLUES FANTASY 8
BABE, HE'S GONE AWAY. . . . . WB BLUES FANTASY 10
MEANS HE'S GONNA LEAVE THIS WORLD. FC GAL'S CRY DYING 8
MEANS HE'S GONNA LEAVE THIS WORLD. FC GAL'S CRY DYING 10
HE'S GOT THOSE 'LECTRIC-SHOCKIN' EYES AN' . . . . FC MA MAN 5
HE PLAYS GOOD WHEN HE'S SOBER . . . FC MA MAN 11
AN' BETTER, BETTER, BETTER WHEN HE'S DRUNK. . . . . FC MA MAN 12
HE'S A FRIEND O' MINE. . . . . . . DK MA LORD 11
WHEN HE'S . . . . FW MAN 14
HE'S TRYING TO RUIN THE GOVERNMENT SP BLD LANDLORD 23
NOW THAT HE'S BURIED - . . . . . . SP BLD OF THE MAN 21
HE'S MY ACE-BOY. . . . . SP DEAD IN THERE 14
HE'S WEARING. . . . . SP INTERNE AT PROV 34
HE'S GOT A GRIN ON HIS FACE. . . . SP ME AND THE MULE 2
HE'S BEEN A MULE SO LONG . . . . . SP ME AND THE MULE 3
HE'S FORGOT ABOUT HIS RACE. . . . . SP ME AND THE MULE 4
BUT HE'S THE ONLY MAN I'LL . . . . SP MIDWINTER BLUES 17
AND HE'S SMARTER THAN HE LOOKS. . . SP NEIGHBOR 10
HE'S A GOOD MAN. . . . . SP NEIGHBOR 14
IN FACT, HE'S A GREAT CAT. . . . . SP NEIGHBOR 16
NOW HE'S LIVIN' . . . . SP NOT A MOVIE 7
YES, HE'S DONE BEEN LEFT. . . . . . SP STONY LONESOME 15
SEND (GOD FORBID - HE'S NOT DEAD LONG ENOUGH!) . . . . PL FINAL CALL 17

HIBBLER'S 1

HIBBLER'S GIVING OUT! . . . . OWT JITNEY 27

HID 3

AND HID HER DEEP IN EARTH. . . . . FW GIRL 10
AND HID IT . . . . FW HEART 15
STRAYHORN HID BACKSTAGE WITH LUTHER $ $ . . . . AYM HORN OF PLENTY 10

HIDDEN 2

HIDE AND ARE HIDDEN . . . . SP LONG TRIP 5
HIDDEN FROM THE SKY . . . . PL WITHOUT BENEFIT 14

HIDE 3

HOLD AND HIDE THY BODY. . . . . . . WB SONGS DARK VIRG 13
LIFT ARMS IN VAIN, RUN, HIDE, DIE: ANS SONG OF SPAIN 60
HIDE AND ARE HIDDEN . . . . SP LONG TRIP 5

HIDES 4

MADE FROM THE HIDES OF BLACKS . . . AYM BIRD IN ORBIT 66
MADE FROM THE HIDES OF BLACKS . . . AYM BIRD IN ORBIT 89
VEILING WHAT THE DARKNESS HIDES. . PL GEORGIA DUSK 4
HER BANDAGE HIDES TWO FESTERING SORES . . . . PL JUSTICE 3

HIDING 2

AND BLUE, HIDING HIS DISCONTENT AS THOUGHTS OF A BETTER LIFE OVERCOME . . . . NM BIG-TIMER MOOD 7
HIDING. . . . . SP AS I GREW OLDER 13

HIGH 35

LIFTS HIGH A DRESS OF SILKEN GOLD. WB JAZZONIA 6
BE A HIGH YALLER. . . . . FC RED SILK STOCK 10
WE BURIED HIM HIGH ON THE WINDY HILL. . . . . DK DEATH SEAMAN 1
THE HIGH SHERIFF'S EYES ARE FILLED WITH HATE. . . . . ANS BLD OZZIE POWEL 7
THE HIGH SHERIFF SHOOTS AND HE SHOOTS TO KILL . . . . ANS BLD OZZIE POWEL 9
NEVER SAW THE HIGH SHERIFF'S GUN . ANS BLD OZZIE POWEL 15
THEY NEVER SAW THE HIGH SHERIFF'S EYES . . . . ANS BLD OZZIE POWEL 19
A WHITE HIGH SHERIFF WHO SHOOTS TO KILL . . . . ANS BLD OZZIE POWEL 27
HIGH IN A MARBLE TOMB. . . . . . . ANS BLDS OF LENIN 2
PULL IT HIGH! . . . . ANS LYNCHING SONG 2
HERE I AM WITH MY HEAD HELD HIGH! ANS SISTER JOHNSON 1
TO WALK A HIGH WIRE . . . . SH ASPIRATION 5
HOW HIGH HAVE YOU GOT TO BE? . . . SH MISSISSIPPI LEV 14
HOW HIGH HAVE YOU GOT TO BE . . . . SH MISSISSIPPI LEV 16
BEHIND YOUR HIGH STONE WALLS - . . FW CONVENT 3
UM-HUH! YOU TALKING HIGH AND MIGHTY. SP BLD LANDLORD 17
A FUNERAL SO HIGH? . . . . SP BLD OF THE MAN 26
IN A HIGH COLD WIND . . . . SP CROSSING 6
TO GET THROUGH HIGH AT TWENTY'S KIND OF LATE - . . . . SP DEFERRED 6
HIGH NOON TEETH . . . . SP DREAM BOOGE VAR 3
IF IT HADN'T A-BEEN SO HIGH . . . . SP LIFE IS FINE 18
HIGH UP THERE! . . . . SP LIFE IS FINE 21
IT WAS HIGH! . . . . SP LIFE IS FINE 22
SOME FOLKS BLAME HIGH PRICES ON THE JEWS. . . . . SP LIKEWISE 12
BEYOND A HIGH TENSION WALL . . . . SP MELLOW 5
HAS KNOWN HIGH WIND-SWEPT MOUNTAINS. SP MEXICAN MARKET 5
HABITUES OF THE HIGH SHUTTERED HOUSES. . . . . SP RUBY BROWN 24
(BRUISED BODY HIGH IN AIR) . . . . SP SONG DARK GIRL 6
LIFT HIGH MY BANNER OUT OF THE DUST. SP THE NEGRO MOTHE 41
HIGH BALLS, LOW BALLS: . . . . . . AYM ASK YOUR MAMA 18
NEW JERSEY HIGH SCHOOL! . . . . . . AYM BIRD IN ORBIT 78
BLOWN SKY HIGH BY MONT PELEE? . . . AYM RIDE, RED, RIDE 14
SOARING HIGH - . . . . PL COLOR 7
A. PHILIP RANDOLPH THE HIGH GRAND WORTHY. . . . . PL CULTURAL EXCHNG 45
YOUR WALL IS TOO HIGH . . . . PL LAST PRINCE 4

HIGHER 5

BUT HIGHER THAN THE SINGING PINES DK ALABAMA EARTH 4
AND PULL HIM HIGHER! . . . . SP BLUE BAYOU 18
AND PULL HIM HIGHER! . . . . SP BLUE BAYOU 21
PRESSURE OF THE BLOOD IS SLIGHTLY HIGHER . . . . AYM JAZZTET MUTED 2
IS SLIGHTLY HIGHER - . . . . AYM JAZZTET MUTED 19

HIGHLY 1

HIGHLY INTEGRATED . . . . AYM HORN OF PLENTY 63

HIGHWAY 1

TO MAKE EACH HIGHWAY . . . . PL FREDRK DOUGLASS 12

HIGH-IN-HEABEN 1

HIGH-IN-HEABEN JESUS. . . . . FC GAL'S CRY DYING 17

HIGH-STEPPIN 1

HIGH-STEPPIN JAG. . . . . SH DEATH IN HARLEM 15

HIGH-YALLER 1

I GOT A HIGH-YALLER. . . . . NM BIG-TIMER POEM 21

HILL 12

AND I SHO HAD A PRETTY GAL, TOO, UP YONDER ON SUGAR HILL. . . . . . NM BROKE 48
WE BURIED HIM HIGH ON THE WINDY HILL. . . . . DK DEATH SEAMAN 1
OF SUGAR HILL? . . . . SH HARLEM SWEETIES 2
DELICIOUS, FINE SUGAR HILL. . . . . SH HARLEM SWEETIES 44
HE SITS ON A HILL . . . . FW JAIME 1
HE SITS ON A HILL . . . . FW JAIME 5
FORGOTTEN WATCH-FIRES ON A HILL SOMEWHERE! . . . . OWT NEGRO SERVANT 6
TO THIS COLLEGE ON THE HILL ABOVE HARLEM. . . . . SP THEME FOR ENG B 9
THE STEPS FROM THE HILL LEAD DOWN INTO HARLEM. . . . . SP THEME FOR ENG B 11
UP THAT STEEP HILL . . . . AYM GOSPEL CHA-CHA 52
UP THERE ON THAT HILL . . . . AYM GOSPEL CHA-CHA 59
CLIMBIN' THAT HILL. . . . . PL DOWN WHERE I AM 10

HILLBILLY 1

PLAY HILLBILLY DIRGES . . . . PL SPECIAL BULLTIN 3

HILLS 6

WANDERERS OF THE HILLS AND SEAS. . WB A FAREWELL 2
YOU WHO LIVE BETWEEN THE HILLS . . WB A FAREWELL 7
GREAT LONELY HILLS. . . . . FW BIG SUR 1
RIDING THE HILLS TONIGHT. . . . . . FW NEW MOON 2
DRIPPED BLOOD OVER THE EASTERN HILLS SP A BLACK PIERROT 8
AND THE HILLS OF THE . . . . PL OCTOBER 16 RAID 10

HIM 64

AIN'T CUT HIM WID NO RAZOR, ... FC BLACK GAL 3
I BOUGHT HIM SUITS O' CLOTHES. . . FC BLACK GAL 10
OH, GOD, I WANTS HIM BACK! . . . . FC BLACK GAL 18
THEY CALLED HIM DO DIRTY . . . . . FC DEATH DO DIRTY 6
AN' DE ONES THAT KILT HIM, - . . . FC DEATH DO DIRTY 31
I GIVE IT TO HIM CAUSE I LOVED HIM FC GYPSY MAN 17
I GIVE IT TO HIM CAUSE I LOVED HIM FC GYPSY MAN 17
WHEN I CUDDLES UP TO HIM . . . . . FC MINNIE SINGS 9
ASK HIM TO GIMME HIS HAND. . . . . FC MOAN 8
FOR HIM . . . . FC SPORT 2
HIM, ASSUMING A FALSE AND BRAGGING SELF-ASSURANCE, AND A PRETENDED NM BIG-TIMER MOOD 8
AND I SAW HIM STANDING THERE, STRAIGHT AND TALL. . . . . NM COLORED SL POEM 37
FOR WHAT COULD I ANSWER HIM, EXCEPT, "IT'S A LIE!" . . . . NM COLORED SL POEM 43

Context	Poem	Line
HE WHO OPPRESSES ME, HIM I DEFY!	NM DARK YOUTH USA	7
AS IF FATE HAD NOT BLED HIM WITH HER KNIFE!	DK BEGGAR BOY	8
WE BURIED HIM HIGH ON THE WINDY HILL,	DK DEATH SEAMAN	1
I FILLED HIM FULL OF HOLES	SH BLD THE KILLER	23
HANDS ON HIM.	SH DEATH IN HARLEM	9
THE CRACKERS WERE IN LOVE WITH HIM.	JC JIM CROW'S LAST	2
THEY LIKED HIM SO WELL THEY COULDN'T STAND	JC JIM CROW'S LAST	3
AT FIRST THEY ARE NICE TO HIM.	FW MIGRATION	5
BUT FINALLY THEY TAUNT HIM	FW MIGRATION	6
AND CALL HIM "NIGGER."	FW MIGRATION	7
HATE HIM, TOO.	FW MIGRATION	9
LAMENT HIM	FW OLD SAILOR	19
TO KILL HIM.	FW SNAKE	7
SENT HIM HOME	OWT DECEASED	2
SAYS, I KNOW IT'S HIM!	OWT HONEY BABE	12
PLEASE DON'T TAKE HIM AWAY!	SP AS BEFITS A MAN	16
AND TELLS HIM STORIES.	SP AUNTSUE'S STORI	5
MADAM TOOK HIM IN.	SP BLD FORTUNE TEL	10
SHE TREATED HIM LIKE	SP BLD FORTUNE TEL	11
GAVE HIM MONEY TO GAMBLE.	SP BLD FORTUNE TEL	13
SHE GAVE HIM BREAD.	SP BLD FORTUNE TEL	14
AND LET HIM SLEEP IN HER	SP BLD FORTUNE TEL	15
NO MONEY TO BURY HIM.	SP BLD OF THE MAN	1
TO BLESS HIM DEAD	SP BLD OF THE MAN	19
AND PRAISE HIM ALIVE.	SP BLD OF THE MAN	20
AND PULL HIM HIGHER!	SP BLUE BAYOU	18
PUT HIM ON A ROPE	SP BLUE BAYOU	20
AND PULL HIM HIGHER!	SP BLUE BAYOU	21
I DON'T SEE HIM MUCH.	SP BUDDY	3
FAILED HIM	SP DANCER	2
THE GIRLS LEFT HIM.	SP DANCER	19
WHO COULDN'T DIG HIM.	SP DEAD IN THERE	19
PLANT HIM NOW -	SP DEAD IN THERE	20
BUT IN THEIR HEARTS THE SLAVES BELIEVED HIM, TOO.	SP FREEDOM'S PLOW	97
KILL HIM - AND LET HIS SOUL RUN WILD!	SP GENIUS CHILD	12
AND I'M GOIN' THERE TO THINK ABOUT HIM.	SP LAMENT OVER LOV	12
I NEVER SEEN HIM BEFORE.	SP MADAM WRONG VIS	2
I DIDN'T ASK HIM	SP MADAM PHONE BIL	14
IF I EVER CATCH HIM,	SP MADAM PHONE BIL	19
NO SOONER HAD I TOLD HIM	SP MADAM WRONG VIS	21
I TOLD HIM, JACKSON,	SP MADAM MIGHT-HAV	21
I FELT LIKE THAT ABOUT HIM.	SP MAMA AND DAUGHT	12
CARRIED HIM OUT FOR DEAD	SP NIGHT FUNERAL	32
WELL, THEY ROCKED HIM WITH ROAD-APPLES	SP NOT A MOVIE	1
THEY HUNG HIM TO A TREE.	SP SOUTHERN MAMMY	14
GRANT HIM YOUR LOVE.	PL CHRIST IN ALA.	9
BUT I CAN'T EAT HIM FOR LUNCH.	PL CROWNS GARLANDS	20
SEND FOR THE PIED PIPER AND LET HIM PIPE THE RATS	PL FINAL CALL	1
SEND FOR LAFAYETTE AND TELL HIM, "HELP! HELP ME!"	PL FINAL CALL	19
THEY KILLED HIM DEAD.	PL LUMUMBA'S GRAVE	12
DON'T LET HIM MAKE A PULP OUT OF ME!	PL WHO BUT TH LORD	11

HIMSELF 9

Context	Poem	Line
SHOULDERS AT FATE, ACCEPTING HIS POSITION - BUT INSIDE HIMSELF UNHAPPY	NM BIG-TIMER MOOD	6
PULLING HIMSELF TOGETHER, BOASTING LOUDLY AGAIN, BUT REALIZING WITHIN THE	NM BIG-TIMER MOOD	11
IN THE CLOTHES OF A MODERN MAN, HE PROCLAIMS HIMSELF.	NM BLACK CLWN MOOD	15
SEEKING A HOME WHERE HE HIMSELF IS FREE.	ANS LET AMERICA BE	4
SHE LEFT THE TEXAS KID SETTIN BY HIMSELF	SH DEATH IN HARLEM	79
HE SUNS HIMSELF	FW OLD SAILOR	15
HE STARTS FIRST WITH HIMSELF	SP FREEDOM'S PLOW	5
THE LORD GOD HIMSELF	PL BOMBINGS DIXIE	5
AND BROWN HIMSELF	PL OCTOBER 16 RAID	19

HIND 1

Context	Poem	Line
PAIN ON HIND LEGS RISING.	SP INTERNE AT PROV	23

HIP 2

Context	Poem	Line
HIP BOOTS	AYM SHADES OF PIG	31
(AND I NEVER HAD A HIP BOOT ON)	AYM SHADES OF PIG	33

HIPS 2

Context	Poem	Line
NIGHT-DARK GIRL OF THE SWAYING HIPS?	WB NUDE YOUNG DANC	6
SHE SNAPS HER FINGERS, SLOWLY SHAKES HER HIPS,	OWT LINCOLN THEATRE	9

HIRE 1

Context	Poem	Line
WHO HIRE FRANCO TO LEAD HIS GANG-HORDES	ANS SONG OF SPAIN	76

HIRIN' 1

Context	Poem	Line
AND DE MAN COME TELLIN' ME THEY AIN'T HIRIN' NO MO' COLORED JUST WHITE.	NM BROKE	45

HIS 164

Context	Poem	Line
WOULD GOD HIS LIPS WERE SWEET!	WB TO LITTLE LOVER	12
AN' HAD CUT HIS GAL	FC DEATH DO DIRTY	8
ASK HIM TO GIMME HIS HAND.	FC MOAN	8
PACKED HIS TRUNK AND LEFT.	FC SUICIDE	2
PACKED HIS TRUNK AND LEFT.	FC SUICIDE	4
CHOKING HIS BREATH	OLD THE CONSUMPTIVE	11
SYNCOPATED MUSIC, TELLING HIS STORY IN A HARD, BRAZEN, CYNICAL FASHION.	NM BIG-TIMER MOOD	1
BOASTING, LIKE A CHEAP BULLY, BUT SUDDENLY LOOKING AHEAD: SHRUGGING HIS	NM BIG-TIMER MOOD	5
SHOULDERS AT FATE, ACCEPTING HIS POSITION - BUT INSIDE HIMSELF UNHAPPY	NM BIG-TIMER MOOD	6
AND BLUE, HIDING HIS DISCONTENT AS THOUGHTS OF A BETTER LIFE OVERCOME	NM BIG-TIMER MOOD	7
STRENGTH HE DOESN'T REALLY FEEL. GAY, LOUD, UNHAPPY JAZZ, BARING HIS	NM BIG-TIMER MOOD	9
TRAGIC EMPTINESS OF HIS LIFE.	NM BIG-TIMER MOOD	12
ECHOES THE FIGHTING "MARSEILLAISE." TEARING OFF HIS CLOWN'S SUIT,	NM BLACK CLWN MOOD	13
CAN A CLOWN HAVE HIS DAY.	NM BLACK CLWN POEM	15
WHO HAS A VISION OF HIS BROTHER KILLED IN FRANCE WHILE FIGHTING FOR THE	NM COLORED SL MOOD	2
WITH HIS FACE FULL OF LIGHT AND FAITH, CONFIDENT THAT A NEW WORLD HAS	NM COLORED SL MOOD	9
AND BOWING HIS HEAD IN SHAME, BECOMES SUDDENLY FIERCE AND ANGRY, THEN HE	NM COLORED SL MOOD	11
OUT OF HIS GRAVE FROM OVER THE SEA,	NM COLORED SL POEM	14
IN HIS SOLDIER'S UNIFORM, AND ALL.	NM COLORED SL POEM	38
THEN HIS DARK FACE SMILED AT ME IN THE NIGHT -	NM COLORED SL POEM	39
DRESSED, CARRYING HIS BOOKS TO SCHOOL.	NM DARK YOUTH USA	1
HIS BURIED BODY LIES -	DK ALABAMA EARTH	3
AND YET HE PLAYS UPON HIS FLUTE A WILD FREE TUNE	DK BEGGAR BOY	7
BUT HIS SOUL WENT OUT TO SEA.	DK DEATH SEAMAN	2
HIS SEA-SOUL SAY TO ME:	DK DEATH SEAMAN	4
HE GIVES ME HIS HAND.	DK MA LORD	4
HIS SOUL ON FIRE,	DK MA LORD	13
HE HAD A MERMAID ON HIS ARM,	DK SAILOR	5
AN ANCHOR ON HIS BREAST,	DK SAILOR	6
AND TATTOOED ON HIS BACK HE HAD	DK SAILOR	7
WHO HIRE FRANCO TO LEAD HIS GANG-HORDES	ANS SONG OF SPAIN	76
HIS ROLL WASN'T SLIM -	SH DEATH IN HARLEM	7
A ROW OF GOLD IN HIS UPPER MOUTH.	SH DEATH IN HARLEM	18
A ROLL OF BILLS IN HIS LEFT-HAND POCKET.	SH DEATH IN HARLEM	19
(DIXIE MAKES HIS MONEY ON TWO-BIT GIN.)	SH DEATH IN HARLEM	32
WITH LOVIN IN HIS HEAD.	SH DEATH IN HARLEM	140
DIXIE RUBBED HIS HANDS AND LAUGHED OUT LOUD -	SH DEATH IN HARLEM	63
ALL UNSUSPECTIN OF THE CHIPPIE ON HIS LEFT -	SH DEATH IN HARLEM	80
HE LED HIS COLORED DELEGATION	JC BLD SAM SOLOMON	46
CATCH THAT JIM CROW BIRD, PULL THE FEATHERS OUT HIS TAIL!	JC JIM CROW'S LAST	16
JIM CROW STARTED HIS LAST STAND.	JC JIM CROW'S LAST	29
SHADOWS VEIL HIS DARKNESS	FW DIMOUT IN HARLM	5
TOOK HIS HEART	FW HEART	2
TOOK HIS HEART	FW HEART	14
WHERE HIS HEART IS	FW HEART	18
TO KEEP THE GALL FROM BITING IN HIS MOUTH,	OWT JUICE JOINT	44
GOD, IN HIS INFINITE WISDOM	LHR ACCEPTANCE	1
TO HIS TWELVE DISCIPLES	LHR BLD MARY'S SON	15
HE GAVE THEM OF HIS BREAD.	LHR BLD MARY'S SON	16
HE GAVE THEM TO DRINK OF HIS WINE.	LHR BLD MARY'S SON	17
HIS BODY AND HIS BLOOD DIVINE!	LHR BLD MARY'S SON	31
HIS BODY AND HIS BLOOD DIVINE!	LHR BLD MARY'S SON	31
HIS BODY AND HIS BLOOD	LHR BLD MARY'S SON	34
HIS BODY AND HIS BLOOD	LHR BLD MARY'S SON	34
HIS WIFE TOOK A PAPER	SP BLD OF THE MAN	9
HIS BUDDIES BROUGHT FLOWERS.	SP BLD OF THE MAN	15
GOD REST HIS SOUL -	SP BLD OF THE MAN	22
HAS TO GIVE HIS MOTHER TEN -	SP BUDDY	5
TO PAY HIS CARFARE, BUY A SUIT,	SP BUDDY	8
HE WALKS LIKE HIS SOLDIERING	SP CASUALTY	3
ON HIS SHOULDERS	SP CATCH	3
BENEATH HIS ARM.	SP CATCH	7
WHERE HIS TWELVE-SHOE LANDS,	SP DREAM BOOGE VAR	8
LOOKS LIKE HIS EYES	SP DREAM BOOGE VAR	9
WHEN A MAN STARTS OUT WITH HIS HANDS	SP FREEDOM'S PLOW	2
AND THE FAITH THAT IS IN HIS HEART -	SP FREEDOM'S PLOW	6

HIS EYES LOOK OUT ON THE WORLD. . . SP FREEDOM'S PLOW 11
WILL HIS FREEDOM TRAIN COME ZOOMIN' DOWN THE TRACK . . . . SP FREEDOM TRAIN 49
HIS NAME WAS JEFFERSON. THERE WERE SLAVES THEN. . . . . SP FREEDOM'S PLOW 96
KILL HIM - AND LET HIS SOUL RUN WILD! . . . . SP GENIUS CHILD 12
I CRIED ON HIS SHOULDER BUT . . . . SP HARD DADDY 7
HE TURNED HIS BACK ON ME. . . . . . SP HARD DADDY 8
CRIED ON HIS SHOULDER BUT . . . . . SP HARD DADDY 9
HE TURNED HIS BACK ON ME. . . . . . SP HARD DADDY 10
I'D SCRATCH OUT BOTH HIS EYES. . . SP HARD DADDY 18
HE ROSE UP ON HIS DYING BED . . . . SP HOPE 1
HIS WIFE LOOKED IT UP IN HER DREAM BOOK . . . . SP HOPE 3
GLEAMS ON HIS FOREHEAD. . . . . . . SP INTERNE AT PROV 36
CELLOPHANES HIS LONG STRIDE. . . . SP INTERNE AT PROV 46
CELLOPHANES HIS FUTURE. . . . . . . SP INTERNE AT PROV 47
CROWN ON HIS HEAD. . . . . SP JUDGMENT DAY 7
JOHN HENRY WITH HIS HAMMER . . . . SP LOVE 5
HIS FACE WAS PALE AND . . . . SP LOVER'S RETURN 3
HIS EYES DIDN'T LOOK JUST RIGHT. . SP LOVER'S RETURN 4
SPENT HIS MONEY ON ME - . . . . . . SP MADAM MIGHT-HAV 10
HE UP AND WENT HIS WAY. . . . . . . SP MAMA AND DAUGHT 14
HE'S GOT A GRIN ON HIS FACE. . . . SP ME AND THE MULE 2
HE'S FORGOT ABOUT HIS RACE. . . . . SP ME AND THE MULE 4
DON'T KNOW'S I'D MIND HIS GOIN' . . SP MIDWINTER BLUES 7
DON'T KNOW'S I'D MIND HIS GOIN' . . SP MIDWINTER BLUES 9
SIGNS HIS NAME . . . . SP MIGRANT 35
ON THE CHECK THAT IS HIS PAY. . . . SP MIGRANT 37
HIS WOMAN AND HIS FRIEND IS DEAD. SP MONROE'S BLUES 2
HIS WOMAN AND HIS FRIEND IS DEAD. SP MONROE'S BLUES 2
CAN'T HARDLY GET HIS BREAD. . . . . SP MONROE'S BLUES 4
HIS LITTLE BLUES IS SAD. . . . . . SP MONROE'S BLUES 6
CAESAR TOLD ME TO KEEP HIS DOOR-STEPS CLEAN. . . . . SP NEGRO 5
WHEN HIS WORK IS DONE . . . . SP NEIGHBOR 5
LETS HIS GLASS . . . . SP NEIGHBOR 23
HIS INSURANCE LAPSED THE OTHER DAY - SP NIGHT FUNERAL 6
FOR HIS HEAD TO LAY. . . . . SP NIGHT FUNERAL 8
BLACK BOY TO HIS GRAVE? . . . . . . SP NIGHT FUNERAL 20
HIS GIRL FRIEND HAD TO PAY. . . . . SP NIGHT FUNERAL 24
AND THE LID SHUT ON HIS HEAD . . . SP NIGHT FUNERAL 28
AT HIS CORNER . . . . SP NIGHT FUNERAL 36
AND WHIPPED HIS HEAD WITH CLUBS . . SP NOT A MOVIE 3
AND HE CRAWLED ON HIS KNEES TO HIS HOUSE . . . . SP NOT A MOVIE 4
AND HE CRAWLED ON HIS KNEES TO HIS HOUSE . . . . SP NOT A MOVIE 4
SIX KNOTS WAS ON HIS HEAD . . . . . SP NOT A MOVIE 12
GRAND MARSHAL IN HIS WHITE SUIT . . SP PARADE 5
TO STRUGGLE BY HIS SELF. . . . . . SP STONY LONESOME 13
AN OLD NEGRO MINISTER CONCLUDES HIS SERMON IN HIS LOUDEST VOICE. . . SP SUNDAY MORNING 1
AN OLD NEGRO MINISTER CONCLUDES HIS SERMON IN HIS LOUDEST VOICE. . . SP SUNDAY MORNING 1
AND THE DEVIL LICKS HIS CHOPS . . . SP SUNDAY MORNING 7
WITH HIS EBONY HANDS ON EACH IVORY KEY . . . . SP THE WEARY BLUES 9
SWAYING TO AND FRO ON HIS RICKETY STOOL . . . . SP THE WEARY BLUES 12
THUMP. THUMP. THUMP. WENT HIS FOOT ON THE FLOOR. . . . . SP THE WEARY BLUES 23
WHILE THE WEARY BLUES ECHOED THROUGH HIS HEAD. . . . . SP THE WEARY BLUES 34
WITH THE TRUMPET AT HIS LIPS . . . SP TRUMPET PLAYER 2
BENEATH HIS EYES . . . . SP TRUMPET PLAYER 4
ABOUT HIS THIGHS. . . . . SP TRUMPET PLAYER 8
WITH THE TRUMPET AT HIS LIPS . . . SP TRUMPET PLAYER 10
FROM THE TRUMPET AT HIS LIPS . . . SP TRUMPET PLAYER 18
FROM THE TRUMPET AT HIS LIPS . . . SP TRUMPET PLAYER 22
IN HIS EYES. . . . . SP TRUMPET PLAYER 28
WITH THE TRUMPET AT HIS LIPS . . . SP TRUMPET PLAYER 34
TO HIS SOUL - . . . . SP TRUMPET PLAYER 40
AS THE TUNE COMES FROM HIS THROAT SP TRUMPET PLAYER 42
TO KNOW HIS . . . . SP UNCLE TOM 11
HIS OWN STRENGTH . . . . SP YOUNG SAILOR 2
AND HIS OWN LAUGHTER. . . . . SP YOUNG SAILOR 3
HIS OWN TODAY . . . . SP YOUNG SAILOR 4
AND HIS OWN HEREAFTER - . . . . . . SP YOUNG SAILOR 5
BIG BOY OPENED HIS MOUTH AND SAID. SP 50 - 50 6
ALIOUNE AIME SEDAR SIPS HIS NEGRITUDE. . . . . AYM BIRD IN ORBIT 23
KING MOUNTS HIS UNICORN . . . . . . AYM BIRD IN ORBIT 25
FOR THE MOON WOULD WHITE HIS WHITENESS . . . . AYM BLUES IN STEREO 17
THREAD STILL PULLS HIS . . . . . . AYM GOSPEL CHA-CHA 22
WITH HIS GLORY. . . . . AYM GOSPEL CHA-CHA 26
WHAT'S HIS NAME. MY COUSIN. . . . . AYM GOSPEL CHA-CHA 41
GOT CHANGE IN HIS LONG POCKET? . . AYM SHOW FARE PLESE 4
THE PANTHER IN HIS DESPERATE BOLDNESS . . . . PL BLACK PANTHER 8
MARY IS HIS MOTHER: . . . . PL CHRIST IN ALA. 4
GOD IS HIS FATHER: . . . . PL CHRIST IN ALA. 7
HIS WORDS JUMP DOWN . . . . PL CORNER MEETING 6
DR. RUFUS CLEMENT HIS CHIEF ADVISER. PL CULTURAL EXCHNG 44
SEND FOR UNCLE TOM ON HIS MIGHTY KNEES. . . . . PL FINAL CALL 28
MIGHT HAVE LOST HIS SOUL. . . . . . PL FREDRK DOUGLASS 6
ON WHICH HE SET HIS FEET. . . . . . PL FREDRK DOUGLASS 9
CHOOSE HIS COMPASS' CHOICE. . . . . PL FREDRK DOUGLASS 13
WHO STICKS A NEEDLE IN HIS ARM . . PL JUNIOR ADDICT 2
HIS NEEDLE AND HIS SPOON. . . . . . PL JUNIOR ADDICT 12
HIS NEEDLE AND HIS SPOON. . . . . . PL JUNIOR ADDICT 12
OF HIS DESPAIR. . . . . PL JUNIOR ADDICT 15
POLLUTES HIS STINKING AIR . . . . . PL JUNIOR ADDICT 21
THAN IS HIS LIVING HERE. . . . . . PL JUNIOR ADDICT 23
HIS BLOOD WAS RED - . . . . PL LUMUMBA'S GRAVE 10
FOR AIR IS HIS GRAVE. . . . . PL LUMUMBA'S GRAVE 16
SUN IS HIS GRAVE. . . . . PL LUMUMBA'S GRAVE 17
SPACE IS HIS GRAVE. . . . . PL LUMUMBA'S GRAVE 19
MY HEART'S HIS GRAVE. . . . . PL LUMUMBA'S GRAVE 20
WHO TOOK HIS GUN. . . . . PL OCTOBER 16 RAID 5
WITH HIS BLOOD . . . . PL OFFICIAL NOTICE 13
THE LAW RAISED UP HIS STICK . . . . PL WHO BUT TH LORD 13

HISS 2

IN THE SNAKE-LIKE HISS OF ITS STREAM JC THE BITTER RIVR 15
WITH THE HISS OF ITS SNAKE-LIKE SONG - . . . . JC THE BITTER RIVR 64

HISTORY 4

FOR MARGIE AND HISTORY . . . . . . OWT BLD MARGE POLIT 31
SAVE THOSE THAT HISTORY BOOKS CREATE. . . . . SP AFRO-AMER FRAG 5
ACROSS THE FIELD OF HISTORY. . . . SP FREEDOM'S PLOW 193
HISTORY SAYS IT'S TIME. . . . . . . SP IN EXPLANATION 30

HIT 9

HIT ME AGAIN. . . . . FC BEALE ST. LOVE 6
HIT 'EM. BONES! . . . . FC CRAP GAME 9
I MEAN FOUR - BEFORE DAYLIGHT - S'POSE TO'VE DONE HIT YO' FIRST STROKE - . . . . NM BROKE 14
GONNA HIT YOU IN THE FACE AND LET YOU FALL! . . . . SH DAYBREAK 2
HIT FOR YOU. . . . . SP MADAM NUMBER WR 8
BE A HIT FOR ME. . . . . SP MADAM NUMBER WR 12
IF I EVER HIT FOR A DOLLAR . . . . SP NUMBERS 1
THEY HIT ME IN THE HEAD . . . . . . PL KU KLUX 13
HIT ME! JAB ME! . . . . PL THIRD DEGREE 1

HITLER 1

IT'S HARD TO BEAT HITLER . . . . . JC HOW ABOUT DIXIE 19

HITLER'S 1

IF YOU WANT TO GET OLD HITLER'S GOAT. . . . . JC JIM CROW'S LAST 23

HO 1

HO . . . HUM! . . . . FC SATURDAY NIGHT 26

HOBNAILED 1

OF THE HOBNAILED BOOT. . . . . . . PL BLACK PANTHER 2

HOEING 2

PLOWING. PLANTING. HOEING. . . . . SP SHARE-CROPPERS 3
DOWN THE LONG HARD ROW THAT I BEEN HOEING . . . . AYM BLUES IN STEREO 34

HOLD 22

HOLD AND HIDE THY BODY. . . . . . . WB SONGS DARK VIRG 13
I HOLD TRAGEDY . . . . WB THE JESTER 2
THE RIVER AND THE MOON HOLD MEMORIES. . . . . FC CLOSING TIME 10
HOLD FAST TO DREAMS . . . . DK DREAMS 1
HOLD FAST TO DREAMS . . . . DK DREAMS 5
ITS PEOPLE'S HEART. TOO SMALL TO HOLD A SOB. . . . . SL TOWN OF SCOTTSB 4
TO HOLD AND GUARD . . . . ANS SONG OF SPAIN 65
BUT THERE ARE THOSE WHO STILL HOLD OUT . . . . JC TO CAPTAIN MULZ 10
HAS TAKEN HOLD. . . . . JC TO CAPTAIN MULZ 27
AND HOLD IT TIGHT. . . . . FW LITTLE SONG 4
FOUR WALLS CAN HOLD . . . . FW WALLS 1
LET YOUR SONGS HOLD ALL THE SUNNY JOYS . . . . OWT JUICE JOINT 19
KEEP YOUR HAND ON THE PLOW! HOLD ON! SP FREEDOM'S PLOW 200
KEEP YOUR HAND ON THE PLOW! HOLD ON! SP FREEDOM'S PLOW 126
THAT SONG MEANT JUST WHAT IT SAID: HOLD ON! . . . . SP FREEDOM'S PLOW 127
KEEP YOUR HAND ON THE PLOW! HOLD ON! SP FREEDOM'S PLOW 129
THE PEOPLE OFTEN HOLD . . . . SP FREEDOM'S PLOW 147
KEEP YOUR HAND ON THE PLOW! HOLD ON! SP FREEDOM'S PLOW 160
KEEP YOUR HAND ON THE PLOW! HOLD ON! SP FREEDOM'S PLOW 191
HOLD A YELLOW GIRL . . . . SP RUBY BROWN 19
WHEN COZY HOUSES HOLD. . . . . . . SP STRANGE HURT 12
AIN'T GOT NOBODY TO HOLD MY HAND - SP 50 - 50 3

HOLDER 1

DIAMOND RING. CIGARETTE HOLDER. AND A CANE. TO THE MUSIC OF PIANO OR NM BIG-TIMER MOOD 1

HOLDING 1

BY HOLDING ITS HEAD . . . . SH SNOB 7

HOLDIN' 2
AND HOLDIN' THINGS TIGHT. . . . . . NM BIG-TIMER POEM 52
AND SHE BEEN HOLDIN' 'EM SO TIGHT
TILL DE EAGLE'S IN TEARS - . . . . NM BROKE 24

HOLDS 3
WITH THE WHITE AND THE BLACK WHOM
NOTHING HOLDS BACK - . . . . . . NM DARK YOUTH USA 24
AND THAT THE SEA HOLDS . . . . . . DK SEA CHARM 10
AND HOLDS OF BOATS, CHICO. . . . . SP GOOD MORNING 10

HOLES 2
BULLET HOLES. . . . . FC DEATH DO DIRTY 34
I FILLED HIM FULL OF HOLES . . . . SH BLD THE KILLER 23

HOLIDAYS 1
EXCEPT ON HOLIDAYS. . . . . SP SHAME ON YOU 5

HOLLAND 1
HOLLAND BULBS IN SPRING . . . . . . AYM HORN OF PLENTY 74

HOLLER 6
SHE COULD MAKE ME HOLLER LIKE A
SISSIE, ... SH ONLY WOMAN BLUS 7
TO HOLLER, CRY, AND MOAN. . . . . . SP AS BEFITS A MAN 4
I WANT THE WOMEN TO HOLLER: . . . . SP AS BEFITS A MAN 15
I'LL HOLLER, BLOW YOUR WHISTLE. . . SP FREEDOM TRAIN 65
THOUGH YOU MAY HEAR ME HOLLER, . . SP LIFE IS FINE 27
YOU WILL HOLLER. . . . . SP SUNDAY MORNING 21

HOLLERED 4
SHE CAST HER EYES ON TEXAS,
HOLLERED, ... SH DEATH IN HARLEM 33
SOMEBODY HOLLERED, ... OWT BLD MARGE POLIT 44
I CAME UP ONCE AND HOLLERED! . . . SP LIFE IS FINE 5
I STOOD THERE AND I HOLLERED! . . . SP LIFE IS FINE 16

HOLLERS 1
SO I HOLLERS, "COM'ERE, BABIES, . . SP SYLVESTER'S BED 23

HOLLY 1
AND HOLLY . . . . FW CAROLINA CABIN 2

HOLLYWOOD 2
(HOLLYWOOD . . . . SP MOVIES 8
AND YOU SING 'EM IN HOLLYWOOD BOWL. SP NOTE COMM THEAT 3

HOLY 3
BEYOND THE HOLY GHOST. . . . . . . AYM SHOW FARE PLESE 30
MOST HOLY BASTARD . . . . PL CHRIST IN ALA. 10
SEND FOR KING ARTHUR TO BRING THE
HOLY GRAIL. . . . . PL FINAL CALL 8

HOME 46
CAUSE HE NEVER DOES COME HOME. . . FC GYPSY MAN 2
HE NEVER DOES COME HOME. . . . . . FC GYPSY MAN 4
CAN I GO HOME WID YUH, SWEETIE? . . FC JAZZ BAND 22
COMES HOME AT NIGHT, - . . . . . . FC WORKIN' MAN 3
I'M THE GUY THE HOME FOLKS CALL - NM BIG-TIMER POEM 3
HOME, KIDS, AND EVERYTHING FINE. . NM BIG-TIMER POEM 46
FOLKS, DOWN YONDER AT HOME. . . . . NM BIG-TIMER POEM 54
SINCE THE COLORED SOLDIERS CAME HOME
FROM FRANCE. . . . . NM COLORED SL POEM 32
WHEN I WAS HOME DE . . . . DK PO' BOY BLUES 1
WHEN I WAS HOME DE . . . . DK PO' BOY BLUES 3
HALF A WORLD AWAY FROM HOME. . . . DK SAILOR 2
SEEKING A HOME WHERE HE HIMSELF IS
FREE. . . . . ANS LET AMERICA BE 4
IN SEARCH OF WHAT I MEANT TO BE MY
HOME - . . . . ANS LET AMERICA BE 46
HOME TODAY! . . . . SH DEATH IN HARLEM 130
COME ON HOME AND BAKE SOME CORN
BREAD, ... SH LETTER 16
WENT HOME TO HER MA. . . . . SH SHAKESPEARE 8
IT MEANS FREEDOM AT HOME, TOO - . . JC HOW ABOUT DIXIE 23
MAKE A HOME. . . . . FW CAROLINA CABIN 22
GO HOME, YOU HUCKS! . . . . OWT BLD MARGE POLIT 41
SENT HIM HOME . . . . OWT DECEASED 2
A NIGGER COMES HOME FROM WORK: . . OWT MAN INTO MEN 1
A NEGRO COMES HOME FROM WORK: . . . OWT MAN INTO MEN 8
A MAN COMES HOME FROM WORK: . . . . OWT MAN INTO MEN 15
WHEN WILL MY GAL BE HOME? . . . . . SP BLD THE GYPSY 4
AND SHE AIN'T COME HOME YET. . . . SP BLD THE GYPSY 15
EVEN IF IT IS MY HOME. . . . . . . SP CROON 3
CARRIES HOME . . . . SP DEAD IN THERE 4
HEAVEN, HEAVEN, IS MY HOME! . . . . SP DEFERRED 39
TO STAY HOME AT ALL. . . . . SP DELINQUENT 4
AT HOME THEY GOT A TRAIN THAT'S
YOURS AND MINE! . . . . SP FREEDOM TRAIN 62
I'LL BRING HOME CHICKEN! . . . . . SP GRADUATION 22
SHE WASN'T HOME NO MORE. . . . . . SP HOMECOMING 4
FLYING HOME . . . . SP KID IN THE PARK 6
CAME BACK HOME LAST NIGHT. . . . . SP LOVER'S RETURN 2
COMIN' HOME TO YOU - . . . . SP LOVER'S RETURN 6
COME HOME TO DIE! . . . . SP LOVER'S RETURN 19
I GOT BACK HOME . . . . SP MIDNIGHT RAFFLE 7
STAYED HOME INSIDE: . . . . SP MIDNIGHT RAFFLE 14
COMING FOR TO CARRY ME HOME. . . . SP MYSTERY 10
DOWN HOME . . . . SP NEIGHBOR 1
COMING HOME. . . . . SP SEASCAPE 8
GO HOME AND WRITE . . . . SP THEME FOR ENG B 2
YOUR THIRD-FLOOR TENANT'S NEVER
HOME. . . . . AYM ASK YOUR MAMA 9
INSTEAD OF COMING HOME TO DECENT DIE AYM HORN OF PLENTY 54
AND NEVER CAME BACK HOME AT ALL . . PL BIRMINGHAM SUND 3
TO GET A NICE HOME . . . . PL LITTLE SNG HOUS 3

HOMELAND 2
NOR FREEDOM IN THIS "HOMELAND OF THE
FREE.") . . . . ANS LET AMERICA BE 16
TO BUILD A "HOMELAND FOR THE FREE." ANS LET AMERICA BE 50

HOMESICK 2
HOMESICK BLUES, LAWD, ... DK HOMESICK BLUES 13
HOMESICK BLUES IS . . . . DK HOMESICK BLUES 15

HOME'S 1
HOME'S JUST AROUND . . . . SP KID IN THE PARK 9

HONEST 2
FOR HONEST WORK . . . . PL MILITANT 8
FOR HONEST DREAMS . . . . PL MILITANT 10

HONEY 28
DON'T YOU, HONEY? . . . . WB CAT AND SAXOPHN 9
HONEY. . . . . WB LENOX AVE MIDNT 3
HONEY. . . . . WB LENOX AVE MIDNT 12
HONEY BABY. . . . . FC MA MAN 17
AN' SHE SAY, HONEY, ... FC NEW CABARET GRL 9
WHEN THEY CALLIN' ME HONEY. . . . . NM BIG-TIMER POEM 68
I SAY, "NOW, BABY, YOU KNOW I AIN'T
GOT NONE, HONEY." . . . . NM BROKE 20
SHAKE YOUR BROWN FEET, HONEY, . . . DK SONG BANJO DANC 1
SHAKE YOUR BROWN FEET, HONEY, . . . DK SONG BANJO DANC 3
GET WAY BACK, HONEY, ... DK SONG BANJO DANC 5
SHAKE YOUR BROWN FEET, HONEY, . . . DK SONG BANJO DANC 10
SHAKE 'EM, HONEY CHILE. . . . . . . DK SONG BANJO DANC 11
SO DANCE WITH SWIFT FEET, HONEY, . DK SONG BANJO DANC 16
DANCE WITH SWIFT FEET, HONEY - . . DK SONG BANJO DANC 18
WHAT'S DE MATTER, HONEY? . . . . . ANS SISTER JOHNSON 2
I SAID, HONEY, ... SH BLD THE KILLER 11
HONEY BABY, SOCK IT! . . . . SH DEATH IN HARLEM 21
HONEY BABE, ... OWT HONEY BABE 1
THAT, HONEY BABE, ... OWT HONEY BABE 7
HONEY, AIN'T YOU HEARD? . . . . . . OWT JITNEY 47
MA DADDY SAYS, HONEY, ... SP HARD DADDY 5
SHE SAID, YOUR FORTUNE, HONEY, . . SP MADAM FORT TELL 17
WHO IS YOUR SUGAR, HONEY? . . . . . SP MAMA AND DAUGHT 5
FOR I'SE STILL GOIN', HONEY, . . . SP MOTHER TO SON 18
OFFERING: A NIGHT WITH ME, HONEY. SP NATCHA 3
HONEY, WHAT DOES YOU NEED? . . . . SP PREFERENCE 8
HONEY! BABY! DON'T GO, DEAR!" . . . SP SYLVESTER'S BED 16
IS HONEY . . . . SP TRUMPET PLAYER 19

HONEY-BROWN 1
TO A HONEY-BROWN DREAM. . . . . . . SH HARLEM SWEETIES 36

HONEY-GOLD 1
HONEY-GOLD BABY . . . . SH HARLEM SWEETIES 7

HONEY-LIPPED 1
HONEY-LIPPED, SYPHILITIC - . . . . SP THE SOUTH 16

HONG 2
DIXIE TO SINGAPORE, CAPE TOWN TO
HONG KONG . . . . SP IN EXPLANATION 10
FROM HARLEM PAST HONG KONG TALKING
BACK. . . . . SP IN EXPLANATION 22

HONOR 4
HONOR AND HUNGER . . . . FW TODAY 3
THE GOVERNMENT MIGHT HONOR YOU. . . SP SHAME ON YOU 3
TO HONOR MODERN MAN - . . . . PL MOTHER IN WAR 8
YOU SAY HE DIED WITH HONOR . . . . PL OFFICIAL NOTICE 7

HONORED 2
HONORED IN A MARBLE TOMB, ... ANS BLDS OF LENIN 18
AND THAT I AM HONORED, TOO, ... PL OFFICIAL NOTICE 9

HOOD 1
SEND FOR ROBIN HOOD TO CLINCH THE
ANTI-POVERTY . . . . PL FINAL CALL 3

HOODED 1
THAT HOODED SERPENTS MAY DANCE, . . PL SPECIAL BULLTIN 4

HOOTIN' 2
HEARD DE OWL A HOOTIN', ... FC GAL'S CRY DYING 1
HEARD DE OWL A HOOTIN', ... FC GAL'S CRY DYING 3

HOPE 13
YOU CAN TAKE THAT JOB AND GO TO - I
HOPE YOU CHOKE. . . . . NM BROKE 37
AND I HOPE YOU'RE MAKING GOOD, AND
DOING FINE - . . . . NM COLORED SL POEM 17

THE HOPE OF MY RACE . . . . NM DARK YOUTH USA 3
I AM THE IMMIGRANT CLUTCHING THE
HOPE I SEEK - . . . . ANS LET AMERICA BE 22
I AM THE YOUNG MAN, FULL OF STRENGTH
AND HOPE, ... ANS LET AMERICA BE 25
FOR WHICH THERE AIN'T NO HOPE. . . . SP ARGUMENT 7
BUT I HOPE IT . . . . SP BLACK MARIA 4
WELL, I HOPE THAT LAMB OF MARY'S . . SP EVENING SONG 11
I HOPE THERE AIN'T NO JIM CROW ON
THE FREEDOM TRAIN. . . . . SP FREEDOM TRAIN 11
I HOPE MY CHILD'LL . . . . SP LAMENT OVER LOV 1
I SAY I HOPE MY CHILD'LL . . . . . . SP LAMENT OVER LOV 3
I HOPE THAT WILD YOUNG SON-OF-A-GUN SP MAMA AND DAUGHT 15
I HAD ONLY HOPE THEN, BUT NOW
THROUGH YOU, ... SP THE NEGRO MOTHE 33

5

HOPES
AND ALL THE HOPES WE'VE HELD . . . ANS LET AMERICA BE 58
MIXED WITH THE HOPES THAT ARE
DROWNED THERE . . . . JC THE BITTER RIVR 14
BUILDER OF HOPES TO BE SMASHED, . . JC THE BITTER RIVR 68
SHE HOPES TO LAY EYES ON YOU
SOMETIME IN LIFE. . . . . SP LETTER 7
MY HOPES THE WIND DONE SCATTERED. PL STILL HERE 2

2

HOPING
HOPING TO FIND THEIR FREEDOM, . . . SP FREEDOM'S PLOW 44
GROPING, HOPING, ... PL QUESTION ANSWER 8

1

HOPPIN'
FIT FER A HOPPIN' TOAD. . . . . SP BOUND NO'TH BLS 24

1

HORIZONS
STRETCHES ITS WIDE HORIZONS . . . . FW THERE 2

4

HORN
A SWORD THRUST, A HORN TIP, ... ANS SONG OF SPAIN 14
AND MOONLIGHT ON ITS HORN . . . . . AYM BIRD IN ORBIT 27
I THOUGHT I HEARD THE HORN OF PLENTY
BLOWING. . . . . AYM BLUES IN STEREO 35
HORN OF PLENTY . . . . AYM HORN OF PLENTY 81

1

HORNE
FATHER BISHOP, EFFENDI, MOTHER
HORNE, ... SP MYSTERY 21

1

HORNS
BORROWED FOR THE HORNS . . . . AYM BLUES IN STEREO 24

1

HORN-RIM
IN HORN-RIM GLASSES, ... AYM ASK YOUR MAMA 53

6

HORSE
HORSE A FANTASY OF DAYS . . . . . . SP FLATTED FIFTHS 17
DAMPALLA WEDO OGOUN AND THE HORSE AYM GOSPEL CHA-CHA 15
SOME HORSE MIGHT . . . . AYM IS IT TRUE? 46
YET THE HORSE WHOSE BACK IS BROKEN AYM IS IT TRUE? 52
WHERE'S THE HORSE . . . . PL MERRY-GO-ROUND 14
HORSE AND HORSEMAN, OUTSIDE! . . . PL WHERE WHEN WHCH 14

1

HORSEMAN
HORSE AND HORSEMAN, OUTSIDE! . . . PL WHERE WHEN WHCH 14

4

HORSES
CRACK WENT THE WHIPS THAT DROVE THE
HORSES . . . . SP FREEDOM'S PLOW 59
LAUNCHED THE BOATS AND WHIPPED THE
HORSES . . . . SP FREEDOM'S PLOW 66
AND HORSES SHOD WITH GOLD . . . . . AYM BLUES IN STEREO 4
RIDE ON BITLESS HORSES . . . . . . PL WHERE WHEN WHCH 9

6

HOT
AND ALL THE WILD HOT MOONS OF THE
JUNGLES SHINE IN MY SOUL. . . . WB FOR PORTRAIT OF 2
I SAID, GO, HOT DAMN! . . . . SH ONLY WOMAN BLUS 22
BEFORE THE HOT NIGHTS OF SUMMER . . SH YOUNG NEGRO GRL 8
WORKING IN THE HOT SUN. . . . . . . SP AUNTSUE'S STORI 7
SOMETIMES, THE ROAD WAS HOT WITH
SUN, ... SP THE NEGRO MOTHE 27
WHEN THE LONG HOT SUMMERS COME . . PL DEATH YORKVILLE 18

6

HOTEL
THE STEAM IN HOTEL KITCHENS, . . . FC BRASS SPITOONS 7
AND THE SMOKE IN HOTEL LOBBIES, . . FC BRASS SPITOONS 8
AND THE SLIME IN HOTEL SPITOONS: . FC BRASS SPITOONS 9
SO I WENT DOWN TOWN TO A HOTEL WHERE
I USED TO WORK AT NIGHT, ... NM BROKE 44
OF THE BRADDOCK HOTEL . . . . OWT BLD MARGE POLIT 6
IN THE DENNISON HOTEL IN JERSEY. . SP ELEVATOR BOY 3

2

HOUND
HOUND DAWG'S BARKIN' . . . . FC GAL'S CRY DYING 7
HOUND DAWG'S BARKIN' . . . . FC GAL'S CRY DYING 9

1

HOUNDS
THE HOUNDS ARE AT YOUR BACK. . . . OWT FLIGHT 4

11

HOUR
MIDNIGHT DANCER OF THE JAZZY HOUR? WB NUDE YOUNG DANC 2
THEN AT THE CLOSING HOUR . . . . . FC SPORT 7
TO SPEND A MEDITATIVE HOUR - . . . OLD TOWER 7
TO BEAUTIFY THIS HOUR, THIS SPRING,
AND ALL THE SPRINGS TO COME . . ANS CHANT MAY DAY 12
100-VOICES: FROM THIS HOUR. . . . . ANS CHANT MAY DAY 36
THEY HAVE FOUND THEIR HOUR. . . . . JC TO CAPTAIN MULZ 24
AN HOUR. . . . . LHR POET TO BIGOT 13
BUT YOUR HOUR IS . . . . LHR POET TO BIGOT 14
COMES THE COLORED HOUR: . . . . . . PL CULTURAL EXCHNG 42
OF THEIR PRISTINE HOUR . . . . . . PL SWEET WORDS RAC 6
BEWARE THE HOUR . . . . PL WARNING 9

4

HOURS
DE TIME IS FOURTEEN HOURS A DAY? . NM BROKE 34
DESPERATE HOURS . . . . FW DANCERS 3
STILL AFTER HOURS POURING DRINKS THE
LAW FORBIDS - . . . . OWT JUICE JOINT 38
TWENTY HOURS . . . . AYM IS IT TRUE? 23

38

HOUSE
MYSELF A HOUSE TO BUY. . . . . . . WB PIERROT 3
MERCEDES IS A JUNGLE-LILY IN A DEATH
HOUSE. . . . . WB TO DARK MERCEDE 1
HOUSE RENT TO PAY. . . . . FC BRASS SPITOONS 22
AND HOUSE RENT TO PAY. . . . . . . FC BRASS SPITOONS 30
NO LAND, NO HOUSE, NO JOB, ... NM BLACK CLWN POEM 34
THIS LITTLE HOUSE IS SUGAR. . . . . DK WINTER SWEEETNS 1
HOUSE IS SO QUIET! . . . LISTEN AT
THEM MICE. . . . . SH BED TIME 12
IN THE DEATH HOUSE. . . . . SH BLD THE KILLER 26
BUT THIS HOUSE IS MIGHTY QUIET! . . SH SUNDAY 10
COULD NOT CALL THEIR HOUSE, THEIR
HOUSE, ... JC TO CAPTAIN MULZ 17
COULD NOT CALL THEIR HOUSE, THEIR
HOUSE, ... JC TO CAPTAIN MULZ 17
CHEAPEST BOARDING HOUSE: . . . . . OWT BOARDING HOUSE 2
CHEAPEST BOARDING HOUSE. . . . . . OWT BOARDING HOUSE 8
CHEAPEST BOARDING HOUSE! . . . . . OWT BOARDING HOUSE 14
I CAN SEE YOUR HOUSE, BABE, ... OWT CURIOUS 1
I CAN SEE YOUR HOUSE, ... OWT CURIOUS 3
WHEN YOU'RE IN YOUR HOUSE, BABY . . OWT CURIOUS 5
OF THIS HOUSE . . . . SP A HOUSE IN TAOS 12
ABOUT THIS HOUSE IN TAOS . . . . . SP A HOUSE IN TAOS 17
IN THIS ONE HOUSE IN TAOS - . . . . SP A HOUSE IN TAOS 20
OF OUR HOUSE IN TAOS. . . . . SP A HOUSE IN TAOS 46
TILL YOU FIX THIS HOUSE UP NEW. . . SP BLD LANDLORD 12
MY OLD MAN DIED IN A FINE BIG HOUSE. SP CROSS 9
IF THE HOUSE IS NOT YET FINISHED, SP FREEDOM'S PLOW 161
TO THE OTHER SIDE OF THE HOUSE . . SP KID SLEEPY 3
MY HOUSE LAST WEEK. . . . . SP MADAM MINISTER 2
HOUSE TO CLEAN. . . . . SP MADAM HER MADAM 4
AND HE CRAWLED ON HIS KNEES TO HIS
HOUSE . . . . SP NOT A MOVIE 4
A MOVIE HOUSE IN HARLEM NAMED AFTER
LINCOLN, ... SP SHAME ON YOU 6
AND IN HER HOUSE MY CHILDREN . . . SP THE SOUTH 27
I'M GOIN' TO THE PO' HOUSE . . . . SP YOUNG GAL'S BLS 7
GOIN' TO THE PO' HOUSE . . . . . . SP YOUNG GAL'S BLS 9
THE PO' HOUSE IS LONELY . . . . . . SP YOUNG GAL'S BLS 13
O, THE PO' HOUSE IS LONELY, ... SP YOUNG GAL'S BLS 15
PAST HUTS THAT HOUSE A MILLION
BLACKS . . . . AYM BLUES IN STEREO 15
IN THE WHITE HOUSE . . . . AYM SHADES OF PIG 41
(AND AIN'T NEVER HAD A BLACK HOUSE) AYM SHADES OF PIG 42
BUT THE HOUSE IS OLD, ... PL LITTLE SNG HOUS 10

1

HOUSED
THAT FED AND HOUSED AND MOVED
AMERICA. . . . . SP FREEDOM'S PLOW 67

6

HOUSES
AND THE SINISTER SHUTTERED HOUSES OF
THE BOTTOMS . . . . SP RUBY BROWN 18
HABITUES OF THE HIGH SHUTTERED
HOUSES. . . . . SP RUBY BROWN 24
WHEN COZY HOUSES HOLD, ... SP STRANGE HURT 12
$40,000 HOUSES - . . . . AYM HORN OF PLENTY 77
YOU GIVE ME SECOND-CLASS HOUSES, . PL BACKLASH BLUES 7
SECOND-CLASS HOUSES . . . . PL BACKLASH BLUES 9

1

HOUSING
ON A TWENTY-STORY HOUSING PROJECT, AYM ODE TO DINAH 79

1

HOVEL
IT AIN'T NOTHIN' BUT A HOVEL. . . . FC WORKIN' MAN 4

61

HOW
HOW QUIET . . . . WB SICK ROOM 1
WELL, ER - ER . . . HOW MUCH DOES
YOU PAY? . . . . NM BROKE 35
LAWD, FOLKSES, HOW MUCH LONGER IS
THIS GONNA LAST? . . . . NM BROKE 59
HOWDY-DO, DAUGHTER! CALEDONIA, HOW
ARE YOU? . . . . NM BROKE 66
HE KNOWED HOW TO PRAY. . . . . . . DK MA LORD 7
AN' I DON'T KNOW HOW TO FLOAT. . . DK WIDE RIVER 6
I NEVER KNOWED HOW . . . . DK WIDE RIVER 11

I WONDER HOW IT FEELS . . . . SH ASPIRATION 1
HOW ABOUT THIS NECKLACE? . . . . . SH BLD PAWNBROKER 5
HOW DE BLUES THEY COME TO BE. . . . SH EVENIN' BLUES 20
HOW DE BLUES THEY COME TO BE - . . SH EVENIN' BLUES 22
I DON'T CARE HOW YOU PLAY 'EM . . . SH HEY-HEY BLUES 17
HOW DID I KNOW WHERE YOU DONE GONE
AT? . . . . SH LETTER 5
HOW HIGH HAVE YOU GOT TO BE? . . . SH MISSISSIPPI LEV 14
HOW HIGH HAVE YOU GOT TO BE . . . . SH MISSISSIPPI LEV 16
I WISH I COULD TELL YOU HOW MUCH I
DON'T CARE . . . . SH SUNDAY 5
HOW FAR YOU GO, NOR HOW LONG YOU
STAY - . . . . SH SUNDAY 6
HOW FAR YOU GO, NOR HOW LONG YOU
STAY - . . . . SH SUNDAY 6
I DON'T KNOW HOW YOU FEEL TODAY - OWT YESTERDAY TODAY 11
HOW SHE COULD GET IN TROUBLE . . . SP BLD OF THE GIRL 3
NO DIFF' NO HOW. . . . . SP DEAD IN THERE 22
HOW DREAMS . . . . SP DREAM 12
BUT NOW WE KNOW HOW IT ALL CAME OUT. SP FREEDOM'S PLOW 135
WE KNOW NOW HOW IT CAME OUT. . . . SP FREEDOM'S PLOW 138
TRUE ANYHOW NO MATTER HOW MANY . . SP IN EXPLANATION 38
THEY'LL SEE HOW BEAUTIFUL I AM . . SP I, TOO 16
HOW CAN YOU FORGET ME? . . . . . . SP LOW TO HIGH 1
HOW CAN YOU FORGET ME . . . . SP LOW TO HIGH 7
HOW CAN YOU FORGET ME, ... SP LOW TO HIGH 10
HOW CAN YOU LOW-RATE ME . . . . . . SP LOW TO HIGH 12
HOW CAN YOU FORGET ME? . . . . . . SP LOW TO HIGH 16
HOW OLD NOBODY KNOWS - . . . . . . SP MYSTERY 12
HOW STILL, ... SP SEA CALM 1
HOW STRANGELY STILL . . . . SP SEA CALM 2
HOW DIXIE PROTECTS . . . . SP SILHOUETTE 9
HOW I COULD PRAISE MY LORD! . . . . SP TESTIMONIAL 4
REMEMBER HOW THE STRONG IN STRUGGLE
AND STRIFE . . . . SP THE NEGRO MOTHE 45
BABY, HOW COME YOU CAN'T SEE ME . . SP ULTIMATUM 1
JOE SAID I WONDER HOW IT WOULD FEEL SP WEST TEXAS 7
HOW THIN AND SHARP IS THE MOON
TONIGHT! . . . . SP WINTER MOON 1
HOW THIN AND SHARP AND GHOSTLY WHITE SP WINTER MOON 2
HEAR THE OLD FOLKS SAY HOW . . . . AYM BIRD IN ORBIT 40
HOW TALL HOW TALL THE CANE GREW . . AYM BIRD IN ORBIT 41
HOW TALL HOW TALL THE CANE GREW . . AYM BIRD IN ORBIT 41
SAY HOW WHITE THE COTTON COTTON . . AYM BIRD IN ORBIT 42
AND OF HOW SOJOURNER HOW SOJOURNER AYM BIRD IN ORBIT 47
AND OF HOW SOJOURNER HOW SOJOURNER AYM BIRD IN ORBIT 47
HOW ABOUT THAT N.A.A.C.P. . . . . . AYM BIRD IN ORBIT 79
THAT DON'T KNOW HOW TO PLAY . . . . AYM BLUES IN STEREO 25
HOW THEY EVER GOT THAT WAY. . . . . AYM BLUES IN STEREO 27
HOW I GOT THERE I DON'T KNOW. . . . AYM GOSPEL CHA-CHA 40
TELL ME HOW LONG - . . . . AYM RIDE, RED, RIDE 4
NO MATTER HOW SANCTIFIED, ... PL BIBLE BELT 7
HOW MANY BULLETS DOES IT TAKE . . . PL DEATH YORKVILLE 3
HOW MANY CENTURIES DOES IT TAKE . . PL DEATH YORKVILLE 5
HOW MANY CENTENNIALS DOES IT TAKE PL DEATH YORKVILLE 15
WONDERING HOW THINGS GOT THIS WAY PL DINNER GUEST ME 10
HOW MANY BULLETS DOES IT TAKE . . . PL DREAM DEFERRED 1
LEARN HOW TO . . . . PL FROSTING 7
HOW CAN ONE MAN BE TEN? . . . . . . PL GHOSTS OF 1619 21
TO SHOW HOW LIBERAL I AM? . . . . . PL NORTHERN LIBERL 10

HOWARD 1
HOWARD COATS. . . . . SP FLATTED FIFTHS 14

HOWDY-DO 2
HOWDY-DO, DAUGHTER! CALEDONIA, HOW
ARE YOU? . . . . NM BROKE 66
HE SAID, HOWDY-DO? . . . . SP MADAM RENT MAN 2

HOWEVER 1
I, HOWEVER, ... LHP POET TO BIGOT 7

HOW-DO-YOU-DO 1
"HOW-DO-YOU-DO?" . . . . SP HEAVEN 10

HOW'D 1
HOW'D A DANCE STRIKE YOU? . . . . . SH DEATH IN HARLEM 44

HUCKS 1
GO HOME, YOU HUCKS! . . . . OWT BLD MARGE POLIT 41

HUG 1
AND I PEACHES UP TO HUG 'EM - . . . SP SYLVESTER'S BED 25

HUH 2
HUH - FOR ALL." . . . . SP CHILDREN'S RYME 24
HUH! - FOR ALL? . . . . PL CHILDREN'S RYME 15

HUM 2
HO . . . HUM! . . . . FC SATURDAY NIGHT 26
OH, HUM! . . . . SP WINE-O 8

HUMAN 4
A HUMAN GETS LONESOME IF THERE AIN'T
TWO. . . . . SH BED TIME 15
WHAT HE SAID MUST BE MEANT FOR EVERY
HUMAN BEING - . . . . SP FREEDOM'S PLOW 107
FLOW OF HUMAN BLOOD IN HUMAN VEINS. SP NEGRO SPEAKS OF 3
FLOW OF HUMAN BLOOD IN HUMAN VEINS. SP NEGRO SPEAKS OF 3

HUMBLE 3
I AM THE PEOPLE, HUMBLE, HUNGRY,
MEAN - . . . . ANS LET AMERICA BE 34
ABOVE A CROWD OF BLACK FOLK, HUMBLE,
MEAN. . . . . OWT LINCOLN THEATRE 4
MEEK, HUMBLE, AND KIND: . . . . . . PL WARNING 3

HUMBLY 1
I STAND MOST HUMBLY . . . . FW WISDOM 1

HUMILIATION 1
THE MUSIC, OVER-BURDENED, BACKING
AWAY ANGRILY, FRANTIC WITH
HUMILIATION . . . . NM BLACK CLWN MOOD 10

HUMOROUS 1
HUMOROUS DEFIANCE, MELANCHOLY JAZZ,
THEN DEFIANCE AGAIN FOLLOWED BY
LOUD . . . . NM BLACK CLWN MOOD 2

HUNCHED 1
NOW, HUNCHED IN THE COLD, ... DK PARISIAN BEGGAR 2

HUNDRED 7
THREE HUNDRED YEARS . . . . NM BLACK CLWN POEM 16
SHE RAKED UP A HUNDRED . . . . . . SP BLD OF THE MAN 13
AND A HUNDRED PRETTY MAMAS . . . . SP SYLVESTER'S BED 7
THREE HUNDRED YEARS AGO IN AFRICA'S
LAND. . . . . SP THE NEGRO MOTHE 8
THREE HUNDRED YEARS IN THE DEEPEST
SOUTH: . . . . SP THE NEGRO MOTHE 17
OR TEN BE A HUNDRED AND TEN? . . . PL GHOSTS OF 1619 22
OR A HUNDRED AND TEN . . . . PL GHOSTS OF 1619 26

HUNG 13
WHAT GREAT FOREST HAS HUNG ITS
PERFUME . . . . WB NUDE YOUNG DANC 3
HUNG ABOUT MY NECK, ... ANS A NEW SONG 19
AND ALL THE FLAGS WE'VE HUNG, . . . ANS LET AMERICA BE 59
FROM ITS IRON BRIDGE HUNG, ... JC THE BITTER RIVR 13
WHERE THE LYNCHED BOYS HUNG, . . . JC THE BITTER RIVR 84
AND HUNG IT . . . . FW HEART 3
THAT THERE HUNG . . . . FW HEART 10
JOHN BROWN WAS HUNG. . . . . SP FREEDOM'S PLOW 117
THEY'VE JUST HUNG A BLACK MAN . . . SP SILHOUETTE 3
THEY'VE HUNG A BLACK MAN . . . . . SP SILHOUETTE 5
THEY HUNG MY BLACK YOUNG LOVER . . SP SONG DARK GIRL 3
THEY HUNG HIM TO A TREE. . . . . . SP SOUTHERN MAMMY 14
THEY'RE HUNG. . . . . PL SLUM DREAMS 12

HUNGER 1
HONOR AND HUNGER . . . . FW TODAY 3

HUNGRY 5
BUT WHEN I WAS HUNGRY. . . . . . . FC DEATH DO DIRTY 11
I AM THE PEOPLE, HUMBLE, HUNGRY,
MEAN - . . . . ANS LET AMERICA BE 34
HUNGRY YET TODAY DESPITE THE DREAM. ANS LET AMERICA BE 35
LEAVES US HUNGRY, RAGGED . . . . . SP SHARE-CROPPERS 9
THE HUNGRY . . . . SP VAGABONDS 3

HUNG'S 1
PLACE WHERE YOUR CLOTHES HUNG'S
EMPTY AND BARE. . . . . SH SUPPER TIME 9

HUNTING 1
STOP HUNTING FOR THE PRICE TAG! . . SH BLD PAWNBROKER 15

HUROK 1
ON BEDLOE'S ISLAND MANAGED BY SOL
HUROK . . . . AYM HORN OF PLENTY 4

HURRIED 1
IF PUSHED BY HURRIED ENTRANCE. . . AYM ODE TO DINAH 119

HURRY 8
HURRY, SWEATING RUNNER! . . . . . . OWT FLIGHT 3
HURRY, BLACK BOY, HURRY! . . . . . OWT FLIGHT 7
HURRY, BLACK BOY, HURRY! . . . . . OWT FLIGHT 7
HURRY UP, BOY! . . . . SP IN EXPLANATION 15
BUT IF HE WASN'T IN A HURRY . . . . SP MIGRANT 38
BETTER HURRY, BETTER HURRY . . . . AYM ODE TO DINAH 103
BETTER HURRY, BETTER HURRY . . . . AYM ODE TO DINAH 103
HURRY UP! . . . . PL CULTURAL EXCHNG 60

HURT 7
THEY DON'T HURT MA FEET, ... DK DRESSED UP 10
FACT THAT I HURT HER, JUDGE, . . . SH BRIEF ENCOUNTER 13
FACT THAT I HURT HER. . . . . SH BRIEF ENCOUNTER 15
LOVE CAN HURT YOU . . . . SP LAMENT OVER LOV 5
WHEN LIFE HURT HER: . . . . SP SPIRITUALS 7
STRANGE HURT SHE KNEW . . . . SP STRANGE HURT 7
NOT ENOUGH TO HURT MY PLAYING $ $ $
$ $ . . . . AYM HORN OF PLENTY 12

Context	Work	Line
HURTS 2		
WHEN IT HURTS YO' HEART YOU	FC GYPSY MAN	23
CAUSE THAT OLD ALARM CLOCK SHO HURTS MY EARS.	SH LETTER	19
HUSBAND 2		
TOLD HER HUSBAND	SH PRESENT	2
CHILDREN SOLD AWAY FROM ME, HUSBAND SOLD, TOO.	SP THE NEGRO MOTHE	15
HUSBANDS 1		
I HAD TWO HUSBANDS.	SP MADAM MIGHT-HAV	1
HUSSY'S 1		
NO! THE HUSSY'S TELLING EVERYBODY -	SP BLD OF THE GIRL	13
HUSTLER 1		
I'M A FIRST CLASS HUSTLER.	NM BIG-TIMER POEM	37
HUSTLIN' 1		
SO I'M HUSTLIN' IN THE NIGHT.	NM BIG-TIMER POEM	12
HUT 1		
I BUILT MY HUT NEAR THE CONGO AND IT LULLED ME TO SLEEP.	SP NEGRO SPEAKS OF	6
HUTS 1		
PAST HUTS THAT HOUSE A MILLION BLACKS	AYM BLUES IN STEREO	15
HYMN 2		
OUT OF SADNESS IT RISES TO DEFIANCE AND DETERMINATION. A HYMN OF FAITH	NM BLACK CLWN MOOD	12
WHOSE TOMORROW SINGS A HYMN	PL BIRMINGHAM SUND	20
HYMNS 1		
AND GRANDMA CANNOT GET HER GOSPEL HYMNS	SP PASSING	3
HYPE 2		
HE'LL NEVER HYPE	SP DEAD IN THERE	8
HYPE NOWHERE!	SP DEAD IN THERE	13
HYPODERMIC 1		
ITS HYPODERMIC NEEDLE	SP TRUMPET PLAYER	39
IBM 1		
IBM ELECTRIC BONGO DRUMS ARE COSTLY.	AYM SHOW FARE PLESE	7
ICEBERGS 1		
WHERE THE PEOPLE ALL ARE ICEBERGS	SP GRADUATION	8
ICEBERG'S 1		
AND ICEBERG'S KITCHEN.	SP GRADUATION	19
ICING 2		
SAVE IN MEMORIES OF GANGRENOUS ICING	AYM ODE TO DINAH	78
THE CHOCOLATE GANGRENOUS ICING OF	AYM ODE TO DINAH	30
ICY 1		
AND I CROSSED AN ICY STREAM	SP CROSSING	10
IDIOT-BRAINED 1		
IDIOT-BRAINED.	SP THE SOUTH	5
IF 144		
IF YOU WILL.	WB THE JESTER	13
I WOULDN'T GO TO HEABEN IF I COULD.	FC BAD MAN	18
IF A SEVEN DON'T COME	FC CRAP GAME	3
AN' IF I CRAPS.	FC CRAP GAME	5
IF DIRTY HAD DE MONEY	FC DEATH DO DIRTY	18
IF I WAS A MULE I'D	FC HARD LUCK	13
IF I WAS A MULE I'D	FC HARD LUCK	15
EVEN IF YOU DO COME FROM GEORGIA.	FC JAZZ BAND	21
SAY IT VERY SLOWLY IF YOU CHOOSE.	FC MAMMY	4
IF MA DADDY DIDN'T LOVE ME	FC MINNIE SINGS	13
IF HE DIDN'T LOVE ME	FC MINNIE SINGS	15
IF HER DADDY AIN'T WHITE	FC NEW CABARET GRL	3
IF HER DADDY AIN'T 'FAY	FC NEW CABARET GRL	15
IF I WASN'T DUMB	FC PRIZE FIGHTER	2
AND IF I DON'T GET YOU GOIN',	NM BIG-TIMER POEM	31
BUT IF I WANTED TO GO STRAIGHT	NM BIG-TIMER POEM	41
TALKIN' 'BOUT "WE'LL WORK FOR 50¢ A DAY, IF WE CAN'T GET NO MO'."	NM BROKE	7
I WOULDN'T PAY HER A PENNY NOW IF I WAS TO CROAK -	NM BROKE	25
EVEN IF I IS BROKE.	NM BROKE	38
SHE WOULD BE ALRIGHT IF SHE WASN'T SO BOW-LEGGED, AND CROSS-EYED.	NM BROKE	64
IF A PRETTY GAL LIKE YOU WAS WILLIN', I'D BITE.	NM BROKE	72
AS IF FATE HAD NOT BLED HIM WITH HER KNIFE!	DK BEGGAR BOY	8
FOR IF DREAMS DIE	DK DREAMS	2
CAUSE IF I DON'T SEE MA BABY	DK WIDE RIVER	17
(IF I'D A-ONLY KNEW IT)	SH ANNOUNCEMENT	10
IF THIS RADIO WAS GOOD I'D GET KDQ	SH BED TIME	1
IF I HAD SOME MONEY I'D STROLL DOWN THE STREET	SH BED TIME	3
OR IF I WASN'T SO DROWSY I'D LOOK UP JOE	SH BED TIME	5
OR IF IT WASN'T SO LATE I MIGHT TAKE A WALK	SH BED TIME	7
A HUMAN GETS LONESOME IF THERE AIN'T TWO.	SH BED TIME	15
IF THERE'S ANYBODY ON THIS EARTH, JUDGE,	SH BRIEF ENCOUNTER	11
I WONDER IF WHITE FOLKS EVER FEEL BAD,	SH DAYBREAK	12
(IT WAS JUST AS IF SOMEBODY	SH DEATH IN HARLEM	97
IF I WAS A SEA-LION	SH DECLARATION	1
IF I WAS A RICH BOY	SH DECLARATION	8
IF I WAS A BIRD I'D	SH DECLARATION	17
BUT IF YOU WAS TO ASK ME	SH EVENIN' BLUES	19
SAYS IF YOU WAS TO ASK ME	SH EVENIN' BLUES	21
SO IF YOU WANT TO KNOW BEAUTY'S	SH HARLEM SWEETIES	41
BUT IF YOU GIMME GOOD CORN WHISKY	SH HEY-HEY BLUES	5
IF YOU CAN WHIP DE BLUES, BOY,	SH HEY-HEY BLUES	7
BOY, IF YOU CAN WHIP DE BLUES,	SH HEY-HEY BLUES	9
IF I HAD SOME SMALL CHANGE	SH IF-ING	1
IF I HAD SOME GREENBACKS	SH IF-ING	5
IF I HAD A MILLION	SH IF-ING	9
AND EVEN IF I DID, I WAS MAD -	SH LETTER	8
AND IF YOU THINK I BEEN TOO MEAN BEFORE,	SH LETTER	12
IF YOUR REPUTATION	SH SNOB	1
I WOULDN'T TAKE YOU BACK IF YOU COME ON YOUR KNEES.	SH SUNDAY	9
STAY AWAY IF YOU WANT TO, AND SEE IF I CARE!	SH SUPPER TIME	10
STAY AWAY IF YOU WANT TO, AND SEE IF I CARE!	SH SUPPER TIME	10
IF I HAD A FIRE I'D MAKE ME SOME TEA	SH SUPPER TIME	11
CAUSE IF I DON'T THEY'LL CUT DOWN MY PAY.	SH SUPPER TIME	14
MAKE YOU WALK LIKE A GHOST IF YOU BOTHER ME ANY MORE.	SH TWILIGHT REVERI	6
IF I JUST HAD A OWL HEAD, OLD OWL HEAD WOULD DO.	SH TWILIGHT REVERI	11
IF I GOT TO FIGHT,	JC BIG BUDDY	5
IF WE'RE FIGHTING TO CREATE	JC BLACK MAN SPEAK	25
IF YOU CARRY THIS THROUGH,	JC BLD SAM SOLOMON	26
IF YOU BELIEVE	JC HOW ABOUT DIXIE	5
IF YOU WANT TO GET OLD HITLER'S GOAT,	JC JIM CROW'S LAST	23
IF YOU KEEP ON,	JC NOTE TO NAZIS	5
BUT IF THEY WERE BLOOD, MOTHER -	FW WHEN ARMIES PAS	14
IF WE WERE	FW WISDOM	5
IF MARGIE POLITE	OWT BLD MARGE POLIT	1
BUT ME - IF I CAN	OWT BOARDING HOUSE	9
IF I WAS ALIVE	OWT FUNERAL	5
IF YOU WANT A GOOD CHICKEN	OWT JITNEY	55
I WONDER IF	OWT TOO BLUE	10
FOR TEARS IF SHE SHOULD CRY.	LHR TESTAMENT	8
IF I WAS YOU.	SP BAD LUCK CARD	12
IF SHE ONLY WOULD.	SP BLD FORTUNE TEL	20
IF I LAND MY FIST ON YOU.	SP BLD LANDLORD	20
THAT IF SHE HAD A CHANCE	SP BLD OF THE GIRL	15
BUT IF I WAS A GYPSY	SP BLD THE GYPSY	22
IF I THOUGHT THOUGHTS IN BED,	SP BLUES AT DAWN	3
IF I RECALL THE DAY BEFORE,	SP BLUES AT DAWN	8
EVEN IF IT IS MY HOME.	SP CROON	3
IF EVER I CURSED MY WHITE OLD MAN	SP CROSS	3
IF EVER I CURSED MY BLACK OLD MOTHER	SP CROSS	5
BUT IT WAS AS IF THEY'D LEFT.	SP CROSSING	4
BUT WAS JUST AS IF THEY'D LEFT.	SP CROSSING	22
BABY, IF YOU LOVE ME	SP DOWN AND OUT	1
IF YOU LOVE ME, BABY,	SP DOWN AND OUT	3
IF YOU'S A WISE WOMAN, HATTIE,	SP EARLY EVENING	11
WORSER IF I WOULD.	SP EARLY EVENING	20
IF I WAS ANYBODY'S SISTER,	SP EVENING SONG	5
IF YOU WANTA GO TO HEABEN	SP FIRE	12
"OR IF IT WOULD," THOUGHT SOME.	SP FREEDOM'S PLOW	121
IF MY CHILDREN ASK ME, DADDY, PLEASE EXPLAIN	SP FREEDOM TRAIN	31
IF THE HOUSE IS NOT YET FINISHED,	SP FREEDOM'S PLOW	161
IF THE FIGHT IS NOT YET WON,	SP FREEDOM'S PLOW	163
(BUT NOBODY KNOWS IF THAT IS SO.)	SP HAVANA DREAMS	4
JUST AS IF YOU WERE DOWN SOUTH.	SP HIGH TO LOW	16
BUT IF SHE WAS TO LISTEN	SP LADY'S BOOGIE	5
IF YOU WANT TO BE HAPPY	SP LAMENT OVER LOV	17
IF THAT WATER HADN'T A-BEEN SO COLD	SP LIFE IS FINE	7
IF IT HADN'T A-BEEN SO HIGH	SP LIFE IS FINE	18
IF YOU GONNA SEE ME DIE.	SP LIFE IS FINE	30
I SAID, IF YOU DO,	SP MADAM CENSUS	15
IF I EVER CATCH HIM,	SP MADAM PHONE BIL	19
IF I DID!	SP MADAM MINISTER	20
IF I LOVE YOU!	SP MADAM HER MADAM	24
IF IT'S MONEY YOU WANT	SP MADAM RENT MAN	25
IF YOU UNDERSTOOD -	SP MAYBE	2
NOW, IF A MAN LOVES A WOMAN	SP MIDWINTER BLUES	11
BUT IF HE WASN'T IN A HURRY	SP MIGRANT	38
IF THE BLUES WOULD LET ME,	SP MISS BLUES'ES	1
IF THE BLUES WOULD LET ME,	SP MISS BLUES'ES	3
IF I EVER HIT FOR A DOLLAR	SP NUMBERS	1

IF THEY CAN: . . . . SP PARADE 17
IF THE WAR HADN'T COME ALONG . . . SP RELIEF 8
IF THESE WHITE FOLKS WANT TO GO AHEAD . . . . SP RELIEF 12
BUT WHO WOULD MISS ME IF I LEFT? . SP REVERIE HARLEM 14
IF YOU'RE GREAT ENOUGH . . . . SP SHAME ON YOU 1
IF YOU'RE NOT ALIVE AND KICKING. . SP SHAME ON YOU 10
JACK. IF YOU GOT TO BE A ROUNDER . SP STREET SONG 1
AND IF UNCLE MAC BRINGS BEER . . . SP SUMMER EVENING 24
IF I JUST HAD A PIANO. . . . . . . SP TESTIMONIAL 1
IF I JUST HAD A ORGAN. . . . . . . SP TESTIMONIAL 2
IF I JUST HAD A DRUM. . . . . SP TESTIMONIAL 3
I WONDER IF IT'S THAT SIMPLE? . . . SP THEME FOR ENG B 6
IF YOU GOT SOMEBODY ELSE. . . . . . SP ULTIMATUM 4
IF I LIVE TO BE A THOUSAND . . . . SP WIDOW WOMAN 17
IF YOU HAD A HEAD AND USED YOUR MIND SP 50 - 50 9
IF I HAVE . . . . AYM ASK YOUR MAMA 28
PERHAPS IF IT BE GOD'S WILL . . . . AYM ASK YOUR MAMA 64
ON WHICH TO RIDE IF MOTORCARS . . . AYM BLUES IN STEREO 5
IF SHOW FARE'S MORE THAN 30¢ ¢ ¢ ¢ ¢ ¢ ¢ ¢ . . . . AYM HORN OF PLENTY 29
IF PUSHED BY HURRIED ENTRANCE. . . AYM ODE TO DINAH 119
IF BORN PREMATURE . . . . AYM ODE TO DINAH 72
WHEN THEY ASK YOU IF YOU KNEW ME. AYM RIDE, RED, RIDE 27
IT WOULD BE TOO BAD IF JESUS . . . PL BIBLE BELT 1
THEY ASKED ME IF MY BLACKNESS. . . PL CULTURAL EXCHNG 33
IF YOU WANT TO SEE ME. . . . . . . PL DOWN WHERE I AM 15
(AND IF NOBODY COMES. SEND FOR ME.) PL FINAL CALL 39
IF I WANTED TO. . . . . PL IMPASSE 2
IF YOU'D JUST TURN ME LOOSE." . . . PL KU KLUX 8
AS IF IT WERE SOME NOBLE THING. . . PL MOTHER IN WAR 1
AS IF FREEDOM'S CAUSE . . . . PL MOTHER IN WAR 3
AS IF THE WEAPONS USED TODAY . . . PL MOTHER IN WAR 5
AS IF TECHNICOLOR BANNERS FLEW . . PL MOTHER IN WAR 7
IF I HAD A HEART OF GOLD. . . . . . PL VARI-COLORED 1
I SAID. O. LORD. IF YOU CAN. . . . PL WHO BUT TH LORD 9
IF YOU HAD KNOWN WHAT I KNOW . . . PL WORDS LIKE FREE 7

IF-ING 1
SO JUST BY IF-ING . . . . SH IF-ING 15

IG 2
DON'T IG ME LIKE YOU DO. . . . . . SH MIDNIGHT CHIPPI 20
PLEASE DON'T IG ME LIKE YOU DO. . . SH MIDNIGHT CHIPPI 22

IGNITE 1
THE DYNAMITE THAT MIGHT IGNITE . . PL BIRMINGHAM SUND 18

IGNORANCE 1
OUT OF THE DARKNESS. THE IGNORANCE. THE NIGHT. . . . . SP THE NEGRO MOTHE 40

IGNORE 1
IGNORE ME - THOUGH I PAY YOUR FEES. SP LOW TO HIGH 15

ILLS 2
TO CURE ILLS OF AFRICA. . . . . . . SP INTERNE AT PROV 13
ALSO ILLS QUITE COMMON . . . . SP INTERNE AT PROV 16

ILLUSION 1
STRIP TICKETS STILL ILLUSION? . . . AYM SHOW FARE PLESE 9

ILLUSIVE 1
WHERE CAME TO BAG'S ILLUSIVE . . . AYM IS IT TRUE? 12

IMMIGRANT 1
I AM THE IMMIGRANT CLUTCHING THE HOPE I SEEK - . . . . ANS LET AMERICA BE 22

IMMORTAL 2
IS IT MUCH TO DIE WHEN IMMORTAL FEET SL SCOTTSBORO 5
IMMORTAL RAIDERS . . . . PL OCTOBER 16 RAID 25

IMPART 1
AND STRENGTH TO OUR LAND IMPART. . NM DARK YOUTH USA 15

IMPEL 1
IMPEL YOU FOREVER UP THE GREAT STAIRS - . . . . SP THE NEGRO MOTHE 50

IMPLEMENT 1
TO IMPLEMENT THE GOLDEN RULE. . . . PL BIRMINGHAM SUND 23

IMPLORING 1
IMPLORING MECCA . . . . SP BE-BOP BOYS 1

IMPORTANT 2
IMPORTANT BEFORE - . . . . OWT BLD MARGE POLIT 22
TAKES UP IMPORTANT MATTERS . . . . SP MIGRANT 28

IMPOTENCE 1
AMOUNT OF IMPOTENCE . . . . SP SAME IN BLUES 20

IMPRISON 1
THEY IMPRISON FREEDOM. . . . . . . JC FREEDOM 6

IMPRISONED 2
THE WIND IMPRISONED IN THE FLESH. ANS NEGRO GHETTO 3
AFRICA IMPRISONED . . . . FW MOTHERLAND 3

IMPRISONING 1
BY IMPRISONING NEHRU . . . . JC FREEDOM 5

INCHES 2
A BLADE TEN INCHES LONG. . . . . . FC SUICIDE 8
A BLADE TEN INCHES LONG. . . . . . FC SUICIDE 10

INDECISION 1
FROM VERY INDECISION . . . . PL FREDRK DOUGLASS 4

INDEEDY 1
YES. INDEEDY. I SHO HAVE MISSED YOU. TOO! . . . . NM BROKE 67

INDENTURED 4
FREE MEN AND INDENTURED SERVANTS. SP FREEDOM'S PLOW 32
SOME WERE INDENTURED HANDS . . . . SP FREEDOM'S PLOW 43
IN INDENTURED HANDS AND ADVENTUROUS HANDS. . . . . SP FREEDOM'S PLOW 51
INDENTURED HANDS. ADVENTUROUS HANDS. SP FREEDOM'S PLOW 62

INDIA 2
INDIA TO GERMANY. . . . . ANS CHANT TOM MOONY 19
BUT INDIA AND CHINA AND HARLEM. TOO. JC JIM CROW'S LAST 13

INDIAN 3
SHUT UP. INDIAN! . . . . SP IN EXPLANATION 49
GEORGE SALLIE COOLIE INDIAN BOY . . SP IN EXPLANATION 51
WE SAW AN INDIAN MERCHANTMAN . . . SP SEASCAPE 7

INDIANS 1
NIAGARA OF THE INDIANS! . . . . . . AYM ODE TO DINAH 46

INDIAN'S 1
THE LAND THAT'S MINE - THE POOR MAN'S. INDIAN'S. NEGRO'S. . . . ANS LET AMERICA BE 65

INDIES 1
YOU FROM THE WEST INDIES. . . . . . SP BROTHERS 2

INDIVIDUAL 2
BUT STOOD. INDIVIDUAL AND ALONE. . JC TO CAPTAIN MULZ 22
OUR BODIES ARE SEPARATE. INDIVIDUAL THINGS. . . . . SP A HOUSE IN TAOS 31

INEZ 2
PLAYED BY INEZ AND TIMME. . . . . . SP PROJECTION 14
BRICKTOP INEZ MABEL MERCER . . . . AYM BIRD IN ORBIT 6

INFECTED 1
INFECTED. . . . . PL SLAVE 11

INFINITE 1
GOD. IN HIS INFINITE WISDOM . . . . LHR ACCEPTANCE 1

INFINITY 1
WILL BECOME INFINITY. . . . . FW THERE 9

INFIRMARY 2
CARELESS. AND HALF-DEFIANT ECHOES OF THE "ST. JAMES INFIRMARY" AS THE NM BIG-TIMER MOOD 2
SING THE ST. JAMES INFIRMARY . . . OWT REQUEST REQUIEM 5

INFORMATION 1
AIN'T YOU GOT NO INFORMATION . . . AYM BIRD IN ORBIT 82

INK 1
THE INK YOU USED . . . . PL OFFICIAL NOTICE 4

INNER 3
INNER HEARTACHES AND LONELINESS TO THE IRONIC GAIETY OF THE MUSIC. THEN . . . . NM BIG-TIMER MOOD 10
MY INNER CRY? . . . . DK MINSTREL MAN 12
WITHIN THE INNER EAR. . . . . PL SWEET WORDS RAC 4

INSANE 1
THINK I WAS INSANE. . . . . SH IF-ING 12

INSIDE 5
SHOULDERS AT FATE. ACCEPTING HIS POSITION - BUT INSIDE HIMSELF UNHAPPY . . . . NM BIG-TIMER MOOD 6
INSIDE . . . . FW CAROLINA CABIN 6
ON TRADE-MARKS INSIDE . . . . SP FLATTED FIFTHS 13
STAYED HOME INSIDE: . . . . SP MIDNIGHT RAFFLE 14
CANDLE INSIDE. . . . . SP 125TH STREET 4

INSISTENCE 1
INSISTENCE BECKON . . . . FW CONVENT 7

INSTALLMENT 1
I NEVER DID LIKE THE INSTALLMENT PLAN . . . . SH PAY DAY 14

INSTANCE 1
FOR INSTANCE, WHAT CAN . . . . . . SP MADAM PHONE BIL 27

INSTEAD 9
AND DICE INSTEAD OF BOOKS WILL DO NM BLACK CLWN POEM 5
LET US BECOME INSTEAD, YOU AND I, ANS OPEN LETTER 21
INSTEAD: MIGRATION INTO FORCE AND POWER - . . . . ANS OPEN LETTER 42
INSTEAD OF TO A SONG. . . . . SH IN TROUBLED KEY 12
INSTEAD OF THAT I'M CRYIN' - . . . SP MISS BLUES'ES 5
INSTEAD OF COMING HOME TO DECENT DIE AYM HORN OF PLENTY 54
BUT LEFT INSTEAD . . . . PL BIRMINGHAM SUND 4
BUT INSTEAD DECIDED TO BE BOLD . . PL FREDRK DOUGLASS 7
AND NEVER UP INSTEAD. . . . . PL VARI-COLORED 16

INSTRUCTOR 2
THE INSTRUCTOR SAID, ... SP THEME FOR ENG B 1
A PART OF YOU, INSTRUCTOR. . . . . SP THEME FOR ENG B 30

INSTRUMENT 1
AN INSTRUMENT . . . . LHR CONSERVATORY 10

INSURANCE 3
CAUSE I HAD A INSURANCE . . . . . . SP MADAM'S PAST HI 14
INSURANCE MAN, HE DID NOT PAY - . . SP NIGHT FUNERAL 5
HIS INSURANCE LAPSED THE OTHER DAY - SP NIGHT FUNERAL 6

INTEGRATED 2
HIGHLY INTEGRATED . . . . AYM HORN OF PLENTY 63
INTEGRATED. . . . . AYM HORN OF PLENTY 80

INTEGRATION 1
SHARP AS INTEGRATION . . . . PL WHERE WHEN WHCH 5

INTEND 1
BUT WE INTEND TO VOTE . . . . JC BLD SAM SOLOMON 35

INTENTION 1
THEY HAD NO INTENTION OF CALLING COOLIES MISTER. . . . . SP IN EXPLANATION 9

INTEREST 1
INTEREST BEYOND CARING? . . . . . . AYM SHOW FARE PLESE 25

INTERESTED 1
HE SAID, I AM INTERESTED . . . . . SP MADAM MINISTER 5

INTERMINABLE 1
WHEN THE AIR IS ONE INTERMINABLE BALL GAME . . . . SP PASSING 2

INTERRACIAL 2
WHOSE DOLLS ARE INTERRACIAL! . . . AYM BIRD IN ORBIT 85
YOUR DOLLS ARE INTERRACIAL. . . . . AYM RIDE, RED, RIDE 25

INTO 55
DROP ONE BY ONE INTO STILLNESS. . . WB SUMMER NIGHT 3
INTO THE COURT-YARD. . . . . WB SUMMER NIGHT 25
INTO THE STILL. . . . . WB TO LITTLE LOVER 5
FROM ONE SIDE TO THE OTHER. BUT NOW A HARSH AND BITTER NOTE CREEPS INTO . . . . NM BLACK CLWN MOOD 9
UNTIL THE WHOLE WORLD FALLS INTO THE HANDS OF . . . . ANS CHANT TOM MOONY 24
INSTEAD: MIGRATION INTO FORCE AND POWER - . . . . ANS OPEN LETTER 42
LEST SOME FRANCO STEAL INTO OUR BACKYARD . . . . ANS SONG OF SPAIN 66
WENT BUSTIN INTO DIXIE'S BOUT ONE A.M. . . . . SH DEATH IN HARLEM 2
CAME TIPPIN INTO DIXIE'S TO GET A VIEW. . . . . SH DEATH IN HARLEM 59
CAME TIPPIN INTO DIXIE'S WITH SMILES ON THEIR FACES. . . . . SH DEATH IN HARLEM 60
BUT MY LOVE MIGHT TURN INTO A KNIFE SH IN TROUBLED KEY 11
AND SHOOT ALL KINDS O' SHELLS INTO YOU. . . . . SP TWILIGHT REVERI 8
BACK INTO THE GRASS - . . . . FW SNAKE 2
AND TURNED INTO RIOT. . . . . OWT BLD MARGE POLIT 16
INTO THIS GIN MILL . . . . OWT JUICE JOINT 15
THE BAND DOWN IN THE PIT BURSTS INTO JAZZ. . . . . OWT LINCOLN THEATRE 6
INTO A NEIGHBORHOOD . . . . OWT RESTRICTIVE 2
HE WENT INTO THE GARDEN . . . . . . LHR BLD MARY'S SON 22
INTO SOME OTHER THING . . . . LHR DEAR LVLY DEATH 5
SO I CREPT AWAY INTO THE NIGHT . . SP A BLACK PIERROT 3
INTO THE WINDLESSNESS - . . . . . . SP A HOUSE IN TAOS 43
INTO THE WINDLESSNESS . . . . SP A HOUSE IN TAOS 45
BEAT BACK INTO THE BLOOD - . . . . SP AFRO-AMER FRAG 7
DOWN INTO THE CLAY. . . . . SP AS BEFITS A MAN 14
INTO A THOUSAND LIGHTS OF SUN, . . SP AS I GREW OLDER 31
INTO A THOUSAND WHIRLING DREAMS . . SP AS I GREW OLDER 32
AND I'LL LOOK INTO THE FUTURE . . . SP BLD THE GYPSY 7
INTO MIDNIGHT RUFFLES . . . . SP BOOGIE 1 A.M. 7
WHIRLS SOFTLY INTO A . . . . SP DANSE AFRICAINE 8
AND YOU RUN INTO YOURSELF . . . . . SP FINAL CURVE 2
INTO FLATTED FIFTHS AND FLATTER BEERS . . . . SP FLATTED FIFTHS 5
DOWN INTO THE EARTH WENT THE PLOW SP FREEDOM'S PLOW 49
AND FAULTILY PUT THEM INTO PRACTICE. SP FREEDOM'S PLOW 151
SPLASH INTO THE RIVERS AND THE SEAS WENT THE BOAT-HULLS . . . . . . SP FREEDOM'S PLOW 57
INTO THE WARP AND WOOF OF AMERICA: SP FREEDOM'S PLOW 167
INTO THAT FURROW THE FREEDOM SEED WAS DROPPED. . . . . SP FREEDOM'S PLOW 194
OPENING INTO CORRIDORS. . . . . . . SP INTERNE AT PROV 43
INTO THE LAPS . . . . SP MELLOW 1
EDGE INTO A SWOON. . . . . SP MOONLIGHT NIGHT 8
INTO A THOUSAND SMILES, ... SP SUNDAY MORNING 6
COME INTO THE CHURCH THIS MORNING, SP SUNDAY MORNING 36
AND FAR INTO THE NIGHT HE CROONED THAT TUNE. . . . . SP THE WEARY BLUES 31
THE STEPS FROM THE HILL LEAD DOWN INTO HARLEM. . . . . SP THEME FOR ENG B 11
INTO LATE FALL . . . . SP WHAT? 2
GETS SHOT RIGHT INTO GLORY. . . . . AYM IS IT TRUE? 53
INTO A MILLION POOLS OF QUARTERS . AYM ODE TO DINAH 56
INTO CLOTH OF DOLLARS . . . . AYM SHOW FARE PLESE 22
MUST TURN INTO . . . . PL ANGOLA QUESTION 9
PUSHED INTO THE CORNER . . . . . . PL BLACK PANTHER 1
PUSHED INTO THE CORNER OF THE . . . PL BLACK PANTHER 3
PUSHED INTO THE CORNER OF . . . . . PL BLACK PANTHER 5
CHANGED INTO "EYE FOR EYE." . . . . PL BLACK PANTHER 7
TO MAKE US ALL INTO PRINCES AND PRINCESSES. . . . . PL FINAL CALL 7
AND BITE INTO THE SANDWICH OF YOUR HEART, ... PL JIM CROW CAR 2
TURNED INTO A BAR: . . . . PL LITTLE SNG HOUS 21

INTRODUCE 1
DELIGHTED! INTRODUCE ME TO EARTHA AYM BIRD IN ORBIT 3

INVENTED 1
STILL TO BE INVENTED. . . . . AYM IS IT TRUE? 15

INVESTIGATED 1
RALPH BUNCHE INVESTIGATED! . . . . AYM BIRD IN ORBIT 75

INVESTIGATE 2
INVESTIGATE THAT SANTA CLAUS . . . AYM BIRD IN ORBIT 84
INVESTIGATE THEM NEGRAS WHO . . . . AYM BIRD IN ORBIT 86

INVESTIGATED 1
AS THOSE INVESTIGATED - . . . . . . PL UN-AMERICAN 6

INVITE 1
I'M GONNA GET UP A POKER GAME AND INVITE THE BOYS. . . . . SH SUNDAY 12

INWARD 1
THE DOOR MARKED LADIES OPENS INWARD AYM ODE TO DINAH 110

IN-BETWEEN 1
(NO IN-BETWEEN TO CHOOSE) . . . . . PL MOTHER IN WAR 11

IODINE 1
A MIST OF IODINE AND ETHER . . . . SP INTERNE AT PROV 44

IRA 7
CA IRA! CA IRA! . . . . AYM RIDE, RED, RIDE 7
CA IRA! CA IRA! . . . . AYM RIDE, RED, RIDE 7
IRA! BOY, IRA! . . . . AYM RIDE, RED, RIDE 9
IRA! BOY, IRA! . . . . AYM RIDE, RED, RIDE 9
SEND FOR ROBESPIERRE TO SCREAM, "CA IRA! CA IRA! . . . . PL FINAL CALL 15
SEND FOR ROBESPIERRE TO SCREAM, "CA IRA! CA IRA! . . . . PL FINAL CALL 15
CA IRA!" . . . . PL FINAL CALL 16

IRELAND 1
OFF THE COAST OF IRELAND . . . . . SP SEASCAPE 1

IRELAND'S 1
FOR I'M THE ONE WHO LEFT DARK IRELAND'S SHORE. . . . . ANS LET AMERICA BE 47

IRENE 1
IRENE AND HELEN ARE AS THEY USED TO BE . . . . AYM BIRD IN ORBIT 21

IRISH 1
POLISH, BOHUNK, IRISH, ... SP MIGRANT 9

IRON 16
FOR THE KIDS WHO DIE ARE LIKE IRON IN THE BLOOD OF THE PEOPLE - . . ANS KIDS WHO DIE 32
TO TASTE THE IRON OF THE KIDS WHO DIE. . . . . ANS KIDS WHO DIE 34
AS IRON . . . . JC ME AND MY SONG 10
AS BLACK IRON . . . . JC ME AND MY SONG 19
AS THE FIRST IRON . . . . JC ME AND MY SONG 30
FROM ITS IRON BRIDGE HUNG. . . . . JC THE BITTER RIVR 13
WHERE THE IRON BRIDGE CROSSES THE STREAM. . . . . JC THE BITTER RIVR 60
IRON CELL. . . . . SP BLD LANDLORD 23
WASH, IRON, AND SCRUB, ... SP MADAM HER MADAM 9
IRON LIFTING IRON . . . . SP MIGRANT 14

Line	Poem	No.
IRON LIFTING IRON	SP MIGRANT	14
MAKES IRON OF CHOCOLATE MUSCLES.	SP MIGRANT	15
IRON LIFTING IRON	SP MIGRANT	16
IRON LIFTING IRON	SP MIGRANT	16
ON THE OLD IRON STOVE WHAT'S COOKING?	PL CULTURAL EXCHNG	27
LIKE RUSTY IRON AND MINT,	PL WHERE WHEN WHCH	3

IRONIC 1

Line	Poem	No.
INNER HEARTACHES AND LONELINESS TO THE IRONIC GAIETY OF THE MUSIC. THEN	NM BIG-TIMER MOOD	10

IS 464

Line	Poem	No.
IT IS NIGHT.	WB AFRAID	5
THAT IS SUNSET IN THE CARIBBEAN.	WB CARIBBEAN SUNST	4
TOMORROW. . . . IS DARKNESS.	WB HARLEM NIGHT CL	20
IS A JAZZ RHYTHM.	WB LENOX AVE MIDNT	2
IS A SOFT BANDANNA HANDKERCHIEF	WB OUR LAND	5
AND NOT THIS LAND WHERE LIFE IS COLD.	WB OUR LAND	7
AND NOT THIS LAND WHERE JOY IS WRONG.	WB OUR LAND	15
IT IS IN THIS SICK ROOM	WB SICK ROOM	2
THE LAST PLAYER-PIANO IS CLOSED.	WB SUMMER NIGHT	4
LAUGHTER IS MY PAIN.	WB THE JESTER	11
MERCEDES IS A JUNGLE-LILY IN A DEATH HOUSE.	WB TO DARK MERCEDE	1
MERCEDES IS A DOOMED STAR.	WB TO DARK MERCEDE	2
MERCEDES IS CHARNEL ROSE.	WB TO DARK MERCEDE	3
IS LIKE A WITHERED FLOWER	WB YOUNG PROSTITUT	2
CAUSE I IS LONG GONE WRONG.	FC A RUINED GAL	5
IS A BROWN MAN'S FIST	FC BEALE ST. LOVE	2
FACT IS YOU WORRIES ME.	FC BLD OF GIN MARY	14
A BRIGHT BOWL OF BRASS IS BEAUTIFUL TO THE LORD.	FC BRASS SPITOONS	32
HER FACE IS PALE	FC CLOSING TIME	2
AN' SAYS YO' BOY IS GETTIN' BEAT.	FC DEATH DO DIRTY	24
LOVE, OH, LOVE IS	FC GYPSY MAN	19
LOVE, OH, LOVE IS	FC GYPSY MAN	21
DE WAY HE SHOCKS ME SHO IS SWEET.	FC MA MAN	6
SHE IS DEATH.	FC MAMMY	2
CHARLIE IS A GAMBLER	FC SATURDAY NIGHT	3
AN' SADIE IS A WHORE.	FC SATURDAY NIGHT	4
WHEN YOU IS	FC SATURDAY NIGHT	19
AND THERE IS NO MUSIC AT ALL	FC SPORT	9
DEATH IS A TOWER	OLD TOWER	1
ONE IS KNOWN BY THE NAME OF DEATH.	OLD TWO THINGS	7
BECAUSE MY MIND IS DULL	NM BLACK CLWN POEM	4
WHEN THE DAY IS THROUGH.	NM BLACK CLWN POEM	7
AND HELPLESSNESS. THE MUSIC IS LIKE A MOURNFUL TOM-TOM IN THE DARK! BUT	NM BLACK CLWN MOOD	11
JUST ONLY PROVIDIN' DE BOSS MAN IS NICE!"	NM BROKE	9
FOLKS SHO IS GETTIN' HARD ON YOU - JUST 'CAUSE YOU BROKE.	NM BROKE	15
SO HERE I IS, BROKE.	NM BROKE	18
DE TIME IS FOURTEEN HOURS A DAY?	NM BROKE	34
EVEN IF I IS BROKE.	NM BROKE	38
LAWD, FOLKSES, HOW MUCH LONGER IS THIS GONNA LAST?	NM BROKE	59
IS I MARRIED? NO, ALL THESE-HERE GIRLS UP NORTH IS TOO LIGHT.	NM BROKE	70
IS I MARRIED? NO, ALL THESE-HERE GIRLS UP NORTH IS TOO LIGHT.	NM BROKE	70
YOU STILL BAKES BISCUITS? FRIED CHICKEN EVERY NIGHT? IS THAT TRUE?	NM BROKE	73
(IS YOU LOOKIN' AT ME, BABY, OR SOME OTHER WAY?)	NM BROKE	76
YES, UM-HUM! YOU SHO IS SWEET! CAN YOU PAY FO' DE LICENSE, DEAR?	NM BROKE	78
THAT IS MY MISSION.	NM DARK YOUTH USA	18
IS MY AMBITION.	NM DARK YOUTH USA	21
WHEN THE NIGHT IS A VAST SOFTNESS	DK AFTR MNY SPRNGS	3
WHAT IS THERE WITHIN THIS BEGGAR LAD	DK BEGGAR BOY	1
IS NOT HE BUT A SHADOW IN THE SUN -	DK BEGGAR BOY	5
LIFE IS A BROKEN-WINGED BIRD	DK DREAMS	3
LIFE IS A BARREN FIELD	DK DREAMS	7
SHO IS FINE.	DK DRESSED UP	6
HOMESICK BLUES IS	DK HOMESICK BLUES	15
IS WIDE WITH LAUGHTER	DK MINSTREL MAN	2
IS DEEP WITH SONG.	DK MINSTREL MAN	4
IS WIDE WITH LAUGHTER.	DK MINSTREL MAN	10
THIS IS WHAT I'M GONNA SING.	DK NIGHT AND MORN	2
THIS IS WHAT I'M GONNA SING:	DK NIGHT AND MORN	4
THIS IS GONNA BE MA SONG.	DK NIGHT AND MORN	8
THIS IS GONNA BE MA SONG:	DK NIGHT AND MORN	10
BUT THIS WORLD IS WEARY	DK PO' BOY BLUES	11
AN' DE ROAD IS HARD AN' LONG.	DK PO' BOY BLUES	12
MA SOUL IS FULL OF COLOR	DK REASONS WHY	3
BUT THAT THE SEA IS STRONG	DK SEA CHARM	5
BUT THAT SEA WIND IS SWEET	DK SEA CHARM	8
THIS LITTLE HOUSE IS SUGAR.	DK WINTER SWEEETNS	1
ITS ROOF WITH SNOW IS PILED.	DK WINTER SWEEETNS	2
IS IT MUCH TO DIE?	SL SCOTTSBORO	4
IS IT MUCH TO DIE WHEN IMMORTAL FEET	SL SCOTTSBORO	5
NONE OF THOSE IS DEAD.)	SL SCOTTSBORO	23
NO SHAME IS WRIT ACROSS ITS FACE -	SL TOWN OF SCOTTSB	2
THE DAY IS PAST.	ANS A NEW SONG	10
THAT DAY IS PAST.	ANS A NEW SONG	16
THAT DAY IS PAST.	ANS A NEW SONG	24
THAT DAY IS PAST	ANS A NEW SONG	33
THE PAST IS DONE!	ANS A NEW SONG	52
RED IS THE ALABAMA ROAD.	ANS BLD OZZIE POWEL	1
WHAT IT IS TO LIVE IN HELL.	ANS BLD OZZIE POWEL	23
AND RED IS THAT ALABAMA ROAD.	ANS BLD OZZIE POWEL	29
NOW MY WORK IS DONE.	ANS BLDS OF LENIN	16
THE WORLD IS OUR ROOM!	ANS BLDS OF LENIN	28
50-VOICES: LIFE IS EVERYWHERE FOR YOU.	ANS CHANT MAY DAY	24
50-VOICES: LIFE IS EVERYWHERE.	ANS CHANT MAY DAY	26
50-VOICES: WHEN THE EARTH IS NEW.	ANS CHANT MAY DAY	30
THIS IS FOR THE KIDS WHO DIE.	ANS KIDS WHO DIE	1
YOU ARE SURE YOURSELVES THAT IT IS COMING -	ANS KIDS WHO DIE	44
SEEKING A HOME WHERE HE HIMSELF IS FREE.	ANS LET AMERICA BE	4
IS CROWNED WITH NO FALSE PATRIOTIC WREATH.	ANS LET AMERICA BE	12
BUT OPPORTUNITY IS REAL, AND LIFE IS FREE.	ANS LET AMERICA BE	13
BUT OPPORTUNITY IS REAL, AND LIFE IS FREE.	ANS LET AMERICA BE	13
EQUALITY IS IN THE AIR WE BREATHE.	ANS LET AMERICA BE	14
AND YET MUST BE - THE LAND WHERE EVERY MAN IS FREE.	ANS LET AMERICA BE	64
AND THIS IS WHAT I SAW:	ANS NEGRO GHETTO	2
AND THIS IS WHAT MOVED IN MY HEART:	ANS NEGRO GHETTO	7
BECAUSE ONE IS BLACK.	ANS OPEN LETTER	30
HERE IS MY HAND.	ANS OPEN LETTER	66
WHAT IS THE SONG OF SPAIN?	ANS SONG OF SPAIN	4
FLAMENCO IS THE SONG OF SPAIN:	ANS SONG OF SPAIN	5
FLAMENCO IS THE SONG OF SPAIN.	ANS SONG OF SPAIN	10
IS THE SONG OF SPAIN.	ANS SONG OF SPAIN	17
PINTURA IS THE SONG OF SPAIN:	ANS SONG OF SPAIN	19
POISON GAS IS SPAIN.	ANS SONG OF SPAIN	35
AND ITS TERROR AND PAIN IS SPAIN.	ANS SONG OF SPAIN	37
OUR SKY IS GRAY.	ANS SONG OF SPAIN	49
IS THE SONG OF SPAIN.	ANS SONG OF SPAIN	83
IS ANOTHER DESIRE.	SH ASPIRATION	6
HOUSE IS SO QUIET! . . . LISTEN AT THEM MICE.	SH BED TIME	12
JUDGE, SHE IS DE WOMAN	SH BRIEF ENCOUNTER	7
SHE IS DE WOMAN, JUDGE.	SH BRIEF ENCOUNTER	9
DE FACT THAT SHE IS DEAD,	SH BRIEF ENCOUNTER	14
FACT THAT SHE IS DEAD -	SH BRIEF ENCOUNTER	16
WHEN THE NIGHT IS YOUNG -	SH DEATH IN HARLEM	25
UH! IT SURE IS AWFUL TO	SH EVIL MORNING	13
FORE IT IS TOO LATE!	SH EVIL MORNING	16
FACT IS, AIN'T GOT A DIME -	SH IF-ING	14
WHEN THIS FLOOD IS OVER.	SH MISSISSIPPI LEV	5
IN THE COMMUNITY IS GOOD	SH SNOB	2
EVERY WAY THEY IS.	SH STATEMENT	3
BUT THIS HOUSE IS MIGHTY QUIET!	SH SUNDAY	10
BUT THE BOYS IS ALL MARRIED! PSHAW!	SH SUNDAY	13
I LOOK IN THE KETTLE, THE KETTLE IS DRY.	SH SUPPER TIME	1
IS JIM CROW FREEDOM THE BEST	JC BLACK MAN SPEAK	19
THAT A NEGRO IS A MAN.	JC BLD SAM SOLOMON	4
CAUSE THE VOTE IS NOT RESTRICTED	JC BLD SAM SOLOMON	11
IS SOMETHING THAT SURELY	JC BLD SAM SOLOMON	15
A NEGRO IS A MAN.	JC BLD SAM SOLOMON	56
THINGS IS BAD -	JC GOOD MORN STLIN	7
LIFT THEIR HEADS AND THINGS IS BAD.	JC GOOD MORN STLIN	30
HAVE MADE UP THEIR MINDS JIM CROW IS THROUGH.	JC JIM CROW'S LAST	14
TO JIM CROW MY PEOPLE IS A PITY.	JC JIM CROW'S LAST	20
OUR BATTLE YET IS FAR FROM WON	JC JIM CROW'S LAST	30
BUT WHEN IT IS, JIM CROW'LL BE DONE.	JC JIM CROW'S LAST	31
THERE IS A BITTER RIVER	JC THE BITTER RIVR	2
THERE IS A BITTER RIVER	JC THE BITTER RIVR	6
BECAUSE MY FACE IS BLACK.	JC THE BITTER RIVR	78
THE CLOCK IS MOVING FORWARD HERE -	JC TO CAPTAIN MULZ	25
AND TYRANNY AGAIN IS BOLD.	JC TO CAPTAIN MULZ	28
ALONE, I KNOW, NO ONE IS FREE.	JC TO CAPTAIN MULZ	35
THERE IS A CREW OF MANY RACES, TOO,	JC TO CAPTAIN MULZ	47
IS THE BOOKER T.	JC TO CAPTAIN MULZ	64
YOUR SHIP IS MANKIND'S DEEPEST DREAM	JC TO CAPTAIN MULZ	67
YOUR SHIP IS FLAGSHIP	JC TO CAPTAIN MULZ	69
YOUR SHIP IS VICTORY.	JC TO CAPTAIN MULZ	73
YOUR SHIP IS	JC TO CAPTAIN MULZ	77
IS NOWHERE.	FW BORDER LINE	8
IT IS NOT WEARINESS	FW BURDEN	1
THAT IS GOOD.	FW CAROLINA CABIN	11
THE WORLD IS GLOOMY.	FW CAROLINA CABIN	13
FOR THE JAIL IS ROUND -	FW CIRCLES	8
IS THERE PEACE	FW CONVENT	2
IN THE DUSK IS WALKING	FW DIMOUT IN HARLM	2
DOWN THE STREET IS WALKING	FW DIMOUT IN HARLM	4
IS WALKING.	FW DIMOUT IN HARLM	18
THE SEA IS DEEP.	FW EXITS	1
A KNIFE IS SHARP.	FW EXITS	2
LOVE IS GIVEN.	FW GIFTS	2
HERE IS THAT SLEEPING PLACE.	FW GRAVE YARD	1

IS

Line	Collection	Poem	Line no.
IS HERE.	FW	GRAVE YARD	6
HERE IS MY HEART!"	FW	HEART	7
WHERE HIS HEART IS	FW	HEART	18
AND IS AFRAID TO PLAY	FW	MIGRATION	3
HE IS A LITTLE DARK BOY	FW	MIGRATION	11
IS TO REMEMBER FRAGRANCE WHERE	FW	REMEMBRANCE	3
IS HEARD.	FW	SILENCE	8
IS ALL,	FW	THERE	5
THIS IS EARTHQUAKE	FW	TODAY	1
WHOSE IS IT, DO YOU KNOW?	FW	WHEN ARMIES PAS	4
WHOSE CAP IT IS, SON,	FW	WHEN ARMIES PAS	6
IT IS NOT BLOOD?	FW	WHEN ARMIES PAS	11
IT IS A RED STAR, MOTHER!	FW	WHEN ARMIES PAS	22
AUGUST 1ST IS	OWT	BLD MARGE POLIT	27
THE GRAVEYARD IS THE	OWT	BOARDING HOUSE	1
THE GRAVEYARD IS THE	OWT	BOARDING HOUSE	7
YOUR HEART IS RIGHT.	OWT	HONEY BABE	4
IS WHAT I LIKE ABOUT YOU.	OWT	HONEY BABE	8
SEE WHAT THIS WEEK'S JIVE IS ALL ABOUT:	OWT	JITNEY	25
THE DUKE IS MELLOW!	OWT	JITNEY	26
THERE IS A GIN MILL ON THE AVENUE	OWT	JUICE JOINT	1
GIN IS SOLD IN GLASSES FINGER-TALL.	OWT	JUICE JOINT	6
THE HEAD OF LINCOLN IS SERENELY TALL	OWT	LINCOLN THEATRE	3
IS WHO I WANT TO SEE.	OWT	LONESOME CORNER	8
THE MAN IS THERE!	OWT	RAID	11
AS HARD AS MY HEAD IS,	OWT	TOO BLUE	12
THIS IS MY BODY	LHR	BLD MARY'S SON	18
AND THIS IS MY BLOOD, HE SAID.	LHR	BLD MARY'S SON	19
THIS IS MY BODY	LHR	BLD MARY'S SON	29
AND THIS IS MY BLOOD!	LHR	BLD MARY'S SON	30
IS ORDINARY.	LHR	CONSERVATORY	6
CHANGE IS THY OTHER NAME.	LHR	DEAR LVLY DEATH	10
BUT YOUR HOUR IS	LHR	POET TO BIGOT	14
MY MOMENT IS	LHR	POET TO BIGOT	16
IS NOT SO STRANGE,	SP	A HOUSE IN TAOS	18
BIRTHING IS HARD	SP	ADVICE	2
AND DYING IS MEAN -	SP	ADVICE	3
IS AFRICA.	SP	AFRO-AMER FRAG	3
IS AFRICA.	SP	AFRO-AMER FRAG	12
IS AFRICA'S	SP	AFRO-AMER FRAG	23
THE ANGELS WINGS IS WHITE AS SNOW,	SP	ANGELS WINGS	1
THE ANGELS WINGS IS WHITE AS SNOW,	SP	ANGELS WINGS	6
BUT THE ANGELS WINGS IS WHITE AS SNOW,	SP	ANGELS WINGS	11
WHITE IS RIGHT,	SP	ARGUMENT	1
BLACK IS FINE!	SP	ARGUMENT	8
THE DARK-FACED CHILD IS QUIET	SP	AUNTSUE'S STORI	23
IS AWFUL, AWFUL HARD.	SP	BAD LUCK CARD	2
THE DREAM IS VAGUE	SP	BEALE STREET	1
THE DREAM IS VAGUE,	SP	BEALE STREET	5
AW, MY HEART IS	SP	BLACK MARIA	7
IS FOR ME.	SP	BLACK MARIA	10
THESE STEPS IS BROKEN DOWN.	SP	BLD LANDLORD	6
TEN BUCKS YOU SAY IS DUE?	SP	BLD LANDLORD	10
DOROTHY'S NAME IS MUD.	SP	BLD OF THE GIRL	8
THERE IS TWO THOUSAND CHILDREN	SP	CHILDREN'S RYME	10
SOME OF THESE YOUNG ONES IS CERT'LY BAD -	SP	CHILDREN'S RYME	17
HASTINGS STREET IS WEARY,	SP	COULD BE	13
ANY PLACE IS DREARY	SP	COULD BE	15
EVEN IF IT IS MY HOME.	SP	CROON	3
ALL I WANT IS	SP	DEFERRED	32
ALL I WANT IS TO SEE	SP	DEFERRED	34
ALL I WANT IS A WIFE WHO WILL	SP	DEFERRED	36
HEAVEN, HEAVEN, IS MY HOME!	SP	DEFERRED	39
WHAT SHE MEANS IS:	SP	DELINQUENT	15
WHERE IS THIS LIGHT	SP	DEMAND	8
AND WHAT IS THIS WIND	SP	DEMAND	10
TOMORROW IS ANOTHER DAY.	SP	DEMOCRACY	12
IS A STRONG SEED	SP	DEMOCRACY	16
CHILE, THESE STEPS IS HARD TO CLIMB.	SP	DIME	1
TILL THE WHITE DAY IS DONE.	SP	DREAM VARIATION	4
THAT IS MY DREAM!	SP	DREAM VARIATION	9
TILL THE QUICK DAY IS DONE.	SP	DREAM VARIATION	13
THAT DEATH IS A DRUM	SP	DRUM	2
IS NO ATOM AT ALL,	SP	DRUM	8
UNTIL TIME IS LOST	SP	DRUM	9
AND THERE IS NO AIR	SP	DRUM	10
IS NOTHING NOWHERE,	SP	DRUM	12
DEATH IS A DRUM,	SP	DRUM	13
WHERE IS THAT SUGAR, HAMMOND,	SP	EARLY EVENING	1
I SAY, WHERE IS THAT SUGAR	SP	EARLY EVENING	3
I WONDER IS THERE NOWHERE A	SP	EARLY EVENING	23
THERE IS NEITHER LIGHT	SP	END	7
THERE IS NO DOOR!	SP	END	10
AND THE FAITH THAT IS IN HIS HEART -	SP	FREEDOM'S PLOW	6
FIRST IN THE HEART IS THE DREAM -	SP	FREEDOM'S PLOW	9
NO MAN IS GOOD ENOUGH	SP	FREEDOM'S PLOW	102
IS THERE BALLOT BOXES ON THE FREEDOM TRAIN?	SP	FREEDOM TRAIN	20
IS THAT THE WAY TO GET ABOARD THE FREEDOM TRAIN?	SP	FREEDOM TRAIN	28
AMERICA IS A DREAM.	SP	FREEDOM'S PLOW	142
THE PEOPLE SAY IT IS PROMISES - THAT WILL COME TRUE.	SP	FREEDOM'S PLOW	144
IS IT FOR REAL - OR JUST A SHOW AGAIN?	SP	FREEDOM TRAIN	46
BUT THERE IS, SOMEWHERE THERE,	SP	FREEDOM'S PLOW	153
IF THE HOUSE IS NOT YET FINISHED,	SP	FREEDOM'S PLOW	161
IF THE FIGHT IS NOT YET WON,	SP	FREEDOM'S PLOW	163
THE PLAN AND THE PATTERN IS HERE,	SP	FREEDOM'S PLOW	165
NO MAN IS GOOD ENOUGH	SP	FREEDOM'S PLOW	169
WHO IS AMERICA? YOU, ME!	SP	FREEDOM'S PLOW	176
NOW IT IS ME HERE, AND YOU THERE.	SP	FREEDOM'S PLOW	85
NOW IT IS THE U.S.A.	SP	FREEDOM'S PLOW	89
FROM THAT SEED A TREE GREW, IS GROWING, WILL EVER GROW.	SP	FREEDOM'S PLOW	195
THAT TREE IS FOR EVERYBODY,	SP	FREEDOM'S PLOW	196
THIS IS A SONG FOR THE GENIUS CHILD.	SP	GENIUS CHILD	1
SING IT SOFTLY, FOR THE SONG IS WILD.	SP	GENIUS CHILD	2
MOON IS SHINING.	SP	HARLEM NIGHT SO	7
NIGHT SKY IS BLUE.	SP	HARLEM NIGHT SO	8
A BAND IS PLAYING.	SP	HARLEM NIGHT SO	12
THE DREAM IS A COCKTAIL AT SLOPPY JOE'S -	SP	HAVANA DREAMS	1
THE DREAM IS THE ROAD TO BATABANO.	SP	HAVANA DREAMS	3
(BUT NOBODY KNOWS IF THAT IS SO.)	SP	HAVANA DREAMS	4
PERHAPS THE DREAM IS ONLY HER FACE -	SP	HAVANA DREAMS	5
HEAVEN IS	SP	HEAVEN	1
HAPPINESS IS	SP	HEAVEN	3
ONE TROUBLE IS YOU:	SP	HIGH TO LOW	3
BUT IS TRUE ANYHOW:	SP	IN EXPLANATION	34
HE IS A GOD.	SP	JOE LOUIS	6
IS DUSTY	SP	JULIET	14
WHERE THE SHADE IS?	SP	KID SLEEPY	4
LOVE IS LIKE WHISKEY,	SP	LAMENT OVER LOV	13
LOVE IS LIKE RED, RED WINE.	SP	LAMENT OVER LOV	14
LOVE IS LIKE WHISKEY,	SP	LAMENT OVER LOV	15
TALL AS A TREE IS TALL,	SP	LAMENT OVER LOV	20
TALL AS A TREE IS TALL.	SP	LAMENT OVER LOV	22
BUT HERE IS FIVE DOLLARS FOR YOU	SP	LETTER	4
HERE. WELL, THAT IS ALL SO I WILL CLOSE.	SP	LETTER	9
LIFE IS FINE!	SP	LIFE IS FINE	31
LIFE IS FINE!	SP	LIFE IS FINE	33
IS DUE TO LAST.	SP	LITTLE GRN TREE	4
IS WAITIN' TO SHELTER ME.	SP	LITTLE GRN TREE	14
THE SEA IS A WILDERNESS OF WAVES,	SP	LONG TRIP	1
THE SEA IS A DESERT OF WAVES,	SP	LONG TRIP	9
LOVE IS A WILD WONDER	SP	LOVE	1
THAT LITTLE SPARK IS LOVE	SP	LOVE	7
IS FLUNG.	SP	LUCK	4
LOVE IS GIVEN,	SP	LUCK	6
YOUR RENT IS DUE.	SP	MADAM RENT MAN	6
OR IS YOUR HEART STONE-COLD?	SP	MADAM MINISTER	8
THE SINK IS BROKE,	SP	MADAM RENT MAN	11
WHERE IS MY FORTUNE AT?	SP	MADAM FORT TELL	15
ALL I WANT IS YOU.	SP	MADAM MIGHT-HAV	18
THINGS IS BAD -	SP	MADAM CHARTY CH	27
MY NAME IS JOHNSON -	SP	MADAM'S PAST HI	1
WHO IS YOUR SUGAR, HONEY?	SP	MAMA AND DAUGHT	5
HE IS THAT YOUNG MAN, MAMA,	SP	MAMA AND DAUGHT	7
THE MOON IS NAKED.	SP	MARCH MOON	1
UNTIL A GLOW IS LIGHTED	SP	MIGRANT	21
AND THE COTTON FIELD IS FRIGHTENED	SP	MIGRANT	23
ON THE CHECK THAT IS HIS PAY.	SP	MIGRANT	37
HIS WOMAN AND HIS FRIEND IS DEAD.	SP	MONROE'S BLUES	2
HIS LITTLE BLUES IS SAD.	SP	MONROE'S BLUES	6
MY WOMAN AND MY FRIEND IS DEAD.	SP	MONROE'S BLUES	8
IS CROCODILE:	SP	MOVIES	7
THE SOUTHERN NIGHT IS FULL OF STARS,	SP	MULATTO	31
THE NIGHT IS BEAUTIFUL,	SP	MY PEOPLE	1
BEAUTIFUL, ALSO, IS THE SUN.	SP	MY PEOPLE	5
HER FEATURES IS ALL RUN TOGETHER	SP	NECESSITY	9
WHICH IS WHY I RECKON I DOES	SP	NECESSITY	11
BLACK AS THE NIGHT IS BLACK,	SP	NEGRO	2
BLACK AS THE NIGHT IS BLACK,	SP	NEGRO	18
WHEN HIS WORK IS DONE	SP	NEIGHBOR	5
HE LOOKS TALLER THAN HE IS	SP	NEIGHBOR	7
HE LOOKS DARKER THAN HE IS, TOO.	SP	NEIGHBOR	9
ANY PLACE THAT IS	SP	ONE-WAY TICKET	5
ANY PLACE THAT IS	SP	ONE-WAY TICKET	13
WHEN THE AIR IS ONE INTERMINABLE - BALL GAME	SP	PASSING	2
THAT IS	SP	QUESTION	3
MY HEART IS ACHING	SP	RELIEF	1
ALL I WANT IS YOU.	SP	SAME IN BLUES	16
BUT MY LOVIN' DAYS IS THROUGH.	SP	SAME IN BLUES	18
THE WATER IS TODAY.	SP	SEA CALM	3
IT IS NOT GOOD	SP	SEA CALM	4
AND THE WORK IS DONE	SP	SHARE-CROPPERS	6
IS SHE WANTS SOME CASH?	SP	SISTER	9
IS ALL YOU KNOW.	SP	SNAIL	4
IS ALL YOU SEE,	SP	SNAIL	6
IS IN THE SONG	SP	SO LONG	2
IS DUSTED WITH DESPAIR.	SP	SONG BILLIE HOL	15
LOVE IS A NAKED SHADOW	SP	SONG DARK GIRL	11
MISS MICHAELMAS IS AT DE MASS	SP	SOUTHERN MAMMY	3
THE NATIONS THEY IS FIGHTIN'	SP	SOUTHERN MAMMY	7
SONG IS A STRONG THING.	SP	SPIRITUALS	5
SONG IS A STRONG THING.	SP	SPIRITUALS	16
O, LITTLE BREATH OF OBLIVION THAT IS NIGHT.	SP	STARS	2
THAT IS NIGHT,	SP	STARS	9

WHERE THE CARNIVAL IS CHRISTIAN. SP SUMMER EVENING 13
THAT TOMORROW IS MONDAY. SP SUMMER EVENING 28
LIFE IS SHORT SP TAMBOURINES 9
BUT GOD IS LONG! SP TAMBOURINES 10
THAT IS THE SOUTH. SP THE SOUTH 17
IS A KINDER MISTRESS. SP THE SOUTH 26
IT'S NOT EASY TO KNOW WHAT IS TRUE
FOR YOU OR ME SP THEME FOR ENG B 16
THIS IS MY PAGE FOR ENGLISH B. SP THEME FOR ENG B 41
IS HONEY SP TRUMPET PLAYER 19
IS ECSTASY SP TRUMPET PLAYER 23
THAT IS LONGING FOR THE MOON SP TRUMPET PLAYER 26
THAT IS LONGING FOR THE SEA SP TRUMPET PLAYER 30
THE SPRING IS NOT SO BEAUTIFUL THERE
\- SP WATER-FRONT STR 1
TO WHERE THE SPRING IS WONDROUS RARE SP WATER-FRONT STR 3
AND LIFE IS GAY. SP WATER-FRONT STR 4
THE SPRING IS NOT SO BEAUTIFUL THERE
\- SP WATER-FRONT STR 5
HER FACE IS LIKE AN ANCIENT CAMEO SP WHEN SUE WEARS 2
OH, THAT LAST LONG RIDE IS A SP WIDOW WOMAN 1
AND THAT FINAL STOP IS A SP WIDOW WOMAN 5
WOMAN LIKE ME IS FREE! SP WIDOW WOMAN 24
HOW THIN AND SHARP IS THE MOON
TONIGHT! SP WINTER MOON 1
IS THE SLIM CURVED CROOK OF THE MOON
TONIGHT! SP WINTER MOON 3
SORRY THAT OLD WAR IS DONE! SP WORLD WAR II 6
WHAT IS MONEY FOR? SP YOUNG SAILOR 8
THE PO' HOUSE IS LONELY SP YOUNG GAL'S BLS 13
AN' THE GRAVE IS COLD. SP YOUNG GAL'S BLS 14
O, THE PO' HOUSE IS LONELY, SP YOUNG GAL'S BLS 15
THE GRAVEYARD GRAVE IS COLD. SP YOUNG GAL'S BLS 16
WHEN LOVE IS GONE WHAT SP YOUNG GAL'S BLS 19
WHEN LOVE IS GONE, O, SP YOUNG GAL'S BLS 21
TROUBLE WITH YOU IS SP 50 - 50 7
IS YOU. AYM ASK YOUR MAMA 20
IS IN ORBIT. AYM BIRD IN ORBIT 31
WHAT TIME IS IT, MAMA? AYM BLUES IN STEREO 28
WHAT TIME IS IT NOW? AYM BLUES IN STEREO 29
WHAT TIME IS IT, MAMA? AYM BLUES IN STEREO 32
WHERE THE GRASS IS GREENER $ $ $ $
$ $ $ AYM HORN OF PLENTY 23
WHERE WINTER'S NAME IS HAWKINS ¢ ¢
¢ ¢ AYM HORN OF PLENTY 27
AND NIAGARA FALLS IS FROZEN ¢ ¢ ¢ ¢
¢ ¢ ¢ AYM HORN OF PLENTY 28
(WHICH LATELY IS STONE NOWHERE) AYM HORN OF PLENTY 32
FOR ONE'S COUNTRY IS YOUR MAMA. AYM HORN OF PLENTY 58
IS ALWAYS FOUR YEARS AYM HORN OF PLENTY 90
YET THE HORSE WHOSE BACK IS BROKEN AYM IS IT TRUE? 52
IS IT TRUE THAT NEGROES - ? AYM IS IT TRUE? 55
PRESSURE OF THE BLOOD IS SLIGHTLY
HIGHER AYM JAZZTET MUTED 2
FROM JUKEBOX JOINTS IS LAID AYM JAZZTET MUTED 11
IS SLIGHTLY HIGHER - AYM JAZZTET MUTED 19
FOR NIAGARA FALLS IS FROZEN AYM ODE TO DINAH 11
WHERE THE PENDULUM IS SWINGING AYM ODE TO DINAH 111
AS IS CUSTOM BELOW ZERO. AYM ODE TO DINAH 12
WHEN NIAGARA FALLS IS FROZEN AYM ODE TO DINAH 23
AMEN IS NOT AN ENDING AYM ODE TO DINAH 123
IS COLORED FOLKS' DEPRESSION. AYM ODE TO DINAH 126
WHAT TIME IS IT NOW? AYM ODE TO DINAH 63
WHAT TIME IS IT NOW? AYM ODE TO DINAH 65
DON'T CARE WHAT TIME IT IS - AYM ODE TO DINAH 66
WHILE NIAGARA FALLS IS FROZEN. AYM ODE TO DINAH 68
WHEN THE ROLL IS CALLED UP YONDER AYM RIDE, RED, RIDE 2
WHERE IS LOTTE LENYA AYM SHADES OF PIG 13
AND WHO IS MACK THE KNIFE AYM SHADES OF PIG 14
AND THE TALMUD IS CORRECTED AYM SHADES OF PIG 24
WHO IS TO JESUIT AYM SHADES OF PIG 26
AS NORTH POLE IS TO SOUTH AYM SHADES OF PIG 27
WHERE THE MASK IS PLACED BY OTHERS AYM SHOW FARE PLESE 6
WHERE THE LIGHTER IS THE DARKER AYM SHOW FARE PLESE 16
IS THE ANSWER TO THE CHILD. AYM SHOW FARE PLESE 19
IS ONE AYM SHOW FARE PLESE 32
BUT IT IS SO - PL ANGOLA QUESTION 14
IS A WHITE BACKLASH. PL BACKLASH BLUES 18
BUT THE WORLD IS BIG, PL BACKLASH BLUES 19
THE WORLD IS BIG AND ROUND, PL BACKLASH BLUES 20
IS DENIED, PL BIBLE BELT 8
IS GLORIFIED. PL BIBLE BELT 10
CHRIST IS A NIGGER, PL CHRIST IN ALA. 1
MARY IS HIS MOTHER: PL CHRIST IN ALA. 4
GOD IS HIS FATHER: PL CHRIST IN ALA. 7
IS GENTLY STEWING. PL CULTURAL EXCHNG 20
WHERE IS THE COLORED LAUNDROMAT PL CULTURAL EXCHNG 24
MARTIN LUTHER KING IS GOVERNOR OF
GEORGIA, PL CULTURAL EXCHNG 43
CULTURE, THEY SAY, IS A TWO-WAY
STREET: PL CULTURAL EXCHNG 58
THE LOBSTER IS DELICIOUS. PL DINNER GUEST ME 15
IS NOT SO BAD. PL DINNER GUEST ME 21
LIFE IS A SYSTEM OF HALF-TRUTHS AND
LIES. PL ELDERLY LEADERS 3
HE IS NOT DEAD. PL FREDRK DOUGLASS 22
TOMORROW IS ANOTHER DAY. PL FREEDOM 12
IS A STRONG SEED PL FREEDOM 16

IS JUST FROSTING PL FROSTING 2
OF THE DOG IS FAST. PL GO SLOW 3
IS HEAVY WITH THE DRUG PL JUNIOR ADDICT 14
THAN IS HIS LIVING HERE. PL JUNIOR ADDICT 23
THAN IT IS TO GET A JOB." PL JUNIOR ADDICT 29
THAT JUSTICE IS A BLIND GODDESS PL JUSTICE 1
IS A THING TO WHICH WE BLACK ARE
WISE: PL JUSTICE 2
YOUR WALL IS TOO HIGH PL LAST PRINCE 4
AND YOUR MOAT IS TOO WIDE - PL LAST PRINCE 5
IS THE JEW PL LENOX AVE. BAR 3
BUT THE HOUSE IS OLD. PL LITTLE SNG HOUS 10
STILL - THERE IS ME! PL LITTLE SNG HOUS 26
FOR AIR IS HIS GRAVE. PL LUMUMBA'S GRAVE 16
SUN IS HIS GRAVE, PL LUMUMBA'S GRAVE 17
MOON IS, STARS ARE, PL LUMUMBA'S GRAVE 18
SPACE IS HIS GRAVE. PL LUMUMBA'S GRAVE 19
WHERE IS THE JIM CROW SECTION PL MERRY-GO-ROUND 3
YOUR SPIT IS MY FACE. PL MILITANT 11
AND SO MY FIST IS CLENCHED PL MILITANT 12
IS PL MOTTO 7
IS ALIVE WITH GHOSTS TODAY. PL OCTOBER 16 RAID 24
THAT MY SON IS DEAD. PL OFFICIAL NOTICE 3
IS THE BLOOD HE BLED. PL OFFICIAL NOTICE 6
IS SEALED. PL OFFICIAL NOTICE 14
WHEN DANGER IS NOT NEAR, PL SWEET WORDS RAC 10
. . . AND HERE IS PL THE DOVE 1
THE FACE OF WAR IS MY FACE. PL THE DOVE 1
EARTH IS BROWN PL THE DOVE 7
IS WHO? PL UN-AMERICAN 12
IS NOT YOUR NAME LIPSHITZ? PL UN-AMERICAN 13
THAT'S WHY MY HEART IS RED. PL VARI-COLORED 8
WHY DOWN SOUTH IS ALWAYS DOWN. PL VARI-COLORED 15
THE FACE OF WAR IS YOUR FACE. PL WAR 2
IS THE FACE PL WAR 4
DEATH IS THE BROOM PL WAR 8
IS WAR. PL WAR 25
AND IT IS WINTER. PL WHERE WHEN WHCH 7
THE RAIN IS LEAD. PL WITHOUT BENEFIT 11

ISLAND 5

I SEE THE ISLAND SP ISLAND 3
I SEE THE ISLAND SP ISLAND 5
MANHATTAN ISLAND WILL WHIRL SP PROJECTION 12
ON BEDLOE'S ISLAND MANAGED BY SOL
HUROK AYM HORN OF PLENTY 4
I MOVED OUT TO LONG ISLAND AYM HORN OF PLENTY 30

ISLANDS 1

10-OTHERS: WORKERS IN THE ISLANDS OF
THE SEA - ANS CHANT MAY DAY 23

ISN'T 2

'CAUSE THAT'S WHAT I DIED FOR -
ISN'T IT, BROTHER?" NM COLORED SL POEM 36
IT ISN'T NICE TO BE NAKED? SP MARCH MOON 10

ISSUE 1

SEND FOR TROTSKY! (WHAT? DON'T
CONFUSE THE ISSUE. PL FINAL CALL 26

IT 302

IT IS NIGHT, WB AFRAID 5
NO, MAKE IT WB CAT AND SAXOPHN 5
DO IT! WB CAT AND SAXOPHN 27
IT IS IN THIS SICK ROOM WB SICK ROOM 2
DON'T KNOW WHY I DO IT BUT FC BAD MAN 11
IT KEEPS ME FROM FEELIN' BLUE. FC BAD MAN 12
YET IT SEEMS LIKE ALWAYS FC BLACK GAL 5
CAN'T HELP IT CAUSE I'M BLACK. FC BLACK GAL 14
I GIVE IT TO HIM CAUSE I LOVED HIM FC GYPSY MAN 17
WHEN IT HURTS YO' HEART YOU FC GYPSY MAN 23
PLAY IT FOR THE LORDS AND LADIES, FC JAZZ BAND 3
PLAY IT, FC JAZZ BAND 9
YOU KNOW IT. FC JAZZ BAND 13
PLAY IT, JAZZ BAND! FC JAZZ BAND 18
SAY IT VERY SOFTLY. FC MAMMY 3
SAY IT VERY SLOWLY IF YOU CHOOSE. FC MAMMY 4
IT SHO WOULD BE SAD. FC MINNIE SINGS 14
PLAY IT ONCE. FC SATURDAY NIGHT 1
DO, IT, MR. CHARLIE, FC SATURDAY NIGHT 27
IT AIN'T NOTHIN' BUT A HOVEL. FC WORKIN' MAN 4
EXCEPT THE NAME EACH GIVES IT - OLD TWO THINGS 9
IT AIN'T SO DEEP: NM BIG-TIMER POEM 2
AND WHOEVER DON'T LIKE IT NM BIG-TIMER POEM 27
AND I SWING IT A-HUMMIN', NM BIG-TIMER POEM 30
BUT DON'T LET IT MATTER TO YOU, NM BIG-TIMER POEM 49
AND FIGHT IT OUT ALONE. NM BIG-TIMER POEM 56
SO I'M TAKIN' IT EASY NM BIG-TIMER POEM 73
OUT OF SADNESS IT RISES TO DEFIANCE
AND DETERMINATION. A HYMN OF
FAITH NM BLACK CLWN MOOD 12
LET IT BE GAY. NM BLACK CLWN POEM 13
WELL, AIN'T NEVER DONE IT, BUT FOR
TO KEEP BODY AND SOUL NM BROKE 29
HAS I DID IT BEFO'? CERTAINLY! NM BROKE 31
'CAUSE THAT'S WHAT I DIED FOR -
ISN'T IT, BROTHER?" NM COLORED SL POEM 36

Line	Book	Poem	Line No.
IT WAS AWFUL - FACING THAT BOY WHO WENT OUT TO DIE.	NM	COLORED SL POEM	42
AND STILL IT CALLS TO ME?	DK	BEGGAR BOY	4
SOFT AS IT BEGAN -	DK	I LOVED FRIEND	5
MA LORD KNOWED WHAT IT WAS TO WORK.	DK	MA LORD	6
WERE IT NOT FOR YOUR EYES.	DK	QUIET GIRL	3
WERE IT NOT FOR YOUR SONGS.	DK	QUIET GIRL	6
IS IT MUCH TO DIE?	SL	SCOTTSBORO	4
IS IT MUCH TO DIE WHEN IMMORTAL FEET	SL	SCOTTSBORO	5
WHAT IT IS TO LIVE IN HELL.	ANS	BLD OZZIE POWEL	23
YOU ARE SURE YOURSELVES THAT IT IS COMING -	ANS	KIDS WHO DIE	44
LET IT BE THE DREAM IT USED TO BE.	ANS	LET AMERICA BE	2
LET IT BE THE DREAM IT USED TO BE.	ANS	LET AMERICA BE	2
LET IT BE THE PIONEER ON THE PLAIN	ANS	LET AMERICA BE	3
LET IT BE THAT GREAT STRONG LAND OF LOVE	ANS	LET AMERICA BE	7
(IT NEVER WAS AMERICA TO ME.)	ANS	LET AMERICA BE	10
THAT'S MADE AMERICA THE LAND IT HAS BECOME.	ANS	LET AMERICA BE	44
I SAY IT PLAIN.	ANS	LET AMERICA BE	76
PULL IT HIGH!	ANS	LYNCHING SONG	2
PULL IT, BOYS.	ANS	LYNCHING SONG	5
SING IT VERY SIMPLY THAT I MIGHT UNDERSTAND.	ANS	SONG OF SPAIN	3
I MUST NOT DO IT AGAIN.	ANS	SONG OF SPAIN	72
I MUST NOT DO IT AGAIN.	ANS	SONG OF SPAIN	74
IT TOOK ALL I HAD.	SH	ANNOUNCEMENT	6
(IF I'D A-ONLY KNEW IT)	SH	ANNOUNCEMENT	10
I WONDER HOW IT FEELS	SH	ASPIRATION	1
OR IF IT WASN'T SO LATE I MIGHT TAKE A WALK	SH	BED TIME	7
I MIGHT AS WELL PUT IT ON IN THE HAY.	SH	BED TIME	10
TWO BUCKS ON IT?	SH	BLD PAWNBROKER	3
I DON'T KNOW WHY IT LOOKS	SH	BLD PAWNBROKER	11
IT AIN'T STOLE.	SH	BLD PAWNBROKER	16
O.K. YOU DON'T WANT IT?	SH	BLD PAWNBROKER	17
WHIP IT, MISS LUCY!	SH	DEATH IN HARLEM	12
DO IT, ARABELLA!	SH	DEATH IN HARLEM	20
HONEY BABY, SOCK IT!	SH	DEATH IN HARLEM	21
AW, PICK IT, MISS LUCY!	SH	DEATH IN HARLEM	27
JAZZ IT SLOW!	SH	DEATH IN HARLEM	28
IT WAS DAY -	SH	DEATH IN HARLEM	138
ROCK IT, ARABELLA,	SH	DEATH IN HARLEM	39
AW, PLUNK IT, MISS LUCY,	SH	DEATH IN HARLEM	56
AW, PLAY IT, MISS LUCY!	SH	DEATH IN HARLEM	74
LUCY WAS A-BASSIN IT, BOOM, BOOM, BOOM.	SH	DEATH IN HARLEM	77
WHILE MISS LUCY PLAYED IT, BOOM, BOOM, BOOM,	SH	DEATH IN HARLEM	91
(IT WAS JUST AS IF SOMEBODY	SH	DEATH IN HARLEM	97
FILL IT UP WITH GAS	SH	DECLARATION	10
IT MUST HAVE BEEN YESTERDAY,	SH	EVIL MORNING	1
(I KNOW IT AIN'T TODAY)	SH	EVIL MORNING	2
UH! IT SURE IS AWFUL TO	SH	EVIL MORNING	13
FORE IT IS TOO LATE!	SH	EVIL MORNING	16
FILL IT UP WITH GAS AND	SH	IF-ING	7
IT COME LAST NIGHT.	SH	LETTER	2
IT TAKES YOU AND IT BREAKS YOU -	SH	LOVE AGAIN BLUS	17
IT TAKES YOU AND IT BREAKS YOU -	SH	LOVE AGAIN BLUS	17
WHY DON'T YOU TRY IT, FOLKS,	SH	OUT OF WORK	23
AND SEE WHAT IT WOULD DO TO YOU?	SH	OUT OF WORK	24
DON'T HAVE TO SHAPE IT A-TALL.	SH	PAY DAY	2
"THIS WEEK I NEED IT ALL."	SH	PAY DAY	4
I'M GONNA GET IT CASHED,	SH	PAY DAY	5
JUST SO IT GOES AWAY FROM HERE.	SH	SIX-BITS BLUES	6
BUT DON'T MAKE IT TOO LONG.	SH	SIX-BITS BLUES	8
DON'T MAKE IT TOO LONG.	SH	SIX-BITS BLUES	10
MAKE IT SHORT AND SWEET, YOUR LOVIN'.	SH	SIX-BITS BLUES	11
IT MIGHT BE MISUNDERSTOOD -	SH	SNOB	4
AND SET DOWN AND DRINK IT, MYSELF AND ME.	SH	SUPPER TIME	12
AND SPLIT IT WIDE!	JC	BIG BUDDY	15
IT WAS DOWN IN MIAMI	JC	BLD SAM SOLOMON	5
THAT MAY BE SO - FOR THOSE WHO WANT IT SO.	JC	GOOD MORN STLIN	25
I MEAN IT WHEN I SAY.	JC	GOOD MORN STLIN	54
IT MEANS FREEDOM AT HOME, TOO -	JC	HOW ABOUT DIXIE	23
BUT WHEN IT IS, JIM CROW'LL BE DONE.	JC	JIM CROW'S LAST	31
SO IT WOULD SEEM.	JC	NOTE TO NAZIS	2
IT GIVES ONLY THE GLINT OF STEEL BARS	JC	THE BITTER RIVR	27
YOU WHO GUIDE IT ON ITS WAY.	JC	TO CAPTAIN MULZ	66
IT IS NOT WEARINESS	FW	BURDEN	1
WHAT IT WAS ALL ABOUT	FW	COMMUNION	2
WHAT IT WAS ALL ABOUT	FW	COMMUNION	4
AND WHEN I TOOK IT	FW	COMMUNION	7
IT FELT GOOD TO SHOUT!	FW	COMMUNION	8
IT HAD NO DIGNITY BEFORE.	FW	HARLEM DANCE HA	1
AND HUNG IT	FW	HEART	3
AND HID IT	FW	HEART	15
AND HOLD IT TIGHT.	FW	LITTLE SONG	4
TOUCHES IT.	FW	SLEEP	5
IT HAS A RED STAR ON IT.	FW	WHEN ARMIES PAS	3
IT HAS A RED STAR ON IT.	FW	WHEN ARMIES PAS	3
WHOSE IS IT, DO YOU KNOW?	FW	WHEN ARMIES PAS	4
WHOSE CAP IT IS, SON,	FW	WHEN ARMIES PAS	6
BUT IT HAS A RED STAR ON IT!	FW	WHEN ARMIES PAS	9
BUT IT HAS A RED STAR ON IT!	FW	WHEN ARMIES PAS	9
IT IS NOT BLOOD?	FW	WHEN ARMIES PAS	11
IT MIGHT HAVE BEEN	FW	WHEN ARMIES PAS	17
IT IS A RED STAR, MOTHER!	FW	WHEN ARMIES PAS	22
FOLKS STARTED TO CRY IT -	OWT	BLD MARGE POLIT	14
IT WASN'T MOTHER'S	OWT	BLD MARGE POLIT	54
IT WERE	OWT	BLD MARGE POLIT	56
I SAID, IT DON'T MAKE NO DIFFERENCE NOHOW.	OWT	STRANGER IN TWN	9
IT WOULD PROBABLY TAKE TWO.	OWT	TOO BLUE	13
IT WAS IN THE SPRING.	LHR	BLD MARY'S SON	1
I WISH IT WOULD	LHR	CONSERVATORY	3
TO MAKE IT EITHER MORE OR LESS.	LHR	DEAR LVLY DEATH	7
WERE IT NOT FOR YOUR EYES.	SP	ARDELLA	3
WERE IT NOT FOR YOUR SONGS.	SP	ARDELLA	6
IT WAS A LONG TIME AGO.	SP	AS I GREW OLDER	1
BUT IT WAS THERE THEN,	SP	AS I GREW OLDER	3
ROSE UNTIL IT TOUCHED THE SKY -	SP	AS I GREW OLDER	15
BUT I HOPE IT	SP	BLACK MARIA	4
LOOKS LIKE SHE COULD'VE KNOWED IT	SP	BLD FORTUNE TEL	19
DON'T YOU 'MEMBER I TOLD YOU ABOUT IT	SP	BLD LANDLORD	3
THROW IT IN THE STREET?	SP	BLD LANDLORD	16
JUST AS THOUGH IT WAS NO SIN -	SP	BLD OF THE GIRL	14
SHE'D DO IT AGIN'!	SP	BLD OF THE GIRL	16
ANYTHING HE WANTS OUT OF IT.	SP	BUDDY	10
IT TAKES TO LIVE.	SP	CONSIDER ME	32
EVEN IF IT IS MY HOME.	SP	CROON	3
IT WAS THAT LONELY DAY, FOLKS,	SP	CROSSING	1
BUT IT WAS AS IF THEY'D LEFT.	SP	CROSSING	4
IT WAS THAT LONELY DAY, FOLKS,	SP	CROSSING	19
OUT WHERE IT MAKES	SP	DEAD IN THERE	21
IT DON'T MAKE SENSE -	SP	DEFERRED	22
IT ALL THE TIME.	SP	DIME	8
LISTEN TO IT CLOSELY:	SP	DREAM BOOGIE	10
TAKE IT AWAY!	SP	DREAM BOOGIE	17
ROLLING LIKE I LIKE IT	SP	EASY BOOGIE	7
EASY LIKE I ROCK IT	SP	EASY BOOGIE	12
BUT I'M GONNA KEEP ON AT IT	SP	EVIL	3
TILL IT DRIVES YOU CRAZY, TOO.	SP	EVIL	4
IT WAS A LONG TIME AGO,	SP	FREEDOM'S PLOW	100
ELSE IT HAD NO MEANING FOR ANYONE.	SP	FREEDOM'S PLOW	108
WHEN IT STOPS IN MISSISSIPPI WILL IT BE MADE PLAIN	SP	FREEDOM TRAIN	21
WHEN IT STOPS IN MISSISSIPPI WILL IT BE MADE PLAIN	SP	FREEDOM TRAIN	21
"OR IF IT WOULD," THOUGHT SOME.	SP	FREEDOM'S PLOW	121
BUT OTHERS KNEW IT HAD TO TRIUMPH.	SP	FREEDOM'S PLOW	122
THAT SONG MEANT JUST WHAT IT SAID: HOLD ON!	SP	FREEDOM'S PLOW	127
OUT OF WAR IT CAME, BLOODY AND TERRIBLE!	SP	FREEDOM'S PLOW	130
BUT IT CAME!	SP	FREEDOM'S PLOW	131
BUT MAYBE THEY EXPLAINS IT ON THE	SP	FREEDOM TRAIN	35
BUT NOW WE KNOW HOW IT ALL CAME OUT.	SP	FREEDOM'S PLOW	136
WE KNOW NOW HOW IT CAME OUT.	SP	FREEDOM'S PLOW	138
MISTER, I THOUGHT IT WERE THE	SP	FREEDOM TRAIN	41
THE POET SAYS IT WAS PROMISES.	SP	FREEDOM'S PLOW	143
HE DIED FOR REAL. IT WARN'T NO SHOW.	SP	FREEDOM TRAIN	44
THE PEOPLE SAY IT IS PROMISES - THAT WILL COME TRUE.	SP	FREEDOM'S PLOW	144
IS IT FOR REAL - OR JUST A SHOW AGAIN?	SP	FREEDOM TRAIN	46
THE G.I.'S WHO FOUGHT WILL SAY, WE WANTED IT SO!	SP	FREEDOM TRAIN	60
BLACK MEN AND WHITE WILL SAY, AIN'T IT FINE?	SP	FREEDOM TRAIN	61
NOW IT IS ME HERE, AND YOU THERE.	SP	FREEDOM'S PLOW	85
NOW IT IS THE U.S.A.	SP	FREEDOM'S PLOW	39
SING IT SOFTLY, FOR THE SONG IS WILD.	SP	GENIUS CHILD	2
SING IT SOFTLY AS EVER YOU CAN -	SP	GENIUS CHILD	3
DOES IT DRY UP	SP	HARLEM	2
DOES IT STINK LIKE ROTTEN MEAT?	SP	HARLEM	6
MAYBE IT JUST SAGS	SP	HARLEM	9
OR DOES IT EXPLODE?	SP	HARLEM	11
AND SOMETIMES IT SEEMS	SP	HIGH TO LOW	8
HIS WIFE LOOKED IT UP IN HER DREAM BOOK	SP	HOPE	3
AND PLAYED IT.	SP	HOPE	4
AND DON'T MEAN HALF IT SAYS -	SP	IN EXPLANATION	33
PUT IT ON A RECORD, LET IT WHIRL,	SP	JUKE BOX LOVE	9
PUT IT ON A RECORD, LET IT WHIRL,	SP	JUKE BOX LOVE	9
AND WHILE WE LISTEN TO IT PLAY,	SP	JUKE BOX LOVE	10
MAMA, IT HAS BEEN RAINING CATS AND DOGS UP	SP	LETTER	8
BUT IT WAS	SP	LIFE IS FINE	9
IT WAS COLD!	SP	LIFE IS FINE	11
IF IT HADN'T A-BEEN SO HIGH	SP	LIFE IS FINE	18
BUT IT WAS	SP	LIFE IS FINE	20
IT WAS HIGH!	SP	LIFE IS FINE	22
IT LOOKS LIKE TO ME	SP	LITTLE GRN TREE	1
IT WAS YESTERDAY MORNING	SP	LITTLE OLD LETT	1
BUT IT MADE ME WISH	SP	LITTLE OLD LETT	7
I TURNED IT OVER.	SP	LITTLE OLD LETT	9
MAYBE IT AIN'T RIGHT -	SP	LIVE LET LIVE	1

O.K.ED IT WHEN? . . . SP MADAM PHONE BIL 3
TO PUT IT DOWN. . . . SP MADAM CENSUS 4
HAS IT BEEN SAVED. . . . SP MADAM MINISTER 7
YOU SAY, I WILL PAY IT - . . . SP MADAM PHONE BIL 10
IT WAS TOO MUCH. . . . SP MADAM HER MADAM 11
HE SAID, I'M GONNA PUT IT . . . SP MADAM CENSUS 13
CAN IT BE . . . SP MADAM HER MADAM 14
I SAID, IT FELT GOOD - . . . SP MADAM MINISTER 19
YOU AIN'T GONNA FIND IT . . . SP MADAM FORT TELL 19
BUT IT WAS A LONG TIME AGO . . . SP MAMA AND DAUGHT 12
IT ISN'T NICE TO BE NAKED? . . . SP MARCH MOON 10
WHICH MAKES IT . . . SP MELLOW 7
I WOULDN'T HAVE DROPPED IT. . . . SP MIDNIGHT RAFFLE 11
AN' PLANT IT AT MY BACK DOOR. . . . SP MIDWINTER BLUES 20
PLANT IT AT MY BACK DOOR. . . . SP MIDWINTER BLUES 22
MOULDS AND MELTS AND MOULDS IT . . . SP MIGRANT 19
IT'S HAD TACKS IN IT. . . . SP MOTHER TO SON 3
I BUILT MY HUT NEAR THE CONGO AND IT LULLED ME TO SLEEP. . . . SP NEGRO SPEAKS OF 6
I LOOKED UPON THE NILE AND RAISED THE PYRAMIDS ABOVE IT. . . . SP NEGRO SPEAKS OF 7
WHO WAS IT SENT . . . SP NIGHT FUNERAL 11
WHEN IT WAS ALL OVER . . . SP NIGHT FUNERAL 27
IT WAS ALL THEIR TEARS THAT MADE . . . SP NIGHT FUNERAL 42
AND TAKE IT WITH ME . . . SP ONE-WAY TICKET 2
AND I PUT IT DOWN IN . . . SP ONE-WAY TICKET 3
AND TAKE IT ON THE TRAIN . . . SP ONE-WAY TICKET 10
AND TAKE IT AWAY . . . SP ONE-WAY TICKET 24
WILL LEAD IT. . . . SP PARADE 6
WILL PRECEDE IT. . . . SP PARADE 8
WILL SPEED IT . . . SP PARADE 15
IT AIN'T FOREVER, GIMME! . . . SP PREFERENCE 14
IT TOOK ME TWO YEARS TO GET ON WPA. SP RELIEF 7
BABY, TAKE IT SLOW. . . . SP SAME IN BLUES 2
IT IS NOT GOOD . . . SP SEA CALM 4
DID IT EVER OCCUR TO YOU, SON, . . . SP SISTER 7
WELL, ANYWAY, IT DON'T HAVE TO BE A MARRIED MAN. . . . SP SISTER 12
DID IT EVER OCCUR TO YOU, BOY, . . . SP SISTER 13
IT WILL AGAIN . . . SP SUMMER EVENING 33
DID NOT THINK IT GOOD! . . . SP S-SSS-SS-SH! 7
THOUGHT IT FUN. . . . SP S-SSS-SS-SH! 21
WHY SHOULD IT BE MY LONELINESS, . . . SP TELL ME 1
WHY SHOULD IT BE MY SONG, . . . SP TELL ME 2
WHY SHOULD IT BE MY DREAM . . . SP TELL ME 3
THEN, IT WILL BE TRUE. . . . SP THEME FOR ENG B 5
BEING ME, IT WILL NOT BE WHITE. . . . SP THEME FOR ENG B 28
BUT IT WILL BE . . . SP THEME FOR ENG B 29
I WILL BE GOD WHEN IT COMES TO YOU. SP TO ARTINA 11
UNTIL IT GLEAMS . . . SP TRUMPET PLAYER 14
BUT IT REQUIRES . . . SP UP-BEAT 11
JOE SAID I WONDER HOW IT WOULD FEEL SP WEST TEXAS 7
WON'T COVER IT ALL - . . . SP WHAT? 4
YOU CALL IT FATE? . . . SP WHAT? SO SOON! 8
I NEVER SEEN IT. . . . AYM ASK YOUR MAMA 25
PERHAPS IF IT BE GOD'S WILL . . . AYM ASK YOUR MAMA 64
WHAT TIME IS IT, MAMA? . . . AYM BLUES IN STEREO 28
WHAT TIME IS IT NOW? . . . AYM BLUES IN STEREO 29
WHAT TIME IS IT, MAMA? . . . AYM BLUES IN STEREO 32
I BOIL A FISH AND SALT IT . . . AYM GOSPEL CHA-CHA 24
GOT THERE! YES, I MADE IT! . . . AYM HORN OF PLENTY 36
WOULD HARDLY WRITE IT IN THE SCRIPT - . . . AYM IS IT TRUE? 50
IS IT TRUE THAT NEGROES - ? . . . AYM IS IT TRUE? 55
WHAT TIME IS IT NOW? . . . AYM ODE TO DINAH 63
WHAT TIME IS IT NOW? . . . AYM ODE TO DINAH 65
DON'T CARE WHAT TIME IT IS - . . . AYM ODE TO DINAH 66
CAN I GET IT NOW? . . . AYM RIDE, RED, RIDE 6
BUT IT IS SO - . . . PL ANGOLA QUESTION 14
IT WOULD BE TOO BAD IF JESUS . . . PL BIBLE BELT 1
BUT SAY IT - . . . PL BIBLE BELT 11
WEAR IT . . . PL COLOR 1
WEAR IT . . . PL COLOR 5
AND HANG IT ABOUT YOUR NECK . . . PL CROWNS GARLANDS 2
WOULD IT RUB OFF? . . . PL CULTURAL EXCHNG 34
AND I'M GONNA PUT THE PURTIEST SONGS IN IT . . . PL DAYBREAK IN ALA 4
I'M GONNA PUT SOME TALL TALL TREES IN IT . . . PL DAYBREAK IN ALA 7
AND RED CLAY EARTH HANDS IN IT . . . PL DAYBREAK IN ALA 17
HOW MANY BULLETS DOES IT TAKE . . . PL DEATH YORKVILLE 3
HOW MANY CENTURIES DOES IT TAKE . . . PL DEATH YORKVILLE 5
HOW MANY CENTENNIALS DOES IT TAKE PL DEATH YORKVILLE 15
HOW MANY BULLETS DOES IT TAKE . . . PL DREAM DEFERRED 1
DOES IT DRY UP . . . PL DREAM DEFERRED 2
DOES IT STINK LIKE ROTTEN MEAT? . . . PL DREAM DEFERRED 6
MAYBE IT JUST SAGS . . . PL DREAM DEFERRED 9
OR DOES IT EXPLODE? . . . PL DREAM DEFERRED 11
AND RIDE THE JIM CROW CAR UNTIL IT SCREAMS . . . PL JIM CROW CAR 3
THAN IT IS TO GET A JOB." . . . PL JUNIOR ADDICT 29
CAN IT BE . . . PL KU KLUX 10
SO IT SEEMS. . . . PL LONG VIEW NEGRO 6
IT EVERYWHERE. . . . PL LUMUMBA'S GRAVE 23
AS IF IT WERE SOME NOBLE THING. . . . PL MOTHER IN WAR 1
I PLAY IT COOL . . . PL MOTTO 1
TO WRITE IT . . . PL OFFICIAL NOTICE 5
BUT SUPPOSE I DON'T WANT IT. . . . PL QUESTION ANSWER 14
WHY TAKE IT? . . . PL QUESTION ANSWER 15
TO REMAKE IT. . . . PL QUESTION ANSWER 16
BUT IT MUST BE AROUND . . . PL STOKELY MALCOLM 4
I DONE FORGOT WHEN IT PASSED . . . PL STOKELY MALCOLM 8
BUT I KNOW IT MUST BE . . . PL STOKELY MALCOLM 11
MAKE ME SAY I DID IT. . . . PL THIRD DEGREE 2
DID YOU NOT CHANGE IT . . . PL UN-AMERICAN 15
IT UPROOTS TREES! . . . PL WARNING 10
AND IT IS WINTER. . . . PL WHERE WHEN WHCH 7

ITS 51

WHAT GREAT FOREST HAS HUNG ITS PERFUME . . . WB NUDE YOUNG DANC 3
LIFTING MY RACE TO ITS RIGHTFUL PLACE . . . NM DARK YOUTH USA 19
ITS ROOF WITH SNOW IS PILED. . . . DK WINTER SWEEETNS 2
AND FROM ITS TINY WINDOW . . . DK WINTER SWEEETNS 3
NO SHAME IS WRIT ACROSS ITS FACE - SL TOWN OF SCOTTSB 2
ITS COURT, TOO WEAK TO STAND AGAINST A MOB. . . . SL TOWN OF SCOTTSB 3
ITS PEOPLE'S HEART, TOO SMALL TO HOLD A SOB. . . . SL TOWN OF SCOTTSB 4
THAT EVEN YET ITS MIGHTY DARING SINGS . . . ANS LET AMERICA BE 42
AND ITS TERROR AND PAIN IS SPAIN. ANS SONG OF SPAIN 37
WITH ITS WINGS OF GOLD FOR WHICH I PAY - . . . ANS SONG OF SPAIN 42
BY HOLDING ITS HEAD . . . SH SNOB 7
TOO LONG HAS THE TASTE OF ITS WATER JC THE BITTER RIVR 4
TOO LONG HAS ITS EVIL POISON . . . JC THE BITTER RIVR 8
AND ITS GALL COATS THE RED OF MY TONGUE, . . . JC THE BITTER RIVR 11
FROM ITS IRON BRIDGE HUNG. . . . JC THE BITTER RIVR 13
IN THE SNAKE-LIKE HISS OF ITS STREAM JC THE BITTER RIVR 15
AND MY GRANDFATHER'S BACK WITH ITS LADDER OF SCARS. . . . JC THE BITTER RIVR 36
NOR THE TASTE OF ITS BITTER BREW. JC THE BITTER RIVR 52
I WAS GIVEN ITS WATER . . . JC THE BITTER RIVR 53
WITH THE HISS OF ITS SNAKE-LIKE SONG - . . . JC THE BITTER RIVR 64
WITH ITS FILTH AND ITS MUD TOO LONG. JC THE BITTER RIVR 74
WITH ITS FILTH AND ITS MUD TOO LONG. JC THE BITTER RIVR 74
AGAIN MANKIND HAS LOST ITS COURSE. JC TO CAPTAIN MULZ 6
BEEN DRIVEN OFF ITS WAY. . . . JC TO CAPTAIN MULZ 7
YOU WHO GUIDE IT ON ITS WAY. . . . JC TO CAPTAIN MULZ 66
FROM ITS MOTHER'S WOMB - . . . FW EARTH SONG 10
STRETCHES ITS WIDE HORIZONS . . . FW THERE 2
TO ANSWER ITS CALL. . . . SP DRUM 5
MAY ITS BRANCHES SPREAD AND ITS SHELTER GROW . . . SP FREEDOM'S PLOW 198
MAY ITS BRANCHES SPREAD AND ITS SHELTER GROW . . . SP FREEDOM'S PLOW 198
UNTIL ALL RACES AND ALL PEOPLES KNOW ITS SHADE. . . . SP FREEDOM'S PLOW 199
DIPLOMA IN ITS NEW FRAME: . . . SP GRADUATION 10
THE DIPLOMA BURSTS ITS FRAME . . . SP GRADUATION 23
AND ITS SANDS ARE FAIR: . . . SP ISLAND 6
WENT DOWN TO NEW ORLEANS, AND I'VE SEEN ITS MUDDY . . . SP NEGRO SPEAKS OF 9
AND HARLEM HAS ITS . . . SP PASSING 9
ITS WHITE WOMANHOOD. . . . SP SILHOUETTE 10
NIGHT WILL PULL ITS SLACK TAUT . . . SP SUMMER EVENING 25
AND WRAP A STRING AROUND ITS FINGER SP SUMMER EVENING 26
AND ITS GRANDMA - . . . SP S-SSS-SS-SH! 18
WITH BLOOD ON ITS MOUTH. . . . SP THE SOUTH 2
THAT NEVER LIFTS ITS HEAD . . . SP TROUBLED WOMAN 11
ITS HYPODERMIC NEEDLE . . . SP TRUMPET PLAYER 39
AND MOONLIGHT ON ITS HORN . . . AYM BIRD IN ORBIT 27
BEYOND ITS MASK OF WHITENESS . . . AYM BLUES IN STEREO 18
AND SO LOSE ITS REPOSE. . . . AYM BLUES IN STEREO 20
ITS BACK: . . . AYM IS IT TRUE? 48
STUMPED ITS TOE - . . . PL AMER HEARTBREAK 3
TASTING ITS BITTERNESS IN MY THROAT, PL MILITANT 5
ITS JAIL. . . . PL OPPRESSION 14
ITS MANURE. . . . PL UN-AMERICAN 23

ITSELF 3

AND SPACE ITSELF . . . SP DRUM 11
ALL BY ITSELF. . . . SP ONE 8
SHOUTS FROM THE EARTH ITSELF . . . AYM BLUES IN STEREO 8

IT'LL 2

I RECKON IT'LL BE . . . SP NOTE COMM THEAT 18
YES, IT'LL BE ME. . . . SP NOTE COMM THEAT 20

IT'S 65

I TELL YOU IT'S AWFUL, WHEN YOU'RE BROKE. . . . NM BROKE 47
IT'S DONE GOT ME SO CRAZY, FEEL LIKE I BEEN TAKIN' COKE. . . . NM BROKE 60
FOR WHAT COULD I ANSWER HIM, EXCEPT, "IT'S A LIE!" . . . NM COLORED SL POEM 43
IT'S A LIE! IT'S A LIE! EVERY WORD THEY SAID. . . . NM COLORED SL POEM 44
IT'S A LIE! IT'S A LIE! EVERY WORD THEY SAID. . . . NM COLORED SL POEM 44
AND IT'S BETTER A THOUSAND TIMES YOU'RE IN FRANCE DEAD. . . . NM COLORED SL POEM 45

Line	Source	Title	No.
AND IT'S A GOOD THING ALL THE BLACK BOYS LYING DEAD	NM	COLORED SL POEM	51
IT'S DE FIRST OF MAY!	ANS	SISTER JOHNSON	4
IT'S DE FIRST OF MAY!	ANS	SISTER JOHNSON	8
IT'S DE FIRST OF MAY!	ANS	SISTER JOHNSON	13
IT'S UNION-MADE.	SH	BLD PAWNBROKER	8
IT'S GOOD LIKE THAT WHEN YOU	SH	DEATH IN HARLEM	29
EVERYBODY'S HAPPY. IT'S A SPENDIN CROWD -	SH	DEATH IN HARLEM	36
I DON'T CARE WHERE IT'S GOIN'	SH	SIX-BITS BLUES	5
IT'S DARK ON THIS STOOP, LAWD! THE SUN'S GONE DOWN!	SH	TWILIGHT REVERI	15
SAM SAID, IT'S TIME TO GO	JC	BLD SAM SOLOMON	8
IT'S HARD TO BEAT HITLER	JC	HOW ABOUT DIXIE	19
AND IT'S TURNED TO STEEL IN MY BLOOD.	JC	THE BITTER RIVR	82
IT'S AN EARTH SONG -	FW	EARTH SONG	1
IT'S A SPRING SONG!	FW	EARTH SONG	4
IT'S SAILING DATE.	FW	SAILING DATE	19
SAYS, I KNOW IT'S HIM!	OWT	HONEY BABE	12
IT'S TIME TO GO.	OWT	RAID	9
TO ME IT'S HERE	OWT	VISITORS	3
TO ME IT'S HERE	OWT	VISITORS	7
TO ME IT'S HELL	OWT	VISITORS	11
IT'S MERCENARY!	LHR	CONSERVATORY	8
IT'S MINE!	SP	ARGUMENT	10
IT'S A WONDER YOU DON'T FALL DOWN.	SP	BLD LANDLORD	8
IT'S HARD TO UNDERSTAND	SP	BLD OF THE GIRL	2
IT'S EIGHT.	SP	BLUE MONDAY	3
AND IT'S MARKED DOWN THAT-A-WAY.	SP	BLUE MONDAY	5
IT'S HARD TO BELIEVE.	SP	DEAD IN THERE	10
FOLKS SAY IT'S NOT JUST	SP	DELINQUENT	7
IT'S A HAPPY BEAT?	SP	DREAM BOOGIE	9
IT'S SUCH A	SP	ENNUI	1
NOW IT'S MANHATTAN, CHICAGO,	SP	FREEDOM'S PLOW	86
PERHAPS IT'S A FAN OF SILVER LACE -	SP	HAVANA DREAMS	6
HELL, NO! IT'S TIME TO TALK BACK NOW!	SP	IN EXPLANATION	29
HISTORY SAYS IT'S TIME.	SP	IN EXPLANATION	30
IT'S SUNNY HERE	SP	KID SLEEPY	5
MADAM, IT'S JUST GOOD LUCK	SP	MADAM FORT TELL	3
IT'S NOT UP TO ME.	SP	MADAM RENT MAN	20
IF IT'S MONEY YOU WANT	SP	MADAM RENT MAN	25
IT'S ALWAYS A STONE -	SP	MADAM MIGHT-HAV	26
IT'S HAD TACKS IN IT.	SP	MOTHER TO SON	3
'CAUSE YOU FINDS IT'S KINDER HARD.	SP	MOTHER TO SON	16
AND IT'S ALL YOUR'N.	SP	PREFERENCE	10
IT'S TRULY	SP	PROJECTION	22
AT CLUB HARLEM IT'S ELEVEN	SP	SEASHORE THROUG	3
AND IT'S IN THE WAY YOU'RE GONE	SP	SO LONG	3
BUT IT'S LIKE A FOREIGN LANGUAGE	SP	SO LONG	4
I WONDER IF IT'S THAT SIMPLE?	SP	THEME FOR ENG B	6
IT'S NOT EASY TO KNOW WHAT IS TRUE FOR YOU OR ME	SP	THEME FOR ENG B	16
SINCE IT'S SNOWING ON THE TV	AYM	ODE TO DINAH	7
CRUMBLES AS IT'S NIBBLED	AYM	ODE TO DINAH	14
AND IT'S FULL OF FOLKS LIKE ME WHO ARE	PL	BACKLASH BLUES	23
IT'S NOT ENOUGH TO MOURN	PL	BOMBINGS DIXIE	1
"IT'S EASIER TO GET DOPE	PL	JUNIOR ADDICT	28
AND IT'S MARKED THERE.	PL	LUMUMBA'S GRAVE	21
IT'S WRONG.	PL	MILITANT	7
IT'S MADE OF PLAIN OLD GEORGIA CLAY.	PL	VARI-COLORED	7
I WONDER WHY IT'S YES TO ME.	PL	VARI-COLORED	11
IT'S HARD TO BLAME ME.	PL	WAR	19
IT'S BEEN SAID	PL	WITHOUT BENEFIT	8

IVAN 1

Line	Source	Title	No.
I AM IVAN, THE PEASANT.	ANS	BLDS OF LENIN	5

IVORY 1

Line	Source	Title	No.
WITH HIS EBONY HANDS ON EACH IVORY KEY	SP	THE WEARY BLUES	9

I-DON'T-WANT-TO-DIE 1

Line	Source	Title	No.
"I-DON'T-WANT-TO-DIE" CRY.	PL	BLACK PANTHER	4

I'D 43

Line	Source	Title	No.
IF I WAS A MULE I'D	FC	HARD LUCK	13
IF I WAS A MULE I'D	FC	HARD LUCK	15
I'D GO AWAY	FC	MINNIE SINGS	16
I'D SHO HAVE THEM BLUES.	FC	MINNIE SINGS	20
AND I'D SAVE MORE THAN I DO NOW.	FC	PRIZE FIGHTER	6
I'D STARVE AND - OH, WELL -	NM	BIG-TIMER POEM	42
AND TOLD ME I'D BETTER PAY HER FOR MY ROOM RENT AND BOARD!	NM	BROKE	22
IF A PRETTY GAL LIKE YOU WAS WILLIN', I'D BITE.	NM	BROKE	72
I WISH I'D NEVER BEEN BORN.	OK	PO' BOY BLUES	24
(IF I'D A-ONLY KNEW IT)	SH	ANNOUNCEMENT	10
IF THIS RADIO WAS GOOD I'D GET KDQ	SH	BED TIME	1
IF I HAD SOME MONEY I'D STROLL DOWN THE STREET	SH	BED TIME	3
OR IF I WASN'T SO DROWSY I'D LOOK UP JOE	SH	BED TIME	5
I'D RATHER DIE WHERE THE BAND'S A-PLAYIN'	SH	CABARET GIRL	3
I'D BUY MYSELF A CAR.	SH	DECLARATION	9
IF I WAS A BIRD I'D	SH	DECLARATION	17
BUT BEFORE I'D BITE A NAIL	SH	EVIL MORNING	7
I'D PULVERIZE YOU.	SH	EVIL MORNING	8
I'D BUY ME A MULE.	SH	IF-ING	2
I'D BUY ME A PACKARD.	SH	IF-ING	6
I'D GET ME A PLANE	SH	IF-ING	10
IF I HAD A FIRE I'D MAKE ME SOME TEA	SH	SUPPER TIME	11
CAUSE I'D TAKE THAT OWL HEAD AND FIRE ON YOU.	SH	TWILIGHT REVERI	12
I'D SAY,	OWT	FUNERAL	6
I'D NEVER BEEN	LHR	CONSERVATORY	12
BUT I'D HATE TO DIE ALL ALONE!	SP	AS BEFITS A MAN	2
GYPSY SAYS I'D KILL MY SELF	SP	BAD LUCK CARD	11
I'D LIKE TO MEET A GOOD FRIEND	SP	BOUND NO'TH BLS	11
I'D LIKE TO TAKE UP BACH.	SP	DEFERRED	48
I'D LIKE TO BUY A STRAIGHTENIN' COMB.	SP	DOWN AND OUT	9
I'D TELL HER, GIMME A PLACE TO SLEEP.	SP	EVENING SONG	6
I'D FLY ON MA MAN AN'	SP	HARD DADDY	17
I'D SCRATCH OUT BOTH HIS EYES.	SP	HARD DADDY	18
BEFORE I'D PAY	SP	MADAM RENT MAN	8
I'D GO TO HADES	SP	MADAM RENT MAN	9
DON'T KNOW'S I'D MIND HIS GOIN'	SP	MIDWINTER BLUES	7
DON'T KNOW'S I'D MIND HIS GOIN'	SP	MIDWINTER BLUES	9
BUT I'D RATHER BE DEAD THAN	SP	YOUNG GAL'S BLS	17
AND I'D LIKE TO MEET THE	AYM	BIRD IN ORBIT	7
I'D BELIEVE IN ANYTHING	PL	KU KLUX	7
I'D JUST AS LEAVE	PL	SWEET WORDS RAC	13
I'D MAKE TOMORROW.	PL	THIRD DEGREE	12
I'D UP AND SELL MY HEART OF GOLD	PL	VARI-COLORED	3

I'LL 57

Line	Source	Title	No.
I'LL CAST MY BLUES ASIDE.	WB	BLUES FANTASY	26
BUT I'LL MISS MA GIN.	FC	BLD OF GIN MARY	20
ELSE I'LL USE HER HEAD	FC	EVIL WOMAN	15
BUT I'LL HAVE MO' SENSE NEXT TIME.	FC	GYPSY MAN	18
'LIEVE I'LL JUMP IN DE RIVER	FC	SUICIDE	13
'LIEVE I'LL JUMP IN DE RIVER	FC	SUICIDE	15
I'LL CUT YOU DOWN COMIN'.	NM	BIG-TIMER POEM	32
YOU SAY I'LL MEET A BAD ENDIN', HEH?	NM	BIG-TIMER POEM	33
AND WHEN I'M DEAD - I'LL KEEP STILL.	NM	BIG-TIMER POEM	36
AND ONE OLD FUNNY BOY SAID, "I'LL WORK AT ANY PRICE	NM	BROKE	8
SO DE MAN SAY, "I'LL GET SOMEBODY ELSE, THEN, TO CLEAN." -	NM	BROKE	17
TOGETHER, RECKON I'LL TRY . . . SHO, I WANTS DE JOB! YES, SIR!	NM	BROKE	30
SO WHEN I GOT READY TO GO, I SAID, "I'LL BE SEEIN' YOU SOON, MARIE."	NM	BROKE	52
I'LL LAY DOWN AN' DIE RIGHT NOW.	OK	WIDE RIVER	18
THEN I'LL GO.	SH	BLD PAWNBROKER	18
I'LL GET 'EM FOR YOU.	SH	BLD THE KILLER	4
SAY! YOU KNOW I BELIEVE I'LL CHANGE MY NAME.	SH	DAYBREAK	9
BELIEVE I'LL DO A LITTLE DANCIN'	SH	EVENIN' BLUES	13
I'LL SING 'EM, TOO.	SH	HEY-HEY BLUES	16
I'LL KEEP RIGHT UP WITH YOU.	SH	HEY-HEY BLUES	18
AND I'LL HEY-HEY-HEY - AND CHEER!	SH	HEY-HEY BLUES	24
I'LL TRY NOT TO BE THAT MEAN NO MORE.	SH	LETTER	13
I'LL MEET YOU AT THE BUS STATION.	SH	LETTER	21
I'LL FIGHT LIKE A MAN.	JC	BIG BUDDY	6
I'LL SING FOR YOU - BUT DROP THAT COLOR BAR.	JC	JIM CROW'S LAST	18
I'LL MAKE MINCE-MEAT	JC	NOTE TO NAZIS	7
I'LL KNOW MY WAY AROUND.	OWT	STRANGER IN TWN	16
YES, I'LL KNOW	OWT	STRANGER IN TWN	17
I'LL LEAVE HER MORE TO NAG ABOUT	LHR	TESTAMENT	11
WELL, THAT'S TEN BUCKS MORE'N I'LL PAY YOU	SP	BLD LANDLORD	11
AND I'LL LOOK INTO THE FUTURE	SP	BLD THE GYPSY	7
I'LL KILL OLD GREELEY.	SP	BLUE BAYOU	13
I'LL NEVER GO TO FRANCE.	SP	DEFERRED	23
SO, SI'L-VOUS PLAIT, I'LL STUDY FRENCH!	SP	DEFERRED	28
THIS WORLD I'LL LEAVE BEHIND	SP	DEFERRED	40
I'LL HAVE A THRONE FOR MINE!	SP	DEFERRED	42
GUESS I'LL QUIT NOW.	SP	ELEVATOR BOY	23
THEN I'LL SHOUT, GLORY FOR THE	SP	FREEDOM TRAIN	63
I'LL HOLLER, BLOW YOUR WHISTLE.	SP	FREEDOM TRAIN	65
I'LL BRING HOME CHICKEN!	SP	GRADUATION	22
I'LL BE AT THE TABLE	SP	I, TOO	9
I'LL BE DOGGED, SWEET BABY,	SP	LIFE IS FINE	29
I'LL HAVE YOU KNOW	SP	MADAM MINISTER	10
I'LL PAY SOME MIND TO YOU.	SP	MADAM FORT TELL	16
BUT I'LL BE DOGGED	SP	MADAM HER MADAM	23
I'LL READ YOUR OTHER PALM.	SP	MADAM FORT TELL	24
I'LL HAVE YOU KNOW	SP	MADAM CENSUS	31
AND I'LL GET ALONG.	SP	MADAM'S PAST HI	22
TURN AROUND - I'LL BRUSH BEHIND.	SP	MAMA AND DAUGHT	6
BUT HE'S THE ONLY MAN I'LL	SP	MIDWINTER BLUES	17
WELL, SON, I'LL TELL YOU:	SP	MOTHER TO SON	1
ELSE I'LL CUT YOU OFF	SP	ULTIMATUM	6
I'LL NEVER DRY THESE TEARS.	SP	WIDOW WOMAN	18
I'LL WANT TO SEE SOMEBODY, TOO.	SP	YOUNG GAL'S BLS	12
BOUQUETS I'LL SEND YOU	AYM	BLUES IN STEREO	2
AND DREAMS I'LL SEND YOU	AYM	BLUES IN STEREO	3

Line	Poem	No.
I'LL SIGN THE	PL THIRD DEGREE	17

I'M 138

Line	Poem	No.
I'M YOUR	WB CAT AND SAXOPHN	19
I'M A BAD, BAD MAN	FC BAD MAN	1
I'M A BAD, BAD MAN.	FC BAD MAN	3
I'M SO BAD I	FC BAD MAN	13
I'M GOIN' TO DE DEVIL AN'	FC BAD MAN	17
CAN'T HELP IT CAUSE I'M BLACK.	FC BLACK GAL	14
I'M TIRED.	FC CLOSING TIME	7
I'M GONNA FILL 'EM UP FULL O'	FC DEATH DO DIRTY	33
I'M JUST GONNA KILL HER	FC EVIL WOMAN	3
I'M BLACK AN' UGLY	FC GAL'S CRY DYING	15
I'M GONNA BE A GYPSY WOMAN	FC GYPSY MAN	5
I'M SO LOW-DOWN I	FC HARD LUCK	17
I'M WAITING FOR MA MAMMY, -	FC MAMMY	1
I'M WAITING FOR MA MAMMY, -	FC MAMMY	5
I'M MIDNIGHT MAD.	FC MINNIE SINGS	12
I'M DEEP IN TROUBLE.	FC MOAN	1
I'M MOANIN', MOANIN',	FC MOAN	10
I'M GONNA KILL MA SELF.	FC SUICIDE	6
I'M GONNA BUY ME A KNIFE WITH	FC SUICIDE	7
I'M A HARD WORKIN' MAN	FC WORKIN' MAN	13
I'M THE GUY THE HOME FOLKS CALL -	NM BIG-TIMER POEM	3
I'M THE BAD EGG, SEE!	NM BIG-TIMER POEM	9
SO I'M HUSTLIN' IN THE NIGHT.	NM BIG-TIMER POEM	12
BUT WHILE I'M LIVIN' - I'M LIVIN'!	NM BIG-TIMER POEM	35
BUT WHILE I'M LIVIN' - I'M LIVIN'!	NM BIG-TIMER POEM	35
AND WHEN I'M DEAD - I'LL KEEP STILL.	NM BIG-TIMER POEM	36
I'M A FIRST CLASS HUSTLER.	NM BIG-TIMER POEM	37
SOMETIMES I'M SETTIN' PRETTY.	NM BIG-TIMER POEM	39
I'M JUST A GOOD-TIMER	NM BIG-TIMER POEM	43
CAUSE I'M ALL RIGHT.	NM BIG-TIMER POEM	50
I'M EATIN' AND LOVIN'.	NM BIG-TIMER POEM	51
I GUESS I KNOW WHAT I'M UP AGAINST.	NM BIG-TIMER POEM	57
SO I'M TAKIN' IT EASY	NM BIG-TIMER POEM	73
I'M JUST A BIG-TIMER.	NM BIG-TIMER POEM	75
BECAUSE I'M POOR AND BLACK AND FUNNY -	NM BLACK CLWN POEM	2
I'M ONLY A CLOWN!	NM BLACK CLWN POEM	58
I'M A MAN!	NM BLACK CLWN POEM	79
COME BAWLIN' ME OUT, 'CAUSE I'M BROKE.	NM BROKE	26
SINCE I'M BROKE.	NM BROKE	55
BUT I CAN'T EVEN BUY A PAPER - I'M SO BROKE.	NM BROKE	61
'CAUSE I'M JUST DYIN' TO TAKE ON THAT THERE MARRIAGE YOKE.	NM BROKE	77
'CAUSE I'M BROKE.	NM BROKE	79
AND I'M STILL JUST A "NIGGER" IN AMERICA TONIGHT.	NM COLORED SL POEM	47
THIS IS WHAT I'M GONNA SING.	DK NIGHT AND MORN	2
THIS IS WHAT I'M GONNA SING:	DK NIGHT AND MORN	4
YET I'M THE ONE WHO DREAMT OUR BASIC DREAM	ANS LET AMERICA BE	39
O, I'M THE MAN WHO SAILED THOSE EARLY SEAS	ANS LET AMERICA BE	45
FOR I'M THE ONE WHO LEFT DARK IRELAND'S SHORE,	ANS LET AMERICA BE	47
BUT I'M WAKIN' UP!	ANS PARK BENCH	7
I'M GONNA DIE!	SH BLD THE KILLER	27
BIG BEN, I'M GONNA BUST YOU BANG UP SIDE THE WALL!	SH DAYBREAK	1
I'M THE ONLY ONE'S GOT TO PILE OUT IN THE COLD.	SH DAYBREAK	6
I'M ABOUT TO LOSE MY MIND.	SH EVENIN' BLUES	6
CAUSE WHEN I'M DANCIN'	SH EVENIN' BLUES	17
I'M GONNA GET IT CASHED.	SH PAY DAY	5
I'M GONNA TELL THE FURNITURE MAN TO COME	SH PAY DAY	11
CAUSE I'M GOING BACK TO ROOMING AND BE A FREE MAN.	SH PAY DAY	16
I'M GONNA RENT ME A CUBBY-HOLE WITH A SINGLE BED.	SH PAY DAY	17
CAUSE I'M SURE ENJOYING MYSELF TODAY!	SH SUNDAY	7
I'M GONNA GET UP A POKER GAME AND INVITE THE BOYS.	SH SUNDAY	12
KEEP FEELING LIKE THIS I'M GONNA START ACTING BAD.	SH TWILIGHT REVERI	4
I'M GONNA SPLIT THIS ROCK	JC BIG BUDDY	14
SAM SOLOMON SAID, I'M	JC BLD SAM SOLOMON	33
AND I'M NOT SO DUMB	JC GOOD MORN STLIN	11
I'M GLAD	JC GOOD MORN STLIN	58
I'M BEAT TO MY KNEES.	JC HOW ABOUT DIXIE	12
I'M TIRED OF SEGREGATION,	JC THE BITTER RIVR	79
I'M TIRED OF THE BITTER RIVER!	JC THE BITTER RIVR	89
I'M EVER SO SURE	FW FAITHFUL ONE	3
I'M GOING TO THE REGAL,	OWT JITNEY	24
I'M GOING SHOPPING NOW, CHILD.	OWT JITNEY	58
OF COURSE, I'M JUST A STRANGER	OWT STRANGER IN TWN	13
AND I'M TOO BLUE	OWT TOO BLUE	16
FOLKS, I'M TELLING YOU,	SP ADVICE	1
I'M LATE -	SP BLUE MONDAY	4
BUT I'M TALKING ABOUT	SP COMMENT ON CURB	6
I'M SORRY FOR THAT EVIL WISH	SP CROSS	7
I WONDER WHERE I'M GONNA DIE,	SP CROSS	11
I'M ALREADY TWO YEARS LATE.	SP DEFERRED	2
I'M GONNA BUY TWO NEW SUITS	SP DEFERRED	30
I DO NOT NEED MY FREEDOM WHEN I'M DEAD.	SP DEMOCRACY	13
HELP ME WHEN I'M DOWN AND OUT.	SP DOWN AND OUT	2
HELP ME WHEN I'M DOWN AND OUT,	SP DOWN AND OUT	4
I'M A PO' GAL	SP DOWN AND OUT	5
I'M HAPPY!	SP DREAM BOOGIE	16
I'M JUST A POOR LOST SHEEP.	SP EVENING SONG	8
BUT I'M GONNA KEEP ON AT IT	SP EVIL	3
I'M GONNA CHECK UP ON THIS	SP FREEDOM TRAIN	15
SOMETIMES WHEN I'M LONELY,	SP HOPE	1
AN' NOW I'M SETTIN' CLEAN AN' BRIGHT	SP JUDGMENT DAY	11
I'M GOIN' DOWN TO THE RIVER	SP LAMENT OVER LOV	7
AND I'M GOIN' THERE TO THINK ABOUT HIM.	SP LAMENT OVER LOV	12
I'M GOIN' UP IN A TOWER	SP LAMENT OVER LOV	19
SO SINCE I'M STILL HERE LIVIN',	SP LIFE IS FINE	23
HE SAYS, "MARY, I'M	SP LOVER'S RETURN	5
WHEN I'M YOU?	SP LOW TO HIGH	8
I'M MAD AND DISGUSTED	SP MADAM PHONE BIL	6
I'M JUST OLD DEATH	SP MADAM WRONG VIS	13
HE SAID, I'M GONNA PUT IT	SP MADAM CENSUS	13
I'M JUST THE AGENT.	SP MADAM RENT MAN	21
I'M GONNA PRAY	SP MADAM MINISTER	25
CAUSE I'M STILL HERE KICKIN'!	SP MADAM WRONG VIS	28
I'M MADAM TO YOU!	SP MADAM CENSUS	32
I'M SMART THAT WAY.	SP MADAM'S PAST HI	4
I'M GOING DOWN THE STREET.	SP MAMA AND DAUGHT	2
I'M LIKE THAT OLD MULE -	SP ME AND THE MULE	5
I'M GONNA BUY ME A ROSE BUD	SP MIDWINTER BLUES	19
SO WHEN I'M DEAD THEY WON'T NEED	SP MIDWINTER BLUES	23
INSTEAD OF THAT I'M CRYIN' -	SP MISS BLUES'ES	5
IN MY HEART I'M CRYING,	SP MISS BLUES'ES	13
I'M JUST MISS BLUES'ES CHILD!	SP MISS BLUES'ES	14
NOW, I'M ALMOST BACK IN THE BARREL AGAIN.	SP RELIEF	10
I'M GOING	SP REQUEST	3
NOW, THROUGH MY CHILDREN, I'M REACHING THE GOAL.	SP THE NEGRO MOTHE	20
AT TWENTY-TWO, MY AGE. BUT I GUESS I'M WHAT	SP THEME FOR ENG B	17
WHEN I'M PAYING YOUR BILLS	SP ULTIMATUM	2
I'M GONNA WALK TO THE GRAVEYARD	SP YOUNG GAL'S BLS	1
CAUSE WHEN I'M DEAD SOME	SP YOUNG GAL'S BLS	5
I'M GOIN' TO THE PO' HOUSE	SP YOUNG GAL'S BLS	7
WHEN I'M OLD AN' UGLY	SP YOUNG GAL'S BLS	11
I'M ALL ALONE IN THIS WORLD, SHE SAID.	SP 50 - 50	1
I'M ASKING, GRANDPA, ASKING.	AYM BIRD IN ORBIT	36
BUT I'M ASKING ANYHOW.	AYM BLUES IN STEREO	31
AND I'M THE ONLY COLORED.	AYM HORN OF PLENTY	35
I'M GONNA LEAVE YOU, MISTER BACKLASH,	PL BACKLASH BLUES	29
I'M GONNA WRITE ME SOME MUSIC ABOUT	PL DAYBREAK IN ALA	2
AND I'M GONNA PUT THE PURTIEST SONGS IN IT	PL DAYBREAK IN ALA	4
I'M GONNA PUT SOME TALL TALL TREES IN IT	PL DAYBREAK IN ALA	7
AND I'M GONNA PUT WHITE HANDS	PL DAYBREAK IN ALA	15
"I'M SO ASHAMED OF BEING WHITE."	PL DINNER GUEST ME	14
I'M GONNA PLANT MY FEET	PL DOWN WHERE I AM	13
I'M MAKIN' A ROAD	PL FLORIDA WORKERS	3
I'M MAKIN' A ROAD	PL FLORIDA WORKERS	9
I'M MAKIN' A ROAD!	PL FLORIDA WORKERS	20
I DO NOT NEED MY FREEDOM WHEN I'M DEAD.	PL FREEDOM	13
I'M STILL HERE!	PL STILL HERE	9

I'S 7

Line	Poem	No.
I'S ALWAYS BEEN A WORKIN' GIRL.	FC BLACK GAL	1
I'S SO WEARY	DK PO' BOY BLUES	23
I'S FRUSTRATED!	SP BAD MORNING	4
A-SHOUTIN', GOD, I'S COMIN' SOON.	SP JUDGMENT DAY	4
AND I KNOW'D I'S DYIN' FAST.	SP SYLVESTER'S BED	18
BUT I'S STILL SWEET PAPA 'VESTER,	SP SYLVESTER'S BED	21
I'S GWINE TO QUIT MA FROWNIN'	SP THE WEARY BLUES	21

I'SE 3

Line	Poem	No.
I'SE BEEN A-CLIMBIN' ON,	SP MOTHER TO SON	9
FOR I'SE STILL GOIN', HONEY,	SP MOTHER TO SON	18
I'SE STILL CLIMBIN',	SP MOTHER TO SON	19

I'VE 22

Line	Poem	No.
DE TROUBLE I'VE HAD." FLINCHING UNDER THE WHIP, THE SPIRITUAL	NM BLACK CLWN MOOD	5
I'VE GONE BACK TO THE WIND AND WAVE.	DK DEATH SEAMAN	8
I'VE DRUNK OF THE BITTER RIVER	JC THE BITTER RIVR	10
I'VE DRUNK AT THE BITTER RIVER	JC THE BITTER RIVR	73
I'VE DRUNK OF THE BITTER RIVER	JC THE BITTER RIVR	81
AND I'VE BEEN WAITING LONG	FW EARTH SONG	2
I'VE BEEN WAITING LONG	FW EARTH SONG	5
AND I'VE BEEN WAITING LONG	FW EARTH SONG	14
NOW AT LAST I'VE GOT A JOB	SP DEFERRED	25
I'VE SEEN THEM COME DARK	SP GOOD MORNING	17
BUT I'VE COME TO CALL	SP MADAM WRONG VIS	7
I'VE KNOWN RIVERS:	SP NEGRO SPEAKS OF	1
I'VE KNOWN RIVERS ANCIENT AS THE WORLD AND OLDER THAN THE	SP NEGRO SPEAKS OF	2

I'VE BEEN A SLAVE: . . . . SP NEGRO 4
I'VE BEEN A WORKER: . . . . SP NEGRO 7
WENT DOWN TO NEW ORLEANS, AND I'VE
SEEN ITS MUDDY . . . . SP NEGRO SPEAKS OF 9
I'VE BEEN A SINGER: . . . . SP NEGRO 10
I'VE KNOWN RIVERS: . . . . SP NEGRO SPEAKS OF 11
I'VE BEEN A VICTIM: . . . . SP NEGRO 14
I'VE WRITTEN, CALLED REPEATEDLY. . AYM ASK YOUR MAMA 7
I'VE HEARD . . . . PL SWEET WORDS RAC 11
I'VE NO WEAPON TO STRIKE BACK . . . PL WHO BUT TH LORD 20

I.W 1
I.W. HARPER . . . . SP SUMMER EVENING 10

JAB 1
HIT ME! JAB ME! . . . . PL THIRD DEGREE 1

JACK 3
JACK. . . . . SH LETTER 23
DO YOU BELIEVE THAT, JACK? . . . . SP ARGUMENT 4
JACK, IF YOU GOT TO BE A ROUNDER . SP STREET SONG 1

JACKET 1
WHOSE JACKET . . . . SP TRUMPET PLAYER 35

JACKIE 2
WILL TEAM UP WITH JACKIE MABLEY, . SP PROJECTION 19
JACKIE WILLIE CAMPANELLA $ $ $ $ $
$ $ $ $ . . . . AYM HORN OF PLENTY 17

JACKSON 3
MARY LULU JACKSON . . . . SP GRADUATION 3
MARY LULU JACKSON. . . . . SP GRADUATION 11
I TOLD HIM, JACKSON. . . . . SP MADAM MIGHT-HAV 21

JACK-LEG 1
A JACK-LEG PREACHER, A PH.D. . . . SP MYSTERY 24

JACK-O'-LANTERN 1
FACE LIKE A JACK-O'-LANTERN. . . . SP 125TH STREET 3

JACK-O'-LANTERNS 2
AMORPHOUS JACK-O'-LANTERNS CAPER . PL CULTURAL EXCHNG 5
FACES LIKE JACK-O'-LANTERNS . . . . PL THIRD DEGREE 5

JADE 1
PURE JADE. . . . . SH BLD PAWNBROKER 6

JAG 1
HIGH-STEPPIN JAG. . . . . SH DEATH IN HARLEM 15

JAGUAR 1
RIDING IN A JAGUAR, SANTA CLAUS, . AYM RIDE, RED, RIDE 30

JAIL 13
EIGHTEEN MONTHS IN JAIL! . . . . . FC BLD OF GIN MARY 17
WON'T BE SO BAD IN JAIL . . . . . . FC BLD OF GIN MARY 19
AN' PUT ME IN JAIL . . . . FC DEATH DO DIRTY 17
8 BLACK BOYS IN A SOUTHERN JAIL. . SL SCOTTSBORO 1
8 BLACK BOYS IN A SOUTHERN JAIL. . SL SCOTTSBORO 28
AND DROVE HER OFF TO JAIL . . . . . SH DEATH IN HARLEM 132
NEHRU SAID, BEFORE HE WENT TO JAIL. JC JIM CROW'S LAST 15
TILL WE'RE IN JAIL. . . . . FW CIRCLES 6
FOR THE JAIL IS ROUND - . . . . . . FW CIRCLES 8
THEY TAKEN MARGIE TO JAIL . . . . . OWT BLD MARGE POLIT 17
JUDGE GIVES NEGRO 90 DAYS IN COUNTY
JAIL . . . . SP BLD LANDLORD 33
DETAINED IN JAIL . . . . SP JAM SESSION 5
ITS JAIL. . . . . PL OPPRESSION 14

JAMAICA 1
UP FROM CUBA HAITI JAMAICA, ... SP GOOD MORNING 11

JAMES 3
CARELESS, AND HALF-DEFIANT ECHOES OF
THE "ST. JAMES INFIRMARY" AS THE NM BIG-TIMER MOOD 2
SING THE ST. JAMES INFIRMARY . . . OWT REQUEST REQUIEM 5
ST. JAMES PRESBYTERIAN . . . . . . SP PROJECTION 7

JAMESTOWN 2
THAT JAMESTOWN MADE . . . . PL AMER HEARTBREAK 5
JAMESTOWN, 1619 TO 1963: . . . . . PL DEATH YORKVILLE 11

JANE 1
OLD JUDGE SAYS, MARY JANE, ... FC BLD OF GIN MARY 6

JAPANESE 1
MARTHA'S GOT A JAPANESE! . . . . . OWT JITNEY 17

JASPER 3
WERE YOU MARRIED BY JOHN JASPER . . AYM BIRD IN ORBIT 37
JOHN JASPER! JESUS! DADDY GRACE! . AYM GOSPEL CHA-CHA 44
JOHN JASPER JESUS . . . . AYM GOSPEL CHA-CHA 57

JAUNDICED 1
JAUNDICED EYES SHOWING . . . . . . PL MISSISSIPPI 15

JAZZ 15
IS A JAZZ RHYTHM, ... WB LENOX AVE MIDNT 2
"JAZZ BOY BLUES." . . . . WB SUMMER NIGHT 6
JAZZ BAND! . . . . FC JAZZ BAND 2
JAZZ BAND! . . . . FC JAZZ BAND 10
PLAY IT, JAZZ BAND! . . . . FC JAZZ BAND 18
JAZZ BAND, JAZZ BAND! . . . . FC MINNIE SINGS 7
JAZZ BAND, JAZZ BAND! . . . . FC MINNIE SINGS 7
BARREL-HOUSE JAZZ, SHOWING-OFF,
STRUTTING ABOUT PROUDLY, BRAGGING
AND . . . . NM BIG-TIMER MOOD 4
STRENGTH HE DOESN'T REALLY FEEL.
GAY, LOUD, UNHAPPY JAZZ, BARING
HIS . . . . NM BIG-TIMER MOOD 9
HUMOROUS DEFIANCE. MELANCHOLY JAZZ.
THEN DEFIANCE AGAIN FOLLOWED BY
LOUD . . . . NM BLACK CLWN MOOD 2
WAS PLAYIN JAZZ FOR A MIDNIGHT
WORLD. . . . . SH DEATH IN HARLEM 11
JAZZ IT SLOW! . . . . SH DEATH IN HARLEM 28
THE BAND DOWN IN THE PIT BURSTS INTO
JAZZ. . . . . OWT LINCOLN THEATRE 6
JAZZ ON THE SOUTH SIDE - . . . . . OWT VISITORS 10
AND JAZZ AND BOOZE. . . . . SP BEALE STREET 4

JAZZERS 4
SIX LONG-HEADED JAZZERS PLAY. . . . WB JAZZONIA 4
SIX LONG-HEADED JAZZERS PLAY. . . . WB JAZZONIA 17
JAZZERS. . . . . FC LAUGHERS 12
JAZZERS DUKE AND DIZZY ERIC DOLPHY
$ $ $ . . . . AYM HORN OF PLENTY 8

JAZZY 1
MIDNIGHT DANCER OF THE JAZZY HOUR? WB NUDE YOUNG DANC 2

JAZZ-BAND 6
DOES A JAZZ-BAND EVER SOB? . . . . WB CABARET 1
ONE SAID SHE HEARD THE JAZZ-BAND SOB WB CABARET 5
JAZZ-BAND, JAZZ-BAND, - . . . . . . WB HARLEM NIGHT CL 2
JAZZ-BAND, JAZZ-BAND, - . . . . . . WB HARLEM NIGHT CL 2
JAZZ-BAND, JAZZ-BAND, - . . . . . . WB HARLEM NIGHT CL 12
JAZZ-BAND, JAZZ-BAND, - . . . . . . WB HARLEM NIGHT CL 12

JAZZ-BAND'S 1
THEY SAY A JAZZ-BAND'S GAY. . . . . WB CABARET 2

JAZZ-BOYS 2
JAZZ-BOYS, JAZZ-BOYS, - . . . . . . WB HARLEM NIGHT CL 18
JAZZ-BOYS, JAZZ-BOYS, - . . . . . . WB HARLEM NIGHT CL 18

JAZZ-TUNED 1
OF THE JAZZ-TUNED NIGHT, ... SP MIDNIGHT DANCER 2

JEANNE 1
JEANNE D' ARC. . . . . SL SCOTTSBORO 17

JEFFERSON 1
HIS NAME WAS JEFFERSON. THERE WERE
SLAVES THEN, ... SP FREEDOM'S PLOW 36

JELLY 1
AND SHE SAT ON HER CHAIR LIKE A
SWEET JELLY ROLL. . . . . SH DEATH IN HARLEM 82

JERDEN 1
I SEED THE RIVER JERDEN . . . . . . SP SYLVESTER'S BED 19

JERICHO 1
GURGLING JERICHO. . . . . SP SUMMER EVENING 17

JERSEY 2
IN THE DENNISON HOTEL IN JERSEY. . SP ELEVATOR BOY 3
NEW JERSEY HIGH SCHOOL! . . . . . . AYM BIRD IN ORBIT 78

JEST 1
YOU JEST A LITTLE BIT O' WOMAN BUT
YOU . . . . SP MORNING AFTER 17

JESTER 1
I AM THE BLACK JESTER. . . . . . . WB THE JESTER 15

JESUIT 1
WHO IS TO JESUIT . . . . AYM SHADES OF PIG 26

JESUS 25
HIGH-IN-HEABEN JESUS, ... FC GAL'S CRY DYING 17
GONNA PRAY TO MA JESUS, ... FC MOAN 7
MA JESUS, ... FC MOAN 17
JESUS, TAKE ME . . . . SH DEATH IN HARLEM 129
TO BE SOUVENIRS OF JESUS, ... LHR PASTORAL 8
AT THE FEET O' JESUS, ... SP FEET O' JESUS 1
AT THE FEET O' JESUS . . . . SP FEET O' JESUS 5
MAMA SAYS, PRAISE JESUS! . . . . . SP GRADUATION 20
MAMA SAYS, PRAISE JESUS! . . . . . SP GRADUATION 25
PRAISE JESUS! . . . . SP GRADUATION 28
O JESUS! . . . . SP JUDGMENT DAY 5
KIND JESUS! . . . . SP JUDGMENT DAY 10
JESUS, LOVER OF MY SOUL! . . . . . SP MYSTERY 5
DO, JESUS! . . . . SP PROJECTION 11

LITTLE JESUS! . . . SP SHOUT 2
I ASKED THE WHITE LORD JESUS . . . SP SONG DARK GIRL 7
SING, C LORD JESUS! . . . SP SPIRITUALS 4
JESUS! . . . SP WHEN SUE WEARS 5
BLCW TRUMPETS, JESUS! . . . SP WHEN SUE WEARS 9
JESUS! . . . SP WHEN SUE WEARS 13
JOHN JASPER! JESUS! DADDY GRACE! . AYM GOSPEL CHA-CHA 44
JOHN JASPER JESUS . . . AYM GOSPEL CHA-CHA 57
DO, JESUS! . . . AYM SHADES OF PIG 43
IT WOULD BE TOO BAD IF JESUS . . . PL BIBLE BELT 1
SEND FOR JESUS TO PREACH THE SERMON
ON THE . . . PL FINAL CALL 10

JET 3
JET AND COCONUT EYES, . . . SP GRADUATION 2
LIKE JET - . . . SP TRUMPET PLAYER 15
WERE JET A CROWN. . . . SP TRUMPET PLAYER 16

JEW 6
AN' SELL 'EM TO DE JEW. . . . FC HARD LUCK 6
JEW TAKES YO' FINE CLOTHES, . . . FC HARD LUCK 7
JEW TAKES YO' FINE CLOTHES, . . . FC HARD LUCK 9
IS THE JEW . . . PL LENOX AVE. BAR 3
ONE JEW, . . . PL LENOX AVE. BAR 5
BORN JEW, . . . PL UN-AMERICAN 11

JEWEL 2
THAT I WERE A JEWEL, . . . WB SONGS DARK VIRG 2
A SHATTERED JEWEL, . . . WB SONGS DARK VIRG 3

JEWELS 2
YET AN ALTAR OF JEWELS, . . . WB POEM 17
AN ALTAR OF SHIMMERING JEWELS, . . WB POEM 18

JEWISH 1
BECOME JEWISH . . . AYM SHADES OF PIG 18

JEWS 5
THE JEWS: . . . SP LIKEWISE 1
JEWS SELL ME THINGS. . . . SP LIKEWISE 8
SOME FOLKS BLAME HIGH PRICES ON THE
JEWS. . . . SP LIKEWISE 12
(SOME FOLKS BLAME TOO MUCH ON JEWS.) SP LIKEWISE 13
JEWS MUST HAVE HEARD . . . SP LIKEWISE 25

JIGABOO 1
A DUMB LITTLE JIGABOO FROM . . . SH DEATH IN HARLEM 16

JIM 25
WE COULDN'T EAT IN RESTAURANTS; HAD
JIM CROW CARS; . . . NM COLORED SL POEM 24
IN A JIM CROW CAR. . . . JC BLACK MAN SPEAK 14
JIM CROW ARMY, . . . JC BLACK MAN SPEAK 17
IS JIM CROW FREEDOM THE BEST . . . JC BLACK MAN SPEAK 19
OLD JIM CROW'S SORROW? . . . JC BLACK MAN SPEAK 28
PROTECTING JIM CROW. . . . JC HOW ABOUT DIXIE 20
THERE WAS AN OLD CROW BY THE NAME OF
JIM. . . . JC JIM CROW'S LAST 1
TO SEE JIM CROW GET OUT OF HAND. . JC JIM CROW'S LAST 4
PEARL HARBOR PUT JIM CROW ON THE
RUN. . . . JC JIM CROW'S LAST 8
HAVE MADE UP THEIR MINDS JIM CROW IS
THROUGH. . . . JC JIM CROW'S LAST 14
CATCH THAT JIM CROW BIRD, PULL THE
FEATHERS OUT HIS TAIL! . . . JC JIM CROW'S LAST 16
TO JIM CROW MY PEOPLE IS A PITY. . JC JIM CROW'S LAST 20
YOU AIN'T TELLING NOTHING BUT YOUR
JIM CROW LIES - . . . JC JIM CROW'S LAST 22
JIM CROW STARTED HIS LAST STAND. . JC JIM CROW'S LAST 29
BUT WHEN IT IS, JIM CROW'LL BE DONE. JC JIM CROW'S LAST 31
THE SOLDIER THROWN FROM A JIM CROW
BUS BEHIND STEEL BARS, . . . JC THE BITTER RIVR 33
GOT A JIM CROW CAR SET ASIDE FOR ME. SP FREEDOM TRAIN 10
I HOPE THERE AIN'T NO JIM CROW ON
THE FREEDOM TRAIN, . . . SP FREEDOM TRAIN 11
WHY THERE'S JIM CROW STATIONS FOR
THE FREEDOM TRAIN? . . . SP FREEDOM TRAIN 32
WHERE THERE NEVER WAS NO JIM CROW
SIGNS NOWHERE, . . . SP FREEDOM TRAIN 54
WITH JIM CROW LAWS, . . . SP ONE-WAY TICKET 17
AND RIDE THE JIM CROW CAR UNTIL IT
SCREAMS . . . PL JIM CROW CAR 3
WHERE IS THE JIM CROW SECTION . . . PL MERRY-GO-ROUND 3
THERE'S A JIM CROW CAR. . . . PL MERRY-GO-ROUND 10
AT JIM CROW LAWS . . . PL NORTHERN LIBERL 19

JIMMY 2
HER GRANDSON'S NAME WAS JIMMY. HE
DIED AT ANZIO. . . . SP FREEDOM TRAIN 43
JIMMY WANTS TO KNOW ABOUT THE . . . SP FREEDOM TRAIN 47

JIM'S 1
BUT SOMETHING HAPPENED, JIM'S
FEATHERS FELL. . . . JC JIM CROW'S LAST 5

JINGO 1
TO THE JINGO CRY . . . PL LAST PRINCE 10

JITNEYS 1
JITNEYS GO BY . . . SP SUMMER EVENING 14

JITTERBUGGING 2
JITTERBUGGING BACK, . . . SH BLD THE SINNER 16
AND STARTS JITTERBUGGING . . . SP PROJECTION 3

JITTERED 1
JITTERED, . . . SP DANCER 13

JIVE 4
AND JIVE SOME OLD BROAD I MIGHT
MEET. . . . SH BED TIME 4
SEE WHAT THIS WEEK'S JIVE IS ALL
ABOUT: . . . OWT JITNEY 25
NO JIVE. . . . PL DEATH YORKVILLE 20
AND DIG ALL JIVE - . . . PL MOTTO 2

JOAN 1
THAT GROWS IN NO-MAN'S LAND, JOAN OF
ARC, AND VARIOUS OTHER WAR-TIME NM COLORED SL MOOD 5

JOB 22
NO LAND, NO HOUSE, NO JOB, . . . NM BLACK CLWN POEM 34
LAST JOB I HAD, WENT TO WORK AT FIVE
IN DE MORNIN', OR LITTLE MO' . . NM BROKE 12
TOGETHER, RECKON I'LL TRY . . . SHO,
I WANTS DE JOB! YES, SIR! . . . NM BROKE 30
YOU CAN TAKE THAT JOB AND GO TO - I
HOPE YOU CHOKE, . . . NM BROKE 37
YOU GOT A GOOD JOB? YES! WELL, I SHO
AM GLAD TO SEE YOU, DEAR! . . . NM BROKE 69
COULD HARDLY FIND A JOB THAT OFFERED
DECENT PAY. . . . NM COLORED SL POEM 21
I PULLED THAT JOB . . . SH BLD THE KILLER 13
BEEN LOOKIN' FOR A JOB . . . SH OUT OF WORK 5
I COULDN'T FIND NO JOB . . . SH OUT OF WORK 7
COULDN'T FIND NO JOB . . . SH OUT OF WORK 9
NOW AT LAST I'VE GOT A JOB . . . SP DEFERRED 25
I GOT A JOB NOW . . . SP ELEVATOR BOY 1
JOB AIN'T NO GOOD THOUGH. . . . SP ELEVATOR BOY 4
MAYBE A GOOD JOB SOMETIMES: . . . SP ELEVATOR BOY 10
OF A JOB IN A FINE OFFICE . . . SP GRADUATION 16
WHEN I TRY TO FIND A JOB . . . PL BACKLASH BLUES 13
TRY TO FIND MYSELF A JOB . . . PL BACKLASH BLUES 15
WE REMEMBER THE JOB WE NEVER HAD, PL HARLEM 12
THAN IT IS TO GET A JOB." . . . PL JUNIOR ADDICT 29
THAN TO GET A JOB - . . . PL JUNIOR ADDICT 31
DAYTIME OR NIGHTIME JOB. . . . PL JUNIOR ADDICT 32
PRE-LIFETIME JOB. . . . PL JUNIOR ADDICT 34

JOBLESS 1
WHILE JOBLESS I STARVE DEAD? . . . PL GO SLOW 14

JOBS 5
UP AND DOWN, AND THEY JUST AIN'T NO
JOBS IN THIS MAN'S TOWN. . . . NM BROKE 3
TRIED TO FIND ONE O' THEM LITTLE
ELEVATOR AND SWITCHBOARD JOBS
THEY USED . . . NM BROKE 41
JOSTLE OF MEN WITH GOOD JOBS . . . OWT MAN INTO MEN 6
GOOD JOBS . . . OWT MAN INTO MEN 13
JOBS ARE JUST CHANCES . . . SP ELEVATOR BOY 6

JOCKO 1
JOCKO BODDIDLY LIL GREENWOOD . . . AYM BIRD IN ORBIT 4

JOE 11
OR IF I WASN'T SO DROWSY I'D LOOK UP
JOE . . . SH BED TIME 5
JOE LOUIS SAID, WE GONNA WIN THIS
WAR . . . JC JIM CROW'S LAST 25
THEY WORSHIPPED JOE. . . . SP JOE LOUIS 1
JOE HAS SENSE ENOUGH TO KNOW . . . SP JOE LOUIS 5
FOR JOE. . . . SP JOE LOUIS 12
JOE . . . SP LETTER 12
JOE LOUIS WORE, . . . SP TO BE SOMEBODY 16
WAS JOE. . . . SP WEST TEXAS 5
JOE SAID I WONDER HOW IT WOULD FEEL SP WEST TEXAS 7
IN ESCROW TO JOE GLASSER. . . . AYM HORN OF PLENTY 82
LISTEN HERE, JOE, . . . PL WITHOUT BENEFIT 1

JOES 1
UNFORGOTTEN JOES AND SUGAR RAYS $ $
$ $ . . . AYM HORN OF PLENTY 19

JOE'S 1
THE DREAM IS A COCKTAIL AT SLOPPY
JOE'S - . . . SP HAVANA DREAMS 1

JOHANNESBURG 1
JOHANNESBURG, WATTS, . . . PL QUESTION ANSWER 3

JOHN 19
SAID SIMPLE JOHN, . . . WB PIERROT 2
SAID SIMPLE JOHN, . . . WB PIERROT 5
SAID SIMPLE JOHN, . . . WB PIERROT 12

SAID SIMPLE JOHN.	WB PIERROT	15
SAID SIMPLE JOHN.	WB PIERROT	22
SAID SIMPLE JOHN.	WB PIERROT	25
JOHN BROWN.	SL SCOTTSBORO	12
WITH JOHN BROWN AT HARPER'S FERRY. NEGROES DIED.	SP FREEDOM'S PLOW	116
JOHN BROWN WAS HUNG.	SP FREEDOM'S PLOW	117
JOHN HENRY WITH HIS HAMMER	SP LOVE	5
NOTHING AT ALL NAMED AFTER JOHN BROWN.	SP SHAME ON YOU	7
WERE YOU MARRIED BY JOHN JASPER	AYM BIRD IN ORBIT	37
AND JOHN BROWN'S WHITE AND LONGER	AYM BIRD IN ORBIT	45
JOHN JASPER! JESUS! DADDY GRACE!	AYM GOSPEL CHA-CHA	44
JOHN JASPER JESUS	AYM GOSPEL CHA-CHA	57
FOR OLD JOHN BROWN WHO KNEW SLAVERY COULDN'T	PL FINAL CALL	22
JOHN BROWN.	PL OCTOBER 16 RAID	3
JOHN BROWN	PL OCTOBER 16 RAID	4
JOHN BROWN.	PL OCTOBER 16 RAID	29

JOHNSON 10

I DRESSED UP ALBERT JOHNSON.	FC BLACK GAL	9
ARABELLA JOHNSON AND THE TEXAS KID	SH DEATH IN HARLEM	1
AND ARABELLA JOHNSON HAD HER	SH DEATH IN HARLEM	8
I SAID. JOHNSON.	SP MADAM CENSUS	5
HE SAID. YOU'RE JOHNSON -	SP MADAM WRONG VIS	17
THAT ALBERTA K. JOHNSON	SP MADAM PHONE BIL	29
MY NAME IS JOHNSON -	SP MADAM'S PAST HI	1
MADAM JOHNSON.	SP MADAM'S CALLING	9
ALBERTA K. JOHNSON -	SP MADAM'S CALLING	19
ALBERTA K. JOHNSON -	SP MADAM'S PAST HI	25

JOIN 2

TURN FROM THE BAR AND JOIN YOU IN YOUR SONG.	OWT JUICE JOINT	22
ROOM IN HELL TO JOIN ME	LHR TESTAMENT	3

JOINED 2

WHO JOINED UP TO FIGHT FOR THE U.S.A.	NM COLORED SL POEM	3
BUT WE HAVE JOINED HANDS -	JC TO CAPTAIN MULZ	36

JOINT 1

DANCE IN THIS JUICE JOINT	OWT JUICE JOINT	47

JOINTS 4

LIGHTS IN THE FISH JOINTS.	SP RAILROAD AVENUE	3
SHAKING THE LIGHTS IN THE FISH JOINTS.	SP RAILROAD AVENUE	26
SEA FOOD JOINTS	SP SEASHORE THROUG	11
FROM JUKEBOX JOINTS IS LAID	AYM JAZZTET MUTED	11

JOKE 1

YOU ALL OUT THERE LAUGHIN'. BUT THAT AIN'T NO JOKE -	NM BROKE	10

JOKER 1

SHE HAD ANOTHER JOKER	SH ANNOUNCEMENT	11

JOMO 1

JOMO IN KENYATTA. . . . STARS.	AYM BIRD IN ORBIT	60

JONES 6

LEWIS JONES BEHIND STEEL BARS.	JC THE BITTER RIVR	30
YOU PUT ME IN MACBETH AND CARMEN JONES	SP NOTE COMM THEAT	9
PO' BUDDY JONES.	SP STONY LONESOME	14
WHEN SUSANNA JONES WEARS RED	SP WHEN SUE WEARS	1
WHEN SUSANNA JONES WEARS RED	SP WHEN SUE WEARS	6
AND THE BEAUTY OF SUSANNA JONES IN RED	SP WHEN SUE WEARS	10

JOSEPHINE 1

BELAFONTE FRISCO JOSEPHINE	AYM BIRD IN ORBIT	5

JOSTLE 6

JOSTLE OF FUR COATS	OWT MAN INTO MEN	2
JOSTLE OF DIRTY COATS	OWT MAN INTO MEN	3
JOSTLE OF WOMEN WHO SHOP	OWT MAN INTO MEN	4
JOSTLE OF WOMEN WHO WORK	OWT MAN INTO MEN	5
JOSTLE OF MEN WITH GOOD JOBS	OWT MAN INTO MEN	6
JOSTLE OF MEN IN THE DITCHES.	OWT MAN INTO MEN	7

JOY 27

JOY TODAY!	WB HARLEM NIGHT CL	21
AH. WE SHOULD HAVE A LAND OF JOY.	WB OUR LAND	13
OF LOVE AND JOY AND WINE AND SONG.	WB OUR LAND	14
AND NOT THIS LAND WHERE JOY IS WRONG.	WB OUR LAND	15
AND THE MOON WAS JOY.	WB TO MIDNIGHT NAN	16
JOY. A BURST OF MUSIC. STRUTTING AND DANCING. THEN SUDDEN SADNESS AGAIN.	NM BLACK CLWN MOOD	3
ONLY IN JOY	NM BLACK CLWN POEM	14
AND JOY. AND LAUGHTER.	ANS KIDS WHO DIE	47
SPREAD SOME JOY!	SH DEATH IN HARLEM	86
A SONG OF JOY.	OWT JUICE JOINT	32
THERE WAS FASTING IN THE STREETS AND JOY.	LHR BLD MARY'S SON	3
SENT TO BRING THE WHOLE WORLD JOY.	LHR BLD MARY'S SON	10
ROCKETS OF JOY	SP GYPSY MELODIES	4
IN JOY BENEATH THE SKY	SP IN TIME SILVER	17
TEARS OF JOY	SP INTERNE AT PROV	31
I WENT TO LOOK FOR JOY.	SP JOY	1
SLIM. DANCING JOY.	SP JOY	2
GAY. LAUGHING JOY.	SP JOY	3
BRIGHT-EYED JOY -	SP JOY	4
AS KEEPS THIS YOUNG NYMPH. JOY!	SP JOY	9
FROM THE TABLES OF JOY.	SP LUCK	2
THE GRAPES OF JOY	SP MIDNIGHT DANCER	8
A NIGGER JOY.	SP MULATTO	24
A NIGGER JOY.	SP MULATTO	42
NOR FUEL FOR THE CLEAN FLAME OF JOY	SP RUBY BROWN	6
AND AIN'T THERE ANY JOY IN THIS TOWN?	SP RUBY BROWN	15
FOR JOY.	SP YOUNG SAILOR	15

JOYS 2

GRIN JUNGLE JOYS.	WB HARLEM NIGHT CL	9
LET YOUR SONGS HOLD ALL THE SUNNY JOYS	OWT JUICE JOINT	19

JUDGE 15

JUDGE WAS SETTIN' THERE.	FC BLD OF GIN MARY	2
JUDGE PIERCE HE SAYS. MARY.	FC BLD OF GIN MARY	5
OLD JUDGE SAYS. MARY JANE.	FC BLD OF GIN MARY	6
JUDGE. WON'T LET ME BE.	FC BLD OF GIN MARY	12
OLD JUDGE SAYS YOU'S A DRUNKARD.	FC BLD OF GIN MARY	13
O. PLEASE SIR. JUDGE. HAVE MERCY!	FC BLD OF GIN MARY	21
OLD HARD-FACED JUDGE SAYS EIGHTEEN MONTHS	FC BLD OF GIN MARY	23
I WAS LOOKIN' FOR A SANDWICH. JUDGE.	SH BRIEF ENCOUNTER	1
I WAS WALKIN' DOWN DE STREET. JUDGE.	SH BRIEF ENCOUNTER	3
JUDGE. SHE IS DE WOMAN	SH BRIEF ENCOUNTER	7
SHE IS DE WOMAN. JUDGE.	SH BRIEF ENCOUNTER	9
IF THERE'S ANYBODY ON THIS EARTH. JUDGE.	SH BRIEF ENCOUNTER	11
FACT THAT I HURT HER. JUDGE.	SH BRIEF ENCOUNTER	13
SHE WAS DE WRONGEST THING. JUDGE.	SH BRIEF ENCOUNTER	17
JUDGE GIVES NEGRO 90 DAYS IN COUNTY JAIL	SP BLD LANDLORD	33

JUICE 2

DANCE IN THIS JUICE JOINT	OWT JUICE JOINT	47
AND DRIPPED THEIR JUICE	SP MIDNIGHT DANCER	9

JUICY 1

JUICY BODIES	SP MULATTO	12

JUKE 1

AND THE SONGS ON THE JUKE BOX	OWT RAID	7

JUKEBOX 3

KING COLE JUKEBOX PAYOLA	AYM ASK YOUR MAMA	42
SEEKING SUBURB WITH NO JUKEBOX	AYM HORN OF PLENTY	69
FROM JUKEBOX JOINTS IS LAID	AYM JAZZTET MUTED	11

JUKEBOXES 1

SUCKED IN BY FAT JUKEBOXES	AYM ODE TO DINAH	52

JULEP 1

HAND ME MY MINT JULEP. MAMMY.	PL CULTURAL EXCHNG	59

JULIE 4

LITTLE JULIE	SP DELINQUENT	1
LITTLE JULIE	SP DELINQUENT	5
LITTLE JULIE	SP DELINQUENT	9
LITTLE JULIE	SP DELINQUENT	13

JUMP 6

BUT JUMP OVERBOARD AN' DROWN.	FC A RUINED GAL	14
'LIEVE I'LL JUMP IN DE RIVER	FC SUICIDE	13
'LIEVE I'LL JUMP IN DE RIVER	FC SUICIDE	15
YOU JUMP OUT OF BED.	OWT HONEY BABE	11
AND THOUGHT I WOULD JUMP DOWN.	SP LIFE IS FINE	15
HIS WORDS JUMP DOWN	PL CORNER MEETING	6

JUMPED 2

SO I JUMPED IN AND SANK.	SP LIFE IS FINE	4
I MIGHT'VE JUMPED AND DIED.	SP LIFE IS FINE	19

JUMPS 1

SCREAM JUMPS OUT	PL THIRD DEGREE	8

JUNE 3

AND THE BREATH OF A ROSE IN JUNE.	WB PIERROT	10
WITH THE BURGHER'S WIFE ONE JUNE.	WB PIERROT	30
IN JUNE.	OK AFTR MNY SPRNGS	2

JUNE-TIME 2

IN THE MIDDLE OF JUNE-TIME	SH YOUNG NEGRO GRL	2
IN THE MIDDLE OF JUNE-TIME	SH YOUNG NEGRO GRL	7

JUNGLE 6

GRIN JUNGLE JOYS.	WB HARLEM NIGHT CL	9

WHAT JUNGLE TREE HAVE YOU SLEPT UNDER. . . . . WB NUDE YOUNG DANC 1
WHAT JUNGLE TREE HAVE YOU SLEPT UNDER. . . . . WB NUDE YOUNG DANC 5
JUNGLE NIGHT. . . . . WB TO MIDNIGHT NAN 6
JUNGLE LOVER. . . . . WB TO MIDNIGHT NAN 13
THROUGH THE JUNGLE OF WHITE DANGER AYM ODE TO DINAH 31

JUNGLES 3

ALL THE TOM-TOMS OF THE JUNGLES BEAT IN MY BLOOD. . . . . WB FOR PORTRAIT OF 1
AND ALL THE WILD HOT MOONS OF THE JUNGLES SHINE IN MY SOUL. . . . WB FOR PORTRAIT OF 2
THEY TOOK ME AWAY FROM THE JUNGLES. WB LAMENT DARK PEO 6

JUNGLE-LILY 1

MERCEDES IS A JUNGLE-LILY IN A DEATH HOUSE. . . . . WB TO DARK MERCEDE 1

JUST 98

JUST A BIT TOO BOLD? . . . . WB JAZZONIA 11
I'M JUST GONNA KILL HER . . . . . . FC EVIL WOMAN 3
NOBODY CARES JUST WHY. . . . . . . FC MOAN 11
JUST GIMME SOME SASS. . . . . NM BIG-TIMER POEM 28
I'M JUST A GOOD-TIMER . . . . NM BIG-TIMER POEM 43
I'M JUST A BIG-TIMER. . . . . NM BIG-TIMER POEM 75
JUST A BLACK CLOWN! . . . . NM BLACK CLWN POEM 54
UP AND DOWN, AND THEY JUST AIN'T NO JOBS IN THIS MAN'S TOWN. . . . . NM BROKE 3
JUST ONLY PROVIDIN' DE BOSS MAN IS NICE!" . . . . NM BROKE 9
FOLKS SHO IS GETTIN' HARD ON YOU - JUST 'CAUSE YOU BROKE. . . . . . NM BROKE 15
BUT THEY GIVIN' 'EM TO SCHOOL BOYS NOW AND PAYIN' JUST ABOUT HALF. NM BROKE 43
AND DE MAN COME TELLIN' ME THEY AIN'T HIRIN' NO MO' COLORED - JUST WHITE. . . . . NM BROKE 45
'CAUSE I'M JUST DYIN' TO TAKE ON THAT THERE MARRIAGE YOKE. . . . NM BROKE 77
WE WERE JUST TWO COLORED BOYS, BROWN AND BLACK. . . . . NM COLORED SL POEM 2
SO NOW I KNOW WE BLACKS ARE JUST LIKE ANY OTHER - . . . . NM COLORED SL POEM 35
AND I'M STILL JUST A "NIGGER" IN AMERICA TONIGHT. . . . . NM COLORED SL POEM 47
JUST LIKE NEW. . . . . DK DRESSED UP 2
JUST BECAUSE I LOVES YOU - . . . . DK REASONS WHY 1
JUST BECAUSE I LOVES YOU . . . . . DK REASONS WHY 5
SCOTTSBORO'S JUST A LITTLE PLACE: SL TOWN OF SCOTTSB 1
THAT I MIGHT, JUST MAYBE, ... ANS PARK BENCH 9
I JUST WANT TO CRY: . . . . ANS SISTER JOHNSON 3
JUST AS THE SKY IN THE . . . . . . SH DEATH IN HARLEM 133
(IT WAS JUST AS IF SOMEBODY . . . . SH DEATH IN HARLEM 97
JUST TO DRIVE MY BLUES AWAY - . . . SH EVENIN' BLUES 14
JUST LOOK AT ME AND SEE! . . . . . SH EVENIN' BLUES 24
JUST PLAY 'EM, PERFESSER, ... SH HEY-HEY BLUES 11
SO JUST BY IF-ING . . . . SH IF-ING 15
WHAT DO YOU MEAN, JUST A LITTLE SPAT? . . . . SH LETTER 4
BUT YOU JUST AS WELL BE HERE WHERE YOU DUE TO LIVE. . . . . SH LETTER 11
SO LET'S JUST FORGET WHAT THIS FUSS WAS ABOUT. . . . . SH LETTER 15
JUST ONE THING AFTER 'NOTHER . . . SH LOVE AGAIN BLUS 5
THIS WHOLE PAY CHECK'S JUST FOR ME. SH PAY DAY 1
WOMEN'S ABOMINATIONS! JUST LIKE A CURSE! . . . . SH PAY DAY 19
JUST SO IT GOES AWAY FROM HERE. . . SH SIX-BITS BLUES 6
IF I JUST HAD A OWL HEAD, OLD OWL HEAD WOULD DO. . . . . SH TWILIGHT REVERI 11
THAT YOU'RE OUR ALLY JUST FOR TODAY. JC GOOD MORN STLIN 24
THAN JUST TODAY. . . . . JC GOOD MORN STLIN 48
FREEDOM'S NOT JUST . . . . JC HOW ABOUT DIXIE 21
OR JUST ANOTHER . . . . FW SAILING DATE 16
BUT SHE AIN'T JUST NOBODY . . . . . OWT BLD MARGE POLIT 23
OF COURSE, I'M JUST A STRANGER . . OWT STRANGER IN TWN 13
JUST AS THOUGH IT WAS NO SIN - . . . SP BLD OF THE GIRL 14
BUT WAS JUST AS IF THEY'D LEFT. . . SP CROSSING 22
WITH NO SENSE, JUST WONDERFUL FEET, SP DANCER 21
FOLKS SAY IT'S NOT JUST . . . . . . SP DELINQUENT 7
JUST AS YOU. . . . . SP DEMOCRACY 21
JOBS ARE JUST CHANCES . . . . SP ELEVATOR BOY 6
I'M JUST A POOR LOST SHEEP. . . . . SP EVENING SONG 8
THAT SONG MEANT JUST WHAT IT SAID: HOLD ON! . . . . SP FREEDOM'S PLOW 127
IS IT FOR REAL - OR JUST A SHOW AGAIN? . . . . SP FREEDOM TRAIN 46
JUST STOPPIN' IN THE FIELDS IN THE BROAD DAYLIGHT, ... SP FREEDOM TRAIN 52
MAYBE IT JUST SAGS . . . . SP HARLEM 9
JUST AS IF YOU WERE DOWN SOUTH. . . SP HIGH TO LOW 16
JUST MAN WOMAN TIRED SAYS: . . . . SP IN EXPLANATION 55
HOME'S JUST AROUND . . . . SP KID IN THE PARK 9
KID SLEEPY, JUST . . . . SP KID SLEEPY 19
RATHER JUST . . . . SP KID SLEEPY 21
JUST MAYBE SHRUG THEIR SHOULDERS. SP LIKEWISE 15
JUST A LITTLE OLD LETTER. . . . . . SP LITTLE OLD LETT 5
JUST A PENCIL AND PAPER. . . . . . SP LITTLE OLD LETT 13
HIS EYES DIDN'T LOOK JUST RIGHT. . SP LOVER'S RETURN 4
JUST LIKE A PAIR O' SHOES - . . . . SP LOVER'S RETURN 10
MADAM, IT'S JUST GOOD LUCK . . . . SP MADAM FORT TELL 3
ON YOU JUST THE SAME. . . . . SP MADAM WRONG VIS 8
JUST MIGHT BE SO. . . . . SP MADAM MIGHT-HAV 8
I'M JUST OLD DEATH . . . . SP MADAM WRONG VIS 13
JUST THAT WAY! . . . . SP MADAM CENSUS 20
I'M JUST THE AGENT. . . . . SP MADAM RENT MAN 21
JUST TO SAY HE LOVES ME! . . . . . SP MADAM PHONE BIL 23
JUST A K . . . . SP MADAM CENSUS 23
JUST LIKE I AM! . . . . SP MADAM CENSUS 28
JUST LIKE THE SONG. . . . . SP MADAM'S PAST HI 20
I COULD JUST AS WELL'VE . . . . . . SP MIDNIGHT RAFFLE 13
I'M JUST MISS BLUES'ES CHILD! . . . SP MISS BLUES'ES 14
HE JUST . . . . SP NEIGHBOR 22
SHINED JUST LIKE A TEAR - . . . . . SP NIGHT FUNERAL 37
I JUST DRAWED MY MONEY TONIGHT . . SP PREFERENCE 9
JUST A HERD OF NEGROES . . . . . . SP SHARE-CROPPERS 1
THEY'VE JUST HUNG A BLACK MAN . . . SP SILHOUETTE 3
JUST AIN'T GOT NO HEART. . . . . . SP SOUTHERN MAMMY 22
JUST AIN'T GOT NO HEART. . . . . . SP SOUTHERN MAMMY 24
TAKE JUST . . . . SP STARS 10
JUST DON'T LET MAMA CATCH YOU . . . SP STREET SONG 3
IF I JUST HAD A PIANO, ... SP TESTIMONIAL 1
IF I JUST HAD A ORGAN, ... SP TESTIMONIAL 2
IF I JUST HAD A DRUM, ... SP TESTIMONIAL 3
JUST DON'T LET YOUR DOG CURB YOU! SP WARNING AUGMENT 14
BUT JUST A PUNCTUATION. . . . . . . AYM ODE TO DINAH 124
JUST WAIT. . . . . AYM ODE TO DINAH 81
JUST WHO DO YOU THINK I AM? . . . . PL BACKLASH BLUES 2
MAYBE IT JUST SAGS . . . . PL DREAM DEFERRED 9
JUST AS YOU. . . . . PL FREEDOM 21
IS JUST FROSTING . . . . PL FROSTING 2
IF YOU'D JUST TURN ME LOOSE." . . . PL KU KLUX 8
"BUT JUST WAIT, CHILE . . . " . . . PL OFFICE BUILDING 11
I'D JUST AS LEAVE . . . . PL SWEET WORDS RAC 13
JUST GO AHEAD AND DIE. . . . . . . PL WITHOUT BENEFIT 13

JUSTICE 3

"LIBERTY AND JUSTICE - . . . . . . SP CHILDREN'S RYME 23
LIBERTY AND JUSTICE - . . . . PL CHILDREN'S RYME 14
THAT JUSTICE IS A BLIND GODDESS . . PL JUSTICE 1

JUVENILE 1

JUVENILE COURT . . . . SP MADAM CHARTY CH 22

J'ACCUSE 1

SEND FOR DREYFUS TO CRY, "J'ACCUSE!" PL FINAL CALL 12

K 13

ALBERTA K. . . . . SP MADAM CENSUS 6
THE K THAT WAY. . . . . SP MADAM CENSUS 8
DOES K STAND FOR? . . . . SP MADAM CENSUS 10
I SAID, K - . . . . SP MADAM CENSUS 11
K - A - Y. . . . . SP MADAM CENSUS 14
MADAM ALBERTA K.? . . . . SP MADAM WRONG VIS 18
ALBERTA K. . . . . SP MADAM CENSUS 18
JUST A K . . . . SP MADAM CENSUS 23
THAT ALBERTA K. JOHNSON . . . . . . SP MADAM PHONE BIL 29
MADAM ALBERTA K. . . . . SP MADAM'S PAST HI 2
ALBERTA K. . . . . SP MADAM'S CALLING 10
ALBERTA K. JOHNSON - . . . . SP MADAM'S CALLING 19
ALBERTA K. JOHNSON - . . . . SP MADAM'S PAST HI 25

KANSAS 2

PAUL ROBESON SAID, OUT IN KANSAS CITY, ... JC JIM CROW'S LAST 19
FROM KANSAS CITY . . . . SP MADAM PHONE BIL 22

KATHERINE 1

KATHERINE DUNHAM AL AND LEON $ $ $ $ $ . . . . AYM HORN OF PLENTY 6

KDQ 1

IF THIS RADIO WAS GOOD I'D GET KDQ SH BED TIME 1

KEEP 34

AND WHEN I'M DEAD - I'LL KEEP STILL. NM BIG-TIMER POEM 36
YOU CAN'T KEEP ME DOWN! . . . . . . NM BLACK CLWN POEM 68
WELL, AIN'T NEVER DONE IT, BUT FOR TO KEEP BODY AND SOUL . . . . . NM BROKE 29
TO KEEP FROM CRYIN' . . . . DK HOMESICK BLUES 17
LET ALL OTHERS KEEP SILENT A MOMENT. ANS A NEW SONG 3
THAT KEEP THE RICH ENTHRONED . . . ANS OPEN LETTER 26
MAKE THIS EARLY MORNING TIME TO KEEP BODY AND SOUL . . . . SH DAYBREAK 7
KEEP ME CAGED UP HERE. . . . . . . SH FREE MAN 8
I'LL KEEP RIGHT UP WITH YOU. . . . SH HEY-HEY BLUES 18
TO KEEP THEM COLD MUDDY WATERS . . SH MISSISSIPPI LEV 17
KEEP FEELING LIKE THIS I'M GONNA START ACTING BAD. . . . . SH TWILIGHT REVERI 4
TO KEEP THE KLAN AWAY) . . . . . . JC GOOD MORN STLIN 56
DON'T KEEP 'EM ALL FOR YOU. . . . . JC HOW ABOUT DIXIE 8
IF YOU KEEP ON. . . . . JC NOTE TO NAZIS 5
OF THOSE WHO WOULD KEEP, OR ONCE MORE MAKE . . . . JC TO CAPTAIN MULZ 31

TO KEEP THE GALL FROM BITING IN HIS
MOUTH. . . . . OWT JUICE JOINT 44
AS THOUGH YOU COULD KEEP. . . . . . SP A HOUSE IN TAOS 27
BUT I'M GONNA KEEP ON AT IT . . . . SP EVIL 3
KEEP YOUR HAND ON THE PLOW! HOLD ON! SP FREEDOM'S PLOW 200
KEEP YOUR HAND ON THE PLOW! HOLD ON! SP FREEDOM'S PLOW 126
KEEP YOUR HAND ON THE PLOW! HOLD ON! SP FREEDOM'S PLOW 129
KEEP YOUR HAND ON THE PLOW! HOLD ON! SP FREEDOM'S PLOW 160
KEEP YOUR HAND ON THE PLOW! HOLD ON! SP FREEDOM'S PLOW 191
KEEP THINKIN' I WON'T BE LONELY . . SP HOPE 3
WELL. THAT O.K. YOU MAY KEEP - . . SP MADAM PHONE BIL 39
CAESAR TOLD ME TO KEEP HIS
DOOR-STEPS CLEAN. . . . . SP NEGRO 5
WHY DOES HE KEEP ON FOOLIN' AROUND
MARIE? . . . . SP SISTER 2
BUT WHY DOES HE KEEP ON FOOLIN'
AROUND MARIE? . . . . SP SISTER 4
BUT I HAD TO KEEP ON TILL MY WORK
WAS DONE: . . . . SP THE NEGRO MOTHE 28
I HAD TO KEEP ON! NO STOPPING FOR ME
- . . . . SP THE NEGRO MOTHE 29
DARES KEEP DOWN THE CHILDREN OF THE
NEGRO MOTHER. . . . . SP THE NEGRO MOTHE 52
KEEP ON A-LOVIN' ME. DADDY. . . . . SP YOUNG GAL'S BLS 23
BUT HEARTS KEEP DOGGED BEATING . . AYM ASK YOUR MAMA 69
TO KEEP FAR-OFF CANARIES . . . . . . AYM ODE TO DINAH 60

KEEPER 2

ONCE YOUR BROTHER'S KEEPER . . . . AYM ODE TO DINAH 84
NOW NOT EVEN KEEPER TO YOUR CHILD - AYM ODE TO DINAH 85

KEEPING 1

THAT'S BEEN KEEPING MY NOSE TO THE
GRINDSTONE. . . . . SH PAY DAY 13

KEEPS 4

IT KEEPS ME FROM FEELIN' BLUE. . . FC BAD MAN 12
AS KEEPS THIS YOUNG NYMPH. JOY! . . SP JOY 9
MY TV KEEPS ON SNOWING. . . . . . . AYM BLUES IN STEREO 37
KEEPS THE GAS ON WHILE THE TV . . . AYM ODE TO DINAH 5

KENTUCKY 1

I FROM KENTUCKY. . . . . SP BROTHERS 3

KENYATTA 2

JOMO IN KENYATTA. . . . STARS. . . . AYM BIRD IN ORBIT 60
KENYATTA RED! CASTRO RED! . . . . . AYM BIRD IN ORBIT 73

KEPT 4

AND KEPT HER THERE. . . . . OWT BLD MARGE POLIT 18
KEPT THE MAYOR . . . . OWT BLD MARGE POLIT 48
I KEPT WISHING I HAD A GIRL-FRIEND OWT STRANGER IN TWN 3
BUT I KEPT TRUDGING ON THROUGH THE
LONELY YEARS. . . . . SP THE NEGRO MOTHE 26

KERRY 1

CUR DOG. FICE DOG. KERRY BLUE - . . SP WARNING AUGMENT 13

KETTLE 2

I LOOK IN THE KETTLE. THE KETTLE IS
DRY. . . . . SH SUPPER TIME 1
I LOOK IN THE KETTLE. THE KETTLE IS
DRY. . . . . SH SUPPER TIME 1

KEY 2

KNOWN THE KEY. . . . . FW OLD SAILOR 12
WITH HIS EBONY HANDS ON EACH IVORY
KEY . . . . SP THE WEARY BLUES 9

KEYS 1

AND THE CLICKING OF THE KEYS . . . SP GRADUATION 14

KICK 3

THEY DON'T KICK . . . . SP COMMENT ON CURB 2
FRANTIC. KICK THEIR DRAFTEE YEARS SP FLATTED FIFTHS 4
HEY! BABA-RE-BOP! MOP! ON A BE-BOP
KICK! . . . . SP LIKEWISE 23

KICKED 4

KICKED HER IN THE FACE.) . . . . . SH DEATH IN HARLEM 98
WHEN A DREAM GETS KICKED AROUND. . SP SAME IN BLUES 32
AND THEN THEY KICKED ME . . . . . . PL KU KLUX 15
DREAMS KICKED ASUNDER. . . . . . . PL QUESTION ANSWER 11

KICKING 1

IF YOU'RE NOT ALIVE AND KICKING. . SP SHAME ON YOU 10

KICKIN' 1

CAUSE I'M STILL HERE KICKIN'! . . . SP MADAM WRONG VIS 28

KICKS 3

YOU KICKS 'EM ROUND AND . . . . . . SP LOVER'S RETURN 11
THE OLD KICKS IN THE BACK. . . . . PL HARLEM 4
THREE KICKS BETWEEN THE LEGS . . . PL THIRD DEGREE 10

KID 16

WHAT WAS THE COVER CHARGE. KID? . . FC CLOSING TIME 14
YOU WOULDN'T KID ME. WOULD YOU? . . ANS SONG OF SPAIN 30
AND FIND SOMEBODY TO KID AND TALK. SH BED TIME 8
ARABELLA JOHNSON AND THE TEXAS KID SH DEATH IN HARLEM 1
BUT THE TEXAS KID. . . . . SH DEATH IN HARLEM 139
SHE LEFT THE TEXAS KID SETTIN BY
HIMSELF . . . . SH DEATH IN HARLEM 79
LISTEN. KID SLEEPY. . . . . SP KID SLEEPY 1
KID SLEEPY SAID. . . . . SP KID SLEEPY 8
LISTEN. KID SLEEPY. . . . . SP KID SLEEPY 10
KID SLEEPY SAID. . . . . SP KID SLEEPY 16
KID SLEEPY. JUST . . . . SP KID SLEEPY 19
SOLID LAND. KID. . . . . SP PORT TOWN 11
THAT LITTLE NEGRO'S MARRIED AND GOT
A KID. . . . . SP SISTER 1
TO KILL A FIFTEEN-YEAR-OLD KID? . . PL DREAM DEFERRED 2
FOR A KID THAT'S BLACK? . . . . . . PL MERRY-GO-ROUND 15
LISTEN HERE. KID. . . . . PL WITHOUT BENEFIT 7

KIDS 25

HOME. KIDS. AND EVERYTHING FINE. . NM BIG-TIMER POEM 46
THIS IS FOR THE KIDS WHO DIE. . . . ANS KIDS WHO DIE 1
FOR KIDS WILL DIE CERTAINLY. . . . ANS KIDS WHO DIE 3
LETTING KIDS DIE. . . . . ANS KIDS WHO DIE 7
KIDS WILL DIE IN THE SWAMPS OF
MISSISSIPPI . . . . ANS KIDS WHO DIE 8
KIDS WILL DIE IN THE STREETS OF
CHICAGO . . . . ANS KIDS WHO DIE 10
KIDS WILL DIE IN THE ORANGE GROVES
OF CALIFORNIA . . . . ANS KIDS WHO DIE 12
ALL KINDS OF KIDS WILL DIE . . . . ANS KIDS WHO DIE 16
WILL LIVE ON WEAVING WORDS TO
SMOTHER THE KIDS WHO DIE. . . . ANS KIDS WHO DIE 24
WILL ALL RAISE THEIR HANDS AGAINST
THE KIDS WHO DIE. . . . . ANS KIDS WHO DIE 29
FOR THE KIDS WHO DIE ARE LIKE IRON
IN THE BLOOD OF THE PEOPLE - . . ANS KIDS WHO DIE 32
TO TASTE THE IRON OF THE KIDS WHO
DIE. . . . . ANS KIDS WHO DIE 34
LISTEN. KIDS WHO DIE - . . . . . . ANS KIDS WHO DIE 37
THROUGH THE KIDS WHO DIE. . . . . . ANS KIDS WHO DIE 51
AND SOME FORGET TO LAUGH WHO STILL
ARE KIDS. . . . . OWT JUICE JOINT 40
THE WHITE KIDS . . . . SP CHILDREN'S RYME 6
THEM WHITE KIDS . . . . SP CHILDREN'S RYME 13
THEN KIDS. . . . . SP DEFERRED 13
THE WAY YOU SEND YOUR KIDS TO SCHOOL SP HIGH TO LOW 10
WHEN THE KIDS LOOK ALL NEW . . . . SP PASSING 7
THOSE SIT-IN KIDS. HE SAID. . . . . AYM BIRD IN ORBIT 71
AND OTHER KIDS LESS MEANER THAN ¢ ¢
¢ ¢ . . . . AYM HORN OF PLENTY 25
THE WHITE KIDS . . . . PL CHILDREN'S RYME 2
THEM WHITE KIDS . . . . PL CHILDREN'S RYME 7
THAT KILL THE KIDS . . . . PL THIRD DEGREE 11

KID'S 2

THE TEXAS KID'S ON A . . . . SH DEATH IN HARLEM 14
THAT KID'S MY BUDDY. . . . . SP BUDDY 1

KILL 22

I'M JUST GONNA KILL HER . . . . . . FC EVIL WOMAN 3
I'M GONNA KILL MA SELF. . . . . . . FC SUICIDE 6
THE HIGH SHERIFF SHOOTS AND HE
SHOOTS TO KILL . . . . ANS BLD OZZIE POWEL 9
A WHITE HIGH SHERIFF WHO SHOOTS TO
KILL . . . . ANS BLD OZZIE POWEL 27
TO KILL THE LIES OF COLOR . . . . . ANS OPEN LETTER 25
UP MILLIONS FOR BOMBS TO KILL A
CHILD - . . . . ANS SONG OF SPAIN 44
DRESSED TO KILL - . . . . SH BLD THE SINNER 2
ALL DRESSED TO KILL - . . . . SH BLD THE SINNER 18
YOU'LL NEVER KILL ME! . . . . JC FREEDOM 14
AND DEEP DETERMINATION GEARED TO
KILL . . . . JC TO CAPTAIN MULZ 51
TO KILL HIM. . . . . FW SNAKE 7
THEY DIDN'T KILL THE SOLDIER. . . . OWT BLD MARGE POLIT 42
NEVER TO KILL - . . . . LHR DEAR LVLY DEATH 3
GYPSY SAYS I'D KILL MY SELF . . . . SP BAD LUCK CARD 11
I'LL KILL OLD GREELEY. . . . . . . SP BLUE BAYOU 13
KILL HIM - AND LET HIS SOUL RUN
WILD! . . . . SP GENIUS CHILD 12
TO KILL ME? . . . . PL DEATH YORKVILLE 4
TO KILL ME. . . . . PL DEATH YORKVILLE 16
TO KILL A FIFTEEN-YEAR-OLD KID? . . PL DREAM DEFERRED 2
THAT KILL THE KIDS . . . . PL THIRD DEGREE 11
SO I KILL YOU. . . . . PL WAR 21
AND YOU KILL ME. . . . . PL WAR 22

KILLED 5

WHO HAS A VISION OF HIS BROTHER
KILLED IN FRANCE WHILE FIGHTING
FOR THE . . . . NM COLORED SL MOOD 2
THEY KILLED A COLORED SOLDIER! . . OWT BLD MARGE POLIT 13
KILLED MARY'S BOY. . . . . LHR BLD MARY'S SON 7
THEY KILLED HIM DEAD. . . . . PL LUMUMBA'S GRAVE 12
KILLED WITH GREAT ELAN. . . . . . . PL MOTHER IN WAR 6

KILLERS 1

O. THIEVES. EXPLOITERS. KILLERS. . ANS A NEW SONG 29

KILLING 1
WIRED FOR KILLING . . . . SP MELLOW 6

KILLING'S 1
AND THE GUN TO DO THE KILLING'S . . AYM IS IT TRUE? 14

KILT 2
THAT NIGHT HE GOT KILT . . . . . . FC DEATH DO DIRTY 21
AN' DE ONES THAT KILT HIM, - . . . FC DEATH DO DIRTY 31

KIN 6
KIN MAKE YOU LOSE YO' 'GINITY. . . FC LISTEN HERE 6
HE KIN PLAY A BANJO. . . . . FC MA MAN 7
LORDY, HE KIN PLUNK, PLUNK, PLUNK. FC MA MAN 8
HE KIN PLAY A BANJO. . . . . FC MA MAN 9
EAGLE-ROCKISH AS I KIN BE! . . . . FC MA MAN 18
HE WAS HER KIN. . . . . SP BLD FORTUNE TEL 12

KIND 19
BE KIND TO ME. . . . . WB DISILLUSION 11
THOSE KIND COME CHEAP IN HARLEM . . WB YOUNG PROSTITUT 4
DEATH, BE KIND . . . . FC CLOSING TIME 13
I TREATS HER KIND BUT . . . . FC EVIL WOMAN 5
BUT HE SHO DO TREAT ME KIND. . . . FC GAL'S CRY DYING 14
BUT HE SHO DO TREAT ME KIND. . . . FC GAL'S CRY DYING 16
CAUSE SHE AIN'T DE RIGHT KIND. . . FC WORKIN' MAN 12
AND ALL THAT KIND O' THING. . . . . NM BIG-TIMER POEM 24
A GAL I THOUGHT WAS KIND. . . . . . DK PO' BOY BLUES 14
A GAL I THOUGHT WAS KIND. . . . . . DK PO' BOY BLUES 16
WHAT KIND OF A WORLD . . . . JC BLACK MAN SPEAK 23
AS THE KIND AND QUIET NIGHT . . . . JC ME AND MY SONG 4
KIND . . . . JC ME AND MY SONG 20
KIND, THOUGHTFUL TO THE FACES THAT ARE WHITE. . . . . OWT NEGRO SERVANT 2
TO GET THROUGH HIGH AT TWENTY'S KIND OF LATE - . . . . SP DEFERRED 6
KIND JESUS! . . . . SP JUDGMENT DAY 10
SOME KIND OF TRICKERATION . . . . . SP WHAT? SO SOON! 4
TOUCHING EVERYBODY WITH KIND FINGERS PL DAYBREAK IN ALA 18
MEEK, HUMBLE, AND KIND: . . . . . . PL WARNING 3

KINDER 3
I FELT KINDER SORRY . . . . SP MADAM MINISTER 28
'CAUSE YOU FINDS IT'S KINDER HARD. SP MOTHER TO SON 16
IS A KINDER MISTRESS. . . . . SP THE SOUTH 26

KINDS 4
ALL KINDS OF KIDS WILL DIE . . . . ANS KIDS WHO DIE 16
AND SHOOT ALL KINDS O' SHELLS INTO YOU. . . . . SH TWILIGHT REVERI 8
ABOUT TWO KINDS O' PISTOLS THAT I AIN'T GOT. . . . . SH TWILIGHT REVERI 10
AND ALL KINDS OF SWING MIKADOS . . SP NOTE COMM THEAT 10

KING 6
OF KING DAVID'S DANCERS, ... FC BRASS SPITOONS 34
KING COLE JUKEBOX PAYOLA . . . . . AYM ASK YOUR MAMA 42
KING MOUNTS HIS UNICORN . . . . . . AYM BIRD IN ORBIT 25
MARTIN LUTHER KING IS GOVERNOR OF GEORGIA. . . . . PL CULTURAL EXCHNG 43
SEND FOR KING ARTHUR TO BRING THE HOLY GRAIL. . . . . PL FINAL CALL 8
BEFORE YOU ARE KING. . . . . PL LAST PRINCE 14

KINGDOM 1
WE'D OPEN UP THE KINGDOM . . . . . FW WISDOM 6

KINGS 4
WHERE NEVER KINGS CONNIVE NOR TYRANTS SCHEME . . . . ANS LET AMERICA BE 8
IN THAT OLD WORLD WHILE STILL A SERF OF KINGS. . . . . ANS LET AMERICA BE 40
EXTRA-LARGE THE KINGS AND QUEENS . AYM JAZZTET MUTED 14
THE FUSE OF CENTURIES OF DRAGON KINGS . . . . PL BIRMINGHAM SUND 19

KINGSTON 1
KINGSTON TOO GOOD WILLING . . . . . AYM ASK YOUR MAMA 48

KINSMEN 1
KINSMEN - YOU AND I. . . . . SP BROTHERS 4

KIPPUR 1
YOM KIPPUR, NO! . . . . SP LIKEWISE 9

KISS 7
SURE. KISS ME, ... WB CAT AND SAXOPHN 11
AND GIVES HER KISS TO NOTHINGNESS. WB TO LITTLE LOVER 11
LET THE RAIN KISS YOU. . . . . . . DK APRIL RAIN SONG 1
WILL KISS YOU AGAIN. . . . . DK PARISIAN BEGGAR 12
BLESSED US WITH A KISS . . . . . . SP FULFILMENT 18
STOOPS TO KISS 12 WEST 133RD. . . . SP PROJECTION 9
ASKED ME FOR A KISS. . . . . SP SUICIDE'S NOTE 3

KISSES 1
COME, DRINK KISSES. . . . . SP NATCHA 6

KISSING 2
KISSING THE NIGHT. . . . . DK LULLABY 18
AND KISSING THE MOON . . . . SP MOONLIGHT NIGHT 6

KITCHEN 7
OR GREASY POTS IN A DIRTY KITCHEN. SP ELEVATOR BOY 20
BRINGS REMAINDERS FROM THE KITCHEN SP GRADUATION 7
AND ICEBERG'S KITCHEN. . . . . . . SP GRADUATION 19
THEY SEND ME TO EAT IN THE KITCHEN SP I, TOO 3
"EAT IN THE KITCHEN," . . . . SP I, TOO 13
KITCHEN FLOOR SQUEAKS. . . . . . . SP MADAM RENT MAN 16
ON THE MONEY FROM A WHITE WOMAN'S KITCHEN? . . . . SP RUBY BROWN 14

KITCHENETTES 1
KITCHENETTES . . . . OWT VISITORS 13

KITCHENS 2
THE STEAM IN HOTEL KITCHENS. . . . FC BRASS SPITOONS 7
WHEN SHE WORKED IN THEIR KITCHENS. SP RUBY BROWN 27

KIVER 1
PUT MA HEAD UN'NEATH DE KIVER. . . FC GAL'S CRY DYING 5

KLAN 4
YOU MAY CALL OUT THE KLAN . . . . . JC BLD SAM SOLOMON 2
THEY CALLED OUT THE KLAN. . . . . . JC BLD SAM SOLOMON 41
GO GET OUT YOUR KLAN - . . . . . . JC BLD SAM SOLOMON 54
TO KEEP THE KLAN AWAY) . . . . . . JC GOOD MORN STLIN 56

KLANSMAN 2
THE LAW'S A KLANSMAN WITH AN EVIL WILL. . . . . ANS BLD OZZIE POWEL 11
A KLANSMAN SAID, "NIGGER, ... PL KU KLUX 17

KLANSMEN 1
WHEN CROOKS AND KLANSMEN . . . . . JC GOOD MORN STLIN 29

KLEAGLE 1
THE DEVIL'S A KLEAGLE WITH AN EVIL WILL. . . . . ANS BLD OZZIE POWEL 25

KLUX 2
THE KU KLUX WAS TOUGH - . . . . . . JC BLD SAM SOLOMON 50
AND THERE AIN'T NO KU KLUX . . . . SP NOT A MOVIE 14

KNEES 5
I WOULDN'T TAKE YOU BACK IF YOU COME ON YOUR KNEES. . . . . SH SUNDAY 9
I'M BEAT TO MY KNEES. . . . . JC HOW ABOUT DIXIE 12
ON THEIR KNEES. . . . . SP GARDEN 7
AND HE CRAWLED ON HIS KNEES TO HIS HOUSE . . . . SP NOT A MOVIE 4
SEND FOR UNCLE TOM ON HIS MIGHTY KNEES. . . . . PL FINAL CALL 28

KNELT 1
AND HE KNELT THERE TO PRAY. . . . . LHR BLD MARY'S SON 23

KNEW 13
(IF I'D A-ONLY KNEW IT) . . . . . . SH ANNOUNCEMENT 10
MEN WHO KNEW NOT WHAT THEY DID . . LHR BLD MARY'S SON 6
BUT IN THEIR HEARTS THE SLAVES KNEW SP FREEDOM'S PLOW 105
AND THE SLAVES KNEW . . . . SP FREEDOM'S PLOW 114
AND NOBODY KNEW FOR SURE . . . . . SP FREEDOM'S PLOW 119
BUT OTHERS KNEW IT HAD TO TRIUMPH. SP FREEDOM'S PLOW 122
NEVER KNEW DUSABLE. . . . . SP MIGRANT 12
I NEVER KNEW . . . . SP PARADE 23
I NEVER KNEW! . . . . SP PARADE 27
STRANGE HURT SHE KNEW . . . . SP STRANGE HURT 7
WHEN THEY ASK YOU IF YOU KNEW ME. AYM RIDE, RED, RIDE 27
FOR OLD JOHN BROWN WHO KNEW SLAVERY COULDN'T . . . . PL FINAL CALL 22
I KNEW THAT THIS WOULD COME." . . . PL NORTHERN LIBERL 5

KNIFE 9
I'M GONNA BUY ME A KNIFE WITH . . . FC SUICIDE 7
GONNA BUY A KNIFE WITH . . . . . . FC SUICIDE 9
AS IF FATE HAD NOT BLED HIM WITH HER KNIFE! . . . . DK BEGGAR BOY 8
A KNIFE IN THE BACK . . . . ANS SONG OF SPAIN 36
BESSIE PULLED A KNIFE. . . . . . . SH DEATH IN HARLEM 104
BUT MY LOVE MIGHT TURN INTO A KNIFE SH IN TROUBLED KEY 11
A KNIFE IS SHARP. . . . . FW EXITS 2
YOU DON'T NEED NO GUN NOR KNIFE - SP LITTLE OLD LETT 14
AND WHO IS MACK THE KNIFE . . . . . AYM SHADES OF PIG 14

KNOCK 2
I KNOCK ON YOUR DOOR . . . . OWT HONEY BABE 9
AND CAN KNOCK THE HADES . . . . . . AYM ODE TO DINAH 117

KNOCKED 3
THE RENT MAN KNOCKED. . . . . SP MADAM RENT MAN 1
A MAN KNOCKED THREE TIMES. . . . . SP MADAM WRONG VIS 1
AND KNOCKED ME DOWN. . . . . PL KU KLUX 14

KNOCKOUT 1
KNOCKOUT! SP TO BE SOMEBODY 19

KNOCKS 2
HE KNOCKS ME OFF MA FEET. FC MA MAN 2
HE KNOCKS ME OFF MA FEET. FC MA MAN 4

KNOTS 1
SIX KNOTS WAS ON HIS HEAD SP NOT A MOVIE 12

KNOW 128
NOR EVER KNOW. WB DISILLUSION 5
WHAT DO YOU KNOW WB HARLEM NIGHT CL 15
ALTHOUGH I DO NOT KNOW. WB YOUNG BRIDE 2
DON'T KNOW WHY I DO IT BUT FC BAD MAN 11
YOU KNOW THAT TUNE FC JAZZ BAND 11
YOU KNOW IT. FC JAZZ BAND 13
I DON'T KNOW FC NEW CABARET GRL 10
I GUESS I KNOW WHAT I'M UP AGAINST. NM BIG-TIMER POEM 57
I SAY, "NOW, BABY, YOU KNOW I AIN'T GOT NONE, HONEY." NM BROKE 20
AND DON'T YOU KNOW THAT OLD WOMAN SWELLED UP LIKE A SPECKLED TOAD NM BROKE 21
WHAT I DON'T KNOW 'BOUT SHOVELIN' COAL, AIN'T NO MO' TO KNOW! NM BROKE 32
WHAT I DON'T KNOW 'BOUT SHOVELIN' COAL, AIN'T NO MO' TO KNOW! NM BROKE 32
I SAID, "BABY, YOU KNOW I LOVES YOU, AND ALL LIKE THAT NM BROKE 50
AW-OO! YONDER COMES A WOMAN I USED TO KNOW WAY DOWN SOUTH. NM BROKE 62
THEY TOLD US AMERICA WOULD KNOW NO BLACK OR WHITE: NM COLORED SL POEM 11
BUT NOW I KNOW WE'VE GOT PLENTY TO DO. NM COLORED SL POEM 23
BUT NOW I KNOW WELL THAT'S NOT OUR SITUATION: NM COLORED SL POEM 28
AND NO LONGER DO WE KNOW THE DARK MISERY NM COLORED SL POEM 30
SO NOW I KNOW WE BLACKS ARE JUST LIKE ANY OTHER - NM COLORED SL POEM 35
CAN'T SEE! AND DON'T KNOW! AND WON'T EVER CARE! NM COLORED SL POEM 53
THAT I CAN NEITHER KNOW NOR UNDERSTAND DK BEGGAR BOY 3
I KNOW, FOR I HEARD, WHEN ALL WAS STILL, DK DEATH SEAMAN 3
YOU DO NOT KNOW DK MINSTREL MAN 15
THEY KNOW DK SEA CHARM 4
THEY KNOW DK SEA CHARM 7
AN' I DON'T KNOW HOW TO FLOAT. DK WIDE RIVER 6
I KNOW FULL WELL NOW ANS A NEW SONG 25
BUT NINE BLACK BOYS KNOW FULL WELL. ANS BLD OZZIE POWEL 21
DOES NOT KNOW ANS CHANT TOM MOONY 11
WE DID NOT KNOW THAT WE WERE BROTHERS. ANS OPEN LETTER 47
NOW WE KNOW! ANS OPEN LETTER 48
WE DID NOT KNOW ANS OPEN LETTER 51
LAWD! DON'T YOU KNOW? ANS SISTER JOHNSON 11
WORKERS, KNOW THAT WE TOO CAN CRY. ANS SONG OF SPAIN 59
I KNOW NOW - ANS UNION 2
I WANT THE WORLD TO KNOW. SH ANNOUNCEMENT 14
TO KNOW. SH ASPIRATION 4
AND START A SKIN GAME WITH SOME CHUMPS I KNOW. SH BED TIME 6
I DON'T KNOW WHY IT LOOKS SH BLD PAWNBROKER 11
YOU KNOW. SH BLD PAWNBROKER 20
SAY! YOU KNOW I BELIEVE I'LL CHANGE MY NAME. SH DAYBREAK 9
BIG TIME SPORTS AND GIRLS WHO KNOW SH DEATH IN HARLEM 37
(I KNOW IT AIN'T TODAY) SH EVIL MORNING 2
SO IF YOU WANT TO KNOW BEAUTY'S SH HARLEM SWEETIES 41
TILL YOU DON'T KNOW RIGHT FROM WRONG. SH HEY-HEY BLUES 12
HOW DID I KNOW WHERE YOU DONE GONE AT? SH LETTER 5
YAL, COME ON BACK - I KNOW YOU WANT TO. SH LETTER 9
DON'T KNOW WHY I BUILD THIS LEVEE SH MISSISSIPPI LEV 7
DON'T KNOW WHY I BUILD THIS LEVEE SH MISSISSIPPI LEV 9
I REALLY DON'T KNOW JC BLACK MAN SPEAK 10
I STILL DON'T KNOW JC GOOD MORN STLIN 12
AND I KNOW YOU KNOW JC GOOD MORN STLIN 53
AND I KNOW YOU KNOW JC GOOD MORN STLIN 53
FOLKS OUGHT TO KNOW JC HOW ABOUT DIXIE 18
ALONE, I KNOW, NO ONE IS FREE. JC TO CAPTAIN MULZ 35
WHOSE IS IT, DO YOU KNOW? FW WHEN ARMIES PAS 4
I DO NOT KNOW FW WHEN ARMIES PAS 5
SON, I DO NOT KNOW. FW WHEN ARMIES PAS 16
TO KNOW WHY: OWT DECEASED 5
SAYS, I KNOW IT'S HIM! OWT HONEY BABE 12
I'LL KNOW MY WAY AROUND. OWT STRANGER IN TWN 16
YES, I'LL KNOW OWT STRANGER IN TWN 17
I DON'T KNOW WHERE TO TURN. OWT TOO BLUE 2
I DON'T KNOW WHERE TO GO. OWT TOO BLUE 3
I DON'T KNOW HOW YOU FEEL TODAY - OWT YESTERDAY TODAY 11
I DON'T KNOW WHAT SP BAD LUCK CARD 9
YOU OUGHT TO KNOW! SP BAR 5
THEN YOU KNOW A NEW DAY'S SP BLACK MARIA 16
YOU'D WANT TO KNOW. SP BLD FORTUNE TEL 4
I KNOW YOU'VE HEARD SP BOOGIE 1 A.M. 2
I KNOW I CAN'T SP CHILDREN'S RYME 8
BUT YOU KNOW. SP DEFERRED 11
YOU KNOW, AS OLD AS I AM. SP DEFERRED 45
THEN YOU KNOW THAT YOU HAVE TURNED SP FINAL CURVE 3
I GOT TO KNOW ABOUT THIS SP FREEDOM TRAIN 29
BUT NOW WE KNOW HOW IT ALL CAME OUT. SP FREEDOM'S PLOW 136
WE KNOW NOW HOW IT CAME OUT. SP FREEDOM'S PLOW 138
JIMMY WANTS TO KNOW ABOUT THE SP FREEDOM TRAIN 47
UNTIL ALL RACES AND ALL PEOPLES KNOW ITS SHADE. SP FREEDOM'S PLOW 199
DON'T KNOW WHY. SP HOPE 2
JOE HAS SENSE ENOUGH TO KNOW SP JOE LOUIS 5
SO MANY GODS DON'T KNOW. SP JOE LOUIS 7
I DON'T KNOW WHAT TO DO." SP LOVER'S RETURN 8
HE SAID, YOU KNOW SP MADAM RENT MAN 5
SOMETIMES YOU DON'T KNOW SP MADAM MIGHT-HAV 6
YOU DON'T KNOW MY NAME. SP MADAM WRONG VIS 6
I'LL HAVE YOU KNOW SP MADAM MINISTER 10
YOU KNOW, ALBERTA, SP MADAM HER MADAM 19
I DON'T KNOW? SP MADAM PHONE BIL 26
I'LL HAVE YOU KNOW SP MADAM CENSUS 31
DON'T YOU KNOW SP MARCH MOON 9
DIDN'T HARDLY KNOW MY MIND. SP MORNING AFTER 2
DIDN'T KNOW MY MIND. SP MORNING AFTER 4
THAT YOU KNOW SP MOVIES 5
I DO NOT KNOW. SP PRAYER 7
I DO NOT KNOW. SP PRAYER 9
I KNOW WHAT RELIEF CAN BE - SP RELIEF 6
KNOW MORE ABOUT THIS PRETTY RUBY BROWN. SP RUBY BROWN 17
IS ALL YOU KNOW. SP SNAIL 4
AND WOULD NOT KNOW SP SO LONG 8
THAT I HAD TO CLIMB, THAT I HAD TO KNOW SP THE NEGRO MOTHE 3
IT'S NOT EASY TO KNOW WHAT IS TRUE FOR YOU OR ME SP THEME FOR ENG B 16
DOES NOT KNOW SP TRUMPET PLAYER 37
TO KNOW HIS SP UNCLE TOM 11
WE DIDN'T KNOW - SP WEST TEXAS 14
YOU KNOW. AYM ASK YOUR MAMA 27
THAT DON'T KNOW HOW TO PLAY AYM BLUES IN STEREO 25
KNOW TOURISTS ONLY FOR AYM GOSPEL CHA-CHA 11
HOW I GOT THERE I DON'T KNOW. AYM GOSPEL CHA-CHA 40
THEY KNOW ME, TOO, DOWNTOWN. AYM HORN OF PLENTY 40
DID I KNOW CHARLIE MINGUS? AYM HORN OF PLENTY 51
BUT SCRIPT-WRITERS WHO KNOW BETTER AYM IS IT TRUE? 49
DON'T KNOW WHY I. PL ANGOLA QUESTION 1
DON'T KNOW WHY I PL ANGOLA QUESTION 8
I KNOW PL ANGOLA QUESTION 16
DID NOT KNOW PL BIRMINGHAM SUND 10
I KNOW I CAN'T PL CHILDREN'S RYME 4
WE KNOW EVERYBODY PL CHILDREN'S RYME 9
YOU KNOW, RIGHT AT CHRISTMAS PL CULTURAL EXCHNG 32
I KNOW I AM PL DINNER GUEST ME 1
CANNOT KNOW, OF COURSE, PL JUNIOR ADDICT 6
NEXT THING YOU KNOW, PL LITTLE SNG HOUS 18
WHAT I DON'T KNOW WHAT I WANT PL STOKELY MALCOLM 3
BUT I KNOW IT MUST BE PL STOKELY MALCOLM 11
AS HAVE SOME FOLKS I KNOW. PL VARI-COLORED 2
DON'T YOU KNOW PL WITHOUT BENEFIT 2
IF YOU HAD KNOWN WHAT I KNOW PL WORDS LIKE FREE 7
YOU WOULD KNOW WHY. PL WORDS LIKE FREE 8

KNOWED 9
KNOWED SOMEBODY'S 'BOUT TO DIE. FC GAL'S CRY DYING 2
KNOWED SOMEBODY'S 'BOUT TO DIE. FC GAL'S CRY DYING 4
MA LORD KNOWED WHAT IT WAS TO WORK. DK MA LORD 6
HE KNOWED HOW TO PRAY. DK MA LORD 7
I NEVER KNOWED HOW DK WIDE RIVER 11
LOOKS LIKE SHE COULD'VE KNOWED IT SP BLD FORTUNE TEL 19
I MIGHT'VE KNOWED SP DIME 7
I KNOWED WE WAS THROUGH! SP MADAM MIGHT-HAV 20
I KNOWED THAT WAS SO. SP MADAM PHONE BIL 24

KNOWIN 1
KNOWIN THEY CAN BUY A DOZEN COLORED PLACES. SH DEATH IN HARLEM 61

KNOWING 5
KNOWING WE ARE NOT FW WISDOM 3
KNOWING ALL THINGS OWT MAN INTO MEN 16
KNOWING SO WELL THE WIND AND THE SUN - SP DEMAND 7
KNOWING WHAT I GOT. SP MIDNIGHT RAFFLE 12
(NOT KNOWING THERE'S A STEINWAY BIGGER, BIGGER) SP TO BE SOMEBODY 3

KNOWLEDGE 2
SEEKING THE KNOWLEDGE THAT RIGHTS ALL WRONG - NM DARK YOUTH USA 17
KNOWLEDGE ACQUIRED BUT THROWN AWAY. JC THE BITTER RIVR 20

KNOWN 11
ONE IS KNOWN BY THE NAME OF DEATH. DLD TWO THINGS 7
AND MAKE YOUR CHOICE KNOWN JC BLD SAM SOLOMON 10
WALLS HAVE BEEN KNOWN FW DUSK 10

KNOWN THE KEY. . . . . FW OLD SAILOR 12
HAS KNOWN HIGH WIND-SWEPT MOUNTAINS. SP MEXICAN MARKET 5
I'VE KNOWN RIVERS: . . . . SP NEGRO SPEAKS OF 1
I'VE KNOWN RIVERS ANCIENT AS THE
WORLD AND OLDER THAN THE . . . . SP NEGRO SPEAKS OF 2
I'VE KNOWN RIVERS: . . . . SP NEGRO SPEAKS OF 11
OF THE NOW KNOWN WORLD: . . . . . . AYM ASK YOUR MAMA 4
OF THE NOW KNOWN WORLD . . . . . . AYM IS IT TRUE? 4
IF YOU HAD KNOWN WHAT I KNOW . . . PL WORDS LIKE FREE 7

KNOWS 22

TOMORROW. . . . WHO KNOWS? . . . . WB HARLEM NIGHT CL 4
BACK BENT AS IN THE FIELDS. THE SLOW
STEP. THE BOWED HEAD. "NOBODY
KNOWS . . . . NM BLACK CLWN MOOD 4
AND THE STRENGTH A STRONG HAND
KNOWS. . . . . DK ALABAMA EARTH 9
SHE KNOWS WHY. . . . . SH BLD THE KILLER 29
CAUSE THE GOOD LORD KNOWS WHAT WE'RE
FIGHTING FOR! . . . . JC JIM CROW'S LAST 26
THAT KNOWS . . . . FW GRIEF 5
BUT THE GOOD LORD KNOWS . . . . . . OWT HONEY BABE 3
AND, GOD KNOWS. . . . . SP ARGUMENT 9
KNOWS THAT AUNT SUE'S STORIES ARE
REAL STORIES. . . . . SP AUNTSUE'S STORI 18
HE KNOWS THAT AUNT SUE NEVER GOT HER
STORIES . . . . SP AUNTSUE'S STORI 19
WE KNOWS EVERYBODY . . . . SP CHILDREN'S RYME 15
(MAYBE - NOBODY KNOWS.) . . . . . . SP HAVANA DREAMS 2
(BUT NOBODY KNOWS IF THAT IS SO.) SP HAVANA DREAMS 4
(QUIEN SABE? WHO REALLY KNOWS?) . . SP HAVANA DREAMS 8
GOD KNOWS . . . . SP HIGH TO LOW 1
ROSCOE KNOWS DARN WELL . . . . . . SP MADAM PHONE BIL 16
LORD KNOWS I WOULD SMILE. . . . . . SP MISS BLUES'ES 2
HOW OLD NOBODY KNOWS - . . . . . . SP MYSTERY 12
AND GOD KNOWS SHE SURE CAN
OVERCHARGE - . . . . SP NECESSITY 10
LORD KNOWS I TRIED . . . . AYM GOSPEL CHA-CHA 46
LORD KNOWS I PRAYED . . . . AYM GOSPEL CHA-CHA 49
LORD KNOWS I CLIMBED . . . . AYM GOSPEL CHA-CHA 55

KNOW'D 1

AND I KNOW'D I'S DYIN' FAST. . . . SP SYLVESTER'S BED 18

KNOW'S 2

DON'T KNOW'S I'D MIND HIS GOIN' . . SP MIDWINTER BLUES 7
DON'T KNOW'S I'D MIND HIS GOIN' . . SP MIDWINTER BLUES 9

KNUCKLES 1

WITH HARD KNUCKLES . . . . FC BEALE ST. LOVE 3

KONG 2

DIXIE TO SINGAPORE, CAPE TOWN TO
HONG KONG . . . . SP IN EXPLANATION 10
FROM HARLEM PAST HONG KONG TALKING
BACK. . . . . SP IN EXPLANATION 22

KOO 1

OOL YA KOO . . . . SP FLATTED FIFTHS 18

KU 2

THE KU KLUX WAS TOUGH - . . . . . . JC BLD SAM SOLOMON 50
AND THERE AIN'T NO KU KLUX . . . . SP NOT A MOVIE 14

K.C 1

18TH AND VINE IN K.C., 63RD IN CHI. AYM ASK YOUR MAMA 32

LA 4

LA MAJA DESNUDA'S . . . . ANS SONG OF SPAIN 23
AQUEL RINCON DE LA MANCHA DE . . . . ANS SONG OF SPAIN 27
MAYOR LA GUARDIA . . . . OWT BLD MARGE POLIT 33
DE SANGRE ES LA GOTA? . . . . AYM RIDE, RED, RIDE 22

LABOR 11

BANNER OF FORCE AND LABOR, STRENGTH
AND UNION. . . . . ANS CHANT TOM MOONY 43
I, A WORKER, LETTING MY LABOR PILE ANS SONG OF SPAIN 43
THE LABOR LEADER BEHIND STEEL BARS. JC THE BITTER RIVR 32
UNDERPAID ME FOR MY LABOR. . . . . JC THE BITTER RIVR 61
THUS TOGETHER THROUGH LABOR. . . . SP FREEDOM'S PLOW 68
LABOR! OUT OF LABOR CAME THE
VILLAGES . . . . SP FREEDOM'S PLOW 70
LABOR! OUT OF LABOR CAME THE
VILLAGES . . . . SP FREEDOM'S PLOW 70
LABOR! OUT OF LABOR CAME THE
ROWBOATS . . . . SP FREEDOM'S PLOW 72
LABOR! OUT OF LABOR CAME THE
ROWBOATS . . . . SP FREEDOM'S PLOW 72
OUT OF LABOR CAME THE FACTORIES. . SP FREEDOM'S PLOW 76
OUT OF LABOR - WHITE HANDS AND BLACK
HANDS - . . . . SP FREEDOM'S PLOW 82

LABORED 1

I AM THE ONE WHO LABORED AS A SLAVE. SP THE NEGRO MOTHE 13

LACE 3

OF CAT-GUT LACE. . . . . SP BOOGIE 1 A.M. 8
PERHAPS IT'S A FAN OF SILVER LACE - SP HAVANA DREAMS 6
OF CAT-GUT LACE. . . . . SP NIGHTMARE BOOGE 12

LACK 2

IN HARLEM'S NO LACK. . . . . SH HARLEM SWEETIES 20
WHAT I LACK. . . . . SP CONSIDER ME 34

LAD 4

WHAT IS THERE WITHIN THIS BEGGAR LAD OK BEGGAR BOY 1
THE THINGS A YOUNG LAD . . . . . . FW MAN 12
BUT SUDDENLY A GUITAR-PLAYING LAD OWT JUICE JOINT 41
LAD TALL AND BROWN . . . . SP COLLEGE FORMAL 5

LADDER 3

YET CLINGING TO THE LADDER. . . . . NM BLACK CLWN POEM 43
AND MY GRANDFATHER'S BACK WITH ITS
LADDER OF SCARS. . . . . JC THE BITTER RIVR 36
LADDER, FLAG, AND AMPLIFIER . . . . PL CORNER MEETING 1

LADIES 3

PLAY IT FOR THE LORDS AND LADIES. FC JAZZ BAND 3
SEVEN LADIES . . . . SP PARADE 1
THE DOOR MARKED LADIES OPENS INWARD AYM ODE TO DINAH 116

LADIES' 3

LADIES' MAIDS. . . . . FC LAUGHERS 8
WHEN ARABELLA WENT TO THE LADIES'
ROOM. . . . . SH DEATH IN HARLEM 78
AND ARABELLA WAS BUSY IN THE LADIES'
ROOM. . . . . SH DEATH IN HARLEM 92

LADS 1

BUT LADS PUT OUT TO SEA . . . . . . SP WATER-FRONT STR 6

LADY 10

A WHITE LADY FAINTED. . . . . SH DEATH IN HARLEM 114
DE LADY I WORK FOR . . . . SH PRESENT 1
A LADY NAMED . . . . FW NIGHT SONG 18
POLICE LADY OR LESBIAN . . . . . . SP CAFE: 3 A.M. 9
SEE THAT LADY . . . . SP LADY'S BOOGIE 1
AND THE LADY FROM THE . . . . SP MADAM CHARTY CH 21
I DIDN'T MEAN TO STUMP MA TOE ON
YOU, LADY. . . . . SP MAGNOLIA FLOWER 9
SAID THE LADY, CAN YOU DO . . . . . SP QUESTION 1
SOUTHERN GENTLE LADY, ... SP SILHOUETTE 1
SOUTHERN GENTLE LADY, ... SP SILHOUETTE 11

LADY'S 1

I BELIEVE MY OLD LADY'S . . . . . . SP WHAT? SO SOON! 1

LAFAYETTE 1

SEND FOR LAFAYETTE AND TELL HIM,
"HELP! HELP ME!" . . . . PL FINAL CALL 19

LAGOS 1

BAHIA LAGOS DAKAR LENOX . . . . . . AYM ASK YOUR MAMA 47

LAID 4

LAID HER DOWN. . . . . SP STONY LONESOME 5
FROM JUKEBOX JOINTS IS LAID . . . . AYM JAZZTET MUTED 11
GOOSE LAID: . . . . PL ELDERLY LEADERS 10
OF BEING LAID OUT COLD AND DEAD. . PL WHO BUT TH LORD 6

LAIN 1

WHERE THE CHRIST CHILD ONCE HAD
LAIN. . . . . AYM ODE TO DINAH 34

LAKE 1

SEATTLE, OAKLAND, SALT LAKE, . . . SP ONE-WAY TICKET 12

LAMB 2

HAD A LITTLE LAMB. . . . . SP EVENING SONG 10
WELL, I HOPE THAT LAMB OF MARY'S . SP EVENING SONG 11

LAMENT 1

LAMENT HIM . . . . FW OLD SAILOR 19

LAMENTED 1

DANCERS BOJANGLES LATE LAMENTED $ $
$ $ . . . . AYM HORN OF PLENTY 5

LAMP 1

COMMENT AGAINST LAMP POST . . . . . SP WHAT? SO SOON! 7

LAND 49

WE SHOULD HAVE A LAND OF SUN, . . . WB OUR LAND 1
AND A LAND OF FRAGRANT WATER . . . WB OUR LAND 3
AND NOT THIS LAND WHERE LIFE IS
COLD. . . . . WB OUR LAND 7
WE SHOULD HAVE A LAND OF TREES, . . WB OUR LAND 8
AND NOT THIS LAND WHERE BIRDS ARE
GREY. . . . . WB OUR LAND 12
AH, WE SHOULD HAVE A LAND OF JOY, WB OUR LAND 13
AND NOT THIS LAND WHERE JOY IS
WRONG. . . . . WB OUR LAND 15
DARK LAND OF DEATH . . . . WB TO LITTLE LOVER 6
NO LAND, NO HOUSE, NO JOB, ... NM BLACK CLWN POEM 34
THAT GROWS IN NO-MAN'S LAND, JOAN OF
ARC, AND VARIOUS OTHER WAR-TIME NM COLORED SL MOOD 5

IN AMERICA'S MAGIC LAND. . . . . . NM DARK YOUTH USA 5
AND STRENGTH TO OUR LAND IMPART. . NM DARK YOUTH USA 15
LET IT BE THAT GREAT STRONG LAND OF
  LOVE . . . . ANS LET AMERICA BE 7
O, LET MY LAND BE A LAND WHERE
  LIBERTY . . . . ANS LET AMERICA BE 11
O, LET MY LAND BE A LAND WHERE
  LIBERTY . . . . ANS LET AMERICA BE 11
I AM THE RED MAN DRIVEN FROM THE
  LAND, ... ANS LET AMERICA BE 21
OF PROFIT, POWER, GAIN, OF GRAB THE
  LAND! . . . . ANS LET AMERICA BE 27
THAT'S MADE AMERICA THE LAND IT HAS
  BECOME. . . . . ANS LET AMERICA BE 44
THE LAND THAT NEVER HAS BEEN YET - ANS LET AMERICA BE 63
AND YET MUST BE - THE LAND WHERE
  EVERY MAN IS FREE. . . . . ANS LET AMERICA BE 64
THE LAND THAT'S MINE - THE POOR
  MAN'S, INDIAN'S, NEGRO'S. . . . ANS LET AMERICA BE 65
WE MUST TAKE BACK OUR LAND AGAIN, ANS LET AMERICA BE 73
THE LAND, THE MINES, THE PLANTS, THE
  RIVERS - . . . . ANS LET AMERICA BE 83
THAT THE LAND MIGHT BE OURS, . . . ANS OPEN LETTER 14
TAKES LAND, ... ANS OPEN LETTER 58
WHY WE OWNS DE LAND! . . . . ANS SISTER JOHNSON 7
TO DRIVE THE FICISTS FROM THE LAND. JC GOOD MORN STLIN 34
NOR THEIR LAND, THEIR LAND - . . . JC TO CAPTAIN MULZ 18
NOR THEIR LAND, THEIR LAND - . . . JC TO CAPTAIN MULZ 18
THE LAND . . . . FW DUSTBOWL 1
THE LAND . . . . FW DUSTBOWL 7
THE LAND . . . . FW DUSTBOWL 11
THIS SONG OF ATAVISTIC LAND, . . . SP AFRO-AMER FRAG 18
IF I LAND MY FIST ON YOU. . . . . . SP BLD LANDLORD 20
AND OVERTURN THE LAND! . . . . . . SP BLD LANDLORD 24
AND OWN THE LAND. . . . . SP DEMOCRACY 9
LAND. . . . . SP DESERT 10
THEY BEGAN TO BUILD OUR LAND. . . . SP FREEDOM'S PLOW 40
THERE WAS A GREAT WOODED LAND, . . SP FREEDOM'S PLOW 140
"YOU ARE A MAN. TOGETHER WE ARE
  BUILDING OUR LAND." . . . . SP FREEDOM'S PLOW 156
LAND CREATED IN COMMON, ... SP FREEDOM'S PLOW 158
SOLID LAND, KID. . . . . SP PORT TOWN 11
THREE HUNDRED YEARS AGO IN AFRICA'S
  LAND. . . . . SP THE NEGRO MOTHE 8
AND THE BROWN LAND . . . . SP YOUNG SAILOR 18
IN MY OWN LAND. . . . . PL ANGOLA QUESTION 7
TO LIVE ON MY OWN LAND. . . . . . . PL ANGOLA QUESTION 13
AND OWN THE LAND. . . . . PL FREEDOM 9
BEGINNING IN SOME OTHER LAND - . . PL JUNIOR ADDICT 9
OF MALAYSIA LAND. . . . . PL LAST PRINCE 3

LANDIN'S 1
AND REACHIN' LANDIN'S. . . . . . . SP MOTHER TO SON 10

LANDLADY 3
LANDLADY 'LOWED TO ME LAST WEEK,
  "SAM, AIN'T YOU GOT NO MONEY?" . NM BROKE 19
I ASKED MY LANDLADY DID I HAVE
  PRIVILEGES. . . . . OWT STRANGER IN TWN 7
MY LANDLADY, SHE SAID, NO! . . . . OWT STRANGER IN TWN 8

LANDLADY'S 1
AND MY LANDLADY'S SO OLD . . . . . SP NECESSITY 8

LANDLORD 5
LANDLORD, LANDLORD, ... SP BLD LANDLORD 1
LANDLORD, LANDLORD, ... SP BLD LANDLORD 1
LANDLORD, LANDLORD, ... SP BLD LANDLORD 5
LANDLORD, LANDLORD, ... SP BLD LANDLORD 5
MAN THREATENS LANDLORD . . . . . . SP BLD LANDLORD 31

LANDS 3
BUT BACKWARD IN THE LANDS WHERE
  FACIST FEAR . . . . JC TO CAPTAIN MULZ 26
WHERE HIS TWELVE-SHOE LANDS, . . . SP DREAM BOOGE VAR 8
IN SOME LANDS . . . . PL OPPRESSION 6

LAND'S 1
AND BEATING THE LAND'S . . . . . . SP MOONLIGHT NIGHT 7

LANE 1
THEY EVEN GOT A SEGREGATED LANE. . SP FREEDOM TRAIN 27

LANG 1
(DEDICATED TO THE MEMORY OF CHARLIE
  LANG AND ERNEST GREEN, ... JC THE BITTER RIVR 1

LANGUAGE 1
BUT IT'S LIKE A FOREIGN LANGUAGE . SP SO LONG 4

LANGUAGES 1
YOU'VE GOT SEVEN LANGUAGES TO SPEAK
  IN . . . . FC JAZZ BAND 19

LANGUID 1
WHOSE LANGUID LEAN BRINGS BACK THE
  SUNNY SOUTH . . . . OWT JUICE JOINT 42

LAP 1
FROM THE SOLID LAP OF EARTH. . . . SP SPIRITUALS 12

LAPS 1
INTO THE LAPS . . . . SP MELLOW 1

LAPSED 1
HIS INSURANCE LAPSED THE OTHER DAY - SP NIGHT FUNERAL 6

LARGE 2
BEICE SAILORS WITH LARGE NOSES . . SP SEASHORE THROUG 1
WHAT WAS SO LARGE . . . . PL LONG VIEW NEGRO 11

LARGER 3
LOOMS LARGER, ... PL LONG VIEW NEGRO 4
SO MUCH LARGER, ... PL LONG VIEW NEGRO 5
LOOK THROUGH THE LARGER END - . . . PL LONG VIEW NEGRO 9

LASSIE 1
BROWN SUGAR LASSIE, ... SH HARLEM SWEETIES 5

LAST 47
THE LAST PLAYER-PIANO IS CLOSED. . WB SUMMER NIGHT 4
THE LAST VICTROLA CEASES WITH THE WB SUMMER NIGHT 5
THE LAST CRYING BABY SLEEPS . . . . WB SUMMER NIGHT 7
DON'T LAST ALL DE TIME. . . . . . . FC CRAP GAME 8
HE TOOK MA LAST THIN DIME. . . . . FC GYPSY MAN 14
HE TOOK MA LAST THIN DIME. . . . . FC GYPSY MAN 16
LAST JOB I HAD, WENT TO WORK AT FIVE
  IN DE MORNIN', OR LITTLE MO' . . NM BROKE 12
LANDLADY 'LOWED TO ME LAST WEEK,
  "SAM, AIN'T YOU GOT NO MONEY?" . NM BROKE 19
AFTER ALL THEM DOLLARS I GIVED HER
  THESE LAST TWO YEARS, ... NM BROKE 23
SHE BOUGHT A NEW HAT LAST WEEK AND
  COME SENDIN' ME THE BILL. . . . . NM BROKE 49
LAWD, FOLKSES, HOW MUCH LONGER IS
  THIS GONNA LAST? . . . . NM BROKE 59
LAST NIGHT IN A DREAM MY BROTHER
  CAME TO ME . . . . NM COLORED SL POEM 13
SAY! ON THE LAST THING I OWN, . . . SH BLD PAWNBROKER 21
IT COME LAST NIGHT. . . . . SH LETTER 2
YOU DE LAST AND ONLY . . . . SH ONLY WOMAN BLUS 23
AIN'T DUE TO LAST. . . . . JC BLD SAM SOLOMON 16
JIM CROW STARTED HIS LAST STAND. . JC JIM CROW'S LAST 29
WAY LAST WEEK? . . . . SP BLD LANDLORD 4
NOW AT LAST I'VE GOT A JOB . . . . SP DEFERRED 25
LAST NIGHT I DREAMT . . . . SP DREAM 1
TILL THE LAST WORMS COME . . . . . SP DRUM 4
TILL THE LAST STARS FALL, ... SP DRUM 6
UNTIL THE LAST ATOM . . . . SP DRUM 7
LATE LAST NIGHT I . . . . SP LATE LAST NIGHT 1
IS DUE TO LAST. . . . . SP LITTLE GRN TREE 4
CAME BACK HOME LAST NIGHT. . . . . SP LOVER'S RETURN 2
MY HOUSE LAST WEEK. . . . . SP MADAM MINISTER 2
I SAID, LAST NIGHT, ... SP MADAM NUMBER WR 3
LAST TIME I TOLD HER, ... SP MADAM CHARTY CH 25
I WAS SO SICK LAST NIGHT I . . . . SP MORNING AFTER 1
SO SICK LAST NIGHT I . . . . SP MORNING AFTER 3
HAD A DREAM LAST NIGHT I . . . . . SP MORNING AFTER 7
I DREMPT LAST NIGHT I . . . . SP MORNING AFTER 9
AND THE LAST PRAYERS BEEN SAID . . SP NIGHT FUNERAL 30
LAST WEEK THEY LYNCHED A COLORED
  BOY. . . . . SP SOUTHERN MAMMY 13
YES, SIR! LONG AS LIFE DO LAST! . . SP SYLVESTER'S BED 22
OH, THAT LAST LONG RIDE IS A . . . SP WIDOW WOMAN 1
YES, THAT LAST LONG RIDE'S A . . . SP WIDOW WOMAN 3
THIS LAST QUARTER OF CENTENNIAL . . AYM ODE TO DINAH 8
THIS LAST QUARTER OF CENTENNIAL: . AYM ODE TO DINAH 93
TO THE LAST FRONTIER . . . . PL ANGOLA QUESTION 5
THEY DO NOT LAST A DAY - . . . . . PL CROWNS GARLANDS 13
LAST. . . . . PL FINAL CALL 23
UNTIL LAST NIGHT. . . . . PL GHOSTS OF 1619 11
LAST NIGHT? . . . . PL GHOSTS OF 1619 12
LAST LITTLE BROWN PRINCE . . . . . PL LAST PRINCE 2
SINCE THE DAY BEFORE LAST . . . . . PL STOKELY MALCOLM 6

LATCH 2
SHE'LL OPEN THE LATCH . . . . FW FAITHFUL ONE 7
TO LATCH ONTO . . . . SP JOE LOUIS 11

LATE 16
TOO LATE! . . . . ANS SONG OF SPAIN 61
OR IF IT WASN'T SO LATE I MIGHT TAKE
  A WALK . . . . SH BED TIME 7
FORE IT IS TOO LATE! . . . . SH EVIL MORNING 16
LATE AT NIGHT . . . . OWT RAID 1
I'M LATE - . . . . SP BLUE MONDAY 4
SOMETIMES WORKING LATE, ... SP CONSIDER ME 19
LATE, ... SP CONSIDER ME 47
I'M ALREADY TWO YEARS LATE. . . . . SP DEFERRED 2
TO GET THROUGH HIGH AT TWENTY'S KIND
  OF LATE - . . . . SP DEFERRED 6
A FEW MINUTES LATE . . . . SP DREAM BOOGE VAR 11
"LATE TO WORK AGAIN," . . . . SP FIRED 4
BUT THE TRAINS ARE LATE. . . . . . SP GOOD MORNING 22
LATE LAST NIGHT I . . . . SP LATE LAST NIGHT 1

INTO LATE FALL . . . SP WHAT? 2
DANCERS BOJANGLES LATE LAMENTED $ $ $ $ . . . AYM HORN OF PLENTY 5
TAKEN LATE IN TIME . . . PL NORTHERN LIBERL 9

LATELY 2
BUT I SHO BEEN LOOKIN' ROUND HARD LATELY FOR WAYS AND MEANS . . . NM BROKE 39
(WHICH LATELY IS STONE NOWHERE) . . AYM HORN OF PLENTY 32

LATER 1
I WOKE UP LITTLE LATER . . . SP SYLVESTER'S BED 9

LATHAM'S 1
SITTING ON OLD MRS. LATHAM'S BACK PORCH . . . SP RUBY BROWN 9

LAUGH 19
THEY LAUGH, . . . WB BLUES FANTASY 5
LAUGH A LOUD, . . . WB BLUES FANTASY 29
LAUGH WITH ME. . . . WB THE JESTER 6
YOU WOULD LAUGH! . . . WB THE JESTER 7
LAUGH AT MY SORROW'S REIGN. . . . WB THE JESTER 14
GIT SOME GIN TO MAKE YOU LAUGH. . . FC HARD LUCK 12
LAUGH - OR TAKE PITY. . . . NM BIG-TIMER POEM 8
YOU LAUGH . . . NM BLACK CLWN POEM 1
SYNCOPATED, DETERMINED TO LAUGH, A BUGLE CALL, GAY, MARTIAL MUSIC. NM BLACK CLWN MOOD 6
LAUGH AND PUSH ME DOWN. . . . NM BLACK CLWN POEM 9
LAUGH AT ME! LAUGH AT ME! . . . NM BLACK CLWN POEM 53
LAUGH AT ME! LAUGH AT ME! . . . NM BLACK CLWN POEM 53
LAUGH AT ME THEN, . . . NM BLACK CLWN POEM 55
WHITE FOLKS, LAUGH! . . . DK NEGRO DANCERS 11
LOUNGERS AT THE BAR LAUGH OUT LOUD. SH DEATH IN HARLEM 35
TO LAUGH IN SUNSHINE . . . FW GIRL 21
AND SOME FORGET TO LAUGH WHO STILL ARE KIDS. . . . OWT JUICE JOINT 40
BUT I LAUGH, . . . SP I, TOO 5
SO I LAUGH . . . SP MOVIES 11

LAUGHED 4
DIXIE RUBBED HIS HANDS AND LAUGHED OUT LOUD - . . . SH DEATH IN HARLEM 63
AND LAUGHED IN RAIN. . . . FW GIRL 4
THE DAY-PEOPLE LAUGHED - . . . FW POPPY FLOWER 3
LAUGHED AND BATHED . . . SP FULFILMENT 7

LAUGHERS 7
LOUD LAUGHERS IN THE HANDS OF FATE - FC LAUGHERS 4
DANCERS AND LAUGHERS. . . . FC LAUGHERS 28
LAUGHERS? . . . FC LAUGHERS 29
YES, LAUGHERS . . . LAUGHERS . . . LAUGHERS - . . . FC LAUGHERS 30
YES, LAUGHERS . . . LAUGHERS . . . LAUGHERS - . . . FC LAUGHERS 30
YES, LAUGHERS . . . LAUGHERS . . . LAUGHERS - . . . FC LAUGHERS 30
LOUD-MOUTHED LAUGHERS IN THE HANDS FC LAUGHERS 31

LAUGHING 8
LAUGHING, . . . WB BLUES FANTASY 27
THE GODS ARE LAUGHING AT US. . . . WB LENOX AVE MIDNT 4
AND THE GODS ARE LAUGHING AT US. . WB LENOX AVE MIDNT 14
PRESS HANDS TOGETHER, LAUGHING AT HER SONG. . . . OWT LINCOLN THEATRE 15
LAUGHING. . . . SP FULFILMENT 21
GAY, LAUGHING JOY, . . . SP JOY 3
HARLEM LAUGHING IN ALL THE WRONG PLACES . . . SP MOVIES 2
THE LAZY, LAUGHING SOUTH . . . SP THE SOUTH 1

LAUGHIN' 2
YOU ALL OUT THERE LAUGHIN', BUT THAT AIN'T NO JOKE - . . . NM BROKE 10
STOP LAUGHIN', STOP LOVIN', STOP LIVIN' - . . . PL STILL HERE 7

LAUGHS 4
THAT LAUGHS AND CRIES AT THE SAME TIME. . . . FC JAZZ BAND 12
I OPENS MA MOUTH AN' LAUGHS. . . . DK HOMESICK BLUES 18
STANDS UP AND LAUGHS . . . JC FREEDOM 11
LAUGHS AT ME, . . . SP MOVIES 9

LAUGHTER 20
THE WILD LAUGHTER . . . WB DISILLUSION 7
TEARS ARE MY LAUGHTER. . . . WB THE JESTER 10
LAUGHTER IS MY PAIN. . . . WB THE JESTER 11
ONLY IN SONG AND LAUGHTER . . . NM BLACK CLWN POEM 10
GOD! GIVE ME LAUGHTER . . . NM BLACK CLWN POEM 23
IS WIDE WITH LAUGHTER . . . DK MINSTREL MAN 2
IS WIDE WITH LAUGHTER, . . . DK MINSTREL MAN 10
AND JOY, AND LAUGHTER, . . . ANS KIDS WHO DIE 47
AND LAUGHTER . . . FW CAROLINA CABIN 10
AND LAUGHTER . . . FW CAROLINA CABIN 19
VEILING SHADOWS CUT BY LAUGHTER . . FW DIMOUT IN HARLM 6
THEN A SILENCE OVER LAUGHTER . . . FW DIMOUT IN HARLM 9
VEILING HARLEM'S LAUGHTER . . . FW DIMOUT IN HARLM 13
SATURDAY LAUGHTER, A BAR, A BED. . SP CONSIDER ME 43
LAUGHTER . . . SP RAILROAD AVENUE 17
LAUGHTER . . . SP RAILROAD AVENUE 20
LAUGHTER . . . SP RAILROAD AVENUE 23
LAUGHTER . . . SP RAILROAD AVENUE 25
AND HIS OWN LAUGHTER, . . . SP YOUNG SAILOR 3
FOR LAUGHTER. . . . SP YOUNG SAILOR 19

LAUNCHED 2
TOGETHER WE HAVE LAUNCHED A SHIP . JC TO CAPTAIN MULZ 39
LAUNCHED THE BOATS AND WHIPPED THE HORSES . . . SP FREEDOM'S PLOW 66

LAUNDROMAT 1
WHERE IS THE COLORED LAUNDROMAT . . PL CULTURAL EXCHNG 24

LAUNDRY 1
AND LAUNDRY I DON'T HAVE MUCH LEFT SP LETTER 3

LAURELS 1
PUT THEIR LAURELS ON YOUR BROW . . PL CROWNS GARLANDS 6

LAVEAU 1
WHO SEDUCED MARIE LAVEAU? . . . AYM GOSPEL CHA-CHA 42

LAW 7
THE SUN BOUND DOWN BY LAW. . . . ANS NEGRO GHETTO 4
STILL AFTER HOURS POURING DRINKS THE LAW FORBIDS - . . . OWT JUICE JOINT 38
HAS NO RECOURSE NOW BUT TO THE LAW? AYM ASK YOUR MAMA 11
SEND FOR OLD MAN MOSES TO LAY DOWN THE LAW. . . . PL FINAL CALL 9
HAS LONG BEEN TRIED AT LAW, . . . PL OCTOBER 16 RAID 20
THAT MAN THEY CALL THE LAW. . . . PL WHO BUT TH LORD 2
THE LAW RAISED UP HIS STICK . . . PL WHO BUT TH LORD 13

LAWD 25
O, LAWD! O, LAWD! . . . FC BLD OF GIN MARY 9
O, LAWD! O, LAWD! . . . FC BLD OF GIN MARY 9
O, LAWD . . . LAWDEE! . . . FC BLD OF GIN MARY 10
O, LAWD HAVE MERCY . . . FC GAL'S CRY DYING 11
LAWD, IN SUNDAY SCHOOL. . . . FC LISTEN HERE 8
LAWD, FOLKSES, HOW MUCH LONGER IS THIS GONNA LAST? . . . NM BROKE 59
HOMESICK BLUES, LAWD, . . . DK HOMESICK BLUES 13
LAWD! DON'T YOU KNOW? . . . ANS SISTER JOHNSON 11
LAWD! . . . SH DEATH IN HARLEM 75
FEELIN' SO SAD, LAWD, . . . SH MIDNIGHT CHIPPI 7
SO SAD, LAWD! . . . SH MIDNIGHT CHIPPI 9
A YEAR AND A DAY, LAWD. . . . SH OUT OF WORK 13
LAWD! I GOT TO FIND ME A WOMAN FOR THE WPA - . . . SH SUPPER TIME 13
IT'S DARK ON THIS STOOP, LAWD! THE SUN'S GONE DOWN! . . . SH TWILIGHT REVERI 15
LAWD, I SAW THE SUN GO DOWN! . . . SP BLUE BAYOU 27
GOIN' DOWN THE ROAD, LAWD, . . . SP BOUND NO'TH BLS 1
DOWN THE ROAD, LAWD, . . . SP BOUND NO'TH BLS 3
LAWD, I HATES TO BE SAD. . . . SP BOUND NO'TH BLS 14
LAWD, THESE THINGS WE WOMEN . . . SP EARLY EVENING 21
LAWD! AND I WANTED TO CRY. . . . SP LOVER'S RETURN 14
LAWD! THAT I WANTED TO CRY. . . . SP LOVER'S RETURN 16
LAWD, HAVE PITY! . . . SP MADAM PHONE BIL 20
LAWD, I WISH I COULD DIE - . . . SP REVERIE HARLEM 13
LAWD! . . . SP SOUTHERN MAMMY 5
WHEN THE LAWD PUT OUT THE LIGHT. . SP SYLVESTER'S BED 26

LAWDEE 1
O, LAWD . . . LAWDEE! . . . FC BLD OF GIN MARY 10

LAWDY 1
HEY, LAWDY, MAMA! . . . SP EASY BOOGIE 10

LAWDY-MERCY 1
LAWDY-MERCY! . . . SP BAD MORNING 3

LAWN 1
AND MY LAWN MOWER . . . AYM HORN OF PLENTY 92

LAWNS 1
SEEKING LAWNS AND SHADE TREES . . . AYM HORN OF PLENTY 71

LAWS 3
BEATING THEM WITH LAWS AND CLUBS AND BAYONETS AND BULLETS . . . ANS KIDS WHO DIE 30
WITH JIM CROW LAWS, . . . SP ONE-WAY TICKET 17
AT JIM CROW LAWS . . . PL NORTHERN LIBERL 19

LAW'S 1
THE LAW'S A KLANSMAN WITH AN EVIL WILL, . . . ANS BLD OZZIE POWEL 11

LAY 7
HE LAY, . . . DLD THE CONSUMPTIVE 7
I'LL LAY DOWN AN' DIE RIGHT NOW. . DK WIDE RIVER 18
I THOUGHT THAT FRIENDSHIP LAY . . . FW MAN 3
HE'LL NEVER LAY A . . . SP DEAD IN THERE 12
SHE HOPES TO LAY EYES ON YOU SOMETIME IN LIFE. . . . SP LETTER 7

Context	Source	Line
FOR HIS HEAD TO LAY.	SP NIGHT FUNERAL	8
SEND FOR OLD MAN MOSES TO LAY DOWN THE LAW.	PL FINAL CALL	9

LAZY 4

Context	Source	Line
IN LAZY FAR-OFF DROWSY SOUTHERN DAYS	OWT JUICE JOINT	11
THE LAZY, LAUGHING SOUTH	SP THE SOUTH	1
HE DID A LAZY SWAY.	SP THE WEARY BLUES	6
HE DID A LAZY SWAY.	SP THE WEARY BLUES	7

LEA 1

Context	Source	Line
AND POLAND'S PLAIN, AND ENGLAND'S GRASSY LEA.	ANS LET AMERICA BE	48

LEAD 5

Context	Source	Line
WHO HIRE FRANCO TO LEAD HIS GANG-HORDES	ANS SONG OF SPAIN	76
WILL LEAD IT.	SP PARADE	6
THE STEPS FROM THE HILL LEAD DOWN INTO HARLEM,	SP THEME FOR ENG B	11
MY HEART'S NOT EVEN LEAD.	PL VARI-COLORED	6
THE RAIN IS LEAD.	PL WITHOUT BENEFIT	11

LEADER 2

Context	Source	Line
THE LABOR LEADER BEHIND STEEL BARS,	JC THE BITTER RIVR	32
A RACE LEADER CRIED.	OWT BLD MARGE POLIT	43

LEADERS 1

Context	Source	Line
COLORED LEADERS	OWT BLD MARGE POLIT	38

LEADS 2

Context	Source	Line
THAT LEADS TO HELL.	SH BLD THE SINNER	4
THE ROAD THAT LEADS	SH BLD THE SINNER	19

LEAF 2

Context	Source	Line
MA HEART'S A FLUTTERING ASPEN LEAF	DK REASONS WHY	7
AND A LEAF OF COLLARD GREEN.	PL CULTURAL EXCHNG	30

LEAK 1

Context	Source	Line
MY ROOF HAS SPRUNG A LEAK.	SP BLD LANDLORD	2

LEAKS 1

Context	Source	Line
AND THE ATTIC LEAKS.	SP MADAM RENT MAN	18

LEAN 2

Context	Source	Line
WALK LEAN	FW TODAY	4
WHOSE LANGUID LEAN BRINGS BACK THE SUNNY SOUTH	OWT JUICE JOINT	42

LEAPING 1

Context	Source	Line
BUT ONE SHARP, LEAPING FLAME	WB SONGS DARK VIRG	17

LEAPS 1

Context	Source	Line
LEAPS CLEAN OVER TO SEVENTH AVENUE	SP PROJECTION	2

LEARN 6

Context	Source	Line
LET US NEW LESSONS LEARN.	ANS OPEN LETTER	32
I LIKE TO WORK, READ, LEARN, AND UNDERSTAND LIFE.	SP THEME FOR ENG B	22
AS I LEARN FROM YOU,	SP THEME FOR ENG B	37
I GUESS YOU LEARN FROM ME -	SP THEME FOR ENG B	38
LEARN HOW TO	PL FROSTING	7
AS I LIVE AND LEARN	PL MOTTO	6

LEARNED 1

Context	Source	Line
OF COURSE, THE WISE AND THE LEARNED	ANS KIDS WHO DIE	19

LEARNING 2

Context	Source	Line
PAIN AND A LEARNING	SP INTERNE AT PROV	5
LEARNING SKILLS OF SURGEONS	SP INTERNE AT PROV	11

LEARNS 1

Context	Source	Line
LEARNS SO SOON	FW MAN	13

LEAST 1

Context	Source	Line
AT LEAST I CAN OFFER THAT.	FC BRASS SPITOONS	39

LEATHER 1

Context	Source	Line
FOOTBALL PLAYERS LEATHER PUNCHERS $ $ $	AYM HORN OF PLENTY	18

LEAVE 19

Context	Source	Line
MEANS HE'S GONNA LEAVE THIS WORLD.	FC GAL'S CRY DYING	8
MEANS HE'S GONNA LEAVE THIS WORLD.	FC GAL'S CRY DYING	10
BUT I HAD TO LEAVE CAUSE	FC GYPSY MAN	11
AND LEAVE ME ROOM.	ANS BLDS OF LENIN	20
DON'T LEAVE ME HERE ALONE.	SH MIDNIGHT CHIPPI	12
AND LEAVE UNCUT THE ROSES	FW REMEMBRANCE	2
STEP, AND LEAVE NO TRACK.	OWT FLIGHT	2
WHAT SHALL I LEAVE MY SON	LHR TESTAMENT	1
WHAT SHALL I LEAVE MY DAUGHTER,	LHR TESTAMENT	5
WHAT SHALL I LEAVE MY WIFE	LHR TESTAMENT	9
I'LL LEAVE HER MORE TO NAG ABOUT	LHR TESTAMENT	11
THIS WORLD I'LL LEAVE BEHIND	SP DEFERRED	40
YOU LEAVE MY NAME	SP MADAM CENSUS	19
YOU BETTER LEAVE -	SP MADAM MIGHT-HAV	22
LEAVE ME AND MY NAME	SP MADAM CENSUS	27
"YOU CAN'T LEAVE US HERE!"	SP SYLVESTER'S BED	14
I'M GONNA LEAVE YOU, MISTER BACKLASH,	PL BACKLASH BLUES	29
AND LEAVE ME STANDIN' HERE.	PL FLORIDA WORKERS	12
I'D JUST AS LEAVE	PL SWEET WORDS RAC	13

LEAVES 10

Context	Source	Line
THE AUTUMN LEAVES	WB POEME D'AUTOMNE	1
LEAVES DE SNOW OUTSIDE	FC MINNIE SINGS	5
MAY ROSE LEAVES	FW FOR DEAD MIMES	2
LEAVES NOTHING	SP BEALE STREET	11
LEAVES THE SUNRISE IN THE SKY -	SP BLACK MARIA	19
NEW LEAVES TO SING	SP IN TIME SILVER	16
THEM COOL GREEN LEAVES	SP LITTLE GRN TREE	13
LEAVES US HUNGRY, RAGGED	SP SHARE-CROPPERS	9
AUTUMN LEAVES IN AUTUMN	AYM HORN OF PLENTY	73
THE VERY ROOM IN WHICH HE LEAVES	PL JUNIOR ADDICT	11

LEAVING 1

Context	Source	Line
AND LEAVING UNTOUCHED THE BOX-CAR	SP RAILROAD AVENUE	28

LED 1

Context	Source	Line
HE LED HIS COLORED DELEGATION	JC BLD SAM SOLOMON	46

LEDA 1

Context	Source	Line
AS LEDA STREW HER CORN	AYM BIRD IN ORBIT	29

LEE 2

Context	Source	Line
'HIND MA FRIEND MISS CORA LEE.	SP YOUNG GAL'S BLS	2
'HIND MA DEAR FRIEND CORA LEE	SP YOUNG GAL'S BLS	4

LEECHES 1

Context	Source	Line
FROM THOSE WHO LIVE LIKE LEECHES ON THE PEOPLE'S LIVES.	ANS LET AMERICA BE	72

LEFT 36

Context	Source	Line
MY MAN'S DONE LEFT ME.	WB BLUES FANTASY	7
MY GOOD MAN'S LEFT ME.	WB BLUES FANTASY	9
BUT PIERROT LEFT PIERRETTE.	WB PIERROT	16
WON'T BE NOTHIN' LEFT	FC SATURDAY NIGHT	15
PACKED HIS TRUNK AND LEFT.	FC SUICIDE	2
PACKED HIS TRUNK AND LEFT.	FC SUICIDE	4
WITH YOUR LEFT.	DK SONG BANJO DANC	9
FOR I'M THE ONE WHO LEFT DARK IRELAND'S SHORE,	ANS LET AMERICA BE	47
AND LEFT POOR BESSIE BLEEDIN	SH DEATH IN HARLEM	121
SHE LEFT THE TEXAS KID SETTIN BY HIMSELF	SH DEATH IN HARLEM	79
ALL UNSUSPECTIN OF THE CHIPPIE ON HIS LEFT -	SH DEATH IN HARLEM	30
LEFT ME BY MYSELF IN A DOUBLE BED.	SH LETTER	7
WHEN SHE LEFT	SH ONLY WOMAN BLUS	21
BUT I AIN'T GOT NO OWL HEAD AND YOU DONE LEFT TOWN	SH TWILIGHT REVERI	13
THAT WOMEN HE HAS LEFT	FW OLD SAILOR	18
LIKE ME LEFT AROUND.	OWT REQUEST REQUIEM	8
THERE AIN'T NO GOOD LEFT	SP BAD LUCK CARD	5
THEN WENT OFF AND LEFT HER.	SP BLD FORTUNE TEL	23
BUT IT WAS AS IF THEY'D LEFT.	SP CROSSING	4
BUT WAS JUST AS IF THEY'D LEFT.	SP CROSSING	22
THE GIRLS LEFT HIM.	SP DANCER	19
ALL THE CORNERS THAT ARE LEFT.	SP FINAL CURVE	4
THE WHITE FOLKS GO LEFT, THE COLORED GO RIGHT -	SP FREEDOM TRAIN	26
MY TRUE LOVE'S LEFT ME	SP LAMENT OVER LOV	11
AND LAUNDRY I DON'T HAVE MUCH LEFT	SP LETTER	3
BUT HE LEFT ME WHEN THE COAL WAS LOW.	SP MIDWINTER BLUES	8
BUT HE LEFT WHEN THE COAL WAS LOW.	SP MIDWINTER BLUES	10
STILL LEFT BY V-J DAY.	SP MIGRANT	29
AND WONDER WHAT YOU GOT LEFT?	SP REVERIE HARLEM	4
BUT WHO WOULD MISS ME IF I LEFT?	SP REVERIE HARLEM	14
SHE DONE LEFT PO' BUDDY	SP STONY LONESOME	12
YES, HE'S DONE BEEN LEFT.	SP STONY LONESOME	15
BUT LEFT INSTEAD	PL BIRMINGHAM SUND	4
WHO LEFT THEIR BLOOD UPON THAT WALL,	PL BIRMINGHAM SUND	16
LEFT BY A STREAK OF SUN,	PL GEORGIA DUSK	6
WHITE FOLKS HAVE LEFT	PL LITTLE SNG HOUS	22

LEFT-HAND 1

Context	Source	Line
A ROLL OF BILLS IN HIS LEFT-HAND POCKET.	SH DEATH IN HARLEM	19

LEGBA 1

Context	Source	Line
MAMACITA! PAPA LEGBA! SHANGO!	AYM GOSPEL CHA-CHA	35

LEGION 1

Context	Source	Line
THE LEGION FROM ENGLEWOOD	AYM BIRD IN ORBIT	77

LEGS 4

Context	Source	Line
LOOK AT YO' LEGS.	FC RED SILK STOCK	4
LOOK AT YO' LEGS.	FC RED SILK STOCK	12
PAIN ON HIND LEGS RISING.	SP INTERNE AT PROV	23
THREE KICKS BETWEEN THE LEGS	PL THIRD DEGREE	10

LEI 1

Context	Source	Line
LIKE A LEI.	PL CROWNS GARLANDS	3

LEMME 2
LEMME ROLL 'EM, BOY. FC CRAP GAME 1
LEMME OUT! OWT JITNEY 23

LEMON 3
STEP-FATHERED BY BLIND LEMON AYM ODE TO DINAH 20
BLIND LEMON. AYM ODE TO DINAH 22
SEND FOR DEAD BLIND LEMON TO SING THE B FLAT PL FINAL CALL 13

LENAS 1
MAKE A GARLAND OF LEONTYNES AND LENAS PL CROWNS GARLANDS 1

LEND 3
WHAT'LL YOU LEND? SH BLD PAWNBROKER 26
WON'T YOU LEND A HAND? JC BIG BUDDY 8
GRANDMA, LEND ME A DIME. SP DIME 2

LENIN 11
LENIN WITH THE FLAG BLOOD RED. SL SCOTTSBORO 21
COMRADE LENIN OF RUSSIA, ANS BLDS OF LENIN 1
MOVE OVER, COMRADE LENIN, ANS BLDS OF LENIN 3
I FOUGHT WITH YOU, COMRADE LENIN. ANS BLDS OF LENIN 7
COMRADE LENIN OF RUSSIA, ANS BLDS OF LENIN 9
MOVE OVER, COMRADE LENIN, ANS BLDS OF LENIN 11
I LIVED FOR YOU, COMRADE LENIN ANS BLDS OF LENIN 15
COMRADE LENIN OF RUSSIA, ANS BLDS OF LENIN 17
MOVE OVER, COMRADE LENIN, ANS BLDS OF LENIN 19
COMRADE LENIN OF RUSSIA ANS BLDS OF LENIN 25
SEND FOR LENIN! (DON'T YOU DARE! - HE CAN'T COME PL FINAL CALL 24

LENOX 10
LENOX AVENUE, WB LENOX AVE MIDNT 11
TO LENOX AVENUE. SP CONSIDER ME 40
OR LENOX AVENUE, SP COULD BE 2
ALSO LENOX AVENUE. SP COULD BE 14
LENOX AVENUE SP DIVE 1
TAKE THE LENOX AVENUE BUSSES, SP JUKE BOX LOVE 4
AND OFF DOWN LENOX AVENUE SP NIGHT FUNERAL 33
DOWN ON LENOX AVENUE THE OTHER NIGHT SP THE WEARY BLUES 4
BAHIA LAGOS DAKAR LENOX AYM ASK YOUR MAMA 47
UPTOWN ON LENOX AVENUE PL PRIME 1

LENYA 1
WHERE IS LOTTE LENYA AYM SHADES OF PIG 13

LEOLA 1
AS LEOLA PASSES BY AYM ASK YOUR MAMA 36

LEON 1
KATHERINE DUNHAM AL AND LEON $ $ $ $ $ AYM HORN OF PLENTY 6

LEONARD 2
LULU SAID TO LEONARD, SP SAME IN BLUES 8
LEONARD SAID TO LULU, SP SAME IN BLUES 10

LEONTYNE 2
WHAT'S SMELLING, LEONTYNE? PL CULTURAL EXCHNG 28
LOVELY LIEDER, LEONTYNE. PL CULTURAL EXCHNG 31

LEONTYNES 1
MAKE A GARLAND OF LEONTYNES AND LENAS PL CROWNS GARLANDS 1

LEONTYNE'S 1
YET LEONTYNE'S UNPACKING. PL CULTURAL EXCHNG 13

LEOPOLD 1
BELGIUM SHADOWS LEOPOLD AYM SHADES OF PIG 2

LESBIAN 1
POLICE LADY OR LESBIAN SP CAFE: 3 A.M. 9

LESS 5
TO MAKE IT EITHER MORE OR LESS. LHR DEAR LVLY DEATH 7
WELL, EVEN LESS ABOUT YOUR SP MADAM PHONE BIL 35
FINDING LESS THAN SOUGHT SP OLD WALT 3
AND OTHER KIDS LESS MEANER THAN ¢ ¢ ¢ ¢ AYM HORN OF PLENTY 25
OR LESS OR MOST - AYM SHOW FARE PLESE 28

LESSER 2
OF LESSER GENIUS. SP DANCER 4
FROM LESSER STARS IN ORBIT $ $ $ $ $ $ $ AYM HORN OF PLENTY 21

LESSONS 1
LET US NEW LESSONS LEARN. ANS OPEN LETTER 32

LEST 2
LEST SOME FRANCO STEAL INTO OUR BACKYARD ANS SONG OF SPAIN 66
LEST THE SONG GET OUT OF HAND. SP GENIUS CHILD 4

LET 72
LET ME FORGET. WB DISILLUSION 13
JUDGE, WON'T LET ME BE. FC BLD OF GIN MARY 12
SO LICKER'LL LET YOU BE. FC BLD OF GIN MARY 16
TILL LICKER'LL LET YOU BE. FC BLD OF GIN MARY 24
GO OUT AN' LET DE WHITE BOYS FC RED SILK STOCK 3
GO OUT AN' LET DE WHITE BOYS FC RED SILK STOCK 11
BUT DON'T LET IT MATTER TO YOU, NM BIG-TIMER POEM 49
AND LET 'EM HAVE MY MONEY, NM BIG-TIMER POEM 66
LET IT BE GAY. NM BLACK CLWN POEM 13
LET THE RAIN KISS YOU. DK APRIL RAIN SONG 1
LET THE RAIN BEAT UPON YOUR HEAD WITH SILVER LIQUID DROPS. DK APRIL RAIN SONG 2
LET THE RAIN SING YOU A LULLABY. DK APRIL RAIN SONG 3
LET ALL OTHERS KEEP SILENT A MOMENT. ANS A NEW SONG 3
LET AMERICA BE AMERICA AGAIN. ANS LET AMERICA BE 1
LET IT BE THE DREAM IT USED TO BE. ANS LET AMERICA BE 2
LET IT BE THE PIONEER ON THE PLAIN ANS LET AMERICA BE 3
LET AMERICA BE THE DREAM THE DREAMERS DREAMED - ANS LET AMERICA BE 6
LET IT BE THAT GREAT STRONG LAND OF LOVE ANS LET AMERICA BE 7
O, LET MY LAND BE A LAND WHERE LIBERTY ANS LET AMERICA BE 11
O, LET AMERICA BE AMERICA AGAIN - ANS LET AMERICA BE 62
LET THE WHITE FOLKS LIVE ANS LYNCHING SONG 3
LET US FORGET WHAT BOOKER-T. SAID, ANS OPEN LETTER 19
LET US BECOME INSTEAD, YOU AND I, ANS OPEN LETTER 21
LET US NEW LESSONS LEARN, ANS OPEN LETTER 32
LET US TOGETHER, SAY: ANS OPEN LETTER 38
LET POWER GROW! ANS OPEN LETTER 50
LET UNION BE ANS OPEN LETTER 55
TO LET YOU LIVE! SH BLD THE KILLER 22
GONNA HIT YOU IN THE FACE AND LET YOU FALL! SH DAYBREAK 2
STAND BACK FOLKSES, LET US SH DEATH IN HARLEM 106
LET ME REPEAT: SH HARLEM SWEETIES 30
LET THE WINDS RISE THEN! JC TO CAPTAIN MULZ 71
LET THE GREAT WAVES BEAT! JC TO CAPTAIN MULZ 72
LET THE GREAT WAVES RISE JC TO CAPTAIN MULZ 75
SHE'LL LET ME IN. FW FAITHFUL ONE 4
TO LET ME PASS, FW SNAKE 4
LET THE GRAVEYARD BE THE OWT BOARDING HOUSE 13
AND LET YOUR SONGS DRIFT THROUGH THE SWINGING DOORS. OWT JUICE JOINT 18
LET YOUR SONGS HOLD ALL THE SUNNY JOYS OWT JUICE JOINT 19
LET THOSE WOMEN WITH THEIR LIPS TOO RED OWT JUICE JOINT 21
WHEN YOU LET ME DOWN - OWT REQUEST REQUIEM 6
LET ME ALONE. LHR CONSERVATORY 4
WHEN THEY LET ME DOWN, SP AS BEFITS A MAN 13
AND LET HIM SLEEP IN HER SP BLD FORTUNE TEL 15
LET THINGS TAKE THEIR COURSE. SP DEMOCRACY 11
AND LET THE CHOIR SING A STORMY SONG SP FATASY PURPLE 3
AND LET THE WHITE VIOLINS WHIR THIN AND SLOW, SP FATASY PURPLE 6
LORDY, LET YO' MERCY SP FEET O' JESUS 3
KILL HIM - AND LET HIS SOUL RUN WILD! SP GENIUS CHILD 12
LET US ROAM THE NIGHT TOGETHER SP HARLEM NIGHT SO 2
LET US ROAM THE NIGHT TOGETHER SP HARLEM NIGHT SO 15
YOU LET ME DOWN - SP HIGH TO LOW 20
PUT IT ON A RECORD, LET IT WHIRL, SP JUKE BOX LOVE 9
AND LET MY FOOL-SELF FALL. SP LAMENT OVER LOV 24
YOU BETTER LET SP MADAM PHONE BIL 12
LET ME BRUSH THE HEM - SP MAMA AND DAUGHT 10
IF THE BLUES WOULD LET ME, SP MISS BLUES'ES 1
IF THE BLUES WOULD LET ME, SP MISS BLUES'ES 3
LET ME TO THY BOSOM FLY! SP MYSTERY 7
A CHANCE TO LET SP PARADE 29
JUST DON'T LET MAMA CATCH YOU SP STREET SONG 3
BELIEVE IN THE RIGHT, LET NONE PUSH YOU BACK. SP THE NEGRO MOTHE 43
AND LET THAT PAGE COME OUT OF YOU - SP THEME FOR ENG B 4
DON'T LET YOUR DOG CURB YOU! SP WARNING AUGMENT 1
DON'T LET YOUR DOG SP WARNING 2
BUT DON'T LET THAT DOG CURB YOU! SP WARNING AUGMENT 4
JUST DON'T LET YOUR DOG CURB YOU! SP WARNING AUGMENT 14
SEND FOR THE PIED PIPER AND LET HIM PIPE THE RATS PL FINAL CALL 1
LET THINGS TAKE THEIR COURSE. PL FREEDOM 11
LET ALL WHO WILL PL MILITANT 1
BUT WON'T LET ME PL PRIME 7
DON'T LET HIM MAKE A PULP OUT OF ME! PL WHO BUT TH LORD 11

LETS 3
AN' LETS ME BE. FC BLACK GAL 8
LETS HIS GLASS SP NEIGHBOR 23
WHERE THE DOORKNOB LETS IN LIEDER PL CULTURAL EXCHNG 15

LETTER 8
DEAR CASSIE: YES, I GOT YOUR LETTER. SH LETTER 1
(A CAPITAL LETTER THERE, SP CONSIDER ME 13
THE LETTER THAT I FOUND THERE SP LITTLE OLD LETT 3
JUST A LITTLE OLD LETTER, SP LITTLE OLD LETT 5
A LITTLE OLD LETTER SP LITTLE OLD LETT 15
OR A ROMAN LETTER? SP MADAM'S CALLING 14
GOD ADDRESSED ME A LETTER. SP PERSONAL 3
YOUR LETTER PL OFFICIAL NOTICE 11

LETTERS 1
IN UPHILL LETTERS — SP MIGRANT 36

LETTING 3
LETTING KIDS DIE. — ANS KIDS WHO DIE 7
I, A WORKER, LETTING MY LABOR PILE — ANS SONG OF SPAIN 43
LETTING MIDNIGHT — SP JAM SESSION 1

LET'S 7
THEN LET'S — WB CAT AND SAXOPHN 25
LET'S SHAKE DAT THING! — FC SATURDAY NIGHT 12
LET'S GET MARRIED RIGHT NOW! YES! WHAT DO YOU SAY? — NM BROKE 75
LET'S GO SEE OLD ABE — DK LINCOLN MONUMNT 1
WHILE THE MUSIC'S PLAYIN LET'S — SH DEATH IN HARLEM 85
SO LET'S JUST FORGET WHAT THIS FUSS WAS ABOUT. — SH LETTER 15
LET'S GO, SWEETIE! — SP PORT TOWN 15

LEVEE 10
BEEN WORKIN' ON DE LEVEE, — SH MISSISSIPPI LEV 1
WORKIN' ON DE LEVEE — SH MISSISSIPPI LEV 3
DON'T KNOW WHY I BUILD THIS LEVEE — SH MISSISSIPPI LEV 7
AND DE LEVEE DON'T DO NO GOOD. — SH MISSISSIPPI LEV 8
DON'T KNOW WHY I BUILD THIS LEVEE — SH MISSISSIPPI LEV 9
WHEN DE LEVEE DON'T DO NO GOOD. — SH MISSISSIPPI LEV 10
LEVEE, LEVEE, — SH MISSISSIPPI LEV 12
LEVEE, LEVEE, — SH MISSISSIPPI LEV 13
LEVEE, LEVEE, — SH MISSISSIPPI LEV 15
LEVEE, LEVEE, — SH MISSISSIPPI LEV 15

LEVY 1
FEEL THE WEIGHT, MR. LEVY, — SH BLD PAWNBROKER 13

LEWIS 2
LEWIS JONES BEHIND STEEL BARS, — JC THE BITTER RIVR 30
NAT-UNDREAMED-OF LEWIS COMBINES — SP FLATTED FIFTHS 11

LIABLE 2
THERE'S LIABLE — SP SAME IN BLUES 26
THERE'S LIABLE TO BE CONFUSION — SP SAME IN BLUES 31

LIARS 1
LIARS USE THOSE WORDS. — SP IN EXPLANATION 39

LIBERAL 1
TO SHOW HOW LIBERAL I AM? — PL NORTHERN LIBERL 10

LIBERTIES 2
OUR SYMBOL OF NEW LIBERTIES. — JC TO CAPTAIN MULZ 42
HE, TOO, A SYMBOL OF NEW LIBERTIES. — JC TO CAPTAIN MULZ 46

LIBERTY 7
O, LET MY LAND BE A LAND WHERE LIBERTY — ANS LET AMERICA BE 11
WHY IN THE NAME OF LIBERTY — JC BLACK MAN SPEAK 11
"LIBERTY AND JUSTICE - — SP CHILDREN'S RYME 23
AMONG THESE LIFE, LIBERTY — SP FREEDOM'S PLOW 34
LIBERTY! — SP IN EXPLANATION 35
LIBERTY AND JUSTICE - — PL CHILDREN'S RYME 14
THERE ARE WORDS LIKE LIBERTY — PL WORDS LIKE FREE 5

LICENSE 1
YES, UM-HUM! YOU SHO IS SWEET! CAN YOU PAY FO' DE LICENSE, DEAR? — NM BROKE 78

LICENSES 1
LICENSES AND SUCH. — SP S-SSS-SS-SH! 11

LICK 3
WHAT'S THE LICK? — SP LIKEWISE 22
WE LICK OUR CHOPS AT BIRMINGHAM — PL NORTHERN LIBERL 2
AND LICK MY CHOPS — PL NORTHERN LIBERL 18

LICKER 7
I TAKES MA MEANNESS AND MA LICKER — FC BAD MAN 5
SEEMS LIKE BAD LICKER, — FC BLD OF GIN MARY 11
GIT A QUART O' LICKER, — FC SATURDAY NIGHT 11
BUT I WAS DRINKING LICKER, — SH BLD THE SINNER 15
THE LICKER — OWT DECEASED 6
I DRUNK SOME BAD LICKER THAT — SP MORNING AFTER 5
AS A BOTTLE OF LICKER — SP ONE 6

LICKER-HEADED 1
TILL THESE LICKER-HEADED ROUNDERS — FC LISTEN HERE 11

LICKER'LL 2
SO LICKER'LL LET YOU BE. — FC BLD OF GIN MARY 16
TILL LICKER'LL LET YOU BE. — FC BLD OF GIN MARY 24

LICKS 1
AND THE DEVIL LICKS HIS CHOPS — SP SUNDAY MORNING 7

LICORICE 1
LICORICE, CLOVE, CINNAMON — SH HARLEM SWEETIES 35

LID 1
AND THE LID SHUT ON HIS HEAD — SP NIGHT FUNERAL 28

LIE 15
FOR WHAT COULD I ANSWER HIM, EXCEPT, "IT'S A LIE!" — NM COLORED SL POEM 43
IT'S A LIE! IT'S A LIE! EVERY WORD THEY SAID. — NM COLORED SL POEM 44
IT'S A LIE! IT'S A LIE! EVERY WORD THEY SAID. — NM COLORED SL POEM 44
8 BLACK BOYS AND ONE WHITE LIE. — SL SCOTTSBORO 3
I LIE DOWN IN THE SHADOW. — SP AS I GREW OLDER 19
THEN SHE STARTED IN TO LIE. — SP BLD THE GYPSY 10
AW, WHAT A LIE! — SP BLD THE GYPSY 13
CAN LIE! — SP DREAM 13
YOU LIE. — SP MADAM CENSUS 16
BUT HE MUST A BEEN TELLIN' A LIE. — SP MIDWINTER BLUES 14
HE MUST A BEEN TELLIN' A LIE. — SP MIDWINTER BLUES 16
THAT'S NO LIE, HE SAID, — SP NEW YORKERS 2
NEITHER TRUTH NOR LIE. — SP RAILROAD AVENUE 22
SO YOU LIE IN YOUR CRADLE — PL LAST PRINCE 8
OUT YONDER YOU'LL LIE: — PL WITHOUT BENEFIT 15

LIEBKNECHT 1
OR THE RIVERS WHERE YOU'RE DROWNED LIKE LIEBKNECHT, — ANS KIDS WHO DIE 42

LIEDER 4
WHERE THE DOORKNOB LETS IN LIEDER — PL CULTURAL EXCHNG 15
LIEDER, LOVELY LIEDER — PL CULTURAL EXCHNG 29
LIEDER, LOVELY LIEDER — PL CULTURAL EXCHNG 29
LOVELY LIEDER, LEONTYNE. — PL CULTURAL EXCHNG 31

LIES 18
A SILENT WOMAN LIES BETWEEN TWO LOVERS - — WB SICK ROOM 4
SO FULL OF LIES. — WB SOLEDAD 7
HIS BURIED BODY LIES - — DK ALABAMA EARTH 3
WHO DON'T BELIEVE IN LIES, AND BRIBES AND CONTENTMENT, — ANS KIDS WHO DIE 17
THE RAPE AND ROT OF GRAFT, AND STEALTH, AND LIES, — ANS LET AMERICA BE 81
TO KILL THE LIES OF COLOR — ANS OPEN LETTER 25
IN UNION LIES OUR STRENGTH. — ANS OPEN LETTER 54
FORGIVE THEM LIES! — SH ONLY WOMAN BLUS 16
YOU AIN'T TELLING NOTHING BUT YOUR JIM CROW LIES - — JC JIM CROW'S LAST 22
SWEEPS YOUR LIES AWAY. — JC THE BITTER RIVR 50
I THINK THE DIFFERENCE LIES — FW BORDER LINE 3
BEEN TELLIN' LIES, — SP FIRE 18
LIES RIGHT IN YOURSELF. — SP MADAM FORT TELL 18
LIES. — PL BLACK PANTHER 12
LIES WRITTEN DOWN — PL CHILDREN'S RYME 11
LIFE IS A SYSTEM OF HALF-TRUTHS AND LIES, — PL ELDERLY LEADERS 3
REMEMBERING THE OLD LIES, — PL HARLEM 3
THE LIES THIEVES SHOCK — PL LUMUMBA'S GRAVE 7

LIFE 64
THE RHYTHM OF LIFE — WB LENOX AVE MIDNT 1
AND NOT THIS LAND WHERE LIFE IS COLD. — WB OUR LAND 7
LIFE AND DEATH, — WB SICK ROOM 5
PART OF MY LIFE. — FC BRASS SPITOONS 10
LIFE — FC SPORT 1
I SHOULD MEET LIFE FACE TO FACE — OLD AESTHETE HARLEM 3
LIFE IN PLACES GENTLER SPEAKING — OLD AESTHETE HARLEM 5
AND FOUND LIFE - STEPPING ON MY FEET! — OLD AESTHETE HARLEM 7
FEELING LIFE GO. — OLD THE CONSUMPTIVE 4
AND BLUE, HIDING HIS DISCONTENT AS THOUGHTS OF A BETTER LIFE OVERCOME — NM BIG-TIMER MOOD 7
TRAGIC EMPTINESS OF HIS LIFE. — NM BIG-TIMER MOOD 12
DRINKIN' LIFE LIKE WINE. — NM BIG-TIMER POEM 18
BUT - AIN'T MY LIFE MINE? — NM BIG-TIMER POEM 20
WE ONLY GOT ONE LIFE — NM BIG-TIMER POEM 71
THE LONG STRUGGLE FOR LIFE: — NM BLACK CLWN POEM 38
OF A FREE LIFE BENEATH OUR GREAT SKY. — NM DARK YOUTH USA 10
A BIT OF CLAY, BROWN, UGLY, GIVEN LIFE? — DK BEGGAR BOY 6
LIFE IS A BROKEN-WINGED BIRD — DK DREAMS 3
LIFE IS A BARREN FIELD — DK DREAMS 7
MA LORD'S LIFE WAS TROUBLE, TOO, — DK MA LORD 8
OPEN WIDE YOUR ARMS TO LIFE, — DK SONG 5
50-VOICES: LIFE IS EVERYWHERE FOR YOU, — ANS CHANT MAY DAY 24
50-VOICES: LIFE IS EVERYWHERE. — ANS CHANT MAY DAY 26
LIFE FOREVER THROUGH THE WORKERS' POWER - — ANS CHANT TOM MOONY 44
THE SONG OF THE NEW LIFE TRIUMPHANT — ANS KIDS WHO DIE 50
BUT OPPORTUNITY IS REAL, AND LIFE IS FREE, — ANS LET AMERICA BE 13
LIFE! — SH BLD PAWNBROKER 25
MY LIFE AIN'T NOTHIN' — SH LOVE AGAIN BLUS 1
I SAY MY LIFE AIN'T NOTHIN' — SH LOVE AGAIN BLUS 3
AND YOUTH AND LIFE — FW CAROLINA CABIN 9
OF LIFE. — FW DANCERS 8

C. DRUMS OF LIFE IN HARLEM AFTER DARK!	OWT	NEGRO SERVANT	15
RIGHT OUT OF HER OWN LIFE.	SP	AUNTSUE'S STORI	22
CALLING LIFE	SP	DRUM	15
AMONG THESE LIFE, LIBERTY	SP	FREEDOM'S PLOW	94
PUTS FORTH NEW LIFE AGAIN.	SP	IN TIME SILVER	3
OF LIFE.	SP	IN TIME SILVER	8
OF LIFE.	SP	IN TIME SILVER	9
OF LIFE!	SP	IN TIME SILVER	10
AND LIFE	SP	IN TIME SILVER	23
OF LIFE	SP	JULIET	8
SHE HOPES TO LAY EYES ON YOU SOMETIME IN LIFE.	SP	LETTER	7
LIFE IS FINE!	SP	LIFE IS FINE	31
LIFE IS FINE!	SP	LIFE IS FINE	33
CAN TAKE A PERSON'S LIFE.	SP	LITTLE OLD LETT	16
FIRST TIME IN MY LIFE	SP	MADAM MIGHT-HAV	11
THE QUIET FADING OUT OF LIFE	SP	MAGNOLIA FLOWER	1
LIFE FOR ME AIN'T BEEN NO CRYSTAL STAIR.	SP	MOTHER TO SON	2
AND LIFE FOR ME AIN'T BEEN NO CRYSTAL STAIR.	SP	MOTHER TO SON	20
I PICK UP MY LIFE	SP	ONE-WAY TICKET	1
I PICK UP MY LIFE	SP	ONE-WAY TICKET	9
I PICK UP MY LIFE	SP	ONE-WAY TICKET	23
PLOWING LIFE AWAY	SP	SHARE-CROPPERS	15
WHEN LIFE HURT HER:	SP	SPIRITUALS	7
PREPARING TO FEAST ON LIFE.	SP	SUNDAY MORNING	8
YES, SIR! LONG AS LIFE DO LAST!	SP	SYLVESTER'S BED	22
IN LIFE BEING CREATED	SP	S-SSS-SS-SH!	3
LIFE IS SHORT	SP	TAMBOURINES	9
STILL BAR YOU THE WAY, AND DENY YOU LIFE -	SP	THE NEGRO MOTHE	46
I LIKE TO WORK, READ, LEARN, AND UNDERSTAND LIFE.	SP	THEME FOR ENG B	22
AND LIFE IS GAY.	SP	WATER-FRONT STR	4
IN MY NATURAL LIFE)	AYM	SHADES OF PIG	39
LIFE IS A SYSTEM OF HALF-TRUTHS AND LIES.	PL	ELDERLY LEADERS	3
BEEN SAVING ALL MY LIFE	PL	LITTLE SNG HOUS	2

LIFE-WAYS 1

NEW LIFE-WAYS MAKE.	ANS	OPEN LETTER	24

LIFE'S 1

BUT REDDER NOW WHERE YOUR LIFE'S BLOOD FLOWED.	ANS	BLD OZZIE POWEL	31

LIFT 9

WORKERS, LIFT NO HAND AGAIN	ANS	SONG OF SPAIN	56
LIFT ARMS IN VAIN, RUN, HIDE, DIE:	ANS	SONG OF SPAIN	60
LIFT THEIR HEADS AND THINGS IS BAD,	JC	GOOD MORN STLIN	30
LIFT THEIR HEADS, TOO, WITH GUN IN HAND	JC	GOOD MORN STLIN	33
AND SWITCH THEIR SKIRTS AND LIFT THEIR STRAIGHTENED HEADS	OWT	JUICE JOINT	23
AND FLOWERS LIFT THEIR HEADS.	SP	IN TIME SILVER	5
LIFT SILKEN WINGS	SP	IN TIME SILVER	13
LIFT HIGH MY BANNER OUT OF THE DUST.	SP	THE NEGRO MOTHE	41
AND LIFT MY HAND	PL	ANGOLA QUESTION	11

LIFTED 1

SHE LIFTED UP HER LIPS	SP	NEW YORKERS	15

LIFTING 3

LIFTING MY RACE TO ITS RIGHTFUL PLACE	NM	DARK YOUTH USA	19
IRON LIFTING IRON	SP	MIGRANT	14
IRON LIFTING IRON	SP	MIGRANT	16

LIFTS 2

LIFTS HIGH A DRESS OF SILKEN GOLD.	WB	JAZZONIA	6
THAT NEVER LIFTS ITS HEAD	SP	TROUBLED WOMAN	11

LIGHT 25

WOULD PALE IN THE LIGHT	WB	POEM	19
PALE IN THE LIGHT	WB	POEM	21
IN THE DOORWAY LIGHT.	FC	CLOSING TIME	3
IS I MARRIED? NO. ALL THESE-HERE GIRLS UP NORTH IS TOO LIGHT.	NM	BROKE	70
WITH HIS FACE FULL OF LIGHT AND FAITH, CONFIDENT THAT A NEW WORLD HAS	NM	COLORED SL MOOD	9
SOFT LIGHT ON THE TABLES.	DK	NEGRO DANCERS	7
DO NOT BE AFRAID OF LIGHT.	DK	SONG	3
TURN ON THE LIGHT AND LOOK REAL GOOD!	SH	SUPPER TIME	3
THE LIGHT OF MY DREAM.	SP	AS I GREW OLDER	14
NO LONGER THE LIGHT OF MY DREAM BEFORE ME.	SP	AS I GREW OLDER	20
CIRCLE OF LIGHT.	SP	DANSE AFRICAINE	9
WHERE IS THIS LIGHT	SP	DEMAND	8
THERE IS NEITHER LIGHT	SP	END	7
THERE WAS LIGHT WHEN THE BATTLE CLOUDS ROLLED AWAY.	SP	FREEDOM'S PLOW	139
BECAME A BRIGHT BALL OF LIGHT	SP	FULFILMENT	10
THE LIGHT ON THE PALMOLIVE BUILDING	SP	INTERNE AT PROV	40
WHERE THERE AIN'T BEEN NO LIGHT.	SP	MOTHER TO SON	13
THE STREET LIGHT	SP	NIGHT FUNERAL	35
QUICKER THAN LIGHT	SP	NIGHTMARE BOOGE	6
WHEN THE LAWD PUT OUT THE LIGHT.	SP	SYLVESTER'S BED	26
YET SHINING LIKE THE SUN WITH LOVE'S TRUE LIGHT.	SP	THE NEGRO MOTHE	6
MAKE OF MY PAST A ROAD TO THE LIGHT	SP	THE NEGRO MOTHE	39
BY THE PALE DULL PALLOR OF AN OLD GAS LIGHT	SP	THE WEARY BLUES	5
AND BY MISTAKE SHOT OUT THE LIGHT.	AYM	ODE TO DINAH	132
FOR LIGHT AND CIVILIZATION	PL	FLORIDA WORKERS	7

LIGHTED 1

UNTIL A GLOW IS LIGHTED	SP	MIGRANT	21

LIGHTER 1

WHERE THE LIGHTER IS THE DARKER	AYM	SHOW FARE PLESE	16

LIGHTNING 2

OF LIGHTNING	FW	BIRTH	7
AND THE LIGHTNING	SP	AFRICA	4

LIGHTS 12

YOUR FACES ARE WHIRLING LIGHTS OF LOVELINESS AND SPLENDOR, TOO.	WB	THE WHITE ONES	4
THE LIGHTS GO OUT	FC	SPORT	8
LIGHTS THE SKY.	JC	GOOD MORN STLIN	14
THE MOVIES END. THE LIGHTS FLASH GAILY ON.	OWT	LINCOLN THEATRE	5
INTO A THOUSAND LIGHTS OF SUN.	SP	AS I GREW OLDER	31
TAKE THE NEON LIGHTS AND MAKE A CROWN.	SP	JUKE BOX LOVE	3
LIGHTS, SAILOR BOY.	SP	PORT TOWN	9
WARM, WHITE LIGHTS.	SP	PORT TOWN	10
LIGHTS IN THE FISH JOINTS.	SP	RAILROAD AVENUE	3
LIGHTS IN THE POOL ROOMS.	SP	RAILROAD AVENUE	4
SHAKING THE LIGHTS IN THE FISH JOINTS.	SP	RAILROAD AVENUE	26
LIGHTS AIN'T COME ON YET.	SP	WONDER	2

LIKE 231

CORN. YOU LIKE	WB	CAT AND SAXOPHN	7
LIKE THE EARTH.	WB	DISILLUSION	3
LIKE THE RAIN.	WB	DISILLUSION	4
LIKE A SWEET VEIL ABOUT YOUR BOWER?	WB	NUDE YOUNG DANC	4
LIKE YOUNG COURTESANS	WB	POEME D'AUTOMNE	6
DESCENDS LIKE A WHITE MIST	WB	SUMMER NIGHT	24
NOW LIKE A LITTLE LONELY WAIF	WB	TO LITTLE LOVER	8
IS LIKE A WITHERED FLOWER	WB	YOUNG PROSTITUT	2
YET IT SEEMS LIKE ALWAYS	FC	BLACK GAL	5
SEEMS LIKE BAD LICKER.	FC	BLD OF GIN MARY	11
BRIGHT POLISHED BRASS LIKE THE CYMBALS	FC	BRASS SPITOONS	33
LIKE THE WINE CUPS OF SOLOMON.	FC	BRASS SPITOONS	35
FEELS LIKE I COULD DIE.	FC	MOAN	14
AN' SHE DON'T LIKE CORN.	FC	NEW CABARET GRL	6
CREEPING LIKE FIRE	DLD	THE CONSUMPTIVE	9
CREEPING LIKE FIRE FROM A SLOW SPARK	DLD	THE CONSUMPTIVE	10
BOASTING, LIKE A CHEAP BULLY, BUT SUDDENLY LOOKING AHEAD: SHRUGGING HIS	NM	BIG-TIMER MOOD	5
SPENDIN' MONEY LIKE WATER.	NM	BIG-TIMER POEM	17
DRINKIN' LIFE LIKE WINE.	NM	BIG-TIMER POEM	18
NOT LIVIN' LIKE I OUGHTER.	NM	BIG-TIMER POEM	19
AND WHOEVER DON'T LIKE IT	NM	BIG-TIMER POEM	27
BUST 'EM LIKE BUBBLES.	NM	BIG-TIMER POEM	60
A GAY AND LOW-DOWN BLUES. COMIC ENTRANCE LIKE THE CLOWNS IN THE CIRCUS.	NM	BLACK CLWN MOOD	1
PACE. "SOMETIMES I FEEL LIKE A MOTHER-LESS CHILE." TURNING FUTILELY	NM	BLACK CLWN MOOD	8
AND HELPLESSNESS. THE MUSIC IS LIKE A MOURNFUL TOM-TOM IN THE DARK! BUT	NM	BLACK CLWN MOOD	11
LIKE THIS WILL I BE:	NM	BLACK CLWN POEM	60
AND DON'T YOU KNOW THAT OLD WOMAN SWELLED UP LIKE A SPECKLED TOAD	NM	BROKE	21
I SAID, "BABY, YOU KNOW I LOVES YOU, AND ALL LIKE THAT	NM	BROKE	50
IT'S DONE GOT ME SO CRAZY, FEEL LIKE I BEEN TAKIN' COKE.	NM	BROKE	60
IF A PRETTY GAL LIKE YOU WAS WILLIN', I'D BITE.	NM	BROKE	72
BLACK BOYS COULDN'T WORK THEN ANYWHERE LIKE THEY CAN	NM	COLORED SL POEM	19
SO NOW I KNOW WE BLACKS ARE JUST LIKE ANY OTHER -	NM	COLORED SL POEM	35
LIKE LITTLE BROWN BUTTERFLIES.	DK	AUTUMN THOUGHT	5
JUST LIKE NEW.	DK	DRESSED UP	2
SUNSHINE SEEMED LIKE GOLD.	DK	PO' BOY BLUES	2
SUNSHINE SEEMED LIKE GOLD.	DK	PO' BOY BLUES	4
LIKE DE WINGS OF A BUTTERFLY.	DK	REASONS WHY	4
LIKE GOD'S HAND.	DK	SEA CHARM	6
LIKE GOD'S BREATH.	DK	SEA CHARM	9
LIKE A FLAME.	DK	YOUTH	3
LIKE A MIGHTY HEART-BEAT AS THEY COME?	SL	SCOTTSBORO	8

Context	Book	Title	Line
WAVES OF RISING AND RE-RISING MASS VOICES. MULTIPLYING LIKE	ANS	CHANT MAY DAY	2
BE LIKE THE FLOWERS.	ANS	CHANT MAY DAY	8
10-VOICES: BE LIKE THE SAP RISING IN THE TREES.	ANS	CHANT MAY DAY	15
FOR THE KIDS WHO DIE ARE LIKE IRON IN THE BLOOD OF THE PEOPLE -	ANS	KIDS WHO DIE	32
OR THE RIVERS WHERE YOU'RE DROWNED LIKE LIEBKNECHT.	ANS	KIDS WHO DIE	42
FROM THOSE WHO LIVE LIKE LEECHES ON THE PEOPLE'S LIVES.	ANS	LET AMERICA BE	72
LIKE WATER DOWN THE STREET,	ANS	NEGRO GHETTO	6
BULLETS LIKE RAIN'S	ANS	SONG OF SPAIN	33
I SURE WOULD LIKE	SH	ASPIRATION	3
I DID NOT ACT LIKE	SH	BLD THE SINNER	11
LIKE A SIEVE.	SH	BLD THE KILLER	24
OVER EVERYTHING LIKE A SHROUD.	SH	CABARET GIRL	2
LIKE A WOMAN IN A DREAM	SH	DEATH IN HARLEM	112
IT'S GOOD LIKE THAT WHEN YOU	SH	DEATH IN HARLEM	29
AND NIGHT LIKE A REEFER-MAN	SH	DEATH IN HARLEM	135
WHAT YOU LIKE TO EAT?	SH	DEATH IN HARLEM	52
AND SHE SAT ON HER CHAIR LIKE A SWEET JELLY ROLL.	SH	DEATH IN HARLEM	82
O' MY FEELING LIKE A DOG	SH	EVIL MORNING	10
RIDE LIKE A FOOL.	SH	IF-ING	4
DON'T IG ME LIKE YOU DO.	SH	MIDNIGHT CHIPPI	20
PLEASE DON'T IG ME LIKE YOU DO.	SH	MIDNIGHT CHIPPI	22
WORKIN' LIKE A TUCK-TAIL DOG.	SH	MISSISSIPPI LEV	2
LIKE A TUCK-TAIL DOG.	SH	MISSISSIPPI LEV	4
GONNA SLEEP LIKE A WATER-LOG.	SH	MISSISSIPPI LEV	6
SHE COULD MAKE ME HOLLER LIKE A SISSIE.	SH	ONLY WOMAN BLUS	7
BARK LIKE A DOG.	SH	ONLY WOMAN BLUS	8
I NEVER DID LIKE THE INSTALLMENT PLAN	SH	PAY DAY	14
WOMEN'S ABOMINATIONS! JUST LIKE A CURSE!	SH	PAY DAY	19
THEY OUGHT TO BE LIKE ME SETTING HERE - FEELING GLAD!	SH	SUNDAY	15
KEEP FEELING LIKE THIS I'M GONNA START ACTING BAD.	SH	TWILIGHT REVERI	4
MAKE YOU WALK LIKE A GHOST IF YOU BOTHER ME ANY MORE.	SH	TWILIGHT REVERI	6
YOU ARE LIKE A WARM DARK DUSK	SH	YOUNG NEGRO GRL	1
YOU ARE LIKE A WARM DARK DUSK	SH	YOUNG NEGRO GRL	6
I'LL FIGHT LIKE A MAN.	JC	BIG BUDDY	6
LOTS OF FOLKS WHO DON'T LIKE YOU	JC	GOOD MORN STLIN	2
AND SEE WHERE SIMPLE WORKING FOLKS LIKE ME	JC	GOOD MORN STLIN	32
I WOULD LIKE TO SEE THOSE FREEDOMS	JC	HOW ABOUT DIXIE	3
LOOKS LIKE BY NOW	JC	HOW ABOUT DIXIE	17
NOW THAT CROW'S BEGUN TO LOOK LIKE HELL.	JC	JIM CROW'S LAST	6
LIKE STROKE	FW	BIRTH	6
LIKE A SQUIRREL IN A CAGE -	FW	CIRCLES	7
LIKE CRIMSON	FW	FOR DEAD MIMES	4
SEEMS LIKE SHE SAID:	FW	GIRL	11
AND LIKE A WAVE THE FLOOR -	FW	HARLEM DANCE HA	7
VEILING HER FACE LIKE A VIRGIN	FW	NEW MOON	6
IS WHAT I LIKE ABOUT YOU.	OWT	HONEY BABE	8
LIKE MY LITTLE GIRL.	OWT	HONEY BABE	16
AND HANDLE EASY LIKE A PURCHASED THING.	OWT	JUICE JOINT	36
LIKE ME LEFT AROUND.	OWT	REQUEST REQUIEM	8
SHRUNKEN LIKE A BALLOON WITHOUT AIR.	SP	A BLACK PIERROT	13
BRIGHT LIKE A SUN -	SP	AS I GREW OLDER	5
SHE TREATED HIM LIKE	SP	BLD FORTUNE TEL	11
LOOKS LIKE SHE COULD'VE KNOWED IT	SP	BLD FORTUNE TEL	19
I'D LIKE TO MEET A GOOD FRIEND	SP	BOUND NO'TH BLS	11
LIKE THEY TRY TO DO YOU BAD.	SP	BOUND NO'TH BLS	18
BUT HE DOESN'T WALK LIKE ONE.	SP	CASUALTY	2
HE WALKS LIKE HIS SOLDIERING	SP	CASUALTY	3
AND THINGS LIKE THAT. BUT NOW, LORD.	SP	CHILDREN'S RYME	3
YOU TALK LIKE	SP	COMMENT ON CURB	1
LIKE AS NOT YOU WON'T.	SP	COULD BE	12
LOOKED LIKE ME.	SP	CROSSING	18
LIKE A WISP OF SMOKE AROUND THE FIRE -	SP	DANSE AFRICAINE	11
I'D LIKE TO TAKE UP BACH.	SP	DEFERRED	48
FOLKS SAY SHE DON'T LIKE	SP	DELINQUENT	3
WAS LIKE A DOUBLE DEATH.	SP	DESIRE	2
GRANDMA ACTS LIKE	SP	DIME	4
I'D LIKE TO BUY A STRAIGHTENIN' COMB.	SP	DOWN AND OUT	9
DARK LIKE ME -	SP	DREAM VARIATION	8
LOOKS LIKE HIS EYES	SP	DREAM BOOGE VAR	9
LIKE A -	SP	DREAM BOOGIE	13
BLACK LIKE ME.	SP	DREAM VARIATION	17
LIKE MARCHING FEET.	SP	EASY BOOGIE	4
ROLLING LIKE I LIKE IT	SP	EASY BOOGIE	7
ROLLING LIKE I LIKE IT	SP	EASY BOOGIE	7
EASY LIKE I ROCK IT	SP	EASY BOOGIE	12
LIKE EVERYTHING ELSE.	SP	ELEVATOR BOY	7
DON'T TURN OUT LIKE I AM.	SP	EVENING SONG	12
LOOKS LIKE WHAT DRIVES ME CRAZY	SP	EVIL	1
SORROW LIKE A SEA.	SP	FEET O' JESUS	2
LIKE THE SKY-MEANING	SP	FULFILMENT	2
LIKE AN OLD GRANDMOTHER.	SP	FULFILMENT	17
FLY LIKE THE EAGLE FLIES.	SP	HARD DADDY	14
FLY LIKE THE EAGLE FLIES.	SP	HARD DADDY	16
LIKE A RAISIN IN THE SUN?	SP	HARLEM	3
OR FESTER LIKE A SORE -	SP	HARLEM	4
DOES IT STINK LIKE ROTTEN MEAT?	SP	HARLEM	6
LIKE A SYRUPY SWEET?	SP	HARLEM	8
LIKE A HEAVY LOAD.	SP	HARLEM	10
AND THINGS LIKE THAT.	SP	IN EXPLANATION	16
LIKE A MULE BROKE TO THE HALTER.	SP	INTERNE AT PROV	25
SHINES LIKE A STAR IN THE EAST.	SP	INTERNE AT PROV	41
LIKE DARKER RIVERS	SP	ISLAND	3
LOVE IS LIKE WHISKEY,	SP	LAMENT OVER LOV	13
LOVE IS LIKE RED, RED WINE.	SP	LAMENT OVER LOV	14
LOVE IS LIKE WHISKEY,	SP	LAMENT OVER LOV	15
LIKE SWEET RED WINE.	SP	LAMENT OVER LOV	16
IT LOOKS LIKE TO ME	SP	LITTLE GRN TREE	1
JUST LIKE A PAIR O' SHOES -	SP	LOVER'S RETURN	10
DOES 'EM LIKE YOU CHOOSE.	SP	LOVER'S RETURN	12
YOU TREAT ME LIKE YOU DAMN WELL PLEASE.	SP	LOW TO HIGH	14
LOOKS LIKE A LIKELY	SP	MADAM NUMBER WR	7
LIKE HE HAD A CHARM.	SP	MADAM WRONG VIS	10
JUST LIKE I AM!	SP	MADAM CENSUS	28
JUST LIKE THE SONG.	SP	MADAM'S PAST HI	20
I FELT LIKE THAT ABOUT HIM.	SP	MAMA AND DAUGHT	12
I'M LIKE THAT OLD MULE -	SP	ME AND THE MULE	5
LIKE I AM.	SP	ME AND THE MULE	8
LIKE PALE PLUMS FROM A TREE	SP	MELLOW	4
LIKE THE PILLOWS OF ALL SWEET DREAMS.	SP	MIDNIGHT DANCER	6
BLACK GAL LIKE ME.	SP	MISERY	13
BLACK GAL LIKE ME	SP	MISERY	14
BABE, YOUR MOUTH WAS OPEN LIKE A WELL.	SP	MORNING AFTER	12
SOUND LIKE A GREAT BIG CROWD.	SP	MORNING AFTER	18
LIKE HELL!	SP	MULATTO	6
BLACK LIKE THE DEPTHS OF MY AFRICA.	SP	NEGRO	3
MY SOUL HAS GROWN DEEP LIKE THE RIVERS.	SP	NEGRO SPEAKS OF	4
MY SOUL HAS GROWN DEEP LIKE THE RIVERS.	SP	NEGRO SPEAKS OF	13
BLACK LIKE THE DEPTHS OF MY AFRICA.	SP	NEGRO	19
SHINED JUST LIKE A TEAR -	SP	NIGHT FUNERAL	37
SO THEY DON'T SOUND LIKE ME.	SP	NOTE COMM THEAT	6
LIKE A DIZZY GILLESPIE TRANSCRIPTION	SP	PROJECTION	13
LIKE A TAUT DRUM.	SP	RAILROAD AVENUE	19
AND GOLDEN LIKE THE SUNSHINE	SP	RUBY BROWN	2
AND THEY RAN SOMETHING LIKE THIS:	SP	RUBY BROWN	12
BUT IT'S LIKE A FOREIGN LANGUAGE	SP	SO LONG	4
BOOTS POLISHED LIKE A MURRAY HEAD,	SP	SUMMER EVENING	6
I FEEL LIKE DANCIN', BABY,	SP	SUNDAY BY COMB	1
I FEEL LIKE DANCIN'!	SP	SUNDAY BY COMB	6
YET SHINING LIKE THE SUN WITH LOVE'S TRUE LIGHT.	SP	THE NEGRO MOTHE	6
GOD PUT A DREAM LIKE STEEL IN MY SOUL.	SP	THE NEGRO MOTHE	19
STAND LIKE FREE MEN SUPPORTING MY TRUST.	SP	THE NEGRO MOTHE	42
BEAUTIFUL, LIKE A WOMAN,	SP	THE SOUTH	13
HE PLAYED THAT SAD RAGGY TUNE LIKE A MUSICAL FOOL.	SP	THE WEARY BLUES	13
HE SLEPT LIKE A ROCK OR A MAN THAT'S DEAD.	SP	THE WEARY BLUES	35
WELL, I LIKE TO EAT, SLEEP, DRINK, AND BE IN LOVE.	SP	THEME FOR ENG B	21
I LIKE TO WORK, READ, LEARN, AND UNDERSTAND LIFE.	SP	THEME FOR ENG B	22
I LIKE A PIPE FOR A CHRISTMAS PRESENT.	SP	THEME FOR ENG B	23
I GUESS BEING COLORED DOESN'T MAKE ME NOT LIKE	SP	THEME FOR ENG B	25
THE SAME THINGS OTHER FOLKS LIKE WHO ARE OTHER RACES.	SP	THEME FOR ENG B	26
LIKE A BAD BOY IN THE CORNER.	SP	TO BE SOMEBODY	7
LIKE AN	SP	TROUBLED WOMAN	6
LIKE A	SP	TROUBLED WOMAN	9
LIKE JET -	SP	TRUMPET PLAYER	15
LIKE YOU OUGHT TO DO,	SP	WARNING AUGMENT	3
AND DREAMS, LIKE ME.	SP	WATER-FRONT STR	8
SHINES LIKE THE EVIL ONE	SP	WEST TEXAS	2
SHINES LIKE THE EVIL ONE	SP	WEST TEXAS	17
HER FACE IS LIKE AN ANCIENT CAMEO	SP	WHEN SUE WEARS	2
BURNS IN MY HEART A LOVE-FIRE SHARP LIKE PAIN.	SP	WHEN SUE WEARS	11
WOMAN LIKE ME IS FREE!	SP	WIDOW WOMAN	24
FACE LIKE A CHOCOLATE BAR	SP	125TH STREET	1
FACE LIKE A JACK-O'-LANTERN,	SP	125TH STREET	3
FACE LIKE SLICE OF MELON,	SP	125TH STREET	5
DRESSED LIKE A TEDDY BOY	AYM	ASK YOUR MAMA	62
BRICKBATS BURST LIKE BUBBLES	AYM	ASK YOUR MAMA	67
STONES BURST LIKE BALLOONS	AYM	ASK YOUR MAMA	68
AND I'D LIKE TO MEET THE	AYM	BIRD IN ORBIT	7
LINCOLN'S LIKE A CLOTHESBRUSH	AYM	BIRD IN ORBIT	46
CHA-CHA LIKE CASTANETS	AYM	GOSPEL CHA-CHA	3
SINGERS LIKE O -	AYM	HORN OF PLENTY	2
SINGERS LIKE ODETTA - AND THAT STATUE	AYM	HORN OF PLENTY	3

Context	Source	Poem	Line
WHO BREAK AWAY LIKE COMETS $ $ $ $ $ $	AYM	HORN OF PLENTY	20
WHERE BLACK SHADOWS MOVE LIKE SHADOWS	AYM	JAZZTET MUTED	4
SEEMS LIKE ONCE I MET YOU	AYM	RIDE, RED, RIDE	31
AND IT'S FULL OF FOLKS LIKE ME WHO ARE	PL	BACKLASH BLUES	23
LIKE A BANNER	PL	COLOR	2
NOT LIKE A SHROUD.	PL	COLOR	4
LIKE A SONG	PL	COLOR	6
LIKE A LEI.	PL	CROWNS GARLANDS	3
RISING OUT OF THE GROUND LIKE A SWAMP MIST	PL	DAYBREAK IN ALA	5
AND FALLING OUT OF HEAVEN LIKE SOFT DEW.	PL	DAYBREAK IN ALA	6
LIKE A RAISIN IN THE SUN?	PL	DREAM DEFERRED	3
OR FESTER LIKE A SORE -	PL	DREAM DEFERRED	4
DOES IT STINK LIKE ROTTEN MEAT?	PL	DREAM DEFERRED	6
LIKE A SYRUPY SWEET?	PL	DREAM DEFERRED	8
LIKE A HEAVY LOAD.	PL	DREAM DEFERRED	10
SCATTERS HATE LIKE SEED	PL	GEORGIA DUSK	10
AND, LIKE AN ATOM BOMB, BURSTS APART.	PL	JIM CROW CAR	4
SHOULD MIX LIKE RAIN	PL	MISSISSIPPI	5
STILL MIX LIKE RAIN	PL	MISSISSIPPI	19
LOOKS LIKE BETWEEN 'EM THEY DONE	PL	STILL HERE	5
FACES LIKE JACK-O'-LANTERNS	PL	THIRD DEGREE	5
LIKE BLOWTORCH.	PL	THIRD DEGREE	9
AND BURST LIKE ROMAN CANDLES.	PL	THIRD DEGREE	14
LIKE WAVES OF SEA	PL	UNDERTOW	11
LIKE YOUR NAME.	PL	WAR	24
LIKE RUSTY IRON AND MINT.	PL	WHERE WHEN WHCH	3
WITH AN EDGE LIKE APARTHEID.	PL	WHERE WHEN WHCH	6
THERE ARE WORDS LIKE FREEDOM	PL	WORDS LIKE FREE	1
THERE ARE WORDS LIKE LIBERTY	PL	WORDS LIKE FREE	5

LIKED 1

Context	Source	Poem	Line
THEY LIKED HIM SO WELL THEY COULDN'T STAND	JC	JIM CROW'S LAST	3

LIKELY 1

Context	Source	Poem	Line
LOOKS LIKE A LIKELY	SP	MADAM NUMBER WR	7

LIKEN 4

Context	Source	Poem	Line
I WOULD LIKEN YOU	DK	QUIET GIRL	1
I WOULD LIKEN YOU	DK	QUIET GIRL	4
I WOULD LIKEN YOU	SP	ARDELLA	1
I WOULD LIKEN YOU	SP	ARDELLA	4

LIKES 2

Context	Source	Poem	Line
I LIKES A WOMAN	SP	PREFERENCE	1
THAT'S WHY I LIKES A OLDER WOMAN	SP	PREFERENCE	11

LIL 1

Context	Source	Poem	Line
JOCKO BODDIDLY LIL GREENWOOD	AYM	BIRD IN ORBIT	4

LINCOLN 8

Context	Source	Poem	Line
ABE LINCOLN DONE SET ME FREE -	NM	BLACK CLWN POEM	30
THE HEAD OF LINCOLN LOOKS DOWN FROM THE WALL	OWT	LINCOLN THEATRE	1
THE HEAD OF LINCOLN IS SERENELY TALL	OWT	LINCOLN THEATRE	3
BUT NOT SO LONG AGO AT THAT, LINCOLN SAID:	SP	FREEDOM'S PLOW	101
I HEARD THE SINGING OF THE MISSISSIPPI WHEN ABE LINCOLN	SP	NEGRO SPEAKS OF	8
ON THE LINCOLN	SP	ONE	3
A MOVIE HOUSE IN HARLEM NAMED AFTER LINCOLN.	SP	SHAME ON YOU	6
SEND FOR LINCOLN, SEND FOR GRANT.	PL	FINAL CALL	29

LINCOLN'S 1

Context	Source	Poem	Line
LINCOLN'S LIKE A CLOTHESBRUSH	AYM	BIRD IN ORBIT	46

LINE 8

Context	Source	Poem	Line
OF PREJUDICE, AND HATE, AND THE FALSE COLOR LINE -	NM	COLORED SL POEM	9
GETS IN LINE TO SEE THE FREEDOM,	SP	FREEDOM TRAIN	38
AND NARY A SIGN OF A COLOR LINE -	SP	FREEDOM TRAIN	57
AND HE CROSSED THAT DIXIE LINE	SP	NOT A MOVIE	6
THE ONES WHO'VE CROSSED THE LINE	SP	PASSING	11
ON MY PARTY LINE -	SP	SAME IN BLUES	23
WE SAW A LINE OF FISHING SHIPS	SP	SEASCAPE	3
ON THE LINE WHOSE ROUTE WAS FREEDOM	AYM	ODE TO DINAH	30

LINKED 1

Context	Source	Poem	Line
YOU HAVE LINKED YOUR HANDS WITH ME.	ANS	OPEN LETTER	46

LION 1

Context	Source	Poem	Line
A TIGER, A LION, AND AN OWL	SP	DELINQUENT	11

LIPPED 1

Context	Source	Poem	Line
POMEGRANATE LIPPED	SH	HARLEM SWEETIES	15

LIPS 20

Context	Source	Poem	Line
BLACK BOYS' LIPS	WB	HARLEM NIGHT CL	8
TO WHAT CLEAN BOY HAVE YOU OFFERED YOUR LIPS?	WB	NUDE YOUNG DANC	8
WOULD GOD HIS LIPS WERE SWEET!	WB	TO LITTLE LOVER	12
CRUSHING THE LIPS.	FC	BEALE ST. LOVE	4
HER LIPS BLOOD RED	FC	CLOSING TIME	4
YOUR LIPS WERE SWEET.	DK	PARISIAN BEGGAR	8
WITH ARROGANT EYES AND SCORNFUL LIPS:	ANS	A NEW SONG	31
FROM THE DARK LIPS	JC	ME AND MY SONG	23
WHEN THE LIPS	FW	SLEEP	1
WHEN THE LIPS	FW	SLEEP	9
LET THOSE WOMEN WITH THEIR LIPS TOO RED	OWT	JUICE JOINT	21
AND CRIES, ALL CARELESS-LIKE FROM REDDENED LIPS!	OWT	LINCOLN THEATRE	10
LIPS	SP	MIDNIGHT DANCER	3
SHE LIFTED UP HER LIPS	SP	NEW YORKERS	15
NOR THE SWEET OF YOUR LIPS ALONE.	SP	TO ARTINA	8
WITH THE TRUMPET AT HIS LIPS	SP	TRUMPET PLAYER	2
WITH THE TRUMPET AT HIS LIPS	SP	TRUMPET PLAYER	10
FROM THE TRUMPET AT HIS LIPS	SP	TRUMPET PLAYER	18
FROM THE TRUMPET AT HIS LIPS	SP	TRUMPET PLAYER	22
WITH THE TRUMPET AT HIS LIPS	SP	TRUMPET PLAYER	34

LIPSHITZ 1

Context	Source	Poem	Line
IS NOT YOUR NAME LIPSHITZ?	PL	UN-AMERICAN	13

LIQUID 2

Context	Source	Poem	Line
LET THE RAIN BEAT UPON YOUR HEAD WITH SILVER LIQUID DROPS.	DK	APRIL RAIN SONG	2
MIXED WITH LIQUID FIRE.	SP	TRUMPET PLAYER	20

LIQUOR 1

Context	Source	Poem	Line
LIQUOR.	WB	CAT AND SAXOPHN	8

LISTEN 31

Context	Source	Poem	Line
LISTEN HERE TO ME.	FC	LISTEN HERE	2
LISTEN HERE TO ME:	FC	LISTEN HERE	4
LISTEN HERE TO ME.	FC	LISTEN HERE	14
BETTER LISTEN TO ME:	FC	LISTEN HERE	16
LISTEN, KIDS WHO DIE -	ANS	KIDS WHO DIE	37
LISTEN:	ANS	OPEN LETTER	13
HOUSE IS SO QUIET! . . . LISTEN AT THEM MICE.	SH	BED TIME	12
LISTEN, BOY.	SH	DEATH IN HARLEM	84
LONESOME SAID, LISTEN!	SH	MIDNIGHT CHIPPI	13
SAID, LISTEN! HEY!	SH	MIDNIGHT CHIPPI	14
LONESOME SAID, LISTEN!	SH	MIDNIGHT CHIPPI	15
WOMAN, LISTEN! SAY!	SH	MIDNIGHT CHIPPI	16
LISTEN AT MY HEARTBEATS TRYING TO THINK.	SH	SUPPER TIME	6
LISTEN AT MY FOOTPRINTS WALKING ON THE FLOOR.	SH	SUPPER TIME	7
LISTEN! I DON'T OWN NO RADIO -	JC	GOOD MORN STLIN	49
SHE SAID, NOW, LISTEN, MISTER,	SP	BLD THE GYPSY	11
LISTEN AT THEM LITTLE VARMINTS!	SP	CHILDREN'S RYME	4
LISTEN!	SP	DEMAND	1
LISTEN CLOSELY:	SP	DREAM BOOGIE	5
LISTEN TO IT CLOSELY:	SP	DREAM BOOGIE	10
LISTEN, COOLIE!	SP	IN EXPLANATION	14
AND WHILE WE LISTEN TO IT PLAY,	SP	JUKE BOX LOVE	10
LISTEN, KID SLEEPY,	SP	KID SLEEPY	1
LISTEN, KID SLEEPY,	SP	KID SLEEPY	10
BUT IF SHE WAS TO LISTEN	SP	LADY'S BOOGIE	5
I SAID, LISTEN,	SP	MADAM RENT MAN	7
LISTEN TO YO' PROPHETS,	SP	SHOUT	1
LISTEN TO YO' SAINTS!	SP	SHOUT	3
STOPS TO LISTEN TO GOSPEL SONGS	SP	SUMMER EVENING	11
LISTEN HERE, JOE,	PL	WITHOUT BENEFIT	1
LISTEN HERE, KID,	PL	WITHOUT BENEFIT	7

LISTENERS' 1

Context	Source	Poem	Line
LOOKING AT LISTENERS' FACES.	PL	CORNER MEETING	5

LISTENING 2

Context	Source	Poem	Line
AND THE DARK-FACED CHILD, LISTENING,	SP	AUNTSUE'S STORI	17
LISTENING TO AUNT SUE'S STORIES.	SP	AUNTSUE'S STORI	25

LITTLE 103

Context	Source	Poem	Line
WHEN THE LITTLE DAWN WAS GREY.	WB	CABARET	6
NOW LIKE A LITTLE LONELY WAIF	WB	TO LITTLE LOVER	8
MA LITTLE, SHORT, SWEET, BROWNSKIN BOY, -	FC	BLACK GAL	17
TO A LITTLE DROWNED GIRL.	FC	CLOSING TIME	15
THAT LITTLE YALLER GAL	FC	NEW CABARET GRL	1
THAT CRAZY LITTLE YALLER GAL	FC	NEW CABARET GRL	13
ONE LITTLE MOMENT	NM	BLACK CLWN POEM	31
LAST JOB I HAD, WENT TO WORK AT FIVE IN DE MORNIN', OR LITTLE MO'	NM	BROKE	12
TRIED TO FIND ONE O' THEM LITTLE ELEVATOR AND SWITCHBOARD JOBS THEY USED	NM	BROKE	41
THE RAIN PLAYS A LITTLE SLEEP-SONG ON OUR ROOF AT NIGHT -	DK	APRIL RAIN SONG	6
LIKE LITTLE BROWN BUTTERFLIES.	DK	AUTUMN THOUGHT	5
MY LITTLE DARK BABY.	DK	LULLABY	2
MY LITTLE EARTH-THING.	DK	LULLABY	3
MY LITTLE LOVE-ONE.	DK	LULLABY	4
MY LITTLE BLACK BABY.	DK	LULLABY	11
OH, LITTLE DARK BABY.	DK	LULLABY	19
THIS LITTLE HOUSE IS SUGAR.	DK	WINTER SWEEETNS	1

Line	Book	Poem	Line no.
SCOTTSBORO'S JUST A LITTLE PLACE:	SL	TOWN OF SCOTTSB	1
DOG-GONE LITTLE MOUSES! I WISH I WAS YOU!	SH	BED TIME	14
AT A BIG PIANO A LITTLE DARK GIRL	SH	DEATH IN HARLEM	10
A DUMB LITTLE JIGABOO FROM	SH	DEATH IN HARLEM	16
BELIEVE I'LL DO A LITTLE DANCIN'	SH	EVENIN' BLUES	13
A LITTLE DANCIN'	SH	EVENIN' BLUES	15
WHAT DO YOU MEAN, JUST A LITTLE SPAT?	SH	LETTER	4
BABY, GIMME A LITTLE LOVIN',	SH	SIX-BITS BLUES	7
A LITTLE LOVIN', BABE, BUT	SH	SIX-BITS BLUES	9
ABOUT THIS LITTLE CABIN	FW	CAROLINA CABIN	4
LITTLE DOLLAR ROSE	FW	CHIPPY	6
A LITTLE SOUTHERN COLORED CHILD	FW	MIGRATION	1
HE IS A LITTLE DARK BOY	FW	MIGRATION	11
LITTLE FRIGHTENED CHILD	FW	MIGRATION	15
LITTLE SHORT	FW	NIGHT SONG	4
LITTLE SHORT	FW	NIGHT SONG	11
LIKE MY LITTLE GIRL.	OWT	HONEY BABE	16
BETWEEN THE LITTLE CLOUDS OF HEAVEN	LHR	PASTORAL	1
FOR LITTLE TEARS OF HEAVEN	LHR	PASTORAL	4
I HAVE DONE SO LITTLE	LHR	POET TO BIGOT	1
AND YOU HAVE DONE SO LITTLE	LHR	POET TO BIGOT	3
A LITTLE LOVING	SP	ADVICE	5
FOR TOO LITTLE PAY -	SP	BLUE BAYOU	10
LISTEN AT THEM LITTLE VARMINTS!	SP	CHILDREN'S RYME	4
LITTLE JULIE	SP	DELINQUENT	1
LITTLE JULIE	SP	DELINQUENT	5
LITTLE JULIE	SP	DELINQUENT	9
LITTLE JULIE	SP	DELINQUENT	13
MAYBE A LITTLE LUCK NOW.	SP	ELEVATOR BOY	8
HAD A LITTLE LAMB.	SP	EVENING SONG	10
LITTLE CULLUD BOYS WITH BEARDS	SP	FLATTED FIFTHS	1
LITTLE CULLUD BOYS WITH FEARS.	SP	FLATTED FIFTHS	3
LITTLE CULLUD BOYS IN BERETS	SP	FLATTED FIFTHS	15
IN LITTLE BANDS TOGETHER.	SP	FREEDOM'S PLOW	37
LONELY LITTLE QUESTION MARK	SP	KID IN THE PARK	1
JUST A LITTLE OLD LETTER.	SP	LITTLE OLD LETT	5
AND I SEE A LITTLE TREE.	SP	LITTLE GRN TREE	10
A LITTLE PIECE DOWN THE ROAD.	SP	LITTLE GRN TREE	11
I SEE A LITTLE TREE.	SP	LITTLE GRN TREE	12
O, LITTLE TREE!	SP	LITTLE GRN TREE	15
A LITTLE OLD LETTER	SP	LITTLE OLD LETT	15
MAKES A LITTLE SPARK.	SP	LOVE	6
THAT LITTLE SPARK IS LOVE	SP	LOVE	7
A LITTLE GIRL CHILD.	SP	MADAM CHARTY CH	2
A LITTLE TIME TO SPEAK?	SP	MADAM MINISTER	4
A LITTLE BOY.	SP	MADAM CHARTY CH	6
POOR LITTLE THINGS.	SP	MADAM CHARTY CH	13
MONROE SINGS A LITTLE BLUES.	SP	MONROE'S BLUES	5
HIS LITTLE BLUES IS SAD.	SP	MONROE'S BLUES	6
MONROE SINGS A LITTLE BLUES -	SP	MONROE'S BLUES	7
YOU JEST A LITTLE BIT O' WOMAN BUT YOU	SP	MORNING AFTER	17
O, YOU LITTLE BASTARD BOY.	SP	MULATTO	16
A LITTLE YELLOW	SP	MULATTO	25
TO LITTLE YELLOW BASTARD BOYS.	SP	MULATTO	36
A LITTLE YELLOW	SP	MULATTO	44
THIS LITTLE OLD FURNISHED ROOM'S	SP	NECESSITY	5
COMBINATE A LITTLE	SP	NUMBERS	7
LITTLE JESUS!	SP	SHOUT	2
THAT LITTLE NEGRO'S MARRIED AND GOT A KID.	SP	SISTER	1
CHEAP LITTLE RHYMES	SP	SLIVER	1
A CHEAP LITTLE TUNE	SP	SLIVER	2
A CHEAP LITTLE TUNE	SP	SLIVER	5
TO CHEAP LITTLE RHYMES	SP	SLIVER	6
LITTLE SNAIL.	SP	SNAIL	1
AIN'T WORTH A LITTLE BIT.	SP	SOUTHERN MAMMY	10
AIN'T WORTH A LITTLE BIT.	SP	SOUTHERN MAMMY	12
O, LITTLE BREATH OF OBLIVION THAT IS NIGHT.	SP	STARS	2
OUT OF THE LITTLE BREATH OF OBLIVION	SP	STARS	8
AND ALL THE LITTLE DEVILS	SP	SUNDAY MORNING	9
I WOKE UP LITTLE LATER	SP	SYLVESTER'S BED	9
LITTLE CULLUD BOYS	SP	TAG	1
WITH THE LITTLE WORDS YOU SAY TO ME.	SP	TO ARTINA	5
LITTLE GIRL	SP	TO BE SOMEBODY	1
LITTLE BOY	SP	TO BE SOMEBODY	14
THEM LITTLE OLD MUTTS	SP	WARNING AUGMENT	9
LITTLE MULES AND DONKEYS SHARE	AYM	ASK YOUR MAMA	76
A LITTLE RUM WITH SUGAR.	AYM	RIDE, RED, RIDE	19
TO EARN A LITTLE CASH,	PL	BACKLASH BLUES	14
TO EARN A LITTLE CASH,	PL	BACKLASH BLUES	16
FOUR LITTLE GIRLS	PL	BIRMINGHAM SUND	1
IN LITTLE GRAVES TODAY AWAIT	PL	BIRMINGHAM SUND	17
FOUR LITTLE GIRLS	PL	BIRMINGHAM SUND	24
THE LITTLE BOY	PL	JUNIOR ADDICT	1
(YET LITTLE CAN	PL	JUNIOR ADDICT	16
LAST LITTLE BROWN PRINCE	PL	LAST PRINCE	2
LITTLE DREAMS	PL	SLUM DREAMS	1

LIVE 35

Line	Book	Poem	Line no.
YOU WHO LIVE BETWEEN THE HILLS	WB	A FAREWELL	7
YOU CAN'T LIVE THAT WAY!	FC	NEW CABARET GRL	22
LIVE THAT WAY!	FC	NEW CABARET GRL	24
WHAT IT IS TO LIVE IN HELL.	ANS	BLD OZZIE POWEL	23
THE OLD AND RICH WILL LIVE ON AWHILE.	ANS	KIDS WHO DIE	4
WILL LIVE ON WEAVING WORDS TO SMOTHER THE KIDS WHO DIE.	ANS	KIDS WHO DIE	24
FROM THOSE WHO LIVE LIKE LEECHES ON THE PEOPLE'S LIVES.	ANS	LET AMERICA BE	72
LET THE WHITE FOLKS LIVE	ANS	LYNCHING SONG	3
I LIVE ON A PARK BENCH.	ANS	PARK BENCH	1
BUT A MAN'S GOT TO LIVE.	SH	BLD PAWNBROKER	19
TO LET YOU LIVE!	SH	BLD THE KILLER	22
BUT YOU JUST AS WELL BE HERE WHERE YOU DUE TO LIVE.	SH	LETTER	11
YOU GOT TO LIVE HERE A YEAR AND A DAY.	SH	OUT OF WORK	12
WHERE I LIVE DOWN IN DIXIE	JC	GOOD MORN STLIN	6
IT TAKES TO LIVE.	SP	CONSIDER ME	72
WAKE UP AND LIVE!	SP	DEAD IN THERE	16
I CANNOT LIVE ON TOMORROW'S BREAD.	SP	DEMOCRACY	14
I LIVE HERE, TOO.	SP	DEMOCRACY	19
THAN TO LIVE SLAVES.	SP	FREEDOM'S PLOW	111
THAN TO LIVE SLAVES.	SP	FREEDOM'S PLOW	173
I GUESS I WILL LIVE ON.	SP	LIFE IS FINE	24
TO LIVE DOWNTOWN	SP	PASSING	12
MIGHT LIVE.	SP	SUNDAY MORNING	42
IN ORDER THAT THE RACE MIGHT LIVE AND GROW.	SP	THE NEGRO MOTHE	4
IF I LIVE TO BE A THOUSAND	SP	WIDOW WOMAN	17
LIVE ALL THAT WHILE IN PARIS	AYM	HORN OF PLENTY	53
DEAD OR LIVE THEIR GHOSTS CAST SHADOWS	AYM	SHADES OF PIG	6
TO LIVE ON MY OWN LAND.	PL	ANGOLA QUESTION	13
I CANNOT LIVE ON TOMORROW'S BREAD.	PL	FREEDOM	14
I LIVE HERE, TOO.	PL	FREEDOM	19
YOU CAN'T LIVE HERE!	PL	GO SLOW	7
AND MEEKLY LIVE	PL	GO SLOW	16
TO ONE WHO WILL NOT LIVE.)	PL	JUNIOR ADDICT	18
AS I LIVE AND LEARN	PL	MOTTO	6
YOU LIVE IN THE BRONX	PL	STOKELY MALCOLM	13
DID I EVER LIVE	PL	STOKELY MALCOLM	16

LIVED 4

Line	Book	Poem	Line no.
I LIVED FOR YOU, COMRADE LENIN	ANS	BLDS OF LENIN	15
RATHER DIE THE WAY I LIVED -	SH	CABARET GIRL	5
SHE LIVED IN SINFUL HAPPINESS	FW	GIRL	1
AND SURE SHE LIVED	FW	GIRL	18

LIVES 6

Line	Book	Poem	Line no.
MA BABY LIVES ACROSS DE RIVER	DK	WIDE RIVER	1
SHE LIVES ACROSS DE RIVER.	DK	WIDE RIVER	3
FROM THOSE WHO LIVE LIKE LEECHES ON THE PEOPLE'S LIVES.	ANS	LET AMERICA BE	72
THE THINGS THEY MADE, NOR THEIR OWN LIVES -	JC	TO CAPTAIN MULZ	21
THEIR LIVES	FW	SAILING DATE	2
ALL THEIR LIVES	SP	NEW YORKERS	8

LIVING 10

Line	Book	Poem	Line no.
BEEN MADE, PROUD AND SMILING, BUT THE LIVING, REMEMBERING WITH A HALF-SOB	NM	COLORED SL MOOD	10
'CAUSE WHEN I WAS LIVING, I DIDN'T HAVE MINE.	NM	COLORED SL POEM	18
WILL RAISE FOR YOU A LIVING MONUMENT OF LOVE.	ANS	KIDS WHO DIE	46
AND I WON'T NEED NO FURNITURE LIVING ALONE -	SH	PAY DAY	15
ABOUT LIVING AND DYING -	FW	BORDER LINE	2
TO WANDER THROUGH THIS LIVING WORLD	FW	REMEMBRANCE	1
LIVING IN ST. ALBANS	AYM	HORN OF PLENTY	59
LIVING 20 YEARS IN 10	AYM	ODE TO DINAH	102
THAN IS HIS LIVING HERE,	PL	JUNIOR ADDICT	23
AND BEAT THE LIVING HELL	PL	WHO BUT TH LORD	14

LIVIN' 10

Line	Book	Poem	Line no.
AND LIVIN' ON GALS.	NM	BIG-TIMER POEM	14
NOT LIVIN' LIKE I OUGHTER.	NM	BIG-TIMER POEM	19
BUT WHILE I'M LIVIN' - I'M LIVIN'!	NM	BIG-TIMER POEM	35
BUT WHILE I'M LIVIN' - I'M LIVIN'!	NM	BIG-TIMER POEM	35
DID YOU EVER TRY LIVIN'	SH	OUT OF WORK	19
I SAY DID YOU EVER TRY LIVIN'	SH	OUT OF WORK	21
SO SINCE I'M STILL HERE LIVIN',	SP	LIFE IS FINE	23
BUT FOR LIVIN' I WAS BORN.	SP	LIFE IS FINE	26
NOW HE'S LIVIN'	SP	NOT A MOVIE	7
STOP LAUGHIN', STOP LOVIN', STOP LIVIN' -	PL	STILL HERE	7

LIZA 4

Line	Book	Poem	Line no.
SHAKE YOUR BROWN FEET, LIZA,	DK	SONG BANJO DANC	20
SHAKE 'EM, LIZA, CHILE,	DK	SONG BANJO DANC	21
SHAKE YOUR BROWN FEET, LIZA,	DK	SONG BANJO DANC	22
SHAKE YOUR BROWN FEET, LIZA,	DK	SONG BANJO DANC	24

LOAD 5

Line	Book	Poem	Line no.
AND A WHOLE TRUCK LOAD OF FLOWERS.	SP	AS BEFITS A MAN	12
TO HELP ME CARRY THIS LOAD.	SP	BOUND NO'TH BLS	6
LIKE A HEAVY LOAD.	SP	HARLEM	10
GRABS A LOAD OF SUNRISE	SP	MIGRANT	10
LIKE A HEAVY LOAD.	PL	DREAM DEFERRED	10

LOADERS 1
LOADERS OF SHIPS. . . . . FC LAUGHERS 14

LOBBIES 1
AND THE SMOKE IN HOTEL LOBBIES, . . FC BRASS SPITOONS 8

LOBBY 1
IN THE LOBBY . . . . OWT BLD MARGE POLIT 5

LOBSTER 1
THE LOBSTER IS DELICIOUS. . . . . . PL DINNER GUEST ME 15

LOCK 3
YOU CAN'T LOCK UP GANDHI, ... JC HOW ABOUT DIXIE 13
GONNA SHUT AN' LOCK MY DOOR . . . . SP CORA 4
WHILE THEY LOCK THE GATE. . . . . . PL GO SLOW 10

LOCKED 2
O, EIGHTEEN MONTHS LOCKED IN! . . . FC BLD OF GIN MARY 18
NOW THEY'VE LOCKED ME . . . . SH BLD THE KILLER 25

LOG 1
AND THEN CUT DOWN DE LOG - . . . . SH ONLY WOMAN BLUS 10

LOMAX 1
BY MOE ASCH OR ALAN LOMAX . . . . . AYM IS IT TRUE? 10

LONDON 1
FROM LOS ANGELES TO LONDON . . . . JC BLACK MAN SPEAK 15

LONE 2
FEELIN' SO SAD AND LONE. . . . . . SH MIDNIGHT CHIPPI 8
SO SAD AND LONE! . . . . SH MIDNIGHT CHIPPI 10

LONELINESS 3
INNER HEARTACHES AND LONELINESS TO THE IRONIC GAIETY OF THE MUSIC. THEN . . . . NM BIG-TIMER MOOD 10
WHEN PIMPS OUT OF LONELINESS CRY: SP SLIVER SERMON 1
WHY SHOULD IT BE MY LONELINESS. . . SP TELL ME 1

LONELY 26
NOW LIKE A LITTLE LONELY WAIF . . . WB TO LITTLE LOVER 8
SITTING LONELY IN THE MARBLE AND THE MOONLIGHT. . . . . DK LINCOLN MONUMNT 3
LOVELY, DARK, AND LONELY ONE. . . . DK SONG 1
GREAT LONELY HILLS. . . . . FW BIG SUR 1
LONELY PEOPLE . . . . FW LITTLE SONG 1
IN THE LONELY NIGHT . . . . FW LITTLE SONG 2
GRAB A LONELY DREAM . . . . FW LITTLE SONG 3
LONELY PEOPLE . . . . FW LITTLE SONG 5
IN THE LONELY DAY . . . . FW LITTLE SONG 6
CARRIED LONELY UP THE AISLE . . . . OWT FUNERAL 1
HATES TO BE LONELY, ... SP BOUND NO'TH BLS 13
SAYS I HATES TO BE LONELY, ... SP BOUND NO'TH BLS 15
HATES TO BE LONELY AN' SAD, ... SP BOUND NO'TH BLS 16
IT WAS THAT LONELY DAY, FOLKS, . . SP CROSSING 1
IT WAS THAT LONELY DAY, FOLKS, . . SP CROSSING 19
IN THIS LONELY . . . . SP DESERT 9
SOMETIMES WHEN I'M LONELY, ... SP HOPE 1
KEEP THINKIN' I WON'T BE LONELY . . SP HOPE 3
LONELY LITTLE QUESTION MARK . . . . SP KID IN THE PARK 1
NOW MY DAYS ARE LONELY, ... SP MISS BLUES'ES 11
LONELY . . . . SP ONE 1
LONELY . . . . SP ONE 5
BUT I KEPT TRUDGING ON THROUGH THE LONELY YEARS. . . . . SP THE NEGRO MOTHE 26
THE PO' HOUSE IS LONELY . . . . . . SP YOUNG GAL'S BLS 13
O, THE PO' HOUSE IS LONELY. . . . . SP YOUNG GAL'S BLS 15
IN LONELY PITY THROUGH THE GEORGIA DUSK . . . . PL GEORGIA DUSK 3

LONESOME 26
STANDIN' BY DE LONESOME RIVERSIDE FC A RUINED GAL 1
PO' LONESOME ME . . . . FC A RUINED GAL 8
O, DE LONESOME RIVERSIDE. . . . . . FC A RUINED GAL 15
A HUMAN GETS LONESOME IF THERE AIN'T TWO. . . . . SH BED TIME 15
GETTING UP IN THE MORNING LONESOME AND SAD? . . . . SH DAYBREAK 13
NOT A SOUL BUT LONESOME BLUE. . . . SH MIDNIGHT CHIPPI 2
NOBODY BUT LONESOME BLUE. . . . . . SH MIDNIGHT CHIPPI 4
I SAID COME HERE, LONESOME, ... SH MIDNIGHT CHIPPI 5
I SAID, PLEASE, MR. LONESOME, . . . SH MIDNIGHT CHIPPI 11
LONESOME SAID, LISTEN! . . . . . . SH MIDNIGHT CHIPPI 13
LONESOME SAID, LISTEN! . . . . . . SH MIDNIGHT CHIPPI 15
I SAID, MR. LONESOME, ... SH MIDNIGHT CHIPPI 19
CRIPPLE MR. LONESOME, ... SH MIDNIGHT CHIPPI 21
LONESOME SAID WHEN A TWO-BIT WOMAN SH MIDNIGHT CHIPPI 23
CRYIN' TO NO LONESOME BLUE! . . . . SH MIDNIGHT CHIPPI 26
CRYIN' TO NO LONESOME BLUE! . . . . SH MIDNIGHT CHIPPI 28
IN THIS GREAT BIG LONESOME TOWN! . SH OUT OF WORK 14
GREAT BIG LONESOME TOWN! . . . . . SH OUT OF WORK 16
OLD LONESOME CORNER! . . . . OWT LONESOME CORNER 5
I NEVER FELT SO LONESOME . . . . . SP LITTLE OLD LETT 11
SO SICK AND LONESOME . . . . SP LOVER'S RETURN 7
OUT TO STONY LONESOME GROUND. . . . SP STONY LONESOME 2
TO STONY LONESOME. . . . . SP STONY LONESOME 4
SHE'S OUT IN STONY LONESOME. . . . SP STONY LONESOME 16
LONESOME . . . . SP STONY LONESOME 20
TO SOME LONESOME PLACE. . . . . . . PL KU KLUX 2

LONG 86
FOR PIERROT LOVED THE LONG WHITE ROAD. . . . . WB PIERROT 7
AND PIERROT RAN DOWN THE LONG WHITE ROAD . . . . WB PIERROT 29
CAUSE I IS LONG GONE WRONG. . . . . FC A RUINED GAL 5
AN' YOU'S A LONG TIME . . . . FC SATURDAY NIGHT 17
ALL NIGHT LONG. . . . . FC SATURDAY NIGHT 24
DRUNK LONG . . . . FC SPORT 15
A BLADE TEN INCHES LONG. . . . . . FC SUICIDE 8
A BLADE TEN INCHES LONG. . . . . . FC SUICIDE 10
THE LONG STRUGGLE FOR LIFE: . . . . NM BLACK CLWN POEM 38
BUT RIGHT LONG THROUGH HERE NOW, I CAN'T 'FORD TO BUY YOU NO HAT." NM BROKE 51
LONG A PART OF THE UNION'S HEART - NM DARK YOUTH USA 11
TO BE WISE AND STRONG, THEN, STUDYING LONG. . . . . NM DARK YOUTH USA 16
SO LONG? . . . . DK MINSTREL MAN 8
I BEEN BLUE ALL NIGHT LONG. . . . . DK NIGHT AND MORN 12
AN' DE ROAD IS HARD AN' LONG. . . . DK PO' BOY BLUES 12
PLAY A LONG TIME, GAL! . . . . . . SH DEATH IN HARLEM 46
THEN WHIP 'EM ALL NIGHT LONG. . . . SH HEY-HEY BLUES 8
THEN WHIP 'EM ALL NIGHT LONG. . . . SH HEY-HEY BLUES 10
SHE HAD LONG BLACK HAIR. . . . . . SH ONLY WOMAN BLUS 13
BUT DON'T MAKE IT TOO LONG. . . . . SH SIX-BITS BLUES 8
DON'T MAKE IT TOO LONG. . . . . . . SH SIX-BITS BLUES 10
HOW FAR YOU GO, NOR HOW LONG YOU STAY - . . . . SH SUNDAY 6
SET ON THE FRONT PORCH AS LONG AS I PLEASE. . . . . SH SUNDAY 8
THAT AS LONG AS YOUR RED STAR . . . JC GOOD MORN STLIN 13
AS LONG AS I AM YOU . . . . JC GOOD MORN STLIN 42
TOO LONG HAS THE TASTE OF ITS WATER JC THE BITTER RIVR 4
TOO LONG HAS ITS EVIL POISON . . . JC THE BITTER RIVR 8
LONG AGO, LONG AGO - THE WHIP AND STEEL BARS - . . . . JC THE BITTER RIVR 37
LONG AGO, LONG AGO - THE WHIP AND STEEL BARS - . . . . JC THE BITTER RIVR 37
I HAVE DRUNK AT THE RIVER TOO LONG: JC THE BITTER RIVR 66
WITH ITS FILTH AND ITS MUD TOO LONG. JC THE BITTER RIVR 74
THERE ARE THOSE, TOO, WHO FOR SO LONG . . . . JC TO CAPTAIN MULZ 16
AND I'VE BEEN WAITING LONG . . . . FW EARTH SONG 2
I'VE BEEN WAITING LONG . . . . . . FW EARTH SONG 5
AND I'VE BEEN WAITING LONG . . . . FW EARTH SONG 14
LONG RESTING PLACE, ... FW GRAVE YARD 2
AND FAR-OFF LONG TOMORROW: . . . . FW MOTHERLAND 2
IN A LONG BOX - . . . . OWT DECEASED 3
BEFORE THIS LONG HEGIRA HAD BEGUN OWT JUICE JOINT 12
SO LONG, ... SP AFRO-AMER FRAG 1
SO LONG, ... SP AFRO-AMER FRAG 10
SO LONG, ... SP AFRO-AMER FRAG 21
A ROW OF LONG TALL MAMAS . . . . . SP AS BEFITS A MAN 7
IT WAS A LONG TIME AGO. . . . . . . SP AS I GREW OLDER 1
GREAT LONG FINGERS . . . . SP DREAM BOOGIE VAR 5
MAYBE NO LUCK FOR A LONG TIME. . . SP ELEVATOR BOY 14
ELEVATOR TOO LONG. . . . . SP ELEVATOR BOY 22
IT WAS A LONG TIME AGO. . . . . . . SP FREEDOM'S PLOW 100
BUT NOT SO LONG AGO AT THAT, LINCOLN SAID: . . . . SP FREEDOM'S PLOW 101
A LONG TIME AGO, BUT NOT TOO LONG AGO. . . . . SP FREEDOM'S PLOW 28
A LONG TIME AGO, BUT NOT TOO LONG AGO. . . . . SP FREEDOM'S PLOW 28
A LONG TIME AGO. . . . . SP FREEDOM'S PLOW 188
A LONG TIME AGO, BUT NOT TOO LONG AGO, A MAN SAID: . . . . SP FREEDOM'S PLOW 90
A LONG TIME AGO, BUT NOT TOO LONG AGO, A MAN SAID: . . . . SP FREEDOM'S PLOW 90
CELLOPHANES HIS LONG STRIDE, . . . SP INTERNE AT PROV 46
WASN'T EVEN ONE PAGE LONG - . . . . SP LITTLE OLD LETT 6
LONG DISTANCE? . . . . SP MADAM PHONE BIL 2
LONG AGO. . . . . SP MADAM MINISTER 12
LONG DISTANCE . . . . SP MADAM PHONE BIL 17
BUT IT WAS A LONG TIME AGO . . . . SP MAMA AND DAUGHT 13
HE'S BEEN A MULE SO LONG . . . . . SP ME AND THE MULE 3
IN LONG RANKS . . . . SP MOONLIGHT NIGHT 2
A LONG, SWEET NIGHT WITH ME. . . . SP NATCHA 4
A LONG, DREAM NIGHT WITH ME. . . . SP NATCHA 7
THAT LONG BLACK HEARSE DONE SPED, SP NIGHT FUNERAL 34
SO LONG . . . . SP SO LONG 1
YOU'RE GONE SO LONG . . . . SP SO LONG 9
SO LONG. . . . . SP SO LONG 10
YES, SIR! LONG AS LIFE DO LAST! . . SP SYLVESTER'S BED 22
BUT GOD IS LONG! . . . . SP TAMBOURINES 10
TO TELL YOU A STORY OF THE LONG DARK WAY . . . . SP THE NEGRO MOTHE 2
LONG AGO . . . . SP UNCLE TOM 9
OH, THAT LAST LONG RIDE IS A . . . SP WIDOW WOMAN 1
YES, THAT LAST LONG RIDE'S A . . . SP WIDOW WOMAN 3
DOWN THE LONG HARD ROW THAT I BEEN HOEING . . . . AYM BLUES IN STEREO 34
A LONG WAY TO BAHIA - . . . . AYM GOSPEL CHA-CHA 39

I MOVED OUT TO LONG ISLAND	AYM HORN OF PLENTY	30
TELL ME HOW LONG -	AYM RIDE, RED, RIDE	4
GOT CHANGE IN HIS LONG POCKET?	AYM SHOW FARE PLESE	4
LONG AGO.	PL AMER HEARTBREAK	6
AND LONG RED NECKS	PL DAYBREAK IN ALA	10
WHEN THE LONG HOT SUMMERS COME	PL DEATH YORKVILLE	18
SEND (GOD FORBID - HE'S NOT DEAD LONG ENOUGH!)	PL FINAL CALL	17
WITHOUT COMPLAINING LOUD AND LONG,	PL MILITANT	4
HAS LONG BEEN TRIED AT LAW,	PL OCTOBER 16 RAID	20
BUT THAT DAY WAS SO LONG	PL STOKELY MALCOLM	7

LONGER 12

LAWD, FOLKSES, HOW MUCH LONGER IS THIS GONNA LAST?	NM BROKE	59
AND NO LONGER DO WE KNOW THE DARK MISERY	NM COLORED SL POEM	30
NO LONGER SHALL YOU SAY	ANS A NEW SONG	30
NOW YOUR WORDS NO LONGER HAVE MEANING -	JC THE BITTER RIVR	65
NO LONGER THE LIGHT OF MY DREAM BEFORE ME.	SP AS I GREW OLDER	20
AS TIME GROWS LONGER UNTIL DAY	SP DRUNKARD	3
AND JOHN BROWN'S WHITE AND LONGER	AYM BIRD IN ORBIT	45
ARE TRIBAL NOW NO LONGER	AYM ODE TO DINAH	77
TRIBAL NOW NO LONGER PAPA MAMA	AYM ODE TO DINAH	82
SHELTERED NOW NO LONGER.	AYM ODE TO DINAH	86
TRIBAL NOW NO LONGER ONE FOR ALL	AYM ODE TO DINAH	88
AND ALL FOR ONE NO LONGER	AYM ODE TO DINAH	89

LONGING 3

BROWN AND WONDERFUL WITH LONGING	SP INTERNE AT PROV	12
THAT IS LONGING FOR THE MOON	SP TRUMPET PLAYER	26
THAT IS LONGING FOR THE SEA	SP TRUMPET PLAYER	30

LONG-HEADED 2

SIX LONG-HEADED JAZZERS PLAY.	WB JAZZONIA	4
SIX LONG-HEADED JAZZERS PLAY.	WB JAZZONIA	17

LONG-TERM 1

WEAVING OUT OF LONG-TERM CREDIT	AYM SHOW FARE PLESE	24

LOOK 35

LOOK AT YO' LEGS.	FC RED SILK STOCK	4
LOOK AT YO' LEGS.	FC RED SILK STOCK	12
LOOK AT ME NOW AND	NM BIG-TIMER POEM	7
LOOK 'EM IN THE FACE AND	NM BIG-TIMER POEM	59
LOOK AT THE STARS YONDER	NM BLACK CLWN POEM	73
OR IF I WASN'T SO DROWSY I'D LOOK UP JOE	SH BED TIME	5
JUST LOOK AT ME AND SEE!	SH EVENIN' BLUES	24
I LOOK IN THE KETTLE, THE KETTLE IS DRY.	SH SUPPER TIME	1
LOOK IN THE BREAD BOX, NOTHING BUT A FLY.	SH SUPPER TIME	2
TURN ON THE LIGHT AND LOOK REAL GOOD!	SH SUPPER TIME	3
LOOK AT THAT WATER DRIPPING IN THE SINK.	SH SUPPER TIME	5
I CAN LOOK WAY ACROSS THE SEA	JC GOOD MORN STLIN	31
NOW THAT CROW'S BEGUN TO LOOK LIKE HELL.	JC JIM CROW'S LAST	6
"LOOK, PASSERS-BY,	FW HEART	6
TO LOOK FOR ONE.	OWT TOO BLUE	17
MADAM COULD LOOK IN YOUR HAND -	SP BLD FORTUNE TEL	1
AND I'LL LOOK INTO THE FUTURE	SP BLD THE GYPSY	7
HIS EYES LOOK OUT ON THE WORLD,	SP FREEDOM'S PLOW	11
LOOK TOO BLACK.	SP HIGH TO LOW	6
I WENT TO LOOK FOR JOY,	SP JOY	1
I LOOK DOWN THE ROAD	SP LITTLE GRN TREE	9
HIS EYES DIDN'T LOOK JUST RIGHT.	SP LOVER'S RETURN	4
WHEN THE KIDS LOOK ALL NEW	SP PASSING	7
AND LOOK TOWARD THE MOUNTAINS.	SP SUNDAY MORNING	18
LOOK AT MY FACE - DARK AS THE NIGHT -	SP THE NEGRO MOTHE	5
LOOK EVER UPWARD AT THE SUN AND THE STARS.	SP THE NEGRO MOTHE	48
LOOK ALL SCRAGGLY AND BAD,	SP WARNING AUGMENT	10
I LOOK AT THE STARS	AYM BIRD IN ORBIT	53
AND THEY LOOK AT THE STARS,	AYM BIRD IN ORBIT	54
LOOK AT ME!	PL FLORIDA WORKERS	2
HEY, BUDDY, LOOK!	PL FLORIDA WORKERS	19
AND LOOK OUT ON THE WORLD	PL HARLEM	19
LOOK ME IN THE FACE -	PL KU KLUX	18
LOOK THROUGH THE LARGER END -	PL LONG VIEW NEGRO	9
LOOK SLOW AT ONE ANOTHER -	PL OCTOBER 16 RAID	12

LOOKED 18

LOOKED ALL AROUND ME,	FC BLD OF GIN MARY	3
I LOOKED AT THEIR BLACK FACES	ANS NEGRO GHETTO	1
LOOKED AT THE BLACKS AND	SH DEATH IN HARLEM	66
LOOKED AT THE BLACKS AND	SH DEATH IN HARLEM	68
LOOKED AT THE BLACKS AND	SH DEATH IN HARLEM	70
SHE LOOKED ACROSS THE PLACE -	SH DEATH IN HARLEM	94
I LOOKED DOWN 31ST STREET,	SH MIDNIGHT CHIPPI	1
NO WAY SHE LOOKED.	SP BLD FORTUNE TEL	28
LOOKED LIKE ME.	SP CROSSING	18
HIS WIFE LOOKED IT UP IN HER DREAM BOOK	SP HOPE	3
YOU LOOKED AT ME CROSS-EYED	SP LATE LAST NIGHT	7
I LOOKED IN MY BOX FOR MAIL.	SP LITTLE OLD LETT	2
I LOOKED AT MY DADDY -	SP LOVER'S RETURN	13
HE LOOKED SO THIN -	SP LOVER'S RETURN	15
FORTUNE TELLER LOOKED IN MY HAND.	SP MADAM FORT TELL	1
WOKE UP AND LOOKED AROUND ME -	SP MORNING AFTER	11
I LOOKED UPON THE NILE AND RAISED THE PYRAMIDS ABOVE IT.	SP NEGRO SPEAKS OF	7
I LOOKED AND I SAW	PL WHO BUT TH LORD	1

LOOKING 4

BOASTING, LIKE A CHEAP BULLY, BUT SUDDENLY LOOKING AHEAD: SHRUGGING HIS	NM BIG-TIMER MOOD	5
A COMPLAINT TO B GIVEN BY A DEJECTED LOOKING FELLOW SHUFFLING ALONG	NM BROKE	1
LOOKING OUT TO SEA	FW JAIME	6
LOOKING AT LISTENERS' FACES.	PL CORNER MEETING	5

LOOKIN' 9

A LOOKIN' ALL SAD	FC NEW CABARET GRL	19
BUT I SHO BEEN LOOKIN' ROUND HARD LATELY FOR WAYS AND MEANS	NM BROKE	39
(IS YOU LOOKIN' AT ME, BABY, OR SOME OTHER WAY?)	NM BROKE	76
LOOKIN' FOR A BOX CAR	DK HOMESICK BLUES	11
I WAS LOOKIN' FOR A SANDWICH, JUDGE,	SH BRIEF ENCOUNTER	1
LOOKIN' FOR ANY OLD THING TO EAT -	SH BRIEF ENCOUNTER	4
BEEN LOOKIN' FOR A JOB	SH OUT OF WORK	5
I WENT LOOKIN' FOR MAGNOLIA FLOWERS	SP MAGNOLIA FLOWER	3
I WENT LOOKIN' FOR MAGNOLIA FLOWERS IN THE DUSK	SP MAGNOLIA FLOWER	5

LOOKS 15

WHEN MA MAN LOOKS AT ME	FC MA MAN	1
WHEN MA MAN LOOKS AT ME	FC MA MAN	3
I DON'T KNOW WHY IT LOOKS	SH BLD PAWNBROKER	11
LOOKS LIKE BY NOW	JC HOW ABOUT DIXIE	17
THE HEAD OF LINCOLN LOOKS DOWN FROM THE WALL	OWT LINCOLN THEATRE	1
LOOKS LIKE SHE COULD'VE KNOWED IT	SP BLD FORTUNE TEL	19
LOOKS LIKE HIS EYES	SP DREAM BOOGE VAR	9
LOOKS LIKE WHAT DRIVES ME CRAZY	SP EVIL	1
IT LOOKS LIKE TO ME	SP LITTLE GRN TREE	1
LOOKS LIKE A LIKELY	SP MADAM NUMBER WR	7
HE SAID, YOUR NAME LOOKS GOOD	SP MADAM'S CALLING	11
HE LOOKS TALLER THAN HE IS	SP NEIGHBOR	7
HE LOOKS DARKER THAN HE IS, TOO.	SP NEIGHBOR	9
AND HE'S SMARTER THAN HE LOOKS,	SP NEIGHBOR	10
LOOKS LIKE BETWEEN 'EM THEY DONE	PL STILL HERE	5

LOOKY 2

LOOKY YONDER	SP DANCER	15
LOOKY YONDER!	SP WONDER	3

LOOMS 1

LOOMS LARGER,	PL LONG VIEW NEGRO	4

LOOSE 1

IF YOU'D JUST TURN ME LOOSE."	PL KU KLUX	8

LORD 52

THE LORD WILL TAKE ME IN.	WB PIERROT	23
A BRIGHT BOWL OF BRASS IS BEAUTIFUL TO THE LORD.	FC BRASS SPITOONS	32
A CLEAN SPITOON ON THE ALTAR OF THE LORD.	FC BRASS SPITOONS	37
LORD, LORD!	FC MOAN	3
LORD, LORD!	FC MOAN	3
O, LORD!	FC MOAN	6
MA LORD!	FC MOAN	9
NO, LORD!	FC MOAN	12
O, LORD!	FC MOAN	15
YES, LORD!	FC MOAN	19
MA LORD AIN'T NO STUCK-UP MAN.	DK MA LORD	1
MA LORD, HE AIN'T PROUD.	DK MA LORD	2
MA LORD KNOWED WHAT IT WAS TO WORK.	DK MA LORD	6
MA LORD AIN'T NO STUCK-UP MAN.	DK MA LORD	10
I SWEAR TO THE LORD	JC BLACK MAN SPEAK	1
CAUSE THE GOOD LORD KNOWS WHAT WE'RE FIGHTING FOR!	JC JIM CROW'S LAST	26
BUT THE GOOD LORD KNOWS	OWT HONEY BABE	3
HE SAID, OH, LORD, THY WILL BE DONE!	LHR BLD MARY'S SON	24
AND TOOK MY LORD AWAY.	LHR BLD MARY'S SON	26
LORD, I WISH I WAS DEAD!	SP BLD OF THE GIRL	12
AND THINGS LIKE THAT. BUT NOW, LORD,	SP CHILDREN'S RYME	3
FIRE, LORD!	SP FIRE	2
FIRE, LORD!	SP FIRE	8
FIRE, LORD!	SP FIRE	15
FIRE, LORD!	SP FIRE	22
I MEANS FIRE, LORD!	SP FIRE	24
LORD, I BEEN A-WAITIN' FOR THE	SP FREEDOM TRAIN	7
LORD IN HEAVEN,	SP JUDGMENT DAY	6
THE LORD WILL SURELY	SP MADAM MINISTER	23
LORD KNOWS I WOULD SMILE.	SP MISS BLUES'ES	2
LORD GOD,	SP PRAYER	8

Context	Poem	Line
ON THAT DAY, LORD.	SP PROJECTION	15
LORD, AIN'T MINE!	SP SAME IN BLUES	25
HAVE MERCY, LORD!	SP SINNER	1
HAVE MERCY, LORD!	SP SINNER	5
I ASKED THE WHITE LORD JESUS	SP SONG DARK GIRL	7
SING, O LORD JESUS!	SP SPIRITUALS	4
SAVE ME, LORD!	SP SUNDAY MORNING	23
AND THE LORD WILL SAY,	SP SUNDAY MORNING	25
THE LORD WILL SAY,	SP SUNDAY MORNING	28
THE LORD WILL SAY,	SP SUNDAY MORNING	31
HOW I COULD PRAISE MY LORD!	SP TESTIMONIAL	4
FOR TO PRAISE MY LORD!	SP TESTIMONIAL	8
BUT I GOT TO GET A NEW ANTENNA, LORD -	AYM BLUES IN STEREO	36
LORD KNOWS I TRIED	AYM GOSPEL CHA-CHA	46
LORD KNOWS I PRAYED	AYM GOSPEL CHA-CHA	49
LORD KNOWS I CLIMBED	AYM GOSPEL CHA-CHA	55
LORD!	AYM SHADES OF PIG	44
THE LORD GOD HIMSELF	PL BOMBINGS DIXIE	5
I SAID, O, LORD, IF YOU CAN,	PL WHO BUT TH LORD	9
BUT THE LORD HE WAS NOT QUICK.	PL WHO BUT TH LORD	12
SO WHO BUT THE LORD	PL WHO BUT TH LORD	21
LORDS 3		
PLAY IT FOR THE LORDS AND LADIES.	FC JAZZ BAND	3
I MADE RICH THE GRANDEES AND LORDS	ANS SONG OF SPAIN	75
AT THE MISTERS, LORDS, GENERALS, VICEROYS,	SP IN EXPLANATION	42
LORDY 3		
LORDY, HE KIN PLUNK, PLUNK, PLUNK.	FC MA MAN	8
LORDY, LET YO' MERCY	SP FEET O' JESUS	3
LORDY! SLEEPIN' BY HERSELF.	SP STONY LONESOME	17
LORD-D-D-D-D-AH 1		
LORD-D-D-D-D-AH!	SP SUNDAY MORNING	22
LORD'S 2		
MA LORD'S LIFE WAS TROUBLE, TOO,	DK MA LORD	8
IN THE SWEET O' MA LORD'S SIGHT -	SP JUDGMENT DAY	12
LOS 2		
FROM LOS ANGELES TO LONDON	JC BLACK MAN SPEAK	15
TO LOS ANGELES, BAKERSFIELD,	SP ONE-WAY TICKET	11
LOSE 9		
KIN MAKE YOU LOSE YO' 'GINITY.	FC LISTEN HERE	6
SHE MADE ME LOSE MA MONEY	DK PO' BOY BLUES	17
AN' ALMOST LOSE MA MIND.	DK PO' BOY BLUES	18
I'M ABOUT TO LOSE MY MIND.	SH EVENIN' BLUES	6
AND SO LOSE ITS REPOSE.	AYM BLUES IN STEREO	20
THERE'S NO WAY NOT TO LOSE.	AYM ODE TO DINAH	114
WHAT DO YOU THINK I GOT TO LOSE?	PL BACKLASH BLUES	26
WHAT YOU THINK I GOT TO LOSE?	PL BACKLASH BLUES	28
MIGHT LOSE.	PL MOTHER IN WAR	15
LOSER 1		
LOSER FROM AN EMPTY POCKET	JC THE BITTER RIVR	69
LOSERS 1		
WINNERS OR LOSERS.	PL PEACE	3
LOSS 1		
THE LOSS	SP BEALE STREET	9
LOST 16		
I LOST MY TREES.	WB LAMENT DARK PEO	7
I LOST MY SILVER MOONS.	WB LAMENT DARK PEO	8
MAYBE YOUR BODIES'LL BE LOST IN A SWAMP.	ANS KIDS WHO DIE	40
AGAIN MANKIND HAS LOST ITS COURSE.	JC TO CAPTAIN MULZ	6
YOU GET LOST IN THE DUSK -	FW DUSK	3
THAT MY SOUL SHOULD NOT BE LOST.	LHR BLD MARY'S SON	33
OF BITTER YEARNINGS LOST	SP AFRO-AMER FRAG	19
UNTIL TIME IS LOST	SP DRUM	9
I'M JUST A POOR LOST SHEEP.	SP EVENING SONG	8
I LOST MY NICKEL.	SP MIDNIGHT RAFFLE	5
I LOST MY TIME.	SP MIDNIGHT RAFFLE	6
AND LOST AS MY NEED.	SP MYSTERY	16
WILL BE LOST!	SP SUNDAY MORNING	35
ON A TRAIN THAT LOST NO PASSENGERS	AYM ODE TO DINAH	29
LOST IN CASTRO'S BEARD?	AYM RIDE, RED, RIDE	12
MIGHT HAVE LOST HIS SOUL.	PL FREDRK DOUGLASS	6
LOT 4		
WITH A LOT O' SPORTY PALS.	NM BIG-TIMER POEM	16
BUT A LOT O' GAWD-KNOWS-WHAT.	SH LOVE AGAIN BLUS	2
BUT A LOT O' GAWD-KNOWS-WHAT.	SH LOVE AGAIN BLUS	4
A WHOLE LOT OF ROOM	SP HOMECOMING	7
LOTS 4		
LOTS OF OLD SCHOOLMATES ARE MARRIED NOW;	NM BIG-TIMER POEM	45
MAKE LOTS O' NOISE.	NM BIG-TIMER POEM	63
LOTS OF FOLKS WHO DON'T LIKE YOU	JC GOOD MORN STLIN	2
THE MISTERS WON'T CALL LOTS OF OTHER FOLKS MISTER.	SP IN EXPLANATION	11
LOTTE 1		
WHERE IS LOTTE LENYA	AYM SHADES OF PIG	13
LOU 1		
AND I THOUGHT ABOUT LOU	SP BLUE BAYOU	5
LOUD 15		
LAUGH A LOUD.	WB BLUES FANTASY	29
LOUD LAUGHERS IN THE HANDS OF FATE -	FC LAUGHERS	4
STRENGTH HE DOESN'T REALLY FEEL. GAY, LOUD, UNHAPPY JAZZ, BARING HIS	NM BIG-TIMER MOOD	9
HUMOROUS DEFIANCE, MELANCHOLY JAZZ. THEN DEFIANCE AGAIN FOLLOWED BY LOUD	NM BLACK CLWN MOOD	2
NOISY AND LOUD.	SH CABARET GIRL	4
ALARM CLOCK HERE RINGING SO DAMN LOUD	SH DAYBREAK	3
LOUNGERS AT THE BAR LAUGH OUT LOUD.	SH DEATH IN HARLEM	35
DIXIE RUBBED HIS HANDS AND LAUGHED OUT LOUD -	SH DEATH IN HARLEM	63
THE PEOPLE DO NOT ALWAYS SAY THINGS OUT LOUD.	SP FREEDOM'S PLOW	145
YOU TALK TOO LOUD.	SP HIGH TO LOW	4
CUSS TOO LOUD.	SP HIGH TO LOW	5
THE WAY YOU SHOUT OUT LOUD IN CHURCH,	SP HIGH TO LOW	13
PLEASE DON'T SNORE SO LOUD.	SP MORNING AFTER	14
PLEASE DON'T SNORE SO LOUD.	SP MORNING AFTER	16
WITHOUT COMPLAINING LOUD AND LONG.	PL MILITANT	4
LOUDEST 1		
AN OLD NEGRO MINISTER CONCLUDES HIS SERMON IN HIS LOUDEST VOICE,	SP SUNDAY MORNING	1
LOUDLY 1		
PULLING HIMSELF TOGETHER, BOASTING LOUDLY AGAIN, BUT REALIZING WITHIN THE	NM BIG-TIMER MOOD	11
LOUD-MOUTHED 1		
LOUD-MOUTHED LAUGHERS IN THE HANDS	FC LAUGHERS	31
LOUIS 5		
JOE LOUIS SAID, WE GONNA WIN THIS WAR	JC JIM CROW'S LAST	25
PLAY THE ST. LOUIS BLUES	OWT REQUEST REQUIEM	1
JOE LOUIS WORE,	SP TO BE SOMEBODY	16
LUMUMBA LOUIS ARMSTRONG	AYM ASK YOUR MAMA	29
DO YOU READ MUSIC? AND LOUIS SAYING $ $	AYM HORN OF PLENTY	11
LOUISIANA 1		
FROM GEORGIA FLORIDA LOUISIANA	SP GOOD MORNING	13
LOUNGE 2		
AND THE WAY YOU LOUNGE ON DOORSTEPS	SP HIGH TO LOW	15
AT THE ELKS CLUB LOUNGE	SP PARADE	7
LOUNGERS 1		
LOUNGERS AT THE BAR LAUGH OUT LOUD.	SH DEATH IN HARLEM	35
LOUNGING 1		
LOUNGING ON A CORNER.	SP RAILROAD AVENUE	14
LOUSY 1		
AND A LOUSY PEACE.	ANS KIDS WHO DIE	18
LOVE 94		
DON'T LOVE NOBODY	WB CAT AND SAXOPHN	12
THE BROKEN HEART OF LOVE,	WB LENOX AVE MIDNT	5
OF LOVE AND JOY AND WINE AND SONG,	WB OUR LAND	14
AND, FAITH, I LOVE HER YET.	WB PIERROT	13
LOVE.	WB POEME D'AUTOMNE	15
OF TOO MANY NIGHTS OF LOVE	WB SOLEDAD	3
AND REST FROM PAIN OF LOVE	WB YOUNG BRIDE	6
LOVE	FC BEALE ST. LOVE	1
LOVE, OH, LOVE IS	FC GYPSY MAN	19
LOVE, OH, LOVE IS	FC GYPSY MAN	19
LOVE, OH, LOVE IS	FC GYPSY MAN	21
LOVE, OH, LOVE IS	FC GYPSY MAN	21
IF MA DADDY DIDN'T LOVE ME	FC MINNIE SINGS	13
IF HE DIDN'T LOVE ME	FC MINNIE SINGS	15
NOBODY TO LOVE ME:	FC SUICIDE	5
I THOUGHT LOVE WAS A DREAM, BUT I SHO HAVE AWOKE -	NM BROKE	54
LOVE - AND CHAINS ARE BROKEN.	DK ALABAMA EARTH	13
AND I LOVE THE RAIN.	DK APRIL RAIN SONG	7
I FELL IN LOVE WITH	DK PO' BOY BLUES	13
FELL IN LOVE WITH	DK PO' BOY BLUES	15
'TWIXT MA LOVE AN' ME.	DK WIDE RIVER	8
'TWIXT MA LOVE AN' ME.	DK WIDE RIVER	10
WILL RAISE FOR YOU A LIVING MONUMENT OF LOVE,	ANS KIDS WHO DIE	46
LET IT BE THAT GREAT STRONG LAND OF LOVE	ANS LET AMERICA BE	7
DEATH AND LOVE AND HEARTBREAK	ANS SONG OF SPAIN	7

Line	Source	No.
BUT MY LOVE MIGHT TURN INTO A KNIFE	SH IN TROUBLED KEY	11
WHAT MAKES LOVE SUCH AN ACHE AND PAIN?	SH LOVE AGAIN BLUS	14
LOVE SUCH AN ACHE AND PAIN?	SH LOVE AGAIN BLUS	16
BUT YOU GOT TO LOVE AGAIN.	SH LOVE AGAIN BLUS	18
AND I WILL LOVE YOU, TOO.	SH MIDNIGHT CHIPPI	6
GIVES LOVE AWAY SHE'S THROUGH.	SH MIDNIGHT CHIPPI	24
ROBE O' LOVE -	SH PRESENT	4
THE CRACKERS WERE IN LOVE WITH HIM.	JC JIM CROW'S LAST	2
LOVE IS GIVEN.	FW GIFTS	2
I THOUGHT THAT LOVE MUST BE	FW MAN	5
IN THE ARMS OF YOUR LOVE -	FW PRAYER	10
NO LOVE FROM ABOVE.	FW PRAYER	12
AND SLEEK-HAIRED BOYS WHO DEAL IN LOVE FOR PAY	OWT LINCOLN THEATRE	14
SHE DID NOT LOVE ME.	SP A BLACK PIERROT	2
SHE DID NOT LOVE ME.	SP A BLACK PIERROT	6
SHE DID NOT LOVE ME.	SP A BLACK PIERROT	11
TO SEEK A NEW BROWN LOVE.	SP A BLACK PIERROT	15
CAUSE YOU DON'T LOVE ME	SP BAD LUCK CARD	1
SHE COULD TELL YOU ABOUT LOVE.	SP BLD FORTUNE TEL	5
THE ONES I LOVE.	SP CORA	6
COULD BE YOU LOVE ME.	SP COULD BE	9
HE WAS NO GOOD AT MAKING LOVE	SP DANCER	7
I DREAMED ABOUT WHEN WE FIRST FELL IN LOVE	SP DEFERRED	9
BABY, IF YOU LOVE ME	SP DOWN AND OUT	1
IF YOU LOVE ME, BABY,	SP DOWN AND OUT	3
CAN YOU LOVE AN EAGLE,	SP GENIUS CHILD	6
CAN YOU LOVE A MONSTER	SP GENIUS CHILD	9
I LOVE YOU.	SP HARLEM NIGHT SO	4
I LOVE YOU.	SP HARLEM NIGHT SO	13
AND FOR YOUR LOVE SONG TONE THEIR RUMBLE DOWN.	SP JUKE BOX LOVE	6
NEVER LOVE A MAN.	SP LAMENT OVER LOV	2
NEVER LOVE A MAN.	SP LAMENT OVER LOV	4
LOVE CAN HURT YOU	SP LAMENT OVER LOV	5
LOVE IS LIKE WHISKEY,	SP LAMENT OVER LOV	13
LOVE IS LIKE RED, RED WINE.	SP LAMENT OVER LOV	14
LOVE IS LIKE WHISKEY,	SP LAMENT OVER LOV	15
YOU GOT TO LOVE ALL THE TIME.	SP LAMENT OVER LOV	18
MY GIRL-FRIEND SEND HER LOVE AND SAY	SP LETTER	6
I COULD'VE DIED FOR LOVE -	SP LIFE IS FINE	25
IN THE ARMS OF YOUR LOVE -	SP LITANY	10
NO LOVE FROM ABOVE.	SP LITANY	12
LOVE IS A WILD WONDER	SP LOVE	1
THAT LITTLE SPARK IS LOVE	SP LOVE	7
LOVE IS GIVEN.	SP LUCK	6
I SAID, DO YOU LOVE ME?	SP MADAM MIGHT-HAV	13
I LOVE YOU SO!	SP MADAM HER MADAM	20
IF I LOVE YOU!	SP MADAM HER MADAM	24
LOVE TILL THE DAY I DIE.	SP MIDWINTER BLUES	18
I LOVE YOU, OH, I LOVE YOU SO -	SP MISS BLUES'ES	9
I LOVE YOU, OH, I LOVE YOU SO -	SP MISS BLUES'ES	9
NATCHA, OFFERING LOVE.	SP NATCHA	1
FOR TEN SHILLINGS OFFERING LOVE.	SP NATCHA	2
OUT OF LOVE.	SP NO REGRETS	1
OUT OF LOVE.	SP NO REGRETS	5
COME HERE, I LOVE YOU.	SP PORT TOWN	7
LOVE ME, DADDY -	SP QUESTION	4
LOVE IS A NAKED SHADOW	SP SONG DARK GIRL	11
FO' TO LOVE YO' DADDY RIGHT!"	SP SYLVESTER'S BED	24
NO SAFETY, NO LOVE, NO RESPECT WAS I DUE.	SP THE NEGRO MOTHE	16
AND I, WHO AM BLACK, WOULD LOVE HER	SP THE SOUTH	18
WELL, I LIKE TO EAT, SLEEP, DRINK, AND BE IN LOVE.	SP THEME FOR ENG B	21
TO LOVE.	SP YOUNG SAILOR	13
WHEN LOVE IS GONE WHAT	SP YOUNG GAL'S BLS	19
WHEN LOVE IS GONE, O,	SP YOUNG GAL'S BLS	21
AND ONE SHOULD LOVE ONE'S COUNTRY	AYM HORN OF PLENTY	57
LOVE THY NEIGHBOR AS THYSELF	AYM HORN OF PLENTY	85
GONNA LOVE YOU ANYHOW	AYM ODE TO DINAH	67
GRANT HIM YOUR LOVE.	PL CHRIST IN ALA.	9
I LOVE RALPH BUNCHE -	PL CROWNS GARLANDS	19

13

LOVED

Line	Source	No.
FOR PIERROT LOVED THE LONG WHITE ROAD,	WB PIERROT	7
AND PIERROT LOVED THE MOON.	WB PIERROT	8
AND PIERROT LOVED A STAR-FILLED SKY.	WB PIERROT	9
AND PIERROT LOVED EACH ONE.	WB PIERROT	18
AND PIERROT LOVED THE MOON.	WB PIERROT	28
I GIVE IT TO HIM CAUSE I LOVED HIM	FC GYPSY MAN	17
THAT HE LOVED SO	OLD THE CONSUMPTIVE	2
I LOVED MY FRIEND.	DK I LOVED FRIEND	1
I LOVED MY FRIEND.	DK I LOVED FRIEND	6
AND WHOEVER LOVED BESSIE WAS	SH DEATH IN HARLEM	126
THEY LOVED ONE ANOTHER TILL	SH DEATH IN HARLEM	89
HE TOLD ME THAT HE LOVED ME	SP MIDWINTER BLUES	13
HE TOLD ME THAT HE LOVED ME.	SP MIDWINTER BLUES	15

1

LOVELESS

Line	Source	No.
IN LOVELESS SLEEP.	WB YOUNG BRIDE	7

4

LOVELINESS

Line	Source	No.
A LOVELINESS	WB POEM	6
YOUR FACES ARE WHIRLING LIGHTS OF LOVELINESS AND SPLENDOR, TOO.	WB THE WHITE ONES	4
FOR YOUR LOVELINESS.	WB TO DARK MERCEDE	8
THIS UNBOUGHT LOVELINESS OF MOON.	SP A HOUSE IN TAOS	28

6

LOVELY

Line	Source	No.
LOVELY, DARK, AND LONELY ONE.	DK SONG	1
DEAR LOVELY DEATH	LHR DEAR LVLY DEATH	1
DEAR LOVELY DEATH.	LHR DEAR LVLY DEATH	9
WE CAN BUY LOVELY THINGS WITH MONEY.	SP A HOUSE IN TAOS	24
LIEDER, LOVELY LIEDER	PL CULTURAL EXCHNG	29
LOVELY LIEDER, LEONTYNE.	PL CULTURAL EXCHNG	31

8

LOVER

Line	Source	No.
JUNGLE LOVER.	WB TO MIDNIGHT NAN	13
NOW, TEXAS WAS A LOVER.	SH DEATH IN HARLEM	87
WAITING FOR A LOVER.	FW NEW MOON	7
DAMN A LOVER	SP LOVER'S RETURN	18
JESUS, LOVER OF MY SOUL!	SP MYSTERY	5
THEY HUNG MY BLACK YOUNG LOVER	SP SONG DARK GIRL	3
YOU WAS A MIGHTY LOVER AND YOU	SP WIDOW WOMAN	13
A MIGHTY LOVER, BABY, CAUSE YOU	SP WIDOW WOMAN	15

4

LOVERS

Line	Source	No.
WAITING FOR THEIR LOVERS.	WB POEME D'AUTOMNE	7
A SILENT WOMAN LIES BETWEEN TWO LOVERS -	WB SICK ROOM	4
WHO SEARCHED FOR LOVERS	WB TO LITTLE LOVER	2
TURN, OH, TURN, DARK LOVERS	AYM IS IT TRUE?	18

10

LOVES

Line	Source	No.
LOVES MY BABY	WB CAT AND SAXOPHN	6
I SAID, "BABY, YOU KNOW I LOVES YOU, AND ALL LIKE THAT	NM BROKE	50
JUST BECAUSE I LOVES YOU -	DK REASONS WHY	1
JUST BECAUSE I LOVES YOU	DK REASONS WHY	5
DE MAN I LOVES HAS	OWT LINCOLN THEATRE	11
NOBODY LOVES A GENIUS CHILD.	SP GENIUS CHILD	5
NOBODY LOVES A GENIUS CHILD.	SP GENIUS CHILD	11
JUST TO SAY HE LOVES ME!	SP MADAM PHONE BIL	23
NOBODY LOVES NOBODY	SP MADAM MIGHT-HAV	27
NOW, IF A MAN LOVES A WOMAN	SP MIDWINTER BLUES	11

1

LOVE-FIRE

Line	Source	No.
BURNS IN MY HEART A LOVE-FIRE SHARP LIKE PAIN.	SP WHEN SUE WEARS	11

1

LOVE-ONE

Line	Source	No.
MY LITTLE LOVE-ONE.	DK LULLABY	4

4

LOVE'S

Line	Source	No.
AND LOVE'S OLD STORY TOLD -	FW CAROLINA CABIN	20
MY TRUE LOVE'S LEFT ME	SP LAMENT OVER LOV	11
CAUSE THE MAN I LOVE'S DONE	SP MISERY	7
YET SHINING LIKE THE SUN WITH LOVE'S TRUE LIGHT.	SP THE NEGRO MOTHE	6

1

LOVIN

Line	Source	No.
WITH LOVIN IN HIS HEAD.	SH DEATH IN HARLEM	140

2

LOVING

Line	Source	No.
A LITTLE LOVING	SP ADVICE	5
AWAKE ALL NIGHT WITH LOVING	SP FIRED	1

11

LOVIN'

Line	Source	No.
YOU WANT LOVIN'	WB TO MIDNIGHT NAN	11
BUT SHE DON'T GIMME LOVIN'	FC WORKIN' MAN	11
I'M EATIN' AND LOVIN',	NM BIG-TIMER POEM	51
STILL I CAN'T HELP LOVIN' YOU.	SH IN TROUBLED KEY	7
SAYS I CAN'T HELP LOVIN' YOU	SH IN TROUBLED KEY	9
BABY, GIMME A LITTLE LOVIN',	SH SIX-BITS BLUES	7
A LITTLE LOVIN', BABE, BUT	SH SIX-BITS BLUES	9
MAKE IT SHORT AND SWEET, YOUR LOVIN'.	SH SIX-BITS BLUES	11
BUT BEING NO GOOD AT LOVIN' -	SP DANCER	18
BUT MY LOVIN' DAYS IS THROUGH.	SP SAME IN BLUES	18
STOP LAUGHIN', STOP LOVIN', STOP LIVIN' -	PL STILL HERE	7

14

LOW

Line	Source	No.
(THE BANJO'S SOBBING LOW)	DK SONG BANJO DANC	17
(THE BANJO'S SOBBING LOW)	DK SONG BANJO DANC	25
BASS SO LOW!	SH DEATH IN HARLEM	30
WHEN YOU SINK SO LOW.	OWT TOO BLUE	5
THE LOW BEATING OF THE TOM-TOMS,	SP DANSE AFRICAINE	1
LOW . . . SLOW	SP DANSE AFRICAINE	3
SLOW . . . LOW -	SP DANSE AFRICAINE	4
AND THE LOW BEATING OF THE TOM-TOMS	SP DANSE AFRICAINE	14
BUT HE LEFT ME WHEN THE COAL WAS LOW.	SP MIDWINTER BLUES	8
BUT HE LEFT WHEN THE COAL WAS LOW.	SP MIDWINTER BLUES	10
SWING LOW, SWEET CHARIOT,	SP MYSTERY	9
THE LOW, OBSEQUIOUS,	SP UNCLE TOM	5
HIGH BALLS, LOW BALLS:	AYM ASK YOUR MAMA	18
LYING LOW, UNPUBLICIZED,	PL MISSISSIPPI	13

1

LOWELL

Line	Source	No.
LOWELL.	PL FINAL CALL	31

LOWER 2

THE PRICES LOWER. . . . SP MADAM'S PAST HI 9
LOWER THE FLAGS . . . PL SPECIAL BULLTIN 1

LOW-DOWN 4

GOT SUCH LOW-DOWN WAYS. . . . FC EVIL WOMAN 10
I'M SO LOW-DOWN I . . . FC HARD LUCK 17
A GAY AND LOW-DOWN BLUES. COMIC ENTRANCE LIKE THE CLOWNS IN THE CIRCUS. . . . NM BLACK CLWN MOOD 1
I BEEN STINKIN'. LOW-DOWN. MEAN. . SP FIRE 6

LOW-RATE 2

SO NOBODY CAN'T LOW-RATE YOU. . . . SH MIDNIGHT CHIPPI 30
HOW CAN YOU LOW-RATE ME . . . SP LOW TO HIGH 12

LPS 1

ON LPS THAT WONDER . . . AYM BLUES IN STEREO 26

LUCK 9

WHEN HARD LUCK OVERTAKES YOU . . . FC HARD LUCK 1
WHEN HARD LUCK OVERTAKES YOU . . . FC HARD LUCK 3
HARD LUCK . . . OWT BLUES ON A BOX 7
MY BAD LUCK CARD. . . . SP BAD LUCK CARD 4
MAYBE A LITTLE LUCK NOW. . . . SP ELEVATOR BOY 8
MAYBE NO LUCK FOR A LONG TIME. . . SP ELEVATOR BOY 14
MADAM. IT'S JUST GOOD LUCK . . . SP MADAM FORT TELL 3
AIN'T HAD NO LUCK . . . SP MADAM CHARTY CH 11
YOU'RE OUT OF LUCK. . . . SP MADAM RENT MAN 26

LUCY 8

WHIP IT. MISS LUCY! . . . SH DEATH IN HARLEM 12
AW. PICK IT. MISS LUCY! . . . SH DEATH IN HARLEM 27
SAYS TO LUCY. . . . SH DEATH IN HARLEM 45
AW. PLUNK IT. MISS LUCY. . . . SH DEATH IN HARLEM 56
AW. PLAY IT. MISS LUCY! . . . SH DEATH IN HARLEM 74
LUCY WAS A-BASSIN IT. BOOM. BOOM. BOOM. . . . SH DEATH IN HARLEM 77
WHILE MISS LUCY PLAYED IT. BOOM. BOOM. BOOM. . . . SH DEATH IN HARLEM 91
ALEXANDER'S QUIT LUCY! . . . OWT JITNEY 51

LUGGED 1

THAT LUGGED THE FIRST WHITE . . . AYM GOSPEL CHA-CHA 16

LULLABY 5

LET THE RAIN SING YOU A LULLABY. . DK APRIL RAIN SONG 3
FOR YOUR LULLABY? . . . DK LULLABY 6
FOR YOUR LULLABY? . . . DK LULLABY 14
FOR YOUR SLEEP-SONG LULLABY! . . . DK LULLABY 25
TO A LULLABY. . . . SP STARS 6

LULLED 1

I BUILT MY HUT NEAR THE CONGO AND IT LULLED ME TO SLEEP. . . . SP NEGRO SPEAKS OF 6

LULU 5

I MISS YOU. LULU. . . . OWT YESTERDAY TODAY 5
MARY LULU JACKSON . . . SP GRADUATION 3
MARY LULU JACKSON. . . . SP GRADUATION 11
LULU SAID TO LEONARD. . . . SP SAME IN BLUES 8
LEONARD SAID TO LULU. . . . SP SAME IN BLUES 10

LUMINOUS 1

THOU ART NOT LUMINOUS . . . WB POEM 16

LUMUMBA 8

LUMUMBA LOUIS ARMSTRONG . . . AYM ASK YOUR MAMA 39
LUMUMBA IN THE CONGO . . . AYM BIRD IN ORBIT 59
WAS SHE FLEEING WITH LUMUMBA? . . . AYM RIDE. RED. RIDE 16
FOR LUMUMBA TO CRY "FREEDOM NOW!" PL FINAL CALL 18
LUMUMBA WAS BLACK . . . PL LUMUMBA'S GRAVE 1
LUMUMBA WAS BLACK . . . PL LUMUMBA'S GRAVE 5
LUMUMBA WAS BLACK. . . . PL LUMUMBA'S GRAVE 9
THEY BURIED LUMUMBA . . . PL LUMUMBA'S GRAVE 13

LUNCH 2

HAS A LUNCH TO CARRY. . . . SP MIGRANT 13
BUT I CAN'T EAT HIM FOR LUNCH. . . PL CROWNS GARLANDS 20

LUNCHES 1

FOR LUNCHES AND CAR FARE? . . . SP KID SLEEPY 15

LUNCH-BOX 1

GET OUT THE LUNCH-BOX OF YOUR DREAMS PL JIM CROW CAR 1

LUSCIOUS 1

STROLL DOWN LUSCIOUS. . . . SH HARLEM SWEETIES 43

LUSH 1

IN THESE LUSH AND THEIVING DAYS . . PL PRIME 3

LUTHER 3

THE REVEREND MARTIN LUTHER . . . AYM BIRD IN ORBIT 24
STRAYHORN HID BACKSTAGE WITH LUTHER $ $ . . . AYM HORN OF PLENTY 10
MARTIN LUTHER KING IS GOVERNOR OF GEORGIA. . . . PL CULTURAL EXCHNG 43

LYE 1

WAS LYE. . . . OWT DECEASED 7

LYING 3

AND IT'S A GOOD THING ALL THE BLACK BOYS LYING DEAD . . . NM COLORED SL POEM 51
LYING IN THE SNOW. . . . FW WHEN ARMIES PAS 2
LYING LOW. UNPUBLICIZED. . . . PL MISSISSIPPI 13

LYIN' 2

AND FORGET THAT THEY LYIN' . . . NM BIG-TIMER POEM 67
UH! I HATES A LYIN' GYPSY . . . SP BLD THE GYPSY 18

LYNCH 5

THEY LYNCH FREEDOM. . . . JC FREEDOM 9
THEY LYNCH ME STILL IN MISSISSIPPI. SP NEGRO 16
WHO LYNCH AND RUN. . . . SP ONE-WAY TICKET 20
ROPE MY NECK - LYNCH ME - . . . PL DEATH YORKVILLE 7
FROM THE SLAVE CHAIN TO THE LYNCH ROPE . . . PL DEATH YORKVILLE 9

LYNCHED 7

EACH FOURTEEN YEARS OLD WHEN LYNCHED TOGETHER BENEATH THE . . . JC THE BITTER RIVR 1
MIXED WITH THE BLOOD OF THE LYNCHED BOYS . . . JC THE BITTER RIVR 12
YOU HAVE LYNCHED MY COMRADES . . . JC THE BITTER RIVR 59
WHERE THE LYNCHED BOYS HUNG. . . . JC THE BITTER RIVR 84
LAST WEEK THEY LYNCHED A COLORED BOY. . . . SP SOUTHERN MAMMY 13
LYNCHED TOMORROW SWAYS. . . . AYM ODE TO DINAH 101
A LYNCHED TOMORROW SWAYS. . . . AYM ODE TO DINAH 99

LYNCHER'S 1

WHEN THE LYNCHER'S ROPE . . . ANS A NEW SONG 18

LYNCHING 2

ON EVERY LYNCHING TREE. A POSTER CRYING FREE . . . ANS OPEN LETTER 44
BY LYNCHING A NEGRO . . . JC FREEDOM 8

L.K 2

SHUT UP. SAYS GERALD L.K. SMITH. . SP IN EXPLANATION 23
GOVERNORS OF SOUTH CAROLINA. GERALD L.K. STRYDOMS. . . . SP IN EXPLANATION 43

MA 95

DAMN MA BLACK OLD MAMMY'S SOUL . . FC A RUINED GAL 17
I TAKES MA MEANNESS AND MA LICKER FC BAD MAN 5
I TAKES MA MEANNESS AND MA LICKER FC BAD MAN 5
I BEATS MA WIFE AN' . . . FC BAD MAN 7
I BEATS MA SIDE GAL TOO. . . . FC BAD MAN 8
BEATS MA WIFE AN' . . . FC BAD MAN 9
BEATS MA SIDE GAL TOO. . . . FC BAD MAN 10
THEN OUT MA DOOR HE GOES. . . . FC BLACK GAL 12
AN' I WANTS MA ALBERT BACK. . . . FC BLACK GAL 16
MA LITTLE. SHORT. SWEET. BROWNSKIN BOY. - . . . FC BLACK GAL 17
BUT I'LL MISS MA GIN. . . . FC BLD OF GIN MARY 20
I GOT MA TAIL CURLED! . . . FC CRAP GAME 2
MA FRIEND O' MINE. . . . FC DEATH DO DIRTY 10
HE'D GO MA BAIL. . . . FC DEATH DO DIRTY 19
MA FRIEND O' MINE. . . . FC DEATH DO DIRTY 25
MA FRIEND O' MINE. . . . FC DEATH DO DIRTY 35
I AIN'T GONNA MISTREAT MA . . . FC EVIL WOMAN 1
PUT MA HEAD UN'NEATH DE KIVER. . . FC GAL'S CRY DYING 5
MA MAN'S A GYPSY . . . FC GYPSY MAN 1
MA MAN'S A GYPSY. - . . . FC GYPSY MAN 3
HE TOOK MA LAST THIN DIME. . . . FC GYPSY MAN 14
HE TOOK MA LAST THIN DIME. . . . FC GYPSY MAN 16
WHEN MA MAN LOOKS AT ME . . . FC MA MAN 1
HE KNOCKS ME OFF MA FEET. . . . FC MA MAN 2
WHEN MA MAN LOOKS AT ME . . . FC MA MAN 3
HE KNOCKS ME OFF MA FEET. . . . FC MA MAN 4
I'M WAITING FOR MA MAMMY. - . . . FC MAMMY 1
I'M WAITING FOR MA MAMMY. - . . . FC MAMMY 5
THAT'S WHERE MA MAN AN' ME GO. . . FC MINNIE SINGS 2
MA MAN AN' ME DANCE. . . . FC MINNIE SINGS 8
IF MA DADDY DIDN'T LOVE ME . . . FC MINNIE SINGS 13
GONNA PRAY TO MA JESUS. . . . FC MOAN 7
MA LORD! . . . FC MOAN 9
MA JESUS. . . . FC MOAN 17
MA SWEET GOOD MAN HAS . . . FC SUICIDE 1
MA SWEET GOOD MAN HAS . . . FC SUICIDE 3
I'M GONNA KILL MA SELF. . . . FC SUICIDE 6
SHALL I CARVE MA SELF OR . . . FC SUICIDE 11
I CALLS FOR MA WOMAN . . . FC WORKIN' MAN 5
I HAD MA CLOTHES CLEANED . . . DK DRESSED UP 1
THEY DON'T HURT MA FEET. . . . DK DRESSED UP 10
MA HEART WAS IN MA MOUTH. . . . DK HOMESICK BLUES 8
MA HEART WAS IN MA MOUTH. . . . DK HOMESICK BLUES 8
HEART WAS IN MA MOUTH. . . . DK HOMESICK BLUES 10
I OPENS MA MOUTH AN' LAUGHS. . . . DK HOMESICK BLUES 18
MA LORD AIN'T NO STUCK-UP MAN. . . DK MA LORD 1
MA LORD. HE AIN'T PROUD. . . . DK MA LORD 2

Context	Source	Line
"YOU MA FRIEND," HE 'LOWED.	DK MA LORD	5
MA LORD KNOWED WHAT IT WAS TO WORK.	DK MA LORD	6
MA LORD'S LIFE WAS TROUBLE, TOO.	DK MA LORD	8
MA LORD AIN'T NO STUCK-UP MAN.	DK MA LORD	10
AN' BE MA FRIEND THROUGH ETERNITY."	DK MA LORD	16
"ME AN' MA BABY'S	DK NEGRO DANCERS	1
"ME AN' MA BABY'S	DK NEGRO DANCERS	13
THIS IS GONNA BE MA SONG.	DK NIGHT AND MORN	8
THIS IS GONNA BE MA SONG:	DK NIGHT AND MORN	10
SHE MADE ME LOSE MA MONEY	DK PO' BOY BLUES	17
AN' ALMOST LOSE MA MIND.	DK PO' BOY BLUES	18
MA SOUL IS FULL OF COLOR	DK REASONS WHY	3
MA HEART'S A FLUTTERING ASPEN LEAF	DK REASONS WHY	7
MA BABY LIVES ACROSS DE RIVER	DK WIDE RIVER	1
'TWIXT MA LOVE AN' ME.	DK WIDE RIVER	8
'TWIXT MA LOVE AN' ME.	DK WIDE RIVER	10
AN' GIT TO MA BABY SOMEHOW.	DK WIDE RIVER	14
GIT TO MA BABY SOMEHOW -	DK WIDE RIVER	16
CAUSE IF I DON'T SEE MA BABY	DK WIDE RIVER	17
WENT HOME TO HER MA.	SH SHAKESPEARE	8
BUT I DRUG MA WINGS	SP ANGELS WINGS	7
O, I DRUG MA WINGS	SP ANGELS WINGS	9
MY MA DIED IN A SHACK.	SP CROSS	10
THE CREDIT MAN'S DONE TOOK MA CLOTHES	SP DOWN AND OUT	7
FIRE GONNA BURN MA SOUL!	SP FIRE	3
FIRE GONNA BURN MA SOUL!	SP FIRE	9
FIRE GONNA BURN MA SOUL!	SP FIRE	16
FIRE GONNA BURN MA SOUL!	SP FIRE	23
FIRE GONNA BURN MA SOUL!	SP FIRE	25
I WENT TO MA DADDY,	SP HARD DADDY	1
WENT TO MA DADDY,	SP HARD DADDY	3
MA DADDY SAYS, HONEY,	SP HARD DADDY	5
I'D FLY ON MA MAN AN'	SP HARD DADDY	17
THEY PUT MA BODY IN THE GROUND,	SP JUDGMENT DAY	1
MA SOUL WENT FLYIN' O' THE TOWN,	SP JUDGMENT DAY	2
IN THE SWEET O' MA LORD'S SIGHT -	SP JUDGMENT DAY	12
I DIDN'T MEAN TO STUMP MA TOE ON YOU, LADY.	SP MAGNOLIA FLOWER	9
I DIDN'T MEAN TO STUMP MA TOE ON YOU.	SP MAGNOLIA FLOWER	13
BOTH AT MA DO'.	SP SYLVESTER'S BED	12
BUT I FELT MA TIME'S A-COMIN',	SP SYLVESTER'S BED	17
AIN'T GOT NOBODY BUT MA SELF.	SP THE WEARY BLUES	20
I'S GWINE TO QUIT MA FROWNIN'	SP THE WEARY BLUES	21
AND PUT MA TROUBLES ON THE SHELF."	SP THE WEARY BLUES	22
'HIND MA FRIEND MISS CORA LEE.	SP YOUNG GAL'S BLS	2
'HIND MA DEAR FRIEND CORA LEE	SP YOUNG GAL'S BLS	4
TO SEE MA OLD AUNT CLEW.	SP YOUNG GAL'S BLS	8
TO SEE MA OLD AUNT CLEW.	SP YOUNG GAL'S BLS	10
SAID, TELL YOUR MA.	AYM ASK YOUR MAMA	14

1
MABEL

Context	Source	Line
BRICKTOP INEZ MABEL MERCER	AYM BIRD IN ORBIT	6

1
MABLEY

Context	Source	Line
WILL TEAM UP WITH JACKIE MABLEY.	SP PROJECTION	19

1
MAC

Context	Source	Line
AND IF UNCLE MAC BRINGS BEER	SP SUMMER EVENING	24

1
MACBETH

Context	Source	Line
YOU PUT ME IN MACBETH AND CARMEN JONES	SP NOTE COMM THEAT	9

3
MACHINE

Context	Source	Line
SO I SAY, "MISTER, I AIN'T NO SWEEPIN' MACHINE."	NM BROKE	16
I AM THE WORKER SOLD TO THE MACHINE.	ANS LET AMERICA BE	32
CIGARETTE MACHINE.	SP TOMORROW	5

1
MACK

Context	Source	Line
AND WHO IS MACK THE KNIFE	AYM SHADES OF PIG	14

5
MAD

Context	Source	Line
I'M MIDNIGHT MAD.	FC MINNIE SINGS	12
THAT MAD MOB	SL SCOTTSBORO	13
AND EVEN IF I DID, I WAS MAD -	SH LETTER	6
I AM EVIL AND MAD.	SP EARLY EVENING	14
I'M MAD AND DISGUSTED	SP MADAM PHONE BIL	6

24
MADAM

Context	Source	Line
I DON'T TURN, MADAM!	CWT JITNEY	39
MADAM COULD LOOK IN YOUR HAND -	SP BLD FORTUNE TEL	1
MADAM TOOK HIM IN.	SP BLD FORTUNE TEL	10
MADAM, IT'S JUST GOOD LUCK	SP MADAM FORT TELL	3
HE SAID, ARE YOU MADAM?	SP MADAM WRONG VIS	3
HE SAID, MADAM,	SP MADAM NUMBER WR	5
MADAM, YOU AIN'T WISE.	SP MADAM FORT TELL	8
I SAID, MADAM,	SP MADAM HER MADAM	13
I SAID, MADAM, TELL ME -	SP MADAM FORT TELL	13
FOR SHE WAS MADAM, TOO -	SP MADAM FORT TELL	14
HE SAID, MADAM, I SWEAR	SP MADAM MIGHT-HAV	17
MADAM ALBERTA K.?	SP MADAM WRONG VIS	18
HE SAID, MADAM,	SP MADAM RENT MAN	19
I SAID, MADAM,	SP MADAM HER MADAM	21
SHE SAID, MADAM! BE CALM -	SP MADAM FORT TELL	22
THE DOCTOR SAID, MADAM,	SP MADAM WRONG VIS	23
HE SAID, MADAM,	SP MADAM RENT MAN	27
THE RUNNER SAID, MADAM,	SP MADAM NUMBER WR	29
I'M MADAM TO YOU!	SP MADAM CENSUS	32
MADAM ALBERTA K.	SP MADAM'S PAST HI	2
THE MADAM STANDS FOR BUSINESS.	SP MADAM'S PAST HI	3
MADAM JOHNSON,	SP MADAM'S CALLING	9
MADAM TO YOU.	SP MADAM'S PAST HI	26
MADAM WALKER	SP SUMMER EVENING	8

1
MADAM'D

Context	Source	Line
MADAM'D THAT WAY.	SP MADAM'S CALLING	12

41
MADE

Context	Source	Line
MADE ME EVERBODY'S FOOL.	FC LISTEN HERE	12
BEEN MADE, PROUD AND SMILING, BUT THE LIVING, REMEMBERING WITH A HALF-SOB	NM COLORED SL MOOD	10
THE WORLD'S BEEN MADE SAFE FOR DEMOCRACY	NM COLORED SL POEM	29
SHE MADE ME LOSE MA MONEY	DK PO' BOY BLUES	17
THAT'S MADE AMERICA THE LAND IT HAS BECOME.	ANS LET AMERICA BE	44
WHO MADE AMERICA,	ANS LET AMERICA BE	66
WORKERS MADE THOSE BOMBS FOR A FACIST SPAIN!	ANS SONG OF SPAIN	46
EXCEPT THAT THEY BE MADE FOR US	ANS SONG OF SPAIN	64
I MADE THOSE BOMBS FOR SPAIN.	ANS SONG OF SPAIN	71
I MADE THOSE BOMBING PLANES.	ANS SONG OF SPAIN	73
I MADE RICH THE GRANDEES AND LORDS	ANS SONG OF SPAIN	75
HAVE MADE UP THEIR MINDS JIM CROW IS THROUGH.	JC JIM CROW'S LAST	14
THE THINGS THEY MADE, NOR THEIR OWN LIVES -	JC TO CAPTAIN MULZ	21
FOLKS MADE A COFFIN	FW GIRL	9
THEY MADE A CROSS	LHR BLD MARY'S SON	27
MADE THEM THAT WAY.	SP CAFE: 3 A.M.	8
UNTIL HE MADE FOLKS SAY,	SP DANCER	14
WHEN IT STOPS IN MISSISSIPPI WILL IT BE MADE PLAIN	SP FREEDOM TRAIN	21
THE SLAVES MADE UP A SONG:	SP FREEDOM'S PLOW	125
ALL THESE HANDS MADE AMERICA.	SP FREEDOM'S PLOW	69
MADE UP A SONG:	SP FREEDOM'S PLOW	130
I MADE DOWN THE BED.	SP HOMECOMING	6
MADE ME TURN RIGHT PALE.	SP LITTLE OLD LETT	4
BUT IT MADE ME WISH	SP LITTLE OLD LETT	7
AND THE SUN HAS MADE	SP MEXICAN MARKET	6
ALMOST MADE ME BLIND.	SP MORNING AFTER	6
I MADE MORTAR FOR THE WOOLWORTH BUILDING.	SP NEGRO	9
I MADE RAGTIME.	SP NEGRO	13
IT WAS ALL THEIR TEARS THAT MADE	SP NIGHT FUNERAL	42
THAT MADE	SP STRANGE HURT	8
HE MADE THAT POOR PIANO MOAN WITH MELODY.	SP THE WEARY BLUES	10
MADE FROM THE HIDES OF BLACKS	AYM BIRD IN ORBIT	66
MADE FROM THE HIDES OF BLACKS	AYM BIRD IN ORBIT	89
GOT THERE! YES, I MADE IT!	AYM HORN OF PLENTY	36
WHERE DINAH'S SONGS ARE MADE	AYM ODE TO DINAH	53
THAT JAMESTOWN MADE	PL AMER HEARTBREAK	5
THAT CHINA MADE AEONS AGO -	PL BIRMINGHAM SUND	9
THAT WHAT CHINA MADE	PL BIRMINGHAM SUND	11
HAVE MADE THEIR DOUGH.	PL OFFICE BUILDING	5
MADE IN ATLANTA.	PL SPECIAL BULLTIN	13
IT'S MADE OF PLAIN OLD GEORGIA CLAY.	PL VARI-COLORED	7

1
MAGI

Context	Source	Line
MAGI ARE STARING.	SP INTERNE AT PROV	39

2
MAGIC

Context	Source	Line
IN AMERICA'S MAGIC LAND.	NM DARK YOUTH USA	5
IN MELLOW MAGIC	SP COLLEGE FORMAL	11

3
MAGNOLIA

Context	Source	Line
I WENT LOOKIN' FOR MAGNOLIA FLOWERS	SP MAGNOLIA FLOWER	3
I WENT LOOKIN' FOR MAGNOLIA FLOWERS IN THE DUSK	SP MAGNOLIA FLOWER	5
AS YET UNFELT AMONG MAGNOLIA TREES.	PL BIRMINGHAM SUND	27

1
MAGNOLIAS

Context	Source	Line
THERE OUGHT TO BE MAGNOLIAS	SP MAGNOLIA FLOWER	10

1
MAGNOLIA-SCENTED

Context	Source	Line
THE MAGNOLIA-SCENTED SOUTH.	SP THE SOUTH	12

1
MAHALIA'S

Context	Source	Line
WHERE THE SONG'S MAHALIA'S DAUGHTER	AYM ODE TO DINAH	19

1
MAHOMET

Context	Source	Line
MAHOMET!	SP MYSTERY	19

1
MAI

Context	Source	Line
AND WHY WOULD MAI (NOT MAY)	AYM SHADES OF PIG	17

2
MAID

Context	Source	Line
YOU GOT A BUTLER AND MAID.	ANS PARK BENCH	6
COULD I RECOMMEND A MAID.	AYM HORN OF PLENTY	97

MAIDENS 1
AND PIERROT THOUGHT ALL MAIDENS FAIR . . . WB PIERROT 19
MAIDS 1
LADIES' MAIDS. . . . FC LAUGHERS 8
MAIL 1
I LOCKED IN MY BOX FOR MAIL. . . . SP LITTLE OLD LETT 2
MAIS 1
MAIS OUI. . . . FC JAZZ BAND 15
MAJA 1
LA MAJA DESNUDA'S . . . ANS SONG OF SPAIN 23
MAJORITY 1
SUDDENLY BECAME MAJORITY . . . PL GHOSTS OF 1619 18
MAKE 65
NO, MAKE IT . . . WB CAT AND SAXOPHN 5
GIT SOME GIN TO MAKE YOU LAUGH. . . FC HARD LUCK 12
KIN MAKE YOU LOSE YO' 'GINITY. . . FC LISTEN HERE 6
I COULD MAKE SIX DOLLARS A DAY . . FC PRIZE FIGHTER 4
MAKE LOTS O' NOISE. . . . NM BIG-TIMER POEM 63
THAT CAN REALLY MAKE ME FREE! . . . NM BLACK CLWN POEM 62
THAT MAKE ME A CLOWN! . . . NM BLACK CLWN POEM 70
FOR HERE I DO NOT MAKE MY BED. . . DK DEATH SEAMAN 6
THEY MAKE RAINBOW WINGS. . . . DK FAIRIES 4
CAN MAKE MY EARTH-BODY FREE. . . . ANS A NEW SONG 28
AND MAKE ME ROOM. . . . ANS BLDS OF LENIN 12
WHO MAKE SURVEYS AND WRITE BOOKS. ANS KIDS WHO DIE 23
AND MAKE AMERICA AGAIN! . . . ANS LET AMERICA BE 86
NEW LIFE-WAYS MAKE. . . . ANS OPEN LETTER 34
WILL I MAKE THEM AGAIN, AND YET AGAIN? . . . ANS SONG OF SPAIN 47
WORKERS, MAKE NO BOMBS AGAIN! . . . ANS SONG OF SPAIN 54
WORKERS, MAKE NO BOMBS AGAIN . . . ANS SONG OF SPAIN 63
MAKE THIS EARLY MORNING TIME TO KEEP BODY AND SOUL . . . SH DAYBREAK 7
SHE COULD MAKE ME HOLLER LIKE A SISSIE. . . . SH ONLY WOMAN BLUS 7
BUT DON'T MAKE IT TOO LONG. . . . SH SIX-BITS BLUES 8
DON'T MAKE IT TOO LONG. . . . SH SIX-BITS BLUES 10
MAKE IT SHORT AND SWEET, YOUR LOVIN'. . . . SH SIX-BITS BLUES 11
I WOULD MAKE A FIRE BUT THERE AIN'T NO WOOD. . . . SH SUPPER TIME 4
IF I HAD A FIRE I'D MAKE ME SOME TEA SH SUPPER TIME 11
MAKE YOU WALK LIKE A GHOST IF YOU BOTHER ME ANY MORE. . . . SH TWILIGHT REVERI 6
DOWN SOUTH YOU MAKE ME RIDE . . . JC BLACK MAN SPEAK 13
AND MAKE YOUR CHOICE KNOWN . . . JC BLD SAM SOLOMON 10
THEN MAKE FINE SPEECHES . . . JC HOW ABOUT DIXIE 15
I'LL MAKE MINCE-MEAT . . . JC NOTE TO NAZIS 7
AND MAKE ME DRINK OF THE BITTER CUP JC THE BITTER RIVR 57
OF THOSE WHO WOULD KEEP, OR ONCE MORE MAKE . . . JC TO CAPTAIN MULZ 31
WE WILL TO MAKE - . . . JC TO CAPTAIN MULZ 55
TO MAKE . . . FW BIRTH 10
MAKE A HOME. . . . FW CAROLINA CABIN 22
ONE MIGHT MAKE A STORY . . . FW MIGRATION 16
AND MAKE EARTH HAPPY . . . FW WISDOM 7
I SAID, IT DON'T MAKE NO DIFFERENCE NOHOW. . . . OWT STRANGER IN TWN 9
DID NOT MAKE ME VERY WISE - . . . LHR ACCEPTANCE 2
TO MAKE IT EITHER MORE OR LESS. . . LHR DEAR LVLY DEATH 7
TO MAKE MY GAL FORGET. . . . SP BLD THE GYPSY 17
ONE DON'T MAKE ENOUGH . . . SP CONSIDER ME 30
IT DON'T MAKE SENSE - . . . SP DEFERRED 22
TRYING TO MAKE HER WHERE-WITH-ALL: SP EVENING SONG 2
TAKE THE NEON LIGHTS AND MAKE A CROWN, . . . SP JUKE BOX LOVE 3
MAKE A DRUMBEAT. . . . SP JUKE BOX LOVE 8
YOU TRYING TO MAKE A . . . SP MADAM HER MADAM 15
TO MAKE THE COTTON YIELD. . . . SP SHARE-CROPPERS 4
TO MAKE THE COTTON YIELD. . . . SP SHARE-CROPPERS 16
AND MAKE OF THOSE YEARS A TORCH FOR TOMORROW. . . . SP THE NEGRO MOTHE 38
MAKE OF MY PAST A ROAD TO THE LIGHT SP THE NEGRO MOTHE 39
I GUESS BEING COLORED DOESN'T MAKE ME NOT LIKE . . . SP THEME FOR ENG B 25
STOP EVERYBODY MUST MAKE. . . . SP WIDOW WOMAN 6
SEA GOURDS MAKE MARACAS OUT OF ME. AYM GOSPEL CHA-CHA 6
MAKE CLAVES OF MY SORROWS . . . AYM GOSPEL CHA-CHA 33
MAKE A SPANGLE OUT OF QUARTERS RINGING . . . AYM ODE TO DINAH 59
MAKE A GARLAND OF LEONTYNES AND LENAS . . . PL CROWNS GARLANDS 1
MAKE A CROWN OF SAMMYS, SIDNEYS, HARRYS. . . . PL CROWNS GARLANDS 4
MAKE HASTE! . . . PL CULTURAL EXCHNG 61
TO MAKE US ALL INTO PRINCES AND PRINCESSES. . . . PL FINAL CALL 7
TO MAKE EACH HIGHWAY . . . PL FREDRK DOUGLASS 12
TRIED TO MAKE ME . . . PL STILL HERE 6
MAKE ME SAY I DID IT. . . . PL THIRD DEGREE 2
I'D MAKE TOMORROW. . . . PL THIRD DEGREE 12
DON'T LET HIM MAKE A PULP OUT OF ME! PL WHO BUT TH LORD 11
THAT ALMOST MAKE ME CRY. . . . PL WORDS LIKE FREE 6
MAKER 1
TROUBLE MAKER!" YOU SAY. . . . JC THE BITTER RIVR 48
MAKES 21
NEXT TIME SHE MAKES ME SORE. . . . FC EVIL WOMAN 4
THE RAIN MAKES STILL POOLS ON THE SIDEWALK. . . . DK APRIL RAIN SONG 4
THE RAIN MAKES RUNNING POOLS IN THE GUTTER. . . . DK APRIL RAIN SONG 5
WHAT MAKES A WOMAN . . . SH ANNOUNCEMENT 7
(DIXIE MAKES HIS MONEY ON TWO-BIT GIN.) . . . SH DEATH IN HARLEM 32
WHAT MAKES LOVE SUCH AN ACHE AND PAIN? . . . SH LOVE AGAIN BLUS 14
TELL ME WHAT MAKES . . . SH LOVE AGAIN BLUS 15
BUT DE WATER STILL MAKES A FLOOD. SH MISSISSIPPI LEV 12
I WONDER WHAT MAKES . . . SP BLD OF THE MAN 25
MAKES ME WORK ALL DAY . . . SP BLUE BAYOU 8
OUT WHERE IT MAKES . . . SP DEAD IN THERE 21
MAKES A GOOD WOMAN CRY. . . . SP EARLY EVENING 6
MAKES A LITTLE SPARK. . . . SP LOVE 6
WHAT MAKES THESE CHARITY . . . SP MADAM CHARTY CH 9
MAKES YOUR NAME TOO SHORT. . . . SP MADAM CENSUS 24
WHICH MAKES IT . . . SP MELLOW 7
MAKES IRON OF CHOCOLATE MUSCLES. . SP MIGRANT 15
MAKES HAMMER BEAT OF DRUM BEAT . . SP MIGRANT 17
MAKES NO DIFFERENCE TO ME - . . . AYM BLUES IN STEREO 30
FROM THE COLD THAT MAKES NIAGARA . AYM ODE TO DINAH 25
WHAT MAKES ME . . . PL IMPASSE 3
MAKING 5
AND I HOPE YOU'RE MAKING GOOD, AND DOING FINE - . . . NM COLORED SL POEM 17
BUT WHEN THE SUN ROSE MAKING . . . DK IRISH WAKE 5
AT MAKING MINCE-MEAT . . . JC NOTE TO NAZIS 3
HE WAS NO GOOD AT MAKING LOVE . . . SP DANCER 7
AND NO GOOD AT MAKING MONEY. . . . SP DANCER 8
MAKIN' 6
MAKIN' ME DIE THIS WAY? . . . SH CABARET GIRL 8
MAKIN' ROUNDS AT NIGHT. . . . SP STREET SONG 4
I'M MAKIN' A ROAD . . . PL FLORIDA WORKERS 3
MAKIN' A ROAD . . . PL FLORIDA WORKERS 5
I'M MAKIN' A ROAD . . . PL FLORIDA WORKERS 9
I'M MAKIN' A ROAD! . . . PL FLORIDA WORKERS 20
MALAN 1
EASTLAND AND MALAN DECEASED . . . AYM SHADES OF PIG 5
MALAYSIA 1
OF MALAYSIA LAND. . . . PL LAST PRINCE 3
MALCOLM 1
DUBOIS (WHEN?) MALCOLM (OH!) SEND FOR STOKELY. . . . PL FINAL CALL 35
MAMA 38
PRAY FOR ME, MAMA! . . . SH BLD THE SINNER 21
BUT YOU CAN'T, PRETTY MAMA, . . . SH FREE MAN 3
BUT YOU'LL NEVER, PRETTY MAMA, . . SH FREE MAN 7
DID MY SWEET MAMA GO? . . . SH SHAKESPEARE 4
THEY SAY YOUR SWEET MAMA . . . SH SHAKESPEARE 7
MAMA, I FOUND THIS SOLDIER'S CAP . FW WHEN ARMIES PAS 1
PAPA, MAMA, . . . SP CONSIDER ME 8
HEY, LAWDY, MAMA! . . . SP EASY BOOGIE 10
MAMA, PORTLY OVEN, . . . SP GRADUATION 6
TELLS HER MAMA SHE'S A TYPIST . . . SP GRADUATION 13
MAMA SAYS, PRAISE JESUS! . . . SP GRADUATION 20
MAMA SAYS, PRAISE JESUS! . . . SP GRADUATION 25
MAMA SAYS, . . . SP GRADUATION 27
DEAR MAMA, . . . SP LETTER 1
MAMA, IT HAS BEEN RAINING CATS AND DOGS UP . . . SP LETTER 8
MAMA, PLEASE BRUSH OFF MY COAT. . . SP MAMA AND DAUGHT 1
HE IS THAT YOUNG MAN, MAMA, . . . SP MAMA AND DAUGHT 7
MAMA, DAD COULDN'T BE STILL YOUNG. SP MAMA AND DAUGHT 17
JUST DON'T LET MAMA CATCH YOU . . . SP STREET SONG 3
I SAID, VOTED FOR YOUR MAMA. . . . AYM BIRD IN ORBIT 17
WHAT TIME IS IT, MAMA? . . . AYM BLUES IN STEREO 28
WHAT TIME IS IT, MAMA? . . . AYM BLUES IN STEREO 32
MAMA MAMACITA PAPA PAPIAMENTO . . . AYM GOSPEL CHA-CHA 14
I SAID, FROM YOUR MAMA! . . . AYM HORN OF PLENTY 48
FOR ONE'S COUNTRY IS YOUR MAMA. . . AYM HORN OF PLENTY 58
I SAID, YES, YOUR MAMA. . . . AYM HORN OF PLENTY 98
I SAID, ASK YOUR MAMA. . . . AYM IS IT TRUE? 56
TRIBAL NOW NO LONGER PAPA MAMA . . AYM ODE TO DINAH 82
I WANT TO GO TO THE SHOW, MAMA. . . AYM ODE TO DINAH 95
TELL ME, MAMA, CAN I GET MY SHOW . AYM SHOW FARE PLESE 1
TELL ME, MAMA, TELL ME, . . . AYM SHOW FARE PLESE 8
TELL ME, TELL ME, MAMA, . . . AYM SHOW FARE PLESE 11
AND THE TELL ME OF THE MAMA . . . AYM SHOW FARE PLESE 18
SHOW FARE, MAMA, PLEASE. . . . AYM SHOW FARE PLESE 35
SHOW FARE, MAMA. . . . AYM SHOW FARE PLESE 36
AND WE BETTER FIND OUT, MAMA, . . . PL CULTURAL EXCHNG 23
I SAID, ASK YOUR MAMA. . . . PL CULTURAL EXCHNG 35
MAMA, DON'T CRY. . . . PL WITHOUT BENEFIT 19

MAMACITA 2
MAMA MAMACITA PAPA PAPIAMENTO . . . AYM GOSPEL CHA-CHA 14
MAMACITA! PAPA LEGBA! SHANGO! . . . AYM GOSPEL CHA-CHA 35

MAMAS 2
A ROW OF LONG TALL MAMAS . . . . . SP AS BEFITS A MAN 7
AND A HUNDRED PRETTY MAMAS . . . . SP SYLVESTER'S BED 7

MAMA'S 1
MAMA'S FRUITCAKE SENT FROM GEORGIA AYM ODE TO DINAH 13

MAMMA 1
MAMMA! . . . . WB CAT AND SAXOPHN 30

MAMMIES 2
AND COLORED CHILDREN HAVE WHITE MAMMIES: . . . . PL CULTURAL EXCHNG 50
DEAR, DEAR DARLING OLD WHITE MAMMIES - . . . . PL CULTURAL EXCHNG 54

MAMMY 8
I'M WAITING FOR MA MAMMY, - . . . . FC MAMMY 1
I'M WAITING FOR MA MAMMY, - . . . . FC MAMMY 5
MAMMY OF THE SOUTH, ... PL CHRIST IN ALA. 5
MAMMY FAUBUS . . . . PL CULTURAL EXCHNG 51
MAMMY EASTLAND . . . . PL CULTURAL EXCHNG 52
MAMMY WALLACE . . . . PL CULTURAL EXCHNG 53
MAMMY FAUBUS! . . . . PL CULTURAL EXCHNG 57
HAND ME MY MINT JULEP, MAMMY. . . . PL CULTURAL EXCHNG 59

MAMMY'S 1
DAMN MA BLACK OLD MAMMY'S SOUL . . FC A RUINED GAL 17

MAN 134
I WAS A RED MAN ONE TIME, ... WB LAMENT DARK PEO 1
I WAS A BLACK MAN, TOO, ... WB LAMENT DARK PEO 3
BE YOUR MAN. . . . . WB TO MIDNIGHT NAN 20
I'M A BAD, BAD MAN . . . . FC BAD MAN 1
I'M A BAD, BAD MAN. . . . . FC BAD MAN 3
AN' SHOT A MAN IN DE BACK. . . . . FC DEATH DO DIRTY 9
PLEASE DON'T TAKE THIS MAN O' MINE. FC GAL'S CRY DYING 18
WHEN MA MAN LOOKS AT ME . . . . . . FC MA MAN 1
WHEN MA MAN LOOKS AT ME . . . . . . FC MA MAN 3
THAT'S WHERE MA MAN AN' ME GO. . . FC MINNIE SINGS 2
MA MAN AN' ME DANCE. . . . . FC MINNIE SINGS 8
MA SWEET GOOD MAN HAS . . . . FC SUICIDE 1
MA SWEET GOOD MAN HAS . . . . FC SUICIDE 3
THAT MAN THAT DONE ME WRONG? . . . FC SUICIDE 12
I'M A HARD WORKIN' MAN . . . . . . FC WORKIN' MAN 13
A MORAL POEM TO BE RENDERED BY A MAN IN A STRAW HAT WITH A BRIGHT BAND, A . . . . NM BIG-TIMER MOOD 1
IN THE CLOTHES OF A MODERN MAN, HE PROCLAIMS HIMSELF. . . . . . . NM BLACK CLWN MOOD 15
I'M A MAN! . . . . NM BLACK CLWN POEM 79
JUST ONLY PROVIDIN' DE BOSS MAN IS NICE!" . . . . NM BROKE 9
AND DE MAN COME TELLIN' ME I BETTER GET THERE AT FO'. . . . . NM BROKE 13
SO DE MAN SAY, "I'LL GET SOMEBODY ELSE, THEN, TO CLEAN." - . . . . NM BROKE 17
AND DE MAN COME TELLIN' ME THEY AIN'T HIRIN' NO MO' COLORED - JUST WHITE. . . . . NM BROKE 45
BACK, AND EYES SHINING, QUIETLY RECALLING THE VISION, THE DEAD MAN SPEAKS . . . . NM COLORED SL MOOD 8
TODAY'S DARK CHILD, TOMORROW'S STRONG MAN: . . . . NM DARK YOUTH USA 2
MA LORD AIN'T NO STUCK-UP MAN. . . DK MA LORD 1
MA LORD AIN'T NO STUCK-UP MAN. . . DK MA LORD 10
"YOU ARE MY SERVANT, BLACK MAN - I, THE FREE!" . . . . ANS A NEW SONG 32
A MAN WITH THE TITLE OF GOVERNOR HAS SPOKEN: . . . . ANS CHANT TOM MOONY 4
A MAN WITH THE TITLE OF GOVERNOR HAS SPOKEN: . . . . ANS CHANT TOM MOONY 6
BUT THE MAN WITH THE TITLE OF GOVERNOR . . . . ANS CHANT TOM MOONY 10
OF COURSE, THE MAN WITH THE TITLE OF GOVERNOR . . . . ANS CHANT TOM MOONY 26
THAT ANY MAN BE CRUSHED BY ONE ABOVE. . . . . ANS LET AMERICA BE 9
I AM THE RED MAN DRIVEN FROM THE LAND, ... ANS LET AMERICA BE 21
I AM THE YOUNG MAN, FULL OF STRENGTH AND HOPE, ... ANS LET AMERICA BE 25
I AM THE MAN WHO NEVER GOT AHEAD, ANS LET AMERICA BE 37
O, I'M THE MAN WHO SAILED THOSE EARLY SEAS . . . . ANS LET AMERICA BE 45
AND YET MUST BE - THE LAND WHERE EVERY MAN IS FREE. . . . . ANS LET AMERICA BE 64
WE'RE MAN TO MAN. . . . . ANS OPEN LETTER 68
WE'RE MAN TO MAN. . . . . ANS OPEN LETTER 58
TREAT A MAN SO BAD? . . . . SH ANNOUNCEMENT 8
AND BE A WHITE MAN THE REST OF MY DAYS! . . . . SH DAYBREAK 11
AND A WOMAN CROSS THE TABLE WHEN A MAN AIN'T BROKE - . . . . SH DEATH IN HARLEM 54
WPA MAN TOLD ME: . . . . SH OUT OF WORK 11
I'M GONNA TELL THE FURNITURE MAN TO COME . . . . SH PAY DAY 11
CAUSE I'M GOING BACK TO ROOMING AND BE A FREE MAN. . . . . SH PAY DAY 16
I'LL FIGHT LIKE A MAN. . . . . . . JC BIG BUDDY 6
TO THE BLACK MAN. . . . . JC BLACK MAN SPEAK 8
THAT A NEGRO IS A MAN. . . . . . . JC BLD SAM SOLOMON 4
EVERY COLORED MAN . . . . JC BLD SAM SOLOMON 18
SAM SOLOMON SAID, A MAN . . . . . . JC BLD SAM SOLOMON 39
A NEGRO IS A MAN. . . . . JC BLD SAM SOLOMON 56
A MAN, SPARE, SWARTHY, STRONG, FOURSQUARE - . . . . JC TO CAPTAIN MULZ 44
IN UNION, YOU, WHITE MAN, ... JC TO CAPTAIN MULZ 59
AND I, BLACK MAN, ... JC TO CAPTAIN MULZ 60
A MAN. . . . . FW MAN 15
DE MAN I LOVES HAS . . . . OWT LINCOLN THEATRE 11
A MAN COMES HOME FROM WORK: . . . . OWT MAN INTO MEN 15
TO THE MAN . . . . OWT MAN INTO MEN 18
THE MAN IS THERE! . . . . OWT RAID 11
CAUSE THERE AIN'T A GOOD MAN . . . OWT REQUEST REQUIEM 7
COME AND GET THIS MAN! . . . . . . SP BLD LANDLORD 22
MAN THREATENS LANDLORD . . . . . . SP BLD LANDLORD 31
WITH A NO-GOOD MAN. . . . . SP BLD OF THE GIRL 4
FOR HER MAN THAT WAS DEAD. . . . . SP BLD OF THE MAN 14
A POOR MAN AIN'T GOT . . . . SP BLD OF THE MAN 27
WHITE MAN . . . . SP BLUE BAYOU 7
THEN A WHITE MAN . . . . SP BLUE BAYOU 11
PUT THE BLACK MAN . . . . SP BLUE BAYOU 16
NEXT TIME A MAN COMES NEAR ME . . . SP CORA 3
MY OLD MAN'S A WHITE OLD MAN . . . SP CROSS 1
IF EVER I CURSED MY WHITE OLD MAN SP CROSS 3
MY OLD MAN DIED IN A FINE BIG HOUSE. SP CROSS 9
DO-RIGHT MAN? . . . . SP EARLY EVENING 24
THE BOSS MAN SAID. . . . . SP FIRED 5
WHEN A MAN STARTS OUT WITH NOTHING, SP FREEDOM'S PLOW 1
WHEN A MAN STARTS OUT WITH HIS HANDS SP FREEDOM'S PLOW 2
WHEN A MAN STARTS OUT TO BUILD A WORLD, ... SP FREEDOM'S PLOW 4
NO MAN IS GOOD ENOUGH . . . . SP FREEDOM'S PLOW 102
TO GOVERN ANOTHER MAN . . . . SP FREEDOM'S PLOW 103
THEN A MAN SAID: . . . . SP FREEDOM'S PLOW 109
HE WAS A COLORED MAN WHO HAD BEEN A SLAVE . . . . SP FREEDOM'S PLOW 112
CAN A COAL BLACK MAN DRIVE THE FREEDOM TRAIN? . . . . SP FREEDOM TRAIN 18
'CAUSE FREEDOM AIN'T FREEDOM WHEN A MAN AIN'T FREE. . . . . SP FREEDOM TRAIN 34
WILL SOME WHITE MAN YELL, GET BACK! SP FREEDOM TRAIN 39
"YOU ARE A MAN. TOGETHER WE ARE BUILDING OUR LAND." . . . . SP FREEDOM'S PLOW 156
NO MAN IS GOOD ENOUGH . . . . SP FREEDOM'S PLOW 169
TO GOVERN ANOTHER MAN . . . . SP FREEDOM'S PLOW 170
A LONG TIME AGO, BUT NOT TOO LONG AGO, A MAN SAID: . . . . SP FREEDOM'S PLOW 90
I'D FLY ON MA MAN AN' . . . . SP HARD DADDY 17
JUST MAN WOMAN TIRED SAYS: . . . . SP IN EXPLANATION 55
NEVER LOVE A MAN. . . . . SP LAMENT OVER LOV 2
NEVER LOVE A MAN. . . . . SP LAMENT OVER LOV 4
GONNA THINK ABOUT MY MAN - . . . . SP LAMENT OVER LOV 23
THE RENT MAN KNOCKED. . . . . . . SP MADAM RENT MAN 1
A MAN KNOCKED THREE TIMES. . . . . SP MADAM WRONG VIS 1
THE CENSUS MAN, ... SP MADAM CENSUS 1
I SAID, WHAT MAN YOU'RE TALKING 'BOUT? . . . . SP MADAM FORT TELL 21
I TOLD THE MAN . . . . SP MADAM'S CALLING 5
WITH A NO-GOOD MAN. . . . . SP MADAM'S PAST HI 13
HE IS THAT YOUNG MAN, MAMA, ... SP MAMA AND DAUGHT 7
MY GOOD MAN TURNED ME DOWN. . . . . SP MIDWINTER BLUES 6
NOW, IF A MAN LOVES A WOMAN . . . . SP MIDWINTER BLUES 11
BUT HE'S THE ONLY MAN I'LL . . . . SP MIDWINTER BLUES 17
CAUSE THE MAN I LOVE'S DONE . . . . SP MISERY 7
FOR A NO-GOOD MAN? . . . . SP MISERY 12
I AM YOUR SON, WHITE MAN! . . . . . SP MULATTO 1
I AM YOUR SON, WHITE MAN! . . . . . SP MULATTO 43
HE'S A GOOD MAN, ... SP NEIGHBOR 14
INSURANCE MAN, HE DID NOT PAY - . . SP NIGHT FUNERAL 5
TO THAT GIRL WHO PAID THE PREACHER MAN - . . . . SP NIGHT FUNERAL 41
RICH OLD WHITE MAN . . . . SP PORTER 9
WHAT MY OTHER MAN CAN'T DO - . . . SP QUESTION 2
BOSS MAN TAKES THE MONEY . . . . . SP SHARE-CROPPERS 7
THEY'VE JUST HUNG A BLACK MAN . . . SP SILHOUETTE 3
THEY'VE HUNG A BLACK MAN . . . . . SP SILHOUETTE 5
I CAN UNDERSTAND - SOME DECENT MAN? SP SISTER 6
WELL, ANYWAY, IT DON'T HAVE TO BE A MARRIED MAN. . . . . SP SISTER 12
SO DOES A MAN. . . . . SP SISTER 16
AND A BLIND MAN PLAYS AN ACCORDION SP SUMMER EVENING 16
THE TAMALE MAN WILL COME BY, . . . SP SUMMER EVENING 23
HE SLEPT LIKE A ROCK OR A MAN THAT'S DEAD. . . . . SP THE WEARY BLUES 35
MAN TO STAY! . . . . SP WEST TEXAS 20
I AIN'T GOT NO MAN. . . . . SP 50 - 50 5
WHEN THE MAN SHOT AT THE WOMAN . . AYM ODE TO DINAH 131
AGAINST MY FELLOW MAN . . . . PL ANGOLA QUESTION 12

SEND FOR OLD MAN MOSES TO LAY DOWN THE LAW. . . . . PL FINAL CALL 9
HOW CAN ONE MAN BE TEN? . . . . . . PL GHOSTS OF 1619 21
NOW WHEN THE MAN AT THE CORNER STORE PL HARLEM 8
THE WHITE MAN SAID, "BOY, ... PL KU KLUX 9
AND FOR BEING A MAN . . . . PL LUMUMBA'S GRAVE 11
TO HONOR MODERN MAN - . . . . PL MOTHER IN WAR 8
THAT MAN THEY CALL THE LAW. . . . . PL WHO BUT TH LORD 2
SAVE ME FROM THAT MAN! . . . . . . PL WHO BUT TH LORD 10
WHY GOD DON'T PROTECT A MAN . . . . PL WHO BUT TH LORD 17

MANAGED 1
ON BEDLOE'S ISLAND MANAGED BY SOL HUROK . . . . AYM HORN OF PLENTY 4

MANCHA 1
AQUEL RINCON DE LA MANCHA DE . . . ANS SONG OF SPAIN 27

MANDALAY 1
MANDALAY . . . . SP NEON SIGNS 6

MANGER 2
WHOSE HAYMOW WAS A MANGER MANGER . AYM ODE TO DINAH 33
WHOSE HAYMOW WAS A MANGER MANGER . AYM ODE TO DINAH 33

MANHATTAN 4
NOW IT'S MANHATTAN, CHICAGO, . . . SP FREEDOM'S PLOW 86
ACROSS THE MIDDLE OF MANHATTAN . . SP GOOD MORNING 6
DUSKY SASH ACROSS MANHATTAN . . . . SP GOOD MORNING 16
MANHATTAN ISLAND WILL WHIRL . . . . SP PROJECTION 12

MANHOOD'S 1
TO MANHOOD'S TRUE RIGHT. . . . . . NM BLACK CLWN POEM 66

MANKIND 2
AGAIN MANKIND HAS LOST ITS COURSE, JC TO CAPTAIN MULZ 6
AND MANKIND. . . . . SP INTERNE AT PROV 15

MANKIND'S 1
YOUR SHIP IS MANKIND'S DEEPEST DREAM JC TO CAPTAIN MULZ 67

MANSIONS 1
IN WHITE PILLARED MANSIONS . . . . PL CULTURAL EXCHNG 46

MANTOVA 1
TO MANTOVA . . . . SP JULIET 13

MANUFACTURED 1
CAME THE MIGHTY PRODUCTS MOULDED, MANUFACTURED. . . . . SP FREEDOM'S PLOW 79

MANURE 2
IN WARM MANURE . . . . PL UN-AMERICAN 5
ITS MANURE. . . . . PL UN-AMERICAN 23

MANY 27
NOW I HERD WITH THE MANY - . . . . WB LAMENT DARK PEO 11
OF TOO MANY NIGHTS OF LOVE . . . . WB SOLEDAD 3
IN MANY MOUTHS - . . . . ANS A NEW SONG 35
THERE IS A CREW OF MANY RACES, TOO, JC TO CAPTAIN MULZ 47
MANY BLOODS - YET ALL OF ONE BLOOD STILL: . . . . JC TO CAPTAIN MULZ 48
WITH TOO MANY . . . . FW FRAGMENTS 5
MANY PLACES . . . . FW OLD SAILOR 2
THERE'S MANY ANOTHER WOMAN . . . . OWT HONEY BABE 13
TURNING THE RICH SOIL WENT THE FLOW IN MANY HANDS . . . . SP FREEDOM'S PLOW 52
CLANG AGAINST THE TREES WENT THE AX IN MANY HANDS . . . . SP FREEDOM'S PLOW 55
TRUE ANYHOW NO MATTER HOW MANY . . SP IN EXPLANATION 38
SO MANY GODS DON'T KNOW. . . . . . SP JOE LOUIS 7
THAT MANY NEGROES . . . . SP PARADE 24
WOULD GIVE HER MANY RARE GIFTS . . SP THE SOUTH 21
RULED MY MANY YEARS. . . . . SP WIDOW WOMAN 14
RULED MY MANY YEARS - . . . . . . SP WIDOW WOMAN 16
MEANS TOO MANY NEGROES . . . . . . AYM HORN OF PLENTY 64
THERE ARE SO MANY CHURCHES . . . . PL BIBLE BELT 3
HOW MANY BULLETS DOES IT TAKE . . . PL DEATH YORKVILLE 3
HOW MANY CENTURIES DOES IT TAKE . . PL DEATH YORKVILLE 5
HOW MANY CENTENNIALS DOES IT TAKE PL DEATH YORKVILLE 15
TOO MANY YEARS . . . . PL DOWN WHERE I AM 1
TOO MANY YEARS . . . . PL DOWN WHERE I AM 5
TOO MANY YEARS . . . . PL DOWN WHERE I AM 9
HOW MANY BULLETS DOES IT TAKE . . . PL DREAM DEFERRED 1
MANY YEARS FREE. . . . . PL OCTOBER 16 RAID 16
SO MANY TIMES BEFORE. . . . . . . PL SWEET WORDS RAC 12

MAN'S 16
MY MAN'S DONE LEFT ME. . . . . . . WB BLUES FANTASY 7
MY GOOD MAN'S LEFT ME. . . . . . . WB BLUES FANTASY 9
IS A BROWN MAN'S FIST . . . . FC BEALE ST. LOVE 2
MA MAN'S A GYPSY . . . . FC GYPSY MAN 1
MA MAN'S A GYPSY, - . . . . FC GYPSY MAN 3
UP AND DOWN, AND THEY JUST AIN'T NO JOBS IN THIS MAN'S TOWN. . . . . NM BROKE 3
THE LAND THAT'S MINE - THE POOR MAN'S, INDIAN'S, NEGRO'S. . . . ANS LET AMERICA BE 65
BUT A MAN'S GOT TO LIVE. . . . . . SH BLD PAWNBROKER 19
WHEN A MAN'S WON A FIGHT IN A BIG MAN'S TOWN - . . . . SH DEATH IN HARLEM 55
WHEN A MAN'S WON A FIGHT IN A BIG MAN'S TOWN - . . . . SH DEATH IN HARLEM 55
BEFORE MAN'S WISDOM. . . . . FW WISDOM 2
MY OLD MAN'S A WHITE OLD MAN . . . SP CROSS 1
THE CREDIT MAN'S DONE TOOK MA CLOTHES . . . . SP DOWN AND OUT 7
THUS THE DREAM BECOMES NOT ONE MAN'S DREAM ALONE. . . . . SP FREEDOM'S PLOW 22
CAN CUT A MAN'S . . . . SP SLIVER 7
COMING FROM A BLACK MAN'S SOUL. . . SP THE WEARY BLUES 15

MAP 1
BLOTS COLORS OFF THE MAP. . . . . . AYM ASK YOUR MAMA 63

MAPLE-SUGAR 1
PEEPS A MAPLE-SUGAR CHILD. . . . . DK WINTER SWEEETNS 4

MARACAS 2
SEA GOURDS MAKE MARACAS OUT OF ME. AYM GOSPEL CHA-CHA 6
IN THE RUM THAT WAFTS MARACAS . . . AYM ODE TO DINAH 16

MARBLE 6
SITTING IN THE MARBLE AND THE MOONLIGHT. . . . . DK LINCOLN MONUMNT 2
SITTING LONELY IN THE MARBLE AND THE MOONLIGHT. . . . . DK LINCOLN MONUMNT 3
HIGH IN A MARBLE TOMB. . . . . . . ANS BLDS OF LENIN 2
ALIVE IN A MARBLE TOMB. . . . . . . ANS BLDS OF LENIN 10
HONORED IN A MARBLE TOMB. . . . . . ANS BLDS OF LENIN 18
SPEAKS FROM THE MARBLE: . . . . . . ANS BLDS OF LENIN 26

MARCH 4
WE MARCH! . . . . DK YOUTH 9
MARCH WITH YOU DOWN TIME'S STREET, SL SCOTTSBORO 6
TONIGHT THE WAVES MARCH . . . . . . SP MOONLIGHT NIGHT 1
BUT MARCH EVER FORWARD, BREAKING DOWN BARS. . . . . SP THE NEGRO MOTHE 47

MARCHED 1
SO WE MARCHED TO THE FRONT, HAPPY TO FIGHT. . . . . NM COLORED SL POEM 12

MARCHING 6
WHEN THE MARCHING FEET OF THE MASSES ANS KIDS WHO DIE 45
MARCHING IN A MASS? . . . . ANS SISTER JOHNSON 10
LIKE MARCHING FEET. . . . . SP EASY BOOGIE 4
MARCHING . . . MARCHING . . . . . . SP PARADE 20
MARCHING . . . MARCHING . . . . . . SP PARADE 20
MARCHING . . . . SP PARADE 21

MARCUS 1
SEND FOR MARCUS GARVEY (WHAT?) SUFI (WHO?) . . . . PL FINAL CALL 33

MARGARET 1
BONDS AND STILL AND MARGARET STILL $ $ . . . . AYM HORN OF PLENTY 15

MARGIE 7
IF MARGIE POLITE . . . . OWT BLD MARGE POLIT 1
THEY TAKEN MARGIE TO JAIL . . . . . OWT BLD MARGE POLIT 17
MARGIE WARN'T NOBODY . . . . OWT BLD MARGE POLIT 21
FOR MARGIE AND HISTORY . . . . . . OWT BLD MARGE POLIT 31
MARGIE POLITE! . . . . OWT BLD MARGE POLIT 46
MARGIE POLITE! . . . . OWT BLD MARGE POLIT 47
TAKEN MARGIE AWAY - . . . . OWT BLD MARGE POLIT 53

MARGIE'S 2
MARGIE'S DAY. . . . . OWT BLD MARGE POLIT 28
MARGIE'S DAY! . . . . OWT BLD MARGE POLIT 57

MARIA 3
MUST BE THE BLACK MARIA . . . . . . SP BLACK MARIA 1
THE BLACK MARIA THAT I SEE - . . . SP BLACK MARIA 3
BLACK MARIA PASSIN' BY . . . . . . SP BLACK MARIA 18

MARIAN 1
SAMMY DAVIS AND MARIAN ANDERSON . . SP PROJECTION 16

MARIE 5
SO WHEN I GOT READY TO GO, I SAID, "I'LL BE SEEIN' YOU SOON, MARIE." NM BROKE 52
WHY DOES HE KEEP ON FOOLIN' AROUND MARIE? . . . . SP SISTER 2
BUT WHY DOES HE KEEP ON FOOLIN' AROUND MARIE? . . . . SP SISTER 4
THE REASON MARIE RUNS AROUND WITH TRASH . . . . SP SISTER 8
WHO SEDUCED MARIE LAVEAU? . . . . . AYM GOSPEL CHA-CHA 42

MARIE'S 1
MARIE'S MY SISTER - NOT MARRIED TO ME - . . . . SP SISTER 3

MARION 1
MARION ANDERSON SAID TO THE DAR. . JC JIM CROW'S LAST 17

MARK 4
SOME MARK . . . . FW BIRTH 9
MARK AUGUST 1ST . . . . OWT BLD MARGE POLIT 29
LONELY LITTLE QUESTION MARK . . . . SP KID IN THE PARK 1
TOMORROW WILL MARK . . . . PL LUMUMBA'S GRAVE 22

MARKED 8
AND IT'S MARKED DOWN THAT-A-WAY. . SP BLUE MONDAY 5
THE BIRMINGHAM STATION'S MARKED COLORED AND WHITE. . . . . SP FREEDOM TRAIN 25
NOT STOPPIN' AT NO STATIONS MARKED COLORED NOR WHITE. . . . . SP FREEDOM TRAIN 51
IN BUSES MARKED NEW YORK . . . . . SP GOOD MORNING 12
IN AN ENVELOPE MARKED: . . . . . . SP PERSONAL 1
IN AN ENVELOPE MARKED: . . . . . . SP PERSONAL 4
THE DOOR MARKED LADIES OPENS INWARD AYM ODE TO DINAH 116
AND IT'S MARKED THERE. . . . . . . PL LUMUMBA'S GRAVE 21

MARKER 2
NOBODY NEEDS A MARKER. . . . . . . AYM ODE TO DINAH 122
BUT HE NEEDS NO MARKER - . . . . . PL LUMUMBA'S GRAVE 15

MARKET 2
TO THE MARKET OF DEATH . . . . . . PL SLAVE 2
TO THE MARKET OF DEATH . . . . . . PL SLAVE 13

MARKETS 1
CAME THE MARTS AND MARKETS, SHOPS AND STORES. . . . . SP FREEDOM'S PLOW 78

MARRIAGE 2
'CAUSE I'M JUST DYIN' TO TAKE ON THAT THERE MARRIAGE YOKE. . . . NM BROKE 77
ABOUT MARRIAGE . . . . SP S-SSS-SS-SH! 10

MARRIED 10
LOTS OF OLD SCHOOLMATES ARE MARRIED NOW: . . . . NM BIG-TIMER POEM 45
IS I MARRIED? NO, ALL THESE-HERE GIRLS UP NORTH IS TOO LIGHT. . . NM BROKE 70
LET'S GET MARRIED RIGHT NOW! YES! WHAT DO YOU SAY? . . . . NM BROKE 75
BUT THE BOYS IS ALL MARRIED! PSHAW! SH SUNDAY 13
BUT NOW MY DAUGHTER'S MARRIED . . . SP DEFERRED 15
THAT LITTLE NEGRO'S MARRIED AND GOT A KID. . . . . SP SISTER 1
MARIE'S MY SISTER - NOT MARRIED TO ME - . . . . SP SISTER 3
WELL, ANYWAY, IT DON'T HAVE TO BE A MARRIED MAN. . . . . SP SISTER 12
WERE YOU MARRIED BY JOHN JASPER . . AYM BIRD IN ORBIT 37
AND WAS PORGY EVER MARRIED . . . . AYM SHADES OF PIG 15

MARROW 1
AND THE MARROW . . . . SP JULIET 6

MARRY 2
TO MARRY. . . . . SP CATCH 13
WOULD I MARRY POCAHONTAS? . . . . . AYM ODE TO DINAH 128

MARSEILLAISE 1
ECHOES THE FIGHTING "MARSEILLAISE." TEARING OFF HIS CLOWN'S SUIT. . NM BLACK CLWN MOOD 13

MARSHAL 1
GRAND MARSHAL IN HIS WHITE SUIT . . SP PARADE 5

MARSHALND 1
SPEAK OF RICE DOWN IN THE MARSHALND AYM BIRD IN ORBIT 43

MARTHA 2
NO, MARTHA, I AIN'T HEARD. . . . . OWT JITNEY 10
OF A MILLION MARTHA ROUNDTREES? . . AYM BIRD IN ORBIT 62

MARTHA'S 1
MARTHA'S GOT A JAPANESE! . . . . . OWT JITNEY 17

MARTIAL 2
SYNCOPATED, DETERMINED TO LAUGH. A BUGLE CALL, GAY, MARTIAL MUSIC. NM BLACK CLWN MOOD 6
UNITED STATES OF AMERICA, MARTIAL MUSIC ON A PIANO, OR BY AN ORCHESTRA. . . . . NM COLORED SL MOOD 3

MARTIN 3
MRS. BETHUNE TOLD MARTIN DIES. . . JC JIM CROW'S LAST 21
THE REVEREND MARTIN LUTHER . . . . AYM BIRD IN ORBIT 24
MARTIN LUTHER KING IS GOVERNOR OF GEORGIA. . . . . PL CULTURAL EXCHNG 43

MARTS 1
CAME THE MARTS AND MARKETS, SHOPS AND STORES. . . . . SP FREEDOM'S PLOW 78

MARVELLOUS 1
NO WONDER WE FIND THEM SUCH MARVELLOUS THINGS! . . . . OK FAIRIES 5

MARY 12
JUDGE PIERCE HE SAYS, MARY. . . . . FC BLD OF GIN MARY 5
OLD JUDGE SAYS, MARY JANE. . . . . FC BLD OF GIN MARY 6
MARY, MARY, MARY, ... SP EVENING SONG 9
MARY, MARY, MARY, ... SP EVENING SONG 9
MARY, MARY, MARY, ... SP EVENING SONG 9
MARY LULU JACKSON . . . . SP GRADUATION 3
MARY LULU JACKSON, ... SP GRADUATION 11
HE SAYS, "MARY, I'M . . . . SP LOVER'S RETURN 5
HAIL, MARY, MOTHER OF GOD! . . . . SP MYSTERY 6
MARY MCLEOD BETHUNE BARRED BY . . . AYM BIRD IN ORBIT 76
ARTHUR CARMEN ALVIN MARY $ $ $ $ $ $ $ $ . . . . AYM HORN OF PLENTY 7
MARY IS HIS MOTHER: . . . . PL CHRIST IN ALA. 4

MARY'S 5
KILLED MARY'S BOY. . . . . LHR BLD MARY'S SON 7
HE WAS MARY'S SON. . . . . LHR BLD MARY'S SON 8
FOR MARY'S BOY. . . . . LHR BLD MARY'S SON 14
FOR MARY'S SON. . . . . LHR BLD MARY'S SON 28
WELL, I HOPE THAT LAMB OF MARY'S . SP EVENING SONG 11

MASK 3
BEYOND ITS MASK OF WHITENESS . . . AYM BLUES IN STEREO 18
WHERE THE MASK IS PLACED BY OTHERS AYM SHOW FARE PLESE 6
THROUGH THE MASK? . . . . PL MISSISSIPPI 16

MASKED 1
MASKED - WITH ONLY . . . . PL MISSISSIPPI 14

MASKS 1
MASKS FOR THE SOUL. . . . . WB THE JESTER 5

MASS 3
WAVES OF RISING AND RE-RISING MASS VOICES, MULTIPLYING LIKE . . . . ANS CHANT MAY DAY 2
MARCHING IN A MASS? . . . . ANS SISTER JOHNSON 10
MISS MICHAELMAS IS AT DE MASS . . . SP SOUTHERN MAMMY 3

MASSES 1
WHEN THE MARCHING FEET OF THE MASSES ANS KIDS WHO DIE 45

MAST 1
FOR CINQUE SAYING, "RUN A NEW FLAG UP THE MAST." . . . . PL FINAL CALL 21

MASTER 1
WHITE MASTER ABOVE . . . . PL CHRIST IN ALA. 8

MASTERS 1
SLAVE MEN AND SLAVE MASTERS, ALL NEW - . . . . SP FREEDOM'S PLOW 33

MASTER'S 1
THEIR MASTER'S . . . . PL ELDERLY LEADERS 9

MATCH 1
FROM THE WING TIP OF A MATCH TIP . AYM JAZZTET MUTED 8

MATERIALS 1
THE EYES SEE THERE MATERIALS FOR BUILDING. . . . . SP FREEDOM'S PLOW 15

MATERNITY 1
MIRACLE MATERNITY: . . . . SP INTERNE AT PROV 22

MATTER 7
BUT DON'T LET IT MATTER TO YOU. . . NM BIG-TIMER POEM 49
HE WON'T MATTER AT ALL. . . . . . . ANS CHANT TOM MOONY 29
WHAT'S DE MATTER, HONEY? . . . . . ANS SISTER JOHNSON 2
WHAT'S DE MATTER, CHILE? . . . . . ANS SISTER JOHNSON 6
NO MATTER WHAT . . . . FW FAITHFUL ONE 9
TRUE ANYHOW NO MATTER HOW MANY . . SP IN EXPLANATION 38
NO MATTER HOW SANCTIFIED. . . . . . PL BIBLE BELT 7

MATTERS 1
TAKES UP IMPORTANT MATTERS . . . . SP MIGRANT 28

MATTER'S 1
THE TRUTH OF THE MATTER'S . . . . . SP 50 - 50 4

MAU 2
A MAU MAU . . . . PL ANGOLA QUESTION 10
A MAU MAU . . . . PL ANGOLA QUESTION 10

MAY 31
MAY I? . . . . FC JAZZ BAND 14
MAY ACCOMPANY THE RECITATION - ECHOING SOFTLY, OVER THERE, THERE'S A ROSE . . . . NM COLORED SL MOOD 4
THAT I MAY WRAP THEM . . . . OK DREAM KEEPER 5
WORKER: THE FIRST OF MAY: . . . . . ANS CHANT MAY DAY 3
10-VOICES: MAY DAY! . . . . ANS CHANT MAY DAY 27
20-VOICES: MAY DAY! . . . . ANS CHANT MAY DAY 28
40-VOICES: MAY DAY! . . . . ANS CHANT MAY DAY 29
IT'S DE FIRST OF MAY! . . . . ANS SISTER JOHNSON 4
IT'S DE FIRST OF MAY! . . . . ANS SISTER JOHNSON 8

IT'S DE FIRST OF MAY! . . . . ANS SISTER JOHNSON 13
YOU MAY CALL OUT THE KLAN . . . . . JC BLD SAM SOLOMON 2
COME WHAT MAY. . . . . JC BLD SAM SOLOMON 24
THAT MAY BE SO - FOR THOSE WHO WANT IT SO. . . . . JC GOOD MORN STLIN 25
MAY ROSE LEAVES . . . . FW FOR DEAD MIMES 2
AND MAY PIERRETTE. . . . . FW FOR DEAD MIMES 6
AND WOMEN. TOO. WHOM ANYONE MAY MEET OWT JUICE JOINT 35
MAY ITS BRANCHES SPREAD AND ITS SHELTER GROW . . . . SP FREEDOM'S PLOW 198
THOUGH YOU MAY HEAR ME HOLLER. . . SP LIFE IS FINE 27
AND YOU MAY SEE ME CRY - . . . . . SP LIFE IS FINE 28
THAT MAY BE TRUE - . . . . SP MADAM HER MADAM 22
WELL. THAT O.K. YOU MAY KEEP - . . SP MADAM PHONE BIL 39
OH. MY DARK CHILDREN. MAY MY DREAMS AND MY PRAYERS . . . . SP THE NEGRO MOTHE 49
MAY ESCAPE THE SPELL OF THE SOUTH. SP THE SOUTH 28
TOMORROW MAY BE . . . . SP TOMORROW 1
MAY MEET BOYS . . . . SP UP-BEAT 7
YOU MAY PLAY FOLKS CHEAP. . . . . . SP WARNING AUGMENT 5
THE FRENCH MAY HAVE THE SECRET. . . AYM IS IT TRUE? 17
AND WHY WOULD MAI (NOT MAY) . . . . AYM SHADES OF PIG 17
YOU MAY BE . . . . PL BIBLE BELT 12
THEY MAY NOT ONLY HAUNT YOU - . . . PL GHOSTS OF 1619 5
THAT HOODED SERPENTS MAY DANCE. . . PL SPECIAL BULLTIN 4

MAYBE 27

AND YOU DON'T MEAN MAYBE. . . . . . WB TO MIDNIGHT NAN 12
WELL. MAYBE I WILL. . . . . NM BIG-TIMER POEM 34
MAYBE. NOW. THERE WILL BE NO MONUMENT FOR YOU . . . . ANS KIDS WHO DIE 38
MAYBE YOUR BODIES'LL BE LOST IN A SWAMP. . . . . ANS KIDS WHO DIE 40
THAT I MIGHT. JUST MAYBE. . . . . . ANS PARK BENCH 9
(MAYBE IN A WHISPER . . . . JC GOOD MORN STLIN 55
MAYBE THE EGG . . . . SP BAR 3
AND MAYBE YOUR FRIENDS'LL . . . . . SP BLD OF THE MAN 7
MAYBE. . . . . SP CONSIDER ME 48
THIS YEAR MAYBE. DO YOU THINK I CAN GRADUATE? . . . . SP DEFERRED 1
BUT MAYBE THIS YEAR I CAN GRADUATE. SP DEFERRED 7
MAYBE NOW I CAN HAVE THAT WHITE ENAMEL STOVE . . . . SP DEFERRED 8
MAYBE I CAN BUY THAT WHITE ENAMEL STOVE! . . . . SP DEFERRED 20
MAYBE A LITTLE LUCK NOW. . . . . . SP ELEVATOR BOY 8
MAYBE NOT. . . . . SP ELEVATOR BOY 9
MAYBE A GOOD JOB SOMETIMES: . . . . SP ELEVATOR BOY 10
MAYBE NO LUCK FOR A LONG TIME. . . SP ELEVATOR BOY 14
BUT MAYBE THEY EXPLAINS IT ON THE SP FREEDOM TRAIN 35
THEN MAYBE FROM THEIR GRAVES IN ANZIO . . . . SP FREEDOM TRAIN 59
MAYBE IT JUST SAGS . . . . SP HARLEM 9
(MAYBE - NOBODY KNOWS.) . . . . . . SP HAVANA DREAMS 2
OR MAYBE THE DREAM'S A VEDADO ROSE - SP HAVANA DREAMS 7
JUST MAYBE SHRUG THEIR SHOULDERS. SP LIKEWISE 15
MAYBE IT AIN'T RIGHT - . . . . . . SP LIVE LET LIVE 1
AND MAYBE WAS I BLIND . . . . . . SP SO LONG 6
BUT MAYBE BEFORE MIDNIGHT . . . . . SP SUMMER EVENING 22
MAYBE IT JUST SAGS . . . . PL DREAM DEFERRED 9

MAYBELL 1

OR BIG MAYBELL TO . . . . AYM SHADES OF PIG 29

MAYOR 2

MAYOR LA GUARDIA . . . . OWT BLD MARGE POLIT 33
KEPT THE MAYOR . . . . OWT BLD MARGE POLIT 48

MAYORS 1

NO MAYORS AND SUCH FOR WHICH COLORED CAN'T VOTE. . . . . SP FREEDOM TRAIN 56

MAYVILLE 1

MAYVILLE HAD NO PLACE TO OFFER HER. SP RUBY BROWN 5

MCLEOD 1

MARY MCLEOD BETHUNE BARRED BY . . . AYM BIRD IN ORBIT 76

MEAGRE 2

OF MY MEAGRE CASH. . . . . JC THE BITTER RIVR 70
HAVE SUCH MEAGRE . . . . LHR POET TO BIGOT 8

MEALIE 1

HAS ALMOST FORGOTTEN MEALIE. . . . AYM ASK YOUR MAMA 58

MEAN 27

AND YOU DON'T MEAN MAYBE. . . . . . WB TO MIDNIGHT NAN 12
I MEAN TENNESSEE. . . . . FC GYPSY MAN 8
I MEAN PLUNK. PLUNK . . . PLUNK. PLUNK. . . . . FC MA MAN 10
I MEAN FOUR - BEFORE DAYLIGHT - S'POSE TO'VE DONE HIT YO' FIRST STROKE - . . . . NM BROKE 14
I AM THE PEOPLE. HUMBLE. HUNGRY. MEAN - . . . . ANS LET AMERICA BE 34
WHAT DO YOU MEAN - . . . . ANS LYNCHING SONG 10
I FEEL SO MEAN I COULD . . . . . . SH EVIL MORNING 5
WHAT DO YOU MEAN. WHY I DIDN'T WRITE? . . . . SH LETTER 3
WHAT DO YOU MEAN. JUST A LITTLE SPAT? . . . . SH LETTER 4
AND IF YOU THINK I BEEN TOO MEAN BEFORE. . . . . SH LETTER 12
I'LL TRY NOT TO BE THAT MEAN NO MORE. . . . . SH LETTER 13
GONNA GO GET MY PISTOL. I MEAN THIRTY-TWO. . . . . SH TWILIGHT REVERI 7
I MEAN IT WHEN I SAY. . . . . JC GOOD MORN STLIN 54
SHOW ME THAT YOU MEAN . . . . JC HOW ABOUT DIXIE 9
ABOVE A CROWD OF BLACK FOLK. HUMBLE. MEAN. . . . . OWT LINCOLN THEATRE 4
AND DYING IS MEAN - . . . . SP ADVICE 3
CAUSE THEY TREAT ME MEAN - . . . . SP CORA 5
THEY ALWAYS TREAT ME MEAN. . . . . SP CORA 7
I BEEN STINKIN'. LOW-DOWN. MEAN. . SP FIRE 6
AND DON'T MEAN HALF IT SAYS - . . . SP IN EXPLANATION 33
SHE WASN'T MEAN - . . . . SP MADAM HER MADAM 2
WHAT YOU MEAN BY THAT? . . . . . . SP MADAM FORT TELL 10
DON'T MEAN NO HARM. . . . . SP MADAM WRONG VIS 12
I DIDN'T MEAN TO STUMP MA TOE ON YOU. LADY. . . . . SP MAGNOLIA FLOWER 9
I DIDN'T MEAN TO STUMP MA TOE ON YOU. . . . . SP MAGNOLIA FLOWER 13
I MEAN . . . . SP ULTIMATUM 8
SINGING YOUR MEAN OLD BACKLASH BLUES. . . . . PL BACKLASH BLUES 30

MEANER 1

AND OTHER KIDS LESS MEANER THAN ¢ ¢ ¢ ¢ . . . . AYM HORN OF PLENTY 25

MEANEST 1

SHE WAS DE MEANEST WOMAN . . . . . SH ONLY WOMAN BLUS 3

MEANING 2

NOW YOUR WORDS NO LONGER HAVE MEANING - . . . . JC THE BITTER RIVR 65
ELSE IT HAD NO MEANING FOR ANYONE. SP FREEDOM'S PLOW 108

MEANIN' 2

NOT MEANIN' TO BE SASSY . . . . . . SP SOUTHERN MAMMY 19
AND NOT MEANIN' TO BE SMART - . . . SP SOUTHERN MAMMY 20

MEANNESS 1

I TAKES MA MEANNESS AND MA LICKER FC BAD MAN 5

MEANS 8

MEANS HE'S GONNA LEAVE THIS WORLD. FC GAL'S CRY DYING 8
MEANS HE'S GONNA LEAVE THIS WORLD. FC GAL'S CRY DYING 10
BUT I 'SHO BEEN LOOKIN' ROUND HARD LATELY FOR WAYS AND MEANS . . . NM BROKE 39
WHY DEMOCRACY MEANS . . . . JC BLACK MAN SPEAK 3
IT MEANS FREEDOM AT HOME. TOO - . . JC HOW ABOUT DIXIE 23
WHAT SHE MEANS IS: . . . . SP DELINQUENT 15
I MEANS FIRE. LORD! . . . . SP FIRE 24
MEANS TOO MANY NEGROES . . . . . . AYM HORN OF PLENTY 64

MEANT 6

IN SEARCH OF WHAT I MEANT TO BE MY HOME - . . . . ANS LET AMERICA BE 46
DAVE MEANT HER NO GOOD. . . . . . . SP BLD FORTUNE TEL 18
WHAT YOUR FUTURE MEANT. . . . . . . SP BLD FORTUNE TEL 30
WHAT HE SAID MUST BE MEANT FOR EVERY HUMAN BEING - . . . . SP FREEDOM'S PLOW 107
THAT SONG MEANT JUST WHAT IT SAID: HOLD ON! . . . . SP FREEDOM'S PLOW 127
THAT WHAT HE SAID WAS ALSO MEANT FOR THEM. . . . . SP FREEDOM'S PLOW 99

MEANWHILE 2

MEANWHILE . . . . AYM IS IT TRUE? 38
MEANWHILE DINAH EATING CHICKEN . . AYM ODE TO DINAH 129

MEAT 4

AN' A STEW O' MEAT. . . . . FC DEATH DO DIRTY 14
DOES IT STINK LIKE ROTTEN MEAT? . . SP HARLEM 6
NOR TAKE THE PLACE OF MEAT OR BREAD PL CROWNS GARLANDS 15
DOES IT STINK LIKE ROTTEN MEAT? . . PL DREAM DEFERRED 6

MECCA 1

IMPLORING MECCA . . . . SP BE-BOP BOYS 1

MECHANICS 2

MECHANICS. . . . . ANS OPEN LETTER 4
MECHANICS NEED REPAIRING . . . . . AYM ODE TO DINAH 10

MEDAL 1

A MEDAL TO YOUR FAMILY - . . . . . PL WITHOUT BENEFIT 16

MEDITATIVE 1

TO SPEND A MEDITATIVE HOUR - . . . OLD TOWER 3

MEEK 1

MEEK. HUMBLE. AND KIND: . . . . . . PL WARNING 3

MEEKLY 1
AND MEEKLY LIVE . . . . PL GO SLOW 16

MEET 15
WON'T MEET NOBODY . . . . FC A RUINED GAL 9
I SHOULD MEET LIFE FACE TO FACE . . OLD AESTHETE HARLEM 3
YOU SAY I'LL MEET A BAD ENDIN', HEH? NM BIG-TIMER POEM 33
AND JIVE SOME OLD BROAD I MIGHT
MEET. . . . . SH BED TIME 4
THAT I DIDN'T WANT TO MEET. . . . . SH BRIEF ENCOUNTER 6
I'LL MEET YOU AT THE BUS STATION. SH LETTER 21
AND MEET THEIR OWN TAIL. . . . . . FW CIRCLES 3
AND WOMEN, TOO, WHOM ANYONE MAY MEET OWT JUICE JOINT 35
I'D LIKE TO MEET A GOOD FRIEND . . SP BOUND NO'TH BLS 11
WHEN THEY MEET THEIR ENDS. . . . . SP NIGHT FUNERAL 16
MIGHT MEET GIRLS . . . . SP UP-BEAT 3
MAY MEET BOYS . . . . SP UP-BEAT 7
AND I'D LIKE TO MEET THE . . . . . AYM BIRD IN ORBIT 7
GRANDPA, WHERE DID YOU MEET MY
GRANDMA? . . . . AYM BIRD IN ORBIT 34
WHERE TWO RIVERS MEET . . . . PL OCTOBER 16 RAID 9

MELANCHOLY 2
HUMOROUS DEFIANCE. MELANCHOLY JAZZ.
THEN DEFIANCE AGAIN FOLLOWED BY
LOUD . . . . NM BLACK CLWN MOOD 2
IN A DEEP SONG VOICE WITH A
MELANCHOLY TONE . . . . SP THE WEARY BLUES 17

MELLOW 6
DEEP AND MELLOW SONG . . . . JC ME AND MY SONG 15
THE DUKE IS MELLOW! . . . . OWT JITNEY 26
WHILE BLUES AS MELLOW AS THE
SOUTHERN AIR . . . . OWT JUICE JOINT 25
YELLOW MELLOW. . . . . SP ARGUMENT 2
IN MELLOW MAGIC . . . . SP COLLEGE FORMAL 11
ROCKING BACK AND FORTH TO A MELLOW
CROON. . . . . SP THE WEARY BLUES 2

MELLOWS 1
MELLOWS TO A GOLDEN NOTE. . . . . . SP TRUMPET PLAYER 44

MELODIES 3
SINGING MINOR MELODIES . . . . . . WB BLUES FANTASY 4
MELODIES. . . . . NM COLORED SL MOOD 6
HEART MELODIES . . . . DK DREAM KEEPER 4

MELODY 2
IN A MELODY NIGHT . . . . SP COLLEGE FORMAL 3
HE MADE THAT POOR PIANO MOAN WITH
MELODY. . . . . SP THE WEARY BLUES 10

MELON 1
FACE LIKE SLICE OF MELON. . . . . . SP 125TH STREET 5

MELT 1
MELT TO WATER ONCE AGAIN . . . . . AYM ODE TO DINAH 36

MELTS 1
MOULDS AND MELTS AND MOULDS IT . . SP MIGRANT 19

MEMORIES 5
THE RIVER AND THE MOON HOLD
MEMORIES. . . . . FC CLOSING TIME 10
OUT OF THE PURPLE AND ROSE OF OLD
MEMORIES . . . . DK FAIRIES 3
NOT EVEN MEMORIES ALIVE . . . . . . SP AFRO-AMER FRAG 4
SAVE IN MEMORIES OF GANGRENOUS ICING AYM ODE TO DINAH 78
EXCEPT IN MEMORIES OF HATE . . . . AYM ODE TO DINAH 90

MEMORY 2
(DEDICATED TO THE MEMORY OF CHARLIE
LANG AND ERNEST GREEN. . . . . . . JC THE BITTER RIVR 1
WHERE THE SMOLDERING MEMORY . . . . SP TRUMPET PLAYER 5

MEMPHIS 2
ONCE I WAS IN MEMPHIS. . . . . . . FC GYPSY MAN 7
ONCE I WAS IN MEMPHIS. . . . . . . FC GYPSY MAN 9

MEN 33
BUT THE WHITE MEN CAME. . . . . . . WB LAMENT DARK PEO 2
BUT THE WHITE MEN CAME. . . . . . . WB LAMENT DARK PEO 4
THE BOOTED, BOOTED FOOL OF SILLY
MEN. . . . . WB THE JESTER 17
MEN TAKES ALL THEY CAN FROM ME . . FC BLACK GAL 6
DON'T YOU FOOL WID NO MEN CAUSE . . FC LISTEN HERE 17
MY YOUNG MEN WITHOUT A VOICE IN THE
WORLD. . . . . ANS A NEW SONG 13
NINE OLD MEN IN WASHINGTON. . . . . ANS BLD OZZIE POWEL 13
NINE OLD MEN SO RICH AND WISE. . . ANS BLD OZZIE POWEL 17
OF WORK THE MEN! OF TAKE THE PAY! ANS LET AMERICA BE 29
RAILWAY MEN. . . . . ANS OPEN LETTER 7
SLAVES OF MEN. . . . . JC TO CAPTAIN MULZ 32
TO SING ABOUT THE MEN WHO'VE DONE
THEM WRONG - . . . . OWT JUICE JOINT 24
WHERE BLACK MEN COME TO DRINK AND
PLAY AND SING. . . . . OWT JUICE JOINT 34
WHERE TWO OLD BROWN MEN STAND BEHIND
THE BAR - . . . . OWT JUICE JOINT 37
JOSTLE OF MEN WITH GOOD JOBS . . . OWT MAN INTO MEN 6
JOSTLE OF MEN IN THE DITCHES. . . . OWT MAN INTO MEN 7
MEN. . . . . OWT MAN INTO MEN 20
MEN WHO KNEW NOT WHAT THEY DID . . LHR BLD MARY'S SON 6
FREE MEN AND INDENTURED SERVANTS. SP FREEDOM'S PLOW 32
SLAVE MEN AND SLAVE MASTERS. ALL NEW
- . . . . SP FREEDOM'S PLOW 33
BRINGING MEN AND DREAMS. WOMEN AND
DREAMS. . . . . SP FREEDOM'S PLOW 36
AND MEN UNITED AS A NATION. . . . . SP FREEDOM'S PLOW 141
BLACK MEN AND WHITE WILL SAY, AIN'T
IT FINE? . . . . SP FREEDOM TRAIN 61
ALL MEN ARE CREATED EQUAL. . . . . SP FREEDOM'S PLOW 168
ALL MEN ARE CREATED EQUAL . . . . . SP FREEDOM'S PLOW 91
OH, MEN TREATS WOMEN . . . . SP LOVER'S RETURN 9
BUT THE WHITE MEN. . . . . SP RUBY BROWN 23
STAND LIKE FREE MEN SUPPORTING MY
TRUST. . . . . SP THE NEGRO MOTHE 42
TWO DOZEN MEN TO THE FLOOR. . . . . SP TO BE SOMEBODY 18
THE MEN CAN ONLY MURMUR . . . . . . AYM ASK YOUR MAMA 37
THAT MEN BE BURNED TO DEATH - . . . PL BOMBINGS DIXIE 7
BECAME FLESH-AND-BLOOD MEN? . . . . PL GHOSTS OF 1619 15
THE DEAD MEN THERE. . . . . PL PEACE 2

MENACED 1
MENACED BY THE WILL . . . . JC TO CAPTAIN MULZ 30

MENDED 1
MENDED. . . . . NM COLORED SL POEM 50

MENTION 1
THE GOOD CHURCH FOLK DO NOT MENTION SP RUBY BROWN 21

MEN'S 2
IN BLOND MEN'S ARMS. . . . . WB HARLEM NIGHT CL 11
DROPPED ON THE MEN'S ROOM FLOOR . . PL UNDERTOW 9

MERCEDES 4
MERCEDES IS A JUNGLE-LILY IN A DEATH
HOUSE. . . . . WB TO DARK MERCEDE 1
MERCEDES IS A DOOMED STAR. . . . . WB TO DARK MERCEDE 2
MERCEDES IS CHARNEL ROSE. . . . . . WB TO DARK MERCEDE 3
MERCEDES. . . . . WB TO DARK MERCEDE 8

MERCENARY 1
IT'S MERCENARY! . . . . LHR CONSERVATORY 8

MERCER 1
BRICKTOP INEZ MABEL MERCER . . . . AYM BIRD IN ORBIT 6

MERCHANTMAN 1
WE SAW AN INDIAN MERCHANTMAN . . . SP SEASCAPE 7

MERCY 6
O, PLEASE SIR, JUDGE, HAVE MERCY! FC BLD OF GIN MARY 21
HAVE MERCY, PLEASE, ON ME! . . . . FC BLD OF GIN MARY 22
O, LAWD HAVE MERCY . . . . FC GAL'S CPY DYING 11
LORDY, LET YO' MERCY . . . . SP FEET O' JESUS 3
HAVE MERCY, LORD! . . . . SP SINNER 1
HAVE MERCY, LORD! . . . . SP SINNER 5

MERCY'S 1
THE ANGEL OF MERCY'S . . . . JC RED CROSS 1

MERE 1
COM' MERE, BOY! . . . . FC BRASS SPITOONS 40

MERGE 1
WHERE THE SHADOWS MERGE WITH SHADOWS AYM ODE TO DINAH 115

MERMAID 3
HE HAD A MERMAID ON HIS ARM. . . . DK SAILOR 5
CARRYING A MERMAID . . . . SP CATCH 2
AND THE MERMAID . . . . SP CATCH 4

MERRY-GO-ROUND 2
ON THIS MERRY-GO-ROUND. . . . . . . PL MERRY-GO-ROUND 4
TO A MERRY-GO-ROUND! . . . . PL MERRY-GO-ROUND 13

MESSAGE 1
I GOT YOUR MESSAGE . . . . PL OFFICIAL NOTICE 2

MESSAGES 1
CAN'T SEND NO MESSAGES THROUGH THE
AIR. . . . . JC GOOD MORN STLIN 50

MET 4
I MET A YELLOW PAPA. . . . . FC GYPSY MAN 13
MET A YELLOW PAPA. . . . . FC GYPSY MAN 15
SEEMS LIKE ONCE I MET YOU . . . . . AYM RIDE, RED, RIDE 31
THE MET. . . . . AYM SHADES OF PIG 30

METAL 1
WEAVING METAL FROM TWO QUARTERS . . AYM SHOW FARE PLESE 21

METAPHYSICALLY 1
(METAPHYSICALLY SPEAKING) . . . . . PL GHOSTS OF 1619 19

METER 1
THE ONE COIN IN THE METER . . . . . AYM ODE TO DINAH 4

METHUSELAH 1
METHUSELAH SIGNS PAPERS W.E.B. . . AYM BIRD IN ORBIT 18

MEXICANS 1
NEGROES AND MEXICANS, ... ANS KIDS WHO DIE 15

MI 1
AY, MI NEGRA! . . . . AYM BIRD IN ORBIT 32

MIAMI 2
IT WAS DOWN IN MIAMI . . . . JC BLD SAM SOLOMON 5
BUT THE NEGROES IN MIAMI . . . . . JC BLD SAM SOLOMON 51

MICE 1
HOUSE IS SO QUIET! . . . LISTEN AT THEM MICE. . . . . SH BED TIME 12

MICHAEL 1
ADELE RAMONA MICHAEL SERVE BAKOKO TEA . . . . AYM BIRD IN ORBIT 20

MICHAELMAS 1
MISS MICHAELMAS IS AT DE MASS . . . SP SOUTHERN MAMMY 3

MIDDLE 6
IN THE MIDDLE OF JUNE-TIME . . . . SH YOUNG NEGRO GRL 2
IN THE MIDDLE OF JUNE-TIME . . . . SH YOUNG NEGRO GRL 7
ACROSS THE MIDDLE OF MANHATTAN . . SP GOOD MORNING 6
IN THE MIDDLE OF THE WINTER, . . . SP MIDWINTER BLUES 1
IN THE MIDDLE OF THE WINTER, . . . SP MIDWINTER BLUES 3
IN THE MIDDLE OF THE . . . . SP RAILROAD AVENUE 7

MIDNIGHT 13
MIDNIGHT, ... WB LENOX AVE MIDNT 13
MIDNIGHT DANCER OF THE JAZZY HOUR? WB NUDE YOUNG DANC 2
I'M MIDNIGHT MAD. . . . . FC MINNIE SINGS 12
WAS PLAYIN JAZZ FOR A MIDNIGHT WORLD. . . . . SH DEATH IN HARLEM 11
INTO MIDNIGHT RUFFLES . . . . SP BOOGIE 1 A.M. 7
IN A MIDNIGHT FACE, ... SP DREAM BOOGE VAR 4
LETTING MIDNIGHT . . . . SP JAM SESSION 1
AND HE GOT THE MIDNIGHT TRAIN . . . SP NOT A MOVIE 5
TWO A.M. MIDNIGHT BY YOUR SELF? . . SP REVERIE HARLEM 2
MIDNIGHT! . . . . SP REVERIE HARLEM 11
BUT MAYBE BEFORE MIDNIGHT . . . . . SP SUMMER EVENING 22
OUT OF THE MIDNIGHT SKY . . . . . . AYM ASK YOUR MAMA 34
AND THE WIND WON'T WAIT FOR MIDNIGHT PL CULTURAL EXCHNG 6

MIEN 1
MIEN GOTT! . . . . FC JAZZ BAND 16

MIGHT 41
MIGHT FALL AT THY FEET, ... WB SONGS DARK VIRG 5
MIGHT WRAP ABOUT THY BODY, ... WB SONGS DARK VIRG 11
THAT ALL MIGHT UNDERSTAND: . . . . NM BLACK CLWN POEM 76
DOES I WANTA? WELL, CAN'T SAY BUT WHAT I MIGHT - . . . . NM BROKE 71
THAT RIGHT MIGHT ABIDE . . . . . . NM DARK YOUTH USA 14
MIGHT NEVER RISE NO MO'. . . . . . DK SONG BANJO DANC 13
MIGHT NEVER RISE NO MO' - . . . . . DK SONG BANJO DANC 15
MIGHT NEVER DANCE NO MO'. . . . . . DK SONG BANJO DANC 19
MIGHT NEVER RISE NO MO'. . . . . . DK SONG BANJO DANC 27
THAT THE LAND MIGHT BE OURS, . . . ANS OPEN LETTER 14
THAT I MIGHT, JUST MAYBE, ... ANS PARK BENCH 9
SING IT VERY SIMPLY THAT I MIGHT UNDERSTAND. . . . . ANS SONG OF SPAIN 3
AND JIVE SOME OLD BROAD I MIGHT MEET. . . . . SH BED TIME 4
OR IF IT WASN'T SO LATE I MIGHT TAKE A WALK . . . . SH BED TIME 7
I MIGHT AS WELL PUT IT ON IN THE HAY. . . . . SH BED TIME 10
BUT MY LOVE MIGHT TURN INTO A KNIFE SH IN TROUBLED KEY 11
I MIGHT NOT FORGET AND I MIGHT NOT FORGIVE. . . . . SH LETTER 10
I MIGHT NOT FORGET AND I MIGHT NOT FORGIVE. . . . . SH LETTER 10
I MIGHT STARVE FOR A YEAR BUT . . . SH OUT OF WORK 17
IT MIGHT BE MISUNDERSTOOD - . . . . SH SNOB 4
ONE MIGHT MAKE A STORY . . . . . . FW MIGRATION 16
IT MIGHT HAVE BEEN . . . . FW WHEN ARMIES PAS 17
SHE MIGHT NOT'VE CUSSED . . . . . . OWT BLD MARGE POLIT 3
SHE MIGHT NOT'VE FELT . . . . OWT BLD MARGE POLIT 7
MIGHT BE THAT YOU'LL COME BACK, . . SP COULD BE 11
JUST MIGHT BE SO. . . . . SP MADAM MIGHT-HAV 8
HE SAID, THAT MIGHT . . . . SP MADAM NUMBER WR 11
AND I THOUGHT I MIGHT . . . . SP MADAM WRONG VIS 14
(OF COURSE, I MIGHT . . . . SP NUMBERS 6
THE GOVERNMENT MIGHT HONOR YOU. . . SP SHAME ON YOU 3
MIGHT LIVE. . . . . SP SUNDAY MORNING 42
IN ORDER THAT THE RACE MIGHT LIVE AND CROW. . . . . SP THE NEGRO MOTHE 4
WHO MIGHT BE PASSING! . . . . SP TO BE SOMEBODY 12
MIGHT MEET GIRLS . . . . SP UP-BEAT 3
AND THE NIGHT MIGHT BE ASTONISHED AYM BLUES IN STEREO 19
SOME HORSE MIGHT . . . . AYM IS IT TRUE? 46
THE DYNAMITE THAT MIGHT IGNITE . . PL BIRMINGHAM SUND 18
MIGHT BE AWAKENED SOMEDAY SOON . . PL BIRMINGHAM SUND 25
MIGHT BE DEAD, ... PL FREDRK DOUGLASS 5
MIGHT HAVE LOST HIS SOUL, ... PL FREDRK DOUGLASS 6
MIGHT LOSE. . . . . PL MOTHER IN WAR 15

MIGHTY 14
WHEN THE NATION CALLED US THAT MIGHTY DAY. . . . . NM COLORED SL POEM 4
LIKE A MIGHTY HEART-BEAT AS THEY COME? . . . . SL SCOTTSBORO 8
OF DOG EAT DOG, OF MIGHTY CRUSH THE WEAK. . . . . ANS LET AMERICA BE 24
THAT EVEN YET ITS MIGHTY DARING SINGS . . . . ANS LET AMERICA BE 42
MUST BRING BACK OUR MIGHTY DREAM AGAIN. . . . . ANS LET AMERICA BE 69
THAT MIGHTY NIGH DROVE ME WILD! . . SH LOVE AGAIN BLUS 12
BUT THIS HOUSE IS MIGHTY QUIET! . . SH SUNDAY 10
MIGHTY TOUCHSTONES OF SONG. . . . . FW BIG SUR 3
SINGING SORROW SONGS ON THE BANKS OF A MIGHTY RIVER . . . . SP AUNTSUE'S STORI 11
UM-HUH! YOU TALKING HIGH AND MIGHTY. SP BLD LANDLORD 17
CAME THE MIGHTY PRODUCTS MOULDED, MANUFACTURED. . . . . SP FREEDOM'S PLOW 79
YOU WAS A MIGHTY LOVER AND YOU . . SP WIDOW WOMAN 13
A MIGHTY LOVER, BABY, CAUSE YOU . . SP WIDOW WOMAN 15
SEND FOR UNCLE TOM ON HIS MIGHTY KNEES. . . . . PL FINAL CALL 28

MIGHT-HAVE-BEEN 1
BUT MY MIGHT-HAVE-BEEN . . . . . . SP MADAM MIGHT-HAV 3

MIGHT'VE 3
I MIGHT'VE KNOWED . . . . SP DIME 7
I MIGHT'VE SUNK AND DIED. . . . . . SP LIFE IS FINE 8
I MIGHT'VE JUMPED AND DIED. . . . . SP LIFE IS FINE 19

MIGRATION 2
FOR ME, NO MORE, THE GREAT MIGRATION TO THE NORTH. . . . . ANS OPEN LETTER 41
INSTEAD: MIGRATION INTO FORCE AND POWER - . . . . ANS OPEN LETTER 42

MIKADOS 1
AND ALL KINDS OF SWING MIKADOS . . SP NOTE COMM THEAT 10

MILES 2
A THOUSAND MILES AWAY. . . . . . . SP MIGRANT 24
MILES AND ELLA AND MISS NINA $ $ $ $ $ $ $ . . . . AYM HORN OF PLENTY 9

MILL 5
MILL HANDS, ... ANS OPEN LETTER 5
THERE IS A GIN MILL ON THE AVENUE OWT JUICE JOINT 1
INTO THIS GIN MILL . . . . OWT JUICE JOINT 15
FOR THE MILL WHEEL TO BE MILL WHEEL AYM IS IT TRUE? 24
FOR THE MILL WHEEL TO BE MILL WHEEL AYM IS IT TRUE? 24

MILLER 1
WHEN DORIE MILLER TOOK GUN IN HAND - JC JIM CROW'S LAST 28

MILLION 10
QUIET FOR A MILLION, MILLION YEARS. DK LINCOLN MONUMNT 5
QUIET FOR A MILLION, MILLION YEARS. DK LINCOLN MONUMNT 5
IF I HAD A MILLION . . . . SH IF-ING 9
BUT I AIN'T GOT A MILLION, ... SH IF-ING 13
I PACK A MILLION BAGS O' SAND . . . SH MISSISSIPPI LEV 11
A MILLION FACES . . . . SP NIGHTMARE BOOGE 3
OF A MILLION MARTHA ROUNDTREES? . . AYM BIRD IN ORBIT 62
PAST HUTS THAT HOUSE A MILLION BLACKS . . . . AYM BLUES IN STEREO 15
INTO A MILLION POOLS OF QUARTERS . AYM ODE TO DINAH 56
OR A MILLION AND TEN . . . . PL GHOSTS OF 1619 24

MILLIONAIRES 1
FOR THE AMERICAN MILLIONAIRES. . . FC JAZZ BAND 6

MILLIONS 6
I SPEAK IN THE NAME OF THE BLACK MILLIONS . . . . ANS A NEW SONG 1
SURELY NOT ME? THE MILLIONS ON RELIEF TODAY? . . . . ANS LET AMERICA BE 53
THE MILLIONS SHOT DOWN WHEN WE STRIKE? . . . . ANS LET AMERICA BE 54
THE MILLIONS WHO HAVE NOTHING FOR OUR PAY? . . . . ANS LET AMERICA BE 55
THE MILLIONS WHO HAVE NOTHING FOR OUR PAY? . . . . ANS LET AMERICA BE 60
UP MILLIONS FOR BOMBS TO KILL A CHILD - . . . . ANS SONG OF SPAIN 44

MILLION-DOLLAR 2
WHEN MILLION-DOLLAR THIEVES . . . . PL PRIME 4
GLORIFY THEIR MILLION-DOLLAR WAYS PL PRIME 5

MIMES 1
O WHITE-FACED MIMES. FW FOR DEAD MIMES 1

MINCE-MEAT 2
AT MAKING MINCE-MEAT JC NOTE TO NAZIS 3
I'LL MAKE MINCE-MEAT JC NOTE TO NAZIS 7

MIND 23
BECAUSE MY MIND IS DULL NM BLACK CLWN POEM 4
AN' ALMOST LOSE MA MIND. DK PO' BOY BLUES 18
NEVER MIND! DON'T BOTHER. SH BLD PAWNBROKER 4
I'M ABOUT TO LOSE MY MIND. SH EVENIN' BLUES 6
SOMETHING IN MY MIND BETTER I FORGOT. SH TWILIGHT REVERI 2
I DON'T PAY YOU NO MIND. JC BLD SAM SOLOMON 30
I DON'T MIND DYING - SP AS BEFITS A MAN 1
I DON'T MIND DYING SP AS BEFITS A MAN 5
BEAR IN MIND SP DRUM 1
THEN THE MIND STARTS SEEKING A WAY. SP FREEDOM'S PLOW 10
THE MIND SEEKS A WAY TO OVERCOME THESE OBSTACLES. SP FREEDOM'S PLOW 17
ON HER MIND - SP LADY'S BOOGIE 4
I'LL PAY SOME MIND TO YOU. SP MADAM FORT TELL 16
I CAN'T GET OFF MY MIND. SP MAMA AND DAUGHT 8
DON'T KNOW'S I'D MIND HIS GOIN' SP MIDWINTER BLUES 7
DON'T KNOW'S I'D MIND HIS GOIN' SP MIDWINTER BLUES 9
DIDN'T HARDLY KNOW MY MIND. SP MORNING AFTER 2
DIDN'T KNOW MY MIND. SP MORNING AFTER 4
IN MY MIND SP SO LONG 5
IF YOU HAD A HEAD AND USED YOUR MIND SP 50 - 50 9
TO BIND MY MIND - CHAIN MY FEET - PL DEATH YORKVILLE 6
THAT COME TO WHITE MIND PL DINNER GUEST ME 5
THEY CHANGE THEIR MIND! PL WARNING 5

MINDING 2
EVERY DETAIL MINDING SP OLD WALT 5
EACH DETAIL MINDING. SP OLD WALT 9

MINDS 1
HAVE MADE UP THEIR MINDS JIM CROW IS THROUGH. JC JIM CROW'S LAST 14

MINE 30
HE WAS A FRIEND O' MINE. FC DEATH DO DIRTY 5
MA FRIEND O' MINE. FC DEATH DO DIRTY 10
GOOD FRIEND O' MINE. FC DEATH DO DIRTY 15
O, FRIEND O' MINE. FC DEATH DO DIRTY 20
MA FRIEND O' MINE. FC DEATH DO DIRTY 25
BEST FRIEND O' MINE. FC DEATH DO DIRTY 30
MA FRIEND O' MINE. FC DEATH DO DIRTY 35
PLEASE DON'T TAKE THIS MAN O' MINE. FC GAL'S CRY DYING 18
BUT - AIN'T MY LIFE MINE? NM BIG-TIMER POEM 20
THAT I CAN CALL MINE. NM BIG-TIMER POEM 48
AND GIVE US THE RIGHTS THAT ARE YOURS AND MINE. NM COLORED SL POEM 10
'CAUSE WHEN I WAS LIVING, I DIDN'T HAVE MINE. NM COLORED SL POEM 18
OLD GAL O' MINE. DK DRESSED UP 8
HE'S A FRIEND O' MINE. DK MA LORD 11
THE LAND THAT'S MINE - THE POOR MAN'S, INDIAN'S, NEGRO'S. ANS LET AMERICA BE 65
WORKERS, MINE NO COLD AGAIN! ANS SONG OF SPAIN 55
MUST PUT THEIR HANDS WITH MINE ANS UNION 6
FLAVOR HARLEM OF MINE! SH HARLEM SWEETIES 28
HER BODY CLOSE TO MINE. FW MAN 6
REDEEM MINE. LHR BLD MARY'S SON 35
NOT MINE. SP A HOUSE IN TAOS 37
IT'S MINE! SP ARGUMENT 10
I'LL HAVE A THRONE FOR MINE! SP DEFERRED 42
FOR THE FREEDOM TRAIN WILL BE YOURS AND MINE! SP FREEDOM TRAIN 58
AT HOME THEY GOT A TRAIN THAT'S YOURS AND MINE! SP FREEDOM TRAIN 62
COME AND BE MINE. SP PORT TOWN 8
LORD, AIN'T MINE! SP SAME IN BLUES 25
I WILL TAKE YOUR HEART FOR MINE. SP TO ARTINA 9
OF GLORY TO YOUR NAME AND MINE AYM BLUES IN STEREO 10
AT THE DAMASK TABLE, MINE. PL DINNER GUEST ME 18

MINERS 1
MINERS. ANS OPEN LETTER 2

MINES 3
THE LAND, THE MINES, THE PLANTS, THE RIVERS - ANS LET AMERICA BE 83
AND THE MINES AND THE FACTORIES AND THE OFFICE TOWERS ANS OPEN LETTER 15
TAKES TOOLS AND BANKS AND MINES. ANS OPEN LETTER 61

MINGLE 2
MINGLE THEMSELVES SOFTLY SP AUNTSUE'S STORI 12
MINGLE THEMSELVES SOFTLY SP AUNTSUE'S STORI 14

MINGLED 3
OF OUR MINGLED BREATH. SP DESIRE 4
MINGLED SP SUBWAY RUSH HOU 1
MINGLED SP SUBWAY RUSH HOU 4

MINGUS 1
DID I KNOW CHARLIE MINGUS? AYM HORN OF PLENTY 51

MINISTER 2
A MINISTER PREACHED - SP BLD OF THE MAN 17
AN OLD NEGRO MINISTER CONCLUDES HIS SERMON IN HIS LOUDEST VOICE. SP SUNDAY MORNING 1

MINOR 1
SINGING MINOR MELODIES WB BLUES FANTASY 4

MINORITY 1
ALTHOUGH MINORITY. PL GHOSTS OF 1619 17

MINT 4
I WASN'T NO MINT. SP MADAM'S CALLING 6
HAND ME MY MINT JULEP, MAMMY. PL CULTURAL EXCHNG 59
THE PAST HAS BEEN A MINT PL HISTORY 1
LIKE RUSTY IRON AND MINT. PL WHERE WHEN WHCH 3

MINTON'S 1
MINTON'S SP NEON SIGNS 4

MINUS 2
ON TWO-BITS MINUS TWO? SH OUT OF WORK 20
ON TWO-BITS MINUS TWO? SH OUT OF WORK 22

MINUTES 1
A FEW MINUTES LATE SP DREAM BOOGE VAR 11

MIRACLE 1
MIRACLE MATERNITY: SP INTERNE AT PROV 22

MIRAGE-LAND 1
TOWARD A MIRAGE-LAND FW JAIME 7

MIRE 2
WITH MY FEET IN THE MIRE SH EVIL MORNING 11
IN THE DIRTY MIRE. SP ANGELS WINGS 8

MIRROR-GO-ROUND 1
MIRROR-GO-ROUND SP SHALIMAR 1

MIRTH 1
OF YOUR MIRTH WB DISILLUSION 8

MISERY 5
THEY'LL BRING YOU MISERY. FC LISTEN HERE 18
AND NO LONGER DO WE KNOW THE DARK MISERY NM COLORED SL POEM 30
SMASHES MISERY. ANS OPEN LETTER 57
'LL EASE MY MISERY. SP MISERY 4
FOR HER MISERY. SP MISERY 16

MISMATED 1
WITH MY SHOES MISMATED. SP BAD MORNING 2

MISS 19
BUT YOU WILL NOT MISS ME, - WB A FAREWELL 6
BUT I'LL MISS MA GIN. FC BLD OF GIN MARY 20
WHIP IT, MISS LUCY! SH DEATH IN HARLEM 12
AW, PICK IT, MISS LUCY! SH DEATH IN HARLEM 27
AW, PLUNK IT, MISS LUCY. SH DEATH IN HARLEM 56
AW, PLAY IT, MISS LUCY! SH DEATH IN HARLEM 74
WHILE MISS LUCY PLAYED IT, BOOM, BOOM, BOOM, SH DEATH IN HARLEM 31
SURE, I MISSED YOUR TRUNK - BUT I DIDN'T MISS YOU. SH LETTER 8
I MISS YOU, LULU, OWT YESTERDAY TODAY 5
I MISS YOU SO BAD - OWT YESTERDAY TODAY 6
I MUST BE MISS BLUES'ES CHILD. SP MISS BLUES'ES 6
I'M JUST MISS BLUES'ES CHILD! SP MISS BLUES'ES 14
MISS YOU, SP PASSING 13
BUT WHO WOULD MISS ME IF I LEFT? SP REVERIE HARLEM 14
MISS GARDNER'S IN HER GARDEN. SP SOUTHERN MAMMY 1
MISS YARDMAN'S IN HER YARD. SP SOUTHERN MAMMY 2
MISS MICHAELMAS IS AT DE MASS SP SOUTHERN MAMMY 3
'HIND MA FRIEND MISS CORA LEE. SP YOUNG GAL'S BLS 2
MILES AND ELLA AND MISS NINA $ $ $ $ $ $ $ AYM HORN OF PLENTY 9

MISSED 3
YES, INDEEDY, I SHO HAVE MISSED YOU, TOO! NM BROKE 67
SURE, I MISSED YOUR TRUNK - BUT I DIDN'T MISS YOU. SH LETTER 8
NEVER MISSED A BITE AYM ODE TO DINAH 130

MISSION 1
THAT IS MY MISSION. NM DARK YOUTH USA 18

MISSIONARIES 1
THE MISSIONARIES NEVER TAUGHT CHINESE PL BIRMINGHAM SUND 21

MISSISSIPPI 10

KIDS WILL DIE IN THE SWAMPS OF MISSISSIPPI . . . . ANS KIDS WHO DIE 8
I GOT HER IN MISSISSIPPI. . . . . . SH ONLY WOMAN BLUS 19
SHUBUTA BRIDGE OVER THE CHICASAWHAY RIVER IN MISSISSIPPI. . . . . . JC THE BITTER RIVR 1
THESE MISSISSIPPI TOWNS AIN'T . . . SP BOUND NO'TH BLS 23
WHEN IT STOPS IN MISSISSIPPI WILL IT BE MADE PLAIN . . . . SP FREEDOM TRAIN 21
I HEARD THE SINGING OF THE MISSISSIPPI WHEN ABE LINCOLN . . SP NEGRO SPEAKS OF 8
THEY LYNCH ME STILL IN MISSISSIPPI. SP NEGRO 16
OR THE WOMB OF MISSISSIPPI? . . . . AYM HORN OF PLENTY 56
TO MISSISSIPPI. . . . . PL MISSISSIPPI 7
IN MISSISSIPPI. . . . . PL MISSISSIPPI 20

MIST 4

DESCENDS LIKE A WHITE MIST . . . . WB SUMMER NIGHT 24
THROUGH SOME VAST MIST OF RACE . . SP AFRO-AMER FRAG 15
A MIST OF IODINE AND ETHER . . . . SP INTERNE AT PROV 44
RISING OUT OF THE GROUND LIKE A SWAMP MIST . . . . PL DAYBREAK IN ALA 5

MISTAKE 4

EVERY PAST MISTAKE . . . . ANS OPEN LETTER 37
THE WORLD WHERE EVERY UGLY PAST MISTAKE . . . . JC TO CAPTAIN MULZ 56
AND BY MISTAKE SHOT OUT THE LIGHT. AYM ODE TO DINAH 132
THE GREAT MISTAKE . . . . PL AMER HEARTBREAK 4

MISTAKEN 1

OR AM I MISTAKEN? . . . . SP MADAM MIGHT-HAV 14

MISTER 21

SO I SAY, "MISTER, I AIN'T NO SWEEPIN' MACHINE." . . . . NM BROKE 16
HEY, MISTER, WAIT! . . . . OWT JITNEY 37
SHE SAID, NOW, LISTEN, MISTER, . . SP BLD THE GYPSY 11
MISTER, I THOUGHT IT WERE THE . . . SP FREEDOM TRAIN 41
TO THE FOLKS CALLED MISTER. . . . . SP IN EXPLANATION 4
YOU SAY YOU THOUGHT EVERYBODY WAS CALLED MISTER? . . . . SP IN EXPLANATION 5
IN DIXIE, OFTEN THEY WON'T CALL NEGROES MISTER. . . . . SP IN EXPLANATION 7
THEY HAD NO INTENTION OF CALLING COOLIES MISTER. . . . . SP IN EXPLANATION 9
THE MISTERS WON'T CALL LOTS OF OTHER FOLKS MISTER. . . . . SP IN EXPLANATION 11
FOLKS WITH NOT EVEN MISTER IN FRONT OF THEIR NAMES . . . . SP IN EXPLANATION 19
TO THOSE CALLED MISTER. . . . . . . SP IN EXPLANATION 21
MISTER BACKLASH, MISTER BACKLASH, PL BACKLASH BLUES 1
MISTER BACKLASH, MISTER BACKLASH, PL BACKLASH BLUES 1
TELL ME, MISTER BACKLASH, ... PL BACKLASH BLUES 3
GREAT BIG WORLD, MISTER BACKLASH, PL BACKLASH BLUES 21
MISTER BACKLASH, MISTER BACKLASH, PL BACKLASH BLUES 25
MISTER BACKLASH, MISTER BACKLASH, PL BACKLASH BLUES 25
TELL ME, MISTER BACKLASH, ... PL BACKLASH BLUES 27
I'M GONNA LEAVE YOU, MISTER BACKLASH, ... PL BACKLASH BLUES 29
I SAID, "MISTER, ... PL KU KLUX 5
MISTER, CAUSE I WANT TO RIDE? . . . PL MERRY-GO-ROUND 5

MISTERS 2

THE MISTERS WON'T CALL LOTS OF OTHER FOLKS MISTER. . . . . SP IN EXPLANATION 11
AT THE MISTERS, LORDS, GENERALS, VICEROYS, ... SP IN EXPLANATION 42

MISTOOK 1

THEY MISTOOK THE GENTLE DEW. . . . LHR PASTORAL 5

MISTREAT 5

I AIN'T GONNA MISTREAT MA . . . . . FC EVIL WOMAN 1
WOMAN THAT COULD MISTREAT ME! . . . SH ONLY WOMAN BLUS 6
WOMAN THAT COULD MISTREAT ME. . . . SH ONLY WOMAN BLUS 12
WOMAN'S GONNA MISTREAT ME. . . . . SH ONLY WOMAN BLUS 18
WOMAN'S GONNA MISTREAT ME. . . . . SH ONLY WOMAN BLUS 24

MISTREATED 2

HE MISTREATED HER TERRIBLE, ... SP BLD FORTUNE TEL 21
BEATEN AND MISTREATED FOR THE WORK THAT I GAVE - . . . . SP THE NEGRO MOTHE 14

MISTRESS 1

IS A KINDER MISTRESS, ... SP THE SOUTH 26

MISUNDERSTOOD 1

IT MIGHT BE MISUNDERSTOOD - . . . . SH SNOB 4

MIX 3

MIX UP A DRINK, ... NM BIG-TIMER POEM 62
SHOULD MIX LIKE RAIN . . . . PL MISSISSIPPI 5
STILL MIX LIKE RAIN . . . . PL MISSISSIPPI 19

MIXED 8

ALL MIXED UP WITH DIMES AND . . . . FC BRASS SPITOONS 28
MIXED WITH THE BLOOD OF THE LYNCHED BOYS . . . . JC THE BITTER RIVR 12
MIXED WITH THE HOPES THAT ARE DROWNED THERE . . . . JC THE BITTER RIVR 14
MIXED WITH BLOOD AND GALL. . . . . JC THE BITTER RIVR 58
(NEGRO SKIPPER OF THE BOOKER T. WASHINGTON SAILING WITH A MIXED CREW) . . . . JC TO CAPTAIN MULZ 1
TILL I GOT MIXED UP . . . . SP MADAM'S PAST HI 12
AND YOU MIXED 'EM UP WITH SYMPHONIES SP NOTE COMM THEAT 4
MIXED WITH LIQUID FIRE. . . . . . . SP TRUMPET PLAYER 20

MIZ 2

THAT PUT DE MIZ ON ME. . . . . . . SH BRIEF ENCOUNTER 8
THAT PUT DE MIZ ON ME. . . . . . . SH BRIEF ENCOUNTER 10

MOAN 6

STARTED IN TO MOAN AN' CRY. . . . . FC GAL'S CRY DYING 6
TO HOLLER, CRY, AND MOAN. . . . . . SP AS BEFITS A MAN 4
GOT TO MOAN AN' GRIEVE? . . . . . . SP FIRE 13
HE MADE THAT POOR PIANO MOAN WITH MELODY. . . . . SP THE WEARY BLUES 10
I HEARD THAT NEGRO SING, THAT OLD PIANO MOAN - . . . . SP THE WEARY BLUES 18
NOT MOAN OR CRY. . . . . PL COLOR 8

MOANER'S 1

SHE NEEDS TO SET ON DE MOANER'S BENCH . . . . SP MYSTERY 3

MOANIN' 4

I'M MOANIN', MOANIN', ... FC MOAN 10
I'M MOANIN', MOANIN', ... FC MOAN 10
MOANIN', MOANIN', ... FC MOAN 13
MOANIN', MOANIN', ... FC MOAN 13

MOAT 1

AND YOUR MOAT IS TOO WIDE - . . . . PL LAST PRINCE 5

MOB 2

THAT MAD MOB . . . . SL SCOTTSBORO 13
ITS COURT, TOO WEAK TO STAND AGAINST A MOB, ... SL TOWN OF SCOTTSB 3

MODERN 3

IN THE CLOTHES OF A MODERN MAN, HE PROCLAIMS HIMSELF. . . . . . . NM BLACK CLWN MOOD 15
TREADING THE MODERN WAY . . . . . . NM DARK YOUTH USA 23
TO HONOR MODERN MAN - . . . . PL MOTHER IN WAR 8

MOE 1

BY MOE ASCH OR ALAN LOMAX . . . . . AYM IS IT TRUE? 10

MOHAMMED 1

PLUS CASSIUS MOHAMMED ALI CLAY. . . PL CROWNS GARLANDS 5

MOLASSES 1

MOLASSES TAFFY, ... SH HARLEM SWEETIES 33

MOLD 1

FOR GRAVEYARD MOLD. . . . . SP BLD OF THE MAN 24

MOLLIE 1

WHILE MOLLIE MOON STREWS SEQUINS . AYM BIRD IN ORBIT 28

MOMENT 4

ONE LITTLE MOMENT . . . . NM BLACK CLWN POEM 31
LET ALL OTHERS KEEP SILENT A MOMENT. ANS A NEW SONG 3
MOMENT, ... LHR POET TO BIGOT 11
MY MOMENT IS . . . . LHR POET TO BIGOT 16

MONDAY 4

THAT OLD BLUE MONDAY . . . . SP BLUE MONDAY 10
MONDAY COMES, ... SP CONSIDER ME 45
THAT TOMORROW IS MONDAY. . . . . . SP SUMMER EVENING 28
MONDAY MORNING'S GONNA BE? . . . . SP SUNDAY BY COMB 5

MONDAY'LL 1

MONDAY'LL GET YOU DOWN. . . . . . . SP BLUE MONDAY 9

MONEY 32

IF DIRTY HAD DE MONEY . . . . FC DEATH DO DIRTY 18
SPENDIN' MONEY LIKE WATER. . . . . NM BIG-TIMER POEM 17
AND LET 'EM HAVE MY MONEY. . . . . NM BIG-TIMER POEM 66
LANDLADY 'LOWED TO ME LAST WEEK, "SAM, AIN'T YOU GOT NO MONEY?" . NM BROKE 19
I CAN'T EVEN GET DE MONEY FOR TO BUY MYSELF A SMOKE. . . . . NM BROKE 46
SHE MADE ME LOSE MA MONEY . . . . . OK PO' BOY BLUES 17
IF I HAD SOME MONEY I'D STROLL DOWN THE STREET . . . . SH BED TIME 3
(DIXIE MAKES HIS MONEY ON TWO-BIT GIN.) . . . . SH DEATH IN HARLEM 32
WE CAN BUY LOVELY THINGS WITH MONEY. SP A HOUSE IN TAOS 24
AND MONEY, AND SUCH. . . . . SP BLD FORTUNE TEL 6
GAVE HIM MONEY TO GAMBLE. . . . . . SP BLD FORTUNE TEL 13
NO MONEY TO BURY HIM. . . . . SP BLD OF THE MAN 1
WILL TAKE GOOD MONEY FROM YOU, . . SP BLD THE GYPSY 19
AND TAKE YOUR MONEY FROM YOU - . . SP BLD THE GYPSY 21
I WOULD TAKE YOUR MONEY, TOO. . . . SP BLD THE GYPSY 23

AND NO GOOD AT MAKING MONEY. . . . SP DANCER 8
NO MONEY AROUND. . . . SP ELEVATOR BOY 5
WHEN MONEY ROLLED IN . . . SP GREEN MEMORY 2
MONEY WAS NEAR. . . . SP GREEN MEMORY 7
CHARITY'S CHECKED MONEY . . . SP INTERNE AT PROV 26
SPENT HIS MONEY ON ME - . . . SP MADAM MIGHT-HAV 10
IF IT'S MONEY YOU WANT . . . SP MADAM RENT MAN 25
I JUST DRAWED MY MONEY TONIGHT . . . SP PREFERENCE 9
ON THE MONEY FROM A WHITE WOMAN'S
KITCHEN? . . . SP RUBY BROWN 14
PAY MORE MONEY TO HER NOW . . . SP RUBY BROWN 25
BOSS MAN TAKES THE MONEY . . . SP SHARE-CROPPERS 7
SINCE THE MONEY THAT COMES IN . . . SP WHAT? 3
WHAT IS MONEY FOR? . . . SP YOUNG SAILOR 8
AND YOUR MONEY, TOO. . . . SP 50 - 50 14
THE MONEY . . . AYM ASK YOUR MAMA 29
THE MONEY THAT THEY'RE WORTH . . . AYM GOSPEL CHA-CHA 12
WHERE DID I GET MY MONEY! . . . AYM HORN OF PLENTY 47

MONEY-LOVING 1
AND THE MONEY-LOVING PREACHERS . . . ANS KIDS WHO DIE 28

MONEY'S 1
AND AGAIN MONEY'S SHORT. . . . NM BIG-TIMER POEM 40

MONOLOGUE 1
A DRAMATIC MONOLOGUE TO BE SPOKEN BY
A PURE-BLOODED NEGRO IN THE WHITE . . . NM BLACK CLWN MOOD 1

MONROE 2
MONROE SINGS A LITTLE BLUES. . . . SP MONROE'S BLUES 5
MONROE SINGS A LITTLE BLUES - . . . SP MONROE'S BLUES 7

MONROE'S 2
MONROE'S FELL ON EVIL DAYS - . . . SP MONROE'S BLUES 1
MONROE'S FELL ON EVIL DAYS. . . . SP MONROE'S BLUES 3

MONSTER 1
CAN YOU LOVE A MONSTER . . . SP GENIUS CHILD 9

MONSTROUS 1
MONSTROUS PITIES . . . FW OLD SAILOR 9

MONT 1
BLOWN SKY HIGH BY MONT PELEE? . . . AYM RIDE, RED, RIDE 14

MONTAGE 2
MONTAGE . . . SP DEFERRED 49
MONTAGE OF A DREAM DEFERRED: . . . SP DIME 3

MONTEREY 1
MONTEREY . . . SP NEON SIGNS 3

MONTHS 7
GWINE GIVE YOU EIGHTEEN MONTHS . . . FC BLD OF GIN MARY 15
EIGHTEEN MONTHS IN JAIL! . . . FC BLD OF GIN MARY 17
O, EIGHTEEN MONTHS LOCKED IN! . . . FC BLD OF GIN MARY 18
OLD HARD-FACED JUDGE SAYS EIGHTEEN
MONTHS . . . FC BLD OF GIN MARY 23
BEEN UP HERE SIX MONTHS - . . . SH EVENIN' BLUES 5
DROPPED OUT SIX MONTHS WHEN I WAS
SEVEN. . . . SP DEFERRED 3
IN MONTHS OF SNOWY WINTER . . . SP STRANGE HURT 11

MONUMENT 3
MAYBE, NOW, THERE WILL BE NO
MONUMENT FOR YOU . . . ANS KIDS WHO DIE 38
WILL RAISE FOR YOU A LIVING MONUMENT
OF LOVE, . . . ANS KIDS WHO DIE 46
GHOSTLY MONUMENT OF WINTER . . . AYM ODE TO DINAH 26

MOOD 1
SO I AIN'T IN NO MOOD . . . SP MADAM MINISTER 32

MOON 47
WHAT STAR-WHITE MOON HAS BEEN YOUR
MOTHER? . . . WB NUDE YOUNG DANC 7
AND PIERROT LOVED THE MOON. . . . WB PIERROT 3
AND PIERROT LOVED THE MOON. . . . WB PIERROT 28
AND THE MOON WAS WHITE. . . . WB TO MIDNIGHT NAN 8
TWO AGAINST THE MOON . . . WB TO MIDNIGHT NAN 15
AND THE MOON WAS JOY. . . . WB TO MIDNIGHT NAN 16
THE RIVER AND THE MOON HOLD
MEMORIES. . . . FC CLOSING TIME 10
MOON, . . . DK LULLABY 15
MOON, . . . DK LULLABY 16
GREAT DIAMOND MOON, . . . DK LULLABY 17
MOON, . . . DK LULLABY 22
MOON, . . . DK LULLABY 24
AND MOON AND SUN . . . FW BIRTH 4
THERE'S A NEW YOUNG MOON . . . FW NEW MOON 1
THERE'S A SPRIGHTLY YOUNG MOON . . . FW NEW MOON 3
THERE'S A HALF-SHY YOUNG MOON . . . FW NEW MOON 5
MOON CAME, . . . FW NIGHT SONG 3
MOON CAME, . . . FW NIGHT SONG 10
MOON CAME, . . . FW NIGHT SONG 17
THE MOON DOESN'T RUN. . . . OWT RESTRICTIVE 7
MOON . . . SP A HOUSE IN TAOS 22
DID YOU ASK FOR THE BEATEN BRASS OF
THE MOON? . . . SP A HOUSE IN TAOS 23
THIS UNBOUGHT LOVELINESS OF MOON. . . . SP A HOUSE IN TAOS 28
THE MOON, . . . SP FULFILMENT 16
OUT OF THE MOON: . . . SP GYPSY MELODIES 3
MOON IS SHINING. . . . SP HARLEM NIGHT SO 7
IN THE WHITE MOON . . . SP INTERNE AT PROV 37
WENT FLYIN' TO THE STARS AN' MOON . . . SP JUDGMENT DAY 3
THE MOON IS NAKED. . . . SP MARCH MOON 1
THE WIND HAS UNDRESSED THE MOON. . . . SP MARCH MOON 2
OFF THE BODY OF THE MOON . . . SP MARCH MOON 4
O SHAMELESS MOON? . . . SP MARCH MOON 8
YOU WERE MY MOON UP IN THE SKY, . . . SP MISS BLUES'ES 7
AND KISSING THE MOON . . . SP MOONLIGHT NIGHT 6
THE MOON OVER THE TURPENTINE WOODS. . . . SP MULATTO 7
IN THE DARK OF THE MOON. . . . SP SILHOUETTE 4
IN THE DARK OF THE MOON . . . SP SILHOUETTE 7
AS A SLIVER OF THE MOON. . . . SP SLIVER 4
COTTON AND THE MOON. . . . SP THE SOUTH 9
THE STARS WENT OUT AND SO DID THE
MOON. . . . SP THE WEARY BLUES 32
THAT IS LONGING FOR THE MOON . . . SP TRUMPET PLAYER 26
HOW THIN AND SHARP IS THE MOON
TONIGHT! . . . SP WINTER MOON 1
IS THE SLIM CURVED CROOK OF THE MOON
TONIGHT! . . . SP WINTER MOON 3
WHILE MOLLIE MOON STREWS SEQUINS . . . AYM BIRD IN ORBIT 28
FOR THE MOON WOULD WHITE HIS
WHITENESS . . . AYM BLUES IN STEREO 17
ON THE BONGO OF THE MOON. . . . AYM GOSPEL CHA-CHA 8
MOON IS, STARS ARE, . . . FL LUMUMBA'S GRAVE 18

MOONEY 13
TOM MOONEY! . . . ANS CHANT TOM MOONY 1
TOM MOONEY! . . . ANS CHANT TOM MOONY 2
TOM MOONEY! . . . ANS CHANT TOM MOONY 3
TOM MOONEY! . . . ANS CHANT TOM MOONY 14
TOM MOONEY! . . . ANS CHANT TOM MOONY 15
TOM MOONEY! . . . ANS CHANT TOM MOONY 16
TOM MOONEY! . . . ANS CHANT TOM MOONY 31
TOM MOONEY. . . . ANS CHANT TOM MOONY 33
TOM MOONEY. . . . ANS CHANT TOM MOONY 35
TOM MOONEY. . . . ANS CHANT TOM MOONY 37
TOM MOONEY. . . . ANS CHANT TOM MOONY 39
TOM MOONEY. . . . ANS CHANT TOM MOONY 41
TOM MOONEY. . . . ANS CHANT TOM MOONY 46

MOONLIGHT 4
SITTING IN THE MARBLE AND THE
MOONLIGHT. . . . DK LINCOLN MONUMNT 2
SITTING LONELY IN THE MARBLE AND THE
MOONLIGHT, . . . DK LINCOLN MONUMNT 3
SILVER MOONLIGHT EVERYWHERE. . . . SP MULATTO 20
AND MOONLIGHT ON ITS HORN . . . AYM BIRD IN ORBIT 27

MOONLIGHT'S 1
WHERE THE MOONLIGHT'S BUT A
SPOTLIGHT . . . SP TRUMPET PLAYER 27

MOONS 4
AND ALL THE WILD HOT MOONS OF THE
JUNGLES SHINE IN MY SOUL. . . . WB FOR PORTRAIT OF 2
I LOST MY SILVER MOONS. . . . WB LAMENT DARK PEO 8
NIGHT OF THE TWO MOONS . . . SP NIGHT FOUR SONG 1
HAS DARK MOONS OF WEARINESS . . . SP TRUMPET PLAYER 3

MOON-GLIMMER 1
AND BROKEN SHAFTS OF MOON-GLIMMER . . . DK AFTR MNY SPRNGS 5

MOP 7
MOP! . . . SP DREAM BOOGIE 20
RE-BOP BE-BOP MOP AND STOP. . . . SP FLATTED FIFTHS 2
HEY! BABA-RE-BOP! MOP! ON A BE-BOP
KICK! . . . SP LIKEWISE 23
BAM! BOP! MOP! . . . SP TO BE SOMEBODY 20
THEN MOP AND I MOP. . . . PL WAR 13
THEN MOP AND I MOP. . . . PL WAR 17
MY MOP IN BLOOD - . . . PL WAR 15

MORAL 1
A MORAL POEM TO BE RENDERED BY A MAN
IN A STRAW HAT WITH A BRIGHT
BAND, A . . . NM BIG-TIMER MOOD 1

MORE 50
GOOD GAL ANY MORE. . . . FC EVIL WOMAN 2
AND I'D SAVE MORE THAN I DO NOW. . . . FC PRIZE FIGHTER 6
O, PLAY SOME MORE. . . . FC SATURDAY NIGHT 3
THAT I CAN STAND MORE. . . . NM BLACK CLWN POEM 24
I CANNOT FIND THEM ANY MORE. . . . DK AFTR MNY SPRNGS 8
THERE'S NOTHING MORE TO SAY. . . . DK I LOVED FRIEND 3
FOR ME, NO MORE, THE GREAT MIGRATION
TO THE NORTH. . . . ANS OPEN LETTER 41
CAR NO MORE. . . . SH ANNOUNCEMENT 16
I'LL TRY NOT TO BE THAT MEAN NO
MORE. . . . SH LETTER 13
THAT PLACE WHERE YOUR TRUNK WAS,
AIN'T NO TRUNK NO MORE. . . . SH SUPPER TIME 8

MAKE YOU WALK LIKE A GHOST IF YOU BOTHER ME ANY MORE. . . . . . . SH TWILIGHT REVERI 6
YOU'RE HALF A WORLD AWAY OR MORE . JC GOOD MORN STLIN 17
ARE WITH YOU MORE . . . . JC GOOD MORN STLIN 47
OF THOSE WHO WOULD KEEP, OR ONCE MORE MAKE . . . . JC TO CAPTAIN MULZ 31
BUT MORE THAN SHIP, ... JC TO CAPTAIN MULZ 41
BUT MORE THAN THESE. . . . . JC TO CAPTAIN MULZ 45
MORE THAN SHIP THEN. . . . . JC TO CAPTAIN MULZ 62
AND MORE THAN CAPTAIN . . . . JC TO CAPTAIN MULZ 65
AND THE SUN GALLOPS NO MORE . . . FW THERE 7
NOW NO MORE. . . . . OWT BLD MARGE POLIT 24
AIN'T NO MORE! . . . . OWT BLUES ON A BOX 8
MORE THAN THAT. . . . . LHR CONSERVATORY 7
TO MAKE IT EITHER MORE OR LESS. . . LHR DEAR LVLY DEATH 7
I'LL LEAVE HER MORE TO NAG ABOUT . LHR TESTAMENT 11
AND TELL YOU MORE THAN . . . . . . SP BLD FORTUNE TEL 3
YOU'LL NEED SIXTY MORE . . . . . . SP BLD OF THE MAN 4
I WOULDN'T GET UP NO MORE - . . . . SP BLUES AT DAWN 9
AIN'T GOT NO HEART NO MORE. . . . . SP CORA 2
ONE MORE BOTTLE OF GIN. . . . . . . SP DEFERRED 33
HAD MORE WOMEN . . . . SP FIRE 19
SHE WASN'T HOME NO MORE. . . . . . SP HOMECOMING 4
I WOULDN'T PLAY NO MORE. . . . . . SP MADAM NUMBER WR 4
AND NOTHING MORE. . . . . SP MADAM CENSUS 12
AIN'T GONNA PLAY NO MORE . . . . . SP MADAM NUMBER WR 22
FOR ONE MORE DOLLAR AND A HALF. . . SP MADAM FORT TELL 27
CAN'T DO - AND MORE, TOO? . . . . . SP MADAM PHONE BIL 30
THEY COST ME MORE . . . . SP MADAM'S CALLING 3
MORE THRILLING. . . . . SP MELLOW 8
SEEKING MORE THAN FOUND. . . . . . SP OLD WALT 4
KNOW MORE ABOUT THIS PRETTY RUBY BROWN. . . . . SP RUBY BROWN 17
HER NAME ANY MORE. . . . . SP RUBY BROWN 22
PAY MORE MONEY TO HER NOW . . . . . SP RUBY BROWN 25
AND WE ARE NOTHING MORE . . . . . . SP SHARE-CROPPERS 12
HE PLAYED A FEW CHORDS THEN HE SANG SOME MORE - . . . . SP THE WEARY BLUES 24
AND SOMEWHAT MORE FREE. . . . . . . SP THEME FOR ENG B 40
BUT THEY GOT MORE SENSE . . . . . . SP WARNING AUGMENT 11
IF SHOW FARE'S MORE THAN 30¢ ¢ ¢ ¢ ¢ ¢ ¢ ¢ . . . . AYM HORN OF PLENTY 23
WAITED TWENTY MORE . . . . AYM IS IT TRUE? 29
"I DON'T WANT TO STUDY WAR NO MORE." PL BLACK PANTHER 6
MORE THAN GERMAN EVER BORE. . . . . PL CULTURAL EXCHNG 16

MORENA 2
AY, MORENA! . . . . AYM BIRD IN ORBIT 33
AY, MORENA, DONDE ESTA? . . . . . . AYM RIDE, RED, RIDE 20

MORE'N 1
WELL, THAT'S TEN BUCKS MORE'N I'LL PAY YOU . . . . SP BLD LANDLORD 11

MORN 2
WEARY EARLY IN DE MORN. . . . . . . DK PO' BOY BLUES 20
EARLY, EARLY IN DE MORN. . . . . . DK PO' BOY BLUES 22

MORNING 24
BEING WALKERS WITH THE DAWN AND MORNING. . . . . DK WALKERS WITH 1
WALKERS WITH THE SUN AND MORNING. DK WALKERS WITH 2
BEING WALKERS WITH THE SUN AND MORNING. . . . . DK WALKERS WITH 6
MAKE THIS EARLY MORNING TIME TO KEEP BODY AND SOUL . . . . SH DAYBREAK 7
GETTING UP IN THE MORNING LONESOME AND SAD? . . . . SH DAYBREAK 13
SHE WENT ONE SUMMER MORNING . . . . FW GIRL 5
I WENT FORTH IN THE MORNING . . . . SP A BLACK PIERROT 14
I DON'T DARE START THINKING IN THE MORNING. . . . . SP BLUES AT DAWN 1
I DON'T DARE START THINKING IN THE MORNING. . . . . SP BLUES AT DAWN 2
SO I DON'T DARE START THINKING IN THE MORNING. . . . . SP BLUES AT DAWN 5
I DON'T DARE REMEMBER IN THE MORNING SP BLUES AT DAWN 6
DON'T DARE REMEMBER IN THE MORNING. SP BLUES AT DAWN 7
SO I DON'T DARE REMEMBER IN THE MORNING. . . . . SP BLUES AT DAWN 10
GOOD MORNING, DADDY! . . . . SP DREAM BOOGIE 1
I SENT YOU THIS MORNING TO BUY? . . SP EARLY EVENING 2
I SENT YOU THIS MORNING TO BUY? . . SP EARLY EVENING 4
GOOD MORNING, DADDY! . . . . SP GOOD MORNING 1
GOOD MORNING, DADDY! . . . . SP ISLAND 11
IT WAS YESTERDAY MORNING . . . . . SP LITTLE OLD LETT 1
SUNDAY MORNING WHERE THE RHYTHM FLOWS. . . . . SP MYSTERY 11
WHERE THE MORNING . . . . SP REQUEST 4
COME INTO THE CHURCH THIS MORNING. SP SUNDAY MORNING 36
THE BABY CAME ONE MORNING. . . . . SP S-SSS-SS-SH! 15
AT MOTHER BETHEL'S IN THE MORNING? AYM BIRD IN ORBIT 35

MORNING'S 1
MONDAY MORNING'S GONNA BE? . . . . SP SUNDAY BY COMB 5

MORNIN' 3
BEEN WALKIN' SINCE FIVE THIS MORNIN'. . . . . NM BROKE 2
LAST JOB I HAD, WENT TO WORK AT FIVE IN DE MORNIN', OR LITTLE MO' . . NM BROKE 12
THIS MORNIN' FOR BREAKFAST . . . . SH EVENIN' BLUES 7
I CHAWED DE MORNIN' AIR. . . . . . SH EVENIN' BLUES 8
THIS MORNIN' FOR BREAKFAST . . . . SH EVENIN' BLUES 9
CHAWED DE MORNIN' AIR. . . . . . . SH EVENIN' BLUES 10
I BROKE MY HEART THIS MORNIN'. . . SP CORA 1
I WOKE UP THIS MORNIN' . . . . . . SP SYLVESTER'S BED 1

MORTAR 1
I MADE MORTAR FOR THE WOOLWORTH BUILDING. . . . . SP NEGRO 9

MOSES 2
MOSES. . . . . SL SCOTTSBORO 16
SEND FOR OLD MAN MOSES TO LAY DOWN THE LAW. . . . . PL FINAL CALL 9

MOSQUITO-NETTING 1
WAS MOSQUITO-NETTING THIN. . . . . SP CROSSING 8

MOSS 1
THERE'S HANGING MOSS . . . . FW CAROLINA CABIN 1

MOST 7
SHE FIGHTS AN' QUARRELS MOST . . . FC EVIL WOMAN 7
I STAND MOST HUMBLY . . . . FW WISDOM 1
AND MY BOY'S MOST GROWN - . . . . . SP DEFERRED 16
THIS MOST STRANGE DREAM. . . . . . SP DREAM 2
BUT MOST OF ALL TO HARLEM . . . . . SP GOOD MORNING 15
OR LESS OR MOST - . . . . AYM SHOW FARE PLESE 28
MOST HOLY BASTARD . . . . PL CHRIST IN ALA. 10

MOTHER 26
WHAT STAR-WHITE MOON HAS BEEN YOUR MOTHER? . . . . WB NUDE YOUNG DANC 7
(FOR A BLACK MOTHER) . . . . DK LULLABY 1
MOTHER WARNED ME. . . . . SH BLD THE SINNER 5
I THOUGHT I SAW RED STARS, MOTHER. FW WHEN ARMIES PAS 12
BUT IF THEY WERE BLOOD, MOTHER - . FW WHEN ARMIES PAS 14
IT IS A RED STAR, MOTHER! . . . . . FW WHEN ARMIES PAS 22
HAS TO GIVE HIS MOTHER TEN - . . . SP BUDDY 5
IF EVER I CURSED MY BLACK OLD MOTHER SP CROSS 5
MY MOTHER CHRISTENED ME . . . . . . SP MADAM CENSUS 17
WHAT'S THE BODY OF YOUR MOTHER? . . SP MULATTO 19
WHAT'S THE BODY OF YOUR MOTHER? . . SP MULATTO 21
HAIL, MARY, MOTHER OF GOD! . . . . SP MYSTERY 6
FATHER BISHOP, EFFENDI, MOTHER HORNE, ... SP MYSTERY 21
DID YOU EVER THINK ABOUT YOUR MOTHER? . . . . SP REVERIE HARLEM 5
I HEARD MY MOTHER SINGING . . . . . SP SPIRITUALS 6
SING, O BLACK MOTHER! . . . . SP SPIRITUALS 15
AND HER MOTHER . . . . SP S-SSS-SS-SH! 6
AND HER MOTHER . . . . SP S-SSS-SS-SH! 13
BUT MOTHER AND CHILD . . . . SP S-SSS-SS-SH! 20
DEEP IN MY BREAST - THE NEGRO MOTHER. . . . . SP THE NEGRO MOTHE 32
DARES KEEP DOWN THE CHILDREN OF THE NEGRO MOTHER. . . . . SP THE NEGRO MOTHE 52
AT MOTHER BETHEL'S IN THE MORNING? AYM BIRD IN ORBIT 35
AND THE MOTHER DRUM OF EARTH . . . AYM GOSPEL CHA-CHA 10
I WANT TO SEE MY MOTHER MOTHER . . AYM RIDE, RED, RIDE 1
I WANT TO SEE MY MOTHER MOTHER . . AYM RIDE, RED, RIDE 1
MARY IS HIS MOTHER: . . . . PL CHRIST IN ALA. 4

MOTHERS 1
MOTHERS PASS. . . . . SP SUMMER EVENING 1

MOTHER-LESS 1
PACE. "SOMETIMES I FEEL LIKE A MOTHER-LESS CHILE." TURNING FUTILELY . . . . NM BLACK CLWN MOOD 8

MOTHER'S 5
MY MOTHER'S CHILD. . . . . SH BLD THE SINNER 12
FROM ITS MOTHER'S WOMB - . . . . . FW EARTH SONG 10
IT WASN'T MOTHER'S . . . . OWT BLD MARGE POLIT 54
AND MY OLD MOTHER'S BLACK. . . . . SP CROSS 2
TO A MOTHER'S SONG. . . . . SP STARS 4

MOTIVATED 1
MOTIVATED BY THE TRUEST . . . . . . PL BLACK PANTHER 10

MOTORCARS 1
ON WHICH TO RIDE IF MOTORCARS . . . AYM BLUES IN STEREO 5

MOTORCYCLE 1
MOTORCYCLE COPS. . . . . SP PARADE 13

MOTTO 1
MY MOTTO. . . . . PL MOTTO 5

MOULD 1
TO MOULD A PLACE . . . . NM DARK YOUTH USA 4

MOULDED 1
CAME THE MIGHTY PRODUCTS MOULDED, MANUFACTURED. . . . . SP FREEDOM'S PLOW 79

MOULDS 2
MOULDS AND MELTS AND MOULDS IT . . SP MIGRANT 19
MOULDS AND MELTS AND MOULDS IT . . SP MIGRANT 19

MOUND 3
COULD BE 5TH & MOUND. . . . . SP COULD BE 5
GRASSLESS MOUND. . . . . SP STONY LONESOME 8
5TH AND MOUND IN CINCI, 63RD IN CHI. AYM ASK YOUR MAMA 5

MOUNT 3
THE SERMON ON THE MOUNT . . . . . . AYM HORN OF PLENTY 83
SINCE WE MOVED UP TO MOUNT VERNON. PL CULTURAL EXCHNG 25
MOUNT. . . . . PL FINAL CALL 11

MOUNTAIN 3
I WENT UP ON A MOUNTAIN . . . . . . SP CROSSING 5
CLIMBING UP A GREAT BIG MOUNTAIN . SP PORTER 7
FIRST WHITE TOURIST UP THE MOUNTAIN AYM GOSPEL CHA-CHA 17

MOUNTAINS 7
THE MOUNTAINS AND THE ENDLESS PLAIN - . . . . ANS LET AMERICA BE 84
GREAT MOUNTAINS. . . . . FW BIG SUR 2
AND MOUNTAINS THAT TAKE WING. . . . SP LOVE 4
HAS KNOWN HIGH WIND-SWEPT MOUNTAINS. SP MEXICAN MARKET 5
THE RISING SHAFTS OF MOUNTAINS. . . SP SPIRITUALS 2
THE MOUNTAINS RISE . . . . SP SPIRITUALS 11
AND LOOK TOWARD THE MOUNTAINS. . . SP SUNDAY MORNING 18

MOUNTS 2
EVER TIME I MOUNTS THIS BENCH . . . FC BLD OF GIN MARY 7
KING MOUNTS HIS UNICORN . . . . . . AYM BIRD IN ORBIT 25

MOURN 2
TO MOURN IN RED - . . . . SP WAKE 2
IT'S NOT ENOUGH TO MOURN . . . . . PL BOMBINGS DIXIE 1

MOURNERS 2
THE MOURNERS GOT UP SMILING. . . . DK IRISH WAKE 7
TELL ALL MY MOURNERS . . . . SP WAKE 1

MOURNFUL 1
AND HELPLESSNESS. THE MUSIC IS LIKE A MOURNFUL TOM-TOM IN THE DARK! BUT . . . . NM BLACK CLWN MOOD 11

MOURNIN' 1
THAT BOY THAT THEY WAS MOURNIN' . . SP NIGHT FUNERAL 38

MOUSES 1
DOG-GONE LITTLE MOUSES! I WISH I WAS YOU! . . . . SH BED TIME 14

MOUTH 21
CRY AT MY GRINNING MOUTH. . . . . . WB THE JESTER 12
IN NO SINGLE MOUTH THE SAME. . . . OLD TWO THINGS 10
AND DIDN'T HAVE SUCH A BIG MOUTH. NM BROKE 65
MA HEART WAS IN MA MOUTH. . . . . DK HOMESICK BLUES 8
HEART WAS IN MA MOUTH. . . . . . . DK HOMESICK BLUES 10
I OPENS MA MOUTH AN' LAUGHS. . . . DK HOMESICK BLUES 18
BECAUSE MY MOUTH . . . . DK MINSTREL MAN 1
BECAUSE MY MOUTH . . . . DK MINSTREL MAN 9
A ROW OF GOLD IN HIS UPPER MOUTH. SH DEATH IN HARLEM 18
BEEN IN MY MOUTH. . . . . JC THE BITTER RIVR 5
TO KEEP THE GALL FROM BITING IN HIS MOUTH. . . . . OWT JUICE JOINT 44
HER MOUTH. . . . . SP JULIET 10
SHE OPENED HER MOUTH. . . . . SP MADAM HER MADAM 17
BABE, YOUR MOUTH WAS OPEN LIKE A WELL. . . . . SP MORNING AFTER 12
WITHOUT GETTING FUR IN MY MOUTH . . SP NECESSITY 7
AND A ROSE PINK MOUTH. . . . . . . SP SUMMER EVENING 4
BUT GOD PUT A SONG AND A PRAYER IN MY MOUTH. . . . . SP THE NEGRO MOTHE 18
WITH BLOOD ON ITS MOUTH. . . . . . SP THE SOUTH 2
BIG BOY OPENED HIS MOUTH AND SAID. SP 50 - 50 6
SILENCE YOUR MOUTH. . . . . PL CHRIST IN ALA. 6
OF THE BLEEDING MOUTH. . . . . . . PL CHRIST IN ALA. 11

MOUTHFUL 1
THAT SAYS A MOUTHFUL . . . . SP IN EXPLANATION 32

MOUTHING 1
WAVING A FLAG AND MOUTHING ROT . . ANS SONG OF SPAIN 68

MOUTHS 2
IN MANY MOUTHS - . . . . ANS A NEW SONG 35
DARK MOUTHS WHERE RED TONGUES BURN ANS A NEW SONG 36

MOVE 11
MOVE OVER, COMRADE LENIN, ... ANS BLDS OF LENIN 3
MOVE OVER, COMRADE LENIN, ... ANS BLDS OF LENIN 11
MOVE OVER, COMRADE LENIN, ... ANS BLDS OF LENIN 19
MOVE ON OVER . . . . ANS PARK BENCH 11
STORM CLOUDS MOVE FAST. . . . . . . ANS SONG OF SPAIN 48
WHEN I MOVE . . . . OWT RESTRICTIVE 1
THAT CAN MOVE, MOVES. . . . . OWT RESTRICTIVE 5
NO SHADOWS THAT MOVE . . . . SP END 4
TO MOVE OUT TO ST. ALBANS $ $ $ $ $ $ $ $ . . . . AYM HORN OF PLENTY 22
WHO MOVE IN UNOBTRUSIVE . . . . . . AYM HORN OF PLENTY 67
WHERE BLACK SHADOWS MOVE LIKE SHADOWS . . . . AYM JAZZTET MUTED 4

MOVED 6
AND THIS IS WHAT MOVED IN MY HEART: ANS NEGRO GHETTO 7
THAT MOVED AND TRANSPORTED AMERICA. SP FREEDOM'S PLOW 58
THAT FED AND HOUSED AND MOVED AMERICA. . . . . SP FREEDOM'S PLOW 67
I MOVED OUT TO LONG ISLAND . . . . AYM HORN OF PLENTY 30
I MOVED OUT EVEN FARTHER FURTHER FARTHER . . . . AYM HORN OF PLENTY 32
SINCE WE MOVED UP TO MOUNT VERNON. PL CULTURAL EXCHNG 25

MOVES 1
THAT CAN MOVE, MOVES. . . . . OWT RESTRICTIVE 5

MOVIE 1
A MOVIE HOUSE IN HARLEM NAMED AFTER LINCOLN. . . . . SP SHAME ON YOU 6

MOVIES 2
WHILE MOVIES ECHO DRAMAS ON THE SCREEN. . . . . OWT LINCOLN THEATRE 2
THE MOVIES END. THE LIGHTS FLASH GAILY ON. . . . . OWT LINCOLN THEATRE 5

MOVING 4
I WATCHED THEM MOVING, MOVING, . . ANS NEGRO GHETTO 5
I WATCHED THEM MOVING, MOVING, . . ANS NEGRO GHETTO 5
THE CLOCK IS MOVING FORWARD HERE - JC TO CAPTAIN MULZ 25
AND WHERE WE'RE MOVING . . . . . . SP DEFERRED 18

MOWER 1
AND MY LAWN MOWER . . . . AYM HORN OF PLENTY 92

MO' 16
BUT I'LL HAVE MO' SENSE NEXT TIME. FC GYPSY MAN 18
TALKIN' 'BOUT "WE'LL WORK FOR 50¢ A DAY, IF WE CAN'T GET NO MO'." . . NM BROKE 7
LAST JOB I HAD, WENT TO WORK AT FIVE IN DE MORNIN', OR LITTLE MO' . . NM BROKE 12
WHAT I DON'T KNOW 'BOUT SHOVELIN' COAL, AIN'T NO MO' TO KNOW! . . NM BROKE 32
AND DE MAN COME TELLIN' ME THEY AIN'T HIRIN' NO MO' COLORED - JUST WHITE. . . . . NM BROKE 45
AND SHE COME TELLIN' ME, SHE AIN'T GOT NO MO' EVENINGS FREE! . . . NM BROKE 53
GOT TWO MO' WAYS. . . . . DK NEGRO DANCERS 2
TWO MO' WAYS TO DO DE CHARLESTON! DK NEGRO DANCERS 3
TWO MO' WAYS TO DO DE CHARLESTON!" DK NEGRO DANCERS 6
GOT TWO MO' WAYS. . . . . DK NEGRO DANCERS 14
TWO MO' WAYS TO DO DE CHARLESTON!" DK NEGRO DANCERS 15
MIGHT NEVER RISE NO MO'. . . . . . DK SONG BANJO DANC 13
MIGHT NEVER RISE NO MO' - . . . . . DK SONG BANJO DANC 15
MIGHT NEVER DANCE NO MO'. . . . . . DK SONG BANJO DANC 19
MIGHT NEVER RISE NO MO'. . . . . . DK SONG BANJO DANC 27
I AIN'T HAPPY NO MO' . . . . SP THE WEARY BLUES 29

MO'N 1
MO'N ANYTHING ELSE CAN. . . . . . . SP LAMENT OVER LOV 6

MR 6
STRUT, MR. CHARLIE. . . . . FC SATURDAY NIGHT 7
DO, IT, MR. CHARLIE. . . . . FC SATURDAY NIGHT 27
FEEL THE WEIGHT, MR. LEVY. . . . . SH BLD PAWNBROKER 13
I SAID, PLEASE, MR. LONESOME, . . . SH MIDNIGHT CHIPPI 11
I SAID, MR. LONESOME, ... SH MIDNIGHT CHIPPI 19
CRIPPLE MR. LONESOME. . . . . SH MIDNIGHT CHIPPI 21

MRS 4
MRS. BETHUNE TOLD MARTIN DIES. . . JC JIM CROW'S LAST 21
HE SAID, MRS.. . . . . SP MADAM CENSUS 21
THAT MRS.. TOO - . . . . SP MADAM CENSUS 30
SITTING ON OLD MRS. LATHAM'S BACK PORCH . . . . SP RUBY BROWN 9

MUCH 21
WELL, ER - ER . . . HOW MUCH DOES YOU PAY? . . . . NM BROKE 25
LAWD, FOLKSES, HOW MUCH LONGER IS THIS GONNA LAST? . . . . NM BROKE 59
IS IT MUCH TO DIE? . . . . SL SCOTTSBORO 4
IS IT MUCH TO DIE WHEN IMMORTAL FEET SL SCOTTSBORO 5
I WISH I COULD TELL YOU HOW MUCH I DON'T CARE . . . . SH SUNDAY 5
SO MUCH PAIN. . . . . FW WALLS 2
SO MUCH SORROW . . . . FW WALLS 6
CHARGE YOU MUCH. . . . . SP BLD FORTUNE TEL 8
I DON'T SEE HIM MUCH. . . . . SP BUDDY 3

HE DIDN'T HAVE MUCH SENSE. . . . . SP DANCER 5
I HAVE AS MUCH RIGHT . . . . SP DEMOCRACY 5
AND LAUNDRY I DON'T HAVE MUCH LEFT SP LETTER 3
(SOME FOLKS BLAME TOO MUCH ON JEWS.) SP LIKEWISE 13
IT WAS TOO MUCH. . . . . SP MADAM HER MADAM 11
EXCEPT THAT HE TALKS TOO MUCH. . . SP NEIGHBOR 15
OF NOT CARING MUCH . . . . SP S-SSS-SS-SH! 9
CARED VERY MUCH! . . . . SP S-SSS-SS-SH! 14
BRING WELFARE CHECKS MUCH SOONER . AYM ODE TO DINAH 73
(AND I NEVER HAD THAT MUCH HAIR) . AYM SHADES OF PIG 36
I HAVE AS MUCH RIGHT . . . . PL FREEDOM 5
SO MUCH LARGER. . . . . PL LONG VIEW NEGRO 5

MUD 8
GOT WINGS IN THE MUD. . . . . JC RED CROSS 2
DARK WITH FILTH AND MUD. . . . . . JC THE BITTER RIVR 7
WITH ITS FILTH AND ITS MUD TOO LONG. JC THE BITTER RIVR 74
TIRED OF FILTH AND MUD. . . . . . . JC THE BITTER RIVR 80
WITH WET AND MUD. . . . . FW WHEN ARMIES PAS 8
SEE! WHEN YOU WIPE THE MUD AWAY. . FW WHEN ARMIES PAS 21
PLANT YOUR TOES IN THE COOL SWAMP
MUD. . . . . OWT FLIGHT 1
DOROTHY'S NAME IS MUD. . . . . . . SP BLD OF THE GIRL 8

MUDDY 5
BOOTS ALL MUDDY WITH SOIL. . . . . ANS BLDS OF LENIN 6
TO KEEP THEM COLD MUDDY WATERS . . SH MISSISSIPPI LEV 17
WENT DOWN TO NEW ORLEANS, AND I'VE
SEEN ITS MUDDY . . . . SP NEGRO SPEAKS OF 9
A-CREEPIN' MUDDY PAST - . . . . . . SP SYLVESTER'S BED 20
ON A MUDDY TRACK . . . . AYM IS IT TRUE? 42

MUFFLED 1
MUFFLED DRUMS IN SWANEE RIVER TEMPO. PL SPECIAL BULLTIN 9

MUGGER 1
THE 15¢ MUGGER BEHIND STEEL BARS. JC THE BITTER RIVR 34

MUG-LIKE 1
THEY SELL BEER FOAMING THERE IN
MUG-LIKE CUPS. . . . . OWT JUICE JOINT 5

MULE 9
IF I WAS A MULE I'D . . . . FC HARD LUCK 13
IF I WAS A MULE I'D . . . . FC HARD LUCK 15
I'D BUY ME A MULE. . . . . SH IF-ING 2
GET ON THAT MULE AND . . . . SH IF-ING 3
LIKE A MULE BROKE TO THE HALTER. . SP INTERNE AT PROV 25
MY OLD MULE. . . . . SP ME AND THE MULE 1
HE'S BEEN A MULE SO LONG . . . . . SP ME AND THE MULE 3
I'M LIKE THAT OLD MULE - . . . . . . SP ME AND THE MULE 5
BUT WHY RIDE ON MULE OR DONKEY . . AYM ASK YOUR MAMA 59

MULES 1
LITTLE MULES AND DONKEYS SHARE . . AYM ASK YOUR MAMA 76

MULTIPLYING 1
WAVES OF RISING AND RE-RISING MASS
VOICES. MULTIPLYING LIKE . . . . ANS CHANT MAY DAY 2

MULZAC 1
CAPTAIN MULZAC. . . . . JC TO CAPTAIN MULZ 63

MUMBLES 1
SAY WHO ARE YOU THAT MUMBLES IN THE
DARK? . . . . ANS LET AMERICA BE 17

MURDERED 1
OR ELSE MURDERED . . . . PL WHO BUT TH LORD 7

MURILLO 1
GOYA, VELASQUEZ, MURILLO. . . . . . ANS SONG OF SPAIN 20

MURMUR 4
AIN'T EVEN HEARD HER MURMUR. . . . SP BLD OF THE GIRL 11
AND MURMUR: . . . . SP SEASHORE THROUG 7
DO NOT SING. NOT EVEN MURMUR. . . . SP SUMMER EVENING 21
THE MEN CAN ONLY MURMUR . . . . . . AYM ASK YOUR MAMA 37

MURMURING 1
MURMURING GENTLY . . . . PL DINNER GUEST ME 12

MURRAY 1
BOOTS POLISHED LIKE A MURRAY HEAD. SP SUMMER EVENING 6

MUSCLES 1
MAKES IRON OF CHOCOLATE MUSCLES. . SP MIGRANT 15

MUSHROOM 1
BEFORE THE MUSHROOM BOMB . . . . . . PL JUNIOR ADDICT 20

MUSIC 27
HEAR DAT MUSIC. . . . . WB TO MIDNIGHT NAN 5
HEAR DAT MUSIC. . . . . WB TO MIDNIGHT NAN 7
AND THERE IS NO MUSIC AT ALL . . . FC SPORT 9
SYNCOPATED MUSIC. TELLING HIS STORY
IN A HARD, BRAZEN, CYNICAL
FASHION. . . . . NM BIG-TIMER MOOD 1
DIAMOND RING, CIGARETTE HOLDER, AND
A CANE, TO THE MUSIC OF PIANO OR NM BIG-TIMER MOOD 1
MUSIC TAKES ON A BLUES STRAIN.
GRADUALLY RETURNING TO A SORT OF NM BIG-TIMER MOOD 3
INNER HEARTACHES AND LONELINESS TO
THE IRONIC GAIETY OF THE MUSIC.
THEN . . . . NM BIG-TIMER MOOD 10
SUIT AND HAT OF A CLOWN, TO THE
MUSIC OF A PIANO, OR AN
ORCHESTRA. . . . . . . NM BLACK CLWN MOOD 1
JOY. A BURST OF MUSIC. STRUTTING AND
DANCING. THEN SUDDEN SADNESS
AGAIN. . . . . NM BLACK CLWN MOOD 3
SYNCOPATED. DETERMINED TO LAUGH. A
BUGLE CALL. GAY. MARTIAL MUSIC. NM BLACK CLWN MOOD 6
THE MUSIC. OVER-BURDENED. BACKING
AWAY ANGRILY. FRANTIC WITH
HUMILIATION . . . . NM BLACK CLWN MOOD 10
AND HELPLESSNESS. THE MUSIC IS LIKE
A MOURNFUL TOM-TOM IN THE DARK!
BUT . . . . NM BLACK CLWN MOOD 11
STRIKE UP THE MUSIC. . . . . NM BLACK CLWN POEM 12
UNITED STATES OF AMERICA. MARTIAL
MUSIC ON A PIANO, OR BY AN
ORCHESTRA. . . . . NM COLORED SL MOOD 3
MUSIC GAY. . . . . DK NEGRO DANCERS 8
NO MUSIC DIDN'T PLAY. . . . . . . SH DEATH IN HARLEM 125
SPAGHETTI AND GIN, MUSIC AND SMOKE. SH DEATH IN HARLEM 53
THE MUSIC GOT THROUGH. . . . . . . SH DEATH IN HARLEM 90
I WANT SOME FINE MUSIC . . . . . . OWT REQUEST REQUIEM 3
HEAR THAT MUSIC PLAYIN' UPSTAIRS? SP BLACK MARIA 6
BUT THAT MUSIC PLAYIN' UPSTAIRS . . SP BLACK MARIA 9
THE MUSIC WRAPS . . . . SP COLLEGE FORMAL 9
THE MUSIC OF A . . . . SP LIKEWISE 26
NO OTHER MUSIC . . . . SP MISERY 3
BUT SENDING MUSIC . . . . SP TO BE SOMEBODY 8
THE MUSIC . . . . SP TRUMPET PLAYER 17
UPON WHAT RIFF THE MUSIC SLIPS . . SP TRUMPET PLAYER 38
SOAKING UP THE MUSIC . . . . AYM BIRD IN ORBIT 68
SOAKING UP THE MUSIC. . . . . AYM BIRD IN ORBIT 91
MUSIC. . . . . AYM BIRD IN ORBIT 92
AND THE MUSIC OF OLD MUSIC'S . . . AYM BLUES IN STEREO 23
AND THE CRY THAT TURNED TO MUSIC . AYM GOSPEL CHA-CHA 31
DO YOU READ MUSIC? AND LOUIS SAYING
$ $ . . . . AYM HORN OF PLENTY 11
IN NEON TOMBS THE MUSIC . . . . . . AYM JAZZTET MUTED 10
ALL THAT MUSIC, ALL THAT DANCING . AYM SHOW FARE PLESE 12
I'M GONNA WRITE ME SOME MUSIC ABOUT PL DAYBREAK IN ALA 2
IN THAT DAWN OF MUSIC WHEN I . . . PL DAYBREAK IN ALA 20

MUSICAL 1
HE PLAYED THAT SAD RAGGY TUNE LIKE A
MUSICAL FOOL. . . . . SP THE WEARY BLUES 13

MUSIC'S 3
(THE MUSIC'S SOFT AND WIL') . . . . DK SONG BANJO DANC 23
WHILE THE MUSIC'S PLAYIN LET'S . . SH DEATH IN HARLEM 85
AND THE MUSIC OF OLD MUSIC'S . . . AYM BLUES IN STEREO 23

MUST 48
I MUST HAVE A PARTING. . . . . . . WB A FAREWELL 5
SHO, THERE MUST BE PEACE. . . . . . FC MOAN 16
MUST BE . . . . FC SPORT 3
I MUST NOT SING YOU OVER-LONG. . . DK PASSING LOVE 2
AND YET MUST BE - THE LAND WHERE
EVERY MAN IS FREE. . . . . ANS LET AMERICA BE 64
MUST BRING BACK OUR MIGHTY DREAM
AGAIN. . . . . ANS LET AMERICA BE 69
WE MUST TAKE BACK OUR LAND AGAIN. ANS LET AMERICA BE 73
WE, THE PEOPLE, MUST REDEEM . . . . ANS LET AMERICA BE 82
I MUST NOT DO IT AGAIN. . . . . . . ANS SONG OF SPAIN 72
I MUST NOT DO IT AGAIN. . . . . . . ANS SONG OF SPAIN 74
I MUST NEVER DO THAT AGAIN. . . . . ANS SONG OF SPAIN 78
I MUST DRIVE THE BOMBERS OUT OF
SPAIN! . . . . ANS SONG OF SPAIN 79
I MUST DRIVE THE BOMBERS OUT OF THE
WORLD! . . . . ANS SONG OF SPAIN 80
I MUST TAKE THE WORLD FOR MY OWN
AGAIN - . . . . ANS SONG OF SPAIN 81
MUST PUT THEIR HANDS WITH MINE . . ANS UNION 6
THAT MUST BE ENDED. . . . . ANS UNION 12
YOU MUST THINK YOU GOT TO WAKE UP A
CROWD! . . . . SH DAYBREAK 4
IT MUST HAVE BEEN YESTERDAY. . . . SH EVIL MORNING 1
MUST HAVE BEEN YESTERDAY . . . . . SH EVIL MORNING 3
MUST ROAM. . . . . FW CAROLINA CABIN 17
I THOUGHT THAT LOVE MUST BE . . . . FW MAN 5
MUST CARE. . . . . OWT RESTRICTIVE 17
MUST BE THE BLACK MARIA . . . . . . SP BLACK MARIA 1
WHAT HE SAID MUST BE MEANT FOR EVERY
HUMAN BEING - . . . . SP FREEDOM'S PLOW 107
JEWS MUST HAVE HEARD . . . . SP LIKEWISE 25
SHE SAID, YOU MUST RECOGNIZE . . . SP MADAM FORT TELL 11
BUT HE MUST A BEEN TELLIN' A LIE. SP MIDWINTER BLUES 14
HE MUST A BEEN TELLIN' A LIE. . . . SP MIDWINTER BLUES 16
I MUST BE MISS BLUES'ES CHILD. . . SP MISS BLUES'ES 6
I MUST SAY . . . . SP PORTER 1

DARK ONES OF TODAY, MY DREAMS MUST COME TRUE:	SP	THE NEGRO MOTHE	34
FATE MUST HAVE	SP	WHAT? SO SOON!	3
RIDE EVERYBODY MUST TAKE.	SP	WIDOW WOMAN	2
RIDE EVERYBODY MUST TAKE.	SP	WIDOW WOMAN	4
STOP EVERYBODY MUST MAKE.	SP	WIDOW WOMAN	6
SHE ANSWERED, BABE, WHAT MUST I DO?	SP	50 - 50	12
MUST BE RED!	AYM	BIRD IN ORBIT	72
MUST I WAIT?	AYM	RIDE, RED, RIDE	5
OR MUST I HESITATE?	AYM	RIDE, RED, RIDE	8
MUST STILL STAND	PL	ANGOLA QUESTION	3
MUST TURN INTO	PL	ANGOLA QUESTION	9
YOU MUST THINK US COLORED FOLKS	PL	BACKLASH BLUES	11
OR RENT THAT I MUST PAY.	PL	CROWNS GARLANDS	16
THEMSELVES MUST STRIKE	PL	FREDRK DOUGLASS	19
AND SO MUST BE	PL	FROSTING	5
THAT MUST NOT BE	PL	HISTORY	3
BUT IT MUST BE AROUND	PL	STOKELY MALCOLM	4
BUT I KNOW IT MUST BE	PL	STOKELY MALCOLM	11

MUSTA 1

SOMETHING MUSTA HAPPENED	SP	BLD THE GYPSY	16

MUST'VE 2

BUT YOU MUST'VE FORGOT	JC	BLD SAM SOLOMON	3
BUT YOU MUST'VE FORGOTTEN	JC	BLD SAM SOLOMON	55

MUTED 1

VOICE OF MUTED TRUMPET,	SP	SONG BILLIE HOL	16

MUTTS 1

THEM LITTLE OLD MUTTS	SP	WARNING AUGMENT	9

MY 460

I GO TO SEEK MY FORTUNE.	WB	A FAREWELL	3
MY MAN'S DONE LEFT ME,	WB	BLUES FANTASY	7
MY GOOD MAN'S LEFT ME,	WB	BLUES FANTASY	9
PACK MY TRUNK AND RIDE.	WB	BLUES FANTASY	21
PACK MY TRUNK AND RIDE.	WB	BLUES FANTASY	24
I'LL CAST MY BLUES ASIDE.	WB	BLUES FANTASY	26
LOVES MY BABY	WB	CAT AND SAXOPHN	6
BUT MY BABY	WB	CAT AND SAXOPHN	10
WANTS MY BABY	WB	CAT AND SAXOPHN	18
BUT MY BABY	WB	CAT AND SAXOPHN	20
ALL THE TOM-TOMS OF THE JUNGLES BEAT IN MY BLOOD,	WB	FOR PORTRAIT OF	1
AND ALL THE WILD HOT MOONS OF THE JUNGLES SHINE IN MY SOUL.	WB	FOR PORTRAIT OF	2
I LOST MY TREES.	WB	LAMENT DARK PEO	7
I LOST MY SILVER MOONS.	WB	LAMENT DARK PEO	8
AH, MY BELOVED ONE, AWAY!	WB	OUR LAND	17
MY BLACK ONE,	WB	POEM	3
MY BLACK ONE,	WB	POEM	9
MY BLACK ONE,	WB	POEM	15
THAT ALL MY SHINING BRILLIANTS	WB	SONGS DARK VIRG	4
THAT ALL MY FOLDS	WB	SONGS DARK VIRG	10
MY SOUL	WB	SUMMER NIGHT	13
TEARS ARE MY LAUGHTER.	WB	THE JESTER	10
LAUGHTER IS MY PAIN.	WB	THE JESTER	11
CRY AT MY GRINNING MOUTH,	WB	THE JESTER	12
LAUGH AT MY SORROW'S REIGN.	WB	THE JESTER	14
PART OF MY LIFE.	FC	BRASS SPITOONS	10
MY GOD!	FC	BRASS SPITOONS	25
MY PEOPLE.	FC	LAUGHERS	5
MY PEOPLE.	FC	LAUGHERS	20
MY PEOPLE.	FC	LAUGHERS	22
MY GOD, I SAYS,	FC	NEW CABARET GRL	21
AND FOUND LIFE - STEPPING ON MY FEET!	OLD	AESTHETE HARLEM	7
MY PEOPLE DISOWNED ME -	NM	BIG-TIMER POEM	11
BUT - AIN'T MY LIFE MINE?	NM	BIG-TIMER POEM	20
ON MY ROAD TO HELL.	NM	BIG-TIMER POEM	44
AND LET 'EM HAVE MY MONEY,	NM	BIG-TIMER POEM	66
BECAUSE MY MIND IS DULL	NM	BLACK CLWN POEM	4
WHITE SPIT IN MY FACE -	NM	BLACK CLWN POEM	48
HERE ARE MY HANDS	NM	BLACK CLWN POEM	61
SMASH MY WAY THROUGH	NM	BLACK CLWN POEM	65
AND TOLD ME I'D BETTER PAY HER FOR MY ROOM RENT AND BOARD!	NM	BROKE	22
MY BROTHER DIED IN FRANCE - BUT I CAME BACK.	NM	COLORED SL POEM	1
AND ME AND MY BROTHER WERE HAPPY AS YOU PLEASE	NM	COLORED SL POEM	6
LAST NIGHT IN A DREAM MY BROTHER CAME TO ME	NM	COLORED SL POEM	13
STURDY I STAND, BOOKS IN MY HAND -	NM	DARK YOUTH USA	1
THE HOPE OF MY RACE	NM	DARK YOUTH USA	3
THAT IS MY MISSION.	NM	DARK YOUTH USA	18
LIFTING MY RACE TO ITS RIGHTFUL PLACE	NM	DARK YOUTH USA	19
IS MY AMBITION.	NM	DARK YOUTH USA	21
PUT NO TOMBSTONE AT MY HEAD,	DK	DEATH SEAMAN	5
FOR HERE I DO NOT MAKE MY BED.	DK	DEATH SEAMAN	6
STREW NO FLOWERS ON MY GRAVE,	DK	DEATH SEAMAN	7
FOR I AM HAPPY WITH MY SEA.	DK	DEATH SEAMAN	10
I LOVED MY FRIEND.	DK	I LOVED FRIEND	1
I LOVED MY FRIEND.	DK	I LOVED FRIEND	6
MY LITTLE DARK BABY,	DK	LULLABY	2
MY LITTLE EARTH-THING,	DK	LULLABY	3
MY LITTLE LOVE-ONE,	DK	LULLABY	4
MY LITTLE BLACK BABY,	DK	LULLABY	11
MY DARK BODY'S BABY,	DK	LULLABY	12
BECAUSE MY MOUTH	DK	MINSTREL MAN	1
AND MY THROAT	DK	MINSTREL MAN	3
I HAVE HELD MY PAIN	DK	MINSTREL MAN	7
BECAUSE MY MOUTH	DK	MINSTREL MAN	9
MY INNER CRY?	DK	MINSTREL MAN	12
BECAUSE MY FEET	DK	MINSTREL MAN	13
WHEN I BOWED MY BACK	ANS	A NEW SONG	8
WHEN I SAW MY CHILDREN UNSCHOOLED,	ANS	A NEW SONG	12
MY YOUNG MEN WITHOUT A VOICE IN THE WORLD,	ANS	A NEW SONG	13
MY WOMEN TAKEN AS THE BODY-TOYS	ANS	A NEW SONG	14
HUNG ABOUT MY NECK,	ANS	A NEW SONG	19
AND THE FIRE SCORCHED MY FEET,	ANS	A NEW SONG	20
ONLY MY OWN HANDS,	ANS	A NEW SONG	26
CAN MAKE MY EARTH-BODY FREE.	ANS	A NEW SONG	28
"YOU ARE MY SERVANT, BLACK MAN - I, THE FREE!"	ANS	A NEW SONG	32
NOW I HAVE FINISHED MY TOIL.	ANS	BLDS OF LENIN	8
NOW MY WORK IS DONE.	ANS	BLDS OF LENIN	16
O, LET MY LAND BE A LAND WHERE LIBERTY	ANS	LET AMERICA BE	11
IN SEARCH OF WHAT I MEANT TO BE MY HOME -	ANS	LET AMERICA BE	46
AND THIS IS WHAT MOVED IN MY HEART:	ANS	NEGRO GHETTO	7
"YOU ARE MY BROTHER, BLACK OR WHITE,"	ANS	OPEN LETTER	39
"YOU ARE MY SISTER - NOW - TODAY!"	ANS	OPEN LETTER	40
HERE IS MY HAND.	ANS	OPEN LETTER	66
HERE I AM WITH MY HEAD HELD HIGH!	ANS	SISTER JOHNSON	1
HERE I GO WITH MY BANNER IN MY HAND!	ANS	SISTER JOHNSON	5
HERE I GO WITH MY BANNER IN MY HAND!	ANS	SISTER JOHNSON	5
I, A WORKER, LETTING MY LABOR FILE	ANS	SONG OF SPAIN	43
I MUST TAKE THE WORLD FOR MY OWN AGAIN -	ANS	SONG OF SPAIN	61
IN MY BUICK!	SH	ANNOUNCEMENT	12
THAT GAL DON'T DRIVE MY	SH	ANNOUNCEMENT	15
THAT BELONGED TO MY FATHER?	SH	BLD PAWNBROKER	2
MY SELF!	SH	BLD PAWNBROKER	24
MY MOTHER'S CHILD.	SH	BLD THE SINNER	12
TOGETHER IN MY BIG OLD DOWN-HOME FRAME.	SH	DAYBREAK	8
SAY! YOU KNOW I BELIEVE I'LL CHANGE MY NAME,	SH	DAYBREAK	9
CHANGE MY COLOR, CHANGE MY WAYS,	SH	DAYBREAK	10
CHANGE MY COLOR, CHANGE MY WAYS,	SH	DAYBREAK	10
AND BE A WHITE MAN THE REST OF MY DAYS!	SH	DAYBREAK	11
HERE'S MY SUGAR-DADDY PAL.	SH	DEATH IN HARLEM	48
I'M ABOUT TO LOSE MY MIND.	SH	EVENIN' BLUES	6
JUST TO DRIVE MY BLUES AWAY -	SH	EVENIN' BLUES	14
TO DRIVE MY BLUES AWAY.	SH	EVENIN' BLUES	16
O' MY FEELING LIKE A DOG	SH	EVIL MORNING	10
WITH MY FEET IN THE MIRE	SH	EVIL MORNING	11
AND MY HEART IN A BOG.	SH	EVIL MORNING	12
GET OUT O' MY SIGHT BE-	SH	EVIL MORNING	15
BUT MY LOVE MIGHT TURN INTO A KNIFE	SH	IN TROUBLED KEY	11
CAUSE THAT OLD ALARM CLOCK SHO HURTS MY EARS.	SH	LETTER	19
MY LIFE AIN'T NOTHIN'	SH	LOVE AGAIN BLUS	1
I SAY MY LIFE AIN'T NOTHIN'	SH	LOVE AGAIN BLUS	3
MY USED-TO-BE -	SH	ONLY WOMAN BLUS	2
DE SHOES WORE OFF MY FEET.	SH	OUT OF WORK	2
DE SHOES WORE OFF MY FEET.	SH	OUT OF WORK	4
THAT'S BEEN KEEPING MY NOSE TO THE GRINDSTONE.	SH	PAY DAY	13
DID MY SWEET MAMA GO?	SH	SHAKESPEARE	4
LISTEN AT MY HEARTBEATS TRYING TO THINK.	SH	SUPPER TIME	6
LISTEN AT MY FOOTPRINTS WALKING ON THE FLOOR.	SH	SUPPER TIME	7
CAUSE IF I DON'T THEY'LL CUT DOWN MY PAY.	SH	SUPPER TIME	14
SOMETHING IN MY MIND BETTER I FORGOT.	SH	TWILIGHT REVERI	2
GONNA GO GET MY PISTOL, I SAID FORTY-FOUR -	SH	TWILIGHT REVERI	5
GONNA GO GET MY PISTOL, I MEAN THIRTY-TWO,	SH	TWILIGHT REVERI	7
STAND BY MY SIDE.	JC	BIG BUDDY	17
I SWEAR TO MY SOUL	JC	BLACK MAN SPEAK	5
BUT AS FOR ME - YOU'RE MY ALLY	JC	GOOD MORN STLIN	26
I'M BEAT TO MY KNEES.	JC	HOW ABOUT DIXIE	12
TO JIM CROW MY PEOPLE IS A PITY.	JC	JIM CROW'S LAST	20
MY SONG	JC	ME AND MY SONG	22
ME AND MY	JC	ME AND MY SONG	33
OF MY DREAM.	JC	NOTE TO NAZIS	4
BEEN IN MY MOUTH.	JC	THE BITTER RIVR	5
POISONED MY BLOOD.	JC	THE BITTER RIVR	9
AND ITS GALL COATS THE RED OF MY TONGUE,	JC	THE BITTER RIVR	11
THAT STRANGLED MY DREAM:	JC	THE BITTER RIVR	17
AND MY GRANDFATHER'S BACK WITH ITS LADDER OF SCARS,	JC	THE BITTER RIVR	36
TO FORCE MY BACK TO THE WALL	JC	THE BITTER RIVR	56

Line	Poem	No.
YOU HAVE LYNCHED MY COMRADES . . .	JC THE BITTER RIVR	59
UNDERPAID ME FOR MY LABOR.	JC THE BITTER RIVR	61
AND SPIT IN THE FACE OF MY DREAM.	JC THE BITTER RIVR	62
OF MY MEAGRE CASH, ...	JC THE BITTER RIVR	70
BECAUSE MY FACE IS BLACK, ...	JC THE BITTER RIVR	78
AND IT'S TURNED TO STEEL IN MY BLOOD.	JC THE BITTER RIVR	82
COATS MY TONGUE.	JC THE BITTER RIVR	86
IN THE PALM OF MY HAND	FW DUSTBOWL	5
MY BODY	FW GIRL	12
HERE IS MY HEART!"	FW HEART	7
LIKE MY LITTLE GIRL.	OWT HONEY BABE	16
GOTTA GET MY TEACHING!	OWT JITNEY	31
WHO WOULD BE MY VERY OWN -	OWT STRANGER IN TWN	4
I ASKED MY LANDLADY DID I HAVE PRIVILEGES.	OWT STRANGER IN TWN	7
MY LANDLADY, SHE SAID, NO!	OWT STRANGER IN TWN	8
I'LL KNOW MY WAY AROUND.	OWT STRANGER IN TWN	16
MY WAY AROUND.	OWT STRANGER IN TWN	18
AS HARD AS MY HEAD IS.	OWT TOO BLUE	12
TO GET YOU OUT OF MY HEAD.	OWT YESTERDAY TODAY	8
SO WHEN MY ACTIONS ARE STUPID . . .	LHR ACCEPTANCE	3
THIS IS MY BODY	LHR BLD MARY'S SON	18
AND THIS IS MY BLOOD, HE SAID. . . .	LHR BLD MARY'S SON	19
MY CROSS FOR YOU	LHR BLD MARY'S SON	20
AND TOOK MY LORD AWAY.	LHR BLD MARY'S SON	26
THIS IS MY BODY	LHR BLD MARY'S SON	29
AND THIS IS MY BLOOD!	LHR BLD MARY'S SON	30
THAT MY SOUL SHOULD NOT BE LOST. . .	LHR BLD MARY'S SON	33
MY MOMENT IS	LHR POET TO BIGOT	16
WHAT SHALL I LEAVE MY SON	LHR TESTAMENT	1
WHAT SHALL I LEAVE MY DAUGHTER, . . .	LHR TESTAMENT	5
THE APPLE OF MY EYE?	LHR TESTAMENT	6
WHAT SHALL I LEAVE MY WIFE	LHR TESTAMENT	9
WHO NAGGED ME TO MY DEATH?	LHR TESTAMENT	10
AND MY HEART WAS BLEEDING, TOO. . .	SP A BLACK PIERROT	9
SO WITH MY ONCE GAY-COLORED SOUL . .	SP A BLACK PIERROT	12
BUT I WANT MY FUNERAL TO BE FINE:	SP AS BEFITS A MAN	6
I HAVE ALMOST FORGOTTEN MY DREAM.	SP AS I GREW OLDER	2
MY DREAM.	SP AS I GREW OLDER	6
BETWEEN ME AND MY DREAM.	SP AS I GREW OLDER	10
THE LIGHT OF MY DREAM.	SP AS I GREW OLDER	14
NO LONGER THE LIGHT OF MY DREAM BEFORE ME.	SP AS I GREW OLDER	20
MY HANDS!	SP AS I GREW OLDER	24
MY DARK HANDS!	SP AS I GREW OLDER	25
FIND MY DREAM!	SP AS I GREW OLDER	27
MY BAD LUCK CARD.	SP BAD LUCK CARD	4
GYPSY SAYS I'D KILL MY SELF	SP BAD LUCK CARD	11
WITH MY SHOES MISMATED.	SP BAD MORNING	2
AW, MY HEART IS	SP BLACK MARIA	7
MY ROOF HAS SPRUNG A LEAK.	SP BLD LANDLORD	2
YOU GONNA CUT OFF MY HEAT?	SP BLD LANDLORD	14
YOU GONNA TAKE MY FURNITURE AND . .	SP BLD LANDLORD	15
IF I LAND MY FIST ON YOU.	SP BLD LANDLORD	20
WHEN WILL MY GAL BE HOME?	SP BLD THE GYPSY	4
PUT SOME SILVER IN MY HAND	SP BLD THE GYPSY	6
TO MAKE MY GAL FORGET.	SP BLD THE GYPSY	17
TAKES MY WOMAN AWAY.	SP BLUE BAYOU	12
NO USE IN MY GOING	SP BLUE MONDAY	1
THEM THOUGHTS WOULD BUST MY HEAD -	SP BLUES AT DAWN	4
THAT KID'S MY BUDDY.	SP BUDDY	1
"ONE - TWO - BUCKLE MY SHOE!" . . .	SP CHILDREN'S RYME	2
ONE BATTED A HARD BALL RIGHT THROUGH MY WINDOW	SP CHILDREN'S RYME	18
AND MY GOLD FISH ET THE CLASS. . .	SP CHILDREN'S RYME	19
OR GIVE MY SUGAR	SP CONSIDER ME	23
MY SUGAR.	SP CONSIDER ME	26
I BROKE MY HEART THIS MORNIN'. . .	SP CORA	1
GONNA SHUT AN' LOCK MY DOOR	SP CORA	4
WHEN YOU PAWNED MY WATCH	SP COULD BE	7
YOU PAWNED MY HEART.	SP COULD BE	8
WITHOUT MY WATCH AND YOU.	SP COULD BE	16
EVEN IF IT IS MY HOME.	SP CROON	3
MY OLD MAN'S A WHITE OLD MAN . . .	SP CROSS	1
AND MY OLD MOTHER'S BLACK.	SP CROSS	2
IF EVER I CURSED MY WHITE OLD MAN	SP CROSS	3
I TAKE MY CURSES BACK.	SP CROSS	4
IF EVER I CURSED MY BLACK OLD MOTHER	SP CROSS	5
MY OLD MAN DIED IN A FINE BIG HOUSE.	SP CROSS	9
MY MA DIED IN A SHACK.	SP CROSS	10
MY FRIENDS WAS ALL AROUND ME . . .	SP CROSSING	3
MY FRIENDS WAS RIGHT THERE WITH ME	SP CROSSING	21
HE'S MY ACE-BOY.	SP DEAD IN THERE	14
BUT NOW MY DAUGHTER'S MARRIED . . .	SP DEFERRED	15
AND MY BOY'S MOST GROWN -	SP DEFERRED	16
MY FURNITURE PAID FOR.	SP DEFERRED	35
HEAVEN, HEAVEN, IS MY HOME!	SP DEFERRED	39
WHEN I GET MY FEET IN GLORY	SP DEFERRED	41
TOUCHING MY BODY OF UTTER DEATH -	SP DEMAND	3
ON MY TWO FEET	SP DEMOCRACY	8
I DO NOT NEED MY FREEDOM WHEN I'M DEAD.	SP DEMOCRACY	13
TO FLING MY ARMS WIDE	SP DREAM VARIATION	1
THAT IS MY DREAM!	SP DREAM VARIATION	9
TO FLING MY ARMS WIDE	SP DREAM VARIATION	10
IN MY SOUL.	SP EASY BOOGIE	8
IN MY BED!	SP EASY BOOGIE	13

Line	Poem	No.
TO DROWN THE RATTLE OF MY DYING BREATH.	SP FATASY PURPLE	4
BENEATH MY HEAD.	SP FIRED	10
NOT MY DREAM ALONE, BUT OUR DREAM.	SP FREEDOM'S PLOW	24
NOT MY WORLD ALONE, ...	SP FREEDOM'S PLOW	25
BUT YOUR WORLD AND MY WORLD. . . .	SP FREEDOM'S PLOW	26
IF MY CHILDREN ASK ME, DADDY, PLEASE EXPLAIN	SP FREEDOM TRAIN	31
WHAT SHALL I TELL MY CHILDREN? . . . YOU TELL ME -	SP FREEDOM TRAIN	33
WHEN MY GRANDMOTHER IN ATLANTA, 83 AND BLACK, ...	SP FREEDOM TRAIN	37
AND I OPENED UP MY DOOR.	SP HOMECOMING	2
DANCE WITH YOU, MY SWEET BROWN HARLEM GIRL.	SP JUKE BOX LOVE	12
I HOPE MY CHILD'LL	SP LAMENT OVER LOV	1
I SAY I HOPE MY CHILD'LL	SP LAMENT OVER LOV	3
MY TRUE LOVE'S LEFT ME	SP LAMENT OVER LOV	11
GONNA THINK ABOUT MY MAN -	SP LAMENT OVER LOV	23
AND LET MY FOOL-SELF FALL.	SP LAMENT OVER LOV	24
SET ON MY STEPS AND CRIED.	SP LATE LAST NIGHT	2
CAUSE YOU BROKE MY HEART IN TWO. .	SP LATE LAST NIGHT	6
AND BROKE MY HEART IN TWO -	SP LATE LAST NIGHT	8
TIME I PAY RENT AND GET MY FOOD . .	SP LETTER	2
MY GIRL-FRIEND SEND HER LOVE AND SAY	SP LETTER	6
I THOUGHT ABOUT MY BABY	SP LIFE IS FINE	14
MY GOOD-TIME DAYS DONE PAST. . . .	SP LITTLE GRN TREE	2
I LOOKED IN MY BOX FOR MAIL. . . .	SP LITTLE OLD LETT	2
DEALT MY BAD-LUCK CARD.	SP LITTLE GRN TREE	8
I WAS IN MY GRAVE AND GONE.	SP LITTLE OLD LETT	8
MY OLD TIME DADDY	SP LOVER'S RETURN	1
I LOOKED AT MY DADDY -	SP LOVER'S RETURN	13
FORTUNE TELLER LOOKED IN MY HAND.	SP MADAM FORT TELL	1
COME TO MY DOOR.	SP MADAM NUMBER WR	2
MY HOUSE LAST WEEK.	SP MADAM MINISTER	2
WANTED MY NAME	SP MADAM CENSUS	3
BUT MY MIGHT-HAVE-BEEN	SP MADAM MIGHT-HAV	3
MY GOODNESS, CENTRAL, ...	SP MADAM PHONE BIL	4
FORTUNE TELLER SQUEEZE MY HAND. . .	SP MADAM FORT TELL	5
YOU DON'T KNOW MY NAME.	SP MADAM WRONG VIS	6
ELSE YOU'LL TAKE OUT MY PHONE? . .	SP MADAM PHONE BIL	11
FIRST TIME IN MY LIFE	SP MADAM MIGHT-HAV	11
MY PHONE ALONE.	SP MADAM PHONE BIL	13
WHERE IS MY FORTUNE AT?	SP MADAM FORT TELL	15
MY MOTHER CHRISTENED ME	SP MADAM CENSUS	17
YOU LEAVE MY NAME	SP MADAM CENSUS	19
REPORT, MY EYE!	SP MADAM CHARTY CH	26
LEAVE ME AND MY NAME	SP MADAM CENSUS	27
MY HEART TO BUST.	SP MADAM MIGHT-HAV	32
NOTHING ABOUT MY	SP MADAM PHONE BIL	33
YOU SAY I GAVE MY O.K.?	SP MADAM PHONE BIL	38
MY NAME IS JOHNSON -	SP MADAM'S PAST HI	1
MY NAME IN PRINT.	SP MADAM'S CALLING	8
TO MY PEDIGREE:	SP MADAM'S CALLING	18
MAMA, PLEASE BRUSH OFF MY COAT. . .	SP MAMA AND DAUGHT	1
TO SEE MY SUGAR-SWEET.	SP MAMA AND DAUGHT	4
I CAN'T GET OFF MY MIND.	SP MAMA AND DAUGHT	8
MY OLD MULE.	SP ME AND THE MULE	1
I PUT MY NICKEL	SP MIDNIGHT RAFFLE	1
I LOST MY NICKEL.	SP MIDNIGHT RAFFLE	5
I LOST MY TIME.	SP MIDNIGHT RAFFLE	6
MY BREAD WASN'T BUTTERED	SP MIDNIGHT RAFFLE	15
MY GOOD MAN TURNED ME DOWN.	SP MIDWINTER BLUES	6
AN' PLANT IT AT MY BACK DOOR. . . .	SP MIDWINTER BLUES	20
PLANT IT AT MY BACK DOOR.	SP MIDWINTER BLUES	22
'LL EASE MY MISERY.	SP MISERY	4
YOU WERE MY MOON UP IN THE SKY. . .	SP MISS BLUES'ES	7
AT NIGHT MY WISHING STAR.	SP MISS BLUES'ES	8
NOW MY DAYS ARE LONELY.	SP MISS BLUES'ES	11
IN MY HEART I'M CRYING.	SP MISS BLUES'ES	13
MY WOMAN AND MY FRIEND IS DEAD. . .	SP MONROE'S BLUES	8
MY WOMAN AND MY FRIEND IS DEAD. . .	SP MONROE'S BLUES	8
DIDN'T HARDLY KNOW MY MIND.	SP MORNING AFTER	2
DIDN'T KNOW MY MIND.	SP MORNING AFTER	4
YOU ARE MY SON!	SP MULATTO	5
NAW, YOU AIN'T MY BROTHER.	SP MULATTO	27
NIGGERS AIN'T MY BROTHER.	SP MULATTO	28
NIGGERS AIN'T MY BROTHER.	SP MULATTO	30
SO THE FACES OF MY PEOPLE.	SP MY PEOPLE	2
SO THE EYES OF MY PEOPLE.	SP MY PEOPLE	4
BEAUTIFUL, ALSO, ARE THE SOULS OF MY PEOPLE.	SP MY PEOPLE	6
JESUS, LOVER OF MY SOUL!	SP MYSTERY	5
AND LOST AS MY NEED.	SP MYSTERY	16
WITHOUT GETTING FUR IN MY MOUTH . .	SP NECESSITY	7
AND MY LANDLADY'S SO OLD	SP NECESSITY	8
BLACK LIKE THE DEPTHS OF MY AFRICA.	SP NEGRO	3
MY SOUL HAS GROWN DEEP LIKE THE RIVERS.	SP NEGRO SPEAKS OF	4
I BUILT MY HUT NEAR THE CONGO AND IT LULLED ME TO SLEEP.	SP NEGRO SPEAKS OF	6
UNDER MY HAND THE PYRAMIDS AROSE.	SP NEGRO	8
I CARRIED MY SORROW SONGS.	SP NEGRO	12
MY SOUL HAS GROWN DEEP LIKE THE RIVERS.	SP NEGRO SPEAKS OF	13
THE BELGIANS CUT OFF MY HANDS IN THE CONGO.	SP NEGRO	15
BLACK LIKE THE DEPTHS OF MY AFRICA.	SP NEGRO	19

YOU'VE TAKEN MY BLUES AND GONE -	SP NOTE COMM THEAT	1
YEP, YOU DONE TAKEN MY BLUES AND GONE.	SP NOTE COMM THEAT	7
YOU ALSO TOOK MY SPIRITUALS AND GONE.	SP NOTE COMM THEAT	8
WITH MY RENT.)	SP NUMBERS	8
I PICK UP MY LIFE	SP ONE-WAY TICKET	1
I PICK UP MY LIFE	SP ONE-WAY TICKET	9
I PICK UP MY LIFE	SP ONE-WAY TICKET	23
I HAVE GIVEN MY ANSWER.	SP PERSONAL	6
ALL MY DAYS	SP PORTER	6
UPON MY HAIR?	SP PRAYER	6
I JUST DRAWED MY MONEY TONIGHT	SP PREFERENCE	9
WHAT MY OTHER MAN CAN'T DO -	SP QUESTION	2
MY HEART IS ACHING	SP RELIEF	1
I SAID TO MY BABY,	SP SAME IN BLUES	1
BUT MY LOVIN' DAYS IS THROUGH.	SP SAME IN BLUES	18
ON MY PARTY LINE -	SP SAME IN BLUES	23
MARIE'S MY SISTER - NOT MARRIED TO ME -	SP SISTER	3
MY GOD!	SP SLIVER SERMON	6
IN MY MIND	SP SO LONG	5
WHAT CAN PURGE MY HEART	SP SONG BILLIE HOL	1
WHAT CAN PURGE MY HEART	SP SONG BILLIE HOL	4
WHAT CAN PURGE MY HEART	SP SONG BILLIE HOL	7
THEY HUNG MY BLACK YOUNG LOVER	SP SONG DARK GIRL	3
SOMETHING STRONG TO PUT MY HANDS ON.	SP SPIRITUALS	3
I HEARD MY MOTHER SINGING	SP SPIRITUALS	6
GONNA RIDE IN MY CHARIOT SOME DAY!	SP SPIRITUALS	8
I BRING YOU MY SONGS	SP SUN SONG	6
THEN MY FRIENDS!	SP SUNDAY MORNING	14
WHY SHOULD IT BE MY LONELINESS,	SP TELL ME	1
WHY SHOULD IT BE MY SONG,	SP TELL ME	2
WHY SHOULD IT BE MY DREAM	SP TELL ME	3
HOW I COULD PRAISE MY LORD!	SP TESTIMONIAL	4
FOR TO PRAISE MY LORD!	SP TESTIMONIAL	8
LOOK AT MY FACE - DARK AS THE NIGHT -	SP THE NEGRO MOTHE	5
CARRYING IN MY BODY THE SEED OF THE FREE.	SP THE NEGRO MOTHE	10
BUT GOD PUT A SONG AND A PRAYER IN MY MOUTH.	SP THE NEGRO MOTHE	18
GOD PUT A DREAM LIKE STEEL IN MY SOUL.	SP THE NEGRO MOTHE	19
NOW, THROUGH MY CHILDREN, I'M REACHING THE GOAL.	SP THE NEGRO MOTHE	20
NOW, THROUGH MY CHILDREN, YOUNG AND FREE,	SP THE NEGRO MOTHE	21
BUT I HAD TO KEEP ON TILL MY WORK WAS DONE:	SP THE NEGRO MOTHE	28
DEEP IN MY BREAST - THE NEGRO MOTHER.	SP THE NEGRO MOTHE	32
DARK ONES OF TODAY, MY DREAMS MUST COME TRUE:	SP THE NEGRO MOTHE	34
REMEMBER MY SWEAT, MY PAIN, MY DESPAIR.	SP THE NEGRO MOTHE	36
REMEMBER MY SWEAT, MY PAIN, MY DESPAIR.	SP THE NEGRO MOTHE	36
REMEMBER MY SWEAT, MY PAIN, MY DESPAIR.	SP THE NEGRO MOTHE	36
REMEMBER MY YEARS, HEAVY WITH SORROW -	SP THE NEGRO MOTHE	37
MAKE OF MY PAST A ROAD TO THE LIGHT	SP THE NEGRO MOTHE	39
LIFT HIGH MY BANNER OUT OF THE DUST.	SP THE NEGRO MOTHE	41
STAND LIKE FREE MEN SUPPORTING MY TRUST.	SP THE NEGRO MOTHE	42
OH, MY DARK CHILDREN, MAY MY DREAMS AND MY PRAYERS	SP THE NEGRO MOTHE	49
OH, MY DARK CHILDREN, MAY MY DREAMS AND MY PRAYERS	SP THE NEGRO MOTHE	49
OH, MY DARK CHILDREN, MAY MY DREAMS AND MY PRAYERS	SP THE NEGRO MOTHE	49
BUT SHE SPITS IN MY FACE.	SP THE SOUTH	19
AND IN HER HOUSE MY CHILDREN	SP THE SOUTH	27
I AM THE ONLY COLORED STUDENT IN MY CLASS.	SP THEME FOR ENG B	10
UP TO MY ROOM, SIT DOWN, AND WRITE THIS PAGE:	SP THEME FOR ENG B	15
AT TWENTY-TWO, MY AGE. BUT I GUESS I'M WHAT	SP THEME FOR ENG B	17
SO WILL MY PAGE BE COLORED THAT I WRITE?	SP THEME FOR ENG B	27
THIS IS MY PAGE FOR ENGLISH B.	SP THEME FOR ENG B	41
TELL ALL MY MOURNERS	SP WAKE	1
IN MY BEIN' DEAD.	SP WAKE	4
I BELIEVE MY OLD LADY'S	SP WHAT? SO SOON!	1
BURNS IN MY HEART A LOVE-FIRE SHARP LIKE PAIN.	SP WHEN SUE WEARS	11
RULED MY MANY YEARS.	SP WIDOW WOMAN	14
RULED MY MANY YEARS -	SP WIDOW WOMAN	16
OH, MY, MY!	SP WORLD WAR II	2
OH, MY, MY!	SP WORLD WAR II	2
MY, MY, MY!	SP WORLD WAR II	4
MY, MY, MY!	SP WORLD WAR II	4
MY, MY, MY!	SP WORLD WAR II	4
MY, MY!	SP WORLD WAR II	8
MY, MY!	SP WORLD WAR II	8
AIN'T GOT NOBODY TO SHARE MY BED.	SP SO - SO	2
AIN'T GOT NOBODY TO HOLD MY HAND -	SP SO - SO	3
MY! . . . MY! MY!	AYM ASK YOUR MAMA	38
MY! . . . MY! MY!	AYM ASK YOUR MAMA	38
MY! . . . MY! MY!	AYM ASK YOUR MAMA	38
GRANDPA, WHERE DID YOU MEET MY GRANDMA?	AYM BIRD IN ORBIT	34
MY TV KEEPS ON SNOWING.	AYM BLUES IN STEREO	37
(AND MY PLANTAINS)	AYM GOSPEL CHA-CHA	25
MAKE SLAVES OF MY SORROWS	AYM GOSPEL CHA-CHA	33
WHAT'S HIS NAME, MY COUSIN,	AYM GOSPEL CHA-CHA	41
NOT ENOUGH TO HURT MY PLAYING $ $ $ $ $	AYM HORN OF PLENTY	12
NOW A NAME! MY NAME - A NAME!	AYM HORN OF PLENTY	45
YET THEY ASKED ME OUT ON MY PATIO	AYM HORN OF PLENTY	46
WHERE DID I GET MY MONEY!	AYM HORN OF PLENTY	47
AND MY LAWN MOWER	AYM HORN OF PLENTY	92
CUTS MY HAIR ON CREDIT.	AYM HORN OF PLENTY	95
THEY RUNG MY BELL TO ASK ME	AYM HORN OF PLENTY	96
TO MY CHAGRIN - NOT EVEN SINGING -	AYM IS IT TRUE?	32
I WANT TO SEE MY MOTHER MOTHER	AYM RIDE, RED, RIDE	1
IN MY NATURAL LIFE)	AYM SHADES OF PIG	39
TELL ME, MAMA, CAN I GET MY SHOW	AYM SHOW FARE PLESE	1
WITH MY PACK	PL ANGOLA QUESTION	4
IN MY OWN LAND.	PL ANGOLA QUESTION	7
AND LIFT MY HAND	PL ANGOLA QUESTION	11
AGAINST MY FELLOW MAN	PL ANGOLA QUESTION	12
TO LIVE ON MY OWN LAND.	PL ANGOLA QUESTION	13
YOU RAISE MY TAXES, FREEZE MY WAGES,	PL BACKLASH BLUES	5
YOU RAISE MY TAXES, FREEZE MY WAGES,	PL BACKLASH BLUES	5
SEND MY SON TO VIETNAM.	PL BACKLASH BLUES	6
THOUGH WORN IN GLORY ON MY HEAD,	PL CROWNS GARLANDS	12
THEY ASKED ME IF MY BLACKNESS,	PL CULTURAL EXCHNG	33
HAND ME MY MINT JULEP, MAMMY.	PL CULTURAL EXCHNG	59
TO BIND MY MIND - CHAIN MY FEET -	PL DEATH YORKVILLE	6
TO BIND MY MIND - CHAIN MY FEET -	PL DEATH YORKVILLE	6
ROPE MY NECK - LYNCH ME -	PL DEATH YORKVILLE	7
I DONE BEAT MY	PL DOWN WHERE I AM	3
DONE BROKE MY ANKLES DOWN.	PL DOWN WHERE I AM	7
I GOT MY FILL.	PL DOWN WHERE I AM	12
I'M GONNA PLANT MY FEET	PL DOWN WHERE I AM	13
HEAR MY VOICE!	PL FREDRK DOUGLASS	15
ON MY TWO FEET	PL FREEDOM	8
I DO NOT NEED MY FREEDOM WHEN I'M DEAD.	PL FREEDOM	13
AND A HALO ON MY HEAD	PL GO SLOW	13
FUTILE OF ME TO OFFER YOU MY HAND.	PL LAST PRINCE	1
BEEN SAVING ALL MY LIFE	PL LITTLE SNG HOUS	2
FOR ME AND MY WIFE.	PL LITTLE SNG HOUS	4
MY PROBLEMS	PL LITTLE SNG HOUS	7
MY WIFE	PL LITTLE SNG HOUS	16
TO MY BLACK SELF.	PL LITTLE SNG HOUS	24
MY HEART'S HIS GRAVE,	PL LUMUMBA'S GRAVE	20
TASTING ITS BITTERNESS IN MY THROAT,	PL MILITANT	5
AND FEELING TO MY VERY SOUL	PL MILITANT	6
YOUR SPIT IS MY FACE.	PL MILITANT	11
AND SO MY FIST IS CLENCHED	PL MILITANT	12
MY MOTTO,	PL MOTTO	5
AND LICK MY CHOPS	PL NORTHERN LIBERL	18
THAT MY SON IS DEAD.	PL OFFICIAL NOTICE	3
I, BLACK, COME TO MY PRIME	PL PRIME	9
MY HOPES THE WIND DONE SCATTERED.	PL STILL HERE	2
THE FACE OF WAR IS MY FACE.	PL THE DOVE	1
BLOOD ON MY SPORT SHIRT	PL THIRD DEGREE	3
AND MY TAN SUEDE SHOES.	PL THIRD DEGREE	4
I'D UP AND SELL MY HEART OF GOLD	PL VARI-COLORED	3
MY HEART'S NOT EVEN LEAD.	PL VARI-COLORED	6
THAT'S WHY MY HEART IS RED.	PL VARI-COLORED	8
YOUR FACE AND MY FACE.	PL WAR	7
I TAKE IN MY HANDS	PL WAR	9
I DIP MY BROOM IN BLOOD,	PL WAR	14
MY MOP IN BLOOD -	PL WAR	15
MY NAME,	PL WAR	22
I HAD VISIONS IN MY HEAD	PL WHO BUT TH LORD	5
ON MY HEARTSTRINGS FREEDOM SINGS	PL WORDS LIKE FREE	3

MYSELF 14

MYSELF A HOUSE TO BUY.	WB PIERROT	3
(I DON'T CARE NOTHIN' 'BOUT HER MYSELF!)	NM BROKE	27
I CAN'T EVEN GET DE MONEY FOR TO BUY MYSELF A SMOKE.	NM BROKE	46
I'D BUY MYSELF A CAR,	SH DECLARATION	9
LEFT ME BY MYSELF IN A DOUBLE BED.	SH LETTER	7
HERE BY MYSELF, I DO AS I PLEASE.	SH SUNDAY	2
CAUSE I'M SURE ENJOYING MYSELF TODAY!	SH SUNDAY	7
AND SET DOWN AND DRINK IT, MYSELF AND ME.	SH SUPPER TIME	12
AND PUT MYSELF AWAY?	OWT TOO BLUE	9
WHEN I WALKED ALL BY MYSELF.	SP CROSSING	2
I WALKED ALL BY MYSELF:	SP CROSSING	20
ME MYSELF!	SP NOTE COMM THEAT	19
SIX OR EIGHT AND TEN YEARS OLDER'N MYSELF.	SP PREFERENCE	2
TRY TO FIND MYSELF A JOB	PL BACKLASH BLUES	15

MYSTERY 6

HAS TASTED MYSTERY.	FW OLD SAILOR	6

BEING MYSTERY.) . . . . SP CONSIDER ME 15
MYSTERY. . . . . SP CONSIDER ME 52
YET OLD AS MYSTERY. . . . . SP MYSTERY 13
THE MYSTERY . . . . SP MYSTERY 25
MYSTERY. . . . . SP SNAIL 9

M'AM 3

NO, M'AM! . . . . SP SOUTHERN MAMMY 11
YES, M'AM! . . . . SP SOUTHERN MAMMY 17
NO, M'AM! . . . . SP SOUTHERN MAMMY 23

NABBED 1

OH, THEY NABBED ARABELLA . . . . . SH DEATH IN HARLEM 131

NAG 1

I'LL LEAVE HER MORE TO NAG ABOUT . LHR TESTAMENT 11

NAGGED 1

WHO NAGGED ME TO MY DEATH? . . . . LHR TESTAMENT 10

NAIL 2

BITE A NAIL IN TWO. . . . . SH EVIL MORNING 6
BUT BEFORE I'D BITE A NAIL . . . . SH EVIL MORNING 7

NAIVE 1

NAIVE. . . . . PL SLUM DREAMS 9

NAKED 8

IN A NAKED . . . . SP DESIRE 8
THE MOON IS NAKED. . . . . SP MARCH MOON 1
AND NOW SHE'S NAKED. . . . . SP MARCH MOON 5
STARK NAKED. . . . . SP MARCH MOON 6
IT ISN'T NICE TO BE NAKED? . . . . SP MARCH MOON 10
LOVE IS A NAKED SHADOW . . . . . . SP SONG DARK GIRL 11
ON A GNARLED AND NAKED TREE. . . . SP SONG DARK GIRL 12
TO WANDER NAKED . . . . SP STRANGE HURT 14

NAME 45

TWO THINGS DESERVE THE NAME. . . . OLD TWO THINGS 2
ONE IS KNOWN BY THE NAME OF DEATH. OLD TWO THINGS 7
AND THE OTHER HAS NO NAME . . . . . OLD TWO THINGS 8
EXCEPT THE NAME EACH GIVES IT - . . OLD TWO THINGS 9
A SUN-DOWN NAME. . . . . DK YOUTH 6
I SPEAK IN THE NAME OF THE BLACK MILLIONS . . . . ANS A NEW SONG 1
THE WORKERS SPEAK THE NAME: . . . . ANS CHANT TOM MOONY 15
BUT REMEMBERED FOREVER WILL BE THE NAME: . . . . ANS CHANT TOM MOONY 30
WILL BE THE NAME: . . . . ANS CHANT TOM MOONY 45
SURE, CALL ME ANY UGLY NAME YOU CHOOSE - . . . . ANS LET AMERICA BE 70
SAY! YOU KNOW I BELIEVE I'LL CHANGE MY NAME. . . . . SH DAYBREAK 9
WITHOUT A NAME. . . . . SH DEATH IN HARLEM 73
HER NAME WAS BESSIE. SHE WAS BROWN AND BOLD. . . . . SH DEATH IN HARLEM 81
WHY IN THE NAME OF LIBERTY . . . . JC BLACK MAN SPEAK 11
THERE WAS AN OLD CROW BY THE NAME OF JIM. . . . . JC JIM CROW'S LAST 1
CHANCE IS THY OTHER NAME. . . . . . LHR DEAR LVLY DEATH 10
WITHOUT A NAME. . . . . SP BEALE STREET 6
DOROTHY'S NAME IS MUD. . . . . . . SP BLO OF THE GIRL 8
HER GRANDSON'S NAME WAS JIMMY. HE DIED AT ANZIO. . . . . SP FREEDOM TRAIN 43
HIS NAME WAS JEFFERSON. THERE WERE SLAVES THEN. . . . . SP FREEDOM'S PLOW 36
OF FRIGHTENING NAME? . . . . SP GENIUS CHILD 10
WILL SPELL THE NAME . . . . SP GRADUATION 15
WITH NO TITLE IN FRONT OF NAME . . SP IN EXPLANATION 54
WANTED MY NAME . . . . SP MADAM CENSUS 3
YOU DON'T KNOW MY NAME. . . . . . . SP MADAM WRONG VIS 6
YOU LEAVE MY NAME . . . . SP MADAM CENSUS 19
MAKES YOUR NAME TOO SHORT. . . . . SP MADAM CENSUS 24
LEAVE ME AND MY NAME . . . . SP MADAM CENSUS 27
MY NAME IS JOHNSON - . . . . SP MADAM'S PAST HI 1
MY NAME IN PRINT. . . . . SP MADAM'S CALLING 8
HE SAID, YOUR NAME LOOKS GOOD . . . SP MADAM'S CALLING 11
SIGNS HIS NAME . . . . SP MIGRANT 35
HER NAME ANY MORE. . . . . SP RUBY BROWN 22
AND HER NAME . . . . SP WEST TEXAS 4
OF GLORY TO YOUR NAME AND MINE . . AYM BLUES IN STEREO 10
WHAT'S HIS NAME, MY COUSIN, ... AYM GOSPEL CHA-CHA 41
WHERE WINTER'S NAME IS HAWKINS ¢ ¢ ¢ ¢ . . . . AYM HORN OF PLENTY 27
NAME IN THE PAPERS EVERY DAY! . . . AYM HORN OF PLENTY 37
NOW A NAME! MY NAME - A NAME! . . . AYM HORN OF PLENTY 45
NOW A NAME! MY NAME - A NAME! . . . AYM HORN OF PLENTY 45
NOW A NAME! MY NAME - A NAME! . . . AYM HORN OF PLENTY 45
TOO BRAVE TO NAME A NAME - . . . . PL UN-AMERICAN 7
TOO BRAVE TO NAME A NAME - . . . . PL UN-AMERICAN 7
IS NOT YOUR NAME LIPSHITZ? . . . . PL UN-AMERICAN 13
MY NAME. . . . . PL WAR 23
LIKE YOUR NAME. . . . . PL WAR 24

NAMED 9

SCHOOLS WILL BE NAMED: . . . . . . ANS CHANT TOM MOONY 32
FARMS WILL BE NAMED: . . . . ANS CHANT TOM MOONY 34
DAMS WILL BE NAMED: . . . . ANS CHANT TOM MOONY 36
SHIPS WILL BE NAMED: . . . . ANS CHANT TOM MOONY 38
FACTORIES WILL BE NAMED: . . . . . ANS CHANT TOM MOONY 40
A LADY NAMED . . . . FW NIGHT SONG 18
A MOVIE HOUSE IN HARLEM NAMED AFTER LINCOLN. . . . . SP SHAME ON YOU 6
NOTHING AT ALL NAMED AFTER JOHN BROWN. . . . . SP SHAME ON YOU 7
IN A TOWN NAMED AFTER STANLEY . . . AYM BLUES IN STEREO 21

NAMES 9

AND THE GENTLEMEN WITH DR. IN FRONT OF THEIR NAMES. . . . . ANS KIDS WHO DIE 21
HAVE ALMOST FORGOTTEN THEIR NAMES SH YOUNG NEGRO GRL 4
THE FOLKS WITH NO TITLES IN FRONT OF THEIR NAMES . . . . SP IN EXPLANATION 1
FOLKS WITH NOT EVEN MISTER IN FRONT OF THEIR NAMES . . . . SP IN EXPLANATION 19
WITH NO TITLES IN FRONT OF THEIR NAMES. . . . . SP IN EXPLANATION 28
THE PEOPLE WITH NO TITLES IN FRONT OF THEIR NAMES . . . . SP IN EXPLANATION 40
IN FRONT OF THEIR NAMES. . . . . . SP IN EXPLANATION 61
GREAT NAMES FOR CROWNS AND GARLANDS! PL CROWNS GARLANDS 17
CHANGED YOUR NAMES. . . . . PL SPECIAL BULLTIN 17

NAN 1

SHAMELESS NAN. . . . . WP TO MIDNIGHT NAN 18

NANIGO 1

TO THE VILLE OF NANIGO. . . . . . . AYM GOSPEL CHA-CHA 38

NARY 5

ANSWERIN' THEM WANT-ADS' NOT NARY BIT O' FUN. . . . . NM BROKE 4
BUT NARY A ONE . . . . OWT HONEY BABE 15
BUT I DIDN'T HAVE NARY ONE. . . . . OWT STRANGER IN TWN 5
NOT NARY ONE A-TALL. . . . . OWT STRANGER IN TWN 6
AND NARY A SIGN OF A COLOR LINE - SP FREEDOM TRAIN 57

NAT 1

NAT TURNER. . . . . SL SCOTTSBORO 19

NATCHA 1

NATCHA, OFFERING LOVE. . . . . . . SP NATCHA 1

NATION 7

WHEN THE NATION CALLED US THAT MIGHTY DAY. . . . . NM COLORED SL POEM 4
IN THE VOTING OF A NATION. . . . . JC BLD SAM SOLOMON 48
OUT OF THE DARKEST DAYS FOR A PEOPLE AND A NATION. . . . . SP FREEDOM'S PLOW 137
AND MEN UNITED AS A NATION. . . . . SP FREEDOM'S PLOW 141
DARK TENTH OF A NATION. . . . . . . SP GOOD MORNING 8
CULLUD NATION! . . . . SP WHAT? SO SOON! 6
OF THE NATION. . . . . PL MISSISSIPPI 12

NATIONS 2

THE NATIONS THEY IS FIGHTIN' . . . SP SOUTHERN MAMMY 7
AND THE NATIONS THEY DONE FIT. . . SP SOUTHERN MAMMY 8

NATION'S 1

YEARS AGO AT THE NATION'S START . . NM DARK YOUTH USA 12

NATURAL 2

IN MY NATURAL LIFE) . . . . AYM SHADES OF PIG 39
AND TOUCHING EACH OTHER NATURAL AS DEW . . . . PL DAYBREAK IN ALA 19

NATURALLY 2

SO, NATURALLY, THERE'S TROUBLE . . SP IN EXPLANATION 58
I SAID, NATURALLY, ... SP MADAM RENT MAN 23

NATURE 2

BUT GOD, NATURE, ... SP CAFE: 3 A.M. 6
NATURE HAS A WAY . . . . SP S-SSS-SS-SH! 8

NAT-UNDREAMED-OF 1

NAT-UNDREAMED-OF LEWIS COMBINES . . SP FLATTED FIFTHS 11

NAVY 1

AND NAVY, TOO - . . . . JC BLACK MAN SPEAK 18

NAW 3

NAW! BUT THEY TRIED! . . . . OWT BLD MARGE POLIT 45
NAW, YOU AIN'T MY BROTHER. . . . . SP MULATTO 27
NAW, HE AIN'T NEITHER. . . . . . . SP NEIGHBOR 13

NEAR 7

UNTIL I CAME TO THIS NEAR STREET . OLD AESTHETE HARLEM 6
RESTING NEAR THE ALTER WHERE . . . OWT FUNERAL 3
NEXT TIME A MAN COMES NEAR ME . . . SP COPA 3
MONEY WAS NEAR. . . . . SP GREEN MEMORY 7
I BUILT MY HUT NEAR THE CONGO AND IT LULLED ME TO SLEEP. . . . . . . SP NEGRO SPEAKS OF 6
SO NEAR . . . . SP SUBWAY RUSH HOU 6
WHEN DANGER IS NOT NEAR, ... PL SWEET WORDS RAC 10

NEARLY 3

AND RENT TIME'S NEARLY HERE. . . . . SP DOWN AND OUT 8
NEARLY DROVE ME WILD. . . . . SP MADAM CHARTY CH 4
NEARLY BROKE ME DOWN. . . . . SP MADAM HER MADAM 12

NEARNESS 1

BUT SUDDEN NEARNESS . . . . FW BURDEN 3

NEATLY 1

A RECITATION TO BE DELIVERED BY A NEGRO BOY, BRIGHT, CLEAN, AND NEATLY . . . . NM DARK YOUTH USA 1

NECK 4

HUNG ABOUT MY NECK, ... ANS A NEW SONG 19
AND HANG IT ABOUT YOUR NECK . . . . PL CROWNS GARLANDS 2
ROPE MY NECK - LYNCH ME - . . . . . PL DEATH YORKVILLE 7
HANGED BY THE NECK, ... PL OCTOBER 16 RAID 21

NECKLACE 2

A NECKLACE OF STARS . . . . OK LULLABY 9
HOW ABOUT THIS NECKLACE? . . . . . SH BLD PAWNBROKER 5

NECKS 1

AND LONG RED NECKS . . . . PL DAYBREAK IN ALA 10

NEED 18

OF GRAB THE GOLD! OF GRAB THE WAYS OF SATISFYING NEED! . . . . . . ANS LET AMERICA BE 28
YOU WOULDN'T NEED TO ASK ME: . . . SH EVENIN' BLUES 23
"THIS WEEK I NEED IT ALL." . . . . SH PAY DAY 4
AND I WON'T NEED NO FURNITURE LIVING ALONE - . . . . SH PAY DAY 15
I DO NOT NEED . . . . FW SILENCE 4
YOU'LL NEED SIXTY MORE . . . . . . SP BLD OF THE MAN 4
I DO NOT NEED MY FREEDOM WHEN I'M DEAD. . . . . SP DEMOCRACY 13
IN A GREAT NEED. . . . . SP DEMOCRACY 18
AN' I NEED A DIME FO' BEER. . . . . SP DOWN AND OUT 10
I NEED A DIME FO' BEER. . . . . . . SP DOWN AND OUT 11
YOU DON'T NEED NO GUN NOR KNIFE - SP LITTLE OLD LETT 14
SO WHEN I'M DEAD THEY WON'T NEED . SP MIDWINTER BLUES 23
AND LOST AS MY NEED. . . . . SP MYSTERY 16
HONEY, WHAT DOES YOU NEED? . . . . SP PREFERENCE 8
BUT I DON'T NEED NO PIANO, ... SP TESTIMONIAL 5
MECHANICS NEED REPAIRING . . . . . AYM ODE TO DINAH 10
I DO NOT NEED MY FREEDOM WHEN I'M DEAD. . . . . PL FREEDOM 13
IN A GREAT NEED. . . . . PL FREEDOM 18

NEEDED 2

NOT WANTED HERE; NOT NEEDED THERE - NM BLACK CLWN POEM 40
BERNICE SAID SHE NEEDED . . . . . . SH BLD THE KILLER 9

NEEDING 1

NEEDING SOMEONE. . . . . WP SUMMER NIGHT 16

NEEDLE 4

ITS HYPODERMIC NEEDLE . . . . SP TRUMPET PLAYER 39
WHO STICKS A NEEDLE IN HIS ARM . . PL JUNIOR ADDICT 2
HIS NEEDLE AND HIS SPOON, ... PL JUNIOR ADDICT 12
WITH A RUSTY NEEDLE . . . . PL SLAVE 10

NEEDLES 1

AND THE SCENT OF PINE NEEDLES . . . PL DAYBREAK IN ALA 8

NEEDS 5

SHE NEEDS. . . . . SP CONSIDER ME 25
SHE NEEDS TO SET ON DE MOANER'S BENCH . . . . SP MYSTERY 3
I NEEDS THIS, THAT, AND THE OTHER. SP PREFERENCE 6
NOBODY NEEDS A MARKER. . . . . . . AYM ODE TO DINAH 122
BUT HE NEEDS NO MARKER - . . . . . PL LUMUMBA'S GRAVE 15

NEFARIOUS 1

FOR NEFARIOUS GAIN? . . . . FL UN-AMERICAN 18

NEGLECT 1

GOT TO NEGLECT SOMETHING, ... SP WHAT? 7

NEGLECTED 1

40-VOICES: NO PART NEGLECTED - . . ANS CHANT MAY DAY 17

NEGRA 1

AY, MI NEGRA! . . . . AYM BIRD IN ORBIT 32

NEGRAS 1

INVESTIGATE THEM NEGRAS WHO . . . . AYM BIRD IN ORBIT 86

NEGRITUDE 1

ALIOUNE AIME SEDAR SIPS HIS NEGRITUDE. . . . . AYM BIRD IN ORBIT 23

NEGRO 24

A DRAMATIC MONOLOGUE TO BE SPOKEN BY A PURE-BLOODED NEGRO IN THE WHITE NM BLACK CLWN MOOD 1
A RECITATION TO BE DELIVERED BY A NEGRO BOY, BRIGHT, CLEAN, AND NEATLY . . . . NM DARK YOUTH USA 1
I AM CHICO, THE NEGRO. . . . . . . ANS BLDS OF LENIN 13
I AM THE NEGRO BEARING SLAVERY'S SCARS. . . . . ANS LET AMERICA BE 20
I AM THE NEGRO, SERVANT TO YOU ALL. ANS LET AMERICA BE 33
THAT A NEGRO IS A MAN. . . . . . . JC BLD SAM SOLOMON 4
A NEGRO IS A MAN. . . . . JC BLD SAM SOLOMON 56
BY LYNCHING A NEGRO . . . . JC FREEDOM 8
NEGRO BLOOD. . . . . JC RED CROSS 4
(NEGRO SKIPPER OF THE ROCKER T. WASHINGTON SAILING WITH A MIXED CREW) . . . . JC TO CAPTAIN MULZ 1
A NEGRO COMES HOME FROM WORK: . . . OWT MAN INTO MEN 8
JUDGE GIVES NEGRO 90 DAYS IN COUNTY JAIL . . . . SP BLD LANDLORD 33
WITH THAT NEGRO NOW. . . . . SP MADAM PHONE BIL 7
I AM A NEGRO: . . . . SP NEGRO 1
I AM A NEGRO: . . . . SP NEGRO 17
AN OLD NEGRO MINISTER CONCLUDES HIS SERMON IN HIS LOUDEST VOICE, . . SP SUNDAY MORNING 1
DEEP IN MY BREAST - THE NEGRO MOTHER. . . . . SP THE NEGRO MOTHE 32
DARES KEEP DOWN THE CHILDREN OF THE NEGRO MOTHER. . . . . SP THE NEGRO MOTHE 52
I HEARD A NEGRO PLAY. . . . . SP THE WEARY BLUES 3
I HEARD THAT NEGRO SING, THAT OLD PIANO MOAN - . . . . SP THE WEARY BLUES 13
THE NEGRO . . . . SP TRUMPET PLAYER 1
THE NEGRO . . . . SP TRUMPET PLAYER 9
THE NEGRO . . . . SP TRUMPET PLAYER 33
THE NEGRO PROBLEM . . . . PL DINNER GUEST ME 2

NEGROES 57

NEGROES AND MEXICANS, ... ANS KIDS WHO DIE 15
NEGROES NEVER VOTED BUT . . . . . . JC BLD SAM SOLOMON 7
BUT THE NEGROES IN MIAMI . . . . . JC BLD SAM SOLOMON 51
WE NEGROES HAVE BEEN SLAVES BEFORE. JC TO CAPTAIN MULZ 33
WITH JOHN BROWN AT HARPER'S FERRY, NEGROES DIED. . . . . SP FREEDOM'S PLOW 116
IN DIXIE, OFTEN THEY WON'T CALL NEGROES MISTER. . . . . SP IN EXPLANATION 7
THAT MANY NEGROES . . . . SP PARADE 24
SUCH NEGROES . . . . SP SEASHORE THROUG 8
JUST A HERD OF NEGROES . . . . . . SP SHARE-CROPPERS 1
THAN A HERD OF NEGROES . . . . . . SP SHARE-CROPPERS 13
IN THE QUARTER OF THE NEGROES . . . AYM ASK YOUR MAMA 35
IN THE QUARTER OF THE NEGROES . . . AYM ASK YOUR MAMA 43
IN THE QUARTER OF THE NEGROES . . . AYM ASK YOUR MAMA 74
IN THE QUARTER OF THE NEGROES . . . AYM BIRD IN ORBIT 10
IN THE QUARTER OF THE NEGROES . . . AYM BIRD IN ORBIT 63
IN THE QUARTER OF THE NEGROES . . . AYM BLUES IN STEREO 13
IN THE QUARTER OF THE NEGROES . . . AYM GOSPEL CHA-CHA 1
IN THE QUARTER OF THE NEGROES . . . AYM GOSPEL CHA-CHA 13
WHERE THE SHADOWS OF THE NEGROES . AYM GOSPEL CHA-CHA 19
IN THE QUARTER OF THE NEGROES ¢ ¢ ¢ ¢ ¢ . . . . AYM HORN OF PLENTY 26
IN THE QUARTER OF THE NEGROES, . . AYM HORN OF PLENTY 44
SHADOW OF THE NEGROES . . . . AYM HORN OF PLENTY 60
IN THE SHADOW OF THE NEGROES - . . AYM HORN OF PLENTY 62
MEANS TOO MANY NEGROES . . . . . . AYM HORN OF PLENTY 64
EVEN FOR THE NEGROES - . . . . . . AYM HORN OF PLENTY 65
THE ONLY NEGROES IN THE BLOCK . . . AYM HORN OF PLENTY 79
IN THE QUARTER OF THE NEGROES . . . AYM IS IT TRUE? 43
NEGROES . . . . AYM IS IT TRUE? 44
NEGROES . . . . AYM IS IT TRUE? 45
IS IT TRUE THAT NEGROES - ? . . . . AYM IS IT TRUE? 55
IN THE NEGROES OF THE QUARTER . . . AYM JAZZTET MUTED 1
IN THE QUARTER OF THE NEGROES . . . AYM JAZZTET MUTED 3
IN THE QUARTER OF THE NEGROES . . . AYM JAZZTET MUTED 6
IN THE QUARTER OF THE NEGROES . . . AYM JAZZTET MUTED 17
TO THE QUARTER OF THE NEGROES . . . AYM ODE TO DINAH 1
IN THE QUARTER OF THE NEGROES . . . AYM ODE TO DINAH 110
TO THIS QUARTER OF THE NEGROES . . AYM ODE TO DINAH 18
QUARTER OF THE NEGROES . . . . . . AYM ODE TO DINAH 41
IN THE QUARTER OF THE NEGROES . . . AYM ODE TO DINAH 49
IN THE QUARTER OF THE NEGROES: . . AYM RIDE, RED, RIDE 3
IN THE QUARTER OF THE NEGROES . . . AYM RIDE, RED, RIDE 10
IN THE QUARTER OF THE NEGROES . . . AYM RIDE, RED, RIDE 29
IN THE QUARTER OF THE NEGROES . . . AYM SHADES OF PIG 1
IN THE QUARTER OF THE NEGROES . . . AYM SHADES OF PIG 7
WHERE NEGROES SING SO WELL . . . . AYM SHADES OF PIG 8
NEGROES SING SO WELL . . . . AYM SHADES OF PIG 9
IN THE QUARTER OF THE NEGROES . . . AYM SHADES OF PIG 21
IN THE QUARTER OF THE NEGROES . . . AYM SHOW FARE PLESE 5
IN THE QUARTER OF THE NEGROES . . . AYM SHOW FARE PLESE 17
DID YOU EVER SEE TEN NEGROES . . . AYM SHOW FARE PLESE 20
WHERE ENTRANCE TO NEGROES, ... PL BIBLE BELT 6
IN THE QUARTER OF THE NEGROES . . . PL CULTURAL EXCHNG 1
IN THE QUARTER OF THE NEGROES . . . PL CULTURAL EXCHNG 14
DREAMING THAT THE NEGROES . . . . . PL CULTURAL EXCHNG 38
WEALTHY NEGROES HAVE WHITE SERVANTS, PL CULTURAL EXCHNG 48
FIFTY NEGROES: . . . . PL LENOX AVE. BAR 6
NEGROES, ... PL WARNING 1

NEGRO'S 4

THE LAND THAT'S MINE - THE POOR MAN'S, INDIAN'S, NEGRO'S. . . . . ANS LET AMERICA BE 65
A NEGRO'S GOT NO BUSINESS ON THE FREEDOM TRACK! . . . . SP FREEDOM TRAIN 40

THAT LITTLE NEGRO'S MARRIED AND GOT A KID.	SP SISTER	1
FOR A NEGRO'S BONES.	SP THE SOUTH	8

NEHRU 2

BY IMPRISONING NEHRU	JC FREEDOM	5
NEHRU SAID, BEFORE HE WENT TO JAIL,	JC JIM CROW'S LAST	15

NEIGH 2

HEY NINNY NEIGH!	SH SHAKESPEARE	1
HEY NINNY NEIGH	SH SHAKESPEARE	5

NEIGHBOR 1

LOVE THY NEIGHBOR AS THYSELF	AYM HORN OF PLENTY	85

NEIGHBORHOOD 2

INTO A NEIGHBORHOOD	OWT RESTRICTIVE	2
TO THE NEIGHBORHOOD CORNER,	PL CROWNS GARLANDS	9

NEIGHBORHOOD'S 1

NEIGHBORHOOD'S CLEAN,	PL LITTLE SNG HOUS	9

NEIGHBORHOOD 1

THE WHOLE NEIGHBORHOOD	PL LITTLE SNG HOUS	23

NEIGHBORS 4

EXCEPT THE NEIGHBORS	SP S-SSS-SS-SH!	5
BUT THE NEIGHBORS	SP S-SSS-SS-SH!	12
THE NEIGHBORS -	SP S-SSS-SS-SH!	17
OUR NEIGHBORS ALL COLORED ARE.	PL LITTLE SNG HOUS	19

NEITHER 15

THAT I CAN NEITHER HEAR NOR FEEL NOR SEE,	DK BEGGAR BOY	2
THAT I CAN NEITHER KNOW NOR UNDERSTAND	DK BEGGAR BOY	3
NEITHER ONE NOR THE OTHER -	JC BLD SAM SOLOMON	34
NEITHER DOES THE SUN.	OWT RESTRICTIVE	8
NEITHER BULLET NOR GUN -	OWT TOO BLUE	15
BEING NEITHER WHITE NOR BLACK?	SP CROSS	12
NEITHER DOES I TREAT YOU GOOD.	SP EARLY EVENING	18
THERE IS NEITHER LIGHT	SP END	7
NEITHER HAD NOBODY DIED.	SP LATE LAST NIGHT	4
I SAID, NEITHER AM I.	SP MADAM RENT MAN	29
ON NEITHER SIDE.	SP MIDNIGHT RAFFLE	16
NAW, HE AIN'T NEITHER.	SP NEIGHBOR	13
NEITHER IN NEWARK ON THE WAY.	SP NOT A MOVIE	11
NEITHER TRUTH NOR LIE.	SP RAILROAD AVENUE	22
NEITHER ORGAN	SP TESTIMONIAL	6

NEON 5

ROSE OF NEON DARKNESS,	FW CHIPPY	1
A NEON ROSE	FW MONTMARTRE	2
TAKE THE NEON LIGHTS AND MAKE A CROWN,	SP JUKE BOX LOVE	3
IN NEON TOMBS THE MUSIC	AYM JAZZTET MUTED	10
IN THIS NEON	PL LENOX AVE. BAR	11

NEST 1

A BLUE BIRD IN A NEST.	DK SAILOR	8

NEVER 75

AND HAVE NEVER SEEN THE SEAS.	WB A FAREWELL	8
AIN'T NEVER BEEN UNKIND.	FC BLACK GAL	4
YET I AIN'T NEVER BEEN NO BAD ONE.	FC BLACK GAL	13
CAUSE HE NEVER DOES COME HOME.	FC GYPSY MAN	2
HE NEVER DOES COME HOME.	FC GYPSY MAN	4
THAT NEVER ENDS.	OLD TOWER	4
WELL, AIN'T NEVER DONE IT, BUT FOR TO KEEP BODY AND SOUL	NM BROKE	29
NEVER DONE NO WRONG.	DK PO' BOY BLUES	8
NEVER DONE NO WRONG.	DK PO' BOY BLUES	10
I WISH I'D NEVER BEEN BORN.	DK PO' BOY BLUES	24
MIGHT NEVER RISE NO MO'.	DK SONG BANJO DANC	13
MIGHT NEVER RISE NO MO' -	DK SONG BANJO DANC	15
MIGHT NEVER DANCE NO MO'.	DK SONG BANJO DANC	19
MIGHT NEVER RISE NO MO'.	DK SONG BANJO DANC	27
I NEVER KNOWED HOW	DK WIDE RIVER	11
NEVER SAW THE HIGH SHERIFF'S GUN	ANS BLD OZZIE POWEL	15
THEY NEVER SAW THE HIGH SHERIFF'S EYES	ANS BLD OZZIE POWEL	19
(AMERICA NEVER WAS AMERICA TO ME.)	ANS LET AMERICA BE	5
WHERE NEVER KINGS CONNIVE NOR TYRANTS SCHEME	ANS LET AMERICA BE	8
(IT NEVER WAS AMERICA TO ME.)	ANS LET AMERICA BE	10
(THERE'S NEVER BEEN EQUALITY FOR ME,	ANS LET AMERICA BE	15
I AM THE MAN WHO NEVER GOT AHEAD,	ANS LET AMERICA BE	37
THE LAND THAT NEVER HAS BEEN YET -	ANS LET AMERICA BE	63
AMERICA NEVER WAS AMERICA TO ME,	ANS LET AMERICA BE	77
I MUST NEVER DO THAT AGAIN.	ANS SONG OF SPAIN	78
NEVER MIND! DON'T BOTHER.	SH BLD PAWNBROKER	4
AND YOU NEVER WOULD SEE ME.	SH DECLARATION	4
YOU NEVER WOULD	SH DECLARATION	6
BUT YOU'LL NEVER, PRETTY MAMA,	SH FREE MAN	7
I NEVER DID LIKE THE INSTALLMENT PLAN	SH PAY DAY	14
NEGROES NEVER VOTED BUT	JC BLD SAM SOLOMON	7
THE FACT WE NEVER VOTED	JC BLD SAM SOLOMON	13
YOU'LL NEVER KILL ME!	JC FREEDOM	14
THAT NEVER COME.	FW JAIME	4
THAT WILL NEVER BE.	FW JAIME	8
I'D NEVER BEEN	LHR CONSERVATORY	12
NEVER TO KILL -	LHR DEAR LVLY DEATH	3
NEVER TO AGREE.	LHR POET TO BIGOT	6
HE KNOWS THAT AUNT SUE NEVER GOT HER STORIES	SP AUNTSUE'S STORI	19
NEVER SEEN YOU BEFORE -	SP BLD FORTUNE TEL	2
HE'LL NEVER HYPE	SP DEAD IN THERE	8
HE'LL NEVER LAY A	SP DEAD IN THERE	12
I'LL NEVER GO TO FRANCE,	SP DEFERRED	23
I AIN'T NEVER	SP DEFERRED	46
WHERE THERE NEVER WAS NO JIM CROW SIGNS NOWHERE,	SP FREEDOM TRAIN	54
NEVER GONNA BOTHER ME.	SP HARD DADDY	12
NEVER LOVE A MAN.	SP LAMENT OVER LOV	2
NEVER LOVE A MAN.	SP LAMENT OVER LOV	4
I NEVER FELT SO LONESOME	SP LITTLE OLD LETT	11
I NEVER SEEN HIM BEFORE.	SP MADAM WRONG VIS	2
AND NEVER TAKING.	SP MADAM MIGHT-HAV	16
NEVER KNEW DUSABLE,	SP MIGRANT	12
AND NEVER OWN NO PARTS	SP NEW YORKERS	10
BE NEVER.	SP NO REGRETS	8
I NEVER KNEW	SP PARADE	23
I NEVER KNEW!	SP PARADE	27
AND WISH SHE'D NEVER BEEN BORN?	SP REVERIE HARLEM	8
THAT NEVER LIFTS ITS HEAD	SP TROUBLED WOMAN	11
I'LL NEVER DRY THESE TEARS.	SP WIDOW WOMAN	18
YET YOU NEVER CAN TELL WHEN A	SP WIDOW WOMAN	23
YOUR THIRD-FLOOR TENANT'S NEVER HOME.	AYM ASK YOUR MAMA	9
I NEVER SEEN IT.	AYM ASK YOUR MAMA	25
AND THE WHITE GOD NEVER GOES	AYM BLUES IN STEREO	16
NEVER MISSED A BITE	AYM ODE TO DINAH	130
(AND I NEVER HAD A HIP BOOT ON)	AYM SHADES OF PIG	33
(AND I NEVER HAD THAT MUCH HAIR)	AYM SHADES OF PIG	36
(AND I NEVER HAD A DIAMOND	AYM SHADES OF PIG	38
(AND AIN'T NEVER HAD A BLACK HOUSE)	AYM SHADES OF PIG	42
AND NEVER CAME BACK HOME AT ALL	PL BIRMINGHAM SUND	3
THE MISSIONARIES NEVER TAUGHT CHINESE	PL BIRMINGHAM SUND	21
I AIN'T NEVER SEEN NOBODY	PL FLORIDA WORKERS	17
WE REMEMBER THE JOB WE NEVER HAD,	PL HARLEM	12
NEVER COULD GET,	PL HARLEM	13
WHAT I HAVE NEVER FOUND	PL STOKELY MALCOLM	2
AND NEVER UP INSTEAD.	PL VARI-COLORED	16

NEVERMORE 1

TO THE NEVERMORE -	FW SAILING DATE	14

NEVER-GET-UP-NO-MORE 1

THAT NEVER-GET-UP-NO-MORE	FW GRAVE YARD	4

NEW 43

UNTIL THE NEW DAWN,	WB SUMMER NIGHT	22
O' GETTIN' A NEW WINTER COAT, OR HAVIN' THAT OLD ONE CLEANED.	NM BROKE	40
SHE BOUGHT A NEW HAT LAST WEEK AND COME SENDIN' ME THE BILL.	NM BROKE	49
WITH HIS FACE FULL OF LIGHT AND FAITH, CONFIDENT THAT A NEW WORLD HAS	NM COLORED SL MOOD	9
JUST LIKE NEW.	DK DRESSED UP	2
I BOUGHT A NEW HAT,	DK DRESSED UP	5
I GOT NEW SHOES -	DK DRESSED UP	9
NEW WORDS ARE FORMED,	ANS A NEW SONG	38
A NEW DREAM FLAMES	ANS A NEW SONG	53
50-VOICES: WHEN THE EARTH IS NEW,	ANS CHANT MAY DAY	30
THE SONG OF THE NEW LIFE TRIUMPHANT	ANS KIDS WHO DIE	50
LET US NEW LESSONS LEARN,	ANS OPEN LETTER	32
NEW LIFE-WAYS MAKE,	ANS OPEN LETTER	34
TUSKEGEE WITH A NEW FLAG ON THE TOWER!	ANS OPEN LETTER	43
AND SEE WHAT COUNT BASIE'S PLAYING NEW.	SH BED TIME	2
OUR SYMBOL OF NEW LIBERTIES.	JC TO CAPTAIN MULZ	42
HE, TOO, A SYMBOL OF NEW LIBERTIES.	JC TO CAPTAIN MULZ	46
THAT GUIDE US TOWARD THE HARBOR OF THE NEW WORLD	JC TO CAPTAIN MULZ	54
STRONG AS THE SHOOTS OF A NEW PLANT,	FW EARTH SONG	8
BRINGS NEW BIRTH.	FW GIRL	13
THERE'S A NEW YOUNG MOON	FW NEW MOON	1
TO SEEK A NEW BROWN LOVE.	SP A BLACK PIERROT	15
THE NEW STRIDE	SP AFRICA	14
THEN YOU KNOW A NEW DAY'S	SP BLACK MARIA	16
AND A NEW DAY,	SP BLACK MARIA	20
YES, A NEW DAY'S	SP BLACK MARIA	21
TILL YOU FIX THIS HOUSE UP NEW.	SP BLD LANDLORD	12
I'M GONNA BUY TWO NEW SUITS	SP DEFERRED	30
TWO NEW SUITS AN'	SP ELEVATOR BOY	12
SLAVE MEN AND SLAVE MASTERS, ALL NEW -	SP FREEDOM'S PLOW	33
TO A NEW WORLD, AMERICA!	SP FREEDOM'S PLOW	34
SEATTLE, NEW ORLEANS,	SP FREEDOM'S PLOW	87
THE PLOW PLOWED A NEW FURROW	SP FREEDOM'S PLOW	192
IN BUSES MARKED NEW YORK	SP GOOD MORNING	12
DIPLOMA IN ITS NEW FRAME:	SP GRADUATION	10

PUTS FORTH NEW LIFE AGAIN. . . . . SP IN TIME SILVER 3
NEW LEAVES TO SING . . . . . . SP IN TIME SILVER 16
ARE NEW. . . . . SP IN TIME SILVER 24
WENT DOWN TO NEW ORLEANS, AND I'VE SEEN ITS MUDDY . . . . SP NEGRO SPEAKS OF 9
WHEN THE KIDS LOOK ALL NEW . . . . SP PASSING 7
(I HEAR NEW YORK, TOO.) ME - WHO? SP THEME FOR ENG B 20
SOAKING UP A NEW HOUSE. . . . . . . SP WINE-O 6
FIRST GRADE IN NEW ORLEANS . . . . AYM BIRD IN ORBIT 9
NEW JERSEY HIGH SCHOOL! . . . . . . AYM BIRD IN ORBIT 78
BUT I GOT TO GET A NEW ANTENNA, LORD - . . . . AYM BLUES IN STEREO 36
WESTPORT AND NEW CANAAN . . . . . . AYM HORN OF PLENTY 61
NEW AND SHINY . . . . AYM HORN OF PLENTY 33
FOR CINQUE SAYING, "RUN A NEW FLAG UP THE MAST." . . . . PL FINAL CALL 21
AND THERE'S A NEW TAX ON CIGARETTES - . . . . PL HARLEM 11

NEWARK 1
NEITHER IN NEWARK ON THE WAY. . . . SP NOT A MOVIE 11

NEWER 1
OF A NEWER DAY. . . . . JC TO CAPTAIN MULZ 70

NEWLY 1
A CLEAN BRIGHT SPITOON ALL NEWLY POLISHED, - . . . . FC BRASS SPITOONS 38

NEWS 3
CAN'T YOU BRING NO BETTER NEWS? . . SP HARD DADDY 6
THE DAILY NEWS . . . . SP LIKEWISE 7
IN THE DAILY NEWS. . . . . PL MOTHER IN WAR 10

NEW-ORLEANS 1
AT HARLAN, RICHMOND, GASTONIA, ATLANTA, NEW-ORLEANS; . . . . . ANS OPEN LETTER 16

NEXT 5
NEXT TIME SHE MAKES ME SORE. . . . FC EVIL WOMAN 4
BUT I'LL HAVE MO' SENSE NEXT TIME. . FC GYPSY MAN 18
NEXT TIME A MAN COMES NEAR ME . . . SP CORA 3
NEXT DAY . . . . SP GONE BOY 5
NEXT THING YOU KNOW. . . . . PL LITTLE SNG HOUS 18

NIAGARA 9
ORIGINAL NIAGARA N.A.A.C.P. . . . . AYM BIRD IN ORBIT 19
AND NIAGARA FALLS IS FROZEN ¢ ¢ ¢ ¢ ¢ ¢ ¢ . . . . AYM HORN OF PLENTY 28
FOR NIAGARA FALLS IS FROZEN . . . . AYM ODE TO DINAH 11
WHEN NIAGARA FALLS IS FROZEN . . . AYM ODE TO DINAH 23
FROM THE COLD THAT MAKES NIAGARA . AYM ODE TO DINAH 25
AND THE ROAR OF NIAGARA . . . . . . AYM ODE TO DINAH 37
NIAGARA OF THE INDIANS! . . . . . . AYM ODE TO DINAH 46
NIAGARA OF THE CONGO! . . . . AYM ODE TO DINAH 47
WHILE NIAGARA FALLS IS FROZEN. . . AYM ODE TO DINAH 68

NIBBLED 1
CRUMBLES AS IT'S NIBBLED . . . . . AYM ODE TO DINAH 14

NICE 4
JUST ONLY PROVIDIN' DE BOSS MAN IS NICE!" . . . . NM BROKE 9
AT FIRST THEY ARE NICE TO HIM. . . FW MIGRATION 5
IT ISN'T NICE TO BE NAKED? . . . . SP MARCH MOON 10
TO GET A NICE HOME . . . . PL LITTLE SNG HOUS 3

NICHOLAS 1
THROUGH A PARK, THEN I CROSS ST. NICHOLAS. . . . . SP THEME FOR ENG B 12

NICKEL 9
A NICKEL. . . . . FC BRASS SPITOONS 12
A NICKEL. . . . . FC BRASS SPITOONS 17
THERE'S BEEN AN EAGLE ON A NICKEL. SP FACT 1
I PUT MY NICKEL . . . . SP MIDNIGHT RAFFLE 1
I LOST MY NICKEL. . . . . SP MIDNIGHT RAFFLE 5
WHEN I DROPPED THAT NICKEL . . . . SP MIDNIGHT RAFFLE 9
VINCT FRANCS NICKEL DIME . . . . . AYM ASK YOUR MAMA 46
WHERE A NICKEL COSTS A DIME. . . . PL PRIME 2
WHERE A NICKEL COSTS A DIME. . . . PL PRIME 11

NICKLE 1
TWO DIMES AND A NICKLE ONLY . . . . SP TOMORROW 3

NIGGER 15
THAT IN THIS NIGGER PLACE. . . . . OLD AESTHETE HARLEM 2
NIGGER! NIGGER! NIGGER! . . . . . . NM BLACK CLWN POEM 51
NIGGER! NIGGER! NIGGER! . . . . . . NM BLACK CLWN POEM 51
NIGGER! NIGGER! NIGGER! . . . . . . NM BLACK CLWN POEM 51
AND I'M STILL JUST A "NIGGER" IN AMERICA TONIGHT. . . . . NM COLORED SL POEM 47
AND CALL HIM "NIGGER." . . . . . . FW MIGRATION 7
A NIGGER COMES HOME FROM WORK: . . OWT MAN INTO MEN 1
OF NIGGER WENCHES . . . . SP MULATTO 13
A NIGGER NIGHT. . . . . SP MULATTO 23
A NIGGER JOY. . . . . SP MULATTO 24
A NIGGER NIGHT. . . . . SP MULATTO 41
A NIGGER JOY. . . . . SP MULATTO 42
CHRIST IS A NIGGER. . . . . PL CHRIST IN ALA. 1
NIGGER CHRIST . . . . PL CHRIST IN ALA. 12
A KLANSMAN SAID, "NIGGER, ... PL KU KLUX 17

NIGGERS 3
NIGGERS AIN'T MY BROTHER. . . . . . SP MULATTO 28
NIGGERS AIN'T MY BROTHER. . . . . . SP MULATTO 30
IN THE SECTION OF THE NIGGERS . . . PL PRIME 10

NIGH 1
THAT MIGHTY NIGH DROVE ME WILD! . . SH LOVE AGAIN BLUS 12

NIGHT 131
IT IS NIGHT. . . . . WB AFRAID 5
HAUNTS ME NIGHT AND DAY. . . . . . WB BLUES FANTASY 12
AND THE WAN NIGHT WORE AWAY. . . . WB CABARET 4
OF THE HARLEM NIGHT . . . . WB SUMMER NIGHT 2
AND THE NIGHT BECOMES . . . . WB SUMMER NIGHT 8
WEARY AS THE TIRED NIGHT. . . . . . WB SUMMER NIGHT 12
IN THE NIGHT . . . . WB TO LITTLE LOVER 3
JUNGLE NIGHT. . . . . WB TO MIDNIGHT NAN 6
NIGHT BLACK BOY. . . . . WB TO MIDNIGHT NAN 14
THAT NIGHT HE GOT KILT . . . . . . FC DEATH DO DIRTY 21
EVER NIGHT. . . . . FC EVIL WOMAN 8
I ASKED HER ONE NIGHT . . . . FC NEW CABARET GRL 7
ALL NIGHT LONG. . . . . FC SATURDAY NIGHT 24
COMES HOME AT NIGHT. - . . . . . . FC WORKIN' MAN 3
ALL NIGHT IN BED . . . . OLD THE CONSUMPTIVE 5
SO I'M HUSTLIN' IN THE NIGHT. . . . NM BIG-TIMER POEM 12
SO I WENT DOWN TOWN TO A HOTEL WHERE I USED TO WORK AT NIGHT. . . . . NM BROKE 44
YOU STILL BAKES BISCUITS? FRIED CHICKEN EVERY NIGHT? IS THAT TRUE? . . . . NM BROKE 73
LAST NIGHT IN A DREAM MY BROTHER CAME TO ME . . . . NM COLORED SL POEM 13
THEN HIS DARK FACE SMILED AT ME IN THE NIGHT - . . . . NM COLORED SL POEM 39
WHEN THE NIGHT IS A VAST SOFTNESS DK AFTR MNY SPRNGS 3
THE RAIN PLAYS A LITTLE SLEEP-SONG ON OUR ROOF AT NIGHT - . . . . . DK APRIL RAIN SONG 6
WINDING THE NIGHT. . . . . DK LULLABY 10
KISSING THE NIGHT. . . . . DK LULLABY 18
NIGHT BLACK BABY. . . . . DK LULLABY 20
NIGHT STARS. . . . . DK LULLABY 23
I BEEN BLUE ALL NIGHT LONG. . . . . DK NIGHT AND MORN 12
TO A NIGHT WITHOUT STARS . . . . . DK QUIET GIRL 2
YOU WHO ARE A CHILD OF NIGHT. . . . DK SONG 4
THE SUN'S GOING DOWN THIS VERY NIGHT - . . . . DK SONG BANJO DANC 14
THE SUN'S GOING DOWN THIS VERY NIGHT - . . . . DK SONG BANJO DANC 26
WE ARE NOT AFRAID OF NIGHT. . . . . DK WALKERS WITH 3
THE NIGHT WAS YOUNG - . . . . SH DEATH IN HARLEM 3
WHEN THE NIGHT IS YOUNG - . . . . . SH DEATH IN HARLEM 25
AND NIGHT LIKE A REEFER-MAN . . . . SH DEATH IN HARLEM 135
THEN WHIP 'EM ALL NIGHT LONG. . . . SH HEY-HEY BLUES 8
THEN WHIP 'EM ALL NIGHT LONG. . . . SH HEY-HEY BLUES 10
IT COME LAST NIGHT. . . . . SH LETTER 2
AS THE GENTLE NIGHT . . . . JC ME AND MY SONG 2
AS THE KIND AND QUIET NIGHT . . . . JC ME AND MY SONG 4
AS THE BLACK NIGHT . . . . JC ME AND MY SONG 21
AS THE BLACK NIGHT . . . . JC ME AND MY SONG 23
YOU REFLECT NO STARS BY NIGHT. . . JC THE BITTER RIVR 24
IN THE NIGHT . . . . FW BIRTH 8
STEALING FROM THE NIGHT . . . . . . FW DANCERS 1
DEATH IN THE NIGHT. . . . . FW FRAGMENTS 3
IN THE LONELY NIGHT . . . . FW LITTLE SONG 2
CUT THE COP THAT NIGHT. . . . . . . OWT BLD MARGE POLIT 4
UP ALL NIGHT! . . . . OWT BLD MARGE POLIT 51
NIGHT SCHOOL! . . . . OWT JITNEY 30
WHERE SINGING BLACK BOYS DANCE AND PLAY EACH NIGHT . . . . OWT JUICE JOINT 2
O, VELDT AT NIGHT! . . . . OWT NEGRO SERVANT 5
O, SAXOPHONES AT NIGHT! . . . . . . OWT NEGRO SERVANT 13
LATE AT NIGHT . . . . OWT RAID 1
SO I CREPT AWAY INTO THE NIGHT . . SP A BLACK PIERROT 3
AND THE NIGHT WAS BLACK, TOO. . . . SP A BLACK PIERROT 4
TO A NIGHT WITHOUT STARS . . . . . SP ARDELLA 7
TO SMASH THIS NIGHT. . . . . SP AS I GREW OLDER 29
WALKING IN THE DEWY NIGHT. . . . . SP AUNTSUE'S STORI 9
OF A SUMMER NIGHT . . . . SP AUNTSUE'S STORI 24
IN THE SHADOW NIGHT . . . . SP CHORD 2
IN A MELODY NIGHT . . . . SP COLLEGE FORMAL 3
A NIGHT FUNERAL . . . . SP DEAD IN THERE 2
BUT NIGHT SCHOOLS TEACH FRENCH. . . SP DEFERRED 24
LAST NIGHT I DREAMT . . . . SP DREAM 1
WHILE NIGHT COMES ON GENTLY. . . . SP DREAM VARIATION 7
NIGHT COMING TENDERLY . . . . SP DREAM VARIATION 16
AWAKE ALL NIGHT WITH LOVING . . . . SP FIRED 1
NIGHT . . . . SP FULFILMENT 14
OUT ALL NIGHT . . . . SP GONE BOY 3
LET US ROAM THE NIGHT TOGETHER . . SP HARLEM NIGHT SO 2
NIGHT SKY IS BLUE. . . . . SP HARLEM NIGHT SO 8
LET US ROAM THE NIGHT TOGETHER . . SP HARLEM NIGHT SO 15
I COULD TAKE THE HARLEM NIGHT . . . SP JUKE BOX LOVE 1
LATE LAST NIGHT I . . . . SP LATE LAST NIGHT 1

CLOSE UP TIGHT THAT NIGHT. . . . . SP LIKEWISE 11
BUT THE PEOPLE OF THE NIGHT . . . . SP LIVE LET LIVE 2
DAY, NIGHT. . . . . SP LONG TRIP 7
NIGHT, DAY. . . . . SP LONG TRIP 8
CAME BACK HOME LAST NIGHT. . . . . SP LOVER'S RETURN 2
I SAID, LAST NIGHT. . . . . SP MADAM NUMBER WR 9
BEFORE NIGHT. . . . . SP MADAM WRONG VIS 16
IN THE RAFFLE OF THE NIGHT. . . . . SP MIDNIGHT RAFFLE 2
OF THE JAZZ-TUNED NIGHT. . . . . . SP MIDNIGHT DANCER 2
'TWAS THE NIGHT BEFO' CHRISTMAS . . SP MIDWINTER BLUES 5
AT NIGHT MY WISHING STAR. . . . . . SP MISS BLUES'ES 8
I WAS SO SICK LAST NIGHT I . . . . SP MORNING AFTER 1
SO SICK LAST NIGHT I . . . . SP MORNING AFTER 3
HAD A DREAM LAST NIGHT I . . . . . SP MORNING AFTER 7
I DREMPT LAST NIGHT I . . . . SP MORNING AFTER 9
THE SOUTHERN NIGHT . . . . SP MULATTO 8
THE SCENT OF PINE WOOD STINGS THE
SOFT NIGHT AIR. . . . . SP MULATTO 18
A NIGGER NIGHT. . . . . SP MULATTO 23
THE SOUTHERN NIGHT IS FULL OF STARS, SP MULATTO 31
GIT ON BACK THERE IN THE NIGHT. . . SP MULATTO 37
A NIGGER NIGHT. . . . . SP MULATTO 41
THE NIGHT IS BEAUTIFUL. . . . . . . SP MY PEOPLE 1
NIGHT AND DAY. . . . . SP MYSTERY 4
OFFERING: A NIGHT WITH ME, HONEY. SP NATCHA 3
A LONG, SWEET NIGHT WITH ME. . . . SP NATCHA 4
A LONG, DREAM NIGHT WITH ME. . . . SP NATCHA 7
BLACK AS THE NIGHT IS BLACK. . . . SP NEGRO 2
BLACK AS THE NIGHT IS BLACK. . . . SP NEGRO 18
NIGHT OF THE TWO MOONS . . . . . . SP NIGHT FOUR SONG 1
NIGHT FUNERAL . . . . SP NIGHT FUNERAL 1
NIGHT OF THE DAY BEFORE YESTERDAY SP NIGHT FOUR SONG 3
NIGHT OF THE FOUR SONGS UNSUNG: . . SP NIGHT FOUR SONG 5
NIGHT FUNERAL . . . . SP NIGHT FUNERAL 9
NIGHT FUNERAL . . . . SP NIGHT FUNERAL 17
NIGHT FUNERAL . . . . SP NIGHT FUNERAL 25
NIGHT FUNERAL . . . . SP NIGHT FUNERAL 45
NOON TILL NIGHT . . . . SP PARADE 22
O, LITTLE BREATH OF OBLIVION THAT IS
NIGHT. . . . . SP STARS 2
THAT IS NIGHT. . . . . SP STARS 9
MAKIN' ROUNDS AT NIGHT. . . . . . . SP STREET SONG 4
NIGHT WILL PULL ITS SLACK TAUT . . SP SUMMER EVENING 25
IN A GREAT . . . BIG . . . NIGHT. SP SYLVESTER'S BED 28
LOOK AT MY FACE - DARK AS THE NIGHT
- . . . . SP THE NEGRO MOTHE 5
I HAD NOTHING, BACK THERE IN THE
NIGHT. . . . . SP THE NEGRO MOTHE 24
OUT OF THE DARKNESS, THE IGNORANCE,
THE NIGHT. . . . . SP THE NEGRO MOTHE 40
DOWN ON LENOX AVENUE THE OTHER NIGHT SP THE WEARY BLUES 4
AND FAR INTO THE NIGHT HE CROONED
THAT TUNE. . . . . SP THE WEARY BLUES 31
A QUEEN FROM SOME TIME-DEAD EGYPTIAN
NIGHT . . . . SP WHEN SUE WEARS 7
NIGHT IN A SEKOU TOURE CAP . . . . AYM ASK YOUR MAMA 61
AND THE NIGHT MIGHT BE ASTONISHED AYM BLUES IN STEREO 19
NIGHT EACH NIGHT COMES NIGHTLY . . AYM BLUES IN STEREO 22
NIGHT EACH NIGHT COMES NIGHTLY . . AYM BLUES IN STEREO 22
IN CURRENT DEMOCRATIC NIGHT. . . . PL DINNER GUEST ME 11
UNTIL LAST NIGHT. . . . . PL GHOSTS OF 1619 11
LAST NIGHT? . . . . PL GHOSTS OF 1619 12
DARK NIGHT . . . . PL OPPRESSION 7

NIGHTIME 1
DAYTIME OR NIGHTIME JOB. . . . . . PL JUNIOR ADDICT 32

NIGHTLY 1
NIGHT EACH NIGHT COMES NIGHTLY . . AYM BLUES IN STEREO 22

NIGHTMARE 1
A NIGHTMARE DREAM: . . . . SP NIGHTMARE BOOGE 5

NIGHTMARES 2
DREAMS AND NIGHTMARES! . . . . . . PL CULTURAL EXCHNG 36
NIGHTMARES, DREAMS, OH! . . . . . . PL CULTURAL EXCHNG 37

NIGHTNESS 1
OF THY NIGHTNESS. . . . . WB POEM 22

NIGHTS 4
OF TOO MANY NIGHTS OF LOVE . . . . WB SOLEDAD 3
BEFORE THE HOT NIGHTS OF SUMMER . . SH YOUNG NEGRO GRL 8
SUMMER NIGHTS ON THE FRONT PORCH . SP AUNTSUE'S STORI 3
WILD, WHITE NIGHTS. . . . . SP PORT TOWN 12

NIGHT-BIRD 2
BUT FOR A WISE NIGHT-BIRD . . . . . SH DEATH IN HARLEM 4
FOR AN OLD NIGHT-BIRD. . . . . . . SH DEATH IN HARLEM 26

NIGHT-DARK 2
NIGHT-DARK GIRL OF THE SWAYING HIPS? WB NUDE YOUNG DANC 6
PLAY YOUR GUITARS, GRINNING
NIGHT-DARK BOYS. . . . . OWT JUICE JOINT 17

NIGHT-GONE 1
A NIGHT-GONE THING. . . . . OK YOUTH 5

NIGHT-PEOPLE 1
BUT THE NIGHT-PEOPLE CRIED. . . . . FW POPPY FLOWER 4

NIGHT-TIME'S 1
NIGHT-TIME'S COMIN' DOWN. . . . . . FC A RUINED GAL 12

NIGHT-TIME 1
AND NIGHT-TIME DRIVES ME WILD. . . SP MISS BLUES'ES 12

NIGHT-VEILED 1
A NIGHT-VEILED GIRL . . . . SP DANSE AFRICAINE 7

NILE 1
I LOOKED UPON THE NILE AND RAISED
THE PYRAMIDS ABOVE IT. . . . . . SP NEGRO SPEAKS OF 7

NINA 1
MILES AND ELLA AND MISS NINA $ $ $
$ $ $ $ . . . . AYM HORN OF PLENTY 9

NINE 3
NINE OLD MEN IN WASHINGTON, ... ANS BLD OZZIE POWEL 13
NINE OLD MEN SO RICH AND WISE, . . . ANS BLD OZZIE POWEL 17
BUT NINE BLACK BOYS KNOW FULL WELL. ANS BLD OZZIE POWEL 21

NINNY 2
HEY NINNY NEIGH! . . . . SH SHAKESPEARE 1
HEY NINNY NEIGH . . . . SH SHAKESPEARE 5

NIXON 1
DID I VOTE FOR NIXON? . . . . AYM BIRD IN ORBIT 16

NKRUMAH 1
NKRUMAH RED! . . . . AYM BIRD IN ORBIT 74

NO 271
NO, MAKE IT . . . . WB CAT AND SAXOPHN 5
WOULDN'T NO GOOD FELLOW . . . . . . WB TO MIDNIGHT NAN 3
WOULDN'T NO GOOD FELLOW . . . . . . WB TO MIDNIGHT NAN 19
CAUSE I AIN'T GOT NO FRIEND. . . . FC A RUINED GAL 10
AIN'T CUT HIM WID NO RAZOR. . . . . FC BLACK GAL 3
YET I AIN'T NEVER BEEN NO BAD ONE. FC BLACK GAL 13
I CAN'T HAVE NO WOMAN'S . . . . . . FC EVIL WOMAN 9
SHO CAN'T FIND NO EASE. . . . . . . FC GYPSY MAN 24
DON'T YOU FOOL WID NO MEN CAUSE . . FC LISTEN HERE 17
NO OTHER GAL'S GOT A CHANCE. . . . FC MINNIE SINGS 10
NO, LORD! . . . . FC MOAN 12
AND THERE IS NO MUSIC AT ALL . . . FC SPORT 9
AND THE OTHER HAS NO NAME . . . . . OLD TWO THINGS 8
IN NO SINGLE MOUTH THE SAME. . . . OLD TWO THINGS 10
WITH NO GAIN - . . . . NM BLACK CLWN POEM 19
NO LAND, NO HOUSE, NO JOB. . . . . NM BLACK CLWN POEM 34
NO LAND, NO HOUSE, NO JOB. . . . . NM BLACK CLWN POEM 34
NO LAND, NO HOUSE, NO JOB. . . . . NM BLACK CLWN POEM 34
NO PLACE TO GO. . . . . NM BLACK CLWN POEM 35
NO SCHOOLS, NO WORK - . . . . NM BLACK CLWN POEM 39
NO SCHOOLS, NO WORK - . . . . NM BLACK CLWN POEM 39
BUT NO! NOT FOREVER . . . . NM BLACK CLWN POEM 59
UP AND DOWN, AND THEY JUST AIN'T NO
JOBS IN THIS MAN'S TOWN. . . . . NM BROKE 3
TALKIN' 'BOUT "WE'LL WORK FOR 50¢ A
DAY, IF WE CAN'T GET NO MO'." . NM BROKE 7
YOU ALL OUT THERE LAUGHIN', BUT THAT
AIN'T NO JOKE - . . . . NM BROKE 10
SO I SAY, "MISTER, I AIN'T NO
SWEEPIN' MACHINE." . . . . NM BROKE 16
LANDLADY 'LOWED TO ME LAST WEEK,
"SAM, AIN'T YOU GOT NO MONEY?" . NM BROKE 19
WHAT I DON'T KNOW 'BOUT SHOVELIN'
COAL, AIN'T NO MO' TO KNOW! . . NM BROKE 32
AND DE MAN COME TELLIN' ME THEY
AIN'T HIRIN' NO MO' COLORED -
JUST WHITE. . . . . NM BROKE 45
BUT RIGHT LONG THROUGH HERE NOW, I
CAN'T 'FORD TO BUY YOU NO HAT." NM BROKE 51
AND SHE COME TELLIN' ME, SHE AIN'T
GOT NO MO' EVENINGS FREE! . . . NM BROKE 53
BUT YOU DON'T SEE NO PRESIDENTS
DYIN' O' GRIEF - . . . . NM BROKE 57
IS I MARRIED? NO, ALL THESE-HERE
GIRLS UP NORTH IS TOO LIGHT. . . NM BROKE 70
THEY TOLD US AMERICA WOULD KNOW NO
BLACK OR WHITE: . . . . NM COLORED SL POEM 11
AND NO LONGER DO WE KNOW THE DARK
MISERY . . . . NM COLORED SL POEM 30
OF BEING HELD BACK, OF HAVING NO
CHANCE - . . . . NM COLORED SL POEM 31
FOR HERE IN THE SOUTH THERE'S NO
VOTES AND NO RIGHT. . . . . . . NM COLORED SL POEM 46
FOR HERE IN THE SOUTH THERE'S NO
VOTES AND NO RIGHT. . . . . . . NM COLORED SL POEM 46
PUT NO TOMBSTONE AT MY HEAD. . . . DK DEATH SEAMAN 5
STREW NO FLOWERS ON MY GRAVE. . . . DK DEATH SEAMAN 7
NO WONDER WE FIND THEM SUCH
MARVELLOUS THINGS! . . . . DK FAIRIES 5
MA LORD AIN'T NO STUCK-UP MAN. . . DK MA LORD 1
MA LORD AIN'T NO STUCK-UP MAN. . . DK MA LORD 10

Line	Source	No.
NO ONE REMEMBERS	DK PARISIAN BEGGAR	7
NEVER DONE NO WRONG.	DK PO' BOY BLUES	8
NEVER DONE NO WRONG.	DK PO' BOY BLUES	10
MIGHT NEVER RISE NO MO'.	DK SONG BANJO DANC	13
MIGHT NEVER RISE NO MO' -	DK SONG BANJO DANC	15
MIGHT NEVER DANCE NO MO'.	DK SONG BANJO DANC	19
MIGHT NEVER RISE NO MO'.	DK SONG BANJO DANC	27
AN' I AIN'T GOT NO BOAT.	DK WIDE RIVER	2
I AIN'T GOT NO BOAT.	DK WIDE RIVER	4
NO SHAME IS WRIT ACROSS ITS FACE -	SL TOWN OF SCOTTSB	2
AND THE OPPRESSORS HAD NO PITY.	ANS A NEW SONG	21
NO LONGER SHALL YOU SAY	ANS A NEW SONG	30
40-VOICES: NO PART NEGLECTED -	ANS CHANT MAY DAY	17
MAYBE, NOW, THERE WILL BE NO MONUMENT FOR YOU	ANS KIDS WHO DIE	38
IS CROWNED WITH NO FALSE PATRIOTIC WREATH.	ANS LET AMERICA BE	12
FOR ME, NO MORE, THE GREAT MIGRATION TO THE NORTH.	ANS OPEN LETTER	41
CUYO NOMBRE NO QUIERO ACORDARME.	ANS SONG OF SPAIN	28
WORKERS, MAKE NO BOMBS AGAIN!	ANS SONG OF SPAIN	54
WORKERS, MINE NO GOLD AGAIN!	ANS SONG OF SPAIN	55
WORKERS, LIFT NO HAND AGAIN	ANS SONG OF SPAIN	56
WORKERS, MAKE NO BOMBS AGAIN	ANS SONG OF SPAIN	63
CAR NO MORE.	SH ANNOUNCEMENT	16
CHINESE? . . . HELL, NO!	SH BLD PAWNBROKER	7
THERE AIN'T NO REASON	SH BLD THE KILLER	21
YOU AIN'T GOT TO WAKE UP NO BODY BUT ME.	SH DAYBREAK	5
NO MUSIC DIDN'T PLAY.	SH DEATH IN HARLEM	125
DIXIE'S AIN'T NO PLACE FOR A GANG THAT'S SLOW.	SH DEATH IN HARLEM	38
NO!	SH DECLARATION	5
IN HARLEM'S NO LACK.	SH HARLEM SWEETIES	20
I'LL TRY NOT TO BE THAT MEAN NO MORE.	SH LETTER	13
GIRLS, DON'T STAND ON NO CORNER	SH MIDNIGHT CHIPPI	25
CRYIN' TO NO LONESOME BLUE!	SH MIDNIGHT CHIPPI	26
I SAY DON'T STAND ON NO CORNER	SH MIDNIGHT CHIPPI	27
CRYIN' TO NO LONESOME BLUE!	SH MIDNIGHT CHIPPI	28
AND DE LEVEE DON'T DO NO GOOD.	SH MISSISSIPPI LEV	8
WHEN DE LEVEE DON'T DO NO GOOD.	SH MISSISSIPPI LEV	10
I COULDN'T FIND NO JOB	SH OUT OF WORK	7
COULDN'T FIND NO JOB	SH OUT OF WORK	9
AND I WON'T NEED NO FURNITURE LIVING ALONE -	SH PAY DAY	15
I WOULD MAKE A FIRE BUT THERE AIN'T NO WOOD.	SH SUPPER TIME	4
THAT PLACE WHERE YOUR TRUNK WAS, AIN'T NO TRUNK NO MORE.	SH SUPPER TIME	8
THAT PLACE WHERE YOUR TRUNK WAS, AIN'T NO TRUNK NO MORE.	SH SUPPER TIME	8
BUT I AIN'T GOT NO OWL HEAD AND YOU DONE LEFT TOWN	SH TWILIGHT REVERI	13
AIN'T NO TELLING WHAT	JC BLD SAM SOLOMON	27
I DON'T PAY YOU NO MIND.	JC BLD SAM SOLOMON	30
LISTEN! I DON'T OWN NO RADIO -	JC GOOD MORN STLIN	49
CAN'T SEND NO MESSAGES THROUGH THE AIR.	JC GOOD MORN STLIN	50
YOU REFLECT NO STARS BY NIGHT.	JC THE BITTER RIVR	24
NO SUN BY DAY.	JC THE BITTER RIVR	25
THE BITTER RIVER REFLECTS NO STARS -	JC THE BITTER RIVR	26
THE BITTER RIVER REFLECTS NO STARS.	JC THE BITTER RIVR	38
NOW YOUR WORDS NO LONGER HAVE MEANING -	JC THE BITTER RIVR	65
FOR ME GIVES BACK NO STARS.	JC THE BITTER RIVR	88
ALONE, I KNOW, NO ONE IS FREE.	JC TO CAPTAIN MULZ	35
WILL HAVE NO PLACE.	JC TO CAPTAIN MULZ	58
WHERE NO WORLDLY DUTY CALLS -	FW CONVENT	5
NO ONE TALKING	FW DIMOUT IN HARLM	15
NO SOUL RETURNS.	FW EXITS	11
NO MATTER WHAT	FW FAITHFUL ONE	9
WITH NO PAIN	FW GIRL	20
NO STRETCHING PLACE.	FW GRAVE YARD	3
NO WAY OF DYING.	FW GRIEF	6
IT HAD NO DIGNITY BEFORE.	FW HARLEM DANCE HA	1
THAT HAD NO DIGNITY BEFORE!	FW HARLEM DANCE HA	8
BUT NO ONE WAS CURIOUS.	FW HEART	8
NO ONE CARED AT ALL	FW HEART	9
NO LOVE FROM ABOVE.	FW PRAYER	12
THE FLOWER NO SCENT ENCLOSES.	FW REMEMBRANCE	4
NO WORDS.	FW SONGS	8
AND THE SUN GALLOPS NO MORE	FW THERE	3
NOW NO MORE.	OWT BLD MARGE POLIT	24
AIN'T NO MORE!	OWT BLUES ON A BOX	8
STEP, AND LEAVE NO TRACK.	OWT FLIGHT	2
NO, I DIDN'T TOUCH HER.	OWT FLIGHT	5
NO, MARTHA, I AIN'T HEARD.	OWT JITNEY	10
MY LANDLADY, SHE SAID, NO!	OWT STRANGER IN TWN	8
I SAID, IT DON'T MAKE NO DIFFERENCE NOHOW.	OWT STRANGER IN TWN	9
WITH NO HEAT	OWT VISITORS	14
THERE AIN'T NO WAY FOR ME	OWT YESTERDAY TODAY	7
FOR WHICH THERE AIN'T NO HOPE.	SP ARGUMENT	7
NO LONGER THE LIGHT OF MY DREAM BEFORE ME.	SP AS I GREW OLDER	20
THERE AIN'T NO GOOD LEFT	SP BAD LUCK CARD	5
DAVE MEANT HER NO GOOD.	SP BLD FORTUNE TEL	18
NO WAY SHE LOOKED.	SP BLD FORTUNE TEL	28
TENANT HELD NO BAIL	SP BLD LANDLORD	32
NO MONEY TO BURY HIM.	SP BLD OF THE MAN	1
NO! THE HUSSY'S TELLING EVERYBODY -	SP BLD OF THE GIRL	13
JUST AS THOUGH IT WAS NO SIN -	SP BLD OF THE GIRL	14
RECKON THERE'S NO CHARGE	SP BLD OF THE MAN	23
NO BUSINESS TO DIE.	SP BLD OF THE MAN	28
NO USE IN MY GOING	SP BLUE MONDAY	1
BUT NO USE DENYING -	SP BLUE MONDAY	8
I WOULDN'T GET UP NO MORE -	SP BLUES AT DAWN	9
AIN'T GOT NO HEART NO MORE.	SP CORA	2
AIN'T GOT NO HEART NO MORE.	SP CORA	2
WAS NO WATER IN A DREAM	SP CROSSING	12
NO PROTECTION FOR THAT STREAM.	SP CROSSING	14
HE WAS NO GOOD AT MAKING LOVE	SP DANCER	7
AND NO GOOD AT MAKING MONEY.	SP DANCER	8
BUT BEING NO GOOD AT LOVIN' -	SP DANCER	18
(WHEN YOU'RE NO GOOD FOR DOUGH THEY GO.)	SP DANCER	20
WITH NO SENSE, JUST WONDERFUL FEET.	SP DANCER	21
DID HE GET ANYWHERE? NO!	SP DANCER	23
NO DIFF' NO HOW.	SP DEAD IN THERE	22
NO DIFF' NO HOW.	SP DEAD IN THERE	22
THERE AIN'T NO STOVE -	SP DEFERRED	19
CHILE, GRANNY AIN'T GOT NO DIME.	SP DIME	6
IS NO ATOM AT ALL.	SP DRUM	8
AND THERE IS NO AIR	SP DRUM	10
I AIN'T GOT NO SUGAR, HATTIE,	SP EARLY EVENING	7
AIN'T GOT NO SUGAR, I	SP EARLY EVENING	9
I AIN'T NO WISE WOMAN, HAMMOND.	SP EARLY EVENING	13
AIN'T NO SENSE IN A GOOD WOMAN	SP EARLY EVENING	15
JOB AIN'T NO GOOD THOUGH.	SP ELEVATOR BOY	4
NO MONEY AROUND.	SP ELEVATOR BOY	5
MAYBE NO LUCK FOR A LONG TIME.	SP ELEVATOR BOY	14
NO CLOCKS ON THE WALL.	SP END	2
AND NO TIME.	SP END	3
NO SHADOWS THAT MOVE	SP END	4
THERE IS NO DOOR!	SP END	10
DON'T HAVE NO EFFECT ON YOU -	SP EVIL	2
BUT THERE AIN'T NO EAGLE	SP FACT	3
NO MAN IS GOOD ENOUGH	SP FREEDOM'S PLOW	102
ELSE IT HAD NO MEANING FOR ANYONE.	SP FREEDOM'S PLOW	108
I HOPE THERE AIN'T NO JIM CROW ON THE FREEDOM TRAIN.	SP FREEDOM TRAIN	11
NO BACK DOOR ENTRANCE TO THE FREEDOM TRAIN.	SP FREEDOM TRAIN	12
NO SIGNS FOR COLORED ON THE FREEDOM TRAIN.	SP FREEDOM TRAIN	13
NO WHITE FOLKS ONLY ON THE FREEDOM TRAIN.	SP FREEDOM TRAIN	14
A NEGRO'S GOT NO BUSINESS ON THE FREEDOM TRACK!	SP FREEDOM TRAIN	40
HE DIED FOR REAL. IT WARN'T NO SHOW.	SP FREEDOM TRAIN	44
NOT STOPPIN' AT NO STATIONS MARKED COLORED NOR WHITE.	SP FREEDOM TRAIN	51
WHERE THERE NEVER WAS NO JIM CROW SIGNS NOWHERE.	SP FREEDOM TRAIN	54
NO WELCOMIN' COMMITTEES, NOR POLITICIANS OF NOTE.	SP FREEDOM TRAIN	55
NO MAYORS AND SUCH FOR WHICH COLORED CAN'T VOTE.	SP FREEDOM TRAIN	56
NO MAN IS GOOD ENOUGH	SP FREEDOM'S PLOW	169
WE SAY, NO!	SP FREEDOM'S PLOW	179
WE SAY, NO!	SP FREEDOM'S PLOW	182
WE SAY, NO!	SP FREEDOM'S PLOW	187
CAN'T YOU BRING NO BETTER NEWS?	SP HARD DADDY	6
SHE WASN'T HOME NO MORE.	SP HOMECOMING	4
THE FOLKS WITH NO TITLES IN FRONT OF THEIR NAMES	SP IN EXPLANATION	1
NO, SON, NOT EVERYBODY.	SP IN EXPLANATION	6
THEY HAD NO INTENTION OF CALLING COOLIES MISTER.	SP IN EXPLANATION	9
HELL NO SHUT UP! SAY THE PEOPLE	SP IN EXPLANATION	27
WITH NO TITLES IN FRONT OF THEIR NAMES.	SP IN EXPLANATION	28
HELL, NO! IT'S TIME TO TALK BACK NOW!	SP IN EXPLANATION	29
TRUE ANYHOW NO MATTER HOW MANY	SP IN EXPLANATION	38
THE PEOPLE WITH NO TITLES IN FRONT OF THEIR NAMES	SP IN EXPLANATION	40
WITH NO TITLE IN FRONT OF NAME	SP IN EXPLANATION	54
NO SHUT UP!	SP IN EXPLANATION	56
HELL NO SHUT UP!	SP IN EXPLANATION	57
BECAUSE OF PEOPLE WITH NO TITLES	SP IN EXPLANATION	60
BUT THE GOSSIPS HAD NO	SP JOE LOUIS	9
YOM KIPPUR, NO!	SP LIKEWISE	9
NO LOVE FROM ABOVE.	SP LITANY	12
YOU DON'T NEED NO GUN NOR KNIFE -	SP LITTLE OLD LETT	14
I WOULDN'T PLAY NO MORE.	SP MADAM NUMBER WR	4
I DON'T PAY NO REVERSED	SP MADAM PHONE BIL	8
AIN'T HAD NO LUCK	SP MADAM CHARTY CH	11
DON'T MEAN NO HARM.	SP MADAM WRONG VIS	12
SHE CRIED, OH, NO!	SP MADAM HER MADAM	18
CAN'T RAISE NO CHILD ON THAT.	SP MADAM CHARTY CH	19
NO SOONER HAD I TOLD HIM	SP MADAM WRONG VIS	21
AIN'T GONNA PLAY NO MORE	SP MADAM NUMBER WR	22
YOU'VE GOT NO TRUST.	SP MADAM MIGHT-HAV	30

SO I AIN'T IN NO MOOD . . . . SP MADAM MINISTER 32
I WASN'T NO MINT. . . . . SP MADAM'S CALLING 6
THAT AIN'T NO TIME TO GO. . . . . . SP MIDWINTER BLUES 12
NO FLOWERS FROM THE STORE. . . . . SP MIDWINTER BLUES 24
NO OTHER MUSIC . . . . SP MISERY 3
LIFE FOR ME AIN'T BEEN NO CRYSTAL
STAIR. . . . . SP MOTHER TO SON 2
AND PLACES WITH NO CARPET ON THE
FLOOR - . . . . SP MOTHER TO SON 6
WHERE THERE AIN'T BEEN NO LIGHT. . SP MOTHER TO SON 13
AND LIFE FOR ME AIN'T BEEN NO
CRYSTAL STAIR. . . . . SP MOTHER TO SON 20
THAT'S NO LIE, HE SAID, ... SP NEW YORKERS 2
AND NEVER OWN NO PARTS . . . . . . SP NEW YORKERS 10
NO REGRETS - . . . . SP NO REGRETS 2
NO REGRETS - . . . . SP NO REGRETS 6
AND THERE AIN'T NO KU KLUX . . . . SP NOT A MOVIE 14
MAYVILLE HAD NO PLACE TO OFFER HER. SP RUBY BROWN 5
UNFORTUNATELY USUALLY NO! . . . . . SP SISTER 11
NO, M'AM! . . . . SP SOUTHERN MAMMY 11
JUST AIN'T GOT NO HEART. . . . . . SP SOUTHERN MAMMY 22
NO, M'AM! . . . . SP SOUTHERN MAMMY 23
JUST AIN'T GOT NO HEART. . . . . . SP SOUTHERN MAMMY 24
NO ROOM FOR FEAR. . . . . SP SUBWAY RUSH HOU 7
BUT I DON'T NEED NO PIANO, ... SP TESTIMONIAL 5
NO SAFETY, NO LOVE, NO RESPECT WAS I
DUE. . . . . SP THE NEGRO MOTHE 16
NO SAFETY, NO LOVE, NO RESPECT WAS I
DUE. . . . . SP THE NEGRO MOTHE 16
NO SAFETY, NO LOVE, NO RESPECT WAS I
DUE. . . . . SP THE NEGRO MOTHE 16
I HAD TO KEEP ON! NO STOPPING FOR ME
- . . . . SP THE NEGRO MOTHE 29
FOR I WILL BE WITH YOU TILL NO WHITE
BROTHER . . . . SP THE NEGRO MOTHE 51
I AIN'T HAPPY NO MO' . . . . SP THE WEARY BLUES 29
NO PLACE TO SLEEP. . . . . SP VAGABONDS 6
CAUSE THERE AIN'T NO SENSE . . . . SP WAKE 3
AIN'T NO PLACE . . . . SP WEST TEXAS 18
I AIN'T GOT NO MAN. . . . . SP 50 - 50 5
YOU AIN'T GOT NO HEAD! . . . . . . SP 50 - 50 8
HAS NO RECOURSE NOW BUT TO THE LAW? AYM ASK YOUR MAMA 11
WHERE NO SHADOW WALKS ALONE . . . . AYM ASK YOUR MAMA 75
AIN'T YOU GOT NO INFORMATION . . . AYM BIRD IN ORBIT 32
MAKES NO DIFFERENCE TO ME - . . . . AYM BLUES IN STEREO 30
SEEKING SUBURB WITH NO JUKEBOX . . AYM HORN OF PLENTY 69
THERE'S NO WAY NOT TO LOSE. . . . AYM ODE TO DINAH 114
ON A TRAIN THAT LOST NO PASSENGERS AYM ODE TO DINAH 29
NO CONDUCTOR AND NO TRAIN. . . . . AYM ODE TO DINAH 43
NO CONDUCTOR AND NO TRAIN. . . . . AYM ODE TO DINAH 43
YET NO PRESENTS DOWN THE CHIMNEY. AYM ODE TO DINAH 74
ARE TRIBAL NOW NO LONGER . . . . . AYM ODE TO DINAH 77
TRIBAL NOW NO LONGER PAPA MAMA . . AYM ODE TO DINAH 82
SHELTERED NOW NO LONGER. . . . . . AYM ODE TO DINAH 86
TRIBAL NOW NO LONGER ONE FOR ALL . AYM ODE TO DINAH 88
AND ALL FOR ONE NO LONGER . . . . . AYM ODE TO DINAH 89
NO SHOW FARE, BABY - . . . . AYM ODE TO DINAH 96
NO MATTER HOW SANCTIFIED, ... PL BIBLE BELT 7
"I DON'T WANT TO STUDY WAR NO MORE," PL BLACK PANTHER 6
WEARS NO DISGUISE. . . . . PL BLACK PANTHER 9
NO TRAINS OR STEAMBOATS GOING - . . PL CULTURAL EXCHNG 12
NO JIVE. . . . . PL DEATH YORKVILLE 20
(NO?) THEN . . . . PL FINAL CALL 36
(AND HAS NO WAY TO UNDERSTAND) . . PL JUNIOR ADDICT 7
BUT HE NEEDS NO MARKER - . . . . . PL LUMUMBA'S GRAVE 15
BUT THERE AIN'T NO BACK . . . . . . PL MERRY-GO-ROUND 12
(NO IN-BETWEEN TO CHOOSE) . . . . . PL MOTHER IN WAR 11
WITH NO ROOTS . . . . PL SLUM DREAMS 4
SINCE NO STEMS . . . . PL SLUM DREAMS 6
NO. . . . . PL UN-AMERICAN 17
I'VE NO WEAPON TO STRIKE BACK . . . PL WHO BUT TH LORD 20

NOBLE 1

AS IF IT WERE SOME NOBLE THING, . . PL MOTHER IN WAR 1

NOBODY 51

DON'T LOVE NOBODY . . . . WB CAT AND SAXOPHN 12
DON'T WANT NOBODY . . . . WB CAT AND SAXOPHN 22
WON'T MEET NOBODY . . . . FC A RUINED GAL 9
NOBODY THERE WAS GOOD TO ME. . . . FC GYPSY MAN 12
NOBODY TO UNDERSTAND. . . . . FC MOAN 2
NOBODY TO UNDERSTAND. . . . . FC MOAN 5
NOBODY CARES JUST WHY. . . . . . . FC MOAN 11
NOBODY TO LOVE ME: . . . . FC SUICIDE 5
BACK BENT AS IN THE FIELDS. THE SLOW
STEP. THE BOWED HEAD. "NOBODY
KNOWS . . . . NM BLACK CLWN MOOD 4
NOBODY WILL CARE - . . . . NM BLACK CLWN POEM 42
BUT I AIN'T GOT NOBODY . . . . DK DRESSED UP 11
NOBODY CARES . . . . DK PARISIAN BEGGAR 3
NOBODY BUT DEATH . . . . DK PARISIAN BEGGAR 11
NOBODY BUT LONESOME BLUE. . . . . . SH MIDNIGHT CHIPPI 4
SO NOBODY CAN'T LOW-RATE YOU. . . . SH MIDNIGHT CHIPPI 30
DON'T HAVE TO HEAR NOBODY SAY. . . SH PAY DAY 3
WHO AM NOBODY. . . . . FW THERE 8
MARGIE WARN'T NOBODY . . . . OWT BLD MARGE POLIT 21
BUT SHE AIN'T JUST NOBODY . . . . . OWT BLD MARGE POLIT 23
NOBODY A-TALL - . . . . OWT STRANGER IN TWN 11
NOBODY CARES ABOUT YOU . . . . OWT TOO BLUE 4
ONCE NOBODY. . . . . SP CONSIDER ME 5
WASN'T NOBODY ON THAT PRAIRIE . . . SP CROSSING 17
NOBODY CARES . . . . SP DELINQUENT 16
NOBODY. . . . . SP DESERT 3
BETTER THAN NOBODY . . . . SP DESERT 8
NOBODY GIVES A DAMN ABOUT. . . . . SP DOWN AND OUT 6
AND NOBODY KNEW FOR SURE . . . . . SP FREEDOM'S PLOW 119
NOBODY LOVES A GENIUS CHILD. . . . SP GENIUS CHILD 5
NOBODY LOVES A GENIUS CHILD. . . . SP GENIUS CHILD 11
(MAYBE - NOBODY KNOWS.) . . . . . . SP HAVANA DREAMS 2
(BUT NOBODY KNOWS IF THAT IS SO.) SP HAVANA DREAMS 4
WASN'T NOBODY GONE. . . . . SP LATE LAST NIGHT 3
NEITHER HAD NOBODY DIED. . . . . . SP LATE LAST NIGHT 4
ON NOBODY ELSE'S SHELF. . . . . . . SP MADAM FORT TELL 20
NOBODY LOVES NOBODY . . . . SP MADAM MIGHT-HAV 27
NOBODY LOVES NOBODY . . . . SP MADAM MIGHT-HAV 27
HOW OLD NOBODY KNOWS - . . . . . . SP MYSTERY 12
"AIN'T GOT NOBODY IN ALL THIS WORLD, SP THE WEARY BLUES 19
AIN'T GOT NOBODY BUT MA SELF. . . . SP THE WEARY BLUES 20
I DON'T WANT NOBODY ELSE AND . . . SP WIDOW WOMAN 19
DON'T NOBODY ELSE WANT ME. . . . . SP WIDOW WOMAN 20
I SAY DON'T WANT NOBODY ELSE . . . SP WIDOW WOMAN 21
AND DON'T NOBODY ELSE WANT ME - . . SP WIDOW WOMAN 22
AIN'T GOT NOBODY TO SHARE MY BED. SP 50 - 50 2
AIN'T GOT NOBODY TO HOLD MY HAND - SP 50 - 50 3
FROM NOBODY AND NOTHING TO WHERE I
AM. . . . . AYM HORN OF PLENTY 39
ME WHO USED TO BE NOBODY. . . . . . AYM HORN OF PLENTY 42
NOBODY NEEDS A MARKER. . . . . . . AYM ODE TO DINAH 122
(AND IF NOBODY COMES, SEND FOR ME.) PL FINAL CALL 39
I AIN'T NEVER SEEN NOBODY . . . . . PL FLORIDA WORKERS 17

NOBODY'LL 1

NOBODY'LL DARE . . . . SP I, TOO 11

NOBODY'S 5

WON'T BE NOBODY'S BRIDE . . . . . . FC A RUINED GAL 4
CAUSE I AIN'T NOBODY'S BEAU. . . . OWT STRANGER IN TWN 10
I AIN'T NOBODY'S BEAU. . . . . . . OWT STRANGER IN TWN 12
BUT NOBODY'S SEEN HER SHED A TEAR. SP BLD OF THE GIRL 9
BUT I AIN'T NOBODY'S SISTER. . . . SP EVENING SONG 7

NOE 1

AND A HEY NONNY NOE! . . . . SH SHAKESPEARE 2

NOHOW 3

AIN'T NOTHIN' TO DO FOR YOU, NOHOW, FC RED SILK STOCK 5
I SAID, IT DON'T MAKE NO DIFFERENCE
NOHOW. . . . . OWT STRANGER IN TWN 9
CHARGES NOHOW. . . . . SP MADAM PHONE BIL 9

NOISE 2

MAKE LOTS O' NOISE. . . . . NM BIG-TIMER POEM 63
THEY OUGHT TO BE SOME NOISE. . . . SH SUNDAY 11

NOISY 1

NOISY AND LOUD. . . . . SH CABARET GIRL 4

NOMBRE 1

CUYO NOMBRE NO QUIERO ACORDARME. . .
. . . . ANS SONG OF SPAIN 28

NONE 9

I SAY, "NOW, BABY, YOU KNOW I AIN'T
GOT NONE, HONEY." . . . . NM BROKE 20
AMERICAN AM I, NONE CAN DENY: . . . NM DARK YOUTH USA 6
NONE OF THOSE IS DEAD.) . . . . . . SL SCOTTSBORO 23
BUT NONE OF THEM PEOPLES . . . . . OWT LONESOME CORNER 7
WITH NONE I HAD. . . . . SP MADAM CHARTY CH 12
I SAID, NONE OF YOUR . . . . SP MADAM MINISTER 15
AND WE GET NONE. . . . . SP SHARE-CROPPERS 8
BELIEVE IN THE RIGHT, LET NONE PUSH
YOU BACK. . . . . SP THE NEGRO MOTHE 43
OR NONE - . . . . PL GHOSTS OF 1619 28

NONNY 1

AND A HEY NONNY NOE! . . . . SH SHAKESPEARE 2

NON-SUBPOENA 1

SEND FOR ADAM POWELL ON A
NON-SUBPOENA DAY. . . . . PL FINAL CALL 37

NOON 2

HIGH NOON TEETH . . . . SP DREAM BOOGE VAR 3
NOON TILL NIGHT . . . . SP PARADE 22

NOR 35

NOR EVER KNOW. . . . . WB DISILLUSION 5
NOR THE SALT TEARS . . . . WB DISILLUSION 9
THAT I CAN NEITHER HEAR NOR FEEL NOR
SEE. . . . . DK BEGGAR BOY 2
THAT I CAN NEITHER HEAR NOR FEEL NOR
SEE. . . . . DK BEGGAR BOY 2
THAT I CAN NEITHER KNOW NOR
UNDERSTAND . . . . DK BEGGAR BOY 3
NOR DAYS OF GLOOM. . . . . DK WALKERS WITH 4
NOR DARKNESS - . . . . DK WALKERS WITH 5

WHERE NEVER KINGS CONNIVE NOR TYRANTS SCHEME . . . . ANS LET AMERICA BE 8
NOR FREEDOM IN THIS "HOMELAND OF THE FREE.") . . . . ANS LET AMERICA BE 16
NOR THEM TWO DIAMOND RINGS . . . . SH PAY DAY 8
HOW FAR YOU GO, NOR HOW LONG YOU STAY - . . . . SH SUNDAY 6
NEITHER ONE NOR THE OTHER - . . . . JC BLD SAM SOLOMON 34
NOR THE TASTE OF ITS BITTER BREW. JC THE BITTER RIVR 52
NOR THEIR LAND, THEIR LAND - . . . JC TO CAPTAIN MULZ 18
THE THINGS THEY MADE, NOR THEIR OWN LIVES - . . . . JC TO CAPTAIN MULZ 21
NOR FATHER'S - . . . . OWT BLD MARGE POLIT 55
NEITHER BULLET NOR GUN - . . . . . OWT TOO BLUE 15
NOR SEEN HER HANG HER HEAD. . . . . SP BLD OF THE GIRL 10
BEING NEITHER WHITE NOR BLACK? . . SP CROSS 12
NOR EVER . . . . SP DEMOCRACY 3
NOR DARK . . . . SP END 8
NOR WRITE THEM DOWN ON PAPER. . . . SP FREEDOM'S PLOW 146
NOT STOPPIN' AT NO STATIONS MARKED COLORED NOR WHITE. . . . . SP FREEDOM TRAIN 51
NO WELCOMIN' COMMITTEES, NOR POLITICIANS OF NOTE. . . . . . . SP FREEDOM TRAIN 55
YOU DON'T NEED NO GUN NOR KNIFE - SP LITTLE OLD LETT 14
OF EARTH NOR SKY . . . . SP NEW YORKERS 11
NEITHER TRUTH NOR LIE. . . . . SP RAILROAD AVENUE 22
NOR FUEL FOR THE CLEAN FLAME OF JOY SP RUBY BROWN 6
NOR DRUM . . . . SP TESTIMONIAL 7
NOR DO I OFTEN WANT TO BE A PART OF YOU. . . . . SP THEME FOR ENG 3 35
NOR THE SWEET OF YOUR LIPS ALONE. SP TO ARTINA 8
NOR WHICH WAY. . . . . SP WEST TEXAS 15
NOR TAKE THE PLACE OF MEAT OR BREAD PL CROWNS GARLANDS 15
NOR EVER . . . . PL FREEDOM 3
NOR SONGS . . . . PL OPPRESSION 4

NORTH 13

IS I MARRIED? NO, ALL THESE-HERE GIRLS UP NORTH IS TOO LIGHT. . . NM BROKE 70
SINCE I COME UP NORTH DE . . . . . OK PO' BOY BLUES 5
FOR ME, NO MORE, THE GREAT MIGRATION TO THE NORTH. . . . . ANS OPEN LETTER 41
FOLKS, I COME UP NORTH . . . . . . SH EVENIN' BLUES 1
CAUSE THEY TOLD ME DE NORTH WAS FINE. . . . . SH EVENIN' BLUES 2
I COME UP NORTH . . . . SH EVENIN' BLUES 3
CAUSE THEY TOLD ME DE NORTH WAS FINE. . . . . SH EVENIN' BLUES 4
THEN GOT PUT BACK WHEN WE COME NORTH. . . . . SP DEFERRED 5
NORTH OF THE PARK. . . . . SP ISLAND 2
NORTH AND EAST - . . . . SP ONE-WAY TICKET 7
NORTH AND WEST - . . . . SP ONE-WAY TICKET 14
GONE UP NORTH. . . . . SP ONE-WAY TICKET 26
SO NOW I SEEK THE NORTH - . . . . . SP THE SOUTH 23
THE COLD-FACED NORTH. . . . . SP THE SOUTH 24
AS NORTH POLE IS TO SOUTH . . . . . AYM SHADES OF PIG 27
ON VACATION? UP NORTH? . . . . . . PL MISSISSIPPI 10
UP NORTH. . . . . PL NORTHERN LIBERL 15
AND HEAD NORTH WITH THE DOUGH. . . PL VARI-COLORED 4

NORTHERN 1

COMES TO A NORTHERN SCHOOL . . . . FW MIGRATION 2

NOSE 1

THAT'S BEEN KEEPING MY NOSE TO THE GRINDSTONE. . . . . SH PAY DAY 13

NOSES 1

BEIGE SAILORS WITH LARGE NOSES . . SP SEASHORE THROUG 1

NOTE 4

FROM ONE SIDE TO THE OTHER. BUT NOW A HARSH AND BITTER NOTE CREEPS INTO . . . . NM BLACK CLWN MOOD 9
BUT BLOW ONE BLARING TRUMPET NOTE OF SUN . . . . SP FATASY PURPLE 7
NO WELCOMIN' COMMITTEES, NOR POLITICIANS OF NOTE. . . . . . . SP FREEDOM TRAIN 55
MELLOWS TO A GOLDEN NOTE. . . . . . SP TRUMPET PLAYER 44

NOTES 1

IN SILVER THREAD AND DIAMOND NOTES SP FLATTED FIFTHS 12

NOTHIN 1

YOU AIN'T GONNA HAVE NOTHIN TO SAY. SP EARLY EVENING 12

NOTHING 24

WITH THE WHITE AND THE BLACK WHOM NOTHING HOLDS BACK - . . . . . . NM DARK YOUTH USA 24
THERE'S NOTHING MORE TO SAY. . . . OK I LOVED FRIEND 3
THE MILLIONS WHO HAVE NOTHING FOR OUR PAY? . . . . ANS LET AMERICA BE 55
THE MILLIONS WHO HAVE NOTHING FOR OUR PAY? . . . . ANS LET AMERICA BE 60
THAT'S NOTHING BUT TRASH. . . . . . SH BLD THE KILLER 12
LOOK IN THE BREAD BOX, NOTHING BUT A FLY. . . . . SH SUPPER TIME 2
YOU AIN'T TELLING NOTHING BUT YOUR JIM CROW LIES - . . . . JC JIM CROW'S LAST 22
ROSE OF NOTHING BUT YESTERDAYS . . FW CHIPPY 4
THERE WHERE NOTHING . . . . FW THERE 5
LEAVES NOTHING . . . . SP BEALE STREET 11
IS NOTHING NOWHERE. . . . . SP DRUM 12
WHEN A MAN STARTS OUT WITH NOTHING, SP FREEDOM'S PLOW 1
AND NOTHING MORE. . . . . SP MADAM CENSUS 12
NOTHING ABOUT MY . . . . SP MADAM PHONE BIL 33
THERE'S NOTHING FOREIGN . . . . . . SP MADAM'S CALLING 17
I DON'T HAVE TO DO NOTHING . . . . SP NECESSITY 3
AMOUNT OF NOTHING . . . . SP SAME IN BLUES 13
NOTHING AT ALL NAMED AFTER JOHN BROWN. . . . . SP SHAME ON YOU 7
AND WE ARE NOTHING MORE . . . . . . SP SHARE-CROPPERS 12
I HAD NOTHING, BACK THERE IN THE NIGHT. . . . . SP THE NEGRO MOTHE 24
I NOURISHED THE DREAM THAT NOTHING COULD SMOTHER . . . . SP THE NEGRO MOTHE 31
AND NOTHING HEREAFTER. . . . . . . SP YOUNG SAILOR 20
FROM NOBODY AND NOTHING TO WHERE I AM. . . . . AYM HORN OF PLENTY 39
NOTHING BUT ANOTHER SHADOW . . . . AYM HORN OF PLENTY 43

NOTHINGNESS 3

AND GIVES HER KISS TO NOTHINGNESS. WB TO LITTLE LOVER 11
IN A NOTHINGNESS . . . . FW EXITS 9
WAITING FOR NOTHINGNESS. . . . . . SP A HOUSE IN TAOS 10

NOTHIN' 16

AIN'T NOTHIN' FOR A RUINED GAL . . FC A RUINED GAL 13
HAD NOTHIN' TO EAT, ... FC DEATH DO DIRTY 12
NOTHIN' FOR YOU TO DO. . . . . . . FC HARD LUCK 2
NOTHIN' FOR YOU TO DO. . . . . . . FC HARD LUCK 4
AIN'T NOTHIN' TO DO FOR YOU, NOHOW. FC RED SILK STOCK 5
WON'T BE NOTHIN' LEFT . . . . FC SATURDAY NIGHT 15
IT AIN'T NOTHIN' BUT A HOVEL. . . . FC WORKIN' MAN 4
AIN'T NOTHIN' BUT A 'HORE. . . . . FC WORKIN' MAN 8
AN' GITS NOTHIN' BUT TROUBLE. . . . FC WORKIN' MAN 16
BUT I AINT GOT NOTHIN' REAL . . . . NM BIG-TIMER POEM 47
(I DON'T CARE NOTHIN' 'BOUT HER MYSELF!) . . . . NM BROKE 27
ALL THIS TALKIN' AIN'T NOTHIN' BUT TINKLIN' SYMBOLS AND SOUNDIN' BRASS: . . . . NM BROKE 58
MY LIFE AIN'T NOTHIN' . . . . SH LOVE AGAIN BLUS 1
I SAY MY LIFE AIN'T NOTHIN' . . . . SH LOVE AGAIN BLUS 3
NOTHIN' TO DO BUT WALK. . . . . . . SP BOUND NO'TH BLS 8
NOTHIN' IN THIS WORLD . . . . SP LITTLE GRN TREE 3

NOT'VE 2

SHE MIGHT NOT'VE CUSSED . . . . . . OWT BLD MARGE POLIT 3
SHE MIGHT NOT'VE FELT . . . . OWT BLD MARGE POLIT 7

NOURISH 1

TO NOURISH THEM. . . . . PL SLUM DREAMS 5

NOURISHED 2

DREAM NOURISHED IN COMMON. . . . . SP FREEDOM'S PLOW 159
I NOURISHED THE DREAM THAT NOTHING COULD SMOTHER . . . . SP THE NEGRO MOTHE 31

NOWHERE 10

DIDN'T HAVE A FRIEND NOWHERE. . . . FC BLD OF GIN MARY 4
DON'T HAVE TO GO NOWHERE. . . . . . SH SUNDAY 4
IS NOWHERE. . . . . FW BORDER LINE 8
HYPE NOWHERE! . . . . SP DEAD IN THERE 13
IS NOTHING NOWHERE. . . . . SP DRUM 12
I WONDER IS THERE NOWHERE A . . . . SP EARLY EVENING 27
WHERE THERE NEVER WAS NO JIM CROW SIGNS NOWHERE. . . . . SP FREEDOM TRAIN 54
WHO HAVE NOWHERE . . . . SP VAGABONDS 4
(WHICH LATELY IS STONE NOWHERE) . . AYM HORN OF PLENTY 32
GOT NOWHERE. . . . . PL DOWN WHERE I AM 8

NO-GOOD 3

WITH A NO-GOOD MAN. . . . . SP BLD OF THE GIRL 4
WITH A NO-GOOD MAN. . . . . SP MADAM'S PAST HI 13
FOR A NO-GOOD MAN? . . . . SP MISERY 12

NO-MAN'S 1

THAT GROWS IN NO-MAN'S LAND, JOAN OF ARC, AND VARIOUS OTHER WAR-TIME NM COLORED SL MOOD 5

NO-OOOO-OOO-OO-O 1

NO-OOOO-OOO-OO-O! . . . . SP SUNDAY MORNING 32

NO'THERN 1

ON THE NO'THERN ROAD. . . . . SP BOUND NO'TH BLS 22

NUDGE 1

NUDGE THEIR DRAFTEE YEARS. . . . . SP TAG 4

NUMBER 6

NUMBER WRITERS. . . . . FC LAUGHERS 16
NUMBER RUNNER . . . . SP MADAM NUMBER WR 1
BUT THE NUMBER THAT DAY . . . . . . SP MADAM NUMBER WR 17
WHERE THE NUMBER NOT ONLY . . . . . SP MADAM NUMBER WR 27

WAS THE NUMBER. . . . . SP RAILROAD AVENUE 12
AND THE NUMBER . . . . AYM ASK YOUR MAMA 16

NUMBER'S 1
YOUR NUMBER'S COMING OUT! . . . . . AYM BLUES IN STEREO 1

NURSE 1
NURSE, PUT HER ON A DIET. . . . . . SP MADAM WRONG VIS 25

NURSES 2
NURSES OF BABIES. . . . . FC LAUGHERS 13
NURSES TURN GLASS DOORKNOBS . . . . SP INTERNE AT PROV 42

NURSES' 1
NURSES' HANDS ON SUTURE. . . . . . SP INTERNE AT PROV 21

NUTS 1
FULL OF NUTS AND SWEET. . . . . . . SP 125TH STREET 2

NYMPH 1
AS KEEPS THIS YOUNG NYMPH, JOY! . . SP JOY 9

N.A.A.C.P 2
ORIGINAL NIAGARA N.A.A.C.P. . . . . AYM BIRD IN ORBIT 19
HOW ABOUT THAT N.A.A.C.P. . . . . . AYM BIRD IN ORBIT 79

O 57
O, WHITE STRONG ONES. . . . . WB THE WHITE ONES 6
O, DE LONESOME RIVERSIDE. . . . . . FC A RUINED GAL 15
O, DE WICKED WATER. . . . . FC A RUINED GAL 16
O, LAWD! O, LAWD! . . . . FC BLD OF GIN MARY 9
O, LAWD! O, LAWD! . . . . FC BLD OF GIN MARY 9
O, LAWD . . . LAWDEE! . . . . FC BLD OF GIN MARY 10
O, EIGHTEEN MONTHS LOCKED IN! . . . FC BLD OF GIN MARY 18
O, PLEASE SIR, JUDGE, HAVE MERCY! FC BLD OF GIN MARY 21
O, GOD, PLEASE! . . . . FC CLOSING TIME 9
O, YOU CAN'T FIND A BUDDY . . . . . FC DEATH DO DIRTY 1
O, FRIEND O' MINE. . . . . FC DEATH DO DIRTY 20
O, LAWD HAVE MERCY . . . . FC GAL'S CRY DYING 11
BABY, O, BABY. . . . . FC MINNIE SINGS 11
O, LORD! . . . . FC MOAN 6
O, LORD! . . . . FC MOAN 15
O, PLAY SOME MORE. . . . . FC SATURDAY NIGHT 2
O, THIEVES, EXPLOITERS, KILLERS. . ANS A NEW SONG 29
O, LET MY LAND BE A LAND WHERE LIBERTY . . . . ANS LET AMERICA BE 11
BEATEN YET TODAY - O, PIONEERS! . . ANS LET AMERICA BE 36
O, I'M THE MAN WHO SAILED THOSE EARLY SEAS . . . . ANS LET AMERICA BE 45
O, LET AMERICA BE AMERICA AGAIN - ANS LET AMERICA BE 62
O, YES. . . . . ANS LET AMERICA BE 75
BECAUSE, O POOR WHITE WORKERS. . . ANS OPEN LETTER 45
O WHITE-FACED MIMES. . . . . FW FOR DEAD MIMES 1
O, IN THIS TAVERN ON THE CITY STREET OWT JUICE JOINT 33
O, TRIBAL DANCE! . . . . OWT NEGRO SERVANT 3
O, DRUMS! . . . . OWT NEGRO SERVANT 4
O, VELDT AT NIGHT! . . . . OWT NEGRO SERVANT 5
O, SONGS THAT DO NOT CARE! . . . . OWT NEGRO SERVANT 7
O, DRUMS OF LIFE IN HARLEM AFTER DARK! . . . . OWT NEGRO SERVANT 15
O, DREAMS! . . . . OWT NEGRO SERVANT 16
O, SONGS! . . . . OWT NEGRO SERVANT 17
O, SAXOPHONES AT NIGHT! . . . . . . OWT NEGRO SERVANT 18
O, SWEET RELIEF FROM FACES THAT ARE WHITE! . . . . OWT NEGRO SERVANT 19
O, I WISH THAT YESTERDAY. . . . . . OWT YESTERDAY TODAY 1
O, WHITE AS SNOW. . . . . SP ANGELS WINGS 2
O, I DRUG MA WINGS . . . . SP ANGELS WINGS 9
ROAD, ROAD, ROAD, O! . . . . SP BOUND NO'TH BLS 19
ROAD, ROAD, ROAD, O! . . . . SP BOUND NO'TH BLS 21
TELL ME, O QUICKLY! DREAM OF ALIVENESS. . . . . SP DEMAND 4
TELL ME, O DREAM OF UTTER ALIVENESS - . . . . SP DEMAND 6
O JESUS! . . . . SP JUDGMENT DAY 5
O, LITTLE TREE! . . . . SP LITTLE GRN TREE 15
O SHAMELESS MOON? . . . . SP MARCH MOON 8
O, UNDERSTAND . . . . SP MISERY 10
O, YOU LITTLE BASTARD BOY. . . . . SP MULATTO 16
O, SWEET AS EARTH. . . . . SP MULATTO 33
SING, O LORD JESUS! . . . . SP SPIRITUALS 4
SING, O BLACK MOTHER! . . . . SP SPIRITUALS 15
O, SWEEP OF STARS OVER HARLEM STREETS. . . . . SP STARS 1
O, LITTLE BREATH OF OBLIVION THAT IS NIGHT. . . . . SP STARS 2
O BLUES! . . . . SP THE WEARY BLUES 11
O BLUES! . . . . SP THE WEARY BLUES 16
O, THE PO' HOUSE IS LONELY. . . . . SP YOUNG GAL'S BLS 15
WHEN LOVE IS GONE, O. . . . . SP YOUNG GAL'S BLS 21
SINGERS LIKE O - . . . . AYM HORN OF PLENTY 2
I SAID, O, LORD, IF YOU CAN. . . . PL WHO BUT TH LORD 9

OAKLAND 1
SEATTLE, OAKLAND, SALT LAKE. . . . SP ONE-WAY TICKET 12

OATH 1
AND YET I SWEAR THIS OATH - . . . . ANS LET AMERICA BE 78

OBITUARIES 1
WRITE OBITUARIES . . . . PL SPECIAL BULLTIN 5

OBLIVION 2
O, LITTLE BREATH OF OBLIVION THAT IS NIGHT. . . . . SP STARS 2
OUT OF THE LITTLE BREATH OF OBLIVION SP STARS 8

OBLIVIOUS 1
OBLIVIOUS TO BLOOD . . . . AYM BIRD IN ORBIT 26

OBSEQUIOUS 1
THE LOW, OBSEQUIOUS. . . . . SP UNCLE TOM 5

OBSTACLES 2
SEE THE DIFFICULTIES, TOO, AND THE OBSTACLES. . . . . SP FREEDOM'S PLOW 16
THE MIND SEEKS A WAY TO OVERCOME THESE OBSTACLES. . . . . SP FREEDOM'S PLOW 17

OCCUR 2
DID IT EVER OCCUR TO YOU, SON. . . SP SISTER 7
DID IT EVER OCCUR TO YOU, BOY. . . SP SISTER 13

OCTOBER 2
OCTOBER 12TH,1942.) . . . . JC THE BITTER RIVR 1
TO A BROKEN SONG IN OCTOBER. . . . FW DUSTBOWL 9

ODETTA 1
SINGERS LIKE ODETTA - AND THAT STATUE . . . . AYM HORN OF PLENTY 3

OFF 28
HE KNOCKS ME OFF MA FEET. . . . . . FC MA MAN 2
HE KNOCKS ME OFF MA FEET. . . . . . FC MA MAN 4
TWO THINGS CAST OFF ALL SHAME. . . OLD TWO THINGS 6
ECHOES THE FIGHTING "MARSEILLAISE." TEARING OFF HIS CLOWN'S SUIT. . NM BLACK CLWN MOOD 13
TEAR OFF THE GARMENTS . . . . NM BLACK CLWN POEM 69
AND DROVE HER OFF TO JAIL . . . . . SH DEATH IN HARLEM 132
DE SHOES WORE OFF MY FEET. . . . . SH OUT OF WORK 2
DE SHOES WORE OFF MY FEET. . . . . SH OUT OF WORK 4
ANYHOW, AWAY OFF THERE. . . . . . . JC GOOD MORN STLIN 52
BEEN DRIVEN OFF ITS WAY. . . . . . JC TO CAPTAIN MULZ 7
THEN WENT OFF AND LEFT HER. . . . . SP BLD FORTUNE TEL 23
YOU GONNA CUT OFF MY HEAT? . . . . SP BLD LANDLORD 14
WHERE I GET OFF AT FIVE. . . . . . SP DEFERRED 26
MAMA, PLEASE BRUSH OFF MY COAT. . . SP MAMA AND DAUGHT 1
I CAN'T GET OFF MY MIND. . . . . . SP MAMA AND DAUGHT 8
OFF THE BODY OF THE MOON . . . . . SP MARCH MOON 4
THE BELGIANS CUT OFF MY HANDS IN THE CONGO. . . . . SP NEGRO 15
AND OFF DOWN LENOX AVENUE . . . . . SP NIGHT FUNERAL 33
OFF THE COAST OF IRELAND . . . . . SP SEASCAPE 1
OFF THE COAST OF ENGLAND . . . . . SP SEASCAPE 5
A THOUSAND YEARS OFF: . . . . SP TOMORROW 2
ELSE I'LL CUT YOU OFF . . . . SP ULTIMATUM 6
BLOTS COLORS OFF THE MAP. . . . . . AYM ASK YOUR MAMA 63
ON THE SOUND WAY OFF THE TURNPIKE - AYM HORN OF PLENTY 34
TO BE CARTED OFF BY BRINK'S. . . . AYM ODE TO DINAH 57
WOULD IT RUB OFF? . . . . PL CULTURAL EXCHNG 34
PEEL OFF THE SKIN. . . . . PL SPECIAL BULLTIN 20
PEEL OFF . . . . PL SPECIAL BULLTIN 22

OFFER 4
AT LEAST I CAN OFFER THAT. . . . . FC BRASS SPITOONS 39
MAYVILLE HAD NO PLACE TO OFFER HER. SP RUBY BROWN 5
ALL YOU GOT TO OFFER . . . . PL BACKLASH BLUES 17
FUTILE OF ME TO OFFER YOU MY HAND. PL LAST PRINCE 1

OFFERED 2
TO WHAT CLEAN BOY HAVE YOU OFFERED YOUR LIPS? . . . . WB NUDE YOUNG DANC 8
COULD HARDLY FIND A JOB THAT OFFERED DECENT PAY. . . . . NM COLORED SL POEM 21

OFFERING 3
NATCHA, OFFERING LOVE. . . . . . . SP NATCHA 1
FOR TEN SHILLINGS OFFERING LOVE. . SP NATCHA 2
OFFERING: A NIGHT WITH ME, HONEY. SP NATCHA 3

OFFICE 6
AND THE MINES AND THE FACTORIES AND THE OFFICE TOWERS . . . . ANS OPEN LETTER 15
TAKES OFFICE TOWERS. . . . . ANS OPEN LETTER 60
OF A JOB IN A FINE OFFICE . . . . . SP GRADUATION 16
IN THE POST OFFICE FOR A RAINY DAY. SP NUMBERS 3
DID YOU TELL HER THAT OUR CREDIT OFFICE . . . . AYM ASK YOUR MAMA 10
PAID AT THE BOX OFFICE . . . . . . AYM SHOW FARE PLESE 15

OFTEN 3
THE PEOPLE OFTEN HOLD . . . . SP FREEDOM'S PLOW 147
IN DIXIE, OFTEN THEY WON'T CALL NEGROES MISTER. . . . . SP IN EXPLANATION 7
NOR DO I OFTEN WANT TO BE A PART OF YOU. . . . . SP THEME FOR ENG B 35

OGOUN 2

DAMBALLA WEDO OGOUN AND THE HORSE AYM GOSPEL CHA-CHA 15
BEDWARD! POCOMANIA! WEDO! OGOUN! . AYM GOSPEL CHA-CHA 36

OH 44

OH, GREAT DARK CITY. . . . . WB DISILLUSION 12
OH, SILVER TREE! . . . . WB JAZZONIA 1
OH, SHINING RIVERS OF THE SOUL! . . WB JAZZONIA 2
OH, SINGING TREE! . . . . WB JAZZONIA 7
OH, SHINING RIVERS OF THE SOUL! . . WB JAZZONIA 8
OH, SHINING TREE! . . . . WB JAZZONIA 14
OH, SILVER RIVERS OF THE SOUL! . . WB JAZZONIA 15
OH, SWEET, AWAY! . . . . WB OUR LAND 16
OH, I AM GOOD, ... WB PIERROT 21
OH, ... WB POEM 8
OH, GOD, I WANTS HIM BACK! . . . . FC BLACK GAL 18
LOVE, OH, LOVE IS . . . . FC GYPSY MAN 19
LOVE, OH, LOVE IS . . . . FC GYPSY MAN 21
OH, YOU GOOD GIRLS, ... FC LISTEN HERE 15
I'D STARVE AND - OH, WELL - . . . . NM BIG-TIMER POEM 42
OH, LITTLE DARK BABY, ... DK LULLABY 19
OH, WITHERED OLD WOMAN . . . . . . DK PARISIAN BEGGAR 9
PULL AT THE ROPE! OH! . . . . ANS LYNCHING SONG 1
OH, THEY NABBED ARABELLA . . . . . SH DEATH IN HARLEM 131
WHERE, OH, WHERE . . . . SH SHAKESPEARE 3
OH, WATER OF THE BITTER RIVER . . . JC THE BITTER RIVR 22
OH, TRAGIC BITTER RIVER . . . . . . JC THE BITTER RIVR 83
OH, FIELDS OF WONDER . . . . FW BIRTH 1
HE SAID, OH, LORD, THY WILL BE DONE! LHR BLD MARY'S SON 24
OH, MEN TREATS WOMEN . . . . SP LOVER'S RETURN 9
SHE CRIED, OH, NO! . . . . SP MADAM HER MADAM 18
I LOVE YOU, OH, I LOVE YOU SO - . . SP MISS BLUES'ES 9
OH, GOD! . . . . SP SLIVER SERMON 5
OH, THEN! OH, THEN! . . . . SP SUNDAY MORNING 15
OH, THEN! OH, THEN! . . . . SP SUNDAY MORNING 15
OH, MY DARK CHILDREN, MAY MY DREAMS AND MY PRAYERS . . . . SP THE NEGRO MOTHE 49
OH! . . . . SP TO BE SOMEBODY 13
OH, THAT LAST LONG RIDE IS A . . . SP WIDOW WOMAN 1
OH, HUM! . . . . SP WINE-O 8
OH, MY, MY! . . . . SP WORLD WAR II 2
TURN, OH, TURN, DARK LOVERS . . . . AYM IS IT TRUE? 18
OH, BARE YOUR BACK! . . . . PL CHRIST IN ALA. 3
NIGHTMARES, DREAMS, OH! . . . . . . PL CULTURAL EXCHNG 37
DUBOIS (WHEN?) MALCOLM (OH!) SEND FOR STOKELY. . . . . PL FINAL CALL 35
OH, TO BE A BEAST, A BIRD, ... PL FREDRK DOUGLASS 16
OH, WHAT SORROW! . . . . PL MISSISSIPPI 1
OH, WHAT PITY! . . . . PL MISSISSIPPI 2
OH, WHAT PAIN . . . . PL MISSISSIPPI 3
OH, RUN, ALL WHO HAVE NOT . . . . . PL SPECIAL BULLTIN 16

OH-OOO-OO-O 1

OH-OOO-OO-O! . . . . SP SUNDAY MORNING 13

OLD 115

DAMN MA BLACK OLD MAMMY'S SOUL . . FC A RUINED GAL 17
OLD JUDGE SAYS, MARY JANE, ... FC BLD OF GIN MARY 6
OLD JUDGE SAYS YOU'S A DRUNKARD. . FC BLD OF GIN MARY 13
OLD HARD-FACED JUDGE SAYS EIGHTEEN MONTHS . . . . FC BLD OF GIN MARY 23
ANY OLD TIME . . . . FC DEATH DO DIRTY 2
LOTS OF OLD SCHOOLMATES ARE MARRIED NOW; . . . . NM BIG-TIMER POEM 45
IN AN OLD SUIT AND A BATTERED HAT, TO THE TUNE OF A SLOW DRAG STOMP NM BROKE 1
AND ONE OLD FUNNY BOY SAID, "I'LL WORK AT ANY PRICE . . . . NM BROKE 8
AND DON'T YOU KNOW THAT OLD WOMAN SWELLED UP LIKE A SPECKLED TOAD NM BROKE 21
O' GETTIN' A NEW WINTER COAT, OR HAVIN' THAT OLD ONE CLEANED. . . NM BROKE 40
AM I TOO OLD TO SEE THE FAIRIES DANCE? . . . . DK AFTR MNY SPRNGS 7
OLD GAL O' MINE. . . . . DK DRESSED UP 8
OUT OF THE PURPLE AND ROSE OF OLD MEMORIES . . . . DK FAIRIES 3
LET'S GO SEE OLD ABE . . . . DK LINCOLN MONUMNT 1
QUIET FOR TEN THOUSAND CENTURIES, OLD ABE. . . . . DK LINCOLN MONUMNT 4
OLD ABE. . . . . DK LINCOLN MONUMNT 11
THAT YOU ARE OLD. . . . . DK PARISIAN BEGGAR 4
OH, WITHERED OLD WOMAN . . . . . . DK PARISIAN BEGGAR 9
NINE OLD MEN IN WASHINGTON, ... ANS BLD OZZIE POWEL 13
NINE OLD MEN SO RICH AND WISE, . . ANS BLD OZZIE POWEL 17
THE OLD AND RICH WILL LIVE ON AWHILE, ... ANS KIDS WHO DIE 4
AND THE OLD AND RICH DON'T WANT THE PEOPLE . . . . ANS KIDS WHO DIE 33
AND FINDING ONLY THE SAME OLD STUPID PLAN. . . . . ANS LET AMERICA BE 23
IN THAT OLD WORLD WHILE STILL A SERF OF KINGS, ... ANS LET AMERICA BE 40
TO SMASH THE OLD DEAD DOGMAS OF THE PAST - . . . . ANS OPEN LETTER 24
AND JIVE SOME OLD BROAD I MIGHT MEET. . . . . SH BED TIME 4
PAWNBROKER, OLD FRIEND - . . . . . . SH BLD PAWNBROKER 22
ANY OLD THING TO EAT. . . . . SH BRIEF ENCOUNTER 2
LOOKIN' FOR ANY OLD THING TO EAT - SH BRIEF ENCOUNTER 4
TOGETHER IN MY BIG OLD DOWN-HOME FRAME. . . . . SH DAYBREAK 8
FOR AN OLD NIGHT-BIRD. . . . . SH DEATH IN HARLEM 26
CAUSE THAT OLD ALARM CLOCK SHO HURTS MY EARS. . . . . SH LETTER 19
HERE I SET WITH A BITTER OLD THOUGHT, ... SH TWILIGHT REVERI 1
YAL, HERE I SET THINKING - A BITTER OLD THOUGHT . . . . SH TWILIGHT REVERI 9
IF I JUST HAD A OWL HEAD, OLD OWL HEAD WOULD DO, ... SH TWILIGHT REVERI 11
AND HERE I SET THINKING WITH A BITTER OLD FROWN. . . . . SH TWILIGHT REVERI 14
OLD JIM CROW'S SORROW? . . . . JC BLACK MAN SPEAK 28
THERE WAS AN OLD CROW BY THE NAME OF JIM. . . . . JC JIM CROW'S LAST 1
AND BE THE SAME OLD CROW HE USED TO BE - . . . . JC JIM CROW'S LAST 10
HE STILL TRIES TO ACT IN THE SAME OLD WAY. . . . . JC JIM CROW'S LAST 12
IF YOU WANT TO GET OLD HITLER'S GOAT, ... JC JIM CROW'S LAST 23
EACH FOURTEEN YEARS OLD WHEN LYNCHED TOGETHER BENEATH THE . . . . . . JC THE BITTER RIVR 1
AND LOVE'S OLD STORY TOLD - . . . . FW CAROLINA CABIN 20
OLD SEAMEN . . . . FW SAILING DATE 7
AND EVIL OLD . . . . OWT BLUES ON A BOX 5
ECHO THE AGE-LESS, AGE-LONG OLD DESPAIR . . . . OWT JUICE JOINT 27
WHERE TWO OLD BROWN MEN STAND BEHIND THE BAR - . . . . OWT JUICE JOINT 37
OLD LONESOME CORNER! . . . . OWT LONESOME CORNER 5
IN THIS STRANGE OLD TOWN - . . . . OWT STRANGER IN TWN 14
I GOT THOSE SAD OLD WEARY BLUES. . OWT TOO BLUE 1
IN THE FLOW OF OLD AUNT SUE'S VOICE, SP AUNTSUE'S STORI 13
I THOUGHT ABOUT OLD GREELEY . . . . SP BLUE BAYOU 4
I'LL KILL OLD GREELEY. . . . . . . SP BLUE BAYOU 13
THAT OLD BLUE MONDAY . . . . SP BLUE MONDAY 10
MY OLD MAN'S A WHITE OLD MAN . . . SP CROSS 1
MY OLD MAN'S A WHITE OLD MAN . . . SP CROSS 1
AND MY OLD MOTHER'S BLACK. . . . . SP CROSS 2
IF EVER I CURSED MY WHITE OLD MAN SP CROSS 3
IF EVER I CURSED MY BLACK OLD MOTHER SP CROSS 5
MY OLD MAN DIED IN A FINE BIG HOUSE. SP CROSS 9
YOU KNOW, AS OLD AS I AM, ... SP DEFERRED 45
LIKE AN OLD GRANDMOTHER, ... SP FULFILMENT 17
JUST A LITTLE OLD LETTER, ... SP LITTLE OLD LETT 5
NOW OLD AGE HAS . . . . SP LITTLE GRN TREE 7
A LITTLE OLD LETTER . . . . SP LITTLE OLD LETT 15
MY OLD TIME DADDY . . . . SP LOVER'S RETURN 1
I'M JUST OLD DEATH . . . . SP MADAM WRONG VIS 13
THE SAME OLD FIX. . . . . SP MADAM NUMBER WR 20
SHALL I USE OLD ENGLISH . . . . . . SP MADAM'S CALLING 13
MY OLD MULE, ... SP ME AND THE MULE 1
I'M LIKE THAT OLD MULE - . . . . . SP ME AND THE MULE 5
HOW OLD NOBODY KNOWS - . . . . . . SP MYSTERY 12
YET OLD AS MYSTERY, ... SP MYSTERY 13
THIS LITTLE OLD FURNISHED ROOM'S . SP NECESSITY 5
AND MY LANDLADY'S SO OLD . . . . . SP NECESSITY 8
THE SAME OLD SPARK! . . . . SP NEW YORKERS 17
OLD PREACHER-MAN . . . . SP NIGHT FUNERAL 21
OLD WALT WHITMAN . . . . SP OLD WALT 1
OLD WALT WENT SEEKING . . . . SP OLD WALT 10
OLD BLACK ME! . . . . SP PARADE 33
RICH OLD WHITE MAN . . . . SP PORTER 9
A BLACK OLD WOMAN CROONS . . . . . SP PRAYER MEETING 5
A BLACK OLD WOMAN CROONS - . . . . SP PRAYER MEETING 8
BUT A OLD WOMAN'LL SAY, ... SP PREFERENCE 7
SITTING ON OLD MRS. LATHAM'S BACK PORCH . . . . SP RUBY BROWN 9
AN OLD NEGRO MINISTER CONCLUDES HIS SERMON IN HIS LOUDEST VOICE, . . SP SUNDAY MORNING 1
BY THE PALE DULL PALLOR OF AN OLD GAS LIGHT . . . . SP THE WEARY BLUES 5
I HEARD THAT NEGRO SING, THAT OLD PIANO MOAN - . . . . SP THE WEARY BLUES 18
DISTILLED FROM OLD DESIRE - . . . . SP TRUMPET PLAYER 24
THEM LITTLE OLD MUTTS . . . . SP WARNING AUGMENT 9
SO WE CRANKED UP OUR OLD FORD . . . SP WEST TEXAS 11
I BELIEVE MY OLD LADY'S . . . . . . SP WHAT? SO SOON! 1
SORRY THAT OLD WAR IS DONE! . . . . SP WORLD WAR II 6
TO SEE MA OLD AUNT CLEW. . . . . . SP YOUNG GAL'S BLS 8
TO SEE MA OLD AUNT CLEW. . . . . . SP YOUNG GAL'S BLS 10
WHEN I'M OLD AN' UGLY . . . . SP YOUNG GAL'S BLS 11
TO BE UGLY AN' OLD. . . . . SP YOUNG GAL'S BLS 18
HEAR THE OLD FOLKS SAY HOW . . . . AYM BIRD IN ORBIT 40
AND THE MUSIC OF OLD MUSIC'S . . . AYM BLUES IN STEREO 23
SINGING YOUR MEAN OLD BACKLASH BLUES. . . . . PL BACKLASH BLUES 30
ON THE OLD IRON STOVE WHAT'S COOKING? . . . . PL CULTURAL EXCHNG 27
DEAR, DEAR DARLING OLD WHITE MAMMIES - . . . . PL CULTURAL EXCHNG 54
DEAR OLD . . . . PL CULTURAL EXCHNG 58

THE OLD, THE CAUTIOUS, THE OVER-WISE -	PL ELDERLY LEADERS	1
SEND FOR OLD MAN MOSES TO LAY DOWN THE LAW.	PL FINAL CALL	9
FOR OLD JOHN BROWN WHO KNEW SLAVERY COULDN'T	PL FINAL CALL	22
SEND FOR HARRIETT TUBMAN, OLD SOJOURNER TRUTH.	PL FINAL CALL	32
REMEMBERING THE OLD LIES.	PL HARLEM	3
THE OLD KICKS IN THE BACK.	PL HARLEM	4
THE OLD "BE PATIENT"	PL HARLEM	5
BUT THE HOUSE IS OLD.	PL LITTLE SNG HOUS	10
OLD PICASSO AND THE DOVE	PL THE DOVE	2
FROM OUR OLD	PL THE DOVE	8
IT'S MADE OF PLAIN OLD GEORGIA CLAY.	PL VARI-COLORED	7
WITH OLD AND NOT TOO GENTLE	PL WHERE WHEN WHCH	15

OLDER 4

OLDER THAN CREED.	SP MYSTERY	14
I'VE KNOWN RIVERS ANCIENT AS THE WORLD AND OLDER THAN THE	SP NEGRO SPEAKS OF	2
THAT'S WHY I LIKES A OLDER WOMAN .	SP PREFERENCE	11
ALTHOUGH YOU'RE OLDER - AND WHITE -	SP THEME FOR ENG B	39

OLDER'N 1

SIX OR EIGHT AND TEN YEARS OLDER'N MYSELF.	SP PREFERENCE	2

OLDEST 1

OF THE OLDEST	PL BLACK PANTHER	11

ONCE 23

ONCE I WAS WISE.	WB THE JESTER	18
ONCE I WAS IN MEMPHIS.	FC GYPSY MAN	7
ONCE I WAS IN MEMPHIS.	FC GYPSY MAN	9
PLAY IT ONCE.	FC SATURDAY NIGHT	1
I WAS ONCE A BLACK CLOWN	NM BLACK CLWN POEM	77
ONCE YOU WERE YOUNG.	DK PARISIAN BEGGAR	1
ONCE YOU WERE BEAUTIFUL.	DK PARISIAN BEGGAR	5
CAN'T DIE BUT ONCE.	JC BLD SAM SOLOMON	40
OF THOSE WHO WOULD KEEP, OR ONCE MORE MAKE	JC TO CAPTAIN MULZ	31
THAT ONCE WAS SUNG BENEATH THE SUN	OWT JUICE JOINT	10
SO WITH MY ONCE GAY-COLORED SOUL .	SP A BLACK PIERROT	12
ONCE SIXTEEN.	SP CONSIDER ME	3
ONCE FIVE, ONCE THREE.	SP CONSIDER ME	4
ONCE FIVE, ONCE THREE.	SP CONSIDER ME	4
ONCE NOBODY.	SP CONSIDER ME	5
AT ONCE!	SP DEFERRED	31
I CAME UP ONCE AND HOLLERED! . . .	SP LIFE IS FINE	5
ONCE I ADOPTED	SP MADAM CHARTY CH	1
DAUGHTER, ONCE UPON A TIME - . . .	SP MAMA AND DAUGHT	9
IN THE EYES ONCE SOFT BENIGHTED . .	SP MIGRANT	22
ONCE IN 1923.	SP RELIEF	5
WALKS ONCE AGAIN.	SP WHEN SUE WEARS	8
TO A BAND THAT ONCE PASSED OVER . .	AYM ODE TO DINAH	27
WHERE THE CHRIST CHILD ONCE HAD LAIN.	AYM ODE TO DINAH	34
MELT TO WATER ONCE AGAIN	AYM ODE TO DINAH	36
ONCE YOUR BROTHER'S KEEPER	AYM ODE TO DINAH	84
SEEMS LIKE ONCE I MET YOU	AYM RIDE, RED, RIDE	31
THAT ONCE PERHAPS WERE EYES. . . .	PL JUSTICE	4

ONE 101

ONE SAID SHE HEARD THE JAZZ-BAND SOB	WB CABARET	5
I WAS A RED MAN ONE TIME.	WB LAMENT DARK PEO	1
AH, MY BELOVED ONE, AWAY!	WB OUR LAND	17
I HAVE ONE WIFE.	WB PIERROT	11
I HAVE ONE WIFE.	WB PIERROT	14
AND PIERROT LOVED EACH ONE.	WB PIERROT	18
WITH THE BURGHER'S WIFE ONE JUNE.	WB PIERROT	30
MY BLACK ONE.	WB POEM	3
MY BLACK ONE.	WB POEM	9
MY BLACK ONE.	WB POEM	15
THOU DARK ONE.	WB SONGS DARK VIRG	6
THOU DARK ONE.	WB SONGS DARK VIRG	14
BUT ONE SHARP, LEAPING FLAME . . .	WB SONGS DARK VIRG	17
THOU DARK ONE.	WB SONGS DARK VIRG	19
DROP ONE BY ONE INTO STILLNESS. . .	WB SUMMER NIGHT	3
DROP ONE BY ONE INTO STILLNESS. . .	WB SUMMER NIGHT	3
IN ONE HAND	WB THE JESTER	1
YET I AIN'T NEVER BEEN NO BAD ONE.	FC BLACK GAL	13
I ASKED HER ONE NIGHT	FC NEW CABARET GRL	7
ONE IS KNOWN BY THE NAME OF DEATH.	OLD TWO THINGS	7
WE ONLY GOT ONE LIFE	NM BIG-TIMER POEM	71
FROM ONE SIDE TO THE OTHER, BUT NOW A HARSH AND BITTER NOTE CREEPS INTO	NM BLACK CLWN MOOD	9
ONE LITTLE MOMENT	NM BLACK CLWN POEM	31
'CAUSE 'FORE YOU GETS THERE, TEN THOUSAND AND ONE	NM BROKE	5
AND ONE OLD FUNNY BOY SAID, "I'LL WORK AT ANY PRICE	NM BROKE	8
O' GETTIN' A NEW WINTER COAT, OR HAVIN' THAT OLD ONE CLEANED. . . .	NM BROKE	40
TRIED TO FIND ONE O' THEM LITTLE ELEVATOR AND SWITCHBOARD JOBS THEY USED	NM BROKE	41
NO ONE REMEMBERS	DK PARISIAN BEGGAR	7
LOVELY, DARK, AND LONELY ONE. . . .	DK SONG	1
8 BLACK BOYS AND ONE WHITE LIE. . .	SL SCOTTSBORO	3
SHALL BE ONE!	ANS A NEW SONG	50
AND BLACK HANDS AND WHITE HANDS CLASPED AS ONE.	ANS KIDS WHO DIE	48
THAT ANY MAN BE CRUSHED BY ONE ABOVE.	ANS LET AMERICA BE	9
YET I'M THE ONE WHO DREAMT OUR BASIC DREAM	ANS LET AMERICA BE	39
FOR I'M THE ONE WHO LEFT DARK IRELAND'S SHORE.	ANS LET AMERICA BE	47
ONE SINGLE HAND	ANS OPEN LETTER	22
BECAUSE ONE IS BLACK.	ANS OPEN LETTER	30
ONE UNION FORM:	ANS OPEN LETTER	35
WENT BUSTIN INTO DIXIE'S BOUT ONE A.M.	SH DEATH IN HARLEM	2
THEY LOVED ONE ANOTHER TILL	SH DEATH IN HARLEM	89
JUST ONE THING AFTER 'NOTHER . . .	SH LOVE AGAIN BLUS	5
TOO FAR TO ONE SIDE.	SH SNOB	8
NEITHER ONE NOR THE OTHER -	JC BLD SAM SOLOMON	34
ALONE, I KNOW, NO ONE IS FREE. . .	JC TO CAPTAIN MULZ	35
MANY BLOODS - YET ALL OF ONE BLOOD STILL:	JC TO CAPTAIN MULZ	48
NO ONE TALKING	FW DIMOUT IN HARLM	15
SHE WENT ONE SUMMER MORNING	FW GIRL	5
BUT NO ONE WAS CURIOUS.	FW HEART	8
NO ONE CARED AT ALL	FW HEART	9
ONE MIGHT MAKE A STORY	FW MIGRATION	16
BUT NARY A ONE	OWT HONEY BABE	15
BUT I DIDN'T HAVE NARY ONE.	OWT STRANGER IN TWN	5
NOT NARY ONE A-TALL.	OWT STRANGER IN TWN	6
ONE BULLET WOULD DO?	OWT TOO BLUE	11
TO LOOK FOR ONE.	OWT TOO BLUE	17
IN THIS ONE HOUSE IN TAOS -	SP A HOUSE IN TAOS	20
BUT ALL ONE SNARL OF SOULS.	SP A HOUSE IN TAOS	40
ONE RUN OVAH YOU	SP BABY	6
A FELLOW CAME ONE DAY.	SP BLD FORTUNE TEL	9
BUT HE DOESN'T WALK LIKE ONE. . . .	SP CASUALTY	2
"ONE - TWO - BUCKLE MY SHOE!" . . .	SP CHILDREN'S RYME	2
ONE BATTED A HARD BALL RIGHT THROUGH MY WINDOW	SP CHILDREN'S RYME	18
ONE DON'T MAKE ENOUGH	SP CONSIDER ME	30
ONE MORE BOTTLE OF GIN.	SP DEFERRED	33
BUT BLOW ONE BLARING TRUMPET NOTE OF SUN	SP FATASY PURPLE	7
THUS THE DREAM BECOMES NOT ONE MAN'S DREAM ALONE.	SP FREEDOM'S PLOW	22
ONE TROUBLE IS YOU:	SP HIGH TO LOW	3
WASN'T EVEN ONE PAGE LONG -	SP LITTLE OLD LETT	6
FOR ONE MORE DOLLAR AND A HALF. . .	SP MADAM FORT TELL	23
YOUR FATHER, YES, HE WAS THE ONE!	SP MAMA AND DAUGHT	11
ONE OF THE PILLARS OF THE TEMPLE FELL.	SP MULATTO	4
WHEN THE AIR IS ONE INTERMINABLE BALL GAME	SP PASSING	2
THE ONE TO STOP 'EM WON'T BE ME. .	SP RELIEF	15
ONE DAY.	SP RUBY BROWN	8
ONE STAR.	SP STARS	11
THE BABY CAME ONE MORNING.	SP S-SSS-SS-SH!	15
I AM THE ONE WHO LABORED AS A SLAVE.	SP THE NEGRO MOTHE	13
OF ONE THE WHITE FOLKS	SP UNCLE TOM	8
SHINES LIKE THE EVIL ONE	SP WEST TEXAS	2
SHINES LIKE THE EVIL ONE	SP WEST TEXAS	17
THAT'S ONE TIME, PRETTY PAPA. . . .	SP WIDOW WOMAN	11
ONE AND THE SAME:	AYM BLUES IN STEREO	11
AND ONE, YES, ONE	AYM GOSPEL CHA-CHA	61
AND ONE, YES, ONE	AYM GOSPEL CHA-CHA	61
AND ONE SHOULD LOVE ONE'S COUNTRY	AYM HORN OF PLENTY	57
THE ONE COIN IN THE METER	AYM ODE TO DINAH	4
OUT OF ONE IN EXIT	AYM ODE TO DINAH	118
TRIBAL NOW NO LONGER ONE FOR ALL .	AYM ODE TO DINAH	88
AND ALL FOR ONE NO LONGER	AYM ODE TO DINAH	89
IS ONE	AYM SHOW FARE PLESE	32
YOU'RE THE ONE.	PL BACKLASH BLUES	31
YES, YOU'RE THE ONE	PL BACKLASH BLUES	32
NOT ONE -	PL CROWNS GARLANDS	14
ONE HANDFUL OF DREAM-DUST	PL DREAM DUST	5
HOW CAN ONE MAN BE TEN?	PL GHOSTS OF 1619	21
OR TEN - OR ONE -	PL GHOSTS OF 1619	27
AND BREAD ONE.	PL HARLEM	10
TO ONE WHO WILL NOT LIVE.)	PL JUNIOR ADDICT	18
ONE JEW.	PL LENOX AVE. BAR	5
ONE SIDE WON.	PL MOTHER IN WAR	13
LOOK SLOW AT ONE ANOTHER -	PL OCTOBER 16 RAID	12

ONES 10

WHITE ONES, BROWN ONES.	WB HARLEM NIGHT CL	14
WHITE ONES, BROWN ONES.	WB HARLEM NIGHT CL	14
O, WHITE STRONG ONES.	WB THE WHITE ONES	6
AN' DE ONES THAT KILT HIM. - . . .	FC DEATH DO DIRTY	31
SOME OF THESE YOUNG ONES IS CERT'LY BAD -	SP CHILDREN'S RYME	17
THE ONES I LOVE.	SP CORA	6
THE ONES WHO'VE CROSSED THE LINE .	SP PASSING	11
DARK ONES OF AFRICA.	SP SUN SONG	5
DARK ONES OF TODAY, MY DREAMS MUST COME TRUE:	SP THE NEGRO MOTHE	34

ESPECIALLY FOR THE FIRST ONES . . . AYM HORN OF PLENTY 65

ONE-BUTTON 1
HAS A FINE ONE-BUTTON ROLL. . . . . SP TRUMPET PLAYER 36

ONE-TIME 1
ONE-TIME SIX-YEAR-OLDS . . . . . . AYM BIRD IN ORBIT 8

ONE-WAY 1
ON A ONE-WAY TICKET - . . . . SP ONE-WAY TICKET 25

ONE'S 5
AND I GUESS THAT ONE'S ALL - . . . NM BIG-TIMER POEM 72
OF OWNING EVERYTHING FOR ONE'S OWN
GREED! . . . . ANS LET AMERICA BE 30
I'M THE ONLY ONE'S GOT TO PILE OUT
IN THE COLD. . . . . SH DAYBREAK 6
AND ONE SHOULD LOVE ONE'S COUNTRY AYM HORN OF PLENTY 57
FOR ONE'S COUNTRY IS YOUR MAMA. . . AYM HORN OF PLENTY 58

ONLY 44
WILL BE THEIR ONLY . . . . WB POEME D'AUTOMNE 14
ONLY DUMB GUYS FIGHT. . . . . FC PRIZE FIGHTER 1
ONLY DUMB GUYS FIGHT. . . . . FC PRIZE FIGHTER 7
WE ONLY GOT ONE LIFE . . . . NM BIG-TIMER POEM 71
ONLY IN SONG AND LAUGHTER . . . . . NM BLACK CLWN POEM 10
ONLY IN JOY . . . . NM BLACK CLWN POEM 14
I'M ONLY A CLOWN! . . . . NM BLACK CLWN POEM 58
JUST ONLY PROVIDIN' DE BOSS MAN IS
NICE!" . . . . NM BROKE 9
AND ONLY IN THE SORROW SONGS . . . ANS A NEW SONG 22
ONLY MY OWN HANDS. . . . . ANS A NEW SONG 26
AND FINDING ONLY THE SAME OLD STUPID
PLAN. . . . . ANS LET AMERICA BE 23
WHEN BOMBS'LL FALL NOT ONLY ON SPAIN
- . . . . ANS SONG OF SPAIN 52
I'M THE ONLY ONE'S GOT TO PILE OUT
IN THE COLD. . . . . SH DAYBREAK 6
BUT SHE'S DE ONLY . . . . SH ONLY WOMAN BLUS 5
CAUSE SHE'S DE ONLY . . . . SH ONLY WOMAN BLUS 11
SHE'S DE ONLY . . . . SH ONLY WOMAN BLUS 17
YOU DE LAST AND ONLY . . . . SH ONLY WOMAN BLUS 23
IT GIVES ONLY THE GLINT OF STEEL
BARS . . . . JC THE BITTER RIVR 27
ONLY HEAVEN. . . . . FW GIFTS 4
ONLY TO CHANGE . . . . LHR DEAR LVLY DEATH 4
ONLY THE THICK WALL. . . . . SP AS I GREW OLDER 22
ONLY THE SHADOW. . . . . SP AS I GREW OLDER 23
IF SHE ONLY WOULD. . . . . SP BLD FORTUNE TEL 20
ONLY THE ELEVATORS . . . . SP ELEVATOR BOY 15
DOWN SOUTH IN DIXIE ONLY TRAIN I
SEE'S . . . . SP FREEDOM TRAIN 9
NO WHITE FOLKS ONLY ON THE FREEDOM
TRAIN. . . . . SP FREEDOM TRAIN 14
AND SOMETIMES ONLY BLUNDERINGLY
EXPRESS THEM. . . . . SP FREEDOM'S PLOW 149
PERHAPS THE DREAM IS ONLY HER FACE - SP HAVANA DREAMS 5
WAS THE ONLY THING I HAD. . . . . . SP HOMECOMING 8
ONLY HEAVEN. . . . . SP LUCK 8
WHERE THE NUMBER NOT ONLY . . . . . SP MADAM NUMBER WR 27
AND THERE WAS ONLY THIS CORNER . . SP MAGNOLIA FLOWER 6
BUT HE'S THE ONLY MAN I'LL . . . . SP MIDWINTER BLUES 17
I HAD ONLY HOPE THEN, BUT NOW
THROUGH YOU. . . . . SP THE NEGRO MOTHE 33
I AM THE ONLY COLORED STUDENT IN MY
CLASS. . . . . SP THEME FOR ENG B 10
TWO DIMES AND A NICKLE ONLY . . . . SP TOMORROW 3
THE MEN CAN ONLY MURMUR . . . . . . AYM ASK YOUR MAMA 37
KNOW TOURISTS ONLY FOR . . . . . . AYM GOSPEL CHA-CHA 11
AND I'M THE ONLY COLORED. . . . . . AYM HORN OF PLENTY 35
THE ONLY NEGROES IN THE BLOCK . . . AYM HORN OF PLENTY 79
ONLY IN THE SEA. . . . . AYM IS IT TRUE? 37
THEY MAY NOT ONLY HAUNT YOU - . . . PL GHOSTS OF 1619 5
MASKED - WITH ONLY . . . . PL MISSISSIPPI 14
SHE THOUGHT THAT ONLY . . . . PL MOTHER IN WAR 12

ONTO 1
TO LATCH ONTO . . . . SP JOE LOUIS 11

OOL 1
OOL YA KOO . . . . SP FLATTED FIFTHS 18

OOP 1
OOP POP-A-DA . . . . SP FLATTED FIFTHS 16

OOP-POP-A-DA 2
OOP-POP-A-DA! . . . . SP CHILDREN'S RYME 25
OOP-POP-A-DA . . . . SP JAM SESSION 6

OPEN 6
OPEN WIDE YOUR ARMS TO LIFE. . . . OK SONG 5
SHE'LL OPEN THE LATCH . . . . FW FAITHFUL ONE 7
WE'D OPEN UP THE KINGDOM . . . . . FW WISDOM 6
THE GATES OPEN - . . . . SP GOOD MORNING 23
BABE, YOUR MOUTH WAS OPEN LIKE A
WELL. . . . . SP MORNING AFTER 12
HAVE DOORS THAT OPEN OUTWARD . . . AYM JAZZTET MUTED 16

OPENED 3
AND I OPENED UP MY DOOR. . . . . . SP HOMECOMING 2
SHE OPENED HER MOUTH. . . . . SP MADAM HER MADAM 17
BIG BOY OPENED HIS MOUTH AND SAID. SP 50 - 50 6

OPENING 1
OPENING INTO CORRIDORS. . . . . . . SP INTERNE AT PROV 43

OPENS 3
WHEN I OPENS DE DOOR. . . . . FC WORKIN' MAN 6
I OPENS MA MOUTH AN' LAUGHS. . . . OK HOMESICK BLUES 18
THE DOOR MARKED LADIES OPENS INWARD AYM ODE TO DINAH 116

OPPORTUNISTIC 1
OPPORTUNISTIC, CONVENIENT EVASION. PL ELDERLY LEADERS 4

OPPORTUNITY 1
BUT OPPORTUNITY IS REAL, AND LIFE IS
FREE. . . . . ANS LET AMERICA BE 13

OPPRESSED 1
BUT ALL THE WHOLE OPPRESSED . . . . ANS UNION 3

OPPRESSES 1
HE WHO OPPRESSES ME, HIM I DEFY! . NM DARK YOUTH USA 7

OPPRESSORS 1
AND THE OPPRESSORS HAD NO PITY. . . ANS A NEW SONG 21

OR 102
OR WHERE I GO. . . . . FC NEW CABARET GRL 12
SHALL I CARVE MA SELF OR . . . . . FC SUICIDE 11
DIAMOND RING, CIGARETTE HOLDER, AND
A CANE, TO THE MUSIC OF PIANO OR NM BIG-TIMER MOOD 1
LAUGH - OR TAKE PITY. . . . . NM BIG-TIMER POEM 8
OR THINKIN' AT ALL? . . . . NM BIG-TIMER POEM 70
SUIT AND HAT OF A CLOWN, TO THE
MUSIC OF A PIANO, OR AN
ORCHESTRA. . . . . . . NM BLACK CLWN MOOD 1
OR A WEARY BLUES. . . . . NM BROKE 1
LAST JOB I HAD, WENT TO WORK AT FIVE
IN DE MORNIN', OR LITTLE MO' . . NM BROKE 12
O' GETTIN' A NEW WINTER COAT, OR
HAVIN' THAT OLD ONE CLEANED. . . NM BROKE 40
(IS YOU LOOKIN' AT ME, BABY, OR SOME
OTHER WAY?) . . . . NM BROKE 76
UNITED STATES OF AMERICA, MARTIAL
MUSIC ON A PIANO, OR BY AN
ORCHESTRA. . . . . NM COLORED SL MOOD 3
THEY TOLD US AMERICA WOULD KNOW NO
BLACK OR WHITE: . . . . NM COLORED SL POEM 11
TO A COLORED BOY'S RISING IN WEALTH
OR STATION - . . . . NM COLORED SL POEM 27
TO BELIEVE AN ANGELO HERNDON, OR
EVER GET TOGETHER. . . . . ANS KIDS WHO DIE 36
OR A PRISON GRAVE, OR THE POTTER'S
FIELD. . . . . ANS KIDS WHO DIE 41
OR A PRISON GRAVE, OR THE POTTER'S
FIELD. . . . . ANS KIDS WHO DIE 41
OR THE RIVERS WHERE YOU'RE DROWNED
LIKE LIEBKNECHT. . . . . ANS KIDS WHO DIE 42
"YOU ARE MY BROTHER, BLACK OR
WHITE," . . . . ANS OPEN LETTER 39
IN A YEAR OR TWO. . . . . ANS PARK BENCH 10
OR IF I WASN'T SO DROWSY I'D LOOK UP
JOE . . . . SH BED TIME 5
OR IF IT WASN'T SO LATE I MIGHT TAKE
A WALK . . . . SH BED TIME 7
DO I SEE A COUPLE? OR DID I COUNT
TWICE? . . . . SH BED TIME 13
A DIAMOND OR TWO. . . . . SH BLD THE KILLER 2
OR COCOA BROWN. . . . . SH HARLEM SWEETIES 14
WALNUT OR COCOA. . . . . SH HARLEM SWEETIES 29
ARE YOU A FOOL OR A DUNCE? . . . . JC BLD SAM SOLOMON 38
YOU'RE HALF A WORLD AWAY OR MORE . JC GOOD MORN STLIN 17
OF THOSE WHO WOULD KEEP, OR ONCE
MORE MAKE . . . . JC TO CAPTAIN MULZ 31
OR DOES SOME STRANGE . . . . FW CONVENT 6
I DO OR SAY. . . . . FW FAITHFUL ONE 10
OR JUST ANOTHER . . . . FW SAILING DATE 16
OR THEY'LL HANG YOU TO A TREE! . . OWT FLIGHT 8
AT SIX O'CLOCK, OR SEVEN, OR EIGHT. OWT NEGRO SERVANT 8
AT SIX O'CLOCK, OR SEVEN, OR EIGHT. OWT NEGRO SERVANT 8
TO MAKE IT EITHER MORE OR LESS. . . LHR DEAR LVLY DEATH 7
OR SOMEBODY . . . . SP CAFE: 3 A.M. 7
POLICE LADY OR LESBIAN . . . . . . SP CAFE: 3 A.M. 9
OR SAVE. . . . . SP CONSIDER ME 22
OR GIVE MY SUGAR . . . . SP CONSIDER ME 23
OR LENOX AVENUE. . . . . SP COULD BE 2
TWO OR THREE THINGS IN THE PAST . . SP DANCER 1
OR SOMEBODY ELSE'S SHOES . . . . . SP ELEVATOR BOY 13
OR GREASY POTS IN A DIRTY KITCHEN. SP ELEVATOR BOY 20
OR AM I STILL A PORTER ON THE
FREEDOM TRAIN? . . . . SP FREEDOM TRAIN 19
"OR IF IT WOULD," THOUGHT SOME. . . SP FREEDOM'S PLOW 121
OR THAT THE UNION WOULD STAND. . . SP FREEDOM'S PLOW 135

IS IT FOR REAL - OR JUST A SHOW AGAIN? . . . SP FREEDOM TRAIN 46
TAME OR WILD? . . . SP GENIUS CHILD 7
WILD OR TAME. . . . SP GENIUS CHILD 8
OR FESTER LIKE A SORE - . . . SP HARLEM 4
OR CRUST AND SUGAR OVER - . . . SP HARLEM 7
OR DOES IT EXPLODE? . . . SP HARLEM 11
OR MAYBE THE DREAM'S A VEDADO ROSE - SP HAVANA DREAMS 7
OR WOULD YOU RATHER. . . . SP KID SLEEPY 18
OR IS YOUR HEART STONE-COLD? . . . SP MADAM MINISTER 8
OR AM I MISTAKEN? . . . SP MADAM MIGHT-HAV 14
OR A ROMAN LETTER? . . . SP MADAM'S CALLING 14
OF THE SEEKING OR THE FINDING. . . . SP OLD WALT 6
SIX OR EIGHT AND TEN YEARS OLDER'N MYSELF. . . . SP PREFERENCE 2
OR EVEN TWO. . . . SP RELIEF 14
OR BITS OF DUST IN EYES . . . SP SONG BILLIE HOL 12
OR IN REVERSE . . . SP SUMMER EVENING 7
HE SLEPT LIKE A ROCK OR A MAN THAT'S DEAD. . . . SP THE WEARY BLUES 35
IT'S NOT EASY TO KNOW WHAT IS TRUE FOR YOU OR ME . . . SP THEME FOR ENG B 16
OR RECORDS - BESSIE, BOP, OR BACH. SP THEME FOR ENG B 24
OR RECORDS - BESSIE, BOP, OR BACH. SP THEME FOR ENG B 24
A QUARTER OR A SHILLING. PARIS - . AYM ASK YOUR MAMA 49
BUT WHY RIDE ON MULE OR DONKEY . . AYM ASK YOUR MAMA 59
IN HARLEM OR THE SOUTH SIDE OF CHICAGO . . . AYM HORN OF PLENTY 55
OR THE WOMB OF MISSISSIPPI? . . . AYM HORN OF PLENTY 56
POOL HALL OR BAR ON CORNER . . . AYM HORN OF PLENTY 70
BY MOE ASCH OR ALAN LOMAX . . . AYM IS IT TRUE? 10
OR SPORTS-WRITERS IN THEIR STORY. AYM IS IT TRUE? 51
OR MUST I HESITATE? . . . AYM RIDE, RED, RIDE 8
GRENADINE GRANADA OR . . . AYM RIDE, RED, RIDE 21
DEAD OR LIVE THEIR GHOSTS CAST SHADOWS . . . AYM SHADES OF PIG 6
OR ZIK TO ALABAMA . . . AYM SHADES OF PIG 28
OR PIG MAYBELL TO . . . AYM SHADES OF PIG 29
OR DO YOU THINK THAT PAPA'S . . . AYM SHOW FARE PLESE 3
ARE THIS OR THAT . . . AYM SHOW FARE PLESE 27
OR LESS OR MOST - . . . AYM SHOW FARE PLESE 28
OR LESS OR MOST - . . . AYM SHOW FARE PLESE 28
NOT MOAN OR CRY. . . . PL COLOR 8
NOR TAKE THE PLACE OF MEAT OR BREAD PL CROWNS GARLANDS 15
OR RENT THAT I MUST PAY. . . . PL CROWNS GARLANDS 16
NO TRAINS OR STEAMBOATS GOING - . . PL CULTURAL EXCHNG 12
OR FESTER LIKE A SORE - . . . PL DREAM DEFERRED 4
OR CRUST AND SUGAR OVER - . . . PL DREAM DEFERRED 7
OR DOES IT EXPLODE? . . . PL DREAM DEFERRED 11
OR TEN BE A HUNDRED AND TEN? . . . PL GHOSTS OF 1619 22
OR A THOUSAND AND TEN? . . . PL GHOSTS OF 1619 23
OR A MILLION AND TEN . . . PL GHOSTS OF 1619 24
OR A HUNDRED AND TEN . . . PL GHOSTS OF 1619 26
OR TEN - OR ONE - . . . PL GHOSTS OF 1619 27
OR TEN - OR ONE - . . . PL GHOSTS OF 1619 27
OR NONE - . . . PL GHOSTS OF 1619 28
OR AN ANGEL WITH WINGS . . . PL GO SLOW 12
DAYTIME OR NIGHTIME JOB. . . . PL JUNIOR ADDICT 32
WINNERS OR LOSERS. . . . PL PEACE 3
WHICH APEAWAY, OR BAR. . . . PL WHERE WHEN WHCH 11
OR STATION WAITING ROOM . . . PL WHERE WHEN WHCH 12
OR ELSE MURDERED . . . PL WHO BUT TH LORD 7

ORANGE 1

KIDS WILL DIE IN THE ORANGE GROVES OF CALIFORNIA . . . ANS KIDS WHO DIE 12

ORBIT 2

IS IN ORBIT. . . . AYM BIRD IN ORBIT 31
FROM LESSER STARS IN ORBIT $ $ $ $ $ $ $ . . . AYM HORN OF PLENTY 21

ORCHESTRA 3

ORCHESTRA. . . . NM BIG-TIMER MOOD 1
SUIT AND HAT OF A CLOWN, TO THE MUSIC OF A PIANO, OR AN ORCHESTRA. . . . NM BLACK CLWN MOOD 1
UNITED STATES OF AMERICA. MARTIAL MUSIC ON A PIANO, OR BY AN ORCHESTRA. . . . NM COLORED SL MOOD 3

ORDER 1

IN ORDER THAT THE RACE MIGHT LIVE AND GROW. . . . SP THE NEGRO MOTHE 4

ORDERS 1

WHAT? YOU GONNA GET EVICTION ORDERS? SP BLD LANDLORD 13

ORDINARY 1

IS ORDINARY. . . . LHR CONSERVATORY 6

ORGAN 3

AND THE ORGAN HAD DONE PLAYED . . . SP NIGHT FUNERAL 29
IF I JUST HAD A ORGAN. . . . SP TESTIMONIAL 2
NEITHER ORGAN . . . SP TESTIMONIAL 6

ORGANIZING 2

ORGANIZING SHARECROPPERS. . . . ANS KIDS WHO DIE 9
ORGANIZING WORKERS. . . . ANS KIDS WHO DIE 11

ORIENTAL 2

IN ORIENTAL CITIES . . . FW OLD SAILOR 7
SPARKLING ORIENTAL WINES . . . SP FLATTED FIFTHS 7

ORIGINAL 2

TO ORIGINAL . . . SP CONSIDER ME 11
ORIGINAL NIAGARA N.A.A.C.P. . . . AYM BIRD IN ORBIT 19

ORLEANS 3

SEATTLE, NEW ORLEANS, . . . SP FREEDOM'S PLOW 87
WENT DOWN TO NEW ORLEANS, AND I'VE SEEN ITS MUDDY . . . SP NEGRO SPEAKS OF 9
FIRST GRADE IN NEW ORLEANS . . . AYM BIRD IN ORBIT 9

ORNETTE 1

ON THE BREATH OF ORNETTE COLEMAN. AYM JAZZTET MUTED 9

OTHER 39

AND IN THE OTHER . . . WB THE JESTER 3
AND IN THE OTHER . . . WB THE JESTER 3
NO OTHER GAL'S GOT A CHANCE. . . . FC MINNIE SINGS 10
AND THE OTHER HAS NO NAME . . . DLD TWO THINGS 8
FROM ONE SIDE TO THE OTHER. BUT NOW A HARSH AND BITTER NOTE CREEPS INTO . . . NM BLACK CLWN MOOD 9
(IS YOU LOOKIN' AT ME, BABY, OR SOME OTHER WAY?) . . . NM BROKE 76
THAT GROWS IN NO-MAN'S LAND. JOAN OF ARC, AND VARIOUS OTHER WAR-TIME NM COLORED SL MOOD 5
SO NOW I KNOW WE BLACKS ARE JUST LIKE ANY OTHER - . . . NM COLORED SL POEM 35
OTHER PEOPLE'S COLD. . . . SH BLD THE KILLER 18
DON'T SNUB THE OTHER FELLOW - . . . SH SNOB 3
NEITHER ONE NOR THE OTHER - . . . JC BLD SAM SOLOMON 34
INTO SOME OTHER THING . . . LHR DEAR LVLY DEATH 5
CHANGE IS THY OTHER NAME. . . . LHR DEAR LVLY DEATH 10
THE OTHER TWO . . . SP BUDDY 7
AS THE OTHER FELLOW HAS . . . SP DEMOCRACY 6
THEN THE HAND SEEKS OTHER HANDS TO HELP. . . . SP FREEDOM'S PLOW 20
THE PEOPLE DO NOT ALWAYS UNDERSTAND EACH OTHER. . . . SP FREEDOM'S PLOW 152
THE WAY, IN OTHER WORDS, . . . SP HIGH TO LOW 19
THE MISTERS WON'T CALL LOTS OF OTHER FOLKS MISTER. . . . SP IN EXPLANATION 11
TO THE OTHER SIDE OF THE HOUSE . . SP KID SLEEPY 3
TO THE OTHER SHORE - . . . SP MADAM NUMBER WR 24
I'LL READ YOUR OTHER PALM. . . . SP MADAM FORT TELL 24
THEM OTHER GIRLS DO . . . SP MADAM PHONE BIL 28
THE OTHER DAY. . . . SP MADAM'S CALLING 2
NO OTHER MUSIC . . . SP MISERY 3
HIS INSURANCE LAPSED THE OTHER DAY - SP NIGHT FUNERAL 6
I NEEDS THIS, THAT, AND THE OTHER. SP PREFERENCE 6
WHAT MY OTHER MAN CAN'T DO - . . . SP QUESTION 2
DOWN ON LENOX AVENUE THE OTHER NIGHT SP THE WEARY BLUES 4
THE SAME THINGS OTHER FOLKS LIKE WHO ARE OTHER RACES. . . . SP THEME FOR ENG B 26
THE SAME THINGS OTHER FOLKS LIKE WHO ARE OTHER RACES. . . . SP THEME FOR ENG B 26
AND OTHER KIDS LESS MEANER THAN ¢ ¢ ¢ ¢ . . . AYM HORN OF PLENTY 25
FROM THE OTHER . . . AYM HORN OF PLENTY 91
ALWAYS TOOK THE OTHER SIDE.) . . . AYM RIDE, RED, RIDE 18
AND TOUCHING EACH OTHER NATURAL AS DEW . . . PL DAYBREAK IN ALA 19
AS THE OTHER FELLOW HAS . . . PL FREEDOM 6
AND SEEKS AN OUT IN OTHER WORLDLY DREAMS. . . . PL JUNIOR ADDICT 3
BEGINNING IN SOME OTHER LAND - . . PL JUNIOR ADDICT 9
IN SOME OTHER SECTION . . . PL MISSISSIPPI 11

OTHERS 8

LET ALL OTHERS KEEP SILENT A MOMENT. ANS A NEW SONG 3
TELLING OTHERS TO GET TOGETHER. . . ANS KIDS WHO DIE 13
TO OTHERS - . . . FW GIFTS 3
BUT OTHERS KNEW IT HAD TO TRIUMPH. SP FREEDOM'S PLOW 122
TO OTHERS . . . SP LUCK 7
OTHERS TAKE A QUARTER STRAIGHT. . . SP TOMORROW 6
WHERE THE MASK IS PLACED BY OTHERS AYM SHOW FARE PLESE 6
AS FOR YOU OTHERS - . . . PL SPECIAL BULLTIN 18

OTHER'S 2

WITHOUT THAT OTHER'S CONSENT. . . . SP FREEDOM'S PLOW 104
WITHOUT THAT OTHER'S CONSENT. . . . SP FREEDOM'S PLOW 171

OUGHT 7

WHEN SHE OUGHT TO PLAY. . . . FC NEW CABARET GRL 20
THEY OUGHT TO BE SOME NOISE. . . . SH SUNDAY 11
THEY OUGHT TO BE LIKE ME SETTING HERE - FEELING GLAD! . . . SH SUNDAY 15
FOLKS OUGHT TO KNOW . . . JC HOW ABOUT DIXIE 18
YOU OUGHT TO KNOW! . . . SP BAR 5
THERE OUGHT TO BE MAGNOLIAS . . . SP MAGNOLIA FLOWER 10
LIKE YOU OUGHT TO DO. . . . SP WARNING AUGMENT 3

OUGHTER 1
NOT LIVIN' LIKE I OUGHTER. . . . . NM BIG-TIMER POEM 19

OUI 1
MAIS OUI. . . . . FC JAZZ BAND 15

OURS 3
THAT THE LAND MIGHT BE OURS. . . . ANS OPEN LETTER 14
BE OURS: . . . . ANS OPEN LETTER 18
ARE OURS! . . . . ANS OPEN LETTER 64

OURSELVES 1
OURSELVES UPSIDE DOWN. . . . . FW CIRCLES 10

OUT 179
THEY DROVE ME OUT OF THE FOREST. . . WB LAMENT DARK PEO 5
AN' SOON AS HE GOT OUT DE BARREL . . FC BLACK GAL 11
THEN OUT MA DOOR HE GOES. . . . . FC BLACK GAL 12
'LL HELP YOU OUT . . . . FC DEATH DO DIRTY 3
OUT FOR A SPREE. . . . . FC JAZZ BAND 8
GO OUT AN' LET DE WHITE BOYS . . . FC RED SILK STOCK 3
GO OUT AN' LET DE WHITE BOYS . . . FC RED SILK STOCK 11
THE LIGHTS GO OUT . . . . FC SPORT 8
SHE'S OUT IN DE STREET, - . . . . FC WORKIN' MAN 7
DIDN'T TURN OUT RIGHT. . . . . NM BIG-TIMER POEM 10
AND FIGHT IT OUT ALONE. . . . . NM BIG-TIMER POEM 56
OUT OF SADNESS IT RISES TO DEFIANCE AND DETERMINATION. A HYMN OF FAITH . . . . NM BLACK CLWN MOOD 12
OUT OF THE SLIME! . . . . NM BLACK CLWN POEM 72
DONE BEAT YOU TO DE PLACE, STANDIN' OUT SIDE DE DO' . . . . NM BROKE 6
YOU ALL OUT THERE LAUGHIN', BUT THAT AIN'T NO JOKE - . . . . NM BROKE 10
COME BAWLIN' ME OUT, 'CAUSE I'M BROKE. . . . . NM BROKE 26
OUT OF HIS GRAVE FROM OVER THE SEA, NM COLORED SL POEM 14
IT WAS AWFUL - FACING THAT BOY WHO WENT OUT TO DIE, ... NM COLORED SL POEM 42
SO I CLIMB TOWARD TOMORROW, OUT OF PAST SORROW, ... NM DARK YOUTH USA 22
AND OUT OF ALABAMA EARTH . . . . DK ALABAMA EARTH 6
BUT HIS SOUL WENT OUT TO SEA. . . . DK DEATH SEAMAN 2
OUT OF THE DUST OF DREAMS . . . . DK FAIRIES 1
OUT OF THE PURPLE AND ROSE OF OLD MEMORIES . . . . DK FAIRIES 3
NOW! COME OUT . . . . DK SONG BAJO DANC 8
20-VOICES: GROW OUT OF THE PASSIVE EARTH. . . . . ANS CHANT MAY DAY 10
UNTIL THE FUTURE BURNS OUT . . . . ANS OPEN LETTER 36
OUT OF THAT BROTHERHOOD . . . . ANS OPEN LETTER 49
I MUST DRIVE THE BOMBERS OUT OF SPAIN! . . . . ANS SONG OF SPAIN 79
I MUST DRIVE THE BOMBERS OUT OF THE WORLD! . . . . ANS SONG OF SPAIN 80
COME TO FIND OUT . . . . SH ANNOUNCEMENT 9
I'M THE ONLY ONE'S GOT TO PILE OUT IN THE COLD, ... SH DAYBREAK 6
A SHOT RANG OUT. . . . . SH DEATH IN HARLEM 103
AND A SHOT RANG OUT. . . . . SH DEATH IN HARLEM 108
AS THE SHOTS RANG OUT. . . . . SH DEATH IN HARLEM 113
AS THE SHOTS RANG OUT. . . . . SH DEATH IN HARLEM 118
WHEN THE SHOTS RANG OUT. . . . . SH DEATH IN HARLEM 123
LOUNGERS AT THE BAR LAUGH OUT LOUD. SH DEATH IN HARLEM 35
DIXIE RUBBED HIS HANDS AND LAUGHED OUT LOUD - . . . . SH DEATH IN HARLEM 63
WHEN SHE COME OUT . . . . SH DEATH IN HARLEM 93
GET OUT O' MY SIGHT BE- . . . . SH EVIL MORNING 15
OUT OF A DREAM. . . . . SH HARLEM SWEETIES 12
DO NOT SELL ME OUT, BABY, ... SH IN TROUBLED KEY 1
PLEASE DO NOT SELL ME OUT. . . . . SH IN TROUBLED KEY 2
DO NOT SELL ME OUT, BABY. . . . . SH IN TROUBLED KEY 3
DO NOT SELL ME OUT. . . . . SH IN TROUBLED KEY 4
YOU TURNED OUT TO BE A DEVIL . . . SH LOVE AGAIN BLUS 11
TURNED OUT SO BAD. . . . . SH MAY DAY 10
YOU MAY CALL OUT THE KLAN . . . . JC BLD SAM SOLOMON 2
AND BE UP AND OUT AND READY . . . . JC BLD SAM SOLOMON 21
THEY CALLED OUT THE KLAN. . . . . JC BLD SAM SOLOMON 41
GO GET OUT YOUR KLAN - . . . . JC BLD SAM SOLOMON 54
TO SEE JIM CROW GET OUT OF HAND. . JC JIM CROW'S LAST 4
CATCH THAT JIM CROW BIRD, PULL THE FEATHERS OUT HIS TAIL! . . . . JC JIM CROW'S LAST 16
PAUL ROBESON SAID, OUT IN KANSAS CITY, ... JC JIM CROW'S LAST 19
OUT OF AFRICA . . . . JC ME AND MY SONG 8
OUT OF AFRICA . . . . JC ME AND MY SONG 14
OUT OF AFRICA . . . . JC ME AND MY SONG 32
OUT OF YOU. . . . . JC NOTE TO NAZIS 8
BUT THERE ARE THOSE WHO STILL HOLD OUT . . . . JC TO CAPTAIN MULZ 10
OUT OF WHICH . . . . FW BIRTH 2
I WAS TRYING TO FIGURE OUT . . . . FW COMMUNION 1
BUT I COULD NOT FIGURE OUT . . . . FW COMMUNION 3
LOOKING OUT TO SEA . . . . FW JAIME 6
OUT THE COP THAT NIGHT. . . . . OWT BLD MARGE POLIT 4
RUNS OUT TOMORROW'S . . . . OWT BLUES ON A BOX 4
GO OUT THERE. . . . . OWT BOARDING HOUSE 12
YOU JUMP OUT OF BED. . . . . OWT HONEY BABE 11
LEMME OUT! . . . . OWT JITNEY 23
HIBBLER'S GIVING OUT! . . . . OWT JITNEY 27
31ST! ALL OUT! . . . . OWT JITNEY 36
OF WHISKEY AS THEY START OUT FOR A BALL. . . . . OWT JUICE JOINT 8
TO GET YOU OUT OF MY HEAD. . . . . OWT YESTERDAY TODAY 8
BEAT OUT OF BLOOD WITH WORDS SAD-SUNG . . . . SP AFRO-AMER FRAG 8
OUT OF ANY BOOK AT ALL, ... SP AUNTSUE'S STORI 20
RIGHT OUT OF HER OWN LIFE. . . . . SP AUNTSUE'S STORI 22
SHE TRIED TO FIND OUT . . . . SP BLD FORTUNE TEL 25
ANYTHING HE WANTS OUT OF IT. . . . SP BUDDY 10
THEN I STOOD OUT ON A PRAIRIE . . . SP CROSSING 15
OUT WHERE IT MAKES . . . . SP DEAD IN THERE 21
DROPPED OUT SIX MONTHS WHEN I WAS SEVEN, ... SP DEFERRED 3
STOMACH STICKING OUT. . . . . SP DELINQUENT 8
HELP ME WHEN I'M DOWN AND OUT. . . SP DOWN AND OUT 2
HELP ME WHEN I'M DOWN AND OUT, . . SP DOWN AND OUT 4
BEATING OUT AND BEATING OUT A - . . SP DREAM BOOGIE 7
BEATING OUT AND BEATING OUT A - . . SP DREAM BOOGIE 7
STEP OUT O' THE BARREL, BOY. . . . SP ELEVATOR BOY 11
DON'T TURN OUT LIKE I AM. . . . . SP EVENING SONG 12
PLEASE REACH OUT YO' HAND. . . . . SP FEET O' JESUS 8
WHEN A MAN STARTS OUT WITH NOTHING, SP FREEDOM'S PLOW 1
WHEN A MAN STARTS OUT WITH HIS HANDS SP FREEDOM'S PLOW 2
WHEN A MAN STARTS OUT TO BUILD A WORLD, ... SP FREEDOM'S PLOW 4
HIS EYES LOOK OUT ON THE WORLD. . . SP FREEDOM'S PLOW 11
OUT OF WAR IT CAME, BLOODY AND TERRIBLE! . . . . SP FREEDOM'S PLOW 130
BUT NOW WE KNOW HOW IT ALL CAME OUT. SP FREEDOM'S PLOW 136
OUT OF THE DARKEST DAYS FOR A PEOPLE AND A NATION, ... SP FREEDOM'S PLOW 137
HEART REACHING OUT TO HEART, . . . SP FREEDOM'S PLOW 38
WE KNOW NOW HOW IT CAME OUT. . . . SP FREEDOM'S PLOW 138
HAND REACHING OUT TO HAND, ... SP FREEDOM'S PLOW 39
THE PEOPLE DO NOT ALWAYS SAY THINGS OUT LOUD, ... SP FREEDOM'S PLOW 145
LABOR! OUT OF LABOR CAME THE VILLAGES . . . . SP FREEDOM'S PLOW 70
LABOR! OUT OF LABOR CAME THE ROWBOATS . . . . SP FREEDOM'S PLOW 72
OUT OF LABOR CAME THE FACTORIES, . SP FREEDOM'S PLOW 76
OUT OF LABOR - WHITE HANDS AND BLACK HANDS - . . . . SP FREEDOM'S PLOW 82
LEST THE SONG GET OUT OF HAND. . . SP GENIUS CHILD 4
OUT ALL NIGHT . . . . SP GONE BOY 3
OUT OF PENN STATION . . . . SP GOOD MORNING 7
OUT OF PENN STATION - . . . . SP GOOD MORNING 21
AND BLOOD ROLLED OUT. . . . . SP GREEN MEMORY 3
OUT OF THE MOON: . . . . SP GYPSY MELODIES 3
I'D SCRATCH OUT BOTH HIS EYES. . . SP HARD DADDY 18
THE WAY YOU SHOUT OUT LOUD IN CHURCH, ... SP HIGH TO LOW 13
OUT ON BAIL . . . . SP JAM SESSION 2
ELSE YOU'LL TAKE OUT MY PHONE? . . SP MADAM PHONE BIL 11
PACK-HORSE OUT OF ME? . . . . SP MADAM HER MADAM 16
YOU'RE OUT OF LUCK. . . . . SP MADAM RENT MAN 26
YOU FIGURE OUT WHY! . . . . SP MADAM CHARTY CH 28
COMES OUT - BUT REPEATS! . . . . SP MADAM NUMBER WR 28
FURTHERMORE, RUB OUT . . . . SP MADAM CENSUS 29
THE QUIET FADING OUT OF LIFE . . . SP MAGNOLIA FLOWER 1
DIDN'T TURN OUT RIGHT. . . . . SP MIDNIGHT RAFFLE 4
AS HE RIDES OUT ON THE PRAIRIE. . . SP MIGRANT 11
CARRIED HIM OUT FOR DEAD . . . . SP NIGHT FUNERAL 32
OUT OF LOVE. . . . . SP NO REGRETS 1
OUT OF LOVE, ... SP NO REGRETS 5
GONE OUT WEST. . . . . SP ONE-WAY TICKET 27
OUT OF SIGHT . . . . SP PARADE 16
WASHED-AND-IRONED-AND-CLEANED-BEST OUT, ... SP PASSING 10
OUT O' THE SEA. . . . . SP PORT TOWN 14
I WOULDN'T BE OUT THE BARREL YET. SP RELIEF 9
I WAS SCARED TO WALK OUT . . . . SP SITUATION 3
WHEN PIMPS OUT OF LONELINESS CRY: SP SLIVER SERMON 1
OUT OF THE LITTLE BREATH OF OBLIVION SP STARS 8
OUT TO STONY LONESOME GROUND. . . . SP STONY LONESOME 2
SHE'S OUT IN STONY LONESOME, . . . SP STONY LONESOME 16
HAVING PREVIOUSLY POINTED OUT THE SINS OF THIS WORLD: . . . . SP SUNDAY MORNING 1
AND HELL BREAKS OUT . . . . SP SUNDAY MORNING 5
GET OUT THEIR BIBS . . . . SP SUNDAY MORNING 10
WHEN THE LAWD PUT OUT THE LIGHT. . SP SYLVESTER'S BED 26
ALL YOU DARK CHILDREN IN THE WORLD OUT THERE, ... SP THE NEGRO MOTHE 35
OUT OF THE DARKNESS, THE IGNORANCE, THE NIGHT. . . . . SP THE NEGRO MOTHE 40
LIFT HIGH MY BANNER OUT OF THE DUST. SP THE NEGRO MOTHE 41
THE STARS WENT OUT AND SO DID THE MOON. . . . . SP THE WEARY BLUES 32
AND LET THAT FACE COME OUT OF YOU - SP THEME FOR ENG B 4
I WILL TAKE YOUR SOUL OUT OF YOUR BODY . . . . SP TO ARTINA 2
AND OUT THE DOOR . . . . SP TO BE SOMEBODY 10
AS OUT OF THE GUTTER . . . . SP UP-BEAT 5
BUT LADS PUT OUT TO SEA . . . . SP WATER-FRONT STR 6
FILLMORE OUT IN FRISCO, 7TH ACROSS THE BAY, ... AYM ASK YOUR MAMA 31

OUT OF THE MIDNIGHT SKY . . . . . . AYM ASK YOUR MAMA 34
YOUR NUMBER'S COMING OUT! . . . . . AYM BLUES IN STEREO 1
SEA GOURDS MAKE MARACAS OUT OF ME. AYM GOSPEL CHA-CHA 6
TO MOVE OUT TO ST. ALBANS $ $ $ $ $
$ $ $ . . . . AYM HORN OF PLENTY 22
I MOVED OUT TO LONG ISLAND . . . . AYM HORN OF PLENTY 30
I MOVED OUT EVEN FARTHER FURTHER
FARTHER . . . . AYM HORN OF PLENTY 33
YET THEY ASKED ME OUT ON MY PATIO AYM HORN OF PLENTY 46
OUT OF ONE IN EXIT . . . . AYM ODE TO DINAH 118
AND BY MISTAKE SHOT OUT THE LIGHT. AYM ODE TO DINAH 132
MAKE A SPANGLE OUT OF QUARTERS
RINGING . . . . AYM ODE TO DINAH 59
WEAVING OUT OF LONG-TERM CREDIT . . AYM SHOW FARE PLESE 24
AND WE BETTER FIND OUT. MAMA. . . . PL CULTURAL EXCHNG 23
RIGHT OUT OF POWER - . . . . PL CULTURAL EXCHNG 41
RISING OUT OF THE GROUND LIKE A
SWAMP MIST . . . . PL DAYBREAK IN ALA 5
AND FALLING OUT OF HEAVEN LIKE SOFT
DEW. . . . . PL DAYBREAK IN ALA 6
'BOUT OUT OF BREATH. . . . . PL DOWN WHERE I AM 11
GATHER OUT OF STAR-DUST . . . . . . PL DREAM DUST 1
AND LOOK OUT ON THE WORLD . . . . . PL HARLEM 19
GET OUT THE LUNCH-BOX OF YOUR DREAMS PL JIM CROW CAR 1
AND SEEKS AN OUT IN OTHER WORLDLY
DREAMS. . . . . PL JUNIOR ADDICT 3
WHO SEEKS AN OUT IN EYES THAT DROOP PL JUNIOR ADDICT 4
SUNRISE OUT OF AFRICA. . . . . . . PL JUNIOR ADDICT 36
THEY TOOK ME OUT . . . . PL KU KLUX 1
SCREAM JUMPS OUT . . . . PL THIRD DEGREE 8
SLIPPING OUT FROM UNDER THEM . . . PL UNDERTOW 10
OF BEING LAID OUT COLD AND DEAD. . PL WHO BUT TH LORD 6
DON'T LET HIM MAKE A PULP OUT OF ME! PL WHO BUT TH LORD 11
OUT OF ME! . . . . PL WHO BUT TH LORD 15
OUT YONDER WHERE . . . . PL WITHOUT BENEFIT 5
OUT THERE WHERE . . . . PL WITHOUT BENEFIT 10
OUT YONDER YOU'LL LIE: . . . . . . PL WITHOUT BENEFIT 15

OUTDONE 1
WERE OUTDONE! . . . . SP S-SSS-SS-SH! 19

OUTSIDE 4
LEAVES DE SNOW OUTSIDE . . . . . . FC MINNIE SINGS 5
OUTSIDE . . . . FW CAROLINA CABIN 12
OUTSIDE THE DOOR. . . . . SP END 9
HORSE AND HORSEMAN. OUTSIDE! . . . PL WHERE WHEN WHCH 14

OUTSIDER 1
WHO'RE YOU. OUTSIDER? . . . . OWT VISITORS 17

OUTWARD 1
HAVE DOORS THAT OPEN OUTWARD . . . AYM JAZZTET MUTED 16

OVAH 1
ONE RUN OVAH YOU . . . . SP BABY 6

OVEN 2
MAMA. PORTLY OVEN. . . . . SP GRADUATION 6
FAR REMOVED FROM BASIC OVEN. . . . SP GRADUATION 17

OVER 46
I DON'T CRY OVER TROUBLES. . . . . NM BIG-TIMER POEM 58
MAY ACCOMPANY THE RECITATION -
ECHOING SOFTLY. OVER THERE.
THERE'S A ROSE . . . . NM COLORED SL MOOD 4
OUT OF HIS GRAVE FROM OVER THE SEA. NM COLORED SL POEM 14
WHEN WE GOT THROUGH FIGHTING. OVER
THERE. AND DYING? . . . . NM COLORED SL POEM 34
OVER THERE . . . . NM COLORED SL POEM 52
WHILE OVER ALABAMA EARTH . . . . . OK ALABAMA EARTH 10
SLIDE ON OVER. DARLING. . . . . . . OK SONG BANJO DANC 7
MOVE OVER. COMRADE LENIN. . . . . . ANS BLDS OF LENIN 3
MOVE OVER. COMRADE LENIN. . . . . . ANS BLDS OF LENIN 11
MOVE OVER. COMRADE LENIN. . . . . . ANS BLDS OF LENIN 19
THAT ALL OVER THE EARTH TODAY . . . ANS CHANT TOM MOONY 12
AND ALL OVER THE WORLD - . . . . . ANS CHANT TOM MOONY 42
MOVE ON OVER . . . . ANS PARK BENCH 11
OVER EVERYTHING LIKE A SHROUD. . . SH CABARET GIRL 2
WHEN THIS FLOOD IS OVER. . . . . . SH MISSISSIPPI LEV 5
FROM WASHIN' OVER ME? . . . . SH MISSISSIPPI LEV 18
ALL OVER THE WORLD. WHO CARE. . . . JC GOOD MORN STLIN 45
TO BE WON OVER THERE. . . . . JC HOW ABOUT DIXIE 22
SHUBUTA BRIDGE OVER THE CHICASAWHAY
RIVER IN MISSISSIPPI. . . . . . JC THE BITTER RIVR 1
THEN A SILENCE OVER LAUGHTER . . . FW DIMOUT IN HARLM 9
SCATTERED ALL OVER THE SNOW. . . . FW WHEN ARMIES PAS 13
THE CRY SPREAD OVER HARLEM . . . . OWT BLD MARGE POLIT 15
I WANT TO GET OVER TO STATE. . . . OWT JITNEY 38
OVER TO THE GRAND. . . . . OWT JITNEY 42
I WALKED ALL OVER THE ZOO AND THE
PARK. . . . . OWT STRANGER IN TWN 1
DRIPPED BLOOD OVER THE EASTERN HILLS SP A BLACK PIERROT 8
OVER THERE? . . . . SP CAFE: 3 A.M. 10
SHIPPED THE WIDE WORLD OVER: . . . SP FREEDOM'S PLOW 81
OR CRUST AND SUGAR OVER - . . . . . SP HARLEM 7
ALL OVER THE WORLD . . . . SP IN EXPLANATION 2
SO ALL OVER THE WORLD TODAY . . . . SP IN EXPLANATION 18
AND OVER ALL THE PLAIN . . . . . . SP IN TIME SILVER 6
SHOPS ALL OVER HARLEM . . . . SP LIKEWISE 10
I TURNED IT OVER. . . . . SP LITTLE OLD LETT 9
TILL I GET OVER . . . . SP MADAM NUMBER WR 23
SNOW ALL OVER THE GROUND. . . . . . SP MIDWINTER BLUES 2
SNOW ALL OVER THE GROUND - . . . . SP MIDWINTER BLUES 4
THE MOON OVER THE TURPENTINE WOODS. SP MULATTO 7
WHEN IT WAS ALL OVER . . . . SP NIGHT FUNERAL 27
LEAPS CLEAN OVER TO SEVENTH AVENUE SP PROJECTION 2
O. SWEEP OF STARS OVER HARLEM
STREETS. . . . . SP STARS 1
TO A BAND THAT ONCE PASSED OVER . . AYM ODE TO DINAH 27
OF THE SOUTH HAVE TAKEN OVER - . . PL CULTURAL EXCHNG 39
OVER FRAISES DU BOIS. . . . . PL DINNER GUEST ME 13
OR CRUST AND SUGAR OVER - . . . . . PL DREAM DEFERRED 7
FOR THE RICH TO SWEEP OVER . . . . PL FLORIDA WORKERS 10

OVERBOARD 1
BUT JUMP OVERBOARD AN' DROWN. . . . FC A RUINED GAL 14

OVERCHARGE 1
AND GOD KNOWS SHE SURE CAN
OVERCHARGE - . . . . SP NECESSITY 10

OVERCOAT 1
SUIT. OVERCOAT. SHOES - . . . . . . SP WHAT? 5

OVERCOME 2
AND BLUE. HIDING HIS DISCONTENT AS
THOUGHTS OF A BETTER LIFE
OVERCOME . . . . NM BIG-TIMER MOOD 7
THE MIND SEEKS A WAY TO OVERCOME
THESE OBSTACLES. . . . . SP FREEDOM'S PLOW 17

OVERLONG 1
OVERLONG? . . . . SP TELL ME 5

OVERNIGHT 1
BUFFALO TO HARLEM'S OVERNIGHT: . . AYM ODE TO DINAH 48

OVERSEAS 1
WE WERE SENT TO TRAINING CAMP. THEN
OVERSEAS - . . . . NM COLORED SL POEM 5

OVERTAKES 2
WHEN HARD LUCK OVERTAKES YOU . . . FC HARD LUCK 1
WHEN HARD LUCK OVERTAKES YOU . . . FC HARD LUCK 3

OVERTIME 1
OVERTIME PAY . . . . SP CONSIDER ME 20

OVERTONES 1
OVERTONES. . . . . WB LENOX AVE MIDNT 7

OVERTURN 1
AND OVERTURN THE LAND! . . . . . . SP BLD LANDLORD 24

OVER-BURDENED 1
THE MUSIC. OVER-BURDENED. BACKING
AWAY ANGRILY. FRANTIC WITH
HUMILIATION . . . . NM BLACK CLWN MOOD 10

OVER-LONG 1
I MUST NOT SING YOU OVER-LONG. . . OK PASSING LOVE 2

OVER-WISE 1
THE OLD. THE CAUTIOUS. THE OVER-WISE
- . . . . PL ELDERLY LEADERS 1

OWE 1
TEN BUCKS YOU SAY I OWE YOU? . . . SP BLD LANDLORD 9

OWL 7
HEARD DE OWL A HOOTIN'. . . . . . . FC GAL'S CRY DYING 1
HEARD DE OWL A HOOTIN'. . . . . . . FC GAL'S CRY DYING 3
IF I JUST HAD A OWL HEAD. OLD OWL
HEAD WOULD DO. . . . . SH TWILIGHT REVERI 11
IF I JUST HAD A OWL HEAD. OLD OWL
HEAD WOULD DO. . . . . SH TWILIGHT REVERI 11
CAUSE I'D TAKE THAT OWL HEAD AND
FIRE ON YOU. . . . . SH TWILIGHT REVERI 12
BUT I AIN'T GOT NO OWL HEAD AND YOU
DONE LEFT TOWN . . . . SH TWILIGHT REVERI 13
A TIGER. A LION. AND AN OWL . . . . SP DELINQUENT 11

OWN 24
THE SEA'S OWN CHILDREN . . . . . . OK SEA CHARM 2
ONLY MY OWN HANDS. . . . . ANS A NEW SONG 26
WORKER: WHEN THE SAP OF YOUR OWN
STRENGTH RISES . . . . ANS CHANT MAY DAY 25
DON'T WANT THE PEOPLE TO GET WISE TO
THEIR OWN POWER. . . . . ANS KIDS WHO DIE 35
OF OWNING EVERYTHING FOR ONE'S OWN
CREED! . . . . ANS LET AMERICA BE 30
I MUST TAKE THE WORLD FOR MY OWN
AGAIN - . . . . ANS SONG OF SPAIN 81
SAY! ON THE LAST THING I OWN. . . . SH BLD PAWNBROKER 21
LISTEN! I DON'T OWN NO RADIO - . . JC GOOD MORN STLIN 49
WHO DID NOT OWN . . . . JC TO CAPTAIN MULZ 20

THE THINGS THEY MADE, NOR THEIR OWN
LIVES - JC TO CAPTAIN MULZ 21
AND MEET THEIR OWN TAIL. FW CIRCLES 3
WHO WOULD BE MY VERY OWN - OWT STRANGER IN TWN 4
RIGHT OUT OF HER OWN LIFE. SP AUNTSUE'S STORI 22
AND OWN THE LAND. SP DEMOCRACY 9
AND NEVER OWN NO PARTS SP NEW YORKERS 10
HIS OWN STRENGTH SP YOUNG SAILOR 2
AND HIS OWN LAUGHTER, SP YOUNG SAILOR 3
HIS OWN TODAY SP YOUNG SAILOR 4
AND HIS OWN HEREAFTER - SP YOUNG SAILOR 5
IN MY OWN LAND. PL ANGOLA QUESTION 7
TO LIVE ON MY OWN LAND. PL ANGOLA QUESTION 13
NOT OF HER OWN DOING - PL CULTURAL EXCHNG 18
AND OWN THE LAND. PL FREEDOM 9
THEIR OWN SWEET TIME TO FLOWER PL SWEET WORDS RAC 2

OWNED 1
OWNED A DECENT RADIO YET? SP DEFERRED 47

OWNING 1
OF OWNING EVERYTHING FOR ONE'S OWN
GREED! ANS LET AMERICA BE 30

OWNS 4
WHY WE OWNS DE LAND! ANS SISTER JOHNSON 7
WHO OWNS THOSE WORDS? AMERICA! SP FREEDOM'S PLOW 175
OWNS THE WORLD. SP PORTER 10
WHO OWNS THE PLACE - PL LENOX AVE. BAR 4

OW-000-00-0 1
OW-000-00-0! SP AS BEFITS A MAN 17

OZIE 27
OZIE, OZIE POWELL. ANS BLD OZZIE POWEL 2
OZIE, OZIE POWELL, ANS BLD OZZIE POWEL 2
OZIE, OZIE POWELL. ANS BLD OZZIE POWEL 4
OZIE, OZIE POWELL. ANS BLD OZZIE POWEL 4
OZIE, OZIE POWELL, ANS BLD OZZIE POWEL 6
OZIE, OZIE POWELL, ANS BLD OZZIE POWEL 6
OZIE, OZIE POWELL. ANS BLD OZZIE POWEL 8
OZIE, OZIE POWELL. ANS BLD OZZIE POWEL 8
BLACK YOUNG OZIE POWELL. ANS BLD OZZIE POWEL 10
OZIE, OZIE POWELL. ANS BLD OZZIE POWEL 12
OZIE, OZIE POWELL. ANS BLD OZZIE POWEL 12
OZIE, OZIE POWELL, ANS BLD OZZIE POWEL 14
OZIE, OZIE POWELL, ANS BLD OZZIE POWEL 14
AIMED AT OZIE POWELL. ANS BLD OZZIE POWEL 16
OZIE, OZIE POWELL, ANS BLD OZZIE POWEL 18
OZIE, OZIE POWELL, ANS BLD OZZIE POWEL 18
STARE AT OZIE POWELL. ANS BLD OZZIE POWEL 20
DON'T THEY, OZIE POWELL? ANS BLD OZZIE POWEL 22
OZIE, OZIE POWELL. ANS BLD OZZIE POWEL 24
OZIE, OZIE POWELL. ANS BLD OZZIE POWEL 24
OZIE, OZIE POWELL, ANS BLD OZZIE POWEL 26
OZIE, OZIE POWELL. ANS BLD OZZIE POWEL 26
BLACK YOUNG OZIE POWELL. ANS BLD OZZIE POWEL 28
OZIE, OZIE POWELL, ANS BLD OZZIE POWEL 30
OZIE, OZIE POWELL, ANS BLD OZZIE POWEL 30
OZIE! OZIE POWELL! ANS BLD OZZIE POWEL 32
OZIE! OZIE POWELL! ANS BLD OZZIE POWEL 32

O' 47
BY DE EDGE O' DE WEARY RIVERSIDE FC A RUINED GAL 11
I BOUGHT HIM SUITS O' CLOTHES, FC BLACK GAL 10
HE WAS A FRIEND O' MINE. FC DEATH DO DIRTY 5
MA FRIEND O' MINE. FC DEATH DO DIRTY 10
AN' A STEW O' MEAT. FC DEATH DO DIRTY 14
GOOD FRIEND O' MINE. FC DEATH DO DIRTY 15
O, FRIEND O' MINE. FC DEATH DO DIRTY 20
MA FRIEND O' MINE. FC DEATH DO DIRTY 25
BEST FRIEND O' MINE. FC DEATH DO DIRTY 30
I'M GONNA FILL 'EM UP FULL O' FC DEATH DO DIRTY 33
MA FRIEND O' MINE. FC DEATH DO DIRTY 35
PLEASE DON'T TAKE THIS MAN O' MINE. FC GAL'S CRY DYING 18
A GLASS O' WHISKEY FC SATURDAY NIGHT 5
AN' A GLASS O' GIN: FC SATURDAY NIGHT 6
GIT A QUART O' LICKER, FC SATURDAY NIGHT 11
WITH A LOT O' SPORTY PALS. NM BIG-TIMER POEM 16
AND ALL THAT KIND O' THING. NM BIG-TIMER POEM 24
MAKE LOTS O' NOISE, NM BIG-TIMER POEM 63
CALL IN A GANG O' WOMEN NM BIG-TIMER POEM 65
SO WHAT'S THE USE O' WORRYIN' NM BIG-TIMER POEM 69
ANSWERIN' THEM WANT-ADS' NOT NARY
BIT O' FUN. NM BROKE 4
O' GETTIN' A NEW WINTER COAT, OR
HAVIN' THAT OLD ONE CLEANED. NM BROKE 40
TRIED TO FIND ONE O' THEM LITTLE
ELEVATOR AND SWITCHBOARD JOBS
THEY USED NM BROKE 41
BUT YOU DON'T SEE NO PRESIDENTS
DYIN' O' GRIEF - NM BROKE 57
OLD GAL O' MINE. OK DRESSED UP 8
HE'S A FRIEND O' MINE. OK MA LORD 11
O' MY FEELING LIKE A DOG SH EVIL MORNING 10
GET OUT O' MY SIGHT BE- SH EVIL MORNING 15
BUT A LOT O' CAWD-KNOWS-WHAT. SH LOVE AGAIN BLUS 2
BUT A LOT O' CAWD-KNOWS-WHAT. SH LOVE AGAIN BLUS 4
I PACK A MILLION BAGS O' SAND SH MISSISSIPPI LEV 11
ROBE O' LOVE - SH PRESENT 4
GIMME SIX-BITS' WORTH O' TICKET SH SIX-BITS BLUES 1
I SAY SIX-BITS' WORTH O' TICKET SH SIX-BITS BLUES 3
AND SHOOT ALL KINDS O' SHELLS INTO
YOU. SH TWILIGHT REVERI 8
ABOUT TWO KINDS O' PISTOLS THAT I
AIN'T GOT. SH TWILIGHT REVERI 10
ROAD'S IN FRONT O' ME, SP BOUND NO'TH BLS 7
ROAD'S IN FRONT O' ME, SP BOUND NO'TH BLS 9
STEP OUT O' THE BARREL, BOY. SP ELEVATOR BOY 11
AT THE FEET O' JESUS, SP FEET O' JESUS 1
AT THE FEET O' JESUS SP FEET O' JESUS 5
MA SOUL WENT FLYIN' O' THE TOWN, SP JUDGMENT DAY 2
IN THE SWEET O' MA LORD'S SIGHT - SP JUDGMENT DAY 12
JUST LIKE A PAIR O' SHOES - SP LOVER'S RETURN 10
YOU JEST A LITTLE BIT O' WOMAN BUT
YOU SP MORNING AFTER 17
OUT O' THE SEA. SP PORT TOWN 14
TO THE TUNE O' THOSE WEARY BLUES. SP THE WEARY BLUES 8

O'CLOCK 1
AT SIX O'CLOCK, OR SEVEN, OR EIGHT, OWT NEGRO SERVANT 8

O.K 3
O.K. YOU DON'T WANT IT? SH BLD PAWNBROKER 17
YOU SAY I GAVE MY O.K.? SP MADAM PHONE BIL 38
WELL, THAT O.K. YOU MAY KEEP - SP MADAM PHONE BIL 39

O.K.ED 2
YOU SAY I O.K.ED SP MADAM PHONE BIL 1
O.K.ED IT WHEN? SP MADAM PHONE BIL 3

PA 1
PA. SP CONSIDER ME 13

PACE 1
PACE. "SOMETIMES I FEEL LIKE A
MOTHER-LESS CHILE." TURNING
FUTILELY NM BLACK CLWN MOOD 8

PACK 5
PACK MY TRUNK AND RIDE. WB BLUES FANTASY 21
PACK MY TRUNK AND RIDE. WB BLUES FANTASY 24
I PACK A MILLION BAGS O' SAND SH MISSISSIPPI LEV 11
FOR US TO PACK UP SP WEST TEXAS 8
GOSPEL SINGERS WHO PANT TO PACK $ $
$ $ AYM HORN OF PLENTY 13

PACKARD 2
A PACKARD CAR. SH BLD THE KILLER 6
I'D BUY ME A PACKARD, SH IF-ING 6

PACKED 2
PACKED HIS TRUNK AND LEFT. FC SUICIDE 2
PACKED HIS TRUNK AND LEFT. FC SUICIDE 4

PACK-HORSE 1
PACK-HORSE OUT OF ME? SP MADAM HER MADAM 16

PADDLE-TAILED 1
THAT STRETCHES PADDLE-TAILED ACROSS
THE FLOOR. SP TO BE SOMEBODY 5

PADDY 1
ANOTHER PADDY. SP DEAD IN THERE 9

PAGE 8
WASN'T EVEN ONE PAGE LONG - SP LITTLE OLD LETT 6
A PAGE TONIGHT. SP THEME FOR ENG B 3
AND LET THAT PAGE COME OUT OF YOU - SP THEME FOR ENG B 4
UP TO MY ROOM, SIT DOWN, AND WRITE
THIS PAGE: SP THEME FOR ENG B 15
HEAR YOU, HEAR ME - WE TWO - YOU,
ME, TALK ON THIS PAGE. SP THEME FOR ENG B 19
SO WILL MY PAGE BE COLORED THAT I
WRITE? SP THEME FOR ENG B 27
THIS IS MY PAGE FOR ENGLISH B. SP THEME FOR ENG B 41
PATRICE AND PATTI PAGE AYM ASK YOUR MAMA 40

PAID 4
MY FURNITURE PAID FOR. SP DEFERRED 35
TO THAT GIRL WHO PAID THE PREACHER
MAN - SP NIGHT FUNERAL 41
PAID AT THE BOX OFFICE AYM SHOW FARE PLESE 15
VERY WELL PAID. PL ELDERLY LEADERS 7

PAIN 31
TROUBLE, PAIN. WB BLUES FANTASY 16
OF YOUR PAIN. WB DISILLUSION 10
THE WEARY, WEARY HEART OF PAIN. - WB LENOX AVE MIDNT 6
AND ALL THREE COVERED WITH A SHEET
OF PAIN. WB SICK ROOM 6
SO FULL OF PAIN AND PASSION, WB SOLEDAD 6
SO FULL OF PAIN AND PASSION. WB SOLEDAD 8
LAUGHTER IS MY PAIN. WB THE JESTER 11
AND REST FROM PAIN OF LOVE WB YOUNG BRIDE 6
SO THAT THE PAIN AND THE SHAME NM BLACK CLWN POEM 27

I HAVE HELD MY PAIN . . . . DK MINSTREL MAN 7
WHIRL IN THE WIND OF PAIN AND
STRIFE. . . . . DK SONG 6
WHOSE SWEAT AND BLOOD, WHOSE FAITH
AND PAIN. . . . . ANS LET AMERICA BE 67
AND ITS TERROR AND PAIN IS SPAIN. ANS SONG OF SPAIN 37
WHAT MAKES LOVE SUCH AN ACHE AND
PAIN? . . . . SH LOVE AGAIN BLUS 14
LOVE SUCH AN ACHE AND PAIN? . . . . SH LOVE AGAIN BLUS 16
AND DIED IN PAIN. . . . . FW GIRL 2
WITH NO PAIN . . . . FW GIRL 20
SO MUCH PAIN, ... FW WALLS 2
THAT FILLS A WOMAN'S AGE-LESS,
AGE-LONG PAIN - . . . . OWT JUICE JOINT 28
ARE TEASING PAIN. . . . . SP DREAM BOOGE VAR 10
PAIN AND A LEARNING . . . . SP INTERNE AT PROV 5
PAIN ON HIND LEGS RISING, ... SP INTERNE AT PROV 23
PAIN TAMED AND SUBSIDING . . . . . SP INTERNE AT PROV 24
AND PAIN . . . . SP JULIET 2
SHE FELT QUEER PAIN . . . . SP STRANGE HURT 2
REMEMBER MY SWEAT, MY PAIN, MY
DESPAIR. . . . . SP THE NEGRO MOTHE 36
WEARINESS AND PAIN . . . . SP TROUBLED WOMAN 5
BURNS IN MY HEART A LOVE-FIRE SHARP
LIKE PAIN. . . . . SP WHEN SUE WEARS 11
AS FORGOTTEN PAIN IN THE QUARTER . AYM ODE TO DINAH 40
OH, WHAT PAIN . . . . PL MISSISSIPPI 3
WHAT SORROW, PITY, PAIN, ... PL MISSISSIPPI 17

PAINTINGS 1
TOROS, FLAMENCO, PAINTINGS, BOOKS - ANS SONG OF SPAIN 38

PAIR 1
JUST LIKE A PAIR O' SHOES - . . . . SP LOVER'S RETURN 10

PAL 2
BE YOUR PAL. . . . . WB TO MIDNIGHT NAN 4
HERE'S MY SUGAR-DADDY PAL. . . . . SH DEATH IN HARLEM 48

PALE 13
WOULD PALE IN THE LIGHT . . . . . . WB POEM 19
PALE IN THE LIGHT . . . . WB POEM 21
WAN AND PALE, ... WB SUMMER NIGHT 23
HER FACE IS PALE . . . . FC CLOSING TIME 2
WORLD, TURN PALE! . . . . SL SCOTTSBORO 2
WORLD, TURN PALE! . . . . SL SCOTTSBORO 29
EAST TURNED PALE . . . . SH DEATH IN HARLEM 134
UNTIL THE STARS PALE AND THE SKY
TURNS BLUE . . . . OWT JUICE JOINT 3
REST AT PALE EVENING . . . . SP DREAM VARIATION 14
MADE ME TURN RIGHT PALE. . . . . . SP LITTLE OLD LETT 4
HIS FACE WAS PALE AND . . . . SP LOVER'S RETURN 3
LIKE PALE PLUMS FROM A TREE . . . . SP MELLOW 4
BY THE PALE DULL PALLOR OF AN OLD
GAS LIGHT . . . . SP THE WEARY BLUES 5

PALLBEARERS 1
AND SIX PALLBEARERS . . . . SP NIGHT FUNERAL 31

PALLOR 1
BY THE PALE DULL PALLOR OF AN OLD
GAS LIGHT . . . . SP THE WEARY BLUES 5

PALM 5
PALM BEACH. . . . . FC BRASS SPITOONS 5
IN THE PALM OF MY HAND . . . . . . FW DUSTBOWL 5
I CROSSED HER PALM WITH SILVER. . . SP BLD THE GYPSY 9
I'LL READ YOUR OTHER PALM. . . . . SP MADAM FORT TELL 24
COME, DRINK PALM WINE. . . . . . . SP NATCHA 5

PALMETTO 1
THROUGH THE PALMETTO THICKET . . . PL FLORIDA WORKERS 6

PALMOLIVE 1
THE LIGHT ON THE PALMOLIVE BUILDING SP INTERNE AT PROV 40

PALMS 2
CRIED AMONG THE PALMS IN AFRICA . . WB AFRAID 3
WHERE THE PALMS AND COCONUTS . . . AYM GOSPEL CHA-CHA 2

PALS 1
WITH A LOT O' SPORTY PALS. . . . . NM BIG-TIMER POEM 16

PANT 1
GOSPEL SINGERS WHO PANT TO PACK $ $
$ $ . . . . AYM HORN OF PLENTY 13

PANTHER 1
THE PANTHER IN HIS DESPERATE
BOLDNESS . . . . PL BLACK PANTHER 8

PAPA 12
I MET A YELLOW PAPA. . . . . FC GYPSY MAN 13
MET A YELLOW PAPA. . . . . FC GYPSY MAN 15
PAPA, MAMA, ... SP CONSIDER ME 8
BUT I'S STILL SWEET PAPA 'VESTER. SP SYLVESTER'S BED 21
THAT'S ONE TIME, PRETTY PAPA. . . . SP WIDOW WOMAN 11
THE PAPA DRUM OF SUN . . . . AYM GOSPEL CHA-CHA 9
MAMA MAMACITA PAPA PAPIAMENTO . . . AYM GOSPEL CHA-CHA 14
MAMACITA! PAPA LEGBA! SHANGO! . . . AYM GOSPEL CHA-CHA 35
TELL ME, PRETTY PAPA, ... AYM ODE TO DINAH 62
PRETTY PAPA, PRETTY PAPA, ... AYM ODE TO DINAH 64
PRETTY PAPA, PRETTY PAPA, ... AYM ODE TO DINAH 64
TRIBAL NOW NO LONGER PAPA MAMA . . AYM ODE TO DINAH 82

PAPA'S 1
OR DO YOU THINK THAT PAPA'S . . . . AYM SHOW FARE PLESE 3

PAPER 8
BUT I CAN'T EVEN BUY A PAPER - I'M
SO BROKE. . . . . NM BROKE 61
HIS WIFE TOOK A PAPER . . . . SP BLD OF THE MAN 9
NOR WRITE THEM DOWN ON PAPER. . . . SP FREEDOM'S PLOW 146
JUST A PENCIL AND PAPER, ... SP LITTLE OLD LETT 13
WHERE THE DOORS ARE DOORS OF PAPER PL CULTURAL EXCHNG 2
IN THE POT BEHIND THE PAPER DOORS PL CULTURAL EXCHNG 26
PAPER . . . . PL THIRD DEGREE 18
PINK PAPER TOWELS . . . . PL UNDERTOW 8

PAPERS 4
WHO PEN EDITORIALS IN THE PAPERS, ANS KIDS WHO DIE 20
I READ IN THE PAPERS ABOUT THE . . SP FREEDOM TRAIN 1
METHUSELAH SIGNS PAPERS W.E.B. . . AYM BIRD IN ORBIT 18
NAME IN THE PAPERS EVERY DAY! . . . AYM HORN OF PLENTY 37

PAPIAMENTO 1
MAMA MAMACITA PAPA PAPIAMENTO . . . AYM GOSPEL CHA-CHA 14

PARADE 5
THEY HAD A PARADE. . . . . JC BLD SAM SOLOMON 42
PLANNING PLANNING A PARADE: . . . . SP PARADE 4
PARADE! . . . . SP PARADE 28
PARADE! . . . . SP PARADE 30
PARADE! . . . . SP PARADE 32

PARALYZED 1
PARALYZED. . . . . FW OLD SAILOR 14

PARECE 1
PARECE UNA RUMBA. . . . . FC JAZZ BAND 17

PARENTS 1
WITH PARENTS THAT DON'T EVEN . . . SP MADAM CHARTY CH 15

PARIS 2
A QUARTER OR A SHILLING, PARIS - . AYM ASK YOUR MAMA 49
LIVE ALL THAT WHILE IN PARIS . . . AYM HORN OF PLENTY 53

PARK 10
I LIVE ON A PARK BENCH. . . . . . . ANS PARK BENCH 1
YOU, PARK AVENUE. . . . . ANS PARK BENCH 2
TO PARK AVENUE? . . . . ANS PARK BENCH 12
THROUGH THE PARK. . . . . OWT NEGRO SERVANT 14
I WALKED ALL OVER THE ZOO AND THE
PARK. . . . . OWT STRANGER IN TWN 1
RUNS TO DIVE IN THE PARK . . . . . SP DIVE 3
NORTH OF THE PARK. . . . . SP ISLAND 2
ON A BENCH IN THE PARK: . . . . . . SP KID IN THE PARK 2
THROUGH A PARK, THEN I CROSS ST.
NICHOLAS, ... SP THEME FOR ENG B 12
PARK AVENUE AT EIGHT . . . . PL DINNER GUEST ME 20

PARKER 1
AND CHARLIE YARDBIRD PARKER . . . . AYM BIRD IN ORBIT 30

PARKWAY 1
OF SOUTH PARKWAY: . . . . OWT JITNEY 2

PARLOR 1
HAIR-DRESSING PARLOR . . . . SP MADAM'S PAST HI 6

PARROTS 1
BOWED DOWN WITH CHATTERING PARROTS WB OUR LAND 10

PART 10
PART OF MY LIFE. . . . . FC BRASS SPITOONS 10
LONG A PART OF THE UNION'S HEART - NM DARK YOUTH USA 11
40-VOICES: NO PART NEGLECTED - . . ANS CHANT MAY DAY 17
TO TAKE THEIR RIGHTFUL PART . . . . JC BLD SAM SOLOMON 47
A SOLDIER TOOK HER PART. . . . . . OWT BLD MARGE POLIT 9
A PART OF YOU, INSTRUCTOR. . . . . SP THEME FOR ENG B 30
YET A PART OF ME, AS I AM A PART OF
YOU. . . . . SP THEME FOR ENG B 32
YET A PART OF ME, AS I AM A PART OF
YOU. . . . . SP THEME FOR ENG B 32
SOMETIMES PERHAPS YOU DON'T WANT TO
BE A PART OF ME. . . . . SP THEME FOR ENG B 34
NOR DO I OFTEN WANT TO BE A PART OF
YOU. . . . . SP THEME FOR ENG B 35

PARTICULAR 1
SAYS THIS PARTICULAR . . . . SP TOMORROW 4

PARTIES 2
THREE PARTIES . . . . SP SAME IN BLUES 22
TWO PARTIES FROM PHILADELPHIA . . . SP SEASHORE THROUG 5

PARTING 1
I MUST HAVE A PARTING. . . . . . . WB A FAREWELL 5

PARTS 1
AND NEVER OWN NO PARTS . . . . . . SP NEW YORKERS 10

PARTY 3
A PARTY OF WHITES FROM FIFTH AVENUE SH DEATH IN HARLEM 58
ON MY PARTY LINE - . . . . SP SAME IN BLUES 23
BUT THAT THIRD PARTY, ... SP SAME IN BLUES 24

PASO 1
BOSTON AND EL PASO - . . . . SP FREEDOM'S PLOW 88

PASS 9
EVER TIME DE TRAINS PASS . . . . . DK HOMESICK BLUES 5
WHEN YOU PASS BY. . . . . DK REASONS WHY 8
TO LET ME PASS. . . . . FW SNAKE 4
FOLKS PASS BY AND STARE - . . . . . OWT FUNERAL 4
PEOPLE PASS BY ME - . . . . OWT LONESOME CORNER 6
I WANT TO PASS THE CIVIL SERVICE. SP DEFERRED 43
YOU PASS THE BUCK. . . . . SP MADAM RENT MAN 24
MOTHERS PASS. . . . . SP SUMMER EVENING 1
WHERE WHITE SHADOWS PASS. . . . . . AYM ODE TO DINAH 50

PASSED 6
A BALL PASSED BY. . . . . SH DEATH IN HARLEM 102
AS OUR SHIP PASSED BY . . . . SP SEASCAPE 2
TO A BAND THAT ONCE PASSED OVER . . AYM ODE TO DINAH 27
HAS PASSED AWAY. . . . . PL OCTOBER 16 RAID 18
WE PASSED THEIR GRAVES: . . . . . . PL PEACE 1
I DONE FORGOT WHEN IT PASSED . . . PL STOKELY MALCOLM 8

PASSENGERS 1
ON A TRAIN THAT LOST NO PASSENGERS AYM ODE TO DINAH 29

PASSERS-BY 1
"LOOK, PASSERS-BY, ... FW HEART 6

PASSES 2
WHEN HE PASSES ON. . . . . LHR TESTAMENT 4
AS LEOLA PASSES BY . . . . AYM ASK YOUR MAMA 36

PASSING 4
PASSING BOYS AND GIRLS . . . . . . SP IN TIME SILVER 19
SEE THE PEOPLE PASSING BY? . . . . SP KID IN THE PARK 3
A PASSING GIRL . . . . SP RAILROAD AVENUE 15
WHO MIGHT BE PASSING! . . . . SP TO BE SOMEBODY 12

PASSIN' 1
BLACK MARIA PASSIN' BY . . . . . . SP BLACK MARIA 18

PASSION 2
SO FULL OF PAIN AND PASSION. . . . WB SOLEDAD 6
SO FULL OF PAIN AND PASSION. . . . WB SOLEDAD 8

PASSIONATE 1
PASSIONATE, CRUEL. . . . . SP THE SOUTH 15

PASSIVE 1
20-VOICES: GROW OUT OF THE PASSIVE EARTH. . . . . ANS CHANT MAY DAY 10

PASSOVER 1
THE PASSOVER HAD COME. . . . . . . LHR BLD MARY'S SON 2

PAST 19
SO I CLIMB TOWARD TOMORROW, OUT OF PAST SORROW. . . . . NM DARK YOUTH USA 22
THE DAY IS PAST. . . . . ANS A NEW SONG 10
THAT DAY IS PAST. . . . . ANS A NEW SONG 16
THAT DAY IS PAST. . . . . ANS A NEW SONG 24
THAT DAY IS PAST . . . . ANS A NEW SONG 33
WITH THE PAST . . . . ANS A NEW SONG 40
THE PAST IS DONE! . . . . ANS A NEW SONG 52
TO SMASH THE OLD DEAD DOGMAS OF THE PAST - . . . . ANS OPEN LETTER 24
EVERY PAST MISTAKE . . . . ANS OPEN LETTER 37
IN THE PAST . . . . JC BLD SAM SOLOMON 14
THE WORLD WHERE EVERY UGLY PAST MISTAKE . . . . JC TO CAPTAIN MULZ 56
TWO OR THREE THINGS IN THE PAST . . SP DANCER 1
FROM HARLEM PAST HONG KONG TALKING BACK. . . . . SP IN EXPLANATION 22
MY GOOD-TIME DAYS DONE PAST. . . . SP LITTLE GRN TREE 2
A-CREEPIN' MUDDY PAST - . . . . . . SP SYLVESTER'S BED 20
MAKE OF MY PAST A ROAD TO THE LIGHT SP THE NEGRO MOTHE 39
PAST HUTS THAT HOUSE A MILLION BLACKS . . . . AYM BLUES IN STEREO 15
HER YESTERDAY PAST GRANDPA - . . . PL CULTURAL EXCHNG 17
THE PAST HAS BEEN A MINT . . . . . PL HISTORY 1

PAT 1
TIRED NOW OF THE PAT ON THE BACK. JC THE BITTER RIVR 76

PATENT-LEATHERED 1
PATENT-LEATHERED NOW . . . . SP TRUMPET PLAYER 13

PATH 1
TO ROUTE EACH PATH . . . . PL FREDRK DOUGLASS 10

PATHS 2
WHERE ALL PATHS GO? . . . . WB HARLEM NIGHT CL 17
DOWN PATHS OF DEATH AND DARKNESS . JC TO CAPTAIN MULZ 8

PATIENCE 2
"WORK, EDUCATION, PATIENCE . . . . JC THE BITTER RIVR 43
CARRIES YOUR "PATIENCE" AWAY . . . JC THE BITTER RIVR 46

PATIENT 2
"WAIT, BE PATIENT," YOU SAY. . . . JC THE BITTER RIVR 39
THE OLD "BE PATIENT" . . . . PL HARLEM 5

PATIO 1
YET THEY ASKED ME OUT ON MY PATIO AYM HORN OF PLENTY 46

PATRICE 1
PATRICE AND PATTI PAGE . . . . . . AYM ASK YOUR MAMA 40

PATRIOT 1
UNDER THE GUISE OF A PATRIOT . . . ANS SONG OF SPAIN 67

PATRIOTIC 1
IS CROWNED WITH NO FALSE PATRIOTIC WREATH. . . . . ANS LET AMERICA BE 12

PATROL 1
PATROL BELL! . . . . SP BLD LANDLORD 26

PATTERN 2
I CATCH THE PATTERN . . . . FW SILENCE 1
THE PLAN AND THE PATTERN IS HERE. SP FREEDOM'S PLOW 165

PATTI 1
PATRICE AND PATTI PAGE . . . . . . AYM ASK YOUR MAMA 40

PAUL 2
PAUL ROBESON SAID, OUT IN KANSAS CITY. . . . . JC JIM CROW'S LAST 19
PAUL ROBESON . . . . SP PROJECTION 18

PAWN 2
PAWN YO' GOLD WATCH . . . . FC SATURDAY NIGHT 9
DIAMONDS IN PAWN . . . . AYM SHADES OF PIC 37

PAWNBROKER 1
PAWNBROKER, OLD FRIEND - . . . . . SH BLD PAWNBROKER 22

PAWNED 2
WHEN YOU PAWNED MY WATCH . . . . . SP COULD BE 7
YOU PAWNED MY HEART. . . . . SP COULD BE 8

PAY 38
GO WHERE THEY WILL PAY YOU WELL . . WB TO DARK MERCEDE 7
HOUSE RENT TO PAY. . . . . FC BRASS SPITOONS 22
AND HOUSE RENT TO PAY. . . . . . . FC BRASS SPITOONS 30
AND TOLD ME I'D BETTER PAY HER FOR MY ROOM RENT AND BOARD! . . . . NM BROKE 22
I WOULDN'T PAY HER A PENNY NOW IF I WAS TO CROAK - . . . . NM BROKE 25
WELL, ER - ER . . . HOW MUCH DOES YOU PAY? . . . . NM BROKE 35
YES, UM-HUM! YOU SHO IS SWEET! CAN YOU PAY FO' DE LICENSE, DEAR? . NM BROKE 78
COULD HARDLY FIND A JOB THAT OFFERED DECENT PAY. . . . . NM COLORED SL POEM 21
OF WORK THE MEN! OF TAKE THE PAY! ANS LET AMERICA BE 29
THE MILLIONS WHO HAVE NOTHING FOR OUR PAY? . . . . ANS LET AMERICA BE 55
THE MILLIONS WHO HAVE NOTHING FOR OUR PAY? . . . . ANS LET AMERICA BE 60
WITH ITS WINGS OF GOLD FOR WHICH I PAY - . . . . ANS SONG OF SPAIN 42
HAD TO PAY HER TICKET. . . . . . . SH ANNOUNCEMENT 5
THIS WHOLE PAY CHECK'S JUST FOR ME. SH PAY DAY 1
AIN'T GONNA PAY A CENT ON THAT RADIO SH PAY DAY 7
CAUSE IF I DON'T THEY'LL CUT DOWN MY PAY. . . . . SH SUPPER TIME 14
I DON'T PAY YOU NO MIND. . . . . . JC BLD SAM SOLOMON 30
AND SLEEK-HAIRED BOYS WHO DEAL IN LOVE FOR PAY . . . . OWT LINCOLN THEATRE 14
WELL, THAT'S TEN BUCKS MORE'N I'LL PAY YOU . . . . SP BLD LANDLORD 11
FOR TOO LITTLE PAY - . . . . SP BLUE BAYOU 10
TO PAY HIS CARFARE, BUY A SUIT. . . SP BUDDY 8
OVERTIME PAY . . . . SP CONSIDER ME 20
TIME I PAY RENT AND GET MY FOOD . . SP LETTER 2
IGNORE ME - THOUGH I PAY YOUR FEES. SP LOW TO HIGH 15
I DON'T PAY NO REVERSED . . . . . . SP MADAM PHONE BIL 8
BEFORE I'D PAY . . . . SP MADAM RENT MAN 8
YOU SAY, I WILL PAY IT - . . . . . SP MADAM PHONE BIL 10
PAY YOU A VISIT . . . . SP MADAM WRONG VIS 15
I'LL PAY SOME MIND TO YOU. . . . . SP MADAM FORT TELL 16
THE COUNTY WON'T PAY ME . . . . . . SP MADAM CHARTY CH 17
BUT I SURE AIN'T GONNA PAY! . . . . SP MADAM PHONE BIL 40

THAN I WANTED TO PAY. . . . . SP MADAM'S CALLING 4
ON THE CHECK THAT IS HIS PAY. . . . SP MIGRANT 37
INSURANCE MAN, HE DID NOT PAY - . . SP NIGHT FUNERAL 5
HIS GIRL FRIEND HAD TO PAY. . . . . SP NIGHT FUNERAL 24
PAY MORE MONEY TO HER NOW . . . . . SP RUBY BROWN 25
OR RENT THAT I MUST PAY. . . . . . PL CROWNS GARLANDS 16
YOU PROFFER ME POOR PAY. . . . . . PL MILITANT 9

PAYING 1
WHEN I'M PAYING YOUR BILLS . . . . SP ULTIMATUM 2

PAYIN' 1
BUT THEY GIVIN' 'EM TO SCHOOL BOYS
NOW AND PAYIN' JUST ABOUT HALF. NM BROKE 43

PAYMENTS 1
PAYMENTS NOT BELATED - . . . . AYM HORN OF PLENTY 78

PAYOLA 1
KING COLE JUKEBOX PAYOLA . . . . . AYM ASK YOUR MAMA 42

PAYS 2
AN' I SHO PAYS DOUBLE . . . . FC WORKIN' MAN 14
SIX DOLLARS A WEEK? WHEE-OOO! YOU
SHO PAYS WELL! . . . . NM BROKE 36

PAY-NIGHTS 1
PAY-NIGHTS A TAXI . . . . OWT NEGRO SERVANT 13

PD 1
WHEN THE PD CAR . . . . OWT BLD MARGE POLIT 52

PEACE 9
SHO, THERE MUST BE PEACE. . . . . . FC MOAN 16
AND A LOUSY PEACE. . . . . ANS KIDS WHO DIE 18
BUT HERE THERE'S PEACE . . . . . . FW CAROLINA CABIN 18
IS THERE PEACE . . . . FW CONVENT 2
PEACE . . . . FW CONVENT 4
THEY ALL BRING PEACE . . . . FW EXITS 5
PEACE! . . . . SP PROJECTION 21
SEEKING PEACE AND QUIET . . . . . . AYM HORN OF PLENTY 72
OF OUR PEACE. . . . . PL JUNIOR ADDICT 27

PEACH-SKINNED 1
PEACH-SKINNED GIRLIE. . . . . SH HARLEM SWEETIES 9

PEARL 2
PEARL HARBOR PUT JIM CROW ON THE
RUN. . . . . JC JIM CROW'S LAST 8
FAILS TO GET PEARL BAILEY. . . . . AYM ODE TO DINAH 6

PEASANT 1
I AM IVAN, THE PEASANT. . . . . . . ANS BLDS OF LENIN 5

PEDALS 1
SCREAMING PEDALS . . . . SP DREAM BOOGIE VAR 7

PEDIGREE 1
TO MY PEDIGREE: . . . . SP MADAM'S CALLING 18

PEEL 4
PEEL OFF THE SKIN. . . . . PL SPECIAL BULLTIN 20
PEEL PEEL . . . . PL SPECIAL BULLTIN 21
PEEL PEEL . . . . PL SPECIAL BULLTIN 21
PEEL OFF . . . . PL SPECIAL BULLTIN 22

PEEPING 1
THE SAVIOUR PEEPING THROUGH. . . . LHR PASTORAL 3

PEEPS 1
PEEPS A MAPLE-SUGAR CHILD. . . . . OK WINTER SWEEETNS 4

PEKING 2
SELMA AND PEKING. . . . . PL UNDERTOW 4
BETWEEN SELMA, PEKING. . . . . . . PL UNDERTOW 12

PELEE 1
BLOWN SKY HIGH BY MONT PELEE? . . . AYM RIDE, RED, RIDE 14

PEN 1
WHO PEN EDITORIALS IN THE PAPERS. ANS KIDS WHO DIE 20

PENCIL 1
JUST A PENCIL AND PAPER. . . . . . SP LITTLE OLD LETT 13

PENDULUM 1
WHERE THE PENDULUM IS SWINGING . . AYM ODE TO DINAH 111

PENN 2
OUT OF PENN STATION . . . . SP GOOD MORNING 7
OUT OF PENN STATION - . . . . SP GOOD MORNING 21

PENNY 1
I WOULDN'T PAY HER A PENNY NOW IF I
WAS TO CROAK - . . . . NM BROKE 25

PEOPLE 50
MY PEOPLE. . . . . FC LAUGHERS 5
MY PEOPLE. . . . . FC LAUGHERS 20
MY PEOPLE. . . . . FC LAUGHERS 22
MY PEOPLE DISOWNED ME - . . . . . . NM BIG-TIMER POEM 11
OF A THIEVING PEOPLE. . . . . ANS A NEW SONG 15
TO FRIGHTEN THE PEOPLE - . . . . . ANS KIDS WHO DIE 31
FOR THE KIDS WHO DIE ARE LIKE IRON
IN THE BLOOD OF THE PEOPLE - . . ANS KIDS WHO DIE 32
AND THE OLD AND RICH DON'T WANT THE
PEOPLE . . . . ANS KIDS WHO DIE 33
DON'T WANT THE PEOPLE TO GET WISE TO
THEIR OWN POWER. . . . . ANS KIDS WHO DIE 35
I AM THE PEOPLE, HUMBLE, HUNGRY,
MEAN - . . . . ANS LET AMERICA BE 34
WE, THE PEOPLE, MUST REDEEM . . . . ANS LET AMERICA BE 82
WHO ARE ALL THEM PEOPLE . . . . . . ANS SISTER JOHNSON 9
THE PEOPLE ARE SPAIN: . . . . ANS SONG OF SPAIN 40
THE PEOPLE BENEATH THAT BOMBING
PLANE . . . . ANS SONG OF SPAIN 41
ON THE PEOPLE. . . . . ANS SONG OF SPAIN 70
A WHOLE SLEW OF PEOPLE . . . . . . SH DEATH IN HARLEM 119
TO JIM CROW MY PEOPLE IS A PITY. . JC JIM CROW'S LAST 20
WHERE TWO PEOPLE . . . . FW CAROLINA CABIN 21
TO SOME PEOPLE . . . . FW GIFTS 1
NOW PEOPLE WONDER . . . . FW HEART 17
LONELY PEOPLE . . . . FW LITTLE SONG 1
LONELY PEOPLE . . . . FW LITTLE SONG 5
PEOPLE PASS BY ME - . . . . OWT LONESOME CORNER 6
NOW AMONGST DECENT PEOPLE. . . . . SP BLD OF THE GIRL 7
THAT HAD NOT FAILED PEOPLE . . . . SP DANCER 3
I TIRE SO OF HEARING PEOPLE SAY. . SP DEMOCRACY 10
OUT OF THE DARKEST DAYS FOR A PEOPLE
AND A NATION. . . . . SP FREEDOM'S PLOW 137
THE PEOPLE SAY IT IS PROMISES - THAT
WILL COME TRUE. . . . . SP FREEDOM'S PLOW 144
THE PEOPLE DO NOT ALWAYS SAY THINGS
OUT LOUD. . . . . SP FREEDOM'S PLOW 145
THE PEOPLE OFTEN HOLD . . . . SP FREEDOM'S PLOW 147
THE PEOPLE DO NOT ALWAYS UNDERSTAND
EACH OTHER. . . . . SP FREEDOM'S PLOW 152
AN ENSLAVED PEOPLE HEADING TOWARD
FREEDOM . . . . SP FREEDOM'S PLOW 189
WHERE THE PEOPLE ALL ARE ICEBERGS SP GRADUATION 8
HELL NO SHUT UP! SAY THE PEOPLE . . SP IN EXPLANATION 27
THE PEOPLE WITH NO TITLES IN FRONT
OF THEIR NAMES . . . . SP IN EXPLANATION 40
SHUT UP, PEOPLE! . . . . SP IN EXPLANATION 44
BECAUSE OF PEOPLE WITH NO TITLES . SP IN EXPLANATION 60
SEE THE PEOPLE PASSING BY? . . . . SP KID IN THE PARK 3
BUT THE PEOPLE OF THE NIGHT . . . . SP LIVE LET LIVE 2
TO SOME PEOPLE . . . . SP LUCK 5
SO THE FACES OF MY PEOPLE. . . . . SP MY PEOPLE 2
SO THE EYES OF MY PEOPLE. . . . . . SP MY PEOPLE 4
BEAUTIFUL, ALSO, ARE THE SOULS OF MY
PEOPLE. . . . . SP MY PEOPLE 6
PEOPLE WHO ARE CRUEL . . . . SP ONE-WAY TICKET 18
BUT THE PEOPLE WILL FORGET - . . . SP SHAME ON YOU 4
BLACK PEOPLE DON'T REMEMBER . . . . SP SHAME ON YOU 8
THAN SOME PEOPLE EVER HAD. . . . . SP WARNING AUGMENT 12
WHERE THE PEOPLE ALL ARE DARKER . . AYM ODE TO DINAH 121
OF BLACK AND WHITE BLACK WHITE BLACK
PEOPLE . . . . PL DAYBREAK IN ALA 14
I TIRE SO OF HEARING PEOPLE SAY. . PL FREEDOM 10

PEOPLES 2
BUT NONE OF THEM PEOPLES . . . . . OWT LONESOME CORNER 7
UNTIL ALL RACES AND ALL PEOPLES KNOW
ITS SHADE. . . . . SP FREEDOM'S PLOW 199

PEOPLE'S 3
ITS PEOPLE'S HEART, TOO SMALL TO
HOLD A SOB. . . . . SL TOWN OF SCOTTSB 4
FROM THOSE WHO LIVE LIKE LEECHES ON
THE PEOPLE'S LIVES. . . . . . . ANS LET AMERICA BE 72
OTHER PEOPLE'S GOLD. . . . . SH BLD THE KILLER 18

PEPSI-COLA 1
HAMBURGERS PEPSI-COLA . . . . AYM ASK YOUR MAMA 41

PERFESSER 1
JUST PLAY 'EM, PERFESSER. . . . . . SH HEY-HEY BLUES 11

PERFUME 2
WHAT GREAT FOREST HAS HUNG ITS
PERFUME . . . . WB NUDE YOUNG DANC 3
OF AN UNKNOWN STRANGE PERFUME . . . SP DESIRE 6

PERHAPS 11
PERHAPS - . . . . FW SAILING DATE 15
EVEN PERHAPS . . . . FW THERE 10
PERHAPS BLOOD . . . . FW WHEN ARMIES PAS 19
PERHAPS THE DREAM IS ONLY HER FACE - SP HAVANA DREAMS 5
PERHAPS IT'S A FAN OF SILVER LACE - SP HAVANA DREAMS 6
SOMETIMES PERHAPS YOU DON'T WANT TO
BE A PART OF ME. . . . . SP THEME FOR ENG B 34
PERHAPS IF IT BE GOD'S WILL . . . . AYM ASK YOUR MAMA 64
THAT ONCE PERHAPS WERE EYES. . . . PL JUSTICE 4
PERHAPS . . . . PL OCTOBER 16 RAID 1
PERHAPS . . . . PL OCTOBER 16 RAID 27

Context	Source	Line
PERHAPS FROM A FIX	PL SLAVE	9
PERPETUALLY 1		
PERPETUALLY THE FLAME.	OLD TWO THINGS	4
PERSIMMON 2		
PERSIMMON BRONZE	SH HARLEM SWEETIES	23
PERSIMMON, BLACKBERRY,	SH HARLEM SWEETIES	38
PERSONAL 3		
PERSONAL	SP PERSONAL	2
PERSONAL	SP PERSONAL	5
WISDOM REDUCED TO THE PERSONAL EQUATION:	PL ELDERLY LEADERS	2
PERSON'S 1		
CAN TAKE A PERSON'S LIFE.	SP LITTLE OLD LETT	16
PETALS 3		
THEIR PETALS DANCE ON THE WIND	DK AUTUMN THOUGHT	4
AND THE ROUGE-BRIGHT PETALS.	FW CHIPPY	3
THE PETALS	FW MONTMARTRE	5
PHARAOH 1		
THAN PHARAOH HAD WIVES.	SP FIRE	20
PHILADELPHIA 1		
TWO PARTIES FROM PHILADELPHIA	SP SEASHORE THROUG	5
PHILIP 1		
A. PHILIP RANDOLPH THE HIGH GRAND WORTHY.	PL CULTURAL EXCHNG	45
PHILLIPS 1		
(NOT ST. PHILLIPS)	SP HIGH TO LOW	14
PHONE 3		
ELSE YOU'LL TAKE OUT MY PHONE?	SP MADAM PHONE BIL	11
MY PHONE ALONE.	SP MADAM PHONE BIL	13
PHONE BILL DOES I CARE!	SP MADAM PHONE BIL	36
PH.D 1		
A JACK-LEG PREACHER, A PH.D.	SP MYSTERY	24
PIANO 10		
DIAMOND RING, CIGARETTE HOLDER, AND A CANE, TO THE MUSIC OF PIANO OR	NM BIG-TIMER MOOD	1
SUIT AND HAT OF A CLOWN, TO THE MUSIC OF A PIANO, OR AN ORCHESTRA.	NM BLACK CLWN MOOD	1
UNITED STATES OF AMERICA, MARTIAL MUSIC ON A PIANO, OR BY AN ORCHESTRA,	NM COLORED SL MOOD	3
AT A BIG PIANO A LITTLE DARK GIRL	SH DEATH IN HARLEM	10
A PLAYER PIANO,	SP RAILROAD AVENUE	9
IF I JUST HAD A PIANO,	SP TESTIMONIAL	1
BUT I DON'T NEED NO PIANO.	SP TESTIMONIAL	5
HE MADE THAT POOR PIANO MOAN WITH MELODY.	SP THE WEARY BLUES	10
I HEARD THAT NEGRO SING, THAT OLD PIANO MOAN -	SP THE WEARY BLUES	18
DREAMING OF A BABY GRAND PIANO	SP TO BE SOMEBODY	2
PICASSO 1		
OLD PICASSO AND THE DOVE	PL THE DOVE	2
PICK 6		
WID A PICK AN' A SHOVEL.	FC WORKIN' MAN	2
AW, PICK THAT RAG!	SH DEATH IN HARLEM	13
AW, PICK IT, MISS LUCY!	SH DEATH IN HARLEM	27
I PICK UP MY LIFE	SP ONE-WAY TICKET	1
I PICK UP MY LIFE	SP ONE-WAY TICKET	9
I PICK UP MY LIFE	SP ONE-WAY TICKET	23
PICKED 2		
PICKED UP ANOTHER WOMAN AND	SH DEATH IN HARLEM	141
WHEN THE COTTON'S PICKED	SP SHARE-CROPPERS	5
PICKING 1		
ON THE CORNER PICKING SPLINTERS	AYM ASK YOUR MAMA	33
PICKIN' 1		
PICKIN' COTTON IN THE FIELD	SP WEST TEXAS	6
PICKIN'S 2		
THE PICKIN'S WEREN'T BAD ON A 133RD.	SH DEATH IN HARLEM	5
THE PICKIN'S WEREN'T BAD -	SH DEATH IN HARLEM	6
PICTURE 1		
AT THE PICTURE SHOW.	AYM ASK YOUR MAMA	24
PIE 1		
PIE OF A TOWN.	SP ISLAND	8
PIECE 1		
A LITTLE PIECE DOWN THE ROAD.	SP LITTLE GRN TREE	11
PIED 2		
SEND FOR THE PIED PIPER AND LET HIM PIPE THE RATS	PL FINAL CALL	1
SEND FOR THE PIED PIPER TO PIPE OUR RATS AWAY.	PL FINAL CALL	38
PIERCE 1		
JUDGE PIERCE HE SAYS, MARY.	FC BLD OF GIN MARY	5
PIERRETTE 2		
BUT PIERROT LEFT PIERRETTE.	WB PIERROT	16
AND MAY PIERRETTE,	FW FOR DEAD MIMES	6
PIERROT 17		
BUT PIERROT WONDERED WHY.	WB PIERROT	6
FOR PIERROT LOVED THE LONG WHITE ROAD,	WB PIERROT	7
AND PIERROT LOVED THE MOON,	WB PIERROT	8
AND PIERROT LOVED A STAR-FILLED SKY,	WB PIERROT	9
BUT PIERROT LEFT PIERRETTE.	WB PIERROT	16
FOR PIERROT SAW A WORLD OF GIRLS,	WB PIERROT	17
AND PIERROT LOVED EACH ONE,	WB PIERROT	18
AND PIERROT THOUGHT ALL MAIDENS FAIR	WB PIERROT	19
FOR PIERROT PLAYED ON A SLIM GUITAR,	WB PIERROT	27
AND PIERROT LOVED THE MOON,	WB PIERROT	28
AND PIERROT RAN DOWN THE LONG WHITE ROAD	WB PIERROT	29
WITH PIERROT.	FW FOR DEAD MIMES	9
PIERROT	FW HEART	1
SO PIERROT	FW HEART	13
I AM A BLACK PIERROT:	SP A BLACK PIERROT	1
I AM A BLACK PIERROT:	SP A BLACK PIERROT	5
I AM A BLACK PIERROT:	SP A BLACK PIERROT	10
PIERROT'S 2		
BUT PIERROT'S STEEPED IN SIN.	WB PIERROT	26
PIERROT'S HEART	FW HEART	11
PIGALLE 2		
PIGALLE:	FW MONTMARTRE	1
FORT DE FRANCE, PLACE PIGALLE	AYM ASK YOUR MAMA	45
PIGGY-BACK 1		
TO RIDE PIGGY-BACK	PL SLAVE	1
PILE 2		
I, A WORKER, LETTING MY LABOR PILE	ANS SONG OF SPAIN	43
I'M THE ONLY ONE'S GOT TO PILE OUT IN THE COLD.	SH DAYBREAK	6
PILED 2		
ITS ROOF WITH SNOW IS PILED.	DK WINTER SWEEETNS	2
SOLD IN SHOPS, PILED IN WAREHOUSES.	SP FREEDOM'S PLOW	30
PILGRIMS 1		
BRINGING PILGRIMS AND PRAYER-MAKERS,	SP FREEDOM'S PLOW	30
PILLARED 1		
IN WHITE PILLARED MANSIONS	PL CULTURAL EXCHNG	46
PILLARS 2		
TO SHAKE THE PILLARS OF THOSE TEMPLES	ANS UNION	7
ONE OF THE PILLARS OF THE TEMPLE FELL.	SP MULATTO	4
PILLOWS 1		
LIKE THE PILLOWS OF ALL SWEET DREAMS,	SP MIDNIGHT DANCER	6
PIMPS 3		
WHEN PIMPS OUT OF LONELINESS CRY:	SP SLIVER SERMON	1
PIMPS IN GRAY GO BY,	SP SUMMER EVENING	5
SOME PIMPS WEAR SUMMER HATS	SP WHAT?	1
PINE 5		
AND TALL STRAIGHT PINE	FW CAROLINA CABIN	3
THE SCENT OF PINE WOOD STINGS THE SOFT NIGHT AIR.	SP MULATTO	18
SHARP PINE SCENT IN THE EVENING AIR.	SP MULATTO	22
PINE WOOD SCENT IN THE EVENING AIR.	SP MULATTO	40
AND THE SCENT OF PINE NEEDLES	PL DAYBREAK IN ALA	8
PINES 1		
BUT HIGHER THAN THE SINGING PINES	DK ALABAMA EARTH	4
PINK 2		
AND A ROSE PINK MOUTH.	SP SUMMER EVENING	4
PINK PAPER TOWELS	PL UNDERTOW	8
PINSCHER 1		
BOUGHT A DOBERMAN PINSCHER.	AYM BIRD IN ORBIT	87
PINTURA 1		
PINTURA IS THE SONG OF SPAIN:	ANS SONG OF SPAIN	19
PIONEER 1		
LET IT BE THE PIONEER ON THE PLAIN	ANS LET AMERICA BE	3

PIONEERS 1
BEATEN YET TODAY - O, PIONEERS! . . ANS LET AMERICA BE 36

PIOUS 1
WITH PIOUS FOLK AND FAIR . . . . . WB A FAREWELL 4

PIPE 4
PIPE OF ETERNITY, ... SP SUNDAY MORNING 4
I LIKE A PIPE FOR A CHRISTMAS PRESENT, ... SP THEME FOR ENG B 23
SEND FOR THE PIED PIPER AND LET HIM PIPE THE RATS . . . . PL FINAL CALL 1
SEND FOR THE PIED PIPER TO PIPE OUR RATS AWAY. . . . . PL FINAL CALL 38

PIPER 2
SEND FOR THE PIED PIPER AND LET HIM PIPE THE RATS . . . . PL FINAL CALL 1
SEND FOR THE PIED PIPER TO PIPE OUR RATS AWAY. . . . . PL FINAL CALL 38

PISTOL 3
ARABELLA DREW HER PISTOL. . . . . . SH DEATH IN HARLEM 99
GONNA GO GET MY PISTOL, I SAID FORTY-FOUR - . . . . SH TWILIGHT REVERI 5
GONNA GO GET MY PISTOL, I MEAN THIRTY-TWO, ... SH TWILIGHT REVERI 7

PISTOLS 2
ABOUT TWO KINDS O' PISTOLS THAT I AIN'T GOT. . . . . SH TWILIGHT REVERI 10
WITH A WOMAN WITH TWO PISTOLS . . . AYM ODE TO DINAH 28

PIT 1
THE BAND DOWN IN THE PIT BURSTS INTO JAZZ. . . . . OWT LINCOLN THEATRE 6

PITIES 1
MONSTROUS PITIES . . . . FW OLD SAILOR 9

PITY 11
LAUGH - OR TAKE PITY. . . . . NM BIG-TIMER POEM 8
AND THE OPPRESSORS HAD NO PITY, . . ANS A NEW SONG 21
TO JIM CROW MY PEOPLE IS A PITY. . JC JIM CROW'S LAST 20
IN THE ARMS OF YOUR PITY . . . . . FW PRAYER 2
IN THE ARMS OF YOUR PITY. . . . . FW PRAYER 8
IN THE ARMS OF YOUR PITY . . . . . SP LITANY 2
IN THE ARMS OF YOUR PITY. . . . . . SP LITANY 8
LAWD, HAVE PITY! . . . . SP MADAM PHONE BIL 20
IN LONELY PITY THROUGH THE GEORGIA DUSK . . . . PL GEORGIA DUSK 3
OH, WHAT PITY! . . . . PL MISSISSIPPI 2
WHAT SORROW, PITY, PAIN. . . . . . PL MISSISSIPPI 17

PLACE 38
THAT IN THIS NIGGER PLACE, ... OLD AESTHETE HARLEM 2
NO PLACE TO GO. . . . . NM BLACK CLWN POEM 35
DONE BEAT YOU TO DE PLACE, STANDIN' OUT SIDE DE DO' . . . . NM BROKE 6
TO MOULD A PLACE . . . . NM DARK YOUTH USA 4
LIFTING MY RACE TO ITS RIGHTFUL PLACE . . . . NM DARK YOUTH USA 19
SCOTTSBORO'S JUST A LITTLE PLACE: SL TOWN OF SCOTTSB 1
THEN THE PLACE WAS EMPTY, ... SH DEATH IN HARLEM 124
IN DIXIE'S PLACE ON 133RD . . . . . SH DEATH IN HARLEM 24
DIXIE'S AIN'T NO PLACE FOR A GANG THAT'S SLOW. . . . . SH DEATH IN HARLEM 38
SHE LOOKED ACROSS THE PLACE - . . . SH DEATH IN HARLEM 94
SETTIN IN HER PLACE! . . . . SH DEATH IN HARLEM 96
THAT PLACE WHERE YOUR TRUNK WAS, AIN'T NO TRUNK NO MORE. . . . . SH SUPPER TIME 8
PLACE WHERE YOUR CLOTHES HUNG'S EMPTY AND BARE. . . . . SH SUPPER TIME 9
WILL HAVE NO PLACE. . . . . JC TO CAPTAIN MULZ 58
HERE IS THAT SLEEPING PLACE, . . . FW GRAVE YARD 1
LONG RESTING PLACE, ... FW GRAVE YARD 2
NO STRETCHING PLACE, ... FW GRAVE YARD 3
PLACE . . . . FW GRAVE YARD 5
50TH PLACE. . . . . OWT JITNEY 49
WITHOUT A PLACE - . . . . SP AFRO-AMER FRAG 20
ANY PLACE IS DREARY . . . . SP COULD BE 15
IN THE FIRST PLACE . . . . SP DANCER 5
IN SOME PLACE OF THE SUN. . . . . . SP DREAM VARIATION 2
I'D TELL HER, GIMME A PLACE TO SLEEP. . . . . SP EVENING SONG 6
THE PLACE WHERE . . . . SP HEAVEN 2
ANY PLACE THAT IS . . . . SP ONE-WAY TICKET 6
ANY PLACE THAT IS . . . . SP ONE-WAY TICKET 13
MAYVILLE HAD NO PLACE TO OFFER HER, SP RUBY BROWN 5
DIGNIFY THE PLACE . . . . SP SEASHORE THROUG 6
PLACE. . . . . SP UNCLE TOM 12
NO PLACE TO SLEEP, ... SP VAGABONDS 6
AIN'T NO PLACE . . . . SP WEST TEXAS 18
YOU'LL SURE STAY IN YOUR PLACE. . . SP WIDOW WOMAN 12
FORT DE FRANCE, PLACE PIGALLE . . . AYM ASK YOUR MAMA 45
NOR TAKE THE PLACE OF MEAT OR BREAD PL CROWNS GARLANDS 15
TO SOME LONESOME PLACE. . . . . . . PL KU KLUX 2
WHO OWNS THE PLACE - . . . . PL LENOX AVE. BAR 4
PLACE. . . . . PL LENOX AVE. BAR 12

PLACED 1
WHERE THE MASK IS PLACED BY OTHERS AYM SHOW FARE PLESE 6

PLACES 6
LIFE IN PLACES GENTLER SPEAKING . . OLD AESTHETE HARLEM 5
KNOWIN THEY CAN BUY A DOZEN COLORED PLACES. . . . . SH DEATH IN HARLEM 61
MANY PLACES . . . . FW OLD SAILOR 2
AND PLACES WITH NO CARPET ON THE FLOOR - . . . . SP MOTHER TO SON 6
HARLEM LAUGHING IN ALL THE WRONG PLACES . . . . SP MOVIES 2
PLACES. . . . . PL CORNER MEETING 9

PLAIN 9
LET IT BE THE PIONEER ON THE PLAIN ANS LET AMERICA BE 3
AND POLAND'S PLAIN, AND ENGLAND'S GRASSY LEA, ... ANS LET AMERICA BE 48
I SAY IT PLAIN, ... ANS LET AMERICA BE 76
THE MOUNTAINS AND THE ENDLESS PLAIN - . . . . ANS LET AMERICA BE 84
WHEN FLOWERS SPREAD THE PLAIN, . . FW GIRL 6
THAT GREW UPON THE PLAIN . . . . . LHR PASTORAL 7
WHEN IT STOPS IN MISSISSIPPI WILL IT BE MADE PLAIN . . . . SP FREEDOM TRAIN 21
AND OVER ALL THE PLAIN . . . . . . SP IN TIME SILVER 6
IT'S MADE OF PLAIN OLD GEORGIA CLAY. PL VARI-COLORED 7

PLAINS 1
ACROSS THE PLAINS OF AMERICA. . . . SP FREEDOM'S PLOW 60

PLAIT 1
SO, SI'L-VOUS PLAIT, I'LL STUDY FRENCH! . . . . SP DEFERRED 28

PLAN 3
AND FINDING ONLY THE SAME OLD STUPID PLAN. . . . . ANS LET AMERICA BE 23
I NEVER DID LIKE THE INSTALLMENT PLAN . . . . SH PAY DAY 14
THE PLAN AND THE PATTERN IS HERE, SP FREEDOM'S PLOW 165

PLANE 3
THE PEOPLE BENEATH THAT BOMBING PLANE . . . . ANS SONG OF SPAIN 41
THE BOMBING PLANE! . . . . ANS SONG OF SPAIN 62
I'D GET ME A PLANE . . . . SH IF-ING 10

PLANES 2
I MADE THOSE BOMBING PLANES. . . . ANS SONG OF SPAIN 73
PLANES FROM PUERTO RICO. . . . . . SP GOOD MORNING 9

PLANE'S 1
A BOMBING PLANE'S . . . . ANS SONG OF SPAIN 31

PLANNING 2
PLANNING PLANNING A PARADE: . . . . SP PARADE 4
PLANNING PLANNING A PARADE: . . . . SP PARADE 4

PLANT 6
STRONG AS THE SHOOTS OF A NEW PLANT, FW EARTH SONG 8
PLANT YOUR TOES IN THE COOL SWAMP MUD. . . . . OWT FLIGHT 1
PLANT HIM NOW - . . . . SP DEAD IN THERE 20
AN' PLANT IT AT MY BACK DOOR, . . . SP MIDWINTER BLUES 20
PLANT IT AT MY BACK DOOR, ... SP MIDWINTER BLUES 22
I'M GONNA PLANT MY FEET . . . . . . PL DOWN WHERE I AM 13

PLANTAINS 1
(AND MY PLANTAINS) . . . . AYM GOSPEL CHA-CHA 25

PLANTATIONS 1
WHITE SHARECROPPERS WORK THE BLACK PLANTATIONS, ... PL CULTURAL EXCHNG 49

PLANTED 3
PLANTED . . . . SP DEMOCRACY 17
THAT PLANTED AND HARVESTED THE FOOD THAT FED . . . . SP FREEDOM'S PLOW 53
PLANTED . . . . PL FREEDOM 17

PLANTING 1
PLOWING, PLANTING, HOEING, ... SP SHARE-CROPPERS 3

PLANTS 2
THE LAND, THE MINES, THE PLANTS, THE RIVERS - . . . . ANS LET AMERICA BE 83
THAT THE PLANTS AND THE ROADS AND THE TOOLS OF POWER . . . . ANS OPEN LETTER 17

PLAY 52
PLAY, PLAY, PLAY! . . . . WB HARLEM NIGHT CL 3
PLAY, PLAY, PLAY! . . . . WB HARLEM NIGHT CL 3
PLAY, PLAY, PLAY! . . . . WB HARLEM NIGHT CL 3
PLAY, PLAY, PLAY! . . . . WB HARLEM NIGHT CL 19

PLAY, PLAY, PLAY!	WB HARLEM NIGHT CL	19
PLAY, PLAY, PLAY!	WB HARLEM NIGHT CL	19
SIX LONG-HEADED JAZZERS PLAY.	WB JAZZONIA	4
SIX LONG-HEADED JAZZERS PLAY.	WB JAZZONIA	17
CORNETS PLAY.	FC CLOSING TIME	11
PLAY THAT THING.	FC JAZZ BAND	1
PLAY IT FOR THE LORDS AND LADIES.	FC JAZZ BAND	3
PLAY IT.	FC JAZZ BAND	9
PLAY IT, JAZZ BAND!	FC JAZZ BAND	18
HE KIN PLAY A BANJO.	FC MA MAN	7
HE KIN PLAY A BANJO.	FC MA MAN	9
WHEN SHE OUGHT TO PLAY.	FC NEW CABARET GRL	20
PLAY IT ONCE.	FC SATURDAY NIGHT	1
O, PLAY SOME MORE.	FC SATURDAY NIGHT	2
FOR ME TO PLAY WITH	NM BLACK CLWN POEM	6
NO MUSIC DIDN'T PLAY.	SH DEATH IN HARLEM	125
PLAY A LONG TIME, GAL!	SH DEATH IN HARLEM	46
AW, PLAY IT, MISS LUCY!	SH DEATH IN HARLEM	74
JUST PLAY 'EM, PERFESSER.	SH HEY-HEY BLUES	11
WHILE YOU PLAY 'EM.	SH HEY-HEY BLUES	13
AND WHILE YOU PLAY 'EM.	SH HEY-HEY BLUES	15
I DON'T CARE HOW YOU PLAY 'EM	SH HEY-HEY BLUES	17
BUT WHEN THE BAND BEGAN TO PLAY.	FW HARLEM DANCE HA	2
AND IS AFRAID TO PLAY	FW MIGRATION	3
PLAY YOUR GUITAR, BOY.	OWT BLUES ON A BOX	1
WHERE SINGING BLACK BOYS DANCE AND PLAY EACH NIGHT	OWT JUICE JOINT	2
PLAY YOUR GUITARS, GRINNING NIGHT-DARK BOYS.	OWT JUICE JOINT	17
WHERE BLACK MEN COME TO DRINK AND PLAY AND SING.	OWT JUICE JOINT	34
PLAY THE ST. LOUIS BLUES	OWT REQUEST REQUIEM	1
DON'T YOU PLAY IN DAT ROAD.	SP BABY	3
ALBERT, DON'T YOU PLAY IN DAT ROAD.	SP BABY	8
WHEN I WAS A CHILE WE USED TO PLAY.	SP CHILDREN'S RYME	1
FOR US TO PLAY WITH.	SP FULFILMENT	11
AND WHILE WE LISTEN TO IT PLAY.	SP JUKE BOX LOVE	10
I USED TO PLAY	SP LITTLE GRN TREE	5
I WOULDN'T PLAY NO MORE.	SP MADAM NUMBER WR	4
AIN'T GONNA PLAY NO MORE	SP MADAM NUMBER WR	22
THEN I CAN PLAY	SP MADAM NUMBER WR	25
PLAY THE BLUES FOR ME.	SP MISERY	1
PLAY THE BLUES FOR ME.	SP MISERY	2
AND UNBOOTED PLAY	SP NEON SIGNS	8
PLAY BACK A CENT.	SP NUMBERS	5
I HEARD A NEGRO PLAY.	SP THE WEARY BLUES	3
DREAMING OF A BABY GRAND TO PLAY	SP TO BE SOMEBODY	4
YOU MAY PLAY FOLKS CHEAP.	SP WARNING AUGMENT	5
THAT DON'T KNOW HOW TO PLAY	AYM BLUES IN STEREO	25
I PLAY IT COOL	PL MOTTO	1
PLAY HILLBILLY DIRGES	PL SPECIAL BULLTIN	3

PLAYBOY 1

PLAYBOY OF THE DAWN.	SP GONE BOY	1

PLAYED 11

FOR PIERROT PLAYED ON A SLIM GUITAR.	WB PIERROT	27
WHILE MISS LUCY PLAYED IT, BOOM, BOOM, BOOM.	SH DEATH IN HARLEM	91
AND PLAYED IT.	SP HOPE	4
AND I PLAYED SO DOG-GONE HARD.	SP LITTLE GRN TREE	6
HE PLAYED A DIME.	SP MADAM NUMBER WR	13
I PLAYED, TOO.	SP MADAM NUMBER WR	14
AND THE ORGAN HAD DONE PLAYED	SP NIGHT FUNERAL	29
PLAYED BY INEZ AND TIMME.	SP PROJECTION	14
HE PLAYED THAT SAD RAGGY TUNE LIKE A MUSICAL FOOL.	SP THE WEARY BLUES	13
HE PLAYED A FEW CHORDS THEN HE SANG SOME MORE -	SP THE WEARY BLUES	24
ON GRAVESTONES DATES ARE PLAYED.	AYM JAZZTET MUTED	13

PLAYER 1

A PLAYER PIANO.	SP RAILROAD AVENUE	9

PLAYERS 1

FOOTBALL PLAYERS LEATHER PUNCHERS $ $ $	AYM HORN OF PLENTY	18

PLAYER-PIANO 1

THE LAST PLAYER-PIANO IS CLOSED.	WB SUMMER NIGHT	4

PLAYIN 2

WAS PLAYIN JAZZ FOR A MIDNIGHT WORLD.	SH DEATH IN HARLEM	11
WHILE THE MUSIC'S PLAYIN LET'S	SH DEATH IN HARLEM	85

PLAYING 4

AND SEE WHAT COUNT BASIE'S PLAYING NEW.	SH BED TIME	2
A BAND IS PLAYING.	SP HARLEM NIGHT SO	12
THE SINGER STOPPED PLAYING AND WENT TO BED	SP THE WEARY BLUES	33
NOT ENOUGH TO HURT MY PLAYING $ $ $ $ $	AYM HORN OF PLENTY	12

PLAYIN' 2

HEAR THAT MUSIC PLAYIN' UPSTAIRS?	SP BLACK MARIA	6
BUT THAT MUSIC PLAYIN' UPSTAIRS	SP BLACK MARIA	9

PLAYS 8

HE PLAYS GOOD WHEN HE'S SOBER	FC MA MAN	11
THE RAIN PLAYS A LITTLE SLEEP-SONG ON OUR ROOF AT NIGHT -	DK APRIL RAIN SONG	6
AND YET HE PLAYS UPON HIS FLUTE A WILD FREE TUNE	DK BEGGAR BOY	7
SOMETIMES A BLACK BOY PLAYS A SONG	OWT JUICE JOINT	9
AND DIG ALL PLAYS.	SP FLATTED FIFTHS	19
AND PUT ON PLAYS ABOUT ME!	SP NOTE COMM THEAT	17
AND A BLIND MAN PLAYS AN ACCORDION	SP SUMMER EVENING	16
ERZULIE PLAYS A TUNE	AYM GOSPEL CHA-CHA	7

PLEASE 24

O, PLEASE SIR, JUDGE, HAVE MERCY!	FC BLD OF GIN MARY	21
HAVE MERCY, PLEASE, ON ME!	FC BLD OF GIN MARY	22
O, GOD, PLEASE!	FC CLOSING TIME	9
PLEASE DON'T TAKE THIS MAN O' MINE.	FC GAL'S CRY DYING	18
AND ME AND MY BROTHER WERE HAPPY AS YOU PLEASE	NM COLORED SL POEM	6
SHE BEGGED ME, PLEASE.	SH BLD THE SINNER	13
PLEASE DO NOT SELL ME OUT.	SH IN TROUBLED KEY	2
I SAID, PLEASE, MR. LONESOME.	SH MIDNIGHT CHIPPI	11
PLEASE DON'T IG ME LIKE YOU DO.	SH MIDNIGHT CHIPPI	22
HERE BY MYSELF, I DO AS I PLEASE.	SH SUNDAY	2
SET ON THE FRONT PORCH AS LONG AS I PLEASE.	SH SUNDAY	8
DEMOCRACY, PLEASE -	JC HOW ABOUT DIXIE	10
PLEASE DON'T TAKE HIM AWAY!	SP AS BEFITS A MAN	16
PLEASE REACH OUT YO' HAND.	SP FEET O' JESUS	8
IF MY CHILDREN ASK ME, DADDY, PLEASE EXPLAIN	SP FREEDOM TRAIN	31
YOU TREAT ME LIKE YOU DAMN WELL PLEASE.	SP LOW TO HIGH	14
I SAID, PLEASE EXPLAIN TO ME	SP MADAM FORT TELL	9
MAMA, PLEASE BRUSH OFF MY COAT.	SP MAMA AND DAUGHT	1
PLEASE DON'T SNORE SO LOUD.	SP MORNING AFTER	14
BABY! PLEASE!	SP MORNING AFTER	15
PLEASE DON'T SNORE SO LOUD.	SP MORNING AFTER	16
SHOW FARE, MAMA, PLEASE.	AYM SHOW FARE PLESE	35
PLEASE!)	PL FINAL CALL	27
SUNRISE, PLEASE COME!	PL JUNIOR ADDICT	38

PLEASED 1

I AIN'T PLEASED!	SP MADAM RENT MAN	28

PLEASURE 1

OF PLEASURE.	FW DANCERS	4

PLEASURED 1

PLEASURED EQUALLY	SP OLD WALT	7

PLEASURES 1

FLESHLY PLEASURES	FW OLD SAILOR	11

PLED 1

WERE PLED ANEW AT SOME HEROIC BAR.	PL MOTHER IN WAR	4

PLENTY 5

'COURSE, YOU HEARS PLENTY 'BOUT THIS-HERE UNEMPLOYMENT RELIEF -	NM BROKE	56
BUT NOW I KNOW WE'VE GOT PLENTY TO DO.	NM COLORED SL POEM	23
PLENTY EYES.	SP UP-BEAT	12
I THOUGHT I HEARD THE HORN OF PLENTY BLOWING.	AYM BLUES IN STEREO	35
HORN OF PLENTY	AYM HORN OF PLENTY	81

PLOW 11

WHOSE HAND AT THE FOUNDRY, WHOSE PLOW IN THE RAIN.	ANS LET AMERICA BE	68
AND DRIVE US TO THE TIME-CLOCK AND THE PLOW	ANS OPEN LETTER	27
KEEP YOUR HAND ON THE PLOW! HOLD ON!	SP FREEDOM'S PLOW	200
KEEP YOUR HAND ON THE PLOW! HOLD ON!	SP FREEDOM'S PLOW	126
KEEP YOUR HAND ON THE PLOW! HOLD ON!	SP FREEDOM'S PLOW	129
DOWN INTO THE EARTH WENT THE PLOW	SP FREEDOM'S PLOW	49
TURNING THE RICH SOIL WENT THE PLOW IN MANY HANDS	SP FREEDOM'S PLOW	52
KEEP YOUR HAND ON THE PLOW! HOLD ON!	SP FREEDOM'S PLOW	160
HELD THE PLOW HANDLES.	SP FREEDOM'S PLOW	64
KEEP YOUR HAND ON THE PLOW! HOLD ON!	SP FREEDOM'S PLOW	191
THE PLOW PLOWED A NEW FURROW	SP FREEDOM'S PLOW	192

PLOWED 1

THE PLOW PLOWED A NEW FURROW	SP FREEDOM'S PLOW	192

PLOWING 3

PLOWING AND REAPING	NM BLACK CLWN POEM	18
PLOWING, PLANTING, HOEING,	SP SHARE-CROPPERS	3
PLOWING LIFE AWAY	SP SHARE-CROPPERS	15

PLUMP 1

THE CROWD APPLAUDS A PLUMP BROWN-SKIN BLEACHED BLONDE	OWT LINCOLN THEATRE	7

PLUMS 1

LIKE PALE PLUMS FROM A TREE	SP MELLOW	4

PLUM-TINTED 1
TO PLUM-TINTED BLACK. . . . . SH HARLEM SWEETIES 18

PLUNK 8
LORDY, HE KIN PLUNK, PLUNK, PLUNK. FC MA MAN 8
LORDY, HE KIN PLUNK, PLUNK. FC MA MAN 8
LORDY, HE KIN PLUNK, PLUNK, PLUNK. FC MA MAN 8
I MEAN PLUNK, PLUNK . . . PLUNK, PLUNK. . . . . FC MA MAN 10
I MEAN PLUNK, PLUNK . . . PLUNK, PLUNK. . . . . FC MA MAN 10
I MEAN PLUNK, PLUNK . . . PLUNK, PLUNK. . . . . FC MA MAN 10
I MEAN PLUNK, PLUNK . . . PLUNK, PLUNK. . . . . FC MA MAN 10
AW, PLUNK IT, MISS LUCY. . . . . . SH DEATH IN HARLEM 56

PLUS 1
PLUS CASSIUS MOHAMMED ALI CLAY. . . PL CROWNS GARLANDS 5

POCAHONTAS 1
WOULD I MARRY POCAHONTAS? . . . . . AYM ODE TO DINAH 128

POCKET 3
A ROLL OF BILLS IN HIS LEFT-HAND POCKET. . . . . SH DEATH IN HARLEM 19
LOSER FROM AN EMPTY POCKET . . . . JC THE BITTER RIVR 69
GOT CHANGE IN HIS LONG POCKET? . . AYM SHOW FARE PLESE 4

POCOMANIA 1
BEDWARD! POCOMANIA! WEDO! OGOUN! . AYM GOSPEL CHA-CHA 36

POEM 2
A MORAL POEM TO BE RENDERED BY A MAN IN A STRAW HAT WITH A BRIGHT BAND, A . . . . NM BIG-TIMER MOOD 1
THE POEM ENDS. . . . . DK I LOVED FRIEND 4

POET 2
A WANDERING POET . . . . FW CAROLINA CABIN 16
THE POET SAYS IT WAS PROMISES. . . SP FREEDOM'S PLOW 143

POINT 1
HAVE PROVEN A POINT . . . . PL NORTHERN LIBERL 8

POINTED 1
HAVING PREVIOUSLY POINTED OUT THE SINS OF THIS WORLD: . . . . . . SP SUNDAY MORNING 1

POINTS 1
COMPASS POINTS. . . . . SP SEASHORE THROUG 13

POISON 4
POISON GAS IS SPAIN. . . . . ANS SONG OF SPAIN 35
TOO LONG HAS ITS EVIL POISON . . . JC THE BITTER RIVR 8
AND A POISON ACID BURNS - . . . . . FW EXITS 3
IN POISON FROM THE FALLOUT . . . . PL JUNIOR ADDICT 26

POISONED 1
POISONED MY BLOOD. . . . . JC THE BITTER RIVR 9

POKER 1
I'M GONNA GET UP A POKER GAME AND INVITE THE BOYS. . . . . SH SUNDAY 12

POLAND'S 1
AND POLAND'S PLAIN, AND ENGLAND'S GRASSY LEA, ... ANS LET AMERICA BE 48

POLE 1
AS NORTH POLE IS TO SOUTH . . . . . AYM SHADES OF PIG 27

POLES 1
FOR THEM POLES AND GREEKS . . . . . SP RELIEF 2

POLICE 5
AND THE BRIBE-REACHING POLICE. . . ANS KIDS WHO DIE 26
POLICE! POLICE! . . . . SP BLD LANDLORD 21
POLICE! POLICE! . . . . SP BLD LANDLORD 21
POLICE LADY OR LESBIAN . . . . . . SP CAFE: 3 A.M. 9
FROM POLICE BRUTALITY. . . . . . . PL WHO BUT TH LORD 18

POLISH 1
POLISH, BOHUNK, IRISH. . . . . . . SP MIGRANT 9

POLISHED 3
BRIGHT POLISHED BRASS LIKE THE CYMBALS . . . . FC BRASS SPITOONS 33
A CLEAN BRIGHT SPITOON ALL NEWLY POLISHED, - . . . . FC BRASS SPITOONS 38
BOOTS POLISHED LIKE A MURRAY HEAD. SP SUMMER EVENING 6

POLISHING 1
POLISHING THE SILVER. . . . . SP RUBY BROWN 10

POLITE 5
IF MARGIE POLITE . . . . OWT BLD MARGE POLIT 1
MARGIE POLITE! . . . . OWT BLD MARGE POLIT 46
MARGIE POLITE! . . . . OWT BLD MARGE POLIT 47
ALL DAY SUBDUED, POLITE. . . . . . OWT NEGRO SERVANT 1
TO PROBE IN POLITE WAY . . . . . . PL DINNER GUEST ME 7

POLITICIANS 1
NO WELCOMIN' COMMITTEES, NOR POLITICIANS OF NOTE. . . . . . . SP FREEDOM TRAIN 55

POLL 1
ABOLISH POLL TAX SO FOLKS CAN VOTE. JC JIM CROW'S LAST 24

POLLS 2
TO THE POLLS ELECTION DAY . . . . . JC BLD SAM SOLOMON 9
TO VOTE AT THE POLLS. . . . . JC BLD SAM SOLOMON 23

POLLUTES 1
POLLUTES HIS STINKING AIR . . . . . PL JUNIOR ADDICT 21

POMEGRANATE 1
POMEGRANATE LIPPED . . . . SH HARLEM SWEETIES 15

POOL 4
A POOL OF FIRE. . . . . SP BLUE BAYOU 23
LIGHTS IN THE POOL ROOMS. . . . . . SP RAILROAD AVENUE 4
ROLLING WHITE BALLS IN THE POOL ROOMS. . . . . SP RAILROAD AVENUE 27
POOL HALL OR BAR ON CORNER . . . . AYM HORN OF PLENTY 70

POOLS 3
THE RAIN MAKES STILL POOLS ON THE SIDEWALK. . . . . DK APRIL RAIN SONG 4
THE RAIN MAKES RUNNING POOLS IN THE GUTTER. . . . . DK APRIL RAIN SONG 5
INTO A MILLION POOLS OF QUARTERS . AYM ODE TO DINAH 56

POOR 18
BECAUSE I'M POOR AND BLACK AND FUNNY - . . . . NM BLACK CLWN POEM 2
I AM THE POOR WHITE, FOOLED AND PUSHED APART. . . . . ANS LET AMERICA BE 19
THE LAND THAT'S MINE - THE POOR MAN'S, INDIAN'S, NEGRO'S. . . . ANS LET AMERICA BE 65
BECAUSE, O POOR WHITE WORKERS, . . ANS OPEN LETTER 45
POOR WORLD. . . . . ANS UNION 4
AND LEFT POOR BESSIE BLEEDIN . . . SH DEATH IN HARLEM 121
FORMERLY THE BEATEN AND THE POOR . JC TO CAPTAIN MULZ 19
IN CHARITY'S POOR CHAIR - . . . . . FW OLD SAILOR 16
RICH AND POOR . . . . OWT BOARDING HOUSE 5
A POOR MAN AIN'T GOT . . . . SP BLD OF THE MAN 27
POOR. . . . . SP ENNUI 4
I'M JUST A POOR LOST SHEEP. . . . . SP EVENING SONG 8
POOR LITTLE THINGS. . . . . SP MADAM CHARTY CH 13
FROM THAT POOR BOY'S FRIENDS - . . SP NIGHT FUNERAL 14
THAT POOR BOY'S . . . . SP NIGHT FUNERAL 43
HE MADE THAT POOR PIANO MOAN WITH MELODY. . . . . SP THE WEARY BLUES 10
YOU PROFFER ME POOR PAY. . . . . . PL MILITANT 9
BEING POOR AND BLACK. . . . . PL WHO BUT TH LORD 19

POOREST 1
THE POOREST WORKER BARTERED THROUGH THE YEARS. . . . . ANS LET AMERICA BE 38

POP 1
HEY, POP! . . . . SP DREAM BOOGIE 18

POPPY 1
AND POPPY COLORED FACES . . . . . . PL DAYBREAK IN ALA 11

POPPY-FLOWER 2
A WILD POPPY-FLOWER . . . . FW POPPY FLOWER 1
A WILD POPPY-FLOWER . . . . FW POPPY FLOWER 5

POPULATE 1
TO POPULATE THE . . . . SP WHAT? SO SOON! 5

POP-A-DA 4
OOP POP-A-DA . . . . SP FLATTED FIFTHS 16
POP-A-DA . . . . SP JAM SESSION 3
POP-A-DA . . . . SP JAM SESSION 9
POP-A-DA! . . . . SP TAG 5

PORCH 3
SET ON THE FRONT PORCH AS LONG AS I PLEASE. . . . . SH SUNDAY 8
SUMMER NIGHTS ON THE FRONT PORCH . SP AUNTSUE'S STORI 3
SITTING ON OLD MRS. LATHAM'S BACK PORCH . . . . SP RUBY BROWN 9

PORGY 2
PORGY AND BESS . . . . AYM ASK YOUR MAMA 23
AND WAS PORGY EVER MARRIED . . . . AYM SHADES OF PIG 15

PORTER 1
OR AM I STILL A PORTER ON THE FREEDOM TRAIN? . . . . SP FREEDOM TRAIN 19

PORTLY 1
MAMA, PORTLY OVEN. . . . . SP GRADUATION 6

PORTRAIT 1
A CUBAN PORTRAIT . . . . WB SOLEDAD 1

POSITION 1
SHOULDERS AT FATE, ACCEPTING HIS POSITION - BUT INSIDE HIMSELF UNHAPPY . . . . NM BIG-TIMER MOOD 6

POSSESS 1
TWO THINGS POSSESS THE POWER. . . . OLD TWO THINGS 1

POSSIBLY 1
WHAT COULD POSSIBLY BE ALL-REET? . SP DANCER 22

POST 2
IN THE POST OFFICE FOR A RAINY DAY. SP NUMBERS 3
COMMENT AGAINST LAMP POST . . . . . SP WHAT? SO SOON! 7

POSTER 1
ON EVERY LYNCHING TREE, A POSTER CRYING FREE . . . . ANS OPEN LETTER 44

POT 2
IN A POT OF COLLARD GREENS . . . . PL CULTURAL EXCHNG 19
IN THE POT BEHIND THE PAPER DOORS PL CULTURAL EXCHNG 26

POTS 1
OR GREASY POTS IN A DIRTY KITCHEN. SP ELEVATOR BOY 20

POTTERY 1
AS POTTERY WITH DOVE . . . . PL THE DOVE 4

POTTER'S 1
OR A PRISON GRAVE, OR THE POTTER'S FIELD. . . . . ANS KIDS WHO DIE 41

POUNDS 1
A THOUSAND POUNDS OF SALT . . . . . LHR TESTAMENT 7

POURING 1
STILL AFTER HOURS POURING DRINKS THE LAW FORBIDS - . . . . OWT JUICE JOINT 38

POWDERED 2
WITH PURPLE POWDERED SKIN. . . . . SP RAILROAD AVENUE 16
THE WHORES ALL POWDERED . . . . . . PL LUMUMBA'S GRAVE 3

POWELL 18
OZIE, OZIE POWELL. . . . . ANS BLD OZZIE POWEL 2
OZIE, OZIE POWELL. . . . . ANS BLD OZZIE POWEL 4
OZIE, OZIE POWELL. . . . . ANS BLD OZZIE POWEL 6
OZIE, OZIE POWELL. . . . . ANS BLD OZZIE POWEL 8
BLACK YOUNG OZIE POWELL. . . . . . ANS BLD OZZIE POWEL 10
OZIE, OZIE POWELL. . . . . ANS BLD OZZIE POWEL 12
OZIE, OZIE POWELL. . . . . ANS BLD OZZIE POWEL 14
AIMED AT OZIE POWELL. . . . . ANS BLD OZZIE POWEL 16
OZIE, OZIE POWELL. . . . . ANS BLD OZZIE POWEL 18
STARE AT OZIE POWELL. . . . . ANS BLD OZZIE POWEL 20
DON'T THEY, OZIE POWELL? . . . . . ANS BLD OZZIE POWEL 22
OZIE, OZIE POWELL. . . . . ANS BLD OZZIE POWEL 24
OZIE, OZIE POWELL. . . . . ANS BLD OZZIE POWEL 26
BLACK YOUNG OZIE POWELL. . . . . . ANS BLD OZZIE POWEL 28
OZIE, OZIE POWELL. . . . . ANS BLD OZZIE POWEL 30
OZIE! OZIE POWELL! . . . . ANS BLD OZZIE POWEL 32
WITH ADAM POWELL FOR CHAUFFEUR . . AYM RIDE, RED, RIDE 32
SEND FOR ADAM POWELL ON A NON-SUBPOENA DAY. . . . . PL FINAL CALL 37

POWER 14
TWO THINGS POSSESS THE POWER. . . . OLD TWO THINGS 1
10-VOICES: BLOOM IN THE STRENGTH OF YOUR UNKNOWN POWER. . . . . . . ANS CHANT MAY DAY 9
60-VOICES: TAKE POWER. . . . . . . ANS CHANT MAY DAY 34
LIFE FOREVER THROUGH THE WORKERS' POWER - . . . . ANS CHANT TOM MOONY 44
DON'T WANT THE PEOPLE TO GET WISE TO THEIR OWN POWER. . . . . ANS KIDS WHO DIE 35
OF PROFIT, POWER, GAIN, OF GRAB THE LAND! . . . . ANS LET AMERICA BE 27
THAT THE PLANTS AND THE ROADS AND THE TOOLS OF POWER . . . . ANS OPEN LETTER 17
INSTEAD: MIGRATION INTO FORCE AND POWER - . . . . ANS OPEN LETTER 42
LET POWER GROW! . . . . ANS OPEN LETTER 50
YOURS HAS BEEN THE POWER . . . . . JC THE BITTER RIVR 55
WITHOUT POWER - . . . . JC TO CAPTAIN MULZ 22
POWER. . . . . LHR POET TO BIGOT 9
TO TILL THE SOIL, AND HARNESS THE POWER OF THE WATERS. . . . . . . SP FREEDOM'S PLOW 19
RIGHT OUT OF POWER - . . . . PL CULTURAL EXCHNG 41

PO' 14
PO' WEARY ME . . . . FC A RUINED GAL 3
PO' LONESOME ME . . . . FC A RUINED GAL 8
ON A PO' BLACK GIRL. . . . . FC GAL'S CRY DYING 12
AN' A PO', PO' GAL CAN SLEEP. . . . FC SUICIDE 18
AN' A PO', PO' GAL CAN SLEEP. . . . FC SUICIDE 18
PO' WEARY ME CAN DO. . . . . SP BAD LUCK CARD 10
I'M A PO' GAL . . . . SP DOWN AND OUT 5
PO' AN' BLACK . . . . SP SINNER 2
SHE DONE LEFT PO' BUDDY . . . . . . SP STONY LONESOME 12
PO' BUDDY JONES. . . . . SP STONY LONESOME 14
I'M GOIN' TO THE PO' HOUSE . . . . SP YOUNG GAL'S BLS 7
GOIN' TO THE PO' HOUSE . . . . . . SP YOUNG GAL'S BLS 9
THE PO' HOUSE IS LONELY . . . . . . SP YOUNG GAL'S BLS 13
C. THE PO' HOUSE IS LONELY. . . . . SP YOUNG GAL'S BLS 15

PRACTICE 4
AND FAULTILY PUT THEM INTO PRACTICE. SP FREEDOM'S PLOW 151
PRACTICE ON A STATE STREET CANCER. SP INTERNE AT PROV 7
PRACTICE ON A STOCKYARDS RUPTURE. SP INTERNE AT PROV 8
PRACTICE ON THE SMALL APPENDIX . . SP INTERNE AT PROV 9

PRAIRIE 3
THEN I STOOD OUT ON A PRAIRIE . . . SP CROSSING 15
WASN'T NOBODY ON THAT PRAIRIE . . . SP CROSSING 17
AS HE RIDES OUT ON THE PRAIRIE. . . SP MIGRANT 11

PRAIRIES 1
PRAIRIES. . . . . SP ONE 4

PRAISE 6
AND PRAISE HIM ALIVE. . . . . SP BLD OF THE MAN 20
MAMA SAYS, PRAISE JESUS! . . . . . SP GRADUATION 20
MAMA SAYS, PRAISE JESUS! . . . . . SP GRADUATION 25
PRAISE JESUS! . . . . SP GRADUATION 28
HOW I COULD PRAISE MY LORD! . . . . SP TESTIMONIAL 4
FOR TO PRAISE MY LORD! . . . . . . SP TESTIMONIAL 8

PRANCING 1
WALKING PROUDLY, ALMOST PRANCING, BUT GRADUALLY SUBDUED TO A SLOW, HEAVY . . . . NM BLACK CLWN MOOD 7

PRAY 9
GONNA PRAY TO MA JESUS. . . . . . . FC MOAN 7
WORK, PRAY, AND FIGHT. . . . . . . NM BLACK CLWN POEM 64
HE KNOWED HOW TO PRAY. . . . . . . OK MA LORD 7
WHITE FOLKS, PRAY! . . . . OK NEGRO DANCERS 12
PRAY FOR ME, MAMA! . . . . SH BLD THE SINNER 21
AND HE KNELT THERE TO PRAY. . . . . LHR BLD MARY'S SON 23
I'M GONNA PRAY . . . . SP MADAM MINISTER 25
WHERE HE COULD NOT PRAY . . . . . . PL BIBLE BELT 4
AND NOT ENOUGH TO PRAY. . . . . . . PL BOMBINGS DIXIE 2

PRAYED 2
I PRAYED . . . . AYM GOSPEL CHA-CHA 48
LORD KNOWS I PRAYED . . . . AYM GOSPEL CHA-CHA 49

PRAYER 3
BECAUSE YOU ARE TO ME A PRAYER . . OK PASSING LOVE 3
WHAT WAS THE USE OF PRAYER. . . . . SP SONG DARK GIRL 8
BUT GOD PUT A SONG AND A PRAYER IN MY MOUTH. . . . . SP THE NEGRO MOTHE 18

PRAYERS 3
SUNDAY PRAYERS SYNCOPATE GLORY. . . SP CONSIDER ME 44
AND THE LAST PRAYERS BEEN SAID . . SP NIGHT FUNERAL 30
OH, MY DARK CHILDREN, MAY MY DREAMS AND MY PRAYERS . . . . SP THE NEGRO MOTHE 49

PRAYER-MAKERS 1
BRINGING PILGRIMS AND PRAYER-MAKERS. SP FREEDOM'S PLOW 30

PREACH 1
SEND FOR JESUS TO PREACH THE SERMON ON THE . . . . PL FINAL CALL 10

PREACHED 3
A MINISTER PREACHED - . . . . SP BLD OF THE MAN 17
WHO PREACHED THAT . . . . SP NIGHT FUNERAL 19
PREACHED THAT BOY AWAY - . . . . . SP NIGHT FUNERAL 22

PREACHER 2
A JACK-LEG PREACHER, A PH.D. . . . SP MYSTERY 24
TO THAT GIRL WHO PAID THE PREACHER MAN - . . . . SP NIGHT FUNERAL 41

PREACHERS 1
AND THE MONEY-LOVING PREACHERS . . ANS KIDS WHO DIE 28

PREACHER-MAN 1
OLD PREACHER-MAN . . . . SP NIGHT FUNERAL 21

PREACHING 1
TONIGHT THERE'S PREACHING! . . . . OWT JITNEY 35

PRECEDE 1
WILL PRECEDE IT. . . . . SP PARADE 8

PRECINCT 1
PRECINCT STATION. . . . . SP BLD LANDLORD 28

PREGNANT 1
PREGNANT AGAIN! . . . . SP WHAT? SO SOON! 2

PREJUDICE 1
OF PREJUDICE, AND HATE, AND THE FALSE COLOR LINE - . . . . NM COLORED SL POEM 9

PREMATURE 1
IF BORN PREMATURE . . . . AYM ODE TO DINAH 72

PREMIER 1
PREMIER DOWNING ACING . . . . AYM SHADES OF PIG 3

PREPARING 1
PREPARING TO FEAST ON LIFE. . . . . SP SUNDAY MORNING 8

PRESBYTERIAN 1
ST. JAMES PRESBYTERIAN . . . . . . SP PROJECTION 7

PRESENT 3
I LIKE A PIPE FOR A CHRISTMAS PRESENT. . . . . SP THEME FOR ENG B 23
BEFORE THE PRESENT BECOMES WHEN . . AYM ODE TO DINAH 104
PRESENT ARMS . . . . PL SPECIAL BULLTIN 11

PRESENTS 1
YET NO PRESENTS DOWN THE CHIMNEY. AYM ODE TO DINAH 74

PRESIDENT 3
BE PRESIDENT. . . . . SP CHILDREN'S RYME 9
OUR PRESIDENT . . . . SP MIGRANT 27
BE PRESIDENT. . . . . PL CHILDREN'S RYME 5

PRESIDENTS 1
BUT YOU DON'T SEE NO PRESIDENTS DYIN' O' GRIEF - . . . . NM BROKE 57

PRESIDENT'S 1
THE PRESIDENT'S FOUR FREEDOMS . . . JC HOW ABOUT DIXIE 1

PRESS 3
PRESS HANDS TOGETHER, LAUGHING AT HER SONG. . . . . OWT LINCOLN THEATRE 15
HEADLINES IN PRESS: . . . . SP BLD LANDLORD 30
IN THE PRESS AND ON THE RADIO AND TV - . . . . PL PRIME 6

PRESSURE 2
PRESSURE OF THE BLOOD IS SLIGHTLY HIGHER . . . . AYM JAZZTET MUTED 2
WHERE THE PRESSURE OF THE BLOOD . . AYM JAZZTET MUTED 18

PRETENDED 1
HIM. ASSUMING A FALSE AND BRAGGING SELF-ASSURANCE. AND A PRETENDED NM BIG-TIMER MOOD 8

PRETTY 15
PRETTY BABY. . . . . WB TO MIDNIGHT NAN 10
YOU'S TOO PRETTY. . . . . FC RED SILK STOCK 7
SOMETIMES I'M SETTIN' PRETTY. . . . NM BIG-TIMER POEM 39
AND I SHO HAD A PRETTY GAL, TOO, UP YONDER ON SUGAR HILL. . . . . . NM BROKE 48
IF A PRETTY GAL LIKE YOU WAS WILLIN', I'D BITE. . . . . NM BROKE 72
BUT YOU CAN'T, PRETTY MAMA, ... SH FREE MAN 3
BUT YOU'LL NEVER, PRETTY MAMA, . . SH FREE MAN 7
I WANT A DOZEN PRETTY WOMEN . . . . SP AS BEFITS A MAN 3
TELL YOU PRETTY STORIES . . . . . . SP BLD THE GYPSY 20
KNOW MORE ABOUT THIS PRETTY RUBY BROWN, ... SP RUBY BROWN 17
AND A HUNDRED PRETTY MAMAS . . . . SP SYLVESTER'S BED 7
THAT'S ONE TIME, PRETTY PAPA, . . . SP WIDOW WOMAN 11
TELL ME, PRETTY PAPA, ... AYM ODE TO DINAH 62
PRETTY PAPA, PRETTY PAPA, ... AYM ODE TO DINAH 64
PRETTY PAPA, PRETTY PAPA, ... AYM ODE TO DINAH 64

PREVAIL 1
PREVAIL - . . . . PL OPPRESSION 9

PREVIOUSLY 1
HAVING PREVIOUSLY POINTED OUT THE SINS OF THIS WORLD: . . . . . . SP SUNDAY MORNING 1

PRE-DRAFT 1
TEEN-AGE, PRE-DRAFT, ... PL JUNIOR ADDICT 33

PRE-LIFETIME 1
PRE-LIFETIME JOB. . . . . PL JUNIOR ADDICT 34

PRICE 2
AND ONE OLD FUNNY BOY SAID, "I'LL WORK AT ANY PRICE . . . . NM BROKE 8
STOP HUNTING FOR THE PRICE TAG! . . SH BLD PAWNBROKER 15

PRICES 3
SOME FOLKS BLAME HIGH PRICES ON THE JEWS. . . . . SP LIKEWISE 12
THE PRICES LOWER. . . . . SP MADAM'S PAST HI 9
PRICES ARE DOUBLED . . . . PL LITTLE SNG HOUS 11

PRIDE 5
TILL BEAUTY AND PRIDE FILLS EACH DARK FACE . . . . NM DARK YOUTH USA 20
PRIDE OF THE TOWN. . . . . SH HARLEM SWEETIES 16
THE BEATEN PRIDE. . . . . SP UNCLE TOM 2
BATHMATS OF PRIDE, ... PL UNDERTOW 6
TETHERED BY SOMETHING WORSE THAN PRIDE, ... PL WHERE WHEN WHCH 10

PRIME 1
I, BLACK, COME TO MY PRIME . . . . PL PRIME 9

PRINCE 1
LAST LITTLE BROWN PRINCE . . . . . PL LAST PRINCE 2

PRINCES 1
TO MAKE US ALL INTO PRINCES AND PRINCESSES. . . . . PL FINAL CALL 7

PRINCESSES 1
TO MAKE US ALL INTO PRINCES AND PRINCESSES. . . . . PL FINAL CALL 7

PRINT 1
MY NAME IN PRINT. . . . . SP MADAM'S CALLING 8

PRINTED 1
I HAD SOME CARDS PRINTED . . . . . SP MADAM'S CALLING 1

PRISON 2
AND THE PRISON WALLS WRAP YOU ABOUT, ANS CHANT TOM MOONY 8
OR A PRISON GRAVE, OR THE POTTER'S FIELD, ... ANS KIDS WHO DIE 41

PRISTINE 1
OF THEIR PRISTINE HOUR . . . . PL SWEET WORDS RAC 6

PRIVATE 1
PRIVATE AFFAIR? . . . . SP MADAM PHONE BIL 34

PRIVILEGES 1
I ASKED MY LANDLADY DID I HAVE PRIVILEGES. . . . . OWT STRANGER IN TWN 7

PROBABLY 1
IT WOULD PROBABLY TAKE TWO. . . . . OWT TOO BLUE 13

PROBE 1
TO PROBE IN POLITE WAY . . . . . . PL DINNER GUEST ME 7

PROBLEM 3
THE NEGRO PROBLEM . . . . PL DINNER GUEST ME 2
TO BE A PROBLEM ON . . . . PL DINNER GUEST ME 19
SOLUTIONS TO THE PROBLEM, ... PL DINNER GUEST ME 22

PROBLEMS 2
WE HAVE OUR PROBLEMS. . . . . SP HIGH TO LOW 24
MY PROBLEMS . . . . PL LITTLE SNG HOUS 7

PROCLAIMS 1
IN THE CLOTHES OF A MODERN MAN, HE PROCLAIMS HIMSELF. . . . . NM BLACK CLWN MOOD 15

PRODUCTIVE 1
AS THE DEEP PRODUCTIVE EARTH . . . JC ME AND MY SONG 6

PRODUCTS 1
CAME THE MIGHTY PRODUCTS MOULDED, MANUFACTURED, ... SP FREEDOM'S PLOW 79

PROFFER 1
YOU PROFFER ME POOR PAY, ... PL MILITANT 9

PROFIT 1
OF PROFIT, POWER, GAIN, OF GRAB THE LAND! . . . . ANS LET AMERICA BE 27

PROFITS 1
TO BUILD UP PROFITS FOR THE RAPE OF SPAIN! . . . . ANS SONG OF SPAIN 57

PROJECT 1
ON A TWENTY-STORY HOUSING PROJECT, AYM ODE TO DINAH 79

PROJECTION 1
PROJECTION OF A DAY! . . . . SP INTERNE AT PROV 30

PROLETARIANS 1
WORKER: PROLETARIANS OF ALL THE WORLD: . . . . ANS CHANT MAY DAY 31

PROMISE 1
BELIE THE BUDDING PROMISE . . . . . PL SWEET WORDS RAC 5

PROMISED 1
YOU PROMISED TO'VE DONE. . . . . . SP MADAM RENT MAN 14

PROMISES 2
THE POET SAYS IT WAS PROMISES. . . SP FREEDOM'S PLOW 143
THE PEOPLE SAY IT IS PROMISES - THAT WILL COME TRUE. . . . . SP FREEDOM'S PLOW 144

PROPAGANDA 1
AND THE RADIO, TOO, FOGGY WITH PROPAGANDA . . . . SP IN EXPLANATION 31

PROPHETS 1
LISTEN TO YO' PROPHETS, ... SP SHOUT 1

PROTECT 2
WHY GOD DON'T PROTECT A MAN . . . . PL WHO BUT TH LORD 17
CAN PROTECT ME? . . . . PL WHO BUT TH LORD 22

PROTECTED 1
I RIDE PROTECTED. . . . . PL SLAVE 14

PROTECTING 1
PROTECTING JIM CROW. . . . . JC HOW ABOUT DIXIE 20

PROTECTION 1
NO PROTECTION FOR THAT STREAM. . . SP CROSSING 14

PROTECTS 1
HOW DIXIE PROTECTS . . . . SP SILHOUETTE 9

PROUD 4
BEEN MADE. PROUD AND SMILING. BUT THE LIVING, REMEMBERING WITH A HALF-SOB . . . . NM COLORED SL MOOD 10
MA LORD, HE AIN'T PROUD. . . . . . DK MA LORD 2
FOR THE PROUD - . . . . PL COLOR 3
SO PROUD THAT SAVAGES . . . . PL NORTHERN LIBERL 7

PROUDLY 3
BARREL-HOUSE JAZZ. SHOWING-OFF. STRUTTING ABOUT PROUDLY, BRAGGING AND . . . . NM BIG-TIMER MOOD 4
WALKING PROUDLY, ALMOST PRANCING. BUT GRADUALLY SUBDUED TO A SLOW, HEAVY . . . . NM BLACK CLWN MOOD 7
CALMLY TELLING THE STORY. PROUDLY AND EXPECTANTLY WITH HEAD UP, SHOULDERS . . . . NM COLORED SL MOOD 7

PROVE 2
TO PROVE SHE WAS A WOMAN WOMAN . . AYM BIRD IN ORBIT 48
TO PROVE SHE WAS A WOMAN? . . . . . AYM BIRD IN ORBIT 50

PROVEN 1
HAVE PROVEN A POINT . . . . PL NORTHERN LIBERL 8

PROVIDIN' 1
JUST ONLY PROVIDIN' DE BOSS MAN IS NICE!" . . . . NM BROKE 9

PROW 1
PROW OF STONE STONE. . . . . AYM GOSPEL CHA-CHA 23

PSEUDONYMS 1
HAVE PSEUDONYMS REVEALED . . . . . PL UN-AMERICAN 8

PSHAW 1
BUT THE BOYS IS ALL MARRIED! PSHAW! SH SUNDAY 13

PTA 1
THEY ASKED ME AT THE PTA . . . . . AYM IS IT TRUE? 54

PUBLIC 2
ON THE PUBLIC WALL. . . . . FW HEART 12
BARED HER BOSOMS, BARED IN PUBLIC AYM BIRD IN ORBIT 49

PUERTO 1
PLANES FROM PUERTO RICO, ... SP GOOD MORNING 9

PULL 8
WILL NOT PULL ME DOWN. . . . . . . NM BLACK CLWN POEM 28
PULL AT THE ROPE! OH! . . . . ANS LYNCHING SONG 1
PULL IT HIGH! . . . . ANS LYNCHING SONG 2
PULL IT, BOYS. . . . . ANS LYNCHING SONG 5
CATCH THAT JIM CROW BIRD, PULL THE FEATHERS OUT HIS TAIL! . . . . . JC JIM CROW'S LAST 16
AND PULL HIM HIGHER! . . . . SP BLUE BAYOU 18
AND PULL HIM HIGHER! . . . . SP BLUE BAYOU 21
NIGHT WILL PULL ITS SLACK TAUT . . SP SUMMER EVENING 25

PULLED 3
I PULLED THAT JOB . . . . SH BLD THE KILLER 13
BESSIE PULLED A KNIFE. . . . . . . SH DEATH IN HARLEM 104
I PULLED BACK THE COVERS, ... SP HOMECOMING 5

PULLING 1
PULLING HIMSELF TOGETHER, BOASTING LOUDLY AGAIN, BUT REALIZING WITHIN THE . . . . NM BIG-TIMER MOOD 11

PULLS 1
THREAD STILL PULLS HIS . . . . . . AYM GOSPEL CHA-CHA 22

PULP 1
DON'T LET HIM MAKE A PULP OUT OF ME! PL WHO BUT TH LORD 11

PULVERIZE 1
I'D PULVERIZE YOU. . . . . SH EVIL MORNING 8

PUNCHERS 1
FOOTBALL PLAYERS LEATHER PUNCHERS $ $ $ . . . . AYM HORN OF PLENTY 18

PUNCTUATION 1
BUT JUST A PUNCTUATION. . . . . . . AYM ODE TO DINAH 124

PURCHASE 2
THERE TO PURCHASE A SLAVE, ... PL SLAVE 3
TO PURCHASE A SLAVE . . . . PL SLAVE 12

PURCHASED 1
AND HANDLE EASY LIKE A PURCHASED THING, ... OWT JUICE JOINT 36

PURE 1
PURE JADE. . . . . SH BLD PAWNBROKER 6

PURE-BLOODED 1
A DRAMATIC MONOLOGUE TO BE SPOKEN BY A PURE-BLOODED NEGRO IN THE WHITE NM BLACK CLWN MOOD 1

PURGE 3
WHAT CAN PURGE MY HEART . . . . . . SP SONG BILLIE HOL 1
WHAT CAN PURGE MY HEART . . . . . . SP SONG BILLIE HOL 4
WHAT CAN PURGE MY HEART . . . . . . SP SONG BILLIE HOL 7

PURITY 1
A PURITY . . . . WB POEM 12

PURPLE 3
OUT OF THE PURPLE AND ROSE OF OLD MEMORIES . . . . DK FAIRIES 3
SWEET AS PURPLE DEW. . . . . SP MIDNIGHT DANCER 4
WITH PURPLE POWDERED SKIN. . . . . SP RAILROAD AVENUE 16

PURPOSES 1
FOR SUBVERSIVE PURPOSES? . . . . . PL UN-AMERICAN 16

PURSUIT 1
AND THE PURSUIT OF HAPPINESS. . . . SP FREEDOM'S PLOW 95

PURTIEST 1
AND I'M GONNA PUT THE PURTIEST SONGS IN IT . . . . PL DAYBREAK IN ALA 4

PUSH 3
LAUGH AND PUSH ME DOWN. . . . . . . NM BLACK CLWN POEM 9
AND PUSH AND SHOVE AND GRAB! . . . OWT JITNEY 57
BELIEVE IN THE RIGHT, LET NONE PUSH YOU BACK. . . . . SP THE NEGRO MOTHE 43

PUSHCARTS 1
PUSHCARTS FOLD AND UNFOLD . . . . . PL CULTURAL EXCHNG 21

PUSHED 6
FOREVER PUSHED DOWN. . . . . NM BLACK CLWN POEM 46
I AM THE POOR WHITE, FOOLED AND PUSHED APART, ... ANS LET AMERICA BE 19
IF PUSHED BY HURRIED ENTRANCE. . . AYM ODE TO DINAH 119
PUSHED INTO THE CORNER . . . . . . PL BLACK PANTHER 1
PUSHED INTO THE CORNER OF THE . . . PL BLACK PANTHER 3
PUSHED INTO THE CORNER OF . . . . . PL BLACK PANTHER 5

PUT 45
AN' PUT ME IN JAIL . . . . FC DEATH DO DIRTY 17
PUT MA HEAD UN'NEATH DE KIVER, . . FC GAL'S CRY DYING 5
PUT ON YO' RED SILK STOCKINGS, . . FC RED SILK STOCK 1
PUT ON YO' RED SILK STOCKINGS, GAL, FC RED SILK STOCK 8
PUT NO TOMBSTONE AT MY HEAD, . . . DK DEATH SEAMAN 5
I PUT 'EM ON BUT . . . . DK DRESSED UP 3
MUST PUT THEIR HANDS WITH MINE . . ANS UNION 6
I MIGHT AS WELL PUT IT ON IN THE HAY. . . . . SH BED TIME 10
THAT PUT DE MIZ ON ME. . . . . . . SH BRIEF ENCOUNTER 3
THAT PUT DE MIZ ON ME. . . . . . . SH BRIEF ENCOUNTER 10
PEARL HARBOR PUT JIM CROW ON THE RUN. . . . . JC JIM CROW'S LAST 8
WE'VE PUT A CAPTAIN ON THAT SHIP'S BRIDGE THERE, ... JC TO CAPTAIN MULZ 43
AND PUT MYSELF AWAY? . . . . OWT TOO BLUE 9
SHE PUT 'EM DOWN. . . . . SP BLD OF THE MAN 12
PUT SOME SILVER IN MY HAND . . . . SP BLD THE GYPSY 6
PUT THE BLACK MAN . . . . SP BLUE BAYOU 16
PUT HIM ON A ROPE . . . . SP BLUE BAYOU 20

THEN GOT PUT BACK WHEN WE COME
NORTH. . . . . SP DEFERRED 5
AND FAULTILY PUT THEM INTO PRACTICE. SP FREEDOM'S PLOW 151
AND TREES PUT FORTH . . . . SP IN TIME SILVER 15
THEY PUT MA BODY IN THE GROUND. . . SP JUDGMENT DAY 1
PUT IT ON A RECORD, LET IT WHIRL, SP JUKE BOX LOVE 9
TO PUT IT DOWN. . . . . SP MADAM CENSUS 4
HE SAID, I'M GONNA PUT IT . . . . . SP MADAM CENSUS 13
NURSE, PUT HER ON A DIET, ... SP MADAM WRONG VIS 25
THE DEPRESSION PUT . . . . SP MADAM'S PAST HI 8
I PUT MY NICKEL . . . . SP MIDNIGHT RAFFLE 1
YOU PUT ME IN MACBETH AND CARMEN
JONES . . . . SP NOTE COMM THEAT 9
AND PUT ON PLAYS ABOUT ME! . . . . SP NOTE COMM THEAT 17
AND I PUT IT DOWN IN . . . . SP ONE-WAY TICKET 3
WHICH CROWN TO PUT . . . . SP PRAYER 5
SOMETHING STRONG TO PUT MY HANDS ON. SP SPIRITUALS 3
THEY DONE PUT CORDELIA . . . . . . SP STONY LONESOME 6
WHEN THE LAWD PUT OUT THE LIGHT. . SP SYLVESTER'S BED 26
BUT GOD PUT A SONG AND A PRAYER IN
MY MOUTH. . . . . SP THE NEGRO MOTHE 18
GOD PUT A DREAM LIKE STEEL IN MY
SOUL. . . . . SP THE NEGRO MOTHE 19
AND PUT MA TROUBLES ON THE SHELF." SP THE WEARY BLUES 22
BUT LADS PUT OUT TO SEA . . . . . . SP WATER-FRONT STR 6
WHEN THEY PUT YOU IN THE GROUND AND SP WIDOW WOMAN 7
I SAY PUT YOU IN THE GROUND AND . . SP WIDOW WOMAN 9
PUT THEIR LAURELS ON YOUR BROW . . PL CROWNS GARLANDS 6
AND I'M GONNA PUT THE PURTIEST SONGS
IN IT . . . . PL DAYBREAK IN ALA 4
I'M GONNA PUT SOME TALL TALL TREES
IN IT . . . . PL DAYBREAK IN ALA 7
AND I'M GONNA PUT WHITE HANDS . . . PL DAYBREAK IN ALA 15
ON THE BUS WE'RE PUT IN THE BACK - PL MERRY-GO-ROUND 11

PUTS 2
PUTS FORTH NEW LIFE AGAIN, ... SP IN TIME SILVER 3
PUTS ON A RED GOWN. . . . . PL LAST PRINCE 13

PYRAMIDS 2
I LOOKED UPON THE NILE AND RAISED
THE PYRAMIDS ABOVE IT. . . . . . SP NEGRO SPEAKS OF 7
UNDER MY HAND THE PYRAMIDS AROSE. SP NEGRO 8

QUAKERS 1
TO THE HAVEN OF WHITE QUAKERS . . . AYM ODE TO DINAH 32

QUALIFY 1
TO QUALIFY AND REGISTER . . . . . . JC BLD SAM SOLOMON 19

QUARRELS 1
SHE FIGHTS AN' QUARRELS MOST . . . FC EVIL WOMAN 7

QUART 1
GIT A QUART O' LICKER. . . . . . . FC SATURDAY NIGHT 11

QUARTER 42
BUY YOU TWO FOR A QUARTER . . . . . SH MIDNIGHT CHIPPI 17
AN EAGLE ON A QUARTER, TOO. . . . . SP FACT 2
OTHERS TAKE A QUARTER STRAIGHT. . . SP TOMORROW 6
FROM THE SHADOWS OF THE QUARTER . . AYM ASK YOUR MAMA 1
IN THE QUARTER OF THE NEGROES . . . AYM ASK YOUR MAMA 35
IN THE QUARTER OF THE NEGROES . . . AYM ASK YOUR MAMA 43
A QUARTER OR A SHILLING. PARIS - . AYM ASK YOUR MAMA 49
IN THE QUARTER OF THE NEGROES . . . AYM ASK YOUR MAMA 74
IN THE QUARTER OF THE NEGROES . . . AYM BIRD IN ORBIT 10
IN THE QUARTER OF THE NEGROES . . . AYM BIRD IN ORBIT 63
IN THE QUARTER OF THE NEGROES . . . AYM BLUES IN STEREO 13
IN THE QUARTER OF THE NEGROES . . . AYM GOSPEL CHA-CHA 1
IN THE QUARTER OF THE NEGROES . . . AYM GOSPEL CHA-CHA 13
IN THE QUARTER OF THE NEGROES ¢ ¢ ¢
¢ ¢ . . . . AYM HORN OF PLENTY 26
IN THE QUARTER OF THE NEGROES. . . AYM HORN OF PLENTY 44
FROM THE SHADOWS OF THE QUARTER . . AYM IS IT TRUE? 1
IN THE QUARTER OF THE NEGROES . . . AYM IS IT TRUE? 43
IN THE NEGROES OF THE QUARTER . . . AYM JAZZTET MUTED 1
IN THE QUARTER OF THE NEGROES . . . AYM JAZZTET MUTED 3
IN THE QUARTER OF THE NEGROES . . . AYM JAZZTET MUTED 6
TO THE QUARTER OF THE NEGROES . . . AYM JAZZTET MUTED 17
IN THE QUARTER OF THE NEGROES . . . AYM ODE TO DINAH 1
THIS LAST QUARTER OF CENTENNIAL . . AYM ODE TO DINAH 8
IN THE QUARTER OF THE NEGROES . . . AYM ODE TO DINAH 110
FROM ANOTHER DISTANT QUARTER . . . AYM ODE TO DINAH 17
TO THIS QUARTER OF THE NEGROES . . AYM ODE TO DINAH 18
IN THE SHADOW OF THE QUARTER . . . AYM ODE TO DINAH 120
AS FORGOTTEN PAIN IN THE QUARTER . AYM ODE TO DINAH 40
QUARTER OF THE NEGROES . . . . . . AYM ODE TO DINAH 41
IN THE QUARTER OF THE NEGROES . . . AYM ODE TO DINAH 49
AS EACH QUARTER CLINKS . . . . . . AYM ODE TO DINAH 55
THIS LAST QUARTER OF CENTENNIAL: . AYM ODE TO DINAH 93
IN THE QUARTER OF THE NEGROES: . . AYM RIDE, RED, RIDE 3
IN THE QUARTER OF THE NEGROES . . . AYM RIDE, RED, RIDE 10
IN THE QUARTER OF THE NEGROES . . . AYM RIDE, RED, RIDE 29
IN THE QUARTER OF THE NEGROES . . . AYM SHADES OF PIG 1
IN THE QUARTER OF THE NEGROES . . . AYM SHADES OF PIG 7
IN THE QUARTER OF THE NEGROES . . . AYM SHADES OF PIG 21
IN THE QUARTER OF THE NEGROES . . . AYM SHOW FARE PLESE 5
IN THE QUARTER OF THE NEGROES . . . AYM SHOW FARE PLESE 17
IN THE QUARTER OF THE NEGROES . . . PL CULTURAL EXCHNG 1
IN THE QUARTER OF THE NEGROES . . . PL CULTURAL EXCHNG 14

QUARTERS 4
INTO A MILLION POOLS OF QUARTERS . AYM ODE TO DINAH 56
MAKE A SPANGLE OUT OF QUARTERS
RINGING . . . . AYM ODE TO DINAH 59
WEAVING METAL FROM TWO QUARTERS . . AYM SHOW FARE PLESE 21
THE HEADS ON THESE TWO QUARTERS . . AYM SHOW FARE PLESE 26

QUEEN 2
A QUEEN FROM SOME TIME-DEAD EGYPTIAN
NIGHT . . . . SP WHEN SUE WEARS 7
SEND FOR THE FAIRY QUEEN WITH A WAVE
OF THE . . . . PL FINAL CALL 5

QUEENS 1
EXTRA-LARGE THE KINGS AND QUEENS . AYM JAZZTET MUTED 14

QUEER 1
SHE FELT QUEER PAIN . . . . SP STRANGE HURT 2

QUESTION 2
LONELY LITTLE QUESTION MARK . . . . SP KID IN THE PARK 1
AND ANSWERS WITH A QUESTION . . . . AYM SHADES OF PIG 23

QUESTIONS 5
I SIMPLY RAISE THESE QUESTIONS . . JC BLACK MAN SPEAK 21
SHE ASKED HERSELF TWO QUESTIONS . . SP RUBY BROWN 11
SEEKING AN ANSWER TO HER QUESTIONS. SP RUBY BROWN 20
ANSWER QUESTIONS ANSWER . . . . . . AYM SHADES OF PIG 22
ANSWERING THE USUAL QUESTIONS . . . PL DINNER GUEST ME 4

QUICK 5
TILL THE QUICK DAY IS DONE. . . . . SP DREAM VARIATION 13
QUICK, SUNRISE, COME - . . . . . . PL JUNIOR ADDICT 19
QUICK, SUNRISE, COME! . . . . PL JUNIOR ADDICT 35
QUICK, COME! . . . . PL JUNIOR ADDICT 37
BUT THE LORD HE WAS NOT QUICK. . . PL WHO BUT TH LORD 12

QUICKER 1
QUICKER THAN LIGHT . . . . SP NIGHTMARE BOOGE 6

QUICKLY 5
BUT BLOW QUICKLY . . . . SP A HOUSE IN TAOS 33
BLOW QUICKLY, WIND, ... SP A HOUSE IN TAOS 41
TELL ME, O QUICKLY! DREAM OF
ALIVENESS, ... SP DEMAND 4
BETWEEN US QUICKLY . . . . SP DESIRE 7
AND THEN SO QUICKLY WILT . . . . . PL SWEET WORDS RAC 3

QUIEN 1
(QUIEN SABE? WHO REALLY KNOWS?) . . SP HAVANA DREAMS 8

QUIERO 1
CUYO NOMBRE NO QUIERO ACORDARME. . .
. . . . ANS SONG OF SPAIN 28

QUIET 14
HOW QUIET . . . . WB SICK ROOM 1
HAS GONE THE QUIET WAY . . . . . . WB TO LITTLE LOVER 4
CAUSE DE RIVER'S QUIET . . . . . . FC SUICIDE 17
QUIET FOR TEN THOUSAND CENTURIES,
OLD ABE. . . . . DK LINCOLN MONUMNT 4
QUIET FOR A MILLION, MILLION YEARS. DK LINCOLN MONUMNT 5
QUIET - . . . . DK LINCOLN MONUMNT 6
HOUSE IS SO QUIET! . . . LISTEN AT
THEM MICE. . . . . SH BED TIME 12
I HATE TO DIE THIS WAY WITH THE
QUIET . . . . SH CABARET GIRL 1
BUT THIS HOUSE IS MIGHTY QUIET! . . SH SUNDAY 10
AS THE KIND AND QUIET NIGHT . . . . JC ME AND MY SONG 4
THE DARK-FACED CHILD IS QUIET . . . SP AUNTSUE'S STORI 23
THE QUIET FADING OUT OF LIFE . . . SP MAGNOLIA FLOWER 1
IN THE QUIET DARKNESS. . . . . . . SP TROUBLED WOMAN 2
SEEKING PEACE AND QUIET . . . . . . AYM HORN OF PLENTY 72

QUIETLY 2
BACK, AND EYES SHINING. QUIETLY
RECALLING THE VISION. THE DEAD
MAN SPEAKS . . . . NM COLORED SL MOOD 8
EAT QUIETLY THE BREAD OF SHAME. . . PL MILITANT 2

QUILT 1
AND CROCHET A QUILT FOR OUR DOUBLE
BED. . . . . SH LETTER 17

QUINCE 1
GLOW OF THE QUINCE . . . . SH HARLEM SWEETIES 21

QUIT 5
I QUIT ALEXANDER! . . . . OWT JITNEY 46
ALEXANDER'S QUIT LUCY! . . . . . . OWT JITNEY 51
QUIT SCHOOL TO WORK - . . . . SP DEFERRED 17
GUESS I'LL QUIT NOW. . . . . SP ELEVATOR BOY 23
I'S GWINE TO QUIT MA FROWNIN' . . . SP THE WEARY BLUES 21

QUITE 5
HAS GROWN QUITE TALL. . . . . SP DELINQUENT 2
HAS GROWN QUITE STOUT. . . . . . . SP DELINQUENT 6
HAS GROWN QUITE WISE - . . . . . . SP DELINQUENT 10
ALSO ILLS QUITE COMMON . . . . . . SP INTERNE AT PROV 16
I CAN QUITE AFFORD TO BE: . . . . . PL NORTHERN LIBERL 12

QUIXOTE 1
DON QUIXOTE! ESPANA! . . . . ANS SONG OF SPAIN 26

RABBI 1
FATHER DIVINE, A RABBI BLACK . . . SP MYSTERY 22

RABBIT 1
YOU CAN TAME A RABBIT. . . . . . . SH FREE MAN 5

RACE 16
FOR THE "CIVILIZED" RACE. . . . . . NM BLACK CLWN POEM 50
THE HOPE OF MY RACE . . . . NM DARK YOUTH USA 3
LIFTING MY RACE TO ITS RIGHTFUL PLACE . . . . NM DARK YOUTH USA 19
RACE AGAINST RACE. . . . . ANS OPEN LETTER 29
RACE AGAINST RACE. . . . . ANS OPEN LETTER 29
OF HATE AND GREED AND RACE . . . . JC TO CAPTAIN MULZ 57
A RACE LEADER CRIED. . . . . OWT BLD MARGE POLIT 43
THROUGH SOME VAST MIST OF RACE . . SP AFRO-AMER FRAG 15
THE COLORED RACE WILL RISE! . . . . SP GRADUATION 26
ME, TRYING TO UPHOLD THE RACE . . . SP HIGH TO LOW 21
HE'S FORGOT ABOUT HIS RACE. . . . . SP ME AND THE MULE 4
DISGRACE THE RACE! . . . . SP SEASHORE THROUG 9
IN ORDER THAT THE RACE MIGHT LIVE AND GROW. . . . . SP THE NEGRO MOTHE 4
WHERE RACE, NOT RELIGION. . . . . . PL BIBLE BELT 9
IN THE GREAT WHITE RACE?" . . . . . PL KU KLUX 4
THE GREAT WHITE RACE." . . . . . . PL KU KLUX 20

RACES 3
THERE IS A CREW OF MANY RACES, TOO. JC TO CAPTAIN MULZ 47
UNTIL ALL RACES AND ALL PEOPLES KNOW ITS SHADE. . . . . SP FREEDOM'S PLOW 199
THE SAME THINGS OTHER FOLKS LIKE WHO ARE OTHER RACES. . . . . SP THEME FOR ENG B 26

RACK 1
OUR OF THE RACK AND RUIN OF OUR GANGSTER DEATH. . . . . ANS LET AMERICA BE 80

RACKET 1
I GUESS I CAN STAND THE RACKET . . NM BIG-TIMER POEM 55

RADICALS 1
AND THE RADICALS IN THAT . . . . . AYM BIRD IN ORBIT 80

RADIO 9
I TURN ON THE RADIO. . . . . NM BIG-TIMER POEM 61
IF THIS RADIO WAS GOOD I'D GET KDQ SH BED TIME 1
AIN'T GONNA PAY A CENT ON THAT RADIO SH PAY DAY 7
LISTEN! I DON'T OWN NO RADIO - . . JC GOOD MORN STLIN 49
OWNED A DECENT RADIO YET? . . . . . SP DEFERRED 47
I HEARD ON THE RADIO ABOUT THE . . SP FREEDOM TRAIN 3
AND THE RADIO, TOO, FOGGY WITH PROPAGANDA . . . . SP IN EXPLANATION 31
ON ACCOUNT OF THE DODGERS ON THE RADIO. . . . . SP PASSING 5
IN THE PRESS AND ON THE RADIO AND TV - . . . . PL PRIME 6

RAFFLE 2
IN THE RAFFLE OF THE NIGHT. . . . . SP MIDNIGHT RAFFLE 2
SOMEHOW THAT RAFFLE . . . . SP MIDNIGHT RAFFLE 3

RAG 1
AW, PICK THAT RAG! . . . . SH DEATH IN HARLEM 13

RAGGED 1
LEAVES US HUNGRY, RAGGED . . . . . SP SHARE-CROPPERS 9

RAGGY 1
HE PLAYED THAT SAD RAGGY TUNE LIKE A MUSICAL FOOL. . . . . SP THE WEARY BLUES 13

RAGTIME 1
I MADE RAGTIME. . . . . SP NEGRO 13

RAIDERS 1
IMMORTAL RAIDERS . . . . PL OCTOBER 16 RAID 25

RAILROAD 7
I GOT A RAILROAD TICKET. . . . . . WB BLUES FANTASY 20
GOT A RAILROAD TICKET. . . . . . . WB BLUES FANTASY 23
DE RAILROAD BRIDGE'S . . . . DK HOMESICK BLUES 1
DE RAILROAD BRIDGE'S . . . . DK HOMESICK BLUES 3
ACROSS THE RAILROAD TRACKS - . . . OWT VISITORS 2
ON RAILROAD AVENUE. . . . . SP RAILROAD AVENUE 2
BY THE RIVER AND THE RAILROAD . . . PL CULTURAL EXCHNG 8

RAILROADS 2
RAILROADS, SHIPS AND DAMS. . . . . ANS OPEN LETTER 62
CAME THE FOUNDRIES, CAME THE RAILROADS. . . . . SP FREEDOM'S PLOW 77

RAILWAY 1
RAILWAY MEN. . . . . ANS OPEN LETTER 7

RAIN 30
LIKE THE RAIN. . . . . WB DISILLUSION 4
TO THE SWISH OF RAIN. . . . . WB LENOX AVE MIDNT 10
LET THE RAIN KISS YOU. . . . . . . DK APRIL RAIN SONG 1
LET THE RAIN BEAT UPON YOUR HEAD WITH SILVER LIQUID DROPS. . . . DK APRIL RAIN SONG 2
LET THE RAIN SING YOU A LULLABY. . DK APRIL RAIN SONG 3
THE RAIN MAKES STILL POOLS ON THE SIDEWALK. . . . . DK APRIL RAIN SONG 4
THE RAIN MAKES RUNNING POOLS IN THE GUTTER. . . . . DK APRIL RAIN SONG 5
THE RAIN PLAYS A LITTLE SLEEP-SONG ON OUR ROOF AT NIGHT - . . . . . DK APRIL RAIN SONG 6
AND I LOVE THE RAIN. . . . . DK APRIL RAIN SONG 7
WHOSE HAND AT THE FOUNDRY, WHOSE PLOW IN THE RAIN. . . . . ANS LET AMERICA BE 68
AND LAUGHED IN RAIN. . . . . FW GIRL 4
AND DANCE IN RAIN. . . . . FW GIRL 22
FROM THE WIND AND RAIN. . . . . . . FW WALLS 4
AND WEARY AS A DROWSY SOUTHERN RAIN OWT JUICE JOINT 26
THEN DROWSY AS THE RAIN . . . . . . OWT JUICE JOINT 45
RAIN . . . . SP A HOUSE IN TAOS 1
THUNDER OF THE RAIN GOD: . . . . . SP A HOUSE IN TAOS 2
THUNDER OF THE RAIN GOD: . . . . . SP A HOUSE IN TAOS 5
THUNDER OF THE RAIN GOD: . . . . . SP A HOUSE IN TAOS 8
UNDER THE THUNDER OF THE RAIN GOD? SP A HOUSE IN TAOS 14
IN TIME OF SILVER RAIN . . . . . . SP IN TIME SILVER 1
IN TIME OF SILVER RAIN . . . . . . SP IN TIME SILVER 11
IN TIME OF SILVER RAIN . . . . . . SP IN TIME SILVER 21
"YOU'LL FIND RAIN BETTER . . . . . SP STRANGE HURT 4
THAN SHELTER FROM THE RAIN." . . . SP STRANGE HURT 5
IN THE FROZEN RAIN. . . . . SP TROUBLED WOMAN 8
AND THE SMELL OF RED CLAY AFTER RAIN PL DAYBREAK IN ALA 9
SHOULD MIX LIKE RAIN . . . . PL MISSISSIPPI 5
STILL MIX LIKE RAIN . . . . PL MISSISSIPPI 19
THE RAIN IS LEAD. . . . . PL WITHOUT BENEFIT 11

RAINBOW 2
THEY MAKE RAINBOW WINGS. . . . . . DK FAIRIES 4
TO CATCH A RAINBOW CRY. . . . . . . SP IN TIME SILVER 14

RAINBOW-SWEET 1
RAINBOW-SWEET THRILL. . . . . SH HARLEM SWEETIES 42

RAINDROP 1
TO A RAINDROP . . . . FW DUSTBOWL 4

RAINING 1
MAMA, IT HAS BEEN RAINING CATS AND DOGS UP . . . . SP LETTER 8

RAINY 1
IN THE POST OFFICE FOR A RAINY DAY. SP NUMBERS 3

RAIN'S 1
BULLETS LIKE RAIN'S . . . . ANS SONG OF SPAIN 33

RAISE 6
WILL ALL RAISE THEIR HANDS AGAINST THE KIDS WHO DIE. . . . . ANS KIDS WHO DIE 29
WILL RAISE FOR YOU A LIVING MONUMENT OF LOVE. . . . . ANS KIDS WHO DIE 46
I SIMPLY RAISE THESE QUESTIONS . . JC BLACK MAN SPEAK 21
THE URGE TO RAISE HELL. . . . . . . OWT BLD MARGE POLIT 8
CAN'T RAISE NO CHILD ON THAT. . . . SP MADAM CHARTY CH 19
YOU RAISE MY TAXES, FREEZE MY WAGES. PL BACKLASH BLUES 5

RAISED 2
I LOOKED UPON THE NILE AND RAISED THE PYRAMIDS ABOVE IT. . . . . . SP NEGRO SPEAKS OF 7
THE LAW RAISED UP HIS STICK . . . . PL WHO BUT TH LORD 13

RAISIN 2
LIKE A RAISIN IN THE SUN? . . . . . SP HARLEM 3
LIKE A RAISIN IN THE SUN? . . . . . PL DREAM DEFERRED 3

RAISING 1
A GIRL WITH ALL THAT RAISING. . . . SP BLD OF THE GIRL 1

RAKED 1
SHE RAKED UP A HUNDRED . . . . . . SP BLD OF THE MAN 13

RALPH 2
RALPH BUNCHE INVESTIGATED! . . . . AYM BIRD IN ORBIT 75
I LOVE RALPH BUNCHE - . . . . PL CROWNS GARLANDS 19

RAMONA 1
ADELE RAMONA MICHAEL SERVE BAKOKO TEA . . . . AYM BIRD IN ORBIT 20

RAMPART 1
COULD BE RAMPART: . . . . SP COULD BE 6

RAN 3
AND PIERROT RAN DOWN THE LONG WHITE ROAD . . . WB PIERROT 29
I RAN AWAY. . . . NM BIG-TIMER POEM 5
AND THEY RAN SOMETHING LIKE THIS: SP RUBY BROWN 12

RANDOLPH 1
A. PHILIP RANDOLPH THE HIGH GRAND WORTHY. . . . PL CULTURAL EXCHNG 45

RANG 5
A SHOT RANG OUT. . . . SH DEATH IN HARLEM 103
AND A SHOT RANG OUT. . . . SH DEATH IN HARLEM 108
AS THE SHOTS RANG OUT. . . . SH DEATH IN HARLEM 113
AS THE SHOTS RANG OUT. . . . SH DEATH IN HARLEM 118
WHEN THE SHOTS RANG OUT. . . . SH DEATH IN HARLEM 123

RANGE 1
WITH BITTER RANGE . . . FW SAILING DATE 3

RANKS 1
IN LONG RANKS . . . SP MOONLIGHT NIGHT 2

RAPE 4
THE RAPE AND ROT OF GRAFT, AND STEALTH, AND LIES. . . . ANS LET AMERICA BE 81
TO BUILD UP PROFITS FOR THE RAPE OF SPAIN! . . . ANS SONG OF SPAIN 57
THOUGHT OF RAPE. . . . SH DEATH IN HARLEM 67
BUT RAPE, ROB, STEAL. . . . PL GHOSTS OF 1619 6

RARE 2
WOULD GIVE HER MANY RARE GIFTS . . SP THE SOUTH 21
TO WHERE THE SPRING IS WONDROUS RARE SP WATER-FRONT STR 3

RARING 2
ARE RARING UP AND TALKING BACK . . SP IN EXPLANATION 3
ARE RARING UP AND TALKING BACK . . SP IN EXPLANATION 20

RATHER 7
I'D RATHER DIE WHERE THE BAND'S A-PLAYIN' . . . SH CABARET GIRL 3
RATHER DIE THE WAY I LIVED - . . . SH CABARET GIRL 5
OR WOULD YOU RATHER. . . . SP KID SLEEPY 18
RATHER JUST . . . SP KID SLEEPY 21
RATHER HAVE WINE? . . . SP PORT TOWN 6
RATHER THAN THE SHADE. . . . SP STRANGE HURT 10
BUT I'D RATHER BE DEAD THAN . . . SP YOUNG GAL'S BLS 17

RATS 3
THERE'S RATS IN THE CELLAR, . . . SP MADAM RENT MAN 17
SEND FOR THE PIED PIPER AND LET HIM PIPE THE RATS . . . PL FINAL CALL 1
SEND FOR THE PIED PIPER TO PIPE OUR RATS AWAY. . . . PL FINAL CALL 38

RATTLE 2
TO DROWN THE RATTLE OF MY DYING BREATH. . . . SP FATASY PURPLE 4
AND SHAKE YOUR RATTLE . . . PL LAST PRINCE 9

RATTLES 1
OF DEATH RATTLES. . . . PL SPECIAL BULLTIN 8

RAYON 1
CINNAMON AND RAYON. . . . SP GRADUATION 1

RAYS 1
UNFORGOTTEN JOES AND SUGAR RAYS $ $ $ $ . . . AYM HORN OF PLENTY 19

RAZOR 1
AIN'T CUT HIM WID NO RAZOR, . . . FC BLACK GAL 3

REACH 2
PLEASE REACH OUT YO' HAND. . . . SP FEET O' JESUS 8
REACH UP YOUR HAND, DARK BOY, AND TAKE A STAR. . . . SP STARS 7

REACHES 2
AND A SONG THAT REACHES THE SKY - ANS KIDS WHO DIE 49
AND I REACHES UP TO HUG 'EM - . . . SP SYLVESTER'S BED 25

REACHING 4
50-VOICES: REACHING ALL THE WORLD. ANS CHANT MAY DAY 18
HEART REACHING OUT TO HEART, . . . SP FREEDOM'S PLOW 38
HAND REACHING OUT TO HAND. . . . SP FREEDOM'S PLOW 39
NOW, THROUGH MY CHILDREN, I'M REACHING THE GOAL. . . . SP THE NEGRO MOTHE 20

REACHIN' 1
AND REACHIN' LANDIN'S, . . . SP MOTHER TO SON 10

READ 7
TO BE READ BY A WORKMAN WITH, FOR BACKGROUND, THE RHYTHMIC . . . ANS CHANT MAY DAY 1
I READ IN THE PAPERS ABOUT THE . . SP FREEDOM TRAIN 1
I'LL READ YOUR OTHER PALM. . . . SP MADAM FORT TELL 24
I COULDN'T READ THEN. I COULDN'T WRITE. . . . SP THE NEGRO MOTHE 23
I LIKE TO WORK, READ, LEARN, AND UNDERSTAND LIFE. . . . SP THEME FOR ENG B 22
DO YOU READ MUSIC? AND LOUIS SAYING $ $ . . . AYM HORN OF PLENTY 11
BELIEVING EVERYTHING SHE READ . . . PL MOTHER IN WAR 9

READY 2
SO WHEN I GOT READY TO GO, I SAID, "I'LL BE SEEIN' YOU SOON, MARIE." NM BROKE 52
AND BE UP AND OUT AND READY . . . JC BLD SAM SOLOMON 21

REAL 9
BUT I AINT GOT NOTHIN' REAL . . . NM BIG-TIMER POEM 47
BUT OPPORTUNITY IS REAL, AND LIFE IS FREE, . . . ANS LET AMERICA BE 13
TURN ON THE LIGHT AND LOOK REAL GOOD! . . . SH SUPPER TIME 3
WAS REAL - . . . FW MAN 8
KNOWS THAT AUNT SUE'S STORIES ARE REAL STORIES. . . . SP AUNTSUE'S STORI 18
HE DIED FOR REAL. IT WARN'T NO SHOW. SP FREEDOM TRAIN 44
IS IT FOR REAL - OR JUST A SHOW AGAIN? . . . SP FREEDOM TRAIN 46
YET GHOSTS SO SOLID, GHOSTS SO REAL PL GHOSTS OF 1619 4
(EVEN VOTE FOR REAL IN ALABAM') . . PL GHOSTS OF 1619 8

REALIZE 1
I REALIZE THE BLESSINGS DENIED TO ME. . . . SP THE NEGRO MOTHE 22

REALIZING 1
PULLING HIMSELF TOGETHER, BOASTING LOUDLY AGAIN, BUT REALIZING WITHIN THE . . . NM BIG-TIMER MOOD 11

REALLY 10
STRENGTH HE DOESN'T REALLY FEEL. GAY, LOUD, UNHAPPY JAZZ, BARING HIS . . . NM BIG-TIMER MOOD 9
THAT CAN REALLY MAKE ME FREE! . . . NM BLACK CLWN POEM 62
I REALLY DON'T KNOW . . . JC BLACK MAN SPEAK 10
REALLY WISE: . . . FW WISDOM 4
(QUIEN SABE? WHO REALLY KNOWS?) . . SP HAVANA DREAMS 8
BUT NOT REALLY . . . SP KID IN THE PARK 12
HE SAID, I REALLY . . . SP MADAM WRONG VIS 11
BIRDS THAT REALLY SING . . . AYM HORN OF PLENTY 76
BIRDS THAT REALLY SING. . . . AYM HORN OF PLENTY 87
REALLY WANT TO - . . . PL IMPASSE 6

REAPING 1
PLOWING AND REAPING . . . NM BLACK CLWN POEM 18

REASON 6
THAT'S DE REASON WHY . . . DK REASONS WHY 2
THAT'S DE REASON WHY . . . DK REASONS WHY 6
THERE AIN'T NO REASON . . . SH BLD THE KILLER 21
THAT WE HAVE GOOD REASON . . . LHR POET TO BIGOT 5
THE REASON MARIE RUNS AROUND WITH TRASH . . . SP SISTER 8
THAT'S THE REASON . . . PL MOTTO 3

REAWAKEN 1
TWO THINGS CAN REAWAKEN . . . DLD TWO THINGS 3

RECALL 2
IF I RECALL THE DAY BEFORE, . . . SP BLUES AT DAWN 8
YOU WILL RECALL . . . PL OCTOBER 16 RAID 28

RECALLING 1
BACK, AND EYES SHINING, QUIETLY RECALLING THE VISION, THE DEAD MAN SPEAKS . . . NM COLORED SL MOOD 8

RECALLS 1
SADLY RECALLS THE ROWS OF WHITE CROSSES IN FRANCE. . . . NM COLORED SL MOOD 12

RECESSION 1
WHITE FOLKS' RECESSION . . . AYM ODE TO DINAH 125

RECITATION 3
A DRAMATIC RECITATION TO BE DONE IN THE HALF-DARK BY A YOUNG BROWN FELLOW . . . NM COLORED SL MOOD 1
MAY ACCOMPANY THE RECITATION - ECHOING SOFTLY, OVER THERE, THERE'S A ROSE . . . NM COLORED SL MOOD 4
A RECITATION TO BE DELIVERED BY A NEGRO BOY, BRIGHT, CLEAN, AND NEATLY . . . NM DARK YOUTH USA 1

RECKON 8
TOGETHER, RECKON I'LL TRY . . . SHO, I WANTS DE JOB! YES, SIR! . . . NM BROKE 30
BUT I RECKON YOU CAN HEAR ME. . . . JC GOOD MORN STLIN 51

I RECKON THE WIND . . . . OWT RESTRICTIVE 16
RECKON THERE'S NO CHARGE . . . . . SP BLD OF THE MAN 23
BUT I RECKON I COULD TREAT YOU . . SP EARLY EVENING 19
HE SAID, I RECKON . . . . SP MADAM WRONG VIS 5
WHICH IS WHY I RECKON I DOES . . . SP NECESSITY 11
I RECKON IT'LL BE . . . . SP NOTE COMM THEAT 18

RECOGNIZE 1
SHE SAID, YOU MUST RECOGNIZE . . . SP MADAM FORT TELL 11

RECOMMEND 1
COULD I RECOMMEND A MAID. . . . . . AYM HORN OF PLENTY 97

RECORD 1
PUT IT ON A RECORD, LET IT WHIRL. SP JUKE BOX LOVE 9

RECORDS 1
OR RECORDS - BESSIE, BOP, OR BACH. SP THEME FOR ENG B 24

RECOURSE 1
HAS NO RECOURSE NOW BUT TO THE LAW? AYM ASK YOUR MAMA 11

RECROSS 1
IN THE DARK SHADOWS THAT CROSS AND
RECROSS . . . . SP AUNTSUE'S STORI 15

RED 45
STAINING THE DARK SEA RED. . . . . WB CARIBBEAN SUNST 3
I WAS A RED MAN ONE TIME. . . . . . WB LAMENT DARK PEO 1
HER LIPS BLOOD RED . . . . FC CLOSING TIME 4
PUT ON YO' RED SILK STOCKINGS. . . FC RED SILK STOCK 1
PUT ON YO' RED SILK STOCKINGS, GAL. FC RED SILK STOCK 8
TILL DE RED DAWN COME. . . . . . . FC SATURDAY NIGHT 28
LENIN WITH THE FLAG BLOOD RED. . . SL SCOTTSBORO 21
DARK MOUTHS WHERE RED TONGUES BURN ANS A NEW SONG 36
RED IS THE ALABAMA ROAD. . . . . . ANS BLD OZZIE POWEL 1
AND RED IS THAT ALABAMA ROAD. . . . ANS BLD OZZIE POWEL 29
I AM THE RED MAN DRIVEN FROM THE
LAND. . . . . ANS LET AMERICA BE 21
THE BELLOWING BULL, THE RED CAPE. ANS SONG OF SPAIN 13
AND THE DEEP RED ROSES BLOOM. . . . SH YOUNG NEGRO GRL 5
THAT AS LONG AS YOUR RED STAR . . . JC GOOD MORN STLIN 13
AND ITS GALL COATS THE RED OF MY
TONGUE. . . . . JC THE BITTER RIVR 11
WARM RED WINE. . . . . FW CAROLINA CABIN 8
IT HAS A RED STAR ON IT. . . . . . FW WHEN ARMIES PAS 3
BUT IT HAS A RED STAR ON IT! . . . FW WHEN ARMIES PAS 9
I THOUGHT I SAW RED STARS, MOTHER. FW WHEN ARMIES PAS 12
IT IS A RED STAR, MOTHER! . . . . . FW WHEN ARMIES PAS 22
LET THOSE WOMEN WITH THEIR LIPS TOO
RED . . . . OWT JUICE JOINT 21
THROUGH THE RED, WHITE, YELLOW SKINS SP A HOUSE IN TAOS 34
TURNS RED AS FIRE. . . . . SP BLUE BAYOU 15
LOVE IS LIKE RED, RED WINE. . . . . SP LAMENT OVER LOV 14
LOVE IS LIKE RED, RED WINE. . . . . SP LAMENT OVER LOV 14
LIKE SWEET RED WINE. . . . . SP LAMENT OVER LOV 16
ON RED HEART BECOME AN ANVIL . . . SP MIGRANT 20
TO MOURN IN RED - . . . . SP WAKE 2
WHEN SUSANNA JONES WEARS RED . . . SP WHEN SUE WEARS 1
WHEN SUSANNA JONES WEARS RED . . . SP WHEN SUE WEARS 6
AND THE BEAUTY OF SUSANNA JONES IN
RED . . . . SP WHEN SUE WEARS 10
MUST BE RED! . . . . AYM BIRD IN ORBIT 72
KENYATTA RED! CASTRO RED! . . . . . AYM BIRD IN ORBIT 73
KENYATTA RED! CASTRO RED! . . . . . AYM BIRD IN ORBIT 73
NKRUMAH RED! . . . . AYM BIRD IN ORBIT 74
BEFORE CHINA WAS EVER RED AT ALL . PL BIRMINGHAM SUND 12
AND THE SMELL OF RED CLAY AFTER RAIN PL DAYBREAK IN ALA 9
AND LONG RED NECKS . . . . PL DAYBREAK IN ALA 10
AND RED CLAY EARTH HANDS IN IT . . PL DAYBREAK IN ALA 17
PUTS ON A RED GOWN. . . . . PL LAST PRINCE 13
HIS BLOOD WAS RED - . . . . PL LUMUMBA'S GRAVE 10
THAT'S WHY MY HEART IS RED. . . . . PL VARI-COLORED 8
I WONDER WHY RED CLAY'S SO RED . . PL VARI-COLORED 9
I WONDER WHY RED CLAY'S SO RED . . PL VARI-COLORED 9
AND WHY THE CLAY'S SO RED. . . . . PL VARI-COLORED 14

REDDEN 1
WOULD REDDEN WITH THEIR BLOOD . . . PL BIRMINGHAM SUND 13

REDDENED 1
AND CRIES, ALL CARELESS-LIKE FROM
REDDENED LIPS! . . . . OWT LINCOLN THEATRE 10

REDDER 2
REDDER NOW WHERE YOUR BLOOD HAS
FLOWED. . . . . ANS BLD OZZIE POWEL 3
BUT REDDER NOW WHERE YOUR LIFE'S
BLOOD FLOWED. . . . . ANS BLD OZZIE POWEL 31

REDDISH-PURPLE 1
A REDDISH-PURPLE IN THE SUN. . . . SP KID SLEEPY 7

REDEEM 2
WE, THE PEOPLE, MUST REDEEM . . . . ANS LET AMERICA BE 82
REDEEM MINE. . . . . LHR BLD MARY'S SON 35

REDUCED 1
WISDOM REDUCED TO THE PERSONAL
EQUATION: . . . . PL ELDERLY LEADERS 2

RED-HOT 1
RED-HOT - THAT'S ME. . . . . NM BIG-TIMER POEM 15

REEFER-MAN 1
AND NIGHT LIKE A REEFER-MAN . . . . SH DEATH IN HARLEM 135

REFLECT 1
YOU REFLECT NO STARS BY NIGHT. . . JC THE BITTER RIVR 24

REFLECTS 2
THE BITTER RIVER REFLECTS NO STARS - JC THE BITTER RIVR 26
THE BITTER RIVER REFLECTS NO STARS. JC THE BITTER RIVR 38

REGAL 1
I'M GOING TO THE REGAL. . . . . . . OWT JITNEY 24

REGISTER 1
TO QUALIFY AND REGISTER . . . . . . JC BLD SAM SOLOMON 19

REGRETS 2
NO REGRETS - . . . . SP NO REGRETS 2
NO REGRETS - . . . . SP NO REGRETS 6

REIGN 2
LAUGH AT MY SORROW'S REIGN. . . . . WB THE JESTER 14
THINKING WE WERE FIGHTING FOR
DEMOCRACY'S TRUE REIGN . . . . . NM COLORED SL POEM 7

RELATED 1
WE'RE RELATED - YOU AND I. . . . . SP BROTHERS 1

RELATION 1
IN RELATION TO THE CHILD. . . . . . AYM ODE TO DINAH 83

RELEASE 1
THAN BRING TODAY'S RELEASE . . . . PL JUNIOR ADDICT 25

RELIEF 9
SOUGHT CALM RELIEF. . . . . WB YOUNG BRIDE 5
'COURSE, YOU HEARS PLENTY 'BOUT
THIS-HERE UNEMPLOYMENT RELIEF - NM BROKE 56
RELIEF WAS FOUND. . . . . ANS A NEW SONG 23
SURELY NOT ME? THE MILLIONS ON
RELIEF TODAY? . . . . ANS LET AMERICA BE 53
O, SWEET RELIEF FROM FACES THAT ARE
WHITE! . . . . OWT NEGRO SERVANT 19
THE RELIEF GAVE FORTY-FOUR. . . . . SP BLD OF THE MAN 2
ON RELIEF WAY ACROSS THE SEA . . . SP RELIEF 3
BECAUSE I WAS ON RELIEF . . . . . . SP RELIEF 4
I KNOW WHAT RELIEF CAN BE - . . . . SP RELIEF 6

RELIGION 1
WHERE RACE, NOT RELIGION. . . . . . PL BIBLE BELT 9

REMAINDERS 1
BRINGS REMAINDERS FROM THE KITCHEN SP GRADUATION 7

REMAKE 1
TO REMAKE IT. . . . . PL QUESTION ANSWER 16

REMEMBER 15
TOO BITTER TO REMEMBER - . . . . . FW CHIPPY 5
IS TO REMEMBER FRAGRANCE WHERE . . FW REMEMBRANCE 3
I DON'T DARE REMEMBER IN THE MORNING SP BLUES AT DAWN 6
DON'T DARE REMEMBER IN THE MORNING. SP BLUES AT DAWN 7
SO I DON'T DARE REMEMBER IN THE
MORNING. . . . . SP BLUES AT DAWN 10
TRYING TO FORGET TO REMEMBER . . . SP DRUNKARD 4
BLACK PEOPLE DON'T REMEMBER . . . . SP SHAME ON YOU 8
REMEMBER MY SWEAT, MY PAIN, MY
DESPAIR. . . . . SP THE NEGRO MOTHE 36
REMEMBER MY YEARS, HEAVY WITH SORROW
- . . . . SP THE NEGRO MOTHE 37
REMEMBER THE WHIP AND THE SLAVER'S
TRACK. . . . . SP THE NEGRO MOTHE 44
REMEMBER HOW THE STRONG IN STRUGGLE
AND STRIFE . . . . SP THE NEGRO MOTHE 45
SURE, WE REMEMBER. . . . . PL HARLEM 7
WE REMEMBER THE JOB WE NEVER HAD. PL HARLEM 12
WE REMEMBER. . . . . PL HARLEM 23
YOU WILL REMEMBER . . . . PL OCTOBER 16 RAID 2

REMEMBERED 1
BUT REMEMBERED FOREVER WILL BE THE
NAME: . . . . ANS CHANT TOM MOONY 30

REMEMBERING 2
BEEN MADE, PROUD AND SMILING, BUT
THE LIVING, REMEMBERING WITH A
HALF-SOB . . . . NM COLORED SL MOOD 10
REMEMBERING THE OLD LIES. . . . . . PL HARLEM 3

REMEMBERS 1
NO ONE REMEMBERS . . . . OK PARISIAN BEGGAR 7

REMOVED 1
FAR REMOVED FROM BASIC OVEN. . . . SP GRADUATION 17

RENAISSANCE 2
THE ROOSEVELT, RENAISSANCE, GEM, ALHAMBRA: . . . . SP MOVIES 1
WITH THE RENAISSANCE. . . . . SP PROJECTION 4

RENDERED 1
A MORAL POEM TO BE RENDERED BY A MAN IN A STRAW HAT WITH A BRIGHT BAND, A . . . . NM BIG-TIMER MOOD 1

RENT 12
HOUSE RENT TO PAY. . . . . FC BRASS SPITOONS 22
AND HOUSE RENT TO PAY. . . . . . FC BRASS SPITOONS 30
AND TOLD ME I'D BETTER PAY HER FOR MY ROOM RENT AND BOARD! . . . . NM BROKE 22
I'M GONNA RENT ME A CUBBY-HOLE WITH A SINGLE BED. . . . . SH PAY DAY 17
AND RENT TIME'S NEARLY HERE. . . . SP DOWN AND OUT 8
TIME I PAY RENT AND GET MY FOOD . . SP LETTER 2
I WISH THE RENT . . . . SP LITTLE LYRIC 1
THE RENT MAN KNOCKED. . . . . SP MADAM RENT MAN 1
YOUR RENT IS DUE. . . . . SP MADAM RENT MAN 6
WITH MY RENT.) . . . . SP NUMBERS 8
WITHOUT YOUR RENT. . . . . SP ULTIMATUM 7
OR RENT THAT I MUST PAY. . . . . . PL CROWNS GARLANDS 16

RENTS 1
(DIXIE RENTS ROOMS AT A BUCK A BREAK.) . . . . SH DEATH IN HARLEM 34

REPAIRING 1
MECHANICS NEED REPAIRING . . . . . AYM ODE TO DINAH 10

REPEAT 1
LET ME REPEAT: . . . . SH HARLEM SWEETIES 30

REPEATEDLY 1
I'VE WRITTEN, CALLED REPEATEDLY. . AYM ASK YOUR MAMA 7

REPEATS 1
COMES OUT - BUT REPEATS! . . . . . SP MADAM NUMBER WR 28

REPORT 2
WANTING A REPORT. . . . . SP MADAM CHARTY CH 24
REPORT, MY EYE! . . . . SP MADAM CHARTY CH 26

REPOSE 1
AND SO LOSE ITS REPOSE. . . . . . . AYM BLUES IN STEREO 20

REPUTATION 2
IF YOUR REPUTATION . . . . SH SNOB 1
BECAUSE A GOOD REPUTATION . . . . . SH SNOB 5

REQUIRES 1
BUT IT REQUIRES . . . . SP UP-BEAT 11

RESPECT 1
NO SAFETY, NO LOVE, NO RESPECT WAS I DUE. . . . . SP THE NEGRO MOTHE 16

RESPECTABLY 1
RESPECTABLY AS EVER. . . . . SP LETTER 11

REST 10
WITHOUT REST IN THE DARKNESS. . . . WB SUMMER NIGHT 11
I TOSS WITHOUT REST . . . . WB SUMMER NIGHT 20
AND REST FROM PAIN OF LOVE . . . . WB YOUNG BRIDE 6
AND BE A WHITE MAN THE REST OF MY DAYS! . . . . SH DAYBREAK 11
BUT THEY ALL BRING REST. . . . . . FW EXITS 4
THEY ALL BRING REST . . . . FW EXITS 8
REST FOREVER . . . . FW FOR DEAD MIMES 8
GOD REST HIS SOUL - . . . . SP BLD OF THE MAN 22
THEN REST AT COOL EVENING . . . . . SP DREAM VARIATION 5
REST AT PALE EVENING . . . . SP DREAM VARIATION 14

RESTAURANTS 1
WE COULDN'T EAT IN RESTAURANTS; HAD JIM CROW CARS; . . . . NM COLORED SL POEM 24

RESTING 3
LONG RESTING PLACE. . . . . FW GRAVE YARD 2
RESTING NEAR THE ALTER WHERE . . . OWT FUNERAL 3
YOU'VE BEEN RESTING AWHILE. . . . . SP AFRICA 2

RESTRICTED 1
CAUSE THE VOTE IS NOT RESTRICTED . JC BLD SAM SOLOMON 11

RESTRICTING 1
RESTRICTING ME - . . . . OWT RESTRICTIVE 11

RESTRICTIVE 1
THEY DRAW UP RESTRICTIVE COVENANTS SP MIGRANT 25

RETURN 2
THOUGH THE RETURN . . . . SP NO REGRETS 7
IN RETURN. . . . . PL MOTTO 9

RETURNING 1
MUSIC TAKES ON A BLUES STRAIN, GRADUALLY RETURNING TO A SORT OF NM BIG-TIMER MOOD 3

RETURNS 1
NO SOUL RETURNS. . . . . FW EXITS 11

REV 1
AFTER REV. BUTLER . . . . SP MADAM MINISTER 30

REVEALED 1
HAVE PSEUDONYMS REVEALED . . . . . PL UN-AMERICAN 8

REVEALS 1
YOUR EVERY STEP REVEALS . . . . . . SP AFRICA 13

REVEREND 3
REVEREND BUTLER CAME BY . . . . . . SP MADAM MINISTER 1
I SAID, REVEREND, ... SP MADAM MINISTER 9
THE REVEREND MARTIN LUTHER . . . . AYM BIRD IN ORBIT 24

REVERSE 1
OR IN REVERSE . . . . SP SUMMER EVENING 7

REVERSED 1
I DON'T PAY NO REVERSED . . . . . . SP MADAM PHONE BIL 8

REVOLT 2
REVOLT! ARISE! . . . . ANS A NEW SONG 47
WHILE REVOLT IN THE RICE FIELDS . . PL LAST PRINCE 12

REVOLUTION 1
FOR THE SAKE OF THE REVOLUTION . . ANS BLDS OF LENIN 23

RE-BOP 3
RE-BOP! . . . . SP DREAM BOOGIE 19
RE-BOP RE-BOP MOP AND STOP. . . . . SP FLATTED FIFTHS 2
SMEARS RE-BOP . . . . SP SHALIMAR 4

RE-RISING 1
WAVES OF RISING AND RE-RISING MASS VOICES, MULTIPLYING LIKE . . . . ANS CHANT MAY DAY 2

RHYMES 2
CHEAP LITTLE RHYMES . . . . SP SLIVER 1
TO CHEAP LITTLE RHYMES . . . . . . SP SLIVER 6

RHYTHM 4
THE RHYTHM OF LIFE . . . . WB LENOX AVE MIDNT 1
IS A JAZZ RHYTHM. . . . . WB LENOX AVE MIDNT 2
SUNDAY MORNING WHERE THE RHYTHM FLOWS. . . . . SP MYSTERY 11
THE RHYTHM . . . . SP TRUMPET PLAYER 21

RHYTHMIC 1
TO BE READ BY A WORKMAN WITH, FOR BACKGROUND, THE RHYTHMIC . . . . ANS CHANT MAY DAY 1

RICE 2
SPEAK OF RICE DOWN IN THE MARSHALND AYM BIRD IN ORBIT 43
WHILE REVOLT IN THE RICE FIELDS . . PL LAST PRINCE 12

RICH 17
NINE OLD MEN SO RICH AND WISE, . . ANS BLD OZZIE POWEL 17
THE OLD AND RICH WILL LIVE ON AWHILE. . . . . ANS KIDS WHO DIE 4
AND THE OLD AND RICH DON'T WANT THE PEOPLE . . . . ANS KIDS WHO DIE 33
THAT KEEP THE RICH ENTHRONED . . . ANS OPEN LETTER 26
I MADE RICH THE GRANDEES AND LORDS ANS SONG OF SPAIN 75
IF I WAS A RICH BOY . . . . SH DECLARATION 8
RICH CREAM COLORED . . . . SH HARLEM SWEETIES 17
RICH . . . . JC ME AND MY SONG 16
AS THE RICH EARTH . . . . JC ME AND MY SONG 26
RICH AND POOR . . . . OWT BOARDING HOUSE 5
WHILE GIRLS WHO WASH RICH WHITE FOLKS CLOTHES BY DAY . . . . . . OWT LINCOLN THEATRE 13
RICH AND STRANGE . . . . SP FLATTED FIFTHS 8
ON THE RICH SOIL OF THE WORLD. . . SP FREEDOM'S PLOW 13
TURNING THE RICH SOIL WENT THE FLOW IN MANY HANDS . . . . SP FREEDOM'S PLOW 52
RICH OLD WHITE MAN . . . . SP PORTER 9
FOR THE RICH TO SWEEP OVER . . . . PL FLORIDA WORKERS 10
RICH FOLKS RIDE - . . . . PL FLORIDA WORKERS 15

RICHARD 1
AND WHY DID RICHARD WRIGHT . . . . AYM HORN OF PLENTY 52

RICHES 1
EARNING RICHES FOR THE WHOLE WORLD SP IN EXPLANATION 53

RICHMOND 1
AT HARLAN, RICHMOND, GASTONIA, ATLANTA, NEW-ORLEANS; . . . . . ANS OPEN LETTER 16

RICHNESS 1
IN THE DAYS OF YOUR RICHNESS . . . SP SUNDAY MORNING 29

RICKETY 1
SWAYING TO AND FRO ON HIS RICKETY STOOL . . . . SP THE WEARY BLUES 12

RICKEYS 1
GIN RICKEYS FOR TWO. . . . . SH DEATH IN HARLEM 42

RICO 1
PLANES FROM PUERTO RICO. . . . . . SP GOOD MORNING 9

RIDE 18
PACK MY TRUNK AND RIDE. . . . . . . WB BLUES FANTASY 21
PACK MY TRUNK AND RIDE. . . . . . . WB BLUES FANTASY 24
RIDE LIKE A FOOL. . . . . SH IF-ING 4
DOWN SOUTH YOU MAKE ME RIDE . . . . JC BLACK MAN SPEAK 13
GONNA RIDE IN MY CHARIOT SOME DAY! SP SPIRITUALS 8
OH, THAT LAST LONG RIDE IS A . . . SP WIDOW WOMAN 1
RIDE EVERYBODY MUST TAKE. . . . . . SP WIDOW WOMAN 2
RIDE EVERYBODY MUST TAKE. . . . . . SP WIDOW WOMAN 4
BUT WHY RIDE ON MULE OR DONKEY . . AYM ASK YOUR MAMA 59
ON WHICH TO RIDE IF MOTORCARS . . . AYM BLUES IN STEREO 5
RICH FOLKS RIDE - . . . . PL FLORIDA WORKERS 15
AND I GET TO SEE 'EM RIDE. . . . . PL FLORIDA WORKERS 16
RIDE SO FINE BEFORE. . . . . PL FLORIDA WORKERS 18
AND RIDE THE JIM CROW CAR UNTIL IT SCREAMS . . . . PL JIM CROW CAR 3
MISTER, CAUSE I WANT TO RIDE? . . . PL MERRY-GO-ROUND 5
TO RIDE PIGGY-BACK . . . . PL SLAVE 1
I RIDE PROTECTED. . . . . PL SLAVE 14
RIDE ON BITLESS HORSES . . . . . . PL WHERE WHEN WHCH 9

RIDES 2
RIDES THE STATE STREET STREET CAR, SP MIGRANT 7
AS HE RIDES OUT ON THE PRAIRIE. . . SP MIGRANT 11

RIDE'S 1
YES, THAT LAST LONG RIDE'S A . . . SP WIDOW WOMAN 3

RIDING 3
RIDING THE HILLS TONIGHT. . . . . . FW NEW MOON 2
RIDING UP AND DOWN. . . . . OWT BLD MARGE POLIT 34
RIDING IN A JAGUAR, SANTA CLAUS, . AYM RIDE, RED, RIDE 30

RIFF 1
UPON WHAT RIFF THE MUSIC SLIPS . . SP TRUMPET PLAYER 38

RIFFS 1
RIFFS, SMEARS, BREAKS. . . . . . . SP EASY BOOGIE 9

RIGHT 45
SHE DON'T DO ME RIGHT. . . . . . . FC EVIL WOMAN 6
CAUSE SHE AIN'T DE RIGHT KIND. . . FC WORKIN' MAN 12
DIDN'T TURN OUT RIGHT. . . . . . . NM BIG-TIMER POEM 10
CAUSE I'M ALL RIGHT. . . . . NM BIG-TIMER POEM 50
TO MANHOOD'S TRUE RIGHT. . . . . . NM BLACK CLWN POEM 66
BUT RIGHT LONG THROUGH HERE NOW, I CAN'T 'FORD TO BUY YOU NO HAT." NM BROKE 51
LET'S GET MARRIED RIGHT NOW! YES! WHAT DO YOU SAY? . . . . NM BROKE 75
NOT RIGHT. . . . . NM COLORED SL POEM 41
FOR HERE IN THE SOUTH THERE'S NO VOTES AND NO RIGHT. . . . . . . NM COLORED SL POEM 46
THAT RIGHT MIGHT ABIDE . . . . . . NM DARK YOUTH USA 14
I'LL LAY DOWN AN' DIE RIGHT NOW. . DK WIDE RIVER 18
STAY ON THE RIGHT TRACK. . . . . . SH BLD THE SINNER 14
RIGHT STRAIGHT TO HELL. . . . . . . SH BLD THE SINNER 20
TILL YOU DON'T KNOW RIGHT FROM WRONG. . . . . SH HEY-HEY BLUES 12
I'LL KEEP RIGHT UP WITH YOU. . . . SH HEY-HEY BLUES 18
WHY NOT END RIGHT NOW . . . . JC BLACK MAN SPEAK 27
NOW - RIGHT HERE! . . . . JC HOW ABOUT DIXIE 24
ALTHOUGH RIGHT NOW, EVEN YET TODAY. JC JIM CROW'S LAST 11
YOUR HEART IS RIGHT. . . . . OWT HONEY BABE 4
WHITE IS RIGHT. . . . . SP ARGUMENT 1
RIGHT OUT OF HER OWN LIFE. . . . . SP AUNTSUE'S STORI 22
ONE BATTED A HARD BALL RIGHT THROUGH MY WINDOW . . . . SP CHILDREN'S RYME 18
MY FRIENDS WAS RIGHT THERE WITH ME SP CROSSING 21
I HAVE AS MUCH RIGHT . . . . SP DEMOCRACY 5
EVERYBODY'S GOT A RIGHT TO BOARD THE FREEDOM TRAIN? . . . . SP FREEDOM TRAIN 22
THE WHITE FOLKS GO LEFT, THE COLORED GO RIGHT - . . . . SP FREEDOM TRAIN 26
WHO DOUBTED THAT THE WAR WOULD END RIGHT, ... SP FREEDOM'S PLOW 133
MADE ME TURN RIGHT PALE. . . . . . SP LITTLE OLD LETT 4
MAYBE IT AIN'T RIGHT - . . . . . . SP LIVE LET LIVE 1
HIS EYES DIDN'T LOOK JUST RIGHT. . SP LOVER'S RETURN 4
LIES RIGHT IN YOURSELF. . . . . . . SP MADAM FORT TELL 18
RIGHT THEN AND THERE . . . . SP MADAM MIGHT-HAV 19
DIDN'T TURN OUT RIGHT. . . . . . . SP MIDNIGHT RAFFLE 4
RIGHT HERE BENEATH GOD'S SKY. . . . SP NEW YORKERS 3
CAN'T BE RIGHT. . . . . SP PARADE 19
BE A ROUNDER RIGHT - . . . . SP STREET SONG 2
FO' TO LOVE YO' DADDY RIGHT!" . . . SP SYLVESTER'S BED 24
BELIEVE IN THE RIGHT, LET NONE PUSH YOU BACK. . . . . SP THE NEGRO MOTHE 43
ASKED ME RIGHT AT CHRISTMAS . . . . AYM BIRD IN ORBIT 69
GETS SHOT RIGHT INTO GLORY. . . . . AYM IS IT TRUE? 53
THEY ASKED ME RIGHT AT CHRISTMAS, AYM ODE TO DINAH 127
YOU KNOW, RIGHT AT CHRISTMAS . . . PL CULTURAL EXCHNG 32
RIGHT OUT OF POWER - . . . . PL CULTURAL EXCHNG 41
I HAVE AS MUCH RIGHT . . . . PL FREEDOM 5
FOR THE FACT THAT WHITE WAS RIGHT PL GHOSTS OF 1619 10

RIGHTFUL 2
LIFTING MY RACE TO ITS RIGHTFUL PLACE . . . . NM DARK YOUTH USA 19
TO TAKE THEIR RIGHTFUL PART . . . . JC BLD SAM SOLOMON 47

RIGHTS 3
AND GIVE US THE RIGHTS THAT ARE YOURS AND MINE. . . . . NM COLORED SL POEM 10
SEEKING THE KNOWLEDGE THAT RIGHTS ALL WRONG - . . . . NM DARK YOUTH USA 17
WITH CERTAIN UNALIENABLE RIGHTS . . . . SP FREEDOM'S PLOW 93

RIM 1
BEYOND THE RIM OF DAY. . . . . . . WB TO LITTLE LOVER 7

RINCON 1
AQUEL RINCON DE LA MANCHA DE . . . ANS SONG OF SPAIN 27

RING 8
AN' DIAMOND RING. . . . . FC SATURDAY NIGHT 10
DIAMOND RING, CIGARETTE HOLDER, AND A CANE, TO THE MUSIC OF PIANO OR NM BIG-TIMER MOOD 1
GOT A DIAMOND RING. . . . . NM BIG-TIMER POEM 22
DON'T YOU HEAR THIS HAMMER RING? . JC BIG BUDDY 11
DON'T YOU HEAR THIS HAMMER RING? . JC BIG BUDDY 13
DON'T YOU HEAR THIS HAMMER RING? . JC BIG BUDDY 19
I WANT A DIAMOND RING. . . . . . . SP SAME IN BLUES 9
DO NOT RING, NOT EVEN MURMUR. . . . SP SUMMER EVENING 21

RINGING 2
ALARM CLOCK HERE RINGING SO DAMN LOUD . . . . SH DAYBREAK 3
MAKE A SPANGLE OUT OF QUARTERS RINGING . . . . AYM ODE TO DINAH 59

RINGS 2
NOR THEM TWO DIAMOND RINGS . . . . SH PAY DAY 8
DIAMOND RINGS . . . . SP LIKEWISE 6

RINNEY 1
I HATES THEM RINNEY YALLER GALS . . FC BLACK GAL 15

RIOT 1
AND TURNED INTO RIOT. . . . . OWT BLD MARGE POLIT 16

RIOTS 1
SHE STARTED THE RIOTS! . . . . . . OWT BLD MARGE POLIT 25

RISE 16
I RISE AGAIN - A BLACK CLOWN. . . . NM BLACK CLWN POEM 11
RISE FROM THE BOTTOM, ... NM BLACK CLWN POEM 71
MIGHT NEVER RISE NO MO'. . . . . . DK SONG BANJO DANC 13
MIGHT NEVER RISE NO MO' - . . . . . DK SONG BANJO DANC 15
MIGHT NEVER RISE NO MO'. . . . . . DK SONG BANJO DANC 27
THAT CAN UNITED RISE . . . . ANS OPEN LETTER 23
LET THE WINDS RISE THEN! . . . . . JC TO CAPTAIN MULZ 71
LET THE GREAT WAVES RISE . . . . . JC TO CAPTAIN MULZ 75
RISE AT DAWNIN' FULL OF FUN? . . . SP BLACK MARIA 13
SAYS, DID YOU EVER SEE THE SUN RISE SP BLACK MARIA 14
THE COLORED RACE WILL RISE! . . . . SP GRADUATION 26
RISE AND ROLL. . . . . SP LONG TRIP 4
THE BRANCHES RISE . . . . SP SPIRITUALS 9
THE MOUNTAINS RISE . . . . SP SPIRITUALS 11
THE WAVES RISE . . . . SP SPIRITUALS 13
BOTH CAN RISE: . . . . SP UP-BEAT 10

RISES 3
OUT OF SADNESS IT RISES TO DEFIANCE AND DETERMINATION. A HYMN OF FAITH . . . . NM BLACK CLWN MOOD 12
WHEN THE SAP RISES IN THE TREES, . ANS CHANT MAY DAY 5
WORKER: WHEN THE SAP OF YOUR OWN STRENGTH RISES . . . . ANS CHANT MAY DAY 25

RISING 6
TO A COLORED BOY'S RISING IN WEALTH OR STATION - . . . . NM COLORED SL POEM 27
WAVES OF RISING AND RE-RISING MASS VOICES, MULTIPLYING LIKE . . . . ANS CHANT MAY DAY 2
10-VOICES: BE LIKE THE SAP RISING IN THE TREES, ... ANS CHANT MAY DAY 15
FAIN ON HIND LEGS RISING, ... SP INTERNE AT PROV 23
THE RISING SHAFTS OF MOUNTAINS. . . SP SPIRITUALS 2

RISING OUT OF THE GROUND LIKE A SWAMP MIST . . . PL DAYBREAK IN ALA 5

RISIN' 2

SUN'S A RISIN'. . . . DK NIGHT AND MORN 7
SUN'S A RISIN'. . . . DK NIGHT AND MORN 9

RIVER 49

DEEP . . . RIVER. . . . FC CLOSING TIME 8
THE RIVER AND THE MOON HOLD MEMORIES. . . . FC CLOSING TIME 10
'LIEVE I'LL JUMP IN DE RIVER . . . FC SUICIDE 13
'LIEVE I'LL JUMP IN DE RIVER . . . FC SUICIDE 15
MA BABY LIVES ACROSS DE RIVER . . . DK WIDE RIVER 1
SHE LIVES ACROSS DE RIVER. . . . DK WIDE RIVER 3
WIDE, WIDE RIVER . . . DK WIDE RIVER 7
WIDE, WIDE RIVER . . . DK WIDE RIVER 9
WIDE A RIVER CAN BE. . . . DK WIDE RIVER 12
GOT TO CROSS THAT RIVER . . . DK WIDE RIVER 13
CROSS THAT RIVER. . . . DK WIDE RIVER 15
SHUBUTA BRIDGE OVER THE CHICASAWHAY RIVER IN MISSISSIPPI. . . . JC THE BITTER RIVR 1
THERE IS A BITTER RIVER . . . JC THE BITTER RIVR 2
THERE IS A BITTER RIVER . . . JC THE BITTER RIVR 6
I'VE DRUNK OF THE BITTER RIVER . . . JC THE BITTER RIVR 10
WHERE I DRANK OF THE BITTER RIVER JC THE BITTER RIVR 16
OH, WATER OF THE BITTER RIVER . . . JC THE BITTER RIVR 22
THE BITTER RIVER REFLECTS NO STARS - JC THE BITTER RIVR 26
THE BITTER RIVER REFLECTS NO STARS. JC THE BITTER RIVR 38
BUT THE SWIRL OF THE BITTER RIVER JC THE BITTER RIVR 41
THE SWIRL OF THE BITTER RIVER . . . JC THE BITTER RIVR 45
THE SWIRL OF THE BITTER RIVER . . . JC THE BITTER RIVR 49
I DID NOT ASK FOR THIS RIVER . . . JC THE BITTER RIVR 51
YOU FORCED ME TO THE BITTER RIVER JC THE BITTER RIVR 63
I HAVE DRUNK AT THE RIVER TOO LONG: JC THE BITTER RIVR 66
I'VE DRUNK AT THE BITTER RIVER . . . JC THE BITTER RIVR 73
TIRED NOW OF THE BITTER RIVER, . . JC THE BITTER RIVR 75
I'VE DRUNK OF THE BITTER RIVER . . JC THE BITTER RIVR 81
OH, TRAGIC BITTER RIVER . . . JC THE BITTER RIVR 83
I'M TIRED OF THE BITTER RIVER! . . JC THE BITTER RIVR 89
SINGING SORROW SONGS ON THE BANKS OF A MIGHTY RIVER . . . SP AUNTSUE'S STORI 11
AND WENT TO THE RIVER. . . . SP FULFILMENT 5
FROM RIVER TO RIVER . . . SP GOOD MORNING 5
FROM RIVER TO RIVER . . . SP GOOD MORNING 5
I'M GOIN' DOWN TO THE RIVER . . . SP LAMENT OVER LOV 7
DOWN TO THE RIVER. . . . SP LAMENT OVER LOV 9
I WENT DOWN TO THE RIVER. . . . SP LIFE IS FINE 1
DID YOU EVER GO DOWN TO THE RIVER - SP REVERIE HARLEM 1
SIT DOWN BY THE RIVER . . . SP REVERIE HARLEM 3
DOWN ON THE HARLEM RIVER: . . . SP REVERIE HARLEM 9
NOW THE STREETS DOWN BY THE RIVER SP RUBY BROWN 16
FROM RIVER TO RIVER. . . . SP SAME IN BLUES 29
FROM RIVER TO RIVER. . . . SP SAME IN BLUES 29
COOL FACE OF THE RIVER . . . SP SUICIDE'S NOTE 2
I SEED THE RIVER JERDEN . . . SP SYLVESTER'S BED 19
ALL SOLD DOWN THE RIVER. . . . AYM BIRD IN ORBIT 52
WHERE AN ANCIENT RIVER FLOWS . . . AYM BLUES IN STEREO 14
BY THE RIVER AND THE RAILROAD . . . PL CULTURAL EXCHNG 8
MUFFLED DRUMS IN SWANEE RIVER TEMPO. PL SPECIAL BULLTIN 9

RIVERS 16

OH, SHINING RIVERS OF THE SOUL! . . WB JAZZONIA 2
OH, SHINING RIVERS OF THE SOUL! . . WB JAZZONIA 8
OH, SILVER RIVERS OF THE SOUL! . . WB JAZZONIA 15
OR THE RIVERS WHERE YOU'RE DROWNED LIKE LIEBKNECHT. . . . ANS KIDS WHO DIE 42
THE LAND, THE MINES, THE PLANTS, THE RIVERS - . . . ANS LET AMERICA BE 83
ON THE RIVERS OF THE WORLD. . . . SP FREEDOM'S PLOW 14
SPLASH INTO THE RIVERS AND THE SEAS WENT THE BOAT-HULLS . . . SP FREEDOM'S PLOW 57
BETWEEN TWO RIVERS. . . . SP ISLAND 1
LIKE DARKER RIVERS . . . SP ISLAND 3
I'VE KNOWN RIVERS: . . . SP NEGRO SPEAKS OF 1
I'VE KNOWN RIVERS ANCIENT AS THE WORLD AND OLDER THAN THE . . . SP NEGRO SPEAKS OF 2
MY SOUL HAS GROWN DEEP LIKE THE RIVERS. . . . SP NEGRO SPEAKS OF 4
I'VE KNOWN RIVERS: . . . SP NEGRO SPEAKS OF 11
ANCIENT, DUSKY RIVERS. . . . SP NEGRO SPEAKS OF 12
MY SOUL HAS GROWN DEEP LIKE THE RIVERS. . . . SP NEGRO SPEAKS OF 13
WHERE TWO RIVERS MEET . . . PL OCTOBER 16 RAID 9

RIVERSIDE 4

STANDIN' BY DE LONESOME RIVERSIDE FC A RUINED GAL 1
STANDIN' BY DE WEARY RIVERSIDE . . FC A RUINED GAL 6
BY DE EDGE O' DE WEARY RIVERSIDE . FC A RUINED GAL 11
O, DE LONESOME RIVERSIDE. . . . FC A RUINED GAL 15

RIVER'S 1

CAUSE DE RIVER'S QUIET . . . FC SUICIDE 17

ROACH 1

A ROACH . . . SP GAUGE 3

ROAD 45

FOR PIERROT LOVED THE LONG WHITE ROAD. . . . WB PIERROT 7
AND PIERROT RAN DOWN THE LONG WHITE ROAD . . . WB PIERROT 29
ON THE VULCAN ROAD . . . WB POEME D'AUTOMNE 4
ON MY ROAD TO HELL. . . . NM BIG-TIMER POEM 44
AN' DE ROAD IS HARD AN' LONG. . . . DK PO' BOY BLUES 12
BROAD ARCH ABOVE THE ROAD WE CAME. DK YOUTH 8
RED IS THE ALABAMA ROAD. . . . ANS BLD OZZIE POWEL 1
AND RED IS THAT ALABAMA ROAD. . . . ANS BLD OZZIE POWEL 29
I WENT DOWN THE ROAD. . . . SH BLD THE SINNER 1
STRAIGHT DOWN THE ROAD . . . SH BLD THE SINNER 3
GOING DOWN THAT ROAD. . . . SH BLD THE SINNER 17
THE ROAD THAT LEADS . . . SH BLD THE SINNER 19
AS DOWN THE ROAD . . . FW CAROLINA CABIN 15
GIVES ME THE COURTESY OF ROAD . . . FW SNAKE 3
DON'T YOU PLAY IN DAT ROAD. . . . SP BABY 3
ALBERT, DON'T YOU PLAY IN DAT ROAD. SP BABY 8
WHAT ROAD HE TOOK. . . . SP BLD FORTUNE TEL 26
GOIN' DOWN THE ROAD, LAWD. . . . SP BOUND NO'TH BLS 1
GOIN' DOWN THE ROAD. . . . SP BOUND NO'TH BLS 2
DOWN THE ROAD, LAWD. . . . SP BOUND NO'TH BLS 3
WAY, WAY DOWN THE ROAD. . . . SP BOUND NO'TH BLS 4
ROAD, ROAD, ROAD, O! . . . SP BOUND NO'TH BLS 19
ROAD, ROAD, ROAD, O! . . . SP BOUND NO'TH BLS 19
ROAD, ROAD, ROAD, O! . . . SP BOUND NO'TH BLS 19
ROAD, ROAD . . . ROAD . . . ROAD, ROAD! . . . SP BOUND NO'TH BLS 20
ROAD, ROAD . . . ROAD . . . ROAD, ROAD! . . . SP BOUND NO'TH BLS 20
ROAD, ROAD . . . ROAD . . . ROAD, ROAD! . . . SP BOUND NO'TH BLS 20
ROAD, ROAD . . . ROAD . . . ROAD, ROAD! . . . SP BOUND NO'TH BLS 20
ROAD, ROAD . . . ROAD . . . ROAD, ROAD! . . . SP BOUND NO'TH BLS 20
ROAD, ROAD, ROAD, O! . . . SP BOUND NO'TH BLS 21
ROAD, ROAD, ROAD, O! . . . SP BOUND NO'TH BLS 21
ROAD, ROAD, ROAD, O! . . . SP BOUND NO'TH BLS 21
ON THE NO'THERN ROAD. . . . SP BOUND NO'TH BLS 22
THE DREAM IS THE ROAD TO BATABANO. SP HAVANA DREAMS 3
THE ROAD . . . SP JULIET 11
I LOOK DOWN THE ROAD . . . SP LITTLE GRN TREE 9
A LITTLE PIECE DOWN THE ROAD. . . . SP LITTLE GRN TREE 11
SOMETIMES, THE ROAD WAS HOT WITH SUN. . . . SP THE NEGRO MOTHE 27
MAKE OF MY PAST A ROAD TO THE LIGHT SP THE NEGRO MOTHE 39
AND WE STARTED DOWN THE ROAD . . . SP WEST TEXAS 12
I'M MAKIN' A ROAD . . . PL FLORIDA WORKERS 3
MAKIN' A ROAD . . . PL FLORIDA WORKERS 5
I'M MAKIN' A ROAD . . . PL FLORIDA WORKERS 9
A ROAD HELPS EVERYBODY. . . . PL FLORIDA WORKERS 14
I'M MAKIN' A ROAD! . . . PL FLORIDA WORKERS 20

ROADS 3

THAT THE PLANTS AND THE ROADS AND THE TOOLS OF POWER . . . ANS OPEN LETTER 17
TO A CROSS ROADS TREE. . . . SP SONG DARK GIRL 4
TO SING ON THE GEORGIA ROADS. . . . SP SUN SONG 7

ROADSIDE 1

TO A ROADSIDE TREE . . . SP SILHOUETTE 6

ROADWAY 1

AS DOWN THE ROADWAY . . . SP IN TIME SILVER 18

ROAD-APPLES 1

WELL, THEY ROCKED HIM WITH ROAD-APPLES . . . SP NOT A MOVIE 1

ROAD'S 2

ROAD'S IN FRONT O' ME. . . . SP BOUND NO'TH BLS 7
ROAD'S IN FRONT O' ME. . . . SP BOUND NO'TH BLS 9

ROAM 3

MUST ROAM. . . . FW CAROLINA CABIN 17
LET US ROAM THE NIGHT TOGETHER . . SP HARLEM NIGHT SO 2
LET US ROAM THE NIGHT TOGETHER . . SP HARLEM NIGHT SO 15

ROAR 4

THE ROAR OF THE SEA. . . . ANS CHANT MAY DAY 2
BUT WHEN YOUR GUNS ROAR. . . . JC GOOD MORN STLIN 18
THEY ROAR FOR ME - . . . JC GOOD MORN STLIN 19
AND THE ROAR OF NIAGARA . . . AYM ODE TO DINAH 37

ROB 1

BUT RAPE, ROB, STEAL. . . . PL GHOSTS OF 1619 6

ROBE 1

ROBE O' LOVE - . . . SH PRESENT 4

ROBERT 1

ON DR. ROBERT WEAVER? . . . AYM BIRD IN ORBIT 83

ROBESON 2

PAUL ROBESON SAID, OUT IN KANSAS CITY, . . . JC JIM CROW'S LAST 19
PAUL ROBESON . . . SP PROJECTION 18

ROBESPIERRE 1

SEND FOR ROBESPIERRE TO SCREAM, "CA IRA! CA IRA! . . . . PL FINAL CALL 15

ROBIN 1

SEND FOR ROBIN HOOD TO CLINCH THE ANTI-POVERTY . . . . PL FINAL CALL 3

ROCK 7

COUPLES ON THE FLOOR ROCK AND SHAKE. SH DEATH IN HARLEM 33
ROCK IT, ARABELLA, ... SH DEATH IN HARLEM 39
I'M GONNA SPLIT THIS ROCK . . . . . JC BIG BUDDY 14
WHEN I SPLIT THIS ROCK, ... JC BIG BUDDY 16
EASY LIKE I ROCK IT . . . . SP EASY BOOGIE 12
HE SLEPT LIKE A ROCK OR A MAN THAT'S DEAD. . . . . SP THE WEARY BLUES 35
THE ROCK ON WHICH FREEDOM . . . . . PL AMER HEARTBREAK 2

ROCKED 1

WELL, THEY ROCKED HIM WITH ROAD-APPLES . . . . SP NOT A MOVIE 1

ROCKETS 1

ROCKETS OF JOY . . . . SP GYPSY MELODIES 4

ROCKING 1

ROCKING BACK AND FORTH TO A MELLOW CROON, ... SP THE WEARY BLUES 2

ROCKIN' 2

EAGLE ROCKIN', ... FC MA MAN 15
DO THAT ROCKIN' STEP. . . . . DK SONG BANJO DANC 6

ROCKS 2

ROCKS THAT BURST ASUNDER . . . . . SP LOVE 3
ROCKS AND THE FIRM ROOTS OF TREES. SP SPIRITUALS 1

RODE 1

AS WE RODE THE FOAM . . . . SP SEASCAPE 6

ROLAND 1

CLUB ROLAND HAYES, ... JC HOW ABOUT DIXIE 14

ROLL 11

LEMME ROLL 'EM, BOY. . . . . FC CRAP GAME 1
TO ROLL ME TO DE SOUTH. . . . . . . DK HOMESICK BLUES 12
HIS ROLL WASN'T SLIM - . . . . . . SH DEATH IN HARLEM 7
A ROLL OF BILLS IN HIS LEFT-HAND POCKET. . . . . SH DEATH IN HARLEM 19
AND SHE SAT ON HER CHAIR LIKE A SWEET JELLY ROLL. . . . . SH DEATH IN HARLEM 82
SO I CAN ROLL ALONG. . . . . SH SIX-BITS BLUES 12
I GOT TO ROLL ALONG! . . . . SH SIX-BITS BLUES 13
THAT EASY ROLL, ... SP EASY BOOGIE 6
RISE AND ROLL, ... SP LONG TRIP 4
HAS A FINE ONE-BUTTON ROLL, ... SP TRUMPET PLAYER 36
WHEN THE ROLL IS CALLED UP YONDER AYM RIDE, RED, RIDE 2

ROLLED 4

THERE WAS LIGHT WHEN THE BATTLE CLOUDS ROLLED AWAY. . . . . . . SP FREEDOM'S PLOW 139
WHEN MONEY ROLLED IN . . . . SP GREEN MEMORY 2
AND BLOOD ROLLED OUT. . . . . SP GREEN MEMORY 3
WHEN I ROLLED THREE 7'S . . . . . . SP SITUATION 1

ROLLING 5

HE SAT UPON THE ROLLING DECK . . . DK SAILOR 1
ROLLING BASS, ... SP DREAM BOOGIE VAR 2
ROLLING LIKE I LIKE IT . . . . . . SP EASY BOOGIE 7
ROLLING BASS, ... SP NIGHTMARE BOOGIE 10
ROLLING WHITE BALLS IN THE POOL ROOMS, ... SP RAILROAD AVENUE 27

ROMAN 2

OR A ROMAN LETTER? . . . . SP MADAM'S CALLING 14
AND BURST LIKE ROMAN CANDLES. . . . PL THIRD DEGREE 14

ROOF 3

THE RAIN PLAYS A LITTLE SLEEP-SONG ON OUR ROOF AT NIGHT - . . . . . DK APRIL RAIN SONG 6
ITS ROOF WITH SNOW IS PILED, . . . DK WINTER SWEEETNS 2
MY ROOF HAS SPRUNG A LEAK. . . . . SP BLD LANDLORD 2

ROOFTOPS 1

THAT HEWED AND SHAPED THE ROOFTOPS OF AMERICA. . . . . SP FREEDOM'S PLOW 56

ROOF-TOPS 1

THE HARLEM ROOF-TOPS . . . . SP HARLEM NIGHT SO 6

ROOM 18

IT IS IN THIS SICK ROOM . . . . . . WB SICK ROOM 2
AND TOLD ME I'D BETTER PAY HER FOR MY ROOM RENT AND BOARD! . . . . NM BROKE 22
AND GIVE ME ROOM. . . . . ANS BLDS OF LENIN 4
AND MAKE ME ROOM. . . . . ANS BLDS OF LENIN 12
AND LEAVE ME ROOM. . . . . ANS BLDS OF LENIN 20
THE WORLD IS OUR ROOM! . . . . . . ANS BLDS OF LENIN 28
WHEN ARABELLA WENT TO THE LADIES' ROOM. . . . . SH DEATH IN HARLEM 78
AND ARABELLA WAS BUSY IN THE LADIES' ROOM. . . . . SH DEATH IN HARLEM 92
ROOM IN HELL TO JOIN ME . . . . . . LHR TESTAMENT 3
ROOM. . . . . SP DESIRE 9
A WHOLE LOT OF ROOM . . . . SP HOMECOMING 7
NO ROOM FOR FEAR. . . . . SP SUBWAY RUSH HOU 7
UP TO MY ROOM, SIT DOWN, AND WRITE THIS PAGE: . . . . SP THEME FOR ENG B 15
THERE'S ALWAYS ROOM, ... SP TO BE SOMEBODY 21
THE VERY ROOM IN WHICH HE LEAVES . PL JUNIOR ADDICT 11
THE VERY ROOM IN WHICH TODAY THE AIR PL JUNIOR ADDICT 13
DROPPED ON THE MEN'S ROOM FLOOR . . PL UNDERTOW 9
OR STATION WAITING ROOM . . . . . . PL WHERE WHEN WHCH 12

ROOMING 2

CAUSE I'M GOING BACK TO ROOMING AND BE A FREE MAN. . . . . SH PAY DAY 16
ROOMING AND EVERYTHING . . . . . . SP DEFERRED 12

ROOMS 3

(DIXIE RENTS ROOMS AT A BUCK A BREAK.) . . . . SH DEATH IN HARLEM 34
LIGHTS IN THE POOL ROOMS. . . . . . SP RAILROAD AVENUE 4
ROLLING WHITE BALLS IN THE POOL ROOMS, ... SP RAILROAD AVENUE 27

ROOM'S 1

THIS LITTLE OLD FURNISHED ROOM'S . SP NECESSITY 5

ROOSEVELT 1

THE ROOSEVELT, RENAISSANCE, GEM, ALHAMBRA: . . . . SP MOVIES 1

ROOTS 3

ROCKS AND THE FIRM ROOTS OF TREES. SP SPIRITUALS 1
FROM THE FIRM ROOTS OF TREES. . . . SP SPIRITUALS 10
WITH NO ROOTS . . . . PL SLUM DREAMS 4

ROPE 7

WHEN THE LYNCHER'S ROPE . . . . . . ANS A NEW SONG 18
PULL AT THE ROPE! OH! . . . . ANS LYNCHING SONG 1
THOUGHT OF A ROPE, ... SH DEATH IN HARLEM 69
ON A ROPE . . . . SP BLUE BAYOU 17
PUT HIM ON A ROPE . . . . SP BLUE BAYOU 20
ROPE MY NECK - LYNCH ME - . . . . . PL DEATH YORKVILLE 7
FROM THE SLAVE CHAIN TO THE LYNCH ROPE . . . . PL DEATH YORKVILLE 9

ROSCOE 1

ROSCOE KNOWS DARN WELL . . . . . . SP MADAM PHONE BIL 16

ROSE 25

OF ROSE AND GOLD, ... WB OUR LAND 6
AND THE BREATH OF A ROSE IN JUNE. WB PIERROT 10
MERCEDES IS CHARNEL ROSE. . . . . . WB TO DARK MERCEDE 3
MAY ACCOMPANY THE RECITATION - ECHOING SOFTLY, OVER THERE, THERE'S A ROSE . . . . NM COLORED SL MOOD 4
OUT OF THE PURPLE AND ROSE OF OLD MEMORIES . . . . DK FAIRIES 3
BUT WHEN THE SUN ROSE MAKING . . . DK IRISH WAKE 5
BECAUSE YOU ARE TO ME A ROSE - . . DK PASSING LOVE 5
TO BLUSH OF THE ROSE. . . . . SH HARLEM SWEETIES 22
ROSE OF NEON DARKNESS, ... FW CHIPPY 1
ROSE OF THE SHARP-THORNED STEM . . FW CHIPPY 2
ROSE OF NOTHING BUT YESTERDAYS . . FW CHIPPY 4
LITTLE DOLLAR ROSE . . . . FW CHIPPY 6
MAY ROSE LEAVES . . . . FW FOR DEAD MIMES 2
A NEON ROSE . . . . FW MONTMARTRE 2
AND THEN THE WALL ROSE, ... SP AS I GREW OLDER 7
ROSE SLOWLY, ... SP AS I GREW OLDER 8
ROSE SLOWLY, SLOWLY, ... SP AS I GREW OLDER 11
ROSE UNTIL IT TOUCHED THE SKY - . . SP AS I GREW OLDER 15
OR MAYBE THE DREAM'S A VEDADO ROSE - SP HAVANA DREAMS 7
HE ROSE UP ON HIS DYING BED . . . . SP HOPE 1
I'M GONNA BUY ME A ROSE BUD . . . . SP MIDWINTER BLUES 19
BUY ME A ROSE BUD, ... SP MIDWINTER BLUES 21
WEATHER AND ROSE . . . . SP SNAIL 3
WEATHER AND ROSE . . . . SP SNAIL 5
AND A ROSE PINK MOUTH. . . . . . . SP SUMMER EVENING 4

ROSES 2

AND THE DEEP RED ROSES BLOOM. . . . SH YOUNG NEGRO GRL 5
AND LEAVE UNCUT THE ROSES . . . . . FW REMEMBRANCE 2

ROT 3

THE RAPE AND ROT OF GRAFT, AND STEALTH, AND LIES, ... ANS LET AMERICA BE 81
WAVING A FLAG AND MOUTHING ROT . . ANS SONG OF SPAIN 68
AND ROT AWAY! . . . . SP MADAM RENT MAN 10

ROTONDE 1

ROTONDE SELECT DUPONT FLORE . . . . AYM ASK YOUR MAMA 51

ROTS 1
ROTS IN HELL TODAY! . . . . SP MAMA AND DAUGHT 16

ROTTEN 2
DOES IT STINK LIKE ROTTEN MEAT? . . SP HARLEM 6
DOES IT STINK LIKE ROTTEN MEAT? . . PL DREAM DEFERRED 6

ROUGE-BRIGHT 1
AND THE ROUGE-BRIGHT PETALS. . . . FW CHIPPY 3

ROUGH 1
ACT ROUGH AND TOUGH. . . . . SP WARNING AUGMENT 6

ROUND 16
ROUND THIS TOWN. - . . . . FC RED SILK STOCK 6
ROUND BY ROUND. . . . . NM BLACK CLWN POEM 44
ROUND BY ROUND. . . . . NM BLACK CLWN POEM 44
ALL THE WORLD ROUND - . . . . NM BLACK CLWN POEM 56
BUT I SHO BEEN LOOKIN' ROUND HARD
LATELY FOR WAYS AND MEANS . . . NM BROKE 39
THE CIRCLES SPIN ROUND . . . . . . FW CIRCLES 1
AND THE CIRCLES SPIN ROUND . . . . FW CIRCLES 2
FOR THE JAIL IS ROUND - . . . . . . FW CIRCLES 8
WITH A ROUND BLACK FACE . . . . . . FW MIGRATION 12
I USED TO GO ROUND THE CORNER. . . OWT LONESOME CORNER 3
YOU KICKS 'EM ROUND AND . . . . . . SP LOVER'S RETURN 11
THE DAY HE CAME ROUND. . . . . . . SP MADAM CENSUS 2
DAY IN. DAY ROUND. . . . . SP MEXICAN MARKET 4
WAS GATHERED ROUND ME. . . . . . . SP SYLVESTER'S BED 4
THE WORLD IS BIG AND ROUND. . . . . PL BACKLASH BLUES 20
BIG AND BRIGHT AND ROUND - . . . . . PL BACKLASH BLUES 22

ROUNDER 3
ROUNDER AND SPORT. . . . . NM BIG-TIMER POEM 38
JACK. IF YOU GOT TO BE A ROUNDER . SP STREET SONG 1
BE A ROUNDER RIGHT - . . . . SP STREET SONG 2

ROUNDERS 2
ROUNDERS. . . . . FC LAUGHERS 15
TILL THESE LICKER-HEADED ROUNDERS FC LISTEN HERE 11

ROUNDS 1
MAKIN' ROUNDS AT NIGHT. . . . . . . SP STREET SONG 4

ROUNDTREES 1
OF A MILLION MARTHA ROUNDTREES? . . AYM BIRD IN ORBIT 62

ROUTE 2
ON THE LINE WHOSE ROUTE WAS FREEDOM AYM ODE TO DINAH 30
TO ROUTE EACH PATH . . . . PL FREDRK DOUGLASS 10

ROW 4
A ROW OF GOLD IN HIS UPPER MOUTH. SH DEATH IN HARLEM 18
A ROW OF LONG TALL MAMAS . . . . . SP AS BEFITS A MAN 7
IN A ROW . . . . SP SITUATION 2
DOWN THE LONG HARD ROW THAT I BEEN
HOEING . . . . AYM BLUES IN STEREO 34

ROWBOATS 1
LABOR! OUT OF LABOR CAME THE
ROWBOATS . . . . SP FREEDOM'S PLOW 72

ROWDY 1
DRUNK AND ROWDY AND GAY! . . . . . SH CABARET GIRL 6

ROWS 1
SADLY RECALLS THE ROWS OF WHITE
CROSSES IN FRANCE. . . . . NM COLORED SL MOOD 12

RUB 2
FURTHERMORE. RUB OUT . . . . SP MADAM CENSUS 29
WOULD IT RUB OFF? . . . . PL CULTURAL EXCHNG 34

RUBBED 1
DIXIE RUBBED HIS HANDS AND LAUGHED
OUT LOUD - . . . . SH DEATH IN HARLEM 63

RUBBER 2
TWINKLE ON THE RUBBER GLOVES . . . SP INTERNE AT PROV 33
IN BILLINGTON'S CHURCH OF RUBBER. AYM HORN OF PLENTY 84

RUBY 1
KNOW MORE ABOUT THIS PRETTY RUBY
BROWN. . . . . SP RUBY BROWN 17

RUE 1
OF RUE FONTAINE. . . . . DK PARISIAN BEGGAR 10

RUFFLES 1
INTO MIDNIGHT RUFFLES . . . . SP BOOGIE 1 A.M. 7

RUFUS 1
DR. RUFUS CLEMENT HIS CHIEF ADVISER. PL CULTURAL EXCHNG 44

RUG 1
FEEL THE RUG OF DIVIDENDS. . . . . PL UNDERTOW 5

RUIN 2
OUR OF THE RACK AND RUIN OF OUR
GANGSTER DEATH. . . . . ANS LET AMERICA BE 80
HE'S TRYING TO RUIN THE GOVERNMENT SP BLD LANDLORD 23

RUINED 1
AIN'T NOTHIN' FOR A RUINED GAL . . FC A RUINED GAL 13

RUINT 1
SHE GREW UP AND GOT RUINT. . . . . SP MADAM CHARTY CH 3

RULE 2
AND THE RULE OF GREED'S UPHELD - . ANS UNION 11
TO IMPLEMENT THE GOLDEN RULE. . . . PL BIRMINGHAM SUND 23

RULED 2
RULED MY MANY YEARS. . . . . SP WIDOW WOMAN 14
RULED MY MANY YEARS - . . . . SP WIDOW WOMAN 16

RUM 2
IN THE RUM THAT WAFTS MARACAS . . . AYM ODE TO DINAH 16
A LITTLE RUM WITH SUGAR. . . . . . AYM RIDE. RED. RIDE 19

RUMBA 1
PARECE UNA RUMBA. . . . . FC JAZZ BAND 17

RUMBLE 6
TO THE RUMBLE OF STREET CARS. . . . WB LENOX AVE MIDNT 9
THE BOOGIE-WOOGIE RUMBLE . . . . . SP BOOGIE 1 A.M. 3
THE BOOGIE-WOOGIE RUMBLE . . . . . SP DREAM BOOGIE 3
AND FOR YOUR LOVE SONG TONE THEIR
RUMBLE DOWN. . . . . SP JUKE BOX LOVE 6
WHEN THE RUMBLE OF DEATH . . . . . SP SUNDAY MORNING 2
DROWNS THE RUMBLE OF THAT TRAIN . . AYM ODE TO DINAH 38

RUN 17
LIFT ARMS IN VAIN. RUN. HIDE. DIE: ANS SONG OF SPAIN 60
PEARL HARBOR PUT JIM CROW ON THE
RUN. . . . . JC JIM CROW'S LAST 8
THE MOON DOESN'T RUN. . . . . OWT RESTRICTIVE 7
BEFORE WE RUN BACK . . . . SP A HOUSE IN TAOS 42
ONE RUN OVAH YOU . . . . SP BABY 6
YOU TOUCH WHEN YOU RUN? . . . . . . SP DEMAND 11
AND YOU RUN INTO YOURSELF . . . . . SP FINAL CURVE 2
BUT HAD RUN AWAY TO FREEDOM. . . . SP FREEDOM'S PLOW 113
KILL HIM - AND LET HIS SOUL RUN
WILD! . . . . SP GENIUS CHILD 12
AND THEN RUN? . . . . SP HARLEM 5
DON'T YOU WANT TO RUN AROUND . . . SP KID SLEEPY 2
THE WATER DON'T RUN. . . . . SP MADAM RENT MAN 12
HER FEATURES IS ALL RUN TOGETHER . SP NECESSITY 9
WHO LYNCH AND RUN. . . . . SP ONE-WAY TICKET 20
AND THEN RUN? . . . . PL DREAM DEFERRED 5
FOR CINQUE SAYING. "RUN A NEW FLAG
UP THE MAST." . . . . PL FINAL CALL 21
OH. RUN. ALL WHO HAVE NOT . . . . . PL SPECIAL BULLTIN 16

RUNG 2
EVEN RUNG THIS BELL ON SUNDAY. YET AYM ASK YOUR MAMA 8
THEY RUNG MY BELL TO ASK ME . . . . AYM HORN OF PLENTY 96

RUNNER 3
HURRY. SWEATING RUNNER! . . . . . . OWT FLIGHT 3
NUMBER RUNNER . . . . SP MADAM NUMBER WR 1
THE RUNNER SAID. MADAM. . . . . . . SP MADAM NUMBER WR 29

RUNNING 1
THE RAIN MAKES RUNNING POOLS IN THE
GUTTER. . . . . DK APRIL RAIN SONG 5

RUNNIN' 2
RUNNIN' AN ELEVATOR . . . . SP ELEVATOR BOY 2
I BEEN RUNNIN' THIS . . . . SP ELEVATOR BOY 21

RUNS 5
ON A TRAIN THAT RUNS SOMEWHERE. . . SH SIX-BITS BLUES 2
ON A TRAIN THAT RUNS SOMEWHERE. . . SH SIX-BITS BLUES 4
RUNS OUT TOMORROW'S . . . . OWT BLUES ON A BOX 4
RUNS TO DIVE IN THE PARK . . . . . SP DIVE 3
THE REASON MARIE RUNS AROUND WITH
TRASH . . . . SP SISTER 8

RUPTURE 1
PRACTICE ON A STOCKYARDS RUPTURE. SP INTERNE AT PROV 8

RUSHES 1
RUSHES DOWN THE DRAIN . . . . SP SUNDAY MORNING 3

RUSHIN 1
WENT RUSHIN FOR THE DOOR . . . . . SH DEATH IN HARLEM 120

RUSSIA 6
COMRADE LENIN OF RUSSIA. . . . . . ANS BLDS OF LENIN 1
COMRADE LENIN OF RUSSIA. . . . . . ANS BLDS OF LENIN 9
COMRADE LENIN OF RUSSIA. . . . . . ANS BLDS OF LENIN 17
COMRADE LENIN OF RUSSIA . . . . . . ANS BLDS OF LENIN 25
RUSSIA TO THE ARGENTINE. . . . . . ANS CHANT TOM MOONY 20
CONGRESS CASES RUSSIA. . . . . . . SP MIGRANT 30

RUSTY 2
- WITH A RUSTY NEEDLE . . . . PL SLAVE 10
- LIKE RUSTY IRON AND MINT. . . . . . PL WHERE WHEN WHCH 3

SABE 1
- (QUIEN SABE? WHO REALLY KNOWS?) . . SP HAVANA DREAMS 8

SACKCLOTH 1
- SACKCLOTH AND ASHES. ANYHOW. . . . PL BOMBINGS DIXIE 3

SACRAMENT 1
- TO TAKE THE SACRAMENT . . . . FW COMMUNION 6

SAD 16
- IT SHO WOULD BE SAD. . . . . FC MINNIE SINGS 14
- A LOOKIN' ALL SAD . . . . FC NEW CABARET GRL 19
- A SAD SONG IN DE AIR. . . . . DK HOMESICK BLUES 2
- A SAD SONG IN DE AIR. . . . . DK HOMESICK BLUES 4
- GETTING UP IN THE MORNING LONESOME AND SAD? . . . . SH DAYBREAK 13
- FEELIN' SO SAD. LAWD. . . . . SH MIDNIGHT CHIPPI 7
- FEELIN' SO SAD AND LONE. . . . . . SH MIDNIGHT CHIPPI 8
- SO SAD. LAWD! . . . . SH MIDNIGHT CHIPPI 9
- SO SAD AND LONE! . . . . SH MIDNIGHT CHIPPI 10
- SETTING HERE THINKING FEELING SAD. SH TWILIGHT REVERI 3
- SOFT SAD BLACK FEET . . . . OWT JUICE JOINT 46
- I GOT THOSE SAD OLD WEARY BLUES. . OWT TOO BLUE 1
- LAWD. I HATES TO BE SAD. . . . . . SP BOUND NO'TH BLS 14
- HATES TO BE LONELY AN' SAD. . . . . SP BOUND NO'TH BLS 16
- HIS LITTLE BLUES IS SAD. . . . . . SP MONROE'S BLUES 6
- HE PLAYED THAT SAD RAGGY TUNE LIKE A MUSICAL FOOL. . . . . SP THE WEARY BLUES 13

SADIE 1
- AN' SADIE IS A WHORE. . . . . FC SATURDAY NIGHT 4

SADISTIC 1
- WITH WEARY SADISTIC EYES . . . . . SP CAFE: 3 A.M. 2

SADLY 1
- SADLY RECALLS THE ROWS OF WHITE CROSSES IN FRANCE. . . . . NM COLORED SL MOOD 12

SADNESS 7
- JOY. A BURST OF MUSIC. STRUTTING AND DANCING. THEN SUDDEN SADNESS AGAIN. . . . . NM BLACK CLWN MOOD 3
- OUT OF SADNESS IT RISES TO DEFIANCE AND DETERMINATION. A HYMN OF FAITH . . . . NM BLACK CLWN MOOD 12
- THEN SADNESS AGAIN - . . . . NM BLACK CLWN POEM 33
- AND THE SADNESS? . . . . SP SONG BILLIE HOL 3
- OF THE SADNESS? . . . . SP SONG BILLIE HOL 6
- OF THE SADNESS . . . . SP SONG BILLIE HOL 8
- FOR THE SADNESS TO BE SORROW. . . . AYM IS IT TRUE? 28

SAD-SUNG 1
- BEAT OUT OF BLOOD WITH WORDS SAD-SUNG . . . . SP AFRO-AMER FRAG 8

SAFARI 1
- NOT YET ON SAFARI. . . . . AYM IS IT TRUE? 11

SAFE 1
- THE WORLD'S BEEN MADE SAFE FOR DEMOCRACY . . . . NM COLORED SL POEM 29

SAFETY 1
- NO SAFETY. NO LOVE. NO RESPECT WAS I DUE. . . . . SP THE NEGRO MOTHE 16

SAGS 2
- MAYBE IT JUST SAGS . . . . SP HARLEM 9
- MAYBE IT JUST SAGS . . . . PL DREAM DEFERRED 9

SAID 160
- ONE SAID SHE HEARD THE JAZZ-BAND SOB WB CABARET 5
- SAID SIMPLE JOHN. . . . . WB PIERROT 2
- SAID SIMPLE JOHN. . . . . WB PIERROT 5
- SAID SIMPLE JOHN. . . . . WB PIERROT 12
- SAID SIMPLE JOHN. . . . . WB PIERROT 15
- SAID SIMPLE JOHN. . . . . WB PIERROT 22
- SAID SIMPLE JOHN. . . . . WB PIERROT 25
- SAID TENNESSEE. . . . . FC GYPSY MAN 10
- AND ONE OLD FUNNY BOY SAID. "I'LL WORK AT ANY PRICE . . . . NM BROKE 8
- I SAID. "BABY. YOU KNOW I LOVES YOU. AND ALL LIKE THAT . . . . NM BROKE 50
- SO WHEN I GOT READY TO GO. I SAID. "I'LL BE SEEIN' YOU SOON. MARIE." NM BROKE 52
- AND SAID TO ME. "BROTHER. YOU'VE GOT YOUR CHANCE. . . . . NM COLORED SL POEM 16
- IT'S A LIE! IT'S A LIE! EVERY WORD THEY SAID. . . . . NM COLORED SL POEM 44
- HE SAID. "SHO YOU'LL COME WID ME . DK MA LORD 15
- WHO SAID THE FREE? NOT ME? . . . . ANS LET AMERICA BE 52
- LET US FORGET WHAT BOOKER-T. SAID. ANS OPEN LETTER 19
- BERNICE SAID SHE WANTED . . . . . . SH BLD THE KILLER 1
- I SAID. BABY. . . . . SH BLD THE KILLER 3
- BERNICE SAID SHE WANTED . . . . . . SH BLD THE KILLER 5
- I SAID. SUGAR. . . . . SH BLD THE KILLER 7
- BERNICE SAID SHE NEEDED . . . . . . SH BLD THE KILLER 9
- I SAID. HONEY. . . . . SH BLD THE KILLER 11
- I SAID TO HELL . . . . SH BLD THE KILLER 19
- I SAID HEY-HEY ON BEER - . . . . . SH HEY-HEY BLUES 20
- I SAID COME HERE. LONESOME. . . . . SH MIDNIGHT CHIPPI 5
- I SAID. PLEASE. MR. LONESOME. . . . SH MIDNIGHT CHIPPI 11
- LONESOME SAID. LISTEN! . . . . . . SH MIDNIGHT CHIPPI 13
- SAID. LISTEN! HEY! . . . . SH MIDNIGHT CHIPPI 14
- LONESOME SAID. LISTEN! . . . . . . SH MIDNIGHT CHIPPI 15
- I SAID. MR. LONESOME. . . . . SH MIDNIGHT CHIPPI 19
- LONESOME SAID WHEN A TWO-BIT WOMAN SH MIDNIGHT CHIPPI 23
- I SAID. GO. HOT DAMN! . . . . SH ONLY WOMAN BLUS 22
- GONNA GO GET MY PISTOL. I SAID FORTY-FOUR - . . . . SH TWILIGHT REVERI 5
- SAM SOLOMON SAID. . . . . JC BLD SAM SOLOMON 1
- SAM SAID. IT'S TIME TO GO . . . . . JC BLD SAM SOLOMON 8
- THE CRACKERS SAID. SAM. . . . . . . JC BLD SAM SOLOMON 25
- THE CRACKERS SAID. BOY. . . . . . . JC BLD SAM SOLOMON 31
- SAM SOLOMON SAID. I'M . . . . JC BLD SAM SOLOMON 33
- THE CRACKERS SAID. SAM. . . . . . . JC BLD SAM SOLOMON 37
- SAM SOLOMON SAID. A MAN . . . . . . JC BLD SAM SOLOMON 39
- SAM SOLOMON SAID. . . . . JC BLD SAM SOLOMON 53
- NEHRU SAID. BEFORE HE WENT TO JAIL. JC JIM CROW'S LAST 15
- MARION ANDERSON SAID TO THE DAR. . JC JIM CROW'S LAST 17
- PAUL ROBESON SAID. OUT IN KANSAS CITY. . . . . JC JIM CROW'S LAST 19
- JOE LOUIS SAID. WE GONNA WIN THIS WAR . . . . JC JIM CROW'S LAST 25
- SEEMS LIKE SHE SAID: . . . . FW GIRL 11
- HE SAID. . . . . FW HEART 5
- SHE SAID. . . . . FW SONGS 3
- I SAID. . . . . FW SONGS 6
- MY LANDLADY. SHE SAID. NO! . . . . OWT STRANGER IN TWN 8
- I SAID. IT DON'T MAKE NO DIFFERENCE NOHOW. . . . . OWT STRANGER IN TWN 9
- AND THIS IS MY BLOOD. HE SAID. . . LHR BLD MARY'S SON 19
- HE SAID. OH. LORD. THY WILL BE DONE! LHR BLD MARY'S SON 24
- I SAID. TELL ME. GYPSY. . . . . . . SP BLD THE GYPSY 3
- GYPSY SAID. SILVER. . . . . SP BLD THE GYPSY 5
- SHE SAID. NOW. LISTEN. MISTER. . . SP BLD THE GYPSY 11
- I SAID. . . . . SP DREAM 11
- DO YOU HEAR WHAT I SAID? . . . . . SP EASY BOOGIE 11
- THE BOSS MAN SAID. . . . . SP FIRED 5
- BUT NOT SO LONG AGO AT THAT. LINCOLN SAID: . . . . SP FREEDOM'S PLOW 101
- WHAT HE SAID MUST BE MEANT FOR EVERY HUMAN BEING - . . . . SP FREEDOM'S PLOW 107
- THEN A MAN SAID: . . . . SP FREEDOM'S PLOW 109
- WHAT FREDERICK DOUGLASS SAID WAS TRUE. . . . . SP FREEDOM'S PLOW 115
- THAT SONG MEANT JUST WHAT IT SAID: HOLD ON! . . . . SP FREEDOM'S PLOW 127
- WHO SAID THOSE THINGS? AMERICANS! SP FREEDOM'S PLOW 174
- A LONG TIME AGO. BUT NOT TOO LONG AGO. A MAN SAID: . . . . SP FREEDOM'S PLOW 90
- THAT WHAT HE SAID WAS ALSO MEANT FOR THEM. . . . . SP FREEDOM'S PLOW 99
- I WAS BORN HERE. HE SAID. . . . . . SP GOOD MORNING 2
- HE SAID A WOMAN'S CRYIN'S . . . . . SP HARD DADDY 11
- SAID: . . . . SP JOE LOUIS 4
- KID SLEEPY SAID. . . . . SP KID SLEEPY 8
- KID SLEEPY SAID. . . . . SP KID SLEEPY 16
- YOU SAID YOU WAS GONNA TAKE ME . . SP LOW TO HIGH 3
- HE SAID. HOWDY-DO? . . . . SP MADAM RENT MAN 2
- FORTUNE TELLER SAID. . . . . SP MADAM FORT TELL 2
- I SAID. WHAT . . . . SP MADAM RENT MAN 3
- HE SAID. HAVE YOU GOT . . . . SP MADAM MINISTER 3
- HE SAID. ARE YOU MADAM? . . . . . . SP MADAM WRONG VIS 3
- I SAID. WHAT'S THE SCORE? . . . . . SP MADAM WRONG VIS 4
- HE SAID. YOU KNOW . . . . SP MADAM RENT MAN 5
- HE SAID. I AM INTERESTED . . . . . SP MADAM MINISTER 5
- HE SAID. I RECKON . . . . SP MADAM WRONG VIS 5
- HE SAID. MADAM. . . . . SP MADAM NUMBER WR 5
- I SAID. JOHNSON. . . . . SP MADAM CENSUS 5
- I SAID. LISTEN. . . . . SP MADAM RENT MAN 7
- FORTUNE TELLER SAID. . . . . SP MADAM FORT TELL 7
- I SAID. PLEASE EXPLAIN TO ME . . . SP MADAM FORT TELL 9
- I SAID. LAST NIGHT. . . . . SP MADAM NUMBER WR 9
- I SAID. REVEREND. . . . . SP MADAM MINISTER 9
- HE SAID. WHAT . . . . SP MADAM CENSUS 9
- SHE SAID. YOU MUST RECOGNIZE . . . SP MADAM FORT TELL 11
- HE SAID. I REALLY . . . . SP MADAM WRONG VIS 11
- HE SAID. THAT MIGHT . . . . SP MADAM NUMBER WR 11
- I SAID. K - . . . . SP MADAM CENSUS 11
- I SAID. MADAM. TELL ME - . . . . . SP MADAM FORT TELL 13
- I SAID. MADAM. . . . . SP MADAM HER MADAM 13
- I SAID. DO YOU LOVE ME? . . . . . . SP MADAM MIGHT-HAV 13
- HE SAID. I'M GONNA PUT IT . . . . . SP MADAM CENSUS 13
- HE SAID. WHAT HAVE YOU . . . . . . SP MADAM MINISTER 13
- I SAID. NONE OF YOUR . . . . SP MADAM MINISTER 15
- I SAID. IF YOU DO. . . . . SP MADAM CENSUS 15
- SHE SAID. YOUR FORTUNE. HONEY. . . SP MADAM FORT TELL 17
- HE SAID. YOU'RE JOHNSON - . . . . . SP MADAM WRONG VIS 17
- HE SAID. MADAM. I SWEAR . . . . . . SP MADAM MIGHT-HAV 17

HE SAID, SISTER . . . . SP MADAM MINISTER 17
I SAID, YES - BUT ALBERTA . . . . . SP MADAM WRONG VIS 19
HE SAID, MADAM, ... SP MADAM RENT MAN 19
I SAID, IT FELT GOOD - . . . . . . SP MADAM MINISTER 19
I SAID, I SWEAR I . . . . SP MADAM NUMBER WR 21
I SAID, WHAT MAN YOU'RE TALKING 'BOUT? . . . . SP MADAM FORT TELL 21
I SAID, MADAM, ... SP MADAM HER MADAM 21
HE SAID, SISTER, ... SP MADAM MINISTER 21
HE SAID, MRS., ... SP MADAM CENSUS 21
SHE SAID, MADAM! BE CALM - . . . . SP MADAM FORT TELL 22
THE DOCTOR SAID, MADAM, ... SP MADAM WRONG VIS 23
I SAID, NATURALLY, ... SP MADAM RENT MAN 23
I SAID, I DON'T . . . . SP MADAM CENSUS 25
I SAID, BETTER BUY TWO - . . . . . SP MADAM WRONG VIS 27
HE SAID, MADAM, ... SP MADAM RENT MAN 27
THE RUNNER SAID, MADAM, ... SP MADAM NUMBER WR 29
I SAID, NEITHER AM I. . . . . SP MADAM RENT MAN 29
HE SAID, IN ME . . . . SP MADAM MIGHT-HAV 29
I SAID, I DON'T WANT . . . . SP MADAM MIGHT-HAV 31
HE SAID, YOUR NAME LOOKS GOOD . . . SP MADAM'S CALLING 11
I SAID, USE AMERICAN. . . . . SP MADAM'S CALLING 15
SAID, WE CAN'T USE YOU . . . . . . SP MADAM'S PAST HI 16
I SAID, ... SP MADAM'S PAST HI 18
SAID A SOOTHIN' SONG, ... SP MISERY 6
I SAID, BABY! BABY! . . . . SP MORNING AFTER 13
THAT'S NO LIE, HE SAID, ... SP NEW YORKERS 2
I WASN'T BORN HERE, SHE SAID, . . . SP NEW YORKERS 4
AND THE LAST PRAYERS BEEN SAID . . SP NIGHT FUNERAL 30
SAID THE LADY, CAN YOU DO . . . . . SP QUESTION 1
I SAID TO MY BABY, ... SP SAME IN BLUES 1
I CAN'T, SHE SAID, I CAN'T! . . . . SP SAME IN BLUES 3
LULU SAID TO LEONARD, ... SP SAME IN BLUES 8
LEONARD SAID TO LULU, ... SP SAME IN BLUES 10
THAT COLORED BOY AIN'T SAID A THING SP SOUTHERN MAMMY 15
THAT SAID, ... SP STRANGE HURT 3
THE INSTRUCTOR SAID, ... SP THEME FOR ENG B 1
JOE SAID I WONDER HOW IT WOULD FEEL SP WEST TEXAS 7
I'M ALL ALONE IN THIS WORLD, SHE SAID, ... SP 50 - 50 1
BIG BOY OPENED HIS MOUTH AND SAID, SP 50 - 50 6
HE SAID, SHARE YOUR BED - . . . . . SP 50 - 50 13
SAID, TELL YOUR MA. . . . . AYM ASK YOUR MAMA 14
I SAID, VOTED FOR YOUR MAMA. . . . AYM BIRD IN ORBIT 17
WHAT SHE SAID ABOUT HER CHILDREN . AYM BIRD IN ORBIT 51
THOSE SIT-IN KIDS, HE SAID, ... AYM BIRD IN ORBIT 71
I SAID, FROM YOUR MAMA! . . . . . . AYM HORN OF PLENTY 48
I SAID, YES, YOUR MAMA. . . . . . . AYM HORN OF PLENTY 98
I SAID, ASK YOUR MAMA. . . . . . . AYM IS IT TRUE? 56
I SAID, ASK YOUR MAMA. . . . . . . PL CULTURAL EXCHNG 35
ANYTHING BUT A SLAVE! HE SAID. . . PL FREDRK DOUGLASS 17
THE FIRST BLOW, HE SAID. . . . . . PL FREDRK DOUGLASS 20
THEY SAID, "DO YOU BELIEVE . . . . PL KU KLUX 3
I SAID, "MISTER, ... PL KU KLUX 5
THE WHITE MAN SAID, "BOY, ... PL KU KLUX 9
A KLANSMAN SAID, "NIGGER, ... PL KU KLUX 17
I SAID, O, LORD, IF YOU CAN, . . . PL WHO BUT TH LORD 9
IT'S BEEN SAID . . . . PL WITHOUT BENEFIT 8

SAIL 1
BUT DREAM SHIPS SAIL AWAY . . . . . SP WATER-FRONT STR 2

SAILBOATS 1
AND THE SAILBOATS AND THE STEAMBOATS. . . . . SP FREEDOM'S PLOW 73

SAILED 1
O, I'M THE MAN WHO SAILED THOSE EARLY SEAS . . . . ANS LET AMERICA BE 45

SAILING 3
(NEGRO SKIPPER OF THE BOOKER T. WASHINGTON SAILING WITH A MIXED CREW) . . . . JC TO CAPTAIN MULZ 1
ON SAILING DATE. . . . . FW SAILING DATE 6
IT'S SAILING DATE. . . . . FW SAILING DATE 19

SAILOR 5
HELLO, SAILOR BOY. . . . . SP PORT TOWN 1
HELLO, SAILOR, ... SP PORT TOWN 3
LIGHTS, SAILOR BOY, ... SP PORT TOWN 9
COME ON, SAILOR, ... SP PORT TOWN 13
THIS STRONG YOUNG SAILOR . . . . . SP YOUNG SAILOR 6

SAILORS 2
WITH GYPSIES AND SAILORS, ... WB A FAREWELL 1
BEIGE SAILORS WITH LARGE NOSES . . SP SEASHORE THROUG 1

SAILS 2
THAT SAILS THESE DANGEROUS SEAS - JC TO CAPTAIN MULZ 40
WITH BILLOWING SAILS THE GALLEONS CAME . . . . SP FREEDOM'S PLOW 35

SAINTS 2
FROM THE SAINTS OF GOD IN CHRIST . SP PASSING 4
LISTEN TO YO' SAINTS! . . . . SP SHOUT 3

SAKE 2
FOR THE SAKE OF THE REVOLUTION . . ANS BLDS OF LENIN 23
FOR YOUR SAKE. . . . . PL OCTOBER 16 RAID 14

SALE 1
NOT FOR SALE. . . . . PL DREAM DUST 6

SALLIE 4
HERE, SALLIE! . . . . SP IN EXPLANATION 13
GEORGE SALLIE COOLIE BOY GETS TIRED SOMETIMES. . . . . SP IN EXPLANATION 17
SHUT UP, SALLIE! . . . . SP IN EXPLANATION 47
GEORGE SALLIE COOLIE INDIAN BOY . . SP IN EXPLANATION 51

SALT 8
NOR THE SALT TEARS . . . . WB DISILLUSION 9
WORK TO SALT . . . . FW LITTLE SONG 7
FROM SALT SEA WATER . . . . FW SAILING DATE 4
A THOUSAND POUNDS OF SALT . . . . . LHR TESTAMENT 7
FOR SPRINKLING SALT . . . . SP JAM SESSION 7
GONNA SALT EVERY DIME AWAY . . . . SP NUMBERS 2
SEATTLE, OAKLAND, SALT LAKE, . . . SP ONE-WAY TICKET 12
I BOIL A FISH AND SALT IT . . . . . AYM GOSPEL CHA-CHA 24

SALTY-COLORED 1
SCENT SALTY-COLORED . . . . SP SEASHORE THROUG 12

SALT'PEANUTS 1
SALT'PEANUTS! . . . . SP CHILDREN'S RYME 28

SALUTES 1
HAND-HIGH SALUTES - HEIL! . . . . . PL SPECIAL BULLTIN 10

SAM 11
LANDLADY 'LOWED TO ME LAST WEEK, "SAM, AIN'T YOU GOT NO MONEY?" . NM BROKE 19
SAM SOLOMON SAID, ... JC BLD SAM SOLOMON 1
SAM SAID, IT'S TIME TO GO . . . . . JC BLD SAM SOLOMON 8
SAM SOLOMON CALLED ON . . . . JC BLD SAM SOLOMON 17
THE CRACKERS SAID, SAM, ... JC BLD SAM SOLOMON 25
SAM SOLOMON ANSWERED, ... JC BLD SAM SOLOMON 29
SAM SOLOMON SAID, I'M . . . . JC BLD SAM SOLOMON 33
THE CRACKERS SAID, SAM, ... JC BLD SAM SOLOMON 37
SAM SOLOMON SAID, A MAN . . . . . . JC BLD SAM SOLOMON 39
BUT SAM SOLOMON . . . . JC BLD SAM SOLOMON 43
SAM SOLOMON SAID, ... JC BLD SAM SOLOMON 53

SAME 15
THAT LAUGHS AND CRIES AT THE SAME TIME. . . . . FC JAZZ BAND 12
IN NO SINGLE MOUTH THE SAME. . . . OLD TWO THINGS 10
NOT THE SAME AS YOU - . . . . NM BLACK CLWN POEM 3
AND FINDING ONLY THE SAME OLD STUPID PLAN. . . . . ANS LET AMERICA BE 23
SAME AS I CAN HEY-HEY ON BEER. . . SH HEY-HEY BLUES 2
SAME AS I CAN HEY-HEY ON BEER. . . SH HEY-HEY BLUES 4
AND BE THE SAME OLD CROW HE USED TO BE - . . . . JC JIM CROW'S LAST 10
HE STILL TRIES TO ACT IN THE SAME OLD WAY. . . . . JC JIM CROW'S LAST 12
BUT NOT AGAIN THE SAME. . . . . . . LHR DEAR LVLY DEATH 8
THE SAME. . . . . SP BEALE STREET 12
ON YOU JUST THE SAME. . . . . SP MADAM WRONG VIS 8
THE SAME OLD FIX. . . . . SP MADAM NUMBER WR 20
THE SAME OLD SPARK! . . . . SP NEW YORKERS 17
THE SAME THINGS OTHER FOLKS LIKE WHO ARE OTHER RACES. . . . . SP THEME FOR ENG B 26
ONE AND THE SAME: . . . . AYM BLUES IN STEREO 11

SAMMY 1
SAMMY DAVIS AND MARIAN ANDERSON . . SP PROJECTION 16

SAMMYS 1
MAKE A CROWN OF SAMMYS, SIDNEYS, HARRYS, ... PL CROWNS GARLANDS 4

SANCTIFIED 1
NO MATTER HOW SANCTIFIED, ... PL BIBLE BELT 7

SAND 6
BLOOD ON THE SAND . . . . ANS SONG OF SPAIN 16
I PACK A MILLION BAGS O' SAND . . . SH MISSISSIPPI LEV 11
TERROR ON THE SAND - . . . . SP DESERT 7
I AM THE CHILD THEY STOLE FROM THE SAND . . . . SP THE NEGRO MOTHE 7
WHERE THE SAND SEEDS AND THE . . . AYM GOSPEL CHA-CHA 5
WHERE THE SEA SAND AND THE SEA GOURDS . . . . AYM GOSPEL CHA-CHA 32

SANDED 1
SANDED, ... SP DANCER 12

SANDINO 1
SANDINO. . . . . SL SCOTTSBORO 25

SANDS 1
AND ITS SANDS ARE FAIR: . . . . . . SP ISLAND 6

SANDWICH 2
I WAS LOOKIN' FOR A SANDWICH. JUDGE. — SH BRIEF ENCOUNTER 1
AND BITE INTO THE SANDWICH OF YOUR HEART. — PL JIM CROW CAR 2

SANG 2
FORGETS HE EVER SANG — OWT JUICE JOINT 31
HE PLAYED A FEW CHORDS THEN HE SANG SOME MORE - — SP THE WEARY BLUES 24

SANGRE 1
DE SANGRE ES LA GOTA? — AYM RIDE. RED. RIDE 22

SANK 1
SO I JUMPED IN AND SANK. — SP LIFE IS FINE 4

SANTA 4
INVESTIGATE THAT SANTA CLAUS — AYM BIRD IN ORBIT 34
SANTA CLAUS. FORGIVE ME. — AYM ODE TO DINAH 69
SANTA CLAUS. FORGIVE ME. — AYM RIDE. RED. RIDE 23
RIDING IN A JAGUAR. SANTA CLAUS. — AYM RIDE. RED. RIDE 30

SAP 3
WHEN THE SAP RISES IN THE TREES. — ANS CHANT MAY DAY 5
10-VOICES: BE LIKE THE SAP RISING IN THE TREES. — ANS CHANT MAY DAY 15
WORKER: WHEN THE SAP OF YOUR OWN STRENGTH RISES — ANS CHANT MAY DAY 25

SASH 1
DUSKY SASH ACROSS MANHATTAN — SP GOOD MORNING 16

SASS 1
JUST GIMME SOME SASS. — NM BIG-TIMER POEM 28

SASSY 1
NOT MEANIN' TO BE SASSY — SP SOUTHERN MAMMY 19

SAT 4
HE SAT. — OLD THE CONSUMPTIVE 3
HE SAT UPON THE ROLLING DECK — DK SAILOR 1
AND SHE SAT ON HER CHAIR LIKE A SWEET JELLY ROLL. — SH DEATH IN HARLEM 82
I SAT THERE SINGING HER — FW SONGS 1

SATIN 2
THE TORN SUIT OF SATIN AND GOLD. — ANS SONG OF SPAIN 15
YET THEY GOT A SATIN BOX — SP NIGHT FUNERAL 7

SATISFIED 4
AND I CAN'T BE SATISFIED. — SP THE WEARY BLUES 26
AND CAN'T BE SATISFIED - — SP THE WEARY BLUES 28
I WILL NOT BE SATISFIED — SP TO ARTINA 4
I WILL NOT BE SATISFIED — SP TO ARTINA 6

SATISFYING 1
OF GRAB THE GOLD! OF GRAB THE WAYS OF SATISFYING NEED! — ANS LET AMERICA BE 28

SATURDAY 3
GIN ON SATURDAY. — FC BRASS SPITOONS 23
SATURDAY AND SUNDAY'S — SP BLUE MONDAY 6
SATURDAY LAUGHTER. A BAR. A BED. — SP CONSIDER ME 43

SAVAGES 1
SO PROUD THAT SAVAGES — PL NORTHERN LIBERL 7

SAVE 11
AND I'D SAVE MORE THAN I DO NOW. — FC PRIZE FIGHTER 6
SAVE THOSE THAT HISTORY BOOKS CREATE. — SP AFRO-AMER FRAG 5
SAVE THOSE THAT SONGS — SP AFRO-AMER FRAG 6
COULDN'T TELL. TO SAVE HER. — SP BLD FORTUNE TEL 31
OR SAVE. — SP CONSIDER ME 22
SAVE ME. LORD! — SP SUNDAY MORNING 23
SAVE ME! — SP SUNDAY MORNING 24
I WILL NOT SAVE YOU NOW! — SP SUNDAY MORNING 33
SAVE IN MEMORIES OF GANGRENOUS ICING — AYM ODE TO DINAH 78
SAVE FOR ANOTHER DAY. — PL BOMBINGS DIXIE 4
SAVE ME FROM THAT MAN! — PL WHO BUT TH LORD 10

SAVED 2
HAS IT BEEN SAVED. — SP MADAM MINISTER 7
AND BE SAVED - — SP SUNDAY MORNING 38

SAVING 1
BEEN SAVING ALL MY LIFE — PL LITTLE SNG HOUS 2

SAVIOUR 1
THE SAVIOUR PEEPING THROUGH. — LHR PASTORAL 3

SAVOY 1
ON THE DAY WHEN THE SAVOY — SP PROJECTION 1

SAW 17
FOR PIERROT SAW A WORLD OF GIRLS. — WB PIERROT 17
AND I SAW HIM STANDING THERE. STRAIGHT AND TALL. — NM COLORED SL POEM 37
WHEN I SAW MY CHILDREN UNSCHOOLED. — ANS A NEW SONG 12
NEVER SAW THE HIGH SHERIFF'S GUN — ANS BLD OZZIE POWEL 15
THEY NEVER SAW THE HIGH SHERIFF'S EYES — ANS BLD OZZIE POWEL 19
AND THIS IS WHAT I SAW: — ANS NEGRO GHETTO 2
I THOUGHT I SAW RED STARS. MOTHER. — FW WHEN ARMIES PAS 12
THEY THOUGHT THEY SAW — LHR PASTORAL 2
AND I SAW THE SUN GO DOWN. — SP BLUE BAYOU 3
AND I SAW THE SUN GO DOWN. — SP BLUE BAYOU 6
I SAW THE SUN GO DOWN. — SP BLUE BAYOU 19
AND I SAW THE SUN GO DOWN. — SP BLUE BAYOU 24
LAWD. I SAW THE SUN GO DOWN! — SP BLUE BAYOU 27
AND EVERYWHERE I SAW — SP DREAM 3
WE SAW A LINE OF FISHING SHIPS — SP SEASCAPE 3
WE SAW AN INDIAN MERCHANTMAN — SP SEASCAPE 7
I LOOKED AND I SAW — PL WHO BUT TH LORD 1

SAXOPHONE 3
AND ETERNITY AN UNBLOWN SAXOPHONE — FC SPORT 12
THE SAXOPHONE — LHR CONSERVATORY 1
THE SAXOPHONE — LHR CONSERVATORY 5

SAXOPHONES 1
O. SAXOPHONES AT NIGHT! — OWT NEGRO SERVANT 18

SAXOPHONE'S 1
THE SAXOPHONE'S — LHR CONSERVATORY 9

SAY 115
BLUES SINGERS SAY. — WB BLUES FANTASY 3
THEY SAY A JAZZ-BAND'S GAY. — WB CABARET 2
SAY! — WB CAT AND SAXOPHN 15
THEY SAY SHE DIED. - — WB YOUNG BRIDE 1
THEY SAY SHE DIED OF GRIEF — WB YOUNG BRIDE 3
SO THEY SAY. — WB YOUNG PROSTITUT 5
SAY IT VERY SOFTLY. — FC MAMMY 3
SAY IT VERY SLOWLY IF YOU CHOOSE. — FC MAMMY 4
AN' SHE SAY. HONEY. — FC NEW CABARET GRL 9
YOU SAY I'LL MEET A BAD ENDIN'. HEH? — NM BIG-TIMER POEM 33
SAY TO ALL FOEMEN: — NM BLACK CLWN POEM 67
SO I SAY. "MISTER. I AIN'T NO SWEEPIN' MACHINE." — NM BROKE 16
SO DE MAN SAY. "I'LL GET SOMEBODY ELSE. THEN. TO CLEAN." - — NM BROKE 17
I SAY. "NOW. BABY. YOU KNOW I AIN'T GOT NONE. HONEY." — NM BROKE 20
WILLING WORKER? UN-UH! YES! WHAT'S THAT YOU SAY? — NM BROKE 33
ALL THESE YEARS YOU SAY YOU BEEN WORKIN' HERE? — NM BROKE 68
DOES I WANTA? WELL. CAN'T SAY BUT WHAT I MIGHT - — NM BROKE 71
LET'S GET MARRIED RIGHT NOW! YES! WHAT DO YOU SAY? — NM BROKE 75
HIS SEA-SOUL SAY TO ME: — DK DEATH SEAMAN 4
THERE'S NOTHING MORE TO SAY. — DK I LOVED FRIEND 3
I CANNOT SAY YOU EVERYWHERE. — DK PASSING LOVE 4
THIS THING TO SAY. — ANS A NEW SONG 5
BITTER WAS THE DAY. I SAY. — ANS A NEW SONG 17
NO LONGER SHALL YOU SAY — ANS A NEW SONG 30
SAY WHO ARE YOU THAT MUMBLES IN THE DARK? — ANS LET AMERICA BE 17
I SAY IT PLAIN. — ANS LET AMERICA BE 76
LET US TOGETHER. SAY: — ANS OPEN LETTER 38
SAY. AIN'T YOU AFRAID — ANS PARK BENCH 8
SAY! ON THE LAST THING I OWN. — SH BLD PAWNBROKER 21
SAY! YOU KNOW I BELIEVE I'LL CHANGE MY NAME. — SH DAYBREAK 9
I SAY MY LIFE AIN'T NOTHIN' — SH LOVE AGAIN BLUS 3
WOMAN. LISTEN! SAY! — SH MIDNIGHT CHIPPI 16
I SAY DON'T STAND ON NO CORNER — SH MIDNIGHT CHIPPI 27
I SAY DID YOU EVER TRY LIVIN' — SH OUT OF WORK 21
DON'T HAVE TO HEAR NOBODY SAY. — SH PAY DAY 3
THEY SAY YOUR SWEET MAMA — SH SHAKESPEARE 7
I SAY SIX-BITS' WORTH O' TICKET — SH SIX-BITS BLUES 3
BUT SAY. BIG BUDDY. — JC BIG BUDDY 7
SAY BIG BUDDY. — JC BIG BUDDY 18
I STILL CAN'T SAY. — JC GOOD MORN STLIN 9
I MEAN IT WHEN I SAY. — JC GOOD MORN STLIN 54
"WAIT. BE PATIENT." YOU SAY. — JC THE BITTER RIVR 39
TROUBLE MAKER!" YOU SAY. — JC THE BITTER RIVR 48
I DO OR SAY. — FW FAITHFUL ONE 10
HARLEMITES SAY — OWT BLD MARGE POLIT 26
I'D SAY. — OWT FUNERAL 6
BABY. SAY WHEN. — OWT RAID 5
DOESN'T SAY WHEN. — OWT RAID 7
WHAT SHALL I SAY? — OWT TOO BLUE 7
YOU CAN SAY — OWT VISITORS 9
SAY NOT SO! — SP BAR 2
TEN BUCKS YOU SAY I OWE YOU? — SP BLD LANDLORD 9
TEN BUCKS YOU SAY IS DUE? — SP BLD LANDLORD 10
YOU AIN'T GONNA BE ABLE TO SAY A WORD — SP BLD LANDLORD 19
SOME FOLKS SAY. — SP CAFE: 3 A.M. 5
UNTIL HE MADE FOLKS SAY. — SP DANCER 14
HE USED TO SAY. — SP DEAD IN THERE 17
WORK WITH ME AND NOT AGAINST ME. SAY. — SP DEFERRED 37
FOLKS SAY SHE DON'T LIKE — SP DELINQUENT 3

FOLKS SAY IT'S NOT JUST . . . . . . SP DELINQUENT 7
I TIRE SO OF HEARING PEOPLE SAY. . SP DEMOCRACY 10
WHAT DID I SAY? . . . . SP DREAM BOOGIE 14
I SAY, WHERE IS THAT SUGAR . . . . SP EARLY EVENING 3
YOU AIN'T GONNA HAVE NOTHIN TO SAY. SP EARLY EVENING 12
THE PEOPLE SAY IT IS PROMISES - THAT WILL COME TRUE. . . . . SP FREEDOM'S PLOW 144
THE PEOPLE DO NOT ALWAYS SAY THINGS OUT LOUD. . . . . SP FREEDOM'S PLOW 145
HALTINGLY AND STUMBLINGLY SAY THEM. SP FREEDOM'S PLOW 150
AND THE TRYING TO SAY. . . . . . . SP FREEDOM'S PLOW 155
THE G.I.'S WHO FOUGHT WILL SAY, WE WANTED IT SO! . . . . SP FREEDOM TRAIN 60
BLACK MEN AND WHITE WILL SAY, AIN'T IT FINE? . . . . SP FREEDOM TRAIN 61
WE SAY, NO! . . . . SP FREEDOM'S PLOW 179
WE SAY, NO! . . . . SP FREEDOM'S PLOW 182
WE SAY, NO! . . . . SP FREEDOM'S PLOW 187
YOU SAY YOU THOUGHT EVERYBODY WAS CALLED MISTER? . . . . SP IN EXPLANATION 5
HELL NO SHUT UP! SAY THE PEOPLE . . SP IN EXPLANATION 27
SAY TO ME. . . . . SP I, TOO 12
"THEY SAY" . . . "THEY SAY" . . . "THEY SAY" . . . . SP JOE LOUIS 8
"THEY SAY" . . . "THEY SAY" . . . "THEY SAY" . . . . SP JOE LOUIS 8
"THEY SAY" . . . "THEY SAY" . . . "THEY SAY" . . . . SP JOE LOUIS 8
"THEY SAY" . . . . SP JOE LOUIS 10
I SAY I HOPE MY CHILD'LL . . . . . SP LAMENT OVER LOV 3
MY GIRL-FRIEND SEND HER LOVE AND SAY SP LETTER 6
FELLOW, SAY? . . . . SP LOW TO HIGH 11
YOU SAY I O.K.ED . . . . SP MADAM PHONE BIL 1
YOU SAY, I WILL PAY IT - . . . . . SP MADAM PHONE BIL 10
JUST TO SAY HE LOVES ME! . . . . . SP MADAM PHONE BIL 23
YOU SAY YOU DON'T CARE . . . . . . SP MADAM PHONE BIL 32
YOU SAY I GAVE MY O.K.? . . . . . . SP MADAM PHONE BIL 38
SO I CAN BRUSH YOUR BACK, I SAY! . SP MAMA AND DAUGHT 21
IN AUSTRALIA, TOO, THEY SAY. . . . SP MIGRANT 26
I MUST SAY . . . . SP PORTER 1
YOUNG GIRL'LL SAY. . . . . SP PREFERENCE 4
BUT A OLD WOMAN'LL SAY. . . . . . . SP PREFERENCE 7
AND FATHER DIVINE WILL SAY IN TRUTH. SP PROJECTION 20
WHORES IN FINAL WEARINESS SAY: . . SP SLIVER SERMON 3
AND THE LORD WILL SAY. . . . . . . SP SUNDAY MORNING 25
THE LORD WILL SAY. . . . . SP SUNDAY MORNING 28
THE LORD WILL SAY. . . . . SP SUNDAY MORNING 31
FOR SHE, THEY SAY. . . . . SP THE SOUTH 25
WITH THE LITTLE WORDS YOU SAY TO ME. SP TO ARTINA 5
THEY SAY. . . . . SP TO BE SOMEBODY 22
I SAY PUT YOU IN THE GROUND AND . . SP WIDOW WOMAN 9
I SAY DON'T WANT NOBODY ELSE . . . SP WIDOW WOMAN 21
WHAT DID SHE SAY? . . . . AYM ASK YOUR MAMA 13
HEAR THE OLD FOLKS SAY HOW . . . . AYM BIRD IN ORBIT 40
SAY HOW WHITE THE COTTON COTTON . . AYM BIRD IN ORBIT 42
BUT SAY IT - . . . . PL BIBLE BELT 11
CULTURE, THEY SAY, IS A TWO-WAY STREET: . . . . PL CULTURAL EXCHNG 58
I TIRE SO OF HEARING PEOPLE SAY. . PL FREEDOM 10
GO SLOW, THEY SAY - . . . . PL GO SLOW 1
AND SAY, "SEE! . . . . PL NORTHERN LIBERL 3
YOU SAY HE DIED WITH HONOR . . . . PL OFFICIAL NOTICE 7
SO FOLKS SAY. . . . . PL STOKELY MALCOLM 14
MAKE ME SAY I DID IT. . . . . PL THIRD DEGREE 2
WILL NOT SAY. . . . . PL WHERE WHEN WHCH 13
SWEET AND WONDERFUL TO SAY. . . . . PL WORDS LIKE FREE 2

SAYING 2
DO YOU READ MUSIC? AND LOUIS SAYING $ $ . . . . AYM HORN OF PLENTY 11
FOR CINQUE SAYING, "RUN A NEW FLAG UP THE MAST." . . . . PL FINAL CALL 21

SAYIN' 1
A GUY WAS SAYIN' . . . . FC DEATH DO DIRTY 28

SAYS 42
SAYS CLORINDA. . . . . FC BEALE ST. LOVE 7
JUDGE PIERCE HE SAYS, MARY. . . . . FC BLD OF GIN MARY 5
OLD JUDGE SAYS, MARY JANE. . . . . FC BLD OF GIN MARY 6
OLD JUDGE SAYS YOU'S A DRUNKARD. . FC BLD OF GIN MARY 13
OLD HARD-FACED JUDGE SAYS EIGHTEEN MONTHS . . . . FC BLD OF GIN MARY 23
AN' SAYS YO' BOY IS GETTIN' BEAT. FC DEATH DO DIRTY 24
MY GOD, I SAYS. . . . . FC NEW CABARET GRL 21
UM-MM! SIGN HERE SAYS THEY WANTS SOMEBODY TO SHOVEL COAL. . . . . NM BROKE 28
SAYS: . . . . ANS LYNCHING SONG 14
SHE SAYS TO THE WAITER. . . . . . . SH DEATH IN HARLEM 41
SAYS TO TEXAS. . . . . SH DEATH IN HARLEM 43
SAYS TO LUCY. . . . . SH DEATH IN HARLEM 45
SAYS TO THE WORLD. . . . . SH DEATH IN HARLEM 47
SAYS IF YOU WAS TO ASK ME . . . . . SH EVENIN' BLUES 21
SAYS I CAN'T HELP LOVIN' YOU . . . SH IN TROUBLED KEY 9
AND SAYS. . . . . JC FREEDOM 13
SAYS, I KNOW IT'S HIM! . . . . . . OWT HONEY BABE 12
GYPSY SAYS I'D KILL MY SELF . . . . SP BAD LUCK CARD 11
SAYS, DID YOU EVER SEE THE SUN RISE SP BLACK MARIA 14
SAYS I HATES TO BE LONELY. . . . . SP BOUND NO'TH BLS 15
SHE SAYS HE CAN HAVE . . . . SP BUDDY 6
SAYS SHE DON'T CARE! . . . . SP DELINQUENT 14
THE POET SAYS IT WAS PROMISES. . . SP FREEDOM'S PLOW 143
MAMA SAYS, PRAISE JESUS! . . . . . SP GRADUATION 20
MAMA SAYS, PRAISE JESUS! . . . . . SP GRADUATION 25
MAMA SAYS. . . . . SP GRADUATION 27
SAYS DADDY I HAVE GOT THE BLUES. . SP HARD DADDY 2
SAYS DADDY I HAVE GOT THE BLUES. . SP HARD DADDY 4
MA DADDY SAYS, HONEY. . . . . SP HARD DADDY 5
SHUT UP, SAYS GERALD L.K. SMITH. . SP IN EXPLANATION 23
SHUT UP, SAYS THE GOVERNOR OF SOUTH CAROLINA. . . . . SP IN EXPLANATION 24
SHUT UP, SAYS THE GOVERNOR OF SINGAPORE. . . . . SP IN EXPLANATION 25
SHUT UP, SAYS STRYDOM. . . . . . . SP IN EXPLANATION 26
HISTORY SAYS IT'S TIME. . . . . . . SP IN EXPLANATION 30
THAT SAYS A MOUTHFUL . . . . SP IN EXPLANATION 32
AND DON'T MEAN HALF IT SAYS - . . . SP IN EXPLANATION 33
JUST MAN WOMAN TIRED SAYS: . . . . SP IN EXPLANATION 55
SAYS DON'T BE 'FRAID . . . . SP JUDGMENT DAY 8
HE SAYS, "MARY, I'M . . . . SP LOVER'S RETURN 5
SAYS THIS PARTICULAR . . . . SP TOMORROW 4
TO SPEND, HE SAYS. . . . . SP YOUNG SAILOR 9
SAYS SUGAR'S GONE UP ANOTHER TWO CENTS. . . . . PL HARLEM 9

SCANTY 1
SELLING HER SCANTY WARES . . . . . SP MEXICAN MARKET 3

SCARED 3
WHO ARE SCARED OF ME . . . . SP ONE-WAY TICKET 21
I WAS SCARED TO WALK OUT . . . . . SP SITUATION 3
I BEEN SCARED AND BATTERED. . . . . PL STILL HERE 1

SCARLET 1
ARE DRESSED IN SCARLET AND GOLD . . WB POEME D'AUTOMNE 5

SCARRED 1
SO DEEPLY SCARRED. . . . . WB SOLEDAD 10

SCARS 2
I AM THE NEGRO BEARING SLAVERY'S SCARS. . . . . ANS LET AMERICA BE 20
AND MY GRANDFATHER'S BACK WITH ITS LADDER OF SCARS. . . . . JC THE BITTER RIVR 36

SCATTER 3
TO SCATTER STAR-DUST IN THEIR EYES. SP GRADUATION 24
AND SCATTER . . . . SP GYPSY MELODIES 2
THE BRIGHT STARS SCATTER EVERYWHERE. SP MULATTO 39

SCATTERED 3
HELPLESS, STUPID, SCATTERED, AND ALONE - AS NOW - . . . . ANS OPEN LETTER 28
SCATTERED ALL OVER THE SNOW. . . . FW WHEN ARMIES PAS 13
MY HOPES THE WIND DONE SCATTERED. PL STILL HERE 2

SCATTERS 1
SCATTERS HATE LIKE SEED . . . . . . PL GEORGIA DUSK 10

SCENT 6
THE FLOWER NO SCENT ENCLOSES. . . . FW REMEMBRANCE 4
THE SCENT OF PINE WOOD STINGS THE SOFT NIGHT AIR. . . . . SP MULATTO 18
SHARP PINE SCENT IN THE EVENING AIR. SP MULATTO 22
PINE WOOD SCENT IN THE EVENING AIR. SP MULATTO 40
SCENT SALTY-COLORED . . . . SP SEASHORE THROUG 12
AND THE SCENT OF PINE NEEDLES . . . PL DAYBREAK IN ALA 8

SCHEME 1
WHERE NEVER KINGS CONNIVE NOR TYRANTS SCHEME . . . . ANS LET AMERICA BE 8

SCHOOL 14
AND THE SCHOOL TEACHERS . . . . . . FC JAZZ BAND 7
LAWD, IN SUNDAY SCHOOL. . . . . . . FC LISTEN HERE 8
ALWAYS IN SUNDAY SCHOOL. . . . . . FC LISTEN HERE 10
BUT THEY GIVIN' 'EM TO SCHOOL BOYS NOW AND PAYIN' JUST ABOUT HALF. NM BROKE 43
DRESSED, CARRYING HIS BOOKS TO SCHOOL. . . . . NM DARK YOUTH USA 1
COMES TO A NORTHERN SCHOOL . . . . FW MIGRATION 2
NIGHT SCHOOL! . . . . OWT JITNEY 30
QUIT SCHOOL TO WORK - . . . . SP DEFERRED 17
THE WAY YOU SEND YOUR KIDS TO SCHOOL SP HIGH TO LOW 10
A SCHOOL TEACHER . . . . SP JOE LOUIS 2
I WENT TO SCHOOL THERE, THEN DURHAM, THEN HERE . . . . SP THEME FOR ENG B 8
NEW JERSEY HIGH SCHOOL! . . . . . . AYM BIRD IN ORBIT 78
WHO WENT TO SUNDAY SCHOOL THAT DAY PL BIRMINGHAM SUND 2
IN CHRISTIAN SUNDAY SCHOOL . . . . PL BIRMINGHAM SUND 22

SCHOOLMATES 1
LOTS OF OLD SCHOOLMATES ARE MARRIED NOW; . . . . NM BIG-TIMER POEM 45

SCHOOLS 7
NO SCHOOLS, NO WORK - . . . . NM BLACK CLWN POEM 39
DIDN'T HAVE ANY SCHOOLS: AND THERE
WERE ALL SORTS OF . . . . NM COLORED SL POEM 25
SCHOOLS WILL BE NAMED: . . . . . . ANS CHANT TOM MOONY 32
BUT NIGHT SCHOOLS TEACH FRENCH. . . SP DEFERRED 24
SCHOOLS ARE BETTER FOR THEIR
CHILDREN $ . . . . AYM HORN OF PLENTY 24
GIVE ME SECOND-CLASS SCHOOLS. . . . PL BACKLASH BLUES 8
AND SECOND-CLASS SCHOOLS. . . . . . PL BACKLASH BLUES 10

SCORCHED 1
AND THE FIRE SCORCHED MY FEET. . . ANS A NEW SONG 20

SCORE 1
I SAID, WHAT'S THE SCORE? . . . . . SP MADAM WRONG VIS 4

SCORN 1
SCORN CRUSHING ME DOWN. . . . . . . NM BLACK CLWN POEM 52

SCORNFUL 1
WITH ARROGANT EYES AND SCORNFUL
LIPS: . . . . ANS A NEW SONG 31

SCOTT 1
TO CONFOUND EVEN HAZEL SCOTT . . . SP TO BE SOMEBODY 11

SCOTTSBORO'S 1
SCOTTSBORO'S JUST A LITTLE PLACE: SL TOWN OF SCOTTSB 1

SCOTTSBORO 1
THE SCOTTSBORO BOYS BEHIND STEEL
BARS. . . . . JC THE BITTER RIVR 29

SCRAGGLY 1
LOOK ALL SCRAGGLY AND BAD. . . . . SP WARNING AUGMENT 10

SCRANTON 1
BUFFALO, SCRANTON. . . . . SP ONE-WAY TICKET 5

SCRAP 1
ON THE SCRAP HEAP OF TIME - . . . . ANS CHANT TOM MOONY 28

SCRATCH 1
I'D SCRATCH OUT BOTH HIS EYES. . . SP HARD DADDY 18

SCRATCHING 1
SCRATCHING IN THE DEAD FIRE'S ASHES SP THE SOUTH 7

SCRATCHY 1
BLOWS A SCRATCHY SOUND. . . . . . . PL CULTURAL EXCHNG 4

SCREAM 3
SOME BEGAN TO SCREAM. . . . . SP DEATH IN HARLEM 110
SEND FOR ROBESPIERRE TO SCREAM, "CA
IRA! CA IRA! . . . . PL FINAL CALL 15
SCREAM JUMPS OUT . . . . PL THIRD DEGREE 8

SCREAMING 1
SCREAMING PEDALS . . . . SP DREAM BOOGE VAR 7

SCREAMS 2
AND RIDE THE JIM CROW CAR UNTIL IT
SCREAMS . . . . PL JIM CROW CAR 3
AND EARS THAT CLOSE TO HARLEM
SCREAMS. . . . . PL JUNIOR ADDICT 5

SCREEN 3
WHILE MOVIES ECHO DRAMAS ON THE
SCREEN. . . . . OWT LINCOLN THEATRE 2
A VELVET SCREEN. . . . . SP FULFILMENT 15
ON THE BIG SCREEN OF THE WELFARE
CHECK . . . . AYM ODE TO DINAH 98

SCRIPT 1
WOULD HARDLY WRITE IT IN THE SCRIPT
- . . . . AYM IS IT TRUE? 50

SCRIPT-WRITERS 1
BUT SCRIPT-WRITERS WHO KNOW BETTER AYM IS IT TRUE? 49

SCRUB 1
WASH, IRON, AND SCRUB. . . . . . . SP MADAM HER MADAM 9

SCUM 2
ALL THE SCUM . . . . FW PRAYER 5
ALL THE SCUM . . . . SP LITANY 5

SEA 38
STAINING THE DARK SEA RED. . . . . WB CARIBBEAN SUNST 3
OUT OF HIS GRAVE FROM OVER THE SEA. NM COLORED SL POEM 14
BUT HIS SOUL WENT OUT TO SEA. . . . DK DEATH SEAMAN 2
FOR I AM HAPPY WITH MY SEA. . . . . DK DEATH SEAMAN 10
SEA CHARM . . . . DK SEA CHARM 1
BUT THAT THE SEA IS STRONG . . . . DK SEA CHARM 5
BUT THAT SEA WIND IS SWEET . . . . DK SEA CHARM 8
AND THAT THE SEA HOLDS . . . . . . DK SEA CHARM 10
THE ROAR OF THE SEA. . . . . ANS CHANT MAY DAY 2
10-OTHERS: WORKERS IN THE ISLANDS OF
THE SEA - . . . . ANS CHANT MAY DAY 23
SWIMMING IN THE SEA. . . . . SH DECLARATION 2
YOU CAN CATCH THE SEA. . . . . . . SH FREE MAN 2
I CAN LOOK WAY ACROSS THE SEA . . . JC GOOD MORN STLIN 31
DARING THE SEA - . . . . JC TO CAPTAIN MULZ 68
THE SEA IS DEEP. . . . . FW EXITS 1
LOOKING OUT TO SEA . . . . FW JAIME 6
THAT CROSS THE SEA. . . . . FW OLD SAILOR 4
FROM SALT SEA WATER . . . . FW SAILING DATE 4
SORROW LIKE A SEA. . . . . SP FEET O' JESUS 2
SHIPS CAME FROM ACROSS THE SEA . . SP FREEDOM'S PLOW 29
THE SEA IS A WILDERNESS OF WAVES. SP LONG TRIP 1
ON THE SEA. . . . . SP LONG TRIP 6
THE SEA IS A DESERT OF WAVES. . . . SP LONG TRIP 9
IN FROM THE SEA! . . . . SP PORT TOWN 2
OUT O' THE SEA. . . . . SP PORT TOWN 14
ON RELIEF WAY ACROSS THE SEA . . . SP RELIEF 3
SEA FOOD JOINTS . . . . SP SEASHORE THROUG 11
FROM THE DEAD WEIGHT OF SEA. . . . SP SPIRITUALS 14
I AM THE DARK GIRL WHO CROSSED THE
WIDE SEA . . . . SP THE NEGRO MOTHE 9
THAT IS LONGING FOR THE SEA . . . . SP TRUMPET PLAYER 30
BUT LADS PUT OUT TO SEA . . . . . . SP WATER-FRONT STP 6
AND THE GREEN SEA . . . . SP YOUNG SAILOR 16
SEA GOURDS MAKE MARACAS OUT OF ME. AYM GOSPEL CHA-CHA 6
WHERE THE SEA SAND AND THE SEA
GOURDS . . . . AYM GOSPEL CHA-CHA 32
WHERE THE SEA SAND AND THE SEA
GOURDS . . . . AYM GOSPEL CHA-CHA 32
ONLY IN THE SEA. . . . . AYM IS IT TRUE? 37
IN A SUPERMARKET SEA. . . . . PL CULTURAL EXCHNG 22
LIKE WAVES OF SEA . . . . PL UNDERTOW 11

SEALED 1
IS SEALED. . . . . PL OFFICIAL NOTICE 14

SEAMEN 1
OLD SEAMEN . . . . FW SAILING DATE 7

SEARCH 1
IN SEARCH OF WHAT I MEANT TO BE MY
HOME - . . . . ANS LET AMERICA BE 46

SEARCHED 1
WHO SEARCHED FOR LOVERS . . . . . . WB TO LITTLE LOVER 2

SEAS 6
WANDERERS OF THE HILLS AND SEAS. . WB A FAREWELL 2
AND HAVE NEVER SEEN THE SEAS. . . . WB A FAREWELL 8
O, I'M THE MAN WHO SAILED THOSE
EARLY SEAS . . . . ANS LET AMERICA BE 45
THAT SAILS THESE DANGEROUS SEAS - JC TO CAPTAIN MULZ 40
SPLASH INTO THE RIVERS AND THE SEAS
WENT THE BOAT-HULLS . . . . . . SP FREEDOM'S PLOW 57
OF THE WIDE SEAS. . . . . SP YOUNG SAILOR 7

SEASONS 2
SEASONS COME, SEASONS GO, ... FW CIRCLES 4
SEASONS COME, SEASONS GO, ... FW CIRCLES 4

SEATTLE 2
SEATTLE, NEW ORLEANS, ... SP FREEDOM'S PLOW 87
SEATTLE, OAKLAND, SALT LAKE, . . . SP ONE-WAY TICKET 12

SEA-LION 1
IF I WAS A SEA-LION . . . . SH DECLARATION 1

SEA-SOUL 1
HIS SEA-SOUL SAY TO ME: . . . . . . DK DEATH SEAMAN 4

SEA'S 2
THE SEA'S OWN CHILDREN . . . . . . DK SEA CHARM 2
WHERE THE SEA'S A BAR-GLASS . . . . SP TRUMPET PLAYER 31

SECOND-CLASS 5
YOU GIVE ME SECOND-CLASS HOUSES. . PL BACKLASH BLUES 7
GIVE ME SECOND-CLASS SCHOOLS. . . . PL BACKLASH BLUES 8
SECOND-CLASS HOUSES . . . . PL BACKLASH BLUES 9
AND SECOND-CLASS SCHOOLS. . . . . . PL BACKLASH BLUES 10
ARE SECOND-CLASS FOOLS. . . . . . . PL BACKLASH BLUES 12

SECRET 1
THE FRENCH MAY HAVE THE SECRET. . . AYM IS IT TRUE? 17

SECTION 3
WHERE IS THE JIM CROW SECTION . . . PL MERRY-GO-ROUND 3
IN SOME OTHER SECTION . . . . PL MISSISSIPPI 11
IN THE SECTION OF THE NIGGERS . . . PL PRIME 10

SECURE 1
SMUG, ALMOST SECURE . . . . PL UN-AMERICAN 2

SEDAR 1
ALIOUNE AIME SEDAR SIPS HIS
NEGRITUDE. . . . . AYM BIRD IN ORBIT 23

SEDUCED 1
WHO SEDUCED MARIE LAVEAU? . . . . . AYM GOSPEL CHA-CHA 42

SEDUCTIVE 1
SEDUCTIVE AS A DARK-EYED WHORE. . . SP THE SOUTH 14

SEE 80
I'M THE BAD EGG, SEE! . . . . NM BIG-TIMER POEM 9
BUT YOU DON'T SEE NO PRESIDENTS
DYIN' O' GRIEF - . . . . NM BROKE 57
YOU GOT A GOOD JOB? YES! WELL, I SHO
AM GLAD TO SEE YOU, DEAR! . . . NM BROKE 69
CAN'T SEE! AND DON'T KNOW! AND WON'T
EVER CARE! . . . . NM COLORED SL POEM 53
AM I TOO OLD TO SEE THE FAIRIES
DANCE? . . . . DK AFTR MNY SPRNGS 7
THAT I CAN NEITHER HEAR NOR FEEL NOR
SEE. . . . . DK BEGGAR BOY 2
LET'S GO SEE OLD ABE . . . . DK LINCOLN MONUMNT 1
CAUSE IF I DON'T SEE MA BABY . . . DK WIDE RIVER 17
NOW WE SEE . . . . ANS OPEN LETTER 53
WORKERS, SEE YOURSELVES AS SPAIN! ANS SONG OF SPAIN 58
AND SEE WHAT COUNT BASIE'S PLAYING
NEW. . . . . SH BED TIME 2
DO I SEE A COUPLE? OR DID I COUNT
TWICE? . . . . SH BED TIME 13
I DIDN'T WANT TO SEE! . . . . SH BRIEF ENCOUNTER 12
AND YOU NEVER WOULD SEE ME. . . . . SH DECLARATION 4
SEE ME. . . . . SH DECLARATION 7
JUST LOOK AT ME AND SEE! . . . . . SH EVENIN' BLUES 24
I EVER DID SEE. . . . . SH ONLY WOMAN BLUS 4
AND SEE WHAT IT WOULD DO TO YOU? . SH OUT OF WORK 24
STAY AWAY IF YOU WANT TO, AND SEE IF
I CARE! . . . . SH SUPPER TIME 10
I STILL CAN'T SEE . . . . JC BLACK MAN SPEAK 2
AND SEE WHERE SIMPLE WORKING FOLKS
LIKE ME . . . . JC GOOD MORN STLIN 32
I WOULD LIKE TO SEE THOSE FREEDOMS JC HOW ABOUT DIXIE 3
TO SEE JIM CROW GET OUT OF HAND. . JC JIM CROW'S LAST 4
SEE! WHEN YOU WIPE THE MUD AWAY. . FW WHEN ARMIES PAS 21
I CAN SEE YOUR HOUSE, BABE. . . . . OWT CURIOUS 1
BUT I CAN'T SEE YOU. . . . . OWT CURIOUS 2
I CAN SEE YOUR HOUSE. . . . . OWT CURIOUS 3
BUT I CAN'T SEE YOU. . . . . OWT CURIOUS 4
SEE WHAT THIS WEEK'S JIVE IS ALL
ABOUT: . . . . OWT JITNEY 25
IS WHO I WANT TO SEE. . . . . OWT LONESOME CORNER 8
NOW I SEE THE THUNDER . . . . SP AFRICA 3
NOW I SEE . . . . SP AFRICA 6
YOU SEE DEM TRUCKS . . . . SP BABY 4
THAT I SEE. . . . . SP BLACK MARIA 2
THE BLACK MARIA THAT I SEE - . . . SP BLACK MARIA 3
SEE THE SUN . . . . SP BLACK MARIA 12
SAYS, DID YOU EVER SEE THE SUN RISE SP BLACK MARIA 14
I DON'T SEE HIM MUCH. . . . . SP BUDDY 3
AND AS FAR AS I COULD SEE . . . . . SP CROSSING 16
ALL I WANT IS TO SEE . . . . SP DEFERRED 34
BABY, COULD YOU SEE YOUR WAY CLEAR? SP DEFERRED 38
YOUR EYES SEE FOREVER? . . . . . . SP DEMAND 9
THE EYES SEE THERE MATERIALS FOR
BUILDING. . . . . SP FREEDOM'S PLOW 15
SEE THE DIFFICULTIES, TOO, AND THE
OBSTACLES. . . . . SP FREEDOM'S PLOW 16
GETS IN LINE TO SEE THE FREEDOM. . SP FREEDOM TRAIN 38
WELL, YOU CAN SEE. . . . . SP HIGH TO LOW 23
I SEE THE ISLAND . . . . SP ISLAND 3
I SEE THE ISLAND . . . . SP ISLAND 5
THEY'LL SEE HOW BEAUTIFUL I AM . . SP I, TOO 16
SEE THE PEOPLE PASSING BY? . . . . SP KID IN THE PARK 3
SEE THE AIRPLANES IN THE SKY? . . . SP KID IN THE PARK 4
SEE THE BIRDS . . . . SP KID IN THE PARK 5
SEE THAT LADY . . . . SP LADY'S BOOGIE 1
AND YOU MAY SEE ME CRY - . . . . . SP LIFE IS FINE 28
IF YOU GONNA SEE ME DIE. . . . . . SP LIFE IS FINE 30
AND I SEE A LITTLE TREE. . . . . . SP LITTLE GRN TREE 10
I SEE A LITTLE TREE. . . . . SP LITTLE GRN TREE 12
DON'T YOU SEE? . . . . SP MADAM RENT MAN 22
BUT I HANKERED TO SEE . . . . SP MADAM'S CALLING 7
TO SEE MY SUGAR-SWEET. . . . . . . SP MAMA AND DAUGHT 4
AND I COULD SEE . . . . SP NIGHTMARE BOOGE 2
THE WHOLE WORLD SEE . . . . SP PARADE 31
FOR THE WORLD TO SEE . . . . SP SILHOUETTE 8
IS ALL YOU SEE. . . . . SP SNAIL 6
I COULD NOT SEE . . . . SP SO LONG 7
I DID NOT SEE YOUR FACE! . . . . . SP SUNDAY MORNING 30
I FEEL AND SEE AND HEAR, HARLEM, I
HEAR YOU: . . . . SP THEME FOR ENG B 18
BABY, HOW COME YOU CAN'T SEE ME . . SP ULTIMATUM 1
TO SEE MA OLD AUNT CLEW. . . . . . SP YOUNG GAL'S BLS 8
TO SEE MA OLD AUNT CLEW. . . . . . SP YOUNG GAL'S BLS 10
I'LL WANT TO SEE SOMEBODY, TOO. . . SP YOUNG GAL'S BLS 12
I WANT TO SEE MY MOTHER MOTHER . . AYM RIDE, RED, RIDE 1
DID YOU EVER SEE TEN NEGROES . . . AYM SHOW FARE PLESE 20
IF YOU WANT TO SEE ME. . . . . . . PL DOWN WHERE I AM 15
AND I GET TO SEE 'EM RIDE. . . . . PL FLORIDA WORKERS 16
A SUNRISE THAT HE CANNOT SEE . . . PL JUNIOR ADDICT 8
AS SOON AS YOU SEE . . . . PL LITTLE SNG HOUS 6
AND SAY, "SEE! . . . . PL NORTHERN LIBERL 3
THEY COULD NOT SEE . . . . PL PEACE 6
WE'LL SEE. . . . . PL WHO BUT TH LORD 23

SEED 11
IS A STRONG SEED . . . . SP DEMOCRACY 16
GUARDING IN THEIR HEARTS THE SEED OF
FREEDOM. . . . . SP FREEDOM'S PLOW 124
GUARDING IN THEIR HEARTS THE SEED OF
FREEDOM. . . . . SP FREEDOM'S PLOW 46
INTO THAT FURROW THE FREEDOM SEED
WAS DROPPED. . . . . SP FREEDOM'S PLOW 194
FROM THAT SEED A TREE GREW, IS
GROWING, WILL EVER GROW. . . . . SP FREEDOM'S PLOW 195
BLACK SEED FOR EYES . . . . SP SUMMER EVENING 3
I SEED THE RIVER JERDEN . . . . . . SP SYLVESTER'S BED 19
CARRYING IN MY BODY THE SEED OF THE
FREE. . . . . SP THE NEGRO MOTHE 10
I WAS THE SEED OF THE COMING FREE. SP THE NEGRO MOTHE 30
IS A STRONG SEED . . . . PL FREEDOM 16
SCATTERS HATE LIKE SEED . . . . . . PL GEORGIA DUSK 10

SEEDS 1
WHERE THE SAND SEEDS AND THE . . . AYM GOSPEL CHA-CHA 5

SEEIN' 1
SO WHEN I GOT READY TO GO, I SAID,
"I'LL BE SEEIN' YOU SOON, MARIE." NM BROKE 52

SEEK 9
I GO TO SEEK MY FORTUNE. . . . . . WB A FAREWELL 3
I AM THE IMMIGRANT CLUTCHING THE
HOPE I SEEK - . . . . ANS LET AMERICA BE 22
EVERY TONE I SEEK . . . . FW SILENCE 7
TO SEEK A STONE . . . . FW SNAKE 6
DARK DANCERS DANCE AND DREAMERS SEEK
A STAR . . . . OWT JUICE JOINT 39
TO SEEK A NEW BROWN LOVE. . . . . . SP A BLACK PIERROT 15
YET YOU SEEK. . . . . SP A HOUSE IN TAOS 26
HER SEEK THE BURNING SUNLIGHT . . . SP STRANGE HURT 9
SO NOW I SEEK THE NORTH - . . . . . SP THE SOUTH 23

SEEKERS 1
ADVENTURERS AND BOOTY SEEKERS. . . SP FREEDOM'S PLOW 31

SEEKING 17
WHEN FOR YEARS, I HAD BEEN SEEKING OLD AESTHETE HARLEM 4
SEEKING THE TRUTH . . . . NM DARK YOUTH USA 9
SEEKING THE KNOWLEDGE THAT RIGHTS
ALL WRONG - . . . . NM DARK YOUTH USA 17
SEEKING A HOME WHERE HE HIMSELF IS
FREE. . . . . ANS LET AMERICA BE 4
THEN THE MIND STARTS SEEKING A WAY. SP FREEDOM'S PLOW 10
SEEKING A GREATER FREEDOM. . . . . SP FREEDOM'S PLOW 42
WENT FINDING AND SEEKING. . . . . . SP OLD WALT 2
SEEKING MORE THAN FOUND. . . . . . SP OLD WALT 4
OF THE SEEKING OR THE FINDING. . . SP OLD WALT 6
IN SEEKING AS IN FINDING. . . . . . SP OLD WALT 8
OLD WALT WENT SEEKING . . . . SP OLD WALT 10
SEEKING AN ANSWER TO HER QUESTIONS. SP RUBY BROWN 20
SEEKING SUBURB WITH NO JUKEBOX . . AYM HORN OF PLENTY 69
SEEKING LAWNS AND SHADE TREES . . . AYM HORN OF PLENTY 71
SEEKING PEACE AND QUIET . . . . . . AYM HORN OF PLENTY 72
IN SEEKING AUTHORITY? . . . . PL GHOSTS OF 1619 20
I HAVE BEEN SEEKING . . . . PL STOKELY MALCOLM 1

SEEKS 7
SHE SEEKS YOUR HAND. . . . . FW SLEEP 4
THE MIND SEEKS A WAY TO OVERCOME
THESE OBSTACLES. . . . . SP FREEDOM'S PLOW 17
THE HAND SEEKS TOOLS TO CUT THE
WOOD. . . . . SP FREEDOM'S PLOW 18
THEN THE HAND SEEKS OTHER HANDS TO
HELP. . . . . SP FREEDOM'S PLOW 20
WHICH SEEKS DEMURELY . . . . PL DINNER GUEST ME 6
AND SEEKS AN OUT IN OTHER WORLDLY
DREAMS. . . . . PL JUNIOR ADDICT 3
WHO SEEKS AN OUT IN EYES THAT DROOP PL JUNIOR ADDICT 4

SEEM 2
SO IT WOULD SEEM. . . . . JC NOTE TO NAZIS 2
WHAT DID NOT SEEM COULD EVER BE: . SP DREAM 4

SEEMED 2
SUNSHINE SEEMED LIKE GOLD. . . . . DK PO' BOY BLUES 2
SUNSHINE SEEMED LIKE GOLD. . . . . DK PO' BOY BLUES 4

SEEMS 7
YET IT SEEMS LIKE ALWAYS . . . . . FC BLACK GAL 5
SEEMS LIKE BAD LICKER. . . . . . . FC BLD OF GIN MARY 11
SEEMS LIKE SHE SAID: . . . . FW GIRL 11
BUT EVER FRIEND YOU FINDS SEEMS . . SP BOUND NO'TH BLS 17
AND SOMETIMES IT SEEMS . . . . . . SP HIGH TO LOW 8
SEEMS LIKE ONCE I MET YOU . . . . . AYM RIDE, RED, RIDE 31
SO IT SEEMS. . . . . PL LONG VIEW NEGRO 6

SEEN 13
AND HAVE NEVER SEEN THE SEAS. . . . WB A FAREWELL 8
AN' SEEN DE AMBULANCE . . . . FC DEATH DO DIRTY 27

(AIN'T SEEN HER IN SIX YEARS! USED TO GO WITH HER, TOO!) . . . . . NM BROKE 63
NEVER SEEN YOU BEFORE - . . . . . . SP BLD FORTUNE TEL 2
BUT NOBODY'S SEEN HER SHED A TEAR. SP BLD OF THE GIRL 9
NOR SEEN HER HANG HER HEAD. . . . . SP BLD OF THE GIRL 10
I SEEN FOLKS TALKIN' ABOUT THE . . SP FREEDOM TRAIN 5
I'VE SEEN THEM COME DARK . . . . . SP GOOD MORNING 17
I NEVER SEEN HIM BEFORE. . . . . . SP MADAM WRONG VIS 2
AND AIN'T SEEN CHRIST YET. . . . . SP MYSTERY 2
WENT DOWN TO NEW ORLEANS, AND I'VE SEEN ITS MUDDY . . . . SP NEGRO SPEAKS OF 9
I NEVER SEEN IT. . . . . AYM ASK YOUR MAMA 25
I AIN'T NEVER SEEN NOBODY . . . . . PL FLORIDA WORKERS 17

SEES 1
I SEES YO' FACE AGAIN. . . . . . . FC BLD OF GIN MARY 8

SEE'S 1
DOWN SOUTH IN DIXIE ONLY TRAIN I SEE'S . . . . SP FREEDOM TRAIN 9

SEGREGATED 1
THEY EVEN GOT A SEGREGATED LANE. . SP FREEDOM TRAIN 27

SEGREGATION 1
I'M TIRED OF SEGREGATION, ... JC THE BITTER RIVR 79

SEKOU 1
NIGHT IN A SEKOU TOURE CAP . . . . AYM ASK YOUR MAMA 61

SELDOM 1
SELDOM BURSTING . . . . AYM ASK YOUR MAMA 70

SELECT 1
ROTONDE SELECT DUPONT FLORE . . . . AYM ASK YOUR MAMA 51

SELF 9
I'M GONNA KILL MA SELF. . . . . . . FC SUICIDE 6
SHALL I CARVE MA SELF OR . . . . . FC SUICIDE 11
MY SELF! . . . . SH BLD PAWNBROKER 24
GYPSY SAYS I'D KILL MY SELF . . . . SP BAD LUCK CARD 11
TWO A.M. MIDNIGHT BY YOUR SELF? . . SP REVERIE HARLEM 2
BY YOUR SELF! . . . . SP REVERIE HARLEM 12
TO STRUGGLE BY HIS SELF. . . . . . SP STONY LONESOME 13
AIN'T GOT NOBODY BUT MA SELF. . . . SP THE WEARY BLUES 20
TO MY BLACK SELF. . . . . PL LITTLE SNG HOUS 24

SELF-ASSURANCE 1
HIM. ASSUMING A FALSE AND BRAGGING SELF-ASSURANCE, AND A PRETENDED NM BIG-TIMER MOOD 8

SELL 8
AN' SELL 'EM TO DE JEW. . . . . . . FC HARD LUCK 6
DO NOT SELL ME OUT, BABY, ... SH IN TROUBLED KEY 1
PLEASE DO NOT SELL ME OUT. . . . . SH IN TROUBLED KEY 2
DO NOT SELL ME OUT, BABY. . . . . . SH IN TROUBLED KEY 3
DO NOT SELL ME OUT. . . . . SH IN TROUBLED KEY 4
THEY SELL BEER FOAMING THERE IN MUG-LIKE CUPS. . . . . OWT JUICE JOINT 5
JEWS SELL ME THINGS. . . . . SP LIKEWISE 8
I'D UP AND SELL MY HEART OF GOLD . PL VARI-COLORED 3

SELLING 1
SELLING HER SCANTY WARES . . . . . SP MEXICAN MARKET 3

SELLS 1
THE GIRL WHO SELLS HER BODY BEHIND STEEL BARS. . . . . JC THE BITTER RIVR 35

SELMA 2
SELMA AND PEKING. . . . . PL UNDERTOW 4
BETWEEN SELMA, PEKING. . . . . . . PL UNDERTOW 12

SEND 34
CAN'T SEND NO MESSAGES THROUGH THE AIR. . . . . JC GOOD MORN STLIN 50
SEND SOME FLOWERS. . . . . SP BLD OF THE MAN 8
THE WAY YOU SEND YOUR KIDS TO SCHOOL SP HIGH TO LOW 10
THEY SEND ME TO EAT IN THE KITCHEN SP I, TOO 3
MY GIRL-FRIEND SEND HER LOVE AND SAY SP LETTER 6
BOUQUETS I'LL SEND YOU . . . . . . AYM BLUES IN STEREO 2
AND DREAMS I'LL SEND YOU . . . . . AYM BLUES IN STEREO 3
TRIUMPHAL ENTRY SEND YOU - . . . . AYM BLUES IN STEREO 7
SEND MY SON TO VIETNAM. . . . . . . PL BACKLASH BLUES 6
SEND FOR THE PIED PIPER AND LET HIM PIPE THE RATS . . . . PL FINAL CALL 1
SEND FOR ROBIN HOOD TO CLINCH THE ANTI-POVERTY . . . . PL FINAL CALL 3
SEND FOR THE FAIRY QUEEN WITH A WAVE OF THE . . . . PL FINAL CALL 5
SEND FOR KING ARTHUR TO BRING THE HOLY GRAIL. . . . . PL FINAL CALL 8
SEND FOR OLD MAN MOSES TO LAY DOWN THE LAW. . . . . PL FINAL CALL 9
SEND FOR JESUS TO PREACH THE SERMON ON THE . . . . PL FINAL CALL 10
SEND FOR DREYFUS TO CRY, "J'ACCUSE!" PL FINAL CALL 12
SEND FOR DEAD BLIND LEMON TO SING THE B FLAT . . . . PL FINAL CALL 13
SEND FOR ROBESPIERRE TO SCREAM, "CA IRA! CA IRA! . . . . PL FINAL CALL 15
SEND (GOD FORBID - HE'S NOT DEAD LONG ENOUGH!) . . . . PL FINAL CALL 17
SEND FOR LAFAYETTE AND TELL HIM, "HELP! HELP ME!" . . . . PL FINAL CALL 19
SEND FOR DENMARK VESEY CRYING, "FREE!" . . . . PL FINAL CALL 20
SEND FOR LENIN! (DON'T YOU DARE! - HE CAN'T COME . . . . PL FINAL CALL 24
SEND FOR TROTSKY! (WHAT? DON'T CONFUSE THE ISSUE. . . . . PL FINAL CALL 26
SEND FOR UNCLE TOM ON HIS MIGHTY KNEES. . . . . PL FINAL CALL 28
SEND FOR LINCOLN, SEND FOR GRANT. PL FINAL CALL 29
SEND FOR LINCOLN, SEND FOR GRANT. PL FINAL CALL 29
SEND FOR FREDERICK DOUGLASS, GARRISON, BEECHER, ... PL FINAL CALL 30
SEND FOR HARRIETT TUBMAN, OLD SOJOURNER TRUTH. . . . . PL FINAL CALL 32
SEND FOR MARCUS GARVEY (WHAT?) SUFI (WHO?) . . . . PL FINAL CALL 33
DUBOIS (WHEN?) MALCOLM (OH!) SEND FOR STOKELY. . . . . PL FINAL CALL 35
SEND FOR ADAM POWELL ON A NON-SUBPOENA DAY. . . . . PL FINAL CALL 37
SEND FOR THE PIED PIPER TO PIPE OUR RATS AWAY. . . . . PL FINAL CALL 38
(AND IF NOBODY COMES, SEND FOR ME.) PL FINAL CALL 39
I SEND CHECKS. . . . . PL NORTHERN LIBERL 16

SENDING 1
BUT SENDING MUSIC . . . . SP TO BE SOMEBODY 8

SENDIN' 1
SHE BOUGHT A NEW HAT LAST WEEK AND COME SENDIN' ME THE BILL. . . . NM BROKE 49

SENDS 2
BY WHAT SENDS . . . . SP CHILDREN'S RYME 5
BY WHAT SENDS . . . . PL CHILDREN'S RYME 1

SENSE 8
BUT I'LL HAVE MO' SENSE NEXT TIME. FC GYPSY MAN 18
HE DIDN'T HAVE MUCH SENSE. . . . . SP DANCER 6
WITH NO SENSE, JUST WONDERFUL FEET. SP DANCER 21
IT DON'T MAKE SENSE - . . . . SP DEFERRED 22
AIN'T NO SENSE IN A GOOD WOMAN . . SP EARLY EVENING 15
JOE HAS SENSE ENOUGH TO KNOW . . . SP JOE LOUIS 5
CAUSE THERE AIN'T NO SENSE . . . . SP WAKE 3
BUT THEY GOT MORE SENSE . . . . . . SP WARNING AUGMENT 11

SENSITIVE 1
THEY WONDERED WAS I SENSITIVE . . . AYM HORN OF PLENTY 49

SENT 12
WE WERE SENT TO TRAINING CAMP, THEN OVERSEAS - . . . . NM COLORED SL POEM 5
SENT HIM HOME . . . . OWT DECEASED 2
SENT TO BRING THE WHOLE WORLD JOY. LHR BLD MARY'S SON 10
SENT! . . . . LHR CONSERVATORY 13
I AIN'T SENT: . . . . SP CHILDREN'S RYME 7
I SENT YOU THIS MORNING TO BUY? . . SP EARLY EVENING 2
I SENT YOU THIS MORNING TO BUY? . . SP EARLY EVENING 4
WAS HEAVEN SENT. . . . . SP LITTLE LYRIC 2
WHO WAS IT SENT . . . . SP NIGHT FUNERAL 11
THE GLOVES THAT SENT . . . . SP TO BE SOMEBODY 17
MAMA'S FRUITCAKE SENT FROM GEORGIA AYM ODE TO DINAH 13
I AIN'T SENT: . . . . PL CHILDREN'S RYME 3

SEPARATE 2
"SEPARATE AS THE FINGERS." . . . . ANS OPEN LETTER 20
OUR BODIES ARE SEPARATE, INDIVIDUAL THINGS. . . . . SP A HOUSE IN TAOS 31

SEPIA 1
ON THIS SEPIA THRILL: . . . . SH HARLEM SWEETIES 4

SEQUINS 1
WHILE MOLLIE MOON STREWS SEQUINS . AYM BIRD IN ORBIT 28

SERENELY 1
THE HEAD OF LINCOLN IS SERENELY TALL OWT LINCOLN THEATRE 7

SERF 1
IN THAT OLD WORLD WHILE STILL A SERF OF KINGS. . . . . ANS LET AMERICA BE 40

SERMON 3
AN OLD NEGRO MINISTER CONCLUDES HIS SERMON IN HIS LOUDEST VOICE, . . SP SUNDAY MORNING 1
THE SERMON ON THE MOUNT . . . . . . AYM HORN OF PLENTY 83
SEND FOR JESUS TO PREACH THE SERMON ON THE . . . . PL FINAL CALL 10

SERPENTS 1
THAT HOODED SERPENTS MAY DANCE. . . PL SPECIAL BULLTIN 4

SERVANT 2
"YOU ARE MY SERVANT, BLACK MAN - I, THE FREE!" . . . . ANS A NEW SONG 32
I AM THE NEGRO, SERVANT TO YOU ALL. ANS LET AMERICA BE 33

SERVANTS 3
SERVANTS. . . . . ANS OPEN LETTER 8
FREE MEN AND INDENTURED SERVANTS. SP FREEDOM'S PLOW 32
WEALTHY NEGROES HAVE WHITE SERVANTS. PL CULTURAL EXCHNG 48

SERVE 2
SERVE - AND HATE WILL DIE UNBORN. DK ALABAMA EARTH 12
ADELE RAMONA MICHAEL SERVE BAKOKO TEA . . . . AYM BIRD IN ORBIT 20

SERVICE 2
I WANT TO PASS THE CIVIL SERVICE. SP DEFERRED 43
DECENT GARBAGE SERVICE . . . . . . AYM HORN OF PLENTY 75

SERVILE 1
THE SLY AND SERVILE GRACE . . . . . SP UNCLE TOM 7

SET 17
ABE LINCOLN DONE SET ME FREE - . . NM BLACK CLWN POEM 30
SET ON THE FRONT PORCH AS LONG AS I PLEASE. . . . . SH SUNDAY 8
AND SET DOWN AND DRINK IT, MYSELF AND ME. . . . . SH SUPPER TIME 12
HERE I SET WITH A BITTER OLD THOUGHT, ... SH TWILIGHT REVERI 1
YAL, HERE I SET THINKING - A BITTER OLD THOUGHT . . . . SH TWILIGHT REVERI 9
AND HERE I SET THINKING WITH A BITTER OLD FROWN. . . . . SH TWILIGHT REVERI 14
I SET DOWN ON A STONE. . . . . . . OWT STRANGER IN TWN 2
WHEN I SET MY FEET IN GLORY . . . . SP DEFERRED 41
I WANT A TELEVISION SET. . . . . . SP DEFERRED 44
GOT A JIM CROW CAR SET ASIDE FOR ME. SP FREEDOM TRAIN 10
SET ON MY STEPS AND CRIED. . . . . SP LATE LAST NIGHT 2
I SET DOWN ON THE BANK. . . . . . . SP LIFE IS FINE 2
DON'T YOU SET DOWN ON THE STEPS . . SP MOTHER TO SON 15
SHE NEEDS TO SET ON DE MOANER'S BENCH . . . . SP MYSTERY 3
SET THERE. . . . . SP NEIGHBOR 24
ON WHICH HE SET HIS FEET. . . . . . PL FREDRK DOUGLASS 9
OF THE COUNTRY CLUB SET. . . . . . PL UNDERTOW 2

SETS 4
AN' THERE SHE SETS A CRYIN' . . . . FC NEW CABARET GRL 17
HE SETS ON A STOOP . . . . SP NEIGHBOR 2
HE SETS IN A BAR WITH A BEER. . . . SP NEIGHBOR 6
AND FREE-DELIVERY TV SETS . . . . . AYM JAZZTET MUTED 12

SETTIN 2
SHE LEFT THE TEXAS KID SETTIN BY HIMSELF . . . . SH DEATH IN HARLEM 79
SETTIN IN HER PLACE! . . . . SH DEATH IN HARLEM 96

SETTING 4
THEY OUGHT TO BE LIKE ME SETTING HERE - FEELING GLAD! . . . . . . SH SUNDAY 15
SETTING HERE THINKING FEELING SAD. SH TWILIGHT REVERI 3
SETTING IN THE WINE-HOUSE . . . . . SP WINE-O 1
SETTING IN THE WINE-HOUSE . . . . . SP WINE-O 5

SETTIN' 6
JUDGE WAS SETTIN' THERE. . . . . . FC BLD OF GIN MARY 2
SOMETIMES I'M SETTIN' PRETTY. . . . NM BIG-TIMER POEM 39
SUN'S A SETTIN'. . . . . DK NIGHT AND MORN 1
SUN'S A SETTIN'. . . . . DK NIGHT AND MORN 3
GYPSY SETTIN' ALL ALONE. . . . . . SP BLD THE GYPSY 2
AN' NOW I'M SETTIN' CLEAN AN' BRIGHT SP JUDGMENT DAY 11

SEVEN 6
IF A SEVEN DON'T COME . . . . FC CRAP GAME 3
YOU'VE GOT SEVEN LANGUAGES TO SPEAK IN . . . . FC JAZZ BAND 19
AT SIX O'CLOCK, OR SEVEN, OR EIGHT, OWT NEGRO SERVANT 8
DROPPED OUT SIX MONTHS WHEN I WAS SEVEN. . . . . SP DEFERRED 3
SEVEN LADIES . . . . SP PARADE 1
AND SEVEN CATS GO FRANTIC. . . . . SP SEASHORE THROUG 4

SEVENTEEN 2
AND THE SEVENTEEN STARS. . . . . . SP NIGHT FOUR SONG 2
AND SEVENTEEN GENTLEMEN . . . . . . SP PARADE 2

SEVENTH 2
LEAPS CLEAN OVER TO SEVENTH AVENUE SP PROJECTION 2
EIGHTH AVENUE, SEVENTH, AND I COME TO THE Y. . . . . SP THEME FOR ENG B 13

SHACK 1
MY MA DIED IN A SHACK. . . . . . . SP CROSS 10

SHADE 6
UNTIL ALL RACES AND ALL PEOPLES KNOW ITS SHADE. . . . . SP FREEDOM'S PLOW 199
WHERE THE SHADE IS? . . . . SP KID SLEEPY 4
RATHER THAN THE SHADE. . . . . . . SP STRANGE HURT 10
SEEKING LAWNS AND SHADE TREES . . . AYM HORN OF PLENTY 71
CUT FROM SHADOWS CUT FROM SHADE . . AYM JAZZTET MUTED 5
DARK SHADOWS BECOME DARKER BY A SHADE . . . . AYM ODE TO DINAH 51

SHADES 1
THE SHADES OF DINAH'S SINGING . . . AYM ODE TO DINAH 58

SHADOW 18
IS NOT HE BUT A SHADOW IN THE SUN - DK BEGGAR BOY 5
SHADOW. . . . . SP AS I GREW OLDER 17
I LIE DOWN IN THE SHADOW. . . . . . SP AS I GREW OLDER 19
ONLY THE SHADOW. . . . . SP AS I GREW OLDER 23
TO BREAK THIS SHADOW . . . . SP AS I GREW OLDER 30
SHADOW FACES . . . . SP CHORD 1
IN THE SHADOW NIGHT . . . . SP CHORD 2
LOVE IS A NAKED SHADOW . . . . . . SP SONG DARK GIRL 11
IN THE SHADOW OF THE CLUNY . . . . AYM ASK YOUR MAMA 55
WHERE NO SHADOW WALKS ALONE . . . . AYM ASK YOUR MAMA 75
NOTHING BUT ANOTHER SHADOW . . . . AYM HORN OF PLENTY 43
SHADOW OF THE NEGROES . . . . AYM HORN OF PLENTY 60
IN THE SHADOW OF THE NEGROES - . . AYM HORN OF PLENTY 62
TO THE SHADOW OF THE BLUES. . . . . AYM ODE TO DINAH 112
IN THE SHADOW OF THE QUARTER . . . AYM ODE TO DINAH 120
IN THE SHADOW OF THE WELFARE . . . AYM ODE TO DINAH 71
IN THE SHADOW OF THE WELFARE . . . AYM ODE TO DINAH 75
OF THE SHADOW OF A DOLLAR . . . . . AYM SHOW FARE PLESE 14

SHADOWS 31
THE SHADOWS . . . . WB SOLEDAD 2
SHADOWS VEIL HIS DARKNESS . . . . . FW DIMOUT IN HARLM 5
SHADOWS VEILING SHADOWS . . . . . . FW DIMOUT IN HARLM 6
SHADOWS VEILING SHADOWS . . . . . . FW DIMOUT IN HARLM 6
VEILING SHADOWS CUT BY LAUGHTER . . FW DIMOUT IN HARLM 8
SHADOWS VEILING SILENCE . . . . . . FW DIMOUT IN HARLM 10
SILENCE VEILING SHADOWS . . . . . . FW DIMOUT IN HARLM 11
SILENCE AND THE SHADOWS . . . . . . FW DIMOUT IN HARLM 12
IN THE DARK SHADOWS THAT CROSS AND RECROSS . . . . SP AUNTSUE'S STORI 15
NO SHADOWS THAT MOVE . . . . SP END 4
FROM THE SHADOWS OF THE QUARTER . . AYM ASK YOUR MAMA 1
WHO TIPS AMONG THE SHADOWS . . . . AYM BIRD IN ORBIT 67
TIPS AMONG THE SHADOWS . . . . . . AYM BIRD IN ORBIT 90
TO THE CITADELLE OF SHADOWS SHADOWS AYM GOSPEL CHA-CHA 18
TO THE CITADELLE OF SHADOWS SHADOWS AYM GOSPEL CHA-CHA 18
WHERE THE SHADOWS OF THE NEGROES AYM GOSPEL CHA-CHA 19
FROM THE SHADOWS OF THE QUARTER . . AYM IS IT TRUE? 1
WHERE BLACK SHADOWS MOVE LIKE SHADOWS . . . . AYM JAZZTET MUTED 4
WHERE BLACK SHADOWS MOVE LIKE SHADOWS . . . . AYM JAZZTET MUTED 4
CUT FROM SHADOWS CUT FROM SHADE . . AYM JAZZTET MUTED 5
DUE TO SMOLDERING SHADOWS . . . . . AYM JAZZTET MUTED 20
SHADOWS SHOW UP SHARPER. . . . . . AYM ODE TO DINAH 3
WHERE THE SHADOWS MERGE WITH SHADOWS AYM ODE TO DINAH 115
WHERE THE SHADOWS MERGE WITH SHADOWS AYM ODE TO DINAH 115
WHERE WHITE SHADOWS PASS. . . . . . AYM ODE TO DINAH 50
DARK SHADOWS BECOME DARKER BY A SHADE . . . . AYM ODE TO DINAH 51
FROM SLABS OF SILVER SHADOWS. . . . AYM ODE TO DINAH 54
BUT BABIES BORN IN SHADOWS . . . . AYM ODE TO DINAH 70
CHOCOLATE BABIES BORN IN SHADOWS . AYM ODE TO DINAH 76
BELGIUM SHADOWS LEOPOLD . . . . . . AYM SHADES OF PIG 2
DEAD OR LIVE THEIR GHOSTS CAST SHADOWS . . . . AYM SHADES OF PIG 6

SHAFTS 2
AND BROKEN SHAFTS OF MOON-GLIMMER DK AFTR MNY SPRNGS 5
THE RISING SHAFTS OF MOUNTAINS. . . SP SPIRITUALS 2

SHAKE 16
LET'S SHAKE DAT THING! . . . . . . FC SATURDAY NIGHT 12
SHAKE 'EM UP AN' SHAKE 'EM UP . . . FC SATURDAY NIGHT 23
SHAKE 'EM UP AN' SHAKE 'EM UP . . . FC SATURDAY NIGHT 23
SHAKE YOUR BROWN FEET, HONEY, . . . DK SONG BANJO DANC 1
SHAKE YOUR BROWN FEET, CHILE. . . . DK SONG BANJO DANC 2
SHAKE YOUR BROWN FEET, HONEY. . . . DK SONG BANJO DANC 3
SHAKE 'EM SWIFT AND WIL' - . . . . DK SONG BANJO DANC 4
SHAKE YOUR BROWN FEET, HONEY, . . . DK SONG BANJO DANC 10
SHAKE 'EM, HONEY CHILE. . . . . . . DK SONG BANJO DANC 11
SHAKE YOUR BROWN FEET, LIZA, . . . DK SONG BANJO DANC 20
SHAKE 'EM, LIZA, CHILE. . . . . . . DK SONG BANJO DANC 21
SHAKE YOUR BROWN FEET, LIZA, . . . DK SONG BANJO DANC 22
SHAKE YOUR BROWN FEET, LIZA, . . . DK SONG BANJO DANC 24
TO SHAKE THE PILLARS OF THOSE TEMPLES . . . . ANS UNION 7
COUPLES ON THE FLOOR ROCK AND SHAKE. SH DEATH IN HARLEM 33
AND SHAKE YOUR RATTLE . . . . PL LAST PRINCE 9

SHAKES 2
SHE SNAPS HER FINGERS, SLOWLY SHAKES HER HIPS. . . . . OWT LINCOLN THEATRE 9
SHAKES HANDS WITH EMMETT TILL. . . AYM ASK YOUR MAMA 66

SHAKING 4

SHAKING THE BARS.	ANS	CHANT TOM MOONY	21
SHAKING THE WALLS.	ANS	CHANT TOM MOONY	22
SHAKING THE EARTH	ANS	CHANT TOM MOONY	23
SHAKING THE LIGHTS IN THE FISH JOINTS.	SP	RAILROAD AVENUE	26

SHALL 14

SHALL I BE WISE AGAIN?	WB	THE JESTER	19
SHALL I CARVE MA SELF OR	FC	SUICIDE	11
WHAT SHALL I SING	DK	LULLABY	5
WHAT SHALL I SING	DK	LULLABY	13
NO LONGER SHALL YOU SAY	ANS	A NEW SONG	30
SHALL BE ONE!	ANS	A NEW SONG	50
WHAT SHALL I DO?	OWT	TOO BLUE	6
WHAT SHALL I SAY?	OWT	TOO BLUE	7
SHALL I TAKE A GUN	OWT	TOO BLUE	8
WHAT SHALL I LEAVE MY SON	LHR	TESTAMENT	1
WHAT SHALL I LEAVE MY DAUGHTER.	LHR	TESTAMENT	5
WHAT SHALL I LEAVE MY WIFE	LHR	TESTAMENT	9
WHAT SHALL I TELL MY CHILDREN? . . . YOU TELL ME -	SP	FREEDOM TRAIN	33
SHALL I USE OLD ENGLISH	SP	MADAM'S CALLING	13

SHAME 7

TWO THINGS CAST OFF ALL SHAME.	OLD	TWO THINGS	6
SO THAT THE PAIN AND THE SHAME	NM	BLACK CLWN POEM	27
AND BOWING HIS HEAD IN SHAME. BECOMES SUDDENLY FIERCE AND ANGRY. THEN HE	NM	COLORED SL MOOD	11
NO SHAME IS WRIT ACROSS ITS FACE -	SL	TOWN OF SCOTTSB	2
AIN'T YOU SHAME?	SH	DEATH IN HARLEM	76
SHAME ON YOU!	SP	SHAME ON YOU	11
EAT QUIETLY THE BREAD OF SHAME.	PL	MILITANT	2

SHAMELESS 3

SHAMELESS GAL.	WB	TO MIDNIGHT NAN	2
SHAMELESS NAN.	WB	TO MIDNIGHT NAN	18
O SHAMELESS MOON?	SP	MARCH MOON	8

SHANGHAI 1

ON STRIKE IN THE STREETS OF SHANGHAI.	ANS	BLDS OF LENIN	22

SHANGO 1

MAMACITA! PAPA LEGBA! SHANGO!	AYM	GOSPEL CHA-CHA	35

SHANKS 1

WITH THEIR SILVER SHANKS.	SP	MOONLIGHT NIGHT	4

SHAPED 1

THAT HEWED AND SHAPED THE ROOFTOPS OF AMERICA.	SP	FREEDOM'S PLOW	56

SHARE 6

DON'T HAVE TO SHARE IT A-TALL.	SH	PAY DAY	2
THEN SHARE 'EM WITH ME -	JC	HOW ABOUT DIXIE	7
ALIKE WILL SHARE.	OWT	BOARDING HOUSE	6
AIN'T GOT NOBODY TO SHARE MY BED.	SP	50 - 50	2
HE SAID. SHARE YOUR BED -	SP	50 - 50	13
LITTLE MULES AND DONKEYS SHARE	AYM	ASK YOUR MAMA	76

SHARECROPPERS 3

ORGANIZING SHARECROPPERS.	ANS	KIDS WHO DIE	9
SHARECROPPERS.	ANS	OPEN LETTER	10
WHITE SHARECROPPERS WORK THE BLACK PLANTATIONS.	PL	CULTURAL EXCHNG	49

SHARE-CROPPER 1

THE VOTELESS SHARE-CROPPER BEHIND STEEL BARS.	JC	THE BITTER RIVR	31

SHARP 9

THE SHARP. SLEET-STUNG	WB	POEME D'AUTOMNE	12
BUT ONE SHARP. LEAPING FLAME	WB	SONGS DARK VIRG	17
A KNIFE IS SHARP.	FW	EXITS	2
AND SHARP AS FLAME.	SP	BEALE STREET	8
SHARP PINE SCENT IN THE EVENING AIR.	SP	MULATTO	22
BURNS IN MY HEART A LOVE-FIRE SHARP LIKE PAIN.	SP	WHEN SUE WEARS	11
HOW THIN AND SHARP IS THE MOON TONIGHT!	SP	WINTER MOON	1
HOW THIN AND SHARP AND GHOSTLY WHITE	SP	WINTER MOON	2
SHARP AS INTEGRATION	PL	WHERE WHEN WHCH	5

SHARPER 1

SHADOWS SHOW UP SHARPER.	AYM	ODE TO DINAH	3

SHARP-THORNED 1

ROSE OF THE SHARP-THORNED STEM	FW	CHIPPY	2

SHATTER 1

HELP ME TO SHATTER THIS DARKNESS.	SP	AS I GREW OLDER	28

SHATTERED 1

A SHATTERED JEWEL.	WB	SONGS DARK VIRG	3

SHE 143

ONE SAID SHE HEARD THE JAZZ-BAND SOB	WB	CABARET	5
SHE	WB	TO LITTLE LOVER	1
SHE WALKS	WB	TO LITTLE LOVER	9
THEY SAY SHE DIED. -	WB	YOUNG BRIDE	1
THEY SAY SHE DIED OF GRIEF	WB	YOUNG BRIDE	3
NEXT TIME SHE MAKES ME SORE.	FC	EVIL WOMAN	4
SHE DON'T DO ME RIGHT.	FC	EVIL WOMAN	6
SHE FIGHTS AN' QUARRELS MOST	FC	EVIL WOMAN	7
SHE IS DEATH.	FC	MAMMY	2
SHE DON'T DRINK GIN	FC	NEW CABARET GRL	5
AN' SHE DON'T LIKE CORN.	FC	NEW CABARET GRL	6
WHERE SHE WAS BORN.	FC	NEW CABARET GRL	8
AN' SHE SAY. HONEY.	FC	NEW CABARET GRL	9
AN' THERE SHE SETS A CRYIN'	FC	NEW CABARET GRL	17
WHEN SHE OUGHT TO PLAY.	FC	NEW CABARET GRL	20
BUT SHE DON'T GIMME LOVIN'	FC	WORKIN' MAN	11
CAUSE SHE AIN'T DE RIGHT KIND.	FC	WORKIN' MAN	12
AND SHE BEEN HOLDIN' 'EM SO TIGHT TILL DE EAGLE'S IN TEARS -	NM	BROKE	24
SHE BOUGHT A NEW HAT LAST WEEK AND COME SENDIN' ME THE BILL.	NM	BROKE	49
AND SHE COME TELLIN' ME. SHE AIN'T GOT NO MO' EVENINGS FREE!	NM	BROKE	53
AND SHE COME TELLIN' ME. SHE AIN'T GOT NO MO' EVENINGS FREE!	NM	BROKE	53
SHE WOULD BE ALRIGHT IF SHE WASN'T SO BOW-LEGGED. AND CROSS-EYED.	NM	BROKE	64
SHE WOULD BE ALRIGHT IF SHE WASN'T SO BOW-LEGGED. AND CROSS-EYED.	NM	BROKE	64
SHE MADE ME LOSE MA MONEY	DK	PO' BOY BLUES	17
SHE LIVES ACROSS DE RIVER.	DK	WIDE RIVER	3
SHE WAS DRIVING ALONE.	SH	ANNOUNCEMENT	2
SHE HAD ANOTHER JOKER	SH	ANNOUNCEMENT	11
BERNICE SAID SHE WANTED	SH	BLD THE KILLER	1
BERNICE SAID SHE WANTED	SH	BLD THE KILLER	5
BERNICE SAID SHE NEEDED	SH	BLD THE KILLER	9
SHE BEGGED ME. PLEASE.	SH	BLD THE SINNER	13
SHE KNOWS WHY.	SH	BLD THE KILLER	29
JUDGE. SHE IS DE WOMAN	SH	BRIEF ENCOUNTER	7
SHE IS DE WOMAN. JUDGE.	SH	BRIEF ENCOUNTER	9
DE FACT THAT SHE IS DEAD.	SH	BRIEF ENCOUNTER	14
FACT THAT SHE IS DEAD -	SH	BRIEF ENCOUNTER	16
SHE WAS DE WRONGEST THING. JUDGE.	SH	BRIEF ENCOUNTER	17
SHE UTTERED A CRY.	SH	DEATH IN HARLEM	100
SHE SAYS TO THE WAITER.	SH	DEATH IN HARLEM	41
SHE GURGLES TO TEXAS.	SH	DEATH IN HARLEM	51
SHE LEFT THE TEXAS KID SETTIN BY HIMSELF	SH	DEATH IN HARLEM	79
HER NAME WAS BESSIE. SHE WAS BROWN AND BOLD.	SH	DEATH IN HARLEM	81
AND SHE SAT ON HER CHAIR LIKE A SWEET JELLY ROLL.	SH	DEATH IN HARLEM	82
SHE CAST HER EYES ON TEXAS. HOLLERED.	SH	DEATH IN HARLEM	83
WHEN SHE COME OUT	SH	DEATH IN HARLEM	93
SHE LOOKED ACROSS THE PLACE -	SH	DEATH IN HARLEM	94
SHE WAS DE MEANEST WOMAN	SH	ONLY WOMAN BLUS	3
SHE COULD MAKE ME HOLLER LIKE A SISSIE.	SH	ONLY WOMAN BLUS	7
SHE COULD CHASE ME UP A TREE	SH	ONLY WOMAN BLUS	9
SHE HAD LONG BLACK HAIR.	SH	ONLY WOMAN BLUS	13
WHEN SHE LEFT	SH	ONLY WOMAN BLUS	21
SHE WANTED A	SH	PRESENT	3
SHE WAITS FOR ME	FW	FAITHFUL ONE	11
SHE LIVED IN SINFUL HAPPINESS	FW	GIRL	1
SHE DANCED IN SUNSHINE	FW	GIRL	3
SHE WENT ONE SUMMER MORNING	FW	GIRL	5
BUT SHE TOLD EVERYBODY	FW	GIRL	7
SHE WAS COMING BACK AGAIN.	FW	GIRL	8
SEEMS LIKE SHE SAID:	FW	GIRL	11
AND SURE SHE LIVED	FW	GIRL	18
SHE SEEKS YOUR HAND.	FW	SLEEP	4
SHE SAID.	FW	SONGS	3
SHE MIGHT NOT'VE CUSSED	OWT	BLD MARGE POLIT	3
SHE MIGHT NOT'VE FELT	OWT	BLD MARGE POLIT	7
BUT SHE AIN'T JUST NOBODY	OWT	BLD MARGE POLIT	23
SHE STARTED THE RIOTS!	OWT	BLD MARGE POLIT	25
SHE SNAPS HER FINGERS. SLOWLY SHAKES HER HIPS.	OWT	LINCOLN THEATRE	9
MY LANDLADY. SHE SAID. NO!	OWT	STRANGER IN TWN	8
FOR TEARS IF SHE SHOULD CRY.	LHR	TESTAMENT	8
SHE DID NOT LOVE ME.	SP	A BLACK PIERROT	2
SHE DID NOT LOVE ME.	SP	A BLACK PIERROT	6
SHE DID NOT LOVE ME.	SP	A BLACK PIERROT	11
AND YOU. SHE. AND I	SP	A HOUSE IN TAOS	9
YOU. SHE. AND I.	SP	A HOUSE IN TAOS	25
SHE COULD TELL YOU ABOUT LOVE.	SP	BLD FORTUNE TEL	5
AND SHE WOULDN'T	SP	BLD FORTUNE TEL	7
SHE TREATED HIM LIKE	SP	BLD FORTUNE TEL	11
SHE GAVE HIM BREAD.	SP	BLD FORTUNE TEL	14
LOOKS LIKE SHE COULD'VE KNOWED IT	SP	BLD FORTUNE TEL	19
IF SHE ONLY WOULD.	SP	BLD FORTUNE TEL	20
STOLE ALL SHE HAD.	SP	BLD FORTUNE TEL	24
SHE TRIED TO FIND OUT	SP	BLD FORTUNE TEL	25
NO WAY SHE LOOKED.	SP	BLD FORTUNE TEL	28
HOW SHE COULD GET IN TROUBLE	SP	BLD OF THE GIRL	3

THE GUY SHE GAVE HER ALL TO . . . . SP BLD OF THE GIRL 5
SHE PUT 'EM DOWN. . . . . SP BLD OF THE MAN 12
SHE RAKED UP A HUNDRED . . . . SP BLD OF THE MAN 13
THAT IF SHE HAD A CHANCE . . . . . SP BLD OF THE GIRL 15
THEN SHE STARTED IN TO LIE. . . . . SP BLD THE GYPSY 10
SHE SAID, NOW, LISTEN, MISTER, . . SP BLD THE GYPSY 11
AND SHE AIN'T COME HOME YET. . . . SP BLD THE GYPSY 15
SHE SAYS HE CAN HAVE . . . . SP BUDDY 6
SHE NEEDS. . . . . SP CONSIDER ME 25
AND WISHED SHE WERE IN HELL. . . . SP CROSS 6
FOLKS SAY SHE DON'T LIKE . . . . . SP DELINQUENT 3
SAYS SHE DON'T CARE! . . . . SP DELINQUENT 14
WHAT SHE MEANS IS: . . . . SP DELINQUENT 15
SHE AIN'T HEARD. . . . . SP DIME 5
SHE SIGHS. . . . . SP GRADUATION 31
SHE WASN'T HOME NO MORE. . . . . . SP HOMECOMING 4
SHE AIN'T GOT BOOGIE-WOOGIE . . . . SP LADY'S BOOGIE 3
BUT IF SHE WAS TO LISTEN . . . . . SP LADY'S BOOGIE 5
SHE HOPES TO LAY EYES ON YOU SOMETIME IN LIFE. . . . . SP LETTER 7
SHE WASN'T MEAN - . . . . SP MADAM HER MADAM 2
SHE GREW UP AND GOT RUINT. . . . . SP MADAM CHARTY CH 3
BUT SHE HAD A TWELVE-ROOM . . . . . SP MADAM HER MADAM 3
SHE SQUINTED UP HER EYES. . . . . . SP MADAM FORT TELL 6
SHE SAID, YOU MUST RECOGNIZE . . . SP MADAM FORT TELL 11
FOR SHE WAS MADAM, TOO - . . . . . SP MADAM FORT TELL 14
SHE SAID, YOUR FORTUNE, HONEY, . . SP MADAM FORT TELL 17
SHE OPENED HER MOUTH. . . . . . . SP MADAM HER MADAM 17
SHE CRIED, OH, NO! . . . . SP MADAM HER MADAM 18
SHE SAID, MADAM! BE CALM - . . . . SP MADAM FORT TELL 22
SHE NEEDS TO SET ON DE MOANER'S BENCH . . . . SP MYSTERY 3
AND GOD KNOWS SHE SURE CAN OVERCHARGE - . . . . SP NECESSITY 10
I WASN'T BORN HERE, SHE SAID. . . . SP NEW YORKERS 4
SHE LIFTED UP HER LIPS . . . . . . SP NEW YORKERS 15
WHEN SHE CONVERSATIONS YOU . . . . SP PREFERENCE 13
SHE WAS YOUNG AND BEAUTIFUL . . . . SP RUBY BROWN 1
AND BECAUSE SHE WAS COLORED . . . . SP RUBY BROWN 4
SHE ASKED HERSELF TWO QUESTIONS . . SP RUBY BROWN 11
WHEN SHE WORKED IN THEIR KITCHENS. SP RUBY BROWN 27
I CAN'T, SHE SAID, I CAN'T! . . . . SP SAME IN BLUES 3
WHY DON'T SHE GET A BOY-FRIEND . . SP SISTER 5
IS SHE WANTS SOME CASH? . . . . . . SP SISTER 9
THAT A WOMAN DOES THE BEST SHE CAN? SP SISTER 14
SHE DONE LEFT PO' BUDDY . . . . . . SP STONY LONESOME 12
SHE FELT QUEER FAIN . . . . SP STRANGE HURT 2
STRANGE HURT SHE KNEW . . . . SP STRANGE HURT 7
BUT SHE SPITS IN MY FACE. . . . . . SP THE SOUTH 19
BUT SHE TURNS HER BACK UPON ME. . . SP THE SOUTH 22
FOR SHE, THEY SAY, ... SP THE SOUTH 25
SHE STANDS . . . . SP TROUBLED WOMAN 1
I'M ALL ALONE IN THIS WORLD, SHE SAID. . . . . SP 50 - 50 1
SHE ANSWERED, BABE, WHAT MUST I DO? SP 50 - 50 12
WHAT DID SHE SAY? . . . . AYM ASK YOUR MAMA 13
TO PROVE SHE WAS A WOMAN WOMAN . . AYM BIRD IN ORBIT 48
TO PROVE SHE WAS A WOMAN? . . . . . AYM BIRD IN ORBIT 50
WHAT SHE SAID ABOUT HER CHILDREN . AYM BIRD IN ORBIT 51
WAS SHE FLEEING WITH LUMUMBA? . . . AYM RIDE, RED, RIDE 16
SHE SPOKE OF SONS AT WAR. . . . . . PL MOTHER IN WAR 2
BELIEVING EVERYTHING SHE READ . . . PL MOTHER IN WAR 9
SHE THOUGHT THAT ONLY . . . . PL MOTHER IN WAR 12

SHED 1
BUT NOBODY'S SEEN HER SHED A TEAR. SP BLD OF THE GIRL 9

SHEEP 2
THE BLACK SHEEP. . . . . NM BIG-TIMER POEM 4
I'M JUST A POOR LOST SHEEP. . . . . SP EVENING SONG 8

SHEET 1
AND ALL THREE COVERED WITH A SHEET OF PAIN. . . . . WB SICK ROOM 6

SHELF 2
ON NOBODY ELSE'S SHELF. . . . . . . SP MADAM FORT TELL 20
AND PUT MA TROUBLES ON THE SHELF." SP THE WEARY BLUES 22

SHELLS 1
AND SHOOT ALL KINDS O' SHELLS INTO YOU. . . . . SH TWILIGHT REVERI 8

SHELTER 4
FOUR WALLS CAN SHELTER . . . . . . FW WALLS 5
MAY ITS BRANCHES SPREAD AND ITS SHELTER GROW . . . . SP FREEDOM'S PLOW 198
IS WAITIN' TO SHELTER ME. . . . . . SP LITTLE GRN TREE 14
THAN SHELTER FROM THE RAIN." . . . SP STRANGE HURT 5

SHELTERED 1
SHELTERED NOW NO LONGER. . . . . . AYM ODE TO DINAH 36

SHEPHERD 1
THAT I WHO AM THY SHEPHERD . . . . SP SUNDAY MORNING 41

SHERIFF 2
THE HIGH SHERIFF SHOOTS AND HE SHOOTS TO KILL . . . . ANS BLD OZZIE POWEL 9
A WHITE HIGH SHERIFF WHO SHOOTS TO KILL . . . . ANS BLD OZZIE POWEL 27

SHERIFF'S 3
THE HIGH SHERIFF'S EYES ARE FILLED WITH HATE. . . . . ANS BLD OZZIE POWEL 7
NEVER SAW THE HIGH SHERIFF'S GUN . ANS BLD OZZIE POWEL 15
THEY NEVER SAW THE HIGH SHERIFF'S EYES . . . . ANS BLD OZZIE POWEL 19

SHE'D 4
SHE'D DO IT AGIN'! . . . . SP BLD OF THE GIRL 16
I BET SHE'D HEAR. . . . . SP LADY'S BOOGIE 6
AND WISH SHE'D NEVER BEEN BORN? . . SP REVERIE HARLEM 8
SHE'D BREAK DOWN DOORS . . . . . . SP STRANGE HURT 13

SHE'LL 3
SHE'LL LET ME IN. . . . . FW FAITHFUL ONE 4
SHE'LL OPEN THE LATCH . . . . FW FAITHFUL ONE 7
SHE'LL BE HERE BY AND BY. . . . . . SP BLD THE GYPSY 12

SHE'S 12
AN' SHE'S GOIN' ON BACK . . . . . . FC EVIL WOMAN 14
SHE'S OUT IN DE STREET, - . . . . . FC WORKIN' MAN 7
GIVES LOVE AWAY SHE'S THROUGH. . . SH MIDNIGHT CHIPPI 24
BUT SHE'S DE ONLY . . . . SH ONLY WOMAN BLUS 5
CAUSE SHE'S DE ONLY . . . . SH ONLY WOMAN BLUS 11
SHE'S DE ONLY . . . . SH ONLY WOMAN BLUS 17
THAN SHE'S GOT BREATH. . . . . . . LHR TESTAMENT 12
TELLS HER MAMA SHE'S A TYPIST . . . SP GRADUATION 13
BECAUSE SHE'S TIRED. . . . . SP GRADUATION 30
AND NOW SHE'S NAKED. . . . . SP MARCH MOON 5
SHE'S OUT IN STONY LONESOME. . . . SP STONY LONESOME 16
AND THE FOUR BELLS SHE'S AWAITING SP SUMMER EVENING 20

SHIELD 1
FOUR WALLS THAT SHIELD . . . . . . FW WALLS 3

SHILLING 2
GOD WILLING DROP A SHILLING . . . . AYM ASK YOUR MAMA 44
A QUARTER OR A SHILLING. PARIS - . AYM ASK YOUR MAMA 49

SHILLINGS 1
FOR TEN SHILLINGS OFFERING LOVE. . SP NATCHA 2

SHIMMERING 2
AN ALTAR OF SHIMMERING JEWELS. . . WB POEM 18
A SHIMMERING, SILKEN GARMENT. . . . WB SONGS DARK VIRG 9

SHIMMERS 1
BY SOUND THAT SHIMMERS - . . . . . SP SONG BILLIE HOL 19

SHINE 4
SUN'S GONNA SHINE . . . . WB BLUES FANTASY 17
AND ALL THE WILD HOT MOONS OF THE JUNGLES SHINE IN MY SOUL. . . . WB FOR PORTRAIT OF 2
TO SHINE, ... SP ELEVATOR BOY 19
TO SHINE. . . . . SP PORTER 12

SHINED 1
SHINED JUST LIKE A TEAR - . . . . . SP NIGHT FUNERAL 37

SHINES 3
SHINES LIKE A STAR IN THE EAST. . . SP INTERNE AT PROV 41
SHINES LIKE THE EVIL ONE . . . . . SP WEST TEXAS 2
SHINES LIKE THE EVIL ONE . . . . . SP WEST TEXAS 17

SHINING 7
OH, SHINING RIVERS OF THE SOUL! . . WB JAZZONIA 2
OH, SHINING RIVERS OF THE SOUL! . . WB JAZZONIA 8
OH, SHINING TREE! . . . . WB JAZZONIA 14
THAT ALL MY SHINING BRILLIANTS . . WB SONGS DARK VIRG 4
BACK, AND EYES SHINING, QUIETLY RECALLING THE VISION, THE DEAD MAN SPEAKS . . . . NM COLORED SL MOOD 8
MOON IS SHINING. . . . . SP HARLEM NIGHT SO 7
YET SHINING LIKE THE SUN WITH LOVE'S TRUE LIGHT. . . . . SP THE NEGRO MOTHE 6

SHINY 1
NEW AND SHINY . . . . AYM HORN OF PLENTY 93

SHIP 8
TOGETHER WE HAVE LAUNCHED A SHIP . JC TO CAPTAIN MULZ 39
BUT MORE THAN SHIP, ... JC TO CAPTAIN MULZ 41
MORE THAN SHIP THEN, ... JC TO CAPTAIN MULZ 62
YOUR SHIP IS MANKIND'S DEEPEST DREAM JC TO CAPTAIN MULZ 67
YOUR SHIP IS FLAGSHIP . . . . JC TO CAPTAIN MULZ 69
YOUR SHIP IS VICTORY. . . . . JC TO CAPTAIN MULZ 73
YOUR SHIP IS . . . . JC TO CAPTAIN MULZ 77
AS OUR SHIP PASSED BY . . . . SP SEASCAPE 2

SHIPPED 1
SHIPPED THE WIDE WORLD OVER: . . . SP FREEDOM'S PLOW 81

SHIPS 8
LOADERS OF SHIPS. . . . . FC LAUGHERS 14
SHIPS WILL BE NAMED: . . . . ANS CHANT TOM MOONY 38
RAILROADS. SHIPS AND DAMS. . . . ANS OPEN LETTER 62
IN SHIPS . . . . . FW OLD SAILOR 3
SHIPS CAME FROM ACROSS THE SEA . . SP FREEDOM'S PLOW 29
WE SAW A LINE OF FISHING SHIPS . . SP SEASCAPE 3
OF SLAVE SHIPS . . . . . SP TRUMPET PLAYER 6
BUT DREAM SHIPS SAIL AWAY . . . . SP WATER-FRONT STR 2

SHIP'S 1
WE'VE PUT A CAPTAIN ON THAT SHIP'S BRIDGE THERE. . . . . JC TO CAPTAIN MULZ 43

SHIRT 1
BLOOD ON MY SPORT SHIRT . . . . . PL THIRD DEGREE 3

SHIVER 1
SHIVER WITH DELIGHT . . . . . PL UN-AMERICAN 4

SHIVERING 1
THE SHIVERING OF . . . . . FC SPORT 4

SHIVERS 1
THE COMMITTEE SHIVERS . . . . . PL UN-AMERICAN 21

SHO 22
BUT HE SHO DO TREAT ME KIND. . . . FC GAL'S CRY DYING 14
BUT HE SHO DO TREAT ME KIND. . . . FC GAL'S CRY DYING 16
SHO CAN'T FIND NO EASE. . . . . FC GYPSY MAN 24
DE WAY HE SHOCKS ME SHO IS SWEET. FC MA MAN 6
IT SHO WOULD BE SAD. . . . . FC MINNIE SINGS 14
I'D SHO HAVE THEM BLUES. . . . . FC MINNIE SINGS 20
SHO. THERE MUST BE PEACE. . . . . FC MOAN 16
AN' I SHO PAYS DOUBLE . . . . . FC WORKIN' MAN 14
UH! I SHO AM TIRED. . . . . NM BROKE 1
FOLKS SHO IS GETTIN' HARD ON YOU - JUST 'CAUSE YOU BROKE. . . . . NM BROKE 15
TOGETHER. RECKON I'LL TRY . . . SHO. I WANTS DE JOB! YES. SIR! . . . NM BROKE 30
SIX DOLLARS A WEEK? WHEE-COO! YOU SHO PAYS WELL! . . . . . NM BROKE 36
BUT I SHO BEEN LOOKIN' ROUND HARD LATELY FOR WAYS AND MEANS . . . NM BROKE 39
AND I SHO HAD A PRETTY GAL. TOO. UP YONDER ON SUGAR HILL. . . . . NM BROKE 48
I THOUGHT LOVE WAS A DREAM. BUT I SHO HAVE AWOKE - . . . . . NM BROKE 54
YES. INDEEDY. I SHO HAVE MISSED YOU. TOO! . . . . . NM BROKE 67
YOU GOT A GOOD JOB? YES! WELL. I SHO AM GLAD TO SEE YOU. DEAR! . . . . NM BROKE 69
YES. UM-HUM! YOU SHO IS SWEET! CAN YOU PAY FO' DE LICENSE. DEAR? . NM BROKE 78
SHO IS FINE. . . . . DK DRESSED UP 6
HE SAID. "SHO YOU'LL COME WID ME . DK MA LORD 15
BABE. YOU SHO CAN GO! . . . . . SH DEATH IN HARLEM 40
CAUSE THAT OLD ALARM CLOCK SHO HURTS MY EARS. . . . . SH LETTER 19

SHOCKS 1
DE WAY HE SHOCKS ME SHO IS SWEET. FC MA MAN 6

SHOD 1
AND HORSES SHOD WITH GOLD . . . . . AYM BLUES IN STEREO 4

SHOE 2
"ONE - TWO - BUCKLE MY SHOE!" . . . SP CHILDREN'S RYME 2
ON THEIR SHOE TIPS. . . . . SP SUMMER EVENING 9

SHOES 15
BUYS SHOES FOR THE BABY. . . . . FC BRASS SPITOONS 21
I GOT NEW SHOES - . . . . . DK DRESSED UP 9
DE SHOES WORE OFF MY FEET. . . . SH OUT OF WORK 2
DE SHOES WORE OFF MY FEET. . . . SH OUT OF WORK 4
WITH MY SHOES MISMATED. . . . . SP BAD MORNING 2
COAT. SHOES. . . . . SP BUDDY 9
AND THE SHOES I WAS WEARING . . . . SP CROSSING 13
OR SOMEBODY ELSE'S SHOES . . . . SP ELEVATOR BOY 18
WHITE SHOES . . . . . SP INTERNE AT PROV 4
JUST LIKE A PAIR O' SHOES - . . . . SP LOVER'S RETURN 10
GIMME YO' SHOES . . . . . SP PORTER 11
SUIT. OVERCOAT. SHOES - . . . . . SP WHAT? 5
THAT GENTLEMAN IN EXPENSIVE SHOES AYM BIRD IN ORBIT 65
THAT GENTLEMAN IN EXPENSIVE SHOES AYM BIRD IN ORBIT 88
AND MY TAN SUEDE SHOES. . . . . PL THIRD DEGREE 4

SHOOK 1
THE LIES THIEVES SHOOK . . . . . PL LUMUMBA'S GRAVE 7

SHOOT 2
AND SHOOT ALL KINDS O' SHELLS INTO YOU. . . . . SH TWILIGHT REVERI 8
WENT TO SHOOT YOUR WAY TO FREEDOM PL OCTOBER 16 RAID 8

SHOOTS 4
THE HIGH SHERIFF SHOOTS AND HE SHOOTS TO KILL . . . . . ANS BLD OZZIE POWEL 9
THE HIGH SHERIFF SHOOTS AND HE SHOOTS TO KILL . . . . . ANS BLD OZZIE POWEL 9
A WHITE HIGH SHERIFF WHO SHOOTS TO KILL . . . . . ANS BLD OZZIE POWEL 27
STRONG AS THE SHOOTS OF A NEW PLANT. FW EARTH SONG 8

SHOP 2
SHOP GIRLS. . . . . ANS OPEN LETTER 6
JOSTLE OF WOMEN WHO SHOP . . . . . OWT MAN INTO MEN 4

SHOPPING 2
I'M GOING SHOPPING NOW. CHILD. . . OWT JITNEY 58
FROM THE BIG GLASS SHOPPING CENTER AYM HORN OF PLENTY 94

SHOPS 3
CAME THE MARTS AND MARKETS. SHOPS AND STORES. . . . . SP FREEDOM'S PLOW 78
SOLD IN SHOPS. PILED IN WAREHOUSES. SP FREEDOM'S PLOW 80
SHOPS ALL OVER HARLEM . . . . . SP LIKEWISE 10

SHORE 3
FOR I'M THE ONE WHO LEFT DARK IRELAND'S SHORE. . . . . ANS LET AMERICA BE 47
TO A WHISKEY SHORE. . . . . FW SAILING DATE 5
TO THE OTHER SHORE - . . . . . SP MADAM NUMBER WR 24

SHORT 7
MA LITTLE. SHORT. SWEET. BROWNSKIN BOY. - . . . . . FC BLACK GAL 17
AND AGAIN MONEY'S SHORT. . . . . NM BIG-TIMER POEM 40
MAKE IT SHORT AND SWEET. YOUR LOVIN'. . . . . SH SIX-BITS BLUES 11
LITTLE SHORT . . . . . FW NIGHT SONG 4
LITTLE SHORT . . . . . FW NIGHT SONG 11
MAKES YOUR NAME TOO SHORT. . . . . SP MADAM CENSUS 24
LIFE IS SHORT . . . . . SP TAMBOURINES 9

SHORTER 2
GET SHORTER AND SHORTER. . . . . OWT RAID 4
GET SHORTER AND SHORTER. . . . . OWT RAID 4

SHOT 8
AN' SHOT A MAN IN DE BACK. . . . . FC DEATH DO DIRTY 9
THE MILLIONS SHOT DOWN WHEN WE STRIKE? . . . . . ANS LET AMERICA BE 54
A SHOT RANG OUT. . . . . SH DEATH IN HARLEM 103
AND A SHOT RANG OUT. . . . . SH DEATH IN HARLEM 108
HE GOT SHOT IN THE BACK . . . . . OWT BLD MARGE POLIT 10
GETS SHOT RIGHT INTO GLORY. . . . AYM IS IT TRUE? 53
WHEN THE MAN SHOT AT THE WOMAN . . AYM ODE TO DINAH 131
AND BY MISTAKE SHOT OUT THE LIGHT. AYM ODE TO DINAH 132

SHOTS 3
AS THE SHOTS RANG OUT. . . . . SH DEATH IN HARLEM 113
AS THE SHOTS RANG OUT. . . . . SH DEATH IN HARLEM 118
WHEN THE SHOTS RANG OUT. . . . . SH DEATH IN HARLEM 123

SHOULD 17
WE SHOULD HAVE A LAND OF SUN. . . . WB OUR LAND 1
WE SHOULD HAVE A LAND OF TREES. . . WB OUR LAND 8
AH. WE SHOULD HAVE A LAND OF JOY. WB OUR LAND 13
I SHOULD MEET LIFE FACE TO FACE . . OLD AESTHETE HARLEM 3
THAT MY SOUL SHOULD NOT BE LOST. . LHR BLD MARY'S SON 33
FOR TEARS IF SHE SHOULD CRY. . . . LHR TESTAMENT 8
THAT THERE SHOULD BE A BARREN GARDEN SP A HOUSE IN TAOS 16
BUT THAT THERE SHOULD BE THREE BARREN HEARTS . . . . . SP A HOUSE IN TAOS 19
WHEN HE SHOULD BE GONE . . . . . SP GONE BOY 6
BUT WE ALL SHOULD BE FREE. . . . SP SOUTHERN MAMMY 16
WE ALL SHOULD BE FREE. . . . . SP SOUTHERN MAMMY 18
AS GREAT ADVENTURES SHOULD . . . . SP S-SSS-SS-SH! 2
WHY SHOULD IT BE MY LONELINESS. . . SP TELL ME 1
WHY SHOULD IT BE MY SONG. . . . . SP TELL ME 2
WHY SHOULD IT BE MY DREAM . . . . . SP TELL ME 3
AND ONE SHOULD LOVE ONE'S COUNTRY AYM HORN OF PLENTY 57
SHOULD MIX LIKE RAIN . . . . . PL MISSISSIPPI 5

SHOULDER 3
I CRIED ON HIS SHOULDER BUT . . . . SP HARD DADDY 7
CRIED ON HIS SHOULDER BUT . . . . SP HARD DADDY 9
AND HAD A CHIP ON SHOULDER? . . . . AYM HORN OF PLENTY 50

SHOULDERS 4
SHOULDERS AT FATE. ACCEPTING HIS POSITION - BUT INSIDE HIMSELF UNHAPPY . . . . . NM BIG-TIMER MOOD 6
CALMLY TELLING THE STORY. PROUDLY AND EXPECTANTLY WITH HEAD UP. SHOULDERS . . . . . NM COLORED SL MOOD 7
ON HIS SHOULDERS . . . . . SP CATCH 3
JUST MAYBE SHRUG THEIR SHOULDERS. SP LIKEWISE 15

SHOUT 5
SHOUT DAT SONG: . . . . . FC SATURDAY NIGHT 22
IT FELT GOOD TO SHOUT! . . . . . FW COMMUNION 8
THEN I'LL SHOUT. GLORY FOR THE . . SP FREEDOM TRAIN 63
THE WAY YOU SHOUT OUT LOUD IN CHURCH. . . . . SP HIGH TO LOW 13

HEAR THOSE WORDS AND SHOUT THEM BACK SP IN EXPLANATION 41
A GOSPEL SHOUT . . . . SP TAMBOURINES 7

SHOUTS 3
SHOUTS ARE WHISPERS CARRYING . . . AYM ASK YOUR MAMA 2
SHOUTS FROM THE EARTH ITSELF . . . AYM BLUES IN STEREO 8
SHOUTS ARE WHISPERS CARRYING . . . AYM IS IT TRUE? 2

SHOVE 1
AND PUSH AND SHOVE AND GRAB! . . . OWT JITNEY 57

SHOVEL 2
WID A PICK AN' A SHOVEL. . . . . . FC WORKIN' MAN 2
UM-MM! SIGN HERE SAYS THEY WANTS SOMEBODY TO SHOVEL COAL. . . . . NM BROKE 28

SHOVELIN' 1
WHAT I DON'T KNOW 'BOUT SHOVELIN' COAL, AIN'T NO MO' TO KNOW! . . NM BROKE 32

SHOW 16
SHOW ME THAT YOU MEAN . . . . JC HOW ABOUT DIXIE 9
WHO CARRIES UGLY THINGS TO SHOW THE SUN? . . . . SP A HOUSE IN TAOS 21
A SHOW. . . . . SP DANCER 26
HE DIED FOR REAL. IT WARN'T NO SHOW. SP FREEDOM TRAIN 44
IS IT FOR REAL - OR JUST A SHOW AGAIN? . . . . SP FREEDOM TRAIN 46
TO SHOW YOU I STILL APPRECIATES YOU. SP LETTER 5
AT THE PICTURE SHOW. . . . . . . AYM ASK YOUR MAMA 24
IF SHOW FARE'S MORE THAN 30¢ ¢ ¢ ¢ ¢ ¢ ¢ ¢ . . . . AYM HORN OF PLENTY 29
SHADOWS SHOW UP SHARPER, ... AYM ODE TO DINAH 3
I WANT TO GO TO THE SHOW, MAMA. . . AYM ODE TO DINAH 95
NO SHOW FARE, BABY - . . . . AYM ODE TO DINAH 96
TELL ME, MAMA, CAN I GET MY SHOW . AYM SHOW FARE PLESE 1
SHOW FARE, MAMA, PLEASE. . . . . . AYM SHOW FARE PLESE 35
SHOW FARE, MAMA. . . . . AYM SHOW FARE PLESE 36
SHOW FARE! . . . . AYM SHOW FARE PLESE 37
TO SHOW HOW LIBERAL I AM? . . . . . PL NORTHERN LIBERL 10

SHOWED 1
GYPSY DONE SHOWED ME . . . . SP BAD LUCK CARD 3

SHOWING 1
JAUNDICED EYES SHOWING . . . . . . PL MISSISSIPPI 15

SHOWING-OFF 1
BARREL-HOUSE JAZZ, SHOWING-OFF, STRUTTING ABOUT PROUDLY, BRAGGING AND . . . . NM BIG-TIMER MOOD 4

SHREDS 1
TORN TO SHREDS BY DYNAMITE . . . . PL BIRMINGHAM SUND 8

SHROUD 2
OVER EVERYTHING LIKE A SHROUD. . . SH CABARET GIRL 2
NOT LIKE A SHROUD. . . . . PL COLOR 4

SHRUG 1
JUST MAYBE SHRUG THEIR SHOULDERS, SP LIKEWISE 15

SHRUGGING 1
BOASTING, LIKE A CHEAP BULLY, BUT SUDDENLY LOOKING AHEAD: SHRUGGING HIS . . . . NM BIG-TIMER MOOD 5

SHRUNKEN 1
SHRUNKEN LIKE A BALLOON WITHOUT AIR, SP A BLACK PIERROT 13

SHUBUTA 1
SHUBUTA BRIDGE OVER THE CHICASAWHAY RIVER IN MISSISSIPPI. . . . . . JC THE BITTER RIVR 1

SHUFFLING 1
A COMPLAINT TO B GIVEN BY A DEJECTED LOOKING FELLOW SHUFFLING ALONG . NM BROKE 1

SHUT 17
GONNA SHUT AN' LOCK MY DOOR . . . . SP CORA 4
SHUT UP, SAYS GERALD L.K. SMITH. . SP IN EXPLANATION 23
SHUT UP, SAYS THE GOVERNOR OF SOUTH CAROLINA. . . . . SP IN EXPLANATION 24
SHUT UP, SAYS THE GOVERNOR OF SINGAPORE. . . . . SP IN EXPLANATION 25
SHUT UP, SAYS STRYDOM. . . . . . SP IN EXPLANATION 26
HELL NO SHUT UP! SAY THE PEOPLE . . SP IN EXPLANATION 27
SHUT UP, PEOPLE! . . . . SP IN EXPLANATION 44
SHUT UP! SHUT UP! . . . . SP IN EXPLANATION 45
SHUT UP! SHUT UP! . . . . SP IN EXPLANATION 45
SHUT UP, GEORGE! . . . . SP IN EXPLANATION 46
SHUT UP, SALLIE! . . . . SP IN EXPLANATION 47
SHUT UP, COOLIE! . . . . SP IN EXPLANATION 48
SHUT UP, INDIAN! . . . . SP IN EXPLANATION 49
SHUT UP, BOY! . . . . SP IN EXPLANATION 50
NO SHUT UP! . . . . SP IN EXPLANATION 56
HELL NO SHUT UP! . . . . SP IN EXPLANATION 57
AND THE LID SHUT ON HIS HEAD . . . SP NIGHT FUNERAL 28

SHUTTERED 2
AND THE SINISTER SHUTTERED HOUSES OF THE BOTTOMS . . . . SP RUBY BROWN 18
HABITUES OF THE HIGH SHUTTERED HOUSES. . . . . SP RUBY BROWN 24

SICK 7
IT IS IN THIS SICK ROOM . . . . . . WB SICK ROOM 2
THE SICK, THE DEPRAVED, ... FW PRAYER 3
AND SICK SILLY SONGS . . . . SP JULIET 4
THE SICK, THE DEPRAVED, ... SP LITANY 3
SO SICK AND LONESOME . . . . SP LOVER'S RETURN 7
I WAS SO SICK LAST NIGHT I . . . . SP MORNING AFTER 1
SO SICK LAST NIGHT I . . . . SP MORNING AFTER 3

SIDE 21
I BEATS MA SIDE GAL TOO. . . . . . FC BAD MAN 8
BEATS MA SIDE GAL TOO. . . . . . . FC BAD MAN 10
FROM ONE SIDE TO THE OTHER. BUT NOW A HARSH AND BITTER NOTE CREEPS INTO . . . . NM BLACK CLWN MOOD 9
DONE BEAT YOU TO DE PLACE, STANDIN' OUT SIDE DE DO' . . . . NM BROKE 6
BIG BEN, I'M GONNA BUST YOU BANG UP SIDE THE WALL! . . . . SH DAYBREAK 1
TOO FAR TO ONE SIDE. . . . . SH SNOB 8
STAND BY MY SIDE. . . . . JC BIG BUDDY 17
ON THE SOUTH SIDE, ... OWT RESTRICTIVE 13
ON THIS SIDE OF THE TRACKS. . . . . OWT VISITORS 4
JAZZ ON THE SOUTH SIDE - . . . . . OWT VISITORS 10
ON THE SOUTH SIDE: . . . . OWT VISITORS 12
TO THE OTHER SIDE OF THE HOUSE . . SP KID SLEEPY 3
ON NEITHER SIDE. . . . . SP MIDNIGHT RAFFLE 16
TRANSFERS TO THE WEST SIDE, ... SP MIGRANT 8
IN HARLEM OR THE SOUTH SIDE OF CHICAGO . . . . AYM HORN OF PLENTY 55
AT EITHER SIDE ARRAYED . . . . . . AYM JAZZTET MUTED 15
ALWAYS TOOK THE OTHER SIDE.) . . . AYM RIDE, RED, RIDE 18
ARE ALL ON YOUR SIDE. . . . . . . PL LAST PRINCE 7
CAN'T SIT SIDE BY SIDE. . . . . . PL MERRY-GO-ROUND 8
CAN'T SIT SIDE BY SIDE. . . . . . PL MERRY-GO-ROUND 8
ONE SIDE WON, ... PL MOTHER IN WAR 13

SIDEWALK 1
THE RAIN MAKES STILL POOLS ON THE SIDEWALK. . . . . DK APRIL RAIN SONG 4

SIDNEYS 1
MAKE A CROWN OF SAMMYS, SIDNEYS, HARRYS, ... PL CROWNS GARLANDS 4

SIEG 1
SIEG . . . . PL SPECIAL BULLTIN 14

SIEVE 2
LIKE A SIEVE. . . . . SH BLD THE KILLER 24
THROUGH THEIR "FREEDOM" SIEVE. . . PL LUMUMBA'S GRAVE 8

SIGHS 1
SHE SIGHS. . . . . SP GRADUATION 31

SIGHT 4
GET OUT O' MY SIGHT BE- . . . . . . SH EVIL MORNING 15
IN THE SWEET O' MA LORD'S SIGHT - SP JUDGMENT DAY 12
OUT OF SIGHT . . . . SP PARADE 16
AN' A SINNER IN YO' SIGHT. . . . . SP SINNER 4

SIGHTED 1
SIGHTED THROUGH THE . . . . PL LONG VIEW NEGRO 2

SIGN 4
UM-MM! SIGN HERE SAYS THEY WANTS SOMEBODY TO SHOVEL COAL. . . . . NM BROKE 28
WILL BE A SIGN. . . . . LHR BLD MARY'S SON 21
AND NARY A SIGN OF A COLOR LINE - SP FREEDOM TRAIN 57
I'LL SIGN THE . . . . PL THIRD DEGREE 17

SIGNAL 1
A SIGNAL DRUM, ... SP DRUM 14

SIGNED 1
SIGNED IN BLOOD, ... PL OFFICIAL NOTICE 12

SIGNS 4
NO SIGNS FOR COLORED ON THE FREEDOM TRAIN, ... SP FREEDOM TRAIN 13
WHERE THERE NEVER WAS NO JIM CROW SIGNS NOWHERE, ... SP FREEDOM TRAIN 54
SIGNS HIS NAME . . . . SP MIGRANT 35
METHUSELAH SIGNS PAPERS W.E.B. . . AYM BIRD IN ORBIT 18

SILENCE 10
EMPTY AS THE SILENCE, ... WB SUMMER NIGHT 14
THEN A SILENCE OVER LAUGHTER . . . FW DIMOUT IN HARLM 9
SHADOWS VEILING SILENCE . . . . . . FW DIMOUT IN HARLM 10
SILENCE VEILING SHADOWS . . . . . . FW DIMOUT IN HARLM 11
SILENCE AND THE SHADOWS . . . . . . FW DIMOUT IN HARLM 12

SILENCE

SILENCE . . . . FW DIMOUT IN HARLM 14
OF YOUR SILENCE . . . . FW SILENCE 2
IN YOUR SILENCE . . . . FW SILENCE 6
GRANDPA, DID YOU FIND HER IN THE TV
SILENCE . . . . AYM BIRD IN ORBIT 61
SILENCE YOUR MOUTH. . . . . PL CHRIST IN ALA. 6

SILENT 3
A SILENT WOMAN LIES BETWEEN TWO
LOVERS - . . . . WB SICK ROOM 4
SO STILL WITH SILENT CRIES. . . . . WB SOLEDAD 11
LET ALL OTHERS KEEP SILENT A MOMENT. ANS A NEW SONG 3

SILENTLY 1
AND SILENTLY TOOK FOR GRANTED . . . SP FREEDOM'S PLOW 98

SILK 2
PUT ON YO' RED SILK STOCKINGS. . . FC RED SILK STOCK 1
PUT ON YO' RED SILK STOCKINGS, GAL. FC RED SILK STOCK 8

SILKEN 4
LIFTS HIGH A DRESS OF SILKEN GOLD. WB JAZZONIA 6
A SHIMMERING, SILKEN GARMENT. . . . WB SONGS DARK VIRG 9
SILKEN BATHROBES WITH GOLD TWINES SP FLATTED FIFTHS 9
LIFT SILKEN WINGS . . . . SP IN TIME SILVER 13

SILLY 2
THE BOOTED, BOOTED FOOL OF SILLY
MEN. . . . . WB THE JESTER 17
AND SICK SILLY SONGS . . . . SP JULIET 4

SILVER 21
OH, SILVER TREE! . . . . WB JAZZONIA 1
OH, SILVER RIVERS OF THE SOUL! . . WB JAZZONIA 15
I LOST MY SILVER MOONS. . . . . . . WB LAMENT DARK PEO 8
LET THE RAIN BEAT UPON YOUR HEAD
WITH SILVER LIQUID DROPS. . . . DK APRIL RAIN SONG 2
OF THIS SILVER BOWL. . . . . SH BLD PAWNBROKER 14
GYPSY SAID, SILVER. . . . . SP BLD THE GYPSY 5
PUT SOME SILVER IN MY HAND . . . . SP BLD THE GYPSY 6
I CROSSED HER PALM WITH SILVER. . . SP BLD THE GYPSY 9
IN SILVER THREAD AND DIAMOND NOTES SP FLATTED FIFTHS 12
TOUCHED SILVER WATER. . . . . SP FULFILMENT 6
PERHAPS IT'S A FAN OF SILVER LACE - SP HAVANA DREAMS 6
IN TIME OF SILVER RAIN . . . . . . SP IN TIME SILVER 1
IN TIME OF SILVER RAIN . . . . . . SP IN TIME SILVER 11
IN TIME OF SILVER RAIN . . . . . . SP IN TIME SILVER 21
WITH THEIR SILVER SHANKS. . . . . . SP MOONLIGHT NIGHT 4
SILVER MOONLIGHT EVERYWHERE. . . . SP MULATTO 20
POLISHING THE SILVER. . . . . SP RUBY BROWN 10
SWEET SILVER TRUMPETS. . . . . . . SP WHEN SUE WEARS 12
AS A SILVER UNICORN . . . . AYM IS IT TRUE? 13
FROM SLABS OF SILVER SHADOWS. . . . AYM ODE TO DINAH 54
IN SILVER CAGES SINGING. . . . . . AYM ODE TO DINAH 61

SIMPLE 11
I WOULD BE SIMPLE AGAIN. . . . . . WB DISILLUSION 1
SIMPLE AND CLEAN . . . . WB DISILLUSION 2
SAID SIMPLE JOHN. . . . . WB PIERROT 2
SAID SIMPLE JOHN. . . . . WB PIERROT 5
SAID SIMPLE JOHN. . . . . WB PIERROT 12
SAID SIMPLE JOHN. . . . . WB PIERROT 15
SAID SIMPLE JOHN. . . . . WB PIERROT 22
SAID SIMPLE JOHN. . . . . WB PIERROT 25
THE TRUTH A SIMPLE HEART HAS HELD DK ALABAMA EARTH 8
AND SEE WHERE SIMPLE WORKING FOLKS
LIKE ME . . . . JC GOOD MORN STLIN 32
I WONDER IF IT'S THAT SIMPLE? . . . SP THEME FOR ENG B 6

SIMPLY 2
SING IT VERY SIMPLY THAT I MIGHT
UNDERSTAND. . . . . ANS SONG OF SPAIN 3
I SIMPLY RAISE THESE QUESTIONS . . JC BLACK MAN SPEAK 21

SIN 4
BUT PIERROT'S STEEPED IN SIN. . . . WB PIERROT 26
JUST AS THOUGH IT WAS NO SIN - . . SP BLD OF THE GIRL 14
FOR SIN TODAY. . . . . SP MADAM MINISTER 33
WHICH SIN TO BEAR? . . . . SP PRAYER 4

SINCE 16
BEEN WALKIN' SINCE FIVE THIS
MORNIN'. . . . . NM BROKE 2
SINCE I'M BROKE. . . . . NM BROKE 55
SINCE THE COLORED SOLDIERS CAME HOME
FROM FRANCE. . . . . NM COLORED SL POEM 32
SINCE I COME UP NORTH DE . . . . . DK PO' BOY BLUES 5
BUT SINCE I GOT TO GET UP AT DAY. SH BED TIME 9
SO SINCE I'M STILL HERE LIVIN'. . . SP LIFE IS FINE 23
SINCE I WAS BORN BLACK. . . . . . . SP LITTLE OLD LETT 12
DONE SINCE THEN? . . . . SP MADAM MINISTER 14
SINCE THEIR DREAM HAS . . . . SP PASSING 15
SINCE THE MONEY THAT COMES IN . . . SP WHAT? 3
SINCE IT'S SNOWING ON THE TV . . . AYM ODE TO DINAH 7
SINCE BUT TWO EXIST . . . . AYM SHOW FARE PLESE 29
SINCE WE MOVED UP TO MOUNT VERNON. PL CULTURAL EXCHNG 25
SINCE HARPERS FERRY . . . . PL OCTOBER 16 RAID 23
SINCE NO STEMS . . . . PL SLUM DREAMS 6
SINCE THE DAY BEFORE LAST . . . . . PL STOKELY MALCOLM 6

SINFUL 1
SHE LIVED IN SINFUL HAPPINESS . . . FW GIRL 1

SING 40
SING 'EM, SISTER! . . . . WB BLUES FANTASY 22
SING EVE'S CHARMS! . . . . WB HARLEM NIGHT CL 13
SING YOUR BLUES SONG. . . . . WB TO MIDNIGHT NAN 9
LET THE RAIN SING YOU A LULLABY. . DK APRIL RAIN SONG 3
WHAT SHALL I SING . . . . DK LULLABY 5
WHAT SHALL I SING . . . . DK LULLABY 13
THIS IS WHAT I'M GONNA SING. . . . DK NIGHT AND MORN 2
THIS IS WHAT I'M GONNA SING: . . . DK NIGHT AND MORN 4
I MUST NOT SING YOU OVER-LONG. . . DK PASSING LOVE 2
THIS SONG TO SING: . . . . ANS A NEW SONG 6
AND SING ME THE SONG OF SPAIN. . . ANS SONG OF SPAIN 2
SING IT VERY SIMPLY THAT I MIGHT
UNDERSTAND. . . . . ANS SONG OF SPAIN 3
I WILL SING 'EM, TOO. . . . . SH HEY-HEY BLUES 14
I'LL SING 'EM, TOO. . . . . SH HEY-HEY BLUES 16
I'LL SING FOR YOU - BUT DROP THAT
COLOR BAR. . . . . JC JIM CROW'S LAST 18
TO SING ABOUT THE MEN WHO'VE DONE
THEM WRONG - . . . . OWT JUICE JOINT 24
WHERE BLACK MEN COME TO DRINK AND
PLAY AND SING. . . . . OWT JUICE JOINT 34
SING THE ST. JAMES INFIRMARY . . . OWT REQUEST REQUIEM 5
AND LET THE CHOIR SING A STORMY SONG SP FATASY PURPLE 3
SING IT SOFTLY, FOR THE SONG IS
WILD. . . . . SP GENIUS CHILD 2
SING IT SOFTLY AS EVER YOU CAN - . SP GENIUS CHILD 3
AND BIRDS SING - . . . . SP HEAVEN 6
NEW LEAVES TO SING . . . . SP IN TIME SILVER 16
I, TOO, SING AMERICA. . . . . SP I, TOO 1
AND STARS THAT SING. . . . . SP LOVE 2
SING A SOOTHIN' SONG. . . . . SP MISERY 5
YOU SING 'EM ON BROADWAY . . . . . SP NOTE COMM THEAT 2
AND YOU SING 'EM IN HOLLYWOOD BOWL. SP NOTE COMM THEAT 3
AND SING ABOUT ME. . . . . SP NOTE COMM THEAT 16
WILL SING A DUET. . . . . SP PROJECTION 17
SING, O LORD JESUS! . . . . SP SPIRITUALS 4
SING, O BLACK MOTHER! . . . . SP SPIRITUALS 15
TO SING ON THE GEORGIA ROADS. . . . SP SUN SONG 7
I HEARD THAT NEGRO SING, THAT OLD
PIANO MOAN - . . . . SP THE WEARY BLUES 18
BIRDS THAT REALLY SING . . . . . . AYM HORN OF PLENTY 76
BIRDS THAT REALLY SING. . . . . . . AYM HORN OF PLENTY 87
WHERE NEGROES SING SO WELL . . . . AYM SHADES OF PIG 8
NEGROES SING SO WELL . . . . AYM SHADES OF PIG 9
SING SO WELL . . . . AYM SHADES OF PIG 10
SEND FOR DEAD BLIND LEMON TO SING
THE B FLAT . . . . PL FINAL CALL 13

SINGAPORE 2
DIXIE TO SINGAPORE, CAPE TOWN TO
HONG KONG . . . . SP IN EXPLANATION 10
SHUT UP, SAYS THE GOVERNOR OF
SINGAPORE. . . . . SP IN EXPLANATION 25

SINGER 3
AND SINGER OF WEARY SONG. . . . . . JC THE BITTER RIVR 72
I'VE BEEN A SINGER: . . . . SP NEGRO 10
THE SINGER STOPPED PLAYING AND WENT
TO BED . . . . SP THE WEARY BLUES 33

SINGERS 11
BLUES SINGERS SAY. . . . . WB BLUES FANTASY 3
DREAM SINGERS. . . . . FC LAUGHERS 1
SINGERS - . . . . FC LAUGHERS 25
GOD! WHAT SINGERS! . . . . FC LAUGHERS 26
SINGERS AND DANCERS. . . . . FC LAUGHERS 27
COME NOW, ALL YOU WHO ARE SINGERS. ANS SONG OF SPAIN 1
SINGERS . . . . AYM HORN OF PLENTY 1
SINGERS LIKE C - . . . . AYM HORN OF PLENTY 2
SINGERS LIKE ODETTA - AND THAT
STATUE . . . . AYM HORN OF PLENTY 3
GOSPEL SINGERS WHO PANT TO PACK $ $
$ $ . . . . AYM HORN OF PLENTY 13
TO THE SINGERS. . . . . PL OPPRESSION 5

SINGING 16
SINGING MINOR MELODIES . . . . . . WB BLUES FANTASY 4
OH, SINGING TREE! . . . . WB JAZZONIA 7
BUT HIGHER THAN THE SINGING PINES DK ALABAMA EARTH 4
WAS SINGING . . . . FW NIGHT SONG 13
I SAT THERE SINGING HER . . . . . . FW SONGS 1
WHERE SINGING BLACK BOYS DANCE AND
PLAY EACH NIGHT . . . . OWT JUICE JOINT 2
SINGING SORROW SONGS ON THE BANKS OF
A MIGHTY RIVER . . . . SP AUNTSUE'S STORI 11
SINGING. . . . . SP HARLEM NIGHT SO 3
SINGING. . . . . SP HARLEM NIGHT SO 16
GO SINGING, TOO. . . . . SP IN TIME SILVER 20
I HEARD THE SINGING OF THE
MISSISSIPPI WHEN ABE LINCOLN . . SP NEGRO SPEAKS OF 8
I HEARD MY MOTHER SINGING . . . . . SP SPIRITUALS 6
TO MY CHAGRIN - NOT EVEN SINGING - AYM IS IT TRUE? 32

THE SHADES OF DINAH'S SINGING . . . AYM ODE TO DINAH 58
IN SILVER CAGES SINGING. . . . . . AYM ODE TO DINAH 61
SINGING YOUR MEAN OLD BACKLASH
BLUES. . . . . PL BACKLASH BLUES 30

SINGLE 3
IN NO SINGLE MOUTH THE SAME. . . . OLD TWO THINGS 10
ONE SINGLE HAND . . . . ANS OPEN LETTER 22
I'M GONNA RENT ME A CUBBY-HOLE WITH
A SINGLE BED. . . . . SH PAY DAY 17

SINGS 6
THAT EVEN YET ITS MIGHTY DARING
SINGS . . . . ANS LET AMERICA BE 42
WHO SINGS THE TROUBLES EVERY WOMAN
HAS. . . . . OWT LINCOLN THEATRE 8
MONROE SINGS A LITTLE BLUES. . . . SP MONROE'S BLUES 5
MONROE SINGS A LITTLE BLUES - . . . SP MONROE'S BLUES 7
WHOSE TOMORROW SINGS A HYMN . . . . PL BIRMINGHAM SUND 20
ON MY HEARTSTRINGS FREEDOM SINGS . PL WORDS LIKE FREE 3

SINISTER 1
AND THE SINISTER SHUTTERED HOUSES OF
THE BOTTOMS . . . . SP RUBY BROWN 18

SINK 3
LOOK AT THAT WATER DRIPPING IN THE
SINK. . . . . SH SUPPER TIME 5
WHEN YOU SINK SO LOW. . . . . OWT TOO BLUE 5
THE SINK IS BROKE. . . . . SP MADAM RENT MAN 11

SINNER 1
AN' A SINNER IN YO' SIGHT. . . . . SP SINNER 4

SINS 1
HAVING PREVIOUSLY POINTED OUT THE
SINS OF THIS WORLD: . . . . . . SP SUNDAY MORNING 1

SIPS 1
ALICUNE AIME SEDAR SIPS HIS
NEGRITUDE. . . . . AYM BIRD IN ORBIT 23

SIR 10
C. PLEASE SIR. JUDGE. HAVE MERCY! FC BLD OF GIN MARY 21
TOGETHER. RECKON I'LL TRY . . . SHO.
I WANTS DE JOB! YES. SIR! . . . NM BROKE 30
YES. SIR. . . . . SP PORTER 2
YES. SIR! . . . . SP PORTER 4
YES. SIR! . . . . SP PORTER 5
YES. SIR! . . . . SP PORTER 13
YES. SIR! LONG AS LIFE DO LAST! . . SP SYLVESTER'S BED 22
YES. SIR. I TOLD HER. . . . . AYM ASK YOUR MAMA 12
BUT YES. SIR. SIR. TO YOU. . . . . PL VARI-COLORED 12
BUT YES. SIR. SIR. TO YOU. . . . . PL VARI-COLORED 12

SIRS 1
OF YES. SIRS! . . . . SP PORTER 8

SISSIE 1
SHE COULD MAKE ME HOLLER LIKE A
SISSIE. . . . . SH ONLY WOMAN BLUS 7

SISTER 8
SING 'EM. SISTER! . . . . WB BLUES FANTASY 22
"YOU ARE MY SISTER - NOW - TODAY!" ANS OPEN LETTER 40
AND SISTER. TOO. . . . . SH BLD THE SINNER 8
IF I WAS ANYBODY'S SISTER. . . . . SP EVENING SONG 5
BUT I AIN'T NOBODY'S SISTER. . . . SP EVENING SONG 7
HE SAID. SISTER . . . . SP MADAM MINISTER 17
HE SAID. SISTER. . . . . SP MADAM MINISTER 21
MARIE'S MY SISTER - NOT MARRIED TO
ME - . . . . SP SISTER 3

SISTERS 1
BROTHERS AND SISTERS. . . . . SP SUNDAY MORNING 37

SIT 4
HERE I SIT . . . . SP BAD MORNING 1
SIT DOWN BY THE RIVER . . . . SP REVERIE HARLEM 3
UP TO MY ROOM. SIT DOWN. AND WRITE
THIS PAGE: . . . . SP THEME FOR ENG B 15
CAN'T SIT SIDE BY SIDE. . . . . . . PL MERRY-GO-ROUND 8

SITS 3
HE SITS ON A HILL . . . . FW JAIME 1
HE SITS ON A HILL . . . . FW JAIME 5
WHO SITS UPON THE GROUND . . . . . SP MEXICAN MARKET 2

SITTING 4
SITTING IN THE MARBLE AND THE
MOONLIGHT. . . . . DK LINCOLN MONUMNT 2
SITTING LONELY IN THE MARBLE AND THE
MOONLIGHT. . . . . DK LINCOLN MONUMNT 3
SITTING ON OLD MRS. LATHAM'S BACK
PORCH . . . . SP RUBY BROWN 9
SITTING ON THEIR WIDE VERANDAS. . . PL CULTURAL EXCHNG 47

SITUATION 1
BUT NOW I KNOW WELL THAT'S NOT OUR
SITUATION: . . . . NM COLORED SL POEM 28

SIT-IN 2
THOSE SIT-IN KIDS. HE SAID. . . . . AYM BIRD IN ORBIT 71
SIT-IN. STAND-IN. STALL-IN. VOTE-IN PL GHOSTS OF 1619 7

SIT-INS 1
WHERE SIT-INS ARE CONDUCTED . . . . AYM BIRD IN ORBIT 11

SIX 13
SIX LONG-HEADED JAZZERS PLAY. . . . WB JAZZONIA 4
SIX LONG-HEADED JAZZERS PLAY. . . . WB JAZZONIA 17
I COULD MAKE SIX DOLLARS A DAY . . FC PRIZE FIGHTER 4
SIX DOLLARS A WEEK? WHEE-OOO! YOU
SHO PAYS WELL! . . . . NM BROKE 36
(AIN'T SEEN HER IN SIX YEARS! USED
TO GO WITH HER. TOO!) . . . . . NM BROKE 63
BEEN UP HERE SIX MONTHS - . . . . . SH EVENIN' BLUES 5
AT SIX O'CLOCK. OR SEVEN. OR EIGHT. OWT NEGRO SERVANT 8
SIX DISCS . . . . SP BE-BOP BOYS 3
DROPPED OUT SIX MONTHS WHEN I WAS
SEVEN. . . . . SP DEFERRED 3
AND SIX PALLBEARERS . . . . SP NIGHT FUNERAL 31
SIX KNOTS WAS ON HIS HEAD . . . . . SP NOT A MOVIE 12
SIX OR EIGHT AND TEN YEARS OLDER'N
MYSELF. . . . . SP PREFERENCE 2
WHO AT THE SORBONNE HAS SIX CLASSES. AYM ASK YOUR MAMA 54

SIXTEEN 3
AND SIXTEEN FISH-TAIL CARS. . . . . SP AS BEFITS A MAN 10
ONCE SIXTEEN. . . . . SP CONSIDER ME 3
SIXTEEN FLOORS ABOVE THE GROUND. . SP LIFE IS FINE 13

SIXTY 1
YOU'LL NEED SIXTY MORE . . . . . . SP BLD OF THE MAN 4

SIX-BITS' 2
GIMME SIX-BITS' WORTH O' TICKET . . SH SIX-BITS BLUES 1
I SAY SIX-BITS' WORTH O' TICKET . . SH SIX-BITS BLUES 3

SIX-YEAR-OLDS 1
ONE-TIME SIX-YEAR-OLDS . . . . . . AYM BIRD IN ORBIT 8

SIZE 1
SUCKER SIZE. . . . . SP TRUMPET PLAYER 32

SI'L-VOUS 1
SO. SI'L-VOUS PLAIT. I'LL STUDY
FRENCH! . . . . SP DEFERRED 28

SKEE 1
SKEE! DADDLE-DE-DO! . . . . SP CHILDREN'S RYME 26

SKEE-DE-DAD 1
SKEE-DE-DAD! DE-DAD! . . . . FC SATURDAY NIGHT 13

SKIES 3
AND TALLER THAN THE SKIES . . . . . DK ALABAMA EARTH 5
AS THE DREAMED OF SKIES. . . . . . FW WISDOM 8
AND GEORGIA SKIES SO BLUE. . . . . PL VARI-COLORED 10

SKILLS 1
LEARNING SKILLS OF SURGEONS . . . . SP INTERNE AT PROV 11

SKIM 1
SKIM EVEN A DIME - . . . . PL PRIME 8

SKIN 7
AND HER SKIN BLUE WHITE. . . . . . FC CLOSING TIME 5
AND START A SKIN GAME WITH SOME
CHUMPS I KNOW. . . . . SH BED TIME 6
HER SKIN SO BROWN. . . . . SP MEXICAN MARKET 7
WITH PURPLE POWDERED SKIN. . . . . SP RAILROAD AVENUE 16
THE SKIN ON YOUR BLACK FACE. . . . PL SPECIAL BULLTIN 19
PEEL OFF THE SKIN. . . . . PL SPECIAL BULLTIN 20
THE SKIN. . . . . PL SPECIAL BULLTIN 23

SKINS 3
WHITE SKINS . . . . OWT MAN INTO MEN 11
BLACK SKINS . . . . OWT MAN INTO MEN 12
THROUGH THE RED. WHITE. YELLOW SKINS SP A HOUSE IN TAOS 34

SKIN'LL 1
AND YOUR SKIN'LL TURN . . . . SP KID SLEEPY 6

SKIPPER 1
(NEGRO SKIPPER OF THE BOOKER T.
WASHINGTON SAILING WITH A MIXED
CREW) . . . . JC TO CAPTAIN MULZ 1

SKIRT 1
SMOOTHS THE SKIRT . . . . SP GRADUATION 4

SKIRTS 1
AND SWITCH THEIR SKIRTS AND LIFT
THEIR STRAIGHTENED HEADS . . . . OWT JUICE JOINT 23

SKY 24
BLOOD COUGHED ACROSS THE SKY. . . . WB CARIBBEAN SUNST 2
AND PIERROT LOVED A STAR-FILLED SKY. WB PIERROT 9
SOMEWHERE IN YO' SKY. . . . . FC MOAN 18
OF A FREE LIFE BENEATH OUR GREAT SKY. . . . . NM DARK YOUTH USA 10
AND A SONG THAT REACHES THE SKY - ANS KIDS WHO DIE 49
OUR SKY IS GRAY. . . . . ANS SONG OF SPAIN 49
JUST AS THE SKY IN THE . . . . . . SH DEATH IN HARLEM 133
LIGHTS THE SKY. . . . . JC GOOD MORN STLIN 14
ACROSS THE SKY. . . . . FW THERE 4
UNTIL THE STARS PALE AND THE SKY TURNS BLUE . . . . OWT JUICE JOINT 3
UP THERE IN THE SKY. . . . . OWT REQUEST REQUIEM 4
ROSE UNTIL IT TOUCHED THE SKY - . . SP AS I GREW OLDER 15
LEAVES THE SUNRISE IN THE SKY - . . SP BLACK MARIA 19
NIGHT SKY IS BLUE. . . . . SP HARLEM NIGHT SO 8
IN JOY BENEATH THE SKY . . . . . . SP IN TIME SILVER 17
SEE THE AIRPLANES IN THE SKY? . . . SP KID IN THE PARK 4
YOU WERE MY MOON UP IN THE SKY. . . SP MISS BLUES'ES 7
RIGHT HERE BENEATH GOD'S SKY. . . . SP NEW YORKERS 3
OF EARTH NOR SKY . . . . SP NEW YORKERS 11
ETCHED AGAINST THE SKY. . . . . . . SP SEASCAPE 4
THE SKY. THE SUN. THE STARS. . . . SP THE SOUTH 11
OUT OF THE MIDNIGHT SKY . . . . . . AYM ASK YOUR MAMA 34
BLOWN SKY HIGH BY MONT PELEE? . . . AYM RIDE. RED. RIDE 14
HIDDEN FROM THE SKY . . . . PL WITHOUT BENEFIT 14

SKYROCKET 1
BARS AND FLOOR SKYROCKET . . . . . PL THIRD DEGREE 13

SKYSCRAPERS 1
WE CRY AMONG THE SKYSCRAPERS . . . WB AFRAID 1

SKY-MEANING 1
LIKE THE SKY-MEANING . . . . SP FULFILMENT 2

SKY'S 1
I WONDER WHY THE SKY'S SO BLUE . . PL VARI-COLORED 13

SLABS 1
FROM SLABS OF SILVER SHADOWS. . . . AYM ODE TO DINAH 54

SLACK 1
NIGHT WILL PULL ITS SLACK TAUT . . SP SUMMER EVENING 25

SLAVE 16
A SLAVE - UNDER THE WHIP. . . . . . NM BLACK CLWN POEM 21
HE WAS A COLORED MAN WHO HAD BEEN A SLAVE . . . . SP FREEDOM'S PLOW 112
SLAVE MEN AND SLAVE MASTERS. ALL NEW - . . . . SP FREEDOM'S PLOW 33
SLAVE MEN AND SLAVE MASTERS. ALL NEW - . . . . SP FREEDOM'S PLOW 33
SOME WERE SLAVE HANDS . . . . SP FREEDOM'S PLOW 45
IN THE FREE HANDS AND THE SLAVE HANDS. . . . . SP FREEDOM'S PLOW 50
FREE HANDS AND SLAVE HANDS. . . . . SP FREEDOM'S PLOW 61
I'VE BEEN A SLAVE: . . . . SP NEGRO 4
I AM THE ONE WHO LABORED AS A SLAVE. SP THE NEGRO MOTHE 13
OF SLAVE SHIPS . . . . SP TRUMPET PLAYER 6
FROM THE SLAVE CHAIN TO THE LYNCH ROPE . . . . PL DEATH YORKVILLE 9
ANYTHING BUT A SLAVE! HE SAID. . . PL FREDRK DOUGLASS 17
THERE TO PURCHASE A SLAVE. . . . . PL SLAVE 3
A SLAVE WHO DIED YOUNG. . . . . . . PL SLAVE 4
A SLAVE WHO DIED YOUNG. . . . . . . PL SLAVE 8
TO PURCHASE A SLAVE . . . . PL SLAVE 12

SLAVERY 2
IN THOSE DARK DAYS OF SLAVERY. . . SP FREEDOM'S PLOW 123
FOR OLD JOHN BROWN WHO KNEW SLAVERY COULDN'T . . . . PL FINAL CALL 22

SLAVERY'S 1
I AM THE NEGRO BEARING SLAVERY'S SCARS. . . . . ANS LET AMERICA BE 20

SLAVER'S 2
BENEATH THE SLAVER'S WHIP. . . . . ANS A NEW SONG 9
REMEMBER THE WHIP AND THE SLAVER'S TRACK. . . . . SP THE NEGRO MOTHE 44

SLAVES 14
SLAVES OF MEN. . . . . JC TO CAPTAIN MULZ 32
WE NEGROES HAVE BEEN SLAVES BEFORE. JC TO CAPTAIN MULZ 33
BLACK SLAVES . . . . SP AUNTSUE'S STORI 6
AND BLACK SLAVES . . . . SP AUNTSUE'S STORI 8
AND BLACK SLAVES . . . . SP AUNTSUE'S STORI 10
THERE WERE SLAVES THEN. TOO. . . . SP FREEDOM'S PLOW 105
BUT IN THEIR HEARTS THE SLAVES KNEW SP FREEDOM'S PLOW 106
THAN TO LIVE SLAVES. . . . . SP FREEDOM'S PLOW 111
AND THE SLAVES KNEW . . . . SP FREEDOM'S PLOW 114
THE SLAVES MADE UP A SONG: . . . . SP FREEDOM'S PLOW 125
THAT THE SLAVES WOULD BE FREE. . . SP FREEDOM'S PLOW 134
THAN TO LIVE SLAVES. . . . . SP FREEDOM'S PLOW 173
HIS NAME WAS JEFFERSON. THERE WERE SLAVES THEN. . . . . SP FREEDOM'S PLOW 96
BUT IN THEIR HEARTS THE SLAVES BELIEVED HIM. TOO. . . . . SP FREEDOM'S PLOW 97

SLEAZY 1
AND THE SLEAZY COURTS. . . . . . . ANS KIDS WHO DIE 25

SLEEK 1
SLEEK BLACK BOYS IN A CABARET. . . WB HARLEM NIGHT CL 1

SLEEK-HAIRED 1
AND SLEEK-HAIRED BOYS WHO DEAL IN LOVE FOR PAY . . . . OWT LINCOLN THEATRE 14

SLEEP 15
IN LOVELESS SLEEP. . . . . WB YOUNG BRIDE 7
AN' A PO'. PO' GAL CAN SLEEP. . . . FC SUICIDE 18
WAITING FOR SLEEP . . . . DLD THE CONSUMPTIVE 6
TO A SLEEP WITHOUT DREAMS . . . . . DK QUIET GIRL 5
I CAN SLEEP SO GOOD WITH YOU AWAY! SH BED TIME 11
GONNA SLEEP LIKE A WATER-LOG. . . . SH MISSISSIPPI LEV 6
AND SLEEP COMES. . . . . FW SLEEP 6
TO A SLEEP WITHOUT DREAMS . . . . . SP ARDELLA 5
AND LET HIM SLEEP IN HER . . . . . SP BLD FORTUNE TEL 15
A WOMAN TO SLEEP WITH. . . . . . . SP ELEVATOR BOY 13
I'D TELL HER. GIMME A PLACE TO SLEEP. . . . . SP EVENING SONG 6
AND SLEEP . . . . SP FULFILMENT 19
I BUILT MY HUT NEAR THE CONGO AND IT LULLED ME TO SLEEP. . . . . . . SP NEGRO SPEAKS OF 6
WELL. I LIKE TO EAT. SLEEP. DRINK. AND BE IN LOVE. . . . . SP THEME FOR ENG B 21
NO PLACE TO SLEEP. . . . . SP VAGABONDS 6

SLEEPING 1
HERE IS THAT SLEEPING PLACE. . . . FW GRAVE YARD 1

SLEEPIN' 1
LORDY! SLEEPIN' BY HERSELF. . . . . SP STONY LONESOME 17

SLEEPS 1
THE LAST CRYING BABY SLEEPS . . . . WB SUMMER NIGHT 7

SLEEPY 6
SLEEPY GIANT. . . . . SP AFRICA 1
LISTEN. KID SLEEPY. . . . . SP KID SLEEPY 1
KID SLEEPY SAID. . . . . SP KID SLEEPY 8
LISTEN. KID SLEEPY. . . . . SP KID SLEEPY 10
KID SLEEPY SAID. . . . . SP KID SLEEPY 16
KID SLEEPY. JUST . . . . SP KID SLEEPY 19

SLEEP-SONG 2
THE RAIN PLAYS A LITTLE SLEEP-SONG ON OUR ROOF AT NIGHT - . . . . . DK APRIL RAIN SONG 6
FOR YOUR SLEEP-SONG LULLABY! . . . DK LULLABY 25

SLEET-STUNG 1
THE SHARP. SLEET-STUNG . . . . . . WB POEME D'AUTOMNE 12

SLEEVE 1
UP YOUR SLEEVE: . . . . SP MADAM MIGHT-HAV 24

SLENDER 1
THE SLENDER TREES . . . . WB POEME D'AUTOMNE 3

SLEPT 3
WHAT JUNGLE TREE HAVE YOU SLEPT UNDER. . . . . WB NUDE YOUNG DANC 1
WHAT JUNGLE TREE HAVE YOU SLEPT UNDER. . . . . WB NUDE YOUNG DANC 5
HE SLEPT LIKE A ROCK OR A MAN THAT'S DEAD. . . . . SP THE WEARY BLUES 35

SLEW 1
A WHOLE SLEW OF PEOPLE . . . . . . SH DEATH IN HARLEM 119

SLICE 1
FACE LIKE SLICE OF MELON. . . . . . SP 125TH STREET 5

SLIDE 1
SLIDE ON OVER. DARLING. . . . . . . DK SONG BANJO DANC 7

SLIGHTLY 2
PRESSURE OF THE BLOOD IS SLIGHTLY HIGHER . . . . AYM JAZZTET MUTED 2
IS SLIGHTLY HIGHER - . . . . AYM JAZZTET MUTED 19

SLIM 5
FOR PIERROT PLAYED ON A SLIM GUITAR. WB PIERROT 27
HIS ROLL WASN'T SLIM - . . . . . . SH DEATH IN HARLEM 7
A TALL. SLIM TREE . . . . SP DREAM VARIATION 15
SLIM. DANCING JOY. . . . . SP JOY 2
IS THE SLIM CURVED CROOK OF THE MOON TONIGHT! . . . . SP WINTER MOON 3

SLIME 2
AND THE SLIME IN HOTEL SPITOONS! . FC BRASS SPITOONS 9

OUT OF THE SLIME! . . . . NM BLACK CLWN POEM 72

SLIP 1
SLIP AND BREAK . . . . AYM IS IT TRUE? 47

SLIPPED 1
SLIPPED AWAY . . . . SH DEATH IN HARLEM 136

SLIPPING 1
SLIPPING OUT FROM UNDER THEM . . . PL UNDERTOW 10

SLIPS 1
UPON WHAT RIFF THE MUSIC SLIPS . . SP TRUMPET PLAYER 38

SLIVER 1
AS A SLIVER OF THE MOON. . . . . . SP SLIVER 4

SLOPPY 1
THE DREAM IS A COCKTAIL AT SLOPPY
JOE'S - . . . . SP HAVANA DREAMS 1

SLOT 1
IN THE SUBWAY SLOT. . . . . SP MIDNIGHT RAFFLE 10

SLOUCH 1
IN GRAY SLOUCH HATS. . . . . PL THIRD DEGREE 6

SLOW 25
CREEPING LIKE FIRE FROM A SLOW SPARK OLD THE CONSUMPTIVE 10
BACK BENT AS IN THE FIELDS. THE SLOW
STEP. THE BOWED HEAD. "NOBODY
KNOWS . . . . NM BLACK CLWN MOOD 4
WALKING PROUDLY. ALMOST PRANCING.
BUT GRADUALLY SUBDUED TO A SLOW.
HEAVY . . . . NM BLACK CLWN MOOD 7
IN AN OLD SUIT AND A BATTERED HAT.
TO THE TUNE OF A SLOW DRAG STOMP NM BROKE 1
JAZZ IT SLOW! . . . . SH DEATH IN HARLEM 28
DIXIE'S AIN'T NO PLACE FOR A GANG
THAT'S SLOW. . . . . SH DEATH IN HARLEM 38
THE SLOW BEATING OF THE TOM-TOMS. SP DANSE AFRICAINE 2
LOW . . . SLOW . . . . SP DANSE AFRICAINE 3
SLOW . . . LOW - . . . . SP DANSE AFRICAINE 4
AND LET THE WHITE VIOLINS WHIR THIN
AND SLOW. . . . . SP FATASY PURPLE 6
BABY. TAKE IT SLOW. . . . . SP SAME IN BLUES 2
GO SLOW. THEY SAY - . . . . PL GO SLOW 1
GO SLOW. I HEAR - . . . . PL GO SLOW 4
GOING SLOW. SLOW. SLOW. . . . . . . PL GO SLOW 17
GOING SLOW. SLOW. SLOW. . . . . . . PL GO SLOW 17
GOING SLOW. SLOW. SLOW. . . . . . . PL GO SLOW 17
SLOW. SLOW. SLOW. . . . . PL GO SLOW 18
SLOW. SLOW. SLOW. . . . . PL GO SLOW 18
SLOW. SLOW. SLOW. . . . . PL GO SLOW 18
SLOW. SLOW. . . . . PL GO SLOW 19
SLOW. SLOW. . . . . PL GO SLOW 19
SLOW. . . . . PL GO SLOW 20
SLOW. . . . . PL GO SLOW 21
SLOW? . . . . PL GO SLOW 22
LOOK SLOW AT ONE ANOTHER - . . . . PL OCTOBER 16 RAID 12

SLOWLY 7
SAY IT VERY SLOWLY IF YOU CHOOSE. FC MAMMY 4
SHE SNAPS HER FINGERS. SLOWLY SHAKES
HER HIPS. . . . . OWT LINCOLN THEATRE 9
ROSE SLOWLY. . . . . SP AS I GREW OLDER 8
SLOWLY. . . . . SP AS I GREW OLDER 9
ROSE SLOWLY. SLOWLY. . . . . SP AS I GREW OLDER 11
ROSE SLOWLY. SLOWLY. . . . . SP AS I GREW OLDER 11
WHIRLS SOFTLY . . . SLOWLY. . . . . SP DANSE AFRICAINE 10

SLUG 1
SLUG ME! BEAT ME! . . . . PL THIRD DEGREE 7

SLY 1
THE SLY AND SERVILE GRACE . . . . . SP UNCLE TOM 7

SMALL 5
ITS PEOPLE'S HEART. TOO SMALL TO
HOLD A SOB. . . . . SL TOWN OF SCOTTSB 4
IF I HAD SOME SMALL CHANGE . . . . SH IF-ING 1
PRACTICE ON THE SMALL APPENDIX . . SP INTERNE AT PROV 9
SO SMALL I CAN'T WHIP A CAT . . . . SP NECESSITY 6
BECOMES SO SMALL . . . . PL LONG VIEW NEGRO 12

SMALL'S 1
SMALL'S . . . . SP NEON SIGNS 9

SMART 4
COLLEGE BOY SMART . . . . SP COLLEGE FORMAL 7
I'M SMART THAT WAY. . . . . SP MADAM'S PAST HI 4
HE AIN'T SMART. . . . . SP NEIGHBOR 11
AND NOT MEANIN' TO BE SMART - . . . SP SOUTHERN MAMMY 20

SMARTER 1
AND HE'S SMARTER THAN HE LOOKS. . . SP NEIGHBOR 10

SMASH 3
SMASH MY WAY THROUGH . . . . NM BLACK CLWN POEM 65
TO SMASH THE OLD DEAD DOGMAS OF THE
PAST - . . . . ANS OPEN LETTER 24
TO SMASH THIS NIGHT. . . . . SP AS I GREW OLDER 29

SMASHED 1
BUILDER OF HOPES TO BE SMASHED. . . JC THE BITTER RIVR 68

SMASHES 1
SMASHES MISERY. . . . . ANS OPEN LETTER 57

SMEARED 1
ARE SMEARED ACROSS . . . . SP JULIET 9

SMEARS 2
RIFFS. SMEARS. BREAKS. . . . . SP EASY BOOGIE 9
SMEARS RE-BOP . . . . SP SHALIMAR 4

SMELL 2
BREATH AND SMELL . . . . SP SUBWAY RUSH HOU 2
AND THE SMELL OF RED CLAY AFTER RAIN PL DAYBREAK IN ALA 9

SMELLING 1
WHAT'S SMELLING. LEONTYNE? . . . . PL CULTURAL EXCHNG 28

SMELTED 1
FIRST SMELTED IN . . . . JC ME AND MY SONG 11

SMILE 6
IN A BOX WITHOUT A SMILE. . . . . . OWT FUNERAL 2
IN YOUR SMILE. . . . . SP AFRICA 5
LORD KNOWS I WOULD SMILE. . . . . . SP MISS BLUES'ES 2
I WOULD SMILE. SMILE. SMILE. . . . SP MISS BLUES'ES 4
I WOULD SMILE. SMILE. SMILE. . . . SP MISS BLUES'ES 4
I WOULD SMILE. SMILE. SMILE. . . . SP MISS BLUES'ES 4

SMILED 1
THEN HIS DARK FACE SMILED AT ME IN
THE NIGHT - . . . . NM COLORED SL POEM 39

SMILES 2
CAME TIPPIN INTO DIXIE'S WITH SMILES
ON THEIR FACES. . . . . SH DEATH IN HARLEM 60
INTO A THOUSAND SMILES. . . . . . . SP SUNDAY MORNING 6

SMILING 2
BEEN MADE. PROUD AND SMILING. BUT
THE LIVING. REMEMBERING WITH A
HALF-SOB . . . . NM COLORED SL MOOD 10
THE MOURNERS GOT UP SMILING. . . . DK IRISH WAKE 7

SMITH 1
SHUT UP. SAYS GERALD L.K. SMITH. . SP IN EXPLANATION 23

SMITTEN 1
SMITTEN BY BEAUTY. . . . . SP A HOUSE IN TAOS 4

SMITTY 1
AND SMITTY HAS NOT CHANGED AT ALL. AYM BIRD IN ORBIT 22

SMOKE 4
AND THE SMOKE IN HOTEL LOBBIES. . . FC BRASS SPITOONS 8
I CAN'T EVEN GET DE MONEY FOR TO BUY
MYSELF A SMOKE. . . . . NM BROKE 46
SPAGHETTI AND GIN. MUSIC AND SMOKE. SH DEATH IN HARLEM 53
LIKE A WISP OF SMOKE AROUND THE FIRE
- . . . . SP DANSE AFRICAINE 11

SMOKED 1
AND SMOKED A CAPSTAN CIGARETTE . . DK SAILOR 3

SMOLDERING 2
WHERE THE SMOLDERING MEMORY . . . . SP TRUMPET PLAYER 5
DUE TO SMOLDERING SHADOWS . . . . . AYM JAZZTET MUTED 20

SMOOTHS 1
SMOOTHS THE SKIRT . . . . SP GRADUATION 4

SMOTHER 2
WILL LIVE ON WEAVING WORDS TO
SMOTHER THE KIDS WHO DIE. . . . ANS KIDS WHO DIE 24
I NOURISHED THE DREAM THAT NOTHING
COULD SMOTHER . . . . SP THE NEGRO MOTHE 31

SMUG 1
SMUG. ALMOST SECURE . . . . PL UN-AMERICAN 2

SNAIL 1
LITTLE SNAIL. . . . . SP SNAIL 1

SNAKE 2
EVEN THE SNAKE . . . . SP DESERT 5
A SNAKE . . . . SP LIVE LET LIVE 4

SNAKE-LIKE 2
IN THE SNAKE-LIKE HISS OF ITS STREAM JC THE BITTER RIVR 15
WITH THE HISS OF ITS SNAKE-LIKE SONG
- . . . . JC THE BITTER RIVR 64

SNAPS 1

Line	Poem	No.
SHE SNAPS HER FINGERS, SLOWLY SHAKES HER HIPS.	OWT LINCOLN THEATRE	9

SNARL 2

Line	Poem	No.
TO THE TERRIBLE SNARL.	SP A HOUSE IN TAOS	36
BUT ALL ONE SNARL OF SOULS.	SP A HOUSE IN TAOS	40

SNORE 2

Line	Poem	No.
PLEASE DON'T SNORE SO LOUD.	SP MORNING AFTER	14
PLEASE DON'T SNORE SO LOUD.	SP MORNING AFTER	16

SNORT 1

Line	Poem	No.
(WITH A SNORT)	SP MADAM CENSUS	22

SNOW 16

Line	Poem	No.
LEAVES DE SNOW OUTSIDE	FC MINNIE SINGS	5
FROZEN WITH SNOW.	DK DREAMS	8
ITS ROOF WITH SNOW IS PILED.	DK WINTER SWEEETNS	2
SNOW.	FW FOR DEAD MIMES	5
LYING IN THE SNOW.	FW WHEN ARMIES PAS	2
SCATTERED ALL OVER THE SNOW.	FW WHEN ARMIES PAS	13
THE ANGELS WINGS IS WHITE AS SNOW.	SP ANGELS WINGS	1
O, WHITE AS SNOW.	SP ANGELS WINGS	2
SNOW.	SP ANGELS WINGS	5
THE ANGELS WINGS IS WHITE AS SNOW.	SP ANGELS WINGS	6
BUT THE ANGELS WINGS IS WHITE AS SNOW.	SP ANGELS WINGS	11
SNOW.	SP ANGELS WINGS	14
SNOW ALL OVER THE GROUND.	SP MIDWINTER BLUES	2
SNOW ALL OVER THE GROUND -	SP MIDWINTER BLUES	4
WHERE TO SNOW NOW ACCLIMATED	AYM ODE TO DINAH	2
SNOW HAS FRIZ ME.	PL STILL HERE	3

SNOWBIRD 1

Line	Poem	No.
TO A SNOWBIRD ON THE WING.	FW DUSTBOWL	10

SNOWING 2

Line	Poem	No.
MY TV KEEPS ON SNOWING.	AYM BLUES IN STEREO	37
SINCE IT'S SNOWING ON THE TV	AYM ODE TO DINAH	7

SNOWY 1

Line	Poem	No.
IN MONTHS OF SNOWY WINTER	SP STRANGE HURT	11

SNUB 1

Line	Poem	No.
DON'T SNUB THE OTHER FELLOW -	SH SNOB	3

SO 212

Line	Poem	No.
SO HARD.	WB FOR PORTRAIT OF	4
SO STRONG.	WB FOR PORTRAIT OF	5
SO COLD.	WB FOR PORTRAIT OF	6
SO FULL OF PAIN AND PASSION.	WB SOLEDAD	6
SO FULL OF LIES.	WB SOLEDAD	7
SO FULL OF PAIN AND PASSION.	WB SOLEDAD	8
SO DEEPLY SCARRED.	WB SOLEDAD	10
SO STILL WITH SILENT CRIES.	WB SOLEDAD	11
SO THEY SAY.	WB YOUNG PROSTITUT	5
CAUSE EVERBODY TELLS ME SO.	FC BAD MAN	2
EVERBODY TELLS ME SO.	FC BAD MAN	4
I'M SO BAD I	FC BAD MAN	13
SO BAD, BAD, BAD I	FC BAD MAN	15
SO LICKER'LL LET YOU BE.	FC BLD OF GIN MARY	16
WON'T BE SO BAD IN JAIL	FC BLD OF GIN MARY	19
I'M SO LOW-DOWN I	FC HARD LUCK	17
SO BEAT DAT DRUM, BOY!	FC SATURDAY NIGHT	21
THAT HE LOVED SO	DLD THE CONSUMPTIVE	2
IT AIN'T SO DEEP:	NM BIG-TIMER POEM	2
SO I'M HUSTLIN' IN THE NIGHT.	NM BIG-TIMER POEM	12
SO DON'T WORRY 'BOUT ME.	NM BIG-TIMER POEM	53
SO WHAT'S THE USE O' WORRYIN'	NM BIG-TIMER POEM	69
SO I'M TAKIN' IT EASY	NM BIG-TIMER POEM	73
SO THAT THE PAIN AND THE SHAME	NM BLACK CLWN POEM	27
SO I SAY, "MISTER, I AIN'T NO SWEEPIN' MACHINE."	NM BROKE	16
SO DE MAN SAY, "I'LL GET SOMEBODY ELSE, THEN, TO CLEAN." -	NM BROKE	17
SO HERE I IS, BROKE.	NM BROKE	18
AND SHE BEEN HOLDIN' 'EM SO TIGHT TILL DE EAGLE'S IN TEARS -	NM BROKE	24
SO I WENT DOWN TOWN TO A HOTEL WHERE I USED TO WORK AT NIGHT,	NM BROKE	44
SO WHEN I GOT READY TO GO, I SAID, "I'LL BE SEEIN' YOU SOON, MARIE."	NM BROKE	52
IT'S DONE GOT ME SO CRAZY, FEEL LIKE I BEEN TAKIN' COKE.	NM BROKE	60
BUT I CAN'T EVEN BUY A PAPER - I'M SO BROKE.	NM BROKE	61
SHE WOULD BE ALRIGHT IF SHE WASN'T SO BOW-LEGGED, AND CROSS-EYED,	NM BROKE	64
SO WE MARCHED TO THE FRONT, HAPPY TO FIGHT.	NM COLORED SL POEM	12
SO NOW I KNOW WE BLACKS ARE JUST LIKE ANY OTHER -	NM COLORED SL POEM	35
SO I CLIMB TOWARD TOMORROW, OUT OF PAST SORROW,	NM DARK YOUTH USA	22
SO LONG?	DK MINSTREL MAN	8
I'S SO WEARY	DK PO' BOY BLUES	23
SO DANCE WITH SWIFT FEET, HONEY,	DK SONG BANJO DANC	16
NINE OLD MEN SO RICH AND WISE,	ANS BLD OZZIE POWEL	17
WHO DREAMT A DREAM SO STRONG, SO BRAVE, SO TRUE,	ANS LET AMERICA BE	41
WHO DREAMT A DREAM SO STRONG, SO BRAVE, SO TRUE,	ANS LET AMERICA BE	41
WHO DREAMT A DREAM SO STRONG, SO BRAVE, SO TRUE,	ANS LET AMERICA BE	41
TREAT A MAN SO BAD?	SH ANNOUNCEMENT	8
SO FROM NOW ON,	SH ANNOUNCEMENT	13
OR IF I WASN'T SO DROWSY I'D LOCK UP JOE	SH BED TIME	5
OR IF IT WASN'T SO LATE I MIGHT TAKE A WALK	SH BED TIME	7
I CAN SLEEP SO GOOD WITH YOU AWAY!	SH BED TIME	11
HOUSE IS SO QUIET! . . . LISTEN AT THEM MICE.	SH BED TIME	12
WORN SO.	SH BLD PAWNBROKER	12
ALARM CLOCK HERE RINGING SO DAMN LOUD	SH DAYBREAK	3
BASS SO LOW!	SH DEATH IN HARLEM	30
AND DRIVE SO FAR, SO FAR.	SH DECLARATION	11
AND DRIVE SO FAR, SO FAR.	SH DECLARATION	11
SO FAR.	SH DECLARATION	14
I FEEL SO MEAN I COULD	SH EVIL MORNING	5
SO IF YOU WANT TO KNOW BEAUTY'S	SH HARLEM SWEETIES	41
SO JUST BY IF-ING	SH IF-ING	15
SO LET'S JUST FORGET WHAT THIS FUSS WAS ABOUT.	SH LETTER	15
FEELIN' SO SAD, LAWD,	SH MIDNIGHT CHIPPI	7
FEELIN' SO SAD AND LONE.	SH MIDNIGHT CHIPPI	8
SO SAD, LAWD!	SH MIDNIGHT CHIPPI	9
SO SAD AND LONE!	SH MIDNIGHT CHIPPI	10
SO NOBODY CAN'T LOW-RATE YOU.	SH MIDNIGHT CHIPPI	30
SO I WENT TO DE WPA.	SH OUT OF WORK	8
SO I WENT TO DE WPA.	SH OUT OF WORK	10
TURNED OUT SO BAD.	SH PAY DAY	10
JUST SO IT GOES AWAY FROM HERE.	SH SIX-BITS BLUES	5
SO I CAN ROLL ALONG.	SH SIX-BITS BLUES	12
YOU TREAT ME SO.	JC BLACK MAN SPEAK	12
BUT THEY'RE NOT SO BAD	JC GOOD MORN STLIN	8
AND I'M NOT SO DUMB	JC GOOD MORN STLIN	11
THAT MAY BE SO - FOR THOSE WHO WANT IT SO,	JC GOOD MORN STLIN	25
THAT MAY BE SO - FOR THOSE WHO WANT IT SO,	JC GOOD MORN STLIN	25
THEY LIKED HIM SO WELL THEY COULDN'T STAND	JC JIM CROW'S LAST	3
ABOLISH POLL TAX SO FOLKS CAN VOTE.	JC JIM CROW'S LAST	24
SO IT WOULD SEEM,	JC NOTE TO NAZIS	2
THERE ARE THOSE, TOO, WHO FOR SO LONG	JC TO CAPTAIN MULZ	16
SO I GAVE UP AND WENT	FW COMMUNION	5
I'M EVER SO SURE	FW FAITHFUL ONE	3
SO PIERROT	FW HEART	13
LEARNS SO SOON	FW MAN	13
HE GLIDES SO SWIFTLY	FW SNAKE	1
SO MUCH PAIN,	FW WALLS	2
SO MUCH SORROW	FW WALLS	6
WHEN YOU SINK SO LOW.	OWT TOO BLUE	5
I MISS YOU SO BAD -	OWT YESTERDAY TODAY	6
SO WHEN MY ACTIONS ARE STUPID	LHR ACCEPTANCE	3
SO THEY BUILT A CROSS	LHR BLD MARY'S SON	13
I HAVE DONE SO LITTLE	LHR POET TO BIGOT	1
AND YOU HAVE DONE SO LITTLE	LHR POET TO BIGOT	3
SO I CREPT AWAY INTO THE NIGHT	SP A BLACK PIERROT	3
SO I WEPT UNTIL THE DAWN	SP A BLACK PIERROT	7
SO WITH MY ONCE GAY-COLORED SOUL	SP A BLACK PIERROT	12
IS NOT SO STRANGE,	SP A HOUSE IN TAOS	18
SO GET YOURSELF	SP ADVICE	4
SO LONG,	SP AFRO-AMER FRAG	1
SO FAR AWAY	SP AFRO-AMER FRAG	2
SO LONG,	SP AFRO-AMER FRAG	10
SO FAR AWAY	SP AFRO-AMER FRAG	11
SO LONG,	SP AFRO-AMER FRAG	21
SO FAR AWAY	SP AFRO-AMER FRAG	22
SAY NOT SO!	SP BAR	2
A FUNERAL SO HIGH?	SP BLD OF THE MAN	26
SO I DON'T DARE START THINKING IN THE MORNING.	SP BLUES AT DAWN	5
SO I DON'T DARE REMEMBER IN THE MORNING.	SP BLUES AT DAWN	10
SO ON BACK	SP CONSIDER ME	10
SO HE TAPPED,	SP DANCER	9
SO, SI'L-VOUS PLAIT, I'LL STUDY FRENCH!	SP DEFERRED	28
KNOWING SO WELL THE WIND AND THE SUN -	SP DEMAND	7
I TIRE SO OF HEARING PEOPLE SAY,	SP DEMOCRACY	10
BEIN TREATED SO BAD.	SP EARLY EVENING	16
SO I WENT ON BACK TO BED -	SP FIRED	7
BUT NOT SO LONG AGO AT THAT, LINCOLN SAID:	SP FREEDOM'S PLOW	101
THE G.I.'S WHO FOUGHT WILL SAY, WE WANTED IT SO!	SP FREEDOM TRAIN	60
(BUT NOBODY KNOWS IF THAT IS SO.)	SP HAVANA DREAMS	4
SO ALL OVER THE WORLD TODAY	SP IN EXPLANATION	18
SO, NATURALLY, THERE'S TROUBLE	SP IN EXPLANATION	58

Line	Source	Title	Line no.
SO MANY GODS DON'T KNOW.	SP	JOE LOUIS	7
DRESSED SO FINE?	SP	LADY'S BOOGIE	2
SO I WAS CRYIN'	SP	LATE LAST NIGHT	9
HERE. WELL. THAT IS ALL SO I WILL CLOSE.	SP	LETTER	9
SO I JUMPED IN AND SANK.	SP	LIFE IS FINE	4
IF THAT WATER HADN'T A-BEEN SO COLD	SP	LIFE IS FINE	7
IF IT HADN'T A-BEEN SO HIGH	SP	LIFE IS FINE	18
SO SINCE I'M STILL HERE LIVIN'.	SP	LIFE IS FINE	23
AND I PLAYED SO DOG-GONE HARD.	SP	LITTLE GRN TREE	6
I NEVER FELT SO LONESOME	SP	LITTLE OLD LETT	11
SO SICK AND LONESOME	SP	LOVER'S RETURN	7
HE LOOKED SO THIN -	SP	LOVER'S RETURN	15
JUST MIGHT BE SO.	SP	MADAM MIGHT-HAV	8
CHILDREN SO BAD?	SP	MADAM CHARTY CH	10
SO TO SPEAK.	SP	MADAM CHARTY CH	20
I LOVE YOU SO!	SP	MADAM HER MADAM	20
I KNOWED THAT WAS SO.	SP	MADAM PHONE BIL	24
SO WE AGREES!	SP	MADAM RENT MAN	30
SO I AIN'T IN NO MOOD	SP	MADAM MINISTER	32
SO I CAN BRUSH YOUR BACK, I SAY!	SP	MAMA AND DAUGHT	21
HE'S BEEN A MULE SO LONG	SP	ME AND THE MULE	3
HER SKIN SO BROWN.	SP	MEXICAN MARKET	7
SO WHEN I'M DEAD THEY WON'T NEED	SP	MIDWINTER BLUES	23
HE WOULDN'T WRITE SO	SP	MIGRANT	39
I LOVE YOU, OH, I LOVE YOU SO -	SP	MISS BLUES'ES	9
BUT YOU HAVE GONE SO FAR!	SP	MISS BLUES'ES	10
I WAS SO SICK LAST NIGHT I	SP	MORNING AFTER	1
SO SICK LAST NIGHT I	SP	MORNING AFTER	3
PLEASE DON'T SNORE SO LOUD.	SP	MORNING AFTER	14
PLEASE DON'T SNORE SO LOUD.	SP	MORNING AFTER	16
SO BOY, DON'T YOU TURN BACK.	SP	MOTHER TO SON	14
SO I LAUGH	SP	MOVIES	11
SO THE FACES OF MY PEOPLE.	SP	MY PEOPLE	2
SO THE EYES OF MY PEOPLE.	SP	MY PEOPLE	4
SO SMALL I CAN'T WHIP A CAT	SP	NECESSITY	6
AND MY LANDLADY'S SO OLD	SP	NECESSITY	8
SO I COME UP HERE.	SP	NEW YORKERS	12
WAS SO DEAR, SO DEAR	SP	NIGHT FUNERAL	39
WAS SO DEAR, SO DEAR	SP	NIGHT FUNERAL	39
SO THEY DON'T SOUND LIKE ME.	SP	NOTE COMM THEAT	6
TO BE SO STILL THAT WAY.	SP	SEA CALM	6
SO DOES A MAN.	SP	SISTER	16
SO LONG	SP	SO LONG	1
YOU'RE GONE SO LONG	SP	SO LONG	9
SO LONG.	SP	SO LONG	10
SO CLOSE	SP	SUBWAY RUSH HOU	3
SO NEAR	SP	SUBWAY RUSH HOU	6
SO AS NOT TO FORGET	SP	SUMMER EVENING	27
SO I HOLLERS, "COM'ERE, BABIES,	SP	SYLVESTER'S BED	23
SO NOW I SEEK THE NORTH -	SP	THE SOUTH	23
THE STARS WENT OUT AND SO DID THE MOON.	SP	THE WEARY BLUES	32
SO WILL MY PAGE BE COLORED THAT I WRITE?	SP	THEME FOR ENG B	27
THE SPRING IS NOT SO BEAUTIFUL THERE -	SP	WATER-FRONT STR	1
THE SPRING IS NOT SO BEAUTIFUL THERE -	SP	WATER-FRONT STR	5
SO WE CRANKED UP OUR OLD FORD	SP	WEST TEXAS	11
SO WHAT WOULD YOU DO?	SP	WHAT?	8
AND SO LOSE ITS REPOSE.	AYM	BLUES IN STEREO	20
SO THE WHITENESS AND THE WATER	AYM	ODE TO DINAH	35
WHERE NEGROES SING SO WELL	AYM	SHADES OF PIG	8
NEGROES SING SO WELL	AYM	SHADES OF PIG	9
SING SO WELL	AYM	SHADES OF PIG	10
SO WELL.	AYM	SHADES OF PIG	11
BUT IT IS SO -	PL	ANGOLA QUESTION	14
AND BEING SO	PL	ANGOLA QUESTION	15
THERE ARE SO MANY CHURCHES	PL	BIBLE BELT	3
"I'M SO ASHAMED OF BEING WHITE."	PL	DINNER GUEST ME	14
IS NOT SO BAD.	PL	DINNER GUEST ME	21
RIDE SO FINE BEFORE.	PL	FLORIDA WORKERS	18
I TIRE SO OF HEARING PEOPLE SAY,	PL	FREEDOM	10
AND SO MUST BE	PL	FROSTING	5
YET GHOSTS SO SOLID, GHOSTS SO REAL	PL	GHOSTS OF 1619	4
YET GHOSTS SO SOLID, GHOSTS SO REAL	PL	GHOSTS OF 1619	4
SO WE STAND HERE	PL	HARLEM	16
SO YOU LIE IN YOUR CRADLE	PL	LAST PRINCE	8
SO MUCH LARGER.	PL	LONG VIEW NEGRO	5
SO IT SEEMS.	PL	LONG VIEW NEGRO	6
WHAT WAS SO LARGE	PL	LONG VIEW NEGRO	11
BECOMES SO SMALL	PL	LONG VIEW NEGRO	12
AND SO MY FIST IS CLENCHED	PL	MILITANT	12
AND SO	PL	NORTHERN LIBERL	1
SO PROUD THAT SAVAGES	PL	NORTHERN LIBERL	7
SO YOUNG.	PL	SLUM DREAMS	10
BUT THAT DAY WAS SO LONG	PL	STOKELY MALCOLM	7
SO FOLKS SAY.	PL	STOKELY MALCOLM	14
AND THEN SO QUICKLY WILT	PL	SWEET WORDS RAC	3
SWEET WORDS SO BRAVE	PL	SWEET WORDS RAC	9
SO MANY TIMES BEFORE.	PL	SWEET WORDS RAC	12
NOT SO.	PL	UN-AMERICAN	19
I WONDER WHY RED CLAY'S SO RED	PL	VARI-COLORED	9
AND GEORGIA SKIES SO BLUE.	PL	VARI-COLORED	10
I WONDER WHY THE SKY'S SO BLUE	PL	VARI-COLORED	13
AND WHY THE CLAY'S SO RED.	PL	VARI-COLORED	14
SO I KILL YOU.	PL	WAR	21
SO WHO BUT THE LORD	PL	WHO BUT TH LORD	21

SOAKING 4

Line	Source	Title	Line no.
SOAKING UP A WINE-SOUSE	SP	WINE-O	2
SOAKING UP A NEW SOUSE.	SP	WINE-O	6
SOAKING UP THE MUSIC	AYM	BIRD IN ORBIT	68
SOAKING UP THE MUSIC.	AYM	BIRD IN ORBIT	91

SOAP 1

Line	Source	Title	Line no.
NOW ARE WHAT THE SOAP BOX	PL	CORNER MEETING	2

SOARING 1

Line	Source	Title	Line no.
SOARING HIGH -	PL	COLOR	7

SOB 3

Line	Source	Title	Line no.
DOES A JAZZ-BAND EVER SOB?	WB	CABARET	1
ONE SAID SHE HEARD THE JAZZ-BAND SOB	WB	CABARET	5
ITS PEOPLE'S HEART, TOO SMALL TO HOLD A SOB.	SL	TOWN OF SCOTTSB	4

SOBBING 2

Line	Source	Title	Line no.
(THE BANJO'S SOBBING LOW)	DK	SONG BANJO DANC	17
(THE BANJO'S SOBBING LOW)	DK	SONG BANJO DANC	25

SOBER 1

Line	Source	Title	Line no.
HE PLAYS GOOD WHEN HE'S SOBER	FC	MA MAN	11

SOCK 1

Line	Source	Title	Line no.
HONEY BABY, SOCK IT!	SH	DEATH IN HARLEM	21

SOFT 9

Line	Source	Title	Line no.
IS A SOFT BANDANNA HANDKERCHIEF	WB	OUR LAND	5
SOFT AS IT BEGAN -	DK	I LOVED FRIEND	5
SOFT LIGHT ON THE TABLES,	DK	NEGRO DANCERS	7
(THE MUSIC'S SOFT AND WIL')	DK	SONG BANJO DANC	23
SOFT AS DUSK THE DARKNESS	FW	DIMOUT IN HARLM	7
SOFT SAD BLACK FEET	OWT	JUICE JOINT	46
IN THE EYES ONCE SOFT BENIGHTED	SP	MIGRANT	22
THE SCENT OF PINE WOOD STINGS THE SOFT NIGHT AIR.	SP	MULATTO	18
AND FALLING OUT OF HEAVEN LIKE SOFT DEW.	PL	DAYBREAK IN ALA	6

SOFTLY 9

Line	Source	Title	Line no.
SAY IT VERY SOFTLY.	FC	MAMMY	3
MAY ACCOMPANY THE RECITATION - ECHOING SOFTLY, OVER THERE, THERE'S A ROSE	NM	COLORED SL MOOD	4
MINGLE THEMSELVES SOFTLY	SP	AUNTSUE'S STORI	12
MINGLE THEMSELVES SOFTLY	SP	AUNTSUE'S STORI	14
WHIRLS SOFTLY INTO A	SP	DANSE AFRICAINE	8
WHIRLS SOFTLY . . . SLOWLY,	SP	DANSE AFRICAINE	10
SING IT SOFTLY, FOR THE SONG IS WILD.	SP	GENIUS CHILD	2
SING IT SOFTLY AS EVER YOU CAN -	SP	GENIUS CHILD	3
BUT SOFTLY	SP	TRUMPET PLAYER	41

SOFTNESS 2

Line	Source	Title	Line no.
WHEN THE NIGHT IS A VAST SOFTNESS	DK	AFTR MNY SPRNGS	3
SUN AND SOFTNESS.	SP	SUN SONG	1

SOGGY 1

Line	Source	Title	Line no.
EVEN SOGGY COUNTRY CLUB	PL	UNDERTOW	7

SOIL 5

Line	Source	Title	Line no.
BOOTS ALL MUDDY WITH SOIL.	ANS	BLDS OF LENIN	6
I AM THE FARMER, BONDSMAN TO THE SOIL.	ANS	LET AMERICA BE	31
ON THE RICH SOIL OF THE WORLD,	SP	FREEDOM'S PLOW	13
TO TILL THE SOIL, AND HARNESS THE POWER OF THE WATERS.	SP	FREEDOM'S PLOW	19
TURNING THE RICH SOIL WENT THE PLOW IN MANY HANDS	SP	FREEDOM'S PLOW	52

SOJOURNER 3

Line	Source	Title	Line no.
AND OF HOW SOJOURNER HOW SOJOURNER	AYM	BIRD IN ORBIT	47
AND OF HOW SOJOURNER HOW SOJOURNER	AYM	BIRD IN ORBIT	47
SEND FOR HARRIETT TUBMAN, OLD SOJOURNER TRUTH.	PL	FINAL CALL	32

SOKOLSKY'S 1

Line	Source	Title	Line no.
IN GEORGE SOKOLSKY'S COLUMN.	AYM	HORN OF PLENTY	36

SOL 1

Line	Source	Title	Line no.
ON BEDLOE'S ISLAND MANAGED BY SOL HUROK	AYM	HORN OF PLENTY	4

SOLD 7

Line	Source	Title	Line no.
I AM THE WORKER SOLD TO THE MACHINE.	ANS	LET AMERICA BE	32
GIN IS SOLD IN GLASSES FINGER-TALL.	OWT	JUICE JOINT	6
SOLD IN SHOPS, PILED IN WAREHOUSES,	SP	FREEDOM'S PLOW	80
CHILDREN SOLD AWAY FROM ME, HUSBAND SOLD, TOO.	SP	THE NEGRO MOTHE	15
CHILDREN SOLD AWAY FROM ME, HUSBAND SOLD, TOO.	SP	THE NEGRO MOTHE	15
ALL SOLD DOWN THE RIVER.	AYM	BIRD IN ORBIT	52
WHEN I GET SOLD:	PL	LITTLE SNG HOUS	12

SOLDIER 7
THE SOLDIER THROWN FROM A JIM CROW BUS BEHIND STEEL BARS. — JC THE BITTER RIVR 33
A SOLDIER TOOK HER PART. — OWT BLD MARGE POLIT 9
THE SOLDIER WERE BLACK. — OWT BLD MARGE POLIT 12
THEY KILLED A COLORED SOLDIER! — OWT BLD MARGE POLIT 13
THEY DIDN'T KILL THE SOLDIER. — OWT BLD MARGE POLIT 42
HE WAS A SOLDIER IN THE ARMY. — SP CASUALTY 1
DON'T BE WEARY, SOLDIER! — SP FREEDOM'S PLOW 164

SOLDIERING 1
HE WALKS LIKE HIS SOLDIERING — SP CASUALTY 3

SOLDIERS 2
SINCE THE COLORED SOLDIERS CAME HOME FROM FRANCE. — NM COLORED SL POEM 32
THE SOLDIERS CAME — LHR BLD MARY'S SON 25

SOLDIER'S 3
IN HIS SOLDIER'S UNIFORM, AND ALL. — NM COLORED SL POEM 38
BUT BROKEN WAS THE SOLDIER'S DREAM, TOO BAD TO BE — NM COLORED SL POEM 49
MAMA, I FOUND THIS SOLDIER'S CAP — FW WHEN ARMIES PAS 1

SOLEDAD 1
SOLEDAD. — WB SOLEDAD 9

SOLID 8
SOLID GONE! — SP GONE BOY 2
SOLID BLACK, — SP PARADE 18
SOLID LAND, KID. — SP PORT TOWN 11
FROM THE SOLID LAP OF EARTH. — SP SPIRITUALS 12
ON SOLID GROUND. — PL DOWN WHERE I AM 14
GHOSTS OF ALL TOO SOLID FLESH, — PL GHOSTS OF 1619 1
YET GHOSTS SO SOLID, GHOSTS SO REAL — PL GHOSTS OF 1619 4
THE SOLID CITIZENS — PL UNDERTOW 1

SOLOMON 8
LIKE THE WINE CUPS OF SOLOMON. — FC BRASS SPITOONS 35
SAM SOLOMON SAID. — JC BLD SAM SOLOMON 1
SAM SOLOMON CALLED ON — JC BLD SAM SOLOMON 17
SAM SOLOMON ANSWERED. — JC BLD SAM SOLOMON 29
SAM SOLOMON SAID, I'M — JC BLD SAM SOLOMON 33
SAM SOLOMON SAID, A MAN — JC BLD SAM SOLOMON 39
BUT SAM SOLOMON — JC BLD SAM SOLOMON 43
SAM SOLOMON SAID. — JC BLD SAM SOLOMON 53

SOLUTIONS 1
SOLUTIONS TO THE PROBLEM. — PL DINNER GUEST ME 22

SOME 72
GIT SOME GIN TO MAKE YOU LAUGH. — FC HARD LUCK 12
AND THEN SOME. — FC JAZZ BAND 20
O, PLAY SOME MORE. — FC SATURDAY NIGHT 2
JUST GIMME SOME SASS. — NM BIG-TIMER POEM 28
(IS YOU LOOKIN' AT ME, BABY, OR SOME OTHER WAY?) — NM BROKE 76
LEST SOME FRANCO STEAL INTO OUR BACKYARD — ANS SONG OF SPAIN 66
IF I HAD SOME MONEY I'D STROLL DOWN THE STREET — SH BED TIME 3
AND JIVE SOME OLD BROAD I MIGHT MEET. — SH BED TIME 4
AND START A SKIN GAME WITH SOME CHUMPS I KNOW. — SH BED TIME 6
SOME BEGAN TO TREMBLE AND — SH DEATH IN HARLEM 109
SOME BEGAN TO SCREAM. — SH DEATH IN HARLEM 110
SPREAD SOME JOY! — SH DEATH IN HARLEM 86
IF I HAD SOME SMALL CHANGE — SH IF-ING 1
IF I HAD SOME GREENBACKS — SH IF-ING 5
COME ON HOME AND BAKE SOME CORN BREAD. — SH LETTER 16
THEY OUGHT TO BE SOME NOISE. — SH SUNDAY 11
IF I HAD A FIRE I'D MAKE ME SOME TEA — SH SUPPER TIME 11
SOME FOLKS THINK — JC FREEDOM 1
SOME FOLKS THINK — JC FREEDOM 4
SOME FOLKS THINK — JC FREEDOM 7
SOME FOLKS TRY TO TELL ME DOWN THIS WAY — JC GOOD MORN STLIN 23
SOME MARK — FW BIRTH 9
SOME WORD — FW BIRTH 11
OR DOES SOME STRANGE — FW CONVENT 6
TO SOME PEOPLE — FW GIFTS 1
SOME OF THESE DAYS — OWT BOARDING HOUSE 3
AND SOME FORGET TO LAUGH WHO STILL ARE KIDS. — OWT JUICE JOINT 40
I WANT SOME FINE MUSIC — OWT REQUEST REQUIEM 3
THERE WERE SOME WHO COULD NOT HEAR. — LHR BLD MARY'S SON 11
AND SOME WERE FILLED WITH FEAR - — LHR BLD MARY'S SON 12
INTO SOME OTHER THING — LHR DEAR LVLY DEATH 5
THROUGH SOME VAST MIST OF RACE — SP AFRO-AMER FRAG 15
SEND SOME FLOWERS. — SP BLD OF THE MAN 8
PUT SOME SILVER IN MY HAND — SP BLD THE GYPSY 6
SOME FOLKS SAY. — SP CAFE: 3 A.M. 5
SOME OF THESE YOUNG ONES IS CERT'LY BAD - — SP CHILDREN'S RYME 17
IN SOME PLACE OF THE SUN. — SP DREAM VARIATION 2
"OR IF IT WOULD," THOUGHT SOME. — SP FREEDOM'S PLOW 121
SOME THERE WERE, AS ALWAYS. — SP FREEDOM'S PLOW 132
WILL SOME WHITE MAN YELL, GET BACK! — SP FREEDOM TRAIN 39
SOME WERE FREE HANDS — SP FREEDOM'S PLOW 41
SOME WERE INDENTURED HANDS — SP FREEDOM'S PLOW 43
SOME WERE SLAVE HANDS — SP FREEDOM'S PLOW 45
SOME FOLKS BLAME HIGH PRICES ON THE JEWS. — SP LIKEWISE 12
(SOME FOLKS BLAME TOO MUCH ON JEWS.) — SP LIKEWISE 13
TO SOME PEOPLE — SP LUCK 5
I'LL PAY SOME MIND TO YOU. — SP MADAM FORT TELL 16
AND BUY HER SOME CHICKEN. — SP MADAM WRONG VIS 26
I HAD SOME CARDS PRINTED — SP MADAM'S CALLING 1
I DRUNK SOME BAD LICKER THAT — SP MORNING AFTER 5
A BOX-CAR SOME TRAIN — SP RAILROAD AVENUE 5
SOME TRAIN HAS FORGOTTEN. — SP RAILROAD AVENUE 29
I CAN UNDERSTAND - SOME DECENT MAN? — SP SISTER 6
IS SHE WANTS SOME CASH? — SP SISTER 9
GONNA RIDE IN MY CHARIOT SOME DAY! — SP SPIRITUALS 8
HE PLAYED A FEW CHORDS THEN HE SANG SOME MORE - — SP THE WEARY BLUES 24
SOME DAWNS — SP TOMORROW 7
THAN SOME PEOPLE EVER HAD. — SP WARNING AUGMENT 12
SOME PIMPS WEAR SUMMER HATS — SP WHAT? 1
SOME KIND OF TRICKERATION — SP WHAT? SO SOON! 4
A QUEEN FROM SOME TIME-DEAD EGYPTIAN NIGHT — SP WHEN SUE WEARS 7
CAUSE WHEN I'M DEAD SOME — SP YOUNG GAL'S BLS 5
SOME HORSE MIGHT — AYM IS IT TRUE? 46
I'M GONNA WRITE ME SOME MUSIC ABOUT — PL DAYBREAK IN ALA 2
I'M GONNA PUT SOME TALL TALL TREES IN IT — PL DAYBREAK IN ALA 7
BEGINNING IN SOME OTHER LAND - — PL JUNIOR ADDICT 9
TO SOME LONESOME PLACE. — PL KU KLUX 2
IN SOME OTHER SECTION — PL MISSISSIPPI 11
AS IF IT WERE SOME NOBLE THING. — PL MOTHER IN WAR 1
WERE PLED ANEW AT SOME HEROIC BAR. — PL MOTHER IN WAR 4
IN SOME LANDS — PL OPPRESSION 6
AS HAVE SOME FOLKS I KNOW. — PL VARI-COLORED 2

SOMEBODY 16
SOMEBODY COMES BY — FC DEATH DO DIRTY 23
SO DE MAN SAY, "I'LL GET SOMEBODY ELSE, THEN, TO CLEAN." - — NM BROKE 17
UM-MM! SIGN HERE SAYS THEY WANTS SOMEBODY TO SHOVEL COAL. — NM BROKE 28
AND FIND SOMEBODY TO KID AND TALK. — SH BED TIME 8
(IT WAS JUST AS IF SOMEBODY — SH DEATH IN HARLEM 97
SOMEBODY YELLED. — OWT BLD MARGE POLIT 35
SOMEBODY YELLED. — OWT BLD MARGE POLIT 40
SOMEBODY HOLLERED. — OWT BLD MARGE POLIT 44
GOT TO FIND SOMEBODY — SP BOUND NO'TH BLS 5
OR SOMEBODY — SP CAFE: 3 A.M. 7
OR SOMEBODY ELSE'S SHOES — SP ELEVATOR BOY 18
SOMEBODY TELL ME ABOUT THIS — SP FREEDOM TRAIN 23
IF YOU GOT SOMEBODY ELSE. — SP ULTIMATUM 4
SOMEBODY — SP WORLD WAR II 11
I'LL WANT TO SEE SOMEBODY, TOO. — SP YOUNG GAL'S BLS 12
ON SOMEBODY ELSE'S — PL FROSTING 3

SOMEBODY'LL 1
BUT SOMEDAY SOMEBODY'LL — SP NOTE COMM THEAT 12

SOMEBODY'S 2
KNOWED SOMEBODY'S 'BOUT TO DIE. — FC GAL'S CRY DYING 2
KNOWED SOMEBODY'S 'BOUT TO DIE. — FC GAL'S CRY DYING 4

SOMEDAY 3
SOMEDAY. — SP DEFERRED 29
BUT SOMEDAY SOMEBODY'LL — SP NOTE COMM THEAT 12
MIGHT BE AWAKENED SOMEDAY SOON — PL BIRMINGHAM SUND 25

SOMEHOW 6
BUT THE DREAM WAS CRUEL - AND BITTER - AND SOMEHOW — NM COLORED SL POEM 40
AN' GIT TO MA BABY SOMEHOW. — DK WIDE RIVER 14
GIT TO MA BABY SOMEHOW - — DK WIDE RIVER 16
SOMEHOW. — JC TO CAPTAIN MULZ 5
STILL AHEAD SOMEHOW. — SP ISLAND 4
SOMEHOW THAT RAFFLE — SP MIDNIGHT RAFFLE 3

SOMEONE 2
NEEDING SOMEONE. — WB SUMMER NIGHT 18
DOUGLASS WAS SOMEONE WHO. — PL FREDRK DOUGLASS 1

SOMETHING 12
SOMETHING. — WB SUMMER NIGHT 19
AND THOUGHT OF SOMETHING — SH DEATH IN HARLEM 72
SOMETHING IN MY MIND BETTER I FORGOT. — SH TWILIGHT REVERI 2
IS SOMETHING THAT SURELY — JC BLD SAM SOLOMON 15
BUT SOMETHING HAPPENED, JIM'S FEATHERS FELL. — JC JIM CROW'S LAST 5
EVERYBODY THAT GAVE SOMETHING — SP BLD OF THE MAN 11
SOMETHING MUSTA HAPPENED — SP BLD THE GYPSY 16
SOMETHING UNDERNEATH — SP DREAM BOOGIE 12
AND THEY RAN SOMETHING LIKE THIS: — SP RUBY BROWN 12
SOMETHING STRONG TO PUT MY HANDS ON. — SP SPIRITUALS 3

GOT TO NEGLECT SOMETHING. . . . . . SP WHAT? 7
TETHERED BY SOMETHING WORSE THAN
PRIDE. . . . . PL WHERE WHEN WHCH 10

SOMETIME 1

SHE HOPES TO LAY EYES ON YOU
SOMETIME IN LIFE. . . . . SP LETTER 7

SOMETIMES 33

SOMETIMES I'M SETTIN' PRETTY. . . . NM BIG-TIMER POEM 39
PACE. "SOMETIMES I FEEL LIKE A
MOTHER-LESS CHILE." TURNING
FUTILELY . . . . NM BLACK CLWN MOOD 8
WE SOMETIMES FIND . . . . FW CIRCLES 9
SOMETIMES . . . . FW DUSK 2
AND SOMETIMES NOT. . . . . FW DUSK 4
BUT SOMETIMES NOT. . . . . FW DUSK 9
SOMETIMES A BLACK BOY PLAYS A SONG OWT JUICE JOINT 9
SOMETIMES WORKING LATE. . . . . . SP CONSIDER ME 19
SOMETIMES . . . . SP DEAD IN THERE 1
MAYBE A GOOD JOB SOMETIMES: . . . . SP ELEVATOR BOY 10
AND SOMETIMES ONLY BLUNDERINGLY
EXPRESS THEM. . . . . SP FREEDOM'S PLOW 149
AND SOMETIMES IT SEEMS . . . . . . SP HIGH TO LOW 8
SOMETIMES WHEN I'M LONELY. . . . . SP HOPE 1
GEORGE SALLIE COOLIE BOY GETS TIRED
SOMETIMES. . . . . SP IN EXPLANATION 17
SOMETIMES I THINK . . . . SP LIKEWISE 24
SOMETIMES A CRUMB FALLS . . . . . . SP LUCK 1
SOMETIMES A BONE . . . . SP LUCK 3
SOMETIMES YOU DON'T KNOW . . . . . SP MADAM MIGHT-HAV 6
AND SOMETIMES GOIN' IN THE DARK . . SP MOTHER TO SON 12
SOMETIMES . . . . SP NEIGHBOR 19
ARE SOMETIMES AS DANGEROUS . . . . SP SLIVER 3
THROAT SOMETIMES. . . . . SP SLIVER 8
SOMETIMES I THINK THAT WHITE FOLKS SP SOUTHERN MAMMY 9
BUT SOMETIMES I THINK THAT WHITE
FOLKS . . . . SP SOUTHERN MAMMY 21
SOMETIMES. THE VALLEY WAS FILLED
WITH TEARS. . . . . SP THE NEGRO MOTHE 25
SOMETIMES. THE ROAD WAS HOT WITH
SUN. . . . . SP THE NEGRO MOTHE 27
SOMETIMES PERHAPS YOU DON'T WANT TO
BE A PART OF ME. . . . . SP THEME FOR ENG B 34
TO THE FARTHEREST CORNERS SOMETIMES AYM IS IT TRUE? 3
THAT SOMETIMES TURN TO FIRE. . . . AYM JAZZTET MUTED 21
SOMETIMES EVEN BURIED WITH OUR
FAMILY. . . . . PL CULTURAL EXCHNG 55
SOMETIMES THERE'S A WIND IN THE
GEORGIA DUSK . . . . PL GEORGIA DUSK 1
SOMETIMES THERE'S BLOOD IN THE
GEORGIA DUSK . . . . PL GEORGIA DUSK 5
SOMETIMES A WIND IN THE GEORGIA DUSK PL GEORGIA DUSK 9

SOMEWHAT 1

AND SOMEWHAT MORE FREE. . . . . . . SP THEME FOR ENG B 40

SOMEWHERE 11

SOMEWHERE . . . . WB BLUES FANTASY 18
SOMEWHERE IN YO' SKY. . . . . FC MOAN 18
I WANTS TO GO SOMEWHERE. . . . . . DK HOMESICK BLUES 6
SOMEWHERE SOUTH. . . . . SH DEATH IN HARLEM 17
ON A TRAIN THAT RUNS SOMEWHERE. . . SH SIX-BITS BLUES 2
ON A TRAIN THAT RUNS SOMEWHERE. . . SH SIX-BITS BLUES 4
FORGOTTEN WATCH-FIRES ON A HILL
SOMEWHERE! . . . . OWT NEGRO SERVANT 6
BUT THERE IS. SOMEWHERE THERE. . . SP FREEDOM'S PLOW 153
TOWN SOMEWHERE . . . . SP KID SLEEPY 13
SOMEWHERE IN THIS DUSK. . . . . . . SP MAGNOLIA FLOWER 11
SOMEWHERE AROUND. . . . . PL STOKELY MALCOLM 12

SOME'N 2

YOU GOT SOME'N ELSE . . . . SP MADAM MIGHT-HAV 23
WHY DIDN'T HE TELL ME SOME'N . . . SP MADAM PHONE BIL 25

SON 18

WHOSE CAP IT IS. SON. . . . . FW WHEN ARMIES PAS 6
SON. I DO NOT KNOW. . . . . FW WHEN ARMIES PAS 16
HE WAS MARY'S SON. . . . . LHR BLD MARY'S SON 8
AND THE SON OF GOD WAS HE - . . . . LHR BLD MARY'S SON 9
FOR MARY'S SON. . . . . LHR BLD MARY'S SON 28
WHAT SHALL I LEAVE MY SON . . . . LHR TESTAMENT 1
SON! . . . SON! . . . . SP CASUALTY 5
SON! . . . SON! . . . . SP CASUALTY 5
NO. SON. NOT EVERYBODY. . . . . . SP IN EXPLANATION 6
YOUR SON BABY . . . . SP LETTER 10
WELL. SON. I'LL TELL YOU: . . . . SP MOTHER TO SON 1
I AM YOUR SON. WHITE MAN! . . . . SP MULATTO 1
YOU ARE MY SON! . . . . SP MULATTO 5
I AM YOUR SON. WHITE MAN! . . . . SP MULATTO 43
DID IT EVER OCCUR TO YOU. SON. . . SP SISTER 7
AZIKIWE'S SON. AMEKA. . . . . . . AYM ASK YOUR MAMA 65
SEND MY SON TO VIETNAM. . . . . . PL BACKLASH BLUES 6
THAT MY SON IS DEAD. . . . . PL OFFICIAL NOTICE 3

SONG 78

OF LOVE AND JOY AND WINE AND SONG. WB OUR LAND 14
SING YOUR BLUES SONG. . . . . WB TO MIDNIGHT NAN 9
SHOUT DAT SONG! . . . . FC SATURDAY NIGHT 22
ONLY IN SONG AND LAUGHTER . . . . . NM BLACK CLWN POEM 10
A SAD SONG IN DE AIR. . . . . DK HOMESICK BLUES 2
A SAD SONG IN DE AIR. . . . . DK HOMESICK BLUES 4
IS DEEP WITH SONG. . . . . DK MINSTREL MAN 4
THIS IS GONNA BE MA SONG. . . . . . DK NIGHT AND MORN 8
THIS IS GONNA BE MA SONG: . . . . . DK NIGHT AND MORN 10
BECAUSE YOU ARE TO ME A SONG . . . DK PASSING LOVE 1
THIS SONG TO SING: . . . . ANS A NEW SONG 6
AND A SONG THAT REACHES THE SKY - ANS KIDS WHO DIE 49
THE SONG OF THE NEW LIFE TRIUMPHANT ANS KIDS WHO DIE 50
AND SING ME THE SONG OF SPAIN. . . ANS SONG OF SPAIN 2
WHAT IS THE SONG OF SPAIN? . . . . ANS SONG OF SPAIN 4
FLAMENCO IS THE SONG OF SPAIN: . . ANS SONG OF SPAIN 5
FLAMENCO IS THE SONG OF SPAIN. . . ANS SONG OF SPAIN 10
TOROS ARE THE SONG OF SPAIN: . . . ANS SONG OF SPAIN 12
IS THE SONG OF SPAIN. . . . . ANS SONG OF SPAIN 17
PINTURA IS THE SONG OF SPAIN: . . . ANS SONG OF SPAIN 19
THE SONG OF SPAIN. . . . . ANS SONG OF SPAIN 24
THAT'S THE SONG OF SPAIN. . . . . . ANS SONG OF SPAIN 29
THE SONG OF SPAIN. . . . . ANS SONG OF SPAIN 32
THE SONG OF SPAIN. . . . . ANS SONG OF SPAIN 34
IS THE SONG OF SPAIN. . . . . ANS SONG OF SPAIN 83
INSTEAD OF TO A SONG. . . . . SH IN TROUBLED KEY 12
SONG . . . . JC ME AND MY SONG 13
DEEP AND MELLOW SONG . . . . JC ME AND MY SONG 15
MY SONG . . . . JC ME AND MY SONG 22
SONG . . . . JC ME AND MY SONG 34
WITH THE HISS OF ITS SNAKE-LIKE SONG
- . . . . JC THE BITTER RIVR 64
AND SINGER OF WEARY SONG. . . . . . JC THE BITTER RIVR 72
MIGHTY TOUCHSTONES OF SONG. . . . . FW BIG SUR 3
TO SONG WITHOUT SOUND. . . . . . . FW BURDEN 4
TO A BROKEN SONG IN OCTOBER. . . . FW DUSTBOWL 9
IT'S AN EARTH SONG - . . . . FW EARTH SONG 1
FOR AN EARTH SONG. . . . . FW EARTH SONG 3
IT'S A SPRING SONG! . . . . FW EARTH SONG 4
FOR A SPRING SONG: . . . . FW EARTH SONG 6
AN EARTH SONG! . . . . FW EARTH SONG 11
A BODY SONG! . . . . FW EARTH SONG 12
A SPRING SONG! . . . . FW EARTH SONG 13
FOR AN EARTH SONG. . . . . FW EARTH SONG 15
A SONG . . . . FW FRAGMENTS 4
A SONG. . . . . FW NIGHT SONG 14
SOMETIMES A BLACK BOY PLAYS A SONG OWT JUICE JOINT 9
TURN FROM THE BAR AND JOIN YOU IN
YOUR SONG. . . . . OWT JUICE JOINT 22
A SONG OF JOY. . . . . OWT JUICE JOINT 32
PRESS HANDS TOGETHER. LAUGHING AT
HER SONG. . . . . OWT LINCOLN THEATRE 15
THERE COMES THIS SONG . . . . SP AFRO-AMER FRAG 16
THIS SONG OF ATAVISTIC LAND. . . . SP AFRO-AMER FRAG 18
AS SONG GROWS STRONGER . . . . . . SP DRUNKARD 2
AND LET THE CHOIR SING A STORMY SONG SP FATASY PURPLE 3
THE SLAVES MADE UP A SONG: . . . . SP FREEDOM'S PLOW 125
THAT SONG MEANT JUST WHAT IT SAID:
HOLD ON! . . . . SP FREEDOM'S PLOW 127
MADE UP A SONG: . . . . SP FREEDOM'S PLOW 190
THIS IS A SONG FOR THE GENIUS CHILD. SP GENIUS CHILD 1
SING IT SOFTLY. FOR THE SONG IS
WILD. . . . . SP GENIUS CHILD 2
LEST THE SONG GET OUT OF HAND. . . SP GENIUS CHILD 4
AND FOR YOUR LOVE SONG TONE THEIR
RUMBLE DOWN. . . . . SP JUKE BOX LOVE 6
JUST LIKE THE SONG. . . . . SP MADAM'S PAST HI 20
SING A SOOTHIN' SONG. . . . . . . SP MISERY 5
SAID A SOOTHIN' SONG. . . . . . . SP MISERY 6
AND THE SONG . . . . SP MYSTERY 27
IS IN THE SONG . . . . SP SO LONG 2
OF THE SONG . . . . SP SONG BILLIE HOL 2
BUT THE SONG . . . . SP SONG BILLIE HOL 5
OF THE SONG? . . . . SP SONG BILLIE HOL 9
SONG IS A STRONG THING. . . . . . SP SPIRITUALS 5
SONG IS A STRONG THING. . . . . . SP SPIRITUALS 16
TO A MOTHER'S SONG. . . . . SP STARS 4
SUN AND THE SONG OF ALL THE
SUN-STARS . . . . SP SUN SONG 3
AND A GOSPEL SONG: . . . . SP TAMBOURINES 8
WHY SHOULD IT BE MY SONG. . . . . . SP TELL ME 2
BUT GOD PUT A SONG AND A PRAYER IN
MY MOUTH. . . . . SP THE NEGRO MOTHE 18
IN A DEEP SONG VOICE WITH A
MELANCHOLY TONE . . . . SP THE WEARY BLUES 17
LIKE A SONG . . . . PL COLOR 6
AND THE SONG . . . . PL OPPRESSION 12

SONGS 22

WERE IT NOT FOR YOUR SONGS. . . . . DK QUIET GIRL 6
AND ONLY IN THE SORROW SONGS . . . ANS A NEW SONG 22
AND ALL THE SONGS WE'VE SUNG . . . ANS LET AMERICA BE 57
SONGS IN THE DARK. . . . . FW SONGS 2
AND LET YOUR SONGS DRIFT THROUGH THE
SWINGING DOORS. . . . . OWT JUICE JOINT 18
LET YOUR SONGS HOLD ALL THE SUNNY
JOYS . . . . OWT JUICE JOINT 19
O. SONGS THAT DO NOT CARE! . . . . OWT NEGRO SERVANT 7
O. SONGS! . . . . OWT NEGRO SERVANT 17
AND THE SONGS ON THE JUKE BOX . . . OWT RAID 3

SAVE THOSE THAT SONGS . . . . SP AFRO-AMER FRAG 6
WERE IT NOT FOR YOUR SONGS. . . . . SP ARDELLA 6
SINGING SORROW SONGS ON THE BANKS OF
A MIGHTY RIVER . . . . SP AUNTSUE'S STORI 11
SONGS THAT BREAK . . . . SP GYPSY MELODIES 1
AND SICK SILLY SONGS . . . . SP JULIET 4
I CARRIED MY SORROW SONGS. . . . . SP NEGRO 12
NIGHT OF THE FOUR SONGS UNSUNG: . . SP NIGHT FOUR SONG 5
STOPS TO LISTEN TO GOSPEL SONGS . . SP SUMMER EVENING 11
I BRING YOU MY SONGS . . . . SP SUN SONG 6
WHERE DINAH'S SONGS ARE MADE . . . AYM ODE TO DINAH 53
BY SONGS UPON THE BREEZE . . . . . PL BIRMINGHAM SUND 26
AND I'M GONNA PUT THE PURTIEST SONGS
IN IT . . . . PL DAYBREAK IN ALA 4
NOR SONGS . . . . PL OPPRESSION 4

SONG'S 1
WHERE THE SONG'S MAHALIA'S DAUGHTER AYM ODE TO DINAH 19

SONS 1
SHE SPOKE OF SONS AT WAR. . . . . . PL MOTHER IN WAR 2

SON-OF-A-GUN 2
WE GONNA BURY THAT SON-OF-A-GUN! . JC JIM CROW'S LAST 32
I HOPE THAT WILD YOUNG SON-OF-A-GUN SP MAMA AND DAUGHT 15

SOON 10
BUT SOON . . . . WB POEME D'AUTOMNE 8
AN' SOON AS HE GOT OUT DE BARREL . FC BLACK GAL 11
SO WHEN I GOT READY TO GO. I SAID.
"I'LL BE SEEIN' YOU SOON. MARIE." NM BROKE 52
LEARNS SO SOON . . . . FW MAN 13
DIMMED TOO SOON. . . . . SP GYPSY MELODIES 5
A-SHOUTIN'. GOD. I'S COMIN' SOON. SP JUDGMENT DAY 4
MIGHT BE AWAKENED SOMEDAY SOON . . PL BIRMINGHAM SUND 25
BUT DESTINED SURE TO FLOOD - AND
SOON - . . . . PL JUNIOR ADDICT 10
AS SOON AS YOU SEE . . . . PL LITTLE SNG HOUS 6
SOON AS YOU SPY . . . . PL LITTLE SNG HOUS 15

SOONER 2
NO SOONER HAD I TOLD HIM . . . . . SP MADAM WRONG VIS 21
BRING WELFARE CHECKS MUCH SOONER . AYM ODE TO DINAH 73

SOOTHIN' 2
SING A SOOTHIN' SONG. . . . . SP MISERY 5
SAID A SOOTHIN' SONG. . . . . SP MISERY 6

SORBONNE 1
WHO AT THE SORBONNE HAS SIX CLASSES. AYM ASK YOUR MAMA 54

SORE 6
NEXT TIME SHE MAKES ME SORE. . . . FC EVIL WOMAN 4
BEATEN AND SORE. . . . . NM BLACK CLWN POEM 22
AND WOUND HER SORE. . . . . FW FAITHFUL ONE 6
OR FESTER LIKE A SORE - . . . . . . SP HARLEM 4
BOTH FISTS SORE. . . . . PL DOWN WHERE I AM 4
OR FESTER LIKE A SORE - . . . . . . PL DREAM DEFERRED 4

SORES 1
HER BANDAGE HIDES TWO FESTERING
SORES . . . . PL JUSTICE 3

SORROW 22
SO I CLIMB TOWARD TOMORROW. OUT OF
PAST SORROW. . . . . NM DARK YOUTH USA 22
AND ONLY IN THE SORROW SONGS . . . ANS A NEW SONG 22
OLD JIM CROW'S SORROW? . . . . . . JC BLACK MAN SPEAK 28
IN HER BITTER SORROW. . . . . FW MOTHERLAND 4
SO MUCH SORROW . . . . FW WALLS 6
SINGING SORROW SONGS ON THE BANKS OF
A MIGHTY RIVER . . . . SP AUNTSUE'S STORI 11
SORROW LIKE A SEA. . . . . SP FEET O' JESUS 2
WAVE OF SORROW. . . . . SP ISLAND 1
WAVE OF SORROW. . . . . SP ISLAND 7
OF SORROW. . . . . SP JULIET 5
I CARRIED MY SORROW SONGS. . . . . SP NEGRO 12
SORROW! SORROW! . . . . SP NIGHT FOUR SONG 6
SORROW! SORROW! . . . . SP NIGHT FOUR SONG 6
SORROW! SORROW! . . . . SP NIGHT FOUR SONG 7
SORROW! SORROW! . . . . SP NIGHT FOUR SONG 7
DO NOT SPEAK OF SORROW . . . . . . SP SONG BILLIE HOL 10
THE SORROW THAT I SPEAK OF . . . . SP SONG BILLIE HOL 14
REMEMBER MY YEARS. HEAVY WITH SORROW
- . . . . SP THE NEGRO MOTHE 37
FOR THE SADNESS TO BE SORROW. . . . AYM IS IT TRUE? 28
OF BLOOD AND SORROW. . . . . PL HISTORY 2
OH. WHAT SORROW! . . . . PL MISSISSIPPI 1
WHAT SORROW. PITY. PAIN. . . . . . PL MISSISSIPPI 17

SORROWS 2
17 SORROWS . . . . AYM ASK YOUR MAMA 15
MAKE CLAVES OF MY SORROWS . . . . . AYM GOSPEL CHA-CHA 33

SORROW'S 1
LAUGH AT MY SORROW'S REIGN. . . . . WB THE JESTER 14

SORRY 3
I'M SORRY FOR THAT EVIL WISH . . . SP CROSS 7
I FELT KINDER SORRY . . . . SP MADAM MINISTER 28
SORRY THAT OLD WAR IS DONE! . . . . SP WORLD WAR II 6

SORT 1
MUSIC TAKES ON A BLUES STRAIN.
GRADUALLY RETURNING TO A SORT OF NM BIG-TIMER MOOD 3

SORTS 1
DIDN'T HAVE ANY SCHOOLS: AND THERE
WERE ALL SORTS OF . . . . NM COLORED SL POEM 25

SOUGHT 2
SOUGHT CALM RELIEF. . . . . WB YOUNG BRIDE 5
FINDING LESS THAN SOUGHT . . . . . SP OLD WALT 3

SOUL 41
AND ALL THE WILD HOT MOONS OF THE
JUNGLES SHINE IN MY SOUL. . . . WB FOR PORTRAIT OF 2
OH. SHINING RIVERS OF THE SOUL! . . WB JAZZONIA 2
OH. SHINING RIVERS OF THE SOUL! . . WB JAZZONIA 8
OH. SILVER RIVERS OF THE SOUL! . . WB JAZZONIA 15
MY SOUL . . . . WB SUMMER NIGHT 13
MASKS FOR THE SOUL. . . . . WB THE JESTER 5
DAMN MA BLACK OLD MAMMY'S SOUL . . FC A RUINED GAL 17
TO WHICH THE SOUL ASCENDS . . . . . OLD TOWER 2
WELL. AIN'T NEVER DONE IT. BUT FOR
TO KEEP BODY AND SOUL . . . . . NM BROKE 29
BUT HIS SOUL WENT OUT TO SEA. . . . DK DEATH SEAMAN 2
HIS SOUL ON FIRE. . . . . DK MA LORD 13
MA SOUL IS FULL OF COLOR . . . . . DK REASONS WHY 3
WITH YOUR STINGY SOUL! . . . . . . SH BLD THE KILLER 20
MAKE THIS EARLY MORNING TIME TO KEEP
BODY AND SOUL . . . . SH DAYBREAK 7
NOT A SOUL BUT LONESOME BLUE. . . . SH MIDNIGHT CHIPPI 2
I SWEAR TO MY SOUL . . . . JC BLACK MAN SPEAK 5
SOUL YEARNS. . . . . FW EXITS 7
NO SOUL RETURNS. . . . . FW EXITS 11
THAT MY SOUL SHOULD NOT BE LOST. . LHR BLD MARY'S SON 33
SO WITH MY ONCE GAY-COLORED SOUL . SP A BLACK PIERROT 12
GOD REST HIS SOUL - . . . . SP BLD OF THE MAN 22
IN MY SOUL. . . . . SP EASY BOOGIE 8
FIRE GONNA BURN MA SOUL! . . . . . SP FIRE 3
FIRE GONNA BURN MA SOUL! . . . . . SP FIRE 9
FIRE GONNA BURN MA SOUL! . . . . . SP FIRE 16
FIRE GONNA BURN MA SOUL! . . . . . SP FIRE 23
FIRE GONNA BURN MA SOUL! . . . . . SP FIRE 25
KILL HIM - AND LET HIS SOUL RUN
WILD! . . . . SP GENIUS CHILD 12
MA SOUL WENT FLYIN' O' THE TOWN. . SP JUDGMENT DAY 2
IN YOUR SOUL. . . . . SP MADAM MINISTER 6
JESUS. LOVER OF MY SOUL! . . . . . SP MYSTERY 5
MY SOUL HAS GROWN DEEP LIKE THE
RIVERS. . . . . SP NEGRO SPEAKS OF 4
MY SOUL HAS GROWN DEEP LIKE THE
RIVERS. . . . . SP NEGRO SPEAKS OF 13
THAT TRIED TO BURN WITHIN HER SOUL. SP RUBY BROWN 7
GOD PUT A DREAM LIKE STEEL IN MY
SOUL. . . . . SP THE NEGRO MOTHE 19
COMING FROM A BLACK MAN'S SOUL. . . SP THE WEARY BLUES 15
I WILL TAKE YOUR SOUL OUT OF YOUR
BODY . . . . SP TO ARTINA 2
I WILL TAKE YOUR SOUL. . . . . . . SP TO ARTINA 10
TO HIS SOUL - . . . . SP TRUMPET PLAYER 40
MIGHT HAVE LOST HIS SOUL. . . . . . PL FREDRK DOUGLASS 6
AND FEELING TO MY VERY SOUL . . . . PL MILITANT 6

SOULS 3
DAMN THEIR SOULS. - . . . . FC DEATH DO DIRTY 32
BUT ALL ONE SNARL OF SOULS. . . . . SP A HOUSE IN TAOS 40
BEAUTIFUL. ALSO. ARE THE SOULS OF MY
PEOPLE. . . . . SP MY PEOPLE 6

SOUND 11
WHEN BEYOND STEEL BARS SOUND THE
DEATHLESS DRUMS . . . . SL SCOTTSBORO 7
AND THE SOUND VIBRATES IN WAVES . . ANS CHANT TOM MOONY 17
TO SONG WITHOUT SOUND. . . . . . . FW BURDEN 4
IN SOUND TRUCKS. . . . . OWT BLD MARGE POLIT 39
OF DANCING SOUND . . . . SP COLLEGE FORMAL 12
SOUND LIKE A GREAT BIG CROWD. . . . SP MORNING AFTER 18
SO THEY DON'T SOUND LIKE ME. . . . SP NOTE COMM THEAT 6
SOUND . . . . SP SHALIMAR 5
BY SOUND THAT SHIMMERS - . . . . . SP SONG BILLIE HOL 19
ON THE SOUND WAY OFF THE TURNPIKE - AYM HORN OF PLENTY 34
BLOWS A SCRATCHY SOUND. . . . . . . PL CULTURAL EXCHNG 4

SOUNDIN' 1
ALL THIS TALKIN' AIN'T NOTHIN' BUT
TINKLIN' SYMBOLS AND SOUNDIN'
BRASS: . . . . NM BROKE 58

SOUNDS 1
THE SOUNDS . . . . WB SUMMER NIGHT 1

SOURCE 1
THE FLAMING SOURCE OF YOUR BRIGHT
BREATH. . . . . SP DEMAND 5

SOUSE 1

SOAKING UP A NEW SOUSE. . . . . . . SP WINE-O 6

SOUTH 38

I BROUGHT HER FROM DE SOUTH . . . . FC EVIL WOMAN 13
AW-OO! YONDER COMES A WOMAN I USED TO KNOW WAY DOWN SOUTH. . . . . NM BROKE 62
FOR HERE IN THE SOUTH THERE'S NO VOTES AND NO RIGHT. . . . . . . NM COLORED SL POEM 46
TO ROLL ME TO DE SOUTH. . . . . . . OK HOMESICK BLUES 12
WHEN THE BIRDS COME BACK FROM THE SOUTH. . . . . ANS CHANT MAY DAY 6
WHITE WORKERS OF THE SOUTH . . . . ANS OPEN LETTER 1
SOMEWHERE SOUTH. . . . . SH DEATH IN HARLEM 17
DOWN SOUTH YOU MAKE ME RIDE . . . . JC BLACK MAN SPEAK 13
FLOWING THROUGH THE SOUTH. . . . . JC THE BITTER RIVR 3
OF SOUTH PARKWAY: . . . . OWT JITNEY 2
WHOSE LANGUID LEAN BRINGS BACK THE SUNNY SOUTH . . . . OWT JUICE JOINT 42
ON THE SOUTH SIDE. . . . . OWT RESTRICTIVE 13
JAZZ ON THE SOUTH SIDE - . . . . . OWT VISITORS 10
ON THE SOUTH SIDE: . . . . OWT VISITORS 12
DOWN SOUTH IN DIXIE ONLY TRAIN I SEE'S . . . . SP FREEDOM TRAIN 9
JUST AS IF YOU WERE DOWN SOUTH. . . SP HIGH TO LOW 16
SHUT UP, SAYS THE GOVERNOR OF SOUTH CAROLINA. . . . . SP IN EXPLANATION 24
GOVERNORS OF SOUTH CAROLINA, GERALD L.K. STRYDOMS. . . . . SP IN EXPLANATION 43
AND NOT SOUTH. . . . . SP ONE-WAY TICKET 15
WAY DOWN SOUTH IN DIXIE . . . . . . SP SONG DARK GIRL 1
WAY DOWN SOUTH IN DIXIE . . . . . . SP SONG DARK GIRL 5
WAY DOWN SOUTH IN DIXIE . . . . . . SP SONG DARK GIRL 9
THREE HUNDRED YEARS IN THE DEEPEST SOUTH: . . . . SP THE NEGRO MOTHE 17
THE LAZY, LAUGHING SOUTH . . . . . SP THE SOUTH 1
THE SUNNY-FACED SOUTH, ... SP THE SOUTH 3
THE CHILD-MINDED SOUTH . . . . . . SP THE SOUTH 6
THE MAGNOLIA-SCENTED SOUTH. . . . . SP THE SOUTH 12
THAT IS THE SOUTH. . . . . SP THE SOUTH 17
MAY ESCAPE THE SPELL OF THE SOUTH. SP THE SOUTH 28
IN HARLEM OR THE SOUTH SIDE OF CHICAGO . . . . AYM HORN OF PLENTY 55
AS NORTH POLE IS TO SOUTH . . . . . AYM SHADES OF PIG 27
MAMMY OF THE SOUTH, ... PL CHRIST IN ALA. 5
OF THE SOUTH. . . . . PL CHRIST IN ALA. 14
OF THE SOUTH HAVE TAKEN OVER - . . PL CULTURAL EXCHNG 39
DOWN SOUTH WHERE I COME FROM . . . PL MERRY-GO-ROUND 6
DOWN SOUTH ON THE TRAIN . . . . . . PL MERRY-GO-ROUND 9
SOUTH . . . . PL OCTOBER 16 RAID 11
WHY DOWN SOUTH IS ALWAYS DOWN. . . PL VARI-COLORED 15

SOUTHERN 12

8 BLACK BOYS IN A SOUTHERN JAIL. . SL SCOTTSBORO 1
8 BLACK BOYS IN A SOUTHERN JAIL. . SL SCOTTSBORO 28
A LITTLE SOUTHERN COLORED CHILD . . FW MIGRATION 1
IN LAZY FAR-OFF DROWSY SOUTHERN DAYS OWT JUICE JOINT 11
WHILE BLUES AS MELLOW AS THE SOUTHERN AIR . . . . OWT JUICE JOINT 25
AND WEARY AS A DROWSY SOUTHERN RAIN OWT JUICE JOINT 26
THE SOUTHERN NIGHT . . . . SP MULATTO 8
THE SOUTHERN NIGHT IS FULL OF STARS. SP MULATTO 31
SOUTHERN GENTLE LADY, ... SP SILHOUETTE 1
SOUTHERN GENTLE LADY, ... SP SILHOUETTE 11
THERE SOUTHERN CONFERENCE? . . . . AYM BIRD IN ORBIT 81
SOUTHERN DOGS HAVE VINDICATED ME - PL NORTHERN LIBERL 4

SOUVENIRS 1

TO BE SOUVENIRS OF JESUS. . . . . . LHR PASTORAL 8

SO-AND-SO 1

DADDY, I WANT SO-AND-SO. . . . . . SP PREFERENCE 5

SO'S 1

SO'S THAT I COULD EAT. . . . . . . SH OUT OF WORK 6

SPACE 2

AND SPACE ITSELF . . . . SP DRUM 11
SPACE IS HIS GRAVE. . . . . PL LUMUMBA'S GRAVE 19

SPAGHETTI 1

SPAGHETTI AND GIN, MUSIC AND SMOKE. SH DEATH IN HARLEM 53

SPAIN 24

AND SING ME THE SONG OF SPAIN. . . ANS SONG OF SPAIN 2
WHAT IS THE SONG OF SPAIN? . . . . ANS SONG OF SPAIN 4
FLAMENCO IS THE SONG OF SPAIN: . . ANS SONG OF SPAIN 5
FLAMENCO IS THE SONG OF SPAIN. . . ANS SONG OF SPAIN 10
TOROS ARE THE SONG OF SPAIN: . . . ANS SONG OF SPAIN 12
IS THE SONG OF SPAIN. . . . . . . ANS SONG OF SPAIN 17
PINTURA IS THE SONG OF SPAIN: . . . ANS SONG OF SPAIN 19
THE SONG OF SPAIN. . . . . ANS SONG OF SPAIN 24
THAT'S THE SONG OF SPAIN. . . . . . ANS SONG OF SPAIN 29
THE SONG OF SPAIN. . . . . ANS SONG OF SPAIN 32
THE SONG OF SPAIN. . . . . ANS SONG OF SPAIN 34
POISON GAS IS SPAIN. . . . . ANS SONG OF SPAIN 35
AND ITS TERROR AND PAIN IS SPAIN. ANS SONG OF SPAIN 37
NOT SPAIN. . . . . ANS SONG OF SPAIN 39
THE PEOPLE ARE SPAIN: . . . . ANS SONG OF SPAIN 40
I BOUGHT THOSE BOMBS FOR SPAIN! . . ANS SONG OF SPAIN 45
WORKERS MADE THOSE BOMBS FOR A FACIST SPAIN! . . . . ANS SONG OF SPAIN 46
WHEN BOMBS'LL FALL NOT ONLY ON SPAIN - . . . . ANS SONG OF SPAIN 52
TO BUILD UP PROFITS FOR THE RAPE OF SPAIN! . . . . ANS SONG OF SPAIN 57
WORKERS, SEE YOURSELVES AS SPAIN! ANS SONG OF SPAIN 58
I MADE THOSE BOMBS FOR SPAIN. . . . ANS SONG OF SPAIN 71
AGAINST SPAIN. . . . . ANS SONG OF SPAIN 77
I MUST DRIVE THE BOMBERS OUT OF SPAIN! . . . . ANS SONG OF SPAIN 79
IS THE SONG OF SPAIN. . . . . ANS SONG OF SPAIN 83

SPANGLE 1

MAKE A SPANGLE OUT OF QUARTERS RINGING . . . . AYM ODE TO DINAH 59

SPARE 2

I GOT EVENIN' AIR TO SPARE. . . . . SH EVENIN' BLUES 12
A MAN, SPARE, SWARTHY, STRONG, FOURSQUARE - . . . . JC TO CAPTAIN MULZ 44

SPARK 4

CREEPING LIKE FIRE FROM A SLOW SPARK OLD THE CONSUMPTIVE 10
MAKES A LITTLE SPARK. . . . . SP LOVE 6
THAT LITTLE SPARK IS LOVE . . . . . SP LOVE 7
THE SAME OLD SPARK! . . . . SP NEW YORKERS 17

SPARKLING 1

SPARKLING ORIENTAL WINES . . . . . SP FLATTED FIFTHS 7

SPAT 1

WHAT DO YOU MEAN, JUST A LITTLE SPAT? . . . . SH LETTER 4

SPATTERED 1

WITH SPATTERED FLESH . . . . PL BIRMINGHAM SUND 6

SPEAK 10

YOU'VE GOT SEVEN LANGUAGES TO SPEAK IN . . . . FC JAZZ BAND 19
I SPEAK IN THE NAME OF THE BLACK MILLIONS . . . . ANS A NEW SONG 1
THE WORKERS SPEAK THE NAME: . . . . ANS CHANT TOM MOONY 13
BEFORE YOU SPEAK. . . . . FW SILENCE 3
A LITTLE TIME TO SPEAK? . . . . . . SP MADAM MINISTER 4
SO TO SPEAK. . . . . SP MADAM CHARTY CH 20
DO NOT SPEAK OF SORROW . . . . . . SP SONG BILLIE HOL 10
THE SORROW THAT I SPEAK OF . . . . SP SONG BILLIE HOL 14
SPEAK OF RICE DOWN IN THE MARSHALND AYM BIRD IN ORBIT 43
SPEAK OF FREDERICK DOUGLASS'S BEARD AYM BIRD IN ORBIT 44

SPEAKER 1

THE SPEAKER CATCHES FIRE. . . . . . PL CORNER MEETING 4

SPEAKING 2

LIFE IN PLACES GENTLER SPEAKING . . OLD AESTHETE HARLEM 5
(METAPHYSICALLY SPEAKING) . . . . . PL GHOSTS OF 1619 19

SPEAKS 3

BACK, AND EYES SHINING, QUIETLY RECALLING THE VISION, THE DEAD MAN SPEAKS . . . . NM COLORED SL MOOD 8
SPEAKS FROM THE MARBLE: . . . . . . ANS BLDS OF LENIN 26
SPEAKS ENGLISH FRENCH SWAHILI . . . AYM ASK YOUR MAMA 57

SPECKLED 1

AND DON'T YOU KNOW THAT OLD WOMAN SWELLED UP LIKE A SPECKLED TOAD NM BROKE 21

SPECTRUM 1

ALL THROUGH THE SPECTRUM . . . . . SH HARLEM SWEETIES 39

SPED 1

THAT LONG BLACK HEARSE DONE SPED. SP NIGHT FUNERAL 34

SPEECHES 1

THEN MAKE FINE SPEECHES . . . . . . JC HOW ABOUT DIXIE 15

SPEED 2

WILL SPEED IT . . . . SP PARADE 15
WITH ALL DELIBERATE SPEED A . . . . AYM ODE TO DINAH 100

SPELL 2

WILL SPELL THE NAME . . . . SP GRADUATION 15
MAY ESCAPE THE SPELL OF THE SOUTH. SP THE SOUTH 28

SPEND 2

TO SPEND A MEDITATIVE HOUR - . . . OLD TOWER 3
TO SPEND, HE SAYS. . . . . SP YOUNG SAILOR 9

SPENDIN 1

EVERYBODY'S HAPPY, IT'S A SPENDIN CROWD - . . . . SH DEATH IN HARLEM 36

SPENDIN' 1
SPENDIN' MONEY LIKE WATER. . . . . NM BIG-TIMER POEM 17

SPENT 1
SPENT HIS MONEY ON ME - . . . . SP MADAM MIGHT-HAV 10

SPILL 1
HAVE YOU DUG THE SPILL . . . . SH HARLEM SWEETIES 1

SPIN 2
THE CIRCLES SPIN ROUND . . . . FW CIRCLES 1
AND THE CIRCLES SPIN ROUND . . . . . FW CIRCLES 2

SPINS 1
AS THE BLACK BOY SPINS . . . . ANS LYNCHING SONG 7

SPIRALS 1
THAT SPIRALS . . . . SP DESERT 6

SPIRITS 1
FOR THE GREAT EARTH SPIRITS . . . . FW JAIME 3

SPIRITUAL 1
DE TROUBLE I'VE HAD." FLINCHING
UNDER THE WHIP. THE SPIRITUAL . NM BLACK CLWN MOOD 5

SPIRITUALS 1
YOU ALSO TOOK MY SPIRITUALS AND
GONE. . . . . SP NOTE COMM THEAT 8

SPIT 3
WHITE SPIT IN MY FACE - . . . . NM BLACK CLWN POEM 48
AND SPIT IN THE FACE OF MY DREAM. JC THE BITTER RIVR 62
YOUR SPIT IS MY FACE. . . . . PL MILITANT 11

SPITOON 2
A CLEAN SPITOON ON THE ALTAR OF THE
LORD. . . . . FC BRASS SPITOONS 37
A CLEAN BRIGHT SPITOON ALL NEWLY
POLISHED. - . . . . FC BRASS SPITOONS 38

SPITOONS 4
CLEAN THE SPITOONS. BOY. . . . . . FC BRASS SPITOONS 1
CLEAN THE SPITOONS. . . . . FC BRASS SPITOONS 6
AND THE SLIME IN HOTEL SPITOONS: . FC BRASS SPITOONS 9
DOLLARS AND CLEAN SPITOONS . . . . FC BRASS SPITOONS 29

SPITS 1
BUT SHE SPITS IN MY FACE. . . . . . SP THE SOUTH 19

SPLASH 2
SPLASH OF COLOR ON CANVASS. . . . . ANS SONG OF SPAIN 21
SPLASH INTO THE RIVERS AND THE SEAS
WENT THE BOAT-HULLS . . . . SP FREEDOM'S PLOW 57

SPLENDOR 1
YOUR FACES ARE WHIRLING LIGHTS OF
LOVELINESS AND SPLENDOR. TOO. . WB THE WHITE ONES 4

SPLINTERS 3
AND SPLINTERS. . . . . SP MOTHER TO SON 4
ON THE CORNER PICKING SPLINTERS . . AYM ASK YOUR MAMA 33
AND SPLINTERS OF HAIL. . . . . . . PL DREAM DUST 4

SPLIT 3
I'M GONNA SPLIT THIS ROCK . . . . . JC BIG BUDDY 14
AND SPLIT IT WIDE! . . . . JC BIG BUDDY 15
WHEN I SPLIT THIS ROCK. . . . . . . JC BIG BUDDY 16

SPLITS 1
THAT SPLITS THE WORLD IN TWO . . . SP CONSIDER ME 37

SPOKE 1
SHE SPOKE OF SONS AT WAR. . . . . . PL MOTHER IN WAR 2

SPOKEN 4
A DRAMATIC MONOLOGUE TO BE SPOKEN BY
A PURE-BLOODED NEGRO IN THE WHITE NM BLACK CLWN MOOD 1
THESE WORDS ARE GENTLY SPOKEN: . . DK ALABAMA EARTH 11
A MAN WITH THE TITLE OF GOVERNOR HAS
SPOKEN: . . . . ANS CHANT TOM MOONY 4
A MAN WITH THE TITLE OF GOVERNOR HAS
SPOKEN: . . . . ANS CHANT TOM MOONY 6

SPOON 1
HIS NEEDLE AND HIS SPOON. . . . . . PL JUNIOR ADDICT 12

SPORT 4
ROUNDER AND SPORT. . . . . NM BIG-TIMER POEM 38
FUN TO SPORT AROUND. . . . . SP BLUE MONDAY 7
TO SPORT AWAY. . . . . SP CONSIDER ME 21
BLOOD ON MY SPORT SHIRT . . . . . . PL THIRD DEGREE 3

SPORTS 1
BIG TIME SPORTS AND GIRLS WHO KNOW SH DEATH IN HARLEM 37

SPORTS-WRITERS 1
OR SPORTS-WRITERS IN THEIR STORY. AYM IS IT TRUE? 51

SPORTY 1
WITH A LOT O' SPORTY PALS. . . . . NM BIG-TIMER POEM 16

SPOTLIGHT 1
WHERE THE MOONLIGHT'S BUT A
SPOTLIGHT . . . . SP TRUMPET PLAYER 27

SPOTS 1
SPOTS WHERE THE BOOTED . . . . . . SP NEON SIGNS 7

SPOTTED 1
GOD! GIVE ME THE SPOTTED . . . . . NM BLACK CLWN POEM 25

SPOTTING 1
SPOTTING FAIRIES. . . . . SP CAFE: 3 A.M. 3

SPREAD 6
SPREAD SOME JOY! . . . . SH DEATH IN HARLEM 86
YOU SPREAD YOUR COLOR BAR. . . . . JC BLACK MAN SPEAK 16
WHEN FLOWERS SPREAD THE PLAIN. . . FW GIRL 6
THE CRY SPREAD OVER HARLEM . . . . OWT BLD MARGE POLIT 15
MAY ITS BRANCHES SPREAD AND ITS
SHELTER GROW . . . . SP FREEDOM'S PLOW 138
UNTIL COLORED FOLKS SPREAD . . . . SP GOOD MORNING 4

SPREADS 1
THE WONDER SPREADS . . . . SP IN TIME SILVER 7

SPREE 1
OUT FOR A SPREE. . . . . FC JAZZ BAND 8

SPRIGHTLY 1
THERE'S A SPRIGHTLY YOUNG MOON . . FW NEW MOON 3

SPRING 12
TO BEAUTIFY THIS HOUR. THIS SPRING.
AND ALL THE SPRINGS TO COME . . ANS CHANT MAY DAY 12
IN SPRING. . . . . FW DUSTBOWL 6
IT'S A SPRING SONG! . . . . FW EARTH SONG 4
FOR A SPRING SONG: . . . . FW EARTH SONG 6
A SPRING SONG! . . . . FW EARTH SONG 13
IT WAS IN THE SPRING. . . . . LHR BLD MARY'S SON 1
HAPPENED IN THE SPRING - . . . . . LHR BLD MARY'S SON 5
WHEN SPRING . . . . SP IN TIME SILVER 22
THE SPRING IS NOT SO BEAUTIFUL THERE
- . . . . SP WATER-FRONT STR 1
TO WHERE THE SPRING IS WONDROUS RARE SP WATER-FRONT STR 3
THE SPRING IS NOT SO BEAUTIFUL THERE
- . . . . SP WATER-FRONT STR 5
HOLLAND BULBS IN SPRING . . . . . . AYM HORN OF PLENTY 74

SPRINGS 1
TO BEAUTIFY THIS HOUR. THIS SPRING.
AND ALL THE SPRINGS TO COME . . ANS CHANT MAY DAY 12

SPRINGTIME 2
OF SPRINGTIME. . . . . FW FRAGMENTS 2
OF SPRINGTIME . . . . PL SLUM DREAMS 2

SPRINKLING 1
FOR SPRINKLING SALT . . . . SP JAM SESSION 7

SPROUT 1
TO SPROUT THEIR BITTER BARRIERS . . PL GEORGIA DUSK 11

SPRUNG 1
MY ROOF HAS SPRUNG A LEAK. . . . . SP BLD LANDLORD 2

SPY 1
SOON AS YOU SPY . . . . PL LITTLE SNG HOUS 15

SQUAD 1
DETECTIVES FROM THE VICE SQUAD . . SP CAFE: 3 A.M. 1

SQUALLING 1
AIDS TRIUMPHANT ENTRY SQUALLING . . SP INTERNE AT PROV 27

SQUARES 1
SQUARES . . . . SP DEAD IN THERE 18

SQUEAKS 1
KITCHEN FLOOR SQUEAKS. . . . . . . SP MADAM RENT MAN 16

SQUEEZE 1
FORTUNE TELLER SQUEEZE MY HAND. . . SP MADAM FORT TELL 5

SQUINTED 1
SHE SQUINTED UP HER EYES. . . . . . SP MADAM FORT TELL 6

SQUIRREL 1
LIKE A SQUIRREL IN A CAGE - . . . . FW CIRCLES 7

ST 9
CARELESS. AND HALF-DEFIANT ECHOES OF
THE "ST. JAMES INFIRMARY" AS THE NM BIG-TIMER MOOD 2
PLAY THE ST. LOUIS BLUES . . . . . OWT REQUEST REQUIEM 1

SING THE ST. JAMES INFIRMARY . . . OWT REQUEST REQUIEM 5
(NOT ST. PHILLIPS) . . . . SP HIGH TO LOW 14
ST. JAMES PRESBYTERIAN . . . . . . SP PROJECTION 7
THROUGH A PARK, THEN I CROSS ST.
NICHOLAS, ... SP THEME FOR ENG B 12
TO MOVE OUT TO ST. ALBANS $ $ $ $ $
$ $ $ . . . . AYM HORN OF PLENTY 22
EVEN FARTHER THAN ST. ALBANS . . . AYM HORN OF PLENTY 31
LIVING IN ST. ALBANS . . . . AYM HORN OF PLENTY 59

STAGE 1
COVERED WAGONS, STAGE COACHES, . . SP FREEDOM'S PLOW 75

STAIN 2
AND THAT OUR DARK BLOOD WOULD WIPE
AWAY THE STAIN . . . . NM COLORED SL POEM 8
THE STEEL OF FREEDOM DOES NOT STAIN. ANS LET AMERICA BE 71

STAINED 2
ALL STAINED . . . . FW WHEN ARMIES PAS 7
SUNSETS STAINED WITH BLOOD . . . . AYM GOSPEL CHA-CHA 29

STAINING 1
STAINING THE DARK SEA RED, ... WB CARIBBEAN SUNST 3

STAIR 2
LIFE FOR ME AIN'T BEEN NO CRYSTAL
STAIR. . . . . SP MOTHER TO SON 2
AND LIFE FOR ME AIN'T BEEN NO
CRYSTAL STAIR. . . . . SP MOTHER TO SON 20

STAIRS 3
IMPEL YOU FOREVER UP THE GREAT
STAIRS - . . . . SP THE NEGRO MOTHE 50
UP THE STAIRS AND DOWN THE STAIRS SP TO BE SOMEBODY 9
UP THE STAIRS AND DOWN THE STAIRS SP TO BE SOMEBODY 9

STALINGRAD 9
GOODMORNING, STALINGRAD! . . . . . JC GOOD MORN STLIN 1
GOODMORNING, STALINGRAD! . . . . . JC GOOD MORN STLIN 5
GOODMORNING, STALINGRAD! . . . . . JC GOOD MORN STLIN 10
GOODMORNING, STALINGRAD! . . . . . JC GOOD MORN STLIN 16
GOODMORNING, STALINGRAD! . . . . . JC GOOD MORN STLIN 22
GOODMORNING, STALINGRAD! . . . . . JC GOOD MORN STLIN 28
STALINGRAD! . . . . JC GOOD MORN STLIN 36
GOODMORNING, STALINGRAD! . . . . . JC GOOD MORN STLIN 57
GOODMORNING, STALINGRAD! . . . . . JC GOOD MORN STLIN 60

STALL 1
AIN'T EVEN GOT A STALL. . . . . . . FC HARD LUCK 18

STALL-IN 1
SIT-IN, STAND-IN, STALL-IN, VOTE-IN PL GHOSTS OF 1619 7

STAND 30
I GUESS I CAN STAND THE RACKET . . NM BIG-TIMER POEM 55
THAT I CAN STAND MORE. . . . . . . NM BLACK CLWN POEM 24
STURDY I STAND, BOOKS IN MY HAND - NM DARK YOUTH USA 1
ITS COURT, TOO WEAK TO STAND AGAINST
A MOB. . . . . SL TOWN OF SCOTTSB 3
AND WORN-OUT ALTARS STAND . . . . . ANS UNION 9
STAND BACK FOLKSES, LET US . . . . SH DEATH IN HARLEM 106
GIRLS, DON'T STAND ON NO CORNER . . SH MIDNIGHT CHIPPI 25
I SAY DON'T STAND ON NO CORNER . . SH MIDNIGHT CHIPPI 27
AIN'T YOU GONNA STAND BY ME? . . . JC BIG BUDDY 2
AIN'T YOU GONNA STAND BY ME? . . . JC BIG BUDDY 4
AIN'T YOU GONNA STAND BY ME? . . . JC BIG BUDDY 9
STAND BY MY SIDE. . . . . JC BIG BUDDY 17
AND TAKE A STAND . . . . JC BLD SAM SOLOMON 20
THEY LIKED HIM SO WELL THEY COULDN'T
STAND . . . . JC JIM CROW'S LAST 3
JIM CROW STARTED HIS LAST STAND. . JC JIM CROW'S LAST 29
I STAND MOST HUMBLY . . . . FW WISDOM 1
WHERE TWO OLD BROWN MEN STAND BEHIND
THE BAR - . . . . OWT JUICE JOINT 37
TO STAND . . . . SP DEMOCRACY 7
HAVE TO STAND! . . . . SP EARLY EVENING 22
AT YO' FEET I STAND. . . . . SP FEET O' JESUS 6
OR THAT THE UNION WOULD STAND, . . SP FREEDOM'S PLOW 135
AMONG ALL WHO STAND ON TWO FEET. . SP INTERNE AT PROV 17
DOES K STAND FOR? . . . . SP MADAM CENSUS 10
BARBECUE STAND . . . . SP MADAM'S PAST HI 11
STAND UP AND TALK ABOUT ME, ... SP NOTE COMM THEAT 13
STAND LIKE FREE MEN SUPPORTING MY
TRUST. . . . . SP THE NEGRO MOTHE 42
MUST STILL STAND . . . . PL ANGOLA QUESTION 3
TO STAND . . . . PL CORNER MEETING 7
TO STAND . . . . PL FREEDOM 7
SO WE STAND HERE . . . . PL HARLEM 16

STANDING 4
THROWING DOWN THE HAT OF A FOOL, AND
STANDING FORTH, STRAIGHT AND
STRONG, ... NM BLACK CLWN MOOD 14
AND I SAW HIM STANDING THERE,
STRAIGHT AND TALL, ... NM COLORED SL POEM 37
A WOMAN STANDING IN THE DOORWAY . . SP EVENING SONG 1
NOT STANDING UPRIGHT . . . . SP TO BE SOMEBODY 6

STANDIN' 5
STANDIN' BY DE LONESOME RIVERSIDE FC A RUINED GAL 1
STANDIN' BY DE WEARY RIVERSIDE . . FC A RUINED GAL 6
I WAS STANDIN' IN DE STREET. . . . FC DEATH DO DIRTY 22
DONE BEAT YOU TO DE PLACE, STANDIN'
OUT SIDE DE DO' . . . . NM BROKE 6
AND LEAVE ME STANDIN' HERE. . . . . PL FLORIDA WORKERS 12

STANDS 4
STANDS UP AND LAUGHS . . . . JC FREEDOM 11
THE MADAM STANDS FOR BUSINESS. . . SP MADAM'S PAST HI 3
SHE STANDS . . . . SP TROUBLED WOMAN 1
STANDS HARLEM - . . . . PL HARLEM 2

STAND-IN 1
SIT-IN, STAND-IN, STALL-IN, VOTE-IN PL GHOSTS OF 1619 7

STANLEY 1
IN A TOWN NAMED AFTER STANLEY . . . AYM BLUES IN STEREO 21

STAR 10
MERCEDES IS A DOOMED STAR. . . . . WB TO DARK MERCEDE 2
THAT AS LONG AS YOUR RED STAR . . . JC GOOD MORN STLIN 13
IT HAS A RED STAR ON IT. . . . . . FW WHEN ARMIES PAS 3
BUT IT HAS A RED STAR ON IT! . . . FW WHEN ARMIES PAS 9
IT IS A RED STAR, MOTHER! . . . . . FW WHEN ARMIES PAS 22
DARK DANCERS DANCE AND DREAMERS SEEK
A STAR . . . . OWT JUICE JOINT 39
SHINES LIKE A STAR IN THE EAST. . . SP INTERNE AT PROV 41
AT NIGHT MY WISHING STAR. . . . . . SP MISS BLUES'ES 8
REACH UP YOUR HAND, DARK BOY, AND
TAKE A STAR. . . . . SP STARS 7
ONE STAR. . . . . SP STARS 11

STARE 2
STARE AT OZIE POWELL. . . . . ANS BLD OZZIE POWEL 20
FOLKS PASS BY AND STARE - . . . . . OWT FUNERAL 4

STARED 1
BESSIE STARED AT BELLA . . . . . . SH DEATH IN HARLEM 111

STARING 1
MAGI ARE STARING. . . . . SP INTERNE AT PROV 39

STARK 1
STARK NAKED. . . . . SP MARCH MOON 6

STARS 42
LOOK AT THE STARS YONDER . . . . . NM BLACK CLWN POEM 73
FILLED WITH BLUE STARS. . . . . . . DK AFTR MNY SPRNGS 4
STARS, ... DK LULLABY 7
STARS, ... DK LULLABY 8
A NECKLACE OF STARS . . . . DK LULLABY 9
STARS, STARS, ... DK LULLABY 21
STARS, STARS, ... DK LULLABY 21
NIGHT STARS, ... DK LULLABY 23
TO A NIGHT WITHOUT STARS . . . . . DK QUIET GIRL 2
AND WHO ARE YOU THAT DRAWS YOUR VEIL
ACROSS THE STARS? . . . . ANS LET AMERICA BE 18
BURN WHITE WITH STARS. . . . . . . SH YOUNG NEGRO GRL 9
YOU REFLECT NO STARS BY NIGHT, . . JC THE BITTER RIVR 24
THE BITTER RIVER REFLECTS NO STARS - JC THE BITTER RIVR 26
THE BITTER RIVER REFLECTS NO STARS. JC THE BITTER RIVR 38
FOR ME GIVES BACK NO STARS. . . . . JC THE BITTER RIVR 88
STARS ARE BORN, ... FW BIRTH 3
I THOUGHT I SAW RED STARS, MOTHER, FW WHEN ARMIES PAS 12
UNTIL THE STARS PALE AND THE SKY
TURNS BLUE . . . . OWT JUICE JOINT 3
TO A NIGHT WITHOUT STARS . . . . . SP ARDELLA 2
TILL THE LAST STARS FALL, ... SP DRUM 6
STARS ARE GREAT DROPS . . . . SP HARLEM NIGHT SO 9
WENT FLYIN' TO THE STARS AN' MOON SP JUDGMENT DAY 3
AND STARS THAT SING, ... SP LOVE 2
FULL OF STARS, ... SP MULATTO 9
GREAT BIG YELLOW STARS. . . . . . . SP MULATTO 10
THE SOUTHERN NIGHT IS FULL OF STARS, SP MULATTO 31
GREAT BIG YELLOW STARS. . . . . . . SP MULATTO 32
THE BRIGHT STARS SCATTER EVERYWHERE. SP MULATTO 39
THE STARS ARE BEAUTIFUL, ... SP MY PEOPLE 3
AND THE SEVENTEEN STARS. . . . . . SP NIGHT FOUR SONG 2
O, SWEEP OF STARS OVER HARLEM
STREETS, ... SP STARS 1
LOOK EVER UPWARD AT THE SUN AND THE
STARS. . . . . SP THE NEGRO MOTHE 48
THE SKY, THE SUN, THE STARS, . . . SP THE SOUTH 11
THE STARS WENT OUT AND SO DID THE
MOON. . . . . SP THE WEARY BLUES 32
I LOOK AT THE STARS . . . . AYM BIRD IN ORBIT 53
AND THEY LOOK AT THE STARS, ... AYM BIRD IN ORBIT 54
STARS AT STARS STARS. . . . . AYM BIRD IN ORBIT 57
STARS AT STARS STARS. . . . . AYM BIRD IN ORBIT 57
STARS AT STARS STARS. . . . . AYM BIRD IN ORBIT 57
JOMO IN KENYATTA. . . . STARS. . . . AYM BIRD IN ORBIT 60
FROM LESSER STARS IN ORBIT $ $ $ $
$ $ $ . . . . AYM HORN OF PLENTY 21
MOON IS, STARS ARE, ... PL LUMUMBA'S GRAVE 18

START 7

Line	Poem	No.
YEARS AGO AT THE NATION'S START	NM DARK YOUTH USA	12
AND START A SKIN GAME WITH SOME CHUMPS I KNOW.	SH BED TIME	6
KEEP FEELING LIKE THIS I'M GONNA START ACTING BAD.	SH TWILIGHT REVERI	4
OF WHISKEY AS THEY START OUT FOR A BALL.	OWT JUICE JOINT	8
I DON'T DARE START THINKING IN THE MORNING.	SP BLUES AT DAWN	1
I DON'T DARE START THINKING IN THE MORNING.	SP BLUES AT DAWN	2
SO I DON'T DARE START THINKING IN THE MORNING.	SP BLUES AT DAWN	5

STARTED 7

Line	Poem	No.
STARTED IN TO MOAN AN' CRY.	FC GAL'S CRY DYING	6
I STARTED FEELING THIS A-WAY.	SH EVIL MORNING	4
JIM CROW STARTED HIS LAST STAND.	JC JIM CROW'S LAST	29
FOLKS STARTED TO CRY IT -	OWT BLD MARGE POLIT	14
SHE STARTED THE RIOTS!	OWT BLD MARGE POLIT	25
THEN SHE STARTED IN TO LIE.	SP BLD THE GYPSY	10
AND WE STARTED DOWN THE ROAD	SP WEST TEXAS	12

STARTER 1

Line	Poem	No.
STARTER!	FC CLOSING TIME	1

STARTS 6

Line	Poem	No.
WHEN A MAN STARTS OUT WITH NOTHING,	SP FREEDOM'S PLOW	1
WHEN A MAN STARTS OUT WITH HIS HANDS	SP FREEDOM'S PLOW	2
WHEN A MAN STARTS OUT TO BUILD A WORLD,	SP FREEDOM'S PLOW	4
HE STARTS FIRST WITH HIMSELF	SP FREEDOM'S PLOW	5
THEN THE MIND STARTS SEEKING A WAY.	SP FREEDOM'S PLOW	10
AND STARTS JITTERBUGGING	SP PROJECTION	3

STARVE 4

Line	Poem	No.
I'D STARVE AND - OH, WELL -	NM BIG-TIMER POEM	42
I FIGHT, I STARVE, I DIE.	ANS BLDS OF LENIN	24
I MIGHT STARVE FOR A YEAR BUT	SH OUT OF WORK	17
WHILE JOBLESS I STARVE DEAD?	PL GO SLOW	14

STAR-DUST 2

Line	Poem	No.
TO SCATTER STAR-DUST IN THEIR EYES.	SP GRADUATION	24
GATHER OUT OF STAR-DUST	PL DREAM DUST	1

STAR-FILLED 1

Line	Poem	No.
AND PIERROT LOVED A STAR-FILLED SKY.	WB PIERROT	9

STAR-WHITE 1

Line	Poem	No.
WHAT STAR-WHITE MOON HAS BEEN YOUR MOTHER?	WB NUDE YOUNG DANC	7

STATE 5

Line	Poem	No.
ON STATE STREET ANY DAY.	SH MIDNIGHT CHIPPI	18
CAUSE I WANT YOU TO STATE	JC BLACK MAN SPEAK	22
I WANT TO GET OVER TO STATE.	OWT JITNEY	38
PRACTICE ON A STATE STREET CANCER,	SP INTERNE AT PROV	7
RIDES THE STATE STREET STREET CAR,	SP MIGRANT	7

STATES 2

Line	Poem	No.
UNITED STATES OF AMERICA. MARTIAL MUSIC ON A PIANO, OR BY AN ORCHESTRA.	NM COLORED SL MOOD	3
ALL, ALL THE STRETCH OF THESE GREAT GREEN STATES -	ANS LET AMERICA BE	85

STATION 8

Line	Poem	No.
TO A COLORED BOY'S RISING IN WEALTH OR STATION -	NM COLORED SL POEM	27
I WENT DOWN TO DE STATION.	DK HOMESICK BLUES	7
WENT DOWN TO DE STATION.	DK HOMESICK BLUES	9
I'LL MEET YOU AT THE BUS STATION.	SH LETTER	21
PRECINCT STATION.	SP BLD LANDLORD	28
OUT OF PENN STATION	SP GOOD MORNING	7
OUT OF PENN STATION -	SP GOOD MORNING	21
OR STATION WAITING ROOM	PL WHERE WHEN WHCH	12

STATIONS 2

Line	Poem	No.
WHY THERE'S JIM CROW STATIONS FOR THE FREEDOM TRAIN?	SP FREEDOM TRAIN	32
NOT STOPPIN' AT NO STATIONS MARKED COLORED NOR WHITE.	SP FREEDOM TRAIN	51

STATION'S 1

Line	Poem	No.
THE BIRMINGHAM STATION'S MARKED COLORED AND WHITE.	SP FREEDOM TRAIN	25

STATUE 1

Line	Poem	No.
SINGERS LIKE ODETTA - AND THAT STATUE	AYM HORN OF PLENTY	3

STAY 15

Line	Poem	No.
FER I CAN'T STAY HERE ALONE.	FC GYPSY MAN	6
OF THOSE COMPELLED TO STAY -	DK IRISH WAKE	4
YOU WILL NOT STAY WHEN SUMMER GOES.	DK PASSING LOVE	6
STAY ON THE RIGHT TRACK.	SH BLD THE SINNER	14
DE BLUES FORGETS TO STAY.	SH EVENIN' BLUES	18
HOW FAR YOU GO, NOR HOW LONG YOU STAY -	SH SUNDAY	6
STAY AWAY IF YOU WANT TO, AND SEE IF I CARE!	SH SUPPER TIME	10
TO STAY HOME AT ALL.	SP DELINQUENT	4
STAY HERE?	SP KID SLEEPY	20
STAY HERE.	SP KID SLEEPY	22
BUT EAT, DRINK, STAY BLACK, AND DIE.	SP NECESSITY	4
AND FAR TOO CLEAN TO STAY THAT WAY.	SP PASSING	8
MAN TO STAY!	SP WEST TEXAS	20
YOU'LL SURE STAY IN YOUR PLACE.	SP WIDOW WOMAN	12
I STAY ALIVE.	PL MOTTO	4

STAYED 1

Line	Poem	No.
STAYED HOME INSIDE:	SP MIDNIGHT RAFFLE	14

STEADY 1

Line	Poem	No.
THAT STEADY BEAT	SP EASY BOOGIE	2

STEAL 2

Line	Poem	No.
LEST SOME FRANCO STEAL INTO OUR BACKYARD	ANS SONG OF SPAIN	66
BUT RAPE, ROB, STEAL,	PL GHOSTS OF 1619	6

STEALING 2

Line	Poem	No.
STEALING FROM THE NIGHT	FW DANCERS	1
STEALING FROM DEATH	FW DANCERS	5

STEALIN' 1

Line	Poem	No.
I BEEN STEALIN',	SP FIRE	17

STEALTH 1

Line	Poem	No.
THE RAPE AND ROT OF GRAFT, AND STEALTH, AND LIES,	ANS LET AMERICA BE	81

STEAM 1

Line	Poem	No.
THE STEAM IN HOTEL KITCHENS,	FC BRASS SPITOONS	7

STEAMBOATS 2

Line	Poem	No.
AND THE SAILBOATS AND THE STEAMBOATS,	SP FREEDOM'S PLOW	73
NO TRAINS OR STEAMBOATS GOING -	PL CULTURAL EXCHNG	12

STEEL 19

Line	Poem	No.
WHEN BEYOND STEEL BARS SOUND THE DEATHLESS DRUMS	SL SCOTTSBORO	7
STRONG ARE THE BARS AND STEEL THE GATE.	ANS BLD OZZIE POWEL	5
AND THE STEEL BARS SURROUND YOU,	ANS CHANT TOM MOONY	7
THE STEEL OF FREEDOM DOES NOT STAIN.	ANS LET AMERICA BE	71
IT GIVES ONLY THE GLINT OF STEEL BARS	JC THE BITTER RIVR	27
AND DARK BITTER FACES BEHIND STEEL BARS:	JC THE BITTER RIVR	28
THE SCOTTSBORO BOYS BEHIND STEEL BARS,	JC THE BITTER RIVR	29
LEWIS JONES BEHIND STEEL BARS,	JC THE BITTER RIVR	30
THE VOTELESS SHARE-CROPPER BEHIND STEEL BARS,	JC THE BITTER RIVR	31
THE LABOR LEADER BEHIND STEEL BARS,	JC THE BITTER RIVR	32
THE SOLDIER THROWN FROM A JIM CROW BUS BEHIND STEEL BARS,	JC THE BITTER RIVR	33
THE 15¢ MUGGER BEHIND STEEL BARS,	JC THE BITTER RIVR	34
THE GIRL WHO SELLS HER BODY BEHIND STEEL BARS,	JC THE BITTER RIVR	35
LONG AGO, LONG AGO - THE WHIP AND STEEL BARS -	JC THE BITTER RIVR	37
TIRED NOW OF THE STEEL BARS	JC THE BITTER RIVR	77
AND IT'S TURNED TO STEEL IN MY BLOOD.	JC THE BITTER RIVR	82
GOD PUT A DREAM LIKE STEEL IN MY SOUL.	SP THE NEGRO MOTHE	19
AND COLD STEEL	PL OPPRESSION	8
THE STEEL WINDS BLOW?	PL WITHOUT BENEFIT	6

STEEP 1

Line	Poem	No.
UP THAT STEEP HILL	AYM GOSPEL CHA-CHA	52

STEEPED 1

Line	Poem	No.
BUT PIERROT'S STEEPED IN SIN.	WB PIERROT	26

STEEPLE 1

Line	Poem	No.
AND DROPPING BOMBS FROM A CHRISTIAN STEEPLE	ANS SONG OF SPAIN	69

STEINWAY 1

Line	Poem	No.
(NOT KNOWING THERE'S A STEINWAY BIGGER, BIGGER)	SP TO BE SOMEBODY	3

STEM 2

Line	Poem	No.
ON A BROKEN STEM.	WB YOUNG PROSTITUT	3
ROSE OF THE SHARP-THORNED STEM	FW CHIPPY	2

STEMS 1

Line	Poem	No.
SINCE NO STEMS	PL SLUM DREAMS	6

STEP 5
- BACK BENT AS IN THE FIELDS. THE SLOW STEP. THE BOWED HEAD. "NOBODY KNOWS . . . NM BLACK CLWN MOOD 4
- DO THAT ROCKIN' STEP. . . . DK SONG BANJO DANC 6
- STEP, AND LEAVE NO TRACK. . . . OWT FLIGHT 2
- YOUR EVERY STEP REVEALS . . . SP AFRICA 13
- STEP OUT O' THE BARREL, BOY. . . . SP ELEVATOR BOY 11

STEPPED 1
- I STEPPED BACK . . . SP MADAM WRONG VIS 9

STEPPERS 1
- BROWN-SKIN STEPPERS . . . DK NEGRO DANCERS 9

STEPPING 1
- AND FOUND LIFE - STEPPING ON MY FEET! . . . OLD AESTHETE HARLEM 7

STEPS 6
- AND I STEPS ON THE GAS. . . . NM BIG-TIMER POEM 26
- THESE STEPS IS BROKEN DOWN. . . . SP BLD LANDLORD 6
- CHILE, THESE STEPS IS HARD TO CLIMB. SP DIME 1
- SET ON MY STEPS AND CRIED. . . . SP LATE LAST NIGHT 2
- DON'T YOU SET DOWN ON THE STEPS . . SP MOTHER TO SON 15
- THE STEPS FROM THE HILL LEAD DOWN INTO HARLEM. . . . SP THEME FOR ENG B 11

STEP-FATHERED 2
- STEP-FATHERED BY BLIND LEMON . . . AYM ODE TO DINAH 20
- STEP-FATHERED BY . . . AYM ODE TO DINAH 21

STEW 1
- AN' A STEW O' MEAT. . . . FC DEATH DO DIRTY 14

STEWING 1
- IS GENTLY STEWING. . . . PL CULTURAL EXCHNG 20

STICK 2
- A STICK . . . SP GAUGE 2
- THE LAW RAISED UP HIS STICK . . . PL WHO BUT TH LORD 13

STICKING 1
- STOMACH STICKING OUT. . . . SP DELINQUENT 8

STICKS 2
- BEATEN WITH SWIFT STICKS . . . FC SPORT 6
- WHO STICKS A NEEDLE IN HIS ARM . . PL JUNIOR ADDICT 2

STILL 52
- SO STILL WITH SILENT CRIES. . . . WB SOLEDAD 11
- STILL AS A WHISPERING HEARTBEAT. . WB SUMMER NIGHT 9
- INTO THE STILL. . . . WB TO LITTLE LOVER 5
- AND WHEN I'M DEAD - I'LL KEEP STILL. NM BIG-TIMER POEM 36
- YOU STILL BAKES BISCUITS? FRIED CHICKEN EVERY NIGHT? IS THAT TRUE? . . . NM BROKE 73
- AND I'M STILL JUST A "NIGGER" IN AMERICA TONIGHT. . . . NM COLORED SL POEM 47
- THE RAIN MAKES STILL POOLS ON THE SIDEWALK. . . . DK APRIL RAIN SONG 4
- AND STILL IT CALLS TO ME? . . . DK BEGGAR BOY 4
- I KNOW, FOR I HEARD, WHEN ALL WAS STILL. . . . DK DEATH SEAMAN 3
- I STILL FEELS BLUE. . . . DK DRESSED UP 4
- IN THAT OLD WORLD WHILE STILL A SERF OF KINGS. . . . ANS LET AMERICA BE 40
- STILL BODY . . . ANS LYNCHING SONG 13
- STILL I CAN'T HELP LOVIN' YOU. . . SH IN TROUBLED KEY 7
- BUT DE WATER STILL MAKES A FLOOD. SH MISSISSIPPI LEV 12
- I STILL CAN'T SEE . . . JC BLACK MAN SPEAK 2
- I STILL CAN'T SAY. . . . JC GOOD MORN STLIN 9
- I STILL DON'T KNOW . . . JC GOOD MORN STLIN 12
- HE STILL TRIES TO ACT IN THE SAME OLD WAY. . . . JC JIM CROW'S LAST 12
- BUT THERE ARE THOSE WHO STILL HOLD OUT . . . JC TO CAPTAIN MULZ 10
- YES, DANGEROUS ARE THE WIDE WORLD'S WATERS STILL. . . . JC TO CAPTAIN MULZ 29
- MANY BLOODS - YET ALL OF ONE BLOOD STILL: . . . JC TO CAPTAIN MULZ 48
- STILL AFTER HOURS POURING DRINKS THE LAW FORBIDS - . . . OWT JUICE JOINT 38
- AND SOME FORGET TO LAUGH WHO STILL ARE KIDS. . . . OWT JUICE JOINT 40
- STILL AND YET . . . SP BUDDY 2
- AND STILL BE TRUE. . . . SP COULD BE 4
- OR AM I STILL A PORTER ON THE FREEDOM TRAIN? . . . SP FREEDOM TRAIN 19
- STILL AHEAD SOMEHOW. . . . SP ISLAND 4
- TO SHOW YOU I STILL APPRECIATES. YOU. SP LETTER 5
- SO SINCE I'M STILL HERE LIVIN', . . SP LIFE IS FINE 23
- CAUSE I'M STILL HERE KICKIN'! . . . SP MADAM WRONG VIS 28
- MAMA, DAD COULDN'T BE STILL YOUNG. SP MAMA AND DAUGHT 17
- STILL LEFT BY V-J DAY. . . . SP MIGRANT 29
- FOR I'SE STILL GOIN', HONEY. . . . SP MOTHER TO SON 18
- I'SE STILL CLIMBIN'. . . . SP MOTHER TO SON 19
- THEY LYNCH ME STILL IN MISSISSIPPI. SP NEGRO 16
- HOW STILL. . . . SP SEA CALM 1
- HOW STRANGELY STILL . . . SP SEA CALM 2
- TO BE SO STILL THAT WAY. . . . SP SEA CALM 6
- BUT I'S STILL SWEET PAPA 'VESTER. SP SYLVESTER'S BED 21
- STILL BAR YOU THE WAY, AND DENY YOU LIFE - . . . SP THE NEGRO MOTHE 46
- THREAD STILL PULLS HIS . . . AYM GOSPEL CHA-CHA 22
- BONDS AND STILL AND MARGARET STILL $ $ . . . AYM HORN OF PLENTY 15
- BONDS AND STILL AND MARGARET STILL $ $ . . . AYM HORN OF PLENTY 15
- STILL TO BE INVENTED. . . . AYM IS IT TRUE? 15
- STRIP TICKETS STILL ILLUSION? . . . AYM SHOW FARE PLESE 9
- THE TV'S STILL NOT WORKING. . . . AYM SHOW FARE PLESE 34
- MUST STILL STAND . . . PL ANGOLA QUESTION 3
- STILL ALIVE? . . . PL DEATH YORKVILLE 17
- STILL I BUY. . . . PL LITTLE SNG HOUS 13
- STILL - THERE IS ME! . . . PL LITTLE SNG HOUS 26
- STILL MIX LIKE RAIN . . . PL MISSISSIPPI 19
- I'M STILL HERE! . . . PL STILL HERE 9

STILLNESS 2
- DROP ONE BY ONE INTO STILLNESS. . . WB SUMMER NIGHT 3
- DO YOU UNDERSTAND THE STILLNESS . . SP A HOUSE IN TAOS 11

STINGS 1
- THE SCENT OF PINE WOOD STINGS THE SOFT NIGHT AIR. . . . SP MULATTO 18

STINGY 1
- WITH YOUR STINGY SOUL! . . . SH BLD THE KILLER 20

STINK 2
- DOES IT STINK LIKE ROTTEN MEAT? . . SP HARLEM 6
- DOES IT STINK LIKE ROTTEN MEAT? . . PL DREAM DEFERRED 6

STINKING 1
- POLLUTES HIS STINKING AIR . . . PL JUNIOR ADDICT 21

STINKIN' 1
- I BEEN STINKIN', LOW-DOWN, MEAN. . SP FIRE 6

STIRS 2
- STIRS YOUR BLOOD. . . . SP DANSE AFRICAINE 5
- STIRS YOUR BLOOD. . . . SP DANSE AFRICAINE 15

STOCK 1
- STOP TO TAKE STOCK. . . . SP MADAM CHARTY CH 16

STOCKINGS 3
- PUT ON YO' RED SILK STOCKINGS, . . FC RED SILK STOCK 1
- PUT ON YO' RED SILK STOCKINGS, GAL. FC RED SILK STOCK 8
- STOCKINGS DOWN. . . . SP HIGH TO LOW 11

STOCKYARDS 1
- PRACTICE ON A STOCKYARDS RUPTURE. SP INTERNE AT PROV 8

STOKELY 2
- DUBOIS (WHEN?) MALCOLM (OH!) SEND FOR STOKELY. . . . PL FINAL CALL 35
- STOKELY. . . . PL STOKELY MALCOLM 15

STOLE 3
- IT AIN'T STOLE. . . . SH BLD PAWNBROKER 16
- STOLE ALL SHE HAD. . . . SP BLD FORTUNE TEL 24
- I AM THE CHILD THEY STOLE FROM THE SAND . . . SP THE NEGRO MOTHE 7

STOMACH 1
- STOMACH STICKING OUT. . . . SP DELINQUENT 8

STOMP 1
- IN AN OLD SUIT AND A BATTERED HAT, TO THE TUNE OF A SLOW DRAG STOMP NM BROKE 1

STONE 14
- STONE BY STONE. . . . SL SCOTTSBORO 15
- STONE BY STONE. . . . SL SCOTTSBORO 15
- IN EVERY BRICK AND STONE, IN EVERY FURROW TURNED . . . ANS LET AMERICA BE 43
- BEHIND YOUR HIGH STONE WALLS - . . FW CONVENT 3
- TO SEEK A STONE . . . FW SNAKE 6
- I SET DOWN ON A STONE. . . . OWT STRANGER IN TWN 2
- A STONE. . . . LHR POET TO BIGOT 15
- TO EACH STONE. . . . SP HEAVEN 9
- STONE ANSWERS BACK. . . . SP HEAVEN 11
- IT'S ALWAYS A STONE - . . . SP MADAM MIGHT-HAV 26
- FAR FROM STONE. . . . AYM ASK YOUR MAMA 73
- PROW OF STONE STONE. . . . AYM GOSPEL CHA-CHA 23
- PROW OF STONE STONE. . . . AYM GOSPEL CHA-CHA 23
- (WHICH LATELY IS STONE NOWHERE) . . AYM HORN OF PLENTY 32

STONES 1
- STONES BURST LIKE BALLOONS . . . AYM ASK YOUR MAMA 68

STONE-COLD 1
- OR IS YOUR HEART STONE-COLD? . . . SP MADAM MINISTER 8

STONY 4
CUT TO STONY LONESOME GROUND. . . . SP STONY LONESOME 2
TO STONY LONESOME. . . . . SP STONY LONESOME 4
SHE'S OUT IN STONY LONESOME. . . . SP STONY LONESOME 16
IN STONY . . . . SP STONY LONESOME 19

STOOD 6
YOU'VE STOOD BETWEEN US WELL. . . . JC GOOD MORN STLIN 35
BUT STOOD, INDIVIDUAL AND ALONE. . JC TO CAPTAIN MULZ 22
I STOOD THERE FEELIN' BLUE - . . . OWT LONESOME CORNER 2
THEN I STOOD OUT ON A PRAIRIE . . . SP CROSSING 15
I STOOD THERE AND I HOLLERED! . . . SP LIFE IS FINE 16
I STOOD THERE AND I CRIED! . . . . SP LIFE IS FINE 17

STOOL 1
SWAYING TO AND FRO ON HIS RICKETY STOOL . . . . SP THE WEARY BLUES 12

STOOLS 1
OF THE BAR STOOLS . . . . FW CHIPPY 7

STOOP 3
IT'S DARK ON THIS STOOP. LAWD! THE SUN'S GONE DOWN! . . . . SH TWILIGHT REVERI 15
HE SETS ON A STOOP . . . . SP NEIGHBOR 2
COMMENT ON STOOP . . . . SP SISTER 15

STOOPS 1
STOOPS TO KISS 12 WEST 133RD. . . . SP PROJECTION 9

STOP 12
STOP HUNTING FOR THE PRICE TAG! . . SH BLD PAWNBROKER 15
WOMEN OF THE STREETS STOP BY FOR SUPS . . . . OWT JUICE JOINT 7
RE-BOP BE-BOP MOP AND STOP. . . . . SP FLATTED FIFTHS 2
STOP TO TAKE STOCK. . . . . SP MADAM CHARTY CH 16
HE DIDN'T STOP IN WASHINGTON . . . SP NOT A MOVIE 9
AND HE DIDN'T STOP IN BALTIMORE . . SP NOT A MOVIE 10
THE ONE TO STOP 'EM WON'T BE ME. . SP RELIEF 15
AND THAT FINAL STOP IS A . . . . . SP WIDOW WOMAN 5
STOP EVERYBODY MUST MAKE. . . . . . SP WIDOW WOMAN 6
STOP LAUGHIN', STOP LOVIN', STOP LIVIN' - . . . . PL STILL HERE 7
STOP LAUGHIN', STOP LOVIN', STOP LIVIN' - . . . . PL STILL HERE 7
STOP LAUGHIN', STOP LOVIN', STOP LIVIN' - . . . . PL STILL HERE 7

STOPPED 1
THE SINGER STOPPED PLAYING AND WENT TO BED . . . . SP THE WEARY BLUES 33

STOPPING 1
I HAD TO KEEP ON! NO STOPPING FOR ME - . . . . SP THE NEGRO MOTHE 29

STOPPIN' 3
NOT STOPPIN' AT NO STATIONS MARKED COLORED NOR WHITE. . . . . SP FREEDOM TRAIN 51
JUST STOPPIN' IN THE FIELDS IN THE BROAD DAYLIGHT. . . . . SP FREEDOM TRAIN 52
STOPPIN' IN THE COUNTRY IN THE WIDE-OPEN AIR . . . . SP FREEDOM TRAIN 53

STOPS 2
WHEN IT STOPS IN MISSISSIPPI WILL IT BE MADE PLAIN . . . . SP FREEDOM TRAIN 21
STOPS TO LISTEN TO GOSPEL SONGS . . SP SUMMER EVENING 11

STORE 2
NO FLOWERS FROM THE STORE. . . . . SP MIDWINTER BLUES 24
NOW WHEN THE MAN AT THE CORNER STORE PL HARLEM 8

STORES 1
CAME THE MARTS AND MARKETS, SHOPS AND STORES. . . . . SP FREEDOM'S PLOW 78

STORE'S 1
THE CANDY STORE'S . . . . PL LITTLE SNG HOUS 20

STORIES 9
AUNT SUE HAS A HEAD FULL OF STORIES. SP AUNTSUE'S STORI 1
AUNT SUE HAS A WHOLE HEART FULL OF STORIES. . . . . SP AUNTSUE'S STORI 2
AND TELLS HIM STORIES. . . . . . . SP AUNTSUE'S STORI 5
AUNT SUE'S STORIES. . . . . SP AUNTSUE'S STORI 16
KNOWS THAT AUNT SUE'S STORIES ARE REAL STORIES. . . . . SP AUNTSUE'S STORI 18
KNOWS THAT AUNT SUE'S STORIES ARE REAL STORIES. . . . . SP AUNTSUE'S STORI 18
HE KNOWS THAT AUNT SUE NEVER GOT HER STORIES . . . . SP AUNTSUE'S STORI 19
LISTENING TO AUNT SUE'S STORIES. . SP AUNTSUE'S STORI 25
TELL YOU PRETTY STORIES . . . . . . SP BLD THE GYPSY 20

STORM 2
STORM CLOUDS MOVE FAST. . . . . . . ANS SONG OF SPAIN 48
THE STORM CLOUDS . . . . SP AFRICA 7

STORMS 1
A THOUSAND STORMS. . . . . FW SAILING DATE 9

STORMY 2
AND LET THE CHOIR SING A STORMY SONG SP FATASY PURPLE 3
IN TIMES OF STORMY WEATHER . . . . SP STRANGE HURT 1

STORY 7
STORY TELLERS. . . . . FC LAUGHERS 2
SYNCOPATED MUSIC. TELLING HIS STORY IN A HARD, BRAZEN, CYNICAL FASHION. . . . . NM BIG-TIMER MOOD 1
CALMLY TELLING THE STORY, PROUDLY AND EXPECTANTLY WITH HEAD UP, SHOULDERS . . . . NM COLORED SL MOOD 7
AND LOVE'S OLD STORY TOLD - . . . . FW CAROLINA CABIN 20
ONE MIGHT MAKE A STORY . . . . . . FW MIGRATION 16
TO TELL YOU A STORY OF THE LONG DARK WAY . . . . SP THE NEGRO MOTHE 2
OR SPORTS-WRITERS IN THEIR STORY. AYM IS IT TRUE? 51

STORY-TELLERS 1
STORY-TELLERS ALL, - . . . . FC LAUGHERS 21

STOUT 1
HAS GROWN QUITE STOUT. . . . . . . SP DELINQUENT 6

STOVE 4
MAYBE NOW I CAN HAVE THAT WHITE ENAMEL STOVE . . . . SP DEFERRED 8
THERE AIN'T NO STOVE - . . . . . . SP DEFERRED 19
MAYBE I CAN BUY THAT WHITE ENAMEL STOVE! . . . . SP DEFERRED 20
ON THE OLD IRON STOVE WHAT'S COOKING? . . . . PL CULTURAL EXCHNG 27

STRAIGHT 8
BUT IF I WANTED TO GO STRAIGHT . . NM BIG-TIMER POEM 41
THROWING DOWN THE HAT OF A FOOL, AND STANDING FORTH, STRAIGHT AND STRONG, ... NM BLACK CLWN MOOD 14
AND I SAW HIM STANDING THERE, STRAIGHT AND TALL. . . . . NM COLORED SL POEM 37
STRAIGHT DOWN THE ROAD . . . . . . SH BLD THE SINNER 3
RIGHT STRAIGHT TO HELL. . . . . . . SH BLD THE SINNER 20
FEEL BAD TWO DAYS STRAIGHT. . . . . SH EVIL MORNING 14
AND TALL STRAIGHT PINE . . . . . . FW CAROLINA CABIN 3
OTHERS TAKE A QUARTER STRAIGHT. . . SP TOMORROW 6

STRAIGHTENED 1
AND SWITCH THEIR SKIRTS AND LIFT THEIR STRAIGHTENED HEADS . . . . OWT JUICE JOINT 23

STRAIGHTENIN' 1
I'D LIKE TO BUY A STRAIGHTENIN' COMB, ... SP DOWN AND OUT 9

STRAIN 1
MUSIC TAKES ON A BLUES STRAIN, GRADUALLY RETURNING TO A SORT OF NM BIG-TIMER MOOD 3

STRAND 1
AND TORN FROM BLACK AFRICA'S STRAND I CAME . . . . ANS LET AMERICA BE 49

STRANGE 15
SUCH A STRANGE DISEASE. . . . . . . FC GYPSY MAN 20
SUCH A STRANGE DISEASE. . . . . . . FC GYPSY MAN 22
STRANGE, ... OLD AESTHETE HARLEM 1
OR DOES SOME STRANGE . . . . FW CONVENT 6
TWISTED AND STRANGE . . . . FW SAILING DATE 1
IN THIS STRANGE OLD TOWN - . . . . OWT STRANGER IN TWN 14
IS NOT SO STRANGE. . . . . SP A HOUSE IN TAOS 18
IN STRANGE UN-NEGRO TONGUE - . . . SP AFRO-AMER FRAG 9
OF AN UNKNOWN STRANGE PERFUME . . . SP DESIRE 6
THIS MOST STRANGE DREAM. . . . . . SP DREAM 2
RICH AND STRANGE . . . . SP FLATTED FIFTHS 8
STRANGE . . . . SP GARDEN 1
STRANGE . . . . SP GARDEN 3
STRANGE . . . . SP GARDEN 5
STRANGE HURT SHE KNEW . . . . SP STRANGE HURT 7

STRANGELY 1
HOW STRANGELY STILL . . . . SP SEA CALM 2

STRANGER 1
OF COURSE, I'M JUST A STRANGER . . OWT STRANGER IN TWN 13

STRANGLED 1
THAT STRANGLED MY DREAM: . . . . . JC THE BITTER RIVR 17

STRAW 3
A MORAL POEM TO BE RENDERED BY A MAN IN A STRAW HAT WITH A BRIGHT BAND, A . . . . NM BIG-TIMER MOOD 1
STRAW . . . . SP GAUGE 4
AND GRASP FOR A STRAW. . . . . . . SP SUNDAY MORNING 20

STRAY 1
THOUGH I WANDER AND STRAY . . . . . FW FAITHFUL ONE 5

STRAYHORN 1
STRAYHORN HID BACKSTAGE WITH LUTHER
$ $ . . . . AYM HORN OF PLENTY 10

STREAK 1
LEFT BY A STREAK OF SUN. . . . . . PL GEORGIA DUSK 6

STREAM 4
IN THE SNAKE-LIKE HISS OF ITS STREAM JC THE BITTER RIVR 15
WHERE THE IRON BRIDGE CROSSES THE
STREAM. . . . . JC THE BITTER RIVR 60
AND I CROSSED AN ICY STREAM . . . . SP CROSSING 10
NO PROTECTION FOR THAT STREAM. . . SP CROSSING 14

STREET 36
TO THE RUMBLE OF STREET CARS. . . . WB LENOX AVE MIDNT 9
AN ENDLESS STREET . . . . WB TO LITTLE LOVER 10
I WAS STANDIN' IN DE STREET. . . . FC DEATH DO DIRTY 22
SHE'S OUT IN DE STREET. - . . . . . FC WORKIN' MAN 7
UNTIL I CAME TO THIS NEAR STREET . OLD AESTHETE HARLEM 6
NOW. IN THE STREET. . . . . DK PARISIAN BEGGAR 6
MARCH WITH YOU DOWN TIME'S STREET. SL SCOTTSBORO 6
LIKE WATER DOWN THE STREET. . . . . ANS NEGRO GHETTO 6
IF I HAD SOME MONEY I'D STROLL DOWN
THE STREET . . . . SH BED TIME 3
I WAS WALKIN' DOWN DE STREET. JUDGE. SH BRIEF ENCOUNTER 3
DOWN IN A CELLAR BACK FROM THE
STREET. . . . . SH DEATH IN HARLEM 23
I LOOKED DOWN 31ST STREET. . . . . SH MIDNIGHT CHIPPI 1
DOWN ON 31ST STREET. . . . . SH MIDNIGHT CHIPPI 3
ON STATE STREET ANY DAY. . . . . . SH MIDNIGHT CHIPPI 18
DOWN ON '33RD STREET . . . . SH STATEMENT 1
DOWN THE STREET YOUNG HARLEM . . . FW DIMOUT IN HARLM 1
DOWN THE STREET IS WALKING . . . . FW DIMOUT IN HARLM 4
DOWN THE STREET YOUNG HARLEM . . . FW DIMOUT IN HARLM 16
TAKE A STREET CAR . . . . OWT JITNEY 41
AND DAWN COMES DOWN THE STREET ALL
WANLY WHITE. . . . . OWT JUICE JOINT 4
ON THIS CITY STREET. . . . . OWT JUICE JOINT 16
O. IN THIS TAVERN ON THE CITY STREET OWT JUICE JOINT 33
ON THE CITY STREET. . . . . OWT JUICE JOINT 48
THROW IT IN THE STREET? . . . . . . SP BLD LANDLORD 16
COULD BE HASTINGS STREET. . . . . . SP COULD BE 1
HASTINGS STREET IS WEARY. . . . . . SP COULD BE 13
DOWN THE STREET . . . . SP HARLEM NIGHT SO 11
PRACTICE ON A STATE STREET CANCER. SP INTERNE AT PROV 7
I'M GOING DOWN THE STREET. . . . . SP MAMA AND DAUGHT 2
RIDES THE STATE STREET STREET CAR. SP MIGRANT 7
RIDES THE STATE STREET STREET CAR. SP MIGRANT 7
THE STREET LIGHT . . . . SP NIGHT FUNERAL 35
23RD AND CENTRAL. 18TH STREET AND
VINE. . . . . AYM ASK YOUR MAMA 6
CULTURE. THEY SAY. IS A TWO-WAY
STREET: . . . . PL CULTURAL EXCHNG 58
AND CAPTURE EVERY STREET . . . . . PL FREDRK DOUGLASS 8
DOWN THE STREET AT ME! . . . . . . PL WHO BUT TH LORD 4

STREETS 10
ON STRIKE IN THE STREETS OF
SHANGHAI. . . . . ANS BLDS OF LENIN 22
KIDS WILL DIE IN THE STREETS OF
CHICAGO . . . . ANS KIDS WHO DIE 10
I WALKED DE STREETS TILL . . . . . SH OUT OF WORK 1
I DONE WALKED DE STREETS TILL . . . SH OUT OF WORK 3
WOMEN OF THE STREETS STOP BY FOR
SUPS . . . . OWT JUICE JOINT 7
THERE WAS FASTING IN THE STREETS AND
JOY. . . . . LHR BLD MARY'S SON 3
THE STREETS ARE DARK. . . . . SP ISLAND 4
ON THEM GOLDEN STREETS . . . . . . SP MADAM NUMBER WR 26
NOW THE STREETS DOWN BY THE RIVER SP RUBY BROWN 16
O. SWEEP OF STARS OVER HARLEM
STREETS. . . . . SP STARS 1

STRENGTH 12
STRENGTH HE DOESN'T REALLY FEEL.
GAY. LOUD. UNHAPPY JAZZ. BARING
HIS . . . . NM BIG-TIMER MOOD 9
AND STRENGTH TO OUR LAND IMPART. . NM DARK YOUTH USA 15
AND THE STRENGTH A STRONG HAND
KNOWS. . . . . DK ALABAMA EARTH 9
10-VOICES: BLOOM IN THE STRENGTH OF
YOUR UNKNOWN POWER. . . . . . . ANS CHANT MAY DAY 9
WORKER: WHEN THE SAP OF YOUR OWN
STRENGTH RISES . . . . ANS CHANT MAY DAY 25
BANNER OF FORCE AND LABOR. STRENGTH
AND UNION. . . . . ANS CHANT TOM MOONY 43
I AM THE YOUNG MAN. FULL OF STRENGTH
AND HOPE. . . . . ANS LET AMERICA BE 25
IN UNION LIES OUR STRENGTH. . . . . ANS OPEN LETTER 54
THE STRENGTH THERE. . . . . SP FREEDOM'S PLOW 7
CAME THE DREAM. THE STRENGTH. THE
WILL. . . . . SP FREEDOM'S PLOW 83
HIS OWN STRENGTH . . . . SP YOUNG SAILOR 2
FOR STRENGTH. . . . . SP YOUNG SAILOR 17

STRENGTHENING 1
20-VOICES: STRENGTHENING EACH
BRANCH. . . . . ANS CHANT MAY DAY 16

STRETCH 1
ALL. ALL THE STRETCH OF THESE GREAT
GREEN STATES - . . . . ANS LET AMERICA BE 85

STRETCHES 2
STRETCHES ITS WIDE HORIZONS . . . . FW THERE 2
THAT STRETCHES PADDLE-TAILED ACROSS
THE FLOOR. . . . . SP TO BE SOMEBODY 5

STRETCHING 1
NO STRETCHING PLACE. . . . . FW GRAVE YARD 3

STREW 2
STREW NO FLOWERS ON MY GRAVE. . . . DK DEATH SEAMAN 7
AS LEDA STREW HER CORN . . . . . . AYM BIRD IN ORBIT 29

STREWS 1
WHILE MOLLIE MOON STREWS SEQUINS . AYM BIRD IN ORBIT 28

STRIDE 2
THE NEW STRIDE . . . . SP AFRICA 14
CELLOPHANES HIS LONG STRIDE. . . . SP INTERNE AT PROV 46

STRIFE 2
WHIRL IN THE WIND OF PAIN AND
STRIFE. . . . . DK SONG 6
REMEMBER HOW THE STRONG IN STRUGGLE
AND STRIFE . . . . SP THE NEGRO MOTHE 45

STRIKE 7
STRIKE UP THE MUSIC. . . . . NM BLACK CLWN POEM 12
ON STRIKE IN THE STREETS OF
SHANGHAI. . . . . ANS BLDS OF LENIN 22
THE MILLIONS SHOT DOWN WHEN WE
STRIKE? . . . . ANS LET AMERICA BE 54
HOW'S A DANCE STRIKE YOU? . . . . . SH DEATH IN HARLEM 44
THEMSELVES MUST STRIKE . . . . . . PL FREDRK DOUGLASS 19
TO STRIKE YOUR FACE. . . . . PL MILITANT 14
I'VE NO WEAPON TO STRIKE BACK . . . PL WHO BUT TH LORD 20

STRIKES 1
STRIKES UP A TUNE ALL GAY AND BRIGHT
AND GLAD . . . . OWT JUICE JOINT 43

STRING 1
AND WRAP A STRING AROUND ITS FINGER SP SUMMER EVENING 26

STRINGS 1
ON THREE STRINGS. . . . . ANS SONG OF SPAIN 9

STRIP 2
WILL STRIP THEIR BODIES BARE . . . WB POEME D'AUTOMNE 10
STRIP TICKETS STILL ILLUSION? . . . AYM SHOW FARE PLESE 9

STROKE 2
I MEAN FOUR - BEFORE DAYLIGHT -
S'POSE TO'VE DONE HIT YO' FIRST
STROKE - . . . . NM BROKE 14
LIKE STROKE . . . . FW BIRTH 6

STROLL 2
IF I HAD SOME MONEY I'D STROLL DOWN
THE STREET . . . . SH BED TIME 3
STROLL DOWN LUSCIOUS. . . . . SH HARLEM SWEETIES 43

STRONG 29
SO STRONG. . . . . WB FOR PORTRAIT OF 5
O. WHITE STRONG ONES. . . . . WB THE WHITE ONES 6
THROWING DOWN THE HAT OF A FOOL. AND
STANDING FORTH. STRAIGHT AND
STRONG. . . . . NM BLACK CLWN MOOD 14
TODAY'S DARK CHILD. TOMORROW'S
STRONG MAN: . . . . NM DARK YOUTH USA 2
TO BE WISE AND STRONG. THEN.
STUDYING LONG. . . . . NM DARK YOUTH USA 16
AND THE STRENGTH A STRONG HAND
KNOWS. . . . . DK ALABAMA EARTH 9
BUT THAT THE SEA IS STRONG . . . . DK SEA CHARM 5
STRONG AND SURE. . . . . ANS A NEW SONG 45
STRONG ARE THE BARS AND STEEL THE
GATE. . . . . ANS BLD OZZIE POWEL 5
40-VOICES: GROW STRONG WITH UNION.
ALL HANDS TOGETHER - . . . . . . ANS CHANT MAY DAY 11
40-VOICES: GROW STRONG. . . . . . . ANS CHANT MAY DAY 33
LET IT BE THAT GREAT STRONG LAND OF
LOVE . . . . ANS LET AMERICA BE 7
WHO DREAMT A DREAM SO STRONG. SO
BRAVE. SO TRUE. . . . . ANS LET AMERICA BE 41
THAT WE WERE STRONG. . . . . ANS OPEN LETTER 52
STRONG AND BLACK . . . . JC ME AND MY SONG 9
STRONG . . . . JC ME AND MY SONG 18
STRONG . . . . JC ME AND MY SONG 29

A MAN, SPARE, SWARTHY, STRONG, FOURSQUARE - . . . . JC TO CAPTAIN MULZ 44
STRONG AS THE BURSTING OF YOUNG BUDS, ... FW EARTH SONG 7
STRONG AS THE SHOOTS OF A NEW PLANT, FW EARTH SONG 8
STRONG AS THE COMING OF THE FIRST CHILD . . . . FW EARTH SONG 9
IS A STRONG SEED . . . . SP DEMOCRACY 16
AND GROW STRONG. . . . . SP I, TOO 7
SOMETHING STRONG TO PUT MY HANDS ON. SP SPIRITUALS 3
SONG IS A STRONG THING. . . . . . . SP SPIRITUALS 5
SONG IS A STRONG THING. . . . . . . SP SPIRITUALS 16
REMEMBER HOW THE STRONG IN STRUGGLE AND STRIFE . . . . SP THE NEGRO MOTHE 45
THIS STRONG YOUNG SAILOR . . . . . . SP YOUNG SAILOR 6
IS A STRONG SEED . . . . PL FREEDOM 16

STRONGER 1
AS SONG GROWS STRONGER . . . . . . SP DRUNKARD 2

STRUGGLE 5
THE LONG STRUGGLE FOR LIFE: . . . . NM BLACK CLWN POEM 38
SUFFER AND STRUGGLE. . . . . NM BLACK CLWN POEM 63
TO STRUGGLE BY HIS SELF. . . . . . SP STONY LONESOME 13
REMEMBER HOW THE STRONG IN STRUGGLE AND STRIFE . . . . SP THE NEGRO MOTHE 45
ABOVE THE STRUGGLE . . . . PL NORTHERN LIBERL 11

STRUGGLING 1
STRUGGLING, FIGHTING, ... PL QUESTION ANSWER 5

STRUT 3
STRUT AND WIGGLE, ... WB TO MIDNIGHT NAN 1
STRUT AND WIGGLE, ... WB TO MIDNIGHT NAN 17
STRUT, MR. CHARLIE, ... FC SATURDAY NIGHT 7

STRUTTING 2
BARREL-HOUSE JAZZ. SHOWING-OFF. STRUTTING ABOUT PROUDLY, BRAGGING AND . . . . NM BIG-TIMER MOOD 4
JOY. A BURST OF MUSIC. STRUTTING AND DANCING. THEN SUDDEN SADNESS AGAIN. . . . . NM BLACK CLWN MOOD 3

STRYDOM 1
SHUT UP, SAYS STRYDOM. . . . . . . SP IN EXPLANATION 26

STRYDOMS 1
GOVERNORS OF SOUTH CAROLINA, GERALD L.K. STRYDOMS. . . . . SP IN EXPLANATION 43

STUCK-UP 2
MA LORD AIN'T NO STUCK-UP MAN. . . DK MA LORD 1
MA LORD AIN'T NO STUCK-UP MAN. . . DK MA LORD 10

STUDENT 3
I AM THE ONLY COLORED STUDENT IN MY CLASS. . . . . SP THEME FOR ENG B 10
TALL BLACK STUDENT . . . . AYM ASK YOUR MAMA 52
BY A STUDENT IN A FEZ . . . . AYM SHADES OF PIG 25

STUDIED 2
THE BOOK STUDIED - BUT USELESS, . . JC THE BITTER RIVR 18
HAS STUDIED VARIED FACES, ... FW OLD SAILOR 5

STUDY 3
ME, I ALWAYS DID WANT TO STUDY FRENCH. . . . . SP DEFERRED 21
SO, SI'L-VOUS PLAIT, I'LL STUDY FRENCH! . . . . SP DEFERRED 28
"I DON'T WANT TO STUDY WAR NO MORE," PL BLACK PANTHER 6

STUDYING 1
TO BE WISE AND STRONG, THEN, STUDYING LONG, ... NM DARK YOUTH USA 16

STUFF 2
FOR ALL THE STUFF . . . . SP CONSIDER ME 31
WHEN YOU'RE FULL OF STUFF. . . . . SP WARNING AUGMENT 8

STUMBLINGLY 1
HALTINGLY AND STUMBLINGLY SAY THEM, SP FREEDOM'S PLOW 150

STUMP 2
I DIDN'T MEAN TO STUMP MA TOE ON YOU, LADY. . . . . SP MAGNOLIA FLOWER 9
I DIDN'T MEAN TO STUMP MA TOE ON YOU. . . . . SP MAGNOLIA FLOWER 13

STUMPED 1
STUMPED ITS TOE - . . . . PL AMER HEARTBREAK 3

STUPID 3
AND FINDING ONLY THE SAME OLD STUPID PLAN. . . . . ANS LET AMERICA BE 23
HELPLESS, STUPID, SCATTERED, AND ALONE - AS NOW - . . . . ANS OPEN LETTER 28
SO WHEN MY ACTIONS ARE STUPID . . . LHP ACCEPTANCE 3

STURDY 2
STURDY I STAND, BOOKS IN MY HAND - NM DARK YOUTH USA 1
AND STURDY WEEDS AND GRASSES . . . FW GIRL 16

STUYVESANT 1
STUYVESANT TOWN? . . . . OWT BLD MARGE POLIT 37

STYLE 1
AIN'T DE STYLE NOW DAYS. . . . . . FC EVIL WOMAN 12

SUB 1
THE BUS, THE SUB - . . . . OWT NEGRO SERVANT 12

SUBDUED 3
WALKING PROUDLY, ALMOST PRANCING, BUT GRADUALLY SUBDUED TO A SLOW, HEAVY . . . . NM BLACK CLWN MOOD 7
ALL DAY SUBDUED, POLITE, ... OWT NEGRO SERVANT 1
SUBDUED AND TIME-LOST . . . . SP AFRO-AMER FRAC 13

SUBMARINES 1
AND SUBMARINES . . . . FW SAILING DATE 11

SUBSIDING 1
PAIN TAMED AND SUBSIDING . . . . . SP INTERNE AT PROV 24

SUBURB 1
SEEKING SUBURB WITH NO JUKEBOX . . AYM HORN OF PLENTY 69

SUBURBIA 1
YES, SUBURBIA . . . . AYM IS IT TRUE? 35

SUBVERSIVE 2
BUT YOUR GIFT BOOKS ARE SUBVERSIVE, AYM RIDE, RED, RIDE 24
FOR SUBVERSIVE PURPOSES? . . . . . PL UN-AMERICAN 16

SUBWAY 1
IN THE SUBWAY SLOT, ... SP MIDNIGHT RAFFLE 10

SUBWAYS 1
TAXIS, SUBWAYS, ... SP JUKE BOX LOVE 5

SUCH 15
GOT SUCH LOW-DOWN WAYS, ... FC EVIL WOMAN 10
SUCH A STRANGE DISEASE. . . . . . . FC GYPSY MAN 20
SUCH A STRANGE DISEASE. . . . . . . FC GYPSY MAN 22
AND DIDN'T HAVE SUCH A BIG MOUTH. NM BROKE 65
NO WONDER WE FIND THEM SUCH MARVELLOUS THINGS! . . . . DK FAIRIES 5
WHAT MAKES LOVE SUCH AN ACHE AND PAIN? . . . . SH LOVE AGAIN BLUS 14
LOVE SUCH AN ACHE AND PAIN? . . . . SH LOVE AGAIN BLUS 15
HAVE SUCH MEAGRE . . . . LHP POET TO BIGOT 8
AND MONEY, AND SUCH. . . . . SP BLD FORTUNE TEL 6
IT'S SUCH A . . . . SP ENNUI 1
NO MAYORS AND SUCH FOR WHICH COLORED CAN'T VOTE, ... SP FREEDOM TRAIN 56
SUCH COMPANY, SUCH COMPANY, ... SP JOY 8
SUCH COMPANY, SUCH COMPANY, ... SP JOY 8
SUCH NEGROES . . . . SP SEASHORE THROUG 8
LICENSES AND SUCH. . . . . SP S-SSS-SS-SH! 11

SUCKED 1
SUCKED IN BY FAT JUKEBOXES . . . . AYM ODE TO DINAH 52

SUCKER 1
SUCKER SIZE. . . . . SP TRUMPET PLAYER 32

SUDDEN 3
JOY. A BURST OF MUSIC. STRUTTING AND DANCING. THEN SUDDEN SADNESS AGAIN. . . . . NM BLACK CLWN MOOD 3
BUT SUDDEN NEARNESS . . . . FW BURDEN 3
THAT AT A SUDDEN CHANGE BECOME . . SP FLATTED FIFTHS 6

SUDDENLY 9
BOASTING, LIKE A CHEAP BULLY, BUT SUDDENLY LOOKING AHEAD: SHRUGGING HIS . . . . NM BIG-TIMER MOOD 5
AND BOWING HIS HEAD IN SHAME, BECOMES SUDDENLY FIERCE AND ANGRY, THEN HE . . . . NM COLORED SL MOOD 11
SUDDENLY THE EARTH WAS THERE, . . . FW HARLEM DANCE HA 3
BUT SUDDENLY A GUITAR-PLAYING LAD OWT JUICE JOINT 41
SUDDENLY . . . . OWT RAID 8
SUDDENLY . . . . SP RAILROAD AVENUE 18
SUDDENLY . . . . SP RAILROAD AVENUE 21
SUDDENLY CATCHING FIRE . . . . . . AYM JAZZTET MUTED 7
SUDDENLY BECAME MAJORITY . . . . . PL GHOSTS OF 1619 18

SUE 4
AUNT SUE HAS A HEAD FULL OF STORIES. SP AUNTSUE'S STORI 1
AUNT SUE HAS A WHOLE HEART FULL OF STORIES. . . . . SP AUNTSUE'S STORI 2
AUNT SUE CUDDLES A BROWN-FACED CHILD TO HER BOSOM . . . . SP AUNTSUE'S STORI 4

HE KNOWS THAT AUNT SUE NEVER GOT HER
STORIES . . . . SP AUNTSUE'S STORI 19

SUEDE 1
AND MY TAN SUEDE SHOES. . . . . . . PL THIRD DEGREE 4

SUE'S 4
IN THE FLOW OF OLD AUNT SUE'S VOICE. SP AUNTSUE'S STORI 13
AUNT SUE'S STORIES. . . . . SP AUNTSUE'S STORI 16
KNOWS THAT AUNT SUE'S STORIES ARE
REAL STORIES. . . . . SP AUNTSUE'S STORI 18
LISTENING TO AUNT SUE'S STORIES. . SP AUNTSUE'S STORI 25

SUFFER 2
SUFFER AND STRUGGLE. . . . . NM BLACK CLWN POEM 63
I SUFFER AFTER . . . . DK MINSTREL MAN 6

SUFFERING 1
THIS SUFFERING FLESH. . . . . LHP DEAR LVLY DEATH 6

SUFI 1
SEND FOR MARCUS GARVEY (WHAT?) SUFI
(WHO?) . . . . PL FINAL CALL 33

SUGAR 19
AND I SHO HAD A PRETTY GAL, TOO, UP
YONDER ON SUGAR HILL. . . . . . NM BROKE 48
THIS LITTLE HOUSE IS SUGAR. . . . . DK WINTER SWEEETNS 1
I SAID, SUGAR, ... SH BLD THE KILLER 7
OF SUGAR HILL? . . . . SH HARLEM SWEETIES 2
BROWN SUGAR LASSIE. . . . . SH HARLEM SWEETIES 5
CARAMEL, BROWN SUGAR. . . . . SH HARLEM SWEETIES 31
DELICIOUS, FINE SUGAR HILL. . . . . SH HARLEM SWEETIES 44
OR GIVE MY SUGAR . . . . SP CONSIDER ME 23
MY SUGAR. . . . . SP CONSIDER ME 26
WHERE IS THAT SUGAR, HAMMOND, . . . SP EARLY EVENING 1
I SAY, WHERE IS THAT SUGAR . . . . SP EARLY EVENING 3
COFFEE WITHOUT SUGAR . . . . SP EARLY EVENING 5
I AIN'T GOT NO SUGAR, HATTIE. . . . SP EARLY EVENING 7
AIN'T GOT NO SUGAR, I . . . . SP EARLY EVENING 9
OR CRUST AND SUGAR OVER - . . . . . SP HARLEM 7
WHO IS YOUR SUGAR, HONEY? . . . . . SP MAMA AND DAUGHT 5
UNFORGOTTEN JOES AND SUGAR RAYS $ $
$ $ . . . . AYM HORN OF PLENTY 19
A LITTLE RUM WITH SUGAR. . . . . . AYM RIDE, RED, RIDE 19
OR CRUST AND SUGAR OVER - . . . . . PL DREAM DEFERRED 7

SUGAR-DADDY 1
HERE'S MY SUGAR-DADDY PAL. . . . . SH DEATH IN HARLEM 48

SUGAR-SWEET 1
TO SEE MY SUGAR-SWEET. . . . . . . SP MAMA AND DAUGHT 4

SUGAR'S 1
SAYS SUGAR'S GONE UP ANOTHER TWO
CENTS. . . . . PL HARLEM 9

SUICIDE 1
CAN COMMIT SUICIDE . . . . SH SNOB 6

SUIT 9
SUIT AND HAT OF A CLOWN, TO THE
MUSIC OF A PIANO, OR AN
ORCHESTRA. . . . . . . NM BLACK CLWN MOOD 1
ECHOES THE FIGHTING "MARSEILLAISE."
TEARING OFF HIS CLOWN'S SUIT. . NM BLACK CLWN MOOD 13
IN AN OLD SUIT AND A BATTERED HAT,
TO THE TUNE OF A SLOW DRAG STOMP NM BROKE 1
THE TORN SUIT OF SATIN AND GOLD. . ANS SONG OF SPAIN 15
CAN I GET TEN ON THIS SUIT . . . . SH BLD PAWNBROKER 9
TO PAY HIS CARFARE, BUY A SUIT. . . SP BUDDY 8
GRAND MARSHAL IN HIS WHITE SUIT . . SP PARADE 5
SUIT, OVERCOAT, SHOES - . . . . . . SP WHAT? 5
FOR A SUIT OF GOOD-TIME WEARING? . AYM SHOW FARE PLESE 23

SUITS 5
I BOUGHT HIM SUITS O' CLOTHES. . . FC BLACK GAL 10
I'M GONNA BUY TWO NEW SUITS . . . . SP DEFERRED 30
TWO NEW SUITS AN' . . . . SP ELEVATOR BOY 12
SUITS . . . . SP LIKEWISE 3
AND THE COUSINS OF THE TOO-THIN
SUITS . . . . PL WHERE WHEN WHCH 8

SULPHUROUS 1
UMBILICAL IN SULPHUROUS CHOCOLATE: AYM ODE TO DINAH 91

SULTRY 1
SULTRY AIR OF FEAR. . . . . PL SWEET WORDS RAC 8

SUMMER 8
FLOWERS ARE HAPPY IN SUMMER. . . . DK AUTUMN THOUGHT 1
YOU WILL NOT STAY WHEN SUMMER GOES. DK PASSING LOVE 6
BEFORE THE HOT NIGHTS OF SUMMER . . SH YOUNG NEGRO GRL 8
SHE WENT ONE SUMMER MORNING . . . . FW GIRL 5
SUMMER NIGHTS ON THE FRONT PORCH . SP AUNTSUE'S STORI 3
OF A SUMMER NIGHT . . . . SP AUNTSUE'S STORI 24
ON SUNNY SUMMER SUNDAY AFTERNOONS IN
HARLEM . . . . SP PASSING 1
SOME PIMPS WEAR SUMMER HATS . . . . SP WHAT? 1

SUMMERS 1
WHEN THE LONG HOT SUMMERS COME . . PL DEATH YORKVILLE 18

SUN 56
WE SHOULD HAVE A LAND OF SUN. . . . WB OUR LAND 1
OF GORGEOUS SUN. . . . . WB OUR LAND 2
AS FLOWERS IN THE SUN. . . . . . . WB PIERROT 20
ALL DAY IN THE SUN . . . . DLD THE CONSUMPTIVE 1
IS NOT HE BUT A SHADOW IN THE SUN - DK BEGGAR BOY 5
BUT WHEN THE SUN ROSE MAKING . . . DK IRISH WAKE 5
BARE YOUR BOSOM TO THE SUN. . . . . DK SONG 2
WALKERS WITH THE SUN AND MORNING. DK WALKERS WITH 2
BEING WALKERS WITH THE SUN AND
MORNING. . . . . DK WALKERS WITH 6
AGAINST THE SUN! . . . . ANS A NEW SONG 54
CUTTING CANE IN THE SUN. . . . . . ANS BLDS OF LENIN 14
THE SUN BOUND DOWN BY LAW. . . . . ANS NEGRO GHETTO 4
AND THE SUN CAME UP AND . . . . . . SH DEATH IN HARLEM 137
NO SUN BY DAY. . . . . JC THE BITTER RIVR 25
AND MOON AND SUN . . . . FW BIRTH 4
AND THE SUN GALLOPS NO MORE . . . . FW THERE 3
THAT ONCE WAS SUNG BENEATH THE SUN OWT JUICE JOINT 10
NEITHER DOES THE SUN. . . . . OWT RESTRICTIVE 8
SUN . . . . SP A HOUSE IN TAOS 15
WHO CARRIES UGLY THINGS TO SHOW THE
SUN? . . . . SP A HOUSE IN TAOS 21
BRIGHT LIKE A SUN - . . . . SP AS I GREW OLDER 5
INTO A THOUSAND LIGHTS OF SUN. . . SP AS I GREW OLDER 31
OF SUN! . . . . SP AS I GREW OLDER 33
WORKING IN THE HOT SUN. . . . . . . SP AUNTSUE'S STORI 7
SEE THE SUN . . . . SP BLACK MARIA 12
SAYS, DID YOU EVER SEE THE SUN RISE SP BLACK MARIA 14
AND I SAW THE SUN GO DOWN. . . . . SP BLUE BAYOU 3
AND I SAW THE SUN GO DOWN. . . . . SP BLUE BAYOU 6
I SAW THE SUN GO DOWN. . . . . . . SP BLUE BAYOU 19
AND I SAW THE SUN GO DOWN. . . . . SP BLUE BAYOU 24
LAWD, I SAW THE SUN GO DOWN! . . . SP BLUE BAYOU 27
KNOWING SO WELL THE WIND AND THE SUN
- . . . . SP DEMAND 7
IN SOME PLACE OF THE SUN. . . . . . SP DREAM VARIATION 2
IN THE FACE OF THE SUN. . . . . . . SP DREAM VARIATION 11
BUT BLOW ONE BLARING TRUMPET NOTE OF
SUN . . . . SP FATASY PURPLE 7
LIKE A RAISIN IN THE SUN? . . . . . SP HARLEM 3
A REDDISH-PURPLE IN THE SUN. . . . SP KID SLEEPY 7
AND THE SUN HAS MADE . . . . SP MEXICAN MARKET 6
BEAUTIFUL, ALSO, IS THE SUN. . . . SP MY PEOPLE 5
AND WATCHES THE SUN GO BY. . . . . SP NEIGHBOR 3
SUN AND SOFTNESS. . . . . SP SUN SONG 1
SUN AND THE BEATEN HARDNESS OF THE
EARTH. . . . . SP SUN SONG 2
SUN AND THE SONG OF ALL THE
SUN-STARS . . . . SP SUN SONG 3
TILL THE SUN GOES DOWN. . . . . . . SP SUNDAY BY COMB 2
ALMOST WITH THE SUN. . . . . SP S-SSS-SS-SH! 16
YET SHINING LIKE THE SUN WITH LOVE'S
TRUE LIGHT. . . . . SP THE NEGRO MOTHE 6
SOMETIMES, THE ROAD WAS HOT WITH
SUN. . . . . SP THE NEGRO MOTHE 27
LOOK EVER UPWARD AT THE SUN AND THE
STARS. . . . . SP THE NEGRO MOTHE 48
THE SKY, THE SUN, THE STARS. . . . SP THE SOUTH 11
DOWN IN WEST TEXAS WHERE THE SUN . SP WEST TEXAS 1
BUT WEST TEXAS WHERE THE SUN . . . SP WEST TEXAS 16
THE PAPA DRUM OF SUN . . . . AYM GOSPEL CHA-CHA 9
LIKE A RAISIN IN THE SUN? . . . . . PL DREAM DEFERRED 3
LEFT BY A STREAK OF SUN. . . . . . PL GEORGIA DUSK 6
SUN IS HIS GRAVE. . . . . PL LUMUMBA'S GRAVE 17
SUN HAS BAKED ME. . . . . PL STILL HERE 4

SUNDAY 14
CHURCH ON SUNDAY. . . . . FC BRASS SPITOONS 24
AND WOMEN AND SUNDAY . . . . FC BRASS SPITOONS 27
LAWD, IN SUNDAY SCHOOL. . . . . . . FC LISTEN HERE 8
ALWAYS IN SUNDAY SCHOOL. . . . . . FC LISTEN HERE 10
ALL DAY SUNDAY DIDN'T EVEN DRESS UP. SH SUNDAY 1
SUNDAY PRAYERS SYNCOPATE GLORY. . . SP CONSIDER ME 44
SUNDAY MORNING WHERE THE RHYTHM
FLOWS. . . . . SP MYSTERY 11
ON SUNNY SUMMER SUNDAY AFTERNOONS IN
HARLEM . . . . SP PASSING 1
ON SUNNY SUNDAY AFTERNOONS . . . . SP PASSING 6
BE SUNDAY. . . . . SP SUMMER EVENING 34
EVEN RUNG THIS BELL ON SUNDAY, YET AYM ASK YOUR MAMA 8
WHO WENT TO SUNDAY SCHOOL THAT DAY PL BIRMINGHAM SUND 2
AND BLOODIED SUNDAY DRESSES . . . . PL BIRMINGHAM SUND 7
IN CHRISTIAN SUNDAY SCHOOL . . . . PL BIRMINGHAM SUND 22

SUNDAY'S 1
SATURDAY AND SUNDAY'S . . . . SP BLUE MONDAY 6

SUNG 2
AND ALL THE SONGS WE'VE SUNG . . . ANS LET AMERICA BE 57
THAT ONCE WAS SUNG BENEATH THE SUN OWT JUICE JOINT 10

SUNK 1
I MIGHT'VE SUNK AND DIED. . . . . . SP LIFE IS FINE 8

SUNLIGHT 2
GLEAMIN' IN THE SUNLIGHT FOR WHITE AND BLACK? . . . . . SP FREEDOM TRAIN 30
HER SEEK THE BURNING SUNLIGHT . . . SP STRANGE HURT 9

SUNNY 6
LET YOUR SONGS HOLD ALL THE SUNNY JOYS . . . . . CWT JUICE JOINT 19
WHOSE LANGUID LEAN BRINGS BACK THE SUNNY SOUTH . . . . . CWT JUICE JOINT 42
IT'S SUNNY HERE . . . . . SP KID SLEEPY 5
ON SUNNY SUMMER SUNDAY AFTERNOONS IN HARLEM . . . . . SP PASSING 1
ON SUNNY SUNDAY AFTERNOONS . . . . SP PASSING 6
BUD IN SUNNY AIR . . . . . PL SLUM DREAMS 3

SUNNY-FACED 1
THE SUNNY-FACED SOUTH. . . . . . SP THE SOUTH 3

SUNRISE 8
LEAVES THE SUNRISE IN THE SKY - . . SP BLACK MARIA 19
GRABS A LOAD OF SUNRISE . . . . . SP MIGRANT 10
THE SUNRISE . . . . . SP SUNDAY BY COMB 4
A SUNRISE THAT HE CANNOT SEE . . . PL JUNIOR ADDICT 8
QUICK, SUNRISE, COME - . . . . . PL JUNIOR ADDICT 19
QUICK, SUNRISE, COME! . . . . . PL JUNIOR ADDICT 35
SUNRISE OUT OF AFRICA. . . . . . PL JUNIOR ADDICT 36
SUNRISE, PLEASE COME! . . . . . PL JUNIOR ADDICT 38

SUNS 1
HE SUNS HIMSELF . . . . . FW OLD SAILOR 15

SUNSET 3
THAT IS SUNSET IN THE CARIBBEAN. . WB CARIBBEAN SUNST 4
SUNSET . . . . . SP FULFILMENT 12
BOSOM TURN ALL GOLDEN IN THE SUNSET. SP NEGRO SPEAKS OF 10

SUNSETS 2
SUNSETS STAINED WITH BLOOD . . . . AYM GOSPEL CHA-CHA 29
WHERE THE SUNSETS BLEED. . . . . . PL GEORGIA DUSK 12

SUNSHINE 8
SUNSHINE SEEMED LIKE GOLD. . . . . DK PO' BOY BLUES 2
SUNSHINE SEEMED LIKE GOLD. . . . . DK PO' BOY BLUES 4
SHE DANCED IN SUNSHINE . . . . . . FW GIRL 3
TO LAUGH IN SUNSHINE . . . . . . FW GIRL 21
IN THE SUNSHINE. . . . . . SP FULFILMENT 8
AND GOLDEN LIKE THE SUNSHINE . . . SP RUBY BROWN 2
DAYS FILLED WITH FIERY SUNSHINE . . SP STRANGE HURT 6
TOMORROW'S SUNSHINE GIVE . . . . . PL JUNIOR ADDICT 17

SUN-DOWN 1
A SUN-DOWN NAME. . . . . . DK YOUTH 6

SUN-STARS 1
SUN AND THE SONG OF ALL THE SUN-STARS . . . . . SP SUN SONG 3

SUN'S 9
SUN'S GONNA SHINE . . . . . WB BLUES FANTASY 17
SUN'S A SETTIN'. . . . . . DK NIGHT AND MORN 1
SUN'S A SETTIN'. . . . . . DK NIGHT AND MORN 3
SUN'S A RISIN'. . . . . . DK NIGHT AND MORN 7
SUN'S A RISIN'. . . . . . DK NIGHT AND MORN 9
SUN'S GOING DOWN THIS EVENING - . . DK SONG BANJO DANC 12
THE SUN'S GOING DOWN THIS VERY NIGHT - . . . . . DK SONG BANJO DANC 14
THE SUN'S GOING DOWN THIS VERY NIGHT - . . . . . DK SONG BANJO DANC 26
IT'S DARK ON THIS STOOP. LAWD! THE SUN'S GONE DOWN! . . . . . SH TWILIGHT REVERI 15

SUPERMARKET 1
IN A SUPERMARKET SEA. . . . . . PL CULTURAL EXCHNG 22

SUPPER 2
BUT THIS EVENIN' FOR SUPPER. . . . SH EVENIN' BLUES 11
DINNER, AND SUPPER, TOO - . . . . . SP MADAM HER MADAM 6

SUPPORT 1
SUPPORT YOUR CAUSE. . . . . . PL NORTHERN LIBERL 17

SUPPORTING 1
STAND LIKE FREE MEN SUPPORTING MY TRUST. . . . . . SP THE NEGRO MOTHE 42

SUPPOSE 2
BUT SUPPOSE . . . . . SP MADAM NUMBER WR 21
BUT SUPPOSE I DON'T WANT IT. . . . PL QUESTION ANSWER 14

SUPPOSED 2
AM I SUPPOSED TO BE GOD. . . . . . PL GO SLOW 11
AM I SUPPOSED TO FORGIVE . . . . . PL GO SLOW 15

SUPS 1
WOMEN OF THE STREETS STOP BY FOR SUPS . . . . . CWT JUICE JOINT 7

SURE 26
SURE. KISS ME. . . . . . WB CAT AND SAXOPHN 11
SURE. . . . . . WB CAT AND SAXOPHN 23
SURE. . . . . . FC JAZZ BAND 23
STRONG AND SURE. . . . . . ANS A NEW SONG 45
YOU ARE SURE YOURSELVES THAT IT IS COMING - . . . . . ANS KIDS WHO DIE 44
SURE. CALL ME ANY UGLY NAME YOU CHOOSE - . . . . . ANS LET AMERICA BE 70
I SURE WOULD LIKE . . . . . SH ASPIRATION 3
UH! IT SURE IS AWFUL TO . . . . . SH EVIL MORNING 13
SURE. I MISSED YOUR TRUNK - BUT I DIDN'T MISS YOU. . . . . . SH LETTER 8
CAUSE I'M SURE ENJOYING MYSELF TODAY! . . . . . SH SUNDAY 7
I'M EVER SO SURE . . . . . FW FAITHFUL ONE 3
FOR SURE THERE GREW FLOWERS . . . . FW GIRL 14
AND SURE SHE LIVED . . . . . FW GIRL 18
ARE YOU SURE . . . . . FW WHEN ARMIES PAS 10
SURE DO! . . . . . SP ARGUMENT 5
SURE BUGS ME: . . . . . SP CHILDREN'S RYME 14
SURE. . . . . . SP DREAM BOOGIE 15
AND NOBODY KNEW FOR SURE . . . . . SP FREEDOM'S PLOW 119
BUT I SURE AIN'T GONNA PAY! . . . . SP MADAM PHONE BIL 40
AND GOD KNOWS SHE SURE CAN OVERCHARGE - . . . . . SP NECESSITY 10
YOU'LL SURE STAY IN YOUR PLACE. . . SP WIDOW WOMAN 12
SURE BUGS ME: . . . . . PL CHILDREN'S RYME 8
SURE. . . . . . PL FLORIDA WORKERS 13
SURE. WE REMEMBER. . . . . . PL HARLEM 7
BUT DESTINED SURE TO FLOOD - AND SOON - . . . . . PL JUNIOR ADDICT 10
ARE YOU SURE? . . . . . PL UN-AMERICAN 20

SURELY 4
SURELY NOT ME? THE MILLIONS ON RELIEF TODAY? . . . . . ANS LET AMERICA BE 57
IS SOMETHING THAT SURELY . . . . . JC BLD SAM SOLOMON 15
WILL SURELY GET YOU DOWN. . . . . . SP BLUE MONDAY 11
THE LORD WILL SURELY . . . . . . SP MADAM MINISTER 23

SURGEONS 1
LEARNING SKILLS OF SURGEONS . . . . SP INTERNE AT PROV 11

SURPASSING 2
SURPASSING BEAUTY. . . . . . WB POEM 7
SURPASSING GOODNESS. . . . . . WB POEM 13

SURPRISE 4
WOULD BE A SURPRISE. . . . . . FC NEW CABARET GRL 4
WOULD BE A SURPRISE. . . . . . FC NEW CABARET GRL 16
THEY HARDLY TAKE GOD BY SURPRISE. LHP ACCEPTANCE 4
SURPRISE. . . . . . SP AFRICA 12

SURROUND 1
AND THE STEEL BARS SURROUND YOU. . ANS CHANT TOM MOONY 7

SURVEYS 1
WHO MAKE SURVEYS AND WRITE BOOKS. ANS KIDS WHO DIE 23

SUSANNA 3
WHEN SUSANNA JONES WEARS RED . . . SP WHEN SUE WEARS 1
WHEN SUSANNA JONES WEARS RED . . . SP WHEN SUE WEARS 6
AND THE BEAUTY OF SUSANNA JONES IN RED . . . . . SP WHEN SUE WEARS 10

SUTURE 1
NURSES' HANDS ON SUTURE. . . . . . SP INTERNE AT PROV 21

SWAHILI 1
SPEAKS ENGLISH FRENCH SWAHILI . . . AYM ASK YOUR MAMA 57

SWAMP 3
MAYBE YOUR BODIES'LL BE LOST IN A SWAMP. . . . . . ANS KIDS WHO DIE 40
PLANT YOUR TOES IN THE COOL SWAMP MUD. . . . . . CWT FLIGHT 1
RISING OUT OF THE GROUND LIKE A SWAMP MIST . . . . . PL DAYBREAK IN ALA 5

SWAMPS 1
KIDS WILL DIE IN THE SWAMPS OF MISSISSIPPI . . . . . ANS KIDS WHO DIE 8

SWANEE 1
MUFFLED DRUMS IN SWANEE RIVER TEMPO. PL SPECIAL BULLTIN 9

SWARTHY 1
A MAN, SPARE, SWARTHY, STRONG, FOURSQUARE - . . . . . JC TO CAPTAIN MULZ 44

SWAY 3
TO SWAY IN THE BREEZE. . . . . . FW GIRL 17
HE DID A LAZY SWAY. . . . . . SP THE WEARY BLUES 6
HE DID A LAZY SWAY. . . . . . SP THE WEARY BLUES 7

SWAYING 2

NIGHT-DARK GIRL OF THE SWAYING HIPS? . . . WB NUDE YOUNG DANC 6
AS EVERY SWAYING . . . . OWT JUICE JOINT 29
SWAYING TO AND FRO ON HIS RICKETY STOOL . . . . SP THE WEARY BLUES 12

SWAYS 2

LYNCHED TOMORROW SWAYS. . . . . AYM ODE TO DINAH 101
A LYNCHED TOMORROW SWAYS. . . . . . . AYM ODE TO DINAH 99

SWEAR 7

AND YET I SWEAR THIS OATH - . . . . . ANS LET AMERICA BE 78
I SWEAR TO THE LORD . . . . JC BLACK MAN SPEAK 1
I SWEAR TO MY SOUL . . . . JC BLACK MAN SPEAK 5
I SWEAR, BY GUM, ... JC BLACK MAN SPEAK 9
THE CHARGES SWEAR. . . . . OWT BLD MARGE POLIT 20
HE SAID, MADAM, I SWEAR . . . . SP MADAM MIGHT-HAV 17
I SAID, I SWEAR I . . . . SP MADAM NUMBER WR 21

SWEAT 3

WHOSE SWEAT AND BLOOD, WHOSE FAITH AND PAIN, ... ANS LET AMERICA BE 67
A CROWN OF SWEAT . . . . SP INTERNE AT PROV 35
REMEMBER MY SWEAT, MY PAIN, MY DESPAIR. . . . . SP THE NEGRO MOTHE 36

SWEATING 1

HURRY, SWEATING RUNNER! . . . . OWT FLIGHT 3

SWEEP 5

THEY SWEEP THE EARTH - . . . . ANS A NEW SONG 46
O, SWEEP OF STARS OVER HARLEM STREETS, ... SP STARS 1
FOR THE RICH TO SWEEP OVER . . . . . PL FLORIDA WORKERS 10
TO SWEEP THE WORLD . . . . PL WAR 10
I SWEEP AND I SWEEP . . . . PL WAR 12
I SWEEP AND I SWEEP . . . . PL WAR 12

SWEEPIN' 1

SO I SAY, "MISTER, I AIN'T NO SWEEPIN' MACHINE." . . . . NM BROKE 16

SWEEPS 1

SWEEPS YOUR LIFE AWAY. . . . . JC THE BITTER RIVR 50

SWEET 43

SWEET ME. . . . . WB CAT AND SAXOPHN 28
LIKE A SWEET VEIL ABOUT YOUR BOWER? . . WB NUDE YOUNG DANC 4
OH, SWEET, AWAY! . . . . WB OUR LAND 16
WOULD GOD HIS LIPS WERE SWEET! . . . WB TO LITTLE LOVER 12
MA LITTLE, SHORT, SWEET, BROWNSKIN BOY, - . . . . FC BLACK GAL 17
SWEET GIRLS, SWEET GIRLS, ... FC LISTEN HERE 1
SWEET GIRLS, SWEET GIRLS, ... FC LISTEN HERE 1
ALL YOU SWEET GIRLS, ... FC LISTEN HERE 3
DE WAY HE SHOCKS ME SHO IS SWEET. . FC MA MAN 6
MA SWEET GOOD MAN HAS . . . . FC SUICIDE 1
MA SWEET GOOD MAN HAS . . . . FC SUICIDE 3
YES, UM-HUM! YOU SHO IS SWEET! CAN YOU PAY FO' DE LICENSE, DEAR? . NM BROKE 78
FOR TO CALL ME SWEET. . . . . DK DRESSED UP 12
YOUR LIPS WERE SWEET. . . . . DK PARISIAN BEGGAR 5
BUT THAT SEA WIND IS SWEET . . . . . DK SEA CHARM 8
BUT SWEET . . . . ANS A NEW SONG 41
DANCIN CLOSE, AND DANCIN SWEET, . . . SH DEATH IN HARLEM 22
BOY, YOU'RE SWEET! . . . . SH DEATH IN HARLEM 50
AND SHE SAT ON HER CHAIR LIKE A SWEET JELLY ROLL. . . . . SH DEATH IN HARLEM 83
SWEET ENOUGH TO EAT. . . . . SH HARLEM SWEETIES 8
ALL THOSE SWEET COLORS . . . . SH HARLEM SWEETIES 27
DID MY SWEET MAMA GO? . . . . SH SHAKESPEARE 4
THEY SAY YOUR SWEET MAMA . . . . . . SH SHAKESPEARE 7
MAKE IT SHORT AND SWEET, YOUR LOVIN', ... SH SIX-BITS BLUES 11
O, SWEET RELIEF FROM FACES THAT ARE WHITE! . . . . OWT NEGRO SERVANT 19
LIKE A SYRUPY SWEET? . . . . SP HARLEM 8
IN THE SWEET O' MA LORD'S SIGHT - SP JUDGMENT DAY 12
DANCE WITH YOU, MY SWEET BROWN HARLEM GIRL. . . . . SP JUKE BOX LOVE 12
LIKE SWEET RED WINE. . . . . SP LAMENT OVER LOV 16
I'LL BE DOGGED, SWEET BABY, ... SP LIFE IS FINE 29
SWEET AS PURPLE DEW, ... SP MIDNIGHT DANCER 4
LIKE THE PILLOWS OF ALL SWEET DREAMS, ... SP MIDNIGHT DANCER 6
O, SWEET AS EARTH, ... SP MULATTO 33
GIVE SWEET BIRTH . . . . SP MULATTO 35
SWING LOW, SWEET CHARIOT, ... SP MYSTERY 9
A LONG, SWEET NIGHT WITH ME. . . . . SP NATCHA 4
SWEET WATERMELON IN A BABY CARRIAGE, SP SUMMER EVENING 2
SWEET GALS WAS A-MOANIN', ... SP SYLVESTER'S BED 5
BUT I'S STILL SWEET PAPA 'VESTER, SP SYLVESTER'S BED 21
SWEET BLUES! . . . . SP THE WEARY BLUES 14
NOR THE SWEET OF YOUR LIPS ALONE. SP TO ARTINA 8
SWEET SILVER TRUMPETS, ... SP WHEN SUE WEARS 12
FULL OF NUTS AND SWEET. . . . . SP 125TH STREET 2
LIKE A SYRUPY SWEET? . . . . PL DREAM DEFERRED 8
SWEET WORDS THAT TAKE . . . . PL SWEET WORDS RAC 1
THEIR OWN SWEET TIME TO FLOWER . . PL SWEET WORDS RAC 2
SWEET WORDS SO BRAVE . . . . PL SWEET WORDS RAC 9
SWEET AND DOCILE, ... PL WARNING 2
SWEET AND WONDERFUL TO SAY. . . . . PL WORDS LIKE FREE 2

SWEETEST 1

AND DREAMED THE SWEETEST DREAM . . SP FIRED 8

SWEETHEART 1

DID YOU EVER THINK ABOUT YOUR SWEETHEART . . . . SP REVERIE HARLEM 7

SWEETIE 3

SWEETIE, AIN'T I? . . . . WB CAT AND SAXOPHN 21
CAN I GO HOME WID YUH, SWEETIE? . . FC JAZZ BAND 22
LET'S GO, SWEETIE! . . . . SP PORT TOWN 15

SWEETNESS 1

FEMININE SWEETNESS . . . . SH HARLEM SWEETIES 19

SWELLED 1

AND DON'T YOU KNOW THAT OLD WOMAN SWELLED UP LIKE A SPECKLED TOAD NM BROKE 21

SWIFT 5

BEATEN WITH SWIFT STICKS . . . . . . FC SPORT 6
SHAKE 'EM SWIFT AND WIL' - . . . . DK SONG BANJO DANC 4
SO DANCE WITH SWIFT FEET, HONEY, . DK SONG BANJO DANC 16
DANCE WITH SWIFT FEET, HONEY - . . DK SONG BANJO DANC 18
SWIFT DYING . . . . SP DESIRE 3

SWIFTLY 1

HE GLIDES SO SWIFTLY . . . . FW SNAKE 1

SWIM 3

I WOULD SWIM TO CHINA . . . . SH DECLARATION 3
AN' I AIN'T GOIN' THERE TO SWIM; . SP LAMENT OVER LOV 8
AIN'T GOIN' THERE TO SWIM. . . . . . SP LAMENT OVER LOV 10

SWIMMER 1

I AIN'T A GOOD SWIMMER . . . . DK WIDE RIVER 5

SWIMMING 1

SWIMMING IN THE SEA. . . . . SH DECLARATION 2

SWING 3

AND I SWING IT A-HUMMIN', ... NM BIG-TIMER POEM 30
SWING LOW, SWEET CHARIOT, ... SP MYSTERY 9
AND ALL KINDS OF SWING MIKADOS . . SP NOTE COMM THEAT 10

SWINGING 2

AND LET YOUR SONGS DRIFT THROUGH THE SWINGING DOORS. . . . . OWT JUICE JOINT 18
WHERE THE PENDULUM IS SWINGING . . AYM ODE TO DINAH 111

SWIRL 4

TO A HEEL TAP AND A SWIRL OF FINGERS ANS SONG OF SPAIN 8
BUT THE SWIRL OF THE BITTER RIVER JC THE BITTER RIVR 41
THE SWIRL OF THE BITTER RIVER . . . JC THE BITTER RIVR 45
THE SWIRL OF THE BITTER RIVER . . . JC THE BITTER RIVR 49

SWISH 1

TO THE SWISH OF RAIN. . . . . WB LENOX AVE MIDNT 10

SWITCH 1

AND SWITCH THEIR SKIRTS AND LIFT THEIR STRAIGHTENED HEADS . . . . OWT JUICE JOINT 23

SWITCHBOARD 1

TRIED TO FIND ONE O' THEM LITTLE ELEVATOR AND SWITCHBOARD JOBS THEY USED . . . . NM BROKE 41

SWITCH-BLADE 2

'CAUSE I CARRIES A SWITCH-BLADE . . NM BIG-TIMER POEM 29
HE USED A SWITCH-BLADE . . . . SP MADAM CHARTY CH 7

SWOON 2

EDGE INTO A SWOON. . . . . SP MOONLIGHT NIGHT 8
DO NOT SWOON. . . . . SP SILHOUETTE 2

SWORD 1

A SWORD THRUST, A HORN TIP, ... ANS SONG OF SPAIN 14

SWORE 1

I HAD SWORE . . . . SP MADAM NUMBER WR 3

SYLVESTER'S 1

"SYLVESTER'S GONNA DIE!" . . . . . . SP SYLVESTER'S BED 6

SYMBOL 2

OUR SYMBOL OF NEW LIBERTIES. . . . JC TO CAPTAIN MULZ 42
HE, TOO, A SYMBOL OF NEW LIBERTIES. JC TO CAPTAIN MULZ 46

SYMBOLS 1
ALL THIS TALKIN' AIN'T NOTHIN' BUT TINKLIN' SYMBOLS AND SOUNDIN' BRASS: . . . . NM BROKE 58

SYMPHONIES 1
AND YOU MIXED 'EM UP WITH SYMPHONIES SP NOTE COMM THEAT 4

SYNCOPATE 1
SUNDAY PRAYERS SYNCOPATE GLORY. . . SP CONSIDER ME 44

SYNCOPATED 3
SYNCOPATED MUSIC. TELLING HIS STORY IN A HARD, BRAZEN, CYNICAL FASHION. . . . . NM BIG-TIMER MOOD 1
SYNCOPATED. DETERMINED TO LAUGH. A BUGLE CALL. GAY, MARTIAL MUSIC. NM BLACK CLWN MOOD 6
DRONING A DROWSY SYNCOPATED TUNE, SP THE WEARY BLUES 1

SYPHILITIC 1
HONEY-LIPPED, SYPHILITIC - . . . . SP THE SOUTH 16

SYRUPY 2
LIKE A SYRUPY SWEET? . . . . SP HARLEM 8
LIKE A SYRUPY SWEET? . . . . PL DREAM DEFERRED 8

SYSTEM 1
LIFE IS A SYSTEM OF HALF-TRUTHS AND LIES, ... PL ELDERLY LEADERS 3

S'POSE 1
I MEAN FOUR - BEFORE DAYLIGHT - S'POSE TO'VE DONE HIT YO' FIRST STROKE - . . . . NM BROKE 14

T 2
(NEGRO SKIPPER OF THE BOOKER T. WASHINGTON SAILING WITH A MIXED CREW) . . . . JC TO CAPTAIN MULZ 1
IS THE BOOKER T., ... JC TO CAPTAIN MULZ 64

TABLE 4
AND A WOMAN CROSS THE TABLE WHEN A MAN AIN'T BROKE - . . . . SH DEATH IN HARLEM 54
I'LL BE AT THE TABLE . . . . SP I, TOO 9
ON A TABLE . . . . SP ONE 7
AT THE DAMASK TABLE, MINE. . . . . PL DINNER GUEST ME 18

TABLES 3
SOFT LIGHT ON THE TABLES, ... DK NEGRO DANCERS 7
FOLKS AT THE TABLES DRINK AND GRIN. SH DEATH IN HARLEM 31
FROM THE TABLES OF JOY, ... SP LUCK 2

TACK 1
FOR A CARPET TACK. . . . . FC EVIL WOMAN 16

TACKS 1
IT'S HAD TACKS IN IT, ... SP MOTHER TO SON 3

TAFFY 1
MOLASSES TAFFY, ... SH HARLEM SWEETIES 33

TAG 1
STOP HUNTING FOR THE PRICE TAG! . . SH BLD PAWNBROKER 15

TAIL 5
I GOT MA TAIL CURLED! . . . . FC CRAP GAME 2
CATCH THAT JIM CROW BIRD, PULL THE FEATHERS OUT HIS TAIL! . . . . . . JC JIM CROW'S LAST 16
AND MEET THEIR OWN TAIL. . . . . . . FW CIRCLES 3
HAD HER TAIL . . . . SP CATCH 5
ON A DREAMER'S TAIL . . . . SP JAM SESSION 8

TAKE 70
THE LORD WILL TAKE ME IN. . . . . . . WR PIERROT 23
PLEASE DON'T TAKE THIS MAN O' MINE. FC GAL'S CRY DYING 18
LAUGH - OR TAKE PITY. . . . . NM BIG-TIMER POEM 8
YOU CAN TAKE THAT JOB AND GO TO - I HOPE YOU CHOKE. . . . . NM BROKE 37
'CAUSE I'M JUST DYIN' TO TAKE ON THAT THERE MARRIAGE YOKE. . . . . NM BROKE 77
GO-VOICES: TAKE POWER. . . . . ANS CHANT MAY DAY 34
OF WORK THE MEN! OF TAKE THE PAY! ANS LET AMERICA BE 29
WE MUST TAKE BACK OUR LAND AGAIN, ANS LET AMERICA BE 73
I MUST TAKE THE WORLD FOR MY OWN AGAIN - . . . . ANS SONG OF SPAIN 81
OR IF IT WASN'T SO LATE I MIGHT TAKE A WALK . . . . SH BED TIME 7
TAKE ME. . . . . SH DEATH IN HARLEM 128
JESUS, TAKE ME . . . . SH DEATH IN HARLEM 129
AND TAKE BACK ALL THEM THINGS WE HAD SH PAY DAY 12
I WOULDN'T TAKE YOU BACK IF YOU COME ON YOUR KNEES. . . . . SH SUNDAY 9
CAUSE I'D TAKE THAT OWL HEAD AND FIRE ON YOU. . . . . SH TWILIGHT REVERI 12
AND TAKE A STAND . . . . JC BLD SAM SOLOMON 20
TO TAKE THEIR RIGHTFUL PART . . . . JC BLD SAM SOLOMON 47
TO TAKE THE SACRAMENT . . . . FW COMMUNION 6
TAKE A STREET CAR . . . . OWT JITNEY 41
SHALL I TAKE A GUN . . . . OWT TOO BLUE 8
IT WOULD PROBABLY TAKE TWO. . . . . . OWT TOO BLUE 13
THEY HARDLY TAKE GOD BY SURPRISE. LHR ACCEPTANCE 4
PLEASE DON'T TAKE HIM AWAY! . . . . . SP AS BEFITS A MAN 16
DON'T TAKE DADDY AWAY! . . . . SP AS BEFITS A MAN 18
YOU GONNA TAKE MY FURNITURE AND . . SP BLD LANDLORD 15
WILL TAKE GOOD MONEY FROM YOU, . . SP BLD THE GYPSY 19
AND TAKE YOUR MONEY FROM YOU - . . SP BLD THE GYPSY 21
I WOULD TAKE YOUR MONEY, TOO. . . . SP BLD THE GYPSY 23
I TAKE MY CURSES BACK. . . . . SP CROSS 4
I'D LIKE TO TAKE UP BACH. . . . . . . SP DEFERRED 48
LET THINGS TAKE THEIR COURSE. . . . SP DEMOCRACY 11
TAKE IT AWAY! . . . . SP DREAM BOOGIE 17
TO TAKE AWAY TO ALABAMA. . . . . . . SP INTERNE AT PROV 6
TAKE ME THERE. . . . . SP ISLAND 8
I COULD TAKE THE HARLEM NIGHT . . . SP JUKE BOX LOVE 1
TAKE THE NEON LIGHTS AND MAKE A CROWN, ... SP JUKE BOX LOVE 3
TAKE THE LENOX AVENUE BUSSES, . . . SP JUKE BOX LOVE 4
TAKE HARLEM'S HEARTBEAT, ... SP JUKE BOX LOVE 7
CAN TAKE A PERSON'S LIFE. . . . . . . SP LITTLE OLD LETT 16
AND MOUNTAINS THAT TAKE WING. . . . SP LOVE 4
YOU SAID YOU WAS GONNA TAKE ME . . SP LOW TO HIGH 3
THEN TAKE CARE OF HER CHILDREN . . SP MADAM HER MADAM 7
ELSE YOU'LL TAKE OUT MY PHONE? . . SP MADAM PHONE BIL 11
STOP TO TAKE STOCK. . . . . SP MADAM CHARTY CH 16
YOU WPA FOLKS TAKE CARE OF YOURSELF - . . . . SP MADAM'S PAST HI 21
YOU GOT TO TAKE ME . . . . SP ME AND THE MULE 7
AND TAKE IT WITH ME . . . . SP ONE-WAY TICKET 2
AND TAKE IT ON THE TRAIN . . . . . . SP ONE-WAY TICKET 10
AND TAKE IT AWAY . . . . SP ONE-WAY TICKET 24
BABY, TAKE IT SLOW. . . . . SP SAME IN BLUES 2
REACH UP YOUR HAND, DARK BOY, AND TAKE A STAR. . . . . SP STARS 7
TAKE JUST . . . . SP STARS 10
THE HARLEM BRANCH Y, WHERE I TAKE THE ELEVATOR . . . . SP THEME FOR ENG B 14
I WILL TAKE YOUR HEART. . . . . SP TO ARTINA 1
I WILL TAKE YOUR SOUL OUT OF YOUR BODY . . . . SP TO ARTINA 2
I WILL TAKE YOUR HEART FOR MINE. . SP TO ARTINA 9
I WILL TAKE YOUR SOUL. . . . . SP TO ARTINA 10
OTHERS TAKE A QUARTER STRAIGHT. . . SP TOMORROW 6
RIDE EVERYBODY MUST TAKE. . . . . . SP WIDOW WOMAN 2
RIDE EVERYBODY MUST TAKE. . . . . . SP WIDOW WOMAN 4
DON'T TAKE THE FIFTH AMENDMENT. . . AYM RIDE, RED, RIDE 28
NOR TAKE THE PLACE OF MEAT OR BREAD PL CROWNS GARLANDS 15
HOW MANY BULLETS DOES IT TAKE . . . PL DEATH YORKVILLE 3
HOW MANY CENTURIES DOES IT TAKE . . PL DEATH YORKVILLE 5
HOW MANY CENTENNIALS DOES IT TAKE PL DEATH YORKVILLE 15
HOW MANY BULLETS DOES IT TAKE . . . PL DREAM DEFERRED 1
LET THINGS TAKE THEIR COURSE. . . . PL FREEDOM 11
WHY TAKE IT? . . . . PL QUESTION ANSWER 15
SWEET WORDS THAT TAKE . . . . PL SWEET WORDS RAC 1
I TAKE IN MY HANDS . . . . PL WAR 9

TAKEN 8
MY WOMEN TAKEN AS THE BODY-TOYS . . ANS A NEW SONG 14
HAS TAKEN HOLD, ... JC TO CAPTAIN MULZ 27
THEY TAKEN MARGIE TO JAIL . . . . . . OWT BLD MARGE POLIT 17
TAKEN MARGIE AWAY - . . . . OWT BLD MARGE POLIT 53
YOU'VE TAKEN MY BLUES AND GONE - . SP NOTE COMM THEAT 1
YEP, YOU DONE TAKEN MY BLUES AND GONE. . . . . SP NOTE COMM THEAT 7
OF THE SOUTH HAVE TAKEN OVER - . . PL CULTURAL EXCHNG 39
TAKEN LATE IN TIME . . . . PL NORTHERN LIBERL 9

TAKES 15
I TAKES MA MEANNESS AND MA LICKER FC BAD MAN 5
MEN TAKES ALL THEY CAN FROM ME . . FC BLACK GAL 6
JEW TAKES YO' FINE CLOTHES, ... FC HARD LUCK 7
JEW TAKES YO' FINE CLOTHES, ... FC HARD LUCK 9
MUSIC TAKES ON A BLUES STRAIN, GRADUALLY RETURNING TO A SORT OF NM BIG-TIMER MOOD 3
TAKES LAND, ... ANS OPEN LETTER 58
TAKES FACTORIES, ... ANS OPEN LETTER 59
TAKES OFFICE TOWERS, ... ANS OPEN LETTER 60
TAKES TOOLS AND BANKS AND MINES, . ANS OPEN LETTER 61
IT TAKES YOU AND IT BREAKS YOU - . SH LOVE AGAIN BLUS 17
TAKES YOUR WORDS AWAY. . . . . . . JC THE BITTER RIVR 42
TAKES MY WOMAN AWAY. . . . . SP BLUE BAYOU 12
IT TAKES TO LIVE. . . . . SP CONSIDER ME 32
TAKES UP IMPORTANT MATTERS . . . . SP MIGRANT 28
BOSS MAN TAKES THE MONEY . . . . . SP SHARE-CROPPERS 7

TAKETH 1
THAT TAKETH ALL THINGS UNDER WING - LHR DEAR LVLY DEATH 2

TAKING 2
AND NEVER TAKING. . . . . SP MADAM MIGHT-HAV 16
BEFORE TAKING BESS TO WIFE . . . . AYM SHADES OF PIG 16

TAKIN' 2
SO I'M TAKIN' IT EASY . . . . NM BIG-TIMER POEM 73
IT'S DONE GOT ME SO CRAZY, FEEL LIKE I BEEN TAKIN' COKE. . . . . . . NM BROKE 60

TALK 10
AND FIND SOMEBODY TO KID AND TALK. . . SH BED TIME 8
YOU CAN TALK ABOUT . . . . OWT VISITORS 1
YOU CAN TALK ABOUT . . . . OWT VISITORS 5
TALK ON - TILL YOU GET THROUGH. . . SP BLD LANDLORD 18
TO COME ALONG AN' TALK. . . . . . . SP BOUND NO'TH BLS 12
YOU TALK LIKE . . . . SP COMMENT ON CURB 1
YOU TALK TOO LOUD. . . . . SP HIGH TO LOW 4
HELL, NO! IT'S TIME TO TALK BACK
NOW! . . . . SP IN EXPLANATION 29
STAND UP AND TALK ABOUT ME. . . . . SP NOTE COMM THEAT 13
HEAR YOU, HEAR ME - WE TWO - YOU,
ME, TALK ON THIS PAGE. . . . . . SP THEME FOR ENG B 19

TALKED 1
I TALKED THAT WAY . . . . SP MADAM MINISTER 29

TALKING 7
NO ONE TALKING . . . . FW DIMOUT IN HARLM 15
UM-HUH! YOU TALKING HIGH AND MIGHTY. SP BLD LANDLORD 17
BUT I'M TALKING ABOUT . . . . SP COMMENT ON CURB 6
ARE RARING UP AND TALKING BACK . . SP IN EXPLANATION 3
ARE RARING UP AND TALKING BACK . . SP IN EXPLANATION 20
FROM HARLEM PAST HONG KONG TALKING
BACK. . . . . SP IN EXPLANATION 22
I SAID, WHAT MAN YOU'RE TALKING
'BOUT? . . . . SP MADAM FORT TELL 21

TALKIN' 3
TALKIN' 'BOUT "WE'LL WORK FOR 50¢ A
DAY, IF WE CAN'T GET NO MO'." . NM BROKE 7
ALL THIS TALKIN' AIN'T NOTHIN' BUT
TINKLIN' SYMBOLS AND SOUNDIN'
BRASS! . . . . NM BROKE 58
I SEEN FOLKS TALKIN' ABOUT THE . . SP FREEDOM TRAIN 5

TALKS 1
EXCEPT THAT HE TALKS TOO MUCH. . . SP NEIGHBOR 15

TALL 24
OF TALL THICK TREES . . . . WR OUR LAND 9
AND I SAW HIM STANDING THERE,
STRAIGHT AND TALL. . . . . NM COLORED SL POEM 37
WHILE A TALL WHITE WOMAN . . . . . SH DEATH IN HARLEM 64
AND TALL STRAIGHT PINE . . . . . . FW CAROLINA CABIN 3
AND TALL YOUNG TREES . . . . FW GIRL 15
BEFORE THE TALL . . . . FW NIGHT SONG 2
BEFORE THE TALL . . . . FW NIGHT SONG 9
BEFORE THE TALL . . . . FW NIGHT SONG 16
THE HEAD OF LINCOLN IS SERENELY TALL OWT LINCOLN THEATRE 3
A ROW OF LONG TALL MAMAS . . . . . SP AS BEFITS A MAN 7
LAD TALL AND BROWN . . . . SP COLLEGE FORMAL 5
TALL AND WISE . . . . SP COLLEGE FORMAL 6
HAS GROWN QUITE TALL. . . . . SP DELINQUENT 2
BENEATH A TALL TREE . . . . SP DREAM VARIATION 6
A TALL, SLIM TREE . . . . SP DREAM VARIATION 15
TALL AS A TREE IS TALL. . . . . . . SP LAMENT OVER LOV 20
TALL AS A TREE IS TALL. . . . . . . SP LAMENT OVER LOV 20
TALL AS A TREE IS TALL. . . . . . . SP LAMENT OVER LOV 22
TALL AS A TREE IS TALL. . . . . . . SP LAMENT OVER LOV 22
TALL BLACK STUDENT . . . . AYM ASK YOUR MAMA 52
HOW TALL HOW TALL THE CANE GREW . . AYM BIRD IN ORBIT 41
HOW TALL HOW TALL THE CANE GREW . . AYM BIRD IN ORBIT 41
I'M GONNA PUT SOME TALL TALL TREES
IN IT . . . . PL DAYBREAK IN ALA 7
I'M GONNA PUT SOME TALL TALL TREES
IN IT . . . . PL DAYBREAK IN ALA 7

TALLER 2
AND TALLER THAN THE SKIES . . . . . DK ALABAMA EARTH 5
HE LOOKS TALLER THAN HE IS . . . . SP NEIGHBOR 7

TALMUD 1
AND THE TALMUD IS CORRECTED . . . . AYM SHADES OF PIC 24

TAMALE 1
THE TAMALE MAN WILL COME BY. . . . SP SUMMER EVENING 23

TAMBOURINES 7
TAMBOURINES! . . . . SP TAMBOURINES 1
TAMBOURINES! . . . . SP TAMBOURINES 2
TAMBOURINES. . . . . SP TAMBOURINES 3
TAMBOURINES . . . . SP TAMBOURINES 5
TAMBOURINES! . . . . SP TAMBOURINES 11
TAMBOURINES! . . . . SP TAMBOURINES 12
TAMBOURINES . . . . SP TAMBOURINES 13

TAME 5
YOU CAN TAME A RABBIT. . . . . SH FREE MAN 5
EVEN TAME A BEAR. . . . . SH FREE MAN 6
TAME OR WILD? . . . . SP GENIUS CHILD 7
WILD OR TAME. . . . . SP GENIUS CHILD 8
WOULD BE TOO TAME - . . . . AYM BLUES IN STEREO 6

TAMED 2
PAIN TAMED AND SUBSIDING . . . . . SP INTERNE AT PROV 24
TAMED DOWN. . . . . SP TRUMPET PLAYER 12

TAN 1
AND MY TAN SUEDE SHOES. . . . . . . PL THIRD DEGREE 4

TANGLED 1
TANGLED IN THAT ANCIENT ENDLESS
CHAIN . . . . ANS LET AMERICA BE 26

TAOS 4
IN TAOS . . . . SP A HOUSE IN TAOS 13
ABOUT THIS HOUSE IN TAOS . . . . . SP A HOUSE IN TAOS 17
IN THIS ONE HOUSE IN TAOS - . . . . SP A HOUSE IN TAOS 20
OF OUR HOUSE IN TAOS. . . . . SP A HOUSE IN TAOS 46

TAP 1
TO A HEEL TAP AND A SWIRL OF FINGERS ANS SONG OF SPAIN 8

TAPE 1
UNTAKEN DOWN ON TAPE - . . . . . . AYM IS IT TRUE? 8

TAPES 1
ON THE TAPES - NOT EVEN FOLKWAYS. AYM IS IT TRUE? 34

TAPPED 1
SO HE TAPPED. . . . . SP DANCER 9

TASTE 5
TO TASTE THE IRON OF THE KIDS WHO
DIE. . . . . ANS KIDS WHO DIE 34
TOO LONG HAS THE TASTE OF ITS WATER JC THE BITTER RIVR 4
WITH YOUR TASTE OF BLOOD AND CLAY. JC THE BITTER RIVR 23
NOR THE TASTE OF ITS BITTER BREW. JC THE BITTER RIVR 52
THE TASTE OF DAY. . . . . SP DRUNKARD 5

TASTED 1
HAS TASTED MYSTERY. . . . . FW OLD SAILOR 6

TASTING 1
TASTING ITS BITTERNESS IN MY THROAT. PL MILITANT 5

TATTERED 1
TATTERED . . . . PL LENOX AVE. BAR 10

TATTOOED 1
AND TATTOOED ON HIS BACK HE HAD . . DK SAILOR 7

TAUGHT 2
TAUGHT WELL . . . . SP UNCLE TOM 10
THE MISSIONARIES NEVER TAUGHT
CHINESE . . . . PL BIRMINGHAM SUND 21

TAUNT 2
BUT FINALLY THEY TAUNT HIM . . . . FW MIGRATION 6
THESE DARK GHOSTS TO TAUNT YOU - . PL GHOSTS OF 1619 3

TAUT 2
LIKE A TAUT DRUM. . . . . SP RAILROAD AVENUE 19
NIGHT WILL PULL ITS SLACK TAUT . . SP SUMMER EVENING 25

TAVERN 1
O, IN THIS TAVERN ON THE CITY STREET OWT JUICE JOINT 33

TAX 2
ABOLISH POLL TAX SO FOLKS CAN VOTE. JC JIM CROW'S LAST 24
AND THERE'S A NEW TAX ON CIGARETTES
- . . . . PL HARLEM 11

TAXES 1
YOU RAISE MY TAXES, FREEZE MY WAGES, PL BACKLASH BLUES 5

TAXI 2
TAXI! . . . . FC CLOSING TIME 6
PAY-NIGHTS A TAXI . . . . OWT NEGRO SERVANT 13

TAXIS 1
TAXIS, SUBWAYS, ... SP JUKE BOX LOVE 5

TE 1
TE DEUM! . . . . SP MYSTERY 18

TEA 2
IF I HAD A FIRE I'D MAKE ME SOME TEA SH SUPPER TIME 11
ADELE RAMONA MICHAEL SERVE BAKOKO
TEA . . . . AYM BIRD IN ORBIT 20

TEACH 1
BUT NIGHT SCHOOLS TEACH FRENCH. . . SP DEFERRED 24

TEACHER 1
A SCHOOL TEACHER . . . . SP JOE LOUIS 2

TEACHERS 1
AND THE SCHOOL TEACHERS . . . . . . FC JAZZ BAND 7

TEACHING 1
GOTTA GET MY TEACHING! . . . . OWT JITNEY 31

TEAM 1

WILL TEAM UP WITH JACKIE MABLEY. . SP PROJECTION 19

TEAR 4

TEAR OFF THE GARMENTS . . . . NM BLACK CLWN POEM 69
BUT NOBODY'S SEEN HER SHED A TEAR. SP BLD OF THE GIRL 9
THE TINGLE OF A TEAR. . . . . SP LADY'S BOOGIE 8
SHINED JUST LIKE A TEAR - . . . . . SP NIGHT FUNERAL 37

TEARING 1

ECHOES THE FIGHTING "MARSEILLAISE."
TEARING OFF HIS CLOWN'S SUIT. . NM BLACK CLWN MOOD 13

TEARLESS 1

THE TEARLESS . . . . SP VAGABONDS 7

TEARS 13

NOR THE SALT TEARS . . . . WB DISILLUSION 9
TEARS ARE MY LAUGHTER. . . . . . . WB THE JESTER 10
AND SHE BEEN HOLDIN' 'EM SO TIGHT
TILL DE EAGLE'S IN TEARS - . . . NM BROKE 24
BETWEEN TEARS AND CRYING. . . . . FW BORDER LINE 4
FOR LITTLE TEARS OF HEAVEN . . . . LHR PASTORAL 4
FOR TEARS IF SHE SHOULD CRY. . . . LHR TESTAMENT 8
TEARS OF JOY . . . . SP INTERNE AT PROV 31
AT THE CROCODILE TEARS . . . . . . SP MOVIES 3
IT WAS ALL THEIR TEARS THAT MADE . SP NIGHT FUNERAL 42
SOMETIMES. THE VALLEY WAS FILLED
WITH TEARS. . . . . SP THE NEGRO MOTHE 25
I'LL NEVER DRY THESE TEARS. . . . . SP WIDOW WOMAN 18
THAT TEARS AND BLOOD . . . . PL MISSISSIPPI 4
THAT TEARS AND BLOOD . . . . PL MISSISSIPPI 18

TEASING 1

ARE TEASING PAIN. . . . . SP DREAM BOOGE VAR 10

TECHNICOLOR 1

AS IF TECHNICOLOR BANNERS FLEW . . PL MOTHER IN WAR 7

TEDDY 1

DRESSED LIKE A TEDDY BOY . . . . . AYM ASK YOUR MAMA 62

TEEN-AGE 1

TEEN-AGE. PRE-DRAFT. . . . . PL JUNIOR ADDICT 33

TEETH 2

AND WHITE TEETH GLEAM - . . . . . . ANS A NEW SONG 37
HIGH NOON TEETH . . . . SP DREAM BOOGE VAR 3

TELEPHONE 1

TO TELEPHONE ME. . . . . SP MADAM PHONE BIL 15

TELESCOPE 2

TELESCOPE OF DREAMS . . . . PL LONG VIEW NEGRO 3
BUT TURN THE TELESCOPE AROUND. . . PL LONG VIEW NEGRO 8

TELEVISION 2

I WANT A TELEVISION SET. . . . . . SP DEFERRED 44
BITTER TELEVISION BLURRED . . . . . SP SONG BILLIE HOL 18

TELL 53

I TELL YOU IT'S AWFUL. WHEN YOU'RE
BROKE. . . . . NM BROKE 47
DIDN'T OUR GOVERNMENT TELL US THINGS
WOULD BE FINE . . . . NM COLORED SL POEM 33
TELL ME. TELL ME. . . . . SH LOVE AGAIN BLUS 13
TELL ME. TELL ME. . . . . SH LOVE AGAIN BLUS 13
TELL ME WHAT MAKES . . . . SH LOVE AGAIN BLUS 15
I WANT TO TELL YOU 'BOUT THAT WOMAN. SH ONLY WOMAN BLUS 1
I'M GONNA TELL THE FURNITURE MAN TO
COME . . . . SH PAY DAY 11
I WISH I COULD TELL YOU HOW MUCH I
DON'T CARE . . . . SH SUNDAY 5
SOME FOLKS TRY TO TELL ME DOWN THIS
WAY . . . . JC GOOD MORN STLIN 23
TO TELL. . . . . FW BIRTH 12
TELL ME. . . . . FW CONVENT 1
TELL ME. WHAT DO YOU DO? . . . . . OWT CURIOUS 6
AND TELL YOU MORE THAN . . . . . . SP BLD FORTUNE TEL 3
SHE COULD TELL YOU ABOUT LOVE. . . SP BLD FORTUNE TEL 5
FRIENDS TRIED TO TELL HER . . . . . SP BLD FORTUNE TEL 17
COULDN'T TELL. TO SAVE HER. . . . . SP BLD FORTUNE TEL 31
I SAID. TELL ME. GYPSY. . . . . . . SP BLD THE GYPSY 3
AND TELL YOU ALL I CAN. . . . . . . SP BLD THE GYPSY 8
TELL YOU PRETTY STORIES . . . . . . SP BLD THE GYPSY 20
TELL ME. O QUICKLY! DREAM OF
ALIVENESS. . . . . SP DEMAND 4
TELL ME. O DREAM OF UTTER ALIVENESS
- . . . . SP DEMAND 6
I'D TELL HER. GIMME A PLACE TO
SLEEP. . . . . SP EVENING SONG 6
TELL ME. BROTHER. . . . . SP FIRE 10
SOMEBODY TELL ME ABOUT THIS . . . . SP FREEDOM TRAIN 23
WHAT SHALL I TELL MY CHILDREN? . . .
YOU TELL ME - . . . . SP FREEDOM TRAIN 33
WHAT SHALL I TELL MY CHILDREN? . . .
YOU TELL ME - . . . . SP FREEDOM TRAIN 33
I SAID. MADAM. TELL ME - . . . . . SP MADAM FORT TELL 13
WHY DIDN'T HE TELL ME SOME'N . . . SP MADAM PHONE BIL 25
WELL. SON. I'LL TELL YOU: . . . . . SP MOTHER TO SON 1
TO TELL THE TRUTH. . . . . SP RELIEF 11
TO TELL YOU A STORY OF THE LONG DARK
WAY . . . . SP THE NEGRO MOTHE 2
TELL ME - . . . . SP ULTIMATUM 5
TELL ALL MY MOURNERS . . . . SP WAKE 1
BUT A DOG CAN TELL . . . . SP WARNING AUGMENT 7
YET YOU NEVER CAN TELL WHEN A . . . SP WIDOW WOMAN 23
DID YOU TELL HER THAT OUR CREDIT
OFFICE . . . . AYM ASK YOUR MAMA 10
SAID. TELL YOUR MA. . . . . AYM ASK YOUR MAMA 14
TELL ME. PRETTY PAPA. . . . . AYM ODE TO DINAH 62
TELL ME HOW LONG - . . . . AYM RIDE. RED. RIDE 4
TELL ME. MAMA. CAN I GET MY SHOW . AYM SHOW FARE PLESE 1
TELL ME FARE FROM YOU? . . . . . . AYM SHOW FARE PLESE 2
TELL ME. MAMA. TELL ME. . . . . . . AYM SHOW FARE PLESE 8
TELL ME. MAMA. TELL ME. . . . . . . AYM SHOW FARE PLESE 8
TELL ME. TELL ME. MAMA. . . . . . . AYM SHOW FARE PLESE 11
TELL ME. TELL ME. MAMA. . . . . . . AYM SHOW FARE PLESE 11
AND THE TELL ME OF THE MAMA . . . . AYM SHOW FARE PLESE 18
TELL ME. MISTER BACKLASH. . . . . . PL BACKLASH BLUES 3
TELL ME. MISTER BACKLASH. . . . . . PL BACKLASH BLUES 27
SEND FOR LAFAYETTE AND TELL HIM.
"HELP! HELP ME!" . . . . PL FINAL CALL 19
WHILE THEY TELL ME . . . . PL GO SLOW 5
I COULD TELL YOU. . . . . PL IMPASSE 1
TO TELL YOU THE TRUTH. . . . . . . PL KU KLUX 8
AND TELL ME YOU BELIEVE IN . . . . PL KU KLUX 19

TELLER 4

FORTUNE TELLER LOOKED IN MY HAND. SP MADAM FORT TELL 1
FORTUNE TELLER SAID. . . . . SP MADAM FORT TELL 2
FORTUNE TELLER SQUEEZE MY HAND. . . SP MADAM FORT TELL 5
FORTUNE TELLER SAID. . . . . SP MADAM FORT TELL 7

TELLERS 2

STORY TELLERS. . . . . FC LAUGHERS 2
WHERE BULLETS ARE THE TELLERS. . . AYM BIRD IN ORBIT 14

TELLING 7

SYNCOPATED MUSIC. TELLING HIS STORY
IN A HARD. BRAZEN. CYNICAL
FASHION. . . . . NM BIG-TIMER MOOD 1
CALMLY TELLING THE STORY. PROUDLY
AND EXPECTANTLY WITH HEAD UP.
SHOULDERS . . . . NM COLORED SL MOOD 7
TELLING OTHERS TO GET TOGETHER. . . ANS KIDS WHO DIE 13
AIN'T NO TELLING WHAT . . . . JC BLD SAM SOLOMON 27
YOU AIN'T TELLING NOTHING BUT YOUR
JIM CROW LIES - . . . . JC JIM CROW'S LAST 22
FOLKS. I'M TELLING YOU. . . . . . . SP ADVICE 1
NO! THE HUSSY'S TELLING EVERYBODY - SP BLD OF THE GIRL 13

TELLIN' 6

AND DE MAN COME TELLIN' ME I BETTER
GET THERE AT FO'. . . . . NM BROKE 12
AND DE MAN COME TELLIN' ME THEY
AIN'T HIRIN' NO MO' COLORED -
JUST WHITE. . . . . NM BROKE 45
AND SHE COME TELLIN' ME. SHE AIN'T
GOT NO MO' EVENINGS FREE! . . . NM BROKE 53
BEEN TELLIN' LIES. . . . . SP FIRE 19
BUT HE MUST A BEEN TELLIN' A LIE. SP MIDWINTER BLUES 14
HE MUST A BEEN TELLIN' A LIE. . . . SP MIDWINTER BLUES 16

TELLS 4

CAUSE EVERBODY TELLS ME SO. . . . . FC BAD MAN 2
EVERBODY TELLS ME SO. . . . . FC BAD MAN 4
AND TELLS HIM STORIES. . . . . . . SP AUNTSUE'S STORI 5
TELLS HER MAMA SHE'S A TYPIST . . . SP GRADUATION 13

TEMPLE 1

ONE OF THE PILLARS OF THE TEMPLE
FELL. . . . . SP MULATTO 4

TEMPLES 1

TO SHAKE THE PILLARS OF THOSE
TEMPLES . . . . ANS UNION 7

TEMPO 1

MUFFLED DRUMS IN SWANEE RIVER TEMPO. PL SPECIAL BULLTIN 9

TEN 20

A BLADE TEN INCHES LONG. . . . . . FC SUICIDE 6
A BLADE TEN INCHES LONG. . . . . . FC SUICIDE 10
'CAUSE 'FORE YOU GETS THERE. TEN
THOUSAND AND ONE . . . . NM BROKE 5
QUIET FOR TEN THOUSAND CENTURIES.
OLD ABE. . . . . DK LINCOLN MONUMNT 4
CAN I GET TEN ON THIS SUIT . . . . SH BLD PAWNBROKER 9
TEN BUCKS YOU SAY I OWE YOU? . . . SP BLD LANDLORD 9
TEN BUCKS YOU SAY IS DUE? . . . . . SP BLD LANDLORD 10
WELL. THAT'S TEN BUCKS MORE'N I'LL
PAY YOU . . . . SP BLD LANDLORD 11
HAS TO GIVE HIS MOTHER TEN - . . . SP BUDDY 5
FOR TEN SHILLINGS OFFERING LOVE. . SP NATCHA 2
SIX OR EIGHT AND TEN YEARS OLDER'N
MYSELF. . . . . SP PREFERENCE 2

- DID YOU EVER SEE TEN NEGROES . . . AYM SHOW FARE PLEASE 20
- HOW CAN ONE MAN BE TEN? . . . . . . PL GHOSTS OF 1619 21
- OR TEN BE A HUNDRED AND TEN? . . . PL GHOSTS OF 1619 22
- OR TEN BE A HUNDRED AND TEN? . . . PL GHOSTS OF 1619 22
- OR A THOUSAND AND TEN? . . . . . . PL GHOSTS OF 1619 23
- OR A MILLION AND TEN . . . . PL GHOSTS OF 1619 24
- ARE BUT A THOUSAND AND TEN . . . . PL GHOSTS OF 1619 25
- OR A HUNDRED AND TEN . . . . PL GHOSTS OF 1619 26
- OR TEN - OR ONE - . . . . PL GHOSTS OF 1619 27

TENANT 1

- TENANT HELD NO BAIL . . . . SP BLD LANDLORD 32

TENANT'S 1

- YOUR THIRD-FLOOR TENANT'S NEVER HOME. . . . . AYM ASK YOUR MAMA 9

TENDERLY 1

- NIGHT COMING TENDERLY . . . . SP DREAM VARIATION 16

TENNESSEE 2

- I MEAN TENNESSEE. . . . . FC GYPSY MAN 8
- SAID TENNESSEE. . . . . FC GYPSY MAN 10

TENSE 1

- TENSE. . . . . ANS A NEW SONG 43

TENSION 1

- BEYOND A HIGH TENSION WALL . . . . . SP MELLOW 5

TENT 1

- FROM A TENT AT THE CORNER . . . . . . SP SUMMER EVENING 12

TENTH 1

- DARK TENTH OF A NATION. . . . . SP GOOD MORNING 3

TERRIBLE 5

- 'S A TERRIBLE THING TO HAVE. . . . . DK HOMESICK BLUES 14
- A TERRIBLE THING TO HAVE. . . . . . . DK HOMESICK BLUES 16
- TO THE TERRIBLE SNARL. . . . . SP A HOUSE IN TAOS 36
- HE MISTREATED HER TERRIBLE. . . . . . SP BLD FORTUNE TEL 21
- OUT OF WAR IT CAME, BLOODY AND TERRIBLE! . . . . SP FREEDOM'S PLOW 130

TERROR 6

- AND ITS TERROR AND PAIN IS SPAIN. ANS SONG OF SPAIN 37
- THE WHITE DEVILS OF THE TERROR . . ANS SONG OF SPAIN 50
- TERROR ON THE SAND - . . . . SP DESERT 7
- AND TERROR. . . . . SP JULIET 3
- AND TERROR COME AGAIN . . . . PL MISSISSIPPI 6
- WHERE HAS TERROR BEEN? . . . . PL MISSISSIPPI 9

TERRORS 1

- BETWEEN ASSORTED TERRORS . . . . . . PL LENOX AVE. BAR 2

TETHERED 1

- TETHERED BY SOMETHING WORSE THAN PRIDE. . . . . PL WHERE WHEN WHCH 10

TEXAS 11

- ARABELLA JOHNSON AND THE TEXAS KID SH DEATH IN HARLEM 1
- THE TEXAS KID'S ON A . . . . SH DEATH IN HARLEM 14
- BUT THE TEXAS KID. . . . . SH DEATH IN HARLEM 139
- SAYS TO TEXAS. . . . . SH DEATH IN HARLEM 42
- WHISPERS TO TEXAS. . . . . SH DEATH IN HARLEM 49
- SHE CURCLES TO TEXAS. . . . . SH DEATH IN HARLEM 51
- SHE LEFT THE TEXAS KID SETTIN BY HIMSELF . . . . SH DEATH IN HARLEM 79
- SHE CAST HER EYES ON TEXAS. HOLLERED. . . . . SH DEATH IN HARLEM 87
- NOW, TEXAS WAS A LOVER. . . . . . . SH DEATH IN HARLEM 37
- DOWN IN WEST TEXAS WHERE THE SUN . SP WEST TEXAS 1
- BUT WEST TEXAS WHERE THE SUN . . . SP WEST TEXAS 16

THAN 44

- AND I'D SAVE MORE THAN I DO NOW. . FC PRIZE FIGHTER 6
- BUT HIGHER THAN THE SINGING PINES DK ALABAMA EARTH 4
- AND TALLER THAN THE SKIES . . . . . DK ALABAMA EARTH 5
- THAN JUST TODAY. . . . . JC GOOD MORN STLIN 48
- BUT MORE THAN SHIP. . . . . JC TO CAPTAIN MULZ 41
- BUT MORE THAN THESE. . . . . JC TO CAPTAIN MULZ 45
- MORE THAN SHIP THEN. . . . . JC TO CAPTAIN MULZ 62
- AND MORE THAN CAPTAIN . . . . JC TO CAPTAIN MULZ 65
- MORE THAN THAT. . . . . LHR CONSERVATORY 7
- THAN SHE'S GOT BREATH. . . . . . . LHR TESTAMENT 12
- AND TELL YOU MORE THAN . . . . SP BLD FORTUNE TEL 3
- BETTER THAN . . . . SP DESERT 2
- BETTER THAN NOBODY . . . . SP DESERT 8
- THAN PHARAOH HAD WIVES. . . . . . . SP FIRE 20
- THAN TO LIVE SLAVES. . . . . SP FREEDOM'S PLOW 111
- THAN TO LIVE SLAVES. . . . . SP FREEDOM'S PLOW 173
- THAN I AWOKE. . . . . SP MADAM WRONG VIS 22
- THAN I WANTED TO PAY. . . . . SP MADAM'S CALLING 4
- OLDER THAN CREED. . . . . SP MYSTERY 14
- I'VE KNOWN RIVERS ANCIENT AS THE WORLD AND OLDER THAN THE . . . . SP NEGRO SPEAKS OF 2
- HE LOOKS TALLER THAN HE IS . . . . SP NEIGHBOR 7
- AND YOUNGER THAN HE AIN'T. . . . . SP NEIGHBOR 8
- HE LOOKS DARKER THAN HE IS, TOO. . SP NEIGHBOR 9
- AND HE'S SMARTER THAN HE LOOKS. . . SP NEIGHBOR 10
- QUICKER THAN LIGHT . . . . SP NIGHTMARE BOOGIE 6
- FINDING LESS THAN SOUGHT . . . . . SP OLD WALT 3
- SEEKING MORE THAN FOUND. . . . . . SP OLD WALT 4
- THAN THEY EVER DID BEFORE. . . . . SP RUBY BROWN 26
- ANY BETTER THAN WHITE. . . . . . . SP SHAME ON YOU 9
- THAN A HERD OF NEGROES . . . . . . SP SHARE-CROPPERS 13
- THAN SHELTER FROM THE RAIN." . . . SP STRANGE HURT 5
- RATHER THAN THE SHADE. . . . . . . SP STRANGE HURT 10
- THAN SOME PEOPLE EVER HAD. . . . . SP WARNING AUGMENT 12
- BUT I'D RATHER BE DEAD THAN . . . . SP YOUNG GAL'S BLS 17
- AND OTHER KIDS LESS MEANER THAN ¢ ¢ ¢ ¢ . . . . AYM HORN OF PLENTY 25
- IF SHOW FARE'S MORE THAN 30¢ ¢ ¢ ¢ ¢ ¢ ¢ ¢ . . . . AYM HORN OF PLENTY 29
- EVEN FARTHER THAN ST. ALBANS . . . AYM HORN OF PLENTY 31
- MORE THAN GERMAN EVER BORE. . . . . PL CULTURAL EXCHNG 16
- THAN IS HIS LIVING HERE. . . . . . PL JUNIOR ADDICT 23
- THAN BRING TODAY'S RELEASE . . . . PL JUNIOR ADDICT 25
- THAN IT IS TO GET A JOB." . . . . . PL JUNIOR ADDICT 29
- THAN TO GET A JOB - . . . . PL JUNIOR ADDICT 31
- THAN TRUTH CAN BE. . . . . PL LONG VIEW NEGRO 7
- TETHERED BY SOMETHING WORSE THAN PRIDE. . . . . PL WHERE WHEN WHCH 10

THANK 2

- THANK GOD-A-MIGHTY! HERE'S THE . . SP FREEDOM TRAIN 67
- BUT, THANK GOD, HE WASN'T DEAD! . . SP NOT A MOVIE 13

THANKSGIVING 1

- THEY ASKED ME AT THANKSGIVING . . . AYM BIRD IN ORBIT 15

THAT-A-WAY 1

- AND IT'S MARKED DOWN THAT-A-WAY. . SP BLUE MONDAY 5

THAY 1

- CATCH THAY JIM CROW BIRD, PULL THE FEATHERS OUT HIS TAIL! . . . . . JC JIM CROW'S LAST 16

THEIR 89

- WAITING FOR THEIR LOVERS. . . . . . WB POEME D'AUTOMNE 7
- WILL STRIP THEIR BODIES BARE . . . WB POEME D'AUTOMNE 10
- WILL BE THEIR ONLY . . . . WB POEME D'AUTOMNE 14
- DAMN THEIR SOULS. - . . . . FC DEATH DO DIRTY 32
- THEIR PETALS DANCE ON THE WIND . . DK AUTUMN THOUGHT 4
- FAIRIES WEAVE THEIR GARMENTS. . . . DK FAIRIES 2
- AND THE GENTLEMEN WITH DR. IN FRONT OF THEIR NAMES. . . . . ANS KIDS WHO DIE 21
- WILL ALL RAISE THEIR HANDS AGAINST THE KIDS WHO DIE. . . . . ANS KIDS WHO DIE 29
- DON'T WANT THE PEOPLE TO GET WISE TO THEIR OWN POWER. . . . . ANS KIDS WHO DIE 35
- I LOOKED AT THEIR BLACK FACES . . . ANS NEGRO GHETTO 1
- THEIR FAR-TOO-HUMBLE FEET. . . . . ANS NEGRO GHETTO 8
- AWAIT THEIR DAY . . . . ANS SONG OF SPAIN 51
- MUST PUT THEIR HANDS WITH MINE . . ANS UNION 6
- CAME TIPPIN INTO DIXIE'S WITH SMILES ON THEIR FACES. . . . . SH DEATH IN HARLEM 60
- HAVE ALMOST FORGOTTEN THEIR NAMES SH YOUNG NEGRO GRL 4
- TO TAKE THEIR RIGHTFUL PART . . . . JC BLD SAM SOLOMON 47
- CALLED THEIR BLUFF. . . . . JC BLD SAM SOLOMON 52
- IN THEIR FACES . . . . JC FREEDOM 12
- LIFT THEIR HEADS AND THINGS IS BAD. JC GOOD MORN STLIN 30
- LIFT THEIR HEADS, TOO, WITH GUN IN HAND . . . . JC GOOD MORN STLIN 33
- HAVE MADE UP THEIR MINDS JIM CROW IS THROUGH. . . . . JC JIM CROW'S LAST 14
- COULD NOT CALL THEIR HOUSE, THEIR HOUSE. . . . . JC TO CAPTAIN MULZ 17
- COULD NOT CALL THEIR HOUSE, THEIR HOUSE. . . . . JC TO CAPTAIN MULZ 17
- NOR THEIR LAND, THEIR LAND - . . . JC TO CAPTAIN MULZ 18
- NOR THEIR LAND, THEIR LAND - . . . JC TO CAPTAIN MULZ 18
- THE THINGS THEY MADE, NOR THEIR OWN LIVES - . . . . JC TO CAPTAIN MULZ 21
- THEY HAVE FOUND THEIR HOUR. . . . . JC TO CAPTAIN MULZ 24
- AND MEET THEIR OWN TAIL. . . . . . FW CIRCLES 3
- THE YEARS BUILD THEIR BARS . . . . FW CIRCLES 5
- THEIR DREAM AWAY. . . . . FW LITTLE SONG 8
- THEIR LIVES . . . . FW SAILING DATE 2
- THEIR CAPTAIN'S . . . . FW SAILING DATE 20
- LET THOSE WOMEN WITH THEIR LIPS TOO RED . . . . OWT JUICE JOINT 21
- AND SWITCH THEIR SKIRTS AND LIFT THEIR STRAIGHTENED HEADS . . . . OWT JUICE JOINT 23
- AND SWITCH THEIR SKIRTS AND LIFT THEIR STRAIGHTENED HEADS . . . . OWT JUICE JOINT 23
- LET THINGS TAKE THEIR COURSE. . . . SP DEMOCRACY 11
- YOU'LL HEAR THEIR FEET . . . . . . SP DREAM BOOGIE 6
- FRANTIC, KICK THEIR DRAFTEE YEARS SP FLATTED FIFTHS 4
- BUT IN THEIR HEARTS THE SLAVES KNEW SP FREEDOM'S PLOW 106
- GUARDING IN THEIR HEARTS THE SEED OF FREEDOM. . . . . SP FREEDOM'S PLOW 124
- HOPING TO FIND THEIR FREEDOM. . . . SP FREEDOM'S PLOW 44
- GUARDING IN THEIR HEARTS THE SEED OF FREEDOM. . . . . SP FREEDOM'S PLOW 46

GREAT THOUGHTS IN THEIR DEEPEST HEARTS . . . . SP FREEDOM'S PLOW 148
THEN MAYBE FROM THEIR GRAVES IN ANZIO . . . . SP FREEDOM TRAIN 39
ENDOWED BY THEIR CREATOR . . . . . SP FREEDOM'S PLOW 92
BUT IN THEIR HEARTS THE SLAVES BELIEVED HIM, TOO. . . . . SP FREEDOM'S PLOW 97
ON THEIR KNEES. . . . . SP GARDEN 7
TO SCATTER STAR-DUST IN THEIR EYES. SP GRADUATION 24
THE FOLKS WITH NO TITLES IN FRONT OF THEIR NAMES . . . . SP IN EXPLANATION 1
FOLKS WITH NOT EVEN MISTER IN FRONT OF THEIR NAMES . . . . SP IN EXPLANATION 19
WITH NO TITLES IN FRONT OF THEIR NAMES. . . . . SP IN EXPLANATION 28
THE PEOPLE WITH NO TITLES IN FRONT OF THEIR NAMES . . . . SP IN EXPLANATION 40
IN FRONT OF THEIR NAMES. . . . . . SP IN EXPLANATION 61
AND FLOWERS LIFT THEIR HEADS, ... SP IN TIME SILVER 5
AND FOR YOUR LOVE SONG TONE THEIR RUMBLE DOWN. . . . . SP JUKE BOX LOVE 6
JUST MAYBE SHRUG THEIR SHOULDERS, SP LIKEWISE 15
AND DRIPPED THEIR JUICE . . . . . . SP MIDNIGHT DANCER 9
WITH THEIR SILVER SHANKS, ... SP MOONLIGHT NIGHT 4
ALL THEIR LIVES . . . . SP NEW YORKERS 8
WHEN THEY MEET THEIR ENDS. . . . . SP NIGHT FUNERAL 16
IT WAS ALL THEIR TEARS THAT MADE . SP NIGHT FUNERAL 42
SINCE THEIR DREAM HAS . . . . SP PASSING 15
WHEN SHE WORKED IN THEIR KITCHENS. SP RUBY BROWN 27
ON THEIR SHOE TIPS. . . . . SP SUMMER EVENING 9
GET OUT THEIR BIBS . . . . SP SUNDAY MORNING 10
BOWED THEIR HEADS TO CRY. . . . . . SP SYLVESTER'S BED 8
NUDGE THEIR DRAFTEE YEARS. . . . . SP TAG 4
WHO CARRY BEAUTIES IN THEIR HEARTS SP WATER-FRONT STR 7
THEIR GRASS WITH UNICORNS. . . . . AYM ASK YOUR MAMA 77
SCHOOLS ARE BETTER FOR THEIR CHILDREN $ . . . . AYM HORN OF PLENTY 24
OR SPORTS-WRITERS IN THEIR STORY. AYM IS IT TRUE? 31
DEAD OR LIVE THEIR GHOSTS CAST SHADOWS . . . . AYM SHADES OF PIG 6
THEIR BLOOD UPON THE WALL . . . . . PL BIRMINGHAM SUND 5
WOULD REDDEN WITH THEIR BLOOD . . . PL BIRMINGHAM SUND 13
WHO LEFT THEIR BLOOD UPON THAT WALL. PL BIRMINGHAM SUND 16
IN THEIR . . . . PL CORNER MEETING 8
PUT THEIR LAURELS ON YOUR BROW . . PL CROWNS GARLANDS 6
SITTING ON THEIR WIDE VERANDAS, . . PL CULTURAL EXCHNG 47
THEIR MASTER'S . . . . PL ELDERLY LEADERS 9
IN THEIR BIG CARS . . . . PL FLORIDA WORKERS 11
LET THINGS TAKE THEIR COURSE. . . . PL FREEDOM 11
TO SPROUT THEIR BITTER BARRIERS . . PL GEORGIA DUSK 11
THROUGH THEIR "FREEDOM" SIEVE. . . PL LUMUMBA'S GRAVE 8
HAVE MADE THEIR DOUGH. . . . . . . PL OFFICE BUILDING 5
WE PASSED THEIR GRAVES: . . . . . . PL PEACE 1
GLORIFY THEIR MILLION-DOLLAR WAYS PL PRIME 5
THEIR OWN SWEET TIME TO FLOWER . . PL SWEET WORDS RAC 2
OF THEIR PRISTINE HOUR . . . . . . PL SWEET WORDS RAC 6
THEY CHANGE THEIR MIND! . . . . . . PL WARNING 5

THEIVING 1

IN THESE LUSH AND THEIVING DAYS . . PL PRIME 3

THELONIOUS 1

(ANCIENT ALTAR OF THELONIOUS) . . . SP NEON SIGNS 5

THEM 50

I HATES THEM RINNEY YALLER GALS . . FC BLACK GAL 15
I'D SHO HAVE THEM BLUES. . . . . . FC MINNIE SINGS 20
ANSWERIN' THEM WANT-ADS' NOT NARY BIT O' FUN. . . . . NM BROKE 4
AFTER ALL THEM DOLLARS I GIVED HER THESE LAST TWO YEARS. . . . . . . NM BROKE 23
TRIED TO FIND ONE O' THEM LITTLE ELEVATOR AND SWITCHBOARD JOBS THEY USED . . . . NM BROKE 41
I CANNOT FIND THEM ANY MORE. . . . DK AFTR MNY SPRNGS 8
THAT I MAY WRAP THEM . . . . DK DREAM KEEPER 5
NO WONDER WE FIND THEM SUCH MARVELLOUS THINGS! . . . . DK FAIRIES 5
BEATING THEM WITH LAWS AND CLUBS AND BAYONETS AND BULLETS . . . . . . ANS KIDS WHO DIE 30
I WATCHED THEM MOVING, MOVING, . . ANS NEGRO GHETTO 5
WHO ARE ALL THEM PEOPLE . . . . . . ANS SISTER JOHNSON 9
WILL I MAKE THEM AGAIN, AND YET AGAIN? . . . . ANS SONG OF SPAIN 47
HOUSE IS SO QUIET! . . . LISTEN AT THEM MICE. . . . . SH BED TIME 12
TO KEEP THEM COLD MUDDY WATERS . . SH MISSISSIPPI LEV 17
FORGIVE THEM LIES! . . . . SH ONLY WOMAN BLUS 16
NOR THEM TWO DIAMOND RINGS . . . . SH PAY DAY 8
AND TAKE BACK ALL THEM THINGS WE HAD SH PAY DAY 12
TO SING ABOUT THE MEN WHO'VE DONE THEM WRONG - . . . . OWT JUICE JOINT 24
BUT NONE OF THEM PEOPLES . . . . . OWT LONESOME CORNER 7
HE GAVE THEM OF HIS BREAD. . . . . LHR BLD MARY'S SON 16
HE GAVE THEM TO DRINK OF HIS WINE. LHR BLD MARY'S SON 17
THEM THOUGHTS WOULD BUST MY HEAD - SP BLUES AT DAWN 4
MADE THEM THAT WAY. . . . . SP CAFE: 3 A.M. 8
LISTEN AT THEM LITTLE VARMINTS! . . SP CHILDREN'S RYME 4
THEM WHITE KIDS . . . . SP CHILDREN'S RYME 17
THEM BOTH AROUND . . . . SP COLLEGE FORMAL 10
NOR WRITE THEM DOWN ON PAPER. . . . SP FREEDOM'S PLOW 146
AND SOMETIMES ONLY BLUNDERINGLY EXPRESS THEM. . . . . SP FREEDOM'S PLOW 149
HALTINGLY AND STUMBLINGLY SAY THEM. SP FREEDOM'S PLOW 150
AND FAULTILY PUT THEM INTO PRACTICE. SP FREEDOM'S PLOW 151
THAT WHAT HE SAID WAS ALSO MEANT FOR THEM. . . . . SP FREEDOM'S PLOW 99
I'VE SEEN THEM COME DARK . . . . . SP GOOD MORNING 17
THEY CALL THEM, HEY GEORGE! . . . . SP IN EXPLANATION 12
HEAR THOSE WORDS AND SHOUT THEM BACK SP IN EXPLANATION 41
THEM COOL GREEN LEAVES . . . . . . SP LITTLE GRN TREE 13
ON THEM GOLDEN STREETS . . . . . . SP MADAM NUMBER WR 26
THEM OTHER GIRLS DO . . . . SP MADAM PHONE BIL 28
THEM TWO FINE CARS? . . . . SP NIGHT FUNERAL 4
THEM FLOWERS CAME . . . . SP NIGHT FUNERAL 13
TO THEM FOLKS THAT BROUGHT THE FLOWERS. . . . . SP NIGHT FUNERAL 40
ALL THEM FACES . . . . SP NIGHTMARE BOOGIE 7
AND ME OF THEM. . . . . SP ONE-WAY TICKET 22
FOR THEM POLES AND GREEKS . . . . . SP RELIEF 2
THEM LITTLE OLD MUTTS . . . . SP WARNING AUGMENT 9
INVESTIGATE THEM NEGRAS WHO . . . . AYM BIRD IN ORBIT 36
THEM WHITE KIDS . . . . PL CHILDREN'S RYME 7
WATCH THEM DROOP, WILT, FADE . . . PL CROWNS GARLANDS 10
TO NOURISH THEM. . . . . PL SLUM DREAMS 5
NOT HEAR THEM . . . . PL SWEET WORDS RAC 14
SLIPPING OUT FROM UNDER THEM . . . PL UNDERTOW 10

THEMSELVES 3

MINGLE THEMSELVES SOFTLY . . . . . SP AUNTSUE'S STORI 10
MINGLE THEMSELVES SOFTLY . . . . . SP AUNTSUE'S STORI 14
THEMSELVES MUST STRIKE . . . . . . PL FREDRK DOUGLASS 19

THEN 84

THEN LET'S . . . . WB CAT AND SAXOPHN 25
AND THEN . . . . WB POEME D'AUTOMNE 11
THEN THEY GOES AN' FINDS A YALLER GAL . . . . FC BLACK GAL 7
THEN OUT MA DOOR HE GOES. . . . . . FC BLACK GAL 12
AND THEN SOME. . . . . FC JAZZ BAND 20
THEN AT THE CLOSING HOUR . . . . . FC SPORT 7
INNER HEARTACHES AND LONELINESS TO THE IRONIC GAIETY OF THE MUSIC. THEN . . . . NM BIG-TIMER MOOD 10
THEN I DON'T HAVE TO THINK. . . . . NM BIG-TIMER POEM 64
HUMOROUS DEFIANCE. MELANCHOLY JAZZ. THEN DEFIANCE AGAIN FOLLOWED BY LOUD . . . . NM BLACK CLWN MOOD 2
JOY. A BURST OF MUSIC. STRUTTING AND DANCING. THEN SUDDEN SADNESS AGAIN. . . . . NM BLACK CLWN MOOD 3
THEN SADNESS AGAIN - . . . . NM BLACK CLWN POEM 33
LAUGH AT ME THEN. . . . . NM BLACK CLWN POEM 55
SO DE MAN SAY, "I'LL GET SOMEBODY ELSE, THEN, TO CLEAN." - . . . . NM BROKE 17
WE WERE SENT TO TRAINING CAMP, THEN OVERSEAS - . . . . NM COLORED SL POEM 5
AND BOWING HIS HEAD IN SHAME, BECOMES SUDDENLY FIERCE AND ANGRY. THEN HE . . . . NM COLORED SL MOOD 11
BLACK BOYS COULDN'T WORK THEN ANYWHERE LIKE THEY CAN . . . . . NM COLORED SL POEM 19
THEN HIS DARK FACE SMILED AT ME IN THE NIGHT - . . . . NM COLORED SL POEM 39
THEN I WOKE UP, AND THE DREAM WAS ENDED - . . . . NM COLORED SL POEM 48
TO BE WISE AND STRONG, THEN, STUDYING LONG, ... NM DARK YOUTH USA 16
WILL BE FORGOTTEN THEN . . . . . . ANS CHANT TOM MOONY 27
THEN I'LL GO. . . . . SH BLD PAWNBROKER 18
THEN THE PLACE WAS EMPTY. . . . . . SH DEATH IN HARLEM 124
THEN WHIP 'EM ALL NIGHT LONG. . . . SH HEY-HEY BLUES 8
THEN WHIP 'EM ALL NIGHT LONG. . . . SH HEY-HEY BLUES 10
AND THEN CUT DOWN DE LOG - . . . . SH ONLY WOMAN BLUS 10
THEN SHARE 'EM WITH ME - . . . . . JC HOW ABOUT DIXIE 7
THEN MAKE FINE SPEECHES . . . . . . JC HOW ABOUT DIXIE 15
MORE THAN SHIP THEN. . . . . JC TO CAPTAIN MULZ 62
LET THE WINDS RISE THEN! . . . . . JC TO CAPTAIN MULZ 71
THEN A SILENCE OVER LAUGHTER . . . FW DIMOUT IN HARLM 5
I WAS A BOY THEN. . . . . FW MAN 1
BUT I WAS A BOY THEN. . . . . FW MAN 10
THEN DROWSY AS THE RAIN . . . . . . OWT JUICE JOINT 45
THEN YOU'RE A DOPE . . . . SP ARGUMENT 6
BUT IT WAS THERE THEN. . . . . . . SP AS I GREW OLDER 3
AND THEN THE WALL ROSE, ... SP AS I GREW OLDER 7
THEN YOU KNOW A NEW DAY'S . . . . . SP BLACK MARIA 16
THEN WENT OFF AND LEFT HER. . . . . SP BLD FORTUNE TEL 23
THEN SHE STARTED IN TO LIE. . . . . SP BLD THE GYPSY 10
THEN A WHITE MAN . . . . SP BLUE BAYOU 11
THEN I STOOD OUT ON A PRAIRIE . . . SP CROSSING 15
THEN GOT PUT BACK WHEN WE COME NORTH. . . . . SP DEFERRED 5
THEN KIDS. . . . . SP DEFERRED 13
THEN REST AT COOL EVENING . . . . . SP DREAM VARIATION 5
THEN YOU KNOW THAT YOU HAVE TURNED SP FINAL CURVE 7
THERE WERE SLAVES THEN, TOO. . . . SP FREEDOM'S PLOW 105

THEN A MAN SAID: . . . . SP FREEDOM'S PLOW 109
THEN THE MIND STARTS SEEKING A WAY. SP FREEDOM'S PLOW 10
THEN THE HAND SEEKS OTHER HANDS TO
HELP. . . . . SP FREEDOM'S PLOW 20
THEN MAYBE FROM THEIR GRAVES IN
ANZIO . . . . SP FREEDOM TRAIN 59
THEN I'LL SHOUT, GLORY FOR THE . . SP FREEDOM TRAIN 63
HIS NAME WAS JEFFERSON. THERE WERE
SLAVES THEN. . . . . SP FREEDOM'S PLOW 96
UNTIL THEN . . . . SP GRADUATION 21
THEN. . . . . SP GRADUATION 29
AND THEN RUN? . . . . SP HARLEM 5
THEN. . . . . SP I, TOO 14
THEN I ADOPTED . . . . SP MADAM CHARTY CH 5
THAT WAS THEN! . . . . SP MADAM PHONE BIL 5
THEN TAKE CARE OF HER CHILDREN . . SP MADAM HER MADAM 7
DONE SINCE THEN? . . . . SP MADAM MINISTER 14
THEN WE BOXED 'EM. . . . . SP MADAM NUMBER WR 15
RIGHT THEN AND THERE . . . . . . SP MADAM MIGHT-HAV 19
THEN I CAN PLAY . . . . SP MADAM NUMBER WR 25
THEN I HAD A . . . . SP MADAM'S PAST HI 10
THEN MY FRIENDS! . . . . SP SUNDAY MORNING 14
OH, THEN! OH, THEN! . . . . SP SUNDAY MORNING 15
OH, THEN! OH, THEN! . . . . SP SUNDAY MORNING 15
THEN EVERYTHING WAS DARKNESS . . . SP SYLVESTER'S BED 27
I COULDN'T READ THEN. I COULDN'T
WRITE. . . . . SP THE NEGRO MOTHE 23
I HAD ONLY HOPE THEN, BUT NOW
THROUGH YOU. . . . . SP THE NEGRO MOTHE 33
HE PLAYED A FEW CHORDS THEN HE SANG
SOME MORE - . . . . SP THE WEARY BLUES 24
THEN, IT WILL BE TRUE. . . . . . . SP THEME FOR ENG B 5
I WENT TO SCHOOL THERE, THEN DURHAM,
THEN HERE . . . . SP THEME FOR ENG B 8
I WENT TO SCHOOL THERE, THEN DURHAM,
THEN HERE . . . . SP THEME FOR ENG B 8
THROUGH A PARK, THEN I CROSS ST.
NICHOLAS. . . . . SP THEME FOR ENG B 12
THEN . . . . SP WINE-O 4
THEN BEFORE YOU CAN WALK . . . . . PL CROWNS GARLANDS 8
AND THEN RUN? . . . . PL DREAM DEFERRED 5
(NO?) THEN . . . . PL FINAL CALL 36
WHAT HAPPENED THEN? . . . . PL GHOSTS OF 1619 13
OF THEN? . . . . PL GHOSTS OF 1619 30
AND THEN THEY KICKED ME . . . . . PL KU KLUX 15
AND THEN SO QUICKLY WILT . . . . . PL SWEET WORDS RAC 3
THEN MOP AND I MOP. . . . . PL WAR 13

THERE 137

JUDGE WAS SETTIN' THERE. . . . . . FC BLD OF SIN MARY 2
BUT WHEN I GOT THERE . . . . FC DEATH DO DIRTY 26
NOBODY THERE WAS GOOD TO ME. . . . FC GYPSY MAN 12
SHO, THERE MUST BE PEACE. . . . . . FC MOAN 16
AN' THERE SHE SETS A CRYIN' . . . . FC NEW CABARET GRL 17
AND THERE IS NO MUSIC AT ALL . . . FC SPORT 9
NOT WANTED HERE; NOT NEEDED THERE - NM BLACK CLWN POEM 40
'CAUSE 'FORE YOU GETS THERE, TEN
THOUSAND AND ONE . . . . NM BROKE 5
YOU ALL OUT THERE LAUGHIN', BUT THAT
AIN'T NO JOKE - . . . . NM BROKE 10
AND DE MAN COME TELLIN' ME I BETTER
GET THERE AT FO'. . . . . NM BROKE 13
'CAUSE I'M JUST DYIN' TO TAKE ON
THAT THERE MARRIAGE YOKE. . . . . NM BROKE 77
MAY ACCOMPANY THE RECITATION -
ECHOING SOFTLY, OVER THERE,
THERE'S A ROSE . . . . NM COLORED SL MOOD 4
DIDN'T HAVE ANY SCHOOLS; AND THERE
WERE ALL SORTS OF . . . . NM COLORED SL POEM 25
WHEN WE GOT THROUGH FIGHTING, OVER
THERE, AND DYING? . . . . NM COLORED SL POEM 34
AND I SAW HIM STANDING THERE,
STRAIGHT AND TALL. . . . . NM COLORED SL POEM 37
OVER THERE . . . . NM COLORED SL POEM 52
TO ALL THE WORLD THERE GOES . . . . DK ALABAMA EARTH 7
WHAT IS THERE WITHIN THIS BEGGAR LAD DK BEGGAR BOY 1
MAYBE, NOW, THERE WILL BE NO
MONUMENT FOR YOU . . . . ANC KIDS WHO DIE 38
A HUMAN GETS LONESOME IF THERE AIN'T
TWO. . . . . SH BED TIME 15
THERE AIN'T NO REASON . . . . . . SH BLD THE KILLER 21
AND THERE WAS BESSIE . . . . SH DEATH IN HARLEM 95
I WOULD MAKE A FIRE BUT THERE AIN'T
NO WOOD. . . . . SH SUPPER TIME 4
ANYHOW, AWAY OFF THERE. . . . . . . JC GOOD MORN STLIN 52
TO BE WON OVER THERE. . . . . . . JC HOW ABOUT DIXIE 22
THERE WAS AN OLD CROW BY THE NAME OF
JIM. . . . . JC JIM CROW'S LAST 1
THERE IS A BITTER RIVER . . . . . JC THE BITTER RIVR 2
THERE IS A BITTER RIVER . . . . . JC THE BITTER RIVR 6
MIXED WITH THE HOPES THAT ARE
DROWNED THERE . . . . JC THE BITTER RIVR 14
BUT THERE ARE THOSE WHO STILL HOLD
OUT . . . . JC TO CAPTAIN MULZ 10
AND THERE ARE THOSE WHO FIGHT . . . JC TO CAPTAIN MULZ 13
THERE ARE THOSE, TOO, WHO FOR SO
LONG . . . . JC TO CAPTAIN MULZ 16
WE'VE PUT A CAPTAIN ON THAT SHIP'S
BRIDGE THERE. . . . . JC TO CAPTAIN MULZ 43
THERE IS A CREW OF MANY RACES, TOO. JC TO CAPTAIN MULZ 47
ABOUT HERE AND THERE - . . . . . . FW BORDER LINE 6
IS THERE PEACE . . . . FW CONVENT 2
FOR SURE THERE GREW FLOWERS . . . . FW GIRL 14
SUDDENLY THE EARTH WAS THERE. . . . FW HARLEM DANCE HA 3
THAT THERE HUNG . . . . FW HEART 10
FROM HERE TO THERE. . . . . FW SAILING DATE 12
THERE. . . . . FW SAILING DATE 21
I SAT THERE SINGING HER . . . . . . FW SONGS 1
THERE ARE . . . . FW SONGS 7
THERE WHERE NOTHING . . . . FW THERE 5
AND KEPT HER THERE. . . . . OWT BLD MARGE POLIT 18
WE'LL ALL BOARD THERE. . . . . . . OWT BOARDING HOUSE 4
GO OUT THERE. . . . . OWT BOARDING HOUSE 12
YOU HAVE TO GET THERE EARLY . . . . OWT JITNEY 56
THERE IS A GIN MILL ON THE AVENUE OWT JUICE JOINT 1
THEY SELL BEER FOAMING THERE IN
MUG-LIKE CUPS. . . . . OWT JUICE JOINT 5
I STOOD THERE FEELIN' BLUE - . . . OWT LONESOME CORNER 2
THE MAN IS THERE! . . . . OWT RAID 11
UP THERE IN THE SKY. . . . . OWT REQUEST REQUIEM 4
CAUSE THERE AIN'T A GOOD MAN . . . OWT REQUEST REQUIEM 7
BUT THE WIND BLOWS THERE. . . . . . OWT RESTRICTIVE 15
THERE AIN'T NO WAY FOR ME . . . . . OWT YESTERDAY TODAY 7
THERE WAS FASTING IN THE STREETS AND
JOY. . . . . LHR BLD MARY'S SON 3
THERE WERE SOME WHO COULD NOT HEAR. LHR BLD MARY'S SON 11
AND HE KNELT THERE TO PRAY. . . . . LHR BLD MARY'S SON 23
THAT THERE SHOULD BE A BARREN GARDEN SP A HOUSE IN TAOS 16
BUT THAT THERE SHOULD BE THREE
BARREN HEARTS . . . . SP A HOUSE IN TAOS 19
THERE COMES THIS SONG . . . . . . SP AFRO-AMER FRAG 16
FOR WHICH THERE AIN'T NO HOPE. . . SP ARGUMENT 7
BUT IT WAS THERE THEN. . . . . . . SP AS I GREW OLDER 3
THERE AIN'T NO GOOD LEFT . . . . . SP BAD LUCK CARD 5
THERE WASN'T A TRACE . . . . SP BLD FORTUNE TEL 27
OVER THERE? . . . . SP CAFE: 3 A.M. 10
THERE IS TWO THOUSAND CHILDREN . . SP CHILDREN'S RYME 10
(A CAPITAL LETTER THERE. . . . . . SP CONSIDER ME 13
MY FRIENDS WAS RIGHT THERE WITH ME SP CROSSING 21
BUT DEAD IN THERE. . . . . SP DEAD IN THERE 11
THERE AIN'T NO STOVE - . . . . . . SP DEFERRED 19
YOU WERE NOT THERE WITH ME! . . . . SP DREAM 5
BUT YOU WERE NOT THERE AT ALL! . . SP DREAM 14
AND THERE IS NO AIR . . . . SP DRUM 10
I WONDER IS THERE NOWHERE A . . . . SP EARLY EVENING 23
THERE ARE . . . . SP END 1
THERE IS NEITHER LIGHT . . . . . . SP END 7
THERE IS NO DOOR! . . . . SP END 10
BUT THERE AIN'T NO EAGLE . . . . . SP FACT 3
THE STRENGTH THERE. . . . . SP FREEDOM'S PLOW 7
THE WILL THERE TO BUILD. . . . . . SP FREEDOM'S PLOW 8
THERE WERE SLAVES THEN, TOO. . . . SP FREEDOM'S PLOW 105
I HOPE THERE AIN'T NO JIM CROW ON
THE FREEDOM TRAIN. . . . . SP FREEDOM TRAIN 11
THE EYES SEE THERE MATERIALS FOR
BUILDING. . . . . SP FREEDOM'S PLOW 15
IS THERE BALLOT BOXES ON THE FREEDOM
TRAIN? . . . . SP FREEDOM TRAIN 20
SOME THERE WERE, AS ALWAYS. . . . . SP FREEDOM'S PLOW 132
THERE WAS LIGHT WHEN THE BATTLE
CLOUDS ROLLED AWAY. . . . . SP FREEDOM'S PLOW 139
THERE WAS A GREAT WOODED LAND, . . SP FREEDOM'S PLOW 140
BUT THE WORD WAS THERE ALWAYS: . . SP FREEDOM'S PLOW 47
BUT THERE IS, SOMEWHERE THERE, . . SP FREEDOM'S PLOW 153
BUT THERE IS, SOMEWHERE THERE, . . SP FREEDOM'S PLOW 153
WHERE THERE NEVER WAS NO JIM CROW
SIGNS NOWHERE. . . . . SP FREEDOM TRAIN 54
NOW IT IS ME HERE, AND YOU THERE. SP FREEDOM'S PLOW 85
HIS NAME WAS JEFFERSON. THERE WERE
SLAVES THEN. . . . . SP FREEDOM'S PLOW 96
TAKE ME THERE. . . . . SP ISLAND 8
THERE - . . . . SP KID IN THE PARK 11
AN' I AIN'T GOIN' THERE TO SWIM; . SP LAMENT OVER LOV 8
AIN'T GOIN' THERE TO SWIM. . . . . SP LAMENT OVER LOV 10
AND I'M GOIN' THERE TO THINK ABOUT
HIM. . . . . SP LAMENT OVER LOV 12
I STOOD THERE AND I HOLLERED! . . . SP LIFE IS FINE 16
I STOOD THERE AND I CRIED! . . . . SP LIFE IS FINE 17
HIGH UP THERE! . . . . SP LIFE IS FINE 21
THE LETTER THAT I FOUND THERE . . . SP LITTLE OLD LETT 3
RIGHT THEN AND THERE . . . . SP MADAM MIGHT-HAV 19
AND THERE WAS ONLY THIS CORNER . . SP MAGNOLIA FLOWER 6
THERE OUGHT TO BE MAGNOLIAS . . . . SP MAGNOLIA FLOWER 10
WHERE THERE AIN'T BEEN NO LIGHT. . SP MOTHER TO SON 13
GIT ON BACK THERE IN THE NIGHT. . . SP MULATTO 37
SET THERE. . . . . SP NEIGHBOR 24
AND THERE AIN'T NO KU KLUX . . . . SP NOT A MOVIE 14
AND AIN'T THERE ANY JOY IN THIS
TOWN? . . . . SP RUBY BROWN 15
A CHANCE WIND BLOWS THERE. . . . . SP SONG BILLIE HOL 13
I HAD NOTHING, BACK THERE IN THE
NIGHT. . . . . SP THE NEGRO MOTHE 24
ALL YOU DARK CHILDREN IN THE WORLD
OUT THERE. . . . . SP THE NEGRO MOTHE 35

AND THERE ARE THOSE WHO FIGHT . . . JC TO CAPTAIN MULZ 13
THERE ARE THOSE, TOO, WHO FOR SO
LONG . . . . JC TO CAPTAIN MULZ 16
WE'VE PUT A CAPTAIN ON THAT SHIP'S
BRIDGE THERE. . . . . JC TO CAPTAIN MULZ 43
THERE IS A CREW OF MANY RACES, TOO. JC TO CAPTAIN MULZ 47
ABOUT HERE AND THERE - . . . . . . FW BORDER LINE 6
IS THERE PEACE . . . . FW CONVENT 2
FOR SURE THERE GREW FLOWERS . . . . FW GIRL 14
SUDDENLY THE EARTH WAS THERE. . . . FW HARLEM DANCE HA 3
THAT THERE HUNG . . . . FW HEART 10
FROM HERE TO THERE. . . . . FW SAILING DATE 12
THERE. . . . . FW SAILING DATE 21
I SAT THERE SINGING HER . . . . . . FW SONGS 1
THERE ARE . . . . FW SONGS 7
THERE WHERE NOTHING . . . . FW THERE 5
AND KEPT HER THERE. . . . . OWT BLO MARGE POLIT 18
WE'LL ALL BOARD THERE. . . . . . . OWT BOARDING HOUSE 4
GO OUT THERE. . . . . OWT BOARDING HOUSE 12
YOU HAVE TO GET THERE EARLY . . . . OWT JITNEY 56
THERE IS A GIN MILL ON THE AVENUE OWT JUICE JOINT 1
THEY SELL BEER FOAMING THERE IN
MUG-LIKE CUPS. . . . . OWT JUICE JOINT 5
I STOOD THERE FEELIN' BLUE - . . . OWT LONESOME CORNER 2
THE MAN IS THERE! . . . . OWT RAID 11
UP THERE IN THE SKY. . . . . OWT REQUEST REQUIEM 4
CAUSE THERE AIN'T A GOOD MAN . . . OWT REQUEST REQUIEM 7
BUT THE WIND BLOWS THERE. . . . . . OWT RESTRICTIVE 15
THERE AIN'T NO WAY FOR ME . . . . . OWT YESTERDAY TODAY 7
THERE WAS FASTING IN THE STREETS AND
JOY. . . . . LHR BLD MARY'S SON 3
THERE WERE SOME WHO COULD NOT HEAR. LHR BLD MARY'S SON 11
AND HE KNELT THERE TO PRAY. . . . . LHR BLD MARY'S SON 23
THAT THERE SHOULD BE A BARREN GARDEN SP A HOUSE IN TAOS 18
BUT THAT THERE SHOULD BE THREE
BARREN HEARTS . . . . SP A HOUSE IN TAOS 19
THERE COMES THIS SONG . . . . SP AFRO-AMER FRAG 16
FOR WHICH THERE AIN'T NO HOPE. . . SP ARGUMENT 7
BUT IT WAS THERE THEN. . . . . . . SP AS I GREW OLDER 3
THERE AIN'T NO GOOD LEFT . . . . . SP BAD LUCK CARD 5
THERE WASN'T A TRACE . . . . SP BLD FORTUNE TEL 27
OVER THERE? . . . . SP CAFE: 3 A.M. 10
THERE IS TWO THOUSAND CHILDREN . . SP CHILDREN'S RYME 10
(A CAPITAL LETTER THERE. . . . . . SP CONSIDER ME 13
MY FRIENDS WAS RIGHT THERE WITH ME SP CROSSING 21
BUT DEAD IN THERE. . . . . SP DEAD IN THERE 11
THERE AIN'T NO STOVE - . . . . . . SP DEFERRED 13
YOU WERE NOT THERE WITH ME! . . . . SP DREAM 5
BUT YOU WERE NOT THERE AT ALL! . . SP DREAM 14
AND THERE IS NO AIR . . . . SP DRUM 10
I WONDER IS THERE NOWHERE A . . . . SP EARLY EVENING 23
THERE ARE . . . . SP END 1
THERE IS NEITHER LIGHT . . . . . . SP END 7
THERE IS NO DOOR! . . . . SP END 10
BUT THERE AIN'T NO EAGLE . . . . . SP FACT 3
THE STRENGTH THERE. . . . . SP FREEDOM'S PLOW 7
THE WILL THERE TO BUILD. . . . . . SP FREEDOM'S PLOW 8
THERE WERE SLAVES THEN, TOO. . . . SP FREEDOM'S PLOW 105
I HOPE THERE AIN'T NO JIM CROW ON
THE FREEDOM TRAIN. . . . . SP FREEDOM TRAIN 11
THE EYES SEE THERE MATERIALS FOR
BUILDING. . . . . SP FREEDOM'S PLOW 15
IS THERE BALLOT BOXES ON THE FREEDOM
TRAIN? . . . . SP FREEDOM TRAIN 20
SOME THERE WERE, AS ALWAYS. . . . . SP FREEDOM'S PLOW 132
THERE WAS LIGHT WHEN THE BATTLE
CLOUDS ROLLED AWAY. . . . . . . SP FREEDOM'S PLOW 139
THERE WAS A GREAT WOODED LAND. . . SP FREEDOM'S PLOW 140
BUT THE WORD WAS THERE ALWAYS: . . SP FREEDOM'S PLOW 47
BUT THERE IS, SOMEWHERE THERE. . . SP FREEDOM'S PLOW 153
BUT THERE IS, SOMEWHERE THERE. . . SP FREEDOM'S PLOW 153
WHERE THERE NEVER WAS NO JIM CROW
SIGNS NOWHERE. . . . . SP FREEDOM TRAIN 54
NOW IT IS ME HERE, AND YOU THERE. SP FREEDOM'S PLOW 85
HIS NAME WAS JEFFERSON. THERE WERE
SLAVES THEN. . . . . SP FREEDOM'S PLOW 96
TAKE ME THERE. . . . . SP ISLAND 8
THERE - . . . . SP KID IN THE PARK 11
AN' I AIN'T GOIN' THERE TO SWIM; . SP LAMENT OVER LOV 8
AIN'T GOIN' THERE TO SWIM. . . . . SP LAMENT OVER LOV 10
AND I'M GOIN' THERE TO THINK ABOUT
HIM. . . . . SP LAMENT OVER LOV 12
I STOOD THERE AND I HOLLERED! . . . SP LIFE IS FINE 16
I STOOD THERE AND I CRIED! . . . . SP LIFE IS FINE 17
HIGH UP THERE! . . . . SP LIFE IS FINE 21
THE LETTER THAT I FOUND THERE . . . SP LITTLE OLD LETT 3
RIGHT THEN AND THERE . . . . SP MADAM NIGHT-HAV 19
AND THERE WAS ONLY THIS CORNER . . SP MAGNOLIA FLOWER 6
THERE OUGHT TO BE MAGNOLIAS . . . . SP MAGNOLIA FLOWER 10
WHERE THERE AIN'T BEEN NO LIGHT. . SP MOTHER TO SON 13
GIT ON BACK THERE IN THE NIGHT. . . SP MULATTO 37
SET THERE. . . . . SP NEIGHBOR 24
AND THERE AIN'T NO KU KLUX . . . . SP NOT A MOVIE 14
AND AIN'T THERE ANY JOY IN THIS
TOWN? . . . . SP RUBY BROWN 15
A CHANGE WIND BLOWS THERE. . . . . SP SONG BILLIE HOL 13
I HAD NOTHING, BACK THERE IN THE
NIGHT. . . . . SP THE NEGRO MOTHE 24

ALL YOU DARK CHILDREN IN THE WORLD
OUT THERE. . . . . SP THE NEGRO MOTHE 35
I WENT TO SCHOOL THERE, THEN DURHAM,
THEN HERE . . . . SP THEME FOR ENG B 8
CAUSE THERE AIN'T NO SENSE . . . . SP WAKE 3
THE SPRING IS NOT SO BEAUTIFUL THERE
- . . . . SP WATER-FRONT STR 1
THE SPRING IS NOT SO BEAUTIFUL THERE
. . . . SP WATER-FRONT STR 5
THERE SOUTHERN CONFERENCE? . . . . AYM BIRD IN ORBIT 31
HOW I GOT THERE I DON'T KNOW. . . . AYM GOSPEL CHA-CHA 40
UP THERE ON THAT HILL . . . . AYM GOSPEL CHA-CHA 39
ALREADY THERE WAS THREE - . . . . . AYM GOSPEL CHA-CHA 30
GOT THERE! YES, I MADE IT! . . . . AYM HORN OF PLENTY 36
THERE ARE SO MANY CHURCHES . . . . PL BIBLE BELT 5
TRYIN' TO GET UP THERE - . . . . . PL DOWN WHERE I AM 6
YOU'RE A-STANDIN' THERE . . . . . . PL KU KLUX 11
STILL - THERE IS ME! . . . . PL LITTLE SNG HOUS 26
AND IT'S MARKED THERE. . . . . . . PL LUMUMBA'S GRAVE 21
BUT THERE AIN'T NO BACK . . . . . . PL MERRY-GO-ROUND 12
THE DEAD MEN THERE. . . . . PL PEACE 2
THERE TO PURCHASE A SLAVE. . . . . PL SLAVE 3
ARE THERE - . . . . PL SLUM DREAMS 7
BECAUSE YOU ARE THERE. . . . . . . PL WAR 17
OUT THERE WHERE . . . . PL WITHOUT BENEFIT 10
THERE ARE WORDS LIKE FREEDOM . . . PL WORDS LIKE FREE 1
THERE ARE WORDS LIKE LIBERTY . . . PL WORDS LIKE FREE 5

THERESA 1

THERESA BELLE ALETHA . . . . SP SUMMER EVENING 18

THERE'RE 1

YET THERE'RE BARS . . . . SP GOOD MORNING 24

THERE'S 32

MAY ACCOMPANY THE RECITATION -
ECHOING SOFTLY, OVER THERE,
THERE'S A ROSE . . . . NM COLORED SL MOOD 4
FOR HERE IN THE SOUTH THERE'S NO
VOTES AND NO RIGHT. . . . . . . NM COLORED SL POEM 46
THERE'S NOTHING MORE TO SAY. . . . OK I LOVED FRIEND 3
(THERE'S NEVER BEEN EQUALITY FOR ME, ANS LET AMERICA BE 15
IF THERE'S ANYBODY ON THIS EARTH,
JUDGE. . . . . SH BRIEF ENCOUNTER 11
THERE'S HANGING MOSS . . . . FW CAROLINA CABIN 1
BUT HERE THERE'S PEACE . . . . . . FW CAROLINA CABIN 18
THERE'S A NEW YOUNG MOON . . . . . FW NEW MOON 1
THERE'S A SPRIGHTLY YOUNG MOON . . FW NEW MOON 3
THERE'S A HALF-SHY YOUNG MOON . . . FW NEW MOON 5
THERE'S MANY ANOTHER WOMAN . . . . OWT HONEY BABE 13
TONIGHT THERE'S PREACHING! . . . . OWT JITNEY 35
RECKON THERE'S NO CHARGE . . . . . SP BLD OF THE MAN 23
THERE'S BEEN AN EAGLE ON A NICKEL, SP FACT 1
WHY THERE'S JIM CROW STATIONS FOR
THE FREEDOM TRAIN? . . . . SP FREEDOM TRAIN 32
SO, NATURALLY, THERE'S TROUBLE . . SP IN EXPLANATION 30
THERE'S RATS IN THE CELLAR, ... SP MADAM RENT MAN 17
THERE'S NOTHING FOREIGN . . . . . . SP MADAM'S CALLING 17
THERE'S A CERTAIN . . . . SP SAME IN BLUES 5
THERE'S LIABLE . . . . SP SAME IN BLUES 28
THERE'S LIABLE TO BE CONFUSION . . SP SAME IN BLUES 31
(NOT KNOWING THERE'S A STEINWAY
BIGGER, BIGGER) . . . . SP TO BE SOMEBODY 3
THERE'S ALWAYS ROOM. . . . . SP TO BE SOMEBODY 21
WHEN THERE'S A UNICORN? . . . . . . AYM ASK YOUR MAMA 60
THERE'S NO WAY NOT TO LOSE. . . . . AYM ODE TO DINAH 114
THERE'S A BAR WITH WINDOWS FROSTED AYM ODE TO DINAH 24
THERE'S . . . . PL ANGOLA QUESTION 19
SOMETIMES THERE'S A WIND IN THE
GEORGIA DUSK . . . . PL GEORGIA DUSK 1
SOMETIMES THERE'S BLOOD IN THE
GEORGIA DUSK . . . . PL GEORGIA DUSK 5
AND THERE'S A NEW TAX ON CIGARETTES
- . . . . PL HARLEM 11
THERE'S A JIM CROW CAR. . . . . . . PL MERRY-GO-ROUND 10
THERE'S A WORLD TO GAIN. . . . . . PL QUESTION ANSWER 12

THESE 23

TILL THESE LICKER-HEADED ROUNDERS FC LISTEN HERE 11
AFTER ALL THEM DOLLARS I GIVED HER
THESE LAST TWO YEARS. . . . . . NM BROKE 23
ALL THESE YEARS YOU SAY YOU BEEN
WORKIN' HERE? . . . . NM BROKE 38
THESE WORDS ARE GENTLY SPOKEN: . . OK ALABAMA EARTH 11
ALL, ALL THE STRETCH OF THESE GREAT
GREEN STATES - . . . . ANS LET AMERICA BE 85
I SIMPLY RAISE THESE QUESTIONS . . JC BLACK MAN SPEAK 21
THAT SAILS THESE DANGEROUS SEAS - JC TO CAPTAIN MULZ 40
BUT MORE THAN THESE. . . . . JC TO CAPTAIN MULZ 45
SOME OF THESE DAYS . . . . OWT BOARDING HOUSE 7
THESE STEPS IS BROKEN DOWN. . . . . SP BLD LANDLORD 6
THESE MISSISSIPPI TOWNS AIN'T . . . SP BOUND NO'TH BLS 23
SOME OF THESE YOUNG ONES IS CERT'LY
BAD - . . . . SP CHILDREN'S RYME 17
CHILE, THESE STEPS IS HARD TO CLIMB. SP DIME 1
LAWD, THESE THINGS WE WOMEN . . . . SP EARLY EVENING 21
THE MIND SEEKS A WAY TO OVERCOME
THESE OBSTACLES. . . . . SP FREEDOM'S PLOW 17
ALL THESE HANDS MADE AMERICA. . . . SP FREEDOM'S PLOW 59

TO ALL THE ENEMIES OF THESE GREAT WORDS: . . . . SP FREEDOM'S PLOW 186
AMONG THESE LIFE, LIBERTY . . . . . SP FREEDOM'S PLOW 94
IN THESE OUR TIMES . . . . SP IN EXPLANATION 59
WHAT MAKES THESE CHARITY . . . . . SP MADAM CHARTY CH 9
I DON'T FOOL WITH THESE YOUNG GIRLS. SP PREFERENCE 3
IF THESE WHITE FOLKS WANT TO GO AHEAD . . . . SP RELIEF 12
I'LL NEVER DRY THESE TEARS. . . . . SP WIDOW WOMAN 18
NOT THESE DAYS. . . . . AYM ODE TO DINAH 37
THE HEADS ON THESE TWO QUARTERS . . AYM SHOW FARE PLESE 26
OF THESE THREE. . . . . AYM SHOW FARE PLESE 31
THESE DARK GHOSTS TO TAUNT YOU - . PL GHOSTS OF 1619 3
IN THESE LUSH AND THEIVING DAYS . . PL PRIME 3

THESE-HERE 1

IS I MARRIED? NO. ALL THESE-HERE GIRLS UP NORTH IS TOO LIGHT. . . NM BROKE 70

THEY 163

THEY LAUGH. . . . . WB BLUES FANTASY 5
THEY SAY A JAZZ-BAND'S GAY. . . . . WB CABARET 2
THEY DROVE ME OUT OF THE FOREST. . WB LAMENT DARK PEO 5
THEY TOOK ME AWAY FROM THE JUNGLES. WB LAMENT DARK PEO 6
GO WHERE THEY WILL PAY YOU WELL . . WB TO DARK MERCEDE 7
THEY SAY SHE DIED, - . . . . WB YOUNG BRIDE 1
THEY SAY SHE DIED OF GRIEF . . . . WB YOUNG BRIDE 3
SO THEY SAY. . . . . WB YOUNG PROSTITUT 5
MEN TAKES ALL THEY CAN FROM ME . . FC BLACK GAL 6
THEN THEY GOES AN' FINDS A YALLER GAL . . . . FC BLACK GAL 7
THEY CALLED HIM DO DIRTY . . . . . FC DEATH DO DIRTY 6
AND FORGET THAT THEY LYIN' . . . . NM BIG-TIMER POEM 67
WHEN THEY CALLIN' ME HONEY. . . . . NM BIG-TIMER POEM 68
UP AND DOWN, AND THEY JUST AIN'T NO JOBS IN THIS MAN'S TOWN. . . . . NM BROKE 3
UM-MM! SIGN HERE SAYS THEY WANTS SOMEBODY TO SHOVEL COAL. . . . . NM BROKE 28
TRIED TO FIND ONE O' THEM LITTLE ELEVATOR AND SWITCHBOARD JOBS THEY USED . . . . NM BROKE 41
BUT THEY GIVIN' 'EM TO SCHOOL BOYS NOW AND PAYIN' JUST ABOUT HALF. NM BROKE 43
AND DE MAN COME TELLIN' ME THEY AIN'T HIRIN' NO MO' COLORED - JUST WHITE. . . . . NM BROKE 45
THEY TOLD US AMERICA WOULD KNOW NO BLACK OR WHITE: . . . . NM COLORED SL POEM 11
BLACK BOYS COULDN'T WORK THEN ANYWHERE LIKE THEY CAN . . . . . NM COLORED SL POEM 19
IT'S A LIE! IT'S A LIE! EVERY WORD THEY SAID. . . . . NM COLORED SL POEM 44
IN AUTUMN THEY DIE AND ARE BLOWN AWAY. . . . . DK AUTUMN THOUGHT 2
THEY DON'T HURT MA FEET, ... DK DRESSED UP 10
THEY MAKE RAINBOW WINGS. . . . . . DK FAIRIES 4
IN THE DARK THEY FELL A-CRYING . . DK IRISH WAKE 1
HAPPY THEY WERE HERE. . . . . . . DK IRISH WAKE 8
THEY KNOW . . . . DK SEA CHARM 4
THEY KNOW . . . . DK SEA CHARM 7
LIKE A MIGHTY HEART-BEAT AS THEY COME? . . . . SL SCOTTSBORO 8
THEY SWEEP THE EARTH - . . . . . . ANS A NEW SONG 46
THEY NEVER SAW THE HIGH SHERIFF'S EYES . . . . ANS BLD OZZIE POWEL 19
DON'T THEY, OZIE POWELL? . . . . . ANS BLD OZZIE POWEL 22
EXCEPT THAT THEY BE MADE FOR US . . ANS SONG OF SPAIN 64
OH, THEY NABBED ARABELLA . . . . . SH DEATH IN HARLEM 131
KNOWIN THEY CAN BUY A DOZEN COLORED PLACES. . . . . SH DEATH IN HARLEM 61
THEY LOVED ONE ANOTHER TILL . . . . SH DEATH IN HARLEM 39
CAUSE THEY TOLD ME DE NORTH WAS FINE. . . . . SH EVENIN' BLUES 2
CAUSE THEY TOLD ME DE NORTH WAS FINE. . . . . SH EVENIN' BLUES 4
HOW DE BLUES THEY COME TO BE. . . . SH EVENIN' BLUES 20
HOW DE BLUES THEY COME TO BE - . . SH EVENIN' BLUES 22
THEY SAY YOUR SWEET MAMA . . . . . SH SHAKESPEARE 7
THEY CUT YOU . . . . SH STATEMENT 2
EVERY WAY THEY IS. . . . . SH STATEMENT 3
THEY OUGHT TO BE SOME NOISE. . . . SH SUNDAY 11
THEY OUGHT TO BE LIKE ME SETTING HERE - FEELING GLAD! . . . . . . SH SUNDAY 15
THEY CALLED OUT THE KLAN. . . . . . JC BLD SAM SOLOMON 41
THEY HAD A PARADE. . . . . JC BLD SAM SOLOMON 42
THEY BURN FREEDOM. . . . . JC FREEDOM 3
THEY IMPRISON FREEDOM. . . . . . . JC FREEDOM 6
THEY LYNCH FREEDOM. . . . . JC FREEDOM 9
THEY ROAR FOR ME - . . . . JC GOOD MORN STLIN 19
THEY WERE GLAD. . . . . JC GOOD MORN STLIN 39
AND THEY . . . . JC GOOD MORN STLIN 46
THEY LIKED HIM SO WELL THEY COULDN'T STAND . . . . JC JIM CROW'S LAST 3
THEY LIKED HIM SO WELL THEY COULDN'T STAND . . . . JC JIM CROW'S LAST 3
THE THINGS THEY MADE, NOR THEIR OWN LIVES - . . . . JC TO CAPTAIN MULZ 21
THEY HAVE FOUND THEIR HOUR. . . . . JC TO CAPTAIN MULZ 24
BUT THEY ALL BRING REST. . . . . . FW EXITS 4
THEY ALL BRING PEACE . . . . FW EXITS 5
THEY ALL BRING REST . . . . FW EXITS 8
AT FIRST THEY ARE NICE TO HIM, . . FW MIGRATION 5
BUT FINALLY THEY TAUNT HIM . . . . FW MIGRATION 6
BUT IF THEY WERE BLOOD, MOTHER - . FW WHEN ARMIES PAS 14
THEY KILLED A COLORED SOLDIER! . . OWT BLD MARGE POLIT 13
THEY TAKEN MARGIE TO JAIL . . . . . OWT BLD MARGE POLIT 17
THEY DIDN'T KILL THE SOLDIER, . . . OWT BLD MARGE POLIT 42
NAW! BUT THEY TRIED! . . . . OWT BLD MARGE POLIT 45
THEY SELL BEER FOAMING THERE IN MUG-LIKE CUPS. . . . . OWT JUICE JOINT 5
OF WHISKEY AS THEY START OUT FOR A BALL. . . . . OWT JUICE JOINT 8
THEY HARDLY TAKE GOD BY SURPRISE. LHR ACCEPTANCE 4
MEN WHO KNEW NOT WHAT THEY DID . . LHR BLD MARY'S SON 6
SO THEY BUILT A CROSS . . . . LHR BLD MARY'S SON 13
THEY MADE A CROSS . . . . LHR BLD MARY'S SON 27
THEY THOUGHT THEY SAW . . . . LHR PASTORAL 2
THEY THOUGHT THEY SAW . . . . LHR PASTORAL 2
THEY MISTOOK THE GENTLE DEW. . . . LHR PASTORAL 5
WHEN THEY LET ME DOWN. . . . . . . SP AS BEFITS A MAN 13
BUT THAT THEY CAME . . . . SP AUNTSUE'S STORI 21
LIKE THEY TRY TO DO YOU BAD. . . . SP BOUND NO'TH BLS 18
THEY DON'T KICK . . . . SP COMMENT ON CURB 2
I EXPECT THEY DO - . . . . SP COMMENT ON CURB 5
CAUSE THEY TREAT ME MEAN - . . . . SP CORA 5
THEY ALWAYS TREAT ME MEAN. . . . . SP CORA 7
(WHEN YOU'RE NO GOOD FOR DOUGH THEY GO.) . . . . SP DANCER 20
THEY EVEN GOT A SEGREGATED LANE. . SP FREEDOM TRAIN 27
BUT MAYBE THEY EXPLAINS IT ON THE SP FREEDOM TRAIN 35
THEY BEGAN TO BUILD OUR LAND. . . . SP FREEDOM'S PLOW 40
THE FREEDOM THAT THEY CARRYIN' ON THIS FREEDOM TRAIN. . . . . . . SP FREEDOM TRAIN 45
AT HOME THEY GOT A TRAIN THAT'S YOURS AND MINE! . . . . SP FREEDOM TRAIN 62
IN DIXIE, OFTEN THEY WON'T CALL NEGROES MISTER. . . . . SP IN EXPLANATION 7
THEY HAD NO INTENTION OF CALLING COOLIES MISTER. . . . . SP IN EXPLANATION 9
THEY CALL THEM, HEY GEORGE! . . . . SP IN EXPLANATION 12
THEY SEND ME TO EAT IN THE KITCHEN SP I, TOO 3
THEY WORSHIPPED JOE. . . . . SP JOE LOUIS 1
"THEY SAY" . . . "THEY SAY" . . . "THEY SAY" . . . . SP JOE LOUIS 8
"THEY SAY" . . . "THEY SAY" . . . "THEY SAY" . . . . SP JOE LOUIS 8
"THEY SAY" . . . "THEY SAY" . . . "THEY SAY" . . . . SP JOE LOUIS 8
"THEY SAY" . . . . SP JOE LOUIS 10
THEY PUT MA BODY IN THE GROUND. . . SP JUDGMENT DAY 1
BUT IN HARLEM THEY DON'T ANSWER BACK. . . . . SP LIKEWISE 14
THEY COST ME MORE . . . . SP MADAM'S CALLING 3
SO WHEN I'M DEAD THEY WON'T NEED . SP MIDWINTER BLUES 23
THEY DRAW UP RESTRICTIVE COVENANTS SP MIGRANT 25
IN AUSTRALIA, TOO, THEY SAY. . . . SP MIGRANT 26
THEY LYNCH ME STILL IN MISSISSIPPI. SP NEGRO 16
UNTIL THEY DIE . . . . SP NEW YORKERS 9
WHERE DID THEY GET . . . . SP NIGHT FUNERAL 3
YET THEY GOT A SATIN BOX . . . . . SP NIGHT FUNERAL 7
WHEN THEY MEET THEIR ENDS. . . . . SP NIGHT FUNERAL 16
THAT BOY THAT THEY WAS MOURNIN' . . SP NIGHT FUNERAL 38
WELL, THEY ROCKED HIM WITH ROAD-APPLES . . . . SP NOT A MOVIE 1
SO THEY DON'T SOUND LIKE ME. . . . SP NOTE COMM THEAT 6
IF THEY CAN: . . . . SP PARADE 17
AND THEY RAN SOMETHING LIKE THIS: SP RUBY BROWN 12
THAN THEY EVER DID BEFORE. . . . . SP RUBY BROWN 26
THEY HUNG MY BLACK YOUNG LOVER . . SP SONG DARK GIRL 3
THE NATIONS THEY IS FIGHTIN' . . . SP SOUTHERN MAMMY 7
AND THE NATIONS THEY DONE FIT. . . SP SOUTHERN MAMMY 8
LAST WEEK THEY LYNCHED A COLORED BOY. . . . . SP SOUTHERN MAMMY 13
THEY HUNG HIM TO A TREE. . . . . . SP SOUTHERN MAMMY 14
THEY DONE TOOK CORDELIA . . . . . . SP STONY LONESOME 1
THEY DONE PUT CORDELIA . . . . . . SP STONY LONESOME 6
YES, THEY ARE YOURS. . . . . SP SUMMER EVENING 30
I AM THE CHILD THEY STOLE FROM THE SAND . . . . SP THE NEGRO MOTHE 7
FOR SHE, THEY SAY. . . . . SP THE SOUTH 25
THEY SAY. . . . . SP TO BE SOMEBODY 22
BUT THEY GOT MORE SENSE . . . . . . SP WARNING AUGMENT 11
WHEN THEY PUT YOU IN THE GROUND AND SP WIDOW WOMAN 7
THEY THROW DIRT IN YOUR FACE. . . . SP WIDOW WOMAN 8
THEY COME ON NOW! . . . . SP WONDER 4
THEY ASKED ME AT THANKSGIVING . . . AYM BIRD IN ORBIT 15
IRENE AND HELEN ARE AS THEY USED TO BE . . . . AYM BIRD IN ORBIT 21
AND THEY LOOK AT THE STARS, ... AYM BIRD IN ORBIT 54
AND THEY WONDER WHERE I BE . . . . AYM BIRD IN ORBIT 55
AND I WONDER WHERE THEY BE. . . . . AYM BIRD IN ORBIT 56
HOW THEY EVER GOT THAT WAY. . . . . AYM BLUES IN STEREO 27
THEY KNOW ME, TOO, DOWNTOWN, . . . AYM HORN OF PLENTY 40
YET THEY ASKED ME OUT ON MY PATIO AYM HORN OF PLENTY 46
THEY WONDERED WAS I SENSITIVE . . . AYM HORN OF PLENTY 49
THEY RUNG MY BELL TO ASK ME . . . . AYM HORN OF PLENTY 96

THEY ASKED ME AT THE PTA . . . . . AYM IS IT TRUE? 54
THEY ASKED ME RIGHT AT CHRISTMAS. AYM ODE TO DINAH 127
WHEN THEY ASK YOU IF YOU KNEW ME. AYM RIDE, RED, RIDE 27
THEY DO NOT LAST A DAY - . . . . . PL CROWNS GARLANDS 13
THEY ASKED ME IF MY BLACKNESS. . . PL CULTURAL EXCHNG 33
CULTURE, THEY SAY, IS A TWO-WAY STREET: . . . . PL CULTURAL EXCHNG 58
THEY CLUTCH AT THE EGG . . . . . . PL ELDERLY LEADERS 8
THEY MAY NOT ONLY HAUNT YOU - . . . PL GHOSTS OF 1619 5
GO SLOW, THEY SAY - . . . . PL GO SLOW 1
WHILE THEY TELL ME . . . . PL GO SLOW 5
WHILE THEY LOCK THE GATE. . . . . . PL GO SLOW 10
THEY TOLD US BEFORE. . . . . PL HARLEM 6
THEY TOOK ME OUT . . . . PL KU KLUX 1
THEY SAID, "DO YOU BELIEVE . . . . PL KU KLUX 3
THEY HIT ME IN THE HEAD . . . . . . PL KU KLUX 13
AND THEN THEY KICKED ME . . . . . . PL KU KLUX 15
THEY KILLED HIM DEAD. . . . . PL LUMUMBA'S GRAVE 12
THEY BURIED LUMUMBA . . . . PL LUMUMBA'S GRAVE 13
AWAY THEY GO: . . . . PL OFFICE BUILDING 6
THEY COULD NOT SEE . . . . PL PEACE 6
LOOKS LIKE BETWEEN 'EM THEY DONE . PL STILL HERE 5
THEY CHANGE THEIR MIND! . . . . . . PL WARNING 5
THAT MAN THEY CALL THE LAW. . . . . PL WHO BUT TH LORD 2

THEY'D 2
BUT IT WAS AS IF THEY'D LEFT. . . . SP CROSSING 4
BUT WAS JUST AS IF THEY'D LEFT. . . SP CROSSING 22

THEY'LL 5
THEY'LL BRING YOU MISERY. . . . . . FC LISTEN HERE 18
CAUSE IF I DON'T THEY'LL CUT DOWN MY PAY. . . . . SH SUPPER TIME 14
OR THEY'LL HANG YOU TO A TREE! . . OWT FLIGHT 8
THEY'LL SEE HOW BEAUTIFUL I AM . . SP I, TOO 16
THEY'LL WANT FLOWERS, TOO. . . . . SP NIGHT FUNERAL 15

THEY'RE 4
BUT THEY'RE NOT SO BAD . . . . . . JC GOOD MORN STLIN 8
TILL THEY'RE THE HEART . . . . . . SP COLLEGE FORMAL 13
THE MONEY THAT THEY'RE WORTH . . . AYM GOSPEL CHA-CHA 12
THEY'RE HUNG. . . . . PL SLUM DREAMS 12

THEY'VE 5
NOW THEY'VE CAGED ME . . . . WB LAMENT DARK PEO 9
NOW THEY'VE LOCKED ME . . . . SH BLD THE KILLER 25
THEY'VE GOT COVENANTS . . . . OWT RESTRICTIVE 10
THEY'VE JUST HUNG A BLACK MAN . . . SP SILHOUETTE 3
THEY'VE HUNG A BLACK MAN . . . . . SP SILHOUETTE 5

THICK 2
OF TALL THICK TREES . . . . WB OUR LAND 9
ONLY THE THICK WALL. . . . . SP AS I GREW OLDER 22

THICKER 1
VOICE GROWS THICKER . . . . SP DRUNKARD 1

THICKET 1
THROUGH THE PALMETTO THICKET . . . PL FLORIDA WORKERS 6

THIEVES 3
O, THIEVES, EXPLOITERS, KILLERS, . ANS A NEW SONG 29
THE LIES THIEVES SHOOK . . . . . . PL LUMUMBA'S GRAVE 7
WHEN MILLION-DOLLAR THIEVES . . . . PL PRIME 4

THIEVING 1
OF A THIEVING PEOPLE. . . . . ANS A NEW SONG 15

THIGHS 3
IN YOUR THIGHS. . . . . SP AFRICA 15
AT HER THIGHS. . . . . SP GRADUATION 5
ABOUT HIS THIGHS. . . . . SP TRUMPET PLAYER 8

THIN 7
HE TOOK MA LAST THIN DIME. . . . . FC GYPSY MAN 14
HE TOOK MA LAST THIN DIME. . . . . FC GYPSY MAN 16
WAS MOSQUITO-NETTING THIN. . . . . SP CROSSING 8
AND LET THE WHITE VIOLINS WHIR THIN AND SLOW. . . . . SP FATASY PURPLE 6
HE LOOKED SO THIN - . . . . SP LOVER'S RETURN 15
HOW THIN AND SHARP IS THE MOON TONIGHT! . . . . SP WINTER MOON 1
HOW THIN AND SHARP AND GHOSTLY WHITE SP WINTER MOON 2

THING 25
PLAY THAT THING. . . . . FC JAZZ BAND 1
LET'S SHAKE DAT THING! . . . . . . FC SATURDAY NIGHT 12
AND ALL THAT KIND O' THING. . . . . NM BIG-TIMER POEM 24
AND IT'S A GOOD THING ALL THE BLACK BOYS LYING DEAD . . . . NM COLORED SL POEM 51
'S A TERRIBLE THING TO HAVE. . . . DK HOMESICK BLUES 14
A TERRIBLE THING TO HAVE. . . . . . DK HOMESICK BLUES 16
A NIGHT-GONE THING. . . . . DK YOUTH 5
THIS THING TO SAY. . . . . ANS A NEW SONG 5
SAY! ON THE LAST THING I OWN. . . . SH BLD PAWNBROKER 21
ANY OLD THING TO EAT. . . . . SH BRIEF ENCOUNTER 2
LOCKIN' FOR ANY OLD THING TO EAT - SH BRIEF ENCOUNTER 4
SHE WAS DE WRONGEST THING, JUDGE. SH BRIEF ENCOUNTER 17
JUST ONE THING AFTER 'NOTHER . . . SH LOVE AGAIN BLUS 5
AND HANDLE EASY LIKE A PURCHASED THING. . . . . OWT JUICE JOINT 36
BUT AN AWFUL THING . . . . LHR BLD MARY'S SON 4
INTO SOME OTHER THING . . . . LHR DEAR LVLY DEATH 5
WAS THE ONLY THING I HAD. . . . . . SP HOMECOMING 8
AND YOU AIN'T DONE A THING . . . . SP MADAM RENT MAN 13
YOU WON'T GET A GODDAMN THING! . . SP SAME IN BLUES 11
THAT COLORED BOY AIN'T SAID A THING SP SOUTHERN MAMMY 15
SONG IS A STRONG THING. . . . . . . SP SPIRITUALS 5
SONG IS A STRONG THING. . . . . . . SP SPIRITUALS 16
IS A THING TO WHICH WE BLACK ARE WISE: . . . . PL JUSTICE 2
NEXT THING YOU KNOW. . . . . PL LITTLE SNG HOUS 18
AS IF IT WERE SOME NOBLE THING. . . PL MOTHER IN WAR 1

THINGS 35
TWO THINGS POSSESS THE POWER. . . . OLD TWO THINGS 1
TWO THINGS DESERVE THE NAME. . . . OLD TWO THINGS 2
TWO THINGS CAN REAWAKEN . . . . . . OLD TWO THINGS 3
TWO THINGS ARE FULL OF WONDER. . . OLD TWO THINGS 5
TWO THINGS CAST OFF ALL SHAME. . . OLD TWO THINGS 6
AND HOLDIN' THINGS TIGHT. . . . . . NM BIG-TIMER POEM 52
DIDN'T OUR GOVERNMENT TELL US THINGS WOULD BE FINE . . . . NM COLORED SL POEM 33
NO WONDER WE FIND THEM SUCH MARVELLOUS THINGS! . . . . DK FAIRIES 5
BUY ME A FEW THINGS. . . . . SH PAY DAY 6
AND TAKE BACK ALL THEM THINGS WE HAD SH PAY DAY 12
THINGS IS BAD - . . . . JC GOOD MORN STLIN 7
LIFT THEIR HEADS AND THINGS IS BAD. JC GOOD MORN STLIN 20
THE THINGS THEY MADE, NOR THEIR OWN LIVES - . . . . JC TO CAPTAIN MULZ 21
IN GROWING THINGS . . . . FW GIRL 19
THE THINGS A YOUNG LAD . . . . FW MAN 12
KNOWING ALL THINGS . . . . OWT MAN INTO MEN 16
THAT TAKETH ALL THINGS UNDER WING - LHR DEAR LVLY DEATH 2
WHO CARRIES UGLY THINGS TO SHOW THE SUN? . . . . SP A HOUSE IN TAOS 21
WE CAN BUY LOVELY THINGS WITH MONEY. SP A HOUSE IN TAOS 24
OUR BODIES ARE SEPARATE, INDIVIDUAL THINGS. . . . . SP A HOUSE IN TAOS 31
AND THINGS LIKE THAT. BUT NOW, LORD, SP CHILDREN'S RYME 3
FOR THE THINGS . . . . SP CONSIDER ME 24
TWO OR THREE THINGS IN THE PAST . . SP DANCER 1
LET THINGS TAKE THEIR COURSE. . . . SP DEMOCRACY 11
LAWD, THESE THINGS WE WOMEN . . . . SP EARLY EVENING 21
THE PEOPLE DO NOT ALWAYS SAY THINGS OUT LOUD. . . . . SP FREEDOM'S PLOW 145
WHO SAID THOSE THINGS? AMERICANS! SP FREEDOM'S PLOW 174
AND THINGS LIKE THAT. . . . . SP IN EXPLANATION 16
JEWS SELL ME THINGS. . . . . SP LIKEWISE 8
POOR LITTLE THINGS, ... SP MADAM CHARTY CH 13
THINGS IS BAD - . . . . SP MADAM CHARTY CH 27
THE SAME THINGS OTHER FOLKS LIKE WHO ARE OTHER RACES. . . . . SP THEME FOR ENG B 26
OUR THINGS . . . . SP WEST TEXAS 3
WONDERING HOW THINGS GOT THIS WAY PL DINNER GUEST ME 10
LET THINGS TAKE THEIR COURSE. . . . PL FREEDOM 11

THINK 28
THEN I DON'T HAVE TO THINK. . . . . NM BIG-TIMER POEM 64
YOU DO NOT THINK . . . . DK MINSTREL MAN 5
YOU MUST THINK YOU GOT TO WAKE UP A CROWD! . . . . SH DAYBREAK 4
THINK I WAS INSANE. . . . . SH IF-ING 12
AND IF YOU THINK I BEEN TOO MEAN BEFORE. . . . . SH LETTER 12
LISTEN AT MY HEARTBEATS TRYING TO THINK. . . . . SH SUPPER TIME 6
SOME FOLKS THINK . . . . JC FREEDOM 1
SOME FOLKS THINK . . . . JC FREEDOM 4
SOME FOLKS THINK . . . . JC FREEDOM 7
I THINK THE DIFFERENCE LIES . . . . FW BORDER LINE 3
I THINK THE DISTANCE . . . . FW BORDER LINE 7
THIS YEAR MAYBE, DO YOU THINK I CAN GRADUATE? . . . . SP DEFERRED 1
YOU THINK . . . . SP DREAM BOOGIE 8
AND I'M GOIN' THERE TO THINK ABOUT HIM. . . . . SP LAMENT OVER LOV 12
GONNA THINK ABOUT MY MAN - . . . . SP LAMENT OVER LOV 23
I TRIED TO THINK BUT COULDN'T. . . SP LIFE IS FINE 3
SOMETIMES I THINK . . . . SP LIKEWISE 24
WHEN YOU THINK YOU GOT BREAD . . . SP MADAM MIGHT-HAV 25
DID YOU EVER THINK ABOUT YOUR MOTHER? . . . . SP REVERIE HARLEM 5
DID YOU EVER THINK ABOUT YOUR SWEETHEART . . . . SP REVERIE HARLEM 7
SOMETIMES I THINK THAT WHITE FOLKS SP SOUTHERN MAMMY 9
BUT SOMETIMES I THINK THAT WHITE FOLKS . . . . SP SOUTHERN MAMMY 21
DID NOT THINK IT GOOD! . . . . . . SP S-SSS-SS-SH! 7
OR DO YOU THINK THAT PAPA'S . . . . AYM SHOW FARE PLESE 3
JUST WHO DO YOU THINK I AM? . . . . PL BACKLASH BLUES 2
WHO DO YOU THINK I AM? . . . . . . PL BACKLASH BLUES 4
YOU MUST THINK US COLORED FOLKS . . PL BACKLASH BLUES 11
WHAT DO YOU THINK I GOT TO LOSE? . PL BACKLASH BLUES 26
WHAT YOU THINK I GOT TO LOSE? . . . PL BACKLASH BLUES 28

THINKING 7

THINKING WE WERE FIGHTING FOR DEMOCRACY'S TRUE REIGN	NM	COLORED SL POEM	7
SETTING HERE THINKING FEELING SAD.	SH	TWILIGHT REVERI	3
YAL. HERE I SET THINKING - A BITTER OLD THOUGHT	SH	TWILIGHT REVERI	9
AND HERE I SET THINKING WITH A BITTER OLD FROWN.	SH	TWILIGHT REVERI	14
I DON'T DARE START THINKING IN THE MORNING.	SP	BLUES AT DAWN	1
I DON'T DARE START THINKING IN THE MORNING.	SP	BLUES AT DAWN	2
SO I DON'T DARE START THINKING IN THE MORNING.	SP	BLUES AT DAWN	5

THINKIN' 2

OR THINKIN' AT ALL?	NM	BIG-TIMER POEM	70
KEEP THINKIN' I WON'T BE LONELY . .	SP	HOPE	3

THIRD 2

BUT THAT THIRD PARTY.	SP	SAME IN BLUES	24
BY THE THIRD DEGREE.	FL	WHO BUT TH LORD	8

THIRD-FLOOR 1

YOUR THIRD-FLOOR TENANT'S NEVER HOME.	AYM	ASK YOUR MAMA	9

THIRTEEN 1

WHEN A CHILE GETS TO BE THIRTEEN .	SP	MYSTERY	1

THIRTY-TWO 1

GONNA GO GET MY PISTOL. I MEAN THIRTY-TWO.	SH	TWILIGHT REVERI	7

THIS 163

I AM AFRAID OF THIS CIVILIZATION -	WB	FOR PORTRAIT OF	3
AND NOT THIS LAND WHERE LIFE IS COLD.	WB	OUR LAND	7
AND NOT THIS LAND WHERE BIRDS ARE GREY.	WB	OUR LAND	12
AND NOT THIS LAND WHERE JOY IS WRONG.	WB	OUR LAND	15
IT IS IN THIS SICK ROOM	WB	SICK ROOM	2
EVER TIME I MOUNTS THIS BENCH . . .	FC	BLD OF GIN MARY	7
MEANS HE'S GONNA LEAVE THIS WORLD.	FC	GAL'S CRY DYING	8
MEANS HE'S GONNA LEAVE THIS WORLD.	FC	GAL'S CRY DYING	10
PLEASE DON'T TAKE THIS MAN O' MINE.	FC	GAL'S CRY DYING	18
AN' DIG ME A GRAVE THIS VERY DAY.	FC	MINNIE SINGS	17
ROUND THIS TOWN. -	FC	RED SILK STOCK	6
THAT IN THIS NIGGER PLACE.	DUD	AESTHETE HARLEM	2
UNTIL I CAME TO THIS NEAR STREET .	DLD	AESTHETE HARLEM	6
LIKE THIS WILL I BE:	NM	BLACK CLWN POEM	50
BEEN WALKIN' SINCE FIVE THIS MORNIN'.	NM	BROKE	2
UP AND DOWN. AND THEY JUST AIN'T NO JOBS IN THIS MAN'S TOWN.	NM	BROKE	3
ALL THIS TALKIN' AIN'T NOTHIN' BUT TINKLIN' SYMBOLS AND SOUNDIN' BRASS:	NM	BROKE	58
LAWD. FOLKSES. HOW MUCH LONGER IS THIS GONNA LAST?	NM	BROKE	59
WHAT IS THERE WITHIN THIS BEGGAR LAD	DK	BEGGAR BOY	1
THIS IS WHAT I'M GONNA SING. . . .	DK	NIGHT AND MORN	2
THIS IS WHAT I'M GONNA SING: . . .	DK	NIGHT AND MORN	4
THIS IS GONNA BE MA SONG.	DK	NIGHT AND MORN	8
THIS IS GONNA BE MA SONG:	DK	NIGHT AND MORN	10
BUT THIS WORLD IS WEARY	DK	PO' BOY BLUES	11
SUN'S GOING DOWN THIS EVENING - . .	DK	SONG BANJO DANC	12
THE SUN'S GOING DOWN THIS VERY NIGHT -	DK	SONG BANJO DANC	14
THE SUN'S GOING DOWN THIS VERY NIGHT -	DK	SONG BANJO DANC	26
THIS LITTLE HOUSE IS SUGAR.	DK	WINTER SWEEETNS	1
I HAVE THIS WORD TO BRING.	ANS	A NEW SONG	4
THIS THING TO SAY.	ANS	A NEW SONG	5
THIS SONG TO SING:	ANS	A NEW SONG	6
TO BEAUTIFY THIS HOUR. THIS SPRING. AND ALL THE SPRINGS TO COME . .	ANS	CHANT MAY DAY	12
TO BEAUTIFY THIS HOUR. THIS SPRING. AND ALL THE SPRINGS TO COME . .	ANS	CHANT MAY DAY	12
100-VOICES: FROM THIS HOUR.	ANS	CHANT MAY DAY	36
THIS IS FOR THE KIDS WHO DIE. . . .	ANS	KIDS WHO DIE	1
NOR FREEDOM IN THIS "HOMELAND OF THE FREE.")	ANS	LET AMERICA BE	16
AND YET I SWEAR THIS OATH -	ANS	LET AMERICA BE	78
AND THIS IS WHAT I SAW:	ANS	NEGRO GHETTO	2
AND THIS IS WHAT MOVED IN MY HEART:	ANS	NEGRO GHETTO	7
IN THIS WORLD BEFORE	SH	ASPIRATION	7
IF THIS RADIO WAS GOOD I'D GET KDS	SH	BED TIME	1
THIS GOLD WATCH AND CHAIN	SH	BLD PAWNBROKER	1
HOW ABOUT THIS NECKLACE?	SH	BLD PAWNBROKER	5
CAN I GET TEN ON THIS SUIT	SH	BLD PAWNBROKER	9
OF THIS SILVER BOWL.	SH	BLD PAWNBROKER	14
IF THERE'S ANYBODY ON THIS EARTH. JUDGE.	SH	BRIEF ENCOUNTER	11
I HATE TO DIE THIS WAY WITH THE QUIET	SH	CABARET GIRL	1
MAKIN' ME DIE THIS WAY?	SH	CABARET GIRL	8
MAKE THIS EARLY MORNING TIME TO KEEP BODY AND SOUL	SH	DAYBREAK	7
THIS MORNIN' FOR BREAKFAST	SH	EVENIN' BLUES	7
THIS MORNIN' FOR BREAKFAST	SH	EVENIN' BLUES	9
BUT THIS EVENIN' FOR SUPPER. . . .	SH	EVENIN' BLUES	11
I STARTED FEELING THIS A-WAY. . . .	SH	EVIL MORNING	4
ON THIS SEPIA THRILL:	SH	HARLEM SWEETIES	4
SO LET'S JUST FORGET WHAT THIS FUSS WAS ABOUT.	SH	LETTER	15
WHEN THIS FLOOD IS OVER.	SH	MISSISSIPPI LEV	5
DON'T KNOW WHY I BUILD THIS LEVEE	SH	MISSISSIPPI LEV	7
DON'T KNOW WHY I BUILD THIS LEVEE	SH	MISSISSIPPI LEV	9
IN THIS GREAT BIG LONESOME TOWN! .	SH	OUT OF WORK	14
A YEAR AND A DAY IN THIS	SH	OUT OF WORK	15
THIS WHOLE PAY CHECK'S JUST FOR ME.	SH	PAY DAY	1
"THIS WEEK I NEED IT ALL."	SH	PAY DAY	4
BUT THIS HOUSE IS MIGHTY QUIET! . .	SH	SUNDAY	10
KEEP FEELING LIKE THIS I'M GONNA START ACTING BAD.	SH	TWILIGHT REVERI	4
IT'S DARK ON THIS STOOP. LAWD! THE SUN'S GONE DOWN!	SH	TWILIGHT REVERI	15
DON'T YOU HEAR THIS HAMMER RING? .	JC	BIG BUDDY	11
DON'T YOU HEAR THIS HAMMER RING? .	JC	BIG BUDDY	13
I'M GONNA SPLIT THIS ROCK	JC	BIG BUDDY	14
WHEN I SPLIT THIS ROCK.	JC	BIG BUDDY	16
DON'T YOU HEAR THIS HAMMER RING? .	JC	BIG BUDDY	19
IF YOU CARRY THIS THROUGH.	JC	BLD SAM SOLOMON	26
SOME FOLKS TRY TO TELL ME DOWN THIS WAY	JC	GOOD MORN STLIN	22
JOE LOUIS SAID. WE GONNA WIN THIS WAR	JC	JIM CROW'S LAST	25
I DID NOT ASK FOR THIS RIVER . . .	JC	THE BITTER RIVR	51
ABOUT THIS LITTLE CABIN	FW	CAROLINA CABIN	4
CONCERNING THIS	FW	MIGRATION	14
TO WANDER THROUGH THIS LIVING WORLD	FW	REMEMBRANCE	1
THIS IS EARTHQUAKE	FW	TODAY	1
MAMA. I FOUND THIS SOLDIER'S CAP .	FW	WHEN ARMIES PAS	1
IN THIS WIDE WIDE WORLD -	OWT	HONEY BABE	14
SEE WHAT THIS WEEK'S JIVE IS ALL ABOUT:	OWT	JITNEY	25
BEFORE THIS LONG HEGIRA HAD BEGUN	OWT	JUICE JOINT	12
INTO THIS GIN MILL	OWT	JUICE JOINT	15
ON THIS CITY STREET.	OWT	JUICE JOINT	16
O. IN THIS TAVERN ON THE CITY STREET	OWT	JUICE JOINT	33
DANCE IN THIS JUICE JOINT	OWT	JUICE JOINT	47
IN THIS STRANGE OLD TOWN -	OWT	STRANGER IN TWN	14
ON THIS SIDE OF THE TRACKS.	OWT	VISITORS	4
THIS IS MY BODY	LHR	BLD MARY'S SON	18
AND THIS IS MY BLOOD. HE SAID. . .	LHR	BLD MARY'S SON	19
THIS IS MY BODY	LHR	BLD MARY'S SON	29
AND THIS IS MY BLOOD!	LHR	BLD MARY'S SON	30
THIS SUFFERING FLESH.	LHR	DEAR LVLY DEATH	6
OF THIS HOUSE	SP	A HOUSE IN TAOS	12
ABOUT THIS HOUSE IN TAOS	SP	A HOUSE IN TAOS	17
IN THIS ONE HOUSE IN TAOS -	SP	A HOUSE IN TAOS	20
THIS UNSOUGHT LOVELINESS OF MOON.	SP	A HOUSE IN TAOS	28
THERE COMES THIS SONG	SP	AFRO-AMER FRAG	16
THIS SONG OF ATAVISTIC LAND. . . .	SP	AFRO-AMER FRAG	18
HELP ME TO SHATTER THIS DARKNESS.	SP	AS I GREW OLDER	28
TO SMASH THIS NIGHT.	SP	AS I GREW OLDER	29
TO BREAK THIS SHADOW	SP	AS I GREW OLDER	30
IN THIS WORLD FOR ME.	SP	BAD LUCK CARD	6
TILL YOU FIX THIS HOUSE UP NEW. . .	SP	BLD LANDLORD	12
COME AND GET THIS MAN!	SP	BLD LANDLORD	22
TO HELP ME CARRY THIS LOAD.	SP	BOUND NO'TH BLS	6
IN THIS BLOCK. I DO BELIEVE! . . .	SP	CHILDREN'S RYME	11
I BROKE MY HEART THIS MORNIN'. . .	SP	CORA	1
THIS YEAR MAYBE. DO YOU THINK I CAN GRADUATE?	SP	DEFERRED	1
BUT MAYBE THIS YEAR I CAN GRADUATE.	SP	DEFERRED	7
THIS WORLD I'LL LEAVE BEHIND . . .	SP	DEFERRED	40
WHERE IS THIS LIGHT	SP	DEMAND	8
AND WHAT IS THIS WIND	SP	DEMAND	10
TODAY. THIS YEAR	SP	DEMOCRACY	2
IN THIS LONELY	SP	DESERT	9
THIS MOST STRANGE DREAM.	SP	DREAM	2
I SENT YOU THIS MORNING TO BUY? . .	SP	EARLY EVENING	2
I SENT YOU THIS MORNING TO BUY? . .	SP	EARLY EVENING	4
I BEEN RUNNIN' THIS	SP	ELEVATOR BOY	21
I'M GONNA CHECK UP ON THIS	SP	FREEDOM TRAIN	15
SOMEBODY TELL ME ABOUT THIS	SP	FREEDOM TRAIN	23
I GOT TO KNOW ABOUT THIS	SP	FREEDOM TRAIN	29
THE FREEDOM THAT THEY CARRYIN' ON THIS FREEDOM TRAIN.	SP	FREEDOM TRAIN	45
THIS IS A SONG FOR THE GENIUS CHILD.	SP	GENIUS CHILD	1
AS KEEPS THIS YOUNG NYMPH. JOY! . .	SP	JOY	9
NOTHIN' IN THIS WORLD	SP	LITTLE GRN TREE	3
THIS WAY?	SP	LOW TO HIGH	13
AND THERE WAS ONLY THIS CORNER . .	SP	MAGNOLIA FLOWER	6
SOMEWHERE IN THIS DUSK.	SP	MAGNOLIA FLOWER	11
THIS ANCIENT HAG	SP	MEXICAN MARKET	1
THIS LITTLE OLD FURNISHED ROOM'S .	SP	NECESSITY	5
I ASK YOU THIS:	SP	PRAYER	1
I ASK YOU THIS:	SP	PRAYER	3
I NEEDS THIS. THAT. AND THE OTHER.	SP	PREFERENCE	6
AND THEY RAN SOMETHING LIKE THIS:	SP	RUBY BROWN	12

AND AIN'T THERE ANY JOY IN THIS TOWN? . . . . SP RUBY BROWN 15
KNOW MORE ABOUT THIS PRETTY RUBY BROWN. . . . . SP RUBY BROWN 17
HAVING PREVIOUSLY POINTED OUT THE SINS OF THIS WORLD: . . . . . . SP SUNDAY MORNING 1
OF THIS WORLD - . . . . SP SUNDAY MORNING 12
COME INTO THE CHURCH THIS MORNING. SP SUNDAY MORNING 36
I WOKE UP THIS MORNIN' . . . . . . SP SYLVESTER'S BED 1
"AIN'T GOT NOBODY IN ALL THIS WORLD. SP THE WEARY BLUES 19
TO THIS COLLEGE ON THE HILL ABOVE HARLEM. . . . . SP THEME FOR ENG B 9
UP TO MY ROOM, SIT DOWN, AND WRITE THIS PAGE: . . . . SP THEME FOR ENG B 15
HEAR YOU, HEAR ME - WE TWO - YOU, ME, TALK ON THIS PAGE. . . . . . SP THEME FOR ENG B 19
THIS IS MY PAGE FOR ENGLISH B. . . SP THEME FOR ENG B 41
SAYS THIS PARTICULAR . . . . SP TOMORROW 4
THIS TROUBLED WOMAN . . . . SP TROUBLED WOMAN 3
THIS STRONG YOUNG SAILOR . . . . . SP YOUNG SAILOR 6
I'M ALL ALONE IN THIS WORLD, SHE SAID. . . . . SP 50 - 50 1
EVEN RUNG THIS BELL ON SUNDAY, YET AYM ASK YOUR MAMA 8
THIS LAST QUARTER OF CENTENNIAL . . AYM ODE TO DINAH 8
TO THIS QUARTER OF THE NEGROES . . AYM ODE TO DINAH 18
THIS LAST QUARTER OF CENTENNIAL: . AYM ODE TO DINAH 33
ARE THIS OR THAT . . . . AYM SHOW FARE PLESE 27
THIS BIRMINGHAM-ON-SUNDAY WALL. . . PL BIRMINGHAM SUND 14
WONDERING HOW THINGS GOT THIS WAY PL DINNER GUEST ME 10
TODAY, THIS YEAR . . . . PL FREEDOM 2
IN THIS NEON . . . . PL LENOX AVE. BAR 11
ON THIS MERRY-GO-ROUND. . . . . . . PL MERRY-GO-ROUND 4
I KNEW THAT THIS WOULD COME." . . . PL NORTHERN LIBERL 5
BY THIS BLOODY YIELD. . . . . PL OFFICIAL NOTICE 10
AND BLAME YOU FOR THIS. . . . . . . PL WAR 16

THIS-A 1
BEING THIS-A WAY! . . . . OWT FUNERAL 8

THIS-HERE 1
'COURSE, YOU HEARS PLENTY 'BOUT THIS-HERE UNEMPLOYMENT RELIEF - NM BROKE 56

THOSE 36
THOSE KIND COME CHEAP IN HARLEM . . WB YOUNG PROSTITUT 4
HE'S GOT THOSE 'LECTRIC-SHOCKIN' EYES AN' . . . . FC MA MAN 5
OF THOSE COMPELLED TO STAY - . . . DK IRISH WAKE 4
NONE OF THOSE IS DEAD.) . . . . . . SL SCOTTSBORO 23
O, I'M THE MAN WHO SAILED THOSE EARLY SEAS . . . . ANS LET AMERICA BE 45
FROM THOSE WHO LIVE LIKE LEECHES ON THE PEOPLE'S LIVES. . . . . . . ANS LET AMERICA BE 72
I BOUGHT THOSE BOMBS FOR SPAIN! . . ANS SONG OF SPAIN 45
WORKERS MADE THOSE BOMBS FOR A FACIST SPAIN! . . . . ANS SONG OF SPAIN 46
I MADE THOSE BOMBS FOR SPAIN. . . . ANS SONG OF SPAIN 71
I MADE THOSE BOMBING PLANES. . . . ANS SONG OF SPAIN 73
TO SHAKE THE PILLARS OF THOSE TEMPLES . . . . ANS UNION 7
ALL THOSE SWEET COLORS . . . . . . SH HARLEM SWEETIES 27
THAT MAY BE SO - FOR THOSE WHO WANT IT SO. . . . . JC GOOD MORN STLIN 25
I WOULD LIKE TO SEE THOSE FREEDOMS JC HOW ABOUT DIXIE 3
BUT THERE ARE THOSE WHO STILL HOLD OUT . . . . JC TO CAPTAIN MULZ 10
AND THERE ARE THOSE WHO FIGHT . . . JC TO CAPTAIN MULZ 13
THERE ARE THOSE, TOO, WHO FOR SO LONG . . . . JC TO CAPTAIN MULZ 16
OF THOSE WHO WOULD KEEP, OR ONCE MORE MAKE . . . . JC TO CAPTAIN MULZ 31
THOSE WHO EXPECT . . . . FW PRAYER 11
LET THOSE WOMEN WITH THEIR LIPS TOO RED . . . . OWT JUICE JOINT 21
I GOT THOSE SAD OLD WEARY BLUES. . OWT TOO BLUE 1
SAVE THOSE THAT HISTORY BOOKS CREATE, ... SP AFRO-AMER FRAG 5
SAVE THOSE THAT SONGS . . . . SP AFRO-AMER FRAG 6
IN THOSE DARK DAYS OF SLAVERY, . . SP FREEDOM'S PLOW 123
WHO SAID THOSE THINGS? AMERICANS! SP FREEDOM'S PLOW 174
WHO OWNS THOSE WORDS? AMERICA! . . SP FREEDOM'S PLOW 175
TO THOSE CALLED MISTER. . . . . . . SP IN EXPLANATION 21
LIARS USE THOSE WORDS. . . . . . . SP IN EXPLANATION 39
HEAR THOSE WORDS AND SHOUT THEM BACK SP IN EXPLANATION 41
THOSE WHO EXPECT . . . . SP LITANY 11
A DIME ON THOSE TWO BOTTLES. . . . SP SUMMER EVENING 29
AND MAKE OF THOSE YEARS A TORCH FOR TOMORROW. . . . . SP THE NEGRO MOTHE 38
TO THE TUNE O' THOSE WEARY BLUES. SP THE WEARY BLUES 8
BY THOSE YET UNINDUCTED . . . . . . AYM BIRD IN ORBIT 12
THOSE SIT-IN KIDS, HE SAID, ... AYM BIRD IN ORBIT 71
AS THOSE INVESTIGATED - . . . . . . PL UN-AMERICAN 6

THOU 8
THOU ART NOT BEAUTIFUL . . . . . . WB POEM 4
YET THOU HAST . . . . WB POEM 5
THOU ART NOT GOOD . . . . WB POEM 10
YET THOU HAST . . . . WB POEM 11
THOU ART NOT LUMINOUS . . . . WB POEM 16
THOU DARK ONE. . . . . WB SONGS DARK VIRG 6
THOU DARK ONE. . . . . WB SONGS DARK VIRG 14
THOU DARK ONE. . . . . WB SONGS DARK VIRG 19

THOUGH 13
EVEN THOUGH YOU DO ME WRONG. . . . SH IN TROUBLED KEY 8
THOUGH YOU DO ME WRONG - . . . . . SH IN TROUBLED KEY 10
THOUGH I GO DRUNKEN . . . . FW FAITHFUL ONE 1
THOUGH I WANDER AND STRAY . . . . . FW FAITHFUL ONE 5
AS THOUGH YOU COULD KEEP, ... SP A HOUSE IN TAOS 27
JUST AS THOUGH IT WAS NO SIN - . . SP BLD OF THE GIRL 14
JOB AIN'T NO GOOD THOUGH. . . . . . SP ELEVATOR BOY 4
THOUGH YOU MAY HEAR ME HOLLER, . . SP LIFE IS FINE 27
IGNORE ME - THOUGH I PAY YOUR FEES. SP LOW TO HIGH 15
THOUGH THE GOODNESS . . . . SP NO REGRETS 3
THOUGH THE RETURN . . . . SP NO REGRETS 7
AS THOUGH I WERE GOD. . . . . SP TO ARTINA 3
THOUGH WORN IN GLORY ON MY HEAD. . PL CROWNS GARLANDS 12

THOUGHT 34
AND PIERROT THOUGHT ALL MAIDENS FAIR WB PIERROT 19
I THOUGHT LOVE WAS A DREAM, BUT I SHO HAVE AWOKE - . . . . NM BROKE 54
A GAL I THOUGHT WAS KIND. . . . . . DK PO' BOY BLUES 14
A GAL I THOUGHT WAS KIND. . . . . . DK PO' BOY BLUES 16
THOUGHT OF RAPE, ... SH DEATH IN HARLEM 67
THOUGHT OF A ROPE. . . . . SH DEATH IN HARLEM 69
THOUGHT OF FLAME. . . . . SH DEATH IN HARLEM 71
AND THOUGHT OF SOMETHING . . . . . SH DEATH IN HARLEM 72
THOUGHT I HAD AN ANGEL-CHILE. . . . SH LOVE AGAIN BLUS 8
THOUGHT I HAD AN ANGEL-CHILE. . . . SH LOVE AGAIN BLUS 10
HERE I SET WITH A BITTER OLD THOUGHT, ... SH TWILIGHT REVERI 1
YAL, HERE I SET THINKING - A BITTER OLD THOUGHT . . . . SH TWILIGHT REVERI 9
THE CRACKERS THOUGHT . . . . JC BLD SAM SOLOMON 49
I THOUGHT THAT FRIENDSHIP LAY . . . FW MAN 3
I THOUGHT THAT LOVE MUST BE . . . . FW MAN 5
I THOUGHT THAT DRUNKENNESS . . . . FW MAN 7
I THOUGHT I SAW RED STARS, MOTHER, FW WHEN ARMIES PAS 12
I THOUGHT YOU WAS HAPPY, TOO. . . . OWT YESTERDAY TODAY 10
THEY THOUGHT THEY SAW . . . . LHR PASTORAL 2
I THOUGHT ABOUT OLD GREELEY . . . . SP BLUE BAYOU 4
AND I THOUGHT ABOUT LOU . . . . . . SP BLUE BAYOU 5
IF I THOUGHT THOUGHTS IN BED, . . . SP BLUES AT DAWN 3
"OR IF IT WOULD," THOUGHT SOME. . . SP FREEDOM'S PLOW 121
MISTER, I THOUGHT IT WERE THE . . . SP FREEDOM TRAIN 41
YOU SAY YOU THOUGHT EVERYBODY WAS CALLED MISTER? . . . . SP IN EXPLANATION 5
I THOUGHT ABOUT MY BABY . . . . . . SP LIFE IS FINE 14
AND THOUGHT I WOULD JUMP DOWN. . . SP LIFE IS FINE 15
AND I THOUGHT I MIGHT . . . . SP MADAM WRONG VIS 14
BUT YOU THOUGHT YOU WOULD. . . . . SP MAYBE 4
THOUGHT I WAS IN HELL. . . . . . . SP MORNING AFTER 8
THOUGHT I WAS IN HELL. . . . . . . SP MORNING AFTER 10
THOUGHT IT FUN. . . . . SP S-SSS-SS-SH! 21
I THOUGHT I HEARD THE HORN OF PLENTY BLOWING. . . . . AYM BLUES IN STEREO 35
SHE THOUGHT THAT ONLY . . . . PL MOTHER IN WAR 12

THOUGHTFUL 1
KIND, THOUGHTFUL TO THE FACES THAT ARE WHITE. . . . . OWT NEGRO SERVANT 2

THOUGHTS 4
AND BLUE, HIDING HIS DISCONTENT AS THOUGHTS OF A BETTER LIFE OVERCOME . . . . NM BIG-TIMER MOOD 7
IF I THOUGHT THOUGHTS IN BED, . . . SP BLUES AT DAWN 3
THEM THOUGHTS WOULD BUST MY HEAD - SP BLUES AT DAWN 4
GREAT THOUGHTS IN THEIR DEEPEST HEARTS . . . . SP FREEDOM'S PLOW 148

THOUSAND 14
'CAUSE 'FORE YOU GETS THERE, TEN THOUSAND AND ONE . . . . NM BROKE 5
AND IT'S BETTER A THOUSAND TIMES YOU'RE IN FRANCE DEAD. . . . . . NM COLORED SL POEM 45
QUIET FOR TEN THOUSAND CENTURIES, OLD ABE. . . . . DK LINCOLN MONUMNT 4
A THOUSAND STORMS, ... FW SAILING DATE 9
A THOUSAND POUNDS OF SALT . . . . . LHR TESTAMENT 7
INTO A THOUSAND LIGHTS OF SUN, . . SP AS I GREW OLDER 31
INTO A THOUSAND WHIRLING DREAMS . . SP AS I GREW OLDER 32
THERE IS TWO THOUSAND CHILDREN . . SP CHILDREN'S RYME 10
A THOUSAND MILES AWAY. . . . . . . SP MIGRANT 24
INTO A THOUSAND SMILES. . . . . . . SP SUNDAY MORNING 6
A THOUSAND YEARS OFF: . . . . SP TOMORROW 2
IF I LIVE TO BE A THOUSAND . . . . SP WIDOW WOMAN 17
OR A THOUSAND AND TEN? . . . . . . PL GHOSTS OF 1619 22
ARE BUT A THOUSAND AND TEN . . . . PL GHOSTS OF 1619 25

THREAD 3
IN SILVER THREAD AND DIAMOND NOTES SP FLATTED FIFTHS 12
TOUSSAINT WITH A THREAD . . . . . . AYM GOSPEL CHA-CHA 21
THREAD STILL PULLS HIS . . . . . . AYM GOSPEL CHA-CHA 22

THREATENS 1

MAN THREATENS LANDLORD . . . . . . SP BLD LANDLORD 31

THREE 18

AND ALL THREE COVERED WITH A SHEET OF PAIN. . . . . WB SICK ROOM 5
THREE HUNDRED YEARS . . . . NM BLACK CLWN POEM 16
ON THREE STRINGS. . . . . ANS SONG OF SPAIN 9
AND WE THREE . . . . SP A HOUSE IN TAOS 3
AND WE THREE . . . . SP A HOUSE IN TAOS 6
BUT THAT THERE SHOULD BE THREE BARREN HEARTS . . . . SP A HOUSE IN TAOS 19
ONCE FIVE, ONCE THREE. . . . . . . SP CONSIDER ME 4
TWO OR THREE THINGS IN THE PAST . . SP DANCER 1
A MAN KNOCKED THREE TIMES. . . . . SP MADAM WRONG VIS 1
I COULD OF HAD THREE - . . . . . . SP MADAM MIGHT-HAV 2
THREE PARTIES . . . . SP SAME IN BLUES 22
WHEN I ROLLED THREE 7'S . . . . . . SP SITUATION 1
'BOUT HALF-PAST THREE. . . . . . . SP SYLVESTER'S BED 2
THREE HUNDRED YEARS AGO IN AFRICA'S LAND. . . . . SP THE NEGRO MOTHE 8
THREE HUNDRED YEARS IN THE DEEPEST SOUTH: . . . . SP THE NEGRO MOTHE 17
ALREADY THERE WAS THREE - . . . . . . AYM GOSPEL CHA-CHA 60
OF THESE THREE. . . . . AYM SHOW FARE PLESE 31
THREE KICKS BETWEEN THE LEGS . . . PL THIRD DEGREE 10

THRILL 3

ON THIS SEPIA THRILL: . . . . SH HARLEM SWEETIES 4
RAINBOW-SWEET THRILL, ... SH HARLEM SWEETIES 42
COPPING A THRILL . . . . SP UP-BEAT 8

THRILLING 1

MORE THRILLING. . . . . SP MELLOW 8

THROAT 4

AND MY THROAT . . . . DK MINSTREL MAN 3
THROAT SOMETIMES. . . . . SP SLIVER 8
AS THE TUNE COMES FROM HIS THROAT SP TRUMPET PLAYER 42
TASTING ITS BITTERNESS IN MY THROAT. PL MILITANT 5

THRONE 1

I'LL HAVE A THRONE FOR MINE! . . . SP DEFERRED 42

THROUGH 51

WHEN DE WORMS GIT THROUGH . . . . . FC SATURDAY NIGHT 16
WHEN THE DAY IS THROUGH. . . . . . NM BLACK CLWN POEM 7
SMASH MY WAY THROUGH . . . . NM BLACK CLWN POEM 65
CALLING THROUGH TIME! . . . . NM BLACK CLWN POEM 74
BUT RIGHT LONG THROUGH HERE NOW, I CAN'T 'FORD TO BUY YOU NO HAT." NM BROKE 51
WHEN WE GOT THROUGH FIGHTING, OVER THERE, AND DYING? . . . . NM COLORED SL POEM 34
AN' BE MA FRIEND THROUGH ETERNITY." DK MA LORD 16
WHEN THE FLOWERS BREAK THROUGH THE EARTH, ... ANS CHANT MAY DAY 4
LIFE FOREVER THROUGH THE WORKERS' POWER - . . . . ANS CHANT TOM MOONY 44
THROUGH THE KIDS WHO DIE. . . . . . ANS KIDS WHO DIE 51
THE POOREST WORKER BARTERED THROUGH THE YEARS. . . . . ANS LET AMERICA BE 38
THE MUSIC GOT THROUGH. . . . . . . SH DEATH IN HARLEM 90
ALL THROUGH THE SPECTRUM . . . . . SH HARLEM SWEETIES 39
GIVES LOVE AWAY SHE'S THROUGH. . . SH MIDNIGHT CHIPPI 24
IF YOU CARRY THIS THROUGH. . . . . JC BLD SAM SOLOMON 26
CAN'T SEND NO MESSAGES THROUGH THE AIR. . . . . JC GOOD MORN STLIN 50
HAVE MADE UP THEIR MINDS JIM CROW IS THROUGH. . . . . JC JIM CROW'S LAST 14
BEFORE YOU'RE THROUGH. . . . . . . JC NOTE TO NAZIS 6
FLOWING THROUGH THE SOUTH. . . . . JC THE BITTER RIVR 3
TO WANDER THROUGH THIS LIVING WORLD FW REMEMBRANCE 1
AND LET YOUR SONGS DRIFT THROUGH THE SWINGING DOORS. . . . . OWT JUICE JOINT 18
YOU'RE THROUGH. . . . . OWT NEGRO SERVANT 9
THROUGH THE PARK. . . . . OWT NEGRO SERVANT 14
THE SAVIOUR PEEPING THROUGH. . . . LHR PASTORAL 3
THROUGH THE RED, WHITE, YELLOW SKINS SP A HOUSE IN TAOS 34
THROUGH SOME VAST MIST OF RACE . . SP AFRO-AMER FRAG 15
ALL THROUGH THE FIRE. . . . . SP ANGELS WINGS 10
BREAK THROUGH THE WALL! . . . . . . SP AS I GREW OLDER 26
TALK ON - TILL YOU GET THROUGH. . . SP BLD LANDLORD 18
ONE BATTED A HARD BALL RIGHT THROUGH MY WINDOW . . . . SP CHILDREN'S RYME 18
TO GET THROUGH HIGH AT TWENTY'S KIND OF LATE - . . . . SP DEFERRED 6
THROUGH COMPROMISE AND FEAR. . . . SP DEMOCRACY 4
THUS TOGETHER THROUGH LABOR. . . . SP FREEDOM'S PLOW 68
WHEN I GOT THROUGH. . . . . SP MADAM HER MADAM 8
I KNOWED WE WAS THROUGH! . . . . . SP MADAM MIGHT-HAV 20
BUT MY LOVIN' DAYS IS THROUGH. . . SP SAME IN BLUES 18
NOW, THROUGH MY CHILDREN, I'M REACHING THE GOAL. . . . . SP THE NEGRO MOTHE 20
NOW, THROUGH MY CHILDREN, YOUNG AND FREE, ... SP THE NEGRO MOTHE 21
BUT I KEPT TRUDGING ON THROUGH THE LONELY YEARS. . . . . SP THE NEGRO MOTHE 26
I HAD ONLY HOPE THEN, BUT NOW THROUGH YOU, ... SP THE NEGRO MOTHE 33
WHILE THE WEARY BLUES ECHOED THROUGH HIS HEAD. . . . . SP THE WEARY BLUES 34
THROUGH A PARK, THEN I CROSS ST. NICHOLAS, ... SP THEME FOR ENG B 12
THROUGH THE JUNGLE OF WHITE DANGER AYM ODE TO DINAH 31
THROUGH THE PALMETTO THICKET . . . PL FLORIDA WORKERS 6
THROUGH COMPROMISE AND FEAR. . . . PL FREEDOM 4
IN LONELY PITY THROUGH THE GEORGIA DUSK . . . . PL GEORGIA DUSK 3
SIGHTED THROUGH THE . . . . PL LONG VIEW NEGRO 2
LOOK THROUGH THE LARGER END - . . . PL LONG VIEW NEGRO 9
THROUGH THEIR "FREEDOM" SIEVE. . . PL LUMUMBA'S GRAVE 8
THROUGH THE MASK? . . . . PL MISSISSIPPI 16
WHEN THE WHITE FOLKS GET THROUGH . PL OFFICE BUILDING 1

THROW 4

THROW IT IN THE STREET? . . . . . . SP BLD LANDLORD 16
THEY THROW DIRT IN YOUR FACE, . . . SP WIDOW WOMAN 8
THROW DIRT IN YOUR FACE. . . . . . SP WIDOW WOMAN 10
WHEN YOU THROW . . . . PL THIRD DEGREE 15

THROWING 1

THROWING DOWN THE HAT OF A FOOL, AND STANDING FORTH, STRAIGHT AND STRONG, ... NM BLACK CLWN MOOD 14

THROWN 2

KNOWLEDGE ACQUIRED BUT THROWN AWAY. JC THE BITTER RIVR 20
THE SOLDIER THROWN FROM A JIM CROW BUS BEHIND STEEL BARS, ... JC THE BITTER RIVR 33

THROWS 2

THROWS HER ENORMOUS ARMS AROUND . . SP PROJECTION 5
THROWS A TOOTHPICK FROM HER WINDOW. SP SUMMER EVENING 19

THRUST 2

A SWORD THRUST, A HORN TIP, ... ANS SONG OF SPAIN 14
AFTER BITTER THRUST OF BEARING . . SP INTERNE AT PROV 28

THUD 1

DROPPED HER WITH A THUD. . . . . . SP BLD OF THE GIRL 6

THUMP 3

THUMP, THUMP, THUMP, WENT HIS FOOT ON THE FLOOR. . . . . SP THE WEARY BLUES 23
THUMP, THUMP, THUMP, WENT HIS FOOT ON THE FLOOR. . . . . SP THE WEARY BLUES 23
THUMP, THUMP, THUMP, WENT HIS FOOT ON THE FLOOR. . . . . SP THE WEARY BLUES 23

THUNDER 6

THUNDER OF THE RAIN GOD: . . . . . SP A HOUSE IN TAOS 2
THUNDER OF THE RAIN GOD: . . . . . SP A HOUSE IN TAOS 5
THUNDER OF THE RAIN GOD: . . . . . SP A HOUSE IN TAOS 8
UNDER THE THUNDER OF THE RAIN GOD? SP A HOUSE IN TAOS 14
NOW I SEE THE THUNDER . . . . . . SP AFRICA 3
THE THUNDER, ... SP AFRICA 9

THUS 2

THUS THE DREAM BECOMES NOT ONE MAN'S DREAM ALONE, ... SP FREEDOM'S PLOW 22
THUS TOGETHER THROUGH LABOR. . . . SP FREEDOM'S PLOW 68

THY 12

OF THY DARKNESS, ... WB POEM 20
OF THY NIGHTNESS. . . . . WB POEM 22
MIGHT FALL AT THY FEET, ... WB SONGS DARK VIRG 5
MIGHT WRAP ABOUT THY BODY, ... WB SONGS DARK VIRG 11
ABSORB THY BODY, ... WB SONGS DARK VIRG 12
HOLD AND HIDE THY BODY, ... WB SONGS DARK VIRG 13
TO ANNIHILATE THY BODY, ... WB SONGS DARK VIRG 18
HE SAID, OH, LORD, THY WILL BE DONE! LHR BLD MARY'S SON 24
CHANCE IS THY OTHER NAME. . . . . . LHR DEAR LVLY DEATH 10
LET ME TO THY BOSOM FLY! . . . . . SP MYSTERY 7
THAT I WHO AM THY SHEPHERD . . . . SP SUNDAY MORNING 41
LOVE THY NEIGHBOR AS THYSELF . . . AYM HORN OF PLENTY 85

THYSELF 1

LOVE THY NEIGHBOR AS THYSELF . . . AYM HORN OF PLENTY 85

TICKET 7

I GOT A RAILROAD TICKET, ... WB BLUES FANTASY 20
GOT A RAILROAD TICKET, ... WB BLUES FANTASY 23
HAD TO PAY HER TICKET. . . . . . . SH ANNOUNCEMENT 5
HERE'S FIVE DOLLARS, CASSIE, BUY A TICKET BACK. . . . . SH LETTER 20
GIMME SIX-BITS' WORTH O' TICKET . . SH SIX-BITS BLUES 1
I SAY SIX-BITS' WORTH O' TICKET . . SH SIX-BITS BLUES 3
ON A ONE-WAY TICKET - . . . . SP ONE-WAY TICKET 25

TICKETS 1

STRIP TICKETS STILL ILLUSION? . . . AYM SHOW FARE PLESE 9

TIGER 1

A TIGER, A LION, AND AN OWL . . . . SP DELINQUENT 11

TIGHT 5

AND HOLDIN' THINGS TIGHT. . . . . . NM BIG-TIMER POEM 52
AND SHE BEEN HOLDIN' 'EM SO TIGHT
TILL DE EAGLE'S IN TEARS - . . . NM BROKE 24
AND HOLD IT TIGHT. . . . . FW LITTLE SONG 4
YOU BRAID YOUR HAIR TOO TIGHT - . . OWT HONEY BABE 2
CLOSE UP TIGHT THAT NIGHT. . . . . SP LIKEWISE 11

TILL 32

TILL LICKER'LL LET YOU BE. . . . . FC BLD OF GIN MARY 24
TILL THESE LICKER-HEADED ROUNDERS FC LISTEN HERE 11
TILL DE DAWN COMES IN. . . . . . . FC SATURDAY NIGHT 8
TILL DE RED DAWN COME. . . . . . . FC SATURDAY NIGHT 28
AND SHE BEEN HOLDIN' 'EM SO TIGHT
TILL DE EAGLE'S IN TEARS - . . . . NM BROKE 24
TILL BEAUTY AND PRIDE FILLS EACH
DARK FACE . . . . NM DARK YOUTH USA 20
80-VOICES: TILL THE FORCES OF THE
EARTH ARE YOURS . . . . ANS CHANT MAY DAY 35
THEY LOVED ONE ANOTHER TILL . . . . SH DEATH IN HARLEM 89
TILL YOU DON'T KNOW RIGHT FROM
WRONG. . . . . SH HEY-HEY BLUES 12
I WALKED DE STREETS TILL . . . . . SH OUT OF WORK 1
I DONE WALKED DE STREETS TILL . . . SH OUT OF WORK 3
TILL WE'RE IN JAIL. . . . . FW CIRCLES 6
TILL YESTERDAY'S . . . . OWT BLUES ON A BOX 2
TILL YOU FIX THIS HOUSE UP NEW. . . SP BLD LANDLORD 12
TALK ON - TILL YOU GET THROUGH. . . SP BLD LANDLORD 18
TILL THEY'RE THE HEART . . . . . . SP COLLEGE FORMAL 13
TILL THE WHITE DAY IS DONE. . . . . SP DREAM VARIATION 4
TILL THE QUICK DAY IS DONE. . . . . SP DREAM VARIATION 13
TILL THE LAST WORMS COME . . . . . SP DRUM 4
TILL THE LAST STARS FALL. . . . . . SP DRUM 6
TILL IT DRIVES YOU CRAZY, TOO. . . SP EVIL 4
TO TILL THE SOIL, AND HARNESS THE
POWER OF THE WATERS. . . . . . . SP FREEDOM'S PLOW 19
DANCE WITH YOU TILL DAY - . . . . . SP JUKE BOX LOVE 11
TILL I GET OVER . . . . SP MADAM NUMBER WR 23
TILL I GOT MIXED UP . . . . SP MADAM'S PAST HI 12
LOVE TILL THE DAY I DIE. . . . . . SP MIDWINTER BLUES 18
NOON TILL NIGHT . . . . SP PARADE 22
TILL THE SUN GOES DOWN. . . . . . . SP SUNDAY BY COMB 2
BUT I HAD TO KEEP ON TILL MY WORK
WAS DONE: . . . . SP THE NEGRO MOTHE 28
FOR I WILL BE WITH YOU TILL NO WHITE
BROTHER . . . . SP THE NEGRO MOTHE 51
SHAKES HANDS WITH EMMETT TILL. . . AYM ASK YOUR MAMA 56
TILL WE . . . . PL FROSTING 6

TIME 66

I WAS A RED MAN ONE TIME, ... WB LAMENT DARK PEO 1
EVER TIME I MOUNTS THIS BENCH . . . FC BLD OF GIN MARY 7
DON'T LAST ALL DE TIME. . . . . . . FC CRAP GAME 8
ANY OLD TIME . . . . FC DEATH DO DIRTY 2
NEXT TIME SHE MAKES ME SORE. . . . FC EVIL WOMAN 4
BUT I'LL HAVE MO' SENSE NEXT TIME. FC GYPSY MAN 16
THAT LAUGHS AND CRIES AT THE SAME
TIME. . . . . FC JAZZ BAND 12
AN' YOU'S A LONG TIME . . . . FC SATURDAY NIGHT 17
CALLING THROUGH TIME! . . . . NM BLACK CLWN POEM 74
DE TIME IS FOURTEEN HOURS A DAY? . NM BROKE 34
EVER TIME DE TRAINS PASS . . . . . DK HOMESICK BLUES 5
OF TIME - . . . . DK LINCOLN MONUMNT 10
ON THE SCRAP HEAP OF TIME - . . . . ANS CHANT TOM MOONY 28
MAKE THIS EARLY MORNING TIME TO KEEP
BODY AND SOUL . . . . SH DAYBREAK 7
BIG TIME SPORTS AND GIRLS WHO KNOW SH DEATH IN HARLEM 37
PLAY A LONG TIME, GAL! . . . . . . SH DEATH IN HARLEM 46
I HAVE A GOOD TIME! . . . . SH IF-ING 16
SAM SAID, IT'S TIME TO GO . . . . . JC BLD SAM SOLOMON 8
IT'S TIME TO GO. . . . . OWT RAID 9
IT WAS A LONG TIME AGO. . . . . . . SP AS I GREW OLDER 1
NEXT TIME A MAN COMES NEAR ME . . . SP CORA 3
IN TIME TO WASH AND DRESS. . . . . SP DEFERRED 27
IT ALL THE TIME. . . . . SP DIME 8
UNTIL TIME IS LOST . . . . SP DRUM 9
AS TIME GROWS LONGER UNTIL DAY . . SP DRUNKARD 3
MAYBE NO LUCK FOR A LONG TIME. . . SP ELEVATOR BOY 14
AND NO TIME. . . . . SP END 3
IT WAS A LONG TIME AGO. . . . . . . SP FREEDOM'S PLOW 100
A LONG TIME AGO, BUT NOT TOO LONG
AGO. . . . . SP FREEDOM'S PLOW 28
A LONG TIME AGO. . . . . SP FREEDOM'S PLOW 183
A LONG TIME AGO, BUT NOT TOO LONG
AGO, A MAN SAID: . . . . SP FREEDOM'S PLOW 90
A WONDERFUL TIME - THE WAR: . . . . SP GREEN MEMORY 1
HELL, NO! IT'S TIME TO TALK BACK
NOW! . . . . SP IN EXPLANATION 29
HISTORY SAYS IT'S TIME. . . . . . . SP IN EXPLANATION 30
IN TIME OF SILVER RAIN . . . . . . SP IN TIME SILVER 1
IN TIME OF SILVER RAIN . . . . . . SP IN TIME SILVER 11
IN TIME OF SILVER RAIN . . . . . . SP IN TIME SILVER 21
YOU GOT TO LOVE ALL THE TIME. . . . SP LAMENT OVER LOV 18
TIME I PAY RENT AND GET MY FOOD . . SP LETTER 2
MY OLD TIME DADDY . . . . SP LOVER'S RETURN 1
A LITTLE TIME TO SPEAK? . . . . . . SP MADAM MINISTER 4
HE WORKED ALL THE TIME. . . . . . . SP MADAM MIGHT-HAV 9
FIRST TIME IN MY LIFE . . . . SP MADAM MIGHT-HAV 11
COME TIME TO DIE. . . . . SP MADAM MINISTER 22
LAST TIME I TOLD HER. . . . . SP MADAM CHARTY CH 25
DAUGHTER, ONCE UPON A TIME - . . . SP MAMA AND DAUGHT 9
BUT IT WAS A LONG TIME AGO . . . . SP MAMA AND DAUGHT 13
I LOST MY TIME. . . . . SP MIDNIGHT RAFFLE 6
THAT AIN'T NO TIME TO GO. . . . . . SP MIDWINTER BLUES 12
BUT ALL THE TIME . . . . SP MOTHER TO SON 8
TO YOU ALL THE TIME. . . . . SP PORTER 3
THAT'S ONE TIME, PRETTY PAPA. . . . SP WIDOW WOMAN 11
WHAT A GRAND TIME WAS THE WAR! . . SP WORLD WAR II 1
WHAT A GRAND TIME WAS THE WAR! . . SP WORLD WAR II 3
WHAT A GRAND TIME WAS THE WAR. . . SP WORLD WAR II 7
ALL THE TIME. . . . . SP 50 - 50 11
WHAT TIME IS IT, MAMA? . . . . . . AYM BLUES IN STEREO 28
WHAT TIME IS IT NOW? . . . . AYM BLUES IN STEREO 29
WHAT TIME IS IT, MAMA? . . . . . . AYM BLUES IN STEREO 32
WHAT TIME NOW? . . . . AYM BLUES IN STEREO 33
AND ELECTION TIME . . . . AYM HORN OF PLENTY 89
WHAT TIME IS IT NOW? . . . . AYM ODE TO DINAH 63
WHAT TIME IS IT NOW? . . . . AYM ODE TO DINAH 65
DON'T CARE WHAT TIME IT IS - . . . AYM ODE TO DINAH 66
TAKEN LATE IN TIME . . . . PL NORTHERN LIBERL 9
THEIR OWN SWEET TIME TO FLOWER . . PL SWEET WORDS RAC 2

TIMELESS 1

TIMELESS WALLS . . . . DK LINCOLN MONUMNT 9

TIMES 5

AND IT'S BETTER A THOUSAND TIMES
YOU'RE IN FRANCE DEAD. . . . . . NM COLORED SL POEM 45
IN THESE OUR TIMES . . . . SP IN EXPLANATION 39
A MAN KNOCKED THREE TIMES. . . . . SP MADAM WRONG VIS 1
IN TIMES OF STORMY WEATHER . . . . SP STRANGE HURT 1
SO MANY TIMES BEFORE. . . . . PL SWEET WORDS RAC 12

TIME-CLOCK 2

AND DRIVE US TO THE TIME-CLOCK AND
THE PLOW . . . . ANS OPEN LETTER 27
THE FORCE THAT BREAKS THE
TIME-CLOCK. . . . . ANS OPEN LETTER 56

TIME-DEAD 1

A QUEEN FROM SOME TIME-DEAD EGYPTIAN
NIGHT . . . . SP WHEN SUE WEARS 7

TIME-LOST 1

SUBDUED AND TIME-LOST . . . . SP AFRO-AMER FRAG 13

TIME'S 3

MARCH WITH YOU DOWN TIME'S STREET. SL SCOTTSBORO 6
AND RENT TIME'S NEARLY HERE. . . . SP DOWN AND OUT 8
BUT I FELT MA TIME'S A-COMIN'. . . SP SYLVESTER'S BED 17

TIMME 1

PLAYED BY INEZ AND TIMME. . . . . . SP PROJECTION 14

TINGLE 1

THE TINGLE OF A TEAR. . . . . SP LADY'S BOOGIE 8

TINKLING 1

TINKLING TREBLE. . . . . SP DREAM BOOGE VAR 1

TINKLIN' 1

ALL THIS TALKIN' AIN'T NOTHIN' BUT
TINKLIN' SYMBOLS AND SOUNDIN'
BRASS: . . . . NM BROKE 56

TINTED 1

WALNUT TINTED . . . . SH HARLEM SWEETIES 13

TINY 3

AND FROM ITS TINY WINDOW . . . . . DK WINTER SWEEETNS 3
AND BELIEVED THE TINY FLOWERS . . . LHR PASTORAL 5
FOUR TINY GIRLS . . . . PL BIRMINGHAM SUND 15

TIP 3

A SWORD THRUST, A HORN TIP, ... ANS SONG OF SPAIN 14
FROM THE WING TIP OF A MATCH TIP . AYM JAZZTET MUTED 8
FROM THE WING TIP OF A MATCH TIP . AYM JAZZTET MUTED 8

TIPPED 1

AND WATCHED THE BLUE WAVES TIPPED
WITH FOAM. . . . . DK SAILOR 4

TIPPIN 2

CAME TIPPIN INTO DIXIE'S TO GET A
VIEW. . . . . SH DEATH IN HARLEM 59
CAME TIPPIN INTO DIXIE'S WITH SMILES
ON THEIR FACES. . . . . SH DEATH IN HARLEM 60

TIPS 3

ON THEIR SHOE TIPS. . . . . SP SUMMER EVENING 9
WHO TIPS AMONG THE SHADOWS . . . . AYM BIRD IN ORBIT 87
TIPS AMONG THE SHADOWS . . . . . . AYM BIRD IN ORBIT 90

TIRE 2

I TIRE SO OF HEARING PEOPLE SAY. . SP DEMOCRACY 10

I TIRE SO OF HEARING PEOPLE SAY. PL FREEDOM 10

TIRED 13

WEARY AS THE TIRED NIGHT. WB SUMMER NIGHT 12
I'M TIRED. FC CLOSING TIME 7
UH! I SHO AM TIRED. NM BROKE 1
TIRED NOW OF THE BITTER RIVER. JC THE BITTER RIVR 75
TIRED NOW OF THE PAT ON THE BACK. JC THE BITTER RIVR 76
TIRED NOW OF THE STEEL BARS JC THE BITTER RIVR 77
I'M TIRED OF SEGREGATION. JC THE BITTER RIVR 79
TIRED OF FILTH AND MUD. JC THE BITTER RIVR 80
I'M TIRED OF THE BITTER RIVER! JC THE BITTER RIVR 83
TIRED OF THE BARS! JC THE BITTER RIVR 90
FOR WHICH THE TIRED FW EXITS 6
THE DESPERATE, THE TIRED, FW PRAYER 4
BECAUSE SHE'S TIRED. SP GRADUATION 30
GEORGE SALLIE COOLIE BOY GETS TIRED SOMETIMES. SP IN EXPLANATION 17
JUST MAN WOMAN TIRED SAYS: SP IN EXPLANATION 55
THE DESPERATE, THE TIRED, SP LITANY 4
AND I AM GETTIN' TIRED! SP SOUTHERN MAMMY 4
I AM GETTIN' TIRED! SP SOUTHERN MAMMY 5
GOT TIRED OF ASKING, WHEN? PL GHOSTS OF 1619 16

TITLE 5

A MAN WITH THE TITLE OF GOVERNOR HAS SPOKEN: ANS CHANT TOM MOONY 4
A MAN WITH THE TITLE OF GOVERNOR HAS SPOKEN: ANS CHANT TOM MOONY 6
BUT THE MAN WITH THE TITLE OF GOVERNOR ANS CHANT TOM MOONY 10
OF COURSE, THE MAN WITH THE TITLE OF GOVERNOR ANS CHANT TOM MOONY 26
WITH NO TITLE IN FRONT OF NAME SP IN EXPLANATION 54

TITLES 4

THE FOLKS WITH NO TITLES IN FRONT OF THEIR NAMES SP IN EXPLANATION 1
WITH NO TITLES IN FRONT OF THEIR NAMES. SP IN EXPLANATION 28
THE PEOPLE WITH NO TITLES IN FRONT OF THEIR NAMES SP IN EXPLANATION 40
BECAUSE OF PEOPLE WITH NO TITLES SP IN EXPLANATION 60

TOAD 2

AND DON'T YOU KNOW THAT OLD WOMAN SWELLED UP LIKE A SPECKLED TOAD NM BROKE 21
FIT FER A HOPPIN' TOAD. SP BOUND NO'TH BLS 24

TOBACCO 1

TOBACCO WORKERS. ANS OPEN LETTER 9

TODAY 33

DANCE TODAY! WB HARLEM NIGHT CL 5
JOY TODAY! WB HARLEM NIGHT CL 21
TODAY. NM COLORED SL POEM 20
THE AMERICAN YOUTH OF TODAY. NM DARK YOUTH USA 25
THAT ALL OVER THE EARTH TODAY ANS CHANT TOM MOONY 12
HUNGRY YET TODAY DESPITE THE DREAM. ANS LET AMERICA BE 35
BEATEN YET TODAY - O, PIONEERS! ANS LET AMERICA BE 56
SURELY NOT ME? THE MILLIONS ON RELIEF TODAY? ANS LET AMERICA BE 53
EXCEPT THE DREAM THAT'S ALMOST DEAD TODAY. ANS LET AMERICA BE 61
"YOU ARE MY SISTER - NOW - TODAY!" ANS OPEN LETTER 40
TODAY. ANS OPEN LETTER 67
HOME TODAY! SH DEATH IN HARLEM 130
(I KNOW IT AIN'T TODAY) SH EVIL MORNING 2
CAUSE I'M SURE ENJOYING MYSELF TODAY! SH SUNDAY 7
THAT YOU'RE OUR ALLY JUST FOR TODAY. JC GOOD MORN STLIN 24
THAN JUST TODAY. JC GOOD MORN STLIN 48
ALTHOUGH RIGHT NOW, EVEN YET TODAY. JC JIM CROW'S LAST 11
TODAY. FW HEART 19
YESTERDAY WAS TODAY! OWT YESTERDAY TODAY 2
TODAY YOU DONE AWAY. OWT YESTERDAY TODAY 4
I DON'T KNOW HOW YOU FEEL TODAY - OWT YESTERDAY TODAY 11
DOWNTOWN TO WORK TODAY. SP BLUE MONDAY 2
TODAY, THIS YEAR SP DEMOCRACY 2
SO ALL OVER THE WORLD TODAY SP IN EXPLANATION 18
AIN'T GOIN' WITH YOU TODAY! SP MADAM WRONG VIS 20
FOR SIN TODAY. SP MADAM MINISTER 33
ROTS IN HELL TODAY! SP MAMA AND DAUGHT 16
THE WATER IS TODAY. SP SEA CALM 3
CHILDREN, I COME BACK TODAY SP THE NEGRO MOTHE 1
DARK ONES OF TODAY, MY DREAMS MUST COME TRUE: SP THE NEGRO MOTHE 34
HIS OWN TODAY SP YOUNG SAILOR 4
AND TODAY? SP YOUNG SAILOR 14
IN LITTLE GRAVES TODAY AWAIT PL BIRMINGHAM SUND 17
TODAY - PL CROWNS GARLANDS 7
TODAY, THIS YEAR PL FREEDOM 2
THE VERY ROOM IN WHICH TODAY THE AIR PL JUNIOR ADDICT 13
TODAY - PL MILITANT 13
AS IF THE WEAPONS USED TODAY PL MOTHER IN WAR 5
IS ALIVE WITH GHOSTS TODAY. PL OCTOBER 16 RAID 24

TODAY'S 2

TODAY'S DARK CHILD, TOMORROW'S STRONG MAN: NM DARK YOUTH USA 2
THAN BRING TODAY'S RELEASE PL JUNIOR ADDICT 25

TOE 3

I DIDN'T MEAN TO STUMP MA TOE ON YOU, LADY. SP MAGNOLIA FLOWER 9
I DIDN'T MEAN TO STUMP MA TOE ON YOU. SP MAGNOLIA FLOWER 13
STUMPED ITS TOE - PL AMER HEARTBREAK 3

TOES 2

TO CINNAMON TOES. SH HARLEM SWEETIES 24
PLANT YOUR TOES IN THE COOL SWAMP MUD. OWT FLIGHT 1

TOGETHER 18

PULLING HIMSELF TOGETHER, BOASTING LOUDLY AGAIN, BUT REALIZING WITHIN THE NM BIG-TIMER MOOD 11
TOGETHER, RECKON I'LL TRY . . . SHO, I WANTS DE JOB! YES, SIR! NM BROKE 30
40-VOICES: GROW STRONG WITH UNION, ALL HANDS TOGETHER - ANS CHANT MAY DAY 11
TELLING OTHERS TO GET TOGETHER. ANS KIDS WHO DIE 13
TO BELIEVE AN ANGELO HERNDON, OR EVER GET TOGETHER. ANS KIDS WHO DIE 36
LET US TOGETHER, SAY: ANS OPEN LETTER 38
TOGETHER IN MY BIG OLD DOWN-HOME FRAME. SH DAYBREAK 8
EACH FOURTEEN YEARS OLD WHEN LYNCHED TOGETHER BENEATH THE JC THE BITTER RIVR 1
TOGETHER WE HAVE LAUNCHED A SHIP JC TO CAPTAIN MULZ 39
TOGETHER. FW TODAY 5
PRESS HANDS TOGETHER, LAUGHING AT HER SONG. OWT LINCOLN THEATRE 15
IN LITTLE BANDS TOGETHER. SP FREEDOM'S PLOW 37
"YOU ARE A MAN. TOGETHER WE ARE BUILDING OUR LAND." SP FREEDOM'S PLOW 156
THUS TOGETHER THROUGH LABOR. SP FREEDOM'S PLOW 68
LET US ROAM THE NIGHT TOGETHER SP HARLEM NIGHT SO 2
LET US ROAM THE NIGHT TOGETHER SP HARLEM NIGHT SO 15
HER FEATURES IS ALL RUN TOGETHER SP NECESSITY 9
GATHERED TOGETHER - SP SUN SONG 4

TOIL 1

NOW I HAVE FINISHED MY TOIL. ANS BLDS OF LENIN 8

TOLD 22

AND TOLD ME I'D BETTER PAY HER FOR MY ROOM RENT AND BOARD! NM BROKE 22
THEY TOLD US AMERICA WOULD KNOW NO BLACK OR WHITE: NM COLORED SL POEM 11
CAUSE THEY TOLD ME DE NORTH WAS FINE. SH EVENIN' BLUES 2
CAUSE THEY TOLD ME DE NORTH WAS FINE. SH EVENIN' BLUES 4
WPA MAN TOLD ME: SH OUT OF WORK 11
TOLD HER HUSBAND SH PRESENT 2
MRS. BETHUNE TOLD MARTIN DIES. JC JIM CROW'S LAST 21
AND LOVE'S OLD STORY TOLD - FW CAROLINA CABIN 20
BUT SHE TOLD EVERYBODY FW GIRL 7
DON'T YOU 'MEMBER I TOLD YOU ABOUT IT SP BLD LANDLORD 3
THE UNDERTAKER TOLD 'EM. SP BLD OF THE MAN 3
BUT THE DEVIL TOLD ME: SP LOVER'S RETURN 17
I TOLD HIM, JACKSON. SP MADAM MIGHT-HAV 21
NO SOONER HAD I TOLD HIM SP MADAM WRONG VIS 21
LAST TIME I TOLD HER. SP MADAM CHARTY CH 25
I TOLD THE MAN SP MADAM'S CALLING 5
YOU TOLD ME THAT YOU DIDN'T. SP MAYBE 3
HE TOLD ME THAT HE LOVED ME SP MIDWINTER BLUES 13
HE TOLD ME THAT HE LOVED ME. SP MIDWINTER BLUES 15
CAESAR TOLD ME TO KEEP HIS DOOR-STEPS CLEAN. SP NEGRO 5
YES, SIR, I TOLD HER. AYM ASK YOUR MAMA 12
THEY TOLD US BEFORE. PL HARLEM 6

TOLE 2

HE TOLE ME I WAS GWINE. DK MA LORD 14
GYPSY DONE TOLE ME - SP BAD LUCK CARD 7

TOM 14

TOM MOONEY! ANS CHANT TOM MOONY 1
TOM MOONEY! ANS CHANT TOM MOONY 2
TOM MOONEY! ANS CHANT TOM MOONY 3
TOM MOONEY! ANS CHANT TOM MOONY 14
TOM MOONEY! ANS CHANT TOM MOONY 15
TOM MOONEY! ANS CHANT TOM MOONY 16
TOM MOONEY. ANS CHANT TOM MOONY 31
TOM MOONEY. ANS CHANT TOM MOONY 33
TOM MOONEY. ANS CHANT TOM MOONY 35
TOM MOONEY. ANS CHANT TOM MOONY 37
TOM MOONEY. ANS CHANT TOM MOONY 39
TOM MOONEY. ANS CHANT TOM MOONY 41
TOM MOONEY. ANS CHANT TOM MOONY 46
SEND FOR UNCLE TOM ON HIS MIGHTY KNEES. PL FINAL CALL 28

TOMB 3

HIGH IN A MARBLE TOMB.	ANS BLDS OF LENIN	2
ALIVE IN A MARBLE TOMB.	ANS BLDS OF LENIN	10
HONORED IN A MARBLE TOMB.	ANS BLDS OF LENIN	18

TOMBS 1

IN NEON TOMBS THE MUSIC	AYM JAZZTET MUTED	10

TOMBSTONE 1

PUT NO TOMBSTONE AT MY HEAD.	DK DEATH SEAMAN	5

TOMORROW 28

TOMORROW. . . . WHO KNOWS?	WB HARLEM NIGHT CL	4
ABOUT TOMORROW	WB HARLEM NIGHT CL	16
TOMORROW. . . . IS DARKNESS.	WB HARLEM NIGHT CL	20
SO I CLIMB TOWARD TOMORROW, OUT OF PAST SORROW,	NM DARK YOUTH USA	22
WE HAVE TOMORROW	DK YOUTH	1
A FREE WORLD TOMORROW,	JC BLACK MAN SPEAK	26
CHARTING TOMORROW.	FW MIGRATION	17
AND FAR-OFF LONG TOMORROW:	FW MOTHERLAND	2
AND HELD FOR TOMORROW.	FW WALLS	8
TOMORROW IS ANOTHER DAY.	SP DEMOCRACY	12
TOMORROW.	SP I, TOO	8
AND THE DAY AFTER TOMORROW,	SP NIGHT FOUR SONG	4
THAT TOMORROW IS MONDAY.	SP SUMMER EVENING	28
AND MAKE OF THOSE YEARS A TORCH FOR TOMORROW.	SP THE NEGRO MOTHE	38
TOMORROW MAY BE	SP TOMORROW	1
WAITING FOR TOMORROW TO COME -	SP WINE-O	3
TOMORROW . . .	SP WINE-O	7
EVERY DAY'S TOMORROW	AYM HORN OF PLENTY	68
TO CATCH UP WITH TOMORROW	AYM IS IT TRUE?	30
LYNCHED TOMORROW SWAYS.	AYM ODE TO DINAH	101
A LYNCHED TOMORROW SWAYS.	AYM ODE TO DINAH	99
WHOSE TOMORROW SINGS A HYMN	PL BIRMINGHAM SUND	20
TOMORROW IS ANOTHER DAY.	PL FREEDOM	12
TRUE OF TOMORROW.	PL HISTORY	4
TOMORROW WILL MARK	PL LUMUMBA'S GRAVE	22
I'D MAKE TOMORROW.	PL THIRD DEGREE	12
THAT TOMORROW	PL WITHOUT BENEFIT	3
TOMORROW YOU'LL BE DEAD	PL WITHOUT BENEFIT	5

TOMORROW'S 6

AN' TOMORROW'S CHILE'LL	FC RED SILK STOCK	9
TODAY'S DARK CHILD, TOMORROW'S STRONG MAN:	NM DARK YOUTH USA	2
RUNS OUT TOMORROW'S	OWT BLUES ON A BOX	4
I CANNOT LIVE ON TOMORROW'S BREAD.	SP DEMOCRACY	14
I CANNOT LIVE ON TOMORROW'S BREAD.	PL FREEDOM	14
TOMORROW'S SUNSHINE GIVE	PL JUNIOR ADDICT	17

TOM-TOM 1

AND HELPLESSNESS. THE MUSIC IS LIKE A MOURNFUL TOM-TOM IN THE DARK! BUT	NM BLACK CLWN MOOD	11

TOM-TOMS 6

ALL THE TOM-TOMS OF THE JUNGLES BEAT IN MY BLOOD,	WB FOR PORTRAIT OF	1
THE LOW BEATING OF THE TOM-TOMS,	SP DANSE AFRICAINE	1
THE SLOW BEATING OF THE TOM-TOMS,	SP DANSE AFRICAINE	2
AND THE TOM-TOMS BEAT.	SP DANSE AFRICAINE	12
AND THE TOM-TOMS BEAT,	SP DANSE AFRICAINE	13
AND THE LOW BEATING OF THE TOM-TOMS	SP DANSE AFRICAINE	14

TONE 4

EVERY TONE I SEEK	FW SILENCE	7
HAS A VULGAR TONE.	LHR CONSERVATORY	2
AND FOR YOUR LOVE SONG TONE THEIR RUMBLE DOWN.	SP JUKE BOX LOVE	6
IN A DEEP SONG VOICE WITH A MELANCHOLY TONE	SP THE WEARY BLUES	17

TONGUE 3

AND ITS GALL COATS THE RED OF MY TONGUE,	JC THE BITTER RIVR	11
COATS MY TONGUE.	JC THE BITTER RIVR	86
IN STRANGE UN-NEGRO TONGUE -	SP AFRO-AMER FRAG	9

TONGUES 2

DARK MOUTHS WHERE RED TONGUES BURN	ANS A NEW SONG	30
IN TONGUES UNANALYZED UNECHOED	AYM IS IT TRUE?	7

TONIGHT 8

AND I'M STILL JUST A "NIGGER" IN AMERICA TONIGHT.	NM COLORED SL POEM	47
RIDING THE HILLS TONIGHT.	FW NEW MOON	2
TONIGHT THERE'S PREACHING!	OWT JITNEY	35
TONIGHT THE WAVES MARCH	SP MOONLIGHT NIGHT	1
I JUST DRAWED MY MONEY TONIGHT	SP PREFERENCE	9
A PACE TONIGHT.	SP THEME FOR ENG B	3
HOW THIN AND SHARP IS THE MOON TONIGHT!	SP WINTER MOON	1
IS THE SLIM CURVED CROOK OF THE MOON TONIGHT!	SP WINTER MOON	3

TOO 120

JUST A BIT TOO BOLD?	WB JAZZONIA	11
I WAS A BLACK MAN, TOO,	WB LAMENT DARK PEO	3
ARE TOO HEAVY WITH COLOR.	WB POEME D'AUTOMNE	2
OF TOO MANY NIGHTS OF LOVE.	WB SOLEDAD	3
FOR YOUR FACES ARE BEAUTIFUL, TOO.	WB THE WHITE ONES	2
YOUR FACES ARE WHIRLING LIGHTS OF LOVELINESS AND SPLENDOR, TOO.	WB THE WHITE ONES	4
I BEATS MA SIDE GAL TOO.	FC BAD MAN	8
BEATS MA SIDE GAL TOO.	FC BAD MAN	10
YOU'S TOO PRETTY.	FC RED SILK STOCK	7
DEAD, TOO.	FC SATURDAY NIGHT	20
AND I SHO HAD A PRETTY GAL, TOO, UP YONDER ON SUGAR HILL.	NM BROKE	48
(AIN'T SEEN HER IN SIX YEARS! USED TO GO WITH HER, TOO!)	NM BROKE	63
YES, INDEEDY, I SHO HAVE MISSED YOU, TOO!	NM BROKE	67
IS I MARRIED? NO, ALL THESE-HERE GIRLS UP NORTH IS TOO LIGHT. . .	NM BROKE	70
THE UNIONS BARRED US; THE FACTORIES, TOO,	NM COLORED SL POEM	22
BUT BROKEN WAS THE SOLDIER'S DREAM, TOO BAD TO BE	NM COLORED SL POEM	49
AM I TOO OLD TO SEE THE FAIRIES DANCE?	DK AFTR MNY SPRNGS	7
MA LORD'S LIFE WAS TROUBLE, TOO,	DK MA LORD	8
EVANGELISTA, TOO,	SL SCOTTSBORO	26
ITS COURT, TOO WEAK TO STAND AGAINST A MOB,	SL TOWN OF SCOTTSB	3
ITS PEOPLE'S HEART, TOO SMALL TO HOLD A SOB.	SL TOWN OF SCOTTSB	4
WORKERS, KNOW THAT WE TOO CAN CRY,	ANS SONG OF SPAIN	59
TOO LATE!	ANS SONG OF SPAIN	61
TOO WELL DEFENDED,	ANS UNION	10
AND SISTER, TOO.	SH BLD THE SINNER	8
BESSIE WAS, TOO.	SH DEATH IN HARLEM	88
FORE IT IS TOO LATE!	SH EVIL MORNING	16
I WILL SING 'EM, TOO.	SH HEY-HEY BLUES	14
I'LL SING 'EM, TOO.	SH HEY-HEY BLUES	16
AND IF YOU THINK I BEEN TOO MEAN BEFORE,	SH LETTER	12
AND I WILL LOVE YOU, TOO.	SH MIDNIGHT CHIPPI	6
BUT DON'T MAKE IT TOO LONG.	SH SIX-BITS BLUES	8
DON'T MAKE IT TOO LONG.	SH SIX-BITS BLUES	10
TOO FAR TO ONE SIDE.	SH SNOB	8
AIN'T THAT TOO BAD?	SH SUNDAY	14
AND NAVY, TOO -	JC BLACK MAN SPEAK	18
LIFT THEIR HEADS, TOO, WITH GUN IN HAND	JC GOOD MORN STLIN	33
IN THE FOUR FREEDOMS, TOO,	JC HOW ABOUT DIXIE	6
IT MEANS FREEDOM AT HOME, TOO -	JC HOW ABOUT DIXIE	23
BUT INDIA AND CHINA AND HARLEM, TOO,	JC JIM CROW'S LAST	13
TOO LONG HAS THE TASTE OF ITS WATER	JC THE BITTER RIVR	4
TOO LONG HAS ITS EVIL POISON	JC THE BITTER RIVR	8
I HAVE DRUNK AT THE RIVER TOO LONG:	JC THE BITTER RIVR	66
WITH ITS FILTH AND ITS MUD TOO LONG.	JC THE BITTER RIVR	74
THERE ARE THOSE, TOO, WHO FOR SO LONG	JC TO CAPTAIN MULZ	16
HE, TOO, A SYMBOL OF NEW LIBERTIES.	JC TO CAPTAIN MULZ	46
THERE IS A CREW OF MANY RACES, TOO,	JC TO CAPTAIN MULZ	47
TOO BITTER TO REMEMBER -	FW CHIPPY	5
WITH TOO MANY	FW FRAGMENTS	5
HATE HIM, TOO,	FW MIGRATION	9
TOO DEAD	OWT DECEASED	4
YOU BRAID YOUR HAIR TOO TIGHT -	OWT HONEY BABE	2
LET THOSE WOMEN WITH THEIR LIPS TOO RED	OWT JUICE JOINT	21
AND WOMEN, TOO, WHOM ANYONE MAY MEET	OWT JUICE JOINT	35
AND I'M TOO BLUE	OWT TOO BLUE	16
I THOUGHT YOU WAS HAPPY, TOO.	OWT YESTERDAY TODAY	10
AND THE NIGHT WAS BLACK, TOO.	SP A BLACK PIERROT	4
AND MY HEART WAS BLEEDING, TOO.	SP A BLACK PIERROT	9
I WOULD TAKE YOUR MONEY, TOO.	SP BLD THE GYPSY	23
AND I WORK TOO HARD	SP BLUE BAYOU	9
FOR TOO LITTLE PAY -	SP BLUE BAYOU	10
WHO WORKS, TOO -	SP CONSIDER ME	28
I LIVE HERE, TOO.	SP DEMOCRACY	19
ELEVATOR TOO LONG.	SP ELEVATOR BOY	22
TILL IT DRIVES YOU CRAZY, TOO.	SP EVIL	4
AN EAGLE ON A QUARTER, TOO.	SP FACT	2
THERE WERE SLAVES THEN, TOO,	SP FREEDOM'S PLOW	105
SEE THE DIFFICULTIES, TOO, AND THE OBSTACLES.	SP FREEDOM'S PLOW	16
A LONG TIME AGO, BUT NOT TOO LONG AGO,	SP FREEDOM'S PLOW	28
A LONG TIME AGO, BUT NOT TOO LONG AGO, A MAN SAID:	SP FREEDOM'S PLOW	30
BUT IN THEIR HEARTS THE SLAVES BELIEVED HIM, TOO,	SP FREEDOM'S PLOW	37
DIMMED TOO SOON.	SP GYPSY MELODIES	5
WE HAVE OUR TROUBLES, TOO -	SP HIGH TO LOW	2
YOU TALK TOO LOUD,	SP HIGH TO LOW	4
CUSS TOO LOUD,	SP HIGH TO LOW	5
LOOK TOO BLACK,	SP HIGH TO LOW	6
TOO, WITH YOU.	SP HIGH TO LOW	25

AND THE RADIO, TOO, FOGGY WITH PROPAGANDA	SP	IN EXPLANATION	31
GO SINGING, TOO.	SP	IN TIME SILVER	20
I, TOO, SING AMERICA.	SP	I, TOO	1
I, TOO, AM AMERICA.	SP	I, TOO	18
(SOME FOLKS BLAME TOO MUCH ON JEWS.)	SP	LIKEWISE	13
WAS TOO GOOD FOR ME.	SP	MADAM MIGHT-HAV	4
DINNER, AND SUPPER, TOO -	SP	MADAM HER MADAM	6
WHAT'S TOO GOOD TO BE TRUE,	SP	MADAM MIGHT-HAV	7
IT WAS TOO MUCH.	SP	MADAM HER MADAM	11
I PLAYED, TOO.	SP	MADAM NUMBER WR	14
FOR SHE WAS MADAM, TOO -	SP	MADAM FORT TELL	14
MAKES YOUR NAME TOO SHORT.	SP	MADAM CENSUS	24
CAN'T DO - AND MORE, TOO?	SP	MADAM PHONE BIL	30
THAT MRS., TOO -	SP	MADAM CENSUS	30
DAY'S WORK, TOO!	SP	MADAM'S PAST HI	24
IN AUSTRALIA, TOO, THEY SAY.	SP	MIGRANT	26
HE LOOKS DARKER THAN HE IS, TOO.	SP	NEIGHBOR	9
EXCEPT THAT HE TALKS TOO MUCH.	SP	NEIGHBOR	15
THEY'LL WANT FLOWERS, TOO,	SP	NIGHT FUNERAL	15
AND FAR TOO CLEAN TO STAY THAT WAY.	SP	PASSING	8
AND FEED ME, TOO?	SP	QUESTION	5
TOO!	SP	SUMMER EVENING	31
CHILDREN SOLD AWAY FROM ME, HUSBAND SOLD, TOO.	SP	THE NEGRO MOTHE	15
(I HEAR NEW YORK, TOO.) ME - WHO?	SP	THEME FOR ENG B	20
AND HAT, TOO!	SP	WHAT?	6
I'LL WANT TO SEE SOMEBODY, TOO.	SP	YOUNG GAL'S BLS	12
AND YOUR MONEY, TOO.	SP	50 - 50	14
KINGSTON TOO GOD WILLING	AYM	ASK YOUR MAMA	48
WOULD BE TOO TAME -	AYM	BLUES IN STEREO	6
YOU BAREFOOT, TOO,	AYM	BLUES IN STEREO	12
THEY KNOW ME, TOO, DOWNTOWN,	AYM	HORN OF PLENTY	40
MEANS TOO MANY NEGROES	AYM	HORN OF PLENTY	64
IT WOULD BE TOO BAD IF JESUS	PL	BIBLE BELT	1
TOO MANY YEARS	PL	DOWN WHERE I AM	1
TOO MANY YEARS	PL	DOWN WHERE I AM	5
TOO MANY YEARS	PL	DOWN WHERE I AM	9
I LIVE HERE, TOO.	PL	FREEDOM	19
GHOSTS OF ALL TOO SOLID FLESH,	PL	GHOSTS OF 1619	1
YOUR WALL IS TOO HIGH	PL	LAST PRINCE	4
AND YOUR MOAT IS TOO WIDE -	PL	LAST PRINCE	5
AND THAT I AM HONORED, TOO,	PL	OFFICIAL NOTICE	9
TOO BRAVE TO NAME A NAME -	PL	UN-AMERICAN	7
WITH OLD AND NOT TOO GENTLE	PL	WHERE WHEN WHCH	15
TOOK 27			
THEY TOOK ME AWAY FROM THE JUNGLES.	WB	LAMENT DARK PEO	6
HE TOOK MA LAST THIN DIME.	FC	GYPSY MAN	14
HE TOOK MA LAST THIN DIME.	FC	GYPSY MAN	16
IT TOOK ALL I HAD.	SH	ANNOUNCEMENT	6
BUT BESSIE TOOK A BULLET TO HER	SH	DEATH IN HARLEM	116
TOOK HER TO ALABAM'.	SH	ONLY WOMAN BLUS	20
WHEN DORIE MILLER TOOK GUN IN HAND -	JC	JIM CROW'S LAST	28
AND WHEN I TOOK IT	FW	COMMUNION	7
TOOK HIS HEART	FW	HEART	2
TOOK HIS HEART	FW	HEART	14
A SOLDIER TOOK HER PART,	OWT	BLD MARGE POLIT	9
AND TOOK MY LORD AWAY.	LHR	BLD MARY'S SON	26
MADAM TOOK HIM IN.	SP	BLD FORTUNE TEL	10
WHAT ROAD HE TOOK.	SP	BLD FORTUNE TEL	26
HIS WIFE TOOK A PAPER	SP	BLD OF THE MAN	9
THE CREDIT MAN'S DONE TOOK MA CLOTHES	SP	DOWN AND OUT	7
AND SILENTLY TOOK FOR GRANTED	SP	FREEDOM'S PLOW	98
TOOK US BOTH IN	SP	FULFILMENT	20
I TOOK THE ELEVATOR	SP	LIFE IS FINE	12
YOU ALSO TOOK MY SPIRITUALS AND GONE.	SP	NOTE COMM THEAT	8
IT TOOK ME TWO YEARS TO GET ON WPA.	SP	RELIEF	7
THEY DONE TOOK CORDELIA	SP	STONY LONESOME	1
DONE TOOK CORDELIA	SP	STONY LONESOME	3
ALWAYS TOOK THE OTHER SIDE.)	AYM	RIDE, RED, RIDE	18
THEY TOOK ME OUT	PL	KU KLUX	1
WHO TOOK HIS GUN.	PL	OCTOBER 16 RAID	5
TOOK TWENTY-ONE COMPANIONS	PL	OCTOBER 16 RAID	6
TOOLS 4			
THAT THE PLANTS AND THE ROADS AND THE TOOLS OF POWER	ANS	OPEN LETTER	17
TAKES TOOLS AND BANKS AND MINES.	ANS	OPEN LETTER	61
TOOLS HANDLED - BUT UNUSED.	JC	THE BITTER RIVR	19
THE HAND SEEKS TOOLS TO CUT THE WOOD.	SP	FREEDOM'S PLOW	18
TOOTHPICK 1			
THROWS A TOOTHPICK FROM HER WINDOW.	SP	SUMMER EVENING	19
TOO-ROUGH 1			
AWAY FROM THE TOO-ROUGH FINGERS	DK	DREAM KEEPER	7
TOO-THIN 1			
AND THE COUSINS OF THE TOO-THIN SUITS	PL	WHERE WHEN WHCH	8
TOP 1			
AT THE TOP.	SP	TO BE SOMEBODY	23
TORCH 1			
AND MAKE OF THOSE YEARS A TORCH FOR TOMORROW.	SP	THE NEGRO MOTHE	38
TORE 1			
THAT TORE THE BASTILE DOWN	SL	SCOTTSBORO	14
TORN 4			
AND TORN FROM BLACK AFRICA'S STRAND I CAME	ANS	LET AMERICA BE	49
THE TORN SUIT OF SATIN AND GOLD.	ANS	SONG OF SPAIN	15
AND BOARDS TORN UP,	SP	MOTHER TO SON	5
TORN TO SHREDS BY DYNAMITE	PL	BIRMINGHAM SUND	8
TOROS 2			
TOROS ARE THE SONG OF SPAIN:	ANS	SONG OF SPAIN	12
TOROS, FLAMENCO, PAINTINGS, BOOKS -	ANS	SONG OF SPAIN	38
TORTURE 2			
YET WHY DO YOU TORTURE ME,	WB	THE WHITE ONES	5
WHY DO YOU TORTURE ME?	WB	THE WHITE ONES	7
TOSS 2			
I TOSS	WB	SUMMER NIGHT	10
I TOSS WITHOUT REST	WB	SUMMER NIGHT	20
TOUCH 5			
NO, I DIDN'T TOUCH HER.	OWT	FLIGHT	5
TOUCH OUR BODIES, WIND.	SP	A HOUSE IN TAOS	30
TOUCH OUR BODIES, WIND,	SP	A HOUSE IN TAOS	32
YOU TOUCH WHEN YOU RUN?	SP	DEMAND	11
WITH THE TOUCH OF YOUR HAND	SP	TO ARTINA	7
TOUCHED 3			
ROSE UNTIL IT TOUCHED THE SKY -	SP	AS I GREW OLDER	15
AND TOUCHED YOU	SP	DREAM	8
TOUCHED SILVER WATER.	SP	FULFILMENT	6
TOUCHES 1			
TOUCHES IT.	FW	SLEEP	5
TOUCHING 3			
TOUCHING MY BODY OF UTTER DEATH -	SP	DEMAND	3
TOUCHING EVERYBODY WITH KIND FINGERS	PL	DAYBREAK IN ALA	18
AND TOUCHING EACH OTHER NATURAL AS DEW	PL	DAYBREAK IN ALA	19
TOUCHSTONES 1			
MIGHTY TOUCHSTONES OF SONG.	FW	BIG SUR	3
TOUGH 2			
THE KU KLUX WAS TOUGH -	JC	BLD SAM SOLOMON	50
ACT ROUGH AND TOUGH.	SP	WARNING AUGMENT	6
TOURE 2			
NIGHT IN A SEKOU TOURE CAP	AYM	ASK YOUR MAMA	61
TOURE DOWN IN GUINEA	AYM	BIRD IN ORBIT	58
TOURIST 1			
FIRST WHITE TOURIST UP THE MOUNTAIN	AYM	GOSPEL CHA-CHA	17
TOURISTS 1			
KNOW TOURISTS ONLY FOR	AYM	GOSPEL CHA-CHA	11
TOUSSAINT 1			
TOUSSAINT WITH A THREAD	AYM	GOSPEL CHA-CHA	21
TOWARD 6			
SO I CLIMB TOWARD TOMORROW, OUT OF PAST SORROW,	NM	DARK YOUTH USA	22
THAT GUIDE US TOWARD THE HARBOR OF THE NEW WORLD	JC	TO CAPTAIN MULZ	54
TOWARD A MIRACE-LAND	FW	JAIME	7
AN ENSLAVED PEOPLE HEADING TOWARD FREEDOM	SP	FREEDOM'S PLOW	169
AND LOOK TOWARD THE MOUNTAINS.	SP	SUNDAY MORNING	18
TOWARD FREEDOM'S GOAL.	PL	FREDRK DOUGLASS	11
TOWELS 1			
PINK PAPER TOWELS	PL	UNDERTOW	8
TOWER 4			
DEATH IS A TOWER	OLD	TOWER	1
TUSKEGEE WITH A NEW FLAG ON THE TOWER!	ANS	OPEN LETTER	43
I'M GOIN' UP IN A TOWER	SP	LAMENT OVER LOV	19
UP IN A TOWER	SP	LAMENT OVER LOV	21
TOWERS 2			
AND THE MINES AND THE FACTORIES AND THE OFFICE TOWERS	ANS	OPEN LETTER	15
TAKES OFFICE TOWERS.	ANS	OPEN LETTER	60
TOWN 22			
ROUND THIS TOWN, -	FC	RED SILK STOCK	6
UP AND DOWN, AND THEY JUST AIN'T NO JOBS IN THIS MAN'S TOWN.	NM	BROKE	3

SO I WENT DOWN TOWN TO A HOTEL WHERE I USED TO WORK AT NIGHT.	NM	BROKE	44
WHEN A MAN'S WON A FIGHT IN A BIG MAN'S TOWN -	SH	DEATH IN HARLEM	55
PRIDE OF THE TOWN.	SH	HARLEM SWEETIES	16
IN THIS GREAT BIG LONESOME TOWN!	SH	OUT OF WORK	14
GREAT BIG LONESOME TOWN!	SH	OUT OF WORK	16
BUT I AIN'T GOT NO OWL HEAD AND YOU DONE LEFT TOWN	SH	TWILIGHT REVERI	13
STUYVESANT TOWN?	OWT	BLD MARGE POLIT	37
IN THIS STRANGE OLD TOWN -	OWT	STRANGER IN TWN	14
IN HARLEM TOWN	SP	COLLEGE FORMAL	4
OF THE WHOLE BIG TOWN	SP	COLLEGE FORMAL	14
DIXIE TO SINGAPORE. CAPE TOWN TO HONG KONG	SP	IN EXPLANATION	10
PIE OF A TOWN.	SP	ISLAND	8
MA SOUL WENT FLYIN' O' THE TOWN.	SP	JUDGMENT DAY	2
TOWN SOMEWHERE	SP	KID SLEEPY	13
AND AIN'T THERE ANY JOY IN THIS TOWN?	SP	RUBY BROWN	15
ALL THE WOMENS IN TOWN	SP	SYLVESTER'S BED	3
IN A TOWN NAMED AFTER STANLEY	AYM	BLUES IN STEREO	21
HE'LL COME TO TOWN.	PL	LAST PRINCE	15
COME AGAIN TO TOWN -	PL	OCTOBER 16 RAID	26
CAPE TOWN. ATLANTA.	PL	QUESTION ANSWER	2

TOWNS 2

THESE MISSISSIPPI TOWNS AIN'T	SP	BOUND NO'TH BLS	23
AND THE TOWNS THAT GREW TO CITIES.	SP	FREEDOM'S PLOW	71

TOY 3

FOR A TOY.	SP	MADAM CHARTY CH	8
WHAT'S A BODY BUT A TOY?	SP	MULATTO	11
WHAT'S A BODY BUT A TOY?	SP	MULATTO	17

TO'VE 2

I MEAN FOUR - BEFORE DAYLIGHT - S'POSE TO'VE DONE HIT YO' FIRST STROKE -	NM	BROKE	14
YOU PROMISED TO'VE DONE.	SP	MADAM RENT MAN	14

TRACE 1

THERE WASN'T A TRACE	SP	BLD FORTUNE TEL	27

TRACK 6

STAY ON THE RIGHT TRACK.	SH	BLD THE SINNER	14
STEP. AND LEAVE NO TRACK.	OWT	FLIGHT	2
A NEGRO'S GOT NO BUSINESS ON THE FREEDOM TRACK!	SP	FREEDOM TRAIN	40
WILL HIS FREEDOM TRAIN COME ZOOMIN' DOWN THE TRACK	SP	FREEDOM TRAIN	49
REMEMBER THE WHIP AND THE SLAVER'S TRACK.	SP	THE NEGRO MOTHE	44
ON A MUDDY TRACK	AYM	IS IT TRUE?	42

TRACKS 2

ACROSS THE RAILROAD TRACKS -	OWT	VISITORS	2
ON THIS SIDE OF THE TRACKS.	OWT	VISITORS	4

TRADE-MARKS 1

ON TRADE-MARKS INSIDE	SP	FLATTED FIFTHS	13

TRAGEDY 4

I HOLD TRAGEDY	WB	THE JESTER	2
BEAT THE DRUMS OF TRAGEDY FOR ME.	SP	FATASY PURPLE	1
BEAT THE DRUMS OF TRAGEDY AND DEATH.	SP	FATASY PURPLE	2
BEAT THE DRUMS OF TRAGEDY FOR ME.	SP	FATASY PURPLE	5

TRAGIC 2

TRAGIC EMPTINESS OF HIS LIFE.	NM	BIG-TIMER MOOD	12
OH. TRAGIC BITTER RIVER	JC	THE BITTER RIVR	83

TRAIN 42

AND WHEN I GET ON THE TRAIN	WB	BLUES FANTASY	25
ON A TRAIN THAT RUNS SOMEWHERE.	SH	SIX-BITS BLUES	2
ON A TRAIN THAT RUNS SOMEWHERE.	SH	SIX-BITS BLUES	4
FOR THE FREEDOM TRAIN.	SP	DREAM BOOGE VAR	12
FREEDOM TRAIN.	SP	FREEDOM TRAIN	2
FREEDOM TRAIN.	SP	FREEDOM TRAIN	4
FREEDOM TRAIN.	SP	FREEDOM TRAIN	6
FREEDOM TRAIN!	SP	FREEDOM TRAIN	8
DOWN SOUTH IN DIXIE ONLY TRAIN I SEE'S	SP	FREEDOM TRAIN	9
I HOPE THERE AIN'T NO JIM CROW ON THE FREEDOM TRAIN.	SP	FREEDOM TRAIN	11
NO BACK DOOR ENTRANCE TO THE FREEDOM TRAIN.	SP	FREEDOM TRAIN	12
NO SIGNS FOR COLORED ON THE FREEDOM TRAIN.	SP	FREEDOM TRAIN	13
NO WHITE FOLKS ONLY ON THE FREEDOM TRAIN.	SP	FREEDOM TRAIN	14
FREEDOM TRAIN.	SP	FREEDOM TRAIN	16
WHO'S THE ENGINEER ON THE FREEDOM TRAIN?	SP	FREEDOM TRAIN	17
CAN A COAL BLACK MAN DRIVE THE FREEDOM TRAIN?	SP	FREEDOM TRAIN	18
OR AM I STILL A PORTER ON THE FREEDOM TRAIN?	SP	FREEDOM TRAIN	19
IS THERE BALLOT BOXES ON THE FREEDOM TRAIN?	SP	FREEDOM TRAIN	20
EVERYBODY'S GOT A RIGHT TO BOARD THE FREEDOM TRAIN?	SP	FREEDOM TRAIN	22
FREEDOM TRAIN!	SP	FREEDOM TRAIN	24
IS THAT THE WAY TO GET ABOARD THE FREEDOM TRAIN?	SP	FREEDOM TRAIN	28
FREEDOM TRAIN!	SP	FREEDOM TRAIN	30
WHY THERE'S JIM CROW STATIONS FOR THE FREEDOM TRAIN?	SP	FREEDOM TRAIN	32
FREEDOM TRAIN.	SP	FREEDOM TRAIN	36
FREEDOM TRAIN!	SP	FREEDOM TRAIN	42
THE FREEDOM THAT THEY CARRYIN' ON THIS FREEDOM TRAIN.	SP	FREEDOM TRAIN	45
FREEDOM TRAIN.	SP	FREEDOM TRAIN	48
WILL HIS FREEDOM TRAIN COME ZOOMIN' DOWN THE TRACK	SP	FREEDOM TRAIN	49
FOR THE FREEDOM TRAIN WILL BE YOURS AND MINE!	SP	FREEDOM TRAIN	58
AT HOME THEY GOT A TRAIN THAT'S YOURS AND MINE!	SP	FREEDOM TRAIN	62
FREEDOM TRAIN!	SP	FREEDOM TRAIN	64
FREEDOM TRAIN!	SP	FREEDOM TRAIN	66
FREEDOM TRAIN!	SP	FREEDOM TRAIN	68
GET ON BOARD OUR FREEDOM TRAIN!	SP	FREEDOM TRAIN	69
AND HE GOT THE MIDNIGHT TRAIN	SP	NOT A MOVIE	5
AND TAKE IT ON THE TRAIN	SP	ONE-WAY TICKET	10
A BOX-CAR SOME TRAIN	SP	RAILROAD AVENUE	5
SOME TRAIN HAS FORGOTTEN.	SP	RAILROAD AVENUE	29
ON A TRAIN THAT LOST NO PASSENGERS	AYM	ODE TO DINAH	29
DROWNS THE RUMBLE OF THAT TRAIN	AYM	ODE TO DINAH	38
NO CONDUCTOR AND NO TRAIN.	AYM	ODE TO DINAH	43
DOWN SOUTH ON THE TRAIN	PL	MERRY-GO-ROUND	9

TRAINING 1

WE WERE SENT TO TRAINING CAMP. THEN OVERSEAS -	NM	COLORED SL POEM	5

TRAINS 3

EVER TIME DE TRAINS PASS	OK	HOMESICK BLUES	5
BUT THE TRAINS ARE LATE.	SP	GOOD MORNING	22
NO TRAINS OR STEAMBOATS GOING -	PL	CULTURAL EXCHNG	12

TRANSCRIPTION 1

LIKE A DIZZY GILLESPIE TRANSCRIPTION	SP	PROJECTION	12

TRANSFERS 1

TRANSFERS TO THE WEST SIDE.	SP	MIGRANT	8

TRANSPORTED 1

THAT MOVED AND TRANSPORTED AMERICA.	SP	FREEDOM'S PLOW	58

TRASH 2

THAT'S NOTHING BUT TRASH.	SH	BLD THE KILLER	12
THE REASON MARIE RUNS AROUND WITH TRASH	SP	SISTER	8

TRAVEL 1

TO TRAVEL ON.	PL	FLORIDA WORKERS	8

TRAVELING 1

AMOUNT OF TRAVELING	SP	SAME IN BLUES	6

TRA-LA-LA-LA 1

WITH A TRA-LA-LA-LA!	SH	SHAKESPEARE	6

TREAD 1

AND FRIGHTENED TREAD.	PL	FREDRK DOUGLASS	3

TREADING 1

TREADING THE MODERN WAY	NM	DARK YOUTH USA	23

TREAT 12

BUT HE SHO DO TREAT ME KIND.	FC	GAL'S CRY DYING	14
BUT HE SHO DO TREAT ME KIND.	FC	GAL'S CRY DYING	16
TREAT A MAN SO BAD?	SH	ANNOUNCEMENT	8
CARAMEL TREAT.	SH	HARLEM SWEETIES	6
A CHOCOLATE TREAT.	SH	HARLEM SWEETIES	32
YOU TREAT ME SO.	JC	BLACK MAN SPEAK	12
CAUSE THEY TREAT ME MEAN -	SP	CORA	5
THEY ALWAYS TREAT ME MEAN.	SP	CORA	7
I DON'T TREAT YOU BAD. HATTIE.	SP	EARLY EVENING	17
NEITHER DOES I TREAT YOU GOOD.	SP	EARLY EVENING	18
BUT I RECKON I COULD TREAT YOU	SP	EARLY EVENING	19
YOU TREAT ME LIKE YOU DAMN WELL PLEASE.	SP	LOW TO HIGH	14

TREATED 3

I TREATED ALBERT FINE.	FC	BLACK GAL	2
SHE TREATED HIM LIKE	SP	BLD FORTUNE TEL	11
BEIN TREATED SO BAD.	SP	EARLY EVENING	16

TREATS 3

I TREATS HER KIND BUT	FC	EVIL WOMAN	5
AN' I TREATS HER FINE.	FC	WORKIN' MAN	10
OH. MEN TREATS WOMEN	SP	LOVER'S RETURN	9

TREBLE 4

TRILLING THE TREBLE . . . . SP BOOGIE 1 A.M. 5
TINKLING TREBLE. . . . . SP DREAM BOOGE VAR 1
WAY UP IN THE TREBLE . . . . SP LADY'S BOOGIE 7
WHIRLING TREBLE . . . . SP NIGHTMARE BOOGE 11

TREE 22

OH, SILVER TREE! . . . . WB JAZZONIA 1
OH, SINGING TREE! . . . . WB JAZZONIA 7
OH, SHINING TREE! . . . . WB JAZZONIA 14
WHAT JUNGLE TREE HAVE YOU SLEPT
UNDER. . . . . WB NUDE YOUNG DANC 1
WHAT JUNGLE TREE HAVE YOU SLEPT
UNDER. . . . . WB NUDE YOUNG DANC 5
ON EVERY LYNCHING TREE, A POSTER
CRYING FREE . . . . ANS OPEN LETTER 44
SHE COULD CHASE ME UP A TREE . . . SH ONLY WOMAN BLUS 9
OR THEY'LL HANG YOU TO A TREE! . . OWT FLIGHT 8
BENEATH A TALL TREE . . . . SP DREAM VARIATION 6
A TALL, SLIM TREE . . . . SP DREAM VARIATION 15
FROM THAT SEED A TREE GREW, IS
GROWING, WILL EVER GROW. . . . . SP FREEDOM'S PLOW 195
THAT TREE IS FOR EVERYBODY, ... SP FREEDOM'S PLOW 196
TALL AS A TREE IS TALL. . . . . . . SP LAMENT OVER LOV 20
TALL AS A TREE IS TALL. . . . . . . SP LAMENT OVER LOV 22
AND I SEE A LITTLE TREE. . . . . . SP LITTLE GRN TREE 10
I SEE A LITTLE TREE. . . . . SP LITTLE GRN TREE 12
O, LITTLE TREE! . . . . SP LITTLE GRN TREE 15
LIKE PALE PLUMS FROM A TREE . . . . SP MELLOW 4
TO A ROADSIDE TREE . . . . SP SILHOUETTE 6
TO A CROSS ROADS TREE. . . . . . . SP SONG DARK GIRL 4
ON A GNARLED AND NAKED TREE. . . . SP SONG DARK GIRL 12
THEY HUNG HIM TO A TREE. . . . . . SP SOUTHERN MAMMY 14

TREES 17

I LOST MY TREES. . . . . WB LAMENT DARK PEO 7
WE SHOULD HAVE A LAND OF TREES, . . WB OUR LAND 8
OF TALL THICK TREES . . . . WB OUR LAND 9
THE SLENDER TREES . . . . WB POEME D'AUTOMNE 3
WHEN THE SAP RISES IN THE TREES, . ANS CHANT MAY DAY 5
10-VOICES: BE LIKE THE SAP RISING IN
THE TREES. . . . . ANS CHANT MAY DAY 15
AND TALL YOUNG TREES . . . . FW GIRL 15
TREES. . . . . FW HARLEM DANCE HA 5
CLANG AGAINST THE TREES WENT THE AX
IN MANY HANDS . . . . SP FREEDOM'S PLOW 55
DISTORTED TREES. . . . . SP GARDEN 4
AND TREES PUT FORTH . . . . SP IN TIME SILVER 15
ROCKS AND THE FIRM ROOTS OF TREES. SP SPIRITUALS 1
FROM THE FIRM ROOTS OF TREES. . . . SP SPIRITUALS 10
SEEKING LAWNS AND SHADE TREES . . . AYM HORN OF PLENTY 71
AS YET UNFELT AMONG MAGNOLIA TREES. PL BIRMINGHAM SUND 27
I'M GONNA PUT SOME TALL TALL TREES
IN IT . . . . PL DAYBREAK IN ALA 7
IT UPROOTS TREES! . . . . PL WARNING 10

TREMBLE 1

SOME BEGAN TO TREMBLE AND . . . . . SH DEATH IN HARLEM 109

TREMBLED 1

THE CASHIER TREMBLED . . . . SH BLD THE KILLER 15

TRIBAL 4

O, TRIBAL DANCE! . . . . OWT NEGRO SERVANT 3
ARE TRIBAL NOW NO LONGER . . . . . AYM ODE TO DINAH 77
TRIBAL NOW NO LONGER PAPA MAMA . . AYM ODE TO DINAH 82
TRIBAL NOW NO LONGER ONE FOR ALL . AYM ODE TO DINAH 88

TRIBUNE'S 1

THE TRIBUNE'S HAIR . . . . SP MIGRANT 31

TRICKERATION 1

SOME KIND OF TRICKERATION . . . . . SP WHAT? SO SOON! 4

TRICKLE 1

A CRIMSON TRICKLE IN THE GEORGIA
DUSK. . . . . PL GEORGIA DUSK 7

TRIED 12

TRIED TO FIND ONE O' THEM LITTLE
ELEVATOR AND SWITCHBOARD JOBS
THEY USED . . . . NM BROKE 41
HE TRIED TO GUARD . . . . SH BLD THE KILLER 17
NAW! BUT THEY TRIED! . . . . OWT BLD MARGE POLIT 45
FRIENDS TRIED TO TELL HER . . . . . SP BLD FORTUNE TEL 17
SHE TRIED TO FIND OUT . . . . SP BLD FORTUNE TEL 25
I TRIED TO THINK BUT COULDN'T. . . SP LIFE IS FINE 3
BECAUSE HE TRIED TO VOTE . . . . . SP NOT A MOVIE 2
THAT TRIED TO BURN WITHIN HER SOUL. SP RUBY BROWN 7
I TRIED . . . . AYM GOSPEL CHA-CHA 45
LORD KNOWS I TRIED . . . . AYM GOSPEL CHA-CHA 46
HAS LONG BEEN TRIED AT LAW. . . . . PL OCTOBER 16 RAID 20
TRIED TO MAKE ME . . . . PL STILL HERE 6

TRIES 2

CAUSE I TRIES TO BE GOOD . . . . . FC WORKIN' MAN 15
HE STILL TRIES TO ACT IN THE SAME
OLD WAY. . . . . JC JIM CROW'S LAST 12

TRILLING 1

TRILLING THE TREBLE . . . . SP BOOGIE 1 A.M. 5

TRIP 1

TRIP. . . . . FW SAILING DATE 17

TRIUMPH 2

WHEN FREEDOM WOULD TRIUMPH. . . . . SP FREEDOM'S PLOW 120
BUT OTHERS KNEW IT HAD TO TRIUMPH. SP FREEDOM'S PLOW 122

TRIUMPHAL 1

TRIUMPHAL ENTRY SEND YOU - . . . . AYM BLUES IN STEREO 7

TRIUMPHANT 2

THE SONG OF THE NEW LIFE TRIUMPHANT ANS KIDS WHO DIE 50
AIDS TRIUMPHANT ENTRY SQUALLING . . SP INTERNE AT PROV 27

TROTSKY 1

SEND FOR TROTSKY! (WHAT? DON'T
CONFUSE THE ISSUE. . . . . PL FINAL CALL 26

TROTTERS 1

GLOBAL TROTTERS BASEBALL BATTERS $
$ $ . . . . AYM HORN OF PLENTY 16

TROUBLE 15

TROUBLE, PAIN. . . . . WB BLUES FANTASY 16
TROUBLE . . . . FC CRAP GAME 7
I'M DEEP IN TROUBLE. . . . . FC MOAN 1
DEEP IN TROUBLE. . . . . FC MOAN 4
AN' GITS NOTHIN' BUT TROUBLE. . . . FC WORKIN' MAN 16
DE TROUBLE I'VE HAD." FLINCHING
UNDER THE WHIP. THE SPIRITUAL . NM BLACK CLWN MOOD 5
MA LORD'S LIFE WAS TROUBLE, TOO, . DK MA LORD 8
TROUBLE EVER DAY. . . . . DK MA LORD 9
ADDED TO DE TROUBLE THAT I GOT. . . SH LOVE AGAIN BLUS 6
TROUBLE MAKER!" YOU SAY. . . . . . JC THE BITTER RIVR 48
HOW SHE COULD GET IN TROUBLE . . . SP BLD OF THE GIRL 3
ONE TROUBLE IS YOU: . . . . SP HIGH TO LOW 3
SO, NATURALLY, THERE'S TROUBLE . . SP IN EXPLANATION 58
TROUBLE . . . . SP TRUMPET PLAYER 43
TROUBLE WITH YOU IS . . . . SP 50 - 50 7

TROUBLED 1

THIS TROUBLED WOMAN . . . . SP TROUBLED WOMAN 3

TROUBLES 5

AN' OUR TROUBLES AT DE DOOR. . . . FC MINNIE SINGS 6
I DON'T CRY OVER TROUBLES. . . . . NM BIG-TIMER POEM 58
WHO SINGS THE TROUBLES EVERY WOMAN
HAS. . . . . OWT LINCOLN THEATRE 8
WE HAVE OUR TROUBLES, TOO - . . . . SP HIGH TO LOW 2
AND PUT MA TROUBLES ON THE SHELF." SP THE WEARY BLUES 22

TRUCK 1

AND A WHOLE TRUCK LOAD OF FLOWERS. SP AS BEFITS A MAN 12

TRUCKED 1

TRUCKED. . . . . SP DANCER 10

TRUCKS 2

IN SOUND TRUCKS. . . . . OWT BLD MARGE POLIT 39
YOU SEE DEM TRUCKS . . . . SP BABY 4

TRUDGING 1

BUT I KEPT TRUDGING ON THROUGH THE
LONELY YEARS. . . . . SP THE NEGRO MOTHE 26

TRUE 22

TO MANHOOD'S TRUE RIGHT. . . . . . NM BLACK CLWN POEM 66
YOU STILL BAKES BISCUITS? FRIED
CHICKEN EVERY NIGHT? IS THAT
TRUE? . . . . NM BROKE 73
THINKING WE WERE FIGHTING FOR
DEMOCRACY'S TRUE REIGN . . . . . NM COLORED SL POEM 7
WHO DREAMT A DREAM SO STRONG, SO
BRAVE, SO TRUE. . . . . ANS LET AMERICA BE 41
WARNED ME TRUE. . . . . SH BLD THE SINNER 6
AND STILL BE TRUE. . . . . SP COULD BE 4
WHAT FREDERICK DOUGLASS SAID WAS
TRUE. . . . . SP FREEDOM'S PLOW 115
THE PEOPLE SAY IT IS PROMISES - THAT
WILL COME TRUE. . . . . SP FREEDOM'S PLOW 144
BUT IS TRUE ANYHOW: . . . . SP IN EXPLANATION 34
TRUE ANYHOW NO MATTER HOW MANY . . SP IN EXPLANATION 38
MY TRUE LOVE'S LEFT ME . . . . . . SP LAMENT OVER LOV 11
WHAT'S TOO GOOD TO BE TRUE. . . . . SP MADAM MIGHT-HAV 7
THAT MAY BE TRUE - . . . . SP MADAM HER MADAM 22
TRUE. . . . . SP NEIGHBOR 21
COME TRUE. . . . . SP PASSING 16
YET SHINING LIKE THE SUN WITH LOVE'S
TRUE LIGHT. . . . . SP THE NEGRO MOTHE 6
DARK ONES OF TODAY, MY DREAMS MUST
COME TRUE: . . . . SP THE NEGRO MOTHE 34
THEN, IT WILL BE TRUE. . . . . . . SP THEME FOR ENG B 5
IT'S NOT EASY TO KNOW WHAT IS TRUE
FOR YOU OR ME . . . . SP THEME FOR ENG B 16

BUT WE ARE, THAT'S TRUE! . . . . . SP THEME FOR ENG B 36
IS IT TRUE THAT NEGROES - ? . . . . AYM IS IT TRUE? 55
TRUE OF TOMORROW. . . . . PL HISTORY 4

TRUEST 1
MOTIVATED BY THE TRUEST . . . . . . PL BLACK PANTHER 10

TRULY 1
IT'S TRULY . . . . SP PROJECTION 22

TRUMPET 7
BUT BLOW ONE BLARING TRUMPET NOTE OF SUN . . . . SP FATASY PURPLE 7
VOICE OF MUTED TRUMPET, ... SP SONG BILLIE HOL 16
WITH THE TRUMPET AT HIS LIPS . . . SP TRUMPET PLAYER 2
WITH THE TRUMPET AT HIS LIPS . . . SP TRUMPET PLAYER 10
FROM THE TRUMPET AT HIS LIPS . . . SP TRUMPET PLAYER 18
FROM THE TRUMPET AT HIS LIPS . . . SP TRUMPET PLAYER 22
WITH THE TRUMPET AT HIS LIPS . . . SP TRUMPET PLAYER 34

TRUMPETS 3
COME WITH A BLAST OF TRUMPETS, . . SP WHEN SUE WEARS 4
BLOW TRUMPETS, JESUS! . . . . SP WHEN SUE WEARS 9
SWEET SILVER TRUMPETS, ... SP WHEN SUE WEARS 12

TRUNK 7
PACK MY TRUNK AND RIDE. . . . . . . WB BLUES FANTASY 21
PACK MY TRUNK AND RIDE. . . . . . . WB BLUES FANTASY 24
PACKED HIS TRUNK AND LEFT. . . . . FC SUICIDE 2
PACKED HIS TRUNK AND LEFT. . . . . FC SUICIDE 4
SURE, I MISSED YOUR TRUNK - BUT I DIDN'T MISS YOU. . . . . SH LETTER 8
THAT PLACE WHERE YOUR TRUNK WAS, AIN'T NO TRUNK NO MORE. . . . . SH SUPPER TIME 8
THAT PLACE WHERE YOUR TRUNK WAS, AIN'T NO TRUNK NO MORE. . . . . SH SUPPER TIME 8

TRUST 3
YOU'VE GOT NO TRUST. . . . . SP MADAM MIGHT-HAV 30
STAND LIKE FREE MEN SUPPORTING MY TRUST. . . . . SP THE NEGRO MOTHE 42
AND HE DIDN'T TRUST . . . . PL LUMUMBA'S GRAVE 2

TRUTH 9
SEEKING THE TRUTH . . . . NM DARK YOUTH USA 9
THE TRUTH A SIMPLE HEART HAS HELD DK ALABAMA EARTH 8
AND FATHER DIVINE WILL SAY IN TRUTH. SP PROJECTION 20
NEITHER TRUTH NOR LIE. . . . . . . SP RAILROAD AVENUE 22
TO TELL THE TRUTH. . . . . SP RELIEF 11
THE TRUTH OF THE MATTER'S . . . . . SP 50 - 50 4
SEND FOR HARRIETT TUBMAN, OLD SOJOURNER TRUTH. . . . . PL FINAL CALL 32
TO TELL YOU THE TRUTH, ... PL KU KLUX 6
THAN TRUTH CAN BE. . . . . PL LONG VIEW NEGRO 7

TRY 10
TOGETHER, RECKON I'LL TRY . . . SHO, I WANTS DE JOB! YES, SIR! . . . NM BROKE 30
I'LL TRY NOT TO BE THAT MEAN NO MORE. . . . . SH LETTER 13
DID YOU EVER TRY LIVIN' . . . . . . SH OUT OF WORK 19
I SAY DID YOU EVER TRY LIVIN' . . . SH OUT OF WORK 21
WHY DON'T YOU TRY IT, FOLKS, . . . SH OUT OF WORK 23
SOME FOLKS TRY TO TELL ME DOWN THIS WAY . . . . JC GOOD MORN STLIN 23
LIKE THEY TRY TO DO YOU BAD. . . . SP BOUND NO'TH BLS 18
BOYS WHO TRY . . . . SP UP-BEAT 2
WHEN I TRY TO FIND A JOB . . . . . PL BACKLASH BLUES 13
TRY TO FIND MYSELF A JOB . . . . . PL BACKLASH BLUES 15

TRYING 10
TRYING TO CLIMB UP. . . . . NM BLACK CLWN POEM 45
LISTEN AT MY HEARTBEATS TRYING TO THINK. . . . . SH SUPPER TIME 6
I WAS TRYING TO FIGURE OUT . . . . FW COMMUNION 1
HE'S TRYING TO RUIN THE GOVERNMENT SP BLD LANDLORD 23
TRYING TO FORGET TO REMEMBER . . . SP DRUNKARD 4
TRYING TO MAKE HER WHERE-WITH-ALL: SP EVENING SONG 2
ALWAYS THE TRYING TO UNDERSTAND, . SP FREEDOM'S PLOW 154
AND THE TRYING TO SAY, ... SP FREEDOM'S PLOW 155
ME, TRYING TO UPHOLD THE RACE . . . SP HIGH TO LOW 21
YOU TRYING TO MAKE A . . . . SP MADAM HER MADAM 15

TRYIN' 1
TRYIN' TO GET UP THERE - . . . . . PL DOWN WHERE I AM 6

TU 2
TU ABUELA, DONDE ESTA? . . . . . . AYM RIDE, RED, RIDE 11
TU ABUELA, DONDE ESTA? . . . . . . AYM RIDE, RED, RIDE 13

TUBMAN 1
SEND FOR HARRIETT TUBMAN, OLD SOJOURNER TRUTH. . . . . PL FINAL CALL 32

TUCK-TAIL 2
WORKIN' LIKE A TUCK-TAIL DOG. . . . SH MISSISSIPPI LEV 2
LIKE A TUCK-TAIL DOG. . . . . SH MISSISSIPPI LEV 4

TULIPS 1
DISTORTED TULIPS . . . . SP GARDEN 6

TUNE 12
YOU KNOW THAT TUNE . . . . FC JAZZ BAND 11
IN AN OLD SUIT AND A BATTERED HAT, TO THE TUNE OF A SLOW DRAG STOMP NM BROKE 1
AND YET HE PLAYS UPON HIS FLUTE A WILD FREE TUNE . . . . DK BEGGAR BOY 7
STRIKES UP A TUNE ALL GAY AND BRIGHT AND GLAD . . . . OWT JUICE JOINT 43
A CHEAP LITTLE TUNE . . . . SP SLIVER 2
A CHEAP LITTLE TUNE . . . . SP SLIVER 5
DRONING A DROWSY SYNCOPATED TUNE, SP THE WEARY BLUES 1
TO THE TUNE O' THOSE WEARY BLUES. SP THE WEARY BLUES 8
HE PLAYED THAT SAD RAGGY TUNE LIKE A MUSICAL FOOL. . . . . SP THE WEARY BLUES 13
AND FAR INTO THE NIGHT HE CROONED THAT TUNE. . . . . SP THE WEARY BLUES 31
AS THE TUNE COMES FROM HIS THROAT SP TRUMPET PLAYER 42
ERZULIE PLAYS A TUNE . . . . AYM GOSPEL CHA-CHA 7

TUNES 1
TUNES. . . . . FW FRAGMENTS 6

TURN 28
DIDN'T TURN OUT RIGHT. . . . . . . NM BIG-TIMER POEM 10
I TURN ON THE RADIO, ... NM BIG-TIMER POEM 61
WORLD, TURN PALE! . . . . SL SCOTTSBORO 2
WORLD, TURN PALE! . . . . SL SCOTTSBORO 29
BUT MY LOVE MIGHT TURN INTO A KNIFE SH IN TROUBLED KEY 11
TURN ON THE LIGHT AND LOOK REAL GOOD! . . . . SH SUPPER TIME 3
DUSK TURN TO DAWN, ... FW DUSK 12
I DON'T TURN, MADAM! . . . . OWT JITNEY 39
TURN FROM THE BAR AND JOIN YOU IN YOUR SONG, ... OWT JUICE JOINT 22
I DON'T KNOW WHERE TO TURN. . . . . OWT TOO BLUE 2
DON'T TURN OUT LIKE I AM. . . . . . SP EVENING SONG 12
WHEN YOU TURN THE CORNER . . . . . SP FINAL CURVE 1
NURSES TURN GLASS DOORKNOBS . . . . SP INTERNE AT PROV 42
AND YOUR SKIN'LL TURN . . . . SP KID SLEEPY 6
MADE ME TURN RIGHT PALE. . . . . . SP LITTLE OLD LETT 4
TURN AROUND - I'LL BRUSH BEHIND. . SP MAMA AND DAUGHT 6
TURN AROUND! . . . . SP MAMA AND DAUGHT 20
DIDN'T TURN OUT RIGHT. . . . . . . SP MIDNIGHT RAFFLE 4
SO BOY, DON'T YOU TURN BACK. . . . SP MOTHER TO SON 14
BOSOM TURN ALL GOLDEN IN THE SUNSET. SP NEGRO SPEAKS OF 10
YOU WILL TURN BACK . . . . SP SUNDAY MORNING 17
YOU WILL TURN BACK . . . . SP SUNDAY MORNING 19
TURN, OH, TURN, DARK LOVERS . . . . AYM IS IT TRUE? 18
TURN, OH, TURN, DARK LOVERS . . . . AYM IS IT TRUE? 18
THAT SOMETIMES TURN TO FIRE. . . . AYM JAZZTET MUTED 21
MUST TURN INTO . . . . PL ANGOLA QUESTION 9
IF YOU'D JUST TURN ME LOOSE." . . . PL KU KLUX 8
BUT TURN THE TELESCOPE AROUND, . . PL LONG VIEW NEGRO 8

TURNED 18
WHOLE WIDE WORLD'S TURNED COLD. . . DK PO' BOY BLUES 6
IN EVERY BRICK AND STONE, IN EVERY FURROW TURNED . . . . ANS LET AMERICA BE 43
AND TURNED DEAD WHITE. . . . . . . SH BLD THE KILLER 16
EAST TURNED PALE . . . . SH DEATH IN HARLEM 134
YOU TURNED OUT TO BE A DEVIL . . . SH LOVE AGAIN BLUS 11
TURNED OUT SO BAD. . . . . SH PAY DAY 10
AND IT'S TURNED TO STEEL IN MY BLOOD. . . . . JC THE BITTER RIVR 82
AND TURNED INTO RIOT. . . . . OWT BLD MARGE POLIT 16
I TURNED . . . . SP DREAM 7
THEN YOU KNOW THAT YOU HAVE TURNED SP FINAL CURVE 3
HE TURNED HIS BACK ON ME. . . . . . SP HARD DADDY 8
HE TURNED HIS BACK ON ME. . . . . . SP HARD DADDY 10
I TURNED IT OVER, ... SP LITTLE OLD LETT 9
MY GOOD MAN TURNED ME DOWN. . . . . SP MIDWINTER BLUES 6
TURNED DEAD WHITE! . . . . SP NIGHTMARE BOOGE 8
TURNED BROWN BY THE AGES. . . . . . SP WHEN SUE WEARS 3
AND THE CRY THAT TURNED TO MUSIC . AYM GOSPEL CHA-CHA 31
TURNED INTO A BAR: . . . . PL LITTLE SNG HOUS 21

TURNER 1
NAT TURNER. . . . . SL SCOTTSBORO 19

TURNING 2
PACE. "SOMETIMES I FEEL LIKE A MOTHER-LESS CHILE." TURNING FUTILELY . . . . NM BLACK CLWN MOOD 8
TURNING THE RICH SOIL WENT THE PLOW IN MANY HANDS . . . . SP FREEDOM'S PLOW 52

TURNIN' 1
AND TURNIN' CORNERS, ... SP MOTHER TO SON 11

TURNPIKE 1
ON THE SOUND WAY OFF THE TURNPIKE - AYM HORN OF PLENTY 34

TURNS 4

UNTIL THE STARS PALE AND THE SKY TURNS BLUE . . . OWT JUICE JOINT 3
TURNS RED AS FIRE. . . . SP BLUE BAYOU 15
TURNS GRAY. . . . SP MIGRANT 32
BUT SHE TURNS HER BACK UPON ME. . . . SP THE SOUTH 22

TURPENTINE 2

AND THE TURPENTINE WOODS. . . . SP MULATTO 3
THE MOON OVER THE TURPENTINE WOODS. SP MULATTO 7

TUSKEGEE 1

TUSKEGEE WITH A NEW FLAG ON THE TOWER! . . . ANS OPEN LETTER 43

TV 6

GRANDPA, DID YOU FIND HER IN THE TV SILENCE . . . AYM BIRD IN ORBIT 61
MY TV KEEPS ON SNOWING. . . . AYM BLUES IN STEREO 37
AND FREE-DELIVERY TV SETS . . . AYM JAZZTET MUTED 12
KEEPS THE GAS ON WHILE THE TV . . . AYM ODE TO DINAH 5
SINCE IT'S SNOWING ON THE TV . . . AYM ODE TO DINAH 7
IN THE PRESS AND ON THE RADIO AND TV - . . . PL PRIME 6

TV'S 1

THE TV'S STILL NOT WORKING. . . . AYM SHOW FARE PLESE 34

TWELVE 2

TO HIS TWELVE DISCIPLES . . . LHR BLD MARY'S SON 15
HE WORKS DOWNTOWN FOR TWELVE A WEEK. SP BUDDY 4

TWELVE-ROOM 1

BUT SHE HAD A TWELVE-ROOM . . . SP MADAM HER MADAM 3

TWELVE-SHOE 1

WHERE HIS TWELVE-SHOE LANDS. . . . SP DREAM BOOGIE VAR 8

TWENTY 4

TWENTY HOURS . . . AYM IS IT TRUE? 23
WAITED TWENTY DAYS . . . AYM IS IT TRUE? 25
WAITED TWENTY YEARS . . . AYM IS IT TRUE? 27
WAITED TWENTY MORE . . . AYM IS IT TRUE? 29

TWENTY-MILE 1

IN A TWENTY-MILE ZONE. . . . SH ANNOUNCEMENT 4

TWENTY-ONE 1

TOOK TWENTY-ONE COMPANIONS . . . PL OCTOBER 16 RAID 6

TWENTY-STORY 1

ON A TWENTY-STORY HOUSING PROJECT. AYM ODE TO DINAH 79

TWENTY-TWO 2

I AM TWENTY-TWO, COLORED, BORN IN WINSTON-SALEM. . . . SP THEME FOR ENG B 7
AT TWENTY-TWO, MY AGE. BUT I GUESS I'M WHAT . . . SP THEME FOR ENG B 17

TWENTY'S 1

TO GET THROUGH HIGH AT TWENTY'S KIND OF LATE - . . . SP DEFERRED 6

TWICE 2

DO I SEE A COUPLE? OR DID I COUNT TWICE? . . . SH BED TIME 13
I CAME UP TWICE AND CRIED! . . . SP LIFE IS FINE 6

TWILIGHT 1

WHERE THE TWILIGHT . . . WB OUR LAND 4

TWINES 1

SILKEN BATHROBES WITH GOLD TWINES SP FLATTED FIFTHS 9

TWINING 1

AND TWINING THE BASS . . . SP BOOGIE 1 A.M. 6

TWINKLE 1

TWINKLE ON THE RUBBER GLOVES . . . SP INTERNE AT PROV 33

TWISTED 1

TWISTED AND STRANGE . . . FW SAILING DATE 1

TWO 71

A SILENT WOMAN LIES BETWEEN TWO LOVERS - . . . WB SICK ROOM 4
TWO AGAINST THE MOON . . . WB TO MIDNIGHT NAN 15
TWO DOLLARS A DAY. . . . FC BRASS SPITOONS 15
TWO DOLLARS . . . FC BRASS SPITOONS 20
TWO THINGS POSSESS THE POWER. . . . OLD TWO THINGS 1
TWO THINGS DESERVE THE NAME. . . . OLD TWO THINGS 2
TWO THINGS CAN REAWAKEN . . . OLD TWO THINGS 3
TWO THINGS ARE FULL OF WONDER. . . OLD TWO THINGS 5
TWO THINGS CAST OFF ALL SHAME. . . OLD TWO THINGS 6
AFTER ALL THEM DOLLARS I GIVED HER THESE LAST TWO YEARS. . . . NM BROKE 23
WE WERE JUST TWO COLORED BOYS, BROWN AND BLACK. . . . NM COLORED SL POEM 2
GOT TWO MO' WAYS. . . . DK NEGRO DANCERS 2
TWO MO' WAYS TO DO DE CHARLESTON! DK NEGRO DANCERS 3
TWO MO' WAYS TO DO DE CHARLESTON!" DK NEGRO DANCERS 6
GOT TWO MO' WAYS. . . . DK NEGRO DANCERS 14
TWO MO' WAYS TO DO DE CHARLESTON!" DK NEGRO DANCERS 15
BETWEEN US TWO. . . . ANS PARK BENCH 4
IN A YEAR OR TWO. . . . ANS PARK BENCH 10
A HUMAN GETS LONESOME IF THERE AIN'T TWO. . . . SH BED TIME 15
TWO BUCKS ON IT? . . . SH BLD PAWNBROKER 3
I BOUGHT TWO WEEKS AGO? . . . SH BLD PAWNBROKER 10
A DIAMOND OR TWO. . . . SH BLD THE KILLER 2
GIN RICKEYS FOR TWO. . . . SH DEATH IN HARLEM 42
BITE A NAIL IN TWO. . . . SH EVIL MORNING 6
FEEL BAD TWO DAYS STRAIGHT. . . . SH EVIL MORNING 14
BUY YOU TWO FOR A QUARTER . . . SH MIDNIGHT CHIPPI 17
ON TWO-BITS MINUS TWO? . . . SH OUT OF WORK 20
ON TWO-BITS MINUS TWO? . . . SH OUT OF WORK 22
NOR THEM TWO DIAMOND RINGS . . . SH PAY DAY 8
ABOUT TWO KINDS O' PISTOLS THAT I AIN'T GOT. . . . SH TWILIGHT REVERI 10
WHERE TWO PEOPLE . . . FW CAROLINA CABIN 21
TWO WARS . . . FW SAILING DATE 10
YOU GIMME TWO. . . . OWT HONEY BABE 6
WHERE TWO OLD BROWN MEN STAND BEHIND THE BAR - . . . OWT JUICE JOINT 37
IT WOULD PROBABLY TAKE TWO. . . . OWT TOO BLUE 13
A HEARSE AND TWO CARS - . . . SP BLD OF THE MAN 6
THE OTHER TWO . . . SP BUDDY 7
"ONE - TWO - BUCKLE MY SHOE!" . . . SP CHILDREN'S RYME 2
THERE IS TWO THOUSAND CHILDREN . . SP CHILDREN'S RYME 10
THAT SPLITS THE WORLD IN TWO . . . SP CONSIDER ME 37
TWO OR THREE THINGS IN THE PAST . . SP DANCER 1
I'M ALREADY TWO YEARS LATE. . . . SP DEFERRED 2
I'M GONNA BUY TWO NEW SUITS . . . SP DEFERRED 30
ON MY TWO FEET . . . SP DEMOCRACY 8
TWO NEW SUITS AN' . . . SP ELEVATOR BOY 12
AMONG ALL WHO STAND ON TWO FEET. . SP INTERNE AT PROV 17
BETWEEN TWO RIVERS. . . . SP ISLAND 1
CAUSE YOU BROKE MY HEART IN TWO. . SP LATE LAST NIGHT 6
AND BROKE MY HEART IN TWO - . . . SP LATE LAST NIGHT 8
I HAD TWO HUSBANDS. . . . SP MADAM MIGHT-HAV 1
I SAID, BETTER BUY TWO - . . . SP MADAM WRONG VIS 27
NIGHT OF THE TWO MOONS . . . SP NIGHT FOUR SONG 1
THEM TWO FINE CARS? . . . SP NIGHT FUNERAL 4
IT TOOK ME TWO YEARS TO GET ON WPA. SP RELIEF 7
OR EVEN TWO. . . . SP RELIEF 14
TWO A.M. MIDNIGHT BY YOUR SELF? . . SP REVERIE HARLEM 2
TWO A.M. . . . SP REVERIE HARLEM 10
SHE ASKED HERSELF TWO QUESTIONS . . SP RUBY BROWN 11
TWO PARTIES FROM PHILADELPHIA . . . SP SEASHORE THROUG 5
A DIME ON THOSE TWO BOTTLES. . . . SP SUMMER EVENING 29
HEAR YOU, HEAR ME - WE TWO - YOU, ME, TALK ON THIS PAGE. . . . SP THEME FOR ENG B 19
TWO DOZEN MEN TO THE FLOOR. . . . SP TO BE SOMEBODY 18
TWO DIMES AND A NICKLE ONLY . . . SP TOMORROW 3
WITH A WOMAN WITH TWO PISTOLS . . . AYM ODE TO DINAH 28
WEAVING METAL FROM TWO QUARTERS . . AYM SHOW FARE PLESE 21
THE HEADS ON THESE TWO QUARTERS . . AYM SHOW FARE PLESE 26
SINCE BUT TWO EXIST . . . AYM SHOW FARE PLESE 29
ON MY TWO FEET . . . PL FREEDOM 8
SAYS SUGAR'S GONE UP ANOTHER TWO CENTS. . . . PL HARLEM 9
HER BANDAGE HIDES TWO FESTERING SORES . . . PL JUSTICE 3
WHERE TWO RIVERS MEET . . . PL OCTOBER 16 RAID 9

TWO-BIT 3

(DIXIE MAKES HIS MONEY ON TWO-BIT GIN.) . . . SH DEATH IN HARLEM 32
LONESOME SAID WHEN A TWO-BIT WOMAN SH MIDNIGHT CHIPPI 23
FACING A TWO-BIT . . . FW CHIPPY 8

TWO-BITS 2

ON TWO-BITS MINUS TWO? . . . SH OUT OF WORK 20
ON TWO-BITS MINUS TWO? . . . SH OUT OF WORK 22

TWO-THREE 1

ABOUT TWO-THREE A.M. . . . OWT HONEY BABE 10

TWO-WAY 1

CULTURE, THEY SAY, IS A TWO-WAY STREET: . . . PL CULTURAL EXCHNG 58

TYPIST 1

TELLS HER MAMA SHE'S A TYPIST . . . SP GRADUATION 13

TYRANNY 1

AND TYRANNY AGAIN IS BOLD. . . . JC TO CAPTAIN MULZ 28

TYRANTS 1

WHERE NEVER KINGS CONNIVE NOR TYRANTS SCHEME . . . ANS LET AMERICA BE 8

UGLINESS 2

IN A CORNER FULL OF UGLINESS. . . . SP MAGNOLIA FLOWER 2
FULL OF UGLINESS. . . . SP MAGNOLIA FLOWER 7

UGLY 8
BLACK AN' UGLY . . . FC GAL'S CRY DYING 17
I'M BLACK AN' UGLY . . . FC GAL'S CRY DYING 15
A BIT OF CLAY, BROWN, UGLY, GIVEN LIFE? . . . DK BEGGAR BOY 6
SURE, CALL ME ANY UGLY NAME YOU CHOOSE - . . . ANS LET AMERICA BE 70
THE WORLD WHERE EVERY UGLY PAST MISTAKE . . . JC TO CAPTAIN MULZ 56
WHO CARRIES UGLY THINGS TO SHOW THE SUN? . . . SP A HOUSE IN TAOS 21
WHEN I'M OLD AN' UGLY . . . SP YOUNG GAL'S BLS 11
TO BE UGLY AN' OLD. . . . SP YOUNG GAL'S BLS 18

UH 3
UH! I SHO AM TIRED. . . . NM BROKE 1
UH! IT SURE IS AWFUL TO . . . SH EVIL MORNING 13
UH! I HATES A LYIN' GYPSY . . . SP BLD THE GYPSY 18

UMBILICAL 1
UMBILICAL IN SULPHUROUS CHOCOLATE: AYM ODE TO DINAH 91

UM-HUH 1
UM-HUH! YOU TALKING HIGH AND MIGHTY. SP BLD LANDLORD 17

UM-HUM 1
YES, UM-HUM! YOU SHO IS SWEET! CAN YOU PAY FO' DE LICENSE, DEAR? . NM BROKE 78

UM-MM 1
UM-MM! SIGN HERE SAYS THEY WANTS SOMEBODY TO SHOVEL COAL. . . . NM BROKE 28

UNA 1
PARECE UNA RUMBA. . . . FC JAZZ BAND 17

UNALIENABLE 1
WITH CERTAIN UNALIENABLE RIGHTS . . . . . SP FREEDOM'S PLOW 93

UNANALYZED 1
IN TONGUES UNANALYZED UNECHOED . . AYM IS IT TRUE? 7

UNAWARES 1
UNAWARES - ASLEEP. . . . SP FIRED 3

UNBINDING 1
BOUNDARIES BIND UNBINDING . . . PL CULTURAL EXCHNG 10

UNBLOWN 1
AND ETERNITY AN UNBLOWN SAXOPHONE FC SPORT 12

UNBOOTED 1
AND UNBOOTED PLAY . . . SP NEON SIGNS 8

UNBORN 1
SERVE - AND HATE WILL DIE UNBORN. DK ALABAMA EARTH 12

UNBOUGHT 1
THIS UNBOUGHT LOVELINESS OF MOON. SP A HOUSE IN TAOS 28

UNCLE 2
AND IF UNCLE MAC BRINGS BEER . . . SP SUMMER EVENING 24
SEND FOR UNCLE TOM ON HIS MIGHTY KNEES. . . . PL FINAL CALL 28

UNCODIFIED 1
UNCODIFIED UNPARSED . . . AYM IS IT TRUE? 6

UNCUT 1
AND LEAVE UNCUT THE ROSES . . . FW REMEMBRANCE 2

UNDECIPHERED 1
UNDECIPHERED AND UNLETTERED . . . AYM IS IT TRUE? 5

UNDER 10
WHAT JUNGLE TREE HAVE YOU SLEPT UNDER, . . . WB NUDE YOUNG DANC 1
WHAT JUNGLE TREE HAVE YOU SLEPT UNDER. . . . WB NUDE YOUNG DANC 5
DE TROUBLE I'VE HAD." FLINCHING UNDER THE WHIP, THE SPIRITUAL . NM BLACK CLWN MOOD 5
A SLAVE - UNDER THE WHIP, . . . NM BLACK CLWN POEM 21
UNDER THE GUISE OF A PATRIOT . . . ANS SONG OF SPAIN 67
THAT TAKETH ALL THINGS UNDER WING - LHR DEAR LVLY DEATH 2
UNDER THE THUNDER OF THE RAIN GOD? SP A HOUSE IN TAOS 14
UNDER MY HAND THE PYRAMIDS AROSE. SP NEGRO 8
WHY NOT GO UNDER? . . . PL QUESTION ANSWER 12
SLIPPING OUT FROM UNDER THEM . . . PL UNDERTOW 10

UNDERNEATH 2
SOMETHING UNDERNEATH . . . SP DREAM BOOGIE 12
UNDERNEATH THAT . . . SP STONY LONESOME 7

UNDERPAID 1
UNDERPAID ME FOR MY LABOR. . . . JC THE BITTER RIVR 61

UNDERSTAND 24
NOBODY TO UNDERSTAND. . . . FC MOAN 2
NOBODY TO UNDERSTAND. . . . FC MOAN 5
THAT ALL MIGHT UNDERSTAND: . . . NM BLACK CLWN POEM 76
THAT I CAN NEITHER KNOW NOR UNDERSTAND . . . DK BEGGAR BOY 3
DO NOT UNDERSTAND. . . . DK SEA CHARM 3
SING IT VERY SIMPLY THAT I MIGHT UNDERSTAND. . . . ANS SONG OF SPAIN 3
I DO NOT UNDERSTAND. . . . ANS SONG OF SPAIN 11
I DO NOT UNDERSTAND. . . . ANS SONG OF SPAIN 18
I CAN'T UNDERSTAND . . . JC BLACK MAN SPEAK 6
I DID NOT UNDERSTAND - . . . FW MAN 2
I DIDN'T UNDERSTAND . . . FW MAN 11
I DO NOT UNDERSTAND . . . FW SONGS 4
UNDERSTAND? . . . OWT JITNEY 40
DO YOU UNDERSTAND THE STILLNESS . . SP A HOUSE IN TAOS 11
I DO NOT UNDERSTAND. . . . SP AFRO-AMER FRAG 17
IT'S HARD TO UNDERSTAND . . . SP BLD OF THE GIRL 2
THE PEOPLE DO NOT ALWAYS UNDERSTAND EACH OTHER. . . . SP FREEDOM'S PLOW 152
ALWAYS THE TRYING TO UNDERSTAND. . SP FREEDOM'S PLOW 154
CAN'T YOU UNDERSTAND. . . . SP MISERY 9
O, UNDERSTAND . . . SP MISERY 10
I CAN UNDERSTAND - SOME DECENT MAN? SP SISTER 8
I LIKE TO WORK, READ, LEARN, AND UNDERSTAND LIFE. . . . SP THEME FOR ENG B 22
(AND HAS NO WAY TO UNDERSTAND) . . PL JUNIOR ADDICT 7
NOW I DO NOT UNDERSTAND . . . PL WHO BUT TH LORD 16

UNDERSTOOD 1
IF YOU UNDERSTOOD - . . . SP MAYBE 2

UNDERTAKER 1
THE UNDERTAKER TOLD 'EM. . . . SP BLD OF THE MAN 3

UNDERTAKER'S 1
THE DOCTOR 'N' UNDERTAKER'S . . . SP SYLVESTER'S BED 11

UNDERTONES 1
UNDERTONES. . . . WB LENOX AVE MIDNT 8

UNDRESSED 1
THE WIND HAS UNDRESSED THE MOON. . SP MARCH MOON 2

UNECHOED 2
IN TONGUES UNANALYZED UNECHOED . . AYM IS IT TRUE? 7
AND THE WHISPERS ARE UNECHOED . . . AYM IS IT TRUE? 33

UNEMPLOYMENT 1
'COURSE, YOU HEARS PLENTY 'BOUT THIS-HERE UNEMPLOYMENT RELIEF - NM BROKE 56

UNFELT 1
AS YET UNFELT AMONG MAGNOLIA TREES. PL BIRMINGHAM SUND 27

UNFOLD 1
PUSHCARTS FOLD AND UNFOLD . . . PL CULTURAL EXCHNG 21

UNFORGOTTEN 1
UNFORGOTTEN JOES AND SUGAR RAYS $ $ $ $ . . . AYM HORN OF PLENTY 19

UNFORTUNATELY 1
UNFORTUNATELY USUALLY NO! . . . SP SISTER 11

UNFREE 1
UNFREE? . . . PL DEATH YORKVILLE 8

UNHAPPY 2
SHOULDERS AT FATE, ACCEPTING HIS POSITION - BUT INSIDE HIMSELF UNHAPPY . . . NM BIG-TIMER MOOD 6
STRENGTH HE DOESN'T REALLY FEEL. GAY, LOUD, UNHAPPY JAZZ, BARING HIS . . . NM BIG-TIMER MOOD 9

UNICORN 4
CONJURES UNICORN. . . . AYM ASK YOUR MAMA 56
WHEN THERE'S A UNICORN? . . . AYM ASK YOUR MAMA 60
KING MOUNTS HIS UNICORN . . . AYM BIRD IN ORBIT 25
AS A SILVER UNICORN . . . AYM IS IT TRUE? 13

UNICORNS 1
THEIR GRASS WITH UNICORNS. . . . AYM ASK YOUR MAMA 77

UNIFORM 1
IN HIS SOLDIER'S UNIFORM, AND ALL. NM COLORED SL POEM 38

UNINDUCTED 1
BY THOSE YET UNINDUCTED . . . AYM BIRD IN ORBIT 12

UNION 7
40-VOICES: GROW STRONG WITH UNION, ALL HANDS TOGETHER - . . . ANS CHANT MAY DAY 11
BANNER OF FORCE AND LABOR, STRENGTH AND UNION. . . . ANS CHANT TOM MOONY 43
ONE UNION FORM: . . . ANS OPEN LETTER 35
IN UNION LIES OUR STRENGTH. . . . ANS OPEN LETTER 54
LET UNION BE . . . ANS OPEN LETTER 55

IN UNION, YOU, WHITE MAN. . . . . . JC TO CAPTAIN MULZ 59

OR THAT THE UNION WOULD STAND. . . SP FREEDOM'S PLOW 135

UNIONS 1

THE UNIONS BARRED US; THE FACTORIES, TOO. . . . . NM COLORED SL POEM 22

UNION-MADE 1

IT'S UNION-MADE. . . . . SH BLD PAWNBROKER 8

UNION'S 1

LONG A PART OF THE UNION'S HEART - NM DARK YOUTH USA 11

UNITED 3

UNITED STATES OF AMERICA. MARTIAL MUSIC ON A PIANO, OR BY AN ORCHESTRA. . . . . NM COLORED SL MOOD 3

THAT CAN UNITED RISE . . . . ANS OPEN LETTER 23

AND MEN UNITED AS A NATION. . . . . SP FREEDOM'S PLOW 141

UNKIND 1

AIN'T NEVER BEEN UNKIND. . . . . . FC BLACK GAL 4

UNKNOWN 2

10-VOICES: BLOOM IN THE STRENGTH OF YOUR UNKNOWN POWER. . . . . . . ANS CHANT MAY DAY 9

OF AN UNKNOWN STRANGE PERFUME . . . SP DESIRE 6

UNLETTERED 1

UNDECIPHERED AND UNLETTERED . . . . AYM IS IT TRUE? 5

UNLIKE 2

UNLIKE BUBBLES . . . . AYM ASK YOUR MAMA 71

UNLIKE BRICKBATS . . . . AYM ASK YOUR MAMA 72

UNLOVING 1

HARD-HEARTED AND UNLOVING! . . . . SH DECLARATION 15

UNLUCKY 1

UNLUCKY AS CAN BE. . . . . SP BAD LUCK CARD 8

UNMARKED 1

IN AN UNMARKED GRAVE. . . . . PL LUMUMBA'S GRAVE 14

UNOBTRUSIVE 1

WHO MOVE IN UNOBTRUSIVE . . . . . . AYM HORN OF PLENTY 67

UNPACKING 1

YET LEONTYNE'S UNPACKING. . . . . . PL CULTURAL EXCHNG 13

UNPARSED 1

UNCODIFIED UNPARSED . . . . AYM IS IT TRUE? 6

UNPUBLICIZED 1

LYING LOW, UNPUBLICIZED. . . . . . PL MISSISSIPPI 13

UNSCHOOLED 1

WHEN I SAW MY CHILDREN UNSCHOOLED, ANS A NEW SONG 12

UNSUNG 1

NIGHT OF THE FOUR SONGS UNSUNG: . . SP NIGHT FOUR SONG 5

UNSUSPECTIN 1

ALL UNSUSPECTIN OF THE CHIPPIE ON HIS LEFT - . . . . SH DEATH IN HARLEM 80

UNTAKEN 1

UNTAKEN DOWN ON TAPE - . . . . . . AYM IS IT TRUE? 8

UNTIL 22

UNTIL THE NEW DAWN. . . . . WB SUMMER NIGHT 22

UNTIL I CAME TO THIS NEAR STREET . OLD AESTHETE HARLEM 6

UNTIL THE WHOLE WORLD FALLS INTO THE HANDS OF . . . . ANS CHANT TOM MOONY 24

UNTIL THE FUTURE BURNS OUT . . . . ANS OPEN LETTER 36

UNTIL THE FORCES OF THE WORLD . . . ANS OPEN LETTER 63

UNTIL WE ALL ARE FREE. . . . . . . JC GOOD MORN STLIN 27

UNTIL THE STARS PALE AND THE SKY TURNS BLUE . . . . OWT JUICE JOINT 3

SO I WEPT UNTIL THE DAWN . . . . . SP A BLACK PIERROT 7

ROSE UNTIL IT TOUCHED THE SKY - . . SP AS I GREW OLDER 15

UNTIL HE MADE FOLKS SAY, ... SP DANCER 14

UNTIL THE LAST ATOM . . . . SP DRUM 7

UNTIL TIME IS LOST . . . . SP DRUM 9

AS TIME GROWS LONGER UNTIL DAY . . SP DRUNKARD 3

UNTIL ALL RACES AND ALL PEOPLES KNOW ITS SHADE. . . . . SP FREEDOM'S PLOW 199

UNTIL 12 - 1 - 2 A.M. . . . . SP GONE BOY 4

UNTIL COLORED FOLKS SPREAD . . . . SP GOOD MORNING 4

UNTIL THEN . . . . SP GRADUATION 21

UNTIL A GLOW IS LIGHTED . . . . . . SP MIGRANT 21

UNTIL THEY DIE . . . . SP NEW YORKERS 9

UNTIL IT GLEAMS . . . . SP TRUMPET PLAYER 14

UNTIL LAST NIGHT. . . . . PL GHOSTS OF 1619 11

AND RIDE THE JIM CROW CAR UNTIL IT SCREAMS . . . . PL JIM CROW CAR 3

UNTOUCHED 1

AND LEAVING UNTOUCHED THE BOX-CAR SP RAILROAD AVENUE 28

UNTRUE 1

HARD-HEARTED AND UNTRUE! . . . . . SH DECLARATION 16

UNUSED 1

TOOLS HANDLED - BUT UNUSED. . . . . JC THE BITTER RIVR 19

UNWITTINGLY 1

UNWITTINGLY. . . . . PL SLAVE 6

UNYIELDING 1

UNYIELDING. . . . . ANS A NEW SONG 44

UN-HUMM-M 1

UN-HUMM-M! . . . YES! . . . . SP MADAM PHONE BIL 37

UN-NEGRO 1

IN STRANGE UN-NEGRO TONGUE - . . . SP AFRO-AMER FRAG 9

UN-UH 1

WILLING WORKER? UN-UH! YES! WHAT'S THAT YOU SAY? . . . . NM BROKE 33

UN'NEATH 1

PUT MA HEAD UN'NEATH DE KIVER. . . FC GAL'S CRY DYING 5

UP 167

I DRESSED UP ALBERT JOHNSON. . . . FC BLACK GAL 9

ALL MIXED UP WITH DIMES AND . . . . FC BRASS SPITOONS 28

I'M GONNA FILL 'EM UP FULL O' . . . FC DEATH DO DIRTY 33

GATHER UP YO' FINE CLOTHES . . . . FC HARD LUCK 5

WHEN I CUDDLES UP TO HIM . . . . . FC MINNIE SINGS 9

SHAKE 'EM UP AN' SHAKE 'EM UP . . . FC SATURDAY NIGHT 23

SHAKE 'EM UP AN' SHAKE 'EM UP . . . FC SATURDAY NIGHT 23

I GUESS I KNOW WHAT I'M UP AGAINST. NM BIG-TIMER POEM 57

MIX UP A DRINK. . . . . NM BIG-TIMER POEM 62

STRIKE UP THE MUSIC. . . . . NM BLACK CLWN POEM 12

TRYING TO CLIMB UP. . . . . NM BLACK CLWN POEM 45

UP AND DOWN, AND THEY JUST AIN'T NO JOBS IN THIS MAN'S TOWN. . . . . NM BROKE 3

AND DON'T YOU KNOW THAT OLD WOMAN SWELLED UP LIKE A SPECKLED TOAD NM BROKE 21

AND I SHO HAD A PRETTY GAL, TOO, UP YONDER ON SUGAR HILL. . . . . . NM BROKE 48

IS I MARRIED? NO, ALL THESE-HERE GIRLS UP NORTH IS TOO LIGHT. . . NM BROKE 70

WHO JOINED UP TO FIGHT FOR THE U.S.A. . . . . NM COLORED SL POEM 3

CALMLY TELLING THE STORY, PROUDLY AND EXPECTANTLY WITH HEAD UP, SHOULDERS . . . . NM COLORED SL MOOD 7

THEN I WOKE UP, AND THE DREAM WAS ENDED - . . . . NM COLORED SL POEM 48

THE MOURNERS GOT UP SMILING. . . . DK IRISH WAKE 7

SINCE I COME UP NORTH DE . . . . . DK PO' BOY BLUES 5

BUT I'M WAKIN' UP! . . . . ANS PARK BENCH 7

UP MILLIONS FOR BOMBS TO KILL A CHILD - . . . . ANS SONG OF SPAIN 44

TO BUILD UP PROFITS FOR THE RAPE OF SPAIN! . . . . ANS SONG OF SPAIN 57

OR IF I WASN'T SO DROWSY I'D LOOK UP JOE . . . . SH BED TIME 5

BUT SINCE I GOT TO GET UP AT DAY, SH BED TIME 9

BIG BEN, I'M GONNA BUST YOU BANG UP SIDE THE WALL! . . . . SH DAYBREAK 1

YOU MUST THINK YOU GOT TO WAKE UP A CROWD! . . . . SH DAYBREAK 4

YOU AIN'T GOT TO WAKE UP NO BODY BUT ME. . . . . SH DAYBREAK 5

GETTING UP IN THE MORNING LONESOME AND SAD? . . . . SH DAYBREAK 13

AND THE SUN CAME UP AND . . . . . . SH DEATH IN HARLEM 137

PICKED UP ANOTHER WOMAN AND . . . . SH DEATH IN HARLEM 141

FILL IT UP WITH GAS . . . . SH DECLARATION 10

FOLKS, I COME UP NORTH . . . . . . SH EVENIN' BLUES 1

I COME UP NORTH . . . . SH EVENIN' BLUES 3

BEEN UP HERE SIX MONTHS - . . . . . SH EVENIN' BLUES 5

KEEP ME CAGED UP HERE. . . . . . . SH FREE MAN 8

I'LL KEEP RIGHT UP WITH YOU. . . . SH HEY-HEY BLUES 18

FILL IT UP WITH GAS AND . . . . . . SH IF-ING 7

AND WAKE ME UP GENTLE WHEN THE DAWN APPEARS . . . . SH LETTER 18

SHE COULD CHASE ME UP A TREE . . . SH ONLY WOMAN BLUS 9

ALL DAY SUNDAY DIDN'T EVEN DRESS UP. SH SUNDAY 1

I'M GONNA GET UP A POKER GAME AND INVITE THE BOYS. . . . . SH SUNDAY 12

AND BE UP AND OUT AND READY . . . . JC BLD SAM SOLOMON 21

STANDS UP AND LAUGHS . . . . JC FREEDOM 11

HAD GIVE YOU UP FOR DEAD. . . . . . JC GOOD MORN STLIN 3

DONE GIVE YOU UP FOR DEAD - . . . . JC GOOD MORN STLIN 38

YOU CAN'T LOCK UP GANDHI. . . . . . JC HOW ABOUT DIXIE 13

HAVE MADE UP THEIR MINDS JIM CROW IS THROUGH. . . . . JC JIM CROW'S LAST 14

SO I GAVE UP AND WENT . . . . FW COMMUNION 5

GATHER UP . . . . FW PRAYER 1

GATHER UP . . . . FW PRAYER 7

GATHER UP . . . . FW PRAYER 9

GO UP THE CANEPLANK	FW SAILING DATE	13
WE'D OPEN UP THE KINGDOM	FW WISDOM	6
RIDING UP AND DOWN.	OWT BLD MARGE POLIT	34
UP ALL NIGHT!	OWT BLD MARGE POLIT	51
CARRIED LONELY UP THE AISLE	OWT FUNERAL	1
STRIKES UP A TUNE ALL GAY AND BRIGHT AND GLAD	OWT JUICE JOINT	43
UP THERE IN THE SKY.	OWT REQUEST REQUIEM	4
UP IN HARLEM -	OWT VISITORS	6
BEAT HER UP BAD.	SP BLD FORTUNE TEL	22
WHEN YOU COME UP YOURSELF	SP BLD LANDLORD	7
TILL YOU FIX THIS HOUSE UP NEW.	SP BLD LANDLORD	12
SHE RAKED UP A HUNDRED	SP BLD OF THE MAN	13
I WOULDN'T GET UP NO MORE -	SP BLUES AT DAWN	9
I WENT UP ON A MOUNTAIN	SP CROSSING	5
WAKE UP AND LIVE!	SP DEAD IN THERE	16
I'D LIKE TO TAKE UP BACH.	SP DEFERRED	48
GOIN' UP AN' DOWN.	SP ELEVATOR BOY	16
UP AN' DOWN.	SP ELEVATOR BOY	17
I'M GONNA CHECK UP ON THIS	SP FREEDOM TRAIN	15
THE SLAVES MADE UP A SONG:	SP FREEDOM'S PLOW	125
MADE UP A SONG:	SP FREEDOM'S PLOW	190
WE GOT UP	SP FULFILMENT	4
UP FROM CUBA HAITI JAMAICA.	SP GOOD MORNING	11
DOES IT DRY UP	SP HARLEM	2
AND I OPENED UP MY DOOR.	SP HOMECOMING	2
HE ROSE UP ON HIS DYING BED	SP HOPE	1
HIS WIFE LOOKED IT UP IN HER DREAM BOOK	SP HOPE	3
ARE RARING UP AND TALKING BACK	SP IN EXPLANATION	3
HURRY UP. BOY!	SP IN EXPLANATION	15
ARE RARING UP AND TALKING BACK	SP IN EXPLANATION	20
SHUT UP. SAYS GERALD L.K. SMITH.	SP IN EXPLANATION	23
SHUT UP. SAYS THE GOVERNOR OF SOUTH CAROLINA.	SP IN EXPLANATION	24
SHUT UP. SAYS THE GOVERNOR OF SINGAPORE.	SP IN EXPLANATION	25
SHUT UP. SAYS STRYDOM.	SP IN EXPLANATION	26
HELL NO SHUT UP! SAY THE PEOPLE	SP IN EXPLANATION	27
SHUT UP. PEOPLE!	SP IN EXPLANATION	44
SHUT UP! SHUT UP!	SP IN EXPLANATION	45
SHUT UP! SHUT UP!	SP IN EXPLANATION	45
SHUT UP. GEORGE!	SP IN EXPLANATION	46
SHUT UP. SALLIE!	SP IN EXPLANATION	47
SHUT UP. COOLIE!	SP IN EXPLANATION	48
SHUT UP. INDIAN!	SP IN EXPLANATION	49
SHUT UP. BOY!	SP IN EXPLANATION	50
NO SHUT UP!	SP IN EXPLANATION	56
HELL NO SHUT UP!	SP IN EXPLANATION	57
DON'T YOU WANT TO GET UP	SP KID SLEEPY	11
WAY UP IN THE TREBLE	SP LADY'S BOOGIE	7
I'M GOIN' UP IN A TOWER	SP LAMENT OVER LOV	19
UP IN A TOWER	SP LAMENT OVER LOV	21
MAMA. IT HAS BEEN RAINING CATS AND DOGS UP	SP LETTER	8
I CAME UP ONCE AND HOLLERED!	SP LIFE IS FINE	5
I CAME UP TWICE AND CRIED!	SP LIFE IS FINE	6
HIGH UP THERE!	SP LIFE IS FINE	21
CLOSE UP TIGHT THAT NIGHT.	SP LIKEWISE	11
GATHER UP	SP LITANY	1
GATHER UP	SP LITANY	7
GATHER UP	SP LITANY	9
UP WITH YOU -	SP LOW TO HIGH	4
SHE GREW UP AND GOT RUINT.	SP MADAM CHARTY CH	3
WHEN YOU GROW UP THE HARD WAY	SP MADAM MIGHT-HAV	5
SHE SQUINTED UP HER EYES.	SP MADAM FORT TELL	6
IT'S NOT UP TO ME.	SP MADAM RENT MAN	20
CALLING ME UP	SP MADAM PHONE BIL	21
UP YOUR SLEEVE:	SP MADAM MIGHT-HAV	24
TILL I GOT MIXED UP	SP MADAM'S PAST HI	12
HE UP AND WENT HIS WAY.	SP MAMA AND DAUGHT	14
THEY DRAW UP RESTRICTIVE COVENANTS	SP MIGRANT	25
TAKES UP IMPORTANT MATTERS	SP MIGRANT	28
YOU WERE MY MOON UP IN THE SKY.	SP MISS BLUES'ES	7
WOKE UP AND LOOKED AROUND ME -	SP MORNING AFTER	11
AND BOARDS TORN UP.	SP MOTHER TO SON	5
SO I COME UP HERE.	SP NEW YORKERS	12
SHE LIFTED UP HER LIPS	SP NEW YORKERS	15
AND YOU MIXED 'EM UP WITH SYMPHONIES	SP NOTE COMM THEAT	4
STAND UP AND TALK ABOUT ME.	SP NOTE COMM THEAT	13
I PICK UP MY LIFE	SP ONE-WAY TICKET	1
I PICK UP MY LIFE	SP ONE-WAY TICKET	9
I AM FED UP	SP ONE-WAY TICKET	16
I PICK UP MY LIFE	SP ONE-WAY TICKET	23
GONE UP NORTH.	SP ONE-WAY TICKET	26
CLIMBING UP A GREAT BIG MOUNTAIN	SP PORTER	7
WILL TEAM UP WITH JACKIE MABLEY.	SP PROJECTION	19
REACH UP YOUR HAND. DARK BOY. AND TAKE A STAR.	SP STARS	7
I WOKE UP THIS MORNIN'	SP SYLVESTER'S BED	1
I WOKE UP LITTLE LATER	SP SYLVESTER'S BED	9
AND I REACHES UP TO HUG 'EM -	SP SYLVESTER'S BED	25
IMPEL YOU FOREVER UP THE GREAT STAIRS -	SP THE NEGRO MOTHE	50
UP TO MY ROOM. SIT DOWN. AND WRITE THIS PAGE:	SP THEME FOR ENG B	15
UP THE STAIRS AND DOWN THE STAIRS	SP TO BE SOMEBODY	9
FOR US TO PACK UP	SP WEST TEXAS	8
SO WE CRANKED UP OUR OLD FORD	SP WEST TEXAS	11
SOAKING UP A WINE-SOUSE	SP WINE-O	2
SOAKING UP A NEW SOUSE.	SP WINE-O	6
SOAKING UP THE MUSIC	AYM BIRD IN ORBIT	68
SOAKING UP THE MUSIC.	AYM BIRD IN ORBIT	91
FIRST WHITE TOURIST UP THE MOUNTAIN	AYM GOSPEL CHA-CHA	17
UP THAT STEEP HILL	AYM GOSPEL CHA-CHA	52
UP THERE ON THAT HILL	AYM GOSPEL CHA-CHA	59
TO CATCH UP WITH TOMORROW	AYM IS IT TRUE?	30
SHADOWS SHOW UP SHARPER.	AYM ODE TO DINAH	3
BORN TO GROW UP WILD -	AYM ODE TO DINAH	87
WHEN THE ROLL IS CALLED UP YONDER	AYM RIDE. RED. RIDE	2
SINCE WE MOVED UP TO MOUNT VERNON.	PL CULTURAL EXCHNG	25
HURRY UP!	PL CULTURAL EXCHNG	60
TRYIN' TO GET UP THERE -	PL DOWN WHERE I AM	6
DOES IT DRY UP	PL DREAM DEFERRED	2
FOR CINQUE SAYING. "RUN A NEW FLAG UP THE MAST."	PL FINAL CALL	21
SAYS SUGAR'S GONE UP ANOTHER TWO CENTS.	PL HARLEM	9
ON VACATION? UP NORTH?	PL MISSISSIPPI	10
UP NORTH.	PL NORTHERN LIBERL	15
HAVING GIVEN UP BREATH -	PL SLAVE	5
UP YOUR	PL STOKELY MALCOLM	17
I'D UP AND SELL MY HEART OF GOLD	PL VARI-COLORED	3
AND NEVER UP INSTEAD.	PL VARI-COLORED	16
THE LAW RAISED UP HIS STICK	PL WHO BUT TH LORD	13

UPHELD 1

AND THE RULE OF GREED'S UPHELD -	ANS UNION	11

UPHILL 1

IN UPHILL LETTERS	SP MIGRANT	36

UPHOLD 1

ME. TRYING TO UPHOLD THE RACE	SP HIGH TO LOW	21

UPON 14

FALL UPON THE EARTH.	DK AFTR MNY SPRNGS	6
LET THE RAIN BEAT UPON YOUR HEAD WITH SILVER LIQUID DROPS.	DK APRIL RAIN SONG	2
AND YET HE PLAYS UPON HIS FLUTE A WILD FREE TUNE	DK BEGGAR BOY	7
HE SAT UPON THE ROLLING DECK	DK SAILOR	1
THAT GREW UPON THE PLAIN	LHR PASTORAL	7
DAUGHTER. ONCE UPON A TIME -	SP MAMA AND DAUGHT	9
WHO SITS UPON THE GROUND	SP MEXICAN MARKET	2
I LOOKED UPON THE NILE AND RAISED THE PYRAMIDS ABOVE IT.	SP NEGRO SPEAKS OF	7
UPON MY HAIR?	SP PRAYER	6
BUT SHE TURNS HER BACK UPON ME.	SP THE SOUTH	22
UPON WHAT RIFF THE MUSIC SLIPS	SP TRUMPET PLAYER	38
THEIR BLOOD UPON THE WALL	PL BIRMINGHAM SUND	5
WHO LEFT THEIR BLOOD UPON THAT WALL.	PL BIRMINGHAM SUND	16
BY SONGS UPON THE BREEZE	PL BIRMINGHAM SUND	26

UPPER 1

A ROW OF GOLD IN HIS UPPER MOUTH.	SH DEATH IN HARLEM	18

UPRIGHT 1

NOT STANDING UPRIGHT	SP TO BE SOMEBODY	6

UPROOTS 1

IT UPROOTS TREES!	PL WARNING	10

UPSET 1

I BEEN UPSET	PL STOKELY MALCOLM	5

UPSIDE 1

OURSELVES UPSIDE DOWN.	FW CIRCLES	10

UPSTAIRS 2

HEAR THAT MUSIC PLAYIN' UPSTAIRS?	SP BLACK MARIA	6
BUT THAT MUSIC PLAYIN' UPSTAIRS	SP BLACK MARIA	9

UPTOWN 2

UPTOWN AND DOWN.	SP SAME IN BLUES	30
UPTOWN ON LENOX AVENUE	PL PRIME	1

UPWARD 1

LOOK EVER UPWARD AT THE SUN AND THE STARS.	SP THE NEGRO MOTHE	48

URANIUM 1

WITH URANIUM DUST.	PL LUMUMBA'S GRAVE	4

URGE 1

THE URGE TO RAISE HELL.	OWT BLD MARGE POLIT	8

US 35

THE GODS ARE LAUGHING AT US.	WB LENOX AVE MIDNT	4
AND THE GODS ARE LAUGHING AT US.	WB LENOX AVE MIDNT	14
WHEN THE NATION CALLED US THAT MIGHTY DAY.	NM COLORED SL POEM	4
AND GIVE US THE RIGHTS THAT ARE YOURS AND MINE.	NM COLORED SL POEM	10
THEY TOLD US AMERICA WOULD KNOW NO BLACK OR WHITE:	NM COLORED SL POEM	11

THE UNIONS BARRED US; THE FACTORIES, TOO. . . . . NM COLORED SL POEM 22
DIDN'T OUR GOVERNMENT TELL US THINGS WOULD BE FINE . . . . NM COLORED SL POEM 33
BRIGHT BEFORE US . . . . DK YOUTH 2
LET US FORGET WHAT BOOKER-T. SAID, ANS OPEN LETTER 19
LET US BECOME INSTEAD, YOU AND I, ANS OPEN LETTER 21
AND DRIVE US TO THE TIME-CLOCK AND THE PLOW . . . . ANS OPEN LETTER 27
LET US NEW LESSONS LEARN, ... ANS OPEN LETTER 32
LET US TOGETHER, SAY: . . . . . . ANS OPEN LETTER 38
BETWEEN US TWO. . . . . ANS PARK BENCH 4
EXCEPT THAT THEY BE MADE FOR US . . ANS SONG OF SPAIN 64
STAND BACK FOLKSES, LET US . . . . SH DEATH IN HARLEM 106
YOU'VE STOOD BETWEEN US WELL, . . . JC GOOD MORN STLIN 35
THAT GUIDE US TOWARD THE HARBOR OF THE NEW WORLD . . . . JC TO CAPTAIN MULZ 54
AIN'T FOR US A-TALL: . . . . SP CHILDREN'S RYME 22
DESIRE TO US . . . . SP DESIRE 1
BETWEEN US QUICKLY . . . . SP DESIRE 7
TO THE ENEMY WHO WOULD CONQUER US FROM WITHOUT, ... SP FREEDOM'S PLOW 178
AND CONQUER US FROM WITHIN, ... SP FREEDOM'S PLOW 181
FOR US TO PLAY WITH, ... SP FULFILMENT 11
BLESSED US WITH A KISS . . . . . . SP FULFILMENT 18
TOOK US BOTH IN . . . . SP FULFILMENT 20
LET US ROAM THE NIGHT TOGETHER . . SP HARLEM NIGHT SO 2
LET US ROAM THE NIGHT TOGETHER . . SP HARLEM NIGHT SO 15
LEAVES US HUNGRY, RAGGED . . . . . SP SHARE-CROPPERS 9
"YOU CAN'T LEAVE US HERE!" . . . . SP SYLVESTER'S BED 14
FOR US TO PACK UP . . . . SP WEST TEXAS 8
YOU MUST THINK US COLORED FOLKS . . PL BACKLASH BLUES 11
AIN'T FOR US A-TALL: . . . . PL CHILDREN'S RYME 13
TO MAKE US ALL INTO PRINCES AND PRINCESSES. . . . . PL FINAL CALL 7
THEY TOLD US BEFORE. . . . . PL HARLEM 6

USE 13

ELSE I'LL USE HER HEAD . . . . . . FC EVIL WOMAN 15
SO WHAT'S THE USE O' WORRYIN' . . . NM BIG-TIMER POEM 69
NO USE IN MY GOING . . . . SP BLUE MONDAY 1
BUT NO USE DENYING - . . . . SP BLUE MONDAY 8
LIARS USE THOSE WORDS. . . . . . . SP IN EXPLANATION 39
"WHAT'S THE USE?" . . . . SP LIKEWISE 16
WHAT'S THE USE . . . . SP LIKEWISE 17
WHAT'S THE USE? . . . . SP LIKEWISE 19
USE IN HARLEM . . . . SP LIKEWISE 21
SHALL I USE OLD ENGLISH . . . . . . SP MADAM'S CALLING 13
I SAID, USE AMERICAN. . . . . SP MADAM'S CALLING 15
SAID, WE CAN'T USE YOU . . . . . . SP MADAM'S PAST HI 16
WHAT WAS THE USE OF PRAYER. . . . . SP SONG DARK GIRL 8

USED 22

I USED TO BE A GOOD CHILE. . . . . FC LISTEN HERE 7
USED TO BE A GOOD CHILE. - . . . . FC LISTEN HERE 9
TRIED TO FIND ONE O' THEM LITTLE ELEVATOR AND SWITCHBOARD JOBS THEY USED . . . . NM BROKE 41
SO I WENT DOWN TOWN TO A HOTEL WHERE I USED TO WORK AT NIGHT, ... NM BROKE 44
AW-GO! YONDER COMES A WOMAN I USED TO KNOW WAY DOWN SOUTH. . . . . NM BROKE 62
(AIN'T SEEN HER IN SIX YEARS! USED TO GO WITH HER, TOO!) . . . . . NM BROKE 63
LET IT BE THE DREAM IT USED TO BE. ANS LET AMERICA BE 2
I USED TO BELIEVE IN YOU, BABY, . . SH IN TROUBLED KEY 5
AND BE THE SAME OLD CROW HE USED TO BE - . . . . JC JIM CROW'S LAST 10
I USED TO WONDER . . . . FW BORDER LINE 1
I USED TO WONDER . . . . FW BORDER LINE 5
I USED TO GO ROUND THE CORNER. . . OWT LONESOME CORNER 3
WHEN I WAS A CHILD WE USED TO PLAY, SP CHILDREN'S RYME 1
HE USED TO SAY. . . . . SP DEAD IN THERE 17
I USED TO PLAY . . . . SP LITTLE GRN TREE 5
HE USED A SWITCH-BLADE . . . . . . SP MADAM CHARTY CH 7
IF YOU HAD A HEAD AND USED YOUR MIND SP 50 - 50 9
IRENE AND HELEN ARE AS THEY USED TO BE . . . . AYM BIRD IN ORBIT 21
ME WHO USED TO BE NOBODY, ... AYM HORN OF PLENTY 42
USED TO BE. . . . . PL CORNER MEETING 3
AS IF THE WEAPONS USED TODAY . . . PL MOTHER IN WAR 5
THE INK YOU USED . . . . PL OFFICIAL NOTICE 4

USED-TO-BE 1

MY USED-TO-BE - . . . . SH ONLY WOMAN BLUS 2

USELESS 1

THE BOOK STUDIED - BUT USELESS. . . JC THE BITTER RIVR 13

USUAL 1

ANSWERING THE USUAL QUESTIONS . . . PL DINNER GUEST ME 4

USUALLY 1

UNFORTUNATELY USUALLY NO! . . . . . SP SISTER 11

UTTER 3

DEAR DREAM OF UTTER ALIVENESS - . . SP DEMAND 2
TOUCHING MY BODY OF UTTER DEATH - SP DEMAND 3
TELL ME, O DREAM OF UTTER ALIVENESS - . . . . SP DEMAND 6

UTTERED 1

SHE UTTERED A CRY. . . . . SH DEATH IN HARLEM 100

U.S.A 5

WHO JOINED UP TO FIGHT FOR THE U.S.A. . . . . NM COLORED SL POEM 3
I FROM THE U.S.A. . . . . SP BROTHERS 6
NOW IT IS THE U.S.A. . . . . SP FREEDOM'S PLOW 89
IN THE U.S.A., ... PL BIBLE BELT 5
OF DARKNESS U.S.A. - . . . . PL DINNER GUEST ME 9

VACATION 1

ON VACATION? UP NORTH? . . . . . . PL MISSISSIPPI 10

VAGUE 3

EMPTY WITH A VAGUE, ... WB SUMMER NIGHT 15
THE DREAM IS VAGUE . . . . SP BEALE STREET 1
THE DREAM IS VAGUE, ... SP BEALE STREET 5

VAIN 1

LIFT ARMS IN VAIN, RUN, HIDE, DIE: ANS SONG OF SPAIN 60

VALLEY 2

I WENT DOWN IN THE VALLEY . . . . . SP CROSSING 9
SOMETIMES, THE VALLEY WAS FILLED WITH TEARS, ... SP THE NEGRO MOTHE 25

VARIED 1

HAS STUDIED VARIED FACES, ... FW OLD SAILOR 5

VARIOUS 1

THAT GROWS IN NO-MAN'S LAND, JOAN OF ARC, AND VARIOUS OTHER WAR-TIME NM COLORED SL MOOD 5

VARMINTS 1

LISTEN AT THEM LITTLE VARMINTS! . . SP CHILDREN'S RYME 4

VARY 1

HARLEM GIRLS VARY - . . . . SH HARLEM SWEETIES 40

VAST 2

WHEN THE NIGHT IS A VAST SOFTNESS DK AFTR MNY SPRNGS 3
THROUGH SOME VAST MIST OF RACE . . SP AFRO-AMER FRAG 15

VAUDEVILLE 1

COMEDIANS IN VAUDEVILLE . . . . . . FC LAUGHERS 17

VEDADO 1

OR MAYBE THE DREAM'S A VEDADO ROSE - SP HAVANA DREAMS 7

VEIL 3

LIKE A SWEET VEIL ABOUT YOUR BOWER? WB NUDE YOUNG DANC 4
AND WHO ARE YOU THAT DRAWS YOUR VEIL ACROSS THE STARS? . . . . ANS LET AMERICA BE 18
SHADOWS VEIL HIS DARKNESS . . . . . FW DIMOUT IN HARLM 5

VEILING 7

SHADOWS VEILING SHADOWS . . . . . . FW DIMOUT IN HARLM 6
VEILING SHADOWS CUT BY LAUGHTER . . FW DIMOUT IN HARLM 8
SHADOWS VEILING SILENCE . . . . . . FW DIMOUT IN HARLM 10
SILENCE VEILING SHADOWS . . . . . . FW DIMOUT IN HARLM 11
VEILING HARLEM'S LAUGHTER . . . . . FW DIMOUT IN HARLM 13
VEILING HER FACE LIKE A VIRGIN . . FW NEW MOON 6
VEILING WHAT THE DARKNESS HIDES. . PL GEORGIA DUSK 4

VEINS 1

FLOW OF HUMAN BLOOD IN HUMAN VEINS. SP NEGRO SPEAKS OF 3

VELASQUEZ 1

GOYA, VELASQUEZ, MURILLO, ... ANS SONG OF SPAIN 20

VELDT 1

O, VELDT AT NIGHT! . . . . OWT NEGRO SERVANT 5

VELVET 1

A VELVET SCREEN. . . . . SP FULFILMENT 15

VERANDAS 1

SITTING ON THEIR WIDE VERANDAS. . . PL CULTURAL EXCHNG 47

VERNON 1

SINCE WE MOVED UP TO MOUNT VERNON. PL CULTURAL EXCHNG 25

VERONA 1

FROM VERONA . . . . SP JULIET 12

VERY 15

SAY IT VERY SOFTLY. . . . . FC MAMMY 3
SAY IT VERY SLOWLY IF YOU CHOOSE. FC MAMMY 4
AN' DIG ME A GRAVE THIS VERY DAY. FC MINNIE SINGS 17
THE SUN'S GOING DOWN THIS VERY NIGHT - . . . . DK SONG BANJO DANC 14
THE SUN'S GOING DOWN THIS VERY NIGHT - . . . . DK SONG BANJO DANC 26

SING IT VERY SIMPLY THAT I MIGHT UNDERSTAND. . . . . ANS SONG OF SPAIN 3
WHO WOULD BE MY VERY OWN - . . . . . OWT STRANGER IN TWN 4
DID NOT MAKE ME VERY WISE - . . . . . LHR ACCEPTANCE 2
THAT'S ALL VERY WELL - . . . . SP MADAM NUMBER WR 30
CARED VERY MUCH! . . . . SP S-SSS-SS-SH! 14
VERY WELL PAID. . . . . PL ELDERLY LEADERS 7
FROM VERY INDECISION . . . . PL FREDRK DOUGLASS 4
THE VERY ROOM IN WHICH HE LEAVES . PL JUNIOR ADDICT 11
THE VERY ROOM IN WHICH TODAY THE AIR PL JUNIOR ADDICT 13
AND FEELING TO MY VERY SOUL . . . . PL MILITANT 6

VESEY 1
SEND FOR DENMARK VESEY CRYING, "FREE!" . . . . PL FINAL CALL 20

VIBRANT 1
HAS A HEAD OF VIBRANT HAIR . . . . SP TRUMPET PLAYER 11

VIBRATES 1
AND THE SOUND VIBRATES IN WAVES . . ANS CHANT TOM MOONY 17

VICE 1
DETECTIVES FROM THE VICE SQUAD . . SP CAFE: 3 A.M. 1

VICEROYS 1
AT THE MISTERS, LORDS, GENERALS, VICEROYS, ... SP IN EXPLANATION 42

VICTIM 1
I'VE BEEN A VICTIM: . . . . SP NEGRO 14

VICTORY 2
YOUR SHIP IS VICTORY, ... JC TO CAPTAIN MULZ 73
THE VICTORY. . . . . PL PEACE 8

VICTROLA 2
THE LAST VICTROLA CEASES WITH THE WB SUMMER NIGHT 5
A VICTROLA. . . . . SP RAILROAD AVENUE 10

VIETNAM 1
SEND MY SON TO VIETNAM. . . . . . . PL BACKLASH BLUES 6

VIEW 1
CAME TIPPIN INTO DIXIE'S TO GET A VIEW. . . . . SH DEATH IN HARLEM 59

VILER 1
WITH VILER DRUGS . . . . PL JUNIOR ADDICT 24

VILLAGES 1
LABOR! OUT OF LABOR CAME THE VILLAGES . . . . SP FREEDOM'S PLOW 70

VILLE 1
TO THE VILLE OF NANIGO. . . . . . . AYM GOSPEL CHA-CHA 38

VINDICATED 1
SOUTHERN DOGS HAVE VINDICATED ME - PL NORTHERN LIBERL 4

VINE 3
COULD BE 18TH & VINE . . . . SP COULD BE 3
23RD AND CENTRAL, 18TH STREET AND VINE. . . . . AYM ASK YOUR MAMA 6
18TH AND VINE IN K.C., 63RD IN CHI. AYM ASK YOUR MAMA 32

VINGT 2
VINGT FRANCS NICKEL DIME . . . . . AYM ASK YOUR MAMA 46
AT THE DOME VINGT FRANCS WILL DO . AYM ASK YOUR MAMA 50

VIOLETS 1
WHEN THE FIRST VIOLETS . . . . . . SH YOUNG NEGRO GRL 3

VIOLINS 1
AND LET THE WHITE VIOLINS WHIR THIN AND SLOW. . . . . SP FATASY PURPLE 6

VIRGIN 3
VEILING HER FACE LIKE A VIRGIN . . FW NEW MOON 6
DAMBALLA WEDO! THE VIRGIN! BEDWARD! AYM GOSPEL CHA-CHA 43
THE VIRGIN . . . . AYM GOSPEL CHA-CHA 53

VIRGINIA 1
VIRGINIA DARE WINE - . . . . SH HARLEM SWEETIES 28

VISION 2
WHO HAS A VISION OF HIS BROTHER KILLED IN FRANCE WHILE FIGHTING FOR THE . . . . NM COLORED SL MOOD 2
BACK, AND EYES SHINING, QUIETLY RECALLING THE VISION. THE DEAD MAN SPEAKS . . . . NM COLORED SL MOOD 8

VISIONS 1
I HAD VISIONS IN MY HEAD . . . . . PL WHO BUT TH LORD 5

VISIT 1
PAY YOU A VISIT . . . . SP MADAM WRONG VIS 15

VOICE 3
AND YET A VOICE FOREVER . . . . . . OK LINCOLN MONUMNT 7
MY YOUNG MEN WITHOUT A VOICE IN THE WORLD, ... ANS A NEW SONG 13
IN THE FLOW OF OLD AUNT SUE'S VOICE, SP AUNTSUE'S STORI 13
VOICE GROWS THICKER . . . . SP DRUNKARD 1
VOICE OF MUTED TRUMPET, ... SP SONG BILLIE HOL 16
AN OLD NEGRO MINISTER CONCLUDES HIS SERMON IN HIS LOUDEST VOICE, . . . SP SUNDAY MORNING 1
IN A DEEP SONG VOICE WITH A MELANCHOLY TONE . . . . SP THE WEARY BLUES 17
HEAR MY VOICE! . . . . PL FREDRK DOUGLASS 15

VOICES 1
WAVES OF RISING AND RE-RISING MASS VOICES, MULTIPLYING LIKE . . . . ANS CHANT MAY DAY 2

VOTE 8
CAUSE THE VOTE IS NOT RESTRICTED . JC BLD SAM SOLOMON 11
TO VOTE AT THE POLLS, ... JC BLD SAM SOLOMON 23
BUT WE INTEND TO VOTE . . . . JC BLD SAM SOLOMON 35
ABOLISH POLL TAX SO FOLKS CAN VOTE. JC JIM CROW'S LAST 24
NO MAYORS AND SUCH FOR WHICH COLORED CAN'T VOTE, ... SP FREEDOM TRAIN 56
BECAUSE HE TRIED TO VOTE . . . . . SP NOT A MOVIE 2
DID I VOTE FOR NIXON? . . . . AYM BIRD IN ORBIT 16
(EVEN VOTE FOR REAL IN ALABAMA) . . PL GHOSTS OF 1619 8

VOTED 4
NEGROES NEVER VOTED BUT . . . . . . JC BLD SAM SOLOMON 7
THE FACT WE NEVER VOTED . . . . . . JC BLD SAM SOLOMON 17
I SAID, VOTED FOR YOUR MAMA. . . . AYM BIRD IN ORBIT 17
VOTED ALL THE DIXIECRATS . . . . . PL CULTURAL EXCHNG 40

VOTELESS 1
THE VOTELESS SHARE-CROPPER BEHIND STEEL BARS, ... JC THE BITTER RIVR 31

VOTES 1
FOR HERE IN THE SOUTH THERE'S NO VOTES AND NO RIGHT. . . . . . . NM COLORED SL POEM 46

VOTE-IN 1
SIT-IN, STAND-IN, STALL-IN, VOTE-IN PL GHOSTS OF 1619 7

VOTING 2
IN THE VOTING OF A NATION. . . . . JC BLD SAM SOLOMON 48
AND IN VOTING NOT GIVE A DAMN . . . PL GHOSTS OF 1619 9

VULCAN 1
ON THE VULCAN ROAD . . . . WB POEME D'AUTOMNE 4

VULGAR 2
YET AS THE VULGAR DANCERS WHIRLED WB CABARET 3
HAS A VULGAR TONE. . . . . LHR CONSERVATORY 2

V-J 1
STILL LEFT BY V-J DAY. . . . . . . SP MIGRANT 29

WAFTS 1
IN THE RUM THAT WAFTS MARACAS . . . AYM ODE TO DINAH 16

WAGES 1
YOU RAISE MY TAXES, FREEZE MY WAGES, PL BACKLASH BLUES 5

WAGGON 2
GIT ME A WAGGON TO HAUL. . . . . . FC HARD LUCK 14
GIT A WAGGON TO HAUL. . . . . FC HARD LUCK 16

WAGONS 2
CAME THE WAGONS AND THE COACHES, . SP FREEDOM'S PLOW 74
COVERED WAGONS, STAGE COACHES, . . SP FREEDOM'S PLOW 75

WAIF 1
NOW LIKE A LITTLE LONELY WAIF . . . WB TO LITTLE LOVER 8

WAILING 1
AND YOU COULD HEAR THE DROWSY WAILING . . . . OK IRISH WAKE 3

WAIT 12
AND WAIT. . . . . OK SONG 9
"WAIT, BE PATIENT," YOU SAY. . . . JC THE BITTER RIVR 39
HEY, MISTER, WAIT! . . . . OWT JITNEY 37
WAIT. . . . . SP TOMORROW 8
JUST WAIT. . . . . AYM ODE TO DINAH 81
GOT TO WAIT - . . . . AYM ODE TO DINAH 92
GOT TO WAIT. . . . . AYM ODE TO DINAH 94
MUST I WAIT? . . . . AYM RIDE, RED, RIDE 5
AND THE WIND WON'T WAIT FOR MIDNIGHT PL CULTURAL EXCHNG 6
OF COURSE, WAIT. . . . . PL DINNER GUEST ME 23
DON'T DEMONSTRATE! WAIT! - . . . . PL GO SLOW 9
"BUT JUST WAIT, CHILE . . . " . . . FL OFFICE BUILDING 11

WAITED 2
WAITED TWENTY DAYS . . . . AYM IS IT TRUE? 26
WAITED TWENTY YEARS . . . . AYM IS IT TRUE? 27

Context	Source	Title	Line
WAITED TWENTY MORE	AYM	IS IT TRUE?	29
WAITER 1			
SHE SAYS TO THE WAITER,	SH	DEATH IN HARLEM	41
WAITERS 1			
WAITERS.	FC	LAUGHERS	11
WAITING 12			
WAITING FOR THEIR LOVERS.	WB	POEME D'AUTOMNE	7
I'M WAITING FOR MA MAMMY, -	FC	MAMMY	1
I'M WAITING FOR MA MAMMY, -	FC	MAMMY	5
WAITING FOR SLEEP	OLD	THE CONSUMPTIVE	6
AND I'VE BEEN WAITING LONG	FW	EARTH SONG	2
I'VE BEEN WAITING LONG	FW	EARTH SONG	5
AND I'VE BEEN WAITING LONG	FW	EARTH SONG	14
WAITING FOR A LOVER.	FW	NEW MOON	7
WAITING FOR NOTHINGNESS.	SP	A HOUSE IN TAOS	10
WAITING FOR TOMORROW TO COME -	SP	WINE-O	3
WAITING - FOR WHAT?	PL	QUESTION ANSWER	9
OR STATION WAITING ROOM	PL	WHERE WHEN WHCH	12
WAITIN' 2			
I BEEN WAITIN' AND A-WAITIN'	SP	OLD THE GYPSY	14
IS WAITIN' TO SHELTER ME.	SP	LITTLE GRN TREE	14
WAITS 2			
SHE WAITS FOR ME	FW	FAITHFUL ONE	11
DARK HARLEM WAITS FOR YOU.	OWT	NEGRO SERVANT	11
WAKE 4			
YOU MUST THINK YOU GOT TO WAKE UP A CROWD!	SH	DAYBREAK	4
YOU AIN'T GOT TO WAKE UP NO BODY BUT ME.	SH	DAYBREAK	5
AND WAKE ME UP GENTLE WHEN THE DAWN APPEARS	SH	LETTER	18
WAKE UP AND LIVE!	SP	DEAD IN THERE	16
WAKING 1			
IN YOUR WAKING EYES:	SP	AFRICA	8
WAKIN' 1			
BUT I'M WAKIN' UP!	ANS	PARK BENCH	7
WALK 18			
TO WALK WITH YOU -	SL	SCOTTSBORO	27
TO WALK A HIGH WIRE	SH	ASPIRATION	5
OR IF IT WASN'T SO LATE I MIGHT TAKE A WALK	SH	BED TIME	7
MAKE YOU WALK LIKE A GHOST IF YOU BOTHER ME ANY MORE.	SH	TWILIGHT REVERI	6
WALK LEAN	FW	TODAY	4
NOTHIN' TO DO BUT WALK.	SP	BOUND NO'TH BLS	8
WALK . . . AN' WALK . . . AN' WALK.	SP	BOUND NO'TH BLS	10
WALK . . . AN' WALK . . . AN' WALK.	SP	BOUND NO'TH BLS	10
WALK . . . AN' WALK . . . AN' WALK.	SP	BOUND NO'TH BLS	10
BUT HE DOESN'T WALK LIKE ONE.	SP	CASUALTY	2
WALK THE DOG AROUND -	SP	MADAM HER MADAM	10
I WAS SCARED TO WALK OUT	SP	SITUATION	3
I'M GONNA WALK TO THE GRAVEYARD	SP	YOUNG GAL'S BLS	1
GONNA WALK TO THE GRAVEYARD	SP	YOUNG GAL'S BLS	3
BODY'LL HAVE TO WALK BEHIND ME.	SP	YOUNG GAL'S BLS	6
THEN BEFORE YOU CAN WALK	PL	CROWNS GARLANDS	8
WALKED 6			
I WALKED DE STREETS TILL	SH	OUT OF WORK	1
I DONE WALKED DE STREETS TILL	SH	OUT OF WORK	3
I WALKED ALL OVER THE ZOO AND THE PARK.	OWT	STRANGER IN TWN	1
WHEN I WALKED ALL BY MYSELF.	SP	CROSSING	2
I WALKED ALL BY MYSELF:	SP	CROSSING	20
HAD HE WALKED WITH WARY FOOT	PL	FREDRK DOUGLASS	2
WALKER 1			
MADAM WALKER	SP	SUMMER EVENING	8
WALKERS 3			
BEING WALKERS WITH THE DAWN AND MORNING.	DK	WALKERS WITH	1
WALKERS WITH THE SUN AND MORNING.	DK	WALKERS WITH	2
BEING WALKERS WITH THE SUN AND MORNING.	DK	WALKERS WITH	6
WALKING 10			
WALKING PROUDLY, ALMOST PRANCING, BUT GRADUALLY SUBDUED TO A SLOW, HEAVY	NM	BLACK CLWN MOOD	7
LISTEN AT MY FOOTPRINTS WALKING ON THE FLOOR.	SH	SUPPER TIME	7
IN THE DUSK IS WALKING	FW	DIMOUT IN HARLM	2
DOWN THE STREET IS WALKING	FW	DIMOUT IN HARLM	4
IS WALKING.	FW	DIMOUT IN HARLM	18
WAS WALKING	FW	NIGHT SONG	6
WALKING IN THE DEWY NIGHT.	SP	AUNTSUE'S STORI	9
WALKING WALKING WALKING	SP	EASY BOOGIE	3
WALKING WALKING WALKING	SP	EASY BOOGIE	3
WALKING WALKING WALKING	SP	EASY BOOGIE	3
WALKIN' 3			
BEEN WALKIN' SINCE FIVE THIS MORNIN'.	NM	BROKE	2
I WAS WALKIN' DOWN DE STREET, JUDGE.	SH	BRIEF ENCOUNTER	3
I WENT WALKIN'	SP	BLUE BAYOU	1
WALKS 4			
SHE WALKS	WB	TO LITTLE LOVER	9
HE WALKS LIKE HIS SOLDIERING	SP	CASUALTY	3
WALKS ONCE AGAIN.	SP	WHEN SUE WEARS	8
WHERE NO SHADOW WALKS ALONE	AYM	ASK YOUR MAMA	75
WALL 19			
FACE THE WALL WITH THE DARK CLOSED GATE.	DK	SONG	7
BIG BEN, I'M GONNA BUST YOU BANG UP SIDE THE WALL!	SH	DAYBREAK	1
TO FORCE MY BACK TO THE WALL	JC	THE BITTER RIVR	56
AGAINST THE WALL.	FW	DUSK	6
AGAINST THE WALL -	FW	DUSK	8
ON A WAYSIDE WALL.	FW	HEART	4
ON THE PUBLIC WALL.	FW	HEART	12
THE HEAD OF LINCOLN LOOKS DOWN FROM THE WALL	OWT	LINCOLN THEATRE	1
AND THEN THE WALL ROSE,	SP	AS I GREW OLDER	7
THE WALL.	SP	AS I GREW OLDER	16
ONLY THE THICK WALL.	SP	AS I GREW OLDER	22
BREAK THROUGH THE WALL!	SP	AS I GREW OLDER	26
FACE TO THE WALL.	SP	DREAM	10
NO CLOCKS ON THE WALL,	SP	END	2
BEYOND A HIGH TENSION WALL	SP	MELLOW	5
THEIR BLOOD UPON THE WALL	PL	BIRMINGHAM SUND	5
THIS BIRMINGHAM-ON-SUNDAY WALL.	PL	BIRMINGHAM SUND	14
WHO LEFT THEIR BLOOD UPON THAT WALL.	PL	BIRMINGHAM SUND	16
YOUR WALL IS TOO HIGH	PL	LAST PRINCE	4
WALLACE 1			
MAMMY WALLACE	PL	CULTURAL EXCHNG	53
WALLS 8			
TIMELESS WALLS	DK	LINCOLN MONUMNT	9
AND THE PRISON WALLS WRAP YOU ABOUT.	ANS	CHANT TOM MOONY	8
SHAKING THE WALLS.	ANS	CHANT TOM MOONY	22
BEHIND YOUR HIGH STONE WALLS -	FW	CONVENT	3
WALLS HAVE BEEN KNOWN	FW	DUSK	10
FOUR WALLS CAN HOLD	FW	WALLS	1
FOUR WALLS THAT SHIELD	FW	WALLS	3
FOUR WALLS CAN SHELTER	FW	WALLS	5
WALNUT 3			
WALNUT TINTED	SH	HARLEM SWEETIES	12
WALNUT OR COCOA,	SH	HARLEM SWEETIES	29
WALNUT RED.	SP	OLD FORTUNE TEL	16
WALT 2			
OLD WALT WHITMAN	SP	OLD WALT	1
OLD WALT WENT SEEKING	SP	OLD WALT	10
WALTER 1			
AND WALTER WHITE	OWT	OLD MARGE POLIT	49
WAN 2			
AND THE WAN NIGHT WORE AWAY.	WB	CABARET	4
WAN AND PALE.	WB	SUMMER NIGHT	23
WAND 1			
WAND	PL	FINAL CALL	6
WANDER 3			
THOUGH I WANDER AND STRAY	FW	FAITHFUL ONE	5
TO WANDER THROUGH THIS LIVING WORLD	FW	REMEMBRANCE	1
TO WANDER NAKED	SP	STRANGE HURT	14
WANDERERS 1			
WANDERERS OF THE HILLS AND SEAS.	WB	A FAREWELL	2
WANDERING 2			
A WANDERING POET	FW	CAROLINA CABIN	16
WANDERING IN THE DUSK.	FW	DUSK	1
WANLY 1			
AND DAWN COMES DOWN THE STREET ALL WANLY WHITE.	OWT	JUICE JOINT	4
WANT 63			
DON'T WANT NOBODY	WB	CAT AND SAXOPHN	22
YOU WANT LOVIN'	WB	TO MIDNIGHT NAN	11
DON'T EVEN WANT TO BE GOOD.	FC	BAD MAN	14
DON'T EVEN WANT TO BE GOOD.	FC	BAD MAN	16
AND THE OLD AND RICH DON'T WANT THE PEOPLE	ANS	KIDS WHO DIE	33
DON'T WANT THE PEOPLE TO GET WISE TO THEIR OWN POWER.	ANS	KIDS WHO DIE	35
I JUST WANT TO CRY:	ANS	SISTER JOHNSON	3
I WANT THE WORLD TO KNOW.	SH	ANNOUNCEMENT	14
O.K. YOU DON'T WANT IT?	SH	OLD PAWNBROKER	17
THAT I DIDN'T WANT TO MEET.	SH	BRIEF ENCOUNTER	6

Context	Book	Poem	Line
I DIDN'T WANT TO SEE!	SH	BRIEF ENCOUNTER	12
SO IF YOU WANT TO KNOW BEAUTY'S	SH	HARLEM SWEETIES	41
YAL, COME ON BACK - I KNOW YOU WANT TO.	SH	LETTER	9
I WANT TO TELL YOU 'BOUT THAT WOMAN,	SH	ONLY WOMAN BLUS	1
STAY AWAY IF YOU WANT TO, AND SEE IF I CARE!	SH	SUPPER TIME	10
CAUSE I WANT YOU TO STATE	JC	BLACK MAN SPEAK	22
THAT MAY BE SO - FOR THOSE WHO WANT IT SO,	JC	GOOD MORN STLIN	25
IF YOU WANT TO GET OLD HITLER'S GOAT,	JC	JIM CROW'S LAST	23
I WANT TO GET OVER TO STATE.	OWT	JITNEY	38
IF YOU WANT A GOOD CHICKEN	OWT	JITNEY	55
IS WHO I WANT TO SEE.	OWT	LONESOME CORNER	8
I WANT SOME FINE MUSIC	OWT	REQUEST REQUIEM	3
I WANT A DOZEN PRETTY WOMEN	SP	AS BEFITS A MAN	3
BUT I WANT MY FUNERAL TO BE FINE:	SP	AS BEFITS A MAN	6
I WANT A FISH-TAIL HEARSE	SP	AS BEFITS A MAN	9
I WANT THE WOMEN TO HOLLER:	SP	AS BEFITS A MAN	15
YOU'D WANT TO KNOW.	SP	BLD FORTUNE TEL	4
ME, I ALWAYS DID WANT TO STUDY FRENCH.	SP	DEFERRED	21
ALL I WANT IS	SP	DEFERRED	32
ALL I WANT IS TO SEE	SP	DEFERRED	34
ALL I WANT IS A WIFE WHO WILL	SP	DEFERRED	36
I WANT TO PASS THE CIVIL SERVICE.	SP	DEFERRED	43
I WANT A TELEVISION SET.	SP	DEFERRED	44
I WANT FREEDOM	SP	DEMOCRACY	20
DON'T YOU WANT TO RUN AROUND	SP	KID SLEEPY	2
DON'T YOU WANT TO GET UP	SP	KID SLEEPY	11
IF YOU WANT TO BE HAPPY	SP	LAMENT OVER LOV	17
ALL I WANT IS YOU.	SP	MADAM MIGHT-HAV	18
IF IT'S MONEY YOU WANT	SP	MADAM RENT MAN	25
I SAID, I DON'T WANT	SP	MADAM MIGHT-HAV	31
THEY'LL WANT FLOWERS, TOO,	SP	NIGHT FUNERAL	15
DADDY, I WANT SO-AND-SO.	SP	PREFERENCE	5
IF THESE WHITE FOLKS WANT TO GO AHEAD	SP	RELIEF	12
I WANT A DIAMOND RING.	SP	SAME IN BLUES	9
ALL I WANT IS YOU.	SP	SAME IN BLUES	16
SOMETIMES PERHAPS YOU DON'T WANT TO BE A PART OF ME.	SP	THEME FOR ENG B	34
NOR DO I OFTEN WANT TO BE A PART OF YOU.	SP	THEME FOR ENG B	35
I DON'T WANT NOBODY ELSE AND	SP	WIDOW WOMAN	19
DON'T NOBODY ELSE WANT ME.	SP	WIDOW WOMAN	20
I SAY DON'T WANT NOBODY ELSE	SP	WIDOW WOMAN	21
AND DON'T NOBODY ELSE WANT ME -	SP	WIDOW WOMAN	22
I'LL WANT TO SEE SOMEBODY, TOO.	SP	YOUNG GAL'S BLS	12
CAUSE I DON'T WANT TO BE BLUE.	SP	YOUNG GAL'S BLS	24
DID I WANT TO EAT WITH WHITE FOLKS?	AYM	BIRD IN ORBIT	70
I WANT TO GO TO THE SHOW, MAMA.	AYM	ODE TO DINAH	95
I WANT TO SEE MY MOTHER MOTHER	AYM	RIDE, RED, RIDE	1
"I DON'T WANT TO STUDY WAR NO MORE,"	PL	BLACK PANTHER	6
IF YOU WANT TO SEE ME.	PL	DOWN WHERE I AM	15
I WANT FREEDOM	PL	FREEDOM	20
REALLY WANT TO -	PL	IMPASSE	6
MISTER, CAUSE I WANT TO RIDE?	PL	MERRY-GO-ROUND	5
BUT SUPPOSE I DON'T WANT IT,	PL	QUESTION ANSWER	14
WHAT I DON'T KNOW WHAT I WANT	PL	STOKELY MALCOLM	3

WANTA 2

Context	Book	Poem	Line
DOES I WANTA? WELL, CAN'T SAY BUT WHAT I MIGHT -	NM	BROKE	71
IF YOU WANTA GO TO HEABEN	SP	FIRE	12

WANTED 11

Context	Book	Poem	Line
BUT IF I WANTED TO GO STRAIGHT	NM	BIG-TIMER POEM	41
NOT WANTED HERE; NOT NEEDED THERE -	NM	BLACK CLWN POEM	40
BERNICE SAID SHE WANTED	SH	BLD THE KILLER	1
BERNICE SAID SHE WANTED	SH	BLD THE KILLER	5
SHE WANTED A	SH	PRESENT	3
THE G.I.'S WHO FOUGHT WILL SAY, WE WANTED IT SO!	SP	FREEDOM TRAIN	80
LAWD! AND I WANTED TO CRY.	SP	LOVER'S RETURN	14
LAWD! THAT I WANTED TO CRY.	SP	LOVER'S RETURN	16
WANTED MY NAME	SP	MADAM CENSUS	3
THAN I WANTED TO PAY.	SP	MADAM'S CALLING	4
IF I WANTED TO,	PL	IMPASSE	2

WANTING 1

Context	Book	Poem	Line
WANTING A REPORT.	SP	MADAM CHARTY CH	24

WANTS 13

Context	Book	Poem	Line
WANTS MY BABY	WB	CAT AND SAXOPHN	18
AN' I WANTS MA ALBERT BACK.	FC	BLACK GAL	16
OH, GOD, I WANTS HIM BACK!	FC	BLACK GAL	18
UM-MM! SIGN HERE SAYS THEY WANTS SOMEBODY TO SHOVEL COAL.	NM	BROKE	28
TOGETHER, RECKON I'LL TRY . . . SHO, I WANTS DE JOB! YES, SIR!	NM	BROKE	30
I WANTS TO GO SOMEWHERE.	DK	HOMESICK BLUES	8
WHO WANTS TO BE FREE.	JC	GOOD MORN STLIN	21
WANTS ME TO COME BACK	FW	DUSTBOWL	2
WANTS ME TO COME BACK	FW	DUSTBOWL	8
WANTS ME	FW	DUSTBOWL	12
ANYTHING HE WANTS OUT OF IT.	SP	BUDDY	10
JIMMY WANTS TO KNOW ABOUT THE	SP	FREEDOM TRAIN	47
IS SHE WANTS SOME CASH?	SP	SISTER	9

WANT-ADS' 1

Context	Book	Poem	Line
ANSWERIN' THEM WANT-ADS' NOT NARY BIT O' FUN.	NM	BROKE	4

WAR 19

Context	Book	Poem	Line
JOE LOUIS SAID, WE GONNA WIN THIS WAR	JC	JIM CROW'S LAST	25
BEFORE THE CIVIL WAR, DAYS WERE DARK,	SP	FREEDOM'S PLOW	118
OUT OF WAR IT CAME, BLOODY AND TERRIBLE!	SP	FREEDOM'S PLOW	130
WHO DOUBTED THAT THE WAR WOULD END RIGHT,	SP	FREEDOM'S PLOW	133
A WONDERFUL TIME - THE WAR:	SP	GREEN MEMORY	1
IF THE WAR HADN'T COME ALONG	SP	RELIEF	8
AND FIGHT ANOTHER WAR,	SP	RELIEF	13
WHAT A GRAND TIME WAS THE WAR!	SP	WORLD WAR II	1
WHAT A GRAND TIME WAS THE WAR!	SP	WORLD WAR II	3
SORRY THAT OLD WAR IS DONE!	SP	WORLD WAR II	6
WHAT A GRAND TIME WAS THE WAR,	SP	WORLD WAR II	7
"I DON'T WANT TO STUDY WAR NO MORE,"	PL	BLACK PANTHER	6
CIVIL WAR CENTENNIAL: 1965.	PL	DEATH YORKVILLE	14
SHE SPOKE OF SONS AT WAR,	PL	MOTHER IN WAR	2
AND THE ECHO OF THE CIVIL WAR	PL	OCTOBER 16 RAID	17
THE FACE OF WAR IS MY FACE.	PL	THE DOVE	1
THE FACE OF WAR IS YOUR FACE.	PL	WAR	2
OF WAR?	PL	WAR	5
IS WAR.	PL	WAR	25

WAREHOUSES 1

Context	Book	Poem	Line
SOLD IN SHOPS, PILED IN WAREHOUSES,	SP	FREEDOM'S PLOW	80

WARES 1

Context	Book	Poem	Line
SELLING HER SCANTY WARES	SP	MEXICAN MARKET	3

WARM 7

Context	Book	Poem	Line
YOU ARE LIKE A WARM DARK DUSK	SH	YOUNG NEGRO GRL	1
YOU ARE LIKE A WARM DARK DUSK	SH	YOUNG NEGRO GRL	6
WARM RED WINE,	FW	CAROLINA CABIN	8
YET WARM AND WAVERING	SP	BEALE STREET	7
WARM, WHITE LIGHTS.	SP	PORT TOWN	10
COLD BRASS IN WARM AIR.	SP	SONG BILLIE HOL	17
IN WARM MANURE	PL	UN-AMERICAN	5

WARMED 1

Context	Book	Poem	Line
THAT WARMED HER BODY.	SP	RUBY BROWN	3

WARMTH 2

Context	Book	Poem	Line
WARMTH, EARTH, WARMTH,	SP	THE SOUTH	10
WARMTH, EARTH, WARMTH,	SP	THE SOUTH	10

WARNED 3

Context	Book	Poem	Line
MOTHER WARNED ME,	SH	BLD THE SINNER	5
WARNED ME TRUE.	SH	BLD THE SINNER	6
FATHER WARNED ME,	SH	BLD THE SINNER	7

WARN'T 2

Context	Book	Poem	Line
MARGIE WARN'T NOBODY	OWT	BLD MARGE POLIT	21
HE DIED FOR REAL. IT WARN'T NO SHOW.	SP	FREEDOM TRAIN	44

WARP 1

Context	Book	Poem	Line
INTO THE WARP AND WOOF OF AMERICA:	SP	FREEDOM'S PLOW	167

WARRIORS 1

Context	Book	Poem	Line
FOR WHITE-ROBED WARRIORS	PL	SPECIAL BULLTIN	6

WARS 1

Context	Book	Poem	Line
TWO WARS	FW	SAILING DATE	10

WARTIME 1

Context	Book	Poem	Line
IN WARTIME WE HAD FUN,	SP	WORLD WAR II	5

WARY 1

Context	Book	Poem	Line
HAD HE WALKED WITH WARY FOOT	PL	FREDRK DOUGLASS	2

WAR-TIME 1

Context	Book	Poem	Line
THAT GROWS IN NO-MAN'S LAND, JOAN OF ARC, AND VARIOUS OTHER WAR-TIME	NM	COLORED SL MOOD	5

WAS 245

Context	Book	Poem	Line
WHEN THE LITTLE DAWN WAS GREY.	WB	CABARET	6
WAS CLEOPATRA GORGEOUS	WB	JAZZONIA	12
I WAS A RED MAN ONE TIME,	WB	LAMENT DARK PEO	1
I WAS A BLACK MAN, TOO,	WB	LAMENT DARK PEO	3
ONCE I WAS WISE.	WB	THE JESTER	18
AND THE MOON WAS WHITE.	WB	TO MIDNIGHT NAN	8
AND THE MOON WAS JOY.	WB	TO MIDNIGHT NAN	16
JUDGE WAS GETTIN' THERE.	FC	BLD OF GIN MARY	2
WHAT WAS THE COVER CHARGE, KID?	FC	CLOSING TIME	14
HE WAS A FRIEND O' MINE.	FC	DEATH DO DIRTY	5
CAUSE HE WAS BLACK	FC	DEATH DO DIRTY	7
BUT WHEN I WAS HUNGRY,	FC	DEATH DO DIRTY	11
I WAS STANDIN' IN DE STREET.	FC	DEATH DO DIRTY	22
A GUY WAS SAYIN'	FC	DEATH DO DIRTY	28
ONCE I WAS IN MEMPHIS,	FC	GYPSY MAN	7

ONCE I WAS IN MEMPHIS,	FC GYPSY MAN	9
NOBODY THERE WAS GOOD TO ME.	FC GYPSY MAN	12
IF I WAS A MULE I'D	FC HARD LUCK	13
IF I WAS A MULE I'D	FC HARD LUCK	15
WHERE SHE WAS BORN.	FC NEW CABARET GRL	8
I WAS ONCE A BLACK CLOWN	NM BLACK CLWN POEM	77
I WOULDN'T PAY HER A PENNY NOW IF I WAS TO CROAK -	NM BROKE	25
I THOUGHT LOVE WAS A DREAM, BUT I 'HO HAVE AWOKE -	NM BROKE	54
IF A PRETTY GAL LIKE YOU WAS WILLIN', I'D BITE.	NM BROKE	72
CERTAINLY, CHILE, I ALWAYS WAS CRAZY 'BOUT YOU!	NM BROKE	74
'CAUSE WHEN I WAS LIVING, I DIDN'T HAVE MINE.	NM COLORED SL POEM	18
BUT THE DREAM WAS CRUEL - AND BITTER - AND SOMEHOW	NM COLORED SL POEM	40
IT WAS AWFUL - FACING THAT BOY WHO WENT OUT TO DIE,	NM COLORED SL POEM	42
THEN I WOKE UP, AND THE DREAM WAS ENDED -	NM COLORED SL POEM	48
BUT BROKEN WAS THE SOLDIER'S DREAM, TOO BAD TO BE	NM COLORED SL POEM	49
I KNOW, FOR I HEARD, WHEN ALL WAS STILL,	DK DEATH SEAMAN	3
MA HEART WAS IN MA MOUTH.	DK HOMESICK BLUES	8
HEART WAS IN MA MOUTH.	DK HOMESICK BLUES	10
MA LORD KNOWED WHAT IT WAS TO WORK.	DK MA LORD	6
MA LORD'S LIFE WAS TROUBLE, TOO,	DK MA LORD	8
HE TOLE ME I WAS GWINE.	DK MA LORD	14
WHEN I WAS HOME DE	DK PO' BOY BLUES	1
WHEN I WAS HOME DE	DK PO' BOY BLUES	3
I WAS A GOOD BOY,	DK PO' BOY BLUES	7
YES, I WAS A GOOD BOY.	DK PO' BOY BLUES	9
A GAL I THOUGHT WAS KIND.	DK PO' BOY BLUES	14
A GAL I THOUGHT WAS KIND.	DK PO' BOY BLUES	16
BITTER WAS THE DAY	ANS A NEW SONG	7
BITTER WAS THE DAY	ANS A NEW SONG	11
BITTER WAS THE DAY, I SAY,	ANS A NEW SONG	17
RELIEF WAS FOUND.	ANS A NEW SONG	23
(AMERICA NEVER WAS AMERICA TO ME.)	ANS LET AMERICA BE	5
(IT NEVER WAS AMERICA TO ME.)	ANS LET AMERICA BE	10
AMERICA NEVER WAS AMERICA TO ME,	ANS LET AMERICA BE	77
SHE WAS DRIVING ALONE,	SH ANNOUNCEMENT	2
IF THIS RADIO WAS GOOD I'D GET KDQ	SH BED TIME	1
DOG-GONE LITTLE MOUSES! I WISH I WAS YOU!	SH BED TIME	14
BUT I WAS BOLD,	SH BLD THE SINNER	9
BUT I WAS DRINKING LICKER,	SH BLD THE SINNER	15
I WAS LOOKIN' FOR A SANDWICH, JUDGE,	SH BRIEF ENCOUNTER	1
I WAS WALKIN' DOWN DE STREET, JUDGE,	SH BRIEF ENCOUNTER	3
SHE WAS DE WRONGEST THING, JUDGE,	SH BRIEF ENCOUNTER	17
THE NIGHT WAS YOUNG -	SH DEATH IN HARLEM	3
WAS PLAYIN JAZZ FOR A MIDNIGHT WORLD.	SH DEATH IN HARLEM	11
THEN THE PLACE WAS EMPTY,	SH DEATH IN HARLEM	124
AND WHOEVER LOVED BESSIE WAS	SH DEATH IN HARLEM	126
IT WAS DAY -	SH DEATH IN HARLEM	138
LUCY WAS A-BASSIN IT, BOOM, BOOM, BOOM,	SH DEATH IN HARLEM	77
HER NAME WAS BESSIE, SHE WAS BROWN AND BOLD.	SH DEATH IN HARLEM	81
HER NAME WAS BESSIE, SHE WAS BROWN AND BOLD.	SH DEATH IN HARLEM	31
NOW, TEXAS WAS A LOVER.	SH DEATH IN HARLEM	87
BESSIE WAS, TOO.	SH DEATH IN HARLEM	38
AND ARABELLA WAS BUSY IN THE LADIES' ROOM.	SH DEATH IN HARLEM	32
AND THERE WAS BESSIE	SH DEATH IN HARLEM	95
(IT WAS JUST AS IF SOMEBODY	SH DEATH IN HARLEM	97
IF I WAS A SEA-LION	SH DECLARATION	1
IF I WAS A RICH BOY	SH DECLARATION	8
IF I WAS A BIRD I'D	SH DECLARATION	17
CAUSE THEY TOLD ME DE NORTH WAS FINE.	SH EVENIN' BLUES	2
CAUSE THEY TOLD ME DE NORTH WAS FINE.	SH EVENIN' BLUES	4
BUT IF YOU WAS TO ASK ME	SH EVENIN' BLUES	19
SAYS IF YOU WAS TO ASK ME	SH EVENIN' BLUES	21
THINK I WAS INSANE.	SH IF-ING	12
AND EVEN IF I DID, I WAS MAD -	SH LETTER	6
SO LET'S JUST FORGET WHAT THIS FUSS WAS ABOUT.	SH LETTER	15
SHE WAS DE MEANEST WOMAN	SH ONLY WOMAN BLUS	3
YOU WAS THE BEST - BUT YOU THE WORST.	SH PAY DAY	20
THAT PLACE WHERE YOUR TRUNK WAS, AIN'T NO TRUNK NO MORE.	SH SUPPER TIME	8
IT WAS DOWN IN MIAMI	JC BLD SAM SOLOMON	5
WAS NOT AFRAID.	JC BLD SAM SOLOMON	44
THE KU KLUX WAS TOUGH -	JC BLD SAM SOLOMON	50
THERE WAS AN OLD CROW BY THE NAME OF JIM.	JC JIM CROW'S LAST	1
I WAS GIVEN ITS WATER	JC THE BITTER RIVR	53
I WAS TRYING TO FIGURE OUT	FW COMMUNION	1
WHAT IT WAS ALL ABOUT	FW COMMUNION	2
WHAT IT WAS ALL ABOUT	FW COMMUNION	4
SHE WAS COMING BACK AGAIN.	FW GIRL	8
SUDDENLY THE EARTH WAS THERE,	FW HARLEM DANCE HA	3
BUT NO ONE WAS CURIOUS.	FW HEART	8
I WAS A BOY THEN.	FW MAN	1
WAS REAL -	FW MAN	8
BUT I WAS A BOY THEN,	FW MAN	10
WAS WALKING	FW NIGHT SONG	6
WAS SINGING	FW NIGHT SONG	13
WAS LYE.	OWT DECEASED	7
IF I WAS ALIVE	OWT FUNERAL	5
THAT ONCE WAS SUNG BENEATH THE SUN	OWT JUICE JOINT	10
YESTERDAY WAS TODAY!	OWT YESTERDAY TODAY	2
YESTERDAY YOU WAS HERE.	OWT YESTERDAY TODAY	3
YESTERDAY I WAS HAPPY.	OWT YESTERDAY TODAY	9
I THOUGHT YOU WAS HAPPY, TOO.	OWT YESTERDAY TODAY	10
IT WAS IN THE SPRING.	LHR BLD MARY'S SON	1
THERE WAS FASTING IN THE STREETS AND JOY,	LHR BLD MARY'S SON	3
HE WAS MARY'S SON,	LHR BLD MARY'S SON	8
AND THE SON OF GOD WAS HE -	LHR BLD MARY'S SON	9
AND THE NIGHT WAS BLACK, TOO.	SP A BLACK PIERROT	4
AND MY HEART WAS BLEEDING, TOO.	SP A BLACK PIERROT	9
IT WAS A LONG TIME AGO.	SP AS I GREW OLDER	1
BUT IT WAS THERE THEN,	SP AS I GREW OLDER	3
IF I WAS YOU.	SP BAD LUCK CARD	12
HE WAS HER KIN.	SP BLD FORTUNE TEL	12
LORD, I WISH I WAS DEAD!	SP BLD OF THE GIRL	12
JUST AS THOUGH IT WAS NO SIN -	SP BLD OF THE GIRL	14
FOR HER MAN THAT WAS DEAD.	SP BLD OF THE MAN	14
A FUNERAL WAS HAD.	SP BLD OF THE MAN	16
BUT IF I WAS A GYPSY	SP BLD THE GYPSY	22
HE WAS A SOLDIER IN THE ARMY,	SP CASUALTY	1
WHEN I WAS A CHILD WE USED TO PLAY,	SP CHILDREN'S RYME	1
IT WAS THAT LONELY DAY, FOLKS,	SP CROSSING	1
MY FRIENDS WAS ALL AROUND ME	SP CROSSING	3
BUT IT WAS AS IF THEY'D LEFT.	SP CROSSING	4
AND THE COAT THAT I WAS WEARING	SP CROSSING	7
WAS MOSQUITO-NETTING THIN.	SP CROSSING	8
AND THE WATER I WAS CROSSING	SP CROSSING	11
WAS NO WATER IN A DREAM	SP CROSSING	12
AND THE SHOES I WAS WEARING	SP CROSSING	13
IT WAS THAT LONELY DAY, FOLKS,	SP CROSSING	19
MY FRIENDS WAS RIGHT THERE WITH ME	SP CROSSING	21
BUT WAS JUST AS IF THEY'D LEFT.	SP CROSSING	22
HE WAS NO GOOD AT MAKING LOVE	SP DANCER	7
DROPPED OUT SIX MONTHS WHEN I WAS SEVEN,	SP DEFERRED	3
A YEAR WHEN I WAS ELEVEN,	SP DEFERRED	4
WAS LIKE A DOUBLE DEATH.	SP DESIRE	2
IF I WAS ANYBODY'S SISTER,	SP EVENING SONG	5
IT WAS A LONG TIME AGO,	SP FREEDOM'S PLOW	100
HE WAS A COLORED MAN WHO HAD BEEN A SLAVE	SP FREEDOM'S PLOW	112
WHAT FREDERICK DOUGLASS SAID WAS TRUE.	SP FREEDOM'S PLOW	115
JOHN BROWN WAS HUNG.	SP FREEDOM'S PLOW	117
THERE WAS LIGHT WHEN THE BATTLE CLOUDS ROLLED AWAY.	SP FREEDOM'S PLOW	139
THERE WAS A GREAT WOODED LAND,	SP FREEDOM'S PLOW	140
HER GRANDSON'S NAME WAS JIMMY. HE DIED AT ANZIO.	SP FREEDOM TRAIN	43
THE POET SAYS IT WAS PROMISES.	SP FREEDOM'S PLOW	143
BUT THE WORD WAS THERE ALWAYS:	SP FREEDOM'S PLOW	47
WHERE THERE NEVER WAS NO JIM CROW SIGNS NOWHERE,	SP FREEDOM TRAIN	54
INTO THAT FURROW THE FREEDOM SEED WAS DROPPED.	SP FREEDOM'S PLOW	194
HIS NAME WAS JEFFERSON. THERE WERE SLAVES THEN,	SP FREEDOM'S PLOW	96
THAT WHAT HE SAID WAS ALSO MEANT FOR THEM.	SP FREEDOM'S PLOW	99
WAS FULFILLED.	SP FULFILMENT	3
I WAS BORN HERE, HE SAID,	SP GOOD MORNING	2
WAS FAR AWAY	SP GREEN MEMORY	5
MONEY WAS NEAR.	SP GREEN MEMORY	7
ALL HER CLOTHES WAS GONE:	SP HOMECOMING	3
WAS THE ONLY THING I HAD.	SP HOMECOMING	8
YOU SAY YOU THOUGHT EVERYBODY WAS CALLED MISTER?	SP IN EXPLANATION	5
WHOSE HAIR WAS GRAY	SP JOE LOUIS	3
BUT IF SHE WAS TO LISTEN	SP LADY'S BOOGIE	5
I WAS CRYIN'	SP LATE LAST NIGHT	5
SO I WAS CRYIN'	SP LATE LAST NIGHT	9
BUT IT WAS	SP LIFE IS FINE	9
IT WAS COLD!	SP LIFE IS FINE	11
BUT IT WAS	SP LIFE IS FINE	20
IT WAS HIGH!	SP LIFE IS FINE	22
BUT FOR LIVIN' I WAS BORN.	SP LIFE IS FINE	26
IT WAS YESTERDAY MORNING	SP LITTLE OLD LETT	1
WAS HEAVEN SENT.	SP LITTLE LYRIC	2
I WAS IN MY GRAVE AND GONE.	SP LITTLE OLD LETT	8
SINCE I WAS BORN BLACK.	SP LITTLE OLD LETT	12
HIS FACE WAS PALE AND	SP LOVER'S RETURN	3
YOU SAID YOU WAS GONNA TAKE ME	SP LOW TO HIGH	3
WAS TOO GOOD FOR ME.	SP MADAM MIGHT-HAV	4
THAT WAS THEN!	SP MADAM PHONE BIL	5
IT WAS TOO MUCH,	SP MADAM HER MADAM	11
I WAS BAPTIZED	SP MADAM MINISTER	11

FOR SHE WAS MADAM, TOO -	SP MADAM FORT TELL	14
WAS 3-2-6 -	SP MADAM NUMBER WR	18
AND WE BOTH WAS IN	SP MADAM NUMBER WR	19
I KNOWED WE WAS THROUGH!	SP MADAM MIGHT-HAV	20
I KNOWED THAT WAS SO.	SP MADAM PHONE BIL	24
AND THERE WAS ONLY THIS CORNER	SP MAGNOLIA FLOWER	6
YOUR FATHER, YES, HE WAS THE ONE!	SP MAMA AND DAUGHT	11
BUT IT WAS A LONG TIME AGO	SP MAMA AND DAUGHT	13
HE WAS YOUNG YESTERDAY.	SP MAMA AND DAUGHT	18
HE WAS YOUNG WHEN HE -	SP MAMA AND DAUGHT	19
BUT HE LEFT ME WHEN THE COAL WAS LOW.	SP MIDWINTER BLUES	8
BUT HE LEFT WHEN THE COAL WAS LOW.	SP MIDWINTER BLUES	10
I WAS SO SICK LAST NIGHT I	SP MORNING AFTER	1
THOUGHT I WAS IN HELL.	SP MORNING AFTER	8
THOUGHT I WAS IN HELL.	SP MORNING AFTER	10
BABE, YOUR MOUTH WAS OPEN LIKE A WELL.	SP MORNING AFTER	12
AS BLACK WAS BORN.	SP MYSTERY	23
I WAS BORN HERE.	SP NEW YORKERS	1
WHO WAS IT SENT	SP NIGHT FUNERAL	11
WHEN IT WAS ALL OVER	SP NIGHT FUNERAL	27
THAT BOY THAT THEY WAS MOURNIN'	SP NIGHT FUNERAL	38
WAS SO DEAR, SO DEAR	SP NIGHT FUNERAL	39
IT WAS ALL THEIR TEARS THAT MADE	SP NIGHT FUNERAL	42
SIX KNOTS WAS ON HIS HEAD	SP NOT A MOVIE	12
WAS THE NUMBER.	SP RAILROAD AVENUE	12
BECAUSE I WAS ON RELIEF	SP RELIEF	4
SHE WAS YOUNG AND BEAUTIFUL	SP RUBY BROWN	1
AND BECAUSE SHE WAS COLORED	SP RUBY BROWN	4
I WAS SCARED TO WALK OUT	SP SITUATION	3
AND MAYBE WAS I BLIND	SP SO LONG	6
WHAT WAS THE USE OF PRAYER.	SP SONG DARK GIRL	8
WAS GATHERED ROUND ME.	SP SYLVESTER'S BED	4
SWEET GALS WAS A-MOANIN',	SP SYLVESTER'S BED	5
BLACK GALS WAS A-BEGGIN',	SP SYLVESTER'S BED	13
THEN EVERYTHING WAS DARKNESS	SP SYLVESTER'S BED	27
NO SAFETY, NO LOVE, NO RESPECT WAS I DUE.	SP THE NEGRO MOTHE	16
SOMETIMES, THE VALLEY WAS FILLED WITH TEARS.	SP THE NEGRO MOTHE	25
SOMETIMES, THE ROAD WAS HOT WITH SUN,	SP THE NEGRO MOTHE	27
BUT I HAD TO KEEP ON TILL MY WORK WAS DONE:	SP THE NEGRO MOTHE	28
I WAS THE SEED OF THE COMING FREE.	SP THE NEGRO MOTHE	30
WAS JOE.	SP WEST TEXAS	5
WHERE WE WAS GOIN'	SP WEST TEXAS	13
YOU WAS A MIGHTY LOVER AND YOU	SP WIDOW WOMAN	13
WHAT A GRAND TIME WAS THE WAR!	SP WORLD WAR II	1
WHAT A GRAND TIME WAS THE WAR!	SP WORLD WAR II	2
WHAT A GRAND TIME WAS THE WAR.	SP WORLD WAR II	7
TO PROVE SHE WAS A WOMAN WOMAN	AYM BIRD IN ORBIT	48
TO PROVE SHE WAS A WOMAN?	AYM BIRD IN ORBIT	50
ALREADY THERE WAS THREE -	AYM GOSPEL CHA-CHA	60
WAS BLACK AS ME.	AYM GOSPEL CHA-CHA	62
THEY WONDERED WAS I SENSITIVE	AYM HORN OF PLENTY	49
ON THE LINE WHOSE ROUTE WAS FREEDOM	AYM ODE TO DINAH	30
WHOSE HAYMOW WAS A MANGER MANGER	AYM ODE TO DINAH	33
WAS SHE FLEEING WITH LUMUMBA?	AYM RIDE, RED, RIDE	16
AND YOUR HAIR WAS BLOWING BACK	AYM RIDE, RED, RIDE	33
AND WAS PORGY EVER MARRIED	AYM SHADES OF PIG	15
BEFORE CHINA WAS EVER RED AT ALL	PL BIRMINGHAM SUND	12
DOUGLASS WAS SOMEONE WHO,	PL FREDRK DOUGLASS	1
FOR THE FACT THAT WHITE WAS RIGHT	PL GHOSTS OF 1619	10
WHAT WAS SO LARGE	PL LONG VIEW NEGRO	11
LUMUMBA WAS BLACK	PL LUMUMBA'S GRAVE	1
LUMUMBA WAS BLACK	PL LUMUMBA'S GRAVE	5
LUMUMBA WAS BLACK.	PL LUMUMBA'S GRAVE	9
HIS BLOOD WAS RED -	PL LUMUMBA'S GRAVE	10
BUT THAT DAY WAS SO LONG	PL STOKELY MALCOLM	7
HE WAS COMING	PL WHO BUT TH LORD	3
BUT THE LORD HE WAS NOT QUICK.	PL WHO BUT TH LORD	12

WASH 3

WHILE GIRLS WHO WASH RICH WHITE FOLKS CLOTHES BY DAY	OWT LINCOLN THEATRE	13
IN TIME TO WASH AND DRESS.	SP DEFERRED	27
WASH, IRON, AND SCRUB.	SP MADAM HER MADAM	9

WASHED-AND-IRONED-AND-CLEANED-BEST 1

WASHED-AND-IRONED-AND-CLEANED-BEST OUT.	SP PASSING	10

WASHINGTON'S 1

(AT BOOKER WASHINGTON'S GRAVE)	DK ALABAMA EARTH	1

WASHINGTON 4

NINE OLD MEN IN WASHINGTON.	ANS BLD OZZIE POWEL	13
(NEGRO SKIPPER OF THE BOOKER T. WASHINGTON SAILING WITH A MIXED CREW)	JC TO CAPTAIN MULZ	1
I BRUSHED THE BOOTS OF WASHINGTON.	SP NEGRO	6
HE DIDN'T STOP IN WASHINGTON	SP NOT A MOVIE	9

WASHIN' 1

FROM WASHIN' OVER ME?	SH MISSISSIPPI LEV	18

WASN'T 17

IF I WASN'T DUMB	FC PRIZE FIGHTER	2
SHE WOULD BE ALRIGHT IF SHE WASN'T SO BOW-LEGGED, AND CROSS-EYED.	NM BROKE	64
OR IF I WASN'T SO DROWSY I'D LOCK UP JOE	SH BED TIME	5
OR IF IT WASN'T SO LATE I MIGHT TAKE A WALK	SH BED TIME	7
HIS ROLL WASN'T SLIM -	SH DEATH IN HARLEM	7
IT WASN'T MOTHER'S	OWT BLD MARGE POLIT	54
THERE WASN'T A TRACE	SP BLD FORTUNE TEL	27
WASN'T NOBODY ON THAT PRAIRIE	SP CROSSING	17
SHE WASN'T HOME NO MORE.	SP HOMECOMING	4
WASN'T NOBODY GONE.	SP LATE LAST NIGHT	3
WASN'T EVEN ONE PACE LONG -	SP LITTLE OLD LETT	6
SHE WASN'T MEAN -	SP MADAM HER MADAM	2
I WASN'T NO MINT.	SP MADAM'S CALLING	6
MY BREAD WASN'T BUTTERED	SP MIDNIGHT RAFFLE	15
BUT IF HE WASN'T IN A HURRY	SP MIGRANT	38
I WASN'T BORN HERE, SHE SAID.	SP NEW YORKERS	4
BUT, THANK GOD, HE WASN'T DEAD!	SP NOT A MOVIE	13

WASTED 1

BE WASTED FOREVER.	SP NO REGRETS	4

WATCH 5

PAWN YO' GOLD WATCH	FC SATURDAY NIGHT	9
THIS GOLD WATCH AND CHAIN	SH BLD PAWNBROKER	1
WHEN YOU PAWNED MY WATCH	SP COULD BE	7
WITHOUT MY WATCH AND YOU.	SP COULD BE	16
WATCH THEM DROOP, WILT, FADE	PL CROWNS GARLANDS	10

WATCHED 3

AND WATCHED THE BLUE WAVES TIPPED WITH FOAM.	DK SAILOR	4
I WATCHED THEM MOVING, MOVING,	ANS NEGRO GHETTO	5
WATCHED HARLEM GROW	SP GOOD MORNING	3

WATCHES 2

WATCHES	SP LIKEWISE	5
AND WATCHES THE SUN GO BY.	SP NEIGHBOR	3

WATCH-FIRES 1

FORGOTTEN WATCH-FIRES ON A HILL SOMEWHERE!	OWT NEGRO SERVANT	6

WATER 30

AND A LAND OF FRAGRANT WATER	WB OUR LAND	3
O, DE WICKED WATER.	FC A RUINED GAL	16
SPENDIN' MONEY LIKE WATER.	NM BIG-TIMER POEM	17
LIKE WATER DOWN THE STREET,	ANS NEGRO GHETTO	6
I CAN HEY ON WATER	SH HEY-HEY BLUES	1
HEY ON WATER	SH HEY-HEY BLUES	3
CAUSE I CAN HEY ON WATER,	SH HEY-HEY BLUES	19
HEY ON WATER	SH HEY-HEY BLUES	21
BUT DE WATER STILL MAKES A FLOOD.	SH MISSISSIPPI LEV	12
LOOK AT THAT WATER DRIPPING IN THE SINK.	SH SUPPER TIME	5
TOO LONG HAS THE TASTE OF ITS WATER	JC THE BITTER RIVR	4
OH, WATER OF THE BITTER RIVER	JC THE BITTER RIVR	22
I WAS GIVEN ITS WATER	JC THE BITTER RIVR	52
THE CALL OF YOUR BITTER WATER	JC THE BITTER RIVR	85
THE BLOOD OF YOUR BITTER WATER	JC THE BITTER RIVR	87
FROM SALT SEA WATER	FW SAILING DATE	4
AND THE WATER I WAS CROSSING	SP CROSSING	11
WAS NO WATER IN A DREAM	SP CROSSING	12
TOUCHED SILVER WATER.	SP FULFILMENT	6
IF THAT WATER HADN'T A-BEEN SO COLD	SP LIFE IS FINE	7
COLD IN THAT WATER!	SP LIFE IS FINE	10
A DESERT OF WATER.	SP LONG TRIP	2
A WILDERNESS OF WATER.	SP LONG TRIP	10
THE WATER DON'T RUN.	SP MADAM RENT MAN	12
THE WATER IS TODAY.	SP SEA CALM	3
FOR WATER	SP SEA CALM	5
CLEAR GREEN CRYSTAL WATER	AYM GOSPEL CHA-CHA	20
SO THE WHITENESS AND THE WATER	AYM ODE TO DINAH	35
MELT TO WATER ONCE AGAIN	AYM ODE TO DINAH	36
COLD WATER ON ME.	PL THIRD DEGREE	16

WATERMELON 1

SWEET WATERMELON IN A BABY CARRIAGE.	SP SUMMER EVENING	2

WATERS 5

TO KEEP THEM COLD MUDDY WATERS	SH MISSISSIPPI LEV	17
ARE THE WESTERN WATERS NOW.	JC TO CAPTAIN MULZ	3
AND ALL THE WATERS OF THE WORLD.	JC TO CAPTAIN MULZ	4
YES, DANGEROUS ARE THE WIDE WORLD'S WATERS STILL.	JC TO CAPTAIN MULZ	23
TO TILL THE SOIL, AND HARNESS THE POWER OF THE WATERS.	SP FREEDOM'S PLOW	19

WATER-LOG 1

GONNA SLEEP LIKE A WATER-LOG.	SH MISSISSIPPI LEV	6

WATTS 1

JOHANNESBURG, WATTS.	PL QUESTION ANSWER	3

WAVE 5

I'VE GONE BACK TO THE WIND AND WAVE.	DK DEATH SEAMAN	8
AND LIKE A WAVE THE FLOOR -	FW HARLEM DANCE HA	7
WAVE OF SORROW.	SP ISLAND	1
WAVE OF SORROW.	SP ISLAND	7
SEND FOR THE FAIRY QUEEN WITH A WAVE OF THE	PL FINAL CALL	5

WAVERING 1

YET WARM AND WAVERING	SP BEALE STREET	7

WAVES 10

AND WATCHED THE BLUE WAVES TIPPED WITH FOAM.	DK SAILOR	4
WAVES OF RISING AND RE-RISING MASS VOICES. MULTIPLYING LIKE	ANS CHANT MAY DAY	2
AND THE SOUND VIBRATES IN WAVES	ANS CHANT TOM MOONY	17
LET THE GREAT WAVES BEAT!	JC TO CAPTAIN MULZ	72
LET THE GREAT WAVES RISE	JC TO CAPTAIN MULZ	75
THE SEA IS A WILDERNESS OF WAVES.	SP LONG TRIP	1
THE SEA IS A DESERT OF WAVES.	SP LONG TRIP	9
TONIGHT THE WAVES MARCH	SP MOONLIGHT NIGHT	1
THE WAVES RISE	SP SPIRITUALS	13
LIKE WAVES OF SEA	PL UNDERTOW	11

WAVING 1

WAVING A FLAG AND MOUTHING ROT	ANS SONG OF SPAIN	68

WAY 77

HAS GONE THE QUIET WAY	WB TO LITTLE LOVER	4
DE WAY HE SHOCKS ME SHO IS SWEET.	FC MA MAN	6
YOU CAN'T LIVE THAT WAY!	FC NEW CABARET GRL	22
LIVE THAT WAY!	FC NEW CABARET GRL	24
SMASH MY WAY THROUGH	NM BLACK CLWN POEM	65
AW-OO! YONDER COMES A WOMAN I USED TO KNOW WAY DOWN SOUTH.	NM BROKE	62
(IS YOU LOOKIN' AT ME. BABY. OR SOME OTHER WAY?)	NM BROKE	76
TREADING THE MODERN WAY	NM DARK YOUTH USA	23
GET WAY BACK. HONEY.	DK SONG BANJO DANC	5
I HATE TO DIE THIS WAY WITH THE QUIET	SH CABARET GIRL	1
RATHER DIE THE WAY I LIVED -	SH CABARET GIRL	5
MAKIN' ME DIE THIS WAY?	SH CABARET GIRL	8
YES. WAY	SH DECLARATION	19
EVERY WAY THEY IS.	SH STATEMENT	3
SOME FOLKS TRY TO TELL ME DOWN THIS WAY	JC GOOD MORN STLIN	23
I CAN LOOK WAY ACROSS THE SEA	JC GOOD MORN STLIN	31
HE STILL TRIES TO ACT IN THE SAME OLD WAY.	JC JIM CROW'S LAST	12
BEEN DRIVEN OFF ITS WAY.	JC TO CAPTAIN MULZ	7
FOR A BETTER WAY -	JC TO CAPTAIN MULZ	12
YOU WHO GUIDE IT ON ITS WAY.	JC TO CAPTAIN MULZ	66
NO WAY OF DYING.	FW GRIEF	6
BEING THIS-A WAY!	OWT FUNERAL	8
I'LL KNOW MY WAY AROUND.	OWT STRANGER IN TWN	16
MY WAY AROUND.	OWT STRANGER IN TWN	18
THERE AIN'T NO WAY FOR ME	OWT YESTERDAY TODAY	7
NO WAY SHE LOOKED.	SP BLD FORTUNE TEL	28
WAY LAST WEEK?	SP BLD LANDLORD	4
WAY. WAY DOWN THE ROAD.	SP BOUND NO'TH BLS	4
WAY. WAY DOWN THE ROAD.	SP BOUND NO'TH BLS	4
MADE THEM THAT WAY.	SP CAFE: 3 A.M.	8
BY WAY OF ARKANSAS	SP CONSIDER ME	39
BABY. COULD YOU SEE YOUR WAY CLEAR?	SP DEFERRED	78
THEN THE MIND STARTS SEEKING A WAY.	SP FREEDOM'S PLOW	10
THE MIND SEEKS A WAY TO OVERCOME THESE OBSTACLES.	SP FREEDOM'S PLOW	17
IS THAT THE WAY TO GET ABOARD THE FREEDOM TRAIN?	SP FREEDOM TRAIN	28
AND THE WAY TO BUILD AMERICA.	SP FREEDOM'S PLOW	84
THE WAY YOU SEND YOUR KIDS TO SCHOOL	SP HIGH TO LOW	10
THE WAY YOU SHOUT OUT LOUD IN CHURCH.	SP HIGH TO LOW	13
AND THE WAY YOU LOUNGE ON DOORSTEPS	SP HIGH TO LOW	15
THE WAY YOU CLOWN -	SP HIGH TO LOW	18
THE WAY. IN OTHER WORDS.	SP HIGH TO LOW	19
WAY UP IN THE TREBLE	SP LADY'S BOOGIE	7
THIS WAY?	SP LOW TO HIGH	13
WHEN YOU GROW UP THE HARD WAY	SP MADAM MIGHT-HAV	5
THE K THAT WAY.	SP MADAM CENSUS	8
JUST THAT WAY!	SP MADAM CENSUS	20
I TALKED THAT WAY	SP MADAM MINISTER	29
I'M SMART THAT WAY.	SP MADAM'S PAST HI	4
MADAM'D THAT WAY.	SP MADAM'S CALLING	12
WEALTHY THAT WAY.	SP MADAM'S PAST HI	17
HE UP AND WENT HIS WAY.	SP MAMA AND DAUGHT	14
BAD THAT WAY.	SP MIGRANT	40
ALL THE WAY FROM AFRICA TO GEORGIA	SP NEGRO	11
NEITHER IN NEWARK ON THE WAY.	SP NOT A MOVIE	11
AND FAR TOO CLEAN TO STAY THAT WAY.	SP PASSING	8
WHICH WAY TO GO?	SP PRAYER	2
ON RELIEF WAY ACROSS THE SEA	SP RELIEF	3
TO BE SO STILL THAT WAY.	SP SEA CALM	6
AND IT'S IN THE WAY YOU'RE GONE	SP SO LONG	3
WAY DOWN SOUTH IN DIXIE	SP SONG DARK GIRL	1
WAY DOWN SOUTH IN DIXIE	SP SONG DARK GIRL	5
WAY DOWN SOUTH IN DIXIE	SP SONG DARK GIRL	9
NATURE HAS A WAY	SP S-SSS-SS-SH!	8
TO TELL YOU A STORY OF THE LONG DARK WAY	SP THE NEGRO MOTHE	2
STILL BAR YOU THE WAY. AND DENY YOU LIFE -	SP THE NEGRO MOTHE	46
NOR WHICH WAY.	SP WEST TEXAS	15
HOW THEY EVER GOT THAT WAY.	AYM BLUES IN STEREO	27
A LONG WAY TO BAHIA -	AYM GOSPEL CHA-CHA	39
ON THE SOUND WAY OFF THE TURNPIKE -	AYM HORN OF PLENTY	34
FAMOUS - THE HARD WAY -	AYM HORN OF PLENTY	38
THERE'S NO WAY NOT TO LOSE.	AYM ODE TO DINAH	114
WAY?	AYM SHADES OF PIG	20
TO PROBE IN POLITE WAY	PL DINNER GUEST ME	7
WONDERING HOW THINGS GOT THIS WAY	PL DINNER GUEST ME	10
(AND HAS NO WAY TO UNDERSTAND)	PL JUNIOR ADDICT	7
WENT TO SHOOT YOUR WAY TO FREEDOM	PL OCTOBER 16 RAID	8
WAY?	PL STOKELY MALCOLM	18

WAYS 11

GOT SUCH LOW-DOWN WAYS.	FC EVIL WOMAN	10
BUT I SHO BEEN LOOKIN' ROUND HARD LATELY FOR WAYS AND MEANS	NM BROKE	39
GOT TWO MO' WAYS.	DK NEGRO DANCERS	2
TWO MO' WAYS TO DO DE CHARLESTON!	DK NEGRO DANCERS	3
TWO MO' WAYS TO DO DE CHARLESTON!"	DK NEGRO DANCERS	6
GOT TWO MO' WAYS.	DK NEGRO DANCERS	14
TWO MO' WAYS TO DO DE CHARLESTON!"	DK NEGRO DANCERS	15
OF GRAB THE GOLD! OF GRAB THE WAYS OF SATISFYING NEED!	ANS LET AMERICA BE	28
CHANGE MY COLOR. CHANGE MY WAYS.	SH DAYBREAK	10
ABOUT FREEDOM'S WAYS.	JC HOW ABOUT DIXIE	16
GLORIFY THEIR MILLION-DOLLAR WAYS	PL PRIME	5

WAYSIDE 1

ON A WAYSIDE WALL.	FW HEART	4

WE 108

WE CRY AMONG THE SKYSCRAPERS	WB AFRAID	1
BECAUSE WE ARE ALONE.	WB AFRAID	4
WE SHOULD HAVE A LAND OF SUN.	WB OUR LAND	1
WE SHOULD HAVE A LAND OF TREES.	WB OUR LAND	8
AH. WE SHOULD HAVE A LAND OF JOY.	WB OUR LAND	13
THAT'S WHERE WE GO. -	FC MINNIE SINGS	4
WE ONLY GOT ONE LIFE	NM BIG-TIMER POEM	71
TALKIN' 'BOUT "WE'LL WORK FOR 50¢ A DAY. IF WE CAN'T GET NO MO'."	NM BROKE	7
WE WERE JUST TWO COLORED BOYS. BROWN AND BLACK.	NM COLORED SL POEM	2
WE WERE SENT TO TRAINING CAMP. THEN OVERSEAS -	NM COLORED SL POEM	5
THINKING WE WERE FIGHTING FOR DEMOCRACY'S TRUE REIGN	NM COLORED SL POEM	7
SO WE MARCHED TO THE FRONT. HAPPY TO FIGHT.	NM COLORED SL POEM	12
WE COULDN'T EAT IN RESTAURANTS; HAD JIM CROW CARS;	NM COLORED SL POEM	24
AND NO LONGER DO WE KNOW THE DARK MISERY	NM COLORED SL POEM	30
WHEN WE GOT THROUGH FIGHTING. OVER THERE. AND DYING?	NM COLORED SL POEM	34
SO NOW I KNOW WE BLACKS ARE JUST LIKE ANY OTHER -	NM COLORED SL POEM	35
WE BURIED HIM HIGH ON THE WINDY HILL.	DK DEATH SEAMAN	1
NO WONDER WE FIND THEM SUCH MARVELLOUS THINGS!	DK FAIRIES	5
WE ARE NOT AFRAID OF NIGHT.	DK WALKERS WITH	3
WE HAVE TOMORROW	DK YOUTH	1
BROAD ARCH ABOVE THE ROAD WE CAME.	DK YOUTH	8
WE MARCH!	DK YOUTH	9
EQUALITY IS IN THE AIR WE BREATHE.	ANS LET AMERICA BE	14
THE MILLIONS SHOT DOWN WHEN WE STRIKE?	ANS LET AMERICA BE	54
WE MUST TAKE BACK OUR LAND AGAIN.	ANS LET AMERICA BE	73
WE. THE PEOPLE. MUST REDEEM	ANS LET AMERICA BE	82
WE DID NOT KNOW THAT WE WERE BROTHERS.	ANS OPEN LETTER	47
WE DID NOT KNOW THAT WE WERE BROTHERS.	ANS OPEN LETTER	47
NOW WE KNOW!	ANS OPEN LETTER	48
WE DID NOT KNOW	ANS OPEN LETTER	51
THAT WE WERE STRONG.	ANS OPEN LETTER	52
NOW WE SEE	ANS OPEN LETTER	53
WHY WE OWNS DE LAND!	ANS SISTER JOHNSON	7
WORKERS. KNOW THAT WE TOO CAN CRY.	ANS SONG OF SPAIN	59
CAUSE WE DANCIN DOWN!	SH DEATH IN HARLEM	57
WE BOUGHT FOR THE WEDDING THAT'S	SH PAY DAY	9
AND TAKE BACK ALL THEM THINGS WE HAD	SH PAY DAY	12
THE FACT WE NEVER VOTED	JC BLD SAM SOLOMON	13
BUT WE INTEND TO VOTE	JC BLD SAM SOLOMON	35
WE WON'T DIE.	JC GOOD MORN STLIN	15
UNTIL WE ALL ARE FREE.	JC GOOD MORN STLIN	27
JOE LOUIS SAID. WE GONNA WIN THIS WAR	JC JIM CROW'S LAST	25
WE GONNA BURY THAT SON-OF-A-GUN!	JC JIM CROW'S LAST	32
WE NEGROES HAVE BEEN SLAVES BEFORE.	JC TO CAPTAIN MULZ	33

WE WILL NOT BE AGAIN. JC TO CAPTAIN MULZ 34
BUT WE HAVE JOINED HANDS - JC TO CAPTAIN MULZ 36
TOGETHER WE HAVE LAUNCHED A SHIP JC TO CAPTAIN MULZ 39
WE WILL TO MAKE - JC TO CAPTAIN MULZ 35
WE SOMETIMES FIND FW CIRCLES 9
KNOWING WE ARE NOT FW WISDOM 3
IF WE WERE FW WISDOM 5
THAT WE HAVE GOOD REASON LHR POET TO BIGOT 5
AND WE THREE SP A HOUSE IN TAOS 3
AND WE THREE SP A HOUSE IN TAOS 6
WE CAN BUY LOVELY THINGS WITH MONEY. SP A HOUSE IN TAOS 24
BEFORE WE RUN BACK SP A HOUSE IN TAOS 42
WHEN I WAS A CHILE WE USED TO PLAY. SP CHILDREN'S RYME 1
WE KNOWS EVERYBODY SP CHILDREN'S RYME 15
THEN GOT PUT BACK WHEN WE COME NORTH. SP DEFERRED 5
I DREAMED ABOUT WHEN WE FIRST FELL IN LOVE SP DEFERRED 9
LAWD, THESE THINGS WE WOMEN SP EARLY EVENING 21
BUT NOW WE KNOW HOW IT ALL CAME OUT. SP FREEDOM'S PLOW 136
WE KNOW NOW HOW IT CAME OUT. SP FREEDOM'S PLOW 138
"YOU ARE A MAN. TOGETHER WE ARE BUILDING OUR LAND." SP FREEDOM'S PLOW 156
THE G.I.'S WHO FOUGHT WILL SAY, WE WANTED IT SO! SP FREEDOM TRAIN 60
WE ARE AMERICA! SP FREEDOM'S PLOW 177
WE SAY, NO! SP FREEDOM'S PLOW 179
WE SAY, NO! SP FREEDOM'S PLOW 182
WE SAY, NO! SP FREEDOM'S PLOW 187
WE GOT UP SP FULFILMENT 4
WE HAVE OUR TROUBLES, TOO - SP HIGH TO LOW 2
WE HAVE OUR PROBLEMS. SP HIGH TO LOW 24
AND WHILE WE LISTEN TO IT PLAY. SP JUKE BOX LOVE 10
WE DIP AND DIVE. SP LONG TRIP 3
THEN WE BOXED 'EM. SP MADAM NUMBER WR 15
AND WE BOTH WAS IN SP MADAM NUMBER WR 19
I KNOWED WE WAS THROUGH! SP MADAM MIGHT-HAV 20
SO WE AGREES! SP MADAM RENT MAN 30
SAID, WE CAN'T USE YOU SP MADAM'S PAST HI 16
WE SAW A LINE OF FISHING SHIPS SP SEASCAPE 3
AS WE RODE THE FOAM SP SEASCAPE 6
WE SAW AN INDIAN MERCHANTMAN SP SEASCAPE 7
AND WE GET NONE. SP SHARE-CROPPERS 8
AS WE WERE BEFORE. SP SHARE-CROPPERS 10
AND WE ARE NOTHING MORE SP SHARE-CROPPERS 12
BUT WE ALL SHOULD BE FREE. SP SOUTHERN MAMMY 16
WE ALL SHOULD BE FREE. SP SOUTHERN MAMMY 18
HEAR YOU, HEAR ME - WE TWO - YOU, ME, TALK ON THIS PAGE. SP THEME FOR ENG B 19
BUT WE ARE, THAT'S TRUE! SP THEME FOR ENG B 36
WE ARE THE DESPERATE SP VAGABONDS 1
SO WE CRANKED UP OUR OLD FORD SP WEST TEXAS 11
AND WE STARTED DOWN THE ROAD SP WEST TEXAS 12
WHERE WE WAS GOIN' SP WEST TEXAS 13
WE DIDN'T KNOW - SP WEST TEXAS 14
IN WARTIME WE HAD FUN. SP WORLD WAR II 5
WE KNOW EVERYBODY PL CHILDREN'S RYME 9
AND WE BETTER FIND OUT, MAMA. PL CULTURAL EXCHNG 23
SINCE WE MOVED UP TO MOUNT VERNON. PL CULTURAL EXCHNG 25
TILL WE PL FROSTING 6
SURE, WE REMEMBER. PL HARLEM 7
WE REMEMBER THE JOB WE NEVER HAD, PL HARLEM 12
WE REMEMBER THE JOB WE NEVER HAD. PL HARLEM 12
SO WE STAND HERE PL HARLEM 16
WE REMEMBER. PL HARLEM 23
IS A THING TO WHICH WE BLACK ARE WISE: PL JUSTICE 2
WE LICK OUR CHOPS AT BIRMINGHAM PL NORTHERN LIBERL 2
BUT WHO ARE WE TO BE PL NORTHERN LIBERL 6
WE PASSED THEIR GRAVES: PL PEACE 1

WEAK 2
ITS COURT, TOO WEAK TO STAND AGAINST A MOB, SL TOWN OF SCOTTSB 3
OF DOG EAT DOG, OF MIGHTY CRUSH THE WEAK. ANS LET AMERICA BE 24

WEALTH 1
TO A COLORED BOY'S RISING IN WEALTH OR STATION - NM COLORED SL POEM 27

WEALTHY 3
WRAPPED IN CHECKS AND WEALTHY. SP GRADUATION 9
WEALTHY THAT WAY. SP MADAM'S PAST HI 17
WEALTHY NEGROES HAVE WHITE SERVANTS. PL CULTURAL EXCHNG 48

WEAPON 1
I'VE NO WEAPON TO STRIKE BACK PL WHO BUT TH LORD 20

WEAPONS 1
AS IF THE WEAPONS USED TODAY PL MOTHER IN WAR 5

WEAR 3
SOME PIMPS WEAR SUMMER HATS SP WHAT? 1
WEAR IT PL COLOR 1
WEAR IT PL COLOR 5

WEARINESS 4
IT IS NOT WEARINESS FW BURDEN 1
WHORES IN FINAL WEARINESS SAY: SP SLIVER SERMON 3
WEARINESS AND PAIN SP TROUBLED WOMAN 5
HAS DARK MOONS OF WEARINESS SP TRUMPET PLAYER 3

WEARING 4
AND THE COAT THAT I WAS WEARING SP CROSSING 7
AND THE SHOES I WAS WEARING SP CROSSING 13
HE'S WEARING. SP INTERNE AT PROV 34
FOR A SUIT OF GOOD-TIME WEARING? AYM SHOW FARE PLESE 23

WEARS 3
WHEN SUSANNA JONES WEARS RED SP WHEN SUE WEARS 1
WHEN SUSANNA JONES WEARS RED SP WHEN SUE WEARS 6
WEARS NO DISGUISE. PL BLACK PANTHER 9

WEARY 31
WEARY. WB BLUES FANTASY 14
WEARY. WB BLUES FANTASY 15
THE WEARY, WEARY HEART OF PAIN. - WB LENOX AVE MIDNT 6
THE WEARY, WEARY HEART OF PAIN. - WB LENOX AVE MIDNT 6
WEARY AS THE TIRED NIGHT. WB SUMMER NIGHT 12
PO' WEARY ME FC A RUINED GAL 3
STANDIN' BY DE WEARY RIVERSIDE FC A RUINED GAL 6
BY DE EDGE O' DE WEARY RIVERSIDE FC A RUINED GAL 11
OR A WEARY BLUES. NM BROKE 1
BUT THIS WORLD IS WEARY OK PO' BOY BLUES 11
WEARY, WEARY, OK PO' BOY BLUES 19
WEARY, WEARY, OK PO' BOY BLUES 19
WEARY EARLY IN DE MORN. OK PO' BOY BLUES 20
WEARY, WEARY, OK PO' BOY BLUES 21
WEARY, WEARY, OK PO' BOY BLUES 21
I'S SO WEARY OK PO' BOY BLUES 23
AND SINGER OF WEARY SONG. JC THE BITTER RIVR 72
OF OUR WEARY CITY FW PRAYER 6
AND WEARY AS A DROWSY SOUTHERN RAIN OWT JUICE JOINT 26
I GOT THOSE SAD OLD WEARY BLUES. OWT TOO BLUE 1
WEARY, WEARY. SP A HOUSE IN TAOS 7
WEARY, WEARY. SP A HOUSE IN TAOS 7
PO' WEARY ME CAN DO. SP BAD LUCK CARD 10
WITH WEARY SADISTIC EYES SP CAFE: 3 A.M. 2
HASTINGS STREET IS WEARY. SP COULD BE 13
DON'T BE WEARY, SOLDIER! SP FREEDOM'S PLOW 134
OF OUR WEARY CITY SP LITANY 6
TO THE TUNE O' THOSE WEARY BLUES. SP THE WEARY BLUES 8
"I GOT THE WEARY BLUES SP THE WEARY BLUES 25
GOT THE WEARY BLUES SP THE WEARY BLUES 27
WHILE THE WEARY BLUES ECHOED THROUGH HIS HEAD. SP THE WEARY BLUES 34

WEATHER 4
WEATHER! FW TODAY 2
WEATHER AND ROSE SP SNAIL 3
WEATHER AND ROSE SP SNAIL 5
IN TIMES OF STORMY WEATHER SP STRANGE HURT 1

WEATHERED 1
WHO'VE WEATHERED FW SAILING DATE 8

WEAVE 1
FAIRIES WEAVE THEIR GARMENTS. OK FAIRIES 2

WEAVER 1
ON DR. ROBERT WEAVER? AYM BIRD IN ORBIT 83

WEAVING 4
WILL LIVE ON WEAVING WORDS TO SMOTHER THE KIDS WHO DIE. ANS KIDS WHO DIE 24
WEAVING METAL FROM TWO QUARTERS AYM SHOW FARE PLESE 21
WEAVING OUT OF LONG-TERM CREDIT AYM SHOW FARE PLESE 24
WEAVING PL LENOX AVE. BAR 1

WEDDING 1
WE BOUGHT FOR THE WEDDING THAT'S SH PAY DAY 9

WEDO 3
DAMBALLA WEDO OGOUN AND THE HORSE AYM GOSPEL CHA-CHA 15
BEDWARD! POCOMANIA! WEDO! OGOUN! AYM GOSPEL CHA-CHA 36
DAMBALLA WEDO! THE VIRGIN! BEDWARD! AYM GOSPEL CHA-CHA 43

WEEDS 1
AND STURDY WEEDS AND GRASSES FW GIRL 16

WEEK 11
LANDLADY 'LOWED TO ME LAST WEEK, "SAM, AIN'T YOU GOT NO MONEY?" NM BROKE 19
SIX DOLLARS A WEEK? WHEE-OOO! YOU SHO PAYS WELL! NM BROKE 36
SHE BOUGHT A NEW HAT LAST WEEK AND COME SENDIN' ME THE BILL. NM BROKE 49
"THIS WEEK I NEED IT ALL." SH PAY DAY 4
WAY LAST WEEK? SP BLD LANDLORD 4
HE WORKS DOWNTOWN FOR TWELVE A WEEK. SP BUDDY 4
MY HOUSE LAST WEEK. SP MADAM MINISTER 2
BUT A FEW BUCKS A WEEK. SP MADAM CHARTY CH 18
LAST WEEK THEY LYNCHED A COLORED BOY. SP SOUTHERN MAMMY 13
AND IN ANOTHER WEEK SP SUMMER EVENING 32

EACH AND EVERY WEEK? SP ULTIMATUM 3

WEEKS 1
I BOUGHT TWO WEEKS AGO? SH BLD PAWNBROKER 10

WEEK'S 1
SEE WHAT THIS WEEK'S JIVE IS ALL ABOUT: OWT JITNEY 25

WEEP 4
WEEP WITH ME. WB THE JESTER 8
YOU WOULD WEEP! WB THE JESTER 9
DO NOT, DO NOT WEEP FOR ME. DK DEATH SEAMAN 9
WEEP. SP VAGABONDS 9

WEIGHT 2
FEEL THE WEIGHT, MR. LEVY. SH BLD PAWNBROKER 13
FROM THE DEAD WEIGHT OF SEA. SP SPIRITUALS 14

WELCOMIN' 1
NO WELCOMIN' COMMITTEES, NOR POLITICIANS OF NOTE. SP FREEDOM TRAIN 55

WELFARE 4
IN THE SHADOW OF THE WELFARE AYM ODE TO DINAH 71
BRING WELFARE CHECKS MUCH SOONER AYM ODE TO DINAH 73
IN THE SHADOW OF THE WELFARE AYM ODE TO DINAH 75
ON THE BIG SCREEN OF THE WELFARE CHECK AYM ODE TO DINAH 98

WELL 43
GO WHERE THEY WILL PAY YOU WELL WB TO DARK MERCEDE 7
WELL, MAYBE I WILL. NM BIG-TIMER POEM 34
I'D STARVE AND - OH, WELL - NM BIG-TIMER POEM 42
WELL, AIN'T NEVER DONE IT, BUT FOR TO KEEP BODY AND SOUL NM BROKE 29
WELL, ER - ER . . . HOW MUCH DOES YOU PAY? NM BROKE 35
SIX DOLLARS A WEEK? WHEE-OOO! YOU SHO PAYS WELL! NM BROKE 36
YOU GOT A GOOD JOB? YES! WELL, I SHO AM GLAD TO SEE YOU, DEAR! NM BROKE 69
DOES I WANTA? WELL, CAN'T SAY BUT WHAT I MIGHT - NM BROKE 71
BUT NOW I KNOW WELL THAT'S NOT OUR SITUATION: NM COLORED SL POEM 28
I KNOW FULL WELL NOW ANS A NEW SONG 25
BUT NINE BLACK BOYS KNOW FULL WELL. ANS BLD OZZIE POWEL 21
TOO WELL DEFENDED. ANS UNION 10
I MIGHT AS WELL PUT IT ON IN THE HAY. SH BED TIME 10
BUT YOU JUST AS WELL BE HERE WHERE YOU DUE TO LIVE. SH LETTER 11
YOU'VE STOOD BETWEEN US WELL. JC GOOD MORN STLIN 35
THEY LIKED HIM SO WELL THEY COULDN'T STAND JC JIM CROW'S LAST 3
AND ME AS WELL. FW BIRTH 5
WELL, THAT'S TEN BUCKS MORE'N I'LL PAY YOU SP BLD LANDLORD 11
AND NOW I WISH HER WELL. SP CROSS 8
KNOWING SO WELL THE WIND AND THE SUN - SP DEMAND 7
WELL, I HOPE THAT LAMB OF MARY'S SP EVENING SONG 11
"WELL! AND YOU?" SP HEAVEN 12
WELL, YOU CAN SEE. SP HIGH TO LOW 23
AND EAT WELL. SP I, TOO 6
HERE. WELL, THAT IS ALL SO I WILL CLOSE. SP LETTER 9
YOU TREAT ME LIKE YOU DAMN WELL PLEASE. SP LOW TO HIGH 14
ROSCOE KNOWS DARN WELL SP MADAM PHONE BIL 16
THAT'S ALL VERY WELL - SP MADAM NUMBER WR 30
WELL, EVEN LESS ABOUT YOUR SP MADAM PHONE BIL 35
WELL, THAT O.K. YOU MAY KEEP - SP MADAM PHONE BIL 39
BABE, YOUR MOUTH WAS OPEN LIKE A WELL. SP MORNING AFTER 12
WELL, SON, I'LL TELL YOU: SP MOTHER TO SON 1
WISHING WELL SP NEON SIGNS 2
WELL, THEY ROCKED HIM WITH ROAD-APPLES SP NOT A MOVIE 1
WELL, ANYWAY, IT DON'T HAVE TO BE A MARRIED MAN. SP SISTER 12
WELL, I LIKE TO EAT, SLEEP, DRINK, AND BE IN LOVE. SP THEME FOR ENG B 21
TAUGHT WELL SP UNCLE TOM 10
WHERE NEGROES SING SO WELL AYM SHADES OF PIG 8
NEGROES SING SO WELL AYM SHADES OF PIG 9
SING SO WELL AYM SHADES OF PIG 10
SO WELL. AYM SHADES OF PIG 11
WELL? AYM SHADES OF PIG 12
VERY WELL PAID. PL ELDERLY LEADERS 7

WELL-FED 1
WELL-FED, DEGREED. PL NORTHERN LIBERL 13

WELL'VE 1
I COULD JUST AS WELL'VE SP MIDNIGHT RAFFLE 13

WENCHES 1
OF NIGGER WENCHES SP MULATTO 13

WENT 57
WENT TO THE CITY. NM BIG-TIMER POEM 6
LAST JOB I HAD, WENT TO WORK AT FIVE IN DE MORNIN', OR LITTLE MO' NM BROKE 12
SO I WENT DOWN TOWN TO A HOTEL WHERE I USED TO WORK AT NIGHT. NM BROKE 44
IT WAS AWFUL - FACING THAT BOY WHO WENT OUT TO DIE. NM COLORED SL POEM 42
BUT HIS SOUL WENT OUT TO SEA. DK DEATH SEAMAN 2
I WENT DOWN TO DE STATION. DK HOMESICK BLUES 7
WENT DOWN TO DE STATION. DK HOMESICK BLUES 9
HE WENT AWAY FROM ME. DK I LOVED FRIEND 2
WHEN HE WENT TO HEABEN. DK MA LORD 12
I WENT DOWN THE ROAD. SH BLD THE SINNER 1
WENT BUSTIN INTO DIXIE'S BOUT ONE A.M. SH DEATH IN HARLEM 2
WENT RUSHIN FOR THE DOOR SH DEATH IN HARLEM 120
WENT TO BED. SH DEATH IN HARLEM 142
WHEN ARABELLA WENT TO THE LADIES' ROOM. SH DEATH IN HARLEM 78
SO I WENT TO DE WPA. SH OUT OF WORK 8
SO I WENT TO DE WPA. SH OUT OF WORK 10
WENT HOME TO HER MA. SH SHAKESPEARE 8
NEHRU SAID, BEFORE HE WENT TO JAIL. JC JIM CROW'S LAST 15
SO I GAVE UP AND WENT FW COMMUNION 5
SHE WENT ONE SUMMER MORNING FW GIRL 5
I WENT DOWN TO THE CORNER. OWT LONESOME CORNER 1
HE WENT INTO THE GARDEN LHR BLD MARY'S SON 22
I WENT FORTH IN THE MORNING SP A BLACK PIERROT 14
THEN WENT OFF AND LEFT HER. SP BLD FORTUNE TEL 23
WHERE DAVE WENT. SP BLD FORTUNE TEL 32
AND WENT AROUND. SP BLD OF THE MAN 10
I WENT TO THE GYPSY'S. SP BLD THE GYPSY 1
I WENT WALKIN' SP BLUE BAYOU 1
I WENT UP ON A MOUNTAIN SP CROSSING 5
I WENT DOWN IN THE VALLEY SP CROSSING 9
SO I WENT ON BACK TO BED - SP FIRED 7
DOWN INTO THE EARTH WENT THE PLOW SP FREEDOM'S PLOW 49
TURNING THE RICH SOIL WENT THE PLOW IN MANY HANDS SP FREEDOM'S PLOW 52
CLANG AGAINST THE TREES WENT THE AX IN MANY HANDS SP FREEDOM'S PLOW 55
SPLASH INTO THE RIVERS AND THE SEAS WENT THE BOAT-HULLS SP FREEDOM'S PLOW 57
CRACK WENT THE WHIPS THAT DROVE THE HORSES SP FREEDOM'S PLOW 59
AND WENT TO THE RIVER. SP FULFILMENT 5
I WENT TO MA DADDY. SP HARD DADDY 1
WENT TO MA DADDY. SP HARD DADDY 3
I WENT BACK IN THE ALLEY SP HOMECOMING 1
I WENT TO LOOK FOR JOY. SP JOY 1
MA SOUL WENT FLYIN' O' THE TOWN. SP JUDGMENT DAY 2
WENT FLYIN' TO THE STARS AN' MOON SP JUDGMENT DAY 3
I WENT DOWN TO THE RIVER. SP LIFE IS FINE 1
WENT AWAY - SP MADAM MINISTER 31
I WENT LOOKIN' FOR MAGNOLIA FLOWERS SP MAGNOLIA FLOWER 3
I WENT LOOKIN' FOR MAGNOLIA FLOWERS IN THE DUSK SP MAGNOLIA FLOWER 5
HE UP AND WENT HIS WAY. SP MAMA AND DAUGHT 14
WENT DOWN TO NEW ORLEANS, AND I'VE SEEN ITS MUDDY SP NEGRO SPEAKS OF 9
WENT FINDING AND SEEKING. SP OLD WALT 2
OLD WALT WENT SEEKING SP OLD WALT 10
THUMP, THUMP, THUMP, WENT HIS FOOT ON THE FLOOR. SP THE WEARY BLUES 23
THE STARS WENT OUT AND SO DID THE MOON. SP THE WEARY BLUES 32
THE SINGER STOPPED PLAYING AND WENT TO BED SP THE WEARY BLUES 33
I WENT TO SCHOOL THERE, THEN DURHAM, THEN HERE SP THEME FOR ENG B 8
WHO WENT TO SUNDAY SCHOOL THAT DAY PL BIRMINGHAM SUND 2
WENT TO SHOOT YOUR WAY TO FREEDOM PL OCTOBER 16 RAID 8

WEPT 1
SO I WEPT UNTIL THE DAWN SP A BLACK PIERROT 7

WERE 52
WERE EVE'S EYES WB JAZZONIA 9
THAT I WERE A JEWEL, WB SONGS DARK VIRG 2
THAT I WERE A GARMENT, WB SONGS DARK VIRG 8
THAT I WERE A FLAME, WB SONGS DARK VIRG 16
WOULD GOD HIS LIPS WERE SWEET! WB TO LITTLE LOVER 12
WE WERE JUST TWO COLORED BOYS, BROWN AND BLACK, NM COLORED SL POEM 2
WE WERE SENT TO TRAINING CAMP, THEN OVERSEAS - NM COLORED SL POEM 5
AND ME AND MY BROTHER WERE HAPPY AS YOU PLEASE NM COLORED SL POEM 6
THINKING WE WERE FIGHTING FOR DEMOCRACY'S TRUE REIGN NM COLORED SL POEM 7
DIDN'T HAVE ANY SCHOOLS; AND THERE WERE ALL SORTS OF NM COLORED SL POEM 25
HAPPY THEY WERE HERE. DK IRISH WAKE 8

ONCE YOU WERE YOUNG. . . . . DK PARISIAN BEGGAR 1
ONCE YOU WERE BEAUTIFUL. . . . . . DK PARISIAN BEGGAR 5
YOUR LIPS WERE SWEET. . . . . DK PARISIAN BEGGAR 8
WERE IT NOT FOR YOUR EYES. . . . . DK QUIET GIRL 3
WERE IT NOT FOR YOUR SONGS. . . . . DK QUIET GIRL 6
WE DID NOT KNOW THAT WE WERE
    BROTHERS. . . . . ANS OPEN LETTER 47
THAT WE WERE STRONG. . . . . ANS OPEN LETTER 52
THEY WERE GLAD. . . . . JC GOOD MORN STLIN 39
THE CRACKERS WERE IN LOVE WITH HIM. JC JIM CROW'S LAST 2
BUT IF THEY WERE BLOOD, MOTHER - . FW WHEN ARMIES PAS 14
IF WE WERE . . . . FW WISDOM 5
THE SOLDIER WERE BLACK. . . . . . . OWT BLD MARGE POLIT 12
IT WERE . . . . OWT BLD MARGE POLIT 56
THERE WERE SOME WHO COULD NOT HEAR. LHR BLD MARY'S SON 11
AND SOME WERE FILLED WITH FEAR - . LHR BLD MARY'S SON 12
WERE IT NOT FOR YOUR EYES. . . . . SP ARDELLA 3
WERE IT NOT FOR YOUR SONGS. . . . . SP ARDELLA 6
AND WISHED SHE WERE IN HELL. . . . SP CROSS 6
YOU WERE NOT THERE WITH ME! . . . . SP DREAM 5
BUT YOU WERE NOT THERE AT ALL! . . SP DREAM 14
THERE WERE SLAVES THEN, TOO. . . . SP FREEDOM'S PLOW 105
BEFORE THE CIVIL WAR, DAYS WERE
    DARK. . . . . SP FREEDOM'S PLOW 118
SOME THERE WERE, AS ALWAYS. . . . . SP FREEDOM'S PLOW 132
MISTER, I THOUGHT IT WERE THE . . . SP FREEDOM TRAIN 41
SOME WERE FREE HANDS . . . . SP FREEDOM'S PLOW 41
SOME WERE INDENTURED HANDS . . . . SP FREEDOM'S PLOW 43
SOME WERE SLAVE HANDS . . . . SP FREEDOM'S PLOW 45
HIS NAME WAS JEFFERSON. THERE WERE
    SLAVES THEN. . . . . SP FREEDOM'S PLOW 95
JUST AS IF YOU WERE DOWN SOUTH. . . SP HIGH TO LOW 16
YOU WERE MY MOON UP IN THE SKY. . . SP MISS BLUES'ES 7
I BATHED IN THE EUPHRATES WHEN DAWNS
    WERE YOUNG. . . . . SP NEGRO SPEAKS OF 5
WERE ON EARTH. . . . . SP PARADE 25
AS WE WERE BEFORE. . . . . SP SHARE-CROPPERS 10
WERE OUTDONE! . . . . SP S-SSS-SS-SH! 19
AS THOUGH I WERE GOD. . . . . SP TO ARTINA 3
WERE JET A CROWN. . . . . SP TRUMPET PLAYER 16
WERE YOU MARRIED BY JOHN JASPER . . AYM BIRD IN ORBIT 37
WERE TO COME BACK BLACK. . . . . . PL BIBLE BELT 2
THAT ONCE PERHAPS WERE EYES. . . . PL JUSTICE 4
AS IF IT WERE SOME NOBLE THING. . . PL MOTHER IN WAR 1
WERE PLED ANEW AT SOME HEROIC BAR. PL MOTHER IN WAR 4

WEREN'T 2

THE PICKIN'S WEREN'T BAD ON A 133RD. SH DEATH IN HARLEM 5
THE PICKIN'S WEREN'T BAD - . . . . SH DEATH IN HARLEM 6

WEST 7

YOU FROM THE WEST INDIES. . . . . . SP BROTHERS 2
TRANSFERS TO THE WEST SIDE. . . . . SP MIGRANT 8
NORTH AND WEST - . . . . SP ONE-WAY TICKET 14
GONE OUT WEST. . . . . SP ONE-WAY TICKET 27
STOOPS TO KISS 12 WEST 133RD. . . . SP PROJECTION 9
DOWN IN WEST TEXAS WHERE THE SUN . SP WEST TEXAS 1
BUT WEST TEXAS WHERE THE SUN . . . SP WEST TEXAS 16

WESTCHESTER 1

WESTCHESTER . . . . PL UNDERTOW 13

WESTERN 1

ARE THE WESTERN WATERS NOW. . . . . JC TO CAPTAIN MULZ 3

WESTPORT 1

WESTPORT AND NEW CANAAN . . . . . . AYM HORN OF PLENTY 61

WET 1

WITH WET AND MUD. . . . . FW WHEN ARMIES PAS 8

WE'D 1

WE'D OPEN UP THE KINGDOM . . . . . FW WISDOM 6

WE'LL 4

TALKIN' 'BOUT "WE'LL WORK FOR 50¢ A
    DAY, IF WE CAN'T GET NO MO'." . NM BROKE 7
WE'LL DO TO YOU. . . . . JC BLD SAM SOLOMON 28
WE'LL ALL BOARD THERE. . . . . . . OWT BOARDING HOUSE 4
WE'LL SEE. . . . . PL WHO BUT TH LORD 23

WE'RE 11

AND WE'RE AFRAID. . . . . WB AFRAID 6
WE'RE MAN TO MAN. . . . . ANS OPEN LETTER 68
WE'RE FIGHTING TO CREATE. . . . . . JC BLACK MAN SPEAK 24
IF WE'RE FIGHTING TO CREATE . . . . JC BLACK MAN SPEAK 25
CAUSE THE GOOD LORD KNOWS WHAT WE'RE
    FIGHTING FOR! . . . . JC JIM CROW'S LAST 26
TILL WE'RE IN JAIL. . . . . FW CIRCLES 6
WE'RE RELATED - YOU AND I. . . . . SP BROTHERS 1
AND WHERE WE'RE MOVING . . . . . . SP DEFERRED 18
BECAUSE WE'RE COLORED. . . . . . . PL HARLEM 15
WHAT WE'RE GONNA DO . . . . PL HARLEM 21
ON THE BUS WE'RE PUT IN THE BACK - PL MERRY-GO-ROUND 11

WE'VE 6

BUT NOW I KNOW WE'VE GOT PLENTY TO
    DO. . . . . NM COLORED SL POEM 23
FOR ALL THE DREAMS WE'VE DREAMED . ANS LET AMERICA BE 56
AND ALL THE SONGS WE'VE SUNG . . . ANS LET AMERICA BE 57
AND ALL THE HOPES WE'VE HELD . . . ANS LET AMERICA BE 58
AND ALL THE FLAGS WE'VE HUNG. . . . ANS LET AMERICA BE 59
WE'VE PUT A CAPTAIN ON THAT SHIP'S
    BRIDGE THERE. . . . . JC TO CAPTAIN MULZ 43

WHAT 147

THAT'S WHAT THE . . . . WB BLUES FANTASY 2
WHAT DO YOU KNOW . . . . WB HARLEM NIGHT CL 15
WHAT JUNGLE TREE HAVE YOU SLEPT
    UNDER. . . . . WB NUDE YOUNG DANC 1
WHAT GREAT FOREST HAS HUNG ITS
    PERFUME . . . . WB NUDE YOUNG DANC 3
WHAT JUNGLE TREE HAVE YOU SLEPT
    UNDER. . . . . WB NUDE YOUNG DANC 5
WHAT STAR-WHITE MOON HAS BEEN YOUR
    MOTHER? . . . . WB NUDE YOUNG DANC 7
TO WHAT CLEAN BOY HAVE YOU OFFERED
    YOUR LIPS? . . . . WB NUDE YOUNG DANC 8
WHAT WAS THE COVER CHARGE, KID? . . FC CLOSING TIME 14
GOD! WHAT DANCERS! . . . . FC LAUGHERS 24
GOD! WHAT SINGERS! . . . . FC LAUGHERS 26
I GUESS I KNOW WHAT I'M UP AGAINST. NM BIG-TIMER POEM 57
WHAT I DON'T KNOW 'BOUT SHOVELIN'
    COAL, AIN'T NO MO' TO KNOW! . . NM BROKE 32
DOES I WANTA? WELL, CAN'T SAY BUT
    WHAT I MIGHT - . . . . NM BROKE 71
LET'S GET MARRIED RIGHT NOW! YES!
    WHAT DO YOU SAY? . . . . NM BROKE 75
'CAUSE THAT'S WHAT I DIED FOR -
    ISN'T IT, BROTHER?" . . . . . . NM COLORED SL POEM 36
FOR WHAT COULD I ANSWER HIM, EXCEPT,
    "IT'S A LIE!" . . . . NM COLORED SL POEM 43
WHAT IS THERE WITHIN THIS BEGGAR LAD DK BEGGAR BOY 1
WHAT SHALL I SING . . . . DK LULLABY 5
WHAT SHALL I SING . . . . DK LULLABY 13
MA LORD KNOWED WHAT IT WAS TO WORK. DK MA LORD 6
THIS IS WHAT I'M GONNA SING. . . . DK NIGHT AND MORN 2
THIS IS WHAT I'M GONNA SING: . . . DK NIGHT AND MORN 4
WONDER WHAT DE BLUES'LL BRING? . . DK NIGHT AND MORN 6
WHAT IT IS TO LIVE IN HELL. . . . . ANS BLD OZZIE POWEL 23
IN SEARCH OF WHAT I MEANT TO BE MY
    HOME - . . . . ANS LET AMERICA BE 46
WHAT DO YOU MEAN - . . . . ANS LYNCHING SONG 10
AND THIS IS WHAT I SAW: . . . . . . ANS NEGRO GHETTO 2
AND THIS IS WHAT MOVED IN MY HEART: ANS NEGRO GHETTO 7
LET US FORGET WHAT BOOKER-T. SAID, ANS OPEN LETTER 19
WHAT IS THE SONG OF SPAIN? . . . . ANS SONG OF SPAIN 4
WHAT MAKES A WOMAN . . . . SH ANNOUNCEMENT 7
AND SEE WHAT COUNT BASIE'S PLAYING
    NEW. . . . . SH BED TIME 2
WHAT YOU LIKE TO EAT? . . . . SH DEATH IN HARLEM 52
WHAT DO YOU MEAN, WHY I DIDN'T
    WRITE? . . . . SH LETTER 7
WHAT DO YOU MEAN, JUST A LITTLE
    SPAT? . . . . SH LETTER 4
SO LET'S JUST FORGET WHAT THIS FUSS
    WAS ABOUT. . . . . SH LETTER 15
WHAT MAKES LOVE SUCH AN ACHE AND
    PAIN? . . . . SH LOVE AGAIN BLUS 14
TELL ME WHAT MAKES . . . . SH LOVE AGAIN BLUS 15
AND SEE WHAT IT WOULD DO TO YOU? . SH OUT OF WORK 24
WHAT KIND OF A WORLD . . . . JC BLACK MAN SPEAK 23
COME WHAT MAY. . . . . JC BLD SAM SOLOMON 24
AIN'T NO TELLING WHAT . . . . JC BLD SAM SOLOMON 27
CAUSE THE GOOD LORD KNOWS WHAT WE'RE
    FIGHTING FOR! . . . . JC JIM CROW'S LAST 26
WHAT IT WAS ALL ABOUT . . . . FW COMMUNION 2
WHAT IT WAS ALL ABOUT . . . . FW COMMUNION 4
NO MATTER WHAT . . . . FW FAITHFUL ONE 9
WHAT ABOUT . . . . OWT BLD MARGE POLIT 36
TELL ME, WHAT DO YOU DO? . . . . . OWT CURIOUS 6
IS WHAT I LIKE ABOUT YOU. . . . . . OWT HONEY BABE 8
SEE WHAT THIS WEEK'S JIVE IS ALL
    ABOUT: . . . . OWT JITNEY 25
WHAT SHALL I DO? . . . . OWT TOO BLUE 6
WHAT SHALL I SAY? . . . . OWT TOO BLUE 7
MEN WHO KNEW NOT WHAT THEY DID . . LHR BLD MARY'S SON 6
WHAT SHALL I LEAVE MY SON . . . . . LHR TESTAMENT 1
WHAT SHALL I LEAVE MY DAUGHTER. . . LHR TESTAMENT 5
WHAT SHALL I LEAVE MY WIFE . . . . LHR TESTAMENT 9
I DON'T KNOW WHAT . . . . SP BAD LUCK CARD 9
WHAT ROAD HE TOOK. . . . . SP BLD FORTUNE TEL 26
WHAT YOUR FUTURE MEANT. . . . . . . SP BLD FORTUNE TEL 30
WHAT? YOU GONNA GET EVICTION ORDERS? SP BLD LANDLORD 17
I WONDER WHAT MAKES . . . . SP BLD OF THE MAN 25
AW, WHAT A LIE! . . . . SP BLD THE GYPSY 13
BY WHAT SENDS . . . . SP CHILDREN'S RYME 5
WHAT DON'T BUG . . . . SP CHILDREN'S RYME 12
WHAT I LACK. . . . . SP CONSIDER ME 34
WHAT COULD POSSIBLY BE ALL-REET? . SP DANCER 22
WHAT SHE MEANS IS: . . . . SP DELINQUENT 15
AND WHAT IS THIS WIND . . . . SP DEMAND 10
WHAT DID NOT SEEM COULD EVER BE: . SP DREAM 4
WHAT DID I SAY? . . . . SP DREAM BOOGIE 14
DO YOU HEAR WHAT I SAID? . . . . . SP EASY BOOGIE 11
LOOKS LIKE WHAT DRIVES ME CRAZY . . SP EVIL 1

WHAT HE SAID MUST BE MEANT FOR EVERY HUMAN BEING - . . . . SP FREEDOM'S PLOW 107
WHAT FREDERICK DOUGLASS SAID WAS TRUE. . . . . SP FREEDOM'S PLOW 115
THAT SONG MEANT JUST WHAT IT SAID: HOLD ON! . . . . SP FREEDOM'S PLOW 127
WHAT SHALL I TELL MY CHILDREN? . . . YOU TELL ME - . . . . SP FREEDOM TRAIN 33
THAT WHAT HE SAID WAS ALSO MEANT FOR THEM. . . . . SP FREEDOM'S PLOW 99
WHAT HAPPENS . . . . SP GOOD MORNING 26
WHAT HAPPENS TO A DREAM DEFERRED? SP HARLEM 1
IN CHINA BEFORE WHAT HAPPENED . . . SP IN EXPLANATION 8
I DON'T KNOW WHAT TO DO." . . . . . SP LOVER'S RETURN 8
I SAID. WHAT . . . . SP MADAM RENT MAN 3
WHAT MAKES THESE CHARITY . . . . . SP MADAM CHARTY CH 9
HE SAID. WHAT . . . . SP MADAM CENSUS 9
WHAT YOU MEAN BY THAT? . . . . . . SP MADAM FORT TELL 10
HE SAID. WHAT HAVE YOU . . . . . . SP MADAM MINISTER 13
I SAID. WHAT MAN YOU'RE TALKING 'BOUT? . . . . SP MADAM FORT TELL 21
FOR INSTANCE. WHAT CAN . . . . . . SP MADAM PHONE BIL 27
KNOWING WHAT I GOT. . . . . SP MIDNIGHT RAFFLE 12
HONEY. WHAT DOES YOU NEED? . . . . SP PREFERENCE 8
WHAT MY OTHER MAN CAN'T DO - . . . SP QUESTION 2
I KNOW WHAT RELIEF CAN BE - . . . . SP RELIEF 6
AND WONDER WHAT YOU GOT LEFT? . . . SP REVERIE HARLEM 4
WHAT CAN A COLORED GIRL DO . . . . SP RUBY BROWN 13
WHAT CAN PURGE MY HEART . . . . . . SP SONG BILLIE HOL 1
WHAT CAN PURGE MY HEART . . . . . . SP SONG BILLIE HOL 4
WHAT CAN PURGE MY HEART . . . . . . SP SONG BILLIE HOL 7
WHAT WAS THE USE OF PRAYER. . . . . SP SONG DARK GIRL 8
WHAT WILL YOU DO? . . . . SP SUNDAY MORNING 16
IT'S NOT EASY TO KNOW WHAT IS TRUE FOR YOU OR ME . . . . SP THEME FOR ENG B 16
AT TWENTY-TWO. MY AGE. BUT I GUESS I'M WHAT . . . . SP THEME FOR ENG B 17
UPON WHAT RIFF THE MUSIC SLIPS . . SP TRUMPET PLAYER 38
SO WHAT WOULD YOU DO? . . . . SP WHAT? 8
WHAT A GRAND TIME WAS THE WAR! . . SP WORLD WAR II 1
WHAT A GRAND TIME WAS THE WAR! . . SP WORLD WAR II 3
WHAT A GRAND TIME WAS THE WAR. . . SP WORLD WAR II 7
WHAT IS MONEY FOR? . . . . SP YOUNG SAILOR 8
WHEN LOVE IS GONE WHAT . . . . . . SP YOUNG GAL'S BLS 19
WHAT CAN A YOUNG GAL DO? . . . . . SP YOUNG GAL'S BLS 22
SHE ANSWERED. BABE. WHAT MUST I DO? SP 50 - 50 12
WHAT DID SHE SAY? . . . . AYM ASK YOUR MAMA 13
WHAT SHE SAID ABOUT HER CHILDREN . AYM BIRD IN ORBIT 51
WHAT TIME IS IT. MAMA? . . . . . . AYM BLUES IN STEREO 28
WHAT TIME IS IT NOW? . . . . AYM BLUES IN STEREO 29
WHAT TIME IS IT. MAMA? . . . . . . AYM BLUES IN STEREO 32
WHAT TIME NOW? . . . . AYM BLUES IN STEREO 33
WHAT TIME IS IT NOW? . . . . AYM ODE TO DINAH 63
WHAT TIME IS IT NOW? . . . . AYM ODE TO DINAH 65
DON'T CARE WHAT TIME IT IS - . . . AYM ODE TO DINAH 65
WHAT DO YOU THINK I GOT TO LOSE? . PL BACKLASH BLUES 26
WHAT YOU THINK I GOT TO LOSE? . . . PL BACKLASH BLUES 28
THAT WHAT CHINA MADE . . . . PL BIRMINGHAM SUND 11
BY WHAT SENDS . . . . PL CHILDREN'S RYME 1
WHAT DON'T BUG . . . . PL CHILDREN'S RYME 6
NOW ARE WHAT THE SOAP BOX . . . . . PL CORNER MEETING 2
WHAT HAPPENS TO A DREAM DEFERRED? PL DREAM DEFERRED 1
SEND FOR TROTSKY! (WHAT? DON'T CONFUSE THE ISSUE. . . . . PL FINAL CALL 26
SEND FOR MARCUS GARVEY (WHAT?) SUFI (WHO?) . . . . PL FINAL CALL 33
VEILING WHAT THE DARKNESS HIDES. . PL GEORGIA DUSK 4
WHAT HAPPENED THEN? . . . . PL GHOSTS OF 1619 13
WHAT WE'RE GONNA DO . . . . PL HARLEM 21
IN THE FACE OF WHAT . . . . PL HARLEM 22
WHAT MAKES ME . . . . PL IMPASSE 3
WHAT I AM. . . . . PL IMPASSE 4
WHAT WAS SO LARGE . . . . PL LONG VIEW NEGRO 11
OH. WHAT SORROW! . . . . PL MISSISSIPPI 1
OH. WHAT PITY! . . . . PL MISSISSIPPI 2
OH. WHAT PAIN . . . . PL MISSISSIPPI 3
WHAT SORROW. PITY. PAIN. . . . . . PL MISSISSIPPI 17
DYING - FOR WHAT? . . . . PL QUESTION ANSWER 6
WAITING - FOR WHAT? . . . . PL QUESTION ANSWER 9
WHAT I HAVE NEVER FOUND . . . . . . PL STOKELY MALCOLM 2
WHAT I DON'T KNOW WHAT I WANT . . . PL STOKELY MALCOLM 3
WHAT I DON'T KNOW WHAT I WANT . . . PL STOKELY MALCOLM 3
WHAT I HAVE NOT FOUND . . . . PL STOKELY MALCOLM 10
WHAT COLOR . . . . PL WAR 3
IF YOU HAD KNOWN WHAT I KNOW . . . PL WORDS LIKE FREE 7

WHAT'LL 1

WHAT'LL YOU LEND? . . . . SH BLD PAWNBROKER 26

WHAT'S 22

SO WHAT'S THE USE O' WORRYIN' . . . NM BIG-TIMER POEM 69
WILLING WORKER? UN-UH! YES! WHAT'S THAT YOU SAY? . . . . NM BROKE 33
WHAT'S DE MATTER. HONEY? . . . . . ANS SISTER JOHNSON 2
WHAT'S DE MATTER. CHILE? . . . . . ANS SISTER JOHNSON 6
WHAT'S THAT? . . . . ANS SONG OF SPAIN 25
WHAT'S WRITTEN DOWN . . . . SP CHILDREN'S RYME 20
"WHAT'S THE USE?" . . . . SP LIKEWISE 16
WHAT'S THE USE . . . . SP LIKEWISE 17
WHAT'S THE USE? . . . . SP LIKEWISE 19
WHAT'S THE HARLEM . . . . SP LIKEWISE 20
WHAT'S THE LICK? . . . . SP LIKEWISE 22
I SAID. WHAT'S THE SCORE? . . . . . SP MADAM WRONG VIS 4
WHAT'S TOO GOOD TO BE TRUE. . . . . SP MADAM MIGHT-HAV 7
WHAT'S THAT. CENTRAL? . . . . SP MADAM PHONE BIL 31
WHAT'S A BODY BUT A TOY? . . . . . SP MULATTO 11
WHAT'S A BODY BUT A TOY? . . . . . SP MULATTO 17
WHAT'S THE BODY OF YOUR MOTHER? . . SP MULATTO 19
WHAT'S THE BODY OF YOUR MOTHER? . . SP MULATTO 21
AND IN EVERYTHING BUT WHAT'S ABOUT ME - . . . . SP NOTE COMM THEAT 11
WHAT'S HIS NAME. MY COUSIN. . . . . AYM GOSPEL CHA-CHA 41
ON THE OLD IRON STOVE WHAT'S COOKING? . . . . PL CULTURAL EXCHNG 27
WHAT'S SMELLING. LEONTYNE? . . . . PL CULTURAL EXCHNG 28

WHAT'VE 1

NOW WHAT'VE I GOT? . . . . SP NEW YORKERS 13

WHEEL 2

FOR THE MILL WHEEL TO BE MILL WHEEL AYM IS IT TRUE? 24
FOR THE MILL WHEEL TO BE MILL WHEEL AYM IS IT TRUE? 24

WHEELS 1

TO DO CART WHEELS? . . . . SH ASPIRATION 2

WHEE-OOO 1

SIX DOLLARS A WEEK? WHEE-OOO! YOU SHO PAYS WELL! . . . . NM BROKE 36

WHEN 199

AND WHEN I GET ON THE TRAIN . . . . WB BLUES FANTASY 25
WHEN THE LITTLE DAWN WAS GREY. . . WB CABARET 6
WHEN DE BOAT COMES IN. . . . . . . FC A RUINED GAL 7
WHEN YOU AIN'T GOT A DIME. . . . . FC DEATH DO DIRTY 4
BUT WHEN I WAS HUNGRY. . . . . . . FC DEATH DO DIRTY 11
AN' WHEN DE COPS GOT ME . . . . . . FC DEATH DO DIRTY 16
BUT WHEN I GOT THERE . . . . FC DEATH DO DIRTY 26
WHEN IT HURTS YO' HEART YOU . . . . FC GYPSY MAN 23
WHEN HARD LUCK OVERTAKES YOU . . . FC HARD LUCK 1
WHEN HARD LUCK OVERTAKES YOU . . . FC HARD LUCK 3
WHEN MA MAN LOOKS AT ME . . . . . . FC MA MAN 1
WHEN MA MAN LOOKS AT ME . . . . . . FC MA MAN 3
HE PLAYS GOOD WHEN HE'S SOBER . . . FC MA MAN 11
AN' BETTER. BETTER. BETTER WHEN HE'S DRUNK. . . . . FC MA MAN 12
WHEN I CUDDLES UP TO HIM . . . . . FC MINNIE SINGS 9
WHEN SHE OUGHT TO PLAY. . . . . . . FC NEW CABARET GRL 20
WHEN DE WORMS GIT THROUGH . . . . . FC SATURDAY NIGHT 16
WHEN YOU IS . . . . FC SATURDAY NIGHT 19
WHEN I OPENS DE DOOR. . . . . FC WORKIN' MAN 6
WHEN FOR YEARS. I HAD BEEN SEEKING OLD AESTHETE HARLEM 4
AND WHEN I'M DEAD - I'LL KEEP STILL. NM BIG-TIMER POEM 36
WHEN THEY CALLIN' ME HONEY. . . . . NM BIG-TIMER POEM 68
WHEN THE DAY IS THROUGH. . . . . . NM BLACK CLWN POEM 7
WHEN YOU'RE BROKE. . . . . NM BROKE 11
I TELL YOU IT'S AWFUL. WHEN YOU'RE BROKE. . . . . NM BROKE 47
SO WHEN I GOT READY TO GO. I SAID. "I'LL BE SEEIN' YOU SOON. MARIE." NM BROKE 52
WHEN THE NATION CALLED US THAT MIGHTY DAY. . . . . NM COLORED SL POEM 4
'CAUSE WHEN I WAS LIVING. I DIDN'T HAVE MINE. . . . . NM COLORED SL POEM 18
WHEN WE GOT THROUGH FIGHTING. OVER THERE. AND DYING? . . . . NM COLORED SL POEM 34
WHEN THE NIGHT IS A VAST SOFTNESS DK AFTR MNY SPRNGS 3
I KNOW. FOR I HEARD. WHEN ALL WAS STILL. . . . . DK DEATH SEAMAN 3
FOR WHEN DREAMS GO . . . . DK DREAMS 6
BUT WHEN THE SUN ROSE MAKING . . . DK IRISH WAKE 5
WHEN HE GOES A-WALKIN' . . . . . . DK MA LORD 3
WHEN HE WENT TO HEABEN. . . . . . . DK MA LORD 12
YOU WILL NOT STAY WHEN SUMMER GOES. DK PASSING LOVE 6
WHEN I WAS HOME DE . . . . DK PO' BOY BLUES 1
WHEN I WAS HOME DE . . . . DK PO' BOY BLUES 3
WHEN YOU PASS BY. . . . . DK REASONS WHY 8
IS IT MUCH TO DIE WHEN IMMORTAL FEET SL SCOTTSBORO 5
WHEN BEYOND STEEL BARS SOUND THE DEATHLESS DRUMS . . . . SL SCOTTSBORO 7
WHEN I BOWED MY BACK . . . . ANS A NEW SONG 8
WHEN I SAW MY CHILDREN UNSCHOOLED. ANS A NEW SONG 12
WHEN THE LYNCHER'S ROPE . . . . . . ANS A NEW SONG 18
WHEN THE FLOWERS BREAK THROUGH THE EARTH. . . . . ANS CHANT MAY DAY 4
WHEN THE SAP RISES IN THE TREES. . ANS CHANT MAY DAY 5
WHEN THE BIRDS COME BACK FROM THE SOUTH. . . . . ANS CHANT MAY DAY 6
WORKER: WHEN THE SAP OF YOUR OWN STRENGTH RISES . . . . ANS CHANT MAY DAY 25
50-VOICES: WHEN THE EARTH IS NEW. ANS CHANT MAY DAY 30
WHEN THE MARCHING FEET OF THE MASSES ANS KIDS WHO DIE 45
THE MILLIONS SHOT DOWN WHEN WE STRIKE? . . . . ANS LET AMERICA BE 54
WHEN BOMBS'LL FALL NOT ONLY ON SPAIN - . . . . ANS SONG OF SPAIN 52

Line	Book	Poem	Line No.
WHEN I COME ACROSS THAT WOMAN	SH	BRIEF ENCOUNTER	5
WHEN THE SHOTS RANG OUT.	SH	DEATH IN HARLEM	123
WHEN THE NIGHT IS YOUNG -	SH	DEATH IN HARLEM	25
IT'S GOOD LIKE THAT WHEN YOU	SH	DEATH IN HARLEM	29
AND A WOMAN CROSS THE TABLE WHEN A MAN AIN'T BROKE -	SH	DEATH IN HARLEM	54
WHEN A MAN'S WON A FIGHT IN A BIG MAN'S TOWN -	SH	DEATH IN HARLEM	55
WHEN ARABELLA WENT TO THE LADIES' ROOM.	SH	DEATH IN HARLEM	78
WHEN SHE COME OUT	SH	DEATH IN HARLEM	93
CAUSE WHEN I'M DANCIN'	SH	EVENIN' BLUES	17
AND WAKE ME UP GENTLE WHEN THE DAWN APPEARS	SH	LETTER	18
WHEN I GOT YOU I	SH	LOVE AGAIN BLUS	7
WHEN I GOT YOU	SH	LOVE AGAIN BLUS	9
LONESOME SAID WHEN A TWO-BIT WOMAN	SH	MIDNIGHT CHIPPI	23
WHEN THIS FLOOD IS OVER.	SH	MISSISSIPPI LEV	5
WHEN DE LEVEE DON'T DO NO GOOD.	SH	MISSISSIPPI LEV	10
WHEN SHE LEFT	SH	ONLY WOMAN BLUS	21
WHEN THE FIRST VIOLETS	SH	YOUNG NEGRO GRL	3
WHEN I SPLIT THIS ROCK.	JC	BIG BUDDY	16
BUT WHEN YOUR GUNS ROAR.	JC	GOOD MORN STLIN	18
WHEN CROOKS AND KLANSMEN	JC	GOOD MORN STLIN	29
I MEAN IT WHEN I SAY.	JC	GOOD MORN STLIN	54
WHEN DORIE MILLER TOOK GUN IN HAND -	JC	JIM CROW'S LAST	28
BUT WHEN IT IS. JIM CROW'LL BE DONE.	JC	JIM CROW'S LAST	31
EACH FOURTEEN YEARS OLD WHEN LYNCHED TOGETHER BENEATH THE	JC	THE BITTER RIVR	1
AND WHEN I TOOK IT	FW	COMMUNION	7
WHEN I COME AGAIN.	FW	FAITHFUL ONE	8
WHEN FLOWERS SPREAD THE PLAIN.	FW	GIRL	6
BUT WHEN THE BAND BEGAN TO PLAY.	FW	HARLEM DANCE HA	2
WHEN HE'S	FW	MAN	14
WHEN THE LIPS	FW	SLEEP	1
WHEN THE LIPS	FW	SLEEP	9
SEE! WHEN YOU WIPE THE MUD AWAY.	FW	WHEN ARMIES PAS	21
WHEN THE PD CAR	OWT	BLD MARGE POLIT	52
WHEN YOU'RE IN YOUR HOUSE. BABY	OWT	CURIOUS	5
WHEN THE WINE'S GONE TO YOUR HEAD	OWT	RAID	2
BABY. SAY WHEN.	OWT	RAID	5
DOESN'T SAY WHEN.	OWT	RAID	7
FOR ME WHEN I DIE.	OWT	REQUEST REQUIEM	2
WHEN YOU LET ME DOWN -	OWT	REQUEST REQUIEM	6
WHEN I MOVE	OWT	RESTRICTIVE	1
WHEN YOU SINK SO LOW.	OWT	TOO BLUE	5
SO WHEN MY ACTIONS ARE STUPID	LHR	ACCEPTANCE	3
WHEN I AM DEAD AND GONE?	LHR	TESTAMENT	2
WHEN HE PASSES ON.	LHR	TESTAMENT	4
WHEN THEY LET ME DOWN.	SP	AS BEFITS A MAN	13
WHEN YOU COME UP YOURSELF	SP	BLD LANDLORD	7
WHEN WILL MY GAL BE HOME?	SP	BLD THE GYPSY	4
WHEN I WAS A CHILE WE USED TO PLAY.	SP	CHILDREN'S RYME	1
WHEN YOU PAWNED MY WATCH	SP	COULD BE	7
WHEN I WALKED ALL BY MYSELF.	SP	CROSSING	2
(WHEN YOU'RE NO GOOD FOR DOUGH THEY GO.)	SP	DANCER	20
DROPPED OUT SIX MONTHS WHEN I WAS SEVEN.	SP	DEFERRED	3
A YEAR WHEN I WAS ELEVEN.	SP	DEFERRED	4
THEN GOT PUT BACK WHEN WE COME NORTH.	SP	DEFERRED	5
I DREAMED ABOUT WHEN WE FIRST FELL IN LOVE	SP	DEFERRED	9
WHEN I SET MY FEET IN GLORY	SP	DEFERRED	41
YOU TOUCH WHEN YOU RUN?	SP	DEMAND	11
I DO NOT NEED MY FREEDOM WHEN I'M DEAD.	SP	DEMOCRACY	13
HELP ME WHEN I'M DOWN AND OUT.	SP	DOWN AND OUT	2
HELP ME WHEN I'M DOWN AND OUT.	SP	DOWN AND OUT	4
WHEN YOU TURN THE CORNER	SP	FINAL CURVE	1
WHEN A MAN STARTS OUT WITH NOTHING.	SP	FREEDOM'S PLOW	1
WHEN A MAN STARTS OUT WITH HIS HANDS	SP	FREEDOM'S PLOW	2
WHEN A MAN STARTS OUT TO BUILD A WORLD.	SP	FREEDOM'S PLOW	4
WHEN FREEDOM WOULD TRIUMPH.	SP	FREEDOM'S PLOW	120
WHEN IT STOPS IN MISSISSIPPI WILL IT BE MADE PLAIN	SP	FREEDOM TRAIN	21
'CAUSE FREEDOM AIN'T FREEDOM WHEN A MAN AIN'T FREE.	SP	FREEDOM TRAIN	34
WHEN MY GRANDMOTHER IN ATLANTA. 83 AND BLACK.	SP	FREEDOM TRAIN	37
THERE WAS LIGHT WHEN THE BATTLE CLOUDS ROLLED AWAY.	SP	FREEDOM'S PLOW	139
WHEN HE SHOULD BE GONE	SP	GONE BOY	6
WHEN MONEY ROLLED IN	SP	GREEN MEMORY	2
SOMETIMES WHEN I'M LONELY.	SP	HOPE	1
WHEN SPRING	SP	IN TIME SILVER	22
WHEN COMPANY COMES.	SP	I. TOO	4
WHEN COMPANY COMES.	SP	I. TOO	10
WHEN I'M YOU?	SP	LOW TO HIGH	8
O.K.ED IT WHEN?	SP	MADAM PHONE BIL	3
WHEN YOU GROW UP THE HARD WAY	SP	MADAM MIGHT-HAV	5
WHEN I GOT THROUGH.	SP	MADAM HER MADAM	8
WHEN YOU THINK YOU GOT BREAD	SP	MADAM MIGHT-HAV	25
HE WAS YOUNG WHEN HE -	SP	MAMA AND DAUGHT	19
WHEN I DROPPED THAT NICKEL	SP	MIDNIGHT RAFFLE	9
BUT HE LEFT ME WHEN THE COAL WAS LOW.	SP	MIDWINTER BLUES	8
BUT HE LEFT WHEN THE COAL WAS LOW.	SP	MIDWINTER BLUES	10
SO WHEN I'M DEAD THEY WON'T NEED	SP	MIDWINTER BLUES	23
WHEN A CHILE GETS TO BE THIRTEEN	SP	MYSTERY	1
I BATHED IN THE EUPHRATES WHEN DAWNS WERE YOUNG.	SP	NEGRO SPEAKS OF	5
I HEARD THE SINGING OF THE MISSISSIPPI WHEN ABE LINCOLN	SP	NEGRO SPEAKS OF	8
WHEN HIS WORK IS DONE	SP	NEIGHBOR	5
BUT WHEN HE DRINKS.	SP	NEIGHBOR	17
WHEN THEY MEET THEIR ENDS.	SP	NIGHT FUNERAL	16
WHEN IT WAS ALL OVER	SP	NIGHT FUNERAL	27
WHEN THE AIR IS ONE INTERMINABLE BALL GAME	SP	PASSING	2
WHEN THE KIDS LOOK ALL NEW	SP	PASSING	7
WHEN SHE CONVERSATIONS YOU	SP	PREFERENCE	13
ON THE DAY WHEN THE SAVOY	SP	PROJECTION	1
ON THAT DAY WHEN ABYSSINIA BAPTIST CHURCH	SP	PROJECTION	5
WHEN SHE WORKED IN THEIR KITCHENS.	SP	RUBY BROWN	27
WHEN A DREAM GETS KICKED AROUND.	SP	SAME IN BLUES	32
WHEN THE COTTON'S PICKED	SP	SHARE-CROPPERS	5
WHEN I ROLLED THREE 7'S	SP	SITUATION	1
WHEN PIMPS OUT OF LONELINESS CRY:	SP	SLIVER SERMON	1
WHEN LIFE HURT HER:	SP	SPIRITUALS	7
WHEN COZY HOUSES HOLD.	SP	STRANGE HURT	12
WHEN THE RUMBLE OF DEATH	SP	SUNDAY MORNING	2
WHEN THE LAWD PUT OUT THE LIGHT.	SP	SYLVESTER'S BED	26
I WILL BE GOD WHEN IT COMES TO YOU.	SP	TO ARTINA	11
WHEN I'M PAYING YOUR BILLS	SP	ULTIMATUM	2
WHEN YOU'RE FULL OF STUFF.	SP	WARNING AUGMENT	8
WHEN SUSANNA JONES WEARS RED	SP	WHEN SUE WEARS	1
WHEN SUSANNA JONES WEARS RED	SP	WHEN SUE WEARS	6
WHEN THEY PUT YOU IN THE GROUND AND	SP	WIDOW WOMAN	7
YET YOU NEVER CAN TELL WHEN A	SP	WIDOW WOMAN	23
CAUSE WHEN I'M DEAD SOME	SP	YOUNG GAL'S BLS	5
WHEN I'M OLD AN' UGLY	SP	YOUNG GAL'S BLS	11
WHEN LOVE IS GONE WHAT	SP	YOUNG GAL'S BLS	19
WHEN LOVE IS GONE. O.	SP	YOUNG GAL'S BLS	21
WHEN THERE'S A UNICORN?	AYM	ASK YOUR MAMA	60
BUT WHEN I GOT	AYM	GOSPEL CHA-CHA	56
WHEN I GOT TO CALVARY	AYM	GOSPEL CHA-CHA	58
BEFORE THE PRESENT BECOMES WHEN	AYM	ODE TO DINAH	104
WHEN YOU'RE 40	AYM	ODE TO DINAH	105
40 WHEN YOU'RE 30	AYM	ODE TO DINAH	107
30 WHEN YOU'RE 20	AYM	ODE TO DINAH	108
20 WHEN YOU'RE 10	AYM	ODE TO DINAH	109
EVEN WHEN YOU'RE WINNING	AYM	ODE TO DINAH	113
WHEN NIAGARA FALLS IS FROZEN	AYM	ODE TO DINAH	23
WHEN THE MAN SHOT AT THE WOMAN	AYM	ODE TO DINAH	131
WHEN THE ROLL IS CALLED UP YONDER	AYM	RIDE. RED. RIDE	2
WHEN THEY ASK YOU IF YOU KNEW ME.	AYM	RIDE. RED. RIDE	27
WHEN I TRY TO FIND A JOB	PL	BACKLASH BLUES	13
WHEN I GET TO BE A COMPOSER	PL	DAYBREAK IN ALA	1
IN THAT DAWN OF MUSIC WHEN I	PL	DAYBREAK IN ALA	20
WHEN THE LONG HOT SUMMERS COME	PL	DEATH YORKVILLE	18
DUBOIS (WHEN?) MALCOLM (OH!) SEND FOR STOKELY.	PL	FINAL CALL	35
I DO NOT NEED MY FREEDOM WHEN I'M DEAD.	PL	FREEDOM	13
GOT TIRED OF ASKING. WHEN?	PL	GHOSTS OF 1619	16
NOW WHEN THE MAN AT THE CORNER STORE	PL	HARLEM	3
WHEN I GET SOLD:	PL	LITTLE SNG HOUS	17
WHEN THE WHITE FOLKS GET THROUGH	PL	OFFICE BUILDING	1
WHEN DAYTIME FOLKS	PL	OFFICE BUILDING	4
WHEN WHITE COLLARS GET DONE.	PL	OFFICE BUILDING	8
WHEN MILLION-DOLLAR THIEVES	PL	PRIME	4
I DONE FORGOT WHEN IT PASSED	PL	STOKELY MALCOLM	8
WHEN DANGER IS NOT NEAR.	PL	SWEET WORDS RAC	10
WHEN YOU THROW	PL	THIRD DEGREE	15
WHEN THE COLD COMES	PL	WHERE WHEN WHCH	1

135

WHERE

Line	Book	Poem	Line No.
WHERE ALL PATHS GO?	WB	HARLEM NIGHT CL	17
WHERE THE TWILIGHT	WB	OUR LAND	4
AND NOT THIS LAND WHERE LIFE IS COLD.	WB	OUR LAND	7
AND NOT THIS LAND WHERE BIRDS ARE GREY.	WB	OUR LAND	12
AND NOT THIS LAND WHERE JOY IS WRONG.	WB	OUR LAND	15
WHERE ON THE BED	WB	SICK ROOM	3
GO WHERE GOLD	WB	TO DARK MERCEDE	4
GO WHERE THEY WILL PAY YOU WELL	WB	TO DARK MERCEDE	7
THAT'S WHERE MA MAN AN' ME GO.	FC	MINNIE SINGS	2
THAT'S WHERE WE GO. -	FC	MINNIE SINGS	4
WHERE SHE WAS BORN.	FC	NEW CABARET GRL	6
WHERE I COME FROM	FC	NEW CABARET GRL	11
OR WHERE I GO.	FC	NEW CABARET GRL	12
WHERE COLD WINDS BLOW.	NM	BLACK CLWN POEM	37
SO I WENT DOWN TOWN TO A HOTEL WHERE I USED TO WORK AT NIGHT.	NM	BROKE	44
DARK MOUTHS WHERE RED TONGUES BURN	ANS	A NEW SONG	36
REDDER NOW WHERE YOUR BLOOD HAS FLOWED.	ANS	BLD OZZIE POWEL	3
BUT REDDER NOW WHERE YOUR LIFE'S BLOOD FLOWED.	ANS	BLD OZZIE POWEL	31

OR THE RIVERS WHERE YOU'RE DROWNED
LIKE LIEBKNECHT. . . . . ANS KIDS WHO DIE 42
SEEKING A HOME WHERE HE HIMSELF IS
FREE. . . . . ANS LET AMERICA BE 4
WHERE NEVER KINGS CONNIVE NOR
TYRANTS SCHEME . . . . ANS LET AMERICA BE 8
O, LET MY LAND BE A LAND WHERE
LIBERTY . . . . ANS LET AMERICA BE 11
AND YET MUST BE - THE LAND WHERE
EVERY MAN IS FREE. . . . . ANS LET AMERICA BE 64
I'D RATHER DIE WHERE THE BAND'S
A-PLAYIN' . . . . SH CABARET GIRL 3
HOW DID I KNOW WHERE YOU DONE GONE
AT? . . . . SH LETTER 5
BUT YOU JUST AS WELL BE HERE WHERE
YOU DUE TO LIVE. . . . . SH LETTER 11
WHERE, OH, WHERE . . . . SH SHAKESPEARE 3
WHERE, OH, WHERE . . . . SH SHAKESPEARE 3
I DON'T CARE WHERE IT'S GOIN' . . . SH SIX-BITS BLUES 5
THAT PLACE WHERE YOUR TRUNK WAS,
AIN'T NO TRUNK NO MORE. . . . . . SH SUPPER TIME 3
PLACE WHERE YOUR CLOTHES HUNG'S
EMPTY AND BARE. . . . . SH SUPPER TIME 9
WHERE I LIVE DOWN IN DIXIE . . . JC GOOD MORN STLIN 6
AND SEE WHERE SIMPLE WORKING FOLKS
LIKE ME . . . . JC GOOD MORN STLIN 32
WHERE I DRANK OF THE BITTER RIVER JC THE BITTER RIVR 16
WHERE THE IRON BRIDGE CROSSES THE
STREAM. . . . . JC THE BITTER RIVR 30
WHERE THE LYNCHED BOYS HUNG. . . . JC THE BITTER RIVR 84
BUT BACKWARD IN THE LANDS WHERE
FACIST FEAR . . . . JC TO CAPTAIN MULZ 26
THE WORLD WHERE EVERY UGLY PAST
MISTAKE . . . . JC TO CAPTAIN MULZ 56
WHERE TWO PEOPLE . . . . FW CAROLINA CABIN 21
WHERE NO WORLDLY DUTY CALLS - . . . FW CONVENT 5
FROM WHERE . . . . FW EXITS 10
WHERE HIS HEART IS . . . . FW HEART 18
IS TO REMEMBER FRAGRANCE WHERE . . FW REMEMBRANCE 3
WHERE DEATH . . . . FW THERE 1
THERE WHERE NOTHING . . . . FW THERE 5
RESTING NEAR THE ALTER WHERE . . . OWT FUNERAL 3
WHERE SINGING BLACK BOYS DANCE AND
PLAY EACH NIGHT . . . . OWT JUICE JOINT 2
WHERE BLACK MEN COME TO DRINK AND
PLAY AND SING. . . . . OWT JUICE JOINT 34
WHERE TWO OLD BROWN MEN STAND BEHIND
THE BAR - . . . . OWT JUICE JOINT 37
WHERE? . . . . OWT RAID 10
I DON'T KNOW WHERE TO TURN. . . . . OWT TOO BLUE 2
I DON'T KNOW WHERE TO GO. . . . . . OWT TOO BLUE 3
WHERE DAVE WENT. . . . . SP BLD FORTUNE TEL 32
WHERE? . . . . SP CAFE: 3 A.M. 11
I WONDER WHERE I'M GONNA DIE. . . . SP CROSS 11
OUT WHERE IT MAKES . . . . SP DEAD IN THERE 21
AND WHERE WE'RE MOVING . . . . . SP DEFERRED 18
WHERE I GET OFF AT FIVE. . . . . . SP DEFERRED 26
WHERE IS THIS LIGHT . . . . SP DEMAND 8
WHERE HIS TWELVE-SHOE LANDS. . . . SP DREAM BOOGE VAR 8
WHERE IS THAT SUGAR, HAMMOND. . . . SP EARLY EVENING 1
I SAY, WHERE IS THAT SUGAR . . . . SP EARLY EVENING 3
WHERE I GO. . . . . SP FATASY PURPLE 10
WHERE THERE NEVER WAS NO JIM CROW
SIGNS NOWHERE. . . . . SP FREEDOM TRAIN 54
WHERE THE PEOPLE ALL ARE ICEBERGS SP GRADUATION 8
THE PLACE WHERE . . . . SP HEAVEN 2
WHERE THE SHADE IS? . . . . SP KID SLEEPY 4
WHERE YOUR FORTUNE'S AT. . . . . . SP MADAM FORT TELL 12
WHERE IS MY FORTUNE AT? . . . . . SP MADAM FORT TELL 15
WHERE THE NUMBER NOT ONLY . . . . SP MADAM NUMBER WR 27
WHERE THERE AIN'T BEEN NO LIGHT. . SP MOTHER TO SON 13
SUNDAY MORNING WHERE THE RHYTHM
FLOWS, ... SP MYSTERY 11
SPOTS WHERE THE BOOTED . . . . . . SP NEON SIGNS 7
WHERE I COME FROM . . . . SP NEW YORKERS 6
WHERE DID THEY GET . . . . SP NIGHT FUNERAL 3
WHERE THE MORNING . . . . SP REQUEST 4
WHERE A BROKEN GLASS . . . . . . SP SHALIMAR 2
WHERE? . . . . SP SONG BILLIE HOL 20
WHERE THE CARNIVAL IS CHRISTIAN. . SP SUMMER EVENING 13
BUT I WONDER WHERE . . . . SP SUNDAY BY COMB 3
THE HARLEM BRANCH Y, WHERE I TAKE
THE ELEVATOR . . . . SP THEME FOR ENG B 14
WHERE THE SMOLDERING MEMORY . . . . SP TRUMPET PLAYER 5
WHERE THE MOONLIGHT'S BUT A
SPOTLIGHT . . . . SP TRUMPET PLAYER 27
WHERE THE SEA'S A BAR-GLASS . . . . SP TRUMPET PLAYER 31
TO WHERE THE SPRING IS WONDROUS RARE SP WATER-FRONT STR 3
DOWN IN WEST TEXAS WHERE THE SUN . SP WEST TEXAS 1
WHERE WE WAS GOIN' . . . . SP WEST TEXAS 13
BUT WEST TEXAS WHERE THE SUN . . . SP WEST TEXAS 16
WHERE NO SHADOW WALKS ALONE . . . . AYM ASK YOUR MAMA 75
WHERE SIT-INS ARE CONDUCTED . . . . AYM BIRD IN ORBIT 11
WHERE BULLETS ARE THE TELLERS. . . AYM BIRD IN ORBIT 14
GRANDPA, WHERE DID YOU MEET MY
GRANDMA? . . . . AYM BIRD IN ORBIT 34
AND THEY WONDER WHERE I BE . . . . AYM BIRD IN ORBIT 55
AND I WONDER WHERE THEY BE. . . . . AYM BIRD IN ORBIT 56
WHERE AN ANCIENT RIVER FLOWS . . . AYM BLUES IN STEREO 14
WHERE THE PALMS AND COCONUTS . . . AYM GOSPEL CHA-CHA 2
WHERE THE SAND SEEDS AND THE . . . AYM GOSPEL CHA-CHA 5
WHERE THE SHADOWS OF THE NEGROES . AYM GOSPEL CHA-CHA 19
WHERE THE SEA SAND AND THE SEA
GOURDS . . . . AYM GOSPEL CHA-CHA 32
WHERE THE GRASS IS GREENER $ $ $ $
$ $ $ . . . . AYM HORN OF PLENTY 23
WHERE WINTER'S NAME IS HAWKINS ¢ ¢
¢ ¢ . . . . AYM HORN OF PLENTY 27
FROM NOBODY AND NOTHING TO WHERE I
AM. . . . . AYM HORN OF PLENTY 39
WHERE DID I GET MY MONEY! . . . . . AYM HORN OF PLENTY 47
WHERE GAME TO BAG'S ILLUSIVE . . . AYM IS IT TRUE? 12
WHERE BLACK SHADOWS MOVE LIKE
SHADOWS . . . . AYM JAZZTET MUTED 4
WHERE THE PRESSURE OF THE BLOOD . . AYM JAZZTET MUTED 18
WHERE TO SNOW NOW ACCLIMATED . . . AYM ODE TO DINAH 2
WHERE THE PENDULUM IS SWINGING . . AYM ODE TO DINAH 111
WHERE THE SHADOWS MERGE WITH SHADOWS AYM ODE TO DINAH 115
WHERE THE SONG'S MAHALIA'S DAUGHTER AYM ODE TO DINAH 19
WHERE THE PEOPLE ALL ARE DARKER . . AYM ODE TO DINAH 121
WHERE THE CHRIST CHILD ONCE HAD
LAIN. . . . . AYM ODE TO DINAH 34
WHERE WHITE SHADOWS PASS. . . . . . AYM ODE TO DINAH 50
WHERE DINAH'S SONGS ARE MADE . . . AYM ODE TO DINAH 53
WHERE NEGROES SING SO WELL . . . . AYM SHADES OF PIG 8
WHERE IS LOTTE LENYA . . . . AYM SHADES OF PIG 13
WHERE THE MASK IS PLACED BY OTHERS AYM SHOW FARE PLESE 6
WHERE THE LIGHTER IS THE DARKER . . AYM SHOW FARE PLESE 16
WHERE HE COULD NOT PRAY . . . . . PL BIBLE BELT 4
WHERE ENTRANCE TO NEGROES, ... PL BIBLE BELT 6
WHERE RACE, NOT RELIGION, ... PL BIBLE BELT 9
WHERE THE DOORS ARE DOORS OF PAPER PL CULTURAL EXCHNG 2
WHERE THE DOORKNOB LETS IN LIEDER PL CULTURAL EXCHNG 15
WHERE IS THE COLORED LAUNDROMAT . . PL CULTURAL EXCHNG 24
FATHER DIVINE (WHERE?) . . . . . . PL FINAL CALL 34
WHERE THE SUNSETS BLEED. . . . . . PL GEORGIA DUSK 12
WHERE IS THE JIM CROW SECTION . . . PL MERRY-GO-ROUND 3
DOWN SOUTH WHERE I COME FROM . . . PL MERRY-GO-ROUND 6
WHERE HAS TERROR BEEN? . . . . . . PL MISSISSIPPI 9
WHERE YOU. . . . . PL NORTHERN LIBERL 21
WHERE TWO RIVERS MEET . . . . . . PL OCTOBER 16 RAID 9
WHERE A NICKEL COSTS A DIME. . . . PL PRIME 2
WHERE A NICKEL COSTS A DIME. . . . PL PRIME 11
OUT YONDER WHERE . . . . PL WITHOUT BENEFIT 5
OUT THERE WHERE . . . . PL WITHOUT BENEFIT 10

WHEREIN 1

WHEREIN THE FALSE GODS DWELL . . . ANS UNION 8

WHEREWITHAL 1

THE WHY AND WHEREWITHAL . . . . . . PL DINNER GUEST ME 8

WHERE-WITH-ALL 1

TRYING TO MAKE HER WHERE-WITH-ALL: SP EVENING SONG 2

WHERE'RE 1

WHERE'RE YOU GOING, DAUGHTER? . . . SP MAMA AND DAUGHT 3

WHERE'S 1

WHERE'S THE HORSE . . . . PL MERRY-GO-ROUND 14

WHICH 22

TO WHICH THE SOUL ASCENDS . . . . . OLD TOWER 2
WITH ITS WINGS OF GOLD FOR WHICH I
PAY - . . . . ANS SONG OF SPAIN 42
OUT OF WHICH . . . . FW BIRTH 2
FOR WHICH THE TIRED . . . . FW EXITS 6
BY WHICH I WISH . . . . LHR CONSERVATORY 11
FOR WHICH THERE AIN'T NO HOPE. . . SP ARGUMENT 7
NO MAYORS AND SUCH FOR WHICH COLORED
CAN'T VOTE, ... SP FREEDOM TRAIN 56
WHICH MAKES IT . . . . SP MELLOW 7
WHICH IS WHY I RECKON I DOES . . . SP NECESSITY 11
WHICH WAY TO GO? . . . . SP PRAYER 2
WHICH SIN TO BEAR? . . . . SP PRAYER 4
WHICH CROWN TO PUT . . . . SP PRAYER 5
NOR WHICH WAY. . . . . SP WEST TEXAS 15
ON WHICH TO RIDE IF MOTORCARS . . . AYM BLUES IN STEREO 5
(WHICH LATELY IS STONE NOWHERE) . . AYM HORN OF PLENTY 32
THE ROCK ON WHICH FREEDOM . . . . . PL AMER HEARTBREAK 2
WHICH SEEKS DEMURELY . . . . PL DINNER GUEST ME 6
ON WHICH HE SET HIS FEET, ... PL FREDRK DOUGLASS 9
THE VERY ROOM IN WHICH HE LEAVES . PL JUNIOR ADDICT 11
THE VERY ROOM IN WHICH TODAY THE AIR PL JUNIOR ADDICT 13
IS A THING TO WHICH WE BLACK ARE
WISE: . . . . PL JUSTICE 2
WHICH AREAWAY, OR BAR, ... PL WHERE WHEN WHCH 11

WHILE 26

BUT WHILE I'M LIVIN' - I'M LIVIN'! NM BIG-TIMER POEM 35
WHO HAS A VISION OF HIS BROTHER
KILLED IN FRANCE WHILE FIGHTING
FOR THE . . . . NM COLORED SL MOOD 2
WHILE OVER ALABAMA EARTH . . . . . DK ALABAMA EARTH 10
IN THAT OLD WORLD WHILE STILL A SERF
OF KINGS, ... ANS LET AMERICA BE 40

WHILE A TALL WHITE WOMAN . . . . . SH DEATH IN HARLEM 64
WHILE THE MUSIC'S PLAYIN LET'S . . SH DEATH IN HARLEM 85
WHILE MISS LUCY PLAYED IT, BOOM,
BOOM, BOOM, ... SH DEATH IN HARLEM 91
WHILE YOU PLAY 'EM, ... SH HEY-HEY BLUES 13
AND WHILE YOU PLAY 'EM, ... SH HEY-HEY BLUES 15
WHILE BLUES AS MELLOW AS THE
SOUTHERN AIR . . . . OWT JUICE JOINT 25
WHILE MOVIES ECHO DRAMAS ON THE
SCREEN. . . . . OWT LINCOLN THEATRE 2
WHILE GIRLS WHO WASH RICH WHITE
FOLKS CLOTHES BY DAY . . . . . . OWT LINCOLN THEATRE 13
WHILE YOU CONTROL . . . . LHR POET TO BIGOT 12
WHILE NIGHT COMES ON GENTLY, . . . SP DREAM VARIATION 7
AND WHILE WE LISTEN TO IT PLAY, . . SP JUKE BOX LOVE 10
WHILE THE WEARY BLUES ECHOED THROUGH
HIS HEAD. . . . . SP THE WEARY BLUES 34
WHILE FROM THE GUTTER . . . . SP UP-BEAT 9
WHILE MOLLIE MOON STREWS SEQUINS . AYM BIRD IN ORBIT 28
LIVE ALL THAT WHILE IN PARIS . . . AYM HORN OF PLENTY 53
KEEPS THE GAS ON WHILE THE TV . . . AYM ODE TO DINAH 5
WHILE NIAGARA FALLS IS FROZEN. . . AYM ODE TO DINAH 68
WHILE THE BITE . . . . PL GO SLOW 2
WHILE THEY TELL ME . . . . PL GO SLOW 5
WHILE THEY LOCK THE GATE. . . . . . PL GO SLOW 10
WHILE JOBLESS I STARVE DEAD? . . . PL GO SLOW 14
WHILE REVOLT IN THE RICE FIELDS . . PL LAST PRINCE 12

WHIP 11
DE TROUBLE I'VE HAD." FLINCHING
UNDER THE WHIP. THE SPIRITUAL . NM BLACK CLWN MOOD 5
A SLAVE - UNDER THE WHIP, ... NM BLACK CLWN POEM 21
BENEATH THE SLAVER'S WHIP. . . . . ANS A NEW SONG 9
WHIP IT, MISS LUCY! . . . . SH DEATH IN HARLEM 12
IF YOU CAN WHIP DE BLUES, BOY, . . SH HEY-HEY BLUES 7
THEN WHIP 'EM ALL NIGHT LONG. . . . SH HEY-HEY BLUES 8
BOY, IF YOU CAN WHIP DE BLUES, . . SH HEY-HEY BLUES 9
THEN WHIP 'EM ALL NIGHT LONG. . . . SH HEY-HEY BLUES 10
LONG AGO, LONG AGO - THE WHIP AND
STEEL BARS - . . . . JC THE BITTER RIVR 37
SO SMALL I CAN'T WHIP A CAT . . . . SP NECESSITY 6
REMEMBER THE WHIP AND THE SLAVER'S
TRACK. . . . . SP THE NEGRO MOTHE 44

WHIPPED 2
LAUNCHED THE BOATS AND WHIPPED THE
HORSES . . . . SP FREEDOM'S PLOW 66
AND WHIPPED HIS HEAD WITH CLUBS . . SP NOT A MOVIE 3

WHIPS 2
CRACK WENT THE WHIPS THAT DROVE THE
HORSES . . . . SP FREEDOM'S PLOW 59
BLAZED TO THE CRACK OF WHIPS . . . SP TRUMPET PLAYER 7

WHIR 1
AND LET THE WHITE VIOLINS WHIR THIN
AND SLOW. . . . . SP FATASY PURPLE 6

WHIRL 9
DANCERS WHIRL. . . . . FC CLOSING TIME 12
WHIRL IN THE WIND OF PAIN AND
STRIFE, ... DK SONG 6
WHIRL OF CHERUB-FACES. . . . . . . ANS SONG OF SPAIN 22
TO WHIRL AND TO DANCE . . . . SP DREAM VARIATION 3
DANCE! WHIRL! WHIRL! . . . . SP DREAM VARIATION 12
DANCE! WHIRL! WHIRL! . . . . SP DREAM VARIATION 12
PUT IT ON A RECORD, LET IT WHIRL, SP JUKE BOX LOVE 9
MANHATTAN ISLAND WILL WHIRL . . . . SP PROJECTION 12
A WHIRL OF WHISTLES BLOWING. . . . PL CULTURAL EXCHNG 11

WHIRLED 1
YET AS THE VULGAR DANCERS WHIRLED WB CABARET 3

WHIRLING 4
IN A WHIRLING CABARET . . . . WB JAZZONIA 16
YOUR FACES ARE WHIRLING LIGHTS OF
LOVELINESS AND SPLENDOR, TOO. . WB THE WHITE ONES 4
INTO A THOUSAND WHIRLING DREAMS . . SP AS I GREW OLDER 32
WHIRLING TREBLE . . . . SP NIGHTMARE BOOGIE 11

WHIRLS 2
WHIRLS SOFTLY INTO A . . . . SP DANSE AFRICAINE 8
WHIRLS SOFTLY . . . SLOWLY, ... SP DANSE AFRICAINE 10

WHISKEY 8
GIN AN' WHISKEY . . . . FC LISTEN HERE 5
A GLASS O' WHISKEY . . . . FC SATURDAY NIGHT 5
TO A WHISKEY SHORE. . . . . FW SAILING DATE 5
OF WHISKEY AS THEY START OUT FOR A
BALL. . . . . OWT JUICE JOINT 8
THAT WHISKEY WILL COOK THE EGG. . . SP BAR 1
WILL COOK THE WHISKEY. . . . . . . SP BAR 4
LOVE IS LIKE WHISKEY, ... SP LAMENT OVER LOV 13
LOVE IS LIKE WHISKEY, ... SP LAMENT OVER LOV 15

WHISKY 2
BUT IF YOU GIMME GOOD CORN WHISKY SH HEY-HEY BLUES 5
BUT GIMME GOOD CORN WHISKY . . . . SH HEY-HEY BLUES 23

WHISPER 1
(MAYBE IN A WHISPER . . . . JC GOOD MORN STLIN 55

WHISPERED 1
ON YOUR BED OF WHISPERED ECHOES: . AYM IS IT TRUE? 19

WHISPERING 1
STILL AS A WHISPERING HEARTBEAT. . WB SUMMER NIGHT 9

WHISPERS 5
WHISPERS TO TEXAS, ... SH DEATH IN HARLEM 49
WHISPERS . . . . FW FRAGMENTS 1
SHOUTS ARE WHISPERS CARRYING . . . AYM ASK YOUR MAMA 2
SHOUTS ARE WHISPERS CARRYING . . . AYM IS IT TRUE? 2
AND THE WHISPERS ARE UNECHOED . . . AYM IS IT TRUE? 33

WHISTLE 2
COPPER'S WHISTLE! . . . . SP BLD LANDLORD 25
I'LL HOLLER, BLOW YOUR WHISTLE, . . SP FREEDOM TRAIN 65

WHISTLES 1
A WHIRL OF WHISTLES BLOWING. . . . PL CULTURAL EXCHNG 11

WHITE 167
WHITE GIRLS' EYES . . . . WB HARLEM NIGHT CL 6
WHITE ONES, BROWN ONES, ... WB HARLEM NIGHT CL 14
BUT THE WHITE MEN CAME. . . . . . . WB LAMENT DARK PEO 2
BUT THE WHITE MEN CAME. . . . . . . WB LAMENT DARK PEO 4
FOR PIERROT LOVED THE LONG WHITE
ROAD, ... WB PIERROT 7
AND PIERROT RAN DOWN THE LONG WHITE
ROAD . . . . WB PIERROT 29
DESCENDS LIKE A WHITE MIST . . . . WB SUMMER NIGHT 24
O, WHITE STRONG ONES, ... WB THE WHITE ONES 6
AND THE MOON WAS WHITE. . . . . . . WB TO MIDNIGHT NAN 8
AND HER SKIN BLUE WHITE. . . . . . FC CLOSING TIME 5
IF HER DADDY AIN'T WHITE . . . . . FC NEW CABARET GRL 3
GO OUT AN' LET DE WHITE BOYS . . . FC RED SILK STOCK 3
GO OUT AN' LET DE WHITE BOYS . . . FC RED SILK STOCK 11
A DRAMATIC MONOLOGUE TO BE SPOKEN BY
A PURE-BLOODED NEGRO IN THE WHITE NM BLACK CLWN MOOD 1
BLACK - IN A WHITE WORLD . . . . . NM BLACK CLWN POEM 36
WHITE SPIT IN MY FACE - . . . . . . NM BLACK CLWN POEM 48
AND DE MAN COME TELLIN' ME THEY
AIN'T HIRIN' NO MO' COLORED -
JUST WHITE. . . . . NM BROKE 45
THEY TOLD US AMERICA WOULD KNOW NO
BLACK OR WHITE: . . . . NM COLORED SL POEM 11
SADLY RECALLS THE ROWS OF WHITE
CROSSES IN FRANCE. . . . . NM COLORED SL MOOD 12
WITH THE WHITE AND THE BLACK WHOM
NOTHING HOLDS BACK - . . . . . . NM DARK YOUTH USA 24
WHITE FOLKS, LAUGH! . . . . DK NEGRO DANCERS 11
WHITE FOLKS, PRAY! . . . . DK NEGRO DANCERS 12
8 BLACK BOYS AND ONE WHITE LIE. . . SL SCOTTSBORO 3
AND WHITE TEETH GLEAM - . . . . . . ANS A NEW SONG 37
AND WHITE WORLD . . . . ANS A NEW SONG 49
A WHITE HIGH SHERIFF WHO SHOOTS TO
KILL . . . . ANS BLD OZZIE POWEL 27
10-VOICES: WHITE WORKERS, ... ANS CHANT MAY DAY 20
BLACK AND WHITE, ... ANS KIDS WHO DIE 2
WHITE AND BLACK, ... ANS KIDS WHO DIE 22
AND BLACK HANDS AND WHITE HANDS
CLASPED AS ONE, ... ANS KIDS WHO DIE 48
I AM THE POOR WHITE, FOOLED AND
PUSHED APART, ... ANS LET AMERICA BE 19
LET THE WHITE FOLKS LIVE . . . . . ANS LYNCHING SONG 3
AND THE WHITE FOLKS DIE. . . . . . ANS LYNCHING SONG 8
THE WHITE FOLKS DIE? . . . . ANS LYNCHING SONG 9
THE WHITE FOLKS DIE? . . . . ANS LYNCHING SONG 11
WHITE WORKERS OF THE SOUTH . . . . ANS OPEN LETTER 1
ANOTHER WHITE OF FACE. . . . . . . ANS OPEN LETTER 31
"YOU ARE MY BROTHER, BLACK OR
WHITE," . . . . ANS OPEN LETTER 39
BECAUSE, O POOR WHITE WORKERS, . . ANS OPEN LETTER 45
WHITE WORKER, ... ANS OPEN LETTER 65
THE WHITE DEVILS OF THE TERROR . . ANS SONG OF SPAIN 50
WHITE AND BLACK, ... ANS UNION 5
AND TURNED DEAD WHITE. . . . . . . SH BLD THE KILLER 16
AND BE A WHITE MAN THE REST OF MY
DAYS! . . . . SH DAYBREAK 11
I WONDER IF WHITE FOLKS EVER FEEL
BAD, ... SH DAYBREAK 12
A WHITE LADY FAINTED. . . . . SH DEATH IN HARLEM 114
WHILE A TALL WHITE WOMAN . . . . . SH DEATH IN HARLEM 64
BURN WHITE WITH STARS. . . . . . . SH YOUNG NEGRO GRL 9
TO WHITE FOLKS ALONE. . . . . JC BLD SAM SOLOMON 12
BLACK WORKERS WITH WHITE WORKERS - JC TO CAPTAIN MULZ 37
IN UNION, YOU, WHITE MAN, ... JC TO CAPTAIN MULZ 59
WITH THE WHITE CHILDREN . . . . . . FW MIGRATION 4
AND A WHITE EMBROIDERED COLLAR. . . FW MIGRATION 13
HAD OF BEEN WHITE . . . . OWT BLD MARGE POLIT 2
BY A WHITE COP - . . . . OWT BLD MARGE POLIT 11
AND WALTER WHITE . . . . OWT BLD MARGE POLIT 49
WHITE FOLKS AIN'T FOR ME. . . . . . OWT FLIGHT 6
AND DAWN COMES DOWN THE STREET ALL
WANLY WHITE. . . . . OWT JUICE JOINT 4

Line	Poem	No.
WHILE GIRLS WHO WASH RICH WHITE FOLKS CLOTHES BY DAY	OWT LINCOLN THEATRE	13
WHITE SKINS	OWT MAN INTO MEN	11
KIND, THOUGHTFUL TO THE FACES THAT ARE WHITE.	OWT NEGRO SERVANT	2
O, SWEET RELIEF FROM FACES THAT ARE WHITE!	OWT NEGRO SERVANT	19
THROUGH THE RED, WHITE, YELLOW SKINS	SP A HOUSE IN TAOS	34
THE ANGELS WINGS IS WHITE AS SNOW.	SP ANGELS WINGS	1
O, WHITE AS SNOW,	SP ANGELS WINGS	2
WHITE	SP ANGELS WINGS	3
THE ANGELS WINGS IS WHITE AS SNOW,	SP ANGELS WINGS	6
BUT THE ANGELS WINGS IS WHITE AS SNOW.	SP ANGELS WINGS	11
WHITE	SP ANGELS WINGS	12
WHITE IS RIGHT,	SP ARGUMENT	1
WHITE MAN	SP BLUE BAYOU	7
THEN A WHITE MAN	SP BLUE BAYOU	11
THE WHITE KIDS	SP CHILDREN'S RYME	6
THEM WHITE KIDS	SP CHILDREN'S RYME	13
FOR WHITE FOLKS	SP CHILDREN'S RYME	21
MY OLD MAN'S A WHITE OLD MAN	SP CROSS	1
IF EVER I CURSED MY WHITE OLD MAN	SP CROSS	3
BEING NEITHER WHITE NOR BLACK?	SP CROSS	12
MAYBE NOW I CAN HAVE THAT WHITE ENAMEL STOVE	SP DEFERRED	8
MAYBE I CAN BUY THAT WHITE ENAMEL STOVE!	SP DEFERRED	20
TILL THE WHITE DAY IS DONE.	SP DREAM VARIATION	4
AND LET THE WHITE VIOLINS WHIR THIN AND SLOW,	SP FATASY PURPLE	6
NO WHITE FOLKS ONLY ON THE FREEDOM TRAIN.	SP FREEDOM TRAIN	14
THE BIRMINGHAM STATION'S MARKED COLORED AND WHITE.	SP FREEDOM TRAIN	25
THE WHITE FOLKS GO LEFT, THE COLORED GO RIGHT -	SP FREEDOM TRAIN	26
WILL SOME WHITE MAN YELL, GET BACK!	SP FREEDOM TRAIN	39
GLEAMIN' IN THE SUNLIGHT FOR WHITE AND BLACK?	SP FREEDOM TRAIN	50
NOT STOPPIN' AT NO STATIONS MARKED COLORED NOR WHITE,	SP FREEDOM TRAIN	51
BLACK MEN AND WHITE WILL SAY, AIN'T IT FINE?	SP FREEDOM TRAIN	61
WHITE HANDS AND BLACK HANDS	SP FREEDOM'S PLOW	63
OUT OF LABOR - WHITE HANDS AND BLACK HANDS -	SP FREEDOM'S PLOW	82
WHITE COATS	SP INTERNE AT PROV	1
WHITE APRONS	SP INTERNE AT PROV	2
WHITE DRESSES	SP INTERNE AT PROV	3
WHITE SHOES	SP INTERNE AT PROV	4
GOLDEN HANDS IN WHITE COAT,	SP INTERNE AT PROV	20
IN THE WHITE MOON	SP INTERNE AT PROV	37
BLACK AND WHITE,	SP ISLAND	5
WHITE GIRLS FALL	SP MELLOW	3
I AM YOUR SON, WHITE MAN!	SP MULATTO	1
YOU AIN'T WHITE.	SP MULATTO	38
I AM YOUR SON, WHITE MAN!	SP MULATTO	43
TURNED DEAD WHITE!	SP NIGHTMARE BOOGE	8
GRAND MARSHAL IN HIS WHITE SUIT	SP PARADE	5
WHITE,	SP PARADE	14
WARM, WHITE LIGHTS,	SP PORT TOWN	10
WILD, WHITE NIGHTS,	SP PORT TOWN	12
RICH OLD WHITE MAN	SP PORTER	9
ROLLING WHITE BALLS IN THE POOL ROOMS,	SP RAILROAD AVENUE	27
IF THESE WHITE FOLKS WANT TO GO AHEAD	SP RELIEF	12
ON THE MONEY FROM A WHITE WOMAN'S KITCHEN?	SP RUBY BROWN	14
BUT THE WHITE MEN,	SP RUBY BROWN	23
ANY BETTER THAN WHITE.	SP SHAME ON YOU	9
ITS WHITE WOMANHOOD.	SP SILHOUETTE	10
I ASKED THE WHITE LORD JESUS	SP SONG DARK GIRL	7
SOMETIMES I THINK THAT WHITE FOLKS	SP SOUTHERN MAMMY	9
BUT SOMETIMES I THINK THAT WHITE FOLKS	SP SOUTHERN MAMMY	21
BLACK AND WHITE	SP SUBWAY RUSH HOU	5
FOR I WILL BE WITH YOU TILL NO WHITE BROTHER	SP THE NEGRO MOTHE	51
BEING ME, IT WILL NOT BE WHITE.	SP THEME FOR ENG B	28
YOU ARE WHITE -	SP THEME FOR ENG B	31
ALTHOUGH YOU'RE OLDER - AND WHITE -	SP THEME FOR ENG B	39
OF ONE THE WHITE FOLKS	SP UNCLE TOM	8
HOW THIN AND SHARP AND GHOSTLY WHITE	SP WINTER MOON	2
SAY HOW WHITE THE COTTON COTTON	AYM BIRD IN ORBIT	42
AND JOHN BROWN'S WHITE AND LONGER	AYM BIRD IN ORBIT	45
DID I WANT TO EAT WITH WHITE FOLKS?	AYM BIRD IN ORBIT	70
AND THE WHITE GOD NEVER GOES	AYM BLUES IN STEREO	16
FOR THE MOON WOULD WHITE HIS WHITENESS	AYM BLUES IN STEREO	17
THAT LUGGED THE FIRST WHITE	AYM GOSPEL CHA-CHA	16
FIRST WHITE TOURIST UP THE MOUNTAIN	AYM GOSPEL CHA-CHA	17
WHITE FOLKS' RECESSION	AYM ODE TO DINAH	125
THROUGH THE JUNGLE OF WHITE DANCER	AYM ODE TO DINAH	31
TO THE HAVEN OF WHITE QUAKERS	AYM ODE TO DINAH	32
WHERE WHITE SHADOWS PASS,	AYM ODE TO DINAH	50
IN THE WHITE HOUSE	AYM SHADES OF PIG	41
IS A WHITE BACKLASH.	PL BACKLASH BLUES	18
THE WHITE KIDS	PL CHILDREN'S RYME	2
THEM WHITE KIDS	PL CHILDREN'S RYME	7
FOR WHITE FOLKS	PL CHILDREN'S RYME	12
WHITE MASTER ABOVE	PL CHRIST IN ALA.	8
IN WHITE PILLARED MANSIONS	PL CULTURAL EXCHNG	46
WEALTHY NEGROES HAVE WHITE SERVANTS,	PL CULTURAL EXCHNG	48
WHITE SHARECROPPERS WORK THE BLACK PLANTATIONS,	PL CULTURAL EXCHNG	49
AND COLORED CHILDREN HAVE WHITE MAMMIES:	PL CULTURAL EXCHNG	50
DEAR, DEAR DARLING OLD WHITE MAMMIES -	PL CULTURAL EXCHNG	54
OF BLACK AND WHITE BLACK WHITE BLACK PEOPLE	PL DAYBREAK IN ALA	14
OF BLACK AND WHITE BLACK WHITE BLACK PEOPLE	PL DAYBREAK IN ALA	14
AND I'M GONNA PUT WHITE HANDS	PL DAYBREAK IN ALA	15
THAT COME TO WHITE MIND	PL DINNER GUEST ME	5
"I'M SO ASHAMED OF BEING WHITE."	PL DINNER GUEST ME	14
FOR THE FACT THAT WHITE WAS RIGHT	PL GHOSTS OF 1619	10
IN THE GREAT WHITE RACE?"	PL KU KLUX	4
THE WHITE MAN SAID, "BOY,	PL KU KLUX	9
THE GREAT WHITE RACE."	PL KU KLUX	20
FOR THE WHITE WORLD'S GUNBOATS	PL LAST PRINCE	6
WHITE FOLKS FLEE -	PL LITTLE SNG HOUS	5
WHITE FOLKS FLY -	PL LITTLE SNG HOUS	14
WHITE FOLKS HAVE LEFT	PL LITTLE SNG HOUS	22
WHITE FOLKS, FLEE!	PL LITTLE SNG HOUS	25
WHITE FOLKS, FLY!	PL LITTLE SNG HOUS	27
WHITE AND COLORED	PL MERRY-GO-ROUND	7
WHITE AND BLACK,	PL OCTOBER 16 RAID	7
WHEN THE WHITE FOLKS GET THROUGH	PL OFFICE BUILDING	1
WHEN WHITE COLLARS GET DONE,	PL OFFICE BUILDING	8
IN WHITE ON CLAY	PL THE DOVE	5
BROWN, BLACK, WHITE -	PL WAR	6

WHITENESS 3

Line	Poem	No.
FOR THE MOON WOULD WHITE HIS WHITENESS	AYM BLUES IN STEREO	17
BEYOND ITS MASK OF WHITENESS	AYM BLUES IN STEREO	19
SO THE WHITENESS AND THE WATER	AYM ODE TO DINAH	35

WHITES 2

Line	Poem	No.
WHITES AND FILIPINOS,	ANS KIDS WHO DIE	14
A PARTY OF WHITES FROM FIFTH AVENUE	SH DEATH IN HARLEM	58

WHITE-FACED 1

Line	Poem	No.
O WHITE-FACED MIMES,	FW FOR DEAD MIMES	1

WHITE-ROBED 1

Line	Poem	No.
FOR WHITE-ROBED WARRIORS	PL SPECIAL BULLTIN	6

WHITMAN 1

Line	Poem	No.
OLD WALT WHITMAN	SP OLD WALT	1

WHOEVER 2

Line	Poem	No.
AND WHOEVER DON'T LIKE IT	NM BIG-TIMER POEM	27
AND WHOEVER LOVED BESSIE WAS	SH DEATH IN HARLEM	126

WHOLE 14

Line	Poem	No.
I AM THE FOOL OF THE WHOLE WORLD.	NM BLACK CLWN POEM	8
WHOLE WIDE WORLD'S TURNED COLD.	DK PO' BOY BLUES	6
UNTIL THE WHOLE WORLD FALLS INTO THE HANDS OF	ANS CHANT TOM MOONY	24
BUT ALL THE WHOLE OPPRESSED	ANS UNION	3
A WHOLE SLEW OF PEOPLE	SH DEATH IN HARLEM	119
THIS WHOLE PAY CHECK'S JUST FOR ME.	SH PAY DAY	1
SENT TO BRING THE WHOLE WORLD JOY.	LHR BLD MARY'S SON	10
AND A WHOLE TRUCK LOAD OF FLOWERS.	SP AS BEFITS A MAN	12
AUNT SUE HAS A WHOLE HEART FULL OF STORIES.	SP AUNTSUE'S STORI	2
OF THE WHOLE BIG TOWN	SP COLLEGE FORMAL	14
A WHOLE LOT OF ROOM	SP HOMECOMING	7
EARNING RICHES FOR THE WHOLE WORLD	SP IN EXPLANATION	53
THE WHOLE WORLD SEE	SP PARADE	31
THE WHOLE NEIGHBORHOOD	PL LITTLE SNG HOUS	23

WHOM 2

Line	Poem	No.
WITH THE WHITE AND THE BLACK WHOM NOTHING HOLDS BACK -	NM DARK YOUTH USA	24
AND WOMEN, TOO, WHOM ANYONE MAY MEET	OWT JUICE JOINT	35

WHORE 2

Line	Poem	No.
AN' SADIE IS A WHORE.	FC SATURDAY NIGHT	4
SEDUCTIVE AS A DARK-EYED WHORE.	SP THE SOUTH	14

WHORES 3

Line	Poem	No.
FOR THE WHORES AND GIGOLOS,	FC JAZZ BAND	5
WHORES IN FINAL WEARINESS SAY:	SP SLIVER SERMON	3
THE WHORES ALL POWDERED	PL LUMUMBA'S GRAVE	3

WHOSE 17

Line	Poem	No.
A DANCING GIRL WHOSE EYES ARE BOLD	WB JAZZONIA	5
WHOSE SWEAT AND BLOOD, WHOSE FAITH AND PAIN.	ANS LET AMERICA BE	67
WHOSE SWEAT AND BLOOD, WHOSE FAITH AND PAIN.	ANS LET AMERICA BE	67

WHOSE HAND AT THE FOUNDRY, WHOSE PLOW IN THE RAIN. . . . . ANS LET AMERICA BE 68
WHOSE HAND AT THE FOUNDRY, WHOSE PLOW IN THE RAIN. . . . . ANS LET AMERICA BE 68
WHOSE IS IT, DO YOU KNOW? . . . . . FW WHEN ARMIES PAS 4
WHOSE CAP IT IS, SON. . . . . . . FW WHEN ARMIES PAS 6
WHOSE? . . . . FW WHEN ARMIES PAS 15
WHOSE LANGUID LEAN BRINGS BACK THE SUNNY SOUTH . . . . CWT JUICE JOINT 42
WHOSE HAIR WAS GRAY . . . . SP JOE LOUIS 3
WHOSE JACKET . . . . SP TRUMPET PLAYER 35
WHOSE DOLLS ARE INTERRACIAL! . . . AYM BIRD IN ORBIT 85
YET THE HORSE WHOSE BACK IS BROKEN AYM IS IT TRUE? 52
ON THE LINE WHOSE ROUTE WAS FREEDOM AYM ODE TO DINAH 30
WHOSE HAYMOW WAS A MANGER MANGER . AYM ODE TO DINAH 33
WHOSE TOMORROW SINGS A HYMN . . . . PL BIRMINGHAM SUND 20
WHOSE BLOOD? . . . EVERYONE'S. . . PL GEORGIA DUSK 8

WHO'D 1
FOR THE DEAD WHO'D GONE AWAY. . . . DK IRISH WAKE 2

WHO'RE 1
WHO'RE YOU, OUTSIDER? . . . . CWT VISITORS 17

WHO'S 1
WHO'S THE ENGINEER ON THE FREEDOM TRAIN? . . . . SP FREEDOM TRAIN 17

WHO'VE 3
WHO'VE WEATHERED . . . . FW SAILING DATE 8
TO SING ABOUT THE MEN WHO'VE DONE THEM WRONG - . . . . CWT JUICE JOINT 24
THE ONES WHO'VE CROSSED THE LINE . SP PASSING 11

WHY 55
BUT PIERROT WONDERED WHY. . . . . . WB PIERROT 6
YET WHY DO YOU TORTURE ME. . . . . WB THE WHITE ONES 5
WHY DO YOU TORTURE ME? . . . . . . WB THE WHITE ONES 7
DON'T KNOW WHY I DO IT BUT . . . . FC BAD MAN 11
NOBODY CARES JUST WHY. . . . . . . FC MOAN 11
THAT'S DE REASON WHY . . . . DK REASONS WHY 2
THAT'S DE REASON WHY . . . . DK REASONS WHY 6
WHY WE OWNS DE LAND! . . . . ANS SISTER JOHNSON 7
I DON'T KNOW WHY IT LOOKS . . . . . SH BLD PAWNBROKER 11
SHE KNOWS WHY. . . . . SH BLD THE KILLER 29
GOD! WHY DID YOU EVER CURSE ME . . SH CABARET GIRL 7
WHAT DO YOU MEAN, WHY I DIDN'T WRITE? . . . . SH LETTER 3
DON'T KNOW WHY I BUILD THIS LEVEE SH MISSISSIPPI LEV 7
DON'T KNOW WHY I BUILD THIS LEVEE SH MISSISSIPPI LEV 9
WHY DON'T YOU TRY IT, FOLKS. . . . SH OUT OF WORK 22
WHY DEMOCRACY MEANS . . . . JC BLACK MAN SPEAK 3
WHY FREEDOM DON'T APPLY . . . . . . JC BLACK MAN SPEAK 7
WHY IN THE NAME OF LIBERTY . . . . JC BLACK MAN SPEAK 11
WHY NOT END RIGHT NOW . . . . JC BLACK MAN SPEAK 27
WHY CARE? . . . . FW SAILING DATE 18
TO KNOW WHY: . . . . OWT DECEASED 5
WHY? . . . . OWT RESTRICTIVE 6
WHY THERE'S JIM CROW STATIONS FOR THE FREEDOM TRAIN? . . . . SP FREEDOM TRAIN 32
DON'T KNOW WHY. . . . . SP HOPE 2
ASK YOU WHY! . . . . SP MADAM MINISTER 24
WHY DIDN'T HE TELL ME SOME'N . . . SP MADAM PHONE BIL 25
YOU FIGURE OUT WHY! . . . . SP MADAM CHARTY CH 28
BUT WHY DON'T YOU BLUSH. . . . . . SP MARCH MOON 7
WHICH IS WHY I RECKON I DOES . . . SP NECESSITY 11
I COME - AND WHY? . . . . SP NEW YORKERS 5
THAT'S WHY I LIKES A OLDER WOMAN . SP PREFERENCE 11
WHY DOES HE KEEP ON FOOLIN' AROUND MARIE? . . . . SP SISTER 2
BUT WHY DOES HE KEEP ON FOOLIN' AROUND MARIE? . . . . SP SISTER 4
WHY DON'T SHE GET A BOY-FRIEND . . SP SISTER 5
WHY SHOULD IT BE MY LONELINESS. . . SP TELL ME 1
WHY SHOULD IT BE MY SONG. . . . . . SP TELL ME 2
WHY SHOULD IT BE MY DREAM . . . . . SP TELL ME 3
BUT WHY RIDE ON MULE OR DONKEY . . AYM ASK YOUR MAMA 59
AND WHY DID RICHARD WRIGHT . . . . AYM HORN OF PLENTY 52
AND WHY WOULD MAI (NOT MAY) . . . . AYM SHADES OF PIG 17
DON'T KNOW WHY I. . . . . PL ANGOLA QUESTION 1
DON'T KNOW WHY I . . . . PL ANGOLA QUESTION 8
THE WHY AND WHEREWITHAL . . . . . . PL DINNER GUEST ME 8
AND WONDER WHY . . . . PL LONG VIEW NEGRO 10
WHY NOT GO UNDER? . . . . PL QUESTION ANSWER 12
WHY TAKE IT? . . . . PL QUESTION ANSWER 15
THAT'S WHY MY HEART IS RED. . . . . PL VARI-COLORED 8
I WONDER WHY RED CLAY'S SO RED . . PL VARI-COLORED 9
I WONDER WHY IT'S YES TO ME. . . . PL VARI-COLORED 11
I WONDER WHY THE SKY'S SO BLUE . . PL VARI-COLORED 13
AND WHY THE CLAY'S SO RED. . . . . PL VARI-COLORED 14
WHY DOWN SOUTH IS ALWAYS DOWN. . . PL VARI-COLORED 15
WHY GOD DON'T PROTECT A MAN . . . . PL WHO BUT TH LORD 17
DON'T ASK ME WHY. . . . . PL WITHOUT BENEFIT 12
YOU WOULD KNOW WHY. . . . . PL WORDS LIKE FREE 8

WICKED 1
O, DE WICKED WATER. . . . . FC A RUINED GAL 16

WID 7
AIN'T CUT HIM WID NO RAZOR. . . . . FC BLACK GAL 3
CAN I GO HOME WID YUH, SWEETIE? . . FC JAZZ BAND 22
DON'T YOU FOOL WID NO MEN CAUSE . . FC LISTEN HERE 17
WID BLUE-GREEN EYES: . . . . FC NEW CABARET GRL 2
WID BLUE-GREEN EYES: . . . . FC NEW CABARET GRL 14
WID A PICK AN' A SHOVEL. . . . . . FC WORKIN' MAN 2
HE SAID, "SHO YOU'LL COME WID ME . DK MA LORD 15

WIDE 23
IS WIDE WITH LAUGHTER . . . . DK MINSTREL MAN 2
IS WIDE WITH LAUGHTER. . . . . . . DK MINSTREL MAN 10
WHOLE WIDE WORLD'S TURNED COLD. . . DK PO' BOY BLUES 6
A WIDE, DEEP DEATH. . . . . DK SEA CHARM 11
OPEN WIDE YOUR ARMS TO LIFE. . . . DK SONG 5
WIDE, WIDE RIVER . . . . DK WIDE RIVER 7
WIDE, WIDE RIVER . . . . DK WIDE RIVER 7
WIDE, WIDE RIVER . . . . DK WIDE RIVER 9
WIDE, WIDE RIVER . . . . DK WIDE RIVER 9
WIDE A RIVER CAN BE. . . . . DK WIDE RIVER 12
AND SPLIT IT WIDE! . . . . JC BIG BUDDY 15
YES, DANGEROUS ARE THE WIDE WORLD'S WATERS STILL. . . . . JC TO CAPTAIN MULZ 29
STRETCHES ITS WIDE HORIZONS . . . . FW THERE 2
IN THIS WIDE WIDE WORLD - . . . . . OWT HONEY BABE 14
IN THIS WIDE WIDE WORLD - . . . . . OWT HONEY BABE 14
TO FLING MY ARMS WIDE . . . . SP DREAM VARIATION 1
TO FLING MY ARMS WIDE . . . . SP DREAM VARIATION 10
SHIPPED THE WIDE WORLD OVER: . . . SP FREEDOM'S PLOW 81
I AM THE DARK GIRL WHO CROSSED THE WIDE SEA . . . . SP THE NEGRO MOTHE 9
OF THE WIDE SEAS. . . . . SP YOUNG SAILOR 7
GRIN THAT WIDE. . . . . SP 125TH STREET 6
SITTING ON THEIR WIDE VERANDAS. . . PL CULTURAL EXCHNG 47
AND YOUR MOAT IS TOO WIDE - . . . . PL LAST PRINCE 5

WIDE-EYED 1
WIDE-EYED . . . . SP GOOD MORNING 19

WIDE-OPEN 1
STOPPIN' IN THE COUNTRY IN THE WIDE-OPEN AIR . . . . SP FREEDOM TRAIN 53

WIFE 12
I HAVE ONE WIFE. . . . . WB PIERROT 11
I HAVE ONE WIFE. . . . . WB PIERROT 14
WITH THE BURGHER'S WIFE ONE JUNE. WB PIERROT 30
I BEATS MA WIFE AN' . . . . FC BAD MAN 7
BEATS MA WIFE AN' . . . . FC BAD MAN 9
WHAT SHALL I LEAVE MY WIFE . . . . LHR TESTAMENT 9
HIS WIFE TOOK A PAPER . . . . SP BLD OF THE MAN 9
ALL I WANT IS A WIFE WHO WILL . . . SP DEFERRED 36
HIS WIFE LOOKED IT UP IN HER DREAM BOOK . . . . SP HOPE 3
BEFORE TAKING BESS TO WIFE . . . . AYM SHADES OF PIG 16
FOR ME AND MY WIFE. . . . . PL LITTLE SNG HOUS 4
MY WIFE . . . . PL LITTLE SNG HOUS 16

WIGGLE 2
STRUT AND WIGGLE. . . . . WB TO MIDNIGHT NAN 1
STRUT AND WIGGLE. . . . . WB TO MIDNIGHT NAN 17

WILD 17
THE WILD LAUGHTER . . . . WB DISILLUSION 7
AND ALL THE WILD HOT MOONS OF THE JUNGLES SHINE IN MY SOUL. . . . WB FOR PORTRAIT OF 2
AND YET HE PLAYS UPON HIS FLUTE A WILD FREE TUNE . . . . DK BEGGAR BOY 7
HEADSTRONG AND WILD. . . . . SH BLD THE SINNER 10
THAT MIGHTY NIGH DROVE ME WILD! . . SH LOVE AGAIN BLUS 12
A WILD POPPY-FLOWER . . . . FW POPPY FLOWER 1
A WILD POPPY-FLOWER . . . . FW POPPY FLOWER 5
SING IT SOFTLY, FOR THE SONG IS WILD. . . . . SP GENIUS CHILD 2
TAME OR WILD? . . . . SP GENIUS CHILD 7
WILD OR TAME. . . . . SP GENIUS CHILD 8
KILL HIM - AND LET HIS SOUL RUN WILD! . . . . SP GENIUS CHILD 12
LOVE IS A WILD WONDER . . . . SP LOVE 1
NEARLY DROVE ME WILD. . . . . SP MADAM CHARTY CH 4
I HOPE THAT WILD YOUNG SON-OF-A-GUN SP MAMA AND DAUGHT 15
AND NIGHT-TIME DRIVES ME WILD. . . SP MISS BLUES'ES 12
WILD, WHITE NIGHTS. . . . . SP PORT TOWN 12
BORN TO GROW UP WILD - . . . . . . AYM ODE TO DINAH 87

WILDERNESS 2
THE SEA IS A WILDERNESS OF WAVES. SP LONG TRIP 1
A WILDERNESS OF WATER. . . . . . . SP LONG TRIP 10

WILLIE 1
JACKIE WILLIE CAMPANELLA $ $ $ $ $ $ $ $ $ . . . . AYM HORN OF PLENTY 17

WILLING 3
WILLING WORKER? UN-UH! YES! WHAT'S THAT YOU SAY? . . . . NM BROKE 33
GOD WILLING DROP A SHILLING . . . . AYM ASK YOUR MAMA 44

KINGSTON TOO GOD WILLING . . . . . AYM ASK YOUR MAMA 48

WILLIN' 1
IF A PRETTY GAL LIKE YOU WAS WILLIN', I'D BITE. . . . . NM BROKE 72

WILT 2
WATCH THEM DROOP, WILT, FADE . . . PL CROWNS GARLANDS 10
AND THEN SO QUICKLY WILT . . . . . PL SWEET WORDS RAC 3

WIL' 2
SHAKE 'EM SWIFT AND WIL' - . . . . DK SONG BANJO DANC 4
(THE MUSIC'S SOFT AND WIL') . . . . DK SONG BANJO DANC 23

WIN 1
JOE LOUIS SAID, WE GONNA WIN THIS WAR . . . . JC JIM CROW'S LAST 25

WIND 28
THEIR PETALS DANCE ON THE WIND . . DK AUTUMN THOUGHT 4
I'VE GONE BACK TO THE WIND AND WAVE. DK DEATH SEAMAN 8
BUT THAT SEA WIND IS SWEET . . . . DK SEA CHARM 8
WHIRL IN THE WIND OF PAIN AND STRIFE. . . . . DK SONG 6
THE WIND IMPRISONED IN THE FLESH, ANS NEGRO GHETTO 3
YOU CAN CATCH THE WIND, ... SH FREE MAN 1
FROM THE WIND AND RAIN. . . . . . . FW WALLS 4
BUT THE WIND BLOWS THERE. . . . . . OWT RESTRICTIVE 15
I RECKON THE WIND . . . . OWT RESTRICTIVE 16
WIND . . . . SP A HOUSE IN TAOS 29
TOUCH OUR BODIES, WIND. . . . . . . SP A HOUSE IN TAOS 30
TOUCH OUR BODIES, WIND. . . . . . . SP A HOUSE IN TAOS 32
BLOW QUICKLY, WIND, ... SP A HOUSE IN TAOS 41
IN A HIGH COLD WIND . . . . SP CROSSING 6
KNOWING SO WELL THE WIND AND THE SUN - . . . . SP DEMAND 7
AND WHAT IS THIS WIND . . . . SP DEMAND 10
THE WIND HAS UNDRESSED THE MOON. . SP MARCH MOON 2
THE WIND HAS BLOWN ALL THE CLOUD-GARMENTS . . . . SP MARCH MOON 3
AS THE WIND . . . . SP ONE 2
A CHANCE WIND BLOWS THERE. . . . . SP SONG BILLIE HOL 13
IN THE WIND. . . . . AYM RIDE, RED, RIDE 34
BLOWING BACK IN THE WIND . . . . . AYM SHADES OF PIG 35
AND THE WIND WON'T WAIT FOR MIDNIGHT PL CULTURAL EXCHNG 6
SOMETIMES THERE'S A WIND IN THE GEORGIA DUSK . . . . PL GEORGIA DUSK 1
SOMETIMES A WIND IN THE GEORGIA DUSK PL GEORGIA DUSK 9
MY HOPES THE WIND DONE SCATTERED. PL STILL HERE 2
WIND . . . . PL WARNING 6
AND THE WIND BLOWS . . . . PL WHERE WHEN WHCH 4

WINDING 1
WINDING THE NIGHT. . . . . DK LULLABY 10

WINDLESSNESS 2
INTO THE WINDLESSNESS - . . . . . . SP A HOUSE IN TAOS 43
INTO THE WINDLESSNESS . . . . SP A HOUSE IN TAOS 45

WINDOW 3
AND FROM ITS TINY WINDOW . . . . . DK WINTER SWEEETNS 3
ONE BATTED A HARD BALL RIGHT THROUGH MY WINDOW . . . . SP CHILDREN'S RYME 18
THROWS A TOOTHPICK FROM HER WINDOW. SP SUMMER EVENING 19

WINDOWS 2
THERE'S A BAR WITH WINDOWS FROSTED AYM ODE TO DINAH 24
WITH A BAR WITH FROSTED WINDOWS . . AYM ODE TO DINAH 42

WINDOW'S 1
BACK WINDOW'S CRACKED. . . . . . . SP MADAM RENT MAN 15

WINDS 6
THE WINTER WINDS . . . . WB POEME D'AUTOMNE 9
WHERE COLD WINDS BLOW. . . . . . . NM BLACK CLWN POEM 37
LET THE WINDS RISE THEN! . . . . . JC TO CAPTAIN MULZ 71
AND THE WINDS BLOW FREE! . . . . . JC TO CAPTAIN MULZ 76
THE WINDS OF WINTER COLD, ... FW CAROLINA CABIN 14
THE STEEL WINDS BLOW? . . . . PL WITHOUT BENEFIT 6

WINDY 1
WE BURIED HIM HIGH ON THE WINDY HILL, ... DK DEATH SEAMAN 1

WIND-BLOWN 1
WIND-BLOWN AUTUMN FLOWER . . . . . SP TROUBLED WOMAN 10

WIND-SWEPT 1
HAS KNOWN HIGH WIND-SWEPT MOUNTAINS, SP MEXICAN MARKET 5

WIND'S 2
IN THE WIND'S FRENETIC FISTS . . . AYM GOSPEL CHA-CHA 4
IN THE WIND'S FRENETIC FISTS. . . . AYM GOSPEL CHA-CHA 34

WINE 14
OF LOVE AND JOY AND WINE AND SONG, WB OUR LAND 14
LIKE THE WINE CUPS OF SOLOMON. . . FC BRASS SPITOONS 35
DRINKIN' LIFE LIKE WINE. . . . . . NM BIG-TIMER POEM 18
VIRGINIA DARE WINE - . . . . SH HARLEM SWEETIES 26
WARM RED WINE, ... FW CAROLINA CABIN 8
IN WINE. . . . . FW MAN 9
HE GAVE THEM TO DRINK OF HIS WINE. LHR BLD MARY'S SON 17
LOVE IS LIKE RED, RED WINE. . . . . SP LAMENT OVER LOV 14
LIKE SWEET RED WINE. . . . . SP LAMENT OVER LOV 16
FINE AS WINE! . . . . SP LIFE IS FINE 32
COME, DRINK PALM WINE. . . . . . . SP NATCHA 5
RATHER HAVE WINE? . . . . SP PORT TOWN 6
AND WINE? . . . . SP YOUNG SAILOR 10
THE WINE DIVINE. . . . . PL DINNER GUEST ME 16

WINED 1
BEING WINED AND DINED, ... PL DINNER GUEST ME 3

WINES 1
SPARKLING ORIENTAL WINES . . . . . SP FLATTED FIFTHS 7

WINE-GOLD 1
GINGER, WINE-GOLD, ... SH HARLEM SWEETIES 37

WINE-HOUSE 2
SETTING IN THE WINE-HOUSE . . . . . SP WINE-O 1
SETTING IN THE WINE-HOUSE . . . . . SP WINE-O 5

WINE-MAIDEN 1
WINE-MAIDEN . . . . SP MIDNIGHT DANCER 1

WINE-SOUSE 1
SOAKING UP A WINE-SOUSE . . . . . . SP WINE-O 2

WINE'S 1
WHEN THE WINE'S GONE TO YOUR HEAD OWT RAID 2

WING 4
TO A SNOWBIRD ON THE WING. . . . . FW DUSTBOWL 10
THAT TAKETH ALL THINGS UNDER WING - LHR DEAR LVLY DEATH 2
AND MOUNTAINS THAT TAKE WING. . . . SP LOVE 4
FROM THE WING TIP OF A MATCH TIP . AYM JAZZTET MUTED 8

WINGS 13
THEY MAKE RAINBOW WINGS. . . . . . DK FAIRIES 4
LIKE DE WINGS OF A BUTTERFLY. . . . DK REASONS WHY 4
WITH ITS WINGS OF GOLD FOR WHICH I PAY - . . . . ANS SONG OF SPAIN 42
GOT WINGS IN THE MUD, ... JC RED CROSS 2
THE ANGELS WINGS IS WHITE AS SNOW, SP ANGELS WINGS 1
THE ANGELS WINGS IS WHITE AS SNOW. SP ANGELS WINGS 6
BUT I DRUG MA WINGS . . . . SP ANGELS WINGS 7
O, I DRUG MA WINGS . . . . SP ANGELS WINGS 9
BUT THE ANGELS WINGS IS WHITE AS SNOW. . . . . SP ANGELS WINGS 11
I WISH I HAD WINGS TO . . . . SP HARD DADDY 13
WISH I HAD WINGS TO . . . . SP HARD DADDY 15
LIFT SILKEN WINGS . . . . SP IN TIME SILVER 13
OR AN ANGEL WITH WINGS . . . . . . PL GO SLOW 12

WINNERS 1
WINNERS OR LOSERS, ... PL PEACE 3

WINNING 1
EVEN WHEN YOU'RE WINNING . . . . . AYM ODE TO DINAH 113

WINSTON-SALEM 1
I AM TWENTY-TWO, COLORED, BORN IN WINSTON-SALEM. . . . . SP THEME FOR ENG B 7

WINTER 8
THE WINTER WINDS . . . . WB POEME D'AUTOMNE 9
O' GETTIN' A NEW WINTER COAT, OR HAVIN' THAT OLD ONE CLEANED. . . NM BROKE 40
THE WINDS OF WINTER COLD, ... FW CAROLINA CABIN 14
IN THE MIDDLE OF THE WINTER, . . . SP MIDWINTER BLUES 1
IN THE MIDDLE OF THE WINTER, . . . SP MIDWINTER BLUES 3
IN MONTHS OF SNOWY WINTER . . . . . SP STRANGE HURT 11
GHOSTLY MONUMENT OF WINTER . . . . AYM ODE TO DINAH 26
AND IT IS WINTER. . . . . PL WHERE WHEN WHCH 7

WINTER'S 1
WHERE WINTER'S NAME IS HAWKINS ¢ ¢ ¢ ¢ . . . . AYM HORN OF PLENTY 27

WIPE 2
AND THAT OUR DARK BLOOD WOULD WIPE AWAY THE STAIN . . . . NM COLORED SL POEM 8
SEE! WHEN YOU WIPE THE MUD AWAY, . FW WHEN ARMIES PAS 21

WIRE 1
TO WALK A HIGH WIRE . . . . SH ASPIRATION 5

WIRED 1
WIRED FOR KILLING . . . . SP MELLOW 6

WISDOM 3
BEFORE MAN'S WISDOM, ... FW WISDOM 2
GOD, IN HIS INFINITE WISDOM . . . . LHR ACCEPTANCE 1
WISDOM REDUCED TO THE PERSONAL EQUATION: . . . . PL ELDERLY LEADERS 2

WISE 15
ONCE I WAS WISE. . . . . WB THE JESTER 18
SHALL I BE WISE AGAIN? . . . . . . WB THE JESTER 19
TO BE WISE AND STRONG, THEN, STUDYING LONG. . . . . NM DARK YOUTH USA 16
NINE OLD MEN SO RICH AND WISE. . . ANS BLD OZZIE POWEL 17
OF COURSE, THE WISE AND THE LEARNED ANS KIDS WHO DIE 19
DON'T WANT THE PEOPLE TO GET WISE TO THEIR OWN POWER. . . . . ANS KIDS WHO DIE 35
BUT FOR A WISE NIGHT-BIRD . . . . . SH DEATH IN HARLEM 4
REALLY WISE: . . . . FW WISDOM 4
DID NOT MAKE ME VERY WISE - . . . . LHR ACCEPTANCE 2
TALL AND WISE . . . . SP COLLEGE FORMAL 6
HAS GROWN QUITE WISE - . . . . SP DELINQUENT 10
IF YOU'S A WISE WOMAN, HATTIE, . . . SP EARLY EVENING 11
I AIN'T NO WISE WOMAN, HAMMOND. . . SP EARLY EVENING 13
MADAM, YOU AIN'T WISE. . . . . . . SP MADAM FORT TELL 8
IS A THING TO WHICH WE BLACK ARE WISE: . . . . PL JUSTICE 2

WISH 17
BUT I WISH I HAD BACK THAT . . . . DK DRESSED UP 7
I WISH I'D NEVER BEEN BORN. . . . . DK PO' BOY BLUES 24
DOG-GONE LITTLE MOUSES! I WISH I WAS YOU! . . . . SH BED TIME 14
I WISH I COULD TELL YOU HOW MUCH I DON'T CARE . . . . SH SUNDAY 5
O, I WISH THAT YESTERDAY, ... OWT YESTERDAY TODAY 1
I WISH IT WOULD . . . . LHR CONSERVATORY 3
BY WHICH I WISH . . . . LHR CONSERVATORY 11
LORD, I WISH I WAS DEAD! . . . . . SP BLD OF THE GIRL 12
I'M SORRY FOR THAT EVIL WISH . . . SP CROSS 7
AND NOW I WISH HER WELL. . . . . . SP CROSS 8
I WISH I HAD WINGS TO . . . . SP HARD DADDY 13
WISH I HAD WINGS TO . . . . SP HARD DADDY 15
I WISH THE RENT . . . . SP LITTLE LYRIC 1
BUT IT MADE ME WISH . . . . SP LITTLE OLD LETT 7
AND WISH SHE'D NEVER BEEN BORN? . . SP REVERIE HARLEM 8
LAWD, I WISH I COULD DIE - . . . . SP REVERIE HARLEM 13
AND I WISH THAT I HAD DIED." . . . SP THE WEARY BLUES 30

WISHED 1
AND WISHED SHE WERE IN HELL, . . . SP CROSS 6

WISHING 3
I KEPT WISHING I HAD A GIRL-FRIEND OWT STRANGER IN TWN 3
AT NIGHT MY WISHING STAR. . . . . . SP MISS BLUES'ES 8
WISHING WELL . . . . SP NEON SIGNS 2

WISP 1
LIKE A WISP OF SMOKE AROUND THE FIRE - . . . . SP DANSE AFRICAINE 11

WITHER 1
TO WITHER IN THE . . . . PL SWEET WORDS RAC 7

WITHERED 5
IS LIKE A WITHERED FLOWER . . . . . WB YOUNG PROSTITUT 2
DRY AND WITHERED, ... DK AUTUMN THOUGHT 3
OH, WITHERED OLD WOMAN . . . . . . DK PARISIAN BEGGAR 9
WITHERED AND DIED. . . . . FW POPPY FLOWER 2
WITHERED AND DIED. . . . . FW POPPY FLOWER 6

WITHIN 7
PULLING HIMSELF TOGETHER, BOASTING LOUDLY AGAIN, BUT REALIZING WITHIN THE . . . . NM BIG-TIMER MOOD 11
WHAT IS THERE WITHIN THIS BEGGAR LAD DK BEGGAR BOY 1
AND CONQUER US FROM WITHIN, ... SP FREEDOM'S PLOW 181
DREAM WITHIN A DREAM. . . . . SP ISLAND 9
THAT TRIED TO BURN WITHIN HER SOUL. SP RUBY BROWN 7
WITHIN - . . . . SP UNCLE TOM 1
WITHIN THE INNER EAR, ... PL SWEET WORDS RAC 4

WITHOUT 23
WITHOUT REST IN THE DARKNESS, . . . WB SUMMER NIGHT 11
I TOSS WITHOUT REST . . . . WB SUMMER NIGHT 20
TO A NIGHT WITHOUT STARS . . . . . DK QUIET GIRL 2
TO A SLEEP WITHOUT DREAMS . . . . . DK QUIET GIRL 5
MY YOUNG MEN WITHOUT A VOICE IN THE WORLD, ... ANS A NEW SONG 13
WITHOUT A NAME. . . . . SH DEATH IN HARLEM 73
I CAN'T GET ALONG WITH YOU, I CAN'T GET ALONG WITHOUT - . . . . . . SH LETTER 14
WITHOUT POWER - ". . . . . JC TO CAPTAIN MULZ 23
TO SONG WITHOUT SOUND. . . . . . . FW BURDEN 4
WITHOUT WONDER . . . . FW SLEEP 7
AND WITHOUT DREAMS. . . . . FW SLEEP 8
IN A BOX WITHOUT A SMILE. . . . . . OWT FUNERAL 2
SHRUNKEN LIKE A BALLOON WITHOUT AIR. SP A BLACK PIERROT 13
WITHOUT A PLACE - . . . . SP AFRO-AMER FRAG 20
TO A NIGHT WITHOUT STARS . . . . . SP ARDELLA 2
TO A SLEEP WITHOUT DREAMS . . . . . SP ARDELLA 5
WITHOUT A NAME. . . . . SP BEALE STREET 6
WITHOUT MY WATCH AND YOU. . . . . . SP COULD BE 16
COFFEE WITHOUT SUGAR . . . . SP EARLY EVENING 5
WITHOUT THAT OTHER'S CONSENT. . . . SP FREEDOM'S PLOW 104
WITHOUT THAT OTHER'S CONSENT. . . . SP FREEDOM'S PLOW 171
TO THE ENEMY WHO WOULD CONQUER US FROM WITHOUT. . . . . SP FREEDOM'S PLOW 178
WITHOUT A DIME. . . . . SP MIDNIGHT RAFFLE 8
WITHOUT GETTING FUR IN MY MOUTH . . SP NECESSITY 7
WITHOUT YOUR RENT. . . . . SP ULTIMATUM 7
WITHOUT A CENT. . . . . SP ULTIMATUM 9
WITHOUT - . . . . SP UNCLE TOM 3
WITHOUT COMPLAINING LOUD AND LONG. PL MILITANT 4

WIVES 1
THAN PHARAOH HAD WIVES. . . . . . . SP FIRE 20

WOE 1
WOE. . . . . PL ANGOLA QUESTION 19

WOKE 4
THEN I WOKE UP, AND THE DREAM WAS ENDED - . . . . NM COLORED SL POEM 48
WOKE UP AND LOOKED AROUND ME - . . . SP MORNING AFTER 11
I WOKE UP THIS MORNIN' . . . . . . SP SYLVESTER'S BED 1
I WOKE UP LITTLE LATER . . . . . . SP SYLVESTER'S BED 9

WOMAN 55
A SILENT WOMAN LIES BETWEEN TWO LOVERS - . . . . WB SICK ROOM 4
CAUSE A BLUE-GUMMED WOMAN . . . . . FC EVIL WOMAN 11
I'M GONNA BE A GYPSY WOMAN . . . . FC GYPSY MAN 5
I CALLS FOR MA WOMAN . . . . FC WORKIN' MAN 5
AND DON'T YOU KNOW THAT OLD WOMAN SWELLED UP LIKE A SPECKLED TOAD NM BROKE 21
AW-OO! YONDER COMES A WOMAN I USED TO KNOW WAY DOWN SOUTH. . . . . NM BROKE 62
OH, WITHERED OLD WOMAN . . . . . . DK PARISIAN BEGGAR 9
WHAT MAKES A WOMAN . . . . SH ANNOUNCEMENT 7
ASK THAT WOMAN - . . . . SH BLD THE KILLER 28
WHEN I COME ACROSS THAT WOMAN . . . SH BRIEF ENCOUNTER 5
JUDGE, SHE IS DE WOMAN . . . . . . SH BRIEF ENCOUNTER 7
SHE IS DE WOMAN, JUDGE, ... SH BRIEF ENCOUNTER 9
LIKE A WOMAN IN A DREAM . . . . . . SH DEATH IN HARLEM 112
A BLACK WOMAN CRIED. . . . . SH DEATH IN HARLEM 115
PICKED UP ANOTHER WOMAN AND . . . . SH DEATH IN HARLEM 141
AND A WOMAN CROSS THE TABLE WHEN A MAN AIN'T BROKE - . . . . SH DEATH IN HARLEM 54
WHILE A TALL WHITE WOMAN . . . . . SH DEATH IN HARLEM 64
WOMAN, LISTEN! SAY! . . . . SH MIDNIGHT CHIPPI 16
LONESOME SAID WHEN A TWO-BIT WOMAN SH MIDNIGHT CHIPPI 23
I WANT TO TELL YOU 'BOUT THAT WOMAN, SH ONLY WOMAN BLUS 1
SHE WAS DE MEANEST WOMAN . . . . . SH ONLY WOMAN BLUS 3
WOMAN THAT COULD MISTREAT ME! . . . SH ONLY WOMAN BLUS 6
WOMAN THAT COULD MISTREAT ME. . . . SH ONLY WOMAN BLUS 12
LAWD! I GOT TO FIND ME A WOMAN FOR THE WPA - . . . . SH SUPPER TIME 13
THERE'S MANY ANOTHER WOMAN . . . . OWT HONEY BABE 13
WHO SINGS THE TROUBLES EVERY WOMAN HAS. . . . . OWT LINCOLN THEATRE 8
THAT WOMAN WHO COULD FORESEE . . . SP BLD FORTUNE TEL 29
TAKES MY WOMAN AWAY. . . . . SP BLUE BAYOU 12
MAKES A GOOD WOMAN CRY. . . . . . . SP EARLY EVENING 6
IF YOU'S A WISE WOMAN, HATTIE, . . SP EARLY EVENING 11
I AIN'T NO WISE WOMAN, HAMMOND. . . SP EARLY EVENING 13
AIN'T NO SENSE IN A GOOD WOMAN . . SP EARLY EVENING 15
A WOMAN TO SLEEP WITH. . . . . . . SP ELEVATOR BOY 13
A WOMAN STANDING IN THE DOORWAY . . SP EVENING SONG 1
JUST MAN WOMAN TIRED SAYS: . . . . SP IN EXPLANATION 55
I WORKED FOR A WOMAN, ... SP MADAM HER MADAM 1
NOW, IF A MAN LOVES A WOMAN . . . . SP MIDWINTER BLUES 11
HIS WOMAN AND HIS FRIEND IS DEAD. SP MONROE'S BLUES 2
MY WOMAN AND MY FRIEND IS DEAD. . . SP MONROE'S BLUES 8
YOU JEST A LITTLE BIT O' WOMAN BUT YOU . . . . SP MORNING AFTER 17
A BLACK OLD WOMAN CROONS . . . . . SP PRAYER MEETING 5
A BLACK OLD WOMAN CROONS - . . . . SP PRAYER MEETING 8
I LIKES A WOMAN . . . . SP PREFERENCE 1
THAT'S WHY I LIKES A OLDER WOMAN . SP PREFERENCE 11
THAT A WOMAN DOES THE BEST SHE CAN? SP SISTER 14
I AM THE WOMAN WHO WORKED IN THE FIELD . . . . SP THE NEGRO MOTHE 11
BEAUTIFUL, LIKE A WOMAN, ... SP THE SOUTH 13
THIS TROUBLED WOMAN . . . . SP TROUBLED WOMAN 3
I HAD A WOMAN . . . . SP WEST TEXAS 3
WOMAN LIKE ME IS FREE! . . . . . . SP WIDOW WOMAN 24
TO PROVE SHE WAS A WOMAN WOMAN . . AYM BIRD IN ORBIT 48
TO PROVE SHE WAS A WOMAN WOMAN . . AYM BIRD IN ORBIT 46
TO PROVE SHE WAS A WOMAN? . . . . . AYM BIRD IN ORBIT 50
WITH A WOMAN WITH TWO PISTOLS . . . AYM ODE TO DINAH 28
WHEN THE MAN SHOT AT THE WOMAN . . AYM ODE TO DINAH 131

WOMANHOOD 1
ITS WHITE WOMANHOOD. . . . . SP SILHOUETTE 10

WOMAN'LL 1
BUT A OLD WOMAN'LL SAY. . . . . . . SP PREFERENCE 7

WOMAN'S 7
I CAN'T HAVE NO WOMAN'S . . . . . . FC EVIL WOMAN 9
WOMAN'S GONNA MISTREAT ME. . . . . SH ONLY WOMAN BLUS 18
WOMAN'S GONNA MISTREAT ME. . . . . SH ONLY WOMAN BLUS 24

THAT FILLS A WOMAN'S AGE-LESS,
AGE-LONG PAIN - . . . . OWT JUICE JOINT 28
HE SAID A WOMAN'S CRYIN'S . . . . . SP HARD DADDY 11
A GOOD WOMAN'S CRYIN' . . . . SP MISERY 11
ON THE MONEY FROM A WHITE WOMAN'S
KITCHEN? . . . . SP RUBY BROWN 14

WOMB 2
FROM ITS MOTHER'S WOMB - . . . . . FW EARTH SONG 10
OR THE WOMB OF MISSISSIPPI? . . . . AYM HORN OF PLENTY 56

WOMEN 17
AND WOMEN AND SUNDAY . . . . FC BRASS SPITOONS 27
CALL IN A GANG O' WOMEN . . . . . . NM BIG-TIMER POEM 65
MY WOMEN TAKEN AS THE BODY-TOYS . . ANS A NEW SONG 14
THAT WOMEN HE HAS LEFT . . . . . . FW OLD SAILOR 18
WOMEN OF THE STREETS STOP BY FOR
SUPS . . . . OWT JUICE JOINT 7
LET THOSE WOMEN WITH THEIR LIPS TOO
RED . . . . OWT JUICE JOINT 21
AND WOMEN, TOO, WHOM ANYONE MAY MEET OWT JUICE JOINT 35
JOSTLE OF WOMEN WHO SHOP . . . . . OWT MAN INTO MEN 4
JOSTLE OF WOMEN WHO WORK . . . . . OWT MAN INTO MEN 5
I WANT A DOZEN PRETTY WOMEN . . . . SP AS BEFITS A MAN 3
I WANT THE WOMEN TO HOLLER: . . . . SP AS BEFITS A MAN 15
WITH DICE AND WOMEN . . . . SP BEALE STREET 3
LAWD, THESE THINGS WE WOMEN . . . . SP EARLY EVENING 21
HAD MORE WOMEN . . . . SP FIRE 19
BRINGING MEN AND DREAMS, WOMEN AND
DREAMS. . . . . SP FREEDOM'S PLOW 36
OH, MEN TREATS WOMEN . . . . SP LOVER'S RETURN 9
AND WOMEN? . . . . SP YOUNG SAILOR 12

WOMENS 2
AIN'T EVEN GONNA DREAM 'BOUT THE
WOMENS I HAD. . . . . SH PAY DAY 18
ALL THE WOMENS IN TOWN . . . . . . SP SYLVESTER'S BED 3

WOMEN'S 1
WOMEN'S ABOMINATIONS! JUST LIKE A
CURSE! . . . . SH PAY DAY 19

WON 5
WHEN A MAN'S WON A FIGHT IN A BIG
MAN'S TOWN - . . . . SH DEATH IN HARLEM 55
TO BE WON OVER THERE. . . . . . . JC HOW ABOUT DIXIE 22
OUR BATTLE YET IS FAR FROM WON . . JC JIM CROW'S LAST 30
IF THE FIGHT IS NOT YET WON. . . . SP FREEDOM'S PLOW 163
ONE SIDE WON. . . . . PL MOTHER IN WAR 13

WONDER 32
TWO THINGS ARE FULL OF WONDER. . . OLD TWO THINGS 5
NO WONDER WE FIND THEM SUCH
MARVELLOUS THINGS! . . . . DK FAIRIES 5
WONDER WHAT DE BLUES'LL BRING? . . DK NIGHT AND MORN 6
I WONDER HOW IT FEELS . . . . SH ASPIRATION 1
I WONDER IF WHITE FOLKS EVER FEEL
BAD. . . . . SH DAYBREAK 12
OH, FIELDS OF WONDER . . . . FW BIRTH 1
I USED TO WONDER . . . . FW BORDER LINE 1
I USED TO WONDER . . . . FW BORDER LINE 5
NOW PEOPLE WONDER . . . . FW HEART 17
WITHOUT WONDER . . . . FW SLEEP 7
I WONDER IF . . . . OWT TOO BLUE 10
THE WONDER. . . . . SP AFRICA 10
IT'S A WONDER YOU DON'T FALL DOWN. SP BLD LANDLORD 8
I WONDER WHAT MAKES . . . . SP BLD OF THE MAN 25
I WONDER WHERE I'M GONNA DIE. . . . SP CROSS 11
I WONDER IS THERE NOWHERE A . . . . SP EARLY EVENING 23
THE WONDER SPREADS . . . . SP IN TIME SILVER 7
WONDER . . . . SP JULIET 1
LOVE IS A WILD WONDER . . . . SP LOVE 1
WONDER BAR . . . . SP NEON SIGNS 1
AND WONDER WHAT YOU GOT LEFT? . . . SP REVERIE HARLEM 4
BUT I WONDER WHERE . . . . SP SUNDAY BY COMB 3
I WONDER IF IT'S THAT SIMPLE? . . . SP THEME FOR ENG B 6
JOE SAID I WONDER HOW IT WOULD FEEL SP WEST TEXAS 7
AND THEY WONDER WHERE I BE . . . . AYM BIRD IN ORBIT 55
AND I WONDER WHERE THEY BE. . . . . AYM BIRD IN ORBIT 56
ON LPS THAT WONDER . . . . AYM BLUES IN STEREO 26
AND WONDER . . . . PL HARLEM 20
AND WONDER WHY . . . . PL LONG VIEW NEGRO 10
I WONDER WHY RED CLAY'S SO RED . . PL VARI-COLORED 9
I WONDER WHY IT'S YES TO ME. . . . PL VARI-COLORED 11
I WONDER WHY THE SKY'S SO BLUE . . PL VARI-COLORED 13

WONDERED 2
BUT PIERROT WONDERED WHY. . . . . . WB PIERROT 6
THEY WONDERED WAS I SENSITIVE . . . AYM HORN OF PLENTY 49

WONDERFUL 5
WITH NO SENSE, JUST WONDERFUL FEET. SP DANCER 21
A WONDERFUL TIME - THE WAR: . . . . SP GREEN MEMORY 1
BROWN AND WONDERFUL WITH LONGING . SP INTERNE AT PROV 12
WONDERFUL! . . . . SP PROJECTION 23
SWEET AND WONDERFUL TO SAY. . . . . PL WORDS LIKE FREE 2

WONDERING 4
WONDERING ABOUT FUR COATS . . . . . OWT MAN INTO MEN 9
WONDERING . . . . SP GOOD MORNING 18
BASIC AND WONDERING . . . . SP MYSTERY 15
WONDERING HOW THINGS GOT THIS WAY PL DINNER GUEST ME 10

WONDROUS 1
TO WHERE THE SPRING IS WONDROUS RARE SP WATER-FRONT STR 3

WON'T 23
WON'T BE NOBODY'S BRIDE . . . . . . FC A RUINED GAL 4
WON'T MEET NOBODY . . . . FC A RUINED GAL 9
JUDGE, WON'T LET ME BE. . . . . . . FC BLD OF GIN MARY 12
WON'T BE SO BAD IN JAIL . . . . . . FC BLD OF GIN MARY 19
WON'T BE NOTHIN' LEFT . . . . FC SATURDAY NIGHT 15
CAN'T SEE! AND DON'T KNOW! AND WON'T
EVER CARE! . . . . NM COLORED SL POEM 53
HE WON'T MATTER AT ALL. . . . . . . ANS CHANT TOM MOONY 29
AND I WON'T NEED NO FURNITURE LIVING
ALONE - . . . . SH PAY DAY 15
WON'T YOU LEND A HAND? . . . . . . JC BIG BUDDY 8
WE WON'T DIE. . . . . JC GOOD MORN STLIN 15
AND YOU WON'T BE . . . . JC GOOD MORN STLIN 41
LIKE AS NOT YOU WON'T. . . . . . . SP COULD BE 12
KEEP THINKIN' I WON'T BE LONELY . . SP HOPE 3
IN DIXIE, OFTEN THEY WON'T CALL
NEGROES MISTER. . . . . SP IN EXPLANATION 7
THE MISTERS WON'T CALL LOTS OF OTHER
FOLKS MISTER. . . . . SP IN EXPLANATION 11
THE COUNTY WON'T PAY ME . . . . . . SP MADAM CHARTY CH 17
SO WHEN I'M DEAD THEY WON'T NEED . SP MIDWINTER BLUES 23
THE ONE TO STOP 'EM WON'T BE ME. . SP RELIEF 15
WON'T BOTHER ME. . . . . SP REQUEST 6
YOU WON'T GET A GODDAMN THING! . . SP SAME IN BLUES 11
WON'T COVER IT ALL - . . . . SP WHAT? 4
AND THE WIND WON'T WAIT FOR MIDNIGHT PL CULTURAL EXCHNG 6
BUT WON'T LET ME . . . . PL PRIME 7

WOOD 5
I WOULD MAKE A FIRE BUT THERE AIN'T
NO WOOD. . . . . SH SUPPER TIME 4
IN THE WOOD. . . . . FW CAROLINA CABIN 5
THE HAND SEEKS TOOLS TO CUT THE
WOOD, ... SP FREEDOM'S PLOW 18
THE SCENT OF PINE WOOD STINGS THE
SOFT NIGHT AIR. . . . . SP MULATTO 18
PINE WOOD SCENT IN THE EVENING AIR. SP MULATTO 40

WOODED 2
ON THE GREAT WOODED WORLD, ... SP FREEDOM'S PLOW 12
THERE WAS A GREAT WOODED LAND, . . SP FREEDOM'S PLOW 140

WOODS 2
AND THE TURPENTINE WOODS. . . . . . SP MULATTO 3
THE MOON OVER THE TURPENTINE WOODS. SP MULATTO 7

WOOF 1
INTO THE WARP AND WOOF OF AMERICA: SP FREEDOM'S PLOW 167

WOOLWORTH 1
I MADE MORTAR FOR THE WOOLWORTH
BUILDING. . . . . SP NEGRO 9

WORD 7
IT'S A LIE! IT'S A LIE! EVERY WORD
THEY SAID. . . . . NM COLORED SL POEM 44
I HAVE THIS WORD TO BRING. . . . . ANS A NEW SONG 4
SOME WORD . . . . FW BIRTH 11
TO HEAR A WORD. . . . . FW SILENCE 5
YOU AIN'T GONNA BE ABLE TO SAY A
WORD . . . . SP BLD LANDLORD 19
BUT THE WORD WAS THERE ALWAYS: . . SP FREEDOM'S PLOW 47
NOT A WORD WRIT ON THE BACK. . . . SP LITTLE OLD LETT 10

WORDS 19
THESE WORDS ARE GENTLY SPOKEN: . . DK ALABAMA EARTH 11
NEW WORDS ARE FORMED. . . . . ANS A NEW SONG 38
WILL LIVE ON WEAVING WORDS TO
SMOTHER THE KIDS WHO DIE, . . . ANS KIDS WHO DIE 24
TAKES YOUR WORDS AWAY. . . . . . . JC THE BITTER RIVR 42
NOW YOUR WORDS NO LONGER HAVE
MEANING - . . . . JC THE BITTER RIVR 65
THE WORDS. . . . . FW SONGS 5
NO WORDS. . . . . FW SONGS 8
BEAT OUT OF BLOOD WITH WORDS
SAD-SUNG . . . . SP AFRO-AMER FRAG 8
WHO OWNS THOSE WORDS? AMERICA! . . SP FREEDOM'S PLOW 175
TO ALL THE ENEMIES OF THESE GREAT
WORDS: . . . . SP FREEDOM'S PLOW 186
THE WAY, IN OTHER WORDS, ... SP HIGH TO LOW 19
LIARS USE THOSE WORDS. . . . . . . SP IN EXPLANATION 39
HEAR THOSE WORDS AND SHOUT THEM BACK SP IN EXPLANATION 41
WITH THE LITTLE WORDS YOU SAY TO ME. SP TO ARTINA 5
HIS WORDS JUMP DOWN . . . . PL CORNER MEETING 6
SWEET WORDS THAT TAKE . . . . PL SWEET WORDS RAC 1
SWEET WORDS SO BRAVE . . . . PL SWEET WORDS RAC 9
THERE ARE WORDS LIKE FREEDOM . . . PL WORDS LIKE FREE 1
THERE ARE WORDS LIKE LIBERTY . . . PL WORDS LIKE FREE 5

WORE 4

AND THE WAN NIGHT WORE AWAY.	WP CABARET	4
DE SHOES WORE OFF MY FEET.	SH OUT OF WORK	2
DE SHOES WORE OFF MY FEET.	SH OUT OF WORK	4
JOE LOUIS WORE.	SP TO BE SOMEBODY	16

WORK 41

I WORK ALL DAY.	WP PIERROT	1
I WORK ALL DAY.	WB PIERROT	4
NO SCHOOLS. NO WORK -	NM BLACK CLWN POEM	39
WORK. PRAY. AND FIGHT.	NM BLACK CLWN POEM	64
TALKIN' 'BOUT "WE'LL WORK FOR 50¢ A DAY. IF WE CAN'T GET NO MO'."	NM BROKE	7
AND ONE OLD FUNNY BOY SAID. "I'LL WORK AT ANY PRICE	NM BROKE	8
LAST JOB I HAD. WENT TO WORK AT FIVE IN DE MORNIN'. OR LITTLE MO'	NM BROKE	12
SO I WENT DOWN TOWN TO A HOTEL WHERE I USED TO WORK AT NIGHT.	NM BROKE	44
BLACK BOYS COULDN'T WORK THEN ANYWHERE LIKE THEY CAN	NM COLORED SL POEM	19
MA LORD KNOWED WHAT IT WAS TO WORK.	DK MA LORD	6
NOW MY WORK IS DONE.	ANS BLDS OF LENIN	16
OF WORK THE MEN! OF TAKE THE PAY!	ANS LET AMERICA BE	29
DE LADY I WORK FOR	SH PRESENT	1
"WORK. EDUCATION. PATIENCE	JC THE BITTER RIVR	43
WORK TO SALT	FW LITTLE SONG	7
A NIGGER COMES HOME FROM WORK:	OWT MAN INTO MEN	1
JOSTLE OF WOMEN WHO WORK	OWT MAN INTO MEN	5
A NEGRO COMES HOME FROM WORK:	OWT MAN INTO MEN	8
A MAN COMES HOME FROM WORK:	OWT MAN INTO MEN	15
MAKES ME WORK ALL DAY	SP BLUE BAYOU	8
AND I WORK TOO HARD	SP BLUE BAYOU	9
DOWNTOWN TO WORK TODAY.	SP BLUE MONDAY	2
TO WORK AT EIGHT.	SP CONSIDER ME	46
QUIT SCHOOL TO WORK -	SP DEFERRED	17
WORK WITH ME AND NOT AGAINST ME. SAY.	SP DEFERRED	37
"LATE TO WORK AGAIN."	SP FIRED	4
TO WORK -	SP GONE BOY	7
AND GO TO WORK DOWN-	SP KID SLEEPY	12
DAY'S WORK. TOO!	SP MADAM'S PAST HI	24
WORK?	SP NECESSITY	1
I DON'T HAVE TO WORK.	SP NECESSITY	2
HAVE TO WORK AFTER ALL.	SP NECESSITY	12
WHEN HIS WORK IS DONE	SP NEIGHBOR	5
FOLKS WORK HARD	SP NEW YORKERS	7
AND THE WORK IS DONE	SP SHARE-CROPPERS	6
BEATEN AND MISTREATED FOR THE WORK THAT I GAVE -	SP THE NEGRO MOTHE	14
BUT I HAD TO KEEP ON TILL MY WORK WAS DONE:	SP THE NEGRO MOTHE	28
I LIKE TO WORK. READ. LEARN. AND UNDERSTAND LIFE.	SP THEME FOR ENG B	22
WHITE SHARECROPPERS WORK THE BLACK PLANTATIONS.	PL CULTURAL EXCHNG	49
YOU CAN'T WORK HERE!	PL GO SLOW	8
FOR HONEST WORK	PL MILITANT	8

WORKED 5

YOU'VE WORKED ALL DAY.	OWT NEGRO SERVANT	10
I WORKED FOR A WOMAN.	SP MADAM HER MADAM	1
HE WORKED ALL THE TIME.	SP MADAM MIGHT-HAV	9
WHEN SHE WORKED IN THEIR KITCHENS.	SP RUBY BROWN	27
I AM THE WOMAN WHO WORKED IN THE FIELD	SP THE NEGRO MOTHE	11

WORKER 13

WORKER AND CLOWN AM I	NM BLACK CLWN POEM	49
WILLING WORKER? UN-UH! YES! WHAT'S THAT YOU SAY?	NM BROKE	33
WORKER: THE FIRST OF MAY:	ANS CHANT MAY DAY	3
WORKER: WORKERS:	ANS CHANT MAY DAY	14
WORKER: ALL WORKERS:	ANS CHANT MAY DAY	19
WORKER: WHEN THE SAP OF YOUR OWN STRENGTH RISES	ANS CHANT MAY DAY	25
WORKER: PROLETARIANS OF ALL THE WORLD:	ANS CHANT MAY DAY	31
I AM THE WORKER SOLD TO THE MACHINE.	ANS LET AMERICA BE	32
THE POOREST WORKER BARTERED THROUGH THE YEARS.	ANS LET AMERICA BE	38
I AM THE BLACK WORKER.	ANS OPEN LETTER	12
WHITE WORKER.	ANS OPEN LETTER	65
I. A WORKER. LETTING MY LABOR PILE	ANS SONG OF SPAIN	43
I'VE BEEN A WORKER:	SP NEGRO	7

WORKERS 25

ON GUARD WITH THE WORKERS FOREVER -	ANS BLDS OF LENIN	27
WORKERS:	ANS CHANT MAY DAY	7
50-VOICES: FOREVER FOR THE WORKERS!	ANS CHANT MAY DAY	13
THE WORKERS SPEAK THE NAME:	ANS CHANT TOM MOONY	13
WORKER: WORKERS:	ANS CHANT MAY DAY	14
WORKER: ALL WORKERS:	ANS CHANT MAY DAY	19
10-VOICES: WHITE WORKERS.	ANS CHANT MAY DAY	20
10-OTHERS: BLACK WORKERS.	ANS CHANT MAY DAY	21
10-OTHERS: YELLOW WORKERS.	ANS CHANT MAY DAY	22
10-OTHERS: WORKERS IN THE ISLANDS OF THE SEA -	ANS CHANT MAY DAY	23
THE WORKERS.	ANS CHANT TOM MOONY	25
ORGANIZING WORKERS.	ANS KIDS WHO DIE	11
WHITE WORKERS OF THE SOUTH	ANS OPEN LETTER	1
TOBACCO WORKERS.	ANS OPEN LETTER	9
ALL WORKERS.	ANS OPEN LETTER	33
BECAUSE. O POOR WHITE WORKERS.	ANS OPEN LETTER	45
WORKERS MADE THOSE BOMBS FOR A FACIST SPAIN!	ANS SONG OF SPAIN	46
WORKERS. MAKE NO BOMBS AGAIN!	ANS SONG OF SPAIN	54
WORKERS. MINE NO GOLD AGAIN!	ANS SONG OF SPAIN	55
WORKERS. LIFT NO HAND AGAIN	ANS SONG OF SPAIN	56
WORKERS. SEE YOURSELVES AS SPAIN!	ANS SONG OF SPAIN	58
WORKERS. KNOW THAT WE TOO CAN CRY.	ANS SONG OF SPAIN	59
WORKERS. MAKE NO BOMBS AGAIN	ANS SONG OF SPAIN	63
BLACK WORKERS WITH WHITE WORKERS -	JC TO CAPTAIN MULZ	37
BLACK WORKERS WITH WHITE WORKERS -	JC TO CAPTAIN MULZ	37

WORKERS' 2

LIFE FOREVER THROUGH THE WORKERS' POWER -	ANS CHANT TOM MOONY	44
A WORKERS' WORLD	ANS SONG OF SPAIN	82

WORKER'S 1

THE WORKER'S WORLD!	ANS A NEW SONG	51

WORKING 6

THAT'S DE WORKING CLASS!	ANS SISTER JOHNSON	12
AND SEE WHERE SIMPLE WORKING FOLKS LIKE ME	JC GOOD MORN STLIN	32
WORKING IN THE HOT SUN.	SP AUNTSUE'S STORI	7
SOMETIMES WORKING LATE.	SP CONSIDER ME	19
BLACK BROWN YELLOW BENT DOWN WORKING	SP IN EXPLANATION	52
THE TV'S STILL NOT WORKING.	AYM SHOW FARE PLESE	24

WORKIN' 6

I'S ALWAYS BEEN A WORKIN' GIRL.	FC BLACK GAL	1
I'M A HARD WORKIN' MAN	FC WORKIN' MAN	13
ALL THESE YEARS YOU SAY YOU BEEN WORKIN' HERE?	NM BROKE	68
BEEN WORKIN' ON DE LEVEE.	SH MISSISSIPPI LEV	1
WORKIN' LIKE A TUCK-TAIL DOG.	SH MISSISSIPPI LEV	2
WORKIN' ON DE LEVEE	SH MISSISSIPPI LEV	3

WORKMAN 1

TO BE READ BY A WORKMAN WITH. FOR BACKGROUND. THE RHYTHMIC	ANS CHANT MAY DAY	1

WORKS 4

I WORKS ALL DAY	FC WORKIN' MAN	1
HE WORKS DOWNTOWN FOR TWELVE A WEEK.	SP BUDDY	4
WHO WORKS. TOO -	SP CONSIDER ME	28
WORKS AT THE FOUNDRY.	SP MIGRANT	4

WORLD 82

FOR PIERROT SAW A WORLD OF GIRLS.	WB PIERROT	17
THE DUMB CLOWN OF THE WORLD.	WB THE JESTER	16
MEANS HE'S GONNA LEAVE THIS WORLD.	FC GAL'S CRY DYING	8
MEANS HE'S GONNA LEAVE THIS WORLD.	FC GAL'S CRY DYING	10
I AM THE FOOL OF THE WHOLE WORLD.	NM BLACK CLWN POEM	8
BLACK - IN A WHITE WORLD	NM BLACK CLWN POEM	36
ALL THE WORLD ROUND -	NM BLACK CLWN POEM	56
CRY TO THE WORLD	NM BLACK CLWN POEM	75
WITH HIS FACE FULL OF LIGHT AND FAITH. CONFIDENT THAT A NEW WORLD HAS	NM COLORED SL MOOD	9
TO ALL THE WORLD THERE GOES	DK ALABAMA EARTH	7
OF THE WORLD.	DK DREAM KEEPER	8
BUT THIS WORLD IS WEARY	DK PO' BOY BLUES	11
HALF A WORLD AWAY FROM HOME.	DK SAILOR	2
WORLD. TURN PALE!	SL SCOTTSBORO	2
WORLD. TURN PALE!	SL SCOTTSBORO	29
MY YOUNG MEN WITHOUT A VOICE IN THE WORLD.	ANS A NEW SONG	13
AND WHITE WORLD	ANS A NEW SONG	49
THE WORKER'S WORLD!	ANS A NEW SONG	51
THE WORLD IS OUR ROOM!	ANS BLDS OF LENIN	28
50-VOICES: REACHING ALL THE WORLD.	ANS CHANT MAY DAY	18
UNTIL THE WHOLE WORLD FALLS INTO THE HANDS OF	ANS CHANT TOM MOONY	24
WORKER: PROLETARIANS OF ALL THE WORLD:	ANS CHANT MAY DAY	31
AND ALL OVER THE WORLD -	ANS CHANT TOM MOONY	42
IN THAT OLD WORLD WHILE STILL A SERF OF KINGS.	ANS LET AMERICA BE	40
UNTIL THE FORCES OF THE WORLD	ANS OPEN LETTER	63
I MUST DRIVE THE BOMBERS OUT OF THE WORLD!	ANS SONG OF SPAIN	80
I MUST TAKE THE WORLD FOR MY OWN AGAIN -	ANS SONG OF SPAIN	81
A WORKERS' WORLD	ANS SONG OF SPAIN	82
POOR WORLD.	ANS UNION	4
I WANT THE WORLD TO KNOW.	SH ANNOUNCEMENT	14
IN THIS WORLD BEFORE	SH ASPIRATION	7
WAS PLAYIN JAZZ FOR A MIDNIGHT WORLD.	SH DEATH IN HARLEM	11
SAYS TO THE WORLD.	SH DEATH IN HARLEM	47

WHAT KIND OF A WORLD JC BLACK MAN SPEAK 23
A FREE WORLD TOMORROW. JC BLACK MAN SPEAK 26
YOU'RE HALF A WORLD AWAY OR MORE JC GOOD MORN STLIN 17
ALL OVER THE WORLD, WHO CARE. JC GOOD MORN STLIN 45
AND ALL THE WATERS OF THE WORLD. JC TO CAPTAIN MULZ 4
THAT GUIDE US TOWARD THE HARBOR OF THE NEW WORLD JC TO CAPTAIN MULZ 54
THE WORLD WHERE EVERY UGLY PAST MISTAKE JC TO CAPTAIN MULZ 56
THE WORLD IS GLOOMY. FW CAROLINA CABIN 13
TO WANDER THROUGH THIS LIVING WORLD FW REMEMBRANCE 1
IN THIS WIDE WIDE WORLD - OWT HONEY BABE 14
SENT TO BRING THE WHOLE WORLD JOY. LHR BLD MARY'S SON 10
IN THIS WORLD FOR ME. SP BAD LUCK CARD 6
THAT SPLITS THE WORLD IN TWO SP CONSIDER ME 37
THIS WORLD I'LL LEAVE BEHIND SP DEFERRED 40
WHEN A MAN STARTS OUT TO BUILD A WORLD. SP FREEDOM'S PLOW 4
HIS EYES LOOK OUT ON THE WORLD. SP FREEDOM'S PLOW 11
ON THE GREAT WOODED WORLD. SP FREEDOM'S PLOW 12
ON THE RICH SOIL OF THE WORLD. SP FREEDOM'S PLOW 13
ON THE RIVERS OF THE WORLD. SP FREEDOM'S PLOW 14
NOT MY WORLD ALONE. SP FREEDOM'S PLOW 25
BUT YOUR WORLD AND MY WORLD. SP FREEDOM'S PLOW 26
BUT YOUR WORLD AND MY WORLD. SP FREEDOM'S PLOW 26
TO A NEW WORLD, AMERICA! SP FREEDOM'S PLOW 34
SHIPPED THE WIDE WORLD OVER: SP FREEDOM'S PLOW 81
FOR ALL AMERICA, FOR ALL THE WORLD. SP FREEDOM'S PLOW 197
ALL OVER THE WORLD SP IN EXPLANATION 2
SO ALL OVER THE WORLD TODAY SP IN EXPLANATION 18
EARNING RICHES FOR THE WHOLE WORLD SP IN EXPLANATION 53
NOTHIN' IN THIS WORLD SP LITTLE GRN TREE 3
I'VE KNOWN RIVERS ANCIENT AS THE WORLD AND OLDER THAN THE SP NEGRO SPEAKS OF 2
THE WHOLE WORLD SEE SP PARADE 31
OWNS THE WORLD. SP PORTER 10
FOR THE WORLD TO SEE SP SILHOUETTE 8
HAVING PREVIOUSLY POINTED OUT THE SINS OF THIS WORLD: SP SUNDAY MORNING 1
OF THIS WORLD - SP SUNDAY MORNING 12
ALL YOU DARK CHILDREN IN THE WORLD OUT THERE. SP THE NEGRO MOTHE 35
"AIN'T GOT NOBODY IN ALL THIS WORLD, SP THE WEARY BLUES 19
I'M ALL ALONE IN THIS WORLD, SHE SAID. SP 50 - 50 1
OF THE NOW KNOWN WORLD: AYM ASK YOUR MAMA 4
OF THE NOW KNOWN WORLD AYM IS IT TRUE? 4
BUT THE WORLD IS BIG. PL BACKLASH BLUES 19
THE WORLD IS BIG AND ROUND, PL BACKLASH BLUES 20
GREAT BIG WORLD, MISTER BACKLASH, PL BACKLASH BLUES 21
TO ALL THE WORLD CRIED, PL FREDRK DOUGLASS 14
AND LOOK OUT ON THE WORLD PL HARLEM 19
A WORLD TO GAIN. PL QUESTION ANSWER 7
A WORLD TO GAIN. PL QUESTION ANSWER 10
THERE'S A WORLD TO GAIN. PL QUESTION ANSWER 13
TO SWEEP THE WORLD PL WAR 10

WORLDLY 2
WHERE NO WORLDLY DUTY CALLS - FW CONVENT 5
AND SEEKS AN OUT IN OTHER WORLDLY DREAMS. PL JUNIOR ADDICT 3

WORLD'S 4
THE WORLD'S BEEN MADE SAFE FOR DEMOCRACY NM COLORED SL POEM 29
WHOLE WIDE WORLD'S TURNED COLD. DK PO' BOY BLUES 6
YES, DANGEROUS ARE THE WIDE WORLD'S WATERS STILL. JC TO CAPTAIN MULZ 29
FOR THE WHITE WORLD'S GUNBOATS PL LAST PRINCE 6

WORMS 2
WHEN DE WORMS GIT THROUGH FC SATURDAY NIGHT 16
TILL THE LAST WORMS COME SP DRUM 4

WORN 2
WORN SO. SH BLD PAWNBROKER 12
THOUGH WORN IN GLORY ON MY HEAD. PL CROWNS GARLANDS 12

WORN-OUT 1
AND WORN-OUT ALTARS STAND ANS UNION 9

WORRIES 1
FACT IS YOU WORRIES ME. FC BLD OF GIN MARY 14

WORRY 2
SO DON'T WORRY 'BOUT ME. NM BIG-TIMER POEM 53
DON'T WORRY 'BOUT ME! SP MADAM'S PAST HI 19

WORRYIN' 1
SO WHAT'S THE USE O' WORRYIN' NM BIG-TIMER POEM 69

WORSE 1
TETHERED BY SOMETHING WORSE THAN PRIDE. PL WHERE WHEN WHCH 10

WORSER 1
WORSER IF I WOULD. SP EARLY EVENING 20

WORSHIPPED 1
THEY WORSHIPPED JOE. SP JOE LOUIS 1

WORST 1
YOU WAS THE BEST - BUT YOU THE WORST. SH PAY DAY 20

WORTH 5
GIMME SIX-BITS' WORTH O' TICKET SH SIX-BITS BLUES 1
I SAY SIX-BITS' WORTH O' TICKET SH SIX-BITS BLUES 3
AIN'T WORTH A LITTLE BIT. SP SOUTHERN MAMMY 10
AIN'T WORTH A LITTLE BIT. SP SOUTHERN MAMMY 12
THE MONEY THAT THEY'RE WORTH AYM GOSPEL CHA-CHA 12

WORTHY 1
A. PHILIP RANDOLPH THE HIGH GRAND WORTHY. PL CULTURAL EXCHNG 45

WOULD 75
I WOULD BE SIMPLE AGAIN. WB DISILLUSION 1
WOULD PALE IN THE LIGHT WB POEM 19
WOULD WB SONGS DARK VIRG 1
WOULD WB SONGS DARK VIRG 7
WOULD WB SONGS DARK VIRG 15
YOU WOULD LAUGH! WB THE JESTER 7
YOU WOULD WEEP! WB THE JESTER 9
WOULD GOD HIS LIPS WERE SWEET! WB TO LITTLE LOVER 12
IT SHO WOULD BE SAD. FC MINNIE SINGS 14
WOULD BE A SURPRISE. FC NEW CABARET GRL 4
WOULD BE A SURPRISE. FC NEW CABARET GRL 16
SHE WOULD BE ALRIGHT IF SHE WASN'T SO BOW-LEGGED, AND CROSS-EYED. NM BROKE 64
AND THAT OUR DARK BLOOD WOULD WIPE AWAY THE STAIN NM COLORED SL POEM 8
THEY TOLD US AMERICA WOULD KNOW NO BLACK OR WHITE: NM COLORED SL POEM 11
DIDN'T OUR GOVERNMENT TELL US THINGS WOULD BE FINE NM COLORED SL POEM 33
I WOULD LIKEN YOU DK QUIET GIRL 1
I WOULD LIKEN YOU DK QUIET GIRL 4
YOU WOULDN'T KID ME, WOULD YOU? ANS SONG OF SPAIN 30
I SURE WOULD LIKE SH ASPIRATION 3
I WOULD SWIM TO CHINA SH DECLARATION 3
AND YOU NEVER WOULD SEE ME. SH DECLARATION 4
YOU NEVER WOULD SH DECLARATION 6
I WOULD DRIVE SH DECLARATION 13
THAT EXTRA DAY WOULD GET ME DOWN. SH OUT OF WORK 18
AND SEE WHAT IT WOULD DO TO YOU? SH OUT OF WORK 24
I WOULD MAKE A FIRE BUT THERE AIN'T NO WOOD. SH SUPPER TIME 4
IF I JUST HAD A OWL HEAD, OLD OWL HEAD WOULD DO. SH TWILIGHT REVERI 11
I WOULD LIKE TO SEE THOSE FREEDOMS JC HOW ABOUT DIXIE 3
SO IT WOULD SEEM. JC NOTE TO NAZIS 2
OF THOSE WHO WOULD KEEP, OR ONCE MORE MAKE JC TO CAPTAIN MULZ 31
THE EVIL FORCES THAT WOULD DESTROY JC TO CAPTAIN MULZ 52
BUT I WOULD GIVE A DAMN. OWT FUNERAL 9
WHO WOULD BE MY VERY OWN - OWT STRANGER IN TWN 4
ONE BULLET WOULD DO? OWT TOO BLUE 11
IT WOULD PROBABLY TAKE TWO. OWT TOO BLUE 13
I WISH IT WOULD LHR CONSERVATORY 3
I WOULD LIKEN YOU SP ARDELLA 1
I WOULD LIKEN YOU SP ARDELLA 4
IF SHE ONLY WOULD. SP BLD FORTUNE TEL 20
I WOULD TAKE YOUR MONEY, TOO. SP BLD THE GYPSY 23
THEM THOUGHTS WOULD BUST MY HEAD - SP BLUES AT DAWN 4
WORSER IF I WOULD. SP EARLY EVENING 20
WHEN FREEDOM WOULD TRIUMPH. SP FREEDOM'S PLOW 120
"OR IF IT WOULD," THOUGHT SOME. SP FREEDOM'S PLOW 121
WHO DOUBTED THAT THE WAR WOULD END RIGHT. SP FREEDOM'S PLOW 133
THAT THE SLAVES WOULD BE FREE. SP FREEDOM'S PLOW 134
OR THAT THE UNION WOULD STAND. SP FREEDOM'S PLOW 135
TO THE ENEMY WHO WOULD CONQUER US FROM WITHOUT. SP FREEDOM'S PLOW 178
TO THE ENEMY WHO WOULD DIVIDE SP FREEDOM'S PLOW 180
OR WOULD YOU RATHER. SP KID SLEEPY 18
AND THOUGHT I WOULD JUMP DOWN. SP LIFE IS FINE 15
BUT YOU THOUGHT YOU WOULD. SP MAYBE 4
IF THE BLUES WOULD LET ME. SP MISS BLUES'ES 1
LORD KNOWS I WOULD SMILE. SP MISS BLUES'ES 2
IF THE BLUES WOULD LET ME. SP MISS BLUES'ES 3
I WOULD SMILE, SMILE, SMILE. SP MISS BLUES'ES 4
WOULD YOU? SP RELIEF 16
BUT WHO WOULD MISS ME IF I LEFT? SP REVERIE HARLEM 14
AND WOULD NOT KNOW SP SO LONG 8
AND I, WHO AM BLACK, WOULD LOVE HER SP THE SOUTH 18
WOULD GIVE HER MANY RARE GIFTS SP THE SOUTH 21
JOE SAID I WONDER HOW IT WOULD FEEL SP WEST TEXAS 7
SO WHAT WOULD YOU DO? SP WHAT? 8
WOULD BE TOO TAME - AYM BLUES IN STEREO 6
FOR THE MOON WOULD WHITE HIS WHITENESS AYM BLUES IN STEREO 17
WOULD HARDLY WRITE IT IN THE SCRIPT - AYM IS IT TRUE? 50
WOULD I MARRY POCAHONTAS? AYM ODE TO DINAH 128

AND WHY WOULD MAI (NOT MAY) . . . . AYM SHADES OF PIG 17
IT WOULD BE TOO BAD IF JESUS . . . PL BIBLE BELT 1
WOULD REDDEN WITH THEIR BLOOD . . . PL BIRMINGHAM SUND 13
WOULD HARDLY DESIRE . . . . PL BOMBINGS DIXIE 6
WOULD IT RUB OFF? . . . . PL CULTURAL EXCHNG 34
WHO WOULD BE FREE . . . . PL FREDRK DOUGLASS 18
I KNEW THAT THIS WOULD COME." . . . PL NORTHERN LIBERL 5
YOU WOULD KNOW WHY. . . . . PL WORDS LIKE FREE 8

WOULDN'T 15
WOULDN'T NO GOOD FELLOW . . . . . . WB TO MIDNIGHT NAN 3
WOULDN'T NO GOOD FELLOW . . . . . . WB TO MIDNIGHT NAN 19
I WOULDN'T GO TO HEABEN IF I COULD. FC BAD MAN 18
I WOULDN'T BE FIGHTIN'. . . . . . FC PRIZE FIGHTER 3
I WOULDN'T PAY HER A PENNY NOW IF I WAS TO CROAK - . . . . NM BROKE 25
YOU WOULDN'T KID ME, WOULD YOU? . . ANS SONG OF SPAIN 30
YOU WOULDN'T NEED TO ASK ME: . . . SH EVENIN' BLUES 23
I WOULDN'T TAKE YOU BACK IF YOU COME ON YOUR KNEES. . . . . SH SUNDAY 9
AND SHE WOULDN'T . . . . SP BLD FORTUNE TEL 7
I WOULDN'T GET UP NO MORE - . . . . SP BLUES AT DAWN 9
I WOULDN'T PLAY NO MORE. . . . . . SP MADAM NUMBER WR 4
WOULDN'T YOU? . . . . SP MADAM NUMBER WR 16
I WOULDN'T HAVE DROPPED IT, ... SP MIDNIGHT RAFFLE 11
HE WOULDN'T WRITE SO . . . . SP MIGRANT 39
I WOULDN'T BE OUT THE BARREL YET. SP RELIEF 9

WOUND 1
AND WOUND HER SORE. . . . . FW FAITHFUL ONE 6

WOVEN 1
WOVEN FROM THE BEGINNING . . . . . SP FREEDOM'S PLOW 166

WPA 7
SO I WENT TO DE WPA. . . . . SH OUT OF WORK 8
SO I WENT TO DE WPA. . . . . SH OUT OF WORK 10
WPA MAN TOLD ME: . . . . SH OUT OF WORK 11
LAWD! I GOT TO FIND ME A WOMAN FOR THE WPA - . . . . SH SUPPER TIME 13
THE WPA . . . . SP MADAM'S PAST HI 15
YOU WPA FOLKS TAKE CARE OF YOURSELF - . . . . SP MADAM'S PAST HI 21
IT TOOK ME TWO YEARS TO GET ON WPA. SP RELIEF 7

WRAP 5
MIGHT WRAP ABOUT THY BODY. . . . . WB SONGS DARK VIRG 11
THAT I MAY WRAP THEM . . . . DK DREAM KEEPER 5
AND THE PRISON WALLS WRAP YOU ABOUT. ANS CHANT TOM MOONY 8
AND WRAP AROUND YOU. . . . . SP JUKE BOX LOVE 2
AND WRAP A STRING AROUND ITS FINGER SP SUMMER EVENING 26

WRAPPED 1
WRAPPED IN CHECKS AND WEALTHY. . . SP GRADUATION 9

WRAPS 1
THE MUSIC WRAPS . . . . SP COLLEGE FORMAL 9

WREATH 2
IS CROWNED WITH NO FALSE PATRIOTIC WREATH. . . . . ANS LET AMERICA BE 12
THAT WREATH OF FLOWERS? . . . . . . SP NIGHT FUNERAL 12

WRIGHT 1
AND WHY DID RICHARD WRIGHT . . . . AYM HORN OF PLENTY 52

WRIT 2
NO SHAME IS WRIT ACROSS ITS FACE - SL TOWN OF SCOTTSB 2
NOT A WORD WRIT ON THE BACK. . . . SP LITTLE OLD LETT 10

WRITE 16
WHO MAKE SURVEYS AND WRITE BOOKS. ANS KIDS WHO DIE 23
WHAT DO YOU MEAN, WHY I DIDN'T WRITE? . . . . SH LETTER 3
NOR WRITE THEM DOWN ON PAPER. . . . SP FREEDOM'S PLOW 146
BUT HE HATED TO WRITE . . . . SP MADAM CENSUS 7
HE WOULDN'T WRITE SO . . . . SP MIGRANT 39
AND WRITE ABOUT ME - . . . . SP NOTE COMM THEAT 14
I COULDN'T READ THEN. I COULDN'T WRITE. . . . . SP THE NEGRO MOTHE 23
GO HOME AND WRITE . . . . SP THEME FOR ENG B 2
UP TO MY ROOM, SIT DOWN, AND WRITE THIS PAGE: . . . . SP THEME FOR ENG B 15
SO WILL MY PAGE BE COLORED THAT I WRITE? . . . . SP THEME FOR ENG B 27
AND I CANNOT WRITE COMMERCIALS - . AYM IS IT TRUE? 31
WOULD HARDLY WRITE IT IN THE SCRIPT - . . . . AYM IS IT TRUE? 50
I'M GONNA WRITE ME SOME MUSIC ABOUT PL DAYBREAK IN ALA 2
AND WRITE ABOUT DAYBREAK . . . . . PL DAYBREAK IN ALA 22
TO WRITE IT . . . . PL OFFICIAL NOTICE 5
WRITE OBITUARIES . . . . PL SPECIAL BULLTIN 5

WRITERS 1
NUMBER WRITERS. . . . . FC LAUGHERS 16

WRITTEN 3
WHAT'S WRITTEN DOWN . . . . SP CHILDREN'S RYME 20
I'VE WRITTEN, CALLED REPEATEDLY. . AYM ASK YOUR MAMA 7
LIES WRITTEN DOWN . . . . PL CHILDREN'S RYME 11

WRONG 14
AND NOT THIS LAND WHERE JOY IS WRONG. . . . . WB OUR LAND 15
CAUSE I IS LONG GONE WRONG. . . . . FC A RUINED GAL 5
THAT MAN THAT DONE ME WRONG? . . . FC SUICIDE 12
SEEKING THE KNOWLEDGE THAT RIGHTS ALL WRONG - . . . . NM DARK YOUTH USA 17
NEVER DONE NO WRONG. . . . . DK PO' BOY BLUES 8
NEVER DONE NO WRONG. . . . . DK PO' BOY BLUES 10
TILL YOU DON'T KNOW RIGHT FROM WRONG. . . . . SH HEY-HEY BLUES 12
EVEN THOUGH YOU DO ME WRONG. . . . SH IN TROUBLED KEY 8
THOUGH YOU DO ME WRONG - . . . . . SH IN TROUBLED KEY 10
TO SING ABOUT THE MEN WHO'VE DONE THEM WRONG - . . . . OWT JUICE JOINT 24
GONE AND DONE ME WRONG . . . . . . OWT LINCOLN THEATRE 12
DONE ME WRONG. . . . . SP MISERY 8
HARLEM LAUGHING IN ALL THE WRONG PLACES . . . . SP MOVIES 2
IT'S WRONG. . . . . PL MILITANT 7

WRONGEST 1
SHE WAS DE WRONGEST THING, JUDGE. SH BRIEF ENCOUNTER 17

W.E.B 1
METHUSELAH SIGNS PAPERS W.E.B. . . AYM BIRD IN ORBIT 18

Y 3
K - A - Y. . . . . SP MADAM CENSUS 14
EIGHTH AVENUE, SEVENTH, AND I COME TO THE Y. . . . . SP THEME FOR ENG B 13
THE HARLEM BRANCH Y, WHERE I TAKE THE ELEVATOR . . . . SP THEME FOR ENG B 14

YA 1
OOL YA KOO . . . . SP FLATTED FIFTHS 18

YAL 2
YAL, COME ON BACK - I KNOW YOU WANT TO. . . . . SH LETTER 9
YAL, HERE I SET THINKING - A BITTER OLD THOUGHT . . . . SH TWILIGHT REVERI 9

YALLER 5
THEN THEY GOES AN' FINDS A YALLER GAL . . . . FC BLACK GAL 7
I HATES THEM RINNEY YALLER GALS . . FC BLACK GAL 15
THAT LITTLE YALLER GAL . . . . . . FC NEW CABARET GRL 1
THAT CRAZY LITTLE YALLER GAL . . . FC NEW CABARET GRL 13
BE A HIGH YALLER. . . . . FC RED SILK STOCK 10

YARD 1
MISS YARDMAN'S IN HER YARD. . . . . SP SOUTHERN MAMMY 2

YARDBIRD 2
AND CHARLIE YARDBIRD PARKER . . . . AYM BIRD IN ORBIT 30
HELP ME, YARDBIRD! . . . . AYM JAZZTET MUTED 22

YARDMAN'S 1
MISS YARDMAN'S IN HER YARD. . . . . SP SOUTHERN MAMMY 2

YEAH 1
YEAH! . . . . PL CROWNS GARLANDS 18

YEAR 12
IN A YEAR OR TWO. . . . . ANS PARK BENCH 10
YOU GOT TO LIVE HERE A YEAR AND A DAY. . . . . SH OUT OF WORK 12
A YEAR AND A DAY, LAWD. . . . . . . SH OUT OF WORK 13
A YEAR AND A DAY IN THIS . . . . . SH OUT OF WORK 15
I MIGHT STARVE FOR A YEAR BUT . . . SH OUT OF WORK 17
THIS YEAR MAYBE, DO YOU THINK I CAN GRADUATE? . . . . SP DEFERRED 1
A YEAR WHEN I WAS ELEVEN, ... SP DEFERRED 4
BUT MAYBE THIS YEAR I CAN GRADUATE. SP DEFERRED 7
TODAY, THIS YEAR . . . . SP DEMOCRACY 2
YEAR BY YEAR GOES BY . . . . SP SHARE-CROPPERS 11
YEAR BY YEAR GOES BY . . . . SP SHARE-CROPPERS 11
TODAY, THIS YEAR . . . . PL FREEDOM 2

YEARNINGS 1
OF BITTER YEARNINGS LOST . . . . . SP AFRO-AMER FRAG 19

YEARNS 1
SOUL YEARNS. . . . . FW EXITS 7

YEARS 33
WHEN FOR YEARS, I HAD BEEN SEEKING OLD AESTHETE HARLEM 4
THREE HUNDRED YEARS . . . . NM BLACK CLWN POEM 16
AFTER ALL THEM DOLLARS I GIVED HER THESE LAST TWO YEARS. . . . . . . NM BROKE 23
(AIN'T SEEN HER IN SIX YEARS! USED TO GO WITH HER, TOO!) . . . . . NM BROKE 63
ALL THESE YEARS YOU SAY YOU BEEN WORKIN' HERE? . . . . NM BROKE 68

YEARS AGO AT THE NATION'S START . . NM DARK YOUTH USA 12
QUIET FOR A MILLION, MILLION YEARS. DK LINCOLN MONUMNT 5
THE POOREST WORKER BARTERED THROUGH
THE YEARS. . . . . ANS LET AMERICA BE 38
A FEW YEARS AGO. . . . . JC BLD SAM SOLOMON 6
EACH FOURTEEN YEARS OLD WHEN LYNCHED
TOGETHER BENEATH THE . . . . . . JC THE BITTER RIVR 1
THE YEARS BUILD THEIR BARS . . . . FW CIRCLES 5
I'M ALREADY TWO YEARS LATE. . . . . SP DEFERRED 2
EIGHTEEN YEARS AGO. . . . . SP DEFERRED 10
FRANTIC, KICK THEIR DRAFTEE YEARS SP FLATTED FIFTHS 4
SIX OR EIGHT AND TEN YEARS OLDER'N
MYSELF. . . . . SP PREFERENCE 2
IT TOOK ME TWO YEARS TO GET ON WPA. SP RELIEF 7
NUDGE THEIR DRAFTEE YEARS. . . . . SP TAG 4
THREE HUNDRED YEARS AGO IN AFRICA'S
LAND. . . . . SP THE NEGRO MOTHE 8
THREE HUNDRED YEARS IN THE DEEPEST
SOUTH: . . . . SP THE NEGRO MOTHE 17
BUT I KEPT TRUDGING ON THROUGH THE
LONELY YEARS. . . . . SP THE NEGRO MOTHE 26
REMEMBER MY YEARS, HEAVY WITH SORROW
- . . . . SP THE NEGRO MOTHE 37
AND MAKE OF THOSE YEARS A TORCH FOR
TOMORROW. . . . . SP THE NEGRO MOTHE 38
A THOUSAND YEARS OFF: . . . . SP TOMORROW 2
RULED MY MANY YEARS. . . . . SP WIDOW WOMAN 14
RULED MY MANY YEARS - . . . . SP WIDOW WOMAN 16
IS ALWAYS FOUR YEARS . . . . AYM HORN OF PLENTY 90
WAITED TWENTY YEARS . . . . AYM IS IT TRUE? 27
LIVING 20 YEARS IN 10 . . . . AYM ODE TO DINAH 102
100 YEARS NOT FREE. . . . . PL DEATH YORKVILLE 13
TOO MANY YEARS . . . . PL DOWN WHERE I AM 1
TOO MANY YEARS . . . . PL DOWN WHERE I AM 5
TOO MANY YEARS . . . . PL DOWN WHERE I AM 9
MANY YEARS FREE. . . . . PL OCTOBER 16 RAID 16

YEE-EE-E-WHO-000-00-0 1

YEE-EE-E-WHO-000-00-0! . . . . . . SH HEY-HEY BLUES 25

YELL 1

WILL SOME WHITE MAN YELL, GET BACK! SP FREEDOM TRAIN 39

YELLED 2

SOMEBODY YELLED. . . . . OWT BLD MARGE POLIT 35
SOMEBODY YELLED. . . . . OWT BLD MARGE POLIT 40

YELLOW 15

I MET A YELLOW PAPA, ... FC GYPSY MAN 13
MET A YELLOW PAPA, ... FC GYPSY MAN 15
10-OTHERS: YELLOW WORKERS, ... ANS CHANT MAY DAY 22
THROUGH THE RED, WHITE, YELLOW SKINS SP A HOUSE IN TAOS 34
YELLOW MELLOW, ... SP ARGUMENT 2
A YELLOW CURTAIN, ... SP FULFILMENT 13
BLACK BROWN YELLOW BENT DOWN WORKING SP IN EXPLANATION 52
GREAT BIG YELLOW STARS. . . . . . . SP MULATTO 10
A LITTLE YELLOW . . . . SP MULATTO 25
GREAT BIG YELLOW STARS. . . . . . . SP MULATTO 32
TO LITTLE YELLOW BASTARD BOYS. . . SP MULATTO 36
A LITTLE YELLOW . . . . SP MULATTO 44
HOLD A YELLOW GIRL . . . . SP RUBY BROWN 19
BLACK, YELLOW, BEIGE, AND BROWN. . PL BACKLASH BLUES 24
AND BLACK HANDS AND BROWN AND YELLOW
HANDS . . . . PL DAYBREAK IN ALA 16

YEP 1

YEP, YOU DONE TAKEN MY BLUES AND
GONE. . . . . SP NOTE COMM THEAT 7

YES 44

YES? . . . . WB CAT AND SAXOPHN 17
YES, I AM GOOD. . . . . WB PIERROT 24
YES, LAUGHERS . . . LAUGHERS . . .
LAUGHERS - . . . . FC LAUGHERS 30
YES, LORD! . . . . FC MOAN 19
TOGETHER, RECKON I'LL TRY . . . SHO,
I WANTS DE JOB! YES, SIR! . . . NM BROKE 30
WILLING WORKER? UN-UH! YES! WHAT'S
THAT YOU SAY? . . . . NM BROKE 33
YES, INDEEDY, I SHO HAVE MISSED YOU,
TOO! . . . . NM BROKE 67
YOU GOT A GOOD JOB? YES! WELL, I SHO
AM GLAD TO SEE YOU, DEAR! . . . NM BROKE 69
LET'S GET MARRIED RIGHT NOW! YES!
WHAT DO YOU SAY? . . . . NM BROKE 75
YES, UM-HUM! YOU SHO IS SWEET! CAN
YOU PAY FO' DE LICENSE, DEAR? . NM BROKE 78
YES, I WAS A GOOD BOY, ... DK PO' BOY BLUES 9
O, YES, ... ANS LET AMERICA BE 75
YES! . . . . SH DECLARATION 12
YES, WAY . . . . SH DECLARATION 19
DEAR CASSIE: YES, I GOT YOUR LETTER. SH LETTER 1
YES, ... SH PRESENT 8
YES, DANGEROUS ARE THE WIDE WORLD'S
WATERS STILL. . . . . JC TO CAPTAIN MULZ 29
YES, I'LL KNOW . . . . OWT STRANGER IN TWN 17
YES, A NEW DAY'S . . . . SP BLACK MARIA 21
I SAID, YES - BUT ALBERTA . . . . . SP MADAM WRONG VIS 19
UN-HUMM-M! . . . YES! . . . . SP MADAM PHONE BIL 37
YOUR FATHER, YES, HE WAS THE ONE! SP MAMA AND DAUGHT 11
YES, IT'LL BE ME. . . . . SP NOTE COMM THEAT 20
YES, SIR, ... SP PORTER 2
YES, SIR! . . . . SP PORTER 4
YES, SIR! . . . . SP PORTER 5
OF YES, SIRS! . . . . SP PORTER 8
YES, SIR! . . . . SP PORTER 13
YES, M'AM! . . . . SP SOUTHERN MAMMY 17
YES, HE'S DONE BEEN LEFT. . . . . . SP STONY LONESOME 15
YES, THEY ARE YOURS, ... SP SUMMER EVENING 30
YES, SIR! LONG AS LIFE DO LAST! . . SP SYLVESTER'S BED 22
YES, THAT LAST LONG RIDE'S A . . . SP WIDOW WOMAN 3
YES, SIR, I TOLD HER. . . . . AYM ASK YOUR MAMA 12
AND ONE, YES, ONE . . . . AYM GOSPEL CHA-CHA 61
GOT THERE! YES, I MADE IT! . . . . AYM HORN OF PLENTY 36
I SAID, YES, YOUR MAMA. . . . . . . AYM HORN OF PLENTY 98
YES, SUBURBIA . . . . AYM IS IT TRUE? 35
YES, YOU'RE THE ONE . . . . PL BACKLASH BLUES 32
YES, EASIER TO GET DOPE . . . . . . PL JUNIOR ADDICT 30
YES ALMOST FORGOT . . . . PL STOKELY MALCOLM 9
YES. . . . . PL UN-AMERICAN 14
I WONDER WHY IT'S YES TO ME, . . . PL VARI-COLORED 11
BUT YES, SIR, SIR, TO YOU. . . . . PL VARI-COLORED 12

YESTERDAY 14

AND YESTERDAY . . . . FC SPORT 13
YESTERDAY . . . . DK YOUTH 4
IT MUST HAVE BEEN YESTERDAY. . . . SH EVIL MORNING 1
MUST HAVE BEEN YESTERDAY . . . . . SH EVIL MORNING 3
DREAM OF YESTERDAY . . . . FW MOTHERLAND 1
GARNERED FROM YESTERDAY . . . . . . FW WALLS 7
O, I WISH THAT YESTERDAY, ... OWT YESTERDAY TODAY 1
YESTERDAY WAS TODAY! . . . . OWT YESTERDAY TODAY 2
YESTERDAY YOU WAS HERE. . . . . . . OWT YESTERDAY TODAY 3
YESTERDAY I WAS HAPPY. . . . . . . OWT YESTERDAY TODAY 9
IT WAS YESTERDAY MORNING . . . . . SP LITTLE OLD LETT 1
HE WAS YOUNG YESTERDAY. . . . . . . SP MAMA AND DAUGHT 18
NIGHT OF THE DAY BEFORE YESTERDAY SP NIGHT FOUR SONG 3
HER YESTERDAY PAST GRANDPA - . . . PL CULTURAL EXCHNG 17

YESTERDAYS 1

ROSE OF NOTHING BUT YESTERDAYS . . FW CHIPPY 4

YESTERDAY'S 1

TILL YESTERDAY'S . . . . OWT BLUES ON A BOX 2

YET 49

YET AS THE VULGAR DANCERS WHIRLED WB CABARET 3
AND, FAITH, I LOVE HER YET. . . . . WB PIERROT 13
YET THOU HAST . . . . WB POEM 5
YET THOU HAST . . . . WB POEM 11
YET AN ALTAR OF JEWELS. . . . . . . WB POEM 17
YET WHY DO YOU TORTURE ME, ... WB THE WHITE ONES 5
YET IT SEEMS LIKE ALWAYS . . . . . FC BLACK GAL 5
YET I AIN'T NEVER BEEN NO BAD ONE. FC BLACK GAL 13
YET CLINGING TO THE LADDER, ... NM BLACK CLWN POEM 43
AND YET HE PLAYS UPON HIS FLUTE A
WILD FREE TUNE . . . . DK BEGGAR BOY 7
AND YET A VOICE FOREVER . . . . . . DK LINCOLN MONUMNT 7
HUNGRY YET TODAY DESPITE THE DREAM. ANS LET AMERICA BE 35
BEATEN YET TODAY - O, PIONEERS! . . ANS LET AMERICA BE 36
YET I'M THE ONE WHO DREAMT OUR BASIC
DREAM . . . . ANS LET AMERICA BE 39
THAT EVEN YET ITS MIGHTY DARING
SINGS . . . . ANS LET AMERICA BE 42
THE LAND THAT NEVER HAS BEEN YET - ANS LET AMERICA BE 63
AND YET MUST BE - THE LAND WHERE
EVERY MAN IS FREE. . . . . ANS LET AMERICA BE 64
AND YET I SWEAR THIS OATH - . . . . ANS LET AMERICA BE 78
WILL I MAKE THEM AGAIN, AND YET
AGAIN? . . . . ANS SONG OF SPAIN 47
ALTHOUGH RIGHT NOW, EVEN YET TODAY, JC JIM CROW'S LAST 11
OUR BATTLE YET IS FAR FROM WON . . JC JIM CROW'S LAST 30
MANY BLOODS - YET ALL OF ONE BLOOD
STILL: . . . . JC TO CAPTAIN MULZ 48
YET YOU SEEK, ... SP A HOUSE IN TAOS 26
ARE THE DRUMS - AND YET . . . . . . SP AFRO-AMER FRAG 14
YET WARM AND WAVERING . . . . SP BEALE STREET 7
AND SHE AIN'T COME HOME YET. . . . SP BLD THE GYPSY 15
STILL AND YET . . . . SP BUDDY 2
OWNED A DECENT RADIO YET? . . . . . SP DEFERRED 47
IF THE HOUSE IS NOT YET FINISHED, SP FREEDOM'S PLOW 161
IF THE FIGHT IS NOT YET WON, . . . SP FREEDOM'S PLOW 163
YET THERE'RE BARS . . . . SP GOOD MORNING 24
AND AIN'T SEEN CHRIST YET, ... SP MYSTERY 2
YET OLD AS MYSTERY, ... SP MYSTERY 13
YET THEY GOT A SATIN BOX . . . . . SP NIGHT FUNERAL 7
I WOULDN'T BE OUT THE BARREL YET. SP RELIEF 9
YET SHINING LIKE THE SUN WITH LOVE'S
TRUE LIGHT. . . . . SP THE NEGRO MOTHE 6
YET A PART OF ME, AS I AM A PART OF
YOU. . . . . SP THEME FOR ENG B 32
YET YOU NEVER CAN TELL WHEN A . . . SP WIDOW WOMAN 23
LIGHTS AIN'T COME ON YET. . . . . . SP WONDER 2
EVEN RUNG THIS BELL ON SUNDAY, YET AYM ASK YOUR MAMA 8
BY THOSE YET UNINDUCTED . . . . . . AYM BIRD IN ORBIT 12
YET THEY ASKED ME OUT ON MY PATIO AYM HORN OF PLENTY 46

NOT YET ON SAFARI. AYM IS IT TRUE? 11
YET THE HORSE WHOSE BACK IS BROKEN AYM IS IT TRUE? 52
YET NO PRESENTS DOWN THE CHIMNEY. AYM ODE TO DINAH 74
AS YET UNFELT AMONG MAGNOLIA TREES. PL BIRMINGHAM SUND 27
YET LEONTYNE'S UNPACKING. PL CULTURAL EXCHNG 13
YET GHOSTS SO SOLID, GHOSTS SO REAL PL GHOSTS OF 1619 4
(YET LITTLE CAN PL JUNIOR ADDICT 16

YIELD 4
TO MAKE THE COTTON YIELD. SP SHARE-CROPPERS 4
TO MAKE THE COTTON YIELD. SP SHARE-CROPPERS 16
BRINGING THE COTTON AND THE CORN TO YIELD. SP THE NEGRO MOTHE 12
BY THIS BLOODY YIELD. PL OFFICIAL NOTICE 10

YOKE 1
'CAUSE I'M JUST DYIN' TO TAKE ON THAT THERE MARRIAGE YOKE. NM BROKE 77

YOM 1
YOM KIPPUR, NO! SP LIKEWISE 9

YONDER 9
FOLKS, DOWN YONDER AT HOME. NM BIG-TIMER POEM 54
LOOK AT THE STARS YONDER NM BLACK CLWN POEM 73
AND I SHO HAD A PRETTY GAL, TOO, UP YONDER ON SUGAR HILL. NM BROKE 48
AW-OO! YONDER COMES A WOMAN I USED TO KNOW WAY DOWN SOUTH. NM BROKE 62
LOOKY YONDER SP DANCER 15
LOOKY YONDER! SP WONDER 3
WHEN THE ROLL IS CALLED UP YONDER AYM RIDE, RED, RIDE 2
OUT YONDER WHERE PL WITHOUT BENEFIT 5
OUT YONDER YOU'LL LIE: PL WITHOUT BENEFIT 15

YORK 2
IN BUSES MARKED NEW YORK SP GOOD MORNING 12
(I HEAR NEW YORK, TOO.) ME - WHO? SP THEME FOR ENG B 20

YORKVILLE 1
TO THE BULLETS OF YORKVILLE. PL DEATH YORKVILLE 10

YOUNG 38
LIKE YOUNG COURTESANS WB POEME D'AUTOMNE 6
A DRAMATIC RECITATION TO BE DONE IN THE HALF-DARK BY A YOUNG BROWN FELLOW NM COLORED SL MOOD 1
ONCE YOU WERE YOUNG. DK PARISIAN BEGGAR 1
MY YOUNG MEN WITHOUT A VOICE IN THE WORLD. ANS A NEW SONG 13
BLACK YOUNG OZIE POWELL. ANS BLD OZZIE POWEL 10
BLACK YOUNG OZIE POWELL. ANS BLD OZZIE POWEL 28
I AM THE YOUNG MAN, FULL OF STRENGTH AND HOPE, ANS LET AMERICA BE 25
THE NIGHT WAS YOUNG - SH DEATH IN HARLEM 3
WHEN THE NIGHT IS YOUNG - SH DEATH IN HARLEM 25
DOWN THE STREET YOUNG HARLEM FW DIMOUT IN HARLM 1
DOWN THE STREET YOUNG HARLEM FW DIMOUT IN HARLM 16
STRONG AS THE BURSTING OF YOUNG BUDS. FW EARTH SONG 7
AND TALL YOUNG TREES FW GIRL 15
THE THINGS A YOUNG LAD FW MAN 12
THERE'S A NEW YOUNG MOON FW NEW MOON 1
THERE'S A SPRIGHTLY YOUNG MOON FW NEW MOON 3
THERE'S A HALF-SHY YOUNG MOON FW NEW MOON 5
AND THE YOUNG SP AFRICA 11
SOME OF THESE YOUNG ONES IS CERT'LY BAD - SP CHILDREN'S RYME 17
FOLLOWS THE YOUNG DOCTOR, SP INTERNE AT PROV 45
AS KEEPS THIS YOUNG NYMPH, JOY! SP JOY 9
HE IS THAT YOUNG MAN, MAMA, SP MAMA AND DAUGHT 7
I HOPE THAT WILD YOUNG SON-OF-A-GUN SP MAMA AND DAUGHT 15
MAMA, DAD COULDN'T BE STILL YOUNG. SP MAMA AND DAUGHT 17
HE WAS YOUNG YESTERDAY. SP MAMA AND DAUGHT 18
HE WAS YOUNG WHEN HE - SP MAMA AND DAUGHT 19
I BATHED IN THE EUPHRATES WHEN DAWNS WERE YOUNG. SP NEGRO SPEAKS OF 5
I DON'T FOOL WITH THESE YOUNG GIRLS. SP PREFERENCE 3
YOUNG GIRL'LL SAY, SP PREFERENCE 4
SHE WAS YOUNG AND BEAUTIFUL SP RUBY BROWN 1
THEY HUNG MY BLACK YOUNG LOVER SP SONG DARK GIRL 3
NOW, THROUGH MY CHILDREN, YOUNG AND FREE, SP THE NEGRO MOTHE 21
THIS STRONG YOUNG SAILOR SP YOUNG SAILOR 6
CAN A YOUNG GAL DO? SP YOUNG GAL'S BLS 20
WHAT CAN A YOUNG GAL DO? SP YOUNG GAL'S BLS 22
A SLAVE WHO DIED YOUNG, PL SLAVE 4
A SLAVE WHO DIED YOUNG, PL SLAVE 8
SO YOUNG, PL SLUM DREAMS 10

YOUNGER 1
AND YOUNGER THAN HE AIN'T. SP NEIGHBOR 8

YOURS 7
AND GIVE US THE RIGHTS THAT ARE YOURS AND MINE. NM COLORED SL POEM 10
80-VOICES: TILL THE FORCES OF THE EARTH ARE YOURS ANS CHANT MAY DAY 35
YOURS HAS BEEN THE POWER JC THE BITTER RIVR 55
NOT YOURS. SP A HOUSE IN TAOS 38
FOR THE FREEDOM TRAIN WILL BE YOURS AND MINE! SP FREEDOM TRAIN 58
AT HOME THEY GOT A TRAIN THAT'S YOURS AND MINE! SP FREEDOM TRAIN 62
YES, THEY ARE YOURS, SP SUMMER EVENING 30

YOUR'N 1
AND IT'S ALL YOUR'N. SP PREFERENCE 10

YOUTH 3
I AM DARK YOUTH NM DARK YOUTH USA 8
THE AMERICAN YOUTH OF TODAY. NM DARK YOUTH USA 25
AND YOUTH AND LIFE FW CAROLINA CABIN 9

YOU'D 3
THE FOLKS WHO HATE YOU'D JC GOOD MORN STLIN 37
YOU'D WANT TO KNOW. SP BLD FORTUNE TEL 4
IF YOU'D JUST TURN ME LOOSE." PL KU KLUX 8

YOU'LL 12
HE SAID, "SHO YOU'LL COME WID ME DK MA LORD 15
BUT YOU'LL NEVER, PRETTY MAMA, SH FREE MAN 7
YOU'LL NEVER KILL ME! JC FREEDOM 14
YOU'LL NEED SIXTY MORE SP BLD OF THE MAN 4
MIGHT BE THAT YOU'LL COME BACK, SP COULD BE 11
YOU'LL HEAR THEIR FEET SP DREAM BOOGIE 6
ELSE YOU'LL TAKE OUT MY PHONE? SP MADAM PHONE BIL 11
"YOU'LL FIND RAIN BETTER SP STRANGE HURT 4
YOU'LL SURE STAY IN YOUR PLACE. SP WIDOW WOMAN 12
YOU'LL BE CALLED BY EASTLAND. AYM RIDE, RED, RIDE 26
TOMORROW YOU'LL BE DEAD PL WITHOUT BENEFIT 9
OUT YONDER YOU'LL LIE: PL WITHOUT BENEFIT 15

YOU'RE 35
WHEN YOU'RE BROKE. NM BROKE 11
I TELL YOU IT'S AWFUL, WHEN YOU'RE BROKE. NM BROKE 47
AND I HOPE YOU'RE MAKING GOOD, AND DOING FINE - NM COLORED SL POEM 17
AND IT'S BETTER A THOUSAND TIMES YOU'RE IN FRANCE DEAD. NM COLORED SL POEM 45
OR THE RIVERS WHERE YOU'RE DROWNED LIKE LIEBKNECHT, ANS KIDS WHO DIE 42
BOY, YOU'RE SWEET! SH DEATH IN HARLEM 50
YOU'RE THE CAUSE SH EVIL MORNING 9
YOU'RE HALF A WORLD AWAY OR MORE JC GOOD MORN STLIN 17
THAT YOU'RE OUR ALLY JUST FOR TODAY. JC GOOD MORN STLIN 24
BUT AS FOR ME - YOU'RE MY ALLY JC GOOD MORN STLIN 26
BEFORE YOU'RE THROUGH, JC NOTE TO NAZIS 6
WHEN YOU'RE IN YOUR HOUSE, BABY OWT CURIOUS 5
YOU'RE THROUGH. OWT NEGRO SERVANT 9
THEN YOU'RE A DOPE SP ARGUMENT 6
(WHEN YOU'RE NO GOOD FOR DOUGH THEY GO.) SP DANCER 20
"YOU'RE FIRED!" SP FIRED 6
YOU'RE ALWAYS GIVING SP MADAM MIGHT-HAV 15
HE SAID, YOU'RE JOHNSON - SP MADAM WRONG VIS 17
I SAID, WHAT MAN YOU'RE TALKING 'BOUT? SP MADAM FORT TELL 21
YOU'RE OUT OF LUCK. SP MADAM RENT MAN 26
IF YOU'RE GREAT ENOUGH SP SHAME ON YOU 1
IF YOU'RE NOT ALIVE AND KICKING, SP SHAME ON YOU 10
AND IT'S IN THE WAY YOU'RE GONE SP SO LONG 3
YOU'RE GONE SO LONG SP SO LONG 9
ALTHOUGH YOU'RE OLDER - AND WHITE - SP THEME FOR ENG B 39
WHEN YOU'RE FULL OF STUFF. SP WARNING AUGMENT 8
AND YOU'RE 50 AYM ODE TO DINAH 105
WHEN YOU'RE 40 AYM ODE TO DINAH 106
40 WHEN YOU'RE 30 AYM ODE TO DINAH 107
30 WHEN YOU'RE 20 AYM ODE TO DINAH 108
20 WHEN YOU'RE 10 AYM ODE TO DINAH 109
EVEN WHEN YOU'RE WINNING AYM ODE TO DINAH 113
YOU'RE THE ONE, PL BACKLASH BLUES 31
YES, YOU'RE THE ONE PL BACKLASH BLUES 32
YOU'RE A-STANDIN' THERE PL KU KLUX 11

YOU'S 4
OLD JUDGE SAYS YOU'S A DRUNKARD. FC BLD OF GIN MARY 13
YOU'S TOO PRETTY. FC RED SILK STOCK 7
AN' YOU'S A LONG TIME FC SATURDAY NIGHT 17
IF YOU'S A WISE WOMAN, HATTIE, SP EARLY EVENING 11

YOU'VE 9
YOU'VE GOT SEVEN LANGUAGES TO SPEAK IN FC JAZZ BAND 19
AND SAID TO ME, "BROTHER, YOU'VE GOT YOUR CHANCE. NM COLORED SL POEM 16
YOU'VE STOOD BETWEEN US WELL. JC GOOD MORN STLIN 35
YOU'VE WORKED ALL DAY. OWT NEGRO SERVANT 10
YOU'VE BEEN RESTING AWHILE. SP AFRICA 2
I KNOW YOU'VE HEARD SP BOOGIE 1 A.M. 2
NOW YOU'VE GOT YOUR CADILLAC, SP LOW TO HIGH 5
YOU'VE GOT NO TRUST. SP MADAM MIGHT-HAV 30
YOU'VE TAKEN MY BLUES AND GONE - SP NOTE COMM THEAT 1

YO' 22

I SEES YO' FACE AGAIN. . . . . . . FC BLD OF GIN MARY 8
AN' SAYS YO' BOY IS GETTIN' BEAT. FC DEATH DO DIRTY 24
WHEN IT HURTS YO' HEART YOU . . . . FC GYPSY MAN 23
GATHER UP YO' FINE CLOTHES . . . . FC HARD LUCK 5
JEW TAKES YO' FINE CLOTHES, ... FC HARD LUCK 7
JEW TAKES YO' FINE CLOTHES, ... FC HARD LUCK 9
KIN MAKE YOU LOSE YO' 'GINITY. . . FC LISTEN HERE 6
SOMEWHERE IN YO' SKY. . . . . FC MOAN 18
PUT ON YO' RED SILK STOCKINGS, . . FC RED SILK STOCK 1
LOOK AT YO' LEGS. . . . . FC RED SILK STOCK 4
PUT ON YO' RED SILK STOCKINGS, GAL. FC RED SILK STOCK 8
LOOK AT YO' LEGS. . . . . FC RED SILK STOCK 12
PAWN YO' GOLD WATCH . . . . FC SATURDAY NIGHT 9
I MEAN FOUR - BEFORE DAYLIGHT - S'POSE TO'VE DONE HIT YO' FIRST STROKE - . . . . NM BROKE 14
LORDY, LET YO' MERCY . . . . SP FEET O' JESUS 3
AT YO' FEET I STAND. . . . . SP FEET O' JESUS 6
PLEASE REACH OUT YO' HAND. . . . . SP FEET O' JESUS 8
GIMME YO' SHOES . . . . SP PORTER 11
LISTEN TO YO' PROPHETS, ... SP SHOUT 1
LISTEN TO YO' SAINTS! . . . . SP SHOUT 3
AN' A SINNER IN YO' SIGHT. . . . . SP SINNER 4
FO' TO LOVE YO' DADDY RIGHT!" . . . SP SYLVESTER'S BED 24

YUH 1

CAN I GO HOME WID YUH, SWEETIE? . . FC JAZZ BAND 22

Y-E-A-H 1

Y-E-A-H! . . . . SP DREAM BOOGIE 21

ZERO 1

AS IS CUSTOM BELOW ZERO. . . . . . AYM ODE TO DINAH 12

ZIK 1

OR ZIK TO ALABAMA . . . . AYM SHADES OF PIG 28

ZONE 1

IN A TWENTY-MILE ZONE. . . . . . . SH ANNOUNCEMENT 4

ZOO 1

I WALKED ALL OVER THE ZOO AND THE PARK. . . . . OWT STRANGER IN TWN 1

ZOOMIN' 1

WILL HIS FREEDOM TRAIN COME ZOOMIN' DOWN THE TRACK . . . . SP FREEDOM TRAIN 49

NUMERICAL KEY-WORDS

00 1

GIMME $25.00 . . . . SP REQUEST 1

000 1

$40,000 HOUSES - . . . . AYM HORN OF PLENTY 77

1 1

UNTIL 12 - 1 - 2 A.M. . . . . SP GONE BOY 4

1ST 2

AUGUST 1ST IS . . . . OWT BLD MARGE POLIT 27
MARK AUGUST 1ST . . . . OWT BLD MARGE POLIT 29

10 2

LIVING 20 YEARS IN 10 . . . . AYM ODE TO DINAH 102
20 WHEN YOU'RE 10 . . . . AYM ODE TO DINAH 109

10-OTHERS 3

10-OTHERS: BLACK WORKERS, ... ANS CHANT MAY DAY 21
10-OTHERS: YELLOW WORKERS, ... ANS CHANT MAY DAY 22
10-OTHERS: WORKERS IN THE ISLANDS OF THE SEA - . . . . ANS CHANT MAY DAY 23

10-VOICES 4

10-VOICES: BLOOM IN THE STRENGTH OF YOUR UNKNOWN POWER, ... ANS CHANT MAY DAY 9
10-VOICES: BE LIKE THE SAP RISING IN THE TREES, ... ANS CHANT MAY DAY 15
10-VOICES: WHITE WORKERS, ... ANS CHANT MAY DAY 20
10-VOICES: MAY DAY! . . . . ANS CHANT MAY DAY 27

100 1

100 YEARS NOT FREE. . . . . PL DEATH YORKVILLE 13

100-VOICES 1

100-VOICES: FROM THIS HOUR. . . . . ANS CHANT MAY DAY 36

100-YEARS 1

100-YEARS EMANCIPATION . . . . . . AYM ODE TO DINAH 9

12 2

UNTIL 12 - 1 - 2 A.M. . . . . SP GONE BOY 4
STOOPS TO KISS 12 WEST 133RD, . . . SP PROJECTION 9

12TH 1

OCTOBER 12TH,1942.) . . . . JC THE BITTER RIVR 1

133RD 5

THE PICKIN'S WEREN'T BAD ON A 133RD. SH DEATH IN HARLEM 5
IN DIXIE'S PLACE ON 133RD . . . . . SH DEATH IN HARLEM 24
ON A 133RD. . . . . SP NOT A MOVIE 8
ON A 133RD. . . . . SP NOT A MOVIE 15
STOOPS TO KISS 12 WEST 133RD, . . . SP PROJECTION 9

15 1

THE 15¢ MUGGER BEHIND STEEL BARS, JC THE BITTER RIVR 34

1619 1

JAMESTOWN, 1619 TO 1963: . . . . . PL DEATH YORKVILLE 11

17 1

17 SORROWS . . . . AYM ASK YOUR MAMA 15

18TH 3

COULD BE 18TH & VINE . . . . SP COULD BE 3
23RD AND CENTRAL, 18TH STREET AND VINE. . . . . AYM ASK YOUR MAMA 6
18TH AND VINE IN K.C., 63RD IN CHI, AYM ASK YOUR MAMA 32

1865 1

EMANCIPATION: 1865 . . . . PL LONG VIEW NEGRO 1

1895 1

HE DIED IN 1895. . . . . PL FREDRK DOUGLASS 21

1933 1

ONCE IN 1933. . . . . SP RELIEF 5

1941 2

DECEMBER 7,1941: . . . . JC JIM CROW'S LAST 7
DECEMBER 7,1941: . . . . JC JIM CROW'S LAST 27

1942 1

OCTOBER 12TH,1942.) . . . . JC THE BITTER RIVR 1

1963 1

JAMESTOWN, 1619 TO 1963: . . . . . PL DEATH YORKVILLE 11

1965 1

CIVIL WAR CENTENNIAL: 1965. . . . . PL DEATH YORKVILLE 14

2 1

UNTIL 12 - 1 - 2 A.M. . . . . SP GONE BOY 4

20 3

LIVING 20 YEARS IN 10 . . . . AYM ODE TO DINAH 102
30 WHEN YOU'RE 20 . . . . AYM ODE TO DINAH 108
20 WHEN YOU'RE 10 . . . . AYM ODE TO DINAH 109

20-VOICES 4

20-VOICES: GROW OUT OF THE PASSIVE EARTH, ... ANS CHANT MAY DAY 10
20-VOICES: STRENGTHENING EACH BRANCH, ... ANS CHANT MAY DAY 16
20-VOICES: MAY DAY! . . . . ANS CHANT MAY DAY 28
20-VOICES: ARISE, ... ANS CHANT MAY DAY 32

23RD 1

23RD AND CENTRAL, 18TH STREET AND VINE. . . . . AYM ASK YOUR MAMA 6

25 1

GIMME $25.00 . . . . SP REQUEST 1

26-GIRL 1

OF 26-GIRL AT THE CORNER, ... SP INTERNE AT PROV 10

3-2-6 1

WAS 3-2-6 - . . . . SP MADAM NUMBER WR 18

30 3

IF SHOW FARE'S MORE THAN 30¢ ¢ ¢ ¢ ¢ ¢ ¢ ¢ . . . . AYM HORN OF PLENTY 29
40 WHEN YOU'RE 30 . . . . AYM ODE TO DINAH 107
30 WHEN YOU'RE 20 . . . . AYM ODE TO DINAH 108

31ST 6

I LOOKED DOWN 31ST STREET, ... SH MIDNIGHT CHIPPI 1
DOWN ON 31ST STREET, ... SH MIDNIGHT CHIPPI 3
31ST, ... OWT JITNEY 5
31ST, ... OWT JITNEY 33
31ST! ALL OUT! . . . . OWT JITNEY 36
31ST, ... OWT JITNEY 64

35TH 4
35TH. — OWT JITNEY 6
35TH. — OWT JITNEY 32
35TH. — OWT JITNEY 43
35TH. — OWT JITNEY 63

39TH 3
39TH. — OWT JITNEY 7
39TH. — OWT JITNEY 29
39TH. — OWT JITNEY 44

40 3
$40,000 HOUSES - — AYM HORN OF PLENTY 77
WHEN YOU'RE 40 — AYM ODE TO DINAH 106
40 WHEN YOU'RE 30 — AYM ODE TO DINAH 107

40-VOICES 4
40-VOICES: GROW STRONG WITH UNION. ALL HANDS TOGETHER - — ANS CHANT MAY DAY 11
40-VOICES: NO PART NEGLECTED - — ANS CHANT MAY DAY 17
40-VOICES: MAY DAY! — ANS CHANT MAY DAY 29
40-VOICES: GROW STRONG. — ANS CHANT MAY DAY 33

409 2
(NOT AT 409) — SP HIGH TO LOW 17
AND 409 EDGECOMBE — SP PROJECTION 8

43RD 4
43RD. — OWT JITNEY 8
DOWN ON 43RD. — OWT JITNEY 12
43RD. — OWT JITNEY 28
43RD. — OWT JITNEY 45

47TH 4
47TH. — OWT JITNEY 13
47TH. — OWT JITNEY 21
47TH. — OWT JITNEY 48
47TH. — OWT JITNEY 62

5TH 2
COULD BE 5TH & MOUND. — SP COULD BE 5
5TH AND MOUND IN CINCI. 63RD IN CHI. — AYM ASK YOUR MAMA 5

50 2
TALKIN' 'BOUT "WE'LL WORK FOR 50¢ A DAY, IF WE CAN'T GET NO MO'." — NM BROKE 7
AND YOU'RE 50 — AYM ODE TO DINAH 105

50TH 1
50TH PLACE. — OWT JITNEY 49

50-VOICES 5
50-VOICES: FOREVER FOR THE WORKERS! — ANS CHANT MAY DAY 13
50-VOICES: REACHING ALL THE WORLD. — ANS CHANT MAY DAY 18
50-VOICES: LIFE IS EVERYWHERE FOR YOU. — ANS CHANT MAY DAY 24
50-VOICES: LIFE IS EVERYWHERE. — ANS CHANT MAY DAY 26
50-VOICES: WHEN THE EARTH IS NEW. — ANS CHANT MAY DAY 30

51ST 2
51ST. — OWT JITNEY 14
51ST. — OWT JITNEY 20

55TH 3
55TH. — OWT JITNEY 15
55TH. — OWT JITNEY 19
55TH. — OWT JITNEY 51

6-0-2 2
6-0-2 — SP MADAM NUMBER WR 6
6-0-2. — AYM ASK YOUR MAMA 17

60-VOICES 1
60-VOICES: TAKE POWER. — ANS CHANT MAY DAY 34

63RD 4
63RD. — OWT JITNEY 16
63RD. — OWT JITNEY 50
5TH AND MOUND IN CINCI. 63RD IN CHI. — AYM ASK YOUR MAMA 5
18TH AND VINE IN K.C.. 63RD IN CHI. — AYM ASK YOUR MAMA 32

7 3
DECEMBER 7,1941: — JC JIM CROW'S LAST 7
DECEMBER 7,1941: — JC JIM CROW'S LAST 27
COME 7! — AYM ASK YOUR MAMA 22

7TH 1
FILLMORE OUT IN FRISCO. 7TH ACROSS THE BAY. — AYM ASK YOUR MAMA 31

7-0-3 1
I DREAMED 7-0-3. — SP MADAM NUMBER WR 10

7-11 1
7-11! — AYM ASK YOUR MAMA 21

7'S 1
WHEN I ROLLED THREE 7'S — SP SITUATION 1

8 3
8 BLACK BOYS IN A SOUTHERN JAIL. — SL SCOTTSBORO 1
8 BLACK BOYS AND ONE WHITE LIE. — SL SCOTTSBORO 3
8 BLACK BOYS IN A SOUTHERN JAIL. — SL SCOTTSBORO 28

8-BALL 1
THE 8-BALL — AYM ASK YOUR MAMA 19

8-ROCK 1
BORN BEHIND THE 8-ROCK. — SP MADAM CHARTY CH 14

80-VOICES 1
80-VOICES: TILL THE FORCES OF THE EARTH ARE YOURS — ANS CHANT MAY DAY 35

83 1
WHEN MY GRANDMOTHER IN ATLANTA, 83 AND BLACK. — SP FREEDOM TRAIN 37

90 1
JUDGE GIVES NEGRO 90 DAYS IN COUNTY JAIL — SP BLD LANDLORD 33

942 1
942 — SP RAILROAD AVENUE 11

COLLOQUIAL CONTRACTIONS

'BOUT 15
KNOWED SOMEBODY'S 'BOUT TO DIE. — FC GAL'S CRY DYING 2
KNOWED SOMEBODY'S 'BOUT TO DIE. — FC GAL'S CRY DYING 4
SO DON'T WORRY 'BOUT ME. — NM BIG-TIMER POEM 53
TALKIN' 'BOUT "WE'LL WORK FOR 50¢ A DAY, IF WE CAN'T GET NO MO'." — NM BROKE 7
(I DON'T CARE NOTHIN' 'BOUT HER MYSELF!) — NM BROKE 27
WHAT I DON'T KNOW 'BOUT SHOVELIN' COAL. AIN'T NO MO' TO KNOW! — NM BROKE 32
'COURSE, YOU HEARS PLENTY 'BOUT THIS-HERE UNEMPLOYMENT RELIEF - — NM BROKE 56
CERTAINLY, CHILE, I ALWAYS WAS CRAZY 'BOUT YOU! — NM BROKE 74
I WANT TO TELL YOU 'BOUT THAT WOMAN. — SH ONLY WOMAN BLUS 1
AIN'T EVEN GONNA DREAM 'BOUT THE WOMENS I HAD. — SH PAY DAY 18
I SAID, WHAT MAN YOU'RE TALKING 'BOUT? — SP MADAM FORT TELL 21
DON'T WORRY 'BOUT ME! — SP MADAM'S PAST HI 19
'BOUT HALF-PAST THREE. — SP SYLVESTER'S BED 2
'BOUT HALF-PAST FO'. — SP SYLVESTER'S BED 10
'BOUT OUT OF BREATH. — PL DOWN WHERE I AM 11

'CAUSE 10
'CAUSE I CARRIES A SWITCH-BLADE — NM BIG-TIMER POEM 29
'CAUSE 'FORE YOU GETS THERE, TEN THOUSAND AND ONE — NM BROKE 5
FOLKS SHO IS GETTIN' HARD ON YOU - JUST 'CAUSE YOU BROKE. — NM BROKE 15
COME BAWLIN' ME OUT, 'CAUSE I'M BROKE. — NM BROKE 26
'CAUSE I'M JUST DYIN' TO TAKE ON THAT THERE MARRIAGE YOKE. — NM BROKE 77
'CAUSE I'M BROKE. — NM BROKE 79
'CAUSE WHEN I WAS LIVING, I DIDN'T HAVE MINE. — NM COLORED SL POEM 18
'CAUSE THAT'S WHAT I DIED FOR - ISN'T IT, BROTHER?" — NM COLORED SL POEM 36
'CAUSE FREEDOM AIN'T FREEDOM WHEN A MAN AIN'T FREE. — SP FREEDOM TRAIN 34
'CAUSE YOU FINDS IT'S KINDER HARD. — SP MOTHER TO SON 16

'COURSE 1
'COURSE, YOU HEARS PLENTY 'BOUT THIS-HERE UNEMPLOYMENT RELIEF - — NM BROKE 56

'EM 41
SING 'EM, SISTER! — WB BLUES FANTASY 22
LEMME ROLL 'EM, BOY. — FC CRAP GAME 1
HIT 'EM, BONES! — FC CRAP GAME 9
I'M GONNA FILL 'EM UP FULL O' — FC DEATH DO DIRTY 33
AN' SELL 'EM TO DE JEW. — FC HARD LUCK 6
SHAKE 'EM UP AN' SHAKE 'EM UP — FC SATURDAY NIGHT 23
SHAKE 'EM UP AN' SHAKE 'EM UP — FC SATURDAY NIGHT 23
LOOK 'EM IN THE FACE AND — NM BIG-TIMER POEM 59
BUST 'EM LIKE BUBBLES. — NM BIG-TIMER POEM 60
AND LET 'EM HAVE MY MONEY. — NM BIG-TIMER POEM 66

AND SHE BEEN HOLDIN' 'EM SO TIGHT
TILL DE EAGLE'S IN TEARS - . . . NM BROKE 24
BUT THEY GIVIN' 'EM TO SCHOOL BOYS
NOW AND PAYIN' JUST ABOUT HALF. NM BROKE 43
I PUT 'EM ON BUT . . . . DK DRESSED UP 7
SHAKE 'EM SWIFT AND WIL' - . . . . DK SONG BANJO DANC 4
SHAKE 'EM, HONEY CHILE. . . . . . . DK SONG BANJO DANC 11
SHAKE 'EM, LIZA, CHILE. . . . . . . DK SONG BANJO DANC 21
I'LL GET 'EM FOR YOU. . . . . SH BLD THE KILLER 4
THEN WHIP 'EM ALL NIGHT LONG. . . . SH HEY-HEY BLUES 8
THEN WHIP 'EM ALL NIGHT LONG. . . . SH HEY-HEY BLUES 10
JUST PLAY 'EM, PERFESSER. . . . . . SH HEY-HEY BLUES 11
WHILE YOU PLAY 'EM. . . . . SH HEY-HEY BLUES 13
I WILL SING 'EM, TOO. . . . . SH HEY-HEY BLUES 14
AND WHILE YOU PLAY 'EM. . . . . . . SH HEY-HEY BLUES 15
I'LL SING 'EM, TOO. . . . . SH HEY-HEY BLUES 16
I DON'T CARE HOW YOU PLAY 'EM . . . SH HEY-HEY BLUES 17
THEN SHARE 'EM WITH ME - . . . . . JC HOW ABOUT DIXIE 7
DON'T KEEP 'EM ALL FOR YOU. . . . . JC HOW ABOUT DIXIE 8
THE UNDERTAKER TOLD 'EM. . . . . . SP BLD OF THE MAN 3
SHE PUT 'EM DOWN. . . . . SP BLD OF THE MAN 12
YOU KICKS 'EM ROUND AND . . . . . . SP LOVER'S RETURN 11
DOES 'EM LIKE YOU CHOOSE. . . . . . SP LOVER'S RETURN 12
THEN WE BOXED 'EM. . . . . SP MADAM NUMBER WR 15
BUT I DIDN'T FIND 'EM. . . . . . . SP MAGNOLIA FLOWER 4
YOU SING 'EM ON BROADWAY . . . . . SP NOTE COMM THEAT 2
AND YOU SING 'EM IN HOLLYWOOD BOWL. SP NOTE COMM THEAT 3
AND YOU MIXED 'EM UP WITH SYMPHONIES SP NOTE COMM THEAT 4
AND YOU FIXED 'EM . . . . SP NOTE COMM THEAT 5
THE ONE TO STOP 'EM WON'T BE ME. . SP RELIEF 15
AND I REACHES UP TO HUG 'EM - . . . SP SYLVESTER'S BED 25
AND I GET TO SEE 'EM RIDE. . . . . PL FLORIDA WORKERS 16
LOOKS LIKE BETWEEN 'EM THEY DONE . PL STILL HERE 5

'FAY 1
IF HER DADDY AIN'T 'FAY . . . . . . FC NEW CABARET GRL 15

'FORD 1
BUT RIGHT LONG THROUGH HERE NOW, I
CAN'T 'FORD TO BUY YOU NO HAT." NM BROKE 51

'FORE 1
'CAUSE 'FORE YOU GETS THERE, TEN
THOUSAND AND ONE . . . . NM BROKE 5

'FRAID 1
SAYS DON'T BE 'FRAID . . . . SP JUDGMENT DAY 8

'GINITY 1
KIN MAKE YOU LOSE YO' 'GINITY. . . FC LISTEN HERE 6

'HIND 2
'HIND MA FRIEND MISS CORA LEE. . . SP YOUNG GAL'S BLS 2
'HIND MA DEAR FRIEND CORA LEE . . . SP YOUNG GAL'S BLS 4

'HORE 1
AIN'T NOTHIN' BUT A 'HORE. . . . . FC WORKIN' MAN 8

'LECTRIC-SHOCKIN' 1
HE'S GOT THOSE 'LECTRIC-SHOCKIN'
EYES AN' . . . . FC MA MAN 5

'LEVEN 1
'LEVEN AIN'T FAR AWAY. . . . . . . FC CRAP GAME 4

'LIEVE 2
'LIEVE I'LL JUMP IN DE RIVER . . . FC SUICIDE 13
'LIEVE I'LL JUMP IN DE RIVER . . . FC SUICIDE 15

'LL 2
'LL HELP YOU OUT . . . . FC DEATH DO DIRTY 3
'LL EASE MY MISERY. . . . . SP MISERY 4

'LOWED 2
LANDLADY 'LOWED TO ME LAST WEEK,
"SAM, AIN'T YOU GOT NO MONEY?" . NM BROKE 19
"YOU MA FRIEND," HE 'LOWED. . . . . DK MA LORD 5

'MEMBER 1
DON'T YOU 'MEMBER I TOLD YOU ABOUT
IT . . . . SP BLD LANDLORD 3

'NOTHER 1
JUST ONE THING AFTER 'NOTHER . . . SH LOVE AGAIN BLUS 5

'N' 1
THE DOCTOR 'N' UNDERTAKER'S . . . . SP SYLVESTER'S BED 11

'S 3
'S A TERRIBLE THING TO HAVE. . . . DK HOMESICK BLUES 14
THE G.I.'S WHO FOUGHT WILL SAY, WE
WANTED IT SO! . . . . SP FREEDOM TRAIN 60
'S GOT TO HEAR A BLUES . . . . . . SP MISERY 15

'SCUSE 2
'SCUSE ME, ... SP MAGNOLIA FLOWER 8
'SCUSE ME, ... SP MAGNOLIA FLOWER 12

'TWAS 1
'TWAS THE NIGHT BEFO' CHRISTMAS . . SP MIDWINTER BLUES 5

'TWIXT 2
'TWIXT MA LOVE AN' ME. . . . . . . DK WIDE RIVER 8
'TWIXT MA LOVE AN' ME. . . . . . . DK WIDE RIVER 10

'VESTER 1
BUT I'S STILL SWEET PAPA 'VESTER. SP SYLVESTER'S BED 21

'33RD 1
DOWN ON '33RD STREET . . . . SH STATEMENT 1

TABLE 2 - STATISTICAL SUMMARY

Word Frequencies in Rank Order

Words Omitted from This Concordance

1 ABIDE
1 ACCEPTING
1 ACID
1 ACTS
1 ADVENTURES
1 AGENT
1 AGREES
1 AL
1 ALI
1 ALL-REET
1 AMEKA
1 AMERICA'D
1 AMPLIFIER
1 ANIMALS
1 ANTENNA
1 APPEAL
1 APPRECIATE
1 ARKANSAS
1 ASCENDS
1 ATAVISTIC
1 AUSTRALIA
1 AWAKENED
1 A-CRYING
1 A-ONLY
1 A-WALKIN'
1 BACKING
1 BAKES
1 BALLOTS
1 BANDS
1 BARBECUE
1 BAR-GLASS
1 BATHMATS
1 BAY
1 BEAST-STRONG
1 BECKON
1 BEGGED
1 BELEAGUERED
1 BELLA
1 BELOW
1 BETHEL'S
1 BINOCULAR
1 BITING
1 BLARING
1 BLESSINGS
1 BLOTS
1 BLUNDERINGLY
1 BODIES'LL
1 BOIL
1 BONDS
1 BOOK-OF-THE-MONTH
1 BORROWED
1 BOUND
1 BOWS
1 BRADDOCK
1 BREAKING
1 BRIDE
1 BRINK'S
1 BROTHER'S
1 BROWN-FACED
1 BUDS
1 BURNED
1 BUTCHER'S
1 CAESAR
1 CALIFORNIA
1 CAMPANELLA
1 CANDLE
1 CAPSTAN
1 CARESSES
1 CARVE
1 CASTANETS
1 CAUTIOUS
1 CENTS
1 CHANG
1 CHARITY
1 CHECKED
1 CHILE'LL
1 CHOCOLATE-CUSTARD
1 CHUMPS
1 CITADELLE
1 CLEANING
1 CLIMBING
1 CLORINDA
1 CLOUD-DUST
1 COCA-COLA
1 COKE
1 COLLECTION
1 COMEDY
1 COMMITTEE
1 COMRADES
1 CONDUCTED
1 CONFUSE
1 CONTROL
1 COOLIES
1 CORNETS
1 COSTLY
1 COUPLES
1 COUSIN
1 CRACKED
1 ABLE
1 ACCLIMATED
1 ACCORDANCE
1 ADDED
1 ADVENTURERS
1 AGIN'
1 AIDS
1 ALAN
1 ALIKE
1 ALRIGHT
1 AMEN-CORNER
1 AMERICAN'S
1 ANCESTORS
1 ANKLES
1 ANVIL
1 APPEARS
1 APPRECIATES
1 AROSE
1 ASPEN
1 ATOMS
1 AUTHORITY
1 AW-DO
1 A-CREEPIN'
1 A-PLAYIN'
1 BABA-RE-BOP
1 BACKGROUND
1 BAKED
1 BALTIMORE
1 BANDANNA
1 BARING
1 BASIE'S
1 BATTED
1 BAYOU'S
1 BEAST
1 BEDLOE'S
1 BEGGAR
1 BELGIUM
1 BELL-BOUY
1 BEN
1 BE-
1 BIRMINGHAM-ON-SUND
1 BITLESS
1 BLAZED
1 BLESSED
1 BLOWTORCH
1 BLURRED
1 BODY'S
1 BOJANGLES
1 BONDSMAN
1 BOOTY
1 BOSTON
1 BOURSE
1 BOW-LEGGED
1 BRAID
1 BREW
1 BRIGHTER
1 BROADWAY
1 BROWNSKIN
1 BRUSHED
1 BUGLE
1 BUSES
1 BUTTERED
1 CAGE
1 CALLIN'
1 CAMPAIGN
1 CANDLES
1 CAPTURED
1 CARELESS-LIKE
1 CASBAH
1 CASTRO'S
1 CEASES
1 CENTENNIALS
1 CHANCES
1 CHARTS
1 CHERUB-FACES
1 CHIMNEY
1 CHOKING
1 CIGARETTES
1 CIVILIZED
1 CLEMENT
1 CLINKS
1 CLOTHESBRUSH
1 CLOVE
1 COCONUTS
1 COLD-WATER
1 COLLARS
1 COMEDIANS
1 COMMERCIALS
1 COM'
1 CONDUCT
1 CONFOUND
1 CONTENTMENT
1 COPPING
1 CORRECTED
1 COTTON'S
1 COURAGE
1 COUSINS
1 CRACKLING
1 ABOARD
1 ACCOMPANY
1 ACRES
1 ADDRESSED
1 ADVISER
1 AGING
1 AIMED
1 ALETHA
1 ALIOUNE
1 ALTER
1 AMENDMENT
1 AMONGST
1 ANCHOR
1 ANNIHILATE
1 ANYBODY'S
1 APPLAUDS
1 AQUEL
1 ARRAYED
1 ASSORTED
1 ATTENTION
1 AVAILABLE
1 AZIKIWE'S
1 A-COIN'
1 A-SASSIN'
1 BACK-SLID
1 BAD-LUCK
1 BAKOKO
1 BAM
1 BANG
1 BARK
1 BASKET
1 BATTLEFIELD
1 BEACH
1 BEATIN'
1 BEECHER
1 BEIN
1 BELGIANS
1 BELLS
1 BERETS
1 BE-BACH
1 BIRTHING
1 BITTERNESS
1 BLEACHED
1 BLONDE
1 BLUE-GUMMED
1 BOARDS
1 BODY'LL
1 BOLDNESS
1 BONGO-BONGO
1 BOOTLEG'S
1 BOTTOMS
1 BOUT
1 BOXED
1 BRAZEN
1 BRIBE-REACHING
1 BRIGHT-EYED
1 BROKEN-WINGED
1 BROW
1 BRUTALITY
1 BULBS
1 BUSSES
1 BUTTERFLY
1 CAKE
1 CALMLY
1 CANARIES
1 CANVASS
1 CAPTAIN'S
1 CARIBBEAN
1 CASHED
1 CASTRO
1 CELEBRITIES
1 CERT'LY
1 CHART
1 CHASE
1 CHICASAWKAY
1 CHINE
1 CHOKE
1 CINCI
1 CLANG
1 CLEOPATRA
1 CLINGING
1 CLOTHED
1 CLOWNS
1 COCONUT
1 COLD-FACED
1 COLUMN
1 COMIC
1 COMPLAINING
1 CONCENTRATED
1 CONFIDENT
1 CONGRESS
1 CONVENIENT
1 COPPER'S
1 CORRUPT
1 COUGHED
1 COURT-YARD
1 COVERS
1 CRADLE
1 ABOMINATIONS
1 ACCORDION
1 ACTION
1 ADELE
1 AFFAIR
1 AGITATOR
1 AINT
1 ALEXANDER
1 ALLEY
1 ALVIN
1 AMERICANS
1 AMORPHOUS
1 ANGELO
1 ANSWERIN'
1 ANYWAY
1 APPLY
1 ARCH
1 ARREST
1 ASSUMING
1 ATTIC
1 AWAITING
1 A-BASSIN
1 A-HUMMIN'
1 A-SHOUTIN'
1 BACKYARD
1 BAGS
1 BALLOONS
1 BAND'S
1 BANNERS
1 BARRIERS
1 BATABANO
1 BATTERS
1 BEARER
1 BEAUTY'S
1 BEERS
1 BELATED
1 BELIEVING
1 BELONGED
1 BESIDES
1 BIG-TIMER
1 BISCUITS
1 BLACKENING
1 BLEEDIN
1 BLOODS
1 BLUES'LL
1 BOAT'S
1 BOG
1 BOMBAY
1 BOOGIED
1 BOOZE
1 BOTTOM
1 BOW
1 BOXING
1 BREASTS
1 BRIBES
1 BRILLIANT
1 BRONZE
1 BROWN'S
1 BUDDIES
1 BULLY
1 BUSTIN
1 BUYS
1 CALEDONIA'S
1 CAMEO
1 CANAAN
1 CAPER
1 CARDS
1 CARRIAGE
1 CASHIER
1 CATCHING
1 CELL
1 CHAGRIN
1 CHARNEL
1 CHATTERING
1 CHIEF
1 CHIP
1 CHORDS
1 CINQUE
1 CLASSES
1 CLEVER
1 CLINCH
1 CLOTH
1 CLUNY
1 COFFIN
1 COLEMAN
1 COMB
1 COMMITTEE'S
1 COMPELLED
1 CONCLUDES
1 CONFERENCE
1 CONJURES
1 COOKS
1 CORDIAL
1 CORRIDORS
1 COUNTS
1 COURTS
1 COZY
1 CRANKED
1 ABSORB
1 ACHIEVE
1 ACTING
1 ADVENTURE
1 AFFORD
1 AGREE
1 AIRPLANES
1 ALEXANDER'S
1 ALLIES
1 AMBULANCE
1 AMERICA'S
1 AMPHITHEATRE
1 ANGRY
1 ANSWERING
1 APPALLS
1 APPLE
1 ARGENTINE
1 ARTIC
1 ASTONISHED
1 ATTUCKS
1 AWAKENING
1 A-BEGGIN'
1 A-MOANIN'
1 A-WAY
1 BACKSTAGE
1 BAILEY
1 BALLOON
1 BAND-MEN
1 BAPTIZED
1 BARTERED
1 BATHROBES
1 BAWLIN'
1 BEARDS
1 BEAUTIFY
1 BEG
1 BELAFONTE
1 BELLOWING
1 BELONG
1 BET
1 BILLINGTON'S
1 BISQUIT
1 BLADES
1 BLEED
1 BLOODIED
1 BLUFF
1 BODDIDLY
1 BOHUNK
1 BOMBS'LL
1 BOOKER-T
1 BOPS
1 BOUNDARIES
1 BOWER
1 BOYS'
1 BREASTED
1 BRICKTOP
1 BRILLIANTS
1 BROOKLYN
1 BROWN-SKINS
1 BUDDING
1 BURDENS
1 BUSY
1 CADILLACS
1 CALEDONIA
1 CAMP
1 CANCER
1 CAPITAL
1 CARELESS
1 CARTED
1 CASSIUS
1 CAT'S
1 CENSUS
1 CHALLENGE
1 CHARMS
1 CHAUFFEUR
1 CHILD-MINDED
1 CHIPPIE
1 CHRISTENED
1 CIRCUSES
1 CLAVES
1 CLICKING
1 CLOCKS
1 CLOUD-GARMENTS
1 CLUTCH
1 COIN
1 COLLAR
1 COMBINES
1 COMMITTEES
1 COMPASS'
1 CONCERNING
1 CONFUSED
1 CONNIVE
1 COOKSTOVES
1 CORDELIA'S
1 COSMIC
1 COUPLE
1 COURTESY
1 CO-RELIGIONISTS
1 CRAP-SHOOTERS

1 CRAWLED
1 CREEP
1 CROON
1 CROWNS
1 CUBA
1 CURIOUS
1 CUSTOM
1 DAD
1 DARES
1 DAVIS
1 DEAL
1 DECREED
1 DEGENERATES
1 DELIGHTED
1 DEMURELY
1 DESERVE
1 DESTROY
1 DEUM
1 DE-DADDLE-DY
1 DIFFICULTIES
1 DIMOUT
1 DISC
1 DISH-WASHERS
1 DIVIDE
1 DODGED
1 DONKEY
1 DOOR-STEPS
1 DOUBT
1 DO-MOVE
1 DRAWED
1 DREAM-DUST
1 DRIFTIN'
1 DROWNS
1 DU
1 DUPONT
1 DWELL
1 EARTHA
1 EARTHQUAKE
1 ECHOING
1 EEEEOOOOO
1 EIGHTY
1 ELEVATORS
1 EMBROIDERED
1 ENDOWED
1 ENJOYING
1 ERIC
1 ESCROW
1 ETCHED
1 EVAPORATION
1 EVICTION
1 EXPLAINS
1 FADE
1 FALLOUT
1 FARMS
1 FASTING
1 FEMININE
1 FEZ
1 FIFTY
1 FILIPINOS
1 FIRE'S
1 FIXED
1 FLATTED
1 FLINCHING
1 FLUNG
1 FOGGY
1 FOOL-SELF
1 FORCED
1 FORM
1 FORTUNE'S
1 FRIDAY
1 FRIZ
1 FRUITS
1 FURNISHED
1 FUTILELY
1 GAMBLIN'
1 GANGSTER
1 GARRISON
1 GEARED
1 GERMAN
1 GILLESPIE
1 GIRLS'
1 GLEAMIN'
1 GLOBAL
1 GOAT
1 GOOSE
1 GOYA
1 GRANDFATHER'S
1 GRAPES
1 GREATER
1 GREED'S
1 GROPING
1 GUISE
1 GYPSY'S
1 HAITI
1 HALF-SHY
1 HAMBURGERS
1 HANGING
1 HARLEMITES
1 CRAWFORD
1 CREPT
1 CROOK
1 CRUCIFIED
1 CUBBY-HOLE
1 CURLED
1 CUTS
1 DAISY
1 DARK-EYED
1 DAVID'S
1 DEALT
1 DEDICATED
1 DEGREED
1 DELIVERED
1 DENMARK
1 DESIRING
1 DESTINED
1 DEVIL'S
1 DE-DAD
1 DIFF'
1 DINED
1 DISCOURAGED
1 DISOWNED
1 DIXIECRATS
1 DOGGIE
1 DOOMED
1 DOORYARD
1 DOUBLED
1 DRAGON
1 DRAW
1 DREAMER'S
1 DRIPPING
1 DRUGS
1 DUET
1 DURBAN
1 EAGLE-ROCKIN'
1 EARTH-THING
1 EASTERN
1 ECSTASY
1 EEEOOOOOO
1 EIGHTH
1 ELITE
1 EMERGING
1 ENGINEER
1 ENORMOUS
1 ERMINE
1 ESPANA
1 ETHER
1 EVASION
1 EXCHANGE
1 EXPLORING
1 FAILS
1 FALLEN
1 FARMERS
1 FAULTILY
1 FENCES
1 FICE
1 FIFTHS
1 FILLMORE
1 FIRED
1 FLAMES
1 FLAVOR
1 FLOAT
1 FLUTTERING
1 FOLDS
1 FOOLS
1 FORD
1 FORMERLY
1 FRAGRANT
1 FRIENDS'LL
1 FRO
1 FRUSTRATED
1 FURTHER
1 GAIETY
1 GAMBLER
1 GARDNER'S
1 GARVEY
1 GEM
1 GERMANY
1 GIMS
1 GITS
1 GLEAM
1 GLOOM
1 GODDESS
1 GOSSIPS
1 GRABS
1 GRANDEES
1 GRASSLESS
1 GREETINGS
1 GRENADINE
1 GROVES
1 GUM
1 G.I
1 HALF-PINT
1 HALL
1 HAND-HIGH
1 HANGED
1 HARLAN
1 CREATOR
1 CRIPPLE
1 CROONED
1 CRUMBLES
1 CUP
1 CURSES
1 CYMBALS
1 DAKAR
1 DARKEST
1 DAWN-TODAY
1 DECCA
1 DEEPLY
1 DEJECTED
1 DEM
1 DENNISON
1 DESNUDA'S
1 DETAINED
1 DEVOUR
1 DIAMONDS
1 DIGNIFY
1 DIRGES
1 DISGUISE
1 DISRUPTOR
1 DOCILE
1 DOGMAS
1 DOORSTEPS
1 DOO-DOO-DOO
1 DOUGLASS'S
1 DRAG
1 DREAMER
1 DREMPT
1 DRONING
1 DRUNKENNESS
1 DUKES
1 DURABLE
1 EAGLE-ROCKISH
1 EARTH-DUST
1 EATIN'
1 EDGECOMBE
1 EFFENDI
1 EL
1 ELKS
1 ENCLOSES
1 ENGLAND
1 ENSLAVED
1 ERNEST
1 ESPECIALLY
1 ETHICAL
1 EVENTUALLY
1 EXIST
1 EXPLOITERS
1 FAINTING
1 FANFARE
1 FARMER
1 FEAST
1 FERTILIZE
1 FICISTS
1 FIGHTERS
1 FINALLY
1 FIRST-CLASS
1 FLAMING
1 FLEEING
1 FLORE
1 FLUTE
1 FOLLOWS
1 FOOTBALL
1 FORE
1 FORMER
1 FRAGILE
1 FRIENDSHIP
1 FROSTING
1 FUEL
1 FURTHERMORE
1 GAILY
1 GAMBLE
1 GARLAND
1 GASTONIA
1 GENERAL
1 GIANT
1 GINGER
1 GIVED
1 GLEE
1 GLORIFY
1 GOD-A-MIGHTY
1 GOTTA
1 GRADE
1 GRANDPA'S
1 GRASP
1 GREENS
1 GRINNED
1 GUARANTEE
1 GUNBOATS
1 HABITUES
1 HALF-DEFIANT
1 HALLS
1 HANDLED
1 HANKERED
1 HARM
1 CREED
1 CROAK
1 CROSSING
1 CRUSH
1 CUR
1 CURTAIN
1 CYNICAL
1 DANCED
1 DARN
1 DAY-PEOPLE
1 DECEASED
1 DEFENDED
1 DELEGATION
1 DEMOCRACY'S
1 DENYING
1 DESPITE
1 DETECTIVES
1 DEWDROP'S
1 DIES
1 DIGNITARIES
1 DISCONTENT
1 DISGRACE
1 DISTILLED
1 DOCKS
1 DOME
1 DOORKNOBS
1 DORIE
1 DOWN-HOME
1 DRAMAS
1 DREAM'S
1 DREW
1 DROPPING
1 DRUNKEN
1 DUNCE
1 DUSTED
1 EAR
1 EARTH-DARK
1 EBECANEEZER
1 EDITORIALS
1 EFFECT
1 ELDERLY
1 ELLA
1 ENDIN'
1 ENGLEWOOD
1 ENTHRONED
1 ERZULIE
1 ESSENCE
1 EUROPE
1 EVERWHERE
1 EXIT
1 EXTRA
1 FAIRY
1 FANNING
1 FAR-TOO-HUMBLE
1 FEATURES
1 FESTERING
1 FIERY
1 FIGHTS
1 FINGER-TALL
1 FISHER
1 FLASH
1 FLESHLY
1 FLOWING
1 FOAMING
1 FOLLOWED
1 FORBIDS
1 FOREHEAD
1 FORMED
1 FREE-DELIVERY
1 FRIED
1 FROWN
1 FULFILLED
1 FUSE
1 GALLOPS
1 GANGPLANK
1 GARLANDS
1 GATES
1 GENTILE
1 GIFTS
1 GIRLIE
1 GIVIN'
1 GLIDES
1 GLORIFIED
1 GOOD-TIMER
1 GOTT
1 GRAFT
1 GRANDMA'S
1 GRAVESTONES
1 GREENER
1 GRINDSTONE
1 GUARDIA
1 GUNS
1 HAG
1 HALF-DARK
1 HALO
1 HANDLE
1 HARD-FACED
1 HARNESS
1 CREEPS
1 CROCHET
1 CROW'LL
1 CRYIN'S
1 CURE
1 CUSSED
1 C.P.T
1 DAR
1 DATES
1 DEAF
1 DECIDED
1 DEFY
1 DELIBERATE
1 DEMONSTRATE
1 DESCENDED
1 DESSALINES
1 DETERMINED
1 DEWY
1 DIET
1 DIMMING
1 DISCIPLES
1 DISGUSTED
1 DIVIDENDS
1 DODGERS
1 DON
1 DOORKNOB
1 DOROTHY'S
1 DOWN-
1 DRANK
1 DREAM-SINGERS
1 DRIFT
1 DROUGHT
1 DRUNKARD
1 DUNHAM
1 DUTY
1 EARNING
1 EARTH-BODY
1 ECHOED
1 EDUCATION
1 EGYPTIAN
1 ELECTRIC
1 EMBROIDERIES
1 ENDING
1 ENGLAND'S
1 EQUALLY
1 ESCAPE
1 ET
1 EVANGELISTA
1 EVERYDAY
1 EXPECTANTLY
1 EXTRA-LARGE
1 FAITHFUL
1 FANTASY
1 FASHION
1 FEES
1 FEVER'S
1 FIFTEEN-YEAR-OLD
1 FIGURINE
1 FINGER
1 FISHING
1 FLATTER
1 FLEW
1 FLUID
1 FOEMEN
1 FONTAINE
1 FORBID
1 FOREIGNER
1 FORTALEZA
1 FREELY
1 FRIGHTEN
1 FROWNIN'
1 FURNISHED-UP
1 FUSS
1 GALLEONS
1 GANG-HORDES
1 GARNERED
1 GAY-COLORED
1 GENTLER
1 GIGOLOS
1 GIRL'LL
1 GLASSER
1 GLINT
1 GOAD
1 GOODBYE
1 GOVERNORS
1 GRAIL
1 GRANDSON'S
1 GREATNESS
1 GREENBACKS
1 GRIP
1 GUINEA
1 GURGLES
1 HAIR-DRESSING
1 HALF-TRUTHS
1 HALTINGLY
1 HANDKERCHIEF
1 HARDNESS
1 HARPER

1 HARPER'S
1 HASTE
1 HAZEL
1 HEARS
1 HEILBRONER
1 HEMMED
1 HERS
1 HIGH-IN-HEABEN
1 HIND
1 HO
1 HOLLAND
1 HOODED
1 HORNS
1 HOVEL
1 HUMBLY
1 HUNTING
1 HUSTLER
1 ICEBERGS
1 IGNORE
1 IMPEL
1 INDEEDY
1 INFORMATION
1 INSTALLMENT
1 INTEGRATION
1 INWARD
1 IRONIC
1 I-DON'T-WANT-TO-DI
1 JAG
1 JAUNDICED
1 JELLY
1 JEWISH
1 JITTERED
1 JOE'S
1 JOSEPHINE
1 JUNGLE-LILY
1 KENTUCKY
1 KILLING'S
1 KIPPUR
1 KNOCKOUT
1 KOO
1 LAGOS
1 LANDLADY'S
1 LANG
1 LATER
1 LAWDY-MERCY
1 LEAKS
1 LEATHER
1 LEFT-HAND
1 LEOLA
1 LESSONS
1 LICENSES
1 LIEBKNECHT
1 LIL
1 LIPSHITZ
1 LOBBY
1 LOOMS
1 LOU
1 LOUNGING
1 LOWELL
1 LUNCHES
1 MAC
1 MAGNOLIA-SCENTED
1 MAIL
1 MALAN
1 MANDALAY
1 MAP
1 MARIE'S
1 MARSEILLAISE
1 MASSES
1 MATERIALS
1 MAYVILLE
1 MEANER
1 MELLOWS
1 MENDED
1 MERCENARY
1 METAL
1 MICHAELMAS
1 MILLER
1 MINORITY
1 MIRTH
1 MISTRESS
1 MOLD
1 MONOLOGUE
1 MOON-GLIMMER
1 MOSQUITO-NETTING
1 MOTORCYCLE
1 MOUTHING
1 MO'N
1 MULZAC
1 MUSCLES
1 MUTTS
1 NANIGO
1 NEARNESS
1 NEGRA
1 NEVER-GET-UP-NO-MO
1 NEW-ORLEANS
1 NIGHT-TIME
1 NIGHTMARE
1 HARRIETT
1 HAVEN
1 HEADLINES
1 HEARTSTRINGS
1 HEIRLOOMED
1 HEMORRHAGE
1 HESITATE
1 HIGHWAY
1 HIRE
1 HOBNAILED
1 HOLLERS
1 HOOD
1 HORSEMAN
1 HOWEVER
1 HUMOROUS
1 HUROK
1 HUT
1 ICEBERG'S
1 ILLUSION
1 IMPLORING
1 INDIES
1 INK
1 INTERMINABLE
1 INTRODUCE
1 IODINE
1 ISLANDS
1 I.W
1 JAGUAR
1 JAZZY
1 JERDEN
1 JIGABOO
1 JOAN
1 JOHANNESBURG
1 JUICY
1 J'ACCUSE
1 KERRY
1 KILLING
1 KITCHENETTES
1 KNOTS
1 K.C
1 LAIN
1 LANDIN'S
1 LANGUAGES
1 LAUNDRY
1 LAWDY
1 LEAPS
1 LEAVING
1 LEGBA
1 LEON
1 LETTERS
1 LICKER-HEADED
1 LIFE-WAYS
1 LINCOLN'S
1 LIQUOR
1 LOBSTER
1 LOOSE
1 LOUDEST
1 LOUNGERS
1 LPS
1 LUSCIOUS
1 MACBETH
1 MAHALIA'S
1 MAIS
1 MALCOLM
1 MANHOOD'S
1 MAPLE-SUGAR
1 MARIAN
1 MARTS
1 MASTER
1 MATTER'S
1 MCLEOD
1 MECCA
1 MELON
1 MENTION
1 MERCE
1 METER
1 MICHAEL
1 MIMES
1 MINOR
1 MISMATED
1 MOANER'S
1 MOLLIE
1 MONSTROUS
1 MOONLIGHT'S
1 MOSS
1 MOTTO
1 MOUTHFUL
1 MUFFLED
1 MUMBLES
1 MUSHROOM
1 NABBED
1 NAT
1 NECKS
1 NEGRITUDE
1 NEVERMORE
1 NIBBLED
1 NIGHT-TIME'S
1 NIGHTIME
1 HARRYS
1 HAWKINS
1 HEADING
1 HEARTBEATS
1 HELPLESSNESS
1 HEMP
1 HEWED
1 HIGHLY
1 HIRIN'
1 HOLDING
1 HONEY-LIPPED
1 HOPPIN'
1 HOUNDS
1 HOW-DO-YOU-DO
1 HUNCHED
1 HURRIED
1 HUTS
1 IDIOT-BRAINED
1 ILLUSIVE
1 IMPLEMENT
1 INDIANS
1 INSANE
1 INTERESTED
1 INVESTIGATED
1 IRELAND'S
1 ISSUE
1 JAB
1 JAMAICA
1 JAZZ-TUNED
1 JERICHO
1 JIM'S
1 JOBLESS
1 JOINT
1 JUKE
1 KATHERINE
1 KEYS
1 KILLERS
1 KIVER
1 KNOW'D
1 LADS
1 LAKE
1 LAND'S
1 LAP
1 LAUNDROMAT
1 LAWNS
1 LEAPING
1 LED
1 LEGION
1 LEONTYNES
1 LEVY
1 LICKS
1 LIFTED
1 LINKED
1 LISTENERS'
1 LOG
1 LOSERS
1 LOUD-MOUTHED
1 LOUSY
1 LUGGED
1 LYE
1 MACK
1 MAHOMET
1 MAJA
1 MAMA'S
1 MANSIONS
1 MARCUS
1 MARKETS
1 MARVELLOUS
1 MASTER'S
1 MATTERS
1 MEALIE
1 MEDAL
1 MELT
1 MERCY'S
1 MESSAGE
1 METHUSELAH
1 MIEN
1 MINDS
1 MINUTES
1 MISSIONARIES
1 MOAT
1 MONDAY'LL
1 MONTEREY
1 MORAL
1 MOTHERS
1 MOULDED
1 MOVES
1 MUGGER
1 MURDERED
1 MUSICAL
1 NAG
1 NATCHA
1 NEEDLES
1 NEGRAS
1 NEWARK
1 NICHOLAS
1 NIGHT-PEOPLE
1 NINA
1 HARSH
1 HAYES
1 HEADSTRONG
1 HEEL
1 HELPLESS
1 HENRY
1 HIBBLER'S
1 HIGH-YALLER
1 HITLER'S
1 HOLDER
1 HONEY-GOLD
1 HORIZONS
1 HOUSING
1 HOW'D
1 HUNGER
1 HUSBANDS
1 HYMNS
1 IF-ING
1 IMMIGRANT
1 IMPRISON
1 INFECTED
1 INSISTENCE
1 INTENTION
1 INVESTIGATED
1 IRELAND
1 IVAN
1 JACK-LEG
1 JANE
1 JAZZ-BAND'S
1 JESTER
1 JINGO
1 JOCKO
1 JOKER
1 JUKEBOXES
1 KDQ
1 KICKIN'
1 KINGSTON
1 KLANSMEN
1 KNOWIN
1 LADY'S
1 LAMENTED
1 LANE
1 LAPSED
1 LAURELS
1 LAW'S
1 LEARNS
1 LEDA
1 LEI
1 LEOPOLD
1 LIARS
1 LICORICE
1 LIGHTER
1 LION
1 LOADERS
1 LOMAX
1 LOSER
1 LOUDLY
1 LOVE-ONE
1 LULLED
1 LYNCHER'S
1 MADAM'D
1 MAI
1 MAJORITY
1 MAMMY'S
1 MANTOVA
1 MARGARET
1 MARSHALNC
1 MASKS
1 MASTERS
1 MAYBELL
1 MEANNESS
1 MEDITATIVE
1 MELTS
1 MERCHANTMAN
1 MESSAGES
1 MEXICANS
1 MIGHT-HAVE-BEEN
1 MINERS
1 MIRACLE
1 MISTOOK
1 MOE
1 MONEY'S
1 MONT
1 MORNING'S
1 MOTIVATED
1 MOURNIN'
1 MOVIE
1 MUG-LIKE
1 MURILLO
1 MUSTA
1 NAIVE
1 NATION'S
1 NEFARIOUS
1 NEIGHBOR
1 NEWER
1 NIGH
1 NIGHT-GONE
1 NIXON
1 HARVESTED
1 HAYMOW
1 HEAP
1 HEH
1 HEM
1 HERNDON
1 HIGH-STEPPIN
1 HILLBILLY
1 HITLER
1 HOLIDAYS
1 HONEY-BROWN
1 HORN-RIM
1 HOUSED
1 HUCKS
1 HUNG'S
1 HUSSY'S
1 IBM
1 IGNITE
1 IMPART
1 IMPRISONING
1 INFINITE
1 INSTANCE
1 INTEND
1 INVITE
1 IRENE
1 IVORY
1 JACKET
1 JAPANESE
1 JEFFERSON
1 JESUIT
1 JITNEYS
1 JOES
1 JOKE
1 JUMPS
1 KEEPING
1 KICKING
1 KINSMEN
1 KLEAGLE
1 KNUCKLES
1 LAFAYETTE
1 LAMENT
1 LANGUAGE
1 LAPS
1 LAWDEE
1 LEADERS
1 LEAST
1 LEECHES
1 LENAS
1 LESBIAN
1 LICENSE
1 LID
1 LIKED
1 LIPPED
1 LOBBIES
1 LONDON
1 LOTTE
1 LOUISIANA
1 LOVIN
1 LUNCH-BOX
1 MABEL
1 MAGI
1 MAIDS
1 MAKER
1 MANAGED
1 MANUFACTURED
1 MARION
1 MARSHAL
1 MASKED
1 MATCH
1 MAYORS
1 MEANEST
1 MEEK
1 MENACED
1 MERCER
1 METAPHYSICALLY
1 MICE
1 MIKADOS
1 MINGUS
1 MIRAGE-LAND
1 MISTAKEN
1 MOHAMMED
1 MONEY-LOVING
1 MOOD
1 MORTAR
1 MOTORCARS
1 MOURNFUL
1 MOWER
1 MULES
1 MURRAY
1 MUTED
1 NAN
1 NAVY
1 NEGLECT
1 NEST
1 NEWLY
1 NIGHT-VEILED
1 NIGHTNESS
1 NKRUMAH

1 NOBLE	1 NOBODY'LL	1 NOE	1 NOISY	1 NOMBRE
1 NONNY	1 NORTHERN	1 NOSE	1 NOTES	1 NOTHIN
1 NOURISH	1 NO-MAN'S	1 NO-OOOO-OOO-OO-O	1 NO'THERN	1 NUDGE
1 NUMBER'S	1 NURSES'	1 NURSE	1 NUTS	1 OAKLAND
1 OATH	1 OBITUARIES	1 OBLIVIOUS	1 OBSEQUIOUS	1 OH-OOO-OO-O
1 OLDEST	1 OLDER'N	1 ONE-WAY	1 ONE-TIME	1 ONE-BUTTON
1 OOL	1 OOP	1 OPPORTUNITY	1 OPPORTUNISTIC	1 OPPRESSES
1 OPPRESSED	1 ORANGE	1 ORDER	1 ORDINARY	1 ORNETTE
1 OUI	1 OURSELVES	1 OUTSIDER	1 OUTWARD	1 OVAH
1 OVERBOARD	1 OVERSEAS	1 OVERLONG	1 OVERCOAT	1 OVERCHARGE
1 OVER-WISE	1 OVER-LONG	1 OVERTURN	1 OVERTONES	1 OVERTIME
1 OWE	1 OWNING	1 OW-OOO-OO-O	1 PA	1 PACE
1 PACK-HORSE	1 PADDY	1 PADDLE-TAILED	1 PAINTINGS	1 PAIR
1 PALLOR	1 PALMOLIVE	1 PALMETTO	1 PANTHER	1 PANT
1 PAPA'S	1 PAPIAMENTO	1 PARALYZED	1 PARENTS	1 PARECE
1 PARKER	1 PARKWAY	1 PARLOR	1 PARROTS	1 PARTICULAR
1 PARTS	1 PARTING	1 PASSIN'	1 PASSERS-BY	1 PASSENGERS
1 PASSOVER	1 PASSIVE	1 PASSIONATE	1 PAT	1 PATENT-LEATHERED
1 PATH	1 PATIO	1 PATROL	1 PATRIOTIC	1 PATRIOT
1 PATRICE	1 PATTI	1 PAWNBROKER	1 PAYIN'	1 PAYING
1 PAYMENTS	1 PAYOLA	1 PC	1 PEACH-SKINNED	1 PEASANT
1 PEDIGREE	1 PEEPS	1 PEEPING	1 PEN	1 PENCIL
1 PENDULUM	1 PENNY	1 PEPSI-COLA	1 PERFESSER	1 PERPETUALLY
1 PERSON'S	1 PHILLIPS	1 PHILIP	1 PHILADELPHIA	1 PH.D
1 PICASSO	1 PICKIN'	1 PICKING	1 PICTURE	1 PIE
1 PIECE	1 PIERCE	1 PIGGY-BACK	1 PILGRIMS	1 PILLARED
1 PILLOWS	1 PINES	1 PINSCHER	1 PINTURA	1 PIONEER
1 PIOUS	1 PITIES	1 PLACED	1 PLAIT	1 PLAINS
1 PLANTATIONS	1 PLANTAINS	1 PLAYER-PIANO	1 PLAYER	1 PLAYBOY
1 PLEASURES	1 PLEASURED	1 PLEASURE	1 PLEASED	1 PLED
1 PLOWED	1 PLUMS	1 PLUMP	1 PLUS	1 POCAHONTAS
1 POCOMANIA	1 POINTS	1 POINTED	1 POINT	1 POKER
1 POLAND'S	1 POLES	1 POLE	1 POLISHING	1 POLITICIANS
1 POLLUTES	1 POLL	1 POMEGRANATE	1 POP	1 POPPY
1 POPULATE	1 PORTRAIT	1 PORTLY	1 PORTER	1 POSITION
1 POSSIBLY	1 POSTER	1 POTS	1 POTTER'S	1 POUNDS
1 POURING	1 PRAIRIES	1 PRAYER-MAKERS	1 PREACHING	1 PREACHERS
1 PREACHER-MAN	1 PRECINCT	1 PREGNANT	1 PREJUDICE	1 PREMATURE
1 PREMIER	1 PRESBYTERIAN	1 PRESENTS	1 PRESIDENTS	1 PRETENDED
1 PREVAIL	1 PRE-DRAFT	1 PRE-LIFETIME	1 PRINCE	1 PRINTED
1 PRINT	1 PRINCESSES	1 PRINCES	1 PRISTINE	1 PRIVATE
1 PRIVILEGES	1 PROBABLY	1 PROBE	1 PROCLAIMS	1 PRODUCTIVE
1 PRODUCTS	1 PROFFER	1 PROFITS	1 PROJECT	1 PROJECTION
1 PROLETARIANS	1 PROMISE	1 PROPAGANDA	1 PROPHETS	1 PROTECTION
1 PROTECTED	1 PROTECTS	1 PROVIDIN'	1 PROW	1 PSEUDONYMS
1 PSHAW	1 PTA	1 PUERTO	1 PULLS	1 PULLING
1 PULVERIZE	1 PUNCHERS	1 PUNCTUATION	1 PURCHASED	1 PURE-BLOODED
1 PURITY	1 PURPOSES	1 PURTIEST	1 PUSHCARTS	1 QUAKERS
1 QUALIFY	1 QUARRELS	1 QUART	1 QUEER	1 QUEENS
1 QUICKER	1 QUIERO	1 QUIEN	1 QUILT	1 QUINCE
1 RABBIT	1 RABBI	1 RACK	1 RADICALS	1 RAG
1 RAGGED	1 RAGTIME	1 RAIDERS	1 RAILWAY	1 RAINY
1 RAINING	1 RAINDROP	1 RAINBOW-SWEET	1 RAISING	1 RAKED
1 RAMONA	1 RAMPART	1 RANDOLPH	1 RANKS	1 RATTLES
1 RAYON	1 RAYS	1 RAZOR	1 REACHIN'	1 REALIZE
1 REALIZING	1 REAPING	1 RECALLS	1 RECALLING	1 RECESSION
1 RECOURSE	1 RECORDS	1 RECORD	1 RECOMMEND	1 RECOGNIZE
1 REDDISH-PURPLE	1 REDDENED	1 REDDEN	1 REDUCED	1 RED-HOT
1 REEFER-MAN	1 REFLECT	1 REGISTER	1 RELATION	1 RELATED
1 RELIGION	1 REMAKE	1 REMAINDERS	1 REMEMBERS	1 REMOVED
1 RENDERED	1 RENTS	1 REPAIRING	1 REPEATEDLY	1 REPEAT
1 REPEATS	1 REPOSE	1 REQUIRES	1 RESPECT	1 RESPECTABLY
1 RESTRICTED	1 RESTRICTIVE	1 RESTRICTING	1 RESTAURANTS	1 RETURNING
1 RETURNS	1 REV	1 REVEALED	1 REVERSED	1 REVEALS
1 REVERSE	1 REVOLUTION	1 RHYTHMIC	1 RICHES	1 RICHNESS
1 RICHMOND	1 RICKEYS	1 RICKETY	1 RIDE'S	1 RIFF
1 RIM	1 RINCON	1 RINNEY	1 RIOT	1 RIOTS
1 RIVER'S	1 ROACH	1 ROADSIDE	1 ROAD-APPLES	1 ROB
1 ROBESPIERRE	1 ROBERT	1 ROBIN	1 ROCKING	1 ROCKETS
1 RODE	1 ROOF-TOPS	1 ROOM'S	1 ROSCOE	1 ROTONDE
1 ROTS	1 ROUGE-BRIGHT	1 ROUGH	1 ROUNDTREES	1 ROUNDS
1 ROWBOATS	1 ROWDY	1 ROWS	1 RUBBED	1 RUBY
1 RUE	1 RUFFLES	1 RUFUS	1 RUG	1 RUINT
1 RUINED	1 RUNNING	1 RUPTURE	1 RUSHIN	1 RUSHES
1 SABE	1 SACKCLOTH	1 SACRAMENT	1 SADIE	1 SADLY
1 SAD-SUNG	1 SAFARI	1 SAFE	1 SAILED	1 SAILBOATS
1 SAIL	1 SALT'PEANUTS	1 SALTY-COLORED	1 SALUTES	1 SAMMY
1 SAMMYS	1 SANCTIFIED	1 SANDINO	1 SANDS	1 SANGRE
1 SASH	1 SASSY	1 SASS	1 SATISFYING	1 SAVAGES
1 SAVIOUR	1 SAVING	1 SAVOY	1 SAXOPHONE'S	1 SAXOPHONES
1 SAYIN'	1 SCANTY	1 SCARRED	1 SCARLET	1 SCATTERS
1 SCHEME	1 SCORNFUL	1 SCORN	1 SCORE	1 SCORCHED
1 SCOTTSBORO	1 SCOTTSBORO'S	1 SCRAGGLY	1 SCRATCHY	1 SCRATCHING
1 SCRAP	1 SCRANTON	1 SCREAMING	1 SCRIPT-WRITERS	1 SCRIPT
1 SCRUB	1 SEAMEN	1 SEARCHED	1 SEARCH	1 SEA-SOUL
1 SEA-LION	1 SECRET	1 SECURE	1 SEDAR	1 SEDUCED
1 SEDUCTIVE	1 SEEDS	1 SEEIN'	1 SEEKERS	1 SEES
1 SEGREGATED	1 SEGREGATION	1 SEKOU	1 SELDOM	1 SELECT
1 SELF-ASSURANCE	1 SELLS	1 SELLING	1 SENDIN'	1 SENDING
1 SENSITIVE	1 SEPIA	1 SEQUINS	1 SERENELY	1 SERF
1 SERPENTS	1 SHACK	1 SHADES	1 SHANKS	1 SHANGO
1 SHANGHAI	1 SHARPER	1 SHARE-CROPPER	1 SHATTER	1 SHATTERED
1 SHED	1 SHELLS	1 SHELTERED	1 SHEPHERD	1 SHIELD
1 SHILLINGS	1 SHIMMERS	1 SHINY	1 SHINED	1 SHIPPED
1 SHIRT	1 SHIVER	1 SHIVERS	1 SHIVERING	1 SHOD
1 SHOOK	1 SHOVELIN'	1 SHOVE	1 SHOWING-OFF	1 SHOWING
1 SHREDS	1 SHRUG	1 SHRUNKEN	1 SHUBUTA	1 SHUFFLING
1 SIDEWALK	1 SIDNEYS	1 SIEG	1 SIGHTED	1 SIGNED

1 SIGNAL
1 SIRS
1 SIXTY
1 SKILLS
1 SKIRTS
1 SLABS
1 SLEET-STUNG
1 SLICE
1 SLIPPED
1 SMALL'S
1 SMILED
1 SMUG
1 SNUB
1 SOGGY
1 SOLUTIONS
1 SONS
1 SOUNDS
1 SO-AND-SO
1 SPEAKER
1 SPENDIN
1 SPIRITS
1 SPOKE
1 SPOTTED
1 SPRINKLING
1 SQUALLING
1 STAINING
1 STARED
1 STATION'S
1 STEEPLE
1 STEPPING
1 STINKING
1 STOOPS
1 STORE'S
1 STRANGER
1 STRETCHING
1 STRONGER
1 STUMPED
1 SUBURB
1 SUFFERING
1 SULPHUROUS
1 SUNS
1 SURGEONS
1 SWARTHY
1 SWEETNESS
1 SWIMMER
1 SWORE
1 SYSTEM
1 TALKED
1 TAPES
1 TATTOOED
1 TEACHER
1 TEARLESS
1 TEMPO
1 TENSE
1 THANKSGIVING
1 THERE'RE
1 THIRTY-TWO
1 THREATENS
1 TICKETS
1 TINGLE
1 TOIL
1 TOO-THIN
1 TOURISTS
1 TRANSPORTED
1 TREADING
1 TRICKERATION
1 TROUBLED
1 TRYIN'
1 TURNER
1 TWENTY-MILE
1 TWISTED
1 TYRANNY
1 UNALIENABLE
1 UNBORN
1 UNDERTONES
1 UNFOLD
1 UNIFORM
1 UNLOVING
1 UNPUBLICIZED
1 UNTRUE
1 UN-UH
1 UPRIGHT
1 USED-TO-BE
1 VARIOUS
1 VEINS
1 VERONA
1 VICTIM
1 VINDICATED
1 VOICES
1 WAGES
1 WAKIN'
1 WANDERERS
1 WAREHOUSES
1 WARTIME
1 WASTED
1 WAVING
1 WEAVER
1 WELCOMIN'
1 SILENTLY
1 SISSIE
1 SIX-YEAR-OLDS
1 SKIM
1 SKYROCKET
1 SLAVERY'S
1 SLEEPIN'
1 SLIDE
1 SLIVER
1 SMARTER
1 SMITH
1 SNAIL
1 SOAP
1 SOKOLSKY'S
1 SOMEBODY'LL
1 SORBONNE
1 SOUNDIN'
1 SO'S
1 SPECTRUM
1 SPENT
1 SPIRALS
1 SPOON
1 SPOTS
1 SPROUT
1 SQUEEZE
1 STALL-IN
1 STAR-FILLED
1 STAYED
1 STEEP
1 STEW
1 STOCKYARDS
1 STOOLS
1 STORES
1 STRANGLED
1 STRETCH
1 STRUGGLING
1 STUYVESANT
1 SUBWAYS
1 SUFI
1 SULTRY
1 SUN-STARS
1 SURVEYS
1 SWEATING
1 SWEETHEART
1 SWISH
1 SYLVESTER'S
1 TACKS
1 TALMUD
1 TAPE
1 TAXES
1 TEACHING
1 TEASING
1 TEMPLES
1 TENTH
1 THAT-A-WAY
1 THERESA
1 THIRTEEN
1 THROWING
1 TIGER
1 TINKLING
1 TOMBSTONE
1 TOP
1 TOUSSAINT
1 TRANSFERS
1 TREAD
1 TRILLING
1 TRUCK
1 TUBMAN
1 TUSKEGEE
1 TWENTY'S
1 TWO-WAY
1 UMBILICAL
1 UNANALYZED
1 UNBOOTED
1 UNDERTAKER'S
1 UNFORTUNATELY
1 UNINDUCTED
1 UNLUCKY
1 UNSCHOOLED
1 UNUSED
1 UN'NEATH
1 UPSET
1 USUALLY
1 VARIED
1 VELASQUEZ
1 VESEY
1 VIETNAM
1 VIOLINS
1 VOTE-IN
1 WAIF
1 WALKER
1 WANLY
1 WARMED
1 WAR-TIME
1 WATCH-FIRES
1 WAYSIDE
1 WEAVE
1 WELL-FED
1 SINISTER
1 SISTERS
1 SIZE
1 SKIN'LL
1 SKYSCRAPERS
1 SLEEK
1 SLEEPING
1 SLIP
1 SLOT
1 SMASHES
1 SMITTY
1 SNAPS
1 SOARING
1 SOL
1 SOMEWHAT
1 SORES
1 SOURCE
1 SPANGLE
1 SPED
1 SPILL
1 SPITS
1 SPORTY
1 SPREE
1 SPRUNG
1 SQUEAKS
1 STALL
1 STARTER
1 STEADY
1 STEINWAY
1 STICKING
1 STOMACH
1 STOPPED
1 STRAIGHTENIN'
1 STRANGELY
1 STRENGTHENING
1 STRYDOMS
1 SUB
1 SUBWAY
1 SUGAR-SWEET
1 SUMMERS
1 SUN-DOWN
1 SUTURE
1 SWEETEST
1 SWELLED
1 SWITCH
1 SYMBOLS
1 TACK
1 TAMALE
1 TAPPED
1 TAXIS
1 TEACHERS
1 TECHNICOLOR
1 TENANT
1 TENT
1 THAY
1 THICKET
1 THIRD-FLOOR
1 THRONE
1 TIME-LOST
1 TINTED
1 TOM-TOM
1 TORCH
1 TOWELS
1 TRANSCRIPTION
1 TREMBLE
1 TRIP
1 TRUDGING
1 TULIPS
1 TWELVE-SHOE
1 TWILIGHT
1 TWO-THREE
1 UM-HUH
1 UNAWARES
1 UNCODIFIED
1 UNDERTAKER
1 UNFORGOTTEN
1 UNION-MADE
1 UNMARKED
1 UNSUSPECTIN
1 UNWITTINGLY
1 UPHILL
1 UPSIDE
1 USUAL
1 VARY
1 VELDT
1 VIBRANT
1 VILER
1 VIOLETS
1 VOTES
1 WAITERS
1 WALLACE
1 WANTING
1 WARP
1 WASHIN'
1 WATER-LOG
1 WEALTH
1 WEEDS
1 WENCHES
1 SINNER
1 SITUATION
1 SKEE
1 SKIPPER
1 SKY-MEANING
1 SLEEK-HAIRED
1 SLENDER
1 SLIPS
1 SLOUCH
1 SMEARED
1 SMOKED
1 SNORT
1 SOBER
1 SOLDIERING
1 SOMETIME
1 SORT
1 SOUSE
1 SPARKLING
1 SPEECHES
1 SPIRITUALS
1 SPLENDOR
1 SPORTS-WRITERS
1 SPREADS
1 SPY
1 SQUINTED
1 STANLEY
1 STARK
1 STEAM
1 STEMS
1 STINGY
1 STONES
1 STORY-TELLERS
1 STRAIGHTENED
1 STRAIN
1 STRING
1 STRYDOM
1 SUBMARINES
1 SUCKED
1 SUGAR-DADDY
1 SUNDAY'S
1 SUPPORT
1 SWAHILI
1 SWEEPS
1 SWIFTLY
1 SWITCHBOARD
1 SYNCOPATE
1 TAG
1 TAN
1 TASTED
1 TE
1 TEAM
1 TEEN-AGE
1 TENANT'S
1 TERRORS
1 THEIVING
1 THICKER
1 THIS-A
1 THUD
1 TIMELESS
1 TIPPED
1 TOOTHPICK
1 TOUCHSTONES
1 TRACE
1 TRAVELING
1 TRIBUNE'S
1 TRIUMPHAL
1 TRUEST
1 TUNES
1 TWELVE-ROOM
1 TWINING
1 TYPIST
1 UM-HUM
1 UNBINDING
1 UNDECIPHERED
1 UNDRESSED
1 UNFREE
1 UNION'S
1 UNOBTRUSIVE
1 UNSUNG
1 UN-HUMM-M
1 UPHOLD
1 UPWARD
1 UTTERED
1 VAUDEVILLE
1 VELVET
1 VIBRATES
1 VILLAGES
1 VIRGINIA
1 VULCAN
1 WAITER
1 WALTER
1 WANT-ADS'
1 WARRIORS
1 WASHINGTON'S
1 WATERMELON
1 WEAPONS
1 WEEKS
1 WEPT
1 SINS
1 SIT-INS
1 SKEE-DE-DAD
1 SKIRT
1 SKY'S
1 SLEEVE
1 SLEW
1 SLIPPING
1 SLUG
1 SMELLING
1 SMOOTHS
1 SNOWBIRD
1 SOCK
1 SOLEDAD
1 SONG'S
1 SORTS
1 SOUVENIRS
1 SPATTERED
1 SPENDIN'
1 SPIRITUAL
1 SPLITS
1 SPOTLIGHT
1 SPRIGHTLY
1 SQUARES
1 STAGE
1 STAND-IN
1 STARING
1 STEALTH
1 STEPPERS
1 STINKIN'
1 STONE-COLD
1 STORMS
1 STRAYHORN
1 STREAK
1 STRIKES
1 STUDYING
1 SUBSIDING
1 SUEDE
1 SUICIDE
1 SUNNY-FACED
1 SUPPORTING
1 SWANEE
1 SWEEPIN'
1 SWIMMING
1 SWORD
1 SYPHILITIC
1 TALKS
1 TANGLED
1 TATTERED
1 TEACH
1 TEARING
1 TELEPHONE
1 TENSION
1 TETHERED
1 THELONIOUS
1 THIEVING
1 THOUGHTFUL
1 THYSELF
1 TIMME
1 TOBACCO
1 TOO-ROUGH
1 TOUCHES
1 TRADE-MARKS
1 TRA-LA-LA-LA
1 TRICKLE
1 TROTTERS
1 TRULY
1 TURNPIKE
1 TWENTY-STORY
1 TWINKLE
1 TYRANTS
1 UNA
1 UNBOUGHT
1 UNDERPAID
1 UNFELT
1 UNICORNS
1 UNKIND
1 UNPARSED
1 UNTOUCHED
1 UN-NEGRO
1 UPPER
1 URGE
1 VAIN
1 VEDADO
1 VERANDAS
1 VICEROYS
1 VILLE
1 VISIT
1 WAFTS
1 WAKING
1 WAND
1 WARES
1 WARS
1 WASHED-AND-IRONED-
1 WAVERING
1 WEATHERED
1 WEEK'S
1 WESTPORT

1 WESTERN	1 WESTCHESTER	1 WET	1 WE'D	1 WHAT'LL
1 WHEE-OOO	1 WHEELS	1 WHEREWITHAL	1 WHERE'S	1 WHERE'RE
1 WHERE-WITH-ALL	1 WHIR	1 WHISPERING	1 WHISPER	1 WHISTLES
1 WHITE-ROBED	1 WHITE-FACED	1 WHITMAN	1 WHO'S	1 WHO'RE
1 WICKED	1 WIDE-OPEN	1 WIDE-EYED	1 WILLIN'	1 WILLIE
1 WIN	1 WINDING	1 WINDOW'S	1 WIND-BLOWN	1 WINDY
1 WINE-MAIDEN	1 WINE-COLD	1 WINES	1 WINED	1 WINE'S
1 WINE-SOUSE	1 WINNING	1 WINSTON-SALEM	1 WINTER'S	1 WIRED
1 WISHED	1 WISP	1 WITHER	1 WIVES	1 WOE
1 WOMANHOOD	1 WOMEN'S	1 WONDROUS	1 WOOF	1 WOOLWORTH
1 WORKMAN	1 WORKER'S	1 WORRYIN'	1 WORRIES	1 WORSE
1 WORST	1 WORSER	1 WORTHY	1 WOVEN	1 WRAPPED
1 WRAPS	1 WRIGHT	1 WRITERS	1 WRONGEST	1 W.E.B
1 YA	1 YARDMAN'S	1 YARD	1 YEAH	1 YEARNS
1 YEE-EE-E-WHO-OOO-O	1 YELL	1 YEP	1 YESTERDAY'S	1 YESTERDAYS
1 YOKE	1 YOM	1 YOUNGER	1 YOUR'N	1 YUH
1 Y-E-A-H	1 ZIK	1 ZONE	1 ZOO	1 ZOOMIN'
1 00	1 1	1 100-YEARS	1 100-VOICES	1 12TH
1 1619	1 17	1 1865	1 1895	1 1942
1 1963	1 1965	1 2	1 23RD	1 25
1 26-GIRL	1 3-2-6	1 50TH	1 60-VOICES	1 7TH
1 7-0-3	1 7-11	1 7'S	1 8-ROCK	1 80-VOICES
1 83	1 90	1 942	1 'COURSE	1 'FAY
1 'FORD	1 'FRAID	1 'GINITY	1 'HORE	1 'LECTRIC-SHOCKIN'
1 'MEMBER	1 'NOTHER	1 'TWAS	1 'VESTER	2 ABUELA
2 ACCOUNT	2 ACHE	2 ACHING	2 ADAM	2 ADVENTUROUS
2 AFTERNOONS	2 AGE	2 AGE-LONG	2 AGE-LESS	2 ALARM
2 ALLY	2 ALREADY	2 ANDERSON	2 ANGEL	2 ANGELES
2 ANGEL-CHILE	2 ANSWERED	2 ANSWERS	2 ANYBODY	2 ANYONE
2 ANZIO	2 APARTHEID	2 APART	2 ARC	2 ARISE
2 ARMY	2 ARTHUR	2 ASHES	2 ASIDE	2 ASLEEP
2 ASUNDER	2 ATLANTIC	2 AUGUST	2 AWAIT	2 AWAKE
2 AWOKE	2 A-BEEN	2 A-WAITIN'	2 BABY'S	2 BAKE
2 BANJO'S	2 BANK	2 BANKS	2 BARED	2 BARKIN'
2 BARRED	2 BATHED	2 BAYOU	2 BEARING	2 BEAU
2 BEGINNING	2 BEIGE	2 BELIEVED	2 BELOVED	2 BENT
2 BESS	2 BETHUNE	2 BEWARE	2 BIGGER	2 BILL
2 BILLS	2 BIND	2 BIRTH	2 BLACKBERRY	2 BLADE
2 BLED	2 BLOOM	2 BLUES'ES	2 BLUSH	2 BOASTING
2 BOATS	2 BOMB	2 BORE	2 BOX-CAR	2 BRAGGING
2 BRANCH	2 BREATHE	2 BREAST	2 BRICKBATS	2 BRIDGE'S
2 BRONX	2 BROOM	2 BROWN-SKIN	2 BUCK	2 BUG
2 BUGS	2 BUILT	2 BUILDER	2 BUNCHE	2 BURSTING
2 BURY	2 BUTTERFLIES	2 CADILLAC	2 CARAMEL	2 CARD
2 CARED	2 CARING	2 CARMEN	2 CARNIVAL	2 CAROLINA
2 CART	2 CASSIE	2 CATS	2 CAT-GUT	2 CENTER
2 CHAIR	2 CHAINS	2 CHARGES	2 CHARGED	2 CHARIOT
2 CHARITY'S	2 CHARM	2 CHAWED	2 CHEER	2 CHI
2 CHICO	2 CHOICE	2 CIRCLES	2 CITIES	2 CLEANED
2 CLEW	2 CLIMBIN'	2 CLOSELY	2 CLOSED	2 CLUBS
2 CLUTCHING	2 COAST	2 COCOA	2 COLLARD	2 COLORS
2 COMMENT	2 COMPROMISE	2 COMPOSER	2 CONQUER	2 CONSENT
2 COOK	2 COOKING	2 COP	2 COPS	2 COSTS
2 COULD'VE	2 COUNT	2 COVERED	2 CREW	2 CROONS
2 CROSS-EYED	2 CROW'S	2 CRUST	2 CRUSHING	2 CRUSHED
2 CUDDLES	2 CULTURE	2 CURSED	2 CURSE	2 CURVED
2 DAILY	2 DAMS	2 DANCER	2 DARING	2 DARK-FACED
2 DAVE	2 DAWG'S	2 DAWNS	2 DAYBREAK	2 DAYTIME
2 DELICIOUS	2 DENIED	2 DEPRESSION	2 DEPRAVED	2 DEPTHS
2 DETAIL	2 DETERMINATION	2 DEVILS	2 DICE	2 DIGNITY
2 DIMES	2 DINAH'S	2 DINAH	2 DINNER	2 DIP
2 DIPLOMA	2 DISEASE	2 DITCHES	2 DIVE	2 DIZZY
2 DOLLS	2 DOORWAY	2 DOVE	2 DO'	2 DRAFTEE
2 DRAMATIC	2 DRESSES	2 DRINKIN'	2 DRINKING	2 DRIPPED
2 DROOP	2 DRUMBEAT	2 DUG	2 DUKE	2 DYNAMITE
2 EAGLE-ROCK	2 EARS	2 EASE	2 EASIER	2 EIGHTY-NINE
2 EITHER	2 ELEVEN	2 ELI	2 EMPTINESS	2 ENAMEL
2 ENTRY	2 ENVELOPE	2 EQUAL	2 EQUALITY	2 ER
2 EVENIN'	2 EVENINGS	2 EVERYBODY'S	2 EVERBODY	2 EVE'S
2 EXPLODE	2 EXPLAIN	2 FACIST	2 FACING	2 FAILED
2 FAINTED	2 FAMILY	2 FAMOUS	2 FARTHEREST	2 FASTER
2 FATHER'S	2 FAUBUS	2 FEARS	2 FEATHERS	2 FERRY
2 FESTER	2 FIFTH	2 FIGHTIN'	2 FINAL	2 FINISHED
2 FIRM	2 FISH-TAIL	2 FLAGS	2 FLEE	2 FLESH-AND-BLOOD
2 FLOORS	2 FLOW	2 FLOWED	2 FLYIN'	2 FOAM
2 FOLKSES	2 FOLKS'	2 FOOLIN'	2 FOREIGN	2 FOREST
2 FORGETS	2 FORTY-FOUR	2 FOUNDRY	2 FOUNDRIES	2 FOURTEEN
2 FRAGRANCE	2 FRANCS	2 FRANCO	2 FRENETIC	2 FRISCO
2 FROSTED	2 FUNNY	2 GAMBLED	2 GANG	2 GANGRENOUS
2 GARMENT	2 GATHERED	2 GAWD-KNOWS-WHAT	2 GENERALS	2 GENTLEMEN
2 GENTLEMAN	2 GERALD	2 GETTING	2 GHOSTLY	2 GHOST
2 GIFT	2 GIRL-FRIEND	2 GIVING	2 GLOW	2 GOAL
2 GOOD-TIME	2 GORGEOUS	2 GOURDS	2 GOVERN	2 GRADUATE
2 GRADUALLY	2 GRANNY	2 GRANT	2 GRASSES	2 GREED
2 GREELEY	2 GREY	2 GRIEF	2 GROWING	2 GUARDING
2 GUIDE	2 GUITARS	2 GUITAR	2 GUYS	2 GYPSIES
2 HADES	2 HAIL	2 HALF-PAST	2 HAMMOND	2 HANDFUL
2 HARD-HEARTED	2 HASTINGS	2 HAST	2 HATS	2 HAUL
2 HAUNT	2 HAVIN'	2 HEARING	2 HEARTBEAT	2 HEARTBREAK
2 HEIL	2 HELLO	2 HEREAFTER	2 HERSELF	2 HEY-HEY-HEY
2 HE'D	2 HIDDEN	2 HIDING	2 HIPS	2 HISS
2 HOLDIN'	2 HOLLYWOOD	2 HOMESICK	2 HOMELAND	2 HONEST
2 HONORED	2 HOOTIN'	2 HOPING	2 HOUND	2 HOWDY-DO
2 HUH	2 HUM	2 HURTS	2 HUSBAND	2 HYMN
2 HYPE	2 ICING	2 IG	2 ILLS	2 IMPORTANT
2 IMPRISONED	2 INCHES	2 INDIA	2 INDIVIDUAL	2 INEZ
2 INFIRMARY	2 INSTRUCTOR	2 INTERRACIAL	2 INTEGRATED	2 INVESTIGATE
2 IT'LL	2 JACKIE	2 JAZZ-BOYS	2 JERSEY	2 JEWELS

2	JITTERBUGGING	2	JOINED	2	JOYS	2	JUICE	2	JUMPED
2	KANSAS	2	KEEPER	2	KENYATTA	2	KETTLE	2	KEY
2	KISSING	2	KITCHENS	2	KLANSMAN	2	KLUX	2	KNOCK
2	KNOW'S	2	KU	2	LACK	2	LAMB	2	LARGE
2	LATCH	2	LATELY	2	LAUGHIN'	2	LAUNCHED	2	LEADER
2	LEADS	2	LEAF	2	LEAN	2	LEARNING	2	LEE
2	LEONTYNE	2	LEONARD	2	LESSER	2	LEWIS	2	LIABLE
2	LIBERTIES	2	LICKER'LL	2	LIFTS	2	LIGHTNING	2	LIKES
2	LISTENING	2	LONE	2	LONG-HEADED	2	LORD'S	2	LOS
2	LOVING	2	LOWER	2	LOW-RATE	2	LUNCH	2	LYIN'
2	LYNCHING	2	L.K	2	MAGIC	2	MAID	2	MAMAS
2	MAMACITA	2	MAMMIES	2	MANGER	2	MANKIND	2	MANURE
2	MARACAS	2	MARGIE'S	2	MARKET	2	MARKER	2	MARRIAGE
2	MARRY	2	MARTHA	2	MARTIAL	2	MAU	2	MAYOR
2	MEAGRE	2	MEANWHILE	2	MEANIN'	2	MECHANICS	2	MELANCHOLY
2	MEMORY	2	MEN'S	2	MERRY-GO-ROUND	2	MIAMI	2	MILES
2	MILLION-DOLLAR	2	MINCE-MEAT	2	MINGLE	2	MINISTER	2	MINUS
2	MIRE	2	MISTERS	2	MISTREATED	2	MIZ	2	MOB
2	MONROE'S	2	MONROE	2	MONTAGE	2	MORENA	2	MORN
2	MOULDS	2	MOUNTS	2	MOURN	2	MOURNERS	2	MOUTHS
2	MOVIES	2	MUST'VE	2	NAIL	2	NATIONS	2	NATURAL
2	NATURE	2	NATURALLY	2	NECKLACE	2	NEEDED	2	NEHRU
2	NEIGH	2	NIGHTMARES	2	NIGHT-BIRD	2	NINNY	2	NOISE
2	NOON	2	NOT'VE	2	NOURISHED	2	NURSES	2	N.A.A.C.P
2	OBSTACLES	2	OCCUR	2	OCTOBER	2	OFFERED	2	OGOUN
2	OOP-POP-A-DA	2	ORBIT	2	ORGANIZING	2	ORIENTAL	2	ORIGINAL
2	OTHER'S	2	OVEN	2	OVERTAKES	2	OVERCOME	2	O.K.ED
2	PACKED	2	PAL	2	PALMS	2	PARTIES	2	PASSES
2	PASSION	2	PATHS	2	PATIENCE	2	PAUL	2	PAWN
2	PAWNED	2	PAYS	2	PEARL	2	PEKING	2	PENN
2	PEOPLES	2	PERFUME	2	PERSIMMON	2	PICKED	2	PIED
2	PIERROT'S	2	PIGALLE	2	PILE	2	PILLARS	2	PINK
2	PIPER	2	PISTOLS	2	PLANNING	2	PLANES	2	PLANTS
2	PLAYIN'	2	PLAYIN	2	POET	2	POPPY-FLOWER	2	PORGY
2	POST	2	POT	2	POWDERED	2	PRAYED	2	PREACHER
2	PRESSURE	2	PRICE	2	PROBLEMS	2	PROMISES	2	PROTECT
2	PROVE	2	PURCHASE	2	PYRAMIDS	2	QUEEN	2	QUESTION
2	QUIETLY	2	RAFFLE	2	RAILROADS	2	RAINBOW	2	RAISIN
2	RAISED	2	RARE	2	RARING	2	RATTLE	2	REACHES
2	READY	2	RECALL	2	REDDER	2	REFLECTS	2	REGRETS
2	REIGN	2	REMEMBERING	2	RENAISSANCE	2	REPUTATION	2	REVOLT
2	RHYMES	2	RICE	2	RIDES	2	RIGHTFUL	2	RINGING
2	RINGS	2	RISIN'	2	ROAD'S	2	ROBESON	2	ROCKS
2	ROCKIN'	2	ROMAN	2	ROOMING	2	ROSES	2	ROTTEN
2	ROUNDERS	2	ROUTE	2	RUB	2	RULE	2	RULED
2	RUM	2	RUNG	2	SAGS	2	SAILS	2	SAILORS
2	SAINTS	2	SAKE	2	SANDWICH	2	SANG	2	SATIN
2	SAVED	2	SAYING	2	SCARS	2	SCREAMS	2	SCUM
2	SEASONS	2	SEA'S	2	SEEMED	2	SEEM	2	SELMA
2	SENDS	2	SEPARATE	2	SERVICE	2	SERVE	2	SERVANT
2	SETTIN	2	SEVENTH	2	SEVENTEEN	2	SHAFTS	2	SHAKES
2	SHEEP	2	SHELF	2	SHIMMERING	2	SHOE	2	SHOOT
2	SHOP	2	SHOPPING	2	SHOVEL	2	SHROUD	2	SHUTTERED
2	SIEVE	2	SILK	2	SIMPLY	2	SINGAPORE	2	SIT-IN
2	SIX-BITS'	2	SLAVERY	2	SLAVER'S	2	SLEEP-SONG	2	SLIGHTLY
2	SMEARS	2	SMELL	2	SMILING	2	SMILES	2	SMOLDERING
2	SNAKE	2	SNAKE-LIKE	2	SNORE	2	SNOWING	2	SOBBING
2	SOLDIERS	2	SOME'N	2	SOMEONE	2	SON-OF-A-GUN	2	SOONER
2	SORROWS	2	SOUGHT	2	SPACE	2	SPARE	2	SPEAKING
2	SPEED	2	SPELL	2	SPIN	2	SPLASH	2	SPRINGTIME
2	STAINED	2	STAIN	2	STAR-DUST	2	STATIONS	2	STATES
2	STEALING	2	STEAL	2	STEAMBOATS	2	STEM	2	STEP-FATHERED
2	STICK	2	STICKS	2	STILLNESS	2	STINK	2	STIRS
2	STOKELY	2	STOPS	2	STORMY	2	STORM	2	STORE
2	STREW	2	STRETCHES	2	STRIDE	2	STRIFE	2	STRIP
2	STROKE	2	STROLL	2	STRUTTING	2	STUDIED	2	STUFF
2	STUMP	2	STURDY	2	SUBVERSIVE	2	SUNG	2	SUNLIGHT
2	SUNSETS	2	SUPPOSE	2	SUPPER	2	SUPPOSED	2	SURPASSING
2	SWAYS	2	SWITCH-BLADE	2	SYMBOL	2	SYRUPY	2	T
2	TAKIN'	2	TAKING	2	TALLER	2	TAMED	2	TAUGHT
2	TAUNT	2	TAUT	2	TAX	2	TAXI	2	TEETH
2	TELESCOPE	2	TELEVISION	2	TELLERS	2	TENNESSEE	2	THEY'D
2	THINKIN'	2	THROWS	2	THRUST	2	TIME-CLOCK	2	TIPPIN
2	TIRE	2	TODAY'S	2	TOES	2	TOLE	2	TONGUES
2	TOROS	2	TORTURE	2	TOSS	2	TOUGH	2	TOURE
2	TOWNS	2	TO'VE	2	TRACKS	2	TRAGIC	2	TRASH
2	TRIUMPHANT	2	TRIUMPH	2	TRUCKS	2	TU	2	TUCK-TAIL
2	TURNING	2	TURPENTINE	2	TWELVE	2	TWENTY-TWO	2	TWICE
2	UNCLE	2	UNDERNEATH	2	UNECHOED	2	UNKNOWN	2	UNLIKE
2	UPSTAIRS	2	UPTOWN	2	VALLEY	2	VAST	2	VICTORY
2	VICTROLA	2	VISION	2	VOTING	2	VULGAR	2	WAGGON
2	WAGONS	2	WAITS	2	WALT	2	WANDERING	2	WANTA
2	WARMTH	2	WARN'T	2	WEAK	2	WEIGHT	2	WEREN'T
2	WHEEL	2	WHIPS	2	WHIPPED	2	WHIRLS	2	WHISKY
2	WHISTLE	2	WHITES	2	WHOM	2	WHORE	2	WIGGLE
2	WILDERNESS	2	WIL'	2	WINDOWS	2	WINDLESSNESS	2	WIND'S
2	WIPE	2	WOMB	2	WOMENS	2	WONDERED	2	WOODS
2	WOODED	2	WORKERS'	2	WORLDLY	2	WORMS	2	WORN
2	WORRY	2	WRIT	2	YAL	2	YARDBIRD	2	YELLED
2	YORK	2	YOURSELVES	2	1ST	2	10	2	12
2	1941	2	5TH	2	50	2	51ST	2	6-C-2
2	'HIND	2	'LIEVE	2	'LL	2	'LOWED	2	'SCUSE
2	'TWIXT	3	ACT	3	AFRICA'S	3	ALABAM'	3	ALIVENESS
3	AMOUNT	3	ANGELS	3	ASHAMED	3	AX	3	AY-LORD
3	BAIL	3	BALLS	3	BASIC	3	BEAR	3	BECAME
3	BELL	3	BERNICE	3	BE-BOP	3	BIRMINGHAM	3	BLOCK
3	BLOODY	3	BLOWN	3	BOARDING	3	BONGO	3	BOOKER
3	BOOTED	3	BOSS	3	BOTTLE	3	BOWL	3	BRAVE

3 BREEZE
3 BURNS
3 CALLS
3 CAUGHT
3 CHANCED
3 CHRISTIAN
3 CLEAR
3 CORDELIA
3 CRUEL
3 DARLING
3 DEFIANCE
3 DISTANT
3 DOUGLASS
3 DRIVES
3 DYIN'
3 ELSE'S
3 ETERNITY
3 FILTH
3 FLOOD
3 FREEDOMS
3 GOODNESS
3 GWINE
3 HEABEN
3 HIDE
3 INNER
3 JACKSON
3 JUNE
3 KINDER
3 LANDLADY
3 LETS
3 LONELINESS
3 LYING
3 MASS
3 MISSED
3 MOUNT
3 NIGGERS
3 OPENS
3 O.K
3 PHONE
3 PLANTED
3 PRAIRIE
3 PRESENT
3 PURGE
3 RECITATION
3 RISES
3 ROOTS
3 SCARED
3 SHARECROPPERS
3 SHOTS
3 SINK
3 SMASH
3 SPEAKS
3 STOLE
3 STUDY
3 SUSANNA
3 SWEETIE
3 THEMSELVES
3 THUMP
3 TOMB
3 TREATS
3 UNITED
3 VIRGIN
3 WANDER
3 WEARS
3 WISDOM
3 10-OTHERS
3 8
4 AMEN
4 BAHIA
4 BEGUN
4 BLOWING
4 BOSOM
4 BROAD
4 BUS
4 CARRIED
4 CIVIL
4 CREDIT
4 DREAMERS
4 EXPECT
4 FILL
4 FUTURE
4 GOD'S
4 GUTTER
4 HARLEM'S
4 HONOR
4 INDENTURED
4 KINGS
4 LEGS
4 LOOKING
4 LOVERS
4 MINT
4 MOONLIGHT
4 NEEDLE
4 NOTE
4 PIPE
4 PRACTICE
4 RHYTHM
4 SATISFIED

3 BROTHERS
3 BURNING
3 CALM
3 CELLAR
3 CHEAPEST
3 CIGARETTE
3 COFFEE
3 COURT
3 CRYSTAL
3 DATE
3 DESERT
3 DOCTOR
3 DOZEN
3 DROWNED
3 EARN
3 EMANCIPATION
3 FAIR
3 FIST
3 FOLK
3 FRIGHTENED
3 GOVERNMENT
3 HAPPENS
3 HEART'S
3 HOLDS
3 INSURANCE
3 JAMES
3 JUNGLES
3 KNOCKED
3 LARGER
3 LETTING
3 LONGING
3 MACHINE
3 MELODIES
3 MIX
3 M'AM
3 NINE
3 OPENED
3 PARTY
3 PIMPS
3 PLOWING
3 PRAYER
3 PRESS
3 PURPLE
3 RESTING
3 ROADS
3 ROUNDER
3 SCATTERED
3 SHERIFF'S
3 SHOULDER
3 SITS
3 SOJOURNER
3 SPIT
3 STOOP
3 STUDENT
3 SWAMP
3 SWIM
3 THIEVES
3 TIME'S
3 TONGUE
3 TRUMPETS
3 UTTER
3 WAITED
3 WASH
3 WEDO
3 WRITTEN
3 18TH
3 'S
4 ARM
4 BANNER
4 BENCH
4 BOAT
4 BOTHER
4 BROTHERHOOD
4 BUST
4 CENTENNIAL
4 CLAUS
4 DADDY-O
4 DRIVEN
4 EYE
4 FORCE
4 GALL
4 GRASS
4 GUY
4 HEARSE
4 HORN
4 JOINTS
4 LA
4 LIEDER
4 LOT
4 LOW-DOWN
4 MISTAKE
4 MOVING
4 NEIGHBORS
4 OFFER
4 PLAYING
4 PROUD
4 ROAR
4 SETS

3 BUBBLES
3 BURSTS
3 CAP
3 CENT
3 CHECK
3 CINNAMON
3 COMMON
3 COVER
3 CUTTING
3 DAWN'S
3 DE-DOP
3 DOGGED
3 DR
3 DROWN
3 EAST
3 ENDLESS
3 FARTHER
3 FIX
3 FOOD
3 FURROW
3 GOWN
3 HAPPINESS
3 HEAT
3 HOLY
3 ITSELF
3 JASPER
3 JUSTICE
3 LACE
3 LAWS
3 LICK
3 LORDY
3 MAGNOLIA
3 MERMAID
3 MODERN
3 NAW
3 NO-GOOD
3 ORCHESTRA
3 PEOPLE'S
3 PISTOL
3 POCKET
3 PRAYERS
3 PRICES
3 PUSH
3 RE-BOP
3 ROAM
3 RUNNER
3 SCREAM
3 SHE'LL
3 SHOUTS
3 SIXTEEN
3 SOLDIER'S
3 SPLINTERS
3 STOPPIN'
3 STUPID
3 SWAY
3 SWING
3 THIGHS
3 TINY
3 TOUCHING
3 TRUST
3 VAGUE
3 WALKERS
3 WATCHED
3 WHORES
3 Y
3 33TH
4 AH
4 ART
4 BARREN
4 BEST
4 BOMBING
4 BREAKS
4 BROUGHT
4 CAB
4 CERTAIN
4 CLIMB
4 DAY'S
4 DROP
4 FALSE
4 FRANTIC
4 GALS
4 GRIN
4 HALLELUJAH
4 HERE'S
4 HORSES
4 JULIE
4 LAD
4 LIKEN
4 LOTS
4 MANHATTAN
4 MIST
4 MRS
4 NEIGHBORHOOD
4 OUTSIDE
4 POISON
4 QUARTERS
4 ROLLED
4 SETTING

3 BUD
3 BUTLER
3 CAPTAIN
3 CENTURIES
3 CHECKS
3 CIRCUS
3 COMMUNITY
3 CREAM
3 DAMBALLA
3 DECEMBER
3 DIFFERENCE
3 DOG-GONE
3 DREAMT
3 DRUG
3 EATING
3 ENDS
3 FED
3 FLAMENCO
3 FOUGHT
3 GLASSES
3 GRAVES
3 HARBOR
3 HERD
3 HUMBLE
3 I'SE
3 JET
3 KICK
3 LADDER
3 LEMON
3 LIFTING
3 LORDS
3 MARTIN
3 MIGHT'VE
3 MOUNTAIN
3 NEARLY
3 OFFERING
3 ORGAN
3 PERSONAL
3 PLANE
3 POLISHED
3 PREACHED
3 PROUDLY
3 RACES
3 RIDING
3 ROOF
3 SAP
3 SERVANTS
3 SHOPS
3 SILENT
3 SKIES
3 SOMEDAY
3 STAIRS
3 STRAW
3 SUBDUED
3 SWAYING
3 SYNCOPATED
3 THREAD
3 TIP
3 TOY
3 TWO-BIT
3 VEIL
3 WALKIN'
3 WEALTHY
3 WHO'VE
3 YOUTH
3 40
4 ALTAR
4 ATLANTA
4 BARREL
4 BLAME
4 BOOGIE-WOOGIE
4 BRIDGE
4 BRUSH
4 CALLING
4 CHAIN
4 COMPANY
4 DEVIL
4 ECHO
4 FEELIN'
4 FREEDOM'S
4 GARDEN
4 GROWS
4 HANDLES
4 HIDES
4 HOURS
4 KEEPS
4 LAUGHED
4 LIVED
4 LOVELINESS
4 MARCH
4 MOMENT
4 MURMUR
4 NICE
4 OWNS
4 POOL
4 RAPE
4 SALLIE
4 SHAKING

3 BUFFALO
3 CAGED
3 CAT
3 CERTAINLY
3 CHOPS
3 CLASS
3 COMPASS
3 CROCODILE
3 DANCIN
3 DEEPEST
3 DIDS
3 DOING
3 DRESS
3 DUSKY
3 ECHOES
3 ENEMY
3 FIGURE
3 FLIES
3 FRAME
3 GLOVES
3 GRINNING
3 HATTIE
3 HE'LL
3 INDIAN
3 JACK-O'-LANTERNS
3 JUKEBOX
3 KICKS
3 LADIES
3 LEND
3 LOCK
3 LUTHER
3 MASK
3 MINES
3 MOUND
3 NEWS
3 OFTEN
3 OURS
3 PETALS
3 PLAN
3 POOLS
3 PRESIDENT
3 PULLED
3 RAN
3 RIGHTS
3 ROOMS
3 SATURDAY
3 SHAMELESS
3 SHORE
3 SINGER
3 SKINS
3 SORRY
3 STOCKINGS
3 STRUT
3 SUDDEN
3 SWEAT
3 TABLES
3 THRILL
3 TOE
3 TRAINS
3 UH
3 VINE
3 WALNUT
3 WEAR
3 WILLING
3 YOU'D
3 55TH
4 ALTHOUGH
4 A-COMIN'
4 BATTLE
4 BLESS
4 BOOTS
4 BRINGS
4 BULLET
4 CANE
4 CIVILIZATION
4 CREATED
4 DISTANCE
4 EGG
4 FEELS
4 FUR
4 GODS
4 GUARD
4 HANG
4 HOLLERED
4 HUMAN
4 KINDS
4 LAZY
4 LIZA
4 LOVE'S
4 MARK
4 MONDAY
4 NECK
4 NIGHTS
4 PEEL
4 POP-A-DA
4 REACHING
4 SANTA
4 SHELTER

4 SHE'D
4 SILKEN
4 SOAKING
4 STANDS
4 SUE
4 TABLE
4 THROAT
4 TRAGEDY
4 UNICORN
4 WEARINESS
4 WING
4 YIELD
4 40-VOICES
5 AHEAD
5 BABIES
5 BIRD
5 CA
5 CHOOSE
5 CONGO
5 CROWD
5 DIVINE
5 DOUGH
5 ELEVATOR
5 FISTS
5 FRIENDS
5 GRAB
5 JEWS
5 LANDLORD
5 LULU
5 MEMORIES
5 NARY
5 PACK
5 PRIDE
5 RANG
5 SLIM
5 STEP
5 THEY'LL
5 TROUBLES
5 WHISPERS
5 WORTH
6 AWFUL
6 BITE
6 BULLETS
6 COAT
6 CROWN
6 DOWNTOWN
6 FAST
6 FORGIVE
6 GRANDPA
6 HEADS
6 HOTEL
6 JOSTLE
6 LEARN
6 MARCHING
6 MILLIONS
6 PASSED
6 PUSHED
6 RUSSIA
6 SHADE
6 SOMEHOW
6 STOOD
6 THUNDER
6 WE'VE
7 ALSO
7 BEYOND
7 CHEAP
7 DRESSED
7 FATE
7 GETS
7 IRA
7 LAW
7 MONTHS
7 OWL
7 ROPE
7 SHINING
7 STORY
7 TICKET
7 WOMAN'S
8 BARE
8 BOTH
8 COATS
8 FEELING
8 FRANCE
8 HAT
8 LINCOLN
8 MEANS
8 OTHERS
8 PULL
8 SHIPS
8 STRAIGHT
8 TONIGHT
8 WHISKEY
9 ARABELLA
9 CATCH
9 DEMOCRACY
9 FACT
9 HEARTS
9 KNOWED

4 SHINE
4 SIN
4 SPARK
4 STARVE
4 SUE'S
4 TAOS
4 THROW
4 TREBLE
4 VOTED
4 WEATHER
4 WOKE
4 YOU'S
4 43RD
5 ANYTHING
5 BALL
5 BONES
5 CARES
5 CHRISTMAS
5 CONSIDER
5 CULLUD
5 DIXIE'S
5 DROVE
5 END
5 FLAG
5 GAME
5 GRAY
5 JOBS
5 LEAD
5 LYNCH
5 MILL
5 NEEDS
5 PALM
5 QUICKLY
5 ROLLING
5 SMALL
5 SUITS
5 THEY'VE
5 U.S.A
5 WITHERED
5 WRAP
6 BASS
6 BOLD
6 BURIED
6 COMIN'
6 DAUGHTER
6 DREAMED
6 FILLED
6 FO'
6 GREW
6 HEAVY
6 HOUSES
6 JUMP
6 LIVES
6 MEANT
6 MOAN
6 PICK
6 RAISE
6 SAND
6 SHARE
6 SORE
6 SUNNY
6 TOMORROW'S
6 WINDS
7 AMERICAN
7 BLACKS
7 CHICAGO
7 DUE
7 FLAME
7 GIVEN
7 I'S
7 LAY
7 MOP
7 RAILROAD
7 SADNESS
7 SHORT
7 STRIKE
7 TRUNK
7 WPA
8 BECOME
8 BOUGHT
8 CORN
8 FELL
8 GATHER
8 HELD
8 LOVER
8 MIXED
8 PAGE
8 SALT
8 SHOT
8 SUNRISE
8 UGLY
8 WINTER
9 BEATEN
9 CHURCH
9 DOLLAR
9 FIELD
9 HIMSELF
9 LIFT

4 SHOULDERS
4 SITTING
4 SPITOONS
4 STONY
4 SURELY
4 TELLS
4 TITLES
4 TRIBAL
4 WAKE
4 WEAVING
4 WONDERING
4 10-VOICES
4 47TH
5 ANYWHERE
5 BASTARD
5 BOY'S
5 CARRIES
5 CLOUDS
5 CRACKERS
5 CURB
5 DOESN'T
5 DRY
5 FACTORIES
5 FOOT
5 GEORGE
5 HAVING
5 KILLED
5 LESS
5 MAD
5 MISERY
5 NEON
5 PARADE
5 QUICK
5 RUNS
5 SOIL
5 TAIL
5 TIMES
5 WATCH
5 WONDERFUL
5 133RD
6 BEGAN
6 BOOM
6 CARRY
6 COOL
6 DESIRE
6 DROPPED
6 FINDING
6 GAIN
6 HAMMER
6 HILLS
6 JAZZ-BAND
6 JUNGLE
6 LOVELY
6 MELLOW
6 MR
6 PLACES
6 REASON
6 SCENT
6 SINGS
6 SPREAD
6 SWEEP
6 TOM-TOMS
6 WORKING
7 AUTUMN
7 BOMBS
7 CRYING
7 DUMB
7 FORTUNE
7 GRAVEYARD
7 KISS
7 LIBERTY
7 MOST
7 RATHER
7 SCHOOLS
7 SLOWLY
7 TALKING
7 UNION
7 YOURS
8 BLIND
8 CHINA
8 EAGLE
8 FELT
8 GIT
8 HURRY
8 LUCY
8 MORNIN'
8 PAPER
8 SELL
8 SISTER
8 SUNSHINE
8 VOICE
9 ALABAMA
9 BEER
9 COMRADE
9 DRUMS
9 FORGOTTEN
9 HIT
9 LOOKIN'

4 SIGHT
4 SMART
4 SPOKEN
4 STOVE
4 SURPRISE
4 TELLER
4 TORN
4 TURNS
4 WALKS
4 WELFARE
4 WORE
4 20-VOICES
4 63RD
5 A-TALL
5 BEATS
5 BUCKS
5 CARRYING
5 CLUB
5 CRAZY
5 DA
5 DONDE
5 EASY
5 FAITH
5 FORTH
5 GETTIN'
5 HOPES
5 KNEES
5 LOUIS
5 MAKING
5 MISTREAT
5 NOBODY'S
5 POLICE
5 QUITE
5 SAILOR
5 STANDIN'
5 TAME
5 TITLE
5 WATERS
5 WOOD
6 ALBERT
6 BIRDS
6 BOWED
6 CHARLIE
6 COUNTRY
6 DESPERATE
6 EIGHT
6 FINGERS
6 GAS
6 HARDLY
6 HOLLER
6 JEW
6 KIN
6 MAKIN'
6 MERCY
6 MYSTERY
6 PLANT
6 RISING
6 SEAS
6 SLEEPY
6 STARTS
6 TELLIN'
6 TOWARD
6 WORKIN'
7 AWHILE
7 CARS
7 DAT
7 DUST
7 FROZEN
7 GREEN
7 KITCHEN
7 MARGIE
7 NEAR
7 READ
7 SEEMS
7 SOLDIER
7 TELLING
7 WARM
8 AFRAID
8 BODIES
8 CHOCOLATE
8 EMPTY
8 FIGHTING
8 GLASS
8 LAUGHING
8 LUMUMBA
8 MUD
8 PLAYS
8 SENSE
8 SOLOMON
8 TAKEN
8 VOTE
9 ALIVE
9 BOX
9 DANCING
9 EARLY
9 GRAND
9 INSTEAD
9 LOSE

4 SIGN
4 SMOKE
4 SPORT
4 STREAM
4 SWIRL
4 THEY'RE
4 TOWER
4 TWENTY
4 WEARING
4 WHIRLING
4 WORLD'S
4 35TH
5 ABE
5 A.M
5 BEAUTY
5 BUILDING
5 CASH
5 COAL
5 CROSSED
5 DANCIN'
5 DOUBLE
5 ELECTION
5 FIELDS
5 FRENCH
5 GOSPEL
5 ISLAND
5 KNOWING
5 LULLABY
5 MARIE
5 MOTHER'S
5 ONE'S
5 POLITE
5 QUIT
5 SECOND-CLASS
5 STATE
5 TASTE
5 TOUCH
5 WAVE
5 WORKED
6 ANYHOW
6 BIT
6 BRASS
6 CLOSE
6 CRIES
6 DIRTY
6 FALLS
6 FLOWER
6 GRANDMA
6 HATES
6 HORSE
6 JONES
6 KING
6 MARBLE
6 MIDDLE
6 OPEN
6 PRAISE
6 RUMBLE
6 SETTIN'
6 SMILE
6 STEPS
6 TERROR
6 TV
6 31ST
7 BECOMES
7 CHANČE
7 DECENT
7 FARE
7 GENTLE
7 HUNDRED
7 LAUGHERS
7 MATTER
7 OUGHT
7 ROCK
7 SHAME
7 START
7 THINKING
7 WITHIN
8 ANCIENT
8 BOOKS
8 CLAY
8 FATHER
8 FIVE
8 GOODMORNING
8 LETTER
8 MAMMY
8 NAKED
8 PLUNK
8 SHIP
8 STATION
8 THOU
8 WALLS
9 ALONG
9 BURN
9 DARE
9 EVERYTHING
9 GUN
9 KNIFE
9 MULE

Freq.	Word
9	NAMED
9	PEACE
9	SHARP
9	SUDDENLY
9	YONDER
10	BLOW
10	CRYIN'
10	FOUND
10	JOHNSON
10	LIVING
10	PARK
10	SPEAK
10	UNDER
11	BABE
11	CRIED
11	FUNERAL
11	LABOR
11	PLAYED
11	SOMEWHERE
11	WE'RE
12	COMING
12	FOUR
12	MARY
12	SPRING
12	WAIT
13	ALMOST
13	DRUM
13	HUNG
13	MOONEY
13	USE
14	BREAD
14	DRINK
14	HELP
14	SLAVES
14	UPON
15	DEAR
15	LOOKS
15	SAME
15	SUCH
15	WOULDN'T
16	BUDDY
16	KID
16	RIVERS
16	SINGING
16	WRITE
17	PIERROT
17	SET
17	WHOSE
18	BROKE
18	NEED
18	ROOM
19	ANY
19	JOHN
19	STEEL
20	ASK
20	LAUGHTER
21	DANCE
21	MUCH
22	DIME
22	HOLD
22	SHO
22	TRUE
22	YO'
24	AIR
24	NEGRO
24	UNDERSTAND
25	KIDS
25	THING
26	LONESOME
27	JOY
28	CHILD
28	TOMORROW
29	BOYS
30	WATER
31	MAY
32	TILL
34	DIDN'T
35	LOOK
36	THOSE
38	SEA
40	BAD
41	MADE
42	COLORED
44	EYES
45	BEFORE
45	RIGHT
47	MOON
49	BLUES
50	MORE
51	THROUGH
53	HEART
56	DIE
57	O
61	HOW
66	TIME
72	LET
75	WOULD
81	AM
9	NIAGARA
9	PRAY
9	SOFTLY
9	SUIT
9	YOU'VE
10	BUILD
10	DANCERS
10	GAVE
10	LADY
10	LOVES
10	REALLY
10	STAR
10	WALKING
11	CANNOT
11	DRIVE
11	GIVES
11	LENIN
11	PLOW
11	SOUND
11	WHIP
12	COULDN'T
12	GROW
12	PAPA
12	STOP
12	WAITING
13	BREAK
13	FALL
13	JAIL
13	PALE
13	WANTS
14	CHILE
14	FORGET
14	MIGHTY
14	STONE
14	WHOLE
15	DIXIE
15	MEET
15	SHOES
15	TAKES
16	AGAINST
16	DAMN
16	LATE
16	SAD
16	SLAVE
17	BAR
17	RICH
17	SHOULD
17	WISH
18	DOOR
18	NORTH
18	SON
19	BED
19	KIND
19	SUGAR
20	BEING
20	LIPS
21	DEEP
21	SIDE
22	DUSK
22	I'VE
22	SORROW
22	UNTIL
23	CLEAN
24	FIND
24	NOTHING
25	CROW
25	LAWD
26	COMES
26	MOTHER
27	MANY
28	HONEY
28	TURN
29	STRONG
31	BLUE
31	PAIN
32	WONDER
34	THOUGHT
35	NOR
37	MUSIC
38	YOUNG
40	BITTER
41	MIGHT
42	STARS
44	OH
45	EVEN
45	ROAD
47	O'
49	FACE
50	THEM
52	LORD
55	INTO
56	SUN
57	WENT
63	ABOUT
69	BOY
72	SOME
77	WAY
82	DREAM
9	NICKEL
9	RADIO
9	SOFT
9	SUN'S
10	ALBERTA
10	CABARET
10	DOLLARS
10	GOES
10	LENOX
10	MARRIED
10	SILENCE
10	STREETS
10	WAVES
11	CHANGE
11	DYING
11	HAIR
11	LOVIN'
11	ROLL
11	TEXAS
12	BAND
12	ENOUGH
12	HATE
12	SHE'S
12	THY
12	WIFE
13	CAR
13	FOREVER
13	K
13	SEEN
13	WINGS
14	CUT
14	GLORY
14	MYSELF
14	SUNDAY
14	WINE
15	DOG
15	NIGGER
15	SLEEP
15	TROUBLE
16	ARMS
16	GEORGIA
16	LOST
16	SHAKE
16	SNOW
17	BORN
17	RUN
17	SHUT
17	WOMEN
18	EAT
18	POOR
18	THREE
19	CALL
19	LAUGH
19	TIRED
20	CHILDREN
20	TEN
21	FLOWERS
21	SILVER
22	EVERY
22	JOB
22	TOLD
22	USED
23	HE'S
24	GOLD
24	OWN
25	DAYS
25	LIGHT
26	FINE
26	SURE
27	MEAN
28	OFF
28	WIND
29	THINK
31	BODY
31	SHADOWS
33	DREAMS
35	GONE
35	THINGS
38	DEATH
39	BIG
40	SING
41	SOUL
42	TRAIN
44	ONLY
45	GREAT
46	HOME
48	EVER
49	LAND
51	GOD
52	PLAY
55	OUR
57	CAN'T
58	BLOOD
63	DID
70	TAKE
73	BEEN
78	GONNA
82	WORLD
9	NONE
9	RELIEF
9	ST
9	TRUTH
10	BACKLASH
10	CLOTHES
10	EVERYWHERE
10	GOLDEN
10	LEVEE
10	MILLION
10	SIR
10	TALK
10	'CAUSE
11	CLOWN
11	EVIL
11	HOUR
11	MOVE
11	SIMPLE
11	WANTED
12	BENEATH
12	FLOOR
12	LIGHTS
12	SOMETHING
12	TREAT
12	YEAR
13	COURSE
13	FRONT
13	KNEW
13	TEARS
13	WORKER
14	DAWN
14	GRAVE
14	PO'
14	THOUSAND
14	YESTERDAY
15	FEEL
15	PRETTY
15	STAY
15	VERY
16	BEHIND
16	GIN
16	NOTHIN'
16	SHOW
16	SOMEBODY
17	BRING
17	SAW
17	TREES
18	AFRICA
18	LIES
18	POWELL
18	TURNED
19	DARKNESS
19	LEAVE
19	WORDS
20	EVERYBODY
21	BARS
21	MAKES
22	ACROSS
22	FIRST
22	KILL
22	TOWN
22	WHAT'S
23	MIND
24	HELL
24	SPAIN
25	JESUS
25	ROSE
26	FULL
27	GAL
27	OZIE
28	ONCE
29	AROUND
30	MINE
31	DADDY
32	THAT'S
33	MEN
35	HEY
35	US
38	MAMA
39	OTHER
41	CAME
41	WORK
43	I'D
44	THAN
45	PUT
46	NAME
48	MUST
49	RIVER
51	ITS
52	STILL
55	WHY
57	I'LL
60	DONE
64	HIM
71	TWO
73	FOLKS
78	SONG
83	DARK
9	PASS
9	SEEK
9	STALINGRAD
9	WHIRL
10	BEATING
10	COLOR
10	FELLOW
10	HEAVEN
10	LIVIN'
10	MISSISSIPPI
10	SOON
10	TRY
11	ABOVE
11	COTTON
11	FOOL
11	KNOWN
11	PITY
11	SINGERS
11	WEEK
12	CITY
12	FLY
12	LONGER
12	SOUTHERN
12	TRIED
12	YOU'LL
13	CROSS
13	HAPPY
13	LOVED
13	THOUGH
14	ASKED
14	DEFERRED
14	GROUND
14	SCHOOL
14	TOM
15	BEAUTIFUL
15	JAZZ
15	REMEMBER
15	STRANGE
15	WISE
16	BELIEVE
16	IRON
16	RACE
16	SINCE
16	WALK
17	EACH
17	SEEKING
17	WASN'T
18	AVENUE
18	LOOKED
18	RIDE
19	ANOTHER
19	FAR
19	MISS
20	ALWAYS
20	GOIN'
21	CORNER
21	MOUTH
22	COLD
22	GIRL
22	KNOWS
22	TREE
22	WHICH
23	WIDE
24	MORNING
24	TALL
25	JIM
25	SLOW
26	HEARD
27	HARD
27	TOOK
28	THESE
29	BETTER
30	STAND
31	LISTEN
32	THERE'S
33	YEARS
35	HIGH
36	STREET
38	PLACE
39	TODAY
41	HAND
41	'EM
43	WELL
44	YES
45	RED
47	LAST
49	AGAIN
50	FREE
51	NOBODY
52	WERE
55	WOMAN
57	NEGROES
61	BABY
64	LIFE
72	FREEDOM
75	NEVER
80	SEE
85	GO

85	HERE	86	LONG	89	THEIR	94	LOVE	95	MA
97	BACK	98	JUST	101	DAY	101	ONE	102	OR
103	LITTLE	105	HAD	108	WE	115	OLD	116	BY
116	SAY	117	COME	120	TOO	122	NOW	124	WILL
128	DE	128	KNOW	130	HAVE	131	NIGHT	133	DO
134	MAN	135	WHERE	137	THERE	142	WHO	143	SHE
144	IF	146	ARE	147	WHAT	148	GOT	155	FROM
156	DOWN	160	SAID	163	THEY	163	THIS	164	HIS
167	AS	167	UP	167	WHITE	168	AT	172	AIN'T
173	BLACK	179	OUT	189	DON'T	199	WHEN	207	HE
212	SO	222	NOT	224	YOUR	231	LIKE	245	WAS
248	BE	271	WITH	302	IT	351	FOR	366	BUT
386	ON	444	THAT	464	IS	746	YOU	813	IN
856	OF	993	TO	1248	I	1280	A	1369	AND

WORDS OMITTED FROM THIS CONCORDANCE

1280 A 2.64%	1369 AND 2.82%	146 ARE .30%	128 DE .26%	351 FOR .72%	1248 I 2.57%	813 IN 1.68%	524 ME 1.08%
222 NOT .46%	122 NOW .25%	856 OF 1.77%	386 ON .80%	55 OUR .11%	444 THAT .92%	32 THAT'S .07%	2383 THE 4.91%
999 TO 2.06%	142 WHO .29%	124 WILL .26%	271 WITH .56%	746 YOU 1.54%	224 YOUR .46%	9 YOURSE .02%	12874 =TOTAL 26.55%